D1710605

Trial Practice Series

TOXIC TORTS

Litigation of Hazardous Substance Cases

G.Z. Nothstein, Esq.

Associate Professor
  University of Denver
  College of Law

SHEPARD'S/McGRAW-HILL
P.O. Box 1235
Colorado Springs, Colorado 80901

McGRAW-HILL BOOK COMPANY
New York ● St Louis ● San Francisco ● Colorado Springs
Auckland ● Bogota ● Hamburg ● Johannesburg ● London
Mexico ● Montreal ● New Delhi ● Panama ● São Paulo
Singapore ● Sydney ● Tokyo ● Toronto

12345678910 SHHI   893210987654

Library of Congress Cataloging in Publication Data

Nothstein, Gary Z.
  Toxic torts.

  (Trial practice series)
  Includes index.
  1. Personal injuries—United States.   2. Hazardous substances—Law and legislation—United States.   3. Actions and defenses—United States.   I. Title.   II. Series.
KF1257.N67 1984   346.7303'8   83-27128
                             347.30638

ISBN 0-07-047454-0

To Emily and Peter—
You make life worth living and loving

Acknowledgments

This book could not have been written without the generous support of the University of Denver College of Law, the firm of Debevoise & Liberman in Washington, D.C., and the major contributions of recognized individuals in the environmental, safety and health fields. In addition to the specific chapter contributors, I would like to acknowledge the assistance of other individuals who contributed in one way or another to the book's publication, including: Morton Corn Ph.D., Director & Professor, Division of Environmental Health Engineering, School of Hygiene & Public Health, The Johns Hopkins University, Baltimore, MD; Kenneth R. Cass, Esq., Allegheny International, Inc., Pittsburgh, PA; Thomas J. Cresswell, Esq., Dow Chemical Corporation, Midland, MI; Kenneth A. Henry, Esq., United States Department of Labor, Chicago, IL; Dennis H. Markusson, Esq., Johns-Manville Corporation, Denver, CO; J.A. Martin, United Technologies Corporation, Hartford, CT; Robert H. Sand, Esq., Allied Corporation, Morristown, N.J.; Jeffrey Teitel, Esq., Ashland Oil Company, Ashland, KY; John W. Whittlesey, Esq., Union Carbide Corporation (formerly) Chappaqua, N.Y.; Michael D. McDowell, Esq., Dravo Corporation, Pittsburgh, PA; John D. Carter, Esq., Bechtel Power Corporation, San Francisco, CA; Nicholas A. Ashford, Ph.D., Massachusetts Institute of Technology, Cambridge, MA; Alexander C. Lipsey, Esq., Kellogg Company, Battle Creek, MI; James T. Carney, Esq., United States Steel Corporation, Pittsburgh, PA; and Thomas P. Kennedy, MD, Professor, Occupational Medicine, The Johns Hopkins University, Baltimore, MD.

G.Z. Nothstein
December, 1983

Preface

Not many years ago, the average member of the health profession could not have correctly defined a toxic tort or indeed a tort of any kind, while in turn most members of the legal profession knew little about asbestos, except that it didn't burn and therefore made good insulation. Today, in all likelihood, most health professionals still cannot define a tort, but may well have appeared in court or have assisted in litigation concerned with a toxic tort. A substantially greater percentage of attorneys has become very familiar with asbestos as well as many other hazardous substances associated with the workplace or the general environment, but many remain relatively uninformed concerning basic occupational and environmental health concepts.

It is difficult to say which professional group will benefit most by this book, for it is clearly designed to be of interest and value to both. *Toxic Torts* certainly belongs in the library of the industrial hygienist or occupational physician, for it has become virtually impossible to practice in either profession without at some time being asked to offer advice or testimony relative to a toxic tort, a workers' compensation claim, or a products liability action. All have much in common, but there are substantial legal differences of which most such health professionals may be unaware. A simple review of the chapter headings of this book should convince most health professionals that the mysterious and sometimes apparently arbitrary procedures encountered in legal actions are actually based on accepted principles, and in any event must be understood and respected by the expert witness, be he or she an industrial hygienist, physician, epidemiologist, engineer, or toxicologist.

Members of the legal profession face even greater problems when attempting to understand and resolve the complex arguments related to evidence presented in most toxic tort cases. Somehow they must grasp the subtleties of an enormous and ever-changing body of scientific and technological knowledge and attempt to resolve chemical, physiological, or toxicologic arguments arising from extremely involved theoretical considerations and a generally inadequate data base. Before addressing the particulars of any case, an attorney must above all be familiar with the general principles which guide the occupational and environmental health specialists and serve to make it possible to prevent occupationally or environmentally induced illnesses or at least to explain them on the basis of sound scientific principles.

It is difficult in a single volume to achieve the objectives intended by the editor, but by the selection of a number of experienced experts from the several professions involved in most toxic litigation, a large measure of success has been realized.

Ralph G. Smith, Ph.D.

Department of Environmental
& Industrial Health

School of Public Health

University of Michigan

Ann Arbor, Michigan

Foreword

The rapid growth in the litigation of hazardous substance injury and illness cases is a phenomenon already well-known to the legal profession and one with which many business executives, to their great chagrin, are rapidly becoming acquainted. The public's concern with toxic torts has recently been heightened by extensive media coverage of the controversy surrounding the Environmental Protection Agency's (EPA) administration of the *Superfund* program (discussed in Chapter 10), including such notable incidents as the dioxin contamination problem at Times Beach, Missouri. Everyone remembers *thalidomide,* but now *Agent Orange, asbestos, DES,* and *dioxin* have become household words. The bankruptcy petition of the Manville Corporation, which arose from countless asbestos lawsuits against the corporation, has made the business community and the public aware of the increasingly significant scope of toxic tort issues. The extensive asbestosis litigation may be only the tip of the proverbial iceberg.

Employee health concerns have grown in the wake of the enactment of the Occupational Safety and Health Act of 1970. This statute has concentrated much of its attention and resources in the occupational health field and has proposed and adopted many new standards aimed at protecting workers from toxic substances. Many more standards regulating potentially toxic chemicals are under consideration by the Occupational Safety and Health Administration (OSHA) and the National Institute of Occupational Safety and Health (NIOSH). Unions are actively seeking revised OSHA exposure standards and access to proprietary information on the ingredients of their employers' products. This rise in employee health concerns will no doubt increase the number of toxic tort cases that employers may face in the coming years.

The government's role in the field of toxic torts has been steadily increasing. This increase is evidenced by Congressional consideration of proposed legislation to compensate individuals who have been exposed to toxic substances and new federal products liability legislation. Several state and local governments have already passed worker *right-to-know* laws which require employers to inform workers of their exposure to hazardous substances. The ultimate roles that government and organized labor will play in the field of toxic torts remains to be seen, but there is little evidence that their roles will be diminishing in the near future.

The rapid growth of toxic tort litigation has resulted in the emergence of new specialists within the legal profession and has increased the demand for qualified industrial health professionals. Because toxic tort litigation is both quite complex and quite expensive, attorneys for both plaintiffs and defendants have begun to seek ways to coordinate the management of these cases. There is little doubt that important legal developments which bear close watching will continue to be generated in this expanding field of law.

Gary Nothstein has performed an important and timely service in preparing this comprehensive examination of the issues involved in the litigation of toxic substance cases. Mr. Nothstein has drawn upon the talents, as contributing authors, of the recognized authorities in the field, who together with him constitute the *Who's Who* in safety and health law and science. Seldom has any single publication been able to marshal together so effectively and comprehensively the medical/legal talents of such a distinguished group of experts. The result is a truly worthwhile publication. Mr. Nothstein's contribution to the field of toxic substance litigation, both as author and editor, has once again established his credentials in the safety and health area. Based on the quality of Mr. Nothstein's past publications, and on my extensive review of this book, I am confident that this important work will be of great value to the legal and medical professions, the academic world, and the business community.

Robert T. Thompson, Sr., Esq.

Chairman of the Executive Committee and
Former Chairman of the Board, The Chamber
of Commerce of the United States of America

Senior Partner, Thompson, Mann
& Hutson, Washington, D.C.,
Greenville, S.C., Atlanta, Ga.,
and New York, N.Y.

Contents

Detailed

13 Allegations *Susan T. Travis, Esq.*

14 Defenses *R.B. Ballanfant, Esq.*

Recognition and Evaluation of Hazards

Stanley M. Pier, Ph.D.*; Sally R. Cowles, M.D.;** Marcus M. Key, M.D.†, & G.Z. Nothstein, Esq.

1

---

* Associate Professor of Environmental Health, School of Public Health, University of Texas Health Science Center, Houston, Texas.

** Assistant Professor, Department of Family Practice and Community Medicine University of Texas Medical School, Houston, Texas.

† Director, City of Houston Health Department; formerly Director, National Institute for Occupational Safety and Health.

§1.01   Introduction

Hazardous conditions can be encountered in both community and occupational settings. The hazardous condition may be of a chemical, physical, mechanical, or biological nature. At present, the overwhelming focus of concern is on chemical agents. This emphasis derives, in part, from the extraordinarily large number of such substances in existence. An exact count of known chemical substances cannot be stated, but there are approximately 5,000,000 organic chemicals and 500,000 inorganic substances. More importantly, approximately 10,000 new chemicals are synthesized in the research laboratories of the world each year, of which about 1,000 enter commerce. It is estimated that approximately 63,000 chemicals are in fairly common use in the United States, with other industrialized societies being similar in this respect.

Toxicity defines the capacity of a chemical to produce injury or harm. Toxicity is as much an inherent characteristic of a chemical as is the color, odor, or boiling point; it is specific to the total molecular conformation and is not adequately defined based on the presence of a particular chemical element. In assessing hazard, toxicity is essential information, but not sufficient information because it does not define the conditions of exposure. *Hazard* defines the probability or possibility that a particular chemical will produce injury or harm under specific conditions of use. Hazard thus considers both toxicity and exposure.

The basic unit of quantification in chemical exposures is the *dose*. The dose considers both concentration or quantity and duration of contact or exposure. *Dosage* is the rate of administration of a given dose and frequently determines the outcome of a given dose. A given dose administered in a single exposure is likely to produce a much greater impact than the same dose divided into many small portions administered over a long period of time. Thus, dose and dosage cannot be considered synonymous terms. The *acute dose* is viewed as a relatively high dose administered over a short period of time. There is also generally a short time period between the exposure (insult) and the onset of effects. The *chronic dose* is characterized by a relatively low dose administered over a long period of time, and frequently with a long time interval between insult and effects, if any. Poisonings, suicides, and the like generally involve acute doses. Community exposures to pollutants and occupational exposures to chemicals tend to fall into the chronic dose category. A problem of major importance associated with the chronic dose situation is the long time span between insult and effect; this interval is frequently referred to as the *latency period* where a disease process is involved. In simple terms, it is the time between exposure and the appearance of symptoms or other markers produced by the development of a disease because of the exposure in question. The long time delay may make it exceedingly difficult to demonstrate an association unequivocally. Latency periods of 10 to 25 years or longer are recognized in the production of lung cancer from cigarette smoking. The development of lung cancer or mesothelioma attributable to asbestos exposure may involve a latency period of approximately 40 years. These problems are dealt with again in the discussion of epidemiology in §1.07.

Data concerning the toxic properties of chemicals or the impacts of other environmental stressors can be obtained from four sources: toxicologic, clinical, occupational, or epidemiologic studies. Volumes have been written about each, and an in-depth discussion of any one is beyond the scope of this review, but it is important to understand the applications of and limitations to these data sources. Thus, they are discussed in summary, with emphasis on the two most widely utilized types of studies.

§1.02 Toxicologic Studies

Toxicologic studies, the most widely employed technique for the assessment of toxicity, may be thought of most simply as the type of evaluation conducted under carefully controlled laboratory conditions on selected test organisms. Laboratory conditions enable the control of most aspects of the test organisms' environmental contacts: food eaten, water drunk, air breathed, contacts permitted, etc. Further observations may be made at varying stages of the investigations; observations may involve behavioral tests, determination of blood chemistry, analyses of excreta (feces, urine, exhaled air), etc. Tissue specimens may be taken for analyses and animals may be sacrificed for the determination of a variety of endpoints. In short, the test organisms selected for toxicologic studies may be subjected to procedures that are absolutely out of the range of possibility of what might be done with humans. However, there is an obvious shortcoming to the utility of even the best of toxicologic investigations. At the termination of such a study, there will have been developed information on the effect or effects of a particular chemical or other exposure on the test organism employed. In most cases, the interest really focuses on the effects of the agent on humans. Thus, a *biological question mark* is left, which is basically the issue of how to extrapolate from data in a mouse or a rat to humans.

There is no single, universally applicable toxicologic test procedure because of the wide variation in the objectives of toxicologic assays. The agent under test may be a consumer product, an industrial chemical, or an environmental contaminant. Forensic toxicology is an important division of the science. Testing may be directed toward the determination of a very wide range of endpoints or effects: lethality, behavioral changes, reproductive impacts, liver toxicity, tumor production, etc. This very great variation in objectives results in the need to select procedures carefully with respect to test organism, route of administration, markers or symptoms, test duration, etc.

Recent years have witnessed the evolution of a subdiscipline of toxicology, *genetic toxicology*. This branch of the science focuses on the impact of agents on genes. Each cell in the body contains chromosomes, made up of genes. At conception, the fertilized egg begins development with information provided in chromosomes, half of which were obtained from each parent. Development is thus an integration of the traits carried by the chromosomes.

Chromosomes are composed of genes in uncounted numbers. The genes are composed of deoxyribonucleic acid (DNA), which is a polymer of nucleotides. The information contained in the genes is a consequence of the sequence and arrangement of the nucleotides in DNA. The genes thus constitute the *blueprint* for cellular or organismic development. And, as with something being built from a blueprint, any change in the information results in a different end product.

The DNA is capable of reaction with chemicals because there are free, chemically reactive groups on the polymeric molecules. The concern of genetic toxicology is the nature and results of these reactions. Any such reaction that alters the genetic information, or *code* as it is frequently called, may change cellular development or behavior and could therefore be considered a *mutation*.

Cellular mutation may be expressed in many ways, many of which may be of no consequence whatever. Other mutations may be highly undesirable with respect to the survival or functioning of the cell. A few may actually be beneficial, though it is generally regarded that beneficial mutations are in the minority of all possible mutations.

In any normally functioning organism, cells are continually dying and being replaced. There is a control over cell replication that is presumably genetically determined so that cellular replacement occurs to the necessary, but not excessive, extent. One possible outcome of a mutation is to destroy this inhibitory mechanism, resulting in the production of a great excess of cells; this excess tissue is known as a *neoplasm*. Thus, the initiation of the neoplastic process can be viewed as but one expression of mutation.

Genetic toxicology has generated a number of terms that are widely, if not always correctly, used. Precision in the use of these terms is important in dealing with current issues.

> **Oncogenic**—a chemical or other agent resulting in the production of a neoplasm, presumably by altering the genetically determined control over cell replication.
>
> **Carcinogenic**—a chemical or other agent resulting in the production of a malignant neoplasm, a cancer. Malignancy implies that individual cells can be released by the neoplasm, picked up in the circulation, blood or lymph, and carried to other body sites where additional neoplasms may be *seeded*. This process is known as *metastasis,* and the neoplasms other than the first or primary lesion are known as *secondary* or *metastatic growths.*
>
> **Tumorigenic**—a chemical or other agent resulting in the production of a nonmalignant or benign neoplasm, a tumor.

Mutagenic—a chemical or other agent resulting in the alteration of the genetic structure in the germ plasm, the sperm in the male or the egg in the female. This results in altered information being carried to the next generation and all future generations. As previously noted, many of the changes may be of no particular significance. Indeed, many will be recessive and not expressed at all. However, if this phenomenon is indeed occurring and if more and more people are being subjected to these chemical alterations to the genetic code, the probability increases that two individuals carrying the same recessive mutated gene will mate. In that event, the probability is one in four that the product of that mating will express the mutation as a dominant trait. It should be clear that if this process is occurring it is both undetectable and irreversible. Mutagenesis thus has major implications for the development, and possibly the survival, of the human species. Oncogenesis, however unfortunate it may be for the affected individual, ceases upon the death of that individual and is therefore without significance with respect to the species.

Teratogenic—a chemical or other agent resulting in the alteration in development of an embryo. Teratogenesis does not imply any imprint on the germ plasm and is not to be confused with mutagenesis. The demonstration of the phenomenon of teratogenesis has important implications with respect to permitting exposures of females to chemical or other teratogens because a chemical or other stress that would have no impact on males could have a definite impact on a pregnant female.

§1.03　—Toxicological Testing

Because of the different objectives of toxicological testing, a wide variety of procedures have been developed to satisfy the different needs. One important variable is the test organism selected. Test species are presented in Table 1-1.

Table 1-1 Toxicologic Test Systems

Microorganisms
Plants
Birds
Rodents
    Rats
    Mice
    Hamsters
    Guinea pigs
    Rabbits
Primates
    Monkeys
    Chimpanzees
Other Mammals
    Cattle
    Pigs
    Man

The selection of the test organism to be employed in a bioassay is based on many considerations. The most important one is the appropriateness of the organism. In order to develop the most valid data, it is desirable to have the best *animal model* possible, an animal model being one in which the outcome is the same as in the human for a given exposure. This implies that the animal should be as close as possible to the human in the ways in which the chemical is contacted, absorbed, and metabolized, as well as resulting in the same physiologic effect or disease outcome. This happy state is rarely achieved.

Other considerations in the selection of the test species include cost, numbers of organisms necessary for statistical reliability of data, complexity of handling the test organisms, lifetime, food requirements, problems in handling excreta, etc. For studies such as those focusing on reproductive effects or mutagenesis, short lifetimes are desirable to permit multigenerational investigations within a reasonable time span.

The economics of toxicologic testing are easily illustrated. If a new chemical were under development, it is virtually certain that a very early stage of toxicologic assay would include what is popularly known as an *Ames Test*. This procedure (really a number of procedures) involving microorganisms is an assay for the mutagenic propensity of chemicals. These tests can be conducted in days or weeks at costs in the hundreds of dollars. Carcinogenesis is viewed by some as a varient of mutagenesis, and any chemical that is mutagenic may also be carcinogenic. If the chemical just determined to be mutagenic were pursued for further development, it might be deemed important to determine whether or not it would in fact be carcinogenic if breathed. A definitive determination of this would likely require an inhalation bioassay. This procedure, involving rats and monkeys, might take as long as four years and require an expenditure in excess of $1 million. This extreme range in time and cost dictates the need to eliminate a dangerous chemical at as early a stage as possible. This need carries with it the danger that a chemical might be prematurely or incorrectly deemed toxic based on assay data that may be inappropriate or false.

An issue of importance in the conduct of bioassays concerns the appropriateness of the administration pathway. Does it make any sense to test a chemical that might be breathed by painting it on the shaved back of a mouse? One view holds that the contact should be as close as possible to the anticipated human exposure. However, in the case of materials expected to be breathed, this would require the very costly inhalation tests. Another view states that any contact that results in the agent entering the organism and being exposed to the biochemical systems of that organism is appropriate. On this basis, compromises to control costs are justifiable. Yet another view maintains that a given chemical is subject to many biochemical pathways depending on the nature of the contact, and therefore all administration pathways provide some useful and appropriate information. Commonly used administration routes are presented in Table 1-2.

Table 1-2 Administration Routes

Cutaneous—via the skin

Subcutaneous—injection under the skin

Ocular—via the eye

Intubation—insertion into the gastrointestinal tract or into the trachea

Ingestion—consumption of food or water

Inhalation—inhaled into the respiratory system

Intramuscular—injected into the tissue

Intraperitoneal—injected into the peritoneal cavity

Intravenous—injected into the blood circulation

Tests may be run with more than one route in order to assure that the chemical will be subjected to multiple metabolic changes, thereby allowing study of the toxicity of the chemical itself and the metabolites or derivatives of that chemical through several biochemical transformations. There are many instances in which a given chemical can be shown to be nontoxic when administered by one route and toxic when administered by another route in the same organism.

Toxicologic assays are conveniently grouped into two broad categories, *in vitro* and *in vivo*. In vitro (literally, in glass) tests involve simple organisms such as bacteria or individual cells. The Ames Test is an example of an in vitro procedure. These procedures tend to be quite rapid and of low cost. In vivo (literally, in life) assays involve complete living animals. These procedures are therefore of longer duration and higher cost.

Toxicologic tests can also be grouped according to duration. Duration of testing is one of the variables to be set based on the objective of the assay. Acute tests (Table 1-3) are generally used to obtain information on the short-term effects such as lethality, skin irritation, and eye irritation. Prolonged tests (Table 1-4) are designed to determine a variety of systemic toxic effects such as liver toxicity, tumor development, metabolic changes, behavioral effects, and others. Chronic testing (Table 1-5) may involve the full lifetime of the test organisms; this kind of testing is necessary to establish long-term impacts such as lung cancer, mutagenesis, teratogenesis, and other phenomena related to long-term exposures to lower levels of toxicants.

Table 1-3 Animal Toxicologic Tests

Acute Tests

1. Single Dose
2. LD_{50} Determination
   A. 24 Hrs. to 7 Days (or longer)
   B. Two Species
   C. Two Administration Routes
3. Topical Effects
   A. Skin
   B. Eye
   C. 24 Hrs. to 7 Days

Table 1-4 Animal Toxicologic Tests

Prolonged Tests

1. Daily Doses
2. Three months
3. Three Dose Levels
4. Selected Administration Routes
5. Two Species
6. Health Evaluations
   A. Weight Change Weekly
   B. Physical Exam Weekly
   C. Blood and Urine Analyses
   D. Function Tests
7. Autopsy

Table 1-5 Animal Toxicologic Tests

Chronic Tests

1. Daily Doses
2. 1-2 Years
3. Two Dose Levels
4. Selected Administration Routes
5. Two Species
6. Health Evaluations
   A. Weight Change Weekly

    C. Blood and Urine Analyses

    D. Function Tests

  7.   Autopsy

  8.   Pathology

§1.04   —Dose Response

Another point at issue relates to the proper dose. If a chemical is expected to be encountered at very low levels in an occupational circumstance, it is appropriate and valid to force very large amounts of chemical into the test animals' gastrointestinal tracts by intubation (see Table 1-2). The rationale for massive doses is usually related to the obvious limitation to the number of test animals that can be used. Give a limited number of test organisms, the likelihood of finding a toxic effect is enhanced by elevated doses. This is probably true, but the question of concern then becomes whether there is a continuum in effect over the dose range, or if there is a level of exposure below which there is no effect at all. This problem is discussed further in §§1.06 and 1.07.

Toxicologic assays seek to establish the consequences of exposure to a chemical or other agent as well as a quantitative relationship between the dose and the effect. Definition of the *dose-effect* or *dose-response* relationship is an essential element in determining those exposures that would be considered safe and those which represent potentially hazardous conditions.

A dose-response curve is shown without quantification in Figure 1-1. The ordinate shows a gradation in responses from zero to lethality. Zero effect in this representation means precisely that: no effect of any kind. This must be

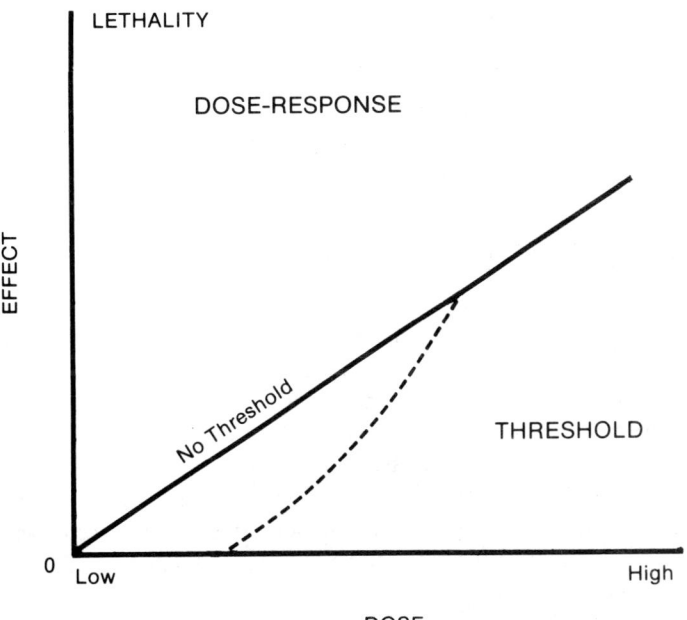

DOSE

distinguished from a subclinical effect, an effect that is there even though technology lacks the ability to detect it.

The solid line labelled *No Threshold* begins at the origin of the plot and increases with increasing dose. The implication of this is that there is some effect, whether or not it can be detected, at the very smallest dose—possibly a single atom or molecule. Thus, there is no dose without effect.

The dashed line, labelled *Threshold,* shows an effect beginning at some dose greater than zero. The point at which this plot is at zero on the effect axis is termed the *threshold dose.* It is therefore clear that there is some level of dose below which there is no effect whatsoever, and anything below the threshold dose would be considered entirely safe.

The shape of the dose-response curve for chemicals is the focus of serious dispute. Many maintain that humans are chemical systems that have evolved in a chemical environment, and that therefore humans have considerable tolerance for chemicals. Chemicals for which human beings have tolerance would be expected to behave in accordance with the threshold model. Many others, however maintain that for chemicals which have genotoxic properties—i.e., chemicals capable of reacting with the components of DNA—there is no safe level of exposure. Such chemicals would behave in accordance with the no-threshold model. By this interpretation, oncogens, mutagens, and teratogens (see §1.02) would fall into the no-safe-exposure category, though the question remains how the judgment would be made that a chemical is genotoxic.

The inability to define the shape of the dose-response curve for chemicals has major implications in terms of regulations covering exposures to chemicals in both community and occupational circumstances. It also presents serious problems in the estimation of risk, an aspect of quantitative toxicology that is at an early stage of development.

In summary, toxicologic studies provide a wealth of data. The primary problem with the results resides in the question of how these data are to be interpreted in terms of human exposures.

§1.05 Clinical Studies

Clinical studies are performed with human subjects, as a result of which the biological question mark discussed in §1.02 is eliminated. In the past, considerable use was made of such studies, involving volunteers, prison inmates, and others. At present, research on human subjects is under such strict control that this source of data is essentially unavailable. Experimentation with humans is limited to such specialized activities as drug trials, and routine exposures of humans to chemicals or other agents suspected of being toxic will almost certainly not be done except under the most extreme circumstances.

Where such data may be available from past experimentation, the limitations of the data should be recognized. In general, clinical exposures involve a small number of subjects. These subjects are almost always healthy adults. The exposures usually extend over a brief time period. Consequently, the results may not be relevant to chronic exposure conditions, nor will they consider the responses of susceptible portions of the population—i.e., aged or inform people, pregnant women, young children, persons with other impairments—who might react more strongly to a given stress.

§1.06 Occupational Exposures

Many of the chemicals and other agents under study at present have been articles of commerce for considerable periods of time. An exposed population therefore exists, and the health status of this population can be studied to obtain information concerning the effects of exposures. It should be understood that this is not the same as human experimentation because the occupational exposures involved have not been intentional.

Occupational exposure data suffer a number of limitations. As with clinical exposures, the population is primarily healthy and adult, again eliminating susceptible segments of the population. Where the exposed individuals have been employed for long periods of time, other aspects of their lifestyles have probably not been monitored or controlled, and this introduces serious confounding factors. The most serious limitation to historic occupational exposure data relates to the quantification of exposure. Although workplace and personal monitoring are commonplace now, this has not been the case for long. In considering exposures that took place more than five to ten years ago, it is likely that there are no good data regarding exposures. It is reasonable to assume that exposures in the past were probably higher than at present, but how much higher cannot be determined. The lack of exposure data renders the definition of a dose-response relationship (see §1.04) much more difficult, if not impossible.

§1.07 Epidemiologic Studies

Epidemiology is the scientific discipline dealing with the study of adverse health effects in human populations. The important difference between epidemiology and other branches of medicine is that epidemiology is concerned with groups of individuals (populations), whereas most other medical disciplines are concerned with individual patients. Another difference is that epidemiology examines not only the patients (hosts) or the adverse health effects, but also the interactions among host, agent, and environment to identify recurring associations. Such associations may help suggest cause (when unknown), potential preventive measures, or important predisposing factors.

Epidemiology can be used to help define the underlying causes, the modes of transmission, and the populations at greater risk for adverse health effects.

Epidemiologic studies can be an excellent source of data for hazard recognition. They often complement and help complete information derived from other sources. Toxicologic studies (§§1.02-1.04) are usually confined to animals, and human case reports (§§1.05-1.06) are often unverified and sporadic. This can make a well controlled and well executed epidemiologic study a major source of human hazard information.

It is important to note, however, that epidemiologic studies are not necessarily the best source for the original recognition of an adverse health effect from a particular toxic exposure. More commonly, an astute clinician becomes suspicious when one or more patients who have had a particular exposure present either an unusual set of symptoms or similar symptoms. If he or she is suspicious enough, these suspicions may be published as a case report in the medical literature, or further cases in the exposed population may be sought. If the suspicions are sustained after further investigation, an epidemiologic study often follows. Epidemiologic studies at such a point are useful because they can generate either further evidence for a causal association between exposure and adverse effect or a refutation of the originally suspected association. An epidemiologic study can never *prove* causation, but it can strongly suggest a causal association.

There are several types of epidemiologic studies, and an understanding of the similarities, differences, and potential pitfalls of each can be important in the evaluation of a potential hazard. In every epidemiologic study, a defined study population is compared with a defined control population. The control population may be the population as a whole or a smaller population not possessing the characteristic feature or features defining the study population. In intervention studies, the study population may act as its own control. In general, most epidemiologic studies are either cross-sectional studies or longitudinal studies.

Cross-Sectional Studies

In a cross-sectional study, descriptive information is obtained about a population at a particular point (cross section) in time. As an example, a cross-sectional study might involve the investigation of workers in a particular textile factory for evidence of respiratory disease compared to workers in a nontextile factory or to the general population. No follow-up over time would occur, and only prevalences of respiratory disease at the time of the study would be identified. Such studies can suggest the presence of previously unrecognized or undocumented hazards, and they can provide the rationale for more extensive and definitive studies.

Cross-sectional studies have several significant limitations which should be recognized if they are to be used effectively. Because they look at essentially an instant frozen in time, they do not necessarily give a true picture of the results of a particular exposure on a population over time. Mortality and morbidity may be grossly underrepresented if mortality or morbidity is severe enough to remove selectively affected members from the study population at an early stage of disease development. If a long latency period exists, as it does for many carcinogens, the age and time after first exposure of those present in the study population can drastically affect results. If, for example, a cross-sectional study of vinyl chloride workers had been done five years after a particular plant opened, it is highly unlikely that any association between exposure to vinyl chloride and angiosarcoma of the liver would have been seen, since the latency period for vinyl chloride-associated angiosarcoma of the liver is over ten years. Similarly, if a disease takes many years to manifest itself and exposure conditions have continuously changed over time, a cross-sectional study may present a very misleading picture if current exposure levels are related to current disease. If, however, the effect is a rapidly occurring one which does not selectively eliminate susceptibles from the study population, a cross-sectional study may well be the most efficient method to assess a possible exposure/effect relationship.

Longitudinal Studies

Longitudinal studies involve obtaining information about a population over time. Longitudinal studies may be prospective or retrospective, case control or cohort in design. A *prospective study* defines a population at a particular point in time and then follows that population forward over a known period of time. A *restospective study* defines a population at a particular point in time and follows that population backward in time for a known period. A *cohort study* defines a population on the basis of a particular characteristic or series of characteristics (e.g., working males born between 1925 and 1945 exposed to asbestos) and follows the population in time. Comparison populations may be the general population, another cohort, or a similar cohort in a different location or with different exposures, etc. A *case-control study* defines a study population based on whether or not a particular outcome is present and compares this population with a population in which the particular outcome is *not* present. Usually, a case-control study is retrospective and a cohort study is prospective. Usually, the population for a case-control study is defined based on the presence of absence of a disease, while the population for a cohort study is defined based on the presence or absence of an exposure. In any case, the purpose of a longitudinal study is to compare two populations over time to determine whether differences exist between them.

If a cohort study comparing a population of people who regularly brush their teeth to a group of people who do not brush their teeth finds a statistically significant increase in new cavities in nonbrushers after five years of observation, the implication is that perhaps tooth brushing in some way protects against cavity formation. Unfortunately, epidemiologic studies of this type are not controlled experiments in which all other aspects can be manipulated by the investigator. Human populations function at times in highly uncontrollable ways so the epidemiologist must be constantly aware of what else may have occurred during the course of the study that may have influenced the outcome. If the brushers also happened to live in an area with natural fluorides in the water or in a town where shortly after the beginning of the study fluoridation was introduced into the water supply, while the nonbrushers were in a low fluoride area, tooth brushing may have had little to do with the results. Since it is known, however, that fluorides, diet, and relative enamel thickness can influence tooth decay, investigators can design studies which are able to examine these variables and at least partially account for their effects. There may be other important variables, however, of which the investigator is totally unaware, and which may lead to spurious associations. The tooth brushing study might have been done in two communities where the predominance of nonbrushers drank water with natural fluoride and the brushers did not. At the end of five years the tooth brushing population is found to have a statistically significant increased number of new cavities. Does tooth brushing cause cavities? If the investigator has controlled for dietary fluorides, she or he may instead be able to demonstrate a strong protective effect of fluorides even when dental hygiene is poor (as in nonbrushers). Statistical associations prove nothing. They may suggest further areas of study, they may contribute to the total body of knowledge about a subject, and they may suggest associations not previously recognized.

Because epidemiologic studies are uncontrolled experiments within free-living human populations, to be of value they must be performed with a great deal of attention to study design, data collection, and analysis, since these can be controlled by the investigator. Study populations must be selected with care to assure that there is comparability in areas other than that specifically under study. (E.g., in the tooth brushing study, the investigator might want identical twins one of whom brushes, the other of whom does not, living in the same house but will settle for classmates of similar age, some of whom brush, others of whom do not, from a single school all living in the same neighborhood with a single water supply.)

Important Issues Regarding Accuracy

The primary limitations of any epidemiologic study lie in the difficulties of selecting valid comparison populations—both study and control. Longitudinal studies are generally more costly than cross-sectional studies. Prospective studies are usually more costly than retrospective studies and also may take an inordinate amount of time and have large numbers of study subjects lost to follow-up. All epidemiologic studies may suffer from unrecognized bias or from poor study design, improper population selection, or careless study implementation. In evaluating longitudinal studies, it is important to look not only at the comparability of study and control populations, but also at what portions of both populations were lost to follow-up, whether selection criteria for the study population were relevantly applied to the control population, whether follow-up methods were similar for populations and of adequate length, whether enough information is actually available to estimate exposure levels, and whether critical information is available or not (e.g., in a study of lung cancer in a particular occupational group, are smoking histories available, and are smoking habits similar in the control population?), as well as several other issues. Do the study results make sense? Are there other studies showing similar results? Is there a dose-response relationship (see §1.04)? Does the exposure always occur before the disease? The more *yes* answers to such questions, the greater confidence one can have in the results and in the assumption that a causal relationship may exist.

§1.08 Occupational Hazards

The potential hazards of the occupational environment (other than biological which is discussed under the heading of environmental contamination, see §1.14) can be grouped conveniently into three major categories:

Chemical Agents—particulates (dusts); gases and vapors; liquids

Physical Agents—noise; temperature extremes (heat and cold); radiation (ionizing and nonionizing); vibration; electrical shock

Mechanical Agents—equipment defects; inadequate protective devices

Another classification basis is also interesting—a classification based on whether or not a possible hazard is evident. The rationale for such a categorization is that an obvious or evident condition is more likely to elicit a protective or corrective response than one which is not evident; the latter potential hazard condition might be termed *insidious*.

On this basis, the evident hazards would be high dust levels, liquids, noise, temperature extremes, vibration, and most mechanical agents. Most exposures to gases and vapors, some finely divided particulates, and radiation would be placed in the insidious category. While it is true that some chemicals have characteristic colors or odors or may trigger some acute response such as respiratory distress, the vast majority of chemicals will not disclose their presence, and this is especially true at the low levels of exposure which are most commonly encountered. Thus, chemical exposures assume great importance.

§1.09 —Chemical Agents: Generally

Human contact with chemicals can occur via three pathways:

Inhalation—agents breathed, entering the respiratory system

Ingestion—agents entering the gastrointestinal tract

Dermal—agents coming into contact with the skin

While it is obvious that a chemical substance on the skin is outside the body, it is less obvious that a chemical in the respiratory system or the gastrointestinal (GI) tract is also still outside the body. The production of any form of systemic intoxication requires that the agent pass one of the protective barriers —lung, GI tract, or skin—a process known as *absorption*. The major exception to this requirement applies to *pneumoconiotic agents,* i.e., particulates that deposit in the lung potentially leading to respiratory disease.

Ingestion-induced intoxications are very rare in the occupational situation because workers usually avoid ingesting the materials with which they work. However, problems can arise indirectly when inadequate hygiene is observed, allowing toxic chemicals to pass from the hands, hair, or clothes of workers to food and beverages that are consumed. Ingestion is, of course, a major problem in suicides and childhood poisonings.

Inhalation is the problem of greatest importance in the occupational setting. This derives from the fact that breathing is a no-option, continuous process, and there are many contaminants in the air being breathed. An adult breaths 10 to 20 cubic meters of air per day, depending on size and level of activity. In most cases, more than one third of this daily volume is breathed during the eight-hour work day. Thus, the volume of air breathed represents a significant multiplier if the air contains even small amounts of toxic agents. All available data also indicate that the more serious diseases, including cancer, arise primarily from inhalation exposures.

Dermal exposures result in the greatest amount of the most common occupational disease, occupational dermatitis. Dermatitis accounts for 30 to 40 per cent of all occupational disease (morbidity), but essentially no deaths (mortality). Thus, while it is a significant problem in terms of numbers of cases, it is not especially serious in terms of disease severity.

Gases, vapors, and particulates (dusts) in the workplace air are subject to inhalation. The term *gas* is applied to any substance that is normally in the gaseous state under ambient conditions of temperature and pressure, whereas a *vapor* is the volatilized portion of a material that is normally in the liquid state under ambient conditions of temperature and pressure. In dealing with inhalation hazards, gases and vapors can be considered the same.

Gases and vapors are at a molecular state of subdivision and are therefore capable of penetration to the deepest reaches of the lung, the alveolar sacs where the primary function of the lung—gas exchange—is accomplished. Therefore, inhaled gases and vapors are very likely to be absorbed.

The ability of a particulate or dust to be inhaled and penetrate the respiratory system is a function of the particle size. Particle size is generally expressed in the units *micron* (μ) or *micrometer* (μm). A micron is one-millionth of a meter, a meter is slightly larger than a yard, and a micrometer is equal to 1/25,400 inch or 40 micro inches.

Large particles are of minimal concern because they are intercepted in uppermost reaches of the respiratory tract. The nasal hairs (cilia) provide an excellent filter mesh, and the air passages afford a tortuous pathway with many sharp turns that cannot be negotiated by large particles in the rapidly flowing air stream, resulting in deposition. The deposition process is facilitated by the nasal mucous which holds onto particles that have deposited by impaction.

Intermediate-sized particles not intercepted in the nasopharyngeal area can flow to the trachea (windpipe) and major bronchi. Deposition is likely there through impaction and sedimentation. A mucous blanket holds deposited particles. Removal of these particles is accomplished by the upward motion induced in the mucous blanket by microscopic cilia in synchronous motion. Particles are returned to the pharyngeal area where they may be expectorated or swallowed.

The particles of greatest concern are in the size range of 0.5 to 3 μm because these are capable of entering the alveoli. A particle depositing in the alveoli may meet one (or more) of several fates. It can be solubilized, rapidly or slowly, in the surface active fluid blanket that coats the lung. Solubilization facilitates absorption, resulting in the soluble material potentially coming into contact with every cell in the body. The particle may simply be deposited. If there is no irritant character to the particle, it may remain there benignly. If the particle has some irritant properties, it may trigger one of the body's primary defense mechanisms, *phagocytosis*. Phagocytosis involves the action of motile cells that scavenge foreign bodies, the action that destroys bacteria or viruses that might otherwise produce infection. This process is also effective against many, but not all, nonviable particles. If phagocytosis is unsuccessful, the irritating particle may trigger the last line of defense, *fibrosis*. Fibrosis is the process whereby the body surrounds an irritating particle with tissue in order to isolate the particle from the lung itself.

The lung is a complex membrane with one primary function, gas exchange. Gas exchange depends on surface area. Fortunately, the normal lung capacity is very much in excess of what is required for adequate oxygenation of blood. Consequently, a great deal of surface area can be obscured by processes such as particle deposition or fibrosis without adverse health effects. Virtually every functioning human being beyond infancy has some degree of particle deposition or fibrosis without significant impact. However, there is a limit to which this can occur, and once that limit is exceeded, too little lung surface area remains for gas exchange and a pulmonary deficit begins. Pulmonary diseases associated with the effects of particle deposition are known as *pneumoconiotic diseases*.

Interestingly, the smallest particles, those less than 0.1 micron in diameter, are of little concern. They are retained in suspension in inspired air through turbulence and Brownian movement and are therefore not likely to deposit. Instead, these very fine particles tend to be exhaled and thereby produce no potential exposures. Particle deposition is pictorially summarized in Figure 1-2 on following page.

§1.10 —Chemical Agents: Effects

There are obviously far too many known and suspected toxic chemicals for a discussion of the effects of each. Rather, the kinds of effects identified as consequences of overexposures to chemicals are described here briefly.

Many chemical overexposures are known to produce *respiratory distress*. Effects include choking, coughing, difficulty in breathing, irritation of the respiratory mucosa, and even death. Some irritating gases and particulates are recognized as being capable of exacerbating bronchitis or asthma, but the role

PARTICULATE DEPOSITION

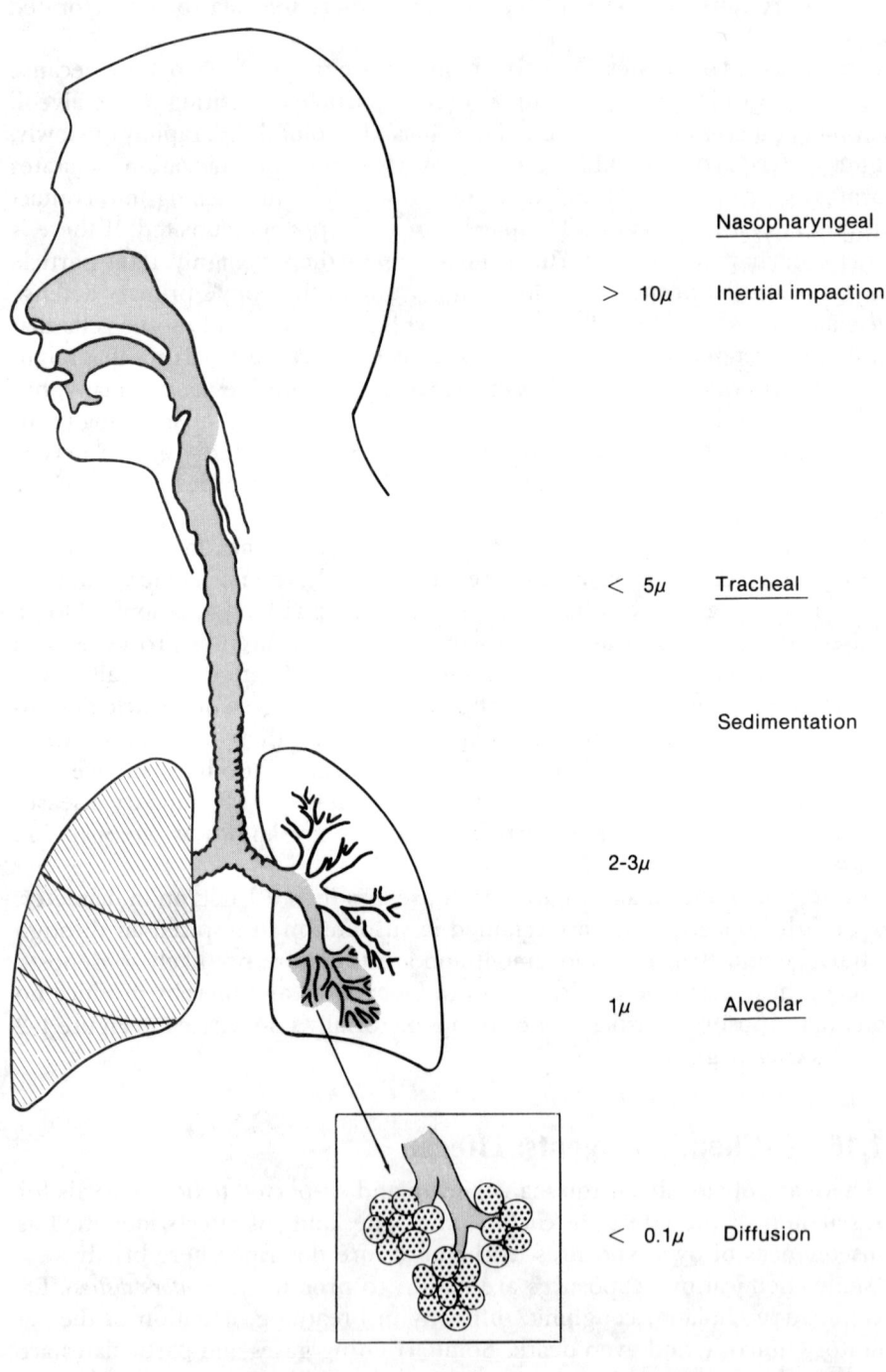

Nasopharyngeal

> 10μ   Inertial impaction

< 5μ   Tracheal

Sedimentation

2-3μ

1μ   Alveolar

< 0.1μ   Diffusion

of these agents in causing these diseases is less clear. While there is little evidence of the causation of asthma by chemical agents, there is a condition known as chemical bronchitis which can be shown to have a chemical exposure etiology.

The majority of forms of respiratory distress produced by chemicals are relatively mild and transient in nature. The symptoms disappear upon the termination of exposure or shortly thereafter; all effects are reversible. However, such is not always the case. Exposure to a toxic agent such as hydrogen sulfide (H_2S) can produce death because this gas at a sufficient concentration will paralyze the respiratory control mechanism. A single exposure to a finely divided fume of cadmium metal or oxide can produce death. Chronic exposures to lower levels have been documented to result in permanent, disabling respiratory disease similar to emphysema.

Dermatitis is the most common occupational disease. Many chemicals, especially in the organic category, have high solvency for fats and oils and can thereby remove these substances which are important to the preservation of the integrity and performance of the skin as a protective barrier. Removal of fats and oils irritate the skin. The skin can also be broken, enabling the entry of microbiological pathogens that can establish infections as secondary problems. The irritation to the skin can also trigger scratching to the degree that can produce breaks in the skin. Some agents are also sensitizers, indicating that repeated exposures will elicit ever more serious responses.

The actions noted in the previous paragraph represent effects of chemicals on the skin. However, there are also chemicals which are capable of passing through the skin and thereby entering the circulation. In such cases, the chemical may be expected to come into contact with all body organs and thereby possibly produce intoxications. In some cases, absorption involves some chemical alteration of the agent.

Narcosis refers to the inducement of sleep. Narcosis can be brought to several levels or depths. Normally this is a transient effect. However, serious secondary problems can ensue. Narcosis can result in falls from heights, contact with moving machinery, contact with high voltages, and the like, any of which could result in death. Another serious problem can occur in confined spaces. These spaces may develop concentrations of narcotic gases or vapors at breathing heights, inducing sleep. These gases or vapors may have densities greater than air, resulting in higher concentrations at floor levels. Concentrations may be high enough to dilute oxygen levels to concentrations below that required to sustain life. Breathing air containing less than 16 per cent oxygen is viewed as presenting a potential hazard to life, even without the presence of toxic agents. If a person is narcotized and then falls to floor level where there may be inadequate oxygen present, death may result from *anoxia.*

Gastroenteritis is generally associated with microbiological agents and is commonly referred to as *food poisoning.* This condition results in nausea, vomiting, and diarrhea. Some chemical agents, notably cadmium and copper, are known to produce a gastroenteritis superficially similar to biologically produced upset. A chemical gastroenteritis generally has a shorter time of onset than one of microbiological etiology. Chemical agents can act within 30 minutes of ingestion, whereas at least six hours is required for enough microorganisms to be present and producing toxin.

The ability of chemical overexposures to produce *neurologic effects* has been recognized for a very long time. Some forms of lead and mercury have been known as neurotoxicants for hundreds of years—over 2,000 years in the case of lead. These materials are capable of reacting with the enzymes involved in neural impulse transmission and exert their toxicities in this fashion.

The recognition of the ability of some chemicals to produce effects manifested at the peripheral nervous system (movement of arms and legs) is much more recent. There is some evidence that hexane, a hydrocarbon previously viewed as quite innocuous, can produce these peripheral nervous system effects. Some ketones are similarly suspect.

Central nervous system (CNS) effects are especially serious. Many are irreversible. CNS effects can progress very slowly, slowly enough to be imperceptible, and enter an irreversible phase before the changes are appreciated. These impacts can produce massive encephalopathies and death, as has been experienced with both lead (Plumbism) and mercury (Minamata Disease).

Some toxicants have *specific organ effects*—that is, they have particular affinities to one or more body organs. Lead tends to seek bone tissue, though lead can be found in every body tissue. Cadmium has special affinities to the bones and kidneys. The amount of cadmium that deposits in the bones is influenced by dietary calcium. Cadmium and calcium are chemically very similar, and where calcium is deficient, cadmium may be incorporated in the bones because of the body's inability to distinguish between the two. Chlorinated hydrocarbons concentrate in the liver, primarily because they are poorly metabolized and therefore survive to encounter the final stages of biochemical processing that occur in the liver (and kidneys).

In some cases, disease will occur in the organs in which the toxicant has concentrated. Accumulation of cadmium in bones results in a much more brittle bone structure than normal. This results in Itai-Itai disease, a condition characterized by bones that are easily deformed and broken under minimal stress. Liver tissue may be extensively damaged by excessive amounts of chlorinated hydrocarbons which enter the circulation through either ingestion or the more common pathway of inhalation.

The nature of *oncogenesis,* encompassing carcinogenesis and tumorigenesis, is defined in §1.02. A range of chemicals has been associated with the induction of these disease processes. Contact with polynuclear aromatic hydrocarbons is associated with increased risk of developing lung or skin cancer. Excessive exposure to vinyl chloride has been shown to produce a relatively uncommon malignancy, liver angiosarcoma. Bladder cancer has been shown epidemiologically to be associated with excessive exposures to aromatic amines. Benzene overexposures appear to be associated with some forms of leukemia. Excessive inhalation of asbestos fibers is associated with lung cancer and mesothelioma.

There are approximately 500 different forms of cancer, considering both cell types and affected organs. Thus, determining causes and effects is not a simple process. It is unlikely that so complex a disease process would have a single cause. The way in which chemical exposures relate to cancer causation is not clearly understood, though at least one theory has been summarized in **§1.02**. A critical question remains just what is meant by the term *overexposure.* It seems unlikely that a single molecule or atom would increase risk significantly— though this is the essence of the current philosophy—because it is virtually certain that everyone had encountered at least one molecule of every carcinogen. The debate over safe levels of exposure for oncogenic chemicals will probably persist for some time into the future, especially as the role of genetics in cancer susceptibility or resistance increases in significance.

The *mutagenic action* (see **§1.02**) of environmental factors has been known for some time. Ultraviolet radiation was demonstrated to be mutagenic in fungi many years ago. Colchicine, a natural product, was found to produce mutations in plants. Many chemicals have been determined to be mutagenic in laboratory assays. However, there is no documented case of mutagenic activity of a chemical in humans, possibly because of the great difficulty in finding such an effect.

The best documented case of a *teratogenic* chemical (see **§1.02**) in humans is presented by the drug Thalidomide. This material was used, very effectively, as a tranquilizer. It was found to interfere with the development of limbs in embryos, but only if the chemical were present in the fetal circulation for a particular period of embryonic development. If the chemical were present outside of this critical time, the teratogenic effect would not be exerted.

High-intensity sound has been found to produce effects such as cleft palates in rodents in laboratory tests. There are some questionable epidemiologic data suggesting that the kinds of sounds experienced in the vicinities of large airports may be associated with congenital anomalies in the offspring of pregnant females living near airports.

One chemical, dibromochloropropane, has been shown to be *spermatotoxic.* Sperm production is inhibited to the extent of resulting in infertility (too few sperm to accomplish fertilization) or sterility (no sperm). To date, no chemical has been found to be toxic to ova (egg cells).

Laboratory tests have shown some chemicals to be *embryotoxic,* resulting in fetal wasteage. If this phenomenon were to exist in humans, this could result in miscarriages. Concern has been expressed over the possible embryotoxic effects of chlorinated hydrocarbons of the types used as surgical anesthetics and any possible consequential impacts on surgeons or surgical nurses who might be pregnant.

At least one point cannot be contested: chemicals can kill. Concentrations or doses required to produce lethality are relatively easy of determination, at least in part because the endpoint is so clear and the onset is so rapid. Chemicals such as hydrogen cyanide (HCN), hydrogen sulfide (H_2S), and nickel carbonyl ($Ni(CO)_4$) are known to be acutely toxic to humans and have been so recognized for a long time. Attention to materials such as TCDD (tetrachlorodibenzodioxin) is more recent, but it is clear that there are many chemicals for which a single overexposure can prove fatal.

The issue over occupational exposures to chemicals can be summarized fairly simply. While there is much honest argument as to what exposure is required to produce disease, there is no doubt but that overexposure to chemicals can produce disease, injury, and death.

§1.11 —Physical Agents

Some of the more common physical agents which can present occupational health hazards include excess heat, excess cold, radiation (including ionizing and nonionizing), excess noise, vibration, excess dust, and electrical shock. Each can produce unique health effects, and each can interact with other hazards in the workplace to produce an otherwise unforeseen adverse health outcome.

Excess heat can produce a variety of disorders ranging from mild discomfort to death. There is a wide range of individual susceptibilities to the effects of heat, so that adverse health effects may at times be seen under conditions normally considered safe according to heat stress tables. Temperature is not the only physical variable determining heat stress levels; humidity and the amount of air movement also play large roles. The higher the humidity and temperature and the less the air movement, the greater the potential problem.

The adverse health effects of excess heat are seen when the body becomes unable to compensate physiologically for increased ambient temperatures. Heat cramps, heat exhaustion, and heat stroke are the three main clinical syndromes seen as a result of exposure to excess heat, but it should be recognized that physiologic effects of heat exposure can be seen in individuals who do *not* develop these syndromes as well. On exposure to increased heat, the heart rate and blood pressure usually increase, exercise tolerance declines, and fatigue occurs much earlier than in a less severe environment. Increased sweating also occurs. Such responses to heat can in turn potentially contribute to the development of a variety of adverse health effects. In susceptible individuals, aggravation or precipitation of a cardiovascular event could occur in response to the increase in blood pressure and heart rate. A greater potential for accidents exists due to the increased likelihood of inattention and slowed reflexes as a result of unaccustomed fatigue. Sweating may lead to unusually slippery control handles or the loss of a firm grip which could in turn contribute to other types of accident or injury. The hot individual is more likely to be irritable and uncomfortable and less likely to consider carefully his or her actions prior to their execution.

Adaptation to excess heat does occur. The first few days of exposure are those in which adverse health effects are most likely to occur, especially if high levels of exertion are required. Within five to seven days, tolerance to heat increases in most individuals, and the physiologic responses seen are much less pronounced.

Burns occur when localized intense heat is applied to the body. Depending on the depth of tissue involvement, burns are medically classified from first degree (only outer layers of skin involved, as in simple sunburn) to third degree (full skin thickness involved with destruction of cutaneous nerves and blood vessels). Severity varies not only with depth of involvement but also with the extent of body area affected.

Some occupations particularly susceptible to the effects of excess heat include workers in forge and foundry operations, ship engine room workers, firefighters, workers in unairconditioned metal frame buildings or enclosures during *heat waves* anywhere or at the beginning of hot weather in southern climates, and outdoor workers during very hot weather—especially if they are exposed against a dark or black background such as a tarred building roof or asphalt pavement.

Excess cold can also produce a variety of disorders, ranging from mild discomfort with shivering to coma and death. As with heat-related disorders, there is a range of individual susceptibilities to cold exposure. Frostbite and chilblains are more localized reactions to excess cold.

Systemically, the body responds to cold in several important ways. Heart rate and blood pressure decrease (after an initial rise in blood pressure). Blood is shunted from the extremities to internal organs. Shivering may occur in the early stages. Decreased sensation of the fingers and toes may lead to increased clumsiness and loss of agility. Subclinical hypothermia can produce slowed reaction times and impaired judgment. Such responses can in turn contribute to other more serious events on the job which may result in accident or injury. Workers at risk include cold storage workers, those who work outside in cold weather (such as farmers, fishermen, and linemen), and those working inside but in unheated environments in cold weather.

Frostbite is the result of localized cold injury to the point of freezing the tissues. Medically, it is classified in a similar way to burns from first degree (superficial outer layer of skin involved) to fourth degree (involving underlying muscle and soft tissues). Areas in which frostbite has previously occurred remain particularly sensitive after recovery to subsequent cold exposure.

Radiation hazards include exposures to the entire electromagnetic spectrum including radiowaves, microwaves, visible light, and ionizing radiation. Sunlight is a major source of nonionizing radiation and can present an occupational hazard to workers working outdoors without protection. In addition to sunburn, skin cancer and malignant melanoma rates are increased in such workers. Fluorescent lighting has recently been suggested as a potential risk factor for malignant melanoma, but this is highly speculative at the present time. Ultraviolet and infrared radiation from a welder's arc can produce an acute sunburn of the cornea known as welder's flash or flashburn (or medically as photokeratitis), and more prolonged unprotected exposure can produce retinal damage and cataracts. Lasers, which are finding increasing applications in industry, pose similar visible light hazards. The concentrated beam created by the laser can produce retinal burns and stimulate cataract formation. Microwave radiation can produce localized or whole body heating and also potentially stimulate cataract formation. Sources of exposure include radar units, heat sealers, diathermy machines, and other microwave generating equipment. Longer wave lengths of the electromagnetic spectrum may also present certain hazards to those exposed, but these have not been well described or documented to date. Debate continues regarding the hazards or lack of hazards associated with living near high-tension power transmission lines and other sources of such nonionizing radiation.

Ionizing radiation is found not only in uranium mines and nuclear power plants, but also in medical centers, smoke detectors, and many, many industries. Radioisotopes are important research tools in both the biological and physical sciences. Radioactive sources are used in industry to perform radiography of key components for quality control or maintenance procedures. They are used, for instance, to log oil wells, to calibrate geiger counters, and to fight cancer. Ionizing radiation, when handled with proper precautions and treated with respect, can be safe and extremely useful. When handled carelessly, just as with many other potent workplace hazards, it can be deadly. The debate over whether low levels of ionizing radiation pose risks for workers so exposed continues with inconclusive results on both sides of the question.

Excess noise is one of the most common physical hazards found in the workplace. The machinery used is often not the only offender. Loudspeaker systems and ventilation systems can also generate noise loud enough to be hazardous to the ear at times. Excess noise will not only produce noise-induced hearing loss (a severe, irreversible disability), it can also create other problems. The body responds to noise with an elevation in blood pressure. Concentration is decreased. Stress is increased. Communication is impaired, with increased potential for misunderstanding instructions. All this can lead to decreased worker effectiveness and increased accidents.

Vibration is another physical hazard present in many workplaces. The sailor, the logger, the construction worker, and the jackhammer operator all share a common exposure to hand-held tools producing localized vibration as well as whole body vibration. The truck driver, the heavy equipment operator, and the farmer all share whole body vibration from the machines they operate. Whole body vibration has been linked to gastrointestinal disorders, sleep disorders, and hemorrhoids, among other disorders; localized vibration has been convincingly linked to vibration white finger disease.

Excess dust, in addition to posing a hazard to machinery and eyes, is another major source of occupational disability through damage to the lungs. Smaller respirable dust particles are inhaled into the lungs with every breath in a dusty environment, and many remain within the lung to produce damage. The type of damage will vary with the amount of dust inhaled and the chemical composition of the dust. Asbestos dust can cause asbestosis, lung cancer, and mesothelioma. Coal dust can cause black lung or coal workers' pneumoconiosis. Silica dust can cause silicosis. Beryllium dust can cause berylliosis. Nuisance dust may contribute to decreased lung function and to the development of chronic bronchitis, although this association is not definitely proven. Allergies to organic materials in dust may also develop and cause acute asthmatic attacks during or up to several hours after exposure.

Smokers, probably partly as a result of a smoking-induced decreased ability to remove foreign particles from the airways, are generally at higher risk in developing dust-related disease than nonsmokers. Nonsmokers may also be affected, however, and excess dust exposures are common in many workplaces today. The farmer, the construction worker, the sandblaster, the miner, the street sweeper, and the factory worker all have the potential for exposure to excess dust if appropriate control measures have not been taken. Respirators can greatly reduce the amount of dust inhaled, but respirators are often extremely uncomfortable, poorly fitted, and difficult to wear for more than short time periods. Engineering controls, where possible, are generally more effective in reducing hazard, but are not always available for feasible. Dust-related diseases remain a major occupational health problem.

Electrical shock is another physical hazard which must be recognized. Cranes are not designed to accommodate direct contact with overhead electrical power lines; backhoes are not protected from encounters with underground power lines. Electricians and other electrical workers are not the only potential casualties from electrical shock hazards. Lock-out and tag-out procedures for electrical equipment have been designed to avoid some of the more common causes of electrical shock accidents, but too often they are ignored. Electrical shock continues to be a cause of on-the-job injury and death in many industries.

Other physical agents presenting occupational hazards include liquids (drownings, slips and falls), lightning, fire, explosion, and hypobaric and hyperbaric pressure. Underillumination and overillumination can also create hazards, as can lack of or too much air movement in the occupational environment. Physical agents can be important factors in the etiology of an accident, injury, or illness and should always be considered in the initial case evaluation.

§1.12 —Mechanical Agents

Occupational injuries from mechanical trauma account for 95 to 98 per cent of workers' compensation costs in the United States. The injuries are described by such familiar terms as lacerations, contusions, amputations, fractures, concussions, penetrating wounds, etc. Transmission of the mechanical force in producing the trauma is generally classified under a system developed by the American National Standards Institute (ANSI) and includes such items as struck by; caught in, under, or between; falls, slips, strains, and sprains; and overexertion.

The human back is especially vulnerable to mechanical trauma when excessive weight is lifted or when lifting is precipitous or improperly done, with resultant injury primarily to muscles and ligaments of the lower back. The associated pain, muscle spasm, and stiffness often make it difficult to diagnose underlying conditions which may be present, such as congenital bony defects in the spine, degenerative disk disease, tumor, etc. Where there is underlying pathology, the trauma may be considered as the precipitating cause rather than the primary cause, but the relative importance of each is frequently debatable.

Repetitive motion trauma is receiving increased recognition as a cause of tendonitis, tenosynovitis, and carpal tunnel syndrome. In many cases the repetitive motion trauma is associated with malposition of the body, especially the hands, wrists, and forearms, in relation to the work being performed.

Vibration, a back-and-forth motion of the body or its parts, is another special example of mechanical trauma. Two forms are described—*whole body vibration* and *segmental vibration*. The effects of whole body vibration, such as that sustained by heavy-equipment operators, are poorly understood, but gastrointestinal disturbances, kidney damage, prostatitis, and bone changes have been reported. Segmental vibration, usually from handheld rotary grinders, chain saws, and pneumatic chippers, is a well-recognized cause of Raynaud's phenomenon, manifested by numbness and whiteness of the fingers, especially in cold weather. There may be further complications such as loss of muscular control, ulcerations of the fingertips, and bony changes.

§1.13   Environmental Contamination

The dangers posed to workers due to occupational hazards are discussed in §§1.08-1.12. In addition, the general public is exposed to dangers from contamination of the environment outside the workplace. These dangers, discussed in §§1.14-1.17, include biological agents, air pollution, water pollution, and hazardous wastes.

§1.14   —Biological Agents

Biological hazards are concerned primarily with the entry of disease-producing infectious agents into the human body. Communicable diseases may be transmitted directly from one person to another by direct contact or discharged aerosols. Sometimes body discharges contaminate foodstuffs or water or infect some other article with which a person has intimate contact. Where the environment may be modified to break the route of transmission from one person to another, such diseases may be prevented.

Animals may be susceptible to or carriers of diseases (zoonoses) which may be transmitted to other animals, and some of these diseases may be transmitted to humans in a manner similar to the transmission of communicable diseases from person to person. Diseases are also transmitted from person to person or from animals to humans by means of other biological agents. In such cases, these agents are *disease vectors*. Among such disease vectors are flies and mosquitoes which may mechanically carry disease-producing microorganisms from human or animal feces to food consumed by humans. Other common disease vectors include fleas, ticks, mites, and cockroaches.

There are other diseases which generally involve close person-to-person contact. Among these are infections of the upper respiratory tract, such as pneumonia, tuberculosis, and common colds. Aerosols composed of droplets discharged upon coughing, sneezing, and breathing convey the organisms from one person to another. This transmission may be aided by the use of common articles, such as drinking glasses, or by the contamination of foods.

Ordinarily, bacteria require moisture, a food medium, and proper temperature and pH to survive any length of time. Drying tends to kill the bacteria.

Communicable diseases can be transmitted by the use of contaminated water for drinking, ablution, and the preparation of food. Water supplies become contaminated by receiving body discharges of humans and animals. Bacteria are normally filtered out of water as it percolates through soils; however, water which follows passageways dissolved in limestone or fissures in rock formations is not filtered. Formations composed entirely of coarse gravels also pass bacteria.

Waterborne illnesses include typhoid and paratyphoid fevers, cholera, bacillary dysentery, amoebic dysentery, and infectious hepatitis. The microorganisms causing these diseases are found in the intestinal and urinary discharges of infected persons. Sometimes persons may be carriers of these organisms—i.e., they discharge the organisms while exhibiting no clinical symptoms of the disease.

Food may be the means for the spread of infectious diseases in several ways. Consumption of the flesh of infected animals, fowl, fish, or shellfish may result in the onset of a disease. Food may simply become contaminated by spraying with aerosols produced by coughing, by handling with hands or equipment contaminated with disease organisms, or by incorporating contaminated water with the food. In some cases, food acts as a medium for the growth of disease organisms, producing large numbers of bacteria or toxins.

Foodborne infections include such diseases as diphtheria and tuberculosis, as well as intestinal diseases like typhoid fever and salmonellosis, dysentery, undulant fever, Q fever, infectious hepatitis, leptospirosis, and botulism. A storage or holding period after contamination of the food during which the bacteria multiply is not required in these cases, although some of the foodborne infections mentioned result from illness in the animal—e.g., the contamination of milk as a result of bovine tuberculosis or undulant fever in cattle.

There are other biological hazards in the environment besides communicable diseases. There are the creatures whose venom is poisonous—e.g., certain snakes, scorpions, black widow spiders, and bees. Various plants, berries, nuts, and roots (e.g., horse chestnuts, toadstools, and castor beans) are poisonous to humans.

Finally, some persons are more seriously affected by communicable diseases than others. This phenomenon may be related to their general state of health, concurrent diseases, physical vitality, natural or acquired immunity, possible inherited factors, diet, environmental conditions, and other factors prevailing at the time of exposure. This is why some persons become carriers but do not show symptoms of the disease; others become ill to varying degrees; and still others die as a result.

§1.15 —Air Pollution

The first references to air pollution can be found in millenia-old writings referring to the "stinking air of Rome." An inkling of what was to come in what is now Los Angeles appears in the mid-sixteenth century journals of Cabrillo.[1] Nonetheless, the modern air pollution problem has undoubtedly been aggravated and changed by virtue of urbanization and industrialization.

It is useful to make a distinction between contamination and pollution. A *contaminant,* be it in air, water, or some other medium, can be defined as a substance that is not a normal or natural constituent of that medium. A contaminant becomes a *pollutant* when it produces some undesired effect, be it esthetic or adverse to health. By these definitions, all pollutants are contaminants, but not all contaminants are pollutants.

Whether the issue is contaminants or pollutants, it obviously involves some degree of degradation from a *pure* state. Thus, the discussion of air pollution must begin with a definition of the composition of pure air. If there is a remaining parcel of pure, dry air left in the world, it would be analyzed as in Table 1-6.

Table 1-6 Composition of Pure, Dry Air

Constituent	Concentration, ppm[1]
Nitrogen, N_2	780,900
Oxygen, O_2	209,400
Argon, A	9,300
Carbon Dioxide, CO_2	315
Neon, Ne	18
Helium, He	5.2
Methane, CH_4	1 - 2
Krypton, Kr	1
Nitrous Oxide, N_2O	0.5
Hydrogen, H_2	0.5
Xenon, Xe	0.08
Nitrogen Dioxide, NO_2	0.02
Ozone, O_3	0.01 -0.04

[1] Parts per million. 10,000 ppm = 1% by volume

The composition presented in Table 1-6 would exist if there were no human activities of any kind. If the tabulation were continued to lower concentrations, the list would include sulfur dioxide from volcanic action and hydrogen sulfide from the anaerobic decomposition of proteins.

Inspection of the table discloses an interesting fact. Several of the natural constituents of air are also air pollutants. For example, methane is the simplest of the hydrocarbons. Hydrocarbons as a class comprised one of the original six *criteria* air pollutants discussed below (though methane itself was excluded).

---

[1] Cabrillo, Journals; see also the poet Horace 65 B.C., who lamented that the shrines of Rome were blackened by smoke.

The source of the natural methane is an aerobic decomposition of protein and evaporation from subterranean hydrocarbon deposits. Nitrogen dioxide (NO_2) is a regulated pollutant as part of the oxides of nitrogen mix. Natural NO_2 comes from photooxidation of the nitrogen oxides formed from the nitrogen and oxygen of the air during electrical discharges—lightning—in the atmosphere. This nitrogen fixation reaction occurs wherever nitrogen and oxygen are subjected to high temperatures and pressures. Ozone is also found in pure air, descending to ground level from the stratospheric ozone layer which is formed from ordinary oxygen by photocatalysis.

Thus there exists the anomolous situation of so-called pure air containing regulated air pollutants. This seeming anomoly can be resolved if it is recognized that air pollution does not imply simply the presence of a particular material but rather a concentration at an undesirable level. With many contaminants or pollutants there is a natural background that must be recognized, along with the fact that problems may ensue when there is a substantial escalation beyond that natural background level. It should follow too that control programs directed toward the total elimination of a given pollutant would be unrealistic if there is a natural background of that material.

Air pollution can produce a number of adverse effects. Visibility impairment was the earliest recognized effect. This may be attributed to airborne particles or to colored gases which interfere with visibility because of reduced light transmission or increased light scattering. Air pollutants can produce material damage because of corrosion, erosion, or deposition of particulate or tarry materials. Agricultural damage has been associated with air pollution through the introduction of acidity or toxic agents, involving both plants and animals. There is clear documentation of the adverse health effects of high levels of air pollution in terms of both morbidity and mortality. Finally, air pollution may be producing climatic changes which have the potential for more far-reaching effects than the foregoing (e.g., Acid Rain).

The Criteria Pollutants

Air pollution research over time resulted in the identification of six pollutants with significance in terms of adverse effects on human health. The federal government undertook research on these pollutants resulting in the issuance of six *criteria documents*, one for each of the pollutants.[2] These pollutants are therefore commonly referred to as the *criteria pollutants.* The criteria documents were intended to review all available literature and catalog the known relationships between exposures and effects. In essence, each criteria document was to result in a dose-response data base (see §1.04) for air pollutants. These data were to be provided to the states, which at that time had the responsibility for the establishment of the air pollution standards—the levels defined in regulations for the control of air pollution. The original criteria pollutants follow.

---

[2] 44 Fed Reg 8202 (Feb 8, 1979). The six air pollutants covered were carbon monoxide, sulfur dioxide, petrochemical oxicants, nitrogen dioxide, and hydrocarbons. See 40 CFR §50.10.

Airborne particulates are responsible for visibility impairment. Some particulates contain toxic components such as lead which could have health implications if inhaled and absorbed. Fine particulates are capable of quite deep penetration of the respiratory system. Particulates frequently have high surface areas with considerable adsorption capability and can thereby adsorb considerable amounts of gaseous material. This adsorption results in a concentration of the gas to greater than ambient air levels and the possibility that the particle will bypass the body's defense mechanisms which might have been effective against the gas. This interaction between particle and gas is known as *potentiation*.

Particulates are emitted by many industrial operations, combustion processes, and activities such as construction and agriculture. In addition, there is a natural background of particulates from windblown soil and urban debris.

Sulfur dioxide (SO_2) and the related compounds sulfur trioxide (SO_3) and sulfuric acid (H_2SO_4) aerosol are known respiratory irritants. Relatively low parts per million level exposures to these agents produce acute effects. The combination of sulfur dioxide and fine particulates is an especially irritating condition. Indeed, all air pollution episodes that have been shown to result in excess human morbidity or mortality have involved the combination of SO_2 and fine particulates. Sulfur dioxide is emitted from many industrial operations including petroleum, chemical, and metallurgical operations. Sulfur dioxide is also produced anywhere sulfur-containing fuels are burned, especially coal.

Carbon monoxide (CO) combines with the blood hemoglobin to produce carboxyhemoglobin (COHb), resulting in a reduced oxygen transportation capability of the blood. Essentially, all individuals have some COHb in the circulation without untoward effect, but an excess is clearly undesirable and potentially dangerous. Persons with cardiovascular or pulmonary impairments are at greater risk than the general population.

Carbon monoxide is emitted by any combustion system operating with a carbonaceous fuel. Automotive equipment, especially gasoline-powered vehicles, are an important source of CO in the urban environment.

At levels encountered in community environments, *hydrocarbons* have no particular health implications. However, hydrocarbons are involved in the complex process leading to the generation of photochemical smog. This process involves hydrocarbons and oxides of nitrogen and catalysis from solar radiation, resulting in the formation of a mixture of chemicals known as *oxidants*. Oxidants are associated with strong eye irritation and other problems typified by the Los Angeles air pollution situation.

Some hydrocarbons have pronounced odors that contribute to the odor problems associated with some industries. Other hydrocarbons, such as ethylene, are highly toxic to plants, resulting in flowering failures. Toxicity to plants is manifested at levels far below that associated with human effects.

Hydrocarbons are emitted from many petroleum production and refining and petrochemical processes. There is also a significant natural background of hydrocarbons from vegetation, especially conifers.

The *oxides of nitrogen* category includes materials such as nitric oxide (NO), nitrogen dioxide (NO_2), which is in equilibrium with nitrogen tetroxide (N_2O_4), and small amounts of nitrogen pentoxide (N_2O_5). Nitrogen dioxide is known to be highly toxic in occupational situations. However, the bulk of evidence indicates that the oxides of nitrogen at the levels found in urban air have no human health impacts. There is a limited amount of data suggesting that low levels of the oxides of nitrogen in highly polluted air may increase susceptibility to infection, though these data are equivocal. Rather, the control of oxides of nitrogen is dictated primarily by the need to restrict the photochemical smog process in which these gases are participants.

Oxides of nitrogen are emitted by all industrial processes involving combustion. The major source of these contaminants is the fixation of the nitrogen in combustion air by high temperatures or pressures.

The standard for *ozone* (O_3) was originally a standard for oxidants. The oxidant standard covered not only ozone but the oxides of nitrogen and a class of chemicals called peroxyacyl nitrates, all of which were generated in the photochemical smog process. Photochemical smog produces an air pollution condition in which eye irritation and damage to vegetation are experienced. Whether ozone pollution is associated with other effects such as pulmonary problems, cardiac problems, or aggravation of asthma remains at issue.

Ozone is not emitted by any industrial activity. Rather, ozone is the product of atmospheric reactions with precursors such as hydrocarbons and oxides of nitrogen.

Subsequent to the issuance of regulations covering the original six criteria pollutants, a regulation covering *lead* was promulgated, based on the known toxicity of lead to the central nervous system. The regulation was the result of special concern for possible effects of low levels of lead on children, interfering with proper neurophysiologic development.

Lead is emitted by lead-based metallurgical operations. A major source of lead is the exhaust of engines using gasolines containing lead antiknock agents. Some airborne lead arises from the weathering of lead-based paints. There is also a natural background of lead attributable to the environmental ubiquity of this element. For most individuals, the overwhelmingly important lead contact is via the diet.

§1.16   —Water Pollution

Any rational discussion of water pollution must be divided into two areas of concern: drinking water and other types of water.

Drinking Water

Few of man's environmental contacts are more critical than drinking water. Consequently, the need to safeguard the quality of *potable* water has been appreciated for a long time. Major outbreaks of waterborne disease have occurred until relatively recent times. Overwhelmingly, these have been associated with microbiological contaminants, but problems attributable to chemical contamination are well documented.

Potable water quality control is accomplished at several levels. The selection of the water source, primarily from a chemical point of view, is the most important determination of water quality. Disinfection is a generally employed technique for most systems for the control of bacterial contamination. As the final element of water quality safeguarding, it is important that contamination from exogenous sources be excluded to the degree possible. Achieving this goal may be relatively simple for a ground water (underground) source but may be much more difficult for surface water sources such as lakes or rivers.

The concentration of toxicants in drinking water has been controlled for many years. The inorganic materials for which there are mandatory standards are arsenic, barium, cadmium, chromium, lead, mercury, nitrate, selenium, silver, and fluoride. Trace quantities of many of these would be found in natural uncontaminated water. However, the objective of these standards is to preclude exogenous contamination such as mercury from chemical operations or nitrate from agricultural use of fertilizers.

More recently, as a result of the wide use of nonbiodegradable organic pesticides which may be toxic to humans, a number of pesticides have been regulated in terms of maximum concentrations in drinking water. Currently, these are endrin, lindane, methoxychlor, toxaphene, 2,4-D, and 2,4,5-T. In most cases, these pesticides have been shown to be carcinogens in animal bioassays; data in humans are either lacking or equivocal.

A more recent concern relates to the presence of the trihalomethanes (THMs) in drinking water. These are single carbon molecules containing three halogen atoms, generally chlorine or bromine. Some of the THMs, such as chloroform (trichloromethane), have been shown to be carcinogenic in animal bioassays at high levels. They appear to be generated by the chlorine treatment of drinking water when the water contains some organic contaminants of particular structures. Some of these organic contaminants may be a consequence of water pollution by industrial or municipal sources, but some clearly are the products of the decomposition of natural vegetation in the water, which generates materials called *humic acids*. Epidemiologic studies of human cancer as it may be related to the consumption of water containing THMs are inconclusive.

In addition to the drinking-water contaminants that have or may have toxic properties, there are other contaminants that would be considered objectionable from an esthetic viewpoint. These include agents that would impart taste, odor, or color to water even if there is no health issue. Commonly encountered materials include traces of hydrogen sulfide that impart a sulfurous taste to water as well as the characteristic odor of rotten eggs, phenols which give a carbolic taste to water, and contaminants such as humic acids or iron salts that result in a yellow-brown or rusty coloration. In the case of phenolic compounds, the problems are rendered potentially greater because, whereas phenolic compounds can be perceived at the parts per million level, chlorinated derivatives which are produced when water is chlorine treated for disinfection can be tasted at the parts per billion concentration level.

Natural Water Systems

Natural water systems, whether saline or fresh, do not consist of pure water, H_2O. Surface waters are in contact with the atmosphere and are thus subject to contamination by whatever may be in the air or precipitate from the atmosphere. Both ground and surface water are in contact with soils, vegetation, and living organisms that contribute chemicals to the water. All of these facts notwithstanding, it is important to control whatever forms of contamination can be controlled to levels that will not interfere with the properties of the water so as to affect adversely the ecosystem dependent upon it.

Waterways are subject to many forms and sources of contamination. Municipal sewage treatment plants discharge effluents to waterways. Many waterways also receive untreated sewage streams. Industrial operations use water for cooling and in chemical and other processes, and this used water may be discharged. Agricultural operations result in the release of fertilizers and pesticides as well as animal excreta to waterways. Vessels may discharge fuels, lubricants, and other wastes. Recreational activities result in some releases. Rainwater that has become contaminated by flowing across fields, industrial plants, or urban areas may reach waterways without any prior treatment. In all, an unpolluted waterway must be considered a rarity.

Water pollution control may be undertaken for a variety of reasons: esthetics, protection of a potable water supply source, safeguarding of recreational amenities, maintenance of the ecosystem, or concern for the introduction of toxic agents into aquatic organisms that might be consumed as food.

Earlier approaches to water pollution regulation recognized different uses for waterways—potable water source, recreation, food source, navigation, and others—and established different quality requirements. A current view is that all waterways should be *fishable and swimmable,* which results in more stringent requirements in many cases.

Types of Waterway Pollutants

The multiplicity of water pollution sources and pollutants originating with these sources means that there are pollutants almost too numerous to describe. However, classes of pollutants and their effects can be summarized briefly.

Oil and grease contaminants produce primarily esthetic degradation in that they may be very unsightly when floating on the water surface. They may also coat shorelines, vegetation, or structures in the water. Oils and greases can also have biological impacts through coating fish gills or water fowl. Water-soluble fractions leached from floating oils and greases can be more toxic than the original material and result in biological effects.

Fine particles tend to become *suspended solids* in water. Though settling will occur eventually through gravity, it can be a slow process. These suspended solids can markedly reduce visibility in water. Should they be colored, a color will be imparted to the water. They can interfere with the respiration of fish and other organisms and can accumulate in filter feeders such as clams and oysters. Should the solids include any toxic agents, this accumulation could render food organisms unsuitable for human consumption. Solids can also stablize any emulsions that might form from floating oils. An excessive amount of suspended solids can reduce the penetration of sunlight into waterways and thus impede photosynthesis of plants, both rooted and floating.

Biochemical oxygen demand (BOD) is an expression of the amount of soluble carbon, usually organic, that is metabolizable by microorganisms in the aquatic system. In essence, it is food for organisms in the lower levels of the food web. The infusion of this metabolizable carbon enables a population explosion of organisms capable of using the particular source. Inasmuch as these organisms require oxygen for metabolism—i.e., they are animals rather than plants—the dissolved oxygen (DO) in the water is consumed at an increasing rate. This DO is also essential to higher organisms such as fish. These higher organisms tend to be more sensitive to reduced oxygen levels than the lower organisms. The reduction in DO levels in a waterway is referred to as oxygen depletion, and oxygen depletion can result in fish kills. The maximum amount of oxygen that can be dissolved in water, or the saturation level, is a function of temperature, with lower temperatures favoring higher DO levels. DO levels greater than about 6 to 10 parts per million (ppm) should be capable of sustaining a fully balanced, healthy ecosystem. When DO levels drop below the 6 ppm level, organisms begin to die selectively, with the most favored organisms usually being most sensitive. Below 2 ppm, only trash fish and benthic (bottom sediment) organisms can thrive, and so DO levels under 2 ppm can have major impacts.

Any biochemical oxygen demand (BOD) infusion resulting in severe oxygen depletion can be extremely harmful. However, BOD infusion without oxygen depletion can be beneficial. If suitable DO levels can be maintained, adding metabolizable carbon will increase the productivity of the waterway: more microorganisms means more plankton, which means more little fish, which leads to more large fish. Thus, the significance of BOD should be evaluated in conjunction with DO rather than by itself.

Many of the modern synthetic organic *pesticides* have a high degree of toxicity toward aquatic organisms. Thus, the appearance of significant levels of such agents in a waterway could produce lethality at several levels of the food web and would therefore be highly undesirable from that standpoint alone. However, many of these pesticides are so insoluble in water that reaching a toxic concentration and producing acute intoxications is not possible. These pesticides may be of concern because of another property manifested by materials such as the organochlorine and carbamate pesticides—the phenomenon of *bioconcentration* or *biomagnification.*

Many of the synthetic pesticides are highly insoluble in water (hydrophobic) and fat-seeking (lipophilic). Thus, when these chemicals are discharged to waterways, they tend to seek lipoid tissues such as those found in plants and animals. These chemicals thereby concentrate in these tissues. As the chemical moves through several levels of the food web from plants to small animals to larger animals, the concentration may increase until it reaches levels significant to an animal high in the food web. Pesticides have thereby affected fish and water fowl, producing phenomena such as reproductive failures because birds produce thin-shelled eggs which cannot be hatched. The phenomenon of bioconcentration in aquatic systems has been documented, and this property of a chemical must be assessed as part of the determination of environmental safety and acceptability.

The category of *metals* covers a large number of materials, many of which are toxic to humans. Metals such as lead, mercury, and cadmium have been linked to environmentally caused diseases. Another metal, chromium, is a suspected human carcinogen. Some metals are subject to biomagnification of the type evidenced by organic pesticides.

There are metals which are not especially toxic to humans, such as aluminum and zinc, which are toxic to fish in the sense of being lethal or producing other adverse impacts such as interference with reproduction. These too must be controlled to assure the integrity of ecosystems.

It has also been demonstrated that materials which enter the environment in a relatively innocuous form may be transformed by environmental components to a noxious form. An example of this is mercury. Elemental mercury, which has been released from chloralkali plants for many years and considered benign in the aquatic environment, has been shown to be transformable by microorganisms in aquatic sediments to the highly toxic methylmercury derivative. Methylmercury compounds are readily concentrated in fish to levels which have proven to be fatal to humans when sufficient amounts of the fish food are consumed.

The conversion of nonliving matter to living material (protoplasm) requires not only carbon, the major energy source, but other elements for the synthesis of protein. The major nutrient elements are nitrogen and phosphorous. Protein synthesis requires adequate amounts of carbon, nitrogen, phosphorous, hydrogen, and oxygen, plus trace elements such as sulfur and a variety of metals.

Obviously, hydrogen and oxygen are abundantly available in aquatic systems, and the trace elements are generally in adequate supply. Carbon may be available in the natural environment or through the infusion of pollutants as expressed by biochemical oxygen demand. Major nutrient elements such as nitrogen or phosphorus must also be available in order for the carbon to be metabolized and converted into protoplasm. Any one of the essential elements could be kinetically limiting—i.e., production of protoplasm will cease when any one of the essential elements is exhausted. Further, if an excess of carbon were available, use of this element would be increased if nitrogen or phosphorus suddenly entered the system as a pollutant. This frequently enables a sudden growth of organisms and is frequently referred to as *eutrophication.* Eutrophication is a natural process which is usually quite slow in unpolluted water systems. Euthrophication can become a serious problem if it becomes a very rapid process stimulated by the introduction of nutrient elements.

Inorganic material other than metals can be serious pollutants, especially if discharged to nonsaline (fresh) water systems. This is a consequence of the fact that most living forms are adapted to either salt or fresh water systems, and many have tolerance to brackish waters. The addition of large amounts of salts to fresh systems could have disasterous results, producing major fish kills. Conversely, a reduction in the salinity of saline systems can also be disastrous. Many kills of oysters occur because of sudden reductions of water salinity around oyster reefs produced by heavy flows of rainwater runoff.

Some inorganic materials have toxic actions. A good example of a toxic ion is fluoride. Other salts have different effects. Sulfides are capable of rapid oxidation in water, resulting in an oxygen depletion phenomenon similar to that produced by BOD, but without the intervention of living organisms. Sulfides are described as producing immediate oxygen demand (IOD) in aquatic systems.

Many living forms are highly temperature sensitive. This is especially true in cold water aquatic systems. *Excessive temperatures* (heat) can produce lethality or lesser effects such as reduced feeding rates, respiration, growth, and reproduction.

Many industrial processes result in liquid effluents at high temperatures. Cold water systems receiving such effluents could be adversely affected if the effluent produced a significant temperature rise in the ambient water. Warm water systems would also be sensitive to cold water discharges, but there are no significant processes producing cold water effluents, so this is not an issue in any practical sense.

The *acid-alkaline balance* of a water system is generally expressed by the pH scale. In the pH scale, pure water is neutral at pH 7. Any solution at a pH greater than 7 would be defined as alkaline or basic, and any solution at a pH lower than 7 would be described as acidic.

Most living forms, and especially those found in aquatic systems, are best adapted to conditions near neutrality. Any major departure from this produces severe stresses on the system and may result in lethality. Aquatic systems appear to thrive in the pH range of about 6 to 9. Consequently, it is important to control the release of acids and bases to maintain the pH in this range. Most natural water systems have considerable amounts of dissolved salts to neutralize acids and/or bases, a property known as *buffering*. Buffering provides a level of tolerance to acid-base changes that would be vastly more abrupt if it did not exist.

§1.17 —Hazardous Wastes

The environmental and health effects of hazardous materials improperly disposed of has been a matter of much contention in recent years. Terms such as *Love Canal, PCBs,* and *dioxin* have become household words, even though the critical issues of the true effects of these agents are anything but resolved. It is evident that any of these is capable of a significant emotional impact, but the physiologic effects of the chemicals on humans is far less clear.

These facts notwithstanding, it is true that chemicals disposed of improperly must be considered as having at least the potential of producing adverse effects. Again it becomes necessary to consider the nature and extent of exposure. As with so many chemicals, the dose-response curve (see §1.04) is undefined.

Intuitively, three potential problem areas can be assumed:

1. Release of chemicals to the air
2. Intrusion of chemicals into water, both surface and ground, through overflows or leaching
3. Occupational exposures by persons handling the waste materials

The problems of assessing these possible hazards is enormously compounded by the fact that many waste materials are poorly defined chemically. Thus, the nature of the exposure may be difficult, if not impossible, to define. Further, the problem of assessing the toxicologic significance of simultaneous exposure to many chemicals remains one of several important poorly answered questions.

Emissions to the air from the operation of waste disposal sites can originate from several practices:

1. Chemicals released when cargos of waste are received and transferred for further treatment or handling within the waste disposal site if these operations are not conducted in an enclosed space
2. Chemicals released when wastes are treated with other chemicals in processes such as thickening
3. Chemicals released through volatilization or wind action where chemicals are stored in open pits without surface covering
4. Chemicals released when wastes are mingled, where the chemical released may be a reaction product—i.e., different from any of the chemicals actually received

In all cases, chemicals may be released in the form of vapors or as aerosols (small droplets or particles). The extent to which a chemical is released to the atmosphere is a function of many factors, the most important of which are conditions of disposal, conditions of handling, ambient temperature, wind conditions, and physical properties of the chemical in question.

Air emissions from waste disposal facilities may be an episodic problem. For example, experience with odor problems indicates that these are episodic rather than continuous phenomena. This is consistent with the nature of waste disposal site operations due to the intermittent delivery of varied cargos. Along with the episodic nature of any air release, it is recognized that the material released at a given episode may be quite different from the material released at any other time. This complicates sampling and analytical problems.

Water, both ground and surface, is certainly subject to contamination in consequence of the operation of waste disposal sites. This is true whether the wastes being handled are solid or liquid.

Surface water is substantially more vulnerable to contamination than is ground water. Contamination of surface water can result from spills or over-flows from disposal pits which receive heavy amounts of rain, flooding, etc. This kind of gross pollution is generally obvious and avoidable.

Ground water and surface water are also subject to less obvious forms of contamination. If chemicals are being disposed of in porous structures, slow passage of a chemical from the disposal point to water can occur. This can occur through the flow of the chemical itself. It can also occur if chemicals can be leached from the disposal point by rain, flooding, etc.

Movement of chemicals through soil is generally rather slow. The extent to which this problem will be experienced depends on a number of factors, important ones of which are porosity of the soil structure, chemical viscosity, solubility of chemical in water, temperature, rainfall rates, and chromatographic properties of the soil.

It is obviously exceedingly difficult to know every aspect of subsurface geology. Consequently, the movement of liquids in the subsurface zone cannot always be predicted with certainty. Problems involve discontinuities in soil composition, unforeseen channels that greatly influence the rate and direction of flow, impermeable zones that direct flow, different chromatographic properties of soils that influence the absorption and chelation of metals, etc.

Persons involved in all stages of the handling of hazardous wastes are subject to contact with such wastes, primarily via the inhalation and dermal routes. These exposures are potentially more significant than in the chemical manufacturing industry because waste handlers are likely to be exposed to a greater diversity of materials and likely to be under poorer controls than in the chemical industry. The consequences of such exposures would be expected to be similar to those wherever chemicals are encountered.

The determination that a waste is hazardous may be based on one or more of several properties of the waste. The definition may be based on the chemical nature of the waste where the composition of the waste is well known and where toxicity data have been developed on that chemical. For instance, if a waste were to be ignitable or flammable, it could be considered hazardous in terms of a fire or explosion possibility.

In many cases, wastes are handled in metal containers such as the ubiquitous 55-gallon drum. Should a waste be corrosive to the metal of which the container is constructed, it would be expected to escape the container in time and thereby intrude into the environment. This could be a basis for the hazardous designation.

Many chemicals are reactive with air, generally with the oxygen component or the moisture always present. Should this be the case, a reaction might produce a more toxic derivative or derivatives than the original chemical. In some cases, an objectionable reaction product might be released to the air. This property could be the basis for a hazardous designation.

Some wastes are designated as hazardous because of the presence of radioactive materials, radionuclides. Sources of ionizing radiation above certain minimum levels must always be handled with the utmost caution. Wastes containing materials with biological activity that might be capable of producing infections in humans or animals would be treated as hazardous. Included would be bacteria, viruses, fungi, spores, and similar materials.

Chemicals and mixtures of chemicals might be considered hazardous by virtue of toxicity. Just what measures of toxicity should be employed is at issue. This is a simple matter when dealing with a pure chemical but can be very complex when dealing with mixtures, especially when the mixtures will change in composition with time and in an unpredictable manner. A key issue concerns the introduction of toxic materials into drinking water supplies when such contamination occurs.

It is obvious that there are manifold opportunities for problems with hazardous wastes. Proper disposal is essential. Proper disposal implies that the waste will remain at the point of disposal, with assurance that intrusion into the air or water environments will not occur.

§1.18 Hazard Recognition and Assessment

Dealing with an actual or presumed hazardous situation requires some form of evaluation. Evaluation requires the recognition of the hazard and the assessment of the hazard in terms of both quality and quantity. The techniques for accomplishing this function in occupational situations are discussed in this section.

In all but the simplest of problems, hazard evaluation will probably require a program of analysis and testing. A sampling and monitoring program is undertaken for a variety of reasons: to identify and perform a quantitative analysis of specific contaminants present in the environment; to determine exposure of workers in response to complaints; to correlate disease and injury with exposures; to determine compliance status with respect to various occupational health hazards; and to design and evaluate the effectiveness of engineering controls installed to minimize exposure. The purpose of the sampling dictates to some extent the sampling strategy which should be used.

The magnitude of chemical and physical stresses can be evaluated in various ways. One form of the evaluation is qualitative, using one or more of the human senses, without taking any actual measurements. Another form of evaluation is quantitative, involving the collection and analysis of ambient samples or those that represent actual exposures. This quantitative evaluation is the most desirable and necessary in many cases, particularly when the purpose of the sampling is to determine compliance with standards or to form the basis for designing and evaluating engineering controls.

The first step in evaluating the occupational environment is to become familiar with particular operations,[3] the type of industrial processes, and the type of materials and contaminants encountered. It should also be determined what protective measures are provided, what controls are being used, and how

---

[3] R.D. Soule, Industrial Hygiene Samples and Analysis, in 1 Patty's Industrial Hygiene and Toxicology, 708 (3d rev ed G.D. Clayton ed 1978).

many workers are exposed to the contaminants generated by the specific job activities. The number of chemical and physical agents capable of producing occupational injuries and illnesses is increasing steadily, and new products that require the use of new raw materials or new combinations of substances are continually being introduced. The responsible hygienist must establish and maintain a list of the chemical and physical agents encountered in his or her particular area of jurisdiction.[4] (The functions of the hygienist are discussed in Chapter 19.) Most often information on these agents can be obtained from the descriptive material provided by suppliers.[5] "Once an inventory is obtained, it is necessary to determine the toxicity of chemical substances. Information of this type can be found in several reference texts on toxicology and industrial hygiene."[6]

Clearly, many potentially hazardous operations can be detected visually. Operations that produce large amounts of dust and fumes can be spotted, although they are not necessarily hazardous.[7] But the absence of visible concentrations of dust and fumes is not a guarantee that a nonhazardous atmosphere exists.[8] In addition to sight, the sense of smell can be used to detect the presence of many vapors and gases.[9] An astonishing amount of information can thus be gleaned by the most flexible and generally applicable of assessment techniques—observation—without the need for sophisticated and expensive instrumentation. The more or less formal approach to this is known as the *walk-through survey*, discussed in **§1.19.**

§1.19   —Walk-Through Survey

The walk-through survey will provide useful information only if it is approached and conducted with a considerable degree of planning and thought. Though it is not necessarily a highly formalized process, it involves a number of steps that must be addressed so that a maximum amount of information can be realized from the effort.

The more that is known about the operation being inspected, the more information will be obtained. It is very useful to understand the processes and operations under way. This understanding is aided by information such as process descriptions and flow sheets, which should be reviewed prior to initiating the survey. As part of this phase, the purpose of the survey should be clearly defined. In the process review, it becomes feasible to determine potential exposures sustained by all occupational groups and operations: materials handling, unit operations, maintenance personnel, office personnel, and others.

---

[4] *Id.* 709.

[5] *Id.*

[6] *Id.*

[7] *Id.*

[8] *Id.*

[9] *Id.*

All must be considered. In the course of the operational review, it also becomes possible to plan for any equipment or instruments that might be needed, as well as for any protective devices that might be required to enable entry into hazardous areas.

Many information sources exist beyond those such as process descriptions which would certainly be considered primary sources. Employee interviews generally unearth a wealth of information. Supervisors, long-term employees, and busy employees usually have most of the useful knowledge. In many cases, previous environmental surveys have been conducted, providing useful historical data. Equipment maintenance records serve to highlight problem areas; a piece of equipment requiring frequent servicing is likely to be a troublesome device. Data from medical records or employee complaints frequently disclose existing or potential problems. Inasmuch as almost no chemical operation remains totally unchanged for long, it is important to trace down process changes or alterations to control systems, since these changes could have important implications in terms of exposures.

The survey should be explained to both management and employees to assure a valid study. There are few things as disconcerting to a working group than a number of white-coated strangers descending on the workplace with mysterious devices performing unexplained functions. Explanations generally engender full cooperation, especially if it is indicated that the effort is directed toward worker health.

In conducting the survey, it can be important to distinguish between normal and unusual activities and operations. Although *typical* operations are of greatest concern, unusual circumstances cannot be ignored because these might result in the most significant exposures.

Environmental sampling may be conducted in the course of the survey. Should this be the case, provision must be made for proper handling of the samples to assure that they will not change in the course of the effort and produce invalid data. Should there be major significant findings made in the course of this phase, they should be discussed immediately and not held for the issuance of a formal report, which might take some time.

Many observations can be made without sophisticated instrumentation, leading to very useful information. No instrumentation is needed to detect a very dusty atmosphere. An unnecessarily dusty environment suggests inadequate attention to the matter of worker protection. The absence of warning signs where they are clearly needed in noisy areas, on rotating machinery, and for other obvious potential hazards is further indication of inadequate attention to health and safety.

The general appearance of the plant is a primary indicator. If the facility is poorly laid out, hot when it need not be so, dirty, lacking in good ventilation devices, and worked in by sloppy employees, it is probably a poorly run plant in all respects, including health and safety. If the plant lacks appropriate protective equipment, affords no evidence of requiring good work practices, and lacks control of obvious environmental problems, there is probably not much interest in health and safety.

Although analytical instrumentation may ultimately be required to quantify some of the problems, sight, smell, and taste can provide substantial information and even range-finding data. In this case, it can be very useful to know the odor thresholds of chemicals expected to be encountered, inasmuch as this will define a concentration range. If toxic chemicals are anticipated, investigators must understand the phenomenon of olfactory fatigue, when a chemical may have desensitized the sense of smell but still be present at possibly dangerous levels.

The walk-through survey should suggest potential chemical exposures. In the chemical processing area, these exposures might involve raw materials, additives, catalysts, solvents, byproducts, and finished products. All of these chemical categories must be considered, rather than just raw materials and finished products. Maintenance activities should receive adequate attention. Maintenance workers may have a greater diversity of exposures by virtue of working on every unit as compared with workers who may have exposure only on a single unit. Persons engaged in packaging finished products as well as those receiving and handling input materials should also be treated adequately. Fugitive emissions, involving leaks from pumps and lines, storage tank vents, sampling points, raw material charging, bulk loading, and packaging must be considered because these are so diverse.

Having defined the potential chemical exposures in terms of type of chemical and possible concentration or dose, it becomes necessary to review the known toxicities of these agents based on published data and to relate the findings to standards.

Combining the two types of data obtained in this phase—potential exposures and toxicities—makes it possible to estimate exposure severity. An exposure or potential exposure may be deemed severe because it involves a large number of persons or because the chemical is of high toxicity. This combination results in establishing a priority rating for the conditions that might require remedial action.

If nothing else, the walk-through survey affords an excellent basis for undertaking the next phase of quantification, which might involve workplace or personal monitoring and even medical surveillance. Most often, however, a potential hazard cannot be evaluated without the aid of special instruments. An additional aspect involved in the qualitative evaluation is an inspection of the types of control measures in use in a particular operation. Thus, only by measurement can the hygienist document the actual level of chemical or physical agents associated with a given operation. Thereafter the strategy used for any given air-sampling program depends to a great extent on the purpose of the study.

Sampling, the quantitative evaluation, is normally conducted for industrial health engineering surveillance, testing or control, health research, or epidemiological purposes. Sampling programs must be tailored to the specific purpose in mind. In order to implement a correct sampling strategy, an industrial hygienist must know: where samples should be obtained; which work areas should be sampled; over how long a period samples should be taken; how many samples are needed; and how samples should be obtained. The choice of sampling locations is dictated by the type of information desired.

§1.20   —Workplace (Environmental) Monitoring

Environmental or workplace monitoring covers the analysis of the workplace for chemicals, noise, radiation, and similar potential hazards. It has the major advantage that one or a few instruments can evaluate a large area, making for economy of expenditures for instrumentation and analyses. The disadvantage is that few, if any, workers spend the entirety of a work shift in a single area. Thus, the characteristics of the workplace may not be a good indicator of the exposure of a given worker.

The workplace may be monitored for a variety of agents: sound levels or sound frequency distributions, radiation, temperature, or chemicals. Chemicals may be in the form of dusts, gases, or vapors. With respect to dusts, it may be necessary to determine not only the quantity of airborne dust, but the particle size distribution as well. Particle size distribution is an important indicator of potential hazard because of the influence of this characteristic on the depth of penetration of the respiratory system.

In some cases, especially for frequently encountered potential hazards, there are automated monitors which are more or less specific for the chemical of concern. This is the simplest of monitoring situations. In other cases, it may be necessary to collect a sample which must be subjected to complicated chemical analyses to determine the level of a particular contaminant. These tasks can involve formidable analytical problems because the contaminant of concern is frequently present at very low concentrations and generally mixed with a very large number of other materials. This leads to the need to exercise care with respect to the representativeness of the sample and selection of analytical methodologies which are appropriate in terms of detection limit, specificity, accuracy, and precision.

Monitoring the work area for surface contamination is called *swipe testing*. Usually a specified area is rubbed with a filter or treated material. The material is then analysed to determine the level of contamination. Specific levels of acceptance are usually determined at each workplace based on the personal protection being employed and the toxicity of the contaminant. The swipe test results indicate only a potential for exposure. In most cases it is a measure of the adequacy of the established work practices or engineering controls and not a representation of worker exposure.

§1.21   —Personal Surveillance

The exposure to chemicals sustained by a worker is best revealed by personal monitoring or surveillance rather than workplace monitoring. Personal monitoring is an attempt to measure as accurately as possible the concentration of a material inhaled or dose of radiation or pressure received by a worker. Through personal monitoring, the monitor is with the worker at all times and takes account of worker movements throughout the work period. Monitoring may be for particulate dusts, gases and vapors, noise, or radiation. Devices for measuring noise and radiation are highly specific. Where it is necessary to monitor dusts or gases, the device worn by the worker is generally a sampling instrument for collection of a material that must be subjected to further analysis.

A key matter that must be addressed is where the sampling device should be placed on the worker's person. In the case of agents which might be inhaled, the device should be placed as close as possible to the nose and would require placement on a helmet, collar, or other support. At times, compromises must be made between ideal placement and convenience.

In the case of monitoring for airborne materials, it is necessary to control air flow rates through the sampling devices so that the analytical data can be converted to an expression of mass per unit volume. This is generally accomplished by an active monitoring system, caled a *sampling pump,* which is carried on the worker's belt where power is provided by batteries. These pumps must be calibrated, and the batteries maintained at charge in order to assure definition of flow rates.

Sampling for dusts is generally done with a filter device. For special contaminants, a size-selecting mechanism may be incorporated in the filter device to enable sampling for particles or fibers of a predetermined size range. In the case of gases and vapors, sampling may be accomplished in a tube containing some adsorbing medium such as charcoal, silica, or synthetic materials. These adsorbents require extraction, elution, or some other means of removing the adsorbed materials from the medium to permit analyses.

Recently, a series of passive samplers have been introduced for a few chemicals. These are worn like a badge and require no air pump. Hence, they are far less bulky and much more convenient. However, the range of application of these devices is much smaller than with air pump sampling systems.

There are several problems with personal samples which have few methods of resolution. The worker's attitude toward the interpretation of the data may cause him or her to overexpose the sampler greatly or to ensure that the sampler is not exposed to any extent. Regardless of the attentiveness of the surveyor to the worker's activity, the sample may not provide useful information for the exposure periods when no sample is worn. Also, the activity being performed the day the sampler is worn may not be consistent with normal operating conditions. Factors such as delay in analysis, improper storage, and incorrect handling can cause a result to be high or low relative to the true value. Unless it can be documented that a high level was the result of contamination, it must be assumed to be an indication of some excessive exposure. All of these errors are subjective and may not be quantifiable. The only field control of the accuracy of the resulting value is the assurance that the sampler had the ability to sample at the stated rate before and after use. The laboratory is the only quantifiable step in developing the accuracy and precision of the exposure level. The chemist and physicist can measure levels far below the levels of concern with excellent precision and accuracy. Unfortunately, this only represents the accuracy and precision of the analysis and not the overall sampling program.

§1.22 —Medical Surveillance (Biological Monitoring)

As opposed to environmental and personal monitoring (see §§1.20-1.21), the extent to which particular workers have absorbed the contaminant must be determined by a clinical measurement of the individuals. Biological monitoring (frequently and incorrectly called *bioassay*) in industrial hygiene is the clinical analysis of tissue, excreta, or response from a worker for a material or its metabolites or condition. While closely related, it is not to be confused with the measurement of biological indicators in medicine where the health status is being evaluated.

There are three schools of thought for the use of biological monitoring. The first is that the measurement of a material or its metabolite in a sample (urine, blood, breath, etc.) from the worker is the only way to calculate the true average exposure or dose of the worker to a material. The second view is that such measurements are so highly variable between workers and within one worker between samplings that the results are meaningless. The third view is that the worker is not a guinea pig; if a problem is found, it is already too late. Depending on the material to which the worker is exposed and the conditions for exposure, it is possible to agree with all three statements. Base-line or unexposed human data are highly variable because it is not known that the normal or unexposed person was not exposed to some degree in the past. Nevertheless, biological monitoring has its place in industrial hygiene, especially when the data are taken from a group of workers exposed essentially at the same rate to the same materials under relatively stable conditions.

The use of a single biological monitoring data point to evaluate an individual exposure situation is neither valid nor consistent with the basis on which background data have been accumulated. Most biological monitoring data were developed on groups to correlate with a predetermined air exposure level; consequently, individual correlations were not practical. Individual data points are valid and practical when metabolic pathways are well developed or where the data are used to monitor work practices or effectiveness of controls.

Urine, breath, blood, and to a lesser extent hair, fingernails, feces, and other tissue have been used as biological samples to monitor specific metabolites or, indirectly, the effected change in another metabolite or response. Considerable effort is being made by industrial hygiene, toxicology, and pharmacodynamic researchers to develop data that will mathematically relate biological monitoring results to the degree of a specific change in the worker's health. In a broad sense, pulmonary function and audimetric tests are forms of biological monitoring; however, in the strict sense, they are measuring the function of an organ and the consequence of an exposure, not the exposure itself.

Medical surveillance alone is a late and relatively ineffective method of hazard recognition and assessment. In conjunction with other measures mentioned in §§1.19-1.21, however, it can provide information not obtainable from other sources. Medical surveillance can also help document the efficacy of a particular control program or identify areas in need of better controls. For example, the appearance of dermatitis in several workers working on a particular process may be first identified by a medical surveillance program in which the results from not only periodic employee examinations but also acute medical visits are examined for trends or unusual clustering of conditions. Workplace follow-up by an industrial hygienist may then identify a recent process change (such as a change in solvent) likely to be the cause of the dermatitis. Implementation of an additional process change (return to old solvent, use of protective equipment, etc.) designed to correct the dermatitis may then occur. Continued medical surveillance can then confirm that no further cases of dermatitis have occurred since the controls were instituted.

It should be emphasized that when a medical surveillance program finds evidence for an adverse health effect in a worker population, it is usually late in the course of events leading to the effect and represents an admission of failure of controls. For chronic or slow-to-manifest conditions such as noise-induced hearing loss or occupational cancer, the controls are more likely to have failed recently, and medical surveillance may be more timely in providing early warning and targets for improved controls.

The human body is marvelously adaptable—up to a point. Several repeated insults are often necessary to push the body beyond that point and produce identifiable evidence of adverse health effects likely to be recognized in a medical surveillance program. Medical surveillance works best when the disease or adverse effect is a known one which is readily recognized or easily and accurately measured. It is far less reliable in situations where an adverse effect has been unrecognized or unsuspected, or where it is not known whether an adverse effect exists or not. In such situations medical examination may detect acute, severe, or unusual effects, but the detection of subtle or more chronic effects is far less likely. Untargeted medical examinations are just as likely to miss an important exposure effect as to find it—just as in other areas of endeavor, one is far more likely to find what one is looking for than what one isn't. This means that when an adverse health effect from a particular exposure is suspected, yet is previously undocumented, the absence of previous documentation does not necessarily refute the suspicion. Medical surveillance programs can usually provide good documentation regarding the presence or absence of known adverse health effects from particular exposures but are likely to be highly unreliable regarding the presence or absence of previously unrecognized adverse health effects from the same exposures. One exception to this general rule arises when the newly suspected adverse health effect is particularly unusual or noteworthy (i.e., impossible to miss on examination), or when by chance the appropriate laboratory test or examination happened to have been routinely performed and the results recorded for an unrelated reason.

An occupational health program in which there is close cooperation and communication among examining physicians, industrial hygienists, and safety personnel, and in which all have first-hand knowledge of the worksite and working conditions, can greatly improve the effectiveness of any medical surveillance. In such a situation, medical surveillance is likely to be carefully targeted and more reliable than where such teamwork is not present. An unusual or previously unrecognized health effect has a far greater chance of being recognized for what it is when the examiner understands the workplace and working conditions. This is particularly true when the exposure in question represents a unique situation because of the particular job being performed and the manner in which it is performed.

Medical surveillance provides but one piece of the information required to recognize and assess an occupational hazard. It can be a useful tool and an excellent adjunct but cannot be relied upon to provide definitive hazard assessment alone.

§1.23 Occupational Standards

Occupational safety and health standards usually have the connotation of being enforceable, but it should be noted that there were voluntary standard-setting organizations, prior to the advent of the Occupational Safety and Health Administration (OSHA), which developed professional and consensus standards intended as guidelines or voluntary codes of practice. Among the organizations developing professional or consensus voluntary standards were the American Standards Association (ASA), now the American National Standards Institute (ANSI), the National Fire Protection Association (NFPA), the American Society for Testing and Materials (ASTM), the American Society of Mechanical Engineers (ASME), and the American Conference of Governmental Industrial Hygienists (ACGIH).

The Occupational Safety and Health Act of 1970[10] authorized the adoption of national consensus standards and established federal standards as start-up standards under OSHA, and accordingly, the Department of Labor adopted a large number of consensus-type safety standards of ANSI and NFPA as well as some 360 of the ACGIH threshold limit values (TLVs) for chemical substances, which had previously been promulgated under the Walsh-Healy Public Contracts Act.[11] Also adopted in the start-up standards were 22 health standards from ANSI. Although the ACGIH TLVs represented 1968 values, the vast majority remain as current OSHA General Industry Standards.[12] Meanwhile, ACGIH has continued its annual review and revision of the TLVs,[13] and today they are generally regarded as the most up-to-date permissible exposure limits available in the United States, as well as in all of the

---

[10] 29 USC §651 *et seq.*

[11] 41 USC §§35-45.

[12] 29 CFR §1910.1000.

[13] American Conference of Governmental & Industrial Hygienists, Documentation of Threshold Limit Values for Chemical Substances and Physical Agents in the Workroom Environment with Intended Changes (1983).

industrialized countries of the free world. It should be noted that ACGIH recommends that the time-weighted average TLVs "should be used as guides in the control of health hazards and should not be used as fine lines between safe and dangerous concentrations." The TLVs presume a relatively healthy work force to begin with and represent an "average concentration for a normal 8 or 10-hour workday and a 40-hour workweek, to which nearly all workers may be repeatedly exposed, day after day, without adverse effect." ACGIH has adopted short-term exposure limits (TLV-STEL) for emergency conditions and ceiling limits (TLV-C) for fast-acting and/or highly irritating substances.

Adoption of new health standards by OSHA has been a slow process, complicated by litigation and court actions. Since the start-up standards, some 20 health standards have been promulgated by OSHA, mostly for carcinogens. Several new or revised OSHA health standards can be expected each year.

In addition to permissible exposure limits for airborne contaminants to the workplace, a number of biological TLVs (Bio-TLVs) are available from AC-GIH, which afford additional protection. The Bio-TLVs were developed in recognition of the facts that some substances have other routes of entry such as ingestion or percutaneous absorption, that accidents may occur, that continuous environmental monitoring is seldom feasible, and that there may be individual susceptibility.

§1.24   Air Quality Standards

The quality of the ambient air is the ultimate measure of the success of air pollution regulation and abatement programs. *Ambient air quality* defines the nature of the air being breathed and is what really matters in influencing human health. Nonetheless, regulations based on ambient air quality standards present difficulties from the legal and regulatory standpoints; who is to be blamed if there is a degradation in air quality below a predetermined level?

Early air pollution control programs vested authority for the establishment of air quality standards in the states. The federal government was responsible for the definition of criteria—the relationships between air composition and health effects—which formed the bases for the standards. Later, as the legal and regulatory structure evolved, the federal government also established the ambient air quality standards. In that process, the concept of having different standards for different land uses or different areas of the country also essentially ended.

Ambient air quality standards have been established at two levels. *Primary standards* are based on human health considerations. *Secondary standards* are designed to protect the public welfare, which encompasses agricultural, esthetic, and similar considerations. In some cases, the same level applies to both standards. An important element in the standards is the averaging time, which varies from hours to to a year—a consequence of the fact that the concentration of a pollutant required to produce an acute effect may be very different from that required to induce a chronic effect.

Primary ambient air quality standards are designed for the maximum level of protection in that they are designed to be *no-effect* concentrations protecting even susceptible populations, such as the elderly and persons with health impairments, for a lifetime of exposure. In this sense, ambient air quality standards differ importantly in philosophy from occupational standards. The establishment of ambient air quality standards specifically excludes economic factors from the process.

In the Clean Air Act amendments of 1977,[14] the concept of prevention of significant deterioration (PSD)[15] was introduced. This provision specified increments (increases) for all criteria pollutants. PSD increments represent the maximum increases that would be permitted in ambient air pollution levels over the existing levels in a given area. These increments are not related to health or other criteria but rather were initially intended to prevent the deterioration in air quality in clean areas of the country.

The original six criteria pollutants (see §1.15) for which ambient air quality standards were issued were particulates, sulfur dioxide, carbon monoxide, hydrocarbons, oxides of nitrogen, and oxidants. The standard for oxidants was later changed and the standard for hydrocarbons eliminated. A standard for airborne lead was issued after the original six criteria pollutants. Standards are promulgated for hazardous chemicals as a need is determined.

Although ambient air quality is the factor of primary concern in air pollution control, it is a difficult approach administratively. A more functional approach is the regulation of emissions. This has resulted in the issuance of *source emission standards.*[16]

Emissions sources may be of the *point* or *multiple* variety. A point source is a more or less single point at which an emission can be identified, such as the stack of an industrial process unit. A multiple source is more complex, such as a parking garage, where the emissions sources are a multiplicity of vehicles. Fugitive emissions from pumps, valves, tanks, etc. in an industrial complex are a special case of multiple sources.

Source emissions standards are technology-based. They consider what can actually be accomplished, with attention to economic elements. The history of emissions standards has been one of increasing strictness as technology improves. The maximum strictness has been exerted in new construction projects where the best technology can be applied at minimum cost when it is incorporated in the original design. These are known as *new source performance standards* (NSPS).[17] They may be based on factors such as amount of raw material used or product produced or energy input. Terms found in these regulations include *best available control technology* (BACT) and *best practical control technology* (BPCT), the latter giving somewhat more weight to economic factors.

A special case of emission standards is covered by the National Emission Standards for Hazardous Air Pollutants (NESHAP). NESHAPs cover any non-

---

[14] 42 USC §7401 *et seq.*

[15] *Id* §§7470-7491.

[16] *Id* §§7521-7524.

[17] *Id* §7411.

criteria air pollutants that may produce serious health impacts. At present, NESHAP standards cover four substances: asbestos, beryllium, mercury, and vinyl chloride.

The administrator of the Environmental Protection Agency has been given wide latitude to add to this list. Other materials under consideration include arsenic, cadmium, chromium, nickel, PCBs, polynuclear aromatic hydrocarbons, and vanadium.

A relatively recent innovation is the *bubble* concept, which treats an industrial complex as a single source of emissions. By this approach, a unit within that complex could be permitted to increase emissions as long as another unit reduces emissions by an equivalent amount, resulting in the same (or less) net emission. The application of the bubble concept could result in air pollution control at lower costs.

§1.25   Water Quality Standards

The control of water pollution has been easier to accomplish than air pollution because the points of pollution are more easily identifiable. Consequently, water pollution control began earlier than management of the air resource.[18]

In the early phases of water management, waterways were classified into various use categories. Inasmuch as this was a local rather than a national program, the categories frequently varied. This approach made good sense both technically and economically, since it was obvious that a potable water source and a river used entirely for navigation did not demand the same quality standards. More recently, the tendency has been to diminish the distinctions, and to control waterways to a higher quality level defined as *fishable and swimmable.*

Ambient water quality is really the factor of concern, and, as with ambient air quality, there are serious problems of regulation and administration. Thus, there is a body of effluent regulation which is intended to guarantee the desired level of ambient water quality.

Ambient water quality must be controlled to certain levels of pH, suspended solids, toxic constituents, and temperature to assure the health of the aquatic ecosystem. Esthetic considerations result in other controls such as floating oil and debris. As noted in **§1.16,** control of toxic agents such as pesticides and metals must consider the bioconcentration aspect as well as the absolute level of toxicant in the water phase.

Effluent control is the effective and obvious approach to water pollution control. Effluent standards cover both the quality and quantity of discharges.[19] Control over the volume is essential to preclude recourse to the oldest approach to pollution abatement: Dilution is the Solution to Pollution.

A given industrial unit or plant generally requires a permit for any water

---

[18] 33 USC §1251 *et seq.*

[19] *Id* §1311.

discharge. The permit defines volume and characteristics for each discharge. Both types of controls often define different levels of contaminants and volume for different averaging times, in order to tolerate fluctuations in operations and upset conditions. Both features of the permit might be tailored to the characteristics of the effluent source and environmental conditions. An integrated permit system must consider the total impact of all pollution sources on the receiving water. Thus, a permit cannot be considered in a vacuum; it must be related to other effluent sources and ambient water quality targets.

The compositional features of the permit are likely to cover factors such as pH, temperature, toxicants, suspended solids, oils and greases, and other characteristics as appropriate. Permits should be related to the pollution source. Indeed, the Environmental Protection Agency (EPA) has issued a series of industry-specific new source performance standards. Again, one finds control levels such as best practicable technology (BPT), best available technology (BAT), and best conventional technology (BCT), representing different relationships between technology and economic factors.

§1.26   Hazardous Waste Standards

Standards governing hazardous wastes currently fall under several governmental organizations. The Environmental Protection Agenty (EPA), the Department of Transportation (DOT), the Occupational Safety and Health Administration (OSHA), and individual states all have hazardous waste regulations which must be followed. The Resource Conservation and Recovery Act (RCRA)[20] also sets hazardous waste handling standards and has resulted in greater responsibilities being placed on the primary manufacturer of a product for its ultimate safe disposal. Standards promulgated pursuant to the authority of the Comprehensive Environmental Response Liability Act (CERLA),[21] also cover the disposal of hazardous wastes into city sewer systems, liquid waste disposal into bodies of water, transportation of hazardous wastes, solid waste disposal of hazardous wastes, incineration, handling of hazardous wastes, and medical monitoring for workers working with hazardous waste.

---

[20] 42 USC §6901 *et seq.*
[21] *Id* §9601 *et seq.*

Occupational and Environmental Exposures

2

Resha M. Putzrath Ph.D.*, Bertram D. Dinman, M.D.**, and Evan E. Campbell†

§2.01 The Occupational Setting

The toxicity of a material and the hygienic standard or threshold limit applying to its use are of considerable interest, but they must not be confused with the hazards of using the material. . . . To plan the preven-

---

* Putzrath & Company; Special Consultant Environ Corporation, Washington, D.C.

** Vice-President Health & Safety, Aluminum Company of America, Pittsburgh, Pennsylvania; formerly President American Academy of Occupational Medicine.

† Corporate Manager of Industrial Hygiene, Diamond Shamrock Corporation, Dallas, Texas; formerly President, American Hygiene Association.

tion of injury or illness from toxic material in industry, it is essential that we have a clear understanding of how these materials enter the body, how they act therein, and how they are eliminated. To understand better these processes, we should understand respiration and circulation and their roles in absorption and elimination. This in turn necessitates comprehension of the gas laws, with an ability to apply them to the solution of gases in liquids and eventually, in the body fluids. We need also to know how different materials act on the body and to understand the different types and degrees of physiological response.[1]

Following this passage, the author of this chapter in *Patty's Industrial Hygiene and Toxicology* went on to cover the topics discussed. This chapter in this book follows up on the chapter in *Patty's* and takes it to its next logical step: the expansion of horizons to consider the particularities of exposures in the occupational and environmental settings.

The corporate health and safety manager has one predominate responsibility: the prevention of physical or mental harm to employees or to potential customers, who use—or misuse—products of the organization. Because such managers usually are technical professionals, they tend to adhere to professional principles of probity, observing the ethical underpinnings of their profession or discipline. Further, their staffs, being similarly composed, behave in a manner that places primacy on their professions' ethical underpinnings, even though such may not be consistent with the short-term fiduciary responsibilities of business managers.

The potentially conflicting points of view are antagonistic only in the abstract. In fact, they are in conflict only among the minority of the corporate community. Just as any community has the usual constellation of saints, ordinary persons, and sinners, so also does the corporate community have a similar distribution. Despite current popular perceptions, the vast majority of corporate officers, managers, and employees find actions that pursue profit at the cost of human lives to be abhorrent. A willingness to market a product which under reasonable conditions of usage could cause harm to either consumer or employee—while not nonexistent—is rare. In those few cases where such products do cause harm, only exceptionally have such untoward consequences arisen out of intent. Rather, there is usually ignorance of such potentially serious consequences. What constitutes adequate pursuit of requisite knowledge of potential hazards in the context of an in-house program is discussed in Chapter 5.

With the recent high visibility and multiplicity of suits against asbestos producers and users, the duty of the manufacturer of any product for use by commerce, industry, or the public is now placed in high relief. The standards of purported performance of a product as well as its safety need to be assayed

---

[1] B. Dinman, *The Mode of Entry and Action of Toxic Materials,* in 1 Patty's Industrial Hygiene and Toxicology 135, ch 6 (3d ed 1978) reprinted by permission of John Wiley & Sons, Inc.

before the product enters channels of commerce. The conditions of use must be anticipated; the possibility for misuse and misadventure must be considered.

In order to meet these responsibilities, corporations require the assistance of technically trained professionals. Thus, to answer the question of potential harm which might arise from a product, the corporation becomes dependent upon a high level of performance of these professionals; it is their corporate responsibility to provide their best opinions of these matters. It is unlikely that such ethically sound professionals will fail to minimize hazards where such exist, or will deny their existence where risk can be found. As professionals, it is the responsibility of these corporate managers to point out the extent and nature of the hazard, the uncertainties and need for further information, how the potential hazard can be minimized or eliminated, and how any residual risk can be communicated to the user or customer. The Material Safety Data Sheet (MSDS) and the warning label represent a minimum, such as the threshold limit values for exposure;[2] the pharmaceutical package insert represents another form of safety warning and information practices. The professional is the source of such corporate informational activities.

When the damage potential or hazard is other than maximal or obvious, the judgmental element inherent in such professional opinions may be disputed by corporate management. It is here that the safety and health professional must define in clear terms the degree and nature of the hazard, the limits and uncertainties of the knowledge, and the seriousness of the possible consequences; to the extent possible these should be assessed in quantitative terms. The balancing of cost and potential profit, while a business determination, cannot and should not be based simply upon the cost elements of such an equation. The human elements as well as corporate credibility need to be considered.

Finally, in the largest context, the corporation has a responsibility to the community as well as to its stockholders. Less than responsible actions ultimately redound against the best interests of both these parties. In a competitive market economy, inadequate product performance eventually becomes apparent; thus, customer rejection of these products results in the loss of markets with the consequent loss to stockholders. The less than egregious cases of corporate negligence may appear to go unpunished more frequently; however, the countervailing force of legal redress tends to militate against even questionable corporate conduct among intelligent managers.

§2.02 —The Property of Materials

The terms materials, compounds, substances, or chemicals as used in this chapter, may be pure chemicals, neat chemicals (as produced chemicals), for-

---

[2] Am Conference of Governmental Indus Hygienists, Threshold Limit Values for Chemical Substances and Physical Agents in the Workplace Environment with Intended Changes for 1983.

mulations of chemicals (usually of a fixed composition which may have some reacted products), mixtures (usually ill-defined compositions), and naturally occurring substances (animal, vegetable, or mineral).

Physical agents may also be toxic. Physical agents can take the form of either ionizing radiation (radiation from a natural or man-made source that produces an alpha, beta, gamma, or x-ray at specific energy levels) and nonionizing radiation (ultraviolet, infrared, etc.). Heat and noise are the results of observations by the body and not agents but a physical response that may cause a physiological change.

Toxic effects of biological agents, primarily of pathogenic organisms, are not a primary consideration of this chapter.

Exposure to materials in the work place can be by contact, inhalation, and ingestion. Specific types of controls and protections are required for each of these and are discussed in Chapter 3. The evaluation of the effectiveness of the controls can be monitored in a variety of ways, depending on the form and properties of the material or physical agent and the source.

Materials in the work place that can cause an exposure of the worker may be solid, liquid, or gas and disbursed in the air or on the worker in similar forms. The physical classifications of materials follow.[3]

Gases are normally those materials that are not condensed to a liquid at 25°C and at atmospheric pressure. It is also usually assumed that these gases obey the physical laws of ideal gases. A contaminant in air as a gas will attemmpt to be evenly distributed throughout the air space rapidly, in contrast to other forms which tend to remain more concentrated or localized at the work station where they are generated.

Vapor is the term sometimes used to designate the gaseous phase of liquids or solids at normal temperatures and pressure. Thus, vapors are also considered to behave as gases when calculations are used to describe their physical behavior in air. Each liquid has its own vapor pressure, which is the property of a liquid to evaporate. Many factors such as surface area, agitation, air turbulence, or air exchange rate at the surface may also affect the evaporation rate.

These two forms of a material in air are normally expressed in terms of the number of parts of the material per million parts of air (ppm). In health, the conditions of 25°C and atmospheric pressure (1 atm, or 760 mm Hg) are often assumed when calculating ppm. One cubic centimeter (1 cm^3) in a cubic meter (1 m^3 or 10^6 cm^3) is one part per million (1 ppm).

Solid materials may be dispensed in air as an aerosol in the form of particulates or fumes. Particulates in air are normally the result of some physical action on the material like grinding, abrading, cutting, or crushing, where fumes are usually the result of combustion or chemical interactions.

When solids are disbursed in air there are two main methods to express their degree of contamination in health matters. The first is amount and the second

---

[3] Portions of **§2.02** have been excerpted from 1 Patty's Industrial Hygiene and Toxicology (3d ed 1978), with consent.

is number—i.e., the weight or mass of solids that may be inhaled or the number of particles that may be inhaled. The mass or weight of a solid disbursed in air is expressed as milligrams per cubic meter of air (mg/m^3) without regard to the particle size or number. Frequently the number, size, or shape of particles in the air is of concern, and this has been expressed in a variety of ways. First, the total number of particles in air may be millions of particles per cubic foot (MPPCF) without reference to particle size. The second way is to describe the particle size distribution by determining the per cent of particles in each of several given, but small, size ranges. From these data the number of particles that may be retained by the lungs can be estimated.

Sampling instruments have been developed to separate the sampled particulates into two factions. When air is drawn through a specially designed particle size separator the particles with an effective diameter of greater than five micrometers ($5\mu m$) of unit density are retained, and those less than $5\mu m$ are captured on a filter. The total amount of the two fractions captured represents the mass as stated above. The amount captured by the filter is described as the amount of respirable mass in air and is also expressed as mg/m^3 or per cent respirable. However, this method does not determine particle shape, a factor that may be critical to determination of toxicity.

Particulate matter can be classified into at least seven forms:[4]

1. **Aerosol**—a dispersion of solid or liquid particles of microscopic size in a gas, e.g., smoke and fog

2. **Dust**—solid particles larger than colloidal and capable of temporary suspension in air or other gases

3. **Fog**—visible aerosols usually formed by condensation

4. **Fumes**—solid particles generated by condensation from the gaseous state, generally after volatilization, often accompanied by a chemical reaction such as oxidation

5. **Mist**—dispersion of liquid particles large enough to be individually visible

6. **Smog**—a combination of smoke and fog

7. **Smoke**—small gasborne particles resulting from incomplete combustion

Liquids and solids disbursed in air are not normally evenly distributed throughout the air space. They tend to fall out of air as the particle mass is large and remain suspended as the mass is smaller. They are in constant motion and can collide to form larger particles, called *agglomerates*. Liquids disbursed in air may evaporate. Liquid and solid particulates in air may absorb or adsorb gases and vapor also present in the air.

When materials in the workplace become classified as contaminants, they may be thereafter classified not only according to their physical state as de-

---

[4] B. Dinman, *The Mode of Entry and Action of Toxic Materials*, in 1 Patty's Industrial Hygiene and Toxicology 136 (3d rev ed G.D. Clayton ed 1978).

scribed above, but also by chemical composition or physiological action. Chemical classifications may vary widely depending on the aspect of the composition to be emphasized. Physiological classification is not entirely satisfactory because, with most materials, the type of physiological action depends on the material's concentration. Although it is often impossible to place materials correctly in a single class, the following have been suggested for occupational exposures:[5]

1. *Irritant materials* are corrosive or vesicant and inflame moist or mucous surfaces

2. *Asphyxiants* are those agents that produce a lack of oxygen and increased carbon dioxide in the blood and tissues

3. *Anesthetics* and *narcotics* have a depressant action on the central nervous system, affecting the blood supply to the brain

4. *Systemic poisons* cause organic injury to the organs, nerves, and hematopoietic systems (There are also several categories of particulate matter which cannot be classified as systemic, but which produce toxic effects)

5. *Sensitizers* are materials that produce or result in an allergic-type reaction in the body

When a contaminant is dispersed in an atmosphere in solid or liquid form as a mist, dust, or fume, its concentration is often expressed on a weight per volume basis. The ppm unit is traditionally used in referring to materials in a gaseous state. Liquids and toxic solids in the air are often expressed as milligrams per cubic meter. Outdoor air contaminants are frequently expressed as grams, milligrams, or micrograms per cubic meter, ounces per thousand cubic feet, pounds per thousand pounds of air, and grains per cubic foot. The ppm (weight to volume) used in water analysis (milligrams per liter) must not be confused with the ppm (volume to volume) unit used in the analysis and expression of atmospheric constituents, although mathematical interconversion between the two units of measure is possible if conditions of measurement are known.

§2.03 —Route and Effect of Materials

All workplaces can expose workers to some material or agent; however, the hazards posed by exposure may be small and may be acceptable by the worker, government, management, and the health professional. The intensity or amount, duration, and resulting health effect of the exposure must also be considered with the route of exposure. The routes of entry in the worker's body may be skin contact with a material or agent, inhalation of a material, or

---

[5] *Id* 137.

ingestion of a material. Good personal hygiene practice, however, usually precludes the ingestion of materials.

Toxic materials in the workplace can be absorbed by means other than inhalation. Many other sources such as contaminated food, tobacco, or beverages can enter the body by ingestion, which can also occur by putting fingers or other contaminated objects into the mouth or licking the lips. Compared with inhalation, however, ingestion generally plays a minor role in the occupational setting in the absorption of most toxic materials into a system.

Although some substances may be absorbed directly through the skin, gaseous and liquid materials may also be absorbed to a limited extent through the skin by way of the air spaces in the hair follicles and the gland cells. Through the sweat gland ducts, any substance may reach the secretory surface of the sweat glands after having passed through the straight and convoluted parts of the ducts. The skin or other organ of a worker may contact a material in liquid, solid, gas, or vapor form or receive some form of energy. The resulting effect on the worker may include:

No effect

Transient sensation

Surface reaction, e.g., burn, corrosion, erythema, vesication

Allergic response

Absorption of the material and some energy forms through the intact skin resulting in:

 Sensitization and upon repeated exposure an allergic reaction

 Localized abnormal changes; ulceration, mutation, or a cancerous lesion

 Metabolised (anabolised and catabolised) products to be: excreted unchanged; complexed; stored and/or excreted with or without health effect; converted to more toxic material; or localized at specific sites where damage may be immediate or delayed

During respiration/inspiration, air is forced (inhaled) into nasal openings or the mouth. The normal functions of respiration are to supply atmospheric oxygen to the blood for distribution to the tissues and to remove carbon dioxide resulting from oxidation within cells. Any gas or vapor in the air which is breathed may pass through the lungs into the blood stream and be distributed throughout the body.

Inhalation of liquids, solids, or gases is one of the most frequent methods of body intake during worker exposure to materials in the workplace. The resulting effects of inhaling a material can be similar to those listed for contact exposure. However, the respiratory mechanism toward aerosols is more complex. While the solubility of a material in an aqueous medium is a factor that must be considered for absorption of compounds into the body insoluable materials may have different but equal or more severe health effects.

§2.04 —Sampling of Materials

Sampling techniques applicable to a substance in a gaseous form, for the most part are similar for particulate contamination of the air as well. There are, however, several aspects of sampling that apply only for particulates because of the wide range in particulate sizes of airborne particles confronting the industrial hygienist in most industrial settings.

"In classifying airborne particulates, the term *aerosol* normally refers to any system of liquid droplets or solid droplets dispersed in a stable aerial suspension. This requires that the particulates remain suspended for significant periods of time."[6] Liquid particulates are sometimes classified into two subgroups, *mists* and *fogs,* depending on particulate size.[7] The larger particles are generally referred to as mists, whereas small particle sizes result in fogs.[8] Solid particulates are usually also divided into categories, the distinction among them being primarily related to particle size.[9] The nature of the airborne particulate dictates to a great extent the manner in which the sampling of the environment is to be accomplished.[10] Concentration of solid particulate matter in air is denoted by weight or the number of particles collected per unit volume of sampled air.[11] The weight of collected material is determined by direct weighing or by appropriate chemical analysis.[12] The number of particles collected is determined by counting particles in a known portion or aliquot of the sample.[13] Particulate shape can be determined by several techniques including direct observation by microscopy.

There are various analytical methods and techniques that have been applied to industrial hygiene samples. The reader is referred to more detailed sources for a better understanding of the analytical requirements of particular substances of interest.[14] Literally dozens of analytical methods are available to the industrial hygienist or analytical chemist for application to specific qualitative and quantitative needs.

Finally, in this respect, it is important to be aware that since the implementation of the Occupational Safety and Health Act,[15] statistical studies for noncompliance are being applied more consistently when environmental data are used to make a decision concerning a worker's exposure to a contaminant.

---

[6] R.D. Soule, *Industrial Hygiene Sampling and Analysis,* in 1 Patty's Industrial Hygiene and Toxicology 750 (3d rev ed G.D. Clayton ed 1978)

[7] *Id.*

[8] *Id.*

[9] *Id.*

[10] *Id* 751.

[11] *Id.*

[12] *Id.*

[13] *Id.*

[14] 1 Patty's Industrial Hygiene and Toxicology chs 4, 17 (3d ed 1978); H.B. Elkins, The Chemistry of Industrial Toxicology (1959).

[15] 29 USC §651 *et seq.*

Statistics are normally oriented towards determining whether compliance or noncompliance exists, with a time-weighted average, ceiling, action, or exclusion standard.[16] Chapter 4 discusses the use of statistics.

§2.05   —Prevention and Response

The optimum point at which corporate response to exposure to hazardous and toxic materials in the workplace should commence is long before the particular product or process exists—i.e., long before hazardous exposure has occurred. In the product research phase analysis should be undertaken of the potentially hazardous nature of the product or its elements or the dangers of the production process, before any decisions on production are made. To the extent that information exists, chemical ingredients, intermediates or products need to be reviewed for toxic potentials at this early developmental stage. Where questions of toxicity persist into the later stages of research and development, more extensive toxicity testing needs to be considered in light of costs, potential profitability, and safety. Since costs for chronic animal tests continually escalate, the expected investment cost must include such test-cost burdens in deciding whether the ultimate returns on production justify the necessary investment in testing. Finally, it needs to be recognized that if such studies are undertaken, even the most adequately executed testing will frequently provide less than unequivocal results. Thus, risk and uncertainty elements even in those best of circumstances will remain to be factored into the cost/benefit determination. Here again the professional has the responsibility for providing the best judgment of hazards.

The range, extent, and nature of toxicity testing procedures are discussed in Chapter 1. It is sufficient to note here that factors such as the range of doses, number of animals and species used, routes of administration, and types of responses studied, proliferate, the nature of research becomes increasingly complex and expensive. Accordingly, whether such investigations are carried out by in-house or outside personnel will be determined by the frequency of occurrence of their need. Thus, chemical producers tend to establish their own in-house capabilities; such resources, however, are not commonly justifiable in other industrial sectors.

Under these circumstances, it becomes incumbent upon corporate health and hazard control managers to define what tests are necessary, how adequate contract laboratories might be, and how well the tests are performed and to participate actively in the translation of results in the context of potential exposures or usages.

The use of the data so generated revolves about their point of application—i.e., within the corporation or within the broad community. Thus, if toxic

---

[16] See A.A. Leidel, Statistical Methods for Determination of Noncompliance with Occupational Health Standards (US DHEW, Publication No 75-159, Cincinnati, Ohio 1975); See also Am Conference of Governmental Indus Hygienists, Documentation of Threshold Values (2d ed 1983).

hazards occur in the course of production, corporate health and industrial hygiene personnel are responsible for setting performance standards for the design of safe work premises, development of appropriate medical/biological and/or environmental surveillance programs, education and instruction concerning hazards and their control or avoidance, and programs for emergency management of mishaps arising from uncontrolled exposures. After establishing such programs, their maintenance or revision as production methods change (which invariably is the case) requires continual diligence; technical and production personnel may tend to disregard or take lightly potential hazards as time passes without incident.

In regard to products or processes utilized outside the corporation, much the same responsibility exists. Here, adequate information of much the same nature must be provided. Recent developments such as material safety data sheets for customers, adequate warning labels, and provision of emergency information resources for the customer or general public have stemmed out of a burgeoning awareness of toxic potentials. (See Chapter 7.) An example of the ultimate degree of involvement by a chemical producer is provided by the contractual constraints that were placed upon users of tetraethyl lead. The producer retained the right of entry at places of customer usage, performed blood lead analyses upon customer employees, and held the right to terminate supply contracts of tetraethyllead where it was inadequately managed with regard to safety and health precautions.

§2.06 —Occupational Toxicology: The Mechanisms of Chemical Intoxication in Industry

Toxic materials are encountered to a variable extent in all industrial sectors. Frequently, only acids or caustics are used; organic or petroleum distillate-based solvents are also commonly used. Beyond these general groups, a highly variegated mix of agents of various chemical families may be encountered.

The hazard (aside from skin, eye, or lung contact with corrosive or irritating agents) inherent to most chemical agents arises from their potential for absorption into the body. Most agents in industry, be they individual elements or their compounds, usually enter the body via inhalation by the lungs. In the case of some organic compounds, these can also pass through the intact skin and thus be absorbed into the body. Entry via the oral ingestion route is not as common a consequence of industrial activity except where contamination of hands and poor personal hygiene occur. For example, the *dusting* of cigarettes in open packages commonly presents a potential for chemical absorption at the workplace. Whichever means of entry occurs, the net result is entry and potential distribution via the blood stream to the various organs of the body.

The site of organ damage may be dependant on the amount of a material absorbed and its specific chemical nature. With regard to the quantitative element, the concept of dose is critical to the understanding of toxicology. The primary determinant of intoxication revolves around the question, "How much of the chemical got into the body and over what period of time?"

Dusts found in the workplace pose potentials for lung damage, depending upon the qualitative or quantitative nature of the dusts as well as the size and shape of the particles. The size and shape of the particles determines how far the particle can penetrate the respiratory system. Particles larger than 5 to 10 microns do not reach the deepest extent of the lungs; they impact largely upon the branchings of the airway conducting tubes where they adsorb the mucus film coating these passages. The cell linings of these passages possess *cilia*, i.e., fine whiplike projections which beat headward and thus propel this mucus film upward as on an escalator. By this process, particulates that are not solubilized by the mucus are carried up and out of the airways for aspiration out of the throat or swallowing. In these cases, damage to the lung may be avoided. However, where such particulates consist of potentially toxic compounds, clearance of the respiratory tract ultimately presents an opportunity for further exposure as these compounds enter the throat and are subsequently swallowed. Phagocytes are cells that engulf some foreign particles which normally pervade the lower respiratory tract, e.g., the lungs. Consider selenium.[17] At low doses, it is a required nutrient. At high doses it is acutely toxic to the nervous system; accumulation of selenium by plants from the soil has caused central nervous system problems in livestock. Other experiments suggest that selenium may help to prevent cancer. Still other results suggest that selenium may cause birth defects. On the basis of which effect should the toxicity (or benefit) of selenium be calculated? Like selenium, most chemicals are toxic at some doses.

The amount of chemical which enters the body via the lungs depends upon how much is dispersed into the air. Thus, if the chemical is heated, more of it may be volatilized and available for lung absorption. Unless the chemical is corrosive, such absorption through the lungs may occur without the subject being aware of it. Processes which generate the chemical in a spray form so that fine mists result also enhance the potential for inhalation. Steps taken to minimize volatilization or to conduct these agents away from the breathing zone (i.e., ventilation) represent typical environmental control procedures.

Regarding the qualitative element in toxicology, the tendency for accumulation in and/or damage of specific organs by specific chemicals has been demonstrated. Thus, the tendency for inorganic lead compounds to depress the formation of red blood cells or affect the central nervous system is well defined. By contrast, although lead accumulates in the liver, the liver is not expected to be the primary site of the major toxic effects. Accordingly, each chemical will produce a specific mix of organ damage and organ sparing which may be dependent on dose or route of exposure; patterns of involvement should follow such patterns to be consistent with a proper diagnosis.

The toxic effect on the body may also arise from the metabolic conversion

---

[17] P.B. Hammond and R.P. Beliles, *Metals*, in Casarett and Doull's Toxicology, (2d ed 1980).

of a material in question. Compounds which are metabolically altered thus will not be found in the body in the same form as the compound may have been encountered in the workplace. Accordingly, knowledge of the metabolic conversions of the compound in question is necessary before analytical investigation of body fluids or substances is undertaken.

The duration of residence of the chemical in the body depends upon a complex of individual factors. One important determinant of the time of bodily residence is the lipid (fat) solubility of the compound. Fat tends to turn over its chemical constituents slowly and tends to hold onto or sequester such chemicals for long periods of time. Although the chemical may be present in fat or fatty parts of an organ for variable periods of time, the presence of such chemicals may or may not be associated with damage. Once more, each chemical is specific in this regard.

After a period of time of residence in the body that may vary from minutes to years, chemicals usually are excreted. If the agent is soluble (or metabolically solubilized) in body fluids, it is largely excreted via the kidneys into the urine. Small amounts may be detected in breast milk, semen, perspiration, or saliva; however, these media are less frequently examined in the occupational setting.

Just as toxicity is determined by dose considerations (see §1.04), the simple presence of chemicals or their metabolites in body tissues does not indicate a toxic effect. Some compounds, e.g., formaldehyde, are normal constituents of the body. Most relevant to diagnosis is the determination that toxic levels of a compound have been exceeded.

The temporal sequence of absorption, metabolism distribution, residence, and excretion must be taken into consideration on a chemical-by-chemical basis. Further, the quantitative elements of atmospheric and body tissues concentration—as well as duration of exposure—may be useful in arriving at a determination of intoxication. An analysis of these qualitative and quantitative considerations leads to the strategy for the assessment of risk of intoxication. Thus, the form and amount present in air as measured by the industrial hygienist represents a significant determinant of risk. The amount of the chemical or its metabolite found in body fluids such as blood or urine, over a defined time period—as determined by the analytical laboratory—may also be critical to the assessment of damage potentials. A knowledge of which organ is at risk also directs attention to tests of that organ's functional status. It should be noted that alterations in function tests represent simply that—i.e., such changes may be caused by other factors and thus such organ function test results are not per se diagnostic of occupational intoxication.

A note of caution is in order regarding the use of laboratory analyses. While organ function tests can be performed at most hospital centers, analyses of bodily tissues for specific toxic chemical elements, compounds, or their metabolites may require use of a specialized laboratory facility skilled in these relatively unusual determinations. Thus, the place of analysis and its experimental history are critical to assessment of such data.

§2.07   Environmental versus Occupational Toxicology

One essential element of difference between environmental and occupational toxicology revolves around the quantitative nature of the chemical exposure. The dose or quantity of chemical encountered is usually much greater in the occupational setting. Since severity of toxicity is dependent on dose, the lower levels of environmental exposure are less likely to cause severe toxic effects. Much of the same application of investigatory techniques and the obtaining of the same measurements of environment and biological tissues are pertinent.

The one element which may enhance susceptibility to damage among a large, general population stems from the fact that such a large population includes the very young, the very old, and the ill. By contrast, the working population consists of relatively fit and healthy individuals. While the particularly susceptible members of the population indeed suffered heavy damage in protracted, severe pollution episodes (e.g., London in 1952 and Donora in 1949),[18] the association of damage to environmental exposures to the general population has also occurred (e.g., minamata). In population exposures other than those resulting in specific and easily recognizable toxic effects, organ effects, efforts have been made to link generalized, multiple, nonspecific conditions to chemical exposures. Allegations which do not clearly relate to the known toxicity of the chemical involved are more difficult to substantiate.

§2.08   The Environmental Setting

In many cases, the effects of exposure to a toxic chemical are easily observed: a patient ingests a medicine and has an adverse reaction, or a worker spills a chemical on his or her skin and suffers a burn or rash. Environmental exposures tend to be more subtle and even may go unnoticed. Effects of such exposure may be considered random events unless appropriate epidemiological studies are performed. Dilute chemicals may cause less severe symptoms whose initial effects, such as fatigue or headaches, may be ignored. Elements within the environment may chemically change the compound; in such cases, symptoms would be unrelated to the original chemical but associated with the altered chemical. Thus, the correlation between exposure and effect may not be direct and may be overlooked. These are but a few of the complex issues that should be considered in every evaluation of potential harm to human health that might result from toxicants in the environment. A basic understanding of environmental toxicology is, therefore, essential for the effective litigation of cases where toxicants have been released into the environment—e.g., hazardous waste leachates, chemical spills, or products of combustion.

In order to discuss problems in environmental toxicology, it is necessary to

---

[18] Ministry of Health, Mortality and Morbidity during the London Fog of December 1952, Reports on Public Health and Related Subjects (1954); Schrenk & Clayton, Air Pollution in Donora, Penna, Public Health Bulletin No 306, GPO Wash, D.C.

define what is meant by the environment. The simplest and most complete definition of the environment is that which is not self, including effects of occupation, nutrition, and lifestyle that are not explicit concerns of this section. This discussion centers on effects of the conventional habitat of humans, excluding such factors as occupation and lifestyle. Occupational exposure is covered in §§2.01-2.06. Aquatic toxicology and ecotoxicology, although important subdisciplines of environmental toxicology, are discussed here tangentially. In keeping with the theme of this volume, the discussion concentrates on more direct effects on human health. Differences in lifestyle, such as smoking, drinking, and fat consumption, have been shown to have a significant influence on susceptibility to disease;[19] however, this complex issue is not a major concern of this chapter.

Even within this limited definition of the environment, the field of environmental toxicology is large.[20] The potential for hazard from each situation varies with the type and amount of the chemical, potential for exposure, and potential population at risk. No document could cover all situations; this chapter raises issues of general concern, develops concepts necessary to understand the complexities of environmental toxicology, and gives some illustrative examples. Even if an exhaustive compendium of environmental toxicology were attempted, it would beg the critical issue: there are few definite answers. Environmental toxicology often deals with low-level exposure of a potentially large population to a chemical which has been in existence for only a few years and whose effect may take decades to manifest itself. In contrast, the toxic effects of the chemicals of interest may have only been examined at high doses in laboratory animals. Thus, assessment of the potential hazard to human

---

[19] Natl Research Council, Diet, Nutrition, and Cancer, Natl Acad Publications, Wash, DC (1982); Doll & Peto, *The Causes of Cancer: Quantitative Estimates of Avoidable Risks of Cancer in the United States Today,* 1981 J Natl Cancer Inst 66, 1193-1308; D.H.K. Lee and P. Kotin, Multiple Factors in the Causation of Environmentally Induced Disease (1972).

[20] The field on environmental toxicology covers a vast area. To attempt to condense it, certain compromises must be made. In order to best serve the purposes of this book, concepts and problems in environmental toxicology will be stressed to provide the reader with the appropriate background to discuss individual cases. Toxicity of specific chemicals, therefore, are not included except as illustrative examples. Several compendia of toxic properties of chemicals are available; among these are the International Agency for Research on Cancer (IARC) Monographs, the National Academy of Sciences series on Medical and Biological Effects of Environmental Pollutants, and the criteria documents on specific chemicals published by various government agencies. Frequently, these and other reviews will be cited as references in place of the primary research articles that would be standard for a similar chapter in a science book. Most lawyers will find these reviews more useful than the primary articles which often do not provide the background for a proper perspective on the field since such knowledge is assumed. Readers of knowledge of biochemistry are encouraged to read the relevant chapters of *Casarett and Doull's Toxicology,* a standard textbook in toxicology. In order to cover most aspects of this field, this chapter must also deal with generalizations. As with all such simplifications, exceptions can be found. Although these are of great interest to toxicologists, their inclusion would tend to confuse novices in this complex field.

health usually involves extrapolation and prediction from observed facts based on previous experience.

§2.09 —Dilute Contamination

When toxicants are released into the environment, the air, water, or soil dilutes the chemicals. Thus, exposures in the environment are often to very dilute chemicals; dilution affects both the toxicity and the fate of the contaminant.

That diluted compounds are less toxic is undisputable. The dose-response curve (see §1.04) for each toxic effect of each toxicant has a positive slope— i.e., toxic effects increase with dose. (See Chapter 4.) However, the toxic effect can change with dose, and low-level continuous exposure may prove insidious. Pollutants in the environment are often measured in small numbers, such as parts per million (ppm), e.g., one part in 1,000,000 or 10^{-6}, parts per billion (ppb), e.g., one part in 1,000,000,000 or 10^{-9}, or even parts per trillion, e.g., one part in 1,000,000,000,000 or 10^{-12}. One part per billion is approximately one second in 35 years; one part per million is one penny in $10,000. Low as they are, however, some chemicals can produce significant toxic effects at these doses. Aflatoxin can cause cancer in animals at one part per billion in their diet.[21] A highly toxic form of dioxin, 2,3,7,8-tetrachlorodibenzo-p-dioxin or 2,3,7,8-TCDD, has been shown to cause serious reproductive problems in rodents which were fed 100 parts per trillion of the chemical in their diet and may cause effects at doses as low as 10 parts per trillion.[22]

The old adage is "Dilution is the Solution to Pollution." This is the basis of waste disposal into rivers, lakes, soil, and air. Since diluted chemicals are less toxic, some problems of pollution are attenuated by dilution. Two assumptions, however, are buried in this adage: that the pollution does not overwhelm the biological system before the compound is rendered less toxic, and that the substance can be degraded by the environment into a less toxic form.

The assumption that the earth can handle dilute compounds depends upon the ability of the earth to replenish itself—i.e., to deal with the waste and decay of the biota it supports. The ability of a body of water or plot of ground to recycle waste, from humans to other species, is directly dependent upon the ability of the plant and animal life found within it to convert that material from a waste into useful nutrients that can support life. Each body of water or patch of land has a finite amount, or burden, of waste it can process into less toxic compounds or sequester in a manner that prevents exposure to living organisms. For example, undiluted wastes can kill the microorganisms which would otherwise feed on the material and, thus, recycle it in the environment. A surplus of nutrients an also present problems by creating a high biochemical

---

[21] Weisberger & Williams, *Chemical Carcinogens,* in Casarett and Doull's Toxicology (2d ed 1980).

[22] M.P. Esposito, T.O. Tiernan & F.E. Dryden, Dioxins, (US EPA Cincinnati, Ohio 1980).

oxygen demand—i.e., the microorganisms using the waste as a nutrient can consume oxygen to the detriment of fish and other aquatic life. If dilution is properly controlled, the environment can handle those pollutants that can be easily degraded. Compounds that are poorly degraded, e.g., some xenobiotics, may not be adequately recycled by dilution. Some of these compounds may be sequestered, e.g., by adsorption to soil. The amount of a chemical that can be adsorbed to soil is also limited, and increasing the amount of chemical applied to a piece of land increases the likelihood of the chemical to desorb or leach the soil.

Since dilution is the direct result of spreading the contamination over a larger area, contamination which originally affects a small area will affect larger areas with the passage of time. For chemicals which are rapidly degraded or metabolized in the environment, the spread of the contamination will be limited by the disappearance of the compound. For more persistent compounds, however, the spread of pollution will continue as the presence of the contamination becomes random with respect to location on the earth.

Unlike direct exposures by medication or in an occupational setting, chemicals that are released into the environment may also be significantly altered, chemically or physically, by interaction with either biological or inanimate sources within the environment before exposure to humans. Any evaluation of the potential for harm to human health must, therefore, account for the potential of the environment to alter the original contamination with time. Forces within the environment may change the contaminant from one compound into another which may be more or less toxic. The change of seasons may affect exposure. Hot weather can increase the volatility of compounds from soils; the rush of rivers in a spring thaw may volatilize chemicals from the water. The environment may act as a sink or a barrier which prevents or severely limits the exposure and thus the potential for harm.

These changes in chemical structure pose several problems in the assessment of a potential hazard. The exposure may be to a mixture of original contaminants as well as degradation products. Compounds to which individuals are exposed may change with time. As the chemicals change, especially if they degrade into normal constituents of the environment, determining the source and nature of the original contamination may become more difficult; thus, sampling, analysis, and prediction of potential for harm is more complex and tenuous than in the occupational setting.

§2.10 —Exposure and Toxicant

As in the law one looks for motive and opportunity, in toxicology one looks for toxicant and exposure. If there is no opportunity for the poison to come in contact with the organism, there is no possible danger to the organism from the poison. The need to demonstrate a potential exposure is vital; however, unlike in the occupational setting, resolving the potential route and amount of exposure in the environmennt is often quite difficult.

When a person is exposed to a toxicant while working or by deliberate ingestion of a drug or other compound, the resulting exposure is comparatively straight forward. Environmental exposures are more difficult to determine. Attempts have been made to model the movement of chemicals through the environment in an effort to understand potential routes of exposure. Interest has also increased in the possibility of monitoring smaller changes in human physiology, e.g., changes in enzyme levels, as a measure of exposure and a potential indicator for exposure.

Environmental exposure must deal with two additional issues. First, toxicants in the environment affect all people, regardless of age, sex, health, or genetic inheritance, some of these groups of people are at higher risk for certain diseases. Second, many compounds occurring naturally in the environment, e.g., mercury, are toxic. For these substances, exposure may be a matter of being in the wrong place at the wrong time.

Epidemiology, the science which has been developed to examine the course of exposures in populations, was developed by study of infectious diseases; the nature of some diseases caused by chemical toxicants in the environment can complicate the design and interpretation of epidemiological studies.[23] Unlike most infectious diseases, the time between exposure and toxic effect may be 10 to 30 years. In this latent period, the exposure responsible for the effect may continue or cease, the victim will be exposed to other chemicals which may enhance or attenuate the course of the disease, and the exposed population may disperse. Epidemiologists can work only with populations and probabilities and not with single individuals. Thus, their results are easiest to obtain and interpret when an exposed population is stable with respect to the time between exposure and onset of disease, as in the case of most infectious diseases. Increased job and residential mobility increases the difficulty for conclusively linking a specific exposure to a given disease. Dilution of toxicants by the environment lowers the exposure and makes detection even more difficult than for higher exposures such as occupational or medicinal.

This is not to imply that all chemical exposures go undetected. Some effects are rapid—e.g., immediate death or birth defects. The effects of these toxicants will be more easily observed. Furthermore, some toxicants produce an effect which is so rare or novel that its appearance in even relatively small numbers gives rise to a high probability of cause and effect relationship. Thus thalidomide, when ingested at the appropriate interval of gestation, produced phocomelia, a foreshortening or absence of an arm or leg.[24] Since this birth defect is normally quite rare, the sudden increase in its prevalance suggested the action of a toxicant with a new or increased exposure. Even in this case, however, not all pregnant women who took thalidomide bore deformed children, for the drug is a teratogen only during a certain time of gestation. If the

---

[23] I.C.T. Nisbet, *Multichemical Contamination: Assessment of Human Exposure*, in Assessment of Multichemical Contamination. (Proceedings of an International Workshop Apr 28-30, 1981 Milan, Italy. Natl Acad Press, Wash, DC 1982).

[24] H.B. Taussig, *A Study of the German Outbreak of Phocomelia. The Thalidomide Syndrome*, JAMA 180, 1106-14 (1962).

deformity had been a more common one, e.g., cleft palate, the side effects of thalidomide might have gone undiscovered for a longer period of time. Similarly, the appearance of a rare form of vaginal cancer in young women was a clue to the effect of diethylstilbestrol (DES) on the developing fetus.[25] It was only after observation of this dramatic disease that the other effects, e.g., effects on developing male fetuses and nonmalignant changes of the vagina, were observed. Vinyl chloride is another example of a chemical which has been implicated as a cause of several cancers, but which was initially brought to light by an observed increase in angiosarcoma of the liver, a rare disease.[26] Even in these cases, much time and effort was required to establish a casual link.

One of the problems associated with latent periods between exposure to the toxic agent and manifestation of the disease is the resultant difficulty in establishing a cause and effect relationship. These difficulties are exemplified by the course of an infectious disease, feline leukemia virus.[27] Like many chemically caused diseases, this virus has a long and variable latent period, i.e., time between exposure and onset of symptoms. Thus, even cats that are exposed at the same time may exhibit symptoms years apart. Pinpointing the time, and therefore, the source of exposure in the environment becomes more difficult. Moreover, like many chemical exposures, not all animals that are exposed contract the disease. Even when located, an environmental exposure might be discounted by its lack of effect on certain animals. Only after the isolation of a virus which could be shown to transmit the disease was the epidemiology of feline leukemia virus understood.

Since an increase in rate of cancer may take decades to manifest itself, other changes in human metabolism or physiology can be monitored to estimate exposure.[28] While monitoring human body tissues and fluids for the presence of a toxicant has been a common practice (e.g., examining hair for the presence of heavy metals or blood for the presence of drugs) the use of physiological changes to monitor exposure to toxicants is in its infancy. Even when changes are observed, much disagreement exists concerning the interpretation of these effects. At the current state of knowledge, such changes cannot be viewed as predictive of future disease. Moreover, some of the short-term effects which can be measured are reversible even if the ultimate damage caused by the exposure is not. Increased enzyme levels may return to normal levels; DNA damage may be repaired; and chemicals may be cleared from the body and, thus, not be detectable in urine or breast milk. The use of these changes as

---

[25] Herbst, Scully, Robboy, Welch & Cole, *Abnormal Development of the Human Genital Tract Following Prenatal Exposure to Diethylstilbestrol,* Origins of Human Cancer, Book A, Cold Springs Harbor Laboratory (1977).

[26] International Agency for Cancer Research, IARC Monographs on the Evaluation of the Carcinogenic Risk of Chemicals to Humans: Some Monomers, Plastics and Synthetic Elasomers, and Acrolein, vol 19 (1979).

[27] Francis & Essex, *Leukemia and Lymphoma: Infrequent Manifestations of Common Viral Infections? A Review,* J Infect Diseases 138, 916-23 (1978).

[28] Meyer, *Liver Dysfunction in Residents Exposed to Leachate from a Toxic Waste Dump,* 48 Envtl Health Persp 9-13 (1983).

monitors for human exposure is gaining increased interest but remains controversial, since the connection between the observed changes and chronic disease has not been well established. Since these effects may be transient and may cease in a finite time after exposure is terminated, it may be necessary to sample the population quickly, before or shortly after the exposure is terminated, by containing the toxicant or by moving the population.

Another concern for environmental contaminants is the demographics of the exposed population.[29] Most occupational exposures are to healthy adults who are generally more resistant to toxic effects. Exposures in the environment also affect sick and/or elderly adults who may have medical problems which make the total effect more hazardous. Smog, for example, is a greater health hazard to people with preexisting pulmonary disease.

Another major concern of environmental exposure is exposure to children, infants, and developing fetuses in utero. The young of animals may differ from adults in the level of some metabolic enzymes.[30] Depending on the mode of action of a toxicant, this difference might increase or decrease the young animal's sensitivity to the chemical. Moreover, children are still growing and developing; toxic effects may be more severe than for an adult. Ingestion of lead by children and exposure to mercury in utero appears to have a significant and irreversible effect on developing nervous systems.[31] Exposures of adults to the same compounds causes neurological damage, but the damage usually is less severe for a given exposure.

Most development occurs between conception and birth. The period of development for the organ systems, called organogenesis, seems especially sensitive to outside influences which may retard or reprogram development.[32] For example, in order to avoid cleft palate, several events must occur in synchrony.[33] If the synchrony between these events is disturbed, the deformation will occur. While social issues with respect to special protection and civil rights of women of reproductive age regarding chemical exposure within the

---

[29] E.B. Hook, *Perspectives in Mutation Epidemiology 2. Epidemiologic and Design Aspects of Studies of Somatic Chromosome Breakage and Sister-Chromatid Exchange,* 99 Mutatation Research 373-382 (1982); White & Froeb, *Small-Airways Dysfunction in Nonsmokers Chronically Exposed to Tobacco Smoke,* New England J Med 302, 720-23 (1980); Blum, Gold, Ames, Kenyon, Jones, Hett, Dougherty, Horning, Dzidic, Carroll, Stillwell & Thenot, *Children Absorb Tris-BP Flame Retardant from Sleepwear: Urine Contains the Mutagenic Metabolite, 2,3-Dibromopropanol.* Sci 201, 1020-23 (1978).

[30] E.J. Calabrese, Pollutants and High Risk Groups (1978).

[31] Neims, Warner, Laughnan & Aranda, *Development of the Hepatic Cytochrome P450 Monoxygenase System,* Ann Rev Pharmacol Toxicol 16, 427-43 (1976)

[32] Natl Research Council, An Assessment of Mercury in the Environment (Natl Acad of Sciences, Wash, DC 1977); Kojima & Fujita, *Summary of Recent Studies in Japan on Methyl Mercury Poisoning,* Toxicology 1, 43-62 (1973); Bakir, Damluji, Amin-Zaki, Murtadha, Khalidi, Al-Rawi, Tikriti, Dhahir, Clarkson, Smith & Doherty, *Methylmercury Poisoning in Iraq,* Sci 181, 230-240 (1973).

[33] R. Wolkowski-Tyl, *Reproductive and Teratogenic Effects: No More Thalidomides?,* in The Pesticide Chemist and Modern Toxicology (ACS Symposium Series 160:115-155 Wash, DC 1981); Wilson, *Current Status of Teratology,* in Handbook of Teratology 47-74 (1977).

workplace must be resolved, exposures of child-bearing women to chemicals within the environment are inevitable.

Exposure to toxicants in the environment is not only the result of man-made pollution. With the exception of xenobiotics which are the deliberate chemical creations of man, chemical toxicants occur naturally in the environment. Some plants and animals produce chemical toxins for protection or food gathering. Certain elements which are toxic in high doses are also required nutrients. Many foods or byproducts of cooking food contain mutagens.[34] The effect of a potential toxicant can be dependent on both level and route of exposure. To repeat an old saw, even water is toxic if inhaled in sufficient quantities.

Elements such as lead occur naturally in the environment. As an element, lead is neither created nor destroyed without changes at the atomic level—e.g., radioactive decay of an unstable isomer. Lead can occur in numerous organic and inorganic compounds, each with its own toxicity. Concentrations of lead to which humans are normally exposed are relatively low, but human activities have increased this exposure. The potential for lead to present a hazard to human health depends on its chemical form and availability. Lead bricks used to shield people from radioactive sources are the antithesis of a health hazard; lead in paint chips eaten by children has been strongly linked to impaired mental development. When lead is added to gasoline in the form of tetraethyl lead, its combustion releases the toxicant into the air. Thus, the activities of humans can dramatically alter exposure to naturally occurring compounds. The fate and distribution, then, of a chemical in the environment is dependent on the physical and chemical properties of the compound and on the characteristics of the environment into which it is released.[35]

As with risk extrapolation models, discussed in Chapter 4, models for estimating exposure have been developed for individual chemicals. The omnipresence of mixtures in the environment can be expected to affect exposure as well as toxicity.[36] For example, soil acts as an affinity column for polycholorinated biphenyls and some pesticides; these chemicals stick to soil and are only slowly leached by pure water. Water in the environment, however, is seldom pure and is frequently contaminated with organic solvents. Pure organic solvents have been shown to release PCBs from the soil.[37] Organic solvents in ground water would be expected to have an effect on the amount and time for release of hydrophobic contaminants from soils.

---

[34] Trasler & Fraser, *Time-Position Relationships*, in Handbook of Teratology (1977).

[35] Nagao, Sugimura & Matsushima, *Environmental Mutagens and Carcinogens*, Ann Rev Genet 12, 117-59 (1978).

[36] Brassell & Eglinton, *Fate of Lipids and Other Organic Compounds in Aquatic Environments*, Assessment of Multichemical Contamination (Proceedings of an International Workshop, Natl Acad Press, Wash, DC 1982); Suffet, *Fate of Pollutants in the Air and Water Environments: A Frame of Reference*, in Fate of Pollutants in the Air and Water Environments, pt 1 (1977); Nisbet & Sarofim, *Rates and Routes of Transport of PCBs in the Environment*, Envtl Health Persp 1, 21-38 (1972).

[37] R.M. Putzrath & E. Eisenstadt, *Implications of Ground Water Contamination on Pollutant Movement and Toxicity*, manuscript in preparation.

§2.11   —The Toxicity of Mixtures

While knowledge of the toxicity of each chemical is important to assessing the hazard posed by any situation, few exposures are to only one chemical. Combinations of chemicals may have toxic effects that differ from the sum of the effects of each chemical taken separately.

More than any other area in toxicology, environmental toxicologists must be concerned with the effects of exposures to mixtures. Mixtures can occur in the environment in at least three ways. First, many pollutants released into the environment are mixtures, e.g., chemicals released as byproducts of combustion. Similarly, few chemicals are used in absolutely pure forms; most consumer products are mixtures and most commercial grade chemicals contain impurities that constitute a mixture. Thus, they are also released into the environment as mixtures. Second, the environment itself mixes contaminants with each other, e.g., leachates from a hazardous waste site, and with compounds that exist naturally in the environment. Finally, as toxicants in the environment are transformed or degraded, each compound becomes a mixture of the original chemical and its byproducts. All of these chemicals may affect each others' toxicity.

Although occupational exposures may also be to mixtures, the number of compounds to which one is exposed is usually limited to number. Furthermore, the amount of each chemical in each exposure is usually confined within specific limits. In the environment, the level of exposure may be constantly changing, both from varying sources of toxicants and from effects of the environment on the chemicals.

Since exposure to toxicants in the environment frequently involves exposure to mixtures, the question becomes how to evaluate the potential health hazard of a complex mixture as contrasted with that of a pure chemical. In addition to the problems that exist for all risk extrapolation, chemicals in a mixture may not act independently. For those chemicals which do affect each other's toxicity, toxic effects are sometimes observed to vary according to the relative ratio of the chemicals and whether exposure to the chemicals is simultaneous or sequential. By definition, carcinogenic promoters have their effect only after exposure to initiators; the effects of repeated exposure to a mixture of initiators and promoters are not well understood.

The chemicals in a mixture may act independently, synergistically, or antagonistically. One chemical may affect the absorption, metabolism, excretion, or distribution of another chemical within an organism. For example, the presence of either organic solvents or surfactants can affect the amount of material absorbed through the skin; increasing exposure increases toxicity. Pollutants may adsorb to particulates in the air; the size of the particulate will determine how deeply the particulate/contaminant is inhaled and which part, if any, of the respiratory system is exposed. While the possibilities are endless, the data to support the concept of interactions are limited and usually involve two or three chemicals rather than more complex mixtures. Moreover, toxicological interactions have usually been studied at high doses rather than at the lower exposures expected in the environment.

Toxicity testing of complex mixtures is a growing field. Much of the testing has centered on short-term tests[38] since they are relatively inexpensive and allow screening of a large number of samples to attempt to determine which mixtures may have important toxicological properties.

While short-term toxicity tests of complex mixtures in environmental samples can suggest potential hazards, their limitations should also be recognized. First, short-term tests only exist for certain toxicological endpoints such as mutagenicity. Mutagenicity, as an indication of damage to DNA, is an important endpoint; many mutagenic compounds are also carcinogenic. Short-term bioassays for other toxic effects, such as damage to the nervous system, do not currently exist. Moreover, complex mixtures may contain substances which interfere with the test system, e.g., one chemical in a mixture may kill the cells in a mutagenesis assay at doses lower than the amount needed for a second chemical to demonstrate a significant mutagenic effect. Partial chemical fractionation, i.e., separating the mixture into its components by chemical properties such as water solubility, may overcome these problems,[39] but it is difficult a priori to determine which fractionation procedures will be useful and whether the sum of the fractions accurately represents the whole. Thus, while short-term assays of environmental mixtures may give some indication of potential hazard, a negative response in such a test cannot easily be interpreted as an absence of hazard.

Given the paucity of data on toxic effects of complex mixtures, expert judgment is often relied upon to estimate hazard. Certain interactions can be suspected although the magnitude of the effect cannot usually be estimated. Also certain chemicals with similar chemical and physiological properties may be considered as a group—e.g., halomethanes, total chlorinated organic compounds, or polycyclic aromatic hydrocarbons. Although this procedure can provide an indication of the potential effect of the combination, it should be remembered that, even when the mode of toxic action for two chemicals is identical, the potency may vary. Moreover, not all compounds in a class have identical effects, e.g., the steroid hormones estrogen and testosterone.

§2.12 —The Importance of Ecotoxicology

Issues in environmental toxicology would not normally be presented without discussion about aquatic toxicology and ecotoxicology.[40] Toxicants can

---

[38] Tucker, Litschgi & Mees, *Migration of Polychlorinated Biphenyls in Soil Induced by Percolating Water,* Bull Envtl Contam Toxicol 13, 86-93 (1975).

[39] Hoffmann, *Mutagenicity Testing in Environmental Toxicology,* Envtl Sci Tech 16, 560A-574A (1982); Natl Research Council, Quality Criteria for Water Reuse, Natl Acad Press, Wash, DC (1982).

[40] Putzrath & Eisenstadt, *Mutagenicity Testing of Complex Mixtures Derived from Human Body Fluid,* Short-Term Bioassays in the Analysis of Complex Environmental Mixtures III (1983); Tabor & Loper, *Separation of Mutagens from Drinking Water using Coupled Bioassay/Analytical Fractionation,* Intl Analyt Chem 8, 197-215 (1980).

harm plants and animals as well as humans. For any given chemical, some organisms are more sensitive than humans and others are more resistant. The dangers posed to the environment vary with the ecosystem. For example, a given toxicant may have a different effect on a salt marsh than a hardwood forest. Effects of ocean dumping of waste or pollutants in streams are most quickly felt by the plants and animals within them. The spread of toxicants may affect the food chain of birds and animals as well as humans.

Since this volume is concerned with litigation involving endangerment to humans, issues involving harm to the environment are not accorded their normal weight. Human beings, however, do not exist in isolation from the environment. Eventually, effects on the environment can affect human life and health.

Ecology has become a sufficiently well publicized issue that most laypersons have heard that life on earth is highly interdependent. While that statement is true, it is not true that all life is absolutely interdependent on all other life. Obviously, certain species, such as dinosaurs, have become extinct and life on earth has continued. Other species, such as human beings, have come into existence, and life on earth existed both before and after their emergence. One problem is that, with limited knowledge, it is not known which of these inter-dependences are essential and, more specifically, which ecosystems are essential for human life.

Since *ecosystem* is a term used to describe the interrelationships between living things and their environment, there is no one ecosystem, but rather a series of ecosystems that vary for each habitat.[41] Since habitats do not have well defined boundaries, ecosystems and food chains are interwoven and inter-dependent. Most natural ecosystems have a built-in redundancy for the same reasons that redundancy is provided in the artificial environment of a space-craft—i.e., to prevent total disaster in the event of a small fluctuation or failure. Thus, each system has a limited ability to buffer changes and adapt to stress. Too much stress may damage the system beyond repair; while it may continue to function for a period of time, it will be more vulnerable to natural fluctua-tions and may break down to the detriment of other ecosystems.

Human life depends on the food chain. Not only can poisoned plants and animals serve as contaminated food, but the death of plants and animals can affect food supplies.[42]

Redistribution of the elements in the earth's crust can also disrupt the food supply. Lead arsenate was used as a pesticide in orchards from the early 1900s until its use was largely superceded by synthetic organic pesticides. The soils in the orchards became contaminated with lead and arsenic; concentrations of

---

[41] A.I. Auerbach & C.W. Gehrs, Environmental Toxicology: Issues, Problems, and Challenges, The Scientific Basis of Toxicity Assessment (1980); Cairns, Jr., *Estimating Hazard,* Bioscience 30, 101-07 (1980).

[42] Woodwell, *Effects of Pollution on the Structure and Physiology of Ecosystems,* Sci 168, 429-33 (1970).

arsenic up to 2,500 parts per million (ppm) were found in some soils.[43] At these concentrations, arsenic can be poisonous to plants, production levels may decrease, and the trees may die. If the field is to be returned to productive use, the topsoil may need to be replaced.

Pollution can cause physical changes in the environment that are detrimental to human health. The effect of chlorofluorocarbons on the ozone layer is still controversial.[44] However, if the worst estimates are true, the destruction of the ozone layer would affect humans in diverse ways. Since the ozone layer filters out much of the ultraviolet light, a reduction of its effect would increase human exposure and increase the rate of skin cancer. Changes in the ozone layer could also affect climate worldwide. Since food crops are delicately dependent on climate, even a slight change in climate could dramatically affect the food supply.

§2.13 Summary

While the complexities presented in this chapter may suggest that little can be said about environmental and occupational toxicology, it must be remembered that scientific proof and legal proof are quite different. Most scientists are careful to delineate that which they consider possible or even highly probable from that which they consider a proven fact. Every scientist has seen hypotheses change as a perfectly reasonable theory dissolves in the light of new evidence. Knowledge about toxicology is dwarfed by ignorance.

Lack of knowledge, however, is not an excuse for inaction, but rather a warning for caution. Limited knowledge can alert to a hazard; the dangers of smoking were suspected long before all the evidence was gathered. When considering potential toxicants with long latent periods, lack of action not only increases exposure but may also leave a legacy of decades of disease after sufficient evidence is produced and exposure has ceased. Caution also precludes hysteria. All actions in life contain risks, and while certain chemicals may be particularly dangerous, not sufficiently useful, and therefore worth a consideration of banning their production, not every substance that tests as positive in one short-term bioassay should be prohibited. Judgments must be made on the basis of the best available data; in retrospect some of these judgments will be wrong. Avoidance of all action, however, would be unconscionable.

---

[43] Natl Research Council, Arsenic (Natl Acad of Sciences, Wash, DC 1977).

[44] Natl Research Council, Halocarbons: Environmental Effects of Chlorofluoromethane Release (Natl Acad of Sciences Wash, DC 1976).

3

Controls and Protections

Robert L. Harris, Jr., Ph.D.* and
G. Z. Nothstein, Esq.

* Professor of Environmental Engineering, School of Public Health, Department of Environmental Sciences and Engineering the University of North Carolina, Chapel Hill, North Carolina.

§3.01   Introduction

The potential for injury or illness associated with exposures to toxic and hazardous materials exists in almost any human activity in modern society. Hazardous materials in air, water, food, soil, or within or on other materials or devices in our surroundings may result in some effect on health or well-being. The numbers and variety of situations involving hazardous materials are very great; the numbers and variety of controls and protections applicable to them are correspondingly great. The information discussed in this chapter deals principally with controls and protections which may be applied in employee work situations. Such controls and protections are those which are ordinarily applied in the practice of industrial hygiene. Because control and protection techniques developed for, and used in, employee work situations are effective in many other situations, for example, in hobby crafts, in household activities, in recreation, in gardening, in pest control, and in environmental control, they are applicable in such endeavors as well. To the extent differences exist, they are discussed in **§3.22.**

Materials may be hazardous in places of work because they can cause illness or injury through inhalation, through ingestion, or through contact with skin, mucous membranes, or eyes. They may also be hazardous because of their flammability or explosion potential. Controls and protections discussed here deal with inhalation, ingestion, and direct contact. Inherent in some of these techniques is control of fire and explosion hazards as well, and some of the control techniques are routinely applied for such purpose.

Traditionally, industrial hygiene practice has been defined as the recognition, evaluation, and control of environmental agents arising in places of work which may cause illness, impairment of health or well-being, or significant discomfort or inefficiency among workers or people in the community.[1] Recognition and evaluation are discussed in Chapter 1. Control, in the context of this definition, includes all of the procedures and techniques which may be used to prevent illness, impairment of health or well-being, or significant discomfort or inefficiency among workers or others in the neighborhood of workplaces.

The types of controls and protections applied to hazardous materials in places of work are ordinarily classified as engineering controls, administrative and work practice controls, and personal protection. These classes of controls and protections are described in the following sections. In addition, a section on professional practice as it relates to control is offered. Professional practice factors are among the measures of quality assurance pertinent to the adequacy of controls and protections applied to specific potential hazards.

There are no clear boundaries to distinguish among the different classes of controls. The Occupational Safety and Health Administration's (OSHA) general industry safety and health standards describe engineering controls by example. In addressing control of occupational diseases caused by contaminat-

---

[1] American Industrial Hygiene Association, Preamble Membership Directory, annual publication AIHA Akron OH (1981).

ed air, the regulation states, "This shall be accomplished as far as feasible by accepted engineering control measures (for example, enclosure or confinement of the operation, general and local ventilation, and substitution of less toxic materials)."[2] In the section which lists air concentration limits for some 400 chemical agents, distinctions are made among classes of control:

> To achieve compliance with paragraph (a) through (d) of this section, [i.e., the tabulations of chemical agents and requirements for their use] administrative or engineering controls must be determined and implemented whenever feasible. When such controls are not feasible to achieve full compliance, protective equipment or any other protective measures shall be used to keep the exposure of employees to air contaminants within the limits prescribed in this section.[3]

This paragraph of the regulation continues, "Any equipment and/or technical measures used for this purpose must be approved for each particular use by a competent industrial hygienist or other technically qualified person." The section on professional practice (§3.17) addresses this important aspect of control.

In February 1983, the United States Department of Labor announced its intention to reexamine its policy of requiring implementation of feasible engineering and administrative or work practice controls in preference to use of personal protective devices for achieving compliance with exposure limits. The objectives of this reexamination are listed as:

1. To explore whether a revised policy will allow employers to institute more cost-effective compliance strategies

2. To investigate whether advances in respirator design, technology, and applications may permit increased reliance on respirators

3. To attempt to identify processes, operations and circumstances appropriate for particular compliance strategies

4. To assess actual workplace conditions and employee health in industries and operations employing different compliance strategies[4]

This reexamination is expected to generate a great amount of interest among representatives of industry, labor, government, and occupational health practitioners.

---

[2] 29 CFR §1910.134(a)(1); *see also id* §1910.95(b).

[3] *Id* §1910.1000(e).

[4] 48 Fed Reg 7473-76 (Feb 22, 1983).

§3.02 Engineering Control

Engineering control of exposure of workers to hazardous materials involves process or equipment design and use aimed specifically at limiting or eliminating the exposure. Categories of engineering control are:

1. *Substitution* of processes, equipment, or materials which limit or eliminate exposures for those which cause or permit exposures

2. *Isolation* of an offending process, device, or material from workers, or of workers from the offending agent

3. *Local exhaust ventilation* to capture hazardous materials at their points of generation, thus preventing their dispersion into working environments

4. *Dilution or general ventilation* which dilutes hazardous materials to acceptable levels at locations occupied by workers

Although not ordinarily listed as categories of engineering control, two additional areas of activity must be considered for successful engineering control of workplace exposures. These are, first, maintenance and housekeeping, and second, education and training; these topics are discussed briefly in this section.

As mentioned in **§3.01**, compliance with Occupational Safety and Health Administration (OSHA) standards for exposure to most regulated hazardous materials requires that administrative or engineering controls must be determined and implemented whenever feasible. The term *feasible* is not specifically defined in the standards.[5] Caplan has proposed a definition of the word *feasible* as used in the context of the applicable standards.[6] Adoption of a definition for this term would be helpful to employers, to regulatory compliance officers, and to design engineers.

§3.03 —Substitution

When the use of a hazardous material is eliminated from a process or operation, it no longer is a hazard to the workers involved. Outright elimination of the use of a hazardous material, when this can be done without adverse effect upon the process or operation involved, is the most effective means of controlling exposure to that agent.

---

[5] 29 CFR §1910.134(a)(1); 29 CFR §1910.95(b); 29 CFR §1910.1000(e).

[6] K.J. Caplan, Philosophy and Management of Engineering Controls; III Patty's Industrial Hygiene and Toxicology ch 18; (1958 2d Rev ed); Theory and Rationale of Industrial Hygiene Practice (L.V. Cralley & L.J. Cralley eds 1979). Recently, the Occupational Safety and Health Review Commission in Sun Ship Inc, 11 OSH Cas (BNA) 1028, 1982 OSHD (CCH) ¶26,353 (1982) and Harmony Blue Granite Co, 11 OSH Cas (BNA) 1277 (1983) interpreted the word feasible as used in the OSHA safety and health standards to mean *achievable* or *capable of being done,* relying on the Supreme Court's decision in American Textile Mfrs Inst v Donovan, 101 S Ct 2478 (1981) to support its determination.

Ordinarily, an agent is involved in a process for a purpose, however, so outright elimination cannot be done without other consequences. Most often, removal of an agent from a process requires substitution of some other agent to serve its purpose. The practice in industrial hygiene is to substitute for a hazardous material one which is nonhazardous or less hazardous, but which will serve the same purpose. A classic example of substitution is the substitution of a nonsilica parting compound for silica flour in the making of foundry molds. Other examples are the substitution of nonberyllium phosphors for beryllium phosphors in the manufacture of fluorescent lamps and the substitution of various other chlorinated and fluorinated hydrocarbons for carbon tetrachloride in solvent applications.

Because hydrocarbon solvents are flammable and explosive, nonflammable carbon tetrachloride was widely used many years ago as a cold cleaning solvent. When the high toxicity of carbon tetrachloride was recognized, other halogenated hydrocarbons were substituted. Now health consequences of exposures to some of these substitute materials have become matters of serious concern. This illustrates the possibility that in substituting materials, one may also inadvertently substitute hazards. Care in selection of substitute materials and vigilance regarding new developments in the toxicology of substitute materials considered to be acceptable at the time of choice are necessary for the successful application of materials substitution as an engineering control method.

Often the source from which a hazardous material is released into a work environment is a specific piece of equipment. Substitution of equipment which does not permit such release for equipment which does is an effective engineering control technique. Substitution of electrically powered lift trucks for gasoline powered ones in a warehouse to eliminate exposures to carbon monoxide is an example. When a hazardous material is inherent in a process— i.e. a reactant or a product—it cannot be eliminated by equipment substitution, but its release into the air may be eliminated or reduced by substitution of equipment. Automated weighing scales substituted for manual scales for the weighing of a hazardous material may eliminate the exposure of an operator, or an electrostatic painting apparatus may greatly reduce the escape of pigments from a spray-painting operation. The systematic evaluation of processes by knowledgeable persons to detect sources from which hazardous materials are released may reveal items of equipment whose substitution can reduce or eliminate exposures.

The substitution of an entire process may sometimes be used to reduce or eliminate exposure to a hazardous material. The use of photographic processes rather than type casting eliminates exposures to lead fume in printing operations, for example. Major process changes are more often dictated by economic and technical considerations, however, than by requirements for control of exposures to hazardous materials. Present day concern for health and safety results in greater attention being given to hazard control in the choice and design of new processes than was the case in earlier years. Clearly, satisfying needs for hazard control in the initial design and construction of a process or facility is much more cost-effective than is postconstruction recognition of a hazard and retrofitting of control.

Substitution, whether it be material, equipment, or process, can seldom be a single action which can be clearly categorized as a single method of control. Many substitutions have elements of other control techniques. The reduction or elimination of exposure to benzene, for example, may be accomplished by the administrative action of purchase specifications which limit the benzene content of solvents. The choice of a piece of enclosed equipment to substitute for one from which hazardous material is released may be an effective means of control because it isolates the material from the workplace.

§3.04 —Isolation

Exposures of workers to hazardous materials may be accomplished by isolating the worker from the material or by isolating the material from the worker.

The use of personal protective equipment is perhaps the most obvious means of isolating a worker from contact with hazardous material. This technique is discussed in §3.16. Engineering means may also be used to isolate workers from hazards. Insulated crane cabs supplied with cleaned, conditioned air are used to isolate crane operators from heat, noise, and air contaminants in steel mills. Insulated air conditioned enclosures around control stations in this and other industries are used to isolate and protect workers from hazards. Although it would be technically possible to isolate workmen from virtually any hazard, in most cases of exposure to hazardous material it would be very expensive to do so, and thus it is not often done. More often the technique of isolation is used to isolate the hazardous material from the workplace.

The most common means for isolating material from a workplace is enclosure. The transportation of materials in pipes, ducts, and closed bins rather than by means of open conveyors or in open vessels represents isolation by enclosure. The handling of materials such as pigments and additives in sealed plastic bags which can be changed without opening into mills or mixers is another form of isolation.

Enclosed processes, exemplified by modern petroleum refineries, effectively isolate materials from workplaces during normal operations. Exposure of workers to hazardous materials in such processes occurs when leaks or spills occur, or when equipment malfunctions and repair or maintenance must be performed. Emergency operations and maintenance and repair have the potential for high exposures of workers to process materials, so preplanning for such in the process design stage and the provision of procedures and equipment to limit exposures when they must be dealt with is needed.

Isolation is the means most often used to prevent contact of workers with stored materials. Closed containers for storage of materials represent isolation. Imposing distance between a material and workers is also isolation. Hazardous materials, for example, sources of radioactivity, kept in remote locations to which access by workers is limited or is denied, are isolated by distance as well as by any container which confines them. In some processes, items of equipment subject to leaks or frequent maintenance, for example, pumps, may be located together (the pump room) in isolation from the rest of the process, thereby reducing exposures of most of the process operators.

§3.05   —Ventilation

Ventilation[7] can be defined as a method for providing control of an environment by strategic use of airflow. The flow of air may be used to provide either heating or cooling of a workplace, to remove a contaminant near its source of release into the environment, to dilute the concentration of a contaminant to acceptable levels, or to replace air exhausted from an enclosure.[8] Ventilation is by far the most important engineering control principle available to the industrial hygienist.[9] Applied either as a general or local control, this principle has industrial significance in at least three applications: the control of heat and humidity primarily for comfort reasons, the prevention of fire and explosions, and most important to the industrial hygienist, the maintenance of concentrations of airborne contaminants at acceptable levels in the workplace.[10]

General Ventilation

The term *general ventilation* normally is applied to the practice of supplying and exhausting large volumes of air throughout a workspace.[11] It is used typically in industry to achieve comfortable work conditions (temperature and humidity control) or to dilute the concentrations of airborne contaminants to acceptable limits throughout the workspace.[12] Properly used, general ventilation can be effective in removing large volumes of heated air or relatively low concentrations of low toxicity contaminants from several decentralized sources.[13]

General ventilation can be provided by either natural or mechanical means; often the best overall result is obtained with a combination of mechanical and natural air supply and exhaust.[14]

Natural ventilation may be provided either by gravitational forces (being motivated primarily by thermal forces of convection) or by anemotive forces (created by differences in wind pressure).[15] These two natural forces operate

---

[7] The first portion of this section, *General Ventilation Concepts,* is excerpted from 1 Patty's Industrial Hygiene and Toxicology, ch 18 (3d Ed 1979), with consent.

[8] Soule, *Industrial Hygiene Engineering Controls,* in Patty's Industrial Hygiene and Toxicology, 174 (3d rev ed, vol 1, G.D. Clayton, ed 1978)

[9] *Id.*

[10] *Id.*

[11] *Id* 778.

[12] *Id.*

[13] *Id.*

[14] *Id.*

[15] *Id.*

together in most cases, resulting in the natural displacement and infiltration of air through windows, doors, walls, floors, and other openings in an industrial building.[16] Unfortunately, the wind currents and thermal convection profiles on which natural ventilation is dependent are erratic and frequently unpredictable.[17] Thus it is perhaps a misnomer to refer to natural ventilation as a *control* method, since to employ this technique requires dependence on, rather than control of, natural forces.[18]

Mechanical ventilation exhausts contaminated air by mechanical means (exhaust fans), with the concomitant use of an appropriate air supply to replace the exhausted air.[19] The best method of achieving this in a modern closed building is to supply air through a system of ductwork, distributing the air into the work areas in a manner that will provide optimum benefit to the worker for both comfort and control of contaminants.[20]

Local Exhaust Ventilation

Local exhaust ventilation may be used to recover process materials, to protect process equipment, to maintain product quality, or to promote good housekeeping, but its most common purpose is to control exposures of workers to hazardous materials. Design specifications and procedures have been developed for a great many industrial operations and are described in a great many books and papers, including the widely used manual, *Industrial Ventilation —A Manual of Recommended Practice*.[21] This manual presents data and information on the design, maintenance, and testing of industrial exhaust ventilation systems. It contains chapters on:

> General principles of ventilation
>
> Dilution ventilation
>
> Ventilation for heat control
>
> Hood design (principles and procedures)
>
> Specific operations (specific hood designs)
>
> Design procedure (balanced systems and blast gate systems)
>
> Make-up and recirculated air
>
> Construction specifications
>
> Testing of ventilation systems
>
> Fans
>
> Air cleaning devices

---

[16] *Id.*

[17] *Id.*

[18] *Id.*

[19] *Id* 779.

[20] *Id.*

[21] Comm on Indus Ventilation, Am Conference of Governmental Indus Hygienists, *Industrial Ventilation—A Manual of Recommended Practice* (17th ed 1982).

The manual is under continuing review and revision by the Committee on Industrial Ventilation, and a new edition has been published every two years for the past three decades.

A major consideration in the design and operation of industrial exhaust ventilation systems is achievement of an acceptable level of hazard control at minimum cost. This generally is accomplished by designing systems which will achieve control with a minimum amount of exhaust air; costs of heating, air conditioning, system ductwork, and to some degree fan operation are related to the air volume exhaust rate. For any particular operation the factor which has the greatest influence on the quantity of air which must be exhausted to achieve control is the hood design. Of the 290 pages of text in the current edition of *Industrial Ventilation,* 151 pages are devoted to hoods.

Discussion of details in exhaust ventilation system design and operation is not undertaken in this chapter. Four general points are to be made, however, about exhaust ventilation systems. First, many, and perhaps most, exhaust ventilation systems are designed by persons who are unacquainted with, or who neglect, good exhaust system design principles and practices. The costs of installing and operating a poorly designed and inefficient system may be as great as, or greater than, those for a well-designed, effective system. This alone is sufficient cause to obtain good design services, but of much greater importance is the likelihood that poorly designed systems will fail to provide adequate protection for workers. The second concern is system maintenance. Even a well-designed system may lose its effectiveness if its maintenance is neglected. Systematic monitoring of the performance of exhaust ventilation systems, and a regular schedule of maintenance, are necessary if dependable control of exposures is to be assured. Third, even a well-designed exhaust ventilation system cannot perform satisfactorily if it is starved for air. It is obvious that air must gain entrance to a space before it can be exhausted, yet many exhaust systems are operated with no conscious provision being made for the supply of make-up air. Make-up air supply should be included in the design and installation of all exhaust ventilation systems. Finally, from the standpoint of regulatory compliance, there may be requirements for exhaust ventilation which are not addressed in references such as *Industrial Ventilation.* Some industrial operations have ventilation requirements specified by the Occupational Safety and Health Administration.[22] It is prudent to review the appropriate regulation when initiating the design of control for any particular operation.

Local exhaust ventilation is intended to capture material at its point of release and prevent its dispersion in workroom air. It cannot be designed to capture only a specified fraction of the emission while the remainder escapes at such rate that exposures will be near, but not exceed, regulatory exposure limits. *Dilution ventilation,* on the other hand, does not have as its purpose the

---

[22] *See generally* 29 CFR §1910.

capture of air contaminants at their points of generation. In dilution ventilation situations, materials are permitted to be released into workspace air, and sufficient ventilation air is provided to dilute the emission to acceptable concentrations. Dilution ventilation is inappropriate as a means of control for point sources of air contaminants—for example, as control for a grinding operation. Local exhaust ventilation is the means of choice for control of such sources. Dilution ventilation is most appropriate for controlling wide-spread low-level emissions such as the relatively slow desorption of an air contaminant from treated fabrics in a sewing room.

Rigorous design of dilution ventilation systems requires knowledge of rates at which air contaminants are being generated. Means for calculating dilution ventilation requirements have been presented in detail.[23] Theoretical concepts of materials' balance and transport, upon which dilution ventilation calculations are based, do not take into account departures from complete and instantaneous mixing of the contaminant and supply air. In practice the theoretical quantity of supply air required to dilute emissions of a contaminant to some design concentration is multiplied by a factor of 3 to 10 to account for these departures. The choice of multiplying factor depends largely on the nature of the contaminant-generating operations and is usually based on literature references and/or the experience of the designer.

Specifications for the design and operation of industrial exhaust ventilation systems have been developed over a period of many years. The general procedure has been to control exposures in places of work and to discharge exhausted air out-of-doors after it has been cleaned sufficiently to meet any air pollution source emission standards. In the past decade, the costs of energy for comfort heating and air conditioning have increased substantially, and the conservation of energy by recirculation of exhaust has become an attractive possibility. At the present time the recirculation of exhaust air should be limited to systems which handle relatively nonhazardous materials which can be effectively collected in available air cleaners. Sawdust of some woods is an example; some woods are sensitizers for allergies, others are essentially non-toxic, and the particles are of such size and character that they can be removed with high efficiency with available air cleaners.

Much attention has been given to extending recirculation to exhaust system air carrying wider ranges of air contaminants. For recirculation of exhaust air used to control exposures to hazardous materials, air-cleaning systems with efficiencies of higher magnitude than those used in meeting emission standards for discharge to the out-of-doors may be necessary. For recirculation, the air cleaning systems would have to be capable of fail-safe operation and be provided with reliable alarms and shut-down features in event of malfunction. Research on various factors which bear on successful recirculation of exhaust

---

[23] R.L. Harris & E.W. Arp, The Emission Inventory; III Patty's Industrial Hygiene and Toxicology, ch 2 (1958 2d rev ed); Theory and Rationale of Industrial Hygiene Practice (L.V. Cralley & L.J. Cralley eds 1979).

air has been reported.[24] Much remains to be done before recirculation of exhaust air used for control of toxic materials can be practiced on a wide scale with confidence that the workers in the space receiving the recirculated air will be protected.

Inadvertent recirculation of exhaust ventilation air may occur under some conditions. Close proximity of make-up air intakes and exhaust ventilation air discharge ducts may result in such recirculation. The same effect may result from failure to provide in system design for make-up air with the consequence that it enters a workplace by uncontrolled infiltration through windows or other openings, perhaps near the discharge plume of an exhaust system. Short discharge stacks which result in downwash of exhaust system discharges so they reenter the building or infiltrate other nearby buildings are a form of inadvertent recirculation. Stringent safeguards with extraordinarily efficient air cleaning are required for controlled recirculation of exhaust air; such recirculation is seldom practiced. Inadvertent recirculation takes place without control and often without recognition; such recirculation is not uncommon.

§3.06 —Maintenance and Housekeeping

The need for the proper maintenance of exhaust ventilation systems to preserve their effectiveness is mentioned in §3.02. Of equal or perhaps greater importance in processes handling hazardous materials is maintenance of processing equipment. Exhaust systems are applied to recognized points of generation of contaminants in workplaces. Malfunction of exhaust systems may be recognized by workers who then are able to take action for their own protection. Leaks from pumps, tank seals, sampling ports, or other process devices resulting from poor maintenance may go unnoticed or be ignored. Neglect of such sources may defeat otherwise effective engineering control of exposures.

General housekeeping is also important in the control of exposures to hazardous materials. This is particularly true if the material of concern is particulate in nature so it settles on surfaces and serves as a secondary source of air contamination when it is disturbed. Good housekeeping not only prevents the accumulation of particulate materials, with the potential for redispersion, but promotes early detection of leaks or spills from process equipment with timely maintenance of repair.

§3.07 —Education and Training

The success of any effort to control a hazard, including engineering control of exposures to hazardous materials, depends to a great extent on knowledge. A particular body of knowledge pertinent to each design problem must be

---

[24] L.J. Partridge, A Recommended Approach to Recirculation of Exhaust Air (US DHEW(NIOSH) Publication No 78-124, Cincinnati, OH 1978); M.L. Holcomb & R.C. Scholz, Evaluation of Air Cleaning and Monitoring Equipment Used in Recirculation Systems (US DHHS (NIOSH) Publication No 81-113, Cincinnati, OH 1981).

accessible to, and used by, the engineers who design a control system; knowledge regarding the nature of the hazard and the functioning of the control system must be possessed by the supervisors who monitor performance of the process and the control system; knowledge regarding the reasons for and performance of the control system must be possessed by the workers who operate and are protected by it; knowledge regarding requirements for and importance of hazard control systems must be possessed by managers who are responsible for providing safe and healthful places of work; and finally, knowledge regarding all aspects of hazard recognition, evaluation, and control is needed by compliance officers and other safety and health professionals who judge the adequacy of hazard control systems and provide advice regarding their design and operation.

Knowledge is gained by formal degree program education, by short course and similar training activities, by use of textbooks and other literature, by obtaining advice of experts, and by experience. Experience alone is an unreliable and costly means of gaining knowledge. Academic training without experience is likely to lead to deficiencies in the design and use of hazard controls. As in other areas of science and technology, a combination of training and experience is the preparation of choice for the design and use of engineering controls for hazardous materials. This matter is addressed further in **§3.17.**

§3.08 Administrative and Work Practice Controls

According to a United States Department of Labor announcement, "Administrative controls include scheduling or rotating assignments so as to reduce individual exposures," and "work practice controls can reduce exposures by modifying the way in which a task is performed."[25] In **§§3.12-3.16,** various administrative actions and work practices which have as their purpose the control of workers' exposures to hazardous materials are discussed. Although on first reading all of them may not appear to fit neatly into the Department of Labor examples, they do bear more directly on the control of exposure by administrative or work practice means than by engineering means or use of personal protective devices. The approaches discussed here are work scheduling, regulation of worker access to exposure areas, prescribed operating procedures, specific job descriptions, behavorial requirements, materials specifications, and labeling.

§3.09 —Work Scheduling

Procedures for administrative control of exposures to toxic and hazardous materials by means of work scheduling are not explicitly described in the Occupational Safety and Health Administration (OSHA) safety and health standards, but such procedures are implicit in the standards' definitions and

---

[25] 48 Fed Reg 7473 (Feb 22, 1983).

formulae.[26] Permissible exposure limits (PELs) for toxic and hazardous substances are expressed either as ceiling concentrations, never to be exceeded, as 8-hour time-weighted average concentrations for 8-hour shifts in a 40-hour work week, or, for some materials, as both ceiling and 8-hour time-weighted average concentrations. Work scheduling may be a means of achieving compliance with ceiling PELs for some workers in some situations and may be used routinely for achieving compliance with 8-hour time-weighted average PELs in other situations.

Work scheduling is not a means of protecting workers from exposures above ceiling values when such exposures occur at unpredictable times. In such situations, other means of protection, such as additional engineering control to eliminate the source of emission or the provision and use of personal protective equipment, are necessary. When predictable excursion of concentrations above ceiling values occur, however, as may be the case in scheduled maintenance and repair of equipment or other such intermittent activities which result in abnormally high concentrations of air contaminants, such activities can be scheduled for times when persons not involved in the work are absent from the workplace, or the absence of such persons can be specifically scheduled. Those workers who are present can be protected with personal protective devices.

Eight-hour time-weighted average exposures are computed as follows:

$$E = (C_1T_1 + C_2T_2 + \ldots + C_nT_n)\,(1/8)$$

Where E is the average exposure concentration over the 8-hour period and T is the duration in hours of exposure at its companion concentration C. This means that exposures at concentrations above the 8-hour time-weighted average PEL for a fraction of a work shift, if combined with periods of exposure to lower concentrations so that the average, E, is less than the PEL, will be in compliance with the standard so long as any applicable ceiling value is not violated. This constitutes the basis for administrative control by work scheduling. When certain tasks, or work in a particular location, involve exposures always less than any applicable ceiling value but greater than the concentration allowable for a full 8-hour shift, administrative control is practiced by limiting hours of work at such tasks or locations, with the remainder of the 8-hour shift devoted to tasks or locations with lower or no exposure so the 8-hour average exposure of any worker does not exceed the 8-hour PEL. This can be accomplished by the rotation of workers for various tasks or workplace locations, or by the scheduling of tasks during the work day.

The foregoing discussion dealt with adjusting work schedules to achieve control. A converse consideration is special control requirements imposed by abnormal work schedules. Eight-hour PELs listed in the safety and health standards and threshold limit values of the American Conference of Govern-

---

[26] 29 CFR §1910.1000.

mental Industrial Hygienists,[27] are applicable to 8-hour work shifts in 40-hour work weeks. The protection of persons exposed over work shifts longer than 8 hours, and/or work weeks longer than 40 hours, requires exposure limits for some materials to be lower than the published 8-hour average values. Procedures for the modification of PELs for exposures longer than 8-hour days or 40-hour weeks have been described by OSHA in Chapter XIII of its *Industrial Hygiene Manual*.[28] The PELs for some materials are ceiling values only, others are intended to prevent acute irritation or discomfort by materials with no known cumulative effects, and still others are based on feasibility or good hygiene practice. The items listed last are identified in Chapter XIII of the OSHA *Industrial Hygiene Manual* and no adjustment of PELs for prolonged exposures is required. Some materials, also identified in Chapter XIII of the *Industrial Hygiene Manual,* exhibit acute toxicity and others exhibit cumulative toxicity. These materials require PEL modifications as follows.

For those identified as having acute toxicity:

$$\text{Equivalent PEL} = \text{8-hour PEL} \left(\frac{\text{8 hours}}{\text{hours of exposure in 1 day}} \right)$$

For those identified as having cumulative toxicity:

$$\text{Equivalent PEL} = \text{8-hour PEL} \left(\frac{\text{40 hours}}{\text{hours of exposure in 1 week}} \right)$$

Compliance with these equivalent PELs limits the dosage (length of exposure time period *times* concentration) of the material to the level intended by the standard.

The *Industrial Hygiene Manual* states that the adjustment equations as reproduced above reflect simplifications of the actual accumulation and removal of toxic agents frrom the body. More rigorous methods for adjusting PELs have been proposed,[29] and, with specific approval, OSHA industrial hygienists who have sufficient data to validate adjustment of 8-hour PEL's by such methods are encouraged to do so.

---

[27] Am Conference of Governmental Indus Hygienists, TLVs-Threshold Limit Values for Chemical Substances and Physical Agents in the Workplace Environment with Intended Charges (annual publication, 1983 Cincinnati, OH 45211).

[28] Modification of PELs for Prolonged Exposure Periods, OSHA, Industrial Hygiene Manual ch XIII, *reported in* Occupational Safety and Health Reporter, BNA Reference File 77:8361 The Bureau of National Affairs, Inc, Washington, DC (July 15, 1982).

[29] Brief & Scala, *Occupational Exposure Limits for Novel Schedules,* American Industrial Hygiene Association J 36, 467 (1975); S.A. Roach, *A Most Rational Basis for Air Sampling Programmes,* Annals Occupational Hygiene 20, 65 (1977); Hickey & Reist, *Application of Occupational Exposure Limits to Unusual Work Schedules,* AIHA J 38, 613 (1977).

§3.10 —Regulated Access

Isolation of workers from locations in which they would be exposed to hazardous materials is a recognized engineering control method. In some cases, implementation of the method may actually be by regulated access or administrative control. When access to a place of exposure is limited by a physical barrier, administrative control may be unnecessary. When access is limited not by physical barriers, but by work rules and/or supervisory actions, the control becomes administrative. The wearing of safety glasses and hard hats as conditions of access to work areas are common in industry. In some situations, the use of respiratory protective devices is required for access. Such requirements may be universally applied to all persons, workers and visitors alike, who wish to enter a work area. In other situations, access may be limited to workers who have special training and who must perform necessary tasks in the controlled area—for example, the operators of a nuclear reactor. In some cases, controlled access may be applied selectively; if personal monitoring reveals that the accumulated exposure of an individual worker has reached some predetermined index value—for example, an accumulated dose of ionizing radiation or of inorganic lead—access to work locations where further exposure could take place may be administratively limited until further periods of exposure are within the range of the acceptable accumulated dose.

§3.11 —Prescribed Operating Procedures

Some industrial establishments develop and use standard operating procedure documents. Such documents contain specific step-by-step operating instructions for a process and may specify the process equipment to be used, conditions of processing (e.g., time, temperature, pressure, etc), materials used, techniques of operation, and instructions for safety and environmental control. The inclusion of instructions relative to the control of exposures to hazardous materials is not universal in standard operating procedures, but when it is done it is a form of administrative control.

Formal written documents do not represent the only form of operating procedures which are applied to the control of exposures to hazardous materials. For example, the adoption of wet methods as a standard work practice to limit the generation and dispersion of dust in some dusty trades is commonly practiced. This, and similar procedures, are effective work practice controls.

§3.12 —Written Job Descriptions

Written job descriptions, like standard operating procedures, are used in some industrial establishments. Job descriptions may list the specific tasks to be done, their sequence, the tools to be used, the means for handling materials and devices, and protective devices to be used in the performance of the job. The description may include instructions for use of engineering controls applicable to the process. Job descriptions represent an administrative means for prescribing specific steps in performance of tasks—for example, the manner may be specified for handling empty shipping containers to minimize the dispersion of dust after their contents have been introduced to process equipment. Such instructions, as well as instructions regarding effective use of engineering controls and personal protective equipment, are an important form of administrative control.

§3.13 —Behavioral Requirements

Constraints on some types of personal behavior of workers have long been practiced in industry and are a form of administrative control. Perhaps the most common form of such control is the prohibition of smoking in locations where a fire or explosion hazard exists. It is not uncommon to prohibit eating or drinking in areas where hazardous materials are handled. The recognition of synergism between exposures to asbestos and smoking, as associated with respiratory disease, has lead to the prohibition of smoking for workers in some asbestos processing and products manufacturing operations. This type of administrative control is unique in that it applies to workers even during times that they are away from their places of work.

§3.14 —Material Specifications

One engineering control technique is the substitution of a less hazardous material for a specified one of greater hazard. In some situations the presence or absence of a hazardous material in a workplace is unrelated to process requirements but is determined only by whether or not the material is a casual component of a mixture used in the process. Examples are the presence of asbestiform fibers in talc or the presence of benzene in solvent naphtha. Administrative means for controlling the presence of such hazardous materials in places of work are purchase specifications. Such specifications can limit the amount of the undesired component in process materials and by this means control the exposure of workers to that component.

§3.15 —Labeling

Labeling is a form of administrative control in that it alerts workers and supervisors to the existence of a potential hazard and may provide instructions for coping with it.[30] Labeling of containers of hazardous materials is commonplace. Labeling may be employed in other ways as well. Limited access and caution signs for work areas where potential hazards exist are labels. Such

---

[30] OSHA has proposed the adoption of a hazardous communication (labeling) standard, 47 Fed Reg 12102 (Mar 19, 1982), and following receipt of comments will publish a final rule in late 1983. (Note: A final rule was published in 48 Fed Reg 53280 (Nov 25, 1983).)

labels may apply at all times to a particular area—for example, to areas where safety glasses or respirators are required—or may be used only when the hazard is temporary, as when maintenance is being performed or when a spill of hazardous material has occurred. Labeling of personal protective equipment is one safeguard against its misuse; for example, labeling helps to prevent the use of a respiratory protective device designed to protect its wearer from dusts and fumes in a work situation which has exposure to gases or vapors.

§3.16   Personal Protection

As stated in §3.01, the Occupational Safety and Health Administration (OSHA) safety and health standards require that administrative and engineering controls must be used for control of exposures to hazardous materials whenever feasible, but that when such controls are not feasible to achieve full compliance, protective equipment or other protective measures shall be used to keep exposures within limits. Also noted in §3.01 is the announcement by the United States Department of Labor of its intention to review this policy. Thus, some change may come in the current OSHA requirement that engineering and administrative or work practice controls be used in preference to personal protective devices to achieve compliance with exposure limits.

General requirements for the application of personal protective equipment are stated in the current OSHA standards as follows:

> Protective equipment, including personal protective equipment for eyes, face, head, and extremities, protective clothing, respiratory devices, and protective shields and barriers, shall be provided, used, and maintained in a sanitary and reliable condition wherever it is necessary by reason of hazards of processes or environment, chemical hazards, radiological hazards, or mechanical irritants encountered in a manner capable of causing injury or impairment in the function of any part of the body through absorption, inhalation or physical contact.[31]

These requirements suggest the types of devices considered in the OSHA standards to be personal protective equipment—i.e., eye protection; respiratory devices; headgear, footwear, and protective garments; and shields and barriers. They also identify the routes of exposure to hazardous materials (absorption, inhalation, or physical contact) for which the devices are intended to provide control.

Safety glasses, goggles, and face shields are used as protection against flying objects which may cause traumatic injury to eyes and as protection against some forms of radiant energy such as that generated by electric arc welding. Eye protection devices are also used to control exposure of the eyes to hazardous materials which cause eye injury by virtue of their chemical composition or temperature. Glasses, goggles, and face shields may be used to protect eyes

---

[31] 29 CFR §1910.132(a). *See also* 29 CFR §§1910.105, 1926.28(a).

from splashes of liquids such as solutions of acids, alkalies, or corrosive salts, solvents, or hot materials. Eye protection may be incorporated in respiratory protective devices (e.g., full face masks and supplied air hoods) and in full coverage protective garments designed to protect the entire body against contamination by hazardous materials.

Respiratory protective devices may be grouped into three main classes: devices which remove particles from ambient air which is then breathed by the wearer; devices which remove one or more gases and/or vapors from ambient air which is then breathed by the wearer; and devices through which satisfactory breathing air is supplied so the wearer does not breathe the ambient atmosphere. Common face pieces for air-cleaning type respirators are half masks which cover only the nose and mouth of the wearer and full face masks which incorporate protective lenses for the eyes as well. Supplied-air respirators may be of either half mask or full face design or may be in the form of a hood which covers the head or the head and shoulders of the wearer. Supplied-air hoods may be integral parts of full-body protective garments.

The air-cleaning components of respiratory protective devices can provide protection only against materials which they are designed to control. Filter elements which are effective for pneumoconiosis-producing dusts provide no protection against gases or vapors. An adsorption cartridge for hydrocarbon vapor will not provide adequate protection against carbon monoxide. It is vital that the air-cleaning elements of respiratory protective devices be those appropriate for protection against the hazardous material to which the wearer is exposed.

A great variety of respiratory protective devices are offered on the market, and detailed discussion of their selection and application is not undertaken here. The National Institute for Occupational Safety and Health (NIOSH) conducts a testing and certification program for respiratory protective devices. The *Certified Equipment List*,[32] published by NIOSH, may be used as a guide in the selection of devices for specific applications. This publication lists certified respiratory protective devices and approved component parts in the following categories:

Self-contained breathing apparatus

Gas masks

Supplied-air respirators

Dust, fume, and mist respirators

Chemical cartridge respirators

Vinyl chloride respirators

---

[32] NIOSH Certified Equipment List as of June 1, 1980 (US DHHS(NIOSH) Publication No 80-144, with Supplement of Oct 1981, US DHHS(NIOSH) Publication No 82-106).

A new edition of the NIOSH Certified Equipment as of February 17, 1983, is in press at the time of this writing.

Protection from absorption of hazardous materials through the skin, or from other injury resulting from direct contact, can be achieved in some degree by appropriate headgear, footwear, and protective clothing. The headgear most often required are hard hats, whose purpose is to protect wearers from injury by falling objects and from other such traumatic injury. Hard hats or other impervious headgear can also be used to protect the head from materials which may be absorbed through the scalp or cause injury by direct contact.

Some jobs require work in places where walking surfaces are wet or are otherwise contaminated with materials with which direct contact is to be avoided. Impervious footwear which keep workers' feet dry and prevent direct contact with hazardous materials are available and should be used in such situations.

When workers must handle materials which are hazardous by skin absorption or direct contact, impervious gloves should be used if other means to prevent direct contact are not provided. Special care is needed in the use of any impervious clothing—especially gloves which are subject to rapid wear—so that they are discarded or repaired when leaks develop. Continued use of gloves or other devices after they are no longer impervious may compound an exposure hazard. Another precaution which should be observed when the use of gloves or boots is required is to choose those of sufficient length or of such cuff design that hazardous materials will not gain entrance at their tops. The wearing of gloves or other devices which are contaminated inside with a hazardous material assures skin contact and almost certainly represents a greater hazard than would be the case if the devices were not used.

In some cases, impervious garments such as aprons, coats, leggings, or sleeves may be necessary to control direct contract with hazardous materials. The choice of the proper combination of boots, gloves, and other garments to control direct contact can be made only when information is available about characteristics of the job and of the hazardous material involved.

Some special cases call for protection of the entire body. When such protection is needed, as might be the case in handling especially infectious material or in dealing with a spill of highly toxic material, the services of specialists should be obtained. A point to be kept in mind about the use of whole body protection from hazardous materials is that, even though the garments may provide effective protection in the course of work, special care is needed in removing them, and in their decontamination or disposal, so that the garments themselves do not become a source of exposure to the wearers or others.

The use of face shields for the protection of eyes and skin from splashes of hazardous materials has been mentioned, and as a general rule the use of impervious garments is the method of choice for personal protection of other parts of the body from direct contact with hazardous materials. In a few work situations, although personal protection may be needed, the use of gloves or other garments may not be practical. In some such cases, some protection may be obtained by use of barrier creams. To be effective, the proper barrier cream for the hazardous material to which the worker is exposed must be used. No barrier cream has universal application. The method of use must also be carefully developed and adhered to faithfully. When barrier creams are considered for use as an alternative to other means of control, it is important that it be done with the advice and under supervision of a dermatologist with experience in industrial practice.

§3.17   Professional Practice

In addressing the control of exposures to toxic and hazardous substances the Occupational Safety and Health Administration (OSHA) safety and health standards state: "Any equipment and/or technical measures used for this purpose must be approved for each particular use by a competent industrial hygienist or other technically qualified person."[33] This provision recognizes the importance of professional practice as a vital part of hazard control and protection of workers, but the OSHA standards do not elaborate further on the matter. Professional practice to satisfy requirements for regulatory compliance is important; of greater importance, however, is professional practice to assure, insofar as possible, that workers are protected from hazards. In this section, aspects of professional practice of industrial hygiene are examined by brief discussion of professional certification, accreditation of academic programs, licensing, governmental compliance and assistance programs, and professional ethics.

The American Board of Industrial Hygiene (ABIH), incorporated in 1960 under the laws of Pennsylvania, is a nonprofit corporation which certifies individuals as to education, experience, and professional ability in the practice of industrial hygiene.[34] Certification may be taken in acoustic, air pollution, chemical, engineering, radiologic, or toxicologic aspects, or in the comprehensive practice of industrial hygiene. Certification may be gained by persons who have education and experience acceptable to the ABIH, and who successfully complete two days of written professional examination.

The educational requirement is graduation from a college acceptable to the ABIH with a degree in industrial hygiene, chemistry, physics, biology, or chemical, mechanical, or sanitary engineering. A degree in another field may be acceptable, but a candidate who wishes to qualify with such a degree must present evidence of the scientific content of the curriculum for ABIH review. A graduate degree in an acceptable field of science or engineering may also satisfy the educational requirement.

At least five years of experience acceptable to the ABIH in the practice of industrial hygiene subsequent to receipt of a baccalaureate degree is required. Special provision is made for admission to examination of nondegree persons

---

[33] 29 CFR §1910.1000(e).

[34] Bulletin of the American Board of Industrial Hygiene, rev Jan 1, 1983 (ABIH Executive Secretary, 302 S Waverly Rd, Lansing MI 48917).

if they have had at least 10 years of experience in professional practice of industrial hygiene acceptable to the ABIH.

When persons satisfy educational and experience requirements, they may be admitted to examination. Written professional examinations are given at one location in the spring and at several locations in the fall each year. Upon successful completion of the one-day core and the one-day comprehensive or aspect examinations, a person becomes a Certified Industrial Hygienist (CIH) and is admitted as a Diplomate to the American Academy of Industrial Hygiene.

Persons who have at least one year of acceptable professional experience and who are otherwise qualified for admission to examination may become an Industrial Hygienist in Training (IHIT) by successful completion of the first-day core examination.

At the beginning of 1983, there were approximately 1700 active Certified Industrial Hygienists and approximately 800 Industrial Hygienists in Training.

The ABIH requires that every six years, each Certified Industrial Hygienist must present evidence of continuing professional qualification for maintenance of his or her certification. A variety of professional activities, including advanced courses in continuing education, qualify for maintenance of certification.

This discussion of ABIH certification is not intended to imply that such certification is necessary for competent professional practice of industrial hygiene. Such is not the case. Certification of an individual by the American Board of Industrial Hygiene is evidence, however, that the board's criteria for professional practice, as outlined briefly above, have been met by that person, and that judged by these criteria he or she has demonstrated professional competence.

The American Board for Engineering and Technology (ABET) is the agency which accredits engineering academic programs in the United States. Curriculum guidelines for ABET accreditation of master's level graduate programs in industrial hygiene engineering have been published.[35] Five universities—Drexel, Johns Hopkins, the University of North Carolina at Chapel Hill, the University of Oklahoma, and the University of Texas at Austin—list ABET-accredited programs in occupational health engineering.[36] Programs at all five institutions are at the master and doctorate levels.

No agency now accredits academic programs in all aspects of industrial hygiene. The American Academy of Industrial Hygiene, in cooperation with the American Industrial Hygiene Association, has under way the development of such an accreditation program. The program is expected to follow closely that of ABET for engineering programs and may be implemented through, or

---

[35] AAEE/ASCE/AEEP, Guide for Environmental Engineering Visitors on ECPD Accreditation Teams (ABET, New York 1979).

[36] P.A. Vesilind, & R.A. Minear, Register of Environmental Engineering Graduate Programs, Assn of Envtl Engg Professors (Ann Arbor Science Publishers, Ann Arbor MI 1981).

with the cooperation of, ABET. No date for implementation of this program has been set.

Accreditation of academic programs helps assure that curricula, facilties, and faculties meet some established minimum requirements for granting degrees in the field of industrial hygiene.

Professional engineering licensing programs are operated by individual states. As is the case for ABIH certification, licensing is achieved by meeting specified criteria for education and experience and by success in professional examination. Specific criteria may vary from state to state. An estimated 25 to 40 per cent of ABIH diplomates have engineering degrees, and of these it is estimated on the basis of an incomplete questionnaire survey that one-half or more have professional engineering licenses. Such licensing is a strong professional credential for an industrial hygienist. It should be pointed out, however, that although basic engineering techniques are applicable to the solution of many industrial hygiene problems, the field does have a specialized body of knowledge, and the mere holding of a professional engineering license does not necessarily qualify a person as an expert in industrial hygiene.

Several federal agencies, all states, and a number of local governments offer some form of compliance assistance to industry and other employers in matters of occupational health. A review of such programs and identification of the governmental agencies engaged in them has been published.[37] Expert consultation, or assistance in identifying such consultation, is available from many of the governmental programs listed to persons who have, or suspect, exposures of workers to hazardous materials in their places of employment.

The American Academy of Industrial Hygiene has adopted a code of ethics for the professional practice of industrial hygiene.[38] This code identifies the elements of professional responsibility and lists the professional industrial hygienists' responsibilities to employees (i.e., to workers), to employers and clients, and to the public. It is noteworthy that one specific responsibility listed in this code is to: "Hold responsibilities to the employer or client subservent to the ultimate responsibility to protect the health of the employees."[39]

Adherence to this code of ethics, coupled with demonstrated professional competence, are major elements of quality assurance in the practice of industrial hygiene for the control of workers' exposures to hazardous materials.

---

[37] Office of the Assistant Secretary for Planning and Evaluation, US DHHS, Protecting Workers' Health: Federal, State and Local Compliance-Assistance Programs (1981).

[38] Roster of Diplomates of the American Academy of Industrial Hygiene, (Annual publication, ABIH, administrative office, 475 Wolf Ledges Parkway, Akron, OH 44311).

[39] Id.

§3.18   The Role of Controls and Protections

Various types of controls and protections for limiting exposures of workers to toxic materials are discussed in §§3.02-3.16. In §§3.19-3.21, some possible roles of such controls and protections in litigation are briefly explored in a very general way. It is recognized that in litigation each case is based on the specific facts related to the matter at issue, and each case is judged on its own merits. Thus, material presented here is not intended to relate to the conduct or outcome of any particular case. Moreover, it is a science viewpoint, not a legal viewpoint.

§3.19   —When Standards Are Met

When a standard, rule, or regulation of a regulatory agency addresses an issue of controls or protections, it may be expected that compliance with all regulatory requirements should give some protection and relief from liability in litigation. Compliance, however, requires careful attention. There are several agencies with toxic substances regulations, and their requirements and assessment methods are not uniform. This nonuniformity poses problems for an establishment to which the regulations of more than one agency apply. This matter is being addressed by the Committee on Institutional Means for Assessment of Risks to Public Health, National Research Council. The committee has developed 10 recommendations on general procedures for achieving uniform toxic substances risk assessment guidelines among federal regulatory agencies.[40] At the present time, careful and systematic assessment of all regulatory requirements applicable to a particular establishment is necessary if one is to be assured that compliance with standards is, in fact, achieved.

Compliance goes beyond the provision of physical facilities for controls and protections. Monitoring of facility performance and surveillance of exposures, with the keeping of complete and defensible records of control actions and exposures, are necessary. Further, workers should be informed, in an understandable way, of the nature and extent of risks and the functions and capabilities of controls and protections which are provided. Misleading assurances of safety when there is a known potential risk, even when controls and protections required by regulations are provided, may negate any liability protection provided by hazard control facilities. Purchase and procurement practices and records are important in this regard. The substitution of a different process material, intentionally or inadvertently, for one expected by workers could be considered misleading regarding a work-related risk. In the same context, incomplete or misleading labeling of substances in the workplace could be considered a discrepancy.

In matters of products liability, manufacturers have been held responsible for a standard of care not required by regulation at the time the product was

---

[40] *Ways Needed to Gauge Health Effects of Hazardous Substances,* 61 Chemical & Engineering News 22-23 (Mar 14, 1983)

made.[41] It is not conceivable that such standard of care may be applied in workplace exposure litigation. It has been reported that workers have begun to sue manufacturers for injuries sustained from using their products in workplaces.[42]

Compliance with standards is not always simple. Efforts to comply should include:

1. Careful, systematic, and continuing review of regulatory requirements, and compliance with all applicable provisions

2. Maintenance of control facilities and surveillance of exposures, with adequate records of these activities

3. Training of workers and understandable disclosures of all known potential risks associated with processes and operations

4. Adequate labeling of materials with proper notification of workers when changes or substitutions of materials take place

§3.20 —When There Is No Specific Standard

Several hundred chemical compounds, common mixtures, and materials are dealt with specifically by standards and regulations. The overwhelming majority of the millions of known compounds, however, are not specifically and individually addressed. Such materials may be considered to be covered under the general duty provision, §5(a)(1) of The Occupational Safety and Health Act, which states that each employer "shall furnish to each of his employees employment and a place of employment which are *free* from *recognized hazards* that are causing or are *likely to cause* death or serious physical harm to his employees."[43] Because the section specifies *recognized hazards,* it may not be construed to cover hazardous materials which have not yet been recognized as such. It is noteworthy, however, that for recognized hazards, the section calls for protection not only from those which cause injury, but from those *likely to cause* injury. Thus, care is required even though there may be no evidence of actual injury.

When no specific standard or regulation applies to exposures to particular substances, the controls and protections provided should meet any applicable industry standard and should be no less protective than would be required for state-of-the-art professional practice of industrial hygiene. Failure to provide such level of protection may lead to allegations of negligence. The history of litigation regarding the professional practice of engineering may be indicative of expectations for professional practice of industrial hygiene in providing

---

[41] Witherell, *The Products-Liability Threat,* Chemical Engineering, Jan 24, 1983, at 72-87.

[42] Goerth, *In Search of Justice in Injury Liability Law,* 52 Occupational Health & Safety 38-42 (Jan 1983).

[43] 29 USC §654 (a)(1) (1970) (emphasis added).

controls and protections. Using engineering practice as a guide,[44] industrial hygienists may expect courts to measure professional performance by what a person with similar knowledge and training would do in the same circumstances, if he or she were a reasonable person. A lower level of performance may be considered negligent. This standard may be applied not only to the industrial hygienist, but to his or her superiors as well. Most industrial hygienists are employees. As such, under the concept of collective responsibility, industrial hygienists' responsibilities for adequacy of controls and protections may be shared by their managers at the various levels of the organizational hierarchy.

When no specific standard is applicable in a matter involving controls and protections, the likelihood of negligence may be reduced by:

1. Meeting applicable industry practice standards for controls and protections

2. Being alert to the development of new standards or regulations which may be applicable

3. Keeping current on recognition of hazards and improvements in controls and protections which may be applicable to work processes or operations of concern

4. Maintaining complete and accurate records of conditions of work, materials used, and performance of control and protections

5. Advising workers in an understandable way of any potential or suspected risks associated with work, and of best practice means for control and protection

Engaging or cooperating in research aimed at defining and controlling any suspected risks not yet recognized as hazards may be viewed as a good faith effort to provide effective controls and protections.

§3.21 —When There Is Compliance But Injury or Illness Occurs

Standards and regulations on controls and protections are intended to protect populations of workers from injury and illness. They are based in part upon available information regarding causal associations—that is, upon observed health effects which result from various levels of exposure. Some individuals may be especially susceptible to some specific agents; this may be because of a preexisting medical condition (e.g., a metabolic dysfunction), a behavorial characteristic (e.g., smoking), or a biologic circumstance (e.g., pregnancy). In such cases, injury may occur even though compliance with specific regulatory requirements for controls and protections is achieved. For some

---

[44] Mingle, & Reagan, *Legal and Moral Responsibilities of the Engineer* Chemical Engineering Progress, Dec 1980, at 15-23.

materials—for example, some carcinogens—there appears to be no threshold, or *safe,* level of exposure, and standards may be set at the lowest detectable level or at the level of best available control. In such cases, the standard may be complied with, but a level of risk may still be associated with residual exposures. For some other materials, standards may require controls and protections against a recognized health effect, yet the material may cause other effects as well, and these effects may occur even though the controls required for compliance with the standard are provided. Such a material might be one which causes direct toxic effect on a person exposed, an effect which is addressed by the standard, but which also causes reproductive effects or teratogenesis affecting the spouse or progeny of the person exposed. In such cases, standards may be met, yet injury may still be a consequence of exposure.

When injury occurs despite compliance with standards intended to protect against such injury, negligence in providing controls and protection would not seem to be an issue, even though liability for the injury may still be litigated. When it is known that specific medical, biological, or behavioral conditions increase risks of exposure to a material, risk of injury may be reduced by limiting or eliminating exposures of susceptible workers to that agent. For example, jobs involving some kinds of exposures might not be assigned to workers who smoke or to fertile or pregnant females.

Compliance with a standard for protection against one toxic effect should not necessarily be considered to be a defense against liability for injury caused by some other toxic effect. In such cases the *reasonable person standard* might be applied as a test for negligence. Steps which may be taken to reduce the likelihood of such injury and liability would seem to be those discussed in **§3.20.**

§3.22   Occupational and Environmental Exposures

As stated in **§3.01** and throughout Chapter 2, the numbers and varieties of situations involving hazardous materials are very great, and the numbers and varieties of controls and protections applicable to them are correspondingly great. The discussions on controls and protections contained in this chapter deal principally with those applicable in employee work situations. Controls and protections against community exposures to toxic materials caused by contamination of air, water, or soil, or by use of hazardous products, require other techniques, but the general principles of compliance with standards, meeting industry practice standards in the absence of regulations, and reasonable persons tests of negligence would seem to apply.

The variety and complexity of environmental problems associated with toxic materials, and the wide-spread publicity and public concern which have been associated with some hazardous materials problems, are generating legislative activity. The numbers and types of laws governing environmental aspects of toxic materials are likely to increase. It is reported that bills providing redress for persons injured by environmental exposures to hazardous materials are gaining higher priority on the legislative agenda.[45] New legislation will alter the nature of tort activity regarding environmental exposures to toxic materials.

For protection against liability for either occupational or environmental exposures, perhaps the most important factor is a true commitment by management to an exemplary, well-documented, systematic, and planned program of controls and protections. Such a program should be kept under continued review as a major responsibility by a top-level management official. One author, writing on products liability, has stated: "No program can confer absolute immunity to liability claims. But a well-run program can reduce their number and intensity, as well as minimize their consequences."[46] This statement is equally applicable to occupational and environmental exposures.

§3.23   Summary

Industrial hygiene practice is the recognition, evaluation, and control of environmental agents which may adversely affect workers or people in the community. Controls and protections under this definition are ordinarily categorized as engineering controls, administrative and work practice controls, and personal protection. There are no sharp boundaries to distinguish between these categories of control; a comprehensive program for the protection of workers is likely to involve elements of all three.

Engineering control includes substitution of processes, equipment, or materials to eliminate or reduce exposures of workers, isolation of offending agents from workers or of workers from offending agents, local exhaust ventilation to capture and prevent dispersion of contaminants into workroom air, and general ventilation to dilute air contaminants to acceptable levels of exposure. To be effective, engineering controls must be properly designed and maintained, and workers and supervisors must understand the purposes of the controls and be trained to recognize and correct or report malfunctions.

Administrative and work practice controls have as their purpose the limiting of workers' exposures to acceptable levels by the scheduling of work, and by controlling materials used in processes and the ways in which jobs are done. When a job involves different tasks having different levels of exposures, the scheduling of tasks so both the peak and average exposures of the worker involved are within acceptable limits is a form of administrative control. Work practices, including regulated access to locations where exposures may occur, control of the way in which tasks are done so hazardous exposures are eliminated or reduced, and constraints on personal behavior, such as smoking, when that behavior constitutes or increases hazard, are commonly used as means of control. As is the case with engineering controls, effective use of administrative

---

[45] Ember, *Legal Remedies for Toxics Victims Begin Taking Shape,* 61 Chemical & Engineering News 11-20 Mar 28, 1983.

[46] Witherell, *The Products-Liability Threat,* Chemical Engineering, Jan 24, 1983, at 72-77.

and work practice controls requires understanding and cooperation of workers and supervisors.

A wide range of personal protective devices are commercially available and are used to limit exposures of workers to hazardous materials. Personal protective devices include such safety devices as hard hats and safety glasses, protective clothing, respirators, and protective shields and barriers. Effectiveness of personal protection as a means of limiting exposures depends not only on the choice of proper devices, but more than any other means of control, on the understanding and cooperation of workers and supervisors. Industrial hygiene practice and government regulatory policy provide that use of personal protection is an acceptable alternative only when control of exposures by engineering and administrative or work practice means is not feasible. The federal Occupational Safety and Health Administration (OSHA) has announced its intention to review its policy in this matter.

The effectiveness of any means of control and protection is largely related to the level of expertise employed in its conception and implementation. The practice of industrial hygiene is based on a specialized body of scientific knowledge and technical information; professional practice requires an understanding of, and ability to apply, such knowledge and information. Criteria intended to identify and promote professionalism and ethical practice have been developed by industrial hygienists. Skillful application of this specialized body of knowledge in professional practice should result in controls and protections which meet applicable standards, and which stand the reasonable person test when there is no specific standard. Such practice, when kept current with constant, well-documented surveillance of the performance of controls, workplace exposures, and materials used, along with an adequately informed and well-trained workforce, should minimize the amount and consequences of litigation for injuries from exposures to toxic substances.

By expert application of proven methods of control and protection, it is possible to accomplish essentially any job, or to work with essentially any material, without injury to the workers involved.

The Diagnosis of Occupational or Environmental Illness & Injury

Resha M. Putzrath, Ph.D.*, Marshal S. Levine, M.D.**, C. Ralph Buncher, Ph.D.†, and G.Z. Nothstein, Esq.

4

§4.01   Introduction

Many deaths, diseases, and even more subtle biochemical abnormalities have been linked to exposures to hazardous and toxic substances during the past several decades. There have also been many firm denials and insistences that

---

*Putzrath & Company; Special Consultant, Environ Corporation, Washington D.C.

**Department of Epidemiology and Preventive Medicine, University of Maryland School of Medicine, Baltimore, Maryland

† Professor of Epidemiology and Biostatistics, Institute of Environmental Health, University of Cincinnati Medical Center, Cincinnati, Ohio.

such relationships do not exist. While it may not, in fact, be too difficult to demonstrate the concept that certain work or environmental situations do result in disease, it is much more difficult to determine the relationship of workplace exposures to disease in any particular individual. This difficulty arises from the fact that many diseases which are induced by or aggravated by exposure to toxic substances are similar to diseases which are not related to that particular toxic exposure. For example, diseases such as chronic lung disease or lung cancer, which may be caused by working with hazardous dusts, may also be due to other factors such as cigarette smoking. These diseases tend to express themselves in the same manner regardless of the precipitating agent, and it is rare that diagnosis of the disease in a particular individual will unequivocally indicate either the causative agent or the source of that agent. We must therefore rely upon other techniques to differentiate illness due to toxic substances from illness occurring in the general population.

The similarity of some diseases caused by exposure to a given chemical with those of other origins has led to much confusion and has led to much confusing discussion, both in and out of court. Before approaching the resolution of this problem, two questions must be answered: What is an occupational or environmental disease, and how does one establish attributability in any particular instance?

§4.02 The Nature of Occupational or Environmental Disease

An *occupational disease* may be defined as a disease or physical defect which occurs among people who perform a particular task, and which does not occur among people who do not perform that task. It is not quite as evident, however, that *any* disease or abnormality, even one which also occurs in the general population, can be termed *occupationally related* if it is found more frequently among a particular group of workers than among their fellows who perform different tasks or work in different locations. The implication is that there is something about that task or work location which itself leads to development of the disease, or which leads to an excess of disease occurring among the workers in question as compared to the general population.

Thus, often that there is nothing particularly unique about a disease or abnormality itself which identifies it as occupational. Rather, any disease or abnormality may be considered potentially to be occupational in origin if it occurs more frequently among certain workers than among the general population, and conversely, any disease may be considered nonoccupational if it does not occur more frequently than among the general population. Again, the distinction between occupational and nonoccupational depends upon the incidence of the disease in the general population and upon the work situation, and it generally cannot be determined directly from characteristics of the disease process, nor from characteristics of the individual affected.

As is the case for occupational disease, any illness or disease which occurs in excess among people who live in a particular environment (i.e., near a factory, near a hazardous waste site, or near a common source of drinking water) may be considered potentially to be an *environmentally related* disease. The toxic substance may be the same in both instances where a disease has been contracted. For example, exposure to a pesticide might be termed occupational if it occurred among workers who manufactured or applied the material. The same exposure might be termed environmental if it occurred among people who lived near the manufacturing plant or were near the area of application. The resulting disease or abnormality would depend upon levels of exposure and, on the whole, might be the same regardless of whether it was labeled as an occupational or environmental exposure.

There are, of course, many similarities and crossovers between occupational and environmental diseases and exposures, and occasionally the terms are used interchangeably. There are some important differences, however, particularly when considering the amount of polluting substance under consideration, the length of time for which people are exposed, or the type of people who may be involved. In the workplace, presumably healthy adult workers may be exposed to potentially toxic substances for only eight or ten hours a day, five days a week for the extent of their working lives. In the general environment, all types of people, old and young, healthy and infirm, may be continually exposed for 24 hours per day. Therefore, standards may differ between the workplace and the general environment. However, the similarities in the nature of the toxic substances of interest, and in the basic concepts of determining attribution of cause, allow the inclusion of environmentally related diseases with those of occupational origin for purposes of this chapter.

§4.03 —Acute Injuries and Illnesses

Classical examples of occupationally related injuries are the amputation which results from getting one's hand caught in a punch press and the acid burn which results from an accidental spill. Generally, there is little question as to what has happened and where it has happened, and there is no question about its relationship to work or of the occupational nature of the injury. In other instances, such as chronic low back pain, the situation may not be quite as obvious, and the main problem becomes how to determine where the trauma occurred which led to the back pain.

Acute illness as well as trauma may also be traced to a specific incident, such as in the case of metal fume fever, which is an illness with some flu-like symptoms resulting from breathing fumes generated by burning zinc or other metals. Again, there is a relatively clear relationship between a work-related event and a health outcome. Although these acute injuries and illnesses are generally straightforward, they may occasionally require considerable detective work to determine the relationship between cause and effect.

§4.04   —Chronic Diseases

During the past quarter of a century, there has been an increase in the incidence of chronic diseases such as lung cancer, liver disease, heart disease, and others. It has been suggested that many of these diseases are related to the man-made environment both within the workplace and in the general community. Chronic diseases may have a long latency period—that is, a long time lag between the beginning of the causative exposure and the onset of the resulting disease—ranging from as short as five years to as long as 25 or more years. This time lag makes determination of the relationship of cause and effect extremely difficult. In addition, chronic diseases may have multiple causes, which fact adds to the difficulty of determining the exact cause. Further, since many of these chronic diseases also occur in the general population, it is difficult to determine with absolute precision whether a particular disease occurring in a particular individual is related to the exposure of concern, or whether it represents the expression of *background* occurrence in the general population.

While short-term, high-dose exposures to toxic substances generally result in acute health effects, chronic diseases often result from long-term, repeated exposures to low levels of toxic material, and therefore no one specific instance can easily be related to these diseases.

§4.05   —Other Health Effects

In addition to the acute injury and illness and the chronic diseases mentioned in §§4.03-4.04, other more subtle health effects may occur. Abnormal pulmonary function tests, abnormal liver function tests, or abnormalities of blood tests have been related to the workplace. These abnormalities may or may not develop into more severe illness. However, when they occur in excess among a working population, the possibility of occupational causation must be considered.

The definition of an occupational disease depends upon the incidence of that disease or abnormality in the working population as compared to a population not performing the same tasks. The *working population* can be defined in general terms—such as those employees working on a particular production process or at a certain plant site—or in more specific terms—such as work with one chemical or work with that chemical at different ambient levels of exposure. The disease itself may also be described in very specific terms, such as *mesothelcoma,* or in such general terms as *headache.*

§4.06   The Nature of the Diagnostic Process

A primary goal of the occupational or environmental health professional is the prevention of the accident or illness which arises out of the conditions of employment or alterations to the environment. In this preoccupation with prevention, the occupational health physician or nurse may differ from some of his or her colleagues in clinical medicine.

The clinician's primary concern frequently is to diagnose illness so that it can be treated, and so that the patient can be returned to normal, healthy status, or as close to that healthy state as possible. Thus, the function of a correct diagnosis for the clinician is to assist in the appropriate treatment of his or her patient. Since the clinician's main concern is often that of treatment, tentative diagnoses may have to be made on the basis of available information, and the clinician may have to proceed without the luxury of complete knowledge. Medical diagnosis, then, is often of an inferential nature, and the diagnosis or the treatment itself may be altered as the disease progresses and more information becomes available. Thus, it is evident that general medical diagnosis requires much art and clinical judgment, and that reasonable people may disagree on the particulars. In fact, different approaches to the same problem may yield similar results.

The occupational physician (and by extension the physician interested in environmental disease) must not only deal with the difficulties of clinical diagnosis and treatment but must also be concerned with identifying the causative agent and its relationship to the workplace, so that the offending substance or situation may be eliminated or controlled. The diagnosis of occupational disease therefore consists of three main elements. These elements may be termed:

1. The medical (clinical) diagnosis
2. The etiological (causative agent) diagnosis
3. The attributability of the disease to the specific workplace or environment

Thus, in a patient with lead poisoning who suffers some paralysis so that he or she cannot extend the hand at the wrist, the medical diagnosis may be *wrist drop* and the etiological diagnosis may be *due to lead poisoning.* The attribution may be that the lead exposure occurred at work, or that it is due to eating acidic food stored in lead-glazed pottery, or that some other exposure is responsible.

The making of an etiological diagnosis and the attribution of underlying cause require different types of information than is generally available to the clinician. Although in the illustration above, determination of blood lead may indicate the etiology of the symptoms, in many instances of occupationally or environmentally related disease, such biological markers of exposure are not available. The physician is thus left with the need to make inferences both as to etiology and attribution, just as he or she must make inferences in order to arrive at the clinical diagnosis itself. Again, considerable art or judgment may be involved. If a patient with lead-induced wrist drop belongs to an occupation that uses lead, the inference is often drawn that there is a causal relationship between occupation and disease. However, the lead exposure in the work location under question may have been very minimal, or it may have been adequately controlled, or appropriate work practices may have been followed.

Additionally, the patient may have had other sources of lead exposure. In such a case, it becomes extremely difficult to determine attributability with certainty.

A more precise approach to attribution depends upon a thorough knowledge of the workplace, the nature of the production process, the nature and degree of potentially toxic exposures, the presence and functioning of engineering controls, the use of personal protective equipment, and the nature of work practices. This information generally is the responsibility of the industrial hygienist, but the nurse or physician must be aware of these facts and have a solid working relationship with the hygienist if an appropriate attribution is to be made. In addition, the physician must be aware of the toxicological relationship of the disease in question to the causative agent and must obtain a good medical and work history of the patient, as well as information on other potential exposures in his or her environment.

An informed inference of attribution can then be made based on this knowledge. This inference can be greatly strengthened (or defended against) by knowledge of the incidence of the disease in the exposed and in the unexposed populations.

Thus, key factors in determining the work-relatedness of a disease in a particular individual are a thorough knowledge of the workplace and a knowledge of the incidence of that disease among his or her fellow workers and among similar individuals not performing the same tasks or not working in the same location. If the disease in question occurs in excess among his or her fellow workers, it may be reasonable to assume that the disease in the individual may be related to his or her occupation. If there is not an excess among his or her colleagues, other relationships should also be investigated.

Information on the incidence of disease in the working population and in a comparison population is available from epidemiological studies, and from appropriately designed medical monitoring programs. In general, epidemiological studies are performed after a problem has arisen and these studies are designed to answer a question phrased as an hypothesis. Medical monitoring may be performed as a routine activity, without a specific hypothesis. Medical monitoring may thus serve as an early warning of problems and may help to determine attribution or to demonstrate the effectiveness of engineering control procedures in preventing the development of excess illness.

§4.07 Epidemiological Studies

Epidemiological studies (discussed in greater detail in Chapter 1), in conjunction with toxicological studies and clinical case reports, are frequently the means by which the original association of disease to toxic exposures is made. Epidemiological studies are also used to establish (or to deny) the probability of the presence of an occupational disease in a particular environment or workplace. The field of epidemiology is broad, but it can be simply defined as the study of the distribution of disease among populations. The rates of disease occurring in various populations are compared, and attempts are made to relate the differences found to factors such as variations in age, race, sex, smoking habits, alcohol consumption, dietary differences, or other factors.

In the workplace, these other factors may be differences in work location, job description, or work with specific substances. In the environment, the other factors may include proximity to the dump site or access to a water system. The goal of these epidemiological studies is to establish whether there is a significant difference between the rates of disease (or death) in the population under study as compared to a control population. For example, excess of disease in the workers studied would suggest a relationship between work and that disease. The lack of an excess suggests the absence of such a relationship.

Epidemiological studies are performed for a variety of reasons, and with a variety of techniques. Those studies done in response to concerns of causality in the workplace may be cross-sectional—i.e., an examination of the situation at one point in time—or longitudinal—i.e., performed over a period of time. Two types of analyses are generally performed. These are the SMR (standardized mortality or morbidity ratio) and the PMR (proportional mortality or morbidity ratio).

§4.08 —Standardized Mortality or Morbidity Ratio

The standardized mortality or morbidity ratio (SMR) is a means of comparing the rates of disease in two different populations. For example, assume that lung cancer occurs at the rate of 200 times per 100,000 workers in a certain plant or occupation, and at the rate of 100 cases per 100,000 people in the general population with the same age distribution. The observed rate in workers is placed over the expected rate in the general population to give a ratio of:

$$\frac{200/100,000}{100/100,000},$$

or an SMR of 2, or 200 per cent. Thus, an SMR of 200 (since SMRs are generally expressed as a percentage) for lung cancer among certain workers indicates that lung cancer occurs twice as frequently among those workers as it does among the general population. In order for this figure to have meaning, consideration must also be made for differences between workers and the general population such as smoking habits, drinking habits, race, sex, section of the country, and other possible confounding variables. Alternatively, the comparison population may be originally chosen on the basis of these characteristics.

Several other factors must be taken into account when using the SMR, such as the *healthy worker effect*. This concept suggests that because those who work must be healthy enough to hold a job, they can be expected to have less disease than occurs in the general population. Thus, although an SMR of 100 may seem to indicate no difference between workers and the general population, because of the healthy worker effect, an SMR of 100 may actually indicate that slightly more disease is present among the workers than might have been anticipated. Care must be taken in invoking the healthy worker effect, however, as not all diseases show this difference, nor do workers of all ages. For example, if a disease such as congenital heart disease or childhood cancer is not compatible with long life, there may be few older people with the disease even in the general population.

Another factor to be considered when using the SMR is the choice of a comparison population. For example, if there are regional differences in the prevalence of a disease, comparison populations chosen from other regions would reflect the regional differences and confuse the occupational effect. For example, if lung cancer were more prevalent in Baltimore, Maryland than in the United States in general, comparison of workers in Baltimore with the United States' population would show an increase of lung cancer in these workers regardless of the work situation. This may, of course, also be a problem if there is a lower local rate of disease than is found nationally.

§4.09 —Proportional Mortality or Morbidity Ratio

Another summary statistic, the proportional mortality or morbidity ratio (PMR), has been used to indicate the presence of an occupational disease among groups of workers. The PMR differs from the standardized mortality or morbidity ratio (SMR) in that the PMR compares percentages of disease rather than rates. That is, it compares the percentage of lung cancer among all other diseases (or deaths) in one population in relation to a comparison population. Assume, for example, that lung cancer accounts for 40 per cent of all deaths in workers and 20 per cent of all deaths in the comparison population. The PMR is determined by placing the observed percentage in workers over the expected percentage in the general population to yield a ratio of:

$$\frac{40\%}{20\%}$$

or a PMR of 2, or 200 per cent. This figure again indicates that lung cancer occurs twice as frequently among workers than might be expected. However, the PMR may be biased by two main factors in addition to those discussed in §4.08 which affect the SMR.

Since the PMR measures the differences in percentage of deaths or diseases in a population (all of which must add up to 100 per cent), an increase in the percentage of one cause of death is reflected as a decrease in other causes of death. For example, if race car drivers have more deaths from accidents, the PMR will indicate fewer deaths from lung cancer regardless of the fact that no change in the rate of lung cancer has occurred.

It may also be difficult to be sure that there is complete information on the number of deaths or diseases which have occurred. For example, people may be more concerned about lung cancer and less concerned about auto accidents. Therefore, they may report lung cancer more rigorously than auto accidents. In view of the proportionate nature of PMR comparisons, such differential ascertainment of disease may cause serious errors in interpretation. Although these problems with the PMR may be overcome by experienced investigators, it is generally preferable to use the SMR.

Epidemiological studies have proven to be a very valuable source of information for determination of the attribution of disease to the workplace, and much of our current knowledge derives from that source. Unfortunately, these studies tend to require a great deal of time, money, and expertise, as well as a suitable test and control population. Furthermore, it may be difficult to apply the findings from one study to a case of interest in a slightly different situation.

§4.10   Medical Monitoring Techniques

The terms *medical monitoring, surveillance,* and *screening* tend to be used interchangeably to indicate the process of examining workers to observe changes in body function in an attempt to identify diseases of occupational or environmental origin. The availability of new computerized techniques for collecting and analyzing data allows investigators to both *screen,* or examine the individual worker for evidence of disease and *monitor* a working population for evidence of health effects resulting from possible exposure to toxic substances. By using aggregate population data and comparing average values and rates of abnormalities, investigators can determine the presence of excess disease and indicate the work-relatedness and attributability of disease. Thus, investigators can monitor a population, in addition to screening the individual.

Groups of workers, or populations, are often defined in terms of *exposure zones.*[1] These zones are not necessarily geographic but indicate the commonality of the work process, of the substances used, or of the level of exposure to these substances. Data are collected from both industrial hygiene and medical monitoring activities and can be analyzed to determine if a relationship exists between work and health effects.

A group of employees working with a respiratory irritant can illustrate these concepts. Assume that 10 employees are working in an exposure zone (Zone B) in which respiratory irritants are found in the ambient air. Sample pulmonary function tests (PFT) on these theoretical workers are displayed in Table 4-1. It is apparent that among this group of 10 workers, three have abnormal PFTs, and they will require appropriate diagnosis and treatment. However, it is difficult to know if these abnormal PFTs are due to the work situation, or to nonoccupational exposures such as cigarette smoking, or to normal background effects in the general population.

In various different circumstances, depending upon the specific work envi-

---

[1] Corn, *Workplace Exposure Zones for Classification of Employee Exposures to Physical and Chemical Agents,* Am Indus Hygiene Assn J 40(1): 47-57 (1979).

ronment and the incidence of abnormal PFTs in comparison populations, analysis of this same set of 10 PFTs in the same sample of workers might:

1. Indicate the work-relatedness of the abnormalities found in this group of employees

2. Indicate subtle early changes which require investigation prior to the onset of overt disease

3. Document the effectiveness of control procedures in preventing occupational illness in this population

Table 4-1 Sample Pulmonary Function Tests

(Zone B)

Employee Number	FEV_1 (Lung Volumes) [Forced Expatory Volume in 1 Second] (% of FVC) [Forced Vital Capacity]
1	82
2	76
3	80
4	62*
5	72
6	64*
7	76
8	62*
9	76
10	84
Total	730
Mean Value	73
Abnormal Results	3*

If we compare the sample of 10 employees (Zone B) with others having less exposure (such as supervisors or workers using the same substance in another process), and also with an unexposed comparison population, tests might generate PFT values and a dose-response or exposure-effect relationship (see §1.04), as recorded in Table 4-2. (These data are simplified for illustration purposes. In actual situations, adjustments would have been made for factors such as variations in age, race, smoking habits, and use of respirators, and consideration would have been made for pre- and post-work shift measurements.)

Table 4-2 Comparison of Pulmonary Function Tests Demonstrating Work-Relatedness of Disease

FEV$_1$ (% of TLV)

Comparison Group	Zone A (Minimal Exposure)	Zone B (Moderate Exposure)
82	86	82
72	76	76
76	72	80
74	74	62*
78	66*	72
86	72	64*
84	64*	72
62*	80	62*
84	78	76
72	82	84

Total	770	750	730
Mean Value	77	75	73
Abnormal Results	1*	2*	3*

Using epidemiologic techniques of comparing and analyzing this monitoring data for a larger sample population, investigators may be able to demonstrate that the abnormal pulmonary function test among the 10 workers is in fact related to working with the irritant dust (Figure 4-1).

Computerized data bases allow investigators to analyze information, in the manner described above, on large groups of employees at regularly scheduled intervals.

In a second example using the same group of 10 workers, but where the comparison populations reflect a different background incidence of pulmonary function abnormalities (Table 4-3), there is no excess of abnormal values, but there is a fall in mean values from what would be expected. Thus this may be an early warning of subtle health effects which are related to the workplace (Figure 4-2).

Figure 4-1 Dose-response relationships demonstrating work-relatedness of disease

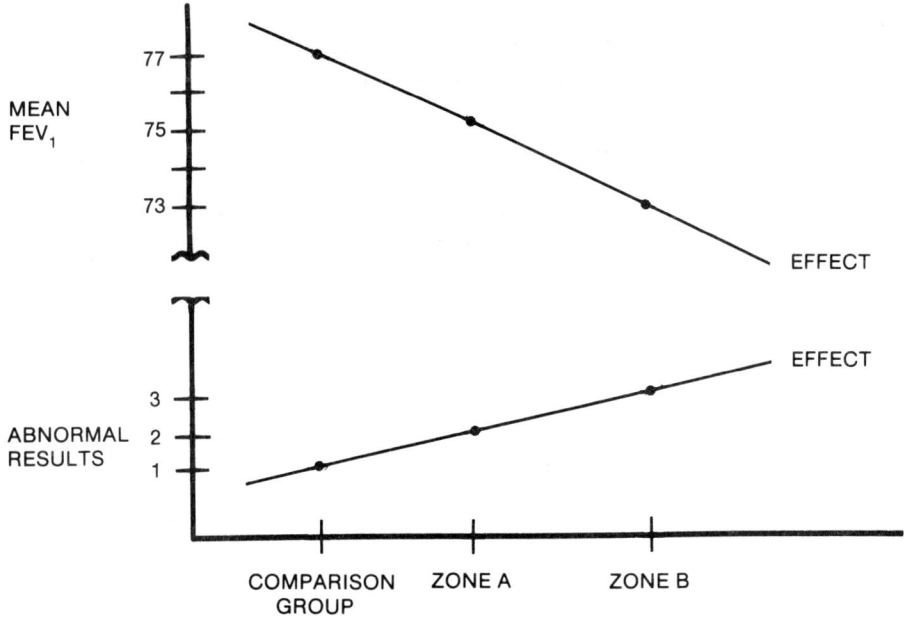

Table 4-3 Comparison of Pulmonary Function Tests Indicating Subtle Physiologic Change

FEV$_1$ (% of FVC)

	Comparison Group	Zone A (Minimal Exposure)	Zone B (Moderate Exposure)
	74	86	82
	66*	76	76
	72	64*	80
	66*	72	62*
	78	66*	72
	86	72	64*
	84	64*	72
	62*	80	62*
	84	78	76
	78	82	84
Total	750	740	730
Mean Value	75	74	73
Abnormal Results	3*	3*	3*

Figure 4-2 Dose-response relationships indicating subtle physiologic change

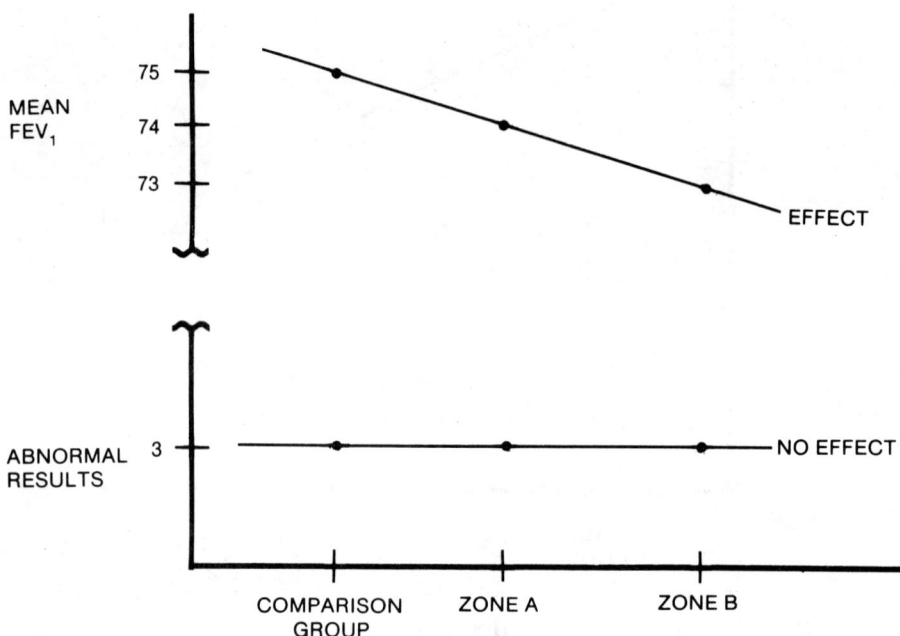

In a third example (Table 4-4), again using the very same group of 10 workers, but with a higher incidence of background abnormalities in the general population, the investigator may not be able to attribute these abnormalities to the workplace at all but must seek some other causative factor (Figure 4-3).

Table 4-4 Comparison of Pulmonary Function Tests Documenting the Adequacy of Control Procedures

FEV₁ (% of FVC)

FEV_1 (% of FVC)

Comparison Group	Zone A (Minimal Exposure)	Zone B (Moderate Exposure)
72	84	82
64*	76	76
72	62*	80
62*	72	62*
76	64*	72
84	72	64*
82	62*	72

	Comparison Group	Zone A (Minimal Exposure)	Zone B (Moderate Exposure)
	62*	80	62*
	80	76	76
	76	82	84
Total	730	730	730
Mean Value	73	73	73
Abnormal Results	3* 3* 3*		

Figure 4-3 Dose-response relationships documenting the adequacy of control procedures

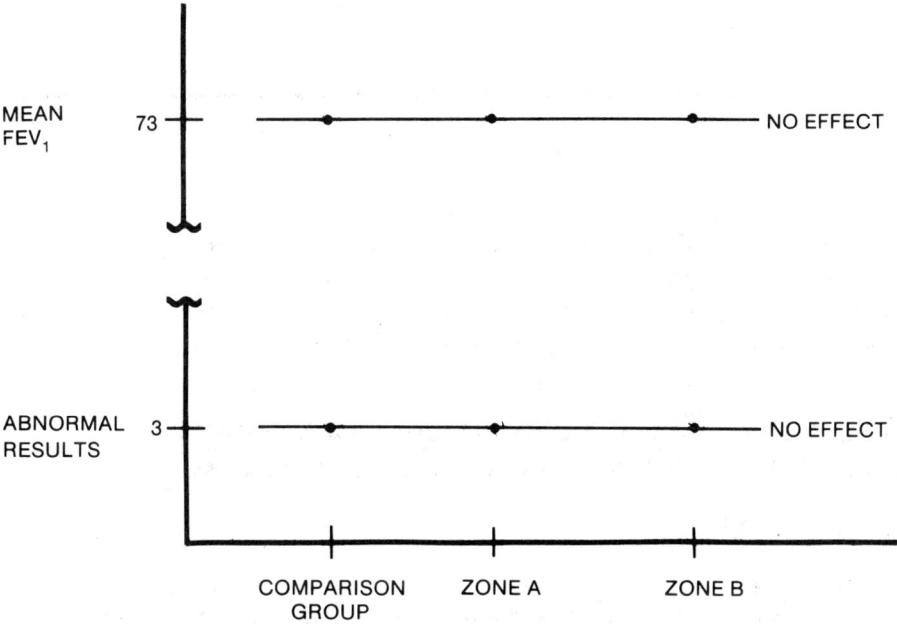

The above examples indicate the manner in which an appropriately designed and analyzed medical monitoring program can be critical in assessing attributability of occupational disease. These medical monitoring programs can be used to gather data routinely, and to prepare reports at regular intervals. These reports can then serve as an audit of the effectiveness of control procedures and can indicate areas of potential concern.

§4.11   Risk Extrapolation

After the investigator determines all possible toxic effects that a compound may produce, several questions exist. Which effects are most likely to occur? What is the probability that any particular disease will be caused by a particular level of exposure? At which doses will a given effect predominate? Risk extrapolations assist in answering such questions by predicting probable outcomes under new circumstances using known effects of studied exposures.

Most toxicological responses are linear over some range of doses. (Linearity involves the shape of the dose-response curve (see §1.04); if the response is directly proportional to the dose for all concentrations, the dose-response curve is linear.) No effect can be linear for all doses, however, since once all animals are affected, increasing the dose cannot increase that effect (although increasing the dose may change the effect).

A threshold is that dose below which a toxic effect is not observed. The concept appears simple: e.g., an amount of aspirin below which the drug is not lethal, or an amount of alcohol below which the person will not be intoxicated. In toxicity testing of animals, thresholds are often expressed as *no observed effect levels* or NOELs.

However, complications for the determination of thresholds arise as soon as specific cases are examined. The lethal dose of aspirin is lower for the average child than the average adult. Even if the dose is expressed as milligrams of the compound per kilogram body weight, the lethal dose of a given chemical will not be exactly the same for each individual and may be significantly lower for hypersensitive individuals. Individuals within a population, such as fetuses, children, or people with a given genetic background, may be at higher risk for a specific chemical. Ingestion of the same amount of alcohol, for example, will affect individuals differently.

Risk extrapolations depend heavily on two factors: known toxic effects of a compound and risk extrapolation models. Obviously, if the only knowledge of toxic effects of a compound is from a poorly executed laboratory study, the results of even the best risk extrapolation will be tenuous. The converse is also true. Excellent data on the effects of a compound on animals are applicable to humans only to the extent that a risk extrapolation model is able to mimic the differences and similarities between humans and the laboratory animal.

Knowledge about the toxic properties of chemicals primarily comes from two sources: epidemiological studies of the consequences of human exposures and laboratory experiments on other organisms. If exposure to a compound has a rapid effect or if the effect is sufficiently strong or unusual, the effects can be observed in a human population. These effects are most easily noticed for high levels of exposure. When a toxicant is released into the environment, however, it is usually diluted. Thus, exposures are to a smaller amount of the chemical, and the risk to an exposed human population must be extrapolated to this lower dose. Furthermore, the amount of information which can be gathered from human exposures is limited and is almost always retrospective.

In order to prevent exposure to potentially dangerous chemicals, toxicologists use animals, plants, or bacteria to observe the chemical's toxic effects on other living things. These results must be interpreted to estimate the potential for harm to humans. Therefore, estimation of the risk posed by exposure to hazardous chemicals generally involves extrapolation of risk from scientific laboratory experiments. These extrapolations usually involve two phases: from high to low dose and from animals to humans. Each process requires the use of models; each issue is surrounded by varying degrees of controversy within the scientific community.[2]

Finally, the difference in the ability to estimate risk and the ability to estimate safety must be recognized. Even if the models were completely accurate, they would only allow assessment above which an effect can be observed. The only guarantee of complete safety from the toxic effects of a chemical occurs with no exposure to that chemical. Beyond that, the question becomes one of what is considered to be *sufficiently safe*. Even when toxicologists agree on test results and risk extraploation models, the concept of a safe dose can be a source of disagreement. The concepts of risk perception and acceptable risk have a literature of their own.

§4.12   Statistical Analysis

Statistical analyses are primarily utilized to analyze a predictor/criterion relationship. The final output of data collection in the conduct of a validity study is a set or distribution of predictor scores and of criterion scores. Such a distribution can be developed for each measure or variable employed in the study. The distributions may take a variety of forms, and the nature of predictor and criterion score distributions is a major determinant of the particular statistical techniques that should be used in the analysis. However, a distribution, where the scores spread out over a range of values, is one where there is a sizeable concentration of scores near the middle with gradually declining frequencies on both sides of the distribution. A common procedure in conducting a statistical summary is to calculate a mean (X) by totalling all of the scores and dividing by the number of subjects (N). In some cases the use of the mean would provide a somewhat distorted picture. In such cases it may be

---

[2] Using different models for risk extrapolation from high to low dose can result in significantly different risks at the lower doses. For example, as reported in the 1981 publication of the National Research Council, *The Health Effects of Nitrate, Nitrite, and N-Nitrosocompounds,* the dose which would result in a risk of 10^2 for the chemical N-nitrosopyrolidine is within a factor of 20 for the one-hit, multistage, and multi-hit models. At a risk of 10^6, however, the doses vary by a factor of 10,000 depending on which model is used; Maugh II, *Chemical Carcinogens: How Dangerous Are Low Doses?* Sci 202, 37-41 (1978); Hoel, *Low-dose and Species-to-Species Extrapolation for Chemically Induced Carcinogenesis,* Banbury Report 1; Assessing Chemical Mutagens: The Risk to Humans (1979).

better to use the middle score or the median. The median is that point on the scale of scores where the frequency above or below is 50 per cent of the total frequency. The mean and median are, of course, identical when the shape of a frequency distribution is perfectly symmetrical, but the median moves more slowly in either direction when scores begin to accumulate which are either extremely high or extremely low.

§4.13   —Statistical Significance and p-Values

Assume that the rate of a particular disease in a group of workers exposed to the chemical *Badstuff* is seven per thousand and the rate in workers not exposed to this chemical is five per thousand. What does this difference indicate? Decades ago, scientists used to judge differences of this variety on a subjective basis. This lead to a great deal of confusion between those observations which were not repeatable—ie, due to random chance—and those observations which were due to causal effects and therefore were repeatable. If the phenomenon is due to chance variation, there is no reason to expect the same phenomenon to be repeated the next time the situation occurs. On the other hand, if chance as the explanation is ruled out, the scientist must assume that the next time the same circumstances come together, he or she will observe the same type of phenomenon. To tell these situations apart, statisticians evolved a series of statistical hypothesis tests which are now routinely used throughout science to separate those events which are likely to be chance phenomena from those events which are likely to be repeatable.

Two key phrases in the science of statistics are *statistical significance* and *p-value.* The p-value, or probability value, is the mathematical probability associated with an event. There is no statistical concept that is easier to misinterpret than p-values. Perhaps this is because of a difference in the way lawyers and statisticans think and come to decisions.

Defining the term *p-value,* can start with what p-values are not. A p-value is not the probability of being correct or the probability that the agent being discussed caused the phenomenon under study. It is logically inconsistant to believe that one could have the information necessary to calculate the probability of being correct without at the same time knowing for certain whether one is correct. In fact, statisticians and other scientists are forced to calculate a different probability which is indirectly related to the question at issue and which hopefully also provides insight into the issue of concern.

A particularly egregious example of the misuse of statistics occurred in the Food and Drug Administration (FDA) handling of the cyclamate issue.[3] The decision used statistical reasoning written by attorneys for the FDA rather than by the FDA's statisticians. The result was so statistically imprecise that the American Statistical Association judged it important enough to send a letter

---

[3] 45 Fed Reg 61474 (Sept 16, 1980).

of objection to the Food and Drug Administration for their misuse of statistical methods.

What probability, then, is being calculated when a p-value is reported? If one completely specifies all of the numbers or, in the technical sense, *parameters* of a situation but still allows for random variation, the probability of all possible outcomes can be calculated. A simple example would be all possible outcomes in the situation of tossing 20 coins. If one specifies the probability of the result being a *head* and the result being a *tail,* a statistician can calculate the probability of tossing exactly 10 heads when tossing 20 coins, or tossing 11 heads or 12 or zero or 20 or any other number. The problem in hypothesis testing in statistics then becomes the challenge of separating out highly likely events from those events which are unlikely. A common situation would be to have the completely specified hypothesis say that there is no difference between those who are exposed to the agent and those who are not (often called a *null hypothesis*), and then calculate the probability of various outcomes in that circumstance.

If the probability of kidney damage is theoretically equal in each of two groups of 20 persons, it would be an unusual event for, say, 18 of 20 cases to have occurred in those exposed to the agent and only three to have occurred in those 20 not exposed. If the probability of this event and those more extreme is perhaps one in a million, most people would be uncomfortable with saying that chance variation explains the current situation. When there is an alternative hypothesis that the agent causes extra cases of kidney disease, statisticians are especially shy in saying they have been chosen to witness this rare one-in-a-million event. Instead, they choose to believe that the hypothesis is not true such that the actual outcome is not such a rare event. Through custom, the value of 0.05, or one in 20, is often accepted as the de facto boundary between those situations for which chance is a reasonable explanation (probabilities >0.05) and those situations for which some alternative is a reasonable explanation (probabilities <0.05).

Each of these situations or conclusions from a hypothesis test must be carefully interpreted. If the probability is <0.05, common usage applies the wording *statistically significant* to this situation. Unfortunately, there are both a technical meaning and a common meaning to these two words. In statistical terminology, nothing more nor less is meant than that the statistical jury went out and decided that in this trial there was a high possibility that the agent was guilty of this single event—i.e., the observation was unlikely to be due to chance. Other evidence and other procedures and issues will be tested in separate (statistical) courtrooms. Following this analogy, there is no reason to think that the event in the first courtroom was necessarily significant in the sense of meaningful and important. This is simply a statistical term to separate out those issues likely due to chance variation from those which need another explanation. These other explanations include the agent being guilty, the evidence being tampered with, and someone miscalculating the statistical test. Obviously, an agent that is a repeat offender, found at a statistically significant level in a number of studies, is more likely to be truly guilty than not.

The other side of the situation also needs explanation. If the probability of an event is > 0.05, this only means that the jury of statistics found a high probability that the agent was not guilty. Clearly, this type of situation can come about for many reasons, including that the agent is really not guilty and that there was insufficient evidence presented to find in the statistical court that the agent was guilty. The latter situation is of particular importance in statistical hypothesis testing. The size of the sample being studied affects statistical significance. The larger the sample size, the more likely one is to pronounce a difference as statistically significant; or in the courtroom analogy, the more persons there are in the neighborhood of a crime, the more likely one is to be able to find witnesses necessary to get a conviction.

One final comment on statistical significance is necessary. The boundary line between events which are statistically significant and those which are not is blurry rather than sharp. The 0.05 point should be thought of as a region rather than a point, even though in some legal proceedings a definitive decision may have to be made. One is discussing a horizon rather than the edge of a flat earth. People do not all see the same horizon because of differences in vision, because of aids to vision, and because of impediments to looking out at the horizon. Statisticians may agree on how to calculate the probability in each individual case, but in a legal situation they may to disagree over which method is to be used in a particular instance.

§4.14   —The Whole Group versus Subgroups

A particularly troublesome issue in statistical inference and thus toxic torts diagnosis is whether the whole group of individuals studied should be at issue or whether some restricted subgroup is the group that is of importance. For example, suppose a study of the health effects of living near a toxic waste dump has been completed. The total study did not find any health effect at a statistically significant level and therefore cannot make a scientific claim of having found any effect justifying legal action. On the other hand, suppose there is a subgroup of individuals, say those males between the ages of 40 and 60 who have lived near the waste dump for three to fifteen years. Suppose that in this group there are found four cases of disease out of the 13 individuals who qualify for this subgroup. First, one must consider statistical significance, since there is a technical point here (see **§4.13**). One may be able to support the contention that the finding in the small subgroup is statistically significant if this were calculated as an a priori hypothesis test. On the other hand, most such subgroups are determined after the data have been analyzed so that the hypothesis is really on an a posteriori basis. In this case, the finding may or may not be statistically significant when the appropriate statistical test is made.

Even if the result is agreed to be statistically significant, there are some who will argue that this particular subgroup was chosen only because of the data and that this one study is not adequate scientific proof of a health hazard. The problem is that any total study can be divided into hundreds or even thousands and, if it was a large enough study, even millions of subgroups. The important question is whether the subgroups consist of those special individuals that are really at hazard to a health harm, or whether this is in reality a construct of the mind because random variation has produced a few extra cases in a group that can be defined by some subgroup charactistics. The situation is basically the same as for any other study but the problem is multiplied by the numerous potential subgroups. In studying the effects of air pollution, one would be more impressed if the effects were found only in a subgroup consisting of those with the lung diseases of asthma and emphysema than if the subgroup were defined by color of hair and number of siblings, since there appears to be more biologic reasoning involved in selecting the former subgroup than the latter subgroup. The advent of computers with the ability to manipulate great quantities of data very rapidly has made it easier for investigators to find effects in one subgroup in a large data set which does not show the same effect as the total group in the study.

§4.15 Summary

An occupational or environmental disease can be defined as any disease which occurs in excess among a group of workers or persons exposed to the same environment in comparison to a control population. The diagnosis of an occupational or environmental disease consists of three separate elements. These are the medical (clinical) diagnosis, the etiological (causative agent) diagnosis, and the attribution of the cause of disease to the specific workplace or exposure site. The attribution of disease to the workplace, for example, depends upon a thorough knowledge of that workplace, the nature and degree of potentially toxic exposures existing there, the control mechanisms in place, and the general relationship of toxic substances to disease.

The attribution of disease to a specific occupational exposure can be greatly strengthened (or defended against) by knowledge of the incidence of that disease in the workers in question, and in comparison with the incidence in a similar but unexposed population. These comparisons may be made from epidemiological studies, or by applying epidemiological and statistical principals to appropriately designed medical monitoring of employees.

In-House Program to Avoid Toxic Tort Litigation

5

Roy Fagin, M.D.*, Neal E. Minahan, Esq.** and James H. Morris†

§5.01 Introduction

The development and expansion of in-house medical, legal, safety, and environmental programs have been the result of a slowly developing awareness of occupational health, safety, and environmental needs of the public. The public's concern is continually fueled by statements from the government, scientific community, and press identifying many chemicals and other agents

---

* Director, Environmental Planning and Control, Grumman Aerospace Corp, Bethpage, New York.

** Staff Counsel, Office of the General Counsel, Raytheon Co, Lexington, Massachusetts.

† Corporate Safety Manager, ACF Industries, Inc., New York, New York.

which cause lung disease, cancer, and mutagenic and teratogenic disorders. Other disease conditions, including skin irritation and nervous disorders, have received increasing recognition as being associated with industrial chemical exposure. If one adds to this coterie of disease a potpourri of life style factors, industrial accidents, and stress-induced illnesses, it is easy to understand the ever-increasing occupational disease costs, the demand for upgrading outmoded workers' compensation laws, and union agitation for improved health benefits, as well as increased environmental concern by the general public.

Developing an effective corporate health, safety, and environmental program requires the proper balancing of many factors, such as a demonstration of need, proper timing, company size, an enlightened management, appropriate corporate culture, political sensitivity and internal politics, organizational flexibility, availability of certain types of personnel, and the necessary financial support, all of which must be placed under a conceptual umbrella entitled *Long-Term Corporate Commitment.*

No company was designed around occupational or environmental health needs. Today there is in many corporations a fragmentation of resources. This is the challenge: to bring together, in an organized fashion, what has been in many companies a dispersal of capabilities as well as a conglomerate of separate corporate entities. The challenge is to form an integrated, multidisciplined program which will bring together a corporation's goals, policies, procedures, manpower, and finances for the development of a unified program of compliance with all federal, state, and local occupational health, safety, and environmental regulations. This organization, when formed, must have the capability of handling present and near term regulations that might deal with the environment as well as with the employee's health and safety. In addition, the program must function within the framework of the company's overhead or cost structure and within the framework of products liability law.

§5.02   Corporate Business Philosophy

In order to organize and maintain a viable in-house program, it is necessary to briefly review corporate organization, business philosophy, management style, and corporate culture. An extensive dissertation on this subject would go far beyond the boundaries of this book. It is nevertheless essential to discuss certain corporate organizational concepts, the relationship between these concepts, and the integration of an in-house program into the corporate strategy.

Corporations were formed around the elegant idea that a group of investors could create a legal and financial entity to make a profit while limiting their personal liability. Originally, it was not recognized that a corporate entity could attain such a size as to become almost city-like in diversity of buildings, scope of business interests, and profound effect on the lives of its employees.

Corporations evolved from solely business enterprises to social institutions with human qualities and a corporate culture. It is within this interaction between a corporation as a business enterprise and a corporation as a social institution that an in-house program must be defined, developed, implemented, maintained, and expanded to meet corporate needs.

Many companies are motivated to solve their business problems only when either a product, manufacturing process, or marketing situation has so seriously deteriorated as to reach a point where an internal company crisis occurs. Many of these companies take pride in their ability to organize a response to critical situations quickly. When the crisis period has passed, the company recedes back into its pattern of not dealing with the external business issues or internal company operations in a planned manner.

Anticipatory management, on the other hand, develops a planned approach to operational problems. When the potential problem area is identified, plans are then developed to solve or control the problem in such a way as to prevent a critical situation from arising.

These divergent management approaches to problem solving must be recognized by company health, safety, and environmental professionals if an effective in-house program is to be planned and implemented. It is more difficult to maintain management's interest in long-term in-house programs when the motivation to face problems is dictated by crisis. However, it is possible to utilize a crisis situation to build in-house programs in building-block fashion. That is, if a crisis occurs concerning a particular health, safety, or environmental situation, a program can be proposed to resolve that difficulty. However, when the crisis is past, it is usually possible to maintain that program at some level of viability. When a crisis occurs again in a different area, another program can be developed to resolve that difficulty. Thus, it is possible over several years' time to build a modest in-house program using a building-block approach, through the advent of various corporate crises that may occur in a variety of health, safety, and environmental areas.

A competitive marketplace demands performance. Marketing specialists and their sales personnel are mandated by management to show immediate sales and profits on products and services. This mandate is based on the prevailing business strategy involving the philosophy of an immediate return on investment. This strategy involves a dynamic day-to-day business operational process in which cash flow, manpower, and other resources are focused on sales volume and the immediacy of profits. Management's attitude is reflected in the here-and-now philosophy. Management is not interested in potential future problems or activities or needs outside the primary focus of the corporation's daily commercial business activities. This scenario is, of course, a gross over-simplification of an important business process. Even so, the fundamental point is that management with a short-term business philosophy will have difficulty with the long-term view required of an in-house medical, environmental, and safety program. On the other hand, a management that develops a balanced business base encompassing a short-term view and long-term product development strategy will more likely be amenable to an in-house program. A long-term strategy in which a return on investment is projected several years into the future is a strategy involving long-term commitments. It is a strategy that requires management to look at all of the corporation's resources as well as the marketplace in planning the company's future. This type of management will more readily accept long-term programs such as an in-house health, safety, and environmental program.

Union Activity

The collective bargaining process can also have a profound effect on the existence and vitality of in-house programs. Historically, at the collective bargaining table, unions have demanded better health and safety programs. In reality, the strategy was to use such a program as a bargaining chip in order to obtain more favorable hourly wage rates.[1] Now, however, union activity has become increasingly dedicated to pressuring management for better industrial health, safety, and environmental programs. Unions have formed health, safety, and environmental organizations within the union headquarters' structure. In some cases, their industrial hygiene staffs monitor particular environments in a variety of corporations. Unions have argued for access to medical data of employees and have fought for the right of workers to be made aware of potential exposures to harmful substances. It is anticipated that union agitation will continue in the direction of forcing management to upgrade and improve in-house occupational health, safety, and environmental programs.

Governmental Scrutiny

Large corporations can come under governmental scrutiny merely by virtue of their size. Whether these intrusions into corporate life are fair or burdensome, management usually develops an appreciation for the regulatory process and the right of the government to regulate and to inspect. Small companies, in many cases, do not have experience in dealing with government agencies and do not appreciate the regulatory authority that federal or state agencies possess. In fact, small companies usually do not have the resources, the knowledge, or the experience to develop proper compliance programs. Therefore, in many cases, nothing is done. In addition, in small companies led by a single entrepreneur, that individual may want to do everything himself or herself. This leads to isolation of the *boss* from the people that work for him or her. The owner may become more hostile to new ideas and become more certain of the righteousness of his or her policies. Thus, the business grows only to a size that can be encompassed by the owner. His or her ignorance of government regulation, his or her isolation from the employees, and his or her certainty that he or she has everything under control leave little room for the development of in-house occupational health, safety, and environmental programs.

---

[1] Provost, *Legal Trends in Occupational Health*, 24 J Occupational Med 115-19 (Feb 1982).

Type of Business

The types of products or goods and services a company produces also play an important role in the existence and scope of in-house programs. Naturally, companies involved in the manufacture or use of large numbers of chemicals or petroleum products would certainly have a need for extensive in-house programs. Companies involved in mining, extracting, and processing minerals would also require in-house programs. Insurance companies and computer companies may not require extensive programs because of the lack of chemical toxicity in their facilities. However, the office environment may present special hazards (e.g., DDT use) which could require health, safety, and environmental programs. Fundamentally, any company with a manufacturing facility should have an in-house program, because the manufacturing facility is usually a major focus for accidents and occupational illnesses. In addition, it is the major area from which industrial chemical waste is generated. With these considerations in mind, it is appropriate to consider the development of an effective in-house program to deal with potential toxic tort litigation.

§5.03   Hazardous Substance Inventory

In order for a corporation to develop proper procedures for dealing with toxic or hazardous substances, it must know the substances with which it is dealing. The cornerstone of such a procedure is the development of a system to identify the substances which are being used in the manufacturing process and which are being incorporated into the company's products.

This type of system, including the updating of information on the manner and extent of use of those substances, allows the company to monitor the use of such substances in the light of developing knowledge of the nature and extent of the toxicity or hazardous properties of the substances being used by the company. Such a system also allows the company to determine which workers or classes of customers may have been exposed to various substances which the company has been using in its processes or its products. The company can then take necessary protective measures and consider the substitution of other substances which are or tend to be less toxic or hazardous than the substances presently being used. Such a system also permits a company to isolate substances which may be responsible for incidents of workers' illnesses in either the short or long term and to take steps at an early stage to minimize exposure to those substances. Such a system allows a company to consider at an early stage whether to shield or enclose certain substances which are incorporated into its products when the company has indications that those substances contain properties which could be considered toxic in the light of developing scientific knowledge or through exposure over long periods of time.

As an added benefit to such a system, the company which is faced with an allegation that it has caused illness in workers, customers, or others by virtue of exposure of those people to substances which have been identified as hazardous may be able to demonstrate that in that company's particular processes or particular products such substances were not in fact used, even though they may be used generally in the industry. Without this system, the company would not be able to establish that such substances were not used, or if such substances were used in a particular process or product, that a particular worker was not working in that part of the production facility in which the particular substance in question was being used, or that the substance was not used in quantities which are sufficiently great to be harmful.

This type of system also enables the company to monitor the balance of quantities of those substances which are purchased and which are used or dissipated in the manufacturing process, incorporated into the products, or ultimately discarded as waste. The ability to monitor the balance of such quantities allows a company to identify situations where such substances may be leaking where such would not otherwise be readily apparent. A company would thus be able to take steps to identify a situation where leaks are occurring or procedures are being improperly practiced in order to minimize and eliminate the leak or unnecessary exposure of persons to the substances. This type of monitoring ability also allows a company to account for the substances which it uses by quantity so that it can better defend against allegations such as that the company is contributing to a ground water contamination problem.

The development of and use of such a system is not without difficulty. Many substances which are used in the manufacturing process are purchased under the trade name of the manufacturer of that substance, and it is not always readily apparent what generic substances are included in the trade-name product. Some manufacturers will not permit its customer to be informed of the generic nature of its trade-name product. In other cases, the manufacturer may require the purchaser to sign a nondisclosure agreement in order to obtain the identification of the substances included under the trade-name product. Even if a company were not able to obtain the generic name of the substances being provided by a manufacturer, it is likely that the development of information concerning the toxicity or hazardous nature of these trade-name products will develop by trade name. For example, many of the substances and chemicals included on the toxic substances inventory compiled by the Environmental Protection Agency (EPA) pursuant to the Toxic Substances Control Act (TSCA)[2] are included by generic name and can therefore be dealt with on that basis. Another problem for the company which manufactures products is that many of the components of that product are purchased on an original equipment manufacturer (OEM) basis. Very often, the company, when it purchases an OEM component, does not know what substances are contained within that component. Nevertheless, a company could request the manufacturer of that component to identify those chemicals which are included within that component and in addition could obtain from the manufacturer a certification or warranty that such chemicals are not toxic or hazardous. Indeed, suppliers often provide such information via material safety data

---

[2] 15 USC §2601.

sheets; many Occupational Safety and Health Administration (OSHA) standards require their use. In fact, the hazard communication standard when promulgated in final form requires the inclusion of such information. (See Chapter 7.)

§5.04   Determination of Toxicity or Hazard

Ideally, a company procedure should include the evaluation of substances which are manufactured, processed, used, or expended by the company to determine whether such substances are toxic or hazardous and to classify such substances by degree of toxicity or hazard. However, as a practical matter, most companies do not have the financial resources or expertise to evaluate the toxicity of chemicals properly. It is usually necessary to depend on toxicity data received from the chemical manufacturer or from governmental sources.

Of course, if the substance is toxic or hazardous, a corporation is regulated in the manufacture, processing, distribution, and in some cases the use of such substances,[3] in transporting such substances or materials,[4] in discarding the waste products of such substances and materials,[5] in the work place,[6] and as to certain consumers.[7] In the first instance, in determining whether a substance or material is toxic or hazardous, a company can look to some of the existing regulations which establish, in some cases with specificity, which substances are toxic or hazardous and at what level they are toxic or hazardous.[8] In other cases, the statutory definition of hazardous or toxic materials or substances is very broad.[9] A company program designed to identify those substances which are toxic and hazardous can, of course, use the more specific substances which have been designated by governmental agencies as toxic or hazardous. This program, to the maximum extent feasible, should also seek to identify to whom and under what circumstances a substance can be toxic or hazardous. It is possible, for example, for an agency to designate a certain substance as toxic or hazardous by type of exposure. One type of substance might be designated as toxic or hazardous if ingested by drinking or consumption, another substance might be toxic or hazardous if inhaled in certain quantities, another substance might be toxic or hazardous if simply physically contacted.

Company management will have to be alert to new scientific information which may indicate that a chemical substance formerly considered nonhazardous is now labeled as a toxic substance. In addition, within the practical reality of corporate financial constraints, scientific experience, and laboratory exper-

---

[3] 15 USC §2601.

[4] Hazardous Materials Transportation Act, 49 USC §1801.

[5] Resource Conservation and Recovery Act, 42 USC §6901.

[6] Occupational Safety and Health Act, 29 USC §651 *et seq.*

[7] Consumer Product Safety Act, 15 USC §2056.

[8] 40 CFR §§116.4, 261.33.

[9] *See, e.g.,* Mass Gen Laws Ann ch 94B §1 (West 1978).

tise, the company program will have to include testing of substances against certain criteria to determine whether those substances are toxic or hazardous.[10]

The company program should also attempt to determine which substances that are being used might be considered to be acutely toxic or hazardous. Guidance for determining what constitutes a high degree of toxicity or hazard can be obtained from the regulations promulgated by various agencies.[11] Many companies have scientific engineering and medical resources within the company to make reasoned judgments on the basis of the degree of toxicity of particular substances. The importance of the designation of substances as acutely toxic or hazardous arises from the need to determine priorities for dealing with these particular substances. It is assumed that a company has a limited amount of resources to commence a program for dealing with each substance, and it is obviously important to set out at the beginning the priorities which need to be addressed.

Once the company program has identified those substances which are toxic and hazardous and set priorities regarding these substances both as to the acuteness of the toxicity or hazard and also as to the pervasiveness of these substances in the workplace or environment, the program must commence with an objective cost-benefit analysis of the desirability or necessity of substituting other substances and the desirability or necessity of making changes in the manufacturing process which will eliminate or reduce the use of the toxic or hazardous substances. A corporate program should be designed to scrutinize continually the substances used in processes to determine available substitutes, and when a company manufactures to a customer's specifications, the company program should also include attempts to change those specifications to allow for the substitution of substances and processes.

Whether a substitute is readily available or not, the corporate program should continue with a method of determining the hidden costs to the company in utilizing these toxic materials. Obviously, the company must consider the increased risk of injury to workers or damage to the environment whenever it chooses to use toxic materials. In addition, however, the company is often required by law or common prudence to include protective measures in the manufacturing process and in the finished products. Many times, additional processes are required to reduce or dilute the extent of the substance in the product or process, and there are also hidden costs required for increased treatment, handling, and disposal of the toxic material. The company program should allow for an examination of these costs to be weighed against the cost of using substitute materials whenever the substitute is not readily available. An examination of the hidden costs in the use of toxic material should also be made whenever new materials or substances are proposed to be incorporated in a product or in the manufacturing process, so that potential substitutes can

---

[10] *See, e.g.,* 40 CFR §261.20.

[11] *See, e.g.,* Toxic Substances Control Act, 15 USC §2603(e); 40 CFR §§61.20-.65; 29 CFR §§1910.1001-.1046.

be examined and utilized, if possible, without incurring the risks and added costs in using or incorporating the toxic or hazardous materials.

§5.05   Reduction of Quantity of Hazardous or Toxic Substances

Whenever a company deals with toxic or hazardous substances or materials, the chance of injury to person or damage to the environment is increased as the quantity of toxic and hazardous materials which pass through the hands of the company increases. While it may be difficult to quantify the increased risk from using such substances and materials in large quantities and the potential liability to the company arising from such use, it nevertheless costs the company money. The company must take steps to protect itself against such liability not only by increasing insurance coverage, but also by adopting additional protective measures to limit its potential liability and the opportunity for accident or illness. When a company uses toxic materials or substances, it is also required by many laws and regulations to perform additional and sometimes costly tasks whenever such materials are handled, transported, used, or disposed. In short, it is expensive for a company to utilize toxic or hazardous materials and substances. If, for example, someone chooses to use a particular material in the manufacturing process which may have advantages in that processing activity or in the product itself, the material should not be allowed to be incorporated until a determination is made by the company of the nature and extent of the toxicity of that material and a total evaluation is made of the hidden costs in increased protective measures and equipment which must be taken in dealing with that material.

Once a decision is made to continue to use certain toxic materials or to include new toxic materials and substances in the manufacturing process, the company must include an evaluation of the methods of manufacture, use, or disposal of toxic material to minimize costs and risks. As previously stated, the greater the quantity of toxic materials used by a company, the greater the risk to the company of liability for illness or accident. The company program, therefore, must look to determine whether those toxic materials can be recycled within the manufacturing process and for how long. The recycling will obviously reduce the quantity of such materials which are being used in the manufacturing process and which are discarded on a one-to-one basis. The reduction in quantity of materials which are discarded obviously reduces the quantity of such waste material in the environment for which the company is responsible, and it also reduces the costs of such disposal and the transportation of such waste product. The company program, therefore, should be flexible enough to examine the cost-benefit ratio between recycling and disposal.

The company program must also include the valuation of materials used and discarded to determine whether any of these materials may be reclaimed. Any procedure for reclamation should obviously include not only an evaluation of whether certain elements in waste products can be extracted which have an inherent value—for example, precious metals—but also should include an evaluation of the types of wastes which are being accumulated for disposal by category.

Certain solvents have a value for recycling purposes even if such solvents are not recycled by the company which creates the waste, and they can theoretically be sold for value to companies who wish to use these solvents for such purposes. Obviously, if the solvents are mixed with other waste, the potential value will be lost to the company and to those persons who would otherwise purchase the solvents for purposes of recycling and resale. The program, therefore, should include an evaluation of methods to segregate waste products being accumulated. In addition, of course, the segregation of waste is required by certain laws and regulations,[12] and the segregation evaluation should occur in any event to prevent a hazardous interaction of various waste materials.

§5.06 Control of Toxic or Hazardous Substances

The company program which is developed to provide for the identification of toxic substances and the evaluation of the nature and extent of their toxicity must also establish procedures for controlling the use of such substances. The goal of such control procedures should be both to comply with existing laws and regulations and to minimize the chances for accident, injury, damage, or unnecessary exposure.

Compliance with laws and regulations is an important part of a company program dealing with toxic or hazardous substances, but compliance with law does not guarantee that the company will be free from liability or responsibility for illness, injury, or damage which may occur as the result of the company's use of toxic or hazardous substances. Laws and regulations also do not always specify in detail how the use of toxic or hazardous substances is to be controlled, how exposure to those substances is to be limited, how the substances are to be labeled or identified, what work practices must be established, and what safeguards must be undertaken. The company is well advised to adopt these practices and procedures which, to the maximum extent economically and technologically feasible, minimize the chance of illness through exposure, injury through accident, or damage to property and the environment through unexpected releases of the substances. It would seem better to budget the cost and expense of a program which minimizes the chance of an unexpected liability than to continue the risk of large and unexpected claims.

In order to support and assist management in giving appropriate policy direction to in-house programs, it is necessary to organize and set in motion an ongoing program for understanding and implementing the various laws and regulations which relate to toxic and hazardous substances. Every individual who is responsible for implementing the company program must have a fundamental understanding of the requirements of the regulations and laws which bear upon his or her area of responsibility. This understanding can be attained

---

[12] 40 CFR §265.177.

only through a training and education program. This education program can include the distribution of copies of the regulations, explanations or interpretations of the regulations, seminars or discussion groups, training films, and myriad other education techniques which a company could choose to utilize. This education program must, of course, be an ongoing program designed to alert and educate relevant personnel to new and changing laws and regulations. It is important to note in this regard that keeping pace with new and changing regulations cannot be left to chance. Some clearly defined mechanism must be established for the collection within the company of the new and changing regulations and the dissemination of the regulations to personnel who will understand the effect of the regulations on the company's activities.

Environmental, safety, and industrial hygiene monitoring and medical data management systems are also essential in managing large multiplant in-house programs. The ability to collect and analyze data comparing individuals with themselves over time and comparing individuals to population groups within the company will further assist company health experts to obtain epidemiological profiles of chemically induced diseases in the company. These data can be used in the development of risk management programs.

Companies can use health risk profiles to make periodic examinations of employees more efficient and effective.[13] In a risk-based medical management plan, cost effectiveness can be achieved by concentrating physical examinations and preventive medical techniques on those employees at greatest risk of illness. These types of risk reduction programs are now being implemented in many areas under titles such as Preventive Medical Programs, Wellness Programs, and Health Management Programs.[14]

§5.07   Hazardous Waste Management Program

In many companies using chemicals in their manufacturing processes, the development of a waste treatment program has become a necessity. Most programs involve the treatment, neutralization, extraction, storage, and then transportation of chemical and material waste. In order to achieve a first-rate waste management program, corporate management should implement as many of the following program elements that are technically feasible and cost effective:

> Altering the source of pollution (the manufacturing process)
>
> Initial separation and concentration of spent chemicals and chemical waste (which renders recovery of individual chemicals much easier)

---

[13] Hogan, & Bernacki, *Developing Job-Related Preplacement Medical Examinations*, 23 J Occupational Med 469-75 (July 1981).

[14] Polakoff, *Pollution Control Can Be Profitable*, 51 Occupational Health & Safety 36-50 (Dec 1982).

Neutralization and detoxification procedures, as well as reclamation of chemicals and metals prior to storage and transportation

Storage and transportation

Hazardous waste exchange programs. "An alternative to the sale of converted waste is waste exchange. One firm's chemical waste may be another company's raw material."[15] Waste exchange between companies can be done through groups of waste exchangers which operate as materials exchangers or brokers. "These exchangers actually bury or accept wastes, analyze waste properties, reprocess if necessary, identify potential users, and sell at a profit."[16]

Disposal, if necessary, in a certified landfill

In many companies, industrial pollution stems from manufacturing or production inefficiencies. The costs of processing the company's waste may not have been included in the original cost analysis of the manufacturing process. Therefore, a process change to reduce waste and the need for its processing may well bring about cost savings as well as reducing the potential costs of noncompliance.

Many times, a company which deals with toxic or hazardous materials must utilize the services of third parties to handle the company's toxic or hazardous materials or substances. Most often, this need arises when the substances must be transported, disposed of, or perhaps sold for reclamation or recycling purposes. In some circumstances—e.g., the Superfund (see Chapter 10)—the generator of hazardous waste can be held liable for cleanup costs expended to clean up abandoned hazardous waste sites maintained by others.[17] In other situations, where toxic or hazardous substances are improperly handled by a company's third-party contractor, those persons who are allegedly damaged by the release of such substances may attempt to hold the company liable on the theory that the company was negligent in choosing the contractor, or otherwise because of allegedly improperly labeled materials or sloppy practices of the contractor which cannot easily be disassociated from those of the company.

A company must therefore be very careful in selecting a contractor to handle its toxic or hazardous substances. In the first instance, the contractor should be selected on the basis of its track record, financial stability, and reputation with governmental agencies and other clients. The contractor should also be required to provide copies of all required licenses or permits for review by the company, together with a representation that the contractor has obtained all required licenses or permits and that such licenses and permits continue to be

---

[15] Polakoff, *Pollution Control Can Be Profitable,* 51 Occupational Health & Safety 36-50 (Dec 1982).

[16] Council on Environmental Quality, Waste Management, Environmental Quality 1981, at 102.

[17] Comprehensive Environmental Response Compensation and Liability Act, 42 USC §9601; 33 CFR §153.203.

held in good standing. The contractor should also be required to list all facilities at which the work will be performed. Since a contractor is normally selected based upon the competence and reputation, the contractor should be expressly prohibited from assigning the work to others without the approval of the company. If other contractors must be used, approval of those contractors should be withheld until those contractors have been reviewed by the company in the same manner as if the company were engaging the subcontractor directly.

Care should also be taken to establish that the contractor is acting as an independent contractor. While the procedures and manner of operation of the contractor should be reviewed, the company should not involve itself in controlling the details of the methods of operation by the contractor.

The contractor should also be required to indemnify and hold the company harmless from and to defend the company against any loss, injury, or damage which may be caused or alleged to be caused by company's toxic or hazardous substances while in the possession or under the control of the contractor. The indemnity, of course, will only be as valuable and effective as the financial ability of the contractor. The contractor, therefore, should be required to maintain insurance in reasonable amounts, including workers' compensation to cover any injury or damage which may result from accident, spill, or exposure to the company's toxic or hazardous substances while the contractor is handling those substances for the company. The company should be a named insured. The insurance should be required to be maintained for the duration of the contractor's activities with a provision for notification to the company before the policy can be cancelled.

§5.08   Safety Considerations

In an industrial environment, the relationship between traumatic injuries and accidents is obvious, due to the fact that the interval of time between the accident and the injury is of short duration. The effect of exposure to hazardous substances often does not follow immediately after the exposure. Diseases that occur from exposure to hazardous substances can, however, occur as a result of unsafe mechanical or physical conditions or acts on the part of one person or other persons. These are direct and approximate causes of diseases that are triggered by exposure to hazardous substances.

It should be pointed out that, unlike traumatic injury-causing situations, some hazardous substances can be handled safely by some people but can actually be unsafe to others who might have an allergy to them. It is very likely that this perspective is true with people who drink alcoholic beverages or smoke. Some people have absolutely no reaction to these two activities, while others can have minor or severe reactions that could eventually lead to death. Also, in some cases, the act of handling the hazardous substance without protective equipment could be termed unsafe, and the possible exposure to the substance can be termed an *unsafe condition*.

There have been many examples in past years of exposure to hazardous substances which, at the time, weren't necessarily considered hazardous. For example, there were times when sandblast operations were not considered very toxic and, therefore, not much thought was given to the protection that is stringently required at present. Sandblasting operations are associated with silicosis, which is an occupational disease, but very little was known about necessary protection, and workers were exposed. The same holds true with lead, asbestos, and radiation. There were some guidelines in reference to protection, but basically, they were very general.

It is safe to assume that the company safety professional was generally aware that exposures were created by certain operations but felt that the majority of these exposures were of the traumatic type. There was normally very little attention paid to the possible hazardous substance exposures from the same operations. Examples are operations such as welding and painting, where the combination of materials, heat, and the mixing of various chemicals provides exposures of which not all effects are immediate.

The safety professional has been somewhat naive in thinking that operations caused more traumatic injuries than occupational diseases and that his or her main concern was to protect people from traumatic injuries. In many cases, the safety professional was not even aware of the exposures from the hazardous substances. His or her thinking was that traumatic injuries were of more importance because they were immediate, and he or she was really not prepared to deal with long-term exposures to hazardous substances which might be causing occupational disease. In fact, his or her records probably did not reflect such exposures.

The safety professional has always spent a great deal of his or her time in the recognition of specific materials, processes, equipment, and personal performance, dealing with exposures from a traumatic point of view and addressing only when necessary an exposure from a hazardous substance point of view.

This problem of exposures to hazardous substances is further complicated by such factors as: susceptibility of the individual and the physical resistance or immunity; lack of complete knowledge relating to the results of exposures to the certain hazardous substances; and the slow development of occupational disease in certain cases. There are also problems due to the nonstandardization of methods for determining the degree of the hazard: the questionable degree of the hazard; the questionable threshold danger limit; and, often, the questionable methods of control and prevention.

The safety professional's point of view toward exposures to hazardous substances has to be the same as that which has existed in the control of accidents. It is necessary to point out that a person's injury as a result of exposure to hazardous substances often cannot be established as definitely as a traumatic injury resulting from an accident. It should also be pointed out that in traumatic injuries, the major cause of accidents and resultant injuries are unsafe acts, which is not the case with exposures to hazardous substances, even though the major cause of such incidents is a lack of knowledge as to what to expect from the substance. The principle or method that a safety professional might use in recognizing, preventing, and dealing with exposures to hazardous substances really does not change as compared to those same principles or methods that have been established in dealing with traumatic injuries. So, there is a definite need for the safety professional to become aware of the exposures from hazardous substances. The professional needs to become knowledgeable of hazardous substances, how to recognize hazardous substances, how to detect the levels of exposures, and how to control hazardous substances. This knowledge must then be incorporated into the overall company program.

§5.09   —Action by the Safety Professional

Are there pathways the safety professional can take to become familiar with the effects of exposures to hazardous substances? The safety professional presumably can use his or her expertise as a means toward detection of hazardous substances. This detection is rather simple.

For example, it is an easy task to detect certain exposures by visual means. Actual oabservation of an operation can determine at the start if the operation produces any active, unknown residue. Is it a mist? Is it a fume? Is it a vapor? What does it smell like? Is it a smell that burns one's nose? Does hearing it produce a noise that hurts the ears? Does it produce a burning effect to the eyes? It is very simple to detect the basic exposures to hazardous substances; but it will take some time in observing the operation over a period of time. The next step would be to review the material safety data sheets. Manufacturers of raw materials are now required to have available to purchasers data sheets that indicate the chemicals that are used in their products, levels of exposures, and safety precautions that shouuld be taken. It is also very important that the safety professional be familiar with all products and processes his or her employer uses and should maintain a current safety data sheet on each and every product.

Once the safety professional accumulates the necessary data on the actual chemicals associated with the product or process and what the threshold limit values are, he or she can then enter into the next stage. This stage entails sampling for actual exposure levels.

In order to determine what the actual exposures are, the safety professional either has to do the sampling himself or herself or has to enlist the help of an industrial hygienist who has such expertise. If his or her company is insured, he or she might utilize the services of his or her workers' compensation insurance carrier's engineering section. If the operations are self-insured, he or she might elect to obtain the services of a consultant who has expertise, or as in many cases, he or she might have one available in-house. Regardless of what method the safety professional elects to use, it is very important that the people doing the actual sampling have the necessary knowledge and can act as qualified witnesses if that becomes necessary. The levels of exposure are determined by the use of various sampling equipment. Instruments for determining the degree of a hazardous substance—for example, in the air—are numerous. There are several types of sampling devices present on the market, and the choice will depend on the level of expertise, the material present in the work-place, the exposure level, the equipment which might be available, and, natu-rally, the time factor.

Once the sampling data indicates there is definitely an exposure to a hazard-ous substance, there need to be a determination of the levels of exposure and the implementation of controls to these exposures. In determining methods of control, there has to be a coordination of efforts among the industrial hygienist, the safety professional, and all personnel responsible for the ad-ministrative and engineering aspects of the products or processes causing exposures. It is also important to remember that if personal protective equip-ment is utilized, periodic physical examinations or medical evaluations might be necessary.

In summary, it is very important to reiterate the primary methods of control of the exposures, discussed more fully in Chapter 3:

1. Substitution
2. Reduction of amounts and frequency of use
3. Control of substance at point of operation
4. Isolation and guarding of personnel involved with the operation

In addition, the safety professional should consider definite controls of unsafe acts through training and discipline and definitely should not forget periodic medical evaluations if necessary or required. Once implementation has taken place and it is found that it does indeed control the levels of exposure to the hazardous substance, audit programs need to be developed.

What part, then, can the safety professional's part in the overall company program play in preventing injuries or illness from exposure to hazardous and toxic substances from reaching the point where they become cases for litiga-tion? First, the safety professional needs the expertise to establish, implement, and audit all programs that cover those operations he or she knows might expose workers to injury or illness. When he or she discovers exposures that could at any time cause injury or illness to the workers, he or she has to address them on a timely basis. The definition of addressing an exposure means that corrective measures will be directed to the proper management. These meas-ures should include a description of exposure, the levels of exposure, and the corrective programs necessary to contain or control the exposures. The re-ports associated with these exposures should include accurate factual data only. They should not include any assumptions, conclusions, or personal opin-ions. It is important that the safety professional keep in mind when document-ing these exposures that any and all material could be subject to subpoena at a later date. Once the exposures are acknowledged, programs should be imple-mented in order to control the exposures, and these should include both engineering and administrative methods, keeping in mind that engineering controls should be considered first. Written documentation should be com-pleted on a timely basis throughout the investigation of any incident.

Recently, and after much pressure, Occupational Safety and Health Administration (OSHA) officials have begun considering the issuance of perform-ance-type regulations that will permit employers to comply with the regulation by whatever resources they have at their disposal. The regulations might per-mit certain administrative controls.[18] This type of performance regulation will undoubtedly place additional burdens on the safety professional in the mainte-nance of complete written documentation, which will be helpful during inspec-tions by regulatory agencies or in the defense of the employer in litigation.

The maintenance of records is very important in dealing with any type of incident. Records are definitely required to be concise, accurate, and, above all, legible. Records become very vital where there is possible exposure to hazardous substances. The OSH Access to Medical and Exposure record regu-lation requires employers to maintain certain records for up to 30 years.[19] However, the safety professional should be aware that records involving cer-tain injuries and illnesses should be maintained in a more complete format and be such that they can be stored in good shape for as long as required by both the employer and regulatory agencies.

The safety professional, in complying with his or her responsibility of acci-dent investigation, should realize from the date of the incident forward that it could become a case that will be litigated whether a suit is filed immediately or in the future. The records that are developed from the date of accident forward should be maintained on durable material and in a safe place. If there are cases of termination or transfer of employees, there should be some meth-od to maintain continuity so that in the event these records need to be re-searched at a much later date, they will be easily accessible and legible. Too many times, as employee turnover occurs, records become lost, gaps develop, and, when most needed, the records are unable to be of any help. In almost every case involving litigation of accidents or illnesses resulting from exposure to hazardous substances, the safety professional becomes a key member of the defense team. It will be his or her job, as employer representative, to gather all records pertaining to the incident, which should include the list of wit-nesses, and he or she could very well become a witness himself or herself. It is very important that the safety professional have a full knowledge of regulato-ry agency standards and regulations and applicable state workers' compensa-tion laws, and that he or she be able to converse at least in general terms with attorneys who might be handling the case.

Experience developed over the years indicates that the safety person becomes a key figure in certain cases involving exposure to hazardous sub-stances. If he or she has the knowledge, the background, the education, and most important, detailed knowledge of a particular case that is being tried, then more than likely, the defense will be very strong.

---

[18] 47 Fed Reg 12092 (Mar 19, 1982).
[19] 29 CFR §1910.20.

§5.10 Reproductive Hazards: Concepts and Policies

Reproductive hazards in the workplace pose a perplexing series of practical problems. From a company viewpoint, corporate medical directors find themselves in the middle, attempting to satisfy conflicting rules and regulations, being concerned for the health and safety of employees, maintaining economically and technologically feasible programs, and dealing with the frustrations of having to face workers' compensation claims.

Within this framework, the company's medical, safety, industrial hygiene, and personnel experts must grapple with the tasks of evaluating risks, properly monitoring the work environment, conducting physical examination programs, counseling employees, and advising management on the policies to be followed, the programs to be developed, the legal issues, and in some cases, the collective bargaining issues to be considered. The safety and health programs that are developed must be practicable, cost effective, and beneficial from the standpoint of protecting the worker, and most importantly, the programs must instill in the worker a sense of confidence that management is acting responsibly and fairly in balancing a person's right to work with the need for protection afforded by feasible health and safety programs.

From the employee viewpoint, the worker finds himself or herself in a dilemma characterized by the need for a well-paying, satisfying, and reasonable job, and by the concern for potential reproductive harm and fetal damage. The degree of employee activism involving suits or requests for Occupational Safety and Health Administration (OSHA) inspections or complaints to the union and the press is determined in general by the employee's perception that management, aided by a capable medical and safety staff and first-line supervisors, is dedicated to protecting the employee from unreasonable risks.

With all these concerns in mind, how then can a company act in a reasonable manner to solve these practical problems? To meet this challenge, management must develop an organized approach to control the problem. Management should bring together a multidisciplined group consisting of representatives from the medical, safety and industrial hygiene, industrial relations, corporate counsel, and manufacturing departments. This group should be given the responsibility for developing and implementing a reproductive hazards control program.

Every aspect of the program must be well documented, and good records must be maintained. The health professional should inventory the workplace for mutagenic and teratogenic chemicals and materials. Each employee should be fully informed of the potential exposure to a teratogenic and/or mutagenic agent. In a number of instances, the company, when presented with the knowledge of a potential employee exposure to reproductive hazards, falls into the trap of a *quick fix*—that is, there is the temptation to resolve the problem quickly by having the employee sign a statement waiving his or her rights. It is important to understand that there is considerable controversy as to whether or not employees can sign away their rights. For all practical purposes, employees cannot sign a statement indicating that they understand the dangers of exposure and that they will neither find fault with the company nor hold the company accountable for chemical injury done to them or to a fetus during the course of their work. In other words, an employee cannot release an employer from liability, especially in regard to workers' compensation claims.

In addition, such an arrangement made between the parent-to-be and the company cannot legally protect the company from suits brought by the child. In other words, any agreement between the mother and the company cannot prevent the child, after birth, from suing the company for an occupationally related developmental condition.[20]

Employees utilizing chemicals and materials with a risk of reproductive harm should have a medical history taken with special emphasis on the reproductive system, social history, and job history. Information such as the normality or abnormality of the menstrual period and the number of pregnancies, abortions, miscarriages, and normal births should be recorded. Health history of children concerning developmental defects should be obtained, and all previous and present illnesses or diseases of the reproductive system should be noted. A prior job history, seeking information concerning chemical exposure to mutagenic/teratogenic agents, must be obtained. A social history, which may unearth hobbies involving exposure to potential mutagenic/teratogenic agents, should also be obtained. Smoking, drinking, and drug histories should be obtained whenever possible.

The employee should be given adequate training and knowledge on how to handle any substance in question. Engineering controls should be instituted to the extent that they are technologically and economically feasible. If technical and economic feasibility is not obtainable, the reasons why must be stated for the record. As far as practicable, work practice or administrative controls must be instituted. Protective equipment for personnel must be used if feasible and practical. However, the elements and the problems associated with this particular step include the following:

1. The equipment may pose a problem for women because almost all types of personnel protective equipment are the results of anthropometric studies done on men for the proper size and fit of the equipment. Thus, women may require personalized or customized protective equipment

2. Technical feasibility is an important concept because it asks the question:

---

[20] Stillman, *The Law in Conflict: Accommodating Equal Employment and Occupational Health Obligations,* 21 J of Occupational Med 599-606 (Sept 1979); see also Nothstein, *Sex Based Considerations of Differentiation in the Workplace,* 26 Vill L Rev 239 (1981); Stoner, *Olin Debates Title VII Applicability to Fetal Rights,* Legal Times, Apr 18, 1983, at 24; Ashford, *Legal Mechanisms for Controlling Reproductive Hazards in the Workplace,* Occupational Health & Safety 10 (Feb 1983); Karrh, *Guidance For The Evaluation Risk Assessment and Control of Chemical Embryo-Fetotoxins,* 23 J Occupational Med 397-99 (June 1981). *See also* Wright v Olin, 697 F2d 1172 (4th Cir 1983), and Zunziga v Kleberg County Hosp, 692 F2d 986 (5th Cir 1983), which are the most important cases to date to discuss the applicability of Title VII of the Civil Rights Act of 1964 to fetal rights in the context discussed above.

Can the particular equipment in question really do the job of protecting the individual? Thus, if no equipment is technically adequate to protect the individual, this fact must be documented

3.   Is the equipment practical? Do the ergonomic or human factors of the job enable the worker to use the equipment? In effect, protective equipment may be available and the equipment may adequately protect the individual, but carrying out the job itself may make it impossible or impractical to use the equipment

As part of a program to control reproductive hazards, when should management exclude workers from their jobs? If the company determines and documents well that all the above administrative mechanisms have been carried out and that technological considerations will not create an adequate protective barrier, then the employee, man or woman, should be excluded from the work area. Such other considerations as a history of abnormal pregnancies or a history of multiple abnormalities in the individual's children can be used as supporting evidence to convince the employees that they may be at greater risk by remaining at their present jobs. However, it is important to note that a history of abnormal pregnancies or a history of abnormalities in the employee's children taken alone, without the support of the plan described above, may not be sufficient to convince the worker, the union, or the Equal Employment Opportunity Commission (EEOC) that job discrimination was not practiced.[21]

Programs utilizing genetic monitoring constitute a new area of testing that holds the promise of being of value in the future for determining any unusual susceptibility of workers to a particular chemical and for use as a biological monitor for workers exposed to known or suspected mutagenic agents.[22] However, at the present time, replication of test data is inconsistent. Furthermore, test results can be easily influenced by test methods as well as by individual life style factors (e.g., drugs, alcohol, or smoking). In addition, test sample analysis is expensive, and test protocols require that periodic samples be taken. Thus, from a practical viewpoint, genetic monitoring tests, although possessing great promise for the future, should at the present time be considered as research tools rather than as standard clinical occupational tests.[23]

Along with any decision to exclude an employee from a work area, the company must consider the development of a system involving reasonable alternative job assignments. This alternative job assignment program may necessarily have to be blended into the collective bargaining arrangements made between management and the unions.

---

[21] See the authorities cited in note 20.

[22] Fabriclant & Legator *Etiology, Role and Detection of Chromosomal Aberrations In Man,* 23 J Occupational Med 617-25 (Sept 1981); Hoffman, *Mutagenicity Testing in Environmental Toxicology* 46 Envtl Sci & Tech 560A-74A (1982).

[23] Dabney, *The Role of Human Genetic Monitoring In The Work Place,* 23 J Occupational Med 626-31 (Sept 1981).

Finally, it is inevitable that any decision not to permit a male or female employee to work at a certain job because the reproductive hazards outweigh the company's ability to neutralize those hazards will be met with strong criticism and possible legal action. Therefore, job exclusion decisions based on a logical, consistent, and well-documented approach to the problem will be more easily defended.

§5.11   Auditing Program Operations

If a company has expended time and money to develop and implement an in-house program, it normally wants to make certain that the program is being implemented properly. Oftentimes, a company will not know whether its program is being implemented properly until it is called upon to evaluate the program as the result of some event—e.g., an accident or spill, some noncompliance with the law, or a claim for injury or illness. The happening of such an event is not the optimum moment to determine the effectiveness of the program; it is far better to adopt a procedure for auditing the program and its implementation. As an example, it is one thing to adopt a program which mandates that safety equipment be worn by employees working within a certain proximity to toxic materials, but if the employees do not wear the equipment and are not being forced by their superiors to wear it, the program in that respect is useless. A procedure, however, where auditors are sent to various parts of the company to monitor compliance will bring to light such implementation failures.

To be effective, the auditors chosen must be familiar with the details of the program, must be competent to evaluate compliance with the program, and must have the ability to report directly to someone who has the authority to impose the necessary discipline to correct any noncompliance with the program. The auditor chosen must also be capable of objectivity. Obviously, as in any auditing function, the auditor must be free from the direct influence of the persons or functions being audited. A company may wish to hire a consulting firm in place of its own employees as auditors or as a periodic independent overseer of the implementation of the program.

Health, safety, and environmental plans, programs, and procedures are of value only if they are properly implemented, if they are adhered to by all employees, and if they truly serve to protect indivudals and the environment. Thus, program audits are very useful in determining the practicality, cost effectiveness, and general utility of individual health, safety, and environmental programs.

Even if a company program provides for an evaluation of preventive measures, there will be occasions of accidents and spills. The program must provide sufficient contingency plans to react to and deal with such accidents and spills. These contingency plans must be in place and properly tuned before the accident or spill occurs. The plans can be founded upon the requirements of the contingency plans which are mandated by law.

§5.12 Manufacturing and Process Control

Under usual circumstances, the planning of a new manufacturing process involves a number of obvious business and technical considerations, including cost, types of equipment, basic materials required, technical feasibility, and other considerations. The process is then placed on line, and production begins. Often, it is only then discovered that some aspect of the system is unsafe or poses a toxic hazard to employees. Safety and industrial hygiene personnel are called to identify and quantify the hazard. Process engineers and facilities personnel then become involved in redesigning, shielding, or isolating the process in order to reduce or eliminate the hazard. In some cases, new work procedures have to be instituted. In other situations, new training programs must be implemented in order to educate the employees regarding the new process changes.

This scenario is replayed on many occasions in companies large and small across the country. Consider the costs of this scenario—the initial cost of designing, developing, and implementing the process; the cost of treating injured employees; the cost of time lost from work; the cost of industrial safety and hygiene surveys; the cost of changing the process to reduce the hazards; and the cost of instituting new procedures and retraining personnel. All these costs could in many cases be significantly reduced if during the manufacturing-planning process environmental, health, and safety specialists were teamed with manufacturing engineers to evaluate the process before the process went on line.

For example, the use of automation and robotics, or computer-aided manufacturing processes, would be highly desirable, not only from a cost perspective, but also from a health, safety, and environmental point of view. Such new systems applied to dangerous operations or to operations involving toxic chemicals should significantly reduce employee hazards. In addition, in-house program costs and workers' compensation payments would be reduced. Employee litigation would also be expected to diminish. Therefore, any new product or manufacturing process under development should have the benefit of an evaluation by occupational health, safety, environmental, and toxicological experts.

§5.13 General Concepts

The last two decades of this century promise to produce much more extensive scientific evidence concerning the association between chemical use and occupational disease. The synergistic effects of multiple low-level exposures may begin to be better understood and quantified. In addition, the effects of ground water contamination and air pollution on health will receive better scientific definition. It is hoped that the hysteria and the emotional reaction to environmental problems in the 1970s will give way to the collection of solid scientific data in the 1980s and 1990s. From a business standpoint, what is the value of having good scientific data? Management will respond in a positive manner if it is given solid evidence that the implementation of health, safety, and environmental programs will protect a valuabale work force against a toxic environment. Management does not like emotion-charged programs which fight phantom threats. Managers are result oriented. If they see a specific, proven need, they will invest in health, safety, and environmental protection because they can see a specific favorable result.

Management must be sold on the idea that health, safety, and environmental professionals should be part of the company's strategic planning team. It is through a team effort that in-house programs can be designed for cost effectiveness, while at the same time providing excellent protection for the company's work force and the environment.

Finally, it is important for companies to join with the scientific community to gather data on chemical exposure and health effects in an organized and scientific manner. It is this type of association that will bring about the accumulation of useful toxicity data which, in turn, will lead to reasonable government regulation, rather than overzealous, ill-founded rules which, in many cases, burden the employer while only affording minimal protection to employees.

6

Workers' Compensation and the Exclusivity Doctrine

G.Z. Nothstein, Esq.

§6.01 Introduction

A major route of exposure to hazardous substances occurs in the occupational setting. Even exposures contracted in the environmental setting may be aggravated by exposures in the workplace—or by an employer's failure to inform an employee of the discovery of a nonoccupational injury or illness. When, whether, and under what circumstances a workers' compensation statute will provide a remedy to an employee for injuries or illnesses resulting from occupational exposure to hazardous substances is the thrust of this chapter. Also discussed is the so-called exclusivity doctrine, which in its present form precludes actions for damages at law (in the context of this book, a toxic tort action) once workers' compensation coverage is established. One exception recognized in varying guises is the *intentional act* idea, which would enable an employee to initiate an action for recovery for the injury or illness suffered—known as the toxic tort.

§6.02 —Coverage of Workers' Compensation Statutes

Prior to the enactment of the various state workers' compensation statutes, an injured employee could sue his or her employer at common law, but recoveries were rare because of the availability of employer defenses such as contributory negligence, assumption of risk, and the fellow-servant doctrine. Workers' compensation was put forth as a means to provide cash benefits and medical assistance to persons who suffered employment-related injuries and illnesses. The need for such state legislation arose because of a steady increase in industrial accidents and the corresponding decrease in available common law remedies for employees' injuries and illnesses. No comprehensive federal law addressed the problem.

Workers' compensation involved a quid pro quo. Employees were guaranteed compensation for nearly all workplace injuries, but they gave up their common law right to sue their employers in tort for damages. Employers were liable to compensate employees for most workplace injuries without regard to negligence or fault but were protected from tort suit by their employees.

The heart of every workers' compensation statute is its coverage formula. A majority of the states, and the federal government in the Longshoremen's and Harbor Workers' Compensation Act,[1] adopted the *arising out of and in the course of employment* formula. Each of the two tests must be independently applied and met before compensation will be allowed.[2] Typical statutory formulations state that:

> Every employer subject to the provisions of this article, shall pay or provide as required herein compensation according to the schedules of this article for the disability or death of his employee resulting from an accidental personal injury sustained by the employee arising out of and in the course of his employment without regard to fault as a cause of such injury.[3]

Compensation shall be payable under this chapter in respect of disability

---

[1] 33 USC §901 *et seq.*

[2] Smith v Travelers Ins Co, 139 Ga App 45, 227 SE2d 868 (1976); Martin v Unified School Dist No 233, 5 Kan 298, 615 P2d 168 (1980).

[3] Md Ann Code art 101, §15 (Michie 1969).

or death of an employee if the disability or death results from an injury arising out of and in the course of employment.[4]

A minority of states and the Federal Employees Compensation Act,[5] however, have different coverage formulas and do not utilize the *arising out of* concept.

Every employer shall be liable for compensation for personal injury to, or for the death of each employee, by an injury in the course of his employment, and such compensation shall be paid in all cases by the employer.[6]

Liability under this chapter shall exist against an employer only where the following conditions concur: (a) Where the employee sustains an injury; (b) Where, at the time of the injury, both the employer and employee are subject to the provisions of this chapter; (c) Where at the time of the injury, the employee is performing service growing out of and incidental to his employment; (d) Where the injury is not intentionally self-inflicted.[7]

Where an injury or illness is shown to be covered under a particular statutory formulation, the natural consequences which flow from the injury or illness likewise are considered to arise out of employment. An injury is said to arise in the course of employment when it takes place within the period of employment, at a place where an employee may reasonably be, and while he or she is fulfilling his or her duties or engaged in doing something incidentally related to employment. The aberrant actions of an employee, whether negligent or willful, are generally immaterial, *unless* they take the form of a deviation from the course of employment; in that event they may become a defense, as embodied in the typical statute.

Every employer subject to this chapter shall in accordance with this chapter, except as otherwise provided in section twenty-five-a-hereof, secure compensation to his employees and pay or provide compensation for their disability or death from injury arising out of and in the course of the employment without regard to fault as a cause of the injury, except that there shall be no liability for compensation under this chapter when the injury has been solely occasioned by intoxication of the injured employee while on duty or by willful intention of the injured employee to bring about the injury or death of himself or another.[8]

Except as excluded by this chapter all employers and employees are subject to the provisions of this chapter. Every such employer is liable for compensation according to the provisions of this chapter and is liable to

---

[4] Fla Stat Ann §440.09 (West 1977).

[5] 5 USC §8102(a).

[6] Pa Stat Ann tit 77, §431 (Purdon 1974).

[7] Wis Stat Ann §102.03 (West 1973).

[8] NY Work Comp Law §10 (McKinney 1957).

pay compensation in every case of personal injury or death of his employee arising out of and in the course of employment without regard to the question of negligence, unless the injury or death was intentionally self-inflicted or when the intoxication of the employee is the proximate cause of the injury.[9]

Although many states initially covered only injuries, which were required to be accidental, general compensation coverage is now provided for *occupational illness and disease* in all but a handful of states. Prior to coverage under the compensation acts, common law actions were not barred as a means of recovery.[10] Now that coverage is provided, oftentimes attempts are made to skirt it, so that a return to the common law remedies can be permitted.

Some diseases and illnesses are caused by short-term exposure whose effects manifest themselves suddenly (e.g., inhaling fumes through a faulty respirator), others are caused by repeated exposure over a period of years, the effects of which are characterized by gradual onset and result (e.g., byssinosis, caused by inhalation of dust from cloth and prevalant among textile workers). Occupational disease is usually defined as any disability arising out of exposure to hazardous or harmful conditons in employment when they are present in a peculiar or increased degree by comparison with other employment or the environment generally. Some states cover it by an expansive use of the term injury, by a separate act or by a catchall provision, such as:

> Every employee, who is injured or who contracts an occupational disease, and the dependents of each employee who is killed, or dies as the result of an occupational disease contracted in the course of employment, wherever such injury has occurred or occupational disease has been contracted, provided the same were not purposely self-inflicted, is entitled to receive [compensation].[11]

> Definitions: (2) "Accident", "injury", or "injuries" includes liability or death resulting from accident or occupational disease as defined in subsection (3) of this section; (3) "Occupational disease" means a disease which results directly from the employment or the conditions under which work was performed, which can be seen to have followed as a natural incident of the work and as a result of the exposure occasioned by the nature of the employment, and which can be fairly traced to the employment as a proximate cause and which does not come from a hazard to which the work would have been equally exposed outside of the employment.[12]

---

[9] Minn Stat Ann §176.021 (West 1982).

[10] Peerless Woolen Mills v Pharr, 74 Ga App 459, 40 SE2d 106 (1946); Donnelly v Minneapolis Mfg Co, 161 Minn 240, 201 NW 305 (1924).

[11] Ohio Rev Code Ann §4123-54 (Page 1955).

[12] Colo Rev Stat §8-41-108 (1973).

What originally set occupational illnesses and diseases apart from injuries was the notion that illnesses and diseases could not be considered to be unexpected (e.g., accidental), since they were recognized and presumably accepted as an inherent hazard of continued exposure to conditions of the particular employment. This *fact* is now soundly rejected. Connected with the notion that occupational disease should be treated differently than occupational injury was the idea that hypersusceptible employees should be beyond coverage of workers' compensation statutes. This idea is now in the process of revision, as most cases now hold that individual weakness is immaterial if the particular condition of employment in fact caused the disability beyond that normally prevailing.[13] Moreover, a disease which is ordinarily nonoccupational may become occupational if work facilitates or aggravates its transmission. There still remain hard questions of proof of the causal relationship, such as whether the work conditions or hazard, as distinct from outside factors, caused the disability.[14]

§6.03   What Is Exclusivity?

With these rather intricate statutory formulations (discussed in **§6.02**) in place, most states provide that where the conditions of compensation exist— i.e., the workers' compensation act is applicable—workers' compensation is then the *exclusive* remedy for the injury or illness of the employee against the employer and its insurance carrier, regardless of the question of negligence and the existence of any other rights and remedies.[15] This is the case even if the injury or illness is not totally compensable under the act. For example, the act may cover the injury or illness, and thus bar common law rights, but may fail to award benefits for the kind of harm suffered or may not adequately cover the degree of harm (e.g., impotency, pain and suffering, psychic damage, stress, or disfigurement).[16] If however, an injury or illness falls outside of the act's coverage, the exclusivity provision would not apply.[17] Thus, before many

---

[13] LeLenko v Wilson H Lee Co, 128 Conn 499, 24 A2d 253 (1943); Bondar v Simmons Co, 23 NJ Super 109, 92 A2d 642 (1952); Herrera v Fluor Utah, Inc, 89 NM 245, 550 P2d 144 (1976).

[14] McAllister v Workmens Comp Bd, 445 P2d 313, 71 Cal Rptr 697 69 C2d 408 (1968); Amoroso v Tubular Cast Prods Mfg Co, 13 NY2d 992, 244 NYS2d 787 (1963).

[15] In a tort action by an employee to recover damages for work-related injury or illness, the employer has the burden of proving the affirmative defense that the employee is entitled only to workers' compensation. DeRosa v Albert F Amling Co, 84 Ill App 3d 64, 404 NE2d 564 (1980).

[16] *See generally* Fetterhof v Western Block Co, 49 AD2d 1001, 373 NYS2d 920 (1975) (impotence); Fisher v Consol Freightways, Inc, 12 Ore App 417, 507 P2d 53 (1973) (pain); Nowell v Stone Mountain Scenic RR, 150 Ga App 201, 257 SE2d 344 (1979) (disfigurement); Tredway v District of Columbia, 403 A2d 732 (DC App 1979), *cert denied*, 101 S Ct 141 (1980) (psychic damage).

[17] *See* Horney v Johnson, 167 Conn 621, 356 A2d 879 (1975); Szydlowski v General Motors Corp, 397 Mich 356, 245 NW2d 26 (1976).

occupational diseases were made compensable, common law suits were not barred for employees who suffered from them.[18] This is illustrative of the quid pro quo concept mentioned in **§6.02.**

There are three general types of exclusivity provisions. The narrow type is contained in the Massachusetts and New Jersey statutes in which the employee waives his or her, and sometimes his or her spouse's, common law rights.[19]

> Such agreement shall be a surrender by the parties thereto of their rights to any other method, form or amount of compensation or determination thereof than as provided in this article and an acceptance of all the provisions of this article, and shall bind the employee and for compensation for *the employee's* death shall bind *the employee's* personal representatives, *surviving spouse* and next of kin, as well as the employer, and those conducting *the employer's* business during bankruptcy or insolvency.[20]

> An employee shall be held to have waived his right of action at common law or under the law of any other jurisdiction in respect to an injury therein occurring, to recover damages for personal injuries if he shall not have given his employer, at the time of his contract of hire, written notice that he claimed such right.[21]

In the California and Michigan type of formulation, the employer's liability to the employee for work-related illness or injury is exclusive; no other liability whatsoever may exist.[22]

> Liability for the compensation provided by this division, in lieu of any other liability whatsoever to any person except as provided in Section 3706, shall, without regard to negligence, exist against an employer for any injury sustained by his employees arising out of and in the course of the employment and for the death of any employee if the injury proximately causes death in those cases where the following conditions of compensation concur.[23]

> Section 131 . . . The right to the recovery of . . . benefits as provided in this act shall be the *employee's* exclusive remedy against the employer. As used in this section and section 827—"employee" includes the person injured, his personal representatives and any other person to whom a claim accrues by reason of the injury to or death of the employee, and "employer" includes his insurer, a service agent to a self-insured employ-

---

[18] *See generally* Davis v Bath Iron Works Corp, 338 A2d 146 (Me 1975); Boniecke v McGraw Edison Co, 485 Pa 163, 401 A2d 345 (1979).

[19] Ferriter v O'Connell's Sons, 413 NE2d 690 (Mass 1980); Ransmeier v Camp Cody, Inc, 117 NJ 736, 378 A2d 752 (1977).

[20] NJ Stat Ann §34:15-8 (West 1978) (emphasis added).

[21] Mass Gen Laws Ann C152 §24 (1958).

[22] *See also* Okla Stat Ann tit 85, §12 (West 1970).

[23] Cal Lab Code §3600 (West 1982).

er, and the accident fund insofar as they furnish, or fail to furnish, safety inspections or safety advisory services incident to providing workmen's compensation insurance or incident to a self-insured employer's liability servicing contact.[24]

Finally, under the broadest formulation, as contained in jurisdictions such as Texas and Missouri, the exclusion covers all actions by any person arising out of his or her employment for any injuries or illnesses suffered.[25]

> Section 3. The employees of a subscriber and the parents of minor employees shall have no right of action against their employer or against any agent, servant or employee of said employer for damages for personal injuries, and the representatives and beneficiaries of deceased employees shall have no right of action against such subscribing employer or his agent, servant or employee for damages for injuries resulting in death, but such employees and their representatives and beneficiaries shall look for compensation solely to the association, as the same is hereinafter provided for.[26]

> The rights and remedies herein granted to an employee shall exclude all other rights and remedies of the employee, his wife, her husband, parents, personal representatives, dependents, heirs or next kin, at common law or otherwise, on account of such accidental injury or death, except such rights and remedies as are not provided for by this chapter.[27]

The second and third types of *exclusive* remedy formulas are the most common, and they bar such actions as those for loss of consortium by spouses[28] and loss of services for minor children. Such actions and remedies are barred

---

[24] Mich Stat Ann §418.131 (Callaghan 1972).

[25] *See also* NY Work Comp Law §11 (McKinney 1957); Iowa Code Ann §85.20 (West 1981); Manscal v American Smelting & Ref Co, 113 Ariz 148, 548 P2d 412 (1976); Collier v Wagner Castings Co, 70 Ill App 3d 233, 388 NE2d 265 (1979), *affd* 81 Ill 2d 229, 408 NE2d 198 (1980).

[26] Tex Code Ann art 8306, §6 (West 1967).

[27] Mo Rev Stat §15.287.120(2) (Vernon 1978).

[28] Smither & Co v Coles, 242 F2d 220 (DC Cir 1957). The court, interpreting the District of Columbia Workers' Compensation Act, §36-501 (West, 1968) held that the exclusive nature of the legislation determines an employer's liability and bars both common law and other statutory liability. The plaintiff's husband was injured and received workers' compensation benefits, but the plaintiff brought an action against the employer asking damages for loss of consortium because of the injury the husband received, alleging negligence on the part of the company. The court, in barring the action, said the law provides that the liability of the employer shall be exclusive in place of all other liability of the employer to the employee, legal representative, husband, or wife. A spouse's right, whether independent—that is, arising directly from tort—or derivative does not come into existence except for the occurrence of an injury to an employee; thus, it is barred. *See also* Williams v Byrd, 242 Ga 80, 247 SE2d 874 (1978); Cockrum v Baumgartner, 449 NE2d 911 (Ill 1983) (action for wrongful birth); Stoneci-

even if the parent or spouse gets no compensation as a substitute for the common law or statutory wrongful death cause of action which was lost. In only the rarest case might it be possible to show that the loss to the spouse, parent, or child was such an independent violation of duty that it is not covered by the exclusive remedy provision.

If the compensable injury or illness is the result of a third party's tortious conduct, an overwhelming majority of states preserve a right against that tortfeasor, since the compensation system was not designed to extend immunity to strangers. In order to avoid a double recovery, an employee must, if he or she recovers, reimburse the employer for the compensation outlay; the employee gets the excess of any damage recovery over the amount of compensation.[29] Persons and entities who are considered to be third parties vary from state to state. Sometimes they include coemployees (a great majority of jurisdictions exclude coemployees from the third party category), physicians whose actions aggravate the injury, the insurance carrier who conducts a negligent safety inspection, governmental instrumentalities, manufacturers, and suppliers.

The third-party action is primarily the employee's cause of action. Sometimes, however, the third party will seek recovery over against a *contributorily negligent* employer for contribution or indemnity when the employer's negligence has caused or contributed to the employee's injury. The majority rule in the states is not to allow such contribution;[30] the minority rule permits limited contribution.[31]

§6.04 Application of the Exclusivity Doctrine

In its simplest and purest form, the exclusivity doctrine precludes common law suits by employees against their employers. In the case of *Silkwood v Kerr-McGee Corp,*[32] the plaintiff was a laboratory analyst at the Kerr-McGee plant in Oklahoma. The plant fabricated fuel pins containing plutonium for use as a

---

pher v Winn Rau Corp, 545 P2d 317 (Kan 1976); Harbeson v Parke Davis, 643 P2d 914 (Wash 1982) (action for wrongful life).

[29] Fuller v Capital Sky Park, 46 Cal App 3d 727, 557 P2d 812, 120 Cal Rptr 131 (1975); Granger v Urda, 44 NY2d 91, 375 NE2d 380, 404 NYS2d 319 (1978).

[30] *See* Montoya v Greenway Aluminum Co, 10 Wash App 630, 519 P2d 22 (1974); AA Equip Inc v Farmorl Inc, 31 Conn Super 322, 330 A2d 99 (1974); Blau Knox Food & Chem Equip Corp v Holmes, 348 So 2d 604 (Fla Dist Ct App 1977); Arcell v Ashland Chem Co, 152 NJ Super 471, 378 A2d 53 (1977); Cutter v Massey-Ferguson Inc, 318 NW2d 554 (Mich Ct App 1982).

[31] *See* Skinner v Reed-Prentice Div Package Mach Co, 70 Ill 2d 1, 374 NE2d 437 (1978). An employee brought a strict liability action in tort against the manufacturer of a machine whose use had injured him. The manufacturer counterclaimed against the employer because the employer misused the product. The court permitted the third party action and contribution from the employer proportionate to his relative degree of fault.

[32] 667 F2d 908 (10th Cir 1981), *revd on other grounds,* __ US __ (Jan 12, 1984).

reactor fuel. Ms. Silkwood became contaminated by plutonium over a nine-day period.

The Oklahoma workers' compensation statute had the *arising out of and in the course of employment* language and further provided that the liability shall be exclusive and in place of all other liability of the employer.[33] In order to invoke this affirmative defense of exclusivity, the employer had the burden of producing evidence sufficient to demonstrate that Ms. Silkwood's injuries were covered by the statute. The method of proving applicability of the statute is the same regardless of whether it is offered by an employee to prove a claim or by an employer to bar an action at common law.

The court said that the Oklahoma compensation law indulges a presumption that a claim for an injury is covered, absent substantial evidence to the contrary. Circumstantial evidence may be used to provide a legal and logical basis for a reasonable inference as to the existence of the fact sought to be proven. If a prima facie case of coverage and hence exclusivity is established by inference, it is incumbent upon the other party to produce reasons for the nonexclusivity of the remedy as to elements of the injuries for which a plaintiff seeks relief.[34] The court then, upon an examination of the circumstantial evidence, determined that Ms. Silkwood's exposure occurred at the job site. Thus, the exposure which caused injury was job related. If cancer had developed from this exposure, it was job related, and the workers' compensation law covered it—exclusively. The court reversed the lower court's award of $500,000 in personal injury tort damages and $10 million in punitive damages to Ms. Silkwood's estate.[35] Only a $5000 property damage award was permitted to stand.

The workers' compensation remedy is not only exclusive as to common law tort actions, it is also exclusive of other statutory rights and remedies. It precludes the employee from recovery against his or her employer under state products liability and wrongful death acts,[36] the Federal Employers Liability Act,[37] the Federal Tort Claims Act,[38] the Mine Safety and Health Act,[39] the Occupational Safety and Health Act,[40] the Outer Continental Shelf Lands

---

[33] Okla Stat Ann 85 §27 (West 1978).

[34] *See generally* Murphy v Owens-Corning Fiberglass Corp, 447 F Supp 557 (D Kan 1977).

[35] Silkwood v Kerr-McGee Corp, 667 F2d 908 (10th Cir 1981).

[36] *See* Jackson v Dravo Corp, 603 F2d 156 (10th Cir 1979); Frith v Harrah South Shore Corp, 92 Nev 447, 552 P2d 337 (1976); Lupovisci v Hunzinger Constr Co, 79 Wis 2d 491, 255 NW2d 590 (1977); Davis v Siloo, Inc, 47 NC App 237, 267 SE2d 354, *cert denied*, 310 NC 234 (1980).

[37] Federal Employers Liability Act, 45 USC §56; Ferreira v Panama Canal Co, 215 F Supp 726 (DDC 1963).

[38] 28 USC §1346(b); Gill v United States, 641 F2d 195 (5th Cir 1981); Boyer v United States, 510 F Supp 1081 (ED Pa 1981).

[39] 30 USC §801 *et seq;* Blessing v United States, 447 F Supp 1160 (ED Pa 1978).

[40] 29 USC §651 *et seq;* Cochran v International Harvester Co, 408 F Supp 598 (WD Ky 1975); Taylor v Brighton Corp, 616 F2d 256 (6th Cir 1980).

Act,[41] and many other acts.

In *Byrd v Fieldcrest Mills, Inc,*[42] the plaintiff alleged that the company's violation of Occupational Safety and Health Administration (OSHA) standards was the proximate cause of the employee's injuries and death; thus, the company was negligent. However, the court held that since the employee died as a result of an accident arising out of and in the course of employment, it was covered under the applicable state workers' compensation act.[43] Moreover, §653(b)(4) of the Occupational Safety and Health Act[44] precludes such a private remedy, for there is no private cause of action under this or similar laws.[45]

Although touched upon briefly in **§6.03,** it should also be noted here that in third-party cases, the exclusivity of workers' compensation statutes acts to preclude indemnification claims against the employer in some jurisdictions. In *Austin v Johns-Manville Sales Corp,*[46] the estate of Ms. Austin filed a wrongful death action under Maine law against the manufacturers of asbestos who had sold it to Austin's employer, Bath Iron Works. Ms. Austin's estate alleged that her disability and death were caused by the inhalation of asbestos dust and fibers contained in the manufacturer's products. Her estate sought damages on the theories of negligence, strict liability, and breach of warranty. One of the manufacturers brought a third-party action against Bath seeking contribution and indemnity. Bath countered that the manufacturer's action was barred by the exclusivity provisions of the Longshoremen's and Harbor Worker's Compensation Act[47] under which Ms. Austin was covered and had received benefits.

The court said the Longshoremen's and Harbor Workers' Compensation Act provision immunizes a compensation-paying employer from third-party contribution claims, at least to the extent that the employer is immune from common law liability to its employees. In addition, the third party is not entitled to have any judgment recovered against it by the employee reduced by the amount of the employer's compensation lien (the pro tanto theory of recovery). Bath would be liable for contribution to the manufacturer only if Bath could be found liable to its employee—that is, if it was guilty of conduct which would take it outside the compensation act.

Finally, it must be noted that even if the exclusivity provisions of a state's workers' compensation law can be overcome, a common law claim can be defeated by utilization of certain defenses, most notably the expiration of the

---

[41] 43 USC §1331 *et seq;* Pure Oil Co v Snipes, 293 F2d 60 (5th Cir 1961).

[42] 496 F2d 1323 (4th Cir 1974).

[43] NC Stat Ann §97-1 *et seq* (Michie 1979).

[44] 29 USC §653(b)(4).

[45] *See* Taylor v United States, — F Supp —, 1981 OSHD ¶25,800 (CCH) (WD Ky 1981); Blessing v United States, 447 F Supp 1160 (ED Pa 1978); Skidmore v Travelers Ins Co, 356 F Supp 676 (ED La), *affd per curium,* 483 F2d 67 (5th Cir 1973).

[46] 508 F Supp 313 (D Me 1981). *See also* Baltimore Transit Co v State, 183 Md 674, 39 A2d 858 (1944).

[47] 33 USC §905.

applicable statute of limitation. For this reason, it is of great importance to determine when the limitations period begins to run in the jurisdiction—at the time employment ends; at the time the illness, injury, or disease is diagnosable or diagnosed or the employee shows symptoms; at the time of last inhalation or exposure; at the time the disease resulting from exposure is discovered or reasonably should have been discovered; at the time of death from the disease; or at some other time.[48] Resolution of this question is also significant with respect to whether and when coverage under standard products liability insurance policies is triggered.

§6.05 Intentional Acts Exception to Exclusivity

An intentional act committed by an employer which causes injury or illness to its employee may become the subject of a common law action for damages on the reasoning that an intentional act is not an *accidental* injury or illness which would fall under the exclusivity provisions of a workers' compensation act. Since the justification for bringing a common law action is the nonaccidental character of the injury or illness, most jurisdictions have held that such liability cannot be predicated upon or caused by the employers *mere* gross, wanton, willful, deliberate, intentional, reckless, culpable, or malicious *negligence, misconduct, or violation of statutory obligation.* It must be an *intentionally* caused injury.

In *Duncan v Perry Packing Co,*[49] an allegation of gross and wanton negligence in improperly grounding a machine did not avoid the exclusivity bar since there was no actual intent to cause injury. It appears, under this traditional approach, that even if the employee's conduct goes beyond aggravated negli-

---

[48] Fearson v Johns-Manville Sales Corp, 489 F Supp 914 (DDC 1981) (the limitations period begins to run from the date cancer from asbestos exposure is discovered); Steinhardt v Johns-Manville Sales Corp, 54 NY2d 1008, 446 NYS2d 244, 430 NE2d 1297 (NY 1981) (must file suit within four years of the last inhalation of asbestos, not after discovery of health problems); Locke v Johns-Manville Sales Corp, 221 Va 951, 275 SE2d 900 (1981) (from the time the worker shows disease symptoms, not from date of last exposure); Anthony v Koppers Co, 50 USLW 2296 (Pa Oct 29, 1981) (from the date of the employee's death, not from date it was discovered exposure may have caused health problems); Newbauer v Owens-Corning Fiberglass Corp, 686 F2d 570 (7th Cir 1982) (cause of action occures when disease becomes diagnosed); Olsen v Bell Tel Laboratories, Inc, 51 USLW 2539 (Mass Feb 15, 1983) (when the victim discovers or should have discovered the disease); O'Stricker v Jim Walter Corp, 447 NE2d 727 (Ohio 1983) (when plaintiff knows or should know injury was asbestos-related).

[49] 162 Kan 79, 174 P2d 78 (1946). The court in Boek v Wong Hing, 180 Minn 470, 471, 231 NW 233, 234 (1930), discussed the difference between extreme negligence and actual intent to injure, stating that it would be a "perversion of the Workmen's Compensation Act's purpose to allow employers immunity from intentional torts. Indeed, it would be travesty on the use of the English language to allow someone who intentionally inflicts an injury on another to call the injury a work accident." *See also* Houston v Bechtel Assoc Prof Corp, 552 F Supp 1094 (DDC 1981) (the exclusivity provision of the Longshoreman Harbor Worker's Compensation Act, 33 USC §901 *et seq.* bars an action based on wanton, willful, reckless or unlawful conduct).

gence—such as knowingly permitting a hazardous condition to exist, failure to warn of the existence of a hazardous condition, misrepresentation of the hazards, willfully failing to furnish a safe and healthful workplace, or willfully violating a safety or health statute such as the Occupational Safety and Health Act or the Mine Safety and Health Act—no common law action will be permitted.[50] This type of conduct cannot be equated with an actual intent to injure, which is deliberately directed at a specific employee.[51] The important and decisive factor is the intentional versus the accidental quality of the specific incident which caused the injury or illness—thus, the deliberate or intentional removal of a safety device *may or may not* cause a later accidental injury. A deliberate thrusting of an employee into an unguarded machine would, however, be an intentional action.

The majority of courts which have considered the requirement of deliberate intent to injure in order to maintain a tort action outside the workers' compensation laws have held that the standard for that intent is very high—i.e., an employer must have deliberately intended to cause injury to a *specific* employee or employees. Nevertheless, as discussed in §6.07, even where courts have applied the traditional standards, there has recently been some indication that courts are becoming dissatisfied with the results. This seems to indicate that in the future, more courts may seek ways to avoid the exclusivity bar of workers' compensation statutes by finding evidence of deliberate intention in a wider variety of circumstances.

For example, a recent California case, *Johns-Manville Products Corp v Contra Costa Superior Court,*[52] held that allegations that an employer's intentional concealment of the risks of employment which caused employees to contract asbestos-related diseases were not sufficient to escape the exclusivity bar of the workers' compensation system. However, allegations that the employer's deliberate concealment of the actual existence of an asbestos-related illness prevented treatment of the disease and caused it to worsen stated a common law cause of action for damages for the intentional aggravation of an injury.

Often, there will be no express statutory exception to the exclusivity rule in workers' compensation acts, and thus, courts are forced to *imply* an exception

---

[50] Wright v FMC Corp, 81 Cal App 3d 554, 146 Cal Rptr 741 (1978) (misrepresentation of the hazard of pesticide chemicals); Yancy v Green, 129 Ga App 705, 201 SE2d 162 (1973) (failure to repair and furnish a safe workplace); Kerrigan v Firestone Tire & Rubber Co, 207 NW2d 578 (Ia 1973) (failure to correct a known defect on a press); Sanford v Presto Mfg Co, 92 NM 746, 594 P2d 1202 (1979) (employer alleged to have intentionally allowed toxic fumes to exist and to have maintained an unsafe workplace); Peterick v State, 22 Wash App 163, 589 P2d 250 (1978) (evasion and violation of safety and health standards.

[51] *Compare* Artonio v Hirsch, 3 AD2d 939, 163 NYS2d 489 (1951) *with* De Coigne v Ludlum Steel Co, 251 AD 662, 297 NYS 636 (1937) (deliberate removal or rendering inoperative of safety guards was not the equivalent of a deliberate intent to injure an employee).

[52] Cal 3d 27 465, 612 P2d 948, 165 Cal Rptr 858 (1980).

for injuries and illnesses caused by an employer's intentional torts.[53] In this situation, however, the courts have generally required allegations and proof of a very high degree of intent on the employer's part to permit the maintenance of a tort action outside the workers' compensation system. In *Mylroie v GAF Corp*,[54] the plaintiff

> charged that GAF falsely and fraudulently stated and represented to plaintiff that she was physically and medically fit for her particular work assignment involving exposure to allegedly carcinogenic chemicals and substances; that from prior medical examinations GAF has actual knowledge that plaintiff was uniquely susceptible to bladder cancer by virtue of constant exposure to carcinogenic substances, yet wantonly and maliciously continued to expose her to those substances; and that GAF fraudulently and carelessly subjected her to carcinogens in persistent and willful violation of safety rules and regulations.[55]

The court held the plaintiff's allegations of intentional tort and fraud insufficient to escape the exclusivity bar of the workers' compensation statute.

> While an intentional tort can give rise to a cause of action outside the ambit of the Workers' Compensation Law, a complaint seeking to neutralize the statute's exclusivity must allege an intentional or deliberate act by the employer directed at causing harm to this particular employee [citations omitted].
>
> For the same reason, the fraud accusations are wanting, for it is not alleged that GAF purposely and specifically intended to cause plaintiff the medical difficulties she foresees.[56]

The Illinois workers' compensation statute[57] also contains no statutory exemption for intentional torts. Nevertheless, one of the few cases where plaintiffs' allegations have been found sufficient to withstand a motion to dismiss arose in *McDaniel v Johns-Manville Sales Corp*.[58] The plaintiffs alleged that defendant's intentional and felonious poisoning, fraud and misrepresentation, and conspiracy to deceive, as a result of which the plaintiffs allegedly developed asbestos-related diseases, constituted intentional torts as to which the plaintiffs

---

[53] *E.g.*, Love v Flour Mills of America, 647 F2d 1058 (10th Cir 1981) (Oklahoma law); Mylroie v GAF Corp, 81 AD2d 994, 440 NYS2d 67 (1980). The theory on which many such suits are allowed to be brought involves a finding that the injury was not an accident and thus not within the scope of employment *E.g.*, Provo v Bunker Hill Co, 393 F Supp 778 (D Idaho 1975).

[54] 440 NYS2d 67, 81 AD2d 994 (App Div 1981).

[55] *Id* 68-69.

[56] *Id.*

[57] Ill Ann Stat §48-138 (West 1969).

[58] 487 F Supp 714 (ND Ill 1978); *see also* Barnson v Foote Mineral Co, CA 80-0119A (D Utah 1981).

could seek damages outside of the workers' compensation statute. The court agreed and denied defendant's motion to dismiss, despite the plaintiff's foreseeable difficulties in proving their allegations.

§6.06   —Statutory Exception for Intentional Acts

In those cases where statutory exceptions exist, there are varying approaches to the removal of the exclusivity bar where an employer's intentional acts cause injury to an employee. Some jurisdictions provide employees with an election of remedies, entitling them to proceed under either the workers' compensation statute or to sue at common law.[59] Other jurisdictions allow employees to sue at common law as an additional remedy.[60] Still other jurisdictions provide a percentage increase in compensation awards over that normally available as a statutory penalty for an employer's willful, intentional, or reckless misconduct, such as a failure to comply with safety and health laws.[61]

The gravity of employer misconduct and the definitions of intent dealt with in the various workers' compensation statutes vary from intentional injury and willful misconduct to gross and wanton negligence. Kentucky, Oregon, Washington, West Virginia, and Maryland have workers' compensation statutes which are common in the use of the term *deliberate intention* as the basis for the removal of the exclusivity bar.[62]

> If injury or death results to a workman from the deliberate intention of his employer to produce such injury or death, the workman, the widow, widower, child or dependent of the workman may take under ORS 656.001 to 656.794, and also have cause for action against the employer, as if such statutes had not been passed, for damages over the amount payable under those statutes.[63]

In states which require a showing of deliberate, intentional injury, the standard is as exacting as in the cases discussed in **§6.05** dealing with intentional torts in the absence of a specific statutory provision on employer misconduct—the intention must be real and deliberate. For example, in Washington: "[T]he employer must have determined to injure an employee and used some means appropriate to that end; . . . there must be a specific intent, not merely careless-

---

[59] *E.g.,* Ariz Rev Stat §23-1022 (West 1970); Ky Rev Stat §342.015 (Michie 1980); Md Ann Code art 101, §44 (Michie 1969); Tex Code Ann Art 8306, §5 (West 1967).

[60] *E.g.,* Or Rev Stat §656.156(2) (1965); Wash Rev Code §51.24.020 (1974); W Va Code §23-4-2 (Michie 1981).

[61] *E.g.,* Ark Stat Ann §81-1310(d) (Bobbs-Merrill 1981); Cal Lab Code §4553 (West 1982); Mass Ann Laws ch 152 §28 (Michie/Law Co-op 1943); Mo Ann Stat §287-120(4) (Vernon 1978); NC Gen Stat §97-12 (Michie 1979).

[62] Ky Rev Stat §342.015(2); Md Ann Code art 101, §44 (Michie 1969); Or Rev Stat §656.156(2) (1965); Wash Rev Code §51.24.020 (West 1974); W Va Code §23-4-2 (Michie 1981).

[63] Or Rev Stat §656.156(2).

ness or negligence, however gross."[64] Under these formulations, the employer must have had a specific intent to injure an employee and must have taken or failed to take action toward that end; mere carelessness or negligence, no matter how gross, is insufficient. The intent to injure in this type of statute need not, however, be an intent to injure a particular employee; it is sufficient that the employer has an intent to injure someone.

A second group of states also provides a statutory exception to the exclusivity of the workers' compensation where the employer acted intentionally but uses different wording than that used by the first group of states. New Jersey's law provides that if an injury is compensable under the workers' compensation system, such compensation is the exclusive remedy for the injury "except for intentional wrong."[65]

Louisiana defines *intent* in the traditional way: "To constitute the requisite intent to result in civil liability, the defendant must have entertained a desire to bring about the result which followed and he should have believed that the result was substantially certain to follow."[66] The statute further provides that nothing in its workers' compensation law shall affect the employer's liability, civil or criminal, resulting from an intentional act.[67] The words *intentional wrong*, according to the only New Jersey decision to date, were interpreted to have their narrowly and commonly understood significance of deliberate intention.[68] However, a recent case from Louisiana has slightly expanded the definition—stating that the intent required by its statute had reference to the consequences of the act rather than the act itself. The court further rejected interpretations by several of the intermediate appellate courts limiting *intentional acts* to those acts where the defendant had entertained a desire to bring about the result which had followed *and* had believed the result was substantially certain to follow. The court stated: "Intent is not, however, limited to consequences which are desired. If the actor knows that the consequences are certain, or substantially certain, to result from his act, and still goes ahead, he is treated by the law as if he had in fact desired to produce the result."[69] As a practical matter then, the court expanded the definition of *intent,* since it required the plaintiff to allege and prove only one part of the intention test.

Finally, employer malfeasance at the level of serious and willful misconduct has often been varyingly applied depending upon the severity of the penalty

---

[64] Wash Rev Code §51.24.020 (West 1974); Briggs v Donovan-Corkery Logging Co, 185 Wash 284, 54 P2d 235 (1936). *See also* Winterroth v Meats, Inc, 10 Wash App 7, 516 P2d 522 (1973); McGray v Davis H Elliott Co, 419 SW2d 542 (Ky App 1967); Weis v Allen, 147 Ore 670, 35 P2d 478 (1934).

[65] NJ Stat Ann §34:15-8 (West 1978).

[66] La Rev Stat Ann §23-1032 (West 1976); Guidry v Aetna Casualty & Surety Co, 359 So 2d 637 (La App 1st Cir 1978), *cert denied,* 362 So 2d 578 (La 1978).

[67] La Rev Stat Ann §23-1033 (West 1976).

[68] Bryan v Jeffers, 103 NJ Super 522, 248 A2d 129 (1968), *cert denied,* 53 NJ 581 (1969); *see also* Copeland v Johns Mansville Products Corp, 492 F Supp 498 (D NJ 1980).

[69] Bazely v Tortorich, 397 So 2d 475 (La 1981).

which results. Two states provide that an employer's *willful misconduct* (Arizona) or *serious and willful misconduct* (California) will remove the bar and subject him or her to penalty. The Arizona statute specifically defines *willful misconduct:* "The term willful misconduct as employed in this section shall be construed to mean an act done knowingly and purposely with the direct object of injuring another."[70] In Arizona, courts have narrowly defined the intent which will exempt an employee from the exclusivity bar, and a heavy burden is imposed because the consequence is to subject the employer to an action at common law.[71]

In California, where the penalty is a percentage increase in the compensation award, the burden on persons asserting the employer misconduct is less onerous. An employer commits willful misconduct when he or she "turns his [or her] mind" to the fact that injury to employees will probably result from his or her acts or omissions yet fails to take appropriate precautions for their safety.[72] Violations of safety and health regulations are oftentimes relied upon as foundations for a charge of serious and willful misconduct.[73]

Finally, in Texas, the compensation act provides exemplary damages for gross negligence. This has been interpreted to mean an entire want of care or conscious indifference.[74] Remaining statutory provisions in other jurisdictions impose penalties not necessarily for misconduct, but for failure to comply with safety and health laws, or to provide safe and healthful workplaces.[75]

The traditional application of the exception, of course, is in assault and battery cases. The weight of authority implies an exception in this limited class of cases where the employer deliberately sets out to injure a specific em-

---

[70] Ariz Rev Stat Ann §23-1022.

[71] Serna v Statewide Contractors, Inc, 6 Ariz App 12, 429 P2d 504 (1967); *contra In re* Paccia's Case, 351 NE2d 546 (Mass App 1976).

[72] Cal Lab Code §4553 (West 1982); Rogers Materials Co v Industrial Accident Commn, 48 Cal Rptr 129, 408 P2d 737 (1965) *disapproved on other grounds;* Levesque v Workmen's Compensation Appeals Bd, 83 Cal Rptr 208, 1 Cal 3d 627, 463 P2d 432 (1970) (*en banc*); *See also* Johns-Manville Sales Corp Private Carriage v Worker's Compensation Appeals Bd, 96 Cal App 2d 923, 158 Cal Rptr 463 (1979). Only West Virginia permits an action at common law to be brought for the reckless, willful, or wanton misconduct of an employer. Even though California uses the term serious and willful misconduct, it only permits a penalty—a percentage increase in the award. It does not permit a tort suit.

[73] American Smelting v Worker's Compensation Appeals Bd, 79 Cal App 3d 615, 144 Cal Rptr 898 (1978); Casillas v SWIG, 628 P2d 329 (NM App 1981); *but see* Abron v Workmen's Compensation Appeals Bd, 34 Cal App 3d 232, 109 Cal Rptr 778 (1973).

[74] Tex Code Ann art 8306, §5 (West 1967); Burk Royalty Co v Walls, 616 SW2d 911 (Tex 1981).

[75] Ark Stat Ann §41-1310(d) (Bobbs-Merrill 1981); Ky Rev Stat §342.165 (Michie 1980). *See* Ryan v NAPA, 266 Ark 802, 586 SW2d 6 (1979); Shimp v New Jersey Bell Tel Co, 145 NJ Super 516, 368 A2d 408 (1976); *but see* Sewell v Bathey Mfg Co, 103 Mich App 732, 303 NW2d 876 (1981).

ployee.[76] An intentional assault by an employer is not an accident covered by workers' compensation. Clearly, if the employer *personally* committed or expressly commanded or authorized the assault, he or she was the active tortfeasor, and a common law suit would be allowed. (The distinction among deliberate and reckless and wanton—e.g., ordering employee to perform a dangerous job—is still important in determining the employers intent.)[77] Even if the employer did not personally commit the assault, a suit would be allowed if the tortfeasor was a person who is realistically the alter ego of the corporation. If, however, the employer acts constructively through an agent—that is, a supervisor committed the assault—even though the employer may have investigated it, a substantial majority of cases bar a damage action against the employer—even though the supervisor could be personally liable to the employee.[78]

§6.07 —Recent Decisions Expanding the Intentional Acts Exception

In *Mandolis v Elkins Industries, Inc*,[79] the plaintiff employee was injured during the course of the employment while operating a table saw which was not equipped with a safety guard. The plaintiff alleged that the employer knew that the operation of the saw without a guard violated federal and state safety rules because the employer had been cited previously for Occupational Safety and Health Act (OSHA) violations. The plaintiff further alleged that the employer actually knew that the saw was dangerous because other employees had previously been injured. Finally, the plaintiff alleged that when he objected to operating the saw without a safety guard, he was threatened with being fired and that another employee who had refused to operate the saw without a guard had actually been fired.

---

[76] 2A Larson, Workmen's Compensation Law §§68.13, 68.21 (1976 & 1982 Supp); Rodriquez v Industrial Commn, 333 NW2d 118 (Ill 1983) (injuries resulting from workplace assault by coemployee are compensable).

[77] *E.g.,* Readinger v Gottschall, 201 Pa Super 134, 191 A2d 694 (1963); Lavin v Goldberg Bldg Material Corp, 274 AD 690, 87 NYS2d 90 (1949), *app denied,* 275 AD 865, 89 NYS2d 523 (1949); Serna v Statewide Contractors Inc, 6 Ariz App 12, 429 P2d 504 (1967); McCray v Davis H Elliott Co 419 SW2d 542 (Ky 1967).

[78] *E.g.,* Burkhart v Wells Elec Corp, 139 Ind App 658, 215 NE2d 879 (1966); Echols v Chattanooga Mercantile Co, 74 Ga App 18, 38 SE2d 675 (1946)(supervisor is fellow employee); Elliot v Brown 569 P2d 1323 (Alaska 1977); Jett v Dunlap, 179 Conn 215, 425 A2d 1263 (1979); Brown v Stauffer Chem Co, 167 Mont 418, 539 P2d 374 (1975) *But see* Lavin v Goldberg Bldg Material Corp, 274 AD 690, 87 NYS2d 90, *app denied,* 275 AD 865, 89 NYS2d 523 (1949) (supervisor is agent of employer, therefore tort suit allowed); Stewart v McLellan's Stores Co, 194 SC 50, 9 SE2d 35 (1940).
In a recent case, Jones v Thomas, 430 So 2d 891 (La 1983), it was held that the exclusivity provisions of the workers' compensation law did not bar an employee from bringing a tort action against his employer for injuries resulting from the intentional act of a coemployee.

[79] 246 SE2d 907 (W Va 1980).

The defendant employer submitted an affidavit denying any deliberate intent to injure plaintiff and moved to dismiss the complaint on the ground that the suit was barred by the exclusivity provision of the workers' compensation law. The West Virginia Supreme Court reversed the trial court's grant of defendant's motion and remanded the case for trial, holding that the phrase "deliberate intent to produce such injury or death" in the state worker's compensation act encompassed *both* "specific intentional torts" *and* "willful, wanton, and reckless misconduct."[80]

The *Mandolis* court's definition of deliberate intent is substantially broader than any other state except California (but with the distinction as noted in §6.07), and expands considerably the type of conduct for which an employer may be subject to tort liability. This decision, which is distinctly out of line with other holdings, has been specifically rejected by several courts.[81] The other states with similar statutory language—Kentucky, Oregon, and Washington—have not had occassion to construe that language since the *Mandolis* decision, but it appears unlikely, based on their past actions, that they would follow such a broad interpretation.

In *Basley v Tortorich*,[82] the Louisiana Supreme Court rejected earlier interpretations by intermediate appellate courts limiting *intentional acts* to acts where the defendant entertained a desire to bring about the result which had followed and believed the result was substantially certain to follow. The Louisiana Supreme Court held that intent encompassed both results which were desired and consequences which were known or substantially certain to result whether or not they were actually desired. (The latter test is distinguished from reckless misconduct where the employer disregards the possibility that his or her act or omission will have certain consequences.)

In *McDaniel v Johns-Manville Sales Corp*,[83] plaintiffs, who claimed they were injured by inhaling asbestos fibers while employed at an asbestos-processing plant, alleged intentional and felonious poisoning, fraud and misrepresentation, and conspiracy to deceive. The district court denied the defendant's motion to dismiss, concluding that under Illinois law, workers' compensation

---

[80] 246 SE2d 911. The court adopted the definition of intent from the Restatement (Second) of Torts §8A (1965): intent means either that the actor desired the consequences of his act, or that he believed the consequences were substantially certain to result from it.

[81] Great Western Sugar Co v District Court, 610 F2d 717 (Mont 1980); Waldrop v Vistron Corp, 391 So 2d 1274 (La Ct App 1980); Houston v Bechtel Assoc Prof Corp, 522 F Supp 1094 (DDC 1981). The only case to date to apply the *Mandolis* interpretation is Belcher v JH Fletcher Co, 498 F Supp 629 (SD WVa 1980) which result, of course, was required by Erie RR Co v Tompkins, 340 US 64 (1938). In February, 1983, West Virginia enacted a statute nullifying a large part of *Mandolis* in that employees no longer may collect punitive damages from their employers; only compensatory damages will be allowed.

[82] 397 So 2d 475 (La 1981).

[83] 487 F Supp 714 (ND Ill 1978).

might not be the exclusive remedy for intentional torts and holding that plaintiffs should be allowed the opportunity to prove their allegations.

In *Blankenship v Cincinnati Milacron Chemicals*,[84] employees of Cincinnati Milacron Chemicals filed a lawsuit against their employer claiming that they had been permanently disabled as a result of exposure to noxious fumes while working. They claimed that their employer *knew* that poisonous fumes in the plant were causing disease and that the company failed to correct the hazardous conditions, failed to warn the employees, failed to provide medical examinations as required by law, and furthermore, failed to report the hazardous conditions to the various state and federal agencies as required by law. The employees also claimed that the employer's conduct constituted intentional, malicious wrongdoing in willful and wanton disregard of the employees' health.

The employer moved to dismiss the lawsuit at the outset, relying upon the Ohio Constitution and the Ohio Workers' Compensation Act, both of which provide that an employer complying with the law shall be immune from lawsuits by employees for injuries or occupational diseases received or contracted in the course of employment.

The Ohio Supreme Court held that the workers' compensation laws do not give employers immunity from lawsuits where an employee claims that the employer intentionally caused the injury. Reasoning that these laws were developed to protect both employees and employers only in the event of *unforeseen, accidental* injuries, the Ohio Supreme Court concluded that *intentional* injuries are outside the scope of the Workers' Compensation Act. The court thus held that the employees could sue in tort for the employer's intentional use of chemicals it knew were hamful and for failure to warn and report on the dangerous conditions. It is important to note that in this out-of-line case, the Ohio Supreme Court did not decide that the facts in *Blankenship* established the employer's intent to harm its employees. Rather, the court decided that the employees must be given the opportunity to prove their cases.

§6.08 —Recent Decisions Narrowly Applying the Intentional Acts Exception

In *Copeland v Johns-Manville Products Corp*,[85] plaintiff employees alleged that their employers were forewarned with knowledge of their imminent peril, yet:

> intentionally, maliciously, willfully, wantonly and with reckless disregard to the health interest of plaintiffs . . . failed to advise plaintiffs of their peril, failed to take proper precautionary steps to protect plaintiffs from

---

[84] 69 Ohio St 2d 608 (1982).

[85] 492 F Supp 498 (DNJ 1980) *See also* Keating v Shell Chem Co, 610 F2d 238 (5th Cir 1980) (extreme negligence is not intention); Phifer v Union Carbide Corp, 492 F Supp 483 (ED Ark 1980) (failure to warn about harmful effects of chemicals is not an actual, specific, and deliberate attempt to harm an employee).

this peril, failed to provide a safe workplace as described [sic] by law, failed to remove plaintiffs from said peril and intentionally withheld information from the plaintiffs about the dangerous conditions in which they worked and the dangerous nature of material to which they were daily exposed and, moreover, failed to advise plaintiffs that they were in fact developing a disease while in the defendants' employ.[86]

Plaintiffs further alleged that their employers' omissions were motivated by a desire to "foster an atmosphere of ignorance" among the employees "in order to insure uninterrupted work and profits," and that the employers' failings proximately injured plaintiffs. The court found that none of the allegations charged a deliberate intent and denied plaintiffs leave to amend their complaint to allege that their employers willfully, wantonly, and with reckless disregard of plaintiffs' health failed to warn plaintiffs of the danger from exposure to asbestos or to take precautions to protect plaintiffs. The federal district court relied on the interpretation of the New Jersey statute by a New Jersey intermediate appellate court which had held that the legislature, in enacting the statute, had used the words *intentional wrong* to mean deliberate intent.[87] The federal district court, however, questioned the New Jersey court's conclusion that the legislature intended such a narrow exception to the exclusivity provision.

In *Austin v Johns-Manville Sales Corp*,[88] plaintiffs sued asbestos manufacturers for wrongful death under the Longshoremen's and Harbor Workers' Compensation Act (LHWCA), alleging negligence, breach of warranty, and strict liability. One of the manufacturer defendants sued the decedents' employer for contribution and indemnity, alleging that the employer willfully, wantonly, recklessly, and negligently failed to exercise due care in the discharge of its duty to protect the health and safety of its employees, that the employer failed to warn its employees of dangers from exposure to asbestos products, that the employer failed to protect its employees from such dangers, and that the employer fraudulently misrepresented and failed to disclose the hazards of exposure to asbestos "for the purpose of inducing them [the employees] to work in the hazardous environment created by the presence of asbestos products." The complaint further charged that physicians employed by the employers had negligently examined, diagnosed, and treated the employees.

The court noted that the employer could be liable to the third-party plaintiff only if it would be liable in a direct action by its employees. Noting that LHWCA covers accidental injury or death, the court distinguished between: (1) accidental injury resulting from gross, wanton, willful, deliberate, intentional, reckless, culpable, or malicious negligence, breach of statute or other misconduct of the employer—which it held fell within the phrase *accidental*

---

[86] 492 F Supp 501.

[87] *Id.*

[88] 508 F Supp 313 (D Me 1981).

injury or death and thus could not be the basis for a common law tort action—and (2) genuine intentional injury:

> While an act to be reckless must be intended by the actor, the actor does not intend to cause the harm which results from it. . . . It is enough that [the actor] realizes or from facts which he knows, should realize that there is a strong probability that harm may result, even though he hopes or even expects that his conduct will prove harmless. *However, a strong probability is a different thing from the substantial certainty without which he cannot be said to intend the harm in which his act results.*[89]

The court found that the complaint made no suggestion that the employer had deliberately intended to harm the employees; therefore no cause of action was stated.

The court also noted that fraudulent misrepresentation was not the same as a deliberate intent to harm. The court distinguished *Johns-Manville Products Corp v Contra Costa Superior Court*[90] on the ground that in *Austin*, the alleged misrepresentation was the concealment from the employees that their health was endangered by asbestos in the work environment. In *Contra Costa*, on the other hand, the misrepresentation consisted of concealing from the employees the fact that they had actually developed an asbestos-related disease, thereby preventing them from obtaining treatment for the disease.[91]

It appears then that the overwhelming majority of the states require that a plaintiff allege and prove that the employer intended that the consequences

---

[89] *Id* 317 (quoting Restatement (Second) of Torts §500 and Comment (1965) (emphasis added)).

[90] 165 Cal Rptr 658, 27 C3d 465, 612 P2d 948 (1980), discussed in **§6.05.**

[91] *See also* Griffin v George's Inc, 589 SW2d 24 (Ark 1979) (allegations of willful and wanton negligence and failure to warn employee of an extreme hazard in the form of an unguarded grain augur did not satisfy the requirement of allegation of deliberate and intentional act with desire to bring about the consequence of the act); Kittell v Vermont Weatherboard Inc, 138 Vt 439, 417 A2d 926 (1980)(allegations that plaintiff, an inexperienced worker, was put to work at a multiple saw from which safety devices had been removed and that plaintiff's injuries were due to the employer's willful and wanton acts were not sufficient since they fell short of alleging genuine intent); Sanford v Presto Mfg Co, 92 NM 743, 594 P2d 1199 (1979)(the claimant sought tort damages against her employer for intentionally allowing a dangerous condition of toxic fumes to exist, which led to the claimant's injury, but recovery was denied); Sewell v Bathey Mfg Co, 103 Mich App 732, 303 NW2d 876 (1981)(allegations of Michigan (MI) OSHA violations did not affect the application of the exclusive-remedy provision of the workers' compensation act); Great Western Sugar Co v District Court, 610 P2d 717 (Mont 1980)(wantonly and maliciously placing plaintiff in a position of danger is not the equivalent of intentional harm); Waldrop v Vistron Corp, 391 So 2d 1274 (La Ct App 1980) (plaintiffs claimed that the employer intentionally, knowingly, and with willful, wanton, and reckless disregard of the employee's safety caused the employee to be exposed to unsafe levels of acrylonitrile even though the employer knew of its dangerous qualities. The court found that nothing in plaintiffs' petition evidenced employer's intent that its employee develop cancer, nor substantial certainty on employer's part that he would develop cancer).

of his or her act or omission be injury to the employee. Allegations that an employer actually knew that working conditions were dangerous, that an employer deliberately used unsafe equipment or failed to provide appropriate safety equipment, that an employer deliberately disregarded safety regulations or warnings of safety inspectors, that an employer deliberately failed to warn employees of a known peril, even that an employer knowingly ordered an employee to perform or acquiesced in his or her performing dangerous work, and even that the employer's motive was to increase profits have all been held insufficient to charge the requisite intent where there was no allegation that the employer intended that his or her employee be injured or killed.[92]

Recently, however, several courts have expressed dissatisfaction with the laws as they exist or have broadened interpretations of those laws so as to permit more tort suits against employers. This may be an indication that courts are finding the compensation provided by the workers' compensation laws inadequate, or that courts find the diseases now appearing in suits to be more serious and more deserving of compensation than earlier industrial accidents. The current case law in this area is almost uniformly favorable to employers. However, there are indications of a shift towards allowing tort recovery by employees. Employers whose conduct is egregious or whose employees allege facts creating great sympathy may start finding themselves subject to tort liability on what were formerly exclusively workers' compensation claims.

§6.09   The Nonphysical Injury Torts Exception

Under the traditional approach to exclusivity, torts such as libel, false imprisonment, malicious prosecution, invasion of privacy, alienation of affections, intentional infliction of emotional distress, fraud, and deceit do not constitute personal injury by accident arising out of and in the course of employment. They would not fall within the basic coverage formula of the typical workers' compensation act, and therefore a common law suit would not be barred.[93]

The tort of intentional infliction of emotional distress has been the subject of much recent litigation; there is still no consensus concerning workers' compensation coverage of emotional injury resulting from an employer's conduct.[94] Similarly, suits involving mental distress resulting from an employer's

---

[92] *See generally* Keating v Shell Chem Co, 610 F2d 238 (5th Cir 1980); McCray v Davis H Elliot Co, 419 SW2d 542 (Ky 1967); Winterroth v Meats Inc, 10 Wash App 7, 516 P2d 522 (1973); Copeland v Johns-Manville Prods Corp, 492 F Supp 498 (DNJ 1980); Foster v Allsop Automatic Inc, 547 P2d 856 (Wash 1976); Southern Wire & Iron Co v Fowler, 217 Ga 727, 124 SE2d 681 (1979); Schlenk v Aerial Contractors Inc, 268 NW2d 466 (ND 1978).

[93] Skelton v WT Grant Co, 331 F2d 593 (5th Cir), *cert denied,* 379 US 830 (1964); Braman v Walthall, 215 Ark 582, 225 SW2d 342 (1949); Hamilton v East Ohio Gas Co, 47 Ohio App 2d 55, 351 NE2d 775 (1975); Foley v Polaroid Corp, 413 NE2d 711 (Mass 1980); Wilkins v West Point Pepperell, Inc, 397 So 2d 115 (Ala 1981).

[94] Cases holding that such an action does not come within the scope of workers' compensation laws and thus is not barred by the exclusivity provision include: Retter

wrongful termination of an employee or delay of workers' compensation benefits have been the subject of much litigation.[95]

To date there appear to be few cases involving exposures to hazardous or toxic substances in which the issues of nonphysical injury and deliberate intention, by means of fraud and deceit, have come into juxtaposition. Most cases involve claims based on employers' intentional misconduct which exposed employees to hazards and caused actual physical injury or illness. Representative cases are discussed in §§6.07-6.08. In the nonphysical injury approach, plaintiffs have had little success so far in successfully framing allegations which will withstand motions to dismiss; but as the cases indicate, there appears to be a gradual shift towards permitting tort recovery by employees under this emerging theory—especially in the occupational disease area.

§6.10 —Recent Decisions Concerning the Nonphysical Injury Tort Exception

A distinction drawn by many cases and commentators on the nonphysical injury exception in connection with occupational disease actions is whether the fraud or deceit precedes and helps produce or aggravate the injury and is thus merged into that action and barred, or whether the fraud or deceit is separate or follows the injury and produces a second additional injury or loss which is cognizable in tort and unaffected by the exclusive remedy provisions. This is a *dual injury* concept.

In *Johns-Manville Products Corp v Contra Costa Superior Court*,[96] plaintiff alleged that the decedent, an employee of Johns-Manville, had been continuously exposed to asbestos during his employment, which exposure had caused him to develop asbestosis. In addition, plaintiff alleged that defendant had known

---

v Allied Chem Corp, 295 F Supp 1360 (DSC 1968), *affd*, 407 F2d 403 (4th Cir 1969); Sullivan v United States, 428 F Supp 79 (ED Wis 1977); and Lagies v Copley, 110 Cal App 3d 958, 168 Cal Rptr 368 (1980). Cases holding that workers' compensation provides the exclusive remedy include: Schroeder v Dayton-Hudson Corp, 456 F Supp 652 (ED Mich 1978); Foley v Polaroid Corp, 413 NE2d 711 (Mass 1980); Cowan v Federal Mogul Corp, 86 Mich App 619, 273 NW2d 487 (1979); and Gater v Tram Video Corp, 93 Cal App 3d 196, 155 Cal Rptr 486 (1979). Some cases have skirted the issue and held that by its very term, the tort is considered *intentional* and thus is not an injury, which requires an accidental quality. Hamilton v East Ohio Gas Co, 47 Ohio App 2d 55, 351 NE2d 775 (1973); Maggio v St Francis Med Center Inc, 391 So 2d 948 (La Ct App 1980).

[95] Cases which allowed common law suits include: Martin v Travelers Ins Co, 497 F2d 329 (1st Cir 1974); Coleman v American Universal Ins Co, 86 Wis 2d 615, 273 NW2d 220 (1979); and Gibson v National Ben Franklin Ins Co, 387 A2d 220 (Me 1978). Cases which hold that workers' compensation is the exclusive remedy include: Whitten v American Mut Liab Ins Co, 468 F Supp 470 (DSC 1977), *affd*, 594 F2d 860 (4th Cir 1979); Young v United States Fidelity & Guaranty Co, 588 SW2d 46 (Mo Ct App 1979); Hicks v Board of Educ, 77 Ill App 3d 974, 397 NE2d 16 (1979); Sandoval v Salt River Project, 117 Ariz 209, 571 P2d 706 (1977).

[96] 165 Cal Rptr 858, 612 P2d 948 (1980).

of the dangers of exposure to asbestos and had known that plaintiff's decedent had actually contracted an asbestos-related disease yet failed to advise him of that condition at a time when he could have obtained medical treatment and avoided a worsening of the disease. The court held that the suit based on the initial contracting of the disease was barred by the exclusivity of the workers' compensation law, but that injury resulting from aggravation of the disease caused by defendant's *fraudulent concealment* of the employee's condition stated a cause of action in tort. The court further noted that plaintiff was entitled to recover damages only for the aggravation of the injury, not for the initial injury, but placed the burden of proving the apportionment of those damages on defendant.[97] (*Note:* If the employer's only misconduct had been in exposing the worker to and then *concealing the hazards* in the work environment, and in failing to provide necessary protection, the only remedy would have been under workers' compensation. However, there were two instances of misconduct and two injuries; the second was concealing the existence of the first which led to additional harm, and thus it was not excluded. The *concealment of the condition after it occurred* was actionable.)

In *Delamotte v Unitcast Division of Midland Ross Corp,*[98] the plaintiff, who had been employed by defendant for 30 years, alleged that from 1952 onward, X-rays taken by defendant as part of periodic physical examinations of employees revealed the existence of pneumoconiosis, and that defendant fraudulently, maliciously, and willfully conspired not to inform plaintiff of his condition. The trial court granted defendant's summary judgment motion on the ground that the Ohio workers' compensation statute provided plaintiff's exclusive remedy against his employer. The appellate court reversed, holding that such *fraud* was an intentional tort by the employer, not a hazard of employment. As such it did not fall within the exclusivity provision of the workers' compensation statute.

The court also advanced the dual capacity doctrine (see §6.11) as an additional ground for its decision. Without extended explanation, the court stated that where the employer undertook physical examinations of its employees, it assumed obligations unrelated to its obligations as an employer.

The use of such a fraud theory was rejected in *Burdette v Burlington Industries, Inc,*[99] where the court held that an allegation that the defendant had fraudulently induced plaintiff to continue working under conditions which were dangerous and which disabled him presented a claim for injuries compensable under the workers' compensation laws. The court stated that "even if plaintiff could prove fraud, we believe that the Act provides his exclusive remedy for all damages resulting from this fraud, which include the contraction of the disease, pain and suffering, medical expenses, emotional distress, and eco-

---

[97] 165 Cal Rptr 862, 612 P2d 951 (1980).
[98] 64 Ohio App 2d 159, 411 NE2d 814 (1978).
[99] CA No 132-87 (EDSC Nov 5, 1981).

nomic loss attributable to the same."[100]

The court, however, did allow plaintiff to sue his employer and the compensation carrier for *conspiracy to deprive* him of his statutory workers' compensation benefit. The court explained that plaintiff would have to prove that the defendants perpetrated a *fraud* which proximately caused him a temporary loss of benefits. His recoverable damages would be those damages attributable to the deprivation of benefits, but not those damages attributable to the disease, nor the amount of full workers' compensation benefits he would otherwise have been entitled to receive.

A recent case, *Henson v Bethlehem Steel Corp,*[101] was filed in the United States District Court for the District of Maryland in September of 1981 claiming $200 million damages. Named as individual defendants, in addition to the corporation, were three medical doctors and one industrial hygienist. The plaintiff employees alleged that they were continually exposed to asbestos over a period of years and that they were *fraudulently induced to continue* their employment without the knowledge that they would be exposed to the probability of developing asbestosis and other life-threatening cancers. The employees further alleged that the medical directors and industrial hygienist *fraudulently concealed* from the employees their affirmative findings which were shown in X-ray examinations, sampling, testing, and workplace monitoring. Moreover, it was alleged that they intentionally defrauded and deprived the employees of various occupational disease benefits available under the workers' compensation laws and that, in doing so, they were outrageous in their deliberate premeditated and willful disregard for human life. The employees further alleged that Bethlehem Steel acquired knowledge through testing, sampling, medical exams, and physical examinations that the work environment created a probability that workers would develop asbestosis, but that the defendants *withheld and concealed* this fact and did not advise nor inform the employees. For this reason, the doctors and industrial hygienist were sued under the theory of a *conspiracy* to deprive the plaintiffs of their civil rights.

In *Neal v Carey Canadian Mines, Ltd,*[102] a former director of the state's Division of Industrial Hygiene testified that he was specifically hired by the asbestos insulation manufacturer to study the problems of asbestos exposure at the company's facilities and to propose an occupational health program in order to decrease the number of worker asbestos exposure claims. As part of his work, the consultant studied the death certificates of workers from the manufacturer's plant and determined that there was a high degree of asbestos-related diseases and an occupational cancer problem in workers formerly employed there. The consultant discussed these problems with the manufacturer's president and employee-relations manager. At that time, he specifically advised these high-ranking corporate officials that there was an occupational cancer risk, that the former workers should be informed that they had a risk

---

[100] *Id.*

[101] CA No K 81-2112 (D Md Sept 5, 1981).

[102] 548 F Supp 357 (ED Pa 1982).

involving occupational cancer, and that they should be placed under medical surveillance for early detection of asbestos-related conditions. Subsequently, the consultant submitted his report to the manufacturer, which report recommended that the workers be warned that they were at risk because of the dangers of exposure to asbestos, that necessary positive measures be taken, and that these workers be placed under medical surveillance for early detection of asbestos-related conditions. Moreover, the consultant recommended a special study of the workers because of important circumstantial evidence of the mortality pattern connected with the workers' exposure to asbestos. For these reasons, according to the court, the evidence was sufficient for the jury to conclude that the manufacturer, through the knowledge and inaction of its highest officials, despite professional and scientific consultation and advice, deliberately intended to injure the workers by choosing to disregard totally and blatantly the consultant's warnings and recommendations that the workers be informed of the risks that they had an asbestos-related condition.

Along this line of reasoning, if an employer negligently fails to disclose to an employee the existence of a *noncompensable* disease, possibly in the course of a medical examination, most cases allow a tort action on the theory that the injury or illness is not employment related.[103] The employer clearly appears to be under such a duty if he or she had knowledge of the condition, its dangerous nature, and if the employee was unaware of the disease or condition.

In all of the cases discussed in this section, under the emerging dual injury theory, plaintiffs still face a formidable burden of proof, but the legal validity of the theory appears to be gaining acceptance.

§6.11   The Dual Capacity Exception to Exclusivity

An employer, normally shielded from tort liability to an employee by the exclusivity bar (see §6.03), may become liable if he or she occupies, in addition to his or her capacity as employer, a second capacity conferring obligations toward his or her employees independently of those imposed on him or her as employer.[104]

Under this theory, an employer may become a third party susceptible to tort liability, *if* he or she possesses a second personality or capacity which is independent from and unrelated to his or her status as an employer and is such that the law will recognize a separate legal entity. If accepted by a majority of jurisdictions, this theory (or, more appropriately, this legal fiction) could eventually spell the demise of the exclusive remedy principle.

---

[103] Blue Bell Globe Mfg Co v Lewis, 200 Miss 685, 27 So 2d 900 (1946); Bednarksi v General Motors Corp, 88 Mich App 482, 276 NW2d 624 (1979); Castner v American Airlines, 78 AD2d 917, 433 NYS2d 512 (1980).

[104] Douglas v E&J Gallo Winery, 69 Cal App 3d 103, 137 Cal Rptr 797 (1977).

In one case, *Mercer v Uniroyal Inc,*[105] a truck driver who was injured because a tire blew out discovered that his employer manufactured the tire. He bought an action in products liability against his employer as a manufacturer and recovered. In another case, *Rosales v Vernon Allstell Press Co,*[106] the employer merely modified a machine, and the employee sued him, albeit unsuccessfully, on products liability as a quasi manufacturer. In *Duprey v Shane,*[107] a chiropractor who treated the workplace injury of his nurse was held liable to her in malpractice due to the negligent aggravation of her injury, because the doctor-patient relationship was distinct from the employer-employee relationship.

A majority of courts have, of course, not accepted this theory—in fact, a Tennessee court resolved the question by stating: "The employer is the employer; not some person other than the employer. It is as simple as that."[108] Perhaps the best way to handle the situation is to employ the theory only in those situations in which it is truly legitimate to do so—when the law clearly and realistically recognizes the duality of legal persons. Thus, while disparaging the way the dual capacity doctrine has been applied to permit suits against employers in their capacities as owners or manufacturers, the court in *Billy v Consolidated Machine Tool Corp,*[109] permitted its use in the situation where the manufacturer of defective equipment which injured an employee had merged with the employee's employer. The employer had assumed the liabilities and obligations of the manufacturer when they merged.

On a related issue, while it is true that protection from common law suits by the application of the exclusivity bar normally extends only to those persons who meet the workers' compensation acts' definitions of *employer,* many jurisdictions, by statute or judicial decision, have extended immunity beyond the direct employer to coemployees,[110] general contractors (to the independent subcontractor's employees),[111] and compensation insurance carriers.[112] More-

---

[105] 49 Ohio App 279, 361 NE2d 492 (1977).

[106] 41 Ill App 3d 787, 354 NE2d 553 (1976).

[107] 39 Cal 2d 781, 249 P2d 8 (1952). *See also* Bell v Industrial Vangas Inc, 110 Cal App 3d 436, 168 Cal Rptr 41 (1980), *affd,* 637 P2d 266, 30 Cal 3d 268, 179 Cal Rptr 30 (1981); Sharp v Gallagher, 94 Ill App 1128, 419 NE2d 443 (1981); Delamotte v Unitcast Div Midland Ross Corp, 64 Ohio App 2d 159, 411 NE2d 814 (1978).

[108] McAllister v Methodist Hosp, 550 SW2d 240, 246 (Tenn 1977). *See also* State v Purdy, 601 P2d 258 (Alaska 1979); Firth v Harrah South Shore Corp, 92 Nev 447, 552 P2d 337 (1976); Cohn v Spinks Indus Inc, 602 SW2d 102 (Tex Civ App 1980); Mapson v Montgomery White Trucks Inc, 357 So 2d 971 (Ala 1978); Noland v Westinghouse Elec Corp, 628 P2d 1123 (Nev 1981); White v EI duPont de Nemours & Co, 523 F Supp 302 (WD Va 1981).

[109] 51 NY2d 152, 432 NYS2d 879 (1980); *cf* Gerger v Campbell, 98 Wis 2d 282 (1980).

[110] *E.g.,* NJ Stat Ann §34:15-8 (West 1978); Ohio Rev Code Ann §4123.741 (Page 1955); Miller v Scott, 339 SW2d 941 (Ky 1960).

[111] *E.g.,* Md Ann Code art 101, §62; Parker v Williams & Madjanik Inc, 267 SE2d 524 (SC 1980).

[112] *E.g.,* Flood v Merchant Mut Ins Co, 230 Md 373, 187 A2d 320 (1963); Donohue v Maryland Cas Co, 363 F2d 442 (4th Cir 1966), *affg,* 248 F Supp 588 (D Md 1965).

over, dual capacity will not be found merely because an employer has several departments or divisions that are separate in their functions and operations.[113]

However, it appears that the parent and subsidiary or affiliated corporation are subject to suit at common law for their actions or breaches of duty as if they were independent third parties.[114] A defendant corporation cannot pierce its own corporate veil to extend employer immunity to holding companies and subsidiaries, since ordinarily, it is the corporation that tries to insist on separateness for its subsidiary—usually a plaintiff is attempting to pierce the corporate veil to reach the deep pocket of the parent. In this situation, for the parent to avoid suit, it would have to disavow the separateness, and that disavowal may disadvantage it later on. There are cases, however, in which courts have found the subsidiary to be completely controlled by the parent, and thus, single identity and immunity were found.[115]

§6.12 —Recent Decisions Concerning the Dual Capacity Exception

In *In re Johns-Manville/Asbestosis Cases,*[116] plaintiffs brought suit against four separate but allied Johns-Manville (JM) corporations seeking to recover for injuries that they or their decedents had suffered from inhaling asbestos while employed by JM Sales. JM Sales moved for dismissal, contending that the suit was barred by the exclusive remedy provision of the Illinois Workers' Compensation Act. The plaintiffs argued that exclusivity should not apply, either because JM had acted in dual capacities as a miner-supplier of asbestos and as a provider of medical care, or because the injuries were committed intentionally. The court acknowledged that Illinois recognized the dual capacity doctrine in strict liability cases but held that it was not applicable here because neither dual capacity allegation asserted a separate legal relationship from JM's relationship as employer. The court did hold, however, that the plaintiffs had sufficiently stated a cause of action for intentional injury when they alleged that JM Sales had adopted a uniform and intentional policy of misrepresenting and concealing the dangers of inhaling asbestos. Accordingly, it held that JM Sales' motion for dismissal under the compensation act would be denied except as

---

But see Unruh v Truck Ins Exch, 7 Cal 3d 616, 498 P2d 1063 (1972); Mager v United Hosp, 88 NJ Super 421, 212 A2d 664 (1965), *affd per curiam,* 46 NJ 398, 217 A2d 325 (1966).

[113] Miller v United States, 307 F Supp 932 (ED Va 1969); Stoddard v Lang-Temco-Vought Inc, 513 F Supp 314 (CD Cal 1980) (interpreting Texas law); Mingin v Continental Can Co, 171 NJ Super 148, 408 A2d 146 (1979).

[114] *E.g.,* Boggs v Blue Diamond Coal Co, 590 F2d 655 (6th Cir 1979), *cert denied,* 444 US 836 (1979); McDaniel v Johns-Manville Sales Corp, 487 F Supp 714 (ND Ill 1978); Tucker v Union Oil Co, 100 Idaho 590, 603 P2d 156 (1979); *but see* Love v Flour Mills of America, 647 F2d 1058 (10th Cir 1981).

[115] Goldberg v Context Indus Inc, 362 So 2d 974 (Fla Dist Ct App 1978); Nicholas v Uniroyal, 399 So 2d 751 (La Ct App 1981).

[116] 511 F Supp 1229 (ND Ill 1981).

to any employees who had collected compensation benefits for asbestosis. The court also held that JM would not be able to pierce its own corporate veils in order to prove that all four corporations were one entity and thus were all the plaintiffs' employer.[117]

The court in *Bell v Industrial Vangas, Inc,*[118] after an extensive review of the dual capacity theory, arrived at a clearly outrageous interpretation which if taken to its logical extreme could destroy the exclusivity principle. In essence, the court said that the exclusivity defense applies only if the duty involved in the accident arose solely from the employment relation.

> If the duty flows solely from the employment relationship and the injury "arises out of" and "during the course of" that employment, then the recited policy considerations behind the exclusive remedy in workers' compensation mandating that the employer be immune from tort liability have viabilty. If, however, an additional concurrent duty flows from an "extra" employer status or a relationship that is distinct from that of employer-employee and invokes a different set of obligations, then a second capacity arises and the employer status is coincidental. The employer should then be treated as any third-party tortfeasor, not immune from a common law tort action.[119]

The court here unfortunately has things backward. If the dual person doctrine is to apply, it must be possible to say that the duty arose solely from the nonemployer person, rather than from the employer person; for only in such a case can the second person be really distinct from the employer person. In other words, it is not enough, as the court seems to think, that the second person imposes additional duties. The duties must be totally separate from and unrelated to those of the employment. In this case, and in most dual capacity cases, the additional duties are inextricably intertwined with those of the employer status. Clearly, despite the court's own inaccurate attempt to include its decision as part of a group trend, its view is not only in the minority (it appears only Ohio is in agreement)[120] but also in the realm of the inconceivable.

Finally, in a very recent case, it was held that the exclusivity provisions of the Colorado workers' compensation law do not bar an employee who was treated for a workplace injury by a company physician from bringing a malpractice action against the physician, since a company doctor may operate in the dual capacity of coemployee and physician.[121]

---

[117] *See also* Kohr v Raybestos Manhattan Inc, 522 F Supp 1070 (ED Pa 1981); Borman v Interlake Inc, 623 SW2d 912 (Ky Ct App 1981); White v EI duPont de Nemours & Co, 523 F Supp 302 (WD Va 1981); Noland v Westinghouse, 628 P2d 1123 (Nev 1981).

[118] 637 P2d 266, 30 Cal 3d 268, 179 Cal Rptr 30 (1981).

[119] *Id* 36.

[120] Guy v Arthur H Thomas Co, 55 OS2d 183, 373 NE2d 488 (1978).

[121] Wright v District Court, 447 P2d 727 (Colo 1983).

§6.13   The Future of Exclusivity

The reasons for the erosion of the exclusivity doctrine appear to be the perceived disparity between workers' compensation benefits and potential tort recoveries,[122] the structure and procedure of some workers' compensation systems which may preclude compensation of occupational diseases, and the difficulties in proving causation and determining when the limitations period begins.[123] A desire to subject a broader class of employer conduct to judicial scrutiny is also a reason for the erosion.[124]

In one article,[125] a proposal was put forth to creat a catalog of carcinogenic substances and their dose-response curves (see §1.04) to be adopted into law by state legislatures. For example, in Illinois, it was discovered that only about 0.1 per cent of the estimated number of victims of job-related diseases in the state received the kind of compensation the workers' compensation program was designed to provide, primarily due to the restrictive statute of limitations.[126] Proof of exposure to a catalogued substance above a specific threshold would create a *rebuttable presumption* that a cancer victim's disease was caused by a given substance. The proposal would facilitate a recovery under tort law where the statute of limitations runs from the date of discovery of the injury, but as articulated the proposal makes no provision for altering workers' compensation time limits. Therefore, benefits would still be unavailable in many cases.

The current litigation situation involving toxic torts is such that the judicial system is unable to adequately handle it, and the 98th Congress will have to face the issue whether a legislative solution is necessary;[127] that is, should the government become involved in the claims of persons suffering from various occupational diseases, and should it foot the bill for toxic torts? Though it is not at all certain that the Johns-Manville and Unarco bankruptcy petitions will pressage a stampede of bankruptcies by other asbestos or toxic substances manufacturers, the sight of the world's largest makers of the substance claiming that the tort system has bankrupted them has given focus to a growing anxiety in Congress. Johns-Manville said its reason for filing for bankruptcy

---

[122] See Comment, *Compensating Victims of Occupational Disease,* 93 Harv L Rev 916, 925 (1980).

[123] *E.g.,* Kutchins, *The Most Exclusive Remedy is No Remedy at All: Worker's Compensation Coverage for Occupational Diseases,* 32 Lab LJ 212, 213 (1981).

[124] See Comment, *Employer Liability in West Virginia Compensation beyond the Law,* 36 Wash & Lee L Rev 151, 163 (1979).

[125] Comment, *Tort Actions for Cancer: Deterrence, Compensation and Environmental Carcinogenesis,* 90 Yale LJ 840 (1981).

[126] *Occ Disease in Illinois: Who's Paying the Bills* (Jan 1982).

[127] In the 97th Congress, several bills and proposals were put forth as a solution to the toxic torts problem, but none were successful, including HR 5735, the Occupational Health Hazards Compensation Act of 1982 (the Miller Bill) which would have been the first step toward federalization of the state workers' compensation system.

was caused by a failure of the judicial system to provide an orderly way to compensate victims of an unexpected health catastrophe.

§6.14 —Occupational Disease

Legislative attention is focused on several occupational disease proposals.[128] The first and most comprehensive, a bill offered in 1982 by Representative George Miller and which was dropped into the hopper again in 1983, HR 3175 (The [Occupational] Asbestos Health Hazards Compensation Act) would pinpoint and tax asbestos manufacturers, their insurance carriers, and employers who use the substance at their workplaces. It proposes creating a pool or fund for the payment of claims that would be administered by the Office of Workers' Compensation Programs of the Department of Labor. The bill provides an exclusive federal administrative remedy that would replace existing tort remedies and would also significantly supplement workers' compensation.

The Labor Department would adjudicate claims using a liberal standard set out in the bill, which provides generous time limits for the lodging of claims. Compensation would generally be paid by the afflicted worker's last employer, with the new fund paying if the employer could prove it was not responsible for the exposure or if the employer has gone out of business. Filing a claim with the Labor Department would in most cases be a workers-only remedy, though there are some exceptions outlined in the Miller proposal. The Miller bill, although it deals initially with occupationally related asbestos diseases, includes a mechanism for expanding the program to cover any disease that afflicts an employee population more heavily than the population as a whole.

An alternative plan offered by a group of manufacturers would also establish a compensation fund, but half of the money for it would be paid by the United States Treasury, on the ground that much of the asbestos used in this country was installed under government orders to fireproof ships built during World War II. Administration of claims under the manufacturers' bill would be left to state workers' compensation boards, with the newly created fund used only to pay supplemental benefits, up to $30,000 per person. The Miller bill has no such cap on payment. Resort to the federally created compensation fund would be an exclusive remedy (thus eliminating the right to sue).

Lack of state action to compensate occupational victims of toxic substances has created a vacuum that is likely to impel the federal government to act. What state action has taken place has mostly been in three areas: establishing state *superfunds* to clean up hazardous waste sites; passing right-to-know laws; and amending workers' compensation laws to revise or remove statutes of limitations and other technical barriers that have prevented occupational disease sufferers from recovering damages.

The question of government financial participation in any compensation

---

[128] See V Legal Times of Washington 32 (Jan 1983); IX New York Law Journal 26 (July 1983).

plan is complicated by litigation over the federal government's own liability for asbestos-caused diseases. Slightly fewer than one-quarter of the World War II shipyard workers were employed by the government. They are eligible either to file tort claims against the government under the Federal Tort Claims Act, or to collect from the government's own workers' compensation program, the Federal Employees Compensation Act. Currently, the United States faces about 13,000 administrative claims and 1,000 suits under the Federal Employees Compensation Act. According to Labor Department figures, the government has paid some $10 million in the past three years to settle claims under these two programs.

Representative Miller's proposal would have no effect on the government claims process. The manufacturers' proposal, however, would pay claims against the government from the same fund that would pay private-sector claims, the fund for which the government would provide half the money.

Either the Miller proposal or the manufacturers' plan would, if passed, shift a great deal of the burden from the federal and state courts to workers' compensation systems. Under current law, in all but a few states, employees who have been injured by asbestos exposure can file workers' compensation claims and collect from their former employers. But workers have generally found that they can recover considerably more by suing asbestos manufacturers.

The two remedies are not necessarily mutually exclusive, but plaintiffs' lawyers frequently counsel against pursuing both courses of action because they fear that evidence produced for a typical workers' compensation claim becomes available to lawyers defending a tort suit based on the same claim.

Both of the congressional draft bills have the potential to affect other toxic tort litigation besides asbestos. They both contain provisions that could create new compensation funds for future occupational diseases as they are discovered.

According to a recent study of asbestos-related claims between 1967 and 1976, employees who filed for workers' compensation received an average settlement of $18,900, while those who filed tort suits that ended in settlements received an average of $72,000, a figure that includes the plaintiff lawyer's fee.[129] Another incentive toward court and away from the workers' compensation system for any claimant is provided by state laws requiring that those who prevail in tort suits involving a matter decided by the workers' compensation system must repay the compensation settlement.

---

[129] Hamilton, Rabinovitz & Szanton, Inc 26 (July 1983). Cutting the Overhead Costs of Resolving Asbestos Claims (1982). The same study predicted that asbestos defendants and insurers will spend a billion dollars a year over the next thirty years defending such suits.

§6.15 —Environmental Release and Products Liability

In the closing months of the Carter administration, the Senate passed a *superfund* bill that would have allowed people injured by hazardous substances to collect from a federal fund and would have established a federal cause of action for suits against those who make or dispose of chemicals. Those provisions were dropped in the final draft because of fierce opposition from the chemical industry.[130]

Instead, Congress limited the superfund to pay for cleanups of abandoned dumps, to be financed by an excise tax on the raw materials used to make industrial chemicals. It also authorized a study of the compensation problem by a committee of representatives of the Associated Trial Lawyers of America (ATLA), the American Bar Association, the American Law Institute, and the National Association of Attorneys General. In the report issued last year by the *Superfund Sec. 301(e) Study Group,* there was renewed legitimacy given to the concept of a no-fault administrative remedy for compensating hazardous waste victims (See Chapter 10).

The committee's report rejected proposals to make the administrative compensation plan an exclusive remedy, recommending instead that judicial discretion and economic incentives be used to encourage claimants to stay out of court. Although the report dealt with the question of compensating people who are victims of hazardous waste spills and leaky dumps, no sense was seen in establishing a host of different compensation schemes for different people who may have been exposed to the same toxic substances simply because one was exposed on the job, another at a dump site, and a third in some other manner.

This particular issue of toxic substances victim compensation is, however, being addressed in two other formats (other than the occupational disease approach discussed in **§6.14**): environmental release bills and products liability proposals. Most of the environmental bills are designed to fill the gap left when provisions for personal injury and property damage recovery were deleted from the superfund act. Senators Stafford, and Mitchell, and Representatives LaFalce and Markey have each introduced legislation to compensate individuals who have been injured by hazardous substances in the air, ground, or water.[131]

The common features of these proposals derive from a shared reliance on superfund concepts and structures. For example, each of them, like the superfund, provides a new *no-fault* administrative compensation remedy. In addition,

---

130 42 USC §9601 *et seq.*

131 Senator Stafford, a Republican from Vermont, introduced S 917; Senator Mitchell, a Democrat from Maine, introduced S 945 and 5946; Representative LaFalce, a Democrat from New York, introduced HR 2482 and HR 2330; and Representative Markey, a Democrat from Massachusetts, introduced HR 2582.

in all but one of the bills,[132] the new administrative remedy, as in the super-fund, is accompanied by a new federal cause of action against persons who release, transport, or arrange for the disposal of hazardous substances.

Each of the bills, like the superfund, leaves existing common law remedies intact. Like the superfund, the bills also focus on environmental rather than occupational exposure and would, therefore, have relatively little impact on workers' compensation programs. Finally, the new administrative remedy provided by each bill is financed, like the current superfund, by a tax imposed on petroleum and specified chemicals.

Beyond these superfund similarities, however, the bills differ substantially—especially in the kinds of compensation they provide, and the use they make of presumptions to determine disease causation.

Variations in the kinds of compensation provided can be illustrated by comparing a few features of several bills. Very broad coverage is provided by the Stafford and LaFalce bills, which would compensate both personal injury and property damage.

The Markey bill and the two Mitchell bills are contrastingly narrow, omitting coverage for property damage and addressing only the problem of personal injury. Indeed, one of the two Mitchell bills (S 945) would cover only the medical expenses associated with personal injury and not lost wages or other damages.

The amount of compensation provided also varies from bill to bill. While most environmental bills set a cap on amounts that may be recovered under the new administrative remedy, the maxima are not uniform.

One bill, although partly environmental in nature, is much more narrowly focused than the superfund-type proposals already described. This is S 921, the bill introduced by Senator Hatch, a Republican from Utah, solely to compensate for injuries caused by nuclear weapons tests and uranium mining. The bill does not create any new administrative compensation mechanism; eligible veterans are compensated through the Veterans Administration and eligible civilians under the Federal Tort Claims Act.

The bills' approaches to the issue of proving disease causation are also varied. While each of the bills (with the exception of S 945, which compensates only for medical expenses) creates presumptions designed to ease the claimant's burden in establishing causation, these presumptions are differently formulated, and the kind of showing necessary to trigger the presumptions is not uniform.

From the standpoint of latent-disease compensation, the most interesting aspect of Senator Hatch's bill is its innovative approach to the issue of causation. Recognizing the difficulties in demonstrating that a particular instance of disease was caused by radiation, the bill provides a sliding scale of maximum recoveries, based upon statistical probabilities that the claimant's radiation exposure caused his or her disease. Finally, the bills also vary in the degree to which the presumptions may be rebutted.

---

[132] HR 2582, introduced by Representative Markey.

Bills recently introduced by Senator Kasten[133] and Representative Shumway[134] would provide no new remedy for environmental or occupational exposure but rather would modify, in a variety of ways, the substantive standards under which plaintiffs would recover under tort law. By *federalizing* the law of products liability and preempting state laws, these bills would, however, have a rather minimal impact on most environmental claims, because the wastes that give rise to these claims are not *products* in the usual sense and would therefore not be covered.

Although either bill, if enacted, would clearly apply to a large number of latent-disease claims, neither bill attempts to resolve the difficult issues of causation underlying such claims. Nor does either bill directly affect a claimant's ability to obtain workers' compensation benefits.

Both bills would, however, affect the relationship between tort and workers' compensation in a variety of ways. Both bills would overrule state court decisions that have, in limited circumstances, both permitted employees who are covered by workers' compensation programs to sue their employers and allowed manufacturers found liable in products liability proceedings to look to employers for contribution to the amounts they have paid. Senator Kasten's proposal, additionally, would require workers first to pursue their workers' compensation remedy before filing a tort claim.

What all of these bills have in common is one deficiency—unless proceedings can be simplified (changing presumptions may increase the likelihood of receipt of compensation but does not simplify proceedings), unless potential plaintiffs can be induced to abandon toxic tort litigation in favor of administrative remedies, and unless insurance coverage issues are resolved, these bills will increase rather than decrease overall costs.

---

[133] Senator Kasten, a Republican from Wisconsin, introduced S 544.
[134] Representative Shumway, a Republican from California, introduced HR 2729.

7

Hazard Identification and Communication

Hugh M. Finneran, Esq.* and
G.Z. Nothstein, Esq.

§7.01 Introduction

In the words of Jean Rostand, "The obligation to endure gives us the right to know."[1] This chapter surveys a representative sampling of federal, state, and local statutes, standards, and regulations which provide means of employee and public access to information about hazardous and toxic substances. The access discussed in this chapter is other than in the context of discovery conducted during or in anticipation of litigation. The legal prescriptions attendant upon these access mechanisms impose upon employers, manufactur-

---

* Senior Counsel Labor, PPG Industries, Inc., Pittsburgh, Pennsylvania
[1] R Carson, Silent Spring 23 (1962).

ers, producers, and suppliers various recordkeeping, reporting, and posting obligations which are described here in general terms. Three charts which set forth the bases for general "duty to inform"; "duty to generate or retain"; and "duty to provide access to various types of hazard information" are reproduced in the Appendix to this chapter.

§7.02   Right-to-Know Laws

Although several states and municipalities have enacted *right-to-know* laws to meet perceived needs for the dissemination of information about toxic and hazardous substances,[2] there unfortunately has been no consistency or uniformity in the legislative responses to date, and still other jurisdictions are presently considering the enactment of right-to-know legislation. The extent of such legislation will probably increase in the foreseeable future, unless there is a definitive movement on the federal level to address the issue. Basically, what all of the laws have in common is the establishment of a comprehensive program for the disclosure of information on hazardous substances, either in the workplace or the general environment, or both.

Essentially, the legislative enactments contain the following basic elements in that they require that employers and/or manufacturers:

1. Identify and report those hazardous and toxic substances present at their places of business

2. Maintain files of basic safety and health information for their employees and/or public use respecting each toxic and hazardous substance

3. Prepare and/or receive hazardous substance information including: chemical name, generic name, trade name, and common name; describe the hazard of the substance (flammability, explosiveness, reactivity); record acute and chronic health risks, potential routes, and symptoms of exposure; and document proper precautions and emergency handling procedures

4. Insure that containers are properly labeled so as to disclose the identity of the contents

---

[2] Cal Lab Code §6360 *et seq* (West 1980); Conn Gen Stat Ann §31-40(c)(West 1980); Conn Pub Act 82-251 (Laws 1982); Mass Ann Laws ch 149 §142A (Michie/Law Co-op 1981); Me Rev Stat Ann tit 2, §1701 *et seq* (1980); Michigan Comp Laws Ann §4808.1011 (1981); NY Labor Law §875 *et seq* (McKinney 1981); Va Code §40.1-51.1 (1982); NJ S 1670/AB 3318 (1983); Alaska Spec Act ch 93 (1983); New Hampshire ch 466 (1982); Ill HB 741 (1983); Rhode Island 161 (Laws 1983); Minn Spec Act ch 316 (1983); Wash Rev Code Ann §§49.17.220, .240 (West 1982); W Va Code §21-3-18(a) (Michie 1982); Wis Stat Ann §101.58 *et seq* (West 1981); Cincinnati Ohio Ordinance 210 (1982); Philadelphia Pa Ordinance 475 (1982); Santa Monica Cal Ord 132 (1981); Hadley, *The Right to Know and The Sensitive Worker: Access to Medical and Exposure Records and Hazard Identification* 3 Ann Am Conf Gov Indus Hygienists 165 (1982); Note, *Occupational Health Risks and the Worker's Right to Know,* 90 Yale LJ 1792 (1981).

5.   Disclose basic information about the dosage, treatment, and emission of substances into the environment and the workplace

6.   Make the required information available through posting, notices, and use of material safety data sheets and keep the information for a period of years

7.   Provide data to public agencies relevant to the planning for emergencies involving hazardous substances

Generally, the laws protect employees (and others) from discipline or discrimination subsequent to their receipt of or access to information, or from refusal to work in areas where they reasonably believe an imminent danger may exist. Although access to information must be provided within a reasonable time or else penalties will be involved, generally the manufacturer, producer, or employer may withhold disclosure of information on a toxic substance if disclosure would reveal a trade secret or compromise a competitive advantage— unless the substance is a carcinogen, mutagen, or teratogen.

One area, which is discussed in §§7.03-7.07, where the laws vary considerably is in the definition and designation of substances that are hazardous or toxic. The difference in treatment means that in some jurisdictions, as few as 300 substances will be covered, whereas in other jurisdictions, upwards of 40,000 substances may be covered. For example, in some states every material on the National Institute for Occupational Safety and Health Registry of Toxic Effects of Chemical Substances (RTECS) must be labeled or covered. This list, however, includes sodium chloride—ordinary table salt—which is not toxic.

Discussed below are the right-to-know laws of five states, which provide a varied overview of the types of provisions currently in effect.

§7.03   —California

The California Hazardous Substances Information Act[3] is applicable to:

1.   All California employers using hazardous substances

2.   All persons who sell hazardous substances to California employers

3.   All manufacturers who produce or sell hazardous substances in the state[4]

Laboratories are exempt if they are under the control of a technically qualified individual, provided the laboratory does not perform quality control analysis for a manufacturing process or produce hazardous substances for commerce.[5] The law, which applies to hazardous substances which are present in the workplace under normal operating conditions or in a reasonably foreseea-

---

[3] Cal Lab Code §6360 *et seq* (West 1981). The act is effective only through January 1, 1986, unless extended.

[4] *Id* §6362.

[5] *Id* §6386. This provision is similar to that contained in other laws.

ble emergency resulting from workplace operations, does not require manufacturers or employers to conduct studies or to develop new information.[6]

The state director of industrial relations is required to develop a list of hazardous substances, and unless a substance is on the director's list, the substance is not subject to the Hazardous Substances Act.[7] In developing the list, it is to be presumed that a substance is potentially hazardous if it is designated:

1. As a human or animal carcinogen by the International Agency for Research on Cancer

2. As a human or animal carcinogen by the Environmental Protection Agency pursuant to the federal Clean Water Act or Clean Air Act

3. As an airborne chemical contaminant by the California Occupational Safety and Health Standards Board

4. As an airborne chemical contaminant by the California director of food and agriculture

5. As a substance for which an information alert has been issued[8]

A substance can be removed from the list if it can be proved that the substance as present occupationally is not potentially hazardous to human health.

Special labeling for hazardous substances is not required. Instead, the manufacturer must provide purchasers with certain information: chemical name and common name; potential for fire, explosion, and reactivity; acute and chronic health effects; route of exposure and symptoms of overexposure; proper precautions in the use of the substance; emergency procedures for clean-up; and a laymen's description of health risks.[9] The manufacturer must include this information on a material data safety sheet and provide the state with a copy for each hazardous substance it manufactures.[10]

The California Occupational Safety and Health Board is required by the act to promulgate standards prescribing the employer's duties toward its employees to ensure that employees have timely access to material safety data sheets and are properly trained concerning exposure to these hazardous substances.[11]

§7.04   —Connecticut

Connecticut has two different statutes which could be considered as right-to-

---

[6] *Id* §6362.

[7] *Id* §6380-81.

[8] *Id* §6382.

[9] *Id* §§6390-6391.

[10] *Id* §6394.

[11] *Id* §6398.

know laws, one of which relates to carcinogenic material in the workplace and the second of which relates to toxic substances.

Under the first law, employers are required to post a list of all carcinogenic substances used or produced in the workplace.[12] Carcinogenic substances include either those specifically listed in the statute or those identified by the commissioner of health. When offering employment to an applicant the employer must give the applicant and on January 1 of each year the employer must give each employee a list of all carcinogenic substances used or produced. The law also provides that each new employee must receive education and training describing the carcinogenic substance, inherent dangers, and means of avoiding harmful effects.

The other law requires education and training for employees exposed to workplace toxic substances.[13] Under this law, each employer must post a sign, at a location readily available to employees, informing the employees of their right to information about toxic substances. On January 1, 1984, and annually thereafter, the employer must furnish the Connecticut Labor Department with a list of toxic substances.

An employee or his or her representative may request in writing information related to the toxic substances. A toxic substance is any substance which has been identified as an air contaminant under the federal Occupational Safety and Health Act (OSHA).[14] The information to be disclosed is comparable to the California law (see **§7.03**) and includes the generic and chemical name, location of exposure, properties, acute and chronic effects to the extent available, emergency treatment, proper operating procedures, and clean-up procedures. If an employee or his or her representative requests data on a toxic substance and the employer does not make it available within five working days, the employer may not make the employee work with the substance.

§7.05 —New York

The New York right-to-know law is very detailed and specific.[15] Interestingly, the law is to remain operative only until such time as the New York commissioner of health determines that there is in effect a federal program which affords substantially similar protection.[16]

The employer is required to post a sign advising employees of their right to information regarding toxic substances found in the workplace, a description of the toxic effects of those substances, and the circumstances under which toxic effects are produced. The employer must furnish the information to the employee or his or her representative upon request. A toxic substance is

---

[12] Conn Gen Stat Ann §31-40(c)(West 1982).

[13] 1982 Conn Pub Acts 82-251.

[14] 29 CFR §1910 Subpt Z.

[15] NY Lab Law §875 *et seq* (McKinney 1981).

[16] *Id* §876(2).

defined as any substance that is listed in the National Institute for Occupational Safety and Health's Registry of Toxic Effects[17] *or* has yielded positive evidence of acute or chronic health hazards in human, animal, or biological testing.

Containers are not required to be labeled, and there is no obligation to conduct independent scientific studies, but the employer must obtain the required information from the manufacturer, the New York State Department of Health, the federal Environmental Protection Agency, or the National Institute of Occupational Safety and Health. The employer must also distribute toxic substance information booklets which can be obtained from the Department of Health.[18]

The law imposes an obligation on manufacturers, importers, formulators, or producers of toxic substances who introduce their products into the state to provide, upon request, specified information of the type usually revealed in material safety data sheets on any toxic substance shipped, transported, or sold in New York.[19] The employer must provide the requested information within 72 hours, exclusive of holidays and weekends. If the employer does not respond within the time period, the employee may not be required to work with the substance until the employer makes the data available.[20]

The law requires every employer to establish an education and training program for employees routinely exposed to toxic substances.[21] The program must commence prior to initial job assignment and annually thereafter. The law also specifies a number of topics regarding health hazards and proper handling of toxic substances that must be addressed in the training program, but the employer may include other additional information. In addition, New York requires the employer to keep records of the names and addresses of employees who have contact with toxic substances and to maintain the records for 40 years.[22] If the employer ceases operation, the records must be sent to the state Department of Health.

§7.06   —West Virginia

Under the West Virginia law, the state labor commissioner must prepare a list of chemical substances and materials which have been determined or are suspected to be hazardous or toxic to health.[23] Any employer of 10 or more employees using or producing any such substance or material must post a warning notice, indicating the name of the hazardous chemical or material and

---

[17] US Dept Health and Human Services (1982).

[18] NY Lab Law §876(2)(McKinney 1981)

[19] *Id* §876(4).

[20] *Id* §§876(7), 880(2).

[21] *Id* §878.

[22] *Id* §879.

[23] W Va Code §21-3-18(a)(1981).

the symptoms of overexposure.[24] In addition, the employer must notify the commissioner of labor, within 10 days, of any employee exposure in excess of the safe exposure level published by the commissioner and must provide a copy of the report to the employee.[25]

The West Virginia law was challenged in *West Virginia Manufacturers Association v West Virginia*[26] on the grounds that:

1. It was defective because it failed to inform those subject to its sanctions of the criminal penalties which may be imposed
2. It was preempted by the federal Occupational Safety and Health Act (OSHA)
3. It was void for vagueness under the Due Process Clause of the Fourteenth Amendment of the United States Constitution
4. It unconstitutionally discriminated among employers and thus violated the Equal Protection Clause of the Constitution

Each of these contentions was rejected by the court.

Of importance was the preemption holding of the court in this case. The national consensus standards adopted by the secretary of labor pursuant to §6(a) of OSHA[27] relate to permissible exposure levels, and these standards do not contain posting or notice requirements similar to West Virginia law. Each of the substances regulated by West Virginia was regulated by a federal standard adopted under §6(a). The court concluded that since there was no federal standard relative to notice and posting of the specific substances regulated by West Virginia, the federal government had not preempted the subject. For example, the West Virginia commissioneer of labor had not sought to regulate asbestos and other substances covered by standards promulgated under §6(b) of OSHA which do have federal posting and notice requirements.

The holding in the case highlights the legal problems which must be overcome before there can be national uniformity in the right-to-know area by means of federal law.[28] This issue is discussed in **§7.11.**

---

[24] *Id* §21-3-18(c).

[25] *Id* §21-3-18(d).

[26] 542 F Supp 1247 (SD WVa 1982), *affd,* — F2d —, 1983 OSHD ¶26,635 (4th Cir 1983).

[27] 29 USC §655(a).

[28] OSHA, in its notice of proposed rulemaking on the hazard communication standard, has added a section to 29 CFR §1910.1200 which attempts to address the preemption question: "This occupational safety and health standard is intended to occupy the field in terms of communicating hazards to employees in the manufacturing sector. Any state which desires to assume responsibility in this area may only do so under the provisions of 18(b) of the Occupational Safety and Health Act (P.L. 91-596, 84 Stat. 1608) which deals with state plans."

§7.07 —Wisconsin

Wisconsin, a state known for its progressive social legislation, adopted a comprehensive right-to-know law in 1982.[29] The law requires employers who use, study, or produce toxic substances or *infectious* agents to post in the workplace a notice informing employees of the employer's obligation, upon request, to provide the following information to the employee or employee representative:

1. Identity of substances to which the employee is exposed or is likely to be exposed
2. Hazards of exposure
3. Precautions when handling the substance[30]

The law contains detailed definitions of the terms *infectious agent, pesticide,* and *toxic substance.*[31] An infectious agent is a bacterial, mycoplasmal, fungal, parasitic, or viral agent identified by the state as causing illness in humans or human fetuses. A pesticide is a substance registered with the federal Environmental Protection Agency or the state Department of Agriculture, Trade and Consumer Protection, and which is designed or intended for agricultural purposes associated with pesticides. Toxic substances include those substances regulated by the federal Occupational Safety and Health Administration (OSHA) under 29 CFR §1910. 1000 Part Z, but the definition excludes: substances in a solid form which do not cause health hazards; consumer products under certain conditions; mixtures of the toxic substance is less than one per cent, or two per cent if the toxic substance is an impurity; substances in a sealed package if the seal remains intact; and waste material regulated by the federal government.

The employer must furnish designated information about toxic substances to the employee or his or her representative within 15 days after a written request is received. Requests related to an infectious agent must be provided within 72 hours after a request by an employee or his or her representative if the agent is present in the workplace on the date of request or was present within 30 days immediately preceding the request. The law also requires data about pesticides to be furnished within 72 hours. Upon request, the state may obtain the same information within the same period of time as the employee. Manufacturers of toxic substances or suppliers of infectious agents sold or transported within Wisconsin must provide employers with the statutorily designated data within 15 days.

Prior to initial assignment, employees who may be routinely exposed to any toxic substance, infectious agent, or pesticide must be educated and trained

---

[29] Wis Stat Ann §101.58 *et seq* (West 1981).
[30] *Id* §101.58(1).
[31] *Id* §101.58.

about these specific substances.[32] The employee must be given additional instruction prior to exposure to other substances. Routine exposure to an infectious agent or pesticide is not defined in the statute. *Routine exposure to any toxic substance,* however, is defined as an exposure of at least 30 days per year to levels exceeding 50 per cent of the federal OSHA permissible exposure or any exposure in excess of 100 per cent of such permissible exposure level, regardless of the exposure period. If the employee is not given the information to which he or she is entitled, he or she may refuse to work with the material until the information is provided.

If the federal government promulgates a hazard communication regulation, a company may apply to the state for an exemption from some of the statutory obligations.

§7.08   Federal Hazard Identification Requirements

There are a multitude of federal statutory and regulatory recordkeeping and reporting requirements relating to toxic or hazardous substances.[33] Due to the volume of regulatory material, the comments in this chapter emphasize the more significant obligations imposed by the Occupational Safety and Health Act (OSHA)[34] and the Toxic Substance Control Act (TSCA)[35] but also provide citations to other pertinent laws which apply to precise industries or products.

§7.09   —Toxic Substance Control Act

The Environmental Protection Agency (EPA) has general regulations governing the access to environmental information.[36] Each environmental statute also includes provisions that require companies to keep records and to provide information in permit applications and reports. Failure to provide such information can result in the imposition of penalties.

The EPA has published an inventory of existing chemical substances, which tracks the reporting requirements of the Toxic Substance Control Act (TSCA),[37] the Resource Conservation and Recovery Act (RCRA),[38] and other

---

[32] *Id* §101.597.

[33] Federal Environmental Pesticide Control Act, 7 USC §136; Federal Water Pollution Control Act, 33 USC §1251 *et seq;* Safe Drinking Water Act, 42 USC §300f *et seq;* Resource Conservation and Recovery Act, *id* §6901 *et seq;* Clean Air Act, *id* §7401 *et seq;* Consumer Product Safety Act, 15 USC §2051 *et seq;* Food Drug and Cosmetic Act, 21 USC §301 *et seq;* Federal Railroad Safety Act, 45 USC §421 *et seq;* Dangerous Cargo Act, 46 USC §170 *et seq;* Ports and Water Safety Act, 4 USC §391(a); Hazardous Material Transportation Act, 49 USC §1801 *et seq;* Fair Packaging & Labeling Act, 15 USC §1451 *et seq;* Federal Insecticide, Fungicide and Rodenticide Act, 7 USC §136 *et seq.*

[34] 29 USC §651 *et seq.* See **§7.10.**

[35] 15 USC §2601 *et seq.* See **§7.09.**

[36] 40 CFR §§2.100-.120; 48 Fed Reg 11270 (Mar 17, 1983).

[37] 42 USC §3007(b).

[38] 15 USC §2608.

environmental statutes;[39] however, the TSCA requirements alone are note-worthy. TSCA imposes on the manufacturer or processor of chemical substances and mixtures a duty to do necessary testing to determine the effects of the substances or mixtures, and the manufacturer or processor may have to submit a premanufacture notice.[40] The items to be included in the premanufacture notice are the chemical composition of the substance, its common or trade name, its proposed or present uses, the quantities of the substances produced, the number of persons exposed, and length of exposure.

Another section of TSCA authorized the EPA administrator to issue rules governing the distribution, use, or processing of chemical substances or mixtures which present an undue risk of injury to health or the environment.[41] The rule can include requirements which would prohibit those activities, limit the quantities produced of the substances, or prohibit manufacture, processing, or distribution for a particular use or in a concentration above a limit set by the EPA on the amount to be applied to particular uses. The rules also can consider labeling and marking with warnings and instructions respecting use, distribution, and disposal.

Moreover, the rules may require manufacturers and processors to make and retain records and monitor and conduct tests which are reasonable and necessary to assure compliance with the requirements. The requirements can prohibit or otherwise regulate any manner or method of commercial use of the substance or mixture. Similarly, the rule can regulate the manner or method of disposal by those persons who dispose of a substance or mixture for commercial purposes. The EPA can also require manufacturers or processors to give notice of an unreasonable risk of injury to distributors and to persons in possession of the substance or mixture or exposed to it. The agency can require public notice of the risk of injury and can require the manufacturer or processor to replace or to repurchase the substance or mixture if a person elects to do so. The EPA may also require companies to submit lists of health and safety studies for chemical substances and mixtures and copies of any studies on the list.

TSCA also authorizes the EPA to require manufacturers or processors other than small manufacturers or processors to maintain records and make them available to the EPA.[42] The information to be reported includes the common trade name, chemical identity, and molecular structure of the chemical substance or mixture. It also can include the categories or proposed categories of

---

[39] 45 Fed Reg 50544 (July 29, 1980).

[40] 15 USC §2603-4.

[41] *Id* §2605.

[42] The EPA is authorized under §2607(a)(3)(B), in consultation with the Small Business Administration to prescribe standards for determining which manufacturers and processors qualify as "small". The EPA may also, by rule, require small manufacturers and processors to submit information on chemical substances or mixtures. §2607(a)(3)(A)(i) and (ii).

use, amounts to be manufactured or processed, and a description of by-products resulting from the manufacture, processing, use, or disposal of the substance. There also must be reporting on all existing data concerning environmental and health effects. Other relevant information to be retained includes the number of individuals who have been or will be exposed to the substance, their places of employment, and the duration of their exposure.

Under TSCA, the administrator is to keep an inventory and publish a list of each chemical substance manufactured or processed in the United States. The list must include those substances subject to premanufacture and new-use notice and is limited to those manufactured or processed in the United States since 1973.

The manufacturer and processor must also keep records of harm to humans or the environment caused by the substance or mixture. These are to include consumer allegations of personal injury or harm to health and reports of occupational disease or injury, and the manufacturer or processor must make them available to the EPA.[43] These records of adverse reactions affecting the health of employees must be retained for a period of 30 years from the date that the reactions were first reported or known by the person maintaining the records. Records of any other adverse reactions must be maintained for a period of five years.

Each company is required to report "immediately" to EPA any information that "reasonably supports the conclusion that [any] substance or mixture [manufactured, processed, or distributed by the company] presents a substantial risk of injury to health or the environment."[44] This vague requirement is enforceable by criminal as well as civil penalties.

Substantial risk information under the EPA policy includes information on human health effects, environmental effects, and emergency incidents of environmental contamination. Reportable information includes not only systematic studies, but also uncontrolled observations, including "a single instance of cancer, birth defects, mutation, death, or serious incapacitation in a human . . . if one (or a few) chemical(s) is strongly implicated."[45] A company is regarded as having obtained such information when any officer or employee capable of appreciating its significance obtains it. From that date, the company has 15 working days to report (except that an immediate report by telephone is required for an emergency incident of environmental contamination). Information need not be reported if it has already been reported to the EPA under other requirements of law, or if it is corroborative of well-established adverse effects already documented in the scientific literature referenced in specified abstract services.

TSCA basically does not apply to toxic substances which will not be used in commerce in the United States. The act exempts from its requirements any substances or mixtures which will be distributed in commerce for export from

---

[43] *Id.*

[44] 15 USC §2607(e).

[45] 43 Fed Reg 11110 (Mar 16, 1978).

the United States. It does require, however, that any such substances or mixtures be properly *labeled* for export. There is an exception, however, to the export exemption if the administrator determines that the substance, mixture, or article presents an unreasonable risk of harm within the United States or to the environment of the United States. In that event, the testing and other requirements of TSCA may apply.

A large amount of highly confidential information must be reported to the EPA under TSCA. This includes information regarding manufacturing processes, the chemical identity of products, product testing programs, and new product plans. Premanufacture notifications are an especially fertile source of confidential information; but such information is also contained in reports required under other sections. The basic rules for protecting confidential information provides that the EPA may not disclose "trade secrets."[46] However, there are several exceptions to the trade secret protection.

Under RCRA, a generator that ships waste off-site must file an annual report with the EPA no later than March 1 for the preceding calendar year.[47] This report must identify the types and quantities of hazardous waste transported off-site and the EPA identification numbers of the transporters and waste facilities involved. Similar reports must be filed for on-site disposal under other provisions of the regulations.

Records developed in complying with Subtitle C[48] (a system for cradle-to-grave management of hazardous waste) must be kept for three years. These include copies of manifests, exception reports, annual reports, and records of testing conducted to determine whether waste is hazardous.

In addition to its tax, clean-up, and liability provisions, the Comprehensive Environmental Response, Compensation and Liability Act (Superfund)[49] includes several significant regulatory provisions. Sections 102 and 103 require the reporting of the release of hazadous substances into the environment, unless the release occurs in accordance with a permit. Until superseded by regulations establishing a new *reportable quantity*, a spill of one pound or any reportable quantity established pursuant to §311(b)(4) of the Clean Water Act[50] must be reported under these provisions.

The pesticides program, which began with the Federal Insecticide, Fungicide and Rodenticide Act (FIFRA)[51] and is now carried on under the Federal Environmental Pesticide Control Act (FEPCA),[52] requires that registered pesticides be properly labeled. The label must be attached to the pesticide, or to its containers or wrappers, as appropriate. The labeling must be able to be attached so that it can be with the pesticide or device at any time. The pesticide

46 15 USC §2613.
47 40 CFR §262.41.
48 40 CFR §262.40.
49 42 USC §9601 *et seq.*
50 33 USC §1251.
51 7 USC §135-K
52 *Id* §136-Y.

is misbranded if its labeling is incomplete or inaccurate, or if the label has any statement or design which is false or misleading, or if the pesticide is in an improper container or a container which imitates the container of another pesticide.

The label also must carry the appropriate registration number. The label must include any word or statement or other information required under the FEPCA, in a manner that is plain and conspicuous, so that it can be read and understood by the ordinary individual under customary conditions of purchase and use. It is also misbranding if the label does not contain directions for use that would be necessary to the purpose or classification for which the product is intended. The label must also have any warning or cautionary statement necessary to protect health and the environment.

Other misbranding practices include the situation when the label does not have an ingredients statement on the immediate package. Similarly, the label must contain a statement of the use classification for which the product is registered. Likewise, the label that is affixed to the container must indicate the name and address of the producer and the registrant or person for whom it was produced, the name or trademark or brand of the pesticide, the net weight, the registration number, and the use classification.

A last element of labeling is that labels of those pesticides that are highly toxic to humans must indicate this toxicity. The indication must include the skull and crossbones, the word *POISON* prominently printed in red against a background of distinctly contrasting color, and a statement of first aid or practical treatment.

§7.10 —Occupational Safety and Health Act

The Occupational Safety and Health Act[53] (OSHA) contains the authority for the promulgation of occupational safety and health identification, reporting, and labeling regulations.[54] Pursuant to this authority, the administrative agency, in its General Industry Standards, has promulgated certain hazard identification, reporting, and labeling obligations; however, the obligations do not apply to all toxic or hazardous substances.[55] Violations of the standards and regulations may result in the imposition of civil penalties.

---

[53] 29 USC §651 *et seq.*

[54] 29 USC §§655(b) & 657(g)(2).

[55] 29 CFR §1910.1001 (asbestos); *id* §1910.1003 (4-Nitrobiphenyl); *id* §1910.1004 (alpha-Naphthylamine); *id* §1910.1006 (methylchloromethyl ether); *id* §1910.1007 (3,-3'-Dichlorobenzidine and its salts); *id* §1910.1008 (bis-Chloromethyl ether); *id* §1910.1009 (beta-Naphthylamine); *id* §1910.1010 (benzidine); *id* §1910.1011 (4-Aminodiphenyl); *id* §1910.1012 (ethyleneimine); *id* §1910.1013 (beta-Propiolactone); *id* §1910.1014 (2-Acetylaminofluorene); *id* §1910.1015 (4-Dimethylaminoazobenzene); *id* §1910.1016 (N-Nitrosodimethylamine); *id* §1910.1017 (vinyl chloride); *id* §1910.1018 (inorganic arsenic); *id* §1910.1025 (lead); *id* §1910.1029 (coke oven emissions); *id* §1910.1043 (cotton dust); *id* §1910.1044 (1,2-dibromo-3-chloropropane); *id* §1910.1045 (acrylonitrile); *id* §1910.96 (ionizing radiation); *id* §1910.103 (hydrogen); *id* §1910.104 (oxygen); *id* §1910.111 (storage and handling of anhydrous ammonia); *id*

§7.11 —Hazard Communication

Recognizing the limited obligations imposed on management to educate employees about the hazards of the chemicals to which they are exposed, the Occupational Safety and Health Administration (OSHA) issued a notice of proposed rulemaking on hazard communication and conducted hearings in 1982.[56] No standard has as yet been promulgated; however, it is anticipated that a final rule will be promulgated in late 1983. OSHA's proposed performance-oriented hazard communication standard is very comprehensive (at least for the workplaces covered); it requires employers to evaluate every chemical in the workplace in order to determine whether or not it is hazardous. These hazards must then be communicated to the employees in a variety of ways. The definition of the term *hazardous* is extremely broad, as are the provisions for labeling, use of material safety data sheets, and training and education.

In regard to the issue of preemption, the Occupational Safety and Health Act does give OSHA some preemptive authority over state laws. States that have chosen to administer OSHA-approved occupational safety and health programs, also known as state-plan states, are treated differently under the act than those states where occupational safety and health is administered by federal OSHA. States with approved state plans have six months after promulgation of the federal standard to either adopt an identical one or an alternative. The state's standard would have to be submitted for review and approval by federal OSHA. OSHA would look at it and not only make sure that it is at least as effective as the federal law, but also, if the state proposed different standards, OSHA would make a determination that there is a compelling need to do so and determine whether the state standard would put an undue burden on interstate commerce. State laws in states without approved state plans could be preempted by the federal standard. In states that do not have their own OSHA-approved occupational safety and health plan, OSHA could preempt state laws that deal with the workers' right to know but could not preempt state laws that deal with other issues.

In determining whether a state standard in a state-plan state will stand in place of OSHA's, three specific issues must be considered. First, the state rule has to be as effective as the federal standard; second, if the state standard is applicable to products which are distributed or used in interstate commerce, there must be a compelling need for the standard if it differs from OSHA; and third, it must not pose an undue burden on interstate commerce.

---

§1910.144 (safety color code for marketing physical hazards); *id* §1910.145 (specifications for accident prevention signs and tags); and *id* §1910.252 (welding, cutting, and brazing).

[56] 47 Fed Reg 12092 (Mar 19, 1982); see generally Nothstein, *The OSHA Labelling Standard: Generically, Inherently and Fatally Flawed,* 5 Natl LJ 35 (Sept 23, 1982). *Note:* A final standard was promulgated at 48 Fed Reg 53280 (Nov 25, 1983).

§7.12 —Access to Medical/Exposure Records

In addition to the hazard communication standard, the Occupational Safety and Health Administration (OSHA) has previously promulgated a rule[57] requiring the preservation of, and access to, employer-maintained exposure and medical records relevant to employees exposed to toxic substances and harmful physical agents and to analyses prepared from employee exposure and medical records. The rule, which is known as the *access rule,* does not obligate an employer to generate records but is a method of obtaining access to existing records. The rule was promulgated for the purpose of improving the detection, treatment, and prevention of occupational illness and disease. To accomplish these objectives, employees, their representatives, and the government were granted the right of access to the designated records.

The access rule applies to all employee exposure records, medical records, and analyses, whether or not the records are related to a specific safety or health standard, and even though the exposure level is below the level of such a standard. Thus, for example, an employee is entitled to access even though his or her exposure is within permissible limits under a particular standard, such as the OSHA lead standard. The rule applies to records and analyses in existence on the effective date of the rule as well as records created after the enactment of the OSHA access rule. OSHA's access rule will be a source of tremendous data relevant to legal, medical, and scientific inquiries relating to employee exposure to toxic substances or harmful physical substances, since the records must be preserved for many years.

OSHA requires the employer, upon request, to assure access for employees and designated representatives to an employee's own medical records.[58] The term *employer* is not restricted to the present employer but is expansively defined to include present, past, and successor employers. Likewise, the term *employee* is not limited to present employees but includes former employees.

The access rule defines an employee *medical record* to mean "a record concerning the health status of an employee which is made or maintained by a physician, nurse, or health care professional."[59] The employer is not however obligated to grant access to:

1. Physical specimens which are routinely discarded as a part of normal medical practice

---

[57] 29 CFR §1910.20; *see also* 46 Fed Reg 40490 (Aug 7, 1981), in which OSHA clarified the employer's obligations with regard to the term *records of similarly situated workers,* and said that the search for such records need not be "heroic" or an "unusually descriptive search," provided the search was made in good faith. Also clarified was the fact that records produced solely in anticipation of litigation—i.e., attorney work product—need not be produced.

[58] 29 CFR §1910.20(e)(2)(ii).

[59] *Id* §1910.20(c)(6)(1). The term includes results of medical examinations and laboratory tests, medical and employment questionnaires or histories, diagnosis, treatment, recommendations, progress notes, and employee complaints.

2. Records regarding health insurance claims if maintained separately from the employer's medical program records, and such records are not accessible to the employer in a manner which enables the employer to identify the employee

3. Records concerning voluntary employee assistance programs, including drug, alcohol, and personal counseling programs, provided such records are segregated from the employer's medical program and its records

The employee has an absolute right of direct access to his or her own records, except in very limited situations. The access rule specifies that the employer's physician can prevent direct access to information regarding a diagnosis of a terminal illness or a psychiatric condition if the employer's physician believes such access could be detrimental to the employee's health;[60] however, even in such a situation, the information must be released to a designated representative who has obtained the employee's written consent.

To preserve confidentiality of medical records and avoid intrusions into matters of privacy, designated representatives have no right to access to medical records unless the particular employee has given the representative a specific written authorization. The specific written authorization must include a general description of the information that is to be provided, the purpose for the release, and the date on which the authorization will expire if the authorization is for less than a year.

OSHA itself has a right of direct access to employee medical records without specific employee authorization, subject to compliance with procedural rules governing such access.[61]

The provision of the access rule concerning employee *exposure records* states: "Each employer shall, upon request, assure the access of each employee and designated representative to employee exposure records relevant to the employer."[62] Exposure records include documents containing information concerning an employee's past and present exposure to toxic substances or harmful physical agents[63] and exposure records of other employees with comparable past or present working conditions. The right of access is not limited to the employee's present workplace but includes workplaces to which the employee is being assigned or transferred.

The employee's designated representative must have a written authorization to examine employee exposure information. However, either OSHA or a certified or designated collective bargaining agent has a right of access to employee exposure records without employee authorization. Moreover, a collective bargaining agent may obtain copies of exposure records even though the same records were previously provided to the employee.

---

60 *Id* §1910.20(e)(2)(ii)(D).

61 *Id* §1910.20(e)(3); *id* §1913.

62 *Id* §1910.20(e)(2).

63 *Id* §1910.20(c)(11) defines toxic substances and harmful physical agents.

In addition, the OSHA access rule authorizes access by employees, designated representatives, and OSHA to *analyses using exposure and medical records*.[64] The definition of analyses is extremely broad and includes:

> Any compilation of data, or any research, statistical or other study based in part on information collected from individual employee exposure or medical records or information collected from health insurance claims records, provided that either the analysis has been reported to the employer or no further work is currently being done by the person responsible for preparing the analysis.[65]

The employer has the responsibility to take necessary precautions to assure that before the analysis is released, any direct, or indirect, employee identifiers are removed from the records. If deletion of the identifiers is not feasible, the analysis need not be provided. The designated representative must have employee authorization for access to the analyses from medical and exposure records, unless the representative is a union, in which situation authorization is not necessary.

The access rule does not obligate employers to generate records or reports or require an employer to monitor or measure employee exposure or to provide medical examinations or surveillance, but once records are created by an employer, for whatever reason, the records must be preserved by the employer. Employer exposure records and analyses must be preserved for at least 30 years, while medical records must be retained for at least the duration of employment, plus 30 years.[66] However, if a specific OSHA standard sets a retention period for exposure and medical records different from the OSHA access rule, the specific provisions of the OSHA standard will control (e.g., cotton dust, lead, alpha-naphthylamine, bis-chlormethyl ether, coke oven emissions, and asbestos).

The access rule, like the proposed hazard communication standard, accords some degree of recognition to industry fears over the disclosure of valuable information such as the percentage of chemicals in a mixture and other proprietary information. Thus, an employer may delete: "any trade secret data which discloses manufacturing processes or discloses the percentage of a chemical substance in a mixture, as long as the employee or designated representative is notified that the information has been deleted."[67] If the deletions impair the evaluation of the location and date of exposure, the employer must provide alternative information to remedy this deficiency. The employer, how-

---

[64] *Id* §1910.20(e)(2)(iii); *id* §1910.20(e)(3).

[65] *Id* §1910.20(c)(2).

[66] *Id* §1910.20(d). Health insurance information need not be retained if kept separate from an employer's medical program. Background data to environmental monitoring or measuring such as worksheets need only be retained from one year under enumerated conditions. Material safety data sheets need not be retained as long as identity of substance is retained.

[67] *Id* §1910.20(g).

ever, cannot delete the chemical or physical agent identities, including chemical names, levels of exposure, or employee health status data contained in the requested records. However, to the degree that proprietary information may be disclosed, the employer has the right to require the employee or his or her designated representative to sign a secrecy agreement.[68]

The access rule survived its first major legal challenge when a district court upheld its validity in *Louisiana Chemical Association v Bingham*.[69] The court held that OSHA had the requisite statutory authority to promulgate the rule, placing emphasis on the purpose and policy of the act. The court stated:

> The rule will serve to establish a primary data base regarding long term exposure to toxic substances and harmful physical agents. Such a pool of information will obviously be of great utility to medical/industrial research in the isolation and identification of latent occupational diseases and health hazards yet unknown . . . . Given the insidious nature and long term effects of many latent occupational diseases, a rule which establishes a data base for medical research . . . bears more than a reasonable relation to a major policy goal of the Act.[70]

Louisiana Chemical Association also held that the access rule did not violate employees' rights of privacy. The court concluded that ample security measures for sensitive identifiable medical information was specified in OSHA procedural rules regulating access. Likewise, the court indicated that the use to be made of the information by OSHA is circumscribed, and there are ample internal security procedures at the agency. The court also concluded that the access rule did not violate the Trade Secrets Act[71] or the National Labor Relations Act[72] and was adopted in compliance with the procedural rules of the Administrative Procedure Act.

Louisiana Chemical Association is the first, but it will probably not be the last, decision concerning the OSHA access rule. Regardless of its legality, the access rule on the surface appears to impose a disparate burden on the more conscientious members of industry who maintain detailed records and analyses

---

[68] For OSHA analysis of the legal considerations relating to the trade secret issue and its conclusion that public policy justified the balance it struck, see 45 Fed Reg at 35274 and 35248-51 (May 21, 1980). Certain modifications to the trade secret provision have been provided, including strengthening the trade secret provisions (from the employer's perspective) by permitting liquidated damage clauses in confidentiality agreements and limiting the requirements of disclosure to only certain categories of highly toxic chemicals. Also proposed is lessening the preservation requirements for records, and redefining the terms *employee, exposure,* and *toxic material.* 47 Fed Reg 30420 (July 13, 1982).

[69] 550 F Supp 1136 (WD La 1982), *on remand from* 657 F2d 777 (5th Cir 1981). The decision has been appealed and is pending.

[70] 550 F Supp at 1141.

[71] 18 USC §1905.

[72] 29 USC §151 *et seq.*

concerning employee exposures, while the less conscientious employers have no records to which access must be granted.

§7.13   National Labor Relations Act

The health and safety of employees are terms and conditions of employment about which employers must bargain with unions.[73] The National Labor Relations Board (NLRB) has long held that employers must furnish unions with information relevant to the union's representation function.[74]

In three cases decided in 1982, referred to as the *Health Trilogy*, the NLRB ruled that the employers involved had violated the National Labor Relations Act (NLRA)[75] by refusing to provide data relating to employee health and safety:

> Few matters can be of greater legitimate concern to individuals in the workplace, and thus to the bargaining agent representing them, than exposure to conditions potentially threatening their health, well being or their very lives. Information of the type sought by [the union] appears reasonably necessary to enable that union to discuss and negotiate in a meaningful fashion on behalf of those whom it represents, for [the union] can hardly be expected to bargain effectively regarding health and safety matters, if it, unlike [the employer] knows neither those substances to which the unit employees are exposed nor the previously identified health problems resulting therefrom.[76]

Included in the requested information to which the NLRB held the unions were entitled were the following:

1. Morbidity and mortality statistics on all past and present employees

2. The generic names of all substances used and produced at the plants

3. Results of clinical and laboratory studies of any employee undertaken by the employer, including the results of toxicological investigations regarding agents to which employees may be exposed

4. Certain health information derived from insurance programs covering employees, as well as information concerning occupational illness and accident data relating to workers' compensation claims

---

[73] Gulf Power Co, 156 NLRB 622, 625 (1966), *enforced,* 384 F2d 82 (5th Cir 1967); San Isabel Elec Inc, 225 NLRB 1073 (1976); G.Z. Nothstein, The Law of Occupational Safety and Health 639-44 (1981), 89-90 (Supp 1983).

[74] SL Allen & Co, 1 NLRB 714 (1936).

[75] 29 USC §151 *et seq.*

[76] Minnesota Mining & Mfg Co, 261 NLRB No 28 (1982); Colgate-Palmolive Co, 261 NLRB No 7 (1982); Borden Chemical, a Division of Borden Inc, 261 NLRB No 6 (1982).

5. A listing of contaminants monitored by the employer, along with a sample protocol

6. A description of the employer's hearing conservation program, including noise level surveys

7. Radiation sources in the plant and a listing of radiation incidents requiring notification of state and federal agencies

8. An indication of plant work areas which exceeded proposed National Institute of Occupational Safety and Health heat standards

9. An outline of the employer's control program to prevent heart disease

Like the Occupational Safety and Health Administration (OSHA) access rule, discussed in **§7.12,** §8(a)(5) of the NLRA does not impose an affirmative obligation on employers to generate safety and health information. The employer's obligation is limited to providing the union with existing data.

The employers contended in the *Health Trilogy* that the physician-patient privilege and employee privacy justified their refusal to provide certain medical records. The NLRB rejected the employers' defense since the unions had indicated that the employers could remove employee names and other identifying information such as clock numbers and social security numbers from the medical records. Likewise, the data could be coded to protect employee privacy interests. The NLRB in *Colgate-Palmolive Co*[77] and *Minnesota Mining & Manufacturing Co*[78] stated that to the extent supplying a union with statistical or aggregate medical data might result in the unavoidable identification of some individual employee's medical information, the union's need for medical data about the work environment outweighed the employees' privacy interests.

With respect to the employers' contention that the disclosure of generic names of substances used and produced at the plants involved in the request would require the employers to disclose trade secrets, the NLRB recognized that the employers might have legitimate proprietary interests concerning some of the substances but realized the unions' need for such information to represent properly the safety and health interests of its members. To accommodate the conflicting needs, the NLRB held that the parties must bargain in good faith regarding the conditions under which the needed information must be disclosed to unions with appropriate safeguards for the employers' legitimate proprietary information. In a recent decision, the United States Court of Appeals for the District of Columbia Circuit upheld the NLRB decisions in the *Health Trilogy*.[79]

The employers had claimed in the appeal of the consolidated cases that the unions failed to document the relevance of the requested safety and health information, since:

[77] 261 NLRB No 7 (1982).
[78] 261 NLRB No 28 (1982).
[79] Oil, Chem & Atomic Workers, Local 6-418 v NLRB, 711 F2d 348 (DC Cir 1983).

1. The union's requests were not motivated by specific problems in their respective plants

2. The mere presence of hazardous substances or conditions within the workplace did not demonstrate the relevance of the requested information

3. The disclosure of a list of hazardous substances or conditions would not aid the unions in performing their bargaining obligations

4. The company's extensive health and safety programs ensured their employees a safe and healthful working environment

The court rejected all four of these arguments, stating that a union's right to relevant information is not dependent upon the existence of some particular controversy or need to dispose of some recognized problem. The assertion that a union must rely on an employer's good intentions concerning questions of safety and health of employees was rejected as fallacious.

In cases where employees admittedly are exposed to a variety of potential hazards and have expressed growing and legitimate concerns over their health and safety, where the unions explain the rationale underlying their requests, and where a pertinent collective bargaining agreement obligates management and union to take specified actions to safeguard employees' safety and health, the relevance of a wide range of information concerning the working environment and employees' health cannot be gainsaid. Under these circumstances, the court stated, safety and health information should be shared fully with unions. The release of exposure and medical data in such cases will also facilitate the identification of workplace hazards, promote meaningful bargaining calculated to reduce those hazards, and enable unions to police the performance of employers' contractual obligations, as well as to carry out their own responsibilities under collective bargaining agreements.

Finally, however, the court reaffirmed its adherence to the Supreme Court's decision in *Detroit Edison Co v NLRB*,[80] which made clear that a union's interest in relevant information will not always outweigh an employer's legitimate and substantial interest in maintaining the confidentiality of such information. The court held that, if conditions can be devised to accommodate both the employer's confidentiality interests in trade secret information and the union's interest in obtaining relevant information, a refusal to disclose under those conditions would not likely violate the NLRA; a balancing of the parties' interests is required.

An employer faced with a request for safety and health data by a union should not *stonewall* the request. The employer should analyze the union's request to determine whether compliance will violate the privacy interest of employees or the employer's trade secrets. A good faith attempt at compliance and bargaining over the request will establish a favorable background if there is later litigation on the question.

---

[80] 440 US 318 (1978).

Employers should not claim too much with reference to trade secret claims. An objective and reasonable posture should be exercised. Employers should rely on a sound technical position supported by scientific personnel, patent attorneys, and those knowledgeable in the law of intellectual property. The union may well accept the employer's disclosure of general data if it reflects a good faith attempt at compliance. In the event the union disagrees and the NLRB must balance the competing interests, the reasonableness of the employer's position will set a favorable position from which to litigate.

§7.14   Freedom of Information Act

The Freedom of Information Act (FOIA)[81] permits private individuals and organizations to obtain certain information in the possession of federal governmental agencies. The scope of this chapter precludes an in-depth study of the law governing the release of information, but an overview is pertinent since there is a wealth of information about toxic and hazardous substances in the possession of federal agencies.[82] A corollary discussion is contained in Chapter 15.

FOIA was enacted to facilitate public access to government data and thereby promote an informed electorate; FOIA is a disclosure act. Nondisclosure of information is the exception.[83] There are, however, nine exemptions to the government's mandatory disclosure obligation.[84] The nine exceptions are:

1. Classified information
2. Internal personnel rules and practices of federal agencies
3. Exemptions specified in other federal statutes
4. Trade secrets and commercial or financial information obtained from a person and privileged or confidential
5. Inter-agency or intra-agency documents which would not be available in litigation with the agency
6. Personal and medical files and similar files which would constitute a clearly unwarranted invasion of personal privacy
7. Investigatory records complied for law enforcement purposes under specified conditions
8. Specified data bearing on the regulation or supervision of financial institutions
9. Geological and geophysical information and data, including maps, concerning wells

---

[81] 5 USC §552.

[82] For a thorough analysis of the subject, see O'Reilly, Federal Information Disclosure (Shepard's/McGraw-Hill 1977).

[83] Chrysler Corp v Brown, 441 US 281, 290-94 (1979).

[84] 5 USC §552(b).

The fourth exemption which excludes from mandatory disclosure trade secrets and commercial or financial information is germane to disclosure of environmental or safety and health information relating to toxic or hazardous substances.

The term *trade secret* is not defined in FOIA; however, it has generally been defined as "any formula, pattern, device or compilation of information which is used in one's business and which gives him an opportunity to obtain an advantage over competitors who do not know or use it."[85] However, the court in *Public Citizen Health Research Group v Food and Drug Administration*[86] rejected this traditional definition of a trade secret. It defined the term as "a secret, commercially valuable plan, formula, process or device that is used for making, preparing, compounding, or processing of trade commodities and that can be said to be the end product of either innovation or substantial effort."[87]

The fourth exemption's second prong requires proof that: (1) the information is:

1. Commercial or financial
2. Obtained from a person
3. Privileged or confidential

Regarding the issue of confidentiality, the usual test is whether disclosure is likely "to cause substantial harm to the competitive position of the person from whom the information was obtained."[88]

The Supreme Court in *Chrysler v Brown*[89] held that FOIA is exclusively a disclosure statute, stating "the Congressional concern was with the agency's need or preference for confidentiality; FOIA by itself protects the submitters' interest in confidentiality only to the extent that this interest is endorsed by the agency collecting the information."[90]

Therefore, to protect a commercial interest, a submitter may have to take affirmative action under the Administrative Procedure Act[91] to protect proprietary information. Although FOIA does not deprive the agency of discretion to disclose materials that are exempt from mandatory disclosure, the Administrative Procedure Act should normally afford a remedy against agency action which is "arbitrary, capricious, an abuse of discretion, or otherwise not in

---

[85] 4 Restatement Second of Torts §757; *see also* Union Oil Co v Federal Power Commn, 542 F2d 1036, 1044 (9th Cir 1976); St Paul's Benevolent Educ & Missionary Inst v United States, 506 F Supp 822, 830 (ND Ga 1980).

[86] 704 F2d 1280 (DC Cir 1983).

[87] *Id* 1286.

[88] National Parks & Conservation Assn v Morton, 498 F2d 765, 770 (DC Cir 1974); Public Citizens Health Research Group v FDA, 704 F2d 1280, 1291 (DC Cir 1983).

[89] 441 US 281 (1979).

[90] *Id* 292-93.

[91] 5 USC §702; Chrysler Corp v Brown, 441 US 281, 317-18 (1979).

accordance with law,"[92] and the submitter is entitled to judicial review of agency action. Since the Federal Trade Secrets Act[93] makes it a crime for a federal employee to disclose trade secrets or other confidential business data, it is reasonable to conclude that a disclosure in violation of the Federal Trade Secrets Act would be an abuse of discretion.

A person either seeking or submitting information to federal agencies should review the particular agencies regulations on disclosure of information to the public. The Occupational Safety and Health Administration[94] and the Environmental Protection Agency[95] have promulgated detailed and explicit regulations concerning requests for information.

---

[92] 5 USC §706(2)(A).

[93] 18 USC §1905.

[94] 29 CFR §70.1 *et seq.*

[95] 40 CFR §2.100 *et seq.*

Appendix to
Chapter Seven

These charts were originally published as part of an article entitled "Framework Provides Path Through Right-to-Know Law," in the October, 1983 edition of Occupational Health and Safety, p. 11 and are reproduced here by specific permission of the authors Nicholas A. Ashford, Associate Professor of Technology and Policy, Director, Center for Policy Alternatives, and Charles C. Caldart, Staff Attorney, Center for Policy Alternatives, Massachusetts Institute of Technology, Cambridge, MA.

The authors plan to republish the chart and prepare a more detailed analysis for the specific laws and regulations referred therein, in a future law review article.

DUTY TO INFORM

ORIGIN OF DUTY	COVERAGE	PARTY REQUIRED TO ACT	TO WHOM DISCLOSED	TYPE OF INFORMATION DISCLOSED	REMEDY FOR NON-COMPLIANCE	TRADE SECRET PROTECTION	MEDICAL CONFIDENTIALITY PROTECTION
Common Law: Products Liability	All workplaces where the substance could reasonably be expected to be put to its intended use	Manufacturer	• Worker • Employer	Scientific: a reasonable appraisal of the risks of exposure	Tort suit of damages resulting from exposure	Application unclear	Not applicable
Common Law: • intentional tort and/or recklessness • duty of care owed to family members of workers	In states where cause of action is valid and workers' compensation laws are not a bar to recovery: all workplaces	Employer	Worker	Scientific: • the fact of exposure • a reasonable appraisal of the risks of exposure	Tort suit for damages resulting from exposure	Application unclear	Not applicable
OSHAct: Section 6(b) standards for particular exposure	All workplaces covered by the standard	Employer	Worker	Depends on specifics of standard. May be: • scientific - effects and/or exposure • legal - worker rights under the standard	Request OSHA inspection/ enforcement under §8(f)(1) of OSHAct	General protection under section 15 of the OSHAct; specific composition of mixtures need not be disclosed	Disclosure of effects information limited to worker's own medical data only
OSHAct: OSHA Employee Access Rule, 29 CFR 1910.20	All workplaces covered by the OSHAct	Employer	Worker	Legal: worker rights under the access rule	Request OSHA inspection/ enforcement	Not applicable	Not applicable
OSHAct: *Proposed* Hazard Communication Rule (as of March 1983)	Chemical manufacturers, importers, and distributors	Chemical manufacturers, importers, and distributors	• Worker • Employer	Scientific information regarding certain toxic chemicals: • ingredients • Material safety data sheet (MSDS) "Toxic" narrowly defined to include only *known* toxins	Request OSHA inspection/ enforcement	Exclusion for any chemical identity employer can substantiate as trade secret, but disclosure to medical professional subject to confidentiality agreement	Not applicable
TSCA: § 8(a), and implementing regulation, 40 CFR 710	Chemical manufacturers, processors, and importers	Chemical manufacturers, processors, and importers	EPA	Scientific information on certain high volume and "priority" chemicals: • exposure data • effects data	EPA enforcement	General protection under §14: no unwarranted EPA disclosure to third parties; specific composition of mixtures need not be disclosed. Precise chemical identities *not* trade secrets	None in statute or regulation
TSCA: § 8(a), and implementing regulation, 40 CFR 710	Chemical manufacturers, processors, and importers	Chemical manufacturers, processors, and importers	EPA	Scientific: *ingredients* of chemicals commercially produced, processed, or imported	EPA enforcement	General protection under § 14: no unwarranted EPA disclosure to third parties; specific composition of mixtures need not be disclosed. Precise chemical identities *not* trade secrets	Not applicable

DUTY TO INFORM

ORIGIN OF DUTY	COVERAGE	PARTY REQUIRED TO ACT	TO WHOM DISCLOSED	TYPE OF INFORMATION DISCLOSED	REMEDY FOR NON-COMPLIANCE	TRADE SECRET PROTECTION	MEDICAL CONFIDENTIALITY PROTECTION
TSCA: § 8(a) and implementing regulation, 40 CFR 712	Chemical manufacturers and processors	Chemical manufacturers and processors	EPA	Scientific: • Ingredients • General exposure and effects informantion only; does not require generation of individual medical or exposure records • Production information	EPA enforcement	General protection under § 14: no unwarranted EPA disclosure to third parties; specific composition of mixtures need not be disclosed. Precise chemical identities *not* trade secrets	Not applicable, as required exposure information is not individualized
TSCA: § 8(d) and implementing regulation 40 CFR 716	Chemical manufacturers and processors	Chemical manufacturers and processors	EPA	Scientific: lists of "reasonably obtainable" health and safety studies for 169 chemicals	EPA enforcement	General protection under § 14: no unwarranted EPA disclosure to third parties; specific composition of mixtures need not be disclosed. Precise chemical identities *not* trade secrets	None in statute or regulation
TSCA: § 8(e)	Chemical manufacturers and processors	Chemical manufacturers and processors	EPA	Scientific: information indicating that a chemical poses a "substantial risk of injury to health"	EPA enforcement	General protection under § 14: no unwarranted EPA disclosure to third parties; specific composition of mixtures need not be disclosed. Precise chemical identities *not* trade secrets	None in statute
NLRA	All workplaces covered by NLRA	Employer	Worker	Legal: existance and nature of right to refuse hazardous work	Claim for unfair labor practice	Not applicable	Not applicable
State Workers' Compensation Laws	Coverage will vary with state	Employer	Worker	Legal: existance and nature of right to file workers' compensation claim	Varies with particular state law	Not applicable	Not applicable
State and local "right to know" laws	Varies with particular statute/ ordinance	Employer	Varies; can be worker and/or chemical user and/or community	Varies; usually at least ingredients information	Varies with particulat statute/ ordinance	Some protection commonly provided, but degree of protection varies	Varies; often will not be applicable

DUTY TO GENERATE AND/OR RETAIN

ORIGIN OF DUTY	NATURE OF DUTY	COVERAGE	PARTY REQUIRED TO ACT	TYPE OF INFORMATION TO BE GENERATED AND/OR RETAINED	REMEDY FOR NON-COMPLIANCE	TRADE SECRET PROTECTION	MEDICAL CONFIDENTIALITY
OSHAct: Section 6(b) standards for particular exposures	Generate and Retain	All workplaces covered by the standard	Employer	Scientific: • Exposure • Effects	Request OSHA Inspection/ Enforcement Under Section 8(f)(1) of the OSHAct	General protection under section 15 of the OSHAct; specific conposition of mixtures need not be disclosed	All such records must be maintained
OSHAct: Worker access rule, 29 CFR 1910.20	Retain if Generated	All workplaces covered by the OSHAct	Employer	Scientific: • Exposure • Effects Pertains to all chemicals listed in RTECHS	Request OSHA Inspection/ Enforcement	Legitimate "process" trade secrets can be excluded, but precise chemical identities must be retained if recorded	All records must be maintained
OSHAct: *Proposed* revision of worker access rule, 47 FR 30,420	Retain if Generated	All workplaces covered by the OSHAct	Employer	Scientific: • Exposure • Effects Pertains only to *known* toxins	Request OSHA Inspection/ Enforcement	If a trade secret can be substantiated, records of precise chemical identity need not be retained	All records must be maintained
TSCA: Section 8(c) and *proposed* reguaftion 45 FR 47008	Generate and Retain (30 years for occupational exposure)	Chemical manufacturers, processors, and distributors	Chemical manufacturers, processors, and distributors	Scientific: information pertaining to "significant adverse reactions" to chemical exposures	EPA Enforcement	General protection under § 14: no unwarranted EPA disclosure to third parties; specific composition of mixtures need not be disclosed. Precise chemical identities *not* trade secrets.	All such records must be maintained
TSCA: Section 8(a) and implementing regulation, 40 CFR 712	Generate and Retain	Chemical manufacturers and processors	Chemical manufacturers and processors	Scientific: • Ingredients • General exposure and effects information only; does not require generation of individual medical or exposure records • Production information	EPA Enforcement	General protection under § 14: no unwarranted EPA disclosure to third parties; specific composition of mixtures need not be disclosed. Precise chemical identities *not* trade secrets.	Not applicable, as required information is not individualized
NLRA: Collective bargaining process	Will depend on wording of collective bargaining agreement; duty exists only if imposed by agreement	Scope of applicable collective bargaining agreement	Employer (where duty exists)	Will depend on wording of collective bargaining agreement; *potential* scope includes both scientific and technological information	Enforcement of collective bargaining agreement under NLRA and any applicable arbitration agreement	Depends on collective bargaining agreement	Depends on collective bargaining agreement
State and local "right to know" laws	Varies; not all such laws and ordinances contain requirements of this nature	Varies with particular statute/ ordinance	Employer (where duty exists)	Varies with particular statute/ ordinance	Varies with particular statute/ ordinance	Some protection commonly provided, but degree of protection varies	Varies with particular statute/ ordinance

RIGHT OF ACCESS

ORIGIN OF RIGHT	COVERAGE	PARTY ENTITLED TO ACT	HOW EXERCISED	TYPE OF INFORMATION SUBJECT TO ACCESS	REMEDY FOR NON-COMPLIANCE	TRADE SECRET PROTECTION	MEDICAL CONFIDENTIALITY PROTECTION
OSHAct: OSHA access to medical records rule, 29 CFR 1913.10	All workplaces covered by the OSHAct	OSHA	"Immediate Access" on OSHA request to employer	All exposure data recorded by employer	OSHA enforcement	No protection on regulation, but presumably information will not be disclosed by OSHA. 29 CFR 70.24	No protection in regulation
OSHAct: Section 20	All workplaces covered by the OSHAct	NIOSH	Administrative subpoena (usually resulting in litigation)	Broad access to scientific information	Court enforcement	As protected by court on a case-by-case basis	As protected by court on a case-by-case basis
TSCA: Section 8(c) and *proposed* implementing regulation, 45 FR 47008	Chemical manufacturers, processors and distributors	EPA	EPA request	Scientific Records of "significant adverse reactions" to chemical exposures	EPA enforcement	General protection under § 14: no unwarranted EPA disclosure to third parties, specific composition of mixtures need not be disclosed Precise chemical identities *not* trade secrets	No specific protection
TSCA: Section 11	Chemical manufacturers, storers, and distributors	EPA	EPA request accompanied by written notice	Potentially broad access to recorded scientific information	EPA enforcement (subpoena power granted by statute)	General protection under §14: no unwarranted EPA disclosure to third parties, specific composition of mixtures need not be disclosed Precise chemical identities *not* trade secrets	No specific protection
State and local "right to know" laws	Varies with particular statute/ordinance	Varies; generally worker and worker representative	Varies with particular statute/ordinance	Varies, generally includes exposure and effects information	Varies with particular statute/ordinance	Some protection commonly provided, but degree of protection varies	Varies with particular statute/ordinance

RIGHT OF ACCESS

ORIGIN OF RIGHT	COVERAGE	PARTY ENTITLED TO ACT	HOW EXERCISED	TYPE OF INFORMATION SUBJECT TO ACCESS	REMEDY FOR NON-COMPLIANCE	TRADE SECRET PROTECTION	MEDICAL CONFIDENTIALITY PROTECTION
OSHAct: Worker access rule, 29 CFR 1910.20	All workplaces covered by the OSHAct	Worker (or worker representative)	Worker (or representative) request to employer; 15 day compliance period	Scientific • Exposure • Effects Pertains to all chemicals listed in RTECS	Request OSHA inspection/ enforcement	"Process" trade secrets can be witheld, but• precise chemical identities must be supplied	Access is limited to one's own medical record; no similar protection for exposure record
OSHAct: *Proposed* revision of worker access rule, 47 FR 30, 420	All workplaces covered by the OSHAct	Worker (or worker representative)	Worker (or representative) request to employer; 15 day compliance period	Scientific: • Exposure • Effects Pertains only to *known* toxins	Request OSHA inspection/ enforcement	If a trade secret can be substantiated, precise chemical identities can be witheld, but generic chemical identities must be provided	Access is limited to one's own medical record; no similar protection for exposure records
OSHAct: *Proposed* hazard communication rule (as of March, 1983)	Chemical manufacturers, importers and distributors	Worker (or worker representative)	Worker (or representative) request to employer	Scientific: • Ingredients • Material Safety Data Sheets (MSDS) Pertains only to *known* toxins	Request OSHA inspection/ enforcement	If a trade secret can be substantiated, precise chemical identities can be witheld, but must be disclosed to medical professionals, subject to confidentiality agreement	Not applicable
NLRA: An *arguable* adjunct to the right to refuse hazardous work under section 7 and 502	All workplaces covered by the NLRA	• Individual worker under section 502 • One or more workers in a nonunion shop under section 7	Unclear; probably worker request to employer	Broad potential for Scientific Information: • Ingredients • Exposure • Effects	Unclear; probably file claim for unfair labor practice	Unclear; NLRA requires balancing between health interests and "legitimate" trade secret interests	Probably limited to one's *own* medical information
NLRA: Collective bargaining process	All workplaces covered by the NLRA	Union	Collective bargaining	Broad access to scientific information; breadth of access to technological information not clear	Claim for unfair labor practice	Unclear: NLRA requires balancing between health interests and "legitimate" trade secret interests	Unclear: Union has unquestionable right of access to medical records where personal identifiers have been removed

8

Standards, Rules, and Regulations in Toxic Tort Litigation

*Joseph A. Darrell, Esq.**

§8.01 Introduction

The violation of a statute or ordinance punishing certain behavior has long been used to establish the *reasonable person* standard of conduct. As the Minnesota Supreme Court noted in *Osborne v McMasters*,[1] liability may be established based upon violation of a statute or ordinance if: (1) the defendant violated the statute or ordinance; (2) the violation proximately caused the injury; (3) the injury was of the character which the statute or ordinance was

---

* Partner, Thelen, Marrin, Johnson, & Bridges, San Francisco, California
[1] 40 Minn 103, 41 NW 543 (1889).

designed to protect; and (4) the injury was to one for whose protection or benefit the statute was enacted.

> [D]efendant's clerk in his drug-store, in the course of his employment as such, sold to plaintiff's intestate a deadly poison without labeling it "Poison," as required by statute: . . . It is now well settled, certainly in this state, that where a statute or municipal ordinance imposes upon any person a specific duty for the protection or benefit of others, if he neglects to perform that duty he is liable to those for whose protection or benefit it was imposed for any injuries of the character which the statute or ordinance was designed to prevent, and which were proximately produced by such neglect. . . . It is immaterial whether the duty is one imposed by the rule of common law requiring the exercise of ordinary care not to injure another, or is imposed by a statute designed for the protection of others. In either case the failure to perform the duty constitutes negligence, and renders the party liable for injuries resulting from it. The only difference is that in the one case the measure of legal duty is to be determined upon common-law principles, while in the other the statute fixes it, so that the violation of the statute constitutes conclusive evidence of negligence, or, in other words, negligence *per se*. The action in the latter case is not a statutory one, nor does the statute give the right of action in any other sense, except that it makes an act negligent which otherwise might not be such, or at least only evidence of negligence. All that the statute does is to establish a fixed standard by which the fact of negligence may be determined. The gist of the action is still negligence, or the non-performance of a legal duty to the person injured.[2]

With very little effort or discussion, courts have expanded the principles applicable to violation of a statute to include violations of agency standards, rules, regulations, and orders. Such an expansion may be arguably suspect, since it fails to distinguish between the nature of a statute—considered, debated, and adopted by a legislative body—and an agency standard or rule—adopted through the administrative process and therefore not subject to the normal and often vigorous give-and-take procedural safeguards of the legislative process. On the other hand, agencies may have better access to expert advice and therefore be more capable than legislatures of promulgating a reasonable standard. In any event, the principles of law applicable to violations of statute are equally applicable to violations of agency standards, rules, regulations, or orders.

A few general principles, applicable to violations of any standard or regulation, are important at the outset. When arguing a defendant's violation of an agency standard or regulation on behalf of a plaintiff and in furtherance of establishing liability, it should be kept in mind that in almost every instance it is not violation of the regulation itself upon which liability is based, but rather

---

[2] *Id* at 103-04, 41 NW at 543-44.

upon the theory that violation of the statute is evidence of defendant's failure to meet a proper standard of care. In other words, the regulation (or statute) usually will not specifically provide for civil liability, and it can be a serious mistake to base one's complaint upon such a *statutory* or *regulatory* cause of action.

For example, in the Safety Appliance Act, Congress specifically established a statutory cause of action for railway workers for injuries resulting from a breach of Interstate Commerce Commission (ICC) safety regulations.[3] In such a case, the employee has a statutory rather than a common law cause of action.[4] While presumably a plaintiff could forego his or her statutory strict liability cause of action and bring a cause of action for negligence,[5] if a plaintiff bases his or her action solely on violation of these ICC regulations, he or she must show noncompliance to win. In addition, a defendant railroad which proves conformity with these ICC regulations wins such a suit—not on the basis of due care, but on the basis of compliance with the statute as a complete defense to such an action.[6]

Such legislative (or administrative) recognition of civil liability, however, is rare. For example, the theory that a private cause of action for violation of standards in the Occupational Safety and Health Act of 1970[7] is impliedly created by that act has been uniformly rejected by the courts.[8]

The more pertinent question, therefore, is whether violation of an agency standard is negligence per se, or whether such violation is simply evidence of negligence. Other questions equally important to the practitioner in this area and discussed in this chapter, include:

1. How a plaintiff can make the most effective use of this tool (see §§8.02-8.07)

2. How a defendant can structure a defense to an attempt to use a violation of a standard to establish or aid in the establishment of liability (see §8.08)

---

[3] Safety Appliance & Boiler Inspection Acts, 27 Stat 531 (1893)(codified as amended at 45 USC §§1-43 (1976)).

[4] *See, e.g.,* Chicago GWRR v Schendel, 267 US 287 (1925).

[5] To do so, however, would enable the defendant to argue compliance with statutory standards as evidence of due care, discussed in §8.09.

[6] Defendant complied with ICC regulations and avoided liability in Auschwitz v Wabash Ry, 346 Ill 190, 178 NE 403 (1931); Mahutga v Minneapolis, St P & SSM Ry, 182 Minn 362, 234 NW 272 (1931); Lancaster v Wight & Allen, 110 Tex 213, 217 SW 1032 (1920); Payne v Albright, 235 SW 288 (Tex Civ App 1921). *Cf* Pennell v Philadelphia & R Ry, 231 US 675 (1914).

[7] 29 USC §651 *et seq;* G. Z. Nothstein, Law of Occupational Safety and Health (1981 & Supp 1983).

[8] *See generally* Jeter v St Regis Paper Co, 507 F2d 973 (5th Cir 1975); Russell v Bartley, 494 F2d 334 (6th Cir 1974); Byrd v Fieldcrest Mills, Inc, 496 F2d 1323 (4th Cir 1974); Knight v Burns, Kirkley & Williams Constr Co, 331 So2d 651 (Ala 1976).

3.   Whether or not compliance with agency standards can be used by a defendant as a defense to tort liability (see **§8.09**)

§8.02   Plaintiffs' Use of Agency Standards

Plaintiff's use of violation of a statute in establishing tort liability has historically been very successful. The great majority of courts have held that if the statute is applicable (designed to protect the class of persons in which plaintiff is included against risk of the type of harm which in fact occurred as a result of the violation) a violation conclusively establishes negligence.[9] Of course, the issue of causal relationship between the violation and the injury to the plaintiff and defenses such as contributory negligence and assumption of risk are issues even in such per se holdings.[10]

California, for example, has arrived at this same result statutorily by providing in its evidence code that a presumption of negligence arises from a violation of a statute, ordinance, or regulation when that violation proximately causes harm of the type the statute was designed to prevent to a person for whose protection such statute was adopted[11] The section gives rise to a "presumption affecting the burden of proof" requiring the defendant to come forward and prove to the trier of fact that it is more probable than not that the violation of the statute was reasonable and justifiable under the circumstances.[12]

However, a number of courts have held that a violation of statute is only evidence of negligence for the jury to weigh.[13] It is this conflict between violation of a statute as negligence per se and violation of a statute as merely evidence of negligence which creates most of the conflict in the Occupational Safety and Health Act (OSH Act) cases.

§8.03   —Occupational Safety and Health Act Violation as Evidence of Negligence

A number of courts have held that a violation of Occupational Safety and Health Act (OSH Act) standards can be used as evidence of negligence.

---

[9] Haines v Carroll, 126 Kan 408, 267 P 982 (1928); Russell v Szczawinaki, 268 Mich 112, 255 NW 731 (1934); Fridley v Brush, 161 Neb 318, 73 NW2d 376 (1955); Metro v Long Transp Co, 387 Pa 354, 127 A2d 716 (1956); Harris v Hendrixson, 25 Tenn App 221, 155 SW2d 876 (1941); Lauson v Town of Fond du Lac, 141 Wis 57, 123 NW 629 (1909). See Prosser, Handbook of Law of Torts ¶36, at 200 (4th ed 1971).

[10] Prosser, *supra* note 9, at 200-01.

[11] Cal Evid Code §669 (West 1981).

[12] *Id* §669 (Law Revision Commn Comment).

[13] Baldwin v City of Norwalk, 95 Conn 1, 112 A 660 (1921); Kendall v City of Des Moines, 183 Iowa 866, 167 NW 684 (1918); Duby v Columbia County, 194 Wis 172, 215 NW 819 (1927). See Prosser, *supra* note 9, at 201.

In *Buhler v Marriot Hotels, Inc,*[14] the court held that while OSH Act does not create a private cause of action, a plaintiff may use OSH Act standards and evidence that they have been violated as evidence of negligence at trial.

In *Watwood v RR Dawson Bridge Co, Inc,*[15] the court held that the complaint did state a cause of action based on a violation of OSH Act. However, the OSH Act violation was not the exclusive basis; the complaint also stated a cause of action based on ordinary negligence.

In *Knight v Burns, Kirkley & Williams Const Co,*[16] the complaint alleged violations of OSH Act. The defendant argued that OSH Act creates no duty on a defendant's part and gives no remedy to plaintiffs. The court held that the plaintiff did not have a private civil remedy under OSH Act, but that under proper circumstances the OSH Act regulations and provisions may be admissible for a jury to consider in determining the standard of care that a defendant should have followed.

In *Disabatino Brothers, Inc v Baio,*[17] the court held that it was proper for the trial court to allow the jury to consider OSH Act regulations as relevant to the proper standard of care required by law. The trial court gave instructions that the guidelines did not create a specific duty. The appellate court stated that the regulations were relevant to assist the jury in determining the proper standard of care.

In *Dunn v Brimer,*[18] in upholding the trial judge's instruction that a violation of the regulations is evidence of negligence to be considered with the other facts and circumstances, the court held that a jury may consider whether a violation of OSH Act standards was negligence.

Finally, in *Brogley v Chambersburg Engineering Co,*[19] a recent case deciding, on first impression, whether under Pennsylvania law OSH Act regulations would be admissible as evidence of negligence, the court stated that Pennsylvania courts had uniformly held admissible other safety codes and regulations intended to enhance safety. Citing cases in other states holding that OSH Act regulations are admissible as a standard of care, the violation of which is evidence of negligence, the court held that the trial judge did not err in allowing an OSH Act regulation into evidence to show the employer's duty of care.

---

[14] 390 F Supp 999 (ED La 1974).
[15] 307 So 2d 692 (Ala 1975).
[16] 331 So 2d 651 (Ala 1976).
[17] 366 A2d 508 (Del 1976).
[18] 537 SW2d 164 (Ark 1976).
[19] 452 A2d 743 (Pa Super 1982).

§8.04 —Occupational Safety and Health Act Violation as Negligence Per Se

A few courts have held that proof of an Occupational Safety and Health Act (OSH Act) violation is negligence per se. Much of the conflict between these cases and cases such as those discussed in §8.03 is centered on interpretation of the following federal OSH Act provision:

> Nothing in this Act shall be construed to supercede or in any manner affect any workman's compensation law or to enlarge or diminish or affect in any other manner the common law or statutory rights, duties, or liabilities of employers under any law with respect to injuries, diseases, or death of employees arising out of, or in the course of, employment.[20]

Although the first case described below did not discuss this statutory language in its finding of negligence per se, the other cases did base their decisions on this language.

In *Arthur v Flota Merchante Gran Centro Americana, SA,*[21] the trial court had instructed the jury that a violation of OSH Act regulations was negligence per se. The court stated that the purpose of the regulations was to promote safety and to establish an unambiguous standard for measuring industrial safety, and that such a purpose was advanced when the court instructs a jury that violation of the regulations is negligence per se if the plaintiff was in the class of persons the regulations were intended to protect, if the regulations were intended to protect against the risk of harm that occurred, and if there is proof that there was a violation of the regulations. This case has, in effect, been overruled by the Fifth Circuit in *Gay v Ocean Transport & Trading Co*[22] and *Brown v Mitsubishi Shintaku Ginko.*[23], which held that the safety & health regulations relied on in those cases, do not automatically impose a duty on persons unless they are acting as employers. In the absence of the existence of such a duty there can be no cause of action based on those regulations.[24]

In *Carroll v Getty Oil Co,*[25] a violation of state OSH Act regulations (adopting federal OSH Act by reference) was alleged. The court stated that conduct in violation of a statute, ordinance, regulation, or rule enacted for the safety of others and having the force of law constitutes negligence per se. The violation of state OSH Act regulations was held to constitute negligence per se under Delaware law.

The court addressed the contention that 29 USC §653(b)(4) expressly for-

---

[20] 29 USC §653(b)(4).

[21] 487 F2d 501 (5th Cir 1973).

[22] 546 F2d 1233 (5th Cir 1977).

[23] 550 F2d 331 (5th Cir 1977). *See also* National Marine Serv Inc v Gulf Oil Co, 433 F Supp 913 (ED La 1977).

[24] Arthur v Flota Merchante, is however still relied on in other jurisdictions. *See* Dravo Corp v Occupational Safety & Health Rev Commn, 613 F2d 1227 (3d Cir 1980).

[25] 498 F Supp 409 (D Del 1980).

bids the use of any alleged violation of OSH Act standards for the purpose of establishing negligence per se. The court followed a Delaware Supreme Court decision in rejecting this contention, which had held that 29 USC §653(b)(4) could have no effect on the Delaware statute and the regulations adopted thereunder since the Delaware statute under which the OSH Act regulations were adopted contained no counterpart to 29 USC §653(b)(4).

In *Wendland v Ridgefield Construction Services, Inc*,[26] the jury had been given an instruction on negligence per se as a result of the establishment of an OSH Act violation. The Connecticut Supreme Court dealt with the question of whether the language of the Connecticut statute, which was identical to 29 USC §653(b)(4), would allow the jury instruction on negligence per se. The court concluded that the application of negligence per se instructions affects common law rights, duties, and liabilities of employers and employees with respect to injuries arising out of and in the course of employment as those terms are used in 29 USC §653(b)(4). Therefore, the court held that the negligence per se instruction was erroneous.

The decision cites other jurisdictions which have reached the same conclusion and states that other courts which have held that an OSH Act violation constitutes negligence per se have not been faced with a statute analogous to 29 USC §653(b)(4) or have failed to take that statute into account. The court did state that OSH Act regulations can be admitted as *evidence* of the standard of care.

§8.05   —A Distinction without a Difference?

As in most tort cases, the goal of the plaintiff in a toxic tort case is to present a persuasive case to the jury. Therefore, whether the trial judge instructs the jury that violation of the agency standard is negligence per se and therefore conclusive on the issue of negligence or simply that such a violation is evidence of negligence may not affect the outcome. Either instruction is likely to have a very persuasive effect on the jury. Plaintiff's counsel may slightly increase his or her chances of winning with a negligence per se instruction but at the same time increase the chances of reversal on appeal, particularly in a jurisdiction which has not yet considered the question.

For example, in a number of safety standard cases, plaintiff's counsel apparently made a strategic error when, after establishing a violation of a safety regulation, he or she successfully argued a negligence per se instruction, only to be reversed on appeal.[27] Therefore, unless plaintiff's counsel is in a jurisdic-

---

[26] 439 A2d 954 (Conn 1981).

[27] Snow v Riggs, 172 Ark 835, 290 SW 591 (1927)(disregard of highway commission rule requiring pedestrians to face traffic); Town of Kirkland v Everman, 217 Ind 683, 29 NE2d 206 (1940); Rodenkirch v Nemnich, 168 SW2d 977 (Mo Ct App 1943)(disregard of highway commission's stop sign); Schumer v Caplin, 241 NY 346, 150 NE 139 (1925)(failure to install safeguards for window washers required by an industrial commission; Matz v JL Curtis Cartage Co, 132 Ohio St 271, 7 NE2d 220 (1937)(violation

tion with a well-established negligence per se rule, or he or she feels compelled to make new law in a jurisdiction which has not yet considered the question, prudence would seem to dictate that the plaintiff should request an instruction that violation of the regulation is only evidence of negligence.

§8.06 —Violation of Food, Drug, and Cosmetic Act as Negligence Per Se

Violations of Food and Drug Administration (FDA) regulations have been held to be negligence per se. Although the Food, Drug, and Cosmetic Act[28] does not create a civil remedy for injured consumers, this act has been held to create an absolute duty, breach of which can result in a strict liability action.

Examples of cases holding a violation of an FDA regulation to be negligence per se in products liability actions include *Lukaszewicz v Ortho Pharmaceutical Corp,*[29] where the regulation promulgated under the Food, Drug, and Cosmetic Act required that, in the case of oral contraceptives, warnings in the form of package inserts be given to the patient as well as the physician. The court held that, under Wisconsin law, violation of the federal regulation was negligence per se, giving rise to strict liability.

In *Orthopedic Equipment Co v Eutsler,*[30] the court stated that although the Food, Drug, and Cosmetic Act does not expressly provide a civil remedy for injured consumers, the statute does impose an absolute duty on manufacturers not to mislabel their products, and the breach of this duty may give rise to civil liability. The court held that a violation of the act is negligence per se under Virginia law and stated that "the majority of American courts which have passed on this question, in cases under state laws resembling the Federal Act, have held violations to be negligence per se."[31]

Finally, in *Gober v Revlon, Inc,*[32] a case involving a fingernail polish base coat, violation of the Food, Drug, and Cosmetic Act was held to be negligence per se under California law.

§8.07 —Violation of Federal Hazardous Substances Act and Toxic Substance Control Act

In *Shatz v Tec Technical Adhesives,*[33] homeowners brought a products liability

---

of Public Utility Commission rules requiring warning flares for trucks stalled on highways).

[28] 21 USC §321 *et seq.*

[29] 510 F Supp 961 (ED Wis 1981).

[30] 276 F2d 455 (4th Cir 1960).

[31] *Id* 461.

[32] 317 F2d 47 (4th Cir 1963).

[33] 415 A2d 1188 (NJ Super 1980); *see also* Steagall v Dot Mfg Corp, 223 Tenn 428,

action against an adhesive manufacturer. The plaintiffs had attempted to show that the adhesive was not labeled in accordance with the regulations adopted under the Federal Hazardous Substances Act,[34] and the trial judge had excluded the evidence. The appellate court held that exclusion of such evidence was highly prejudicial error and stated that a violation of the statute and the regulations under it was evidence of negligence.

In *Johnson v Koppers Co*,[35] an action was brought against manufacturers, producers, retailers, and merchants of coke-processing equipment and chemicals used by United States Steel Company. The plaintiffs alleged they were exposed to fumes, particles, and dust, including but not limited to asbestos, and brought suit under the Occupational Safety and Health Act (OSH Act)[36] and for violation of the requirements of the Toxic Substance Control Act,[37] among other theories.

The court held that neither OSH Act nor the Toxic Substance Control Act created a civil action under which damages could be recovered. The court stated that the Toxic Substance Control Act "grants authority to the administrator of the Environmental Protection Agency to regulate dangerous chemical substances but it in no way creates a civil action."[38] The court did not reach the issue of whether the alleged violations of the Toxic Substance Control Act could be evidence of negligence.

§8.08   Defending against an Allegation of Violation of Agency Standards

After answering the threshold question of whether the standard was violated, a defendant faced with use of an agency standard by a plaintiff should ask:

1. Is the plaintiff in the class of persons which the standard was designed to protect

2. Was the harm suffered the type which the standard was designed to prevent

3. Did the violation proximately cause the injury

Analogizing to violation of statute cases, a plaintiff cannot base an action against a railroad which runs a train on a Sunday, in violation of a statute prohibiting such activity, solely on the violation of that statute without other

---

446 SW2d 515 (1969).

[34] 15 USC §§1, 1262(b).

[35] 524 F Supp 1182 (ND Ohio 1981).

[36] 29 USC §651 *et seq.*

[37] 15 USC §§1, 2605.

[38] 524 F Supp 1182, 1189 (ND Ohio 1981).

evidence of negligence.[39] The interest to be protected here is that of the state or the community, not the plaintiff. Likewise, a statute providing that dangerous machinery must be guarded may be interpreted only for the benefit of employees and not others entering the building.[40] However, some statutes, such as those requiring druggists to label poisons, may be so broad that the class of those to be protected extends to anyone likely to be injured by the violation.[41]

The leading case on the requirement that the hazard which occurred be the one the statute was designed to prevent is *Gorris v Scott*,[42] where a statute required that animals shipped by boat be kept in separate pens to avoid the spread of disease. Plaintiff's sheep were swept overboard because they were not in pens, but the court held the violation of statute did not make defendant liable because the damage was of such a nature as was not contemplated at all by the statute, and as to which it was not intended to confer any benefit on plaintiffs.

Even if all of the above criteria are met by the plaintiff, defense counsel can still argue that the agency standard, while appropriate to compel enforcement, is nevertheless inappropriate as a basis to respond to injury in damages. The argument is that the focus of many regulations is to ensure safety, not establish reasonable standards of precaution, so that application of the standard may lead to liability without fault. For example, in *Phillip v Britannia Hygenic Laundry Co*[43], plaintiff argued to the King's Bench that violation of traffic regulations which required that cars be kept in such condition as not to cause, or be likely to cause, danger was negligence per se. The defect in the defendant's lorry was undiscovered, and the axle broke in spite of reasonable precaution. Although enforcement of the safety standards by the administrator of the traffic regulations would have been appropriate, the court refused to hold that violation of the regulation was negligence per se.

A fertile area for defense counsel may be the argument that the defendant had no notice of the standard and therefore should not be held answerable in damages for its violation. Although in most cases the court would find that a defendant knew or should have the known of the regulation, in *Ursbrung v Winter Garden Co*[44], the court held that the defendant was not chargeable with violating an unpublished regulation requiring elevator shaft guards. The de-

---

[39] Tingle v Chicago B & Q RR, 60 Iowa 333, 14 NW 320 (1882); Prosser, Handbook of Law of Torts ¶36, at 193 (4th ed 1971).

[40] Prosser, *supra* note 39, at 194. Gibson v Leonard, 143 Ill 182, 32 NE 182 (1892); Alsaker v De Graff Lumber Co, 234 Minn 280, 48 NW2d 431 (1951); Kelly v Henry Muhs Co, 71 NJL 358, 59 A 23 (1904). *Cf* Davy v Greenlaw, 101 NH 134, 135 A2d 900 (1957)(limiting those entitled to protection); Aldworth v FW Woolworth Co, 295 Mass 344, 3 NE2d 1008 (1936).

[41] Osborne v McMasters, 40 Minn 103, 41 NW 543 (1889).

[42] 9 LR—Ex 125 (1874).

[43] [1923] 2 KB 832.

[44] 183 AD 718, 169 NYS 738 (1st Dept 1918).

fendant was nevertheless found to be negligent for violating other shaft-guarding rules which apparently were published.

From a plaintiff's standpoint, the argument can be made that even justifiable ignorance of a regulation is not necessarily a defense to its use. Plaintiff may still argue that the regulation is evidence of the existence of a potentially dangerous condition and the practicality of using safeguards to reduce the danger.[45]

Another possible defense is an attack on the validity or soundness of the regulation itself. Theories for an attack on an administrative measure as arbitrary and capricious are complicated and beyond the scope of this chapter,[46] but a thorough defense counsel should carefully analyze the availability of such a defense when the procedural or substantive validity of a standard, rule, or regulation appears doubtful.

Another defense raised by defendants in products liability actions has been called the *state of the art* defense. The argument is that the manufacturer used the best technology reasonably available and feasible for use at the time of manufacture. This defense has been codified in many jurisdictions. For instance, an Arizona statute states:

> In any products liability action, a defendant shall not be liable if the defendant proves that any of the following apply: 1) the defect in the product is alleged to result from inadequate design or fabrication; or 2) the plans or designs for the products or the methods and techniques of manufacturing, inspecting, testing and labeling the product conformed with the state of the art at the time the product was first sold by the defendant.[47]

This concept of *state of the art* may also embrace the theory that the government regulations define the state of the art. Colorado has enacted a statute which creates a rebuttable presumption of no negligence if government regulations were complied with, and conversely, a rebuttable presumption of negligence if they were not.

> Presumptions. (1) In any product liability action, it shall be rebuttably presumed that the product which caused the injury, death, or property damage was not defective and that the manufacturer or seller thereof was not negligent if the product:
> (a) Prior to sale by the manufacturer, conformed to the state of the art, as distinguished from industry standards, applicable to such product in existence at the time of sale; or

[45] Morris, *The Role of Administrative Safety Measures In Negligence Actions*, 28 Tex L Rev 143, 151 (1949).

[46] See e.g. Gellhorn, Cases on Administrative Law chs X-XI (2d ed 1947); and Davis, *Non Reviewable Administrative Action*, 96 U Pa L Rev 749 (1948).

[47] Ariz Rev Stat Ann §12-683 (West 1978).

(b) Complied with, at the time of sale by the manufacturer, any applicable code, standard, or regulation adopted or promulgated by the United States or by this state, or by any agency of the United States or of this state.

(2) In like manner, noncompliance with a government code, standard, or regulation existing and in effect at the time of sale of the product by the manufacturer which contributed to the claim or injury shall create a rebuttable presumption that the product was defective or negligently manufactured.

(3) Ten years after a product is first sold for use or consumption, it shall be rebuttably presumed that the product was not defective and that the manufacturer or seller thereof was not negligent and that all warnings and instructions were proper and adequate.[48]

This statute seems by far the most explicit on the issue; however, other states have enacted similar provisions.[49]

§8.09 Compliance with Agency Standards

Traditionally, courts have held that even if a violation of a statute is evidence of negligence, compliance with it is not always due care.[50] For example, a defendant cannot avoid liability by arguing that he or she complied with a statute requiring a hand signal on a left turn, when he or she was otherwise negligent by failing to slow down, to keep a proper lookout, and to proceed with reasonable care.[51] The statutory standard has been held to be a minimum, and the defendant may be negligent by failing to take additional precautions required of a reasonable person. In addition, at least one commentator has argued that safety standards may be less protective of an employee than what a jury might find to be reasonable care for an employer.[52]

The unanimous view, however, seems to be that compliance with agency standards should at least be admitted as evidence of due care,[53] thus shifting

---

[48] Colo Rev Stat §13-21-403 (1977)

[49] NH Rev Stat Ann §507-D:4 (1978); (1979) ND Sess Laws 1075.

[50] Prosser, Handbook of Law of Torts ¶36, at 203 (4th ed 1971), which lists the courts adhering to this proposition.

[51] Curtis v Perry, 171 Wash 542, 18 P2d 840 (1933); cf Peterson v Salt River Project Agricultural Implementation & Power Dist, 96 Ariz 1, 391 P2d 567 (1964)(red flag on end of towed long pole); Caviote v Shen, 116 Conn 569, 165 A 788 (1933)(parking car on highway in a fog with tail light on); Mitchell v Hotel Berry Co, 34 Ohio App 259, 171 NE 39 (1929)(requirements as to hotel exists in case of fire).

[52] Brodeur, *Annals of Industry—Casualties of the Workplace*, New Yorker, Nov 5, 1973, at 92.

[53] See generally Morris, *The Role of Administrative Safety Measures in Negligence Actions*, 28 Tex L Rev 143, 159 (1949), which summarizes the courts which constitute this unanimous viewpoint.

the burden to the plaintiff to prove that the defendant's reliance upon the standard did not constitute due care under the circumstances.

At least one commentator[54] has opined that because the Occupational Safety and Health Act's general duty clause[55] may require more than reasonable conduct,[56] compliance with that general duty clause as a practical matter absolves an employer from liability for negligence. The point made is that an employer would therefore rarely use compliance with the general duty clause as a defense since it would be easier to show simply that he or she exercised reasonable care.

Probably the best judicial discussion of the applicability and effect of compliance with government regulations in toxic tort litigation is the Oklahoma district court's analysis in *Silkwood v Kerr-McGee Corp.*[57] The suit was brought as a personal injury case for damages caused by the escape of plutonium from the Kerr-McGee facility. In that case, the defendant, Kerr-McGee, argued that compliance with *operational regulations* (those relating to the conduct and operation of the facility) was conclusive evidence of nonnegligent conduct and therefore a bar to a claim of ordinary negligence. Alternatively, the defendant argued that substantial compliance with these operational guidelines barred any award of punitive damages. The defendant also argued that if the *exposure limit* regulations (those which set the maximum permissible exposure limits for different workers) were met, a jury could not find actual injury, that even if actual injury occurred within those limits the defendant could not be held liable in damages because federal law permitted the exposure limit, and that punitive damages could not be awarded if the exposure limit was not exceeded.

In rejecting the defendant's argument that compliance was a complete bar to recovery, the district court said:

> Had this Court instructed the jury that substantial compliance with governmental regulations would bar an award of actual damages in the area of nuclear power, the Court would have paved a new road in jurisprudence that heretofore has not existed in any other comparable area of the law. Liability for operators and manufacturers of aircraft represents a situation analogous to that in the instant case. The federal government has occupied the field of regulating aircraft, and no aircraft may fly in this country without a federal certification of its airworthiness.

* * * *

[54] Miller, *The Occupational Safety and Health Act of 1970 and the Law of Torts,* 38 Law & Contemp Probs 42 (Duke Univ 1973).

[55] 29 USC §654(a)(1): "Each employer shall furnish to each of his employees employment and a place of employment which are free from recognized hazards that are causing or are likely to cause death or serious physical harm to his employees."

[56] *See* National Realty & Constr Co v OSHRC, 489 F2d 1257, 1265 n34 (DC Cir 1973). Furthermore, the court there said that "employers have a general duty to do virtually everything possible to prevent and repress hazardous conduct by employees." *Id* 1268.

[57] 485 F Supp 566 (WD Okla 1979), *reversed on other grounds,* 667 F2d 908 (10th Cir 1981), *revd,* __ US __ (Jan 13, 1984).

It is commonly the rule in the field of aviation law that a defendant's complete compliance with governmental safety regulations is only some evidence of the defendant's exercise of reasonable care, but it is not conclusive. Evidence of compliance is therefore admissible for consideration by the jury, but it does not bind the jury to find that a defendant's conduct was reasonable under the circumstances.[58]

Also, analogizing to the drug manufacture and distribution industry, the court said:

> The same principles obtain in the field of drug manufacture and distribution, another field where a governmental agency has promulgated a vast and extensive network of administrative regulations designed to insure public safety. It is typically the rule that compliance with federal laws and regulations concerning a drug does not in itself absolve a manufacturer of liability for injury caused by that drug. *Salmon v. Parke, Davis & Co.,* 520 F.2d 1359 (4th Cir. 1975), citing, 1 Frumer & Friedman, Products Liability, §8.07[1]. A defendant's compliance with these government regulations is admissible before the jury as some evidence of the exercise of reasonable care, but it is not conclusive or binding on the jury. *Brick v. Barnes-Hines Pharmaceutical Co.,* 428 F. Supp. 496, 498 (D.D.C. 1977); *Chambers v. G.D. Searle & Co.,* 441 F. Supp. 377, 383 (D.Md. 1975)(compliance with FDA requirements on required warning not conclusive on adequacy of warning), aff'd, 567 F.2d 269 (4th Cir. 1977); *Gonzales v. Virginia-Carolina Chemical Co.,* 239 F.Supp. 567, 575 (E.D.S.C.1965).
>
> Thus, strict liability may be imposed on a defendant for failure to warn adequately even though full compliance with all government regulations and requirements in production and marketing is demonstrated . . . .[59]

The court followed with a very extensive exposition of the cases and treatises on this subject and concluded with the holding that compliance was also not a bar to imposition of punitive damages. The court said that the existence of wanton conduct depends upon the tortfeasor's mental attitude at the time of the conduct and that a tortfeasor could have that culpable mental attitude despite compliance with government regulations. Using an example of a drug manufacturer who distributed a drug approved for distribution and marketing by the Food and Drug Administration (FDA) despite his or her knowledge that it would cause blindness, and an example of an airplane manufacturer who sold an aircraft certified by the Federal Aviation Administration (FAA) as airworthy despite the manufacturer's knowledge of defects, the court noted that a nuclear licensee who was aware of defects which rendered likely repeated exposures of employees to plutonium might be liable for punitive damages for failure to

---

[58] 485 F Supp at 577-78 (citations omitted).
[59] *Id* 578.

make necessary changes, regardless of whether government regulations required those changes to be made.[60]

§8.10   Summary and Application of Principles

The principles of law applicable to violation of statutes are equally applicable to violation of agency standards, rules, regulations, or orders. In particular, the long-established judicial principle establishing the *reasonable person* standard of conduct in tort cases is applicable. It is important to note, however, that liability is not based on violation of the standard itself but rather upon the theory that the violation is evidence of defendant's failure to meet a proper standard of care. Only a few statutes create a cause of action for violation of the statute, and a plaintiff should be careful to base his or her case on the theory that the violation is simply evidence of negligence.

The cases are in conflict over whether violation of an agency standard is negligence per se, or whether such violation is simply evidence of negligence. When in a jurisdiction in which the rule is unsettled, the safer approach on behalf of a plaintiff is to argue for a jury instruction that such a failure is merely evidence of negligence, since the practical impact upon the jury may be just as great as arguing negligence per se.

A defendant faced with use of an agency standard by a plaintiff should analyze, in addition to whether the standard was violated, whether:

1.   The plaintiff is in the class of persons which the standard was designed to protect

2.   Whether the harm suffered was the type which the standard was designed to prevent

3.   Whether the violation proximately caused the injury.

In addition, affirmative defenses such as inappropriate application of the regulation, no notice of the standard, an attack on the validity of the regulation itself, and the so-called state of the art defense are also available. Finally, while compliance with agency standards is not a complete defense, it can be evidence of due care and is certainly likely to be persuasive with a jury.

---

[60] *Id* 854.

9

Unique Hazardous Waste Issues in the Occupational Setting

Barbara D. Little, Esq.*

---

* Senior Environmental Counsel, Browning Ferris Industries, Inc., Houston, Texas.

§9.01   Introduction

The area of environmental protection in the 1980s has been dominated by laws, regulations, and litigation involving the comprehensive management of hazardous waste, and the response to spill events involving releases of hazardous substances, and concerning remedies for long-term releases of hazardous substances from past disposal and handling of hazardous and toxic substances.

In 1976, Congress enacted the Resource Conservation and Recovery Act (RCRA),[1] and the federal government was authorized for the first time to

---

[1] 42 USC §§6901-6987 (1977 & Supp 1978-1981); Pub L No 94-580 (1978); Pub L

establish a comprehensive program for the *cradle-to-grave* management of hazardous waste. Federal environmental laws had concentrated on regulation of discharges to the air and surface waters, which ironically increased the problem of disposal of hazardous waste from the systems designed to remove pollutants from such discharges, such as biotreaters and flue gas-scrubbing systems.

In order to address both the acute effects of spills of hazardous and toxic substances into the environment and the chronic effects of long-term releases of hazardous substances into the environment from past disposal activities, Congress enacted in 1980 the Comprehensive Environmental Response, Compensation and Liability Act (CERCLA),[2] known widely as *Superfund.* CERCLA created a fund from a tax on petroleum and petrochemical feedstocks to be utilized by the federal government to clean up immediate spills as well as chronic pollution of the environment.[3] The Superfund is discussed more fully in Chapter 10.

In response to these laws and the regulatory schemes engendered thereby, there has been a rapid transformation of the business of waste collection, transportation, and disposal, and the creation of a new business to evaluate and provide remedies for releases of toxic and hazardous materials into the environment. This chapter discusses examples of the unique problems of worker exposure, safety, and protection arising in the context of RCRA and Superfund, in the following areas:

1.   The collection, transportation, and disposal of waste
2.   Response to spill events
3.   Remedial activities at Superfund sites

The chapter also discusses theories of statutory and common law liability relating to:

1.   Remedies available to the plaintiff/employee for actions of the federal government in spill response or Superfund remedial action
2.   Remedies available to the plaintiff/employee against employers and third parties for injuries in the course of transportation, disposal, spill response, or remedial actions for hazardous sites

§9.02   Occupational Safety and Health Administration Regulation of Toxic and Hazardous Substances

The purpose of the Occupational Safety and Health Act (OSH Act)[4] is to

No 96-482 (1980 Amendments); Pub L No 96-463 (Used Oil Recycling Act of 1980, Amendment).

   [2] 42 USC §§9601-9657 (Supp 1981)(originally enacted Pub L No 96-510.

   [3] Hazardous Substance Response Revenue Act of 1980, 26 USC §1 *et seq* (Supp 1981).

   [4] 29 USC §651 *et seq* (originally enacted Pub L No 91-596 (1970).

"assure so far as possible every working man and woman in the Nation safe and healthful working conditions."[5] To implement this primary purpose, the Occupational Safety and Health Administration (OSHA) is authorized to establish health and safety standards which are "reasonably necessary or appropriate to provide safe or healthful environment in places of employment."[6] When mandating the development of industrial safety standards, Congress also recognized the need to address the uniquely pernicious problem of worker exposures to *toxic materials* and *harmful physical agents*. Therefore, §6(b)(5) was enacted to deal with these special risks by establishing standards:

> to the extent feasible, on the basis of the best available evidence, that no employee will suffer material impairment of health or functional capacity even if such employee has regular exposure to the hazard . . . for the period of his working life . . . in addition to the attainment of the highest degree of health and safety protection for the employee, other considerations shall be the latest available scientific data in the field, feasibility of the standards, and the experience gained under this and other health and safety laws.[7]

Although the federal courts have held that no private cause of action under the OSH Act is available to an employee because of an OSH Act violation,[8] such a violation may well support a claim of gross negligence or malfeasance to provide tort remedies in addition to workers' compensation benefits.[9] The OSH Act also provides workers with the ability to make direct complaints to OSHA without reprisal against the employee. Workers are to be provided a copy of occupational safety and health standards, regulations, and requirements applicable to their employment.[10] The employee may request that the National Institute for Occupational Safety and Health (NIOSH) perform a workplace evaluation to see if safety and health hazards exist, and he or she may file safety and health complaints with OSHA.[11] The worker may remain anonymous in making such requests. Workers may not be fired or discriminated against because they have made complaints to their employers, to OSHA or other safety and health agencies, or to their unions regarding working conditions.[12] The employee may refuse to work when confronted with a hazard that is imminently dangerous and may not be fired for such refusal. All of these

---

[5] 29 USC §651(b).
[6] 29 USC §652(8).
[7] 29 USC §655(b)(5).
[8] Rogers v Frito-Lay, 611 F2d 1074 (5th Cir 1980).
[9] See §9.34; ch 8.
[10] 29 USC §657(c).
[11] 29 USC §657(f).
[12] 29 USC §660(c).

provisions become critical in the area of hazardous substance response actions, since, by definition, many such response actions are imminently dangerous.

The occupational safety and health standards for general industry[13] consist of subparts A through Z. Generally speaking, the relevant ones of these subparts address the following categories:

1. Safety provisions applicable to workplaces generally, such as emergency plans, fire protection plans, medical services and first aid, sanitation, accident prevention, ventilation, and noise requirements (subparts E, G, J, K, L, S)

2. Standards applicable to the use of certain equipment and machinery, such as industrial stairs, ladders, man-lifters, personal protective equipment, and hand-powered tools (subparts D, F, I, M, N, O, P)

3. Standards applicable to specific industries (subparts B, Q, R, T)

4. Standards applicable to the handling of hazardous materials (Subpart H)

5. Exposure standards, protective requirements and monitoring requirements for certain listed chemicals, and access to employee exposure and medical records (subparts C and Z)

The focus of this chapter is compliance with the *Subpart Z* standards, so-called because they are contained at Part 1910, subpart Z of title 29 of the Code of Federal Regulations. The attention of OSHA in recent years has been directed to the area of exposure to toxic and hazardous substances, especially in regard to the issue of increased cancer risks due to workplace exposures. Subpart Z imposes on the employer the duties to conduct inspections and investigations, to inform employees, and to keep records. Accurate records must be maintained of employee exposures to potentially toxic materials or harmful physical agents.[14] Employees must have the opportunity to observe and to have access to records of such monitoring.[15] The employer must notify an employee if he or she has been exposed to concentrations at or exceeding levels set by a standard and must inform employees of corrective action being taken.[16]

---

[13] 29 CFR Pt 1910.

[14] 29 USC §657(c)(3).

[15] OSH Act §6(b)(7), 29 USC §655(b)(7). Effective August 21, 1980, each worker (or representative with written consent) may examine and copy an employer's records of exposure to toxic materials, personal medical records, and analyses based on these records. Access must be provided no later than 15 days after a request. Exposure records include environmental and certain biological monitoring information as well as material safety data sheets. 29 CFR §1910.20(a)-(e) & (g)-(f).

[16] 29 CFR §1910.20. Exposure notification requirements are specific to each standard contained in 29 CFR 1910, subpt Z. For instance, if any employee is found to have been exposed at any time to airborne concentrations of asbestos fibers in excess of the exposure limits, he or she must be notified in writing of the exposure as soon as practicable, but no later than five days after the finding. The employee must also be timely notified of the corrective action being taken.

In the manufacturing industry, it is generally feasible to determine with specificity the types of machinery, general working conditions, materials handled, and chemical exposures which are present in a particular work area. For instance, the six high-volume human carcinogens in Table 9-1 are found most commonly in the occupations designated:

Table 9-1

Chemical	Occupations at Risk[17]
Acrylonitrile	Chemical workers and plastic workers
Carbon Tetrachloride	Dry cleaning and machinists
Ethylene Oxide	Hospital workers, laboratory workers, fumigators
Beryllium	Beryllium workers, defense and aerospace industry, nuclear industry
Cadmium	Electrical workers, painters, battery plant and alloy workers
Vinyl Chloride	Plastics industry

The problem of applying various OSHA standards to the industrial waste disposal and cleanup business is the difficulty in determining the types, levels, and lengths of exposure to the various subpart Z chemicals. The difficulty arises because of the numerous chemicals and combinations of chemicals which may be present in particular waste streams for transportation and disposal, in spill events, or at abandoned chemical waste sites. Combinations and the location of chemicals present the dual unknown danger of the chemicals present and the reaction of those chemicals in a particular environment.

The enactment of the Resource Conservation and Recovery Act (RCRA),[18] by requiring a more detailed identification of chemicals present in the waste stream destined for disposal, at least provides a preliminary tool for determining what exposures are present at which times. Similarly, labeling requirements for hazardous materials transportation supplies valuable information for spill response actions. The management problems of providing various worker protection devices and limiting employee exposures when numerous chemical substances are involved pose challenging problems which are discussed in the context of the generation, transportation, and disposal of wastes,

---

[17] P. Cole & M. Goldman, Persons at High Risk of Cancer (J. Fraumeni ed 1975); US Dept of Health, Education & Welfare, Occupational Diseases (1977); Toxicology (I. Casarett & J. Douall eds 1975): G. Waldbott, Health Effects of Environmental Pollutants (1978); International Agency for Research on Cancer, Chemicals and Industrial Processes Associated with Cancer in Humans (Supp to vols 1-20 1979).

[18] 42 USC §§6901-6987.

response to emergency spill events, and Superfund[19] cleanup response actions. See §§9.16-9.31.

§9.03 Resource Conservation and Recovery Act and Department of Transportation Preemption of Occupational Safety and Health Administration Requirements

Whenever another regulatory agency exercises plenary authority over an industry, the issue arises whether the applicability of Occupational Safety and Health Administration (OSHA) regulations is preempted by such plenary regulatory scheme. Section 4(b)(1) of the Occupational Safety and Health Act (OSH Act)[20] provides in pertinent part that: "Nothing in this Act shall apply to working conditions of employees with respect to which other Federal agencies . . . exercise statutory authority to prescribe or enforce standards or regulations affecting occupational safety or health."[21] The general principle underlying this provision of the OSH Act is that the exemption is activated by statutory authority in another agency and an actual exercise of such authority by the agency.[22] The exemption does not strip OSHA of its regulatory authority where such other agency has regulatory authority but has not implemented the authority.[23] The preemptive authority has been greatly narrowed by subsequent decisions so that unless a regulatory agency has acted to regulate a specific working condition, OSHA rules still apply. A given working condition has been defined in terms of a particular "hazard" or "surrounding."[24]

Since the primary focus of the Resource Conservation and Recovery Act (RCRA)[25] and Department of Transportation (DOT) regulations[26] governing the storage, treatment, disposal, and transportation of hazardous wastes is the protection of the public health and welfare and the environment rather than specific employee protection, few, if any, of the OSHA standards would be preempted. The DOT requirements for hours of service discussed in §9.11 and

---

[19] Comprehensive Environmental Response, Compensation and Liability Act, 42 USC §§9601-9657.

[20] 29 USC §651 *et seq.*

[21] 29 USC §653(b)(1).

[22] Southern Pac Transp Co v Usery, 539 F2d 386, 389 (5th Cir 1976).

[23] Southern Ry v OSHRC, 539 F2d 335, 336 (4th Cir), *cert denied,* 429 US 999 (1976).

[24] *Id* 391; Columbia Gas, Inc v Marshall, 636 F2d 913 (3d Cir 1980); PBR Inc v Secretary of Labor, 643 F2d 890 (1st Cir 1981).

[25] 42 USC §§6901-6987.

[26] Motor Carrier Safety Regulations, 49 CFR pts 300-397, apply generally to the safety of employee drivers while on the highway. The Hazardous Materials Regulations, 49 CFR pts 106, 107, 171-179, and 397, provide detailed identification requirements for hazardous substances being transported by description on shipping papers and requirements for marking, labeling, and placarding of wastes as to their hazardous properties.

other *on highway* operating requirements would be an example of such non preemptive regulations. There is nothing in the RCRA or DOT regulations that specifically establishes exposure limits to certain chemicals, as subpart Z of the OSHA regulations[27] requires. So, under the standard of regulation of a specific *hazard* in a workplace, the subpart Z standards would clearly be applicable to the transportation, storage, treatment, and disposal of hazardous waste.

§9.04   Worker Protection in the Management of Hazardous Wastes

The Resource Conservation and Recovery Act (RCRA)[28] is directed toward protection of the general public health and environment rather than specifically toward worker protection, but certain provisions of RCRA have an impact on worker protection. Pursuant to the RCRA regulations,[29] the first duty of characterizing a waste stream belongs to the generator of the waste. The first step is to determine whether the material in question is a *solid waste*—that is, whether it is garbage, refuse, or sludge, or other waste material which may be or will be discarded.[30] The second step is to determine whether the waste will be designated as a *hazardous waste.* It can exhibit one of four characteristics— ignitability, corrosivity, reactivity, or extraction procedure toxicity[31] (certain metals, pesticides)—or it can be specifically listed in any one of three lists— hazardous wastes from nonspecific sources, hazardous wastes from specific sources, and discarded commercial products from manufacturing chemical intermediates and their off-specification species.[32]

---

[27] 29 CFR pt 1910, subpt Z. See **§9.02.**

[28] 42 USC §§6901-6987.

[29] The first substantial regulations implementing RCRA were promulgated May 19, 1980, 45 Fed Reg 33066-33588, in which the Environmental Protection Agency (EPA) established hazardous waste identification procedures, and basic operating requirements for generators, transporters, and disposers of hazardous wastes. Since the May 19, 1980, promulgation, there have been hundreds of amendments and additions to these basic regulations. The comprehensive design, operating, and permit requirements for land disposal facilities were promulgated July 26, 1982, 47 Fed Reg 32274-32386. Certain useful references to the major RCRA regulations between May 19, 1980, and July 26, 1982, are contained at 47 Fed Reg 32276-77.

[30] 40 CFR §262.11, 45 Fed Reg 33142 (May 19, 1980).

[31] 40 CFR §§261.21-.24, 47 Fed Reg 33121-22 (Aug 2, 1982).

[32] 40 CFR §§261.30-.33; 47 Fed Reg 33122-27 (Aug 2, 1982).

§9.05 —Resource Conservation and Recovery Act Waste Characterization: The Need to Quantify Subpart Z Substances

The manifest system imposed by subpart B of part 262 of the Resource Conservation and Recovery Act (RCRA)[33] regulations requires that the generator make the basic identification (see **§9.04**) of the type of waste on the manifest.[34] However, the information that is required by the regulations to be included on the manifest[35] is generally not sufficient to characterize the waste adequately in terms of chemical constituents to assure that persons handling the wastes will not be exposed to levels in violation of the Occupational Safety and Health Administration (OSHA)[36] subpart Z[37] standards. Therefore, the prudent waste disposer, prior to accepting a contract for disposal of a waste stream, should require data from the generator which adequately characterise such waste stream, as well as a representative sample of the waste stream for an independent analysis by the disposal company (or an outside analytical laboratory).

This analysis should not only determine the proper methods for handling, detoxifying, solidifying, disposing, and otherwise rendering the waste less hazardous, but the procedure should also provide sufficient information regarding the characteristics of the waste to determine the handling procedures and protective equipment necessary to assure that workers transporting and disposing of the waste will be properly protected pursuant to OSHA standards. Further, a chemical analysis of the waste stream must be detailed enough to ascertain the presence of any materials listed in Table Z-1, Z-2, or Z-3 of the OSHA Subpart Z regulations to extrapolate exposure risk monitoring requirements, both environmental monitoring and personnel monitoring, and appropriate warnings and labeling. The extrapolation of exposure risks is a complicated process because of the many variables involved. The presence of a certain subpart Z substance would have to be calculated in a range of values, with exposure levels based on the maximum value in the range, since waste streams will not be totally consistent. Additionally, vapor pressures, handling techniques, temperature, humidity, and other specific site factors will have to

---

[33] 42 USC §§6901-6987.

[34] 40 CFR §262.20; 47 Fed Reg 33143 (Aug 2, 1982).

[35] The basic manifest requirements are general. 40 CFR §262.21 requires as to the description of the wastes:

    1. The description of the waste(s) (e.g., proper shipping name, etc.) required by regulations of the Department of Transportation in 49 CFR §§172.101, .202 and .203

    2. The total quantity of each hazardous waste by units of weight or volume, and the type and number of containers as loaded into or onto the transport vehicle

These requirements are extremely general and would not necessarily require the identification of even the critical 23 subpt Z substances.

[36] 29 USC §651 *et seq.*

[37] 29 CFR pt 1910, subpt Z, see **§9.02.**

be evaluated and levels calculated to take into account variable environmental conditions.

As stated, the initial waste characterization is done on a sample provided by the generator, which is supposed to be representative of the waste, and it is the generator's duty to provide a correct representative sample and assure that the entire waste stream will basically conform to the sample. However, despite contractual obligations which can put the burden of any nonconformity back onto the generator, the prudent disposer must also have some method of spot checking the waste as it comes into the gate of the facility to assure that it conforms to the original waste characterization data sheet.

§9.06   —Exclusions from Resource Conservation and Recovery Act Which Increase Risks of Worker Exposure to Hazardous Substances

The Resource Conservation and Recovery Act (RCRA)[38] provides certain specific exclusions from the definition of *solid waste*[39] and from the definition of *hazardous waste*[40] which pose problems for the waste collection, transportation, and disposal industry in general. Excluded from the definition of *solid waste* are:

> domestic sewage, any mixture of domestic sewage and other waste that passes through a sewer system to a publicly-owned treatment works for treatment, industrial wastewater discharges that are point source discharges subject to regulation under Section 402 of the Clean Water Act, irrigation return flows, and source, special nuclear or by-product material as defined by the Atomic Energy Act of 1984, as amended.[41]

The exclusion from the definition of *solid waste* which causes the greatest problem is the exclusion for wastes which are mixed with domestic sewage and which pass through a sewer system to a publicly owned treatment works (POTW). Because they are unregulated, that is, excluded from the definition of solid waste, materials such as chlorinated hydrocarbons may be disposed of through floor drains into a sewer system that eventually goes to a POTW.

There is no federal regulatory requirement, although in some instances the

---

[38] 42 USC §§6901-6987.

[39] 40 CFR §261.4(a), 45 Fed Reg 33120 (May 19, 1980); major exclusions are domestic wastes, wastes to publicly owned treatment works, and industrial wastewater discharges subject to regulation under §402 of the Clean Water Act, 33 USC §§1251-1376.

[40] 40 CFR §261.4(b), 45 Fed Reg 33120 (May 19, 1980); major exclusions are for agricultural activities, mining overburden when returned to the mine site, flyash waste, and drilling fluids and other wastes associated with production of crude oil, natural gas, or geothermal energy.

[41] 40 CFR §261.4(b), 45 Fed Reg 33120 (May 19, 1980).

POTW has contract requirements, for the industrial user to fully characterize the nature or quantity of such waste streams, since the pretreatment regulations pursuant to the Clean Water Act[42] require only the evaluation of the toxic pollutants,[43] and most of the specific requirements are not yet effective.[44] This loophole in the law presents dangers to those persons operating POTWs, since the POTW does not have the adequate data to completely evaluate the risk of exposure to its employees. The industries utilizing POTWs for their waste streams which contain hazardous or toxic chemicals should be aware of their exposure to lawsuits brought by employees of the POTW who have been damaged by chemical substances present in the industrial waste streams. The employee of the POTW may successfully claim that the industrial POTW user was negligent in failing to inform the POTW of the presence of certain chemicals and the risks posed thereby. Although the employee is usually limited in his or her remedy against the POTW to a workers' compensation claim, in most states the worker could bring a civil suit for negligence against the industrial user on a theory of negligent failure to warn or a theory of strict liability.[45]

Within the definition of *hazardous waste,* certain wastes are excluded from the definition by statute—i.e., fly ash waste, bottom ash wastes, and other wastes generated primarily from the combustion of coal or other fossil fuels; any solid waste associated with the exploration, development, or production of crude oil, natural gas, and geothermal energy; any solid waste from the extraction, beneficiation, and processing of ores and minerals; and cement kiln dust waste.[46] Since these materials are outside of the regulatory scheme, there is no force of law requiring generators of these materials to characterize them adequately prior to disposal. Thus, persons employed in the transportation of waste, at the hazardous waste facilities, and at sanitary landfulls may be exposed to lead, benzene, and even radioactive materials commonly present in this type of waste.

The RCRA regulatory exclusion which presents the most immediate danger to persons involved in the collection and disposal of waste is the *small quantity*

---

[42] 33 USC §1317.

[43] 33 USC §1317(a)(1), 129 substances.

[44] On June 26, 1978, the Environmental Protection Agency (EPA) promulgated the General Pretreatment Regulations establishing general mechanisms for controlling introduction of wastes into POTWs. 43 Fed Reg 27736-27773. Following promulgation, industry and environmental groups challenged the regulations, and on January 28, 1981, a settlement agreement was entered between industry groups and the EPA. After general postponements of the original effective date of March 13, 1981, and a lawsuit by environmental groups challenging the delays, only portions of the general pretreatment regulations were made effective on January 31, 1982. 47 Fed Reg 4518. However, the critical provisions relating to pass-through of toxic pollutants (40 CFR §403.3(i)), the definition of *interference,* the §403.3(n) definition of *pass-through,* and §403.7, revision of categorical pretreatment standards to reflect POTW removal of toxic pollutants, were indefinitely postponed. Additionally, most of the specific pretreatment standards for 21 classes of industries, iron and steel, organic chemicals, etc. are not yet effective.

[45] See §9.34.

[46] 42 USC §6921.

generator exemption. Pertinent provisions of the RCRA regulations exempt from control those generators who produce less than 1,000 kilograms of hazardous waste monthly, a bit more than one ton a month.[47] Since such generators are not required by regulation either to segregate or to identify such wastes, the present lack of regulation of small quantities of hazardous waste exposes refuse haulers and operators of resource recovery facilities and sanitary landfills to unnecessary and sometimes catastrophic risks. Unfortunately it is not uncommon for receptacles designated by the disposal company for only nonhazardous waste to contain quantities of a reactive, ignitable, or otherwise toxic waste that pose very grave and unforeseeable dangers to persons engaged in the waste hauling and disposal industry. General safety factors in handling waste can go only so far to protect workers when risks are unknowable and unforeseeable. Contractual relationships with generators, although they may exclude generators from disposing any quantities of hazardous waste commingled with sanitary wastes, are not in themselves sufficient to prevent the initial harm to the worker, although they may provide some indemnity to the disposal company for the harm caused by the presence of such hazardous waste.

The RCRA reauthorization bills[48] pending in Congress present as a major issue the possible regulation of small quantities of hazardous waste at least to require all businesses and industries which produce hazardous waste to notify waste transporters of the general characteristics—ignitability, reactivity, corrosivity, toxicity—of their waste streams. Since the generator could be liable in actions brought by injured employees of waste companies for negligent failure to warn, the generating industry should not be opposed to at least notifying the transporter and disposer of the presence of a hazardous waste in any quantity.

§9.07   Department of Transportation Requirements Relating to Employee Protection

The Department of Transportation hazardous materials regulations[49] provide some closure of the small quantity Resource Conservation and Recovery Act (RCRA)[50] regulatory loophole discussed in **§9.06,** since their coverage is expansive, requiring the identification, labeling, and marking of hazardous materials which include the class of hazardous wastes and do not specifically provide an exemption for small quantities.

---

[47] 40 CFR §261.5.

[48] Numerous bills have been introduced to amend RCRA. The major ones are: HR 2867 (Florio-D, NJ); HR 2478 (Florio-D, NJ & Dingell-D Mich); HR 1700 (Breaux-D, La); HR 2407 (Rinaldo-R, NJ); HR 1670 (Subquist-R, Tenn); S 1363 (Hart-D, Colo); S 208 (Mikulski-D, Md).

[49] 48 CFR pts 106, 107, 171-179, & 397.

[50] 42 USC §§6901-6987.

§9.08 —Motor Carrier Safety Regulations and Hazardous Material Regulations

There are two basic sets of regulations which cover the transportation of hazardous materials and wastes. The Motor Carrier Act of 1935[51] originally made it the duty of the Interstate Commerce Commission (ICC) to exercise authority over common and contract carriers. The Bureau of Motor Carrier Safety was established within the ICC. The first Motor Carrier Safety Regulations were effective in 1937.[52] Then in 1966, the Department of Transportation Act[53] established the Department of Transportation (DOT) and transferred all safety functions (railroad, motor carrier, and hazardous materials) of the ICC to the new DOT. The Federal Highway Administration was given motor carrier safety responsibilities. The Transportation Safety Act of 1974[54] centralized in the DOT authority to promulgate and enforce hazardous materials regulations for all modes of transportation. The DOT now has the consolidated authority to establish safety requirements for all motor carriers and motor vehicles, as well as establishing any safety aspect of labeling, marking, placarding, and routing of hazardous materials.

Thus, the federal Motor Carrier Safety Regulations[55] apply generally to the safety of workers while on the highways. The regulations are extremely detailed and therefore, as to on-the-road operation, supercede Occupational Safety and Health Administration (OSHA) requirements under the principle of preemption discussed in §9.03. The Hazardous Materials Regulations[56] provide detailed identification requirements for hazardous substances in materials being transported, by requiring description on shipping papers and marking, labeling, and placarding of wastes as to their hazardous properties— explosive, flammable, poisonous, organic peroxide, radioactive, corrosive, etc. Generally, the Motor Carrier Safety Regulations are more attuned to the safety and qualification of the employee driver, while the Hazardous Materials Regulations relate to proper identification and labeling, proper containers, and proper carriage of hazardous materials.

§9.09 —Application of Motor Carrier Safety Regulations

As stated in §9.03, the primary focus of the Department of Transportation (DOT) regulations is the protection of the public health and welfare and the environment rather than specific employee protection; however, many of the requirements do incidentally provide worker safety and health protection. The

---

[51] 49 USC §305.

[52] 49 CFR pts 300-397.

[53] 49 USC §§1234-1235.

[54] 49 USC §1471 *et seq.*

[55] 49 CFR pts 300-397.

[56] *Id* pts 106, 107, 171-179, & 397.

Motor Carrier Safety Regulations (MCSR)[57] impose operating and safety practices by which companies engaged in waste transportation must abide. While Occupational Safety and Health Administration (OSHA) regulations do apply to the motor carrier industry, they are applicable only to off-highway operations because of the operation of §4(b)(1) of the Occupational Safety and Health Act (OSH Act),[58] and the MCSR apply while the vehicle is on the highway.

The requirements of the MCSR place responsibilities for compliance with the regulations on both the employee driver and the company. Where the employee driver is charged with compliance with the requirement, the regulations make the company responsible for requiring driver compliance.

> Whereas in Parts 390-397 of the subchapter a duty is prescribed for a driver where a prohibition is imposed upon him, it shall be the duty of the motor carrier to require observance of such prescription or prohibition; and, if the motor carrier is himself a driver, he shall likewise be bound thereby.[59]

§9.10 —Medical History and Monitoring of Employees

The first step in employee driver protection is the qualification of the driver. Part 391 of the Motor Carrier Safety Regulations (MCSR)[60] requires specific investigation and inquiries in the employment applications and qualification tests as well as physical examinations prior to employment. The provisions of §391.41 relating to physical qualifications for drivers, although designed primarily to assure the physical ability and competence of the driver, are also important factors relating to the exposure to certain chemicals. In addition to the prescribed tests of §391.43 for the medical examination of the employee, prior to employing an individual in a hazardous waste transportation capacity, a complete epidemiological and toxicological work-up should be done to be able to detect any changes in the presence of certain chemicals in the blood level, urine, tissues, chromosone structures, etc., which could indicate past damage due to exposure to chemicals. The MCSR require specific findings for blood pressure, neurological examinations, and urinalysis and neurological tests which could be relatively easily expanded to provide background data on the condition of the worker. From a legal viewpoint, as well as protection for the worker, the background data is essential to the employer who may be faced with future lawsuits regarding alleged chemical exposures. Background data increase the employer's ability to prove that the worker's illness or injury was

---

[57] 49 CFR pts 300-397.
[58] 29 USC §154(b)(1).
[59] 49 CFR §§390-392.
[60] 49 CFR pts 300-397.

due to a preexisting condition. The MCSR require medical examinations every 24 months, which is also a useful period to review the worker's condition for any possible exposure effects.

Sections 392.3, 392.4, and 392.5 of the MCSR detail specific conditions under which a driver is prohibited from operating a vehicle and the company is prohibited from requiring or permitting a driver to operate such vehicle:

1. When the driver's ability or alertness is impaired or likely to be impaired due to fatigue, illness, or other causes

2. When driver possesses, is under the influence of, or is using a narcotic, amphetamine, or other dangerous substance

3. If a driver consumes or is under the influence of an intoxicating beverage within four hours before going on duty or is in the possession of or consumes an intoxicating beverage while on duty.

§9.11 —Motor Carrier Safety: Hours of Service Regulations

Some of the more complex and most often violated of the Motor Carrier Safety Regulations (MCSR)[61] are those that deal with hours of service. Part 395 of the regulations imposes three basic limitations—the 10-hours driving time rule; the 15-hours on-duty/driving time rule; and the 60 or 70 maximum hours service rule. Again, the duty to comply with these regulations falls on the company to direct their employees properly. The most frequent types of MCSR citations and fines are imposed for violation of the Part 395 hours of service requirements. The regulations allow a maximum of 10 hours of driving, after which a driver must have at least 8 consecutive hours off-duty before he or she can drive again.[62]

1. A maximum on-duty period of 15 hours is allowed, after which a driver must have at least 8 consecutive hours of rest before he or she can again drive.[63] This rule does not conflict with the 10-hour driving rule as it applies to the total time on duty. Regardless of whether he or she has been driving or not, once a driver has been on duty 15 hours without rest, he or she cannot drive again until he or she has had 8 hours off-duty

2   The drivers are restricted to 60 hours on-duty in any 7 consecutive days, or if working every day in the week, a maximum 70 hours on-duty in any 8 consecutive days

In order to enforce these regulations, the MCSR require the keeping of a driver's daily log.

---

[61] 49 CFR pts 300-397.

[62] *Id* §395.3(a)

[63] *Id.*

§9.12 —Protection and Safety Equipment

The Motor Carrier Safety Regulations (MCSR)[64] further detail maintenance standards for equipment and carrying of emergency equipment, including employee protection safety devices. The MCSR prescribe different safety equipment for the carriage of various substances, but transporters of hazardous wastes should carry, at a minimum, personal protection kits for each individual in the truck, hard hat, monogoggles (regulation safety glasses), face shields, rubber boots, slicker suits and gloves, full face respirators with organic/acid vapor canisters, industrial-type first aid kit, two sets of triangular load reflectors, safety road flares, round point shovels, flashlights, lanterns, and ballines (to rope off area), Ph paper, 1-14 range, dry chemical fire extinguisher, explosimeter (testing instrument regarding explosiveness), Scott Air Pack for each employee, organic absorbant, a copy of *Fire Protection Guide on Hazardous Materials,* and a copy of *Pocket Guide to Chemical Hazards.*

§9.13 Overlapping Authority of the Environmental Protection Agency and the Department of Transportation

Both the Environmental Protection Agency (EPA) and the Department of Transportation (DOT) have the authority to regulate the transportation of hazardous wastes. The Resource Conservation and Recovery Act (RCRA)[65] requires that the two agencies coordinate their regulatory programs to preclude potential conflict between them.[66] Therefore, the EPA's May 19, 1980, hazardous waste transporter regulations[67] and the DOT's May 22, 1980, hazardous waste transporter regulations[68] cross-refer to each other as to marking, labeling, and placarding requirements which are essential for identification of the wastes and to provide notification to all persons of the basic characteristics of the waste being transported. There is also a Memorandum of Understanding between the DOT and the EPA (June 29, 1980) which sets forth the agencies' respective enforcement responsibilities.

One area in which the duplicative requirements of the EPA and the DOT has created some problem is that the regulatory scope of the DOT's requirements is more comprehensive than that of the EPA. The DOT broadly regulates the transportation of hazardous materials which include all product materials as well as *wastes* which are regulated under RCRA. Additionally, a waste substance may be listed as a *hazardous material* under the DOT regulations and may not be listed as a *hazardous waste* under the EPA regulations. A primary example of

---

[64] 49 CFR pts 300-397.
[65] 42 USC §§6901-6987.
[66] 42 USC §6905.
[67] 40 CFR §26310 (Note).
[68] 49 CFR §171.3.

this anomaly is the *small quantity* hazardous waste exemptions of the RCRA regulations, discussed in **§9.06.**

The issue is whether hazardous waste which is exempted as a small quantity pursuant to 40 CFR §261.5 is also exempted from the DOT requirements. The definition of *hazardous waste* at 49 CFR §171 of the DOT regulations does not conflict in that the definition includes "any material that is subject to the hazardous waste manifest requirements of the EPA specified in 40 CFR Part 262," which includes the small quantity exemption. Although this definition of *waste* is consistent, the material is still a *hazardous material* or *hazardous substance* pursuant to the DOT definitions. The transporter must consult the DOT tables (discussed in **§9.14**) and determine the hazard class of the material and then determine what, if any, amounts are exempted by the DOT, and what, if any, packaging requirements are applicable. The exempted reportable quantities (RQ) of a hazardous substance under the DOT regulations differ from the exempted small quantity amounts under RCRA.

§9.14   —Use of Department of Transportation Hazardous Materials Tables

The Department of Transportation (DOT) Hazardous Materials Tables[69] are essential to the task of determining the types of materials to which an employee may be exposed. Each person who offers a hazardous material for transportation and each carrier who transports such material has the responsibility of assuming that each substance listed in the tables which is present in the shipment is correctly identified, and if a reportable quantity—i.e., the quantity of which a spill must be reported—is established for the material, the material must be so marked. The Hazardous Materials Table includes all of the hazardous wastes listed pursuant to the Resource Conservation and Recovery Act (RCRA)[70] as well as all of the hazardous substances listed pursuant to the Comprehensive Environmental Response, Compensation and Liability Act (CERCLA),[71] for a total of approximately 2,400 different hazardous materials. The requirement to identify these materials and quantities of such materials provides a better basis than the RCRA manifest, discussed in **§9.05,** for determining concentrations of a particular subpart Z[72] substance.

Since pursuant to DOT's regulations the shipper (i.e., generator) has the responsibility to mark, label, and package properly hazardous materials for transportation, it is important that the generator not rely on the RCRA hazardous waste exemption discussed in **§9.06.** If employees of the waste transportation or disposal company or other third parties are damaged, violation of the DOT requirement could be deemed to be negligence per se.

---

[69] 49 CFR pt 172.

[70] 42 USC §§6901-6987.

[71] *Id* §§9601-9657, also known as *Superfund.*

[72] 29 CFR pt 1910, subpt Z. See **§9.02.**

244 HAZARDOUS WASTE ISSUES

In contracts for transportation of wastes, the transporter should require that the generator warrant that the wastes which are hazardous wastes, hazardous materials, or hazardous substances meet all Environmental Protection Agency (EPA) manifest requirements as well as DOT container, labeling, marking, and placarding requirements, not only for the legal purpose of having recourse against the generator, but to assure sufficient information to discharge the transporter's duty to provide proper notification to and protection for the employees and to respond properly in the event of a spill of the transported material.

§9.15 —Resource Conservation and Recovery Act Transportation/Regulations: Mixing of Hazardous Wastes

The Resource Conservation and Recovery Act (RCRA)[73] regulations address one problem which is common in the transport of waste which affects the safety of the worker—the mixing of hazardous waste loads by containerization. Often, waste bulk loads are consolidated at transfer stations into larger bulk loads for economic reasons. This practice can present a problem if the transporter does not properly test waste before mixing or does not characterize such wastes after consolidation. Reactions of chemical substances may create exposures to new chemicals not present in any of the original waste streams which were consolidated.

The RCRA transporter regulations[74] subject a transporter to all the requirements applicable to generators if the transporter mixes hazardous wastes with other hazardous wastes or with nonhazardous wastes. The transporter then is obligated to characterize the waste, manifest the waste, and assume full responsibility as the generator of the waste. Imposing the responsibility as generator discourages the practice of consolidating waste streams.

§9.16 Resource Conservation and Recovery Act Requirements Relating to Employee Protection during Waste Disposal

Although there are various methodologies for storing, treating, and ultimate disposal of wastes—incineration, deep-well injection, landfilling—certain Resource Conservation and Recovery Act (RCRA)[75] operating requirements which relate to worker protection are applicable to all types of hazardous waste management.

---

[73] 42 USC §§6901-6987.
[74] 40 CFR §263.10.
[75] 42 USC §§6901-6987.

§9.17 —Waste Analysis Plans

The operating requirements of the Resource Conservation and Recovery Act (RCRA)[76] regulations applicable to hazardous waste storage, treatment, and disposal facilities requiring waste analysis plans provide the basic structure of assuring conformity of characterization of a particular waste stream. Analysis of a representative sample of a waste is required prior to acceptance.[77] Although, pursuant to §262.11 of the RCRA regulations applicable to generators, it is the generator's responsibility to characterize the waste stream, if the generator does not supply adequate information, and the owner/operator of a hazardous waste management facility chooses to accept a hazardous waste, then the owner/operator is responsible for obtaining the information pursuant to §265.13(2).

Further, after the intial analysis of a waste stream, the analysis must be repeated as necessary to insure accuracy. At the minimum:

1. Analysis must be repeated if the owner/operator is notified or has reason to believe that the process or operation generating the hazardous wastes has changed

2. The owner/operator must inspect, and, if necessary, analyze each hazardous waste shipment received at the facility to determine whether it matches the identity of the waste specified on the accompanying manifest or shipping paper and full analysis must be performed if a discrepancy in kind (rather than volume) is found

3. The owner/operator must have a written waste analysis plan. At a minimum, the plan must specify the limits for which each hazardous waste stream received at the facility is to be analyzed and the rationale supporting the selection of such limits. The plan must also specify test methods, sampling methods, and frequency of analyses

Although there are no RCRA requirements, the waste analysis plan should also include the analyses for the subpart Z[78] chemicals originally identified in the waste characterization analysis, especially if the concentration of such chemicals may vary sufficiently to affect exposure levels. The specific waste analysis plan required by RCRA regulations[79] should be expanded to include the requisite analysis for the subpart Z chemicals, and both types of analyses should be readily available.

It is essential that specific procedures be followed in handling wastes. Specific procedures should be a part of the written waste analysis plan, and all employees at the hazardous waste management facility involved in the receipt of wastes should be carefully trained in such procedures.

---

[76] 42 USC §§6901-6987.
[77] 40 CFR §265.13.
[78] 29 CFR pt 1910, subpt Z. See **§9.02.**
[79] 40 CFR §265.13.

The transport vehicle should be initially stopped at the gate of the facility to assure that the driver has the proper manifest form and Department of Transportation (DOT) shipping papers and to verify that the site is correctly identified as the shipment destination. If the site is not identified as the shipment destination, or if the driver cannot furnish a manifest and DOT shipping papers, the shipment should not be admitted to the site. In addition to the liability pursuant to RCRA for acceptance of nonmanifested wastes,[80] receipt into the facility of unidentified wastes creates the risk of unknown exposures.

Preparation for receipt of wastes during a particular day should be made as much in advance as possible. Since there must be prior analysis of a representative sample of the waste stream prior to acceptance for disposal, the facility should have a complete characterization of the waste and the principal subpart Z constituents contained in the waste well in advance of the arrival of the shipment at the facility. There should be a receipt schedule for the waste streams detailing as precisely as possible the type of wastes, their quantity, and the general time of expected arrival. Shipments of waste should be scheduled, insofar as possible, to allow necessary changes in protective equipment and monitoring devices.

If the manifest and shipping papers are in order, the vehicle must still be checked to verify that the waste conforms to the waste characterization originally supplied by the generator. This process should take place in a segregated area accessible to the authorized technical personnel and situated so that if a spill occurs, the spill may be contained. The authorized technical personnel should thoroughly check the generator and transporter portions of the manifest for completeness, content, and consistency; then they should verify that the following records exist for a shipment:

1. The Waste Characterization Data Sheet which was prepared for that waste stream on the representative sample of the waste stream prior to the agreement with the generator to accept the waste

2. The laboratory pretreatment and disposal recommendation for the waste

3. The established work practice, personal protective equipment, warning signs, and environmental and personal monitoring required by Subpart Z standards for the waste stream

All persons who will be handling the wastes should be required to read the manifest and shipping papers and acknowledge that they understand the type of materials present in the waste stream, the proper techniques for handling and disposal, and the proper protective equipment and practices to be utilized for the waste. This method of providing specific notification and instruction not only complies with Occupational Safety and Health Administration

---

[80] 42 USC §6925.

(OSHA) requirements to notify and instruct but also provides excellent defenses to a suit for failure to warn of hazards or to supervise properly.

The site technical personnel should obtain a representative sample of the waste shipment for on-site analysis to determine that the material contained in the truck conforms with the waste described on the Waste Characterization Data Sheet. The proper confirmatory test should include ignitability, water solubility, corrosivity, radioactivity, acid compatibility, alkali compatibility, free liquidity, and reactivity. Since the technical personnel verifying the waste stream are the first to come into contact with the waste stream, such personnel should be equipped with appropriate personal protective equipment and monitoring devices during the sampling and analysis of the waste, as a means of testing to determine if the exposure levels to the subpart Z materials correspond with the determination made on the initial sample of the waste.

§9.18 —Inspection Requirements

The general inspection requirements applicable to hazardous waste facilities require frequent inspections for malfunction, deterioration of systems, and discharges.[81] A written schedule must be developed for inspecting monitoring equipment, security devices, and operating or structural equipment. Areas subject to spills, such as loading and unloading areas, must be inspected daily when in use. Container storage areas must be inspected at least weekly for leaks or evidence of corrosion.[82] Diked areas and vegetation around the dikes must be inspected at least weekly to detect leaks or deterioration.[83] These periodic inspections, besides preventing releases to the environment, protect against unforeseen exposures to workers. In conducting inspections, workers should be equipped with accessible protective clothing and respirators in the event a spill or leak is discovered.

§9.19 —Personnel Training

The Resource Conservation and Recovery Act (RCRA)[84] provides detailed requirements for personnel training designed to ensure that facility personnel are able to respond effectively to emergencies by familiarity with emergency procedures, equipment, and systems. By May 19, 1981, all employees at hazardous waste facilities were to have completed a training program. New employees or employees assigned to a new facility or a new position at a facility must complete training within six months. Such employees must not work in unsupervised positions until they have completed training. Annual reviews of training programs are required. The facility must maintain records of training

---

[81] 40 CFR §265.15.
[82] *Id* §265.164.
[83] *Id* §265.226.
[84] 42 USC §§6901-6987.

and job experience of current personnel until closure of the facility. Training records on former employees must be kept for at least three years from the date the employee last worked at the facility.[85]

These training programs are essential from a legal viewpoint since they could be key facors in proving or disproving that an employee had adequate training to perform his or her duties safely and that he or she was or was not informed adequately of the nature of the materials to which he or she had potential exposure, which is required under various state worker right-to-know laws as well as Occupational Safety and Health Administration (OSHA) subpart Z regulations.[86]

§9.20 —Ignitable, Reactive, or Incompatible Waste

Special requirements are applicable to the handling of ignitable, reactive, and incompatible wastes.[87] During the handling of ignitable or reactive wastes, smoking and open flames must be confined to specially designated locations. *No Smoking* signs must be conspicuously placed wherever there is a hazard from ignitable or reactive wastes. The treatment, storage, and disposal of ignitable or reactive wastes and the mixture or commingling of incompatible wastes must be conducted so that they do not:

1.　Generate extreme heat, pressure, fire, or an explosive or violent reaction

2.　Produce uncontrolled toxic waste, fumes, mists, or gases in sufficient quantities to threaten human health

3.　Produce uncontrolled flammable fumes or gases in sufficient quantities to pose a risk of fire or explosion

4.　Through other like means threaten human health or the environment

An interesting legal issue is whether the handling of a waste material in a manner so that the subpart Z[88] maximum exposure limit for a chemical substance is exceeded would constitute violation of this general Resource Conser-

---

[85] 40 CFR §265.16(e).

[86] 29 CFR pt 1910, subpt Z. See **§9.02.** The issue of right-to-know laws at both the worker and public level promises to be a major issue in state and local politics. The laws require detailed identification and explanation of chemical identities of substances to which workers are exposed in order to protect workers from exposures to chemicals with potential chronic health hazards. The laws are being spawned because of the position of worker groups that the OSHA standards are not adequate and not sufficiently enforced to provide necessary protection. For a detailed discussion of right-to-know laws, see **§§7.02-7.07.**

[87] 40 CFR §§265.281-.282.

[88] 29 CFR §1910.1000, subpt Z. See **§9.02.**

vation and Recovery Act (RCRA)[89] standard—i.e., whether it would threaten human health or the environment.

§9.21   —Contingency Plans and Emergency Procedures

The Resource Conservation and Recovery Act (RCRA)[90] imposes comprehensive requirements for contingency plans and emergency procedures, which require written plans and at least one emergency coordinator on the premises, or available within a short period of time, with responsibility for coordinating emergency response measures.

In emergency situations, workers are potentially exposed to acute injuries from caustic or acidic burns, respiratory failure, and/or suffocation due to toxic vapors. A program must be established to deal with controlling the discharge or other emergency event, while providing maximum protection to employees. The emergency coordinator is the key person for coordinating emergency response at a hazardous waste management site, and the individual with this responsibility should be highly trained in chemical reactions, emergency first aid, protective equipment operation and designation, etc. The failure to have a fully trained emergency coordinator and back-up coordinators who are readily available at all times could result in serious liability for injuries suffered by employees due to inadequate emergency training. Emergency exit routes, equipment, alarms, communication, and protective equipment must be reviewed with all employees in regularly scheduled meetings. A waste disposal site poses such a variety of exposures that the following safety equipment and personal protective equipment should be readily available:

1. Stationary and portable safety showers and eye baths; portable units are pressurized tanks with 15 minutes of water supply

2. Supplied air units capable of supplying virgin air by means of a pressure-demand tank, hose, and mask unit in toxic atmospheres for up to 60 minutes

3. Emergency oxygen units capable of supplying pure oxygen by means of a constant-flow tube and mouthpiece unit for up to 30 minutes; to be used in revival capacity only and not in toxic atmospheres

4. Vacuum truck with capability of transporting large volumes of water and replenishing its own pumping system from any available water source

5. Bulldozers for earth moving

6. Absorbent material to assist in spill containment and control, flotation spill containment boom

---

[89] 42 USC §§6901-6987.
[90] 42 USC §§6901-6987.

7.   Chemical splash suits, acid suits, fire suits, heat-resistant gloves, chemical-resistant gloves, and boots

8.   Cannister and cartridge gas respirators, particulate respirators

9.   Safety shields, goggles and safety glasses, protective ear inserts, hard hats, fire blankets

The emergency coordinator should require that all local, state, and federal response agencies provide specific contacts, and that such agencies be thoroughly familiar with the emergency response plan for the facility.

§9.22   Compliance with Occupational Safety and Health Administration Subpart Z Requirements at Hazardous Waste Management Facilities

In many ways the operation of a facility for the treatment and disposal of hazardous wastes presents the most difficult problems for compliance with Occupational Safety and Health Administration (OSHA) subpart Z standards.[91] Enormous complexities arise for a hazardous waste management facility which accepts a variety of waste materials of heterogeneous composition and employs varying technologies for the neutralization, solidification, and ultimate disposal by landfilling, deep-well injection, or incineration. A waste management facility will receive numerous waste streams of widely varying composition over the course of an eight-hour workday. Additionally, the waste streams received will vary greatly from day to day and week to week. The facility may receive a few waste streams from a particular generator so that the same type of waste stream can be expected on a regular basis, but many wastes may be received only once every month or quarter—such as sludges from a biotreater which are removed only at certain intervals. Other waste streams, such as those from spill events are one-time events.

§9.23   —Inapplicability of the Eight-Hour Time Weighted Average

The Occupational Safety and Health Administration (OSHA) subpart Z[92] toxic and hazardous substance standards are designed to be applicable to manufacturing processes where chemical exposures are generally specific and consistent. Therefore, the exposure standards are based on an eight-hour work shift during a 40-hour week. Since a particular waste stream is generally not handled every day, it is arguable that the eight-hour time weighted averages

---

[91] 29 CFR §1910.1000, subpt Z. See **§9.02.**
[92] 29 CFR §1910.1000, subpt Z. See **§9.02.**

standards contained in subpart Z[93] are legally not applicable at hazardous waste disposal facilities, since there would never be eight hours of exposure per day over a 40-hour work week. However, the ceiling exposure values are clearly applicable, and the disposal industry faces the complex task of determining the particular substances and combinations of substances and exposure concentrations to which a particular worker may be exposed each day.

§9.24 —Engineering and Work Practice Controls

Subpart Z[94] requires that compliance with the exposure limits is to be achieved primarily by engineering and work practice controls. Engineering and work practice controls are to be used to reduce and maintain employee exposures to a particular substance at or below permissible exposure limits, *except* "to the extent that the *employer* establishes that these controls are not feasible."[95] Although certain engineering controls, such as inflatable structures to enclose certain waste processes to control airborne emissions and to reduce the number of persons exposed, and enclosed loading and unloading systems, are feasible, the nature of the waste-handling process is such that, in large part, personal protective devices such as respirators must be relied on for exposure control.

At all facilities handling hazardous wastes, all employees, including supervisory personnel who have any contact or potential contact with waste materials, should be processed through a decontamination room. All personnel should be provided uniforms and, as necessary, individualized protective equipment, such as respiratory protection equipment, with a proper fit. The decontamination room should have strict controls for complete segregation from clean changing areas. Personnel reporting to work should be issued work clothes and protective gear appropriate for each day's work area, determined by the waste characterization for the waste received during the day. Because of the varying nature of waste received, the protective equipment may vary from day to day.

After being in a contaminated area, persons should discard work clothes into special hampers, then shower and undergo other specialized decontamination if necessary. Special attention should be given to hands and fingernails to assure that all wastes have been removed. The decontamination room should have separate air conditioning and a separate drain system for the showers. Employees who have been working in a contaminated area should not be eating, drinking, or smoking, or engaged in any other activity which increases the possibility of incidental ingestion of toxic substances. Separate toilet facilities should be provided for persons working in contaminated areas. In no event should any employee who has been in a contaminated area be allowed to wear

---

[93] For instance, most of the materials in 29 CFR §1910.1000, Table Z-1.

[94] 29 CFR §1910.1000, subpt Z. See **§9.02**

[95] 29 CFR §1910.1000(e) (emphasis added).

home outer clothing or shoes which have potentially come into contact with hazardous substances. Incidental exposure to children or pregnant women and other persons particularly susceptible to toxic materials could cause harm and subject a company to liability for injuries caused from such exposure.

There is a major problem as to proper decontamination of protective gear and clothing. The normal method of sending uniforms to an industrial cleaning establishment may require a duty to inform the cleaning establishment of the types of chemical constituents on the clothing. This may be a very difficult task because of the wide variety of chemicals which could be present. Waste water from decontamination of splash suits and protective boots should be handled as a chemical waste and not commingled with ordinary sanitary wastes.

§9.25   —Identification of and Protection from Toxic Exposures

Beyond the basic protective measures discussed in §9.24, a waste disposal site must consider specific exposures associated with each step in the waste disposal process. For example, at a facility utilizing only the landfilling of wastes, the following activities are usually involved:

1. Waste receipt, laboratory testing, and verification

2. Neutralization of caustic or acidic waste streams

3. Solidification of liquids or semisolids prior to landfilling

4. Landfilling in secure disposal cells

5. Transfer of waste materials from various treatment or storage phases to final disposal

6. Decontamination of off-site waste transportation vehicles and on-site vehicles and equipment

The waste receipt, treatment, and disposal process presents the challenge of determining the types of exposures, exposure levels, duration, and location likely at each phase of waste handling from receipt and testing of the waste at the on-site laboratory to final disposal. Each employee whose work will involve exposure to the particular substance should be initially monitored to determine exposure levels. During the initial monitoring, maximum protective equipment, including appropriate respirators, should be provided unless there is sufficient reason to believe that the exposure will be well below the maximum exposure level established for that particular substance. For instance, the maximum exposure level for vinyl chloride is one part per million (1 ppm) averaged over any eight-hour period,[96] and no concentration is to exceed 5

---

[96] 29 CFR §1910.1017(c)(1).

ppm for 15 minutes.[97] Potential exposure levels will vary at each stage of the waste-handling process—testing and verification, loading of waste, treatment processes, transfer processes, and final disposal.

For example, if a facility were to receive, for the first time, a waste stream containing 5,000 ppm vinyl chloride, it would be assumed that all persons with any contact with the waste stream should be wearing an open-circuit, self-contained breathing apparatus, pressure-demand type with full face piece, as required by 29 CFR §1910.1017(g)(4)(i) for exposures to vinyl chloride of unknown amounts or above 3,600 ppm. Personal monitoring could be conducted to establish the precise levels of exposure for each employee to determine the type of respiratory equipment needed for his or her particular job. After the initial monitoring, if exposures were in excess of 1 ppm averaged over the eight-hour work day, a program of routine monitoring would have to be established pursuant to 29 CFR §1910.1017(d)(2).

The Occupational Safety and Health Administration (OSHA) regulations are problematic for the waste disposal industry since they assume daily or routine exposures to a substance. The regulations require that once it has been determined that there is employee exposure in excess of the action level, which is based on the eight-hour time weighted average over a 40-hour work week (see §9.23), monitoring and measurement must be repeated not less than quarterly.[98] Monitoring cannot be discontinued for any employee unless at least two consecutive monitoring determinations, made *not less than* five working days apart, show exposures for that employee at or below the action level.[99] A waste disposal facility may not receive a particular waste stream, such as the hypothetical 5,000 ppm vinyl chloride stream, more than once every two months, but the vinyl chloride standard nevertheless requires a program of monitoring and medical surveillance for each employee exposed, without regard to use of respirators, to vinyl chloride in excess of the action levels.[100]

§9.26 —Industrial Cleaning Services

One of the primary businesses of waste disposal is providing on-site capability to an industrial facility to clean out tank bottoms and biotreater sludges and to perform surface impoundments catalyst cleaning and other cleaning on the generator's site involving the removal of hazardous waste from a particular unit. The biggest problem in complying with Occupational Safety and Health Administration (OSHA) requirements in these situations is to compel the manufacturing facility to provide adequate information so that the company performing the cleaning operation can assure that OSHA standards are being met.

---

[97] *Id* §1910.1017(c)(2).
[98] *Id* §1910.1017(d)(2).
[99] *Id* §1019.1017(d)(2)(iii).
[100] *Id* §1910(k).

The Occupational Safety and Health Act (OSH Act)[101] does not apply to relations between the owner of a workplace and a worker who is the employee of an independent contractor.[102] In industrial cleaning operations, the company performing the cleaning is generally an independent contractor. Because the OSH Act does not impose a separate duty to employees of the independent contractor, it is essential that the contract for industrial cleaning services clearly require the industrial facility to inform the cleaning company adequately of all potential exposures to which employees may be subject.

§9.27   Subpart Z Compliance during Spill Response

Under the Occupational Safety and Health Administration (OSHA) Subpart Z requirements,[103] the most critical aspect of employee and public protection during spills is the existence of a detailed spill prevention and control plan which can be implemented quickly and of which all employees are informed. It is the duty of the company to develop the spill control plan and provide proper training to all employees to implement such plan.

§9.28   —Spill Reporting Requirements

Spill events are the instances posing the greatest threat of acute exposure to toxic and hazardous substances to personnel engaged in spill response as well as the public in the vicinity of the spill, and therefore, procedures for spill control are addressed in numerous sets of regulations. The Transportation Safety Act of 1974,[104] and the Hazardous Materials Regulations[105] require specific emergency procedures as well as spill contingency plan and reporting requirements. Overlapping requirements for spill contingency plans and reporting are also contained in the Resource Conservation and Recovery Act (RCRA)[106] regulations,[107] the Comprehensive Environmental Response, Compensation and Liability Act (CERCLA),[108] and the Clean Water Act.[109]

The most critical step in spill control is prompt and effective reporting to

---

[101] 29 USC §651 *et seq.*

[102] Cochran v International Harvester Co, 408 F Supp 598, 5 OSHC 1385 (WD Ky 1975); *see also* Brennan v Gilles & Cotting Inc, 504 F2d 1255 (4th Cir 1974)(general contractor is not jointly responsible with subcontractor for safety of subcontractor's employees); Bloomfield Mechanical Contracting, Inc v Secretary of Labor, 519 F2d 1257 (3d Cir 1975).

[103] 29 CFR pt 1910, subpt Z. See **§9.02.**

[104] 49 USC §1471 *et seq.*

[105] 49 CFR pts 106, 107, 171-179, and 397.

[106] 42 USC §§6901-6987.

[107] 40 CFR subpt D-Contingency Plan and Emergency Procedures.

[108] 42 USC §§9601-9657

[109] 43 USC §1331.

the agencies best equipped to respond to a spill. Accordingly, the central report center for any spill of a toxic or hazardous substance is the National Response Center. Subpart C of part 263 of RCRA regulations[110] requires that if *any* discharge of hazardous waste occurs during transportation, the transporter must give notice as required by 49 CFR §171, and §171.17 of the Hazardous Materials Regulations[111] requires reporting of a discharge of a *reportable quantity,* from one package or from one transport vehicle if not packaged, into or upon navigable waters or adjoining shorelines to the United States Coast Guard National Response Center. The regulations under §311 of the Clean Water Act similarly require reporting of spills of reportable quantities of hazardous substances to navigable waters.[112] CERCLA is broader than all of these acts, requiring reporting of a release of the comprehensive list of hazardous substances whether onto the land, into the air, or into the water. CERCLA establishes an initial list of 696 different substances and provides the Environmental Protection Agency (EPA) with authority to list additional substances.[113] Discharges of hazardous substances in reportable quantities must be immediately reported to the National Response Center. Failure to report such discharges is punishable by a fine of not more than $10,000 or imprisonment for not more than one year, or both.[114]

Section 103.(a) of CERLA provides that:

> Any person in charge of a vessel or an offshore or an onshore facility shall, as soon as he has knowledge of any release (other than a federally permitted release) of a hazardous substance from such vessel or facility in quantities equal to or greater than those determined pursuant to section 102 of this title, immediately notify the National Response Center established under the Clean Water Act of such release. The National Response Center shall convey the notification expeditiously to all appropriate Government agencies, including the Governor of any affected State.[115]

For purposes of reporting, the *person in charge* is considered to be the individual in charge at the scene of the spill—i.e., a plant manager, a tugboat captain, a service station operator, etc. The person in charge may delegate someone else to make the necessary reports, but that individual, as well as any corporate officer, may be held criminally liable if the discharge is not reported. The court in *Apex Oil Co v United States*[116] held both the employee and his corporate employer criminally liable for failure to report a spill. The employee's knowl-

---

[110] 40 CFR §263.
[111] 49 CFR §171.17.
[112] 33 USC §1251 *et seq.*
[113] 42 USC §9602(a).
[114] 42 USC §9603(b).
[115] 42 USC §9603(a).
[116] 530 F2d 1291 (8th Cir), *cert denied,* 429 US 827 (1976).

edge was attributed to the corporation. In *United States v Mackin*,[117] a tank truck driver who, while filling his truck, neglected to detect an overflowing storage tank owned by another company, was held not to be in charge for purposes of notification. The facility owner was deemed to have the duty of report. Ownership alone may trigger the notification liability.

The requirement to *immediately notify* as soon as a person has knowledge of a release of a hazardous substance has been interpreted in cases involving §311 of the Clean Water Act[118] to require reporting even before the substance actually reaches navigable waters, if the spiller should have known the substance would reach such waters.

A *reportable quantity* of a hazardous substance is defined by the regulation in terms of pounds of the substance discharged over a 24-hour period.[119] Initially a one pound limitation was set on all substances until regulations were promulgated setting specific quantities. From December 1980 to May 1983 this unrealistic one-pound rule was in effect. On May 25, 1983, the Environmental Protection Agency (EPA) finally promulgated notification quantities, many of which were increased to 100 pounds.[120] The designations of substances include any isomers and hydrates as well as any solutions and mixtures containing these substances. In the case of solutions or mixtures, only that portion of the mixture composed of the hazardous substance is to be considered for

---

[117] 388 F Supp 478 (D Mass 1975).

[118] 43 USC §1321. In United States v Kennecott Copper, 523 F2d 821 (9th Cir 1975), Kennecott appealed a criminal conviction for failure to notify promptly. The facts were that a pipeline broke at a Kennecott facility in Arizona during the night of November 30. The oil flowed over a period of time about two miles into a pond and eventually in small quantity to the Gila River. No oil spill was reported until December 3 when small sheen patches were observed in the Gila River. Kennecott was deemed to have known of the spill when it discovered the broken pipe and was held criminally liable since the company did not immediately notify the National Response Center. The Ninth Circuit upheld the conviction, stating that if Kennecott had called the National Response Center "reasonably promptly," such as on the morning of December 1, it would have met its duties.

United States v Ashland Oil & Transp, 504 F2d 1317 (6th Cir 1974), presented a similar issue when the company had knowledge of the spill and did not report sufficiently promptly. The original spill occurred in what Ashland classified as a nonnavigable area which led to a navigable water. Ashland *knew* the spill had occurred by 7:00 p.m., February 20, but since the water was not reached, did not report until 10:00 a.m., February 21. Ashland was held criminally liable for failure to immediately notify.

The important issue is that both Kennecott and Ashland were held to have *known* of the spill before it actually reached navigable waters. The standard pursuant to §311 by these cases is a *knew or should have known* standard. For example, if a tank was showing a product loss and the product contained one or more of the §311 hazardous substances, and if a person familiar with the operation would reasonably assume that the product had reached a ditch leading to waters of the United States, an immediate notification would be required at the time of the discovery of the leak. Waiting until tests of the water showed evidence of a reportable quantity of a hazardous substance would probably be found to be too late.

[119] 40 CFR pt 302.

[120] *Id*, 48 Fed Reg 23552-23602 (May 25, 1983).

purposes of discharge reporting.[121] The spill prevention control and counter measures (SPCC) plan should identify areas where spills are most likely—i.e., material transfer areas, roads along which materials are carried, tanks, etc. SPCC plans require diking around tanks and other potential spill areas to contain the spills in areas where the nature of the spilled substance can be predetermined—i.e., around storage tanks or containers of specific substances, and the appropriate personal safety equipment can be identified in advance.

In spills occurring during transportation, if the material is properly marked, labeled, and quantified as required by Department of Transportation (DOT) regulations,[122] there will be a reasonable amount of information regarding the substance available to determine what protective equipment should be utilized. It is essential that the determination of correct protective equipment be made quickly. These decisions could be greatly facilitated by the use of a computer system, which if provided data regarding specific chemicals, quantities, and general environmental conditions (temperature, wind, humidity, etc.) could provide a listing of protective equipment based on a data base of past spill events and exposure extrapolation models.

One useful source of information to determine the exact nature of a chemical spill is the Chemical Emergency Transportation Center (CHEMTREC), which offers advice to response officials from industry experts regarding accidents involving their particular products.

§9.29   Subpart Z Compliance during Clean-Up

Abandoned waste sites present the threat of both acute and chronic exposure to hazardous substances. At the initial analysis of the site, personnel engaged in the sampling process, in handling containers, and in soil analysis have a high risk of unknown and acute exposure. Therefore, maximum protective equipment should be employed during the initial site investigation.

Under subpart Z[123] of the Occupational Safety and Health Administration (OSHA) regulations, it is the responsibility of the on-scene coordinator to arrange for the proper methods of determining potential exposures at a site and to assure the presence of proper operating procedures and protective equipment. The on-scene coordinator (OSC) is defined as the federal official designated by the Environmental Protection Agency (EPA) or the Coast Guard (or a state official acting pursuant to a contract or cooperative agreement) to coordinate and direct federal responses to spill events or to longer term remedial actions at sites.[124] When there is a release from any vessel or facility

---

[121] 40 CFR pt 302.

[122] 49 CFR pt 172.

[123] 29 CFR pt 1910, subpt Z. See **§9.02.**

[124] National Oil and Hazardous Substances Contingency Plan, 40 CFR §300.33, 47 Fed Reg 31208 (July 16, 1982).

of the Department of Defense, the OSC is designated by the Department of Defense. The National Contingency Plan[125] provides for regions within the United States, and OSCs are to be designated for each region. The EPA is to assign the OSCs for response and remedial actions for releases from hazardous waste management facilities.

Even in a private clean-up action, if that action is to be consistent with the National Contingency Plan, the OSC has the overall duty to assure that clean-up personnel are not exposed to hazardous substances and that the clean-up is being conducted properly. The potential liability of the federal government for the failure of the OSC to properly protect personnel engaged in hazardous waste clean-up is discussed in §§9.35-9.37.

§9.30   —Initial Site Operations

The first matter that must be addressed in any site clean-up is the assessment of the hazardous conditions presented by the site and selection of proper safety measures to protect personnel. In some instances, such as the clean-up of a chemical manufacturing pond where the types of chemicals placed in the pond are definitely known, the nature of the hazardous substances located at a particular site will be sufficiently certain to select protective equipment. However, the most common type case to date in Comprehensive Environmental Response Compensation and Liability Act (CERCLA)[126] clean-up actions is the remedying of abandoned waste sites. Records are rarely sufficient to know with any accuracy what chemicals may be present. The lack of knowledge precludes selection of protective equipment by normal methods, so the initial entry should include fully encapsulating suits and contained breathing apparatus.

After first entry, immediate tests for atmospheric hazards—such as low oxygen content of the air, presence of subpart Z substances,[127] explosive potential, etc.—should be conducted. No general site clean-up should commence until adequate testing has been done to determine exposure levels as they may vary in different conditions—such as high heat increasing volatility or rain or high humidity increasing the risk of pyrophoric reaction.

§9.31   —Ongoing Remedial Activities

Once the proper characterization has been made, extreme care must still be utilized when excavating, removing liquids from areas, exposing sludges, etc., since a new release is possible during these activities. Of course, emergency equipment similar to that described in §9.30 should be available on-site. Since the exposures normally do not vary drastically after the initial characterization, if properly performed, the protection of workers involved in hazardous waste

---

[125] *Id.*

[126] 42 USC §§9601-9657.

[127] 29 CFR pt 1910, subpt Z. See **§9.02.**

clean-up is less problematic than the operation of a hazardous waste management facility where new or different waste streams are frequently received.

§9.32 Statutory and Common Law Liability

Despite the complexity and difficulty of complying with subpart Z standards,[128] it is essential that a company engaged in the transportation and/or disposal of hazardous wastes, in providing industrial cleaning services, in responding to spill events, or in providing remedial action at waste sites establish a program implementing reasonable measures to identify and characterize the nature, frequency, and level of exposure to the subpart Z substances. The procedure for identifying and characterizing the risk must be efficient enough to take into account numerous variable factors and to extrapolate quickly reasonably accurate exposure ranges. Whether for an emergency spill response or the day-to-day operation of a hazardous waste management system, a computer system to extrapolate exposure data, as well as to provide the necessary recordkeeping of employee training, monitoring, and medical records, would be the most efficient system. Once the potential exposures have been identified, feasible engineering controls and work practices must be established, and where such controls are not feasible, proper protective respirators and clothing must be provided.

Failure to have a program that complies with the Occupational Safety and Health Act (OSH Act)[129] can expose the company not only to the various penalties under the OSH Act, but also to exposure to substantial liability from civil suits by employees. Although the OSH Act does not provide a private remedy to an individual employee, a serious OSH Act violation may be sufficient evidence of gross negligence or intentional tort to allow a plaintiff employee to maintain a damage suit above and beyond the workers' compensation laws.[130]

Additionally, it is not uncommon for an employee of a company engaged in hazardous waste disposal or clean-up of a hazardous substance spill to bring suit against the generator of the waste or the manufacturer of the hazardous substance if there was a failure to warn of the presence of substances, of which the generator or manufacturer is in the best position to know. In the area of clean-up of hazardous waste spills or remedial efforts at abandoned hazardous waste sites where the nature of material is unknown, the doctrines of ultrahazardous activity may be applied. This doctrines imposes higher standards of care and greater duties to provide protection.

Finally, an employee who can come into contact with hazardous substances may inadvertently cause exposure to his or her family or others if there are not strict procedures regarding changing of clothes and decontamination. In such

---

[128] 29 CFR pt 1910, subpt Z. See **§9.02.**
[129] 29 USC §651 *et seq;* OSHA Instr. CPL 2-2.37.
[130] See **ch 6** for a discussion of workers' compensation issues.

cases, an employer could be liable for injuries to a member of an employee's family. For example, the daily exposure of a pregnant woman while washing her husband's work clothes which were contaminated with highly fetotoxic substances could result in substantial liability for the employer of the husband.

§9.33 Citations and Penalties

Section 17 of the Occupational Safety and Health Act (OSH Act)[131] establishes a series of penalties which depend upon the seriousness of the violation:

1. **Willful or repeated violation**—Any employer who willfully or repeatedly violates the OSH Act may be assessed a civil penalty of not more than $10,000 for each violation. If an employer is convicted of a willful violation that has resulted in the death of an employee, the offense is punishable by a fine of not more than $10,000 or by imprisonment of up to six months or both. A second conviction doubles these maximum penalties

2. **Serious violation**—Any employer who commits a serious violation in which there is substantial probability that death or serious physical harm could result, and if the employer knew or should have known of such a hazard, shall be fined $1,000 for each violation.

3. **Nonserious violation**—Any employer who commits a violation that has a direct relationship to job safety and health but probably would not cause death or serious physical harm may be fined up to $1,000 for each violation.

4. **Failure to correct violation**—Any employer who fails to correct, within the specified time period, a violation for which a citation has been issued may be fined up to $1,000 per day, for each day the violation continues.

The most common OSH Act violations in the disposal, spill response, or clean-up areas—all of which may also be grounds for a negligence claim by the plaintiff employee—are:

1. Failure of the employer to instruct each employee regarding the recognition and avoidance of unsafe conditions and regarding the regulations applicable to his or her work environment to control or eliminate any hazards or other exposure to illness or injury

2. Failure of employer to identify and advise employees as to specific hazards and provide necessary protective equipment

3. Failure of employer to assure adequacy of protective equipment, including maintenance and sanitation

---

[131] 29 USC §668; see generally G.Z. Nothstein, The Law of Occupational Safety and Health 347 (1981).

4. Failure of employer to provide proper medical surveillance and monitoring

§9.34 Tort Remedies

In addition to the statutory penalties discussed in §9.33, the violation of an Occupational Safety and Health Administration (OSHA) standard when coupled with the death or serious injury (whether acute—such as burns—or chronic—such as cancer) of an employee can subject the employer to tort claims above and beyond normal workers' compensation systems.

State workers' compensation systems are statutorily created schemes that allow employees to receive compensation for injuries or death resulting from activities within the course of their employment without regard to fault. In compensation to the employer, once the workers' compensation claim is satisfied, the employer is granted a tort immunity to lawsuits for common law damages. The immunity from tort and the predetermined compensation due for particular damages claimed by the employee allow predictable workers' compensation insurance plans which become an identifiable cost of doing business.

In recent years the concept of the absolute, exclusive remedy of the workers' compensation benefit for an injured employee has been eroded by two theories of law. The first theory is applicable where the employer's conduct was willful or based upon an intentional tort which warrants punitive damages. The second theory applies where the employer possesses a dual capacity in relation to the employee. For a more detailed discussion of this subject, see Chapter 6.

Liability of the Federal Government in Spill Response and Long-Term Remedial Actions

§9.35 Comprehensive Environmental Response, Compensation and Liability Act Requirements for Employee Protection

The Comprehensive Environmental Response, Compensation and Liability Act (CERCLA)[132] covers both the emergency spill of a hazardous substance and the long-term release of any hazardous substances into the environment. The act addresses spills or releases to any medium—the land, air, or water. Moreover, it covers spills of any substance designated toxic or hazardous by the other environmental laws—the Clean Water Act,[133] the Clean Air Act,[134]

---

[132] 42 USC §§9601-9657.

[133] 33 USC §§1251-1376.

[134] 42 USC §§7401-7642.

the Resource Conservation and Recovery Act (RCRA),[135] and the Toxic Substances Control Act (TSCA).[136] Therefore, CERCLA has eclipsed the other regulatory schemes for spill response and clean-up and is the primary mechanism for governmental response actions, with the exception of oil spills since crude oil products are currently excluded[137] and covered only in the event of discharges to navigable waters under the Clean Water Act. Therefore, CERCLA (also known as Superfund) and the regulations promulgated thereunder —i.e., the National Contingency Plan[138]—are a useful scope of inquiry of the potential liability of governmental entities when conducting Superfund removal or remedial actions.

CERCLA specifically requires that a regulatory scheme—i.e., the National Contingency Plan—be provided to protect the health and safety of employees involved in response actions.

> The President acting through the Administrator of the Environmental Protection Agency, the Secretary of Transportation, the Administrator of Occupational Safety and Health Administration, and the Director of the National Institute for Occupational Safety and Health shall study and, not later than two years after the enactment of this Act, shall modify the national contingency plan to provide for the protection of the health and safety of employees involved in response actions.[139]

CERCLA was enacted in December of 1980, so the employee safety and health provisions were due in December of 1982. The Environmental Protection Agency (EPA), National Institute of Occupational Safety and Health (NIOSH), Occupational Safety and Health Administration (OSHA), and United States Coast Guard, pursuant to a Memorandum of Understanding,[140] issued a minimal 22-page preliminary guidance NIOSH Worker Bulletin, *Hazardous Waste Sites and Hazardous Substance Emergencies,* which in very general terms describes possible exposures and personal protective equipment, but the bulletin is clearly inadequate to meet the mandate of §301(f).

The safety and health plans under CERCLA are to apply to contractors and subcontractors of the EPA performing clean-up by contract.

---

[135] 42 USC §§6901-6987.

[136] 15 USC §§2601-2629.

[137] "The term [hazardous substance] does not include petroleum, including crude oil or any fraction thereof which is not otherwise specifically listed or designated as a hazardous substance under subparagraphs (A) through (F) of this one paragraph, and the term does not include natural gas, natural gas liquids, liquified natural gas, or synthetic gas useable for fuel (or mixtures of natural gas and such synthetic gas). 42 USC §9601 (14).

[138] 40 CFR §300.

[139] 42 USC §9603(c).

[140] AD-75-F2A09.

[I]n awarding contracts to any person engaged in response actions, the President [or his representative] or the State, pursuant to a contract entered into under subsection (d) of this section, shall require compliance with Federal health and safety standards established under section 301(f) of this Act by contractors and subcontractors as a condition of such contracts.[141]

The only provisions in the National Contingency Plan[142] which address the health and safety protection of response personnel are §300.57 and §300.71, which require that the on-scene coordinator (OSC)(see §9.29):

> should be aware of threats to human health and safety and shall ensure that persons entering the response area use proper precautions, procedures and equipment and that they possess proper training. Federal local plans shall identify sources of information on anticipated hazards, precautions, and requirements to protect personnel during response operations.[143] . . . Responsibility for the safety of all Federal employees rests with the heads of these agencies. Accordingly, each Federal employee on the scene must be apprised of and conform with OSHA regulations and other requirements deemed necessary by the OSC. All private contractors who are working on-site must conform to applicable provisions of the Occupational Safety and Health Act and standards deemed necessary by the OSC.[144]

It is the duty of the OSC, who is appointed under the National Contingency Plan, and who may be a federal official or a state official,[145] to assure that the response action to a spill or hazardous waste clean-up is conducted properly. The OSC has the ultimate responsibility to determine which of the subpart Z[146] substances may be present, in what concentrations, and employ such controls, monitoring, and personal protective equipment as required by OSHA.

One issue is the potential liability of the federal government where, due to improper control by the federal government's OSC, clean-up personnel are damaged by exposure to toxic or hazardous substances during a spill removal or hazardous site remedial action. Section 107(d) of CERCLA provides:

> No person shall be liable under this title for damages as a result of actions taken or omitted in the course of rendering care, assistance or advice in accordance with the National Contingency Plan or at the direction of an

---

[141] 42 USC §9604(f).
[142] 40 CFR §300.6 (definitions); 47 Fed Reg 31205 (July 16, 1982).
[143] 40 CFR §300.57.
[144] 40 CFR §300.71.
[145] 40 CFR §300.72.
[146] 29 CFR pt 1910, subpt Z. See §9.02.

on-scene coordinator appointed under such a plan with respect to an incident creating a danger to public health or welfare or the environment as a result of any release of a hazardous substance or the threat thereof. This subsection shall not preclude liability for damages as the result of gross negligence or intentional misconduct on the part of such person. For the purposes of the preceding sentence, reckless, willful, or wanton misconduct shall constitute gross negligence.[147]

This exculpatory *good samaritan* provision has not yet been an issue in any Superfund action. The exemption from liability provision is limited to damages under title I of CERCLA. The only damage provisions in title I are §107(a)—"Damages for injury to, destruction of, or loss of natural resources, including the reasonable costs of assessing such injury, destruction, or loss resulting from such release."[148]—and, for failure to provide proper removal or remedial action upon an administrative order pursuant to §104 or §106 of the act, a person may be liable under §107(c)(3) for "[p]unitive damages in an amount at least equal to, and not more than three times, the amount of any costs incurred by the Fund as a result of such failure to take proper action."[149] Therefore, this good samaritan exclusion of §107(d) would not insulate an OSC for failure to identify correctly and to provide proper protection to workers against exposure to toxic and hazardous substances. Since federal agencies are subject to the sanctions imposed by OSHA, the EPA, in conducting or supervising a spill response or hazardous waste site clean-up, could be found to be in violation of the subpart Z standard.

§9.36   The Federal Employees' Compensation Act Remedy

The direct federal employee of the Environmental Protection Agency (EPA) or the United States Coast Guard would have an expeditious remedy against the respective agency for failure to identify adequately and provide protective equipment and measures against exposure to hazards during the course of a clean-up action. The Federal Employees' Compensation Act (FECA)[150] provides a comprehensive compensation system affording federal employees an expeditious administrative remedy for injuries or damage incurred in their employment. In essence, FECA is the equivalent of workers' compensation schemes for private industry in that the remedy provided is both limited and generally exclusive. The liability imposed by FECA is expressly made to take the place of all other liability of the government to an employee for damages for injury or death, whether the proceeding is a civil action or an administrative

---

[147] 42 USC §9607(d).

[148] *Id* §9607(a).

[149] *Id* §9607(c)(3).

[150] 5 USC §8101 *et seq.*

or judicial proceeding under a workers' compensation or federal tort liability statute.[151] Generally, there has not been erosion of the exclusivity of the FECA remedy, which has been evidenced in state workers' compensation schemes, to allow further recovery in the event of gross negligence or intentional tort by the federal government as employer or on the basis of the dual capacity doctrine, discussed in Chapter 6.

However, FECA does not supersede or in any way abrogate the right of a federal employee to proceed in an action in tort, or any other common law or statutory remedy, or right of indemnity against a third party[152] or against negligent fellow federal employees.[153] Thus, if during the clean-up of a chemical spill occurring during the transportation of product X, if the DOT shipping paper, labels, marking, or other descriptive information provided by the manufacturer of product X failed to identify correctly or adequately the presence of a certain hazardous substance, and because of the inadequate or incorrect information, the on-scene coordinator (OSC) did not provide respirators to protect the employee from dangerous exposure levels, the federal employee could have a tort claim against the manufacturer in addition to any compensation received under FECA.

Similarly, if the OSC negligently failed to characterize or protect against a particular hazardous exposure, the injured federal employee could proceed under a common law claim against the OSC personally.[154] There is some precedent that the OSC could then proceed against the United States for recovery of contribution or indemnity.[155] If an employee successfully makes a third-party claim, the government is entitled to a refund or credit of up to four-fifths of the compensation paid.[156]

§9.37   The Federal Tort Claims Act Remedy

To date, most Superfund[157] priority waste site remedial actions and many hazardous substance spill response actions have been performed primarily by third-party contractors to the Environmental Protection Agency (EPA) or the United States Coast Guard. However, the on-scene coordinators (OSCs) are usually direct employees of the EPA or the Coast Guard. An injured subcontract employee would have a remedy under the Federal Tort Claims Act

---

[151] 5 USC §8101.

[152] Tredway v District of Columbia, 402 A2d 732 (DC Ct App 1979), *cert denied,* 444 US 867 (1979).

[153] Allman v Hanley, 302 F2d 559 (5th Cir 1962).

[154] Kiker v Estep, 444 F Supp 563 (ND Ga 1978).

[155] Wallenius Bremen GMBH v United States, 409 F2d 994 (4th Cir), *cert denied,* 398 US 958 (1970), *contra* Newport Air Park Inc v United States, 419 F2d 342 (1st Cir 1969).

[156] 5 USC §8132.

[157] Comprehensive Environmental Response, Compensation and Liability Act, 42 USC §§9601-9657 (CERCLA or Superfund).

(FTCA),[158] which basically waives the government's sovereign immunity and provides suit against the United States to the same extent as against a private individual.

Generally, if an OSC failed to comply with one of the OSHA Subpart Z standards,[159] the employee of the contracting company could proceed under the FTCA. It is important to note that there is some authority that the United States does not become liable merely because its conduct, if committed by a private person, would have contravened a statute, rule, or regulation so as to make that individual liable in tort.[160]

There are two basic exclusions from the coverage of the FTCA which could preclude an employee of a contractor from recovering for exposures during clean-up activity. Section 2680(a) excludes any claim based on either an act or omission of a government employee exercising due care in the execution of a statute or regulation, whether valid or not, *or* the exercise or performance or the failure to exercise or perform a discretionary function or duty on the part of a federal agency or government employee, whether or not the discretion is abused. In the first case, if the federal employee exercised due care—i.e., was not negligent—the claim would be excluded from FTCA recovery. Therefore, it is likely that a claim that hazardous substance spill clean-up is an abnormally dangerous activity and that therefore, the on-scene coordinator should be held strictly liable even though he or she was not negligent, would be denied as within this statutory exclusion.

It has been held that ownership of an inherently dangerous substance by the United States is not, in itself, sufficient to impose liability on the government for injuries caused by the substance.[161] This is based on the concept that some kind of negligence is required, and there is no liability without fault under the FTCA. The principle raises the interesting question of whether the federal government as the generator of a hazardous substance or the owner/operator of a site where hazardous wastes have come to be located could be sued under the FTCA provisions under the strict liability provisions of §107 of CERCLA,[162] since owner/operators as well as generators and transporters who selected the site for disposal are strictly liable for clean-up costs. This issue becomes especially important since there are federal facilities, such as the Rocky Mountain Arsenal and Red Rocks Arsenal, which would clearly be Superfund sites if privately owned. An interesting question is, in the absence of negligence, does the federal government have sovereign immunity against strict liability provisions of other federal statutes, such as §311 of the Clean

---

[158] 28 USC §2680.

[159] 29 CFR pt 1910, subpt Z. See **§9.02.**

[160] United States v Gregory, 300 F2d 11 (10th Cir 1982).

[161] Mahoney v United States, 220 F Supp 823, (ED Tenn 1963), *affd*, 339 F2d 605 (6th Cir 1964).

[162] 42 USC §9607.

Water Act[163] or §107 of CERCLA?[164] In *Bartholomae Corp v United States*,[165] the plaintiff could not recover under the FTCA on the basis of strict liability for building damage caused by nuclear detonations carried out by the Atomic Energy Commission. Although violation of an Occupational Safety and Health Administration (OSHA) standard may be enough to subject a private employer to a gross negligence or intentional tort claim to override the employer's immunity under workers' compensation statutes, violation of an OSHA standard by the on-scene coordinator of the EPA or the Coast Guard may not be enough to support the FTCA action. It has been held that violation by an agency of a particular statute or regulation, where the purpose of the statute or regulation is protection of the public, may not be enough, by itself, to perfect a federal tort claim.[166] Denial of an FTCA claim based on a negligence per se violation of OSHA statute would be so anomolous that it seems likely that now the federal government *would* be held liable on the basis of negligence per se for violation of an OSHA standard, especially in the area of toxic and hazardous substance exposures under subpart Z.[167]

The *discretionary function or duty* exclusion applicable to both federal agencies and employees has been much debated. It could be argued that a particular clean-up performed pursuant to a specific program, such as the National Contingency Plan,[168] would be a discretionary action and no FTCA action would lie. Liability for damage resulting from nuclear testing has been held barred as within the discretionary exclusion,[169] but failure to warn residents of impending tests does not constitute an exercise of discretion.[170]

Another possible exclusion involves independent contractors. A contractor of an agency is expressly *not* an employee of the agency for whose acts the federal government may be liable.[171]

Most CERCLA spill response and site remedial actions are conducted by independent contractors, and in any FTCA proceeding the government will interpose the defense that the action was caused by the independent contractor and thus the federal government cannot be liable. There is some precedent for a claim of the *dangerous instrumentality* exception to the exclusion from liability for acts of an independent contractor. This *dangerous instrumentality* exception is especially appropriate to the hazardous spill response or site clean-up action.

---

[163] 33 USC §1321.

[164] 42 USC §9607.

[165] 253 F2d 716 (9th Cir 1957); *see also* Dalehite v United States, 346 US 15, *rehg denied*, 346 US 841 (1953); and Strangi v United States, 211 F2d 305 (5th Cir 1954).

[166] Wheelson v United States, 184 F Supp 81 (ND Cal 1963); *but see* Wilsweed Mink Ranch v United States, 218 F Supp 67 (D Minn 1963).

[167] 29 CFR pt 1910, subpart Z. See **§9.02.**

[168] 40 CFR §300.33.

[169] Blaber v United States, 212 F Supp 95 (EDNY 1962), *affd*, 332 F2d 629 (2d Cir 1964).

[170] Bullock v United States, 133 F Supp 885 (D Utah 1962).

[171] 28 USC §2671.

The theory behind the exception is that when the nature of the particular work is so dangerous that dangers may arise in the normal course of the work unless special preventative measures are taken, there is a nondelegable duty of the employer to see that such preventative measures are taken. In the situation where the duty to evaluate the risk of exposure to toxic or hazardous substances and to provide protective measures and equipment has been delegated to an independent clean-up contractor by the EPA or the Coast Guard, the agency could be held liable under this dangerous instrumentality doctrine even though the negligent act was that of the independent contractor.[172]

---

[172] *See* Pierce v United States, 142 F Supp 721 (ED Tenn 1955), *affd*, 235 F2d 466 (6th Cir 1956).

10 Superfund Issues*

Edmond B. Frost, Esq.†

* Grateful acknowledgement is made to the able assistance of Frank Cross, Esq., Kirkland & Ellis, Washington D.C. in the preparation of this chapter.
† Partner, Kirkland & Ellis, Washington, D.C.

§10.16   Administrative Orders

Victim Compensation

§10.17   Compensation for Toxic Tort Victims

Introduction to the Operation of Superfund

§10.01   Clean-Up Authority and Resources

The Comprehensive Environmental Response, Compensation and Liability Act,[1] commonly known as *Superfund,* establishes broad federal authority to clean up releases of hazardous substances into the environment. Congress provided this authority to respond to situations when a hazardous substance was spilled,—e.g., during transportation—and when abandoned hazardous waste disposal sites present a hazard from a release. While this chapter focuses on the disposal site clean-up provisions, which are central to Superfund, the act also expands on the oil and hazardous waste spill clean-up authority already contained in §311 of the Federal Water Pollution Control Act.[2] The latter provisions should not be overlooked but are beyond the scope of this chapter.

By authorizing government clean-up, Superfund represents a departure from most environmental legislation which typically authorize the government to go to court or to issue regulations compelling private parties to take action to protect the environment. By contrast, Superfund provides the authority and resources for the federal government to clean up a spill or a site itself and then seek reimbursement.

Congress recognized, however, that it was not in a position to direct precisely how the available clean-up resources should be managed, and it delegated this job to the president and the Environmental Protection Agency (EPA) under §105 of Superfund.[3] In order to provide a well-managed clean-up program, §105 provides for a revised National Contingency Plan (NCP) to set clean-up priorities and to establish criteria for cost-effective clean-up. In addition, §105 specifically requires that all "response to and actions to minimize damage from hazardous substance releases shall, to the greatest extent possible, be in accordance with the provisions of the plan."[4]

The first step under the NCP is the preparation of a priority list of 400 sites "designated individually" from "throughout the United States," which are to be known as the "top priority among known response targets."[5] The list is to be developed according to "[c]riteria and priorities . . . based upon relative risk

---

[1] Pub L No 96-510, 94 Stat 2767 (1980) (codified at 42 USC §9601 *et seq*).

[2] 33 USC §1321.

[3] 42 USC §9605.

[4] *Id.*

[5] *Id* §9605(8)(B).

or danger to public health or welfare or the environment. . . ."[6] The purpose of the list is to direct and focus the national clean-up effort on "those facilities and sites or other releases which appear to warrant remedial actions."[7] Once these *top priority* sites are identified, §105 requires that the NCP provide "means of assuring that remedial action measures are cost-effective. . . ."[8]

With the NCP as the touchstone, the statute sets forth an orderly procedure for implementing a clean-up program that is cost-effective and sets priorities. Section 104(a)(1) of Superfund[9] authorizes the president[10] to take "removal" or "remedial" action whenever there is a release or threatened release of certain substances. While §104(a) clean-up is limited by the availability of state matching funds and may not exceed $1 million, supplemental authority to deal with emergency conditions is provided in §104(c). That section authorizes further clean-up operations when there is an "immediate risk to public health or welfare or the environment," and Superfund clean-up is necessary to mitigate the danger.[11]

Congress was aware that the clean-up operations authorized by §§104 and 105 could be quite costly and therefore created the Hazardous Substance Response Trust Fund (Fund) to finance government clean-ups. Revenues for the Fund come primarily from a tax on petroleum products and certain chemicals.[12] By the time the taxing authority terminates in September 1985, the Fund will have collected $1.6 billion.[13] In addition, the Fund will be continually replenished through reimbursement actions, as described in **§10.02.**

§10.02   Liability Provisions

In addition to government clean-up authority, Superfund[14] creates a new regime of liability for the costs of hazardous waste clean-up. Once the government has used its §104 clean-up authority,[15] it may attempt to recover under §107 of the act its costs incurred.[16]

Section 107 imposes liability on four categories of defendants:

---

[6] *Id* §9605(8)(A).

[7] S Rep No 848, 96th Cong, 2d Sess 60 (1980), *reprinted in* 1980 US Code Cong & Ad News 6119.

[8] 42 USC §9605(7).

[9] *Id* §9604(a)(1).

[10] President Reagan has delegated his powers under *Superfund* to a number of federal agencies. Exec Order No 12316, 46 Fed Reg 42237 (Aug 20, 1981).

[11] 42 USC §9604(c).

[12] *Id* §9631.

[13] *Id.*

[14] Comprehensive Environmental Response, Compensation and Liability Act, 42 USC §9601 *et seq*, commonly known as *Superfund.*

[15] *Id* §9604. The clean-up authority under this provision is described in **§10.01.**

[16] 42 USC §9607.

1. The owner and operator of a site where a release has occurred or is threatened

2. Past owners and operators who were involved in disposal activities

3. Transporters who selected the disposal site

4. Any other person who arranged for the disposal of hazardous substances at the site

These parties may be liable for any government cleanup costs that are "not inconsistent with the national contingency plan"[17] and for certain damages for destruction of natural resources.

Superfund also seeks to encourage private waste site clean-up, and §107 imposes liability in this circumstance as well. The above-named defendants may be liable to private parties for their "necessary costs of response incurred . . . consistent with the national contingency plan."[18]

Finally, liability may be imposed by government action to compel private party clean-up pursuant to Superfund §106(a).[19] That section authorizes the president to bring suit to require abatement of an "imminent and substantial endangerment" resulting from a release or threatened release of a hazardous substance. Section 106(a) also grants the president authority to issue administrative orders to require private abatement of a release or threatened release of a hazardous substance.

§10.03   Ancillary Provisions

While the provisions discussed in §§10.01 and 10.02 constitute the most significant elements of Superfund,[20] several other provisions are important to the operation of the statute. Sections 111[21] and 112[22] are especially significant because they authorize payments from the Hazardous Substance Response Trust Fund (Fund.)[23]

Section 111 allows the Fund to pay for the reimbursement of private clean-up costs as well as government operations. Section 112 sets forth the procedures for making a claim against the Fund. Together, these sections reflect Congress' desire to encourage private clean-up by compensating parties who voluntarily have accepted responsibility for removal and remedial actions.

---

[17] *Id.*

[18] *Id.*

[19] *Id* §9606(a).

[20] Comprehensive Environmental Response, Compensation and Liability Act, 42 USC §9601 *et seq,* commonly known as *Superfund.*

[21] *Id* §9611.

[22] *Id* §9612.

[23] Congress created the Fund in *id* §9631.

Superfund §301[24] is also noteworthy because it requires a number of reports and studies on the operation of Superfund. Included are reports on the effectiveness of the act and the adequacy of the Fund, sites for future waste storage, the adequacy of legal remedies for hazardous-waste-related injuries, and measures for assessing natural resource damages. The §301 studies are intended to form the basis for Congress to "reexamine the situation" in later years and to make whatever changes are necessary in the Superfund.[25]

Site Identification

§10.04   National Priorities List

The first step in hazardous waste clean-up under Superfund[26] is the identification of sites where a release or threatened release necessitates response actions. Section 103 requires certain private parties to notify the Environmental Protection Agency (EPA) of a disposal site or spill involving hazardous substances.[27] A critical element in the identification process is the government's National Priorities List,[28] issued pursuant to the National Contingency Plan (NCP).

The NCP's priorities list is to consist of 400 sites selected from "throughout the United States" which are to be known as the "top priority."[29] The list is to be chosen according to "[c]riteria and priorities . . . based upon relative risk or danger to public health or welfare or the environment. . . ."[30] The function of the National Priorities List is to direct and focus Superfund clean-up efforts on the sites and releases that present the greatest potential hazard.[31]

The EPA's proposed list is based on a *scoring* of hazardous waste disposal sites according to a *Hazard Ranking System* also known as the MITRE model.[32] The Hazard Ranking System provides a rough measure of the risk presented by a site based on an evaluation of the toxicity of the constituents of the site, the pathways of release (e.g., air or surface water), and the potentially exposed

---

[24] *Id* §9651.

[25] HR Rep No 1016, pt II, 96th Cong, 2d Sess 5 (1980), *reprinted in* 5 US Code Cong & Ad News 6151.

[26] Comprehensive Environmental Response, Compensation and Liability Act, 42 USC §9601 *et seq*, commonly known as *Superfund*.

[27] *Id* §9603.

[28] See **§10.01.**

[29] 42 USC §9605(8)(B).

[30] *Id* §9605(8)(A).

[31] S Rep No 848, 96th Cong, 2d Sess 60 (1980), *reprinted in* 5 US Code Cong & Ad News 6119.

[32] *See* 47 Fed Reg 58476 (Dec 30, 1982).

population.[33]

This system, however, suffers from a number of significant and widely recognized shortcomings. Although the Hazard Ranking System is probably adequate to draw very general conclusions about the hazard posed by a site, it involves considerable subjectivity and lacks the precision necessary to represent an accurate assessment of risk.[34] Consequently, the EPA's site scores should be relied on cautiously and only after independent investigation. The EPA's final list continues to employ the model but has revised the scores for certain sites.[35]

The National Priorities List itself also lacks any automatic clean-up or liability consequences. Rather, the list "serve[s] primarily informational purposes. . . . [It] does not in itself reflect a judgment of the activities of [an] owner or operator, it does not require those persons to undertake any action, nor does it assign liability to any person."[36] Conversely, "[a]bsence from the NPL [National Priorities List] does not preclude enforcement actions,"[37] and the EPA has brought Superfund actions to compel clean-up on unlisted sites.[38]

Nonetheless, the National Priorities List has an important effect on Superfund response actions liability. The EPA is likely to insist upon clean-up of the highest priority sites, and when private action is not forthcoming, the government probably will clean up the site itself and sue to recover its costs.[39]

§10.05   Release of a Hazardous Substance

Although the National Priorities List[40] is likely to be an important factor in the selection of disposal sites for clean-up, Superfund[41] also authorizes prompt response to spills and permits cleanup of unlisted sites. Thus, the National Priorities List is not specifically referred to as a condition for Superfund response activities. Rather, §104 government clean-up may proceed when there has been a release or threatened release of a "hazardous substance" into "the environment."[42] Section 104 is also triggered by a release or threatened release of a pollutant or contaminant (i.e., a substance not designated as hazard-

---

[33] *See* 47 Fed Reg 31219 (July 16, 1982) (App A to National Contingency Plan).

[34] *See, e.g.,* Selection of Hazardous Waste Sites for Superfund Funding, Workshop sponsored by Subcomm on Department of Housing and Urban Development of Senate Comm on Appropriations (Mar 19-20, 1982).

[35] *See* 48 Fed Reg 40658 (Sept 8, 1983).

[36] S Rep No 848, *supra* note 31.

[37] 47 Fed Reg 58478 (Dec 30, 1982).

[38] *See, e.g.,* United States v Conservation Chem Co, Civ No 82-0983-CV-W-5 (WD Mo, complaint filed Nov 22, 1982).

[39] 47 Fed Reg 58478-79 (Dec 30, 1982).

[40] See §§10.01, 10.04.

[41] Comprehensive Environmental Response, Compensation and Liability Act, 42 USC §9601 *et seq,* commonly known as *Superfund.*

[42] *Id* §9604.

ous) which presents an "imminent and substantial danger" to public health or welfare or the environment.[43] Section 106's emergency relief may be invoked only when the release or threatened release is from a "facility," involves a hazardous substance, *and* presents an "imminent and substantial endangerment."[44]

All these terms have a specific meaning defined by the act itself. *Release,* for example, means virtually any escape into the environment, including "any spilling, leaking, pumping, pouring, emitting, emptying, discharging, injecting, escaping, leaching, dumping, or disposing. . . ."[45] *Facility* is also defined very broadly to mean "any site or area where a hazardous substance has been deposited, stored, disposed of, or placed, or otherwise come to be located" and specifically includes a "building" as well as any "well, pit, pond, lagoon, impoundment, ditch, landfill, storage container," etc.[46] *Hazardous substance* is defined more narrowly and precisely[47] to include substances already identified as hazardous under certain provisions of the Clean Water Act,[48] the Clean Air Act,[49] the Resource Conservation and Recovery Act,[50] and the Toxic Substances Control Act.[51] An important exception to this list exists for certain categories of substances that are specifically exempted from the above statutory lists. For example, wastes "from the extraction, beneficiation, and processing of ores and minerals" are exempted from the Resource Conservation and Recovery Act list of hazardous substances, pending further study.[52] As such, they are also outside the definition of *hazardous waste* under Superfund.[53]

§10.06 Imminent and Substantial Endangerment

In contrast to Superfund[54] §104,[55] which authorizes government response to any hazardous substance release, private clean-up under §106[56] may be compelled only where a release may present an "imminent and substantial endangerment." In selecting this term, Congress was well aware of the "tre-

---

[43] *Id.*

[44] *Id* §9606.

[45] *Id* §9601(22).

[46] *Id* §9601(9).

[47] *Id* §9601(14).

[48] 33 USC §§1251-1376.

[49] 42 USC §§7401-7642.

[50] *Id* §§6901-6987.

[51] 15 USC §§2601-2629.

[52] 42 USC §6901(b)(3)(A).

[53] *Id* §9601(14)(c).

[54] Comprehensive Environmental Response, Compensation and Liability Act, 42 USC §9601 *et seq,* commonly known as *Superfund.*

[55] *Id* §9604.

[56] *Id* §9606.

mendous burden of proof associated with an imminent hazard action."[57] Section 106(c) itself describes its authority as one of "emergency response."

Imminent and substantial endangerment is a term of art, used in numerous environmental statutes prior to Superfund. Decisions under these statutes make clear that "while the *risk* of harm must be 'imminent,' the harm itself need not be."[58] Under the Safe Drinking Water Act,[59] for example, such an endangerment exists "when there is an imminent likelihood of the introduction into drinking water of contaminants that may cause health damage after a period of latency."[60]

In determining whether a given risk is substantial, courts have relied on an analysis of the "reciprocal elements of risk and harm, or probability and severity."[61] Thus, "the public health may properly be found endangered both by a lesser risk of a greater harm and by a greater risk of a lesser harm."[62]

As the first Superfund case to address the issue makes clear, however, proof of imminent and substantial endangerment requires a showing that a truly significant risk is present.[63] Like analogous provisions in prior environmental statutes, §106 may not "be used in cases where the risk of harm is remote in time [or] completely speculative in nature."[64] Relief under this provision is appropriate only when there is "a substantial likelihood that contaminants capable of causing adverse health effects will be ingested by consumers if preventive action is not taken."[65] In *Reilly Tar*, the court found that an imminent and substantial endangerment was successfully alleged because cancer-causing substances had entered and would continue to enter the water supplies of several cities.

Thus, to show an imminent and substantial endangerment to public health under §106, the government must show imminent exposure of the population to substances causing adverse health effects. Because hazardous substances by nature will cause adverse health effects, most §106 cases will focus on the *exposure* issue. The existence of a *release* is not sufficient, however, and the government must show imminent exposure to hazardous concentrations of a substance before §106 relief is warranted.

---

[57] Subcommittee on Oversight of Government Management of Senate Comm on Governmental Affairs, 96th Cong, 2d Sess, Report on Hazardous Waste Management and the Implementation of the Resource Conservation and Recovery Act 29 (Comm Print 1980).

[58] HR Rep No 1185, 93d Cong, 2d Sess 35-36 (1974), *reprinted in* 4 US Code Cong & Ad News 6454 (Safe Drinking Water Act); 42 USC §300(f).

[59] 42 USC §300(f) *et seq.*

[60] 42 USC §300(i); HR Rep No 1185, *supra* note 58.

[61] Ethyl Corp v EPA, 541 F2d 1, 18 (DC Cir), *cert denied*, 426 US 941 (1976).

[62] 541 F2d at 18.

[63] United States v Reilly Tar & Chem Corp, 546 F Supp 1100 (D Minn 1982).

[64] *Id* 1109.

[65] *Id* 1110.

Clean-up Operations

§10.07 Settlement and Private Clean-up

Superfund[66] establishes voluntary clean-up as a preferred means of remedying conditions at abandoned waste sites. Prior to government clean-up, Superfund §104 calls upon the Environmental Protection Agency (EPA) to make the initial determination of whether "removal and remedial action will be done properly by the owner or operator of the vessel or facility from which the release or threat of release emanates, or by any other responsible party."[67]

The genesis of this provision is §311 of the Clean Water Act.[68] Under that section, the government may clean up a spill only "[i]f the owner or operator fails to do so."[69] Thus, "the policy behind the [Federal Water Pollution Control Act] FWPCA" is one that "encourages owners and operators of oil facilities to promptly and efficiently clean up any oil spills."[70] Many spills are cleaned up voluntarily, thus enabling response actions to take place expeditiously, with a minimum of *red tape* and delay.

This approach is not only consistent with the general judicial principle of encouraging settlement,[71] it also avoids the administrative and legal costs involved in potentially time-consuming litigation. Furthermore, private parties, especially those in the chemical industry, often have specialized technical and engineering knowledge that will be useful in conducting a safe and effective clean-up. Thus, it is generally recognized that private response actions will usually be more efficient than those performed by the government.[72]

Recognizing the benefits of private clean-up, Superfund settlements have provided for clean-up of numerous sites, on terms acceptable to the affected parties. These settlements have typically involved generators agreeing to finance clean-up of a multigenerator disposal site to which they sent wastes.

In these settlements, costs have often been allocated according to the relative volume of wastes sent to the site. Thus, a generator who sent 20 per cent of the total wastes disposed at a site would be responsible for 20 per cent of the necessary clean-up costs.

In exchange for such agreements, the government has entered into a covenant not to sue or take administrative action against the settling companies concerning the covered response actions. In some settlements, the govern-

---

[66] Comprehensive Environmental Response, Compensation and Liability Act, 42 USC §9601 *et seq*, commonly known as *Superfund.*

[67] 42 USC §9604(a)(1).

[68] 33 USC §1321.

[69] S Rep No 351, 91st Cong, 1st Sess 17-18 (1969), *reprinted in* 1 US Code Cong & Ad News 1682.

[70] Anglo Fabrics, Co v United States, No 279-77, slip op at 15, 23 (Ct Cl Jan 9, 1981).

[71] *See, e.g.,* Burger, Warren E, 1982 Year-End Report on the Judiciary, 8-9 (1982).

[72] *See* Chemical Applications Co, v Home Indem Co, 425 F Supp 777, 779 (D Mass 1977).

ment has also agreed to protect settlers from being required to make any further payments for a covered clean-up in excess of the settlement. Any contribution recovery by a nonsettling party is to be subtracted from the amount due to the government under the agreement.

Settling companies, in turn, have promised not to bring any claims against the government or the Hazardous Substance Response Trust Fund[73] regarding operations covered by the settlement. The settlements are all clear that they do not release any nonsettling third parties from liability, and the government has expressed its intent to seek relief against nonsettling responsible persons.

§10.08   The National Contingency Plan and Its Coverage

In some respects, Superfund's[74] centerpiece is the National Contingency Plan (NCP), which establishes the procedures for setting priorities and defining the nature and scope of clean-up operations. Superfund §105[75] sets forth the requirements for the NCP.

Response measures authorized under Superfund include *removal* and *remedial* actions. A removal action is "that initial response . . . which after discovery must be undertaken quickly to protect or prevent actual or potential injury."[76] Remedial action, by contrast, "involves the more permanent, costly measures which may be necessary after the need for emergency action has terminated."[77]

Under Superfund, all "response to . . . hazardous substance releases shall, to the greatest extent possible, be in accordance with the provisions of the plan,"[78] which is to "effectuate the responsibilities and powers created by this Act."[79] The legislative history emphasizes that the NCP is central to Superfund clean-up. The final debates on the act stress that Superfund "is to be substantially keyed to the national contingency plan."[80]

---

[73] Congress created the Hazardous Substance Response Trust Fund in 42 USC §9631.

[74] Comprehensive Environmental Response, Compensation and Liability Act, 42 USC §9601 *et seq,* commonly known as *Superfund.*

[75] 42 USC §9605.

[76] S Rep No 848, 96th Cong, 2d Sess 53 (1980), *reprinted in* 5 US Code Cong & Ad News 6119.

[77] *Id* 54.

[78] 42 USC §9605. Section 104 of the act requires that removal and remedial actions be "consistent with the National Contingency Plan." 42 USC §9604(a)(1). Section 106(c) calls for enforcement guidelines that are "to the extent practicable . . . consistent with the national hazardous substance response plan," 42 USC §9606(c), and §107 limits reimbursement actions to expenses "consistent with" or "not inconsistent with" the plan. 42 USC §9607(a).

[79] 42 USC §9605.

[80] 126 Cong Rec S15007 (daily ed Nov 24, 1980) (statement of Sen Stafford from colloquy between Sens Stafford and Helms).

Indeed, the application of the NCP to all response actions is emphasized throughout Superfund. The Senate report on Superfund's predecessor bill states that "removal and remedial actions should be in accordance with the plan to the greatest extent possible."[81] Section 107 authorizes government recovery of only those costs that are "not inconsistent with the national contingency plan."[82]

The NCP also governs private response actions compelled by §106. By its terms, the NCP covers private response actions to "determine the level of clean-up to be sought through enforcement efforts."[83] The legislative history also confirms that the NCP applies even to administrative orders for removal or remedial action, and that the inconsistency of such an order with the NCP could be raised as a defense for failure to comply with the order.[84]

§10.09   Requirements of the National Contingency Plan

A clean-up authorized by the National Contingency Plan (NCP)[85] begins with a preliminary site assessment, which evaluates "the magnitude of the hazard" and "the source and nature of the release."[86] The assessment and further federal action may be terminated by a number of circumstances, including a determination that the "amount released does not warrant Federal response" or that a "party responsible for the release, or any other person, is providing appropriate response."[87]

When an "immediate and significant risk of harm to human life or health or to the environment" is found[88] and appropriate response action is not being taken, the NCP authorizes certain "defensive . . . immediate removal actions."[89] Because these removal actions are short-term responses to emergency situations, the expenditures for and duration of removal actions are statutorily limited.

Thus, removal expenditures are restricted to $1 million or any lesser amount that is spent within six months.[90] These limits may be exceeded only when "continued response actions are immediately required to prevent, limit, or mitigate an emergency," there is an "immediate risk," and timely assistance

---

[81] S Rep No 848, *supra* note 76.

[82] 42 USC §9607(a)(4)(A).

[83] 40 CFR §300.68(c); 47 Fed Reg 31180, 31216 (July 16, 1982).

[84] 126 Cong Rec S15008 (daily ed Nov 24, 1980) (statement of Sen Stafford from colloquy between Sens Stafford and Simpson).

[85] See **§10.08.**

[86] 40 CFR §300.64(a).

[87] *Id* §300.64(c).

[88] *Id* §300.65(a).

[89] *Id* §300.65(b).

[90] 42 USC §9604(c)(1).

will not otherwise be provided.[91] Immediate removal actions must be terminated when the site no longer meets acute hazard criteria.[92] Due to the short-term, emergency nature of this relief, it is not subject to all of the substantive and procedural requirements that govern subsequent remedial actions. Even removal actions must, however, rely "on established technology when feasible and cost-effective."[93]

Remedial actions provide a more costly, long-lasting response to abandoned disposal sites. Federal remedial action requires prior consultation with any affected state, and the state must enter a cooperative agreement, assuring, inter alia, that it will pay 10 per cent of all costs.[94]

Cost-effectiveness is the paramount consideration in evaluating remedial actions. Senator Stafford, a key architect of Superfund,[95] elaborated:

> [C]onsiderations of the relationship between the costs and the benefits of a particular response action are an essential part of both the national contingency plan, to be developed under section 105, and the selection of remedial and response actions under section 104.[96]

Likewise, Senator Dole stressed that the act "imposes limits on the discretion of those administering the response mechanism, to insure that reasonably cost-efficient actions are taken."[97]

The NCP also limits remedial actions to sites on the National Priorities List.[98] Furthermore, remedial actions must comply with detailed substantive and procedural requirements to evaluate alternative remedial measures based on cost-effectiveness and feasibility.[99] In sum, the National Contingency Plan plays a central role in Superfund clean-up and, therefore, in defining the magnitude of potential liability.

Recovery of Clean-Up Costs

§10.10   Causation

Site owners and operators, transporters, and those who merely arranged for disposal are potentially resonsible for certain clean-up costs under Super-

---

[91] *Id.*

[92] 40 CFR §300.65(c).

[93] *Id* §300.61(c)(4).

[94] 42 USC §9604(c)(3).

[95] Comprehensive Environmental Response, Compensation and Liability Act, 42 USC §9601 *et seq*, commonly known as *Superfund.*

[96] 126 Cong Rec S15007 (daily ed Nov 24, 1980) (remarks of Sen Stafford).

[97] 126 Cong Rec S14982 (daily ed Nov 24, 1980) (remarks of Sen Dole).

[98] 40 CFR §300.68(a). See §§10.01 & 10.04.

[99] 40 CFR §300.68(g), (h), (i).

fund.[100] Before any given person from these categories may actually be held liable, however, a plaintiff must show that the person caused the release or threatened release necessitating the response costs.

Under Superfund §107, a party is only liable when his or her actions "cause the incurrence of response costs."[101] The legislative history of Superfund elaborates on this requirement. Thus, the House report on Superfund's predecessor bill explained that "the usual common law principles of causation, including those of proximate causation, should govern the determination of whether a defendant 'caused or contributed' to a release or threatened release."[102] Plaintiffs, therefore, "must demonstrate a causal or contributory nexus between the acts of the defendant and the conditions which necessitated response action."[103]

Noteworthy, too, is a provision that was never adopted. Earlier bills would have authorized personal injury recovery for medical expenses and would have explicitly relaxed traditional standards of causation.[104] Yet even this bill did not relax the requirements for strict proof that the named defendant caused the release; rather, only the standard of proof for showing that the release caused the plaintiff's injury would have been lightened.[105]

Decisions under §311 of the Clean Water Act[106] further illustrate the dimensions of the analogous Superfund causation requirement. Although there are no explicit causation conditions in §311, courts have required proof that the defendant caused the discharge in question. In *United States v Tex-Tow, Inc,*[107] the court held that "causation is required even under a strict liability statute" and demanded proof that the defendant's actions were both the "cause in fact" and "legal cause" of a spill.[108] In other §311 cases, the government has used dye tests and chemical, spectrographic, and chromatographic analyses to prove causation by showing that oil spills came from the defendants' facilities.[109]

Like the Clean Water Act, plaintiffs under Superfund must link defendants' wastes to the release: "The Government can sue a defendant under the bill only for those costs and damages that it can prove were caused by the defen-

---

[100] Comprehensive Environmental Response, Compensation and Liability Act, 42 USC §9601 *et seq,* commonly known as *Superfund.*

[101] *Id* §9607(a)(4).

[102] HR Rep No 1016, pt I, 96th Cong, 2d Sess 33 (1980), *reprinted in* 5 US Code Cong & Ad News 6119.

[103] *Id* 34.

[104] S 1480, §4(c), 96th Cong, 2d Sess (1980), 165 Cong Rec V126 (Nov 24, 1980).

[105] S 1480, §4(c)(3)(A), 96th Cong, 2d Sess (1980), 165 Cong Rec V126 (Nov 24, 1980).

[106] 33 USC §1321.

[107] 589 F2d 1310 (7th Cir 1978).

[108] *Id* 1313-14.

[109] *See, e.g.,* United States v Malitovsky Cooperage Co, 472 F Supp 454 (WD Pa 1979); United States v Slade, Inc, 447 F Supp 638 (ED Tex 1978).

dant's conduct."[110] Early decisions have thus applied "the concept of intervening cause to the [Superfund] action."[111] To show causation, a plaintiff should do more than allege that a party sent wastes to a site. Rather, according to Prosser, he or she:

> must introduce evidence which affords a reasonable basis for the conclusion that it is more likely than not that the conduct of the defendant was a substantial factor in bringing about the result. A mere possibility of such causation is not enough; and when the matter remains one of pure speculation or conjecture, or the probabilities are at best evenly balanced, it becomes the duty of the court to direct a verdict for the defendant.[112]

When a defendant is a transporter or generator, for example, a plaintiff should show that the wastes transported or generated by that defendant are still present on the site and that those same wastes are being released or threaten a release necessitating clean-up operations.

§10.11   Standard of Liability

In many cases, Superfund[113] imposes a strict liability standard on defendants. This standard is not inflexibly written into law, however, and in at least some multiparty situations, a negligence standard may be appropriate.

The original Superfund bills introduced in the House and the Senate provided expressly for strict liability.[114] The final act deleted this provision and replaced it by "specifying the standard of liability under section 311 of the Clean Water Act."[115] At least some Senators believed that §311 imposed a strict liability standard. Thus, Senator Randolph referred to the §311 precedent as "a standard of strict liability."[116]

Senator Stafford, however, emphasized that the liability system should be tempered by considerations of fault, at least in some circumstances. He explained that the predecessor bills "had strict liability provisions, but they were severely pared down."[117] According to Stafford, the final compromise bill was "not an embodiment of other forms of no fault liability or innovative Federal

---

[110] 126 Cong Rec S15004 (daily ed Nov 24, 1980) (remarks of Sen Helms).

[111] Ohio v Goergeoff, 562 F Supp 1300, 1306 (ND Ohio 1983).

[112] Prosser, The Law of Torts 241 (4th ed 1971).

[113] Comprehensive Environmental Response, Compensation and Liability Act, 42 USC §9601 *et seq*, commonly known as *Superfund.*

[114] S 1480, *supra* note 104, at §4(a); HR 7020, §3071(a).

[115] 33 USC §1321; 126 Cong Rec S14964 (daily ed Nov 24, 1980) (remarks of Sen Stafford).

[116] *Id* S14967 (remarks of Sen Randolph).

[117] *Id* S14967 (remarks of Sen Stafford).

intrusion into the law now developing within individual State jurisdiction[s]."[118]

The intended result is a hybrid standard of liability. As Congress suggested, the courts have regularly held that the nominal standard of liability under §311, and therefore under Superfund, is strict liability.[119] In a simple situation with only one potentially responsible party, liability probably will be strict.

When several parties may share responsibility for a release, however, §311 decisions have considered negligence issues. In such cases, negligent parties have been held liable and nonnegligent parties exonerated, despite the nominal strict liability standard.[120]

Perhaps more significant, §311 of the Clean Water Act imposes liability only on the owner or operator of a vessel or facility and therefore does not directly address the proper liability standard for transporters or generators under Superfund. In contrast to some potential Superfund defendants, the findings of strict liability under §311 "came in the context of determining the liability of parties intimately involved in the challenged pollution activity."[121]

This issue was most clearly addressed in *City of Philadelphia v Stepan Chemical Co.*[122] There, the court observed that the usual standard of liability under both §311 and Superfund is strict. The court went on, though, to suggest that:

> Superfund's strict liability standards should be confined to those parties who engaged in substantial and purposeful hazardous waste disposal activity for commercial profit after the enactment of this statute. Automatic application of strict liability to parties whose conduct was substantially unrelated to the present danger posed by the hazardous waste release or who did not obtain commercial benefit from their conduct, does not appear to be compelled by the environmental concerns which gave rise to Superfund.[123]

This standard would be consistent with common law decisions, which generally have not applied strict liability to off-site generators.[124] Moreover, as discussed in **§10.12,** relative negligence is a primary factor in apportioning any liability for damages among Superfund defendants.

---

[118] *Id* S15018.

[119] *See* Steuart Transp Co v Allied Towing Corp, 596 F2d 609, 613 (4th Cir 1979); Sabine Towing & Transp Co v United States, 16 Envt Rep Cas (BNA) 2081, 2082 (Ct Cl 1981).

[120] *See* United States v M/V Big Sam, 505 F Supp 1029 (ED La 1981), *affd in part, revd in part,* 681 F2d 451 (5th Cir 1982), *cert denied,* 103 S Ct 3112 (1983); Valley Towing Serv v SS American Wheat, Civ No 75-363 (ED La Jan 23, 1980).

[121] Dore, *The Standard of Civil Liability for Hazardous Waste Disposal Activity: Some Quirks of Superfund,* 57 Notre Dame Law 260, 276 (Dec 1981).

[122] 544 F Supp 1135 (ED Pa 1982).

[123] *Id* 1143 n 10 (dicta).

[124] *See, e.g.,* Ewell v Petro Processors of Louisiana, Inc, 364 So 2d 604 (La Ct App 1978), *cert denied,* 366 So 2d 575 (La 1979).

§10.12   Apportionment of Liability

The early Superfund[125] proposals not only called for strict liability but also would have imposed joint and several liability for all clean-up costs on any named defendant. This requirement became the source of substantial controversy, however, and was deleted from the final act.

The predecessor bill,[126] with joint and several liability, could not pass the Senate. Its sponsor, Senator Stafford, noted that many of his colleagues perceived the bill "as punitive and unnecessarily rigorous."[127] Senator Helms emphasized that the earlier bill had received "well-deserved criticism," because the standards of liability were "grossly unfair."[128]

Consequently, a compromise bill was drafted, which eventually became law. Numerous senators stessed that the elimination of joint and several liability was a "concession" essential to passage.[129] The significance of this deletion is uncertain, however. Some senators appeared to believe that the final bill *precluded* joint and several liability, a view that finds support in the development of the final legislation.[130] Even the predecessor bills provided for apportionment of damages in numerous circumstances,[131] and these bills are best viewed as a hybrid *joint and several/apportionment* system. Because even this partial apportionment system was considered too severe, there is reason to believe Congress intended to rule out even the possibility of joint and several liability.

Nonetheless, some Congressmen suggested that joint and several liability might still be applied in "appropriate circumstances," such as "where several persons have often contributed to an indivisible harm."[132] Senator Randolph thus explained the deletion of joint and several liability not as a "rejection of the standards in the earlier bill," but rather as a "recognition of the difficulty in prescribing in statutory terms liability standards which will be applicable in individual cases."[133]

Even if the latter interpretation of Superfund's legislative history is adopted, apportionment, and not joint and several liability, should generally be the rule. The common law imposes joint and several liability only in certain narrowly defined situations, such as where defendants have acted together in tortious conspiracy or where the harm suffered is *indivisible*.

Although the latter sitatuion might theoretically describe some Superfund

---

[125] Comprehensive Environmental Response, Compensation and Liability Act, 42 USC §9601 *et seq,* commonly known as *Superfund.*

[126] HR 5790.

[127] 126 Cong Rec S14967 (daily ed Nov 24, 1980) (remarks of Sen Stafford).

[128] *Id* S15004 (remarks of Sen Helms).

[129] *See, e.g., id* S14967 (remarks of Sen Stafford), S14980 (remarks of Sen Cohen), S14967 (remarks of Sen Randolph).

[130] *See id* S15004.

[131] *See* HR 7020, §3071(a)(3), 126 Cong Rec No 169 (Dec 3, 1980); S1480, §4(f)(4), 96th Cong, 2d Sess, 126 Cong Rec No 165 (Nov 24, 1980).

[132] 126 Cong Rec H11787 (daily ed Dec 3, 1980) (remarks of Rep Florio).

[133] *Id* S14964 (daily ed Nov 24, 1980) (remarks of Sen Randolph)

cases, it is not favored. Prosser has noted that "entire liability will be imposed only where there is no reasonable alternative."[134] Similarly, the Restatement establishes the presumption that "[i]f two or more persons, acting independently, tortiously cause distinct harms or a single harm for which there is a reasonable basis for division according to the contribution of each, each is subject to liability only for the portion that he has himself caused."[135]

Under this standard, environmental pollution cases arising at common law are "regarded by the courts as capable of some rough apportionment according to the extent to which each defendant has contributed, and [accordingly] . . . each will be liable only for his proportionate share of the harm."[136] The Restatement (Second) of Torts adopts a similar position.[137]

Multiple defendant hazardous waste cases decided to date are too few to enable a confident answer to this question.[138] Perhaps the clearest indication that clean-up costs are generally divisible, and therefore apportionable, is provided by the settlement agreements signed to date by the government. These settlement decisions have apportioned damages among generators roughly in proportion to the parties' percentage of the volume of waste sent to the site.[139]

This *relative volume of waste* approach is likely to be used by the courts in apportioning damages as well. Courts may also turn to the legislative history for guidance in apportionment. Superfund's predecessor bills, which included joint and several liability, also provided for apportionment in many cases. The factors to be considered in apportionment included the amount of hazardous waste, its degree of toxicity, the degree of care exercised by the parties, and the degree of cooperation with government officials.[140]

Where some responsible parties are not before the court, either because

---

[134] Prosser, The Law of Torts 314 (4th ed 1971).

[135] Restatement (Second) of Torts §881 (1975).

[136] Prosser, *supra* note 134, at 608.

[137] Restatement (Second) of Torts §433A, comment d (1975).

[138] *See, e.g.,* United States v Vertac Chem Corp, 489 F Supp 870 (ED Ark 1980); New Jersey v Chemical & Pollution Sci, Inc, 2 Chemical & Radiation Waste Litigation Rep 673 (NJ Super 1981).

[139] *See, e.g., In re,* Stauffer Chemical Company, Westport, Conn, EPA Docket No 82-1070 (May 25, 1982); United States v South Carolina Recycling and Disposal, Inc, Civ No 80-1274-6 (DSC) Settlement Agreement and Release.

Notwithstanding this legislative and common law support for apportionment, recent district court decisions have held that superfund liability is presumptively indivisible, and therefore joint and several unless defendants can themselves prove apportionment. *See, e.g.,* United States v A & F Materials, No 83-3123 (SB Ill 1984); United States v Conservation Chem Co, No 82-0983-CV-W-5 (WD Mo 1984); United States v Chem-Dyne, No C-1-82-40 (SD Ohio 1983); United States v Wade, No 79-1462 (ED Pa 1983). Even if these decisions stand up and defendants are unable to prove apportionment, the harshness of joint and several liability will be mitigated by a right to contribution from other parties who may be liable.

[140] HR 7020, §3071(a)(3)(B), 126 Cong Rec No 169 (Dec 3, 1980); S 1480, §4(f)(4), 96th Cong, 2d Sess, 126 Cong Rec No 165 (Nov 24, 1980).

they cannot be identified or because they have gone out of business, the Hazardous Substance Response Trust Fund[141] would pay their share of the costs. This approach is supported by the House report which states that "if one of the parties is ordered to take actions which result in his expenditure of more than that which he establishes to be his proportionate share, he may recover the excess amount from the fund."[142]

While these provisions were not passed and are in no sense binding, they suggest the following approach in apportioning damages. As among various generators, costs may be apportioned based on that portion of response costs caused by each, which may be determined simply by the quantity of wastes deposited by each generator at the site. As among a generator, transporter, and site owner and operator, relative negligence may play a larger role.

If a court rejects the statutory argument presented above and finds clean-up costs to be indivisible, it may impose joint and several liability under Superfund. Even in this circumstance, however, a defendant should have a right to contribution from other parties who may be liable.

Indeed, §107 of Superfund itself appears to authorize such a contribution action.[143] That section, as discussed above, permits private parties to go to court to recover response costs from other potentially liable parties. Because Congress did not contemplate imposing joint and several liability, it probably did not intend this provision as a contribution right. Nonetheless, contribution actions generally should fall within the statutory requirements for §107 recovery.

However, even if the statute did not explicitly provide for contribution, such a right would still exist under federal or state common law. Although the Supreme Court has on several occasions declined to create a federal common law right of contribution, it has so acted due to the absence of evidence in those cases that Congress meant to create such a right.[144]

Under Superfund, however, those Representatives who supported joint and several liability also supported a right of contribution. A letter introduced in the House debates from the Justice Department suggests that Superfund defendants have "the right to seek contribution from any other person responsible for a release or threat of release."[145] Representative Florio suggested that "the bill would encourage the further development of a Federal common law."[146] Thus, the legislative history of Superfund indicates that the courts

---

[141] Congress created the Hazardous Substance Response Trust Fund in 42 USC §9631.

[142] HR Rep No 1016, pt I, 96th Cong, 2d Sess 29 (1980), *reprinted in* 5 US Code Cong & Ad News 6119.

[143] 42 USC §9607.

[144] *See, e.g.,* Northwest Airlines v Transport Workers Union of America, 451 US 77 (1981); Texas Indus, Inc v Radcliff Materials, 451 US 630 (1981).

[145] 126 Cong Rec H11788 (daily ed Dec 3, 1980).

[146] *Id* H11787 (remarks of Rep Florio).

were intended to fill in the gaps of the statute with federal common law rules, including contribution.

Historically, a federal common law right to contribution has been created in Clean Water Act §311 cases,[147] in admiralty cases,[148] and in various other contexts.[149] And even in the absence of such a federal common law right, most defendants could sue for contribution under state law. The vast majority of states now recognize a right to contribution, many by statute.[150] Whatever the source of such a right, courts are likely to base the amount of contribution owed on such factors as the relative fault of the parties and their relative share in causing the release or threatened release necessitating clean-up.[151]

§10.13   Natural Resource Damage

Section 107 of Superfund[152] also authorizes recovery of "damages for injury to, destruction of, or loss of natural resources," and the "reasonable costs of assessing such injury."[153] Federal officials designated under the National Contingency Plan (NCP) are to assess natural resource damages, and their assessment is given presumptive weight.[154] In turn, §301 directs the president to "promulgate regulations for the assessment of damages for injury to, destruction of, or loss of natural resources."[155]

Important limitations are placed on the recovery of natural resource damages. Section 107(f) provides that "liability shall be to the United States Government and to any State," for recovery of these damages, but a private person is not authorized to sue.[156] Moreover, the statutory definition of natural resources includes only resources "belonging to, managed by, held in trust by, appertaining to, or otherwise controlled by the United States . . . any State or local government, or any foreign government."[157] Thus, the federal and state governments are the only proper plaintiffs in natural resource damage actions, and they may recover only for damage to public resources.

The §301 regulations are not yet issued, but Superfund itself provides considerable guidance for measuring natural resource losses. For *minor releases,*

---

[147] *See* Valley Towing Service v SS American Wheat, Civ No 75-363 (ED La Jan 23, 1980).

[148] *See* United States v Reliable Transfer Co, 421 US 397 (1975).

[149] *See, e.g.,* Gomes v Brodhurst, 394 F2d 465 (3d Cir 1967).

[150] See Robinson, *Multiple Causation in Tort Law: Reflections on the DES Cases,* 68 Va L Rev 713, 716 n 12 (Apr 1982).

[151] See Robinson, Multiple Causation in Tort Law, 12 ULA 53 (1982).

[152] Comprehensive Environmental Response, Compensation and Liability Act, 42 USC §9601 *et seq,* commonly known as *Superfund.*

[153] *Id* §9607(a)(4)(C).

[154] *Id* §9611(h).

[155] *Id* §9651(c)(1).

[156] *Id* §9607(f).

[157] *Id* §9601(16).

Congress intended that assessments should "rely on a combination of habitat values, tables of values for individual species, and previously conducted surveys and laboratory studies, related to units of discharge or units of affected area."[158]

By contrast, for substantial natural resource damage, Congress mandated a "site-specific damage assessment," including "extensive fieldwork."[159] Congress recognized that "procedures for these types of monetary cost assessments are sometimes hard to define," but the Environmental Protection Agency (EPA) was directed to "make a decision as to which are the most accurate and efficient."[160]

The latter condition sets out an overriding principle of natural resource damage liability—that economic values, rather than some intangible, inherent value of an animal or a tree, must be used. Senator Simpson gave a detailed analysis of the factors that should be considered in measuring natural resource damages:

> [R]ehabilitation should be planned and cost effective—those are sound principles of public administration. I also trust that the traditional legal rules for calculating of damages for injury in tort will be observed as part of cost effectiveness. For example, the law achieves cost effectiveness by awarding the difference in value before and after the injury, and where the injured interest can be restored to its original condition for less than the difference in value, the cost [of] restoration is used.[161]

Likewise, the Senate report on S. 1480, the bill from which Superfund's natural resource damage provisions evolved, stressed that "actions to restore, rehabilitate, or replace natural resources under the provisions of this Act be accomplished in the most cost-effective manner possible."[162]

As Senator Simpson observed and the act provides, the common law employs the most *cost-effective* approach, measuring damages in terms of the reduced value of land or the market value of products damaged or destroyed. Restoration costs in excess of this net reduction in value are not granted. Where restoration costs are less than the net reduction in value, however, the efficient measure of damages is the cost of restoring the resources.

When injured or destroyed natural resources have an independent economic value of their own, such as marketable timber or fish in a hatchery, the measure of damages is the value of the destroyed resources.[163] When the destroyed resources lack their own economic value, the virtually unanimous common law

---

[158] S Rep No 848, 96th Cong, 2d Sess 86 (1980), *reprinted in* 5 US Code Cong & Ad News 6119.

[159] *Id.*

[160] *Id.*

[161] 126 Cong Rec S15008 (daily ed Nov 24, 1980) (remarks of Sen Simpson).

[162] S Rep No 848, *supra* note 158, at 85.

[163] *See, e.g.,* Chevron Oil Co v Snellgrove, 175 So 2d 471, 474 (Miss 1965); State Dept of Fisheries v Gillette, 27 Wash App 815, 820, 621 P2d 764, 768 (Wash Ct App 1980).

rule is that damages should be measured by the reduction in the market value of the land to which they are attached.[164]

An exception to this general rule exists where the injured or destroyed natural resources can be restored to their original condition for less cost than the market value of the land, in which case replacement costs are granted.[165] Where restoration costs exceed the reduction in land value, however, they are an inappropriate measure of damages.[166] In addition, when restoration costs are used, only cost-effective restoration may be allowed.[167] Moreover, any damages are to be tempered by consideration of the "ability of the ecosystem or resource to recover" on its own.[168]

Section 106 Emergency Relief

§10.14 Statutory Prerequisites to Relief

Section 106 is the emergency provision of Superfund,[169] authorizing the Environmental Protection Agency (EPA) to go to court to compel relief when the agency "determines that there may be an imminent and substantial endangerment to the public health or welfare or the environment because of an actual or threatened release of a hazardous substance from a facility."[170] In addition, the EPA may take "other action," including the issuance of "such orders as may be necessary to protect public health and welfare and the environment."[171]

Section 106 provides virtually no detail as to the standards for these actions, however, and the threshold question is whether that section is substantive or merely confers jurisdiction upon the federal courts. A similar controversy has arisen under the closely analogous, "imminent and substantial endangerment" provision of §7003 of the Resource Conservation and Recovery Act (RCRA).[172] The early RCRA decisions held that §7003 was solely jurisdictional and just allowed the government to go into federal court and prosecute actions

---

[164] *See, e.g.*, Fiske v Moczik, 329 So 2d 35, 37 (Fla Dist Ct App 1976); Atlas Chem Indus, Inc v Anderson, 524 SW2d 681, 687 (Tex 1975).

[165] *See, e.g.*, Watkins v FMC Corp, 531 P2d 505 (Wash Ct App 1975).

[166] *See, e.g.*, Maldonado v Connecticut Light & Power Co, 31 Conn Supp 536, 328 A2d 120 (Conn 1974).

[167] *See, e.g.*, Farny v Bestfield Builders, Inc, 391 A2d 212, 214 (Del 1978).

[168] 42 USC §9651(c)(2).

[169] Comprehensive Environmental Response, Compensation and Liability Act, 42 USC §9601 *et seq*, commonly known as *Superfund.*

[170] *Id* §9606(a).

[171] *Id.*

[172] 42 USC §6973.

under federal common law.[173]

Subsequent to these decisions, however, the Supreme Court decided *City of Milwaukee v Illinois,*[174] which held that the Clean Water Act's[175] detailed requirements preempted any federal common law in the field. This decision, known as *Milwaukee II,* cast doubt that any federal common law of hazardous waste disposal survived the enactments of RCRA and Superfund. More recent RCRA §7003 cases have dismissed federal common law claims in light of *Milwaukee II* and have allowed §7003 claims to proceed by attributing substantive standards to that section.[176]

Early Superfund cases have followed this approach as well. In *United States v Outboard Marine Corp,*[177] the court held that Superfund §106 carried "certain substantive requirements."[178] While conceding that the section was vague, the decision held that the interpretation that §106 was solely jurisdictional "seems to be foreclosed by Milwaukee II."[179]

It thus seems likely that §106 will be considered substantive as well as jurisdictional. What is not clear is what exactly are the section's substantive standards. One unambiguous standard, found on the face of §106, is that the government demonstrate that there may be an imminent and substantial endangerment at the site. A second standard is that the requirements of the National Contingency Plan be satisfied.

The third, and perhaps the most important, standard of §106 is that relief be consistent with the public interest and the equities of the case. This condition reaffirms the principles that courts apply general equitable principles to government requests for injunctions and invokes public interest balancing considerations, such as those found in the common law of nuisance. Thus, the term *equities of the case,* as used in the bankruptcy laws, has been used as support for courts to apply "the principles and rules of equity jurisprudence."[180]

By applying these principles, as well as traditonal canons of statutory construction, courts can derive standards for §106 actions. In *United States v Wade,*[181] the court held that nonnegligent off-site generators were not proper defendants under §106. In so doing, the court relied primarily on the act's legislative history and its conclusion that Congress intended that §107[182] be the statute's remedy against off-site generators. The government has strongly

---

[173] *See* United States v Solvents Recovery Service, 496 F Supp 1127 (D Conn 1980); United States v Midwest Solvent Recovery, 484 F Supp 138 (D Ind 1980).

[174] 451 US 304 (1981).

[175] 33 USC §§1251-1376.

[176] United States v Price, 523 F Supp 1055 (DNJ 1981); United States v Diamond Shamrock Corp, 17 Envt Rep Cas (BNA) 1329 (ND Ohio 1981).

[177] 18 Envt Rep Cas (BNA) 1087 (ND Ill 1982).

[178] *Id* 1090.

[179] *Id.*

[180] Pepper v Litton, 308 US 295, 304-05 (1939).

[181] 546 F Supp 785 (ED Pa 1982).

[182] 42 USC §9606.

challenged this ruling, and at least one decision, *United States v Price*,[183] has held that off-site generators are strictly liable under §106.

Regardless of whether the *Wade* holding stands up as an absolute bar to generator liability under §106, general equitable principles should limit the liability of nonnegligent off-site generators under §106. Equity is reluctant to enjoin parties who bear a "remote relationship" to the hazard in question or who have "no knowledge or control" over the situation.[184] Furthermore, courts generally will not enjoin defendants who do not own the operations to which an injunction would be directed.[185]

There is an argument that the list of defendants in §107 should be read into §106, which lacks any facial clue as to who may be proper defendants. Given the absence of any clear statutory guidance, however, the better course is for courts to use the traditional equitable principles, specifically referred to in §106, to determine who may be proper defendants in specific cases.

Equitable principles impose other limits on §106 relief as well. At equity, a court will issue an injunction only after "balancing" the "equities and hardships" involved.[186] Equity "balances the conveniences of the parties and possible injuries to them according[ly] as they may be affected by the granting or withholding of the injunction."[187]

The Supreme Court has elaborated on the importance of this balancing of interests:

> Our society and its governmental instrumentalities, having been less than alert to the needs of our environment for generations, have now taken protective steps. These developments, however praiseworthy, should not lead courts to exercise equitable powers loosely or casually whenever a claim of "environmental damage" is asserted. . . . The decisional process for judges is one of balancing and it is often a most difficult task.[188]

This process involves, inter alia, a determination of whether the costs of an injunction are justified by its benefits.[189]

The application of equity principles under §106 may, in appropriate cases, also give rise to certain traditional defenses. The government, for example, may be denied relief due to *unclean hands* if it has itself participated in creating the hazard.[190]

---

[183] Civ No 80-4104 (DNJ July 28, 1983).

[184] *See, e.g.,* Naughton v Bevilacqua, 605 F2d 586, 589 (1st Cir 1979).

[185] *See, e.g.,* Greenhouse v Greco, 368 F Supp 736 (WD La 1973); United States v Gulf-State Theaters, 256 F Supp 549 (ND Miss 1966).

[186] Dobbs, Remedies 52 (1973).

[187] Yakus v United States, 321 US 414 at 440 (1944).

[188] Aberdeen & Rockfish RR v SCRAP, 409 US 1207, 1217-18 (1972).

[189] Boomer v Atlantic Cement Co, 26 NY2d 219, 257 NE2d 870, 309 NYS2d 312, (1970), *affd sub nom,* Kinley v Atlantic Cement Co, 42 AD2d 496 (3d Dept 1973).

[190] *See, e.g.,* Precision Instrument Mfg Co v Automotive Co, 324 US 806, 814 (1945); United States v Georgia Pac, 421 F2d 92 (9th Cir 1970).

§10.15   Adequacy of Legal Remedies

Perhaps the most important condition on use of §106[191] of Superfund,[192] grounded both in equitable and statutory requirements, is the requirement that the government demonstrate the inadequacy of its legal remedies before receiving injunctive relief. Under equitable principles, an injunction may issue only when a plaintiff has shown the inadequacy of his or her legal remedies.

In *Weinberger v Romero-Barcelo*,[193] the Supreme Court held that this require-ment applies even when a federal statute authorizes injunctive relief, as does §106. Under this principle, the government must show that its remedies, including §104 clean-up[194] and §107 reimbursement,[195] are inadequate in the specific case.

In construing the injunctive relief authority of the Clean Water Act,[196] the Court stressed that it "has repeatedly held that the basis for injunctive relief in the federal courts has always been irreparable injury and the inadequacy of legal remedies."[197] In its holding, the Court characterized an injunction as an *extraordinary remedy* and declined to issue an injunction due to the plaintiffs' failure to demonstrate irreparable injury. In this connection, the Court ob-served: "An injunction is not the only means of ensuring compliance. The [Federal Water Pollution Control Act] FWPCA itself, for example, provides for fines and criminal penalties."[198] Since the plaintiffs had made no attempt to demonstrate the inadequacy of these remedies, injunctive relief was denied.

The adequacy of legal remedies under Superfund is even clearer than under the Clean Water Act.[199] The Clean Water Act's fines and criminal penalties are, at best, incentives to undertake clean-up. The Superfund §104 authority for the government to clean up is much broader and far more adequate. In most cases, the government can accomplish everything under §104 that it could under §106. Only in unique circumstances where there is ongoing disposal or where a defendant is specially qualified to undertake clean-up itself should §106 be invoked. Indeed, in early §106 cases, courts have directed the govern-ment to employ its legal remedies in lieu of injunctive relief.[200]

The legislative history of analogous provisions further confirms that §106 authority should only be used when other clean-up alternatives are inadequate. The House Report on the "imminent and substantial endangerment" provi-

---

[191] 42 USC §9606.

[192] Comprehensive Environmental Response, Compensation and Liability Act, 42 USC §9601 *et seq*, commonly known as *Superfund*.

[193] 456 US 305 (1982).

[194] 42 USC §9604.

[195] *Id* §9607.

[196] 33 USC §§1251-1376.

[197] 456 US at 312.

[198] *Id* 314.

[199] 33 USC §§1251-1376.

[200] *See* United States v Wade, 546 F Supp 785 (ED Pa 1982).

sion of the Safe Drinking Water Act,[201] for example, stressed the limits inherent in its authorization of relief:

> In using the words "imminent and substantial endangerment to the health of persons," the Committee intends that this broad administrative authority not be used when the system of regulatory authorities provided elsewhere in the bill could be used adequately to protect the public health.[202]

The House report on 108 of the Clean Air Act,[203] the original "imminent and substantial endangerment" provision, likewise emphasized that it was "not intended as a substitute procedure for chronic or generally recurring pollution problems, which should be dealt with under the other provisions of the act."[204]

Cases under the Resource Conservation and Recovery Act (RCRA)[205] §7003[206] have made the same point. Thus, the court in *United States v Solvents Recovery Service*[207] held that "situations which do not present true emergencies are better dealt with through the more comprehensive, if more cumbersome, provisions of RCRA and the EPA regulations promulgated thereunder than in an action under section 7003."[208] *United States v Hardage*[209] employed a similar interpretation of the RCRA, limiting §7003 to "that sort of emergency situation in which application of the general provisions of the Act" would be inadequate to protect the public health.[210]

Both equitable principles and legislative history suggest that Superfund §106 should be used only when other legal remedies are inadequate. Unlike many statutes, Superfund contains its own built-in legal remedy in §104, authorizing government clean-up, and §107, providing for reimbursement. Thus, in most cases, the government should have an adequate legal remedy under Superfund, and §106 should be unavailable.

In some limited circumstances, however, §106 relief would be appropriate. Section 104 may be an inadequate legal remedy, for example, when state matching funds are unavailable or when the $1 million ceiling on Hazardous Substance Response Trust Fund (Fund)[211] expenditures has been reached.[212]

---

[201] 42 US §§300f-j.

[202] HR Rep No 1185, 93d Cong, 2d Sess 35 (1974), *reprinted in* 4 US Code Cong & Ad News 6454.

[203] 42 USC §7608.

[204] HR Rep No 728, 90th Cong, 1st Sess 119 (1967), *reprinted in* 4 US Code Cong & Ad News 1368.

[205] 42 USC §§6901-6987.

[206] 42 USC §6973.

[207] 496 F Supp 1127 (D Conn 1980).

[208] *Id* 1143 n 29.

[209] Civ No 80-1031-W (WD Okla Sept 29, 1982).

[210] *Id*, slip op at 3.

[211] Congress created the Fund in 42 USC §9631.

[212] 42 USC §9604(c)(1).

In the future, if the Fund were ever exhausted, §106 might be required to ensure clean-up of a site. There is no indication, however, that Congress intended §106 to be used routinely for site clean-up when §104 clean-up is available.

§10.16   Administrative Orders

Section 106[213] of Superfund[214] also authorizes the issuance of administrative orders to compel clean-up. While the statute does not expressly incorporate the standards discussed in §§10.14 and 10.15 in the administrative orders authority, imposing such requirements is the only reasonable construction of the section.

First, §106 explicitly refers to administrative orders as "other action under this section," thereby referring to the requirements outlined above. Second, failure to apply the general §106 substantive standards to administrative orders would raise grave constitutional issues under the delegation doctrine. Absent the standards noted in §§10.14 and 10.15, there would be no "intelligible principle" to guide administrative decisions, as required by *Panama Refining Co v Ryan*.[215]

Finally, the administrative order authority is potentially a summary, ex parte proceeding. As such, it logically should have a higher threshold requirement, reserved for cases where a site presents such a dire emergency that immediate action is required.

In addition to the lack of substantive requirements for administrative orders, §106 provides no procedural requirements for such orders, nor have the Environmental Protection Agency's (EPA) §106 guidelines established any procedures for the issuance of administrative orders.[216]

Targets of an administrative order are guaranteed a hearing by the Fifth Amendment's due process clause. The nature and timing of this hearing, however, depend on a balancing test that takes into account:

> first, the private interest that will be affected by the official action; second, the risk of an erroneous deprivation of such interest through the procedures used, and the probable value, if any, of additional or substitute procedural safeguards; and finally, the Government's interest, including the function involved and the fiscal and administrative burdens that the

---

[213] 42 USC §9606.

[214] Comprehensive Environmental Response, Compensation and Liability Act, 42 USC §9601 *et seq*, commonly known as *Superfund.*

[215] 293 US 388, 401 (1935).

[216] See EPA, Interim Superfund Removal Guidance (July 28, 1981); Section 106(c) Guidelines, 47 Fed Reg 20664 (June 14, 1982).

additional or substitute procedural requirement would entail.[217]

It is clear that the opportunity for a hearing "must be granted at a meaningful time and in a meaningful manner."[218] Targets of administrative orders may succeed in applying the above balancing test to compel a hearing before the EPA before any administrative order may issue.

The automatic right to a preorder administrative hearing, however, is by no means clear. In *Ewing v Mytinger & Casselberry*,[219] the Supreme Court held that the Food and Drug Administration did not need to grant companies a hearing prior to seizing articles as misbranded. The Court characterized the physical seizure as "merely the statutory prerequisite to the bringing of a lawsuit," and emphasized that "only property rights are concerned."[220]

If, however, a party's due process right to a hearing is denied by the agency, it must be fulfilled in judicial review. As a constitutional matter, when no administrative hearing has been held, a party has a right to de novo judicial review.[221] In addition, the Administrative Procedure Act[222] would require de novo judicial review when no hearing was available before the agency.[223]

Moreover, de novo judicial review of administrative orders will be available if the agency has conducted an *inadequate* preorder hearing. While there is a presumption against such de novo review,[224] it may be required where the agency failed to conduct an adversary hearing, including oral testimony and cross-examination.[225] In short, if parties are not given a fair opportunity to challenge an administrative order in an administrative hearing, they will receive such an opportunity in de novo judicial review.

If a party does not receive a preorder hearing, however, it may face a difficult decision as to whether to comply with the order prior to judicial review. Under §107(c)(3),[226] any person who is liable for release of a hazardous substance and who fails "without sufficient cause" to take removal or remedial action in compliance with a §106 order is liable for punitive damages "in an amount at least equal to, and not more than three times," the clean-up costs incurred by the Hazardous Substance Response Trust Fund (Fund).[227] An important issue, therefore, is the question of what constitutes "sufficient cause" for refusing to comply with an order.

---

[217] Mathews v Eldridge, 424 US 319, 335 (1976).

[218] Armstrong v Manzo, 380 US 545, 552 (1965).

[219] 339 US 594 (1950).

[220] *Id* 598, 599.

[221] United States v International Harvester, 387 F Supp 1338 (DDC 1974).

[222] 5 USC §551 *et seq.*

[223] First Natl Bank v Saxon, 352 F2d 267 (4th Cir 1965), *affd sub nom* First Natl Bank v Walker Bank & Trust Co, 385 US 252 (1966).

[224] Camp v Pitts, 411 US 138, 141-42 (1973).

[225] Brown v United States, 396 F2d 989, 994-95 (Ct Cl 1968).

[226] 42 USC §9607(c)(3).

[227] Congress created the Fund in 42 USC §9631.

The legislative history includes one reliable indicator that contesting an order in good faith is a sufficient cause for noncompliance. In the Senate floor debate on the day of Superfund's passage, Senator Simpson engaged Senator Stafford in a colloquy to establish legislative history on the treble damage provision. Senator Stafford stated that Congress' intent was that

> "sufficient cause" would encompass defenses such as the defense that the person who was the subject of the President's order was not the party responsible under the act for the release of the hazardous substance. It would certainly be unfair to assess punitive damages against a party who for good reason believed himself not to be the responsible party.[228]

The Senator mentioned several other examples of sufficient cause for noncompliance as well: if there were "substantial facts in question" at the time of the order, or if the party lacked the financial or technical resources necessary to comply, punitive damages either should not be assessed or should be mitigated in the interest of justice.[229]

Senator Stafford did not pretend to be exhaustive in his list of circumstances that constituted sufficient cause for failure to comply with an order. His use of *such as* indicates that he was merely citing examples of a category of valid reasons for failure to conduct the response ordered.

In short, if a party has a good faith serious dispute with the EPA concerning an issue of fact on which the order is based—for example, over the toxicity of a substance or the composition of a waste site—punitive damages should not be levied. This result would be consistent with other analogous statutes that contain multiple damage provisions. These other acts have applied punitive damages only for willful violations of statutory provisions.[230]

Victim Compensation

§10.17   Compensation for Toxic Tort Victims

On July 30, 1983, the study group created pursuant to §301(e)[231] of Superfund[232] submitted to Congress its recommendations for the improvement of legal remedies available to persons injured by exposure to releases of hazard-

---

[228] 126 Cong Rec S15008 (daily ed Nov 24, 1980) (remarks of Sen Stafford).

[229] *Id.*

[230] *See, e.g.,* 29 USC §626 (Age Discrimination in Employment Act); Dean v American Sec Ins, 559 F2d 1036, 1039 (5th Cir 1977), *cert denied,* 434 US 1066 (1978).

[231] 42 USC §9651(e).

[232] Comprehensive Environmental Response, Compensation and Liability Act, 42 USC §9601 *et seq,* commonly known as *Superfund* or *CERCLA.*

ous wastes.[233] Those recommendations proposed extensive changes to the existing compensation system for persons injured by releases of hazardous substances, including the creation of a new federally supervised compensation system and a new *superfund* for the payment of such compensation. This new federal agency and fund constitute the study group's response to its mandate to evaluate the adequacy of existing remedies for compensation of persons injured by releases of hazardous waste of the type which have occurred in well-publicized incidents at Love Canal, New York; Times Beach, Missouri; and the James River (following the release of kepone at Hopewell, Virginia).

The Superfund §301(e) study group was created as a compromise measure to address concerns of the congressional sponsors of CERCLA in 1980. The 1980 Senate bill[234] which was eventually enacted originally proposed the creation of a federal cause of action for persons injured by releases of hazardous substances. Opposition to such a cause of action resulted in a compromise under which the substantive provisions of CERCLA (establishing a *superfund* to finance federal responses to the release or threatened release of hazardous substances) would be supplemented by the creation of a study group to consider further the problems of compensation for persons injured by such releases.

In broad outline, the study recommends a *two-tier* system of remedies for persons injured or suffering damage due to the release of a hazardous substance.

One half of this scheme—the study's so-called Tier II system—is in essence not new at all. The study recommends that toxic tort victims continue to be able to bring direct civil actions—whether in tort, trespass, or nuisance—against parties who have allegedly injured them. Although the study recommends modernization in certain of the traditional problem areas in toxic torts litigation—such as the adoption of statutes of limitations employing a *discovery* rule and the adoption of a standard of strict liability for parties *responsible* for a release—the study group was content to recommend that the various states undertake this modernization. Thus, implementation by Congress of the study group's recommendations regarding state causes of action would result in no change in existing remedies.

The study group's Tier I proposal would constitute a significant addition to the existing toxic tort compensation system. Under the Tier I system, injured persons would have the option of pursuing a new, federally created administrative remedy similar to that available under existing workers' compensation systems for traumatic, work-related injuries, and also similar to the compensation system established by Congress for black lung victims in 1969. Administration of this system would be delegated to qualifying states, much as

---

[233] 97th Cong, 2d Sess, Injuries and Damages from Hazardous Wastes—Analysis and Improvement of Legal Remedies: A Report to Congress in Compliance with §301(e) of the Comprehensive Environmental Response, Compensation and Liability Act of 1980 (Pub L No 96-510), (Comm Print).

[234] S 1480, 97th Cong, 2d Sess, 126 Cong Rec No 165 (Nov 24, 1980).

programs under the Clean Air Act[235] and Clean Water Act[236] are currently delegated.

The Tier I system is intended by the study group to provide a speedy and effective means of compensation for persons injured by releases now covered by CERCLA—i.e., generally, releases from *old* hazardous waste sites, and releases resulting from breaches of the Resource Conservation and Recovery Act's (RCRA)[237] *cradle-to-grave* system of regulating the generation, transport, treatment, storage, and disposal of hazardous wastes. The proposed Tier I system would allow injured persons to seek compensation for medical costs and lost earnings (not to exceed $2,000 per month) as well as death benefits. (Other compensation—such as for pain and suffering, property damage, and punitive damages—would be available only through a separate legal action under the Tier II system.)

The speed and effectiveness of the Tier I system would derive largely from two main attributes. First, injured persons would recover directly from a special federal fund similar to the existing superfund for the prevention and remedy of releases of hazardous substances. The study group recommends that the compensation fund be financed by a tax on hazardous waste generators and disposers. The study group also recommended further consideration of the question whether the class of industries contributing to the current superfund should be expanded.

By gaining access to the Tier I system, victims would avoid the need to select the proper party or parties responsible for a release and would avoid the risks of evaluating any judgments obtained. Generally, the fund would have a right of subrogation of the claimant's cause of action against the responsible parties.

Second, the Tier I system would be based on a relaxed standard of proof for causation of injury. Although this proposal is controversial, the study group intended that the use of certain presumptions for proof of causation of injuries would allow the Tier I system to process large numbers of cases without the delays typical of litigation. In addition, the study group believed that the use of these presumptions would make it economically feasible for claimants with relatively modest claims to seek compensation.

In general, proof of causation of injuries associated with hazardous substances has proved to be one of the most difficult elements of a toxic torts case. The causal link between certain diseases or injuries—such as asbestosis among persons exposed to asbestos fibers—may on occasion be clear and easily demonstrated. Far more frequently, however, the causal link between an individual's injury and the hazardous substance to which he or she has been exposed is far more tenuous. Typically, the injury appears long after exposure to the substance, and sometimes long after exposure has ceased. Moreover, the disease—e.g., a cancer—may be caused by events other than exposure to hazardous waste, so that it is difficult to distinguish between claimants suffer-

---

[235] 42 USC §§7401-7642.

[236] 33 USC §§1251-1376.

[237] 42 USC §§6901-6987.

ing an injury resulting from *natural* causes and claimants who would not have been injured except for exposure to a hazardous substance. Finally, even where proof suggesting a causal link between exposure and injury is theoretically available, such proof may be so difficult or expensive to muster in individual cases that claims brought on a case-by-case basis will effectively be barred.

These difficulties are not merely legal in nature: they reflect the existing scientific uncertainty over the extent to which exposure to hazardous wastes actually causes injuries—a point subject to considerable debate today. Because scientists currently lack sufficient understanding of the etiology of many diseases possibly caused by exposure to hazardous waste, there is no easy solution to the problem of causation in compensation cases. Generally, the result of this uncertainty is that the party on whom the burden of proof is imposed will be at a tremendous disadvantage. Thus, the study group's treatment of causation will undoubtedly be seen as a litmus test of the study group's *tilt* or leaning toward either those who must pay compensation or those who seek it.

Despite criticism from a significant minority of its members, the study group recommends that a claimant may elect to seek remedies under *both* the Tier I and Tier II systems. The study group would, however, bar any double recovery of damages. In addition, the study proposes that judges in subsequent Tier II actions have the discretion to assess costs against a claimant whose Tier II claim does not result in an award exceeding the amount received in a Tier I proceeding by at least 25 per cent.

11 Theories of Liability

Lynn E. Pollan, Esq.*

* Assistant Counsel and Assistant Secretary, Bunge Corp., New York, New York.

§11.01   Introduction

In our jurisprudence, the courts are often the arbiters of social policy. Whenever they determine that the burden of a loss should be shifted from the plaintiff to the defendant as a consequence of the activities of the latter, they decide and implement broad questions of policy. In the area of toxic torts, society's concept of what constitutes acceptable conduct has dramatically changed in recent years, and the courts have not only responded to this change but have often led the way.

Redress for a toxic tort is normally sought under the following theories of liability: negligence, warranty, strict liability, misrepresentation and concealment, trespass, and nuisance. Absolute liability is just emerging as an avenue of recovery. To list these theories, however, is to suggest that they are each separate and independent avenues of recovery. In fact, they overlap; they expand to encompass new conduct; and they retract when a higher court or legislature overrules a ground-breaking decision.

Recently, the courts have greatly facilitated the ability to gain a redress under these theories by allowing the *offensive* use of collateral estoppel and by developing approaches for imposing liability when the tortfeasor is unknown. These approaches include enterprise liability, concert of action liability, market share liability, and product-line liability.

This chapter addresses the theories of liability available to toxic tort plaintiffs and the approaches that courts are using to allocate responsibility—not solely to wrongdoers but also to those who are in the best financial position to shoulder the responsibility and remedy the wrong prospectively. Problems associated with private causes of action created by statute (including workers' compensation) and the problems defendants face in allocating liability among themselves or in passing it on to insurance carriers are not discussed in this chapter.

§11.02   Negligence

Most toxic tort actions are not brought exclusively on the theory of negligence. The plaintiff bears a higher burden of proof in a negligence action than in a strict liability or breach of warranty action. The Restatement (Second) of Torts defines negligence as "conduct which falls below the standard established by law for the protection of others against unreasonable risk of harm."[1] The elements of a cause of action in negligence are:

1. A duty or standard of conduct imposed by law for the protection of others against unreasonable risk of harm

2. Defendant's failure to comply with that standard

3. Sufficient causal connection between the defendant's conduct and the plaintiff's injury for the law to impose liability—*proximate cause*

---

[1] Restatement (Second) of Torts §282, at 9 (1965).

4.   Actual loss or damage to the plaintiff[2]

Often, negligence may not be provable, as in the case of a manufacturer of electric transformers which used a fluid containing PCBs many years ago, at a time when the health hazards of PCBs were unknown. Another disadvantage of a negligence cause of action is that the plaintiff is subject to more affirmative defenses than in a strict liability or breach of warranty action.[3]

Nevertheless, if the facts exist, negligence should be pleaded in conjunction with all other available theories of liability. Proving a case of negligence to a jury might well result in a greater financial recovery than proof of breach of warranty or strict liability, which might appear not to justify as great an award of damages. In certain circumstances, it may turn out to be the only theory upon which the plaintiff can succeed. Generally, neither strict liability nor breach of warranty will furnish a basis for recovery where the injury did not result from a product. For example, in many states the furnishing of blood is deemed a *service,* not a product. The plaintiff who has contracted serum hepatitis from blood transfusions is precluded from bringing his or her action in strict liability or for breach of warranty in these states.[4] The plaintiff may, however, attempt to establish that the hospital or blood bank was negligent in failing to use reasonable care and diligence in obtaining and testing blood. Similarly, the administration of radiation treatment has not been considered the sale of a product for strict liability or warranty purposes.[5]

In suits involving professional malpractice, the plaintiff is usually limited to a claim for negligence. A toxic tort case that typifies the courts' reluctance to apply strict liability or warranty theories of liability to professionals is *La Rossa v Scientific Design.*[6] The defendant there had contracted with decedent's employer to design, engineer, and supervise the construction and initial operation of a plant for the manufacture of phthalic anhydride. To start up the plant, pellets coated with vanadium were loaded into a reactor. The defendant supplied the pellets and was responsible for supervising the loading operation. Plaintiff alleged that her husband died from cancer occasioned by his exposure to vanadium dust during the loading process. The court affirmed the dismissal of the breach of warranty counts because "[t]hose who hire [experts] . . . are not justified in expecting infallibility, but can expect only reasonable care and competence. They purchase service, not insurance."[7]

---

[2] W. Prosser, The Law of Torts §30, at 143-44 (4th ed 1971).

[3] Defenses are discussed in **ch 14.**

[4] *E.g.,* Samuels v Health & Hosps Corp, 591 F2d 195 (2d Cir 1979) (applying New York law); Cramer v Queen of Angels Hosp, 62 Cal App 3d 812, 133 Cal Rptr 339 (Ct App 1976); Steinik v Doctors Hosp, 82 Misc 2d 97, 368 NYS2d 767 (Sup Ct 1975); Morse v Riverside Hosp, 44 Ohio App 2d 422, 339 NE2d 846 (Ct App 1974); Foster v Memorial Hosp Assn, 219 SE2d 916 (W Va 1975).

[5] Pitler v Michael Reese Hosp, 92 Ill App 3d 739, 415 NE2d 1255 (1980).

[6] 402 F2d 937 (3d Cir 1968) (applying New Jersey law).

[7] *Id* 943 (quoting Gagne v Bertran, 43 Cal 2d 481, 489, 275 P2d 15, 21 (1954)).

The *La Rossa* court justified the distinction between products and professional services because in the case of a product, the consumer relies for his or her safety entirely on the manufacturer, due to the disparity in position and bargaining power. It is unduly difficult for the consumer to trace back along the channel of trade for the origin of the defect and pinpoint an act of negligence and the mass producer of a product should bear the responsibility of an insurer as a matter of public policy. One can question the court's first two distinctions: a patient depends entirely upon his or her physician; a client depends on his or her attorney; indeed, most professionals enjoy a disparity in position and bargaining power. Hence, it can be equally difficult to pinpoint a professional's act of negligence. In the context of the *La Rossa* facts, one can also question the last distinction: the defendant had supplied the pellets which had been manufactured by its subsidiary.

Even in a products liability case, it makes good sense to plead a negligence cause of action, particularly if the slightest doubt exists whether the plaintiff can proceed on his or her other liability theories. In non-products liability cases—such as professional malpractice, improper management of toxic dump sites, improper pesticide application, and the like—negligence may be the most viable predicate for recovery.

§11.03 —The Standard of Care in General

Before a plaintiff can get to a jury on the issue of negligence, he or she must establish that, as a matter of law, the defendant owed a duty to exercise care. (In one guise or another, this element is common to all theories of liability.) There are two questions here: to whom is the duty owed and what is the duty owed? The first question had given rise to the debate over privity. Until *McPherson v Buick Motor Co*,[8] the general rule had been that the original seller of goods was not liable if his or her defective product caused injury to anyone other than the immediate purchaser. In *McPherson*, Justice Cardozo reasoned that by mass-marketing a car, the manufacturer assumed a duty of care to the consumer, because harm was foreseeable if care were not exercised and because it was foreseeable that these people were likely to use or be exposed to the product. The rule applies to sellers as well as manufacturers. In *McPherson*, liability was imposed on the car's manufacturer even though the injury was caused by a defective wheel manufactured by another party. The requirement of privity in products liability cases has been abolished in all states.[9]

---

[8] 217 NY 382, 111 NE 1050 (1916).

[9] See W. Prosser, The Law of Torts §96, at 643 (4th ed 1971). As late as 1962, the Supreme Court of Mississippi had not accepted the *McPherson* decision. In *Cox v Laws*, 244 Miss 696, 145 So 2d 703 (1962), it allowed a widow to sue a drug store for the death of her husband caused by using a nonprescription penicillin ointment. Instead of abolishing privity, the court applied two exceptions to privity: the *inherently dangerous product* exception and the exception for violation of a statute designed for the protection of the public, in that case the Federal Food, Drug & Cosmetic Act.

In non-products liability cases, whether the defendant owes a duty to the plaintiff is a difficult threshold question. Even before *McPherson* was decided, there were exceptions to privity. Where the defendant's activity or article was considered imminently dangerous to another who had no notice of its danger-ous nature and qualities, the defendant would be held liable to the injured person unless he or she could prove that he or she exercised reasonable care.[10] Today, most courts employ a very broad standard for determining to whom the defendant owes a duty. The limitations on the boundaries of a defendant's liability in negligence are two-fold, based upon the foreseeability of the nature of the danger to the type of person put in danger.

In negligence, the standard of care owed another is only reasonable care to protect against a foreseeable and unreasonable risk of harm.[11] There are at least three variables in determining what constitutes reasonable care:

1. The probability that an accident will occur
2. The gravity of the injury which is likely if it does occur
3. The cost of precautions to prevent the accident[12]

These variables have been formulated many different ways and lie at the core of any risk-utility analysis.

In a toxic tort case, variable (1), the probability of an accident is analyzed from the perspective of the reasonable person at the time of defendant's conduct under all the circumstances and not "with the wisdom born of the event."[13] For this reason, the first victims of a particular toxic tort will some-times be left remediless. After the first illnesses or injuries are brought to the defendant's attention, the probability of an accident, variable (1), is easier to establish. The delimma is how to protect the earliest plaintiffs. Variable (2), the gravity of the injury, will often weigh heavily in favor of the toxic tort plaintiff. Courts may still balk, however, at imposing liability upon a defendant due to variables (1) and (3) because of the sometimes unknown risks of defen-dant's conduct at the time it was first undertaken (particularly in light of the long latency periods for many toxic agents) and the unavailability of, or enor-mity of the expense of, precautions to prevent the accident (such as the finding of safe ways of disposing of spent nuclear fuel). In many cases, however, the cost of precautions to prevent the accident can be rendered minimal by giving adequate warning of the danger. In this manner, variable (3) can often be resolved in the plaintiff's favor.

---

[10] *See* Huset v JI Case Threshing Mach Co, 120 F Supp 865 (8th Cir 1903); Cox v Laws, 244 Miss 696, 145 So2d 703 (1962).

[11] *See* Borel v Fibreboard Paper Prods Corp, 493 F2d 1076, 1088 (5th Cir 1973), *cert denied*, 419 US 869 (1974).

[12] United States v Carroll Towing Co, 159 F2d 169, 173 (2d Cir 1947). For a more elaborate statement of the variables, *see* Restatement (Second) of Torts §293, at 58 (1965).

[13] Greene v Sibley, Lindsay & Curr Co, 257 NY 190, 192, 177 NE 416, 417 (1931).

What constitutes reasonable care is affected by the character of the actor. Thus, in many toxic tort cases, because the defendants are manufacturers, professional entities, or others with special expertise in the activities they conduct, they are expected to exercise a higher degree of care than the ordinary, prudent person.

Borel v Fibreboard Paper Products Corp,[14] a leading asbestos case, addressed the duty of an expert: "[A]t a minimum he must keep abreast of scientific knowledge, discoveries, and advances and is presumed to know what is imparted thereby. But even more importantly, a manufacturer has a duty to test and inspect his product."[15] Even though none of the manufacturers in the asbestos insulation industry had provided warnings regarding the dangerous qualities of their products prior to 1974, the *Borel* court observed that a manufacturer cannot rely unquestioningly on others to alert the public to a danger in its product. This observation is equally valid for experts who are not manufacturers. Once on notice of a risk, the expert cannot continue *business as usual* even if others in his or her industry do so, if their conduct (a failure to warn in *Borel*) is careless or dangerous.

§11.04   —Duty to Warn

Breach of the duty to warn is probably the standard of care relied upon most frequently in toxic tort cases. It is common to the theories of negligence, warranty, strict liability, and misrepresentation—with a few distinctions among them. Even if the technology does not exist or it is prohibitively expensive to eliminate the danger of a toxic agent and the toxic agent is too useful to society to prohibit its creation or use, the providing of a warning is neither impossible nor prohibitively expensive. Thus, duty-to-warn cases illustrate the principle that the amount of care that the defendant must take is commensurate with the risk of harm.

According to the Restatement (Second) of Torts, liability for failure to warn arises if the manufacturer or supplier:

1. Knew or had reason to know that the product is or is likely to be dangerous for the use for which it was supplied

2. Had no reason to believe that those who use the product would have realized its dangerous condition

3. Failed to exercise reasonable care to inform the user of its dangerous condition or of the facts which made it likely to be dangerous.[16]

The duty to warn in negligence is not limited to manufacturers and suppliers

---

[14] 493 F2d 1076 (5th Cir 1973).

[15] *Id* 1089-90. *See* Restatement (Second), *supra* note 12, §289(b), at 41, and §299A, at 73; W. Prosser, *supra* note 9, §32, at 161.

[16] Restatement (Second) of Torts §388, at 300-01 (1965).

of products. It arises whenever, under all the circumstances, an ordinary, prudent person (or expert) would have given a warning to protect another person against a foreseeable and unreasonable risk of harm.

Because the manufacturer is expected to keep abreast of the current state of knowledge, its duty to warn continues even after sale whenever it learns of a danger inherent in the product.[17] Although most cases so holding tend to be strict liability cases (where the manufacturer has more incentive to issue warnings as defects come to its attention), the duty is also continuous in negligence cases in which the probability that an accident will occur is present (variable (1) described in **§11.03**), the gravity of the injury is substantial (variable (2)), and the burden of warning users of the danger is not substantial (variable (3)).[18] Since experts are also required to keep abreast of developments in their fields, it is similarly valid to impose upon them a continuing duty to warn their clients of dangers that come to their attention whenever the three variables are met.[19]

The duty to warn is actually composed of two separate duties—a duty to give adequate and comprehensible instructions for safe use and a duty to warn of dangers inherent in improper use.[20] The recent trend of cases is to require that for a warning to be adequate, it must be effective. It must be calculated to reach and be noticeable to and comprehensible by the user of the product and to any others within the foreseeable ambit of danger.[21] Even if a warning is adequate, moreover, its efficacy can be eroded by negligent overpromotion of the product (e.g., letters minimizing the dangers and promotional materials containing no reference to the harmful side effects) according to the California

---

[17] *See* Lindsay v Ortho Pharmaceutical Corp, 637 F2d 87, 91 (2d Cir 1980) (a strict liability case applying New York law and involving injury from oral contraceptives); Ferrigno v Eli Lilly & Co, 175 NJ Super 551, 420 A2d 1305 (Law Div 1980) (a strict liability case involving injury from DES); McKee v Moore, 648 P2d 21, 23-24 (Okla 1982) (a strict liability case involving injury from use of an IUD).

[18] *See* Jones v Bender Welding & Mach Works, Inc, 581 F2d 1331 (9th Cir 1978).

[19] *See* Mink v University of Chicago, 460 F Supp 713, 720 (ND Ill 1978).

[20] Gutowski v M & R Plastics & Coating, Inc, 60 Mich App 499, 231 NW2d 456 (Ct App 1975) (warnings regarding TDI hazards and use were found adequate); Seibel v Symons Corp, 221 NW2d 50 (ND 1974). Restatement (Second), *supra* note 16, §388, comment h, at 304-05. It may be incumbent upon counsel litigating a products liability matter to fully explore the issue of optional equipment, meaning safety and health controls, devices or equipment that are not standard but which are offered for sale by the product manufacturer or vendor at an extra charge. Often, the seller's failure to include such devices as standard equipment, or its failure to adequately apprise the customer of the availability of this option, may result in liability. Alternatively, the customer's failure to purchase such equipment, after being given a meaningful opportunity to do so, may result in an unfavorable verdict. *See* Bliss v Tenneco, 64 AD2d 204, 409 NYS2d 874 (4th Dept 1978); Wagner v International Harvester Co, 611 F2d 224 (8th Cir 1979); Marchant v Lorain Div of Koehring, 251 SE2d 189 (SC 1979).

[21] *See* Jackson v Coast Paint & Lacquer Co, 499 F2d 809, 814 (9th Cir 1974); DArienzo v Clairol, Inc, 125 NJ Super 224, 310 A2d 106 (Law Div 1973); Restatement (Second), *supra* note 16, §388, comment n, at 307-08 (1965).

Supreme Court in *Stevens v Parke, Davis & Co.*[22]

Courts are loathe to find a warning adequate as a matter of law. Whether the manufacturer of TRI, a solvent with toxic vapors, had given an adequate warning when it informed the *employer* of the plaintiff's decedent of its product's dangerous properties but *not* that it could cause death was held to be a jury issue in *Dougherty v Hooker Chemical Corp.* [23] The fact that the decedent's employer was aware of TRI's dangerous propensities and that it could cause death did not, as a matter of law, relieve the manufacturer of its duty to warn the ultimate user. Similarly, in *First National Bank, Albuquerque v Nor-Am Agricultural Products Inc,*[24] the appellate court reversed the trial court's grant of summary judgment to the defendant on the issue of the adequacy of the warning. In this case, the plaintiffs alleged that grain treated with Panogen-15, a grain seed disinfectant, was fed to hogs and caused injuries to the central nervous systems of children who later ate the hog meat. The label warned that it was poisonous and that it should not be used on feed. The court determined that material issues of fact existed that had to be decided by a jury, such as whether employees of the grain processor who used the Panogen-15 should have been warned that the poison might be communicated through the meat of livestock to human beings.

Prescription drugs are a notable exception to the requirement that the ultimate user be warned. The manufacturer's duty is to warn the prescribing and treating physicians, not the patient, unless the Food and Drug Administration has mandated otherwise. The physician acts as the "learned intermediary between the manufacturer and the consumer because he is in the best position to evaluate the patient's needs, assess the benefits and risks of a particular therapy, and to supervise its use."[25]

No one need to give notice of that which is obvious or generally known. In such cases the duty to warn never arises. This situation is different from cases where the duty to warn exists as to the general public, but the plaintiff is a knowledgeable user. In these cases, the issue of negligence is usually sent to the jury along with the instruction that they can consider the extent of plaintiff's knowledge of the danger in determining whether the defendant adequate-

---

[22] 9 Cal 3d 51, 507 P2d 653, 107 Cal Rptr 45 (1973). *Accord,* Salmon v Parke, Davis & Co, 520 F2d 1359 (4th Cir 1975); Lindquist v Ayerst Laboratories, Inc, 227 Kan 308, 607 P2d 1339 (1980); Spinden v Johnson & Johnson, 177 NJ Super 605, 427 A2d 597 (App Div), *cert denied,* 87 NJ 376, 434 A2d 1061 (1981); Whitley v Cubberly, 24 NC App 204, 210 SE2d 289 (Ct App 1974).

[23] 540 F2d 174 (3d Cir 1976). *See also* Jackson v Coast Paint & Lacquer Co, 499 F2d 809, at 812-13 (9th Cir 1974); Borel v Fibreboard Paper Prods Corp, 493 F2d 1076, 1091-92 (5th Cir 1973). (Both cases reject the defense of intervening cause, holding that is is the employer's responsibility to warn of the risk of harm.)

[24] 88 NM 74, 537 P2d 682 (Ct App), *cert denied,* 88 NM 29, 536 P2d 1085 (1975).

[25] McKee v Moore, 648 P2d 21, 24 (Okla 1982). *See also* Lindsay v Ortho Pharmaceutical Corp, 637 F2d 87, 91-92 (2d Cir 1980); Hoffman v Sterling Drug, Inc, 485 F2d 132, 142 (3d Cir 1973); Dunkin v Syntex Laboratories, Inc, 443 F Supp 121 (WD Tenn 1977).

ly fulfilled its duty to warn.[26] Cases in which courts have taken from the jury the issue of whether the defendant adequately discharged its duty to warn are few and far between.

§11.05 —Negligent Misrepresentation

Negligent misrepresentation is similar to a failure to warn. Instead of omitting information, the defendant has given false or misleading information. The negligence alleged is the failure to use reasonable care in ascertaining the accuracy of the information or in the manner of communicating it. The plaintiff must show that his or her reliance upon the false or misleading information was reasonable,[27] an element not required in failure-to-warn cases. However, it is not necessary for the plaintiff to prove that the defendant intended that he or she rely on the misrepresentation. This is an element of an action for fraudulent misrepresentation, discussed in **§11.18.**

Although the court did not label the case as one of negligent misrepresentation, in *United States v Aretz,*[28] the Georgia Supreme Court ruled that the United States government could be liable in negligence because the government had reclassified an illuminant from a class 2 fire hazard to a Class 7 explosive but had failed to communicate the change in classification to its defense contractor. When a fire broke out in a building in which loose illuminant material was being stored, an explosion occurred in which 29 employees of the contractor were killed and 50 were injured. The plaintiffs alleged the elements of negligent misrepresentation—a false statement, carelessness in the failure to correct it, justifiable reliance on the part of the plaintiffs, and causation. This case demonstrates that a defendant who may not otherwise owe a duty to inform the plaintiff may incur that duty if he or she transmits inaccurate information.

Negligent misrepresentation used to be alleged with greater frequency against manufacturers because it was an exception to the requirement of privity.[29] It is generally disfavored by courts because it encompasses such a broad spectrum of activity, much of it entirely innocent, and disfavored by plaintiffs because it carries the extra burden of proving justifiable reliance.

---

[26] *See, e.g.,* Billiar v Minnesota Mining & Mfg Co, 623 F2d 240, 245 (2d Cir 1980); First Natl Bank v Nor-Am Agr Prods, Inc, 88 NM 74, 537 P2d 682 (Ct App), *cert denied,* 88 NM 29, 536 P2d 1085 (1975).

[27] English v Lehigh City Auth, 286 Pa Super 312, 336-38, 428 A2d 1343, 1356-57 (Super Ct 1981) (reliance upon a list of hazardous work which omitted sewage sampling was not established and would have been unreasonable); Restatement (Second) of Torts §311, at 106 (1965).

[28] 248 Ga 19, 280 SE2d 345 (1981), answering questions certified in Aretz v United States, 635 F2d 485 (5th Cir 1981). (The Fifth Circuit suggested the theory of negligent misrepresentation when it listed authorities for the Georgia Supreme Court to consider.)

[29] *See, e.g.,* Gibbs v Procter & Gamble Mfg Co, 51 Ill App 2d 469, 476, 201 NE2d 473, 477 (1964).

§11.06 —Duties to Inspect, Test, and Design

> This is a day of synthetic living, when to an ever-increasing extent our population is dependent upon mass producers for its food and drink, its cures and complexions, its apparel and gadgets. These no longer are natural or simple products but complex ones whose composition and qualities are often secret. Such a dependent society must exact greater care than in more simple days and must require from manufacturers or producers increased integrity and caution as the only protection of its safety and well-being. Purchasers cannot try out drugs to determine whether they kill or cure. . . . Where experiment or research is necessary to determine the presence or the degree of danger, the product must not be tried out on the public, nor must the public be expected to possess the facilities or the technical knowledge to learn for itself of inherent but latent dangers. The claim that a hazard was not foreseen is not available to one who did not use foresight appropriate to his enterprise.[30]

Since manufacturers with expertise relating to toxic agents are held to a higher standard of care, it follows that a manufacturer who fails properly to test, inspect, or design his or her product will be liable in negligence if that failure results in injury to the plaintiff. Similar principles are applicable to the duties to test, inspect, and design with due care. These duties extend not only to the product but also to its container, whenever inspection, testing, or design is reasonably necessary to insure that the product is safe for its intended use and for any reasonably foreseeable emergency use.

What constitute reasonable design, inspection, and testing are questions of fact. The more likely it is that a substance will be dangerous unless carefully made, the higher the standard of care to which the manufacturer will be held.[31] Thus, in *Tinnerholm v Parke Davis & Co*,[32] the trial court, sitting as trier of fact, held the defendant manufacturer negligent for failing to test Quadrigen adequately. Its tests failed to disclose that the drug could cause severe brain damage, but they had disclosed problems of instability and potency unpredictability. The court stated that these problems, plus the known potential for one of the drug's components to cause fatal reactions, suggested further tests were needed, including tests under market conditions.

Drayton v Jiffee Chemical Corp[33] demonstrates the shortcomings of a negligence action as opposed to a warranty or strict liability action. The district court, sitting as trier of fact, found the manufacturer of a liquid drain cleaner negligent in designing a product for home use which contained a 26 per cent

---

[30] Dalehite v United States, 346 US 15, 51-52 (1953) (Jackson, J., dissenting).

[31] Restatement (Second) of Torts §298, comment b, at 68-69, and §395, comments d & e, at 327-28 (1965).

[32] 285 F Supp 432, 446-51 (SDNY 1968), *affd on other grounds*, 411 F2d 48 (2d Cir 1969).

[33] 395 F Supp 1081 (ND Ohio 1975), *affd on other grounds*, 591 F2d 352 (6th Cir 1978).

solution of lye (capable of dissolving skin tissue) and for failing to test the cleaner to determine its effect on human tissue. The drain cleaner had spilled on an infant, severely burning her face. On appeal, these findings were criticized because, among other things, the evidence tended to show that the liquid drain cleaner was safer than others. The appellate court noted that under the negligence rule in Ohio (and elsewhere), it is not the manufacturer's duty to design the best possible product or even one that is accident-proof or fool-proof, but one that is safe for its intended use. The manufacturer is not an insurer of his or her product under the negligence standard.[34]

In negligence, only reasonable testing or inspection is required. If the danger is already known, there is no further duty to test; if tests are not practical or economically feasible or would not have disclosed the latent defect, the manufacturer will not be held to have breached his or her duty.[35] The mere seller of a product of a responsible manufacturer which is still in its original container has no independent duty to warn, test, or inspect unless he or she knows or has reason to know that the product is dangerously defective, such as when there has been a complaint or recall.[36]

§11.07 —Duties Arising from Statutes and Regulations

To the extent that the lack of clearly enunciated standards has deterred environmental tort litigation in the past, the recent increase in statutes and regulations which impose standards of conduct regarding the environment, health, and safety should aid plaintiffs significantly in defining what constitutes negligence. Equally important, the statutes and regulations and the activities of the enforcement agencies have created greater awareness in the public and the judiciary of the risk of dangers from pollutants emanating from such sources as nuclear energy plants, chemical plants, and toxic waste sites, as well as the gravity of those dangers and the foreseeability of the risks.

Statutes and regulations can have an impact on the standard of care in a variety of ways, from creating a private right of action (expressly or by judicial

---

[34] 591 F2d at 357-58. See also W. Prosser, The Law of Torts §96, at 644-45 (4th ed 1971).

[35] See Brick v Barnes-Hines Pharmaceutical Co, 428 F Supp 496 (DDC 1977) (because liver damage was a well known side effect of Isoniazid, the manufacturer violated no duty to plaintiff in failing to conduct further studies); Lindquist v Ayerst Laboratories, Inc, 227 Kan 308, 607 P2d 1339 (1980) (without substantial proof that tests would have produced more conclusive results regarding the dangers of repeated use of Fluothane, an anaesthetic, within a short period of time, the trial court did not err in failing to give a charge on the manufacturer's duty to test); Warvel v Michigan Community Blood Center, 74 Mich App 440, 253 NW2d 791 (Ct App 1977) (no negligence for failure to test where no accurate test exists to establish whether serum hepatitis is present in a donor's blood).

[36] See Bathory v Procter & Gamble Distrib Co, 306 F2d 22 (6th Cir 1962).

implication)[37] to precluding it,[38] and from establishing absolute liability[39] or negligence per se[40] to merely furnishing some evidence of negligence[41] or furnishing none at all.[42] The impact of a statute or regulation varies greatly from state to state and from statute to statute (and from regulation to regulation).

A statute which creates a private right of action can become an obstacle if the case does not fall neatly into its requirements. The Louisiana Civil Code defined a duty and provided a remedy to the neighbors of a hazardous waste disposal site against the site's owner in *Ewell v Petro Processors Inc.*[43] Toxic chemicals had migrated to the neighbors' property due to the improper construction of several dump pits and leakage from them. But the court refused to impose any standard higher than the code's negligence standard because the evidence did not show that the disposal of toxic substances could not have been done safely. The court also refused to hold any of the dump's customers

---

[37] *E.g.,* Texas & Pac Ry v Rigsby, 241 US 33, 39-40 (1916) (a railroad employee injured as a result of his employer's failure to comply with the Federal Safety Appliance Act could bring a private action even though the statute did not expressly provide such a remedy).

[38] *E.g.,* Middlesex City Sewerage Auth v Sea Clammers, 453 US 1 (1981) (in enacting the Federal Water Pollution Control Act, 33 USC §1256, and the Marine Protection, Research and Sanctuaries Act, 16 USC §1431 *et seq,* Congress intended to foreclose implied private actions); *but cf* Smith v Western Elec Co, 643 SW2d 10 (Mo Ct App 1982) (existence of federal Occupational Safety and Health Act, 29 USC §651 *et seq,* does not preclude private action to enforce employer's common law duty under Missouri law to provide a safe place in which to work—in this case, an office area free of tobacco smoke).

[39] *E.g.,* Texas & Pac Ry v Rigsby, 241 US 33 (1916) (because the liability was absolute, evidence of plaintiff's negligence was immaterial); McCallie v New York Cent RR, 23 Ohio App 2d 152, 261 NE2d 179 (Ct App 1969) (failure to place warning signs at railroad crossings in violation of statute gave rise to absolute liability).

[40] *E.g.,* Gibson v Worley Mills, Inc, 614 F2d 464 (5th Cir), *modified on other grounds,* 620 F2d 567 (5th Cir 1980) (violation of federal and state laws in sale of seed containing toxic bindweed seed was negligence per se since laws were designed to protect plaintiff's class and to prevent the type of hazard and resulting damage to land that had occurred); Perry Creek Cranberry Corp v Hopkins Agr Chem Co, 29 Wis 2d 429, 139 NW2d 96 (1966) (failure to abide by the Wisconsin Economic Poisons Act in the labeling of malathion was negligence per se, and presence of disclaimer on labels was no defense); *but cf* Otto v Specialties, Inc, 386 F Supp 1240 (ND Miss 1974) (applying Mississippi law, the court held that negligence per se would not be inferred from a violation of the Occupational Safety and Health Act and that such evidence was inadmissible).

[41] *E.g.,* Monroe v New York, 67 AD2d 89, 414 NYS2d 718 (1979) (breach of duty to furnish workers a reasonably safe place to work, a duty recognized by New York's Labor Law, constitutes only some evidence of negligence).

[42] *E.g.,* Otto v Specialties, Inc, 386 F Supp 1240 (ND Miss 1974).

[43] 364 So2d 604 (La Ct App 1978). La Civ Code Ann arts 667, 669 (West 1980). *Contra* Schexnayder v Bunge Corp, 508 F2d 1069 (5th Cir 1975) (holding that the code imposes a strict liability standard; the case involved alleged injuries to property from grain dust emanating from defendants' grain elevators).

(not covered by the code's provisions) liable unless the plaintiffs could prove that the customer had dumped the toxic agents that had migrated onto plaintiffs' property, was aware of the leakage from the pits, and still continued to dump hazardous materials at the site.

Intention behind the Statute

Whether a private cause of action will be inferred from a statute depends upon whether the plaintiff is a member of the class for whose benefit the statute was enacted; whether the statute was enacted to protect the particular interest which is invaded and to protect against the kind of hazard which occurred and the kind of harm that resulted; whether the legislature intended to create or deny such a remedy; whether it is consistent with the underlying scheme of the statute to imply such a remedy; whether it is a cause of action traditionally or statutorily relegated to another forum; and, most importantly, whether the common law of the jurisdiction favors the inference of a private remedy.[44] Ever since *Cort v Ash*,[45] the federal courts have placed more emphasis on whether Congress *intended* for a private cause of action to exist and less on whether common law principles and public policy warrant such an inference.

In recent cases, the existence of federal environmental and safety legislation has inhibited the development of private common law remedies. Two recent examples are *Middlesex City Sewerage Authority v National Sea Clammers*,[46] where a private association of fishermen was precluded from suing several governmental authorities for polluting the New York harbor and surrounding waters because a pervasive federal statutory scheme existed, and *California v Sierra Club*,[47] where a private environmental group was precluded from enforcing the Rivers and Harbors Appropriation Act of 1899 and enjoining the construction of a California water project because the act was not enacted for the plaintiffs' especial benefit and Congress gave no indication that it intended to provide a private remedy. And in *National Women's Health Network v AH Robins Co*,[48] both preclusion of a private remedy and federal preemption under the Federal Food, Drug and Cosmetic Act were employed to dismiss an action for remedial equitable relief in the form of a worldwide recall of intrauterine contraceptive devices. A violation of the duty to warn users of oral contraceptives via package inserts, a regulatory requirement under the same act, however, was held to be negligence per se under Wisconsin law in *Lukaszewicz v Ortho Pharmaceutical Corp*.[49] One distinction between these seemingly inconsistent decisions is that in *Nat Women's Health Network*, the plaintiffs sought to enforce the act as private

---

[44] *See* Cort v Ash, 422 US 66, 78 (1975); Restatement (Second) of Torts §§286-288, at 25-32 (1965); W. Prosser, The Law of Torts §36, at 192-97 (4th ed 1971).

[45] 422 US 66 (1975).

[46] 453 US 1 (1981).

[47] 451 US 287 (1981). The Rivers and Harbors Appropriation Act is contained at 33 USC §401 *et seq.*

[48] 545 F Supp 1177 (D Mass 1982).

[49] 510 F Supp 961 (ED Wis 1981).

attorneys general; in *Lukaszewics,* the plaintiff sought merely to make evidentiary use of the act to obtain a personal judgment. (The lesson may be that plaintiffs who try to usurp governmental functions incur judicial disfavor.)

Whether the plaintiff was a member of the class for whose protection the regulation was intended was at issue in *Williams v Hill Mfg Co.*[50] The court struck the portion of the complaint which alleged that the manufacturer of Xylene, an explosive chemical, had breached a duty owed the plaintiff when it negligently and improperly labeled a drum of the chemical under Department of Transportation regulations. The court determined that the regulations are intended to protect people while shipments are in transit; here the plaintiff was injured in a postshipment explosion which resulted when plaintiff used a torch to cut the end off an empty drum of Xylene. *Sinclair Prairie Oil Co v Stell*[51] is a less troublesome decision. In that case, a statute which provided that no one should permit oil waste or salt water to run into any pool or stream used for watering livestock was clearly not intended for the protection of plaintiffs' decedent, who drowned in a pool of salt water and oil when his car plunged from a bridge into the pool. The statute was intended to protect cattle against the hazard of drinking polluted water, not motorists from drowning in it.

It is generally quite difficult for a plaintiff to persuade a court that a governmental unit owes a special duty to him or her, as opposed to the general public, particularly if the negligence alleged is the failure to conduct a reasonable inspection in its enforcement of a statute.[52] However, in a narrowly drawn decision, *Lorshbough v Buzzle,*[53] the Minnesota Supreme Court allowed plaintiffs, whose property had been damaged by a dump fire, to proceed with a negligence suit against the county on the basis that it had violated Pollution Control Agency regulations in its solid waste disposal operations and that it had actual knowledge of the dangerous condition that was created by the dump.

Effect of Violation

Once a court determines that the plaintiff is entitled to the benefit of a statute, the consequences of that determination vary from state to state, from case to case, and from statute to statute. In most states, the unexcused violation

---

[50] 489 F Supp 20 (DSC 1980).

[51] 190 Okla 344, 124 P2d 255 (1942).

[52] *See* Cracraft v St Louis Park, 279 NW2d 801 (Minn 1979) (city did not owe plaintiffs, whose child was injured by a chemical explosion at school, a special duty to inspect for fire code violations); O'Connor v New York, 51 USLW 2513 (NY Ct App Feb 23, 1983) (No 10); *but see* Blessing v United States, 447 F Supp 1160 (ED Pa 1978) (under Pennsylvania's *good Samaritan* rule, plaintiffs might be able to plead a cause of action against the Occupational Safety and Health Administration for conducting an inspection in a negligent manner).

[53] 258 NW2d 96 (Minn 1977).

of a statute or regulation is considered negligence per se.[54] But even what that means can vary. In some cases, negligence per se is tantamount to absolute liability, because it is imposed without regard to fault or the causal relationship between the violation and the injury.[55] If, under state law, the violation of a statute or regulation is some evidence of negligence or creates a presumption of negligence, the issue is one for the trier of fact.

The enactment of so many regulations in the past decade may be causing courts to be more circumspect in finding negligence per se. Nevertheless, even if the statute or regulation is introduced to the jury merely as some evidence of negligence, a plaintiff can derive significant psychological advantage from it. During summation, the point can be made (if appropriate) that the statute or regulation defines only a *minimum* standard of conduct.

§11.08 —Proximate Cause

A barrier to recovery in any toxic tort case is establishing the causal relationship between the defendant's conduct and the plaintiff's injury. (The problem is not limited to negligence actions since proximate cause is an element in almost all torts.) Long latency periods, the unforeseen effect of conduct undertaken years ago by persons unknown, the exposure of the plaintiff to many harmful elements over the years, and loss or spoliation of evidence tend to obscure causation. Limitations of scientific knowledge are part of the difficulty. How does one prove the extent of the plaintiff's exposure and the effects of that exposure to a court's satisfaction?[56] In toxic tort litigation particularly, there is often little proof of cause and effect, and courts tend to be skeptical of statistical correlations.[57] In time, these problems of proof may be solved by

---

[54] W. Prosser, *supra* note 44, §36, at 200 (4th ed 1971).

[55] *See, e.g.,* Sloan v Coit Intl, Inc, 292 So 2d 15 (Fla 1974) (violation of a statute requiring certificates of employment for minors constituted negligence per se without regard to the causal relationship between the violation and the child's injury—other courts might label this absolute liability). *See also* Douglas v Smith, 578 F2d 1169 (5th Cir 1978) (supplier of gas could be held liable for delivering gas to an unlicensed dealer in violation of a Georgia regulation if it knew or should have known the dealer was unlicensed; proximate cause existed because there was sufficient likelihood of the occurrence of harm in some manner from any delivery to an unlicensed dealer according to the court).

[56] Further discussion of proof of causation problems, from a scientific perspective, is contained in **ch 2.**

[57] *See, e.g.,* Lartigue v RJ Reynolds Tobacco Co, 317 F2d 19, 22-23 (5th Cir), *cert denied,* 375 US 865 (1963) (verdict for defendant affirmed because plaintiff failed to persuade jury that decedent's lung cancer was caused by his smoking); Mahoney v United States, 220 F Supp 823, 841 (ED Tenn 1963), *affd,* 339 F2d 605 (6th Cir 1964) (plaintiffs' exposures to radioactive radiation and toxic gases not shown to be sufficient to cause lymphatic leukemia, and the cause of Hodgkin's disease is unknown); Garner v Hecla Mining Co, 19 Utah 2d 367, 371, 431 P2d 794, 797 (1967) (despite evidence of higher than average incidence of lung cancer in uranium miners and that decedent had 34 times as much lead-210 in his bones as the average nonminer, plaintiff failed to establish

science; however, the test of proximate cause requires neither absolute medical certainty nor that the defendant's activity be the sole cause of the injury.

The difficulty of proving proximate cause is compounded by the tendency of some courts and lawyers to blur the distinction between proximate cause and legal cause, the standard of care by which the defendant's conduct is measured. (E.g., if injury is unlikely to arise from certain conduct, should a reasonable man refrain from such conduct?) Proximate cause is a fact issue, however, not a *duty* issue and thus should be left to the trier of fact. If it is more probable than not that the injury was caused by the defendant, albeit on the basis of circumstantial evidence, the element of proximate cause has been satisfied.[58] If the defendant's action or inaction was a "substantial contributing factor" in causing the injury, the trier of fact may find for the plaintiff.[59]

The issue of proximate cause is frequently raised in failure-to-warn cases due to the often tenuous causal connection between that failure and the plaintiff's injury. A case in point is *DeLuryea v Winthrop Laboratories.*[60] The plaintiff became dependent upon Talwin, a prescription drug manufactured by defendant, and she administered it to herself by injections. Over years of use, the injections caused damage to tissue, and she sued the defendant for inadequately warning the medical profession of the danger involved. The jury's verdict for plaintiff was upheld on appeal. The treating physician's testimony that the drug's warnings were inadequate because premarketing animal studies had revealed tissue damage, without any testimony from the prescribing physicians that they would have acted differently if different warnings had been given, sufficed to send the issue of causation to the jury. The court noted that the jury may infer that the doctors would have heeded the warning and altered their course of treatment had an adequate warning been given.

The boundaries of proximate cause are defined not only by causal relationship but also by legal policy, which may shift or allocate responsibility. Means of allocating responsibility, without proving that the defendant caused the

---

decedent's cancer resulted from an occupational disease); Clark v State Workmens Compensation Commr, 155 W Va 726, 731-32, 187 SE2d 213, 216 (1972) (because the causes of myeloblastic leukemia are unknown, plaintiff's four exposures to carcinogens were not shown to be the proximate cause); Olson v Federal Am Partners, 567 P2d 710 (Wyo 1977) (plaintiff failed to prove with medical certainty that decedent's cancer was caused by exposures to uranium radiation while in defendant's employ· his smoking habit could have been the cause or could have had a synergizing effect). *See also* Ginsberg & Weiss, *Common Law Liability for Toxic Torts: A Phantom Remedy,* 9 Hofstra L Rev 859, 922-24 (1981); Comment, *Tort Actions for Cancer: Deterrence, Compensation, and Enviromental Carcinogensis,* 90 Yale LJ 840, 847-55 (1981).

[58] *See* Bathory v Procter & Gamble Distrib Co, 306 F2d 22, 25-26 (6th Cir 1962); Borel v Fibreboard Paper Prods Corp, 493 F2d 1976, 1094 (8th Cir 1973), *cert denied,* 419 US 869 (1974); Moran v Johns-Manville Sales Corp, 691 F2d 811, 814 (6th Cir 1982); W. Prosser, The Law of Torts §41, at 242 (4th ed 1971).

[59] Neal v Carey Canadian Mines, Ltd, 548 F Supp 357, 370 (ED Pa 1982). *See also* Borel v Fibreboard Paper Prods Corp, 493 F2d 1076, 1094 (5th Cir 1973), *cert denied,* 419 US 869 (1974); Restatement (Second) of Torts §431, at 428 (1965).

[60] 697 F2d 222 (8th Cir 1983).

injury via concerted action or market share liability, are discussed in §§11.20 and 11.23. Intervening or superseding cause and unforeseeability of risk are defenses which can absolve the defendant from responsibility.

§11.09   —Actual Loss or Damage

The fourth and last element of a negligence cause of action is that the plaintiff must suffer actual loss or damage. (This element is indispensable to all actions, except that where irreparable injury is threatened, one may seek injunctive relief.) The policy behind this requirement is the prevention of fraudulent and vexatious lawsuits. Usually, emotional injuries alone are not compensable. *Payton v Abbott Labs* [61] provides an extensive historical overview of recovery for infliction of emotional distress. In this case, daughters whose mothers had ingested diethylstilbestrol (DES) sought to recover for their emotional injuries engendered by the greater statistical likelihood that they would suffer abnormalities of their reproductive organs than would the general population. The Massachusetts Supreme Court's four-to-three majority held that in order to recover, the plaintiffs had to prove that they suffered physical harm manifested by objective symptomatology and that a reasonable person would have suffered emotional distress under the same circumstances. The dissenters argued that under the circumstances, there were sufficient indicia of the genuineness of the claims that the issue should be submitted to the trier of fact. Certain of these women faced expensive and traumatic periodic examinations to check for DES-induced abnormalities.

§11.10   Express and Implied Warranties

The warranty theory of liability is usually available only where a product is the source of the injury. Strict liability tends to overshadow warranty as a theory of recovery because virtually every warranty case can also be brought in strict liability, and strict liability is not subject to such warranty defenses as lack of notice, lack of privity, and disclaimer.[62]

Express warranty was an early detour around the negligence requirement that the plaintiff prove that the defendant was *at fault*.[63] It is available if the defendant has made a positive assertion of fact to the plaintiff or the public

---

[61] 386 Mass 540, 437 NE2d 171, 174-180 (1982). For other toxic tort cases concerning absence of physical harm, *see* Silkwood v Kerr-McGee Corp, 667 F2d 908, 919 (10th Cir 1981), *appeal pending*, 51 USLW 3508 (US Jan 11, 1983) (No 81-2159); Mink v University of Chicago, 460 F Supp 713, 720 (ND Ill 1978). *See also* Restatement (Second) of Torts §436A, at 461 (1965).

[62] *See* Pearson v Franklin Laboratories, Inc, 254 NW2d 133 (SD 1977).

[63] Baxter v Ford Motor Co, 168 Wash 456, 12 P2d 409, *affd per curiam on rehg*, 168 Wash 465, 15 P2d 1118 (1932) (express statement in sales literature that windshield was shatterproof rendered manufacturer liable regardless of negligence or its knowledge of the statement's falsity).

concerning its product which is not true, the plaintiff learns of and relies upon the fact, and the plaintiff is injured as a result. As discussed in §11.06, in *Drayton v Jiffee Chemical Corp*,[64] the appellate court rejected the negligence portion of the trial court's decision because the manufacturer was not obligated to produce a foolproof drain cleaner. Defendant's advertisements, however, stated that "Liquid-plumr" was safe and showed a human hand swishing water in a sink. Together they created an express warranty that the product was safe for human contact. An infant badly burned when the drain cleaner spilled on her face was allowed to recover upon the defendant's express warranty of safeness. Although expressing skepticism over the landlady's and parents' self-serving statements that the product was safe, the court found that the testimony could be credited because it is the nature of such advertising to encourage and persuade the consumer to buy and use the product. In commenting upon the defendant's intervening cause defense, the court observed: "Accidental spillage during normal use was at least a reasonably foreseeable concern. It was surely within the range of proofs for the [trial] court to have concluded that the defendant's false assurances of safe use were intended to allay public concern as an inducement to purchase the product."[65] The court referred to Ohio's enactment of UCC §2-313, which codifies *contract* law regarding express warranties in sales, but based its decision on Ohio products liability tort law, which no longer required privity.[66]

The implied warranties of merchantability and fitness for intended purpose are an amalgam of tort and contract law. A plaintiff can recover without proof of negligence on the defendant's part if a product has been marketed to the public, the product is defective or not fit for its intended purpose at the time of sale, and the user is injured as a consequence of the defect or unfitness.[67] Failure-to-warn cases are frequently premised upon implied warranty. The product is not deemed merchantable if "the directions and warnings as a whole do not adequately inform the user of the potential dangers."[68] Thus in *Reid v Eckerds Drugs, Inc*,[69] the plaintiff, who suffered burns when he lit a match after spraying himself with an antiperspirant, was not required to prove a defect in the *contents* of the aerosol can. The case was allowed to go to the jury on the sufficiency of the labeling.

---

[64] 591 F2d 352 (6th Cir 1978).

[65] *Id* 361.

[66] Ohio Rev Code Ann §§1301-1309 (Page 1979).

[67] *See, e.g.*, Borel v Fibreboard Paper Prods Corp, 493 F2d 1076, 1091 (5th Cir 1973), *cert denied*, 419 US 869 (1974) (asbestos insulation material); Greenman v Yuba Power Prods, Inc, 59 Cal 2d 57, 377 P2d 897, 27 Cal Rptr 697 (1963) (defective power tool); *but cf* Flinn v Sun Oil Co, 96 Mich App 59, 292 NW2d 484 (1980) (jury's verdict against plaintiff on her implied warranty theory that propane gas should have been adequately odorized to warn of leakage was upheld).

[68] Reid v Eckerds Drugs, Inc, 40 NC App 476, 480, 253 SE2d 344, 347 (1979). For codification of contract law on the implied warranty of merchantability and fitness for intended purpose, *see* UCC §§2-314, 2-315 (1977).

[69] 40 NC App 476, 253 SE2d 344 (1979).

Proof of foreseeability of the danger is usually not required in express warranty cases where the warranty covers the danger. For instance, in *All-O-Matic Industries, Inc v Southern Specialty Paper Co,*[70] the defendant assured plaintiff that its filter paper could not ignite. When it did ignite in a rare second exothermic reaction, the trial court erred in instructing the jury that if such a reaction was unforeseeable by a reasonable and prudent manufacturer, the defendant would not be liable.

Foreseeability becomes relevant if the defendant alleges that the prior express warranty has been overcome by a warning label, as in *Drayton v Jiffee.*[71] The issue for the jury becomes whether it was foreseeable that the label would not be effective.

Foreseeability plays a larger role in implied warranty cases. Implicit in the concept that goods must be fit for the ordinary purposes for which they are used is that the manufacturer's liability is limited to his or her product's foreseeable uses. This is not a *fault* concept; the manufacturer's conduct is not under scrutiny. Here, foreseeability acts as a line, drawn by courts, to keep warranty (and strict liability) cases from becoming absolute liability cases.

Because the warranty theory in tort borrowed from contract law in its development, it has been saddled with such contract notions as privity and the requirement that reasonable notice of the defect be given to the seller. In *Greenman v Yuba Power Products, Inc,*[72] the California Supreme Court did away with the notice requirement, explaining why it is inappropriate in tort: Such actions are not dependent on contract law; the consumer is seldom knowledgeable in such business practices; and he or she is usually not in privity with the manufacturer. A few courts, however, still require that the plaintiff give notice of the defect to the seller.[73]

The requirement of privity in warranty cases may be dead, but it is not completely buried. In *Starling v Seaboard Coast Line RR,*[74] an implied warranty case involving asbestos products, a federal district court applying Georgia law refused to perform the last rites on Georgia's requirement of privity between the manufacturer and the injured party.

§11.11   Strict Liability

Strict liability is a recent common law development designed to make industry in this technologically complex age more responsive to the public welfare by allowing private individuals to recover damages against manufacturers without regard to fault. To date, strict liability has been limited to the products of

---

[70] 49 AD2d 935, 374 NYS2d 331 (1975).

[71] 591 F2d 352, 360-61 (6th Cir 1978).

[72] 59 Cal 2d 57, 377 P2d 897, 27 Cal Rptr 697 (1963).

[73] *E.g.,* Wagmeister v AH Robins Co, 64 Ill App 3d 964, 382 NE2d 23 (1978); Wenner v Gulf Oil Corp, 264 NW2d 374, 378 n 1 (Minn 1978).

[74] 533 F Supp 183, 191-92 (SD Ga 1982).

industry and the abnormally dangerous commercial activities of industry and not to the waste products of its activities. There has, however, been considerable advocacy for such extension.[75] The genesis of strict liability stems from two separate sources: first, the "non-natural uses of lands" theory of *Rylands v Fletcher*,[76] more accurately labeled *absolute liability;* and second, the inherently dangerous consumer product theory which started with such products as food, drugs, and automobiles and achieved respectability in the 1960s after it was incorporated as §402A of the Restatement (Second) of Torts.[77]

§11.12   —Strict Products Liability

Section 402A[78] imposes liability, without regard to fault or privity, upon one who sells a "product in a defective condition unreasonably dangerous to the user or consumer . . . if (a) the seller is engaged in the business of selling such a product, and (b) it is expected to and does reach the user or consumer without substantial change in the condition in which it is sold."[79] Proximate cause and damage or loss from injury are elements of this action, but contributory negligence is not a defense, except in the narrow sense of assumption of the risk.[80]

Strict products liability is generally limited to the relationship between sellers of products and their users or consumers and not to isolated or incidental sales.[81] Raw materials such as asbestos have been held to be products for strict liability purposes even though they will undergo further processing before reaching the ultimate user.[82] A few cases have extended its scope to hybrid sale-service situations—such as a beauty parlor operator who applies a permanent wave solution to a patron's hair—to rental-bailment situations—such as an establishment that rents tools and equipment to the public—and to mass

---

[75] *E.g.,* Bridgeton v BP Oil, Inc, 146 NJ Super 169, 177, 369 A2d 49, 53-54 (Law Div 1976) (in dictum, the court advocated the extension of strict liability to an oil spill because of the hazardous nature of defendant's commercial activities and the statutory prohibitions against pollution); Ginsberg & Weiss, *Common Law Liability for Toxic Torts: A Phantom Remedy,* 9 Hofstra L Rev 859, 902-04 (1981); Note, *Strict Liability for Generators, Transporters, and Disposers of Hazardous Wastes,* 64 Minn L Rev 949, 952-59 (1980).

[76] LR 3 HL 330 (1868).

[77] Restatement (Second) of Torts §402A, at 347-48 (1965).

[78] Restatement (Second) of Torts §402A, at 347-48 (1965).

[79] *Id.*

[80] W. Prosser, The Law of Torts §103, at 670-71 (4th ed 1971); Restatement (Second), *supra* note 77, §402A, comment n, at 356.

[81] Lancaster v WA Hartzell & Assocs, 54 Or App 886, 637 P2d 150 (1981), *review denied,* 292 Or 722 (1982) (sale of wood stain incidental to sale of furniture is not subject to strict liability).

[82] Neal v Carey Canadian Mines, Ltd, 548 F Supp 357, 372 (ED Pa 1982). Hammond v North Am Asbestos Corp, 105 Ill App 3d 1033, 435 NE2d 540 (1982).

manufacturers of residences—such as a developer of residential lots.[83] These cases do not appear to have started a trend.

Consistent with Comment 1 to §402A of the Restatement (Second) of Torts, the scope of the phrase *user or consumer* has not been narrowly construed to preclude recovery by those injured through a user or consumer: Children who ate the meat of hogs that had been fed Panogen-15 treated grain and daughters of women who took DES have been allowed to proceed under strict liability.[84]

Most toxic tort cases alleging strict products liability are failure-to-warn cases. The duty to warn in strict liability is similar to the duty in negligence except that it arises when an unreasonably dangerous product is sold in a defective condition—i.e., without warnings—regardless of whether the defendant knew or had reason to know that the agent was dangerous. In strict liability, the focus is on the condition of the product, and not on the conduct of the defendant.[85]

Failure-to-warn cases fall either into the "unavoidably unsafe products" category discussed in Comment k to §402A[86] or the "unreasonably dangerous without adequate warnings" category discussed in comment j.[87] *Unavoidably unsafe products* are those which cannot be rendered safe for their intended and ordinary use in the present state of human knowledge, such as drugs with known serious side effects which are sufficiently beneficial to justify their continued marketing and use. As to these products, Comment k to §402A states:

> Such a product, properly prepared, and accompanied by proper directions and warning, is not defective, nor is it unreasonably dangerous. . . . The seller of such products, again with the qualification that they are properly prepared and marketed, and proper warning is given, where the situation calls for it, is not to be held to strict liability for unfortunate consequences attending their use, merely because he has undertaken to supply the public with an apparently useful and desirable product, attended with a known but apparently reasonable risk.[88]

---

[83] McClaflin v Bayshore Equip Rental Co, 274 Cal App 2d 446, 79 Cal Rptr 337 (1969); Avner v Longridge Estates, 272 Cal App 2d 607, 77 Cal Rptr 633 (1969); Newmark v Gimbels Inc, 54 NJ 585, 258 A2d 697 (1962). See discussion in **§11.02.**

[84] Restatement (Second), *supra* note 78, §402A, comment 1, at 354-55; First Natl Bank, Albuquerque v Nor-Am Agr Prods, Inc, 88 NM 74, 85-87, 537 P2d 682, 693-94, (Ct App 1975), *cert denied,* 88 NM 29, 536 P2d 1085 (1975). *See also* Sindell v Abbott Laboratories, 26 Cal 3d 588, 607 P2d 924, 163 Cal Rptr 132, *cert denied,* 449 US 912 (1980) (issue of "consumer" not discussed, but strict liability was applied to manufacturers of DES for injuries that resulted to daughters of DES users).

[85] Dougherty v Hooker Chem Corp, 540 F2d 174, 177-78 (3d Cir 1976); Jackson v Coast Paint & Lacquer Co, 499 F2d 509, 812 (9th Cir 1974).

[86] Restatement (Second), *supra* note 78, §402A, comment k, at 353-54.

[87] *Id* comment j, at 353.

[88] *Id* comment k, at 353-54.

Other products, such as certain paints and glues, are safe for their intended and ordinary use, provided adequate directions or warnings are given. As to these products, Comment j to §402A states:

> In order to prevent the product from being unreasonably dangerous, the seller may be required to give directions or warning, on the container, as to its use. . . . Where, however, the product contains an ingredient to which a substantial number of the population are allergic, and the ingredient is one whose danger is not generally known, or if known is one which the consumer would reasonably not expect to find in the product, the seller is required to give warning against it, if he has knowledge, or by the application of reasonable, developed human skill and foresight should have knowledge, of the presence of the ingredient and the danger.[89]

Comments j and k have engendered considerable debate and conflicting case law over just what the plaintiff has to prove in a strict liability failure-to-warn case and over how it differs from a negligence failure-to-warn case. Is the defendant liable regardless of fault if the warnings fail to mention a danger of which the defendant did not know or have reason to know? Comment j's answer would be *no*. Comment k does not answer the question, but it refers to the "present state of human knowledge," suggesting that the answer would be *no*. The resolution of the question can be approached at least three ways: The plaintiff bears the burden of establishing the danger was foreseen or foreseeable to the defendant; foreseeability is a defense; or foreseeability is not germane at all.

§11.13 —Case Law on Strict Products Liability

The Fifth Circuit Court of Appeals in *Borel v Fibreboard*[90] and the Illinois Supreme Court in *Woodill v Parke Davis & Co*[91] both held that the plaintiff must prove that the danger was reasonably foreseeable as a proper limitation on the manufacturer's strict liability for the failure to warn of an inherent danger. The *Borel* court believed that the requirement of foreseeability in strict liability cases "coincides with the standard of due care in negligence cases."[92] In *Woodill*, the Illinois Supreme Court rejected a similar position, argued by the plaintiffs, that the requirement of foreseeability in strict liability improperly places the focus of inquiry upon the conduct of the manufacturer. The *Woodill* court stated that the focus is still on the nature of the product and the adequacy of the warning; the test of foreseeability in strict liability is objective, rather than subjective

---

[89] *Id* comment j, at 353.

[90] Borel v Fibreboard Paper Prods, Inc, 493 F2d 1076 (5th Cir 1973), *cert denied,* 419 US 869 (1974).

[91] 79 Ill 2d 26, 32-37, 402 NE2d 194, 197-99 (1980).

[92] 493 F2d at 1088.

> The inquiry becomes whether the manufacturer, because of the "present state of human knowledge" . . . , knew or should have known of the danger presented by the use or consumption of a product. Once it is established that knowledge existed in the industry of the dangerous propensity of the manufacturer's product, then the plaintiff must establish that the defendant did not warn, in an adequate manner, of the danger.[93]

The distinction between the negligence standard (what a reasonable manufacturer would have foreseen) and the strict liability standard of *Woodill* has become blurred because courts hold manufacturers to the higher standards of experts who are presumed to know of developments in their field.

In *Beshada v Johns-Manville Products Corp*,[94] an asbestos case, the Supreme Court of New Jersey indicated that foreseeability is not germane; in strict liability, unlike negligence, the defendant may not rely on the *state of the art* defense. (The *state of the art* defense is the counterpart to foreseeability, but the burden of proof is on the defendant.) The New Jersey Supreme Court has previously held that the defendant's knowledge of its product's dangerous nature is presumed in strict liability cases and is no longer a part of plaintiff's burden of proof.[95]

In a major departure from the risk-utility balance drawn by §402A,[96] the *Beshada* decision held that if a product is unsafe, the manufacturer must compensate its victims regardless of the state of technology. The court based its departure on a consideration of the policies and goals underlying New Jersey's strict liability rules—in particular, risk spreading, accident avoidance, and simplification of the fact-finding process. *Beshada* comes close to imposing absolute liability. (Cause in fact is still required, which is not the case in some absolute liability contexts such as the imposition of liability for violating the child labor statute in *Sloan v Coit International, Inc.*)[97] Whether other courts will follow the bold lead of the New Jersey Supreme Court and regard the balance they have drawn between risk and utility as better suited to accomplishing their states' policies or consider it more appropriate for their legislatures to tackle the issue, the case will generate extensive debate.[98]

---

[93] 79 Ill 2d at 35, 402 NE2d at 198 (citation omitted).

[94] 90 NJ 191, 447 A2d 539 (1982).

[95] Freund v Cellofilm Properties, Inc, 87 NJ 229, 432 A2d 925 (1981); *see also* Phillips v Kimwood Mach Co, 269 Or 485, 525 P2d 1033 (1974).

[96] Restatement (Second) of Torts §402A, at 347-48 (1965).

[97] 292 So 2d 15 (Fla 1974).

[98] The debate has already begun: E.g., Platt & Platt, *Moving from Strict to Absolute Liability*, Natl LJ, Jan 17, 1983, at 15; Birnbaum & Wrubel, *NJ High Court Blazes New Path in Holding a Manufacturer Liable*, Natl LJ, Jan 24, 1983, at 24.

§11.14 —Abnormally Dangerous Activities

As awareness of the dangers of pollution has grown, American courts have become more receptive to the theory of strict liability adopted in England in *Rylands v Fletcher*[99] which imposes liability for the harm caused by defendant's activities if he or she has undertaken a dangerous, nonnatural use of land. The Restatement (Second) of Torts[100] has sought to broaden the nature of activities encompassed from the original Restatement of Torts' language of "ultrahazardous activity"[101] to "abnormally dangerous activity."[102] Liability is imposed if the harm that occurs is of the type that makes the activity abnormally dangerous, even though the defendant "has exercised *utmost* care to prevent the harm."[103] In determining whether an activity is abnormally dangerous, §520 of the Restatement (Second) of Torts lists as the factors to consider:

(a) existence of a high degree of risk of some harm to the person, land or chattels of others;
(b) likelihood that the harm that results from it will be great;
(c) inability to eliminate the risk by the exercise of reasonable care;
(d) extent to which the activity is not a matter of common usage;
(e) inappropriateness of the activity to the place where it is carried on; and
(f) extent to which its value to the community is outweighed by its dangerous attributes.[104]

The determination of whether an activity is abnormally dangerous involves a risk-utility balancing, as factor (f) indicates, much like the balancing test used in nuisance cases. Consequently, it lies within the province of the court, and not the jury, to make the determination.[105]

The Restatement (Second) of Torts coupled with the greater awareness of dangers to the environment, has affected the willingness of courts to consider certain activities to be abnormally dangerous. For instance, in *Silkwood v Kerr-McGee Corp*,[106] the court appears to have been persuaded by the highly regulated nature of the nuclear energy industry and by the Restatement (Second) of

---

[99] LR 3 HL 338 (1868). See **§11.11.**

[100] Restatement (Second) of Torts (1965).

[101] Restatement of Torts §519, at 41 (1938).

[102] Restatement (Second) of Torts §519, at 34 (1977).

[103] Restatement (Second) of Torts §519, at 34 (1965) (emphasis added). *See also* Loe v Lenhardt, 227 Or 242, 251, 362 P2d 312, 318 (1961) (strict liability imposed upon aerial crop sprayer for damages caused to adjoining field notwithstanding exercise of utmost care; although theory of liability was labeled *trespass,* the court's focus was on the extra hazardous nature of defendant's activity).

[104] Restatement (Second), *supra* note 99, §520, at 36.

[105] *Id* comment 1, at 42-43.

[106] 667 F2d 908 (10th Cir 1981), *appeal pending,* 51 USLW 3508 (US Jan 11, 1983) (No 81-2159), *revd,* __ US __ (Jan 13, 1984).

Torts that the use of plutonium is an abnormally dangerous activity. Unlike absolute liability, however, the court considered the key to imposing liability to be foreseeability: "It is surely foreseeable and within the scope of the abnormal risk that radiation contamination will occur from contact with plutonium that escapes a nuclear fuel plant."[107]

The plaintiff's burden is not light in these cases, however. For example, in *Doundoulakis v Town of Hempstead*,[108] the New York Court of Appeals opined that defendants' hydraulic dredging and landfilling operations could be considered an abnormally dangerous activity but remanded for further evidence on factors (a), (b), and (c) of §520's six factors. Moreover, if the court finds that the risk could be eliminated by reasonable care, it may limit plaintiff to a negligence theory.[109]

Since a balancing test is used, if defendant's type of activity is prevalent in the area or of great economic value to the community, the court need not impose strict liability. In 1936, the Texas Supreme Court in *Turner v Big Lake Oil Co*[110] held that water retention in reservoirs and oil drilling were not nonnatural uses of land in Texas. By contrast, in *Cities Service Co v State*,[111] a Florida court, citing changes in our society since frontier days, relied upon the draft of §§519 and 520 of the Restatement (Second) of Torts to hold the generator of phosphatic slime waste strictly liable when its reservoir broke. It did so despite the prevalence of defendant's type of commercial activity in that area of Florida.

Despite problems of proof and the uncertainty of outcome inherent in the balancing test of §520, if an injury arises from activities such as genetic engineering, use of radioactive materials, or disposal of highly toxic wastes (PCB's, dioxin, and spent nuclear fuel, to name a few), a strict liability count for carrying on an abnormally dangerous activity should be considered.

§11.15 Trespass to Land and Nuisance

Trespass and nuisance focus upon the invasion of plaintiff's property rights, rather than upon the nature of defendant's activities. The law on these two theories varies significantly from state to state, and no attempt is made to summarize or harmonize the differences. Trespass and nuisance deserve men-

---

[107] *Id* 921; *see also* **Restatement** (Second), *supra* note 100, §520, comment g, at 38.

[108] 42 NY2d 440, 368 NE2d 24, 398 NYS2d 401 (1977).

[109] *See, e.g.,* Ewell v Petro Processors, Inc, 364 So 2d 604 (La Ct App 1978).

[110] 128 Tex 155, 96 SW2d 221 (1936). The theory of strict liability is recognized in Texas, although it appears to blend the concepts of trespass, nuisance, and abnormally dangerous activities. *See, e.g.,* Atlas Chem Indus, Inc v Anderson, 514 SW2d 309 (Tex Ct Civ App 1974), *affd,* 524 SW2d 681 (Tex 1975) (the case was submitted to the jury on negligence, but in dictum the Court of Civil Appeals stated that strict liability was applicable where defendant's discharges of process water containing lignite and other wastes polluted a creek and destroyed vegetation).

[111] 312 So 2d 799 (Fla Ct App 1975).

tion because many toxic torts involve environmental injury to plaintiff's property rights.

§11.16 —Trespass

Trespass requires the direct physical invasion of another's right to the exclusive possession of his or her property and subjects the trespasser to strict liability if it is intentional or the result of an abnormally dangerous activity.[112] A few courts have abandoned the requirement of a physical invasion of visible proportions. In *Martin v Reynolds Metals Co,*[113] invisible flouridic compounds emanated from defendant's plant and landed on plaintiffs' property, contaminating the water and forage and poisoning their livestock. The court held that the particulates' intrusion constituted a trespass, observing that in this atomic age, distinctions based upon physical size are meaningless.

An intentional invasion occurs "when the defendant acts for purpose of causing [the invasion] or knows that it is resulting or is substantially certain to result from his conduct."[114] If intention is present, negligence is not material, as *Langford v Kraft*[115] demonstrates. There a Texas court held a professional engineer liable for the nonnegligent design of a drainage system which diverted surface waters onto the plaintiff's lands.

It can be difficult for a plaintiff to establish that the defendant had the requisite intent. In a continuing trespass situation, such as presented in *Martin v Reynolds Metals Co,* however, once the plaintiff has complained to the defendant about the intrusion of toxic substances, the argument can be made that all further intrusions are intentional.[116]

§11.17 —Nuisance

Private nuisance can be distinguished from trespass by the nature of the interest invaded—the private use and enjoyment of one's land, rather than the possession. It covers a broader range of invasions than trespass, but the interference must be significant, unreasonable, and intentional or otherwise action-

---

[112] Restatement (Second) of Torts §158, at 277, and §162, at 291-92 (1965).

[113] 221 Or 86, 342 P2d 790, *cert denied,* 362 US 918 (1960). *See also* Smith v Lockheed Propulsion Co, 247 Cal App 2d 774, 56 Cal Rptr 128 (Dist Ct 1967) (seismic vibrations caused by defendant's rocket firing tests could constitute actionable trespass in California, which has abolished the distinction between direct and indirect injury).

[114] Houston v Renault, Inc, 431 SW2d 322, 325 (Tex 1968).

[115] 551 SW2d 392 (Tex Ct Civ App 1977), *affd,* 565 SW2d 223 (Tex 1978).

[116] The problem is how to compensate the plaintiff for damages suffered *before* the defendant is put on notice. *E.g.,* Phillips v Sun Oil Co, 307 NY 328, 121 NE2d 249 (1954) (trespass action dismissed where there was nothing to show that the defendant knew or had been put on notice that gasoline was escaping from its underground tank and polluting plaintiff's water well).

able—it is not actionable in and of itself.[117] Nuisance cases have equity origins and offer equitable remedies. The court will weigh the value of the defendant's activities to the community against the private harm they cause, and the results will not always be pleasing to the plaintiff.

For example, in *Boomer v Atlantic Cement Co,*[118] the New York Court of Appeals balanced the injuries to the plaintiffs' property caused by the dirt, smoke, and vibration emanating from defendant's cement plant against the value of defendant's activities, which represented an investment in excess of $45 million and the employment of over 300 people. Rather than grant the injunction against defendant's operations, it applied the wisdom of Solomon: An injunction would be granted only if the defendant did not pay permanent damages to plaintiffs for their present and future economic losses. But in exchange for those payments, the defendant would receive a *permanent* servitude over plaintiffs' lands.

One limitation of the nuisance theory for environmental litigation is that the present owner of the offending site will not be liable for the often massive expenses of clean-up if he or she did not cause the nuisance but merely learned about it after acquiring the property and has done nothing to remedy it. On the other hand, a prior owner who has created a nuisance does not escape liability simply by selling the property.[119] The trick, then, is to find the prior owner before the statute of limitations expires and before the proceeds of the sale are spent. Another limitation, inherent in the balancing process, is that the defendant will not be held liable if the nature of his or her use is reasonable for that particular area.

Public nuisance is "an unreasonable interference with a right common to the general public."[120] Although typically only the government has standing to enforce the rights of the public, a private right of action may be afforded if the plaintiff suffers harm of a different kind and degree than the general public.[121] In *National Sea Clammers Association v City of New York,*[122] an organization of

---

[117] Restatement (Second) of Torts §821F, at 105, and §822, at 108 (1979); W Prosser, The Law of Torts §87, at 577-82 (4th ed 1971); *see also* State v Exxon Corp, 151 NJ Super 464, 482, 376 A2d 1339, 1348 (Ch Div 1977) (discussion of nuisance theory in a waste disposal case).

[118] 26 NY2d 219, 257 NE2d 870, 309 NYS2d 312 (1970).

[119] State v Exxon, 151 NJ Super 464, 483-85, 376 A2d 1339, 1349-50 (Ch Div 1977). *See also* State v Ole Olsen, Ltd, 38 AD2d 967, 331 NYS2d 761 (App Div 1972), *affd,* 35 NY2d 979, 324 NE2d 886, 365 NYS2d 528 (1975) (developers of homes, rather than subsequent purchasers, were required to abate the nuisance they created by installing inadequate sewage disposal systems). The Comprehensive Environmental Response, Compensation, and Liability Act of 1980, 42 USC §960, *et seq,* better known as the Superfund law, resolves the issue of who will pay the costs of abatement. It is discussed in **ch 9 and 10.**

[120] Restatement (Second) *supra* note 116, §821B, at 87 (1979)

[121] *Id* §821C, at 94, and §821C, comment b, at 95-96; United States Steel Corp v Save Sand Key, Inc, 303 So 2d 9 (Fla 1974).

[122] 616 F2d 1222 (3d Cir 1980), *modified sub nom* Middlesex City Sewerage Auth v National Sea Clammers Assn, 453 US 1 (1981).

fishermen sought standing to enjoin the dumping of sewage and other waste materials into New York harbor under various federal statutes and the federal common law of nuisance, which had recently been recognized by the Supreme Court in *Illinois v City of Milwaukee*.[123] The Third Circuit held that the association had standing to sue on the public nuisance claim because the injury to its members' livelihood was sufficiently individual. The victory, however, was pyrrhic because the Supreme Court then held that the federal common law of nuisance in the area of ocean pollution had been fully preempted by statutes which afford no private remedies. *National Sea Clammers* holds out the possibility that citizens' groups, which are in a far better position than private individuals to finance environmental litigation, can sue under the law of public nuisance to enjoin an environmental tort. The other lesson of *National Sea Clammers* is that the chances of success are meager, because such suits face a barrage of statutory preemption, standing, and jurisdictional challenges.

§11.18   Fraudulent Misrepresentation and Concealment

The elements of fraudulent misrepresentation are:

1. A misrepresentation of fact

2. Defendant's knowledge or belief that his or her representation is false or absence of belief that his or her representation is true—*scienter*

3. Defendant's intention to induce the plaintiff to act or refrain from action in reliance upon the misrepresentation

4. Plaintiff's justifiable reliance upon the misrepresentation

5. Damage or loss caused by such reliance[124]

Fraudulent concealment requires, instead of the first element in the list, that the defendant has prevented the plaintiff from acquiring material information. The defendant is regarded as having represented the nonexistence of the matter to plaintiff. Otherwise, the elements of the cause of action are the same.[125]

Merely glancing at all the elements a plaintiff must prove to establish fraudulent misrepresentation or concealment should supply the reason why there are few reported cases where the plaintiff has prevailed in the toxic tort area. The

---

[123] 406 US 91 (1972). For a discussion of a possible application of the federal common law of nuisance, see Lind, *Umbrella Equities: Use of the Federal Common Law of Nuisance to Catch the Fall of Acid Rain*, 21 Urb L Ann 143 (1981).

[124] Restatement (Second) of Torts §526, at 59, and §557A, at 149; (1939); W. Prosser, The Law of Torts §105, at 685-86 (4th ed 1971). Negligent misrepresentations and omissions are covered in **§11.05;** and presentations and omissions are covered in **§11.05;** and warranty liability and strict liability for innocent misrepresentations are covered in **§§21.10** and **21.11,** respectively.

[125] Restatement (Second), *supra* note 124, §550, at 118.

enticements are the recovery of punitive damages, the longer statutes of limitations, and the avoidance of the exclusivity of workers' compensation remedies.[126] Most of the cases involve drugs and similar consumer products where the defendant has advertised the product as safe, despite knowledge that it was not, or has failed to report certain dangerous properties of the product which were known to him or her.[127] When the product's label contains warnings or disclaimers in conflict with defendant's representations, the plaintiff may have difficulty proving justifiable reliance.[128] Defendant's intent to induce the plaintiff may be inferred from its advertising to the public or the medical profession.[129]

The availability of generous discovery from defendants and governmental agencies may aid a plaintiff in establishing defendant's knowledge or belief that his or her statement was false. The lag time between defendant's uncovering a defect or danger with its product and the disclosure of that information to the public raises interesting questions: What representations has the defendant made to the public in that interim? Do not the defendant's earlier public statements about the product, now determined to be erroneous, form the basis of fraudulent concealment if prompt disclosure of the new evidence is not made?

Fraudulent concealment and misrepresentation allegations are being raised in asbestos litigation. Punitive damages were recovered in *Neal v Carey Canadian Mines, Ltd*[130] against Johns-Manville, an asbestos supplier, and against the successor to the plaintiffs' employer. Among the theories presented to the jury was intentional failure to warn—in other words, fraudulent misrepresentation and concealment. Plaintiffs' proof on this theory included:

1. Johns-Manville continually failed to warn users of hazards associated with the inhalation of asbestos fibers (concealment), despite overwhelming knowledge of those hazards since the 1940s (scienter)

2. Plaintiffs' employer became aware of those hazards in the early 1960s

---

[126] Workers' compensation and the exclusivity doctrine are discussed in **ch 6.**

[127] *E.g.,* Wennerholm v Stanford Univ School of Med, 20 Cal 2d 713, 128 P2d 522 (1942) (false representation that drug for obesity was harmless where defendant knew otherwise); Toole v Richardson-Merrell Inc, 251 Cal App 2d 689, 60 Cal Rptr 398 (1967) (plaintiff developed cataracts from using trysaranol, which defendant marketed after withholding adverse test results from the Food and Drug Administration, and concerning which defendant made false statements to the Food and Drug Administration and the medical profession); Miller v New Zealand Ins Co, 98 So 2d 544 (La Ct App 1957) (misrepresentation that a cleaning fluid could be used on enamel basins); Throckmorton v MFA Central Cooperative, 462 SW2d 138 (Mo Ct App 1970) (blender of hog feed knowingly used bad corn in the feed and misrepresented that there was nothing wrong with it).

[128] *See, e.g.,* Miller v New Zealand Ins Co, 98 So2d 544 (La Ct App 1957); Gibson v California Spray-Chem Corp, 29 Wash 2d 611, 188 P2d 316 (1948).

[129] Toole v Richardson-Merrell Inc, 251 Cal App 2d 689, 60 Cal Rptr 398 (1962).

[130] 548 F Supp 357 (ED Pa 1982).

(scienter) but took no action despite the recommendations of a company physician (concealment)

3. Plaintiffs were not aware of the dangers until many years after the termination of their employment (justifiable reliance)

4. Plaintiffs would have quit their work or taken other precautionary measures during the course of their employment had they known of the dangers (the court labeled this evidence of "proximate cause,"[131] but it also goes to establishing the materiality of the concealed and misrepresented facts and reliance)

5. Plaintiffs suffered asbestos-related conditions arising out of their exposure to asbestos fibers at work (causation, which defendants had conceded, and damages)

The element of defendant's intention to induce is not mentioned in the district court's opinion, but presumably the suppliers sought to induce plaintiffs to continue using the products, and the employer sought to induce plaintiffs to continue working for it.[132] As between the employer and those employees who had already left their employment when the employer learned of the hazards, the issue of inducement is somewhat troublesome. Can it be presumed that the failure to warn former employees was intended to induce them not to alert active employees and encourage them to quit?

§11.19 Liability Where the Tortfeasor's Identity Is Uncertain

Unlike the typical tort case in which the plaintiff can identify the culprit who struck the plaintiff or the plaintiff's car, the identity of the defendant in toxic tort cases is frequently unascertainable. Whose DES caused Ms. Sindell's adenosis?[133] In grappling with the problem of how to compensate the innocent victim, the courts have expanded upon existing theories of liability and have fashioned a few more.

§11.20 —Conspiracy or Concerted Action

Conspiracy and fraud are often alleged together in one breath, as though they represent distinct tort theories. They do not. Fraud refers to fraudulent misrepresentation, and concerted action (which is conspiracy renamed to minimize its cloak-and-dagger connotation) derives from the criminal law concept

---

[131] *Id* at 361.

[132] *See, e.g.,* Starling v Seaboard Coast Line R Co, 533 F Supp 183, 192-93 (SD Ga 1982) (plaintiffs were allowed to proceed in a suit against an asbestos manufacturer where the defendant's intention was alleged to be to induce the workers to continue to use asbestos products).

[133] Sindell v Abbott Labs, 26 Cal 3d 588, 607 P2d 924, 163 Cal Rptr 132 (1980).

of aiding and abetting. "All those who, in pursuance of a common plan or design to commit a tortious act, actively take part in it, or further it by cooperation, or who lend aid or encouragement to the wrongdoer, or ratify and adopt his acts done for their benefit" are jointly and severally liable.[134] Plaintiff need not prove which defendant's product was the cause in fact of injury. "Liability is imposed on all because all have joined in breaching their duty of care to plaintiff . . . ."[135] A common plan or design may be implied from the conduct itself, without ever being expressed in words. Moreover, negligent conduct, in the form of advice or encouragement to act, can make one a member of the concerted action and thereby liable for its consequences.[136]

Bichler v Eli Lilly & Co[137] demonstrates the potency of the concerted action concept and the breadth of its reach. In *Bichler,* the plaintiff could not establish that Lilly had manufactured the DES taken by her mother. There was no proof of cause in fact. However, under the concerted action instruction that the trial court gave, the jury was permitted to infer that an implied agreement existed between Lilly and other DES manufacturers from the evidence of the consciously parallel behavior of DES manufacturers in marketing it for human pregnancy problems without first conducting tests on pregnant mice to determine its effects and effectiveness. The jury was also permitted to infer, from the evidence of Lilly's leadership in filing new drug applications to the Food and Drug Administration, that Lilly substantially encouraged the other 140 manufacturers to market DES without adequately testing it. The New York Court of Appeals held that there was sufficient evidence to hold Lilly liable.[138]

Other courts have rejected concerted action liability where only parallel or

---

[134] W. Prosser, The Law of Torts §47, at 292 (4th ed 1971). *See also* Restatement (Second) of Torts §876, at 315 (1979).

[135] Abel v Eli Lilly & Co, 94 Mich App 59, 72, 289 NW2d 20, 25 (1979).

[136] Restatement (Second) *supra* note 134, §876, comment a, at 316, comment d, at 317. A recent case entitled Henson v Bethelehem Steel Corporation, CA No K81-2112, was filed in the United States District Court for the District of Maryland in September 1981 claiming $200 million damages. Named as individual defendents, in addition to the corporation, were three medical doctors and one industrial hygienist. The plaintiff employees alleged that they were continually exposed to asbestos over a period of years and that they were fraudulently induced to continue their employment without the knowledge that they would be exposed to the probability of developing asbestosis and other life-threatening cancers.

The employees further alleged that Bethlehem Steel acquired knowledge through testing, sampling, medical exams, and physical examinations that the work environment created a probability that the workers would develop asbestosis, but that the defendants withheld and concealed this fact and did not advise nor inform the employees for this reason; the doctors and industrial hygienist were sued under the theory of a conspiracy to deprive the plaintiffs of their civil rights.

[137] 55 NY2d 571, 436 NE2d 182, 450 NYS2d 766 (1982).

[138] The *Bichler* decision is susceptible to narrow construction, however, because the defendant failed to preserve many issues for review, including the correctness of the trial court's instruction on concerted action.

Other issues that were not preserved for appeal and, thus, not decided were whether the plaintiff pleaded a cause of action or proved a prima facie case, whether plaintiff's imitative conduct is shown because, as the California Supreme Court noted in *Sindell v Abbott Laboratories*,[139] it "would expand the doctrine far beyond its intended scope and would render virtually any manufacturer liable for the defective products of an entire industry, even if it could be demonstrated that the product which caused the injury was not made by the defendant."[140] How useful the concerted action doctrine will be in other toxic tort areas is debatable. The DES situation may be the exception, rather than the rule. Unlike most new drugs, DES was not a proprietary drug, so industry collaboration was present to a greater degree than usual, and DES drugs were generically prescribed from a standard formula.

§11.21 —Alternative Liability

Under the concept of alternative liability, if two or more individuals each act tortiously, independently of one another, and one of them causes injury to the plaintiff, but the plaintiff cannot identify which, joint and several liability will be imposed on all tortfeasors except those who can absolve themselves.[141] In sum, the burden of proof regarding cause in fact shifts to the defendants. Major limitations of this approach from a plaintiff's perspective are that the plaintiff must join all the tortfeasors, and he or she must show that each acted tortiously towards him or her. As the court observed in *Abel v Eli Lilly & Co*, a DES case which proceeded under alternative liability, plaintiffs still "bear a heavy, perhaps . . . an insuperable, burden of proof. . . ."[142]

Anderson v Somberg[143] represents an exceptional factual situation in which a plaintiff was able to succeed on alternative liability. While plaintiff was lying unconscious on an operating table, the tip of a forceps being used by the surgeon broke off. Unsuccessful efforts were made to retrieve the tip. The plaintiff joined everyone who might have been liable for his injury, and as to each, he could show some liability, whether strict liability or negligence. In *Ferrigno v Eli Lilly & Co*,[144] the court relied upon *Anderson v Somberg* to shift the

---

recovery against Lilly should be limited to its market share, whether other DES manufacturers were necessary parties, and whether the trial court's charge on plaintiff's burden of proof was in error.

[139] 26 Cal 3d 588, 607 P2d 924, 163 Cal Rptr 132, *cert denied*, 449 US 912 (1980).

[140] 26 Cal 3d at 605, 607 P2d at 933, 163 Cal Rptr at 141; *see also* Ryan v Eli Lilly & Co, 514 F Supp 1004 (D SC 1981); Payton v Abbott Labs, 386 Mass 540, 437 NE2d 171, 189 n 16 (1982); Lyons v Premo Pharmaceutical Labs, Inc, 170 NJ Super 183, 406 A2d 185 (App Div 1979), *cert denied*, 82 NJ 267, 412 A2d 774 (1979).

[141] Summers v Tice, 33 Cal 2d 80, 199 P2d 1 (1948); Abel v Eli Lilly & Co, 94 Mich App 59, 259 NW2d 20 (1979); Restatement (Second) of Torts §433B (3), at 441-42 (1965).

[142] 94 Mich App 59, 76, 289 NW2d 20, 26 (1979).

[143] 67 NJ 291, 228 A2d 1, *cert denied*, 423 US 929 (1975).

[144] 175 NJ Super 551, 420 A2d 1305 (Law Div 1980).

burden "from inculpation to exculpation" in a DES suit.[145] Although all the defendants who were joined could, arguably, be held strictly liable for any injury their products caused plaintiffs, the reliance upon *Anderson* was not entirely valid. Only 22 manufacturers out of a few hundred were joined.

§11.22   —Enterprise Liability

Despite all that has been written about enterprise, or industry-wide, liability, courts have not been persuaded to adopt it.[146] The concept, an amalgam of concerted action and alternative liability, was proposed but not employed in *Hall v EI DuPont de Nemours & Co.*[147] In *Hall,* the children injured by exploding blasting caps were unable to identify the specific manufacturer of those caps. Instead, plaintiffs sued the six United States manufacturers of such caps and their trade industry. If proved, plaintiffs' allegations would show that the defendants had industry-wide awareness of, control over, and capacity to reduce or affect the risks of blasting caps. Thus, they had a duty to minimize those risks. The court stated that if plaintiffs demonstrated a breach of this duty, they would not have to prove direct causation. The burden of proof would shift to each defendant to prove that its product did not cause the injury. Any defendant who could not do so would be subjected to liability.

Enterprise liability has the appeal of simple fairness. Who should bear the cost—the innocent victim who cannot identify the culpable manufacturer or the industry which is in a far better position to spread the risk? But should the innocent defendant be required to prove his or her innocence, which he or she may be in no better position than the plaintiff to do, or bear the liability simply because the plaintiff chose to sue him or her? Even the *Hall* court acknowledged that the concept may be suited only to tightly knit industries composed of a small number of members.[148] The *Sindell v Abbott Labs*[149] decision also notes that some industries are so closely regulated that all its members may erroneously appear to be acting as one.[150]

§11.23   —Market Share Liability

In *Sindell v Abbott Labs,*[151] the Supreme Court of California departed from

---

[145] *Id* at 553, 420 A2d at 1307.

[146] *E.g,* Sindell v Abbott Labs, 26 Cal 3d 588, 607, 607 P2d 924, 933, 163 Cal Rptr 132, 141 (1980), *cert denied,* 449 US 912 (1980); Sterling v Seaboard Coast Line R Co, 533 FSupp 183, 187 (SD Ga 1982); Comment, *DES and a Proposed Theory of Enterprise Liability,* 46 Fordham L Rev 963 (1978); Comment, *Market Share Liability: An Answer to the DES Causation Problem,* 94 Harv L Rev 668 (1980).

[147] 345 F Supp 353 (ED NY 1972). *Hall* was a consolidation of several suits, but none of the cases consolidated appear to have been tried on the basis of enterprise liability.

[148] *Id* 378.

[149] 26 Cal 3d 588, 607 P2d 924, 163 Cal Rptr 132, *cert denied,* 449 US 912 (1980).

[150] *Id* 609-10, 607 P2d at 935, 163 Cal Rptr at 143.

[151] 26 Cal 3d 588, 607 P2d 924, 163 Cal Rptr 132, *cert denied,* 449 US 912 (1980).

traditional tort principles of causation and the apportionment of damages. (A strong dissent and a more four-to-three majority may be indicative of the extent of that departure.) The court borrowed selectively from the theories of enterprise liability, alternative liability, and concerted liability in an attempt to cure some of their shortcomings and fashioned a new market share theory. *Sindell* states that causation—the likelihood that any one of the defendants supplied the DES that plaintiff's mother took—can be apportioned by the percentage of the DES market that that defendant held.[152] According to the court, if a "substantial share" of the DES suppliers are joined, the injustice of shifting the burden of proof of causation to defendants would be significantly diminished.[153] This theory represents a modification of prior theories of liability because the plaintiff need no longer sue every member of the industry—i.e., everyone who could be liable. The *Sindell* court also dispensed with the element of proof in enterprise liability that the defendants be shown to have exercised joint control of risks. Also, unlike prior theories, under market share liability a defendant who can not exculpate itself will be held liable for only that portion of the judgment which its share of the market represents.

Apart from criticizing the majority for abandoning the element of cause in fact, the dissent in *Sindell* argued the decision was not just: A *large* manufacturer may bear extensive liability, despite his or her lack of culpability, because he or she is visible, solvent, and amenable to process in California and thus will be sued more often than *small* manufacturers. A *small* manufacturer who is culpable may escape liability entirely or, at worst, will only bear a small fraction of the loss. In addition, one can foresee in such tort cases the kinds of problems regarding discovery and proof concerning market share that have made antitrust litigation notorious.[154]

The market share theory has had a cool reception from other courts.[155] Massachusetts rejected it in *Payton v Abbott Labs*.[156] Discovery was allowed on the issue of market share, without determining its applicability, in *Hardy v Johns-Manville Sales Corp*.[157]

§11.24 —Product Line and Successor Liability

Although it is admittedly beyond the scope of this topic to discuss imposition of liability where the tortfeasor's identity *is* known, the recent trend of courts to liberalize the circumstances under which liability will be imposed upon

---

[152] *Id* at 611-12, 607 P2d at 937, 163 Cal Rptr at 145.

[153] *Id* at 612, 607 P2d at 937, 163 Cal Rptr at 145.

[154] 26 Cal 3d at 614, 607 P2d at 939, 163 Cal Rptr at 148 (Richardson, J, dissenting).

[155] *See, e.g.*, Starling v Seaboard Coast Line R Co, 533 F Supp 183 (SD Ga 1982); Ryan v Eli Lilly & Co, 514 FSupp 1004 (DSC 1981); Namm v Charles E Frosst & Co, 178 NJ Super 19, 427 A2d 1121 (App Div 1981).

[156] 386 Mass 540, 437 NE2d 171 (1982).

[157] 509 F Supp 1353 (ED Tex 1981), *revd on other grounds*, 681 F2d 334 (5th Cir 1982).

successor corporations and other entities under the *product line* rule can spell the difference between obtaining a judgment and collecting upon it.[158]

§11.25   Offensive Collateral Estoppel

Ever since *Borel v Fibreboard*,[159] attorneys have debated whether the decision of issues in that asbestos case (and, for example, *Bichler v Eli Lilly*[160] in the area of DES) should preclude defendants from relitigating those issues under the doctrine of offensive collateral estoppel. Some courts, inundated with asbestos and DES cases, have found the concept of offensive collateral estoppel attractive because it can promote judicial economy and spare plaintiffs the considerable expense of submitting proofs on issues already decided in other cases.

The foundations for the debate are two United States Supreme Court decisions, *Blonder-Tongue Laboratories Inc v University of Illinois Foundation*[161] and *Parklane Hosiery Co v Shore*.[162] In *Blonder-Tongue,* the Supreme Court departed from the rigid requirements of mutuality in the defensive use of collateral estoppel. The defendant who had been sued for patent infringement was allowed to preclude the plaintiff, whose patent had previously been held invalid in another action against another defendant, from relitigating the issue of patent validity unless the plaintiff could demonstrate that a full and fair opportunity to pursue the claim was not presented the first time.

Parklane, a securities case, permitted a new plaintiff to use collateral estoppel *offensively* to preclude a defendant from relitigating issues previously resolved against it in a prior suit brought by another plaintiff, provided that the defendant had had a full and fair opportunity to litigate the issues in the prior action. The Supreme Court opined that offensive collateral estoppel "will likely increase rather than decrease the total amount of litigation, since potential plaintiffs will have everything to gain and nothing to lose by not intervening in the first action."[163] Nevertheless, the Supreme Court granted trial courts broad discretion to determine when offensive collateral estoppel should be applied and mentioned some of the circumstances a court should consider, such as:

---

[158] *See, e.g.,* Amader v Pittsburgh Corning Corp, 546 F Supp 1033 (ED Pa 1982); Ray v Alad Corp, 19 Cal 3d 22, 560 P2d 3, 136 Cal Rptr 574 (1977); Ramirez v Amsted Indus, Inc, 86 NJ 332, 431 A2d 811 (1981); Nieves v Bruno Sherman Corp, 86 NJ 361, 431 A2d 826 (1981); Tift v Forage King Indus, Inc, 108 Wis 2d 72, 322 NW2d 14 (1982).

[159] Borel v Fibreboard Paper Prods, Inc, 493 F2d 1076 (5th Cir 1973), *cert denied,* 419 US 869 (1974).

[160] Bichler v Eli Lilly & Co, 55 NY2d 571, 436 NE2d 182, 450 NYS2d 766 (1982), discussed in **§11.20.**

[161] 402 US 313 (1971).

[162] 439 US 322 (1979).

[163] *Id* 330.

1. Whether the defendant in the first action had an incentive to defend vigorously—was he or she sued for small or nominal damages and could he or she foresee future suits?

2. Have there been other judgments inconsistent with the one asserted as the basis for estoppel?

3. Was the earlier forum inconvenient, or did it deny defendant procedural opportunities that could cause a different result?

4. Could plaintiff have easily joined in the earlier action?

Soon after *Parklane,* in *Flatt v Johns-Manville Sales Corp,*[164] a strict liability action, a federal district court used the *Borel* verdict as the basis for estopping Johns-Manville (a *Borel* defendant) and Certain-Teed (not a *Borel* defendant) from litigating two issues—the unreasonably dangerous nature of their asbestos-containing pipes and the causal connection between asbestos dust and mesothelioma. (The court also ruled against defendants on these issues "as a matter of law.")[165] Johns-Manville was also precluded from relitigating the fact of its manufacture and distribution of asbestos-containing pipes; Certain-Teed was not. The court found that these issues were identical to issues actually litigated in *Borel,* and that their determination against defendants was necessary and essential to the judgment in *Borel.* Other courts have used collateral estoppel based on *Borel* in a similar fashion, but not against a defendant such as Certain-Teed, which had never litigated or lost an asbestos case on the merits.[166]

In *Hardy v Johns-Manville Sales Corp,*[167] the Fifth Circuit overturned the district court's use of offensive collateral estoppel premised on *Borel* and criticized *Flatt* because the *Borel* judgment is ambiguous as to what issues were "necessarily decided;"[168] because there had been subsequent judgments inconsistent with the *Borel* verdict; because it is very doubtful that, in 1973, the *Borel* defendants could have foreseen their multimillion dollar exposure; and, as to non-*Borel* defendants, because the use of offensive collateral estoppel violates their due process guarantee of a full and fair opportunity to litigate.

The *Hardy* decision does not preclude the use of offensive collateral estoppel based upon other asbestos litigation judgments or its use in other massive toxic tort litigation; nor does it end the debate. The verdict against DES manufactur-

---

[164] 488 F Supp 836 (ED Tex 1980).

[165] *Id* 837.

[166] Bertrand v Johns-Mansville Sales Corp, 529 F Supp 539 (D Minn 1982); Amader v Johns-Manville Corp, 541 F Supp 1384 (ED Pa 1982); Mooney v Fibreboard Corp, 485 F Supp 242 (ED Tex 1980). *But see* McCarty v Johns-Manville Sales Corp, 502 F Supp 335 (SD Miss 1980) (applying Mississippi law, which still requires mutuality of the parties); Tretter v Johns-Manville Corp, 88 FRD 329 (ED Mo 1980) (inconsistent judgments had been obtained by defendant); Newmark v Gimbels Inc, 54 NJ 585, 258 A2d 697 (1969).

[167] 681 F2d 334 (5th Cir 1982).

[168] *Id* 337.

ers in *Bichler v Eli Lilly* was allowed to be used for offensive collateral estoppel purposes in *Kaufman v Eli Lilly & Co*[169] and was rejected for such purposes in both *Sardell v Eli Lilly & Co*[170] and *Wetherill v University of Chicago*.[171]

In the right case, the use of offensive collateral estoppel can be extremely valuable to a plaintiff. There is growing reluctance among courts to apply it, however, especially since it tends to proliferate litigation (particularly in forums that allow it), rather than promote judicial economy.[172] Additionally, defendants in massive tort situations have become acutely aware of the implications of *Parklane* and litigate fully any case with *Borel*-type potential. The likelihood of an appeal and the danger of a reversal should be considerations when a plaintiff decides whether to seek summary judgment on the basis of offensive collateral estoppel.

---

[169] No 21234/76 (NY Sup Ct, Oct 25, 1982) (relitigation of the defect issue precluded as to the *Bichler* defendant; however, non-*Bichler* defendants were severed to avoid prejudice at trial).

[170] No 18268-77 (NY Sup Ct, Oct 15, 1982) (use of offensive collateral estoppel premised on *Bichler* denied because *Bichler* was affirmed on procedural grounds, leaving the validity of its verdict under New York law uncertain, and because there had been subsequent inconsistent verdicts).

[171] 548 F Supp 66 (ND Ill 1982) (the *Bichler* record was not submitted to the trial court, thus an accurate discernment of what facts were necessarily established in the Bichler trial was not possible).

[172] It was this concern that recently prompted the Ohio Supreme Court in Goodson v McDonough Power Equip, Inc, 2 Ohio St 3d 193, 443 NE2d 978 (1983), to decline to follow the growing number of jurisdictions that have abrogated the rule of mutuality and permitted the assertion of offensive collateral estoppel.

12 Remedies

Thomas H. Barnard, Esq. *

§12.01 Introduction

One of the great principles of the common law is that the existence of any right is defined by the existence of a remedy.[1] The uniform experience of

---

* Partner, Squire, Sanders & Dempsey, Cleveland, Ohio.

[1] As Chief Justice Holt observed, if a person has a right, he or she must "have a means to vindicate and maintain it, and a remedy if he is injured in the exercise and enjoyment of it; and, indeed it is a vain thing to imagine a right without a remedy; for want of right and want of remedy are reciprocal." Ashby v White, 92 Eng Rep 126, 136 (1703).

mankind has amply shown that without a prompt and efficient remedy, even the most sacred and elaborately defined rights amount to little.

The remedies available in hazardous substance litigation are still being defined, both by legislation and by litigation. In general, injured parties may look to three areas for redress: state and federal administrative agencies; litigation in state and federal courts; and, to the extent the hazards are work-related, to labor organization involvement in plant safety.

Each of these avenues of relief offers its own kind of remedy, and each has its own goals and limitations. Each should be considered in attempting to resolve a particular hazardous waste situation.

§12.02   Administrative Remedies

Administrative agencies at the state and federal levels are of two kinds: those which enforce regulatory statutes, either on their own initiative or at the complaint of others; and those which adjudicate individual claims and provide compensation for losses. Among the former are the Occupational Safety and Health Administration (OSHA) and the Environmental Protection Agency (EPA). Among the latter are the state workers' compensation agencies.

The regulatory agencies, while they have broad powers to prevent harmful uses of toxic substances or to punish those who violate the statutes, generally cannot compensate victims directly or order transgressors to provide compensation. The investigations these agencies conduct and the data they collect, however, can often be invaluable to the plaintiff bringing a private action. Violations of statutes or agency regulations, established by administrative action, can substantially ease the plaintiff's burden of establishing liability.

The compensation-type agencies, on the other hand, generally act only upon the specific complaints of harmed individuals, provide procedures for resolving those complaints, and provide compensation to individuals whose complaints are found valid. Such compensation is usually paid from a government fund financed by the industry responsible for the harm. Individuals recovering from these funds are usually barred from seeking other compensation through litigation.

A third type of agency program has also been developed in the past few years to deal with the catastrophic consequences of toxic chemical pollution. These are the so-called superfunds which have been established by the federal government and by several states. These agencies are hybrids. They are aimed at remedying situations which, while relatively few in number, are extremely devastating to the community involved. Such programs are generally aimed at providing funds to clean up a specific toxic site quickly and are only secondarily concerned with compensating the losses of individuals or regulating the activities of those who produce, use, and dispose of toxic chemicals.

§12.03 —Federal Regulatory Agencies

Numerous federal statutes in the environmental field have given powers to federal agencies to remedy toxic waste pollution. Chief among these agencies is the Environmental Protection Agency (EPA), which was created by executive order in 1970 to centralize the federal government's environmental activities.[2] As to employment-related exposure to toxic substances, the Occupational Safety and Health Administration (OSHA) has significant enforcement powers.

There are at least half a dozen laws on the books under which the EPA can regulate hazardous and toxic wastes. Although attention has largely shifted to the so-called Superfund act[3] since its passage, there are numerous other laws which give the EPA alternative or complementary powers.

Refuse Act

The oldest statute, which is not actually a regulatory statute, is the Refuse Act of 1899.[4] This act makes it a federal crime to deposit any "refuse matter of any kind" in any navigable body of water, including the banks or tributaries of any such body. The act has been interpreted as imposing strict liability;[5] in addition to the fines and jail sentences provided for by the law,[6] courts have imposed orders to clean up violations.[7]

Clean Water Act and Safe Drinking Water Act

Under both the Clean Water Act[8] and the Safe Drinking Water Act,[9] the EPA has broad administrative powers to control hazardous wastes which might affect water quality. Under the Clean Water Act, the EPA may set effluent emission levels and standards with regard to toxic pollutants.[10] Violations of these standards are prohibited.[11] Either an appropriate state agency or the EPA may enforce the act, with both civil and criminal penalties possible.[12]

---

[2] Reorg Plan No 3 of 1970, 1970 US Code Cong & Ad News 6322.

[3] Comprehensive Environmental Response, Compensation and Liability Act, 42 USC §§9601-9657.

[4] 33 USC §407.

[5] United States v White Fuel Corp, 498 F2d 619 (1st Cir 1974); United States v American Cyanimid Co, 354 F Supp 1202 (SDNY), *affd,* 480 F2d 1132 (2d Cir 1973).

[6] 33 USC §411 provides that violation of the Refuse Act is a misdemeanor, and punishable by fine of not more than $2,500 nor less than $500, and/or imprisonment of not more than 30 days. One-half of the fine may be paid to the person reporting the violation.

[7] Wyandotte Transp Co v United States, 389 US 191, 197-202 (1967).

[8] 33 USC §1251 *et seq.*

[9] 42 USC §§300f to 300j-10.

[10] 33 USC §1317.

[11] *Id* (d).

[12] *Id* §1319.

Liability is limited, however, to *point source* discharges of pollutants; runoff or leaching of chemicals into bodies of water is not covered.[13] In some cases, however, runoff has given rise to liability where it has formed channels.[14] Under the Safe Drinking Water Act, the EPA sets national standards for drinking water, with primary enforcement by the states.[15] If the state does not act, however, or if there is "imminent and substantial endangerment to the health of persons," the EPA may issue emergency orders or seek civil penalties.[16]

Clean Air Act

The Clean Air Act[17] also authorizes administrative abatement orders or court action by the EPA where a pollutant poses an imminent hazard.[18] In at least two cases, the EPA has relied upon the act to remedy the escape of toxic fumes from hazardous waste facilities.[19]

Acts Aimed at Hazardous Wastes and Toxic Substances

Several acts aimed principally at hazardous wastes give the EPA more specific authority over toxic substances. These are the Resource Conservation and Recovery Act (RCRA),[20] the Toxic Substances Control Act (TSCA),[21] and the Comprehensive Environmental Response, Compensation and Liability Act (*Superfund* or CERCLA).[22]

Resource Conservation and Recovery Act

The Resource Conservation and Recovery Act (RCRA) completely revised the Solid Waste Disposal Act and established the Office of Solid Waste in the EPA.[23] Subchapter III of RCRA deals with hazardous waste management. The act requires the EPA to establish a list of hazardous waste substances and to establish standards for generators, transporters, and disposers of such wastes.[24] A system of federal permits is set up to regulate facilities which process, transport, or dispose of hazardous wastes.[25] A manifest system re-

---

13 *Id* §1362(12).

14 United States v Vertac Chem Corp, 489 F Supp 870 (ED Ark 1980).

15 42 USC §§300g-1, -2.

16 33 USC §300i.

17 42 USC §7401 *et seq.*

18 42 USC §7603.

19 United States v 2001, Inc, Civ No 80-0771 (ED La, filed Mar 5, 1980); United States v Dusek, Civ No B80-110 (SD Tex, filed May 5, 1980).

20 42 USC §6901 *et seq.*

21 15 USC §2601 *et seq.*

22 42 USC §9601 *et seq.*

23 *Id* §6911.

24 *Id* §§6921-6924.

25 *Id* §6925.

quires *cradle-to-grave* records of all toxic substances.[26] The EPA may seek compliance with the act or regulations by administrative order or by a civil action in district court.[27] In additon to seeking "appropriate relief, including a temporary or permanent injunction," the EPA may collect civil penalties of up to $25,000 per day.[28] Criminal penalties are also available against any person who knowingly operates without a permit or makes a false statement to the EPA in connection with any matter under the act.[29] The act also authorizes the EPA to assist states in developing their own hazardous waste programs.[30]

RCRA provides for a civil action by any citizen against the EPA or other governmental agency for failing to perform a duty under the act, or against any person who violates the act or a regulation under it.[31] The EPA must be given 60 days' notice before the action can be brought, and the action cannot be brought if the EPA or a state is already pursuing an action against the violator. Attorneys' fees and court costs may be awarded to a successful plaintiff.[32]

Toxic Substances Control Act

The Toxic Substances Control Act (TSCA)[33] is more broadly aimed at the whole subject of toxic substances than is RCRA, which deals primarily with the disposal of wastes. The EPA has not used TSCA as frequently as RCRA, however, and with the passage of Superfund, one commentator has suggested that "TSCA will remain a clearly subordinate tool for hazardous waste enforcement."[34]

TSCA requires industry testing and reporting of chemical substances where the EPA finds that certain conditions, relating to possible toxicity or widespread exposure, are met.[35] The act gives the EPA broad power to establish regulations over the manufacture and disposal of toxic chemicals.[36]

For failure to comply with any requirement of TSCA or a regulation issued thereunder, the EPA may seek civil penalties of up to $25,000 per day or criminal penalties.[37] Where the situation poses an imminent hazard, the EPA may seek an immediate seizure of the hazardous substance and/or injunctive relief against any person involved in the manufacture, distribution, or disposal

---

[26] *Id* §§6922-6924.

[27] *Id* §6928.

[28] *Id.*

[29] *Id.*

[30] *Id* §§6926, 6929, 6931.

[31] *Id* §6972.

[32] *Id* (e).

[33] 15 USC §2601 *et seq.*

[34] Mott, *Liability for Clean-Up of Inactive Hazardous Waste Disposal Sites,* in Practising Law Institute, Hazardous Waste Litigation 33 (Mott, Chairman 1981).

[35] 15 USC §§2603, 2604, 2607.

[36] *Id* §2605.

[37] *Id* §2615.

of the substance.[38] Relief can take the form of an injunction, or if the hazardous substance has been sold, an order that the defendant notify purchasers and the public of the risk posed by the product, recall it, and replace it.[39]

TSCA also permits citizen actions against violators or against the EPA if it fails to act.[40] In addition, citizens may petition the EPA to issue, amend, or repeal a regulation issued under the act.[41] The act also prohibits any employer from discharging or discriminating against any employee who brings a suit under the act, gives testimony, or otherwise aids in carrying out the purposes of the act.[42]

Superfund

The most recent addition to the regulatory arsenal, Superfund (CERCLA), requires detailed record keeping by any facility which stores hazardous substances, and prompt notification to the EPA of incidents involving the escape of such substances into the environment.[43] The EPA is to prepare a national contingency plan to deal with such incidents.[44] The attorney general may bring an action to abate imminent hazards, and the president may issue such orders as are necessary to protect the public health and welfare and the environment.[45]

The federal government may initiate whatever emergency measures are necessary to see that a hazardous waste situation is remedied.[46] After the emergency has passed, the government may look to all persons involved in the transportation and disposal of the hazardous wastes, who meet the criteria of the act, for clean-up and response costs and for the value of natural resources destroyed as a result of releases of hazardous substances.[47] The only permitted defenses are that the violation is caused by an act of God or war, or that it is the result of the act of a third party, provided the defendant exercised due care and took precautions against the foreseeable acts of the third party.[48]

Occupational Safety and Health Act

Where the hazard is not to the environment in general but rather to the

---

[38] *Id* §2616.

[39] *Id.*

[40] *Id* §2619.

[41] *Id* §2620.

[42] *Id* §2622.

[43] 42 USC §9603.

[44] *Id* §9605.

[45] *Id* §9606.

[46] *Id* §9604.

[47] *Id* §9607.

[48] *Id* (b).

workplace, the Occupational Safety and Health Act (OSH Act),[49] administered by the Occupational Safety and Health Administration (OSHA), becomes the key federal regulatory statute. The OSH Act requires every employer to furnish a workplace free from recognized hazards and to comply with safety and health standards promulgated under the act.[50] Such standards may be promulgated without complying with the Administrative Procedure Act[51] when employees are exposed to "grave danger from exposure" to toxic substances.[52]

If an employer fails to comply with the OSH Act or the safety standards promulgated under it, it may be cited for the violation and subjected to civil and/or criminal penalties through administrative proceedings.[53] In addition, the secretary of labor may bring an action in federal court to have an employer enjoined from continuing an imminent danger—i.e., any practice or condition which could reasonably cause death or serious physical harm before the danger can be eliminated through the administrative process.[54] Employers are prohibited from discharging or discriminating against an employee because the employee makes a complaint under the act, testifies in a proceeding under the act, or exercises any rights under the act.[55] The secretary is authorized to file suit on behalf of any employee who has been subject to discrimination.[56]

The National Institute of Occupational Safety and Health (NIOSH), which was established to conduct research and to draft safety and health standards, publishes annually a list of toxic substances.[57] OSHA has adopted standards for many toxic substances, including air contaminants,[58] various carcinogens such as vinyl chloride,[59] inorganic arsenic,[60] lead,[61] benzene,[62] coke oven emissions,[63] DBCP,[64] and acrylonitrile.[65] Beyond this, the OSH Act provides that

---

[49] 29 USC §651 *et seq.*

[50] *Id* §654. See generally, G. Z. Nothstein, The Law of Occupational Safety & Health (1981); M. A. Rothstein, Occupational Safety and Health Law (1978).

[51] 5 USC §6551 *et seq.*

[52] 29 USC §655(c). Under this authority, OSHA established standards for certain carcinogenic chemicals. 29 CFR §§1910.1017-.1102.

[53] 29 USC §§658, 666.

[54] *Id* §662.

[55] *Id* §660(c).

[56] *Id.*

[57] NIOSH, Dept of Health & Human Services, Public Health Service, Center for Disease Control, Registry of Toxic Effects of Chemical Substances (R. J. Lewis & R. L. Tatken eds 1982 ed) (United States Government Printing Office.).

[58] 29 CFR §1910.1000.

[59] *Id* §§1910.1017-.1102.

[60] *Id* §1910.1018.

[61] *Id* §1910.1025.

[62] *Id* §1910.1028.

[63] *Id* §1910.1029.

[64] *Id* §1910.1044.

[65] *Id* §1910.1045.

an employer or an authorized employee representative may request the Department of Health & Human Services to determine if a substance normally found in the workplace is toxic at the concentrations usually encountered. The secretary is to inform both sides of his or her determination.[66] Employers may be required to measure and report the level of exposure of employees to toxic substances.

§12.04   —State Regulatory Agencies

All of the three major federal laws (discussed in §12.03) dealing with the hazardous waste problem make provisions for state involvement in the regulatory process. Both the Toxic Substances Control Act (TSCA)[67] and the Resource Conservation and Recovery Act (RCRA)[68] provide for the development of state plans and programs and for federal grants to states which meet the federal requirements.[69] The Comprehensive Environmental Response, Compensation and Liability Act (Superfund or CERCLA)[70] explicitly allows states to impose additional requirements or liability with respect to hazardous substances.[71]

Most states have enacted laws setting up programs to regulate hazardous wastes. These statutes vary widely from state to state. Most provide that the state department which oversees environmental affairs shall adopt regulations and standards for the control of hazardous wastes.[72] A system for licensing producers, transporters, and disposers of hazardous wastes is usually provided.[73] Violation of the act or regulations issued thereunder is usually made a crime.[74] Civil penalties and injunctions to enforce the law are usually available at the petition of a state official, and criminal penalties consisting of fines of $10,000 to $25,000 and jail sentences of six months to five years are not uncommon.[75]

---

[66] 29 USC §669(2)(5).

[67] 15 USC §2601 *et seq.*

[68] 42 USC §6901 *et seq.*

[69] RCRA: 42 USC §§6941-6949; TSCA: 15 USC §2627.

[70] 42 USC §9601 *et seq.*

[71] *Id* §9614.

[72] *E.g.,* California Hazardous Waste Control Act, Cal Health & Safety Code §25150 (West 1982) (State Department of Health); District of Columbia Hazardous Waste Management Act, DC Code §6-525 (West 1983) (Mayor); Michigan Hazardous Waste Management Act, Mich Comp Laws §299.526 (West 1983) (Department of Natural Resources).

[73] *E.g.,* Massachusetts Hazardous Waste Management Act, Mass General Laws ch 216, §7 (West 1982); New York Industrial Hazardous Waste Management Act, NY Envtl Conserv Law §27-0905 *et seq.* (McKinney 1982).

[74] *E.g.,* Cal Health & Safety Code §25189.5 (West 1982); Mich Comp Laws §299.548 (West 1983).

[75] *E.g.,* DC Code Ann §§6-530—6-531 (West 1983) (injunction at suit of city; maximum criminal penalty $10,000 and/or six months); Mass General Laws Ann ch 21C,

Fewer states have laws regulating the siting of hazardous waste facilities. Such laws typically provide for a commission of officials and citizens to study and rule upon all applications to build new hazardous waste disposal facilities within the state.[76] Often, public hearings must be held and developers must compile and make public a great deal of information about location, operation, and intended use of such a facility.[77] The Massachusetts siting act requires study by both a state council and a "local assessment committee."[78] The developer and the local committee are required to reduce to writing in the form of a contract the terms and conditions upon which the facility is to operate.[79]

Even fewer states have adopted superfund programs comparable to CER-CLA. Like the federal act, these state laws generally do not provide for direct compensation to individuals, but there are exceptions. These programs are discussed in more detail in §12.06.

§12.05 —Workers' Compensation

Persons injured by exposure to toxic substances in the course of their employment must consider the workers' compensation acts which have been adopted in all states. If the injury is found to be covered by such an act, the amount which the injured person may collect will be limited by law. If the injury is found to be compensable, private damage actions are barred and instead compensation is paid, usually from a state fund, according to a schedule established by law.[80] The workers' compensation law will, in that case, be the employee's sole source of redress.

However, there are several theories by which an employee injured by exposure to toxic substances can seek to bypass the workers' compensation system. Some states allow the willful act or misconduct of the employer to give rise to an ordinary tort suit.[81] Thus, it has been held that where an employer knew that employees were being exposed to toxic chemicals and failed to correct the situation or warn the employees or report the situation to the appropriate authorities, a cause of action for an intentional tort was stated, and the workers'

§10 (West 1982) (injunction at suit of state; civil penalty $25,000 per day; maximum criminal penalty $25,000 and/or five years); Mich Comp Laws §299.548 (West 1983) (injunction and damages to natural resources at suit of state; civil penalty $25,000; maximum criminal penalty $25,000 and/or one year for first offense, $50,000 and/or two years for subsequent offenses).

[76] *E.g.,* New York Industrial Siting Hazardous Waste Facilities Act, NY Envtl Conserv Law §17-1101 *et seq* (McKinney 1982).

[77] *E.g.,* Massachusetts Hazardous Waste Facility Siting Act, Mass General Laws Ann ch 21D, §8 (West 1982).

[78] *Id.*

[79] Mass General Laws Ann ch 21D, §§12-13 (West 1982).

[80] Millus & Gentile, Workers' Compensation Law and Insurance, 47 (2d ed 1980).

[81] Or Rev Stat §656.018(3)(a) (1983); West Va Code §23-2-62 (Michie 1982).

compensation law did not bar the suit.[82] Some states hold that employees may resort to a tort remedy when the employer fails to comply with a statutory safety requirement for the protection of employees.[83]

If an employer fails to inform an employee of the existence of a disease caused by exposure to toxic substances in the workplace, the employee may, in some jurisdictions, bypass the workers' compensation system and sue the employer directly for the aggravation of the injury caused by the employee's failure to seek medical treatment.[84]

Another way to avoid the limitation of the workers' compensation laws is to seek relief from a third party. Unless the specific act provides otherwise, it has generally been held that workers' compensation acts do not bar tort suits by employees against third parties who cause them injury in the workplace.[85] Thus, if the injured employee can find a third party liable for the injury (such as the manufacturer of a toxic chemical),[86] he or she may be able to avoid the limitations of the workers' compensation system.

§12.06 —Superfund Acts

Because existing laws in many cases were found to be inadequate to deal with the immediate hazards posed by toxic waste dumps, Congress and several states have enacted what have been dubbed *superfund acts.* These acts provide a fund, administered by the Environmental Protection Agency (EPA) or a comparable state agency, to be used to pay for the immediate costs of cleaning up the hazard. After the danger has been remedied, the agency may sue the parties responsible for the toxic waste discharge for reimbursement to the fund.

The acts vary in their provisions for remedying the losses incurred by individuals. Under the federal Comprehensive Environmental Response, Compensation and Liability Act (CERCLA),[87] any individual may recover "any necessary costs" incurred in responding to the improper release or disposal

---

[82] Blankenship v Cincinnati Milacron Chems, Inc, 69 Ohio St 2d 608, 433 NE2d 572 (1981), *cert denied,* 103 S Ct 127 (1982).

[83] Converse v State, 181 Misc 113, 41 NYS2d 245 (1943); Mike v Borough of Aliquippa, 279 Pa Super 382, 421 A2d 251 (1980) Depre v Pacific Coast Forge Co, 151 Wash 430, 276 P 89 (1929).

[84] Johns-Manville Products Corp v Superior Court, 27 Cal 3d 465, 612 P2d 948, 165 Cal Rptr 858 (1980); Wojcik v Aluminum Co of America, 18 Misc 2d 740, 183 NYS2d 351 (1959); Delamotte v Unitcast Div of Midland Ross Corp, 64 Ohio App 2d 159, 411 NE2d 814 (1978).

[85] Millus & Gentile, *supra,* note 80, at 169.

[86] Arnstein v Manufacturing Chemists Assn, 414 F Supp 12 (ED Pa 1976); Parzini v Center Chem Co, 136 Ga App 396, 221 SE2d 475 (1975); Gutowski v M&R Plastics & Coating, Inc, 60 Mich App 499, 231 NW2d 456 (1975).

[87] 42 USC §9601 *et seq.*

of a hazardous substance.[88] The persons liable include the owner and operator of a facility transporting or storing hazardous substances, any party who arranges for another party to transport or dispose of hazardous substances, and any party who accepts hazardous substances for transportation or disposal.[89]

Remedies available to private litigants under CERCLA, however, are limited. The act's main goal is the immediate clean-up of hazardous waste situations, not the compensation of individuals.[90] Thus, an individual may recover only "necessary costs of response" and even then only if they are "consistent with the national contingency plan" for hazardous waste control.[91] Congress specifically eliminated provisions from the original bill which would have made the polluters jointly and severally liable for medical expenses and property damage.[92] As CERCLA presently stands, only the federal and state governments may recover damages for injury to property.[93]

Those states which have their own superfund acts, however, sometimes give private litigants greater remedies.[94] The New Jersey Spill Compensation and Control Act is an example of such a law.[95] It creates a state fund to pay immediate clean-up costs, which is reimbursed by the persons responsible

---

[88] 42 USC §9607(a)(4)(B).

[89] *Id* §9607(a).

[90] Ginsberg & Weiss, *Common Law Liability for Toxic Torts: A Phantom Remedy,* 9 Hofstra L Rev 859, 931 (1981).

[91] 42 USC §9607(a)(4)(B).

[92] City of Philadelphia v Stepan Chem Co, 544 F Supp 1135, 1142 n 9 (ED Pa 1982).

[93] 42 USC §9607(f).

[94] The following states have funds for the emergency clean-up of hazardous wastes:

Alabama— Ala Code §§22-30-23, 23-30-9 (Michie 1982)

Arizona— Ariz Rev Stat Ann §36-2805 (West 1981)

Colorado— Colo Rev Stat §29-22-105 (Michie 1980)

Connecticut— Conn Gen Stat Ann §25-54ee(d) (West 1980)

Florida— Fla Stat §403.725(1) (West 1978)

Georgia— Ga Code §43-2909(4) (Michie 1983)

Illinois— Ill Ann Stat ch 111-1/2, §1022.2 (Smith-Hurd 1980)

Louisiana— La Rev Stat Ann §§30:1143, 30:1149 (West 1979)

Maryland— Md Nat Res Code Ann §81-413.2(f) (Michie 1983)

Michigan— Mich Comp Laws Ann §299.543 (West 1983)

New Hampshire— NH Rev Stat Ann §§47-B:3, 147-B:6 (Equity 1981)

New Jersey— NJ Stat Ann §58:10-23.11 (West 1972)

New Mexico— NM Stat Ann §74-4-8 (Michie 1979)

New York— NY Envtl Conserv Law §27-1301 (McKinney 1982)

North Carolina— NC Gen Stat §143-215.87 (Michie 1978)

Oregon— Or Rev Stat §459.600 (1983)

Pennsylvania— Pa Stat Ann tit 35, §6018.701 (Purdon 1981)

Tennessee— Tenn Code Ann §53-6.308 (Michie 1981)

Wisconsin— Wisc Stat Ann §144.441 (West 1982)

[95] NJ Stat Ann §§58:10-23.11 *et seq* (West 1977).

when sued by the state.[96] In addition, the New Jersey act also provides that the fund is strictly liable for all clean-up costs and "all direct and indirect damages" including but not limited to: real or personal property damage, including loss of income; the cost of restoring or replacing damaged natural resources; loss of local tax revenues caused by the damage; and interest on money borrowed to ameliorate the effects of the discharge.[97] Claims for such damage are paid by the state fund. The state may then seek reimbursement from the parties responsible for these costs.[98] It is not clear whether the New Jersey law provides recovery for medical expenses.[99]

As is typical with such laws, both CERCLA and the New Jersey act explicitly preserve the right of private individuals to any other civil remedy available to them.[100] CERCLA, however, has been cited to support a holding that Congress has preempted the right a private litigant may have had under the federal common law of nuisance.[101]

§12.07   Private Litigation Remedies

Administrative remedies, as noted in §§12.02-12.06, generally act to ameliorate a particular hazardous waste situation which threatens the public health and safety. The remedy is either an administrative order, having the force of law, requiring that a particular situation be corrected, or litigation brought by the agency to enforce a public right. Litigation remedies, on the other hand, are generally aimed at compensating individuals who have been directly harmed by such a situation.

The two remedies generally available to vindicate individual rights in the area of toxic tort litigation are money damages and equitable relief. Both may be based on either statutory or common law theories of liability.

§12.08   —Statutory Remedies

Statutes may provide a plaintiff with a remedy for a toxic tort in three ways. First, a statute may explicitly create a cause of action. Second, a court may imply a private right of action from a regulatory statute which is silent on private enforcement. Finally, a court may hold that violation of a regulatory statute which does not otherwise give rise to liability is negligence per se, thereby easing considerably a plaintiff's burden of proving negligence. If liabil-

---

[96] *Id* §§58:10-23.11f, .11g.

[97] *Id* §58:10-23.11g(2).

[98] *Id* §58:10-23.11q.

[99] Although the broad language of §58:10-23.11g(a) would seem to include damages for personal injuries, the examples given by act make no mention of personal injuries.

[100] CERCLA: 42 USC §9614(a); New Jersey act: NJ Stat Ann §58:10-23.11v (West 1977).

[101] City of Philadelphia v Stepan Chem Co, 544 F Supp 1135 (ED Pa 1982).

ity can be established in any one of these ways, a plaintiff can recover compensatory damages and, if the statute allows and the other requirements for their award are met, punitive damages and equitable relief as well.

A few states have explicitly created statutory causes of action in favor of persons injured by hazardous wastes. Alaska's statute is perhaps the broadest.[102] It provides that a person in control of a hazardous substance is strictly liable for damage to persons or property caused by the escape of the hazardous substance onto the land or water of another.[103]

The Rhode Island Hazardous Waste Management Act imposes liability for "all damages, losses, or injuries" resulting from disposal of hazardous waste, if the waste is disposed of in an unauthorized manner or at an unauthorized location.[104] North Dakota[105] and North Carolina[106] have also enacted provisions allowing recovery for personal injuries caused by hazardous wastes.

Although no federal statute creates a private cause of action for toxic torts, and most states do not have such a statute, that fact does not mean that such actions are foreclosed. The courts have in many cases in the past few years held that a variety of regulatory statutes give rise to liability by implying a private cause of action for damages. In determining whether a statute will support an implied private right of action, the court looks to the intent of the legislative body enacting the statute.[107]

Because it is rare that the legislative intent is clearly expressed, the courts look to various other factors. In analyzing federal statutes, the Supreme Court has declared the following four factors to be relevant:

1. Whether the plaintiff is within the class of persons intended to be protected by the statute

2. Whether the legislative history indicates an intent to create or deny a private right of action

3. Whether a private right of action would be consistent with the purpose of the act

4. Whether the cause of action is one traditionally relegated to state law[108]

State courts generally consider factors similar to the first three of these when interpreting state statutes.[109]

---

[102] Alaska Stat §46.03.822 (Michie 1976).

[103] *Id.* Damages include "injury to or loss of persons or property, real or personal. . . ." Alaska Stat §46.03.824.

[104] RI Gen Laws tit 23 §19.1-22 (Bobbs-Merrill 1978).

[105] ND Cent Code §32-40-01 *et seq* (Smith 1979).

[106] NC Gen Stat §§143-215.77(18), .93 (Michie 1980).

[107] Touche Ross & Co v Redington, 442 US 560, 568 (1979).

[108] Cort v Ash, 422 US 66, 78 (1975).

[109] Scroggins v Allstate Ins Co, 74 Ill App 3d 1027, 393 NE2d 718 (1979); Falmouth Hosp v Lopes, 376 Mass 580, 382 NE2d 1042 (1971).

Several federal environmental statutes which might otherwise provide a remedy for toxic torts have been found not to imply a private right of action.[110] Others contain provisions for private actions which limit the relief which may be sought to injunctive enforcement of duties imposed by the act, plus attorneys' fees.[111] Thus, private actions seeking damages must generally proceed on the basis of state-created causes of action.

The final manner in which a statute may support a claim for damages is through use of the negligence per se doctrine. This doctrine permits an injured party to show conclusively a defendant's negligence by showing that the defendant violated a safety statute.[112] The plaintiff must generally be within the class of persons intended to be protected by the statute, and the harm caused by the defendant's violation must be the kind sought to be prevented by the statute.[113] See Chapter 8.

Either a state or a federal statute or administrative regulation promulgated thereunder may be relied upon to establish the standard of care under negligence per se.[114] In particular, the federal Resource Conservation and Recovery Act,[115] the Toxic Substances Control Act,[116] the Comprehensive Environmental Response, Compensation and Liability Act,[117] and the regulations promulgated under these acts all provide a multitude of requirements for the handling of toxic and hazardous wastes, violations of which might be held to give rise to negligence per se.

§12.09 —Common Law Remedies

Liability for toxic torts has been based on a number of different common law theories of liability. Because different causes of action entitle a successful plaintiff to different remedies, the choice of theories on which to sue may prove quite important.

In general, the four common law torts upon which liability can be predicated are: negligence, strict liability, trespass, and nuisance. Money damages are

---

[110] Middlesex County Sewage Auth v National Sea Clammers Assn, 453 US 1 (1981) (Federal Water Pollution Control Act); City of Philadelphia v Stepan Chem Co, 544 F Supp 1135 (ED Pa 1982) (Clean Water Act).

[111] The Toxic Substances Control Act, 15 USC §2619, authorizes private actions to enforce the act, not to collect damages. The Resource Conservation and Recovery Act has a similar provision, 42 USC §6972.

[112] W. Prosser, The Law of Torts 190-204 (4th ed 1971).

[113] *Id.*

[114] *See* Good Fund Ltd 1972 v Church, 540 F Supp 519 (D Colo 1982) (EPA guidelines for safe levels of radioactivity on lands surrounding nuclear weapons factory are conclusive as to whether plaintiff was harmed; court does not have the expertise to fashion its own standard of care).

[115] 42 USC §§6901-6987.

[116] 15 USC §§2601-2629.

[117] 42 USC §§9601-9657.

available in all; although punitive damages are generally not available for negligence or strict liability. These causes of action are created by state law, and their elements are treated elsewhere.[118]

Emerging as new weapons in toxic tort litigation are two additional common law theories of liability. The first of these, the emergence of a federal common law of environmental torts, has been prevented from developing fully by cases holding that the spate of federal environmental legislation has preempted the field of federal common law.[119] The other development, still in its nascent stage, may prove more fruitful. This is the creation of a new *environmental tort* or *environmental cause of action,* recognized by at least one New York court.[120]

§12.10 —Equitable Remedies

Equitable remedies developed historically in the English Court of Chancery to counter the rigidity of the common law and its one balm for every hurt: money damages. They are characterized as being discretionary in nature and are tailored to meet the contours of the situation they are meant to remedy. They are governed by fundamental principles of fairness and justice and seek to "do equity" to all parties to the action.[121]

Equitable relief may be coupled with damages and declaratory relief, or it may be sought by itself. Equitable remedies may also be sought at any time before trial to preserve the status quo and to prevent the controversy from becoming moot before it can be heard on its merits.[122]

The principal equitable remedies of use in toxic waste litigation are the temporary restraining order and preliminary and permanent injunctions. These devices can be used to prevent a party from creating a potentially hazardous situation or to compel the abatement and clean-up of one that already exists. The granting of a provisional remedy before trial is governed principally by Rule 64 of the Federal Rules of Civil Procedure and the case law which has developed under it. The granting of final equitable relief is governed by the substantive law of the theory on which such relief is sought and on general principles of equity jurisprudence.

---

[118] See **ch 11.**

[119] The Supreme Court recognized a federal common law action in Illinois v City of Milwaukee, 406 US 91 (1972), but held the common law preempted by statute in City of Milwaukee v Illinois, 451 US 304 (1981). The lower courts have also had difficulty in this area. *Compare* United States v Solvent Recovery Service, 496 F Supp 1127 (D Conn 1980) (upholding federal common law cause of action) with City of Philadelphia v Stepan Chem Co, 544 F Supp 1135 (ED Pa 1982) and United States v Price, 523 F Supp 1055 (DNJ 1981), *affd,* 688 F2d 204 (3d Cir 1982) (finding preemption).

[120] Casco v Gotbaum, 67 Misc 2d 205, 323 NYS2d 742 (1971), *revd on other grounds,* 38 2d 955, 331 NYS2d 507 (1972). The court held that allegations of malicious pollution or contamination of the environment support a suit for injunctive relief and compensatory and punitive damages.

[121] Dobbs, Remedies, 25-26 (1973).

[122] *Id* 106.

Rule 64 authorizes both temporary restraining orders and preliminary injunctions to preserve the status quo pending trial. The principal difference between the two is that a temporary restraining order is meant to be an emergency measure when there is not sufficient time to hear arguments on both sides. It cannot extend beyond 10 days.[123] A preliminary injunction, granted after notice to the adverse party and a hearing, may extend for as long as the controversy is pending before the court.[124] Often, if a preliminary injunction is granted, the delay and added expense it entails will cause the opposing party to cancel the plans or end the activity which provoked the lawsuit.

To obtain preliminary relief in the federal courts four considerations must be balanced:

1. The threat of harm to the plaintiff
2. The hardship imposed on the defendant by the order
3. The probability that the plaintiff will succeed on the merits
4. The public interest[125]

State courts have also looked to these factors, or similar considerations, in granting or denying preliminary relief.[126] In addition, to obtain a temporary restraining order, the party seeking the order must show facts demonstrating that immediate and irreparable harm will result if the order is not granted; counsel must certify the efforts made, if any, to contact the opposing party; and counsel must provide reasons why notice should not be required.[127]

One further requirement bears careful consideration by a party either seeking or opposing preliminary relief. This is the requirement in Rule 65(e) that the applicant post security, "in such sum as the court deems proper," for any damages the opposing party may suffer by the granting of relief. Even if the relief requested is granted, if the security required is in an amount which cannot be met, the application for relief will be effectively defeated. Many courts, realizing that litigants in environmental cases are representing principles greater than personal gain, have waived the requirement altogether or required only nominal bond.[128]

Permanent injunctive relief granted as part of a judgment at the conclusion of the case can either enjoin the defendant from doing an action found to be

---

[123] Fed R Civ P 65(b).

[124] Fed R Civ P 65(a).

[125] Lundgrin v Claytor, 619 F2d 61 (10th Cir 1980); Elkanem v Health & Hosp Corp of Marion City, 589 F2d 316 (7th Cir 1978).

[126] Adams v Ohio Dept of Health, 5 Ohio Ops 3d 148, 356 NE2d 324 (Common Pleas 1976).

[127] Fed R Civ P 65(b).

[128] West Virginia Highlands Conservancy v Island Creek Coal Co, 441 F2d 232 (4th Cir 1971); Citizens for Responsible Area Growth v Adams, 477 F Supp 994 (DNH 1979); Highland Coop v Lansing, 492 F Supp 1372 (WD Mich 1980).

inimical to the environment or can affirmatively order the defendant to perform an act, such as cleaning up a chemical waste dump, or ordering an administrative agency, such as the Environmental Protection Agency (EPA), to perform a duty required of it under an applicable statute.[129] Where such a result is provided for by statute, the terms of the statute govern, but otherwise the injunctive relief is governed by equitable principles.

§12.11 —Class Actions

Class actions allow the common claims of large numbers of people to be resolved by one court action. Several named, or representative, plaintiffs bring the suit on behalf of themselves and on behalf of all other persons who have suffered the same damage. It is especially suited to claims arising out of toxic chemical accidents because such accidents often involve everyone living in the vicinity of the occurrence. By means of a class action, the plaintiffs can seek to remedy the damage done to the entire community.

The prosecution of a class action, however, entails special procedures and considerations which can stymie an environmental lawsuit unless the plaintiffs carefully think them through and comply with them. This puts an extra burden on counsel seeking to bring a class action. The requirements that must be satisfied to bring a class action, and the procedures that must be followed in prosecuting a class action, are principally found in Rule 23 of the Federal Rules of Civil Procedure and are discussed in detail in Chapter 15.

It has been said that the "difference between success and failure in environmental litigation"[130] often depends on how carefully the class is defined. A class which is overinclusive stands the risk of having members who do not share common questions of fact or law, who do not have claims or defenses which are typical of the other class members, and whose interests would not be *fairly and adequately* represented by the named parties. On the other hand, a class too narrowly defined might fail to remedy fully the environmental problem which is at the heart of the suit.

Nevertheless, the class need not be defined with mathematical certainty. Where the environment in a given locality has been harmed, a class defined geographically to include all persons in the danger area may be proper.[131] The fact that minority of persons within a defined class may not support the action

---

[129] Wood v Picillo, 443 A2d 1244 (RI 1982) (injunction to prevent further dumping and to order dumper to pay for clean-up and removal of toxic chemicals already dumped). For authority for injunctions to order EPA to comply with statute, see 15 USC §2619; 42 USC §6972.

[130] 1 Yannacone & Cohen, Environmental Rights and Remedies, 363 (1971).

[131] *In re* Three Mile Island, 87 FRD 433 (MD Pa 1980) (class of all property owners within 25 miles of nuclear plant); Biechele v Norfolk & W Ry Co, 309 F Supp 354 (ND Ohio 1969) (class defined in air pollution case as all persons living within area polluted by prevailing winds).

does not prevent the action from being maintained as a class action.[132] Even classes which include "unborn generations" which will be harmed by environmental degredation have been upheld.[133] On the other hand, a class of "all Georgia citizens having an economic interest in the production, supply and delivery of pure food" was held too broad,[134] as was a class of "all Texas citizens who are for the orderly development of Texas Parks and Recreational Facilities."[135]

In federal court actions, the Supreme Court has curbed class actions brought for money damages by requiring that each named plaintiff and each member of the class must meet the jurisdictional amount requirement of 28 USC §§1331-1332.[136] On the other hand, where declaratory and injunctive relief are sought instead of damages, each member of the class does not have to meet the jurisdictional amount. In such cases, the value of the project sought to be enjoined, the costs of the harm, or the value of the result to the defendant is examined to see if the jurisdictional amount is met.[137]

Once a legitimate class has been defined, the suit must still meet one or more of the three criteria listed in Rule 23(b) before it can be maintained as a class action. (See Chapter 15.)

On which of these three criteria or theories counsel seeks to predicate a class action is important, because different rules govern the subsequent procedure of the action.

If the action is brought pursuant to Rule 23(b)(3), each class member must meet the jurisdictional amount (if damages are sought), each member must be given "the best notice practicable under the circumstances" of the suit, and each member must be given the option to be excluded from the suit, or to enter an appearance through his or her own counsel.[138] However, if the action is brought under Rule 23(b)(2) for equitable relief only, none of these requirements need be met. Where the class is of more than a small size, the notice requirements can be burdensome, although the courts have been creative in devising methods of notification which allow class actions to survive.[139]

---

[132] Norwalk CORE v Norwalk Redevelopment Agency, 395 F2d 920 (2d Cir 1968); Nolop v Volpe, 333 F Supp 1364 (DSD 1971) (80% of class supported action).

[133] Cape May County Chapter, Inc, Izaak Walton League v Macchia, 329 F Supp 504, 514 (DNJ 1971).

[134] Sevanda, Inc v Irwin, 10 Envt Rep Cas (BNA) 2065 (ND Ga 1976).

[135] Johnson v Russell, 3 Envt Rep Cas (BNA) 1523, 1525 (WD Tex 1971).

[136] Zahn v International Paper Co, 414 US 291 (1973).

[137] River v Richmond Metropolitan Auth, 359 F Supp 611 (ED Va), affd, 481 F2d 1280 (4th Cir 1973); Citizens for Clean Air v Corps of Engineers, 349 F Supp 696 (SDNY 1972).

[138] Fed R Civ P 23(c)(2).

[139] Although individual notice to each class member whose name and address is reasonably ascertainable is required, Eisen v Carlisle & Jacquelin, 417 US 156 (1974), individual notice can be combined with notice by publication where individual notice is not possible. Payton v Abbott Labs, 86 FRD 351 (D Mass 1980); Bullock v Estate of Kircher, 84 FRD 1 (DNJ 1979).

Once the class has been defined and the theory on which the suit will proceed has been decided, counsel for the class should move aggressively to have the action certified as a class action and to meet the notice requirements or other orders the court may enter for management of the case pursuant to Rule 23(d). Failure of counsel to act promptly may result in the court finding that the representative parties are not capable of adequately representing the class.[140]

Before bringing a class action, the parties should be aware of the fact that once certified, the representative parties lose a measure of control over the conduct of the suit. The suit must be managed not only for their best interests but also for the best interests of the class. Thus, it may not be dismissed or compromised without approval of the court, and the court may require that all class members be given notice and be allowed to comment on any proposed dismissal or settlement of the suit.[141]

§12.12   Labor Organization Involvement

In any hazardous waste situation arising in the workplace, one of the most important sources of relief for the employee is through a labor organization. Although not every employer is unionized, a significant amount of the industry in America which generates and processes toxic and hazardous substances is covered by union agreements.

The first line of redress for employees is through the collective bargaining process. By bargaining, the employer can be bound to standards of safety and to specified procedures for enforcing those standards. The bargaining agreement can provide for benefits to employees comensurate with the risks they take and for special compensation, such as medical benefits, for those injured. The bargaining agreement can also provide for mechanisms, such as safety committees and grievance procedures, to monitor and enforce safety standards in the workplace.

Finally, if the union fails to live up to its duty to represent the employees fairly or if it is negligent in performing a duty it undertakes in the bargaining agreement, the union itself may be liable to its individual members.

§12.13   —Collective Bargaining

Both the courts and the National Labor Relations Board (NLRB) have held that safety practices and procedures are a mandatory subject for collective bargaining.[142] Thus, an employer must bargain in good faith over safety issues when requested to by a union. This is so even though legislation, such as the

---

[140] Lau v Standard Oil Co, 70 FRD 526 (ND Cal 1975).

[141] Fed R Civ P 23(e).

[142] NLRB v Gulf Power Co, 384 F2d 822 (5th Cir 1967).

Occupational Safety and Health Act (OSH Act),[143] may already impose duties on employers in this regard.

Occupational safety and health clauses appeared in more than 85 per cent of the collective agreements examined in one study and in all the mining, chemical, rubber, paper, and fabricated metals contracts examined.[144] Such contract provisions deal with a myriad of particulars, but the most common provisions relate to general statements of responsibility for safety;[145] requirements that the company comply with safety laws;[146] requirements that the company furnish safety equipment and first aid;[147] requirements for employee physicals;[148] and provisions for accident investigations and safety committees.[149] In addition, many contracts contain explicit provisions dealing with especially hazardous working conditions.[150]

Provisions dealing with hazardous working conditions generally prohibit such conditions, permit employees to refuse to work under such conditions, and provide procedures for the determination of when such conditions exist.[151]

Bargaining agreements may also require that specific safety rules be observed by management or employees, or both. Sometimes the agreement will spell out in general or specific terms particular safety rules. Other agreements adopt by reference government or industry safety guidelines or establish procedures for employer-employee committees to develop specific rules.

Bargaining agreements can impose obligations on employees to maintain safe working conditions. The most common provisions require that workers obey all safety rules, report all injuries, use all safety equipment and devices, and report all unsafe working conditions. The agreements also often provide for disciplinary action for violation of plant safety rules.

A contract clause which is gaining in popularity provides that a union representative may accompany government safety and health inspectors on tours of the workplace. Such clauses may also require that the union representative be paid for the time he or she spends on such activity[152] and that the company provide special training for such union representative.

A variety of measures are included in bargaining agreements to enforce safety provisions. The use of safety committees and the grievance procedure

---

[143] 29 USC §651 *et seq.*

[144] 2 BNA, Collective Bargaining Negotiations and Contracts 95:1 (1981).

[145] *Id* 95:121.

[146] *Id.*

[147] *Id* 95:123.

[148] *Id* 95:301.

[149] *Id* 95:361 and 95:181.

[150] *Id* 95:241.

[151] *Id.*

[152] Although OSHA regulations require that a union representative be allowed to accompany inspectors, 29 USC §657(e), 29 CFR §§1903.8, .10, regulations formerly requiring *walk-around pay* have been repealed. 46 Fed Reg 28,842 (Mar 13, 1981).

is discussed elsewhere.[153] Other typical provisions require management to publish the safety rules in a booklet and/or to post them on a bulletin board, require management to designate an individual on each shift as the *safety person* to enforce safety rules, require the union to cooperate in the enforcement of safety rules, and make violations of safety rules subject to the disciplinary process or just cause for discharge.

Other contractual safety provisions cover purchase and use of safety devices and clothing, require that the company retain safety consultants, and require that the company conduct safety inspections and audits, including air and water sampling for toxic substances.

§12.14 —Safety Committees

In any plant where toxic or hazardous materials are handled, a committee of employees and supervisors can go far to resolving employee safety concerns while at the same time allowing management the freedom it needs to operate efficiently. Many collective bargaining agreements provide for such *safety committees,* which are composed of various numbers of union and employer representatives. Sometimes the committee is made up solely of bargaining unit members, and sometimes it contains a neutral member selected jointly by the other members. Provision is often made for regular meetings and for employee-members to be paid for their time.

The authority of such committees is as varied as the bargaining agreements which established them. Some do no more than make suggestions to management concerning safety matters.[154] Others have the authority to shut down any operation which a majority of the committee agrees is unsafe.[155] Common powers given to such committees include establishing minimum safety standards, promoting safety awareness, investigating worker complaints, and overseeing compliance with state and federal regulations.

Collective bargaining agreements which provide for safety committees frequently allow disputes not resolved by the committee to be taken up by the grievance procedure, often at a higher initial level than other grievances.

Sometimes a bargaining agreement will spell out in detail the procedures to be followed by a safety committee in conducting its activities. The more authority such a committee is given, the more important it is that the contract

---

[153] See §12.15.

[154] The contract between Dravo Corp and the United Steelworkers provides that the committee shall cooperate with the safety engineer to prevent accidents and "make recommendations from time to time on the subject of safety." 2 BNA, Collective Bargaining Negotiations and Contracts, 95:183 (1981).

[155] The contract between Superior Plating, Inc and the International Union of Electricians provides that "[t]the Safety Committee may shut down a machine or operation which a majority of the committee (a quorum shall be four (4) members) agrees is unsafe." *Id* 95:184.

be explicit in defining the procedures to be followed by the committee and the procedures to be followed in appealing decisions of the committee.

Although ordinarily a union safety committee does not undertake to guarantee employees a safe workplace, depending upon the language of the contract, it may be held that the union has assumed a duty to the employees.[156] In such a case, the union might be found liable for injuries to employees.

§12.15 —Grievance Procedures and Arbitration

Collective bargaining agreements may provide exclusive or nonexclusive procedures for their enforcement. The most common pattern is for a multistep grievance procedure culminating in binding arbitration. The arbitration award may then be enforced by the courts.

In the context of safety matters, the usual grievance procedure may be invoked to enforce duties imposed by the collective bargaining agreement. Often, however, the agreement will provide that safety disputes be expedited by bypassing the initial steps of the grievance procedure. Sometimes, the arbitration step will be explicitly omitted so that plant management may retain ultimate control over safety conditions.

There are numerous arbitrators' decisions dealing with the subject of plant safety. As they are generally limited to the contract terms actually before the arbitrator, they are of limited application. Arbitrators have developed some general rules, however, which even in the absence of specific contractual language protect employees.

Where the contract is silent on the issue, arbitrators have ruled that management may promulgate and enforce reasonable health and safety rules.[157] Where the contract calls on the employer to use reasonable efforts to provide a safe working environment, the employer need not eliminate every hazard[158] but may do more than the contractual minimum if it wishes.[159]

Employees have an inherent obligation to protect themselves and their fellow employees.[160] Safety rules which have been adequately communicated to the employees may be enforced by a progressive discipline scheme, including discharge.[161] Strict compliance may be required, especially where the company's operations are inherently hazardous.[162]

Normally, employees are required to obey the orders of supervisors and resort to the grievance process if they feel the orders are objectionable. But

---

[156] See §12.16.

[157] Nu-Ply Corp, 50 Lab Arb (BNA) 985 (1968); Lone Star Steel Co, 48 Lab Arb (BNA) 1094 (1967).

[158] Brooklyn Union Gas Co, 47 Lab Arb (BNA) 425 (1966).

[159] Bethlehem Steel Co, 41 Lab Arb (BNA) 211 (1963).

[160] General Elec Co, 31 Lab Arb (BNA) 386 (1958).

[161] American Potash & Chem Corp, 64-1 Arb Rep (CCH) ¶8356 (1963); Mobil Chem Co, 71 Lab Arb (BNA) 535 (1978) (employees may be required to wear dosimeters).

[162] Eastern Air Lines, Inc, 44 Lab Arb (BNA) 549 (1965).

arbitrators recognize an important exception to this *work now—grieve later* doctrine where the order objected to would place the employee in an abnormally hazardous situation.[163] In determining whether an employee may invoke this exception to disobey a superior's command, arbitrators generally look to whether a *reasonable person* would have feared for his or her safety in the employee's position.

The most common use of arbitration is to settle the meaning of disputed terms in a contract. The interpretations of general contract clauses prohibiting unsafe or hazardous working conditions are obvious sources of disagreement between management and labor. In one arbitration dealing with the exposure of workers to toxic chemicals, the union contended that a clause requiring the employer to take "all reasonable and necessary precautions" for employee safety required the company to install monitoring equipment to check levels of exposure and to disclose the generic names of all chemicals to which workers were exposed. The company responded that it met all government regulations, that safety was solely the company's prerogative, that the contract required them to do no more than they were doing, and that the technology was not available to do more extensive monitoring. The arbitrator held that the union was entitled to a list, by generic names, of the chemicals used and manufactured at the plant. He reasoned that what might be *reasonable* under the contract may be broader than what government regulations require. However, the arbitrator declined to rule on the issue of additional monitoring, stating that until the union had a list of the chemicals involved it was impossible for both parties to debate the issue intelligently.[164]

The range of remedies which an arbitrator may employ to rectify a meritorious grievance is very broad. As in the case described above, an arbitrator may order a party to perform a particular act, such as disclosing the nature of the hazard. In another case, an arbitrator ordered the removal of an asbestos ceiling which was found to violate a provision that teachers "shall not be required to work under unsafe or hazardous conditions."[165] If the complaining employee has been suspended or fired, an arbitrator may order that lost pay and benefits be restored and/or that the employee be rehired.[166] Of course, the contract may specify remedies for its violation, but even in the absence of

---

[163] Sperry Rand Corp, 51 Lab Arb (BNA) 709 (1968); US Plywood-Champion Papers, Inc, 50 Lab Arb (BNA) 115 (1968). Under the Occupational Safety and Health Act (OSHA), 29 USC §651 *et seq*, an employee may refuse to perform a job where there is a reasonable apprehension of serious injury if there is no reasonable alternative. Whirlpool Corp v Marshall, 445 US 1 (1979).

[164] Ciba-Geigy Corp, 61 Lab Arb (BNA) 438 (1973). *Compare* Eaton Corp, 73 Lab Arb (BNA) 729 (1979) (employee not entitled to job transfer where exposure to chemicals in her present job causes rash, as she could cite no contract provision requiring such a transfer).

[165] Hoboken Bd of Educ, 75 Lab Arb (BNA) 988 (1980).

[166] Borg-Warner Corp, 72 Lab Arb (BNA) 184 (1979).

an express provision, an arbitrator may award damages for a violation.[167]

§12.16 Remedies against Unions

In exchange for the legal protections afforded them, labor unions are under a duty to afford fair representation to all their members.[168] In addition, a union may have a duty to exercise reasonable care in carrying out duties it assumes under a collective bargaining agreement.[169] Where a union breaches these duties, it is liable to harmed members for the damages they sustain. On the other hand, neither employers nor unions may be held liable under state law for breach of the collective bargaining agreement because federal labor law has preempted the field.[170]

To breach its duty of *fair representation,* a union must do more than merely act negligently. It must act in a manner which is "arbitrary, discriminatory or in bad faith.[171] An individual employee has no right to expect the union to take a particular grievance to arbitration[172] or to seek a particular result at the bargaining table.[173]

In one case, plaintiffs developed asbestosis and pneumoconiosis as a result of exposure to asbestos in the workplace. They argued that because health and safety are mandatory bargaining subjects, the union breached its duty of fair representation by not bargaining over the asbestos hazard to which the plaintiffs were exposed. The court upheld summary judgment for the union on the grounds that such an interpretation of the labor laws would fly in the face of congressional intent and would pervert the bargaining process.[174] Thus, a union is not generally liable for failing to create a safe working environment at the bargaining table.

A second theory of liability, however, has resulted in findings of union liability. Under this approach, the union is charged with exercising reasonable care in carrying out the duties to enforce safety rules it assumes under a bargaining agreement. If it fails to discharge that duty, it is liable to the

---

[167] San Antonio Air Logistic Center, 73 Lab Arb (BNA) 1074 (1979); Sterling Regal, Inc, 72 Lab Arb (BNA) 1186 (1979).

[168] Ford Motor Co v Huffman, 345 US 330 (1953). This duty is implicit in §9(a) of the National Labor Relations Act, 29 USC §159(a). Vaca v Sipes, 386 US 171, 177 (1967).

[169] Dunbar v United Steelworkers, 100 Idaho 523, 602 P2d 21 (1979), *cert denied,* 446 US 983 (1980); Helton v Hake, 564 SW2d 313 (Mo Ct App), *cert denied,* 423 US 959 (1978). *Compare* Bryant v United Mine Workers, 467 F2d 1 (6th Cir 1972), *cert denied,* 410 US 930 (1973), and House v Mine Safety Appliances Co, 417 F Supp 939 (D Idaho 1976).

[170] San Diego Unions v Garmon, 359 US 236 (1959); Garner v Teamsters Union, 346 US 485 (1953).

[171] Vaca v Sipes, 386 US 171, 190 (1967).

[172] *Id* 191.

[173] Carollo v Forty-Eight Insulation, Inc, 252 Pa Super 422, 381 A2d 990 (1977).

[174] *Id.*

employee. In one case, a union and its steward were found liable for wrongful death where an employee erecting a building came in contact with a high-tension line and was electrocuted. The bargaining agreement specifically prohibited work in the area of such lines unless the lines were insulated or the power was turned off. The same part of the agreement stated that the union steward "shall see that the provisions of these working rules are complied with" and that "the employer is in no way responsible for the performance of these functions by the steward."[175] In this situation, the court held the union had assumed the duty of protecting the workplace from the danger which killed the worker. The court distinguished other cases holding unions not liable on two grounds. First, some of the other cases were based on the duty of fair representation. Second, other cases did not have the explicit contractual provisions present in this case. Addressing the issue of federal preemption, the court held that the suit was based *on negligence,* not on breach of contract, and therefore was not preempted.

In another case, a mine accident took 91 lives, and the survivors brought wrongful death actions against the union. Reversing a summary judgment in favor of the union, the Idaho Supreme Court held that where a union undertakes a safety program and then negligently fails to carry it out, it is not protected by the federal preemption doctrine. The court held that either preemption does not apply at all or there is an exception to the doctrine where the union is charged with wrongful death.[176]

§12.17 Remedies against the Government

Victims of toxic waste pollution generally receive little in the way of direct compensation from the government under the major federal statutes.[177] One remedy besides those statutes, however, may be a suit for compensatory damages under the Federal Tort Claims Act (FTCA).[178] Government liability under the FTCA may be predicated either on the theory that the government itself created the hazardous waste problem, or, having undertaken supervision of toxic waste disposal, the government has failed to exercise reasonable care in performing this undertaking.

The FTCA does not create a new cause of action against the government. Rather, it waives the defense of sovereign immunity as to certain torts. Thus, a plaintiff suing under the FTCA must still prove his or her case in the same

---

[175] Helton v Hake, 564 SW2d 313, 317 (Mo Ct App), *cert denied,* 439 US 959 (1978).

[176] Dunbar v United Steelworkers, 100 Idaho 523, 602 P2d 21 (1979), *cert denied,* 446 US 983 (1980). *Compare* Bryant v United Mine Workers, 467 F2d 1 (6th Cir 1972), *cert denied,* 410 US 930 (1973), and House v Mine Safety Appliances Co, 417 F Supp 939 (D Idaho 1976).

[177] See §12.03.

[178] 28 USC §§2671-2680. Prejudgment interest and punitive damages are not available under the FTCA. 28 USC §2674.

way as against any other defendant.[179] Furthermore, the FTCA contains several major exceptions.[180] In toxic tort litigation, the "discretionary function"[181] and the "incident to military activities"[182] exceptions are most likely to be raised.

Two major government programs have given rise to claims that the government itself has committed toxic torts. These are the government's program of atomic testing in the 1950s and the use of toxic defoliants during the Vietnam War. Although the decisions in these cases have largely been against the plaintiffs, two recent cases suggest change toward government liability may be appearing.

The atomic testing cases have involved two classes of plaintiffs—soldiers who were intentionally exposed to atomic blasts in order to test their ability to function afterwards and civilians in the vicinity of the blasts who were exposed to fallout. The cases involving soldiers have uniformly held that the *Feres* doctrine,[183] which prevents soldiers from bringing suit for any injury incident to a military activity, precludes suit by the soldiers.[184] Similarly, the wives[185] of the soldiers and their children born with genetic defects are barred from bringing suit.[186] One court has suggested, however, that if the government first learned of the danger of exposure to fallout after the soldier was discharged and thereafter failed to warn him, there might be a postservice negligent act not barred by *Feres*.[187]

The *Feres* doctrine also barred governmental liability in suits brought by Vietnam War veterans alleging exposure to the herbicide Agent Orange. In that case, the soldiers sued the chemical's manufacturers on a theory of products liability, and the manufacturers filed third-party claims against the

---

[179] Dalehite v United States, 346 US 15, 17 (1953).

[180] 28 USC §2680.

[181] *Id* §2680(a) provides that the government is not liable for the

act or omission of an employee of the Government, exercising due care, in the execution of a statute or regulation, whether or not such statute or regulation be valid, or based upon the exercise or performance or the failure to exercise or perform a discretionary function . . . whether or not the discretion involved be abused.

[182] *Id* §2680(j) provides that the FTCA does not apply to "combatant activities . . . during time of war." Judicial decisions have substantially expanded this exception. *See, e.g.,* Feres v United States, 340 US 135 (1950); *In re* Agent Orange Prods Liab Litigation, 506 F Supp 757 (EDNY 1980).

[183] Feres v United States, 340 US 135 (1950).

[184] Laswell v Brown, 683 F2d 261 (8th Cir 1982); but see Johnson v United States, 711 F2d 1066 (9th Cir 1983).

[185] Jaffe v United States, 663 F2d 1226 (3d Cir 1981) (en banc).

[186] Lombard v United States, 690 F2d 215 (DC Cir 1982); Monaco v United States, 661 F2d 129 (9th Cir 1981).

[187] Broudy v United States, 661 F2d 125 (9th Cir 1981).

government. The district court held the government was wholly immune from liability.[118]

Where such suits are barred, the soldier and his family are limited to the veteran's benefits provided by Congress, or to such relief as Congress sees fit to provide by way of a private relief bill.[189]

When civilians sued for damage from atomic tests, the initial results were that such suits were barred by the *discretionary function* exception to the FTCA.[190] Similarly, the discretionary function exception has been invoked to bar suits arising out of asbestos exposure.[191] Two recent cases, however, suggest this is about to change. In *Allen v United States,*[192] nearly 1,000 persons brought suit for injuries caused by fallout from atomic testing. After a lengthy analysis of the discretionary function exception, the court denied the government's motion to dismiss. In light of the record before it, the court found there was not enough evidence to decide the issue.[193] And in *Bulloch v United States,*[194] a 1956 judgment in favor of the government in a nuclear fallout case was vacated when newly revealed evidence showed that the government had intentionally deceived the plaintiffs and the court as to the effects of fallout.

Where the government has not itself created the toxic hazard, it may still be possible to sue under the FTCA on a theory that the government has assumed a duty to protect the plaintiff from exposure to toxic pollution.[195] Although no cases dealing with toxic wastes have invoked this theory, one case held that when the government undertook to maintain a lighthouse, it assumed a duty

---

[188] *In re* Agent Orange Prods Liab Litigation, 506 F Supp 762 (EDNY 1980). An additional obstacle to the soldiers' direct suit against the government is the requirement of 28 USC §2401(b) that each individual soldier file a claim before bringing suit. Neither the government nor the court can dispense with this requirement, even if it is unduly burdensome in the context of a class action. *Id,* 506 F Supp 757 (EDNY 1980).

In Keene Corp v United States, 700 F2d 836 (2d Cir 1983), the dismissal of a third-party claim against the government for 14,000 asbestos-related claims was affirmed because adequate claims had not been presented to the government. *See also* Johns-Manville Sales Corp v United States, 690 F2d 721 (9th Cir 1982).

[189] Laswell v Brown, 683 F2d 261, 269-70 (8th Cir 1982).

[190] Bartholomae Corp v United States, 253 F2d 716 (9th Cir 1957). *See also* Harris v United States, 205 F2d 765 (10th Cir 1953) (government spraying of herbicide does not give rise to liability because decision to spray is a discretionary function); Note, *The Nevada Proving Ground: An Asylum for Sovereign Immunity?* 12 Sw U L Rev 627 (1980-81). Other cases denied recovery against the government because plaintiffs could not prove causation. Kuhne v United States, 267 F Supp 649 (ED Tenn 1967); Bulloch v United States, 145 F Supp 824 (D Utah 1956).

[191] Stewart v United States, 486 F Supp 178 (CD Ill 1980).

[192] 527 F Supp 476 (D Utah 1981).

[193] However, the court allowed the government to renew its motion at trial after further development of the evidence. 527 F Supp at 492.

[194] 95 FRD 123 (D Utah 1982).

[195] Comment, *Establishing Liability for the Damages from Hazardous Wastes: An Alternative Route for Love Canal Plaintiffs,* 31 Cath U L Rev 273 (1982).

to maintain it in a nonnegligent manner.[196] It has been suggested that by virtue of RCRA,[197] TSCA,[198] CERCLA,[199] and Public Health Service Act of 1944[200] the government may have assumed the same duty in regard to the disposal of toxic wastes.[201] Thus, if the government is negligent once it undertakes to clean up a toxic waste dump, it may be liable for its negligence under the FTCA.

---

[196] Indian Towing Co v United States, 350 US 61 (1955). *Compare* First Natl Bank v United States, 552 F2d 370 (10th Cir 1977) (no liability for approving label and registration for fungicide which subsequently entered food chain).

[197] Resource Conservation and Recovery Act, 42 USC §6901 *et seq.*

[198] Toxic Substances Control Act, 15 USC §2601 *et seq.*

[199] Comprehensive Environmental Response, Compensation and Liability Act, 42 USC §9601 *et seq.*

[200] 42 USC §241 *et seq.*

[201] Comment *supra* note 195, at 276.

13 Allegations
Susan T. Travis, Esq.*

§13.01 Introduction

Although, on the surface, this chapter appears to duplicate to some extent the contents of Chapters 11 and 12, it attempts to deal with the subject matter in a practical rather than a theoretical framework by considering a plaintiff's allegations and the problems which may arise in stating a claim for injuries or illnesses from exposure to toxic substances. Since many lawsuits end in dismissal due to the omission of an essential element, this chapter provides a guide to the necessary allegations for the plaintiff's attorney and also assists defendant's counsel by providing an understanding of the plaintiff's counsel's thought processes.

This chapter is divided into several major areas:

1. Identification of the plaintiff
2. Identification of the injury
3. Identification of the defendant

---

* Attorney, Office of the General Counsel, Xerox Corp., Rochester, New York.

4.   Examination of the elements to be pleaded for each legal theory utilized

5.   Review of the damages

In order to formulate successful allegations, the first requirement is to identify the plaintiff. Is it the person directly exposed to the toxic substance, or is it a spouse, child, parent, or heir? What was the person's role: a worker, a consumer, a tenant, a veteran, or a resident? Next, the type of injury must be identified and pleaded. In most toxic tort cases, a disease, a mental disorder, or a genetic disorder is the identifiable injury. Next to be identified is the substance that injured the plaintiff, and thereafter it must be determined, at least preliminary, who was responsible for the exposure: an employer, a landlord, a manufacturer, a merchant, or the government. If it is discovered that several entities caused damage to the plaintiff, it must be determined who introduced the substance into commerce and who exposed the victim to the toxic substance. These questions may be the most difficult to answer and the most crucial to the success of the claim. The last major areas of concern in formulating pleadings are what legal theories are to be pursued in the action—i.e., negligence, intentional tort, strict liability, fraud, or conspiracy—and what damages should be claimed. Each necessary element must be alleged to survive the predictable motion to dismiss brought by the defendant, because proper planning of allegations requires anticipation of probable defenses, as discussed in Chapter 14.

§13.02   Identification of the Plaintiff

The plaintiff in a toxic tort case conceivably could be any person, for in today's society, toxic substances exist in the workplace, in the neighborhood, and in the home. Most toxic substance cases originate with a product placed in commerce that causes harm and injury to a person or persons. With approximately 70,000 toxic chemicals already in existance and over 1,000 new chemicals formulated each year, the potential for harm is enormous. The scientific progress of the twentieth century has left a trail of industrial disease and affliction on workers, their families, consumers, and innocent bystanders. Industrial advances have caused a massive health problem that was neither contemplated nor expected.

One of the first items to investigate in forumulating a complaint is who, in addition to the present, obvious victim, may be a potential plaintiff. In *Hinkie v United States,*[1] a former serviceman's wife, his son, and estate of his deceased son sued the United States for negligent exposure of that serviceman to harmful radiation which allegedly caused chromosomal damage to him and the other military personnel who were exposed. The *Hinkie* plaintiffs alleged that the exposure caused the sons to suffer birth defects and the wife to suffer miscarriages and mental anguish. Mr. Hinkie was one of hundreds of Army

---

[1] 524 F Supp 277 (ED Pa 1981).

servicemen ordered to Camp Desert Rock, Nevada, to participate in nuclear testing programs. The court in *Hinkie* recognized the plaintiff's right to an independent claim as civilian members of the serviceman's family and held that:

> If the Hinkies were related to a civilian working for the government or for defendant REECO, [Inc.,] they would not be barred as members of that civilian family from stating a cause of action for injuries caused by chromosomal damage to the civilian against the U.S. under the FTCA [Federal Tort Claims Act]. Similarly, if a nuclear testing accident caused personal injuries to civilians, the civilians themselves would have a cause of action under the FTCA. In those cases, liability would be determined by state tort law. . . . We see no reason for a different result in this case.[2]

In traditional products liability suits, the victims are usually counted in the hundreds. By comparison, potential toxic tort victims are counted in the hundreds of thousands or even in the millions. Thousands of military personnel were exposed to radiation in the *Teapot Dome* series of nuclear tests in the 1950s. The military personnel and residents near nuclear testing sites continue to allege permanent health injuries as a result of the government's testing.[3] Military personnel were exposed to Agent Orange and dioxin in Vietnam in the 1960s and 1970s. These soldiers and their families allege health injuries resulting from exposures in the Vietnam swamps in over 300 suits filed as of 1982.[4] Millions of military personnel and their families seek relief from the government, manufacturers, and distributors of Agent Orange.

In the Love Canal situation, dozens of families have been displaced. The Love Canal plaintiffs experienced elevated levels of miscarriages, birth defects, cancers, and other diseases. The entire community is a potential plaintiff to recover for health injuries, loss of property usage, and emotional distress.[5] In the Three Mile Island nuclear accident, the entire metropolitan area around the nuclear power plant may have been adversely affected. These plaintiffs include property owners seeking compensation for the loss of use and enjoyment of their property.[6] Exposure to kepone (Hopewell, Virginia) and dioxin (Times Beach, Missouri), was another problem that affected *communities of persons,* as possible plaintiffs.

---

[2] *Id* 283, (citation omitted). The Federal Tort Claims Act is found at 28 USC §§ 2671-2680.

[3] *See, e.g.,* Hinkie v United States, 524 F Supp 277 (Ed Pa 1981), and see unsuccessful attempts to sue the government in Monaco v United States, 661 F2d 129 (9th Cir 1981), and Jaffee v United States, 663 F2d 1226 (3d Cir 1981).

[4] *In re* Agent Orange, 475 F Supp 128 (EDNY 1979) and 506 F Supp 762 (EDNY 1981).

[5] *See, e.g.,* Snyder v Hooker Chem, 104 Misc 2d 735, 78 AD92, 429 NYS2d 153 (Sup Ct Niagara 1980) (class action application involving numerous defendants and various causes of action).

[6] *In re* Three Mile Island, 87 FRD 433 (MD Pa 1980).

Asbestos may be the toxic substance named in more lawsuits than any other single substance; thousands of lawsuits have been filed by plant workers, shipyard workers, and insulators.[7] Most of these toxic tort plaintiffs come from the occupational setting: employees, former employees, or relatives of employees. Other toxic tort plaintiffs include: a doctor suing a drug manufacturer for failing to warn adequately against the effects of drug usage;[8] an infant's representative alleging child poisoning by methanol;[9] and an individaul claiming an addiction to paint thinner.[10]

Hazardous waste site litigants are a newer breed of plaintiff. The Environmental Protection Agency (EPA) has estimated that approximately 1,500 homesites in the nation may be exposed to health hazards of a serious nature with another 30,000 to 40,000 exposed to health hazards of a less urgent nature. Abandoned waste sites scattered throughout the United States expose large segments of the population to toxic substances. The deterioration of these waste sites results in leached chemicals contaminating air, water, and soil. The task of waste site litigants to make proper allegations is more difficult than an employee's task, since the causation trail is more difficult for a waste site plaintiff to discover. Chemical contacts are more remote and frequently involve exposure to multiple substances from multiple sources. These facts complicate the chain of proof of causation.

§13.03   Alternatives to Individual Tort Action

The courts and legislators have been forced to balance a plaintiff's right to his or her day in court against the practical problems posed by the filing of thousands of cases and insufficient judicial resources, personnel, and facilities. Suits arising from massive and often politically delicate toxic contamination can overwhelm the trial court system. The sheer volume of cases in recent years has created new issues and novel attempts to solve the overloading of court calendars.

Upon identification of the victim, it is probably soon discovered that his or her injuries are not unique. Almost every toxic tort plaintiff is one of many who has been exposed to a substance and damaged by that exposure. Counsel should evaluate the case to determine if a class action approach would serve the victim's interest or if the claim would be stronger if pleaded alone. The initial reaction is to favor a class action, since the cost of complicated litigation may be spread over many plaintiffs. The magnitude of legal and scientific issues requires massive efforts few individual litigants can afford. Class action

---

[7] *See, e.g.,* McDaniel v Johns-Manville, 487 F Supp 714 (ND Ill 1978); Johns-Manville Prod Corp v Contra Costa Superior Court, 27 Cal 3d 465, 612 P2d 948, 165 Cal Rptr 858 (1980); Neubauer v Owens-Corning Fiberglass, 686 F2d 570 (7th Cir 1982).

[8] Oksenholt v Lederle Laboratories, 51 Or App 419, 625 P2d 1357 (1982), *appeal filed,* 51 USLW 2406 (Jan 18, 1983).

[9] Mico Mobile Sales v Skyline Corp, 97 Idaho 408, 546 P2d 54 (1975).

[10] Wenk v Glidden Paint, 106 Wis 2d 18, 318 NW2d 26 (1982).

certification is a procedural device that may prove efficient and economical for toxic tort cases.

The shortfall of class action consolidation lies in certification problems, especially for tort actions. Products liability litigators generally reject class action procedures; health injuries are individual injuries. Traditionally, individual injuries resulting from a common occurence were not considered appropriate for class action certification; this subject is discussed in more detail in Chapters 12 and 15.

In addition, and as an alternative to the use of the class action, the Pennsylvania judiciary established a special nonjury calendar to hear the individual cases and expedite their resolution. The court in *Pittsburgh Corning v Bradly*[11] described the situation:

> In an attempt to deal with the problems created by the influx of asbestos litigation, the Court of Common Pleas of Philadelphia created a separate asbestos docket in 1976, and several judges—currently six—were assigned to hear asbestos cases. Thus far, however, fewer than twenty-five cases have been tried to verdict, all by jury, with each case lasting an average of two or three weeks. Attempts to achieve settlements have been hampered by the presence of fifteen to thirty defendant companies in each asbestos suit, and in recent years virtually no asbestos cases have been settled. In the face of this steadily increasing caseload, the Court of Common Pleas of Philadelphia promulgated Philadelphia General Court Regulation 82-5, effective July 12, 1982.[12]

The court, facing a challenge to the new system, defended its resolution and held

> that a program of initial non-jury trials for asbestos litigation in the Court of Common Please of Philadelphia does not unduly burden the parties' right to a trial by jury, but rather may serve to avoid intolerable delay in the vast majority of asbestos cases. Petitioner's challenge on this ground must be rejected. So, too, we must reject petitioner's contention that, by applying only to asbestos cases, the program of initial non-jury trials is violative of the Equal Protection Clause of the Fourteenth Amendment to the United States Constitution and Article III, section 32 of the Pennsylvania Constitution. There is a manifest need for an effective procedure to facilitate the prompt disposition of the growing backlog of asbestos cases in the Court of Common Please of Philadelphia, and the procedure chosen is clearly related to the paramount goal of achieving timely justice.[13]

---

[11] Slip op Doc No 81-1423 (Sup Ct Pa Dec 14, 1982).

[12] *Id* 2.

[13] *Id* 3.

The cost and volume of toxic victim cases have also forced Congress to consider several avenues of legislative relief, which are discussed in Chapters 6 and 10.

§13.04   The Injury or Illness

In order to identify the defendant properly, a clear diagnosis of the plaintiff's illness or injury is required, as well as identification of the cause of the injury (or illness), the period when the injury occurred, and the person who caused the exposure that resulted in the injury. Each step is taken as a link in the chain required to plead a prima facie case. The injury would be identified by the medical community on the basis of exhibited symptoms, testing, and diagnosis. The identity of the substance involved in the injury must then be discovered and named in the complaint.

The ability to identify a medically diagnosable injury or illness is an important element of a plaintiff's claim. As in all injury cases, the burden is on the plaintiff to prove that the injury or illness resulted from exposure to the suspected toxic substance. In a standard accident tort action, the injury, its cause, and its origin are easy to identify. In the toxic tort arena, the medically diagnosed injury is the first in a series of difficult facts to discover and allege. The latency period associated with many toxic substance diseases is a major hurdle in the causation chain. The latency period involved may mask the effects of the toxic substance for years and often may shield the offenders from liability. Little or no medical and scientific data may be available to explain the latency period or to identify the toxic substances.

If the disease is unique to a chemical exposure, the association should be relatively clear. Asbestosis is an example, since actual asbestos fibers may be found in the injured person. In *Flatt v Johns-Manville*,[14] the court held as matter of law that asbestosis was caused by asbestos exposure, yet the more frequent situation is the reliance on medical testimony and statistical evidence where association between substance and disease is unclear. Toxic tort litigation adds to the dilemma posed by the use of statistical evidence when a plaintiff has been exposed to multiple pollutants. Was the plaintiff's lung cancer the result of exposure to asbestos or a result of his or her smoking habits? Was the auto mechanic's lung damage due to exposure to brake fluid fumes, carbon dioxide, gasoline, or anitfreeze?

Cancer is the most difficult disease to trace since the medical community is so baffled by its cause. Therefore, cancer is a good example to illustrate a plaintiff's difficulties in identifying the substance causing the injury. The most common cancer is the environmental cancer caused by drugs (DES, birth control pills), chemicals (asbestos, kepone), dust, gas by-product fumes, radiation, and tobacco. There is significant medical data linking environmental cancers to these substances. However, a major causation problem arises when

---

[14] 488 F Supp 836 (SD Tex 1980).

the substance causing the injury comes from several sources. In *Borel v Fibreboard Products*,[15] an insulation worker brought an action against 11 manufacturers of asbestos insulation. After 33 years on the job and heavy exposure to asbestos, he contracted cancer and asbestosis. There was little doubt that his injury was the result of inhaling asbestos dust during his exposure to the defendants' products. Yet, it was impossible to determine *which* defendant caused the injury. The court held that the effect of the exposure was cumulative, and that sufficient circumstantial evidence was produced to conclude that each defendant contributed to the injury.

Even though a strong connection between exposure to the toxic substance and the injury may have been established, the allegation task is not complete. The quantum of exposure required (if known) should be alleged to avoid a quick dismissal for missing a causal link. For example, the plaintiff who alleges a birth defect based on the ingestion of a drug during pregnancy could assure the court through careful allegations that when the drug was ingested the injury resulted, and that the fetal development impaired was in fact in its critical stages when ingestion occurred.

Once allegations are formulated to describe the diagnosed injury and the substance causing that injury, the next step in formulating the complaint is to determine if there is adequate proof of *causation*. Can a link be established between the injury or illness and an identifiable defendant or chain of defendants? Demonstration of causation means reliance again on medical evidence, and again uncertainty can hamper a plaintiff's case. While the complaint need not allege absolute certainty, the plaintiff must *initially* establish a reasonable probability. Specific expert testimony by a physician should establish a strong likelihood of causation. The physician's testimony together with biomedical, epidemiological, and toxicological evidence may be enough to take the case to the fact-finder. In *Fitzgerald v AL Burbank Co*,[16] a showing of a "reasonable probability that the proper care would have prevented death"[17] was sufficient to take the case to a jury. An experienced physician with expertise in environmental medicine may be able to establish a medical probability sufficient to establish plaintiff's prima facie case.

Allegations concerning causation and accrual create the greatest problems and are perhaps the biggest factors separating standard products liability cases from toxic tort cases. Proof of a defect in a toxic tort situation is difficult because of the degree of scientific uncertainty and medical imprecision concerning the harms caused by toxic substances. Since a new scientific age of discovery concerning toxic substances is just beginning, the complexity of toxic substance cases, the sheer volume of cases, and the unique characteristics of these cases due to medical and scientific uncertainties have created a considerable dilemma for the courts and the legislatures.

---

[15] 493 F2d 1073 (5th Cir 1973), *cert denied,* 419 US 869 (1974).

[16] 451 F2d 670 (2d Cir 1981).

[17] *Id* 681.

§13.05   Limitations Periods

Once the plaintiff and his or her injury are identified, the next critical determination is *when* the injury or illness occured. A survey of state statutes regarding tort actions indicates that limitations periods generally run from one to six years. These periods generally begin to run at one of the following points in time:

1.   The existence of *all* elements of the cause of action
2.   The existence of *some* of the elements of the cause of action
3.   Upon discovery of the injury or illness

The jurisdictions available in which to bring the action and the specific language of the applicable statutes within those jurisdictions must be properly evaluated prior to initiating the action. Furthermore, even if the case is brought in federal court, state law will most likely be applied.

Toxic tort litigation is similar to other products liability suits in several ways:

1.   A business entity places a product into the stream of commerce
2.   That product creates an unacceptable risk and causes injury
3.   The accident and accrual are easy to determine
4.   Injury and diagnosis are contemporaneous with the trauma

The toxic tort situation differs, however, in two key aspects. A toxic substance generally exposes a greater number of people to harm and frequently involves a lag time between the manufacture and the injury. Twenty or thirty years may elapse from the initial exposure to symptom manifestation, followed by recognition of the disease and diagnosis.

The particular statute applicable to the fact situation and the theories proposed should first be identified. The key to any plaintiff's case is to plead a cause of action and bring that action within the applicable statute of limitations. This evaluation usually involves both statutory interpretation and conflicts of law resolution. Tort statutes of limitations are commonly applied in products liability cases and have been frequently applied in toxic substance litigation. Numerous concepts with respect to when a statute of limitation begins to run have confronted the courts. Does the statute begin to run when the defendant breaches a duty to the plaintiff, when a plaintiff is first exposed or injured, when the plaintiff is last injured, when the plaintiff is aware (or should be aware) of the exposure or injury, or when the plaintiff is aware of the full extent of the injury?

The foremost problem with statutes of limitations is their rigidity. Statutory time limits often fly in the face of the equities that are an essential part of the common law tort system. As stated in *Chase Security Corp v Donaldson:*[18] "they [statutes of limitations] are by definition arbitrary, and their operation does not

---

[18] 325 US 304 (1945).

discriminate between the just and the unjust claim, or the avoidable and un-avoidable delay . . . They represent a public policy about the privilege to litigate."[19] Therefore, courts have become increasingly involved, especially in the environmental litigation area, in interpreting statutes of limitations applicable to plaintiff's actions. In general, the statutes begin to run when the plaintiff's cause of action accrues, but in the absence of a statutory definition, it will be the court's determination as to when accrual takes place.[20] The inventiveness of the plaintiff's bar and the apparent willingness of the courts have, however, created new exceptions to this generalization. The defendant's bar argues, often successfully, that the date of accrual is the plaintiff's initial exposure or at the worst, the date the first tissue changes occur. A more detailed discussion of the use of statutes of limitations as defenses is contained in Chapters 6 and 14.

Generally there are three periods to consider:

1.   The date of first exposure to the toxic or hazardous substance
2.   The date when the injury process began, regardless of whether the plaintiff is aware of the injury
3.   The date when the plaintiff knew or reasonable should have known that the injuries had occurred

The strictest of these standards was applied in *Thornton v Roosevelt Hospital*,[21] in which the New York Court of Appeals adhered to the strict standard of injury occurring when the exposure occurs. As a direct result of the *Thornton* decision, courts in New York are dismissing numerous asbestos cases as time-barred where the plaintiffs discovered their injuries years after their initial exposure to asbestos products.[22] The problem with this approach is that it bars most plaintiffs' toxic tort claims before an illness is discovered or diagnosed. (The United States Supreme Court has noted the unreasonableness associated with considering the date of last exposure as the date of accrual in an latent disease situation in *Urie v Thompson*,[23] which recognizes the inequities of imposing a harsh interpretation of the statute of limitations in a toxic tort situation.)

A softer view of the accrual issue was taken by the Supreme Court of Alabama in a radiation exposure case. The court refused to adopt a discovery theory yet concluded that the plaintiff's cause of action did not being to accrue until the last exposure to the radiation.[24] The New York and Alabama cases, while significant, appear to be against the general weight of authority that has rejected the strict application of the exposure accrual rule.

---

[19] *Id* 314.

[20] *See* Raymond v Eli Lilly & Co, 371 A2d 170 (NH 1977).

[21] 47 NY2d 920, 419 NYS2d 487, 393 NE2d 481 (1979).

[22] *See, e.g.,* Rosenberg v Johns-Manville Prods Corp, NO 9913/78 (NY Sup Ct Nov 15, 1978).

[23] 337 US 163 (1949).

[24] *See* Garrett v Raytheon Co, 368 So 2d 516 (Ala 1979).

In recognition of an extended lag time, most courts have held that the plaintiff's statute of limitations should not begin to run until there is some knowledge of the existence of the injury and have adopted a *discovery rule*.[25] The court in *Karajala v Johns-Manville*,[26] for example, stated:

> There is rarely a magic moment when one exposed to asbestos can be said to have contracted asbestosis; the exposure is more in the nature of a continuing tort. It is when the disease manifests itself in a way which supplies some evidence of causal relationship to the manufactured product that the public interest in limiting the time for asserting a claim attaches and the statute of limitations will begin to run.[27]

The Supreme Court of Virginia recently adopted a more modern discovery rule under which the limitation period commences when the plaintiff learns or should have learned of the injury.[28] The court took the discovery rule an extra step by holding that the statute begins to run from the date a latent disease is determined to hurt the plaintiff. This date is identified by medical evidence. Obviously, such a determination is a factual one, and depending on the evidence, the date may coincide with the time of the exposure or the time of complete discovery or may fall somewhere between those two dates.

The trend toward use of the discovery of the injury rule has been followed in New York as recently as January 1983. In *Lindsey v AH Robins Co*,[29] the Appellate Division, Second Department, held that the cause of action accrued at the onset of the infection which produced the physical injury rather than at the time of the insertion of the intrauterine device (IUD) manufactured by defendant. The court carefully analyzed the *Thornton* decision and held

> that an IUD which facilitates infection is significantly different from dust, asbestos particles, a dangerous dye or authoriumdioxide substance which directly and immediately act upon the body causing injury and that the date of onset of injury rather than the date of insertion is the accrual date to be used for computing the limitation of the time for bringing suit in this kind of case.[30]

While the second department was mandated to follow the New York Court of Appeals decision in *Thornton*, it distinguished the *Lindsey* case on its facts. This

---

[25] *See, e.g.*, Karajala v Johns-Manville, 523 F2d 155 (8th Cir 1975); Harig v Johns-Manville, 284 Md 78, 394 A2d 299 (1978); Borel v Fibreboard Paper Prods Corp, 493 F2d 1073 (5th Cir 1973), *cert denied*, 419 US 869 (1974).

[26] 523 F2d 155 (8th Cir 1975).

[27] *Id* 160.

[28] *See, e.g.*, Fenton v. Danaceau, 220 Va 1, 255 SE2d 349 (1979). *See also* Locke v Johns-Manville, 221 Va 951, 275 SE2d 900 (1981).

[29] 459 NYS2d 158 (2d Dept 1983).

[30] *Id* 160.

decision is significant by analogy to the trend of other states in balancing the equities of the litigants.

A plaintiff may have to search for novel, expansive allegations in order to avoid a statutory bar to recovery. Examples include allegations concerning fraudulent concealment, issue preclusion, estoppel, the defendant's absence from the jurisdiction, and disability in the form of infancy, military service, or incapacity. Still other examples include allegations of continuing or secondary exposure, continuing duty to warn, continuing exposure, and continuing negligence.[31]

§13.06   The Defendant

Once the plaintiff, the injury, and the cause thereof have been determined, the next key questions are who introduced the substance into commerce and who exposed the injured party to the substance. Special issues regarding manufacturers and employers are discussed in **§13.07.** The defendant may be the government, the manufacturer, the distributor or supplier, the company doctor, the employer or individual corporate officers, or some combination thereof. The causation chain must be developed to identify the *potential* defendants and the possible defenses; obstacles to that chain must also be evaluated. Costs and complications of multiple defendants should also be considered. A pragmatic assessment of tactics, costs, and probability of success should be made before defendants are named. Allegations may be directed at one party and inadvertently foreclose relief from another. For example, the duty to warn users of product dangers may be placed upon a manufacturer, yet that duty to warn may not pass to the employer. In addition, an employer may defend a cause of action based on the workers' compensation exclusivity doctrine, discussed in Chapter 6. To preserve a cause of action against both the manufacturer and the employer, the complaint should allege a duty to warn by the manufacturer and, if applicable, an intentional or wanton violation by the employer.

Strict Liability and Duty to Warn

Manufacturers, dealers, and retailers are all subject to liability for selling any defective product which is considered to be unreasonably dangerous to the user or consumer. This liability is imposed under a theory of strict products liability.[32] Any entity in a chain between the manufacturer and the ultimate consumer may be a supplier and a named defendant. The supplier of a toxic substance, if he or she knows or should know of the dangerousness of the substance, must take reasonable care to inform users that the product may be

---

[31] *See, e.g.,* Karajala v Johns-Manville, 523 F2d 155 (8th Cir 1975); Holdridge v Heyer-Schulte Corp, 440 F Supp 1088 (NDNY 1977).

[32] *See, e.g.,* Pan-Alaska Fisheries v Marine Constr, 565 F2d 1129 (9th Cir 1977).

dangerous. In *Dougherty v Hooker Chemical*[33] the court stated that "if the danger involved in the ignorant use of a particular chattel is very great, it may be that the supplier does not exercise reasonable care in entrusting the communication of the necessary information even to a person whom he has good reason to believe to be careful."[34] This decision indicates that a supplier may be held liable when his or her warning about nonobvious dangers of his or her product does not reach the ultimate user.[35] A supplier with knowledge of a nonobvious danger or defect who does not warn of the danger or defects is therefore a potential defendant or third-party defendant. Taken one step further, a supplier who buys a product from a manufacturer and then markets it as his or her own may be held to the same standard of care as a manufacturer.[36] In asbestos litigation, for example, the supplier who bought asbestos products from any manufacturer and then labeled those products with his or her own label may be liable on the same basis as the manufacturer.

Concert of Action

Still another option to consider is an allegation of *concert of action* to join more defendants in the case. Plaintiffs are damaged by a toxic substance, yet they are often unable to identify the specific manufacturer involved. The concert of action and market share liability theories, discussed in Chapter 11, are an attempt to solve the problem of specific tortfeasor identification. The traditional concert of action theory required a plaintiff to prove that the defendants acted in concert or pursuant to some common scheme or design. This theory has been extended and modified in toxic tort litigation. The appropriateness of the concert of action and market share liability theories in toxic tort cases is an open issue being argued before the courts. In *Payton v Abbott Laboratories*,[37] for example, the court found no evidence to invoke the concert of action theory, and in *Ryan v Eli Lilly Co*,[38] the court rejected the plaintiff's attempt to use theories of conspiracy, alternative liability, concert of action, and substantial market share liability. Some case law, however, supports the proposition that where a plaintiff cannot, through no fault of his or her own, specifically identify one of several tortfeasors, the doctrine of alternative liabilities should shift the burden of proof to deny causation to the defendants.[39]

---

[33] 540 F2d 174 (3d Cir 1976).

[34] *Id* 179.

[35] *See also* Reyes v Wyeth Laboratories, 498 F2d 1264 (5th Cir), *cert denied,* 419 US 869 (1974).

[36] See Restatement (Second) of Torts §400.

[37] 83 FRD 382 (D Mass 1979); *see* Lyons v Premo Pharmaceutical Laboratories, 170 NJ Super 183, 406 A2d 185 (AD 1979).

[38] 514 F Supp 1004 (DSC 1981).

[39] *See, e.g.,* Bichler v Eli Lilly & Co, 79 AD2d 317, 436 NYS2d 625 (1st Dept 1981) and Sindell v Abbott Laboratories, 26 Cal 3d 588, 607 P2d 924, 163 Cal Rptr 132, *cert denied,* 449 US 912 (1980) (rejecting the concert of action theory and adopting the substantial market share liability theory).

Insurance Companies as Defendants

Plaintiffs have also taken an innovative approach in considering suits against insurance companies by alleging that the insurance company performed or failed to performed an act which caused harm to the plaintiff. The insurance company then becomes a potential defendant. In *Evans v Liberty Mutual Insurance Co*,[40] the plaintiff failed to plead an independent duty on the part of the insurer. An employee was injured while attempting to dismantle a box-cutting machine. Plaintiff alleged that the insurance company's negligence in failing to inspect the machine adequately and failing to warn the plaintiff of the dangerous nature resulted in the injury. In affirming a directed verdict for the insurance company, the court held that the plaintiff must show that the carrier's action *increased* the risk of harm to the plaintiff. In *Hill v United States Fidelity and Guaranty Co*,[41] the plaintiff successfully pleaded an independent cause of action against the insurer. The complaint alleged that the insurance company made periodic inspections and recommendations on safety issues. The defendant relied on these inspections and recommendations. The complaint alleged a duty on the part of the insurance company to exercise reasonable care, and the court found that this duty imposed potential liability on the insurer.

The Employer

The logical target of any employee's claim is the employer. In an attempt to circumvent the standard workers' compensation bar to joining an employer as a common law tort defendant, plaintiffs often attempt to invoke a dual capacity or dual status theory.[42] Another approach to circumvent the workers' compensation exclusion and identify additional defendants is utilization of the subsidiary/parent argument. This argument asks the court to examine the relationship between the wholly owned subsidiary and the parent company to determine whether the parent company is indeed the true employer.[43]

The most commonly utilized allegations to avoid the employer's workers' compensation defense are the allegations of intentional, wanton conduct[44] and

---

[40] 398 F2d 665 (3d Cir 1968).

[41] 428 F2d 112 (5th Cir), *cert denied*, 400 US 1008 (1970).

[42] In Kottis v United States Steel Corp, 543 F2d 22 (7th Cir), *cert denied*, 430 US 916 (1976) the court rejected the dual status argument; *but see* Smith v Metropolitan Sanitary Dist, 396 NE2d 524 (Ill 1979) where the court held that the suit could be maintained at common law since the cause of the injury was not a tool furnished by the defendant, but was equipment leased in a joint venture.

[43] *See, e.g.,* Strickland v Textron, 433 F Supp 326 (DSC 1977); *but see* Lathom v Technar, Inc, 390 F Supp 1031 (D Tenn 1974) where the court rejected the subsidiary/parent analysis to support a single employer theory. The court held that the plaintiff could sue the parent company in a common law action.

[44] *See, e.g.,* Copeland v Johns-Manville, 492 F Supp 498 (DNJ 1980) and Mylorie v GAF, 81 AD2d 994, 440 NYS2d 67 (1981) where an unsuccessful plaintiff failed to plead a proper cause of action. The court stated that "while an intentional tort can give rise to a cause of action outside the ambit of the Worker's Compensation Law, a

postservice tortious actions.[45] Obviously, dissatisfaction with the workers' compensation system for tort liability remedies has created innovative allegation approaches to join defendants in common law tort actions. Employers argue that deficiencies in the award system should be addressed by state legislatures and not by judicial loopholes. Workers' compensation as an exclusionary device and the exceptions to that doctrine are handled more completely in Chapter 6.

The Federal Government

When considering the federal government as a potential defendant in a toxic tort lawsuit, three critical defenses may require attention in the allegations. These three stumbling blocks involve sovereign immunity, intramilitary im-

---

complaint seeking to ventalize the statute's exclusivity must allege an intentional or deliberate act by the employer directed at causing harm to this particular employee." 81 AD2d at 995 (citations omitted). *But see* Sletzer v Isaacson, 147 NJ Super 308, 371 A2d 304 (1977) allowing the employee to maintain an action at law to recover for intentional wrongs committed by the employer, and Blankenship v Cincinnati Milicron Chems, 69 Ohio St 2d 608, 610 (1982), where the plaintiff alleged that the defendant had "knowledge of the noxious characteristics and failed to correct said conditions . . . and such failure . . . was intentional, malicious and in willful and wanton disregard of the health of . . . appellants." The court held that appellants should be given an opportunity to prove their allegations that their employer committed an intentional tort causing them injury. *See also* Wade v Johnson Controls, Inc, slip op CA No F248-81, P3 (2d Cir 1982), where the court, quoting from the complaint, ordered the case remanded for trial, since the plaintiffs stated a cause of action against their employer:

> 9. Nevertheless, in intentional disregard of such conditions and intentional disregard for the health and safety of its employees and with specific intent to cause injury to its (plaintiff-employees) . . . , defendant Globe Union: (a) knowingly caused and allowed its air exchange and purification systems to cease operation and thereby exposed its workers . . . to toxic levels of lead particulate for a period of time in excess of six months: (b) knowingly failed to head the levels of lead particulate, and failed to repair or replace its defective air exchange and purification systems and thereby intentionally subjected its employees . . . to levels of lead particulate which were known to be hazardous to health . . . ; (c) knowingly failed to warn its employees . . . of the altered levels of lead particulate then present in the air within the factory and of the substantial health risk thereby created; [and] (d) knowingly failed to advise its employees . . . that their physical and clinical symptoms were produced by acute lead poisoning at the point in time before lead concentrations . . . had reached a level which would produce permanent injury and disability.

Slip op at 3.
The court emphasized that the complaint catalogued the employer's acts of omission and commission that contributed to the injuries. The allegations sufficed to show the specific intent to injure the employees and thereby avoided the exclusionary provisions of the Workers' Compensation Act.

[45] *See, e.g.,* United States v Brown, 348 US 110 (1954); Thornwell v United States, 471 F Supp 344 (DDC 1979) (postdischarge negligence of government); *but see* Lombard v United States, 690 F2d 215 (DC Cir 1982) (declaring postservice failure to warn to be barred by Feres doctrine, Feres v United States, 340 US 135 (1950)).

munity, and the so-called Nuremberg defense proposed by government contractors. These defenses are discussed in Chapters 12 and 14, but a plaintiff who brings an action against a governmental entity should be aware of their existence and include special allegations to overcome or avoid them. First and perhaps foremost is the *sovereign immunity* hurdle. Pursuant to the Federal Tort Claim Act (FCTA)[46]

> a tort claim against the United States shall be forever barred unless it is presented in writing to the appropriate federal agency within two years after such claim accrues or unless action is begun within six months after the date of mailing by certified or registered mail, of notice of final denial of the claim by the agency to which it was presented.[47]

This requirement is jurisdictional in nature. Therefore, the plaintiff's complaint should contain allegations indicating full compliance with this statute. The plaintiff should allege the filing of the claim with the appropriate agency within two years of the accrual of the cause of action. Under the FTCA, the statute commences to run from the point at which the plaintiff's knowledge of his or her injury and its cause is sufficient to justify placing the burden of inquiry upon him or her as to its legal consequence. In *Sweet v United States,*[48] a serviceman's claim against the United States for injuries allegedly sustained as a result of postdischarge negligence was barred by the two-year statute of limitations. The court held that the cause of action accrued prior to 1978 when the serviceman, who had long believed that his nervous condition was linked to a drug he received in the military's experiment, was informed that he had ingested LSD. The issue of accrual is significant and should be alleged carefully to comply with the statutory requirements.

The filing requirements of the FTCA are individual requirements. Each potential plaintiff's facts concerning the accrual of the action and notice of its causation are unique. Therefore, individual filings are mandatory. In the *In re Agent Orange Product Liability Litigation,*[49] the court could not provide a simplified procedure for permitting the filing of a single notice of claim in satisfaction of the administrative requirement for claims against the government. Each plaintiff was required to file his or her notice of claim to comply with the requirements of the FTCA. In *Allen v United States,*[50] each individual plaintiff was required to file a notice of claim, and each individual was entitled to a determination concerning the application of the statute of limitations to his or her claim. The court held that information provided by the mass media concerning

---

[46] 28 USC §§2671-2680.

[47] *Id* §2671(b).

[48] 528 F Supp 1068 (DSD 1981), *affd,* 687 F2d 246 (8th Cir 1982); *see also* Schnurman v United States, 490 F Supp 429 (ED Va 1980), where plaintiff's cause of action was time barred.

[49] 506 F Supp 757 (EDNY 1981).

[50] 527 F Supp 476 (D Utah 1981).

the effects of radioactive fallout from the Nevada testing program was not substantive or persuasive enough to justify imputing sufficient knowledge to all plaintiffs.

The plaintiff's allegations must also consider the *intramilitary immunity* defense. This immunity, an extension of the sovereign immunity doctrine, applies to service personnel injured during the course of their military service. In *Feres v United States,*[51] the Supreme Court held that service personnel may not sue the United States government for injuries arising out of or incident to military service. The *Feres* doctrine has also barred third-party actions, most frequently claims of family members, where the claims derive from the service-related incident.[52] Therefore, any allegations of postservice injuries or malpractice must be alleged carefully to avoid the intramilitary immunity defense. In *Thornwell v United States,*[53] for example, a serviceman successfully alleged a separate cause of action for negligence relating to conduct after his discharge. The court held that *Feres* barred recovery for damages relating to the original administration of the drug LSD but allowed recovery for the subsequent post-service negligence.

The third potential defense requiring attention when framing the plaintiff's allegations is the so-called *Nuremburg or government contract* defense. Utilizing this defense, government contractors have attempted to hide behind the sovereign immunity protection of the United States government. The government contract defense, to the extent that it exists, provides the manufacturer with the same cloak of sovereign immunity that protects the government. The defense relies on the premise that the toxic or hazardous substances were manufactured at the express direction of the government, that the government dictated the terms of the agreement, and that the government dictated the specifications for the chemical composition as well as the manufacturing procedures.[54]

It is incumbent upon a plaintiff to frame his or her allegations carefully in order to avoid application of this Nuremburg defense. If this defense is adopted in the courts, it will absolve manufacturers of many of the duties normally

---

[51] Feres v United States, 340 US 135 (1950).

[52] Monaco v United States, 661 F2d 129 (9th Cir 1981) (alleged genetic injuries to the child resulting from in-service exposure to radiation by parent); Jaffee v United States, 663 F2d 1226 (3d Cir 1981) (wife's claim stemming from husband's service-related injuries); *In re* Agent Orange Prod Liab Litigation, 506 F Supp 762 (EDNY 1980) (claims of genetically-deformed children of servicemen exposed to herbicides in Vietnam).

[53] 471 F Supp 344 (DDC 1979) (a serviceman was given LSD and did not learn of that fact until 16 years later); *but see* Lombard v United States, 690 F2d 215 (DC Cir 1982) (plaintiff could not avoid the application of the Feres doctrine). *See also,* Johnson v United States, 711 F2d 1066 (9th Cir 1983).

[54] In a recently filed action, Johns-Manville sued the United States, alleging that the government knew during World War II that workers involved in wartime shipbuilding were being exposed to dangerous levels of asbestos dust, yet failed to correct the hazardous conditions or inform asbestos manufacturers. Johns-Manville Corp v United States, No. 465-836 (Ct Cl July 19, 1983).

imposed on the makers and sellers of products. Plaintiffs will be foreclosed from recovery against both the government as the user and the manufacturer as the producer and seller.

Summary

Clearly, the availability of potential defendants in a toxic tort litigation may be limited only by the imagination and creativity of the plaintiffs. Careful allegations and prior planning are essential to avoid multiple attacks for dismissal. The government has its intramilitary exclusion, the employer has the workers' compensation exclusion, and the manufacturer may have a causation or state of the art defense. Each potential defense may be challenged through careful allegations and subsequent proof.

§13.07 Contribution and Indemnity

Assuming that a plaintiff brings suit against a third-party manufacturer or supplier, and assuming further that the plaintiff is an employee who is successful, what, if any, is the employer's exposure to the third party in the event that the third party brings suit against the employer seeking contribution or indemnification? Several courts have considered and addressed this situation.

The majority of the courts that have considered the *contribution* argument have rejected it, reasoning that since the employer cannot be liable in tort for injury to its own employee, then it cannot be held jointly liable with a third party for injury to that same employee.[55] However, such immunity of the employer, together with the concomitant doctrine that an employer may have subrogation rights to an employee's claim against a supplier to the extent of the compensation paid, have been eroded in recent years.[56] Some states, notably New York and Illinois,[57] permit contribution by an employer whose negligence contributed to the damages.

The *indemnity* issue is more complex and clouded. Numerous theories of indemnity have been discussed by the courts, and in several jurisdictions the courts have upheld third-party indemnification. When there is an express contract of indemnification between an employer and a third party, the general

---

[55] Dessler v Baurie Mach Works, 501 F2d 617 (8th Cir 1974); Skinner v Reed-Prentice Div Package Mach Co, 70 Ill2d 1, 374 NE2d 437 (1977) (dissenting opinion). Denial of contribution is also based on the fact that an employer and a supplier do not have the same liability to an injured employee. This would appear to be another way of asserting the exclusivity of the remedy provided by the workers' compensation statutes.

[56] At common law, no contribution among joint tortfeasors was allowed. Merryweather v Nixon, 101 Eng Rep 1337 (1879). This doctrine has been substantially eroded both by statute and by judicial pronouncement in recent years; only nine states still apply the rule. The Uniform Contribution Among Tortfeasors Act, 29 USC §1032 has been a major influence in this trend.

[57] Dole v Dow Chem Corp, 130 NY2d 143, 282 NE2d 288 (1972); Skinner v Reed-Prentice Div, 70 Ill 2d 1, 374 NE2d 437 (1977), *cert denied*, 436 US 946 (1978); Rock v Reed-Prentice Div Pkg, Mach Co, 39 NY2d 34, 382 NYS2d 720, 346 NE2d 520 (1976).

rule is that the courts uphold the contractual relationship.[58]

Other states allow a reduction in damages recovered against a supplier by the amount of workers' compensation benefits paid.[59] The employer can assert a lien in most jurisdictions against any third-party judgment in order to assure reimbursement of the workers' compensation benefits paid in those states which permit subrogation; but the authorities are split on whether, in the event of a reduction in judgment, an employer may actually assert a lien.[60] Where there is no express contract, however, some courts have nevertheless upheld a claim for indemnity based on theories of a common law right to indemnity, an independent duty or obligation owed to a third party, or a special legal relationship (e.g., agency, contract, or statute) which sets up a primary-secondary liability situation.[61]

In any case, most states do not allow the impleading or joining of an employer as a third-party defendant in an action brought against a supplier by an employee of another.[62] However, a separate obligation of a supplier to an employer (or vice versa) will give rise to grounds for indemnification in about four-fifths of the states.[63] Indemnification is generally available without fault attributable to the indemnitor; but contribution, permitted in some jurisdictions, generally depends on apportionment of a loss caused by the negligence of both parties in the matter.[64]

However, the general rule remains that a third-party supplier cannot in most states recover contribution or indemnity against an employer in the absence of an express agreement or a special relationship from which an agreement can be implied; while an employer can recover by way of subrogation from a supplier the amounts paid out to an injured employee in workers' compensation benefits.[65]

---

[58] Pittsburgh-Des Moines Steel Co v American Sur Co, 365 F2d 412 (10th Cir 1966); Lambertson v Cincinnati Corp, 312 Minn 114, 257 NW2d 1679 (1977).

[59] Jacobsen v Dahlberg, 464 P2d 298 (Colo 1970); Powell v Interstate Waterway, Inc, 300 A2d 241 (1972); Pan-American Petroleum Corp v Maddix Well Serv, 568 P2d 522 (1978).

[60] Dawson v Contractors Transp Corp, 467 F2d 727 (DC Cir 1972); Santisteven v Dow Chem Corp, 362 F Supp 646 (D Nev 1973); McClesky v Nobel Corp, 2 Kan App2d 240, 577 P2d 830 (1978); Stark v Posh Constr Co, 192 Pa Super 409, 162 A2d 9 (1960); North Carolina Gen Stat § 97-10 2(i) (Michie 1972).

[61] For cases dealing with these concepts, see United States Fidelity & Guar Co v Kaiser Gypsum Co, 273 Or 162, 539 P2d 1065 (1975); Ryan Stevedoring Co v Pan Atlantic SS Corp, 350 US 124 (1956); Arcell v Ashland Chem Co, 152 NJ Super 471, 378 A2d 53 (1977).

[62] Beach v M&N Modern Hydraulic Press Co, 428 F Supp 956 (D Kan 1977).

[63] Sen Rep No 600, 97th Cong 2d Sess 45 S2631, 3 US Code Cong & Admin News 2018.

[64] Jacobsen v Dahlberg, __ Colo __, 464 P2d 298 (1970); Powell v Interstate Waterway, Inc, 300 A2d 241 (Del Sup Ct 1972); Pan-American Petroleum Corp v Maddix Well Serv, 568 P2d 522 (1978).

[65] Pittsburgh-Des Moines Steel Co v American Sur Co, 365 F2d 412 (10th Cir 1966); Lambertson v Cincinnati Corp, 312 Minn 114, 257 NW2d 1679 (1977).

The New York rule is to the contrary. Indeed, a recent case[66] held that in a suit for contribution against an employer by a supplier, the former's insurance carrier must defend the action, even though the policy excluded liability for indemnity. The court held that contribution was not a mere partial indemnity.

§13.08   Legal Theories and Remedies

Each theory of liability has independent elements, and every element must be alleged in the complaint. The relevant legal theories and manner of remedies are discussed in detail in the preceding chapters. Most toxic tort cases are founded on common law theories of negligence, breach of warranty, products liability, and strict liability. In choosing the causes of action to be pleaded, each theory has advantages and disadvantages. The plaintiff may be tempted to recite a litany of grievances committed by the named defendants. Caution is advised to not plead items that are inapplicable or unprovable.

The duty to warn means that a defendant will be liable for his or her failure to provide adequate warnings with his or her product. The allegation of failure to warn, or insufficient warning, may be part of any of the traditional common law tort theories—indeed, it may be the most common thread of the toxic tort allegations. It may also be the best argument for imposing liability on a defendant. The specificity, adequacy, and effectiveness of the warning are factual issues for the fact-finder. As observed in *Walsh v National Seeding Co,*[67] "almost every product liability case has a potential issue of failure to warn."[68] In addition, the duty to warn does not end with the sale of the product. Courts have held that a continuing duty to warn may exist until users are told of the danger and how to avoid the danger.[69]

The adequacy of a warning is a central issue in determining whether a product is unreasonably dangerous for strict liability purposes. It is a factual issue central to any toxic tort case.

Allegations utilizing a failure-to-warn theory should include assertions that the warning inadequately indicated the scope of the danger. The plaintiff should allege that the warning did not communicate the extent or seriousness of the harm that could result from misuse. The claim should allege that the physical aspects of the warning were inadequate to alert a reasonably prudent person to the danger, and that the means to convey the warning was inadequate—i.e., the manufacturer's warning was not conveyed to the user. The

---

[66] Insurance Co of N Am v Dayton Tool & Die Works, __ NY2d __ (Dec 8, 1982). A general release by a seller to one tortfeasor will bar action against others. *See* Clark v Zimmer Co, 290 F2d 849 (1st Cir 1961); Montgomery Ward v McKesson & Robbins, 285 NYS2d 461, 29 AD2d 629 (1969) (allowed a specific restoration of rights to control). *See* Grumman v IBM, 429 NYS2d 921, 77 AD2d 582 (1980).

[67] 411 F Supp 564 (D Mass 1976).

[68] *Id* 568.

[69] *See, e.g.,* Davis v Wyeth Laboratories, 399 F2d 121 (9th Cir 1968).

court in *Bristol Meyers Co v Gonzales*[70] identified the following factors as relevant:

1. The form of the warning must be reasonably expected to catch the attention of the reasonably prudent person in the circumstances for its use

2. The content of the warning must be of such a nature as to be comprehensible to the average physician and convey a fair indication of the nature and extent of the danger

3. The warning must have a degree of intensity that would cause a reasonable physician to exercise the caution commensurate with the potential danger

4. The warning should contain a clear cautionary statement setting forth the exact nature of the dangers involved

Recent litigation in failure-to-warn cases has focused on the state of the art issue—i.e., imputing knowledge of the dangerous characteristics of a product to the defendant. Defendants argue, in asbestos cases especially, that knowledge of the dangers of asbestos did not become known until the mid-1960s. Obviously, a factual dispute arises as to when the defendants knew or should have known of the hazards associated with the product. The plaintiffs, in these cases, rely on a line of cases that impute knowledge of the dangerous character of the product to the defendant.[71] Disposing of the state of the art defense would, in essence, impose absolute liability on manufacturers regardless of the available technology at the time of manufacture. The New Jersey Supreme Court in *Beshada v Johns-Manville Products Corp*[72] evaluated whether the defendants in a products liability case based on strict liability for failure to warn may raise a state of the art defense. In an order striking that defense the court held: "[W]e impose strict liability because it is unfair for the distributor of a defective product not to compensate its victims. As between those innocent victims and the distributors, it is the distributors—and the public which consumes their products—which should bear the unforeseen costs of the product."[73]

In New Jersey, at least, absolute liability in the area of failure to warn has been imposed. This extension of the traditional rule is encouraging for plaintiffs, discouraging for defendants, and unresolved in most jurisdictions.

Allegations of failure to warn are not limited to manufacturers. Servicemen allege a postdischarge failure on the part of the government to warn servicemen of the hazards involved in service radiation exposure, the use of Agent Orange, the use of dioxin, and other toxic exposures involved with the federal

---

[70] 548 SW2d 416, 418-20 (Tex Civ App 1976), *revd on other grounds,* 561 SW2d 801 (Tex 1978).

[71] *See, e.g.,* Freund v Cellofilm Properties, 87 NJ 229, 432 A2d 925 (1981).

[72] 90 NJ 191, 447 A2d 539 (1982).

[73] Beshada v Johns-Manville Prod Corp, 447 A2d 539, 559, 90 NJ 191, 217 (1982); *but see* Reed v Tiffin Motor Homes, 697 F2d 1192 (4th Cir 1982).

government.[74] Employees also allege failure to warn by employers and a continuing duty to warn of health hazards associated with employment exposures.[75]

§13.09 Damages

Last, but not least important, allegations concerning damages, which are discussed more extensively in Chapter 17, must be included in the complaint. In a toxic tort complaint, damages generally include both compensatory and punitive damages, and the allegations would be analogous to those in traditional tort actions. The major difference for the defendant's consideration is the size of the claim, not the nature of the claim. Toxic substance exposures result in harm to health, property, and resources. Damages could include recovery for property, interference with the use of real property, medical expenses, lost wages, pain, suffering, and mental anguish.[76] Compensatory damage awards against Johns-Manville, for example, have exceeded $9 million in just 65 cases.[77]

The granting of monetary relief in a tort action is generally the province of the fact-finder. Plaintiff must, however, allege and prove the damages claimed with some amount of certainty. Mere speculation is insufficient, but absolute certainty is unnecessary.[78] Some plaintiffs commence their actions without a diagnosable harm to state timely claims in jurisdictions utilizing exposure dates as accrual dates for purposes of the statute of limitations.[79] These toxic tort plaintiffs are *at risk,* and their damage claims are speculative. At-risk litigants rely on allegations of mental anguish and *cancerphobia* to recover before physical symptoms exhibit themselves. This approach requires that allegations of the defendant's intentional conduct be included in the complaint.[80] In *Ferrera v Gallachio,*[81] the New York Court of Appeals declared that "freedom

---

[74] *See In re* Agent Orange Prod Liab Litig, 475 F Supp 928 (EDNY 1979); Thornwell v United States, 471 F Supp 344 (D DC 1979).

[75] *See, e.g.,* McDaniel v Johns-Manville, 487 F Supp 714 (ND Ill 1978); Blankenship v Cincinnati Milicron, 69 Ohio St 2d 608 (1982); *but see* unsuccessful plaintiff attempts in Welden v Celotex, 695 F2d 67 (3d Cir 1982) and Phifer v Union Carbide, 492 F Supp 482 (ED Ark 1980).

[76] *See, e.g., In re* Three Mile Island, 87 FRD 433 (MD Pa 1980); Oulette v International Paper, 87 FRD 476 (D Vt 1980).

[77] See Manville Annual Report (1982).

[78] *See, e.g.,* Smith v Pittston, 203 Va 711, 127 SE 79 (1962) (apportioned damages among pollutants).

[79] See **§13.05.**

[80] *See, e.g.,* Harris v Jones, 281 Md 560, 380 A2d 611 (1977); Ferrara v Gallachio, 5 NY2d 16, 152 NE2d 249, 176 NYS2d 996 (1958); Battalia v State, 10 NY2d 237, 201 NYS2d 34 (1961).

[81] Ferrara v Gallachio, 5 NY2d 16, 176 NYS2d 996 (1958).

from mental anguish is a protected interest in this state."[82] Therefore, the plaintiff's action for an at-risk situation may stand when the allegations are carefully formulated to include the intentional conduct of the defendant.

Monetary relief may also include punitive damages.[83] Punitive damages are allegedly claimed to deter future misconduct by products liability defendants. Yet, the appropriateness of punitive damage awards in products liability cases is subject to challenge. In *Roginsky v Richardson-Merrell*,[84] the court analyzed the issues involved when confronted by claims arising from the manufacturer and distributor of a drug developed to lower blood cholesterol. The court's warning of the dangers associated with punitive damages in the wake of a multitude of claims arising from a single cause of action were ignored, however, when the volume of cases against *Richardson-Merrell* did not materialize. In *Moran v Johns-Manville*,[85] for example, the court upheld a punitive damage award against Manville. The warning in *Richardson-Merrell*, the bankruptcy litigation of Manville, and the multitude of claims arising out of a single cause of action— i.e., asbestos manufacturing—lend credence to the position that punitive damages may be inappropriate in the toxic tort area.

Damage allegations, like other allegations, must be carefully framed to avoid the successful attack from the defendants that they are speculative, unfounded claims. The intent of the common law tort action is to compensate an injured plaintiff for the injury. Punitive damages as a deterrent are ill advised in toxic substance situations, since the deterrent is frequently a rationale for less medical research and fewer industrial tests. Therefore, deterrent tends to counter the desired results of research and warning supported by punitive damage proponents.

---

[82] *Id* 21.

[83] *See, e.g., In re* "Dalkon Shield" IUD Products, 526 F Supp 887 (ND Cal 1981) reviewed slip op CA No 82-1812 (9th Cir 1982).

[84] 378 F2d 832 (2d Cir 1967).

[85] Moran v Johns-Manville, slip op CA No 82-K113 (6th Cir 1982).

14 Defenses*
R.B. Ballanfant, Esq.†

§14.01 Introduction

The topic of defenses in degenerative disease litigation reflects the lack of coherence with which the judicial system has addressed these issues. The failure to warn issue under strict liability is the principal approach to liability in these cases, but the issue of whether this was the appropriate judicial approach has never been carefully addressed by courts, which frequently corre-

  * Grateful acknowledgement is made to J. A. Berlanga, Shell Oil Company, Houston, Texas, for his able assistance in the preparation of this chapter.

  † Counsel and Head of Complex Tort Litigation Section, Shell Oil Company, Houston, Texas.

late strict liability with absolute liability despite articulated statements to the contrary. This chapter, because of limitations as to length, can not address the myriad specific issues that have or may arise in degenerative disease litigation, but it attempts to describe in broad terms that the courts recognize that legitimate public policy reasons dictate limitations of liability, that sometimes public policy demands that not every member of a product distribution system bear liability under every circumstance, and that even the consumer under certain circumstances must shoulder some or all of the burden of a loss.

§14.02 Statutes of Limitations and Statutes of Repose

A discussion of the two defense concepts of statutes of limitations and statutes of repose is difficult because of the vague definitions attached to both concepts and the nuances of the statutes of the individual states.[1] This discussion does not address legislative enactments limiting the time within which a party may bring its cause of action after accrual as defined under the laws of individual states. This section discusses statutes of repose, which may be broadly defined as legislative enactments banning causes of action prior to their accrual.

Statutes of repose have gained in popularity over the course of the last 20 years as the judicial system has rearranged the familiar landscape of tort liability. Two groups which previously sought legislative relief through enactment of statutes of repose were architects and doctors. Challenges to those statutes have resulted in a spectrum of results reflective of different statutory language and different state constitutions.[2] In recent years, states have begun to enact statutes of repose directed at products liability claims.[3]

Several state supreme courts have considered the constitutionality of their respective products liability statutes of repose. The North Carolina Supreme Court, as had been its practice with other statutes of repose, chose not to address the issue.[4] The Indiana Supreme Court, as it had done with other statutes of repose, upheld the constitutionality of the products liability statute of repose.[5] The Oregon Supreme Court, without really addressing the consti-

---

[1] McGovern, *The Variety, Policy and Constitutionality of Product Liability Statutes of Repose,* 30 Am UL Rev 579-641 (1981) Essentially, the prevailing rule is that statutes of limitations are statutes of repose which are based in part on the proposition that persons who *sleep* upon their rights may lose them. They are also designed to compel the exercise of a right of action within a reasonable time in order to suppress stale or fraudulent claims. Elkins v Derby, 12 Cal3d 410, 525 P2d 81, 115 Cal Rptr 641 (1980).

[2] McGovern, *supra* note 1, at 622.

[3] *Id* 638.

[4] Bolick v American Barmag Corp, 306 NC 364, 293 SE2d 416 (NC 1982); NC Gen Stat §1-50(6) (Michie 1969).

[5] Dague v Piper Aircraft Corp, 418 NE2d 207 (Ind 1981); Ind Code §33-1-1.5-5 (Burns §34-4-20A-5).

tutional issues, applied a statute of repose.[6] This treatment by the Oregon Supreme Court is consistent with the approach it had taken toward similar statutes of repose. Federal district courts in Tennessee and Illinois have upheld the products liability statutes of repose.[7]

The Florida Supreme Court, without extensive discussion, followed the authority flowing from the architects and contractors statute of repose cases and held the Florida statute of repose unconstitutional.[8] The Florida Supreme Court did not discuss whether the statute of repose might apply to strict products liability, which was not a cause of action recognized in Florida at the time its constitution was adopted, but the court held that the statute of repose would not apply to negligence causes of action which existed at common law. This silence by the court on strict liability may reflect that this issue was not before the court and may have to be raised in a future case.

The Alabama Supreme Court, in striking down that state's statute of repose, did not contrast that result with its upholding of such statutes pertaining to doctors.[9] Moreover, the Alabama Supreme Court premised its opinion on its own determination that no insurance crisis existed, therefore no relationship existed between the statute and the social ill addressed by the legislature. The underlying validity of this judicial approach is thrown in question by the actions of three asbestos manufacturers filing for bankruptcy within a year of its decision.[10] This contrast between the court's stated perception that no crisis existed and the actual filing of bankruptcy by three asbestos manufacturers emphasizes the very points commentators have articulated that courts are routinely relying on stated and unstated social policies without an adequate factual basis to support the result they reach.[11]

The constitutionality of statutes of repose in products liability law appears to be following the trend in each state set by that particular state's treatment of similar statutes of repose. A national statute of repose would cut this Gordian knot, since the United States Supreme Court has recognized the right of a legislature to modify common law.[12]

---

[6] Dortch v AH Robins Co, 650 P2d 1046 (Or 1982); Or Rev Stat §30.905 (1981).

[7] Gonzalez v Federal Press Corp, 94 FRD 206 (ND Ill 1982); Kline v JI Case Co, 520 F Supp 564 (ND Ill 1981); Buckner v GAF Corp, 495 F Supp 351 (ED Tenn 1979), *affd mem*, 695 F2d 1980 (6th Cir 1981).

[8] Diamond v ER Squibb & Sons, 397 So 2d 671 (Fla 1981); Fla Stat Ann §95.031(2)(West 1977).

[9] *Compare* Lankford v Sullivan, Long & Hagerty, 416 So 2d 996 (Ala 1982) *with* Thomas v Niemann, 397 So 2d 90 (Ala 1982) *and* Sellars v Edwards, 265 So 2d 438 (Ala 1972); Ala Code §6-5-502 (1981).

[10] Comment, *The Manville Bankruptcy: Mass Tort Claims in Chapter 11 Proceedings,* 96 Harv L Rev 1121 (1983); NY Times Oct 30, 1982 at 37, col 1.

[11] McGovern, *supra* note 1.

[12] Liberty Warehouse Co v Burley Tobacco Growers Co-op Mktg Assn, 276 US 71 (1928).

§14.03   Conduct of the Plaintiff as a Defense

The judicial treatment of the plaintiff's conduct in negligence cases is governed by statutory and common law principles as developed in each state. In strict liability actions, the judiciary has emphasized the role of the product and has ignored or treated cursorily the respective conduct of the parties. In an adversary judicial system which has historically attempted to balance the respective interests of all litigants and those of society at large, the shift away from this historic and well-justified balancing approach has bred confusion and chaos when courts have addressed issues pertaining to the conduct of plaintiffs as compared to those of multiple tortfeasors in strict liability cases.

This confusion was created by Comment n to the Restatement (Second) of Torts §402A, which states in part:

> Since the liability with which this Section deals is not based upon negligence of the seller, but is strict liability, the rule applied to strict liability cases . . . applies. Contributory negligence of the plaintiff is not a defense when such negligence consists merely in a failure to discover the defect in the product, or to guard against the possibility of its existence. On the other hand the form of contributory negligence which consists in voluntarily and unreasonably proceeding to encounter a known danger and commonly passes under the name of assumption of risk, is a defense under this Section as in other cases of strict liability. If the user or consumer discovers the defect and is aware of the danger, and nevertheless proceeds unreasonably to make use of the product and is injured by it, he is barred from recovery.

Concurrently with the judicial consideration of contributory negligence in strict liability as proposed in the Restatement, courts and state legislatures have been considering and adopting the concept of comparative fault. The confluence of these two developing legal theories has complicated the submission of strict liability cases to the jury as well as the entry of judgment based upon jury verdicts.

§14.04   —Contributory Negligence

Many states have either not determined how to treat the conduct of the plaintiff in a §402A[13] case or have not fully discussed the ramifications of treating the plaintiff's conduct as proposed in the Restatement (Second) of Torts. For several years, the Texas Supreme Court has substantially adopted the position of the Restatement (Second) of Torts §402A. The treatment of these issues by the Texas courts is illustrative of the legal issues in states following the Restatement's formulation.[14] The Texas court rejected misuse

---

[13] Restatement (Second) of Torts §402(A) (1975).

[14] General Motors Corp v Hopkins, 548 SW2d 344, 349-52 (Tex 1977). An extensive

as a defense where the product was dangerous for its foreseeable use; however, the court recognized the defense where unforeseeable misuse was a concurring proximate cause of the damaging event. In conjunction with this treatment of the plaintiff's conduct as a potential limitation to the plaintiff's recovery, the Texas Supreme Court refused to apply its statutory comparative fault statute to strict liability cases.

Several cases demonstrated the pernicious ramifications of this interpretation by the Texas Supreme Court of the Restatement (Second) of Torts.[15] While not allowing defenses of comparison of fault or indemnity or contribution, the courts recognized the inequities created by their analysis and invited legislative action to resolve this dilemma created by a *judicial* adoption of strict liability and by their unwillingness to resolve the legal conflict they had created. The Texas Supreme Court, in following Comment n of § 402A of the Restatement (Second) of Torts, adopted assumption of the risk as a defense to a strict liability action.[16] The defense of assumption of the risk would act as a complete bar to recovery.[17] This line of Texas cases is illustrative of the treatment of the plaintiff's conduct in a strict liability case as articulated in the Restatement (Second) of Torts. Finally, the Texas Supreme Court recognized the inequities of following the Restatement (Second) of Torts position under systems which provided for comparative fault and adopted a comparative fault system in products liability cases.[18]

§14.05 —Comparative Fault

Other states in considering allocation of loss in strict liability causes of action have addressed the question of the plaintiffs' conduct and have adopted a form of comparative fault. The California Supreme Court considered the theoretical arguments that strict liability focused on the product and not the conduct of the parties and that, therefore, negligence concepts such as contributory negligence and comparative fault should not apply. The California Supreme Court rejected these arguments against the application of comparative fault.[19] Moreover, the California court recognized that defenses such as assumption of risk were a complete bar to a plaintiff's recovery as treated under traditional negligence principles and under the Restatement (Second) of Torts §402A, but that under a comparative fault system such defenses would be merged into com-

---

discussion of the statutes of contributory negligence or comparative fault in each state is contained in Heft & Heft, Comparative Negligence Manual (1971).

[15] Bell Helicopter Corp v Bradshaw, 594 SW2d 519 (Tex Civ App 1979); General Motors Corp v Simmons, 558 SW2d 855 (Tex 1977).

[16] Henderson v Ford Motor Co, 519 SW2d 87, 90-91 (Tex 1975).

[17] Farley v M&M Cattle Co, 529 SW2d 751, 759 (Tex 1975).

[18] Duncan v Cessna Aircraft Co, 621 SW2d 702 (Tex 1983).

[19] Daly v General Motors Corp, 575 F2d 1162 (Cal 1978).

parative fault.[20] This same approach had already been adopted by Alaska[21] and Florida.[22] Some states have dealt with the issue of comparative fault by statute.[23] The statute has been interpreted as applying to actions in strict liability as well as negligence.[24] The evolution of comparative fault doctrines and strict liability in California and Texas reflects the contrast that has developed in judicial analyses of Comment n to §402A of the Restatement (Second) of Torts.

§14.06 State of the Art

The concept of *state of the art* survives as a defense in most jurisdictions. *State of the art* has been defined in the contexts of defective design and warning cases. For each type of case, the evidentiary nature of the concept changes to suit the nature of the inquiry. The major impact upon the state of the art defense has been provided by the incorporation of strict liability analysis under §402A of the Restatement (Second) of Torts. Section 402A provides as follows:

> **§402A. Special Liability of Seller of Product for Physical Harm to User or Consumer.**
>
> (1) One who sells any product in a defective condition unreasonably dangerous to the user or consumer or to his property is subject to liability for physical harm thereby caused to the ultimate user or consumer, or to his property, if
>> (a) the seller is engaged in the business of selling such a product
>> (b) it is expected to and does reach the user or consumer without substantial change in the conditions in which it is sold.
>
> (2) The rule stated in Subsection (1) applies although
>> (a) *the seller has exercised all possible care in the* preparation and sale of this product, and
>> (b) the user or consumer has not bought the product from or entered into any contractual relation with the seller.[25]

The imposition of liability regardless of the care used by the seller in preparation and sale of the product has limited the applicability of the defense. Nevertheless, this section and §14.07 serve to highlight the significant aspects of the state of the art defense that are still vital in negligence actions and in most states that have adopted the Restatement approach for strict liability.

Design cases generally use the term *state of the art* to refer simply to the

---

[20] *Id* 1167, 1169.

[21] Butaud v Suburban Marine & Sporting Goods, Inc, 555 P2d 42 (Alaska 1976).

[22] West v Caterpillar Tractor Co, 336 So 2d 80 (Fla 1976).

[23] Miss Code Ann §11-7-15 (West 1972).

[24] Edwards v Sears Roebuck & Co, 512 F2d 276 (5th Cir 1975).

[25] Restatement (Second) of Torts §402A (1975).

custom and practice of an industry.[26] The sources used by litigants to establish custom and practice of an industry often take the form of written publications by recognized industrial associations and regulations promulgated by governmental entities.[27] Where no published standards exist, the evidence to establish industry custom or practice consists of the manufacturing techniques of other manufacturers producing the same product. Some courts, however, draw a distinction in design cases between *custom* and *state of the art* as those terms are used in strict liability and negligence cases. The Texas Supreme Court considers *custom* and *state of the art* to be equivalent only when evidence of compliance with the custom is used to negate negligence.[28] When the action is one based on strict liability, *state of the art* means the "technological environment at the time of manufacture which includes scientific knowledge, economic feasibility, and practicalities of implementation."[29] Thus, state of the art bears directly on the feasibility of a safer design in strict liability cases.[30] In a strict liability failure-to-warn case, the concept of state of the art relates to evidence offered to determine whether the manufacturer knew or should have known of dangers associated with a particular product and whether such information was adequately conveyed to the consumer or user of the product.[31] The knowledge of the manufacturer is judged against the knowledge of the experts in the field.[32] Manufacturers are held to the knowledge and skill of an expert and must keep abreast of scientific knowledge, discoveries, and advances.[33] The concept of state of the art has evolved from a definition of mere industry custom and practice to one which embraces elements of scientific knowledge, economy, and practicality of design. The importance of the definition becomes apparent as the interplay between negligence and strict liability is examined.

§14.07   —State of the Art in Strict Liability Cases

A minority of jurisdictions do not permit the defendant to raise the defense of state of the art in a strict liability case. The New Jersey Supreme Court in *Beshada v Johns-Manville Product Corp,*[34] held that the state of the art defense was inapplicable in a failure-to-warn case where the defendant sought to assert that it could not be held responsible for injuries due to dangers that were not scientifically discoverable at the time the product was manufactured. The

---

[26] Smith v Minster Mach Co, 669 F2d 628, 633 (10th Cir 1982).

[27] Rexrode v American Laundry Press Co, 674 F2d 826 (10th Cir 1982).

[28] Boatland of Houston, Inc v Bailey, 609 SW2d 743, 748 (Tex 1980).

[29] *Id.*

[30] *Id.*

[31] Borel v Fibreboard Paper Prods Corp, 493 F2d 1076 (5th Cir 1973), *cert denied,* 419 US 869 (1974).

[32] *Id;* Moran v Johns-Manville, 691 F2d 811 (6th Cir 1982).

[33] *Id.*

[34] 447 A2d 539 (NJ 1982).

Beshada court said that the state of the art defense was a negligence concept and was therefore irrelevant in a strict liability action. To bolster its decision, the court looked to a variety of policy considerations which have traditionally provided the underpinnings for strict liability but clearly noted the conflict between negligence and strict liability when the reasonableness of the defendant's conduct is offered to explain the manufacturer's failure to provide adequate warnings. The court's decision requires the fact-finder to consider the dangerous characteristics of a product without reference to what excuse the defendant might proffer for being unaware of such characteristics.[35] While the *Beshada* decision is a recent judicial pronouncement on the incompatibility between strict liability and state of the art considerations, the New Jersey Supreme Court is not the first to disallow state of the art as a defense. Twelve years earlier, the Illinois Supreme Court in *Cunningham v MacNeal Memorial Hospital*[36] held a hospital strictly liable for injuries caused by serum hepatitis virus in whole blood used in a transfusion. While medical science did not have a means to detect serum hepatitis in whole blood, the court ruled that permitting a defense to strict liability based on the inability of a defendant to detect impurities in the product would signal a return to negligence theories. The court stated that the impurity of the product made it defective.[37] A later case in the same state[38] extended the concept to a defective design case and held that the state of the art—"what the rest of the industry had done to make their products safe"—was inapplicable to a strict liability case.[39]

The Supreme Court of New Jersey, however, has limited the applicability of *Beshada*. In *O'Brien v Muskin Corp*,[40] the court concluded that state of the art evidence is "relevant to risk-utility analysis and admissible in a strict liability case involving a defectively designed product."[41] In a design defect case, the plaintiff must establish the existence of a defect. The standard cited with approval by the court to establish a defect is "risk-utility analysis."[42] Such an analysis the court admits relies on negligence principles since the reasonableness of the manufacturer's conduct is considered. State of the art defined as "the level of technological expertise and scientific knowledge" is therefore a relevant consideration.[43] *O'Brien* suggests that *Beshada* was decided on the facts of that particular case and clearly permits state of the art evidence in design defect cases.[44] An appellate court in New Jersey has noted a further limitation on *Beshada* in a warnings case involving a pharmaceutical product. In *Feldman*

---

[35] *Id* 546.
[36] 266 NE2d 897 (Ill 1970).
[37] *Id* 904.
[38] Gelsumino v EW Bliss Co, 295 NE2d 110 (Ill App Ct 1973).
[39] *Id* 113.
[40] 94 NJ 169 (1982)
[41] *Id* 171.
[42] *Id* 171.
[43] *Id* 172.
[44] *Id* 173.

v Lederle Laboratories,[45] the court relied upon Comments j and k of §402A, Restatement (Second) of Torts[46] to rule that strict liability principles do not apply to "unavoidably unsafe" products such as drugs.[47] Strict liability cases involving drugs are not ordinary products liability cases. Therefore, negligence principles, including concepts like state of the art, govern the liability of drug manufacturers.

Other jurisdictions following a strict liability approach permit state of the art evidence in connection with the feasibility of a safer design.[48] *State of the art* refers to the technology existing in the industry at the time when the product is manufactured. As such, state of the art is transformed into custom with elements of feasibility and is a factor to be considered as relevant proof on the issue of feasibility of an alternative design.[49] A duty of care in design, while sounding like a negligence concept, rests on feasibility considerations of a safer design "consonant with the state of the art."[50] Manufacturers are not held liable for a specific design if the technology to produce that design is not available.[51] The minimum burden on the manufacturer is to use existing skill and knowledge to manufacture a product.[52] Even when a technology is available, factors related to economy and practicality of design must be examined in deciding whether a product has an unreasonably dangerous design defect.[53] Regardless of the state of the art (technology or custom), at some point a product can have a certain degree of dangerousness which is not to be tolerated.[54] Some courts, however, do not consider evidence of existing technology relevant in a strict liability case. An appellate court in Missouri so stated in *Cryts v Ford Motor Co*[55] but in doing so was careful to point out that the evidence did not support the defendant's contention that a particular design was the safest possible given the existing technology.[56] A case which has departed from the standard analysis in design cases is *Carter v Johns-Manville.*[57] In *Carter,* a federal court held that in a design defect case governed by Texas law, a state

[45] 11 Prod Safety & Liab Rep (BNA) 438 (May 10, 1983).

[46] Restatement (Second) of Torts §402A Comments j, k (1975).

[47] 11 Prod Safety & Liab Rep (BNA) 438 (May 10, 1983).

[48] Smith v Minster Mach Co, 669 F2d 628 (10th Cir 1982); Boatland of Houston, Inc v Bailey, 609 SW2d 743 (Tex 1980).

[49] Smith v Minster Mach Co, 669 F2d 628, 634 (10th Cir 1982); Haas v United Techs Corp, 450 A2d 1173 (Del 1982).

[50] Bean v Volkswagenwerk Aktiengesellschaft, 440 NE2d 426, 429 (Ill App Ct 1982); Vanskike v ACF Indus, 665 F2d 188, 195 (8th Cir 1981).

[51] Rexrode v American Landing Press Co, 674 F2d 826 (10th Cir 1982).

[52] Smith v Minster Mach Co, 669 F2d 628, 628 (10th Cir 1982).

[53] Starr v J Hacker Co, 688 F2d 78 (8th Cir 1982).

[54] Roach v Kononen, 525 P2d 125 (Or 1974); Phillips v Kimwood Mach Co, 525 P2d 1033 (Or 1974).

[55] 571 SW2d 683, 687 (Mo Ct App 1978).

[56] *Id.*

[57] 557 F Supp 1317 (ED Tex 1983).

of the art defense to a lack of warning depends on a showing of unfeasibility to include a warning on the product. The court also stated that unfeasibility of a warning was not a defense, but merely a consideration to weigh in the balance of danger and utility. Generally, in strict liability design cases, state of the art evidence is considered in the feasibility determination that underlies the balancing between the utility and gravity of injury from use of a product.[58] Feasibility of design inevitably leads to consideration of state of the art issues.[59]

In cases involving the adequacy of a warning, strict liability jurisdictions consider state of the art evidence in order to establish the adequacy of the warning that should be provided by the manufacturers.[60] The nature of a warning to be given about a particular product depends on the state of the knowledge of experts in a given professional field. Testimony relating to the state of the art in a failure-to-warn case involving a drug or a product like asbestos consists of expert testimony dealing with the existence of scientific literature which document the hazards associated with the product.[61] Actual knowledge or imputed knowledge of the scientific literature creates a duty to insure that information related to the hazards associated with a product is disseminated.[62] Such an inquiry focuses upon the reasonableness of the manufacturer's conduct, contrary to §402A of the Restatement (Second) of Torts.[63] Other cases impose a duty upon the seller to warn only of those dangers that are reasonably foreseeable.[64] Comment k to §402A of the Restatement bases the rationale for the distinction on the need to market "unavoidable unsafe products" because of the important benefits derived from the use of the product.[65] Nevertheless, the manufacturer or seller still has the duty to warn of the dangers adequately.[66]

The definition of *state of the art* varies when examined in the context of design and warnings cases. Initially, the term simply referred to industry custom and practice in the design and manufacture of products. However, with the advent of strict liability, that definition was expanded in order to consider the feasibility of using safer or different designs in light of economy, practicality, and

---

[58] Haas v United Techs Corp, 450 A2d 1173 (Del 1982).

[59] Boatland of Houston, Inc v Bailey, 609 SW2d 743, 743 (Tex 1980).

[60] *E.g.,* Greenman v Yuba Power Prods, Inc, 59 Cal 2d 57, 377 P2d 897, 27 Cal Rptr 697 (S Ct 1963); Phipps v General Motors Corp, 278 MD 337, 363 A2d 955 (1976); Zaleskie v Joyce, 333 A2d 110 (Vt 1975); Morningstar v Black & Decker Mfg Co, 253 SE2d 666 (W Va 1979); Restatement (Second) of Torts §402A (1975).

[61] Borel v Fibreboard Paper Prods Corp, 493 F2d 1073 (5th Cir 1973), *cert denied,* 419 US 869 (1974); Hardy v Johns-Manville, 681 F2d 334 (5th Cir 1982); Moran v Johns-Manville, 691 F2d 811 (6th Cir 1982).

[62] Muhlenberg v Upjohn Co, 320 NW2d 358 (Mich Ct App 1982).

[63] Beshada v Johns-Manville Prod Corp, 90 NJ 191, 447 A2d 539 (1982).

[64] Borel v Fibreboard Paper Prods Corp, 493 F2d 1073 (5th Cir 1973), *cert denied,* 419 US 869 (1974).

[65] Restatement (Second) of Torts §402A comment k (1975).

[66] Borel v Fibreboard Paper Prods Corp, 493 F2d 1073 (5th Cir 1973), *cert denied,* 419 US 869 (1974).

availability of technology. When the judicial inquiry concerns the issue of an adequate warning, *state of the art* refers to the knowledge of experts in a particular field. And, while the manufacturer may avoid liability for claims arising out of the use of his or her product because he or she gave an adequate warning, the manufacturer is held to the knowledge and skill of an expert in fashioning an appropriate warning. While some courts have curtailed this defense because of its appearance as a negligence concept,[67] others continue to judge the absence or sufficiency of a warning in view of the state of scientific knowledge available at the time product was sold or placed in stream of commerce.[68]

§14.08   Identification Defense

Historically, a plaintiff was required to identify the tortfeasor in order to prevail in a tort action. In toxic tort actions where the exposure to the alleged causative agent was either distant in time or was to a multiplicity of chemicals, the plaintiff has been confronted with a difficult burden. To circumvent this essential concept of well-settled tort law, several theories such as alternative liability, concert of action, market share liability, and enterprise liability have been proposed by commentators. These theories have not been widely embraced by courts.

The California Supreme Court considered these various theories and found under the pleadings that it would decline to apply alternative liability, concert of action, and enterprise liability as vitiating the need for plaintiff to identify a specific tortfeasor; however, the court refused to dismiss the plaintiff's case on a demurrer and permitted the plaintiff to attempt to craft a market share theory of liability to relieve her of the identification burden.[69] In another case, a Michigan court of appeals[70] permitted the plaintiff to attempt to pursue a concert of action theory. The Michigan court relied principally on the California case of *Summers v Tice*[71] as authority for its decision.[72] The New York Court of Appeals is the other principal authority supporting a theory of vicarious liability.[73] While the New York court upheld a judgment in favor of the plaintiff, it did so on the basis that the defendant did not properly object to the instructions to the jury or properly preserve its own requests for jury instructions. The New York Court of Appeals (the highest court in the state) expressly stated it was not deciding the case on the merits.[74]

---

[67] *E.g.*, Cryts v Ford Motor Co, 571 SW2d 683 (Mo Ct App 1978); Cantu v John Deere Co, 603 P2d 839 (Wash Ct App 1979).

[68] *E.g.*, Spurlin v General Motors Corp, 528 F2d 612 (5th Cir 1976).

[69] Sindell v Abbott Laboratories, 607 P2d 924 (Cal 1980).

[70] Abel v Eli Lilly & Co, 289 NW2d 20 (Mich Ct App 1980).

[71] 199 P2d 1 (Cal 1948).

[72] 289 NW2d at 23.

[73] Bichler v Eli Lilly & Co, 55 NY2d 571, 436 NE2d 182 (NY 1982).

[74] *Id* 189.

These three decisions have been heavily criticized,[75] and each of the three, due to reasons of procedure or adequacy of the pleadings are subject to question as to the extent to which they represent the ultimate disposition of the necessity of identification of the tortfeasor in their respective states. However, a defendant in each of these states or any state following this minority view should object to the submission of a products liability cause of action to the jury under any of these theories, because the *Sindell* court[76] premised its holding that a cause of action may have been stated on the *Summers v Tice* rationale that as between an innocent plaintiff and a *negligent* defendant, the latter should bear the cost of injury. Each of the courts which adopt a theory of vicarious liability strongly rely[77] upon the *Summers v Tice* rationale, which applies to a negligent defendant but would not be pertinent to a strict liability theory which is not premised on the conduct of a defendant.

The Massachusetts Supreme Court, while choosing not to write on this ultimate issue, emphasized that it was negligent conduct under *Summers v Tice* that furnished the justification for shifting the burden of proof on the identification issue to the defendant, and that in cases allowing the plaintiff to proceed, the plaintiff had sued all of the negligent tortfeasors who might have caused his injury.[78] If this line of analysis is followed, an inability to identify the specific tortfeasor in a case involving a generic product would not be an absolute bar to a negligence cause of action but would be a bar to a strict liability cause of action.

Subsequent to the application of the *Sindell* rationale by the California Supreme Court, several jurisdictions have considered and rejected these theories abrogating the necessity of identifying the tortfeasor. The federal district courts for Florida,[79] South Carolina,[80] and Georgia[81] have considered and rejected these novel theories of vicarious liability. Furthermore, intermediate appellate courts in New Jersey and Tennessee have rejected these theories after a summary judgment motion[82] and a motion to dismiss for failure to state a cause of action.[83] The Massachusetts Supreme Court considered this issue

---

[75] Cases which criticized *Sindell Abel,* and which state the traditional burden of proof laws should apply include: Gray v United States, 445 F Supp 337 (SD Tex 1978); Ryan v Eli Lilly & Co, 514 F Supp 1004 (DSC 1981).

[76] Sindell v Abbott Laboratories, 607 P2d at 924.

[77] Cases which rely on *Summers* and *Sindell* include: Hardy v Johns-Manville Sales Corp, 509 F Supp 1353 (ED Tex 1981); Bichler v Eli Lilly & Co, 79 AD2d 317, 436 NYS2d 625 (1981), *affd,* 55 NY2d 571, 436 NE2d 182, 450 NYS2d 766 (1982).

[78] Payton v Abbott Laboratories, 437 NE2d 171 (Mass 1982).

[79] Morton v Abbott Laboratories, 538 F Supp 593 (MD Fla 1982).

[80] Ryan v Eli Lilly & Co, 514 F Supp 1004 (DSC 1981).

[81] Starling v Seaboard Coast Line, 533 F Supp 193 (SD Ga 1982).

[82] Namm v Charles E Frosst & Co, 178 NJ Super 19, 427 A2d 1121 (App Div 1981).

[83] Davis v Yearwood, 612 SW2d 917 (Tenn Ct App 1980), *appeal denied,* 68 ABA 577 (Tenn 1981).

on certification from the United States district court in *Payton*.[84] The *Payton* court criticized the vicarious liability theory advanced by the plaintiffs and articulated public policy arguments why that particular theory should not be adopted. However, the court stated that it was not foreclosing some relaxation of the identification requirement under "appropriate circumstances" and expressly refused to give a definitive answer.[85]

In some instances, plaintiffs are not only unable to identify a specific manufacturer but also are unable to identify a specific chemical as the causative agent. In that context, *Davis v Yearwood*[86] is significant because not only was the plaintiff unable to identify the specific tortfeasor, but out of 15 different chemicals, the plaintiff was also unable to identify the specific chemical which was supposed to be the causative agent. In light of that particular failing in the plaintiff's case, the appellate court sustained a dismissal of the cause of action.[87]

§14.09 Bulk Seller Defense

The Restatement (Second) of Torts and Prosser have recognized the bulk sale defense. Dean Prosser states:

> [It] is ordinarily not reasonably to be expected that one who knows that a chattel is dangerous will pass it on to another without a warning. Where the buyer is notified of the danger, or discovers it for himself, and delivers the product without warning, it usually has been held that the responsibility is shifted to him, and that his negligence supersedes the liability of the seller.[88]

Comment n to § 388 of the Restatement (Second) of Torts acknowledges the viability of this defense:

> There is necessarily some chance that information given to the third person will not be communicated by him to those who are to use the chattel. This chance varies with the circumstances existing at the time the chattel is turned over to the third person, or permission is given to him to allow others to use it. These circumstances include the known or knowable character of the third person and may also include the purpose for which the chattel is given. *Modern life would be intolerable unless one were*

[84] Payton v Abbott Laboratories, 437 NE2d 171 (Mass 1982).
[85] *Id* 173.
[86] 612 SW2d 917 (Tenn Ct App 1980), *appeal denied,* 68 ABA 577 (Tenn 1981).
[87] *Id* 920.
[88] W. Prosser, Law of Torts §102 at 667-68 (4th ed 1971).

permitted to rely to a certain extent on others' doing what they normally do, particularly if it is their duty to do so.[89]

The applicability of the bulk seller defense has been accepted by courts which have considered it in those situations where the supplier sells its product in bulk and that product is repackaged for sale. The leading early case which discusses the bulk seller defense in a negligence context[90] involved a situation where a bulk supplier of liquid petroleum gas added an odor to its product; however, the odorant was destroyed by a chemical reaction in the storage tank. The court, relying upon the bulk delivery of the product, absolved the supplier of liability.[91] The court also acknowledged the pertinence of the sophisticated user defense, discussed in §§14.10-14.12, since the trial court found that trade publications described the chemical reaction which deodorized the gas and that the plaintiff knew or should have known of the possibility of this chemical reaction.[92] The same result has been reached by a court that faced the issue in a suit premised on strict liability as well as negligence.[93] The same principle has been applied in the chemical distribution chain, under both negligence and strict liability theories.[94]

The most significant decision reaching a contrary result occurred in Arizona.[95] However, the pertinence of that opinion is questionable, since the defendant was not only the bulk supplier of the xylene in question but also the supplier of the containers. The basis of the bulk seller defense is the inability of the manufacturer to control the packaging and, through the packaging, the extent of the warning communicated to the ultimate user. Indeed, in the situation where the packaging is also supplied by the bulk seller of the contents, the bulk sale defense should not be applicable.

The bulk seller defense must always be distinguished from the sophisticated user defense, which is discussed in §§14.10-14.12. Courts do not always appreciate that the bulk seller defense is founded upon the inability of the manufacturer to warn the intermediate entity's customers or employees of potential dangers because the sale is in bulk and is not based on the actual or implied knowledge of the user.[96]

The strength of the bulk seller defense also rests on the language in the Restatement that the supplier may rely on others performing a duty which is

---

[89] Restatement (Second) of Torts §388 comment n (1975).

[90] Parkinson v California Co, 255 F2d 265 (10th Cir 1958).

[91] *Id.*

[92] *Id* 269.

[93] Jones v Hittle Serv Inc, 219 Kan 627, 549 P2d 1383 (1976).

[94] Morris v Shell Oil Co, 467 SW2d 39 (Mo 1971); Shell Oil Co v Harrison, 425 So 2d 67 (1st Fla Dist Ct App 1983). *See also* Zunck v Gulf Oil Corp, 224 So 2d 386 (Fla Dist Ct App 1969).

[95] Shell Oil Co v Gutierrez, 119 Ariz 426, 581 P2d 271 (Ariz 1978).

[96] Restatement (Second) of Torts §388 comment n (1975).

placed on them.[97] In the context of an employer-manufacturer or of an intermediate manufacturer, those entities are charged with the knowledge of an expert and have an independent duty to disseminate warning information to the exposed individuals.[98]

§14.10 Sophisticated User Defense

The sophisticated user defense is premised upon §388 of the Restatement (Second) of Torts, which states:

> One who supplies directly or through a third person a chattel for another to use is subject to liability to those whom the supplier should expect to use the chattel with the consent of the other or to be endangered by its probable use, for physical harm caused by the use of the chattel in the manner for which and by a person for whose use it is supplied, if the supplier
>> (a) knows or had reason to know that the chattel is or is likely to be dangerous for the use for which it is supplied and
>> (b) has no reason to believe that those for whose use the chattel is supplied will realize its dangerous condition, and
>> (c) fails to exercise reasonable care to inform them of its dangerous condition or the fact which make it likely to be dangerous.[99]

Section 388 of the Restatement (Second) of Torts originated in the 1934 version of the Restatement of Torts, but did not receive a great deal of comment during the time period between the first and second Restatements of Torts. The principal case interpreting the original §388 was *Hopkins v EI Dupont de Nemours & Co.*[100] That court determined whether the plaintiff had to prove that the sophisticated employer (in that case the contractor who used dynamite) did not have adequate information about the increased hazard which, in the opinion of the plaintiff's expert, existed when the hole was loaded. Neither DuPont nor the employer had previously been aware of the actual circumstances which would lead to the type of injury that occurred in *Hopkins,* though both were aware of the potential of such an accident. The case is significant because the court held that DuPont, as manufacturer, had no duty to warn of a potential hazard when the knowledge or opportunity to gain

---

[97] Courts which have rejected the bulk seller defense: Davis v Wyeth Laboratories, Inc, 399 F2d 121 (9th Cir 1968); West v Broderick Rope Co, 197 NW2d 202 (Iowa 1972).

[98] Borel v Fibreboard Paper Prods Corp, 493 F2d 1076, 1089-90 (5th Cir 1973), *cert denied,* 419 US 869 (1974); Reed v Pennwalt, 591 P2d 478, 481-82 (Wash Ct App 1979); *accord In re* Related Asbestos Cases, 543 F Supp 1142 (ND Cal 1982).

[99] Restatement (Second) of Torts §388 (1975) (emphasis added); see also *id* comments k, l, and n.

[100] 212 F2d 623 (3d Cir 1954).

knowledge of the sophisticated employer was similar to that of the manufacturer.

The Restatement (Second) of Torts retained §388. The United States Court
of Appeals for the Tenth Circuit[101] applied §388 in holding that the supplier
did not have a legal duty to warn of the dangers in a product where the
technical knowledge of both the supplier and the sophisticated user is equal.
Both the *Marker* case as well as the predecessor case of *Hopkins* were negligence
cases that did not involve the application of the sophisticated user defense to
a products liability claim. Subsequently, the doctrine has been applied in both
strict liability and negligence contexts by several courts.[102] In some of these
cases, the courts have held that the sophisticated user should have known of
the dangers;[103] whereas in other cases, the courts have found that the sophisticated user actually knew of the hazards that existed with the use of the
product.[104] Courts upholding the sophisticated user defense have not distinguished between the situation where the sophisticated user actually knew
about the specific dangers of the compounds or equipment and the situation
where he or she should have known about such dangers.

The question remains whether a sophisticated user must be a manufacturer
with its own safety program, such as that found in *Reed v Pennwalt,*[105] or if the
concepts can be applied to an ultimate consumer who has knowledge greater
than that of the average consumer. An opinion which does not effectively
distinguish between the obligations of a sophisticated user and those of the
manufacturer is *Ziglar v EI DuPont de Nemours & Co.*[106] In that case, the court
found that a conduit retailer had no duty to warn a person, who in his or her
occupation regularly used the particular product, about general dangers that
should be known to such a regular user.[107] However, the court did not reach
the same conclusion regarding the manufacturer. Instead, the court held the
manufacturer to a greater duty than the retail conduit under the same facts.[108]
The *Ziglar* case may have turned upon the inadequate recommendations pertaining to first aid for overexposure to a product which could have been

---

[101] Marker v Universal Oil Prods Co, 250 F2d 603 (10th Cir 1957).

[102] Jacobson v Colorado Fuel & Iron Corp, 409 F2d 1263 (9th Cir 1969); Martinez
v Dixie Carriers Inc, 529 F2d 457 (5th Cir 1976); Bradco v Youngstown Sheet & Tube
Co, 532 F2d 501 (5th Cir 1976); Reed v Pennwalt Corp, 22 Wash App 718, 591 P2d
478 (Wash Ct App 1979); Rost v CF&I Steel Corp, 616 P2d 383 (Mont 1980); Marshall
v HK Ferguson Co, 623 F2d 882 (4th Cir 1980); Shanks v AFE Indus, 416 NE2d 833
(Ind 1981); Strong v EI DuPont de Nemours & Co, 667 F2d 682 (8th Cir 1981).

[103] Strong v Du Pont, 667 F2d 684; Bradco v Youngstown, 532 F2d 505; Shanks v
AFE Indus, 416 NE2d 838; Marshall v HK Ferguson Co, 623 F2d 891; Rost v CFI Steel,
616 P2d 685; Reed v Pennwalt, 591 P2d 490.

[104] Jacobson v Colorado Fuel & Iron Corp, 409 F2d 1268; Hopkins v Du Pont, 212
F2d at 630.

[105] Reed v Pennwalt Corp, 22 Wash App 718, 591 P2d 478 (Wash Ct App 1979).

[106] 53 NC App 147, 280 SE2d 510 (1981).

[107] *Id* 514.

[108] *Id* 514.

mistaken for potable water but was instead a lethal poison. The Fifth Circuit, in a case which did not mention the sophisticated user defense, exculpated a defendant when the intended user was a trained or knowledgeable professional.[109] Therefore, a manufacturer whose product is used by consumers whose knowledge of product dangers is greater than a layman may be able to utilize the sophisticated user defense.

§14.11 —Erroneous Application of the Theory

Cases where the sophisticated user defense has been accepted should be contrasted with the cases wherein the courts have not relieved the manufacturer of a duty to warn employees of a sophisticated user.[110] These cases should be discussed individually because in refusing to apply the sophisticated user defense, these appellate courts seem to misconstrue §388 of the Restatement (Second) of Torts. In *Barnes v Litton Industrial Products*,[111] the court specifically found that the dentist in that case, Dr. Hurowitz, was a sophisticated user.[112] However, Dr. Hurowitz testified that he did not know of the dangerous properties of the alcohol which caused the plaintiff's blindness;[113] therefore, the court held that the sophisticated user defense did not apply. It appears that the *Barnes* court has confused the requirements of §388 and has implied an actual knowledge standard not found in the Restatement (Second) of Torts. An actual knowledge standard would be that the sophisticated user must actually know of the dangerous properties of a product and not communicate them to the employees. However, §388 explicitly provides that the sophisticated user either must know or should know of the properties of the dangerous product. In the *Barnes* case, Litton specified on its package that the product was for professional dental use only; therefore a dentist such as Dr. Hurowitz would have the burden of ascertaining and conveying to the actual user or employee the potential dangers presented by the product.

The Third Circuit Court of Appeals in *Dougherty v Hooker Chemical Corp*[114] enumerated several reasons why that court felt Hooker's invocation of §388 was erroneous.[115] However, the *Dougherty* court appears to have confused various bulk seller cases with the sophisticated user defense and did not recognize the distinctions between the two defenses.[116] Specifically, the court found that Hooker could not properly assume that Boeing would communicate what-

---

[109] Helene Curtis Indus Inc v Pruitt, 385 F2d 841, 858-64 (5th Cir 1967).

[110] Barnes v Litton Indus, 555 F2d 1184 (4th Cir 1977); Dougherty v Hooker Chem Corp, 540 F2d 174 (3d Cir 1976); Russell v GAF Corp, 422 A2d 989 (DC 1980).

[111] 555 F2d 1184 (4th Cir 1977).

[112] *Id* 1186 n 5.

[113] *Id* 1187.

[114] 540 F2d 174 (3d Cir 1976).

[115] *Id* 180.

[116] *Id* 181. The bulk seller defense is discussed in **§14.09.**

ever knowledge it had acquired from Hooker to its employees.[117] The court then attempted to find that this was an issue to be decided by a jury. This decision appears to contradict the explicit provisions of §388, which state that a supplier is required to warn only when he or she has no reason to believe that those who are supplied the chattel will realize its dangerous condition and appears to reject the reasoning of cases like *Jacobson*,[118] *Martinez*,[119] and *Reed.* [120] These cases specifically held that an employer who has a safety program and sufficient technical expertise to apprise itself of the dangers of a product may be relied upon by a supplier to provide sufficient warnings and instructions for use to its employees.

The same erroneous reasoning was utilized by the District of Columbia Court of Appeals in *Russell v GAF Corp*,[121] which specifically found that *Hopkins*[122] and *Jacobson*[123] did not apply because the facts did not disclose that the employee's actual supervisor had received the warning.[124] Again, while admitting that the warnings had been conveyed to the plaintiff's employer (a sophisticated user),[125] the court did not find that they had actually reached the supervising personnel. Such a decision is in conflict with §388 of the Restatement (Second) of Torts as well as with the majority view in the case law. Moreover, the *Russell* case can be distinguished from other sophisticated user cases in that it did not involve a bulk sale of a fungible chemical, but rather individual sheets of corrugated asbestos cement upon which the court seemed to believe an individual warning could have been affixed; therefore, the court's decision may be explained on the basis of the confusion between the supplier's bulk sale obligations to the public at large and the supplier's obligations to a sophisticated user.

§14.12   —Support for the Theory

Public policy grounds support the sophisticated user defense. The defense appropriately places a burden upon modern employers who should have extensive health and safety departments to ascertain independently which products pose potential hazards, and then to implement engineering controls and to provide direct warnings to each employee. Several courts have noted the impossibility of the supplier to warn the individual employee directly, to supervise the individual employee, and to implement engineering controls in

---

[117] 540 F2d at 181 n 10.

[118] Jacobson v Colorado Fuel & Iron Corp, 409 F2d 1263 (9th Cir 1969).

[119] Martinez v Dixie Carriers, Inc, 529 F2d 457 (5th Cir 1976).

[120] Reed v Pennwalt Corp, 591 P2d 478 (Wash Ct App 1979).

[121] 422 A2d 989 (DC 1980).

[122] Hopkins v EI Du Pont de Nemours & Co, 212 F2d 623 (3d Cir 1954).

[123] Jacobson v Colorado Fuel & Iron Corp, 409 F2d 1263 (9th Cir 1969).

[124] 422 A2d at 991.

[125] *Id* 993.

another company's facility.[126] These obligations appropriately rest upon the industrial entity directly operating the facility which can evaluate the hazards that products and equipment pose to its employees.

This industrial hygiene burden is placed on employers by state and federal occupational health and safety laws.[127] A fundamental premise in many duty-to-warn cases is that a manufacturer is charged with the knowledge of an expert in the fields of science and medicine pertaining to his or her product; therefore, industrial manufacturers making products or using a product in their manufacturing process are charged with the knowledge of an expert under existing strict liability concepts, thereby relieving a supplier of a duty to warn consumers.[128] Furthermore, in the area of chemicals which have potential toxic properties, placing the burden upon the sophisticated user would encourage companies who are in possession of toxicological data and medical data to publish such data in independent professional journals. Such toxicological information could be discovered and utilized by sophisticated users to fulfill the user's duty under §388 of the Restatement (Second) of Torts[129] and appropriate occupational statutes. In addition, since many of these commercial relationships develop or conclude over long periods of time, the extreme burden should not be placed on the manufacturer to ascertain new developments continually and to distribute new information as to potential toxic hazards which are disclosed in the public literature, because these developments are equally available to any conscientious health and safety personnel employed by a sophisticated user.

Where courts have not relieved suppliers as a matter of law, they have recognized that the sophisticated user defense is a matter to be determined by a jury.[130] To the extent that courts have analyzed the sophisticated user defense, it has been in the context of a superseding cause.[131] If this issue is submitted to the jury, §388 of the Restatement (Second) of Torts places the burden of proof on the plaintiff even though the issue concerns a defense. As such, it is a defense upon which a favorable finding by the fact-finder would be a complete bar to recovery. Alternatively, the negligence of the employer could be submitted to the jury under comparative fault, and the defendant supplier would be responsible only for its percentage of fault.[132]

---

[126] E.g., Posey v Clark Equip Co, 237 F2d 560 (7th Cir 1969); Bemis Co, Inc v Rubush, CCH Prod Liab Rptr ¶9130 (Ind S Ct 1981); Powell v Bliss Co, 529 F Supp 48 (ED Pa 1981).

[127] E.g., 29 USC §656; Md Ann Code art 89, §28 *et seq* (Michie 1979); Cal Lab Code §§6300-7990 (West 1981).

[128] Dougherty v Hooker Chem Corp, 540 F2d 174 (3d Cir 1976).

[129] Restatement (Second) of Torts §388 (1975). This provision is quoted in **§14.10.**

[130] *Id* 179; Ionmar Compania Naviera, SA v Olin Corp, 666 F 2d 897, 904 (5th Cir 1982).

[131] Rost v CF&I Steel Corp, 616 P2d 383, 386 (Mont 1980).

[132] Varela v American Petrofina, 644 SW2d 903 (Tex Civ App 1983).

§14.13   Medical Causation

Frequently, plaintiffs allege causation of an injury or illness by an exposure to a chemical where there is little or questionable support for such an association in the published literature. A principle defense to such a case is that the plaintiff's proffered expert testimony is not based upon a principle generally accepted in the medical community and therefore should be excluded.

A medical conclusion can be given only if the medical principle on which it is based is generally accepted in the pertinent medical field. This legal principle was first articulated in *Frye v United States*.[133] That court, which first excluded expert testimony, held that:

> Just when a scientific principle crosses the line between the experimental and demonstrable stages is difficult to define. Somewhere in this twilight zone the evidential force of the principle must be recognized, and while courts will go a long way in admitting expert testimony deduced from a well recognized scientific principle or discovery, the thing from which the deduction is made must be sufficiently established to have gained general acceptance in the field to which it belongs.[134]

This evidence principle of long standing has been broadly adopted and is still followed.[135] This evidence principle in a personal injury context is clearly stated in *Puhl v Milwaukee Automobile Ins Co*.[136]

> There is no testimony that the generally recognized medical authorities on Mongolism have agreed what causes this deformity. When scientific or medical theories or explanations have not crossed the line and become an accepted *medical* fact, opinions based thereon are no stronger or convincing than the theories. While this Court has gone a long way in admitting expert testimony deduced from well-recognized scientific and medical principles or discoveries, nevertheless the facts from which the opinion is made must be sufficiently established to have gained general acceptance in the particular *medical field* in which they belong.[137]

This principle was recently applied in a California case involving a chronic

---

[133] 293 F 1014 (DC Cir 1923).

[134] *Id* 1014.

[135] United States v Tranowski, 659 F2d 750 (7th Cir 1981); United States v Kilgus, 571 F2d 508 (9th Cir 1978); United States v Brown, 557 F2d 541 (6th Cir 1977); State v Mena, 128 Ariz 226, 624 P2d 1274 (1981); People v Kelly, 549 P2d 1240, 129 Cal Rptr 144 (1976); Coppolino v State, 223 So 2d 68 (Fla Dist Ct App 1968); Kaminski v State, 63 So 2d 339 (Fla 1953); People v Tait, 99 Mich App 19, 24, 297 NE2d 853, 856-57 (Mich Ct App 1980); State v Mack, 292 NW2d 764 (Minn 1980); D'Arc v D'Arc, 157 NJ Super 553, 385 A2d 278 (1978); People v Williams, 6 NY2d 18, 24, 159 NE2d 549, 554 (NY 1959).

[136] 8 Wis 2d 343, 99 NW2d 163 (Wis 1960).

[137] *Id* 169 (emphasis added).

exposure resulting in a degenerative disease.[138] That trial court specifically excluded the plaintiff's proffered testimony on cancer causation because of the lack of a developed epidemiological data base and a developed scientific consensus that DBCP, the chemical at issue, actually caused cancer in a specific, identifiable human organ. Further recognition by courts of this crucial point of evidence would have potentially profound impact in the area of degenerative disease litigation.

§14.14   Compliance with Specifications of Third Parties

Manufacturers of products in design defect cases often plead the intervention of third parties in the design or product specification process as a defense in strict liability or negligence cases. The most dramatic application of such a defense is illustrated in the Agent Orange products liability litigation.[139] The Agent Orange case, however, involves product specifications supplied by the government in the context of an activity uniquely within the governmental section—i.e., acquisitions of weapons of war. Nevertheless, even in the nongovernmental context, the participation of the purchaser in the design of the product offers the manufacturer a defense.

The government contract defense[140] has received a great deal of scrutiny in the Agent Orange litigation. In *Agent Orange II,* Judge George Pratt laid down the essential elements to be addressed in the defense. In order to succeed on such a defense the defendant must prove:

> 1. That the government established the specifications for [the product];
> 2. That [the product] manufactured by the defendant met the government's specifications in all material respects; and 3. That the government knew as much as or more than the defendant about the hazards to people that accompanied use of [the product].[141]

The government contract defense applies under theories of negligence, strict products liability, and warranty, and it defeats liability which might otherwise exist.[142]

The policy underlying the defense was highlighted by Judge Pratt in *Agent Orange I,* where he noted that:

---

[138] Chemical Exposure Cases, Judicial Council Coordination Proceeding Number 985, Superior Court in and for the County and City of San Francisco (1982).

[139] *In re* "Agent Orange" Product Liability Litigation, 506 F Supp 762 (EDNY 1980)(Agent Orange I); *In re* "Agent Orange" Product Liability Litigation, 534 F Supp 1046 (EDNY 1982) (Agent Orange II).

[140] The Supreme Court first recognized the defense in Yearsly v Ross Constr Co, 309 US 18 (1940).

[141] *Agent Orange II,* 534 F Supp at 1055.

[142] *Id.*

First, tort liability principles properly seek to impose liability on the wrongdoer whose act or omission caused the injury, not on the otherwise innocent contractor whose only role in causing the injury was the proper performance of a plan supplied by the government. . . .

Second, the policy considerations that lend continuing vitality to governmental immunity argue for "extension" of that freedom from liability to some government contractors. As one court put it: "To impose liability on the contractor (for the government's planning failures) would render the Government immunity . . . meaningless, for if the contractor was held liable, contract prices to the Government would be increased to cover the contractor's risk of loss from possible harmful effects of complying with decisions of [governmental] officers authorized to make policy judgments."[143]

In *Koutsoubous v Boeing Vertol, Division of the Boeing Co,*[144] the trial court denied a motion for summary judgment by the defendant manufacturer of a helicopter for the Navy. James Koutsoubous was one of three Navy crewmen killed in a training flight during a simulated rescue mission. The plaintiff, Koutsoubous' father, brought an action against the manufacturer on a theory of strict liability. The court denied a motion for summary motion based on the defendants' failure to meet their burden of proof on what Judge Pratt called a "central question"[145]—whether the government knew as much as or more than the defendants about the hazards involved.

The defense was also addressed in *Brown v Caterpillar Tractor Co,*[146] On appeal, the Third Circuit reversed the granting of summary judgment for the defendant manufacturer. In doing so, the court admitted that it was predicting that the contractor defense would apply under Pennsylvania law in the context of negligence, strict liability, and warranty theories.[147] *Brown* involved an action by a reservist injured while riding a bulldozer manufactured by the defendant according to government specifications. The court reversed the judgment based on an inadequate record on the question of compliance with the contract specifications and knowledge of the dangers by the parties. The clear implication from the limited treatment received by the contractor defense after the

---

[143] *Agent Orange I,* 506 F Supp at 793-94 (citation omitted).

[144] 553 F Supp 340 (EDNY 1982).

[145] *Id* 345.

[146] 696 F2d 246 (3d Cir 1982). *Brown* cites numerous examples of cases providing different rationales for the defense, such as:

1. The need to reduce government costs for goods and services
2. The desire for a defense akin to vicarious sovereign immunity
3. Military necessity for a contractor supplier in time of war
4. The fact that liability of contractor would not deter government

Id 250 n 9.

[147] *Id* 249.

Agent Orange litigation is that the factual underpinnings of the defense must be clearly demonstrated before the defense can succeed.

An early case involving compliance with specifications provided by a third party is *Ryan v Feeney & Sheehan Building Co.*[148] Although *Ryan* involved specifications provided by the government, the principles laid down by the *Ryan* court are applied in cases between private litigants.[149] The facts of the case involved the construction of a canopy by the defendant for a building which later collapsed and killed a person. The defendant builder constructed a building according to the specifications provided by the government and its authorized architect. In affirming the judgment for the defendant, the court considered the builder's decision to follow the plans and specifications in light of the builder's obligation to use average skill and ordinary prudence to notice obvious defects in design.[150] The *Ryan* rationale was articulated in *Spangler v Kranco*,[151] involving contract specifications provided by a nongovernmental entity.

> We find additional support for the action of the district judge in the principle that the products liability rule holding a manufacturer liable does not apply where the product has been manufactured in accordance with the plans and specifications of the purchaser except when such plans are so obviously dangerous that they should not reasonably be followed.[152]

A number of cases have involved the liability of a manufacturer of component parts for injuries to a *purchaser*. In *Orien Insurance Corp v United States Technologies Corp*,[153] the trial court granted a component manufacturer's motion for summary judgment based on its reliance on a third party's specification. The court referred to the expertise of the assembler of the product as a reason for relieving the component manufacturer of liability. In considering the strict liability count, the court said that

> no public policy can be served by imposing a civil penalty on a manufacturer of specialized parts for a highly technical machine according to the specifications supplied by one who is expert at assembling these technical machines, who does so without questioning the plans or warning the

---

[148] 145 NE 321, 239 NY 43 (1924).

[149] East Hampton Dewitt Corp v State Farm Mutual Ins Co, 490 F2d 1244 (2d Cir 1973); Hunter v Quality Homes, 68 A2d 623 (Del 1949); Hunt v Blasius, 55 Ill App 14, 1211 Dec 813, 370 NE2d 621 (1977); Arnold v Edelman, 375 SE2d 172 (S Ct Mo 1964); Bush v Albert D Wardell Contractors, 528 P2d 217 (Mont 1974).

[150] 145 NE at 323.

[151] 481 F2d 373 (4th Cir 1973) (failure to equip a crane with warning devices to be activated when crane was operated justified when crane built in accordance with purchaser's specifications and plans did not demonstrate obvious danger).

[152] *Id* 375 (citations omitted).

[153] 502 F Supp 173 (ED Pa 1980).

ultimate user. The effect of such a decision on component parts manufacturers would be enormous. They would be forced to retain private experts to review an assembler's plans and to evaluate the soundness of the
proposed use of the manufacturer's parts. The added cost of such a
procedure both financially and in terms of stifled innovation outweighs
the public benefit of giving plaintiffs an additional pocket to look to for
recovery. I believe the better view is to leave the liability for design
defects where it belongs and where it now is with the originator and
implementer of the design the assembler of the finished product.[154]

Another decision from the Eastern District in Pennsylvania, *Lesnefsky v Fisher
& Porter Co*,[155] granted a motion for summary judgment for a manufacturer
who built a control panel for a brewery mash cooker that injured a brewery
employee.

The law does not impose a duty on the manufacturer of parts produced
in compliance with specifications provided by an experienced purchaser-
user to undertake an independent safety investigation concerning their
intended use. It was not unreasonable as a matter of law for Fischer &
Porter to rely on the specifications provided by the experienced brewery.[156]

A case of recent vintage which appears to create a higher duty for component
parts manufacturers is *Michalco v Cooke Color & Chemical Corp*.[157] The Supreme
Court of New Jersey held that an independent contractor who undertakes to
rebuild part of a machine according to specifications can be strictly liable to
the foreseeable users of the machine for breach of its duty to make the machine
safe.[158] Although *Michalko* speaks in terms of a duty to a foreseeable user, the
end result of the decision is akin to the result in *Ryan*. The builder or manufacturer must make an independent judgment concerning the design of a product
built to someone else's specifications. While *Ryan* does speak in terms of
detecting obvious defects using average skill and ordinary prudence,[159] *Mi-*

---

[154] *Id* 178.

[155] 527 F Supp 951 (ED Pa 1981).

[156] *Id* 956 (citations omitted). An interesting variation on the matter of the specification of component parts by a purchaser is seen in Weggen v Elwell Parker Elec Co, 527
F Supp 951 (ED Pa 1981). In *Weggen*, the court granted a motion for summary judgment
and held that a purchaser's intrusion into the design process for the manufacture of a
truck may give rise to an independent duty requiring the purchaser to use due care in
design and specification of component parts under a theory of indemnity. While the
case does not talk about a product specification defense as to the plaintiff, the defendant
may be in a position to shift his or her loss to the employer-purchaser via indemnity.

[157] 91 NJ 386 (1982).

[158] *Id.*

[159] 145 NE 326.

chalko gives no such guidance in establishing the standard of care to be followed.

The defense of compliance with governmental or nongovernmental contract specifications for the manufacture of a product has a basic theme. That theme centers around legal and policy considerations permitting those parties who do not provide the design or specifications for a product to be relieved from liability. Government contractors avoid liability for the reason that the sovereign controls their performance by contract. In a similar vein, private manufacturers can rely on the purchaser's greater expertise to provide a safe design unless a design defect is obvious to the average manufacturer. The end result is to place the ultimate responsibility on the party with the greatest control over the nature of the product to be manufactured.

§14.15   Discontinued Product Defense

At the heart of strict liability lies the intellectual justification that the manufacturer is better able to afford the cost of an injury than an injured party.[160] Dean Prosser, in his landmark commentary on products liability, discounted the risk-spreading argument as a justification for imposition of strict liability because he felt it did not answer the foundational liability question as to what group should bear a loss.[161] Dean Prosser cited these alternative justifications:

1. The public interest in maximizing the protection of human life, health, and safety

2. The implied warranty of safety given by a supplier who should not avoid responsibility because the supplier had no contract with the consumer

3. The judicial economy of short-circuiting the necessity of establishing the warranties in a chain of distribution

In a degenerative disease case where the product is no longer sold or no longer sold in the same form or for the same purpose, the fundamental question arises as to whether any of these justifications exist for the imposition of strict liability. Courts should recognize a defense to a strict liability cause of action under these circumstances. None of the stated justifications for applying strict liability apply to this type of litigation. Since the traditional sales limitations to negligence actions are no longer recognized, the second and third justifications cited by Dean Prosser have no applicability. As to discontinued products, Dean Prosser's interest in the maximum possible protection of the consuming public has already been achieved if the product is no longer sold, because any additional danger no longer exists to the public. Furthermore, the

---

[160] Greenman v Yuba Power Prods Inc, 377 P2d 897, 901, 27 Cal Rptr 697, 701 (1962); Escola v Coca Cola Bottling Co, 150 P2d 436, 441 (Cal 1944).

[161] Prosser, *The Assault upon the Citadel (Strict Liability to the Consumer)*, 69 Yale L Rev 1099, 1121 (1960).

public interest justification relied upon by Dean Prosser would be better served if removal of dangerous products from the market were legally encouraged by the judicial process by permitting a potential defendant a defense if the defendant undertakes action consistent with the public interest.

Finally, the most frequently cited justification by courts for strict liability—i.e., cost spreading—does not apply if the product is no longer being sold, since there can be no cost spreading by the manufacturer. Thoughtful jurists are beginning to recognize the distinctions that exist between traumatic injury cases and degenerative disease cases.[162] As jurists address the truly complex issues which exist in the area of degenerative disease, many of the fundamental principles such as the pertinency of strict liability to these causes of action will have to be challenged.

---

[162] Wilson v Johns-Manville Sales Corp, 684 F2d Ill (DC Cir 1982); Starling v Seaboard Coast Line RR, 533 F Supp 813, 190 (SD Ga 1982).

15

Pleadings and Discovery*

Willis J. Goldsmith, Esq.†

* Grateful acknowledgment is made of the able assistance of David D. Kadue, Esq., Seyfarth, Shaw, Fairweather & Geraldson, Washington, D.C., in the preparation of this chapter.

† Partner, Jones, Day, Reavis & Pogue, Washington, D.C.

§15.01   Introduction

This chapter discussed the principles of pleading and discovery that are most commonly pertinent to toxic substance litigation. The sections below discuss the complaint, responsive pleadings, third-party practice, class actions, and matters relating to discovery.

§15.02   The Complaint

A well-pleaded complaint states the factual basis for the court's jurisdiction, the identity of the parties, one or more theories of recovery, and a prayer for relief. In federal practice, and in most states, the plaintiff need only prepare a short and plain statement of the plaintiff's claim and generally is given liberal leave to amend the complaint. Nevertheless, to survive a motion to dismiss, these matters eventually must be stated with enough specificity to inform the defendant what the plaintiff intends to show at trial. Specific allegations should be stated in separate paragraphs and apart from legal conclusions to minimize the defendant's ability to make general denials.

§15.03   —Jurisdiction

To have power to adjudicate a dispute, a court must have jurisdiction over both the subject matter of the suit and the parties. Accordingly, the complaint must state the basis of the court's jurisdiction. Insofar as subject matter jurisdiction is concerned, toxic substance litigation, based upon state law theories such as negligence, strict liability, and breach of warranty, may be commenced in the appropriate state court of general jurisdiction. Subject matter jurisdiction over such an action also exists in any federal court where there is diversity of citizenship between the parties and an amount in controversy in excess of $10,000.[1] Diversity of citizenship requires complete diversity, meaning that none of the parties on one side of the lawsuit may be a citizen of the same state as a party on the other side of the lawsuit.[2] A corporation is a citizen of its state

---

[1] 28 USC §1332.

[2] Strawbridge v Curtiss, 3 Cranch 267 (1806). See generally 13 C Wright, A Miller & E Cooper, Federal Practice and Procedure: Jurisdiction §3605 (1976). In a class action, the rule of complete diversity applies only to named parties.

of incorporation and of the state in which it has its principal place of business.[3]
Thus, an allegation of diversity jurisdiction in federal district court could read:

> Plaintiff is a citizen of Virginia. Defendant is a corporation with its place
> of incorporation and its principal place of business in Maryland. The
> jurisdiction of this Court is based upon diversity of citizenship and the
> amount in controversy, which exceeds ten thousand dollars ($10,000),
> exclusive of interests and costs.

It should be noted that in a multiplaintiff lawsuit, each plaintiff's claim should
exceed $10,000 for purposes of diversity.[4]

In addition to subject matter jurisdiction, the court must have jurisdiction
over the parties (in personam jurisdiction). Regardless of whether the suit is
brought in state or federal court, jurisdiction over the parties is a matter of
state statute and constitutional due process.[5] Many states have statutes which
permit service of process on a foreign corporation alleged to have committed
a tortious act or omission in the forum state.[6] Virginia's juridictional statute,
for example, authorizes the exercise of personal jurisdiction over a defendant
as to a cause of action arising from any one of several enumerated activities
of that person in Virginia, including:

1. Transacting any business
2. Contracting to supply services or things
3. Causing tortious injury by an act or omission
4. Causing tortious injury in Virginia by an act or omission outside Virginia
   if the defendant regularly does or solicits business, or engages in any
   other persistent course of conduct, or derives substantial revenue from
   goods used or consumed or services rendered, in Virginia
5. Causing injury in Virginia through breach of warranty made in the sale
   of goods outside Virginia when the defendant might reasonably have
   expected the plaintiff to use, consume, or be affected by the goods in
   Virginia, provided that the defendant also regularly does or solicits
   business, or engages in any other persistent course of conduct, or derives substantial revenue from goods used or consumed or services
   rendered in Virginia
6. Having an interest in, using, or possessing real property in Virginia

---

[3] 28 USC §1332(c).

[4] Zahn v International Paper Co, 414 US 291 (1973).

[5] Absent a federal basis for personal jurisdiction, the personal jurisdiction of federal
courts sitting in diversity depends upon the law of the state in which the court sits. *See*
28 USC §1652; Insurance Corp of Ireland v Compagnie des Bauxites, 102 S Ct 2099,
2109 (1982) (Powell, J, concurring).

[6] Va Code §8.01-328.1 (Michie Supp 1982). See generally Sutton, *Today's Long-Arm
and Products Liability: A Plea for a Contemporary Notion of Fair Play and Substantial Justice,* 41
Ins Counsel J 88 (1974) (collecting statutes).

7.   Contracting to insure any person, property, or risk located within Virginia at the time of contracting

Service upon an absent corporation in such circumstances may be achieved by serving the state official who is designated by the applicable statute.[7]

Although the complaint should be drafted with the relevant state statute in mind, literal compliance with the statute may still leave the defendant with a jurisdictional defense based upon the constitutional requirements of due process. The Supreme Court has permitted the exercise of jurisdiction over a foreign corporation only if it has had certain minimum contacts with the forum state.[8] Thus, in addition to any allegation specifying the site of plaintiff's injury or damages, a reasonably supportable allegation concerning the defendant's contacts with the state through such activities as property ownership, shipping, selling, advertising, telephoning, mailing, ownership, or previous litigation may be advisable.

§15.04   —Parties

The complaint must identify the parties. Toxic substance litigation by its nature tends to involve multiple parties on each side of the lawsuit. On the plaintiffs' side, there is often a large class of persons affected, such as insulation workers exposed to asbestos, veterans exposed to defoliants, or women whose mothers took a popular antimiscarriage drug. Additional plaintiffs are possible even in an individual case. The spouse of the plaintiff, for example, may have a derivative action based in loss of consortium[9] and may have an independent cause of action for exposure to toxic materials the original plaintiff had inad-

---

[7] *E.g.*, Va Code §8.01-329 (Michie Supp 1982) (secretary of commonwealth made statutory agent of nonresident party).

[8] The assertion of jurisdiction over a nonresident defendant has been the subject of several Supreme Court decisions. *E.g.*, Insurance Corp of Ireland, v Compagnie des Bauxites, 102 S Ct 2099 (1982) (when defendant refuses to comply with plaintiff's discovery requests aimed to show factual basis for personal jurisdiction, court may deem established the facts necessary to support constitutional exercise of jurisdiction); World-Wide Volkswagon Corp v Woodson, 444 US 286 (1980) (although defendant's product allegedly caused injury in a foreign state, it was unconstitutional for the forum state to assert jurisdiction because with respect to the forum state the nonresident defendant carried on no activity, closed no sales, performed no services, availed itself of no benefit of state law, solicited no business, and directed no advertising); Hanson v Denckla, 357 US 235 (1958) (nonresident of state who does not consent to personal jurisdiction may be sued only if minimal contacts with forum state are shown); International Shoe Co v Washington, 326 US 310 (1945) (jurisdiction constitutionally asserted if defendant's activities establish sufficient contacts or ties with forum state to make jurisdiction reasonable and just, according to our traditional conception of fair play and justice). With specific respect to products liability cases, see Annot, 19 ALR3d 13 (1968) (in personam jurisdiction over nonresident manufacturer or seller under long-arm statutes).

[9] *E.g.*, Gillig v Bymart Tintair, Inc, 16 FRD 393 (SDNY 1954) (husband suing for loss of services and consortium).

vertently carried home from work. Multiple defendants are also the norm. In a toxic tort suit, as in any products liability suit, there is a broad range of possible defendants, including manufacturers, distributors, advertisers, retailers, insurance companies, unions, government inspectors, landowners, and health care providers.[10]

The prime candidate as a defendant is usually the party that manufactured the toxic substance. In many cases, however, identification of the manufacturer may be impossible because the toxic substance may not be uniquely attributable to one manufacturer and the typically long latency period of a toxic substances effect may make its source impossible to discern by reliance on memory or existing records. Accordingly, plaintiffs may be unable to identify the makers of various generic drugs, the companies responsible for dumping various toxic substances at a waste disposal site,[11] and the manufacturers who actually made the various asbestos products to which a worker has been exposed over many years.[12] This inability to identify is often fatal, for the general rule is that a complaint is vulnerable to a motion to dismiss if it does not identify the defendant as the party actually responsible for the particular harmful agent that injured the plaintiff.[13]

Nevertheless, in some jurisdictions and under some circumstances, the plaintiff, although unable to identify the party who actually made or sold the toxic substance causing the injury, may be able to plead a theory of recovery against one or more defendants who sold the substance during the relevant time period.[14] Most of the cases in this category have involved diethylstilbestol (DES), a drug said to cause cancer in women years after their mothers ingested the drug during pregnancy. The leading DES case is *Sindell v Abbott Laborato-*

---

[10] See McGovern, *Toxic Substances Litigation in the Fourth Circuit,* 16 Univ Richmond L Rev 247 (1982).

[11] See generally Note, *Unearthing Defendants in Toxic Waste Litigation: Problems of Liability and Identification,* 19 San Diego L Rev 891 (1982).

[12] *See, e.g.,* Hardy v Johns-Manville Sales Corp, 509 F Supp 1353 (ED Tex 1981).

[13] *See* Morton v Abbott Laboratories, 538 F Supp 593 (MD Fla 1982) (DES, Florida law); Mizell v Eli Lilly & Co, 526 F Supp (DSC 1981) (DES, South Carolina law); Gray v United States, 445 F Supp 337 (D Tex 1978) (DES, Texas law); Rockett v Pepsi Cola Bottling Co, 460 SW2d 737 (Mo Ct App 1970) (no evidence that defendant made and sold the particular bottle of poisoned soda imbibed by plaintiff). See generally Annot, 51 ALR3d 1344 (1973) (necessity and sufficiency of identification of defendant as manufacturer or seller of product alleged to have caused injury).

[14] Many commentators have addressed this situation. *E.g.,* Lamarca, *Market Share Liability, Industry-Wide Liability, Alternative Liability and Concert of Action: Modern Legal Concepts Reserving Liability for Defective But Unidentifiable Products,* 31 Drake L Rev 61 (1982); Newcomb, *Market Share Liability for Defective Products: An Ill-Advised Remedy for the Problem of Identification,* 76 NW LJ 300 (1981); Robinson, *Multiple Causation in the Tort Law: Reflections on the DES Cases,* 68 Va L Rev 713 (1982); Comment, *DES and a Proposed Theory of Enterprise Liability,* 46 Fordham L Rev 963 (1978); Note, *Market Share Liability: An Answer to the DES Causation Problem,* 94 Harv L Rev 668 (1981); Comment, *The DES Dilemma: An Analysis of Recent Decisions,* 52 Miss LJ 199 (1982); Comment, *Unearthing Defendants in Toxic Waste Litigation: Problems of Liability and Identification,* 19 San Diego L Rev 891 (1982); Note, *Industry Wide Liability,* 13 Suffolk L Rev 980 (1979).

ries,[15] in which the California Supreme Court recognized four means of maintaining a suit even though the defendant actually causing plaintiff's injury cannot be identified:

1.   Alternative liability
2.   Concert of action
3.   Industry-wide liability
4.   Market share liability[16]

Although these means of maintaining an action are discussed more fully in Chapter 11, a brief mention of their bases is included in this chapter.

Alternative liability requires independent torts by each of two or more actors, only one of which may actually have caused the plaintiff's injury. If invoked, this theory requires each defendant to disprove that it caused the injury by, for example, proving that it did not manufacture the toxic substance in question during the relevant period. Alternative liability requires joinder of all or virtually all of the manufacturers in the industry, an often impossible task.[17]

Concert of action as a theory of liability is based on the Restatement (Second) of Torts §876, Under this approach, the California Supreme Court has held that express agreement is not necessary; tacit agreement is enough.[18] Concert of action makes a defendant liable even if it did not make the substance that actually caused the plaintiff's injury.[19]

---

[15] 26 Cal 3d 588, 607 P2d 924, 163 Cal Rptr 132, *cert denied,* 449 US 912 (1980).

[16] On the allegations before it, however, the court in *Sindell* held that only market share liability would be appropriate. A prerequisite to any of these theories would seem to be plaintiff's inability to identify the defendant causing him or her harm. *See* Lyons v Premo Pharmaceutical Labs, Inc, 170 NJ Super 185, 406 A2d 189 (App Div 1979) (alternative liability and industry-wide liability theories not applicable where plaintiff has identified and settled with particular company that made the DES ingested by plaintiff's mother).

[17] The *Sindell* court rejected the appropriateness of alternative liability on the facts before it because the plaintiff had sued only a few of the 200 manufacturers of DES. 26 Cal 3d at 603, 607 P2d at 931, 163 Cal Rptr at 141. *Accord* Morton v Abbott Laboratories, 538 F Supp 593 (MD Fla 1982) (alternative liability theory inapplicable where plaintiffs admittedly cannot show that one of the named defendants caused the injury); Namm v Charles E Frosst Co, 178 NJ Super 19, 427 A2d 1121 (App Div 1981) (alternative liability rejected where complaint names only 74 of 300 companies). *But see* Abel v Eli Lilly & Co, 94 Mich App 59, 289 NW2d 20 (1980) (plaintiffs may maintain action on alternative liability theory by showing that one or more of the defendants made the DES ingested by plaintiffs' mothers).

[18] Sindell v Abbott Laboratories, 26 Cal 3d 588, 606 P2d 924, 163 Cal Rptr 132 (1980).

[19] *See* Abel v Eli Lilly & Co, 94 Mich App 59, 289 NW2d 20 (1979) (concerted negligence by DES manufacturers could make all liable even though only one directly caused the injury). DES plaintiffs prevailed before a jury on a concert of action theory in Bichler v Eli Lilly & Co, 55 NY2d 571, 436 NE2d 182, 450 NYS2d 766 (1982), but

Industry-wide liability may also be a theory for a plaintiff to consider. The basic allegation under this theory is that plaintiff's injury is the result of a deficient industry-wide safety standard to which the defendants concertedly adhered.[20] This theory is likely to be useful only where plaintiff can show that the number of manufacturers is small and that the defendants have jointly delegated standard-making authority to a trade association. The court in *Sindell* rejected the theory's application in the DES context because of the large number of manufacturers, the failure to allege that standard-making authority had been delegated to an association, and the fact that a pervasive standard-making role had already been assumed by the federal Food and Drug Administration.[21]

Potentially the most significant of these means of pleading a case against a defendant whom the plaintiff cannot precisely identify as the responsible tortfeasor is market share liability. Under market share liability, each defendant is held liable according to its relative share of the appropriate market unless it demonstrates that it could not have made the product causing plaintiff's injuries.[22] Like industry-wide liability, however, market share liability, even where accepted as a viable theory, may be limited to allegations of defective design or failure to warn and might not extend to peculiar manufacturing defects.[23]

In a still more extreme case, a plaintiff may not only be unable to identify the responsible manufacturer but also be unable to identify the responsible product. He or she may be a victim of exposure to substances at a toxic waste site, for example, where many toxic materials were dumped. It has been suggested that in such a case a plaintiff unable to identify the particular product

---

the New York Court of Appeals effectively reserved its judgment on the point because the defendant's failure to contest the theory at trial made the concert of action theory the law of the case.

[20] *E.g.,* Hall v EI DuPont de Nemours & Co, 345 F Supp 353 (EDNY 1972) (entire blasting cap industry and its trade association liable, absent proof of lack of causation, once plaintiff shows cap was made by one of the defendants and that each defendant by adhering to industry's safety standards breached its duty of care to plaintiff). See Note, *Industry-Wide Liability,* 13 Suffolk U L Rev 980 (1979); Comment, *DES and a Proposed Theory of Enterprise Liability,* 46 Fordham L Rev 963 (1978).

[21] 26 Cal 3d at 609, 607 P2d at 935, 163 Cal Rptr at 143. *See also* Morton v Abbott Laboratories, 538 F Supp 593 (MD Fla 1982) (industry-wide liability inappropriate in DES case, where number of manufacturers is large and there is no industry-wide delegation of safety functions to a trade association); Namm v Charles E Frosst & Co, 178 NJ Super 19, 427 A2d 1121 (App Div 1981) (industry-wide liability too drastic a change to be adopted by intermediate court).

[22] Sindell v Abbott Laboratories, 26 Cal 3d 588, 607 P2d 924, 163 Cal Rptr 132 (1980). *See also* Hardy v Johns-Manville Sales Corp, 509 F Supp 1353 (ED Tex 1981) (preliminary holding, asbestos), *revd on other grounds,* 681 F2d 334 (5th Cir 1981). *But see* Morton v Abbott Laboratories, 538 F Supp 593 (MD Fla 1982) (granting defendants' motion for summary judgment and rejecting market share liability, Florida law); Mizell v Eli Lilly & Co, 526 F Supp 589 (DSC 1981) (same, South Carolina law).

[23] See LaMarca, *Market Share Liability, Industry-Wide Liability, Alternative Liability and Concert of Action: Modern Legal Concepts Preserving Liability for Defective But Unidentifiable Products,* 31 Drake L Rev 61 (1982).

causing him or her injury should nevertheless be able to maintain a suit by
pleading and showing that the defendants he or she has joined account for a
substantial share of the risk that the hazardous substances at the dump site
represent.[24]

§15.05   —Pleading Theories of Liability

The specificity with which a theory of liability must be alleged in a toxic tort
suit varies with the pleading rules of the jurisdiction in question. In federal
practice and in state jurisdictions adopting *notice pleading* requirements, it is
sufficient to set forth a short and plain statement of the plaintiff's claim which
may be amended upon motions which are freely granted when "justice so
requires."[25] A course nevertheless favored by many attorneys is to identify and
allege at the outset the elements of every theory of liability that reasonably may
be supported. Possible theories of toxic tort liability include negligence,
breach of warranty (express and implied), deceit, misrepresentation, conspiracy, nuisance, and strict tort liability. One commentator has identified over 20
separate approaches to toxic tort recovery.[26] The bulk of toxic tort cases,
however, are based on the theory that the defendant failed to give adequate
warnings or instructions, which may be actionable either in negligence or in
strict liability in tort. The theory in strict liability is that inadequate warnings
were a defect that made the product in question unreasonably dangerous.[27]

A well-pleaded complaint will state the factual basis for each element of each
asserted cause of action, rather than simply stating these elements in conclusory terms.[28] For example, a count in negligence against a manufacturer of a
toxic substance needs to allege facts to show defendant's duty to plaintiff,
defendant's breach of that duty, and a causal relationship between the breach
and plaintiff's injury. More specifically, the complaint might allege that the
defendant made, tested, and sold the substance, that the plaintiff purchased
the substance or was a person likely either to use it or to be exposed to it during
its use, and that defendant knew or should have known that the substance, if
not properly manufactured, tested, distributed, and labeled, would cause damage of the kind plaintiff has suffered. The complaint should then state the
manner of the breach—e.g., inadequacies and negligence in design, in testing,

---

[24] Comment, *Unearthing Defendants in Toxic Waste Litigation: Problems of Liability and Identification,* 19 San Diego L Rev 891 (1982).

[25] Fed R Civ P 15(a).

[26] McGovern, *Toxic Substances Litigation in the Fourth Circuit,* 16 U Richmond L Rev 247, 268 (1982).

[27] *E.g.,* Dalke v Upjohn Co, 555 F2d 245 (9th Cir 1977) (tetracycline-based drug); Borel v Fiberboard Paper Prods Corp, 493 F2d 1076 (5th Cir 1973), *cert denied,* 419 US 860 (1974) (asbestos).

[28] *See, e.g.,* Myers v Montgomery Ward & Co, 253 Md 282, 252 A2d 855 (1969) (general averment of negligence is inadequate as a mere legal conclusion in a complex case where breach of duty is not obvious).

in responding to warnings or complaints, in recommending use of the product, in labeling, in warning, and in other respects. The complaint should next state that the breach caused the plaintiff's injury and identify the nature of plaintiff's damages.[29]

§15.06   —Punitive Damages

In addition to the usual request for compensatory damages, the complaint may include a request for punitive damages. Such damages are available in a large majority of jurisdictions upon a finding of malice or willful, wanton, or reckless disregard of the safety of others. Facts supporting such a finding include corporate knowledge of a product's dangers, knowledge by corporate agents that the product has harmed others, undue delay in remedying the defect or in issuing adequate warnings, and fraudulent corporate behavior.[30] A claim for punitive damages may support discovery inquiries into the defendant's net worth.[31]

§15.07   The Defendant's Responsive Pleading

As in any other litigation, the defendant in a toxic tort case has several procedural options to consider in response to a complaint. In federal practice, a number of defenses may be raised by motion in advance of filing an answer. These include a lack of in personam jurisdiction, improper venue,[32] insufficiency of process, and insufficiency of service of process. In federal practice, these defenses must be raised in any preanswer motion, or they will be waived.[33] If no such motion is made, these defenses must be asserted in the answer. The most commonly raised defenses include the statute of limitations, assumption of risk, contributory or comparative negligence, the medical or scientific state of the art, and supervening negligence based upon the conduct of a third party, such as the plaintiff's employer or the government. These defenses are discussed in Chapter 14. Defenses considered to be affirmative

---

[29] For illustrative allegations in various theories potentially applicable in toxic torts litigation, *see e.g.,* 12 Am Jur *Trials* §§54-60 (1966); Toxic Torts (P. Rheingold, N. Landau, M. Kanavan eds 1977); 3A L. Frumor & M. Friedman, Products Liability § 46.02 (1982).

[30] *See, e.g.,* Owen, *Punitive Damages in Products Liability Litigation,* 78 Mich L Rev 1257 (1976); Parnell, *Manufacturers of Toxic Substances: Tort Liability and Punitive Damages,* 17 Forum 947 (1982); Note, *Punitive Damages Awards in Strict Products Liability Litigation: The Doctrine, the Debate, the Defenses,* 42 Ohio St LJ 771 (1981); Annot, 29 ALR3d 1021 (1970) (allowance of punitive damages in products liability case).

[31] See Note, *Pretrial Discovery of Net Worth in Punitive Damages Cases,* 54 S Cal L Rev 1141 (1981).

[32] *See* 28 USC §1391(a) (civil action wherein jurisdiction is founded only on diversity of citizenship may, except as otherwise provided by law, be brought only in the judicial district where all plaintiffs or all defendants reside, or in which the claim arose).

[33] *See* Fed R Civ P 12(b).

defenses under the pleading rules of the forum jurisdiction must be pleaded or they may be considered waived. In federal courts, affirmative defenses include assumption of risk, contributory negligence, and the statute of limitations,[34] all of which will be necessary to consider in a toxic tort defense.

The nonresident defendant corporation sued in state court by plaintiffs of a citizenship diverse to that of the defendant will want to consider whether it may remove the action to federal court.[35] The defendant may then move for a change of venue—transfer to another federal district court more convenient to the parties.[36]

Out of the ordinary defenses may be provided by a state statute.[37] In Minnesota, for example, a nonmanufacturer defendant, by certifying the identity of the manufacturer of the product in question, may in certain circumstances gain dismissal of a claim in strict liability in tort once the plaintiff, exercising due diligence, has sued and obtained jurisdiction over the manufacturer.[38]

Class Actions

§15.08   General Requirements

Toxic substance litigation typically involves simultaneous lawsuits. There are a broad variety of methods through which the costs of this multiple litigation may be reduced or avoided. Such methods include:

1.   Transfer and consolidation of the actions[39]
2.   Permissive joinder of plaintiffs[40]
3.   Transfer of multidistrict litigation for coordinated or consolidated pretrial proceedings[41]

---

[34] *See* Fed R Civ P 8(c).

[35] *See* 28 USC §1441(a) (civil action in state court of which federal court has original jurisdiction may be removed upon timely action of defendant).

[36] *See* 28 USC §1404(a) (federal district court may transfer case to another district for convenience of parties and witnesses, in the interest of justice).

[37] See generally Buchanan, *Product Liability Defenses Under the Model Uniform Product Liability Act and State Legislation*, 15 Forum 813 (1980).

[38] Minn Stat Ann §444.41 (West Supp 1982).

[39] Fed R Civ P 42(a). *See, e.g.,* Kershaw v Sterling Drug, Inc, 415 F2d 1009 (5th Cir 1969) (consolidation of cases where there were common questions concerning drug company's duty to warn, nature of warnings, and drug's causation of eye disease).

[40] Fed R Civ P 20 (joinder permitted if rights asserted in respect of same series of transactions or occurrences and if any common question of law or fact will arise in the action).

[41] *See* 28 USC §1407 (transfer by judicial panel for coordinated or consolidated pretrial proceedings if actions involve common fact question and if transfer would be convenient for parties and witnesses and would promote just and efficient conduct of actions). *See, e.g., In re* Agent Orange Prod Liab Litig, 475 F Supp 928 (EDNY 1979)

4.   The use of collateral estoppel to preclude relitigation of certain common issues by a party against whom the issue was decided in a prior litigation[42]

5.   The streamlining of pretrial proceedings by order of court or voluntary cooperation among the parties

6.   Certification of a class action, permitting a class of plaintiffs or defendants to proceed through a representative or representatives

A class action may be maintained if, among other things, the trial court finds that it is superior to other means of managing multiple litigation.

Parties must consider a number of factors in deciding whether to propose or oppose certification of a class. From the plaintiff's perspective, the basic advantages to a class action include the sharing of litigation expenses, greater bargaining leverage with defendants, a broader scope of discovery, and the tolling of the statute of limitations for class members. The individual plaintiff, however, may see his or her interests compromised to some extent in favor of the interest of the class as a whole. For example, the plaintiff may be represented by an attorney he or she did not select, in a forum he or she does not prefer, and be unable to reach his or her own settlement with the defendant without notice to the class and approval by the court. Although the plaintiffs' advantages are disadvantages for the defendant, defendants will not necessarily choose to oppose class certification. They also will derive some benefits from a class action, such as unified discovery and trial. The defendant will also gain the potential benefit of having any judgment or settlement binding on all class members who have not excluded themselves from the class.[43]

Allegations in a class action complaint should track the language of the applicable class action rule. In some federal courts, that course is encouraged by local court rule.[44] To maintain a class action, the plaintiff generally must

---

(issues arising in consolidated Agent Orange ligitation); *In re* Swine Flu Immunization Prods Liab Litig, 446 F Supp 224 (JPMDL 1978) (consolidation for substantial common fact questions concerning development and testing despite some opposition from parties). *But see In re* Asbestos Insulation Material Prods Liab Litig, 431 F Supp 906 (JPMDL 1977) (transfer inappropriate where the only common fact questions related to the state of scientific knowledge concerning risk of asbestos exposure, where unique fact questions abounded, and where parties were virtually unanimous in opposition to transfer).

[42] *See* Parklane Hosiery Co v Shore, 439 US 322 (1979) (affirming offensive use of collateral estoppel); Ezagui v Dow Chem Corp, 598 F2d 727 (2d Cir 1979) (defendant estopped to relitigate prior adjudication that warnings it provided concerning its drug were not adequate). See generally L. Frumer & M. Friedman, Products Liability §46.03 (1982) (plaintiff's affirmative use of collateral estoppel). *Cf* Payton v Abbott Laboratories, 83 FRD 382, 392 (D Mass 1979) (collateral estoppel not viable alternative to class action because not available in Massachusetts absent mutuality of parties).

[43] See H. Newberg, Newberg on Class Actions §§1010-1012 (Shepard's/McGraw-Hill 1977).

[44] *See, e.g.,* Local Rule 3.6 of the Southern District of Ohio, requiring allegations of the identity of the class and its size, the basis on which the named class representatives are alleged to be adequate representatives, the common issues of fact and law, and the

allege and prove that the class exists, that he or she is a member of it, and that the class satisfies the elements stated in the applicable class rule. Rule 23 of the Federal Rules of Civil Procedure, the substance of which has been adopted or modified by most of the states,[45] permits one or more named plaintiffs to sue or be sued on behalf of a class and provides, in pertinent part, as follows:

(a) *Prerequisites to a Class Action.* If (1) the class is so numerous that joinder of all members is impracticable, (2) there are questions of law or fact common to the class, (3) the claims or defenses of the representative parties are typical of the claims or defenses of the class, and (4) the representative parties will fairly and adequately protect the interests of the class.

(b) *Class Actions Maintainable.* An action may be maintained as a class action if the prerequisites of subdivision (a) are satisfied, and in addition:

(1) the prosecution of separate actions by or against individual members of the class would create a risk of

(A) inconsistent or varying adjudications with respect to individual members of the class which would establish incompatible standards of conduct for the party opposing the class, or

(B) adjudications with respect to individual members of the class which would as a practical matter be dispositive of the interests of the other members not parties to the adjudications or substantially impair or impede their ability to protect their interests; or

(2) the party opposing the class has acted or refused to act on grounds generally applicable to the class, thereby making appropriate final injunctive relief or corresponding declaratory relief with respect to the class as a whole; or

(3) the court finds that the questions of law or fact common to the members of the class predominate over any questions affecting only individual members, and that a class action is superior to other available methods for the fair and efficient adjudication of the controversy.

In addition to the foregoing requirements, in a diversity action each member of the class must satisfy the $10,000 jurisdiction amount.[46] Moreover, Rule 23(b)(3) class members have a right to exclude themselves from the class and, under Rule 23(c)(2), must be given the best notice of the class action that is "practicable" under the circumstances.

Under Rule 23(c)(1), the trial court is to determine by order, as "soon as

---

basis for finding that common issues predominate and that the class action is superior to other methods of managing the litigation.

[45] Newberg, in a state-by-state analysis of class actions, lists 33 states as having adopted or modified the current federal class action rule, including Florida, Illinois, Indiana, Massachusetts, New Jersey, New York, Ohio, Pennsylvania, and Texas. H. Newberg, Newberg on Class Actions §1210b (Shepard's/McGraw Hill 1977 & Supp).

[46] Zahn v International Paper Co, 414 US 291 (1973); Yandle v PPG Indus, Inc, 65 FRD 566, 570 (ED Tex 1974).

practicable" after the commencement of a class action, whether a class action may be maintained. The order may be modified any time before the decision on the merits. The plaintiff may file a motion to certify the class, or the defendant may initiate matters by filing a motion to deny certification.

To maintain a class action, the plaintiff must allege and show the four elements of Rule 23(a) and, in addition, at least one of the alternative requirements of Rule 23(b).[47] The Rule 23(a) requirements are interpreted as follows.

Numerosity

The numerosity requirement is met if the class is so large that joinder of all members is impracticable. Generally speaking, fewer than 20 class members make a number too small, while more than 40 make a number sufficiently large. Relevant to this inquiry is the size of the class and its geographical dispersion. The complaint should indicate, then, the number of class members, their dispersion, and the impracticability of joinder.[48]

Commonality

The complaint should also identify, in a nonexclusive listing, the questions of law or fact common to the class (commonality). These might include such issues as whether the defendant was negligent in its manufacture, testing, or labeling of a particular toxic substance and whether it is liable for punitive damages because of its conduct.

Typicality

The complaint should also state that the claims of the representatives of the class are typical of the claims of the other members of the class. Typicality does not require total identity of interest,[49] but it does require that the common issues be about as important to the representatives' claim as those issues are to the claims of other class members.[50]

Adequacy of Representation

The last prerequisite of Rule 23(a) is that the class representatives fairly and adequately represent the class interests. Adequacy of representation is essential in that class members may be bound by an adverse judgment, unless they

---

[47] For an in-depth discussion of the requisites of a class action, see 3B Moore's Federal Practice ¶23.00 *et seq* (2d ed 1982); H. Newberg, Newberg on Class Actions §1100 *et seq* (Shepard's/McGraw-Hill 1977).

[48] 3B Moore, *supra* note 47, at ¶23.05.

[49] *E.g.,* Payton v Abbott Labs, 83 FRD 382 (D Mass 1979) (various class representatives can represent class with respect to varying statutes of limitations).

[50] *See, e.g.,* Amswiss Intl Corp v Heublein, Inc, 69 FRD 633 (ND Ga 1975) (claims of class representative not typical if they would require substantially more or less proof than would be required by other members of class).

can thereafter show that their rights were not adequately protected.[51] Adequacy of representation depends upon a variety of factors, including the qualifications of counsel for the class representative, the absence of conflicts between the interests of class representatives and other class members, the unlikelihood that the suit is collusive, and the financial ability of the class representatives to bear the initial costs of suit.[52] In some cases, conflicts may be avoided by pleading the existence of subclasses as provided in Rule 23(c)(4). Each subclass may be represented by a different representative.

§15.09   Toxic Tort Suits

Courts have tended to disfavor class actions in products liability cases, and particularly in toxic tort litigation. The chief difficulty is that even with a large number of plaintiffs suing a single defendant for exposure to the same toxic substance, it is difficult to satisfy the requirements of Rule 23(b) of the Federal Rules of Civil Procedure, discussed in **§15.08**. In addition to the Rule 23(a) requirements, a class action complaint must allege satisfaction of at least one of the subsections of Rule 23(b). Each of the subsections poses its own difficulty. Subsection (b)(1)(A)—referring to the danger of establishing incompatible standards for the defendant—is not likely to apply in any damage action because the award of damages to some class members and the denial of damages to others typically does not establish incompatible standards of conduct for the defendant.[53]

Subsection (b)(1)(B)—referring to the risk that separate adjudications could, as a practical matter, substantially impede the interests of absent class members—has been invoked in mass tort situations where the total amount of punitive damages has been alleged to exceed the ability of the defendant to pay, but courts have been reluctant to certify a (b)(1)(B) class absent a showing that actual liability will exceed the defendant's net worth. In *Abed v AH Robins Co*,[54] for example, the Ninth Circuit reversed the (b)(1)(B) certification of a nationwide punitive damages class of Dalkon Shield users even though it presented common questions as to what the defendant knew and published about its product. Although acknowledging that subsection (b)(1)(B) was meant to govern *limited fund* cases—where defendant's payment of early claims would make it unable to pay later claims—the court held that the record must

---

[51] *See* Hansberry v Lee, 311 US 32 (1940).

[52] Payton v Abbott Laboratories, 83 FRD 382 (D Mass 1979) (listing factors); Elster v Alexander, 74 FRD 503 (ND Ga 1976) (defendant entitled to discover plaintiff's financial ability to prosecute interests of the class vigorously).

[53] *See, e.g., In re* Agent Orange Prod Liab Litig, 506 F Supp 762 (1980) (*incompatible standards* does not refer to inconsistency of paying damages to some claimants and not to others; class of Agent Orange plaintiffs will not be certified on this ground), *revd on other grounds*, 635 F2d 987 (2d Cir 1981), *cert denied*, 454 US 1128 (1981); Payton v Abbott Labs, 83 FRD 382 (D Mass 1979) (same).

[54] 693 F2d 847 (9th Cir 1982).

establish that earlier awards will *inescapably* affect later awards. On the record before it, the court found insufficient evidence concerning the defendant's actual assets, insurance coverage, settlement experience, and continuing exposure.[55]

Subsection (b)(2) is also of limited utility in a typical toxic tort suit. Subsection (b)(2)—referring to the defendant's action or inaction on grounds "generally applicable to the class"—relates primarily to cases seeking injunctive relief. Although toxic tort plaintiffs often seek such relief—DES plaintiffs, for example, have asked for injunctive relief in the form of notice, examination, research, and treatment for the benefit of class members[56]—subsection (b)(2) "does not extend to cases in which the appropriate final relief relates exclusively or predominantly to money damages."[57]

Most toxic tort class actions will be certified, if at all, on the basis of Rule 23(b)(3). Maintenance of a (b)(3) suit requires two special findings: first, predominance of common issues over individual issues; and second, superiority of the class action over other available methods of litigation. Rule 23 makes four factors *pertinent to the findings:*

1. The class members' interests in individual control of the litigation

2. The extent and nature of related litigation already involving class members

3. The merits of concentrating the claims in one particular forum

4. The difficulties in managing the class action

The *predominance* requirement essentially turns on whether common issues, such as the defendant's negligence, can be separated from individual issues, such as damages. An examination of other ongoing litigation may indicate the extent to which common issues predominate. The danger the predominance requirement is meant to avoid is "degenerat[ion] . . . into multiple lawsuits separately tried."[58]

The *superiority* requirement draws more evenly from all four of the pertinent factors. Individual adjudication may be thought superior to a toxic tort class action in part because of the individual's especially strong interest in the personal aspects of the suit.[59] The existence of ongoing litigation on the same

---

[55] *Id* 853. *See also In re* Agent Orange Prod Liab Litig, 506 F Supp 762 (EDNY 1980) (no certification of Rule 23(b)(1)(B) class because plaintiffs did not show likely insolvency of defendant), *revd on other grounds*, 635 F2d 987 (2d Cir), *cert denied*, 452 US 1128 (1981); Payton v Abbott Labs, 83 FRD 382 (D Mass 1979) (numerous plaintiffs and large ad damnum clause do not guarantee (b)(1)(B) certification).

[56] *E.g.*, Ryan v Eli Lilly & Co, 84 FRD 230 (DSC 1979).

[57] *See e.g.*, Payton v Abbott Labs, 83 FRD 382 (D Mass 1979) (no certification of DES class under Rule 23(b)(2) since final relief relates predominately to money damages).

[58] 28 USC Rule 23, Notes of Advisory Committee on Rules, 1966 Amendment.

[59] *See, e.g.*, Hobbs v Northeast Airlines, Inc, 50 FRD 76 (ED Pa 1970).

subject matter may also be a reason to deny certification of a class.[60] The final factor—difficulties in management—will be relevant when the class is so large that the class representatives and their attorneys are unable to identify and notify class members and determine their damages.[61] Into the superiority determination will also go a comparison of the other alternative methods of managing the litigation, such as multidistrict transfer and permissive joinder.

Several aspects peculiar to toxic tort litigation make the *predominance* hurdle of Rule 23(b)(3) particularly difficult to surmount. One is that with respect to a toxic tort, there is rarely a single event causing harm, such as there would be in a mass accident. There is, therefore, no single act of negligence applicable to each class member. Rather, each plaintiff may have been subjected to a different degree of exposure to the toxic substance in question, with a different degree of knowledge and appreciation of the risk of that exposure. These differences could raise individual issues with respect to causation, assumption of risk and contributory negligence, or misuse. In addition, because exposure has occurred over time, there may be multiple defendants as well as multiple plaintiffs, with each defendant raising defenses possibly peculiar to it, such as the applicability of statutes of limitations, the adequacy of warnings, and the state of medical knowledge concerning the toxic substance in question.

Another hindrance to a class action especially prominent in toxic tort litigation is the fact that the plaintiff class may well consist of persons who have been exposed to toxic doses of a hazardous substance but have not yet developed a disease.[62] In light of the potential res judicata effect of a class action on absent class members, a court might be moved by the prospect that persons yet uninjured may neglect to exclude themselves from a class action where they would insist upon handling their claims individually if their personal injuries had manifested themselves.[63]

§15.10 —Specific Cases Involving Class Actions in Toxic Tort Litigation

Class certification was denied in *Rosenfeld v AH Robins Co,*[64] which, although

---

[60] *E.g.,* Snyder v Hooker Chem & Plastics Corp, 104 Misc 2d 876, 429 NYS2d 153 (NY Sup Ct 1980) (class certification denied where plaintiffs' attorneys represented only 24 of 1,254 Love Canal claimants who had brought actions, a fact indicating interest of class members in individually controlling their claims). *Cf* Payton v Abbott Laboratories, 83 FRD 382 (D Mass 1979) (fact that of more than 13,000 class members only 10 had brought individual suit mitigated in favor of certifying class action).

[61] See 3B Moore's Federal Practice ¶¶23.05[1], 23.45[4-4] (2d ed 1982).

[62] *See, e.g.,* Payton v Abbott Laboratories, 83 FRD 382 (D Mass 1979) (class of DES-exposed women who have not developed uterine or vaginal cancer); Yandle v PPG Indus, Inc, 65 FRD 566 (ED Tex 1974) (asbestos-exposed workers who have not yet contracted asbestosis or lung cancer).

[63] Yandle v PPG Indus, Inc, 65 FRD 566 (ED Tex 1974).

[64] 63 AD2d 11, 407 NYS2d 196, *appeal dismissed,* 46 NY2d 731, 385 NE2d 1301, 413 NYS2d 374 (1978). For a thorough discussion of this case, see Note, *Class Action in A*

not a toxic tort case, has implications for toxic tort class actions. Applying a New York rule similar to Rule 23 of the Federal Rules of Civil Procedure, the *Rosenfeld* court determined that plaintiffs could not maintain a class action for damages resulting from the use of the Dalkon Shield, an allegedly defective birth control device, because plaintiffs had failed to show that common issues predominated over the need for individual determinations of liability. With respect to the plaintiffs' strict liability allegations, the court held that each class member would have to prove that the cause of her injury was the defect in defendants' product, rather than her own conduct, her physician's conduct, or her own peculiar physique. With respect to the plaintiffs' breach of warranty claim, the court held that each individual would have to prove individually her detrimental reliance on a false representation by the defendant. The court distinguished the case before it from the typical *mass tort* suit, where several plaintiffs are injured by a single cause, such as an airplane crash. The court acknowledged that some issues were common, such as whether the Dalkon Shield was defective and whether defendant had falsely represented it, but thought that the limited scope of these issues made the economic advantage of class litigation relatively small.

A somewhat similar approach was taken in *Snyder v Hooker Chemicals & Plastics Corp*,[65] in which the court denied certification of a class of persons injured by exposure to toxic materials dumped at the Love Canal site in New York state. Although acknowledging that the various actions had a common denominator —injury from exposure to Love Canal toxic waste—the court noted that plaintiffs relied on various theories of liability, and that each case might call for individual handling on questions of causation, manifestation, and extent of injury. A class action was not superior, the court concluded, to the pretrial consolidation and coordination devices already being used.

In *Yandle v PPF Industries, Inc*,[66] the court declined to certify a class of asbestos plant employees, primarily because the plaintiffs had failed to show that they met the Rule 23(b)(3) requirements of predominance and superiority. With respect to predominance, the court noted that over 10 years the class members had various degrees of exposure to asbestos, and that some probably had occupational diseases when they entered their employment with the defendant. Other issues peculiar to individual plaintiffs included their knowledge concerning the danger of breathing asbestos dust, whether they were given respirators, and whether they used them. These issues, plus the fact that the nine defendants in the case were alleging differing affirmative defenses, convinced the court that common issues did not predominate. The court concluded that a superior method of adjudication would be to freely allow intervention

---

Products Liability Context: The Predomination Requirement and Cause-in-Fact, 7 Hofstra L Rev 859 (1979). *See also* Abed v AH Robins Co, 693 F2d 847 (9th Cir 1982) (reversing Rule 23(b)(3) certification of Dalkon Shield class because consolidated discovery and use of test cases would be equally efficacious).

[65] 104 Misc 2d 735, 429 NYS2d 153 (NY Sup Ct 1980).

[66] 65 FRD 566 (ED Tex 1974).

and follow the procedures set forth in the Manual for Complex and Multidistrict Litigation.

Similarly, in *Ryan v Eli Lilly & Co*,[67] the court denied certification of a DES class because plaintiff failed to show that common issues predominated:

> [T]he length of exposure, the reason for the drug's use, the specific chemical formulation of the drug, the state of the art at the time of consumption or the manufacturer's knowledge of synthetic estrogen's carcinogenic effect and possible medical result in the absence of estrogens are all specific points going toward proximate causation which will require proof for each individual class member.[68]

Bifurcation of the case into a class action for liability and individual actions for damages would not solve the predominance problems, the court reasoned, because the liability issue alone required individual proof for each plaintiff.

Defendant class actions in a toxic tort litigation are even less likely to be certified. Defendants, with a natural incentive to shift liability to codefendants, are unlikely to have an adequate representative with defenses typical of those of the class.[69]

Notwithstanding the general reluctance to certify a toxic tort class, the court in *Payton v Abbott Labs*[70] conditionally certified, "with respect to particular issues," as authorized by Rule 23(c)(4)(A), a plaintiff class of women who were exposed to DES in utero, who resided in Massachusetts, and who had not yet developed DES-related cancer.[71] As to the 23(b)(3) issues of predominance and superiority, the court noted plaintiffs' claim that over 90 per cent of trial time in prior DES suits was devoted to the common issue of whether and when the defendants knew or should have known of the damages of DES exposure. The use of collateral estoppel was not available as an alternative to a class action, the court noted, because in Massachusetts the party to be estopped

---

[67] 84 FRD 230 (DSC 1979).

[68] *Id* 233.

[69] *E.g.*, Payton v Abbott Labs, 83 FRD 382 (D Mass 1979).

[70] *Id.*

[71] *Id.* The issues certified for class treatment included:

1. Whether being placed at greater risk of developing cancer was compensable under Massachusetts law
2. Whether defendants were negligent in making and selling DES as a prevention of miscarriages
3. Whether defendants may be held strictly liable to the plaintiffs
4. Whether defendants engaged in a joint enterprise or as a combination or conspiracy to produce and market DES
5. Whether, in the absence of conspiracy, combination, or joint enterprise, defendants may be held liable to a class member who cannot identify the maker of the DES to which she was exposed
6. Whether statutes of limitations bar claims under plaintiffs' various theories, and for which periods of time

must have been a party to the earlier action in which the issue was litigated. With each new plaintiff or defendant, the opposing party would be free to relitigate issues previously decided. Finally, the court reasoned that the number of individual suits already brought by class members—10—was insignificant in comparison with the estimated size of the class.

Further support for a toxic tort class action under limited circumstances appears in *In re "Agent Orange" Product Liability Litigation,*[72] in which the court granted plaintiffs' motion to certify a class under Rule 23(b)(3). The court emphasized that the litigation was at an early stage, where issues such as the possible liability of the federal government affected all plaintiffs equally. Accordingly, individual plaintiffs had little interest in individual control of their cases. It was also important, the court reasoned, that virtually all pending Agent Orange litigation was already before the court under multidistrict litigation procedures. The court acknowledged that the decertification of the class was a possibility, however, in later stages of litigation where issues of individual causation and damages may come to predominate.

Third-Party Claims

§15.11   Actions in Indemnity and Contribution

A defendant in a toxic tort suit will consider bringing an *action over* in an attempt to shift some or all of its liability to another party which has either agreed to be held responsible or arguably should be held responsible because of its conduct or its relationship with the defendant. Generally, this action either may be a part of the original action, by cross-claim against a codefendant[73] or impleader of a new party,[74] or by a separate action brought after the initial action has terminated.

The theories of third-party liability are basically two: indemnity and contribution. In its purest form, *indemnity* is a common law principle under which the full liability of one party, the indemnitee, is shifted to another party, the indemnitor. *Contribution,* by contrast, is a tort principle under which joint liability is apportioned among tortfeasors, either equally or in proportion to fault. Contribution did not exist at common law,[75] and its substantive and procedural rules are generally set forth in state statutes, such as versions of the Uniform Contribution Among Tortfeasors Act. Another difference worth noting is that

---

[72] 506 F Supp 762 (EDNY), *revd on other grounds,* 635 F2d 987 (2d Cir 1980), *cert denied,* 454 US 1128 (1981).

[73] *See* Fed R Civ P 13(g) (pleading may state cross-claim that coparty is or may be liable to cross-claimant for all or part of claim asserted in the action against cross-claimant).

[74] *See* Fed R Civ P 14(a) (defending party, as third-party plaintiff, may serve complaint on nonparty who is or may be liable to third-party plaintiff for all or part of the plaintiff's claim against him or her).

[75] W. Prosser, Law of Torts §50 (4th ed 1971).

indemnity is an action not only for the amount recovered by the primary plaintiff but for the expenses and attorneys' fees expended in defending the original action.[76]

Indemnity may be either express or implied. Indemnity is ordinarily sought from those located *upstream* in the line of distribution—e.g., a distributor seeking indemnity from a manufacturer—but it may be sought *downstream* as well.[77] The clearest case for indemnity is where there is an express contract by which one party has agreed to save and hold harmless another party with respect to liability growing out of specified activities.[78] A case of express indemnity is simply a matter of pleading that the acts of which the plaintiff complains fall within the terms of a contract of indemnification between the defendant indemnitee and the indemnitor. An express contract of indemnity will usually shift liability, even where it is clear that the indemnitee has been at fault, unless such a contract is shown to be contrary to the public policy of the state.[79] Contracts of indemnification are construed strictly, however, and to be effective must show expressly and unequivocally that the indemnitee is not to be indemnified for the consequences of his or her own fault.[80]

More commonly, indemnity is a matter of contract implied in fact or in law upon the basis of a relationship between the parties or a difference in character and degree between the culpability of each party's conduct with respect to the injury suffered by the plaintiff. Implied indemnity typically operates in favor of the party whose negligence was *passive* or *secondary* and against the party whose negligence was *active* or *primary*.[81] The meanings applied to those terms vary from jurisdiction to jurisdiction. In some jurisdictions, indemnity is said to be available only to the indemnitee who is made liable because of imputed

---

[76] *E.g.*, Insurance Co of N Am v King, 340 So 2d 1175 (Fla Dist Ct App 1976); Warren v McLarth Steel Corp, 911 Mich App 496, 314 NW2d 666 (1982); Hunter v Ford Motor Co, 37 AD2d 335, 325 NYS2d 469 (1971).

[77] White v Johns-Manville Corp, 662 F2d 234 (4th Cir 1981) (asbestos manufacturer sought to establish purchaser-employer's implied duty to manufacturer to use due care in handling asbestos products; theory rejected under Virginia law); Davis v FMC Corp, 537 F Supp 466 (CD Ill 1982) (upholding sufficiency of third-party complaint by manufacturer against purchaser-employer; Illinois law).

[78] *E.g.*, American Agriculture Chem Co v Tampa Armature Works, Inc, 315 F2d 856 (5th Cir 1963) (indemnitee entitled to indemnity despite its negligence pursuant to contract clearly and unequivocally establishing right to indemnity; Florida law).

[79] *See, e.g.*, Maryville Acad v Loeb Rhoades & Co, 530 F Supp 1061 (D Ill 1981) (contract of indemnification with respect to negligence is lawful under both Illinois and New York law).

[80] *See, E.g.*, Price v Shell Oil Co, 2 Cal 3d 245, 466 P2d 722, 85 Cal Rptr 178 (1970).

[81] *See, e.g.*, Glover v Johns-Manville Corp, 662 F2d 225 (4th Cir 1981) (whether under admiralty or Virginia law, liability for which asbestos manufacturers sought indemnity could only arise from allegations of original complaint sounding in active negligence thus precluding action for indemnity); L. Fruman & M. Friedman, Products Liability §44 (1980); 28 ALR3d 943 (1969) (right to indemnity or contribution in products liability).

or vicarious liability rather than any personal negligence.[82] In other jurisdictions, indemnity is available even to an actually negligent tortfeasor if its negligence was only *passive,* a term that may sometimes depend on whether it was a primary or secondary cause of the damages for which indemnity is sought.[83] An indemnitee liable on theory of strict liability in tort may be held to be *actively* negligent for purposes of securing indemnity on a negligence claim, even though strict liability does not necessarily entail negligence.[84] On the other hand, an indemnitee actively negligent, although unable to secure indemnity on a theory of negligence, may be able to secure indemnity on a theory of strict liability in tort or warranty. For example, in *Liberty Mutual Insurance Co v Williams Machine & Tool Co,*[85] the Illinois Supreme Court held that negligence is not a part of any strict liability action, including a strict liability action brought in indemnity, and that actively negligent conduct on the indemnitee's part would, therefore, not be a bar to indemnification based on strict liability.

Some courts have heralded a trend toward a merger of implied indemnity and contribution. The New York Court of Appeals effected a radical change in *Dole v Dow Chemical Co,*[86] an indemnity case which discarded the all-or-nothing rule of indemnity and the passive-active distinction on which that rule rested. Announcing a rule of "partial indemnification," the court held that where a third party is found to have been responsible for part of the negligence for which the defendant is made liable, the defendant may recover for that part against the third party. Subsequently, the California Supreme Court similarly modified its common law indemnity doctrine to permit partial indemnity among concurrent tortfeasors on a comparative fault basis.[87]

A defendant who is considering an action against a third party based upon the same theory as the plaintiff is pursuing should consider *vouching in* the prospective indemnitor. Vouching-in consists of notifying the prospective indemnitor of the litigation's existence and informing the prospective indemnitor that if it does not join the defense it will be bound by the determinations necessarily adjudicated.[88] Vouching-in with respect to a warranty suit is provided for in UCC §2-607(5)(a).

---

[82] *E.g.,* Toman v Underwriters Laboratories, Inc, 532 F Supp 1017 (D Mass 1982) (indemnitee must be entirely free from negligence; Massachusetts law); McCain Mfg Corp v Rockwell Intl Corp, 528 F Supp 524 (DSC 1981) (no right to indemnity for one whose personal negligence, albeit passive, contributed to injury for which he has been held liable; South Carolina law).

[83] *E.g.,* Chesapeake & Ohio RR v Illinois Central Gulf RR, 564 F2d 222 (7th Cir 1977) (Illinois law).

[84] *E.g.,* Symons v Mueller Co, 526 F2d 13 (10th Cir 1975) (party held strictly liable is an active tortfeasor and thus foreclosed from pursuing indemnity; Kansas law).

[85] 62 Ill 2d 77, 338 NE2d 857 (Ill 1975).

[86] 30 NY2d 143, 331 NYS2d 382, 282 NE2d 299 (1972).

[87] American Motorcycle Assn v Superior Court, 20 Cal 3d 578, 578 P2d 899, 146 Cal Rptr 182 (1978).

[88] *See, e.g.,* Barber-Greene Co v Browning Co, 357 F2d 31 (8th Cir 1966) (Nebraska law).

§15.12   Effect of Workers' Compensation

When, as is often the case, the victim of toxic exposure is an employee whose exposure occurred in the course of his or her employment, the employee typically has a statutory right to workers' compensation benefits from the employer without having to prove that the employer was at fault.[89] These benefits are limited, however, and the workers' compensation statutes typically protect the employer, through an *exclusivity clause,* from any action the employee might bring in tort.[90] Accordingly, the employee may seek to recover his or her full damages from other parties, such as manufacturers or sellers of the toxic substance. If the employee is successful, the employer is generally entitled to recoup the workers' compensation benefits it has paid.[91]

The third-party practice question that arises in this context is whether the manufacturer may bring an action over against the employer. For example, an asbestos manufacturer liable to a pipefitter exposed to asbestos products in a shipyard might seek indemnity or contribution from the employer on the ground that the employer negligently failed to instruct its employees in the product's use.[92] Generally, workers' compensation statutes bar any action in contribution, on the theory that by virtue of the exclusivity clause, the employer cannot be jointly liable in tort and, therefore, cannot be a joint tortfeasor liable for contribution.[93] The availability of implied indemnity, on the other hand, is a closer question. Although most jurisdictions have declined to allow implied indemnity simply because the negligence of the third-party plaintiff was passive while that of the employer was active,[94] indemnity has been allowed where the third-party plaintiff can demonstrate that the injury in question resulted from the breach of an independent duty the employer owed to the third party.[95]

---

[89] See generally **ch 6.**

[90] 2A A. Larson, The Law of Workmen's Compensation §65 (1982).

[91] *Id* §71.

[92] *See, e.g.,* White v Johns-Manville Corp, 662 F2d 234 (4th Cir 1981).

[93] 2A A. Larson, *supra* note 90, §76.20. *But see* Lambertson v Cincinnati Corp, 312 Minn 114, 257 NW2d 679 (1977) (employer liable in contribution for its proportional fault, up to amount of workers' compensation liability, despite lack of common liability traditionally required for contribution); Dole v Dow Chem Co, 30 NY2d 143, 282 NE2d 288, 331 NYS2d 382 (1972) (allowing employer to be sued on quasi-contribution theory).

[94] 2A A. Larson, *supra* note 90, at §76.81 (great majority of cases reject indemnity absent contract or special relationship such as lessor-lessee).

[95] *E.g.,* Rabon v Automatic Fasteners, Inc, 672 F2d 1231 (5th Cir 1982) (employer could be required to indemnify manufacturer and distributor on theory that employer accepted responsibility for cooperating in discharging indemnitee's duty to warn of product's dangers and then breached its duty); *Cf In re* General Dynamics Asbestos Cases, 539 F Supp 1106 (D Conn 1982) (employer-purchaser not liable in indemnity

Discovery

§15.13   In General

Although obviously important in any lawsuit, discovery is crucial in toxic tort litigation because information vital to the plaintiff's claim or the defendant's defense is typically in possession of the other party. A basic objective of the plaintiff's discovery of the bases of liability is to inquire into the defendant's knowledge of the hazard created by its toxic substance and the means by which the defendant could have reduced or avoided that hazard. A basic objective of the defendant's discovery is to inquire into the existence of other possible causes of the plaintiff's injury, the plaintiff's own knowledge of the hazard presented by the toxic substance, the date at which any cause of action accrued, the degree to which the plaintiff has already been compensated from other sources, and the basis of the plaintiff's claim for damages. In addition, once counsel are thoroughly familiar with the case, it is imperative for each side to discover the identity of the other side's experts expected to testify and a summary of what their testimony will be.

General categories of information either side might seek are presented in outline form in §§15.14 and 15.15.[96]

§15.14   Plaintiff's Discovery

Items which a plaintiff would want to obtain in discovery are listed in this section in outline form.

Jurisdiction

Volume of the defendant's products shipped into forum state

---

because manufacturer did not allege that employer took on exclusive responsibility for designing, assembling, and ensuring safety of product). See generally Weisgall, *Product Liability in the Workplace: The Effects of Workers' Compensation on the Rights and Liabilities of Third Parties,* 1977 Wis L Rev 1035; Note, *Dual Capacity Doctrine: Third-Party Liability of Employer-Manufacturer in Products Liability Litigation* 12 Ind L Rev 553 (1979); Annot, 100 ALR3d 350 (1980) (modern status of effect of state workers' compensation act on right of third party tortfeasor to contribution or indemnity from employer of injured or killed worker).

[96] See generally Hare, *Discovery in the Products Liability Case,* 16 Trial 42 (Nov 1980); Kirsch, *In Preparation for the Products Liability Case,* 37 Bench & Bar 35 (Dec 1980); Levy, *The Preliminary Handling of Chemical and Toxic Tort Cases,* 26 Prac Law 43 (Oct 1980). Sample interrogatories and other discovery forms adaptable to toxic tort litigation appear in Toxic Torts (P. Rheingold, N. Landau, M. Kanavan eds 1977); 4 D. Danner, Pattern Interrogatories: Products Liability (1972) (defendants' and plaintiffs' interrogatories); L. Frumer & M. Friedman, Products Liability §47.04 (asbestos case interrogatories); J. Kelner, Personal Injury: Successful Litigation Techniques 1-439 (1981) (court orders and deposition transcript in toxic tort cases).

Persons in state receiving shipments

Distributors who ship the defendant's products to forum state

Advertisements or solicitations directed to forum state

Correspondence and telephone calls between the defendant and the forum state

Property interests of the defendant in forum state

Contracts by the defendant executed or performed in forum state

Litigation in forum state involving the defendant as party

Taxes paid by the defendant in forum state

Trips by the defendant's employees in forum state

History of Substance's Manufacture or Sale

Chemical composition and identifying characteristics of substance in question and of products in which it is placed

Names under which sold or used

All entities in line of distribution of product; all parties whom the defendant alleges to be responsible for the plaintiff's injuries

How the defendant's product may be distinguished from competitors' and all manufacturers making similar products

First commercial use of substance and by whom

All intended or expected uses of substances

Development and by whom

Company memos and correspondence concerning substance

How tested and by whom

Express warranties and advertisements made concerning the defendant's products containing the substance, including all media used to promote the product

Defendant's Knowledge of Potential Danger

The defendant's awareness of potential dangers posed by the substance, studies made to learn of dangers or studies relied upon to conclude there was no danger

Warning or instructions given and to whom, when given, and by whom

Studies or tests to determine health risk of substance

Governmental safety regulations considered in development and sale of the product

Submissions concerning the substance given by the defendant to any government agency; results of all government investigation of the substance in question

Statutes and regulations governing manufacture, sale, and use of the defendant's product

Changes in design or marketing of product, and the reasons for them

Investigation of means considered to make use of product more safe—such as engineering controls, protective equipment, minimizing amount of toxic material, and discovering nontoxic substitutes

Means of quality control used in the manufacture of the product

All claims filed against the defendant alleging harm from the substance (workers' compensation; other claims)

Methods used in monitoring of exposure and medical surveillance of users

All organizations to which the defendant belongs that participate in researching the substance in question, setting standards for same, or communicating with government employees regarding same

All pertinent books and publications in the defendant's library

All persons in charge of product safety

All testimony by employees, officers, or persons retained for that purpose in any litigation or in any public hearing

Other

The defendant's liability insurance coverage

The defendant's assets and net worth

§15.15 Defendant's Discovery

Items which a defendant would want to obtain in discovery are listed in this section in outline form.

Basis of Plaintiff's Claim

The facts upon which the plaintiff claims he or she has been damaged by the defendant's substance

Every person who has knowledge of the plaintiff's injuries or from whom the plaintiff or his or her representatives have taken a statement

All persons to whom the plaintiff has complained of the injuries now complained of, with dates, identities, and substance of complaint

All statements made by the plaintiff's pertaining to the circumstances of this action

Plaintiff's Exposure to Toxic Substance

The circumstances of exposure

The plaintiff's experience with similar products

The means by which the plaintiff identified the toxic substance as defendant's

Training and written or oral warnings provided by the plaintiff's employer with respect to exposure

The plaintiff's ability to understand and control product

Union membership and receipt of literature discussing the toxic substance in question

Plaintiff's Medical and Occupational History

Name, address, birth date, physical description, and Social Security number

Physical history of natural parents and children

Complete school and job history including compensation, nature of job, and whether any toxic substance was involved

All accidents, serious illnesses, operations, mental or physical abnormalities, and relationship, if any, to damages now claimed

The plaintiff's workers' compensation filings, if any

All applications for insurance

Each medical problem alleged to be related to this action, with date it became manifest

All medical treatments, hospital records, laboratory tests, and medical surveillance reports

For each medical condition, date of diagnosis, if any, person making diagnosis, therapy prescribed, progress of therapy, and degree to which the plaintiff cooperated

Use of tobacco, alcohol, or other drugs

Hobbies, diet, and lifestyle

Damages

How medical condition has altered the plaintiff's lifestyle

Total time lost from employment because of injuries identified in complaint

Dates for which the plaintiff had doctor's excuse

Damages sought for loss of earning capacity

Any experts employed for purpose of testimony

Itemized charges for medical services and medicine

Date of each payment and person to whom paid

All claims for benefits from insurance companies or from federal, state, or local government, with description of benefits, amounts and dates of payments, and names of payors

The means and scope of discovery are matters of procedural rules. In federal courts, Rules 26 through 37 of the Federal Rules of Civil Procedure govern these matters. These rules, adopted to expand the use of discovery, have been adopted verbatim or in substance by a large number of jurisdictions.[97]

§15.16 Means of Discovery

Discovery may be sought by a wide variety of means, including oral or written depositions, written interrogatories, production of documents or things, permission to enter property to inspect, physical and mental examination, and requests to admit facts, to admit applications of law to fact, or to verify the genuineness of documents. The use of these methods may be limited by the trial court's protective order or by local rules, some of which, for example, limit the number of interrogatories that may be used in the absence of good cause to use more.

Some discovery may occur even prior to commencement of suit. A plaintiff may, for example, be able to obtain a list of potential defendants informally by requesting it of a prospective defendant who, by supplying the list, can hope to persuade the plaintiff to sue a more responsible defendant. Prospective parties may also use formal preaction discovery in the form of a deposition under Rule 27 of the Federal Rules of Civil Procedure, which authorizes such a procedure to perpetuate testimony upon the filing of a verified petition in the federal district in which the expected adverse party resides. Rule 27 makes this procedure available where the petitioner is "presently unable to bring [an action] or cause it to be brought" and where the court is "satisfied that the perpetuation of testimony may prevent a failure or delay of justice." The procedure is particularly helpful to a prospective defendant when the prospective plaintiff is dying. The deposition testimony may later be admissible as evidence at trial if the deponent is dead or unable to testify because of illness.[98]

The attorney for any party may move for a conference on the subject of discovery, proposing a schedule of discovery and limitations thereon, if the parties have been unable to agree on a plan of discovery. The court may also order such a conference on its own motion.[99] The discovery conference is ordinarily reserved for complex discovery problems, however, with relatively narrow discovery disputes being resolved by resort to protective orders or orders to compel discovery.[100]

---

[97] For a state-by-state analysis, see 11 Bender's Forms of Discovery App (A. Sann & S. Bellman eds 1982).

[98] Fed R Civ P 32(a)(3).

[99] Id 26(f).

[100] E.g., McClurrey v Jos Schlitz Brewing Co, 504 F Supp 1264 (ED Wis 1981).

§15.17   Scope of Discovery

Substantively, discovery under the federal rules and similarly liberal state rules extends, presumptively at least, to any nonpriviledged matter that is either relevant to the subject matter of the action or "appears reasonably calculated to lead to the discovery of admissible evidence."[101] Material within this definition must be produced even though the information is already known to the receiving party and even if discovery would be burdensome, unless the party from whom discovery is sought can show that it needs protection from annoyance, embarrassment, oppression, or undue burden or expense.[102] An exception may apply to the production of documents, in that Rule 34 of the Federal Rules of Civil Procedure formerly required *good cause* for the production of documents, a requirement that many states continue to impose.[103]

In the event that a party breaches its duty to provide discovery, a broad array of discovery sanctions are available, including the award of costs, the deeming of certain facts established, and in extreme cases, the entry of judgment against the offending party.[104] Limits to the scope of discovery generally are litigated in the context of the nonmoving party's motion for a protective order[105] or the moving party's motion for an order compelling discovery or for sanctions.[106]

§15.18   Other Complaints or Injuries

Discovery by the plaintiff in virtually every toxic tort case includes interrogatories requesting information on any other complaint that the defendant has received concerning the toxic substance in question. Thus, the defendant might be served with interrogatories asking the defendant to identify, for each person who has claimed to be injured by defendant's toxic substance, the complainant, complainant's attorney, the date of injury, and nature of the injury alleged in the complaint. The discovery also inquires into whether lawsuits were filed in connection with any of these complaints and asks the defendant to identify and to produce, by way of a request for production of documents, any discovery the defendant produced in any such litigation. The defendant is also asked to disclose the identity of any expert witnesses that prior complainants have retained.

Through this means, the plaintiff may be able to obtain information valuable to his or her lawsuit. For example, the plaintiff's counsel may learn the identity

---

[101] Fed R Civ P 26(b).

[102] *Id* 26(c), 37(a)(2).

[103] See 11 Bender's Forms of Discovery 2-11 (A. Sann & S. Bellman eds 1972). The former *good cause* requirement is discussed in Moore's Federal Practice ¶34.08 (2d ed 1982).

[104] *See* Fed R Civ P 37(b).

[105] *Id* 26(c).

[106] *Id* 37(a).

of expert witnesses and of other plaintiff's attorneys who have analyzed or handled similar claims. The previous discovery may also be a direct aid to the plaintiff as evidence in his or her case, to the extent that it consists of admissions or information that the plaintiff may authenticate or verify through a request for admission. The plaintiff also may move to make the prior discovery a part of the record.[107]

Discovery of prior complaints has generally been allowed on the ground that they are relevant, directly or indirectly, to the issues of whether the defendant had notice of its products' dangerous properties and whether the product caused the plaintiff's injuries. Thus, in *Tytel v Richardson-Merrill, Inc,*[108] in which the plaintiffs alleged harm from their consumption of the defendant's drug, the court directed the defendant to answer interrogatories inquiring into the number of claims by persons claiming to have sustained personal injury as a result of using the drug and asking the defendant to identify all doctors, attorneys, litigation, and expert witnesses associated with the claims. The court held that the information sought might aid the plaintiffs in demonstrating that their injuries were caused by the drug and not by any peculiar sensitivities which they might have had. Moreover, even if the information requested were to be held inadmissible at the trial, the court found that "the testimony sought appears reasonably calculated to lead to the discovery of admissible evidence."[109] The court noted, however, that it might be favorable to limiting discovery in this regard if full compliance with these interrogatory requests were shown to be "unduly burdensome."[110]

---

[107] *See, e.g.,* Baldwin-Montrose Chem Co v Rothbert, 37 FRD 354 (SDNY 1964) (reading Fed R Civ P 26(d) and 42(a) to order use of discovery provided in one action in second action involving common questions of law or fact). See generally Lubin & Crowe, *An Effective Approach to the Preparation of a Product Liability Case,* Boston Bar J 14 (Feb 1982).

[108] 37 FRD 351 (SDNY 1965).

[109] *Id* 354.

[110] *Id. See also* Kozlowski v Sears, Roebuck & Co, 73 FRD 73 (D Mass 1976) (information concerning similar accidents involving allegedly defective pajamas subject to discovery notwithstanding claim of undue burden); Hess v Pittsburgh Steel Foundry & Mach Co, 49 FRD 271 (WD Pa 1970) (correspondence between defendant grinding wheel manufacturer and other companies concerning complaints and correspondence with defendant on ways to correct release of fumes and chemicals from polyurethane-bounded grinding wheels); Bowen v Whitehall Laboratories, Inc, 41 FRD 359 (SDNY 1966) (prior complaints received by defendant from other users of its product, *Heet,* complaints discoverable because they "could conceivably aid plaintiff to establish that defendant had knowledge of the dangerous nature of the product and possibly lead to the discovery of other evidence relating to the products' effect on its users;" complaints after plaintiff's lawsuit also discoverable as "they might lead to discovery of other evidence pointing out how the products work [and] . . . whether plaintiff's injuries were caused by his own peculiar susceptibilities . . . or followed upon the use of the product itself"); Cohen v Proctor & Gamble Distrib Co, 18 FRD 301 (D Del 1955) (prior complaints relevant to manufacturer's knowledge of dangerous qualities of detergent in question); Gillig v Bymart-Tintair, Inc, 16 FRD 393 (SDNY 1954) (plaintiff injured by hair dye may discover prior claims and suits of similar nature since they may lead to proof that defendant should have known its product was dangerous).

The request for information concerning other complaints may be so broad that the defendant may secure limitations on discovery. For example, in *Farnum v Bristol-Myers Co*,[111] where a plaintiff sought information on prior complaints from users of defendant's deodorant, the order of discovery was limited to disclosure of complaints of the same nature and to a period prior to defendant's use of a new formula and its institution of a warning not to use its product on broken skin or if a rash develops.[112] Moreover, it has been held that a defendant need not disclose whether it has settled other complaints or for how much.[113]

§15.19   Confidential Information

There are certain exceptions to the generally broad scope of discovery. First, discovery extends only to nonprivileged information. To the extent that information or documents would not be admissible at trial because they fall within a common law or statutory privilege, such as the attorney-client privilege or the physician-patient privilege, they are not discoverable at all. The toxic tort plaintiff alleging personal injuries typically will be held to waive his or her physician-patient privilege as to his or her injuries by virtue of bringing suit.[114] A second category covers material that is not privileged but is of such a nature that the party seeking discovery must show its need for the information and, in certain cases, its unavailability through means other than discovery. The principal examples of this kind of information are work product (discussed in §15.20), experts' testimony (discussed in §15.21), and trade secrets (discussed in §15.22).

§15.20   —Work Product

Work product—matters prepared in anticipation of litigation—is entitled to an absolute or qualified immunity to discovery, depending on its nature. A privilege applies to the "mental impressions, conclusions, opinions, or legal theory of an attorney or other representative of a party concerning the litiga-

---

[111] 107 NH 165, 219 A2d 277 (1966).

[112] *Id* 167, 219 A2d at 279-80. *See also* Proctor & Gamble Distrib Co v Superior Court, 268 P2d 199 (Cal App 1954) (detergent *Cheer* not shown to be similar enough to detergent *Tide* to justify reliance on complaints about one product to support user's claim as to the other).

[113] *E.g.,* Cohen v Proctor & Gamble Distrib Co, 18 FRD 301 (D Del 1955) (defendant need not disclose settlement of other complaints made by user of defendant's detergent).

[114] See generally Annot, 21 ALR3d 912 (1968) (commencing action involving physical condition of plaintiff or decedent as waiving physician-patient privilege as to discovery). *See also* Fed R Civ P 35 (court may order physical examination on party whose physical condition is in controversy).

tion."[115] A qualified protection applies to "documents and tangible things" prepared in anticipation for litigation for a party's representative.[116] These items are discoverable only upon a showing by the party seeking them that there is a "substantial need" to obtain them and an inability without "undue hardship" to obtain substantial equivalents of the items by other means.[117]

A threshold issue in work product controversies is whether the material in question was prepared for litigation, as opposed to being prepared in the regular course of the defendant's business. In *Fibron Products, Inc v Hooker Chemical Corp*,[118] the plaintiff was denied discovery of the investigatory report prepared by the defendant's employees after examining an explosion involving the defendant's liquid resin. The court held that this record was work product because it was not a record kept in the regular course of manufacturing and delivering resin.[119] On the other hand, accident reports filed by employees of a company as part of a normal business routine are not work product even if the company was on notice that a claim was likely.[120]

An issue arising in the case of the frequently sued defendant is whether the plaintiff may discover items that were work product in an already terminated litigation. Courts generally have held that the work product immunity from discovery should continue, especially if the present case and the prior case are closely related in parties or subject matter.[121]

§15.21 —Discovery of Facts Known and Opinions Held by Experts

Discovery of the opposing parties' experts is essential in a toxic tort case. The principal issue in such litigation is typically one of causation. While this issue is often well within the ken of a lay fact-finder in a traditional tort case, causation in a toxic tort case is often a matter of probability based upon expert medical testimony. In a lung cancer case brought by an asbestos worker, for example, medical opinion will be necessary to establish or refute the proposition that the plaintiff's lung cancer is a result of asbestos exposure as opposed to cigarette smoking or some occupational cause of cancer other than asbestos exposure. It is important to discover opposing expert opinion both to prepare for an intelligent cross-examination and to help prepare one's own experts.

---

[115] Fed R Civ P 26(b)(3).

[116] *Id.*

[117] *Id.* The rule is essentially a codification of the Supreme Court's decision in Hickman v Taylor, 329 US 495 (1947).

[118] 26 Misc 2d 779, 206 NYS2d 659 (NY Sup Ct 1960).

[119] *See also* McDougall v Dunn, 468 F2d 468 (4th Cir 1972); Burlington Indus v Exxon Corp, 65 FRD 26 (D Md 1974); Spaulding v Denton, 68 FRD 342 (D Del 1975).

[120] Virginia Elec & Power Co v Sun Shipbuilding & Dry Dock Co, 68 FRD 397 (ED Va 1975).

[121] See generally 41 ALR Fed 123 (1979) (attorney's work product privilege as applied to documents prepared in anticipation of terminated litigation).

In the federal courts, discoverability of expert opinion and underlying facts is governed by Rule 26(b)(4) of the Federal Rules of Civil Procedure. Prior to the rule, an expert opinion and its underlying facts were sometimes shielded from discovery as being privileged or protected as work product.[122] The rule removed these protections from the facts known and opinions held by an expert, but only as to experts expected to testify at trial. As to these experts, the opposing party may use interrogatories to obtain the expert's identity, the subject matter of his or her expected testimony, the substance of the facts and opinions on which the expert is expected to testify, and a summary of the grounds for each opinion. Further discovery, such as by deposition, may be had upon motion. An expert witness who is not identified in response to an interrogatory generally may not be called upon to testify at trial.[123] Although the rule mentions only the expert's identity, it can be argued that a party may also discover the expert's qualifications, as part of his or her identity, in order to advance the rule's purpose of aiding preparation for cross-examination.[124]

Upon discovering an adverse expert's qualifications and the basis of his or her testimony, a party may wish to make a pretrial motion to preclude the testimony of that expert witness at trial. Rule 104 of the Federal Rules of Evidence and the Manual for Complex and Multidistrict Litigation suggest that the admissibility of expert opinion may be tested prior to trial, although for tactical reasons counsel may wish to take the chance of reserving admissibility until the time of trial.[125]

As to the class of experts not expected to testify, discovery of facts and opinions may be had only upon a showing of "exceptional circumstances" under which it would be "impracticable" for the party seeking discovery to obtain the information by other means.[126] This provision for the nontestifying expert is explained as a balance between the desire to sharpen the issues at trial and the need to minimize the unfairness of having one party use another party's experts to prepare his or her own case.[127]

An arguable exception to the general protection for nontestifying experts applies to regular employees of a party.[128] For example, in *Virginia Electric & Power Co v Sun Shipbuilding & Dry Dock Co*,[129] the court reasoned that a regular employee who is also an expert could be deposed as an ordinary party witness

---

[122] *E.g.,* American Oil Co v Pennsylvania Petroleum Prods Co, 23 FRD 680 (DRI 1959) (chemical analysis privileged); Cold Metal Process Co of America, 7 FRD 684 (D Mass 1947) (x-ray analysis part of work product).

[123] Tabatchnick v GD Searle & Co, 67 FRD 49 (DNJ 1975) (plaintiff suing oral contraceptives manufacturer could not call upon expert witness whose identity was disclosed only after trial began and not in response to defendant's interrogatories).

[124] *See, e.g.,* Clark v General Motors Corp, 20 Fed Rules Serv 2d 679 (D Mass 1975).

[125] See Berens, *Pretrial Challenges to Expert Testimony,* 8 Litigation 27 (Summer 1982).

[126] Fed R Civ P 26(b)(4).

[127] *See, e.g.,* Grinnell Corp v Hackett, 70 FRD 326 (DRI 1976).

[128] See generally L. Frumer & M. Friedman, Products Liability §48.02 (1980).

[129] 68 FRD 397 (ED Va 1975).

"if his contact with the case is not in his capacity as an impartial observer, but is instead going about his duties as a loyal employee."[130] On the other hand, the court in *Seiffer v Topsy's International, Inc,*[131] held that an in-house expert was entitled to the protection of a nontestifying expert notwithstanding his regular employee status. In any event, an employee who has gained his or her knowledge or opinions in the ordinary course of business and not in anticipation of litigation would be to that extent subject to discovery as an ordinary witness, for Rule 26(b)(4) applies only to facts and opinions "acquired or developed in anticipation of litigation or for trial."

§15.22 —Trade Secrets

Trade secrets constitute another category of information which, while not absolutely protected from discovery, enjoys a qualified protection in that the moving party generally must show a special need for the information and an inability to acquire it elsewhere. Moreover, any disclosure that is required may be conditioned by the observance of safeguards to prevent widespread disclosure.

A toxic tort plaintiff is often interested in the defendant's product formulas and processes and customer lists, which may be directly or indirectly relevant to issues such as causation and the defendant's knowledge of dangers of its product. Disclosure of these items, however, obviously could undermine the defendant's competitive position in its industry. A party seeking to protect such items from discovery should move for a protective order, which a court may grant either by rule or by exercise of its own discretion. Rule 26(c)(7) of the Federal Rules of Civil Procedure, for example, provides that the trial court, "for good cause shown," may order that "a trade secret or other confidential research, development, or commercial information not be disclosed or be disclosed in a designated way."

A threshold question is whether the information sought qualifies as a trade secret or other confidential information deserving special protection from discovery. For example, in *Harrington Manufacturing Co v Powell Manufacturing Co,*[132] a customer list was discoverable because it was held not to be a trade secret under state law.

If the material being sought constitutes a trade secret, courts require the plaintiff to make a showing that the information is relevant and material or, more stringently, that the information is essential to the plaintiff's case.[133]

---

[130] *Id* 399.

[131] 69 FRD 69 (D Kan 1975).

[132] 26 NC App 414, 216 SE2d 379, *cert denied,* 288 NC 242, 217 SE2d 679 (1975).

[133] Tymko v K-Mart Discount Stores, Inc, 75 AD2d 987, 429 NYS2d 119 (1980) (formula of defendant's tanning lotion "material and necessary" to plaintiff's theories of negligent mixing and negligent design, but disclosure limited by order to parties, counsel, experts, and officers of the court); Farnum v Bristol Myers Co, 219 A2d 277 (NH 1966) (trade secrets such as ingredients in defendant's deodorant formula not

Some courts may go still further and require a showing that the information sought is not available through other means.[134]

Disclosure of a trade secret may be limited to certain particulars and may be subjected to special safeguards to limit the scope of dissemination. For example, in *Farnum v Bristol-Myers Co*,[135] a deodorant manufacturer was required to disclose the ingredients of its product, but not the percentage of each ingredient by volume or weight.[136] And in *McLaughlin v GD Searle, Inc*,[137] disclosure of trade secrets of a birth control pill manufacturer was limited by court order to counsel working on the case, experts reasonably necessary for preparation, and any court supervising the disclosure.[138]

§15.23   Freedom of Information Act

When information relevant to a toxic tort suit is believed to be held by a federal or state agency, the federal Freedom of Information Act (FOIA)[139] or a state freedom of information act may be used as a supplement to the ordinary rules of discovery.[140] For example, in a drug case, the plaintiff might be able to buttress his or her allegation of inadequate warnings of danger with records in the possession of the federal Food and Drug Administration (FDA).[141] An FOIA request may also be used, of course, to verify the accuracy and thoroughness of the defendant's responses to discovery requests.

Although not designed as a means of discovery, FOIA provides access to agency records regardless of whether the person requesting records is a liti-

---

absolutely protected but ordinarily not discoverable "except in case of urgent necessity, and subject to protective orders by the court when justice so requires").

[134] *See, e.g.,* Cronin v Pierce & Stevens Chem Corp, 366 AD2d 764, 321 NYS2d 239 (1971) (discovery disallowed as to density, flammability, and combustibility of defendant's floor-finishing products because defendant asserted they were trade secrets and because plaintiff could obtain information from her own expert and analysis); Bleacher v Bristol Myers Co, 163 A2d 526 (Del 1960) (manufacturer's secret process or formula need not be revealed unless clearly relevant, necessary to plaintiff's case, and not available through other means). See generally Annot, 17 ALR2d 383 (1951) (discovery or inspection of trade secrets).

[135] 107 NH 185, 219 A2d 277 (1966).

[136] *See also* Hyman v Revlon Prods Corp, 227 AD 118, 100 NYS2d 937 (1950) (discovery permitted as to ingredients of cosmetic, but not as to defendant's formula used in the product's manufacture, unless adequate analysis not available).

[137] 38 AD2d 810, 328 NYS2d 899 (1972).

[138] *See also* Bristol Myers Co v District Court, 161 Colo 354, 422 P2d 373 (1967) (confidential documents relating to defendant's drug *Kantrex* to be protected by arrangement made by clerk of court).

[139] 5 USC §552.

[140] See generally Levine, *Using The Freedom of Information Act as a Discovery Device,* 36 Bus Law 45 (1980).

[141] See, e.g., Forde & Kennelly, *The Preparation of a Drug-Caused Injury Case,* 1976 Trial Law Guide 409, 414-16 (FDA records contained evidence that defendant's drug created danger of specific adverse side effects).

gant. Section 552(a)(3) of FOIA requires full agency disclosure upon a request reasonably describing the records sought and upon compliance with the agency's rules regarding the time, place, and fees governing disclosure, except to the extent that the information fails within one of nine statutory exemptions.[142] If the agency in question refuses or otherwise fails to produce the requested data, the requester may file an action in federal district court to compel disclosure.[143]

In certain cases, a person, such as a defendant corporation, may bring a reverse FOIA suit to prevent disclosure.[144] The submitter may not itself enforce an exemption, however; only the agency can do that. That is, the FOIA exemptions are permissive rather than mandatory, and even persons who have submitted information to the government with the expectation that it would be kept confidential may not prevent agency disclosure by a suit to enforce one or more of FOIA's exemptions.[145] Nevertheless, a party affected by a proposed disclosure of information may challenge the disclosure as an abuse of agency discretion under the Administrative Procedure Act.[146]

The FOIA exemptions of greatest potential significance in a toxic tort context are Exemption 4, the trade secret exemption, and Exemption 3, the *another statute* exemption. While the FOIA exemptions are not mandatory, they may be relied upon by a court to determine whether the agency's disclosure would abuse its discretion.[147] One prominent statute under Exemption 3 is the Trade

---

[142] The nine exemptions, listed in 5 USC §552, are:

1. Classified national defense or foreign policy secrets
2. Information related solely to "internal personnel rules" and agency practices
3. Information specifically exempted from disclosure by another statute
4. "[T]rade secrets and commercial or financial information obtained from a person and privileged or confidential"
5. Agency memoranda not available to a party, other than an agency, in litigation with the agency
6. Personnel, medical, and similar files whose disclosure "would constitute a clearly unwarranted invasion of personal privacy"
7. Certain investigatory records compiled for law enforcement purposes
8. Information concerning regulation of financial institutions
9. Geological and geophysical information concerning wells

Id (b).

[143] *Id* §552(a)(4).

[144] The agency often consults the submitter of requested information where an exemption might apply. *See, e.g.,* 21 CFR §20.45 (situations in which confidentiality is uncertain) (FDA FOIA regulation).

[145] *See* Chrysler Corp v Brown, 441 US 281 (1979). (FOIA affords no private right of action to enjoin agency disclosure of material within one of FOIA's nine exemptions).

[146] 5 USC §552. Chrysler Corp v Brown, 441 US 281 (1979) (agency decision to disclose may be reviewed at behest of aggrieved party under abuse of discretion standard).

[147] *See, e.g.,* Pennzoil Corp v PPC, 534 F2d 627 (5th Cir 1976) (Exemption 4 used to delineate scope of agency's discretion in proposed disclosure of information regarding natural gas reserves).

Secrets Act,[148] which makes it a crime for a federal government employee to disclose information coming to him or her in the course of his or her employment that relates to "trade secrets, processes, operations," unless such disclosure is authorized by some statute other than FOIA. For all practical purposes, the incorporation of the Trade Secrets Act through Exemption 3 may be coextensive with Exemption 4.[149]

Another statute relevant to disclosure by federal agencies is the Toxic Substances Control Act,[150] under which corporations are required to file information with the Environmental Protection Agency. Section 2613(a) of the act makes FOIA Exemption 4 mandatory, subject to certain exceptions.[151]

---

[148] 18 USC §1905.
[149] *See* Chrysler Corp v Brown, 441 US 281 (1979).
[150] 15 USC §2601 *et seq.*
[151] *Id* §2613(a).

16

Burdens of Proof*

D. Alan Rudlin, Esq.†

---

* The author would like to express his deep appreciation to David Dreifus, an associate in the Hunton & Williams' Raleigh, North Carolina office, and to Alfred R. Light, an associate in the Richmond office of Hunton & Williams, for their contributions and editorial assistance with this chapter.

† Partner, Hunton & Williams, Richmond, Virginia.

§16.01   Introduction

This chapter discusses burdens of proof in toxic substance injury and illness litigation. Victims of exposure to toxic substances often seek redress in workers' compensation actions or products liability actions against their employers or the manufacturers of the substances allegedly causing the injury. Because of the difficulty in establishing causation, however, many potential plaintiffs tend to rely on private medical insurance, Social Security, or other forms of compensation that do not require the identification of a responsible party or proof of causation.[1]

The burden of proof in workers' compensation cases is controlled by statute and varies from jurisdiction to jurisdiction. Therefore, burdens of proof in workers' compensation cases are difficult to discuss generally. The issue of toxic tort causation, particularly cancer causation, is frequently presented in workers' compensation actions, however. Those cases are discussed in §§16.02-16.11, to the extent the issues presented have general application to the issue of causation in civil litigation. In addition, approaches to the *reform* of causation rules in toxic tort cases often follow pathways which have been experimented with in workers' compensation cases—e.g., the use of statutory presumptions of compensability.[2]

In theory, the burden of proof in a toxic tort products liability action is no different than it is in any other civil action. The plaintiff must prove his or her case by a *preponderance of the evidence.* In order to do this, the plaintiff must present evidence that leads a jury to find that the existence of a contested fact is more probable than its nonexistence.[3] The burden of proof can be divided into two elements. The plaintiff is usually faced with the *burden of producing evidence* on each contested issue and also bears the risk of failing to convince the trier of fact that the facts are as he or she contends (the *burden*

---

[1] See, e.g., National Science Foundation, Compensation for Victims of Toxic Pollution—Assessing the Scientific Knowledge Base (PRA Research Report 83-6) 36-41, 92-93 (Mar 1983).

[2] See, e.g., Superfund Section 301(e) Study Group, Senate Comm on Environment and Public Works, 97th Cong, 2d Sess, Injuries and Damages from Hazardous Wastes—Analysis and Improvement of Legal Remedies 213-39 (Comm Print No 97-12, 1982) [(hereinafter referred to as the Superfund §301(e) Report)]; Trauberman, Statutory Reform of "Toxic Torts;" Relieving Legal, Scientific and Economic Burdens on the Chemical Victim (1983); S 917, 98th Cong, 1st Sess, 129 Cong Rec S 397 (Daily ed) (Mar 24, 1983); S 946, 98th Cong, 1st Sess, 129 Cong Rec S 3973 (Daily ed) (Mar 24, 1983); HR Rep No 2482, 98th Cong, 1st Sess, 129 Cong Rec Daily ed H 1992 (Apr 12, 1983); HR Rep No 2582, 98th Cong, 1st Sess (1983); HR Rep No 3175, 98th Cong, 129 Cong Rec Daily ed H 3430 1st Sess (May 26, 1983); cf Min HR Rep No 76, (enacted May 10, 1983) (prohibition of directed verdict on issue of causation).

[3] McCormick on Evidence, §339 (2d ed 1972).

of persuasion).[4] The following discussion of burdens of proof is concerned with the burden of presenting evidence rather than with the burden of persuasion.[5]

As a practical matter, the burden of proof in a toxic tort action is frequently more difficult to satisfy than in the typical negligence action. A toxic tort suit usually involves manufacturing activities (or other facts relating to exposure) as well as issues of adequacy of warning that are often far removed in both time and space from the manifestation of the injury. This factor often imposes a greater burden on both the plaintiff and the defendant to ferret out evidence to support their respective sides of the claim, and both plaintiff and defendant are more likely to have to rely on expert witnesses to supply missing evidence of causation.

Regardless of whether a plaintiff proceeds under a theory of negligence, breach of warranty, or strict liability, to recover compensatory damages in a toxic substance products liability case he or she must prove:

1. Exposure to a toxic substance connected with the defendant
2. Injury or illness to the plaintiff
3. A causal connection between the exposure and the injury
4. A measurement of the damages

In addition, the plaintiff must also show a duty on the part of the defendant to the plaintiff and a breach of that duty.[6]

There are two burden of proof problems that are particularly important in toxic substance litigation: causation in fact and product identification. Frequently, the inability of a plaintiff to establish causation in fact or to prove that the defendant produced the substance causing the injury results in the plaintiff's inability to recover damages in a traditional tort action. This situation has caused many commentators to suggest radical changes in the burdens of proof regarding causation in fact and product identification in toxic substance litigation.[7] Some courts have begun to shift the burden of proof to defendants to

---

[4] *Id.*

[5] *Id.* As McCormick notes, the burden of persuasion is more academic than real.

[6] W. Prosser, The Law of Torts §30 (4th ed 1971).

[7] See, e.g., Note, *Establishing Causation in Chemical Exposure Cases: The Precursor Symptoms Theory,* 35 Rutgers L Rev 163 (1982), which presents a theory of causation based on circumstantial evidence for plaintiffs who are otherwise unable to prove causation. The author suggests that proof of five elements would permit a plaintiff to rely on circumstantial evidence to establish causation:
   a. prolonged exposure to a chemical in its range of undemonstrable toxicity occurred;
   b. the level of exposure to the chemical in the undemonstrable range is associated with precursor symptoms and abnormalities;
   c. the plaintiff had or has precursor symptoms, or abnormalities associated with exposure to the chemical in the undemonstrable range of exposure;
   d. the plaintiff has an illness which is associated with exposure to a chemical in the demonstrable range of exposure and which is associated with the presence of the precursor symptoms or diseases; and

exculpate themselves from liability on selected issues after the plaintiff has met some relaxed threshold showing.[8] This area of the law is in transition. Certain barriers to recovery have broken down, and others are under attack. In some areas, trends appear to be emerging.[9] In other areas, the problems have been identified, but courts as yet have not squarely confronted them.[10]

Causation

§16.02   Proof

Causation in fact is an essential element of any personal injury action. If the plaintiff is unable to prove that the defendant is the cause in fact of plaintiff's injury, the plaintiff is not entitled to recover damages from the defendant.[11]

---

e. the length of time elapsed between exposure, the onset and duration of the precursor symptoms, and the ultimate development of the disease for which compensation is sought, is within the range of what has been observed for the onset of similar diseases or malignancies.

Id 190.

See also Note, *Tort Actions for Cancer: Deterrence, Compensation, and Environmental Carcinogensis,* 90 Yale L J 840 (1981) (author recommends the adoption of a list of carcinogenic substances and their dose-response curves by a federal agency in a rule-making procedure; once a cancer victim demonstrates exposure by the defendant to a threshold amount of a listed carcinogen, the burden of proof would shift to the defendant to prove that the exposure was not the cause of the plaintiff's cancer); Soble, *A Proposal for the Administrative Compensation of Victims of Toxic Substance Pollution: A Model Act,* 14 Harv J on Legis 683 (1977) (proposes a legislative solution to the problems of causation by creating rebuttable presumptions in favor of claimants and shifting the burden of proof to the defendants); Note, *DES and a Proposed Theory of Enterprise Liability,* 46 Fordham L Rev 963 (1978) (suggests shifting the burden of proof to the defendants in DES cases to exculpate themselves from liability). See also Trauberman, Statutory Reform of "Toxic Torts;" Relieving Chemical, Scientific and Economic Burdens on the Chemical Victim (EL1, 1983); Superfund §301(e) Report, *supra* note 2; National Science Foundation, *supra* note 1.

[8] There may be a trend in cases involving injury from the drug DES to shift the burden of proof to the defendants to show that they were not responsible for manufacturing the drug taken by a plaintiff's mother once the plaintiff has demonstrated that DES has caused the injury. *See* Sindell v Abbott Laboratories, 26 Cal 3d 588, 607 P2d 924, 163 Cal Rptr 132, *cert denied,* 449 US 812 (1980); Abel v Eli Lilly & Co, 94 Mich App 59, 289 NW2d 20 (1980); Bichler v Eli Lilly & Co, 79 AD2d 317, 436 NYS2d 625 (1981), *affd* 55 NY2d 571, 436 NE2d 182, 450 NYS2d 776 (1982); Ferrigno v Eli Lilly & Co, 175 NJ Super 551, 420 A2d 1305 (L Div 1980).

[9] *See* cases cited in note 8.

[10] The problem of plaintiffs' inability to establish causation in cancer cases has been extensively discussed. See articles cited in note 7. To date, the courts have not resolved this dilemma, and neither has science. See R. Shelton, Defending Cancer Litigation: The Causation Defense, for the Defense 8 (Jan 1, 1982).

[11] W. Prosser, The Law of Torts §41 (4th ed 1971). It should be remembered that

In many types of toxic substance litigation, the plaintiff has little problem proving causation in fact. For example, if the plaintiff is burned by acid in a drain cleaner[12] or is overcome by fumes from a highly toxic chemical,[13] it is relatively easy to establish that the exposure caused injury. Causation is often not disputed in such cases. Rather, the issue becomes one of liability, with questions such as: was the product defective, was the product unreasonably dangerous, was the use of the product by the plaintiff foreseeable, or was there intervening negligence on the part of the plaintiff making his or her activity rather than the defendant's the legal cause of the injury? While the plaintiff may be unable to recover, it is usually not due to the inability to prove causation in fact. In such cases, the injury, the identity of the toxic substance, the manufacturer of the substance, and the causal connection between the substance and the injury are all easy to prove.

There are many cases, however, in which causation in fact cannot be established by a plaintiff who clearly has an injury or illness. There are numerous examples. Toxic chemicals may leak into the groundwater from a chemical dump and pollute an individual's well.[14] If a number of manufacturers have deposited waste in the dump site for many years, it is virtually impossible for the plaintiff to prove which of the manufacturers is responsible for the pollution of his or her well by the leaking chemicals.

The same plaintiff whose well water is polluted by chemicals leaking from the dump may also become ill from drinking the water. He or she may develop

---

there is a distinction between the concepts of causation in fact and proximate causation. The former, as its name suggests, is concerned with the factual question of what caused an injury. It is often referred to as *but for* or *significant contribution* causation. A determination of proximate causation may involve equitable considerations, such as foreseeability, or a *cost/benefit* analysis of risk. See generally Note, *Toxic Substance Contamination: The Risk-Benefit Approach to Causation Analysis,* 14 Mich J L Reform 53 (1980).

[12] *See* Drayton v Jiffee Chem Corp, 395 F Supp 1081 (ND Ohio 1975), *affd,* 591 F2d 352 (5th Cir 1978).

[13] *See* Tampa Drug Co v Wait, 103 So 2d 603 (Fla 1958).

[14] This has been alleged to be the situation that has occurred at Love Canal in Niagara County, New York. Toxic chemicals buried in the 1940s and 1950s by Hooker Chemical Company have leaked into the groundwater and polluted hundreds of homes. The state of New York evacuated the entire area, purchased 239 homes, and spent more than $20 million in an effort to contain the migration of the hazardous waste. Residents of the area claim to have suffered a much higher than normal incidence of spontaneous abortions, congenital defects, and cancer. See Ginsberg & Weiss, *Common Law Liability for Toxic Torts: A Phantom Remedy,* 9 Hofstra L Rev 859 (1981). However, Hooker resisted the sale of Love Canal to the school district and clearly warned the purchasers of what was buried there. Also, a 1980 chromosome study which alarmed Love Canal residents has been discredited. See, e.g., Havender, *Assessing and Controlling Risks,* in Bardach & Kagen, Social Regulation: Strategies for Reform 21, 47, 50-51 (1982); Kolata, *Love Canal: False Alarm Caused by Botched Study,* 208 Science 1239 (Jan 13, 1980); Holden, *Love Canal Residents Under Stress,* 208 Science 1242 (Jan 13, 1980); Studies Show Conflicting Health Views of Residents Exposed to Love Canal Site, 14 Envir Rep (BNA) 128 (May 27, 1983).

cancer or other illnesses that he or she believes were a result of the exposure to the toxins in the well, or he or she may develop illnesses from other causes. If the plaintiff seeks to recover damages for his or her illness, he or she will face additional hurdles.

For example, while he or she may be able to prove that the chemicals found in the well have been shown to cause cancer in laboratory animals, he or she will still have to establish that the chemical causes cancer in humans and that his or her cancer was caused by exposure to the chemical. While he or she may be able to establish the first point, it is extremely difficult to establish the latter point because the specific causes for most forms of cancer are unknown. Most types of cancer are associated with many different causes. The plaintiff may be aided if he or she can show that there is a statistically significant correlation between exposure to the type of chemical found in his or her well and the type of cancer from which he or she suffers, but he or she will still be faced with the burden of proving that his or her individual cancer was actually caused by exposure to the chemical in the well. In addition, the studies establishing the causative correlation may be flawed. In this situation, the plaintiff may be faced with a burden of proof he or she cannot meet.[15]

Thus, the permutations of burden of proof and causation issues multiply almost geometrically as factual circumstances shift slightly. If a defendant produces a substance or pollutant, the resulting diseases from the pollutant may be linked by either epidemiological studies (based on human experience) or animal studies (based on extrapolation) to the particular pollutant. There may also be additional pollutants in a geographical area that interact synergistically to cause a disease, or there may be multiple toxic exposures unique to different individuals (e.g., smoking, asbestos insulation or lead paint in dwellings, or radiation exposure through frequent X-rays, through microwaves, or through high-altitude flying). In short, the potential problems of proving cau-

---

[15]   A tragedy involving residents living near Hemlock, Michigan presents a current illustration of this dilemma. Hemlock area residents allege that reinjection wells used for disposal of by-products of chemical manufacture have caused contamination of their well-water. The people in the area have suffered considerable health effects, including miscarriages, tumors, and nervous system disorders. State authorities have concluded, however, that insufficient evidence exists to establish a causal link between the complaints and private well water, notwithstanding official statements that the high incidence of health disorders in the Hemlock area is hard to explain. The Hemlock victims face virtually insurmountable barriers to relief, due to problems in proving the existence of toxic substances in their well water, in determining the movement of groundwaters, and the need for extensive and possibly unobtainable medical studies.

Note, *supra* note 11, at 54. On the possible abuses in the use of statistical studies to establish legal causation, see Dickson, *Medical Causation By Statistics*, 17 Forum 792 (1982). Two good analyses of the present scientific methodologies for establishing causation are National Research Council, Risk Assessment in the Federal Government: Managing the Process (1983) and Congressional Research Service, 98th Cong, 1st Sess, A Review of Risk Assessment Methodologies (Comm Print 1983).

sation are enormously varied and frequently complex as a scientific and factual matter.

§16.03 Immediate Injury

Exposure to toxic substances may cause injuries in a number of different ways. Exposure may cause immediate injury ranging from nausea to death. Immediate injury may be permanent or temporary. Exposure may cause no immediate injury, but injury may manifest itself years later after a prolonged latency period in the form of cancer.[16] These differences may be due to a substance having a high level of *acute toxicity* that causes damage shortly after exposure, or they may be due to the substance having a relatively benign acute toxicity, but a very potent *chronic toxicity*—i.e., causing injury after continued exposure over time. In the latter case, proving causation in fact may be quite difficult, and there may be troublesome statute of limitations problems. In the former case, however, proof of causation is usually relatively simple.

Tampa Drug Co v Wait[17] is an example of immediate injury caused by exposure to a toxic substance. The plaintiff's husband purchased a gallon of carbon tetrachloride technical[18] to use as a floor cleaner. The label attached to the bottle warned that the vapor from carbon tetrachloride was harmful and instructed the user to use it with adequate ventilation and to avoid prolonged or repeated breathing of vapor or contact with skin. The label also warned not to take the carbon tetrachloride internally.

While using the product to clean the floors of their home, the plaintiff's husband was overcome by fumes from the carbon tetrachloride, and he died two weeks later. The decedent was using the carbon tetrachloride in a room that was adequately ventilated (three windows and an outside door were open). The decedent also had a helper who was using the carbon tetrachloride in the same fashion. The helper suffered no ill effects from the carbon tetrachloride, even though he continued to use the product after decedent fell ill.

Notwithstanding the fact that the decedent had even less exposure to the carbon tetrachloride than his helper, causation in fact of decedent's death was not an issue. The court stated:

> It is clear from the record that this chemical can produce harmful results, even death, when taken internally, when the vapor therefrom is breathed excessively or when the skin is subjected to prolonged contact with it. The effect of excessive exposure in any one of the three forms is that the circulatory system becomes saturated with the toxic vapors with the result

---

[16] For example, asbestosis, mesothelioma, or lung cancer caused by exposure to asbestos may not manifest itself until 30 years or more after the exposure. See Selikoff, *Asbestos Disease in the United States,* in Toxic Torts 140 (Reingold ed 1977).

[17] 103 So 2d 603 (Fla 1958).

[18] Carbon tetrachloride technical is 100% pure carbon tetrachloride that has not been diluted with any other substance. *Id* 605.

that the kidneys and liver completely deteriorate. When this happens, of course, death results as it did in the instant case.[19]

The principal disputed issue was whether the warning on the label was adequate and, if not, whether the defendant's failure to warn of the dangers associated with the use of carbon tetrachloride was negligent. The court ruled that the plaintiff met her burden of proof on these issues and affirmed the judgment in her favor.[20]

Most immediate-injury cases involve exposure to a known substance that produces a known injury. Usually, the major disputed issue in these cases is the applicable standard of care. Many immediate-injury cases involve voluntary exposure to the defendant's products, with an unanticipated result,[21] as was the case in *Tampa Drug Co.*[22] Many cases do not involve a voluntary exposure by the plaintiff, however. For example, in *Owens v United States,*[23] the plaintiff's cattle pond was poisoned by insecticide. The insecticide was applied to a neighbor's land by employees of the United States Department of Agriculture (USDA). During a rainstorm, the insecticide washed into a creek bed and drained into the plaintiff's pond. Shortly after the rainstorm, agents of the USDA tested the plaintiff's pond and found that it was poisoned with insecticide. At the expense of the government, a fence was erected on the plaintiff's property enclosing the creek and pond and about 10 to 15 acres of his land.

The plaintiff brought suit under the Federal Tort Claims Act,[24] charging that the USDA negligently used powdered insecticide in close proximity to the creek.[25] The government admitted that the pond was poisoned with insecticide

---

[19] *Id* 605-06.

[20] As to the burden of proof on the issue of liability the court stated:

> The burden remains on one who claims a negligent failure to warn of an inherent danger to prove that the distributor knew, or by the exercise of reasonable care should have known, of the potential danger and in the reasonable course of his business should be able to foresee the possible uses of the commodity as well as the potential damage or injury that might result from such use.

Id 609.

[21] *See e.g.,* Drayton v Jiffee Chem Corp, 395 F Supp 1081 (ND Ohio 1975), *affd,* 591 F2d 352 (6th Cir 1978). In *Drayton,* the plaintiff suffered severe disfiguring burns when a drain cleaner sold for residential use was accidently spilled on her face by her father. The district court found the defendant liable on theories of negligence, breach of express and implied warranty, and strict liability and awarded $1,620,000 in damages to the plaintiff, who was seven years old at the time of trial. On appeal, the court upheld the finding of liability, but only on the theory of breach of express warranty, and reduced the damage award by almost $1 million.

[22] Tampa Drug Co v Wait, 103 So 2d 603 (Fla 1958).

[23] 294 F Supp 400 (SD Ala 1968).

[24] 28 USC §1346(b).

[25] As damages, the plaintiff claimed the loss of his pond, the loss of good pasture land, the costs of drilling a well to supply his cattle with water, and the costs of additional feed. In addition, the plaintiff claimed that the loss of acreage and the resulting greater concentration of his cattle was the direct cause of his cattle contracting brucellosis,

and admitted that the fence was constructed to keep the cattle from the area. Thus causation in fact was conceded: the plaintiff's pond had been poisoned by insecticide applied by defendant on the adjoining property. The government denied liability, however, on the grounds that it was not negligent and that an act of God (an unusually heavy rainstorm) caused the insecticide to poison plaintiff's pond. The court defined the plaintiff's burden of proof:

> In an action by a person in possession of real property against the United States Government for damages caused by the alleged negligence of employees of the Government in failing to exercise due care in the application of a poisonous insecticide, the burden is upon the person in possession to show there was a breach of the duty to exercise due care and that the breach of the duty by the Government was the cause of the plaintiff's injury or loss.[26]

The court determined that the USDA was negligent in using powdered insecticide near the banks of a creek and that the rainstorm was not an intervening act of God because it was foreseeable. The plaintiff was permitted to recover for damages to his property.[27]

§16.04 Delayed Injury

In many cases, exposure to a toxic substance does not cause immediate injury. For example, a single exposure to asbestos dust may have no effect on an individual for years but may eventually result in asbestosis or lung cancer. The latency period for asbestosis may be 30 years or more. Exposure to a toxic substance in small amounts may produce no immediate injury, but the cumulative effect of repeated exposures may eventually produce serious injury.

Proving causation is more difficult in cases in which the injury is not immediate because the causal connection is not as clear. In some instances, causation may be apparent, but in other cases it will be vigorously disputed. Proof of causation in this type of case always depends on expert medical testimony. If both sides present experts on the question of causation, a jury question is presented. In order to sustain the burden of proof necessary to avoid a directed verdict on causation, the plaintiff must present evidence showing that it is more

---

known as *bangs disease,* approximately 16 months after his pond had been poisoned. 294 FSupp at 402-03.

[26] *Id* 403.

[27] The court refused to allow plaintiff any damages for loss of his cattle from bangs disease, however. The court stated:

> The Court finds no causal connection with the Government's negligence in April, 1964, and the cattle's subsequent contact with the bangs disease in July 1965. The time element between the chemical application and the first indication of the bangs disease is far too remote for any causal connection with the Government's action.

Id 405. Thus, the plaintiff failed to prove *proximate cause,* as opposed to *causation in fact.*

likely than not that his or her injury was caused by the defendant. Where there have been multiple exposures to different toxic or other injury-causing substances, the burden of proof on causation (i.e., does X cause Y?) may become a burden of proof regarding apportionment (how much of Y is caused by X?).

In *Roberts v United States*,[28] the plaintiff was exposed to a toxic substance, ethylene glycol, from February through April of 1957. Plaintiff worked as a mechanic, testing hydraulic arresting gear for leaks. He tested the gears by filling them with ethylene glycol and bleeding them to release residual air. Whenever Mr. Roberts opened the gears to test for leaks, ethylene glycol mist was released and came in contact with his head, shoulders, face, chest, arms, and stomach.

The plaintiff first began to experience problems with his vision in June 1957. His eyesight steadily deteriorated, and he was forced to quit his job in December 1957. At the time of trial, plaintiff was virtually blind, suffered from other nerve and organic disorders, and was permanently and totally incapacitated. Plaintiff alleged his injuries were the result of his exposure to ethylene glycol.

At trial, defendants denied causation. The defendants argued that the only empirical evidence about exposure to ethylene glycol showed that internal injury, primarily kidney damage, could result from oral ingestion. There was no evidence, defendants argued, showing that ethylene glycol could cause the injuries from which the plaintiff suffered, or that the manner in which plaintiff was exposed could cause any damage at all.

The plaintiff presented three medical experts who testified that his injuries were caused by his exposure to ethylene glycol. The defendants argued that this testimony was insufficient as a matter of law because the plaintiff's experts all admitted the only cases of injury from ethylene glycol of which they knew resulted from oral ingestion. The defendants also argued that testimony concerning experiments in which rats were exposed to ethylene glycol mist was not probative. The court rejected these arguments, holding that the question of causation was for the jury:

> Each [of plaintiff's experts] had an impressive background and substantial experience in dealing with disorders caused by toxic substances. Each was familiar with literature on the toxic effects of ethylene glycol when orally ingested. Dr. Brieger had performed experiments in which rats were subjected to ethylene glycol mist. While neither knew cases, other than of oral ingestion, in which ethylene glycol had neurotoxic effects, both concluded that plaintiff's disorder was a toxic disease of his nervous system caused by exposure to ethylene glycol. This testimony was for the jury. It was not destroyed because their only experience or knowledge had been with cases of oral ingestion.[29]

The court noted that the defendants conceded that ethylene glycol was toxic

---

[28] 316 F2d 489 (3d Cir 1963).
[29] *Id* 492.

and that there was significant evidence that exposure to ethylene glycol mist was hazardous. The plaintiff's and the defendants' experts differed mainly in the conclusions they drew concerning the type and quantity of exposure and the effects of exposure. The court submitted the case to the jury on a failure-to-warn theory. The jury returned a $210,000 verdict for the plaintiff that was upheld on appeal.

Toxic tort litigation frequently presents cases of first impression concerning the effects of particular chemicals. The defendants in *Roberts* argued, in effect, that the plaintiff should not be allowed to recover because there was no scientific evidence of an injury such as he suffered being caused by ethylene glycol. This argument raises the question of *foreseeability* or *proximate cause* and not the question of causation in fact.[30] If a plaintiff produces evidence that exposure to a toxic substance caused his or her injury, his or her burden of presenting evidence is met, and a jury question is presented.

Although proof of causation in delayed-injury cases is more difficult than in immediate-injury cases, the plaintiff is often able to present enough evidence to get to the jury. Cases of this type in which plaintiffs have carried their burdens of proof include an airplane crash allegedly caused by the pilot's prolonged exposure to crop dust,[31] a heart attack suffered after prolonged

---

[30] *See* Olgers v Sika Chem Corp, 437 F2d 90 (4th Cir 1971). Plaintiffs' decedent died of aplastic anemia alleged to have been caused by prolonged exposure to the vapors, fumes, and dust of an epoxy bonding material produced by the defendant. The jury returned a $150,000 verdict for the plaintiff. The Fourth Circuit stated:

> Admittedly, prior to the trial, there was no known case of aplastic anemia's being caused by the components of defendant's product, singly or in combination, but there was sufficient evidence from which the jury could find that defendant should have anticipated that serious injury could result from any failure to warn adequately. This was enough as to the issue of foreseeability.

Id 91.

[31] Gonzalez v Virginia-Carolina Chem Co, 239 F Supp 567 (EDSC 1965), was an action for injuries suffered in the crash of a crop-dusting plane by the pilot. The plaintiff claimed the crash was caused by prolonged exposure to the defoliant he was using to dust crops. The plaintiff, an experienced crop-dusting pilot, had been dusting crops with a defoliant known as Folex for three or four days prior to his crash. On the day of the crash, plaintiff was suddenly overcome by nausea and dizziness and was unable to control his airplane. When the plane crashed, the hopper carrying the defoliant burst open and the plaintiff was covered with Folex. In addition to the physical injuries suffered in the crash, plaintiff suffered severe systemic shock as a result of his exposure to the chemical in the Folex, which made it more difficult to treat his physical injuries. The shock from exposure to the defoliant was itself life-threatening. Plaintiff's recovery from his physical injuries was incomplete because the systemic shock prevented doctors from operating for several days.

At trial, the evidence showed that the active ingredient in Folex was tributyl phosphorotrithioite, a highly toxic organic phosphorous compound. The evidence showed that exposure to small amounts of the substance over a period of several days could have a cumulative effect, causing the nausea and dizziness the plaintiff suffered immediately before he lost control of his airplane. In addition, the evidence showed that exposure to Folex in large quantities, such as occurred when the plane crashed and the dust was dumped all over him, could cause life-threatening systemic shock. The court

exposure to benzene,[32] brain damage suffered from alleged exposure to an insecticide,[33] and dermatitis allegedly caused by exposure to permanent wave solution.[34] Simply because the plaintiff meets the burden of producing evidence, however, does not mean the burden of persuasion has been satisfied.[35]

---

determined that the plaintiff's injuries were caused by his exposure to the defendant's product. The court determined that the warning provided on the defoliant was inadequate as a matter of law and that the defendant had breached the common law duty to the plaintiff to test the defoliant adequately for its possible toxic effect on humans. In addition, the court found that the defendant had no knowledge of an antidote for the symptoms caused by long exposure to its product. The court awarded $40,000 to the plaintiff.

[32] Smith v Ithaca Corp, 612 F2d 215 (5th Cir 1980), affirmed the district court's finding that the plaintiff's husband suffered a heart attack as a result of extended exposure to benzene fumes. The decedent was a crewman on a tanker known as the SS V.A. FOGG for 161 days. During 41 days of that time, the tanker was transporting benzene. Two days after he was discharged from the FOGG, the decedent suffered a fatal heart attack.

The decedent suffered from a preexisting heart condition. The plaintiff established through expert testimony that benzene is a toxic substance and that sufficient concentrations of benzene vapors are harmful. The fumes are a toxic poison affecting heart disorders and arteriosclerosis. An expert testified that benzene fumes would have had an aggravating effect on the decedent's underlying cardiovascular condition. A medical toxicologist testified that six to eight weeks of exposure to benzene could precipitate the chronic effects of poisoning.

The plaintiff's theory of liability was that the defendant negligently exposed her husband to benzene fumes for an extended period of time. The district court found that the decedent had been exposed to benzene fumes for 41 days and entered judgment for the plaintiff. The defendant challenged a number of the court's findings, including the finding that Mr. Smith was exposed to benzene fumes for at least 41 days. The defendant contended that the only times Mr. Smith could have been exposed to benzene fumes were the nine days when the ship was either loading, discharging, or cleaning the benzene tanks. It argued this was insufficient exposure to benzene to have any effect on a person's heart.

There was testimony from a crew member of the FOGG that during the time of Mr. Smith's employment, benzene fumes were present in the ship's quarters constantly and that benzene fumes entered the ship's ventilation system and remained in the air. The court found that failure to prevent benzene fumes from getting into the ship's ventilation system was negligence and rendered the vessel unseaworthy under general maritime law. This verdict was upheld on appeal.

[33] Skogen v Dow Chem Co, 375 F2d 692 (8th Cir 1967). The plaintiff alleged that his 13- and 16-year-old sons suffered brain damage as a result of exposure to an insecticide manufactured by the defendant. The plaintiff produced two experts who testified that the boys' injuries were the result of organo-phosphate poisoning caused by exposure to the defendant's insecticide. The defendant presented overwhelming evidence that showed that the boys' injuries were caused by viral encephalitis and not organo-phosphate poisoning. In addition, the defendant presented evidence showing that the chemical in the insecticide had an extremely low level of toxicity for humans, thereby making adverse reactions in humans extremely unlikely. The case was submitted to the jury, which found no causal connection between exposure to the insecticide and the boys' injuries.

[34] McDougle v Woodward & Lothrop, Inc, 312 F2d 21 (4th Cir 1963).

[35] See Skogen v Dow Chem Co, 375 F2d 692 (8th Cir 1967), discussed in note 33.

§16.05   Future Injury

A more interesting question than those discussed in §§16.03 and 16.04 is presented when the plaintiff seeks to recover for possible future injuries. Very few cases of this type have been litigated because of the necessarily speculative nature of the proof. Plaintiffs cannot prove with certainty whether they will suffer any future injuries.

At least one court has allowed recovery for possible future injury on the theory that the plaintiff's increased risk of contracting cancer is a present injury. In *Coover v Painless Parker, Dentist*,[36] the plaintiff brought an action for personal injury caused by overexposure to X-rays by her dentist. The plaintiff suffered severe burns on the side of her face as a result of the overexposure. In addition to claiming damages for the burns to her face, the plaintiff also claimed damages on the theory that her overexposure to the X-rays increased her likelihood of developing cancer. After a verdict for the plaintiff, the defendant argued that all testimony as to the possibility of plaintiff developing cancer was purely conjectural and that it was error to have submitted that issue to the jury.[37] The court held that increased risk of cancer was a proper element of damages and was properly considered by the jury. The court stated:

> Appellant argues that the evidence as to the possibility of cancer is wholly conjectural and uncertain, and that that element could not have rightfully been considered by the jury. The court instructed the jury that they were to consider as elements of damage only such physical injury as they may find the plaintiff is certain to suffer in the near future. If we assume that respondent's skin condition was considered by the jury, it by no means follows that this was improper. While the actual condition of cancer may have been conjectural and uncertain, the record contains positive evi-

---

[36] 105 Cal App 110, 286 P 1048 (1930). *See also In re* Three Mile Island Litigation, Civ No 79-9763 (MD Pa Dec 27, 1982) (permitting claim for "chromosomal damage and increased risk of cancer" to go forward).

[37] The plaintiff presented a medical expert who testified as follows about the possibility of the plaintiff's developing cancer.

> Q. In the event the sensory nerves have been destroyed, in this portion of the face that is burned or impaired, what would be the natural consequence of such a condition, in other words, what effect would that have on Mrs. Coover?
> A. The most important sequela from a dermatological standpoint is the possibility of carcinoma—of a cancer.
> In reply to questions by the court, he testified as follows:
> Q. I had more particular reference to the possibility of developing cancer.
> A. You say does it always? Not always.
> Q. It may happen that she can go on through life without that occurring, I suppose?
> A. It is possible, but we do find many times, carcinoma developing upon the scars of X-ray burns, in all our literature they speak of that as a very likely sequela, it is the thing to be guarded against and to be watched.

Id at 114, 286 P at 1049.

dence that a condition actually exists which makes this dread disease much more likely. We think this predisposition in itself is some damage, and, when caused by the wrongful act of another, it is an interference with the normal and natural conditions and rights of the other, which must be held to be a real and not a fanciful element of damage. The necessity of constantly watching and guarding against cancer, as testified to by the physician, is an obligation and a burden that the defendant had no right to inflict upon the plaintiff.[38]

In contrast to *Coover* is *Hahn v McDowell*,[39] in which a jury verdict for the plaintiff was reversed because two doctors were allowed to testify that the plaintiff should have a scar on his left leg removed and replaced with a skin graft because it was possible that cancer might develop in the site of the scar. The court held that this testimony was purely speculative and was improperly admitted. The court stated:

> Both expert witnesses were permitted, over the objection of the defendant, to testify that there was a possibility of cancer developing in the site of the scar. Neither doctor gave it as his opinion that such development was reasonably certain to result, nor even that it would probably result from the injury. We think the evidence was clearly incompetent and prejudicial. It is undoubtedly true that in an action to recover damages for personal injuries testimony of experts as to the future consequences which are expected to follow the injury are competent, but to authorize such evidence, however, the apprehended consequences must be such as in the ordinary course of nature, are reasonably certain to ensue. It is not enough for the doctor to testify to the possibility of a certain result; his testimony should show that it is reasonably certain to follow the injury. Consequences which are contingent, speculative, or merely possible are not proper to be considered by the jury in ascertaining the damages, for it would be plainly unjust to compel one to pay damages for results that may or may not ensue and which are merely problematical.[40]

The problem with recovery for future injury in toxic substance litigation is the difficulty of proving that future injury will occur. Although some courts may allow recovery for future injuries, there must be proof that the future injuries are reasonably likely to occur. Recovery is usually denied if the evidence shows no more than a possibility of future injury.[41]

The uncertain boundary of the current frontier of causation raises the con-

---

[38] *Id* at 115, 286 P at 1050.

[39] 349 SW2d 479 (Mo Ct App 1961).

[40] *Id* 482. *Hahn* was not a toxic substance case. Rather, the plaintiff suffered a burn in an automobile accident. The reasoning of the court would have equal application to a toxic tort case, however. Evidence of the statistical probability of a plaintiff developing cancer would be subject to the same objection raised by the defendant in *Hahn*.

[41] See Annot, 75 ALR3d 9 (1977).

cern whether courts will follow the reasoning of the *Coover* case and permit recovery for plaintiffs who argue they are probable *cancer candidates* as a result of exposure to a toxic substance. The liability exposure from such a trend is virtually limitless, given the fact that it is impossible to prove that a person will not (or even is unlikely) to contract cancer. The potential monetary exposure is similarly enormous, given the phobia of the public (which makes up the jury setting the damages awards) about cancer and the increasing tendency of juries to impose large verdicts against the business and other institutional defendants that will be the target defendants in toxic tort litigation.

Further questions abound. Should a plaintiff have to prove that he or she is likely to contract cancer or some other form of injury or diseases in the future (i.e., more than 50 per cent probability), or will it suffice for a plaintiff to show that he or she is more likely to contract the disease after the exposure than he or she was before the exposure (keeping in mind, for example, that the average probability of contracting cancer in America is one in four, with varying other probabilities according to different demographic characteristics)?[42] What, if anything, is to be done about the windfall to plaintiffs who recover but never thereafter realize the injury for which they have already been compensated? Similarly, should there be any concern for the windfalls that occur when a compensated plaintiff develops a disease such as cancer, yet the cause may or will not have been in fact the plaintiff's past exposure to the toxic substance that was the subject of the lawsuit?

Regardless of the answers to these important questions of legal and social policy, there may be less concern about the related issue of recovery for the negligent infliction of emotional distress—i.e., fear of a future disease such as cancer. In such cases, which are discussed in §16.06 if proper evidence is admitted to establish that the plaintiff's fear is genuine and has resulted from the toxic exposure, then logically the recovery is for a current real injury (i.e., emotional distress) and not a future speculative one. This result would be valid, it would seem, even if the fear is neurotic (i.e., irrational), although that question directly leads to the issue of foreseeability and proximate cause. Should the defendant have foreseen an irrational reaction by the plaintiff, or does the *eggshell skull* or hypersensitive plaintiff theory apply? Moreover, if the plaintiff's neurosis was developed by reading or hearing of imagined speculative harms in media coverage, has the exposure genuinely been the proximate cause of the emotional distress?

These questions must await future treatment by the courts, but it seems clear that these developments currently present creative plaintiffs with opportunities for new theories of causation, while presenting potential defendants with what may become diminished forms of defenses to toxic tort claims.

---

[42] See United States Congress, Office of Technology Assessment, Assessment of Technologies for Determining Cancer Risks from the Environment (June 1981).

§16.06   Cancer

There have been relatively few cases that have litigated the question of whether exposure to a particular toxic substance is the cause of a plaintiff's present cancer condition. Most of the cases that have addressed this issue are workers' compensation cases. Perhaps one of the reasons there are so few cases in this area is the inherent problem of proving what causes cancer and the existence of multiple causes in individual cases. These are questions that have not been resolved by the scientific and medical communities and to which there are understandably no definitive legal answers. Although there are statistical correlations between exposure to certain toxic substances and various forms of cancer, it is virtually impossible in most cases to say with any degree of certainty that a specific toxic substance exposure caused any individual case of cancer.[43] Moreover, although scientists and physicians have been willing to opine on cancer causation theories in a regulatory setting, these types of presumptions, while appropriate for preventative public policy decisions, are far less valid for use in civil litigation where the critical question is not how to prevent cancer risks from various substances, but whether a cancer has been or is likely to be caused by a particular substance.[44]

---

[43] This problem is illustrated in the radiation injury situation, a fairly common type of exposure:

> Scientists do not agree as to the causal connection between irradiation and some cancers. This is true of strontium-90 and bone cancer, and also of iodine-131 and cancer of the thyroid. The relationship between long-delayed leukemia and overexposure to at least high level radiation, however, is undisputed. The painful disabling and, eventually, fatal effects of leukemia are well recognized and the case for compensation seems obvious. Unfortunately, such injuries are not only long delayed but also in particular cases the connection with radiation is difficult to show with sufficient legal or scientific certainty to be acceptable under existing rules. In the first place, the connection can be measured only by a statistical increase in the incidence of the disease. Allowing damages relatively soon after exposure for any future possibility of occurrence of leukemia is a gamble unacceptable for an enlightened legal system. If suit should be delayed until the disease manifests itself, causal relationship to radiation is still impossible to prove with any degree of certainty for the specific case. This results from the fact that such diseases are non-specific as to cause; no differentiation can be made between radiation-caused leukemia and leukemia arising from those other forces which account for the natural incidence of this disease.

Estep, *Radiation Injuries and Statistics: The Need for a New Approach to Injury Litigation,* 59 Mich L Rev 259, 266-67 (1960). A few types of human cancer are said to be so rare as to permit, on the basis of animal studies, the inference that a certain substance was likely the cause of the particular cancer. An example of this theory is a type of liver carcinoma that some scientists link directly to exposure to polyvinylchloride. Currently, however, few substances are believed to leave any kind of medical *footprint* to permit a causal connection with a specific manifestation of cancer.

[44] The rationale for permitting reasoned speculation as to cancer causation in a public health and regulatory policy context is discussed in a number of publications. Good examples include: Scientific Bases for Identification of Potential Carcinogens and Estimation of Risks, 44 Fed Reg 39858 (July 6, 1979); Chemical Contaminants: Safety and Risk Assessment, in Drinking Water and Health (National Academy of Science 1978);

As in other types of toxic substance cases, a plaintiff can usually get to the jury if he or she produces expert testimony that his or her cancer was *probably* caused by exposure to a toxic substance. The problem is that in most cases the evidence shows only that exposure *possibly* caused the plaintiff's cancer. This is usually insufficient to present a jury question.

§16.07 —Recent Decisions: Cigarettes

The issue of cancer causation was addressed and resolved in favor of the plaintiffs in two cases against cigarette manufacturers. The defendants were found to have no liability, however, because the jury found that they were either not negligent or had not breached a warranty to the plaintiff. In both cases, however, the issue of causation was submitted to the jury, and the jury found that the plaintiffs' lung cancer had been caused by smoking the defendants' cigarettes.

In *Pritchard v Liggett & Myers Tobacco Co*,[45] the Third Circuit reversed a directed verdict in favor of the defendant on the issue of causation. The court of appeals held that the plaintiff had presented sufficient evidence of causation to raise a jury question. The plaintiff presented five medical experts who testified that his lung cancer was caused by smoking. The court held that the testimony of the plaintiff's experts that cigarette smoking caused cancer was sufficient to raise a jury question. On remand the jury found, in answer to a special interrogatory, that the plaintiff's lung cancer was caused by his cigarette smoking. The finding of causation was not disturbed when the case was appealed for a second time.[46]

Similarly, in *Green v American Tobacco Co*,[47] a jury found that cigarette smoking was a proximate cause of the plaintiff's lung cancer. In this case, each side presented eight expert witnesses to testify that cigarette smoking either did or did not cause cancer. The court of appeals held that the trial court properly submitted the question of causation to the jury.

It is not clear whether the experts in either *Pritchard* or *Green* testified that the plaintiffs' cancer was actually caused by cigarette smoking or simply that cigarette smoking caused cancer in many instances. What is clear from these cases is that a plaintiff will be permitted to go to the jury if his or her expert witnesses make out a prima facie case of causation. The jury will then be left to sort out the legal resolution of the conflicting scientific opinions expressed by the various experts.

Decision Making for Regulating Chemicals in the Environment (National Academy of Science 1975); Perspectives on Benefit-Risk Decision Making (National Academy of Engineering, 1972).

[45] 295 F2d 292 (3d Cir 1961).

[46] *See* Pritchard v Liggett & Myers Tobacco Co, 350 F2d 479 (3d Cir 1965), *cert denied*, 382 US 987 (1966).

[47] 304 F2d 70 (5th Cir 1962).

§16.08 —Recent Decisions: Workers' Compensation

Parker v Employers Mutual Liability Insurance Company of Wisconsin [48] was a workers' compensation action to recover for cancer that the plaintiff alleged was caused by his employment. The plaintiff worked as a handler of radioactive material and a production operator assembling nuclear weapons for a period of four and one-half years. During the course of his employment, he developed cancer, and he died after the trial. The plaintiff claimed that his cancer was caused by his exposure to radioactive material at his job. In reversing a jury verdict for the plaintiff, the Texas Supreme Court held that the plaintiff had failed to establish a probable connection between his exposure to radiation and his cancer.

The plaintiff's burden of proof in a case in which cancer is allegedly caused by exposure to a toxic substance is a strict one. The court in *Parker* noted that is was extremely difficult to determine the cause of any particular cancer because the etiology of cancer is unknown. A plaintiff can still get to the jury, however, if he or she produces expert testimony that there was a *reasonable probability* that his or her disease was caused by exposure to a particular substance:

> [P]robabilities of causation articulated by scientific experts have been deemed sufficient to allow a plaintiff to proceed to the jury. For while a scientific training conceives of anything as possible, coincidence can be measured and generalizations similar to but not the same as uniform physical laws can be drawn from the probability of a result following a cause. In fact, the relationship between cause and its effect per se without theoretical explanation, can be nothing more than probable relationships between particulars. But this probability must, in equity and justice, be more than coincidence before there can be deemed sufficient proof for the plaintiff to go to the jury. [49]

In discussing the specific evidence presented by the plaintiff in the case, the court determined that the nature of the testimony presented by the plaintiff was not that his exposure to radiation was the probable cause of his cancer, but merely that his exposure to radiation was a possible cause. The court stated: "It is clear that there was no evidence at trial of causal connection between cancer and radiation in the expert testimony per se other than the possibility of such a connection. Indeed, the plaintiff's efforts were directed towards only establishing a possibility, not a probability." [50] Since the plaintiff was not able to produce evidence showing anything other than that his exposure to radiation was a *possible* cause of his cancer, the court held that the

---

[48] 440 SW2d 43 (Tex 1969).

[49] *Id* 46.

[50] *Id* 47.

plaintiff had failed to meet his burden of proving causation and reversed the award in his favor.[51]

Miller v National Cabinet Co[52] involved a claim for workers' compensation death benefits. The decedent died from leukemia, allegedly caused by exposure to benzene during his employment as a piano finisher. The court ruled that there was insufficient evidence that decedent's exposure to benzene was the cause of his leukemia. The plaintiff presented the testimony of a medical expert who stated that the incidence of leukemia was much higher in persons who had been exposed to benzene than in the population as a whole. He was unable to testify, however, that the decedent's exposure to benzene was the cause of his leukemia. The court held that this was simply insufficient evidence of causation to uphold an award in favor of the plaintiff. The court noted that it was extremely rare for a plaintiff to recover when the disease from which the plaintiff or the plaintiff's decedent was suffering was cancer:

> The courts have been confronted before with cancer cases, and this is not likely to be the last. This is not an isolated situation. Questions of causation are common to actions based on warranty, tort or workmen's compensation proceedings. . . . There appear to be no decisions upholding causation in so complex a variety of the disease as leukemia. The cancer decisions in the courts where recovery has been allowed have dealt almost entirely with trauma, and there only in instances where the trauma occurred in the spot in the body where the pre-existing cancer was and the symptoms of its aggravation were immediately apparent. . . . In all of those cases the immediacy of the symptoms of aggravation of the cancer by a traumatic injury suffered in the area where the cancer was located was accepted as a substitute for scientific evidence or understanding of

---

[51] The court stated:

> There is nothing in the record to suggest that the experts hypothesized the probable effect of the factual circumstances at bar on the complex etiological theory of radiation induced cancer. If the experts cannot predict probability in these situations, it is difficult to see how courts can expect a jury of laymen to be able to do so.

> This requirement does in some instances place extraordinary burdens of proof on claimants. But once the theory of causation leaves the realm of lay knowledge for esoteric scientific theories, the scientific theory must be more than a possibility to the scientists who created it. For to the scientific mind, all things are possible. And with all things possible, citizens would have no reasoned protection from the speculations of courts and juries.

Id 49. Note that Senator Hatch (R-Utah) has introduced a bill [S 921, 98th Cong, 1st Sess (1983)], which would provide partial compensation to "victims" where the "probability of causation" is above 10% but less than 50%. The bill builds its computation upon probability tables being developed by the Department of Health & Human Services under Pub L No 97-414, the "Orphan Drug" Act. 15 USC §1274; 96 Stat 2049 (Jan 4, 1983).

[52] 8 NY2d 277, 168 NE2d 811, 204 NYS2d 129 (1960).

cause and effect. Absent that, damage claims of this nature have been dismissed on the law for lack of evidence of causation.[53]

The court in *Miller* specifically stated that it would not shift the burden of proof to the defendant simply because it was difficult for the plaintiff to prove causation. A plaintiff must produce evidence showing that his or her disease was probably caused by exposure to a certain substance. It is not sufficient for a plaintiff to present evidence that his or her disease was possibly caused by such exposure. The court stated:

> Such a doctrine [allowing a showing that exposure possibly causes cancer to satisfy the burden of proof] would overturn the rule that the burden is on the party asserting that a disease is based on actionable facts to prove causation. . . . It would mean that, wherever such a cause is possible, the burden rests on the opposite party to prove that the disease resulted from something else. Consequently, for so long as the causes of the disease are unknown to medical science, the claimant or plaintiff can always recover—if the trier of the fact is favorably disposed—since no one can prove that the disease had other causes. This is a perversion of the normal rule that the disease must have resulted from the occupation and that the burden of proving causation is upon the party asserting it. The law does not intend that the less that is known about a disease the greater shall be the opportunity of recovery in court.[54]

In *Garner v Heckla Mining Co,*[55] the plaintiff brought a workers' compensation action to recover benefits for the death of her husband. The decedent had been a uranium miner for over 20 years. The cause of his death was lung cancer, allegedly caused by his long exposure to radon gas. Plaintiff introduced statistical evidence showing that there was a much higher than average incidence of lung cancer in uranium miners. An autopsy of the decedent showed that he had 34 times as much lead-210, a by-product of radon gas, in his bones as did the average non-uranium miner. Although the court did not discuss the evidence in detail, it appears that the plaintiff presented a strong case showing a high statistical correlation between lung cancer and uranium mining. Nonetheless, the court denied recovery because there was no proof that this particular decedent's lung cancer was caused by exposure to radon gas.

The court in *Garner* noted that the incidence of lung cancer among heavy cigarette smokers is 30 to 50 per cent higher than in nonsmokers and commented that decedent smoked a pack of cigarettes a day for over 20 years.

---

[53] *Id* at 285-86, 168 NE2d at 815, 204 NYS2d at 135.

[54] *Id* at 168 NE2d at 817-18, 289, 294 NYS2d at 138, *Cf* "Superfund Section 301(e) Study Group," Senate Comm. on Environment and Public Works, 97th Cong, 2d Sess, Injuries and Damages from Hazardous Wastes—Analysis and Improvement of Legal Remedies at 299-300 ("This can lead to the *reductio ad absurdum* that if causation is not provable at all, then there must be a claim-saving presumption") (statement of Judge Charles D. Breitel).

[55] 19 Utah 2d 367, 431 P2d 794 (1967).

While not stating the obvious conclusion from these facts, it is apparent the court thought the decedent's smoking was as likely a cause of his lung cancer as exposure to radon gas.[56] The court essentially determined that until there can be conclusive scientific evidence concerning the cause of cancer, no one suffering from cancer will be able to recover.[57]

In *Olson v Federal American Partners*,[58] the Wyoming Supreme Court reached the same conclusion as the Utah court in *Garner*. The decedent was a cigarette-smoking uranium miner who died from lung cancer. Recovery was denied because of the plaintiff's failure to establish causation. The court noted that the most the evidence showed was that the decedent's cancer might have been induced by radiation from uranium mining.[59]

Plaintiffs have not been totally unsuccessful in recovering for cancer allegedly caused by exposure to toxic substances. However, most of these cases have been workers' compensation actions. Courts that have allowed recovery have merely required a showing that employment-related exposure to a toxic substance was a contributing, rather than the sole cause of the decedent's cancer. Thus, courts in California,[60] New Jersey,[61] West Virginia,[62] and Arkansas[63]

---

[56] The court stated:

> Under our statutes and long established decisional law there are insuperable obstacles to the granting of the relief sought by plaintiff on this appeal: it was their burden to show affirmatively and to so persuade the Commission that Mr. Garner's death resulted from a disease caused by his occupation . . . . While it seems logical that the unusually high incidence of lung cancer in uranium miners would indicate in the same ratio the higher probability than otherwise that such was the cause of the disease, it nevertheless falls short of compelling a finding that such was the cause in any individual case. For illustration, in a more commonly known field: the fact that the incidence of lung cancer in heavy cigarette smokers is 30% to 50% higher than in nonsmokers does not necessarily compel the conclusion that any individual smoker's case of lung cancer resulted from cigarette smoking. The disease also arises quite independently of and therefore apparently from other causes than cigarette smoking. Incidentally on the subject of cigarettes, it was shown that Mr. Garner himself had smoked a package a day for about 20 years.

Id at 370-71, 431 P2d at 796-97.

[57] *Id* at 370, 431 P2d at 796.

[58] 567 P2d 710 (Wyo 1977).

[59] While both the *Olson* and *Garner* courts relied, at least in part, on the fact that the decedents were heavy smokers, it does not appear that the results would have been any different had the decedents not smoked. Although that fact would have made it statistically more likely that the decedents' lung cancer was caused by radon gas, it would not have eliminated the uncertainty about the actual cause.

[60] McAllister v Workmen's Comp Appeals Bd, 69 Cal 2d 408, 445 P2d 313, 71 Cal Rptr 697 (1968). The widow of a fireman sought benefits on the grounds that his exposure to toxic smoke during his 32 years as a fireman caused his lung cancer. The court held that the plaintiff should recover because the necessary showing was only a reasonable probability of industrial causation. The fact that decedent smoked a pack of cigarettes a day did not bar the plaintiff's recovery.

> We cannot doubt that the more smoke decedent inhaled—from whatever source —the greater the danger of his contracting lung cancer. His smoking increased

have allowed workers' compensation recovery for lung cancer when the plaintiff showed only that exposure to a toxic substance *could* have caused the decedent's lung cancer. It is quite unlikely that the causation evidence produced in any of these cases would be sufficient to satisfy the plaintiff's burden of proof in a third-party action against a manufacturer.[64]

---

that danger, just as did his employment. Given the present state of medical knowledge, we cannot say whether it was the employment or the cigarettes which "actually" caused the disease; we can only recognize that both contributed substantially to the likelihood of his contracting lung cancer. As we noted, however, in *Employers, etc. Ins. Co. of Wis.* v. *Industrial Acc. Com.,* (1953) 41 Cal.2d 676, 680 [263 P.2d 4], the decedent's employment need only be a "contributing cause" of his injury. And in *Bethlehem Steel Co.* v. *Industrial Acc. Com., supra,* 21 Cal.2d 742, 744, we pointed out a particular instance of this principle when we stated that it was enough that "the employee's risk of contracting the disease by virtue of the employment must be materially greater than that of the general public." Thus in *Bethlehem* we allowed an award to an employee who contracted a contagious eye disease, since he had shown that the disease was more common at his place of employment than among the public.

Although decedent's smoking may have been inadvisable, respondents offer no reason to believe that the likelihood of contracting lung cancer from the smoking was so great that the danger could not have been materially increased by exposure to the smoke produced by burning buildings.

Id at 418-19, 445 P2d at 318-19, 71 Cal Rptr at 702-03.

[61] Bolger v Chris Anderson Roofing Co, 112 NJ Super 383, 271 A2d 451 (1970), *affd,* 117 NJ Super 497, 285 A2d 228 (AD 1971). The court upheld a compensation award to a roofer suffering from lung cancer. He was exposed to fumes from pitch, tar, and asphalt at his job for 23 years. Plaintiff also smoked. The court held that:

Where an employer contends that he is not legally responsible for petitioner's total disability and seeks to attribute the disability of the injured employee to causes for which he is not responsible, the burden of proof in that regard is on the employer.

. . . Factually, the Court must also find from the evidence that whether the smoking contributed to the end result or not, petitioner's exposure to pitch, tar and asphalt contributed in a major way to the onset or precipitation of the lung cancer.

Id at 394-95, 271 A2d at 458 (citing in part Wexler v Lambrecht Foods, 64 NJ Super 489, 166 A2d 576 (App Div 1960)).

[62] Powell v State Workmen's Comp Commr, 273 SE2d 832 (W Va 1980). This case involved a compensation claim for asbestos-caused lung cancer. The causal connection between exposure to asbestos and lung cancer is clear. The court held that a claimant in a workers' compensation case must bear the burden of proving his or her case, but that it is not necessary to prove to the exclusion of all else the causal connection between the injury and the employment.

[63] Scobey v Southern Lumber Co, 218 Ark 671, 238 SW2d 640 (1951). In this case, the court apparently shifted the burden of proof to the defendant to disprove causation. The decedent worked in a lumber mill for 24 years and was exposed to emery dust, fumes, and sawdust on a daily basis. The expert testimony was only that exposure to emery dust might be capable of causing lung cancer. The court reversed a denial of benefits, holding there was not substantial evidence to support the lower court's determination that the exposure had not caused plaintiff's cancer.

[64] For an overview of workers' compensation cases dealing with cancer, see Annot,

§16.09 —Recent Decisions: Asbestos

There are a few toxic substances that a plaintiff can more easily prove was the cause in fact of a particular type of cancer. One of these is asbestos. Exposure to asbestos dust can cause several diseases, including asbestosis, mesothelioma, and lung cancer. Asbestosis is a lung disorder caused by the inhalation of asbestos fibers. It is not malignant or necessarily fatal. There is thought to be a relationship between the amount and duration of exposure and the manifestation and severity of asbestosis. The latency period for asbestosis averages between 10 and 25 years.

Mesothelioma is a form of lung cancer caused by exposure to asbestos. The latency period may be even longer than for asbestosis. There is no relationship between duration and amount of exposure and mesothelioma. Asbestos exposure is the only cause.

Other forms of lung cancer are different. There is a much higher incidence of lung cancer among asbestos workers than among the general public. With the exception of mesothelioma, however, the cause of lung cancer is nonspecific. Therefore, an asbestos worker suffering from one of these other types of lung cancer will only be able to show an increased risk by exposure to asbestos.

The leading asbestos case is *Borel v Fibreboard Paper Products Corp.*[65] The plaintiff was an insulation worker exposed to asbestos dust from 1936 to 1969. The plaintiff discovered in 1969 that he was suffering from asbestosis and mesothelioma. He sued 11 manufacturers to whose products he was exposed during those years.

The plaintiff settled with four defendants before trial, and a fifth was dismissed because there was no evidence that the plaintiff had ever been exposed to its products. The case against the remaining defendants was tried, and the jury returned a verdict for the plaintiff. The evidence showed overwhelmingly that asbestos was the cause of asbestosis and mesothelioma.[66] The issue that was contested was not causation. The defendants argued instead they should not have been held strictly liable for failure to warn of the dangers associated with asbestos. They argued the danger from inhaling asbestos was not foreseeable until 1968, long after the plaintiff contracted his illnesses. This argument was rejected. The court held that asbestos insulation was an unreasonably dangerous product and that harm from its use was foreseeable as early as the 1930s. The verdict against the defendants was affirmed on appeal.[67]

It is not known how many asbestos plaintiffs have recovered damages for their injuries. It is estimated that there were approximately 20,000 asbestos

19 ALR4th 639 (1983). Issues of workers' compensation and the exclusivity doctrine are discussed in **ch. 6.**

[65] 493 F2d 1076 (5th Cir 1973), *cert denied,* 419 US 869 (1974).

[66] *Id* 1083-85.

[67] *See also* Karjala v Johns-Manville Prods Corp, 523 F2d 155 (8th Cir 1975) (jury verdict for asbestos plaintiff affirmed); Beshada v Johns-Manville Corp, 90 NJ 191, 447 A2d 539 (1982) (adopting a duty to warn of unknown and unknowable risks of asbestos).

cases pending at the time Johns-Manville declared bankruptcy in 1982.[68]

§16.10 —Recent Decisions: DES

The preceding section noted that causation is not the major problem in asbestos cases. Causation is also apparently not the major problem in DES cases. DES (diethystilbestrol) is a synthetic estrogen that was used widely for the prevention of miscarriages in the 1950s and 1960s. Use of DES has been linked to cancer in the daughters of women who took the drug while pregnant. While DES plaintiffs have had great difficulty establishing the identity of the manufacturer of the product taken by their mothers,[69] they apparently have little problem establishing DES as the cause in fact of their cancer.

In *Bichler v Eli Lilly & Co*,[70] a $492,842.39 jury verdict for the plaintiff was affirmed. The defendant appealed the finding of liability on a number of grounds. The defendant did not argue, however, that there was insufficient evidence of a causal connection between DES and the plaintiff's cancer. It may be assumed, therefore, that the evidence of causation could not be seriously challenged on appeal.

The same situation was presented in *Needham v White Laboratories, Inc.*[71] In this case, an $800,000 jury verdict was reversed because certain evidence was improperly admitted. This evidence went to the issue of liability, however, not causation. Again, the defendant did not argue that DES did not cause the plaintiff's cancer. Rather, the defendant argued that it did not know and should not have been required to know of the dangerous qualities of DES at the time it was marketed. This is essentially the same type of defense asserted by some asbestos and Agent Orange manufacturers. See **§14.14.**

---

[68] National Science Foundation, Compensation for Victims of Toxic Pollution—Assessing the Scientific Knowledge Base, Addendum (PRA Research Report 83-8), at 3; *see* Hardy v Johns-Manville Sales Corp, 681 F2d 334, 347 (5th Cir 1982). Several asbestos manufacturers have sought protection under Chapter 11 of the Bankruptcy Act. National Science Foundation, Addendum, at 3.

[69] See §§**16.13-16.15.**

[70] 79 AD2d 317, 436 NYS2d 625 (1981), *affd*, 55 NY2d 571, 436 NE2d 182, 450 NYS2d 776 (1982).

[71] 639 F2d 394 (7th Cir), *cert denied*, 454 US 927 (1981). In Mink v University of Chicago, No 77-C-1432 (ND Ill Mar 24, 1983), a jury in March 1983 rejected the plaintiff's claim that her mother's use of DES made her a future cancer candidate and a current sufferer of cancerphobia. The plaintiff did have some physical consequences from DES (a cervical ridge), but there was apparently no evidence of an actual precancerous condition or that she sought medical treatment of her psychological fears. The *Mink* case was the first of hundreds of noncancer DES cases to go to trial, and the decision has been appealed. See Note, 69 ABA J 725 (June 1983).

§16.11 —Future Trends

What seems clear as a trend from the cases on cancer causation discussed in §§16.07-16.10 is a tendency of the courts to engage in fairly undefined causative inferences that result in liability for defendants. The epidemiological evidence on human carcinogens is sparse, thus leaving room for a court and jury to roam at will through the statistical inferences offered by expert witnesses based on nonhuman data. Often, animal research is relied upon as a basis of proving causation, using dose extrapolation theories[72] to establish probability. In such cases, counsel must be careful to evaluate in detail the background facts of the animal studies, such as:

1. Whether the animals were tested in accordance with correct Environmental Protection Agency (EPA) laboratory guidelines (e.g., not in the

---

[72] The concept of dose extrapolation is essentially the use of statistical inferences from animal studies to predict a cancer risk in humans. Animals are tested at *maximum tolerated doses*—that is, the greatest possible dose that stops just short of being lethal. The doses are given continuously over relatively limited time periods. Based on these results in animals at high doses, a projection of risk (*extrapolation*) is made for low doses. The justification for this is that: (1) there is a statistical necessity—i.e., given a small number of animals, there must exist a large tumor rate to be helpful; (2) there is uncertainty at low levels, and thus there is no safety threshold for public safety given the theory that cancer may be caused by a single exposure (or *hit*), and the possibility of hypersensitive individuals. Expressed more simply, the regulatory philosophy is to be safe rather than sorry, and to err conservatively by overprotection.

While this approach may be justifiable as a political policy judgment for the benefit of the general public in a regulatory setting, it lacks force in application as proof of current or future cancer for a specific individual in a civil lawsuit. The concept of the linear dose-response used to extrapolate (see **§1.04**) is that the probability of a cancer event is proportional to exposure, even through etiology and the nature of events is unknown. That is, as has been observed by critics of the theory, if 100 aspirins yield a lethal dose, there is not a 1% chance of dying from one aspirin or, in a lighter vein, if a Mercedes costs $30,000, there is not a 50% chance of buying it for $15,000.

More critically, the extrapolation from high to low doses may fail to account for a number of potentially invalidating factors, such as

1. Difference in *transport* of a substance in humans versus animals (i.e., body size tends to determine the distribution rate)
2. *Repair* differences (massive doses in animals cause continuous injuries for which physical reserves cannot compensate in restoring)
3. Tolerance or detoxification (humans may excrete or metabolize a substance that animals do not)
4. In lower doses over longer times, individuals would tend to die of other causes first
5. Unlike laboratory animals, humans are not genetically homogenous, nor do they live under controlled environmental conditions
6. Animals generally eat more of their percentage of body weight in food, and thus, extrapolations from animal data can overstate the risks.

same location as other animals receiving other types of toxic substances)[73]

2. The length of the study (cancer predictions, which are related more to chronic toxicity than acute toxicity, may not be valid if the doses given to animals were very large and given over a very short period of time)

3. Whether the pathologist's finding of cancer was based on the view that the cellular change was merely neoplastic (changes in cell shapes), or whether some finding of malignancy or metastasis was required

4. Whether the sample size was adequate to permit valid statistical inferences

5. Whether the type of laboratory animal used was subject to recognized or unusual tumor tendencies[74]

In addition, defense counsel should develop the causation defense that cancer may be the product of more than exposure to the client's product. A study recently concluded by two British epidemiologists at Oxford University concluded that the causes of cancer are extremely varied, including infection (10 per cent), sexual factors (7 per cent), occupation (4 per cent), alcohol (3 per cent), geography (3 per cent), environmental pollution (2 per cent), medical treatment (1 per cent), food additives (1 per cent), industrial products (1 per cent), tobacco (30 per cent), and diet (10-70 per cent range).[75] Thus, a particular plaintiff's cancer may have a plethora of possible causes depending on the plaintiff's background, occupation, and habits, and only careful discovery will reveal the extent of these other possible causes.[76]

While it is difficult to predict how courts will respond to the scientific frontier of causation issues, a recent California state court decision, *Arnett, et al v*

---

[73] *See, e.g.,* Nonclinical Laboratory Studies: Good Laboratory Practice Regulations, 43 Fed Reg 59986 (Dec 22, 1978).

[74] See, e.g., Tomatis, Partensky & Montesano, *The Predictive Value of Mouse Liver Tumor Induction in Carcinogenity Testing—A Literature Survey,* 12 Intl J Cancer 1 (1973).

[75] R. Doll & R. Peto, 66 Journal of the National Cancer Institute (June 1981).

[76] There is also emerging scientific evidence that cancer is a rare biological event that is the cumulation of a series of other rare biological events, which have to be evoked by certain stimulants in the right amounts and at precise times. Under this theory of cancer as a multisequential process, carcinogens are classified as *initiators* and *promoters.* Initiators are rare, extremely potent carcinogens whereby a single exposure will produce cancer (this is essentially the philosophy behind the American regulatory view of the *single hit* or *zero dose* safety level for regulating potential carcinogens.) The vast majority of other potential carcinogens are promoters, which in order to cause cancer require exposure in a certain order and at specific times, including exposure after an initiator has been applied. This theory also notes the importance of the human body's repair ability—i.e., the ability to avoid contracting cancer by the biological cell repair that occurs if the exposure is neither too acute nor for too long a period of time. Lawyers should be aware of this and other scientific and medical theories in order to develop the kind of direct and cross-examination of experts that will be required in a cancer causation case.

Dow Chemical Co,[77] may provide clear guidance on both the future cancer theory (the *increased risk* claim) and the fear of cancer theory (*cancerphobia* claim). In *Arnett,* the trial judge denied the increased cancer risk claims as a matter of law and permitted the cancerphobia claim to be submitted to the jury.

The plaintiffs in *Arnett* were seven male workers at a California chemical plant where DBCP[78] was manufactured into commercial grade pesticides. The plaintiffs alleged that DBCP caused fertility problems. Based on laboratory tests that showed DBCP was an animal carcinogen, the plaintiffs also claimed compensation for an increased risk of cancer and for present emotional distress due to a fear of future cancer_(cancerphobia). After a cogent review of the medical and scientific evidence on the etiology of cancer and the reliability of extrapolation of human cancer risks from animal studies, the trial court found that while it was possible for a jury to find that DBCP was a potential human carcinogen, it was impossible for plaintiffs to establish whether they would individually contract cancer. As a consequence, the court held as a matter of law that risk of cancer was not a "proper element of damages for the jury to assess." As the court said:

> The developments at the very frontier of science do not provide reasonably probably predictions. There is no definitive epidemiological evidence to verify the mathematical calculation of quantitative risk assessment. While the animal test results and *in vitro* studies present the possibility that DBCP *may* be a human carcinogen, such an extrapolation does not reach the requisite level of acceptance within the scientific community to justify legal reliance. To award damages based on a mere mathematical probability would significantly undercompensate those who actually do develop cancer and would be a windfall to those who do not.
>
> There has always existed a considerable lag between advances and discoveries in scientific fields and their acceptance as evidence in a court proceeding. . . . Judicial caution in this area is preferable since "Lay jurors tend to give considerable weight to '[s]cientific' evidence when presented by 'experts' with impressive credentials." There is a "misleading aura of certainty which often envelops a new scientific process, obscuring its currently experimental nature . . . 'scientific' proof may in some instances assume a posture of mystic infallibility in the eyes of a jury."
>
> Based on the analysis above, the jury in this case could not have sufficiently reliable date regarding individual cancer risk assessment of these various plaintiffs to make an intelligent award. They would be required

---

[77] Slip op 82-901S (Sup Ct Cal Mar 21, 1983). As reported in the Chemical & Radiation Waste Litigation Reporter (Vol 6, No 3, Aug 1983), the jury in Arnett awarded the plaintiffs a total of $4.9 million in compensatory damages, which were nevertheless said to be for decreased sperm count rather than cancerphobia.

[78] *DBCP* is the acronym for 1, 2-dibromo-3-chloropropane.

to speculate on future developments without the reliable prediction or degree of certainty required by our system of tort law.[79]

With respect to the cancerphobia theory, the trial judge initially observed that courts should proceed cautiously in permitting emotional distress claims:

> Despite the Law's recognition of fear as a debilitating emotional injury worthy of redress under certain circumstances, the spectre of unlimited liability from an army of plaintiffs parading their tumescent fears into the courtroom supported by a corps of psychiatrists has resulted in proper judicial restraint in this area.[80]

After this cautionary observation, however, the court, citing the two other reported cases that permitted recovery for cancerphobia,[81] became the third court to allow such claims. In so holding, the court first found that five evidentiary *guarantees of genuiness* existed to support plaintiffs' claim.[82] The court then established that to permit recovery, the plaintiffs must prove four elements:

1. A serious fear of cancer
2. The fear was caused by exposure to DBCP
3. The fear is reasonable
4. The defendants are "legally responsible" for the exposure to DBCP— i.e., there exists an independent basis of liability such as negligence or strict liability

Interestingly, in discussing the reasonableness requirement, the court held that while the plaintiffs need not prove to a reasonable medical certainty their likelihood of developing cancer, they must establish that their fear is objectively based.[83]

---

[79] Arnett v Dow Chemical, slip op at 15-16.

[80] *Id,* slip op at 19.

[81] *See* Ferrara v Galluchio, 5 NY2d 16, 152 NE2d 249 2d 996, 176 NYS2d 996 (1958) (patient's radiation burn led to fears); Lorenc v Chemirad Corp, 37 NJ 56, 179 A2d 401 (1962) (chemical burns to physician led to fears).

[82] The five factors were:

> (1) All plaintiffs were workers from a specific site with verifiable injuries consisting of sterility or decreased sperm counts;
> (2) The injuries described above are deemed "emotionally changed conditions";
> (3) A biopsy-verified toxic insult to the testes was deemed likely to cause concern of other latent problems;
> (4) All plaintiffs were subjected to substantial media publicity linking DBCP to cancer and sterility; and
> (5) Many plaintiffs had been told by doctors that they should have regular cancer check-ups because of increased risks.

[83] In *Arnett,* the evidence of such objectivity included letters to the plaintiffs from doctors, scientific articles, congressional hearings, and media reports discussing DBCP's carcinogenicity, animal test results, and actual cancer cases of other workers in the plant.

Perhaps the most innovative aspect of the *Arnett* decision was the court's protection of plaintiffs' future cancer claims by the extraction from the defendants of a waiver of any future contention that plaintiffs improperly split their cause of action or violated any statute of limitations. Thus, the court reserved jurisdiction for the plaintiffs to sue in the future should they develop cancer and be able to trace it to DBCP. In a similar vein, there is a developing theory of remedies, often brought in *mass tort* class actions, that seeks the class certification of a *medical detection* class.[84] This proposal seeks to require defendants to fund the monitoring, through medical surveys and examinations, of the members of the affected class over years into the future for the purpose of detecting latent defects due to toxic exposures. If this proposed device succeeds, it may result in defendants' subsidizing the development of potential plaintiffs' claims until actual injuries can be established.

Product Identification

§16.12 In General

Assuming that a plaintiff can establish that exposure to a particular toxic substance was the cause in fact of his or her injury, the plaintiff is still faced with the problem of identifying the responsible party. It has traditionally been a defense in a products liability action that the plaintiff has failed to carry the burden of proof in establishing causation if the plaintiff's evidence does not identify the defendant as the manufacturer or seller of the product causing the injury.[85] In toxic substance litigation, it is often difficult to identify the party responsible for manufacturing the product that caused the plaintiff's injury.

The problem of identifying the maker of the product that injured the plaintiff occurs most frequently in cases in which there is a long latency period between the exposure and the manifestation of a disease. The issue has been litigated most frequently in cases involving exposure to asbestos or DES. In each instance, large numbers of manufacturers produced essentially identical generic products. Identification of the particular defendant responsible for the plaintiffs' injuries is usually impossible.

Product identification can become an issue in much simpler cases as well. For example, in *Drayton v Jiffee Chemical Corp*,[86] the plaintiff was severely burned when a drain cleaner was accidentally spilled on her face by her father. The

---

It is worth noting that *Arnett* would permit evidence as to increased risk of cancer to go to the jury, under the rationale of proving the reasonableness of the cancerphobia. Thus, a jury could possibly inflate its award for cancerphobia if it were persuaded that there was some increased future cancer risk.

[84] *See, e.g., In re* Three Mile Island Litigation, 87 FRD 433, 435 (MD Pa 1980).

[85] See Annot, 51 ALR3d 1344 (1973).

[86] 395 F Supp 1081 (ND Ohio 1975), *affd,* 591 F2d 352 (6th Cir 1978).

defendant denied liability,[87] argued that the sole proximate cause of the plaintiff's injury was her father's act of spilling the drain cleaner,[88] and denied that it manufactured the drain cleaner that caused the plaintiff's injury.

The plaintiff claimed her injuries were caused by *Liquid-plumr,* a product manufactured by the defendant. Liquid-plumr contained a solution of approximately 26 per cent sodium hydroxide, or lye. The bottle of drain cleaner that was spilled on plaintiff's face was thrown out shortly after the accident and was never recovered. The plaintiff established the identity of Liquid-plumr by the testimony of her mother and father and their landlady, who had originally purchased the drain cleaner. In addition the plaintiff's expert testified that her injuries were consistent with exposure to lye.

The defendant argued that the plaintiff had not been injured by Liquid-plumr, but rather by a similar product known as *Mister Plumber,* which was composed of 92 to 93 per cent sulfuric acid. The defendant's expert testified that the plaintiff's injuries were more consistent with exposure to sulfuric acid than to lye. Evidence showed that the method that the plaintiff's father used to clean the clogged sink was more consistent with the instructions on a package of Mister Plumber than those for Liquid-plumr. In addition, the evidence showed the first aid measures taken immediately after the plaintiff was burned were consistent with the instructions on Mister Plumber and inconsistent with the Liquid-plumr instructions. Despite this evidence, the trial court found as a matter of fact that the plaintiff's injuries were caused by Liquid-plumr. This finding was not disturbed on appeal.[89]

§16.13   The DES Litigation

Drayton v Jiffee Chemical Corp[90] illustrates that the problem of product identification can arise in the most straightforward type of toxic substance products liability litigation. The classic problem with product identification is presented in DES cases. DES (diethylstilbestrol) is an artificial estrogen developed in the

---

[87] The plaintiff's theories of liability included negligent failure to warn, breach of express and implied warranties, and strict liability. The district court, sitting without a jury, found defendant liable on all theories and awarded $1,620,000 in damages. On appeal, liability was upheld only for breach of express warranty and the damage award was reduced by almost $1,000,000.

[88] The court found that the actions of the plaintiff's father did not constitute intervening cause because they were foreseeable, 591 F2d at 360-61.

[89] The court stated:

> Under these circumstances, giving "due regard . . . to the opportunity of the trial court to judge of the credibility of the witnesses," Rule 52(a), Fed. R. Civ. P., we are unable to hold that the trial judge's finding of fact that the product involved was Liquid-plumr, manufactured by defendant Jiffee Chemical Corporation, was clearly erroneous.

Id 356.

[90] 395 F Supp 1111 (ND Ohio 1975), *affd,* 591 F2d 352 (6th Cir 1978), discussed in **§16.12.**

1930s. DES was first approved by the federal Food and Drug Administration (FDA) in 1947 for use in the prevention of miscarriages. Between the years 1947 and 1971, DES was manufactured by hundreds of drug companies and was widely prescribed for millions of pregnant women. In 1971, DES was linked to the development of cancer in the daughters of women who took the drug while pregnant.[91] The FDA banned DES for use in the prevention of miscarriages in 1971.

Hundreds of suits have been filed against DES manufacturers by women who were exposed to the drug in utero. It is commonly alleged that the defendant's insufficiently tested DES and sold it without warning of possible dangers when they knew, or should have known, it was both ineffective to prevent miscarriages and unsafe for use by pregnant women.

The major barrier faced by the plaintiffs in DES litigation has been the inability to identify the specific manufacturer of the drug taken by their mothers. DES was a fungible drug manufactured by over 300 drug companies.[92] Due to the long latency period for DES-related cancer,[93] it is virtually impossible for the plaintiffs to identify the manufacturer that produced the drug taken by their mothers.[94] The defendant drug companies have successfully defended many cases on the ground that the plaintiff was unable to identify any particular defendant as the manufacturer of the drugs taken by her mother.

For example, in *Ryan v Eli Lilly & Co*,[95] the court granted summary judgment for the defendant because the plaintiff was unable to identify the manufacturer of the DES taken by her mother nearly 28 years earlier. The court stated: "It is elementary that in any action claiming injury from a product, the plaintiff must show causal connection between the defendant manufacturer and that product. The defendant manufacturer must be identified with the specific

---

[91] DES has been linked with clear-cell adenocarcinoma of the vagina and uterus. This form of cancer was quite rare prior to its development in women exposed to DES. DES also has been linked with precancerous condition known as adenosis, which is tissue placed abnormally on the cervix and vagina. See Note, *DES and a Proposed Theory of Enterprise Liability*, 46 Fordham L Rev, 963, 965-66 (1978).

[92] Despite the fact that over 300 companies manufactured DES, it is estimated that five or six major companies accounted for 90 per cent of the market. The largest single producer was Eli Lilly & Co. *Id* 977.

[93] The latency period for DES related cancer is between 10 and 20 years.

[94] With the passage of over 20 years in most cases, the records that could establish the identity of the manufacturer have been destroyed. Doctors normally did not prescribe the drug of a particular manufacturer. The only records that could identify the source of the drug are records from the pharmacy that filled the prescription, assuming plaintiffs' mothers can remember where their prescriptions were filled. To date, cases have involved exposure to the drug in the 1950s, and adequate records do not exist. *See* Bichler v Eli Lilly & Co, 79 AD2d 317, 436 NYS2d 625 (1981), *affd* 55 NYS2d 571, 436 NE2d 182, 450 NYS2d 776 (1982); Ryan v Eli Lilly & Co, 514 F Supp 1004 (DSC 1981).

[95] 514 F Supp 1004 (DSC 1981).

instrumentality that allegedly caused the injury."[96] The court held that the plaintiff had failed to meet the threshold burden of maintaining her action, which was identifying the manufacturer of the drug and establishing causation in fact. The court rejected the plaintiff's attempt to rely on alternative theories of liability that would have relieved her of the burden of proving the identity of the manufacturer of the drug taken by her mother. These theories included conspiracy, concert of action, alternative liability, enterprise liability, and market share liability.[97] A similar result has been reached in a number of other cases.[98]

§16.14   —*Sindell*

A number of courts have fashioned remedies for DES victims, despite the plaintiff's inability to identify a particular culpable defendant. In so doing, the burden of proof has been shifted to the defendants to exonerate themselves from liability. The leading case is *Sindell v Abbott Laboratories*.[99] The plaintiff

---

[96] *Id* 1006.

[97] The court stated:

The unequivocal law of South Carolina is [that] the plaintiff in a negligence action has not only the burden of proving negligence but also the burden of proving that the injury or damage was caused by the actionable conduct of the particular defendant. Thus in *Messier* v. *Adickes*, 251 S.C. 268, 161 S.E.2d 845 (1968), a judgment for plaintiff was reversed because

where the cause of plaintiff's injury may be as reasonably attributed to an act for which defendant is not liable as to one for which he is liable, plaintiff has failed to carry the burden of establishing that his injuries were the proximate result of defendant's negligence.

See also Elledge v. *Pepsi Cola Bottling Company*, 252 N.C. 337, 113 S.E.2d 435 (1960). The Supreme Court of South Carolina has not carved out any exceptions to this tradional rule. The Court places the burden of proof of proximate cause squarely on the plaintiff. Application of this burden-shifting theory would violate established public policy and fundamental principles of tort law and procedure in this state in a variety of ways. This Court declines to apply this theory in the present case

Id 1018-19.

[98] *See, e.g.,* Gray v United States, 445 F Supp 337 (SD Tex 1978). In awarding summary judgment for the defendant due to the plaintiff's inability to prove that the defendant manufactured the drug taken by her mother, the court said: "It is a fundamental principle of products liability law that a plaintiff must prove, as an essential element of his case, that a defendant manufacturer actually made the particular product which caused injury." *Id* 338.

Other DES cases in which summary judgment has been granted for the defendants due to plaintiffs' inability to identify the manufacturer include Pipon v Burroughs-Wellcome Co, 532 F Supp 637 (DNJ 1982); Morton v Abbott Laboratories, 538 F Supp 593 (MD Fla 1982); Payton v Abbott Labs, 512 F Supp 1031 (D Mass 1981); Mizel v Eli Lilly & Co, 526 F Supp 589 (DSC 1981); Namm v Charles E Frosst & Co, 178 NJ Super 19, 427 A2d 1121 (App 1981).

[99] 26 Cal 3d 588, 607 P2d 924, 163 Cal Rptr 132, *cert denied,* 449 US 912 (1980).

there sued the five largest manufacturers of DES, who were allegedly responsible for 90 per cent of the market. The trial court granted summary judgment for the defendants on the ground that the plaintiff was unable to identify the manufacturer of the DES taken by her mother. On appeal, the plaintiff argued she was entitled to recover under one of three theories, despite the fact that she was unable to identify the manufacturer of the DES taken by her mother. All three theories would have shifted the burden of proof to the defendants to show affirmatively that they did not manufacturer the DES taken by the plaintiff's mother. The court rejected all of plaintiff's theories but developed its own *market share* theory that shifted the burden of proof to the defendants.

The first theory advanced by the plaintiff was alternative liability, classically illustrated by *Summers v Tice*.[100] The rule established by *Summers* is that if the plaintiff is able to establish wrongdoing on the part of all defendants but is unable to prove which of the defendants' wrongful acts caused the plaintiff's injuries, the burden of proof shifts to the defendants to absolve themselves from liability.[101] The court rejected this theory because only five of the hundreds of DES manufacturers were before the court. The court held that alternative liability could not apply unless all potential wrongdoers were before the court.[102]

The plaintiff's second theory was concert of action, based on §876 of the Restatement (Second) of Torts.[103] The plaintiff argued that the defendants

---

[100] 32 Cal 2d 85, 89, 199 P2d 1, 3 (1948).

[101] The plaintiff in *Summers* was injured in a hunting accident. Two hunters negligently fired in the plaintiff's direction at the same time. Although the plaintiff could show both defendants were negligent, the plaintiff could not show which of the defendants actually caused the injury. The court shifted the burden of proof to the defendants, because the defendants were in a better position to offer evidence to determine who caused the injury.

[102] The court rejected application of *Summers* for two reasons. First, not all manufacturers of DES were before the court. Therefore, there was the chance that actual wrongdoers might escape liability. Second, there was no evidence that defendants were in a better position to prove who actually manufactured the DES taken by plaintiff's mother. *Cf* "Superfund Section 301(e) Study Group," Senate Comm on Environmental and Public Works, 97th Cong, 2d Sess, Injuries from Hazardous Wastes—Analysis and Improvement of Legal Remedies 56-59 (Comm Print No 97-12, 1982) [hereinafter cited as Superfund §301(e) Report].

[103] The Restatement (Second) of Torts §876 (19–) provides:

> Persons acting in concert for harm resulting to a third person from the tortious conduct of another one is subject to liability if he
>
> (a) does a tortious act in concert with the other or pursuant to a common design with him, or
>
> (b) knows that the other's conduct constitutes a breach of duty and gives substantial assistance or encouragement to the other so to conduct himself, or
>
> (c) gives substantial assistance to the other in accomplishing a tortious result and his own conduct, separately considered, constitutes a breach of duty to the third person.

Cf Superfund §301(e) Report, at 56.

acted together to design, promote, and manufacture DES. The court rejected this theory because plaintiff failed to allege that defendants aided and encouraged one another to test DES inadequately and to provide inadequate warnings, or that there was a tacit understanding or common plan to do so.

The third theory relief argued by the plaintiffs was the theory of enterprise liability developed in *Hall v EI DuPont de Menours & Co.*[104] The court rejected this theory of liability also, primarily because *Hall* specifically suggested that the theory of enterprise liability would not be applicable to the drug industry where there were large numbers of small manufacturers. *Hall* involved blasting caps and there were only six manufacturers in the United States, all of whom were before the court.

Despite the fact that the court rejected all of the plaintiff's theories of liability, the court did not leave the plaintiff without a remedy. The court developed its own theory of liability known as *market share,* based on an extension of the *Summers v Tice* doctrine of alternative liability. The court's decision was clearly based on public policy grounds:

> In our contemporary complex industrialized society, advances in science and technology create fungible goods which may harm consumers and which cannot be traced to any specific producer. The response of the courts can be either to adhere rigidly to prior doctrine, denying recovery to those injured by such products, or to fashion remedies to meet these changing needs. Just as Justice Traynor in his landmark concurring opinion in *Escola* v. *Coca Cola Bottling Company* (1944) 24 Cal. 2d 453, 467-468, 150 P.2d 436, recognized that in an era of mass production and complex marketing methods the traditional standard of negligence was insufficient to govern the obligations of manufacturer to consumer, so should we acknowledge that some adaptation of the rules of causation and liability may be appropriate in these recurring circumstances. . . .
>
> The most persuasive reason for finding plaintiff states a cause of action is that advanced in *Summers:* as between an innocent plaintiff and negligent defendants, the latter should bear the cost of the injury. Here, as in *Summers,* plaintiff is not at fault in failing to provide evidence of causation, and although the absence of such evidence is not attributable to the

---

[104] 345 F Supp 353 (EDNY 1972). *Cf* Superfund §301(e) Report, at 59-62. While the enterprise liability theory is closely related to the market share theory, they are different. The former postulates that each defendant making up the relevant industry (such as the six blasting cap manufacturers in *Hall*) should contribute an *equal* share of damages to a plaintiff, since the harm would have been caused by their *industry.* This theory necessarily requires that all possible defendants—i.e., all members of the industry—be before the court. Thus, the practical application of this theory is limited to industries that consist of a relatively small number of manufacturers. By contrast, the market share theory would require only one member of the relevant industry to be before the court, and that defendant's share would be apportioned according to its share of the market. This theory of liability to avoid problems of proof of causation for plaintiffs has more logical, if not equitable, symmetry to it than the as-yet unaccepted enterprise theory.

defendants either, their conduct in marketing a drug the effects of which are delayed for many years played a significant role in creating the unavailability of proof.

From a broader policy standpoint, defendants are better able to bear the cost of injury resulting from the manufacture of a defective product. . . . The manufacturer is in the best position to discover and guard against defects in its products and to warn of harmful effects; thus, holding it liable for defects and failure to warn of harmful effects will provide an incentive to product safety. . . . These considerations are particularly significant where medication is involved, for the consumer is virtually helpless to protect himself from serious, sometimes permanent, sometimes fatal, injuries caused by deleterious drugs.[105]

The court held that the burden of proving causation should not be shifted to the defendants on a strict *Summers* theory because not all manufacturers of DES were before the court. If *Summers* were strictly applied, there was a possibility that one or more of the defendants would have been held liable for the entire amount of damages, and the responsible manufacturer might have escaped liability altogether. The court determined that the reasonable approach in this case was to approach the question of liability based on the percentage of DES manufactured by each defendant. The court held that the plaintiff must join a *substantial percentage* of the market. The court did not define substantial percentage but suggested that it could be less than 75 per cent. The court stated:

> Each defendant will be held liable for the proportion of the judgment represented by its share of that market unless it demonstrates that it could not have made the product which caused plaintiff's injuries. . . . Once plaintiff has met her burden of joining the required defendants, they in turn may cross-complain against other DES manufacturers, not joined in the action, which they can allege might have supplied the injury-causing product.
>
> Under this approach, each manufacturer's liability would approximate its responsibility for the injuries caused by its own products.[106]

Sindell has clearly paved the way for DES plaintiffs in California, although most courts to date have specifically declined to follow the California court's lead.[107] In virtually all cases in which the plaintiffs have survived a motion for summary judgment based on their inability to identify the manufacturer of the drug taken by their mothers, the courts have shifted the burden of proof to the defendants. However, no other court has adopted outright the market share theory of liability. Other courts have extended traditional theories, however,

---

[105] 26 Cal 3d at 610-11, 607 P2d at 936, 163 Cal Rptr at 144.
[106] *Id* at 612, 607 P2d at 937, 163 Cal Rptr at 145.
[107] See §16.13.

to shift the burden of proof to the defendants. Thus, the defendants in DES cases have been forced to prove that they could not have manufactured the drug taken by the plaintiffs' mother under the theory of alternative liability, concert of action, and a hybrid of alternative liability and market share.

§16.15 —Other Cases

In *Abel v Eli Lilly & Co*,[108] the court allowed the case to proceed on the theory of alternative liability. The plaintiffs joined as defendants all manufacturers that distributed DES in Michigan during the years the plaintiffs' mothers took DES. The court held that since all potential tortfeasors were before the court, the plaintiffs could proceed on the theory of alternative liability.[109] The court held that it was appropriate to shift the burden of disproving causation to the defendant once the defendant's wrongful conduct had been established.[110]

The court specifically outlined the plaintiffs' burden of proof to establish alternative liability:

> They [plaintiffs] must establish by a preponderance of the evidence that each defendant breached its duty of care in producing the product, that the harm to each plaintiff was the result of ingestion of DES by her mother, and that one or more of the named defendants manufactured the DES so ingested. Each plaintiff must carry her burden as to these defendants in order to recover. Should plaintiffs fail to carry their burden as to any or all defendants, they will suffer the consequences.[111]

The court held that if a plaintiff failed to prove that all of the defendants breached a duty, the plaintiff could not recover from any defendant because of the possibility of holding the wrong defendant liable. If, however, a plaintiff proved that all of the defendants breached a duty, the burden of proof was

---

[108] 94 Mich App 59, 289 NW2d 20 (1980).

[109] Alternative liability involves independent acts by two or more tortfeasors, all of whom have acted wrongfully, but only one of whom has injured the plaintiff. Joint and several liability is imposed, not because all are responsible for the damage, but because it is impossible to tell which one is responsible. A defendant is free to absolve himself or herself of liability, even if it is shown that he or she acted wrongfully, by proving that his or her wrongful act was not the cause of plaintiff's injury. *See* Summers v Tice, 33 Cal 2d 80, 199 P2d 1 (1948).

[110] The court stated:

> Plaintiffs must establish that they suffered a certain amount of damage at the hands of defendants, all of whom are tortfeasors. Should plaintiffs succeed in establishing that defendants are alternatively liable for this amount of damages, defendants are left to apportion the damages among themselves. Each defendant is free to present proofs absolving itself from liability as to any particular plaintiff or as to all plaintiffs. Defendants are also free to implead any third party whom they believe liable for all or part of the damages.

94 Mich App at 76, 289 NW2d at 26.

[111] *Id* at 76-77, 289 NW2d at 26-27.

shifted to the defendants for each to show that its product was not the cause of the plaintiff's injury. The court reasoned that as between an innocent plaintiff and a wrongdoer, the burden of uncertainty should fall on the wrongdoer. The court stated: "[I]f injustice is inevitable, the burden should fall on the wrongdoer rather than on the innocent plaintiff."[112]

In *Bichler v Eli Lilly & Co*,[113] the court upheld a $493,000 jury verdict against the defendant based on a finding that Eli Lilly had acted in concert[114] with other drug companies to manufacture and market DES, and that all the drug companies had failed to test DES adequately. This verdict was upheld despite the fact that the jury found the plaintiff had failed to show that Eli Lilly manufactured the drug taken by her mother. The court explained the reason it was relaxing the plaintiff's burden of proof:

> This court recognizes, as did the courts in California and Michigan, that identification problems arise both as the result of the passage of time as well as the result of industry practice. The specific problems presented by the widespread use of generic drugs, which render identification almost impossible to the user, let alone the ultimately harmed person, plus the absence of any uniform requirement for pharmacies to keep and maintain records over extended periods, cannot be permitted to prevent valid recoveries not to allow some manufacturers to escape their liability altogether by means of this shroud of anonymity. We of this court, too, adhere to the view of Dean Pound that "[t]he law must be stable but must not stand still."[115]

In *Ferrigno v Eli Lilly & Co*,[116] a New Jersey trial court held that the plaintiff could rely on alternative liability, despite the fact that not all manufacturers of DES were joined as defendants. The court stated that for policy reasons it was appropriate to shift the burden to the defendants to exonerate themselves from liability. The court rejected the theories of enterprise liability, concert of

---

[112] *Id* at 76, 289 NW2d at 26.

[113] 79 AD2d 317, 436 NYS2d 625, (1981), *affd*, 55 NY2d 571, 436 NE2d 182 (1982), 450 NYS2d 776.

[114] The trial court gave the following charge on concert of action:

Thus, if you find the defendant and the other drug companies either consciously paralleled each other in failing to test DES on pregnant mice, as a result of some implied understanding, or that they acted independently of each other in failing to do such testing, but that such independent actions had the effect of substantially aiding or encouraging the failure to test by the others, then you should find that the defendant wrongfully acted in concert with the other drug manufacturers in the testing and marketing of DES for use in accidents of pregnancy. Of course, you must also have found that it was wrongful for the defendant and the other drug companies not to have tested DES in pregnant mice because of the state of knowledge that was available to them in 1953.

79 AD2d at 323, 436 NYS2d at 631.

[115] *Id* at 328-29, 436 NYS2d at 632.

[116] 175 NJ Super 551, 420 A2d 1305 (LDV 1980).

action, and market share. The court held, however, that to the extent the defendants failed to exculpate themselves from liability, damages would be apportioned on the basis of market share. Joint and several liability would not be imposed, contrary to the usual procedure in alternative liability cases.[117] It should be noted, however, that a New Jersey appellate court[118] and a United States district court applying New Jersey law[119] have specifically declined to follow *Ferrigno*. Both courts held that the plaintiffs could not proceed under alternative liability and granted summary judgment for the defendants.

§16.16   The Asbestos Litigation

Product identification has also been an issue in asbestos litigation. In certain cases, the problem has not been determining who manufactured the products to which the plaintiff was exposed, but rather determining which exposure caused the plaintiff's injuries. In *Borel v Fibreboard Paper Products Corp*,[120] the plaintiff sued 11 manufacturers of asbestos insulation materials used by him

---

[117] The court discussed in some detail the elements of proof required of a plaintiff to prevail against a manufacturer of DES. To recover under the theory of strict liability the plaintiff must show:

1.   That her mother took DES
2.   That DES causes cancer in the children of women who took the drug while pregnant
3.   That the cancer or other condition of the plaintiff was caused by the DES taken by her mother. (The court stated that present day scientific knowledge would be admissible on the second and third elements)
4.   Identification of the particular product. This could be accomplished either by identifying the specific drug company which manufactured the DES taken by the plaintiff's mother or by establishing alternative liability. In order to establish alternative liability, plaintiff had to show that each defendant marketed or manufactured DES that was sold in New Jersey prior to the time the plaintiff's mother took it, and the defendant produced the drug for use as a miscarriage preventative

The next issue is whether DES was apparently a useful and desirable product. If the plaintiff shows that DES was not an apparently useful and desirable product at the time it was taken by the plaintiff's mother, assuming that the burdens outlined above have been met, the plaintiff will automatically recover under strict liability. If, on the other hand, DES did appear to be a reasonable and useful drug at the time it was manufactured, the plaintiff will have to show that there was a medically recognizable risk associated with the drug at the time it was produced. If the plaintiff establishes that the marketing and use of DES was not justified with its medically recognizable risk, she will prevail under strict liability. If a jury determines that the apparent usefulness outweighed the risk, however, plaintiff must establish that either the drugs were not properly prepared or they were negligently marketed. To establish the former, the plaintiff has to present evidence relating to the adequacy of tests performed by the defendants prior to the manufacture of DES. To establish the latter, plaintiff has to show that the drugs were marketed without proper warnings and directions.

[118] Namm v Charles E Frosst & Co, 178 NJ Super 19, 427 A2d 1121 (App Div 1981).

[119] Pipon v Burroughs-Wellcome Co, 532 F Supp 637 (DNJ 1982).

[120] 493 F2d 1076 (5th Cir 1973), *cert denied*, 419 US 869 (1974).

during his working career. He settled with four defendants before trial, and the court directed a verdict as to a fifth because the plaintiff failed to show he had ever been exposed to a product of that company. A jury returned a verdict against the six remaining defendants.

The plaintiff had worked with asbestos insulation from 1936 to 1969. In 1969, he discovered he was suffering from asbestosis and mesothelioma and brought suit in that year. The plaintiff died before trial. Two of the defendants argued that their products could not possibly have caused Borel's injuries because he was not exposed to them until 1962 and 1966, respectively. These defendants relied on the fact that the latency period for asbestosis is usually at least 10 years, and plaintiff had been exposed to their products for less than that amount of time. The court rejected this argument.

> In the instant case, it is impossible, as a practical matter, to determine with absolute certainty which particular exposure to asbestos dust resulted in injury to Borel. It is undisputed, however, that Borel contracted asbestosis from inhaling asbestos dust and that he was exposed to the products of all the defendants on many occasions. It was also established that the effect of exposure to asbestos dust is cumulative, that is, each exposure may result in an additional and separate injury. We think, therefore, that on the basis of strong circumstantial evidence the jury could find that each defendant was the cause in fact of some injury to Borel.
>
> Relying on expert testimony that asbestosis does not usually manifest itself until fifteen, twenty, or even twenty-five years after initial exposure, Pittsburgh Corning Company and Armstrong Cork Company contend that they cannot be liable because Borel was not exposed to their products until after 1962 and 1966 respectively. As we have pointed out, however, the length of this latent period varies according to individual idiosyncrasy, duration and intensity of exposure, and the type of asbestos used; in some cases the effect of the exposure may manifest itself in less than five or ten years. Thus, even the most recent exposures could have added to or accelerated Borel's overall condition.[121]

---

[121] *Id* 1094. Earlier in the opinion, the court stated:

> The medical testimony adduced at trial indicates that inhaling asbestos dust in industrial conditions, even with relatively light exposure, can produce the disease of asbestosis. The disease is difficult to diagnose in its early stages because there is a long latent period between initial exposure and apparent effect. This latent period may vary according to individual idiosyncrasy, duration and intensity of exposure, and the type of asbestos used. In some cases, the disease may manifest itself in less than ten years after initial exposure. In general, however, it does not manifest itself until ten to twenty-five or more years after initial exposure. This latent period is explained by the fact that asbestos fibers, once inhaled, remain in place in the lung, causing a tissue reaction that is slowly progressive and apparently irreversible. Even if no additional asbestos fibers are inhaled, tissue changes may continue undetected for decades. By the time the disease is diagnosable, a considerable period of time has elapsed since the date of the injurious

In a recent case,[122] a federal court in Texas held that the market share liability theory of *Sindell*[123] could apply to asbestos litigation. This court's ruling is of particular significance because there are over 3000 asbestos cases in the eastern district of Texas alone. The key to *Sindell* is a problem of proof—the inability of the plaintiff to identify the precise causative agent. Asbestos plaintiffs face the same problem as DES plaintiffs: the length of the latency period makes precise proof of causation virtually impossible:

> [I]t is impossible for the plaintiff to isolate the precise exposure or identify the manufacturer's product which caused his disease. In mesothelioma, the problem of identification is largely due to its long latent period. The cumulative nature of asbestosis is basically inconsistent with the legal concept of proof of a precise causative agent.[124]

In the Fifth Circuit, testimony of the plaintiff or his or her coworkers regarding use of a particular product has been accepted as circumstantial evidence of causation in asbestos cases. The district court noted that:

> [I]n the ten years since the trial of Borel, we have been imposing a kind of *Sindell* liability. The proof of causation as related to a particular Defendant's product has been, of necessity, limited to a worker's own testimony and testimony of co-workers who rely on memory with regard to products used over a twenty or thirty year period. Yet, for years, this is all that has been required of plaintiffs.[125]

The court held that *Sindell* would be applicable to asbestos cases. Aside from the policy reasons for shifting the burden of proof to defendants, market share liability would alleviate the unfairness of a pro rata approach to apportionment of damages. When several producers are held jointly and severally liable, a pro

---

exposure. Furthermore, the effect of the disease may be cumulative since each exposure to asbestos dust can result in additional tissue changes. A worker's present condition is the biological product of many years of exposure to asbestos dust, with both past and recent exposures contributing to the overall effect. All of these factors combine to make it impossible, as a practical matter, to determine which exposure or exposures to asbestos dust caused the disease.

A second disease, mesothelioma, is a form of lung cancer caused by exposure to asbestos. It affects the pleural and peritoneal cavities, and there is a similarly long period between initial contact and apparent effect. As with asbestosis, it is difficult to determine which exposure to asbestos dust is responsible for the disease.

Id 1083.

[122] Hardy v Johns-Manville Sales Corp, 509 F Supp 1353 (ED Tex 1981), *revd in part on other grounds*, 681 F2d 334 (5th Cir 1982) (reversed on collateral estoppel, not market share theory).

[123] Sindell v Abbott Laboratories, 26 Cal 3d 588, 607 P2d 924, 163 Cal Rptr 132, *cert denied*, 449 US 912 (1980), discussed in §16.14.

[124] 509 F Supp at 1358.

[125] *Id.*

rata apportionment results in unfairness to small producers and a windfall to large producers. "Market share liability cures this inherent defect, and results in apportionment which bears some relationship to causative fault."[126]

Thus, there appears to be a growing trend among courts to shift the burden of proof to the defendants in toxic substance litigation. In cases where a plaintiff can prove that a group of defendants acted wrongfully and that the plaintiff was injured as a result of the acts of some or all of the defendants, courts have shown a willingness to shift the burden to the defendants to exculpate themselves. This shifting of the burden will necessarily result in some defendants being held liable in some cases in which their products were not the cause of the injury.[127] Courts presumably are willing to make this social policy judgment because the alternative, which is the denial of a remedy for an injured party, is deemed unacceptable. There also is a trend in a similar direction in state legislatures through enactment of statutory presumptions of causation.[128]

Other Issues

§16.17   In-Court Experiments

Use of in-court experiments is an effective method of proof. Parties involved in toxic substance litigation may desire to use in-court experiments to demonstrate particular qualities of certain chemicals. Often the experiment may be designed to show that a certain substance could or could not have been the cause of the plaintiff's injuries.

Experimental evidence is generally admissible if it is relevant and probative. In *Wolf v Proctor & Gamble Co,*[129] the defendant sought to exclude the performance of an in-court experiment by the plaintiff's expert. The plaintiffs claimed that use of Rely tampons manufactured by the defendant caused toxic shock syndrome in the users. The experiment was designed to show that an enzyme

---

[126] *Id* 1358-59. *Compare* Prelick v Johns-Manville Corp, 531 F Supp 96 (WD Pa 1982), in which the court refused to apply *Sindell* because the plaintiff was able to identify some of the manufacturers to whose product he was exposed. "We conclude, therefore, that where, as here, the plaintiff is able to identify at least one manufacturer or supplier whose product caused plaintiff's injury, the 'Sindell' or 'enterprise' theory is inapplicable." *Id* 98.

[127] See Fischer, *Products Liability—An Analysis of Market Share Liability,* 34 Vand L Rev 1623 (1981); Gillick, *The Essence of Enterprise Liability, or the True Meaning of "We're All in this Together,"* 16 Forum 979 (1981).

[128] *E.g.,* Minn HR 76, enacted May 10, 1983 for hazardous waste injuries; *see* HR 2482, 98th Cong, 1st Sess, 129 Cong Rec H-1992 (Apr 12, 1982); HR 2582, 98th Cong, 1st Sess, 129 Cong Rec H-2114 (Apr 18, 1983); S 917, 98th Cong, 1st Sess, 129 Cong Rec S-3972 (Mar 24, 1983); and S 946, 98th Cong, 1st Sess, 129 Cong Rec S-3973 (Mar 24, 1983).

[129] 555 F Supp 613 (DNJ 1982).

found in the vagina would liquify into glucose when added to a component of Rely tampons. The experiment was intended to illustrate the plaintiffs' expert's theory that the staph infection associated with toxic shock syndrome was caused by glucose acting as food for staph bacteria. This would result in an increased production of staph toxins, which in turn could combine with other factors to cause toxic shock syndrome.

In a motion in limine, the defendant objected to the demonstration on the grounds that: first, it would not be performed under conditions substantially similar to conditions found in the human vagina; and second, its probative value would be substantially outweighed by the danger of unfair prejudice and confusion. The court held that the experiment was clearly relevant to the demonstration of the expert's theory and the plaintiffs' theory of causation. While the court noted that there would clearly be differences between the conditions of the experiment and the conditions found in the vagina, it held that the differences could either be explained to the jury or would be obvious. The court noted that the basic purpose of the experiment was to demonstrate that an ingredient found in Rely tampons is capable of being broken down into glucose when exposed to an enzyme found in the vagina. Therefore, the in-court demonstration was both relevant and probative.

The court also rejected the defendants' claim that the effect of the experiment would be highly prejudicial. The court noted that this experiment was not psychologically charged and would not have an emotional impact on the jury. The court ruled that the experiment could be performed in the court.[130] There is little doubt that other types of in-court experiments can be utilized to great effect by either plaintiffs or defendants.

In *Drayton v Jiffee Chemical Corp*,[131] the trial court denied the defendant's request to perform an in-court experiment. The defendant sought to compare the effects of two different drain cleaners on clothing. The defendant argued this would have showed that its product did not cause the plaintiff's injury. The court denied permission to conduct the experiment. While this may appear to be an abuse of discretion, two facts make the court's decision more understandable. First, the case was tried to the judge without a jury, and the defendant presented other evidence to prove which drain cleaner caused the injury. Second, although there had been extensive pretrial discovery, the defendant never raised the claim of product misidentification until the middle of the trial. Under these circumstances, the Sixth Circuit said the trial court's refusal to allow the experiment was not an abuse of discretion.[132]

---

[130] *Id* 626-27.

[131] 395 F Supp 1081 (ND Ohio 1975), *affd*, 591 F2d 352 (6th Cir 1978).

[132] The court stated:

Defendant urges that the trial court abused its discretion in failing to permit an in-court demonstration comparing the effects of both Mister Plumber and Liquid-plumr upon clothing. Defendant insists that the test would have demonstrated the different properties of lye and sulfuric acid and thus might have convinced the trial judge as finder of fact that the injury stemmed from a sulfuric acid solution

§16.18 Collateral Estoppel

The offensive use of collateral estoppel presents an interesting question in toxic substance litigation. In certain types of toxic substance litigation, the same issues are presented in every case and the same parties are the defendants in most cases.[133] The plaintiffs may seek to use offensive, nonmutual collateral estoppel to avoid having to reprove issues which have already been litigated. Courts may be tempted to apply collateral estoppel in order to avoid *reinventing the wheel* in similar cases. The defendants no doubt will vigorously oppose the use of collateral estoppel, since if applied it would prevent litigation of an issue that might defeat recovery.

To date, only one court has attempted to apply offensive collateral estoppel in toxic substances litigation, but the trial court's determination was reversed on appeal.[134] The United States District Court for the Eastern District of Texas, where there are over 3000 asbestos plaintiffs with suits pending, applied offensive collateral estoppel in an attempt to "avoid reinventing the asbestos liability wheel in every case."[135] A year earlier, in *Flatt v Johns-Manville Sales Corp,*[136] the same district court outlined the elements of proof for plaintiffs in asbestos cases:

> [P]laintiffs have the burden of proving by a preponderance of the evidence the following elements:
>
> 1. Defendants manufactured, marketed, sold, distributed, or placed in the stream of commerce products containing asbestos.
> 2. Products containing asbestos are unreasonably dangerous.
> 3. Asbestos dust is a competent producing cause of mesothelioma.
> 4. Decedent was exposed to defendant's products.
> 5. The exposure was sufficient to be a producing cause of mesothelioma.

---

and not from its product. It is true that defendant had entered a general denial that its product was involved. Nevertheless, in spite of extensive pretrial discovery over a period of several years, the particular claim of product misidentification was made for the first time in the middle of the trial. Under such circumstances, we cannot hold that the trial judge abused his discretion in refusing to permit the test. The case must, therefore, proceed upon the premise that the product which caused minor plaintiff's injuries was, in fact, Liquid-plumr and that it consisted of a 26% solution of sodium hydroxide, or lye.

591 F2d at 356-57.

[133] This is particularly true in asbestos and DES litigation, discussed in §§16.09-16.10 and §§16.13-16.16. The same manufacturers are consistently defendants in most lawsuits.

[134] Hardy v Johns-Manville Sales Corp, 509 F Supp 1353 (ED Tex 1981), *revd,* 681 F2d 334 (5th Cir 1982).

[135] 509 F Supp at 1357.

[136] 488 F Supp 836 (ED Tex 1980).

6. Decedent contracted mesothelioma.

7. Plaintiffs suffered damages.[137]

In *Hardy v Johns-Manville Sales Corp*,[138] the district court held, on the basis of *Borel v Fibreboard Paper Products Corp*,[139] that defendants were precluded from offering proof on the second and third elements in the list provided in *Flatt*. In an omnibus order, the district court held that *Borel* established as a matter of law:

1.   Insulation products containing asbestos as a generic ingredient are "unavoidably unsafe products"[140]

2.   Asbestos is a competent producing cause of mesothelioma and asbestosis

3.   No warnings were issued by any asbestos insulation manufacturers prior to 1964

4.   The "warning standard" was not met by the *Borel* defendants in the period from 1964 through 1969[141]

The order applied to all defendants, regardless of whether they were defendants in *Borel*.

The Fifth Circuit reversed, both as to the non-*Borel* and the *Borel* defendants. The court held that the non-*Borel* defendants did not share an identity of interest with the *Borel* defendants sufficient to constitute privity. The fact that all defendants manufactured asbestos-containing products does not constitute privity. The court also rejected the argument the non-*Borel* defendants' interests had been virtually represented by the defendants in *Borel*. This ruling is unexceptional.

The Fifth Circuit's ruling as to *Borel* defendants raises different questions, however. The court determined that the verdict in *Borel* was ambiguous, that there have been verdicts for the defendants in other cases, and that the application of collateral estoppel would be unfair because of the unforeseeability that the small $68,000 liability at stake in *Borel* could lead to potential multimillion dollar liability in later cases. It appears that the court's ruling may have been reached because of its tacit belief that application of collateral estoppel was unfair in asbestos cases, and the court accordingly held that the traditional elements of collateral estoppel had not been met.

Application of offensive collateral estoppel is both problematic and tempting in toxic substance litigation. The plaintiffs will contend it is logical that once a scientific fact is established, the same issue should not be relitigated countless times. Hence, the plaintiffs will argue, offensive use of collateral

---

137 *Id* 838.

138 509 F Supp 1353 (ED Tex 1981), *revd,* 681 F2d 334 (5th Cir 1982).

139 493 F2d 1076 (5th Cir 1973), *cert denied,* 419 US 869 (1974).

140 *Id* 1081.

141 *Id* 1081.

estoppel will result in judicial economy, as well as consistent treatment of injured parties. Clearly, if there is an advance in scientific knowledge, litigation should not be foreclosed. Part of the problem lies in the fact that what facts are found in any particular case often depends more on the skill of the attorneys than it does on anything else. Collateral estoppel at this point is more a possibility than a reality in toxic tort litigation. How the doctrine will be utilized remains to be see.[142]

§16.19 Summary

While the field of toxic torts promises to be one of the most fertile areas of litigation in the coming decade, it also seems clear that the issue of the burden of proof on causation will be one of the most vigorously contested areas, and one that will change most quickly over the years as courts accept scientific advances or create evidentiary policies of their own. Lawyers for plaintiffs and defendants will need to become exceptionally skilled in the medical and scientific aspects of disease causation theories. Judges or legislatures will have to resolve the current uncertainties about the issues of latent injuries and product identification. Perhaps as importantly, lawyers must consider the opportunities and obligations they have, on the one hand, to individuals to provide assistance in identifying legitimate causes of action through the development of creative causation theories, and on the other hand, to corporations to provide preventative counseling to avoid creating a potential cause of action and to minimize liability from anticipated future causation theories.

---

[142] See discussion at "Superfund Section 301(e) Study Group," Senate Comm. on Environment and Public Works, 97th Cong, 2d Sess, Injuries and Damages from Hazardous Wastes—Analysis and Improvement of Legal Remedies 213-33 (Comm Print No 97-12, 1982), recommending that causation *presumptions* be created in federal agency rules in lieu of reliance on litigation in test cases (i.e., collateral estoppel).

17

Damages*

Arthur F. Roeca, Esq.†

---

* The author wishes to express his appreciation to Robert J. Lombardi, University of Hawaii, William S. Richardson School of Law, Class of 1985, and to Darryl Taira, University of Southern California, School of Law, Class of 1984, for their excellent research and invaluable assistance.

† Partner, Case, Kay & Lynch, Honolulu, Hawaii.

§17.01   —Introduction

In a toxic tort case, the plaintiff will recover no damages simply because he or she or his or her property may have been exposed to a toxic substance. Rather, a plaintiff must prove there has been an actual injury from an exposure to the toxic substance of such a nature that it has manifested itself as of the time of trial or is reasonably expected to manifest itself within the normal life expectancy of the plaintiff. Thus, in respect to proof of the elements of damages, the toxic tort case is similar to other personal injury or property damage cases. In any toxic tort case where damages for personal injuries are claimed, the plaintiff must prove by competent medical testimony that the particular plaintiff, within reasonable medical certainty or probability, has sustained such an injury from exposure to the specific toxic substance and not simply that there might possibly have been or will be injurious consequences. This reasoning applies equally in those cases involving property damages.

This chapter discusses the standards, rules, and processes used generally by the courts to measure compensation for personal injuries and property damage. In addition, the subject of punitive damages in the context of toxic torts is discussed, including whether punitive damages should be permitted in toxic tort litigation and, if so, under what circumstances and according to what burden of proof.

Standards and Elements of Damages Generally

§17.02   Reasonable Certainty Requirement

Traditionally, courts imposed a harsh standard of proof upon a plaintiff which required that both the nature and extent of the plaintiff's damages be established with certainty. It was believed that such a standard would preclude the jury from awarding money damages based upon speculation or conjecture.[1] Damages "must be certain, both in their nature and in respect to the cause from which they proceed,"[2] and injury and compensatory damages resulting must be shown with certainty and not left to conjecture or speculation.[3]

---

[1] See generally McCormick, Handbook on the Law of Damages ch 4 (1935).

[2] Moran Towing Corp v MA Gammino Constr Co, 244 F Supp 729 (DRI 1965), *vacated on other grounds*, 363 F2d 108 (1st Cir 1966), *on remand*, 292 F Supp 134 (DRI 1968), *affd in part & remanded in part*, 409 F2d 917 (1st Cir 1969).

[3] Swartz v Steele, 42 Ohio App 2d 1, 325 NE2d 910 (1974).

More recently, courts in most states have modified the harshness of the certainty rule by stating that damages need be proved only with *reasonable certainty,* removing the notion of exactness or mathematical certainty.[4] At a minimum, the term *reasonable certainty* means that damages must be taken out of the area of speculation; however, where it cannot be shown with reasonable certainty that any damages resulted from the defendant's actions, there can be no recovery.[5] Of course, the plaintiff is permitted to establish his or her damages inferentially, relying upon circumstantial evidence wherever necessary.[6]

Generally speaking, where damages may be attributed to more than one of several causes, the plaintiff must prove with reasonable certainty the proportional amount of his or her damages attributable to the particular defendant.

> There can be no recovery where speculation or conjecture must be resorted to in order to determine what caused the damage complained of. . . . When there is evidence of damage from several causes, as to a portion of which a defendant cannot be held liable, the burden is on plaintiff to present evidence which will show "within a reasonable degree of certainty" the share of damages for which a defendant is responsible.[7]

This rule is particularly significant in toxic tort cases where the plaintiff's injury may or may not be attributed to exposure to a particular defendant's product. As the case law makes clear, a defendant cannot be held liable for any injuries that were sustained by plaintiff as a result of a preexisiting condition. Rather, a plaintiff is entitled to recover damages only if the evidence establishes with a reasonable degree of certainty which of his or her present and future injuries are attributable to a particular toxic substance as distinguished from any preexisting condition or conditions related to some other toxic substance or some other cause. However, it is also well-established in tort law that a negligent defendant may be liable for any aggravation of a preexisting condition. Such conditions include a concealed physical condition, such as a latent disease, and aggravation results in liability even though the defendant was in no way responsible for the preexisting condition.[8]

The courts recognize a distinction between the quality of proof necessary to

[4] Stanley Co of Am v Hercules Powder Co, 16 NJ 295, 108 A2d 616 (1954); Taylor v Kaufhold, 368 Pa 538, 84 A2d 347 (1951); Barnes v Graham Virginia Quarries, Inc, 204 Va 414, 132 SE2d 395 (1963).

[5] Straughan v Tsouvulos, 246 Md 242, 228 A2d 300 (1967); Hale v Fawcett, 214 Va 583, 202 SE2d 923 (1974); United States Trust Co v O'Brien, 143 NY 284, 38 NE 266 (1894); California Press Mfg Co v Stafford Packing Co, 192 Cal 479, 221 P 345 (1923); Illinois Power & L Corp v Peterson, 322 Ill 342, 153 NE 577 (1926); Cates v Sparkman, 73 Tex 619, 11 SW 846 (1889).

[6] Roan v Johnson, 38 Ala App 209, 84 So 2d 379 (1955); Lach v Fleth, 361 Pa 340, 64 A2d 821 (1949).

[7] Hale v Fawcett, 214 Va 583, 202 SE2d 923, 925 (1974).

[8] Prosser, Law of Torts §43 (4th ed 1971).

establish that a plaintiff is entitled to some damages and the measure of proof necessary to enable the jury to establish the amount required to compensate the plaintiff.[9] Thus, courts no longer follow the antiquated rule restricting a plaintiff's recovery to matters susceptible to exact calculation of a pecuniary value,[10] and now, as long as the fact and cause of damages are proven with reasonable certainty, a plaintiff is no longer required to show exact or accurate proof as to the extent of injury and amount of damages.[11]

In view of the latency period associated with toxic substance injuries and their complications, the rule of certainty places a burden upon the plaintiff to prove that some part of his or her symptoms or disabilities are attributable to a particular product, rather than to some prior or subsequent history of sustained exposure to someone else's product. Absent this proof, the plaintiff will fail to meet his or her burden, and most courts would direct a verdict in favor of the defendant.

With regard to future injuries resulting from exposure to a particular toxic substance, the plaintiff also has the burden to quantify the amount of his or her injury. Testimony which fails to specify the nature and extent of future injuries with sufficient specificity will generally be considered too abstract and therefore insufficient to establish the damage element of a plaintiff's claim.

§17.03   Avoidable Consequences and Mitigation

Another well-recognized principle of tort law is that a party cannot recover damages flowing from consequences which that party could reasonably have avoided.[12] Prior to the general application of comparative negligence principles, the doctrine of avoidable consequences and failure to mitigate damages could totally wipe out a plaintiff's damage claim much like proof of contributory negligence or assumption of the risk. This was because courts likened the doctrine of avoidable consequences to an extension of the proximate cause principle: if the plaintiff could have reasonably avoided the damages which resulted, the activity of the defendant could no longer be considered the proximate cause of those damages.[13] The corollary to this doctrine is that the

[9] Wolverine Upholstery Co v Ammerman, 1 Mich App 235, 135 NW2d 572 (1965).

[10] Stuart v Western Union Tel Co, 66 Tex 580, 18 SW 351 (1885).

[11] Wakeman v Wheeler & W Mfg Co, 101 NY 205, 4 NE 264 (1886); Dallman Co v Southern Heater Co, 262 Ca App 2d 582, 68 Cal Rptr 873 (1968); Stott v Johnston, 36 Cal 2d 864, 229 P2d 348 (1951); King v Gerold, 109 Cal App 2d 316, 240 P2d 710 (1952); Friedman v Parkway Baking Co, 147 Pa Super 552, 24 A2d 157 (1942).

[12] Bomberger v McKelvey, 35 Cal 2d 607, 220 P2d 729 (1950); Olsen v United States Fidelity & Guaranty Co, 230 NY 31, 128 NE 908 (1920); Haywood v Massie, 188 Va 176, 49 SE2d 281 (1948); Hall v Paine, 224 Mass 62, 112 NE 153 (1916); Galveston H & SAR Co v Zantzinger, 92 Tex 365, 48 SW 563 (1898); Rich v Daily Creamery Co, 296 Mich 270, 296 NW 253 (1941); McClelland v Climax Hosiery Mills, 252 NY 347, 169 NE 605 (1930).

[13] Wabash RR Co v Campbell, 219 Ill 312, 76 NE 346 (1905); McClelland v Climax Hosiery Mills, 252 NY 347, 169 NE 106 (1930).

person who reasonably attempts to minimize his or her damages can recover the expenses incurred, and often those further damages which result from a reasonable effort to minimize damages.

In attempting to mitigate damages, the injured person need not take extraordinary efforts or do what is unreasonable or impracticable; reasonable diligence and ordinary care are all that is required to allow full recovery of all damages caused by the defendant's wrongful activity.[14] Stated differently, the consequences of the injury are recoverable whenever the injured party acts with such care and diligence as a person of ordinary prudence would use under the circumstances. The reasonableness of efforts to minimize damages are determined by rules of common sense, good faith, and fair dealing.[15] In the personal injury setting, the doctrine of mitigation is often expressed in terms of duty—the person who has been injured through the tortious activity of another has the duty to exercise reasonable care and diligence to avoid loss or to minimize the consequences of the injury.[16] If the nature of an injury caused by the tortious activity is such as to render medical or surgical treatment reasonably necessary, it has been held that damages will not be awarded for those injuries which would have been avoided by securing the medical or surgical aid of a physician of ordinary skill and experience.[17] In any event, damages will be decreased under the doctrine only where it is shown that a reasonably prudent person would have followed proper medical advice and the particular injured person did not, and that failure resulted in the worsening of his or her physical condition.[18] In determining whether a given plaintiff acted reasonably in failing to submit to medical treatment that would have reduced his or her injury, courts have considered various factors, including risk

[14] Valencia v Shell Oil Co, 23 Cal 2d 840, 147 P2d 558 (1944); Fruehauf Trailer Co v Lydick, 325 Ill App 28, 59 NE2d 551 (1945).

[15] Kleinclaus v Marin Realty Co, 94 Cal App 2d 733, 211 P2d 582 (1949); Hall v Paine, 224 Mass 62, 112 NE 153 (1916).

[16] Liddle v Collins Constr Co, 283 SW2d 474 (Mo 1955); Alberti v New York, LHigh & Western RR Co, 118 NY 77, 23 NE 35 (1889); Vallo v United States Exp Co, 147 Pa 404, 23 A 594 (1892); Chesapeake & Ohio RR Co v Paris, 111 Va 41, 68 SE 398 (1910); Glasgow v Metropolitan Street R Co, 191 Mo 347, 89 SW 915 (1905); Lorenc v Chemirad Corp, 37 NJ 56, 179 A2d 401 (1962); Bordanaro v Burstiner, 2 Misc 176, 151 NY2d 450 (1956); Bartunek v Koch, 404 Pa 1, 170 A2d 563 (1961); Collova v Mutual Serv Casualty Ins Co, 8 Wis 2d 535, 99 NW2d 740 (1959); Chicago City R Co v Saxby, 213 Ill 274, 72 NE 755 (1904); Intermill v Heumesser, 391 P2d 684 (Colo 1964).

[17] Marshall v Ransome Concrete Co, 33 Cal App 782, 166 P 846 (1917); Stipp v Tsutomi Karasawa, 318 SW2d 172 (Mo 1958); Leitzell v Delaware, Lehigh & Western RR Co, 232 Pa 475, 81 A 543 (1911); Collova v Mutual Serv Casualty Ins Co, 8 Wis 2d 535, 99 NW2d 740 (1959).

[18] Franco v Fujimoto, 47 Hawaii 408, 390 P2d 740 (1964); Intermill v Heumesser, 391 P2d 684 (Colo 1964); Delude v Raasakka, 42 Mich App 665, 202 NW2d 508 (1972), revd on other grounds, 391 Mich 296, 215 NW2d 685 (1974); Yarrow v United States, 309 F Supp 922 (SDNY 1970); Lopez v Prestige Casualty Co, 53 Wis 2d 25, 191 NW 2d 908 (1971).

of pain,[19] probablility of cure,[20] and the expense of medical treatment.[21] In *Lorenc v Chemirad Corp,*[22] the jurors were instructed as follows:

> The refusal to accept an operation is not unreasonable . . . . unless it is free from danger to life and health and extraordinary suffering and, according to the best medical and surgical opinion, offers a reasonable prospect of restoration and relief from disability. And reasonableness of refusal is a question of fact for you ladies and gentlemen of the jury to determine, whether or not the [plaintiff's] refusal to submit to a skin graft was reasonable on the grounds that it was dangerous to his life and health and worked extraordinary suffering.[23]

§17.04 Value

In a personal injury action, a plaintiff is entitled to recover for all the natural and proximate consequences of the defendant's wrongful act or omission. Compensable items include pain and suffering, loss of earnings (including, if proper, loss of profits), ill health or disability naturally resulting from the wrong or injury, subsequent aggravations of the injury that are proximately traceable to the original wrong, and any other compensable damage recognized by law that can be reasonably said to have occurred as a proximate consequence of the tortious conduct.[24] Damages such as pain and suffering are difficult to measure; however, items such as the value of lost time or loss of services permit more elaborate quantitative analyses. One measure of the value of lost time is the determination of what the plaintiff's services would have been worth during the time he or she was incapacitated by the injury, considering the income, health, age, education and background of the plaintiff.[25] Other items of *special damages* claimed in the action, including medical expenses and loss of earnings, are also capable of and require some quantifiable proof before recovery will be allowed.

---

[19] Meding v Robinson, 52 Del 299, 157 A2d 254 (1950), *affd,* 52 Del 578, 163 A2d 272 (1960).

[20] Clearwater v McClury, 157 So 2d 545 (Fla Dist Ct App 1968); Downs v Scott, 201 Pa Super 278, 191 A2d 908 (1963).

[21] Andrus v Security Ins Co, 161 So 2d 113 (La Ct App), *cert denied,* 246 La 81, 163 So 2d 358 (1964).

[22] Lorenc v Chemirad Corp, 37 NJ 56, 179 A2d 401 (1962).

[23] *Id* at 59, 179 A2d at 403.

[24] King v Cooney-Eckstein Co, 66 Fla 246, 63 So 659 (1913).

[25] Bonneau v North Shore RR Co, 152 Cal 406, 93 P 106 (1907); Smith v Blue Ridge Transp Co, 172 Md 42, 191 A 66 (1937); Sibley v Nason, 196 Mass 125, 81 NE 887 (1907); Reynolds v St Louis Transit Co, 189 Mo 408, 88 SW 50 (1905); Kowalke v Farmers Mut Auto Ins Co, 3 Wis 2d 389, 88 NW2d 747 (1958); Seymour v House, 305 SW2d 1 (Mo 1957); Barnes v Danville Street Rd & Light Co, 235 Ill 566, 85 NE 921 (1908); Maxwell v Wanik, 290 Mich 106, 287 NW 396 (1939); Neumann v Metropolitan Tobacco Co, 20 Misc 2d 1013, 189 NYS2d 600 (1959).

Compensable value has another connotation in the personal injury setting. Tort law recognizes certain relationships as being worthy of legal protection such that unprivileged interference may bring into play the protection of the tort law. For example, the injury to a husband could conceivably give rise to the wife's cause of action for loss of consortium, and vice versa; similarly, in some states, a parent witnessing his or her child struck and killed by a negligent driver creates a cause of action in favor of the parent against the negligent driver for emotional distress.[26] However, were that parent to observe someone else's child being struck by the same negligent driver, there would be no legally compensable injury, although the emotional shock and trauma caused by witnessing the death of a child may be identical. In this sense, the term *value* also means those elements of damage which are recognized by our evolving system of tort law as having legal significance. Therefore, such harm or injury justifies compensation provided the other elements of the tort have been established.

Compensatory Damages

§17.05 Lost Wages and Impairment to Earning Capacity

If, as a result of exposure to a toxic substance, an individual is prevented from engaging in his or her usual employment, virtually every court will allow him or her to include a claim for loss of earnings as an element of compensatory damages.[27] If, on the other hand, the plaintiff's injury does not prevent him or her from continuing his or her employment and earning his or her full salary, no compensatory damages can be awarded for mere loss of time.[28] Recovery is also allowed for loss of future earnings discounted to present value.[29] When the plaintiff claims damages for loss of future earnings, an

---

[26] Taylor v Vallenluga, 171 Cal App 2d 107, 399 P2d 310 (1959); Schurk v Christensen, 80 Wash 2d 652, 497 P2d 937 (1972); Dillon v Legg, 68 Cal 2d 728, 441 P2d 912, 69 Cal Rptr 72 (1968); D'Amicol v Alvarez Shipping Co, 31 Conn Sup 164, 326 A2d 129 (1973).

[27] King v Southern Pac Co, 109 Cal 96, 41 P 786 (1895); Arizona Title Ins & Trust Co v O'Malley Lumber Co, 14 Ariz App 486, 484 P2d 639 (1971); Barnes v Danville Street Power & Light Co, 235 Ill 566, 85 NE 921 (1908); Maxwell v Wanik, 290 Mich 106, 287 NW 396 (1939); Neumann v Metropolitan Tobacco Co, 20 Misc 2d 1013, 189 NYS2d 600 (1959); Hoge v Anderson, 200 Va 364, 106 SE2d 121 (1958); Greater Westchester Homeowners Asn v Los Angeles, 26 Cal 3d 86, 603 P2d 1329, 160 Cal Rptr 733 (1979); Flamm v Noble, 296 NY 262, 72 NE2d 886 (1947); Mayflower Invest Co v Stephens, 345 SW2d 786 (Tex Civ App 1960); McCloskey v Ryder, 138 Pa 383, 21 A 148 (1891).

[28] King v Southern Pac Co, 109 Cal 96, 41 P 786 (1895); Kendrick v Towle, 60 Mich 363, 27 NW 567 (1896).

[29] Parker v Brinson Constr Co, 78 So 2d 873 (Fla 1955); Cochran v Boston, 211 Mass 171, 97 NE 1100 (1912); Fitzpatrick v Ritzenhein, 367 Mich 326, 116 NW2d 894 (1962); D'Amico v Cariglia, 330 Mass 246, 112 NE2d 807 (1953); Sylvania Electric Prod, Inc v Barker (Mass), 228 F2d 842 (1st Cir 1955), *cert denied*, 350 US 988 (1956).

instruction in terms of reduction to present net worth is essential. In some cases, the court's instructions provide the jury with the formula to compute present value, while other courts feel that the means of computation is something reasonably known to jurors and accordingly hold that it is not necessary to provide the jury with the formula.[30] A recommended instruction convering the present worth of future wage loss is as follows:

> If the jury should find that the plaintiff is entitled to a verdict, and further find that the evidence in the case establishes either: (1) a reasonable likelihood of future medical expense, or (2) a reasonable likelihood of loss of future earnings, then it becomes the duty of the jury to ascertain the present worth in dollars of such future damage, since the award of future damages necessarily requires that payment be made now for a loss that will not actually be sustained until some future date.
>
> Under these circumstances, the result is that the plaintiff will in effect be reimbursed in advance of the loss, and so will have the use of money which he would not have received until some future date, but for the verdict.
>
> In order to make a reasonable adjustment for the present use, interest free, of money representing a lump sum payment of anticipated future loss, the law requires that the jury discount, or reduce to its present worth, the amount of the anticipated future loss, by taking (1) the interest rate or return which the plaintiff could reasonably be expected to receive on an investment of the lump sum payment, together with (2) the period of time over which the future loss is reasonably certain to be sustained; and then reduce, or in effect deduct from the total amount of anticipated future loss whatever that amount would be reasonably certain to earn or return, if invested at such rate of interest over such future period of time; and include in the verdict an amount for only the present worth—the reduced amount—of the total anticipated future loss.
>
> As already explained to you, this computation is readily made by using the socalled "present-worth" tables, which the court has judicially noticed and received in evidence in this case.[31]

Where the plaintiff has not been totally disabled, but his or her earnings capacity has been impaired, he or she is entitled to recover the diminution of earnings capacity.[32] Where the diminished earnings capacity will continue into

---

[30] Brem v United States Fidelity & Guar Co, 206 A2d 404 (DC App 1964); Cohen v Fair Lawn Dairies, Inc, 86 NJ Super 206, 206 A2d 585 (1964); United Power Co v Matheny, 81 Ohio St 204, 90 NE 154 (1909); Thompson v H Rouw Co, 237 SW2d 662 (Tex Civ App 1951); Hiss v Griedberg, 201 Va 572, 112 SE2d 871 (1960).

[31] 3 Devitt & Blackmar, Federal Jury Practice and Instructions §8513 (3d ed 1977).

[32] Stikney v Goward, 161 Minn 457, 201 NW 630 (1925); Grayson v Irvmar Realty Corp, 7 AD2d 436, 184 NYS2d 33 (1959); Connolly v Pre-Mixed Concrete Co, 49 Cal 2d 483, 319 P2d 343 (1957); Matthews v Mumey, 15 Ohio App 2d 5, 238 NE2d 825 (1968); Nisbet v Medaglia, 356 Mass 580, 254 NE2d 782 (1969); Delph v Ammons, 239

the future but is not permanent, recovery is allowed for the entire time during which the injury will in all likelihood cause loss;[33] however, if the impairment is permanent, recovery will be allowed for the entire work-life expectancy of the plaintiff.[34] As with all items of damages, the plaintiff has the burden of proof of introducing evidence showing what his or her earning power was and the extent to which it has been impaired.[35] The extent of the diminution of impairment is generally arrived at by considering the nature and extent of the plaintiff's business, profession, or employment, his or her skill or ability in his or her occupation or profession, and the loss or diminution of his or her capacity to pursue his or her business or occupation, and by comparing what he or she was capable of earning at or before the time of the injury with what he or she was capable of earning after it occurred.[36]

§17.06   General Damages: Pain and Suffering

The law is clear that an award for pain and suffering is a proper element in a plaintiff's recovery for personal physical injuries tortiously inflicted.[37] Recovery may also include damages for pain and suffering incident to a surgical operation or medical treatment reasonably required by the injury.[38]

It is also well-settled that in an action for personal injuries, future pain and suffering on the part of the injured person constitute a proper element of damages which may be allowed, provided there is the requisite certainty or

---

Md 662, 212 A2d 504 (1965); Canning v Hannaford, 372 Mich 41, 127 NW2d 851 (1964); Baker v Norris, 248 SW2d 870 (Mo App 1952); Bone v General Motors Corp, 322 SW2d 916 (Mo 1959); Nawrocki v Hawkeye Sec Ins, Co, 83 Mich App 135, 268 NW2d 317 (1978); Mullis v Miami, 60 So 2d 174 (Fla 1952).

[33] Kowalke v Farmers Mut Auto Ins Co, 3 Wis 2d 389, 88 NW2d 747 (1958); Augustus v Goodrum, 224 Ky 558, 6 SW2d 703, (1928).

[34] Fournier v Zinn, 257 Mass 575, 154 NE 268 (1926); Bartlebaugh v Pennsylvania RR Co, 150 Ohio St 387, 82 NE2d 853 (1907); Littman v Bell Tel Co, 315 Pa 370, 172 A 687 (1934).

[35] Huus v Ringo, 76 ND 763, 39 NW2d 505 (1949); Louisville & Norfolk Co v Dougherty, 170 Ky 10, 185 SW 114 (1916).

[36] Stynes v Boston Elev RR, 206 Mass 75, 91 NE 998 (1910); Bierbach v Goodyear Rubber Co, 54 Wis 208, 11 NW 514 (1882); Chicago & J El RR Co v Spence, 213 Ill 220, 72 NE 796 (1904); Rosenkranz v Lindell RR Co, 108 Mo 9, 18 SW 890 (1891); Goodhart v Pennsylvania RR, 177 Pa 1, 35 A 191 (1896).

[37] Roedder v Rowley, 28 Cal 2d 820, 172 P2d 353 (1946); Fordon v Bender, 363 Mich 124, 108 NW2d 896 (1961); Faught v Washam, 329 SW2d 588 (Mo 1959); Thompson v Iannuzzi, 403 Pa 329, 169 A2d 777 (1961); Jones v Fisher, 42 Wis 2d 209, 166 NW2d 175 (1969); Reale v Wayne Township, 132 NJ Super 100, 332 A2d 236 (1975); Holmes v New York, 269 AD 95, 54 NYS2d 289, affd 295 NY 615, 64 NW2d 449 (1945); Oglesby v Cleveland, 181 NE2d 289 (Ohio Ct App 1962); Capelouto v Kaiser Foundation Hospitals, 7 Cal 3d 889, 500 P2d 880, 103 Cal Rptr 856 (1972).

[38] Pretzer v California Transit Co, 211 Cal 202, 294 P 382 (1931); Di Leo v Dolinsky, 129 Conn 203, 27 A2d 126 (1942).

probability that such pain and suffering will result.[39] This is true even though the future pain and suffering is not permanent, as long as the plaintiff is able to prove that it is certain or probable to continue for some time and beyond the date of the trial.[40] There is a difference among the jurisdictions as to whether future pain and suffering must be established as a reasonable certainty[41] or as a reasonable probability.[42]

Unlike recovery for future earnings, a recovery for future pain and suffering is not reduced to present value. The reasoning against such reduction has been variously expressed,[43] but it was aptly stated in *Chicago & Northwest Railroad Co v Candler*:[44]

> Neither the plaintiff in the case nor anyone else in the world has ever established a standard of value for these ills. The only proof ever received to guide the jury in determining the amount of the allowance they should make is, broadly stated, the nature and extent of the injury, its effect and results. They are instructed to allow a reasonable sum as compensation, and determining what is reasonable under the evidence to be guided by their observation, experience and sense of fairness and right. At the best the allowance is an estimated sum determined by the intelligence and conscience of the jury, and we are convinced that a jury would be much more likely to return a just verdict, considering the estimated life as one single period, than if it should attempt to reach a verdict by dividing the life into yearly periods, setting yearly estimates, and then reducing the estimates to their present value. The arbitrariness and artificiality of such

---

[39] Cochran v Boston, 211 Mass 171, 97 NE 1100 (1912); Laskowski v People's Ice Co, 203 Mich 186, 168 NW 940 (1918); Hurst v Chicago, Burlington & Quincy RR Co, 280 Mo 566, 219 SW 566 (1920); Feeney v Long Island RR, 116 NY 375, 22 NE 402 (1889); Wallace v Pennsylvania RR, 222 Pa 556, 71 A 1086 (1909); Fisher v Coastal Transp Co, 149 Tex 224, 230 SW2d 522, (1950); Yerkes v Northern Pac RR, 112 Wis 184, 88 NW 33 (1901); Hailes v Gonzales, 207 Va 612, 151 SE2d 388 (1966).

[40] Du Cate v Brighton, 133 Wis 628, 114 NW 103 (1907); Skullety v Humphreys, 247 Or 450, 431 P2d 278 (1967).

[41] Adams v Atchison, Topeka & Santa Fe RR, 280 SW2d 84 (Mo 1955); Feeney & Long Island RR, 116 NY 375, 22 NE 402, (1889); Haase v Ryan, 100 Ohio App 285, 136 NE2d 406 (1955); Kowalke v Farmers Mut Auto Ins Co, 3 Wis 2d 389, 88 NW2d 747 (1958).

[42] Coll v Sherry, 29 NJ 166, 148 A2d 481 (1959); Wallace v Pennsylvania RR, 222 Pa 556, 71 A 1086 (1909); Lake Shore & MSR Co v Frantz, 127 Pa 297, 18 A 22 (1889); Fisher v Coastal Trans Co, 149 Tex 224, 230 SW2d 522 (1950).

[43] Chicago & NW RR v Candler, 283 F 881 (8th Cir 1922); Taylor v Denver & Rio Grande Western RR, 438 F2d 351 (10th Cir 1971); McCray v Illinois Cent RR, 12 Ill App 2d 425, 139 NE2d 817 (1957); Stark v Lehigh Foundries, Inc, 388 Pa 1, 130 A2d 123 (1957); Missouri Pac RR v Handley, 341 SW2d 203 (Tex Civ App 1960).

[44] 283 F 881 (8th Cir 1982).

a method is so apparent that to require a jury to apply it would, we think, be an absurdity.[45]

In *Braddock v Seaboard Airline Railroad Company*,[46] the Florida Supreme Court reversed a trial court's decision to reduce an award of future pain and suffering to cash value and in so doing stated:

> The Rule does not seek to instruct a jury in the process by which they shall determine the amount of damages for pain and suffering. Jurors know the nature of pain, embarrassment and inconvenience, and they also know the nature of money. Their problem of equating the two to afford reasonable and just compensation calls for a high order of human judgment, and the law has provided no better yardstick for their guidance than their enlightened conscience. Their problem is not one of mathematical calculation but involves an exercise of their sound judgment of what is fair and right. The problem is often further complicated by the fact that the pain and suffering are yet to be suffered and thus even further removed from exact calculation and certain measurement. But further uncertainty does not change the problem from one of judgment to one of calculation. It still rests within the enlightened conscience of the jury. We think, therefore, that the aspect of present compensation for future pain is merely one of the subjective elements of the problem, and is not a process of mathematical calculation of present value, such as must be applied to periodic future pecuniary losses.[47]

§17.07 —Discretion in Setting Value

There is no fixed rule or standard whereby damages for pain and suffering can be measured. It is universally recognized that jurors, and trial judges as well, may use their personal experiences and knowledge in arriving at the amount of damages to be awarded under the facts of a particular case, and that damages may be awarded for pain, anxiety, inconvenience, annoyance, interference with the comfort of the plaintiff and his or her family, and disadvantage suffered by reason of the defendant's acts. As to such elements of damage, the amount of compensation is not susceptible to proof in dollars and cents but must be left to the sound discretion of a trial court, to be ascertained after consideration of all the facts and circumstances established in the case. The amount of damages to be awarded in a particular case is ordinarily a question of fact, entirely within the province of the jury, especially where the law furnishes no rule for their measurement.[48] Finally, only where a verdict is so

---

[45] *Id* 884.

[46] 80 So 2d 662 (Fla 1955).

[47] *Id* 668.

[48] Herb v Hallowell, 304 Pa 128, 154 A 582 (1931); Affett v Milwaukee & Suburban Transp Corp, 11 Wis 2d 604, 106 NW2d 274 (1960); Botta v Brunner, 26 NJ 82, 138 A2d 713 (1958); Wood v Davenport, 127 Cal App 2d 247, 273 P2d 564 (1954); Caley

grossly disproportionate to any reasonable limit of compensation warranted by the facts as to shock the sense of justice and raise a strong presumption that it is based on prejudice or passion rather than sober judgment, will a court vacate the jury's verdict. In *Texas Construction Service Co v Allen* [49] the defendant appealed from a jury verdict awarding damages to a worker for injuries sustained to his eyes when lime sprayed from the defendant company's truck came in contact with them. In that case, the jury awarded the plaintiff $500,000, and the defendant contended that the award was excessive and that the trial court should have granted a remittitur. In affirming the jury verdict, the court of appeals stated:

> The general rule is that on appeal the finding of a jury will not be disturbed on the ground of excessiveness if there is any probative evidence to sustain the award. The Appellate Court should not substitute its judgment for that of the jury unless the record indicates that the jury was influenced by passion, prejudice or improper motive. If, after such a review of the evidence, the court finds that the award is so excessive that it shocks the conscience of the Appellate Court, a remittitur is proper. . . . Even if the award seems to be high, both the jury and the Appellate Court are entitled to consider the effects of inflation and increasing value of the dollar. . . . [The defendant] argues that the amount of damages in this case, $500,000, is "usually the kind of damages associated with herniated discs, catastrophic multiple injuries and extended custodial care." Each case must stand on its own. It is proper to compare the awards in other cases from other courts to determine if, after meeting all of the other tests of excessiveness, it shocks the conscience of the court. The mere fact that an award is large is no indication of passion, prejudice or improper motive. [50]

In *Quade v Hartfield Enterprises, Inc,* [51] the plaintiff appealed from an order granting remittitur after a jury awarded her $680,000 in damages. In affirming the remittitur, the court stated:

> In the instant case, while the record does indicate prolonged pain, the existence of a surgical scar, curtailment of sporting activities and a less satisfying sex life for [the plaintiff], we are not convinced that $680,000 is the figure that reasonable minds might deem just compensation for such damages. We find that the trial court's conscience was properly shocked at the jury's damage award. We agree that the court's figure of

---

v Manicke, 24 Ill 2d 390, 182 NE2d 206 (1962); Smithey v Sinclair Refining Co, 203 Va 142, 122 SE2d 872 (1961); Butts v Ward, 227 Wis 287, 279 NW 6 (1938); Sharpe v Munoz, 256 SW2d 890 (Tex Civ App 1953).

[49] 639 SW2d 810 (Tex App 1982).

[50] *Id* 812.

[51] 327 NW2d 343 (Mich Ct App 1982).

$250,000 represents just compensation for the damages, both present and future, incurred by [the plaintiff] in the instant case.[52]

Finally, in *Norwood v Lazarus,*[53] the appellate court affirmed a jury verdict in favor of a child who was injured by ingesting lead-based paint on the defendant landlord's premises. The defendants claimed that the verdict of $9,350 in damages was so excessive as to indicate bias and prejudice on the part of the jury. In affirming, the court of appeals stated:

> Plaintiff had a toxic condition that, if untreated, could result in brain damage. She was required to submit to blood tests on a regular basis so that her condition could be monitored. She went to the clinic on some 21 occasions. The condition required hospitalization on three occasions for a total of 23 days. Treatment consisted of injections of calcium bersanate. Clearly plaintiff suffered an injury which required treatment.
>
> There was an injury to plaintiff. The trial court made a determination that the award of the jury was not so excessive as to show bias and prejudice on the part of the jury. We may not disturb the finding of the trial court.[54]

§17.08   Mental/Emotional Distress

The traditional rule, based upon considerations of policy, is that there is no recovery for the negligent infliction of emotional or mental distress alone.[55] The older cases contain the broad statement that there is no duty to refrain from the negligent infliction of mental distress.[56] Thus the paramount issue may be characterized as one of duty: whether the plaintiff's interest in freedom from mental distress is entitled to legal protection from defendant's conduct. Duty, however, is a legal conclusion which depends upon the "sum total of those considerations of policy which lead the law to say that the particular plaintiff is entitled to protection."[57]

The interest in freedom from the negligent infliction of mental distress has been protected whenever the courts were persuaded that the dangers of fraudulent claims and undue liability of the defendant were outweighed by assurances of "genuine and serious" mental distress.[58] In drawing exceptions to the rule of no recovery, the courts have found such assurances in an accom-

---

[52] *Id* 344.

[53] 634 SW2d 584 (Mo Ct App 1982).

[54] *Id* 589.

[55] Lynch & Knight, 9 HL Cas 577, 578, 11 Eng Rep 854 (1861); Spade v Lynn & Boston RR, 172 Mass 488, 52 NE 747 (1899).

[56] Spade v Lynn & Boston RR, 172 Mass 488, 52 NE 747 (1899); Waube v Warrington, 216 Wis 603, 258 NW 497 (1935).

[57] Prosser, The Law of Torts §53, at 325–26 (4th ed 1971).

[58] *Id* §55, at 330

panying physical injury or impact, close to the cause of action, or in a special factual pattern.[59]

A number of recent cases, however, have held that damages for mental anguish will be allowed in a proper case even though not accompanied by physical injury.[60]

§17.09 —Cancerphobia

Some courts have held that the mental anguish and anxiety about a possible future disease or condition is a proper element of damages where that anguish or anxiety accompanies a physical injury, at least if the disease or condition might reasonably be expected to result from the injury. For example, *Ferrara v Galluchio* [61] involved a medical malpractice case brought by a patient who had received excessive x-ray treatments from defendants. As a result of the treatments, scabs formed and lasted several months, leaving the shoulder with a permanently marginated area of skin. Approximately two years after the treatments, the plaintiff was referred by her attorney to a dermatologist for examination. The dermatologist told the plaintiff to be sure to have her shoulder checked every six months because the area of the burn might become cancerous. During the trial, this statement of the dermatologist was introduced not for the purpose of proving the plaintiff would develop cancer but for the purpose of establishing that there was a basis for plaintiff's mental anxiety. In affirming the judgment for the plaintiff, the appellate court stated:

> There was a real connection between the ultimate damage and the original wrong. The employment of the dermatologist must be regarded as a natural consequence of the original wrongdoers' tort because the necessity for such employment was imposed upon the plaintiff by the original wrongdoers' fault and because the plaintiff, an unprofessional person, did all that she could do, or at least, in the conditions obtaining, what she had a right to do, when she employed a dermatologist to treat and heal her injury. The original wrong certainly occasioned the examination and treatment by the dermatologist. He prescribed a substance to

---

[59] Kirksey v Jernigan, 45 So 2d 188 (Fla 1950); Spade v Lynn & Boston RR, 168 Mass 285, 47 NE 88 (1897); Lombard v Lennox, 155 Mass 70, 28 NE 1125 (1891); Butler v Lomelo, 355 So 2d 1208 (Fla Dist Ct App 1977); DiMare v Creci, 58 Cal 2d 292, 373 P2d 860, 23 Cal Rptr 772 (1962); Green v Floe, 28 Wash 2d 620, 183 P2d 771 (1947).

[60] Zepeda v Zepeda, 41 Ill App 2d 240, 190 NE2d 849 (1963); Battala v State, 10 NY2d, 176 NE2d 729, 219 NYS2d 34 (1961); Rodrigues v State, 52 Hawaii 156, 472 P2d 509 (1970); Charlie Stuart Oldsmobile, Inc v Smith, 171 Ind App 315, 357 NE2d 247 (1976), *rehearing,* 369 NE2d 947 (1977); Dillon v Legg, 441 P2d 912, 69 Cal Rptr 72 (1968); Housh v Peth, 99 Ohio App 485, 135 NE2d 340 (1955), *affd,* 165 Ohio St 35, 133 NE2d 340 (1956); Colla v Mandella, 1 Wis 2d 594, 85 NW2d 345 (1957); Howard v Lecher, 42 NY2d 109, 366 NE2d 64, 397 NYS2d 363 (1977); Molien v Kaiser Foundation Hosp, 27 Cal 3d 916, 616 P2d 813, 167 Cal Rptr 831 (1980).

[61] 5 NY2d 16, 152 NE2d 249 (1958).

be used by plaintiff for the burn. Had such substance aggravated plaintiff's injury no one could doubt, under the present state of our law, the original wrongdoers would be responsible for the resulting damage to its full extent, *including additional mental anguish caused plaintiff.* The only difference here is that the latter treatment by the dermatologist did not aggravate the physical injury inflicted by the original wrongdoers but, rather, increased only the mental anguish attendant upon such injury. We perceive no sound reason for drawing a distinction between the two situations. The dermatologist apparently thought it essential as part of his treatment as a protective measure for plaintiff to advise her to have her shoulder checked every six months because of the possibility of cancer. Under our law the risk of such advise and its effect upon the plaintiff must be borne by the wrongdoers who started the chain of circumstances without which the cancer phobia would not have developed.

This case is somewhat novel, of course, in that it appears to be the first case in which a recovery has been allowed against the original wrongdoer for purely mental suffering arising from information the plaintiff received from a doctor to whom she went for treatment of the original injury. We have concluded, however, that under the circumstances of the case such recovery was justified.[62]

Similarly, in *Lorenc v Chemirad, Corp,*[63] the New Jersey Supreme Court recognized the validity of a damage claim for both the probability of future cancer and for the neurosis based upon *cancerphobia,* the plaintiff's fear of developing cancer. In *Lorenc,* the plaintiff suffered severe burns to his hands from ethylene imine which allegedly had been improperly packaged by the defendant. The skin on the injured hand subsequent to the accident would intermittently break down, and there was also chronic ulceration. The plaintiff, a medical doctor who was somewhat knowledgeable in this area, became apprehensive about the possibility of malignancy.

On appeal from a verdict in the plaintiff's favor, the defendant charged that it was improper for the jury to have considered the testimony relating to the plaintiff's anxiety and the probability of malignancy. The New Jersey Supreme Court held that although a different jury might have rejected the plaintiff's claim of future cancer that was probable to result, the plaintiff had narrowly framed the issue so as to preclude a court from dismissing the claim as a matter of law.

So, although, if we were acting as original triers of the fact, we might have rejected the claim of probable resulting cancer, as distinguished from a neurosis based on a fear of development of that disease, we cannot say that there was no justification for a finding favorable to plaintiff regarding

---

[62] Ferrara v Galluchio, 5 NY2d 16, 152 NE2d 249, 252-53 (1958) (emphasis added).
[63] 37 NJ 56, 179 A2d 401 (1962).

its probable future onset. In addition, there is no way of knowing from the verdict whether the jury accepted the suggestion of probably future cancer, or simply allowed some compensation for the plaintiff's fear of the development of that disease. And with respect to compensation for a malignancy, the trial court instructed the jury that in order to make an award therefore, they must find, by the greater weight of the believable evidence, that plaintiff has shown "he will probably develop malignancy because of this injury."[64]

Toxic tort litigation often involves situations in which there is a greatly increased risk of contracting cancer as a result of an extended exposure to a toxic substance. The modern trend to allow plaintiffs to state causes of action for *cancerphobia* should have widespread effects on the number of cases filed in our courts. The plaintiffs will be entitled to introduce evidence consisting of scientific reports indicating the increased probability of contracting a specific disease among a particular group of workers on the ground that it is relevant to the claims of probably resulting disease and loss of well-being. Consider the impact that a cause of action based on fear of developing a toxic substance disease will have on the current litigation: with the extended latency period one would expect that virtually all persons who have had any significant exposure to a toxic substance during their lives will immediately file suit to obtain present benefits rather than wait to see whether, in fact, they contract the illness. To date, few courts have retreated from a modern trend to permit novel tort actions and any change in this area will probably come from litigation.

§17.10 Loss of Consortium

At common law, a wife could not recover for loss of her husband's services by the act of a third party for the starkly simple reason that she had no independent legal existence of her own[65] and hence had no right to such services in the first place. In the United States, the current rule in a majority of states is that a wife has an action for loss of consortium when her husband is injured by the negligent act of another.[66] Where the husband is injured through the negligence or other tort of his employer, or an agent of his employer, his wife's recovery for loss of consortium has usually been denied where her husband's recovery of workers' compensation benefits is the exclusive remedy against the employer.

---

[64] Lorenc v Chemirad Corp, 37 NJ 56, 179 A2d 401, 411 (1962); *see also* Figlar v Gordon, 53 A2d 645 (Conn 1947), where the court concluded that anxiety about the occurrence of a disease is a present fact which can support an award of present damages.

[65] 1 Blackstone, Commentaries 442.

[66] Rodriguez v Bethlehem Steel Corp, 12 Cal 3d 382, 525 P2d 699, 115 Cal Rptr 765 (1974).

Hammond v North American Asbestos Corp[67] is a recent example of an award of compensatory damages for loss of consortium stemming from an asbestos-related injury. In *Hammond,* the plaintiff, the wife of an asbestos worker who contracted asbestosis, sued North American Asbestos Corp for loss of consortium on a theory, *inter alia,* of strict liability. A jury verdict in favor of the plaintiff was entered on the loss of consortium claim in the amount of $125,000. In affirming the jury's award, the appellate court noted that there was evidence of medical expenses in the amount of $33,000, that at the time of the suit, Charles Hammond was 54 years old and in declining health, that his health would continue to deteriorate, and that additional and substantial medical expenses would be incurred. The deterioration of Mr. Hammond's health would, likewise, have an influence on those other elements of the marital relationship compensible in a consortium action.[68]

The *Hammond* court also considered whether punitive damages should be awarded in an action for loss of consortium. Since the wife's cause of action depended in large part upon evidence concerning her husband's employment and *his* resulting injuries, the court declined to extend punitive damages to actions for loss of consortium.[69] Accordingly, a $375,000 punitive damages verdict was reversed.

§17.11 Cost of Past and Future Medical Care

The plaintiff is allowed to recover for the reasonable value of medical services that are reasonably necessary. The proper measure of damages is not the expenses or liability incurred, but the reasonable value of medical services.[70] Such items as medicines, medical attendants, hospital services, and nursing care are included in this element.[71] Finally, recovery is also allowed for the present value of future medical expenses which are shown to be reasonably

---

[67] 105 Ill App 3d 1033, 435 NE2d 540 (1982).

[68] *Id* at 1040, 435 NE2d at 547.

[69] *Id.*

[70] Seitz v Seitz, 35 Wis 2d 282, 151 NW2d 86 (1967); Johnston v Long, 30 Cal 2d 54, 181 P2d 645 (1947); Tomey v Dyson, 76 Cal App 2d 212, 172 P2d 739 (1946); Goodhart v Pennsylvania RR, 177 Pa 1, 35 A 191 (1896); Guerra v Balestrieri, 127 Cal App 2d 511, 274 P2d 443 (1954); American Natl Bank & Trust Co v Peoples Gas Light & Coke Co, 42 Ill App 2d 163, 191 NE2d 628 (1963); Rodgers v Boynton, 315 Mass 279, 52 NE2d 576 (1943); Murphy v SS Kresge Co, 205 SW2d 252 (Mo Ct App 1947); Goodhart v Pennsylvania RR, 177 Pa 1, 35 A 191 (1896); Texas & Norfolk RR v Barham, 204 SW2d 205 (Tex Civ App 1947).

[71] Balian v Ogussian, 277 Mass 525, 179 NE 232 (1931); Price v Metropolitan Street RR, 220 Mo 435, 119 SW 932 (1909); Seifert v Milwaukee & Suburban Transp Corp, 4 Wis 2d 623, 91 NW2d 236 (1958); Langnehs v Parmelee, 427 SW2d 223 (Ky 1968); Publix Cab Co v Colorado Natl Bank, 139 Colo 205, 338 P2d 702 (1959); Roth v Chatlos, 97 Conn 282, 116 A 332 (1922); Large v Williams, 154 Cal App 2d 315, 315 P2d 919 (1957); Tomey v Dyson, 76 Cal App 2d 212, 172 P2d 739 (1946); Sibley v Nason, 196 Mass 125, 81 NE 877 (1907); Britton v Dube, 154 Me 319, 147 A2d 452 (1958).

certain to be incurred in the future because of the defendant's tortious conduct.[72]

§17.12   Wrongful Death and Survival Actions

Wrongful death statutes are to be distinguished from survival statutes. The latter have been separately enacted to abrogate the common law rule that an action for tort faded at the death of either the injured person or the tortfeasor. Survival statutes permit the deceased's estate to prosecute any claims for personal injury the *deceased* would have had, but for his or her death. They do not permit recovery for harm suffered by the deceased's family as a result of his or her death.[73] The underlying reasons for survival statutes have been summarized by Professor Harper:

> At early common law, the personal representative could not be sued for a tort committed by the decedent during his lifetime. From early notions of the untransmittability of blame—and the quasi-criminal nature of early tort law must not be forgotten—to the crystalization of the maxim actio personalis moritur cum persona, the common law was developed without exception, and the rule was uniform that tort actions died with the parties, either wrongdoer or injured party. There was, then, no survival of a right of action either in favor of or against an executor or administrator until statutes modified somewhat the rule of dependability upon the lives of the original parties to the wrong.[74]

In contrast to the survival of a decedent's cause of action, most wrongful death statutes have been construed to create an independent cause of action in favor of the decedent's dependants.[75] *Sea-Land Services v Gaudet* [76] involved a claim for wrongful death under the Maritime Wrongful Death Act. Mr. Gaudet suffered severe injuries while working as a longshoreman aboard a vessel. Mr. Gaudet brought a lawsuit for personal injuries in which he recovered $140,000 for his permanent disability, physical agony, and loss of earn-

---

[72] Hailes v Gonzales, 207 Va 612, 151 SE2d 388 (1966); Buswell v San Francisco, 89 Cal App 2d 123, 200 P2d 115 (1949); Cassidy v Constantine, 269 Mass 56, 168 NE 169 (1929); Petty v Kansas City Pub Serv Co, 355 Mo 824, 198 SW2d 684 (1946); Barger v Green, 255 SW2d 127 (Mo Ct App 1953); Feeney v Long Island RR, 116 NY 375, 22 NE 402 (1889); Rice v Hill, 315 Pa 166, 172 A 289 (1934).

[73] Murphy v Martin Oil Co, 56 Ill 2d 423, 308 NE2d 583 (1974); Mattyasovszky v West Towns Bus Co, 21 Ill App 3d 46, 313 NE2d 496 (1974); Sea-Land Servs, Inc v Gaudet, 414 US 573, *rehg denied,* 415 US 986 (1974); Thorton v Insurance Co of N Am, 287 So 2d 262 (Miss 1973); Fisher v Missoula White Pine Sash Co, 518 P2d 795 (Mont 1974).

[74] F. Harper, Law of Torts 673-74 (1933) *quoted in* 2 F. Harper & F. James, Law of Torts §24.1 n 2 (1956).

[75] 2 F. Harper & F. James, Law of Torts §24.2 (1956).

[76] 414 US 573 (1974). Death on High Seas Act, 46 USC §§761-68; Federal Employers Liability Act, 45 USC §§151-60.

ings. He died shortly after the lawsuit was terminated. Mrs. Gaudet then instituted her wrongful death action for damages suffered by her. Based upon her husband's prior recovery, the district court dismissed Mrs. Gaudet's suit on grounds of res judicata and failure to state a claim. Based upon a 1970 Supreme Court decision,[77] the Fifth Circuit Court of Appeals reversed, holding that Mrs. Gaudet's cause of action for wrongful death was separate and apart from Mr. Gaudet's cause of action for personal injury.[78] In a five to four decision, the Supreme Court affirmed.

In writing for the majority, Justice Brennan held that: (1) the maritime wrongful death action based on unseaworthiness could be maintained even though the decedent, prior to his death, had recovered from the shipowner in the personal injury action, since the wrongful death remedy involved a different cause of action than the decedent's personal injury action, and thus was not precluded by res judicata; (2) under the maritime wrongful death remedy, the decedent's dependants could recover damages for their loss of support, services, and society, as well as for funeral expenses; and (3) the doctrine of collateral estoppel precluded recovery in the wrongful death action of damages for loss of support insofar as such damages would overlap the decedent's prior recovery in his personal injury action for loss of future wages. Justice Powell's dissenting opinion pointed out the potential for double recovery created by the majority opinion:

> Mr. Gaudet's judgment was given by a jury. It would be unrealistic to assume that that verdict was restricted to an objective measurement of Gaudet's lost earnings plus the "value" of his pain and suffering. In all likelihood, Gaudet's award reflected an element of the jury's concern for a permanently disabled working man. As anyone who has tried jury cases knows, jury sympathy commonly overcomes a theoretical inability to recover for such intangibles as loss of society. If Mrs. Gaudet is then allowed to recover in her subsequent lawsuit the full value, whatever that is, of her loss of love, attention, care, affection, companionship, comfort, and protection, she will be given a second opportunity to benefit from the imprecision built into any award for injuries that cannot be measured objectively, the Gaudet family may well then receive substantially more than just compensation for its injuries.
>
> One expression of jury sympathy is commonplace, despite its conflicts with the damages principles that in theory control. But certainly two opportunities for jury sympathy cross the line between benignity and bonanza and should not be sanctioned.[79]

The implications of the *Gaudet* decision in toxic tort litigation are that in any

---

[77] Moragne v States Marine Lines, 398 US 375 (1970), *overruling* The Harrisburg, 119 US 199 (1886).

[78] 463 F2d 1331, 1332 (5th Cir 1972).

[79] 414 US at 609-10.

case involving an injured party who institutes an action on his or her own behalf, obtains a favorable result, and then succumbs to the toxic illness, a new cause of action comes to life in favor of his or her surviving spouse and dependants, as defined in the applicable wrongful death statute.

§17.13   Property Damage

In early 1983, the Los Angeles Unified School District filed suit against certain members of the asbestos industry alleging that the companies failed to test properly the asbestos materials used in the school district's heating and cooling systems. The lawsuit claims that the defendants manufactured asbestos knowing that it would be distributed to the public without inspecting it for a defect. The complaint alleges that the defendants' tortious conduct caused damage to the property owned and leased by the school district. The complaint prays for damages in excess of $250 million for the replacement of some of the buildings, property damage, building repair, and compensation for warning individuals who have come into contact with the material.

There will be a multitude of toxic tort claims filed involving property damage claims, particularly damage to real property. There have been numerous reports of entire communities who have been forced to leave their homes and businesses because of the presence of dioxin. Unless these problems are addressed at the state and national levels to provide compensation, the victims will have to rely on our tort system to obtain compensation for these property damages.

Out tort law provides that one whose interest in real property has been injured by the tortious act or omission of another is entitled to those damages which will compensate him or her for the injury sustained.[80] This principle has been translated into two rules of damages.

1. *Diminution of Value Rule:* The injured party is entitled to recover the difference between the value of the real property immediately before and immediately after the injury.[81] This rule normally applies wherever the injury is deemed to be permanent or where the damage cannot be expressed in specific items of injury

2. *Restoration or Cost of Repair Rule:* The injured party is entitled to recover

---

[80] Givens v Markall, 51 Cal App 2d 374, 124 P2d 839 (1942); Holcombe v Superior Oil Co, 213 La 684, 35 So 2d 457 (1948); Hamilton v Fant, 422 SW2d 495 (Tex Civ App 1967); Hanna v Martin, 49 So 2d 585 (Fla 1950); Sampson Const Co v Brusowankin, 218 Md 458, 147 A2d 430 (1958).

[81] Western U Tel Co v Ring, 102 Md 677, 62 A 801 (1906); Curtis v Fruin-Dolnon Contracting Co, 363 Mo 676, 253 SW2d 158 (1952); Rempfer v Deerfield Packing Corp, 4 NJ 135, 72 A2d 204 (1950); Pickens v Harrison, 151 Tex 562, 252 SW2d 575 (1952).

the cost of repairing the real estate by restoring it to its condition immediately prior to the injury.[82]

In selecting between the two general rules, the courts will normally select the method which will result in the lower amount of damages.[83] In addition to the two types of compensation listed above, the plaintiff may also recover the value of use of the land and of any annoyance and discomfort caused by the tortious conduct.[84]

Punitive Damages

§17.14   Policy Considerations

Punitive damages have been a controversial topic since its inception in England in the mid-18th century.[85] Advocates argue that punitive damages serve important dual functions—i.e., to punish the willful wrongdoer and to deter others from similar wrongdoing in the future.[86] It is also argued that the financial lure of a punitive damage award induces otherwise reluctant plaintiffs to bring willful wrongdoers to justice; this is the *private attorney general* argument. Finally, advocates assert that punitive damage awards provide compensation to plaintiffs whose damages exceed those for which the law allows recovery.[87]

On the other end of the spectrum, opponents argue that punitive damages should never be allowed in civil cases, particularly in products liability cases.[88] This position is based upon the development of punitive damages in cases involving the one-to-one relationship found in torts, such as battery. Such interpersonal relationships do not exist in the mass manufacturing of products. Opponents also assert: that the specter of huge compensatory damages verdicts is a sufficient threat to meet the objectives of punishment and deterrence; even though the products liability setting always involves a corporate defendant and even though the judgment is usually backed by insurance, the ultimate cost is borne by either the innocent stockholders, the consumer, or both; that offsetting a plaintiff's litigation expenses is not an appropriate function of

---

[82] Dandoy v Oswald Bros Paving Co, 113 Cal App 570, 298 P 1030 (1931); Samson Constr Co v Brusowankin, 218 Md 458, 147 A2d 430 (1958); Wheelock v Noonan, 108 NY 179, 15 NE 67 (1888); Jones v Monroe Elec Co, 350 Pa 539, 39 A2d 569 (1944).

[83] Ferraro v Lyles Constr Co, 102 Cal App 3d 33, 162 Cal Rptr 238 (1980).

[84] Dussel v Kaufman Constr Co, 398 Pa 369, 157 A2d 740 (1960); Price v Dickson 317 SW2d 156 (Ky 1958); Tripp v Bagley, 75 Utah 42, 282 P 1026 (1929).

[85] Wilkes v Wood, 2 Wils KB 203, 95 Eng Rep 766 (1763).

[86] Corloy, Should Punitive Damages Be Abolished—A Statement For The Negative, ABA Proceedings, Section on Insurance, Negligence and Compensation Law 292, 293 (1965).

[87] Owen, *Punitive Damages in Products Liability Litigation*, 74 Mich L Rev 1257 (1976).

[88] Courtney & Cavieo, *Punitive Damages: When Are They Justifiable?*, 18 Trial 52 (Aug 1982).

civil litigation; and finally, that multiple awards of punitive damages to multiple plaintiffs amounts to excessive punishment.[89]

Presently, a majority of jurisdictions allow punitive damages in civil cases. Only nine jurisdictions depart in some degree from this view. Several of these states equate punitive with compensatory damages while others only allow limited, statutory applications.[90]

§17.15   The Elements of a Punitive Damages Claim

In general, phrases such as *willful, wanton misconduct, reckless or conscious disregard for the safety of others,* and *oppressive, fraudulent, malicious, or outrageous conduct* have been used by courts and legislatures to describe the conduct justifying the imposition of punitive damages. Professor McCormick described the requisite misbehavior in the following manner:

> Since these damages are assessed for punishment and not for reparation, a positive element of conscious wrongdoing is alwasy required. It must be shown either that the defendant was actuated by ill will, malice, or evil motive (which may appear by direct evidence of such motive, or from the inherent character of the tort itself, or from the oppressive character of his conduct, sometimes called "circumstances of aggravation"), or by fraudulent disregard of the rights of others. "Gross negligence" is a somewhat ambiguous expression. In the sense of extreme carelessness merely, it would probably not suffice, but only when it goes further and amounts to conscious indifference to harmful consequences.[91]

California has codified this misbehavior in part of Article 3 of its Civil Code as follows:

> §3294 [When permitted] (a) In an action for the breach of an obligation not arising from a contract, where the defendant has been guilty of oppression, fraud or malice, the plaintiff, in addition to the actual damages, may recover damages for the sake of example and by way of punishing the defendant.
>
> (b) An employer shall not be liable for damages pursuant to subdivision (a), based upon acts of an employee of the employer, unless the employer had advance knowledge of the unfitness of the employee and employed him or her with a conscious disregard of the rights or safety of others or authorized or ratified the wrongful conduct for which the damages are awarded or was personally guilty of oppression, fraud, or malice. With respect to a corporate employer, the advance knowledge and conscious

---

[89] Ghiardi & Kircher, Punitive Damages, Law and Practice (1982).

[90] *Id.*

[91] McCormick, Handbook of the Law of Damages §79, at 280-82 (1935).

disregard, authorization, ratification or act of appression, fraud or malice must be on the part of an officer, director, or managing agent of the corporation.

(c) As used in this section, the following definitions shall apply:

(1) "Malice" means conduct which is intended by the defendant to cause injury to the plaintiff or conduct which is carried on by the defendant with a conscious disregard of the rights or safety of others.

(2) "Oppression" means subjecting a person to cruel and unjust hardship in conscious disregard of that person's rights.

(3) "Fraud" means an intentional misrepresentation, deceit, or concealment of a material fact known to the defendant with the intention on the part of the defendant of thereby depriving a person of property or legal rights or otherwise causing injury.[92]

Although various terms are used to describe the misconduct that justifies an award of punitive damages, there is a conceptual uniformity among all jurisdictions. Basically, the conduct described falls into two broad categories. The first category is behavior in which the defendant manifestly desires to harm the plaintiff or in which the defendant knows that it is substantially certain that such harm will occur as a result of his or her actions. The malice and ill will of such conduct are closely related to the intentional torts of assault and battery which formed the roots of the doctrine of punitive damages and are easily distinguishable from the concept of mere negligence. The second category includes situations where the defendant knows or has reason to know that his or her conduct creates an unreasonable risk of harm and that there is a strong probability that such harm will result, yet the defendant ignores these facts and proceeds with his or her conduct in reckless disregard of the consequences.[93]

One commentator, in a recent review of products liability cases, has elaborated further on the second category by creating three subcategories as applicable to product manufacturers only:

1. Fraudulent-type misconduct

2. Failure to acquire sufficient product safety information via tests, inspections, or post-marketing safety monitoring

3. Failure to remedy an excessively dangerous condition known to exist in a product by altering its design, adding warnings, or recalling the product[94]

---

[92] Cal Civil Code §3294 (Deering 1983).

[93] Ghiardi & Kircher, Punitive Damages, Law and Practice (1982).

[94] Owen, *Punitive Damages in Products Liability Litigation,* 74 Mich L Rev 1257, 1361 (1976).

§17.16 —Cases on Elements of a Punitive Damages Claim

The now infamous *Richardson-Merrell* MER-29 litigation is a classic example of mass tort claims involving an element of fraudulent misconduct which caused serious personal injuries on a nationwide scale and eventually led to at least three awards of punitive damages that were affirmed on appeal.[95] Richardson—Merrell manufactured pharmaceuticals and marketed MER-29, a drug purported to reduce blood cholesterol levels and to aid in the treatment of arteriosclerosis. Even though the company's own experiments showed abnormal blood changes and eye opacities in animals, the defendant marketed it as "virtually nontoxic and remarkably free from side effects even on prolonged clinical use."[96] In addition, the company fictionalized data and misrepresented facts to both the medical profession and the Food and Drug Administration (FDA). Even after the harmful effects were discovered, the company refused to change its position and bitterly fought the FDA's recall of the drug. As a result, thousands of persons were injured, including 490 reported cases of cataracts.[97]

In determining whether adequate testing or quality control has been used by a manufacturer, a fine distinction must be drawn between what would normally be considered mere negligence and conduct which is sufficiently egregious to warrant an award of punitive damages. One court has held that before punitive damages can be awarded against a product manufacturer, the manufacturer's testing and quality control procedures must be found to be so inadequate that an inference of complete indifference to the risk of harm created may be drawn.[98] In that case, an IUD had been clinically tested for an average indwelling time of 5.5 months. The defendant, A.H. Robbins Co, knew that normal, foreseeable use of the IUD would be for indwelling times beyond 5.5 months and yet failed to conduct tests to determine the fitness of the device under those conditions. The device was marketed by the manufacturer with full knowledge that the normal indwelling time of the device substantially exceeded its premarketing test conditions. There was no information communicated to the public or the FDA to warn against extended indwelling periods. When is was established that, on extended indwelling, the device both failed to prevent the plaintiff's pregnancy and perforated her uterine wall, the jury awarded punitive damages.[99]

Other examples of products liability cases in which punitive damages have been awarded for the failure to warn of known dangers are found in *Hoffman*

---

[95] Toole v Richardson-Merrell, Inc, 251 Cal App 2d 689, 60 Cal Rptr 398 (1967); Ostopowitz v Richardson-Merrell Co, No 58-79-1963 (NY Sup Ct Jan 11, 1967).

[96] Toole v Richardson-Merrell, Inc, 251 Cal App 2d 689, 696, 60 Cal Rptr 398, 405 (1967).

[97] *Id* 408, 698.

[98] Deemer v AH Robbins Co, No C-26420 (Dist Co Sedgwick County) (*appeal filed,* No 48, 504 (Kan Aug 23, 1976)).

[99] Deemer v AH Robbins, Co, slip op at 7.

v Sterling Drugs, Inc,[100] and more recently in *Neal v Carey Canadian Mines, Ltd.*[101] *Hoffman* is a borderline case in which the manufacturer produced a drug marketed as Aralan whose use resulted in severe retinal damage. The manufacturer, upon discovering the danger, informed physicians by mailing or personally delivering product cards and promotional brochures containing the necessary warning. The court allowed the question of punitive damages to reach the jury by concluding that Sterling's "failure to take action reasonably calculated to warn physicians of a risk of great magnitude was in reckless disregard of the public health."[102] The award of punitive damages is questionable because the defendant's conduct does not fit into either of the two general categories of misconduct discussed above, and appears to have been mere negligence. One can only assume that the court gave great weight to evidence that since the magnitude of harm was great with a potential for widespread effect upon many people, the threshold level of unacceptable behavior would be lowered.

More failure-to-warn products liability situations are the celebrated asbestos cases brought against the Johns-Manville Corporation[103] and other manufacturers and distributors of asbestos products. It has been alleged, and proven to the satisfaction of some juries, that Johns-Manville Corporation's safety officer first became aware of the health dangers involved with inhalation of asbestos in 1947. Dr. Smith, Johns-Manville's medical director, had conducted extensive research and authored several papers on the dangers of asbestos inhalation during the late 1940's and early 1950's. In late 1952 or early 1953, Dr. Smith recommended to high-ranking Johns-Manville corporate officials that appropriate warnings be placed on all asbestos containers. The recommendation was ignored. Dr. Smith continued to suggest that warnings be affixed to all asbestos containers but these suggestions were ignored. No warnings were given until 1964.[104] In *Neal v Carey Canadian Mines, Inc,* the court concluded that this evidence was sufficient to support an award of punitive damages because "Johns-Manville engaged in outrageous conduct by exhibiting a reckless indifference to the health and well-being of plaintiff."[105]

The foregoing cases involved conduct which can be characterized as fraudulent on the part of the manufacturer. This is to be distinguished from mere negligence based on two factors: first, knowledge of the risk and magnitude of injury; second, armed with such knowledge, the refusal or failure to deter-

---

[100] Hoffman v Sterling Drug, Inc, 374 F Supp 850 (ED Pa 1975).

[101] Neal v Carey Canadian Mines, Ltd, 548 F Supp 357 (ED Pa 1982).

[102] Hoffman v Sterling Drug, 374 F Supp 850, 851 (ED Pa 1975).

[103] *E.g.,* Neal v Carey Canadian Mines, 548 F Supp 357 (ED Pa 1982); *In re* Related Asbestos Cases, 543 F Supp 1152 (ND Cal 1982); Janssens v John-Manville Sales Corp, No 79-9659-CA (Fla July 31, 1981).

[104] Neal v Carey Canadian Mines, 548 F Supp 357, 375 (ED Pa 1982).

[105] *Id* 376.

mine the seriousness of the danger or to reduce it to an acceptable level before offering a product for sale to the public.[106]

§17.17 Problems Posed by Punitive Damages Awards in Toxic Substance Litigation

In large part, the problems posed by punitive damages in toxic substance litigation are common in cases involving the broader category of products liabilities litigation—e.g., compatibility of the traditional notion of punitive damages doctrine with modern theories of strict products liability and warranty; imputing conduct warranting punitive damages under agency theories; and the issue of insurance coverage for punitive damages. Two problems, though, which are particularly germane to today's toxic torts are the potential for a single product causing mass disaster litigation and the long latency periods displayed before the injury manifests itself.

Today, it is recognized that a single product can lead to mass products liability litigation involving a potential redistribution of millions of dollars to compensate victims of toxic substances. Modern manufacturing capabilities of the industrial nations together with an incredibly complex and efficient marketing system have created worldwide distribution capabilities. Superimposed over this economic system are the emerging tort doctrines of strict products liability and the very real potential of being sued by multiple plaintiffs for harm caused by a defective product. The specter of financial ruin at the hands of multiple plaintiffs claiming hundreds of millions of dollars in punitive damages first crystalized in the early 1960's in the MER-29 litigation, discussed in §17.16. Following the discovery of fraudulent behavior which led to the marketing of this particularly hazardous drug, over 1,500 personal injury actions were brought against the manufacturer. Although only three cases resulted in punitive damages awards[107] the real potential for bankruptcy at the hands of multiple plaintiffs was finally recognized. In *Roginsky v Richardson-Merrell, Inc,*[108] Judge Friendly noted that legal difficulties engendered by multiple awards are "staggering," involving such abuses as "catastrophic" and "overkill" awards, haphazard awarding of punitive damages and the potential bankruptcy of the business.

The notion that allowing individual claims for punitive damages in multiple-plaintiff litigation is counterproductive to society has been echoed by other courts, the defense bar, and the insurance industry. Whatever good may conceivably be derived from deterring future wrongdoing by awarding one plaintiff among thousands punitive damages, it is more probably outweighed by the harm to society as a whole in having productive segments of the economy

---

[106] Owen, *Punitive Damages in Products Liability Litigation,* 74 Mich L Rev 1257, 1362 (1976).

[107] Roginsky v Richardson-Merrell, Inc, 378 F2d 832 (2d Cir 1967); Toole v Richardson-Merrell, Inc, 251 Cal App 2d 689, 60 Cal Rptr 398 (1967); Ostopowitz v Richardson-Merrell, Co, No 58-79-1963 (NY Jan 11 1967).

[108] Roginsky v Richardson-Merrell, Inc, 378 F2d 832, 838-41 (2d Cir 1967).

crippled or exterminated by civil suits.[109] Most defendant manufacturers have asserted, without success, that such multiple recovery is violative of their fundamental due process and double jeopardy rights.[110] Finally, commentators have argued that it is simply illogical to punish a manufacturer more than once for a single wrongful act.[111]

As discussed in Chapters 1 and 4, injuries from toxic substances usually involve long latency periods between initial exposure and the time when the illness manifests itself. During the interim between the initial exposure and diagnosis, continuous exposure to toxic substances has been known to cause irreversible diseases such as asbestos cancer, arteriosclerosis, and pneumoconiosis (black lung).[112] The asbestos litigation provides an excellent example of toxic substance litigation involving irreversible progress and sometimes terminal illnesses with a latency period of between 10 to 40 years depending upon the dose and duration of exposure. In the asbestos litigations, the plaintiffs' proof of *conscious disregard* on the part of the asbestos industry comes in the form of informal memoranda and letters which were purportedly written by high corporate officials back in the 1930s and 1940s, which purportedly indicate that there was knowledge in the industry during that period of time of a possible or existing asbestos hazard. The tort concept of strict liability did not come into being until 1963[113] and was not adopted in most jurisdictions until the mid-1960s or early 1970s. By the 1970s, most asbestos manufacturers had taken measures to warn those exposed to asbestos of the health hazards associated with the product, yet individuals who were exposed to the asbestos prior to 1970 began to develop asbestos-related diseases.

In the vast majority of the asbestos litigation, the plaintiff was employed in a shipyard during World War II and worked in an atmosphere permeated by asbestos dust. In most jurisdictions, the courts allow the juries to determine whether the defendant's conduct during the 1930s and 1940s rises to the level of *conscious disregard for safety* so as to justify imposing punitives in the 1980s.

The task is made even more difficult because it is almost impossible for the jury to divest itself of what by today's standards is common knowledge or acceptable, reasonable behavior. Modern society's awareness and concern about environmental pollution, health hazards, and the ever-advancing state of medical technology are difficult to set aside when viewing in hindsight a problem that first arose 40 years ago. One commentator has aptly summed up the difficulty:

It is a laborsome task to take a jury back those same 20 or more years,

---

[109] Marey v Freight Line Corp, 451 F Supp 955 (ND Tex 1978).

[110] Neal v Carey Canadian Mines, Ltd, 548 F Supp 357, 376 (ED Pa 1982).

[111] Parnell, *Manufacturers of Toxic Substances, Tort Liability and Punitive Damages,* 17 Forum 947 (1982).

[112] Trauberman, *Compensating Victims of Toxic Substances Pollution: An Analysis of Existing Federal Statutes,* 5 Harv Envtl L Rev 1 (1981).

[113] Parnell, *supra* note 111, at 966.

arm them with the information then available, and ask them to plot the course of conduct for a defendant manufacturer, disregarding the medical state of the art as it exists in 1982. Yet, unless this task is accomplished, the manufacturer risks absorbing repeated punitive damages awards.[114]

§17.18 Punitive Damages in Strict Products Liability Cases

Jurisdictions are divided as to whether or not punitive damages may be awarded in strict liability cases. In both *Beshada v Johns-Manville Products Corp*[115] and *Gold v Johns-Manville Sales Corp,*[116] the New Jersey Supreme Court held that an action based on strict products liability cannot support a claim for punitive damages. In *Gold,*[117] the court stated that while a large award of punitive damages would encourage more cautious behavior by the defendant, it would not encourage asbestos producers as a class to research the risks involved with their products, but rather it would only teach them to eschew learning of the research of others.

However, in *Grimshaw v Ford Motor Co,*[118] the California Supreme Court found ample evidence to support the finding of malice and thus affirmed the award of punitive damages in a products liability suit arising out of an automobile accident involving a Ford Pinto.

In summary, practioners should be aware of the differences in this area of the law and the subsequent developments regarding this issue.

§17.19 Control of the Amount

The measurement and control of punitive damages presents considerable difficulties, especially in mass disaster litigation in which emotion may play a definitive role. The traditional standards to measure the punitive damage award are stated in the Restatement (Second) of Torts §908(2).[119] In considering whether to impose punitive damages, the trier of fact "may consider the character of the defendant's act, the nature and extent of the harm to the plaintiff that the defendant caused or intended to cause, and the wealth of the defendant." Although whether to assess punitive awards is clearly within the sound discretion of the trier of fact,[120] punitive damages are not considered

---

[114] Parnell, *supra* note 111, at 967.

[115] Beshada v Johns-Manville Products Corp, 90 NJ 191, 447 A2d 539 (1982).

[116] Gold v Johns-Manville Sales Corp, 553 F Supp 482 (D NJ 1982).

[117] *Id* 484.

[118] Grimshaw v Ford Motor Co, 119 Cal App 3d 757, 174 Cal Rptr 348 (1981).

[119] Restatement (Second) of Torts, § 908(2) (1975).

[120] Toole v Richardson-Merrell, Inc, 251 Cal App 2d 689, 60 Cal Rptr 398 (1967); *In re* Related Asbestos Cases, 543 F Supp 1152 (ND Cal 1982); State *ex rel* Young v Crookham, 290 Or 61, 618 P2d 1257 (1980).

to be a matter of right; thus, the jury may withhold them even where they find the requisite misbehavior.[121] A majority of jurisdictions allow evidence of the financial status of the defendant[122] to assist the jury in determing the amount of damages necessary to punish the defendant. In many cases, this principle has been effectively explained by counsel for plaintiff during the closing argument by describing experiences that are common to most jurors. The analogy he or she might use may go something like this:

> If a 10-year-old boy delivering newspapers on his bicycle were to ride his bicycle intentionally into a 5-year-old boy, thus injuring that 5-year-old, I think anyone would agree that the newspaperboy should be punished. The newspaperboy earns $5.00 per week. In order to make an example so that the newspaperboy does not do this again a punishment of $10.000, or two weeks pay, seems reasonable. For two weeks, he will think about the injury he caused to the plaintiff and maybe prevent this from ever happening again. Indeed, two weeks pay is less than 5 per cent of his annual salary. Now, in this case you are about to decide, defendant ABC Multi-National Corporation has annual earnings in excess of $10 billion. . . .

However, at least one court has rejected this notion that the net worth of the defendant is relevant in products liability cases, reasoning that it is only relevant in cases "where a tort is committed by and against individuals; a one-on-one situation."[123] Besides the wealth of the defendant, courts provide little guidance in the way of jury instructions beyond reiterating the two remaining factors indicated in the Restatement.[124]

Other factors sometimes taken into consideration in determining whether to impose punitive damages are as follows:

1. Whether there is an award of compensatory damages (often considered a prerequisite to recovery of punitive damages)[125]

2. Whether the high-level management is involved (considered by a number of courts to be a critical prerequisite for finding the corporation vicariously liable for the acts of its employees)[126]

3. Whether the defendant manufacturer will be allowed to inform the jury of defendant's heavy involvement in related litigation along with its

---

[121] State *ex rel* Young v Crookham, 290 Or 61, 618 P2d 1268 (1980).

[122] Ghiardi, & Kircher, Punitive Damages, Law and Practice 105 (1982) (Ghiardi).

[123] Hoffman v Sterling Drug, Inc, 374 F Supp 850, 857 (ED Pa 1975).

[124] Ghiardi & Kircher, *supra* note 122, at 111.

[125] *Id* 108.

[126] Toole v Richardson-Merrell, Inc, 251 Cal App 2d 689, 60 Cal Rptr 398 (1967); Neal v Carey Canadian Mines, Ltd, 548 F Supp 357 (ED Pa 1982).

potential exposure to other plaintiffs[127]

4. Whether the amount of punitive damages should be reasonably related to the amount of actual damages suffered by the plaintiff [128]

A review of the general standards along with these additional considerations makes it clear that the calculation of the punitive damage award by the jury is still far from precise. As long as the current tort system is in effect, it is unlikely that it will ever become more precise, because of the subjective judgments that must be made along with the general nature of the goals of punishment and deterrence that the punitive damage award serves.

Besides enacting legislation to limit the recovery of punitive damages, the only control over the size of the punitive damage award is to have judicial review of the award. It is within the sound discretion of the trial or appellate court, if the award is deemed excessive, to reduce the award or to order a new trial. In the past, trial judges were hesitant to tamper with a punitive damage award because it represented the community's outrage. The increasing awareness for the potential abuse via excessive verdicts has encouraged the bench to begin to scrutinize such awards. A good example of the effectiveness of this tool is the MER-29 cases, discussed in **§17.16.** In *Toole,*[129] an award of $500,000 was reduced to $250,000, while in *Ostopowitz,*[130] the punitive damage award was cut from $8.5 million to $1 million. An even more dramatic example of this control is found in the recent products liability case of *Grimshaw v Ford Motor Co.*[131] In *Grimshaw,* the jury awarded $124 million in punitive damages for severe burn injuries that were sustained due to the allegedly defective design of the Ford Pinto gas tank. The trial court's reduction to $3 million was affirmed on appeal.

Several commentators suggest that punitive damages will be applied in a more principled manner if the judge, rather than the jury, were to measure the award.[132] The proposition, on it face, has several appealing characteristics. The decisions as to the liability for punitive damages would remain with the jury, thereby preserving its sanctity as the trier of fact. Relieving the jury of assessing the amount of the award, though, would reduce the possibility that passion or prejudice would result in an inflated verdict or in overkill, as in the case of mass disaster litigation. In addition, the judge has far greater experience in criminal proceedings involving punishment and is potentially more

---

[127] 548 F Supp 357, 388 (ED Pa 1982).

[128] Hoffman v Sterling Drugs, 374 F Supp 850, 851 (ED Pa 1975); Neal v Carey Canadian Mines, Ltd, 548 FSupp 357 (ED Pa 1982); Toole v Richardson-Merrell, Inc, 251 Cal App 2d 689, 60 Cal Rptr 398 (1967).

[129] Toole v Richardson-Merrell, Inc, 251 Cal App 2d 689, 60 Cal Rptr 398 (1967).

[130] Ostopowitz v Richardson-Merrell, Co, No 58-79-1963 (NY Sup Ct Jan 11, 1967).

[131] Grimshaw v Ford Motor Co, 119 Cal App 3d 757, 174 Cal Rptr 348 (1981).

[132] Owen, *Punitive Damages in Products Liability Litigation,* 74 Mich L Rev 1257 (1976); Mallor & Roberts, *Punitive Damages, Towards a Principled Approach,* 31 Hastings LJ 639 (1980).

aware of the social policies and economics involved in meting out such punitive awards. Finally, the judge might review evidence which might not normally be admissible because of its prejudicial effect. All in all, this seems to be a very practical solution to overkill in punitive damage awards. The policy considerations underlying the punitive damage award would be well-served, and yet the financial destruction of a corporate defendant at the hands of multiple plaintiffs could be averted.

Other suggested controls include: consolidating multiple claims; limiting the total number of awards to be recovered from a single defendant; limiting the amount of any one particular award;[133] allowing the jury to assess one punitive award to be held and appropriately distributed among all successful plaintiffs;[134] and finally, the proposing of the fairly novel idea of *add-on punishments* (any subsequent award of punitive damages after the first will be limited to the difference between the present award and the most recent prior award).[135]

The most obvious difficulty with any of the proposed solutions is that, for them to be effective, it is essential that they be uniformly applied throughout the country. Obviously, it is impracticable to expect such change to be brought about by judicial decision. The more likely approach would be uniform or federal legislation. Until that occurs, the present system of compensating plaintiffs and punishing wrongdoers on a case-by-case basis will continue.

---

[133] Ghiardi & Kircher, *supra* note 122, at 105.

[134] Roginsky v Richardson-Merrell, Inc, 378 F2d, 832, 839 (2d Cir 1967).

[135] Schulkin, *Mass Liability and Punitive Damages Overkill,* 30 Hastings LJ 1797 (1979).

18

The Use of Experts in Toxic Tort Litigation*

J.C. McElveen, Esq†

§18.01 Introduction

More often than not, toxic tort litigation involves complex scientific issues. As a result, the legal profession is required to call upon experts who are highly specialized in particular scientific and medical areas. It is not enough that the toxic tort litigator is skilled in the art of advocacy and persuasion. Counsel must also be skilled in the selection and use of scientific advisors and expert witnesses.

Although the purpose of this chapter is to describe the use and selection of experts in toxic tort litigation, much of the advice presented herein is germane

---

  * Grateful acknowledgment is made to Deborah H.W. Raisher, Esq., Seyfarth, Shaw, Fairweather & Geraldson, Washington, D.C., for her able assistance in the preparation of this chapter.
  † Partner, Jones, Day, Reavis & Pogue, Washington, D.C.

to the use and selection of experts in any type of litigation. Comments especially relevant to toxic tort litigation are provided where appropriate.

Experts serve critical purposes in both the pretrial and trial phases of a toxic tort case. In the pretrial phase of a case, they are particularly helpful in assessing the value of a potential claim. For the plaintiff, experts provide a valuable service by evaluating whether a claim is worth pursuing. Conversely, experts assist defendants in determining the chances of successfully defending a claim or the wisdom of settling a claim.

Experts who are incorporated into the legal scheme early in the case can suggest avenues of further scientific inquiry, evidence which should be obtained, and additional experts who should be consulted on particular issues in question. Early involvement of experts also facilitates the lawyer's educational process. Experts are invaluable educational resources for attorneys who endeavor to become fully conversant with the scientific and technical complexities of each case.

During the trial phase of a case, of course, experts move beyond their roles as advisors and educators. They become responsible for interpreting and clarifying technical information and, frequently, for giving opinions on the issues at hand.

Not all experts consulted during the life of a particular case will testify at trial. Counsel, as early as possible, should define and document the role an expert is to play. Delineation of the expert's role clarifies the applicable scope of discovery. Experts employed in anticipation of litigation or for trial preparation are subject to different and more limited discovery rules than are experts to be called as trial witnesses.[1] Clarification of the role an expert will play also

---

[1] Federal Rules of Civil Procedure—General Provisions Governing Discovery Rule 26(b)(4) Trial Preparation: Experts. Discovery of facts known and opinions held to experts, otherwise discoverable under the provisions of subdivision (b)(1) of this rule and acquired or developed in anticipation of litigation or for trial, may be obtained only as follows:

(A)(i) A party may through interrogatories require any other party to identify each person whom the other party expects to call as an expert witness at trial, to state the subject matter of which the expert is expected to testify, and to state the substance of the facts and opinions to which the expert is expected to testify and a summary of the grounds for each opinion; (ii) Upon motion, the court may order further discovery by other means, subject to such restrictions as to scope and such provisions, pursuant to subdivision (b)(4)(C) of this rule, concerning fees and expenses as the court may deem appropriate.

(B) A party may discover facts known or opinions held by an expert who has been retained or specially employed by another party in anticipation of litigation or preparation for trial and who is not expected to be called as a witness at trial, only as provided in Rule 35(b) or upon a showing of exceptional circumstances under which it is impracticable for the party seeking discovery to obtain facts or opinions on the same subject by other means.

(C) Unless manifest injustice would result, (i) the court shall require that the party seeking discovery pay the expert a reasonable fee for time spent in responding to discovery under subdivisions (b)(4)(A)(ii) and (b)(4)(B) of this rule; and (ii) with respect to discovery obtained under subdivision (b)(4)(A)(ii) of this rule the

dictates selection criteria used by counsel in hiring the expert. For example, physical characteristics and mannerisms of an expert become an important consideration only when the expert will be called as a witness, not when the expert will be used solely in pretrial preparation.

§18.02 Selection

The selection of an expert witness is an important task requiring skill and experience. Too frequently, counsel accepts the recommendation of others without giving serious consideration to the importance of the selection. The selection process should focus on a number of critical criteria. The first obvious selection criterion is expertise in a field useful in proving or disproving the case.

Toxic tort litigation requires experts from numerous academic fields, including but not limited to medical specialists, chemists, epidimiologists, process engineers, industrial hygienists, and environmental scientists. Of particular import in toxic tort litigation are experts in toxicology—the scientific study of poisons, their detection, effects, and treatment.

An obvious resource for obtaining names of potential experts is the client. Often, the client is involved in the same field or industry and is able to judge the qualifications and technical abilities of potential experts better than the attorney. The client should also be involved in the selection of the expert because the expert, like the attorney, is going to represent the client and many have an enormous impact on the outcome of the litigation.

Counsel's search for expert witnesses should also include a conscientious attempt to tap the wealth of expertise within the federal government. Telephone calls to the public information offices of federal research and regulatory agencies such as the Food and Drug Administration or the National Institute of Health often uncover names of experts in the field of interest.

Other sources for locating toxicologists and other experts include universities, local and state agencies, private forensic laboratories, and the American Academy of Forensic Sciences. A host of professional organizations and associations have evolved in the area of toxicology, as well as other fields, and may provide useful leads in finding toxic tort experts.[2]

The fact that an expert will serve as a witness rather than as just a pretrial advisor does not severely limit the pool of possible experts. The Federal Rules of Evidence[3] and many similar state statutes and rules give lawyers broad

---

court may require, and with respect to discovery obtained under subdivision (b)(4)(B) of this rule the court shall require, the party seeking discovery to pay the other party a fair portion of the fees and expenses reasonably incurred by the latter party in obtaining facts and opinions from the expert.

[2] 1 Houts, Baselt & Cravey, Courtroom Toxicology §§5.07-.16 (1981).

[3] Rule 702 of the Federal Rules of Civil Procedure provides:

If scientific, technical, or other specialized knowledge will assist the trier of fact to understand the evidence or to determine a fact in issue, a witness qualified as

discretion in choosing their expert witnesses. To testify as an expert, a witness need only be qualified "by knowledge, skill, experience, training or education."[4] Although this definition of *expert witness* is broad, the attorney should not choose just anyone who exhibits knowledge or skill in the specialty required by the case. The weight the jury or judge will give to the expert's testimony will often hinge on the expert's credentials. Many toxic tort cases become a battle of the experts. Thus, attorneys should try to assemble experts with the most impressive backgrounds possible in an attempt to boost the expert's credibility vis-a-vis opposing experts in the eyes of the fact finder.

Stature can be determined by reviewing objective indicia such as degrees, licenses, and positions held, professional publications, committee appointments, prior consulting experience, eminent professional societies of which the expert is a member, and a history of honors in the field.

The best experts are generally people who are full-time practitioners in a relevant field. As witnesses, practitioners are especially convincing when they testify about their own observations, experiments, and analysis. This first-hand knowledge is much more persuasive testimony than conclusions drawn from others' work. Professional witnesses, for the most part, are regarded with suspicion and are often lacking in credibility because juries perceive them as hired guns, willing to testify for the highest bidder.[5]

If counsel plans to use the expert at trial, the expert's temperament, appearance, and demeanor are important factors. An expert's appearance and mannerisms may make him or her an unsuitable witness, in spite of sterling professional and academic credentials. This is particularly true if he or she is likely to antagonize the trier of fact. Moreover, counsel should take care to select expert witnesses who are able to tolerate rigorous cross-examination without anger, emotion, overstatement, or collapse.

Finally, counsel should avoid selecting experts with obvious biases. In the long run, the most effective witness is one who rigorously maintains scientific impartiality and objectivity.

---

an expert by knowledge, skill, experience, training, or education, may testify thereto in the form of an opinion or otherwise.

[4] *Id.* In toxic tort cases, not all expert witnesses must be chemists or toxicologists. For example, in Gober v Revlon Inc, 317 F2d 47 (4th Cir 1963), a dermatologist was qualified to testify to the reaction of humans to certain chemicals. The expert's lack of qualifications as a chemist went to the weight of his testimony, not to its admissibility. Experts need not have experience which mirrors the exact issue at hand. The experience, however, should be sufficiently similar so that extrapolation from that experience to the case is reasonable. For example, in a case involving surface exposure to ethylene glycol, an expert with experience in oral ingestion was qualified to testify. Roberts v United States, 316 F2d 489 (3d Cir 1963). Similarly, an expert who conducted toxicity tests with laboratory animals was qualified to testify concerning the effect of toxic exposure on humans. *Id.*

[5] Ostroff, Experts: A Few Fundamentals, Litigation 8(3) (Winter 1982).

§18.03   Contacting the Experts

The lawyer's first contact with the expert is usually by telephone or letter. The primary purpose of this overture is to determine whether the expert can help the lawyer and whether the expert wants to be involved in the case. In the initial contact, the attorney should relate the hazardous or toxic agent involved and the names of the parties, and should ascertain the expert's interest and availability to talk further.

The first face-to-face conference is the point at which both the attorney and expert most likely decide whether to continue the relationship. If both agree, the lawyer should broach the subject of fees—hourly and daily charges, mileage, travel expenses, courtroom appearances, and the like. The agreement should be reduced to writing, preferably in the form of a letter to the expert.[6]

Attorneys often find a contract for services useful to clarify the agreement between the expert and the client. Where a contract is used, it should describe the services the expert is expected to perform—i.e., review published scientific articles and/or reports; monitor scientific literature; provide consultation services in a particular field; inspect named premises; testify before judicial, administrative, and executive bodies; etc. It should also list billing rates where appropriate, as well as billing arrangements, travel and hotel accommodations and the like. Of particular import are contract provisions which restrict the expert from providing services to other parties during the pendency of the case. In addition, the contract should include a provision stating that all information disclosed by the party pursuant to the contract shall be used exclusively in the pending case or on appeal and shall not be divulged or otherwise revealed to or discussed with persons other than the contracting party or without advance permission from the party.

The inclusion of provisions restricting the expert's assistance to other parties in the case and divulging information revealed are of particular use if the attorney decides not to use the expert's services once the expert is retained. An attorney may so decide for numerous reasons. Whether or not the parting is amicable, the attorney wants some assurance that the expert cannot share damaging information with other parties in the action. These contractual provisions provide, at least in part, that assurance.

As a practical matter, attorneys must ascertain whether the expert is willing to meet agreed deadlines. An expert's failure to analyze records and to prepare reports in a timely manner simply complicates the attorney's job. By obtaining a time commitment in advance, the attorney can ameliorate potential problems.

The attorney should also find out whether the expert who is willing to participate extensively in pretrial preparation is willing to take the stand at trial. This cannot be assumed. Those experts who regard the witness stand with fear and dread often make less than satisfactory witnesses. Thus, it is better to ascertain early in the working relationship the expert's feelings with

---

[6] 1 Houts, Baselt & Cravey, Courtroom Toxicology §5.17 (1981).

respect to the courtroom, thereby avoiding unpleasant surprise as trial date approaches.

Use of Experts

§18.04   Duty and Breach

Toxic tort actions generally take two forms: negligence and strict liability. Traditional negligence theory requires the plaintiff to show that the defendant had a duty to the plaintiff which was breached and that the breach caused the plaintiff's injury.

Expert witnesses are particularly useful in the plaintiff's effort to show that the defendant employer, manufacturer, distributor, or seller had a duty to the plaintiff. In many cases, the existence of a duty hinges on whether the dangers associated with the defendant's product or occupational process were foreseeable at the time the plaintiff was exposed. It is here, at the foreseeability stage, that counsel can use experts to great advantage.

Prior to trial, experts can search the medical literature to determine when the medical community first recognized the dangers of exposure to the toxic product or process in question. Defendant manufacturers, distributors, and sellers are presumed to know the current state of the medical and scientific art relating to their products and manufacturing techniques.[7] Thus, from the point that the medical community suspects adverse toxic effects, the dangers are foreseeable and defendants have an affirmative duty to warn workers and consumers of the risks associated with exposure.[8] By presenting the studies in chronological order in juxtaposition to the plaintiff's exposure or injury, experts can attest to the foreseeability of the plaintiff's injury and prove the existence of a duty on a defendant's part. Once the existence of a duty is established, the plaintiff's counsel simply needs to show the defendant's failure to warn or take steps to make safe in order to show a breach of the duty.[9]

---

[7] *See* Love v Wolf, 226 Cal 2d 378, 398, 38 Cal Rptr 183, 197 (1964) (where the court held Parke-Davis, a pharmaceutical company, to an expert standard and deemed the company to know of the articles of nationwide dissemination concerning the aftermath of use of the drug). *See also* Stromsodt v Parke-Davis & Co, 257 F Supp 991 (DND 1966), *affd*, 411 F2d 1390 (8th Cir 1969); Tinnerhold v Parke-Davis & Co, 285 F Supp 432 (SDNY 1968), *affd*, 411 F2d 48 (2d Cir 1969); Holbrook v Rose, 458 SW2d 155 (1970).

[8] Love v Wolf, 226 Cal 2d 378, 396, 38 Cal Rptr 183, 196 (1964) (where the plaintiff produced an expert witness to attest to the existence of 30 to 40 reports published in medical journals on the tendency of the drug to cause chronic bone marrow failure so as to establish the foreseeability of the plaintiff's anemia and the breach of the defendant's duty to warn consumers of dangers consonant with these studies).

[9] New York cases have consistently held that a manufacturer's knowledge of special risks of harm attendant upon normal use of his or her product imposes a duty upon the manufacturer to warn adequately of those risks. *See e.g.,* Ezagui v Dow Chem Corp, 598 F2d 727 (2d Cir 1979); Donigi v American Cyanamid Co, 43 NY2d 935, 374 NE2d 1245, 403 NYS2d 894 (1978), *affg* 57 AD2d 760, 394 NYS2d 422 (1977).

Industrial hygienists are particularly useful in showing what steps the defendant could reasonably have taken to avoid a breach of duty.

Even absent medical evidence demonstrating foreseeability, defendants may still have a duty to pretest and evaluate products before marketing and to conduct ongoing medical surveillance once the product is introduced or the process is in use.[10]

Obviously, the defendants in negligence cases can use experts to show that the plaintiffs' injuries were not foreseeable and that the defendants, therefore, had no duty to take the steps the plaintiffs suggests were the defendants' obligation. Once again, a defendant's experts can whittle away at the plaintiff's duty evidence by presenting medical evidence confirming that on the date of the plaintiff's injurious exposure, adverse effects were not forseeable.

A defendant can also use experts to attest to the reasonableness of the defendant's efforts to test, warn, and take precautions to avoid injury and, thereby, to fullfill whatever duty it might have to its workers and the purchasing public.[11]

Where the toxic tort action is based on a strict liability or products liability theory, foreseeability has sometimes been an issue, as has been the reasonableness of the defendant's actions. Where courts have considered foreseeability and reasonableness relevant to such cases, expert witnesses have played useful roles, just as in traditional negligence actions.

The modern trend, however, in strict liability cases appears to ignore foreseeability and the reasonableness of the defendant's conduct. Instead, liability attaches by virtue of the unreasonably or abnormally dangerous nature of the product or process, itself, not the fault of the defendant.[12] In such cases, expert testimony as to foreseeability would not be relevant since the defendant's duty is not really at issue.

---

[10] *See* Presbry v Gillette Co, 105 Ill App 3d 1082, 435 NE2d 513 (1982) (where the company conducted an extensive premarketing testing program on adverse effects of antiperspirants, as well as ongoing postmarketing studies).

[11] For example, in Presbry v Gillette Co, 105 Ill App 3d 1082 (1982) the defendant used an expert toxicologist, a medical review officer for Gillette, to attest to Gillette's efforts to meet its duty to consumers. The toxicologist testified to the company's program to review the product for safety prior to marketing by checking medical literature in the field, reports of adverse reactions, reports on the product, ingredients, or individual chemicals which the product contained, testing information, and applicable government regulations. The expert also testified to Gillette's premarketing animal 14-day acute studies to determine toxicity and the level of skin, eye, and lung irritation and 90-day subacute tests to ascertain toxic effects following dermal application and inhalation.

[12] Beshada v Eagle Picher Indus, 90 NJ 191, 447 A2d 539 (1982) (where the New Jersey Supreme Court held irrelevant the medical community's awareness or ignorance of the dangers of asbestos in a products liability action) and City of Bridgeton v BP Oil Inc, 146 NJ Super 169, 369 A2d 49 (1981) (where the court imposed strict liability on a defendant for storage of hazardous substances which caused damages).

§18.05   Causation

The outcome of most toxic tort cases hinges on proof of causation. Experts are the key to proving causation. The proof process is essentially a three-step process aimed at showing exposure to a toxic agent, the plaintiff's injury, and relationship between the two. Experts play important roles at each step.

§18.06   —Exposure

Step one, proving exposure, is, itself, a two-part task. Counsel must first identify the toxic agent and then describe the plaintiff's exposure to the toxin. Chemists, process engineers, industrial hygientists, geophysicists, and environmental scientists are particularly useful for both purposes.

Identification of the toxic agent in occupational toxic tort actions is simplified if the case involves an industrial process which has been linked with excessive rates of chronic disease and cancer. Process-related exposures which have been identified as high cancer risks include rubber curing, tanning, metallic and nonmetallic mining, metal smelting and processing, petrochemical processing, and coke-oven steel production.[13] Where the case involves such a process, experts can attest to the high-risk nature of the process, the studies which have been conducted, and the results of such studies. Epidemiologists and statisticians may be particularly useful in analyzing such studies and indicating why they believe that the plaintiff is or is not in the group which is the subject of the study, and why the study is a valid one or why it is not.

Where a high risk is not involved, identification of the causal agent may be more difficult. In the pretrial stage, epidemiologists, industrial hygienists, chemists, and environmental scientists are useful in conducting chemical analyses of products and environmental monitoring of workplaces to identify toxic components. At trial, expert witnesses can attest to the existence or absence of these toxic agents and the hazards such agents do or do not present.[14]

Where chemical analysis is not possible, identification of a particular toxic product may be possible through documentation contained in invoices, purchase orders of manufacturers, formulators, middlemen, and sellers, environmental monitoring data, and company records such as advertising brochures, insurance reports, annual reports, SEC filings, interrogatories in other actions, and invoices for printed warning labels.[15] Obtaining such documentation may be complicated by the passage of time between the toxic exposure, the ultimate injury, and the commencement of litigation. The use of trade names or nondescriptive labels and the accidental or deliberate destruction of documents can

---

[13] S.S. Epstein, & J.B. Swartz, Nature 289, 127 (1981).

[14] Roberts v United States, 316 F2d 489 (3d Cir 1963) (where experts testified concerning the hazards of exposure to ethylene gycol).

[15] Epstein, Role of the Scientist in Toxic Tort Case Preparation, Trial 40 (July 1981).

also make the identification process a difficult one.[16] Experts are of utmost importance in reviewing such documentation. Their task, or course, is to review the documents with an eye toward gathering circumstantial evidence to prove the existence or absence of the toxic product.

Once the toxic agent is identified, counsel for the plaintiff must show the plaintiff's exposure to that agent. Proof of exposure requires detailed personal and occupational histories. Personal histories are generally provided by the plaintiff. They commence at birth and include residential, educational, and marital details, as well as lifestyle. Experts, as a general rule, play no role in assembling personal histories. They do, however, play a significant pretrial role in documenting occupational histories. Occupational histories disclose in chronological order the duration and characteristics of each occupational incident whether full-time or part-time. Where occupational toxic exposure is the subject of the claim, expert witnesses such as chemical engineers, process engineers, and industrial hygientists can attest to the existence of the toxic product and the nature of the plaintiff's exposure to it both in qualitative and quantitative terms. Experts can also attest to industrial exposure standards and compare the defendant's work practices with those standards.

In addition, medical experts can confirm or contest the alleged exposure by conducting chemical analysis of body fluids or tissues to ascertain the presence or absence of the casual agent or markers of its presence, such as the bilateral pleural plagues or disphramatic calcification of asbestos exposure.

§18.07 —Injury

After having identified the toxic product and the plaintiff's exposure to it, the second step in proving causation is describing the plaintiff's injury. The purpose at this stage is to diagnose and define the adverse effect. Experts at this stage are generally medical doctors such as internists, neurologists, pathologists, and surgeons.

This step focuses on a detailed medical history of the plaintiff. The medical history, like the personal and occupational histories, is a chronological cataloguing of all illnesses and treatments, however unrelated they may seem to the claim. The medical history also includes all medical records of hospitalizations, examinations, and laboratory tests. This history should also include occupational medical records.

Prior to trial, medical experts assist the attorney by describing what records to obtain, reviewing the records, conducting examinations, diagnosing the disease or adverse effect, recommending further independent examinations or tests where accuracy or objectivity is questionable, and, where appropriate, recommending specific autopsy procedures and analytical tests to be performed.

At trial, medical experts attest to the plaintiff's injuries or the deleterious

---

[16] *Id.*

effects alleged to be the result of toxic exposure.[17] Experts who are consulted for such purposes should not be pressed to render opinions on causality, particularly where such opinions go beyond their areas of expertise. Generally, clinicians are primarily trained to diagnose and treat medical problems, not to propose the cause for such problem. They may not be qualified to render such opinions and should not be depended on for causal testimony.

§18.08   —Linking Injury to Toxic Agent

The third step in proving causation is to link the injury or adverse effect to the toxic agent. The type of expert required to demonstrate the causal link between the injury and the toxic substance will vary from case to case, depending on the type of disease class into which the plaintiff's injuries fall. Diseases in toxic tort litigation generally fall into two categories:

1.   Work-related—known cause diseases
2.   Diseases of unknown cause

In the first category, work-related—known cause diseases, diagnosis of the disease shows the causation. Cases involving diseases such as asbestosis, bysinossis, or silicosis are typical examples. In such cases, the battle centers on the actual diagnosis of the disease, because once diagnosis is established, the cause is also established. These cases pit clinician against clinician, pathologist against pathologist, and radiologist against radiologist, each explaining the tests used to obtain the raw data from which he or she reached the diagnosis. The experts war over the raw data obtained or, where they agree on the raw data obtained, they war over the interpretation of the raw data and the ultimate conclusory diagnosis. Little need exists for epidemiological evidence showing that the exposure to the toxic substance probably caused the disease. For example, no argument exists over whether exposure to asbestos can cause asbestosis. The question is whether the plaintiff, in fact, has asbestosis. However, in close cases testimony about the dose-response relationship[18] (if the appropriate dose is known) may influence the trier of fact regarding the likelihood that the plaintiff has the disease.

In the second category of cases, diseases of unknown cause, clinicians agree on the diagnosis, but they battle over the cause of the agreed-upon disease. An example of such a case might be lung cancer. In such a case, clinical experts are useful in describing the symptoms and giving their diagnoses. However, the most important experts in these cases are those who can gather and present epidemiological evidence which explores the possible etiologies and defines the probability that exposure to the defendant's toxic product or hazardous

---

[17] Tinnerholm v Parke Davis & Co, 285 F Supp 432 (SDNY 1968), *affd,* 411 F2d 48 (2d Cir 1969) (where physician described child's spasticity and retarded mental development thought to be the result of pertussis-vaccine encephalopathy).

[18] See §1.04.

workplace caused the disease.[19]

The causal expert is critical here in helping counsel assemble medical evidence from which the causal relationship may be inferred. The inferences are generally based on toxicological and epidemiological studies involving the alleged causal agent. Prior to trial, counsel, with the assistance of experts, should thoroughly search the published literature for all relevant studies. Experts often know of relevant studies and are generally skilled in accessing such studies through scientific data bases. Experts can also recommend and help search additional sources of unreported studies, such as the files of the appropriate state and federal regulatory agencies and of the manufacturers, distributors, sellers, trade associations, and insurance companies.

An epidemiologist, who specializes in the study of the distribution and determinants of diseases and injuries in human populations, is an obvious choice for these tasks. At trial, the best expert witness is one who has actually conducted a epidemiological study involving the toxic agent or the type of workplace in which the plaintiff works. However, a clinician who can attest to epidemiological studies of others can also fill this role.

Defendants usually attack the plaintiff's causation evidence by ascribing the injury or disease to genetic or lifestyle factors rather than to the toxic exposure.[20] This is an uphill fight for the defendant expert because the plaintiff can generally recover even if lifestyle or genetic factors played a contributory role in the disease. Although the expert's efforts may not result in avoidance of liability, they may be effective in mitigating damages.

§18.09 Preparing the Expert

As noted throughout this chapter, not all experts used during the course of a particular case will testify at trial. If the expert does testify, counsel must remember that the expert is an expert only in his or her field of endeavor. The scientific expert is not an expert in trial technique. The prudent attorney should, therefore, prepare the expert witness for trial just as the attorney would a lay witness.

Initial instructions should concern the expert's behavior and demeanor on the stand and before the trier of fact. It is important, though sometimes uncomfortable, to remind the expert to conduct himself or herself with humili-

---

[19] Lovich v Army, 81 Ohio App 317, 75 NE2d 459 (1947) (where the chief of the subdivision of communicable diseases of the city's health department, who had investigated the typhoid fever epidemic in an institution, testified that one of the food handlers in the institution was a typhoid carrier, thereby eliminating other possible etiologies); Diaz v Eli Lilly & Co, 14 Mass App Ct 448, 440 NE2d 518 (1982) (where the defendant's expert, a professor of ophthalmology and neurology challenged the diagnosis of toxic optic atrophy and listed several possible etiologies which had not been eliminated).

[20] Grinnell v Charles Pfizer & Co, 274 Cal 2d 424, 79 Cal Rptr 369 (1969) (use of experts to show polio not vaccine-induced).

ty and to avoid an air of condescension before or toward the trier of fact and opposing counsel.

The attorney should point out the need for a balanced presentation which combines humility with firm intellectual reasoning. The expert may at times use technical vocabulary. The attorney should remind the expert, however, that the purpose of expert testimony is to assist the trier of fact in understanding the scientific issues at hand and that this purpose is best served if the expert translates technical terms into vocabulary that the ordinary lay person understands. The expert should be encouraged, where possible, to use examples and analogies which people encounter in their everyday lives.

With respect to the expert's testimony in direct examination, one or two days before trial, the attorney should prepare the witness by rehearsing the questions counsel will ask and the desired responses. The witness can even assist counsel in phrasing some questions which will elicit the desired testimony.

The purpose of such preparation will cement in the expert's mind the essential theory of the case and familiarize the expert with the trial procedures. Such preparation will allay some anxiety when the expert finally takes the stand at trial. The expert should be cautioned to testify in terms of *reasonable medical or scientific probabilities* rather than weak common expressions like *may have* or *is consistent with*. Finally, care should be taken not to overrehearse or to turn the expert's testimony into what appears to be a canned presentation.

Counsel should also prepare the expert for cross-examination. The expert should clearly understand that opposing counsel's purpose will be to debunk the expert's theories and opinions, to expose the expert's biases and to attack his credibility. The expert should be cautioned to be polite and to avoid the appearance of anger even when subjected to less than courteous interrogation. Counsel should anticipate the questions opposing counsel will ask and assist the witness in preparing responses which are honest but undamaging to the theory the expert is hired to expose.

In sum, experts and expert witnesses are critical figures in toxic tort litigation. Toxic tort litigators who are skilled in the selection and use of experts are a giant step ahead of the uninitiated in this area.

§18.10   The Opponent's Expert

It should always be remembered that cross-examination of the other side's expert witness is no substitute for counsel's own expert's opinion. Never assume you can get an admission from the other side's expert that will form a part of the proof of your own case. Even if you are in possession of information that the opposition's expert has agreed with your point before, the best you can do if that expert disagrees with the proposition now is to show a prior inconsistent statement. The finder of fact is entitled to believe the witness's present statement in the face of a prior inconsistent statement. This is especially easy if the witness is able to say he or she has come into possession of more recent scientific information that has resulted in a modification of the earlier opinion.

Cross-examination, however, can be very effective, but advance preparation is a must. In these days of extensive pretrial discovery and, in many cases, experts who are courtroom veterans, a startling admission by an expert witness is almost unheard of. Three cross-examination fundamentals are:

1. Try to know as much as possible about the witness's purported area of expertise

2. Try to read everything the witness has written on the subject about which he or she is testifying

3. Try to obtain and read as much of the witness's prior testimony as possible

Once cross-examination begins, do not try for the grandstand *coup-de-gras* —the question that will destroy the witness's credibility once and for all. It will almost never come. Be satisfied to chip away at the witness.

Begin with the witness's curriculum vitae (CV). Ask for CVs as early as possible in the discovery for all identified expert witnesses. Study it. Where can you score some points? Is the witness board-certified in an area of medicine directly relevant to the inquiries in this case? Has the witness written in areas about which he or she is testifying? Is the CV inflated by listing abstracts and then the articles which resulted from the abstracts? Is there an inordinate amount of material *in press* or *submitted for publication?* Find out who underwrote the grants that permitted the witness's research. However, as in all areas of cross-examination, do not talk just to hear yourself talk. Do not give the witness an opportunity to reiterate to the jury an otherwise gilt-edged set of credentials on cross-examination. However, do not be afraid to probe beneath the surface of an otherwise impressive-looking resume—just do it before you stand up in court to ask the questions of the witness.

Listen carefully to the direct examination. Does the witness say anything that is inconsistent with your own understanding of the mechanism of action of the toxin in question, or of the physiological or pathological response of the human body? If you are trying a case involving an organ system, you must, insofar as is possible, understand the way that system operates physiologically before you can understand what has gone wrong with the system and how those effects have probably occurred. Also, to the extent possible, understand the tests which are done to measure the function of these body systems. For example, in any pulmonary disease case, you should know the tests designed to show the volumes of the lungs and the flow rates of air in and out of the lung (spirometry). You should know the fundamentals of blood chemistry and the mechanisms of the transfer of oxygen and carbon dioxide across the blood-gas barrier, and you should know the tests that demonstrate whether those mechanisms are working (arterial blood gases and the diffusion test). You should know what should happen when the organism is stressed, with exercise, what should happen, and what does happen in your case—and you should know how these tests are done and how they should not be done. In any case involving X-ray or CAT scan findings, you should know what different techniques are designed to show and are not designed to show.

If the witness says anything different from what you know to be the case, as to performing tests, the reliability of tests, physiologic responses, or mechanisms of action, chip away at those points, *provided* you know you can support your position by reference to a treatise, or you know your own expert witness is prepared to testify differently from the opposition's expert and has evidence to support himself or herself.

Use treatises to cross-examine the witness, but do not use them any more than absolutely necessary. Excessive use of treatises bores jurors and they lose interest. Above all, do not get into philosophical discussions with the witness. Stay as crisp and clear as possible. Get in and get out. Neither beat a dead horse nor keep trying forever to get the witness to concede a point.

Finally, to the extent possible, use the witness's own prior statements (in court or on paper) against him or her. However, once you get the inconsistency on the record, do not ask him or her to explain why he or she said something then and something else now. Too many expert witnesses will be able to do so. Leave the discrepancy hanging and go on to something else. Let the other side come back for rehabilitation. Do not do it yourself.

§18.11   Use of Scientific Treatises and Medical Literature

A problem related to the use of expert witnesses is the extent to which scientific treatises and medical literature may be used to bolster or impeach the testimony of the expert witness. In toxic tort litigation, as in any other area of litigation in which experts play a prominent role, scientific and medical literature also play an important role. Such evidence can be an invaluable weapon in the attorney's arsenal.[21] Moreover, a thorough review and understanding of the relevant scientific and medical literature will enable one to select, prepare, and use an expert better so as to evaluate, prepare, and try a case more efficiently and effectively.

In all but a few jurisdictions, scientific and medical literature is inadmissible, under the hearsay rule, as proof of the truth of the statement contained therein.[22] A number of states, however, have by statute, rule, or judicial decision rendered *learned treatises* admissible as substantive evidence under certain conditions.[23]

---

[21] Kapp, *Medical Books as Evidence: An Attorney's Introduction to the Literature,* 55 Fla BJ 795 (1981).

[22] Wigmore, Evidence in Trials at Common Law §§1690, 1696 (1932); McCormick, Handbook of the Law of Evidence §321 (Cleary 2d ed) (1972).

[23] *See,* Ark Stat Ann §28-1001, Rule 803(18) (1977); Idaho Code §9-402 (1978); Kan Stat Ann §60-460 (cc) (1976); NC Gen Stat §8.40.1 (1981); Wis Stat §908.03(18) (1974); Lane v Otts, 412 So 2d 254 (Ala 1982); Heilman v Snyder, 520 SW2d 321 (Ky 1975).

Recognizing the view of commentators, which generally favored the admissibility of learned treatises,[24] the Federal Rules of Evidence provide that learned treatises are admissible and substantive evidence as long as two conditions are satisfied.[25] First, the statements must be introduced only during the course of direct or cross-examination of an expert witness. Second, the learned treatise must be established as a reliable authority, either by the testimony or admission of the witness, by other expert testimony or by judicial notice.[26] The portion of the treatise quoted may be read into evidence but may not be received as an exhibit and thus does not go to the jury.[27]

In virtually all jurisdictions, learned treatises are admissible to some extent on cross-examination of an expert witness.[28] The jurisdictions vary, however, as to when learned treatises may be used for this purpose. Some jurisdictions require that the witness first expressly state on direct or cross-examination that he or she relied on the treatise. Other jurisdictions require only that the witness acknowledge the treatise as an authority. A few permit the use of a learned treatise, even without reliance or acknowledgment by the witness, as long as its authoritativeness is established by proof or judicial notice.[29] Again, as with learned treatises admissible as substantive evidence, the trial judge has

---

[24] See Advisory Committee Note to Rule 803(18) of the Federal Rules of Evidence.

[25] Rule 803(18) provides an exception to the hearsay note for learned treatises:

Learned Treatises.—To the extent called to the attention of an expert witness upon cross-examination or relied upon by him in direct examination, statements contained in published treatises, periodicals, or pamphlets on a subject of history, medicine, or other science or art, established as a reliable authority by the testimony or admission of the witness or by other expert testimony or by judicial notice. If admitted, the statements may be read into evidence but may not be received as exhibits.

[26] Courts have wide discretion in ruling on the reliability and admissibility generally of a proffered learned treatise. *See, e.g.,* Johnson v William C Ellis & Sons Iron Works, 609 F2d 820 (5th Cir 1980) (safety codes and standards are admissible when prepared by organizations formed for chief purpose of promoting safety); Lane v Otts, 412 So 2d 254 (Ala 1982) (although experts testified that journal was standard and trustworthy, there was no evidence that article contained within the journal was standard); Shepherd v State, 270 Ark 457, 605 SW2d 414 (1980) (statement from book compiled by expert editor admissible notwithstanding failure to identify author of the statement); Obrien v Angley, 63 Ohio St 2d 159, 407 NE2d 490 (1980) (editorial in Journal of the American Medical Association was not admissible where it was primarily an expression of opinion concerning a controversial subject posing litigation risks for medical profession); Mazzaro v Paull, 372 Mass 645, 363 NE2d 509 (1977) (no abuse of discretion in excluding copy of Directory of Medical Specialists, which plaintiff sought to introduce to establish expertise of authors of various medical treatises); see generally, Imwinkelried, *The Use of Learned Scientific Treatises Under Federal Rule of Evidence 803(18),* 18 Trial 56 (Feb 1982).

[27] *Cf* Cross v Huttenlocher, 43 CLJ 7 (Conn 1981) (if medical treatise is recognized as authoritative and it influenced or tended to confirm expert's opinion, relevant portions thereof may be admitted into evidence in exercise of trial court's discretion).

[28] 6 Wigmore §1700; McCormick §321; Annot, 60 ALR2d 77 (1969).

[29] 6 Wigmore § 1700-02; McCormick § 321-22.

wide discretion in allowing the use of learned treatises on cross-examination, depending on their reliability, relevancy, and possible prejudicial impact.

At trial, whether admissible as substantive evidence or on the cross-examination of an expert, scientific and medical literature can be an important tool. The use of scientific and medical literature, in effect, "permits the proponent to array the world's leading experts against the opposition. . . . The proponent, in effect, displays the texts on the counsel table as an army of experts."[30]

The use of scientific and medical literature is not, however, without drawbacks. Principal among these is the technical nature of the language in which it is written. As one commentator has stated:

> The texts are normally written for scientific readers and frequently cluttered with technical terms. It is true that the expert on the stand can explain difficult terms, but it is far better to find a passage without technical terms. The proponent should seek passages written in simple language; as soon as the expert on the stand reads the passage, it should be evident to the jurors that the passage directly corroborates the witness's testimony. It may be impressive to read passage after passage from learned works, but if those passages contain unfamiliar terms, the result may be confusion. The proponent should be selective in choosing passages for admission under the learned treatise exception.[31]

These considerations are particularly important in those jurisdictions, including the federal courts, where portions of learned treatises may be read to the jury but not received as exhibits.

Use of Treatises before Trial

While the use of scientific and medical literature at trial is indeed important, often overlooked is the importance of this data prior to trial. Expert literature should be reviewed even prior to the selection and retention of an expert to provide the attorney with a basic familiarity with the subject matter. A number of sources of data, both government and private, exist on issues involved in toxic tort cases.[32]

A basic familiarity with the subject matter enables the attorney, at least preliminarily, to evaluate the risks and rewards of bringing or defending a lawsuit. Although the attorney is rarely in a position to judge the ultimate outcome of a case from such a review, it may at least disclose that potential litigation will be hard-fought and costly.

Familiarity with the subject matter also facilitates the selection of an expert, since the informed attorney better understands the likely issues in the case and knows what type of expert is needed. The literature may reveal persons in the

---

[30] Scientific and Expert Evidence 47 (E. Imwinkelried ed, 2d ed 1981).

[31] *Id* 47-48.

[32] See *Where To Look For Help On A Case*, Natl Law J Mar 21, 1983, at 38, col 2; Kapp, *Medical Books as Evidence: An Attorney's Introduction to the Literature*, 55 Fla BJ 795 (1981).

field who have written on the precise issue in the case, or it may reveal persons who are widely recognized as leading authorities. The impact of presenting as an expert witness one who *wrote the book* on a particular subject is obvious.

Once the expert is retained, a thorough familiarity and understanding of the literature will enable the attorney to utilize the expert's knowledge more effectively and efficiently. The attorney able to speak and understand the expert's *language* is better able to educate and better able to evaluate the strengths and weaknesses of the expert's opinions and conclusions and those of the opponent's experts. Equally important, the attorney is able to work with the expert to translate his or her opinions and conclusions, without a loss of scientific accuracy, into terms understandable to lay persons.

In addition to providing the attorney with a thorough understanding of the subject matter on which the expert has been retained, the use of scientific and medical literature is essential in working with the expert to evaluate and prepare the case for trial. The attorney should impress upon the expert that at this stage he or she is interested in all support for and against his or her client's position. All literature, both pro and con, on the subject on which the expert will testify should be closely examined. The expert's explanations for texts, articles, and studies which reach conclusions opposite to his or hers should be carefully scrutinized to insure that he or she is being totally objective. Furthermore, his or her explanations or attempts to distinguish these differing conclusions should be in clear and concise terms, understandable to a lay person.

The scientific and medical literature which purports to support the expert's opinions and conclusions should also be carefully scrutinized. The attorney must explain to the expert that the use of such literature is not indicative of a lack of confidence in his or her testimony, but rather it is necessary to attack the adversary's expert and negate any suggestion from the adversary that the expert's opinions are not supported by other experts in the field. The attorney must convince the expert of the need to point out any and all weaknesses in such literature prior to trial. Should such a weakness be pointed out by the adversary's counsel, particularly after the literature has been offered on direct examination in support of the expert, the jury or judge is at best likely to have serious doubts as to the expert's objectivity and give little weight to his or her testimony.

Finally, prior to trial, the attorney should utilize the discovery process to prepare to respond to scientific and medical literature likely to be introduced by the adversary. The attorney should discover any articles, studies, or reports on which the adversary's expert will rely or which he or she claims support his or her opinions and conclusions. Discovery should also be made into any writings done by the adversary's expert. At trial, the opposing expert should not be allowed to depart from the opinions and conclusions stated in these writings and, if possible, they should be used against him or her.

In sum, scientific and medical literature can be a most valuable tool in both the preparation and trial of a toxic tort case and should be carefully examined at the earliest stage possible.

Health Professionals as Experts

19

Harold R. Imbus, M.D.*, C. Ralph Buncher, Ph.D.**, William L. Dyson, Ph.D.†; John A. Thomas, Ph.D.,‡ G.Z. Nothstein, Esq.

* President, Health & Hygiene Inc., Greensboro, North Carolina; formerly Medical Director, Burlington Industries.

** Professor of Epidemiology & Biostatistics, Institute of Enviromental Health, University of Cincinnati Medical Center, Cincinnati, Ohio.

† Vice-President, Industrial Hygiene, Health & Hygiene Inc., Greensboro, North Carolina.

‡ Vice-President, Life Sciences, Travenol Laboratories, Morton Grove, Illinois; formerly Professor of Pharmacology & Toxicology, West Virginia University School of Medicine.

§19.01   Overview

Torts arise from injuries and illnesses, real or imagined. Hence, any discussion of toxic torts cannot avoid a discussion of toxic injuries and illnesses. Toxic hazards are numerous and diverse; biological systems respond in complex ways; and our scientific understanding of these matters, though growing, remains limited. Given the heterogeneity of circumstances and actual harm alleged in each case, must then every tort action be viewed as unique unto itself? Or, in addition to the legal theories relied upon, are there common *themes* which run among them? In particular, what can be said of the injuries and illnesses acknowledgedly so varied, which set tort actions in motion? What unifying focus do they provide?

First, it may be observed that all *injuries, illnesses,* or *diseases,* terms that are used more or less interchangeably throughout this chapter, fall within the broad scope of medicine and/or science. Toxic injuries or diseases may be distinguished from other injuries and diseases by etiology, but generally they share the symptoms, signs, and test findings common to injuries and diseases of nontoxic origin. Mesothelioma and hepatic angiosarcoma stand apart because the occurrence of these highly unusual cancers does suggest specific culprit agents—i.e., asbestos and vinyl chloride monomer, respectively. Similarly, numbness in a particular pattern over the face may be recognized as a toxic effect of stilbamidine, an antimony-containing drug used to treat parasites. Such examples of truly distinctive toxic injuries are few in number. By contrast, many agents can and do cause chronic obstructive pulmonary disease like that seen in smokers or those with the *naturally* occurring alph-1 antitrypsin deficiency; many agents can and do cause peripheral neuropathies comparable to ones seen in alcoholics and diabetics; many agents can and do cause cancers of the same type seen in the general population. So, clinical considerations rarely separate toxic injuries and diseases from the rest of medicine, and ordinary clinical approaches often fail to resolve what may be key issues when compensation claims are contested in court, considered by an insurance carrier, or weighed in other forums.

What does distinguish toxic injuries and diseases from their nontoxic counterparts are the particular medical and scientific questions which must be asked when they are alleged. What, if any, are the causal links between the cited hazard and the putative harm? What, in fact, is this harm? The importance of reliable answers is obvious.

The medical/scientific expert can be called upon to address questions of causality and at times breach of duty. An epidemiologist may opine about the likelihood of a causal nexus based on inferences from certain observations in the subject case or similar ones. A toxicologist can comment upon what is known concerning the properties and effects of the hazard of interest. An industrial hygienist, engineer, or comparable professional may establish the relevant details of exposure history. In some cases, physicians can weigh questions of causality from the perspective of their own expertise.

When *causality* is extended to include such closely related matters as apportionment of the damages, the expert's role grows. In assessing the nature and extent of any evident harm done the claimant, the expert must consider whether more than one cause or more than one injury may have been responsible for the current condition. After proper evaluation, it may be possible for him or her to identify an occupational asthma, incriminate a specific allergen, and separate the effects of smoking from those of another exposure. Such determinations and conclusions are not always attempted because they are difficult to make and not important in every context. Furthermore, when specific attention is not called to these matters in the beginning, they may be overlooked, and the opportunity to answer vital questions may be lost.

Whatever harm has been done, which is understood to mean some untoward effect upon human health or general well-being rather than an environmental consequence (such as an injury to plant or animal life or degradation of our esthetic surroundings), it must be described and analyzed. Injury and illness assessment is primarily the expert's responsibility, though unfortunately few are prepared for the task. Proper performance of the expert's job entails general identification of the ill effect or effects, proper categorization (i.e., diagnosis), quantification (i.e., rating the impairment), and, when possible, specification of current and future implications for health and well-being (i.e., prognosis). Each component to injury and illness assessment might profitably be considered at length. Because the recognition and diagnostic labeling of toxic injuries is discussed in Chapter 4, only brief attention is devoted to these aspects here.

The World Health Organization has suggested at least four categories into which occupational diseases may be grouped. Enlarging that schema to include toxic injuries generally, there are: diseases or injuries that are exclusively occupational or environmental in nature (e.g., coalworker's pneumoconiosis); those for which occupational and/or environmental exposures can be counted as possible causative factors (e.g., bronchogenic carcinoma); those in which occupation and/or environment may play a contributing role in complex situations (e.g., chronic bronchitis); and those wherein occupational or environmental hazards may aggravate a preexisting disease (e.g., asthma).

The expert who testifies about toxic injuries and illnesses should appreciate all that is implied by those terms, and ideally he or she has some knowledge of relevant toxic hazards and exposure circumstances. He or she should recognize that many of the diseases or injuries are multifactorial in origin and evident only after a variable period of time. When the latencies are short or the temporal relationship of exposure and effect are striking (e.g., *Monday morning asthma,* a feature of byssinosis, or textile workers' disease), the etiology or cause may be virtually certain. When latencies are long, as with many cancers and complications of asbestosis exposure, the causation may be more problematic. In addition, certain injuries may be missed altogether because of their infrequent or *negative* expression—e.g., effects on fertility (failure to conceive), on a developing fetus (deformities), or on reproductive organs (damage to future offspring).

Whatever may be concluded about causation or apportionment, the expert must assess the supposed ill effects himself or herself, seeking an objective, comprehensive statement as to their exact nature and severity. Thus, he or she undertakes to determine what impairment exists.

§19.02 —Writings and Studies: Impairment

As Lindgren concluded in 1965, the evaluation of impairment deserves more attention than it has received, especially when compensation is at stake. "It is surprising," he wrote, "that the medical literature dealing with this aspect of medical activity is scant and that the few available articles deal with definitions, legal aspects, and problems of causal relationship."[1] One can find much about the prevention, recognition, and treatment of diseases in a vast body of scientific writings, while one must search diligently there for guidelines to the objective assessment of physical impairments associated with these same diseases. Perhaps prompted by increasing concern with the function of compensation systems, which demand carefully defined, scientifically sound approaches to the assessment of physical impairment if they are to be equitable, articles have begun to appear on this subject, especially in the pulmonary literature.

To gain a conceptual understanding of *impairment* and the related, but distinct, term *disability,* the model suggested by Hatch should be considered: "a distinction is made between impairment and disability, the two scales representing, respectively, the underlying disturbance of the system and the consequence of such disturbance in terms of identifiable disease."[2] Starting with normal health, the individual progresses, for one reason or another, along the scale of impairment and of disability, ultimately to death. Early departures from health (impairment) are accompanied by little disability. In the beginning, normal homeostatic processes insure adequate adjustment to offset stress, and for a distance beyond this early zone of change, compensatory processes similarly maintain the overall function of the system without serious disability. Further increments in impairment beyond the limits of compensatory processes, however, are accompanied by rapidly increasing increments in

---

[1] B.W. Lindgren, Statistical Theory p. 80-81 (1965).

[2] F.E. Hatch, Impairment 193 (1971).

disability, and the individual moves into the region of sickness and disability, terminating in death.

Clearly, this is a theoretical construct. Rarely, if ever, can the complexities of the relationship between humans and the environment contemplated by Hatch be represented by an exact dose-response curve (see §1.04). However, the abstraction is useful nonetheless, and it leads naturally enough to a consideration of formal definitions.

In its Guides to the Evaluation of Permanent Impairments, the American Medical Association said of permanent impairment:

> This is a purely medical condition. Permanent impairment is any anatomic or functional abnormality or loss after maximal medical rehabilitation has been achieved, which abnormality or loss the physician considers stable or nonprogressive at the time evaluation is made. It is always a basic consideration in the evaluation of permanent disability.[3]

Permanent disability is distinguished as not a purely medical condition. A patient is permanently disabled or under a permanent disability when his actual or presumed ability to engage in gainful activity is reduced or absent because of impairment which, in turn, may or may not be combined with other factors. A permanent condition is found to exist if no fundamental or marked change can be expected in the future.

Many others use similar definitions of these terms. Gaensler and Wright suggest that *impairment* be used to mean reduction of the body or organ function and *disability* to indicate a lack of ability for a certain level of specific type of performance.[4] Generally, impairment reflects an anatomic or functional abnormality, which persists after appropriate therapy and with no reasonable prospect of improvement. It may or may not be stable at the time the evaluation is made. If severe, it frequently precludes gainful employment. It is always a basic consideration in the evaluation of disability. *Disability* is a term that indicates the total effect of impairment upon a patient's life. It is affected by such diverse factors as age, gender, education, economic and social environment, and energy requirements of the occupation. Two people with an identical impairment may be differently affected in their life situations. The *rating of health impairment* falls within the province of a physician's expertise to quantitate, while *determination of disability* is an administrative decision that requires consideration of many nonmedical as well as medical variables.

Because various definitions of these terms exist, note must be taken of often subtle, but important, distinctions when they are employed in different contexts. In compensation law, a usual requirement for disability is that of decrement in occupational performance function, although even absent reduced occupational performance, deficits in nonoccupational performance function

---

[3] Journal of American Medical Assn 173, No 9, 123 (1978).

[4] E.A. Gaensler & N.V. Wright, Functional Disability 192-97 (1973).

may qualify as compensable impairment under some circumstances and also establish entitlement to disability compensation.

§19.03 —Determining Disability

Under most state workers' compensation statutes, compensable disability is "inability, as the result of a work connected injury, to perform or obtain work suitable to the claimant's qualifications and training."[5] Thus, *disability* is synonymous with *loss of earning power*, the degree determined by a comparison of preinjury earnings with postinjury earning ability. No matter how impairing the injury, if still able to perform his or her regular job or another one with earnings equal to or greater than those received before the injury, the affected individual is not disabled. When able to perform alternative work at a lesser rate of earning than that received before the injury, the individual is viewed as *partially disabled.* Only when there is no work for which he or she is medically and vocationally qualified is the injured employee considered *totally disabled.*

If an expert confines himself or herself to assessment of injury or disease, to determining to the best of his or her ability the nature and extent of any associated impairment, or to determining the disturbance in functional capacities, he or she will in general fulfill his or her duties. However, it is important for him or her to understand something of what is involved in various compensation remedies, since there may be a substantially different emphases in each. For example, Social Security Disability Insurance largely ignores casuality as an issue, while workers' compensation benefits may be contingent on a showing of work-relatedness; and workers' compensation may allow benefits only for impairment that diminishes occupational performance, and thus earnings capacities, while tort claims may additionally weigh the much broader possibilities of adverse effects that are outside the occupational scope. Because there is often a long period of time between the exposure and the onset of impairment, the relationship between the two must not be missed. It is often difficult to identify retrospectively the extent and duration of exposure. The importance of estimating dose varies with the disease; for instance, asbestosis is probably dose-related, but mesothelioma is not.

Exposures to a given agent may have occurred in a nonoccupational setting. For instance, asbestos fibers are very common in the urban environment, and the finding of asbestos fibers in the lungs of city dwellers should not imply occupational exposure.

Smoking both predisposes an individual to and independently causes many of the same disease processes as do occupational agents.

The evidence of causality in many occupational diseases is epidemiologic: a high statistical association between an exposure and a disease. While the evidence may be very firm that the risk of an individual is statistically very high,

---

[5] Conn Gen Stat Ann § 31-295 (West 1977); Fla Stat Ann §§440.02, 440.15 (West 1978); Mass Code §71-3-3 (1972); Okla Stat Ann art 85 §3 (West 1979).

this is much less direct *proximate causation* than would be the case in a traumatic accident.

With this general background, the utilization of experts to assist in sorting out the problems attendant upon injuries and diseases of the sort which may prompt toxic tort actions can be considered.

§19.04   The Physician

The physician expert in toxic litigation must be prepared for a number of problems. A thorough analysis of the case is often difficult because vital medical or environmental data may be missing. The present status of litigation may impede obtaining some of the evaluations which the physician believes are necessary. Often previous medical and environmental evaluations are not done by those who are knowledgeable of the interaction between human health and environment. Scientific information regarding the alleged hazard or toxin may be inadequate. Finally, the physician expert in toxic litigation must be prepared for even more controversy than is evident in other medical litigation.

§19.05   —Controversial Aspects of Human Toxic Injury and Illness

There are few more controversial areas in medical science than the question of causality of disease after toxic exposure. This can be very frustrating for both physician and attorney, for it is not unlikely to find two well-qualified physicians taking positions 180 degrees apart. There are many reasons for this, some of the more important of which are discussed in this section.

Knowledge of the results of exposure to toxic substances is often at best very incomplete. Data may have been developed using animals, but they do not necessarily apply to human experience. Frequently, there will be no recorded case of a human illness resulting from exposure to a specific substance. The question then becomes whether this is the *first case*. In such an uncertain area, physicians, depending upon their background, training, and philosophical inclination, can take quite different positions.

Much of the current knowledge regarding human disease experience from toxic exposure rests upon animal studies and epidemiology. Though these sciences are helpful, application of the knowledge gained from them to single cases is fraught with difficulties. Perhaps nothing illustrates some of the difficulties and controversies of interpreting epidemiologic data better than the National Academy of Science's report on bysinossis.[6] *Bysinossis* is a chronic disease resulting from cotton dust exposure which may result in chronic obstructive pulmonary disease. However, it is extremely difficult clinically and even pathologically to differentiate it from other forms of chronic obstructive

---

[6] National Research Council, Committee on Byssinosis, Byssinosis; Clinical and Research Issues, Wash, D.C. (Natl Acad Press 1982).

pulmonary disease. Though some epidemiologic studies indicate an increased incidence of chronic obstructive pulmonary disease among cotton workers, some think that the evidence is very unclear. The National Academy report concludes there is no epidemiologic or other proof that would withstand rigorous scientific scrutiny that there is a chronic disease in relation to cotton dust exposure.

With environmentally induced diseases, physicians and other scientists associated with the problem tend to become polarized. One need only review the controversy regarding some of the recent Occupational Safety and Health Administration (OSHA) standards such as cotton dust,[7] asbestos,[8] and carcinogens[9] in order to appreciate this. Simply put, there is a parade of physicians and other scientific experts who are the most knowledgeable in their fields disagreeing profoundly.

In fact, this topic was the subject of a recent congressional hearing conducted by Congressman Albert Gore of Tennessee. Congressman Gore believes that there has grown up in America an advocacy science, wherein scientists are oriented toward and even tilt their research and interpretation of research in accordance with their affiliations and sources of income.[10] Unfortunately, this oversimplifies the issue. Affiliation may influence interpretation, however, the question arises which comes first, the chicken or the egg? That is, does a particular scientist tend to affiliate with an organization because of a viewpoint at which he or she has independently arrived, or is his or her viewpoint *shaded* by the organization? Whatever the reason, there are marked differences of opinion in the medical community regarding environmental and occupational toxic issues. Many of them are brought about by our uncertainties of scientific fact in the new and evolving sciences of environmental and occupational medicine, toxicology, and epidemiology.

Most physicians have very little training and experience in clinical toxicology. Thus, an outstanding cardiologist, pulmonologist, nephrologist, or neurologist, who is fully competent to evaluate and treat diseases of the heart, lungs, kidneys, and nervous system, may have only a vague appreciation or experience in dealing with toxic exposures as they relate to these or other organ systems.

Generally, even those physicians who may have some knowledge of toxic exposures have very little appreciation of quantitative aspects of such exposures. Physicians are trained to deal with oral and injected dosages. They are usually experienced in determining the toxic dose of a therapeutic drug by

[7] Occupational Safety and Health Administration, Occupational Exposure to Cotton Dust, 43 Fed Reg 27350 (June 23, 1978).

[8] Brodeur, *Annals of Industry—Casualties of the Workplace,* The New Yorker, Oct 29, 1973, at 74; 29 CFR §1910-1001.

[9] Occupational Safety and Health Administration Identification, Classification and Regulation of Potential Carcinogens, 45 Fed Reg 5002 (Jan 22, 1980).

[10] Committee on Science and Technology, House of Representatives, Wash DC (Sept 22, 1982).

these routes. However, for a nontherapeutic toxic substance absorbed by inhalation or by skin absorption, physicians have very little experience and knowledge in quantifying the exposure or appreciating the different toxicologic manifestations as they relate to route of exposure.

§19.06   —Diagnosis Differential

Most cases resulting in litigation after toxic substance exposure are not simple and clear-cut. On the one hand, an obvious case of lead or mercury poisoning can be readily diagnosed and evaluated by physicians with proper training and experience, and such cases are relatively clear-cut. However, more common is the case of lead exposure in a person who has a preexisting or some other predisposition to renal, gastrointestinal, or nervous system disease. Therefore, the litigation may resolve around ordinary diseases of life which may have been caused, aggravated, or in no way related to a toxic exposure but which follow such an exposure. Such diseases may be indistinguisable from diseases which occur in the population. An example is bronchiogenic carcinoma, a type of cancer which is more common in certain occupational exposures such as asbestos,[11] uranium mining,[12] and others.[13] However, when such a case occurs following an exposure, it is common to find that the individual also smokes cigarettes, which is a known risk factor for the development of bronchiogenic carcinoma. Much lung cancer is indistinguisable as to whether it is caused by the working environment or by nonoccupational environmental factors such as smoking.

Cancer, fibrosis, emphysema, and bronchitis are all responses of the lung to various pollutants. These are not specific responses and may be caused by a variety of insults. On the other hand, high exposures to asbestos may create the relatively specific response of asbestosis which is characteristic of the exposure.[14] However, such specific responses are in the minority. The lung has only a limited number of responses that it can make to environmental pollutants. Therefore, it is natural that a so-called ordinary disease of life can also be environmentally induced or aggravated.

In view of these problems, it is quite clear why even very well-qualified physicians can have marked differences of opinion. Due to our limited knowledge of these diseases and our present system of settling toxic litigation, it behooves each side to select a very well-qualified physician. This well-qualified physician can assist the attorney in developing the medical aspects of his or her case presentation if that physician has an opinion which is based upon sound

---

11 Irving J. Selikoff, M.D., E. Cuyler Hammond, Sc.D., & Jacob Churg, M.D. *Asbestos Exposure, Smoking, and Neoplasia,* JAMA, 204 No 2, 106 (Apr 8, 1968).

12 S. Jablon, *Radiation, Persons at High Risk of Cancer—An Approach to Cancer Etiology and Control* 151 (Joseph F. Fraumeni, Jr., ed 1975)

13 Bertram D. Dinman, M.D., Sc.D. *The Nature of Occupational Cancer* (Charles C. Thomas ed, Springfield, Ill).

14 William Keith C. Morgan, Occupational Lung Diseases (1975).

principles of medicine, anatomy, physiology, and toxicology. Unfortunately, all too frequently, physicians who neither have sufficient training or experience are utilized as experts. Some, however, are nevertheless willing to render a strong and inflexible opinion.

§19.07 —Determining Services to Be Rendered

In order to utilize the physician expert effectively, it is necessary to determine the needs for the case. These usually fall into the categories discussed below.

A thorough medical review of the case should be undertaken by a physician who has had experience in dealing with toxic exposures. For best results, all medical material should be reviewed—not just hospital discharge summaries. To the extent feasible, it is preferable to have raw data instead of interpretations thereof.

In addition to the expert in environmental or occupational medicine, it may be necessary to have the case reviewed by an expert in the speciality in which the disease occurs. This review can provide an insight from a physician who deals with similar diseases and can place the disease in perspective. For example, the neurosurgeon sees brain tumors in people from all walks of life and can provide his or her perspective on a tumor that is alleged to be caused by a toxic exposure.

A thorough review of literature related to the toxic substance is required in order to address the major questions with respect to causality:

1. Is the substance capable of producing this type of toxic effect
2. What is its target organ
3. Has exposure been sufficient to produce the effect

The industrial hygienist can assist in quantifying the exposure. The specialist in toxicology or environmental or occupational medicine can provide assistance in evaluating the quantitative aspects of the exposure in relationship to the alleged injury. One of the most difficult areas for the nonmedical person to understand is quantification of exposure of toxic materials. The names arsenic, cyanide, and formaldehyde evoke characteristic responses of impending catastrophe when an individual is so exposed. What is not realized is that arsenic is an ubiquitous substance that people are exposed to continuously; similarily, with cyanide people get a certain nontoxic dosage when eating almonds; and formaldehyde is naturally present in human bodies and in the environment. Only if the exposure is quantified and and put in perspective in relation to ordinary exposures to the substance can it be determined whether or not the substance in the quantity to which the individual was exposed was capable of producing the injury or illness. This quantification is unfortunately frequently bypassed in testimony.

Every toxic substance case has certain key issues, which may be medical and/or legal. The experienced medical expert can readily define key medical issues. These issues revolve around the making of the diagnosis and the question of the toxin as a causive factor.[15] However, what may be a key medical issue may not be the key legal issue. As the medical issues are defined by the medical expert, the attorney is better able to combine the legal issues with these medical issues and develop an overall strategy of dealing with the case.

The physician expert can also prepare questions for the attorney to ask of the parties to the action and of other experts. This is best done after reviewing medical evaluations or depositions of physician experts who will be called upon to testify. Appropriate questions will bring to light certain strong or weak points in the testimony.

The examination of the patient and the rendering of an opinion regarding diagnosis and cause of injury and illness are the traditional areas where physician experts have been used in medical/legal cases. The attorney may wish to have an examination by a physician other than the one who has already examined or treated the patient. In such case, he or she selects an expert who may be the same or different physician who is assisting in the items above.

The final point is the preparation and use of a physician, as a witness, who not only is expert in the field but is articulate and presents himself or herself well. The physician to be used as an expert may be the same physician used in several of the other steps described above or may be someone entirely different. Sometimes, the physician who can be of greatest assistance in preparing the case may not have many of the desirable features for being an expert witness.

It is very important that the attorney identify those services he or she wishes the physician expert to provide and select the appropriate physician or physicians for each of them. Obviously, satisfying all of the above needs may necessitate utilization of more than one expert.

§19.08 —Sources of Information on Expert Physician Qualifications

There are a number of sources for finding physicians who are expert in toxic exposures. Attorneys who have been involved in highly specialized types of litigation such as that involving asbestos, DES, cotton dust, or coke-oven emissions soon learn who the experts are in the field. In these highly specialized and emotional environmental issues, there often develops a polarization among the physician experts—namely, one group becoming known as proplaintiff, and another, as prodefendant. Attorneys are often aware of the viewpoints and relative expertise of certain physicians.

A physician who specializes in toxicology or occupational or environmental medicine who has had experience or knowledge of particular toxic issues will frequently know who the key specialists are in a particular area. Even if the

---

[15] Harold R. Imbus, Clinical Aspects of Occupational Medicine. Occupational Medicine—Principles and Practical Applications 89 (Carl Zenz, M.D., Sc.D., ed). (1980).

physician is not particularly familiar with the field, he or she can often identify certain authors who are well-known in the field.

By identifying the principal scientists associated with a certain toxic substance, the attorney can not only determine who they are but can also get a reasonable idea of their viewpoints. In addition, certain directories, associations, and organizations may be able to assist in the search.[16]

A number of trade associations have developed experience with medical experts in particular areas.[17] For example, the American Textile Manufacturers' Institute would be familiar with physicians who have been involved with the problem of byssinosis; the American Petroleum Institute should be familiar with physicians who have been involved with questions of toxicity from benzene; and the Formaldehyde Institute maintains a list of experts in formaldehyde. The American Industrial Health Council has been actively involved in the issue of chemical carcinogenesis and has lists of experts who have played a role therein. Obviously, in the use of trade associations as a source of expert witnesses, the attorney would expect primarily to be able to obtain information regarding physicians who have been helpful to the industry side of these issues. However, just as with trade associations, labor unions often have had extensive experience with particular toxic substance issues. For example, the Amalgamated Clothing and Textile Workers Union of America is familiar with experts on byssinosis who would represent their viewpoint. The Rubber Workers Union, the Oil, Chemical and Atomic Workers Union, and the Industrial Union Department of the AFL-CIO have been involved in numerous Occupational Safety and Health Administration (OSHA) standard promulgation challenges with particular issues such as asbestos, benzene, cotton dust, and coke-oven emission and could be helpful in providing names of physicians.[18]

§19.09   The Industrial Hygienist

Despite the term *industrial* in the title *industrial hygiene,* the practice of industrial hygiene is not confined to industry. The earliest studies in radiological health and air pollution were conducted by industrial hygienists. In recent years, industrial hygienists have been concerned with the health aspects of product safety and indoor air pollution. Specific examples of such concerns

---

[16] Marquis, Who's Who, Directory of Medical Specialists (21st ed 1983-1984). Marquis, Who's Who, 1983; American Occupational Medical Association, American Occupational Medical Association Membership Directory (Arlington Heights, Ill 1983; American Academy of Occupational Medicine, American Academy of Occupational Medicine Membership Directory (Chicago 1983); American Medical Association, American Medical Directory (Chicago 1983); American Industrial Hygiene Association, Industrial Hygiene Consultants (Akron, Ohio Jan 1983); Society for Occupational and Environmental Health, Wash DC.

[17] National Trade and Professional Associations of the United States (1983).

[18] Bureau of National Affairs, Directory of US Labor Organizations (1982-83 ed).

include formaldehyde emissions in manufactured homes and the reside levels found in homes treated with pesticides.

The activities necessary to determine health effects in these situations are the same as those in industry, and the methodologists are essentially the same. Therefore, it is a logical extension of the industrial hygiene practice.

§19.10   —The Basic Equation

In toxic substances litigation, the contest between equal and opposite experts with doctoral degrees often comes down to a question of risk. Risk is onsidered to be the likelihood or probability that an adverse health effect will occur in a given set of circumstances.[19] The basic toxicity of a substance is only one factor in the assessment of risk. Other factors include the health of the individual, the frequency and duration of exposure, and the environmental conditions under which exposure occurs. The determination of likelihood that an adverse health effect was caused by exposure to an environmental contaminant considering all factors is the central issue.

There are many professional disciplines which are involved in risk assessment. These include physicians, toxicologists, epidemiologists, chemists, pharmacologists, and others. To see what part an industrial hygienist can play in the determination of risk, it is useful to think of the following equation: **Toxic (Hazardous) Substance + A Susceptible Individual + Excessive Exposure = An Adverse Health Effect.** While this equation is oversimplified, it does delineate those elements necessary for an adverse health effect to occur.

In general, it is the purview of the toxicologist to determine whether a substance is potentially hazardous. Through animal studies, he or she provides toxicity data which show the intrinsic hazard potential of the substance. This potential exists wherever the substance exists and does not change. It is expressed in terms such as *oral LD50*—the oral dose at which 50 per cent of the test animals die—and is a relative rather than absolute measure. If a distinctly different chemical entity with a lower toxic potential is substituted, the risk may decrease.

Only physicians are qualified to discuss the susceptibility of individuals to toxic substances in detail. Their training uniquely qualifies them to give opinions on whether a substance is more hazardous to a child than to an adult or to an individual with a preexisting condition as opposed to one who does not have such a condition. The classic example of a difference in individual susceptibility is smoking. Many people know of someone who is elderly and who has smoked two packs of cigarettes per day for the last 35 years with no apparent effect. Unfortunately, this is the element of the risk equation with the weakest scientific basis, and physicians have been relunctant to question one another's opinion. Too often, toxic substances cases are decided on the believability of

[19] National Institute for Occupationsl Safety and Health: A Recommended Standard . . . An Identification System for Occupationally Hazardous Materials 50 (DHEW (NIOSH) Pub No 75-126, USDHEW/CDC/NIOSH, Cincinnati, Ohio 1975).

a physician expressing an opinion about the individual's susceptibility to the effects of a toxic substance rather than a full consideration of the other elements involved. It is difficult to prove a negative, and physicians are reluctant to say that an adverse health condition was not caused or exacerbated by exposure to the toxic substance.

§19.11 —Role of Industrial Hygiene

The third element of the basic equation contained in §19.10—excessive exposure—describes the central role of the industrial hygienist in toxic substance cases. It is apparent that without exposure there can be no health effect caused by a substance. A total lack of exposure is seldom the case, however, Increasing analytical sophistication allows a showing that some exposure occurs in most cases. The question is: how much? Industrial hygienists use analytical techniques to quantify the extent of exposure, which can then be compared to regulatory limits or to past experience to judge the likelihood of adverse effects.

In addition to the amount of a toxic substance to which a person is exposed, several other factors are important. These include the duration of exposure, the frequency of exposure, the route of contact (whether by ingestion, inhalation, or contact with the skin), and the presence of other toxic substances which might cause similar effects. The industrial hygienist is trained to observe these factors and assess their risk implications. Industrial hygienists can also determine those environmental factors such as temperature and ventilation which might increase or decrease the potential exposure.

Consulting chemists and engineering testing firms are possible alternatives to industrial hygienists in determining excessive exposure. In certain cases, such as those involving highly toxic chemicals like dioxin, where the determination of the presence of the toxic substances may be all that is necessary, using such testers might be adequate. However, in those cases where the extent of exposure is important and a broader health perspective is necessary, the expertise of an industrial hygienist would be desirable. Specifically, the industrial hygienist has extensive training in the measurement of trace quantities of toxic substances, particularly in the air. He or she is aware of the limits and fallabilities of such measurements. An industrial hygienist can also assess the environment in question to determine the likelihood of other toxic substances being present which might cause similar health effects. This assessment is based on his or her knowledge of toxicology rather than analytical chemistry. Lastly, industrial hygienists have extensive experience in characterizing exposure in terms other than the amount to which a person is exposed.

It is recognized that the basic equation described in §19.10 defines the role of various experts too sharply. There is a large overlap in the knowledge possessed by various health professionals involved with toxic substance cases. For example, the industrial hygienist may have as extensive an understanding about the toxicology of a given substance as the toxicologist. Likewise, the physician may be knowledgeable about alternative environmental factors, such as pathogens, about which the industrial hygienist would have limited knowledge. Choosing an expert to play the central role in a toxic substance case is difficult.

In general, the selection of the key professional depends upon the allegations being made. The attorney must state the case clearly. If nephrotoxicity is alleged, for example, it is the quantity of the toxic substance or its metabolites reaching the kidney which is of importance, rather than the quantity to which the person is exposed. In this case, the toxicologist would be the key expert because of his or her knowledge of metabolism and excretion. Another example might be where a medical etiology unrelated to exposure to the toxic substance is suspected. In this case, the physician would be the key expert.

The industrial hygienist becomes the key figure when it is necessary to establish the level of exposure with some precision or to differentiate the contributions of multiple toxic substances in a complex environment. Industrial hygiensts should also be selected to provide the attorney with a broader health perspective in those cases where environmental rather than medical etiology is suspected.

§19.12   —Locating the Industrial Hygiene Expert

Most industrial hygienists work for large corporations.[20] The majority of the Fortune 500 companies have one or more industrial hygienists on their staffs. For cases involving such companies or the unions which represent employees of such companies, in-house expertise should be considered first. This consideration is important primarily because the staff industrial hygienist has intimate knowledge of the manufacturing or production processes involved, the health experience of workers potentially exposed to a toxic substance, and the toxicological literature available regarding the company's products. The staff industrial hygienist may have also done exposure monitoring and have those data available. Where concerns of bias and believability are not paramount, it is highly advantageous to use the in-house industrial hygienist's expertise.

For those cases where in-house expertise is not available or it is considered necessary to use an outsider, locating the *right* industrial hygienist is important. There are three potential sources:

1.   Industrial hygienists in insurance companies

2.   University faculty who teach industrial hygiene

3.   Private consultants in the field of industrial hygiene

Each of these groups has certain limitations. Insurance company industrial hygienists are generally interested in loss control rather than overall risk assessment, and they frequently have the least experience in industrial hygiene.

---

[20] K.D. Blehm, Demographic Data from the 1981 Membership Survey, American Industrial Hygiene Association Journal 43(6): A-47 - A-52 (1982).

Academicians in industrial hygiene, while highly qualified, are generally interested in research projects and their ability to respond quickly is limited. Private consultants in industrial hygiene tend to fall into two groups, entrepreneurial and retired, both with limited resources.

The American Industrial Hygiene Association Journal publishes a list of consultants in industrial hygiene twice annually.[21] This list includes most private consultants, insurance companies whose staffs are available on a fee-for-service basis, and some but not all academicians in industrial hygiene. This list includes in indication of the area of specialization or expertise claimed by those listed. Such indications are important because many specialties of industrial hygiene, such as noise and ergonomics, have little to do with toxic substances. Even when expertise in areas related to toxic substances, such as toxicology and industrial medicine, are listed, they should be accepted only with caution.

Probably the largest number of industrial hygiene experts not employed by large corporations and not included in the semiannual consultants listing are those in academia. The faculty at schools which teach industrial hygiene represent an excellent source of expertise. However, no systematic listing of their specialties is available, and the search for the right expert would be random in nature.

§19.13 —Use of the Industrial Hygienist

Toxic substance cases often begin with adverse health effects alleged to have been caused by exposure to the substance. From an industrial hygiene standpoint, the initial questions to be answered are whether or not the substance was present, whether the individual could have been exposed, what the extent of the exposure was, and whether the health claims correlate with the known effects from exposure to the substance. The industrial hygienist can assist the attorney in obtaining objective information in response to these questions.

The first method of obtaining this information is what is known as a walkthrough survey, discussed in §1.19. If the physical environment is available, the industrial hygienist should actually walk through it making a list of all possible contributors of toxic contaminants. This list might include chemical products used, combustion products, emissions from operations such as welding and soldering, and potential contributions from adjacent areas. Preliminary assessment of environmental conditions such as temperature, ventilation, the number of potential contaminant sources, and the use of protective equipment is noted. Where the physical environment is not available, this information has to be generated through memory. Having the industrial hygienist available to question those trying to recall such information would be useful to the attorney.

At this stage, the difficulty of dealing with trade-name products becomes

---

[21] Industrial Hygiene Consultants American Industrial Hygiene Association Journal (listed twice annually in January and July).

apparant. Most chemical products are not used as single entities and are not identified by generic nomenclature. The product manufacturer must be contacted for information. The manufacturer often responds by supplying a technical data sheet or a material safety data sheet. Industrial hygienists have had experience in reading and interpreting the information provided on these data sheets. If the information is not complete or specific, the industrial hygienist can assist the attorney in obtaining additional information from the manufacturer. Further, industrial hygienists experienced in dealing with toxic substances are familiar with those chemicals and chemical groups generally encountered in various types of products. They intuitively look for the presence of certain chemicals in certain operations or environments.

Once the toxic substances which are potentially available are identified by chemical name, a rough correlation with the alleged health effects can be made. This is where the breadth of understanding about the potential effects of toxic substances by different routes of contact is important. For example, if allergic respiratory sensitization is alleged, the industrial hygienist would know that isocyanates are possible causative agents, whereas solvents such as alcohols and ketones, although they may be present, are not likely to cause sensitization reactions. The number of potential contaminants which possibly could have caused the health effect can be narrowed considerably.

All of the above assumes that the offending contaminant is unknown or not specifically identified. Some cases start by the allegation of a health effect from a specific chemical—for instance, nausea and headaches from pesticide treatments in a home. In either case, the industrial hygienist can do exposure monitoring to determine the extent of contact with the specifically identified contaminant or the narrowed list of possible contaminants. For the above example, the industrial hygienist might be asked to monitor the level of the pesticide existing in the home after treatment. One accurate measurement may be worth a thousand expert opinions, so exposure monitoring is an important service.

Once monitoring data are obtained, the industrial hygienist can assist the attorney in interpreting these data with respect to the claimed health effects. He or she can relate the exposure levels to existing standards and regulations and to known effects from the substance reported in the literature. Comparison may be made with permissible exposure limites established by the Occupational Safety and Health Administration (OSHA), threshold limit values recommended by the American Conference of Governmental Industrial Hygienists, workplace environment exposure limits recommended by the American Industrial Hygiene Association, ambient air quality standards established by the Environmental Protection Agency (EPA), recommendations made by the National Academy of Sciences, and internal limits established by companies. In addition to gathering objective data and information on exposure, the expert industrial hygienist is able to critique the date, sampling, analytical method, and other information gathered by the opposition.

Based upon personal experience in gathering exposure data, the industrial hygienist should be able to help the attorney formulate and ask questions which demystify the data presented by the opposition to represent the extent of exposure. For example, the statistics of sampling are very complex.[22] To claim that a single sample represents any more than the likely exposure at one point in space and time requires a number of assumptions. These assumptions can be attacked by the knowledgeable industrial hygienist.

To increase his or her chances of prevailing in a case, the attorney should be thoroughly familiar with all literature relating to the question being litigated. Industrial hygiene literature pertinent to toxic substance cases is extensive. The expert industrial hygienist should be able to assist the attorney in finding both published and unpublished information sources. At a minimum, he or she can guide the attorney to standard references and literature on toxic substances[23] and review materials obtained during case preparation and discovery.

Just as attorneys attempt to avoid the actual trial of a case whenever possible, most expert industrial hygienists prefer not to provide testimony. The primary reason is that expert testimony generally requires advocacy of a position rather than investigation of the facts. Ideally, they would prefer to develop opinions based on the evidence available and advocate that position regardless of whether it meets the requirements of the plaintiff or the defendant. Practically, this ideal is seldom met. The careful attorney realizes that advocacy may ultimately be necessary and selects his or her expert on that basis. Most industrial hygienists who testify have learned that it is necessary to be known as either a plaintiff's witness or a defendant's witness.

On the witness stand, the industrial hygienist should not be expected to

---

[22] N. A. Leidel, K. A. Busch, & J. R. Lynch, Occupational Exposure Sampling Strategy Manual (DHEW (NIOSH) Pub No 77-173 DHEW-CDC-NIOSH, Cincinnati, Ohio 1977). D.G. Taylor, Coordinator, NIOSH Manual of Analytical Methods, vols, 1-7 DHEW-CDC-NIOSH, Cincinnati, OH (1971).

[23] These references include:

1. NIOSH, Registry of Toxic Effects of Chemical Substances, US Dept of Health and Human Services, Public Health Service Center for Disease Control, Sept, 1980, US GPO, Cincinnati, Ohio.
2. M.M. Key, Occupational Diseases, A Guide to Their Recognition US Dept of HEW (rev ed 1977).
3. Gleason, Clinical Toxicology of Commercial Products
4. American Conference of Governmental Industrial Hygienists, Documentation of Threshold Limit Values for Exposure to Contaminants in the Workplace & Intended Charges for 1983 (Cincinnati, Ohio).
5. American Industrial Hygiene Association, Hygienic Guide Series.
6. Proctor & Hughes, Chemical Hazards in the Workplace (1977).
7. Sax, Dangerous Properties of Industrial Materials.
8. Patty's Industrial Hygiene and Toxicology, Volume 2A (G.D. Clayton ed, 3d rev ed 1980).
9. W.A. Burgess, Recognition of Health Hazards in Industry (1981).

Much literature in the filed of toxic substances is available through computer-based search systems. These include: Medline, Toxline, Environmental Bibliography, NIH-EPA Chemical Information System, Toxicology Data Bank, and RTECS (*Registry of Toxic Effects of Chemical Substances*).

testify outside his or her central area of expertise—namely, characterization of the environment and the general effects of toxic substances on humans. The opposing attorney will attempt to draw the industrial hygienist into a diagnosis of the effects of the toxic substance on the particular individual involved or a detailed discussion of the metabolism and body burden of the toxic substance. While the expert industrial hygienist may know a great deal about these subjects, he or she and his or her attorney should be hesitant about his or her response to such questions. As indicated by the basic equation presented in **§19.10,** those subjects are the ares of expertise of the physician and the toxicologist.

Another area where the attorney might reasonably expect the industrial hygienist to testify is in the use of sampling and analytical methods to determine the extent of exposure. Such testimony is particularly useful if the industrial hygienist has made such a determination for the attorney or if it is necessary to review a determination made for the opposition. The National Institute for Occupational Safety & Health Manual of Analytical Method[24] is the basic reference of air sampling methods in industrial hygiene. The methods recommended in this manual have been validated and are defensible. The expert industrial hygienist knows, however, that failure reports on the methods do exist and that better-developed and better-documented methods are sometimes available and should be used. For example, the NIOSH methods might not cover the range of contaminant concentration necessary for indoor air pollution sampling. Such nuances can be covered in industrial hygiene testimony.

Finally, the expert industrial hygienist should be able to interpret exposure monitoring results fully. Such interpretation would include but not be limited to a comparison with existing standards. The industrial hygienist should be able to discuss the basis for setting a standard on a toxic substance and the health effects expected when such limits are approached or exceeded. This expertise of the industrial hygienist should be differentiated from that of the physician. The industrial hygienist knows the effects of chemicals on a normal population, whereas the physician should be able to discuss the effect of the toxic substance on the individual person involved in the case.

§19.14   Epidemiologists and Biostatisticians

Epidemiologists study the distributions of and trends in disease rates in groups of people with the goal of finding the etiology (or causative agents) in the disease process. Once the causative sequence is known, steps can be taken to prevent the disease—for example, bone abscesses developed in some workers leading to the loss of use of the jawbone and other clinical problems. By the early 1900s, epidemiological investigation made it clear that those who made phosphorus matches were at risk for this disease to such an extent that

---

[24] Directory on Online Information Resources (7th ed 1981).

the condition was called by the workers *phossy jaw*.[25] This relationship was demonstrated in workers both in other countries and in the United States. Sulphur matches were too expensive to be an economical but safe substitute. A federal tax was instituted on phosphorus but not sulphur matches (the Esch law)[26] with the result that the safer sulphur matches replaced phosphorus matches in the marketplace, causing better health for those concerned.

Etiology is well-studied in many of these cases. For example, there are abundant data to show that the primary cause of the current lung cancer epidemic in men and women is cigarette smoking.[27] Air pollution has a relatively minor effect. In those who have been exposed to asbestos, usually based on the occupation of the person involved, that exposure is a major contributor to respiratory cancer, especially if the person is a cigarette smoker. Many other occupational and environmental causes of lung cancer are known and proven to varying degrees. To the epidemiologist, the greatest proportion of cases are caused by cigarettes, followed by asbestos, followed by all other causes. On the other hand, the individual and therefore the individual's attorney may be most interested in just one of the other causes.

§19.15 —Who are Epidemiologists?

Who becomes an epidemiologist? Epidemiologists are trained in colleges of medicine and in schools of public health. Many epidemiologists have a medical degree but many others do not. Many epidemiologists specialize in a single disease category such as cancer or diabetes or respiratory disease or congenital malformations, but other epidemiologists study a broad spectrum of diseases. The degrees held by epidemiologists vary from the Doctor of Philosophy (PhD) degree to a Doctor of Science (ScD) to a Doctor of Public Health (DPH) and a smattering of other initials.

Epidemiologists have traditionally been employed by governments concerned with the health of their citizens. Originally, this occupation dealt primarily with infectious diseases, and then the same methods were applied to chronic diseases. More recently, epidemiologists have been more concerned with occupational and environmental issues in health matters. Much funding for epidemiology comes from the National Institutes of Health of the Department of Health and Human Services of the United States. Other funding for epidemiological research has been supplied through the political process, such as government programs in maternal and child health, sickle cell anemia, toxic wastes, and hypertension, and in the programs of private foundations. Government-employed epidemiologists are frequently physicians, especially at the

---

[25] A. Hamilton, Exploring the Dangerous Trades (1943).

[26] 16 USC §791 *et seq.*

[27] Smoking and Health A report of the Surgeon General (DHEW Pub No (PHS) 79-50066, US Gov Printing Office, Wash DC, 1979).

state level, because of the dual role of practicing medicine and doing epidemiology.

One of the largest employers of epidemiologists is academia. Training departments in medical colleges and schools of public health educate and provide new experiences to those who will be the new practitioners. The faculties of these institutions also tend to do research work sponsored by governments, private foundations industry, labor unions, and others.

In the last decade, epidemiologists have been found more commonly in the industrial world as major corporations have found the need for one or more epidemiologists to explore issues of occupational and environmental health. At the same time, private consultants have provided some of the same expertise. When an attorney is looking for an epidemiologist to do some work, the usual source is either a private consultant or an academic epidemiologist acting either privately or in the name of the institution. There is no single list of epidemiologists.

Of what use is an epidemiologist in a toxic tort case? On the plaintiff's side, an epidemiologist can help establish the *relationship* between the exposure of interest and the medical facts claimed by the plaintiff. The epidemiologist is the expert who is qualified to evaluate the studies that have been done as to their quality, sufficiency, and intrepretation. The clinician (physician) is responsible for the diagnosis of each of the individuals involved. The toxicologist is an expert concerning the animal data, the metabolic pathways, and the pharmacology of the exposure agents. The industrial hygientist is trained to comment on exposure levels and their measurement if measurements are available. The epidemiologist is the one person who can synthesize the total human experience based on the training and expertise within the discipline.

On the defendant's side, the epidemiologist can point out the limitations of each of the studies. What are the defects in any particular study? What are the subtle characteristics which stand out to the professional evaluating the study and therefore should stand out to a judge or jury who is trying to evaluate the importance of this evidence? Is the comparison group valid? Were the groups at equal risk of getting the disease aside from the agent of interest?

As is usual in most scientific disciplines, there is a great deal of jargon that is used, but there is no reason why all of epidemiology cannot be translated into ordinary English. In fact, nonprofessionals seem to believe that they understand epidemiological relationships to a greater extent than the other disciplines mentioned, apparently because the material is closer to the experience of ordinary individuals. The professional epidemiologist can point out the subtleties of the epidemiological relationships and their interpretation so that the judge or jury can intrepret the evidence only as far as the science will allow. For example, there are a set of rules of cause-and-effect reasoning in epidemiology (discussed in §19.20) based on the teachings of philosophers over the ages and experience with successful epidemiologic research.

Epidemiologists are scientists who are required in their own discipline to speak very carefully of a relationship and to qualify their statements carefully if they are not to be criticized by their colleagues. This leads to a tendency to have the speech habits of equivocation. These speech habits convince other scientists more completely but often leave the lay public confused. For example, a statement such as "there appear to be six cases of this disease in this group, but Dr. Smith's classification would exclude one of these cases, and for a second case we did not have tissue confirmation, and a third had an unusual rash" is not as convincing to most people as "I found six cases of the disease." Epidemiologists are also prone to say "the evidence leads to this conclusion. On the other hand, another interpretation is. . . ." Clear communication between the epidemiologist and attorney about the bounds of statements that can be made and an explanation to the epidemiologist of the requirement for simple and definitive statements can lead to better communication in a legal proceeding.

§19.16 —Who Are Biostatisticians?

A related discipline to epidemiology is biostatistics. Biostatisticians study the statistical methods used in designing and analyzing epidemiological studies. The exact boundaries between these two fields are blurred. Some persons do both epidemiology and biostatistics, while others work exclusively in the field of doing the studies (epidemiology) or the field of analytic methods (biostatistics).

Biostatisticans tend to be mathematically inclined individuals who deal with the multitudinous data concerning the health of the population. The persons are concerned with recording data on health, storing that data, analyzing them, and determining the mathematical meaning of the individual health encounters. Biostatisticians are concerned with variability in data to differentiate chance findings in a data set from causal events. If three persons in the same workplace have leukemia, is this an example of a common event and thus a source of disease, or is chance variation an adequate explanation of the phenomenon? Biostatisticians have developed the probability-based methodology necessary to make proper inferences from observed health events. Epidemiologists make use of these biostatistical methods, sometimes by collaboration with biostatisticians and sometimes by making direct use of the methods as part of their own proficiency.

If this were a simple world, biostatisticians would be the purely methodological individuals who took numbers and drew objective conclusions from them. Epidemiologists would be the persons who drew medical conclusions from the objective facts based on their personal input. In fact, many individuals assume both of these rules. Moreover, there is a certain degree of subjectivity to both of these disciplines so that an attorney talking with two different professionals may get two different accounts of what are the true facts. One problem is that many individuals do not make a strict practice of discerning what are actual facts based on some observations, what are assumptions based on the way the world is supposed to work, and what are conclusions based on some model of reality.

§19.17   The Nature of Epidemiological Evidence

What is the nature of epidemiological evidence? Epidemiological scientists observe differences in rates of disease that are associated with differences in some risk factor or factors. In addition, there are always several other important factors which either must be shown not to vary between the risk groups or if they are different must be accounted for in the analysis. These other variables are called *covariates, risk modifiers,* or *confounding factors.*

The most convincing type of scientific evidence is based on controlled experiments in either animals or humans. A description of them provides an informative contrast to epidemiological studies. In a controlled experiment, the scientist maintains the risk factor of interest at different levels in the two or more groups at hand but keeps all other factors equal in the groups being compared. For example, a study of the effect of some pollutant in animals would involve a control group of animals which is not exposed to the pollutant and one or more other groups which are exposed to various levels of the pollutant. Other factors such as age, weight, diet, enzyme levels, etc. are adjusted to be equal. In an animal experiment, this is arranged by randomly allocating the groups, which means that the groups are allocated based on a toss of the dice (or computer simulation of ideal dice) so that the groups do not differ on the average in any other factor than the one or ones of interest in the experiment.

The analogous situation in epidemiology would mean that residents are randomly allocated as to whether they live near the source of pollution or far away from it. Other examples would mean random allocation of new employees to various job locations, random allocation based on using a dangerous appliance or not, and random allocation of medical treatment. Clearly, most of these situations are only theoretical and do not exist in the real world. The most common exception is clinical trials in which various medical treatments, expecially pharmaceutical preparations, are randomly allocated to those who agree to participate in such a study.

The epidemiologist attempts to find situations which simulate these types of scientific conditions by some real-life situation which has some of the characteristics of a designed study. For example, workers in different occupations may be compared to each other or persons who live near a pollution source may be compared to those who live far from it. Thus, epidemiology usually involves *observational studies* in which the study subjects and their characteristics are observed but not controlled.

One advantage of an epidemiological study is that the expermiental unit is a human, rather than a laboratory animal from which one must extrapolate in order to predict the effects that would occur in a human. In animal experiments, such as those in toxicology, large doses of the agent are used to reduce the number of animals needed to produce measurable effects. In some experiments, these doses are unrealistic, especially if the animal metabolizes the agent through different biochemical pathways at higher doses. Doses in epidemiological studies are by definition appropriate since they have actually occurred with the humans of concern. The sample size in an epidemiological study is frequently in the thousands, which would be a very large and unusual experiment in an animal study.

The principal complication with an epidemiological study is that the *other factors* have been controlled in only the most rudimentary way in comparison with a designed study. For example, by design one tries to find persons with the same age distribution in each group. In this way, age andother risk factors are balanced. One can also balance after the fact in a statistical analysis. Journal articles sometimes say that factors have been controlled by use of a statistical model, but experience with this type of control is still too small to know if it is effective in a particular case. Although there are these obvious trade-offs in obtaining new and valid knowledge, each type of study has much to offer, and the combination of study results frequently provides a clearer picture of the true situation.

Lawyers and epidemiologists sometimes have a different perception of what makes good evidence. In law, a single dramatic event frequently becomes important evidence, while in epidemiology, much important evidence consists of a continual, routine exposure to an agent often at a relatively low level. Thus, an epidemiologist finds it important that an individual was exposed to a noisy machine for his or her whole working career, drank three cups of coffee every day for the last 30 years, smoked half a pack of cigarettes a day for 35 years, and has been exposed to a dusty environment near his or her home for the last 40 years.

Scientists working in epidemiology and biostatistics usually consider the totality of information when trying to draw a conclusion about the cause of a disease. Obviously, various individuals put a different weight on each of the studies or bits of evidence based on their backgrounds and beliefs. For example, some will rate information from animal studies as important, while others will say that information is not important in a particular instance. Is information from a study of rats on bladder cancer caused by saccharine of importance if there exists adequate human information? Others will consider the methodology in a particular human epidemiology study to be weak and will therefore downgrade the importance of that study. The process is fundamentally different from the legal process which says that certain information may be admissible and other information is not.

While admissibility and hearsay evidence and other issues are important in legal proceedings, the epidemiological scientist feels cheated if not allowed to make a personal judgement about each of the studies that may be relevant to the issue at hand. Epidemiologists are judge-jurors who demand to see all possibly relevant evidence. The epidemiologist thinks that she or he must consider each study even if ultimately the study is not thought to be of much importance. Thus, it is particularly difficult to ask an epidemiologist before a trial to indicate just which studies will be considered in the forthcoming proceeding. For example, consider the case of a scientist who will discuss causes of congenital malformations when the case is concerned with a pregnant woman being exposed to anesthetic gases. There will be a list of key studies which are important. In addition, most epidemiologists will wish to know about and refer to other studies which shed light on problems of malformations even if anesthetic gases were not considered in those studies. These different viewpoints sometimes cause problems with communication between an epidemiologist and an attorney.

Legal and epidemiological conclusions can also be very different. Epidemiologists would consider it ludicrous to learn that women have won law suits because they were struck on the breast and six months later developed breast cancer at that spot, since this sequence of events is contrary to the accepted model of multiyear or even several decade intervals between causation and the appearance of cancer. On the other hand, epidemiologists would find it equally difficult to believe that someone who smoked the same brand of cigarettes for the last 40 years and develops lung cancer would not have the opportunity to be compensated, since the cause and effect are so well documented and so clear. In much epidemiology, especially in that of environmental and occupational cases, there will not be any dramatic exposure or events to which to point—just long-term chronic exposures to agents known to cause problems or thought to cause problems in higher dosages.

§19.18 —Designs of Epidemiological Studies

Epidemiology studies tend to take on one of three basic designs. These are cross-sectional studies, case-control studies, and cohort studies. Each is described below.

Cross-Sectional Studies

A *cross-sectional* study is a one-time look at the sample of people of concern. For example, an employer could have the hearing of each of its employees tested during the first week of October. Then the employer and employees would know what portion of those tested had some sort of hearing impairment during that week. The rate of impairment would be called a prevalence rate to indicate that it is the disease rate in the population at that time consisting of both older and newer cases. The single clinical examination does not indicate how long those who are hearing-impaired have been impaired. Some of the individuals exhibiting ill health would be recently diagnosed cases of disease, while others would be long-term cases. Cross-sectional studies are designed to indicate only current status without any implication of the timing of the disease. With this information, an epidemiologist could compare the work group to information published about other groups to show whether the rate of hearing loss is high in this workplace. In like manner, subgroups within the workplace could be compared, which might serve to reveal that those working in sheet metal stamping have twice the rate of hearing difficulties as those in the finishing and trim areas.

Perceptive readers have already considered the question of possible biases in one-time data. These biases might lead one to obtain results consistent with a causal relationship, which would make it appear that the workplace caused the hearing losses. A major problem with cross-sectional studies is that information on the timing of the events becomes important if one is to intrepret the information epidemiologically. In the case cited, the epidemiologist would need to know the work history of the persons involved, showing, for example, how many years each worker spent on each of the jobs, how long the worker had a hearing defect if it was not first discovered at the cross-sectional examination, and whether there were any special programs such as a *hire-the-handicapped* program which might have caused more workers with hearing difficulties to be hired. Questionnaires used in conjunction with a cross-sectional study often provide some of this information. Alternatively, one can carry out one of the other two forms of epidemiological study which more explicitly take into account the time dimension of exposure and disease.

Case-Control Studies

Frequently, new areas of study in epidemiology are opened up because of the results of a *case-control* study. In this type of study, persons who are diseased, called *cases,* are found in hospital or other clinical records and another group of persons who are free from the disease, called the *control group* or *comparison group* or *referent group,* are identified to provide a comparison with those who have the disease. After the cases and referent groups are identified, the people in each group are asked about the prior exposure of interest. In this sense, these studies tend to be retrospective, starting with the health status of the individuals now and looking back in time to find their exposure status at some time in the past.

For example, a dermatologist may believe that the lesions seen in some of her women patients are due to exposure from a solvent found in their workplace. She could identify a series of 25 women in her records with the diagnosis of interest and compare those persons to a different series of 25 persons with other lesions. Then, on a follow-up visit, a questionnaire could be given to each of these 50 women. A good questionnaire would seek information about demographic background, other known genetic and environmental risk factors for the dermatological condition, a complete work history showing employer and specific jobs held at that workplace with specific dates involved, any exposure to the solvents of interest both at work as well as in the home and other environments, and information on other risk factors that might modify the disease. If 12 of the 25 women with the skin condition and only three of those in the referent series had exposure to the solvents of interest, this would provide strong evidence that the solvents are involved with the skin disease. On the other hand, if the workplace were an unhappy one and legal proceedings had already started concerning the solvent, many epidemiologists would be concerned that the self-reporting of exposure would not provide the objective evidence concerning actual exposure. To avoid this problem, most epidemiologists would prefer to verify the self-reported information through another record system, in this case company or union records of where each woman worked which were recorded prior to the skin disease epidemic.

Cohort Studies

An alternative epidemiological design is the *cohort* study, which starts with the exposure of interest and then goes forward in time to find out which individuals developed the disease. In the example under discussion, the women exposed to the solvent could be identified and the exposure levels quantified. This would identify those persons not exposed as well as yield levels of exposure for each of those who are exposed, and these women would then constitute the cohort or group of persons of interest in this study. After the exposure status and other information of interest along the lines mentioned above were recorded, each woman would be followed to see if she developed the skin lesions of interest. Thus, cohort studies proceed foward in time from exposure to the disease, or prospectively. With this design, one obtains a true rate of new disease in the population, called an *incidence rate*. A limitation on the cohort study is the requirement for a very large cohort in order for enough cases of the disease to occur to draw a conclusion. For example, if a cancer has an incidence rate of one per thousand per year in the working group, it will require many thousands of workers and/or many years before a sufficient number of cases have accumulated to test for a suspected exposure.

Case-control studies tend to be much quicker to accomplish than cohort studies, much less expensive, and therefore often done first in epidemiological research. Cohort studies tend to be more definitive and to include more meaningful exposure data, but they can be prohibitively expensive and even impossible in the case of a rare disease. Moreover, in a cohort study, one must maintain contact with each member of the cohort for several years until sufficient cases of the disease have accumulated for an analysis.

A variant on the above designs is the cohort study done as an historical prospective study. In occupational studies especially, one can define a cohort of workers by their exposure to the agents of interest based on historical records such as 20- 20-year-old work records. Then, the workers can be followed to see if they are living or dead, and if dead, to find the underlying cause of death. Such occupational mortality studies have helped elucidate causes of disease such as the cases of bladder cancer caused by certain dyes.

§19.19 —Epidemiological Characteristics of a Legal Dispute

What are the epidemiological characteristics of a dispute on its way to court? Many cases of interest have a small amount of epidemiological evidence consisting of one or two or three studies pointing in the direction of harm claimed by the plaintiff. A frequent situation arises when there is an established body of epidemiological literature which someone is trying to extend in the case at hand. For example, while asbestos is well known to cause respiratory cancer, a plaintiff and attorney may wish to extend this finding to salivary gland cancer even though there is little or no direct evidence in the epidemiological literature on such a relationship. The other extension is in the amount of the agent necessary to cause harm. For example, while ionizing radiation is well known and proven to cause harm in high doses, was the small dose in a particular case sufficient to have caused the harm that is being claimed?

Those relationships which have been repeated in many epidemiological studies and have been determined to be causal by many investigators frequently do not reach a courtroom. The history of these situations have already involved some court cases. The new plaintiffs presumably settle out of court or at least do not have to establish the same factual basis again. Most epidemiologists will be on the same side of the issue and one will even be able to find such examples written up in textbooks, as established fact. Obviously, as in all fields, there are a few epidemiologists who will argue against even well-established relationships; thus, an attorney could find such an individual to help to make a case in the courtroom. Clearly, there are many instances in which the plaintiff must establish that the risk factors actually occurred to that individual although the epidemiology is well established. These cases are of great importance but do not involve important epidemiological considerations.

Epidemiologists, like other humans, spread out across the spectrum of how much evidence is required before one should believe that a relationship is real or proven. Those epidemiologists who work with plaintiffs' attorneys generally seem to require less evidence before they become convinced. They are willing to extrapolate from animal data to human data, to conclude that a theory is true if some evidence concurs with it, and to believe the one study that shows the relationship and ignore the two studies which do not show any relation. They would argue that errors in an epidemiological study tend to make it less sensitive—that is, less able to find a relationship even if it is there. Thus, failure to find a relationship when at least one other investigator did is an admission that the study was insufficiently sensitive to be able to observe that the agent caused the disease.

For those who do not want to depend on subjective opinions, objective fact argues that one can use the appropriate biostatistical formula to show how large a difference could have been found given the size of the epidemiological study based on the problems of chance (random) variation. On the other hand, lack of sensitivity because of classification errors (e.g., certain workers did not work in the room where the exposure occurred and were classified as nonexposed when in reality they were exposed since they frequently walk through the room on their way to lunch) is another source of variation. Although misclassification is not due to chance variation, it is still subject to analytical calculation and comments on how much misclassification would have been necessary to produce the event observed. In spite of this opportunity, bias due to misclassification in the study and other such factors are usually the topic of subjective discussions with few or no statistical facts to help decide on the importance of variation from the true circumstances.

Those epidemiologists who testify for defendants generally require more evidence before they are willing to believe a relationship exists. They would argue that the subject is unproven since there were biases in the study working in favor of finding a relationship between exposure and disease, or that the investigator incorrectly applied statistical tests and resulting probability values (p-values) by analyzing as if there was only one hypothesis being tested, when in fact there were numerous hypotheses being tested simultaneously in the same study, and that the negative studies must be taken into account since they provide evidence that the original relationship was only a chance variation and can not be repeated. Thus, after reviewing the pertinent information, this epidemiologist pronounces the conclusion to be unproved and does not believe that harm came to the plaintiff through this agent.

§19.20   —Cause-and-Effect Relationships

Fortunately, in epidemiology, there is an accepted set of rules for proving whether a cause-and-effect relationship exists. Unfortunately, there is no agreement on how important each rule is relative to the others, and obviously, there will be disagreement over how convincing the evidence is to fulfill each of these requirements. The first causal factor to be considered is the *relative risk of the disease* for those exposed compared to those who are not. The higher the relative risk, the more likely the relation is a primary cause of the disease. This concept and its background is explained in the next paragraphs.

Suppose that of 2,000 workers exposed to Chemical X, eight of them have been diagnosed for lung cancer in the past year. Another group of 2,000 workers exposed to the same chemical yielded only one case of lung cancer in the past year. The ratio of these two incidence rates is by definition the relative risk—in this instance, eight-to-one. One can only assert that the risk is due to the exposure if other important factors are equivalent in the two groups or have been made to be equivalent through proper biostatistical adjustment of the data. Thus, one would be concerned that the age distribution is the same in each of these two groups, that the cigarette smoking status is the same in the two groups, and that other factors such as socio-economic status are comparable in the two groups.

Typical relative risks for well-established epidemiologic risk factors are ten-to-one for cigarette smoking causing lung cancer, ten-to-one for working topside on a coke oven causing lung cancer, thirty-to-one or greater for angiosarcoma of the liver caused by vinyl chloride monomer, and thirty-to-one or greater for mesothelioma caused by asbestos exposure. Typically, risks of three-to-one and higher are indicative of a causal relationship. Relative risks of two-to-one and lower (towards a risk of one which indicates no excess risk) are problematic. For example, a risk of 1.6-to-one can be due to a causal factor, but it can also be due to some subtle biasing factor or other modifying factor which is unequal in the two groups being compared. While these same biasing and modifying problems are also at work when the relative risk is three-to-one or greater, at the higher level these factors only tend to reduce the risk (say from eight-to-one down to six-to-one). When the relative risk is three-to-one or greater, one can show both mathematically and by experience that bias and modifying factors are not sufficient to remove the conclusion that the agent is a causal risk factor for the disease. If the risk is less than two-to-one, alternatives to causal risk must be considered more completely and eliminated. The range between a risk of two-to-one and three-to-one is intermediate.

One should also be aware of the practical meaning underlying these relative risks. In a group of workers exposed to a relative risk of ten-to-one, the epidemiologists are saying that nine of the ten cases are due to that particular risk factor, and the other case would have occurred for all of the other, usual reasons. Therefore, a randomly chosen individual in that higher-risk group has a probability of 90 per cent that the disease was caused by that risk factor. This difference in the incidence rates is called the *attributable risk*. If the relative risk is two-to-one, only 50 per cent of the cases in the higher-risk group will be due to that risk factor. If the relative risk is 1.5-to-one, the data are saying that only one-third of the cases subjected to the excess risk will have gotten the disease because of that particular risk; the remaining two-thirds of such persons became diseased for the same reasons as all the rest of the citizenry, even if the relationship to the causal factor is accepted in the courtroom.

An interesting legal and epidemiological trend is that recent cases appear to be based on smaller relative risks. Therefore, the other factors causing the same diseases have become more and more important. The present and future of epidemiology should be much more involved with multifactorial causation.[28]

---

[28] A classic case in epidemiology was first published by a London physician by the name of Percivall Potts about 200 years ago. Percivall Potts, Chirurgical Observations Relative to Cancer of the Scrotum, *reprinted in* CA—A Cancer Journal for Clinicians, 24:110-116 (1974). Potts noted that scrotal cancer was particularly common in boys who had been working as chimney sweeps in London. It is now known that the polyaromatic hydrocarbons in soot are carcinogenic chemicals. Animal experiments have shown that rubbing this soot on tender skins such as that of the scrotum will, after prolonged exposure, result in a clinical cancer. This example is frequently cited in a variety of contexts.

A more interesting question concerns whether this was a general finding, and thus raises the issue of multifactor etiology. As pointed out by Sir Richard Doll, after Potts published his finding concerning cases of scrotal cancer in chimney sweeps, the results were accepted in Britain but not in other European countries, since the level of risk was not duplicated elsewhere. Doll, *Potts and the prospects for prevention*, Brit J Cancer, 32:263-72, (1975). This raises questions of differences between the exposure of chimney sweeps in London and elsewhere. A number of differences can be found, such as the fuel used and the shape of chimneys. One important new factor is thus discovered. In Germany, chimney sweeps routinely bathed each and every day; in London, the interval between baths for chimney sweeps was approximately five years. Thus, in addition to the questions about exposure status, one must add concerns about personal hygiene if a true understanding of the causal relationship is to be obtained. On assumes that this interaction of chemical and hygiene is part of the general status of disease etiology and that more and more of our epidemiology will be concerned with these multiple causes of disease. Major areas of concern at this time are the genetic background of each individual and his or her diet/nutritional status.

Multifactorial causation brings up a host of new legal problems, since some persons will argue that the worker is responsible for the disease because of poor personal hygiene, while others will argue that the occupation must be made safe regardless of

The second major criterion of whether a relationship is causal or not is *repeatability*. There are many possible explanations for a single study which shows a relationship between an exposure factor and a disease, including the causal explanation. On the other hand, if there are several different studies and they involve different occupational or environmental groups, they involve different epidemiological designs, they involve different geographic areas, they were done by different investigators, and they involve different potential confounding factors, yet they all have the same basic exposure factor and the same basic disease, then based on this repeatability of the relationship, epidemiologists and other persons are moved towards believing in a causal relationship between the exposure factor and the disease.

A *dose-response relationship* (see §1.04) is another criterion for a causal relation. The simplest exposure situation is a yes-or-no dichotomy in the risk factor, often called *ever* exposure versus *never* exposure in epidemiology, and an increased risk of disease. It is far more convincing to see a natural progression of disease—that is, more disease with a greater dose of the exposure factor. For example, workers who made a bad chemical every day should show more of the disease of interest than those who only worked with the chemical occasionally, and the latter should have more disease than those who rarely came in contact with the chemical, and these in turn should have more disease than those who never came in contact with that chemical (if all other factors are equal). Actual quantitative industrial hygiene measurements are even better than the qualitative exposures mentioned. Often, when measurements are not available, the investigator resorts to surrogate factors. Thus, one can compare those workers who were exposed for many years to those workers who were exposed for only a few years to those not exposed. Controlled laboratory experiments with causal agents can easily demonstrate a progression of disease with increasing dose of the true exposure agent. In like manner, epidemiological studies that demonstrate that increasing dose produces more disease are more convincing of a causal relationship than studies which compare only exposed and nonexposed. Some other causal agent might be more common in the exposed than the nonexposed according to the thoughts of the epidemiologist trying to evaluate alternative explanations, but this third factor is unlikely to mimic the increasing dose levels of the agent being studied.

Another important criterion of a causal relationship is *biological feasibility*. A citizen who complains that spots on her skin were caused by the light that she sees from a nearby street light would not be considered to have shown biological feasibility, since for the visible light spectrum no such affect has been demonstrated in humans or in animals. If measurements were made to show that ultraviolet light was at an unusually high level from the street light, the relationship would be considered biological feasible, since other skin effects

---

the personal hygiene of the worker. The special expertise of the epidemiolgist is to find out about the interactions of the two or more causative mechanisms (is the disease caused by one or the other or only in the presence of both?) and to provide the facts of causation so that others may argue questions of responsibility and liability.

are known to be caused by ultraviolet light in humans and in animals. In like manner, it is a natural extension to believe that workers exposed to chemical B have had the disease caused by it if B is a variety of chemical A which has already been shown by abundant epidemiological data to cause the same disease. Another example would concern a different site of the disease caused by the same agent—for example, if chemical A causes colon cancer, it is biologically feasible to believe that it also may cause rectal cancer.

Discussions of these and other criteria of causation can be found in most textbooks on epidemiology.[29]

§19.21   The Toxicologist

Society has become more attuned to and concerned about hazardous waste problems and human risk factors associated with toxic drugs and chemicals. This increased awareness has been precipitated by accidental exposure to highly toxic substances. Large-scale hazardous waste spills and/or disposal dump sites have also contributed to an adversary atmosphere and to litigation. Very frequently, the fear of the unknown or the potential long-range toxic effects of a chemical has spurred an associated emotionalism. Because the toxic effects of a chemical may not manifest its pathologic consequences until several decades have elapsed, such fears or concerns are warranted. Thus, while asbestos added to sailor safety aboard ships during World War II, its long-term effects leading to the production of lung tumors in shipbuilding workers was not appreciated or understood. It is one thing to recognize the acute toxic effects of organophosphate pesticide exposure, but a far different thing to experience chemically induced disease states, such as asbestosis, that do not occur until 20 to 30 years after exposure. Cause-and-effect relationships are reasonably clear-cut in some instances of chemically induced pathologic states, whereas in other cases, the etiology remains very obscure or remote.

With thousands of chemicals available in various commercial products, it is not always possible to identify conclusively the specific toxic agents. Even when a particular chemical can be identified as the causative agent in a particular syndrome, there is still the possibility of chemical-to-chemical interaction. A drug, for example, can exert a specific therapeutic effect, but in the presence of another drug (drugs, of course, are chemicals), can modify the desired therapeutic effect. These drug interactions, like chemical interactions, can often complicate, or even mask a distinct biological effect. Usually, the more peculiar or rare the particular toxicological action of a chemical, the more likely that it can be identified or associated with the causative agent. For example, formaldehyde and a multitude of other allergens produce a variety of nonspecific ear, nose, and throat symptoms, which make it very difficult to single

---

[29] G. Friedman, Primer of Epidemiology (McGraw-Hill Book Company 1980); A. M. Lilienfeld & D. E. Lilienfeld, Foundations of Epidemiology, (1980); B. MacMahon & T. F. Pugh, Epidemiology, Principles and Methods (1970); J. S. Mausner, & A. K. Bahn, Epidemiology: An Introductory Text (1974).

out the causative agent. Conversely, asbestos causes such a rare type of lung cancer (e.g., mesothelioma) that it can usually be readily identified as the causative agent, despite the long latency of its cancer-producing actions.

Advances in methodologies in chemical detection and more sensitive techniques of analyses of poisonous agents have improved the credibility of forensic pathology and the toxicological sciences. Analytical chemistry has witnessed considerable advances in sophisticated and sensitive instrumentation. The advent of mass spectroscopy and different techniques of chromatography has become commonplace in the detection of various substances, even in the parts per billion (ppb) range. Of course, it is one thing to detect chemically or physically the presence of a substance either in the environment or in the body, and another to establish its biological or toxicological effects or consequences.

It should be apparent that toxicology is becoming increasingly important in litigation involving hazardous toxic substances. Toxicology, as a scientific discipline, can seek to provide necessary factual underpinnings in such cases. The toxicologist can provide information about the chemical characteristics of the substance and to what extent it potentially invades animals, humans, and the environment. Information, usually quite technical, can be assimilated by the toxicologist, leading to risk estimates and perhaps to the extent of exposure to a toxic substance. It should be the responsibility of the toxicologist to explain such technical information and on what basis opinions and/or projections can be made for fully assessing risks to humans and their environment. Oftentimes, this entails the extrapolation of toxicity data obtained from experimental animals and situations that do not necessarily correspond to real-life conditions. Despite such difficulties, the toxicologist, along with other health professionals, should attempt to clarify such technical complexities that ultimately lead to some reasonable resolvement of the issue.

§19.22 —Sources of Information on the Toxicologist

Obtaining the individual scientist most appropriate for a trial or hearing involving a given chemical is difficult. Certainly, a well-published expert within a given field of toxicological sciences represents an obvious candidate. However, some discretion must be exercised in such a selection process, since the most prolific scientific writer does not necessarily make the best expert witness. Some argument could also be made for the more generalized approach in contrast to the highly specialized individual, particularly when a jury consists mostly of nonscientists. Most university or medical school libraries can perform computerized literature searches on a given chemical that includes author citations.

Aside from attempting to identify a specific expert toxicologist witness through some personal contact or by author citations in peer-reviewed scientific biomedical journals, many universities or medical centers have academic programs in toxicology. Oftentimes, contacting the chairperson of the particular department or the academic program director can aid in identifying a faculty member who is not only knowledgeable in a particular area of toxicology, but also willing to consult or participate in a trial or hearing. While most academic programs are administratively within schools of medicine, some programs are also situated in schools of pharmacy, veterinary medicine, and public health. In the case of toxicological expertise residing with a school of public health, it is frequently seen that such expertise is more closely allied to epidemiology. Since pharmacology (not to be confused with pharmacy) is an integral subject in any medical school curriculum, and since pharmacology concerns itself with the adverse effects of chemicals and drugs, it is also a source for identifying a toxicologist. Some universities or medical schools possess departments entitled *Pharmacology* and *Toxicology.*

Seeking a qualified toxicologic expert may involve contacting a particular scientific society. Many of these professional societies have subspecialty groups of toxicologic expertise. For example, the Society of Toxicology (SOT) has subspecialty groups in reproductive toxicology, in genetics, and in heavy metals. The American Society for Pharmacology & Experimental Toxicology (AS-PET) has subspecialty groups in environmental toxicology and in drug (chemical) metabolism.

Certification and specialty boards have been an integral part of medicine and veterinary medicine, but such added qualifications are relatively new to the field of toxicology. Perhaps, in an effort to bring some focus upon the qualifications of those persons considering themselves to be toxicologists, there has been, within the past five years, the formation of at least seven separate accrediting organizations.[30]

In summary, the following criteria might be used to assess the quality of the toxicologic expert:

1. Formal academic training (e.g. toxicology, pharmacology, etc,), usually Ph.D., M.D., or D.V.M.

2. Current professional activities (e.g., editorial boards, governmental scientific panels)

3. Current professional society memberships (e.g., SOT, ASPET, Teratology Society)

4. Current publications in peer-reviewed scientific journals

30

1. American Academy of Clinical Toxicology
2. American Board of Medical Toxicology
3. American Board of Toxicology
4. American Board of Veterinary Toxicology
5. American College of Toxicology
6. American College of Veterinary Pathology
7. American College of Veterinary Toxicologists.

§19.23   —Investigation, Certainty, and Expectations

It is possible for the expert witness to be an original investigator or researcher within an area of toxicological expertise, and to advocate his or her scientific opinion. This type of expert undoubtedly brings more credibility to scientific opinion than the mere advocate. There is, of course, a danger that the researcher-advocate has studied the problem too thoroughly and has an accumulated scientific bias, regardless how well intentioned. On the other hand, sometimes the advocate-only expert suffers a credibility deficit brought on by emotionalism that pertains to the technical area.

If an issue cannot be completely resolved on its technical information, and many, unfortunately cannot be, prudence must be exercised in taking on the role of an advocate. Technical opinions and appropriate extrapolations are often necessary, but some reasonable expression of scientific underpinnings must be present. Seldom, in complicated toxicological issues, are all of the necessary data points available. Information about the duration and exposure (dose) are often sketchy, and the expert may have to offer a scientific opinion. Remember that toxicology is a science, and the more quantification there is in the data base, the more defensible the scientific opinion. For example, it is easier to describe a chemically induced teratologic effect in quantifiable terms than it is to testify about a chemical that produced a psychological or a stress-related phenomena.

There is usually an element of scientific uncertainty in most toxicological issues. Only rarely is there the opportunity to weigh scientific evidence on all facets of the toxicological issue. Frequently, the toxicological data is obtained from animal studies, and appropriate extrapolations must be made to human exposure conditions. No one denies the difficulties involved in such extrapolations, but a defense based solely upon species differences is ill advised. If animals can be used as models to test the therapeutic efficacy of potential drugs, these same relationships can prevail in assessing adverse effects in animals and their subsequent extrapolation to humans.

Scientific uncertainty can be minimized if the particular literature contains research protocols that are well designed and if the biological variables are quantitative. There is no substitute for a good experimental design, complete with a statistically valid number of samples. Lack of acute or even subacute toxicological data in humans can sometimes be bolstered by a combination of comparable toxicological findings in animals and some epidemiological studies in humans.

A fundamental concept in toxicology is that referred to as dose-response (discussed in §1.04)—the more clear-cut this dose-response relationship, the more the scientific certainty. For any given chemical exposure, the scientific uncertainty of its effects lessen with an increasing knowledge of the agent's dose, its duration of exposure, its mode of administration, its possible biotransformation or metabolism, and whether it accumulates in the body. Thus, a complete toxicokinetic profile of a given chemical, or even a closely related chemical prototype, can do much to reduce the scientific uncertainties related to a particular incident involving a toxic substance.

Ideally, scientific expectations should coincide with the expectations of the client. Presumably, the expert witness possesses the appropriate scientific information and convictions to defend his or her opinion. The expectations are most often realized if the attorney involved has some technical background or insight into the toxicological issues. Short of this, there must be a close technical dialogue between the witness and the attorney.

Expectation should seldom exceed the scientific underpinnings of the toxicological issue—the more precise the relevant technical information, the greater the chances of a favorable outcome. The more precise the toxicologic information is, the greater the chances are at arriving at reasonable risk-benefit assessments. Finally, the expectations or the outcome will be more favorable if trial-related emotionalism can be diffused, and relevant and readily understood examples of the magnitude of the toxicological issue, or its lack of magnitude, are put into proper perspective.

In conclusion, it is important to note that definitions or perceptions of just what constitutes an expert toxicologist may vary. For example, a person trained in embryology may be considered a teratologist and even a toxicologist. A person knowledgeable in allergic or immunoreactive phenomena would most likely be trained in microbiology or immunology, and yet not necessarily be considered a toxicologist. It is quite possible that a marine biologist may prove to be the most qualified to testify on shellfish toxins, yet not necessarily be a so-called card-carrying toxicologist. From this small number of examples, it should be evident that there is considerable diversity in what might be construed as a qualified expert in the toxicologic sciences. Nevertheless, the majority of toxicologic efforts are derived from a reasonably focused scientific base. The qualifications need not be compromised, since there are many formally trained toxicologists whose specific scientific expertise will resolve the complex issues involving the actions of chemicals on biological events.

§19.24   Evaluating the Expert

Once the process of screening potential experts has been completed, the attorney needs to evaluate further the potential usefulness of the expert. Experts, like any other human beings, have their strengths and weaknesses; it is probably impossible to get someone who is strong in all areas involved in the toxic substance problem. Honesty, dignity, and personal appearance are obvious personal factors of importance.[31] Obviously, also of great importance are credibility and qualifications.

Credibility or believability are personal characteristics of the expert and his or her background. Obviously, credibility also depends on qualifications, but unfortunately the expert can be highly qualified and still not be credible.

---

[31] Curran, The Physician as Expert (1974).

Personal characteristics of course include the demeanor of the witness—whether he or she is arrogant, pedantic, officious, or lecturing, or whether he or she is humble, relates to ordinary people, and tries to teach.

Curran states: "The witness should be modest not only in stating his qualifications as an expert but in his attitude toward other experts, particularly opposing experts. He should not disparage an opinion given by another expert."[32] The attitude that says, "I am a doctor and it is so because I say it is so," has characterized some experts and does not serve them well in dealing with those persons who have to weigh all aspects of a situation. The attitude of the expert toward those who know less about the subject than himself or herself is important. Obviously, the expert must be very calm in spite of rigorous cross-examination and attempts to impeach his or her testimony. It is also very helpful to have someone who is articulate and capable of explaining a position. Regardless of whether the expert is working for the plaintiff or defendant, it is important that the expert be concerned with the plight of the plaintiff. Although the expert may not agree with the plaintiff's contention, to be credible he or she must be able to empathize with the plaintiff's situation and realize how the litigation arose.

In addition to these personal characteristics, credibility also depends upon background and present status. An expert who has worked full-time with a labor union may obviously be regarded as tending to favor the plaintiff, while one who has worked with a large industry may be regarded as favoring the defendant. Experts from academic and government backgrounds are generally tended to be regarded as less biased and, though often without substance, the factfinder may share this opinion. It is important regardless of the association of the expert—company, labor union, government, etc.—that he or she have an appreciation of all sides of the issue.

While credibility depends upon many factors other than qualifications, the ultimate in credibility and ability to assist in the case is the qualification of the expert. How can the attorney evaluate the expert's qualifications?

Other experts, especially those who specialize in the field which is going to be involved, often know of the expert's qualifications and competency. The expert himself or herself should provide the attorney with a copy of his or her curriculum vitae. This will, of course, provide information regarding training, past work experience, publications, professional societies, and other interests. Obviously, the curriculum vitae which is prepared by the expert will tend to show him or her in the best possible light. Nevertheless, there are certain key points which the attorney should seek.

A number of major specialty boards, disciplines, and certifications exist, and within them a number of subspecialties. In order to be certified, the expert must normally have taken prescribed training, usually have minimum experience requirements, and pass a difficult examination—usually both oral and written. Certification indicates that the expert has the prerequisite training, experience, and knowledge in a particular specialty. Obviously, certification

---

[32] *Id.*

does not indicate his or her qualifications as a witness or indicate that he or she has had experience with the particular issue involved. It does indicate, however, that the expert is considered by his peers to be qualified to practice in a particular speciality.

In order to be considered a specialist in a particular field, an expert need not always be certified; he or she may still be board-eligible. These experts have all of the training and experience requirements but may have never taken the certification examination. There are many very competent specialists who fall in this category, especially some older persons who have been very successful in their fields and felt that it was not a particular advantage to take the time-consuming and expensive certification examination.

Another category of experts who are not board certified includes those fairly recently completing their training requirements but which have not attained the requisite experience. Because of their recent training and knowledge, they may in some cases be very helpful even though not certified. They have the advantage of usually being very up-to-date in the latest developments in their field. They may especially be useful in developing background, reviewing depositions, etc.

The institution wherein the expert was trained may be important, since, obviously, training in a prestigious institution creates a certain amount of credibility and usually indicates good qualifications. However, it is important to identify institutions which are well-known for particular areas.

A review should be made of the publications of the expert, and the attorney would do well to review not only the titles but also to read the articles to determine the basic thought processes of the expert. The expert should have copies of articles to send to the attorney.

Obviously, the expert should be licensed in the state in which he or she is practicing, but not necessarily in the state in which he or she is to testify. Nevertheless, factfinders often appear to give more credibility to the local expert from their own state or city.

§19.25   The Hired Gun Syndrome

An expert may find that working with attorneys is attractive financially and professionally. Also, it is quite natural for the attorney to seek an expert with a particular viewpoint to assist him or her with the case. There may then be the temptation for the expert to *tilt* his or her viewpoint to that which he or she perceives would please the attorney or help the case. If the expert does not truly hold the viewpoints which he or she will be espousing as a witness, this may become readily apparent to a factfinder, especially upon cross-examination. The expert is then viewed as a *hired gun*—one who will, for a price, say whatever someone else wishes him to say. This risk is even greater when the expert will be testifying on behalf of a client such as a large corporation in defense of a claim by a citizen plaintiff. Some experts testify very frequently within a geographical area or jurisdiction and become known to judges, workers' compensation commissioners, and hearing officers as representing a specific viewpoint, and they therefore risk being labeled as biased.

Another way for an expert to be labeled with the hired gun syndrome is to have a sizeable portion of his or her income from the source that he or she is representing in the trial. Experts who work full-time for a particular company, association, or union often have difficulty with credibility when testifying on an issue in which their employer has interest. Often, a local expert, who may have very little qualification in the particular issue in question, will be more credible than the out-of-town expert. Though this may be unfortunate, it indicates that there may be cases when it is best to use the true expert to acquaint the local expert witness with the issues, rather than having the expert testify directly.

Though there is always the danger of the expert being labeled with the *hired gun* epithet, it is normally the case that attorneys, when interwiewing an expert relative to a particular issue, really wish to know what the expert's deeply held viewpoint is with respect to that issue. Attorneys are not interested in having the expert shade his or her viewpoint to meet their needs, for to do so may render the expert useless. It is certainly better for the attorney to determine if the viewpoint of the expert meets his or her needs than for the viewpoint to be altered supposedly to meet those needs. The sincerely held viewpoint skillfully articulated will make the witness credible. The advocate actively promotes a specific, sometimes biased, but sincerely held viewpoint, whereas the hired gun will espouse any viewpoint for convenience or monetary gain. To avoid the hired gun syndrome, the ideal witness would be a local or regional expert who is truly an expert and outstanding in his or her field, who shares a viewpoint with the side with which he or she is working, and who for the most part is so busy with other matters that testifying is of little benefit to him or her economically. Rarely are all of these characteristics be found in the same person. Perhaps somewhere between the hired gun and the ideal candidate is where most expert witnesses fall.

It is important to have an understanding about fees in advance. This understanding should cover not only the tangible aspects of the expert's work—such as actual testimony, time in conference, and examinations—but should also cover additional work such as research, preparing reports, and reviewing cases. With respect to the latter, the only work product may be telephone calls or a better insight into the overall case and the results may not be tangible, but time has been spent and it should be understood in advance that reimbursement will be made for this type of service. The expert should keep a detailed account of the amount of time, date, place, and the work that is being done on the case in order to document the fees.

Another element of professional fees is payment method. Since the nature of the legal process tends to be very prolonged, attorneys are often accustomed to reimbursement at the end of the process. Most experts will wish to send a statement about the time that the work product is delivered. In the event of a prolonged case involving research, analysis, and review, statements may be sent monthly, based upon the hours involved. This billing arrangement should be cleared in advance so that the attorney will reimburse the expert even though the case has not been completed. Experts do not work on a contingency basis; they therefore expect payment in a timely manner regardless of the outcome of the case.

Just as experts do in practice, they may adjust their fees in accordance with the needs of the case. If an expert is generally sympathetic to a plaintiff's cause—and if the plaintiff has little money—it may be appropriate for the attorney to ask the expert to work at a reduced or rather low fee. In cases of defense or where an industry—particularly a large industry—is involved, it is normally understood that funds are available and the expert witnesses are to be fully reimbursed for their work. Most attorneys must, of course, clear the retention of an expert with their client. This is important and this information should be conveyed to the expert so that he or she will be aware that the client or ultimate payor of the fees will honor his or her request.

§19.26   Sources of Technical Data

Potential sources of technical data are so numerous that the basic problem becomes one of sifting through them to find appropriate, useful materials. Modern data accessing systems make data sources available even to the attorney and expert located in remote areas. The attorney or expert who is to be involved in toxic litigation should identify a nearby source of technical publication. Fortunately, there are several index-type publications which list relevant literature by subject matter.[33]

It is also very simple to obtain access to on-line data bases in the medical, epidemilogical, and toxicological areas, directly through the officer computer with the telephone modem. Another method requiring no capital outlay gathers data through the library source and data base services.

In addition to using a library or a private computer terminal for data retrieval, there are a number of commercial systems which specialize in searches and document retrieval. Such services will do a search in a timely manner upon request and also retrieve documents as specified from the search. Though somewhat more expensive than other sources, they often have the advantage of saving time for the busy attorney or expert, and many of them assist in the retrieval of documents that would otherwise be quite difficult to obtain.

It must be noted that there are several problems with all literature-indexing services and computer data base systems. The data base systems may be limited in time; for example, some go back only five years. However, an even greater limitation is the fact that these systems depend primarily upon published material. There are numerous unpublished documents such as federally contracted research, which may never be published but are important in the decision-making process of federal agencies. Some of these documents are

---

[33] Medline, Toxline, Registry of Toxic Effects of Chemical Substances.

available by request or under the Freedom of Information Act,[34] as described in Chapter 7.

Currently, there are a number of computer-based literature retrieval systems in the biological and chemical sciences. Some of these scientific retrieval systems are more useful than others with respect to their assimilation of toxicological information. When using such retrieval systems, the use of key terms or identifiers is particularly important, since many chemicals masquerade under a variety of names or synonyms. A knowledge of the substance's chemical name, its common name, its generic name, or its trade name is particularly beneficial in obtaining a complete retrieval of information. Sometimes, the chemical itself will be only one of a number of ingredients in a commercial product and hence may have still another separate trade name. When resorting to a computer-based information retrieval system, it is important to remember that the use of print-out abstracts (and their contents) are only as good as the author's ability to write a concise summary and the computer programmer's ability to exploit key terms for the retrieval system.

§19.27   Dealing With the Expert

It is important that the expert and the attorneys who are working on a case form an harmonious relationship. It is also important that the attorney ascertain the expert's views regarding the case and then utilize these beliefs to the best advantage. The presentation of the expert's findings and opinions may be assisted and even changed somewhat by the attorney, but the attorney should never try to have the expert alter his or her basic viewpoint.

Both sides in an action have the right to present a thorough and scientific exposition which represents their best interests. Each side has the right to scrutinize the presentation of the other side, and to demonstrate the weaknesses of the opponent's presentation. Both in actual testimony and in pretrial investigation, the expert can be of great assistance. A carefully developed presentation based upon available scientific evidence is the foundation for both sides of the case. All aspects of the case should be investigated—clinical, toxicological, or environmental—and such investigation by both sides can prepare the case in the best light for that side.

Many experts have a distate for advocacy and advocates. Nevertheless, on a controversial subject, an expert may develop a viewpoint which he or she believes is based upon his or her scientific analysis of the issue. To espouse this viewpoint with reasonable forcefulness, he or she may verge on advocacy. In itself, this should not impeach the scientific analysis and credentials of the witness. On the other hand, advocacy which is based upon an emotional or political view point, without scientific basis, is not only readily apparent to the other side but also unbecoming to the expert. The expert needs to differentiate between these two aspects of advocacy, but remaining completely neutral is not

---

[34] 5 USC §552.

necessarily the nature of our legal system, and indeed it is not even the nature of our system of scientific debate. A summary of what is needed is a careful formulation of an opinion based upon scientific reality and a forceful and articulate exposition of that opinion, with a willingness to defend this opinion.

As with any other working relationship, it is important that the attorney and the expert know what to expect of one another; it is important that the attorney determine just what help he or she wants from the expert, and the expert to determine what help can be given. Though many attorneys are primarily interested in the expert as a witness, this is only one of the areas wherein the expert can be useful. It may be a mistake for the attorney to utilize the expert only as a witness without involving him or her in other aspects of the case. To constrain the expert may keep important pieces of information about the case from him or her and may render him or her much less helpful than he or she would be if he or she understood a broader view of the situation.

A frank discussion of mutual expectations is very beneficial to both parties. In addition to expectations regarding the work task, it is important to arrive at understanding and expectations regarding the working relationship. Some of the real difficulties in working together is that both the expert and the attorney are usually quite busy and subject to unscheduled demands. Experts are often bothered by the *hurry up and wait* feature with which attorneys often deal with experts and other witnesses. Once the date is set for trial or a deposition, suddenly all those who are working with the attorney are placed under great pressure to meet the deadline. At the last minute, the anticipated event may be cancelled, and an expert who has juggled his or her schedule and cancelled appointments to get ready for and to appear at the deposition or trial finds that he or she is not needed for the forseeable future. Many of these situations are beyond the control of the attorney. However, to the extent that they can be controlled and at least to the extent that the expert can be brought into the picture and understand, it will help to minimize any friction that may occur.

Normally, experts are used to seeing the results and having feedback regarding their work. Frequently, attorneys provide little feedback or follow-up. The expert does not know whether he or she should forget about the case or whether his or her lack of recent communication from the attorney is simply due to delays in the legal system. The expert is generally reluctant to check with the attorney, as this may be misconstrued, and therefore he or she does not know what to expect in the future. Suddenly, after many months, the attorney may call and wish for information with great haste.

Since there is so little scientific knowledge about certain issues, and since it may be necessary for the expert to spend considerable time in researching these issues, it is important to have an understanding of the mutual expectations in this regard. Does the attorney wish the expert to spend additional time on research and evaluation? This can result in numerous hours spent in the library reviewing articles, etc. Another area of importance is to reach an understanding regarding communications.

When the expert is doing an examination, a test, or other research and later appearing as a witness, a written report is needed and expected. In this case, punctuality and completeness is quite important. There should be an understanding of the scope of the report. Reports which consist of opinions without supporting data do not serve anyone well.

Since medicine and science are not exact, the expert must render an opinion. The opinion, however, should be supported by science and logic; alternatives and opposing viewpoints and findings should be discussed. Recommendations should be made.

Once the report is rendered, the attorney may wish to discuss it further with the expert. The report may be inadequate and not fully serve the needs of the case. In such cases, this fact should be explained, and the expert should be asked to amplify or clarify. Obviously, no attempt should be made to have the expert to change his or her fundamental opinion of the case—other than to allow him or her to evaluate it further in the light of additional information.

20 Mass Tort Issues

Michael V. Corrigan, Esq.*

---

* Partner, Simpson, Thatcher & Bartlett, New York, New York.

§20.01   Introduction

The catastrophic consequences of mass tort litigation were dramatically revealed in August of 1982 when Johns-Manville Corporation, faced with thousands of asbestos-related damage actions, filed its petition for bankruptcy reorganization. Manville's decision to take all its tort troubles to a single court for treatment symbolizes a phenomenon apparent in all litigation involving allegedly harmful products or substances which are widely distributed and used. In such big cases, there is an almost irresistible force compelling their removal from the arena of traditional products liability litigation. Mass tort cases are so huge, so complex, and are becoming so frequent that the resulting pressure on the judicial system has forced it to take radical steps to reduce such litigation to manageable proportions. As one district court has observed:

> The latter half of the twentieth century has witnessed a virtual explosion in the frequency and number of lawsuits filed to redress injuries caused by a single product manufactured for use on a national level. Indeed, certain products have achieved such national notoriety due to their tremendous impact on the consuming public, that the mere mention of their names—Agent Orange, Asbestos, DES, MER/29, Dalkon Shield —conjure images of massive litigation, corporate stonewalling, and infrequent yet prevalent, "big money" punitive damage awards.
>
> In a complex society such as ours, the phenomenon of numerous persons suffering the same or similar injuries as a result of a single pattern of misconduct on the part of a defendant is becoming increasingly frequent.
>
> The judicial system's response to such repetitive litigation has often been blind adherence to the common law's traditional notion of civil litigation as necessarily private dispute resolution.[1]

The four major mass tort cases discussed in this chapter reflect efforts to mitigate immense problems by dealing with individual lawsuits on some form of group basis. Although some of these efforts have originated on the plaintiffs' side (by the use of the class action in the *Agent Orange* litigation and the invocation of offensive collateral estoppel in the *DES* litigation), the Manville

---

[1] *In re* Northern Dist of Cal "Dalkon Shield" IUD Prod Liab Litig, 426 F Supp 887, 892 (ND Cal 1981).

bankruptcy step illustrates that the defendants also may have a reluctant interest in housing huge matters such as the asbestos litigation under one roof. Moreover, even when the litigants themselves seem willing to fight their battles on a case-by-case basis, the courts may not tolerate it, as illustrated by the court's sua sponte certification (subsequently reversed) of a nationwide punitive damages class action in the *Dalkon Shield* litigation. By analyzing the issues of class actions, collateral estoppel, punitive damages, and bankruptcy tort claims within the factual framework of these mass tort cases, it is possible to gain an appreciation for a judiciary struggling with lawsuits which threaten to overwhelm its resources. Such an analysis is the purpose of this chapter.

§20.02   Agent Orange Litigation and Liability Class Actions

Mass tort cases generally involve numerous claims for similar injuries arising from the wide distribution of an identical product or substance. Because the product and the type of harm it is claimed to cause are often common to many claims, the utility of the class action device to manage the suits, or parts thereof, has been examined by a number of courts.

Mass tort class actions have not fared well, however, particularly in the appellate courts, which are a step removed from the calendar problems facing trial judges. Of the four mass tort cases discussed in this chapter, only one, the one involving Agent Orange, has proceeded on a nationwide class basis with respect to any issue, and that has not been subjected to appellate review. The basic obstacle to certification of a mass tort class for liability purposes is the fact that the common issues frequently do not predominate over individual questions such as the time frame and circumstances of each plaintiff's use of or exposure to the product involved, causation matters, and legal questions such as statutes of limitations and strict liability rules, which may vary from state to state. These matters have led courts to deny class action status in the asbestos and Dalkon Shield litigation,[2] or to limit certification to residents of one state, as was done by one court in the DES litigation.[3] The Agent Orange litigation, therefore, stands alone among the major mass tort cases in utilizing the class action on a national basis.

§20.03   —The Agent Orange Claims

The Agent Orange litigation consists of thousands of personal injury or wrongful death claims by veterans and their families arising out of the use of

---

[2] *See e.g.,* Abed v AH Robins Co, 693 F2d 847 (9th Cir 1982); Yandle v PPG Indus, 65 FRD 566 (ED Tex 1974); Rosenfeld v AH Robins Co, 63 AD2d 11, 407 NYS2d 196 (1978).

[3] Payton v Abbott Labs, 83 FRD 382 (D Mass 1979). Other courts have declined to certify a class in DES litigation. *See e.g.,* Ryan v Eli Lilly & Co, 84 FRD 230 (DSC 1979); Mink v University of Chicago, 460 F Supp 713 (ND Ill 1978).

phenoxy herbicides as a weapon of war during the Vietnam conflict.[4] These herbicides, most often identified by the military as Agent Orange, were generally sprayed from the air in an effort to defoliate forested areas in order to deny cover to opposing forces. American soldiers who handled the herbicides or who were deployed in the areas of the spray missions were exposed to Agent Orange, which contained, as a by-product of its manufacturing process, small amounts of the toxic substance dioxin. Some veterans now believe that a wide variety of health problems, including cancers, liver disorders, and birth defects experienced by them or their family members are attributable to their combat exposure to that dioxin. In the format of a class action pending in the federal Eastern District of New York, these veterans seek to impose responsibility for their injuries and for the injuries of other Vietnam servicemen on the various companies which supplied the herbicides to the military under contracts with the United States government, primarily on the theory that the defendants allegedly failed to warn the government or its soldiers of dangers associated with dioxin contamination.[5]

§20.04 —Role of the Government

The government itself stands in the middle of the litigation. It contracted with the defendants to procure Agent Orange and it made the decisions with respect to its use and application in connection with the movement of troops in combat areas. The district court has observed that:

> Overarching the entire dispute is a feeling on both sides that whatever existing law and procedures may technically require, fairness, justice and equity in this unprecedented controversy demand that the government assume responsibility for the harm caused our soldiers and their families by its use of Agent Orange in southeast Asia.[6]

The government is not, however, a party to the Agent Orange litigation. It cannot be sued directly by the plaintiffs because in *Feres v United States,*[7] the Supreme Court held that the government has not waived its sovereign immunity with respect to claims by members of the armed forces arising out of their military service. Moreover, in *Stencel Aero Engineering Corp v United States,*[8] the Supreme Court extended the *Feres* doctrine to bar third-party claims against the government. The court has therefore dismissed third-party actions which the defendants had instituted against the government, holding that these attempts to seek contribution or indemnity are barred under *Feres* and *Stencel.*[9]

---

[4] *In re* Agent Orange Prod Liab Litig, 506 F Supp 762 (EDNY 1980).

[5] *Id.*

[6] *In re* Agent Orange Prod Liab Litig, 506 F Supp 762, 784 (EDNY 1980).

[7] 340 US 135 (1950).

[8] 421 US 666 (1977).

[9] 506 F Supp at 774.

§20.05 —Subject Matter Jurisdiction

One of the unique aspects of *Agent Orange*[10] is that, unlike most other mass tort cases, it is currently being litigated exclusively in the federal court system despite the absence of federal question jurisdiction. The first cases commenced were filed as class actions in federal courts. In addition to diversity of citizenship, the complaints sought to invoke federal question jurisdiction on a number of theories, including the application of a federal common law of products liability. As other cases followed, including state court actions removed to federal court, the Judicial Panel on Multidistrict Litigation transferred them to the Eastern District of New York and assigned the task of coordinating the pretrial proceedings to Judge George C. Pratt. The defendants subsequently challenged the assertion of federal question jurisdiction, and contended that federal common law was in applicable to the litigation. Judge Pratt denied the defendants' motion to dismiss, but the Second Circuit reversed, holding that since Congress had not formulated a national policy to deal with the conflicting interests of veterans and military suppliers, it would be improper for the judiciary to resolve the conflict under a uniform federal common law of product liability.[11]

§20.06 —Conditional Class Action

The decision of the Second Circuit[12] left diversity of citizenship as the sole basis for continued subject matter jurisdiction in the federal courts, and posed difficult manageability problems for the lower court. Among these were:

1. **Diversity problems.** Approximately 3,400 plaintiffs from most of the 50 states had brought 167 separate suits naming as many as 19 defendants with differing degrees of involvement in the supply of Agent Orange to the government. Variations among the states' products liability standards, causation rules, and damage principles could lead to equally varying results in individual cases.

2. **Causation issues.** Agent Orange was used in Southeast Asia for a period of seven years. Types and extent of exposure differed, and the injuries claimed vary substantially. There is a substantial question as to whether Agent Orange is capable of causing any of the injuries alleged.

3. **Legal questions.** "The litigation presents numerous questions of law that lie at the frontier of modern tort jurisprudence. Among them are questions of enterprise liability, strict products liability, liability for inju-

---

[10] *In re*, Agent Orange Prod Liab Litig, 506 F Supp 762 (EDNY 1980).

[11] *In re* Agent Orange Prod Liab Litig, 637 F2d 987 (2d Cir 1980), *cert denied sub nom* Chapman v Dow Chem Co, 454 US 1128 (1981).

[12] *In re* Agent Orange Prod Liab Litig, 637 F2d 987 (2d Cir 1980), *cert denied sub nom* Chapman v Dow Chem Co, 454 US 1128 (1981).

ries that appear long after original exposure to the offending substance, and liability for so-called genetic injuries."[13]

In trying to decide how best to streamline such an inherently unwieldly litigation in light of the Second Circuit decision, Judge Pratt acknowledged that "[m]anaging this case under diversity of citizenship principles is by far the more difficult route to travel. . . ."[14] The court found a number of alternatives wanting because they would either require numerous trials or would fail to account for claims as yet unfiled, thereby impeding a "just, speedy and inexpensive determination" of the controversy.[15] The court decided that initial management of the cases by way of a class action was feasible and appropriate, despite what it termed the "technical and procedural problems that have arisen with the class action device [which] have proved particularly troublesome in the context of mass tort cases."[16]

In conditionally certifying a class, Judge Pratt overcame the major obstacle which has deterred other courts from taking this step in mass tort cases by finding that common questions predominated over questions affecting only individual class members. Tracking the rubric of Rule 23(b)(3) of the Federal Rules of Civil Procedure, the court found that:

1.   Class members had a minimal interest in controlling the prosecution of individual actions. "Indeed, the problems inherent in every one of the individual actions are so great that it is doubtful if a single plaintiff represented by a single attorney pursuing an individual action could every succeed."[17]

2.   Virtually all pending litigation concerning Agent Orange was already before the court by virtue of multidistricting procedures.[18]

3.   "[T]he difficulties likely to be encountered by managing these actions as a class action are significantly outweighed by the truly overwhelming problems that would attend any other management device chosen."[19]

Although the court selected the class action as an apt tool for *managing* a mass tort litigation, it did not hold that it was appropriate for *deciding* all liability issues. Rather, the court expressly limited its certification to the early resolution of the defendants' government contract defense, where "the issues under consideration concern the relationship between the defendants and the gov-

---

[13] *In re* Agent Orange Prod Liab Litig, 506 F Supp 762, 783 (EDNY 1980).
[14] *Id.* 783 n 30.
[15] *Id* 784.
[16] *Id* 785.
[17] *Id* 790.
[18] *Id* 790-91.
[19] *Id* 791.

ernment, issues that impact equally on every plaintiff's claim."[20]

The court therefore granted the plaintiffs' motion for conditional class action certification under Rule 23(b)(3) of the Federal Rules of Civil Procedure. As defined, the class is nationwide in scope, consisting of "persons who claim injury from exposure to Agent Orange and their spouses, children and parents who claim direct or derivative injury therefrom."[21] Under this definition of the class, plaintiffs' counsel purport to represent some 2.4 million veterans.

§20.07 —Government Contract Defense

Although Judge Pratt recognized that conditional certification of a nationwide class in a mass tort diversity case does not eliminate state law questions which might be dispositive of individual claims (such as the bar of statutes of limitations),[22] he did isolate one legal issue common to all claims which could appropriately be tried on a class basis. This issue involves the validity of the government contract defense asserted by the defendants. The gravamen of the defense, which some have labeled the *Nuremberg defense,* is that a supplier of war material should not be obligated to question the military's requirements or specifications for weaponry, nor should he or she be held responsible for the government's creation of or failure to perceive a risk to its own soldiers. The court recognized that if the factual elements of the defense were to be established by any defendant, it would terminate the entire litigation as against that defendant.[23]

In a subsequent opinion, Judge Pratt set forth the elements of the defense which the defendants would be required to prove.[24] A defendant would be entitled to judgment in its favor if it proved that it met specifications established by the government and that the government knew as much as or more than the defendant about the hazards associated with Agent Orange. The most significant element of the defense as described by the court is the contractor's limited duty to warn the government of risks known to the supplier but not known to the government.[25]

This failure-to-warn element of the government contract defense is a significantly narrower concept than the failure-to-warn test generally applicable in products cases, for it is restricted to an examination of *actual* knowledge possessed by the defendants and the government.[26] Questions relating to what the defendants or the government *should* have known concerning the allegedly hazardous potential of Agent Orange are limited under this definition. Thus,

---

[20] *Id* 790.

[21] *Id* 788.

[22] *In re* Agent Orange Prod Liab Litig, 506 F Supp 762, 790 (EDNY 1980).

[23] *Id* 796.

[24] *In re* Agent Orange Prod Liab Litig, 534 F Supp 1046, 1053-58 (EDNY 1982).

[25] *Id* 1055.

[26] *Id* 1057.

for example, in the context of this defense, no independent duty of testing is imposed on the defendants. Negligence on the part of a defendant or the government in failing to acquire knowledge of such hazards does not defeat the defense, for a supplier's duty is limited to his or her obligation "to inform the military of *known* risks attendant to a particular weapon that it supplies, so as to provide the military with at least an opportunity fairly to balance the weapon's risks and benefits."[27]

In an opinion read from the bench on May 12, 1983, the court granted motions for summary judgment made by some of the *Agent Orange* defendants, finding that the government knew more about dioxin and its contamination of Agent Orange than did these defendants.[28] As to certain other defendants, however, summary judgment was denied because there are triable issues of fact on the issue of relative knowledge.[29]

In conditionally certifying a class action for the purpose of litigating the government contract defense, the court had envisioned an early, separate trial of that issue, anticipating that should the defendants prevail at that trial, the entire litigation would come to an end before the parties undertook the enormous amount of discovery required to prepare for trial of the merits of the underlying claims.[30] Having disposed of the summary judgment motions, however, the court reconsidered the matter and decided that as to the remaining defendants, there should be but one trial in which the government contract defense issues would be merged with the general liability question of negligent failure to warn about Agent Orange.[31]

The implications of conducting one class trial of both legal issues are significant. Subsumed within the concept of negligent failure to warn is the double causation question—i.e., *can* Agent Orange cause harm and, if so, *did* it cause the harm complained of by a particular veteran? The theoretical capability of a product to injure persons has never been presented to a jury in a nationwide class action context. Accordingly, if the court formally certifies a class for this

---

[27] *Id* 1055 (emphasis added).

[28] *In re* Agent Orange Prod Liab Litig, MDL No 381 (EDNY May 12, 1983) transcript 5127.

[29] *Id* transcript 5128.

[30] 506 F Supp at 796; May 12, 1983 transcript 5130.

[31] Transcript p 5131-36. The court concluded that the evidence developed in connection with the summary judgment motions had revealed that the level of dioxin contamination in Agent Orange was an important factor in resolving both the government contract defense and the questions of negligent failure to warn. If the level of contamination contained in a particular defendant's Agent Orange were determined to be *safe* by the trier of fact, that defendant would prevail not only under the government contract defense, but also would succeed against the claim of defective product. If, on the other hand, the amount of dioxin contained in the defoilant were deemed to be *unsafe,* and a defendant failed to disclose pertinent information to the government, that defendant would lose its government contract defense, yet could still prevail on the general liability issue if its failure to disclose would not have affected the military's decisions about utilizing the product. See transcript 5134-35.

purpose in *Agent Orange,* a major new chapter in the history of mass tort litigation will have been written.

§20.08   Dalkon Shield Litigation and Punitive Damages Class Actions

The spectre of multiple punitive damages awards in mass tort cases was raised in 1967 by Judge Friendly in the MER-29 litigation. In *Roginsky v Richardson-Merrell, Inc,*[32] the judge wrote extensive dicta on the subject in which he observed that the "legal difficulties engendered by claims for punitive damages on the part of hundreds of plaintiffs are staggering. . . . We have the gravest difficulty in perceiving how claims for punitive damages in such a multiplicity of actions throughout the nation can be so administered as to avoid overkill."[33] Since no legal principle restricts the number of punitive damages awards which could be imposed on a mass tort defendant, the judge foresaw the possibility of a company being punished, in toto, far beyond any reasonable limit, as well as the likelihood that early plaintiffs would "strip the cupboard bare" for later plaintiffs who would have uncollectible judgments.[34] He concluded that: "the apparent impracticability of imposing an effective ceiling on punitive awards in hundreds of suits in different courts may result in an aggregate which, when piled on large compensatory damages, could reach catastrophic amounts."[35]

This potential for corporate catastrophe never came to pass in the MER-29 litigation. Only eleven of the approximately 1500 claims against Richardson-Merrell were tried to verdict, and only three resulted in punitive damages awards.[36] Accordingly, a number of courts have dismissed Judge Friendly's comments as hypothetical only, and one commentator observed that if the MER-29 litigation was an example, "then the threat of bankrupting a manufacturer with punitive damage awards in mass disaster litigation appears to be more theoretical than real."[37] Even the case of Johns-Manville, where the actual imposition of punitive damages and the threat of more was a primary factor prompting the company to seek refuge under the bankruptcy laws, has evoked little appellate sympathy. In *Moran v Johns-Manville Sales Corp,*[38] the asbestos producer relied on Judge Friendly's views in arguing that it will not be punished, but rather destroyed, by a multitude of punitive damage awards. Nevertheless, the Sixth Circuit, while characterizing Judge Friendly's dicta as

---

[32] 378 F2d 832 (2d Cir 1967).

[33] *Id* 839.

[34] *Id* 840.

[35] *Id* 841.

[36] Owen, *Punitive Damages in Products Liability Litigation,* 74 Mich L Rev 1257, 1324 (1976).

[37] *Id* 1324-25. *But see,* Owen, *Problems in Assessing Punitive Damages Against Manufacturers of Defective Products,* 49 Chi L Rev 1 (1982).

[38] 691 F2d 811 (6th Cir 1982).

an "interesting essay," held that relief, if any, is a legislative function.[39]

Absent legislative action, however, trial judges handling mass cases continue to be confronted by the enormous management problems raised in *Roginsky.* Although he did not mention punitive damages class actions, Judge Friendly did touch upon one possible solution:

> If there was any way in which all cases could be assembled before a single court, as in a limitation proceeding in admiralty, it might be possible for a jury to make one award to be held for appropriate distribution among all successful plaintiffs, although even as to this the difficulties are apparent.[40]

A trial judge's recent espousal of the class action as a device for solving these punitive damages problems in the *Dalkon Shield* litigation, discussed below, is thus a natural outgrowth of Judge Friendly's views.

§20.09   —The Dalkon Shield Claims

A.H. Robins, a company whose net worth is slightly over $280 million, faces over 1600 suits from women who claim a variety of injuries from their use of the Dalkon Shield intrauterine device.[41] These suits seek compensatory damages of over $500 million and claim punitive damages in excess of $2.3 billion.[42]

In 1975, cases brought in federal court were transferred to a single district for coordinated pretrial proceedings, and when completed they were remanded to their transferor districts.[43] As a result, District Judge Spencer Williams of the Northern District of California has 165 Dalkon Shield cases pending for trial before him.[44] After presiding over one jury trial which lasted nine weeks, the court observed that the "monumental problems" of the litigation reflect "the obvious inability of our traditional mode of case-by-case litigation to deal with repetitive litigation of the same underlying facts,"[45] and that "any attempts to try all these cases would bankrupt the district court's calendar and result in a tedium of repetition lasting well into the next century."[46]

After concluding he had the power to do so on his own motion, Judge Williams certified two class actions: first, a nationwide class of all plaintiffs seeking to recover punitive damages, and second, a statewide liability class

---

[39] *Id* 814.

[40] 378 F2d at 839-40 n 11.

[41] *In re* Northern Dist of Cal "Dalkon Shield" IUD Prod Liab Litig, 526 F Supp 887, 892-93 (ND Cal 1981), *Preliminary opinion,* 521 F Supp 1188, 1193 (ND Cal 1981).

[42] 526 F Supp at 893.

[43] 521 F Supp at 1190.

[44] 526 F Supp at 893.

[45] 521 F Supp at 1191.

[46] 526 F Supp at 893.

consisting of all persons having filed suit against A.H. Robins in the California federal courts.[47] On a certified interlocutory appeal to the Ninth Circuit, the district court was reversed on both counts.[48] The opinions of both courts with respect to the punitive damages class are discussed in §§20.10-20.11.

§20.10 —Nationwide Punitive Damages Class Action: District Court Opinion

The district court observed that two jury verdicts for punitive damages ($75,000 and $6.2 million) had already been entered against A.H. Robins[49] and, citing *Roginsky*,[50] expressed straightforward reasons for sua sponte certification of a punitive damages class action:

> It is clear that the amount of punitive damages sought far exceeds the available net worth of the company. This fact poses two very real threats if actions on this issue continue on an individual basis: 1) The company will be unable to respond to claims for punitive damages due to actual or constructive bankruptcy; or 2) At some point in the future, courts could rule that the aggregate sum already assessed against the defendant company in punitive damages was such that as a matter of law the company had been sufficiently punished and therefore punitive damage claims would be dismissed as a matter of law.[51]

The court viewed its paramount responsibility to be the collective interests of the plaintiffs in equal access to a punitive damages recovery fund as opposed to the individual interest of each plaintiff's attorney in securing a separate punitive damage award,[52] observing that: "The potential for the constructive bankruptcy of A.H. Robins, a company whose net worth is $280,394,000.00, raises the unconscionable possibility that large numbers of plaintiffs who are not first in line at the courthouse door will be deprived of a practical means of redress."[53]

Concluding that "[i]n mass tort liability situations the inequity and harmful effect of civil punitive damages are multiplied many times over,"[54] the court

---

[47] *Id* 896.

[48] 693 F2d 847 (9th Cir 1982).

[49] *In re* Northern Dist of Cal "Dalkon Shield" IUD Prod Liab Litig, 526 F Supp 887, 892-93 (ND Cal 1981), *preliminary opinion*, 521 F Supp 1188, 1193 (ND Cal 1981).

[50] Roginsky v Richardson-Merrell, Inc, 375 F2d 832 (2d Cir 1967), discussed in **§20.08.**

[51] *In re* Northern Dist of Cal "Dalkon Shield" IUD Prod Liab Litig, 521 F Supp 1188, 1193 (ND Cal 1981).

[52] *Id* 1192.

[53] *Id* 1191; *In re* Northern Dist of Cal "Dalkon Shield" IUD Prod Liab Litig, 526 FSupp 887, 893 (ND Cal 1981).

[54] 526 FSupp at 898.

found that the requirements of Rule 23(a) of the Federal Rules of Civil Procedure had been met and certified a nationwide class under Rule 23(b)(1)(B),[55] to be composed of all persons who have asserted claims for punitive damages against A.H. Robins relating to the Dalkon Shield.[56] The creation of such a class, the members of which would have equal potential access to the limited fund available as contemplated by Rule 23(b)(1)(B), seemed to the district court to be the most equitable way to deal with these claims, despite objections from various plaintiffs' counsel that exhaustion of the fund was not a certainty, that the court did not have subject matter or personal jurisdiction over nonresident plaintiffs who opposed such a class, and that there were conflicts among the states regarding the manner in which punitive damages are to be awarded.

§20.11 —Nationwide Punitive Damages Class Action: Court of Appeals Opinion

While voicing some sympathy for the district court's approach to the punitive damages question discussed in **§20.10,** the Ninth Circuit reversed Judge Williams' decision and decertified the class.[57] Although "not necessarily ruling out the class action tool as a means for expediting multi-party product liability actions,"[58] the court determined that even if the specific requirements of Rule 23(b)(1)(B) of the Federal Rules of Civil Procedure had been met, the more general requirements of commonality, typicality, and adequacy of representation set forth in Rule 23(a) had not been satisfied in the case before it. The court held:

1. That A.H. Robins' knowledge of the safety of its product, what information may have been withheld from the public, and when that information existed presented uncommon questions

2. That the 50 states apply varying punitive damage standards

3. That since no plaintiff supported class certification, no one could be said to have a claim typical of others

4. That none of the plaintiffs' counsel on appeal was willing to serve as class counsel, rendering it difficult to assume the adequacy of unwanted lead counsel appointed by the court[59]

The court also agreed with the plaintiffs that since the present record did not inescapably lead to the conclusion that punitive damage awards would result in the consequences perceived by the district court, and since no eviden-

---

[55] *Id* 895.

[56] *Id* 921.

[57] Abed v AH Robins Co, 693 F2d 847, 857 (9th Cir 1982), *cert denied,* 103 S Ct 817 (1983).

[58] *Id* 857.

[59] *Id* 850-51.

tiary hearing had been held to receive proof of Robins' financial position, insurance coverage, and settlement experience, a Rule 23(b)(1)(B) class should not have been certified even if the requirements of Rule 23(a) had been met.[60]

§20.12   —The Trial Judge's Viewpoint

In addressing a judges' conference in December of 1982, Judge Williams took note of the avalanche of mass tort suits descending on the courts and argued that the class action is the best device available to manage such cases, in light of the competing interests of the plaintiffs, the defendants, and the courts themselves.[61] The judge acknowledged that the plaintiffs' counsel are primary opponents of class treatment but argued that their opposition ignored the primary function of the class action as a method to foster judicial economy and efficiency.[62]

The judge also addressed what he termed the "unarticulated antipathy and aversion"[63] displayed by appellate courts towards the use of class actions in mass tort litigation and specifically criticized the Ninth Circuit's treatment of the punitive damages class in the *Dalkon Shield* litigation.[64] The judge reiterated his view that the award of punitive damages in one case necessarily affects the potential recovery in a later case and stated that when the assets of a company are exceeded by the punitive damages claimed, the assets should constitute the limited fund contemplated by Rule 23(b)(1) of the Federal Rules of Civil Procedure. He disagreed with the Ninth Circuit's imposition of the requirement that separate punitive damage awards must *inescapably* affect later awards, since Rule 23(b) speaks only of the *risk* of such a happenstance.[65]

§20.13   —The Plaintiff's Viewpoint

Personal injury cases have traditionally been prosecuted on a contingent fee basis. Counsel for the plaintiff in effect makes a personal investment in the case and shares with his or her client any settlement or damage award. In normal circumstances, the plaintiff's attorney has no desire to reduce the value of his or her investment by sharing it with others, nor does he or she perceive any economic advantage in pooling the verdict potential inherent in his or her claim with other claimants similarly situated, or with those whose claim is so small as to make it unlikely to be brought, even on a contingent fee basis.

---

[60] *Id* 851-52.

[61] Mass Tort Class Actions: Are They Going, Going, Gone (paper delivered by Judge Spencer M. Williams at the Fifteenth Transferee Judges' Conference on Dec 8-9, 1982 in Carefree, Ariz [hereinafter Williams Speech].

[62] Williams Speech *supra* note 57, at 9-10.

[63] Williams Speech *supra* note 57, at 11.

[64] Williams Speech, *supra* note 57 at 15-16.

[65] Williams Speech, *supra* note 57 at 16.

Accordingly, unless counsel can be assured of playing a leading role (and thus receive a substantial share of court-awarded counsel fees), he or she is unlikely to seek class action certification. The desire to pursue cases on an individual basis is even greater when the potential for punitive damages exists, since those cases which reach trial first have the best chance to recover punitive damages before the defendant's ability to pay becomes threatened by bankruptcy.

§20.14   —The Defendant's Viewpoint

The defendants normally oppose any attempts at class action certification. Despite the heavy cost of litigating on a case-by-case basis (whereby some cases will probably be won and others lost), the traditional thinking is that certification of a class increases the overall risk to a defendant by including claims which would not otherwise be brought, and by presenting the possibility of a class wide determination of liability by a single court or jury. When the stakes are high, as in most mass tort litigation, a defendant is normally unwilling to place all his or her eggs in one basket. These considerations do not necessarily apply with equal force to the potential for punitive damages. Absent class action treatment, a defendant faces the distinct possibility of being punished many times over for the same wrong, with the threat of bankruptcy as a result. To the extent the class action device holds out the possibility of a limited fund to cap liability for punitive damages, it has an attraction for a mass tort defendant.

§20.15   —Future for Punitive Damages Class Actions

As recently as 1976, there were only three appellate cases sustaining jury awards of punitive damages in products liability suits.[66] The largest such award was $250,000. Since then, such awards have numbered in the hundreds, and several have been in the multimillion dollar range. Some attorneys active on the plaintiffs' side in the mass tort field have recently begun to advocate pooling of resources as a useful method of prosecuting claims which are national in scope. As the impact of these developments becomes felt at the trial court level around the country, the utilization of the punitive damages class action will continue to receive heightened attention. As Judge Williams observed,[67] "[D]espite the few recent appellate setbacks, the impetus for future

---

[66] Toole v Richard-Merrill Inc, 251 Cal App 2d 689, 60 Cal Rptr 398 (1967) ($250,000); Gillham v Admiral Corp, 523 F2d 102 (6th Cir 1975), *cert denied,* 424 US 913 (1976) ($10,000); Moore v Jewell Tea Co, 116 Ill App 2d 109, 253 NE2d 636 (1969), *affd,* 46 Ill 2d 288, 263 NE2d 103 (1970) ($10,000); Owen, *Problems in Assessing Damages Against Manufacturers of Defective Products,* 49 Chi L Rev 1, 2-3 n 9 (1982).

[67] Mass Tort Class Actions: Are They Going, Going, Gone (paper delivered by Judge Spencer M. Williams at the Fifteenth Transferee Judges' Conference on Dec 8-9, 1982 in Carefree, Ariz) at 18.

class actions is growing, not abating, at the trial court level, as judges become acutely aware of the need for some coordinated treatment of these mass filings."

§20.16 Collateral Estoppel and the DES Litigation

When it is clear that a specific issue has been resolved against a party who had a full and fair opportunity to litigate the matter, he or she and those in privity with him or her are precluded by the doctrine of collateral estoppel from relitigating that issue in a subsequent action. The purpose of the doctrine is to promote judicial economy by foreclosing repetitious litigation of previously decided questions.[68]

Since mass torts by their nature entail hundreds or perhaps thousands of claims, judicial resources are taxed to their utmost, and the pressures to dispose of cases in an efficient manner are formidable. In the absence of class action certification, the potential use of *offensive* collateral estoppel to facilitate the disposition of large numbers of actions by eliminating general liability issues is receiving increased attention by trial judges. Recent appellate decisions have shown, however, that it is difficult to apply the elements of the doctrine in mass tort litigation without sacrificing fundamental rights in the name of judicial economy.

§20.17 —The DES Claims

An estimated one thousand suits have been brought against Eli Lilly & Company and other pharmaceutical manufacturers by *DES daughters,* many of whom claim to have contracted cervical cancer as a result of their mother's use of the drug DES during pregnancy to prevent miscarriage. In most of these suits, the plaintiff is unable to identify the manufacturer who supplied the DES used by her mother. The plaintiffs have pursued a number of theories to overcome this obstacle to the traditional causation-in-fact requirement in tort litigation.

Bichler v Eli Lilly & Co[69] was the first trial of a DES case in the United States. The plaintiff, unable to prove that the DES ingested by her mother was produced by Lilly, sought to impose liability on a *concert of action* theory, contending that Lilly's failure to perform adequate testing of the drug was a result of concerted action with other drug manufacturers which rendered the product defective, no matter who actually supplied the DES used by the plaintiff's mother.[70] The jury was instructed that consciously parallel behavior of the drug companies in securing Food and Drug Administration (FDA) approval to market DES as a miscarriage preventative could, without more, permit the

---

[68] Parklane Hosiery Co v Shore, 439 US 322, 332 (1979).

[69] 79 AD2d 317, 436 NYS2d 625 (1st Dept 1981).

[70] *Id.*

inference of an implied agreement not to conduct appropriate tests on pregnant mice. The jury was also instructed that it could find that Lilly's failure to conduct these tests substantially aided and encouraged other DES manufacturers to do likewise, without any express agreement among them.

The jury returned a $500,000 verdict in favor of the plaintiff, finding by way of a special verdict that a reasonably prudent manufacturer would have tested the drug on pregnant mice and would not have marketed the drug on the basis of the test results. Under the charge given to it, the jury also found that Lilly and other drug manufacturers acted in concert with each other, thereby eliminating the requirement that the plaintiff identify Lilly as the actual producer of the drug.

The verdict was affirmed by the New York Court of Appeals.[71] The court sustained the trial court's instructions on the ground that proper exception thereto had not been taken and concluded that the evidence supported the verdict under the instructions as given. While the court's opinion appears to sanction, in general terms, the application of a concert of action theory to DES litigation, the narrow basis on which the charge was upheld leaves some doubt as to the validity of the concert of action instructions and the proof requirements of such a theory in subsequent cases.

Predictably, numerous DES plaintiffs have sought to use *Bichler* to estop Lilly collaterally from relitigating the issues resolved aginst it by the *Bichler* jury. Most of these efforts have been unsuccessful. In at least one case, however, *Bichler* has been given offensive collateral estoppel effect. In *Kaufman v Eli Lilly & Co*,[72] the judge who presided over the *Bichler* trial granted partial summary judgment in favor of the plaintiff. The court found that the issues and theory of recovery were the same in both cases, and that Lilly had a full and fair opportunity to contest those issues in *Bichler*. The court also rejected Lilly's contentions that the *Bichler* verdict was inconsistent with DES decisions in other states, finding that *Bichler* was the first DES case to be tried, that the facts in other cases were different, and that the law in other states was not the same as New York's. The court therefore held: "From the standpoint of avoiding the possibility of inconsistent results in the same jurisdiction, and the conservation of judicial manpower without unfairness to the parties this is a logical and appropriate case in which to apply the doctrine of collateral estoppel."[73]

Bichler and *Kaufman* combined suggest the possibility of foreclosing a manufacturer from defending his or her product after he or she loses one case, even if the manufacturer did not make the product involved in that case. If *Kaufman* is sustained on appeal, the two cases taken together could have important consequences not only for DES litigation in New York, but for other mass tort litigation as well. Some of the principal elements of the estoppel doctrine as applied in *Kaufman* and as treated in other mass tort cases are summarized in §§20.18-20.24.

---

[71] 55 NY2d 571, 436 NE2d 182, 450 NYS2d 766 (1982).
[72] 116 Misc 2d 351, 455 NYS2d 329 (Sup Ct 1982).
[73] *Id.*

§20.18 —Issue Identity

The doctrine of collateral estoppel is devoted to issue preclusion. The party asserting estoppel must show, inter alia, that the issue to be concluded is identical to the one litigated in the prior action. The critical ultimate issue in any products liability litigation is whether the product is *defective* or *unreasonably dangerous*. The potential application of collateral estoppel to mass tort cases thus has tremendous significance, for it presents the theoretical possibility of eliminating the central liability questions in hundreds of subsequent cases once an adverse verdict on that issue is rendered against the manufacturer.

The doctrine, however, has the capacity to work tremendous unfairness, particularly when attempts are made to give preclusive effects to judgments which have not clearly resolved the issue of *defect*. It is for this reason that collateral estoppel is inappropriate where the prior judgment is ambiguous. It is essential, therefore, that the previous judgment be scrutinized carefully before any preclusive effect is given to it. If the judgment could have been based on more than one distinctive issue, each such issue may be litigated again.

In *Kaufman*,[74] the court found the issues to be identical with those in *Bichler*,[75] holding that:

> [I]t is difficult to conceive of two cases which could be more similar from a factual standpoint: In each case the plaintiff, a female, allegedly contracted cancer of the cervix upon reaching puberty, as a result of her mother's ingestion of DES in 1953 or early 1954 while pregnant with plaintiff. In each case the plaintiff, because of the passage of time, is unable to identify the manufacturer of the DES her mother took. And in each case plaintiff seeks to recover on the basis of the same alleged wrongdoing by Lilly, and upon the same theory, *i.e.*, concerted action.[76]

The court also determined that the specific findings of the *Bichler* jury were necessary prerequisites to the ultimate verdict in that case and would be equally necessary to a resolution of the *Kaufman* case. Accordingly, the court ruled that Lilly was bound by the following facts:

1. DES was not reasonably safe in the treatment of accidents during pregnancy when it was ingested by plaintiff's mother

2. When plaintiff's mother ingested DES, Lilly should have foreseen that DES might cause cancer in the offspring of pregnant women who took it

3. A reasonably prudent drug manufacturer would have tested DES on pregnant mice before marketing it

---

[74] 116 Misc 2d 351, 455 NYS2d 329 (Sup Ct 1982).

[75] Bichler v Eli Lilly & Co, 56 NY2d 571, 436 NE2d 182, 450 NYS2d 776 (1982).

[76] 116 Misc 2d 351, 455 NYS2d 329 (Sup Ct 1982).

4. Such tests would have shown that DES causes cancer in the offspring of pregnant mice

5. Knowing that DES causes cancer in the offspring of pregnant mice, a reasonably prudent drug manufacturer would not have marketed DES for use in treating accidents during pregnancy

6. Lilly and other drug manufacturers acted in concert with each other in the testing and marketing of DES for use in treating accidents during pregnancy

Preclusion of these issues limits the liability aspect of the *Kaufman* case to a trial on the issue of whether DES was the proximate cause of the plaintiff's cancer. If upheld on appeal, *Kaufman* also foretells similar preclusion in other New York DES cases against Lilly, dramatically illustrating the potential impact of the first verdict in favor of a plaintiff in a mass tort litigation.

§20.19   —Inconsistent Verdicts

A mass tort defendant, confronted with numerous but separate claims, may successfully defend many of the cases on the merits yet run the risk of having his or her first unsuccessful defense operate as a bar to further litigation on the central question of whether his or her product is in fact defective or unreasonably dangerous. The unfairness engendered by the automatic application of collateral estoppel in such circumstances is illustrated by Professor Currie's well-known example as cited by the Supreme Court in *Parklane Hosiery Co v Shore*:[77]

> A railroad collision injures 50 passengers all of whom bring separate actions against the railroad. After the railroad wins the first 25 suits, a plaintiff wins in suit 26. Professor Currie argues that offensive use of collateral estoppel should not be applied so as to allow plaintiffs 27 through 50 automatically to recover.[78]

The existence of inconsistent verdicts is thus a strong argument against the use of collateral estoppel. In *Hardy v Johns-Manville Sales Corp*,[79] the Fifth Circuit applied Professor Currie's example to the asbestos litigation, observing that "[o]ne jury's determination should not, merely because it comes later in time, bind another jury's determination of an issue over which there are equally reasonable resolutions of doubt."[80]

Approximately 70 asbestos cases had been tried at the time of the *Hardy* appeal. About half of those resulted in verdicts in favor of the defendants. At

---

[77] 439 US 322 (1979).

[78] *Id* 331 n 14.

[79] 681 F2d 334 (5th Cir 1982).

[80] *Id* 346.

least one of those cases represented a determination that the asbestos products involved were not unreasonably dangerous. The others were ambiguous in terms of discrete issues resolved. The Fifth Circuit held that under these circumstances, the trial court's selection of an early asbestos decision (upholding a jury verdict of defect) to work an estoppel was arbitrary and erroneous.

Inconsistency of verdicts has resulted in the denial of collateral estoppel in other mass tort contexts. In *Erbeck v United States*,[81] the court refused to preclude the government from litigating the adequacy of warnings given by it in connection with the swine flu immunization program. Although a previous case resulted in a judgment against the government on precisely this issue, earlier decisions were in favor of the government. Citing *Parklane Hosiery*, the court in *Erbeck* held: "The inconsistency of opinions where multiple parties are suing one defendant in similar (albeit not identical) fact situations is the exact instance where it would be unfair for the trial court to allow the use of offensive collateral estoppel against defendant."[82]

These decisions indicate that the first trial on the merits is the most important one from a collateral estoppel viewpoint. If the defendant loses that first case, he or she will not have a argument regarding verdict inconsistency when the plaintiff in the second case invokes collateral estoppel. If the issue of defect has been unambiguously and necessarily resolved in the first trial and is squarely presented again, the defendant will not be able to show nonidentity of issues. Unless other circumstances exist to show that the defendant did not have a full and fair opportunity to litigate the question of defect (or any other material issue) at the first trial, he or she may face the prospect that he or she will be limited to contesting matters such as individual causation and damages in what may turn out to be thousands of cases.

This is precisely the dilemma facing Lilly by virtue of the *Kaufman* decision,[83] for the court rejected Lilly's argument that the verdict in *Bichler*[84] is inconsistent with *subsequent* DES decisions:

> This is not a situation where a number of plaintiffs have successively tried DES cases against Lilly and lost, the issues in each case having been resolved in Lilly's favor, and a plaintiff is then finally successful, and subsequent plaintiffs seek to rely upon collateral estoppel on the basis of the successful plaintiff's verdict. So far as this court is aware, the Bichler case was the first trial of a DES case in the United States. To date it is still the only DES case that has been tried in New York State. Every case cited by Lilly in which collateral estoppel on the basis of Bichler was rejected, was in a foreign jurisdiction. In each case the court cited as the basis for its refusal to apply the doctrine the fact that its law differed from the applicable law in New York; or that it did not have before it the trial

---

[81] 533 F Supp 444 (SD Ohio 1982).
[82] *Id* 447.
[83] Kaufman v Eli Lilly & Co, 2 Prod Liab Rep (CCH) ¶9441 (NY Sup Ct 1982).
[84] Bichler v Eli Lilly & Co, 56 NY2d 571, 436 NE2d 182, 450 NYS2d 776 (1982).

record or pleadings in the Bichler case; or the facts were different from those in Bichler. None of those factors are here present.[85]

§20.20   —Full and Fair Opportunity to Litigate

Before offensive collateral estoppel can be applied, the practical realities of the prior litigation maust be examined to determine whether issue in question was fully and fairly contested: "The point of the inquiry, of course, is not to decide whether the prior determination should be vacated but to decide whether it should be given conclusive effect beyond the case in which it was made . . . ."[86]

> A comprehensive list of the various factors which should enter into a determination whether a party has had his day in court would include such considerations as the size of the claim, the forum of the prior litigation, the use of initiative, the extent of the litigation, the competence and experience of counsel, the availability of new evidence, indications of a compromise verdict, differences in the applicable law and foreseeability of future litigation.[87]

Some of the factors set forth above have been litigated in mass tort cases.

§20.21   —Vigor of Defense

If a defendant goes to trial in a personal injury case without realizing that he or she may have encountered only the tip of a massive products liability litigation iceberg, he or she can hardly be expected to defend the case with the vigor he or she would employ had he or she known that an adverse verdict would bind him or her in many future cases.

It was this lack of foreseeability which caused the *Hardy* court[88] to conclude that: "[E]ven if the *Borel* verdict had been unambiguous and the sole verdict issued on point, application of collateral estoppel would still be unfair . . . because it is very doubtful that these defendants could have foreseen that their $68,000 liability to plaintiff *Borel* would foreshadow multimillion dollar asbestos liability."[89]

Certainly a defendant has little incentive to defend vigorously an action for a relatively small amount of damages when other lawsuits are not on the

---

[85] New York LJ, Oct 29, 1982 at 3.

[86] Gilberg v Barbieri, 53 NY 285, 292, 441 NYS2d 49, 51, 423 NE2d 807, 809 (1982).

[87] Schwartz v Public Admr, 24 NY2d 65m 72, 246 NE2d 725, 729, 298 NYS2d 955, 961 (1969).

[88] Hardy v Johns-Manville Sales Corp, 681 F2d 334 (5th Cir 1982).

[89] *Id* 346.

horizon. As the Fifth Circuit noted, however, "the matter is relative."[90] Indeed, in *Kaufman*[91] the court observed that at the time of the *Bichler*[92] trial, there were a substantial number of DES cases pending against Lilly throughout the country and found that Lilly was fully aware of the significance of *Bichler*. Whether other similar lawsuits could have been foreseen, or their magnitude assessed, are themselves factual questions which may not easily be resolved in other mass tort situations.

§20.22 —Compromise Verdict

A verdict which is the product of jury compromise cannot be used for collateral estoppel purposes, since the judgment is not based on a fair determination of the issues.[93] Proving compromise is difficult, however. In *Kaufman*,[94] Lilly argued that the *Bichler*[95] verdict may have been compromised because two of the jurors allegedly agreed to vote for liability if the others would agree to reduce the size of the damage award and sought leave to depose the jurors to establish this fact. The trial judge denied Lilly's motion on the ground that to permit such depositions would violate the New York rule against the impeachment of a jury verdict.[96]

§20.23 —Privity and Estoppel of Nonparties

Due process requires that collateral estoppel be applied only against a party or someone in privity to the prior judgment.[97] The trial court in *Hardy*[98] applied estoppel against defendants who were not parties to the *Borel*[99] judgment by expanding the concept of privity to include all members of the industry which produced the generic product, asbestos, which was the subject of the *Borel* trial. The district court reached this result by first deciding that Texas law supports the adoption of some form of industry-wide liability as set forth in *Sindell v Abbott Laboratories*.[100] The court then concluded[101] that under this

---

[90] *Id* 347.

[91] Kaufman v Eli Lilly & Co, 2 Prod Liab Rep (CCH) ¶9441 (NY Sup Ct 1982).

[92] Bichler v Eli Lilly & Co, 56 NY2d 571, 436 NE2d 182, 450 NYS2d 776 (1982).

[93] Schwartz v Public Admr, 24 NY2d 65, 72, 246 NE2d 725, 729, 298 NYS2d 955, 961 (1969).

[94] Kaufman v Eli Lilly & Co, 2 Prod Liab Rep (CCH) ¶9441 (NY Sup Ct 1982).

[95] Bichler v Eli Lilly & Co, 56 NY2d 571, 436 NE2d 182, 450 NYS2d 776 (1982).

[96] Kaufman v Eli Lilly & Co, 116 Misc 2d 351, 455 NYS2d 329 (Sup Ct 1982).

[97] Parklane Hosiery Co v Shore, 439 US 322, 332 (1979); Hardy v Johns-Manville Sales Corp, 681 F2d 334, 364 (5th Cir 1982).

[98] Hardy v Johns-Manville Sales Corp, 681 F2d 334 (5th Cir 1982).

[99] Borel v Fibreboard Paper Prod Corp, 493 F2d 1073 (5th Cir 1973), *cert denied*, 419 US 869 (1974).

[100] 26 Cal 3d 588, 607 P2d 924, 163 Cal Rptr 132, *cert denied*, 449 US 912 (1980).

[101] *Id* at 591, 607 P2d at 927, 163 Cal Rptr at 135.

theory of liability, the asbestos manufacturers who were not defendants in *Borel* shared an indentity of interest with the *Borel* defendants sufficient to establish privity with them.

The Fifth Circuit reversed, holding that "the trial court's actions here transgress the bounds of due process," observing that "the fact that all the non-*Borel* defendants, like the *Borel* defendants, are engaged in the manufacture of asbestos-containing products does not evince privity among the parties."[102]

The Fifth Circuit adhered to the basic *control* requirement of collateral estoppel privity. Membership in an industry does not mean that a litigation against some members is controlled by others. Since the nonparty industry members cannot fairly be said to have had their day in court, a judgment against their competitors cannot foreclose them from contesting charges that the product sold by them is defective.

Despite the fact that *concert of action* necessarily implies participation by other industry members, the court in *Kaufman*[103] declined to extend its collateral estoppel ruling to Lilly's codefendants and severed the action as against them, finding that: "[T]o require the other drug manufacturers to be tried by a jury which has been advised of the findings against Lilly arising as a result of collateral estoppel would be highly prejudicial to them."[104]

§20.24 —Future of Collateral Estoppel

The doctrine of collateral estoppel was not developed to cure the problems inherent in mass tort cases. Its application to this kind of litigation has proven to be a difficult problem which is beginning to generate its own body of law.

One of the major drawbacks to the widespread employment of collateral estoppel in mass tort cases is the contests over the applicability of the doctrine in a particular case may consume so much litigation time and judicial attention as to detract from the true merits of the issue to be resolved. At least one court has taken note of the fact that the inquiry necessary to determine whether estoppel should apply may undermine the goal of judicial economy which the doctrine is meant to foster. In *Goodson v McDonough Power Equipment, Inc,*[105] the Ohio Supreme Court declined to abandon the requirement of mutuality in product liability cases involving claims of defective design:

> Upon a review and consideration of this process which is applied in federal and other jurisdictions which have adopted nonmutuality as a general rule for collateral estoppel, we must conclude that there is within such procedure the suggestion that time-consuming and costly investigations may well be necessitated into collateral issues that may be essential-

---

[102] Hardy v Johns-Manville Sales Corp, 681 F2d 334, 340 (5th Cir 1982).

[103] Kaufman v Eli Lilly & Co, 2 Prod Liab Rep ¶9441 (NY Sup Ct 1982).

[104] *Id* 3.

[105] 2 Ohio St 3d 193, 443 NE2d 978 (1983).

ly irrelevant to the actual issues between the parties then present before the court. It seems that these procedures would often offset any savings derived from collateral estoppel, and may indeed increase the total amount of litigation, negating one of the prime supportive arguments, i.e., the economy of the judicial process.[106]

Since a collateral estoppel skirmish can be decisive of an entire mass tort battle, it is safe to predict that courts which disregard the *Goodson* caveat will continue to face issue preclusion questions as mass tort litigation grows.

§20.25   Bankruptcy and the Asbestos Litigation

Even if a mass tort defendant successfully avoids the impact of class action certification or offensive collateral estoppel and sustains relatively few punitive damage awards, the company has no control over suits likely to arise in the future. To the extent that a widely distributed product is allegedly capable of causing harm many years after its sale or use, the sheer number of prospective claims is potentially catastrophic to the product manufacturer. The significance of such a dilemma became dramatically apparent in August of 1982, when the Johns-Manville Corporation, which is a defendant in thousands of asbestos-related damages actions, filed a petition for reorganization under Chapter 11 of the Bankruptcy Code.[107]

Prior to filing its petition, Manville had been reasonably successful in the defense of 16,500 existing asbestos cases. The plaintiffs' attempts to obtain class action certification[108] and to employ offensive collateral estoppel[109] have been denied. Punitive damages were awarded in 10 cases, averaging $616,000 per case.[110] The company remains financially sound, with a net worth of $1.2 billion, and is capable of dealing with those claims which are presently pending.[111] Manville, however, estimates that at least another 30,000 claims will be filed against it through the beginning of the twenty-first century.[112] The reorganization petition was filed as a result of the threat of prospective insolvency posed by these anticipated claims.

The use of the Bankruptcy Code by a solvent company to obtain relief from present and future mass tort claims has generated considerable controversy. As a result, the bankruptcy laws themselves are receiving unprecedented atten-

---

[106] *Id* 198, 443 NE2d at 983-84.

[107] 11 USC §101 *et seq.* Two other asbestos producers, UNR Industries, Inc and Amatex Corp, have also filed reorganization. See Comment, *The Manville Bankruptcy: Treating Mass Tort Claims in Chapter 11 Procedures,* 96 Harv L Rev 1121 (1983).

[108] Yandle v PPG Indus, 65 FRD 566 (ED Tex 1974).

[109] Hardy v Johns-Manville Sales Corp, 681 F2d 334 (5th Cir 1982).

[110] Comment, *The Manville Bankruptcy: Treating Mass Tort Claims in Chapter 11 Proceedings,* 96 Harv L Rev 1121, 1132 n 54 (1983).

[111] *Id* 1121 n 4.

[112] *Id* 1122 n 7.

tion from mass tort litigants. Three significant issues currently being litigated in the asbestos reorganization proceedings are:

1. The requirement that a bankruptcy petition be filed in good faith
2. The scope of the automatic stay in bankruptcy
3. The extent to which tort claimants (existing and potential) can be dealt with by the Bankruptcy Court.

§20.26 —Good Faith

The current Bankruptcy Code became effective on October 1, 1979, replacing the Bankruptcy Act of 1898 (Bankruptcy Act).[113] The Bankruptcy Code provides for reorganization under Chapter 11[114] and liquidations under Chapter 7. A case under the Bankruptcy Code may be commenced voluntarily by the debtor[115] or involuntarily by creditors of the debtor.[116]

Under the old Bankruptcy Act, in order to file a petition for a reorganization, it was necessary for the petition to state that the corporation was insolvent or unable to pay its debts as they matured.[117] There is no such requirement in the voluntary filing section of the Bankruptcy Code. It is "no longer . . . necessary for a Chapter 11 debtor to allege insolvency or inability to pay its debts as they mature as was the case under the [prior] Act."[118] The petition of Johns-Manville Corporation, filed on August 26, 1982, merely states that the petitioner is qualified to file this petition and is entitled to the benefits of Title 11, United States Code as a voluntary debtor.

A committee representing the interests of asbestos claimants has moved to dismiss the Manville petition, contending that it was filed in bad faith as part of a long-standing corporate policy designed to prevent full compensation to

---

[113] The Bankruptcy Code was adopted under the authority of Article I, Section 8, clause 4 of the United States Constitution, which vests Congress with the power "to establish . . . uniform Laws on the subject of Bankruptcies throughout the United States."

[114] See generally Anderson, Chapter 11 Reorganization (Shepard's/McGraw-Hill 1983).

[115] Bankruptcy Code §301, 11 USC §301.

[116] Bankruptcy Code §303, 11 USC §303. Generally, an involuntary case can be commenced by three or more creditors holding, in the aggregate, at least $5,000 of unsecured claims (which are not contingent as to liability). Bankruptcy Code §303(b), 11 USC §303(b). The petitioning creditors, in an involuntary case, must prove that the debtor is generally not paying its debts as they become due or that within the preceding 120 days, a custodian was appointed to take charge of substantially all of the debtor's property. Bankruptcy Code §303(h), 11 USC §303(h).

[117] Bankruptcy Act §130 (ch X), former 11 USC §323, §323 (ch XI), former 11 USC §§201, 501, 701 & 801 §423 (ch XII), former 11 USC §401.

[118] P. Murphy, Creditors' Rights in Bankruptcy §3.02, at 3-2 (Shepard's/McGraw-Hill 1981).

victims of asbestos exposure. Under §1112(b) of the Bankruptcy Code,[119] a court may dismiss a petition "for cause." At least one court has held that this section gives the court the power to dismiss a petition not filed in good faith.[120] Another court has held that " '[g]ood faith' must . . . be viewed as an implicit prerequisite to the filing or continuation of a proceeding under Chapter 11 of the Code."[121]

Under the prior bankruptcy law, the issue of good faith filings frequently involved the formation of the debtor entity immediately prior to the filing.[122] However, so-called bad faith filings were not limited to that circumstance and "can be summarized as conduct which is inconsistent with underlying purposes and contemplation of the reorganization and rehabilitation process and constitutes a perversion of legislative intent."[123]

The mere fact that a solvent company files a petition solely to obtain protection from *pending* litigation does not appear to constitute a perversion of legislative intent. An example of a situation where litigation was the cause of a filing is *In re Alton Telegraph Printing Co.*[124] A $9 million libel judgment had been obtained against the debtor, and other similar suits were pending. The debtor filed for reorganization under Chapter 11. Although the debtor had not been able to obtain a bond to forestall execution of the adverse judgment pending the appeal, the provisions of §362(a)[125] automatically stayed execution of the judgment. Shortly after the filing, the judgment creditor sought to have the case dismissed for not having been filed in good faith. The bankruptcy court upheld the filing on the grounds that "the debtor was forced into filing a Chapter 11 bankruptcy petition in order to preserve its status as an ongoing concern and protect its employees and its creditors while the claims against it are litigated."[126]

In an affidavit accompanying its bankruptcy petition, Manville characterized its filing as an "economic imperative" based on its conclusion "that the potential future impact . . . of pending *and future asbestos cases* could and probably will exceed Manville's ability to pay and finance the continuing operation of Manville's businesses."[127] Central to Manville's resort to Chapter 11 is its estimate that *future* cases could result in liabilities of not less than $2 billion over the next 20 years.[128]

No court has yet decided whether a petition by a solvent company based on

[119] 11 USC §1112(b).

[120] *In re* Alton Telegraph Printing Co, 5 Collier Bankr Cas 2d 236 (Bankr SD Ill 1981).

[121] *In re* Victory Constr Co, 1 Collier Bankr Cas 2d 655, 667 (Bankr CD Cal 1981).

[122] Gaffney, Bankruptcy Petition Filed in Bad Faith, 12 UCCLJ 205 (1980).

[123] *In re* Victory Constr Co, Collier Bankr Cas 2d 655, 667 (Bankr CD Cal 1981).

[124] 5 Collier Bankr Cas 2d 236 (Bankr SD Ill 1981).

[125] 11 USC §326(a), discussed in **§20.27.**

[126] 5 Collier Bankr Cas 2d at 241.

[127] *Id* (emphasis added).

[128] *In re* Johns-Manville Corp, Bankr L Rep (CCH) ¶69,022, at 81,776 (Bankr SDNY Jan 10, 1983).

estimated future litigation to be brought by presently unknown claimants can be dismissed for lack of good faith. Congress did not consider this question when it adopted the Bankruptcy Code. The asbestos claimants' pending motion to dismiss challenges the validity of Manville's estimates of future asbestos liability and contends that the filing was motivated solely by Manville's desire to avoid paying just compensation to present asbestos victims. Certainly, the question of whether it is likely that Manville will face insolvency in the reasonably foreseeable future is a pivotal one.[129] In any event, the decision on this motion will have important consequences for any mass tort defendant considering availing itself of the bankruptcy sanctuary.

§20.27 —Automatic Stay

The immediate attraction of the bankruptcy laws to a defendant in pending or threatened litigation is the automatic stay which issues upon the filing of a petition under Chapter 11 and which normally continues until the reorganization proceedings are completed.

Section 362(a) of the Bankruptcy Code provides that the filing of a voluntary or involuntary petition operates as an immediate and automatic stay against, among other things, "the commencement or continuation . . . of a judicial, administrative, or other proceeding against the debtor. . . ."[130] The legislative history of the Bankruptcy Reform Act[131] confirms the central importance and broad scope of the automatic stay provision:

> The automatic stay is one of the fundamental debtor protections provided by the bankruptcy laws. It gives the debtor a breathing spell from his creditors. It stops all collection efforts, all harassment, and all foreclosure actions. It permits the debtor to attempt a repayment or reorganization plan, or simply to be relieved of the financial pressures that drove him into bankruptcy.[132]

When Manville filed its petition in August of 1982, it immediately obtained the benefit of §362(a). All asbestos actions to which it is a party were automatically stayed as against Manville, and new actions against it were precluded. Because Manville is the nation's largest asbestos producer, the impact of this stay on the other parties to these actions is of critical importance. The plaintiffs are deprived of their principal target defendant, and the remaining codefendants (who no longer have viable cross-claims against Manville) become more visible to the triers of fact. Virtually every one of the thousands of asbestos

---

[129] See, e.g., Comment, *The Manville Bankruptcy: Treating Mass Tort Claims in Chapter 11 Proceedings,* 96 Harv L Rev 1121, 1126-28 (1983).

[130] 11 USC §326(a).

[131] Pub L No 95-598, 92 Stat 2549 (1978).

[132] S Rep No 989, 95th Cong, 2d Sess 54-55, *reprinted in* 1978 US Code Cong & Ad News 5787, 5840-41.

cases pending or about to be commenced throughout the country is affected by the stay.

While the plaintiffs have fought the stay by moving to dismiss Manville's petition, Manville's codefendants have attacked the scope of the stay itself. These asbestos suppliers moved in the Bankruptcy Court for an order extending the stay so as to encompass them, requesting the Court to use its equitable power under §105[133] to prevent irreparable injury.[134] In support of their motion, the codefendants cited a number of consequences flowing from the stay in favor of Manville alone:

> First, they allege that there will be a multiplicity of actions resulting in an increased risk of inconsistent verdicts and a great increase in litigation costs to the co-defendants. Second, they claim that the asbestos lawsuits contain issues of comparative negligence, apportionment among joint tortfeasors, and primary and secondary liability with respect to sellers of asbestos products and suppliers of raw asbestos itself. They argue that without Manville as a party to the litigation, each defendant will not be able fairly to determine its share of liability. Third, the co-defendants contend that their ability to obtain discovery and production of documents from Manville has been severely impaired by Manville's filing. Fourth, they argue that long-established coordinated defense efforts between Manville and the co-defendants will be devastated if the relief sought is not granted. Finally, the co-defendants point out that Manville is currently in litigation with a number of insurance companies regarding questions of insurance coverage of asbestos-related claims. See *e.g., Johns-Manville Corp. v. Home Insurance Company,* No. 765226 (Calif. Sup. Ct., San Francisco County). The co-defendants urge that should it be established that Manville is covered by insurance for some or all of the asbestos claims, then Manville's defense of those cases in the courts in which they arose would be able to go forward without a substantial detrimental effect on property of the estate.[135]

The codefendants have urged that if, on the other hand, the stay were broadened so as to bar proceedings against any asbestos supplier, perhaps the whole asbestos problem could be solved:

> The co-defendants have argued at various times during these proceedings that this court consider their plea that a universal stay will have the effect of creating an atmosphere within the Manville reorganization that could accomodate [sic] an industry-wide solution of the entire asbestos

---

[133] §105(a) provides: "The bankruptcy court may issue any order, process or judgment that is necessary or appropriate to carry out the provisions of this title." 11 USC §105(a).

[134] *In re* Johns-Manville Corp, Bankr L Rep (CCH) ¶69,022, at 81,776-77 (Bankr SDNY Jan 10, 1983).

[135] *Id* 81,783.

health-related problem. They hypothesize a suspension of the enormous litigation nationwide which would facilitate the creation of: a superfund or pool to which they, the insurance industry and Manville would contribute; and, a delivery system to the health claimants. To the extent that the co-defendants' purported goal is to join in the creation of an expedient, efficient and fair compensatory delivery system to asbestos victims, their aim is indeed laudable, notwithstanding their self-advancing motivations. The co-defendants assert that extending the stay will shift the focus from asbestos lawsuits and render the asbestos claimants more amenable to cooperate with the debtors and others, including the insurance industry, to achieve a successful reorganization that could include present claimants, as well as future victims who have not as yet manifested symptoms of asbestos-related disease. Indeed, this suspension of the litigation might well serve the purposes urged by the co-defendants.[136]

The Bankruptcy Court nevertheless denied the motion. Ruling that §362 applies only to the debtor and that as a joint tortfeasor Manville was not, as a matter of law, an indispensable party to asbestos litigation, the court held that the propriety of extending the stay to others was a matter "properly lodged with each individual trial court."[137] The court observed that a number of district courts had already denied applications to broaden the stay in asbestos cases pending before them, and that while a few others had entered such stays, they had chosen to do so for reasons unrelated to §362.[138]

The court also rejected the argument that §105 of the Bankruptcy Code empowered the court to provide injunctive relief not otherwise available under §362.[139] The court found that no showing of irreparable harm to the bankruptcy estate had been made and that harm to the codefendants was outweighed by the hardship to asbestos plaintiffs, who "will certainly suffer by the total frustration of their opportunity for a day in court."[140]

The court also declined to lift the stay to permit asbestos lawsuits to proceed to the point of judgment with Manville as a party, an alternative proposed by the codefendants and joined in by the asbestos claimants. Although §362 permits a modification of the automatic stay for cause, the court held that the modification sought would defeat the entire purpose of the reorganization proceeding filed by Manville by "vitiating Manville's breathing spell and frustrating Manville's attempts at formulating a reorganization plan. . . ."[141]

Manville's codefendants sought relief from the Bankruptcy Court's order by filing a petition for writs of prohibition and mandamus in the United States Supreme Court. The moving parties contended that the Court's decision in the

---

[136] *Id* 81,777.
[137] *Id* 81,782.
[138] *Id* 81,780.
[139] *Id* 81,782.
[140] *Id* 81,784.
[141] *Id* 81,786.

Marathon Pipe Line[142] case, which declared that the Bankruptcy Reform Act unconstitutionally granted jurisdiction to bankruptcy judges, deprived the Bankruptcy Court of the power to enforce the automatic stay. On February 22, 1983, the Supreme Court denied the petition,[143] thus leaving the stay intact and permitting asbestos cases to be tried without Manville.

In the first asbestos case to go to trial after Manville filed its petition, the jury returned a verdict in favor of all the remaining defendants, apparently having found that although the plaintiff had been exposed to their products as well as Manville's, it was Manville's asbestos which caused the plaintiff's injury.[144]

§20.28 —Tort Claimants

There are three types of tort claimants who might exist in a mass tort bankruptcy situation:

1. An actual plaintiff (Category 1 Claimant)
2. A claimant who has been allegedly injured, which injury has allegedly manifested itself, but who has not commenced a lawsuit (Category 2 Claimant)
3. A claimant who has been exposed to an allegedly injurious condition, but which injury has not manifested itself (Category 3 Claimant)

Under prior law, an unliquidated or contingent claim would not be allowed and dealt with in a proceeding under the bankruptcy act "if the court shall determine that it is not capable of liquidation or of reasonable estimation or that such liquidation or estimation would unduly delay the administration of the estate or any proceeding under this Act."[145] In a case under the old bankruptcy act, Category 3 Claimants would probably not have been dealt with, on the ground that their claims were not capable of liquidation or reason-

---

[142] Northern Pipeline Constr Co v Marathon Pipe Line Co, 102 S Ct 2858 (1982).

[143] 103 S Ct 1237 (1983).

[144] See NY Times, Oct 30, 1982, at 37, col 1. Manville itself has not secured complete protection by virtue of the automatic stay. In a companion decision, Judge Lifland limited the scope of the stay to no more than 25 key Manville employees named as defendants and subject to discovery in asbestos suits. *In re Johns-Manville Corp,* Bankr L Rep (CCH) ¶69,021, at 81,768-69 (Bankr SDNY Jan 10, 1983). The court did, however, stay the prosecution of a securities class action against certain Manville officers and directors brought shortly after the bankruptcy petition was filed. An adverse judgment in that action would pose a serious threat to the debtor's estate, the court held, since Manville's by-laws require it to indemnify these officers and directors for litigation expenses and liability judgments, and because of the threat of collateral estoppel against Manville itself as a controlling nonparty to the litigation. *Id* 81,770. In addition, the burdensome discovery requirements of that litigation would conflict with the pressing obligations of these executives in formulating a reorganization plan. *Id.*

[145] Bankruptcy Act of 1898, §57(d), former 11 USC §93(d).

able estimation. Even if claims of Category 1 and 2 Claimants could, in theory, have been liquidated or reasonably estimated, they would have been dealt with in the bankruptcy proceeding only if liquidation or reasonable estimation of those claims would not have unduly delayed the proceeding.

The current Bankruptcy Code[146] appears to take a different approach. Section 101(4) defines *claim* to mean:

> (A) right to payment, whether or not such right is reduced to judgment, liquidated, unliquidated, fixed, contingent, matured, unmatured, disputed, undisputed, legal, equitable, secured or unsecured; or
>
> (B) right to an equitable remedy for breach of performance if such breach gives rise to a right to payment, whether or not such right to an equitable remedy is reduced to judgment, fixed, contingent, matured, unmatured, disputed, undisputed, secured or unsecured.[147]

The legislative history of the Bankruptcy Code states that: "The effect of the definition [of claim] is a significant departure from present law. . . . By this broadest possible definition . . . , the bill contemplates that all legal obligations of the debtor, no matter how remote or contingent, will be able to be dealt with in the bankruptcy case."[148] In this connection, §502(c) provides that: "There shall be estimated for purposes of allowance . . . (1) any contingent or unliquidated claim, fixing or liquidation of which, as the case may be, would unduly delay the closing of the case. . . ."[149]

Under §101(11) of the Bankruptcy Code, a *debt* is a "liability on a claim,"[150] and under §1131(d), if a debtor reorganizes under Chapter 11, it is discharged from all of its debts that arose prior to the court's confirmation of the plan of reorganization.[151] Thus, the interplay of the definition of claim and the discharge provisions give effect to the apparent intent of Congress to "permit the broadest possible relief in the bankruptcy court."[152] In addition, it should be noted that the discharge granted to a reorganized company is effective against a creditor whether or not he or she has filed a proof of claim.[153]

It would seem relatively clear that claims of Category 1 and 2 Claimants could be covered by the definition of *claim* under the Bankruptcy Code, subject to any due process requirement of notice of the need to file a proof of claim.

---

[146] Bankruptcy Reform Act of 1978, Pub L No 95-598, 92 Stat 2549, codified at title 11, USC.

[147] 11 USC §101(4).

[148] Senate Report 989, 95th Cong, 2d Sess 21-22 (1978) [hereinafter cited as Senate Report]; House of Representatives Report 595, 95th Cong, 1st Sess 309 (1977) [hereinafter cited as House Report].

[149] 11 USC §502(c).

[150] 11 USC §101(11).

[151] 11 USC §113(d). A discharge is not available if the debtor liquidates or does not engage in business after confirmation. *Id* §§1141(d)(3), 727(a)(1).

[152] Senate Report *supra* note 148, at 22; House Report *supra* note 148, at 309.

[153] Senate Report *supra* note 148, at 129; House Report *supra* note 148, at 418.

Although claims of Category 3 Claimants could also be said to be covered by the literal wording of the Bankruptcy Code's definition of claims, inclusion of such claimants raises significant due process problems due to the fact that no injury has yet manifested itself, and hence such unidentifiable claimants are not yet aware of their rights.

In the first decision dealing with this issue, District Judge William I. Hart has held in the UNR bankruptcy that it would be impermissible to adopt a reorganization plan which would bind Category 3 Claimants.[154] In that proceeding, UNR applied for the appointment of a legal representative for *Unknown Putative Asbestos-Related Claimants,* contending that such a representative must be given the power to bind prospective claimants so that their claims could be discharged in bankruptcy. The alternative, urged UNR, was liquidation of the company and the elimination of any assets to satisfy judgments on 30,000 to 120,000 claims estimated to be filed over the next 40 years.

The district court found it did not have the equitable power to grant the relief sought. It concluded that a putative asbestos plaintiff does not have a claim cognizable under the Bankruptcy Code, since a claim cannot arise until the plaintiff knows or should have known about the injury.[155] The court also held that no *contingent* claims existed, because the contingency referred to in the Code must arise from a prior *contractual* relationship with the debtor.[156]

Judge Hart concluded that a contrary ruling on his part would yield results not contemplated by Congress:

> The debtors suggest the definition of "contingent claim" includes the future claims of the putative claimants. This position is untenable. If the debtors were correct, then any manufacturer of a potentially dangerous product would be able to file a petition under Title 11 followed by an application such as this, asking that a legal representative be appointed to protect the interests and negotiate a plan (including the discharge of all future claims) for those who some day might be injured by a product placed into the stream of commerce by the manufacturer—debtor. Bankruptcy courts would be forced to speculate as to the future dangerousness of and damages caused by any product which some day (after a discharge in bankruptcy) might be found to harm someone.[157]

The court also analogized the problem before it to the difficulties inherent in the use of class actions in mass tort cases. Noting that courts "have been nearly uniformly reluctant to certify classes in mass tort actions" because common questions do not predominate,[158] the court found it "would be impossible for one legal representative to represent adequately the claims of tens

---

[154] *In re* UNR Indus, Nos 82B9841-51 (ND Ill Mar 25, 1983).

[155] *Id* 18.

[156] *Id.*

[157] *Id.* 11.

[158] *Id* 14-15.

of thousands of future claimants"[159] and that the due process problems of notifying persons to be bound "are insurmountable."[160]

The court reached its decision fully aware of the consequences of the denial of UNR's application: "The Court is not unaware that in refusing to approve of a procedure by which the rights of the putative claimants would be adjudicated and cut off, the putative claimants may wind up with judgments against corporations left with only one asset: a corporate charter."[161]

Should the rationale of the UNR decision be applied to the Manville bankruptcy, the company would likewise be unable to discharge the future claims which prompted it to file its petition and the bankruptcy route would lose its attraction for other mass tort defendants. Moreover, there remains a substantial question as to whether even *pending* tort claims can be the subject of a reorganization under the Bankruptcy Code as it is currently written. On June 28, 1982, the United States Supreme Court decided *Northern Pipeline Construction Co v Marathon Pipe Line Co*,[162] in which a majority of the justices concluded that the Bankruptcy Code violates Article III of the Constitution insofar as it empowers bankruptcy judges, who lack the Article III attributes of life tenure and protection against salary diminution, to decide purely state law claims over the objection of one of the litigants. At least one district court, in applying *Northern Pipeline,* has held that the bankruptcy court, as presently constituted, has no constitutional authority to entertain, over the plaintiffs' objections, some 160 products liability claims pending against the debtor.[163] Accordingly, unless and until Congress passes new legislation to cure the constitutional problems which presently exist in the Bankruptcy Code, a bankruptcy judge assigned to a mass tort reorganization proceeding may be powerless to deal with the very claims which caused the petition to be filed.

§20.29 Conclusion

The American judicial system has not provided any special method to deal with the onset of mass tort litigation. Private dispute resolution, particularly in the personal injury field, has nearly always proceeded on a case-by-case basis. The problems inherent in litigations over products such as asbestos, Agent Orange, DES, or the Dalkon Shield are such, however, that use of the traditional individual lawsuit verges on practical impossibility. The pressures which mass tort cases impose on judges and litigants alike are enormous, and it is certain that the legal issues discussed in this chapter will be the subject of further litigation and controversy, at least until such time as a vehicle for fairly

---

[159] *Id.*

[160] *Id.*

[161] *Id* 18.

[162] 102 S Ct 2858 (1982).

[163] *In re* White Motor Credit Corp, 23 BR 276 (ND Ohio 1982).

and efficiently adjudicating these enormously complicated tort matters is found.

21 In-House Management of Toxic Tort Litigation*

Edward D. Tanenhaus, Esq.†

§21.01 Overview

Traditionally, civil third-party, administrative, and workers' compensation toxic substance litigation has been defended on a mutually exclusive basis by most corporations. As a general rule, civil litigation has been overseen nationally by one or more outside law firms, while administrative and workers' compensation claims have been monitored by an independent administrative claims service or by corporate employees at the local plant level.

---

* The contribution of John G. O'Brien, Esq., Associate Counsel to GAF Corporation is gratefully acknowledged by the author. The author also wishes to acknowledge the assistance of Jerold Oshinsky, Esq., a member of Anderson, Baker, Kill & Olick, Washington, D.C., in the preparation of §§21.10-21.11.

† Partner, Munves, Tanenhaus & Storch; formerly Associate Counsel and Litigation Director, GAF Corporation, New York, New York.

Many corporations, however, now recognize that the mishandling of one or more types of toxic substance actions can have serious, long-term ramifications. Thus, as a cornerstone of their overall strategy, a number of companies are hiring an in-house toxic tort litigation director and an in-house workers' compensation coordinator. These attorneys, with their respective staffs, form a toxic tort defense team.[1]

This legal unit works hand-in-hand with local outside counsel to insure that the handling of civil toxic tort litigation and workers' compensation claims conform to the company's national defense strategy. The objective of this in-house coordinated litigation program is the retention and subsequent supervision of high-quality legal counsel dedicated to the reduction of defense costs, preservation of the corporation's rights and defenses, and implementation of the company's insurance coverages.

§21.02   Coordination of Toxic Substance Actions

The primary benefit derived from the use of an in-house staff for toxic tort management is the coordination of toxic substance actions. Various aspects of this coordination are discussed in the following sections. Specifically, reducing costs and effort is discussed in §21.03; preserving the corporation's rights is discussed in §21.04; administration of third-party suits is discussed in §21.05; protecting corporate confidentiality is discussed in §21.06; and coordination of workers' compensation proceedings is covered in §21.07.

§21.03   —Reducing Costs and Effort

Latent toxic substance injuries, initially discovered among a corporation's plant workers, eventually may manifest themselves in the general population. Therein lies the potential for future civil third-party litigation. The preparation for this contingency provides the initial opportunity for the in-house litigation director and workers' compensation coordinator to implement long-term cost efficiencies which can inure to the benefit of the corporation in its defense of both types of actions.

One of the first cost-saving measures that should be taken is to retain, if possible, the same law firm in each jurisdiction to handle both the civil litigation and the workers' compensation proceedings. The major benefit to utilizing counsel in this dual capacity is to reduce the learning curve substantially.

---

[1] Carrying the in-house coordination effort one step further, certain companies, often depending upon the nature of their industry or the type of toxic substance involved, have entered into *Non-Aggression Defense Pacts* which, in the name of joint defense, address the issues of mutual retention of attorneys, the sharing of costs and responsibilities, and the tolling of cross-claims and third-party complaints. See Sheridan, *Sindell and its Sequelae -or- From a Defendant's Perspective, How to Manage Multiple-Party Litigation Under Nontraditional Theories of Litigation,* The Forum, Vol XVII, No 14 (Spring 1982).

The firm, regardless of the type of claim it was first retained to defend, becomes quickly and intimately familiar with the company's personnel, manufacturing facilities, product lines, and markets, as well as the in-house legal department's work habits and idiosyncrasies. Furthermore, outside counsel will develop an expertise in the forensic aspects of the claim which often overlap both types of litigation. Finally, to the in-house counsel, this arrangement assures that discovery and other tactical and strategic decisions are being carried out in a consistent manner in all jurisdictions.

At times, an insurance company may want the right to choose counsel. Because the overall quality of local counsel is so important to the success of any strategy, the corporation's right to choose its own defense counsel should be negotiated into its insurance contracts.

Another area to be considered in effectuating cost containment is the retention of an independent toxicologist to assist in the more complex aspects of a new or unique case. Many times, the toxicologist's work product in a compensation claim yields significant results which can be used to lay the groundwork for the defense of subsequent civil litigation.[2] The conclusions reached may also allay fears concerning older products which may not have been tested under today's more exacting standards.

Finally, major cost benefits can be achieved by the documentation and implementation of insurance coverage. This is a sizeable project requiring extensive in-house coordination.[3] The program involves both the litigation director and the workers' compensation coordinator conferring on a regular basis about coverage positions and policy defenses raised by the company's carriers. As an example, a comprehensive general liability carrier on risks during the 1960s, 1970s or 1980s may be asserting an *expected and intended* policy defense on recently submitted civil toxic tort claims.[4] This same insurer, however, may have written the company's workers' compensation insurance during the 1930s, 1940s or 1950s. Under these circumstances, the insurer not only may have been aware of the potential for or the existence of certain occupational diseases, but it also may have carried out on-site health and safety inspections upon which the company relied for its industrial hygiene data. The in-house exchange of information on this subject, therefore, could provide vital facts necessary to defeat this policy defense and, thus, prevent the loss of substantial insurance coverage.

---

[2] These considerations also apply to the retention of independent medical experts, examining physicians, epidemiologists and hygienists.

[3] See §§21.08-21.12.

[4] Under standard policy language *occurrence* is generally defined as "an accident, including injurious exposure to conditions, which results, during the policy period, in bodily injury or property damage *neither expected nor intended* from the standpoint of the insured." (Emphasis added.) Keene Corp v Insurance Co of N Am, 667 F2d 1034 (DC Cir 1981), *cert denied,* 455 US 1007 (1982).

§21.04 —Preserving the Corporation's Rights

Several developing areas of the law require active coordination between members of the toxic tort defense team. These include statutory subrogation actions, direct civil actions by employees against their employers or coworkers, and the potential use of collateral estoppel.

A number of states permit an employer or insurance carrier to commence a civil subrogation action under their workers' compensation acts.[5] In general, these statutes permit an employer to commence a civil third-party action in the name of those employees, who, after receiving compensation awards and appropriate statutory notice, fail to commence a suit against third parties who may be liable for their damages and against whom the employer could otherwise assert a statutory compensation lien.[6] The amount recoverable by the employer, however, is usually limited by statute, with any recovery over and above the compensation payments going directly to the employee.

On the one hand, this type of action appears to provide an attractive means of recouping a corporation's compensation payments. On the other hand, there has been limited reported use of this action, primarily due to several tactical considerations. These include the unusual role of a corporation prosecuting an action as a toxic tort plaintiff, the potential difficulty in obtaining full cooperation from plant personnel, and the possibility of a defendant uncovering materials which then become available for the prosecution of cross-claims in civil third-party litigation.

Another area of concern are recent court decisions which have expanded the employee's right to bring a direct action against his or her employer.[7] Some

---

[5] See Weisgall, *Product Liability in the Workplace: The Effect of Workers Compensation on the Rights and Liabilities of Third Parties,* 1977 Wis L Rev 1035.

[6] A typical statutory provision is NJ Stat Ann §34:15-40 (West 1981) which, in pertinent part, states:

> (f) When an injured employee or his dependents fail within 1 year of the accident to either effect a settlement with the third person . . . or institute proceedings for recovery of damages for his injuries and loss against the third person, the employer . . . , 10 days after a written demand on the injured employee or his dependents, can either effect a settlement with the third person . . . or institute proceedings against the third person for the recovery of damages for the injuries and loss sustained by such injured employee or his dependents . . . .
>
> . . . If a settlement is effected . . . or a judgment is recovered . . . and if the amount secured . . . is in excess of the employer's obligation to the employee or his dependents and the expense of suit, such excess shall be paid to the employee or his dependents. The legal action contemplated hereinabove shall be a civil action at law in the name of the injured employee or by the employer . . . in the name of the employee. . . .

[7] *See* Bell v Industrial Vangas, Inc, 30 Cal 3d 268, 637 P2d 266, 179 Cal Rptr 30 (1981); Duprey v Shane, 39 Cal 3d 781, 249 P2d 8 (1952); Birnbaum & Wrubel, *Workers' Compensation and the Employer's Immunity Shield: Recent Exceptions to Exclusivity,* 5 J Prod Liab 1 (1982). See **ch 6** for a more detailed discussion of workers' compensation and the exclusivity doctrine.

cases have been based upon theories of intentional tort[8] or dual capacity.[9] Others have sustained causes of action against subsidiaries or other entities lacking statutory immunity[10] or permitted direct claims against corporate officers and coemployees.[11] Consequently, in devising a workers' compensation defense strategy, the plan should be thoroughly reviewed with an eye toward eliminating the possibility of a situation which allows an employee to bring a subsequent civil action based upon one or more of these theories.

The in-house attorneys must also be prepared to deal with situations arising out of an action brought by their own employee against a third party. Potentially, the most dangerous is the civil suit in which an employee sues a supplier, who, in turn, takes extensive discovery of the corporate employer in an attempt to prove supervening cause, the elements of a dual capacity claim, or to establish grounds for a third-party complaint based upon indemnification or contribution.

Often, ancillary discovery arising out of this type of action is accepted routinely by the corporation. This policy should not be continued because of the potential use of collateral estoppel which can, under appropriate circumstances, be used offensively or defensively to bar the relitigation of specifically determined issues.[12] Thus, attorneys representing the corporation as a non-

---

[8] Blankenship v Cincinnati Milacron Chems, Inc, 69 Ohio St 2d 608, 433 NE2d 572 (1982); Johns-Manville Prods Corp v Contra Costa Super Ct, 27 Cal 3d 465, 612 P2d 948, 165 Cal Rptr 858 (1980). *See also* Mylroie v GAF Corp, 81 AD2d 994, 440 NYS2d 67 (1981), *affd,* 55 NY2d 893, 433 NE2d 1269 (1982).

[9] Bell v Industrial Vangas, Inc, 30 Cal 3d 268, 637 P2d 266, 179 Cal Rptr 30 (1981); Duprey v Shane, 39 Cal 2d 781, 249 P2d 8 (1952). California has recently eliminated the dual capacity doctrine except in those situations involving an injury aggravated by the fraudulent conduct of the employer, Cal Lab Code §3602(a), (b) (West 1982).

[10] Monroe v Monsanto Co, 531 F Supp 426 (DSC 1982); Mingin v Continental Can Co, 171 NJ Super 148, 408 A2d 146 (1979). *Compare* Strickland v Textron, 433 F Supp 326 (DSC 1977).

[11] Fireman's Fund Am Ins Co v Coleman, 394 So 2d 334 (Ala 1980); Grantham v Denke, 359 So 2d 785 (Ala 1978). But cf Gerger v Campbell, 98 Wis 2d 282, 297 NW2d 183 (1980).

[12] Collateral estoppel is the doctrine of *issue preclusion.* It may be used offensively, under appropriate circumstances, to preclude a party which has lost in a prior action from relitigating issues which have already been determined against it. Parklane Hosiery Co v Shore, 439 US 322 (1979). Defensively, a plaintiff who lost in a prior action may be barred by a new defendant from relitigating previously determined issues. Blonder-Tongue Labs v University of Ill Found, 402 US 313 (1971). See C. Wright & D. Miller, Federal Practice and Procedure §4402 (1981).
The doctrine of collateral estoppel is premised upon the assumption that the party against whom it is sought to be used had a *full and fair opportunity* to litigate the first action. Factors included in this determination are "the size of the claim, the forum of the prior litigation, the use of initiative, the extent of the litigation, the competence and experience of counsel, the availability of new evidence, indications of a compromise verdict, differences in the applicable law and foreseeability of future litigation." Schwartz v Public Admin of Co of Bronx, 24 NY2d 65, 72, 246 NE2d 725, 729, 298 NYS2d 955, 962. (1969). See also Restatement (Second) of Judgments §27 (1969).
The use of offensive collateral estoppel was recently sanctioned in a DES action,

party witness must be aware of the drastic impact which a finding of supervening cause or the establishment of facts sufficient to prove either a dual capacity claim or a sophisticated user defense[13] could have on subsequent civil actions.

§21.05 —Administration of Civil Third-Party Suits

The in-house toxic tort litigation director[14] has the responsibility of coordinating five major areas:

1. Senior Management's need to know
2. Middle management's extensive involvement in the toxic substance litigation process
3. Protection of corporate confidentiality
4. Requirements of local counsel for facts and strategic guidance
5. Utilization of the company's comprehensive general liability insurance coverage

Members of senior management abhor surprises; they do not want to read it first in *The Wall Street Journal.* Moreover, they are empowered with the corporation's final settlement authority.[15] Thus, it is as unrealistic as it is unfair to ask or expect senior management to respond instantaneously to a plaintiff's demand on the courthouse steps or a judge's attempt at midtrial settlement. Senior executives, therefore, should not only receive regular updates concerning the nationwide status of the company's toxic tort litigation, but also a synopsis of significant cases as settlement negotiations proceed or trials draw near.

Kaufman v Eli Lilly & Co, 2 Prod Liab Rep (CCH) ¶9441 (NYSup Ct NY 1982), but denied in an asbestos-related injury action, Hardy v Johns-Manville Sales Corp, 681 F2d 334 (5th Cir 1982).

[13] The original manufacturer or processor may be relieved of the duty to warn "where the purchaser or the user has certain knowledge or sophistication, professionally or otherwise, in regard to the product." Poland v Beaird-Poulan, 483 F Supp 1256, 1264 (WD La 1980). The duty is minimized where the user is a member of a trade or profession in which the dangers are generally known and later use, by a person with less training or experience, is a matter of foreseeability. Littlehale v EI Dupont de Nemours & Co, 380 F2d 274, 276 (2d Cir 1967). Apparently linked to the elements of superceding intervening cause (Restatement (Second) of Torts §442 (1975), the Restatement (Second) of Torts §338 (1975) looks to the reasonableness of a manufacturer's or supplier's belief that the purchaser (employer) will warn the ultimate user (employee). In other words, the issue of knowledge in this three-party situation is focused upon the intermediate purchaser or employer rather than upon the end user.

[14] While active coordination between civil and workers' compensation toxic tort litigation may provide the corporation with a number of long-term benefits, it should not be overlooked that the in-house management of these types of cases requires separate and distinct legal skills.

[15] *E.g.,* Del Code Ann §142(a), (b) (Michie 1975). *See also* §§102(b)(1), 109(b), & 14(a).

A substantial portion of the in-house litigator's time is devoted to communicating with middle management personnel. This group's decisions, made with respect to buying insurance, maintaining plants, enforcing safety and health standards, and placing the company's finished products in the marketplace, have the greatest potential effect on the future outcome of the company's toxic tort litigation.[16] It is this segment of the corporate infrastructure, moreover, which is most often barraged with pretrial discovery demands, while, at the same time, most heavily relied upon by senior management to increase the company's sales and profits.

An effort must therefore be made to spare middle management the daily rigors of toxic tort litigation. As a practical matter, once a key employee has been deposed, his or her deposition should be offered for use in other jurisdictions. Furthermore, when witnesses from within the corporation are subpoenaed or otherwise identified for the first time, they should be contacted by outside counsel only after an appropriate introduction from the corporate legal department. Subsequent direct contact with outside counsel should, if practical, be kept to a minimum. In some cases, however, the outside counsel's ability to prepare the case properly will require substantial and continued information that can only be provided by middle management personnel. Finally, when a new or unique case arises, it should be met with one, all-inclusive factual inquiry. The results of this investigation should remain under the control of the in-house legal department, which can disseminate portions to local counsel as needed.

An area sensitive to any corporation is former employees. Some may have left the company under less than favorable circumstances. Others may be suffering from occupational diseases and prosecuting their own claims against the company. Several rules to be followed when dealing with these potential witnesses are:

1. Keep track of their whereabouts at all times within the confines of their rights of privacy

2. Learn the circumstances surrounding their termination or separation

3. Be aware of their current health and the status of any health-related claims

4. Conduct an interview as soon as a factual connection is established between them and a particular type of case

5. Have initial contact made by a fellow employee still with the company, not by outside counsel

6. Request that they speak only through the legal department or the com-

---

[16] Corporate groups fitting this description include: environmental engineering, financial services, marketing, occupational health and safety, plant managers and personnel directors, public relations, research and development, risk management, and sales.

pany's outside counsel (although the ability to enforce this request is very questionable since they may be represented by counsel of their own)

7. Understand their limitations and anxieties

8. Recognize and come to grips early on with real or potential *skeletons in the closet*

There are a number of guidelines available to assist a corporation in coordinating the handling of litigation with outside counsel. The goal is to retain control over the litigation while allowing local counsel to render advice concerning local law, recommended settlement values, and proposed trial strategy. These guidelines include:

1. Move quickly to retain counsel in a new jurisdiction. Bring local counsel up to speed with *starter kits* and a corporate *open-door* policy. Update factual memoranda on a regular basis

2. Humanize the company. Dignify the role of junior attorneys, paralegals, and administrative assistants

3. Encourage active communication among all local counsel. Use the strengths of one firm to satisfy the needs of other counsel throughout the country

4. Look to share expenses and responsibilities with codefendants.[17] A codefendant, however, is always a potential adversary. A group effort, therefore, is only as good as the competence and trustworthiness of the participants[18]

5. Discourage *roadshows.* One counsel can more than adequately cover a multijurisdiction deposition or document production

6. Work with judges to streamline pretrial discovery and to prevent last-minute introduction of previously undiscovered evidence[19]

7. Make local counsel feel that they are working *with* in-house counsel. In insured situations, local counsel's undivided loyalty is owed to the insured, not to the carrier[20]

---

[17] See Sheridan, A Strategy for Defending Multi-Defendant Lawsuits, Toxic Torts Defense Tactics and Techniques Q1 (Defense Research Institute Inc ed 1983); Schultz, Guiding Principles for Cooperation in the Defense of Multi-Party Litigation, For the Defense (July 1982).

[18] The joint defense privilege protects from disclosure confidential legal communications between codefendants and their attorneys, Abraham Constr Corp v Armco Steel Corp, 559 F2d 250, 253 (5th Cir 1977). See also Wilson, *Using the Joint Defense Privilege,* Natl LJ, Vol 5, No 27 (1983).

[19] See Standing Order for Asbestos Cases in the Eastern District of Texas, Beaumont Division (July 7, 1982); Standing Order *In re:* Asbestosis Cases (DSC Feb 24, 1981) (Chapman, J).

[20] American Employers Ins Co v Globe Aircraft Inc, 205 Misc 1066, 1086, 131 NYS2d 393, 401-02 (NY Sup Ct 1954); Model Code of Professional Repsonsibility Canon 5 (1979).

Successful representation in toxic tort litigation, therefore, requires that local counsel possess a thorough understanding of the client's past and present operations. By necessity, this must include knowledge of the method and manner by which decisions were made, of how groups or divisions were structured and interrelated, and of the company's product lines and markets. Local counsel must be provided also with the means to gather this information in an expeditious and unencumbered manner.

§21.06 —Protecting Corporate Confidentiality

It is imperative that the status of privileged corporate material be maintained in a least three distinct areas:

1. Confidential legal communications between corporate employees
2. The preparation and dissemination of documents
3. The protection of the litigation computer data base

In many situations, middle management personnel may question or openly disagree with restrictions placed upon them by the legal department. However, with respect to protecting corporate confidentiality, diligence and strict adherence to the principles enunciated in case law is the only means to prevent inadvertent disclosure and a successful claim of waiver.

In *Upjohn Co v United States*,[21] the Supreme Court "laid to rest suggestions that house counsel are to be treated differently from outside counsel with respect to activities in which they are engaged as attorneys."[22] *Upjohn* "made clear that the attorney-client privilege applies to communications made by corporate employees concerning matters pertinent to the job tasks, regardless of echelon, if sought by the corporation's attorney in order to formulate and render legal advice to the corporation."[23]

While declining "to lay down a broad rule or series of rules to govern all conceivable future questions in this area,"[24] the Court in *Upjohn* stated that the in-house attorney-client privilege required:

1. A confidential communication
2. At the direction or under the auspices of the employee's corporate superior
3. To an in-house attorney, acting at that time in a legal capacity

---

[21] 449 US 383 (1981).

[22] *In re* LTV Secs Litigation, 89 FRD 595, 601 (ND Tex 1981).

[23] *Id* 602.

[24] 449 US at 386. The Supreme Court, relying upon Hickman v Taylor, 329 US 495 (1947) and Fed R Civ P 26(b)(3), invoked the work product doctrine to protect mental impressions, conclusions, opinions, and legal theories of Upjohn's general counsel. 449 US at 400.

4. To secure legal advice from counsel

5. Made with an awareness of its legal implications[25]

It must be remembered, however, that the courts will construe the attorney-client privilege "no more broadly than is necessary to effectuate its purpose."[26] Thus, "the burden of proof is on the individual [or corporation] asserting the privilege to establish the elements necessary to support a claim of privilege."[27]

In the course of its daily operations, a corporation may be called upon to provide information which falls squarely within the attorney-client privilege or is protected by the work product doctrine. In certian situations, the corporation might well be tempted to disclose information in its protected form in response to an investigation by a governmental agency, in buying or renewing insurance, in satisfying an auditor's inquiry, or in complying with the requirement to make full and complete disclosure in a public or private document.

This disclosure, however, is not without substantial risk,[28] since the protection afforded privileged materials may well be lost once they are used for a purpose other than the seeking and rendering of legal advice.[29] As stated in *John Doe Corp v United States:* [30]

A claim that a need for confidentiality must be respected in order to

---

[25] 449 US at 394. In its holding, the Supreme Court specifically rejected the "control group" test which had previously been applied in certain jurisdictions to determine the scope and applicability of the attorney-client privilege in corporate situations.

[26] Cohen v Uniroyal, 80 FRD 480, 483 (ED Pa 1978).

[27] United States v Kelly, 569 F2d 928, 938 (5th Cir), *cert denied,* 439 US 829 (1978); Weinstein & Berger, Weinstein's Evidence ¶503(b)[04] (1980).

[28] For example, in United States v AT&T, 642 F2d 1285 (DC Cir 1980) the United States Court of Appeals for the District of Columbia elaborated upon the attorney-client privilege and the work product doctrine and the voluntary disclosure of materials otherwise protected by each:

> *The attorney-client privilege exists* to protect confidential communications, to assure the client that any statements he makes in seeking legal advice will be kept strictly confidential between him and his attorney; in effect, *to protect the attorney-client relationship.* Any voluntary disclosure by the holder of such a privilege is inconsistent with the confidential relationship and thus waives the privilege.
>
> By contrast, the *work product privilege* does not exist to protect a confidential relationship, but rather *to promote the adversary system by safeguarding the fruits of an attorney's trial preparation from the discovery attempts of the opponent.*
>
> . . . .
>
> A disclosure made in the pursuit of such trial preparation, and not inconsistent with maintaining secrecy against opponents, should be allowed without waiver of the privilege. We conclude, then, that *while the mere showing of a voluntary disclosure to a third person will generally suffice to show waiver of the attorney-client privilege, it should not suffice in itself for waiver of the work product privilege.*

642 F2d at 1299 (footnotes and citations omitted; emphasis in original).

[29] Permian Corp v United States, 665 F2d 1214 (DC Cir 1981).

[30] 675 F2d 482 (2d Cir 1982).

facilitate the seeking and rendering of informed legal advice is not consistent with selective disclosure when the claimant decides that the confidential materials can be put to other beneficial purposes. . . . The fact that they were originally compiled by attorneys is irrelevant because they are serving a purpose other than the seeking and rendering of legal advice.

. . . .

In the corporate context, restricting internal inquiries about particular matters to corporate counsel in the name of giving and receiving of legal advice will afford the benefits of the privilege only so long as those inquiries and the responses they generate are used only for the designated purposes. Once a corporate decision is made to disclose them for commercial purposes, no matter what the economic imperatives, the privilege is lost, not because of the voluntariness or involuntariness, but because the need for confidentiality served by the privilege is inconsistent with such disclosure.[31]

The sheer volume of information generated by toxic substance litigation lends itself to the creation of a computer-supported data base. In essence, it involves a system which is tailor-made at the outset, expandable by necessity, and protected from discovery by an adversary.[32]

A distinction must be drawn between computer-generated records used and maintained in the ordinary course of a company's business and the computerized retrieval data base which is designed by an attorney for the purpose of assisting in the prosecution or defense of litigation. The disclosure of the former group of documents during the course of pretrial discovery and trial preparation has been generally allowed pursuant to rule or statute.[33] The discovery of an adversary's litigation support or trial preparation materials, however, is far more restricted and is allowed only upon a showing of waiver or a unique, unusual, or extraordinary set of circumstances.[34]

No matter how well a data retrieval program functions, it could prove worthless, if not entirely self-defeating, if it were discoverable. In order to protect

---

[31] *Id* 489.

[32] This section is not intended as a practical guide to the creation of an automated data retrieval system. Works on that subject which should be consulted include, Computers & The Law, ABA Sec Science & Tech (CCH 3d ed 1981) and Madden, Information Management in Complex Litigation, Litigation, Vol 4, No 3 (Spring 1978).

[33] Fed R Civ P 34, Advisory Committee Note, 48 FRD 487, 527 (1970); Fed R Evid 803(b) (Hearsay Exceptions [Records of regularly conducted activity]), 901(8) (Requirement of Authentication or Identification [Ancient documents or data compilation]) and 1001(1) (Contents of Writings, Recordings, and Photographs [Writings and Recordings]).

[34] *See* Pearl Brewing Co v Joseph Schlitz Brewing Co, 415 F Supp 1122 (SD Tex 1976), in which the production of certain computer data was compelled in order to permit a party to support or refute the conclusions of an expert trial witness. In National Union Elec Corp v Matsushita Elec Indus Co, 494 F Supp 1257 (ED Pa 1980), the plaintiff was required to produce a portion of its computer-readable tape after using it to generate answers to interrogatories.

the litigation data base, the development of the program must not only be under an attorney's direct control, but the project, when completed, must clearly reflect that fact. Ideally, a general description of the program should convince a judge that the program is a result of an attorney's deliberative thought processes and that to order disclosure would reveal the legal theories or subjective mental impression of the attorney.[35]

§21.07 —Coordination of Workers' Compensation Proceedings

In an effort to curb the substantial rise in workers' compensation costs, a growing number of corporations have transferred the supervision of these claims from their personnel, employee benefit, or risk management departments to the legal department. There, under the auspices of a workers' compensation coordinator, the following issues are handled on a regular basis:

1. Case strategy
2. Whether to insure or self-insure
3. Implementation of insurance coverage
4. Recovery of compensation payments

The workers' compensation coordinator must establish a nationwide strategy which can function successfully within the context of the various and varied state workers' compensation systems. In formulating this plan, it must be remembered that workers' compensation is basically a no-fault system. Trials are difficult to win, since factual findings and legal issues are liberally construed for the claimant.[36] There is often a marked difference, moreover, in the settlement and trial values of a claim. Generally, a corporation should consider trying only those cases intended to stem a flood of dubious claims, to enforce the statute of limitations, or to allocate liability among several employers.

In many states, there is often a lengthy wait while a claim works its way through the workers' compensation system to a final hearing. Thus, a claimant's attorney with similar occupational disease claims arising out of one or more of the company's plant locations may be receptive to a long-term formula

---

[35] *In re* IBM Peripheral, MDC No 163-RM (ND Cal 1975); Montrose Chem Corp v Train, 491 F2d 63 (DC Cir 1974); Sherman & Kinnard, *The Development, Discovery, and Use of Computer Systems in Achieving Efficiency in Litigation,* 79 Colum L Rev 267 (1979); Fromholz, *Discovery, Evidence, Confidentiality and Security Problems Associates with the Use of Computer-Based Litigation Support Systems,* 1977 Wash ULQ 445 (1977).

[36] "The proceedings . . . are more 'free wheeling,' not only in the quantum of proof necessary to establish a claim, but also in the nature of evidence and procedural rules that are followed." Young & Co v Shea, 397 F2d 185, 188 (5th Cir 1968). *See also* LaFranchi v Industrial Accident Commn, 213 Cal 675, 3 P2d 305 (1931); Wilson v General Motors Corp, 298 NY 468, 84 NE2d 781 (1949); Dunn v Trego, 279 Pa 518, 124 A 174 (1924).

for disposition of multiple cases. To the corporation, such an agreement can result in a setting of more accurate reserves and a meaningful reduction in legal expenses.

Once a settlement policy has been adopted, the coordinator must see to it that judgments are postured in the least prejudicial terms possible. Particular attention should be paid to the designation of the disability in the order for compensation. By citing as broad a disability as possible, a subsequent claim for a particular condition may be foreclosed due to the running of the applicable statute of limitations.

Several states permit a claim to be reopened, within certain statutory limits, until total disability is reached.[37] This is accomplished by alleging an increase in the disability for which the employee has previously received an award. To avoid this, cases in which the claimant has left the employ of the company or in which there is no further exposure by the employee to the particular irritant should be settled on a dismissal basis.

A strategy should also be devised to deal with voluntary payments when the question of compensability is not in issue. In certain jurisdictions, if an employer commences compensation payments within a certain period of time after receiving notice of injury, the claimant's attorney is not entitled to a fee, even if a claim has been filed.[38] This saving can be further enhanced where there is an offset for social security payments, pension benefits, and disability payments.

Finally, because many states base their benefits upon the rates in effect or salary earned at the time of last exposure,[39] the coordinator should be conversant with the claimant's duties and the substances to which he or she was exposed. The difference between past and present benefit schedules may often be substantial.

Whether to Self-Insure

One of the most critical recommendations a workers' compensation coordinator must make is whether to insure or self-insure for workers' compensation liability. In reaching this decision, it must first be determined if self-insurance is permitted in those states in which the corporation maintains plants. The next consideration is the corporation's ability to absorb or retain future losses. This projection is based upon loss probability and loss retention studies read in conjunction with other factors such as cost elements (excess insurance, allocated expenses, surety bonds, and guaranty funds), administrative charges (loss control and claims handling), taxes and assessments, and the corporation's current and anticipated size. A final point is the corporation's tax rate. In most instances, insurance premiums can be expensed immediately

---

[37] Cal Lab Code §5410 (West 1982); NJ Stat Ann §34:15-27 (West 1981); NY Work Comp Law §22 (McKinney 1982); 77 Pa Cons Stat Ann §834 (Purdon 1982).

[38] *See* NJ Stat Ann §34:15-64 (West 1981).

[39] *See* MD Ann Code art 101, §23(b) (Michie 1983).

while self-insured reserves cannot.[40] Generally, the closer a corporation's tax rate is to zero, the greater the advantage of self-insurance.

Additional savings may be realized when a corporation self-administers its own program instead of delegating this role to a service organization or insurance carrier. Self-administration may lead to a more dedicated effort by plant and management personnel, because they know that their success in implementing safety programs for occupational exposure and in the handling of related claims will have an impact on the bottom-line results for both their facility and the corporation. This is especially true where a policy provides for a high self-retention level. A company, therefore, should negotiate this right into the insurance contract.

Coverage and Types of Policies

Generally, coverage under workers' compensation policies is triggered when the last exposure occurred during the policy period. The company's historic policy register must therefore be consulted in order to determine, on a case-by-case basis, which carrier should be placed on notice. A corporation should not neglect to make claims for reimbursement against excess workers' compensation policies since the older ones have relatively low self-insured retentions and can provide an excellent means to limit losses.

Most corporations purchase two types of workers' compensation excess coverage. The first is specific excess insurance coverage—a form of catastrophe insurance. Upon reaching the self-insured retention for the policy, the carrier assumes liability for a fixed amount above the retention level. For occupational disease cases, some policies provide coverage only until the total dollar amount paid on all claims above the retention level reaches a fixed dollar figure. At that point, the specific excess is exhausted.

The second type of policy is aggregate excess insurance. This coverage involves all the little claims which do not reach the retention level in the specific excess policy. The amounts paid in these cases are added together with the self-insured retention from the specific excess claims. After the aggregate policy retention level is reached, all further compensation payments for the policy period are reimbursed by the excess carrier. When the specific or aggregate excess coverages are exhausted, most workers' compensation insurance programs provide for the risk to shift to the corporation's umbrella coverage.

Recouping Payments

One method for an employer to recoup occupation-related toxic substance losses—*e.g.* compensation payments—is to pursue civil third—party subrogation rights. The mechanics of a statutory subrogation action are discussed in

---

[40] *See* Treas Reg §1.461-1(a)(3)(i). But reserves may be taken as an expense when an accrual system of accounting is used. *See* Kaiser Steel Corp v United States, 50 AFTR2d 82-6020 (Ct Cl 1980).

an earlier section.[41] A corporation should also pursue its statutory lien rights in common law cases which have been filed by employees against third parties. Local statutes should be consulted, since some jurisdictions require the filing of a formal notice of lien on the common law defendants to protect the employer's interest in any civil recovery.[42]

Finally, an employer should attempt to have compensation claims placed on inactive status until the civil action proceeds to settlement or judgment. A claimant may be satisfied with the civil recovery and dismiss the compensation claim. This can be more easily accomplished when the civil litigation and compensation claims are being prosecuted by the same attorney.

§21.08   Documentation and Implementation of Insurance Coverage

Critical to a corporation's ability to deal with toxic tort claims is the obtaining of full defense and indemnification from its insurers under comprehensive general liability, workers' compensation, excess, and umbrella policies.

Many companies, however, are not aware of all of the coverages against which they may make a claim. The reasons for this may include sloppy internal recordkeeping, confusion resulting from mergers or acquisitions, a lack of cooperation by former brokers, or a less than good faith attitude exhibited by one or more carriers. Furthermore, companies often confuse, particularly with respect to workers' compensation, the concept of being *self-insured* with the status of being *uninsured.*

Discovering forgotten coverages involves imagination, skill, persistence, and luck. Effecting and implementing those coverages, however, may require litigation. Declaratory relief actions in toxic tort insurance situations deal, among other things, with issues of notice, proof of policy terms and conditions, breach of defense and indemnification obligations, and the interpretation of triggers and scope of coverage. The central coverage dispute is often joined by a claim against the carriers for bad faith[43] and punitive damages.

§21.09   —Finding and Documenting Insurance Coverage

In order to assure that it has taken every step possible to uncover its insurance policies—or secondary evidence of policy terms and conditions—a corporation should undertake an in-depth historical insurance audit. This project

---

[41] See §21.04.

[42] *See* NJ Stat Ann §34:15-40 (West 1981).

[43] *Bad faith* may be based upon a failure to defend or indemnify, to conduct a proper investigation, to accept a settlement within policy limits, to engage in settlement negotiations, or to inform the insured of possibility of settlement. Young v American Casualty Co, 416 F2d 906, 910-11 (2d Cir 1969).

should be directed by the legal department, utilizing the skills of the company's risk manager, its past and present brokers, and an independent insurance archaeologist.

The goal of the audit is to recreate, interpret, and understand the corporation's overall insurance program. A thorough audit could uncover many millions of dollars in previously unrealized coverages. An audit involves the review of policies, declaration sheets, policy slips, merger and acquisition documents, and old case files for documentation concerning coverages. Also, any persons, inside or outside the corporation, who may have known how policies were purchased, the manner by which claims were submitted to and coordinated with brokers or carriers, or where insurance-related documents were stored, should be interviewed.

Finally, the scope of the audit should include a search for both general comprehensive and workers' compensation coverages. Often, they were placed by the same brokers, written by the same underwriters, shared the same upper layers of coverage and stored by the company, or its predecessors, in the same basements, warehouses, or archives. Each type of coverage thus provides an excellent source of leads to additional policies.

It can be argued that a corporation is perfectly capable of carrying out an insurance audit entirely on its own. However, in potentially litigious situations, many avenues are not fully open to a company in search of its policies. Thus, the use of an independent insurance archaeologist becomes essential in completing the investigation.

Insurance archaeology [44] is the practice of reconstructing and analyzing an insured's past coverages. It is performed by an insurance archaeologist who, like his or her scientific counterpart, begins with the present and digs down to the past. Insurance is evolutionary in nature, and present forms of coverage can disclose a great deal about forgotten coverages.

The insurance archaeologist's most important role is to establish a working relationship with the insured's present and past domestic and foreign brokers. It is this group which is not only the best source of documentation but also possesses an oral history concerning the insured's past coverages and insurance affiliations. The role of the insurance archaeologist must be nonadversarial. His or her credibility rests upon the fact that neither he or she nor his or her firm will later pursue his or her earlier leads in a subsequent insurance coverage litigation.

Once the insurance archaeologist has exhausted all potential leads, new and old coverages should be catalogued by policy period, carrier, broker, and types of coverage. The policies and secondary documentation are then analyzed based upon such items as deductibles, self-insured retentions, and aggregate limits to determine how the primary and excess coverages interrelate during a particular policy period. The information is then further refined to determine how types of coverages such as comprehensive general liability and workers'

---

[44] The author wishes to acknowledge the contribution of Mr. Randolph Fields, Barrister, of the Middle Temple, on the subject of insurance archaeology.

compensation may dovetail at excess levels or under umbrella policies. As this analysis progresses, it should include a detailed checklist of key insuring clauses, exclusions, and other language which might effect the triggers or scope of coverage.

Upon the completion of the historic insurance audit, a corporation will have the ability to reflect upon its entire insurance program and to understand and make claims for the full coverage to which it is entitled.

§21.10 —Effecting and Utilizing Insurance Coverage

Those civil third-party toxic tort suits which lead to insurance coverage litigation generally involve claims in which many years have passed between exposure to the harmful substance—inhalation, ingestion, or contamination—and the ability to make a competent medical diagnosis or other scientific determination confirming the existence of a disease or other injury.[45] The insurance policies sued upon are, for the most part, standard comprehensive general liability policies which were issued to an insured, usually the present corporation or its predecessor, by many different insurance carriers who were on the risk at different times during the years of injury.

The threshold questions addressed in these coverage disputes focus upon the obligations of the insurers to defend and indemnify their policyholder. With minor variation, the standard policy language before the courts, states:

> [t]he [insurance] company will pay on behalf of the insured all sums which the insured shall become legally obligated to pay as damages because of bodily injury . . . to which this insurance applies, caused by an occurrence, and the [insurance] company shall have the right and duty to defend any suit against the insured seeking damages on account of such bodily injury . . . even if any of the allegations of the suit are groundless, false or fraudulent . . . .[46]

---

[45] *E.g., asbestos,* Keene Corp v Insurance Co of N Am, 667 F2d 1034 (DC Cir 1981), *cert denied,* 455 US 1007 (1982); *DES,* Schering Corp v Home Ins Co, 544 F Supp 613 (EDNY 1982), *revd on other grounds,* Nos 83-7056, 83-7102 (2d Cir June 21, 1983); *radioactive chemicals,* Tenneco Chems, Inc v Continental Cas Co, No 78 Civ 2188 (SDNY May 16, 1979); Tenneco Chems, Inc v Employers Mut Liab Ins Co, [1977] Fire & Casualty Cas (CCH) ¶77-940 (SDNY 1977); Tenneco Chems, Inc v Employers Mut Liab Ins Co, [1968], Fire & Casualty Cas (CCH) ¶68-984 (SDNY 1968); *silicosis,* American Mut Liab Ins Co v Agricola Furnace Co, 236 Ala 535, 183 So 677 (1938); *toxic waste,* Argonaut Ins Co v Occidental Petroleum Corp, No 40229 (NY Sup Ct 1980).

[46] As stated by the United States Court of Appeals for the District of Columbia in Keene Corp v Insurance Co of N Am, 667 F2d at 1039:

> "Bodily injury" is defined as "bodily injury, sickness or disease sustained by any person" . . . and "occurrence" is defined as "an accident including injurious exposure to conditions, which results, during the policy period, in bodily injury . . . neither expected nor intended from the standpoint of the insured." (Record cites omitted.).

The significance of this standard policy language is that it appears to enunciate both the trigger and scope of insurance coverage.[47] The trigger of coverage is the event or condition which determines whether a policy responds to a specific claim. The scope of coverage defines the extent of a carrier's obligation once the policy has been triggered.

When confronted with a strict reading of the standard policy language, it would appear that the intended trigger of coverage is *bodily injury* occurring during the policy period and that once the policy is triggered, the carrier would be required to pay *all sums* which the insured may become *legally obligated to pay* as a result of the underlying toxic tort claim. This standard policy language, however, has been the basis of various theories of coverage advanced by insureds and insurers alike.

The principle dispute, particularly in toxic tort bodily injury situations, arises over the issue of *when* an injury occurs within the meaning of the policy language. The earliest advanced theories were those of exposure versus manifestation—the former interpreted as an injurious contact with the toxic substance and the latter generally defined as when resulting injury becomes capable of a competent medical diagnosis. Therefor, either the carriers on the risk during the periods of exposure or the carrier on the risk at the time of manifestation would be obligated to the insured for defense and indemnification.

These theories have been expanded recently to include theories of *double* and *triple* triggers of coverage. Furthermore, the courts have begun to include in their decisions a resolution of more specific issues, including an analysis of the unlimited duty to defend.

§21.11   —Cases on Exposure versus Manifestation

The first major coverage action to address the exposure versus manifestation issue discussed in **§21.10** was *Insurance Co of North America v Forty-Eight Insulations, Inc.*[48] The basis for the adoption of the exposure theory was enunciated by the Sixth Circuit as follows:

> "Bodily injury" should be construed to include the tissue damage which takes place upon initial inhalation of asbestos. That is both a literal

---

[47] This standard policy language was apparently drafted under the auspices of insurance industry associations including The National Bureau of Casualty Underwriters, The Mutual Insurance Rating Bureau and, as of 1972, The Insurance Services Office. See Wendorff, *The New Standard Comprehensive General Liability Insurance Policy,* 1966 ABA Sec Insur Neglig & Comp Law Proc 250, 254. In American Home Prods Corp v Liberty Mut Ins Co, No 80 Civ 5653 (SDNY June 15, 1983), the court determined that no distinction was warranted between accident and occurrence policies for the purpose of defining the trigger of coverage. The trigger of coverage was held to be injury-in-fact or a real but undiscovered injury.

[48] 451 F Supp 1231 (ED Mich 1978), *affd,* 633 F2d 1212 (6th Cir 1980), *affd on rehg,* 657 F2d 814 (6th Cir), *cert denied,* 454 US 1109 (1981), *rehg denied,* 455 US 1009 (1982).

construction of the policy language and the construction which maximizes coverage. It is also the construction which, we think, best represents what the contracting parties intended.[49]

In rejecting the manifestation theory, the court stated:

> The thrust of the appellants' arguments is that we should apply a uniform manifestation rule in all cases, including this one, and not be concerned with medical intricacies. We see no evidence that this is what the parties meant.
>
> . . . .
>
> The policies themselves show what the insurance industry contemplated by cumulative trauma cases. Since 1962, each of the policies in question has included in its definition of "occurrence" a provision referring to continuous or repeated exposure to conditions which result in injury. There is strong evidence that coverage of diseases such as asbestosis was contemplated. Indeed, appellants openly admit that this is true. There is no similar provision in the policies restricting coverage to when asbestosis manifests itself. The insurance industry doubtless did not foresee the extent of the liability problem asbestosis cases would present. However, that in itself is no basis for construing the contract the way the appellants want.[50]

Shortly after the Sixth Circuit's opinion in *Forty-Eight Insulations,* The Fifth Circuit Court of Appeals also adopted the exposure theory in *Porter v American Optical Corp.*[51] The court's reliance upon *Forty-Eight Insulations* in its opinion is clear:

> We might prolong this already lengthy opinion by paragraphing or rephrasing the Sixth Circuit [*Forty-Eight*] opinion. We are content to say that we agree with its reasoning and result. Under the terms of the policies presently before us, we reject the "manifestation" theory. We accept the "injurious exposure" theory and the logically consequent rule of proration of liability for insurance carriers who were on the coverage while the injured party was exposed to the asbestos hazards which resulted in illness and death.[52]

Another *exposure* decision is *Commercial Union Insurance Co v Pittsburgh Corning Corp.*[53] The importance of that decision, however, is not only its holding that the "carrier must indemnify for asbestos injury caused by exposure during the

---

[49] 633 F2d at 1223.

[50] *Id* (footnotes omitted).

[51] 641 F2d 1128 (5th Cir), *cert denied,* 454 US 1109 (1981). *See also* Commercial Union Ins Co v Sepco Corp, CA No 81-G-1215-S (ND Ala Feb 22, 1983).

[52] 641 F2d at 1145.

[53] 553 F Supp 425 (ED Pa 1981).

policy period,"[54] but also in its determination that the duty to defend under certain policy language continues beyond the exhaustion of the policy limits.[55]

In *Eagle-Picher Industries v Liberty Mutual Insurance Co*,[56] the First Circuit Court of Appeals adopted the manifestation theory of coverage. While modifying the district court's definition of manifestation to mean "the date when the asbestos-related disease became reasonably capable of medical diagnosis,"[57] the circuit court relied upon the following language of the lower court:

> [T]o characterize as injury the minimal changes which occur in some people some time after exposure is not a supportable use of the word "injury" in the context of a liability insurance policy.
>
> In the present case, the Court is . . . faced with one construction which would provide coverage, and another which would leave Eagle-Picher uninsured. Here [comparing *Forty-Eight*] however, it is the manifestation theory which is likely to maximize the coverage provided to Eagle-Picher in the underlying lawsuits. As the earlier discussion demonstrates, this court's adoption of the manifestation theory is grounded on a finding that the relevant text of the insurance policies, as explained by the medical evidence, dictates manifestation.[58]

Recently, courts have extended the earlier holdings of exposure and manifestation cases to provide even greater potential coverage to an insured. Although it may be argued that the *double* trigger of coverage espoused in *Schering Corporation v Home Insurance Co*,[59] a DES coverage action, makes short shrift of the exposure theory, it does on the one hand recognize an injury as of the date of initial exposure and, on the other hand, gives far greater coverage than the manifestation theory alone. The court, having found "inapposite decisions construing CGL [Comprehensive General Liability] policies in the context of asbestos-related diseases,"[60] held:

> Proximity of origin and notice of injury will vary according to the nature of the harm. Some personal injuries covered by the policies at issue involve simultaneous notice and origin of harm, such as mental anguish, shock and humiliation. But years may separate inception and manifestation and manifestation of other covered harms, such as bodily injury or disease, particularly carcinomas. As the gap widens, either origin or no-

---

[54] *Id* 434.

[55] *Id. See* American Employers Ins Co v Goble Aircraft Inc, 205 Misc 1066, 131 NYS2d 393 (NY Sup Ct 1954).

[56] 523 F Supp 110 (D Mass 1981), *affd*, 682 F2d 12 (1st Cir 1982), *cert denied*, __ US __ (1983). For a DES case advancing the manifestation theory, *see* American Motorists Ins Co v ER Squibb & Sons, 95 Misc 2d 222, 406 NYS2d 658 (NY Sup Ct Co 1978).

[57] 628 F2d at 25.

[58] 523 F Supp at 118.

[59] 544 F Supp 613 (EDNY 1982), *revd on other grounds*, 712 F2d 4 (2d Cir 1983).

[60] *Id* 617.

tice may necessarily fall outside the purchased period of insurance. To uphold the policies' purpose of indemnification and the reasonable expectation of the insured, the Court concludes that either inception or discovery of injury may trigger Home's coverage obligations.

. . . Home must indemnify Schering for the latter's excess liability on account of personal injuries caused by prenatal exposure to dienestrol from which personal injury unexpectedly arises, *i.e.,* either originates or is discovered by the individual claimant during the policy periods . . . .[61]

The most far-reaching of all coverage cases to date has been *Keene Corp v Insurance Co of North America,*[62] which provides a *triple trigger* of coverage. In essence, the holding provides for one continuous injury trigger which begins with the first harmful exposure, continues through the cumulative injury stage (referred to as *exposure in residence*) and ends with manifestation or death, whichever occurs first. As stated by the United States Court of Appeals for the District of Columbia:

[E]ach insurer on the risk between the initial exposure and the manifestation of disease is liable to Keene for indemnification and defense costs.[63]

. . . .

[E]ach policy has a built-in trigger of coverage. Once triggered, each policy covers Keene's liability. There is nothing in the policies that provides for a reduction of the insurer's liability if an injury occurs only in part during a policy period. As we interpret the policies, they cover Keene's entire liability once they are triggered. That interpretation is based on the terms of the policies themselves.[64]

---

61 *Id* 622.

62 667 F2d 1034 (DC Cir 1981), *cert denied,* 455 US 1007, *rehg denied,* 456 US 951 (1982). Although constantly under attack from the insurance industry, *Keene,* based upon its record, appears to be supported by:
1. The standard policy language
2. Insurance industry documents and related testimony
3. Medical evidence of how and when an injury occurs
4. A number of earlier decisions dealing with insurance coverage for long-term injuries in a nonasbestos context

See Oshinsky, Gilbert & Shulman, Trigger and Scope of Coverage under Comprehensive General Liability Insurance Policies in Toxic Substance Cases, Legal Notes & Viewpoints Q, Vol 3 No 1 (Nov 1982). *See also* Crown, Cork & Seal Co v Aetna Cas & Sur Co, No 1292 (Pa Ct CP Aug 2, 1983). *Compare* Sandoz, Inc v Employer's Liab Assur Corp, 554 F Supp 257 (DNJ 1983) in which the court, recognizing that New Jersey law was applied in *Forty-Eight,* nonetheless adopted the injury theory of coverage.

63 667 F2d at 1041.

64 *Id* 1048. The *Keene* Court in its opinion states:
Thus initially, the full insurance obligation to Keene must be divided among the insurers whose policies are triggered based on the facts brought out in the tort suit against Keene. . . . [T]he insurance obligations can be allocated among all the insurers whose policies are found to cover a particular injury.
667 F2d at 1051 (footnote omitted).

§21.12   —Relationship between the Insurer and the Insured

It is vital that in-house litigators, the corporation's risk management department, and the company's insurance brokers work together to submit claims in a timely fashion and to cooperate fully with the carrier at all stages of the claims handling procedure. To do otherwise could result in the denial of the claim for defense and indemnification purposes.

The question whether notice to the carrier is sufficient depends upon its being timely and adequately descriptive. The purpose of the notice requirement is to give the insurer an opportunity to investigate the occurrence while the facts are still clear in the minds of all concerned. It rests upon the current availability of witnesses and evidence.[65] The description to be included within the notice should give "all that anyone could ask for by way of information that was available at the time."[66] As a general rule, the issue of sufficiency is governed by which jurisdiction's law governs the interpretation of the insurance contract.

It is virtually impossible to predict what amount of time must have passed between the occurrence and notice to the carrier for a court to deem it *late notice.* Usually, it is a jury question with the burden on the insured to establish a *reasonable, sufficient,* or *good faith* excuse.[67] In certain jurisdictions, however, the burden is upon the insurer to demonstrate prejudice.[68]

Finally, the insured has a duty to cooperate with the insurer at all times during the claims handling procedure. It is the policyholder's obligation to make a frank disclosure to the insurer of all relevant and material facts in its possession regarding the claim.[69]

§21.13   Conclusion

The in-house management of civil third-party and workers' compensation litigation involves a number of similar functions and overlapping responsibili-

---

[65] Granite State Minerals v American Ins Co, 435 F Supp 159 (D Mass 1977); Stonewall Ins Co v Moorby, 298 A2d 826 (Vt 1972).

[66] Liberty Mut Ins Co v Haecker Indus, 326 F Supp 489, 491 (ED Pa 1971).

[67] Deso v London & Lancashire Ind Co, 3 NY2d 127, 143 NE2d 889, 164 NYS2d 689 (1957); Kason v City of New York, 83 Misc 2d 810, 373 NYS2d 456 (NY Sup Ct 1975) (citing Security Mut Ins Co v Acker-Fitzsimmons Corp, 31 NY2d 436, 292 NE2d 76, 340 NYS2d 397 (1972)); *see also* Annot, 24 ALR3d 1007 (1969). Property insurance: Insured's ignorance of loss or casualty, cause of damage, coverage or existence of policy, or identity of insurer, as affecting or excusing compliance with requirements, as to time for giving notice, making proof of loss, or bringing action against insurer.

[68] Comment, *The Materiality of Prejudice to the Insurer as a Result of the Insured's Failure to Give Timely Notice,* 74 Dick L Rev 260 (1969-70).

[69] Car & General Ins Co v Goldstein, 179 F Supp 888 (SDNY 1959), *affd,* 277 F2d 162 (2d Cir 1960); Coleman v New Amsterdam Cas Co, 247 NY 271 (1928).

ties. These include accountability to senior management, responsiveness to local counsel, implementation of insurance coverage, and a close daily coordination of each type of claim so as to prevent one from prejudicially affecting the other. The goal of this effort is to promote meaningful cost effectiveness without sacrificing high-quality legal representation. It is a difficult, but necessary, task if the company's long-term national defense strategy is to be successful.

22 Trial Strategy/Case Management*

Steven R. McCown, Esq.†

---

* The author wishes to gratefully acknowledge the assistance of Ronald A. Manthey, Esq., Jenkens & Gilchrist, Dallas, Texas in the preparation of this chapter.

† Partner, Jenkens & Gilchrist, Dallas, Texas.

§22.01   Introduction

The stakes are high when a toxic tort case matures to trial. The trial often decides the fate of a product or process and has an impact on users or those who claim to have been harmed by the product or process, on a company, on an industry, or even on the local, regional, or national economy. Many times, the primary product or process of a company or industry may be at issue. If the product or process involves a dominant employer or industry in an area, potential claimants may involve the majority of the local population. Local, regional, or national politics may be involved, whether through official governmental intervention, political pressure, or legislative reaction. Often, media attention may be focused on the trial.

Although many toxic tort cases can be managed conceptually as sophisticated personal injury or products liability cases, the subjective, emotional reactions to the toxic tort case must be recognized. Strong public and official reaction is often the case where there are claims of danger to the environment and populace. This is especially true where catastrophic results may have occurred.

Within this type of charged environment, decisions concerning trial strategy and case management are extremely important and often determinative on the outcome of the trial. Because toxic tort litigation mandates sophisticated technical and scientific responses, extra effort must be made to insure that these responses will be understood in a rational, unemotional manner by the trier of fact. It is this that distinguishes toxic tort litigation from ordinary personal injury or products liability cases.

This chapter is not, by necessity, an attempt to provide an in-depth analysis on trial strategy and case management of toxic tort litigation. Many excellent treatises, books, articles, and seminars have examined, in detail, these subjects. However, this chapter deals with broad, practical issues facing outside counsel in toxic tort litigation.

§22.02   Coordination with the Client

Because toxic tort litigation is complex factually, legally, and, often, politically, a high level of coordination of the case must be established between the client and outside counsel.

Initially, it is essential to develop effective lines of communication with the client. One individual or group should be designated within the client's organization with whom outside counsel can rely for needed information, people, support, and decision-making. This individual is typically in-house counsel or a corporate official responsible for claims, litigation, operations, etc. The parameters of the need-to-know circle must be established, and the company should inform outside counsel who is to receive copies of correspondence, pleadings, notices, etc. Care must be taken to insure the protection of the attorney-client privilege and the preservation of attorney work product. Guidelines should be established for responses to inquiries from the public, media, and political entities.

Because of the technical and scientific complexity of toxic tort litigation, outside counsel must have access to a wide variety of personnel within the client's organization. These include public relations, marketing and sales people, engineering and technical people, production and management representatives, and many more, not only in a company's headquarters but also in regional or branch offices. Often, a variety of viewpoints and information can be obtained from the varied sources, especially individuals located in branch or regional offices who may have more *hands-on* experience with a product or process in issue. However, efficient utilization of such sources must be made so as not to burden an entire organization with litigation support. This is where coordination between outside counsel and the client is most essential—balancing the needs of defense with the day-to-day operations of the organization. The decision is best a joint one of outside counsel and the client, with both defense and organizational needs kept in mind.

Because of the tremendous effort from outside counsel and the client that must be devoted to the defense of toxic tort litigation, early commitment by both must be made to the defense of the case. Employees must be made aware of the seriousness of the pending litigation and its potential ramifications. Likewise, the company should expect from outside counsel devotion of effort commensurate with the seriousness of the case. This commitment will avoid the development of attitudes such as the case is *someone else's problem or responsibility* or that the case is *spurious,* with the resulting feeling that the needed preparation and devotion of time is not productive and interferes with normal operations. Effective coordination and communication between the company and outside counsel will avoid this often fatal attitude.

Of initial importance is the education of outside counsel regarding the client's business (past and present), organizational and decision-making structure, products, and processes. Outside counsel also must be familiar with the industry and environment in which the company operates. A myopic view by outside counsel of the client often results in the failure to discover useful information that can humanize an organization. For example, although the product or process involved in the toxic tort litigation may be viewed by the public in a bad light, other company products or processes may be universally accepted and, indeed, proclaimed. This type of information can be crucial in overcoming inherent prejudices against the client as an entity. Another use of this information may involve a specific product or process. Although it may have very toxic results on people or the environment when misused, when properly used the benefits to society may greatly outweigh the risks. This type of information can overcome fear or prejudice against the specific product or process.

Next, outside counsel must be educated, thoroughly, on the involved substance or process. Here, use of in-house personnel and in-house experts, technical or otherwise, is important. Often, these individuals were involved in the development of the involved product or process and can provide invaluable insight into the issues involved. Moreover, good witnesses, both expert and not, come from these groups of individuals. They can also provide names of independent witnesses, expert and otherwise, with knowledge of the product or process in issue.

Education of outside counsel can include many things. Demonstrations and inspections are important. Disclosure of all documents is essential. These documents may include any written material or literature available, such as technical designs, manuals, advertisements, research, testing and development, and industry publications, standards, or practices, if any. Also, relevant governmental regulations, standards, or laws need to be ascertained and the company's interaction, contacts, correspondence, or required governmental reports, etc. with regulatory agencies must be examined. Design, manufacture, suppliers and subcontractors, marketing and distribution processes, and use of dealers or wholesalers must be identified or explained. Past problems, complaints, or similar litigation should be analyzed and discussed. Competitor's like experiences should be analyzed. Postincident changes or modifications should be disclosed and discussed. The most cost-effective resource a company can have is a litigation *manual* prepared from past, similar litigation experiences. This tool, if effectively prepared and used, can draw on the wealth of experience form previous litigation and avoid reinventing the wheel with each new case.

Coordination is also essential where potential witnesses involve former employees. Outside counsel must be aware of former employees who, for whatever reason, may be sources of adverse testimony. Likewise, *friendly* former employees may make excellent witnesses due to their impartiality. Relationships and contacts with them, by necessity, must come directly (at least initially) from the client.

Access to physical evidence and documents is another area of needed coordination. Within the company's organization, outside counsel should have access to the sources of physical evidence and documents relevant to the case. The custody and control of these matters are crucial, especially in light of the well-accepted principle that missing documents, except those subject to reasonable retention programs, often are viewed as having been deliberately destroyed.

Finally, the practical considerations of trial dictate the need for coordination between outside counsel and the client. Often, the trial is located in an area not convenient to witnesses. Vacations and other plans are interrupted. Coordination of travel arrangements, accommodations, etc. is essential to a smooth trial. Not only does good coordination and planning help to alleviate many of the anxieties developed about the trial by witnesses, it also insures an efficient and orderly presentation of witnesses.

§22.03   Is the Case in the *Right* Court?

As diverse as our country is, geographically and politically, in which court a plaintiff chooses to file a toxic tort case is often the most critical choice made.

It is no secret to either the plaintiff's or the defendant's counsel that some jurisdictions are known for their liberal or conservative viewpoints towards personal injury and related cases. Moreover, this philosophy can change between the state and federal courts sitting in the identical geographical area. Additionally, practical considerations often dictate that outside counsel analyze whether the forum chosen by the plaintiff is such that a fair trial will be available or whether a defense will be impractical, burdensome, or costly. Two tools are available in the federal forum to deal with such issues—removal and change of venue.

§22.04   —Removal

The federal law of removal[1] permits defendants to have actions that are originally filed in state court removed to federal court for trial. Many of the stated purposes for removal are rooted in historical conflicts, such as the animosity between the original states. Important factors in toxic tort litigation are local judicial attitudes, whether state judges are elected or appointed, and the area from which jurors are drawn. Moreover, availability of the federal rules of procedure and evidence, as contrasted to state rules, may be crucial to case strategy. Whatever the rationale for removal, however, of primary consideration is the tactical and practical advantages brought about by having the case heard in federal rather than state court.

Removal is based on the premise that defendants have a right to a federal forum on certain issues and under limited conditions, thereby depriving a state from having its courts decide the issue. The federal courts have recognized the conflict and, as a result, the general removal statutes are strictly construed against removal.[2]

The federal district court must have jurisdiction to hear the cause of action pending in the state court.[3] Not only must the district court have original jurisdiction to hear the action, but its jurisdiction is also derivative; it cannot hold any greater jurisdiction over the matter than existed in the state court.[4] Lack of subject matter jurisdiction in either the federal or state court will, as a rule, prevent the federal court from ruling on the dispute.[5]

---

[1] 28 USC §§1441-1451; Fed R Civ P 81.

[2] Shamrock Oil & Gas Corp v Sheets, 313 US 100 (1941); Illinois v Kerr-McGee Chem Corp, 677 F2d 571 (7th Cir), *cert denied,* 103 S Ct 469 (1982).

[3] *See, e.g.,* Snow v Ford Motor Co, 561 F2d 787 (9th Cir 1977).

[4] Liquid Carriers Corp v American Marine Corp, 375 F2d 951 (2d Cir 1967).

[5] Jacobson v Tahoe Regional Planning Agency, 566 F2d 1353 (9th Cir 1977), *revd in part on other grounds sub nom* Lake County Estates Inc v Tahoe Regional Planning Agency, 440 US 391 (1979). Removal is a statutory creation and its construction is based on federal law. Shamrock Oil & Gas Corp v Sheets, 313 US 100 (1941); Illinois v Kerr-McGee Chem Corp, 677 F2d 571 (7th Cir 1982). Unlike changes of venue under 28 USC §1404, see **§§22.06-22.07,** the decision to allow the defendant to remove the action to federal court is not based on convenience, interests of the parties, or judicial economy. Once the statutory prerequisites are met, removal is automatic. Thermtron Prods, Inc v Hermansdorfer, 423 US 336 (1976).

The federal statute provides:

(a) Except as otherwise expressly provided by Act of Congress, any civil action brought in a State court of which the district courts of the United States have original jurisdiction, may be removed by the defendant or the defendants, to the district court of the United States for the district and division embracing the place where such action is pending.

(b) Any civil action of which the district courts have original jurisdiction founded on a claim or right arising under the Constitution, treaties or laws of the United States shall be removable without regard to the citizenship or residence of the parties. Any other such action shall be removable only if none of the parties in interest properly joined and served as defendants is a citizen of the State in which such action is brought.

(c) Whenever a separate and independent claim or cause of action, which would be removable if sued upon alone, is joined with one or more otherwise nonremovable claims or causes of action, the entire case may be removed and the district court may determine all issues therein, or, in its discretion, may remand all matters not otherwise within its original jurisdiction.[6]

Section 1441(a) grants authority to remove civil actions, but it has limitations which are construed narrowly. The first restriction is found in the language quoted above which states: "Except as otherwise expressly provided by Act of Congress. . . ." Given that removal is a statutory creation, Congress can give but may also withdraw authority.[7] Next, the action must be civil as opposed to criminal; it must be *brought;* and the action must be in a *state court* as opposed to an administrative tribunal. Interpretation of these terms is governed by federal law; the state's designation of any particular action as civil or criminal is not controlling.[8] These particular terms are given broad, functional interpretations. For instance, when distinguishing state courts from administrative tribunals, the federal courts look to the nature of the action, whether it is inter partes, and whether—regardless of the name given to the decision-making body—the tribunal has a judicial function as opposed to an executive or implementing function.[9] The essential point to remember is that while the individual requirements of each phrase must be met before removal will be finally approved, the courts will not be restricted by the form of the action but rather will look to its substance.

The federal district court must have original jurisdiction over the civil action brought in the state court. Such original jurisdiction may come from a federal

---

[6] 28 USC §1441.

[7] *See* 28 USC §1445(c), which prohibits removal of civil actions arising under state workers' compensation laws.

[8] Road Dist v St Louis & SW Ry, 257 US 547 (1922).

[9] *See* Floeter v CW Transport, Inc, 597 F2d 1110 (7th Cir 1979) (contains a discussion of the term "state court").

question arising under the laws of the United States,[10] diversity jurisdiction,[11] or any specific grant of jurisdictional authority. While §1441 both expands and restricts certain provisions of original jurisdiction for removal purposes, it is critical in any removal action to show that the action could have been brought originally in federal district court.[12]

The courts look to the plaintiff's pleadings to determine if all the requirements for original jurisdiction exist. However, many courts will also look to the defendant's petition for removal to ascertain whether a proper amount in controversy exists.[13] Moreover, courts will not allow the plaintiff to plead out a necessary federal question issue by phrasing it in state common law or statutory terms simply to avoid removal.[14]

The jurisdiction of the federal court is derivative. Consequently, the district court gains only what subject matter jurisdiction the state court had.[15] While

---

[10] 28 USC §1331.

[11] 28 USC §1332.

[12] McCarty v Amoco Pipeline Co, 595 F2d 389 (7th Cir 1979).

[13] *See,* Redevelopment Auth v City of Hope N Med Center, 383 F Supp 813 (ED Pa 1974). The normal rule for removal of diversity cases is that there must be over $10,000 in controversy. Further, the plaintiffs must, as a rule, be suing for over $10,000 on each cause of action. Thus, one may not remove a case under simple diversity just because several distinct claims add up to over $10,000. This is true regardless of whether one plaintiff has multiple claims that are separate and distinct or several plaintiffs join together in one suit; the dollar amounts cannot be aggregated. Zahn v International Paper Co, 414 US 291 (1973). However, where one plaintiff sues for over $10,000 on one separate and independent claim, other joined actions or claims by separate plaintiffs—even though under the jurisdiction limit—may also be removed from the state court.

The principle that allows the federal court to accept related state law issues where the suit is originally brought in federal court is pendent or ancillary jurisdiction. United Mine Workers v Gibbs, 382 US 715 (1966) (pendent jurisdiction over state and federal claims form a common nucleus of operative facts); Moore v New York Cotton Exch, 270 US 593 (1926) (authority to resolve related and necessary state claim in resolution of entire case). These doctrines are, for all practical purposes, combined for use in removal of state court cases in the statutory grant of jurisdiction found at 28 USC §1441(c). §1441(c) permits the removal of all joined causes of actions between the plaintiff and the named defendants as long as one separate and independent cause of action satisfies the court's original jurisdiction. Northside Iron & Metal Co Inc v Dobson & Johnson, Inc, 483 F2d 798 (5th Cir 1973); Hermann v Braniff Airways, 308 F Supp 1094 (SDNY 1969); Johns-Manville Sales Corp v Chicago Title & Trust Co, 261 F Supp 905 (ND Ill 1966). This grant of jurisdictional power permits the courts to hear all the joined causes of action related to a particular matter regardless of whether all the defendants are sued for over $10,000 or whether all the plaintiffs have claims in excess of $10,000. Thus, even though some claims are for less than $10,000, the entire case can be removed to federal court. *See* Abing v Pain, Webber, Jackson & Curtis, 538 F Supp 1193 (D Minn 1982). *But see* Gamble v Central of Ga Ry, 486 F2d 781 (5th Cir 1973) (holding Fed Emp Liability Act 45 USC §56 is not to be removed, even under §1441(c)).

[14] Illinois v Kerr-McGee Chem Corp, 677 F2d 571 (7th Cir 1982).

[15] Wamp v Chattanooga Housing Auth, 527 F2d 595 (6th Cir 1975), *cert denied,* 425 US 992 (1976); Jacobson v Tahoe Regional Planning Agency, 566 F2d 1353 (9th Cir 1977).

this rule appears obvious at first, consider it as applied to the situation where a federal question is raised in a state court that does not have jurisdiction over the matter. Had the action been filed in federal district court originally, jurisdiction would have existed; but application of the derivative jurisdiction rule requires dismissal of the action on removal. The logic of this application of the rule has been challenged, but appears to have continued vitality.[16]

Finally, §1441(a) allows the action to be removed by the defendant and states that proper venue will exist in the federal district court "embracing the place where such action is pending." The proper party to remove the action is the defendant, and, again, which party is truly the defendant will be determined by federal law.[17] Normally, the authority to petition for removal is given only to the defendants that the plaintiff brought into the suit.[18] However, several courts allow defendants of cross-claims and third-party claims to remove the action if they state a separate and independent claim under §1441(a).[19] If there is more than one defendant, all must join in the petition for removal unless they are only nominal or unnecessary parties.[20] but where a separate and independent claim under §1441(c) is the basis for the removal, only the defendants to that claim must join.[21]

§22.05   —Limits to Removal

Section 1442(b)[22] further delineates the conditions and terms under which the district courts have removal powers. First, where the district court has original jurisdiction "founded on a claim or right arising under the Constitution," the action is removable regardless of the citizenship or residence of the parties.[23] The location or citizenship of the parties is not important because the purpose of this provision is to allow for the trial of federal questions in federal court. Note once again that the court must have original jurisdiction. This restriction is illustrated by statutes where Congress has required the plaintiff to chose his or her forum—either state or federal but not both. Should he or she file in state court originally, no jurisdiction exists in the federal court,

---

[16] *See* Ice Projects, Inc v World Hockey Assn, 443 F Supp 483 (ED Pa 1977); 1A J. Moore, B. Ringle & J. Wicker, Moore's Federal Practice ¶0.157 [3.-2] (2d ed 1983).

[17] Chicago RI&PR Co v Stude, 346 US 574 (1954).

[18] Lowe's of Montgomery, Inc v Smith, 432 F Supp 1008 (MD Ala 1977) (full discussion of principle that removal is limited to plaintiffs or defendants—third-party claims are insufficient).

[19] *See* Marsh Inv Corp v Langford, 652 F2d 583 (5th Cir 1981), *cert denied,* 454 US 1163 (1982).

[20] Bradley v Maryland Casualty Co, 382 F2d 415 (8th Cir 1967).

[21] *See generally* PP Farmers' Elevator Co v Farmers Elevator Mut Ins Co, 395 F2d 546 (7th Cir 1968); Nowell v Nowell, 272 F Supp 298 (D Conn 1967).

[22] 28 USC §1441(b), quoted in **§22.04.**

[23] Federal Deposit Ins Corp v Otero, 598 F2d 627 (1st Cir 1979).

and removal is not authorized under this part of §1441(b).[24]

The determination of whether a federal question exists is based on the normal factors a district court considers when ascertaining jurisdiction over a suit initially filed in federal court. The well-pleaded rule applies and the defendant is limited to the plaintiff's pleadings. He or she cannot add a federal question to the case through a petition for removal.[25] Naturally, the federal issue—i.e., one where the case will stand or fall on the interpretation of a federal statute, right, etc.—should be an essential element to the case.[26] Once established, however, the court may remove not only the federal issue but also other causes of action under pendant jurisdiction.[27]

The other portion of §1441(b) works to restrict the removal of cases that may otherwise have been removable based on original jurisdiction alone. The normal requirements of diversity jurisdiction[28] apply (complete diversity between plaintiffs and defendants, over $10,000 in controversy, etc.), but two additional elements are added. First, the statute denies the court the power to remove on the basis of diversity where one of "the parties in interest properly joined and served as defendants is a citizen of the State in which such action is brought."[29] Thus, even with complete diversity, if one of the defendants is a resident of the state in which the action is filed, the action cannot be removed.[30] Further, the nonresident defendants also may not remove the action under §1441(a) or (b) based on these facts because of the requirement that all defendants join in the motion. Second, for purposes of removal, diversity must be established both at the time of the state suit and the motion to remove. If diversity cannot be shown at either point, removal cannot be based on diversity under §1441(a) or (b).[31]

Unlike §1441(b), §1441(c) (quoted in **§22.04**), in effect, expands what matters the district court may remove by allowing the court to remove otherwise nonremovable actions which are properly joined with an independent claim or cause of action that is removable.[32] Two aspects of §1441(c) warrant explanation. The first is what constitutes a separate and independant claim or cause of action; the second is whether the authority to remove actions that are otherwise nonremovable extends to every nonremovable action regardless of the reason it cannot be removed independently.

---

[24] *See, e.g.,* Federal Employer Liability Act, 45 USC §56.

[25] Milligan v Milligan, 484 F2d 446 (8th Cir 1973); Illinois v Kerr-McGee Chem Corp, 677 F2d 571 (7th Cir 1982).

[26] Gully v First Natl Bank in Meridan, 299 US 109 (1936).

[27] Wilson v Intercollegiate (Big Ten) Conference Athletic Assn, 668 F2d 962 (7th Cir), *cert denied,* 103 S Ct 70 (1982).

[28] 28 USC §1332.

[29] 28 USC §1441(b).

[30] Martin v Snyder, 148 US 663 (1893); American Oil Co v Egan, 357 F Supp 610 (D Minn 1973).

[31] Kaneshrio v North Am Co for Life & Health Ins, 496 F Supp 452 (D Hawaii 1980).

[32] Herrmann v Braniff Airways, 308 F Supp 1094 (SDNY 1969).

A separate and independent claim or cause of action is one with a separate and distinct cause of action. A claim is not independent simply because two defendants are sued for the same injury or wrong to a plaintiff. This is best explained by way of example. Where a plaintiff or plaintiffs sue the defendants for both personal injury and slander, the actions are distinct causes of actions with different proof, evidence, and legal considerations. The defendants may separate the causes of actions for purposes of §1441(c). By way of contradistinction, a plaintiff who suffers one wrong—e.g., an injury—but sues multiple defendants for recovery is suing on only one cause of action. The defendants cannot simply divide themselves in order to avail themselves of §1441(c). In the example of the injury, there is only one cause of action; therefore, there is no separate and independent cause of action.[33]

The plaintiff's pleadings are determinative of whether a separate and independent cause of action exists.[34] However, some circuits have permitted the cross-claims of a third-party defendant to qualify as the separate and independent claim.[35] Note also that the restriction to the plaintiff's pleadings for purposes of removal under §1441 does not apply to the special removal provision of §§1442-1444. Under the special provisions, the entity or person is given the right to remove; it is the identity of the party rather than the nature of the action that is controlling.

Finally, recognizing that certain matters brought up with the entire case may be inappropriate for resolution in the federal district court, the statute permits the court to remand "all matters not otherwise within its original jurisdiction."[36] This allows the court to determine the equities of the situation and the public interest in deciding whether to try matters it would not otherwise have been able to hear because of a lack of jurisdiction. Particular attention is paid to those issues which are of vital interest to the state.[37]

Beyond the statutory prerequisites to removal which are discussed in this and the preceding sections, there are issues involving: when to file the petition to remove (timeliness), waiver (improper venue), choice of law, and other procedural requirements. These issues are beyond the scope of this chapter, but reference to the statute and interpreting cases should be made since compliance with the statutory prerequisites is mandatory for a valid removal.

§22.06 —Venue

Venue questions resolve the issue of where the case is to be tried. Strategical and tactical goals can be served through venue procedures; forum-shopping

---

[33] Union Planters Natl Bank v CBS, Inc, 557 F2d 84 (6th Cir 1977).

[34] Great N Ry v Alexander, 246 US 276 (1918); Scott v Metropolitan Life Ins Co, 450 F Supp 801 (WD Okla 1978).

[35] Marsh Inv Corp v Langford, 652 F2d 583 (5th Cir 1981), *cert denied,* 454 US 1163 (1982).

[36] 28 USC §1441(c).

[37] *See* Louisiana Power & Light Co v City of Thibodaux, 360 US 25 (1959).

can be thwarted. The relative expense and convenience of forums can also be analyzed.

The applicable statutory provisions relative to venue are 28 USC §§1391 (venue), 1404 (change of venue), 1406 (cure or waiver of defects), and 1407 (multidistrict litigation). Section 1404(a) states: "For the convenience of parties and witnesses, in the interest of justice, a district court may transfer any civil action to any other district or division where it might have been brought."[38] This provision is not designed to cure improper venue. It is intended to allow federal courts to transfer actions to other courts where appropriate. Unlike §1406, which deals with improper venue, a motion to transfer under §1404(a) does not have to be included in a motion under Rule 12(b) of the Federal Rules of Civil Procedure or be lost. Consequently, a motion to transfer may be raised at any time.

Section 1404(a) is limited to transferring actions between districts or divisions of the United States district courts. In this way, it is also different from the common law doctrine of forum non conveniens, which allows for dismissal of the action, and is, therefore, governed by different standards.

Section 1404(a) is a procedural tool designed "to prevent the waste of 'time, energy and money' and 'to protect litigants, witnesses and the public against unnecessary inconvenience and expense'. . . ."[39] At least one court has stated that the section's purposes are to give the defendant an equal footing in the case and to avoid forum-shopping.[40] Efficiency of the judicial proceeding is commonly set forth as a primary function of the statute.[41]

The enactment of §1404(a) brought about significant changes from what existed under the doctrine of forum non conveniens; it removes dismissal as an option available to the district court under §1404(a)—only transfer is authorized.

The Supreme Court, in one of its early reviews of the changes, stated:

> When Congress adopted §1404(a), it intended to do more than just codify the existing law on *forum non' conveniens*. . . . As a consequence, we believe that Congress, by the term "for the convenience of parties and witnesses, in the interest of justice," intended to permit courts to grant transfers upon a lesser showing of inconvenience. This is not to say that the relevant factors have changed or that the plaintiff's choice of forum is not to be considered, but only that the discretion to be exercised is broader.[42]

Since that time, the statute has been construed liberally, giving district courts broad discretion. No one factor, including the plaintiff's choice of forum, is

---

[38] 28 USC §1404(a).

[39] Van Dusen v Barrack, 376 US 612, 616 (1964).

[40] Torres v Steamship Rasario, 125 F Supp 496 (SDNY 1954).

[41] Jacobs v Lancaster, 526 F Supp 767 (WD Okla 1981).

[42] Norwood v Kirkpatrick, 349 US 29, 32 (1955).

controlling, whereas under forum non conveniens certain rules were rather rigidly applied.[43]

As distinct from §1404, §1406 allows a district court to dismiss or transfer an action "which is filed . . . laying venue in the *wrong* division or district. . . ."[44] Thus, unlike §1404(a), the purpose of §1406 is to permit, in the interest of justice, an action to proceed where, without a transfer, it could not otherwise.[45] Because of the different purposes—convenience of the parties under §1404 versus curing improper venue under §1406—different standards and procedures apply. These distinctions should be noted.

Venue is determined either by the specific terms of the statute under which one is bringing an action, or under 28 USC §1391, which provides for proper venue in diversity cases, when suing a corporation, etc. Assuming a plaintiff files in a district which is not proper under §1391, the defendant may make a motion to dismiss for improper venue. The timing of this motion or objection is governed by Rules 12(b) and (h) of the Federal Rules of Civil Procedure, which dictate that the defense must be raised in a timely manner or it will be lost. This must be contrasted with §1404, where a motion to transfer may be raised at any time. Should the defense not be raised in a timely fashion, venue is waived.[46]

Where an objection to venue is raised in a timely fashion, the district court, under §1406(a), may transfer the action rather than dismiss it where an alternate forum with proper venue and jurisdiction is available.[47] Moreover, even though the statute reads: "laying venue in the *wrong* division,"[48] several courts have ruled that the action may be transferred regardless of whether venue is proper or improper in the transferor court.[49]

Finally, depending on which section is chosen, the substantive law applied to the merits of the case will vary. Under §1404(a), the substantive law is governed by the state in which the action was filed; however, under §1406(a), the substantive law will come from the state in which the transferee court with proper venue and jurisdiction is located. The conflicting results are rooted in the notion that the plaintiff should receive the benefit of the substantive law he or she originally selected as long as his or her action was proper there

---

[43] *See* Van Dusen v Barrack, 376 US 612 (1964); Codex Corp v Milgo Elec Corp, 553 F2d 735 (1st Cir), *cert denied*, 434 US 860 (1977); Time, Inc v Manning, 366 F2d 690 (5th Cir 1966).

[44] 28 USC §1406(a) (emphasis added).

[45] *See generally* Goldlawr v Heiman, 369 US 463 (1962).

[46] 28 USC §1406(b), Concession Consultants, Inc v Mirisch, 355 F2d 369 (2d Cir 1966).

[47] Nation v United States Govt, 512 F Supp 121 (SD Ohio 1981).

[48] 28 USC §1406(a) (emphasis added).

[49] *See* Ellis v Great Southwestern Corp, 464 F2d 1099, 1103-07 (5th Cir 1981) (ruling that §1406(a) may be used regardless of improper venue and discussing split in case law on the issue). But see 15 C. Wright, A. Miller & E. Cooper, Federal Practice and Procedure §3827, at 171-72 (1976). (contention that the two transfer sections, §§1404 and 1406, must be distinguished by whether venue is proper or improper.)

(§1404) but should not be able to gain an advantage by filing in a forum with improper venue and then having it transferred (§1406).[50]

§22.07 —Procedures and Requirements for Transfer of Venue

Transfers of venue are requested by motion. Both the defendant and the plaintiff may make a motion to transfer, or the court may act sua sponte.[51] Third parties are generally viewed as not having standing to object to venue, but courts will often consider the arguments of a third party without first ruling on his or her standing.[52] As stated in **§22.06,** the motion may be made at any time, as long as the court still has jurisdiction over the matter.

A motion cannot be granted to transfer the action until a federal district court has the case properly before it.[53] However, most courts have ruled that in personam jurisdiction need not exist over the defendant in the transferor court in order for the action to be transferred to a court with proper in personam jurisdiction.[54] The court may, in any event, deny such a motion in the interest of justice.[55]

Section 1404(a) restricts the transfer of civil actions to "any other district or division where it might have been brought."[56] The transferee court must have subject matter jurisdiction, personal jurisdiction, and proper venue. Further, the Supreme Court has ruled transfer cannot be made to a court where defects in venue or personal jurisdiction can only be cured by the defendant's waiver of his personal rights; the transferee court must be one where the plaintiff could have brought the suit as a matter of right.[57] Thus, proper venue and in personam jurisdiction must exist in the transferee court before the action can

---

[50] Van Dusen v Barrack, 376 US 612 (1964); Ellis v Great Southwestern Corp, 464 F2d 1099 (5th Cir 1981); Martin v Stokes, 623 F2d 469 (6th Cir 1980).

[51] *See* American Standard, Inc v Bendix Corp, 487 F Supp 254 (WD Mo 1980) (plaintiff may make motion for transfer); National Acceptance Co of Am v Wechsler, 489 F Supp 642 (ND Ill 1980) (court may raise issue on own initiative).

[52] See generally 15 C. Wright, A. Miller & E. Cooper, Federal Practice and Procedure, §3844, at 208-16 (1976).

[53] Gulf Oil Corp v Gilbert, 330 US 501 (1947); James v Daley & Lewis, 406 F Supp 645 (D Del 1976). *But see* Lamar v American Basketball Assn, 468 F Supp 1198 (SDNY 1979) (both personal jurisdiction and proper venue were lacking New York, but action transferred to state where both would exist).

[54] *See, e.g.,* United States v Berkowitz, 328 F2d 358 (3d Cir), *cert denied,* 379 US 821 (1964). *But see* Martin v Stokes, 623 F2d 469 (6th Cir 1980) (§1404(a) is applicable only where both personal jurisdiction and venue are proper).

[55] *See* Brown v Grimm, 624 F2d 58 (7th Cir 1980) (motion denied where an action was filed without in personam jurisdiction and only a few days were left before expiration of statute of limitations).

[56] 28 USC §1404(a).

[57] Hoffman v Blaski, 364 US 335, 343-44 (1960); *see also* Foster-Milburn Co v Knight, 181 F2d 949 (2d Cir 1950).

be transferred.[58] Note that the transferor court need not have in personam jurisdiction to transfer the action. The determination of whether the action might have been brought in the transferee court is made at the time of the filing of the action.[59]

Venue must be proper in the transferee court, which is a requirement that has some significance when suing a corporation. Section 1391(c) states that "a corporation may be sued in any judicial district in which it is incorporated or licensed to do business or is doing business, and such judicial district shall be regarded as the residence of such corporation for venue purposes."[60] The issue that must be resolved before suit is filed is whether, simply because a corporation is incorporated in a state and may or may not be doing business in each of the state's districts, a corporation can be sued in any of the federal districts of that state or must be sued only in the districts where it is actually doing business. The courts have split on the issue because of the varying importance given to the fact the corporation is empowered to conduct business in every part of the state regardless of whether it exercises the power.[61]

Section 1404(a) permits the transfer of any *civil action*. The term *civil action* has been held to include almost any action regardless of special venue provisions.[62] Transfer has been held to be within the district court's discretion in most cases; however, there are exceptions where the district court must address the issues presented and cannot transfer.[63]

Another action that may not be transferred is a matter in rem, an action taken directly against a thing, such as a ship, rather than against a person, where it is the only basis for the court's jurisdiction. However, when the case involves matters with both in personam and in rem jurisdiction, the court may join both

---

[58] *In re* Pope, 580 F2d 620 (DC Cir 1978); McLouth Steel Corp v Jewell Coal & Coke Co, 432 F Supp 10 (ED Tenn 1976).

[59] *In re* Fine Paper Antitrust Litig, 685 F2d 810 (3d Cir 1982); International Patent Dev Corp v Wyomont Partners, 489 F Supp 266 (D Nev 1980). Many concerns over whether problems with venue and personal jurisdiction in the transferee court will bar the transfer of the action are readily resolved through use of special venue provisions such as in the Clayton Act, 15 USC §22, or through state long-arm statutes. Be aware, however, of statutory provisions that limit where a particular matter may be heard. *See, e.g.,* Rice v Disabled Am Veterans, 295 F Supp 131 (DDC 1968) (local jurisdictional provision of District's Code, D C C E §11-521, limits actions to federal district courts in the District of Columbia).

[60] 28 USC §1391(c); Van Dusen v Barrack, 376 US 612 (1964).

[61] Rather than list each district's decision, one should refer to Educational Dev Corp v Econom Co, 376 F Supp 287 (ND Okla 1974) (may be sued only in district where corporation is conducting business); Johnstone v York County Gas Co, 193 F Supp 709 (ED Pa 1961) (contrary view); Annot, 12 ALR Fed 938 (for a discussion of the various holdings on the issue) (1972).

[62] United States v National City Lines, 334 US 573 (1948) (the plaintiff's wide choice of forums under the Clayton Act can nevertheless be affected by the defendant's motion to transfer under §1404(a)).

[63] *See, e.g.,* Aacon Auto Transp, Inc v Ninfo, 490 F2d 83 (2d Cir 1974).

as a single civil action for transfer purposes.[64]

The leading and still controlling decision on what factors are applied in deciding whether a transfer of a civil action is proper is *Gulf Oil Corp v Gilbert*.[65] A balancing test was announced in which both the private parties' and the public's interests are weighed in reaching the decision on a motion to transfer. The factors listed in the opinion (and restated below) were announced prior to the adoption of §1404(a) but are still used, with varying degrees of significance attached to each item, in the analysis of a motion under §1404(a). Each motion is decided on the facts of the case and the decision rests with the sound discretion of the district court.[66] The factors to be considered are:

1. Convenience to the parties
2. Convenience of the witnesses
3. Relative ease of access to sources of proof
4. Availability of process to compel attendance of unwilling witnesses
5. The costs of obtaining willing witnesses
6. Practical problems of obtaining an expeditious and inexpensive trial
7. The plaintiff's privilege of choosing a forum
8. The interests of justice, which can include scheduling problems, the public interest in having a case tried in a particular forum and other matters of judicial economy[67]

The plaintiff's privilege to select the forum is a critical consideration, but as the Supreme Court held in *Norwood v Kirkpatrick*,[68] unlike under the existing doctrine of forum non conveniens, the plaintiff's choice of forum is not controlling; however, it is to be given consideration in the analysis of all the factors.[69] The courts have since that time formulated various means of giving proper weight to the plaintiff's choice of forum. Most courts state that the plaintiff's choice of forum is to be respected and will not be disturbed unless the movant establishes the balance in its favor. The verbiage used by the courts varies from: "[T]he plaintiff's selected forum should not be lightly disturbed unless the balance tips strongly in favor of the defendant;"[70] to simply: "[The] burden of establishing that [the] action should be transferred rests with the

---

[64] Continental Grain Co v FBL-585, 364 US 19 (1960).

[65] 330 US 501 (1947).

[66] Codex Corp v Milgo Elec Corp, 553 F2d 735 (1st Cir), *cert denied,* 434 US 860 (1977).

[67] 330 US 501, 508 (1947). *See* Saminsky v Occidental Petroleum Corp, 373 F Supp 257 (SDNY 1974); Schneider v Sears, 265 F Supp 257 (SDNY 1967); see also C. Wright, A. Miller & E. Cooper, Federal Practice and Procedure §§3847-3854 (1976).

[68] 349 US 29 (1955).

[69] *Id* 32.

[70] Culbertson v Ford Motor Co, Inc, 531 F Supp 406, 409 (ED Pa 1982).

moving party.''[71] However, where the court finds that the plaintiff's choice of forum is not related to the convenience of the plaintiff or his or her home's location, less weight is given to his or her choice.[72] Regardless of the standard, the plaintiff's choice is protected by the universal rule that the movant bears the burden of establishing that both private and public interests require the case to be transferred.[73]

The public interest factor includes such matters as delay, a belief that the public at the situs of the cause of action has an interest in the outcome of the case, judicial economy, court dockets, the ability of the jury to understand the complex issues of choice of law, and so forth.[74] Arguments on the public interest involved in a transfer should not be overlooked, since often the parties will have equally compelling reasons to support or oppose the motion. The court must then look to factors outside the parties' convenience for the decision.

Contractual clauses dictating the forum in which a matter is to be heard are given strong weight by courts, but the contractual agreement is not controlling. The moving party may attack the clause as being unjust, as requiring huge expense with little or no countervailing benefit to the plaintiff, or as not in the interest of justice.[75]

To conclude, the common law doctrine of forum non conveniens is still vibrant. As noted in **§22.06,** one of its main differences from transfer motions under §1404(a) is the authority of the district court to dismiss the action. The doctrine and the application of the *Gilbert* balancing test were recently discussed in *Piper Aircraft Co v Reyno.*[76]

§22.08   Multidistrict Litigation

Given the nature of toxic tort litigation, once a danger is discovered and publicized by the media, numerous suits may be brought to recover damages for injuries, real and imagined, caused by the particular hazard. The offending product or process may also have been widely distributed and, therefore, so

---

[71] Oudes v Block, 516 F Supp 13, 14 (DDC 1981).

[72] *See* Hotel Constructors, Inc v Seagrave Corp, 543 F Supp 1048 (ND Ill 1982) (plaintiff's choice has less significance where forum lacks significant contacts with underlying cause of action); Bloom v AH Pond Co, Inc, 519 F Supp 1162 (SD Fla 1981) (defendant's constitutional and statutory rights will be carefully reviewed where defendant is forced to defend at a remote site).

[73] *See, e.g.,* Raymond E Danto Assoc v Arthur D Little, Inc, 316 F Supp 1350 (ED Mich 1970); Kisko v Penn Central Transp Co, 408 F Supp 984, 986-87 (MD Pa 1976) (mere assertions of inconvenience as insufficient; motion must contain facts and evidence to support the motion to transfer).

[74] *See generally* American Standard, Inc v Bendrix Corp, 487 F Supp 254 (WD Mo 1980); Bertnick v Home Fed Sav & Loan Assn, 337 F Supp 968 (WD Va 1972).

[75] *See In re* Fireman's Fund Ins Co, 588 F2d 93 (5th Cir 1979); Copperweld Steel Co v Demag-Mannesmann-Bohler, 578 F2d 953 (3d Cir 1978).

[76] 454 US 235 (1981), *rehg denied,* 455 US 928 (1982).

will the potential claimants. The inventor, producer, distributor, and retailors will consequently be exposed to numerous, factually similar lawsuits all across the country. Naturally, this is not a welcomed event, since numerous individual suits may well lead to inconsistent procedures, rulings, and jury verdicts. Moreover, assuming a class action is not filed or the claimants are unable to meet the requirements of such, the key defendants will face repeated trials and the costs associated therewith.

A partial solution to this dilemma is found in the authority of federal courts to coordinate or consolidate pretrial proceedings.[77] Where several suits are filed and they all contain one or more common facts, the actions may be transferred to any district court for pretrial proceedings. The statutorily mandated notice and hearing procedures to determine the propriety of such a consolidation may be initiated by any of the parties to the common suits.[78] One of the valuable aspects of this provision is that it saves judicial resources through consolidation. Thus, where suits involving common facts are filed in several districts, the panel on multidistrict litigation, created by the statute to rule on such transfers, may initiate the proceedings on its own motion.[79]

The standard for approving transfers for coordinated or consolidated pretrial proceedings is stated in §1407(a) as: "Such transfers shall be made by the judicial panel on multidistrict litigation authorized by this section upon its determination that transfers for such proceedings will be for the convenience of parties and witnesses and will promote the just and efficient conduct of such actions." Such a broad standard vests considerable discretion in the panel, especially when one considers that the panel's decisions are reviewable only by extraordinary writ pursuant to 28 USC §1651.[80]

In one case involving multidistrict litigation over alleged injuries from asbestos, the judicial panel ruled a transfer would not serve the interests of justice even though the litigation involved 103 actions in 19 different districts. In this decision, *In re Asbestos & Asbestos Insulation Material Products Liability Litigation*,[81] the panel found too many individual differences in the cases to approve consolidation. The actions included both factory workers producing the material and tradesmen installing and working with the materials; the actions were in various stages of litigation from initial filing to near completion of discovery; individual causation issues predominated because of the different locations, exposure times, and individual characteristics of the plaintiffs; and the defendants' individual liability differed considerably because of the varying duties to warn, knowledge of the dangers, etc. Against all these individual characteristics, the panel found that the state of medical and scientific knowledge at any particular time was the only common aspect among all the cases. Given the fact that such information was widely known and available, the panel found: "The

---

[77] 28 USC §1407.

[78] 28 USC §1407(c)(ii).

[79] 28 USC §1407(c)(i).

[80] 28 USC §1407(e).

[81] 431 F Supp 906 (JPMDL 1977).

common need for this literature is therefore not a significant justification for a transfer."[82]

Factors considered by the panel included:

1. The number and significance of common questions of fact
2. Whether failing to consolidate would permit inconsistent and conflicting class actions to form
3. A balancing of the judicial savings from consolidation versus the forfeiture of judicial time already expended in many of the cases
4. The fact many of the cases in any single district already involved common factual patterns more homogeneous than those in the proposed consolidation
5. The virtually unanimous opposition to the transfer

The last factor, the court pointed out, was only a factor and was not controlling. The panel is authorized to transfer the actions even if there were universal opposition.[83]

Multidistrict litigation should be remembered as a possible means of consolidating actions, at least at the pretrial stage, where a class action is not possible or not tactically advantageous. The issue should be addressed early, since it will be important to show the court that the consolidation will result in a substantial savings of time and effort to the judiciary. Multidistrict litigation should not be used if numerous individual distinctions weigh against both the interests of justice and the convenience of the parties. Furthermore, multidistrict litigation coordinates and consolidates litigation resources, a result which may not be desirable in certain circumstances.

§22.09   Mass Torts

A situation somewhat related to multidistrict litigation occurs in mass tort cases.[84] Numerous plaintiffs may sue for a single incident of exposure to a toxic substance. It is easy to imagine this potential exposure if, for example, a manufacturer's toxic substance was released into a city's drinking supply. In such situations, counsel for both the plaintiffs and the defendants face the same problem of how to try efficiently and effectively all the individual claims. A class action may not be feasible because of the lack of commonality among the injured parties. For instance, causation may be a very large element of each individual case, assuming the toxic substance affects individuals differently depending the amount of time of exposure, the individual's weight or age, etc.

A possible, if somewhat unique, solution, should the parties be agreeable and the court amenable, is the test case approach. In this approach, the plain-

---

[82] *Id* 910.
[83] *Id.*
[84] See **ch 20.**

tiffs, the defendants and the court find representative plaintiffs, for the lead trial on liability. These representative plaintiffs would, naturally, have to include individuals representing each of the general characteristics that are important. If a distinction exists as to harm done to adults as opposed to children, a representative from each group would have to be included in the test case. Assuming this is workable, the trial could then proceed in an effort to establish or disprove liability as to each group and each defendant. If liability is established, the parties could then set up a mechanism to adjudicate the amount of the individual claims of the rest of the plaintiffs. However, this may not be necessary since once liability has been found as to any particular group, settlement of the rest of the plaintiffs in that group may be forthcoming. Obviously, there are difficulties with this approach—not the least of which would be convincing the individual plaintiffs to agree to have their particular claims adjudicated on the basis of someone else's injury. Given the difficulty and expense of trying the vast number of individual cases, however, the test case approach is worth being considered as an alternative.

§22.10 Case Theory

Toxic tort litigation demands a highly refined theory of the case. Dealing in complex legal, technical, scientific, and factual issues, the ultimate *theme* or theory to be presented to the trier of fact must be designed to handle these issues in a manner understandable to the court and the jury. This ultimate theory evolves from the approach to the particular case, keeping in mind prejudices and weaknesses of the case.

Because of the overlap of disciplines in toxic tort litigation, the case theory depends upon which discipline or mix of disciplines is chosen to pursue or to defend the case. For example, it may be important not to stress factual issues and emphasize technical or scientific issues. This approach is important where the facts may be prejudicial, such as widespread harm to the environment. A technical or scientific approach may de-emphasize the seemingly prejudicial factual setting, minimizing its impact. Some cases mandate emphasis of facts, technology, and science. Other cases, by necessity, require emphasis of legal principles which limit or prevent liability. Here the interrelationship between the factual foundations involving the legal issues must be underscored.

There are recognized defenses available to a company in toxic tort litigation.[85] These can be categorized, generally, as follows:

1. Intervening clause[86]
2. State of the art[87]

---

[85] See **ch 14.**
[86] See Restatement (Second) of Torts §§442-453 (1965).
[87] *Id* §402A.

3. Assumption of risk[88]
4. Sophisticated user defense[89]
5. Misuse[90]
6. Contributory negligence[91]
7. Comparative negligence[92]
8. No prima facie case—i.e., the product or process is safe

These defenses, if applicable, should be incorporated into the overall case theory.

Whatever approach to the case theory is chosen, the entire case, from jury selection through closing argument, should emphasize and give continued support to the theory. This continuity insures maximum exposure and support for the theory which must be accepted in order to prevail.

Whatever theory is chosen, care must be taken to present it in as clear and concise a manner as practicable. This is especially true in technical and scientific defenses. Companies often feel that a purely technical or scientific defense is the best defense. This type of defense results from technical or scientific experience with a product or process. A defense too steeped in technical or scientific terms can bewilder or confuse courts and juries. By attempting, if possible, to keep technical or scientific defenses simple, one can be sure of being understood by the court and jury.

Courts and juries cannot be viewed as computers in which complex, technical, or scientific facts can be fed and the correct decision reached. To the contrary, the judicial system is designed, through its restrictive rules and procedures, to reduce complex issues to a simple yes-or-no decision—usually implicitly meaning right or wrong. There are, however, situations where sophisticated courts and juries can understand complex, technical, or scientific defense presentations. In such situations, a case theory should be developed to take advantage of this sophistication. The advantage here is that the court and jury will be able to see the case as the company views it and to decide the case impartially, rather than based on an emotional reaction to the plaintiff's suffering.

Whenever possible, a case theory which is affirmative is desirable. Courts and juries tend to react favorably to a well-designed presentation which focuses on the positive characteristics of the product or process in issue. This can include a history of the product or process, why it came into existence, what the company or industry went through to develop it, how it works, and what it does for society. This approach attempts to impress upon the fact-

---

[88] *Id* §496A.
[89] *See, e.g.,* Martinez v Dixie Carriers, Inc, 529 F2d 457 (5th Cir 1976).
[90] See Restatement (Second) of Torts §395 comment, 402A comment b (1965).
[91] See Restatement (Second) of Torts §§463-496 (1965).
[92] *See, e.g.,* Tex Rev Civ Stat art 2212a (Vernon 1971).

finder the virtues of the product or process, especially where a major investment was made to insure the safety of the product or process. Use of this
approach demands an *upbeat,* positive approach to the case. In such situations,
the case theory must be implemented by witnesses who believe in the product
or process and are not defensive about it or the situation that lead to the case.

§22.11   Practical Considerations in Final Trial Preparation

In complex toxic tort litigation, it is essential to be prepared not only for the
trial but for the many collateral matters that often occur. Of foremost consideration is the preparation of witnesses for testimony. This should be done as
close as possible to trial with some minimal time left between preparation and
trial for fine-tuning. Preparation must include actual dress rehearsals, not just
summaries of testimony to be given. Potential cross-examination must also be
rehearsed. This rehearsal should be repeated until counsel and witness are
completely comfortable with questions and answers. All witnesses should be
prepared to be called as adverse witnesses by the opposition. Witnesses should
be made familiar with courtroom procedure, demeanor, and etiquette, including proper conduct while in the presence of the court and jury. Witnesses
should also be familiar with the procedures and mechanics of exhibit introduction and what to do when objections are made. Finally, witnesses must be told
to *speak* to the court and jury. Eye contact with the court and jury is essential
in the overall assessment of credibility. An example of this has occurred many
times in personal injury litigation. Jurors have found against parties on the
mere fact that a crucial witness would look down or would not look at the jury
while testifying, thereby destroying the credibility of the entire case.

In particularly complex or important cases, entire mock trials are sometimes
used to assess the case's impact on mock juries. Utilization of such procedures
should be weighed carefully. If the use is discovered and disclosed to the jury,
there may be an impact on the jury's assessment of the credibility of the overall
case.

Organization of evidence is crucial to the smooth presentation of the case.
Often in complex toxic tort litigation, many exhibits are required. The better
organized the exhibits, the less time is wasted. Additionally, efficient handling
of exhibits exudes preparation and confidence. There is nothing worse than
breaking the train of important testimony on a crucial issue by counsel fum-
bling through stacks of documents or exhibits trying to find the appropriate
one. One additional aid which is helpful in complex cases is to provide the
court with its own complete set of exhibits (or reproductions, photographs, etc.
of demonstrative exhibits) appropriately organized, marked, and bound in
some fashion. This *personalized* exhibit package attracts the court's attention
(often to the detriment of the adversary's case) and helps focus and organize
the complex case in the mind of the court.

An important pretrial aid is submission of a *truly brief* trial brief on the law
and facts applicable to the case. Often filed shortly before the first day of trial,

this trial brief will assist the court and its staff in understanding the complex legal concepts as applied to the evidence and will assist in structuring the court's charge to the jury. Additionally, evidentiary issues which may arise during the trial can be included in the brief for reference by the court at the appropriate time. More importantly, the trial brief can help influence the court's opening remarks and comments to the jury. The jury will often follow the court's lead.

A final pretrial aid is the motion in limine. In jury trials, even though admonished by the court to the contrary, the jury often views in-court efforts to suppress the introduction of evidence or testimony as an attempt to hide something damaging to the case. Curiosity grows, as does the perception that the moving party is not being open and candid in its case. Motions in limine allow for the resolution of these matters prior to the trial and avoid the build-up of unnecessary prejudice by the jury.

A motion in limine is a preliminary motion made before anyone addresses the jury. The motion is made to prevent prejudicial evidence, or any reference to such evidence, from ever reaching the jury. This motion is most important in toxic tort litigation where the litigant believes certain evidence will improperly influence the trier of fact by sympathy, emotion, prejudice, etc. to such an extent that limiting or corrective instructions will not eliminate the taint—in fact, such instruction may only magnify the negative effect.[93]

From a practical point of view, the litigator should take great care in drafting the motion in limine. It must limit both the opposing party and counsel, prohibit any reference to both the motion and the excluded evidence during voir dire or at any time the jury is present, foreclose any attempts of opposing counsel to identify the issue by asking for documents related to the issue while the jury is in the courtroom, and, finally, restrict all arguments over the breadth of the order to discussions at the bench outside the hearing of the jury. The issues not to be addressed must be identified in sufficient detail to put counsel on notice but also must be noted in general terms so that the motion will include all related matters. Proper drafting will foreclose counsel's attempts to pass the information to the jury without directly raising the issues.

A final practical matter to consider is the selection of the company representative. This individual plays two roles. The individual is important to be available for questioning and input on matters during the trial. In all trials, matters arise that are either surprises or collateral issues. With regard to such matters that raise issues directly involved with the company, this individual should have sufficient knowledge either to respond when such situations may occur or be able to contact appropriate individuals within the company to obtain quick responses. Additionally, and probably more important, this individual will be the personification of the company to the court and jury. To the extent possible, a local representative of the company is an appropriate choice. This is

[93] While not specially provided for in the Federal Rules of Evidence or the Federal Rules of Civil Procedure, reference should be made to the Federal Rules of Evidence, Rules 104 & 403-411, which generally authorize courts to entertain motions in limine.

especially true where regional differences may be important or when dealing with a rural court and jury. The individual chosen must be presentable and capable of humanizing the company. The company representative should be present during all phases of the trial, if possible. These include jury selection, opening argument, the presentation of all evidence and witnesses and closing argument. The company representative should maintain an alert and interested attitude, including making occassional eye contact with the court and jury. The company representative does not have to be a witness in the matter, but it does help if the company representative can be involved in some stage of the testimony so the court and jury can hear the individual speak and have a chance to assess credibility. This will further humanize the company, especially when the individual's family and background or additional connections with regional or local situations can be explained to the court and jury.

§22.12   Jury Selection

Jury selection is one of the most important stages of any litigation. Further, jury selection is an inexact procedure and science. These facts exacerbate complex toxic tort litigation.

Two important goals are to be accomplished in jury voir dire.[94] First, an attempt must be made to identify individuals on the jury panel which satisfy a previously selected jury profile. The jury profile will help seat jurors that may, by occupation, natural bias, or other factors, be most favorable to the outcome sought in the trial. The second goal, one often overlooked, involves conditioning of the jury. Carefully selected voir dire can condition the jury panel to the case theory utilized and elicit commitments from the jury panel to view the case through the case theory, assuming the evidence develops as represented in voir dire. For example, voir dire can be structured to obtain commitments from prospective jurors that if the evidence shows that a product or process was not defective as contended, that the jurors will decide a case in a company's favor, regardless of whether an emotional factual situation exists.

Voir dire varies from jurisdiction to jurisdiction. Some voir dire is unlimited and resembles closing arguments. Others are severely restricted, with the court conducting the entire voir dire and counsel limited to the filing of suggested voir dire for the court's consideration for use. There are many variations in between.

Federal juries are selected in accordance with procedures outlined in 28 USC §1861 *et seq.* Sections 1861-1866 prescribe the methods of identifying potential jurors, ascertaining their qualifications, and then selecting and summoning the jury panels for trial. In addition to the procedures employed by the court clerks and judges to secure a qualified panel, the rules of procedure

---

[94] *Voir Dire*—the term literally translated means *to speak the truth.* The phrase denotes the preliminary examination made of one presented as a prospective witness or juror to determine bias, competency, interest, etc. Black's Law Dictionary 1746 (4th ed 1979).

provide for the exclusion of jurors by counsel on both sides. This may be accomplished by either challenging the selection procedures for the panel (§ 1867) or by challenging the individual juror (§ 1870). An individual juror may be challenged for cause or favor or be removed from the panel by means of a peremptory challenge.

One may challenge the jury by attacking a federal district court's procedures used in selecting the panel. This must be done before voir dire examination or within seven days after the party discovers or should have discovered through the exercise of due diligence the "grounds of substantial failure to comply with the provisions of this title . . . ."[95] Counsel is permitted to review the juror qualification forms to support his or her basis of attack.

A more common means of attacking the panel or individual jurors is through peremptory challenges or for cause. Section 1870[96] permits a minimum of three peremptory challenges to each party. Where there are numerous defendants and/or plaintiffs, the court may group the defendants or the plaintiffs as a single party. Where this occurs, additional peremptory challenges may be granted to each party to be exercised jointly or severally by multiple parties.[97] The method by which the peremptory challenges are exercised is left to the sound discretion of the trial judge.[98] One need not state the reason for a peremptory challenge; thus, normally these are reserved until after the jurors have been attacked for cause.

A juror may be challenged for cause or favor where, among other reasons: there is a blood or other close relationship between the juror and one of the parties or witnesses; where the juror has a pecuniary interest in the outcome of the case; where there is a clear bias for or against a party or an issue in the case; etc.[99] The trial judge determines the validity of all challenges for cause or favor,[100] and he or she has wide discretion in ruling on each challenge. Only where there is a "manifest abuse of such discretion" will an appeals court reverse the trial judge's decision.[101] A juror should always be removed where he or she would judge the credibility of witnesses on improper grounds such as their creed.[102] However, a mere challenge on the basis of improper factors is insufficient. The counsel challenging for cause must put forth evidence to support his or her assertion.[103]

Peremptory challenges and those for cause are made after voir dire—unlike

---

[95] 28 USC § 1876.

[96] 28 USC § 1870.

[97] *See* John Long Trucking, Inc v Greear, 421 F2d 125 (10th Cir 1970).

[98] *See* Gafford v Star Fish & Oyster Co, 475 F2d 767 (5th Cir 1973).

[99] *See* Darbin v Nourse, 664 F2d 1109 (9th Cir 1981) (contains discussions of difference between challenges for cause and peremptory challenges).

[100] 28 USC § 1870.

[101] Vanskike v ACF Indus, 665 F2d 188 (8th Cir 1981), *cert denied,* 455 US 1000 (1982).

[102] United States v Robinson, 485 F2d 1157 (3d Cir 1973).

[103] *Cf* United States v Grose, 525 F2d 1115 (7th Cir 1975), *cert denied,* 424 US 973 (1976).

challenges to the selection procedures. Thus, a thorough examination of a juror's background and biases through voir dire or otherwise is essential to support a challenge.[104]

Regardless of the procedures used, basic information about the jury panel must be obtained. This information is based on a carefully conceived jury profile. Development of this profile comes from a complete understanding of the case and case theory as applied to the jury panel. Often, investigation of community attitudes and opinions must be made. Personal investigation of individual prospective jurors may be appropriate, depending upon the amount of information about prospective jurors provided by the court to counsel prior to jury selection. The use of local counsel where lead counsel is not local is almost mandatory in such situations. Finally, if circumstances warrant, use of a psychologist or psychiatrist to prepare psychological jury profiles and even observe the jury panel may be appropriate.

Generally, voir dire should elicit, in addition to normal background information about the jurors, the following information:

1. Attitude and knowledge of the company and its industry in general; attitude toward the plaintiff

2. Attitude, knowledge, and use of the product or process involved

3. Attitude, knowledge, and use of similar products or processes

4. Attitude and knowledge of similar cases

5. Attitude and knowledge of the situation at hand

6. Contacts with the company and use of other products and processes that the company manufactures or uses

7. Educational, technical, and scientific background of jurors and family

8. Health of jurors' family and friends, especially when diseases such as cancer, asbestosis, etc. are involved. Personal habits such as smoking may be important to learn, especially in such cases as asbestosis where some relationship may exist between the disease and the habit[105]

9. Attitude of jurors toward such diseases as cancer or asbestosis

10. Attitude towards environmental issues, especially where chemicals such as herbicides and pesticides are involved or where hazordous wastes are an issue

11. Accountability for actions. An attempt must be made to obtain the juror's attitude toward the defenses available such as misuse and failure to follow warnings, etc

---

[104] *See* Atlas Roofing Mfg Co v Parnell, 409 F2d 119 (5th Cir 1969); *see also* Darbin v Nourse, 664 F2d 1109 (9th Cir 1981).

[105] Neal v Carey Canadian Mines, Ltd, 548 F Supp 357, 381 (ED Pa 1982); Startling v Seaboard Coast Line RR, 533 F Supp 183, 191 (SD Ga 1982); United States v Reserve Mining Co, 380 F Supp 11, 41 (D Minn), *remanded,* 498 F2d 1073 (8th Cir 1974).

Jury profiles are difficult to prepare but some general guidelines can be utilized. From the company's point of view in toxic tort litigation, favorable jurors come from the ranks of management, owners of businesses, engineers, technical and scientific types, and the spouses of these groups. Additionally, physicians, professionals, farmers, teachers, pilots, and those in the middle income brackets are generally favorable. Experienced jurors (i.e., those that have served before) tend to be more conservative the next time they serve.

§22.13   Opening Statement

The opening statement is the first opportunity to communicate formally with the court and jury in a toxic tort case. If the generally accepted rule of primacy is followed, the opening statement can be crucial to the outcome of the case. The rule of primacy teaches that what a jury hears first will usually be accepted as credible. The plaintiffs have the right to proceed first since they carry the burden of proof. This makes the defense's opening statement even more important.

Opening statements should never be waived or delayed until the defense puts on its case in chief. This is even more true in toxic tort litigation, where emotions and sympathy may cloud the facts. The defense must present its case theory to the court and jury prior to the presentation of the plaintiff's evidence in order for the court and jury to cast themselves in an investigatorial, fact-finding role as opposed to receiving evidence passively. The opening statement must be the device that gives the jury the tools to analyze, question, or reject evidence.

Two important goals are to be achieved in an opening statement. First, the court and jury must be informed about the product and process involved in the litigation and the company involved. These include such things as the development of the product or process, including safety engineering and testing, and benefits to society. The company should also be identified and its record as a good citizen and achievements and concerns for safety and the environment emphasized. Second, the case theory must be explained and outlined to the court and jury, including the company's view of the facts. Depending upon the theory chosen, care must be taken to explain complex or technical defenses and to outline facts supportive of the case theory and those which question opposing theories. This is especially true if circumstances show that a technical or scientific approach to the case will be necessary. Letting the court and jury know in advance that they will be required to sift through complex technical or scientific evidence will ease their uncertainty. Often jurors will rise to the challenge and not let such theories intimidate them. For example, if a toxicologist will offer crucial testimony in the case, what a toxicologist is and does and how toxicology is relevant to the case should be explained to the court and jury. Where serious injury or damage has occurred, the opening statement must directly confront the emotional and sympathy issues and focus attention on the case theory.

While opening statements must be flexible to respond to the other side's opening statement, proper preparation should result in a concise, accurate and interesting opening statement. Where evidentiary issues will result in a lengthy and detailed record, the opening statement should attempt to summarize the expected evidence and identify key exhibits and witnesses, especially experts. Finally, in conjunction with conditioning, if possible, during voir dire, the jury should be reminded to reserve its decision on the issues presented in the case until after all the evidence has been presented.

§22.14   Presentation of Evidence

Counsel's choice of the order of presentation of evidence in toxic tort litigation does not differ from other litigation—it is important to lead with a strong witness and also to close with one.

The order of presentation of evidence will be governed by case theory. If expert witnesses are crucial to the case theory, experts should testify either first or last. To ensure a comprehensive presentation of evidence, some sequence should exist to the order chosen. For example, if the issues cover a long period of time, a chronological sequence may be the easiest for the court and jury to assimilate. A disjunctive presentation can confuse or surprise, resulting in an inability to comprehend the case theory. Thus, to the extent practicable, attention should be given to the sequence chosen.

§22.15   —Fact Witnesses

Choosing individuals to present facts to a court and jury is crucial. Often, no latitude exists as to those who must testify. For example, the only eyewitness to an important event may have to be called to testify, regardless of the individual's potential for making a credible impression. Where latitude does exist, individuals should be chosen based on their ability to be perceived as credible. When fact witnesses come from within the company, local and regional differences should be taken in account. *Rank-and-file* employees, as opposed to management, can be effective witnesses with rural or blue collar juries, if competency to testify exists. Where possible, use of witnesses with no interest in the outcome of the litigation should be considered. If such individuals are reliable, they can make effective *tie-breakers* on disputed factual issues.

Preparation of factual witnesses is as important as the preparation of expert witnesses. Factual witnesses that are company employees must be aware that they are viewed by jurors to be representatives of the company, regardless of whether they agree with this viewpoint. Factual witnesses, in addition to extensive preparation for direct and cross-examination applicable to any witness, should be warned to avoid flippant or off-the-cuff remarks, battles of wits with opposing attorneys, and demeanor which indicates insensitivity or callousness. Moreover, care should be taken concerning cost-benefit analyses of safety devices or testing to avoid the pitfall that profit dictated safety consciousness.

Some general rules apply to all witnesses. These include instructions such as:

1. Listen to all questions carefully and respond honestly and succinctly
2. Do not volunteer, explain, or justify answers unless necessary
3. When a question is not understood ask it to be repeated or clarified
4. Do not speculate as to the meaning of questions—this guessing game is always lost by the witness
5. Give only personal knowledge, avoiding a guess, speculation, or opinion not based on personal knowledge
6. Answer "I don't know" without hesitation if that is the true case
7. Never argue with counsel or the court
8. Never become involved during counsel's objections to testimony, wait for instructions from the court prior to preceding with testimony
9. Tell the truth

For cases in federal forums, fact witnesses can take on an added dimension. A fact witness may give testimony under the Federal Rules of Evidence in the form of opinions instead of being restricted to a simple recital of the facts. This marks a substantial departure from common law, where a layperson was deemed to be unqualifed to speculate as to the cause of something or state an opinion on matters such as whether an individual was inebriated. The Federal Rules of Evidence are designed to facilitate the transfer of helpful information to the jury in whatever form is most effective, as long as certain prerequisites are met. These prerequisites or limitations on opinion testimony for both the expert and lay witness are imposed in order to guarantee a degree of reliability and relevancy. Reliability is assured by prescribing the acceptable bases for the opinion testimony and by requiring a requisite level of competency or expertise before one may testify as an expert.[106]

Rule 701 of the Federal Rules of Evidence permits a fact witness to testify by offering his or her opinion where such opinion is "(a) rationally based on the perception of the witness and (b) helpful to a clear understanding of his testimony or the determination of a fact in issue." The witness must have personal knowledge, and the offered opinion must be helpful to the jury. These criteria limit mere speculations on events that the witness has no actual knowledge of or experience with, as well as allow the trial judge to limit mere oath battles between the opposing sides.

§22.16   —Expert Witnesses

Toxic tort litigation is often decided by expert witness testimony. Thus, the selection, preparation, and handling of expert witnesses is crucial.[107]

Expert witnesses in toxic tort litigation can come from many educational

---

[106] Fed R Evid 701-703 advisory committee note.

[107] See **chs 18-19.**

disciplines. Typical specialties are epidemiology, industrial hygiene, pathology, safety and human engineering, toxicology, and microbiology. All engineering and technical fields are often relied upon to supply technical testimony.

Many factors must be considered in selecting expert witnesses. The credibility of the expert is crucial. Not only are credentials and experience important, but acceptance by the court and jury must be considered. For example, where possible, local experts should be used. For example, where possible, local experts should be used. Also, consideration should be given to use of lay experts as opposed to academic experts. For example, a well-respected local electrician may be more credible than a professor of electrical engineering from a university, assuming the capacity to testify exists. In-house experts may also be useful. Although objectivity may be questioned, a credible, qualified in-house expert may be more than sufficient.

Experts with prior trial experience should be examined closely to avoid impeachment as being biased to one side. Additionally, prior testimony must be reviewed to ensure consistency of opinion. Prior trial experience can be a positive factor due to experience obtained by giving depositions and testifying at trial; however, care should be taken to avoid situations where the expert has come to view the trial as a battle of wits with opposing counsel. Jurors pick up on this trait rather easily and resent the expert trying to *show off* by his or her testimony.

Finally, it is essential to have, if possible, an expert with a pleasing demeanor and appearance with an ability to translate complicated scientific or medical terms to layman's terms. An expert that is not understood by the court and jury is a waste of time and effort. Toxic tort cases often, by definition, require explanation of complicated products and processes in scientific or medical terms. Although some complexity cannot be avoided, it is essential to explain in simple terms. For example, instead of explaining the complex process of how a herbicide interrupts photosynthesis in a plant by the production of peroxide when the herbicide contacts green plant tissue which results in the ultimate destruction of cellular matter, the expert may explain that the herbicide, on contact, stops the plant's ability to produce food and thus kills it. It is this simplification of complex terminology that will win the confidence, the respect, and the vote of the jury.

Preparing the expert witness for trial is similar to the preparation of fact witnesses with additional burdens. The expert must be familiar with the case theory and harmonize his or her testimony with it. If testifying about a product or process, the expert must be totally familiar with it, its formation, uses, applicable warnings, instructions, etc. The expert should be familiar with subsequent testing or similar cases involving the product or process. All government regulations or industry standards should be reviewed and familiarized. The expert should refresh his or her memory on his or her previous testimony and depositions, his or her deposition in the pending case, and all previous articles, books, etc. he or she has published. If testing, demonstrations, or experiments are to be used at trial, the expert should become familiar with these matters and how they were performed. Finally, the expert should be thoroughly familiar with the opposing expert's testimony and the opposing case theory. These include the testimony and deposition of opposing experts and any opposing opinions in the literature or government regulation.

Expert witness testimony in toxic tort litigation can be conclusive to the litigation's outcome due to the wide latitude given expert testimony by the Federal Rules of Evidence. Experts, as defined in Rule 702, may offer their opinions where their "scientific, technical, or other specialized knowledge will assist the trier of fact to understand the evidence or to determine a fact in issue. . . ." The witness may be qualified as an expert "by knowledge, skill, experience, training, or education. . . ." Thus, experts may testify on matters dealing with their specialties even if their expertise was gained simply by operating in that area for a certain period of time. The opinion offered must be helpful to the trier of fact. Thus, if the jury is able to understand the data or come to a sound conclusion without the help of the expert, the expert's testimony may be excluded regardless of his or her recognized knowledge. Finally, the expert may testify in the "form of an opinion or otherwise." This phrase permits the introduction of the expert's testimony on recognized principles or theories in his or her field without having the expert state an opinion of the case. This may help the trier of fact apply the facts of the case to the announced principles in coming to a conclusion. In short, there is no need for the expert to state an opinion in response to a hypothetical question or even state an opinion on the facts of the particular case in order to admit properly the testimony of that expert.[108]

The expert may testify in the form of an opinion, but he or she is limited as to the permissible bases for his or her opinion. Under the rules, he or she may testify from facts he or she perceives or is made aware of at or before the hearing.[109] This translates into three situations. The expert may testify based on:

1. His or her personal observation of the event or person
2. Facts made known to him or her at the trial through the use of a hypothetical question or by listening to the evidence presented
3. Facts made known to him or her prior to the hearing

For example, a doctor may testify as to his or her opinion on the extent of damages and the cause of injury based on his or her review of the patient's medical file prior to the hearing or trial. The evidence relied upon by the expert need not be admissible at trial if the evidence is "of a type reasonably relied upon by experts in the particular field in forming opinions or inferences upon the subject. . . ."[110] Since doctors normally rely upon charts, x-rays, and

---

[108] Fed R Evid 702 advisory committee note.
[109] Fed R Evid 703.
[110] *Id.*

the like, reliance upon such to form his or her opinion is permissible even if the charts could not be introduced otherwise.

Naturally, opposing counsel will want to know upon what the expert is basing his or her opinion. He or she will want to make certain that the full history was presented in addition to making sure that accurate facts were given to the expert. This is particularly significant where the expert gives his or her opinion based on facts given to him or her prior to the trial. Under the rules, opposing counsel best obtain this data through discovery, since Rule 705 permits an expert to give his or her opinion without first stating the underlying facts upon which he or she relied. In fact, the expert is not required to state the basis of his or her opinion unless the judge orders it or it is brought out in cross-examination. Since the basis for the opinion should already be known through discovery, only the weaknesses in the facts or analysis need be exposed during cross examination. Of course, it is not good practice on direct examination to have the expert state only his or her conclusions since it is much more credible evidence if the jury understands how a result is reached.

Finally, no longer must the witness, lay or expert, stay away from an opinion on the "ultimate issue."[111] Thus, a witness can render an opinion on the ultimate issue in a toxic tort case—i.e., whether the product or process was defective, whether it caused the injury, etc. The expert witness may offer an opinion as long as the criteria of Rules 701 through 703 are met. One of those requirements is that the opinion be helpful to the jury. Opinions on particular factual issues or conclusions to be drawn from complex facts may indeed be helpful to the jury. On the other hand, opinions on mere guilt or innocence are not very helpful to an understanding of the facts, since such opinions merely suggest the desired result rather than a means of reaching a decision or explaining complex data. Therefore, such opinions will be excluded.[112]

§22.17   —Live Testimony versus Depositions

Live testimony is almost always preferable to the reading of deposition testimony to the jury. Live testimony allows the court and jury to evaluate personally witness credibility. However, circumstances do not always permit or warrant live testimony. This may be especially true in toxic tort litigation, where important fact and expert witnesses may be unavailable for trial. Thus, to insure that relevant testimony is not excluded, depositions can be used.

Depositions can be used at trial either for impeachment or as substantive evidence. Rule 32 of the Federal Rules of Civil Procedure outlines the proper uses of depositions, objections to their admissibility, and the effects of errors or irregularities in depositions. Rules 801 and 804 of the Federal Rules of Evidence are also applicable, since these rules generally define the circum-

---

[111] Fed R Evid 706.
[112] Fed R Evid 704 advisory committee notes.

stances when an out-of-court statement is not hearsay and thus may be used as substantive evidence.

Subsection (a) of Rule 32 provides general guidance on the use of depositions at trial. More particular guidance is provided in subsections (a)(1) through (a)(4) on the introduction of depositions into evidence and other uses in specific situations. Subsection (a) reads:

> (a) Use of Depositions. At the trial or upon the hearing of a motion or an interlocutory proceeding, any part or all of a deposition, so far as admissible under the rules of evidence applied as though the witness were then present and testifying, may be used against any party who was present or represented at the taking of the deposition or who had reasonable notice thereof, in accordance with any of the following provisions: . . .

The primary importance of the rule is that it permits the admission of depositions. Because of the language: "as though the witness were then present and testifying," depositions are admissible even though a technical objection could be made that the deposition violates the hearsay rule. This exception, however, applies only to the deposition itself. Hearsay objections may still be made to particular questions and answers contained in the text. This is also true of any other objections that may be made under the rules of evidence since the deposition may be used only "so far as admissible under the rules of evidence."

The rest of Rule 32 delineates when, by whom, against whom, and for what purposes the deposition may be introduced at trial. Subsection (a) states the deposition may be used against any *party* who was present at, represented at, or had reasonable notice of the deposition. Thus, a party who is joined after the deposition was taken is not a party against whom the deposition can be used. This factor can be critical when joined as a party late in a case. Note, however, that subsection (a)(4) permits the use of a deposition against a substituted party.

§22.18 —Specific Requirements for use of Depositions under Rule 32(a)

Beyond the limitation to use depositions only against parties (as discussed in §22.17), Rule 32 of the Federal Rules of Civil Procedure limits the use of the deposition to the provisions of subsections (a)(1) through (a)(4). The permissible uses are broad but each contains specific limitations which must be followed.

Rule 32(a)(1) states: "Any deposition may be used by any party for the purpose of contradicting or impeaching the testimony of deponent as a witness, or for any other purpose permitted by the Federal Rules of Evidence." Prior to the addition in 1980 of the last clause of Rule 32(a)(1), many courts limited the use of depositions against nonparties to impeachment purposes only. Thus, the party offering the deposition could not use it as substantive evidence. Such rulings were contrary to Rule 801 of the Federal Rules of Evidence which makes the prior inconsistent statements of witnesses, as well as the statements of agents made in the scope of their employment and during their relationship with the principal, admissible as substantive evidence. Thus, the amendment in 1980 clarified the role for the use of a deposition of a witness who is not a party.[113]

Rule 32(a)(2) reads:

> (2) The deposition of a party or of anyone who at the time of taking the deposition was an officer, director, or managing agent, or person designated under Rule 30(b)(6) or 31(a) to testify on behalf of a public or private corporation, partnership or association or governmental agency which is a party may be used by an adverse party for any purpose.

A deposition of a party, a person designated by a private or public corporation to testify on its behalf, officers, managing agents, etc., may be used for any purpose, including using it as substantive evidence. This result is in line with Rule 801(d)(2) which makes admissions by party-opponents nonhearsay.[114] The limitations applied are that the deposition can be used only by an adverse party,[115] and that the designated person, managing agent, etc., must have been engaged in that role at the time of the deposition.[116] An advantage to using depositions under this subsection is that the deposition may be used in lieu of or in addition to the party's testimony at trial without any showing of unavailability. Objections as to cumulative testimony and irrelevancy are still available.[117]

Subsection (a)(3) of Rule 32 permits the use of depositions as follows:

> (3) The deposition of a witness, whether or not a party, may be used by any party for any purpose if the court finds: (A) that the witness is dead; or (B) that the witness is at a greater distance than 100 miles from the place of trial or hearing, or is out of the United States unless it appears that the absence of the witness was procured by the party offering the deposition; or (C) that the witness is unable to attend or testify because of age, illness, infirmity, or imprisonment; or (D) that the party offering the deposition has been unable to procure the attendance of the witness by subpoena; or (E) upon application and notice, that such exceptional circumstances exist as to make it desirable, in the interest of justice and

---

[113] Fed R Civ P 32(a)(1) advisory committee note (1980 Amendment, Apr 29, 1980).

[114] Fenstermacher v Philadelphia Natl Bank, 493 F2d 333 (3d Cir 1974).

[115] Miles v Continental Can Co, 31 FR Serv 2d 242 (WDNY 1981).

[116] *See generally* King & King Enter v Champlin Petroleum Co, 657 F2d 1147, 1164 (10th Cir 1981), *cert denied*, 454 US 1164 (1982).

[117] Fey v Walston & Co, 493 F2d 1036 (7th Cir 1974); *In re* Checkmate Stereo & Elecs, Ltd, 34 FR Serv 2d 1177 (EDNY 1982).

with due regard to the importance of presenting the testimony of witnesses orally in open court, to allow the deposition to be used.

The rule permits the use of depositions in lieu of actual testimony at trial under the listed situations.

Two of the conditions set forth in subsection (a)(3) warrant discussion. First, the exception for a witness more than 100 miles from the place of the trial applies where the witness does not work, live, or happen to be within a hundred miles at the time the deposition is offered. The rule is not designed to be coextensive with the subpoena power of the court; rather, it is aimed at not inconveniencing one who is simply not within a hundred miles of the courthouse.[118]

The other condition discussed here is the *exceptional circumstances* clause of subpart (E). The courts have used this clause to permit the introduction of a deposition whenever justice dictates. This requirement sometimes translates to situations where critical evidence cannot otherwise be introduced.[119]

In addition to the listed conditions under which the deposition can be used in lieu of live testimony, subsection (a)(4) allows for the use of depositions obtained for an earlier trial where the witness is presently unavailable as that term is defined in Rule 804 of the Federal Rules of Evidence. The party against whom the deposition is offered must have had an opportunity and similar motive to develop testimony from the deponent at the time of the deposition.[120]

Finally, subsection (a)(4) deals with the use of depositions obtained during a previous proceeding that is being offered in a subsequent trial or proceeding. It states:

> [A]nd, when an action has been brought in any court of the United States or of any State and another action involving the same subject matter is afterward brought between the same parties or their representative or successors in interest, all depositions lawfully taken and duly filed in the former action may be used in the latter as if originally taken therefor.

The two trials must involve the same subject matter—at least to the extent that the adverse party would have recognized the same issues in each case.[121] While the parties need not be the same, they must be similar in interest—i.e. successors—before the deposition can be entered into evidence against a party in the subsequent proceeding. Also, one should distinguish this provision from the language in (a)(4) which permits depositions to be used where the witness is

---

[118] United States v International Business Machs Corp, 90 FRD 377, 32 FR Serv 2d 1510 (SDNY 1981); Mark IV Prop Inc v Club Dev & Mgmt Corp, 32 FR Serv 2d 1172 (SD Cal 1981).

[119] Comeaux v TL James & Co, 666 F2d 294 (5th Cir 1982).

[120] Fed R Civ P 32(a)(4) advisory committee note (1980 Amendment, Apr 29, 1980).

[121] Hub v Sun Valley Co, 682 F2d 776 (9th Cir 1982).

unavailable. **Here, unavailability** is not required. For instance, without **regard**
to availability, **the deposition** from an earlier trial may be used in a **subsequent**
trial where the **deponent was** the managing agent of a corporation that is **a**
party.

One other aspect of subsection (a)(4) is the provision that an adverse party
may require **the party offering** only a part of a deposition to offer the whole
in the interest of fairness to both sides. This simply permits the opposing party
to prevent a distorted position from **reaching the jury.**

§22.19 —Other Limitations on Use of Depositions

In addition to the requirements discussed in **§§22.17** and **22.18,** the other
sections of Rule 32 of the **Federal Rules of Civil Procedure** deal with objections
to admissibility (section (b)) **and the effects** of errors and irregularities in
depositions (section (d)). With **regard to section (b),** the primary rule is that,
for the most part, objections to **questions or testimony** in the deposition are
made at the trial when the deposition is **offered into evidence.** The objections
will be treated as if the witness were **there testifying at the time** of the objection.
Exceptions to this rule are found at Rule **32(d)(3). Subsection (d)(3)** requires
objections to be raised at the deposition regarding **the** form of questions,
irregularities in taking the deposition, **competency of the** witnesses, and other
matters "which might be obviated, removed or cured if promptly presented."
Failure to raise an objection that could have been cured, etc., results in a waiver
of the objection.

Finally, consideration of the use of deposition **summaries** should be considered. Normally, depositions are read into the record **in** question and answer
form, with counsel reading the questions and an **associate, sitting in the witness**
stand, reading the answers. This allows for **appropriate objections to be**
made.[122] Some courts allow deposition testimony to **be summarized and mere-**
ly read to the jury if proper advance notice of **the summary** with transcript
sources to the deposition are given to the opposing counsel to allow effective
objections to be made to the summary testimony.

§22.20 —Demonstrative Evidence

Demonstrative evidence[123] is evidence that exists, is **tangible,** or in short, is
a real thing. It is something one can hold, see, or feel for himself or herself

---

[122] Many courts require line-by-line identification of deposition testimony to be used
at trial prior to the commencement of the trial.

[123] Demonstrative evidence, for purposes of §22.20, includes illustrative or visual
aides, real evidence, and traditional demonstrative evidence. Normally, illustrative or
visual aids are not introduced into evidence but used to assist testimony. If not introduced as evidence, generally the jury will not be allowed to take the aid into the jury
room, and it does not become a part of the record. They can, however, be properly
admitted into evidence if appropriate.

rather than simply hear another's impressions through testimony. Thus, a chart, a photograph, a model, the product itself, and a demonstration are examples of demonstrative evidence. Introduction of such evidence is favored because the trier of fact gains a first-hand impression that, in many cases, will stay longer than mere words.

There is no single rule on demonstrative evidence. Rather, the Federal Rules of Evidence on relevance,[124] authentication and identification,[125] and contents of writings, recordings, and photographs[126] all apply in determining whether a piece of evidence is admissible. Generally, demonstrative evidence must satisfy four evidentiary requirements: the relevance, authenticity, hearsay, and best-evidence rules.

Demonstrative evidence must be shown to be what it purports to be—that is, it must be identified. The identification requirement may generally be found at Federal Rules of Evidence Rule 901. It states that "requirement of authentication or identification as a condition precedent to admissibility is satisfied by evidence sufficient to support a finding that the matter in question is what its proponent claims." If the object is unique and not easily subject to modifications, a witness may describe it on the stand as the one he or she saw. If the object is fungible, such as a drug, a more elaborate explanation will be necessary to establish that the item was present at the scene of the event. A chain of custody may have to be established that traces the exact item from the scene to the courtroom.[127]

Where the object is not in court but rather pictures of it are introduced, counsel must show that what is depicted can be relied upon as being what exists or existed. A witness may testify that it is an accurate depiction of what he or she saw. However, all this proves is that the witness' memory and the photograph agree. To introduce it as what in fact exists, the witness must testify as to the process and safeguards used to ensure an accurate reproduction. This method is particularly significant for the introduction of X-rays, since rarely will one be able to say he or she saw the bone or tissue and that the X-rays accurately depict the bone structure.[128]

Beyond the issue of identification, the demonstrative evidence must be helpful to the jury and not be so prejudicial as to merit exclusion. Thus, color photographs of a victim may not be allowed, whereas black and white photos may be permitted, based on the objection that the color will inflame the jury.[129]

With regard to writings or photographs, Rules 1002 and 1004 of the Federal Rules of Evidence require that originals be introduced unless they are unavailable for reasons other than those purposefully caused by the proponent in bad

---

[124] Fed R Evid 104, 401.

[125] Fed R Evid 901.

[126] Fed R Evid 1001 *et seq.*

[127] *See* Fed R Evid 901(b) for other examples of how to identify and authenticate a particular item.

[128] *See* Fed R Evid 901(b)(a) for a further discuussion of this method.

[129] Fed R Evid 104, 401, 403.

faith. An original of a photograph, however, is defined as the negative and prints made from the negative.[130] Further, duplicates are admissible unless there is a genuine question about the authenticity of the original or it would be unfair to introduce the duplicate in lieu of the original.[131]

In toxic tort litigation, demonstrative evidence is even more important. For example, if the adequacy of safety warnings or instructions are in issue, blow-ups of the applicable labels, pamphlets, etc. are quite useful in drawing the attention of the fact-finder to emphasized language. Models of products and processes (or the products and processes themselves) are also useful, sometimes essential, to a proper understanding of the facts and case theory. Other examples of useful demonstrative evidence are experiments, maps, diagrams, drawings, and charts. Motion pictures, overhead projectors, and video recordings are also beneficial. Video recordings are especially persuasive with juries, given society's preoccupation with television.

Although demonstrative evidence is persuasive with the fact-finder, care must be taken in several areas. Too many demonstrative exhibits lessen their impact; save demonstrative evidence for the most crucial issues. Further, avoid elaborate and expensive models, experiments, etc. These only confirm the *deep pocket* theory. Finally, insure that demonstrative evidence used is simple and to the point; if it is too complicated or elaborate, the purpose of the demonstrative piece of evidence—to explain concisely where words fail—is lost. Demonstrative evidence should be big enough to be easily viewed by the jury and witness at the same time or constructed where it can be passed to the jury for easy handling and inspection.

As long as a proper foundation is laid,[132] demonstrative evidence can be, next to expert witness testimony, the most important tactic used in toxic tort litigation.

§22.21 Submitting the Case to the Jury

The manner and procedure for submission of a toxic tort case to a jury for decision varies according to local statute, rule, and procedure. Because of the complex nature of toxic tort litigation and the emotional atmosphere in which the litigation takes place, the use of special verdicts or interrogatories for submission of the case to the jury should be considered. This method allows counsel to guide the jury in the resolution of particular factual matters as opposed to allowing the jury to find, generally, in favor of one party or the other. Since juries generally are instructed not to take into account the effect of their answers, emotional or volatile disputes can be defused by use of special verdicts or interrogatories.

---

[130] Fed R Evid 1001.

[131] Fed R Evid 1003.

[132] See generally McCormick's Handbook of the Law of Evidence, 524-42 (E. Cleary ed 2d ed 1972); Fed R Evid 104, 401, 901, 1001, advisory committee note.

Jury findings may be in the form of special verdicts or general verdicts accompanied by answers to interrogatories. Either way, the findings of fact help the court and the parties ascertain what the jury has concluded as to certain factual issues. Further, in the case of general verdicts, the factual findings reveal whether such conclusions are consistent with the verdict rendered. This insight into the jury's analysis of the case is important in determining whether the jury understood the law as instructed. If the jury failed to comprehend the law, the matter may be resubmitted or the verdict corrected in some fashion to ensure that the findings of fact are consistent with the law in rendering a judgment.[133]

The federal courts have developed specific procedures for jury instructions. Rule 49 of the Federal Rules of Civil Procedure authorizes the court to submit special verdicts or interrogatories to the jury. No standard is set forth to determine when the judge should submit either form to the jury. The decision is within the discretion of the trial judge.[134] However, the cases suggest that such verdicts should be used where there are large and complex cases with numerous factual issues involved or where developing areas of the law have not been tested and one wants the jury's exact findings for purposes of appeal[135]—that is, in most toxic tort cases.

Rule 49 is more explicit, however, with reference to how the factual issues should be presented, what kind of issues may be submitted, the effect of not submitting a particular issue to the jury, and the method of reconciling inconsistent answers to interrogatories with the rendered verdict.

Rule 49(a) deals with special verdicts. Under the rule, the court presents the jury with "written questions susceptible of categorical or other brief answer . . . or it [the court] may use such other method of submitting the issues and requiring the written findings thereon as it deems most appropriate." The court must give the jury "such explanation and instruction concerning the matter thus submitted as may be necessary to enable the jury to make its findings upon each issue." Failure to instruct on the law where the matter submitted contains a joint issue of fact and law constitutes error.[136] The formulation of the issues is within the trial judge's discretion, but the court is to ensure that the special verdicts cover all the relevant issues.[137] The court is further under an obligation to permit counsel to review and comment on the special verdicts before they are submitted to the jury,[138] but once the jury retires with the special verdicts, failure to request an issue by counsel amounts

---

[133] Eichmann v Dennis, 347 F2d 978, 982 (3d Cir 1965)(discussion of value of special verdicts and interrogatories).

[134] Sadowski v Bombardier, Ltd, 539 F2d 615 (7th Cir 1976).

[135] *See* Berkey Photo, Inc v Eastman Kodak Co, 603 F2d 263 (2d Cir 1979), *cert denied,* 444 US 1093 (1980).

[136] Jackson v King, 223 F2d 714 (5th Cir 1955).

[137] Kornicki v Calmar S S Corp, 460 F2d 1134 (3d Cir 1972).

[138] Smith v Danyo, 585 F2d 83 (3d Cir 1978).

to a waiver of the right to a jury trial on that issue.[139] In such a situation, the trial judge may make a specific finding; or, should he or she fail to do so, the necessary finding will be deemed to be consistent with the judgment on the special verdict.[140] Finally, counsel must object to the form or wording of the special verdict prior to the entry of judgment on the verdict or else the objection is waived.[141]

Another means of obtaining specific factual determinations by the jury, while still leaving the general verdict with the trier of fact, is covered in Rule 49(b), General Verdict Accompanied by Answer to Interrogatories. The court presents the jury with written interrogatories on issues necessary to the verdict along with forms for a general verdict. The rules on the scope of the trial judge's discretion and the necessary instructions on legal issues that are applicable to special verdicts apply equally here.

An important difference between special and general verdicts, however, is the rendering of a verdict by the jury. Naturally, conflicts may occur between specific findings and the final result. Rule 49(b) states that if the interrogatories and the verdict are harmonious, a judgment upon the verdict should be entered per Rule 58 of the Federal Rules of Civil Procedure. When the answers are consistent with each other but one or more is inconsistent with the general verdict, "judgment may be entered pursuant to Rule 58 in accordance with the answers, notwithstanding the general verdict, or the court may return the jury for further consideration of its answers and verdict or may order a new trial."[142] Where there are inconsistencies among the answers as well as with the general verdict, no judgment can be entered. The jury must resolve the conflict or a new trial will be ordered.

When reviewing the written factual answers, whether by special verdicts or interrogatories, the court is required, if at all possible, to reconcile any conflict to a result which makes the answers consistent. Such an effort is constitutionally required by the Seventh Amendment right to a trial by jury.[143] The standard is that the trial judge should look to any view that brings about a logical and probable decision on the relevant issues submitted to the jury. If this cannot be done, there can be no judgment.[144] Considering the multitude of ways inconsistencies could arise, it is imperative for both counsel and the trial judge to prepare special verdicts and written interrogatories in such a way as to avoid conflicts based on mere form or wording. Further, limiting the number of interrogatories submitted to only those factual issues essential to the verdict will reduce the probability of finding inconsistencies. The potential for time-

---

[139] Fed R Civ P 49.

[140] *Id* 49.

[141] *See* Frankel v Burke's Excavating, Inc, 397 F2d 167 (3d Cir 1968) (involving written interrogatories).

[142] Fed R Civ P 49(b).

[143] Atlantic & Gulf Stevedores, Inc v Ellerman Lines, Ltd, 369 US 355 (1962).

[144] *See* Griffin v Matherne, 471 F2d 911 (5th Cir 1973) (involving conflict between answers to special verdicts).

consuming resolutions of conflicts and the possibility of a new trial are two sound reasons for vesting considerable authority in the trial judge with regard to both the drafting of and the initial decision whether to submit special verdicts or interrogatories. This is especially true in toxic tort litigation, where cases may take weeks to try.

§22.22   Closing Argument

A toxic tort case cannot be won with closing argument. Jury studies have shown that closing arguments do not result in wholesale conversions from deciding a case for one party to another. Given the existence of emotional issues or facts that evoke sympathy, closing argument must draw on commitments obtained from the jury during voir dire and the opening statement, the case theory, and from analysis of the court's jury instructions and interrogatories in light of the facts.

Closing argument should assist the jury in summarizing the evidence to be able to answer the interrogatories within the confines of the court's instructions. Not only is this a useful approach to defuse emotion and sympathy, it appeals to the orderly resolution of the issues presented and is a *comfortable* release from what may seem to the jury to be an overwhelming task. However, closing arguments should not be a mere summary of the evidence. Since all cases have issues which deserve argument as opposed to summary, the closing argument should focus on these issues to give the jury the psychological support it will need to reach an appropriate verdict. Closing argument should be persuasive, consistent with the opening statement and the evidence, forceful and coherent. The case theory must be conclusively sold resulting in a jury's response to the special interrogatories that compels a favorable finding.[145]

---

[145] Counsel should be aware of the procedures and general requirements for motions for directed verdicts, judgments n.o.v. and new trials, Rules 50, 59, Federal Rules of Civil Procedure, and relief from judgments, Rule 60, Federal Rules of Civil Procedure.

23 Case Settlement*

David J. Mahoney, Esq.†

§23.01 Introduction

Imagine sitting in your office on a blustering November morning, with the *New York Times* turned to page 15, and in bold print you read, "Gasoline fumes spur 112 families to flee." Upon reading further you learn that anywhere from 75,000 to 200,000 gallons of gasoline leaked out of your client's underground storage facilities over the last few months. Concurrent with your feelings of anxiety, dizziness, nausea, and body aches, your telephone begins its incessant ring; clients demand your advice, presence, and legal mysticism to salvage another impossible situation.

As the days progress, your client's technical people have estimated the total product lost is close to 200,000 gallons from several sources besides your client's. Additionally, they inform you that benzene, toluene, and xylene (*BXT*) are present in the groundwater, and these very contaminants have

---

* Grateful acknowledgment is made to Brian Saunders, Esq., Exxon Company, U.S.A., Linden, New Jersey in the preparation of this chapter.

† Senior Counsel, Exxon Company, U.S.A., Linden, New Jersey.

shown up in the municipal well field which supplies drinking water to the surrounding area.

Municipal, state, and federal agencies, along with individuals, are clamoring for your client's head. Corporate responsibility, abatement, tortious injury, public image, and federal environmental legislation are phrases which become entwined in your daily lexicon.

If that scenario is not familiar, consider this: Your client, along with eleven waste generators and Waste Inc, the owner-operator of two hazardous waste disposal sites, is sued by the United States on behalf of the Environmental Protection Agency (EPA), seeking a preliminary and permanent injunction to remedy an alleged imminent hazardous condition at the Waste Inc sites resulting from the deposition in dangerous concentrations of chlorinated hydrocarbons, heavy metals, and other toxic chemicals. Clearly, the government seeks to hold generators liable for the improper distribution of hazardous waste deposited with the independent disposal contractor.

The EPA has requested injunctive relief requiring the responsible parties:

1. To terminate intentional discharges from the sites

2. To desist from placing new waste on the sites

3. To clean up both the surface and groundwater contamination occasioned by the two sites pursuant to a plan approved by the EPA and the court

4. As a part of the clean up plan, to sample, test, analyze, and dispose properly of removed waste

5. To pay to the United States $10,000 a day per defendant for each day pollutants were illegally discharged from the two sites

As counsel for one of the subject generators, you are confronted with the following quagmire:

1. Waste Inc has abandoned the subject sites and therefore could not perform any of the site maintenance set forth in the preliminary injunction

2. Your company is very sensitive to the social and public affairs ramifications of waste disposal; injury to the company's goodwill and public reputation will have deep-felt economic effects

3. Holding pond levees are continuously eroding and heavy rains increase the probability of runoff

4. Your site does not qualify for the Superfund priority list[1] and the state superfund is financially bankrupt; accordingly, there is no governmental action to remedy or to clean up the problem

---

[1] *Superfund* refers to the Comprehensive Environmental Response, Compensation and Liability Act, 42 USC §9601 *et seq*, discussed in **chs 9** and **10**.

5.   Litigation is estimated to take anywhere from three to six years

6.   A site assessment conducted by the EPA uncovers accelerated seepage into the underlying aquifer, and seepage caused by erosion of a levee on the northern perimeter of Site #2 was traced entering a navigable body of water. This body of water has traditionally served as a hotbed of activity during the summer months for swimmers, fishers, and other lovers of aquatic sports

The two scenarios set forth above are basically true and not the demonic conception of some law school professor.[2] For practitioners in the hazardous waste and toxic tort arena, these are commonplace problems.[3] Resolution of these problems may affect the financial viability of companies involved.[4] An additional connector between the examples is that each represents the two levels on which hazardous waste and toxic tort matters must be handled. First, one encounters governmental pressures, whether federal, state, or municipal. Derived from broad, sweeping legislation, this pressure's primary focus is the achievement of clean-up and the imposition of liability for the cost of clean-up on the responsible parties. The next level is the potential or actual plethora of tort actions for personal injury occasioned by the generation, handling, or storage of hazardous waste substances. At each level, the impetus to negotiate an out-of-court settlement drastically differs. This chapter addresses issues associated with handling the factual situations mentioned above and attempts to formulate a strategy to protect oneself from the ever-growing liability associated with hazardous substances.

§23.02   Impetus to Settle

Since the passage of major environmental legislation, the tendency to settle claims rather than engage in protracted expensive litigation has placed the courts in the uncharacteristic situation of approving settlements as opposed to deciding all the issues associated with the enforcement of the legislation. Avoidance of protracted, expensive litigation and the considerations involved in quickly and economically resolving sizable potential liabilities are two of the most important factors which provide a strong inducement for compromise and settlement. Certainly, these factors are just two of many that a practitioner will consider prior to initiating or considering the settlement-negotiation pro-

[2] The subject examples have been altered slightly to protect corporate and individual confidentiality concerns.

[3] The following cases offer examples of the type of problem dealt with on a daily basis by practitioners in this area: United States v Chem-Dyne Corp, 12 Envtl L Rep 30, 26 (SD Ohio Aug 26, 1982); United States v South Carolina Recycling & Disposal Corp, No 80-1274-6 (DSC Mar 23, 1982); United States v Spectron, Inc, No 80-1552 (D Md Apr 1, 1982).

[4] See Saginaw & Weinstein, *The Manville Bankruptcy: Will Asbestos Victims Get Their Day in Court?*, 19 Trial 76 (No 4, 1983).

cess. In the environmental arena, there may be other normative factors which serve as inducements for compromise and settlement.

§23.03   —Statutory Clean-Up: Inability to Avoid Responsibility

The recent explosion of federal and state legislation relating to human health and environmental issues is probably the single most important element to consider in negotiating statutory clean-up agreements.[5] While the vast majority of this legislative boom concerns itself with permits and standards for industry, the federal Superfund legislation and its state *offspring* have specifically addressed the issue of the imposition of clean-up responsibility.[6] These

---

[5] On the federal level, this *alphabet soup* of statutes includes:

1.   The Superfund Act or the Comprehensive Environmental Response, Compensation and Liability Act of 1980 (CERCLA), 42 USC §9601 *et seq,* Pub L No 96-510, 94 Stat 2767 (Dec 11, 1980)
2.   The Uranium Mill Tailings Radiation Control Act of 1978 (UMTRCA); 42 USC §2014 *et seq,* Pub L No 95-604, 92 Stat 3021 (Nov 8, 1978)
3.   The Surface Mine Control and Reclamation Act of 1977 (SMCRA); 30 USC §1201 *et seq,* Pub L No 95-87, 91 Stat 445 (Aug 3, 1977)
4.   The Resource Conservation and Recovery Act of 1976 (RCRA); 42 USC §6901 *et seq,* Pub L No 94-580, 90 Stat 2795 (Oct 21, 1976)
5.   The Toxic Substances Control Act of 1976 (TSCA); 15 USC §2601 *et seq,* Pub L No 94-469, 90 Stat 2003 (Oct 11, 1976)
6.   The Safe Drinking Water Act of 1974 (SDWA); 42 USC §201 *et seq,* Pub L No 93-523, 85 Stat 1660 (Dec 16, 1974)
7.   The Hazardous Materials Transportation Act (HMTA); 49 USC §1471 *et seq,* Pub L No 93-633, 88 Stat 2156 (Jan 3, 1975), *amended,* 49 USC §1801 *et seq*
8.   The Federal Water Pollution Control Act (FWPCA); 33 USC §1251 *et seq,* Pub L No 92-500, 86 Stat 816 (Oct 18, 1972)
9.   The Consumer Product Safety Act of 1972 (CPSA); 15 USC §2051 *et seq,* Pub L No 92-573 86 Stat 1207 (Oct 27, 1972)
10.   The Federal Environmental Pollution Control Act Amendments of 1972 to the Federal Insecticide, Fungicide and Rodenticide Act (FIFRA); 7 USC §136 *et seq,* Pub L No 96-539, 94 Stat 3194 (Dec 17, 1980)
11.   The Poisonous Prevention Packaging Act of 1970 (PPPA); 15 USC 1471 *et seq,* Pub L No 92-516, 86 Stat 998 (Oct 21, 1972)
12.   The Occupational Safety and Health Act of 1970 (OSHA); 29 USC §661 *et seq,* Pub L No 95-251, 92 Stat 183 (Mar 27, 1978)
13.   The Clean Air Act Amendments of 1970 (CAA); 42 USC §§4362, 7401, 7551, Pub L No 95-95, 91 Stat 685 (Aug 7, 1977)
14.   The National Environmental Policy Act of 1970 (NEPA); 42 USC §4343 *et seq,* Pub L No 94-52, 89 Stat 258 (July 3, 1975)

[6] Comprehensive Environmental Response, Compensation and Liability Act of 1980 (CERCLA) 42 USC §§9601-9657 (1980), commonly known as *Superfund;* see the following state legislation:

Florida: Pollutant Spill Prevention and Control Act, Fla Stat Ann §376.12 *et seq,* (West Supp 1981); *see also* Florida House Bill 47-B, Water Quality Assurance Act of 1983

statutes provide for the creation of a fund, financed primarily by industry, to clean up improperly disposed hazardous waste where responsible parties cannot be determined or are insolvent. In situations where responsible parties can be identified and are solvent, Superfund legislation provides for recovery of clean-up costs or the imposition of clean-up responsibility upon the parties deemed to have caused the damage.[7]

Historically, with the passage of the Resource Conservation and Recovery Act (RCRA)[8] in 1976, a decided shift in the federal legislative response was evident. Pursuant to RCRA, the Environmental Protection Agency (EPA) was granted authority to control hazardous waste sites by establishing an elaborate regulatory scheme and by bringing lawsuits to abate imminent hazards.[9] In support of this enforcement scheme, Congress enacted CERCLA, which expands the EPA's authority to bring suit or issue administrative orders to abate hazards.[10] With. the passage of CERCLA, hazardous waste problems entered a new era. CERCLA established a $1.6 billion dollar *Response* fund,[11] the purpose of which was to finance prompt government clean-up of hazardous waste sites prior to any assessment of liability.[12] The response fund is replenished

---

New Jersey: New Jersey Spillage Compensation Fund, NJ Stat Ann §58:10-23.11 *et seq* (West Supp 1980)

North Carolina: The North Carolina Oil Pollution control Act of 1973, NC Gen Stat §143.215.76 *et seq,* (1978)

New Hampshire: Hazardous Waste Cleanup Fund, NH Rev Stat Ann §147-A *et seq* (1981)

Maryland: State Hazardous Substance Control Fund, Md Ann Code ch 240, §2 (1982)

California: Hazardous Substance Account Act of 1981, Cal Legis Serv 2609, 2619-2620 (West 1981); Cal Health & Safety Code §§25186, 25300-25395 (Deering 1981)

[7] 42 USC §§9604, 9606, 9607.

[8] 42 USC §6901 *et seq.*

[9] 42 USC §6921 (identified harmful substances are placed on an official list; EPA is then required to develop criteria for the substances); see Committee on Environmental Controls, *ABA Section of Corporation, Banking and Business Law, The Resource Conservation and Recovery Act of 1976—The Newest Environmental Sleeper,* 33 Bus Law 2555 (July 1978); 42 USC §§6922-6924 (generators, transporters, and disposers must keep detailed records of hazardous substance handling; permits are required for owner or operators of treatment, storage, or disposal facilities); *Id* §§6928, 6973; Skaff, *The Emergency Powers in the Environmental Protection Statutes: A Suggestion for a Unified Emergency Provision,* 3 Harv Envtl L Rev 298 (1979)(detailed discussion of the scope of RCRA powers).

[10] 42 USC §§9601-9657.

[11] *Id* §9631.

[12] *Id* §9605. This provision required revision of the national contingency plan to establish procedures and standards for responding to hazardous waste releases, including methods for discovering, investigating, and cleaning up waste sites. This revision was finally accomplished pursuant to court order. See 13 Envt Rep (BNA) 364-65 (1982); 47 Fed Reg 31,180 (July 16, 1982).

pursuant to the liability assessment provisions.[13] The government (i.e., the EPA) is authorized to sue responsible private parties to recover the clean-up costs the fund has expended or expects to expend in cleaning up targeted sites.[14] As a result of this provision, recovery may be sought from waste generators,[15] dumpsite owners and operators,[16] and parties transporting waste materials.[17] Hence, as a result of CERCLA's liability assessment provisions, corporate generators, pursuant to the *deep pocket* theory, will most likely he held financially responsible for clean-up costs.[18] This responsibility may extend to action occurring prior to the enacting of CERCLA because of the retroactivity of the statute.[19] The federal Superfund liability provision[20] is discussed in Chapter 10.

Specific defenses to liability are set forth in CERCLA and include:

1.   An act of God

2.   An act of war

3.   An act of omission by a wholly unrelated third party

4.   Any combination of the foregoing[21]

While CERCLA does not explicitly establish a strict liability standard, some form of strict liability is presently being used.[22] Indeed, many commentators

---

[13] 42 USC §9607.

[14] *Id* §9605.

[15] *Id* §9607(a)(3)

[16] *Id* §9607(a)(2).

[17] *Id* §9607(a)(4). Even though CERCLA permits recovery against the several responsible parties and also permits recovery of natural resources damages, the legislative history of the act is clear in not providing a private cause of action for personal damages. See Meyer, *Compensating Hazardous Waste Victims: RCRA Insurance Regulations and a Not So "Super" Fund Act,* 11 Envtl L 689, 701 (1981).

[18] *See, e.g.,* United States v Reilly Tar & Chem Corp, No 80-469 (D Minn Sept 4, 1980); United States v Vertac Chem Corp, No 80-109 (ED Ark Mar 4, 1980); United States v Chem-Dyne Corp, 12 Envtl L Rep 30 (SD Ohio Aug 26, 1982); United States v South Carolina Recycling & Disposal Corp, No 80-1274-6 (DSC Mar 23, 1982); United States v Spectron, Inc, No 80-1552 (D Md Apr 1, 1982).

[19] See Note, *Generator Liability Under Superfund for Clean-up of Abandoned Hazardous Waste Dumpsites,* 130 U Pa L Rev 5 (1982).

[20] 42 USC §9607(a).

[21] *Id* §9607(a)(4)(c).

[22] *Id* §9601(32) defines liability as the standard applicable under §311 of the Clean Water Act (CWA), 33 USC §1321. The following cases have construed this provision of the CWA as creating strict liability: United States v LeBoeuf Bros Towing Co, 621 F2d 787 (5th Cir 1980); Stewart Transp Co v Allied Towing, 596 F2d 609 (4th Cir 1979); United States v Hollywood Marine, 16 Envt Rep Cas (BNA) 2180 (SD Tex 1981); Sabine Towing & Transp Co v United States, 16 Envt Rep Cas (BNA) 2081 (Ct Cl 1981). Accordingly, this strict liability standard may apply to the federal Superfund liability assessment provision.

contend that strict liability is the appropriate standard under CERCLA.[23] However, further insight reveals that the CERCLA standard is a hybrid from the common law definition in that it is tempered by considerations of fault.[24]

Armed with the federal CERCLA example, numerous states have taken the initiative and passed legislation addressing the issue of financial responsibility for hazardous waste. Some states provide legislatively for general hazardous waste emergencies. The creation of special hazardous waste trust funds to facilitate clean-up and restoration is one mechanism designed to assure that adequate funds exist for such incidents. Other states either provide for direct liability or subject violators to massive civil penalties. Regardless of the form of state involvement, it is clear that liability for clean-up operations is substantial.[25]

New York's Industrial Hazardous Waste Management Act[26] authorizes the Department of Environmental Conservation "to clean up or return to its original state any area where hazardous wastes were disposed."[27] Monies for clean-up and restoration activities are generated pursuant to New York's elaborate assessment program.[28]

New Jersey's Spill Compensation and Control Act[29] provides for a *superfund* to insure compensation for clean-up costs and property damages associated with the discharge of hazardous substances.[30]

---

[23] See e.g., Hinds, *Liability Under Federal Law for Hazardous Waste Injuries,* 6 Harv Envtl L Rev 1, 26 (1982); Note, *SUPERFUND: Conscripting Industry Support for Environmental Cleanup,* 9 Ecology LQ 524, 541 (1981).

[24] In Philadelphia v Stepan Chem Co, 544 F Supp 1135 (ED Pa 1982), Judge Ditter in dicta expounded the strict liability limitation accordingly:

> It is clear, however, that Superfund's strict liability standards should be confined to those parties who engaged in substantial and purposeful hazardous waste disposal activity for commercial profit after the enactment of this statute. Automatic application of strict liability to parties whose conduct was substantially unrelated to the present danger posed by the hazardous waste release or who did not obtain commercial benefit from their conduct, does not appear to be compelled by the environmental concerns which gave rise to Superfund.

544 F Supp at 1147. See also, Dore, *The Standard of Civil Liability for Hazardous Waste Disposal Activity: Some Quirks of Superfund,* 57 Notre Dame Law 260,276 (1981).

[25] See, *Congressional Research Service of the Library of Congress, Comm on Environment and Public Works, US Senate, 96th Cong, 13th Sess, Six Case Studies of Compensation for Toxic Substances Pollution (June 1980).*

[26] NY Envtl Conserv Law §27-0900 *et seq.* (McKinney Supp 1978). Financial responsibility remains with generator, transporter, or disposer of hazardous substances. *Id* §27-1301.

[27] *Id* §27-0916.

[28] *Id* §27-0923.

[29] NJ Stat Ann §58:10-23 (West 1977). New Jersey provides for an absolute right of recovery against the responsible party. *Id* §58:10-23q.

[30] *Id.*

Pursuant to Maryland's State Hazardous Substance Control Fund,[31] a fund was established for the "emergency removal or mitigation" of the effect of hazardous substances.[32] The fund provides for reimbursement by the party responsible for the existence of any hazardous condition.[33]

Florida presently holds a person jointly and severally liable to the state for any damages to the environment as well as for clean-up costs.[34] Illinois, within its Environmental Protection Act,[35] has created a Hazardous Waste Fund[36] authorized:

> for the purpose of taking whatever preventive or corrective action is necessary or appropriate in circumstances certified by the Governor and the Director to exist at sites in which hazardous wastes have been stored or disposed which will or may cause an immediate or long-term danger to the environment or to the public health. . . .[37]

Additionally, violation of Illinois' Environmental Protection Act[38] can subject the violator to substantial civil penalties.[39]

Another impetus to settle in the clean-up arena is to insure the best possible economic resolution of the problem. While it is clear that both the public and corporate interest in mitigating potential hazards is unquestioned, the issue of determining the most cost effective remedial activity can serve as an impetus to settle. The pertinent issues are restoration versus abatement, or simply *what is the acceptable or tolerable level of risk?* The manner in which these issues are addressed will inexorably determine the cost-effectiveness of a particular settlement.[40]

---

[31] Md Pub Health Code Ann §7-218 *et seq* (1982); Md Ann Code ch 240, §2 (1982).

[32] *Id* §7-220.

[33] *Id* §7-221.

[34] *See* Fla Stat Ann §403.141 (West 1976) (Public Health Law), authorized by Fla Stat Ann §403.011 (West 1976). Florida is presently seeking passage of a comprehensive superfund bill which closely parallels New Jersey's Spill Fund statute.

[35] Ill Stat Ann ch 111 1/2, §§1001-1045 (Smith-Hurd 1978).

[36] *Id* §1022 *et seq.*

[37] *Id* §1022-2(d).

[38] Ill Stat Ann ch 111 1/2, §§1001-1045 (Smith Hurd 1978).

[39] *Id* §1042.

[40] Recently, the EPA notified two major marketers of gasoline that soluble hydrocarbons, specifically benzene, toluene, and xylene (BTX) had been identified contaminating the groundwater and drinking water supplies of a particular housing development. The EPA's nonsettlement position was simple—namely, aquifer restoration. Viewing this solution as inefficient and costly, the two marketers proposed to abate the contamination by constructing a series of interceptor wells to prevent further migration of BTX. Additionally, this proposal called for groundwater from the interceptor wells to be pumped out, thus aerating the contaminants out of the discharge water. The water would then be surface-discharged without the BTX contaminants. It is estimated that the EPA's nonsettlement position was anywhere from 10 to 20 times more expensive than the proposal offered by the interested parties.

§23.04   —Avoidance of a Determination of Violation

The final reason for settlement is the avoidance of the risk of being found in violation of a federal or state statute. While the violation of federal law should be a sufficient reason in itself to settle, when considered with the booming area of personal injury claims growing out of the exposure to hazardous substances in the environment, its importance significantly increases. In settling any hazardous substance incident, appropriate nonadmission of liability language is often included. While a particular settlement may leave some uncertainty over the nature and extent of the remedial action one must undertake, agreement should always be reached regarding clear and concise nonadmission language. Hence, a definite benefit accrues when settlement is the resolution mechanism—that is, the absence of any finding of a violation of a federal or state statute, standard or regulation.

In order for a toxic tort litigant in the personal injury arena to prove the causal links necessary for recovery, four important conditions must be met.[41] First, the plaintiff must substantiate the presence of significant quantities of the hazardous substance/pollutant alleged to have caused injury. Second, the plaintiff must show exposure to the substance/pollutant. Third, the plaintiff must identify the source of the contaminant and show a breach of due care by the defendant. Fourth, the plaintiff must demonstrate the effect of the substance/pollutant in causing injury.

A determination, administratively or judicially, that an environmental statute was violated may serve as proof of some of the elements set forth above—specifically, the question of whether a breach of a duty of care existed.[42] Certainly, any administrative or judicial finding may answer the first and second conditions set forth above.[43] Clearly this is true in the occupational safety and health area; thus, once the stated purposes of the two areas of law are the same—e.g. protection of the individual's health—it is reasonable to assume the same analysis will apply in the environmental area. The test to be used is a threefold one:

---

[41] See Soble, *A Proposal for the Administrative Compensation of Victims of Toxic Substances Pollution: A Model Act,* 14 Harv J on Legis 683, 706, 739 (1977).

[42] See **ch 8.**

[43] An analogy can be drawn to the way courts have considered OSHA (Occupational Safety and Health Act, 29 USC §661 *et seq*) violations as evidence of negligence. The legislative Purpose of OSHA—to protect workers from hazardous conditions and elements in the workplace—is somewhat similar to the expressed legislative purpose underlying federal and state environmental legislation, 29 USC §652. In several cases it has been held or recognized that a fact-finder may consider OSHA (including regulations) violations as bearing on the duty of care required by a defendant in a negligence suit. *See, e.g.,* Buhler v Marriott Hotels, Inc, 390 F Supp 999 (D La 1974); Watwood v RR Dawson Bridge Co, 293 Ala 578, 307 So 2d 692 (1979); Dunn v Brimer, 537 SW2d 164 (Ark 1976); Disabatino Bros v Baio, 366 A2d 508 (Del Super Ct 1976). While there is no current support for this approach in personal injury cases, it may become a developing area of toxic tort litigation.

1. Sufficient proof of violation

2. The statute or regulation was to protect the plaintiff

3. The type of risk involved to be protected against was the same[44]

This final point on the impetus to settle clean-up situations involving the effect of findings of violation of a statute appropriately leads into the next area of discussion, namely, the impetus to settle personal injury claims.

§23.05 Personal Injury Claims: Settle What?

In an article in the April 1983 issue of *Trial* magazine it is asserted that "a major event occurring during the last ten years has been American industry's now-total commitment to fight toxic tort cases, regulations or standards on whatever front is involved."[45] Implicit in this statement is a perception that American industry is committed to fight toxic tort claims and not to seek settlement as a resolution.

Certainly, the existence of the resolve set forth in the article is not conducive to an environment of settlement. Public awareness of the potential health problems associated with exposure to hazardous substances has increased dramatically in the past several years. This increased awareness has certainly evidenced itself in a rapid increase in personal injury claims occasioned by exposure to hazardous substances. As a consequence, corporate counsel must be intimately familiar with the impact and ramifications of statutes and common law as they affect private personal injury litigation. Previously, the impetus to settle was reasoned as follows:

1. Legal economy

2. Controlling the extent and scope of liability

3. The avoidance of findings of statutory liability

In the private injury context, the impetus to settle is virtually nonexistent. Legal elements of proof make settlement prior to the full adjudication of the issue both costly and dangerous. The prevailing legal standards of proof are difficult for a plaintiff to meet in the context of personal hazardous waste injury suits. The next two sections, §§**23.06** and **23.07,** explore common law proof barriers and the existence of state statutory compensation assistance.

---

[44] JA Arthur v Flota Mercante Gran Centro SA, 487 F2d 561, 564 (5th Cir 1973). The various courts have differed as to the weight to be given, varying from negligence per se to evidence of negligence. See cases cited in G. Nothstein, The Law of Safety and Health 550, 580 (1981 & Supp 1983); D.J. Mahoney, Remarks at ABA National Institute, Section Labor Relations Law (Apr 29-30, 1976) (available in Proceedings of the ABA National Institute on Occupational Safety and Health Law).

[45] Keller, *Toxic Tort Litigation: The Management Challenge,* 19 Trial 52 (1983).

§23.06   —State Statutory Compensation Assistance

Currently, there are only two states that legislatively provide compensation for personal injuries associated with exposure to hazardous substances.[46] In California, the Carpenter-Presley-Tanner Hazardous Substance Account Act of 1981[47] has as its legislative intent to "[c]ompensate persons, under certain circumstances, for out of pocket medical expenses and lost wages or business income resulting from injuries proximately caused by exposure to release of hazardous substances."[48] Pursuant to this enactment, California has established a Hazardous Substance Compensation Account,[49] from which the state compensates persons under certain circumstances for all uninsured, out-of-pocket medical expenses and 80 per cent of uninsured actual lost wages or business income for up to three years from the date of discovery of the loss, not to exceed $15,000 per year.[50] The act creates an administrative body to review claims and to provide written responses. No compensation or decision is admissible as evidence of any issue of fact or law, administratively or in court.[51] In exchange for this, any claimant receiving compensation under the fund must subrogate all rights to recover such loss to the state. The Attorney General's office is then required to commence an action to recover any amount paid in compensation from any party who is liable.[52]

The California State Board of Control has as its administrative standard the following minimum requirements:

1. Verification of claim
2. Description of the hazardous substance which was released and is responsible for the injuries or illnesses
3. Certification of dates and place of release
4. Certification of injury, illness, and medical history of the claimant
5. The claimant's income (in order to compute pecuniary loss)[53]

Based on the information set forth above, the board is mandated to render a final decision on whether the loss incurred was proximately caused by the identified release of or exposure to hazardous substances.

In Alaska, the legislature undertook a vastly different approach. Alaska has

---

[46] California and Alaska are the only states which provide a legislative alternative to the common law rules.

[47] California Hazardous Substance-Account Act of 1981, Cal Legis Serv 2609, 2619-20 (West 1981); Cal Health & Safety Code §§25186, 25300-25395 (Deering 1981).

[48] *Id* §25301(b).

[49] *Id* §253781 *et seq.*

[50] *Id* §25375.

[51] *Id* §25379.

[52] *Id* §25380.

[53] *Id* §25380.

expressly recognized a right of recovery in state court for personal injuries suffered by private persons as a result of hazardous substance releases.

Sec. 46.03.822 Strict liability for the discharge of Hazardous Substances.

To the extent not otherwise preempted by federal law, a person owning or having control over a hazardous substance which enters in or upon the waters, surface or subsurface lands of the state is strictly liable, without regard to fault, for the damages to persons or property, public or private, caused by the entry. In an action to recover damages, the person is relieved from strict liability, without regard to fault, if he can prove

(1) that the hazardous substance to which the damages relate entered in or upon the waters, surface or subsurface lands of the state solely as a result of

(A) an act of war,

(B) an intentional act or a negligent act of a third party, other than a party (or its employees) in privity of contract with, or employed by, the person,

(C) negligence on the part of the United States government or the State of Alaska, or

(D) an act of God; and

(2) in relation to (1)(B), (C) or (D) of this section, that he discovered the entry of the hazardous substance in or upon the waters, surface or subsurface lands of the state and began operations to contain and clean up the hazardous substance within a reasonable period of time.[54]

. . .

Sec. 46.03.824 Damages.

Damages include but are not limited to injury to or loss of persons or property, real or personal, loss of income, loss of the means of producing income, or the loss of an economic benefit.[55]

This statutory language creates a strict liability system through which persons injured by the *entry of a hazardous substance* may bring suit for compensatory damages. Recovery for potential future damages may be recovered under the damage provision if proven.

Despite Alaska's removal of the fault component as an obstacle to toxic tort plaintiffs, victims still are not guaranteed recovery. Since hazardous substance personal injury cases are handled as personal injury cases, most potential plaintiffs continue to falter at other evidentiary and substantive hurdles. Proof of causation and injury, along with statute of limitations problems, continues to thwart toxic tort plaintiffs in Alaska.

Finally, in discussing how the Alaskan legislature handled the issue of personal injury claims growing out of hazardous substance release or exposure,

---

[54] Alaska Strict Liability for the Discharge of Hazardous Substances ch 122, §1 (1972); amend ch 260, §13 (1976); tit 46, ch 3, §46.03.822 (1982).

[55] *Id* §46.03.824.

reference is made to part (2) of §46.03.822. In this part, the legislature clearly conditioned the limited defenses to strict liability upon the defendant's reasonable commencement of clean-up operations. Hence, a nonnegligent generator is afforded additional protection from personal injury suits if the defendant timely commences clean-up or abatement operations. While the imposition of strict liability in Alaska may be an impetus to settle personal injury claims growing out of the release of a hazardous substance, this provision attaches a high premium upon prompt clean-up activity. For a nonnegligent generator in Alaska, avoidance of personal injury lawsuits should become one of the factors considered in developing a clean up strategy as previously discussed.

§23.07   —Common Law Standard of Proof: Impossible Hurdles?

Private hazardous waste lawsuits are discussed in this section in broad, general terms. For the practioner, it is clear that since potential claimants will continue to bring suits for private damages in state courts, an in-depth understanding of the particular state tort law, especially in the areas of legal causation, proof of injury, and statutes of limitations, is essential. This section does not attempt to explore fully state tort rules, since this is the subject of Chapter 11. Rather, in very broad terms, this section identifies the general common law obstacles to recovery and how these obstacles work as a disincentive to settlement of suits for injuries from exposure to hazardous wastes and toxic substances.

Hurdle #1—Causation

Traditionally, the common law firmly places the burden of proving legal causation upon the plaintiff.[56] Initially, the plaintiff must demonstrate by a preponderance of the evidence that the defendant's action was a "substantial factor" in causing the alleged injury.[57] The plaintiff must establish a cause-in-fact connection between the defendant's action and the plaintiff's injury.[58] Recovery of damages against a defendant in a hazardous waste injury suit by a plaintiff depends greatly on the plaintiff's ability to meet the heavy burden of proving that a particular exposure to a hazardous substance *directly* caused the claimed injury.[59]

In most jurisdictions, the essential causal connection cannot be met by a showing of slight probability or mere possibility of causation, even though

---

[56] W. Prosser The Law of Torts §41, at 241 (4th ed 1971).

[57] W. Prosser, *supra,* note 56, at §41; Restatement (Second) of Torts §431, at 428 (1965); *see also* Hamil v Bashline, 243 Pa Super 227, 364 A2d 1366 (1976), *overruling,* Hamil v Bashline, 224 Pa Super 407, 307 A2d 57 (1975).

[58] W. Prosser, *supra* note 56, at §41; *see also* Restatement (Second) of Torts §§430-453 (1965).

[59] W. Prosser, *supra* note 56, at §43, at 263-64.

scientifically supportable.[60] Additionally, it is legally insufficient for the plaintiff to show that exposure merely increased the risk of suffering harm.[61] Many plaintiffs in the hazardous tort area are nonsuited (directed verdicts, etc.) because the issue of causation is premised on conjecture or speculation and not fact.[62] To prove the necessary causal link, one commentator has offered the following four elements which a plaintiff must meet:

1.   Substantiate the presence of significant amounts of the hazardous substance which allegedly caused injury

2.   Reconstruct the exposure from origin to the plaintiff

3.   Identify the source of the pollutant and show breach of duty of care

4.   Demonstrate the effect of the pollutant upon the plaintiff [63]

The problems inherent for plaintiffs are numerous. Namely, in most exposure cases, there are several generators and several pollutants involved. Not only must a plaintiff demonstrate that a specific pollutant is the cause of particular symptoms, he or she must also remove doubt that there are not other causes, not attributable to a hazardous substance, which led to the particular symptoms. If the very existence of the pollutants is alleged to have caused injury, the plaintiff continues to bear the burden of showing each pollutant's contribution to the alleged symptoms. While the common law theory of liability may vary from state to state, the major obstacle to recovery of compensatory damages for hazardous waste victims remains proof of legal causation.[64]

In summary, hazardous waste and toxic substance injuries have several characteristics which thwart the plaintiff's ability to meet the test of legal causation. Multiple causal agents and multiple effects, unclear exposure paths, and the phenomena of long-latency periods accentuate the epidemiological uncertainty of hazardous waste injury. The common law requires a high degree of certainty, not the statistically significant association between exposure and injury with which one is faced in most toxic injury cases.

Presently, either the *substantial factor* or *but for*[65] concept of causation which is followed by most state courts mandates that most defendants answer the plaintiff's complaint with the defense that the defendant's acts or omissions

---

[60] *Id* §43, at 242.

[61] Hamil v Bashline, 243 Pa Super 227, 314 A2d 1366 (1976).

[62] W. Prosser, *supra* note 56, at §43; *see also* McMahon v Young, 442 Pa 484, 276 A2d 534 (1971).

[63] Soble, *A Proposal for the Administrative Compensation of Victims of Toxic Substances Pollution: A Model Act,* 14 Harv J on Legis 683,738 (1977).

[64] For further information, see, e.g., Note, *Strict Liability and Hazardous Wastes,* 16 New Eng L Rev (1981); Note, *Liability for Generators of Hazardous Waste: The Failure of Existing Enforcement Mechanisms,* 69 Geo LJ 1047 (1981); Note, *Hazardous Wastes: Preserving the Nuisance Remedy,* 33 Stan L Rev 675 (1981).

[65] W. Prosser, *supra* note 56 at §38, at 208.

were neither the cause in fact nor the legal cause of any alleged exposure to materials or the plaintiff's alleged injuries.

Hurdle #2—Proof of Injury

The common law traditionally requires that the plaintiff provide proof of injury as a necessary element to a private right of action for personal damages.[66] State courts have shown a reluctance to find the plaintiff's proof of injury sufficient when that proof is based on transitory or legally insufficient medical conditions.[67] The right to maintain a cause of action does not *accrue* until the claimant can show a legally provable injury.[68] Courts generally require manifestation of an injury with sufficient certainty before considering it as proof in court.[69] Accordingly, proof of a potential or future threat of physical harm will not be sufficient to sustain a cause of action for personal injury.[70] There has been a traditional reluctance to award compensatory damages for *at-risk*[71] injuries in negligence cases. Prosser adequately describes the rule as "[n]ominal damages, to vindicate a technical right, cannot be recovered in a negligence action, where no actual loss has occurred. The threat of future harm, not yet realized, is not enough."[72]

Not all persons exposed to hazardous substances will immediately contract disease or cancer. Presently, no method exists to predict in advance which exposed individuals will develop physical maladies. In most cases, hazardous substance injuries manifest themselves after long latency periods, following months or years of chronic or routine exposure to relatively low levels.[73] Moreover, the scientific and medical communities are at odds over what is an absolutely *safe* level of exposure.

The result of the common law's approach for addressing *actual,* not *prospective,* injuries has forced many plaintiffs to allege and prove a present injury caused by exposure to hazardous substances, based upon medically detectable symptoms. Unfortunately, most claims rest entirely on alleged harmful expo-

---

[66] For a discussion of the common law principles involved and the few reported state cases, see *Note, An Analysis of Common Law and Statutory Remedies for Hazardous Waste Injuries,* 12 Rut-Cam LJ 117 (1980).

[67] Schenebeck v Sterling Drug, Inc, 473 F2d 919 (8th Cir 1970); Sterling Drug, Inc v Cornish, 370 F2d 83 (8th Cir 1966); Young v Clinchfield RR, 288 F2d 499 (4th Cir 1961).

[68] W. Prosser, *supra,* note 56, at §30, at 146-47.

[69] Bridgford v United States, 550 F2d 978, 982 (4th Cir 1977); Louisville & Nashville RR v Saltzer, 151 Va 165, 144 SE 456 (1978).

[70] See Note, *An Analysis of Common Law and Statutory Remedies for Hazardous Waste Injuries,* 12 Rut Cam LJ 117 (1980).

[71] In the context of this discussion, *at-risk* refers to injuries which have not manifested themselves physically.

[72] W. Prosser, *supra* note 56, at §43.

[73] See Senkan & Stauffer, *The Difficulties at Defining Hazardous Waste,* 84 Tech Rev 40 (1981); S. Epstein the Politics of Cancer 2 (1978); see also B. Brown, Laying Waste— The Poisoning of America By Toxic Chemicals 293 (1980).

sures absent a physical manifestation of effect, but providing a prediction of future harm. Courts armed with the common law have addressed this approach in a harsh and unyielding fashion. The Fourth Circuit in *Sides v Richard Machine Works, Inc,*[74] reasoned that, "If harm had not ensued, there would have been no tort and nothing to sue on."[75] Hence, plaintiffs exposed without incurring immediate injury are subject to the common law principle that a legal injury does not result until a harm evidences itself. Combined with state statute of limitations problems, some plaintiffs may experience an insurmountable legal obstacle to recovery.

Hurdle #3—Long Latency Period

The long latency period involved in most hazardous waste exposure cases presents plaintiffs with insurmountable problems depending on the limitation rules in a particular jurisdiction.[76] Some jurisdictions hold that a cause of action accrues for limitations purposes at the time of exposure to the hazard.[77] Still others focus on when the injury is discovered or should have been discovered.[78] Finally, a small minority of jurisdictions hold that the statute of limitations does not begin to run until the injured party is able to or should reasonably be able to ascertain a causal connection between the injury and exposure to a hazardous substance.[79]

Modern case law reflects a continuing movement towards the discovery rule.[80] In jurisdictions relying on the discovery rule, the plaintiffs will still be faced with a wide variety of rules. An example of the restrictive approach was expressed by the Eighth Circuit in *Karjula v Johns-Manville Products Corp:*[81] "[T]he plaintiff's claim arises when the harm to his person becomes evident . . . . The statute doesn't commence to run against [the plaintiff] until he has contracted the disease . . . . and the process of contracting the disease does not cease until physical impairment manifests itself."[82]

Hence, plaintiffs must expect the limitations period to commence from the time the plaintiff discovers the fact of injury. Other jurisdictions have liberalize

---

[74] 406 F2d 445 (4th Cir 1969).

[75] *Id* 446.

[76] For a more expansive review of state statutes of Limitation and rules, see 51 Am Jur 2d *Limitation of Actions* §§31-36, (1970); Hutton, *Statute of Limitations and Radiation Injury,* 23 Tenn L Rev 278 (1954).

[77] Thornton v Roosevelt Hosp, 47 NY2d 780, 391 NE2d 1002, 417 NYS2d 920 (1979).

[78] Wilson v Johns-Manville Sales Corp 684 F2d 111 (DC Cir 1982); Borel v Fibreboard Paper Prods Corp, 493 F2d 1076 (5th Cir 1973), *cert denied,* 419 US 869 (1974).

[79] Caron v United States, 548 F2d 355 (1st Cir 1976)(applying Michigan Law); Gilbert v Jones, 563 SW2d 212 (Tenn Ct App 1974).

[80] Roman v AH Robins Co, 518 F2d 970 (5th Cir 1975) (Texas law); Frank Cooke, Inc v Horwitz, Mass App Ct Adv Sh 1197, 406 NE2d 678 (1980).

[81] 523 F2d 155 (8th Cir 1975).

[82] *Id* 159.

the discovery rule by requiring that the plaintiff discover the facts supporting the cause of action, not just injury. In liberalizing the discovery rule, courts are quick to note that facts essential to legal causation are not imperative; rather, those facts demonstrating responsibility on someone's part places the plaintiff on notice, thus commencing the limitations period.[83]

In summary, as a sharp contrast to the clean-up context, the impetus to settle cases in the private injury context is obviously missing because of the legal proof difficulties faced by plaintiffs. Common law principles of legal causation, proof of injury, and statutes of limitations pose practical problems to plaintiffs in the private injury area. Until common law barriers are removed, or until the hazardous injury bar undertakes closer scrutiny of the prima facie and proof elements of plaintiffs' cases, defendants will continue to exhibit an unwillingness to participate in settlement efforts.

§23.08   How to Approach Settlement?

The issues associated with the settlement of hazardous substance cases are highly complex and require careful consideration. In the majority of hazardous waste clean-up cases, the impetus to settle exists on both sides. The Supreme Court has expressed a balancing approach in remedying environmental problems which weighs the costs and feasibility of clean-up with the nature and extent of the harm to be corrected.[84] It is this balancing approach which is the linchpin of clean up negotiations.

In 1981, William A. Sullivan, Jr., Enforcement Counsel of the Environmental Protection Agency (EPA), circulated an internal memorandum to the EPA's regional counsels, enforcement division directors, and Superfund[85] coordinators setting forth the agency's position regarding future settlements.[86] (It

---

[83] Cadieux v International Tel & Tel Corp 593 F2d 142 (1st Cir 1979).

[84] *See* Aberdeen & Rockfish RR v Scrap, 409 US 1207, 1217-18 (1972) where the Court states:

> Our society and its governmental instrumentalities having been less than alert to the needs of our environment for generations, have now taken protective steps. These developments, however praiseworthy, should not lead courts to exercise equitable powers loosely or casually whenever a claim of environmental damage is asserted. . . . The decisional process of judges is one of balancing and is often the most difficult task.

See also United States v Vertae Chem Corp, 489 F Supp 870, 886-89 (1980).

[85] Comprehensive Environmental Response, Compensation and Liability Act, 42 USC §9601 *et seq* (CERCLA), discussed in **chs 9 & 10.**

[86] Memorandum from William A. Sullivan Jr., Enforcement Counsel, Guidance on Hazardous Waste Site Settlement Negotiations, reprinted in Hazardous Waste Litigation 1982 341-45 (PLI 1982).

> The party or parties to the agreement should—in the Agency's opinion—be virtually certain to comply with its terms and possess the financial capability to do so.
>
> How the potentially hazardous site or a party's involvement with the site came

should be kept in mind, however, that there may be insufficient time to work out an agreement in true *emergency* situations. In an emergency situation, once federal clean-up has commenced, it will not ordinarily be halted pending completion of discussions concerning the terms and conditions of a possible agreement).[87]

Additionally, seven general principles were expounded in the memorandum to serve as a guide in structuring settlements. First, the details and timing of the clean-up by the responsible party or parties should be explicitly stated. Second, inclusion of *saving clause* language allowing the EPA to revoke if non-compliance is found is required. Third, total releases should be avoided until the responsible party or parties commit to total clean-up. Fourth, in the event total releases are negotiated, the EPA must be certain that the responsible parties' *buy-out* represents the parties' *fair share* of the total clean-up. This requires the EPA to understand fully the scope and expense of clean-up. Fifth, in no event should releases be for more than civil liability under CERCLA. Sixth, settlement agreements should explicitly protect the EPA's right against *nonsettling* responsible parties. Seventh, agreements reached after filing of a civil court action should be pursuant to a consent decree. If settlement is reached prior to filing, the agreement should be pursuant to a consent order.

These are the EPA's views on clean up negotiations; do the practical results in several negotiated settlements bear out these views?

In *Seymour Recycling*[88] and *United States v Wade*,[89] settling parties received a full release from surface of groundwater claims in exchange for a fixed monetary contribution. In each case there were nonsettling responsible parties upon whom the risk of additional liability for clean-up costs were placed. Conversely, in *United States v Duracell*,[90] the absence of nonsettling responsible parties

---

to the attention of the government. (Parties volunteering information not previously available to government authorities might prove to be better candidates for negotiating agreements than parties who are not "volunteers").

The manner in which the party responded to government "notice" of potential involvement in a hazardous waste site problem.

Some major advantage to the Agency should be apparent in pursuing an "agreement" rather than other available formats. (For example, in the Inmont agreement, the private party agreed to finance and assume full responsibility and liability for completing clean-up. Where the nature of the problem and the capabilities of the responsible party permit, EPA will generally prefer that clean-up be undertaken by the responsible party rather than the government.)

The likelihood and degree to which future federal management or supervision of site clean-up will be required. Generally speaking, negotiated agreements would appear to be more appropriate in short-term "removal" situations rather than in the more involved and many-phased "remedial" actions.

[87] *Id* 342-43.

[88] Seymour Recycling, 5 Chem & Rad Waste Lit Rep 95 (SD Ind 1982). Twenty-four settling defendants paid $7.7 million for a total *buy-out* of liability.

[89] 3 Chemical & Radiation Waste Litig Rep 566 (ED Pa 1981).

[90] 1 Hazardous Waste Litig Rep 1817, 1822 (MD Tenn 1982)(government retained right to: "bring a subsequent action for injunctive or similar relief concerning the site

resulting in a settlement which gave the government the right to seek additional funds if needed.

Recently, in *United States v Velsicol Chemical Corp,*[91] an elaborate remedial plan was negotiated which detailed the specific actions step-by-step. The form of *activity* settlement is by far the most common. The existence of cost ceiling provisions is essential to avoidance of the *blank check* approach. A variation on the activity obligation approach is the use of environmental performance standards. *United States v Spectron, Inc*[92] is a prime example of responsible parties agreeing to meet certain designated performance standards in conducting clean-up operations. This approach provides to the settling party or parties a mechanism with which to gauge the extent of the obligation assumed. It also provides more definitive protection to the public.

The vast majority of negotiated settlements in the clean-up/response area have sought a finite and reasonable ceiling to the settling defendant's obligations. Growing sophistication in fashioning settlement agreements has slowly led all parties involved towards maximizing the goals of the parties involved.

§23.09 When to Settle? When to Fight

These are two sides of the same question. The judgments necessary to answer this question, at least in the hazardous waste area, require the lawyer handling the case to have a sound understanding of both his or her client's resources and his or her client's contribution to a state or federal clean-up operation.

The crucial fact to know is whether the client is a major or minor contributor. In order to determine whether the client is an operator, transporter, or generator, a calculation of the total volume of material at a site must be done. After that is accomplished, the toxicity of the material must be examined and a judgment (bringing to bear whatever scientific resources are available) made as to the portion of the problem for which the client is credibly responsible. The difference between *toxicity* as a test of responsibility versus *volume* can only be made on a case-by-case basis.[93] Next, counsel should examine how many

---

including, but not limited to, an action seking additional funds for work contemplated by or of the type contemplated by this decree and seeking rehabilitation of Beech Creek.")

[91] No 82-10303 (ED Mich Nov 8, 1982) (consent judgment).

[92] No 80-1552 (D Md Mar 25, 1982) (settlement decree).

[93] At some contamination sites, the harm done is divisible because methods of treatment of substances differ. For example, removal of benzene, toluene, and the various xylenes from water is relatively simple by aeration. If the water contains chlorinated hydrocarbons like ethylene chloride, chemical treatment at a much higher expense is needed. The physical structures required to collect leachate or remove groundwater are needed no matter which contaminant is present, and the cost is not easily divisible. Various methods to apportion a contributor's percentage liability based on volume and/or toxicity will vary from site to site. At most locations, however, the common law notion of indivisible harm will be the position taken by an agency.

other operators, transporters, or cogenerators have material at the site. If the number is large and the client's volume is low, chances are that the client is a minor contributor. If the client is one of only a few participants at a site, or its waste is high in volume and/or toxicity, the client is probably a major contributor.

Major contributors have three primary reasons to settle:

1. Economic use of resources
2. Control of the cost of clean-up
3. Removal of the Environmental Protection Agency (EPA) or the state or local agency as an adversary

Economic use of resources is the cliche of avoiding the expense of a fight. Fees for attorneys, experts, and consultants, as well as the client's own time, can be saved by entering into an agreement. As a practical matter, the client may decide to spend its money to buy peace and to limit financial exposure.

The risk of unknown clean-up costs is a Damoclean sword. By settling, however, a party can participate in a discussion with the agency as to what is to be required as abatement or removal at the site.

Control of the cost of clean-up is a slippery proposition. When a major contributor assumes responsibility for cleaning up a site, the ultimate cost is often unknown. The advantage of assuming responsibility is the ability to control contractors and, most importantly, the ability to help determine how much clean-up is necessary at the site. How clean is clean? Although the agency will look over the shoulder of the party responsible for clean-up, that party has the best bargaining position to determine the amount of clean-up which is necessary at the site.

As discussed in **§23.09,** the EPA and state agencies in negotiating settlement agreements increasingly prefer performance standards which a responsible party must meet. The extent and scope of these standards will greatly affect the cost-effectiveness of a particular settlement. Performance standards should be avoided in favor of an agreement which looks to the effectiveness of the method of abatement used in the clean-up. Due to the political difficulties in defining acceptable or tolerable levels of risk, standards may be unreasonably high. Thus, determinations of how clean is clean are often affected by factors well beyond the control of the parties' negotiating settlement (i.e. public interest groups, political realities).

Removing the resources of the EPA or a state agency from a case can be a tactical and financial advantage. Personal injury plaintiffs often rely on an agency as a resource for generating data necessary to meet the legal requirements of causality. If an early settlement with an agency is achieved, private injury plaintiffs are left to their own resources in developing the necessary factual and scientific data. The preferred position of a major participant at a site is to limit up-front costs and potential liability by settling and taking an active role in the clean-up of the site. In some instances, a major participant may find itself in a situation where some form of abatement activity is essential to mitigation of damages. This situation may occur prior to reaching at least a technical meeting of the minds on the concept of settlement. The immediate and long-term benefits from rapidly initiating an abatement program with or without the EPA's approval is a positive argument in a participant's favor if and when an enforcement action is undertaken. Of course, not all clients have the resources to undertake a clean-up operation without help from others. In a situation where a small business finds itself as a major contributor, becoming part of a group is often the best protection of its interests. Many Superfund[94] sites have borrowed from the products liability area in the formation of contributor groups which are organized to fund the clean-up and to negotiate with the EPA. Participation is time-consuming and can lead to a compromise as to clean-up commitments with which a client may not be happy. The group is, however, able to speak to the thorny issues at a waste site necessary to be resolved in order to reach a settlement with an agency.

Not settling is perceived by many clients as being very risky. The ultimate cost of the clean-up is not within their control nor is there any guarantee as to their share of the cost. Nevertheless, if the client's contribution is small at a site, not settling may be an advantage.

The site clean-up may have proceeded to a point where the costs are known and a settlement is less of an open-ended risk, at which point the client could better assess the cost of settling. This may be balanced against an agency action. Holding out from participation in settlement negotiations where the client thinks the coalition will do a good job of negotiating will conserve the client's time and resources until the group cuts an acceptable deal with the agency. The risk inherent with this position is that nonsettling contributors may find themselves absorbing contingent clean-up liabilities around which settling contributors have negotiated.[95] Furthermore, small contributors may want to develop the facts as to their participation fully in order to see if there are defenses to being a responsible party.

The decision to settle or to fight is clearly made on a case-by-case basis. Since the likelihood of being found to be a responsible party is high, settlement becomes an economic decision and a matter of timing. Early settlement tends to give the client more control over the ultimate cost of the site. This course is, on balance, usually the best for a major contributor with a large stake in the cost of clean-up. Smaller firms can settle by joining coalitions of other contributors and cutting a deal with the agency.

Requiring the agency and ultimately cocontributors to prove their cases is an option forced on major contributors unable to agree as to the type of clean-up. Also, minor contributors have a perception that their share of the cost is small and the risk of litigation acceptable.

---

[94] Comprehensive Environmental Response, Compensation and Liability Act, 42 USC §9601 *et seq*, discussed in **ch 10.**

[95] See United States v Wade, 3 Chemical Radiation Waste Litig Rep 566 (ED Pa 1981) and United States v Duracell, 1 Hazardous Waste Litig Rep 1817 (MD Tenn 1982) for settlements in which nonsettling participants assumed contingent liability risk.

If the EPA's interpretation of Superfund liability as joint and several is upheld,[96] the minor contributor can be held accountable for the full cost. Thus, a minor contributor's risk is theoretically the same as that of a major contributor. The best way to prevail if a client's percentage responsibility at a site is small may be to negotiate a small share of a settlement.

Of course, fighting may be a tactic to gain time for a better evaluation of the cost of clean-up. Also, fighting may enable a client to win some points from the agency as to clean-up requirements. These considerations can only be made site-by-site.

Current case law is lacking as to the actual cost to nonsettling parties of site clean-ups. Until the law is established, settlement appears to be the only cost-effective option open to most contributors. The form and elements to be settled will become more standard as experience is gained in this area.

For the reasons developed in §23.02, some defendants in a personal injury lawsuit may never perceive settlement as a viable alternative. Any consideration of settlement must balance the plaintiff's potential recovery against the substantial legal fees necessary to defend and the possible effects of losing a lawsuit. In the personal injury area one loss can precipitate an avalanche of personal injury lawsuits, similar to industry's experience in the products liability area.[97] Being a two-edged sword, public pronouncement of settlement can often precipitate numerous frivolous and unmeritorious lawsuits.

Until a plaintiff demonstrates the ability to present a prima facie case, the cost of litigation is minimal. Once the prima facie hurdle has been met, a defendant may incur significant litigation expenses.

Based on the above, management's posture should be to assess during discovery, the plaintiff's ability to meet the prima facie barrier. This assessment is accomplished by getting as much information as possible from the plaintiff. Extensive discovery through interrogatories will provide the defendant's counsel with the data necessary to assess the plaintiff's ability to present a prima facie case. Once a prima facie case is shown, the defendant should assess the case as any other personal injury lawsuit.

§23.10   Innovations

Throughout this chapter, discussion has focused on what can be done to protect and maximize the resources of companies when faced with hazardous substance litigation. This final section explores an innovative approach advocates may want to consider to maximize their goals.

Recently, a major marketer-producer of gasoline was faced with the following factual situation: A municipal water supply was tested by state water quality

---

[96] See Rodburg, Apportionment of Damages in Hazardous Waste Litigation, *reprinted in,* Hazardous Waste Litigation 1982, 183-213 (PLI 1982).

[97] The Johns-Manville situation, growing out of the plaintiffs' success in Borel v Fibreboard Paper Prods Corp, 493 F2d 1076 (5th Cir 1973), *cert denied,* 419 US 869 (1974), is the prime example.

personnel and was found to contain soluble hydrocarbons, specifically, benzene, toluene, and xylene (BTX). Immediately, the municipality's governing body moved rapidly to abate the problem by discontinuing use of the polluted municipal water well field and contracting the purchase of adequate drinking water on a long-term basis. Concurrent with this action, the municipality contacted the state environmental protection agency to seek assistance in funding and to investigate the causing agents of the problem. All marketers of gasoline in the vicinity of the well field were contacted and requested to provide the state agency and/or the municipality with either recent storage tank pressure test data or inventory verification data disproving the existence of leakage. Review of spill reports filed with the appropriate agency uncovered the fact that four major marketers had reported substantial spills in the months preceding discovery of BTX in the municipal well field. The municipality, through its attorney, contacted each marketer expressing its intent to seek reimbursement from all contributors to the problem.[98]

In responding to the municipality's attorney, one marketer undertook an extensive internal investigation of the problem. This investigation resulted in information which resulted in facilitating settlement negotiations. The approach to settlement was simple-by being the first, this marketer wanted to reap the appropriate bargaining leverage. Accordingly, its settlement had to be the best or at least equal to any subsequent settling party. To accomplish this goal, the parties after more than a year of negotiating agreed on fashioning a *Mary Carter*[99] type of settlement agreement which provided the appropriate protection. This agreement placed a ceiling upon the maximum liability of the alleged responsible party and further provided for a reduction or exhaustion of recovery based on judgment or settlement with other responsible parties. Nonsettling responsible parties have since been faced with a $4 million clean-up response lawsuit.

Mary Carter is a generic name given to settlement agreements whereby a partially responsible party or parties place a limit upon liability. The amount agreed upon is related to the recovery achieved against other responsible parties. State jurisdictions are divided on the legality of Mary Carter agreements,[100] with the majority either being silent or allowing them.

---

[98] The state clean-up statute gives private or municipal parties a right to seek reimbursement in state court for any and all monies expended in cleaning up any discharge of hazardous substances into the state's natural resources.

[99] Name taken from the case Booth v Mary Carter Paint Co, 202 So 8 (Fla Dist Ct App 1967), *overruled on other grounds,* Ward v Ochoa, 284 So 2d 385 (Fla 1973).

[100] The following jurisdictions have affirmed the use of "Mary Carter" agreements:

Alabama: Anderson v Kemp, 279 Ala 321, 184 So 2d 832 (1966)

Arizona: Tucson v Gallagher, 108 Ariz 140, 493 P2d 1197 (1972); Glendale v Bradshaw, 16 Ariz App 483, 494 P2d 383 (1972)

Florida: Ward v Ochoa, 284 So 2d 385 (Fla 1973); Maule Indus v Roundtree, 264 So 2d 445 (Fla Dist Ct App 1972), *revd on other grounds,* 284 So 2d 385 (Fla 1973)

Illinois: Gatto v Walgreen Drug Co, 61 Ill 2d 513, 357 NE2d 23 (1975); Schell

While it is not suggested that Mary Carter agreements are appropriate in every clean-up response case, it is clear that in cash buy-out situations when nonsettling parties exist, such an agreement may provide an additional measure of protection. For a responsible party, this settlement mechanism will assure equitable participation by all identified responsible parties. Additionally, if the harm is subsequently found divisible, the settling party has limited liability as far as clean-up costs and the possibility of recoupment of funds in excess of its determined involvement.

In the personal injury area, increased flexibility and alteration of common law principles will greatly affect the success of personal injury claims. As these changes unfold, due to the political pressure exerted by a growing group of uncompensated victims, defense practioners will need to develop innovative methods of assessing and settling these cases. Until that time arrives, most defense practitioners will be relatively comfortable in handling cases in the time-proven method of the personal injury realm.

---

v Albrecht, 65 Ill App 3d 989, 383 NE2d 15 (1978). *Accord* Reese v Chicago Burlington & Quinch Ry, 55 Ill 2d 356, 303 NE2d 382 (1973)

Louisiana: Daniel v Penrod Drilling Co, 393 F Supp 1056 (ED La 1975)(full disclosure during discovery must occur to validate the agreement)

Maryland: General Motors Corp v Lahocki, 286 Md 714, 410 A2d 1039 (1980)

New Hampshire: Bedford School District v Caron Constr Co, 116 NH 800, 367 A2d 1051 (1976); Arapage v Odell, 114 NH 684, 327 A2d 717 (1974)

Oregon: Grillo v Burke's Paint Co, 551 P2d 449 (Or 1976)

South Dakota: Degen v Bayman, 86 SD 598, 200 NW2d 134 (1972)

Tennessee: Florow v Louisville & Nashville RR, 502 F Supp 1 (MD Tenn 1979)

Glossary

A

Ablution   an act of washing or cleansing.

Acute dose   a relatively high dose administered over a short period of time.

Adsorption   a diffusion process whereby certain gases are retained selectively on the surface, or in the pores of interstices of specially prepared solids; used in the separation of mixtures and product improvement.

Alveolus   a small cavity or pit, as a socket for a tooth; an air cell of the lungs.

Ames Test   a procedure (really a number of procedures) involving microorganisms which is an assay for the mutagenic propensity of chemicals.

Anesthetics & narcotics   materials which have a depressant action on the central nervous system, affecting the blood supply to the brain.

Anoxia   an effect caused by agents that produce oxygen lack and increased carbon dioxide tension in the blood and tissues.

Aromatic amines   substances that cause systemic intoxication by way of cutaneous penetration (e.g. through the skin).

Asphyxiants   those agents that produce a lack of oxygen and increased carbon dioxide in the blood and tissues.

B

Bioassay   the determination of the potency or concentration of a compound by its effect upon animals as compared with a chemical or physical assay.

Biochemical oxygen demand (BOD)   an expression of the amount of soluble carbon, usually organic, that is metabolizable by microorganisms in an aquatic system.

Brownian movement   the peculiar rapid vibratory movement exhibited by the microscopic particles of both organic and inorganic substances when suspended in a fluid.

Byssinosis   an occupational respiratory disease of cotton, flax and hemp workers.

C

Carcinogenic   a chemical or other agent resulting in the production of a malignant neoplasm, a cancer. Malignancy implies that individual cells can be released by the neoplasm, picked up in the circulation, blood or lymph, and carried to other body sites where additional neoplasms may be seeded. This process is known as metastasis, and the neoplasms other than the first or primary lesion are known as secondary or metastatic growths.

Carpal tunnel syndrome   results from the compression of the median nerve in the wrist producing paresthesia in the hand and pain in the wrist.

Chelation   to combine with so as to form a chelate ring (heterocyclic) - a metal ion and two or more polar groupings of a single molecule.

Chilblains   a sore produced by exposure of the feet or hands to cold.

Chronic dose   a relatively low dose administered over a long period of time.

Cilia   fine whiplike projections which beat headward and thus propel mucus film upward through air passages as on an escalator.

Cutaneous   via the skin.

D

Dosage   rate of administration of a given dose.

Dose   basic unit of quantification in chemical exposures.

E

Encephalopathy   any disease of the brain.

Entropy   an inactive or static condition.

Erythema   abnormal redness of the skin due to inflamation.

Eutrophication   increased use of carbon if nitrogen or phosphorus suddenly enters a system as a pollutant, which frequently enables a sudden growth of organisms.

F

Fibrosis the process whereby the body surrounds an irritating particle with tissue in order to isolate the particle from the lung itself.

H

Hazard the probability or possibility that a particular chemical will produce injury or harm under specific conditions of use.

I

Impaction a sudden change in direction in airflow and the momentum of dust particles which causes the particles to impact against a flat surface.

Ingestion consumption of food or water.

Inhalation inhaled into the respiratory system.

Intramuscular injected into the tissue.

Intraperitoneal injected into the peritoneal cavity.

Intravenous injected into the blood circulation.

Intubation insertion into the gastrointestinal tract or into the trachea.

Irritant materials materials which are corrosive or vesicant and inflame moist or mucous surfaces.

Isocyanates a salt or ester of isocyonic acid.

K

Ketones a compound containing the carbonyl group (CO) doubly united with carbon; a colorless, volatile liquid with a pungent etheral odor.

L

Latency period interval between insult and effect.

Leptospirosis   a certain infection with parasites, which normally live in mammals.

Liver angiosarcoma   a rare, malignant neoplasm occurring in the liver.

M

Malignant melanoma   malignant tumor containing dark pigment.

Mesothelioma   a rare neoplasm (tumor) derived from the lining cells of the pleura (rib) and peritoneum.

Minamata disease   described in Japan caused by eating fish contaminated with mercury causing a neurological disorder.

Mutagenic   a chemical or other agent resulting in the alteration of the genetic structure in the germ plasm, the sperm in the male or the egg in the female, resulting in altered information being carried to the next generation and all future generations.

Mutation   change in cellular development or behavior as a result of chemical reaction that alters genetic information.

N

Nasopharyngeal area   upper part of the pharynx, continuous with the nasal passage.

Neoplasm   excess tissue resulting from a mutation; new growth, tumor.

Nephrotoxicity   poisonous to the kidney.

O

Ocular   via the eye.

Oncogenic   a chemical or other agent resulting in the production of a neoplasm, presumably by altering the genetically determined control over cell replication.

P

Pathogens   a pathogenic (disease causing) organism or virus.

Percutaneous   effected or performed through the skin without incision.

Phagocytosis the action of motile cells that scavenge foreign bodies, the action that destroys bacteria or viruses that might otherwise produce infection.

Pharyngeal area of/pertaining to the pharynx.

Phenolic compounds colorless, or pinkish compound produced by the destructive distillation of many organic substances as wood, coal, etc.

Plumbism lead poisoning.

Pneumoconiotic agents particulates that deposit in the lung potentially leading to respiratory disease.

Pneumoconiotic diseases pulmonary diseases associated with the effects of particle deposition.

Polymer of nucleotides large molecules built up by the repetition of small, simple chemical units - in this case, any of a class of compounds consisting of a carbohydrate combined with a purine (parent substance of adenine, guanine) or pyrimidine (a heterocyclic substance) base and phosphoric acid.

Polynuclear aromatic hydrocarbons multi-clear, pungent (spicy odor) compound containing only hydrogen and carbon.

Potentiation interaction between particle and gas.

Pyrophoric reaction light producing, igniting spontaneously.

Q

Q-fever an acute disease characterized by sudden onset of fever, headache, malaise and interstitial pneumonitis.

R

Raynaud's disease disease of vasomotor (denoting the nerves) system in which parts of the body, especially the extremities become pale, cold, painful and in some cases, gangrenous.

S

Salmonellosis slightly contagious disease of swine caused by salmonella.

Sensitizers materials that produce or result in an allergic-type reaction in the body.

Solubilize to render soluble.

Subclinical hypothermia   denoting a period prior to the appearance of the manifest symptoms of subnormal temperature of the body.

Subcutaneous   injection under the skin.

Surfactant   a surface-active agent.

Systemic intoxication   poisoning relating or common to a system as a whole (the body) in distinction from local death.

Systemic poisons   materials which cause organic injury to the organs, nerves, and hematopoietic systems.

T

Tenosynovitis   inflammation of a synovial (transparent, viscid) membrane around the tendon.

Teratogenic   a chemical or other agent resulting in the alteration in development of an embryo. Teratogenesis does not imply any imprint on the germ plasm and is not to be confused with mutagenesis.

Toxicity   the capacity of a chemical to produce injury or harm.

Tumorigenic   a chemical or other agent resulting in the production of a nonmalignant or benign neoplasm, a tumor.

U

Undulant fever   a long persisting disease characterized by undulating or remittent fever, perspiration, pain and swelling.

V

Vesication   process of blistering.

Vibration white finger disease   disease caused by a nutritional myopathy (selenium deficiency) of young animals manifested by shaking and soreness.

W

Wrist-drop   paralysis of the extensor muscles of the hand, causing inability to hold the hand out, palm down, in line with the forearm.

Cases

A

Aacon Auto Transp, Inc v Ninfo, 490 F2d 83 (2d Cir 1974) §22.07

AA Equip Inc v Farmorl Inc, 31 Conn Super 322, 330 A2d 99 (1974) §6.03

Abed v AH Robins Co, 693 F2d 847 (9th Cir 1982), *cert denied*, 103 S Ct 817 (1983) §§15.09, 15.10, 20.02, 20.09, 20.11

Abel v Eli Lilly & Co, 94 Mich App 59, 289 NW2d 20 (1979) §§11.20, 11.21, 14.08, 15.04, 16.01, 16.15

Aberdeen & Rockfish RR v SCRAP, 409 US 1207 (1972) §§10.14, 23.08

Abing v Pain, Webber, Jackson & Curtis, 538 F Supp 1193 (D Minn 1982) §22.04

Abraham Constr Corp v Armco Steel Corp, 559 F2d 250 (5th Cir 1977) §21.05

Abron v Workmen's Compensation Appeals Bd, 34 Cal App 3d 232, 109 Cal Rptr 778 (1973) §6.06

Adams v Atchison, Topeka & Santa Fe RR, 280 SW2d 84 (Mo 1955) §17.06

Adams v Ohio Dept of Health, 5 Ohio Ops 3d 148, 356 NE2d 324 (Common Pleas 1976) §12.10

Affett v Milwaukee & Suburban Transp Corp, 11 Wis 2d 604, 106 NW2d 274 (1960) §17.07

Agent Orange, *In re*, 506 F Supp 762 (EDNY 1980), *revd on other grounds*, 635 F2d 987 (2d Cir 1980), *cert denied*, 454 US 1128 (1981) §§13.02, 13.06, 14.14, 15.09, 15.10, 20.04, 20.05, 20.06, 20.07

Agent Orange, *In re*, 475 F Supp 128 (EDNY 1979) §§13.02, 13.08, 15.08

Agent Orange Prod Liab Litig, *In re*, MDL No 381 (EDNY May 12, 1983) §20.07

Agent Orange Product Liability Litig, *In re*, 534 F Supp 1046 (EDNY 1982) §§14.14, 20.07

Agent Orange Prods Liab Litig, *In re*, 506 F Supp 757 (EDNY 1980) §§12.17, 13.06

Fruehauf Trailer Co v Lydick, 325
Ill App 28, 59 NE2d 551 (1945)
§17.03

Frye v United States, 293 F 1014
(DC Cir 1923) §14.13

Fuller v Capital Sky Park, 46 Cal
App 3d 727, 120 Cal Rptr 131
(1975) §6.03

G

Gafford v Star Fish & Oyster Co,
475 F2d 767 (5th Cir 1973)
§22.12

Gagne v Bertran, 43 Cal 2d 481,
275 P2d 15 (1954) §11.02

Galveston H & SAR Co v
Zantzinger, 92 Tex 365, 48 SW
563 (1898) §17.03

Gamble v Central of Ga Ry, 486
F2d 781 (5th Cir 1973) §22.04

Garner v Hecla Mining Co, 19 Utah
2d 367, 431 P2d 794 (1967)
§§11.08, 16.08

Garner v Teamsters Union, 346 US
485 (1953) §12.16

Garrett v Raytheon Co, 368 So 2d
516 (Ala 1979) §13.05

Gater v Tram Video Corp, 93 Cal
App 3d 196, 155 Cal Rptr 486
(1979) §6.09

Gatto v Walgreen Drug Co, 61 Ill
2d 513, 357 NE2d 23 (1975)
§23.10

Gay v Ocean Transport & Trading
Co, 546 F2d 1243 (5th Cir 1977)
§8.04

Gelsumino v EW Bliss Co, 295
NE2d 110 (Ill App Ct 1973)
§14.07

General Dynamics Asbestos Cases,
In re, 539 F Supp 1106 (D Conn
1982) §15.12

General Elec Co, 31 Lab Arb (BNA)
386 (1958) §12.15

General Motors Corp v Hopkins,
548 SW2d 344 (Tex 1977)
§14.04

General Motors Corp v Lahocki,
286 Md 714, 410 A2d 1039
(1980) §23.10

General Motors Corp v Simmons,
558 SW2d 855 (Tex 1977)
§14.04

Gerger v Campbell, 98 Wis 2d 282,
297 NW2d 183 (1980) §§6.11,
21.04

Gibbs v Procter & Gamble Mfg Co,
51 Ill App 2d 469, 201 NE2d 473
(1964) §11.05

Gibson v California Spray-Chem
Corp, 29 Wash 2d 611, 188 P2d
316 (1948) §11.18

Gibson v Leonard, 143 Ill 182, 32
NE 182 (1892) §8.08

Gibson v National Ben Franklin Ins
Co, 387 A2d 220 (Me 1978)
§6.09

Gibson v Worley Mills, Inc, 614 F2d
464 (5th Cir), modified on other
grounds, 620 F2d 567 (5th Cir
1980) §11.07

Gilberg v Barbieri, 53 NY 285, 441
NYS2d 49, 423 NE2d 807 (1982)
§20.20

Gilbert v Jones, 563 SW2d 212
(Tenn Ct App 1974) §23.07

Gill v United States, 641 F2d 195
(5th Cir 1981) §6.04

Gillig v Bymart Tintair, Inc, 16 FRD
393 (DNY 1954) §§15.04, 15.18

Givens v Markall, 51 Cal App 2d
374, 124 P2d 839 (1942) §17.13

Glasgow v Metropolitan Street R
Co, 191 Mo 347, 89 SW 915
(1905) §17.03

M

N

1301, 413 NYS2d 374 (1978) §§**15.10, 20.02**

Rosenkranz v Lindell R Co, 108 Mo 9, 18 SW 890 (1891) §**17.05**

Rost v CF&I Steel Corp, 616 P2d 383 (Mont 1980) §§**14.10, 14.12**

Roth v Chatlos, 97 Conn 282, 116 A 332 (1922) §**17.11**

Russell v Bartley, 494 F2d 334 (6th Cir 1974) §**8.01**

Russell v GAF Corp, 422 A2d 989 (DC 1980) §**14.11**

Russell v Szczawinaki, 268 Mich 112, 255 NW 731 (1934) §**8.02**

Ryan v Eli Lilly & Co, 514 F Supp 1004 (D SC 1981) §§**11.20, 11.23, 13.06, 14.08, 16.13**

Ryan v Eli Lilly & Co, 84 FRD 230 (DSC 1979) §§**15.09, 15.10, 20.02**

Ryan v Feeney & Sheehan Building Co, 145 NE 321 (1924) §**14.14**

Ryan v NAPA, 266 Ark 802, 586 SW2d 6 (1979) §**6.06**

Ryan Stevedoring Co v Pan Atlantic SS Corp, 350 US 124 (1956) §**13.07**

Rylands v Fletcher, LR 3 HL 330 (1868) §§**11.11, 11.14**

S

Sabine Towing & Transp Co v United States, 16 Envt Rep Cas (BNA) 2081 (Ct Cl 1981) §§**10.11, 23.03**

Sadowski v Bombardier, Ltd, 539 F2d 615 (7th Cir 1976) §**22.21**

St Paul's Benevolent Educ & Missionary Inst v United States, 506 F Supp 822 (ND Ga 1980) §**7.14**

Salmon v Parke, Davis & Co, 520 F2d 1359 (4th Cir 1975) §**11.04**

Saminsky v Occidental Petroleum Corp, 373 F Supp 257 (SDNY 1974) §**22.07**

Sampson Const Co v Brusowankin, 218 Md 458, 147 A2d 430 (1958) §**17.13**

Samuels v Health & Hosps Corp, 591 F2d 195 (2d Cir 1979) §**11.02**

San Antonio Air Logistic Center, 73 Lab Arb (BNA) 1074 (1979) §**12.15**

San Diego Unions v Garmon, 359 US 236 (1959) §**12.16**

Sandoval v Salt River Project, 117 Ariz 209, 571 P2d 706 (1977) §**6.09**

Sandoz, Inc v Employer's Liab Assur Corp, 554 F Supp (DNJ 1983) §**21.11**

Sanford v Presto Mfg Co, 92 NM 746, 594 P2d 1202 (1979) §§**6.05, 6.08**

San Isabel Elec Inc, 225 NLRB 1073 (1976) §**7.13**

Santisteven v Dow Chem Corp, 362 F Supp 646 (D Nev 1973) §**13.07**

Sardell v Eli Lilly & Co, No 18268-77 (NY Sup Ct, Oct 15, 1982) §**11.25**

Schell v Albrecht, 65 Ill App 3d 989, 383 NE2d 15 (1978) §**23.10**

Schenebeck v Sterling Drug, Inc, 473 F2d 919 (8th Cir 1970) §**23.07**

Schering Corp v Home Ins Co, 544 F Supp 613 (EDNY 1982), *revd on other grounds,* 712 F2d 4 (2d Cir 1983) §§**21.10, 21.11**

Schexnayder v Bunge Corp, 508 F2d 1069 (5th Cir 1975) §**11.07**

V

Valley Towing Serv v SS American Wheat, Civ No 75-363 (ED La Jan 23, 1980) §§**10.11, 10.12**

Vallo v United States Exp Co, 147 Pa 404, 23 A 594 (1892) §**17.03**

Van Dusen v Barrack, 376 US 612 (1964) §**22.06**

Vanskike v ACF Indus, 665 F2d 188 (8th Cir 1981), *cert denied*, 455 US 1000 (1982) §§**14.07, 22.12**

Varela v American Petrofina, 644 SW2d 903 (Tex Civ App 1983) §**14.12**

Victory Constr Co, *In re*, Collier Bankr Cas 2d 655 (Bankr CD Cal 1981) §**20.26**

Virginia Elec & Power Co v Sun Shipbuilding & Dry Dock Co, 68 FRD 397 (Ed Va 1975) §§**15.20, 15.21**

W

Wabash R Co v Campbell, 219 Ill 312, 76 NE 346 (1905) §**17.03**

Wade v Johnson Controls, Inc, slip op (2d Cir 1982) §**13.06**

Wagmeister v AH Robins Co, 64 Ill App 3d 964, 382 NE2d 23 (1978) §**11.10**

Wagner v International Harvester Co, 611 F2d 224 (8th Cir 1979) §**11.04**

Wakeman v Wheeler & W Mfg Co, 101 NY 205, 4 NE 264 (1886) §**17.02**

Waldrop v Vistron Corp, 391 So 2d 1274 (La Ct App 1980) §§**6.07, 6.08**

Wallace v Pennsylvania R Co, 222 Pa 556, 71 A 1086 (1909) §**17.06**

Wallenius Bremen GMBH v United States, 409 F2d 994 (4th Cir), *cert denied*, 398 US 958 (1970) §**9.36**

Walsh v National Seeding Co, 411 F Supp 564 (D Mass 1976) §**13.08**

Wamp v Chattanooga Housing Auth, 527 F2d 595 (6th Cir 1975), *cert denied*, 425 US 992 (1976) §**22.04**

Ward v Ochoa, 284 So 2d 385 (Fla 1973) §**23.10**

Warren v McLarth Steel Corp, 911 Mich App 496, 314 NW2d 666 (1982) §**15.11**

Warvel v Michigan Community Blood Center, 74 Mich App 440, 253 NW2d 791 (Ct App 1977) §**11.06**

Watkins v FMC Corp, 531 P2d 505 (Wash Ct App 1975) §**10.13**

Watwood v RR Dawson Bridge Co, 307 So 2d 692 (Ala 1975) §§**8.03, 23.04**

Waube v Warrington, 216 Wis 603, 258 NW 497 (1935) §**17.08**

Weggen v Elwell Parker Elec Co, 527 F Supp 951 (1981) §**14.14**

Weinberger v Romero-Barcelo, 456 US 305 (1982) §**10.15**

Weis v Allen, 147 Ore 670, 35 P2d 478 (1934) §**6.06**

Welden v Celotex, 695 F2d 67 (3d Cir 1982) §**13.08**

Wendland v Ridgefield Const Services, Inc, 439 A2d 954 (Conn 1981) §**8.04**

Wenk v Glidden Paint, 106 Wis 2d 18, 318 NW2d 26 (1982) §**13.02**

Wenner v Gulf Oil Corp, 264 NW2d 374 (Minn 1978) §**11.10**

Wennerholm v Stanford Univ School of Med, 20 Cal 2d 713, 128 P2d 522 (1942) §**11.18**

Statutes

State Statutes

Alabama

Alaska

Alaska Stat §46.03.824 (Michie
  1976) **§12.08**
Alaska Special Act ch 93 (1983)
  §7.02

Arizona

Ariz Rev Stat Ann §12-683 **§8.08**
Ariz Rev Stat §23-1022 **§6.06**
Ariz Rev Stat Ann §36-2805 (West
  1981) **§12.06**

Arkansas

Ark Stat Ann §28-1001, Rule
  803(18) **§18.11**
Ark Stat Ann §41-1310(d) **§6.06**

California

Cal Civil Code §3294 (Deering
  1983) **§17.15**
Cal Evid Code §669 **§8.02**
Cal Health & Safety Code §25150
  (West 1982) **§12.04**
Cal Health-Safety Code §25186
  (Deering 1981) **§§23.03, 23.05**
Cal Health & Safety Code §25189.5
  (West 1982) **§12.04**
Cal Health & Safety Code
  §§25300-25395 (Deering 1981)
  §§23.03, 23.05
Cal Health & Safety Code
  §25301(b) **§23.05**
Cal Health & Safety Code §25371 *et
  seq* (Deering 1981) **§23.05**
Cal Health & Safety Code §25375
  (Deering 1981) **§23.05**
Cal Health & Safety Code §25379
  (Deering 1981) **§23.05**
Cal Health & Safety Code §25380
  (Deering 1981) **§23.05**

Cal Lab Code §3600 (West 1981)
  §6.03
Cal Lab Code §3602(a) **§21.04**
Cal Lab Code §3602(b) **§21.04**
Cal Lab Code §4553 **§6.06**
Cal Lab Code §5410 **§21.07**
Cal Lab Code §6360 *et seq* (West
  1981) **§§7.02, 7.03**
Cal Lab Code §6362 (West) **§7.03**
Cal Lab Code §6380-81 (West)
  §7.03
Cal Lab Code §6382 (West) **§7.03**
Cal Lab Code §6386 (West) **§7.03**
Cal Lab Code §§6390-6391 (West)
  §7.03
Cal Lab Code §6394 (West) **§7.03**
Cal Lab Code §6398 (West) **§7.03**

Colorado

Colo Rev Stat §8-41-108 **§6.02**
Colo Rev Stat §13-21-403 (1977)
  §8.08
Colo Rev Stat §29-22-105 (Michie
  1980) **§12.06**

Connecticut

Conn Gen Stat Ann §25-54ee(d)
  (West 1980) **§12.06**
Conn Gen Stat Ann §31-40(c) (West
  1980) **§§7.02, 7.04**

Delaware

Del Corp Law Ann §142(a) & (b)
  §21.05

District of Columbia

DC Code Ann §6-525 (West 1983)
  §12.04
DC Code Ann §§6-530—6-531
  (West 1983) **§12.04**

Florida

Fla Stat Ann §376.12 *et seq* (West Supp 1981) **§23.03**

Fla Stat Ann §403.011 (West 1976) **§23.03**

Fla Stat Ann §403.141 (West 1979) **§23.03**

Fla Stat §403.725(1) (West 1978) **§12.06**

Fla Stat Ann §440.09 (West) **§6.02**

Georgia

Ga Code §43-2909(4) (Michie 1983) **§12.06**

Idaho

Idaho Code §9-402 **§18.11**

Illinois

Ill Stat Ann ch 111-1/2, §§1001-1045 (Smith-Hurd 1978) **§23.03**

Ill Stat Ann ch 111-1/2, §1022 *et seq* (Smith-Hurd 1978) **§23.03**

Ill Ann Stat ch 111-1/2 §1022.2 (Smith-Hurd) **§12.06**

Ill Stat Ann ch 111-1/2, §1022-2(d) (Smith-Hurd 1978) **§23.03**

Ill Stat Ann ch 111-1/2, §1042 (Smith-Hurd 1978) **§23.03**

Iowa

Iowa Code Ann §85 20 (West) **§6.03**

Kansas

Kan Stat Ann §60-460(cc) **§18.11**

Kentucky

Ky Rev Stat §23-1022 **§6.06**

Ky Rev Stat §342.015(2) **§6.06**

Ky Rev Stat §342.165 **§6.06**

Louisiana

La Rev Stat Ann §23-1032 (West 1979) **§6.06**

La Rev Stat Ann §§30:1143, 30:1149 (West 1979) **§12.06**

Maine

Me Rev Stat Ann tit 2, §1701 *et seq* (1980) **§7.02**

Maryland

Md Ann Code art 101, §15 **§6.02**

Md Ann Code art 101, §23(b) **§21.07**

Md Ann Code art 101, §44 **§6.06**

Md Ann Code art 101, §62 **§6.11**

Md Ann Code ch 240, §2 (1982) **§23.03**

Md Nat Res Code Ann §81-413.2(f) (Michie 1983) **§12.06**

Md Pub Health Code Ann §7-218 *et seq* **§23.03**

Md Pub Health Code Ann §7-220 **§23.03**

Md Pub Health Code Ann §7-221 **§23.03**

Massachusetts

Mass Ann Laws ch 149 §142A (Michie/Law Co-op 1981) **§7.02**

Mass Ann Laws ch 152 §28 (Michie/Law Co-op 1981) **§6.06**

Mass Gen Laws Ann ch 21C, §10 (West 1982) **§12.04**

Mass General Laws Ann ch 21D, §8 (West 1982) **§12.04**

Mass General Laws Ann ch 21D, §§12-13 (West) **§12.04**

Mass Gen Laws Ann ch 94B §1
(West 1978) **§5.04**

Mass General Laws ch 216, §7
(West 1982) **§12.04**

Michigan

Mich Comp Laws §299.526 (West
1983) **§12.04**

Mich Comp Laws Ann §299.543
(West 1983) **§12.06**

Mich Comp Laws §299.548 **§12.04**

Mich Comp Laws §599.548 **§12.04**

Mich Comp Laws Ann §4808.1011
(1981) **§7.02**

Mich Stat Ann §418.131 (Callaghan)
§6.03

Minnesota

Minn Stat Ann §544.41 (West Supp
1982) **§15.07**

Mississippi

Miss Code Ann §11-7-15 (1972)
§14.05

Missouri

Mo Ann Stat §287-120(4) (Vernon)
§6.06

Mo Rev Stat §15,287.120(2) **§6.03**

New Hampshire

NH Rev Stat Ann §§47-B:3, 147-B:6
(Equity 1981) **§12.06**

NH Rev Stat Ann §147-A *et seq*
(1981) **§23.03**

NH Rev Stat Ann §507-D:4 (1978)
§8.08

New Jersey

NJ Stat Ann §34:15-8 (West)
§§6.03, 6.06, 6.11

NJ Stat Ann §34:15-27 (West)
§21.07

NJ Stat Ann §34:15-40 (West)
§§21.04, 21.07

NJ Stat Ann §34:15-64 (West)
§21.07

NJ Stat Ann §58:10-23.11 (West
1972) **§23.03**

NJ Stat Ann §58:10-23q (West)
§23.03

NJ Stat Ann §58:10-23.11 *et seq*
(West 1977) **§§12.06, 23.03**

NJ Stat Ann §58:10-23.11 (West)
§12.06

NJ Stat Ann §58:10-23.11f (West)
§12.06

NJ Stat Ann §58:10-23.11g (West)
§12.06

NJ Stat Ann §58:10-23.11g(a)
(West) **§12.06**

NJ Stat Ann §58:10-23.11g(2)
(West) **§12.06**

NJ Stat Ann §58.10-23.11q (West)
§12.06

NJ Stat Ann 58:10-23.11v (West
1977) **§12.06**

New Mexico

NM Stat Ann §74-4-8 (Michie 1979)
§12.06

New York

NY Envtl Conserv Law §27-0900 *et
seq* **§23.03**

NY Envtl Conserv Law §17-0905 *et
seq* (McKinney 1982) **§12.04**

NY Envtl Conserv Law §27-0916
§23.03

NY Envtl Conserv Law §27-0923
§23.03

NY Envtl Conserv Law §17-1101 *et
seq* (McKinney 1982) **§12.04**

NY Envtl Conserv Law §27-1301
(McKinney 1982) §§**12.06, 23.03**

NY Lab Law §875 *et seq* (McKinney
1981) §§**7.02, 7.05**

NY Lab Law §876(2) (McKinney)
§7.05

NY Lab Law §876(4) (McKinney)
§7.05

NY Lab Law §876(7) (McKinney
1981) **§7.05**

NY Lab Law §878 (McKinney)
§7.05

NY Lab Law §879 (McKinney)
§7.05

NY Lab Law §880(2) (McKinney)
§7.05

NY Work Comp Law §10
(McKinney) **§6.02**

NY Work Comp Law §11
(McKinney) **§6.03**

NY Work Comp Law §22
(McKinney 1982) **§21.07**

North Carolina

NC Gen Stat §8.40.1 **§18.11**

NC Gen Stat §143.215.76 *et seq*
(Michie 1978) **§23.03**

NC Gen Stat §143-215.77(18)
(Michie 1980) **§12.08**

NC Gen Stat §143-215.87 **§12.06**

NC Gen Stat §143-215.93 **§12.08**

NC Rev Stat §97-10-2(i) **§13.07**

North Dakota

ND Cent Code §32-40-01 *et seq*
(Smith 1979) **§12.08**

Ohio

Ohio Rev Code Ch 1301-1309
(Page 1979) **§11.10**

Ohio Rev Code Ann §23-54 **§6.02**

Ohio Rev Code Ann §4123.741
§6.11

Oklahoma

Okla Stat Ann tit 85, §12 (West)
§6.03

Oregon

Or Rev Stat §459.600 (1983) **§12.06**

Or Rev Stat §656.018(3)(a) (1983)
§12.05

Or Rev Stat §656.156(2) **§6.06**

Pennsylvania

Pa Stat Ann tit 35, §6018.701
(Purdon 1981) **§12.06**

Pa Stat Ann tit 77, §431 (Purdon)
§6.02

Rhode Island

RI Gen Laws tit 23 §19.1-22
(Bobbs-Merrill 1978) **§12.08**

Tennessee

Tenn Code Ann §53-6308 (Michie
1981) **§12.06**

Texas

Tex Code Ann art 8306, §6 **§6.03**

Tex Rev Civ Stat art 2212a
(Vernon) **§22.10**

Tex Rev Civ Stat Ann art 8306, §5
§6.06

Virginia

Va Code §8.01-328.1 (Michie Supp
1982) **§15.03**

Va Code §8.01-329 (Michie Supp
1982) **§15.03**

Va Code §40.1-51.1 (Michie) **§7.02**

Washington

Wash Rev Code Ann §§49.17.220, .240 (West 1982) **§7.02**

Wash Rev Code §51.24.020 (1974) **§6.06**

West Virginia

W Va Code §21-3-18(a) (1981) **§§7.02, 7.06**

W Va Code §21-3-18(c) **§7.06**

W Va Code §21-3-18(d) **§7.06**

W Va Code §23-2-62 (Michie 1982) **§12.05**

W Va Code §23-4-2 **§6.06**

Wisconsin

Wis Stat Ann §101.58 *et seq* (West) **§§7.02, 7.07**

Wis Stat Ann §101.58 (West 1981) **§7.07**

Wis Stat Ann §101.581(1) (West 1981) **§7.07**

Wis Stat Ann §101.597 (West) **§7.07**

Wis Stat Ann §102.03 (West) **§6.02**

Wis Stat Ann §144.441 (West 1982) **§12.06**

Wis Stat §908.03(18) **§18.11**

Code of Federal Regulations

Federal Rules of Civil Procedure

Federal Register

Index

A

ACTIONS
  Class §§12.11, 13.04, 15.08,
    20.02, 20.06, 20.08-20.14
  Consolidation and coordination
    §22.07
  Coordination with client §22.02
  Individual §13.04
  Multidistrict litigation §22.07
  Removal §§22.04, 22.05
  Settlement. See SETTLEMENT
  Theory of Case §22.09
  Trial Strategy §22.01 *et seq*
AGENT ORANGE §§20.02-20.07
AGENTS
  Biological §1.14
  Chemical §§1.09, 1.10
  Environmental §§1.13-1.17
  Material. See MATERIALS
  Physical §1.11
  Mechanical §1.12
ALLEGATIONS
  Damages §13.09
  Defendants §14.06
  –employers §6.01 *et seq*
  –government §9.35
  –injury/illness §13.04
  –insurance company §14.06
  –limitations §13.05

ALLEGATIONS, *continued*
  –manufacturers §§11.22-11.24
  –victims, identification §13.02
ASBESTOS §§16.16, 20.25-20.28

B

BANKRUPTCY §§20.25-20.28
BIOSTATISTICS §19.17
BURDENS OF PROOF
  Generally §17.01
  Damages §17.02
  In-court experiments §16.17
  Liability, theories of
    §§16.13-16.15
  Product identification §16.11
  Worker's compensation §16.01

C

CANCER §§16.06-16.11
CAUSATION
  Generally §§19.01-19.03, 19.18
  Cancer §§16.06-16.11
  Defenses §14.13
  Experts, use of §§16.04,
    18.05-18.08

The George MacDonald Treasury

The Princess and the Goblin

The Princess and Curdie

The Light Princess

Phantastes

The Giant's Heart

At the Back of the North Wind

The Golden Key

Lilith

By

George MacDonald

The George MacDonald Treasury

The Princess and the Goblin

The Princess and Curdie

The Light Princess

Phantastes

The Giant's Heart

At the Back of the North Wind

The Golden Key

Lilith

By

George MacDonald

Edited By

Glenn Kahley

Table of Contents

Book One

The Princess And The Goblin

ᘓᘗᘔᘒ

1. WHY THE PRINCESS HAS A STORY ABOUT HER

There was once a little princess whose father was king over a great country full of mountains and valleys. His palace was built upon one of the mountains, and was very grand and beautiful. The princess, whose name was Irene, was born there, but she was sent soon after her birth, because her mother was not very strong, to be brought up by country people in a large house, half castle, half farmhouse, on the side of another mountain, about half-way between its base and its peak.

The princess was a sweet little creature, and at the time my story begins was about eight years old, I think, but she got older very fast. Her face was fair and pretty, with eyes like two bits of night sky, each with a star dissolved in the blue. Those eyes you would have thought must have known they came from there, so often were they turned up in that direction. The ceiling of her nursery was blue, with stars in it, as like the sky as they could make it. But I doubt if ever she saw the real sky with the stars in it, for a reason which I had better mention at once.

These mountains were full of hollow places underneath; huge caverns, and winding ways, some with water running through them, and some shining with all colors of the rainbow when a light was taken in. There would not have been much known about them, had there not been mines there, great deep pits, with long galleries and passages running off from them, which had been dug to get at the ore of which the mountains were full. In the course of digging, the miners came upon many of these natural caverns. A few of them had far-off openings out on the side of a mountain, or into a ravine.

Now in these subterranean caverns lived a strange race of beings, called by some gnomes, by some kobolds, by some goblins. There was a legend current in the country that at one time they lived above ground, and were very like other people. But for some reason or other, concerning which there were different legendary theories, the king had laid what they thought too severe taxes upon them, or had required observances of them they did not like, or had begun to treat them with more severity, in some way or other, and impose stricter laws; and the consequence was that they had all disappeared from the face of the country. According to the legend, however, instead of going to some other country, they had all taken refuge in the subterranean caverns, whence they never came out but at night, and then seldom showed themselves in any numbers, and never to many people at once. It was only in the least frequented and most difficult parts of the mountains that they were said to gather even at night in the open air. Those who had caught sight of any of them said that they had greatly altered in the course of generations; and no wonder, seeing they lived away from the sun, in cold and wet and dark places. They were now, not ordinarily ugly, but either absolutely hideous, or ludicrously grotesque both in face and form. There was no invention, they said, of the most lawless imagination expressed by pen or pencil, that could surpass the extravagance of their appearance. But I suspect those who said so had mistaken some of their animal companions for the goblins themselves - of which more by and by. The goblins themselves were not so far removed from the human as such a description would imply. And as they grew misshapen in body they had grown in knowledge and cleverness, and now were able to do things no mortal could see the possibility of. But as they grew in cunning, they grew in mischief, and their great delight was in every way they could think of to annoy the people who lived in the open-air storey above them. They had enough of affection left for each other to preserve them from being absolutely cruel for cruelty's sake to those that came in their way; but still they so heartily cherished the ancestral grudge against those who occupied their former possessions and especially against the descendants of the king who had caused their expulsion, that they sought every opportunity of tormenting them in ways that were as odd as their inventors; and although dwarfed and misshapen, they had strength equal to their cunning. In the process of time they had got a king and a government of their own, whose chief business, beyond their own simple affairs, was to devise trouble for their neighbors. It will now be pretty evident why the little princess had never seen the sky at night. They were much too afraid of the goblins to let her out of the house then, even in company with ever so many attendants; and they had good reason, as we shall see by and by.

2. The Princess Loses Herself

I have said the Princess Irene was about eight years old when my story begins. And this is how it begins.

One very wet day, when the mountain was covered with mist which was constantly gathering itself together into raindrops, and pouring down on the roofs of the great old house, whence it fell in a fringe of water from the eaves all round about it, the princess could not of course go out. She got very tired, so tired that even her toys could no longer amuse her. You would wonder at that if I had time to describe to you one half of the toys she had. But then, you wouldn't have the toys themselves, and that makes all the difference: you can't get tired of a thing before you have it. It was a picture, though, worth seeing - the princess sitting in the nursery with the sky ceiling over her head, at a great table covered with her toys. If the artist would like to draw this, I should advise him not to meddle with the toys. I am afraid of attempting to describe them, and I think he had better not try to draw them. He had better not. He can do a thousand things I can't, but I don't think he could draw those toys. No man could better make the princess herself than he could, though – leaning with her back bowed into the back of the chair, her head hanging down, and her hands in her lap, very miserable as she would say herself, not even knowing what she would like, except it were to go out and get thoroughly wet, and catch a particularly nice cold, and have to go to bed and take gruel. The next moment after you see her sitting there, her nurse goes out of the room.

Even that is a change, and the princess wakes up a little, and looks about her. Then she tumbles off her chair and runs out of the door, not the same door the nurse went out of, but one which opened at the foot of a curious old stair of worm-eaten oak, which looked as if never anyone had set foot upon it. She had once before been up six steps, and that was sufficient reason, in such a day, for trying to find out what was at the top of it.

Up and up she ran - such a long way it seemed to her! - until she came to the top of the third flight. There she found the landing was the end of a long passage. Into this she ran. It was full of doors on each side. There were so many that she did not care to open any, but ran on to the end, where she turned into another passage, also full of doors. When she had turned twice more, and still saw doors and only doors about her, she began to get frightened. It was so silent! And all those doors must hide rooms with nobody in them! That was dreadful. Also the rain made a great trampling noise on the roof. She turned and started at full speed, her little footsteps echoing through the sounds of the rain - back for the stairs and her safe nursery. So she thought, but she had lost herself long ago. It doesn't follow that she was lost, because she had lost herself, though.

She ran for some distance, turned several times, and then began to be afraid. Very soon she was sure that she had lost the way back. Rooms everywhere, and no stair! Her little heart beat as fast as her little feet ran, and a lump of tears was growing in her throat. But she was too eager and perhaps too frightened to cry for some time. At last her hope failed her. Nothing but passages and doors everywhere! She threw herself on the floor, and burst into a wailing cry broken by sobs.

She did not cry long, however, for she was as brave as could be expected of a princess of her age. After a good cry, she got up, and brushed the dust from her frock. Oh, what old dust it was!

Then she wiped her eyes with her hands, for princesses don't always have their handkerchiefs in their pockets, any more than some other little girls I know of. Next, like a true princess, she resolved on going wisely to work to find her way back: she would walk through the passages, and look in every direction for the stair. This she did, but without success. She went over the same ground again an again without knowing it, for the passages and doors were all alike. At last, in a corner, through a half-open door, she did see a stair. But alas! it went the wrong way: instead of going down, it went up. Frightened as she was, however, she could not help wishing to see where yet further the stair could lead. It was very narrow, and so steep that she went on like a four-legged creature on her hands and feet.

3. THE PRINCESS AND - WE SHALL SEE WHO

When she came to the top, she found herself in a little square place, with three doors, two opposite each other, and one opposite the top of the stair. She stood for a moment, without an idea in her little head what to do next. But as she stood, she began to hear a curious humming sound. Could it be the rain? No. It was much more gentle, and even monotonous than the sound of the rain, which now she scarcely heard. The low sweet humming sound went on, sometimes stopping for a little while and then beginning again. It was more like the hum of a very happy bee that had found a rich well of honey in some globular flower, than anything else I can think of at this moment. Where could it come from? She laid her ear first to one of the doors to hearken if it was there - then to another. When she laid her ear against the third door, there could be no doubt where it came from: it must be from something in that room. What could it be? She was rather afraid, but her curiosity was stronger than her fear, and she opened the door very gently and peeped in. What do you think she saw? A very old lady who sat spinning.

Perhaps you will wonder how the princess could tell that the old lady was an old lady, when I inform you that not only was she beautiful, but her skin was smooth and white. I will tell you more. Her hair was combed back from her forehead and face, and hung loose far down and all over her back. That is not much like an old lady - is it? Ah! but it was white almost as snow. And although her face was so smooth, her eyes looked so wise that you could not have helped seeing she must be old. The princess, though she could not have told you why, did think her very old indeed - quite fifty, she said to herself. But she was rather older than that, as you shall hear.

While the princess stared bewildered, with her head just inside the door, the old lady lifted hers, and said, in a sweet, but old and rather shaky voice, which mingled very pleasantly with the continued hum of her wheel:

'Come in, my dear; come in. I am glad to see you.'

That the princess was a real princess you might see now quite plainly; for she didn't hang on to the handle of the door, and stare without moving, as I have known some do who ought to have been princesses but were only rather vulgar little girls. She did as she was told, stepped inside the door at once, and shut it gently behind her.

'Come to me, my dear,' said the old lady.

And again the princess did as she was told. She approached the old lady - rather slowly, I confess - but did not stop until she stood by her side, and looked up in her face with her blue eyes and the two melted stars in them.

'Why, what have you been doing with your eyes, child?' asked the old lady.

'Crying,' answered the princess.

'Why, child?'

'Because I couldn't find my way down again.'

'But you could find your way up.'

'Not at first - not for a long time.'

'But your face is streaked like the back of a zebra. Hadn't you a handkerchief to wipe your eyes with?'

'No.'

'Then why didn't you come to me to wipe them for you?'

'Please, I didn't know you were here. I will next time.'

'There's a good child!' said the old lady.

Then she stopped her wheel, and rose, and, going out of the room, returned with a little silver basin and a soft white towel, with which she washed and wiped the bright little face. And the princess thought her hands were so smooth and nice!

When she carried away the basin and towel, the little princess wondered to see how straight and tall she was, for, although she was so old, she didn't stoop a bit. She was dressed in black velvet with thick white heavy-looking lace about it; and on the black dress her hair shone like silver. There was hardly any more furniture in the room than there might have been in that of the poorest old woman who made her bread by her spinning. There was no carpet on the floor - no table anywhere - nothing but the spinning-wheel and the chair beside it. When she came back, she sat down and without a word began her spinning once more, while Irene, who had never seen a spinning-wheel, stood by her side and looked on. When the old lady had got her thread fairly going again, she said to the princess, but without looking at her:

'Do you know my name, child?'

'No, I don't know it,' answered the princess.

'my name is Irene.'

'That's my name!' cried the princess.

'I know that. I let you have mine. I haven't got your name. You've got mine.'

'How can that be?' asked the princess, bewildered. 'I've always had my name.'

'Your papa, the king, asked me if I had any objection to your having it; and, of course, I hadn't. I let you have it with pleasure.'

'It was very kind of you to give me your name - and such a pretty one,' said the princess.

'Oh, not so very kind!' said the old lady. 'A name is one of those things one can give away and keep all the same. I have a good many such things. Wouldn't you like to know who I am, child?'

'Yes, that I should - very much.'

'I'm your great-great-grandmother,' said the lady.

'What's that?' asked the princess.

'I'm your father's mother's father's mother.'

'Oh, dear! I can't understand that,' said the princess.

'I dare say not. I didn't expect you would. But that's no reason why I shouldn't say it.'

'Oh, no!' answered the princess.

'I will explain it all to you when you are older,' the lady went on. 'But you will be able to understand this much now: I came here to take care of you.'

'Is it long since you came? Was it yesterday? Or was it today, because it was so wet that I couldn't get out?'

'I've been here ever since you came yourself.'

'What a long time!' said the princess. 'I don't remember it at all.'

'No. I suppose not.'

'But I never saw you before.'

'No. But you shall see me again.'

'Do you live in this room always?'

'I don't sleep in it. I sleep on the opposite side of the landing. I sit here most of the day.'

'I shouldn't like it. My nursery is much prettier. You must be a queen too, if you are my great big grand-mother.'

'Yes, I am a queen.'

'Where is your crown, then?' 'In my bedroom.'

'I should like to see it.'

'You shall some day - not today.'

'I wonder why nursie never told me.'

'Nursie doesn't know. She never saw me.'

'But somebody knows that you are in the house?'

'No; nobody.'

'How do you get your dinner, then?'

'I keep poultry - of a sort.'

'Where do you keep them?'

'I will show you.'

'And who makes the chicken broth for you?'

'I never kill any of MY chickens.'

'Then I can't understand.'

'What did you have for breakfast this morning?' asked the lady.

'Oh! I had bread and milk, and an egg - I dare say you eat their eggs.'

'Yes, that's it. I eat their eggs.'

'Is that what makes your hair so white?'

'No, my dear. It's old age. I am very old.'

'I thought so. Are you fifty?'

'Yes - more than that.'

'Are you a hundred?'

'Yes - more than that. I am too old for you to guess. Come and see my chickens.'

Again she stopped her spinning. She rose, took the princess by the hand, led her out of the room, and opened the door opposite the stair. The princess expected to see a lot of hens and chickens, but instead of that, she saw the blue sky first, and then the roofs of the house, with a multitude of the loveliest pigeons, mostly white, but of all colors, walking about, making bows to each other, and talking a language she could not understand. She clapped her hands with delight, and up rose such a flapping of wings that she in her turn was startled.

'You've frightened my poultry,' said the old lady, smiling.

'And they've frightened me,' said the princess, smiling too. 'But what very nice poultry! Are the eggs nice?'

'Yes, very nice.'

'What a small egg-spoon you must have! Wouldn't it be better to keep hens, and get bigger eggs?'

'How should I feed them, though?'

'I see,' said the princess. 'The pigeons feed themselves. They've got wings.'

'Just so. If they couldn't fly, I couldn't eat their eggs.'

'But how do you get at the eggs? Where are their nests?'

The lady took hold of a little loop of string in the wall at the side of the door and, lifting a shutter, showed a great many pigeon-holes with nests, some with young ones and some with eggs in them. The birds came in at the other side, and she took out the eggs on this side. She closed it again quickly, lest the young ones should be frightened.

'Oh, what a nice way!' cried the princess. 'Will you give me an egg to eat? I'm rather hungry.'

'I will some day, but now you must go back, or nursie will be miserable about you. I dare say she's looking for you everywhere.'

'Except here,' answered the princess. 'Oh, how surprised she will be when I tell her about my great big grand-grand-mother!'

'Yes, that she will!' said the old lady with a curious smile. 'Mind you tell her all about it exactly.'

'That I will. Please will you take me back to her?'

'I can't go all the way, but I will take you to the top of the stair, and then you must run down quite fast into your own room.'

The little princess put her hand in the old lady's, who, looking this way and that, brought her to the top of the first stair, and thence to the bottom of the second, and did not leave her till she saw her half-way down the third. When she heard the cry of her nurse's pleasure at finding her, she turned and walked up the stairs again, very fast indeed for such a very great grandmother, and sat down to her spinning with another strange smile on her sweet old face.

About this spinning of hers I will tell you more another time.

Guess what she was spinning.

4. WHAT THE NURSE THOUGHT OF IT

'Why, where can you have been, princess?' asked the nurse, taking her in her arms. 'It's very unkind of you to hide away so long. I began to be afraid -' here she checked herself.

'What were you afraid of, nursie?' asked the princess.

'Never mind,' she answered. 'Perhaps I will tell you another day. Now tell me where you have been.'

'I've been up a long way to see my very great, huge, old grandmother,' said the princess.

'What do you mean by that?' asked the nurse, who thought she was making fun.

'I mean that I've been a long way up and up to see my great grandmother. Ah, nursie, you don't know what a beautiful mother of grandmothers I've got upstairs. She is such an old lady, with such lovely white hair - as white as my silver cup. Now, when I think of it, I think her hair must be silver.'

'What nonsense you are talking, princess!' said the nurse.

'I'm not talking nonsense,' returned Irene, rather offended. 'I will tell you all about her. She's much taller than you, and much prettier.'

'Oh, I dare say!' remarked the nurse.

'And she lives upon pigeons' eggs.'

'Most likely,' said the nurse.

'And she sits in an empty room, spin-spinning all day long.'

'Not a doubt of it,' said the nurse.

'And she keeps her crown in her bedroom.'

'Of course - quite the proper place to keep her crown in. She wears it in bed, I'll be bound.' 'She didn't say that. And I don't think she does. That wouldn't be comfortable - would it? I don't think my papa wears his crown for a night-cap. Does he, nursie?'

'I never asked him. I dare say he does.'

'And she's been there ever since I came here - ever so many years.'

'Anybody could have told you that,' said the nurse, who did not believe a word Irene was saying.

'Why didn't you tell me, then?'

'There was no necessity. You could make it all up for yourself.'

'You don't believe me, then!' exclaimed the princess, astonished and angry, as she well might be.

'Did you expect me to believe you, princess?' asked the nurse coldly. 'I know princesses are in the habit of telling make-believes, but you are the first I ever heard of who expected to have them believed,' she added, seeing that the child was strangely in earnest.

The princess burst into tears.

'Well, I must say,' remarked the nurse, now thoroughly vexed with her for crying, 'it is not at all becoming in a princess to tell stories and expect to be believed just because she is a princess.'

'But it's quite true, I tell you.'

'You've dreamt it, then, child.'

'No, I didn't dream it. I went upstairs, and I lost myself, and if I hadn't found the beautiful lady, I should never have found myself.'

'Oh, I dare say!'

'Well, you just come up with me, and see if I'm not telling the truth.'

'Indeed I have other work to do. It's your dinnertime, and I won't have any more such nonsense.'

The princess wiped her eyes, and her face grew so hot that they were soon quite dry. She sat down to her dinner, but ate next to nothing. Not to be believed does not at all agree with princesses: for a real princess cannot tell a lie. So all the afternoon she did not speak a word. Only when the nurse spoke to her, she answered her, for a real princess is never rude - even when she does well to be offended.

Of course the nurse was not comfortable in her mind - not that she suspected the least truth in Irene's story, but that she loved her dearly, and was vexed with herself for having been cross to her. She thought her crossness was the cause of the princess's unhappiness, and had no idea that she was really and deeply hurt at not being believed. But, as it became more and more plain during the evening in her every motion and look, that, although she tried to amuse herself with her toys, her heart was too vexed and troubled to enjoy them, her nurse's discomfort grew and grew. When bedtime came, she undressed and laid her down, but the child, instead of holding up her little mouth to be kissed, turned away from her and lay still. Then nursie's heart gave way altogether, and she began to cry. At the sound of her first sob the princess turned again, and held her face to kiss her as usual. But the nurse had her handkerchief to her eyes, and did not see the movement.

'Nursie,' said the princess, 'why won't you believe me?'

'Because I can't believe you,' said the nurse, getting angry again.

'Ah! then, you can't help it,' said Irene, 'and I will not be vexed with you any more. I will give you a kiss and go to sleep.'

'You little angel!' cried the nurse, and caught her out of bed, and walked about the room with her in her arms, kissing and hugging her.

'You will let me take you to see my dear old great big grandmother, won't you?' said the princess, as she laid her down again.

'And you won't say I'm ugly, any more - will you, princess?'

'Nursie, I never said you were ugly. What can you mean?'

'Well, if you didn't say it, you meant it.'

'Indeed, I never did.'

'You said I wasn't so pretty as that -'

'As my beautiful grandmother - yes, I did say that; and I say it again, for it's quite true.'

'Then I do think you are unkind!' said the nurse, and put her handkerchief to her eyes again.

'Nursie, dear, everybody can't be as beautiful as every other body, you know. You are very nice-looking, but if you had been as beautiful as my grandmother -'

'Bother your grandmother!' said the nurse.

'Nurse, that's very rude. You are not fit to be spoken to till you can behave better.' The princess turned away once more, and again the nurse was ashamed of herself.

'I'm sure I beg your pardon, princess,' she said, though still in an offended tone. But the princess let the tone pass, and heeded only the words.

'You won't say it again, I am sure,' she answered, once more turning towards her nurse. 'I was only going to say that if you had been twice as nice-looking as you are, some king or other would have married you, and then what would have become of me?'

'You are an angel!' repeated the nurse, again embracing her. 'Now,' insisted Irene, 'you will come and see my grandmother - won't you?'

'I will go with you anywhere you like, my cherub,' she answered; and in two minutes the weary little princess was fast asleep.

5. THE PRINCESS LETS WELL ALONE

When she woke the next morning, the first thing she heard was the rain still falling. Indeed, this day was so like the last that it would have been difficult to tell where was the use of It. The first thing she thought of, however, was not the rain, but the lady in the tower; and the first question that occupied her thoughts was whether she should not ask the nurse to fulfill her promise this very morning, and go with her to find her grandmother as soon as she had had her breakfast. But she came to the conclusion that perhaps the lady would not be pleased if she took anyone to see her without first asking leave; especially as it was pretty evident, seeing she lived on pigeons' eggs, and cooked them herself, that she did not want the household to know she was there. So the princess resolved to take the first opportunity of running up alone and asking whether she might bring her nurse. She believed the fact that she could not otherwise convince her she was telling the truth would have much weight with her grandmother.

The princess and her nurse were the best of friends all dressing-time, and the princess in consequence ate an enormous little breakfast.

'I wonder, Lootie' - that was her pet name for her nurse - 'what pigeons' eggs taste like?' she said, as she was eating her egg - not quite a common one, for they always picked out the pinky ones for her.

'We'll get you a pigeon's egg, and you shall judge for yourself,' said the nurse. 'Oh, no, no!' returned Irene, suddenly reflecting they might disturb the old lady in getting it, and that even if they did not, she would have one less in consequence.

'What a strange creature you are,' said the nurse - 'first to want a thing and then to refuse it!'

But she did not say it crossly, and the princess never minded any remarks that were not unfriendly.

'Well, you see, Lootie, there are reasons,' she returned, and said no more, for she did not want to bring up the subject of their former strife, lest her nurse should offer to go before she had had her grandmother's permission to bring her. Of course she could refuse to take her, but then she would believe her less than ever.

Now the nurse, as she said herself afterwards, could not be every moment in the room; and as never before yesterday had the princess given her the smallest reason for anxiety, it had not yet come into her head to watch her more closely. So she soon gave her a chance, and, the very first that offered, Irene was off and up the stairs again.

This day's adventure, however, did not turn out like yesterday's, although it began like it; and indeed to- day is very seldom like yesterday, if people would note the differences - even when it rains. The princess ran through passage after passage, and could not find the stair of the tower. My own suspicion is that she had not gone up high enough, and was searching on the second instead of the third floor. When she turned to go back, she failed equally in her search after the stair. She was lost once more.

Something made it even worse to bear this time, and it was no wonder that she cried again. Suddenly it occurred to her that it was after having cried before that she had found her grandmother's stair. She got up at once, wiped her eyes, and started upon a fresh quest.

This time, although she did not find what she hoped, she found what was next best: she did not come on a stair that went up, but she came upon one that went down. It was evidently not the stair she had come up, yet it was a good deal better than none; so down she went, and was singing merrily before she reached the bottom. There, to her surprise, she found herself in the kitchen. Although she was not allowed to go there alone, her nurse had often taken her, and she was a great favorite with the servants. So there was a general rush at her the moment she appeared, for every one wanted to have her; and the report of where she was soon reached the nurse's ears. She came at once to fetch her; but she never suspected how she had got there, and the princess kept her own counsel.

Her failure to find the old lady not only disappointed her, but made her very thoughtful. Sometimes she came almost to the nurse's opinion that she had dreamed all about her; but that fancy never lasted very long. She wondered much whether she should ever see her again, and thought it very sad not to have been able to find her when she particularly wanted her. She resolved to say nothing more to her nurse on the subject, seeing it was so little in her power to prove her words.

6. THE LITTLE MINER

The next day the great cloud still hung over the mountain, and the rain poured like water from a full sponge. The princess was very fond of being out of doors, and she nearly cried when she saw that the weather was no better. But the mist was not of such a dark dingy grey; there was light in it; and as the hours went on it grew brighter and brighter, until it was almost too brilliant to look at; and late in the afternoon the sun broke out so gloriously that Irene clapped her hands, crying:

'See, see, Lootie! The sun has had his face washed. Look how bright he is! Do get my hat, and let us go out for a walk. Oh, dear! oh, dear! how happy I am!'

Lootie was very glad to please the princess. She got her hat and cloak, and they set out together for a walk up the mountain; for the road was so hard and steep that the water could not rest upon it, and it was always dry enough for walking a few minutes after the rain ceased. The clouds were rolling away in broken pieces, like great, overwoolly sheep, whose wool the sun had bleached till it was almost too white for the eyes to bear. Between them the sky shone with a deeper and purer blue, because of the rain. The trees on the roadside were hung all over with drops, which sparkled in the sun like jewels. The only things that were no brighter for the rain were the brooks that ran down the mountain; they had changed from the clearness of crystal to a muddy brown; but what they lost in color they gained in sound - or at least in noise, for a brook when it is swollen is not so musical as before. But Irene was in raptures with the great brown streams tumbling down everywhere; and Lootie shared in her delight, for she too had been confined to the house for three days.

At length she observed that the sun was getting low, and said it was time to be going back. She made the remark again and again, but, every time, the princess begged her to go on just a little farther and a little farther; reminding her that it was much easier to go downhill, and saying that when they did turn they would be at home in a moment. So on and on they did go, now to look at a group of ferns over whose tops a stream was pouring in a watery arch, now to pick a shining stone from a rock by the wayside, now to watch the flight of some bird. Suddenly the shadow of a great mountain peak came up from behind, and shot in front of them. When the nurse saw it, she started and shook, and catching hold of the princess's hand turned and began to run down the hill.

'What's all the haste, nursie?' asked Irene, running alongside of her.

'We must not be out a moment longer.'

'But we can't help being out a good many moments longer.'

It was too true. The nurse almost cried. They were much too far from home. It was against express orders to be out with the princess one moment after the sun was down; and they were nearly a mile up the mountain! If His Majesty, Irene's papa, were to hear of it, Lootie would certainly be dismissed; and to leave the princess would break her heart. It was no wonder she ran. But Irene was not in the least frightened, not knowing anything to be frightened at. She kept on chattering as well as she could, but it was not easy.

'Lootie! Lootie! why do you run so fast? It shakes my teeth when I talk.'

'Then don't talk,' said Lootie.

'But the princess went on talking. She was always saying: 'Look, look, Lootie!' but Lootie paid no more heed to anything she said, only ran on.

'Look, look, Lootie! Don't you see that funny man peeping over the rock?'

Lootie only ran the faster. They had to pass the rock, and when they came nearer, the princess saw it was only a lump of the rock itself that she had taken for a man.

'Look, look, Lootie! There's such a curious creature at the foot of that old tree. Look at it, Lootie! It's making faces at us, I do think.'

Lootie gave a stifled cry, and ran faster still - so fast that Irene's little legs could not keep up with her, and she fell with a crash. It was a hard downhill road, and she had been running very fast - so it was no wonder she began to cry. This put the nurse nearly beside herself; but all she could do was to run on, the moment she got the princess on her feet again.

'Who's that laughing at me?' said the princess, trying to keep in her sobs, and running too fast for her grazed knees.

'Nobody, child,' said the nurse, almost angrily.

But that instant there came a burst of coarse tittering from somewhere near, and a hoarse indistinct voice that seemed to say: 'Lies! lies! lies!'

'Oh!' cried the nurse with a sigh that was almost a scream, and ran on faster than ever.

'Nursie! Lootie! I can't run any more. Do let us walk a bit.'

'What am I to do?' said the nurse. 'Here, I will carry you.'

She caught her up; but found her much too heavy to run with, and had to set her down again. Then she looked wildly about her, gave a great cry, and said:

'We've taken the wrong turning somewhere, and I don't know where we are. We are lost, lost!'

The terror she was in had quite bewildered her. It was true enough they had lost the way. They had been running down into a little valley in which there was no house to be seen.

Now Irene did not know what good reason there was for her nurse's terror, for the servants had all strict orders never to mention the goblins to her, but it was very discomposing to see her nurse in such a fright. Before, however, she had time to grow thoroughly alarmed like her, she heard the sound of whistling, and that revived her. Presently she saw a boy coming up the road from the valley to meet them. He was the whistler; but before they met his whistling changed to singing. And this is something like what he sang:

'Ring! dod! bang!

Go the hammers' clang!

Hit and turn and bore!

Whizz and puff and roar!

Thus we rive the rocks,

Force the goblin locks. -

See the shining ore!

One, two, three -

Bright as gold can be!

Four, five, six -

Shovels, mattocks, picks!

Seven, eight, nine -

Light your lamp at mine.

Ten, eleven, twelve -

Loosely hold the helve.

We're the merry miner-boys,

Make the goblins hold their noise.'

'I wish you would hold your noise,' said the nurse rudely, for the very word goblin at such a time and in such a place made her tremble. It would bring the goblins upon them to a certainty, she thought, to defy them in that way. But whether the boy heard her or not, he did not stop his singing.

'Thirteen, fourteen, fifteen -

This is worth the siftin';

Sixteen, seventeen, eighteen -

There's the match, and lay't in.

Nineteen, twenty -

Goblins in a plenty.'

'Do be quiet,' cried the nurse, in a whispered shriek. But the boy, who was now close at hand, still went on.

'Hush! scush! scurry!

There you go in a hurry!

Gobble! gobble! goblin!

There you go a wobblin';

Hobble, hobble, hobblin' -

Cobble! cobble! cobblin'!

Hob-bob-goblin! -

Huuuuuh!'

'There!' said the boy, as he stood still opposite them. 'There! that'll do for them. They can't bear singing, and they can't stand that song. They can't sing themselves, for they have no more voice than a crow; and they don't like other people to sing.'

The boy was dressed in a miner's dress, with a curious cap on his head. He was a very nice-looking boy, with eyes as dark as the mines in which he worked and as sparkling as the crystals in their rocks. He was about twelve years old. His face was almost too pale for beauty, which came of his being so little in the open air and the sunlight - for even vegetables grown in the dark are white; but he looked happy, merry indeed - perhaps at the thought of having routed the goblins; and his bearing as he stood before them had nothing clownish or rude about it.

'I saw them,' he went on, 'as I came up; and I'm very glad I did. I knew they were after somebody, but I couldn't see who it was. They won't touch you so long as I'm with you.'

'Why, who are you?' asked the nurse, offended at the freedom with which he spoke to them.

'I'm Peter's son.'

'Who's Peter?'

'Peter the miner.'

'I don't know him.'

'I'm his son, though.'

'And why should the goblins mind you, pray?'

'Because I don't mind them. I'm used to them.'

'What difference does that make?'

'If you're not afraid of them, they're afraid of you. I'm not afraid of them. That's all. But it's all that's wanted - up here, that is. It's a different thing down there. They won't always mind that song even, down there. And if anyone sings it, they stand grinning at him awfully; and if he gets frightened, and misses a word, or says a wrong one, they - oh! don't they give it him!' 'What do they do to him?' asked Irene, with a trembling voice.

'Don't go frightening the princess,' said the nurse.

'The princess!' repeated the little miner, taking off his curious cap. 'I beg your pardon; but you oughtn't to be out so late. Everybody knows that's against the law.'

'Yes, indeed it is!' said the nurse, beginning to cry again. 'And I shall have to suffer for it.'

'What does that matter?' said the boy. 'It must be your fault. It is the princess who will suffer for it. I hope they didn't hear you call her the princess. If they did, they're sure to know her again: they're awfully sharp.'

'Lootie! Lootie!' cried the princess. 'Take me home.'

'Don't go on like that,' said the nurse to the boy, almost fiercely. 'How could I help it? I lost my way.'

'You shouldn't have been out so late. You wouldn't have lost your way if you hadn't been frightened,' said the boy. 'Come along. I'll soon set you right again. Shall I carry your little Highness?'

'Impertinence!' murmured the nurse, but she did not say it aloud, for she thought if she made him angry he might take his revenge by telling someone belonging to the house, and then it would be sure to come to the king's ears. 'No, thank you,' said Irene. 'I can walk very well, though I can't run so fast as nursie. If you will give me one hand, Lootie will give me another, and then I shall get on famously.'

They soon had her between them, holding a hand of each.

'Now let's run,' said the nurse.

'No, no!' said the little miner. 'That's the worst thing you can do. If you hadn't run before, you would not have lost your way. And if you run now, they will be after you in a moment.'

'I don't want to run,' said Irene.

'You don't think of me,' said the nurse.

'Yes, I do, Lootie. The boy says they won't touch us if we don't run.'

'Yes, but if they know at the house that I've kept you out so late I shall be turned away, and that would break my heart.'

'Turned away, Lootie! Who would turn you away?'

'Your papa, child.'

'But I'll tell him it was all my fault. And you know it was, Lootie.'

'He won't mind that. I'm sure he won't.'

'Then I'll cry, and go down on my knees to him, and beg him not to take away my own dear Lootie.'

The nurse was comforted at hearing this, and said no more. They went on, walking pretty fast, but taking care not to run a step.

'I want to talk to you,' said Irene to the little miner; 'but it's so awkward! I don't know your name.'

'My name's Curdie, little princess.'

'What a funny name! Curdie! What more?'

'Curdie Peterson. What's your name, please?'

'Irene.'

'What more?'

'I don't know what more. What more is my name, Lootie?'

'Princesses haven't got more than one name. They don't want it.'

'Oh, then, Curdie, you must call me just Irene and no more.'

'No, indeed,' said the nurse indignantly. 'He shall do no such thing.'

'What shall he call me, then, Lootie?'

'Your Royal Highness.' 'My Royal Highness! What's that? No, no, Lootie. I won't be called names. I don't like them. You told me once yourself it's only rude children that call names; and I'm sure Curdie wouldn't be rude. Curdie, my name's Irene.'

'Well, Irene,' said Curdie, with a glance at the nurse which showed he enjoyed teasing her; 'it is very kind of you to let me call you anything. I like your name very much.'

He expected the nurse to interfere again; but he soon saw that she was too frightened to speak. She was staring at something a few yards before them in the middle of the path, where it narrowed between rocks so that only one could pass at a time.

'It is very much kinder of you to go out of your way to take us home,' said Irene. 'I'm not going out of my way yet,' said Curdie. 'It's on the other side of those rocks the path turns off to my father's.'

'You wouldn't think of leaving us till we're safe home, I'm sure,' gasped the nurse.

'Of course not,' said Curdie.

'You dear, good, kind Curdie! I'll give you a kiss when we get home,' said the princess.

The nurse gave her a great pull by the hand she held. But at that instant the something in the middle of the way, which had looked like a great lump of earth brought down by the rain, began to move. One after another it shot out four long things, like two arms and two legs, but it was now too dark to tell what they were. The nurse began to tremble from head to foot. Irene clasped Curdie's hand yet faster, and Curdie began to sing again:

'One, two -

Hit and hew!

Three, four -

Blast and bore!

Five, six -

There's a fix!

Seven, eight -

Hold it straight!

Nine, ten -

Hit again!

Hurry! scurry!

Bother! smother!

There's a toad

In the road!

Smash it!

Squash it!

Fry it!

Dry it!

You're another!

Up and off!

There's enough! -

Huuuuuh!'

As he uttered the last words, Curdie let go his hold of his companion, and rushed at the thing in the road as if he would trample it under his feet. It gave a great spring, and ran straight up one of the rocks like a huge spider. Curdie turned back laughing, and took Irene's hand again. She grasped his very tight, but said nothing till they had passed the rocks. A few yards more and she found herself on a part of the road she knew, and was able to speak again.

'Do you know, Curdie, I don't quite like your song: it sounds to me rather rude,' she said.

'Well, perhaps it is,' answered Curdie. 'I never thought of that; it's a way we have. We do it because they don't like it.'

'Who don't like it?'

'The cobs, as we call them.'

'Don't!' said the nurse.

'Why not?' said Curdie.

'I beg you won't. Please don't.'

'Oh! if you ask me that way, of course, I won't; though I don't a bit know why. Look! there are the lights of your great house down below. You'll be at home in five minutes now.'

Nothing more happened. They reached home in safety. Nobody had missed them, or even known they had gone out; and they arrived at the door belonging to their part of the house without anyone seeing them. The nurse was rushing in with a hurried and not over-gracious good night to Curdie; but the princess pulled her hand from hers, and was just throwing her arms round Curdie's neck, when she caught her again and dragged her away.

'Lootie! Lootie! I promised a kiss,' cried Irene.

'A princess mustn't give kisses. It's not at all proper,' said Lootie.

'But I promised,' said the princess.

'There's no occasion; he's only a miner-boy.'

'He's a good boy, and a brave boy, and he has been very kind to us. Lootie! Lootie! I promised.'

'Then you shouldn't have promised.'

'Lootie, I promised him a kiss.'

'Your Royal Highness,' said Lootie, suddenly grown very respectful, 'must come in directly.'

'Nurse, a princess must not break her word,' said Irene, drawing herself up and standing stock-still.

Lootie did not know which the king might count the worst - to let the princess be out after sunset, or to let her kiss a miner-boy. She did not know that, being a gentleman, as many kings have been, he would have counted neither of them the worse. However much he might have disliked his daughter to kiss the miner-boy, he would not have had her break her word for all the goblins in creation. But, as I say, the nurse was not lady enough to understand this, and so she was in a great difficulty, for, if she insisted, someone might hear the princess cry and run to see, and then all would come out. But here Curdie came again to the rescue.

'Never mind, Princess Irene,' he said. 'You mustn't kiss me tonight. But you shan't break your word. I will come another time. You may be sure I will.'

'Oh, thank you, Curdie!' said the princess, and stopped crying.

'Good night, Irene; good night, Lootie,' said Curdie, and turned and was out of sight in a moment.

'I should like to see him!' muttered the nurse, as she carried the princess to the nursery.

'You will see him,' said Irene. 'You may be sure Curdie will keep his word. He's sure to come again.'

'I should like to see him!' repeated the nurse, and said no more. She did not want to open a new cause of strife with the princess by saying more plainly what she meant. Glad enough that she had succeeded both in getting home unseen, and in keeping the princess from kissing the miner's boy, she resolved to watch her far better in future. Her carelessness had already doubled the danger she was in. Formerly the goblins were her only fear; now she had to protect her charge from Curdie as well.

7. THE MINES

Curdie went home whistling. He resolved to say nothing about the princess for fear of getting the nurse into trouble, for while he enjoyed teasing her because of her absurdity, he was careful not to do her any harm. He saw no more of the goblins, and was soon fast asleep in his bed.

He woke in the middle of the night, and thought he heard curious noises outside. He sat up and listened; then got up, and, opening the door very quietly, went out. When he peeped round the corner, he saw, under his own window, a group of stumpy creatures, whom he at once recognized by their shape. Hardly, however, had he begun his 'One, two, three!' when they broke asunder, scurried away, and were out of sight. He returned laughing, got into bed again, and was fast asleep in a moment.

Reflecting a little over the matter in the morning, he came to the conclusion that, as nothing of the kind had ever happened before, they must be annoyed with him for interfering to protect the princess. By the time he was dressed, however, he was thinking of something quite different, for he did not value the enmity of the goblins in the least. As soon as they had had breakfast, he set off with his father for the mine.

They entered the hill by a natural opening under a huge rock, where a little stream rushed out. They followed its course for a few yards, when the passage took a turn, and sloped steeply into the heart of the hill. With many angles and windings and branchings-off, and sometimes with steps where it came upon a natural gulf, it led them deep into the hill before they arrived at the place where they were at present digging out the precious ore. This was of various kinds, for the mountain was very rich in the better sorts of metals. With flint and steel, and tinder-box, they lighted their lamps, then fixed them on their heads, and were soon hard at work with their pickaxes and shovels and hammers. Father and son were at work near each other, but not in the same gang - the passages out of which the ore was dug, they called gangs — for when the lode, or vein of ore, was small, one miner would have to dig away alone in a passage no bigger than gave him just room to work - sometimes in uncomfortable cramped positions. If they stopped for a moment they could hear everywhere around them, some nearer, some farther off, the sounds of their companions burrowing away in all directions in the inside of the great mountain — some boring holes in the rock in order to blow it up with gunpowder, others shoveling the broken ore into baskets to be carried to the mouth of the mine, others hitting away with their pickaxes. Sometimes, if the miner was in a very lonely part, he would hear only a tap-tapping, no louder than that of a woodpecker, for the sound would come from a great distance off through the solid mountain rock.

The work was hard at best, for it is very warm underground; but it was not particularly unpleasant, and some of the miners, when they wanted to earn a little more money for a particular purpose, would stop behind the rest and work all night. But you could not tell night from day down there, except from feeling tired and sleepy; for no light of the sun ever came into those gloomy regions. Some who had thus remained behind during the night, although certain there were none of their companions at work, would declare the next morning that they heard, every time they halted for a moment to take breath, a tap-tapping all about them, as if the mountain were then more full of miners than ever it was during the day; and some in consequence would never stay overnight, for all knew those were the sounds of the goblins. They worked only at night, for the miners' night was the goblins' day. Indeed, the greater number of the miners were afraid of the goblins; for there were strange stories well known amongst them of the treatment some had received whom the goblins had surprised at their work during the night. The more courageous of them, however, amongst them Peter Peterson and Curdie, who in this took after his father, had stayed in the mine all night again and again, and although they had several times encountered a few stray goblins, had never yet failed in driving them away. As I have indicated already, the chief defense against them was verse, for they hated verse of every kind, and some kinds they could not endure at all. I suspect they could not make any themselves, and that was why they disliked it so much. At all events, those who were most afraid of them were those who could neither make verses themselves nor remember the verses that other people made for them; while those who were never afraid were those who could make verses for themselves; for although there were certain old rhymes which were very effectual, yet it was well known that a new rhyme, if of the right sort, was even more distasteful to them, and therefore more effectual in putting them to flight.

Perhaps my readers may be wondering what the goblins could be about, working all night long, seeing they never carried up the ore and sold it; but when I have informed them concerning what Curdie learned the very next night, they will be able to understand.

For Curdie had determined, if his father would permit him, to remain there alone this night - and that for two reasons: first, he wanted to get extra wages that he might buy a very warm red petticoat for his mother, who had begun to complain of the cold of the mountain air sooner than usual this autumn; and second, he had just a faint hope of finding out what the goblins were about under his window the night before.

When he told his father, he made no objection, for he had great confidence in his boy's courage and resources.

'I'm sorry I can't stay with you,' said Peter; 'but I want to go and pay the parson a visit this evening, and besides I've had a bit of a headache all day.'

'I'm sorry for that, father,' said Curdie.

'Oh, it's not much. You'll be sure to take care of yourself, won't

you?'

'Yes, father; I will. I'll keep a sharp look-out, I promise you.' Curdie was the only one who remained in the mine. About six o'clock the rest went away, everyone bidding him good night, and telling him to take care of himself; for he was a great favorite with them all.

'Don't forget your rhymes,' said one.

'No, no,' answered Curdie.

'It's no matter if he does,' said another, 'for he'll only have to make a new one.'

'Yes: but he mightn't be able to make it fast enough,' said another; 'and while it was cooking in his head, they might take a mean advantage and set upon him.'

'I'll do my best,' said Curdie. 'I'm not afraid.' 'We all know that,' they returned, and left him.

8. THE GOBLINS

For some time Curdie worked away briskly, throwing all the ore he had disengaged on one side behind him, to be ready for carrying out in the morning. He heard a good deal of goblin-tapping, but it all sounded far away in the hill, and he paid it little heed. Towards midnight he began to feel rather hungry; so he dropped his pickaxe, got out a lump of bread which in the morning he had laid in a damp hole in the rock, sat down on a heap of ore, and ate his supper. Then he leaned back for five minutes' rest before beginning his work again, and laid his head against the rock. He had not kept the position for one minute before he heard something which made him sharpen his ears. It sounded like a voice inside the rock. After a while he heard it again. It was a goblin voice – there could be no doubt about that - and this time he could make out the words.

'Hadn't we better be moving?' it said.

A rougher and deeper voice replied:

'There's no hurry. That wretched little mole won't be through tonight, if he work ever so hard. He's not by any means at the thinnest place.'

'But you still think the lode does come through into our house?' said the first voice.

'Yes, but a good bit farther on than he has got to yet. If he had struck a stroke more to the side just here,' said the goblin, tapping the very stone, as it seemed to Curdie, against which his head lay, 'he would have been through; but he's a couple of yards past it now, and if he follow the lode it will be a week before it leads him in. You see it back there - a long way. Still, perhaps, in case of accident it would be as well to be getting out of this. Helfer, you'll take the great chest. That's your business, you know.'

'Yes, dad,' said a third voice. 'But you must help me to get it on my back. It's awfully heavy, you know.'

'Well, it isn't just a bag of smoke, I admit. But you're as strong as a mountain, Helfer.'

'You say so, dad. I think myself I'm all right. But I could carry ten times as much if it wasn't for my feet.'

'That is your weak point, I confess, my boy.' 'Ain't it yours too, father?'

'Well, to be honest, it's a goblin weakness. Why they come so soft, I declare I haven't an idea.'

'Specially when your head's so hard, you know, father.'

'Yes my boy. The goblin's glory is his head. To think how the fellows up above there have to put on helmets and things when they go fighting! Ha! ha!'

'But why don't we wear shoes like them, father? I should like it - especially when I've got a chest like that on my head.'

'Well, you see, it's not the fashion. The king never wears shoes.'

'The queen does.'

'Yes; but that's for distinction. The first queen, you see – I mean the king's first wife - wore shoes, of course, because she came from upstairs; and so, when she died, the next queen would not be inferior to her as she called it, and would wear shoes too. It was all pride. She is the hardest in forbidding them to the rest of the women.'

'I'm sure I wouldn't wear them - no, not for - that I wouldn't!' said the first voice, which was evidently that of the mother of the family. 'I can't think why either of them should.'

'Didn't I tell you the first was from upstairs?' said the other. 'That was the only silly thing I ever knew His Majesty guilty of. Why should he marry an outlandish woman like that-one of our natural enemies too?'

'I suppose he fell in love with her.'

'Pooh! pooh! He's just as happy now with one of his own people.'

'Did she die very soon? They didn't tease her to death, did they?'

'Oh, dear, no! The king worshipped her very footmarks.'

'What made her die, then? Didn't the air agree with her?'

'She died when the young prince was born.'

'How silly of her! We never do that. It must have been because she wore shoes.'

'I don't know that.'

'Why do they wear shoes up there?'

'Ah, now that's a sensible question, and I will answer it. But in order to do so, I must first tell you a secret. I once saw the queen's feet.'

'Without her shoes?'

'Yes - without her shoes.'

'No! Did you? How was it?'

'Never you mind how it was. She didn't know I saw them. And what do you think! - they had toes!'

'Toes! What's that?'

'You may well ask! I should never have known if I had not seen the queen's feet. just imagine! the ends of her feet were split up into five or six thin pieces!'

'Oh, horrid! How could the king have fallen in love with her?'

'You forget that she wore shoes. That is just why she wore them. That is why all the men, and women too, upstairs wear shoes. They can't bear the sight of their own feet without them.'

'Ah! now I understand. If ever you wish for shoes again, Helfer, I'll hit your feet - I will.'

'No, no, mother; pray don't.'

'Then don't you.'

'But with such a big box on my head -'

A horrid scream followed, which Curdie interpreted as in reply to a blow from his mother upon the feet of her eldest goblin.

'Well, I never knew so much before!' remarked a fourth voice.

'Your knowledge is not universal quite yet,' said the father. 'You were only fifty last month. Mind you see to the bed and bedding. As soon as we've finished our supper, we'll be up and going. Ha! ha! ha!'

'What are you laughing at, husband?'

'I'm laughing to think what a mess the miners will find themselves in - somewhere before this day ten years.'

'Why, what do you mean?'

'Oh, nothing.'

'Oh, yes, you do mean something. You always do mean something.'

'It's more than you do, then, wife.'

'That may be; but it's not more than I find out, you know.'

'Ha! ha! You're a sharp one. What a mother you've got, Helfer!'

'Yes, father.'

'Well, I suppose I must tell you. They're all at the palace consulting about it tonight; and as soon as we've got away from this thin place I'm going there to hear what night they fix upon. I should like to see that young ruffian there on the other side, struggling in the agonies of -'

He dropped his voice so low that Curdie could hear only a growl. The growl went on in the low bass for a good while, as inarticulate as if the goblin's tongue had been a sausage; and it was not until his wife spoke again that it rose to its former pitch.

'But what shall we do when you are at the palace?' she asked.

'I will see you safe in the new house I've been digging for you for the last two months. Podge, you mind the table and chairs. I commit them to your care. The table has seven legs - each chair three. I shall require them all at your hands.'

After this arose a confused conversation about the various household goods and their transport; and Curdie heard nothing more that was of any importance.

He now knew at least one of the reasons for the constant sound of the goblin hammers and pickaxes at night. They were making new houses for themselves, to which they might retreat when the miners should threaten to break into their dwellings. But he had learned two things of far greater importance. The first was, that some grievous calamity was preparing, and almost ready to fall upon the heads of the miners; the second was - the one weak point of a goblin's body; he had not known that their feet were so tender as he had now reason to suspect. He had heard it said that they had no toes: he had never had opportunity of inspecting them closely enough, in the dusk in which they always appeared, to satisfy himself whether it was a correct report. Indeed, he had not been able even to satisfy himself as to whether they had no fingers, although that also was commonly said to be the fact. One of the miners, indeed, who had had more schooling than the rest, was wont to argue that such must have been the primordial condition of humanity, and that education and handicraft had developed both toes and fingers - with which proposition Curdie had once heard his father sarcastically agree, alleging in support of it the probability that babies' gloves were a traditional remnant of the old state of things; while the stockings of all ages, no regard being paid in them to the toes, pointed in the same direction. But what was of importance was the fact concerning the softness of the goblin feet, which he foresaw might be useful to all miners. What he had to do in the meantime, however, was to discover, if possible, the special evil design the goblins had now in their heads.

Although he knew all the gangs and all the natural galleries with which they communicated in the mined part of the mountain, he had not the least idea where the palace of the king of the gnomes was; otherwise he would have set out at once on the enterprise of discovering what the said design was. He judged, and rightly, that it must lie in a farther part of the mountain, between which and the mine there was as yet no communication. There must be one nearly completed, however; for it could be but a thin partition which now separated them. If only he could get through in time to follow the goblins as they retreated! A few blows would doubtless be sufficient - just where his ear now lay; but if he attempted to strike there with his pickaxe, he would only hasten the departure of the family, put them on their guard, and perhaps lose their involuntary guidance. He therefore began to feel the wall With his hands, and soon found that some of the stones were loose enough to be drawn out with little noise.

Laying hold of a large one with both his hands, he drew it gently out, and let it down softly.

'What was that noise?' said the goblin father.

Curdie blew out his light, lest it should shine through.

'It must be that one miner that stayed behind the rest,' said the mother.

'No; he's been gone a good while. I haven't heard a blow for an hour. Besides, it wasn't like that.'

'Then I suppose it must have been a stone carried down the brook inside.' 'Perhaps. It will have more room by and by.'

Curdie kept quite still. After a little while, hearing nothing but the sounds of their preparations for departure, mingled with an occasional word of direction, and anxious to know whether the removal of the stone had made an opening into the goblins' house, he put in his hand to feel. It went in a good way, and then came in contact with something soft. He had but a moment to feel it over, it was so quickly withdrawn: it was one of the toeless goblin feet. The owner of it gave a cry of fright.

'What's the matter, Helfer?' asked his mother.

'A beast came out of the wall and licked my foot.'

'Nonsense! There are no wild beasts in our country,' said his father.

'But it was, father. I felt it.' 'Nonsense, I say. Will you malign your native realms and reduce them to a level with the country upstairs? That is swarming with wild beasts of every description.'

'But I did feel it, father.'

'I tell you to hold your tongue. You are no patriot.'

Curdie suppressed his laughter, and lay still as a mouse - but no stiller, for every moment he kept nibbling away with his fingers at the edges of the hole. He was slowly making it bigger, for here the rock had been very much shattered with the blasting.

There seemed to be a good many in the family, to judge from the mass of confused talk which now and then came through the hole; but when all were speaking together, and just as if they had bottle-brushes - each at least one - in their throats, it was not easy to make out much that was said. At length he heard once more what the father goblin was saying.

'Now, then,' he said, 'get your bundles on your backs. Here, Helfer, I'll help you up with your chest.'

'I wish it was my chest, father.'

'Your turn will come in good time enough! Make haste. I must go to the meeting at the palace tonight. When that's over, we can come back and clear out the last of the things before our enemies return in the morning. Now light your torches, and come along. What a distinction it is, to provide our own light, instead of being dependent on a thing hung up in the air - a most disagreeable contrivance - intended no doubt to blind us when we venture out under its baleful influence! Quite glaring and vulgar, I call it, though no doubt useful to poor creatures who haven't the wit to make light for themselves.'

Curdie could hardly keep himself from calling through to know whether they made the fire to light their torches by. But a moment's reflection showed him that they would have said they did, inasmuch as they struck two stones together, and the fire came.

9. THE HALL OF THE GOBLIN PALACE

A sound of many soft feet followed, but soon ceased. Then Curdie flew at the hole like a tiger, and tore and pulled. The sides gave way, and it was soon large enough for him to crawl through. He would not betray himself by rekindling his lamp, but the torches of the retreating company, which he found departing in a straight line up a long avenue from the door of their cave, threw back light enough to afford him a glance round the deserted home of the goblins. To his surprise, he could discover nothing to distinguish it from an ordinary natural cave in the rock, upon many of which he had come with the rest of the miners in the progress of their excavations. The goblins had talked of coming back for the rest of their household gear: he saw nothing that would have made him suspect a family had taken shelter there for a single night. The floor was rough and stony; the walls full of projecting corners; the roof in one place twenty feet high, in another endangering his forehead; while on one side a stream, no thicker than a needle, it is true, but still sufficient to spread a wide dampness over the wall, flowed down the face of the rock. But the troop in front of him was toiling under heavy burdens. He could distinguish Helfer now and then, in the flickering light and shade, with his heavy chest on his bending shoulders; while the second brother was almost buried in what looked like a great feather bed. 'Where do they get the feathers?' thought Curdie; but in a moment the troop disappeared at a turn of the way, and it was now both safe and necessary for Curdie to follow them, lest they should be round the next turning before he saw them again, for so he might lose them altogether. He darted after them like a greyhound. When he reached the corner and looked cautiously round, he saw them again at some distance down another long passage. None of the galleries he saw that night bore signs of the work of man - or of goblin either. Stalactites, far older than the mines, hung from their roofs; and their floors were rough with boulders and large round stones, showing that there water must have once run. He waited again at this corner till they had disappeared round the next, and so followed them a long way through one passage after another. The passages grew more and more lofty, and were more and more covered in the roof with shining stalactites.

It was a strange enough procession which he followed. But the strangest part of it was the household animals which crowded amongst the feet of the goblins. It was true they had no wild animals down there - at least they did not know of any; but they had a wonderful number of tame ones. I must, however, reserve any contributions towards the natural history of these for a later position in my story.

At length, turning a corner too abruptly, he had almost rushed into the middle of the goblin family; for there they had already set down all their burdens on the floor of a cave considerably larger than that which they had left. They were as yet too breathless to speak, else he would have had warning of their arrest. He started back, however, before anyone saw him, and retreating a good way, stood watching till the father should come out to go to the palace.

Before very long, both he and his son Helfer appeared and kept on in the same direction as before, while Curdie followed them again with renewed precaution. For a long time he heard no sound except something like the rush of a river inside the rock; but at length what seemed the far-off noise of a great shouting reached his ears, which, however, presently ceased. After advancing a good way farther, he thought he heard a single voice. It sounded clearer and clearer as he went on, until at last he could almost distinguish the words. In a moment or two, keeping after the goblins round another corner, he once more started back - this time in amazement.

He was at the entrance of a magnificent cavern, of an oval shape, once probably a huge natural reservoir of water, now the great palace hall of the goblins. It rose to a tremendous height, but the roof was composed of such shining materials, and the multitude of torches carried by the goblins who crowded the floor lighted up the place so brilliantly, that Curdie could see to the top quite well. But he had no idea how immense the place was until his eyes had got accustomed to it, which was not for a good many minutes. The rough projections on the walls, and the shadows thrown upwards from them by the torches, made the sides of the chamber look as if they were crowded with statues upon brackets and pedestals, reaching in irregular tiers from floor to roof. The walls themselves were, in many parts, of gloriously shining substances, some of them gorgeously colored besides, which powerfully contrasted with the shadows. Curdie could not help wondering whether his rhymes would be of any use against such a multitude of goblins as filled the floor of the hall, and indeed felt considerably tempted to begin his shout of 'One, two, three!', but as there was no reason for routing them and much for endeavoring to discover their designs, he kept himself perfectly quiet, and peering round the edge of the doorway, listened with both his sharp ears.

At the other end of the hall, high above the heads of the multitude, was a terrace-like ledge of considerable height, caused by the receding of the upper part of the cavern- wall. Upon this sat the king and his court: the king on a throne hollowed out of a huge block of green copper ore, and his court upon lower seats around it. The king had been making them a speech, and the applause which followed it was what Curdie had heard. One of the court was now addressing the multitude. What he heard him say was to the following effect: 'Hence it appears that two plans have been for some time together working in the strong head of His Majesty for the deliverance of his people. Regardless of the fact that we were the first possessors of the regions they now inhabit; regardless equally of the fact that we abandoned that region from the loftiest motives; regardless also of the self-evident fact that we excel them so far in mental ability as they excel us in stature, they look upon us as a degraded race and make a mockery of all our finer feelings. But, the time has almost arrived when - thanks to His Majesty's inventive genius - it will be in our power to take a thorough revenge upon them once for all, in respect of their unfriendly behavior.'

'May it please Your Majesty -' cried a voice close by the door, which Curdie recognized as that of the goblin he had followed.

'Who is he that interrupts the Chancellor?' cried another from near the throne.

'Glump,' answered several voices.

'He is our trusty subject,' said the king himself, in a slow and stately voice: 'let him come forward and speak.'

A lane was parted through the crowd, and Glump, having ascended the platform and bowed to the king, spoke as follows:

'Sire, I would have held my peace, had I not known that I only knew how near was the moment, to which the Chancellor had just referred.

In all probability, before another day is past, the enemy will have broken through into my house - the partition between being even now not more than a foot in thickness.'

'Not quite so much,' thought Curdie to himself.

'This very evening I have had to remove my household effects; therefore the sooner we are ready to carry out the plan, for the execution of which His Majesty has been making such magnificent preparations, the better. I may just add, that within the last few days I have perceived a small outbreak in my dining-room, which, combined with observations upon the course of the river escaping where the evil men enter, has convinced me that close to the spot must be a deep gulf in its channel. This discovery will, I trust, add considerably to the otherwise immense forces at His Majesty's disposal.'

He ceased, and the king graciously acknowledged his speech with a bend of his head; whereupon Glump, after a bow to His Majesty, slid down amongst the rest of the undistinguished multitude. Then the Chancellor rose and resumed.

'The information which the worthy Glump has given us,' he said, 'might have been of considerable import at the present moment, but for that other design already referred to, which naturally takes precedence. His Majesty, unwilling to proceed to extremities, and well aware that such measures sooner or later result in violent reactions, has excogitated a more fundamental and comprehensive measure, of which I need say no more. Should His Majesty be successful - as who dares to doubt? - then a peace, all to the advantage of the goblin kingdom, will be established for a generation at least, rendered absolutely secure by the pledge which His Royal Highness the prince will have and hold for the good behavior of her relatives. Should His Majesty fail - which who shall dare even to imagine in his most secret thoughts? - then will be the time for carrying out with rigor the design to which Glump referred, and for which our preparations are even now all but completed. The failure of the former will render the latter imperative.'

Curdie, perceiving that the assembly was drawing to a close and that there was little chance of either plan being more fully discovered, now thought it prudent to make his escape before the goblins began to disperse, and slipped quietly away.

There was not much danger of meeting any goblins, for all the men at least were left behind him in the palace; but there was considerable danger of his taking a wrong turning, for he had now no light, and had therefore to depend upon his memory and his hands. After he had left behind him the glow that issued from the door of Glump's new abode, he was utterly without guide, so far as his eyes were concerned.

He was most anxious to get back through the hole before the goblins should return to fetch the remains of their furniture. It was not that he was in the least afraid of them, but, as it was of the utmost importance that he should thoroughly discover what the plans they were cherishing were, he must not occasion the slightest suspicion that they were watched by a miner.

He hurried on, feeling his way along the walls of rock. Had he not been very courageous, he must have been very anxious, for he could not but know that if he lost his way it would be the most difficult thing in the world to find it again. Morning would bring no light into these regions; and towards him least of all, who was known as a special rhymester and persecutor, could goblins be expected to exercise courtesy. Well might he wish that he had brought his lamp and tinder-box with him, of which he had not thought when he crept so eagerly after the goblins! He wished it all the more when, after a while, he found his way blocked up, and could get no farther. It was of no use to turn back, for he had not the least idea where he had begun to go wrong. Mechanically, however, he kept feeling about the walls that hemmed him in. His hand came upon a place where a tiny stream of water was running down the face of the rock. 'What a stupid I am!' he said to himself. 'I am actually at the end of my journey! And there are the goblins coming back to fetch their things!' he added, as the red glimmer of their torches appeared at the end of the long avenue that led up to the cave. In a moment he had thrown himself on the floor, and wriggled backwards through the hole. The floor on the other side was several feet lower, which made it easier to get back. It was all he could do to lift the largest stone he had taken out of the hole, but he did manage to shove it in again. He sat down on the ore-heap and thought.

He was pretty sure that the latter plan of the goblins was to inundate the mine by breaking outlets for the water accumulated in the natural reservoirs of the mountain, as well as running through portions of it. While the part hollowed by the miners remained shut off from that inhabited by the goblins, they had had no opportunity of injuring them thus; but now that a passage was broken through, and the goblins' part proved the higher in the mountain, it was clear to Curdie that the mine could be destroyed in an hour. Water was always the chief danger to which the miners were exposed. They met with a little choke-damp sometimes, but never with the explosive firedamp so common in coal-mines. Hence they were careful as soon as they saw any appearance of water. As the result of his reflections while the goblins were busy in their old home, it seemed to Curdie that it would be best to build up the whole of this gang, filling it with stone, and clay or lie, so that there should be no smallest channel for the water to get into. There was not, however, any immediate danger, for the execution of the goblins' plan was contingent upon the failure of that unknown design which was to take precedence of it; and he was most anxious to keep the door of communication open, that he might if possible discover what the former plan was. At the same time they could not resume their intermitted labors for the inundation without his finding it out; when by putting all hands to the work, the one existing outlet might in a single night be rendered impenetrable to any weight of water; for by filling the gang entirely up, their embankment would be buttressed by the sides of the mountain itself.

As soon as he found that the goblins had again retired, he lighted his lamp, and proceeded to fill the hole he had made with such stones as he could withdraw when he pleased. He then thought it better, as he might have occasion to be up a good many nights after this, to go home and have some sleep.

How pleasant the night air felt upon the outside of the mountain after what he had gone through in the inside of it! He hurried up the hill without meeting a single goblin on the way, and called and tapped at the window until he woke his father, who soon rose and let him in. He told him the whole story; and, just as he had expected, his father thought it best to work that lode no farther, but at the same time to pretend occasionally to be at work there still in order that the goblins might have no suspicions. Both father and son then went to bed and slept soundly until the morning.

10. THE PRINCESS'S KING-PAPA

The weather continued fine for weeks, and the little princess went out every day. So long a period of fine weather had indeed never been known upon that mountain. The only uncomfortable thing was that her nurse was so nervous and particular about being in before the sun was down that often she would take to her heels when nothing worse than a fleecy cloud crossing the sun threw a shadow on the hillside; and many an evening they were home a full hour before the sunlight had left the weather-cock on the stables. If it had not been for such odd behavior Irene would by this time have almost forgotten the goblins. She never forgot Curdie, but him she remembered for his own sake, and indeed would have remembered him if only because a princess never forgets her debts until they are paid.

One splendid sunshiny day, about an hour after noon, Irene, who was playing on a lawn in the garden, heard the distant blast of a bugle. She jumped up with a cry of joy, for she knew by that particular blast that her father was on his way to see her. This part of the garden lay on the slope of the hill and allowed a full view of the country below. So she shaded her eyes with her hand and looked far away to catch the first glimpse of shining amour. In a few moments a little troop came glittering round the shoulder of a hill. Spears and helmets were sparkling and gleaming, banners were flying, horses prancing, and again came the bugle-blast which was to her like the voice of her father calling across the distance: 'Irene, I'm coming.'

On and on they came until she could clearly distinguish the king. He rode a white horse and was taller than any of the men with him. He wore a narrow circle of gold set with jewels around his helmet, and as he came still nearer Irene could discern the flashing of the stones in the sun. It was a long time since he had been to see her, and her little heart beat faster and faster as the shining troop approached, for she loved her king-papa very dearly and was nowhere so happy as in his arms. When they reached a certain point, after which she could see them no more from the garden, she ran to the gate, and there stood till up they came, clanging and stamping, with one more bright bugle-blast which said: 'Irene, I am come.'

By this time the people of the house were all gathered at the gate, but Irene stood alone in front of them. When the horsemen pulled up she ran to the side of the white horse and held up her arms. The king stopped and took her hands. In an instant she was on the saddle and clasped in his great strong arms.

I wish I could describe the king so that you could see him in your mind. He had gentle, blue eyes, but a nose that made him look like an eagle. A long dark beard, streaked with silvery lines, flowed from his mouth almost to his waist, and as Irene sat on the saddle and hid her glad face upon his bosom it mingled with the golden hair which her mother had given her, and the two together were like a cloud with streaks of the sun woven through it. After he had held her to his heart for a minute he spoke to his white horse, and the great beautiful creature, which had been prancing so proudly a little while before, walked as gently as a lady - for he knew he had a little lady on his back - through the gate and up to the door of the house. Then the king set her on the ground and, dismounting, took her hand and walked with her into the great hall, which was hardly ever entered except when he came to see his little princess. There he sat down, with two of his counselors who had accompanied him, to have some refreshment, and Irene sat on his right hand and drank her milk out of a wooden bowl curiously carved.

After the king had eaten and drunk he turned to the princess and said, stroking her hair:

'Now, my child, what shall we do next?'

This was the question he almost always put to her first after their meal together; and Irene had been waiting for it with some impatience, for now, she thought, she should be able to settle a question which constantly perplexed her.

'I should like you to take me to see my great old grandmother.'

The king looked grave And said:

'What does my little daughter mean?'

'I mean the Queen Irene that lives up in the tower - the very old lady, you know, with the long hair of silver.'

The king only gazed at his little princess with a look which she could not understand.

'She's got her crown in her bedroom,' she went on; 'but I've not been in there yet. You know she's there, don't you?'

'No,' said the king, very quietly.

'Then it must all be a dream,' said Irene. 'I half thought it was; but I couldn't be sure. Now I am sure of it. Besides, I couldn't find her the next time I went up.'

At that moment a snow-white pigeon flew in at an open window and settled upon Irene's head. She broke into a merry laugh, cowered a little, and put up her hands to her head, saying:

'Dear dovey, don't peck me. You'll pull out my hair with your long claws if you don't mind.'

The king stretched out his hand to take the pigeon, but it spread its wings and flew again through the open window, when its Whiteness made one flash in the sun and vanished. The king laid his hand on his princess's head, held it back a little, gazed in her face, smiled half a smile, and sighed half a sigh.

'Come, my child; we'll have a walk in the garden together,' he said.

'You won't come up and see my huge, great, beautiful grandmother, then, king-papa?' said the princess.

'Not this time,' said the king very gently. 'She has not invited me, you know, and great old ladies like her do not choose to be visited without leave asked and given.'

The garden was a very lovely place. Being upon a Mountainside there were parts in it where the rocks came through in great masses, and all immediately about them remained quite wild. Tufts of heather grew upon them, and other hardy mountain plants and flowers, while near them would be lovely roses and lilies and all pleasant garden flowers. This mingling of the wild mountain with the civilized garden was very quaint, and it was impossible for any number of gardeners to make such a garden look formal and stiff.

Against one of these rocks was a garden seat, shadowed from the afternoon sun by the overhanging of the rock itself. There was a little winding path up to the top of the rock, and on top another seat; but they sat on the seat at its foot because the sun was hot; and there they talked together of many things. At length the king said:

'You were out late one evening, Irene.'

'Yes, papa. It was my fault; and Lootie was very sorry.'

'I must talk to Lootie about it,' said the king.

'Don't speak loud to her, please, papa,' said Irene. 'She's been so afraid of being late ever since! Indeed she has not been naughty. It was only a mistake for once.'

'Once might be too often,' murmured the king to himself, as he stroked his child's head.

I can't tell you how he had come to know. I am sure Curdie had not told him. Someone about the palace must have seen them, after all.

He sat for a good while thinking. There was no sound to be heard except that of a little stream which ran merrily out of an opening in the rock by where they sat, and sped away down the hill through the garden. Then he rose and, leaving Irene where she was, went into the house and sent for Lootie, with whom he had a talk that made her cry. When in the evening he rode away upon his great white horse, he left six of his attendants behind him, with orders that three of them should watch outside the house every night, walking round and round it from sunset to sunrise. It was clear he was not quite comfortable about the princess.

11. THE OLD LADY'S BEDROOM

Nothing more happened worth telling for some time. The autumn came and went by. There were no more flowers in the garden. The wind blew strong, and howled among the rocks. The rain fell, and drenched the few yellow and red leaves that could not get off the bare branches. Again and again there would be a glorious morning followed by a pouring afternoon, and sometimes, for a week together, there would be rain, nothing but rain, all day, and then the most lovely cloudless night, with the sky all out in full-blown stars - not one missing. But the princess could not see much of them, for she went to bed early. The winter drew on, and she found things growing dreary. When it was too stormy to go out, and she had got tired of her toys, Lootie would take her about the house, sometimes to the housekeeper's room, where the housekeeper, who was a good, kind old woman, made much of her - sometimes to the servants' hall or the kitchen, where she was not princess merely, but absolute queen, and ran a great risk of being spoiled. Sometimes she would run off herself to the room where the men-at-arms whom the king had left sat, and they showed her their arms and accoutrements and did what they could to amuse her. Still at times she found it very dreary, and often and often wished that her huge great grandmother had not been a dream.

One morning the nurse left her with the housekeeper for a while. To amuse her she turned out the contents of an old cabinet upon the table. The little princess found her treasures, queer ancient ornaments, and many things the use of which she could not imagine, far more interesting than her own toys, and sat playing with them for two hours or more. But, at length, in handling a curious old-fashioned brooch, she ran the pin of it into her thumb, and gave a little scream with the sharpness of the pain, but would have thought little more of it had not the pain increased and her thumb begun to swell. This alarmed the housekeeper greatly. The nurse was fetched; the doctor was sent for; her hand was poulticed, and long before her usual time she was put to bed. The pain still continued, and although she fell asleep and dreamed a good many dreams, there was the pain always in every dream. At last it woke her up.

The moon was shining brightly into the room. The poultice had fallen off her hand and it was burning hot. She fancied if she could hold it into the moonlight that would cool it. So she got out of bed, without waking the nurse who lay at the other end of the room, and went to the window. When she looked out she saw one of the men-at-arms walking in the garden with the moonlight glancing on his armor. She was just going to tap on the window and call him, for she wanted to tell him all about it, when she bethought herself that that might wake Lootie, and she would put her into her bed again. So she resolved to go to the window of another room, and call him from there. It was so much nicer to have somebody to talk to than to lie awake in bed with the burning pain in her hand. She opened the door very gently and went through the nursery, which did not look into the garden, to go to the other window. But when she came to the foot of the old staircase there was the moon shining down from some window high up, and making the worm-eaten oak look very strange and delicate and lovely. In a moment she was putting her little feet one after the other in the silvery path up the stair, looking behind as she went, to see the shadow they made in the middle of the silver. Some little girls would have been afraid to find themselves thus alone in the middle of the night, but Irene was a princess.

As she went slowly up the stair, not quite sure that she was not dreaming, suddenly a great longing woke up in her heart to try once more whether she could not find the old lady with the silvery hair. 'If she is a dream,' she said to herself, 'then I am the likelier to find her, if I am dreaming.'

So up and up she went, stair after stair, until she Came to the many rooms - all just as she had seen them before. Through passage after passage she softly sped, comforting herself that if she should lose her way it would not matter much, because when she woke she would find herself in her own bed with Lootie not far off. But, as if she had known every step of the way, she walked straight to the door at the foot of the narrow stair that led to the tower.

'What if I should real reality-really find my beautiful old grandmother up there!' she said to herself as she crept up the steep steps.

When she reached the top she stood a moment listening in the dark, for there was no moon there. Yes! it was! it was the hum of the spinning-wheel! What a diligent grandmother to work both day and night! She tapped gently at the door.

'Come in, Irene,' said the sweet voice.

The princess opened the door and entered. There was the moonlight streaming in at the window, and in the middle of the moonlight sat the old lady in her black dress with the white lace, and her silvery hair mingling with the moonlight, so that you could not have told which was which. 'Come in, Irene,' she said again. 'Can you tell me what I am spinning?'

'She speaks,' thought Irene, 'just as if she had seen me five minutes ago, or yesterday at the farthest. - No,' she answered; 'I don't know what you are spinning. Please, I thought you were a dream. Why couldn't I find you before, great-great-grandmother?'

'That you are hardly old enough to understand. But you would have found me sooner if you hadn't come to think I was a dream. I will give you one reason though why you couldn't find me. I didn't want you to find me.'

'Why, please?'

'Because I did not want Lootie to know I was here.'

'But you told me to tell Lootie.'

'Yes. But I knew Lootie would not believe you. If she were to see me sitting spinning here, she wouldn't believe me, either.'

'Why?'

'Because she couldn't. She would rub her eyes, and go away and say she felt queer, and forget half of it and more, and then say it had been all a dream.'

'Just like me,' said Irene, feeling very much ashamed of herself.

'Yes, a good deal like you, but not just like you; for you've come again; and Lootie wouldn't have come again. She would have said, No, no - she had had enough of such nonsense.'

'Is it naughty of Lootie, then?'

'It would be naughty of you. I've never done anything for Lootie.'

'And you did wash my face and hands for me,' said Irene, beginning to cry.

The old lady smiled a sweet smile and said:

'I'm not vexed with you, my child - nor with Lootie either. But I don't want you to say anything more to Lootie about me. If she should ask you, you must just be silent. But I do not think she will ask you.'

All the time they talked the old lady kept on spinning.

'You haven't told me yet what I am spinning,' she said.

'Because I don't know. It's very pretty stuff.'

It was indeed very pretty stuff. There was a good bunch of it on the distaff attached to the spinning-wheel, and in the moonlight it shone like - what shall I say it was like? It was not white enough for silver - yes, it was like silver, but shone grey rather than white, and glittered only a little. And the thread the old lady drew out from it was so fine that Irene could hardly see it. 'I am spinning this for you, my child.'

'For me! What am I to do with it, please?'

'I will tell you by and by. But first I will tell you what it is. It is spider-web - of a particular kind. My pigeons bring it me from over the great sea. There is only one forest where the spiders live who make this particular kind - the finest and strongest of any. I have nearly finished my present job. What is on the rock now will be enough. I have a week's work there yet, though,' she added, looking at the bunch.

'Do you work all day and all night, too, great-great-great-great-grandmother?' said the princess, thinking to be very polite with so many greats.

'I am not quite so great as all that,' she answered, smiling almost merrily. 'If you call me grandmother, that will do. No, I don't work every night - only moonlit nights, and then no longer than the moon shines upon my wheel. I shan't work much longer tonight.'

'And what will you do next, grandmother?' 'Go to bed. Would you like to see my bedroom?'

'Yes, that I should.'

'Then I think I won't work any longer tonight. I shall be in good time.'

The old lady rose, and left her wheel standing just as it was. You see there was no good in putting it away, for where there was not any furniture there was no danger of being untidy.

Then she took Irene by the hand, but it was her bad hand and Irene gave a little cry of pain. 'My child!' said her grandmother, 'what is the matter?'

Irene held her hand into the moonlight, that the old lady might see it, and told her all about it, at which she looked grave. But she only said: 'Give me your other hand'; and, having led her out upon the little dark landing, opened the door on the opposite side of it. What was Irene's surprise to see the loveliest room she had ever seen in her life! It was large and lofty, and dome-shaped. From the centre hung a lamp as round as a ball, shining as if with the brightest moonlight, which made everything visible in the room, though not so clearly that the princess could tell what many of the things were. A large oval bed stood in the middle, with a coverlid of rose color, and velvet curtains all round it of a lovely pale blue. The walls were also blue - spangled all over with what looked like stars of silver.

The old lady left her and, going to a strange-looking cabinet, opened it and took out a curious silver casket. Then she sat down on a low chair and, calling Irene, made her kneel before her while she looked at her hand. Having examined it, she opened the casket, and took from it a little ointment. The sweetest odor filled the room - like that of roses and lilies - as she rubbed the ointment gently all over the hot swollen hand. Her touch was so pleasant and cool that it seemed to drive away the pain and heat wherever it came.

'Oh, grandmother! it is so nice!' said Irene. 'Thank you; thank you.'

Then the old lady went to a chest of drawers, and took out a large handkerchief of gossamer-like cambric, which she tied round her hand.

'I don't think I can let you go away tonight,' she said. 'Would you like to sleep with me?'

'Oh, yes, yes, dear grandmother,' said Irene, and would have clapped her hands, forgetting that she could not.

'You won't be afraid, then, to go to bed with such an old woman?'

'No. You are so beautiful, grandmother.'

'But I am very old.'

'And I suppose I am very young. You won't mind sleeping with such a very young woman, grandmother?'

'You sweet little pertness!' said the old lady, and drew her towards her, and kissed her on the forehead and the cheek and the mouth. Then she got a large silver basin, and having poured some water into it made Irene sit on the chair, and washed her feet. This done, she was ready for bed. And oh, what a delicious bed it was into which her grandmother laid her! She hardly could have told she was lying upon anything: she felt nothing but the softness.

The old lady having undressed herself lay down beside her.

'Why don't you put out your moon?' asked the princess.

'That never goes out, night or day,' she answered. 'In the darkest night, if any of my pigeons are out on a message, they always see my moon and know where to fly to.'

'But if somebody besides the pigeons were to see it – somebody about the house, I mean - they would come to look what it was and find you.'

'The better for them, then,' said the old lady. 'But it does not happen above five times in a hundred years that anyone does see it.

The greater part of those who do take it for a meteor, wink their eyes, and forget it again. Besides, nobody could find the room except I pleased. Besides, again - I will tell you a secret – if that light were to go out you would fancy yourself lying in a bare garret, on a heap of old straw, and would not see one of the pleasant things round about you all the time.'

'I hope it will never go out,' said the princess.

'I hope not. But it is time we both went to sleep. Shall I take you in my arms?'

The little princess nestled close up to the old lady, who took her in both her arms and held her close to her bosom.

'Oh, dear! this is so nice!' said the princess. 'I didn't know anything in the world could be so comfortable. I should like to lie here for ever.'

'You may if you will,' said the old lady. 'But I must put you to one trial-not a very hard one, I hope. This night week you must come back to me. If you don't, I do not know when you may find me again, and you Will soon want me very much.' 'Oh! please, don't let me forget.'

'You shall not forget. The only question is whether you will believe I am anywhere - whether you will believe I am anything but a dream. You may be sure I will do all I can to help you to come. But it will rest with yourself, after all. On the night of next Friday, you must come to me. Mind now.'

'I will try,' said the princess.

'Then good night,' said the old lady, and kissed the forehead which lay in her bosom.

In a moment more the little princess was dreaming in the midst of the loveliest dreams - of summer seas and moonlight and mossy springs and great murmuring trees, and beds of wild flowers with such odors as she had never smelled before. But, after all, no dream could be more lovely than what she had left behind when she fell asleep.

In the morning she found herself in her own bed. There was no handkerchief or anything else on her hand, only a sweet odor lingered about it. The swelling had all gone down; the prick of the brooch had vanished - in fact, her hand was perfectly well.

12. A Short Chapter About Curdie

Curdie spent many nights in the mine. His father and he had taken Mrs. Peterson into the secret, for they knew mother could hold her tongue, which was more than could be said of all the miners' wives.

But Curdie did not tell her that every night he spent in the mine, part of it went in earning a new red petticoat for her.

Mrs. Peterson was such a nice good mother! All mothers are nice and good more or less, but Mrs. Peterson was nice and good all more and no less. She made and kept a little heaven in that poor cottage on the high hillside for her husband and son to go home to out of the low and rather dreary earth in which they worked. I doubt if the princess was very much happier even in the arms of her huge great-grandmother than Peter and Curdie were in the arms of Mrs. Peterson. True, her hands were hard and chapped and large, but it was with work for them; and therefore, in the sight of the angels, her hands were so much the more beautiful. And if Curdie worked hard to get her a petticoat, she worked hard every day to get him comforts which he would have missed much more than she would a new petticoat even in winter. Not that she and Curdie ever thought of how much they worked for each other: that would have spoiled everything.

When left alone in the mine Curdie always worked on for an hour or two at first, following the lode which, according to Glump, would lead at last into the deserted habitation. After that, he would set out on a reconnoitering expedition. In order to manage this, or rather the return from it, better than the first time, he had bought a huge ball of fine string, having learned the trick from Hop-o'-my-Thumb, whose history his mother had often told him. Not that Hop-o'-my-Thumb had ever used a ball of string - I should be sorry to be supposed so far out in my classics - but the principle was the same as that of the pebbles. The end of this string he fastened to his pickaxe, which figured no bad anchor, and then, with the ball in his hand, unrolling it as he went, set out in the dark through the natural gangs of the goblins' territory. The first night or two he came upon nothing worth remembering; saw only a little of the home-life of the cobs in the various caves they called houses; failed in coming upon anything to cast light upon the foregoing design which kept the inundation for the present in the background. But at length, I think on the third or fourth night, he found, partly guided by the noise of their implements, a company of evidently the best sappers and miners amongst them, hard at work. What were they about? It could not well be the inundation, seeing that had in the meantime been postponed to something else. Then what was it? He lurked and watched, every now and then in the greatest risk of being detected, but without success. He had again and again to retreat in haste, a proceeding rendered the more difficult that he had to gather up his string as he returned upon its course. It was not that he was afraid of the goblins, but that he was afraid of their finding out that they were watched, which might have prevented the discovery at which he aimed. Sometimes his haste had to be such that, when he reached home towards morning, his string, for lack of time to wind it up as he 'dodged the cobs', would be in what seemed most hopeless entanglement; but after a good sleep, though a short one, he always found his mother had got it right again. There it was, wound in a most respectable ball, ready for use the moment he should want it!

'I can't think how you do it, mother,' he would say.

'I follow the thread,' she would answer - 'just as you do in the mine.' She never had more to say about it; but the less clever she was with her words, the more clever she was with her hands; and the less his mother said, the more Curdie believed she had to say. But still he had made no discovery as to what the goblin miners were about.

13. THE COBS' CREATURES

About this time the gentlemen whom the king had left behind him to watch over the princess had each occasion to doubt the testimony of his own eyes, for more than strange were the objects to which they would bear witness. They were of one sort - creatures - but so grotesque and misshapen as to be more like a child's drawings upon his slate than anything natural. They saw them only at night, while on guard about the house. The testimony of the man who first reported having seen one of them was that, as he was walking slowly round the house, while yet in the shadow, he caught sight of a creature standing on its hind legs in the moonlight, with its forefeet upon a window-ledge, staring in at the window. Its body might have been that of a dog or wolf, he thought, but he declared on his honor that its head was twice the size it ought to have been for the size of its body, and as round as a ball, while the face, which it turned upon him as it fled, was more like one carved by a boy upon the turnip inside which he is going to put a candle than anything else he could think of. It rushed into the garden. He sent an arrow after it, and thought he must have struck it; for it gave an unearthly howl, and he could not find his arrow any more than the beast, although he searched all about the place where it vanished. They laughed at him until he was driven to hold his tongue, and said he must have taken too long a pull at the ale-jug.

But before two nights were over he had one to side with him, for he, too, had seen something strange, only quite different from that reported by the other. The description the second man gave of the creature he had seen was yet more grotesque and unlikely. They were both laughed at by the rest; but night after night another came over to their side, until at last there was only one left to laugh at all his companions. Two nights more passed, and he saw nothing; but on the third he came rushing from the garden to the other two before the house, in such an agitation that they declared - for it was their turn now - that the band of his helmet was cracking under his chin with the rising of his hair inside it. Running with him into that part of the garden which I have already described, they saw a score of creatures, to not one of which they could give a name, and not one of which was like another, hideous and ludicrous at once, gamboling on the lawn in the moonlight. The supernatural or rather sub-natural ugliness of their faces, the length of legs and necks in some, the apparent absence of both or either in others, made the spectators, although in one consent as to what they saw, yet doubtful, as I have said, of the evidence of their own eyes - and ears as well; for the noises they made, although not loud, were as uncouth and varied as their forms, and could be described neither as grunts nor squeaks nor roars nor howls nor barks nor yells nor screams nor croaks nor hisses nor mews nor shrieks, but only as something like all of them mingled in one horrible dissonance. Keeping in the shade, the watchers had a few moments to recover themselves before the hideous assembly suspected their presence; but all at once, as if by common consent, they scampered off in the direction of a great rock, and vanished before the men had come to themselves sufficiently to think of following them.

My readers will suspect what these were; but I will now give them full information concerning them. They were, of course, household animals belonging to the goblins, whose ancestors had taken their ancestors many centuries before from the upper regions of light into the lower regions of darkness. The original stocks of these horrible creatures were very much the same as the animals now seen about farms and homes in the country, with the exception of a few of them, which had been wild creatures, such as foxes, and indeed wolves and small bears, which the goblins, from their proclivity towards the animal creation, had caught when cubs and tamed. But in the course of time all had undergone even greater changes than had passed upon their owners. They had altered - that is, their descendants had altered - into such creatures as I have not attempted to describe except in the vaguest manner - the various parts of their bodies assuming, in an apparently arbitrary and self-willed manner, the most abnormal developments. Indeed, so little did any distinct type predominate in some of the bewildering results, that you could only have guessed at any known animal as the original, and even then, what likeness remained would be more one of general expression than of definable conformation. But what increased the gruesomeness tenfold was that, from constant domestic, or indeed rather family association with the goblins, their countenances had grown in grotesque resemblance to the human.

No one understands animals who does not see that every one of them, even amongst the fishes, it may be with a dimness and vagueness infinitely remote, yet shadows the human: in the case of these the human resemblance had greatly increased: while their owners had sunk towards them, they had risen towards their owners. But the conditions of subterranean life being equally unnatural for both, while the goblins were worse, the creatures had not improved by the approximation, and its result would have appeared far more ludicrous than consoling to the warmest lover of animal nature. I shall now explain how it was that just then these animals began to show themselves about the king's country house.

The goblins, as Curdie had discovered, were mining on - at work both day and night, in divisions, urging the scheme after which he lay in wait. In the course of their tunneling they had broken into the channel of a small stream, but the break being in the top of it, no water had escaped to interfere with their work. Some of the creatures, hovering as they often did about their masters, had found the hole, and had, with the curiosity which had grown to a passion from the restraints of their unnatural circumstances, proceeded to explore the channel. The stream was the same which ran out by the seat on which Irene and her king-papa had sat as I have told, and the goblin creatures found it jolly fun to get out for a romp on a smooth lawn such as they had never seen in all their poor miserable lives. But although they had partaken enough of the nature of their owners to delight in annoying and alarming any of the people whom they met on the mountain, they were, of course, incapable of designs of their own, or of intentionally furthering those of their masters.

For several nights after the men-at-arms were at length of one mind as to the fact of the visits of some horrible creatures, whether bodily or spectral they could not yet say, they watched with special attention that part of the garden where they had last seen them. Perhaps indeed they gave in consequence too little attention to the house. But the creatures were too cunning to be easily caught; nor were the watchers quick-eyed enough to descry the head, or the keen eyes in it, which, from the opening whence the stream issued, would watch them in turn, ready, the moment they should leave the lawn, to report the place clear.

14. THAT NIGHT WEEK

During the whole of the week Irene had been thinking every other moment of her promise to the old lady, although even now she could not feel quite sure that she had not been dreaming. Could it really be that an old lady lived up in the top of the house, with pigeons and a spinning-wheel, and a lamp that never went out? She was, however, none the less determined, on the coming Friday, to ascend the three stairs, walk through the passages with the many doors, and try to find the tower in which she had either seen or dreamed her grandmother.

Her nurse could not help wondering what had come to the child – she would sit so thoughtfully silent, and even in the midst of a game with her would so suddenly fall into a dreamy mood. But Irene took care to betray nothing, whatever efforts Lootie might make to get at her thoughts. And Lootie had to say to herself: 'What an odd child she is!' and give it up. At length the longed-for Friday arrived, and lest Lootie should be moved to watch her, Irene endeavored to keep herself as quiet as possible. In the afternoon she asked for her doll's house, and went on arranging and rearranging the various rooms and their inhabitants for a whole hour. Then she gave a sigh and threw herself back in her chair. One of the dolls would not sit, and another would not stand, and they were all very tiresome. Indeed, there was one would not even lie down, which was too bad. But it was now getting dark, and the darker it got the more excited Irene became, and the more she felt it necessary to be composed.

'I see you want your tea, princess,' said the nurse: 'I will go and get it. The room feels close: I will open the window a little. The evening is mild: it won't hurt you.'

'There's no fear of that, Lootie,' said Irene, wishing she had put off going for the tea till it was darker, when she might have made her attempt with every advantage.

I fancy Lootie was longer in returning than she had intended; for when Irene, who had been lost in thought, looked up, she saw it was nearly dark, and at the same moment caught sight of a pair of eyes, bright with a green light, glowering at her through the open window. The next instant something leaped into the room. It was like a cat, with legs as long as a horse's, Irene said, but its body no bigger and its legs no thicker than those of a cat. She was too frightened to cry out, but not too frightened to jump from her chair and run from the room.

It is plain enough to every one of my readers what she ought to have done - and indeed, Irene thought of it herself; but when she came to the foot of the old stair, just outside the nursery door, she imagined the creature running up those long ascents after her, and pursuing her through the dark passages - which, after all, might lead to no tower! That thought was too much. Her heart failed her, and, turning from the stair, she rushed along to the hall, whence, finding the front door open, she darted into the court pursued - at least she thought so - by the creature. No one happening to see her, on she ran, unable to think for fear, and ready to run anywhere to elude the awful creature with the stilt-legs. Not daring to look behind her, she rushed straight out of the gate and up the mountain. It was foolish indeed - thus to run farther and farther from all who could help her, as if she had been seeking a fit spot for the goblin creature to eat her in his leisure; but that is the way fear serves us: it always sides with the thing we are afraid of.

The princess was soon out of breath with running uphill; but she ran on, for she fancied the horrible creature just behind her, forgetting that, had it been after her such long legs as those must have overtaken her long ago. At last she could run no longer, and fell, unable even to scream, by the roadside, where she lay for some time half dead with terror. But finding nothing lay hold of her, and her breath beginning to come back, she ventured at length to get half up and peer anxiously about her. It was now so dark she could see nothing. Not a single star was out. She could not even tell in what direction the house lay, and between her and home she fancied the dreadful creature lying ready to pounce upon her. She saw now that she ought to have run up the stairs at once. It was well she did not scream; for, although very few of the goblins had come out for weeks, a stray idler or two might have heard her. She sat down upon a stone, and nobody but one who had done something wrong could have been more miserable. She had quite forgotten her promise to visit her grandmother. A raindrop fell on her face. She looked up, and for a moment her terror was lost in astonishment. At first she thought the rising moon had left her place, and drawn nigh to see what could be the matter with the little girl, sitting alone, without hat or cloak, on the dark bare mountain; but she soon saw she was mistaken, for there was no light on the ground at her feet, and no shadow anywhere. But a great silver globe was hanging in the air; and as she gazed at the lovely thing, her courage revived. If she were but indoors again, she would fear nothing, not even the terrible creature with the long legs! But how was she to find her way back? What could that light be? Could it be -? No, it couldn't. But what if it should be - yes - it must be - her great-great-grandmother's lamp, which guided her pigeons home through the darkest night! She jumped up: she had but to keep that light in view and she must find the house. Her heart grew strong. Speedily, yet softly, she walked down the hill, hoping to pass the watching creature unseen. Dark as it was, there was little danger now of choosing the wrong road. And - which was most strange - the light that filled her eyes from the lamp, instead of blinding them for a moment to the object upon which they next fell, enabled her for a moment to see it, despite the darkness. By looking at the lamp and then dropping her eyes, she could see the road for a yard or two in front of her, and this saved her from several falls, for the road was very rough. But all at once, to her dismay, it vanished, and the terror of the beast, which had left her the moment she began to return, again laid hold of her heart. The same instant, however, she caught the light of the windows, and knew exactly where she was. It was too dark to run, but she made what haste she could, and reached the gate in safety. She found the house door still open, ran through the hall, and, without even looking into the nursery, bounded straight up the stair, and the next, and the next; then turning to the right, ran through the long avenue of silent rooms, and found her way at once to the door at the foot of the tower stair.

When first the nurse missed her, she fancied she was playing her a trick, and for some time took no trouble about her; but at last, getting frightened, she had begun to search; and when the princess entered, the whole household was hither and thither over the house, hunting for her. A few seconds after she reached the stair of the tower they had even begun to search the neglected rooms, in which they would never have thought of looking had they not already searched every other place they could think of in vain. But by this time she was knocking at the old lady's door.

15. WOVEN AND THEN SPUN

'Come in, Irene,' said the silvery voice of her grandmother.

The princess opened the door and peeped in. But the room was quite dark and there was no sound of the spinning-wheel. She grew frightened once more, thinking that, although the room was there, the old lady might be a dream after all. Every little girl knows how dreadful it is to find a room empty where she thought somebody was; but Irene had to fancy for a moment that the person she came to find was nowhere at all. She remembered, however, that at night she spun only in the moonlight, and concluded that must be why there was no sweet, bee-like humming: the old lady might be somewhere in the darkness. Before she had time to think another thought, she heard her voice again, saying as before: 'Come in, Irene.' From the sound, she understood at once that she was not in the room beside her. Perhaps she was in her bedroom. She turned across the passage, feeling her way to the other door. When her hand fell on the lock, again the old lady spoke:

'Shut the other door behind you, Irene. I always close the door of my workroom when I go to my chamber.'

Irene wondered to hear her voice so plainly through the door: having shut the other, she opened it and went in. Oh, what a lovely haven to reach from the darkness and fear through which she had come! The soft light made her feel as if she were going into the heart of the milkiest pearl; while the blue walls and their silver stars for a moment perplexed her with the fancy that they were in reality the sky which she had left outside a minute ago covered with rain clouds.

'I've lighted a fire for you, Irene: you're cold and wet,' said her grandmother.

Then Irene looked again, and saw that what she had taken for a huge bouquet of red roses on a low stand against the wall was in fact a fire which burned in the shapes of the loveliest and reddest roses, glowing gorgeously between the heads and wings of two cherubs of shining silver. And when she came nearer, she found that the smell of roses with which the room was filled came from the fire-roses on the hearth. Her grandmother was dressed in the loveliest pale blue velvet, over which her hair, no longer white, but of a rich golden color, streamed like a cataract, here falling in dull gathered heaps, there rushing away in smooth shining falls. And ever as she looked, the hair seemed pouring down from her head and vanishing in a golden mist ere it reached the floor. It flowed from under the edge of a circle of shining silver, set with alternated pearls and opals. On her dress was no ornament whatever, neither was there a ring on her hand, or a necklace or carcanet about her neck. But her slippers glimmered with the light of the Milky Way, for they were covered with seed-pearls and opals in one mass. Her face was that of a woman of three-and-twenty.

The princess was so bewildered with astonishment and admiration that she could hardly thank her, and drew nigh with timidity, feeling dirty and uncomfortable. The lady was seated on a low chair by the side of the fire, with hands outstretched to take her, but the princess hung back with a troubled smile.

'Why, what's the matter?' asked her grandmother. 'You haven't been doing anything wrong - I know that by your face, though it is rather miserable. What's the matter, my dear?'

And she still held out her arms.

'Dear grandmother,' said Irene, 'I'm not so sure that I haven't done something wrong. I ought to have run up to you at once when the long-legged cat came in at the window, instead of running out on the mountain and making myself such a fright.'

'You were taken by surprise, my child, and you are not so likely to do it again. It is when people do wrong things willfully that they are the more likely to do them again. Come.'

And still she held out her arms.

'But, grandmother, you're so beautiful and grand with your crown on; and I am so dirty with mud and rain! I should quite spoil your beautiful blue dress.'

With a merry little laugh the lady sprung from her chair, more lightly far than Irene herself could, caught the child to her bosom, and, kissing the tear-stained face over and over, sat down with her in her lap.

'Oh, grandmother! You'll make yourself such a mess!' cried Irene, clinging to her.

'You darling! do you think I care more for my dress than for my little girl? Besides - look here.'

As she spoke she set her down, and Irene saw to her dismay that the lovely dress was covered with the mud of her fall on the mountain road. But the lady stooped to the fire, and taking from it, by the stalk in her fingers, one of the burning roses, passed it once and again and a third time over the front of her dress; and when Irene looked, not a single stain was to be discovered.

'There!' said her grandmother, 'you won't mind coming to me now?'

But Irene again hung back, eying the flaming rose which the lady held in her hand.

'You're not afraid of the rose - are you?' she said, about to throw it on the hearth again. 'Oh! don't, please!' cried Irene. 'Won't you hold it to my frock and my hands and my face? And I'm afraid my feet and my knees want it too.' 'No, answered her grandmother, smiling a little sadly, as she threw the rose from her; 'it is too hot for you yet. It would set your frock in a flame. Besides, I don't want to make you clean tonight.

I want your nurse and the rest of the people to see you as you are, for you will have to tell them how you ran away for fear of the long-legged cat. I should like to wash you, but they would not believe you then. Do you see that bath behind you?'

The princess looked, and saw a large oval tub of silver, shining brilliantly in the light of the wonderful lamp.

'Go and look into it,' said the lady.

Irene went, and came back very silent with her eyes shining.

'What did you see?' asked her grandmother.

'The sky, and the moon and the stars,' she answered. 'It looked as if there was no bottom to it.'

The lady smiled a pleased satisfied smile, and was silent also for a few moments. Then she said:

'Any time you want a bath, come to me. I know you have a bath every morning, but sometimes you want one at night, too.'

'Thank you, grandmother; I will - I will indeed,' answered Irene, and was again silent for some moments thinking. Then she said: 'How was it, grandmother, that I saw your beautiful lamp - not the light of it only - but the great round silvery lamp itself, hanging alone in the great open air, high up? It was your lamp I saw - wasn't it?'

'Yes, my child - it was my lamp.'

'Then how was it? I don't see a window all round.'

'When I please I can make the lamp shine through the walls – shine so strong that it melts them away from before the sight, and shows itself as you saw it. But, as I told you, it is not everybody can see it.'

'How is it that I can, then? I'm sure I don't know.'

'It is a gift born with you. And one day I hope everybody will have it.'

'But how do you make it shine through the walls?'

'Ah! that you would not understand if I were to try ever so much to make you - not yet - not yet. But,' added the lady, rising, 'you must sit in my chair while I get you the present I have been preparing for you. I told you my spinning was for you. It is finished now, and I am going to fetch it. I have been keeping it warm under one of my brooding pigeons.'

Irene sat down in the low chair, and her grandmother left her, shutting the door behind her. The child sat gazing, now at the rose fire, now at the starry walls, now at the silver light; and a great quietness grew in her heart. If all the long-legged cats in the world had come rushing at her then she would not have been afraid of them for a moment. How this was she could not tell – she only knew there was no fear in her, and everything was so right and safe that it could not get in.

She had been gazing at the lovely lamp for some minutes fixedly: turning her eyes, she found the wall had vanished, for she was looking out on the dark cloudy night. But though she heard the wind blowing, none of it blew upon her. In a moment more the clouds themselves parted, or rather vanished like the wall, and she looked straight into the starry herds, flashing gloriously in the dark blue. It was but for a moment. The clouds gathered again and shut out the stars; the wall gathered again and shut out the clouds; and there stood the lady beside her with the loveliest smile on her face, and a shimmering ball in her hand, about the size of a pigeon's egg.

'There, Irene; there is my work for you!' she said, holding out the ball to the princess.

She took it in her hand, and looked at it all over. It sparkled a little, and shone here and there, but not much. It was of a sort of grey-whiteness, something like spun glass.

'Is this all your spinning, grandmother?' she asked.

'All since you came to the house. There is more there than you think.'

'How pretty it is! What am I to do with it, please?'

'That I will now explain to you,' answered the lady, turning from her and going to her cabinet. She came back with a small ring in her hand. Then she took the ball from Irene's, and did something with the ring - Irene could not tell what.

'Give me your hand,' she said. Irene held up her right hand.

'Yes, that is the hand I want,' said the lady, and put the ring on the forefinger of it.

'What a beautiful ring!' said Irene. 'What is the stone called?'

'It is a fire-opal.' 'Please, am I to keep it?'

'Always.' 'Oh, thank you, grandmother! It's prettier than anything I ever saw, except those - of all colors-in your - Please, is that your crown?'

'Yes, it is my crown. The stone in your ring is of the same sort - only not so good. It has only red, but mine have all colors, you see.'

'Yes, grandmother. I will take such care of it! But -' she added, hesitating.

'But what?' asked her grandmother.

'What am I to say when Lootie asks me where I got it?'

'You will ask her where you got it,' answered the lady smiling.

'I don't see how I can do that.'

'You will, though.'

'Of course I will, if you say so. But, you know, I can't pretend not to know.'

'Of course not. But don't trouble yourself about it. You will see when the time comes.'

So saying, the lady turned, and threw the little ball into the rose fire.

'Oh, grandmother!' exclaimed Irene; 'I thought you had spun it for me.'

'So I did, my child. And you've got it.'

'No; it's burnt in the fire!'

The lady put her hand in the fire, brought out the ball, glimmering as before, and held it towards her. Irene stretched out her hand to take it, but the lady turned and, going to her cabinet, opened a drawer, and laid the ball in it.

'Have I done anything to vex you, grandmother?' said Irene pitifully.

'No, my darling. But you must understand that no one ever gives anything to another properly and really without keeping it. That ball is yours.'

'Oh! I'm not to take it with me! You are going to keep it for me!'

'You are to take it with you. I've fastened the end of it to the ring on your finger.'

Irene looked at the ring.

'I can't see it there, grandmother,' she said.

'Feel - a little way from the ring - towards the cabinet,' said the lady.

'Oh! I do feel it!' exclaimed the princess. 'But I can't see it,' she added, looking close to her outstretched hand.

'No. The thread is too fine for you to see it. You can only feel it. Now you can fancy how much spinning that took, although it does seem such a little ball.'

'But what use can I make of it, if it lies in your cabinet?'

'That is what I will explain to you. It would be of no use to you - it wouldn't be yours at all if it did not lie in my cabinet. Now listen. If ever you find yourself in any danger - such, for example, as you were in this same evening - you must take off your ring and put it under the pillow of your bed. Then you must lay your finger, the same that wore the ring, upon the thread, and follow the thread wherever it leads you.'

'Oh, how delightful! It will lead me to you, grandmother, I know!'

'Yes. But, remember, it may seem to you a very roundabout way indeed, and you must not doubt the thread. Of one thing you may be sure, that while you hold it, I hold it too.'

'It is very wonderful!' said Irene thoughtfully. Then suddenly becoming aware, she jumped up, crying:

'Oh, grandmother! here have I been sitting all this time in your chair, and you standing! I beg your pardon.'

The lady laid her hand on her shoulder, and said:

'Sit down again, Irene. Nothing pleases me better than to see anyone sit in my chair. I am only too glad to stand so long as anyone will sit in it.'

'How kind of you!' said the princess, and sat down again.

'It makes me happy,' said the lady.

'But,' said Irene, still puzzled, 'won't the thread get in somebody's way and be broken, if the one end is fast to my ring, and the other laid in your cabinet?'

'You will find all that arrange itself. I am afraid it is time for you to go.'

'Mightn't I stay and sleep with you tonight, grandmother?' 'No, not tonight. If I had meant you to stay tonight, I should have given you a bath; but you know everybody in the house is miserable about you, and it would be cruel to keep them so all night. You must go downstairs.'

'I'm so glad, grandmother, you didn't say "Go home," for this is my home. Mayn't I call this my home?'

'You may, my child. And I trust you will always think it your home. Now come. I must take you back without anyone seeing you.'

'Please, I want to ask you one question more,' said Irene. 'Is it because you have your crown on that you look so young?'

'No, child,' answered her grandmother; 'it is because I felt so young this evening that I put my crown on. And I thought you would like to see your old grandmother in her best.'

'Why do you call yourself old? You're not old, grandmother.'

'I am very old indeed. It is so silly of people - I don't mean you, for you are such a tiny, and couldn't know better - but it is so silly of people to fancy that old age means crookedness and witheredness and feebleness and sticks and spectacles and rheumatism and forgetfulness! It is so silly! Old age has nothing whatever to do with all that. The right old age means strength and beauty and mirth and courage and clear eyes and strong painless limbs. I am older than you are able to think, and -'

'And look at you, grandmother!' cried Irene, jumping up and flinging her arms about her neck. 'I won't be so silly again, I promise you. At least - I'm rather afraid to promise - but if I am, I promise to be sorry for it - I do. I wish I were as old as you, grandmother. I don't think you are ever afraid of anything.'

'Not for long, at least, my child. Perhaps by the time I am two thousand years of age, I shall, indeed, never be afraid of anything. But I confess I have sometimes been afraid about my children - sometimes about you, Irene.'

'Oh, I'm so sorry, grandmother! Tonight, I suppose, you mean.'

'Yes - a little tonight; but a good deal when you had all but made up your mind that I was a dream, and no real great-great-grandmother. You must not suppose I am blaming you for that. I dare say you could not help it.'

'I don't know, grandmother,' said the princess, beginning to cry. 'I can't always do myself as I should like. And I don't always try. I'm very sorry anyhow.'

The lady stooped, lifted her in her arms, and sat down with her in her chair, holding her close to her bosom. In a few minutes the princess had sobbed herself to sleep. How long she slept I do not know. When she came to herself she was sitting in her own high chair at the nursery table, with her doll's house before her.

16. THE RING

The same moment her nurse came into the room, sobbing. When she saw her sitting there she started back with a loud cry of amazement and joy. Then running to her, she caught her in her arms and covered her with kisses.

'My precious darling princess! where have you been? What has happened to you? We've all been crying our eyes out, and searching the house from top to bottom for you.'

'Not quite from the top,' thought Irene to herself; and she might have added, 'not quite to the bottom', perhaps, if she had known all. But the one she would not, and the other she could not say. 'Oh, Lootie! I've had such a dreadful adventure!' she replied, and told her all about the cat with the long legs, and how she ran out upon the mountain, and came back again. But she said nothing of her grandmother or her lamp.

'And there we've been searching for you all over the house for more than an hour and a half!' exclaimed the nurse. 'But that's no matter, now we've got you! Only, princess, I must say,' she added, her mood changing, 'what you ought to have done was to call for your own Lootie to come and help you, instead of running out of the house, and up the mountain, in that wild, I must say, foolish fashion.'

'Well, Lootie,' said Irene quietly, 'perhaps if you had a big cat, all legs, running at you, you might not exactly know what was the wisest thing to do at the moment.'

'I wouldn't run up the mountain, anyhow,' returned Lootie.

'Not if you had time to think about it. But when those creatures came at you that night on the mountain, you were so frightened yourself that you lost your way home.'

This put a stop to Lootie's reproaches. She had been on the point of saying that the long-legged cat must have been a twilight fancy of the princess's, but the memory of the horrors of that night, and of the talking-to which the king had given her in consequence, prevented her from saying what after all she did not half believe - having a strong suspicion that the cat was a goblin; for she knew nothing of the difference between the goblins and their creatures: she counted them all just goblins.

Without another word she went and got some fresh tea and bread and butter for the princess. Before she returned, the whole household, headed by the housekeeper, burst into the nursery to exult over their darling. The gentlemen-at-arms followed, and were ready enough to believe all she told them about the long-legged cat. Indeed, though wise enough to say nothing about it, they remembered, with no little horror, just such a creature amongst those they had surprised at their gambols upon the princess's lawn.

In their own hearts they blamed themselves for not having kept better watch. And their captain gave orders that from this night the front door and all the windows on the ground floor should be locked immediately the sun set, and opened after upon no pretence whatever. The men-at-arms redoubled their vigilance, and for some time there was no further cause of alarm.

When the princess woke the next morning, her nurse was bending over her. 'How your ring does glow this morning, princess! - just like a fiery rose!' she said.

'Does it, Lootie?' returned Irene. 'Who gave me the ring, Lootie? I know I've had it a long time, but where did I get it? I don't remember.'

'I think it must have been your mother gave it you, princess; but really, for as long as you have worn it, I don't remember that ever I heard,' answered her nurse.

'I will ask my king-papa the next time he comes,' said Irene.

17. SPRINGTIME

The spring so dear to all creatures, young and old, came at last, and before the first few days of it had gone, the king rode through its budding valleys to see his little daughter. He had been in a distant part of his dominions all the winter, for he was not in the habit of stopping in one great city, or of visiting only his favorite country houses, but he moved from place to place, that all his people might know him. Wherever he journeyed, he kept a constant look-out for the ablest and best men to put into office; and wherever he found himself mistaken, and those he had appointed incapable or unjust, he removed them at once. Hence you see it was his care of the people that kept him from seeing his princess so often as he would have liked. You may wonder why he did not take her about with him; but there were several reasons against his doing so, and I suspect her great-great-grandmother had had a principal hand in preventing it. Once more Irene heard the bugle-blast, and once more she was at the gate to meet her father as he rode up on his great white horse.

After they had been alone for a little while, she thought of what she had resolved to ask him. 'Please, king-papa,' she said, 'Will you tell me where I got this pretty ring? I can't remember.'

The king looked at it. A strange beautiful smile spread like sunshine over his face, and an answering smile, but at the same time a questioning one, spread like moonlight over Irene's. 'It was your queen-mamma's once,' he said.

'And why isn't it hers now?' asked Irene.

'She does not want it now,' said the king, looking grave.

'Why doesn't she want it now?'

'Because she's gone where all those rings are made.'

'And when shall I see her?' asked the princess.

'Not for some time yet,' answered the king, and the tears came into his eyes.

Irene did not remember her mother and did not know why her father looked so, and why the tears came in his eyes; but she put her arms round his neck and kissed him, and asked no more questions.

The king was much disturbed on hearing the report of the gentlemen-at-arms concerning the creatures they had seen; and I presume would have taken Irene with him that very day, but for what the presence of the ring on her finger assured him of. About an hour before he left, Irene saw him go up the old stair; and he did not come down again till they were just ready to start; and she thought with herself that he had been up to see the old lady. When he went away he left other six gentlemen behind him, that there might be six of them always on guard.

And now, in the lovely spring weather, Irene was out on the mountain the greater part of the day. In the warmer hollows there were lovely primroses, and not so many that she ever got tired of them. As often as she saw a new one opening an eye of light in the blind earth, she would clap her hands with gladness, and unlike some children I know, instead of pulling it, would touch it as tenderly as if it had been a new baby, and, having made its acquaintance, would leave it as happy as she found it. She treated the plants on which they grew like birds' nests; every fresh flower was like a new little bird to her. She would pay visits to all the flower-nests she knew, remembering each by itself. She would go down on her hands and knees beside one and say: 'Good morning! Are you all smelling very sweet this morning? Good-bye!' and then she would go to another nest, and say the same. It was a favorite amusement with her. There were many flowers up and down, and she loved them all, but the primroses were her favorites.

'They're not too shy, and they're not a bit forward,' she would say to Lootie. There were goats too about, over the mountain, and when the little kids came she was as pleased with them as with the flowers. The goats belonged to the miners mostly-a few of them to Curdie's mother; but there were a good many wild ones that seemed to belong to nobody. These goblins counted theirs, and it was upon them partly that they lived. They set snares and dug pits for them; and did not scruple to take what tame ones happened to be caught; but they did not try to steal them in any other manner, because they were afraid of the dogs the hill-people kept to watch them, for the knowing dogs always tried to bite their feet. But the goblins had a kind of sheep of their own - very queer creatures, which they drove out to feed at night, and the other goblin creatures were wise enough to keep good watch over them, for they knew they should have their bones by and by.

18. Curdie's Clue

Curdie was as watchful as ever, but was almost getting tired of his ill success. Every other night or so he followed the goblins about, as they went on digging and boring, and getting as near them as he could, watched them from behind stones and rocks; but as yet he seemed no nearer finding out what they had in view. As at first, he always kept hold of the end of his string, while his pickaxe, left just outside the hole by which he entered the goblins' country from the mine, continued to serve as an anchor and hold fast the other end. The goblins, hearing no more noise in that quarter, had ceased to apprehend an immediate invasion, and kept no watch.

One night, after dodging about and listening till he was nearly falling asleep with weariness, he began to roll up his ball, for he had resolved to go home to bed. It was not long, however, before he began to feel bewildered. One after another he passed goblin houses, caves, that is, occupied by goblin families, and at length was sure they were many more than he had passed as he came. He had to use great caution to pass unseen - they lay so close together. Could his string have led him wrong? He still followed winding it, and still it led him into more thickly populated quarters, until he became quite uneasy, and indeed apprehensive; for although he was not afraid of the cobs, he was afraid of not finding his way out. But what could he do? It was of no use to sit down and wait for the morning - the morning made no difference here. It was dark, and always dark; and if his string failed him he was helpless. He might even arrive within a yard of the mine and never know it. Seeing he could do nothing better he would at least find where the end of his string was, and, if possible, how it had come to play him such a trick. He knew by the size of the ball that he was getting pretty near the last of it, when he began to feel a tugging and pulling at it. What could it mean? Turning a sharp corner, he thought he heard strange sounds. These grew, as he went on, to a scuffling and growling and squeaking; and the noise increased, until, turning a second sharp corner, he found himself in the midst of it, and the same moment tumbled over a wallowing mass, which he knew must be a knot of the cobs' creatures. Before he could recover his feet, he had caught some great scratches on his face and several severe bites on his legs and arms. But as he scrambled to get up, his hand fell upon his pickaxe, and before the horrid beasts could do him any serious harm, he was laying about with it right and left in the dark. The hideous cries which followed gave him the satisfaction of knowing that he had punished some of them pretty smartly for their rudeness, and by their scampering and their retreating howls, he perceived that he had routed them. He stood for a little, weighing his battle-axe in his hand as if it had been the most precious lump of metal - but indeed no lump of gold itself could have been so precious at the time as that common tool - then untied the end of the string from it, put the ball in his pocket, and still stood thinking. It was clear that the cobs' creatures had found his axe, had between them carried it off, and had so led him he knew not where. But for all his thinking he could not tell what he ought to do, until suddenly he became aware of a glimmer of light in the distance. Without a moment's hesitation he set out for it, as fast as the unknown and rugged way would permit. Yet again turning a corner, led by the dim light, he spied something quite new in his experience of the underground regions - a small irregular shape of something shining. Going up to it, he found it was a piece of mica, or Muscovy glass, called sheep-silver in Scotland, and the light flickered as if from a fire behind it. After trying in vain for some time to discover an entrance to the place where it was burning, he came at length to a small chamber in which an opening, high in the wall, revealed a glow beyond. To this opening he managed to scramble up, and then he saw a strange sight.

Below sat a little group of goblins around a fire, the smoke of which vanished in the darkness far aloft. The sides of the cave were full of shining minerals like those of the palace hall; and the company was evidently of a superior order, for every one wore stones about head, or arms, or waist, shining dull gorgeous colors in the light of the fire. Nor had Curdie looked long before he recognized the king himself, and found that he had made his way into the inner apartment of the royal family. He had never had such a good chance of hearing something. He crept through the hole as softly as he could, scrambled a good way down the wall towards them without attracting attention, and then sat down and listened. The king, evidently the queen, and probably the crown prince and the Prime Minister were talking together. He was sure of the queen by her shoes, for as she warmed her feet at the fire, he saw them quite plainly.

'That will be fun!' said the one he took for the crown prince. It was the first whole sentence he heard.

'I don't see why you should think it such a grand affair!' said his stepmother, tossing her head backward.

'You must remember, my spouse,' interposed His Majesty, as if making excuse for his son, 'he has got the same blood in him. His mother -'

'Don't talk to me of his mother! You positively encourage his unnatural fancies. Whatever belongs to that mother ought to be cut out of him.'

'You forget yourself, my dear!' said the king.

'I don't,' said the queen, 'nor you either. If you expect me to approve of such coarse tastes, you will find yourself mistaken. I don't wear shoes for nothing.'

'You must acknowledge, however,' the king said, with a little groan, 'that this at least is no whim of Harelip's, but a matter of State policy. You are well aware that his gratification comes purely from the pleasure of sacrificing himself to the public good.

Does it not, Harelip?'

'Yes, father; of course it does. Only it will be nice to make her cry. I'll have the skin taken off between her toes, and tie them up till they grow together. Then her feet will be like other people's, and there will be no occasion for her to wear shoes.'

'Do you mean to insinuate I've got toes, you unnatural wretch?' cried the queen; and she moved angrily towards Harelip. The councilor, however, who was betwixt them, leaned forward so as to prevent her touching him, but only as if to address the prince.

'Your Royal Highness,' he said, 'possibly requires to be reminded that you have got three toes yourself - one on one foot, two on the other.'

'Ha! ha! ha!' shouted the queen triumphantly. The councilor, encouraged by this mark of favor, went on.

'It seems to me, Your Royal Highness, it would greatly endear you to your future people, proving to them that you are not the less one of themselves that you had the misfortune to be born of a sun-mother, if you were to command upon yourself the comparatively slight operation which, in a more extended form, you so wisely meditate with regard to your future princess.'

'Ha! ha! ha!' laughed the queen louder than before, and the king and the minister joined in the laugh. Harelip growled, and for a few moments the others continued to express their enjoyment of his discomfiture.

The queen was the only one Curdie could see with any distinctness. She sat sideways to him, and the light of the fire shone full upon her face. He could not consider her handsome. Her nose was certainly broader at the end than its extreme length, and her eyes, instead of being horizontal, were set up like two perpendicular eggs, one on the broad, the other on the small end. Her mouth was no bigger than a small buttonhole until she laughed, when it stretched from ear to ear - only, to be sure, her ears were very nearly in the middle of her cheeks.

Anxious to hear everything they might say, Curdie ventured to slide down a smooth part of the rock just under him, to a projection below, upon which he thought to rest. But whether he was not careful enough, or the projection gave way, down he came with a rush on the floor of the cavern, bringing with him a great rumbling shower of stones.

The goblins jumped from their seats in more anger than consternation, for they had never yet seen anything to be afraid of in the palace. But when they saw Curdie with his pick in his hand their rage was mingled with fear, for they took him for the first of an invasion of miners. The king notwithstanding drew himself up to his full height of four feet, spread himself to his full breadth of three and a half, for he was the handsomest and squarest of all the goblins, and strutting up to Curdie, planted himself with outspread feet before him, and said with dignity:

'Pray what right have you in my palace?'

'The right of necessity, Your Majesty,' answered Curdie. 'I lost my way and did not know where I was wandering to.'

'How did you get in?'

'By a hole in the mountain.'

'But you are a miner! Look at your pickaxe!'

Curdie did look at it, answering:

'I came upon it lying on the ground a little way from here. I tumbled over some wild beasts who were playing with it. Look, Your Majesty.' And Curdie showed him how he was scratched and bitten.

The king was pleased to find him behave more politely than he had expected from what his people had told him concerning the miners, for he attributed it to the power of his own presence; but he did not therefore feel friendly to the intruder.

'You will oblige me by walking out of my dominions at once,' he said, well knowing what a mockery lay in the words.

'With pleasure, if Your Majesty will give me a guide,' said Curdie.

'I will give you a thousand,' said the king with a scoffing air of magnificent liberality.

'One will be quite sufficient,' said Curdie.

But the king uttered a strange shout, half halloo, half roar, and in rushed goblins till the cave was swarming. He said something to the first of them which Curdie could not hear, and it was passed from one to another till in a moment the farthest in the crowd had evidently heard and understood it. They began to gather about him in a way he did not relish, and he retreated towards the wall. They pressed upon him.

'Stand back,' said Curdie, grasping his pickaxe tighter by his knee.

They only grinned and pressed closer. Curdie bethought himself and began to rhyme.

'Ten, twenty, thirty -
You're all so very dirty!
Twenty, thirty, forty -
You're all so thick and snorty!
'Thirty, forty, fifty -
You're all so puff-and-snifty!
Forty, fifty, sixty -
Beast and man so mixty!
'Fifty, sixty, seventy -

Mixty, maxty, leaventy!

Sixty, seventy, eighty -

All your cheeks so slaty!

'Seventy, eighty, ninety,

All your hands so flinty!

Eighty, ninety, hundred,

Altogether dundred!'

The goblins fell back a little when he began, and made horrible grimaces all through the rhyme, as if eating something so disagreeable that it set their teeth on edge and gave them the creeps; but whether it was that the rhyming words were most of them no words at all, for, a new rhyme being considered the more efficacious, Curdie had made it on the spur of the moment, or whether it was that the presence of the king and queen gave them courage, I cannot tell; but the moment the rhyme was over they crowded on him again, and out shot a hundred long arms, with a multitude of thick nailless fingers at the ends of them, to lay hold upon him. Then Curdie heaved up his axe. But being as gentle as courageous and not wishing to kill any of them, he turned the end which was square and blunt like a hammer, and with that came down a great blow on the head of the goblin nearest him. Hard as the heads of all goblins are, he thought he must feel that. And so he did, no doubt; but he only gave a horrible cry, and sprung at Curdie's throat. Curdie, however, drew back in time, and just at that critical moment remembered the vulnerable part of the goblin body. He made a sudden rush at the king and stamped with all his might on His Majesty's feet. The king gave a most un-kingly howl and almost fell into the fire. Curdie then rushed into the crowd, stamping right and left. The goblins drew back, howling on every side as he approached, but they were so crowded that few of those he attacked could escape his tread; and the shrieking and roaring that filled the cave would have appalled Curdie but for the good hope it gave him. They were tumbling over each other in heaps in their eagerness to rush from the cave, when a new assailant suddenly faced him - the queen, with flaming eyes and expanded nostrils, her hair standing half up from her head, rushed at him. She trusted in her shoes: they were of granite - hollowed like French sabots. Curdie would have endured much rather than hurt a woman, even if she was a goblin; but here was an affair of life and death: forgetting her shoes, he made a great stamp on one of her feet. But she instantly returned it with very different effect, causing him frightful pain, and almost disabling him. His only chance with her would have been to attack the granite shoes with his pickaxe, but before he could think of that she had caught him up in her arms and was rushing with him across the cave. She dashed him into a hole in the wall, with a force that almost stunned him. But although he could not move, he was not too far gone to hear her great cry, and the rush of multitudes of soft feet, followed by the sounds of something heaved up against the rock; after which came a multitudinous patter of stones falling near him. The last had not ceased when he grew very faint, for his head had been badly cut, and at last insensible.

When he came to himself there was perfect silence about him, and utter darkness, but for the merest glimmer in one tiny spot. He crawled to it, and found that they had heaved a slab against the mouth of the hole, past the edge of which a poor little gleam found its way from the fire. He could not move it a hairbreadth, for they had piled a great heap of stones against it. He crawled back to where he had been lying, in the faint hope of finding his pickaxe, But after a vain search he was at last compelled to acknowledge himself in an evil plight. He sat down and tried to think, but soon fell fast asleep.

19. GOBLIN COUNSELS

He must have slept a long time, for when he awoke he felt wonderfully restored - indeed almost well - and very hungry. There were voices in the outer cave.

Once more, then, it was night; for the goblins slept during the day and went about their affairs during the night.

In the universal and constant darkness of their dwelling they had no reason to prefer the one arrangement to the other; but from aversion to the sun-people they chose to be busy when there was least chance of their being met either by the miners below, when they were burrowing, or by the people of the mountain above, when they were feeding their sheep or catching their goats. And indeed it was only when the sun was away that the outside of the mountain was sufficiently like their own dismal regions to be endurable to their mole eyes, so thoroughly had they become unaccustomed to any light beyond that of their own fires and torches.

Curdie listened, and soon found that they were talking of himself.

'How long will it take?' asked Harelip.

'Not many days, I should think,' answered the king. 'They are poor feeble creatures, those sun-people, and want to be always eating. We can go a week at a time without food, and be all the better for it; but I've been told they eat two or three times every day! Can you believe it? They must be quite hollow inside - not at all like us, nine-tenths of whose bulk is solid flesh and bone. Yes – I judge a week of starvation will do for him.' 'If I may be allowed a word,' interposed the queen, - 'and I think I ought to have some voice in the matter -'

'The wretch is entirely at your disposal, my spouse,' interrupted the king. 'He is your property. You caught him yourself. We should never have done it.'

The queen laughed. She seemed in far better humor than the night before.

'I was about to say,' she resumed, 'that it does seem a pity to waste so much fresh meat.'

'What are you thinking of, my love?' said the king. 'The very notion of starving him implies that we are not going to give him any meat, either salt or fresh.'

'I'm not such a stupid as that comes to,' returned Her Majesty. 'What I mean is that by the time he is starved there will hardly be a picking upon his bones.'

The king gave a great laugh.

'Well, my spouse, you may have him when you like,' he said. 'I don't fancy him for my part. I am pretty sure he is tough eating.'

'That would be to honor instead of punish his insolence,' returned the queen. 'But why should our poor creatures be deprived of so much nourishment? Our little dogs and cats and pigs and small bears would enjoy him very much.'

'You are the best of housekeepers, my lovely queen!' said her husband. 'Let it be so by all means. Let us have our people in, and get him out and kill him at once. He deserves it. The mischief he might have brought upon us, now that he had penetrated so far as our most retired citadel, is incalculable. Or rather let us tie him hand and foot, and have the pleasure of seeing him torn to pieces by full torchlight in the great hall.'

'Better and better!' cried the queen and the prince together, both of them clapping their hands. And the prince made an ugly noise with his hare-lip, just as if he had intended to be one at the feast.

'But,' added the queen, bethinking herself, 'he is so troublesome. For poor creatures as they are, there is something about those sun-people that is very troublesome. I cannot imagine how it is that with such superior strength and skill and understanding as ours, we permit them to exist at all. Why do we not destroy them entirely, and use their cattle and grazing lands at our pleasure?

Of course we don't want to live in their horrid country! It is far too glaring for our quieter and more refined tastes. But we might use it as a sort of outhouse, you know. Even our creatures' eyes might get used to it, and if they did grow blind that would be of no consequence, provided they grew fat as well. But we might even keep their great cows and other creatures, and then we should have a few more luxuries, such as cream and cheese, which at present we only taste occasionally, when our brave men have succeeded in carrying some off from their farms.'

'It is worth thinking of,' said the king; 'and I don't know why you should be the first to suggest it, except that you have a positive genius for conquest. But still, as you say, there is something very troublesome about them; and it would be better, as I understand you to suggest, that we should starve him for a day or two first, so that he may be a little less frisky when we take him out.'

'Once there was a goblin Living in a hole; Busy he was cobblin' A shoe without a sole.

'By came a birdie: "Goblin, what do you do?" "Cobble at a sturdie Upper leather shoe."

'"What's the good o' that, Sir?" Said the little bird. "Why it's very Pat, Sir - Plain without a word.

'"Where 'tis all a hole, Sir, Never can be holes: Why should their shoes have soles, Sir, When they've got no souls?"'

'What's that horrible noise?' cried the queen, shuddering from pot-metal head to granite shoes.

'I declare,' said the king with solemn indignation, 'it's the sun-creature in the hole!'

'Stop that disgusting noise!' cried the crown prince valiantly, getting up and standing in front of the heap of stones, with his face towards Curdie's prison. 'Do now, or I'll break your head.'

'Break away,' shouted Curdie, and began singing again:

'Once there was a goblin, Living in a hole -'

'I really cannot bear it,' said the queen. 'If I could only get at his horrid toes with my slippers again!' 'I think we had better go to bed,' said the king.

'It's not time to go to bed,' said the queen.

'I would if I was you,' said Curdie.

'Impertinent wretch!' said the queen, with the utmost scorn in her voice.

'An impossible if,' said His Majesty with dignity.

'Quite,' returned Curdie, and began singing again:

'Go to bed, Goblin, do. Help the queen Take off her shoe.

'If you do, It will disclose A horrid set Of sprouting toes.'

'What a lie!' roared the queen in a rage.

'By the way, that reminds me,' said the king, 'that for as long as we have been married, I have never seen your feet, queen. I think you might take off your shoes when you go to bed! They positively hurt me sometimes.'

'I will do as I like,' retorted the queen sulkily.

'You ought to do as your own hubby wishes you,' said the king.

'I will not,' said the queen.

'Then I insist upon it,' said the king.

Apparently His Majesty approached the queen for the purpose of following the advice given by Curdie, for the latter heard a scuffle, and then a great roar from the king.

'Will you be quiet, then?' said the queen wickedly.

'Yes, yes, queen. I only meant to coax you.'

'Hands off!' cried the queen triumphantly. 'I'm going to bed. You may come when you like. But as long as I am queen I will sleep in my shoes. It is my royal privilege. Harelip, go to bed.'

'I'm going,' said Harelip sleepily.

'So am I,' said the king.

'Come along, then,' said the queen; 'and mind you are good, or I'll -'

'Oh, no, no, no!' screamed the king in the most supplicating of tones.

Curdie heard only a muttered reply in the distance; and then the cave was quite still.

They had left the fire burning, and the light came through brighter than before. Curdie thought it was time to try again if anything could be done. But he found he could not get even a finger through the chink between the slab and the rock. He gave a great rush with his shoulder against the slab, but it yielded no more than if it had been part of the rock. All he could do was to sit down and think again.

By and by he came to the resolution to pretend to be dying, in the hope they might take him out before his strength was too much exhausted to let him have a chance. Then, for the creatures, if he could but find his axe again, he would have no fear of them; and if it were not for the queen's horrid shoes, he would have no fear at all. Meantime, until they should come again at night, there was nothing for him to do but forge new rhymes, now his only weapons. He had no intention of using them at present, of course; but it was well to have a stock, for he might live to want them, and the manufacture of them would help to while away the time.

20. IRENE'S CLUE

That same morning early, the princess woke in a terrible fright. There was a hideous noise in her room - creatures snarling and hissing and rocketing about as if they were fighting. The moment she came to herself, she remembered something she had never thought of again - what her grandmother told her to do when she was frightened. She immediately took off her ring and put it under her pillow. As she did so she fancied she felt a finger and thumb take it gently from under her palm. 'It must be my grandmother!' she said to herself, and the thought gave her such courage that she stopped to put on her dainty little slippers before running from the room. While doing this she caught sight of a long cloak of sky-blue, thrown over the back of a chair by the bedside. She had never seen it before but it was evidently waiting for her. She put it on, and then, feeling with the forefinger of her right hand, soon found her grandmother's thread, which she proceeded at once to follow, expecting it would lead her straight up the old stair. When she reached the door she found it went down and ran along the floor, so that she had almost to crawl in order to keep a hold of it. Then, to her surprise, and somewhat to her dismay, she found that instead of leading her towards the stair it turned in quite the opposite direction. It led her through certain narrow passages towards the kitchen, turning aside ere she reached it, and guiding her to a door which communicated with a small back yard. Some of the maids were already up, and this door was standing open. Across the yard the thread still ran along the ground, until it brought her to a door in the wall which opened upon the Mountainside. When she had passed through, the thread rose to about half her height, and she could hold it with ease as she walked. It led her straight up the mountain.

The cause of her alarm was less frightful than she supposed. The cook's great black cat, pursued by the housekeeper's terrier, had bounced against her bedroom door, which had not been properly fastened, and the two had burst into the room together and commenced a battle royal. How the nurse came to sleep through it was a mystery, but I suspect the old lady had something to do with it.

It was a clear warm morning. The wind blew deliciously over the Mountainside. Here and there she saw a late primrose but she did not stop to call upon them. The sky was mottled with small clouds.

The sun was not yet up, but some of their fluffy edges had caught his light, and hung out orange and gold-colored fringes upon the air. The dew lay in round drops upon the leaves, and hung like tiny diamond ear-rings from the blades of grass about her path.

'How lovely that bit of gossamer is!' thought the princess, looking at a long undulating line that shone at some distance from her up the hill. It was not the time for gossamers though; and Irene soon discovered that it was her own thread she saw shining on before her in the light of the morning. It was leading her she knew not whither; but she had never in her life been out before sunrise, and everything was so fresh and cool and lively and full of something coming, that she felt too happy to be afraid of anything.

After leading her up a good distance, the thread turned to the left, and down the path upon which she and Lootie had met Curdie. But she never thought of that, for now in the morning light, with its far outlook over the country, no path could have been more open and airy and cheerful. She could see the road almost to the horizon, along which she had so often watched her king-papa and his troop come shining, with the bugle- blast cleaving the air before them; and it was like a companion to her. Down and down the path went, then up, and then down and then up again, getting rugged and more rugged as it went; and still along the path went the silvery thread, and still along the thread went Irene's little rosy-tipped forefinger. By and by she came to a little stream that jabbered and prattled down the hill, and up the side of the stream went both path and thread. And still the path grew rougher and steeper, and the mountain grew wilder, till Irene began to think she was going a very long way from home; and when she turned to look back she saw that the level country had vanished and the rough bare mountain had closed in about her. But still on went the thread, and on went the princess. Everything around her was getting brighter and brighter as the sun came nearer; till at length his first rays all at once alighted on the top of a rock before her, like some golden creature fresh from the sky. Then she saw that the little stream ran out of a hole in that rock, that the path did not go past the rock, and that the thread was leading her straight up to it. A shudder ran through her from head to foot when she found that the thread was actually taking her into the hole out of which the stream ran. It ran out babbling joyously, but she had to go in.

She did not hesitate. Right into the hole she went, which was high enough to let her walk without stooping. For a little way there was a brown glimmer, but at the first turn it all but ceased, and before she had gone many paces she was in total darkness. Then she began to be frightened indeed. Every moment she kept feeling the thread backwards and forwards, and as she went farther and farther into the darkness of the great hollow mountain, she kept thinking more and more about her grandmother, and all that she had said to her, and how kind she had been, and how beautiful she was, and all about her lovely room, and the fire of roses, and the great lamp that sent its light through stone walls. And she became more and more sure that the thread could not have gone there of itself, and that her grandmother must have sent it. But it tried her dreadfully when the path went down very steep, and especially When she came to places where she had to go down rough stairs, and even sometimes a ladder. Through one narrow passage after another, over lumps of rock and sand and clay, the thread guided her, until she came to a small hole through which she had to creep. Finding no change on the other side, 'Shall I ever get back?' she thought, over and over again, wondering at herself that she was not ten times more frightened, and often feeling as if she were only walking in the story of a dream. Sometimes she heard the noise of water, a dull gurgling inside the rock. By and by she heard the sounds of blows, which came nearer and nearer; but again they grew duller, and almost died away. In a hundred directions she turned, obedient to the guiding thread.

At last she spied a dull red shine, and came up to the mica window, and thence away and round about, and right, into a cavern, where glowed the red embers of a fire. Here the thread began to rise. It rose as high as her head and higher still. What should she do if she lost her hold? She was pulling it down: She might break it! She could see it far up, glowing as red as her fire-opal in the light of the embers.

But presently she came to a huge heap of stones, piled in a slope against the wall of the cavern. On these she climbed, and soon recovered the level of the thread only however to find, the next moment, that it vanished through the heap of stones, and left her standing on it, with her face to the solid rock. For one terrible moment she felt as if her grandmother had forsaken her. The thread which the spiders had spun far over the seas, which her grandmother had sat in the moonlight and spun again for her, which she had tempered in the rose-fire and tied to her opal ring, had left her - had gone where she could no longer follow it - had brought her into a horrible cavern, and there left her! She was forsaken indeed!

'When shall I wake?' she said to herself in an agony, but the same moment knew that it was no dream. She threw herself upon the heap, and began to cry. It was well she did not know what creatures, one of them with stone shoes on her feet, were lying in the next cave. But neither did she know who was on the other side of the slab.

At length the thought struck her that at least she could follow the thread backwards, and thus get out of the mountain, and home. She rose at once, and found the thread. But the instant she tried to feel it backwards, it vanished from her touch. Forwards, it led her hand up to the heap of stones - backwards it seemed nowhere. Neither could she see it as before in the light of the fire. She burst into a wailing cry, and again threw herself down on the stones.

21. THE ESCAPE

As the princess lay and sobbed she kept feeling the thread mechanically, following it with her finger many times up to the stones in which it disappeared. By and by she began, still mechanically, to poke her finger in after it between the stones as far as she could. All at once it came into her head that she might remove some of the stones and see where the thread went next. Almost laughing at herself for never having thought of this before, she jumped to her feet. Her fear vanished; once more she was certain her grandmother's thread could not have brought her there just to leave her there; and she began to throw away the stones from the top as fast as she could, sometimes two or three at a handful, sometimes taking both hands to lift one. After clearing them away a little, she found that the thread turned and went straight downwards. Hence, as the heap sloped a good deal, growing of course wider towards its base, she had to throw away a multitude of stones to follow the thread. But this was not all, for she soon found that the thread, after going straight down for a little way, turned first sideways in one direction, then sideways in another, and then shot, at various angles, hither and thither inside the heap, so that she began to be afraid that to clear the thread she must remove the whole huge gathering. She was dismayed at the very idea, but, losing no time, set to work with a will; and with aching back, and bleeding fingers and hands, she worked on, sustained by the pleasure of seeing the heap slowly diminish and begin to show itself on the opposite side of the fire. Another thing which helped to keep up her courage was that, as often as she uncovered a turn of the thread, instead of lying loose upon the stone, it tightened up; this made her sure that her grandmother was at the end of it somewhere.

She had got about half-way down when she started, and nearly fell with fright. Close to her ears as it seemed, a voice broke out singing:

'Jabber, bother, smash!

You'll have it all in a crash.

Jabber, smash, bother!

You'll have the worst of the pother.

Smash, bother, jabber! -'

Here Curdie stopped, either because he could not find a rhyme to 'jabber', or because he remembered what he had forgotten when he woke up at the sound of Irene's labors, that his plan was to make the goblins think he was getting weak. But he had uttered enough to let Irene know who he was.

'It's Curdie!' she cried joyfully.

'Hush! hush!' came Curdie's voice again from somewhere. 'Speak softly.'

'Why, you were singing loud!' said Irene.

'Yes. But they know I am here, and they don't know you are. Who are you?'

'I'm Irene,' answered the princess. 'I know who you are quite well. You're Curdie.'

'Why, how ever did you come here, Irene?'

'My great-great-grandmother sent me; and I think I've found out why. You can't get out, I suppose?'

'No, I can't. What are you doing?'

'Clearing away a huge heap of stones.'

'There's a princess!' exclaimed Curdie, in a tone of delight, but still speaking in little more than a whisper. 'I can't think how you got here, though.'

'my grandmother sent me after her thread.'

'I don't know what you mean,' said Curdie; 'but so you're there, it doesn't much matter.'

'Oh, yes, it does!' returned Irene. 'I should never have been here but for her.'

'You can tell me all about it when we get out, then. There's no time to lose now,' said Curdie.

And Irene went to work, as fresh as when she began.

'There's such allot of stones!' she said. 'It will take me a long time to get them all away.'

'How far on have you got?' asked Curdie.

'I've got about the half away, but the other half is ever so much bigger.'

'I don't think you will have to move the lower half. Do you see a slab laid up against the wall?'

Irene looked, and felt about with her hands, and soon perceived the outlines of the slab.

'Yes,' she answered, 'I do.'

'Then, I think,' rejoined Curdie, 'when you have cleared the slab about half-way down, or a bit more, I shall be able to push it over.'

'I must follow my thread,' returned Irene, 'whatever I do.'

'What do you mean?' exclaimed Curdie. 'You will see when you get out,' answered the princess, and went on harder than ever.

But she was soon satisfied that what Curdie wanted done and what the thread wanted done were one and the same thing. For she not only saw that by following the turns of the thread she had been clearing the face of the slab, but that, a little more than half-way down, the thread went through the chink between the slab and the wall into the place where Curdie was confined, so that she could not follow it any farther until the slab was out of her way. As soon as she found this, she said in a right joyous whisper:

'Now, Curdie, I think if you were to give a great push, the slab would tumble over.'

'Stand quite clear of it, then,' said Curdie, 'and let me know when you are ready.'

Irene got off the heap, and stood on one side of it. 'Now, Curdie!' she cried.

Curdie gave a great rush with his shoulder against it. Out tumbled the slab on the heap, and out crept Curdie over the top of it.

'You've saved my life, Irene!' he whispered.

'Oh, Curdie! I'm so glad! Let's get out of this horrid place as fast as we can.'

'That's easier said than done,' returned he.

'Oh, no, it's quite easy,' said Irene. 'We have only to follow my thread. I am sure that it's going to take us out now.'

She had already begun to follow it over the fallen slab into the hole, while Curdie was searching the floor of the cavern for his pickaxe.

'Here it is!' he cried. 'No, it is not,' he added, in a disappointed tone. 'What can it be, then? I declare it's a torch. That is jolly! It's better almost than my pickaxe. Much better if it weren't for those stone shoes!' he went on, as he lighted the torch by blowing the last embers of the expiring fire.

When he looked up, with the lighted torch casting a glare into the great darkness of the huge cavern, he caught sight of Irene disappearing in the hole out of which he had himself just come.

'Where are you going there?' he cried. 'That's not the way out. That's where I couldn't get out.'

'I know that,' whispered Irene. 'But this is the way my thread goes, and I must follow it.'

'What nonsense the child talks!' said Curdie to himself. 'I must follow her, though, and see that she comes to no harm. She will soon find she can't get out that way, and then she will come with me.'

So he crept over the slab once more into the hole with his torch in his hand. But when he looked about in it, he could see her nowhere. And now he discovered that although the hole was narrow, it was much longer than he had supposed; for in one direction the roof came down very low, and the hole went off in a narrow passage, of which he could not see the end. The princess must have crept in there. He got on his knees and one hand, holding the torch with the other, and crept after her. The hole twisted about, in some parts so low that he could hardly get through, in others so high that he could not see the roof, but everywhere it was narrow – far too narrow for a goblin to get through, and so I presume they never thought that Curdie might. He was beginning to feel very uncomfortable lest something should have befallen the princess, when he heard her voice almost close to his ear, whispering:

'Aren't you coming, Curdie?'

And when he turned the next corner there she stood waiting for him.

'I knew you couldn't go wrong in that narrow hole, but now you must keep by me, for here is a great wide place,' she said.

'I can't understand it,' said Curdie, half to himself, half to Irene.

'Never mind,' she returned. 'Wait till we get out.'

Curdie, utterly astonished that she had already got so far, and by a path he had known nothing of, thought it better to let her do as she pleased. 'At all events,' he said again to himself, 'I know nothing about the way, miner as I am; and she seems to think she does know something about it, though how she should passes my comprehension. So she's just as likely to find her way as I am, and as she insists on taking the lead, I must follow. We can't be much worse off than we are, anyhow.' Reasoning thus, he followed her a few steps, and came out in another great cavern, across which Irene walked in a straight line, as confidently as if she knew every step of the way. Curdie went on after her, flashing his torch about, and trying to see something of what lay around them. Suddenly he started back a pace as the light fell upon something close by which Irene was passing. It was a platform of rock raised a few feet from the floor and covered with sheepskins, upon which lay two horrible figures asleep, at once recognized by Curdie as the king and queen of the goblins. He lowered his torch instantly lest the light should awake them. As he did so it flashed upon his pickaxe, lying by the side of the queen, whose hand lay close by the handle of it.

'Stop one moment,' he whispered. 'Hold my torch, and don't let the light on their faces.'

Irene shuddered when she saw the frightful creatures, whom she had passed without observing them, but she did as he requested, and turning her back, held the torch low in front of her. Curdie drew his pickaxe carefully away, and as he did so spied one of her feet, projecting from under the skins. The great clumsy granite shoe, exposed thus to his hand, was a temptation not to be resisted. He laid hold of it, and, with cautious efforts, drew it off. The moment he succeeded, he saw to his astonishment that what he had sung in ignorance, to annoy the queen, was actually true: she had six horrible toes. Overjoyed at his success, and seeing by the huge bump in the sheepskins where the other foot was, he proceeded to lift them gently, for, if he could only succeed in carrying away the other shoe as well, he would be no more afraid of the goblins than of so many flies. But as he pulled at the second shoe the queen gave a growl and sat up in bed. The same instant the king awoke also and sat up beside her.

'Run, Irene!' cried Curdie, for though he was not now in the least afraid for himself, he was for the princess.

Irene looked once round, saw the fearful creatures awake, and like the wise princess she was, dashed the torch on the ground and extinguished it, crying out:

'Here, Curdie, take my hand.'

He darted to her side, forgetting neither the queen's shoe nor his pickaxe, and caught hold of her hand, as she sped fearlessly where her thread guided her. They heard the queen give a great bellow; but they had a good start, for it would be some time before they could get torches lighted to pursue them. Just as they thought they saw a gleam behind them, the thread brought them to a very narrow opening, through which Irene crept easily, and Curdie with difficulty.

'Now,' said Curdie; 'I think we shall be safe.'

'Of course we shall,' returned Irene. 'Why do you think so?' asked Curdie.

'Because my grandmother is taking care of us.'

'That's all nonsense,' said Curdie. 'I don't know what you mean.'

'Then if you don't know what I mean, what right have you to call it nonsense?' asked the princess, a little offended.

'I beg your pardon, Irene,' said Curdie; 'I did not mean to vex you.'

'Of course not,' returned the princess. 'But why do you think we shall be safe?'

'Because the king and queen are far too stout to get through that hole.'

'There might be ways round,' said the princess.

'To be sure there might: we are not out of it yet,' acknowledged Curdie.

'But what do you mean by the king and queen?' asked the princess. 'I should never call such creatures as those a king and a queen.'

'Their own people do, though,' answered Curdie.

The princess asked more questions, and Curdie, as they walked leisurely along, gave her a full account, not only of the character and habits of the goblins, so far as he knew them, but of his own adventures with them, beginning from the very night after that in which he had met her and Lootie upon the mountain. When he had finished, he begged Irene to tell him how it was that she had come to his rescue. So Irene too had to tell a long story, which she did in rather a roundabout manner, interrupted by many questions concerning things she had not explained. But her tale, as he did not believe more than half of it, left everything as unaccountable to him as before, and he was nearly as much perplexed as to what he must think of the princess. He could not believe that she was deliberately telling stories, and the only conclusion he could come to was that Lootie had been playing the child tricks, inventing no end of lies to frighten her for her own purposes.

'But how ever did Lootie come to let you go into the mountains alone?' he asked.

'Lootie knows nothing about it. I left her fast asleep - at least I think so. I hope my grandmother won't let her get into trouble, for it wasn't her fault at all, as my grandmother very well knows.'

'But how did you find your way to me?' persisted Curdie.

'I told you already,' answered Irene; 'by keeping my finger upon my grandmother's thread, as I am doing now.'

'You don't mean you've got the thread there?'

'Of course I do. I have told you so ten times already. I have hardly - except when I was removing the stones - taken my finger off it. There!' she added, guiding Curdie's hand to the thread, 'you feel it yourself - don't you?'

'I feel nothing at all,' replied Curdie. 'Then what can be the matter with your finger? I feel it perfectly. To be sure it is very thin, and in the sunlight looks just like the thread of a spider, though there are many of them twisted together to make it - but for all that I can't think why you shouldn't feel it as well as I do.'

Curdie was too polite to say he did not believe there was any thread there at all. What he did say was:

'Well, I can make nothing of it.'

'I can, though, and you must be glad of that, for it will do for both of us.'

'We're not out yet,' said Curdie.

'We soon shall be,' returned Irene confidently. And now the thread went downwards, and led Irene's hand to a hole in the floor of the cavern, whence came a sound of running water which they had been hearing for some time.

'It goes into the ground now, Curdie,' she said, stopping.

He had been listening to another sound, which his practiced ear had caught long ago, and which also had been growing louder. It was the noise the goblin-miners made at their work, and they seemed to be at no great distance now. Irene heard it the moment she stopped.

'What is that noise?' she asked. 'Do you know, Curdie?'

'Yes. It is the goblins digging and burrowing,' he answered.

'And you don't know what they do it for?'

'No; I haven't the least idea. Would you like to see them?' he asked, wishing to have another try after their secret.

'If my thread took me there, I shouldn't much mind; but I don't want to see them, and I can't leave my thread. It leads me down into the hole, and we had better go at once.'

'Very well. Shall I go in first?' said Curdie.

'No; better not. You can't feel the thread,' she answered, stepping down through a narrow break in the floor of the cavern. 'Oh!' she cried, 'I am in the water. It is running strong - but it is not deep, and there is just room to walk. Make haste, Curdie.'

He tried, but the hole was too small for him to get in.

'Go on a little bit he said, shouldering his pickaxe. In a few moments he had cleared a larger opening and followed her. They went on, down and down with the running water, Curdie getting more and more afraid it was leading them to some terrible gulf in the heart of the mountain. In one or two places he had to break away the rock to make room before even Irene could get through – at least without hurting herself. But at length they spied a glimmer of light, and in a minute more they were almost blinded by the full sunlight, into which they emerged. It was some little time before the princess could see well enough to discover that they stood in her own garden, close by the seat on which she and her king-papa had sat that afternoon. They had come out by the channel of the little stream. She danced and clapped her hands with delight.

'Now, Curdie!' she cried, 'won't you believe what I told you about my grandmother and her thread?'

For she had felt all the time that Curdie was not believing what she told him.

'There! - don't you see it shining on before us?' she added.

'I don't see anything,' persisted Curdie.

'Then you must believe without seeing,' said the princess; 'for you can't deny it has brought us out of the mountain.'

'I can't deny we are out of the mountain, and I should be very ungrateful indeed to deny that you had brought me out of it.'

'I couldn't have done it but for the thread,' persisted Irene.

'That's the part I don't understand.'

'well, come along, and Lootie will get you something to eat. I am sure you must want it very much.'

'Indeed I do. But my father and mother will be so anxious about me, I must make haste - first up the mountain to tell my mother, and then down into the mine again to let my father know.'

'Very well, Curdie; but you can't get out without coming this way, and I will take you through the house, for that is nearest.'

They met no one by the way, for, indeed, as before, the people were here and there and everywhere searching for the princess. When they got in Irene found that the thread, as she had half expected, went up the old staircase, and a new thought struck her. She turned to Curdie and said:

'My grandmother wants me. Do come up with me and see her. Then you will know that I have been telling you the truth. Do come – to please me, Curdie. I can't bear you should think what I say is not true.'

'I never doubted you believed what you said,' returned Curdie. 'I only thought you had some fancy in your head that was not correct.' 'But do come, dear Curdie.'

The little miner could not withstand this appeal, and though he felt shy in what seemed to him a huge grand house, he yielded, and followed her up the stair.

22. The Old Lady and Curdie

Up the stair then they went, and the next and the next, and through the long rows of empty rooms, and up the little tower stair, Irene growing happier and happier as she ascended. There was no answer when she knocked at length at the door of the workroom, nor could she hear any sound of the spinning-wheel, and once more her heart sank within her, but only for one moment, as she turned and knocked at the other door.

'Come in,' answered the sweet voice of her grandmother, and Irene opened the door and entered, followed by Curdie.

'You darling!' cried the lady, who was seated by a fire of red roses mingled with white. 'I've been waiting for you, and indeed getting a little anxious about you, and beginning to think whether I had not better go and fetch you myself.'

As she spoke she took the little princess in her arms and placed her upon her lap. She was dressed in white now, and looking if possible more lovely than ever.

'I've brought Curdie, grandmother. He wouldn't believe what I told him and so I've brought him.'

'Yes - I see him. He is a good boy, Curdie, and a brave boy. Aren't you glad you've got him out?'

'Yes, grandmother. But it wasn't very good of him not to believe me when I was telling him the truth.'

'People must believe what they can, and those who believe more must not be hard upon those who believe less. I doubt if you would have believed it all yourself if you hadn't seen some of it.'

'Ah! yes, grandmother, I dare say. I'm sure you are right. But he'll believe now.'

'I don't know that,' replied her grandmother.

'Won't you, Curdie?' said Irene, looking round at him as she asked the question. He was standing in the middle of the floor, staring, and looking strangely bewildered. This she thought came of his astonishment at the beauty of the lady. 'Make a bow to my grandmother, Curdie,' she said.

'I don't see any grandmother,' answered Curdie rather gruffly.

'Don't see my grandmother, when I'm sitting in her lap?' exclaimed the princess.

'No, I don't,' reiterated Curdie, in an offended tone.

'Don't you see the lovely fire of roses - white ones amongst them this time?' asked Irene, almost as bewildered as he.

'No, I don't,' answered Curdie, almost sulkily.

'Nor the blue bed? Nor the rose-colored counterpane? - Nor the beautiful light, like the moon, hanging from the roof?'

'You're making game of me, Your Royal Highness; and after what we have come through together this day, I don't think it is kind of you,' said Curdie, feeling very much hurt.

'Then what do you see?' asked Irene, who perceived at once that for her not to believe him was at least as bad as for him not to believe her.

'I see a big, bare, garret-room - like the one in mother's cottage, only big enough to take the cottage itself in, and leave a good margin all round,' answered Curdie.

'And what more do you see?'

'I see a tub, and a heap of musty straw, and a withered apple, and a ray of sunlight coming through a hole in the middle of the roof and shining on your head, and making all the place look a curious dusky brown. I think you had better drop it, princess, and go down to the nursery, like a good girl.'

'But don't you hear my grandmother talking to me?' asked Irene, almost crying.

'No. I hear the cooing of a lot of pigeons. If you won't come down, I will go without you. I think that will be better anyhow, for I'm sure nobody who met us would believe a word we said to them. They would think we made it all up. I don't expect anybody but my own father and mother to believe me. They know I wouldn't tell a story.'

'And yet you won't believe me, Curdie?' expostulated the princess, now fairly crying with vexation and sorrow at the gulf between her and Curdie.

'No. I can't, and I can't help it,' said Curdie, turning to leave the room.

'What shall I do, grandmother?' sobbed the princess, turning her face round upon the lady's bosom, and shaking with suppressed sobs.

'You must give him time,' said her grandmother; 'and you must be content not to be believed for a while. It is very hard to bear; but I have had to bear it, and shall have to bear it many a time yet. I will take care of what Curdie thinks of you in the end. You must let him go now.'

'You're not coming, are you?' asked Curdie.

'No, Curdie; my grandmother says I must let you go. Turn to the right when you get to the bottom of all the stairs, and that will take you to the hall where the great door is.'

'Oh! I don't doubt I can find my way - without you, princess, or your old grannie's thread either,' said Curdie quite rudely.

'Oh, Curdie! Curdie!'

'I wish I had gone home at once. I'm very much obliged to you, Irene, for getting me out of that hole, but I wish you hadn't made a fool of me afterwards.'

He said this as he opened the door, which he left open, and, without another word, went down the stair. Irene listened with dismay to his departing footsteps. Then turning again to the lady:

'What does it all mean, grandmother?' she sobbed, and burst into fresh tears.

'It means, my love, that I did not mean to show myself. Curdie is not yet able to believe some things. Seeing is not believing – it is only seeing. You remember I told you that if Lootie were to see me, she would rub her eyes, forget the half she saw, and call the other half nonsense.'

'Yes; but I should have thought Curdie -'

'You are right. Curdie is much farther on than Lootie, and you will see what will come of it. But in the meantime you must be content, I say, to be misunderstood for a while. We are all very anxious to be understood, and it is very hard not to be. But there is one thing much more necessary.'

'What is that, grandmother?'

'To understand other people.'

'Yes, grandmother. I must be fair - for if I'm not fair to other people, I'm not worth being understood myself. I see. So as Curdie can't help it, I will not be vexed with him, but just wait.'

'There's my own dear child,' said her grandmother, and pressed her close to her bosom.

'Why weren't you in your workroom when we came up, grandmother?' asked Irene, after a few moments' silence.

'If I had been there, Curdie would have seen me well enough. But why should I be there rather than in this beautiful room?'

'I thought you would be spinning.'

'I've nobody to spin for just at present. I never spin without knowing for whom I am spinning.'

'That reminds me - there is one thing that puzzles me,' said the princess: 'how are you to get the thread out of the mountain again? Surely you won't have to make another for me? That would be such a trouble!'

The lady set her down and rose and went to the fire. Putting in her hand, she drew it out again and held up the shining ball between her finger and thumb.

'I've got it now, you see,' she said, coming back to the princess, 'all ready for you when you want it.'

Going to her cabinet, she laid it in the same drawer as before.

'And here is your ring,' she added, taking it from the little finger of her left hand and putting it on the forefinger of Irene's right hand.

'Oh, thank you, grandmother! I feel so safe now!'

'You are very tired, my child,' the lady went on. 'Your hands are hurt with the stones, and I have counted nine bruises on you. Just look what you are like.'

And she held up to her a little mirror which she had brought from the cabinet. The princess burst into a merry laugh at the sight. She was so draggled with the stream and dirty with creeping through narrow places, that if she had seen the reflection without knowing it was a reflection, she would have taken herself for some gipsy child whose face was washed and hair combed about once in a month. The lady laughed too, and lifting her again upon her knee, took off her cloak and night-gown. Then she carried her to the side of the room. Irene wondered what she was going to do with her, but asked no questions - only starting a little when she found that she was going to lay her in the large silver bath; for as she looked into it, again she saw no bottom, but the stars shining miles away, as it seemed, in a great blue gulf. Her hands closed involuntarily on the beautiful arms that held her, and that was all.

The lady pressed her once more to her bosom, saying:

'Do not be afraid, my child.'

'No, grandmother,' answered the princess, with a little gasp; and the next instant she sank in the clear cool water.

When she opened her eyes, she saw nothing but a strange lovely blue over and beneath and all about her. The lady, and the beautiful room, had vanished from her sight, and she seemed utterly alone. But instead of being afraid, she felt more than happy – perfectly blissful. And from somewhere came the voice of the lady, singing a strange sweet song, of which she could distinguish every word; but of the sense she had only a feeling - no understanding. Nor could she remember a single line after it was gone. It vanished, like the poetry in a dream, as fast as it came. In after years, however, she would sometimes fancy that snatches of melody suddenly rising in her brain must be little phrases and fragments of the air of that song; and the very fancy would make her happier, and abler to do her duty.

How long she lay in the water she did not know. It seemed a long time - not from weariness but from pleasure. But at last she felt the beautiful hands lay hold of her, and through the gurgling water she was lifted out into the lovely room. The lady carried her to the fire, and sat down with her in her lap, and dried her tenderly with the softest towel. It was so different from Lootie's drying. When the lady had done, she stooped to the fire, and drew from it her night-gown, as white as snow.

'How delicious!' exclaimed the princess. 'It smells of all the roses in the world, I think.'

When she stood up on the floor she felt as if she had been made over again. Every bruise and all weariness were gone, and her hands were soft and whole as ever.

'Now I am going to put you to bed for a good sleep,' said her grandmother.

'But what will Lootie be thinking? And what am I to say to her when she asks me where I have been?'

'Don't trouble yourself about it. You will find it all come right,' said her grandmother, and laid her into the blue bed, under the rosy counterpane.

'There is just one thing more,' said Irene. 'I am a little anxious about Curdie. As I brought him into the house, I ought to have seen him safe on his way home.'

'I took care of all that,' answered the lady. 'I told you to let him go, and therefore I was bound to look after him. Nobody saw him, and he is now eating a good dinner in his mother's cottage far up in the mountain.'

'Then I will go to sleep,' said Irene, and in a few minutes she was fast asleep.

23. CURDIE AND HIS MOTHER

Curdie went up the mountain neither whistling nor singing, for he was vexed with Irene for taking him in, as he called it; and he was vexed with himself for having spoken to her so angrily. His mother gave a cry of joy when she saw him, and at once set about getting him something to eat, asking him questions all the time, which he did not answer so cheerfully as usual. When his meal was ready, she left him to eat it, and hurried to the mine to let his father know he was safe. When she came back, she found him fast asleep upon her bed; nor did he wake until his father came home in the evening.

'Now, Curdie,' his mother said, as they sat at supper, 'tell us the whole story from beginning to end, just as it all happened.'

Curdie obeyed, and told everything to the point where they came out upon the lawn in the garden of the king's house.

'And what happened after that?' asked his mother. 'You haven't told us all. You ought to be very happy at having got away from those demons, and instead of that I never saw you so gloomy. There must be something more. Besides, you do not speak of that lovely child as I should like to hear you. She saved your life at the risk of her own, and yet somehow you don't seem to think much of it.'

'She talked such nonsense' answered Curdie, 'and told me a pack of things that weren't a bit true; and I can't get over it.'

'What were they?' asked his father. 'Your mother may be able to throw some light upon them.'

Then Curdie made a clean breast of it, and told them everything.

They all sat silent for some time, pondering the strange tale. At last Curdie's mother spoke.

'You confess, my boy,' she said, 'there is something about the whole affair you do not understand?'

'Yes, of course, mother,' he answered. 'I cannot understand how a child knowing nothing about the mountain, or even that I was shut up in it, should come all that way alone, straight to where I was; and then, after getting me out of the hole, lead me out of the mountain too, where I should not have known a step of the way if it had been as light as in the open air.' 'Then you have no right to say what she told you was not true. She did take you out, and she must have had something to guide her: why not a thread as well as a rope, or anything else? There is something you cannot explain, and her explanation may be the right one.'

'It's no explanation at all, mother; and I can't believe it.'

'That may be only because you do not understand it. If you did, you would probably find it was an explanation, and believe it thoroughly. I don't blame you for not being able to believe it, but I do blame you for fancying such a child would try to deceive you. Why should she? Depend upon it, she told you all she knew. Until you had found a better way of accounting for it all, you might at least have been more sparing of your judgment.'

'That is what something inside me has been saying all the time,' said Curdie, hanging down his head. 'But what do you make of the grandmother? That is what I can't get over. To take me up to an old garret, and try to persuade me against the sight of my own eyes that it was a beautiful room, with blue walls and silver stars, and no end of things in it, when there was nothing there but an old tub and a withered apple and a heap of straw and a sunbeam! It was too bad! She might have had some old woman there at least to pass for her precious grandmother!'

'Didn't she speak as if she saw those other things herself, Curdie?'

'Yes. That's what bothers me. You would have thought she really meant and believed that she saw every one of the things she talked about. And not one of them there! It was too bad, I say.'

'Perhaps some people can see things other people can't see, Curdie,' said his mother very gravely. 'I think I will tell you something I saw myself once - only Perhaps You won't believe me either!'

'Oh, mother, mother!' cried Curdie, bursting into tears; 'I don't deserve that, surely!'

'But what I am going to tell you is very strange,' persisted his mother; 'and if having heard it you were to say I must have been dreaming, I don't know that I should have any right to be vexed with you, though I know at least that I was not asleep.'

'Do tell me, mother. Perhaps it will help me to think better of the princess.'

'That's why I am tempted to tell you,' replied his mother. 'But first, I may as well mention that, according to old whispers, there is something more than common about the king's family; and the queen was of the same blood, for they were cousins of some degree. There were strange stories told concerning them - all good stories - but strange, very strange. What they were I cannot tell, for I only remember the faces of my grandmother and my mother as they talked together about them. There was wonder and awe - not fear - in their eyes, and they whispered, and never spoke aloud. But what I saw myself was this: Your father was going to work in the mine one night, and I had been down with his supper. It was soon after we were married, and not very long before you were born. He came with me to the mouth of the mine, and left me to go home alone, for I knew the way almost as well as the floor of our own cottage. It was pretty dark, and in some parts of the road where the rocks overhung nearly quite dark. But I got along perfectly well, never thinking of being afraid, until I reached a spot you know well enough, Curdie, where the path has to make a sharp turn out of the way of a great rock on the left-hand side. When I got there, I was suddenly surrounded by about half a dozen of the cobs, the first I had ever seen, although I had heard tell of them often enough. One of them blocked up the path, and they all began tormenting and teasing me in a way it makes me shudder to think of even now.'

'If I had only been with you!' cried father and son in a breath.

The mother gave a funny little smile, and went on.

'They had some of their horrible creatures with them too, and I must confess I was dreadfully frightened. They had torn my clothes very much, and I was afraid they were going to tear myself to pieces, when suddenly a great white soft light shone upon me. I looked up. A broad ray, like a shining road, came down from a large globe of silvery light, not very high up, indeed not quite so high as the horizon - so it could not have been a new star or another moon or anything of that sort. The cobs dropped persecuting me, and looked dazed, and I thought they were going to run away, but presently they began again. The same moment, however, down the path from the globe of light came a bird, shining like silver in the sun. It gave a few rapid flaps first, and then, with its wings straight out, shot, sliding down the slope of the light. It looked to me just like a white pigeon. But whatever it was, when the cobs caught sight of it coming straight down upon them, they took to their heels and scampered away across the mountain, leaving me safe, only much frightened. As soon as it had sent them off, the bird went gliding again up the light, and the moment it reached the globe the light disappeared, just as if a shutter had been closed over a window, and I saw it no More. But I had no more trouble with the cobs that night or ever after.'

'How strange!' exclaimed Curdie.

'Yes, it was strange; but I can't help believing it, whether you do or not,' said his mother.

'It's exactly as your mother told it to me the very next morning,' said his father.

'You don't think I'm doubting my own mother?' cried Curdie. 'There are other people in the world quite as well worth believing as your own mother,' said his mother. 'I don't know that she's so much the fitter to be believed that she happens to be your mother, Mr. Curdie. There are mothers far more likely to tell lies than the little girl I saw talking to the primroses a few weeks ago. If she were to lie I should begin to doubt my own word.'

'But princesses have told lies as well as other people,' said Curdie.

'Yes, but not princesses like that child. She's a good girl, I am certain, and that's more than being a princess. Depend upon it you will have to be sorry for behaving so to her, Curdie. You ought at least to have held your tongue.'

'I am sorry now,' answered Curdie.

'You ought to go and tell her so, then.'

'I don't see how I could manage that. They wouldn't let a miner boy like me have a word with her alone; and I couldn't tell her before that nurse of hers. She'd be asking ever so many questions, and I don't know how many the little princess would like me to answer. She told me that Lootie didn't know anything about her coming to get me out of the mountain. I am certain she would have prevented her somehow if she had known it. But I may have a chance before long, and meantime I must try to do something for her. I think, father, I have got on the track at last.'

'Have you, indeed, my boy?' said Peter. 'I am sure you deserve some success; you have worked very hard for it. What have you found out?'

'It's difficult, you know, father, inside the mountain, especially in the dark, and not knowing what turns you have taken, to tell the lie of things outside.'

'Impossible, my boy, without a chart, or at least a compass,' returned his father.

'Well, I think I have nearly discovered in what direction the cobs are mining. If I am right, I know something else that I can put to it, and then one and one will make three.'

'They very often do, Curdie, as we miners ought to be very well aware. Now tell us, my boy, what the two things are, and see whether we can guess at the same third as you.'

'I don't see what that has to do with the princess,' interposed his mother.

'I will soon let you see that, mother. Perhaps you may think me foolish, but until I am sure there, is nothing in my present fancy, I am more determined than ever to go on with my observations. Just as we came to the channel by which we got out, I heard the miners at work somewhere near - I think down below us. Now since I began to watch them, they have mined a good half-mile, in a straight line; and so far as I am aware, they are working in no other part of the mountain. But I never could tell in what direction they were going. When we came out in the king's garden, however, I thought at once whether it was possible they were working towards the king's house; and what I want to do tonight is to make sure whether they are or not. I will take a light with me -'

'Oh, Curdie,' cried his mother, 'then they will see you.'

'I'm no more afraid of them now than I was before,' rejoined Curdie, 'now that I've got this precious shoe. They can't make another such in a hurry, and one bare foot will do for my purpose. Woman as she may be, I won't spare her next time. But I shall be careful with my light, for I don't want them to see me. I won't stick it in my hat.'

'Go on, then, and tell us what you mean to do.'

'I mean to take a bit of paper with me and a pencil, and go in at the mouth of the stream by which we came out. I shall mark on the paper as near as I can the angle of every turning I take until I find the cobs at work, and so get a good idea in what direction they are going. If it should prove to be nearly parallel with the stream, I shall know it is towards the king's house they are working.'

'And what if you should? How much wiser will you be then?'

'Wait a minute, mother dear. I told you that when I came upon the royal family in the cave, they were talking of their prince - Harelip, they called him - marrying a sun-woman - that means one of us - one with toes to her feet. Now in the speech one of them made that night at their great gathering, of which I heard only a part, he said that peace would be secured for a generation at least by the pledge the prince would hold for the good behavior of her relatives: that's what he said, and he must have meant the sun-woman the prince was to marry. I am quite sure the king is much too proud to wish his son to marry any but a princess, and much too knowing to fancy that his having a peasant woman for a wife would be of any great advantage to them.'

'I see what you are driving at now,' said his mother.

'But,' said his father, 'our king would dig the mountain to the plain before he would have his princess the wife of a cob, if he were ten times a prince.'

'Yes; but they think so much of themselves!' said his mother. 'Small creatures always do. The bantam is the proudest cock in my little yard.'

'And I fancy,' said Curdie, 'if they once got her, they would tell the king they would kill her except he consented to the marriage.'

'They might say so,' said his father, 'but they wouldn't kill her; they would keep her alive for the sake of the hold it gave them over our king. Whatever he did to them, they would threaten to do the same to the princess.'

'And they are bad enough to torment her just for their own amusement - I know that,' said his mother.

'Anyhow, I will keep a watch on them, and see what they are up to,' said Curdie. 'It's too horrible to think of. I daren't let myself do it. But they shan't have her - at least if I can help it. So, mother dear - my clue is all right - will you get me a bit of paper and a pencil and a lump of pease pudding, and I will set out at once. I saw a place where I can climb over the wall of the garden quite easily.'

'You must mind and keep out of the way of the men on the watch,' said his mother.

'That I will. I don't want them to know anything about it. They would spoil it all. The cobs would only try some other plan – they are such obstinate creatures! I shall take good care, mother. They won't kill and eat me either, if they should come upon me. So you needn't mind them.'

His mother got him what he had asked for, and Curdie set out. Close beside the door by which the princess left the garden for the mountain stood a great rock, and by climbing it Curdie got over the wall. He tied his clue to a stone just inside the channel of the stream, and took his pickaxe with him. He had not gone far before he encountered a horrid creature coming towards the mouth. The spot was too narrow for two of almost any size or shape, and besides Curdie had no wish to let the creature pass. Not being able to use his pickaxe, however, he had a severe struggle with him, and it was only after receiving many bites, some of them bad, that he succeeded in killing him with his pocket-knife. Having dragged him out, he made haste to get in again before another should stop up the way.

I need not follow him farther in this night's adventures. He returned to his breakfast, satisfied that the goblins were mining in the direction of the palace - on so low a level that their intention must, he thought, be to burrow under the walls of the king's house, and rise up inside it - in order, he fully believed, to lay hands on the little princess, and carry her off for a wife to their horrid Harelip.

24. IRENE BEHAVES LIKE A PRINCE

When the princess awoke from the sweetest of sleeps, she found her nurse bending over her, the housekeeper looking over the nurse's shoulder, and the laundry- maid looking over the housekeeper's. The room was full of women-servants; and the gentlemen-at-arms, with a long column of servants behind them, were peeping, or trying to peep in at the door of the nursery.

'Are those horrid creatures gone?' asked the princess, remembering first what had terrified her in the morning.

'You naughty, naughty little princess!' cried Lootie.

Her face was very pale, with red streaks in it, and she looked as if she were going to shake her; but Irene said nothing – only waited to hear what should come next.

'How could you get under the clothes like that, and make us all fancy you were lost! And keep it up all day too! You are the most obstinate child! It's anything but fun to us, I can tell you!'

It was the only way the nurse could account for her disappearance.

'I didn't do that, Lootie,' said Irene, very quietly.

'Don't tell stories!' cried her nurse quite rudely.

'I shall tell you nothing at all,' said Irene.

'That's just as bad,' said the nurse.

'Just as bad to say nothing at all as to tell stories?' exclaimed the princess. 'I will ask my papa about that. He won't say so. And I don't think he will like you to say so.'

'Tell me directly what you mean by it!' screamed the nurse, half wild with anger at the princess and fright at the possible consequences to herself.

'When I tell you the truth, Lootie,' said the princess, who somehow did not feel at all angry, 'you say to me "Don't tell stories": it seems I must tell stories before you will believe me.'

'You are very rude, princess,' said the nurse.

'You are so rude, Lootie, that I will not speak to you again till you are sorry. Why should I, when I know you will not believe me?' returned the princess. For she did know perfectly well that if she were to tell Lootie what she had been about, the more she went on to tell her, the less would she believe her.

'You are the most provoking child!' cried her nurse. 'You deserve to be well punished for your wicked behavior.'

'Please, Mrs. Housekeeper,' said the princess, 'will you take me to your room, and keep me till my king-papa comes? I will ask him to come as soon as he can.'

Every one stared at these words. Up to this moment they had all regarded her as little more than a baby.

But the housekeeper was afraid of the nurse, and sought to patch matters up, saying:

'I am sure, princess, nursie did not mean to be rude to you.'

'I do not think my papa would wish me to have a nurse who spoke to me as Lootie does. If she thinks I tell lies, she had better either say so to my papa, or go away. Sir Walter, will you take charge of me?'

'With the greatest of pleasure, princess,' answered the captain of the gentlemen-at-arms, walking with his great stride into the room.

The crowd of servants made eager way for him, and he bowed low before the little princess's bed. 'I shall send my servant at once, on the fastest horse in the stable, to tell your king-papa that Your Royal Highness desires his presence. When you have chosen one of these under-servants to wait upon you, I shall order the room to be cleared.'

'Thank you very much, Sir Walter,' said the princess, and her eye glanced towards a rosy-cheeked girl who had lately come to the house as a scullery-maid.

But when Lootie saw the eyes of her dear princess going in search of another instead of her, she fell upon her knees by the bedside, and burst into a great cry of distress.

'I think, Sir Walter,' said the princess, 'I will keep Lootie. But I put myself under your care; and you need not trouble my king-papa until I speak to you again. Will you all please to go away? I am quite safe and well, and I did not hide myself for the sake either of amusing myself, or of troubling my people. Lootie, will you please to dress me.'

25. CURDIE COMES TO GRIEF

Everything was for some time quiet above ground. The king was still away in a distant part of his dominions. The men-at-arms kept watching about the house. They had been considerably astonished by finding at the foot of the rock in the garden the hideous body of the goblin creature killed by Curdie; but they came to the conclusion that it had been slain in the mines, and had crept out there to die; and except an occasional glimpse of a live one they saw nothing to cause alarm.

Curdie kept watching in the mountain, and the goblins kept burrowing deeper into the earth. As long as they went deeper there was, Curdie judged, no immediate danger.

To Irene the summer was as full of pleasure as ever, and for a long time, although she often thought of her grandmother during the day, and often dreamed about her at night, she did not see her. The kids and the flowers were as much her delight as ever, and she made as much friendship with the miners' children she met on the mountain as Lootie would permit; but Lootie had very foolish notions concerning the dignity of a princess, not understanding that the truest princess is just the one who loves all her brothers and sisters best, and who is most able to do them good by being humble towards them. At the same time she was considerably altered for the better in her behavior to the princess. She could not help seeing that she was no longer a mere child, but wiser than her age would account for. She kept foolishly whispering to the servants, however - sometimes that the princess was not right in her mind, sometimes that she was too good to live, and other nonsense of the same sort.

All this time Curdie had to be sorry, without a chance of confessing, that he had behaved so unkindly to the princess. This perhaps made him the more diligent in his endeavors to serve her. His mother and he often talked on the subject, and she comforted him, and told him she was sure he would some day have the opportunity he so much desired. Here I should like to remark, for the sake of princes and princesses in general, that it is a low and contemptible thing to refuse to confess a fault, or even an error. If a true princess has done wrong, she is always uneasy until she has had an opportunity of throwing the wrongness away from her by saying: 'I did it; and I wish I had not; and I am sorry for having done it.' So you see there is some ground for supposing that Curdie was not a miner only, but a prince as well. Many such instances have been known in the world's history.

At length, however, he began to see signs of a change in the proceedings of the goblin excavators: they were going no deeper, but had commenced running on a level; and he watched them, therefore, more closely than ever. All at once, one night, coming to a slope of very hard rock, they began to ascend along the inclined plane of its surface. Having reached its top, they went again on a level for a night or two, after which they began to ascend once more, and kept on at a pretty steep angle. At length Curdie judged it time to transfer his observation to another quarter, and the next night he did not go to the mine at all; but, leaving his pickaxe and clue at home, and taking only his usual lumps of bread and pease pudding, went down the mountain to the king's house. He climbed over the wall, and remained in the garden the whole night, creeping on hands and knees from one spot to the other, and lying at full length with his ear to the ground, listening. But he heard nothing except the tread of the men-at-arms as they marched about, whose observation, as the night was cloudy and there was no moon, he had little difficulty in avoiding. For several following nights he continued to haunt the garden and listen, but with no success.

At length, early one evening, whether it was that he had got careless of his own safety, or that the growing moon had become strong enough to expose him, his watching came to a sudden end. He was creeping from behind the rock where the stream ran out, for he had been listening all round it in the hope it might convey to his ear some indication of the whereabouts of the goblin miners, when just as he came into the moonlight on the lawn, a whizz in his ear and a blow upon his leg startled him. He instantly squatted in the hope of eluding further notice. But when he heard the sound of running feet, he jumped up to take the chance of escape by flight. He fell, however, with a keen shoot of pain, for the bolt of a crossbow had wounded his leg, and the blood was now streaming from it. He was instantly laid Hold of by two or three of the men-at-arms. It was useless to struggle, and he submitted in silence.

'It's a boy!' cried several of them together, in a tone of amazement. 'I thought it was one of those demons. What are you about here?'

'Going to have a little rough usage, apparently,' said Curdie, laughing, as the men shook him.

'Impertinence will do you no good. You have no business here in the king's grounds, and if you don't give a true account of yourself, you shall fare as a thief.'

'Why, what else could he be?' said one.

'He might have been after a lost kid, you know,' suggested another.

'I see no good in trying to excuse him. He has no business here, anyhow.'

'Let me go away, then, if you please,' said Curdie.

'But we don't please - not except you give a good account of yourself.'

'I don't feel quite sure whether I can trust you,' said Curdie.

'We are the king's own men-at-arms,' said the captain courteously, for he was taken with Curdie's appearance and courage.

'Well, I will tell you all about it - if you will promise to listen to me and not do anything rash.'

'I call that cool!' said one of the party, laughing. 'He will tell us what mischief he was about, if we promise to do as pleases him.'

'I was about no mischief,' said Curdie. -

But ere he could say more he turned faint, and fell senseless on the grass. Then first they discovered that the bolt they had shot, taking him for one of the goblin creatures, had wounded him.

They carried him into the house and laid him down in the hall. The report spread that they had caught a robber, and the servants crowded in to see the villain. Amongst the rest came the nurse. The moment she saw him she exclaimed with indignation:

'I declare it's the same young rascal of a miner that was rude to me and the princess on the mountain. He actually wanted to kiss the princess. I took good care of that - the wretch! And he was prowling about, was he? Just like his impudence!' The princess being fast asleep, she could misrepresent at her pleasure.

When he heard this, the captain, although he had considerable doubt of its truth, resolved to keep Curdie a prisoner until they could search into the affair. So, after they had brought him round a little, and attended to his wound, which was rather a bad one, they laid him, still exhausted from the loss of blood, upon a mattress in a disused room - one of those already so often mentioned – and locked the door, and left him. He passed a troubled night, and in the morning they found him talking wildly. In the evening he came to himself, but felt very weak, and his leg was exceedingly painful. Wondering where he was, and seeing one of the men-at-arms in the room, he began to question him and soon recalled the events of the preceding night. As he was himself unable to watch any more, he told the soldier all he knew about the goblins, and begged him to tell his companions, and stir them up to watch with tenfold vigilance; but whether it was that he did not talk quite coherently, or that the whole thing appeared incredible, certainly the man concluded that Curdie was only raving still, and tried to coax him into holding his tongue. This, of course, annoyed Curdie dreadfully, who now felt in his turn what it was not to be believed, and the consequence was that his fever returned, and by the time when, at his persistent entreaties, the captain was called, there could be no doubt that he was raving. They did for him what they could, and promised everything he wanted, but with no intention of fulfillment. At last he went to sleep, and when at length his sleep grew profound and peaceful, they left him, locked the door again, and withdrew, intending to revisit him early in the morning.

26. The Goblin-Miners

That same night several of the servants were having a chat together before going to bed.

'What can that noise be?' said one of the housemaids, who had been listening for a moment or two.

'I've heard it the last two nights,' said the cook. 'If there were any about the place, I should have taken it for rats, but my Tom keeps them far enough.'

'I've heard, though,' said the scullery-maid, 'that rats move about in great companies sometimes. There may be an army of them invading us. I've heard the noises yesterday and today too.'

'It'll be grand fun, then, for my Tom and Mrs. Housekeeper's Bob,' said the cook. 'They'll be friends for once in their lives, and fight on the same side. I'll engage Tom and Bob together will put to flight any number of rats.'

'It seems to me,' said the nurse, 'that the noises are much too loud for that. I have heard them all day, and my princess has asked me several times what they could be. Sometimes they sound like distant thunder, and sometimes like the noises you hear in the mountain from those horrid miners underneath.'

'I shouldn't wonder,' said the cook, 'if it was the miners after all. They may have come on some hole in the mountain through which the noises reach to us. They are always boring and blasting and breaking, you know.'

As he spoke, there came a great rolling rumble beneath them, and the house quivered. They all started up in affright, and rushing to the hall found the gentlemen-at-arms in consternation also. They had sent to wake their captain, who said from their description that it must have been an earthquake, an occurrence which, although very rare in that country, had taken place almost within the century; and then went to bed again, strange to say, and fell -fast asleep without once thinking of Curdie, or associating the noises they had heard with what he had told them. He had not believed Curdie. If he had, he would at once have thought of what he had said, and would have taken precautions. As they heard nothing more, they concluded that Sir Walter was right, and that the danger was over for perhaps another hundred years. The fact, as discovered afterwards, was that the goblins had, in working up a second sloping face of stone, arrived at a huge block which lay under the cellars of the house, within the line of the foundations.

It was so round that when they succeeded, after hard work, in dislodging it without blasting, it rolled thundering down the slope with a bounding, jarring roll, which shook the foundations of the house. The goblins were themselves dismayed at the noise, for they knew, by careful spying and measuring, that they must now be very near, if not under the king's house, and they feared giving an alarm. They, therefore, remained quiet for a while, and when they began to work again, they no doubt thought themselves very fortunate in coming upon a vein of sand which filled a winding fissure in the rock on which the house was built. By scooping this away they came out in the king's wine cellar. No sooner did they find where they were, than they scurried back again, like rats into their holes, and running at full speed to the goblin palace, announced their success to the king and queen with shouts of triumph.

In a moment the goblin royal family and the whole goblin people were on their way in hot haste to the king's house, each eager to have a share in the glory of carrying off that same night the Princess Irene.

The queen went stumping along in one shoe of stone and one of skin.

This could not have been pleasant, and my readers may wonder that, with such skilful workmen about her, she had not yet replaced the shoe carried off by Curdie. As the king, however, had more than one ground of objection to her stone shoes, he no doubt took advantage of the discovery of her toes, and threatened to expose her deformity if she had another made. I presume he insisted on her being content with skin shoes, and allowed her to wear the remaining granite one on the present occasion only because she was going out to war.

They soon arrived in the king's wine cellar, and regardless of its huge vessels, of which they did not know the use, proceeded at once, but as quietly as they could, to force the door that led upwards.

27. THE GOBLINS IN THE KING'S HOUSE

When Curdie fell asleep he began at once to dream. He thought he was ascending the Mountainside from the mouth of the mine, whistling and singing 'Ring, dod, bang!' when he came upon a woman and child who had lost their way; and from that point he went on dreaming everything that had happened to him since he thus met the princess and Lootie; how he had watched the goblins, how he had been taken by them, how he had been rescued by the princess; everything, indeed, until he was wounded, captured, and imprisoned by the men-at-arms. And now he thought he was lying wide awake where they had laid him, when suddenly he heard a great thundering sound.

'The cobs are coming!' he said. 'They didn't believe a word I told them! The cobs'll be carrying off the princess from under their stupid noses! But they shan't! that they shan't!'

He jumped up, as he thought, and began to dress, but, to his dismay, found that he was still lying in bed.

'Now then, I will!' he said. 'Here goes! I am up now!'

But yet again he found himself snug in bed. Twenty times he tried, and twenty times he failed; for in fact he was not awake, only dreaming that he was. At length in an agony of despair, fancying he heard the goblins all over the house, he gave a great cry. Then there came, as he thought, a hand upon the lock of his door. It opened, and, looking up, he saw a lady with white hair, carrying a silver box in her hand, enter the room. She came to his bed, he thought, stroked his head and face with cool, soft hands, took the dressing from his leg, rubbed it with something that smelt like roses, and then waved her hands over him three times. At the last wave of her hands everything vanished, he felt himself sinking into the profoundest slumber, and remembered nothing more until he awoke in earnest.

The setting moon was throwing a feeble light through the casement, and the house was full of uproar. There was soft heavy multitudinous stamping, a clashing and clanging of weapons, the voices of men and the cries of women, mixed with a hideous bellowing, which sounded victorious. The cobs were in the house! He sprang from his bed, hurried on some of his clothes, not forgetting his shoes, which were armed with nails; then spying an old hunting-knife, or short sword, hanging on the wall, he caught it, and rushed down the stairs, guided by the sounds of strife, which grew louder and louder.

When he reached the ground floor he found the whole place swarming.

All the goblins of the mountain seemed gathered there. He rushed amongst them, shouting:

'One, two,

Hit and hew!

Three, four,

Blast and bore!'

And with every rhyme he came down a great stamp upon a foot, cutting at the same time their faces - executing, indeed, a sword dance of the wildest description. Away scattered the goblins in every direction - into closets, up stairs, into chimneys, up on rafters, and down to the cellars. Curdie went on stamping and slashing and singing, but saw nothing of the people of the house until he came to the great hall, in which, the moment he entered it, arose a great goblin shout. The last of the men-at-arms, the captain himself, was on the floor, buried beneath a wallowing crowd of goblins. For, while each knight was busy defending himself as well as he could, by stabs in the thick bodies of the goblins, for he had soon found their heads all but invulnerable, the queen had attacked his legs and feet with her horrible granite shoe, and he was soon down; but the captain had got his back to the wall and stood out longer. The goblins would have torn them all to pieces, but the king had given orders to carry them away alive, and over each of them, in twelve groups, was standing a knot of goblins, while as many as could find room were sitting upon their prostrate bodies. Curdie burst in dancing and gyrating and stamping and singing like a small incarnate whirlwind.

'Where 'tis all a hole, sir, Never can be holes: Why should their shoes have soles, sir, When they've got no souls?

'But she upon her foot, sir, Has a granite shoe: The strongest leather boot, sir, Six would soon be through.'

The queen gave a howl of rage and dismay; and before she recovered her presence of mind, Curdie, having begun with the group nearest him, had eleven of the knights on their legs again.

'Stamp on their feet!' he cried as each man rose, and in a few minutes the hall was nearly empty, the goblins running from it as fast as they could, howling and shrieking and limping, and cowering every now and then as they ran to cuddle their wounded feet in their hard hands, or to protect them from the frightful stamp-stamp of the armed men. And now Curdie approached the group which, in trusting in the queen and her shoe, kept their guard over the prostrate captain. The king sat on the captain's head, but the queen stood in front, like an infuriated cat, with her perpendicular eyes gleaming green, and her hair standing half up from her horrid head. Her heart was quaking, however, and she kept moving about her skin-shod foot with nervous apprehension. When Curdie was within a few paces, she rushed at him, made one tremendous stamp at his opposing foot, which happily he withdrew in time, and caught him round the waist, to dash him on the marble floor. But just as she caught him, he came down with all the weight of his iron-shod shoe upon her skin-shod foot, and with a hideous howl she dropped him, squatted on the floor, and took her foot in both her hands. Meanwhile the rest rushed on the king and the bodyguard, sent them flying, and lifted the prostrate captain, who was all but pressed to death. It was some moments before he recovered breath and consciousness.

'Where's the princess?' cried Curdie, again and again.

No one knew, and off they all rushed in search of her.

Through every room in the house they went, but nowhere was she to be found. Neither was one of the servants to be seen. But Curdie, who had kept to the lower part of the house, which was now quiet enough, began to hear a confused sound as of a distant hubbub, and set out to find where it came from. The noise grew as his sharp ears guided him to a stair and so to the wine cellar. It was full of goblins, whom the butler was supplying with wine as fast as he could draw it.

While the queen and her party had encountered the men-at-arms, Harelip with another company had gone off to search the house. They captured every one they met, and when they could find no more, they hurried away to carry them safe to the caverns below. But when the butler, who was amongst them, found that their path lay through the wine cellar, he bethought himself of persuading them to taste the wine, and, as he had hoped, they no sooner tasted than they wanted more. The routed goblins, on their way below, joined them, and when Curdie entered they were all, with outstretched hands, in which were vessels of every description from sauce pan to silver cup, pressing around the butler, who sat at the tap of a huge cask, filling and filling. Curdie cast one glance around the place before commencing his attack, and saw in the farthest corner a terrified group of the domestics unwatched, but cowering without courage to attempt their escape. Amongst them was the terror-stricken face of Lootie; but nowhere could he see the princess. Seized with the horrible conviction that Harelip had already carried her off, he rushed amongst them, unable for wrath to sing any more, but stamping and cutting with greater fury than ever.

'Stamp on their feet; stamp on their feet!' he shouted, and in a moment the goblins were disappearing through the hole in the floor like rats and mice. They could not vanish so fast, however, but that many more goblin feet had to go limping back over the underground ways of the mountain that morning.

Presently, however, they were reinforced from above by the king and his party, with the redoubtable queen at their head. Finding Curdie again busy amongst her unfortunate subjects, she rushed at him once more with the rage of despair, and this time gave him a bad bruise on the foot. Then a regular stamping fight got up between them, Curdie, with the point of his hunting-knife, keeping her from clasping her mighty arms about him, as he watched his opportunity of getting once more a good stamp at her skin-shod foot. But the queen was more wary as well as more agile than hitherto.

The rest meantime, finding their adversary thus matched for the moment, paused in their headlong hurry, and turned to the shivering group of women in the corner. As if determined to emulate his father and have a sun-woman of some sort to share his future throne, Harelip rushed at them, caught up Lootie, and sped with her to the hole. She gave a great shriek, and Curdie heard her, and saw the plight she was in. Gathering all his strength, he gave the queen a sudden cut across the face with his weapon, came down, as she started back, with all his weight on the proper foot, and sprung to Lootie's rescue. The prince had two defenseless feet, and on both of them Curdie stamped just as he reached the hole. He dropped his burden and rolled shrieking into the earth. Curdie made one stab at him as he disappeared, caught hold of the senseless Lootie, and having dragged her back to the corner, there mounted guard over her, preparing once more to encounter the queen.

Her face streaming with blood, and her eyes flashing green lightning through it, she came on with her mouth open and her teeth grinning like a tiger's, followed by the king and her bodyguard of the thickest goblins. But the same moment in rushed the captain and his men, and ran at them stamping furiously. They dared not encounter such an onset. Away they scurried, the queen foremost. Of course, the right thing would have been to take the king and queen prisoners, and hold them hostages for the princess, but they were so anxious to find her that no one thought of detaining them until it was too late.

Having thus rescued the servants, they set about searching the house once more. None of them could give the least information concerning the princess. Lootie was almost silly with terror, and, although scarcely able to walk would not leave Curdie's side for a single moment. Again he allowed the others to search the rest of the house - where, except a dismayed goblin lurking here and there, they found no one - while he requested Lootie to take him to the princess's room. She was as submissive and obedient as if he had been the king.

He found the bedclothes tossed about, and most of them on the floor, while the princess's garments were scattered all over the room, which was in the greatest confusion. It was only too evident that the goblins had been there, and Curdie had no longer any doubt that she had been carried off at the very first of the inroad. With a pang of despair he saw how wrong they had been in not securing the king and queen and prince; but he determined to find and rescue the princess as she had found and rescued him, or meet the worst fate to which the goblins could doom him.

28. Curdie's Guide

Just as the consolation of this resolve dawned upon his mind and he was turning away for the cellar to follow the goblins into their hole, something touched his hand. It was the slightest touch, and when he looked he could see nothing. Feeling and peering about in the grey of the dawn, his fingers came upon a tight thread. He looked again, and narrowly, but still could see nothing. It flashed upon him that this must be the princess's thread. Without saying a word, for he knew no one would believe him any more than he had believed the princess, he followed the thread with his finger, contrived to give Lootie the slip, and was soon out of the house and on the mountainside - surprised that, if the thread were indeed the grandmother's messenger, it should have led the princess, as he supposed it must, into the mountain, where she would be certain to meet the goblins rushing back enraged from their defeat. But he hurried on in the hope of overtaking her first. When he arrived, however, at the place where the path turned off for the mine, he found that the thread did not turn with it, but went straight up the mountain. Could it be that the thread was leading him home to his mother's cottage? Could the princess be there? He bounded up the mountain like one of its own goats, and before the sun was up the thread had brought him indeed to his mother's door. There it vanished from his fingers, and he could not find it, search as he might.

The door was on the latch, and he entered. There sat his mother by the fire, and in her arms lay the princess, fast asleep.

'Hush, Curdie!' said his mother. 'Do not wake her. I'm so glad you're come! I thought the cobs must have got you again!'

With a heart full of delight, Curdie sat down at a corner of the hearth, on a stool opposite his mother's chair, and gazed at the princess, who slept as peacefully as if she had been in her own bed. All at once she opened her eyes and fixed them on him.

'Oh, Curdie! you're come!' she said quietly. 'I thought you would!'

Curdie rose and stood before her with downcast eyes.

'Irene,' he said, 'I am very sorry I did not believe you.'

'Oh, never mind, Curdie!' answered the princess. 'You couldn't, you know. You do believe me now, don't you?'

'I can't help it now. I ought to have helped it before.'

'Why can't you help it now?'

'Because, just as I was going into the mountain to look for you, I got hold of your thread, and it brought me here.'

'Then you've come from my house, have you?'

'Yes, I have.'

'I didn't know you were there.'

'I've been there two or three days, I believe.'

'And I never knew it! Then perhaps you can tell me why my grandmother has brought me here? I can't think. Something woke me - I didn't know what, but I was frightened, and I felt for the thread, and there it was! I was more frightened still when it brought me out on the mountain, for I thought it was going to take me into it again, and I like the outside of it best. I supposed you were in trouble again, and I had to get you out. But it brought me here instead; and, oh, Curdie! your mother has been so kind to me - just like my own grandmother!'

Here Curdie's mother gave the princess a hug, and the princess turned and gave her a sweet smile, and held up her mouth to kiss her.

'Then you didn't see the cobs?'asked Curdie.

'No; I haven't been into the mountain, I told you, Curdie.'

'But the cobs have been into your house - all over it - and into your bedroom, making such a row!'

'What did they want there? It was very rude of them.'

'They wanted you - to carry you off into the mountain with them, for a wife to their prince Harelip.'

'Oh, how dreadful' cried the princess, shuddering.

'But you needn't be afraid, you know. Your grandmother takes care of you.'

'Ah! you do believe in my grandmother, then? I'm so glad! She made me think you would some day.'

All at once Curdie remembered his dream, and was silent, thinking.

'But how did you come to be in my house, and me not know it?' asked the princess.

Then Curdie had to explain everything - how he had watched for her sake, how he had been wounded and shut up by the soldiers, how he heard the noises and could not rise, and how the beautiful old lady had come to him, and all that followed.

'Poor Curdie! to lie there hurt and ill, and me never to know it!' exclaimed the princess, stroking his rough hand. 'I would have come and nursed you, if they had told me.'

'I didn't see you were lame,' said his mother.

'Am I, mother? Oh - yes - I suppose I ought to be! I declare I've never thought of it since I got up to go down amongst the cobs!'

'Let me see the wound,' said his mother.

He pulled down his stocking - when behold, except a great scar, his leg was perfectly sound!

Curdie and his mother gazed in each other's eyes, full of wonder, but Irene called out:

'I thought so, Curdie! I was sure it wasn't a dream. I was sure my grandmother had been to see you. Don't you smell the roses? It was my grandmother healed your leg, and sent you to help me.'

'No, Princess Irene,' said Curdie; 'I wasn't good enough to be allowed to help you: I didn't believe you. Your grandmother took care of you without me.'

'She sent you to help my people, anyhow. I wish my king-papa would come. I do want so to tell him how good you have been!'

'But,' said the mother, 'we are forgetting how frightened your people must be. You must take the princess home at once, Curdie - or at least go and tell them where she is.'

'Yes, mother. Only I'm dreadfully hungry. Do let me have some breakfast first. They ought to have listened to me, and then they wouldn't have been taken by surprise as they were.'

'That is true, Curdie; but it is not for you to blame them much. You remember?'

'Yes, mother, I do. Only I must really have something to eat.'

'You shall, my boy - as fast as I can get it,' said his mother, rising and setting the princess on her chair.

But before his breakfast was ready, Curdie jumped up so suddenly as to startle both his companions.

'Mother, mother!' he cried, 'I was forgetting. You must take the princess home yourself. I must go and wake my father.'

Without a word of explanation, he rushed to the place where his father was sleeping. Having thoroughly roused him with what he told him he darted out of the cottage.

29. Masonwork

He had all at once remembered the resolution of the goblins to carry out their second plan upon the failure of the first. No doubt they were already busy, and the mine was therefore in the greatest danger of being flooded and rendered useless - not to speak of the lives of the miners. When he reached the mouth of the mine, after rousing all the miners within reach, he found his father and a good many more just entering. They all hurried to the gang by which he had found a way into the goblin country. There the foresight of Peter had already collected a great many blocks of stone, with cement, ready for building up the weak place - well enough known to the goblins. Although there was not room for more than two to be actually building at once, they managed, by setting all the rest to work in preparing the cement and passing the stones, to finish in the course of the day a huge buttress filling the whole gang, and supported everywhere by the live rock. Before the hour when they usually dropped work, they were satisfied the mine was secure.

They had heard goblin hammers and pickaxes busy all the time, and at length fancied they heard sounds of water they had never heard before. But that was otherwise accounted for when they left the mine, for they stepped out into a tremendous storm which was raging all over the mountain. The thunder was bellowing, and the lightning lancing out of a huge black cloud which lay above it and hung down its edges of thick mist over its sides. The lightning was breaking out of the mountain, too, and flashing up into the cloud. From the state of the brooks, now swollen into raging torrents, it was evident that the storm had been storming all day.

The wind was blowing as if it would blow him off the mountain, but, anxious about his mother and the princess, Curdie darted up through the thick of the tempest. Even if they had not set out before the storm came on, he did not judge them safe, for in such a storm even their poor little house was in danger. Indeed he soon found that but for a huge rock against which it was built, and which protected it both from the blasts and the waters, it must have been swept if it was not blown away; for the two torrents into which this rock parted the rush of water behind it united again in front of the cottage - two roaring and dangerous streams, which his mother and the princess could not possibly have passed. It was with great difficulty that he forced his way through one of them, and up to the door.

The moment his hand fell on the latch, through all the uproar of winds and Waters came the joyous cry of the princess:

'There's Curdie! Curdie! Curdie!'

She was sitting wrapped in blankets on the bed, his mother trying for the hundredth time to light the fire which had been drowned by the rain that came down the chimney. The clay floor was one mass of mud, and the whole place looked wretched. But the faces of the mother and the princess shone as if their troubles only made them the merrier. Curdie burst out laughing at the sight of them.

'I never had such fun!' said the princess, her eyes twinkling and her pretty teeth shining. 'How nice it must be to live in a cottage on the mountain!'

'It all depends on what kind your inside house is,' said the mother.

'I know what you mean,' said Irene. 'That's the kind of thing my grandmother says.'

By the time Peter returned the storm was nearly over, but the streams were so fierce and so swollen that it was not only out of the question for the princess to go down the mountain, but most dangerous for Peter even or Curdie to make the attempt in the gathering darkness.

'They will be dreadfully frightened about you,' said Peter to the princess, 'but we cannot help it. We must wait till the morning.'

With Curdie's help, the fire was lighted at last, and the mother set about making their supper; and after supper they all told the princess stories till she grew sleepy. Then Curdie's mother laid her in Curdie's bed, which was in a tiny little garret-room. As soon as she was in bed, through a little window low down in the roof she caught sight of her grandmother's lamp shining far away beneath, and she gazed at the beautiful silvery globe until she fell asleep.

30. THE KING AN THE KISS

The next morning the sun rose so bright that Irene said the rain had washed his face and let the light out clean. The torrents were still roaring down the side of the mountain, but they were so much smaller as not to be dangerous in the daylight. After an early breakfast, Peter went to his work and Curdie and his mother set out to take the princess home. They had difficulty in getting her dry across the streams, and Curdie had again and again to carry her, but at last they got safe on the broader part of the road, and walked gently down towards the king's house. And what should they see as they turned the last corner but the last of the king's troop riding through the gate!

'Oh, Curdie!' cried Irene, clapping her hands right joyfully,' my king-papa is come.'

The moment Curdie heard that, he caught her up in his arms, and set off at full speed, crying: come on, mother dear! The king may break his heart before he knows that she is safe.'

Irene clung round his neck and he ran with her like a deer. When he entered the gate into the court, there sat the king on his horse, with all the people of the house about him, weeping and hanging their heads. The king was not weeping, but his face was white as a dead man's, and he looked as if the life had gone out of him. The men-at-arms he had brought with him sat with horror-stricken faces, but eyes flashing with rage, waiting only for the word of the king to do something - they did not know what, and nobody knew what. The day before, the men-at-arms belonging to the house, as soon as they were satisfied the princess had been carried away, rushed after the goblins into the hole, but found that they had already so skillfully blockaded the narrowest part, not many feet below the cellar, that without miners and their tools they could do nothing. Not one of them knew where the mouth of the mine lay, and some of those who had set out to find it had been overtaken by the storm and had not even yet returned. Poor Sir Walter was especially filled with shame, and almost hoped the king would order his head to be cut off, for to think of that sweet little face down amongst the goblins was unendurable.

When Curdie ran in at the gate with the princess in his arms, they were all so absorbed in their own misery and awed by the king's presence and grief, that no one observed his arrival. He went straight up to the king, where he sat on his horse.

'Papa! papa!' the princess cried, stretching out her arms to him; 'here I am!'

The king started. The color rushed to his face. He gave an inarticulate cry. Curdie held up the princess, and the king bent down and took her from his arms. As he clasped her to his bosom, the big tears went dropping down his cheeks and his beard. And such a shout arose from all the bystanders that the startled horses pranced and capered, and the armor rang and clattered, and the rocks of the mountain echoed back the noises. The princess greeted them all as she nestled in her father's bosom, and the king did not set her down until she had told them all the story. But she had more to tell about Curdie than about herself, and what she did tell about herself none of them could understand - except the king and Curdie, who stood by the king's knee stroking the neck of the great white horse. And still as she told what Curdie had done, Sir Walter and others added to what she told, even Lootie joining in the praises of his courage and energy.

Curdie held his peace, looking quietly up in the king's face. And his mother stood on the outskirts of the crowd listening with delight, for her son's deeds were pleasant in her ears, until the princess caught sight of her.

'And there is his mother, king-papa!' she said. 'See - there. She is such a nice mother, and has been so kind to me!'

They all parted asunder as the king made a sign to her to come forward. She obeyed, and he gave her his hand, but could not speak.

'And now, king-papa,' the princess went on, 'I must tell you another thing. One night long ago Curdie drove the goblins away and brought Lootie and me safe from the mountain. And I promised him a kiss when we got home, but Lootie wouldn't let me give it him. I don't want you to scold Lootie, but I want you to tell her that a princess must do as she promises.' 'Indeed she must, my child - except it be wrong,' said the king. 'There, give Curdie a kiss.'

And as he spoke he held her towards him.

The princess reached down, threw her arms round Curdie's neck, and kissed him on the mouth, saying: 'There, Curdie! There's the kiss I promised you!'

Then they all went into the house, and the cook rushed to the kitchen and the servants to their work. Lootie dressed Irene in her shiningest clothes, and the king put off his armor, and put on purple and gold; and a messenger was sent for Peter and all the miners, and there was a great and a grand feast, which continued long after the princess was put to bed.

31. THE SUBTERRANEAN WATERS

The king's harper, who always formed a part of his escort, was chanting a ballad which he made as he went on playing on his instrument - about the princess and the goblins, and the prowess of Curdie, when all at once he ceased, with his eyes on one of the doors of the hall. Thereupon the eyes of the king and his guests turned thitherward also. The next moment, through the open doorway came the princess Irene. She went straight up to her father, with her right hand stretched out a little sideways, and her forefinger, as her father and Curdie understood, feeling its way along the invisible thread. The king took her on his knee, and she said in his ear:

'King-papa, do you hear that noise?'

'I hear nothing,' said the king.

'Listen,' she said, holding up her forefinger.

The king listened, and a great stillness fell upon the company. Each man, seeing that the king listened, listened also, and the harper sat with his harp between his arms, and his finger silent upon the strings.

'I do hear a noise,' said the king at length - 'a noise as of distant thunder. It is coming nearer and nearer. What can it be?'

They all heard it now, and each seemed ready to start to his feet as he listened. Yet all sat perfectly still. The noise came rapidly nearer.

'What can it be?' said the king again.

'I think it must be another storm coming over the mountain,' said Sir Walter.

Then Curdie, who at the first word of the king had slipped from his seat, and laid his ear to the ground, rose up quickly, and approaching the king said, speaking very fast:

'Please, Your Majesty, I think I know what it is. I have no time to explain, for that might make it too late for some of us. Will Your Majesty give orders that everybody leave the house as quickly as possible and get up the mountain?'

The king, who was the wisest man in the kingdom, knew well there was a time when things must be done and questions left till afterwards. He had faith in Curdie, and rose instantly, with Irene in his arms. 'Every man and woman follow me,' he said, and strode out into the darkness.

Before he had reached the gate, the noise had grown to a great thundering roar, and the ground trembled beneath their feet, and before the last of them had crossed the court, out after them from the great hall door came a huge rush of turbid water, and almost swept them away. But they got safe out of the gate and up the mountain, while the torrent went roaring down the road into the valley beneath.

Curdie had left the king and the princess to look after his mother, whom he and his father, one on each side, caught up when the stream overtook them and carried safe and dry.

When the king had got out of the way of the water, a little up the mountain, he stood with the princess in his arms, looking back with amazement on the issuing torrent, which glimmered fierce and foamy through the night. There Curdie rejoined them.

'Now, Curdie,' said the king, 'what does it mean? Is this what you expected?'

'It is, Your Majesty,' said Curdie; and proceeded to tell him about the second scheme of the goblins, who, fancying the miners of more importance to the upper world than they were, had resolved, if they should fail in carrying off the king's daughter, to flood the mine and drown the miners. Then he explained what the miners had done to prevent it. The goblins had, in pursuance of their design, let loose all the underground reservoirs and streams, expecting the water to run down into the mine, which was lower than their part of the mountain, for they had, as they supposed, not knowing of the solid wall close behind, broken a passage through into it. But the readiest outlet the water could find had turned out to be the tunnel they had made to the king's house, the possibility of which catastrophe had not occurred to the young miner until he had laid his ear to the floor of the hall.

What was then to be done? The house appeared in danger of falling, and every moment the torrent was increasing.

'We must set out at once,' said the king. 'But how to get at the horses!'

'Shall I see if we can manage that?' said Curdie.

'Do,' said the king.

Curdie gathered the men-at-arms, and took them over the garden wall, and so to the stables. They found their horses in terror; the water was rising fast around them, and it was quite time they were got out. But there was no way to get them out, except by riding them through the stream, which was now pouring from the lower windows as well as the door. As one horse was quite enough for any man to manage through such a torrent, Curdie got on the king's white charger and, leading the way, brought them all in safety to the rising ground.

'Look, look, Curdie!' cried Irene, the moment that, having dismounted, he led the horse up to the king.

Curdie did look, and saw, high in the air, somewhere about the top of the king's house, a great globe of light shining like the purest silver.

'Oh!' he cried in some consternation, 'that is your grandmother's lamp! We must get her out. I will go an find her. The house may fall, you know.'

'My grandmother is in no danger,' said Irene, smiling.

'Here, Curdie, take the princess while I get on my horse,' said the king.

Curdie took the princess again, and both turned their eyes to the globe of light. The same moment there shot from it a white bird, which, descending with outstretched wings, made one circle round the king an Curdie and the princess, and then glided up again. The light and the pigeon vanished together.

'Now, Curdie!' said the princess, as he lifted her to her father's arms, 'you see my grandmother knows all about it, and isn't frightened. I believe she could walk through that water and it wouldn't wet her a bit.'

'But, my child,' said the king, 'you will be cold if you haven't Something more on. Run, Curdie, my boy, and fetch anything you can lay your hands on, to keep the princess warm. We have a long ride before us.'

Curdie was gone in a moment, and soon returned with a great rich fur, and the news that dead goblins were tossing about in the current through the house. They had been caught in their own snare; instead of the mine they had flooded their own country, whence they were now swept up drowned. Irene shuddered, but the king held her close to his bosom. Then he turned to Sir Walter, and said: 'Bring Curdie's father and mother here.'

'I wish,' said the king, when they stood before him, 'to take your son with me. He shall enter my bodyguard at once, and wait further promotion.'

Peter and his wife, overcome, only murmured almost inaudible thanks. But Curdie spoke aloud.

'Please, Your Majesty,' he said, 'I cannot leave my father and mother.'

'That's right, Curdie!' cried the princess. 'I wouldn't if I was you.'

The king looked at the princess and then at Curdie with a glow of satisfaction on his countenance.

'I too think you are right, Curdie,' he said, 'and I will not ask you again. But I shall have a chance of doing something for you some time.'

'Your Majesty has already allowed me to serve you,' said Curdie.

'But, Curdie,' said his mother, 'why shouldn't you go with the king? We can get on very well without you.'

'But I can't get on very well without you,' said Curdie. 'The king is very kind, but I could not be half the use to him that I am to you. Please, Your Majesty, if you wouldn't mind giving my mother a red petticoat! I should have got her one long ago, but for the goblins.'

'As soon as we get home,' said the king, 'Irene and I will search out the warmest one to be found, and send it by one of the gentlemen.'

'Yes, that we will, Curdie!' said the princess. 'And next summer we'll come back and see you wear it, Curdie's mother,' she added. 'Shan't we, king-papa?'

'Yes, my love; I hope so,' said the king.

Then turning to the miners, he said: 'Will you do the best you can for my servants tonight? I hope they will be able to return to the house tomorrow.'

The miners with one voice promised their hospitality. Then the king commanded his servants to mind whatever Curdie should say to them, and after shaking hands with him and his father and mother, the king and the princess and all their company rode away down the side of the new stream, which had already devoured half the road, into the starry night.

32. THE LAST CHAPTER

All the rest went up the mountain, and separated in groups to the homes of the miners. Curdie and his father and mother took Lootie with them. And the whole way a light, of which all but Lootie understood the origin, shone upon their path. But when they looked round they could see nothing of the silvery globe.

For days and days the water continued to rush from the doors and windows of the king's house, and a few goblin bodies were swept out into the road.

Curdie saw that something must be done. He spoke to his father and the rest of the miners, and they at once proceeded to make another outlet for the waters. By setting all hands to the work, tunneling here and building there, they soon succeeded; and having also made a little tunnel to drain the water away from under the king's house, they were soon able to get into the wine cellar, where they found a multitude of dead goblins - among the rest the queen, with the skin-shoe gone, and the stone one fast to her ankle - for the water had swept away the barricade, which prevented the men-at-arms from following the goblins, and had greatly widened the passage. They built it securely up, and then went back to their labors in the mine.

A good many of the goblins with their creatures escaped from the inundation out upon the mountain. But most of them soon left that part of the country, and most of those who remained grew milder in character, and indeed became very much like the Scotch brownies. Their skulls became softer as well as their hearts, and their feet grew harder, and by degrees they became friendly with the inhabitants of the mountain and even with the miners. But the latter were merciless to any of the cobs' creatures that came in their way, until at length they all but disappeared.

The rest of the history of The Princess and Curdie must be kept for another volume.

Book Two

The Princess And Curdie

ೞ৪ಬ

1. THE MOUNTAIN

Curdie was the son of Peter the miner. He lived with his father and mother in a cottage built on a mountain, and he worked with his father inside the mountain.

A mountain is a strange and awful thing. In old times, without knowing so much of their strangeness and awfulness as we do, people were yet more afraid of mountains. But then somehow they had not come to see how beautiful they are as well as awful, and they hated them - and what people hate they must fear. Now that we have learned to look at them with admiration, perhaps we do not feel quite awe enough of them. To me they are beautiful terrors.

I will try to tell you what they are. They are portions of the heart of the earth that have escaped from the dungeon down below, and rushed up and out. For the heart of the earth is a great wallowing mass, not of blood, as in the hearts of men and animals, but of glowing hot, melted metals and stones. And as our hearts keep us alive, so that great lump of heat keeps the earth alive: it is a huge power of buried sunlight - that is what it is.

Now think: out of that cauldron, where all the bubbles would be as big as the Alps if it could get room for its boiling, certain bubbles have bubbled out and escaped - up and away, and there they stand in the cool, cold sky - mountains. Think of the change, and you will no more wonder that there should be something awful about the very look of a mountain: from the darkness - for where the light has nothing to shine upon, much the same as darkness – from the heat, from the endless tumult of boiling unrest - up, with a sudden heavenward shoot, into the wind, and the cold, and the star shine, and a cloak of snow that lies like ermine above the blue-green mail of the glaciers; and the great sun, their grandfather, up there in the sky; and their little old cold aunt, the moon, that comes wandering about the house at night; and everlasting stillness, except for the wind that turns the rocks and caverns into a roaring organ for the young archangels that are studying how to let out the pent-up praises of their hearts, and the molten music of the streams, rushing ever from the bosoms of the glaciers fresh born.

Think, too, of the change in their own substance - no longer molten and soft, heaving and glowing, but hard and shining and cold. Think of the creatures scampering over and burrowing in it, and the birds building their nests upon it, and the trees growing out of its sides, like hair to clothe it, and the lovely grass in the valleys, and the gracious flowers even at the very edge of its armor of ice, rich embroidery of the garment below, and the rivers galloping down the valleys in a tumult nite and green! And along with all these, think of the terrible precipices down which the traveler may fall and be lost, and the frightful gulfs of blue air cracked in the glaciers, and the dark profound lakes, covered like little arctic oceans with floating lumps of ice.

All this outside the mountain! But the inside, who shall tell what lies there? Caverns of awfullest solitude, their walls miles thick, sparkling with ores of gold or silver, copper or iron, tin or mercury, studded perhaps with precious stones - perhaps a brook, with eyeless fish in it, running, running ceaselessly, cold and babbling, through banks crusted with carbuncles and golden topazes, or over a gravel of which some of the stones arc rubies and emeralds, perhaps diamonds and sapphires - who can tell? – and whoever can't tell is free to think - all waiting to flash, waiting for millions of ages - ever since the earth flew off from the sun, a great blot of fire, and began to cool.

Then there are caverns full of water, numbingly cold, fiercely hot - hotter than any boiling water. From some of these the water cannot get out, and from others it runs in channels as the blood in the body: little veins bring it down from the ice above into the great caverns of the mountain's heart, whence the arteries let it out again, gushing in pipes and clefts and ducts of all shapes and kinds, through and through its bulk, until it springs newborn to the light, and rushes down the Mountainside in torrents, and down the valleys in rivers - down, down, rejoicing, to the mighty lungs of the world, that is the sea, where it is tossed in storms and cyclones, heaved up in billows, twisted in waterspouts, dashed to mist upon rocks, beaten by millions of tails, and breathed by millions of gills, whence at last, melted into vapor by the sun, it is lifted up pure into the air, and borne by the servant winds back to the mountaintops and the snow, the solid ice, and the molten stream.

Well, when the heart of the earth has thus come rushing up among her children, bringing with it gifts of all that she possesses, then straightway into it rush her children to see what they can find there. With pickaxe and spade and crowbar, with boring chisel and blasting powder, they force their way back: is it to search for what toys they may have left in their long-forgotten nurseries? Hence the mountains that lift their heads into the clear air, and are dotted over with the dwellings of men, are tunneled and bored in the darkness of their bosoms by the dwellers in the houses which they hold up to the sun and air.

Curdie and his father were of these: their business was to bring to light hidden things; they sought silver in the rock and found it, and carried it out. Of the many other precious things in their mountain they knew little or nothing. Silver ore was what they were sent to find, and in darkness and danger they found it. But oh, how sweet was the air on the mountain face when they came out at sunset to go home to wife and mother! They did breathe deep then!

The mines belonged to the king of the country, and the miners were his servants, working under his overseers and officers. He was a real king - that is, one who ruled for the good of his people and not to please himself, and he wanted the silver not to buy rich things for himself, but to help him to govern the country, and pay the ones that defended it from certain troublesome neighbors, and the judges whom he set to portion out righteousness among the people, that so they might learn it themselves, and come to do without judges at all. Nothing that could be got from the heart of the earth could have been put to better purposes than the silver the king's miners got for him. There were people in the country who, when it came into their hands, degraded it by locking it up in a chest, and then it grew diseased and was called mammon, and bred all sorts of quarrels; but when first it left the king's hands it never made any but friends, and the air of the world kept it clean.

About a year before this story began, a series of very remarkable events had just ended. I will narrate as much of them as will serve to show the tops of the roots of my tree.

Upon the mountain, on one of its many claws, stood a grand old house, half farmhouse, half castle, belonging to the king; and there his only child, the Princess Irene, had been brought up till she was nearly nine years old, and would doubtless have continued much longer, but for the strange events to which I have referred.

At that time the hollow places of the mountain were inhabited by creatures called goblins, who for various reasons and in various ways made themselves troublesome to all, but to the little princess dangerous. Mainly by the watchful devotion and energy of Curdie, however, their designs had been utterly defeated, and made to recoil upon themselves to their own destruction, so that now there were very few of them left alive, and the miners did not believe there was a single goblin remaining in the whole inside of the mountain.

The king had been so pleased with the boy - then approaching thirteen years of age - that when he carried away his daughter he asked him to accompany them; but he was still better pleased with him when he found that he preferred staying with his father and mother. He was a right good king and knew that the love of a boy who would not leave his father and mother to be made a great man was worth ten thousand offers to die for his sake, and would prove so when the right time came. As for his father and mother, they would have given him up without a grumble, for they were just as good as the king, and he and they understood each other perfectly; but in this matter, not seeing that he could do anything for the king which one of his numerous attendants could not do as well, Curdie felt that it was for him to decide. So the king took a kind farewell of them all and rode away, with his daughter on his horse before him.

A gloom fell upon the mountain and the miners when she was gone, and Curdie did not whistle for a whole week. As for his verses, there was no occasion to make any now. He had made them only to drive away the goblins, and they were all gone - a good riddance - only the princess was gone too! He would rather have had things as they were, except for the princess's sake. But whoever is diligent will soon be cheerful, and though the miners missed the household of the castle, they yet managed to get on without them. Peter and his wife, however, were troubled with the fancy that they had stood in the way of their boy's good fortune. It would have been such a fine thing for him and them, too, they thought, if he had ridden with the good king's train. How beautiful he looked, they said, when he rode the king's own horse through the river that the goblins had sent out of the hill! He might soon have been a captain, they did believe! The good, kind people did not reflect that the road to the next duty is the only straight one, or that, for their fancied good, we should never wish our children or friends to do what we would not do ourselves if we were in their position. We must accept righteous sacrifices as well as make them.

2. THE WHITE PIGEON

When in the winter they had had their supper and sat about the fire, or when in the summer they lay on the border of the rock-margined stream that ran through their little meadow close by the door of their cottage, issuing from the far-up whiteness often folded in clouds, Curdie's mother would not seldom lead the conversation to one peculiar personage said and believed to have been much concerned in the late issue of events.

That personage was the great-great-grandmother of the princess, of whom the princess had often talked, but whom neither Curdie nor his mother had ever seen. Curdie could indeed remember, although already it looked more like a dream than he could account for if it had really taken place, how the princess had once led him up many stairs to what she called a beautiful room in the top of the tower, where she went through all the - what should he call it? – the behavior of presenting him to her grandmother, talking now to her and now to him, while all the time he saw nothing but a bare garret, a heap of musty straw, a sunbeam, and a withered apple. Lady, he would have declared before the king himself, young or old, there was none, except the princess herself, who was certainly vexed that he could not see what she at least believed she saw.

As for his mother, she had once seen, long before Curdie was born, a certain mysterious light of the same description as one Irene spoke of, calling it her grandmother's moon; and Curdie himself had seen this same light, shining from above the castle, just as the king and princess were taking their leave. Since that time neither had seen or heard anything that could be supposed connected with her. Strangely enough, however, nobody had seen her go away. If she was such an old lady, she could hardly be supposed to have set out alone and on foot when all the house was asleep. Still, away she must have gone, for, of course, if she was so powerful, she would always be about the princess to take care of her.

But as Curdie grew older, he doubted more and more whether Irene had not been talking of some dream she had taken for reality: He had heard it said that children could not always distinguish betwixt dreams and actual events. At the same time there was his mother's testimony: what was he to do with that? His mother, through whom he had learned everything, could hardly be imagined by her own dutiful son to have mistaken a dream for a fact of the waking world.

So he rather shrank from thinking about it, and the less he thought about it, the less he was inclined to believe it when he did think about it, and therefore, of course, the less inclined to talk about it to his father and mother; for although his father was one of those men who for one word they say think twenty thoughts, Curdie was well assured that he would rather doubt his own eyes than his wife's testimony.

There were no others to whom he could have talked about it. The miners were a mingled company - some good, some not so good, some rather bad - none of them so bad or so good as they might have been; Curdie liked most of them, and was a favorite with all; but they knew very little about the upper world, and what might or might not take place there. They knew silver from copper ore; they understood the underground ways of things, and they could look very wise with their lanterns in their hands searching after this or that sign of ore, or for some mark to guide their way in the hollows of the earth; but as to great-great-grandmothers, they would have mocked Curdie all the rest of his life for the absurdity of not being absolutely certain that the solemn belief of his father and mother was nothing but ridiculous nonsense. Why, to them the very word 'great-great-grandmother' would have been a week's laughter! I am not sure that they were able quite to believe there were such persons as great-great-grandmothers; they had never seen one. They were not companions to give the best of help toward progress, and as Curdie grew, he grew at this time faster in body than in mind - with the usual consequence, that he was getting rather stupid - one of the chief signs of which was that he believed less and less in things he had never seen. At the same time I do not think he was ever so stupid as to imagine that this was a sign of superior faculty and strength of mind. Still, he was becoming more and more a miner, and less and less a man of the upper world where the wind blew. On his way to and from the mine he took less and less notice of bees and butterflies, moths and dragonflies, the flowers and the brooks and the clouds. He was gradually changing into a commonplace man.

There is this difference between the growth of some human beings and that of others: in the one case it is a continuous dying, in the other a continuous resurrection. One of the latter sort comes at length to know at once whether a thing is true the moment it comes before him; one of the former class grows more and more afraid of being taken in, so afraid of it that he takes himself in altogether, and comes at length to believe in nothing but his dinner: to be sure of a thing with him is to have it between his teeth.

Curdie was not in a very good way, then, at that time. His father and mother had, it is true, no fault to find with him and yet – and yet - neither of them was ready to sing when the thought of him came up. There must be something wrong when a mother catches herself sighing over the time when her boy was in petticoats, or a father looks sad when he thinks how he used to carry him on his shoulder. The boy should enclose and keep, as his life, the old child at the heart of him, and never let it go. He must still, to be a right man, be his mother's darling, and more, his father's pride, and more. The child is not meant to die, but to be forever fresh born.

Curdie had made himself a bow and some arrows, and was teaching himself to shoot with them. One evening in the early summer, as he was walking home from the mine with them in his hand, a light flashed across his eyes. He looked, and there was a snow-white pigeon settling on a rock in front of him, in the red light of the level sun. There it fell at once to work with one of its wings, in which a feather or two had got some sprays twisted, causing a certain roughness unpleasant to the fastidious creature of the air.

It was indeed a lovely being, and Curdie thought how happy it must be flitting through the air with a flash - a live bolt of light. For a moment he became so one with the bird that he seemed to feel both its bill and its feathers, as the one adjusted the other to fly again, and his heart swelled with the pleasure of its involuntary sympathy. Another moment and it would have been aloft in the waves of rosy light - it was just bending its little legs to spring: that moment it fell on the path broken-winged and bleeding from Curdie's cruel arrow.

With a gush of pride at his skill, and pleasure at his success, he ran to pick up his prey. I must say for him he picked it up gently - perhaps it was the beginning of his repentance. But when he had the white thing in his hands its whiteness stained with another red than that of the sunset flood in which it had been revelling – ah God! who knows the joy of a bird, the ecstasy of a creature that has neither storehouse nor barn! - when he held it, I say, in his victorious hands, the winged thing looked up in his face - and with such eyes! - asking what was the matter, and where the red sun had gone, and the clouds, and the wind of its flight. Then they closed, but to open again presently, with the same questions in them.

And as they closed and opened, their look was fixed on his. It did not once flutter or try to get away; it only throbbed and bled and looked at him. Curdie's heart began to grow very large in his bosom. What could it mean? It was nothing but a pigeon, and why should he not kill a pigeon? But the fact was that not till this very moment had he ever known what a pigeon was. A good many discoveries of a similar kind have to be made by most of us. Once more it opened its eyes - then closed them again, and its throbbing ceased. Curdie gave a sob: its last look reminded him of the princess - he did not know why. He remembered how hard he had labored to set her beyond danger, and yet what dangers she had had to encounter for his sake: they had been saviors to each other - and what had he done now? He had stopped saving, and had begun killing! What had he been sent into the world for? Surely not to be a death to its joy and loveliness. He had done the thing that was contrary to gladness; he was a destroyer! He was not the Curdie he had been meant to be!

Then the underground waters gushed from the boy's heart. And with the tears came the remembrance that a white pigeon, just before the princess went away with her father, came from somewhere - yes, from the grandmother's lamp, and flew round the king and Irene and himself, and then flew away: this might be that very pigeon! Horrible to think! And if it wasn't, yet it was a white pigeon, the same as this. And if she kept a great Many pigeons - and white ones, as Irene had told him, then whose pigeon could he have killed but the grand old princess's? Suddenly everything round about him seemed against him. The red sunset stung him; the rocks frowned at him; the sweet wind that had been laving his face as he walked up the hill dropped - as if he wasn't fit to be kissed any more. Was the whole world going to cast him out? Would he have to stand there forever, not knowing what to do, with the dead pigeon in his hand? Things looked bad indeed. Was the whole world going to make a work about a pigeon - a white pigeon? The sun went down. Great clouds gathered over the west, and shortened the twilight. The wind gave a howl, and then lay down again. The clouds gathered thicker. Then came a rumbling. He thought it was thunder. It was a rock that fell inside the mountain. A goat ran past him down the hill, followed by a dog sent to fetch him home. He thought they were goblin creatures, and trembled. He used to despise them. And still he held the dead pigeon tenderly in his hand.

It grew darker and darker. An evil something began to move in his heart. 'What a fool I am!' he said to himself. Then he grew angry, and was just going to throw the bird from him and whistle, when a brightness shone all round him. He lifted his eyes, and saw a great globe of light - like silver at the hottest heat: he had once seen silver run from the furnace. It shone from somewhere above the roofs of the castle: it must be the great old princess's moon! How could she be there? Of course she was not there! He had asked the whole household, and nobody knew anything about her or her globe either. It couldn't be! And yet what did that signify, when there was the white globe shining, and here was the dead white bird in his hand? That moment the pigeon gave a little flutter. 'It's not dead!' cried Curdie, almost with a shriek. The same instant he was running full speed toward the castle, never letting his heels down, lest he should shake the poor, wounded bird.

3. THE MISTRESS OF THE SILVER MOON

When Curdie reached the castle, and ran into the little garden in front of it, there stood the door wide open. This was as he had hoped, for what could he have said if he had had to knock at it? Those whose business it is to open doors, so often mistake and shut them! But the woman now in charge often puzzled herself greatly to account for the strange fact that however often she shut the door, which, like the rest, she took a great deal of unnecessary trouble to do, she was certain, the next time she went to it, to find it open. I speak now of the great front door, of course: the back door she as persistently kept wide: if people could only go in by that, she said, she would then know what sort they were, and what they wanted. But she would neither have known what sort Curdie was, nor what he wanted, and would assuredly have denied him admittance, for she knew nothing of who was in the tower. So the front door was left open for him, and in he walked. But where to go next he could not tell. It was not quite dark: a dull, shineless twilight filled the place. All he knew was that he must go up, and that proved enough for the present, for there he saw the great staircase rising before him. When he reached the top of it, he knew there must be more stairs yet, for he could not be near the top of the tower. Indeed by the situation of the stairs, he must be a good way from the tower itself. But those who work well in the depths more easily understand the heights, for indeed in their true nature they are one and the same; miners are in mountains; and Curdie, from knowing the ways of the king's mines, and being able to calculate his whereabouts in them, was now able to find his way about the king's house. He knew its outside perfectly, and now his business was to get his notion of the inside right with the outside.

So he shut his eyes and made a picture of the outside of it in his mind. Then he came in at the door of the picture, and yet kept the picture before him all the time - for you can do that kind of thing in your mind - and took every turn of the stair over again, always watching to remember, every time he turned his face, how the tower lay, and then when he came to himself at the top where he stood, he knew exactly where it was, and walked at once in the right direction.

On his way, however, he came to another stair, and up that he went, of course, watching still at every turn how the tower must lie. At the top of this stair was yet another - they were the stairs up which the princess ran when first, without knowing it, she was on her way to find her great-great-grandmother. At the top of the second stair he could go no farther, and must therefore set out again to find the tower, which, as it rose far above the rest of the house, must have the last of its stairs inside itself.

Having watched every turn to the very last, he still knew quite well in what direction he must go to find it, so he left the stair and went down a passage that led, if not exactly toward it, yet nearer it. This passage was rather dark, for it was very long, with only one window at the end, and although there were doors on both sides of it, they were all shut. At the distant window glimmered the chill east, with a few feeble stars in it, and its like was dreary and old, growing brown, and looking as if it were thinking about the day that was just gone. Presently he turned into another passage, which also had a window at the end of it; and in at that window shone all that was left of the sunset, just a few ashes, with here and there a little touch of warmth: it was nearly as sad as the east, only there was one difference - it was very plainly thinking of tomorrow.

But at present Curdie had nothing to do with today or tomorrow; his business was with the bird, and the tower where dwelt the grand old princess to whom it belonged. So he kept on his way, still eastward, and came to yet another passage, which brought him to a door. He was afraid to open it without first knocking. He knocked, but heard no answer. He was answered nevertheless; for the door gently opened, and there was a narrow stair - and so steep that, big lad as he was, he, too, like the Princess Irene before him, found his hands needful for the climbing. And it was a long climb, but he reached the top at last - a little landing, with a door in front and one on each side. Which should he knock at?

As he hesitated, he heard the noise of a spinning wheel. He knew it at once, because his mother's spinning wheel had been his governess long ago, and still taught him things. It was the spinning wheel that first taught him to make verses, and to sing, and to think whether all was right inside him; or at least it had helped him in all these things. Hence it was no wonder he should know a spinning wheel when he heard it sing - even although as the bird of paradise to other birds was the song of that wheel to the song of his mother's.

He stood listening, so entranced that he forgot to knock, and the wheel went on and on, spinning in his brain songs and tales and rhymes, till he was almost asleep as well as dreaming, for sleep does not always come first. But suddenly came the thought of the poor bird, which had been lying motionless in his hand all the time, and that woke him up, and at once he knocked.

'Come in, Curdie,' said a voice.

Curdie shook. It was getting rather awful. The heart that had never much heeded an army of goblins trembled at the soft word of invitation. But then there was the red-spotted white thing in his hand! He dared not hesitate, though. Gently he opened the door through which the sound came, and what did he see? Nothing at first - except indeed a great sloping shaft of moonlight that came in at a high window, and rested on the floor. He stood and stared at it, forgetting to shut the door.

'Why don't you come in, Curdie?' said the voice. 'Did you never see moonlight before?'

'Never without a moon,' answered Curdie, in a trembling tone, but gathering courage.

'Certainly not,' returned the voice, which was thin and quavering: 'I never saw moonlight without a moon.'

'But there's no moon outside,' said Curdie.

'Ah! but you're inside now,' said the voice.

The answer did not satisfy Curdie; but the voice went on.

'There are more moons than you know of, Curdie. Where there is one sun there are many moons - and of many sorts. Come in and look out of my window, and you will soon satisfy yourself that there is a moon looking in at it.'

The gentleness of the voice made Curdie remember his manners. He shut the door, and drew a step or two nearer to the moonlight.

All the time the sound of the spinning had been going on and on, and Curdie now caught sight of the wheel. Oh, it was such a thin, delicate thing - reminding him of a spider's web in a hedge. It stood in the middle of the moonlight, and it seemed as if the moonlight had nearly melted it away. A step nearer, he saw, with a start, two little hands at work with it. And then at last, in the shadow on the other side of the moonlight which came like silver between, he saw the form to which the hands belonged: a small withered creature, so old that no age would have seemed too great to write under her picture, seated on a stool beyond the spinning wheel, which looked very large beside her, but, as I said, very thin, like a long-legged spider holding up its own web, which was the round wheel itself She sat crumpled together, a filmy thing that it seemed a puff would blow away, more like the body of a fly the big spider had sucked empty and left hanging in his web, than anything else I can think of.

When Curdie saw her, he stood still again, a good deal in wonder, a very little in reverence, a little in doubt, and, I must add, a little in amusement at the odd look of the old marvel. Her grey hair mixed with the moonlight so that he could not tell where the one began and the other ended. Her crooked back bent forward over her chest, her shoulders nearly swallowed up her head between them, and her two little hands were just like the grey claws of a hen, scratching at the thread, which to Curdie was of course invisible across the moonlight. Indeed Curdie laughed within himself, just a little, at the sight; and when he thought of how the princess used to talk about her huge, great, old grandmother, he laughed more. But that moment the little lady leaned forward into the moonlight, and Curdie caught a glimpse of her eyes, and all the laugh went out of him.

'What do you come here for, Curdie?' she said, as gently as before.

Then Curdie remembered that he stood there as a culprit, and worst of all, as one who had his confession yet to make. There was no time to hesitate over it.

'Oh, ma'am! See here,' he said, and advanced a step or two, holding out the pigeon.

'What have you got there?' she asked.

Again Curdie advanced a few steps, and held out his hand with the pigeon, that she might see what it was, into the moonlight. The moment the rays fell upon it the pigeon gave a faint flutter. The old lady put out her old hands and took it, and held it to her bosom, and rocked it, murmuring over it as if it were a sick baby.

When Curdie saw how distressed she was he grew sorrier still, and said: 'I didn't mean to do any harm, ma'am. I didn't think of its being yours.'

'Ah, Curdie! If it weren't mine, what would become of it now?' she returned. 'You say you didn't mean any harm: did you mean any good, Curdie?'

'No,' answered Curdie.

'Remember, then, that whoever does not mean good is always in danger of harm. But I try to give everybody fair play; and those that are in the wrong are in far more need of it always than those who are in the right: they can afford to do without it. Therefore I say for you that when you shot that arrow you did not know what a pigeon is. Now that you do know, you are sorry. It is very dangerous to do things you don't know about.'

'But, please, ma'am - I don't mean to be rude or to contradict you,' said Curdie, 'but if a body was never to do anything but what he knew to be good, he would have to live half his time doing nothing.'

'There you are much mistaken,' said the old quavering voice. 'How little you must have thought! Why, you don't seem even to know the good of the things you are constantly doing. Now don't mistake me. I don't mean you are good for doing them. It is a good thing to eat your breakfast, but you don't fancy it's very good of you to do it. The thing is good, not you.'

Curdie laughed.

'There are a great many more good things than bad things to do. Now tell me what bad thing you have done today besides this sore hurt to my little white friend.' While she talked Curdie had sunk into a sort of reverie, in which he hardly knew whether it was the old lady or his own heart that spoke. And when she asked him that question, he was at first much inclined to consider himself a very good fellow on the whole. 'I really don't think I did anything else that was very bad all day,' he said to himself. But at the same time he could not honestly feel that he was worth standing up for. All at once a light seemed to break in upon his mind, and he woke up and there was the withered little atomy of the old lady on the other side of the moonlight, and there was the spinning wheel singing on and on in the middle of it!

'I know now, ma'am; I understand now,' he said. 'Thank you, ma'am, for spinning it into me with your wheel. I see now that I have been doing wrong the whole day, and such a many days besides! Indeed, I don't know when I ever did right, and yet it seems as if I had done right some time and had forgotten how. When I killed your bird I did not know I was doing wrong, just because I was always doing wrong, and the wrong had soaked all through me.'

'What wrong were you doing all day, Curdie? It is better to come to the point, you know,' said the old lady, and her voice was gentler even than before.

'I was doing the wrong of never wanting or trying to be better. And now I see that I have been letting things go as they would for a long time. Whatever came into my head I did, and whatever didn't come into my head I didn't do. I never sent anything away, and never looked out for anything to come. I haven't been attending to my mother - or my father either. And now I think of it, I know I have often seen them looking troubled, and I have never asked them what was the matter. And now I see, too, that I did not ask because I suspected it had something to do with me and my behavior, and didn't want to hear the truth. And I know I have been grumbling at my work, and doing a hundred other things that are wrong.'

'You have got it, Curdie,' said the old lady, in a voice that sounded almost as if she had been crying. 'When people don't care to be better they must be doing everything wrong. I am so glad you shot my bird!'

'Ma'am!' exclaimed Curdie. 'How can you be?'

'Because it has brought you to see what sort you were when you did it, and what sort you will grow to be again, only worse, if you don't mind. Now that you are sorry, my poor bird will be better. Look up, my dovey.'

The pigeon gave a flutter, and spread out one of its red-spotted wings across the old woman's bosom.

'I will mend the little angel,' she said, 'and in a week or two it will be flying again. So you may ease your heart about the pigeon.'

'Oh, thank you! Thank you!' cried Curdie. 'I don't know how to thank you.'

'Then I will tell you. There is only one way I care for. Do better, and grow better, and be better. And never kill anything without a good reason for it.'

'Ma'am, I will go and fetch my bow and arrows, and you shall burn them yourself.'

'I have no fire that would burn your bow and arrows, Curdie.'

'Then I promise you to burn them all under my mother's porridge pot tomorrow morning.'

'No, no, Curdie. Keep them, and practice with them every day, and grow a good shot. There are plenty of bad things that want killing, and a day will come when they will prove useful. But I must see first whether you will do as I tell you.'

'That I will!' said Curdie. 'What is it, ma'am?'

'Only something not to do,' answered the old lady; 'if you should hear anyone speak about me, never to laugh or make fun of me.'

'Oh, ma'am!' exclaimed Curdie, shocked that she should think such a request needful.

'Stop, stop,' she went on. 'People hereabout sometimes tell very odd and in fact ridiculous stories of an old woman who watches what is going on, and occasionally interferes. They mean me, though what they say is often great nonsense. Now what I want of you is not to laugh, or side with them in any way; because they will take that to mean that you don't believe there is any such person a bit more than they do. Now that would not be the case - would it, Curdie?'

'No, indeed, ma'am. I've seen you.'

The old woman smiled very oddly.

'Yes, you've seen me,' she said. 'But mind,' she continued, 'I don't want you to say anything - only to hold your tongue, and not seem to side with them.'

'That will be easy,' said Curdie,' now that I've seen you with my very own eyes, ma'am.'

'Not so easy as you think, perhaps,' said the old lady, with another curious smile. 'I want to be your friend,' she added after a little pause, 'but I don't quite know yet whether you will let me.'
'Indeed I will, ma'am,' said Curdie.

'That is for me to find out,' she rejoined, with yet another strange smile. 'in the meantime all I can say is, come to me again when you find yourself in any trouble, and I will see what I can do for you - only the canning depends on yourself. I am greatly pleased with you for bringing me my pigeon, doing your best to set right what you had set wrong.'

As she spoke she held out her hand to him, and when he took it she made use of his to help herself up from her stool, and - when or how it came about, Curdie could not tell - the same instant she stood before him a tall, strong woman - plainly very old, but as grand as she was old, and only rather severe-looking. Every trace of the decrepitude and witheredness she showed as she hovered like a film about her wheel, had vanished. Her hair was very white, but it hung about her head in great plenty, and shone like silver in the moonlight. Straight as a pillar she stood before the astonished boy, and the wounded bird had now spread out both its wings across her bosom, like some great mystical ornament of frosted silver.

'Oh, now I can never forget you!' cried Curdie. 'I see now what you really are!'

'Did I not tell you the truth when I sat at my wheel?' said the old lady.

'Yes, ma'am,' answered Curdie.

'I can do no more than tell you the truth now,' she rejoined. 'It is a bad thing indeed to forget one who has told us the truth. Now go.'

Curdie obeyed, and took a few steps toward the door. 'Please, ma'am - what am I to call you?' he was going to say; but when he turned to speak, he saw nobody. Whether she was there or not he could not tell, however, for the moonlight had vanished, and the room was utterly dark. A great fear, such as he had never before known, came upon him, and almost overwhelmed him. He groped his way to the door, and crawled down the stair - in doubt and anxiety as to how he should find his way out of the house in the dark. And the stair seemed ever so much longer than when he came up. Nor was that any wonder, for down and down he went, until at length his foot struck a door, and when he rose and opened it, he found himself under the starry, moonless sky at the foot of the tower.

He soon discovered the way out of the garden, with which he had some acquaintance already, and in a few minutes was climbing the mountain with a solemn and cheerful heart. It was rather dark, but he knew the way well. As he passed the rock from which the poor pigeon fell wounded with his arrow, a great joy filled his heart at the thought that he was delivered from the blood of the little bird, and he ran the next hundred yards at full speed up the hill. Some dark shadows passed him: he did not even care to think what they were, but let them run. When he reached home, he found his father and mother waiting supper for him.

4. Curdie's Father and Mother

The eyes of the fathers and mothers are quick to read their children's looks, and when Curdie entered the cottage, his parents saw at once that something unusual had taken place. When he said to his mother, 'I beg your pardon for being so late,' there was something in the tone beyond the politeness that went to her heart, for it seemed to come from the place where all lovely things were born before they began to grow in this world. When he set his father's chair to the table, an attention he had not shown him for a long time, Peter thanked him with more gratitude than the boy had ever yet felt in all his life. It was a small thing to do for the man who had been serving him since ever he was born, but I suspect there is nothing a man can be so grateful for as that to which he has the most right.

There was a change upon Curdie, and father and mother felt there must be something to account for it, and therefore were pretty sure he had something to tell them. For when a child's heart is all right, it is not likely he will want to keep anything from his parents. But the story of the evening was too solemn for Curdie to come out with all at once. He must wait until they had had their porridge, and the affairs of this world were over for the day.

But when they were seated on the grassy bank of the brook that went so sweetly blundering over the great stones of its rocky channel, for the whole meadow lay on the top of a huge rock, then he felt that the right hour had come for sharing with them the wonderful things that had come to him. It was perhaps the loveliest of all hours in the year. The summer was young and soft, and this was the warmest evening they had yet had - dusky, dark even below, while above, the stars were bright and large and sharp in the blackest blue sky. The night came close around them, clasping them in one universal arm of love, and although it neither spoke nor smiled, seemed all eye and ear, seemed to see and hear and know everything they said and did. It is a way the night has sometimes, and there is a reason for it. The only sound was that of the brook, for there was no wind, and no trees for it to make its music upon if there had been, for the cottage was high up on the mountain, on a great shoulder of stone where trees would not grow.

There, to the accompaniment of the water, as it hurried down to the valley and the sea, talking busily of a thousand true things which it could not understand, Curdie told his tale, outside and in, to his father and mother. What a world had slipped in between the mouth of the mine and his mother's cottage! Neither of them said a word until he had ended.

'Now what am I to make of it, Mother? it's so strange!' he said, and stopped.

'It's easy enough to see what Curdie has got to make of it, isn't it, Peter?' said the good woman, turning her face toward all she could see of her husband's.

'it seems so to me,' answered Peter, with a smile which only the night saw, but his wife felt in the tone of his words. They were the happiest couple in that country, because they always understood each other, and that was because they always meant the same thing, and that was because they always loved what was fair and true and right better, not than anything else, but than everything else put together.

'Then will you tell Curdie?' said she.

'You can talk best, Joan,' said he. 'You tell him, and I will listen - and learn how to say what I think,' he added.

'I,' said Curdie, 'don't know what to think.'

'it does not matter so much,' said his mother. 'If only you know what to make of a thing, you'll know soon enough what to think of it. Now I needn't tell you, surely, Curdie, what you've got to do with this?'

'I suppose you mean, Mother,' answered Curdie, 'that I must do as the old lady told me?'

'That is what I mean: what else could it be? Am I not right, Peter?'

'Quite right, Joan,' answered Peter, 'so far as my judgment goes. It is a very strange story, but you see the question is not about believing it, for Curdie knows what came to him.'

'And you remember, Curdie,' said his mother, 'that when the princess took you up that tower once before, and there talked to her great-great-grandmother, you came home quite angry with her, and said there was nothing in the place but an old tub, a heap of straw - oh, I remember your inventory quite well! - an old tub, a heap of straw, a withered apple, and a sunbeam. According to your eyes, that was all there was in the great, old, musty garret. But now you have had a glimpse of the old princess herself!'

'Yes, Mother, I did see her - or if I didn't -' said Curdie very thoughtfully - then began again. 'The hardest thing to believe, though I saw it with my own eyes, was when the thin, filmy creature that seemed almost to float about in the moonlight like a bit of the silver paper they put over pictures, or like a handkerchief made of spider threads, took my hand, and rose up. She was taller and stronger than you, Mother, ever so much! - at least, she looked so.'

'And most certainly was so, Curdie, if she looked so,' said Mrs. Peterson.

'Well, I confess,' returned her son, 'that one thing, if there were no other, would make me doubt whether I was not dreaming, after all, wide awake though I fancied myself to be.'

'Of course,' answered his mother, 'it is not for me to say whether you were dreaming or not if you are doubtful of it yourself; but it doesn't make me think I am dreaming when in the summer I hold in my hand the bunch of sweet peas that make my heart glad with their color and scent, and remember the dry, withered-looking little thing I dibbled into the hole in the same spot in the spring. I only think how wonderful and lovely it all is. It seems just as full of reason as it is of wonder. How it is done I can't tell, only there it is! And there is this in it, too, Curdie - of which you would not be so ready to think - that when you come home to your father and mother, and they find you behaving more like a dear, good son than you have behaved for a long time, they at least are not likely to think you were only dreaming.'

'Still,' said Curdie, looking a little ashamed, 'I might have dreamed my duty.'

'Then dream often, my son; for there must then be more truth in your dreams than in your waking thoughts. But however any of these things may be, this one point remains certain: there can be no harm in doing as she told you. And, indeed, until you are sure there is no such person, you are bound to do it, for you promised.'

'it seems to me,' said his father, 'that if a lady comes to you in a dream, Curdie, and tells you not to talk about her when you wake, the least you can do is to hold your tongue.'

'True, Father! Yes, Mother, I'll do it,' said Curdie.

Then they went to bed, and sleep, which is the night of the soul, next took them in its arms and made them well.

5. THE MINERS

It much increased Curdie's feeling of the strangeness of the whole affair, that, the next morning, when they were at work in the mine, the party of which he and his father were two, just as if they had known what had happened to him the night before, began talking about all manner of wonderful tales that were abroad in the country, chiefly, of course, those connected with the mines, and the mountains in which they lay. Their wives and mothers and grandmothers were their chief authorities. For when they sat by their firesides they heard their wives telling their children the selfsame tales, with little differences, and here and there one they had not heard before, which they had heard their mothers and grandmothers tell in one or other of the same cottages.

At length they came to speak of a certain strange being they called Old Mother Wotherwop. Some said their wives had seen her. It appeared as they talked that not one had seen her more than once. Some of their mothers and grandmothers, however, had seen her also, and they all had told them tales about her when they were children. They said she could take any shape she liked, but that in reality she was a withered old woman, so old and so withered that she was as thin as a sieve with a lamp behind it; that she was never seen except at night, and when something terrible had taken place, or was going to take place - such as the falling in of the roof of a mine, or the breaking out of water in it.

She had more than once been seen - it was always at night – beside some well, sitting on the brink of it, and leaning over and stirring it with her forefinger, which was six times as long as any of the rest. And whoever for months after drank of that well was sure to be ill. To this, one of them, however, added that he remembered his mother saying that whoever in bad health drank of the well was sure to get better. But the majority agreed that the former was the right version of the story- for was she not a witch, an old hating witch, whose delight was to do mischief? One said he had heard that she took the shape of a young woman sometimes, as beautiful as an angel, and then was most dangerous of all, for she struck every man who looked upon her stone-blind.

Peter ventured the question whether she might not as likely be an angel that took the form of an old woman, as an old woman that took the form of an angel. But nobody except Curdie, who was holding his peace with all his might, saw any sense in the question. They said an old woman might be very glad to make herself look like a young one, but who ever heard of a young and beautiful one making herself look old and ugly?

Peter asked why they were so much more ready to believe the bad that was said of her than the good. They answered, because she was bad. He asked why they believed her to be bad, and they answered, because she did bad things. When he asked how they knew that, they said, because she was a bad creature. Even if they didn't know it, they said, a woman like that was so much more likely to be bad than good. Why did she go about at night? Why did she appear only now and then, and on such occasions? One went on to tell how one night when his grandfather had been having a jolly time of it with his friends in the market town, she had served him so upon his way home that the poor man never drank a drop of anything stronger than water after it to the day of his death. She dragged him into a bog, and tumbled him up and down in it till he was nearly dead.

'I suppose that was her way of teaching him what a good thing water was,' said Peter; but the man, who liked strong drink, did not see the joke.

'They do say,' said another, 'that she has lived in the old house over there ever since the little princess left it. They say too that the housekeeper knows all about it, and is hand and glove with the old witch. I don't doubt they have many a nice airing together on broomsticks. But I don't doubt either it's all nonsense, and there's no such person at all.'

'When our cow died,' said another, 'she was seen going round and round the cow house the same night. To be sure she left a fine calf behind her - I mean the cow did, not the witch. I wonder she didn't kill that, too, for she'll be a far finer cow than ever her mother was.'

'My old woman came upon her one night, not long before the water broke out in the mine, sitting on a stone on the hillside with a whole congregation of cobs about her. When they saw my wife they all scampered off as fast as they could run, and where the witch was sitting there was nothing to be seen but a withered bracken bush. I made no doubt myself she was putting them up to it.'

And so they went on with one foolish tale after another, while Peter put in a word now and then, and Curdie diligently held his peace. But his silence at last drew attention upon it, and one of them said:

'Come, young Curdie, what are you thinking of?'

'How do you know I'm thinking of anything?' asked Curdie.

'Because you're not saying anything.'

'Does it follow then that, as you are saying so much, you're not thinking at all?' said Curdie.

'I know what he's thinking,' said one who had not yet spoken; 'he's thinking what a set of fools you are to talk such rubbish; as if ever there was or could be such an old woman as you say! I'm sure Curdie knows better than all that comes to.'

'I think,' said Curdie, 'it would be better that he who says anything about her should be quite sure it is true, lest she should hear him, and not like to be slandered.'

'But would she like it any better if it were true?' said the same man. 'If she is What they say - I don't know - but I never knew a man that wouldn't go in a rage to be called the very thing he was.'

'if bad things were true of her, and I knew it,' said Curdie, 'I would not hesitate to say them, for I will never give in to being afraid of anything that's bad. I suspect that the things they tell, however, if we knew all about them, would turn out to have nothing but good in them; and I won't say a word more for fear I should say something that mightn't be to her mind.'

They all burst into a loud laugh.

'Hear the parson!' they cried. 'He believes in the witch! Ha! ha!'

'He's afraid of her!'

'And says all she does is good!'

'He wants to make friends with her, that she may help him to find the silver ore.'

'Give me my own eyes and a good divining rod before all the witches in the world! And so I'd advise you too, Master Curdie; that is, when your eyes have grown to be worth anything, and you have learned to cut the hazel fork.' Thus they all mocked and jeered at him, but he did his best to keep his temper and go quietly on with his work. He got as close to his father as he could, however, for that helped him to bear it. As soon as they were tired of laughing and mocking, Curdie was friendly with them, and long before their midday meal all between them was as it had been.

But when the evening came, Peter and Curdie felt that they would rather walk home together without other company, and therefore lingered behind when the rest of the men left the mine.

6. THE EMERALD

Father and son had seated themselves on a projecting piece of rock at a corner where three galleries met - the one they had come along from their work, one to the right leading out of the mountain, and the other to the left leading far into a portion of it which had been long disused. Since the inundation caused by the goblins, it had indeed been rendered impassable by the settlement of a quantity of the water, forming a small but very deep lake, in a part where there was a considerable descent.

They had just risen and were turning to the right, when a gleam caught their eyes, and made them look along the whole gallery. Far up they saw a pale green light, whence issuing they could not tell, about halfway between floor and roof of the passage. They saw nothing but the light, which was like a large star, with a point of darker color yet brighter radiance in the heart of it, whence the rest of the light shot out in rays that faded toward the ends until they vanished. It shed hardly any light around it, although in itself it was so bright as to sting the eyes that beheld it. Wonderful stories had from ages gone been current in the mines about certain magic gems which gave out light of themselves, and this light looked just like what might be supposed to shoot from the heart of such a gem.

They went up the old gallery to find out what it could be. To their surprise they found, however, that, after going some distance, they were no nearer to it, so far as they could judge, than when they started. It did not seem to move, and yet they moving did not approach it. Still they persevered, for it was far too wonderful a thing to lose sight of, so long as they could keep it. At length they drew near the hollow where the water lay, and still were no nearer the light. Where they expected to be stopped by the water, however, water was none: something had taken place in some part of the mine that had drained it off, and the gallery lay open as in former times.

And now, to their surprise, the light, instead of being in front of them, was shining at the same distance to the right, where they did not know there was any passage at all. Then they discovered, by the light of the lanterns they carried, that there the water had broken through, and made an entrance to a part of the mountain of which Peter knew nothing. But they were hardly well into it, still following the light, before Curdie thought he recognized some of the passages he had so often gone through when he was watching the goblins.

After they had advanced a long way, with many turnings, now to the right, now to the left, all at once their eyes seemed to come suddenly to themselves, and they became aware that the light which they had taken to be a great way from them was in reality almost within reach of their hands.

The same instant it began to grow larger and thinner, the point of light grew dim as it spread, the greenness melted away, and in a moment or two, instead of the star, a dark, dark and yet luminous face was looking at them with living eyes. And Curdie felt a great awe swell up in his heart, for he thought he had seen those eyes before.

'I see you know me, Curdie,' said a voice.

'if your eyes are you, ma'am, then I know you,' said Curdie. 'But I never saw your face before.'

'Yes, you have seen it, Curdie,' said the voice. And with that the darkness of its complexion melted away, and down from the face dawned out the form that belonged to it, until at last Curdie and his father beheld a lady, beautiful exceedingly, dressed in something pale green, like velvet, over which her hair fell in cataracts of a rich golden color. It looked as if it were pouring down from her head, and, like the water of the Dustbrook, vanishing in a golden vapor ere it reached the floor. It came flowing from under the edge of a coronet of gold, set with alternated pearls and emeralds. In front of the crown was a great emerald, which looked somehow as if out of it had come the light they had followed. There was no ornament else about her, except on her slippers, which were one mass of gleaming emeralds, of various shades of green, all mingling lovelily like the waving of grass in the wind and sun. She looked about five-and-twenty years old. And for all the difference, Curdie knew somehow or other, he could not have told how, that the face before him was that of the old princess, Irene's great-great-grandmother.

By this time all around them had grown light, and now first they could see where they were. They stood in a great splendid cavern, which Curdie recognized as that in which the goblins held their state assemblies. But, strange to tell, the light by which they saw came streaming, sparkling, and shooting from stones of many colors in the sides and roof and floor of the cavern - stones of all the colors of the rainbow, and many more. It was a glorious sight - the whole rugged place flashing with colors - in one spot a great light of deep carbuncular red, in another of sapphirine blue, in another of topaz yellow; while here and there were groups of stones of all hues and sizes, and again nebulous spaces of thousands of tiniest spots of brilliancy of every conceivable shade. Sometimes the colors ran together, and made a little river or lake of lambent, interfusing, and changing tints, which, by their variegation, seemed to imitate the flowing of water, or waves made by the wind.

Curdie would have gazed entranced, but that all the beauty of the cavern, yes, of all he knew of the whole creation, seemed gathered in one centre of harmony and loveliness in the person of the ancient lady who stood before him in the very summer of beauty and strength. Turning from the first glance at the circuadjacent splendor, it dwindled into nothing as he looked again at the lady. Nothing flashed or glowed or shone about her, and yet it was with a prevision of the truth that he said,

'I was here once before, ma'am.'

'I know that, Curdie,' she replied.

'The place was full of torches, and the walls gleamed, but nothing as they do now, and there is no light in the place.'

'You want to know where the light comes from?' she said, smiling.

'Yes, ma'am.'

'Then see: I will go out of the cavern. Do not be afraid, but watch.'

She went slowly out. The moment she turned her back to go, the light began to pale and fade; the moment she was out of their sight the place was black as night, save that now the smoky yellow-red of their lamps, which they thought had gone out long ago, cast a dusky glimmer around them.

7. WHAT IS IN A NAME?

For a time that seemed to them long, the two men stood waiting, while still the Mother of Light did not return. So long was she absent that they began to grow anxious: how were they to find their way from the natural hollows of the mountain crossed by goblin paths, if their lamps should go out? To spend the night there would mean to sit and wait until an earthquake rent the mountain, or the earth herself fell back into the smelting furnace of the sun whence she had issued - for it was all night and no faintest dawn in the bosom of the world.

So long did they wait un-revisited, that, had there not been two of them, either would at length have concluded the vision a home-born product of his own seething brain. And their lamps were going out, for they grew redder and smokier! But they did not lose courage, for there is a kind of capillary attraction in the facing of two souls, that lifts faith quite beyond the level to which either could raise it alone: they knew that they had seen the lady of emeralds, and it was to give them their own desire that she had gone from them, and neither would yield for a moment to the half doubts and half dreads that awoke in his heart.

And still she who with her absence darkened their air did not return. They grew weary, and sat down on the rocky floor, for wait they would - indeed, wait they must. Each set his lamp by his knee, and watched it die. Slowly it sank, dulled, looked lazy and stupid. But ever as it sank and dulled, the image in his mind of the Lady of Light grew stronger and clearer. Together the two lamps panted and shuddered. First one, then the other went out, leaving for a moment a great, red, evil-smelling snuff. Then all was the blackness of darkness up to their very hearts and everywhere around them. Was it? No. Far away - it looked miles away - shone one minute faint point of green light - where, who could tell? They only knew that it shone. It grew larger, and seemed to draw nearer, until at last, as they watched with speechless delight and expectation, it seemed once more within reach of an outstretched hand. Then it spread and melted away as before, and there were eyes - and a face - and a lovely form – and lo! the whole cavern blazing with lights innumerable, and gorgeous, yet soft and interfused - so blended, indeed, that the eye had to search and see in order to separate distinct spots of special color.

The moment they saw the speck in the vast distance they had risen and stood on their feet. When it came nearer they bowed their heads. Yet now they looked with fearless eyes, for the woman that was old yet young was a joy to see, and filled their hearts with reverent delight. She turned first to Peter.

'I have known you long,' she said. 'I have met you going to and from the mine, and seen you working in it for the last forty years.'

'How should it be, madam, that a grand lady like you should take notice of a poor man like me?' said Peter, humbly,

but more foolishly than he could then have understood.

'I am poor as well as rich,' said she. 'I, too, work for my bread, and I show myself no favor when I pay myself my own wages. Last night when you sat by the brook, and Curdie told you about my pigeon, and my spinning, and wondered whether he could believe that he had actually seen me, I heard what you said to each other. I am always about, as the miners said the other night when they talked of me as Old Mother Wotherwop.'

The lovely lady laughed, and her laugh was a lightning of delight in their souls.

'Yes,' she went on, 'you have got to thank me that you are so poor, Peter. I have seen to that, and it has done well for both you and me, my friend. Things come to the poor that can't get in at the door of the rich. Their money somehow blocks it up. It is a great privilege to be poor, Peter - one that no man ever coveted, and but a very few have sought to retain, but one that yet many have learned to prize. You must not mistake, however, and imagine it a virtue; it is but a privilege, and one also that, like other privileges, may be terribly misused. Had you been rich, my Peter, you would not have been so good as some rich men I know. And now I am going to tell you what no one knows but myself: you, Peter, and your wife both have the blood of the royal family in your veins. I have been trying to cultivate your family tree, every branch of which is known to me, and I expect Curdie to turn out a blossom on it. Therefore I have been training him for a work that must soon be done. I was near losing him, and had to send my pigeon. Had he not shot it, that would have been better; but he repented, and that shall be as good in the end.'

She turned to Curdie and smiled.

'Ma'am,' said Curdie, 'may I ask questions?'

'Why not, Curdie?'

'Because I have been told, ma'am, that nobody must ask the king questions.'

'The king never made that law,' she answered, with some displeasure. 'You may ask me as many as you please - that is, so long as they are sensible. Only I may take a few thousand years to answer some of them. But that's nothing. Of all things time is the cheapest.'

'Then would you mind telling me now, ma'am, for I feel very confused about it - are you the Lady of the Silver Moon?'

'Yes, Curdie; you may call me that if you like. What it means is true.'

'And now I see you dark, and clothed in green, and the mother of all the light that dwells in the stones of the earth! And up there they call you Old Mother Wotherwop! And the Princess Irene told me you were her great-great-grandmother! And you spin the spider threads, and take care of a whole people of pigeons; and you are worn to a pale shadow with old age; and are as young as anybody can be, not to be too young; and as strong, I do believe, as I am.'

The lady stooped toward a large green stone bedded in the rock of the floor, and looking like a well of grassy light in it. She laid hold of it with her fingers, broke it out, and gave it to Peter. 'There!' cried Curdie. 'I told you so. Twenty men could not have done that. And your fingers are white and smooth as any lady's in the land. I don't know what to make of it.'

'I could give you twenty names more to call me, Curdie, and not one of them would be a false one. What does it matter how many names if the person is one?'

'Ah! But it is not names only, ma'am. Look at what you were like last night, and what I see you now!'

'Shapes are only dresses, Curdie, and dresses are only names. That which is inside is the same all the time.'

'But then how can all the shapes speak the truth?'

'it would want thousands more to speak the truth, Curdie; and then they could not. But there is a point I must not let you mistake about. It is one thing the shape I choose to put on, and quite another the shape that foolish talk and nursery tale may please to put upon me. Also, it is one thing what you or your father may think about me, and quite another what a foolish or bad man may see in me. For instance, if a thief were to come in here just now, he would think he saw the demon of the mine, all in green flames, come to protect her treasure, and would run like a hunted wild goat. I should be all the same, but his evil eyes would see me as I was not.'

'I think I understand,' said Curdie.

'Peter,' said the lady, turning then to him, 'you will have to give up Curdie for a little while.' 'So long as he loves us, ma'am, that will not matter - much.'

'Ah! you are right there, my friend,' said the beautiful princess. And as she said it she put out her hand, and took the hard, horny hand of the miner in it, and held it for a moment lovingly.

'I need say no more,' she added, 'for we understand each other - you and I, Peter.'

The tears came into Peter's eyes. He bowed his head in thankfulness, and his heart was much too full to speak.

Then the great old, young, beautiful princess turned to Curdie.

'Now, Curdie, are you ready?' she said.

'Yes, ma'am,' answered Curdie.

'You do not know what for.'

'You do, ma'am. That is enough.'

'You could not have given me a better answer, or done more to prepare yourself, Curdie,' she returned, with one of her radiant smiles. 'Do you think you will know me again?'

'I think so. But how can I tell what you may look like next?'

'Ah, that indeed! How can you tell? Or how could I expect you should? But those who know me well, know me whatever new dress or shape or name I may be in; and by and by you will have learned to do so too.'

'But if you want me to know you again, ma'am, for certain sure,' said Curdie, 'could you not give me some sign, or tell me something about you that never changes - or some other way to know you, or thing to know you by?'

'No, Curdie; that would be to keep you from knowing me. You must know me in quite another way from that. It would not be the least use to you or me either if I were to make you know me in that way. It would be but to know the sign of me - not to know me myself. It would be no better than if I were to take this emerald out of my crown and give it to you to take home with you, and you were to call it me, and talk to it as if it heard and saw and loved you. Much good that would do you, Curdie! No; you must do what you can to know me, and if you do, you will. You shall see me again in very different circumstances from these, and, I will tell you so much, it may be in a very different shape. But come now, I will lead you out of this cavern; my good Joan will be getting too anxious about you. One word more: you will allow that the men knew little what they were talking about this morning, when they told all those tales of Old Mother Wotherwop; but did it occur to you to think how it was they fell to talking about me at all? It was because I came to them; I was beside them all the time they were talking about me, though they were far enough from knowing it, and had very little besides foolishness to say.'

As she spoke she turned and led the way from the cavern, which, as if a door had been closed, sank into absolute blackness behind them. And now they saw nothing more of the lady except the green star, which again seemed a good distance in front of them, and to which they came no nearer, although following it at a quick pace through the mountain. Such was their confidence in her guidance, however, and so fearless were they in consequence, that they felt their way neither with hand nor foot, but walked straight on through the pitch-dark galleries. When at length the night of the upper world looked in at the mouth of the mine, the green light seemed to lose its way among the stars, and they saw it no more.

Out they came into the cool, blessed night. It was very late, and only starlight. To their surprise, three paces away they saw, seated upon a stone, an old country-woman, in a cloak which they took for black. When they came close up to it, they saw it was red.

'Good evening!' said Peter.

'Good evening!' returned the old woman, in a voice as old as herself.

But Curdie took off his cap and said:

'I am your servant, Princess.'

The old woman replied:

'Come to me in the dove tower tomorrow night, Curdie - alone.'

'I will, ma'am,' said Curdie.

So they parted, and father and son went home to wife and mother - two persons in one rich, happy woman.

8. CURDIE'S MISSION

The next night Curdie went home from the mine a little earlier than usual, to make himself tidy before going to the dove tower. The princess had not appointed an exact time for him to be there; he would go as near the time he had gone first as he could. On his way to the bottom of the hill, he met his father coming up. The sun was then down, and the warm first of the twilight filled the evening. He came rather wearily up the hill: the road, he thought, must have grown steeper in parts since he was Curdie's age. His back was to the light of the sunset, which closed him all round in a beautiful setting, and Curdie thought what a grand-looking man his father was, even when he was tired. It is greed and laziness and selfishness, not hunger or weariness or cold, that take the dignity out of a man, and make him look mean.

'Ah, Curdie! There you are!' he said, seeing his son come bounding along as if it were morning with him and not evening.

'You look tired, Father,' said Curdie.

'Yes, my boy. I'm not so young as you.'

'Nor so old as the princess,' said Curdie.

'Tell me this,' said Peter, 'why do people talk about going downhill when they begin to get old? It seems to me that then first they begin to go uphill.'

'You looked to me, Father, when I caught sight of you, as if you had been climbing the hill all your life, and were soon to get to the top.' 'Nobody can tell when that will be,' returned Peter. 'We're so ready to think we're just at the top when it lies miles away. But I must not keep you, my boy, for you are wanted; and we shall be anxious to know what the princess says to you- that is, if she will allow you to tell us.'

'I think she will, for she knows there is nobody more to be trusted than my father and mother,' said Curdie, with pride.

And away he shot, and ran, and jumped, and seemed almost to fly down the long, winding, steep path, until he came to the gate of the king's house.

There he met an unexpected obstruction: in the open door stood the housekeeper, and she seemed to broaden herself out until she almost filled the doorway.

'So!' she said, 'it's you, is it, young man? You are the person that comes in and goes out when he pleases, and keeps running up and down my stairs without ever saying by your leave, or even wiping his shoes, and always leaves the door open! Don't you know this is my house?'

'No, I do not,' returned Curdie respectfully. 'You forget, ma'am, that it is the king's house.'

'That is all the same. The king left it to me to take care of - and that you shall know!'

'Is the king dead, ma'am, that he has left it to you?' asked Curdie, half in doubt from the self-assertion of the woman.

'Insolent fellow!' exclaimed the housekeeper. 'Don't you see by my dress that I am in the king's service?'

'And am I not one of his miners?'

'Ah! that goes for nothing. I am one of his household. You are an out-of-doors laborer. You are a nobody. You carry a pickaxe. I carry the keys at my girdle. See!'

'But you must not call one a nobody to whom the king has spoken,' said Curdie.

'Go along with you!' cried the housekeeper, and would have shut the door in his face, had she not been afraid that when she stepped back he would step in ere she could get it in motion, for it was very heavy and always seemed unwilling to shut. Curdie came a pace nearer. She lifted the great house key from her side, and threatened to strike him down with it, calling aloud on Mar and Whelk and Plout, the menservants under her, to come and help her. Ere one of them could answer, however, she gave a great shriek and turned and fled, leaving the door wide open.

Curdie looked behind him, and saw an animal whose gruesome oddity even he, who knew so many of the strange creatures, two of which were never the same, that used to live inside the mountain with their masters the goblins, had never seen equaled. Its eyes were flaming with anger, but it seemed to be at the housekeeper, for it came cowering and creeping up and laid its head on the ground at Curdie's feet. Curdie hardly waited to look at it, however, but ran into the house, eager to get up the stairs before any of the men should come to annoy - he had no fear of their preventing him. Without halt or hindrance, though the passages were nearly dark, he reached the door of the princess's workroom, and knocked.

'Come in,' said the voice of the princess.

Curdie opened the door - but, to his astonishment, saw no room there. Could he have opened a wrong door? There was the great sky, and the stars, and beneath he could see nothing only darkness!

But what was that in the sky, straight in front of him? A great wheel of fire, turning and turning, and flashing out blue lights!

'Come in, Curdie,' said the voice again.

'I would at once, ma'am,' said Curdie, 'if I were sure I was standing at your door.'

'Why should you doubt it, Curdie?'

'Because I see neither walls nor floor, only darkness and the great sky.' 'That is all right, Curdie. Come in.'

Curdie stepped forward at once. He was indeed, for the very crumb of a moment, tempted to feel before him with his foot; but he saw that would be to distrust the princess, and a greater rudeness he could not offer her. So he stepped straight in - I will not say without a little tremble at the thought of finding no floor beneath his foot. But that which had need of the floor found it, and his foot was satisfied.

No sooner was he in than he saw that the great revolving wheel in the sky was the princess's spinning wheel, near the other end of the room, turning very fast. He could see no sky or stars any more, but the wheel was flashing out blue - oh, such lovely sky-blue light! - and behind it of course sat the princess, but whether an old woman as thin as a skeleton leaf, or a glorious lady as young as perfection, he could not tell for the turning and flashing of the wheel.

'Listen to the wheel,' said the voice which had already grown dear to Curdie: its very tone was precious like a jewel, not as a jewel, for no jewel could compare with it in preciousness.

And Curdie listened and listened.

'What is it saying?' asked the voice.

'It is singing,' answered Curdie.

'What is it singing?'

Curdie tried to make out, but thought he could not; for no sooner had he got hold of something than it vanished again.

Yet he listened, and listened, entranced with delight.

'Thank you, Curdie, said the voice.

'Ma'am,' said Curdie, 'I did try hard for a while, but I could not make anything of it.'

'Oh yes, you did, and you have been telling it to me! Shall I tell you again what I told my wheel, and my wheel told you, and you have just told me without knowing it?'

'Please, ma'am.'

Then the lady began to sing, and her wheel spun an accompaniment to her song, and the music of the wheel was like the music of an Aeolian harp blown upon by the wind that bloweth where it listeth. Oh, the sweet sounds of that spinning wheel! Now they were gold, now silver, now grass, now palm trees, now ancient cities, now rubies, now mountain brooks, now peacock's feathers, now clouds, now snowdrops, and now mid-sea islands. But for the voice that sang through it all, about that I have no words to tell. It would make you weep if I were able to tell you what that was like, it was so beautiful and true and lovely. But this is something like the words of its song:

The stars are spinning their threads, and the clouds are the dust that flies, And the suns are weaving them up For the time when the sleepers shall rise.

The ocean in music rolls, and gems are turning to eyes, and the trees are gathering souls for the day when the sleepers shall rise.

The weepers are learning to smile, and laughter to glean the sighs; Burn and bury the care and guile, for the day when the sleepers shall rise.

Oh, the dews and the moths and the daisy red, the larks and the glimmers and flows! The lilies and sparrows and daily bread, and the something that nobody knows!

The princess stopped, her wheel stopped, and she laughed. And her laugh was sweeter than song and wheel; sweeter than running brook and silver bell; sweeter than joy itself, for the heart of the laugh was love.

'Come now, Curdie, to this side of my wheel, and you will find me,' she said; and her laugh seemed sounding on still in the words, as if they were made of breath that had laughed.

Curdie obeyed, and passed the wheel, and there she stood to receive him! - fairer than when he saw her last, a little younger still, and dressed not in green and emeralds, but in pale blue, with a coronet of silver set with pearls, and slippers covered with opals that gleamed every color of the rainbow. It was some time before Curdie could take his eyes from the marvel of her loveliness. Fearing at last that he was rude, he turned them away; and, behold, he was in a room that was for beauty marvelous! The lofty ceiling was all a golden vine, Whose great clusters of carbuncles, rubies, and chrysoberyls hung down like the bosses of groined arches, and in its centre hung the most glorious lamp that human eyes ever saw - the Silver Moon itself, a globe of silver, as it seemed, with a heart of light so wondrous potent that it rendered the mass translucent, and altogether radiant.

The room was so large that, looking back, he could scarcely see the end at which he entered; but the other was only a few yards from him - and there he saw another wonder: on a huge hearth a great fire was burning, and the fire was a huge heap of roses, and yet it was fire. The smell of the roses filled the air, and the heat of the flames of them glowed upon his face. He turned an inquiring look upon the lady, and saw that she was now seated in an ancient chair, the legs of which were crusted with gems, but the upper part like a nest of daisies and moss and green grass.

'Curdie,' she said in answer to his eyes, 'you have stood more than one trial already, and have stood them well: now I am going to put you to a harder. Do you think you are prepared for it?'

'How can I tell, ma'am,' he returned, 'seeing I do not know what it is, or what preparation it needs? Judge me yourself, ma'am.'

'It needs only trust and obedience,' answered the lady.

'I dare not say anything, ma'am. If you think me fit, command me.'

'it will hurt you terribly, Curdie, but that will be all; no real hurt but much good will come to you from it.'

Curdie made no answer but stood gazing with parted lips in the lady's face.

'Go and thrust both your hands into that fire,' she said quickly, almost hurriedly.

Curdie dared not stop to think. It was much too terrible to think about. He rushed to the fire, and thrust both of his hands right into the middle of the heap of flaming roses, and his arms halfway up to the elbows. And it did hurt! But he did not draw them back. He held the pain as if it were a thing that would kill him if he let it go - as indeed it would have done. He was in terrible fear lest it should conquer him.

But when it had risen to the pitch that he thought he could bear it no longer, it began to fall again, and went on growing less and less until by contrast with its former severity it had become rather pleasant. At last it ceased altogether, and Curdie thought his hands must be burned to cinders if not ashes, for he did not feel them at all. The princess told him to take them out and look at them. He did so, and found that all that was gone of them was the rough, hard skin; they were white and smooth like the princess's.

'Come to me,' she said.

He obeyed and saw, to his surprise, that her face looked as if she had been weeping.

'Oh, Princess! What is the matter?' he cried. 'Did I make a noise and vex you?'

'No, Curdie, she answered; 'but it was very bad.'

'Did you feel it too then?'

'Of course I did. But now it is over, and all is well. Would you like to know why I made You put your hands in the fire?' Curdie looked at them again - then said:

'To take the marks of the work off them and make them fit for the king's court, I suppose.'

'No, Curdie,' answered the princess, shaking her head, for she was not pleased with the answer. 'It would be a poor way of making your hands fit for the king's court to take off them signs of his service. There is a far greater difference on them than that. Do you feel none?'

'No, ma'am.'

'You will, though, by and by, when the time comes. But perhaps even then you might not know what had been given you, therefore I will tell you. Have you ever heard what some philosophers say - that men were all animals once?'

'No, ma'am.'

'it is of no consequence. But there is another thing that is of the greatest consequence - this: that all men, if they do not take care, go down the hill to the animals' country; that many men are actually, all their lives, going to be beasts. People knew it once, but it is long since they forgot it.'

'I am not surprised to hear it, ma'am, when I think of some of our miners.'

'Ah! But you must beware, Curdie, how you say of this man or that man that he is traveling beastward. There are not nearly so many going that way as at first sight you might think. When you met your father on the hill tonight, you stood and spoke together on the same spot; and although one of you was going up and the other coming down, at a little distance no one could have told which was bound in the one direction and which in the other. Just so two people may be at the same spot in manners and behavior, and yet one may be getting better and the other worse, which is just the greatest of all differences that could possibly exist between them.'

'But ma'am,' said Curdie, 'where is the good of knowing that there is such a difference, if you can never know where it is?'

'Now, Curdie, you must mind exactly what words I use, because although the right words cannot do exactly what I want them to do, the wrong words will certainly do what I do not want them to do. I did not say you can never know. When there is a necessity for your knowing, when you have to do important business with this or that man, there is always a way of knowing enough to keep you from any great blunder. And as you will have important business to do by and by, and that with people of whom you yet know nothing, it will be necessary that you should have some better means than usual of learning the nature of them. 'Now listen. Since it is always what they do, whether in their minds or their bodies, that makes men go down to be less than men, that is, beasts, the change always comes first in their hands – and first of all in the inside hands, to which the outside ones are but as the gloves. They do not know it of course; for a beast does not know that he is a beast, and the nearer a man gets to being a beast the less he knows it. Neither can their best friends, or their worst enemies indeed, see any difference in their hands, for they see only the living gloves of them. But there are not a few who feel a vague something repulsive in the hand of a man who is growing a beast.

'Now here is what the rose-fire has done for you: it has made your hands so knowing and wise, it has brought your real hands so near the outside of your flesh gloves, that you will henceforth be able to know at once the hand of a man who is growing into a beast; nay, more - you will at once feel the foot of the beast he is growing, just as if there were no glove made like a man's hand between you and it.

'Hence of course it follows that you will be able often, and with further education in zoology, will be able always to tell, not only when a man is growing a beast, but what beast he is growing to, for you will know the foot - what it is and what beast's it is. According, then, to your knowledge of that beast will be your knowledge of the man you have to do with. Only there is one beautiful and awful thing about it, that if any one gifted with this perception once uses it for his own ends, it is taken from him, and then, not knowing that it is gone, he is in a far worse condition than before, for he trusts to what he has not got.'

'How dreadful!' Said Curdie. 'I must mind what I am about.'

'Yes, indeed, Curdie.'

'But may not one sometimes make a mistake without being able to help it?'

'Yes. But so long as he is not after his own ends, he will never make a serious mistake.'

'I suppose you want me, ma'am, to warn every one whose hand tells me that he is growing a beast - because, as you say, he does not know it himself.'

The princess smiled.

'Much good that would do, Curdie! I don't say there are no cases in which it would be of use, but they are very rare and peculiar cases, and if such come you will know them. To such a person there is in general no insult like the truth. He cannot endure it, not because he is growing a beast, but because he is ceasing to be a man. It is the dying man in him that it makes uncomfortable, and he trots, or creeps, or swims, or flutters out of its way – calls it a foolish feeling, a whim, an old wives' fable, a bit of priests' humbug, an effete superstition, and so on.'

'And is there no hope for him? Can nothing be done? It's so awful to think of going down, down, down like that!'

'Even when it's with his own will?'

'That's what seems to me to make it worst of all,' said Curdie.

'You are right,' answered the princess, nodding her head; 'but there is this amount of excuse to make for all such, remember - that they do not know what or how horrid their coming fate is. Many a lady, so delicate and nice that she can bear nothing coarser than the finest linen to touch her body, if she had a mirror that could show her the animal she is growing to, as it lies waiting within the fair skin and the fine linen and the silk and the jewels, would receive a shock that might possibly wake her up.'

'Why then, ma'am, shouldn't she have it?'

The princess held her peace.

'Come here, Lina,' she said after a long pause.

From somewhere behind Curdie, crept forward the same hideous animal which had fawned at his feet at the door, and which, without his knowing it, had followed him every step up the dove tower. She ran to the princess, and lay down flat at her feet, looking up at her with an expression so pitiful that in Curdie's heart it overcame all the ludicrousness of her horrible mass of incongruities. She had a very short body, and very long legs made like an elephant's, so that in lying down she kneeled with both pairs. Her tail, which dragged on the floor behind her, was twice as long and quite as thick as her body. Her head was something between that of a polar bear and a snake. Her eyes were dark green, with a yellow light in them. Her under teeth came up like a fringe of icicles, only very white, outside of her upper lip. Her throat looked as if the hair had been plucked off. It showed a skin white and smooth.

'Give Curdie a paw, Lina,' said the princess.

The creature rose, and, lifting a long foreleg, held up a great doglike paw to Curdie. He took it gently. But what a shudder, as of terrified delight, ran through him, when, instead of the paw of a dog, such as it seemed to his eyes, he clasped in his great mining fist the soft, neat little hand of a child! He took it in both of his, and held it as if he could not let it go. The green eyes stared at him with their yellow light, and the mouth was turned up toward him with its constant half grin; but here was the child's hand! If he could but pull the child out of the beast! His eyes sought the princess. She was watching him with evident satisfaction.

'Ma'am, here is a child's hand!' said Curdie.

'Your gift does more for you than it promised. It is yet better to perceive a hidden good than a hidden evil.'

'But,' began Curdie.

'I am not going to answer any more questions this evening,' interrupted the princess. 'You have not half got to the bottom of the answers I have already given you. That paw in your hand now might almost teach you the whole science of natural history – the heavenly sort, I mean.'

'I will think,' said Curdie. 'But oh! please! one word more: may I tell my father and mother all about it?'

'Certainly - though perhaps now it may be their turn to find it a little difficult to believe that things went just as you must tell them.'

'They shall see that I believe it all this time,' said Curdie.

'Tell them that tomorrow morning you must set out for the court - not like a great man, but just as poor as you are. They had better not speak about it. Tell them also that it will be a long time before they hear of you again, but they must not lose heart. And tell your father to lay that stone I gave him at night in a safe place - not because of the greatness of its price, although it is such an emerald as no prince has in his crown, but because it will be a news-bearer between you and him. As often as he gets at all anxious about you, he must take it and lay it in the fire, and leave it there when he goes to bed. In the morning he must find it in the ashes, and if it be as green as ever, then all goes well with you; if it have lost color, things go ill with you; but if it be very pale indeed, then you are in great danger, and he must come to me.'

'Yes, ma'am,' said Curdie. 'Please, am I to go now?'

'Yes,' answered the princess, and held out her hand to him.

Curdie took it, trembling with joy. It was a very beautiful hand - not small, very smooth, but not very soft - and just the same to his fire-taught touch that it was to his eyes. He would have stood there all night holding it if she had not gently withdrawn it.

'I will provide you a servant,' she said, 'for your journey and to wait upon you afterward.'

'But where am I to go, ma'am, and what am I to do? You have given me no message to carry, neither have you said what I am wanted for. I go without a notion whether I am to walk this way or that, or what I am to do when I get I don't know where.'

'Curdie!' said the princess, and there was a tone of reminder in his own name as she spoke it, 'did I not tell you to tell your father and mother that you were to set out for the court? And you know that lies to the north. You must learn to use far less direct directions than that. You must not be like a dull servant that needs to be told again and again before he will understand. You have orders enough to start with, and you will find, as you go on, and as you need to know, what you have to do. But I warn you that perhaps it will not look the least like what you may have been fancying I should require of you. I have one idea of you and your work, and you have another. I do not blame you for that – you cannot help it yet; but you must be ready to let my idea, which sets you working, set your idea right. Be true and honest and fearless, and all shall go well with you and your work, and all with whom your work lies, and so with your parents - and me too, Curdie,' she added after a little pause.

The young miner bowed his head low, patted the strange head that lay at the princess's feet, and turned away. As soon as he passed the spinning wheel, which looked, in the midst of the glorious room, just like any wheel you might find in a country cottage – old and worn and dingy and dusty - the splendor of the place vanished, and he saw but the big bare room he seemed at first to have entered, with the moon - the princess's moon no doubt - shining in at one of the windows upon the spinning wheel.

9. HANDS

Curdie went home, pondering much, and told everything to his father and mother. As the old princess had said, it was now their turn to find what they heard hard to believe. if they had not been able to trust Curdie himself, they would have refused to believe more than the half of what he reported, then they would have refused that half too, and at last would most likely for a time have disbelieved in the very existence of the princess, what evidence their own senses had given them notwithstanding.

For he had nothing conclusive to show in proof of what he told them. When he held out his hands to them, his mother said they looked as if he had been washing them with soft soap, only they did smell of something nicer than that, and she must allow it was more like roses than anything else she knew. His father could not see any difference upon his hands, but then it was night, he said, and their poor little lamp was not enough for his old eyes. As to the feel of them, each of his own hands, he said, was hard and horny enough for two, and it must be the fault of the dullness of his own thick skin that he felt no change on Curdie's palms.

'Here, Curdie,' said his mother, 'try my hand, and see what beast's paw lies inside it.' 'No, Mother,' answered Curdie, half beseeching, half indignant, 'I will not insult my new gift by making pretence to try it. That would be mockery. There is no hand within yours but the hand of a true woman, my mother.'

'I should like you just to take hold of my hand though,' said his mother. 'You are my son, and may know all the bad there is in me.'

Then at once Curdie took her hand in his. And when he had it, he kept it, stroking it gently with his other hand.

'Mother,' he said at length, 'your hand feels just like that of the princess.'

'What! My horny, cracked, rheumatic old hand, with its big joints, and its short nails all worn down to the quick with hard work - like the hand of the beautiful princess! Why, my child, you will make me fancy your fingers have grown very dull indeed, instead of sharp and delicate, if you talk such nonsense. Mine is such an ugly hand I should be ashamed to show it to any but one that loved me. But love makes all safe - doesn't it, Curdie?'

'Well, Mother, all I can say is that I don't feel a roughness, or a crack, or a big joint, or a short nail. Your hand feels just and exactly, as near as I can recollect, and it's not more than two hours since I had it in mine - well, I will say, very like indeed to that of the old princess.'

'Go away, you flatterer,' said his mother, with a smile that showed how she prized the love that lay beneath what she took for its hyperbole. The praise even which one cannot accept is sweet from a true mouth. 'If that is all your new gift can do, it won't make a warlock of you,' she added.

'Mother, it tells me nothing but the truth,' insisted Curdie, 'however unlike the truth it may seem. It wants no gift to tell what anybody's outside hands are like. But by it I know your inside hands are like the princess's.'

'And I am sure the boy speaks true,' said Peter. 'He only says about your hand what I have known ever so long about yourself, Joan. Curdie, your mother's foot is as pretty a foot as any lady's in the land, and where her hand is not so pretty it comes of killing its beauty for you and me, my boy. And I can tell you more, Curdie. I don't know much about ladies and gentlemen, but I am sure your inside mother must be a lady, as her hand tells you, and I will try to say how I know it. This is how: when I forget myself looking at her as she goes about her work - and that happens often as I grow older - I fancy for a moment or two that I am a gentleman; and when I wake up from my little dream, it is only to feel the more strongly that I must do everything as a gentleman should. I will try to tell you what I mean, Curdie. If a gentleman - I mean a real gentleman, not a pretended one, of which sort they say there are a many above ground - if a real gentleman were to lose all his money and come down to work in the mines to get bread for his family - do you think, Curdie, he would work like the lazy ones? Would he try to do as little as he could for his wages? I know the sort of the true gentleman pretty near as well as he does himself. And my wife, that's your mother, Curdie, she's a true lady, you may take my word for it, for it's she that makes me want to be a true gentleman. Wife, the boy is in the right about your hand.'

'Now, Father, let me feel yours,' said Curdie, daring a little more.

'No, no, my boy,' answered Peter. 'I don't want to hear anything about my hand or my head or my heart. I am what I am, and I hope growing better, and that's enough. No, you shan't feel my hand. You must go to bed, for you must start with the sun.'

It was not as if Curdie had been leaving them to go to prison, or to make a fortune, and although they were sorry enough to lose him, they were not in the least heartbroken or even troubled at his going.

As the princess had said he was to go like the poor man he was, Curdie came down in the morning from his little loft dressed in his working clothes. His mother, who was busy getting his breakfast for him, while his father sat reading to her out of an old book, would have had him put on his holiday garments, which, she said, would look poor enough among the fine ladies and gentlemen he was going to. But Curdie said he did not know that he was going among ladies and gentlemen, and that as work was better than play, his workday clothes must on the whole be better than his play day Clothes; and as his father accepted the argument, his mother gave in. When he had eaten his breakfast, she took a pouch made of goatskin, with the long hair on it, filled it with bread and cheese, and hung it over his shoulder. Then his father gave him a stick he had cut for him in the wood, and he bade them good-bye rather hurriedly, for he was afraid of breaking down. As he went out he caught up his mattock and took it with him. It had on the one side a pointed curve of strong steel for loosening the earth and the ore, and on the other a steel hammer for breaking the stones and rocks. Just as he crossed the threshold the sun showed the first segment of his disc above the horizon.

10. THE HEATH

He had to go to the bottom of the hill to get into a country he could cross, for the mountains to the north were full of precipices, and it would have been losing time to go that way. Not until he had reached the king's house was it any use to turn northwards. Many a look did he raise, as he passed it, to the dove tower, and as long as it was in sight, but he saw nothing of the lady of the pigeons.

On and on he fared, and came in a few hours to a country where there were no mountains more - only hills, with great stretches of desolate heath. Here and there was a village, but that brought him little pleasure, for the people were rougher and worse mannered than those in the mountains, and as he passed through, the children came behind and mocked him.

'There's a monkey running away from the mines!' they cried. Sometimes their parents came out and encouraged them.

'He doesn't want to find gold for the king any longer – the lazybones!' they would say. 'He'll be well taxed down here though, and he won't like that either.'

But it was little to Curdie that men who did not know what he was about should not approve of his proceedings. He gave them a merry answer now and then, and held diligently on his way. When they got so rude as nearly to make him angry, he would treat them as he used to treat the goblins, and sing his own songs to keep out their foolish noises. Once a child fell as he turned to run away after throwing a stone at him. He picked him up, kissed him, and carried him to his mother. The woman had run out in terror when she saw the strange miner about, as she thought, to take vengeance on her boy. When he put him in her arms, she blessed him, and Curdie went on his way rejoicing.

And so the day went on, and the evening came, and in the middle of a great desolate heath he began to feel tired, and sat down under an ancient hawthorn, through which every now and then a lone wind that seemed to come from nowhere and to go nowhither sighed and hissed. It was very old and distorted. There was not another tree for miles all around. It seemed to have lived so long, and to have been so torn and tossed by the tempests on that moor, that it had at last gathered a wind of its own, which got up now and then, tumbled itself about, and lay down again.

Curdie had been so eager to get on that he had eaten nothing since his breakfast. But he had had plenty of water, for many little streams had crossed his path. He now opened the wallet his mother had given him, and began to eat his supper. The sun was setting. A few clouds had gathered about the west, but there was not a single cloud anywhere else to be seen.

Now Curdie did not know that this was a part of the country very hard to get through. Nobody lived there, though many had tried to build in it. Some died very soon. Some rushed out of it. Those who stayed longest went raving mad, and died a terrible death. Such as walked straight on, and did not spend a night there, got through well and were nothing the worse. But those who slept even a single night in it were sure to meet with something they could never forget, and which often left a mark everybody could read. And that old hawthorn Might have been enough for a warning – it looked so like a human being dried up and distorted with age and suffering, with cares instead of loves, and things instead of thoughts. Both it and the heath around it, which stretched on all sides as far as he could see, were so withered that it was impossible to say whether they were alive or not.

And while Curdie ate there came a change. Clouds had gathered over his head, and seemed drifting about in every direction, as if not 'shepherded by the slow, unwilling wind,' but hunted in all directions by wolfish flaws across the plains of the sky. The sun was going down in a storm of lurid crimson, and out of the west came a wind that felt red and hot the one moment, and cold and pale the other. And very strangely it sang in the dreary old hawthorn tree, and very cheerily it blew about Curdie, now making him creep close up to the tree for shelter from its shivery cold, now fan himself with his cap, it was so sultry and stifling. It seemed to come from the deathbed of the sun, dying in fever and ague.

And as he gazed at the sun, now on the verge of the horizon, very large and very red and very dull - for though the clouds had broken away a dusty fog was spread all over the disc - Curdie saw something strange appear against it, moving about like a fly over its burning face. This looked as if it were coming out of the sun's furnace heart, and was a living creature of some kind surely; but its shape was very uncertain, because the dazzle of the light all around melted the outlines.

It was growing larger, it must be approaching! It grew so rapidly that by the time the sun was half down its head reached the top of the arch, and presently nothing but its legs were to be seen, crossing and re-crossing the face of the vanishing disc.

When the sun was down he could see nothing of it more, but in a moment he heard its feet galloping over the dry crackling heather, and seeming to come straight for him. He stood up, lifted his pickaxes and threw the hammer end over his shoulder: he was going to have a fight for his life! And now it appeared again, vague, yet very awful, in the dim twilight the sun had left behind. But just before it reached him, down from its four long legs it dropped flat on the ground, and came crawling towards him, wagging a huge tail as it came.

11. LINA

It was Lina. All at once Curdie recognized her - the frightful creature he had seen at the princess's. He dropped his pickaxes and held out his hand. She crept nearer and nearer, and laid her chin in his palm, and he patted her ugly head. Then she crept away behind the tree, and lay down, panting hard. Curdie did not much like the idea of her being behind him. Horrible as she was to look at, she seemed to his mind more horrible when he was not looking at her. But he remembered the child's hand, and never thought of driving her away. Now and then he gave a glance behind him, and there she lay flat, with her eyes closed and her terrible teeth gleaming between her two huge forepaws.

After his supper and his long day's journey it was no wonder Curdie should now be sleepy. Since the sun set the air had been warm and pleasant. He lay down under the tree, closed his eyes, and thought to sleep. He found himself mistaken, however. But although he could not sleep, he was yet aware of resting delightfully.

Presently he heard a sweet sound of singing somewhere, such as he had never heard before - a singing as of curious birds far off, which drew nearer and nearer. At length he heard their wings, and, opening his eyes, saw a number of very large birds, as it seemed, alighting around him, still singing. It was strange to hear song from the throats of such big birds.

And still singing, with large and round but not the less birdlike voices, they began to weave a strange dance about him, moving their wings in time with their legs. But the dance seemed somehow to be troubled and broken, and to return upon itself in an eddy, in place of sweeping smoothly on.

And he soon learned, in the low short growls behind him, the cause of the imperfection: they wanted to dance all round the tree, but Lina would not permit them to come on her side.

Now curdie liked the birds, and did not altogether like Lina. But neither, nor both together, made a reason for driving away the princess's creature. Doubtless she had been the goblins' creature, but the last time he saw her was in the king's house and the dove tower, and at the old princess's feet. So he left her to do as she would, and the dance of the birds continued only a semicircle, troubled at the edges, and returning upon itself.

But their song and their motions, nevertheless, and the waving of their wings, began at length to make him very sleepy. All the time he had kept doubting whether they could really be birds, and the sleepier he got, the more he imagined them something else, but he suspected no harm.

Suddenly, just as he was sinking beneath the waves of slumber, he awoke in fierce pain. The birds were upon him - all over him – and had begun to tear him with beaks and claws. He had but time, however, to feel that he could not move under their weight, when they set up a hideous screaming, and scattered like a cloud. Lina was among them, snapping and striking with her paws, while her tail knocked them over and over. But they flew up, gathered, and descended on her in a swarm, perching upon every part of her body, so that he could see only a huge misshapen mass, which seemed to go rolling away into the darkness. He got up and tried to follow, but could see nothing, and after wandering about hither and thither for some time, found himself again beside the hawthorn. He feared greatly that the birds had been too much for Lina, and had torn her to pieces. In a little while, however, she came limping back, and lay down in her old place. Curdie also lay down, but, from the pain of his wounds, there was no sleep for him. When the light came he found his clothes a good deal torn and his skin as well, but gladly wondered why the wicked birds had not at once attacked his eyes. Then he turned, looking for Lina. She rose and crept to him. But she was in far worse plight than he - plucked and gashed and torn with the beaks and claws of the birds, especially about the bare part of her neck, so that she was pitiful to see. And those worst wounds she could not reach to lick.

'Poor Lina!' said Curdie, 'you got all those helping me.'

She wagged her tail, and made it clear she understood him. Then it flashed upon Curdie's mind that perhaps this was the companion the princess had promised him. For the princess did so many things differently from what anybody looked for! Lina was no beauty certainly, but already, the first night, she had saved his life.

'Come along, Lina,' he said, 'we want water.'

She put her nose to the earth, and after snuffing for a moment, darted off in a straight line. Curdie followed. The ground was so uneven, that after losing sight of her many times, at last he seemed to have lost her altogether. In a few minutes, however, he came upon her waiting for him. Instantly she darted off again. After he had lost and found her again many times, he found her the last time lying beside a great stone. As soon as he came up she began scratching at it with her paws. When he had raised it an inch or two, she shoved in first her nose and then her teeth, and lifted with all the might of her neck.

When at length between them they got it up, there was a beautiful little well. He filled his cap with the clearest and sweetest water, and drank. Then he gave to Lina, and she drank plentifully. Next he washed her wounds very carefully. And as he did so, he noted how much the bareness of her neck added to the strange repulsiveness of her appearance. Then he bethought him of the goatskin wallet his mother had given him, and taking it from his shoulders, tried whether it would do to make a collar of for the poor animal. He found there was just enough, and the hair so similar in color to Lina's, that no one could suspect it of having grown somewhere else.

He took his knife, ripped up the seams of the wallet, and began trying the skin to her neck. It was plain she understood perfectly what he wished, for she endeavored to hold her neck conveniently, turning it this way and that while he contrived, with his rather scanty material, to make the collar fit. As his mother had taken care to provide him with needles and thread, he soon had a nice gorget ready for her. He laced it on with one of his boot laces, which its long hair covered. Poor Lina looked much better in it. Nor could any one have called it a piece of finery. If ever green eyes with a yellow light in them looked grateful, hers did.

As they had no longer any bag to carry them in, Curdie and Lina now ate what was left of the provisions. Then they set out again upon their journey. For seven days it lasted. They met with various adventures, and in all of them Lina proved so helpful, and so ready to risk her life for the sake of her companion, that Curdie grew not merely very fond but very trustful of her; and her ugliness, which at first only moved his pity, now actually increased his affection for her. One day, looking at her stretched on the grass before him, he said:

'Oh, Lina! If the princess would but burn you in her fire of roses!'

She looked up at him, gave a mournful whine like a dog, and laid her head on his feet. What or how much he could not tell, but clearly she had gathered something from his words.

12. MORE CREATURES

One day from morning till night they had been passing through a forest. As soon as the sun was down Curdie began to be aware that there were more in it than themselves. First he saw only the swift rush of a figure across the trees at some distance. Then he saw another and then another at shorter intervals. Then he saw others both farther off and nearer. At last, missing Lina and looking about after her, he saw an appearance as marvelous as herself steal up to her, and begin conversing with her after some beast fashion which evidently she understood.

Presently what seemed a quarrel arose between them, and stranger noises followed, mingled with growling. At length it came to a fight, which had not lasted long, however, before the creature of the wood threw itself upon its back, and held up its paws to Lina. She instantly walked on, and the creature got up and followed her. They had not gone far before another strange animal appeared, approaching Lina, when precisely the same thing was repeated, the vanquished animal rising and following with the former. Again, and yet again, and again, a fresh animal came up, seemed to be reasoned and certainly was fought with and overcome by Lina, until at last, before they were out of the wood, she was followed by forty-nine of the most grotesquely ugly, the most extravagantly abnormal animals imagination can conceive. To describe them were a hopeless task.

I knew a boy who used to make animals out of heather roots. Wherever he could find four legs, he was pretty sure to find a head and a tail. His beasts were a most comic menagerie, and right fruitful of laughter. But they were not so grotesque and extravagant as Lina and her followers. One of them, for instance, was like a boa constrictor walking on four little stumpy legs near its tail. About the same distance from its head were two little wings, which it was forever fluttering as if trying to fly with them. Curdie thought it fancied it did fly with them, when it was merely plodding on busily with its four little stumps. How it managed to keep up he could not think, till once when he missed it from the group: the same moment he caught sight of something at a distance plunging at an awful serpentine rate through the trees, and presently, from behind a huge ash, this same creature fell again into the group, quietly waddling along on its four stumps.

Watching it after this, he saw that, when it was not able to keep up any longer, and they had all got a little space ahead, it shot into the wood away from the route, and made a great round, serpentine alone in huge billows of motion, devouring the ground, undulating awfully, galloping as if it were all legs together, and its four stumps nowhere. In this mad fashion it shot ahead, and, a few minutes after, toddled in again among the rest, walking peacefully and somewhat painfully on its few fours.

From the time it takes to describe one of them it will be readily seen that it would hardly do to attempt a description of each of the forty-nine. They were not a goodly company, but well worth contemplating, nevertheless; and Curdie had been too long used to the goblins' creatures in the mines and on the mountain, to feel the least uncomfortable at being followed by such a herd. On the contrary, the marvelous vagaries of shape they manifested amused him greatly, and shortened the journey much.

Before they were all gathered, however, it had got so dark that he could see some of them only a part at a time, and every now and then, as the company wandered on, he would be startled by some extraordinary limb or feature, undreamed of by him before, thrusting itself out of the darkness into the range of his ken. Probably there were some of his old acquaintances among them, although such had been the conditions of semi-darkness, in which alone he had ever seen any of them, that it was not like he would be able to identify any of them.

On they marched solemnly, almost in silence, for either with feet or voice the creatures seldom made any noise. By the time they reached the outside of the wood it was morning twilight. Into the open trooped the strange torrent of deformity, each one following Lina. Suddenly she stopped, turned towards them, and said something which they understood, although to Curdie's ear the sounds she made seemed to have no articulation. Instantly they all turned, and vanished in the forest, and Lina alone came trotting lithely and clumsily after her master.

13. THE BAKER'S WIFE

They were now passing through a lovely country of hill and dale and rushing stream. The hills were abrupt, with broken chasms for watercourses, and deep little valleys full of trees. But now and then they came to a larger valley, with a fine river, whose level banks and the adjacent meadows were dotted all over with red and white kine, while on the fields above, that sloped a little to the foot of the hills, grew oats and barley and wheat, and on the sides of the hills themselves vines hung and chestnuts rose.

They came at last to a broad, beautiful river, up which they must go to arrive at the city of Gwyntystorm, where the king had his court. As they went the valley narrowed, and then the river, but still it was wide enough for large boats. After this, while the river kept its size, the banks narrowed, until there was only room for a road between the river and the great Cliffs that overhung it. At last river and road took a sudden turn, and lo! a great rock in the river, which dividing flowed around it, and on the top of the rock the city, with lofty walls and towers and battlements, and above the city the palace of the king, built like a strong castle. But the fortifications had long been neglected, for the whole country was now under one king, and all men said there was no more need for weapons or walls. No man pretended to love his neighbor, but every one said he knew that peace and quiet behavior was the best thing for himself, and that, he said, was quite as useful, and a great deal more reasonable. The city was prosperous and rich, and if everybody was not comfortable, everybody else said he ought to be.

When Curdie got up opposite the mighty rock, which sparkled all over with crystals, he found a narrow bridge, defended by gates and portcullis and towers with loopholes. But the gates stood wide open, and were dropping from their great hinges; the portcullis was eaten away with rust, and clung to the grooves evidently immovable; while the loop holed towers had neither floor nor roof, and their tops were fast filling up their interiors. Curdie thought it a pity, if only for their old story, that they should be thus neglected. But everybody in the city regarded these signs of decay as the best proof of the prosperity of the place. Commerce and self-interest, they said, had got the better of violence, and the troubles of the past were whelmed in the riches that flowed in at their open gates.

Indeed, there was one sect of philosophers in it which taught that it would be better to forget all the past history of the city, were it not that its former imperfections taught its present inhabitants how superior they and their times were, and enabled them to glory over their ancestors. There were even certain quacks in the city who advertised pills for enabling people to think well of themselves, and some few bought of them, but most laughed, and said, with evident truth, that they did not require them. Indeed, the general theme of discourse when they met was, how much wiser they were than their fathers.

Curdie crossed the river, and began to ascend the winding road that led up to the city. They met a good many idlers, and all stared at them. It was no wonder they should stare, but there was an unfriendliness in their looks which Curdie did not like. No one, however, offered them any molestation: Lina did not invite liberties. After a long ascent, they reached the principal gate of the city and entered.

The street was very steep, ascending toward the palace, which rose in great strength above all the houses. Just as they entered, a baker, whose shop was a few doors inside the gate, came out in his white apron, and ran to the shop of his friend, the barber, on the opposite side of the way. But as he ran he stumbled and fell heavily. Curdie hastened to help him up, and found he had bruised his forehead badly. He swore grievously at the stone for tripping him up, declaring it was the third time he had fallen over it within the last month; and saying what was the king about that he allowed such a stone to stick up forever on the main street of his royal residence of Gwyntystorm! What was a king for if he would not take care of his people's heads! And he stroked his forehead tenderly. 'Was it your head or your feet that ought to bear the blame of your fall?' asked Curdie.

'Why, you booby of a miner! My feet, of course,' answered the baker.

'Nay, then,' said Curdie, 'the king can't be to blame.'

'Oh, I see!' said the baker. 'You're laying a trap for me. Of course, if you come to that, it was my head that ought to have looked after my feet. But it is the king's part to look after us all, and have his streets smooth.'

'Well, I don't see, said Curdie, 'why the king should take care of the baker, when the baker's head won't take care of the baker's feet.'

'Who are you to make game of the king's baker?' cried the man in a rage.

But, instead of answering, Curdie went up to the bump on the street which had repeated itself on the baker's head, and turning the hammer end of his mattock, struck it such a blow that it flew wide in pieces. Blow after blow he struck until he had leveled it with the street.

But out flew the barber upon him in a rage. 'What do you break my window for, you rascal, with your pickaxe?'

'I am very sorry,' said Curdie. 'It must have been a bit of stone that flew from my mattock. I couldn't help it, you know.'

'Couldn't help it! A fine story! What do you go breaking the rock for - the very rock upon which the city stands?'

'Look at your friend's forehead,' said Curdie. 'See what a lump he has got on it with falling over that same stone.'

'What's that to my window?' cried the barber. 'His forehead can mend itself; my poor window can't.'

'But he's the king's baker,' said Curdie, more and more surprised at the man's anger.

'What's that to me? This is a free city. Every man here takes care of himself, and the king takes care of us all. I'll have the price of my window out of you, or the exchequer shall pay for it.'

Something caught Curdie's eye. He stooped, picked up a piece of the stone he had just broken, and put it in his pocket.

'I suppose you are going to break another of my windows with that stone!' said the barber.

'Oh no,' said Curdie. 'I didn't mean to break your window, and I certainly won't break another.'

'Give me that stone,' said the barber.

Curdie gave it him, and the barber threw it over the city wall.

'I thought you wanted the stone,' said Curdie.

'No, you fool!' answered the barber. 'What should I want with a stone?'

Curdie stooped and picked up another.

'Give me that stone,' said the barber.

'No,' answered Curdie. 'You have just told me you don't want a stone, and I do.'

The barber took Curdie by the collar.

'Come, now! You pay me for that window.'

'How much?' asked Curdie.

The barber said, 'A crown.' But the baker, annoyed at the heartlessness of the barber, in thinking more of his broken window than the bump on his friend's forehead, interfered.

'No, no,' he said to Curdie; 'don't you pay any such sum. A little pane like that cost only a quarter.'

'Well, to be certain,' said Curdie, 'I'll give a half.' For he doubted the baker as well as the barber. 'Perhaps one day, if he finds he has asked too much, he will bring me the difference.'

'Ha! ha!' laughed the barber. 'A fool and his money are soon parted.'

But as he took the coin from Curdie's hand he grasped it in affected reconciliation and real satisfaction. In Curdie's, his was the cold smooth leathery palm of a monkey. He looked up, almost expecting to see him pop the money in his cheek; but he had not yet got so far as that, though he was well on the road to it: then he would have no other pocket.

'I'm glad that stone is gone, anyhow,' said the baker. 'It was the bane of my life. I had no idea how easy it was to remove it. Give me your pickaxes young miner, and I will show you how a baker can make the stones fly.'

He caught the tool out of Curdie's hand, and flew at one of the foundation stones of the gateway. But he jarred his arm terribly, scarcely chipped the stone, dropped the mattock with a cry of pain, and ran into his own shop. Curdie picked up his implement, and, looking after the baker, saw bread in the window, and followed him in. But the baker, ashamed of himself, and thinking he was coming to laugh at him, popped out of the back door, and when Curdie entered, the baker's wife came from the bake house to serve him. Curdie requested to know the price of a certain good-sized loaf.

Now the baker's wife had been watching what had passed since first her husband ran out of the shop, and she liked the look of Curdie. Also she was more honest than her husband. Casting a glance to the back door, she replied:

'That is not the best bread. I will sell you a loaf of what we bake for ourselves.' And when she had spoken she laid a finger on her lips. 'Take care of yourself in this place, MY son,' she added. 'They do not love strangers. I was once a stranger here, and I know what I say.' Then fancying she heard her husband, 'That is a strange animal you have,' she said, in a louder voice.

'Yes,' answered Curdie. 'She is no beauty, but she is very good, and we love each other. Don't we, Lina?'

Lina looked up and whined. Curdie threw her the half of his loaf, which she ate, while her master and the baker's wife talked a little. Then the baker's wife gave them some water, and Curdie having paid for his loaf, he and Lina went up the street together.

14. THE DOGS OF GWYNTYSTORM

The steep street led them straight up to a large market place with butchers' shops, about which were many dogs. The moment they caught sight of Lina, one and all they came rushing down upon her, giving her no chance of explaining herself. When Curdie saw the dogs coming he heaved up his mattock over his shoulder, and was ready, if they would have it so. Seeing him thus prepared to defend his follower, a great ugly bulldog flew at him. With the first blow Curdie struck him through the brain and the brute fell dead at his feet. But he could not at once recover his weapon, which stuck in the skull of his foe, and a huge mastiff, seeing him thus hampered, flew at him next.

Now Lina, who had shown herself so brave upon the road thither, had grown shy upon entering the city, and kept always at Curdie's heel. But it was her turn now. The moment she saw her master in danger she seemed to go mad with rage. As the mastiff jumped at Curdie's throat, Lina flew at him, seized him with her tremendous jaws, gave one roaring grind, and he lay beside the bulldog with his neck broken. They were the best dogs in the market, after the judgment of the butchers of Gwyntystorm. Down came their masters, knives in hand.

Curdie drew himself up fearlessly, mattock on shoulder, and awaited their coming, while at his heel his awful attendant showed not only her outside fringe of icicle teeth, but a double row of right serviceable fangs she wore inside her mouth, and her green eyes flashed yellow as gold. The butchers, not liking the look of either of them or of the dogs at their feet, drew back, and began to remonstrate in the manner of outraged men.

'Stranger,' said the first, 'that bulldog is mine.'

'Take him, then,' said Curdie, indignant.

'You've killed him!'

'Yes - else he would have killed me.'

'That's no business of mine.'

'No?'

'No.'

'That makes it the more mine, then.'

'This sort of thing won't do, you know,' said the other butcher.

'That's true,' said Curdie. 'That's my mastiff,' said the butcher.

'And as he ought to be,' said Curdie.

'Your brute shall be burned alive for it,' said the butcher.

'Not yet,' answered Curdie. 'We have done no wrong. We were walking quietly up your street when your dogs flew at us. If you don't teach your dogs how to treat strangers, you must take the consequences.'

'They treat them quite properly,' said the butcher. 'What right has any one to bring an abomination like that into our city? The horror is enough to make an idiot of every child in the place.'

'We are both subjects of the king, and my poor animal can't help her looks. How would you like to be served like that because you were ugly? She's not a bit fonder of her looks than you are – only what can she do to change them?'

'I'll do to change them,' said the fellow.

Thereupon the butchers brandished their long knives and advanced, keeping their eyes upon Lina.

'Don't be afraid, Lina,' cried Curdie. 'I'll kill one - you kill the other.'

Lina gave a howl that might have terrified an army, and crouched ready to spring. The butchers turned and ran.

By this time a great crowd had gathered behind the butchers, and in it a number of boys returning from school who began to stone the strangers. It was a way they had with man or beast they did not expect to make anything by. One of the stones struck Lina; she caught it in her teeth and crunched it so that it fell in gravel from her mouth. Some of the foremost of the crowd saw this, and it terrified them. They drew back; the rest took fright from their retreat; the panic spread; and at last the crowd scattered in all directions. They ran, and cried out, and said the devil and his dam were come to Gwyntystorm. So Curdie and Lina were left standing unmolested in the market place. But the terror of them spread throughout the city, and everybody began to shut and lock his door so that by the time the setting sun shone down the street, there was not a shop left open, for fear of the devil and his horrible dam. But all the upper windows within sight of them were crowded with heads watching them where they stood lonely in the deserted market place.

Curdie looked carefully all round, but could not see one open door. He caught sight of the sign of an inn, however, and laying down his mattock, and telling Lina to take care of it, walked up to the door of it and knocked. But the people in the house, instead of opening the door, threw things at him from the windows. They would not listen to a word he said, but sent him back to Lina with the blood running down his face. When Lina saw that she leaped up in a fury and was rushing at the house, into which she would certainly have broken; but Curdie called her, and made her lie down beside him while he bethought him what next he should do.

'Lina,' he said, 'the people keep their gates open, but their houses and their hearts shut.'

As if she knew it was her presence that had brought this trouble upon him, she rose and went round and round him, purring like a tigress, and rubbing herself against his legs.

Now there was one little thatched house that stood squeezed in between two tall gables, and the sides of the two great houses shot out projecting windows that nearly met across the roof of the little one, so that it lay in the street like a doll's house. In this house lived a poor old woman, with a grandchild. And because she never gossiped or quarreled, or chaffered in the market, but went without what she could not afford, the people called her a witch, and would have done her many an ill turn if they had not been afraid of her.

Now while Curdie was looking in another direction the door opened, and out came a little dark-haired, black-eyed, gypsy-looking child, and toddled across the market place toward the outcasts. The moment they saw her coming, Lina lay down flat on the road, and with her two huge forepaws covered her mouth, while Curdie went to meet her, holding out his arms. The little one came straight to him, and held up her mouth to be kissed. Then she took him by the hand, and drew him toward the house, and Curdie yielded to the silent invitation.

But when Lina rose to follow, the child shrank from her, frightened a little. Curdie took her up, and holding her on one arm, patted Lina with the other hand. Then the child wanted also to pat doggy, as she called her by a right bountiful stretch of courtesy, and having once patted her, nothing would serve but Curdie must let her have a ride on doggy. So he set her on Lina's back, holding her hand, and she rode home in merry triumph, all unconscious of the hundreds of eyes staring at her foolhardiness from the windows about the market place, or the murmur of deep disapproval that rose from as many lips.

At the door stood the grandmother to receive them. She caught the child to her bosom with delight at her courage, welcomed Curdie, and showed no dread of Lina. Many were the significant nods exchanged, and many a one said to another that the devil and the witch were old friends. But the woman was only a wise woman, who, having seen how Curdie and Lina behaved to each other, judged from that what sort they were, and so made them welcome to her house. She was not like her fellow townspeople, for that they were strangers recommended them to her.

The moment her door was shut the other doors began to open, and soon there appeared little groups here and there about a threshold, while a few of the more courageous ventured out upon the square - all ready to make for their houses again, however, upon the least sign of movement in the little thatched one.

The baker and the barber had joined one of these groups, and were busily wagging their tongues against Curdie and his horrible beast.

'He can't be honest,' said the barber; 'for he paid me double the worth of the pane he broke in my window.'

And then he told them how Curdie broke his window by breaking a stone in the street with his hammer. There the baker struck in.

'Now that was the stone,' said he, 'over which I had fallen three times within the last month: could it be by fair means he broke that to pieces at the first blow? Just to make up my mind on that point I tried his own hammer against a stone in the gate; it nearly broke both my arms, and loosened half the teeth in my head!'

15. Derba and Barbara

Meantime the wanderers were hospitably entertained by the old woman and her grandchild and they were all very comfortable and happy together. Little Barbara sat upon Curdie's knee, and he told her stories about the mines and his adventures in them. But he never mentioned the king or the princess, for all that story was hard to believe. And he told her about his mother and father, and how good they were. And Derba sat and listened. At last little Barbara fell asleep in Curdie's arms, and her grandmother carried her to bed.

It was a poor little house, and Derba gave up her own room to Curdie because he was honest and talked wisely. Curdie saw how it was, and begged her to allow him to lie on the floor, but she would not hear of it.

In the night he was waked by Lina pulling at him. As soon as he spoke to her she ceased, and Curdie, listening, thought he heard someone trying to get in. He rose, took his mattock, and went about the house, listening and watching; but although he heard noises now at one place now at another, he could not think what they meant for no one appeared. Certainly, considering how she had frightened them all in the day, it was not likely any one would attack Lina at night. By and by the noises ceased, and Curdie went back to his bed, and slept undisturbed.

In the morning, however, Derba came to him in great agitation, and said they had fastened up the door, so that she could not get out. Curdie rose immediately and went with her: they found that not only the door, but every window in the house was so secured on the outside that it was impossible to open one of them without using great force. Poor Derba looked anxiously in Curdie's face. He broke out laughing.

'They are much mistaken,' he said, 'if they fancy they could keep Lina and a miner in any house in Gwyntystorm - even if they built up doors and windows.'

With that he shouldered his mattock. But Derba begged him not to make a hole in her house just yet. She had plenty for breakfast, she said, and before it was time for dinner they would know what the people meant by it.

And indeed they did. For within an hour appeared one of the chief magistrates of the city, accompanied by a score of soldiers with drawn swords, and followed by a great multitude of people, requiring the miner and his brute to yield themselves, the one that he might be tried for the disturbance he had occasioned and the injury he had committed, the other that she might be roasted alive for her part in killing two valuable and harmless animals belonging to worthy citizens. The summons was preceded and followed by flourish of trumpet, and was read with every formality by the city marshal himself.

The moment he ended, Lina ran into the little passage, and stood opposite the door.

'I surrender,' cried Curdie.

'Then tie up your brute, and give her here.'

'No, no,' cried Curdie through the door. 'I surrender; but I'm not going to do your hangman's work. If you want my dog, you must take her.'

'Then we shall set the house on fire, and burn witch and all.'

'It will go hard with us but we shall kill a few dozen of you first,' cried Curdie. 'We're not the least afraid of you.' With that Curdie turned to Derba, and said:

'Don't be frightened. I have a strong feeling that all will be well. Surely no trouble will come to you for being good to strangers.'

'But the poor dog!' said Derba.

Now Curdie and Lina understood each other more than a little by this time, and not only had he seen that she understood the proclamation, but when she looked up at him after it was read, it was with such a grin, and such a yellow flash, that he saw also she was determined to take care of herself. 'The dog will probably give you reason to think a little more of her ere long,' he answered. 'But now,' he went on, 'I fear I must hurt your house a little. I have great confidence, however, that I shall be able to make up to you for it one day.'

'Never mind the house, if only you can get safe off,' she answered. 'I don't think they will hurt this precious lamb,' she added, clasping little Barbara to her bosom. 'For myself, it is all one; I am ready for anything.'

'It is but a little hole for Lina I want to make,' said Curdie. 'She can creep through a much smaller one than you would think.'

Again he took his mattock, and went to the back wall.

'They won't burn the house,' he said to himself. 'There is too good a one on each side of it.'

The tumult had kept increasing every moment, and the city marshal had been shouting, but Curdie had not listened to him. When now they heard the blows of his mattock, there went up a great cry, and the people taunted the soldiers that they were afraid of a dog and his miner. The soldiers therefore made a rush at the door, and cut its fastenings.

The moment they opened it, out leaped Lina, with a roar so unnaturally horrible that the sword arms of the soldiers dropped by their sides, paralyzed with the terror of that cry; the crowd fled in every direction, shrieking and yelling with mortal dismay; and without even knocking down with her tail, not to say biting a man of them with her pulverizing jaws, Lina vanished - no one knew whither, for not one of the crowd had had courage to look upon her.

The moment she was gone, Curdie advanced and gave himself up. The soldiers were so filled with fear, shame, and chagrin, that they were ready to kill him on the spot. But he stood quietly facing them, with his mattock on his shoulder; and the magistrate wishing to examine him, and the people to see him made an example of, the soldiers had to content themselves with taking him. Partly for derision, partly to hurt him, they laid his mattock against his back, and tied his arms to it.

They led him up a very steep street, and up another still, all the crowd following. The king's palace-castle rose towering above them; but they stopped before they reached it, at a low-browed door in a great, dull, heavy-looking building.

The city marshal opened it with a key which hung at his girdle, and ordered Curdie to enter. The place within was dark as night, and while he was feeling his way with his feet, the marshal gave him a rough push. He fell, and rolled once or twice over, unable to help himself because his hands were tied behind him.

It was the hour of the magistrate's second and more important breakfast, and until that was over he never found himself capable of attending to a case with concentration sufficient to the distinguishing of the side upon which his own advantage lay; and hence was this respite for Curdie, with time to collect his thoughts. But indeed he had very few to collect, for all he had to do, so far as he could see, was to wait for what would come next. Neither had he much power to collect them, for he was a good deal shaken.

In a few minutes he discovered, to his great relief, that, from the projection of the pick end of his mattock beyond his body, the fall had loosened the ropes tied round it. He got one hand disengaged, and then the other; and presently stood free, with his good mattock once more in right serviceable relation to his arms and legs.

16. The Mattock

While the magistrate reinvigorated his selfishness with a greedy breakfast, Curdie found doing nothing in the dark rather tiresome work. It was useless attempting to think what he should do next, seeing the circumstances in which he was presently to find himself were altogether unknown to him. So he began to think about his father and mother in their little cottage home, high in the clear air of the open Mountainside, and the thought, instead of making his dungeon gloomier by the contrast, made a light in his soul that destroyed the power of darkness and captivity.

But he was at length startled from his waking dream by a swell in the noise outside. All the time there had been a few of the more idle of the inhabitants about the door, but they had been rather quiet. Now, however, the sounds of feet and voices began to grow, and grew so rapidly that it was plain a multitude was gathering. For the people of Gwyntystorm always gave themselves an hour of pleasure after their second breakfast, and what greater pleasure could they have than to see a stranger abused by the officers of justice?

The noise grew till it was like the roaring of the sea, and that roaring went on a long time, for the magistrate, being a great man, liked to know that he was waited for: it added to the enjoyment of his breakfast, and, indeed, enabled him to eat a little more after he had thought his powers exhausted.

But at length, in the waves of the human noises rose a bigger wave, and by the running and shouting and outcry, Curdie learned that the magistrate was approaching.

Presently came the sound of the great rusty key in the lock, which yielded with groaning reluctance; the door was thrown back, the light rushed in, and with it came the voice of the city marshal, calling upon Curdie, by many legal epithets opprobrious, to come forth and be tried for his life, inasmuch as he had raised a tumult in His Majesty's city of Gwyntystorm, troubled the hearts of the king's baker and barber, and slain the faithful dogs of His Majesty's well-beloved butchers.

He was still reading, and Curdie was still seated in the brown twilight of the vault, not listening, but pondering with himself how this king the city marshal talked of could be the same with the Majesty he had seen ride away on his grand white horse with the Princess Irene on a cushion before him, when a scream of agonized terror arose on the farthest skirt of the crowd, and, swifter than flood or flame, the horror spread shrieking. In a moment the air was filled with hideous howling, cries of unspeakable dismay, and the multitudinous noise of running feet. The next moment, in at the door of the vault bounded Lina, her two green eyes flaming yellow as sunflowers, and seeming to light up the dungeon. With one spring she threw herself at Curdie's feet, and laid her head upon them panting. Then came a rush of two or three soldiers darkening the doorway, but it was only to lay hold of the key, pull the door to, and lock it; so that once more Curdie and Lina were prisoners together.

For a few moments Lina lay panting hard: it is breathless work leaping and roaring both at once, and that in a way to scatter thousands of people. Then she jumped up, and began snuffing about all over the place; and Curdie saw what he had never seen before - two faint spots of light cast from her eyes upon the ground, one on each side of her snuffing nose. He got out his tinder box – a miner is never without one - and lighted a precious bit of candle he carried in a division of it just for a moment, for he must not waste it.

The light revealed a vault without any window or other opening than the door. It was very old and much neglected. The mortar had vanished from between the stones, and it was half filled with a heap of all sorts of rubbish, beaten down in the middle, but looser at the sides; it sloped from the door to the foot of the opposite wall: evidently for a long time the vault had been left open, and every sort of refuse thrown into it. A single minute served for the survey, so little was there to note.

Meantime, down in the angle between the back wall and the base of the heap Lina was scratching furiously with all the eighteen great strong claws of her mighty feet.

'Ah, ha!' said Curdie to himself, catching sight of her, 'if only they will leave us long enough to ourselves!'

With that he ran to the door, to see if there was any fastening on the inside. There was none: in all its long history it never had had one. But a few blows of the right sort, now from the one, now from the other end of his mattock, were as good as any bolt, for they so ruined the lock that no key could ever turn in it again. Those who heard them fancied he was trying to get out, and laughed spitefully. As soon as he had done, he extinguished his candle, and went down to Lina.

She had reached the hard rock which formed the floor of the dungeon, and was now clearing away the earth a little wider. Presently she looked up in his face and whined, as much as to say, 'My paws are not hard enough to get any farther.'

'Then get out of my way, Lina,' said Curdie, and mind you keep your eyes shining, for fear I should hit you.'

So saying, he heaved his mattock, and assailed with the hammer end of it the spot she had cleared.

The rock was very hard, but when it did break it broke in good-sized pieces. Now with hammer, now with pick, he worked till he was weary, then rested, and then set to again. He could not tell how the day went, as he had no light but the lamping of Lina's eyes. The darkness hampered him greatly, for he would not let Lina come close enough to give him all the light she could, lest he should strike her. So he had, every now and then, to feel with his hands to know how he was getting on, and to discover in what direction to strike: the exact spot was a mere imagination.

He was getting very tired and hungry, and beginning to lose heart a little, when out of the ground, as if he had struck a spring of it, burst a dull, gleamy, lead-colored light, and the next moment he heard a hollow splash and echo. A piece of rock had fallen out of the floor, and dropped into water beneath. Already Lina, who had been lying a few yards off all the time he worked, was on her feet and peering through the hole. Curdie got down on his hands and knees, and looked. They were over what seemed a natural cave in the rock, to which apparently the river had access, for, at a great distance below, a faint light was gleaming upon water. If they could but reach it, they might get out; but even if it was deep enough, the height was very dangerous. The first thing, whatever might follow, was to make the hole larger. It was comparatively easy to break away the sides of it, and in the course of another hour he had it large enough to get through.

And now he must reconnoitre. He took the rope they had tied him with - for Curdie's hindrances were always his furtherance – and fastened one end of it by a slipknot round the handle of his pickaxes then dropped the other end through, and laid the pickaxe so that, when he was through himself, and hanging on the edge, he could place it across the hole to support him on the rope. This done, he took the rope in his hands, and, beginning to descend, found himself in a narrow cleft widening into a cave. His rope was not very long, and would not do much to lessen the force of his fall - he thought to himself - if he should have to drop into the water; but he was not more than a couple of yards below the dungeon when he spied an opening on the opposite side of the cleft: it might be but a shadow hole, or it might lead them out. He dropped himself a little below its level, gave the rope a swing by pushing his feet against the side of the cleft, and so penduled himself into it. Then he laid a stone on the end of the rope that it should not forsake him, called to Lina, whose yellow eyes were gleaming over the mattock grating above, to watch there till he returned, and went cautiously in. It proved a passage, level for some distance, then sloping gently up. He advanced carefully, feeling his way as he went. At length he was stopped by a door - a small door, studded with iron. But the wood was in places so much decayed that some of the bolts had dropped out, and he felt sure of being able to open it. He returned, therefore, to fetch Lina and his mattock. Arrived at the cleft, his strong miner arms bore him swiftly up along the rope and through the hole into the dungeon. There he undid the rope from his mattock, and making Lina take the end of it in her teeth, and get through the hole, he lowered her - it was all he could do, she was so heavy. When she came opposite the passage, with a slight push of her tail she shot herself into it, and let go the rope, which Curdie drew up.

Then he lighted his candle and searching in the rubbish found a bit of iron to take the place of his pickaxe across the hole. Then he searched again in the rubbish, and found half an old shutter. This he propped up leaning a little over the hole, with a bit of stick, and heaped against the back of it a quantity of the loosened earth. Next he tied his mattock to the end of the rope, dropped it, and let it hang. Last, he got through the hole himself, and pulled away the propping stick, so that the shutter fell over the hole with a quantity of earth on the top of it. A few motions of hand over hand, and he swung himself and his mattock into the passage beside Lina.

There he secured the end of the rope, and they went on together to the door.

17. THE WINE CELLAR

He lighted his candle and examined it. Decayed and broken as it was, it was strongly secured in its place by hinges on the one side, and either lock or bolt, he could not tell which, on the other. A brief use of his pocket-knife was enough to make room for his hand and arm to get through, and then he found a great iron bolt - but so rusty that he could not move it.

Lina whimpered. He took his knife again, made the hole bigger, and stood back. In she shot her small head and long neck, seized the bolt with her teeth, and dragged it, grating and complaining, back. A push then opened the door. It was at the foot of a short flight of steps. They ascended, and at the top Curdie found himself in a space which, from the echo to his stamp, appeared of some size, though of what sort he could not at first tell, for his hands, feeling about, came upon nothing. Presently, however, they fell on a great thing: it was a wine cask.

He was just setting out to explore the place thoroughly, when he heard steps coming down a stair. He stood still, not knowing whether the door would open an inch from his nose or twenty yards behind his back. It did neither. He heard the key turn in the lock, and a stream of light shot in, ruining the darkness, about fifteen yards away on his right.

A man carrying a candle in one hand and a large silver flagon in the other, entered, and came toward him. The light revealed a row of huge wine casks, that stretched away into the darkness of the other end of the long vault. Curdie retreated into the recess of the stair, and peeping round the corner of it, watched him, thinking what he could do to prevent him from locking them in. He came on and on, until Curdie feared he would pass the recess and see them. He was just preparing to rush out, and master him before he should give alarm, not in the least knowing what he should do next, when, to his relief, the man stopped at the third cask from where he stood. He set down his light on the top of it, removed what seemed a large vent-peg, and poured into the cask a quantity of something from the flagon. Then he turned to the next cask, drew some wine, rinsed the flagon, threw the wine away, drew and rinsed and threw away again, then drew and drank, draining to the bottom. Last of all, he filled the flagon from the cask he had first visited, replaced then the vent-peg, took up his candle, and turned toward the door.

'There is something wrong here!' thought Curdie.

'Speak to him, Lina,' he whispered.

The sudden howl she gave made Curdie himself start and tremble for a moment. As to the man, he answered Lina's with another horrible howl, forced from him by the convulsive shudder of every muscle of his body, then reeled gasping to and fro, and dropped his candle. But just as Curdie expected to see him fall dead he recovered himself, and flew to the door, through which he darted, leaving it open behind him. The moment he ran, Curdie stepped out, picked up the candle still alight, sped after him to the door, drew out the key, and then returned to the stair and waited. In a few minutes he heard the sound of many feet and voices. Instantly he turned the tap of the cask from which the man had been drinking, set the candle beside it on the floor, went down the steps and out of the little door, followed by Lina, and closed it behind them.

Through the hole in it he could see a little, and hear all. He could see how the light of many candles filled the place, and could hear how some two dozen feet ran hither and thither through the echoing cellar; he could hear the clash of iron, probably spits and pokers, now and then; and at last heard how, finding nothing remarkable except the best wine running to waste, they all turned on the butler and accused him of having fooled them with a drunken dream. He did his best to defend himself, appealing to the evidence of their own senses that he was as sober as they were. They replied that a fright was no less a fright that the cause was imaginary, and a dream no less a dream that the fright had waked him from it.

When he discovered, and triumphantly adduced as corroboration, that the key was gone from the door, they said it merely showed how drunk he had been - either that or how frightened, for he had certainly dropped it. In vain he protested that he had never taken it out of the lock - that he never did when he went in, and certainly had not this time stopped to do so when he came out; they asked him why he had to go to the cellar at such a time of the day, and said it was because he had already drunk all the wine that was left from dinner. He said if he had dropped the key, the key was to be found, and they must help him to find it. They told him they wouldn't move a peg for him. He declared, with much language, he would have them all turned out of the king's service. They said they would swear he was drunk.

And so positive were they about it, that at last the butler himself began to think whether it was possible they could be in the right. For he knew that sometimes when he had been drunk he fancied things had taken place which he found afterward could not have happened. Certain of his fellow servants, however, had all the time a doubt whether the cellar goblin had not appeared to him, or at least roared at him, to protect the wine. In any case nobody wanted to find the key for him; nothing could please them better than that the door of the wine cellar should never more be locked. By degrees the hubbub died away, and they departed, not even pulling to the door, for there was neither handle nor latch to it.

As soon as they were gone, Curdie returned, knowing now that they were in the wine cellar of the palace, as indeed, he had suspected. Finding a pool of wine in a hollow of the floor, Lina lapped it up eagerly: She had had no breakfast, and was now very thirsty as well as hungry. Her master was in a similar plight, for he had but just begun to eat when the magistrate arrived with the soldiers. If only they were all in bed, he thought, that he might find his way to the larder! For he said to himself that, as he was sent there by the young princess's great-great-grandmother to serve her or her father in some way, surely he must have a right to his food in the Palace, without which he could do nothing. He would go at once and reconnoitre.

So he crept up the stair that led from the cellar. At the top was a door, opening on a long passage dimly lighted by a lamp. He told Lina to lie down upon the stair while he went on. At the end of the passage he found a door ajar, and, peering through, saw right into a great stone hall, where a huge fire was blazing, and through which men in the king's livery were constantly coming and going. Some also in the same livery were lounging about the fire. He noted that their colors were the same as those he himself, as king's miner, wore; but from what he had seen and heard of the habits of the place, he could not hope they would treat him the better for that.

The one interesting thing at the moment, however, was the plentiful supper with which the table was spread. It was something at least to stand in sight of food, and he was unwilling to turn his back on the prospect so long as a share in it was not absolutely hopeless. Peeping thus, he soon made up his mind that if at any moment the hall should be empty, he would at that moment rush in and attempt to carry off a dish. That he might lose no time by indecision, he selected a large pie upon which to pounce instantaneously. But after he had watched for some minutes, it did not seem at all likely the chance would arrive before suppertime, and he was just about to turn away and rejoin Lina, when he saw that there was not a person in the place. Curdie never made up his mind and then hesitated. He darted in, seized the pie, and bore it swiftly and noiselessly to the cellar stair.

18. The King's Kitchen

Back to the cellar Curdie and Lina sped with their booty, where, seated on the steps, Curdie lighted his bit of candle for a moment. A very little bit it was now, but they did not waste much of it in examination of the pie; that they effected by a more summary process. Curdie thought it the nicest food he had ever tasted, and between them they soon ate it up. Then Curdie would have thrown the dish along with the bones into the water, that there might be no traces of them; but he thought of his mother, and hid it instead; and the very next minute they wanted it to draw some wine into. He was careful it should be from the cask of which he had seen the butler drink.

Then they sat down again upon the steps, and waited until the house should be quiet. For he was there to do something, and if it did not come to him in the cellar, he must go to meet it in other places. Therefore, lest he should fall asleep, he set the end of the helve of his mattock on the ground, and seated himself on the cross part, leaning against the wall, so that as long as he kept awake he should rest, but the moment he began to fall asleep he must fall awake instead. He quite expected some of the servants would visit the cellar again that night, but whether it was that they were afraid of each other, or believed more of the butler's story than they had chosen to allow, not one of them appeared.

When at length he thought he might venture, he shouldered his mattock and crept up the stair. The lamp was out in the passage, but he could not miss his way to the servants' hall. Trusting to Lina's quickness in concealing herself, he took her with him.

When they reached the hall they found it quiet and nearly dark. The last of the great fire was glowing red, but giving little light. Curdie stood and warmed himself for a few moments: miner as he was, he had found the cellar cold to sit in doing nothing; and standing thus he thought of looking if there were any bits of candle about. There were many candlesticks on the supper table, but to his disappointment and indignation their candles seemed to have been all left to burn out, and some of them, indeed, he found still hot in the neck.

Presently, one after another, he came upon seven men fast asleep, most of them upon tables, one in a chair, and one on the floor. They seemed, from their shape and color, to have eaten and drunk so much that they might be burned alive without wakening. He grasped the hand of each in succession, and found two ox hoofs, three pig hoofs, one concerning which he could not be sure whether it was the hoof of a donkey or a pony, and one dog's paw. 'A nice set of people to be about a king!' thought Curdie to himself, and turned again to his candle hunt. He did at last find two or three little pieces, and stowed them away in his pockets. They now left the hall by another door, and entered a short passage, which led them to the huge kitchen, vaulted and black with smoke. There, too, the fire was still burning, so that he was able to see a little of the state of things in this quarter also.

The place was dirty and disorderly. In a recess, on a heap of brushwood, lay a kitchen-maid, with a table cover around her, and a skillet in her hand: evidently she too had been drinking. In another corner lay a page, and Curdie noted how like his dress was to his own. In the cinders before the hearth were huddled three dogs and five cats, all fast asleep, while the rats were running about the floor. Curdie's heart ached to think of the lovely child-princess living over such a sty. The mine was a paradise to a palace with such servants in it.

Leaving the kitchen, he got into the region of the sculleries. There horrible smells were wandering about, like evil spirits that come forth with the darkness. He lighted a candle - but only to see ugly sights. Everywhere was filth and disorder. Mangy turnspit dogs were lying about, and grey rats were gnawing at refuse in the sinks. It was like a hideous dream. He felt as if he should never get out of it, and longed for one glimpse of his mother's poor little kitchen, so clean and bright and airy. Turning from it at last in miserable disgust, he almost ran back through the kitchen, re-entered the hall, and crossed it to another door.

It opened upon a wider passage leading to an arch in a stately corridor, all its length lighted by lamps in niches. At the end of it was a large and beautiful hall, with great pillars. There sat three men in the royal livery, fast asleep, each in a great armchair, with his feet on a huge footstool. They looked like fools dreaming themselves kings; and Lina looked as if she longed to throttle them. At one side of the hall was the grand staircase, and they went up. Everything that now met Curdie's eyes was rich - not glorious like the splendors of the mountain cavern, but rich and soft – except where, now and then, some rough old rib of the ancient fortress came through, hard and discolored. Now some dark bare arch of stone, now some rugged and blackened pillar, now some huge beam, brown with the smoke and dust of centuries, looked like a thistle in the midst of daisies, or a rock in a smooth lawn.

They wandered about a good while, again and again finding themselves where they had been before. Gradually, however, Curdie was gaining some idea of the place. By and by Lina began to look frightened, and as they went on Curdie saw that she looked more and more frightened. Now, by this time he had come to understand that what made her look frightened was always the fear of frightening, and he therefore concluded they must be drawing nigh to somebody.

At last, in a gorgeously painted gallery, he saw a curtain of crimson, and on the curtain a royal crown wrought in silks and stones. He felt sure this must be the king's chamber, and it was here he was wanted; or, if it was not the place he was bound for, something would meet him and turn him aside; for he had come to think that so long as a man wants to do right he may go where he can: when he can go no farther, then it is not the way. 'Only,' said his father, in assenting to the theory, 'he must really want to do right, and not merely fancy he does. He must want it with his heart and will, and not with his rag of a tongue.' So he gently lifted the corner of the curtain, and there behind it was a half-open door. He entered, and the moment he was in, Lina stretched herself along the threshold between the curtain and the door.

19. THE KING'S CHAMBER

He found himself in a large room, dimly lighted by a silver lamp that hung from the ceiling. Far at the other end was a great bed, surrounded with dark heavy curtains. He went softly toward it, his heart beating fast. It was a dreadful thing to be alone in the king's chamber at the dead of night. To gain courage he had to remind himself of the beautiful princess who had sent him.

But when he was about halfway to the bed, a figure appeared from the farther side of it, and came towards him, with a hand raised warningly. He stood still. The light was dim, and he could distinguish little more than the outline of a young girl. But though the form he saw was much taller than the princess he remembered, he never doubted it was she. For one thing, he knew that most girls would have been frightened to see him there in the dead of the night, but like a true princess, and the princess he used to know, she walked straight on to meet him. As she came she lowered the hand she had lifted, and laid the forefinger of it upon her lips. Nearer and nearer, quite near, close up to him she came, then stopped, and stood a moment looking at him.

'You are Curdie,' she said.

'And you are the Princess Irene,' he returned.

'Then we know each other still,' she said, with a sad smile of pleasure. 'You will help me.'

'That I will,' answered Curdie. He did not say, 'If I can'; for he knew that what he was sent to do, that he could do. 'May I kiss your hand, little Princess?'

She was only between nine and ten, though indeed she looked several years older, and her eyes almost those of a grown woman, for she had had terrible trouble of late.

She held out her hand.

'I am not the little princess any more. I have grown up since I saw you last, Mr. Miner.'

The smile which accompanied the words had in it a strange mixture of playfulness and sadness. 'So I see, Miss Princess,' returned Curdie; 'and therefore, being more of a princess, you are the more my princess. Here I am, sent by your great-great-grandmother, to be your servant. May I ask why you are up so late, Princess?'

'Because my father wakes so frightened, and I don't know what he would do if he didn't find me by his bedside. There! he's waking now.'

She darted off to the side of the bed she had come from.

Curdie stood where he was.

A voice altogether unlike what he remembered of the mighty, noble king on his white horse came from the bed, thin, feeble, hollow, and husky, and in tone like that of a petulant child:

'I will not, I will not. I am a king, and I will be a king. I hate you and despise you, and you shall not torture me!'

'Never mind them, Father dear,' said the princess. 'I am here, and they shan't touch you. They dare not, you know, so long as you defy them.'

'They want my crown, darling; and I can't give them my crown, can I? For what is a king without his crown?' 'They shall never have your crown, my king,' said Irene. 'Here it is - all safe. I am watching it for you.'

Curdie drew near the bed on the other side. There lay the grand old king - he looked grand still, and twenty years older. His body was pillowed high; his beard descended long and white over the crimson coverlid; and his crown, its diamonds and emeralds gleaming in the twilight of the curtains, lay in front of him, his long thin old hands folded round it, and the ends of his beard straying among the lovely stones. His face was like that of a man who had died fighting nobly; but one thing made it dreadful: his eyes, while they moved about as if searching in this direction and in that, looked more dead than his face. He saw neither his daughter nor his crown: it was the voice of the one and the touch of the other that comforted him. He kept murmuring what seemed words, but was unintelligible to Curdie, although, to judge from the look of Irene's face, she learned and concluded from it.

By degrees his voice sank away and the murmuring ceased, although still his lips moved. Thus lay the old king on his bed, slumbering with his crown between his hands; on one side of him stood a lovely little maiden, with blue eyes, and brown hair going a little back from her temples, as if blown by a wind that no one felt but herself; and on the other a stalwart young miner, with his mattock over his shoulder. Stranger sight still was Lina lying along the threshold - only nobody saw her just then.

A moment more and the king's lips ceased to move. His breathing had grown regular and quiet. The princess gave a sigh of relief, and came round to Curdie.

'We can talk a little now,' she said, leading him toward the middle of the room. 'My father will sleep now till the doctor wakes him to give him his medicine. It is not really medicine, though, but wine. Nothing but that, the doctor says, could have kept him so long alive. He always comes in the middle of the night to give it him with his own hands. But it makes me cry to see him wake up when so nicely asleep.'

'What sort of man is your doctor?' asked Curdie.

'Oh, such a dear, good, kind gentleman!' replied the princess. 'He speaks so softly, and is so sorry for his dear king! He will be here presently, and you shall see for yourself. You will like him very much.'

'Has your king-father been long ill?' asked Curdie.

'A whole year now,' she replied. 'Did you not know? That's how your mother never got the red petticoat my father promised her. The lord chancellor told me that not only Gwyntystorm but the whole land was mourning over the illness of the good man.'

Now Curdie himself had not heard a word of His Majesty's illness, and had no ground for believing that a single soul in any place he had visited on his journey had heard of it. Moreover, although mention had been made of His Majesty again and again in his hearing since he came to Gwyntystorm, never once had he heard an allusion to the state of his health. And now it dawned upon him also that he had never heard the least expression of love to him. But just for the time he thought it better to say nothing on either point.

'Does the king wander like this every night?' he asked.

'Every night,' answered Irene, shaking her head mournfully. 'That is why I never go to bed at night. He is better during the day - a little, and then I sleep - in the dressing room there, to be with him in a moment if he should call me. It is so sad he should have only me and not my mamma! A princess is nothing to a queen!'

'I wish he would like me,' said Curdie, 'for then I might watch by him at night, and let you go to bed, Princess.'

'Don't you know then?' returned Irene, in wonder. 'How was it you came? Ah! You said my grandmother sent you. But I thought you knew that he wanted you.'

And again she opened wide her blue stars.

'Not I,' said Curdie, also bewildered, but very glad.

'He used to be constantly saying - he was not so ill then as he is now - that he wished he had you about him.'

'And I never to know it!' said Curdie, with displeasure.

'The master of the horse told papa's own secretary that he had written to the miner-general to find you and send you up; but the miner-general wrote back to the master of the horse, and he told the secretary, and the secretary told my father, that they had searched every mine in the kingdom and could hear nothing of you. My father gave a great sigh, and said he feared the goblins had got you, after all, and your father and mother were dead of grief. And he has never mentioned you since, except when wandering. I cried very much. But one of my grandmother's pigeons with its white wing flashed a message to me through the window one day, and then I knew that my Curdie wasn't eaten by the goblins, for my grandmother wouldn't have taken care of him one time to let him be eaten the next. Where were you, Curdie, that they couldn't find you?'

'We will talk about that another time, when we are not expecting the doctor,' said Curdie.

As he spoke, his eyes fell upon something shining on the table under the lamp. His heart gave a great throb, and he went nearer. Yes, there could be no doubt - it was the same flagon that the butler had filled in the wine cellar.

'It looks worse and worse!' he said to himself, and went back to Irene, where she stood half dreaming.

'When will the doctor be here?' he asked once more - this time hurriedly.

The question was answered - not by the princess, but by something which that instant tumbled heavily into the room. Curdie flew toward it in vague terror about Lina.

On the floor lay a little round man, puffing and blowing, and uttering incoherent language. Curdie thought of his mattock, and ran and laid it aside.

'Oh, dear Dr Kelman!' cried the princess, running up and taking hold of his arm; 'I am so sorry!' She pulled and pulled, but might almost as well have tried to set up a cannon ball. 'I hope you have not hurt yourself?'

'Not at all, not at all,' said the doctor, trying to smile and to rise both at once, but finding it impossible to do either.

'If he slept on the floor he would be late for breakfast,' said Curdie to himself, and held out his hand to help him.

But when he took hold of it, Curdie very nearly let him fall again, for what he held was not even a foot: it was the belly of a creeping thing. He managed, however, to hold both his peace and his grasp, and pulled the doctor roughly on his legs - such as they were.

'Your Royal Highness has rather a thick mat at the door,' said the doctor, patting his palms together. 'I hope my awkwardness may not have startled His Majesty.'

While he talked Curdie went to the door: Lina was not there.

The doctor approached the bed.

'And how has my beloved king slept tonight?' he asked.

'No better,' answered Irene, with a mournful shake of her head.

'Ah, that is very well!' returned the doctor, his fall seeming to have muddled either his words or his meaning. 'When we give him his wine, he will be better still.'

Curdie darted at the flagon, and lifted it high, as if he had expected to find it full, but had found it empty.

'That stupid butler! I heard them say he was drunk!' he cried in a loud whisper, and was gliding from the room.

'Come here with that flagon, you! Page!' cried the doctor. Curdie came a few steps toward him with the flagon dangling from his hand, heedless of the gushes that fell noiseless on the thick carpet.

'Are you aware, young man,' said the doctor, 'that it is not every wine can do His Majesty the benefit I intend he should derive from my prescription?'

'Quite aware, sir, answered Curdie. 'The wine for His Majesty's use is in the third cask from the corner.'

'Fly, then,' said the doctor, looking satisfied.

Curdie stopped outside the curtain and blew an audible breath – no more; up came Lina noiseless as a shadow. He showed her the flagon.

'The cellar, Lina: go,' he said.

She galloped away on her soft feet, and Curdie had indeed to fly to keep up with her. Not once did she make even a dubious turn. From the king's gorgeous chamber to the cold cellar they shot. Curdie dashed the wine down the back stair, rinsed the flagon out as he had seen the butler do, filled it from the cask of which he had seen the butler drink, and hastened with it up again to the king's room.

The little doctor took it, poured out a full glass, smelt, but did not taste it, and set it down. Then he leaned over the bed, shouted in the king's ear, blew upon his eyes, and pinched his arm: Curdie thought he saw him run something bright into it. At last the king half woke. The doctor seized the glass, raised his head, poured the wine down his throat, and let his head fall back on the pillow again. Tenderly wiping his beard, and bidding the princess good night in paternal tones, he then took his leave. Curdie would gladly have driven his pick into his head, but that was not in his commission, and he let him go. The little round man looked very carefully to his feet as he crossed the threshold.

'That attentive fellow of a page has removed the mat,' he said to himself, as he walked along the corridor. 'I must remember him.'

20. COUNTERPLOTTING

Curdie was already sufficiently enlightened as to how things were going, to see that he must have the princess of one mind with him, and they must work together. It was clear that among those about the king there was a plot against him: for one thing, they had agreed in a lie concerning himself; and it was plain also that the doctor was working out a design against the health and reason of His Majesty, rendering the question of his life a matter of little moment. It was in itself sufficient to justify the worst fears, that the people outside the palace were ignorant of His Majesty's condition: he believed those inside it also - the butler excepted - were ignorant of it as well. Doubtless His Majesty's councilors desired to alienate the hearts of his subjects from their sovereign. Curdie's idea was that they intended to kill the king, marry the princess to one of themselves, and found a new dynasty; but whatever their purpose, there was treason in the palace of the worst sort: they were making and keeping the king incapable, in order to effect that purpose- The first thing to be seen to, therefore, was that His Majesty should neither eat morsel nor drink drop of anything prepared for him in the palace. Could this have been managed without the princess, Curdie would have preferred leaving her in ignorance of the horrors from which he sought to deliver her. He feared also the danger of her knowledge betraying itself to the evil eyes about her; but it must be risked and she had always been a wise child.

Another thing was clear to him - that with such traitors no terms of honor were either binding or possible, and that, short of lying, he might use any means to foil them. And he could not doubt that the old princess had sent him expressly to frustrate their plans.

While he stood thinking thus with himself, the princess was earnestly watching the king, with looks of childish love and womanly tenderness that went to Curdie's heart. Now and then with a great fan of peacock feathers she would fan him very softly; now and then, seeing a cloud begin to gather upon the sky of his sleeping face, she would climb upon the bed, and bending to his ear whisper into it, then draw back and watch again - generally to see the cloud disperse. In his deepest slumber, the soul of the king lay open to the voice of his child, and that voice had power either to change the aspect of his visions, or, which was better still, to breathe hope into his heart, and courage to endure them.

Curdie came near, and softly called her.

'I can't leave Papa just yet,' she returned, in a low voice.

'I will wait,' said Curdie; 'but I want very much to say something.'

In a few minutes she came to him where he stood under the lamp.

'Well, Curdie, what is it?' she said.

'Princess,' he replied, 'I want to tell you that I have found why your grandmother sent me.'

'Come this way, then,' she answered, 'where I can see the face of my king.'

Curdie placed a chair for her in the spot she chose, where she would be near enough to mark any slightest change on her father's countenance, yet where their low-voiced talk would not disturb him. There he sat down beside her and told her all the story - how her grandmother had sent her good pigeon for him, and how she had instructed him, and sent him there without telling him what he had to do. Then he told her what he had discovered of the state of things generally in Gwyntystorm, and especially what he had heard and seen in the palace that night.

'Things are in a bad state enough,' he said in conclusion - 'lying and selfishness and inhospitality and dishonesty everywhere; and to crown all, they speak with disrespect of the good king, and not a man knows he is ill.'

'You frighten me dreadfully,' said Irene, trembling.

'You must be brave for your king's sake,' said Curdie.

'Indeed I will,' she replied, and turned a long loving look upon the beautiful face of her father. 'But what is to be done? And how am I to believe such horrible things of Dr Kelman?'

'My dear Princess,' replied Curdie, 'you know nothing of him but his face and his tongue, and they are both false. Either you must beware of him, or you must doubt your grandmother and me; for I tell you, by the gift she gave me of testing hands, that this man is a snake. That round body he shows is but the case of a serpent. Perhaps the creature lies there, as in its nest, coiled round and round inside.'

'Horrible!' said Irene.

'Horrible indeed; but we must not try to get rid of horrible things by refusing to look at them, and saying they are not there. Is not your beautiful father sleeping better since he had the wine?'

'Yes.'

'Does he always sleep better after having it?'

She reflected an instant.

'No; always worse - till tonight,' she answered.

'Then remember that was the wine I got him - not what the butler drew. Nothing that passes through any hand in the house except yours or mine must henceforth, till he is well, reach His Majesty's lips.'

'But how, dear Curdie?' said the princess, almost crying.

'That we must contrive,' answered Curdie. 'I know how to take care of the wine; but for his food - now we must think.' 'He takes hardly any,' said the princess, with a pathetic shake of her little head which Curdie had almost learned to look for.

'The more need,' he replied, 'there should be no poison in it.' Irene shuddered. 'As soon as he has honest food he will begin to grow better. And you must be just as careful with yourself, Princess,' Curdie went on, 'for you don't know when they may begin to poison you, too.'

'There's no fear of me; don't talk about me,' said Irene. 'The good food! How are we to get it, Curdie? That is the whole question.'

'I am thinking hard,' answered Curdie. 'The good food? Let me see - let me see! Such servants as I saw below are sure to have the best of everything for themselves: I will go an see what I can find on their table.'

'The chancellor sleeps in the house, and he and the master of the king's horse always have their supper together in a room off the great hall, to the right as you go down the stairs,' said Irene. 'I would go with you, but I dare not leave my father. Alas! He scarcely ever takes more than a mouthful. I can't think how he lives! And the very thing he would like, and often asks for – a bit of bread - I can hardly ever get for him: Dr Kelman has forbidden it, and says it is nothing less than poison to him.'

'Bread at least he shall have,' said Curdie; 'and that, with the honest wine, will do as well as anything, I do believe. I will go at once and look for some. But I want you to see Lina first, and know her, lest, coming upon her by accident at any time, you should be frightened.'

'I should like much to see her,' said the princess.

Warning her not to be startled by her ugliness, he went to the door and called her.

She entered, creeping with downcast head, and dragging her tail over the floor behind her. Curdie watched the princess as the frightful creature came nearer and nearer. One shudder went from head to foot, and next instant she stepped to meet her. Lina dropped flat on the floor, and covered her face with her two big paws. It went to the heart of the princess: in a moment she was on her knees beside her, stroking her ugly head, and patting her all over.

'Good dog! Dear ugly dog!' she said.

Lina whimpered.

'I believe,' said Curdie, 'from what your grandmother told me, that Lina is a woman, and that she was naughty, but is now growing good.' Lina had lifted her head while Irene was caressing her; now she dropped it again between her paws; but the princess took it in her hands, and kissed the forehead betwixt the gold-green eyes.

'Shall I take her with me or leave her?' asked Curdie.

'Leave her, poor dear,' said Irene, and Curdie, knowing the way now, went without her.

He took his way first to the room the princess had spoken of, and there also were the remains of supper; but neither there nor in the kitchen could he find a scrap of plain wholesome-looking bread. So he returned and told her that as soon as it was light he would go into the city for some, and asked her for a handkerchief to tie it in. If he could not bring it himself, he would send it by Lina, who could keep out of sight better than he, and as soon as all was quiet at night he would come to her again. He also asked her to tell the king that he was in the house. His hope lay in the fact that bakers everywhere go to work early. But it was yet much too early. So he persuaded the princess to lie down, promising to call her if the king should stir.

21. THE LOAF

His Majesty slept very quietly. The dawn had grown almost day, and still Curdie lingered, unwilling to disturb the princess.

At last, however, he called her, and she was in the room in a moment. She had slept, she said, and felt quite fresh. Delighted to find her father still asleep, and so peacefully, she pushed her chair close to the bed, and sat down with her hands in her lap.

Curdie got his mattock from where he had hidden it behind a great mirror, and went to the cellar, followed by Lina. They took some breakfast with them as they passed through the hall, and as soon as they had eaten it went out the back way.

At the mouth of the passage Curdie seized the rope, drew himself up, pushed away the shutter, and entered the dungeon. Then he swung the end of the rope to Lina, and she caught it in her teeth. When her master said, 'Now, Lina!' she gave a great spring, and he ran away with the end of the rope as fast as ever he could. And such a spring had she made, that by the time he had to bear her weight she was within a few feet of the hole. The instant she got a paw through, she was all through.

Apparently their enemies were waiting till hunger should have cowed them, for there was no sign of any attempt having been made to open the door. A blow or two of Curdie's mattock drove the shattered lock clean from it, and telling Lina to wait there till he came back, and let no one in, he walked out into the silent street, and drew the door to behind them. He could hardly believe it was not yet a whole day since he had been thrown in there with his hands tied at his back.

Down the town he went, walking in the middle of the street, that, if any one saw him, he might see he was not afraid, and hesitate to rouse an attack on him. As to the dogs, ever since the death of their two companions, a shadow that looked like a mattock was enough to make them scamper. As soon as he reached the archway of the city gate he turned to reconnoitre the baker's shop, and perceiving no sign of movement, waited there watching for the first.

After about an hour, the door opened, and the baker's man appeared with a pail in his hand. He went to a pump that stood in the street, and having filled his pail returned with it into the shop. Curdie stole after him, found the door on the latch, opened it very gently, peeped in, saw nobody, and entered. Remembering perfectly from what shelf the baker's wife had taken the loaf she said was the best, and seeing just one upon it, he seized it, laid the price of it on the counter, and sped softly out, and up the street. Once more in the dungeon beside Lina, his first thought was to fasten up the door again, which would have been easy, so many iron fragments of all sorts and sizes lay about; but he bethought himself that if he left it as it was, and they came to find him, they would conclude at once that they had made their escape by it, and would look no farther so as to discover the hole. He therefore merely pushed the door close and left it. Then once more carefully arranging the earth behind the shutter, so that it should again fall with it, he returned to the cellar.

And now he had to convey the loaf to the princess. If he could venture to take it himself, well; if not, he would send Lina. He crept to the door of the servants' hall, and found the sleepers beginning to stir. One said it was time to go to bed; another, that he would go to the cellar instead, and have a mug of wine to waken him up; while a third challenged a fourth to give him his revenge at some game or other.

'Oh, hang your losses!' answered his companion; 'you'll soon pick up twice as much about the house, if you but keep your eyes open.'

Perceiving there would be risk in attempting to pass through, and reflecting that the porters in the great hall would probably be awake also, Curdie went back to the cellar, took Irene's handkerchief with the loaf in it, tied it round Lina's neck, and told her to take it to the princess.

Using every shadow and every shelter, Lina slid through the servants like a shapeless terror through a guilty mind, and so, by corridor and great hall, up the stair to the king's chamber.

Irene trembled a little when she saw her glide soundless in across the silent dusk of the morning, that filtered through the heavy drapery of the windows, but she recovered herself at once when she saw the bundle about her neck, for it both assured her of Curdie's safety, and gave her hope of her father's. She untied it with joy, and Lina stole away, silent as she had come. Her joy was the greater that the king had waked up a little before, and expressed a desire for food - not that he felt exactly hungry, he said, and yet he wanted something. If only he might have a piece of nice fresh bread! Irene had no knife, but with eager hands she broke a great piece from the loaf, and poured out a full glass of wine. The king ate and drank, enjoyed the bread and the wine much, and instantly fell asleep again.

It was hours before the lazy people brought their breakfast. When it came, Irene crumbled a little about, threw some into the fireplace, and managed to make the tray look just as usual.

In the meantime, down below in the cellar, Curdie was lying in the hollow between the upper sides of two of the great casks, the warmest place he could find. Lina was watching. She lay at his feet, across the two casks, and did her best so to arrange her huge tail that it should be a warm coverlid for her master.

By and by Dr Kelman called to see his patient; and now that Irene's eyes were opened, she saw clearly enough that he was both annoyed and puzzled at finding His Majesty rather better. He pretended however to congratulate him, saying he believed he was quite fit to see the lord Chamberlain: he wanted his signature to something important; only he must not strain his mind to understand it, whatever it might be: if His Majesty did, he would not be answerable for the consequences. The king said he would see the lord Chamberlain, and the doctor went.

Then Irene gave him more bread and wine, and the king ate and drank, and smiled a feeble smile, the first real one she had seen for many a day. He said he felt much better, and would soon be able to take matters into his own hands again. He had a strange miserable feeling, he said, that things were going terribly wrong, although he could not tell how. Then the princess told him that Curdie had come, and that at night, when all was quiet for nobody in the palace must know, he would pay His Majesty a visit. Her great-great-grandmother had sent him, she said. The king looked strangely upon her, but the strange look passed into a smile clearer than the first, and Irene's heart throbbed with delight.

22. THE LORD CHAMBERLAIN

At noon the lord Chamberlain appeared. With a long, low bow, and paper in hand, he stepped softly into the room. Greeting His Majesty with every appearance of the profoundest respect, and congratulating him on the evident progress he had made, he declared himself sorry to trouble him, but there were certain papers, he said, which required his signature - and therewith drew nearer to the king, who lay looking at him doubtfully. He was a lean, long, yellow man, with a small head, bald over the top, and tufted at the back and about the ears. He had a very thin, prominent, hooked nose, and a quantity of loose skin under his chin and about the throat, which came craning up out of his neck cloth. His eyes were very small, sharp, and glittering, and looked black as jet. He had hardly enough of a mouth to make a smile with. His left hand held the paper, and the long, skinny fingers of his right a pen just dipped in ink.

But the king, who for weeks had scarcely known what he did, was today so much himself as to be aware that he was not quite himself; and the moment he saw the paper, he resolved that he would not sign without understanding and approving of it. He requested the lord Chamberlain therefore to read it. His Lordship commenced at once but the difficulties he seemed to encounter, and the fits of stammering that seized him, roused the king's suspicion tenfold. He called the princess.

'I trouble His Lordship too much,' he said to her: 'you can read print well, my child - let me hear how you can read writing. Take that paper from His Lordship's hand, and read it to me from beginning to end, while my lord drinks a glass of my favorite wine, and watches for your blunders.'

'Pardon me, Your Majesty,' said the lord Chamberlain, with as much of a smile as he was able to extemporize, 'but it were a thousand pities to put the attainments of Her Royal Highness to a test altogether too severe. Your Majesty can scarcely with justice expect the very organs of her speech to prove capable of compassing words so long, and to her so unintelligible.'

'I think much of my little princess and her capabilities,' returned the king, more and more aroused. 'Pray, my lord, permit her to try.'

'Consider, Your Majesty: the thing would be altogether without precedent. It would be to make sport of statecraft,' said the lord Chamberlain.

'Perhaps you are right, my lord,' answered the king, with more meaning than he intended should be manifest, while to his growing joy he felt new life and power throbbing in heart and brain. 'So this morning we shall read no further. I am indeed ill able for business of such weight.'

'Will Your Majesty please sign your royal name here?' said the lord Chamberlain, preferring the request as a matter of course, and approaching with the feather end of the pen pointed to a spot where there was a great red seal.

'Not today, my lord,' replied the king.

'It is of the greatest importance, Your Majesty,' softly insisted the other.

'I descried no such importance in it,' said the king.

'Your Majesty heard but a part.'

'And I can hear no more today.'

'I trust Your Majesty has ground enough, in a case of necessity like the present, to sign upon the representation of his loyal subject and Chamberlain? Or shall I call the lord chancellor?' he added, rising.

'There is no need. I have the very highest opinion of your judgment, my lord,' answered the king; 'that is, with respect to means: we might differ as to ends.'

The lord Chamberlain made yet further attempts at persuasion; but they grew feebler and feebler, and he was at last compelled to retire without having gained his object. And well might his annoyance be keen! For that paper was the king's will, drawn up by the attorney-general; nor until they had the king's signature to it was there much use in venturing farther. But his worst sense of discomfiture arose from finding the king with so much capacity left, for the doctor had pledged himself so to weaken his brain that he should be as a child in their hands, incapable of refusing anything requested of him: His Lordship began to doubt the doctor's fidelity to the conspiracy.

The princess was in high delight. She had not for weeks heard so many words, not to say words of such strength and reason, from her father's lips: day by day he had been growing weaker and more lethargic. He was so much exhausted, however, after this effort, that he asked for another piece of bread and more wine, and fell fast asleep the moment he had taken them.

The lord Chamberlain sent in a rage for Dr Kelman. He came, and while professing himself unable to understand the symptoms described by His Lordship, yet pledged himself again that on the morrow the king should do whatever was required of him.

The day went on. When His Majesty was awake, the princess read to him - one storybook after another; and whatever she read, the king listened as if he had never heard anything so good before, making out in it the wisest meanings. Every now and then he asked for a piece of bread and a little wine, and every time he ate and drank he slept, and every time he woke he seemed better than the last time. The princess bearing her part, the loaf was eaten up and the flagon emptied before night. The butler took the flagon away, and brought it back filled to the brim, but both were thirsty and hungry when Curdie came again. Meantime he and Lina, watching and waking alternately, had plenty of sleep. In the afternoon, peeping from the recess, they saw several of the servants enter hurriedly, one after the other, draw wine, drink it, and steal out; but their business was to take care of the king, not of his cellar, and they let them drink. Also, when the butler came to fill the flagon, they restrained themselves, for the villain's fate was not yet ready for him. He looked terribly frightened, and had brought with him a large candle and a small terrier - which latter indeed threatened to be troublesome, for he went roving and sniffing about until he came to the recess where they were. But as soon as he showed himself, Lina opened her jaws so wide, and glared at him so horribly, that, without even uttering a whimper, he tucked his tail between his legs and ran to his master. He was drawing the wicked wine at the moment, and did not see him, else he would doubtless have run too.

When suppertime approached, Curdie took his place at the door into the servants' hall; but after a long hour's vain watch, he began to fear he should get nothing: there was so much idling about, as well as coming and going. It was hard to bear - chiefly from the attractions of a splendid loaf, just fresh out of the oven, which he longed to secure for the king and princess. At length his chance did arrive: he pounced upon the loaf and carried it away, and soon after got hold of a pie.

This time, however, both loaf and pie were missed. The cook was called. He declared he had provided both. One of themselves, he said, must have carried them away for some friend outside the palace. Then a housemaid, who had not long been one of them, said she had seen someone like a page running in the direction of the cellar with something in his hands. Instantly all turned upon the pages, accusing them, one after another. All denied, but nobody believed one of them: Where there is no truth there can be no faith.

To the cellar they all set out to look for the missing pie and loaf. Lina heard them coming, as well she might, for they were talking and quarrelling loud, and gave her master warning. They snatched up everything, and got all signs of their presence out at the back door before the servants entered. When they found nothing, they all turned on the chambermaid, and accused her, not only of lying against the pages, but of having taken the things herself. Their language and behavior so disgusted Curdie, who could hear a great part of what passed, and he saw the danger of discovery now so much increased, that he began to devise how best at once to rid the palace of the whole pack of them. That, however, would be small gain so long as the treacherous officers of state continued in it. They must be first dealt with. A thought came to him, and the longer he looked at it the better he liked it.

As soon as the servants were gone, quarrelling and accusing all the way, they returned and finished their supper. Then Curdie, who had long been satisfied that Lina understood almost every word he said, communicated his plan to her, and knew by the wagging of her tail and the flashing of her eyes that she comprehended it. Until they had the king safe through the worst part of the night, however, nothing could be done.

They had now merely to go on waiting where they were till the household should be asleep. This waiting and waiting was much the hardest thing Curdie had to do in the whole affair. He took his mattock and, going again into the long passage, lighted a candle end and proceeded to examine the rock on all sides. But this was not merely to pass the time: he had a reason for it. When he broke the stone in the street, over which the baker fell, its appearance led him to pocket a fragment for further examination; and since then he had satisfied himself that it was the kind of stone in which gold is found, and that the yellow particles in it were pure metal. If such stone existed here in any plenty, he could soon make the king rich and independent of his ill-conditioned subjects. He was therefore now bent on an examination of the rock; nor had he been at it long before he was persuaded that there were large quantities of gold in the half-crystalline white stone, with its veins of opaque white and of green, of which the rock, so far as he had been able to inspect it, seemed almost entirely to consist. Every piece he broke was spotted with particles and little lumps of a lovely greenish yellow - and that was gold. Hitherto he had worked only in silver, but he had read, and heard talk, and knew, therefore, about gold. As soon as he had got the king free of rogues and villains, he would have all the best and most honest miners, with his father at the head of them, to work this rock for the king. It was a great delight to him to use his mattock once more. The time went quickly, and when he left the passage to go to the king's chamber, he had already a good heap of fragments behind the broken door.

23. DR KELMAN

As soon as he had reason to hope the way was clear, Curdie ventured softly into the hall, with Lina behind him. There was no one asleep on the bench or floor, but by the fading fire sat a girl weeping. It was the same who had seen him carrying off the food, and had been so hardly used for saying so. She opened her eyes when he appeared, but did not seem frightened at him.

'I know why you weep,' said Curdie, 'and I am sorry for you.'

'It is hard not to be believed just because one speaks the truth,' said the girl, 'but that seems reason enough with some people. My mother taught me to speak the truth, and took such pains with me that I should find it hard to tell a lie, though I could invent many a story these servants would believe at once; for the truth is a strange thing here, and they don't know it when they see it. Show it them, and they all stare as if it were a wicked lie, and that with the lie yet warm that has just left their own mouths! You are a stranger,' she said, and burst out weeping afresh, 'but the stranger you are to such a place and such people the better!'

'I am the person,' said Curdie, whom you saw carrying the things from the supper table.' He showed her the loaf. 'If you can trust, as well as speak the truth, I will trust you. Can you trust me?'

She looked at him steadily for a moment.

'I can,' she answered.

'One thing more,' said Curdie: 'have you courage as well as truth?'

'I think so.'

'Look my dog in the face and don't cry out. Come here, Lina.'

Lina obeyed. The girl looked at her, and laid her hand on Lina's head.

'Now I know you are a true woman,' said Curdie. 'I am come to set things right in this house. Not one of the servants knows I am here. Will you tell them tomorrow morning that, if they do not alter their ways, and give over drinking, and lying, and stealing, and unkindness, they shall every one of them be driven from the palace?'

'They will not believe me.'

'Most likely; but will you give them the chance?'

'I will.'

'Then I will be your friend. Wait here till I come again.'

She looked him once more in the face, and sat down.

When he reached the royal chamber, he found His Majesty awake, and very anxiously expecting him. He received him with the utmost kindness, and at once, as it were, put himself in his hands by telling him all he knew concerning the state he was in. His voice was feeble, but his eye was clear, although now and then his words and thoughts seemed to wander. Curdie could not be certain that the cause of their not being intelligible to him did not lie in himself. The king told him that for some years, ever since his queen's death, he had been losing heart over the wickedness of his people. He had tried hard to make them good, but they got worse and worse. Evil teachers, unknown to him, had crept into the schools; there was a general decay of truth and right principle at least in the city; and as that set the example to the nation, it must spread.

The main cause of his illness was the despondency with which the degeneration of his people affected him. He could not sleep, and had terrible dreams; while, to his unspeakable shame and distress, he doubted almost everybody. He had striven against his suspicion, but in vain, and his heart was sore, for his courtiers and councilors were really kind; only he could not think why none of their ladies came near his princess. The whole country was discontented, he heard, and there were signs of gathering storm outside as well as inside his borders. The master of the horse gave him sad news of the insubordination of the army; and his great white horse was dead, they told him; and his sword had lost its temper: it bent double the last time he tried it! - only perhaps that was in a dream; and they could not find his shield; and one of his spurs had lost the rowel.

Thus the poor king went wandering in a maze of sorrows, some of which were purely imaginary, while others were truer than he understood. He told how thieves came at night and tried to take his crown, so that he never dared let it out of his hands even when he slept; and how, every night, an evil demon in the shape of his physician came and poured poison down his throat. He knew it to be poison, he said, somehow, although it tasted like wine.

Here he stopped, faint with the unusual exertion of talking.

Curdie seized the flagon, and ran to the wine cellar.

In the servants' hall the girl still sat by the fire, waiting for him. As he returned he told her to follow him, and left her at the chamber door until he should rejoin her. When the king had had a little wine, he informed him that he had already discovered certain of His Majesty's enemies, and one of the worst of them was the doctor, for it was no other demon than the doctor himself who had been coming every night, and giving him a slow poison.

'So!' said the king. 'Then I have not been suspicious enough, for I thought it was but a dream! Is it possible Kelman can be such a wretch? Who then am I to trust?'

'Not one in the house, except the princess and myself,' said Curdie.

'I will not go to sleep,' said the king.

'That would be as bad as taking the poison,' said Curdie. 'No, no, sire; you must show your confidence by leaving all the watching to me, and doing all the sleeping Your Majesty can.'

The king smiled a contented smile, turned on his side, and was presently fast asleep. Then Curdie persuaded the princess also to go to sleep, and telling Lina to watch, went to the housemaid. He asked her if she could inform him which of the council slept in the palace, and show him their rooms. She knew every one of them, she said, and took him the round of all their doors, telling him which slept in each room. He then dismissed her, and returning to the king's chamber, seated himself behind a curtain at the head of the bed, on the side farthest from the king. He told Lina to get under the bed, and make no noise.

About one o'clock the doctor came stealing in. He looked round for the princess, and seeing no one, smiled with satisfaction as he approached the wine where it stood under the lamp. Having partly filled a glass, he took from his pocket a small phial, and filled up the glass from it. The light fell upon his face from above, and Curdie saw the snake in it plainly visible. He had never beheld such an evil countenance: the man hated the king, and delighted in doing him wrong.

With the glass in his hand, he drew near the bed, set it down, and began his usual rude rousing of His Majesty. Not at once succeeding, he took a lancet from his pocket, and was parting its cover with an involuntary hiss of hate between his closed teeth, when Curdie stooped and whispered to Lina.

'Take him by the leg, Lina.' She darted noiselessly upon him. With a face of horrible consternation, he gave his leg one tug to free it; the next instant Curdie heard the one scrunch with which she crushed the bone like a stick of celery. He tumbled on the floor with a yell.

'Drag him out, Lina,' said Curdie. Lina took him by the collar, and dragged him out. Her master followed her to direct her, and they left the doctor lying across the lord Chamberlain's door, where he gave another horrible yell, and fainted.

The king had waked at his first cry, and by the time Curdie re-entered he had got at his sword where it hung from the centre of the tester, had drawn it, and was trying to get out of bed. But when Curdie told him all was well, he lay down again as quietly as a child comforted by his mother from a troubled dream. Curdie went to the door to watch.

The doctor's yells had aroused many, but not one had yet ventured to appear. Bells were rung violently, but none were answered; and in a minute or two Curdie had what he was watching for. The door of the lord Chamberlain's room opened, and, pale with hideous terror, His Lordship peeped out. Seeing no one, he advanced to step into the corridor, and tumbled over the doctor. Curdie ran up, and held out his hand. He received in it the claw of a bird of prey - vulture or eagle, he could not tell which.

His Lordship, as soon as he was on his legs, taking him for one of the pages abused him heartily for not coming sooner, and threatened him with dismissal from the king's service for cowardice and neglect. He began indeed what bade fair to be a sermon on the duties of a page, but catching sight of the man who lay at his door, and seeing it was the doctor, he fell upon Curdie afresh for standing there doing nothing, and ordered him to fetch immediate assistance. Curdie left him, but slipped into the King's chamber, closed and locked the door, and left the rascals to look after each other. Ere long he heard hurrying footsteps, and for a few minutes there was a great muffled tumult of scuffling feet, low voices and deep groanings; then all was still again.

Irene slept through the whole - so confidently did she rest, knowing Curdie was in her father's room watching over him.

24. THE PROPHECY

Curdie sat and watched every motion of the sleeping king. All the night, to his ear, the palace lay as quiet as a nursery of healthful children. At sunrise he called the princess.

'How has His Majesty slept?' were her first words as she entered the room.

'Quite quietly,' answered Curdie; 'that is, since the doctor was got rid of.' 'How did you manage that?' inquired Irene; and Curdie had to tell all about it.

'How terrible!' she said. 'Did it not startle the king dreadfully?'

'It did rather. I found him getting out of bed, sword in hand.'

'The brave old man!' cried the princess.

'Not so old!' said Curdie, 'as you will soon see. He went off again in a minute or so; but for a little while he was restless, and once when he lifted his hand it came down on the spikes of his crown, and he half waked.'

'But where is the crown?' cried Irene, in sudden terror.

'I stroked his hands,' answered Curdie, 'and took the crown from them; and ever since he has slept quietly, and again and again smiled in his sleep.'

'I have never seen him do that,' said the princess. 'But what have you done with the crown, Curdie?' 'Look,' said Curdie, moving away from the bedside.

Irene followed him - and there, in the middle of the floor, she saw a strange sight. Lina lay at full length, fast asleep, her tail stretched out straight behind her and her forelegs before her: between the two paws meeting in front of it, her nose just touching it behind, glowed and flashed the crown, like a nest of the humming birds of heaven.

Irene gazed, and looked up with a smile.

'But what if the thief were to come, and she not to wake?' she said. 'Shall I try her?' And as she spoke she stooped toward the crown.

'No, no, no!' cried Curdie, terrified. 'She would frighten you out of your wits. I would do it to show you, but she would wake your father. You have no conception with what a roar she would spring at my throat. But you shall see how lightly she wakes the moment I speak to her. Lina!'

She was on her feet the same instant, with her great tail sticking out straight behind her, just as it had been lying.

'Good dog!' said the princess, and patted her head. Lina wagged her tail solemnly, like the boom of an anchored sloop. Irene took the crown, and laid it where the king would see it when he woke.

'Now, Princess,' said Curdie, 'I must leave you for a few minutes. You must bolt the door, please, and not open it to any one.'

Away to the cellar he went with Lina, taking care, as they passed through the servants' hall, to get her a good breakfast. In about one minute she had eaten what he gave her, and looked up in his face: it was not more she wanted, but work. So out of the cellar they went through the passage, and Curdie into the dungeon, where he pulled up Lina, opened the door, let her out, and shut it again behind her. As he reached the door of the king's chamber, Lina was flying out of the gate of Gwyntystorm as fast as her mighty legs could carry her.

'What's come to the wench?' growled the menservants one to another, when the chambermaid appeared among them the next morning. There was something in her face which they could not understand, and did not like.

'Are we all dirt?' they said. 'What are you thinking about? Have you seen yourself in the glass this morning, miss?'

She made no answer.

'Do you want to be treated as you deserve, or will you speak, you hussy?' said the first woman-cook. 'I would fain know what right you have to put on a face like that!' 'You won't believe me,' said the girl.

'Of course not. What is it?'

'I must tell you, whether you believe me or not,' she said.

'Of course you must.'

'It is this, then: if you do not repent of your bad ways, you are all going to be punished - all turned out of the palace together.'

'A mighty punishment!' said the butler. 'A good riddance, say I, of the trouble of keeping minxes like you in order! And why, pray, should we be turned out? What have I to repent of now, your holiness?'

'That you know best yourself,' said the girl.

'A pretty piece of insolence! How should I know, forsooth, what a menial like you has got against me! There are people in this house - oh! I'm not blind to their ways! - but every one for himself, say I! Pray, Miss judgment, who gave you such an impertinent message to His Majesty's household?'

'One who is come to set things right in the king's house.'

'Right, indeed!' cried the butler; but that moment the thought came back to him of the roar he had heard in the cellar, and he turned pale and was silent.

The steward took it up next. 'And pray, pretty prophetess,' he said, attempting to chuck her under the chin, 'what have I got to repent of?'

'That you know best yourself,' said the girl. 'You have but to look into your books or your heart.'

'Can you tell me, then, what I have to repent of?' said the groom of the chambers. 'That you know best yourself,' said the girl once more. 'The person who told me to tell you said the servants of this house had to repent of thieving, and lying, and unkindness, and drinking; and they will be made to repent of them one way, if they don't do it of themselves another.'

Then arose a great hubbub; for by this time all the servants in the house were gathered about her, and all talked together, in towering indignation.

'Thieving, indeed!' cried one. 'A pretty word in a house where everything is left lying about in a shameless way, tempting poor innocent girls! A house where nobody cares for anything, or has the least respect to the value of property!'

'I suppose you envy me this brooch of mine,' said another. 'There was just a half sheet of note paper about it, not a scrap more, in a drawer that's always open in the writing table in the study! What sort of a place is that for a jewel? Can you call it stealing to take a thing from such a place as that? Nobody cared a straw about it. It might as well have been in the dust hole! If it had been locked up - then, to be sure!'

'Drinking!' said the chief porter, with a husky laugh. 'And who wouldn't drink when he had a chance? Or who would repent it, except that the drink was gone? Tell me that, Miss Innocence.'

'Lying!' said a great, coarse footman. 'I suppose you mean when I told you yesterday you were a pretty girl when you didn't pout? Lying, indeed! Tell us something worth repenting of! Lying is the way of Gwyntystorm. You should have heard Jabez lying to the cook last night! He wanted a sweetbread for his pup, and pretended it was for the princess! Ha! ha! ha!'

'Unkindness! I wonder who's unkind! Going and listening to any stranger against her fellow servants, and then bringing back his wicked words to trouble them!' said the oldest and worst of the housemaids. 'One of ourselves, too! Come, you hypocrite! This is all an invention of yours and your young man's, to take your revenge of us because we found you out in a lie last night. Tell true now: wasn't it the same that stole the loaf and the pie that sent you with the impudent message?'

As she said this, she stepped up to the housemaid and gave her, instead of time to answer, a box on the ear that almost threw her down; and whoever could get at her began to push and bustle and pinch and punch her. 'You invite your fate,' she said quietly.

They fell furiously upon her, drove her from the hall with kicks and blows, hustled her along the passage, and threw her down the stair to the wine cellar, then locked the door at the top of it, and went back to their breakfast.

In the meantime the king and the princess had had their bread and wine, and the princess, with Curdie's help, had made the room as tidy as she could - they were terribly neglected by the servants. And now Curdie set himself to interest and amuse the king, and prevent him from thinking too much, in order that he might the sooner think the better. Presently, at His Majesty's request, he began from the beginning, and told everything he could recall of his life, about his father and mother and their cottage on the mountain, of the inside of the mountain and the work there, about the goblins and his adventures with them.

When he came to finding the princess and her nurse overtaken by the twilight on the mountain, Irene took up her share of the tale, and told all about herself to that point, and then Curdie took it up again; and so they went on, each fitting in the part that the other did not know, thus keeping the hoop of the story running straight; and the king listened with wondering and delighted ears, astonished to find what he could so ill comprehend, yet fitting so well together from the lips of two narrators.

At last, with the mission given him by the wonderful princess and his consequent adventures, Curdie brought up the whole tale to the present moment. Then a silence fell, and Irene and Curdie thought the king was asleep. But he was far from it; he was thinking about many things. After a long pause he said:

'Now at last, my children, I am compelled to believe many things I could not and do not yet understand - things I used to hear, and sometimes see, as often as I visited my mother's home. Once, for instance, I heard my mother say to her father - speaking of me - "He is a good, honest boy, but he will be an old man before he understands"; and my grandfather answered, "Keep up your heart, child: my mother will look after him." I thought often of their words, and the many strange things besides I both heard and saw in that house; but by degrees, because I could not understand them, I gave up thinking of them. And indeed I had almost forgotten them, when you, my child, talking that day about the Queen Irene and her pigeons, and what you had seen in her garret, brought them all back to my mind in a vague mass. But now they keep coming back to me, one by one, every one for itself; and I shall just hold my peace, and lie here quite still, and think about them all till I get well again.'

What he meant they could not quite understand, but they saw plainly that already he was better.

'Put away my crown,' he said. 'I am tired of seeing it, and have no more any fear of its safety.' They put it away together, withdrew from the bedside, and left him in peace.

25. The Avengers

There was nothing now to be dreaded from Dr Kelman, but it made Curdie anxious, as the evening drew near, to think that not a soul belonging to the court had been to visit the king, or ask how he did, that day. He feared, in some shape or other, a more determined assault. He had provided himself a place in the room, to which he might retreat upon approach, and whence he could watch; but not once had he had to betake himself to it.

Towards night the king fell asleep. Curdie thought more and more uneasily of the moment when he must again leave them for a little while. Deeper and deeper fell the shadows. No one came to light the lamp. The princess drew her chair close to Curdie: she would rather it were not so dark, she said. She was afraid of something - she could not tell what; nor could she give any reason for her fear but that all was so dreadfully still.

When it had been dark about an hour, Curdie thought Lina might have returned; and reflected that the sooner he went the less danger was there of any assault while he was away. There was more risk of his own presence being discovered, no doubt, but things were now drawing to a crisis, and it must be run. So, telling the princess to lock all the doors of the bedchamber, and let no one in, he took his mattock, and with here a run, and there a halt under cover, gained the door at the head of the cellar stair in safety. To his surprise he found it locked, and the key was gone. There was no time for deliberation. He felt where the lock was, and dealt it a tremendous blow with his mattock. It needed but a second to dash the door open. Someone laid a hand on his arm.

'Who is it?' said Curdie.

'I told you they wouldn't believe me, sir,' said the housemaid. 'I have been here all day.'

He took her hand, and said, 'You are a good, brave girl. Now come with me, lest your enemies imprison you again.'

He took her to the cellar, locked the door, lighted a bit of candle, gave her a little wine, told her to wait there till he came, and went out the back way.

Swiftly he swung himself up into the dungeon. Lina had done her part. The place was swarming with creatures - animal forms wilder and more grotesque than ever ramped in nightmare dream. Close by the hole, waiting his coming, her green eyes piercing the gulf below, Lina had but just laid herself down when he appeared. All about the vault and up the slope of the rubbish heap lay and stood and squatted the forty-nine whose friendship Lina had conquered in the wood. They all came crowding about Curdie.

He must get them into the cellar as quickly as ever he could. But when he looked at the size of some of them, he feared it would be a long business to enlarge the hole sufficiently to let them through. At it he rushed, hitting vigorously at the edge with his mattock. At the very first blow came a splash from the water beneath, but ere he could heave a third, a creature like a tapir, only that the grasping point of its proboscis was hard as the steel of Curdie's hammer, pushed him gently aside, making room for another creature, with a head like a great club, which it began banging upon the floor with terrible force and noise. After about a minute of this battery, the tapir came up again, shoved Clubhead aside, and putting its own head into the hole began gnawing at the sides of it with the finger of its nose, in such a fashion that the fragments fell in a continuous gravelly shower into the water. In a few minutes the opening was large enough for the biggest creature among them to get through it. Next came the difficulty of letting them down: some were quite light, but the half of them were too heavy for the rope, not to say for his arms. The creatures themselves seemed to be puzzling where or how they were to go. One after another of them came up, looked down through the hole, and drew back. Curdie thought if he let Lina down, perhaps that would suggest something; possibly they did not see the opening on the other side. He did so, and Lina stood lighting up the entrance of the passage with her gleaming eyes.

One by one the creatures looked down again, and one by one they drew back, each standing aside to glance at the next, as if to say, Now you have a look. At last it came to the turn of the serpent with the long body, the four short legs behind, and the little wings before. No sooner had he poked his head through than he poked it farther through - and farther, and farther yet, until there was little more than his legs left in the dungeon. By that time he had got his head and neck well into the passage beside Lina. Then his legs gave a great waddle and spring, and he tumbled himself, far as there was betwixt them, heels over head into the passage.

'That is all very well for you, Mr. Legserpent!' thought Curdie to himself; 'but what is to be done with the rest?' He had hardly time to think it, however, before the creature's head appeared again through the floor. He caught hold of the bar of iron to which Curdie's rope was tied, and settling it securely across the narrowest part of the irregular opening, held fast to it with his teeth. It was plain to Curdie, from the universal hardness among them, that they must all, at one time or another, have been creatures of the mines.

He saw at once what this one was after. The beast had planted his feet firmly upon the floor of the passage, and stretched his long body up and across the chasm to serve as a bridge for the rest. Curdie mounted instantly upon his neck, threw his arms round him as far as they would go, and slid down in ease and safety, the bridge just bending a little as his weight glided over it. But he thought some of the creatures would try the legserpent's teeth.

One by one the oddities followed, and slid down in safety. When they seemed to be all landed, he counted them: there were but forty-eight. Up the rope again he went, and found one which had been afraid to trust himself to the bridge, and no wonder! for he had neither legs nor head nor arms nor tail: he was just a round thing, about a foot in diameter, with a nose and mouth and eyes on one side of the ball. He had made his journey by rolling as swiftly as the fleetest of them could run. The back of the legserpent not being flat, he could not quite trust himself to roll straight and not drop into the gulf. Curdie took him in his arms, and the moment he looked down through the hole, the bridge made itself again, and he slid into the passage in safety, with Ballbody in his bosom.

He ran first to the cellar to warn the girl not to be frightened at the avengers of wickedness. Then he called to Lina to bring in her friends.

One after another they came trooping in, till the cellar seemed full of them. The housemaid regarded them without fear.

'Sir,' she said, 'there is one of the pages I don't take to be a bad fellow.'

'Then keep him near you,' said Curdie. 'And now can you show me a way to the king's chamber not through the servants' hall?'

'There is a way through the chamber of the colonel of the guard,' she answered, 'but he is ill, and in bed.'

'Take me that way,' said Curdie.

By many ups and downs and windings and turnings she brought him to a dimly lighted room, where lay an elderly man asleep. His arm was outside the coverlid, and Curdie gave his hand a hurried grasp as he went by. His heart beat for joy, for he had found a good, honest, human hand.

'I suppose that is why he is ill,' he said to himself.

It was now close upon suppertime, and when the girl stopped at the door of the king's chamber, he told her to go and give the servants one warning more.

'Say the messenger sent you,' he said. 'I will be with you very soon.'

The king was still asleep. Curdie talked to the princess for a few minutes, told her not to be frightened whatever noises she heard, only to keep her door locked till he came, and left her.

26. THE VENGEANCE

By the time the girl reached the servants' hall they were seated at supper. A loud, confused exclamation arose when she entered. No one made room for her; all stared with unfriendly eyes. A page, who entered the next minute by another door, came to her side.

'Where do you come from, hussy?' shouted the butler, and knocked his fist on the table with a loud clang.

He had gone to fetch wine, had found the stair door broken open and the cellar door locked, and had turned and fled. Among his fellows, however, he had now regained what courage could be called his. 'From the cellar,' she replied. 'The messenger broke open the door, and sent me to you again.'

'The messenger! Pooh! What messenger?'

'The same who sent me before to tell you to repent.'

'What! Will you go fooling it still? Haven't you had enough of it?' cried the butler in a rage, and starting to his feet, drew near threateningly.

'I must do as I am told,' said the girl.

'Then why don't you do as I tell you, and hold your tongue?' said the butler. 'Who wants your preachments? If anybody here has anything to repent Of, isn't that enough - and more than enough for him - but you must come bothering about, and stirring up, till not a drop of quiet will settle inside him? You come along with me, young woman; we'll see if we can't find a lock somewhere in the house that'll hold you in!'

'Hands off, Mr. Butler!' said the page, and stepped between.

'Oh, ho!' cried the butler, and pointed his fat finger at him. 'That's you, is it, my fine fellow? So it's you that's up to her tricks, is it?'

The youth did not answer, only stood with flashing eyes fixed on him, until, growing angrier and angrier, but not daring a step nearer, he burst out with a rude but quavering authority:

'Leave the house, both of you! Be off, or I'll have Mr. Steward to talk to you. Threaten your masters, indeed! Out of the house with you, and show us the way you tell us of!'

Two or three of the footmen got up and ranged themselves behind the butler.

'Don't say I threaten you, Mr. Butler,' expostulated the girl from behind the page. 'The messenger said I was to tell you again, and give you one chance more.'

'Did the messenger mention me in particular?' asked the butler, looking the page unsteadily in the face.

'No, sir,' answered the girl.

'I thought not! I should like to hear him!'

'Then hear him now,' said Curdie, who that moment entered at the opposite corner of the hall. 'I speak of the butler in particular when I say that I know more evil of him than of any of the rest. He will not let either his own conscience or my messenger speak to him: I therefore now speak myself. I proclaim him a villain, and a traitor to His Majesty the king. But what better is any one of you who cares only for himself, eats, drinks, takes good money, and gives vile service in return, stealing and wasting the king's property, and making of the palace, which ought to be an example of order and sobriety, a disgrace to the country?'

For a moment all stood astonished into silence by this bold speech from a stranger. True, they saw by his mattock over his shoulder that he was nothing but a miner boy, yet for a moment the truth told notwithstanding. Then a great roaring laugh burst from the biggest of the footmen as he came shouldering his way through the crowd toward Curdie.

'Yes, I'm right,' he cried; 'I thought as much! This messenger, forsooth, is nothing but a gallows bird - a fellow the city marshal was going to hang, but unfortunately put it off till he should be starved enough to save rope and be throttled with a pack thread. He broke prison, and here he is preaching!' As he spoke, he stretched out his great hand to lay hold of him. Curdie caught it in his left hand, and heaved his mattock with the other. Finding, however, nothing worse than an ox hoof, he restrained himself, stepped back a pace or two, shifted his mattock to his left hand, and struck him a little smart blow on the shoulder. His arm dropped by his side, he gave a roar, and drew back.

His fellows came crowding upon Curdie. Some called to the dogs; others swore; the women screamed; the footmen and pages got round him in a half circle, which he kept from closing by swinging his mattock, and here and there threatening a blow.

'Whoever confesses to having done anything wrong in this house, however small, however great, and means to do better, let him come to this corner of the room,' he cried. None moved but the page, who went toward him skirting the wall. When they caught sight of him, the crowd broke into a hiss of derision.

'There! See! Look at the sinner! He confesses! Actually confesses! Come, what is it you stole? The barefaced hypocrite! There's your sort to set up for reproving other people! Where's the other now?'

But the maid had left the room, and they let the page pass, for he looked dangerous to stop. Curdie had just put him betwixt him and the wall, behind the door, when in rushed the butler with the huge kitchen poker, the point of which he had blown red-hot in the fire, followed by the cook with his longest spit. Through the crowd, which scattered right and left before them, they came down upon Curdie. Uttering a shrill whistle, he caught the poker a blow with his mattock, knocking the point to the ground, while the page behind him started forward, and seizing the point of the spit, held on to it with both hands, the cook kicking him furiously.

Ere the butler could raise the poker again, or the cook recover the spit, with a roar to terrify the dead, Lina dashed into the room, her eyes flaming like candles. She went straight at the butler. He was down in a moment, and she on the top of him, wagging her tail over him like a lioness.

'Don't kill him, Lina,' said Curdie.

'Oh, Mr. Miner!' cried the butler.

'Put your foot on his mouth, Lina,' said Curdie. 'The truth Fear tells is not much better than her lies.'

The rest of the creatures now came stalking, rolling, leaping, gliding, hobbling into the room, and each as he came took the next place along the wall, until, solemn and grotesque, all stood ranged, awaiting orders.

And now some of the culprits were stealing to the doors nearest them. Curdie whispered to the two creatures next him. Off went Ballbody, rolling and bounding through the crowd like a spent cannon shot, and when the foremost reached the door to the corridor, there he lay at the foot of it grinning; to the other door scuttled a scorpion, as big as a huge crab. The rest stood so still that some began to think they were only boys dressed up to look awful; they persuaded themselves they were only another part of the housemaid's and page's vengeful contrivance, and their evil spirits began to rise again. Meantime Curdie had, with a second sharp blow from the hammer of his mattock, disabled the cook, so that he yielded the spit with a groan. He now turned to the avengers.

'Go at them,' he said.

The whole nine-and-forty obeyed at once, each for himself, and after his own fashion. A scene of confusion and terror followed. The crowd scattered like a dance of flies. The creatures had been instructed not to hurt much, but to hunt incessantly, until everyone had rushed from the house. The women shrieked, and ran hither and thither through the hall, pursued each by her own horror, and snapped at by every other in passing. If one threw herself down in hysterical despair, she was instantly poked or clawed or nibbled up again.

Though they were quite as frightened at first, the men did not run so fast; and by and by some of them finding they were only glared at, and followed, and pushed, began to summon up courage once more, and with courage came impudence. The tapir had the big footman in charge: the fellow stood stock-still, and let the beast come up to him, then put out his finger and playfully patted his nose. The tapir gave the nose a little twist, and the finger lay on the floor.

Then indeed did the footman run. Gradually the avengers grew more severe, and the terrors of the imagination were fast yielding to those of sensuous experience, when a page, perceiving one of the doors no longer guarded, sprang at it, and ran out. Another and another followed. Not a beast went after, until, one by one, they were every one gone from the hall, and the whole crew in the kitchen.

There they were beginning to congratulate themselves that all was over, when in came the creatures trooping after them, and the second act of their terror and pain began. They were flung about in all directions; their clothes were torn from them; they were pinched and scratched any- and everywhere; Ballbody kept rolling up them and over them, confining his attentions to no one in particular; the scorpion kept grabbing at their legs with his huge pincers; a three-foot centipede kept screwing up their bodies, nipping as he went; varied as numerous were their woes. Nor was it long before the last of them had fled from the kitchen to the sculleries.

But thither also they were followed, and there again they were hunted about. They were bespattered with the dirt of their own neglect; they were soused in the stinking water that had boiled greens; they were smeared with rancid dripping; their faces were rubbed in maggots: I dare not tell all that was done to them. At last they got the door into a back yard open, and rushed out. Then first they knew that the wind was howling and the rain falling in sheets. But there was no rest for them even there. Thither also were they followed by the inexorable avengers, and the only door here was a door out of the palace: out every soul of them was driven, and left, some standing, some lying, some crawling, to the farther buffeting of the waterspouts and whirlwinds ranging every street of the city. The door was flung to behind them, and they heard it locked and bolted and barred against them.

27. More Vengeance

As soon as they were gone, Curdie brought the creatures back to the servants' hall, and told them to eat up everything on the table. It was a sight to see them all standing round it - except such as had to get upon it - eating and drinking, each after its fashion, without a smile, or a word, or a glance of fellowship in the act. A very few moments served to make everything eatable vanish, and then Curdie requested them to clean house, and the page who stood by to assist them.

Every one set about it except Ballbody: he could do nothing at cleaning, for the more he rolled, the more he spread the dirt. Curdie was curious to know what he had been, and how he had come to be such as he was: but he could only conjecture that he was a gluttonous alderman whom nature had treated homeopathically. And now there was such a cleaning and clearing out of neglected places, such a burying and burning of refuse, such a rinsing of jugs, such a swilling of sinks, and such a flushing of drains as would have delighted the eyes of all true housekeepers and lovers of cleanliness generally.

Curdie meantime was with the king, telling him all he had done. They had heard a little noise, but not much, for he had told the avengers to repress outcry as much as possible; and they had seen to it that the more anyone cried out the more he had to cry out upon, while the patient ones they scarcely hurt at all.

Having promised His Majesty and Her Royal Highness a good breakfast, Curdie now went to finish the business. The courtiers must be dealt with. A few who were the worst, and the leaders of the rest, must be made examples of; the others should be driven to the street.

He found the chiefs of the conspiracy holding a final consultation in the smaller room off the hall. These were the lord Chamberlain, the attorney-general, the master of the horse, and the king's private secretary: the lord chancellor and the rest, as foolish as faithless, were but the tools of these.

The housemaid had shown him a little closet, opening from a passage behind, where he could overhear all that passed in that room; and now Curdie heard enough to understand that they had determined, in the dead of that night, rather in the deepest dark before the morning, to bring a certain company of soldiers into the palace, make away with the king, secure the princess, announce the sudden death of His Majesty, read as his the will they had drawn up, and proceed to govern the country at their ease, and with results: they would at once levy severer taxes, and pick a quarrel with the most powerful of their neighbors. Everything settled, they agreed to retire, and have a few hours' quiet sleep first - all but the secretary, who was to sit up and call them at the proper moment. Curdie allowed them half an hour to get to bed, and then set about completing his purgation of the palace.

First he called Lina, and opened the door of the room where the secretary sat. She crept in, and laid herself down against it. When the secretary, rising to stretch his legs, caught sight of her eyes, he stood frozen with terror. She made neither motion nor sound. Gathering courage, and taking the thing for a spectral illusion, he made a step forward. She showed her other teeth, with a growl neither more than audible nor less than horrible. The secretary sank fainting into a chair. He was not a brave man, and besides, his conscience had gone over to the enemy, and was sitting against the door by Lina.

To the lord Chamberlain's door next, Curdie conducted the legserpent, and let him in.

Now His Lordship had had a bedstead made for himself, sweetly fashioned of rods of silver gilt: upon it the legserpent found him asleep, and under it he crept. But out he came on the other side, and crept over it next, and again under it, and so over it, under it, over it, five or six times, every time leaving a coil of himself behind him, until he had softly folded all his length about the lord Chamberlain and his bed. This done, he set up his head, looking down with curved neck right over His Lordship's, and began to hiss in his face.

He woke in terror unspeakable, and would have started up but the moment he moved, the legserpent drew his coils closer, and closer still, and drew and drew until the quaking traitor heard the joints of his bedstead grinding and gnarring. Presently he persuaded himself that it was only a horrid nightmare, and began to struggle with all his strength to throw it off. Thereupon the legserpent gave his hooked nose such a bite that his teeth met through it - but it was hardly thicker than the bowl of a spoon; and then the vulture knew that he was in the grasp of his enemy the snake, and yielded.

As soon as he was quiet the legserpent began to untwist and re-twist, to uncoil and recoil himself, swinging and swaying, knotting and relaxing himself with strangest curves and convolutions, always, however, leaving at least one coil around his victim. At last he undid himself entirely, and crept from the bed. Then first the lord Chamberlain discovered that his tormentor had bent and twisted the bedstead, legs and canopy and all, so about him that he was shut in a silver cage out of which it was impossible for him to find a way. Once more, thinking his enemy was gone, he began to shout for help. But the instant he opened his mouth his keeper darted at him and bit him, and after three or four such essays, he lay still.

The master of the horse Curdie gave in charge to the tapir. When the soldier saw him enter - for he was not yet asleep - he sprang from his bed, and flew at him with his sword. But the creature's hide was invulnerable to his blows, and he pecked at his legs with his proboscis until he jumped into bed again, groaning, and covered himself up; after which the tapir contented himself with now and then paying a visit to his toes.

As for the attorney-general, Curdie led to his door a huge spider, about two feet long in the body, which, having made an excellent supper, was full of webbing. The attorney-general had not gone to bed, but sat in a chair asleep before a great mirror. He had been trying the effect of a diamond star which he had that morning taken from the jewel room. When he woke he fancied himself paralyzed; every limb, every finger even, was motionless: coils and coils of broad spider ribbon bandaged his members to his body, and all to the chair. In the glass he saw himself wound about with slavery infinite. On a footstool a yard off sat the spider glaring at him.

Clubhead had mounted guard over the butler, where he lay tied hand and foot under the third cask. From that cask he had seen the wine run into a great bath, and therein he expected to be drowned. The doctor, with his crushed leg, needed no one to guard him.

And now Curdie proceeded to the expulsion of the rest. Great men or underlings, he treated them all alike. From room to room over the house he went, and sleeping or waking took the man by the hand. Such was the state to which a year of wicked rule had reduced the moral condition of the court, that in it all he found but three with human hands. The possessors of these he allowed to dress themselves and depart in peace. When they perceived his mission, and how he was backed, they yielded.

Then commenced a general hunt, to clear the house of the vermin. Out of their beds in their night clothing, out of their rooms, gorgeous chambers or garret nooks, the creatures hunted them. Not one was allowed to escape. Tumult and noise there was little, for fear was too deadly for outcry. Ferreting them out everywhere, following them upstairs and downstairs, yielding no instant of repose except upon the way out, the avengers persecuted the miscreants, until the last of them was shivering outside the palace gates, with hardly sense enough left to know where to turn.

When they set out to look for shelter, they found every inn full of the servants expelled before them, and not one would yield his place to a superior suddenly leveled with himself. Most houses refused to admit them on the ground of the wickedness that must have drawn on them such a punishment; and not a few would have been left in the streets all night, had not Derba, roused by the vain entreaties at the doors on each side of her cottage, opened hers, and given up everything to them. The lord Chancellor was only too glad to share a mattress with a stable boy, and steal his bare feet under his jacket.

In the morning Curdie appeared, and the outcasts were in terror, thinking he had come after them again. But he took no notice of them: his object was to request Derba to go to the palace: the king required her services. She need take no trouble about her cottage, he said; the palace was henceforward her home: she was the king's chatelaine over men and maidens of his household. And this very morning she must cook His Majesty a nice breakfast.

28. THE PREACHER

Various reports went undulating through the city as to the nature of what had taken place in the palace. The people gathered, and stared at the house, eyeing it as if it had sprung up in the night. But it looked sedate enough, remaining closed and silent, like a house that was dead. They saw no one come out or go in. Smoke arose from a chimney or two; there was hardly another sign of life. It was not for some little time generally understood that the highest officers of the crown as well as the lowest menials of the palace had been dismissed in disgrace: for who was to recognize a lord chancellor in his nightshirt? And what lord Chancellor would, so attired in the street, proclaim his rank and office aloud? Before it was day most of the courtiers crept down to the river, hired boats, and betook themselves to their homes or their friends in the country. It was assumed in the city that the domestics had been discharged upon a sudden discovery of general and unpardonable peculation; for, almost everybody being guilty of it himself, petty dishonesty was the crime most easily credited and least easily passed over in Gwyntystorm.

Now that same day was Religion day, and not a few of the clergy, always glad to seize on any passing event to give interest to the dull and monotonic grind of their intellectual machines, made this remarkable one the ground of discourse to their congregations. More especially than the rest, the first priest of the great temple where was the royal pew, judged himself, from his relation to the palace, called upon to 'improve the occasion', for they talked ever about improvement at Gwyntystorm, all the time they were going down hill with a rush.

The book which had, of late years, come to be considered the most sacred, was called The Book of Nations, and consisted of proverbs, and history traced through custom: from it the first priest chose his text; and his text was, 'Honesty Is the Best Policy.' He was considered a very eloquent man, but I can offer only a few of the larger bones of his sermon.

The main proof of the verity of their religion, he said, was that things always went well with those who profess it; and its first fundamental principle, grounded in inborn invariable instinct, was, that every One should take care of that One. This was the first duty of Man. If every one would but obey this law, number one, then would every one be perfectly cared for - one being always equal to one. But the faculty of care was in excess of need, and all that overflowed, and would otherwise run to waste, ought to be gently turned in the direction of one's neighbor, seeing that this also wrought for the fulfilling of the law, inasmuch as the reaction of excess so directed was upon the director of the same, to the comfort, that is, and well-being of the original self. To be just and friendly was to build the warmest and safest of all nests, and to be kind and loving was to line it with the softest of all furs and feathers, for the one precious, comfort-loving self there to lie, revelling in downiest bliss. One of the laws therefore most binding upon men because of its relation to the first and greatest of all duties, was embodied in the Proverb he had just read; and what stronger proof of its wisdom and truth could they desire than the sudden and complete vengeance which had fallen upon those worse than ordinary sinners who had offended against the king's majesty by forgetting that 'Honesty Is the Best Policy'?

At this point of the discourse the head of the legserpent rose from the floor of the temple, towering above the pulpit, above the priest, then curving downward, with open mouth slowly descended upon him. Horror froze the sermon-pump. He stared upward aghast. The great teeth of the animal closed upon a mouthful of the sacred vestments, and slowly he lifted the preacher from the pulpit, like a handful of linen from a washtub, and, on his four solemn stumps, bore him out of the temple, dangling aloft from his jaws. At the back of it he dropped him into the dust hole among the remnants of a library whose age had destroyed its value in the eyes of the chapter. They found him burrowing in it, a lunatic henceforth - whose madness presented the peculiar feature, that in its paroxysms he jabbered sense.

Bone-freezing horror pervaded Gwyntystorm. If their best and wisest were treated with such contempt, what might not the rest of them look for? Alas for their city! Their grandly respectable city! Their loftily reasonable city! Where it was all to end, who could tell!

But something must be done. Hastily assembling, the priests chose a new first priest, and in full conclave unanimously declared and accepted that the king in his retirement had, through the practice of the blackest magic, turned the palace into a nest of demons in the midst of them. A grand exorcism was therefore indispensable.

In the meantime the fact came out that the greater part of the courtiers had been dismissed as well as the servants, and this fact swelled the hope of the Party of Decency, as they called themselves. Upon it they proceeded to act, and strengthened themselves on all sides.

The action of the king's bodyguard remained for a time uncertain. But when at length its officers were satisfied that both the master of the horse and their colonel were missing, they placed themselves under the orders of the first priest. Every one dated the culmination of the evil from the visit of the miner and his mongrel; and the butchers vowed, if they could but get hold of them again, they would roast both of them alive. At once they formed themselves into a regiment, and put their dogs in training for attack.

Incessant was the talk, innumerable were the suggestions, and great was the deliberation. The general consent, however, was that as soon as the priests should have expelled the demons, they would depose the king, and attired in all his regal insignia, shut him in a cage for public show; then choose governors, with the lord chancellor at their head, whose first duty should be to remit every possible tax; and the magistrates, by the mouth of the city marshal, required all able-bodied citizens, in order to do their part toward the carrying out of these and a multitude of other reforms, to be ready to take arms at the first summons.

Things needful were prepared as speedily as possible, and a mighty ceremony, in the temple, in the market place, and in front of the palace, was performed for the expulsion of the demons. This over, the leaders retired to arrange an attack upon the palace.

But that night events occurred which, proving the failure of their first, induced the abandonment of their second, intent. Certain of the prowling order of the community, whose numbers had of late been steadily on the increase, reported frightful things. Demons of indescribable ugliness had been espied careering through the midnight streets and courts. A citizen - some said in the very act of housebreaking, but no one cared to look into trifles at such a crisis - had been seized from behind, he could not see by what, and soused in the river. A well-known receiver of stolen goods had had his shop broken open, and when he came down in the morning had found everything in ruin on the pavement. The wooden image of justice over the door of the city marshal had had the arm that held the sword bitten off. The gluttonous magistrate had been pulled from his bed in the dark, by beings of which he could see nothing but the flaming eyes, and treated to a bath of the turtle soup that had been left simmering by the side of the kitchen fire. Having poured it over him, they put him again into his bed, where he soon learned how a mummy must feel in its cerements.

Worst of all, in the market place was fixed up a paper, with the king's own signature, to the effect that whoever henceforth should show inhospitality to strangers, and should be convicted of the same, should be instantly expelled the city; while a second, in the butchers' quarter, ordained that any dog which henceforth should attack a stranger should be immediately destroyed. It was plain, said the butchers, that the clergy were of no use; they could not exorcise demons! That afternoon, catching sight of a poor old fellow in rags and tatters, quietly walking up the street, they hounded their dogs upon him, and had it not been that the door of Derba's cottage was standing open, and was near enough for him to dart in and shut it ere they reached him, he would have been torn in pieces. And thus things went on for some days.

29. BARBARA

In the meantime, with Derba to minister to his wants, with Curdie to protect him, and Irene to nurse him, the king was getting rapidly stronger. Good food was what he most wanted and of that, at least of certain kinds of it, there was plentiful store in the palace. Everywhere since the cleansing of the lower regions of it, the air was clean and sweet, and under the honest hands of the one housemaid the king's chamber became a pleasure to his eyes. With such changes it was no wonder if his heart grew lighter as well as his brain clearer. But still evil dreams came and troubled him, the lingering result of the wicked medicines the doctor had given him. Every night, sometimes twice or thrice, he would wake up in terror, and it would be minutes ere he could come to himself. The consequence was that he was always worse in the morning, and had loss to make up during the day. While he slept, Irene or Curdie, one or the other, must still be always by his side.

One night, when it was Curdie's turn with the king, he heard a cry somewhere in the house, and as there was no other child, concluded, notwithstanding the distance of her grandmother's room, that it must be Barbara. Fearing something might be wrong, and noting the king's sleep more quiet than usual, he ran to see. He found the child in the middle of the floor, weeping bitterly, and Derba slumbering peacefully in bed. The instant she saw him the night-lost thing ceased her crying, smiled, and stretched out her arms to him. Unwilling to wake the old woman, who had been working hard all day, he took the child, and carried her with him. She clung to him so, pressing her tear-wet radiant face against his, that her little arms threatened to choke him.

When he re-entered the chamber, he found the king sitting up in bed, fighting the phantoms of some hideous dream. Generally upon such occasions, although he saw his watcher, he could not dissociate him from the dream, and went raving on. But the moment his eyes fell upon little Barbara, whom he had never seen before, his soul came into them with a rush, and a smile like the dawn of an eternal day overspread his countenance; the dream was nowhere, and the child was in his heart. He stretched out his arms to her, the child stretched out hers to him, and in five minutes they were both asleep, each in the other's embrace.

From that night Barbara had a crib in the king's chamber, and as often as he woke, Irene or Curdie, whichever was watching, took the sleeping child and laid her in his arms, upon which, invariably and instantly, the dream would vanish. A great part of the day too she would be playing on or about the king's bed; and it was a delight to the heart of the princess to see her amusing herself with the crown, now sitting upon it, now rolling it hither and thither about the room like a hoop. Her grandmother entering once while she was pretending to make porridge in it, held up her hands in horror-struck amazement; but the king would not allow her to interfere, for the king was now Barbara's playmate, and his crown their plaything.

The colonel of the guard also was growing better. Curdie went often to see him. They were soon friends, for the best people understand each other the easiest, and the grim old warrior loved the miner boy as if he were at once his son and his angel. He was very anxious about his regiment. He said the officers were mostly honest men, he believed, but how they might be doing without him, or what they might resolve, in ignorance of the real state of affairs, and exposed to every misrepresentation, who could tell? Curdie proposed that he should send for the major, offering to be the messenger. The colonel agreed, and Curdie went - not without his mattock, because of the dogs.

But the officers had been told by the master of the horse that their colonel was dead, and although they were amazed he should be buried without the attendance of his regiment, they never doubted the information. The handwriting itself of their colonel was insufficient, counteracted by the fresh reports daily current, to destroy the lie. The major regarded the letter as a trap for the next officer in command, and sent his orderly to arrest the messenger. But Curdie had had the wisdom not to wait for an answer.

The king's enemies said that he had first poisoned the good colonel of the guard, and then murdered the master of the horse, and other faithful councilors; and that his oldest and most attached domestics had but escaped from the palace with their lives – not all of them, for the butler was missing. Mad or wicked, he was not only unfit to rule any longer, but worse than unfit to have in his power and under his influence the young princess, only hope of Gwyntystorm and the kingdom.

The moment the lord chancellor reached his house in the country and had got himself clothed, he began to devise how yet to destroy his master; and the very next morning set out for the neighboring kingdom of Borsagrass to invite invasion, and offer a compact with its monarch.

30. PETER

At the cottage in the mountain everything for a time went on just as before. It was indeed dull without Curdie, but as often as they looked at the emerald it was gloriously green, and with nothing to fear or regret, and everything to hope, they required little comforting. One morning, however, at last, Peter, who had been consulting the gem, rather now from habit than anxiety, as a farmer his barometer in undoubtful weather, turned suddenly to his wife, the stone in his hand, and held it up with a look of ghastly dismay.

'Why, that's never the emerald!' said Joan.

'It is,' answered Peter; 'but it were small blame to any one that took it for a bit of bottle glass!'

For, all save one spot right in the centre, of the most intense and brilliant green, it looked as if the color had been burnt out of it.

'Run, run, Peter!' cried his wife. 'Run and tell the old princess. It may not be too late. The boy must be lying at death's door.'

Without a word Peter caught up his mattock, darted from the cottage, and was at the bottom of the hill in less time than he usually took to get halfway.

The door of the king's house stood open; he rushed in and up the stair. But after wandering about in vain for an hour, opening door after door, and finding no way farther up, the heart of the old man had well-nigh failed him. Empty rooms, empty rooms! – desertion and desolation everywhere.

At last he did come upon the door to the tower stair. Up he darted. Arrived at the top, he found three doors, and, one after the other, knocked at them all. But there was neither voice nor hearing. Urged by his faith and his dread, slowly, hesitatingly, he opened one. It revealed a bare garret room, nothing in it but one chair and one spinning wheel. He closed it, and opened the next - to start back in terror, for he saw nothing but a great gulf, a moonless night, full of stars, and, for all the stars, dark, dark! - a fathomless abyss. He opened the third door, and a rush like the tide of a living sea invaded his ears. Multitudinous wings flapped and flashed in the sun, and, like the ascending column from a volcano, white birds innumerable shot into the air, darkening the day with the shadow of their cloud, and then, with a sharp sweep, as if bent sideways by a sudden wind, flew northward, swiftly away, and vanished. The place felt like a tomb. There seemed no breath of life left in it.

Despair laid hold upon him; he rushed down thundering with heavy feet. Out upon him darted the housekeeper like an ogress-spider, and after her came her men; but Peter rushed past them, heedless and careless - for had not the princess mocked him? - and sped along the road to Gwyntystorm. What help lay in a miner's mattock, a man's arm, a father's heart, he would bear to his boy.

Joan sat up all night waiting his return, hoping and hoping. The mountain was very still, and the sky was clear; but all night long the miner sped northward, and the heart of his wife was troubled.

31. THE SACRIFICE

Things in the palace were in a strange condition: the king playing with a child and dreaming wise dreams, waited upon by a little princess with the heart of a queen, and a youth from the mines, who went nowhere, not even into the king's chamber, without his mattock on his shoulder and a horrible animal at his heels; in a room nearby the colonel of his guard, also in bed, without a soldier to obey him; in six other rooms, far apart, six miscreants, each watched by a beast-jailer; ministers to them all, an old woman and a page; and in the wine cellar, forty-three animals, creatures more grotesque than ever brain of man invented. None dared approach its gates, and seldom one issued from them.

All the dwellers in the city were united in enmity to the palace. It swarmed with evil spirits, they said, whereas the evil spirits were in the city, unsuspected. One consequence of their presence was that, when the rumor came that a great army was on the march against Gwyntystorm, instead of rushing to their defenses, to make new gates, free portcullises and drawbridges, and bar the river, each band flew first to their treasures, burying them in their cellars and gardens, and hiding them behind stones in their chimneys; and, next to rebellion, signing an invitation to His Majesty of Borsagrass to enter at their open gates, destroy their king, and annex their country to his own.

The straits of isolation were soon found in the palace: its invalids were requiring stronger food, and what was to be done? For if the butchers sent meat to the palace, was it not likely enough to be poisoned? Curdie said to Derba he would think of some plan before morning.

But that same night, as soon as it was dark, Lina came to her master, and let him understand she wanted to go out. He unlocked a little private postern for her, left it so that she could push it open when she returned, and told the crocodile to stretch himself across it inside. Before midnight she came back with a young deer.

Early the next morning the legserpent crept out of the wine cellar, through the broken door behind, shot into the river, and soon appeared in the kitchen with a splendid sturgeon. Every night Lina went out hunting, and every morning Legserpent went out fishing, and both invalids and household had plenty to eat. As to news, the page, in plain clothes, would now and then venture out into the market place, and gather some.

One night he came back with the report that the army of the king of Borsagrass had crossed the border. Two days after, he brought the news that the enemy was now but twenty miles from Gwyntystorm.

The colonel of the guard rose, and began furbishing his armor - but gave it over to the page, and staggered across to the barracks, which were in the next street. The sentry took him for a ghost or worse, ran into the guardroom, bolted the door, and stopped his ears. The poor colonel, who was yet hardly able to stand, crawled back despairing.

For Curdie, he had already, as soon as the first rumor reached him, resolved, if no other instructions came, and the king continued unable to give orders, to call Lina and the creatures, and march to meet the enemy. If he died, he died for the right, and there was a right end of it. He had no preparations to make, except a good sleep.

He asked the king to let the housemaid take his place by His Majesty that night, and went and lay down on the floor of the corridor, no farther off than a whisper would reach from the door of the chamber. There, -with an old mantle of the king's thrown over him, he was soon fast asleep.

Somewhere about the middle of the night, he woke suddenly, started to his feet, and rubbed his eyes. He could not tell what had waked him. But could he be awake, or was he not dreaming? The curtain of the king's door, a dull red ever before, was glowing a gorgeous, a radiant purple; and the crown wrought upon it in silks and gems was flashing as if it burned! What could it mean? Was the king's chamber on fire? He darted to the door and lifted the curtain. Glorious terrible sight!

A long and broad marble table, that stood at one end of the room, had been drawn into the middle of it, and thereon burned a great fire, of a sort that Curdie knew - a fire of glowing, flaming roses, red and white. In the midst of the roses lay the king, moaning, but motionless. Every rose that fell from the table to the floor, someone, whom Curdie could not plainly see for the brightness, lifted and laid burning upon the king's face, until at length his face too was covered with the live roses, and he lay all within the fire, moaning still, with now and then a shuddering sob.

And the shape that Curdie saw and could not see, wept over the king as he lay in the fire, and often she hid her face in handfuls of her shadowy hair, and from her hair the water of her weeping dropped like sunset rain in the light of the roses. At last she lifted a great armful of her hair, and shook it over the fire, and the drops fell from it in showers, and they did not hiss in the flames, but there arose instead as it were the sound of running brooks.

And the glow of the red fire died away, and the glow of the white fire grew grey, and the light was gone, and on the table all was black - except the face of the king, which shone from under the burnt roses like a diamond in the ashes of a furnace.

Then Curdie, no longer dazzled, saw and knew the old princess. The room was lighted with the splendor of her face, of her blue eyes, of her sapphire crown. Her golden hair went streaming out from her through the air till it went off in mist and light. She was large and strong as a Titaness. She stooped over the table-altar, put her mighty arms under the living sacrifice, lifted the king, as if he were but a little child, to her bosom, walked with him up the floor, and laid him in his bed. Then darkness fell.

The miner boy turned silent away, and laid himself down again in the corridor. An absolute joy filled his heart, his bosom, his head, his whole body. All was safe; all was well. With the helve of his mattock tight in his grasp, he sank into a dreamless sleep.

32. THE KING'S ARMY

He woke like a giant refreshed with wine.

When he went into the king's chamber, the housemaid sat where he had left her, and everything in the room was as it had been the night before, save that a heavenly odor of roses filled the air of it. He went up to the bed. The king opened his eyes, and the soul of perfect health shone out of them. Nor was Curdie amazed in his delight.

'Is it not time to rise, Curdie?' said the king.

'It is, Your Majesty. Today we must be doing,' answered Curdie.

'What must we be doing today, Curdie?'

'Fighting, sire.'

'Then fetch me my armor - that of plated steel, in the chest there. You will find the underclothing with it.'

As he spoke, he reached out his hand for his sword, which hung in the bed before him, drew it, and examined the blade.

'A little rusty!' he said, 'but the edge is there. We shall polish it ourselves today - not on the wheel. Curdie, my son, I wake from a troubled dream. A glorious torture has ended it, and I live. I know now well how things are, but you shall explain them to me as I get on my armor. No, I need no bath. I am clean. Call the colonel of the guard.'

In complete steel the old man stepped into the chamber. He knew it not, but the old princess had passed through his room in the night.

'Why, Sir Bronzebeard!' said the king, 'you are dressed before me! You need no valet, old man, when there is battle in the wind!'

'Battle, sire!' returned the colonel. 'Where then are our soldiers?'

'Why, there and here,' answered the king, pointing to the colonel first, and then to himself. 'Where else, man? The enemy will be upon us ere sunset, if we be not upon him ere noon. What other thing was in your brave brain when you donned your armor, friend?'

'Your Majesty's orders, sire,' answered Sir Bronzebeard.

The king smiled and turned to Curdie.

'And what was in yours, Curdie, for your first word was of battle?'

'See, Your Majesty,' answered Curdie; 'I have polished my mattock. If Your Majesty had not taken the command, I would have met the enemy at the head of my beasts, and died in comfort, or done better.'

'Brave boy!' said the king. 'He who takes his life in his hand is the only soldier. You shall head your beasts today. Sir Bronzebeard, will you die with me if need be?'

'Seven times, my king,' said the colonel.

'Then shall we win this battle!' said the king. 'Curdie, go and bind securely the six, that we lose not their guards. Can you find me a horse, think you, Sir Bronzebeard? Alas! they told me my white charger was dead.'

'I will go and fright the varletry with my presence, and secure, I trust, a horse for Your Majesty, and one for myself.'

'And look you, brother!' said the king; 'bring one for my miner boy too, and a sober old charger for the princess, for she too must go to the battle, and conquer with us.'

'Pardon me, sire,' said Curdie; 'a miner can fight best on foot. I might smite my horse dead under me with a missed blow. And besides that, I must be near to my beasts.'

'As you will,' said the king. 'Three horses then, Sir Bronzebeard.'

The colonel departed, doubting sorely in his heart how to accoutre and lead from the barrack stables three horses, in the teeth of his revolted regiment.

In the hall he met the housemaid.

'Can you lead a horse?' he asked. 'Yes, sir.'

'Are you willing to die for the king?'

'Yes, sir.'

'Can you do as you are bid?'

'I can keep on trying, sir.'

'Come then. Were I not a man I would be a woman such as you.'

When they entered the barrack yard, the soldiers scattered like autumn leaves before a blast of winter. They went into the stable unchallenged - and lo! in a stall, before the colonel's eyes, stood the king's white charger, with the royal saddle and bridle hung high beside him!

'Traitorous thieves!' muttered the old man in his beard, and went along the stalls, looking for his own black charger. Having found him, he returned to saddle first the king's. But the maid had already the saddle upon him, and so girt that the colonel could thrust no finger tip between girth and skin. He left her to finish what she had so well begun, and went and made ready his own. He then chose for the princess a great red horse, twenty years old, which he knew to possess every equine virtue. This and his own he led to the palace, and the maid led the king's.

The king and Curdie stood in the court, the king in full armor of silvered steel, with a circlet of rubies and diamonds round his helmet. He almost leaped for joy when he saw his great white charger come in, gentle as a child to the hand of the housemaid. But when the horse saw his master in his armor, he reared and bounded in jubilation, yet did not break from the hand that held him. Then out came the princess attired and ready, with a hunting knife her father had given her by her side. They brought her mother's saddle, splendent with gems and gold, set it on the great red horse, and lifted her to it. But the saddle was so big, and the horse so tall, that the child found no comfort in them.

'Please, King Papa,' she said, 'can I not have my white pony?'

'I did not think of him, little one,' said the king. 'Where is he?'

'In the stable,' answered the maid. 'I found him half starved, the only horse within the gates, the day after the servants were driven out. He has been well fed since.'

'Go and fetch him,' said the king.

As the maid appeared with the pony, from a side door came Lina and the forty-nine, following Curdie.

'I will go with Curdie and the Uglies,' cried the princess; and as soon as she was mounted she got into the middle of the pack.

So out they set, the strangest force that ever went against an enemy. The king in silver armor sat stately on his white steed, with the stones flashing on his helmet; beside him the grim old colonel, armed in steel, rode his black charger; behind the king, a little to the right, Curdie walked afoot, his mattock shining in the sun; Lina followed at his heel; behind her came the wonderful company of Uglies; in the midst of them rode the gracious little Irene, dressed in blue, and mounted on the prettiest of white ponies; behind the colonel, a little to the left, walked the page, armed in a breastplate, headpiece, and trooper's sword he had found in the palace, all much too big for him, and carrying a huge brass trumpet which he did his best to blow; and the king smiled and seemed pleased with his music, although it was but the grunt of a brazen unrest. Alongside the beasts walked Derba carrying Barbara - their refuge the mountains, should the cause of the king be lost; as soon as they were over the river they turned aside to ascend the Cliff, and there awaited the forging of the day's history. Then first Curdie saw that the housemaid, whom they had all forgotten, was following, mounted on the great red horse, and seated in the royal saddle.

Many were the eyes unfriendly of women that had stared at them from door and window as they passed through the city; and low laughter and mockery and evil words from the lips of children had rippled about their ears; but the men were all gone to welcome the enemy, the butchers the first, the king's guard the last. And now on the heels of the king's army rushed out the women and children also, to gather flowers and branches, wherewith to welcome their conquerors.

About a mile down the river, Curdie, happening to look behind him, saw the maid, whom he had supposed gone with Derba, still following on the great red horse. The same moment the king, a few paces in front of him, caught sight of the enemy's tents, pitched where, the cliffs receding, the bank of the river widened to a little plain.

33. THE BATTLE

He commanded the page to blow his trumpet; and, in the strength of the moment, the youth uttered a right warlike defiance.

But the butchers and the guard, who had gone over armed to the enemy, thinking that the king had come to make his peace also, and that it might thereafter go hard with them, rushed at once to make short work with him, and both secure and commend themselves. The butchers came on first - for the guards had slackened their saddle girths - brandishing their knives, and talking to their dogs. Curdie and the page, with Lina and her pack, bounded to meet them. Curdie struck down the foremost with his mattock. The page, finding his sword too much for him, threw it away and seized the butcher's knife, which as he rose he plunged into the foremost dog. Lina rushed raging and gnashing among them. She would not look at a dog so long as there was a butcher on his legs, and she never stopped to kill a butcher, only with one grind of her jaws crushed a leg of him. When they were all down, then indeed she flashed among the dogs.

Meantime the king and the colonel had spurred toward the advancing guard. The king clove the major through skull and collar bone, and the colonel stabbed the captain in the throat. Then a fierce combat commenced - two against many. But the butchers and their dogs quickly disposed of, up came Curdie and his beasts. The horses of the guard, struck with terror, turned in spite of the spur, and fled in confusion. Thereupon the forces of Borsagrass, which could see little of the affair, but correctly imagined a small determined body in front of them, hastened to the attack. No sooner did their first advancing wave appear through the foam of the retreating one, than the king and the colonel and the page, Curdie and the beasts, went charging upon them. Their attack, especially the rush of the Uglies, threw the first line into great confusion, but the second came up quickly; the beasts could not be everywhere, there were thousands to one against them, and the king and his three companions were in the greatest possible danger.

A dense cloud came over the sun, and sank rapidly toward the earth. The cloud moved all together, and yet the thousands of white flakes of which it was made up moved each for itself in ceaseless and rapid motion: those flakes were the wings of pigeons. Down swooped the birds upon the invaders; right in the face of man and horse they flew with swift-beating wings, blinding eyes and confounding brain. Horses reared and plunged and wheeled. All was at once in confusion. The men made frantic efforts to seize their tormentors, but not one could they touch; and they out doubled them in numbers. Between every wild clutch came a peck of beak and a buffet of pinion in the face. Generally the bird would, with sharp-clapping wings, dart its whole body, with the swiftness of an arrow, against its singled mark, yet so as to glance aloft the same instant, and descend skimming; much as the thin stone, shot with horizontal cast of arm, having touched and torn the surface of the lake, ascends to skim, touch, and tear again. So mingled the feathered multitude in the grim game of war. It was a storm in which the wind was birds, and the sea men. And ever as each bird arrived at the rear of the enemy, it turned, ascended, and sped to the front to charge again.

The moment the battle began, the princess's pony took fright, and turned and fled. But the maid wheeled her horse across the road and stopped him; and they waited together the result of the battle.

And as they waited, it seemed to the princess right strange that the pigeons, every one as it came to the rear, and fetched a compass to gather force for the re-attack, should make the head of her attendant on the red horse the goal around which it turned; so that about them was an unintermittent flapping and flashing of wings, and a curving, sweeping torrent of the side-poised wheeling bodies of birds. Strange also it seemed that the maid should be constantly waving her arm toward the battle. And the time of the motion of her arm so fitted with the rushes of birds, that it looked as if the birds obeyed her gesture, and she was casting living javelins by the thousand against the enemy. The moment a pigeon had rounded her head, it went off straight as bolt from bow, and with trebled velocity.

But of these strange things, others besides the princess had taken note. From a rising ground whence they watched the battle in growing dismay, the leaders of the enemy saw the maid and her motions, and, concluding her an enchantress, whose were the airy legions humiliating them, set spurs to their horses, made a circuit, outflanked the king, and came down upon her. But suddenly by her side stood a stalwart old man in the garb of a miner, who, as the general rode at her, sword in hand, heaved his swift mattock, and brought it down with such force on the forehead of his charger, that he fell to the ground like a log. His rider shot over his head and lay stunned. Had not the great red horse reared and wheeled, he would have fallen beneath that of the general.

With lifted saber, one of his attendant officers rode at the miner. But a mass of pigeons darted in the faces of him and his horse, and the next moment he lay beside his commander.

The rest of them turned and fled, pursued by the birds.

'Ah, friend Peter!' said the maid; 'thou hast come as I told thee! Welcome and thanks!'

By this time the battle was over. The rout was general. The enemy stormed back upon their own camp, with the beasts roaring in the midst of them, and the king and his army, now reinforced by one, pursuing. But presently the king drew rein.

'Call off your hounds, Curdie, and let the pigeons do the rest,' he shouted, and turned to see what had become of the princess.

In full panic fled the invaders, sweeping down their tents, stumbling over their baggage, trampling on their dead and wounded, ceaselessly pursued and buffeted by the white-winged army of heaven. Homeward they rushed the road they had come, straight for the borders, many dropping from pure fatigue, and lying where they fell. And still the pigeons were in their necks as they ran. At length to the eyes of the king and his army nothing was visible save a dust cloud below, and a bird cloud above. Before night the bird cloud came back, flying high over Gwyntystorm. Sinking swiftly, it disappeared among the ancient roofs of the palace.

34. JUDGMENT

The king and his army returned, bringing with them one prisoner only, the lord Chancellor. Curdie had dragged him from under a fallen tent, not by the hand of a man, but by the foot of a mule.

When they entered the city, it was still as the grave. The citizens had fled home. 'We must submit,' they cried, 'or the king and his demons will destroy us.' The king rode through the streets in silence, ill-pleased with his people. But he stopped his horse in the midst of the market place, and called, in a voice loud and clear as the cry of a silver trumpet, 'Go and find your own. Bury your dead, and bring home your wounded.' Then he turned him gloomily to the palace. Just as they reached the gates, Peter, who, as they went, had been telling his tale to Curdie, ended it with the words:

'And so there I was, in the nick of time to save the two princesses!'

'The two princesses, Father! The one on the great red horse was the housemaid,' said Curdie, and ran to open the gates for the king.

They found Derba returned before them, and already busy preparing them food. The king put up his charger with his own hands, rubbed him down, and fed him.

When they had washed, and eaten and drunk, he called the colonel, and told Curdie and the page to bring out the traitors and the beasts, and attend him to the market place.

By this time the people were crowding back into the city, bearing their dead and wounded. And there was lamentation in Gwyntystorm, for no one could comfort himself, and no one had any to comfort him. The nation was victorious, but the people were conquered.

The king stood in the centre of the market place, upon the steps of the ancient cross. He had laid aside his helmet and put on his crown, but he stood all armed beside, with his sword in his hand. He called the people to him, and, for all the terror of the beasts, they dared not disobey him. Those, even, who were carrying their wounded laid them down, and drew near trembling.

Then the king said to Curdie and the page:

'Set the evil men before me.'

He looked upon them for a moment in mingled anger and pity, then turned to the people and said:

'Behold your trust! Ye slaves, behold your leaders! I would have freed you, but ye would not be free. Now shall ye be ruled with a rod of iron, that ye may learn what freedom is, and love it and seek it. These wretches I will send where they shall mislead you no longer.'

He made a sign to Curdie, who immediately brought up the legserpent. To the body of the animal they bound the lord Chamberlain, speechless with horror. The butler began to shriek and pray, but they bound him on the back of Clubhead. One after another, upon the largest of the creatures they bound the whole seven, each through the unveiling terror looking the villain he was. Then said the king:

'I thank you, my good beasts; and I hope to visit you ere long. Take these evil men with you, and go to your place.'

Like a whirlwind they were in the crowd, scattering it like dust. Like hounds they rushed from the city, their burdens howling and raving.

What became of them I have never heard.

Then the king turned once more to the people and said, 'Go to your houses'; nor vouchsafed them another word. They crept home like chidden hounds.

The king returned to the palace. He made the colonel a duke, and the page a knight, and Peter he appointed general of all his mines. But to Curdie he said:

'You are my own boy, Curdie. My child cannot choose but love you, and when you are grown up - if you both will - you shall marry each other, and be king and queen when I am gone. Till then be the king's Curdie.'

Irene held out her arms to Curdie. He raised her in his, and she kissed him.

'And my Curdie too!' she said.

Thereafter the people called him Prince Conrad; but the king always called him either just Curdie, or my miner boy.

They sat down to supper, and Derba and the knight and the housemaid waited, and Barbara sat at the king's left hand. The housemaid poured out the wine; and as she poured for Curdie red wine that foamed in the cup, as if glad to see the light whence it had been banished so long, she looked him in the eyes. And Curdie started, and sprang from his seat, and dropped on his knees, and burst into tears. And the maid said with a smile, such as none but one could smile:

'Did I not tell you, Curdie, that it might be you would not know me when next you saw me?' Then she went from the room, and in a moment returned in royal purple, with a crown of diamonds and rubies, from under which her hair went flowing to the floor, all about her ruby- slippered feet. Her face was radiant with joy, the joy overshadowed by a faint mist as of unfulfilment. The king rose and kneeled on one knee before her. All kneeled in like homage. Then the king would have yielded her his royal chair. But she made them all sit down, and with her own hands placed at the table seats for Derba and the page. Then in ruby crown and royal purple she served them all.

35. THE END

The king sent Curdie out into his dominions to search for men and women that had human hands. And many such he found, honest and true, and brought them to his master. So a new and upright court was formed, and strength returned to the nation.

But the exchequer was almost empty, for the evil men had squandered everything, and the king hated taxes unwillingly paid. Then came Curdie and said to the king that the city stood upon gold. And the king sent for men wise in the ways of the earth, and they built smelting furnaces, and Peter brought miners, and they mined the gold, and smelted it, and the king coined it into money, and therewith established things well in the land.

The same day on which he found his boy, Peter set out to go home. When he told the good news to Joan, his wife, she rose from her chair and said, 'Let us go.' And they left the cottage, and repaired to Gwyntystorm. And on a mountain above the city they built themselves a warm house for their old age, high in the clear air.

As Peter mined one day, at the back of the king's wine Cellar, he broke into a cavern crusted with gems, and much wealth flowed there from, and the king used it wisely.

Queen Irene - that was the right name of the old princess – was thereafter seldom long absent from the palace. Once or twice when she was missing, Barbara, who seemed to know of her sometimes when nobody else had a notion whither she had gone, said she was with the dear old Uglies in the wood. Curdie thought that perhaps her business might be with others there as well. All the uppermost rooms in the palace were left to her use, and when any one was in need of her help, up thither he must go. But even when she was there, he did not always succeed in finding her. She, however, always knew that such a one had been looking for her.

Curdie went to find her one day. As he ascended the last stair, to meet him came the well-known scent of her roses; and when he opened the door, lo! there was the same gorgeous room in which his touch had been glorified by her fire! And there burned the fire - a huge heap of red and white roses. Before the hearth stood the princess, an old grey-haired woman, with Lina a little behind her, slowly wagging her tail, and looking like a beast of prey that can hardly so long restrain itself from springing as to be sure of its victim. The queen was casting roses, more and more roses, upon the fire. At last she turned and said, 'Now Lina!' - and Lina dashed burrowing into the fire. There went up a black smoke and a dust, and Lina was never more seen in the palace.

Irene and Curdie were married. The old king died, and they were king and queen. As long as they lived Gwyntystorm was a better city, and good people grew in it. But they had no children, and when they died the people chose a king. And the new king went mining and mining in the rock under the city, and grew more and more eager after the gold, and paid less and less heed to his people. Rapidly they sank toward their old wickedness. But still the king went on mining, and coining gold by the pail full, until the people were worse even than in the old time. And so greedy was the king after gold, that when at last the ore began to fail, he caused the miners to reduce the pillars which Peter and they that followed him had left standing to bear the city. And from the girth of an oak of a thousand years, they chipped them down to that of a fir tree of fifty.

One day at noon, when life was at its highest, the whole city fell with a roaring crash. The cries of men and the shrieks of women went up with its dust, and then there was a great silence.

Where the mighty rock once towered, crowded with homes and crowned with a palace, now rushes and raves a stone-obstructed rapid of the river. All around spreads a wilderness of wild deer, and the very name of Gwyntystorm had ceased from the lips of men.

Book Three

The Light Princess

☙

1. WHAT! NO CHILDREN?

Once upon a time, so long ago that I have quite forgotten the date, there lived a king and queen who had no children.

And the king said to himself, "All the queens of my acquaintance have children, some three, some seven, and some as many as twelve; and my queen has not one. I feel ill-used." So he made up his mind to be cross with his wife about it. But she bore it all like a good patient queen as she was. Then the king grew very cross indeed. But the queen pretended to take it all as a joke, and a very good one too.

"Why don't you have any daughters, at least?" said he. "I don't say sons; that might be too much to expect."

"I am sure, dear king, I am very sorry," said the queen.

"So you ought to be," retorted the king; "you are not going to make a virtue of that, surely."

But he was not an ill-tempered king, and in any matter of less moment would have let the queen have her own way with all his heart. This, however, was an affair of state.

The queen smiled.

"You must have patience with a lady, you know, dear king," said she.

She was, indeed, a very nice queen, and heartily sorry that she could not oblige the king immediately.

The king tried to have patience, but he succeeded very badly. It was more than he deserved, therefore, when, at last, the queen gave him a daughter-as lovely a little princess as ever cried.

2. WON'T I, JUST?

The day drew near when the infant must be christened. The king wrote all the invitations with his own hand. Of course somebody was forgotten.

Now it does not generally matter if somebody is forgotten, only you must mind who. Unfortunately, the king forgot without intending to forget; and so the chance fell upon the Princess

Makemnoit, which was awkward. For the princess was the king's own sister; and he ought not to have forgotten her. But she had made herself so disagreeable to the old king, their father, that he had forgotten her in making his will; and so it was no wonder that her brother forgot her in writing his invitations. But poor relations don't do anything to keep you in mind of them. Why don't they? The king could not see into the garret she lived in, could he?

She was a sour, spiteful creature. The wrinkles of contempt crossed the wrinkles of peevishness, and made her face as full of wrinkles as a pat of butter. If ever a king could be justified in forgetting anybody, this king was justified in forgetting his sister, even at a christening. She looked very odd, too. Her forehead was as large as all the rest of her face, and projected over it like a precipice. When she was angry her little eyes flashed blue. When she hated anybody, they shone yellow and green. What they looked like when she loved anybody, I do not know; for I never heard of her loving anybody but herself, and I do not think she could have managed that if she had not somehow got used to herself. But what made it highly imprudent in the king to forget her was-that she was awfully clever. In fact, she was a witch; and when she bewitched anybody, he very soon had enough of it; for she beat all the wicked fairies in wickedness, and all the clever ones in cleverness. She despised all the modes we read of in history, in which offended fairies and witches have taken their revenges; and therefore, after waiting and waiting in vain for an invitation, she made up her mind at last to go without one, and make the whole family miserable, like a princess as she was.

So she put on her best gown, went to the palace, was kindly received by the happy monarch, who forgot that he had forgotten her, and took her place in the procession to the royal chapel. When they were all gathered about the font, she contrived to get next to it, and throw something into the water; after which she maintained a very respectful demeanor till the water was applied to the child's face. But at that moment she turned round in her place three times, and muttered the following words, loud enough for those beside her to hear:-

"Light of spirit, by my charms,

Light of body, every part,

Never weary human arms-

Only crush thy parents' heart!"

They all thought she had lost her wits, and was repeating some foolish nursery rhyme; but a shudder went through the whole of them notwithstanding. The baby, on the contrary, began to laugh and crow; while the nurse gave a start and a smothered cry, for she thought she was struck with paralysis: she could not feel the baby in her arms. But she clasped it tight and said nothing.

The mischief was done.

3. SHE CAN'T BE OURS

Her atrocious aunt had deprived the child of all her gravity. If you ask me how this was effected, I answer, "In the easiest way in the world. She had only to destroy gravitation." For the princess was a philosopher, and knew all the ins and outs of the laws of gravitation as well as the ins and outs of her boot-lace. And being a witch as well, she could abrogate those laws in a moment; or at least so clog their wheels and rust their bearings, that they would not work at all. But we have more to do with what followed than with how it was done.

The first awkwardness that resulted from this unhappy privation was, that the moment the nurse began to float the baby up and down, she flew from her arms towards the ceiling. Happily, the resistance of the air brought her ascending career to a close within a foot of it. There she remained, horizontal as when she left her nurse's arms, kicking and laughing amazingly. The nurse in terror flew to the bell, and begged the footman, who answered it, to bring up the house-steps directly. Trembling in every limb, she climbed upon the steps, and had to stand upon the very top, and reach up, before she could catch the floating tail of the baby's long clothes.

When the strange fact came to be known, there was a terrible commotion in the palace. The occasion of its discovery by the king was naturally a repetition of the nurse's experience. Astonished that he felt no weight when the child was laid in his arms, he began to wave her up and-not down, for she slowly ascended to the ceiling as before, and there remained floating in perfect comfort and satisfaction, as was testified by her peals of tiny laughter. The king stood staring up in speechless amazement, and trembled so that his beard shook like grass in the wind. At last, turning to the queen, who was just as horror-struck as himself, he said, gasping, staring, and stammering,

"She can't be ours, queen!"

Now the queen was much cleverer than the king, and had begun already to suspect that "this effect defective came by cause."

"I am sure she is ours," answered she. "But we ought to have taken better care of her at the christening. People who were never invited ought not to have been present."

"Oh, ho!" said the king, tapping his forehead with his forefinger, "I have it all. I've found her out. Don't you see it, queen? Princess Makemnoit has bewitched her."

"That's just what I say," answered the queen.

"I beg your pardon, my love; I did not hear you.-John! bring the steps I get on my throne with."

For he was a little king with a great throne, like many other kings.

The throne-steps were brought, and set upon the dining-table, and John got upon the top of them. But he could not reach the little princess, who lay like a baby-laughter-cloud in the air, exploding continuously.

"Take the tongs, John," said his Majesty; and getting up on the table, he handed them to him.

John could reach the baby now, and the little princess was handed down by the tongs.

4. WHERE IS SHE?

One fine summer day, a month after these her first adventures, during which time she had been very carefully watched, the princess was lying on the bed in the queen's own chamber, fast asleep. One of the windows was open, for it was noon, and the day so sultry that the little girl was wrapped in nothing less ethereal than slumber itself. The queen came into the room, and not observing that the baby was on the bed, opened another window. A frolicsome fairy wind, which had been watching for a chance of mischief, rushed in at the one window, and taking its way over the bed where the child was lying, caught her up, and rolling and floating her along like a piece of flue, or a dandelion-seed, carried her with it through the opposite window, and away. The queen went downstairs, quite ignorant of the loss she had herself occasioned.

When the nurse returned, she supposed that her Majesty had carried her off, and, dreading a scolding, delayed making inquiry about her. But hearing nothing, she grew uneasy, and went at length to the queen's boudoir, where she found her Majesty.

"Please, your Majesty, shall I take the baby?" said she.

"Where is she?" asked the queen.

"Please forgive me. I know it was wrong."

"What do you mean?" said the queen, looking grave.

"Oh! don't frighten me, your Majesty!" exclaimed the nurse, clasping her hands.

The queen saw that something was amiss, and fell down in a faint. The nurse rushed about the palace, screaming, "My baby! my baby!"

Every one ran to the queen's room. But the queen could give no orders. They soon found out, however, that the princess was missing, and in a moment the palace was like a beehive in a garden; and in one minute more the queen was brought to herself by a great shout and a clapping of hands. They had found the princess fast asleep under a rose-bush, to which the elvish little wind-puff had carried her, finishing its mischief by shaking a shower of red rose-leaves all over the little white sleeper. Startled by the noise the servants made, she woke, and, furious with glee, scattered the rose-leaves in all directions, like a shower of spray in the sunset.

She was watched more carefully after this, no doubt; yet it would be endless to relate all the odd incidents resulting from this peculiarity of the young princess. But there never was a baby in a house, not to say a palace, that kept the household in such constant good-humor, at least below-stairs. If it was not easy for her nurses to hold her, at least she made neither their arms nor their hearts ache. And she was so nice to play at ball with! There was positively no danger of letting her fall. They might throw her down, or knock her down, or push her down, but couldn't let her down. It is true, they might let her fly into the fire or the coal-hole, or through the window; but none of these accidents had happened as yet. If you heard peals of laughter resounding from some unknown region, you might be sure enough of the cause. Going down into the kitchen, or the room, you would find Jane and Thomas, and Robert and Susan, all and sum, playing at ball with the little princess. She was the ball herself, and did not enjoy it the less for that. Away she went, flying from one to another, screeching with laughter. And the servants loved the ball itself better even than the game. But they had to take some care how they threw her, for if she received an upward direction, she would never come down again without being fetched.

5. What Is To Be Done?

But above-stairs it was different. One day, for instance, after breakfast, the king went into his counting-house, and counted out his money.

The operation gave him no pleasure.

"To think," said he to himself, "that every one of these gold sovereigns weighs a quarter of an ounce, and my real, live, flesh-and-blood princess weighs nothing at all!"

And he hated his gold sovereigns, as they lay with a broad smile of self-satisfaction all over their yellow faces.

The queen was in the parlor, eating bread and honey. But at the second mouthful she burst out crying, and could not swallow it. The king heard her sobbing. Glad of anybody, but especially of his queen, to quarrel with, he clashed his gold sovereigns into his money-box, clapped his crown on his head, and rushed into the parlor.

"What is all this about?" exclaimed he. "What are you crying for, queen?"

"I can't eat it," said the queen, looking ruefully at the honey-pot.

"No wonder!" retorted the king. "You've just eaten your breakfast—two turkey eggs, and three anchovies."

"Oh, that's not it!" sobbed her Majesty. "It's my child, my child!"

"Well, what's the matter with your child? She's neither up the chimney nor down the draw-well. Just hear her laughing."

Yet the king could not help a sigh, which he tried to turn into a cough, saying-

"It is a good thing to be light-hearted, I am sure, whether she be ours or not."

"It is a bad thing to be light-headed," answered the queen, looking with prophetic soul far into the future.

"'Tis a good thing to be light-handed," said the king.

"'Tis a bad thing to be light-fingered," answered the queen.

"'Tis a good thing to be light-footed," said the king.

"'Tis a bad thing-" began the queen; but the king interrupted her.

"In fact," said he, with the tone of one who concludes an argument in which he has had only imaginary opponents, and in which, therefore, he has come off triumphant-"in fact, it is a good thing altogether to be light-bodied."

"But it is a bad thing altogether to be light-minded," retorted the queen, who was beginning to lose her temper.

This last answer quite discomfited his Majesty, who turned on his heel, and betook himself to his counting-house again. But he was not half-way towards it, when the voice of his queen overtook him.

"And it's a bad thing to be light-haired," screamed she, determined to have more last words, now that her spirit was roused.

The queen's hair was black as night; and the king's had been, and his daughter's was, golden as morning. But it was not this reflection on his hair that arrested him; it was the double use of the word light. For the king hated all witticisms, and punning especially. And besides, he could not tell whether the queen meant light haired or light heired; for why might she not aspirate her vowels when she was ex-aspirated herself?

He turned upon his other heel, and rejoined her. She looked angry still, because she knew that she was guilty, or, what was much the same, knew that he thought so.

"My dear queen," said he, "duplicity of any sort is exceedingly objectionable between married people of any rank, not to say kings and queens; and the most objectionable form duplicity can assume is that of punning."

"There!" said the queen, "I never made a jest, but I broke it in the making. I am the most unfortunate woman in the world!"

She looked so rueful, that the king took her in his arms; and they sat down to consult.

"Can you bear this?" said the king.

"No, I can't," said the queen.

"Well, what's to be done?" said the king.

"I'm sure I don't know," said the queen. "But might you not try an apology?"

"To my old sister, I suppose you mean?" said the king.

"Yes," said the queen.

"Well, I don't mind," said the king.

So he went the next morning to the house of the princess, and, making a very humble apology, begged her to undo the spell. But the princess declared, with a grave face, that she knew nothing at all about it. Her eyes, however, shone pink, which was a sign that she was happy. She advised the king and queen to have patience, and to mend their ways. The king returned disconsolate. The queen tried to comfort him.

"We will wait till she is older. She may then be able to suggest something herself. She will know at least how she feels, and explain things to us."

"But what if she should marry?" exclaimed the king, in sudden consternation at the idea.

"Well, what of that?" rejoined the queen. "Just think! If she were to have children! In the course of a hundred years the air might be as full of floating children as of gossamers in autumn."

"That is no business of ours," replied the queen. "Besides, by that time they will have learned to take care of themselves."

A sigh was the king's only answer.

He would have consulted the court physicians; but he was afraid they would try experiments upon her.

6. SHE LAUGHS TOO MUCH

Meantime, notwithstanding awkward occurrences, and griefs that she brought upon her parents, the little princess laughed and grew—not fat, but plump and tall. She reached the age of seventeen, without having fallen into any worse scrape than a chimney; by rescuing her from which, a little bird-nesting urchin got fame and a black face. Nor, thoughtless as she was, had she committed anything worse than laughter at everybody and everything that came in her way. When she was told, for the sake of experiment, that General Clanrunfort was cut to pieces with all his troops, she laughed; when she heard that the enemy was on his way to besiege her papa's capital, she laughed hugely; but when she was told that the city would certainly be abandoned to the mercy of the enemy's soldiery - why, then she laughed immoderately. She never could be brought to see the serious side of anything. When her mother cried, she said,-

"What queer faces mamma makes! And she squeezes water out of her cheeks? Funny mamma!"

And when her papa stormed at her, she laughed, and danced round and round him, clapping her hands, and crying,-

"Do it again, papa. Do it again! It's such fun! Dear, funny papa!"

And if he tried to catch her, she glided from him in an instant, not in the least afraid of him, but thinking it part of the game not to be caught. With one push of her foot, she would be floating in the air above his head; or she would go dancing backwards and forwards and sideways, like a great butterfly. It happened several times, when her father and mother were holding a consultation about her in private, that they were interrupted by vainly repressed outbursts of laughter over their heads;

and looking up with indignation, saw her floating at full length in the air above them, whence she regarded them with the most comical appreciation of the position.

One day an awkward accident happened. The princess had come out upon the lawn with one of her attendants, who held her by the hand. Spying her father at the other side of the lawn, she snatched her hand from the maid's, and sped across to him. Now when she wanted to run alone, her custom was to catch up a stone in each hand, so that she might come down again after a bound. Whatever she wore as part of her attire had no effect in this way: even gold, when it thus became as it were a part of herself, lost all its weight for the time. But whatever she only held in her hands retained its downward tendency. On this occasion she could see nothing to catch up but a huge toad, that was walking across the lawn as if he had a hundred years to do it in. Not knowing what disgust meant, for this was one of her peculiarities, she snatched up the toad and bounded away. She had almost reached her father, and he was holding out his arms to receive her, and take from her lips the kiss which hovered on them like a butterfly on a rosebud, when a puff of wind blew her aside into the arms of a young page, who had just been receiving a message from his Majesty. Now it was no great peculiarity in the princess that, once she was set a going, it always cost her time and trouble to check herself. On this occasion there was no time. She must kiss - and she kissed the page. She did not mind it much; for she had no shyness in her composition; and she knew, besides, that she could not help it. So she only laughed, like a musical box. The poor page fared the worst. For the princess, trying to correct the unfortunate tendency of the kiss, put out her hands to keep her off the page; so that, along with the kiss, he received, on the other cheek, a slap with the huge black toad, which she poked right into his eye. He tried to laugh, too, but the attempt resulted in such an odd contortion of countenance, as showed that there was no danger of his pluming himself on the kiss. As for the king, his dignity was greatly hurt, and he did not speak to the page for a whole month.

I may here remark that it was very amusing to see her run, if her mode of progression could properly be called running. For first she would make a bound; then, having alighted, she would run a few steps, and make another bound. Sometimes she would fancy she had reached the ground before she actually had, and her feet would go backwards and forwards, running upon nothing at all, like those of a chicken on its back. Then she would laugh like the very spirit of fun; only in her laugh there was something missing. What it was, I find myself unable to describe. I think it was a certain tone, depending upon the possibility of sorrow - morbidezza, perhaps. She never smiled.

7. TRY METAPHYSICS.

After a long avoidance of the painful subject, the king and queen resolved to hold a council of three upon it; and so they sent for the princess. In she came, sliding and flitting and gliding from one piece of furniture to another, and put herself at last in an armchair, in a sitting posture. Whether she could be said to sit, seeing she received no support from the seat of the chair, I do not pretend to determine.

"My dear child," said the king, "you must be aware by this time that you are not exactly like other people."

"Oh, you dear funny papa! I have got a nose, and two eyes, and all the rest. So have you. So has mamma."

"Now be serious, my dear, for once," said the queen.

"No, thank you, mamma; I had rather not."

"Would you not like to be able to walk like other people?" said the king. "No indeed, I should think not. You only crawl. You are such slow coaches!"

"How do you feel, my child?" he resumed, after a pause of discomfiture.

"Quite well, thank you."

"I mean, what do you feel like?"

"Like nothing at all, that I know of."

"You must feel like something."

"I feel like a princess with such a funny papa, and such a dear pet of a queen-mamma!"

"Now really!" began the queen; but the princess interrupted her.

"Oh yes," she added, "I remember. I have a curious feeling sometimes, as if I were the only person that had any sense in the whole world."

She had been trying to behave herself with dignity; but now she burst into a violent fit of laughter, threw herself backwards over the chair, and went rolling about the floor in an ecstasy of enjoyment. The king picked her up easier than one does a down quilt, and replaced her in her former relation to the chair. The exact preposition expressing this relation I do not happen to know.

"Is there nothing you wish for?" resumed the king, who had learned by this time that it was quite useless to be angry with her.

"Oh, you dear papa!-yes," answered she.

"What is it, my darling?"

"I have been longing for it-oh, such a time! Ever since last night."

"Tell me what it is."

"Will you promise to let me have it?"

The king was on the point of saying Yes, but the wiser queen checked him with a single motion of her head.

"Tell me what it is first," said he.

"No no. Promise first."

"I dare not. What is it?"

"Mind, I hold you to your promise.-It is-to be tied to the end of a string-a very long string indeed, and be flown like a kite. Oh, such fun! I would rain rose-water, and hail sugar-plums, and snow Whipped-cream, and – and – and -"

A fit of laughing checked her; and she would have been off again over the floor, had not the king started up and caught her just in time. Seeing nothing but talk could be got out of her, he rang the bell, and sent her away with two of her ladies-in-waiting.

"Now, queen," he said, turning to her Majesty, "what is to be done?"

"There is but one thing left," answered she. "Let us consult the college of Metaphysicians."

"Bravo!" cried the king; "we will."

Now at the head of this college were two very wise Chinese philosophers-by name, Hum-Drum and Kopy-Keck. For them the king sent; and straightway they came. In a long speech he communicated to them what they knew very well already-as who did not?-namely, the peculiar condition of his daughter in relation to the globe on which she dwelt; and requested them to consult together as to what might be the cause and probable cure of her infirmity. The king laid stress upon the word, but failed to discover his own pun. The queen laughed; but Hum-Drum and Kopy-Keck heard with humility and retired in silence.

The consultation consisted chiefly in propounding and supporting, for the thousandth time, each his favorite theories. For the condition of the princess afforded delightful scope for the discussion of every question arising from the division of thought - in fact, of all the Metaphysics of the Chinese Empire. But it is only justice to say that they did not altogether neglect the discussion of the practical question, what was to be done.

Hum-Drum was a Materialist, and Kopy-Keck was a spiritualist. The former was slow and sententious; the latter was quick and flighty: the latter had generally the first word; the former the last.

"I reassert my former assertion," began Kopy-Keck, with a plunge. "There is not a fault in the princess, body or soul; only they are wrong put together. Listen to me now, Hum-Drum, and I will tell you in brief what I think. Don't speak. Don't answer me. I won't hear you till I have done. - At that decisive moment, when souls seek their appointed habitations, two eager souls met, struck, rebounded, lost their way, and arrived each at the wrong place. The soul of the princess was one of those, and she went far astray. She does not belong by rights to this world at all, but to some other planet, probably Mercury. Her proclivity to her true sphere destroys all the natural influence which this orb would otherwise possess over her corporeal frame. She cares for nothing here. There is no relation between her and this world.

"She must therefore be taught, by the sternest compulsion, to take an interest in the earth as the earth. She must study every department of its history-its animal history; its vegetable history; its mineral history; its social history; its moral history; its political history; its scientific history; its literary history; its musical history; its artistical history; above all, its metaphysical history. She must begin with the Chinese dynasty and end with Japan. But first of all she must study geology, and especially the history of the extinct races of animals - their natures, their habits, their loves, their hates, their revenges. She must -"

"Hold, h-o-o-old!" roared Hum-Drum. "It is certainly my turn now. My rooted and insubvertible conviction is, that the causes of the anomalies evident in the princess's condition are strictly and solely physical. But that is only tantamount to acknowledging that they exist. Hear my opinion.- From some cause or other, of no importance to our inquiry, the motion of her heart has been reversed. That remarkable combination of the suction and the force-pump works the wrong way – I mean in the case of the princess: it draws in where it should force out, and forces out where it should draw in. The offices of the auricles and the ventricles are subverted. The blood is sent forth by the veins, and returns by the arteries. Consequently it is running the wrong way through all her corporeal organism-lungs and all. Is it then at all mysterious, seeing that such is the case, that on the other particular of gravitation as well, she should differ from normal humanity? My proposal for the cure is this:-

"Phlebotomize until she is reduced to the last point of safety. Let it be affected, if necessary, in a warm bath. When she is reduced to a state of perfect asphyxy, apply a ligature to the left ankle, drawing it as tight as the bone will bear. Apply, at the same moment, another of equal tension around the right wrist. By means of plates constructed for the purpose, place the other foot and hand under the receivers of two air-pumps. Exhaust the receivers. Exhibit a pint of French brandy, and await the result."

"Which would presently arrive in the form of grim death," said Kopy-Keck.

"If it should, she would yet die in doing our duty," retorted Hum-Drum.

But their Majesties had too much tenderness for their volatile offspring to subject her to either of the schemes of the equally unscrupulous philosophers. Indeed, the most complete knowledge of the laws of nature would have been unserviceable in her case; for it was impossible to classify her. She was a fifth imponderable body, sharing all the other properties of the ponderable.

8. Try A Drop Of Water.

Perhaps the best thing for the princess would have been to fall in love. But how a princess who had no gravity could fall into anything is a difficulty - perhaps the difficulty. As for her own feelings on the subject, she did not even know that there was such a beehive of honey and stings to be fallen into. But now I come to mention another curious fact about her.

The palace was built on the shore of the loveliest lake in the world; and the princess loved this lake more than father or mother. The root of this preference no doubt, although the princess did not recognize it as such, was, that the moment she got into it, she recovered the natural right of which she had been so wickedly deprived-namely, gravity. Whether this was owing to the fact that water had been employed as the means of conveying the injury, I do not know. But it is certain that she could swim and dive like the duck that her old nurse said she was. The manner in which this alleviation of her misfortune was discovered was as follows:

One summer evening, during the carnival of the country, she had been taken upon the lake by the king and queen, in the royal barge. They were accompanied by many of the courtiers in a fleet of little boats. In the middle of the lake she wanted to get into the Lord Chancellor's barge, for his daughter, who was a great favorite with her, was in it with her father. Now though the old king rarely condescended to make light of his misfortune, yet, happening on this occasion to be in a particularly good humor, as the barges approached each other, he caught up the princess to throw her into the chancellor's barge. He lost his balance, however, and, dropping into the bottom of the barge, lost his hold of his daughter; not, however, before imparting to her the downward tendency of his own person, though in a somewhat different direction; for, as the king fell into the boat, she fell into the water. With a burst of delightful laughter she disappeared in the lake. A cry of horror ascended from the boats. They had never seen the princess go down before. Half the men were under water in a moment; but they had all, one after another, come up to the surface again for breath, when-tinkle, tinkle, babble, and gush! came the princess's laugh over the water from far away. There she was, swimming like a swan. Nor would she come out for king or queen, chancellor or daughter. She was perfectly obstinate.

But at the same time she seemed more sedate than usual. Perhaps that was because a great pleasure spoils laughing. At all events, after this, the passion of her life was to get into the water, and she was always the better behaved and the more beautiful the more she had of it. Summer and winter it was quite the same; only she could not stay so long in the water when they had to break the ice to let her in. Any day, from morning till evening in summer, she might be descried – a streak of white in the blue water-lying as still as the shadow of a cloud, or shooting along like a dolphin; disappearing, and coming up again far off, just where one did not expect her. She would have been in the lake of a night, too, if she could have had her way; for the balcony of her window overhung a deep pool in it; and through a shallow reedy passage she could have swum out into the wide wet water, and no one would have been any the wiser. Indeed, when she happened to wake in the moonlight she could hardly resist the temptation. But there was the sad difficulty of getting into it.

She had as great a dread of the air as some children have of the water. For the slightest gust of wind would blow her away; and a gust might arise in the stillest moment. And if she gave herself a push towards the water and just failed of reaching it, her situation would be dreadfully awkward, irrespective of the wind; for at best there she would have to remain, suspended in her night-gown, till she was seen and angled for by someone from the window.

"Oh! if I had my gravity," thought she, contemplating the water, "I would flash off this balcony like a long white sea-bird, headlong into the darling wetness. Heigh-ho!"

This was the only consideration that made her wish to be like other people.

Another reason for her being fond of the water was that in it alone she enjoyed any freedom. For she could not walk out without a cortege, consisting in part of a troop of light horse, for fear of the liberties which the wind might take with her. And the king grew more apprehensive with increasing years, till at last he would not allow her to walk abroad at all without some twenty silken cords fastened to as many parts of her dress, and held by twenty noblemen. Of course horseback was out of the question. But she bade good-bye to all this ceremony when she got into the water.

And so remarkable were its effects upon her, especially in restoring her for the time to the ordinary human gravity, that Hum-Drum and Kopy-Keck agreed in recommending the king to bury her alive for three years; in the hope that, as the water did her so much good, the earth would do her yet more. But the king had some vulgar prejudices against the experiment, and would not give his consent. Foiled in this, they yet agreed in another recommendation; which, seeing that the one imported his opinions from China and the other from Thibet, was very remarkable indeed. They argued that, if water of external origin and application could be so efficacious, water from a deeper source might work a perfect cure; in short, that if the poor afflicted princess could by any means be made to cry, she might recover her lost gravity.

But how was this to be brought about? Therein lay all the difficulty-to meet which the philosophers were not wise enough. To make the princess cry was as impossible as to make her weigh. They sent for a professional beggar; commanded him to prepare his most touching oracle of woe; helped him, out of the court charade-box, to whatever he wanted for dressing up; and promised great rewards in the event of his success. But it was all in vain. She listened to the mendicant artist's story, and gazed at his marvelous make-up, till she could contain herself no longer, and went into the most undignified contortions for relief, shrieking, positively screeching with laughter.

When she had a little recovered herself, she ordered her attendants to drive him away, and not give him a single copper; whereupon his look of mortified discomfiture wrought her punishment and his revenge, for it sent her into violent hysterics, from which she was with difficulty recovered.

But so anxious was the king that the suggestion should have a fair trial, that he put himself in a rage one day, and, rushing up to her room, gave her an awful whipping. Yet not a tear would flow. She looked grave, and her laughing sounded uncommonly like screaming-that was all. The good old tyrant, though he put on his best gold spectacles to look, could not discover the smallest cloud in the serene blue of her eyes.

9. PUT ME IN AGAIN.

It must have been about this time that the son of a king, who lived a thousand miles from Lagobel, set out to look for the daughter of a queen. He traveled far and wide, but as sure as he found a princess, he found some fault in her. Of course he could not marry a mere woman, however beautiful; and there was no princess to be found worthy of him. Whether the prince was so near perfection that he had a right to demand perfection itself, I cannot pretend to say. All I know is, that he was a fine, handsome, brave, generous, well-bred, and well-behaved youth, as all princes are.

In his wanderings he had come across some reports about our princess; but as everybody said she was bewitched, he never dreamed that she could bewitch him. For what indeed could a prince do with a princess that had lost her gravity? Who could tell what she might not lose next? She might lose her visibility, or her tangibility; or, in short, the power of making impressions upon the radical sensorium; so that he should never be able to tell whether she was dead or alive. Of course he made no further inquiries about her.

One day he lost sight of his retinue in a great forest. These forests are very useful in delivering princes from their courtiers, like a sieve that keeps back the bran. Then the princes get away to follow their fortunes. In this they have the advantage of the princesses, who are forced to marry before they have had a bit of fun. I wish our princesses got lost in a forest sometimes.

One lovely evening, after wandering about for many days, he found that he was approaching the outskirts of this forest; for the trees had got so thin that he could see the sunset through them; and he soon came upon a kind of heath. Next he came upon signs of human neighborhood; but by this time it was getting late, and there was nobody in the fields to direct him.

After traveling for another hour, his horse, quite worn out with long labor and lack of food, fell, and was unable to rise again. So he continued his journey on foot. At length he entered another wood–not a wild forest, but a civilized wood, through which a footpath led him to the side of a lake. Along this path the prince pursued his way through the gathering darkness. Suddenly he paused, and listened. Strange sounds came across the water. It was, in fact, the princess laughing. Now there was something odd in her laugh, as I have already hinted, for the hatching of a real hearty laugh requires the incubation of gravity; and perhaps this was how the prince mistook the laughter for screaming. Looking over the lake, he saw something white in the water; and, in an instant, he had torn off his tunic, kicked off his sandals, and plunged in. He soon reached the white object, and found that it was a woman. There was not light enough to show that she was a princess, but quite enough to show that she was a lady, for it does not want much light to see that.

Now I cannot tell how it came about, - whether she pretended to be drowning, or whether he frightened her, or caught her so as to embarrass her, - but certainly he brought her to shore in a fashion ignominious to a swimmer, and more nearly drowned than she had ever expected to be; for the water had got into her throat as often as she had tried to speak.

At the place to which he bore her, the bank was only a foot or two above the water, so he gave her a strong lift out of the water, to lay her on the bank. But, her gravitation ceasing the moment she left the water, away she went up into the air, scolding and screaming.

"You naughty, naughty, NAUGHTY, NAUGHTY man!" she cried.

No one had ever succeeded in putting her into a passion before. When the prince saw her ascend, he thought he must have been bewitched, and have mistaken a great swan for a lady. But the princess caught hold of the topmost cone upon a lofty fir. This came off; but she caught at another, and, in fact, stopped herself by gathering cones, dropping them as the stocks gave way. The prince, meantime, stood in the water, staring, and forgetting to get out. But the princess disappearing, he scrambled on shore, and went in the direction of the tree. There he found her climbing down one of the branches towards the stem. But in the darkness of the wood, the prince continued in some bewilderment as to what the phenomenon could be; until, reaching the ground, and seeing him standing there, she caught hold of him, and said, -

"I'll tell papa."

"Oh no, you won't!" returned the prince.

"Yes, I will," she persisted. "What business had you to pull me down out of the water, and throw me to the bottom of the air? I never did you any harm."

"Pardon me. I did not mean to hurt you."

"I don't believe you have any brains; and that is a worse loss that your wretched gravity. I pity you."

The prince now saw that he had come upon the bewitched princess, and had already offended her. But before he could think what to say next, she burst out angrily, giving a stamp with her foot that would have sent her aloft again but for the hold she had of his arm, -

"Put me up directly."

"Put you up where, you beauty?" asked the prince.

He had fallen in love with her almost, already; for her anger made her more charming than any one else had ever beheld her; and, as far as he could see, which certainly was not far, she had not a single fault about her, except, of course, that she had not any gravity. No prince, however, would judge of a princess by weight. The loveliness of her foot he would hardly estimate by the depth of the impression it could make in the mud.

"Put you up where, you beauty?" asked the prince.

"In the water, you stupid!" answered the princess.

"Come, then," said the prince.

The condition of her dress, increasing her usual difficulty in walking, compelled her to cling to him; and he could hardly persuade himself that he was not in a delightful dream, notwithstanding the torrent of musical abuse with which she overwhelmed him. The prince being therefore in no hurry, they came upon the lake at quite another part, where the bank was twenty-five feet high at least; and when they had reached the edge, he turned towards the princess, and said, -

"How am I to put you in?"

"That is your business," she answered, quite snappishly. "You took me out - put me in again."

"Very well," said the prince; and, catching her up in his arms, he sprang with her from the rock. The princess had just time to give one delighted shriek of laughter before the water closed over them. When they came to the surface, she found that, for a moment or two, she could not even laugh, for she had gone down with such a rush, that it was with difficulty she recovered her breath. The instant they reached the surface -

"How do you like falling in?" said the prince.

After some effort the princess panted out, -

"Is that what you call falling in?"

"Yes," answered the prince, "I should think it a very tolerable specimen."

"It seemed to me like going up," rejoined she.

"My feeling was certainly one of elevation too," the prince conceded.

The princess did not appear to understand him, for she retorted his question: -

"How do you like falling in?" said the princess.

"Beyond everything," answered he; "for I have fallen in with the only perfect creature I ever saw."

"No more of that: I am tired of it," said the princess.

Perhaps she shared her father's aversion to punning.

"Don't you like falling in, then?" said the prince.

"It is the most delightful fun I ever had in my life," answered she. "I never fell before. I wish I could learn. To think I am the only person in my father's kingdom that can't fall!"

Here the poor princess looked almost sad.

"I shall be most happy to fall in with you any time you like," said the prince, devotedly.

"Thank you. I don't know. Perhaps it would not be proper. But I don't care. At all events, as we have fallen in, let us have a swim together."

"With all my heart," responded the prince.

And away they went, swimming, and diving, and floating, until at last they heard cries along the shore, and saw lights glancing in all directions. It was now quite late, and there was no moon.

"I must go home," said the princess. "I am very sorry, for this is delightful."

"So am I," returned the prince. "But I am glad I haven't a home to go to - at least, I don't exactly know where it is."

"I wish I hadn't one either," rejoined the princess; "it is so stupid! I have a great mind," she continued, "to play them all a trick. Why couldn't they leave me alone? They won't trust me in the lake for a single night!-You see where that green light is burning? That is the window of my room. Now if you would just swim there with me very quietly, and when we are all but under the balcony, give me such a push - up you call it - as you did a little while ago, I should be able to catch hold of the balcony, and get in at the window; and then they may look for me till to-morrow morning!"

"With more obedience than pleasure," said the prince, gallantly; and away they swam, very gently.

"Will you be in the lake to-morrow night?" the prince ventured to ask.

"To be sure I will. I don't think so. Perhaps," was the princess's somewhat strange answer.

But the prince was intelligent enough not to press her further; and merely whispered, as he gave her the parting lift, "Don't tell." The only answer the princess returned was a roguish look. She was already a yard above his head. The look seemed to say, "Never fear. It is too good fun to spoil that way."

So perfectly like other people had she been in the water, that even yet the prince could scarcely believe his eyes when he saw her ascend slowly, grasp the balcony, and disappear through the window. He turned, almost expecting to see her still by his side. But he was alone in the water. So he swam away quietly, and watched the lights roving about the shore for hours after the princess was safe in her chamber. As soon as they disappeared, he landed in search of his tunic and sword, and, after some trouble, found them again. Then he made the best of his way round the lake to the other side. There the wood was wilder, and the shore steeper-rising more immediately towards the mountains which surrounded the lake on all sides, and kept sending it messages of silvery streams from morning to night, and all night long. He soon found a spot whence he could see the green light in the princess's room, and where, even in the broad daylight, he would be in no danger of being discovered from the opposite shore. It was a sort of cave in the rock, where he provided himself a bed of withered leaves, and lay down too tired for hunger to keep him awake. All night long he dreamed that he was swimming with the princess.

10. LOOK AT THE MOON.

Early the next morning the prince set out to look for something to eat, which he soon found at a forester's hut, where for many following days he was supplied with all that a brave prince could consider necessary. And having plenty to keep him alive for the present, he would not think of wants not yet in existence. Whenever Care intruded, this prince always bowed him out in the most princely manner.

When he returned from his breakfast to his watch-cave, he saw the princess already floating about in the lake, attended by the king or queen-whom he knew by their crowns-and a great company in lovely little boats, with canopies of all the colors of the rainbow, and flags and streamers of a great many more. It was a very bright day, and soon the prince, burned up with the heat, began to long for the cold water and the cool princess. But he had to endure till twilight; for the boats had provisions on board, and it was not till the sun went down that the gay party began to vanish. Boat after boat drew away to the shore, following that of the king and queen, till only one, apparently the princess's own boat, remained. But she did not want to go home even yet, and the prince thought he saw her order the boat to the shore without her. At all events, it rowed away; and now, of all the radiant company, only one white speck remained. Then the prince began to sing.

And this is what he sang:-

"Lady fair,

Swan-white,

Lift thine eyes

Banish night

By the might

Of thine eyes.

Snowy arms,

Oars of snow,

Oar her hither,

Plashing low.

Soft and slow,

Oar her hither.

Stream behind her

O'er the lake,

Radiant whiteness!

In her wake

Following, following for her sake,

Radiant whiteness!

Cling about her,

Waters blue;

Part not from her,

But renew

Cold and true

Kisses round her.

Lap me round,

Waters sad

That have left her;

Make me glad,

For ye had

Kissed her ere ye left her."

Before he had finished his song, the princess was just under the place where he sat, and looking up to find him. Her ears had led her truly.

"Would you like a fall, princess?" said the prince, looking down.

"Ah! there you are! Yes, if you please, prince," said the princess, looking up.

"How do you know I am a prince, princess?" said the prince.

"Because you are a very nice young man, prince," said the princess.

"Come up then, princess."

"Fetch me, prince."

The prince took off his scarf, then his sword-belt, then his tunic, and tied them all together, and let them down. But the line was far too short. He unwound his turban, and added it to the rest, when it was all but long enough; and his purse completed it. The princess just managed to lay hold of the knot of money, and was beside him in a moment. This rock was much higher than the other, and the splash and the dive were tremendous. The princess was in ecstasies of delight, and their swim was delicious.

Night after night they met, and swam about in the dark clear lake; where such was the prince's gladness, that (whether the princess's way of looking at things infected him, or he was actually getting light-headed) he often fancied that he was swimming in the sky instead of the lake. But when he talked about being in heaven, the princess laughed at him dreadfully.

When the moon came, she brought them fresh pleasure. Everything looked strange and new in her light, with an old, withered, yet unfading newness. When the moon was nearly full, one of their great delights was, to dive deep in the water, and then, turning round, look up through it at the great blot of light close above them, shimmering and trembling and wavering, spreading and contracting, seeming to melt away, and again grow solid. Then they would shoot up through the blot; and lo! there was the moon, far off, clear and steady and cold, and very lovely, at the bottom of a deeper and bluer lake than theirs, as the princess said.

The prince soon found out that while in the water the princess was very like other people. And besides this, she was not so forward in her questions or pert in her replies at sea as on shore. Neither did she laugh so much; and when she did laugh, it was more gently. She seemed altogether more modest and maidenly in the water than out of it. But when the prince, who had really fallen in love when he fell in the lake, began to talk to her about love, she always turned her head towards him and laughed. After a while she began to look puzzled, as if she were trying to understand what he meant, but could not-revealing a notion that he meant something. But as soon as ever she left the lake, she was so altered, that the prince said to himself, "If I marry her, I see no help for it: we must turn merman and mermaid, and go out to sea at once."

11. Hiss!

The princess's pleasure in the lake had grown to a passion, and she could scarcely bear to be out of it for an hour. Imagine then her consternation, when, diving with the prince one night, a sudden suspicion seized her that the lake was not so deep as it used to be. The prince could not imagine what had happened. She shot to the surface, and, without a word, swam at full speed towards the higher side of the lake. He followed, begging to know if she was ill, or what was the matter. She never turned her head, or took the smallest notice of his question. Arrived at the shore, she coasted the rocks with minute inspection. But she was not able to come to a conclusion, for the moon was very small, and so she could not see well. She turned therefore and swam home, without saying a word to explain her conduct to the prince, of whose presence she seemed no longer conscious. He withdrew to his cave, in great perplexity and distress.

Next day she made many observations, which, alas! strengthened her fears. She saw that the banks were too dry; and that the grass on the shore, and the trailing plants on the rocks, were withering away. She caused marks to be made along the borders, and examined them, day after day, in all directions of the wind; till at last the horrible idea became a certain fact - that the surface of the lake was slowly sinking.

The poor princess nearly went out of the little mind she had. It was awful to her to see the lake, which she loved more than any living thing, lie dying before her eyes. It sank away, slowly vanishing. The tops of rocks that had never been seen till now, began to appear far down in the clear water. Before long they were dry in the sun. It was fearful to think of the mud that would soon lie there baking and festering, full of lovely creatures dying, and ugly creatures coming to life, like the unmaking of a world. And how hot the sun would be without any lake! She could not bear to swim in it any more, and began to pine away. Her life seemed bound up with it; and ever as the lake sank, she pined. People said she would not live an hour after the lake was gone.

But she never cried.

Proclamation was made to all the kingdom, that whosoever should discover the cause of the lake's decrease, would be rewarded after a princely fashion. Hum-Drum and Kopy-Keck applied themselves to their physics and metaphysics; but in vain. Not even they could suggest a cause.

Now the fact was that the old princess was at the root of the mischief. When she heard that her niece found more pleasure in the water than anyone else out of it, she went into a rage, and cursed herself for her want of foresight.

"But," said she, "I will soon set all right. The king and the people shall die of thirst; their brains shall boil and frizzle in their skulls before I will lose my revenge."

And she laughed a ferocious laugh, that made the hairs on the back of her black cat stand erect with terror.

Then she went to an old chest in the room, and opening it, took out what looked like a piece of dried seaweed. This she threw into a tub of water. Then she threw some powder into the water, and stirred it with her bare arm, muttering over it words of hideous sound, and yet more hideous import. Then she set the tub aside, and took from the chest a huge bunch of a hundred rusty keys, that clattered in her shaking hands. Then she sat down and proceeded to oil them all. Before she had finished, out from the tub, the water of which had kept on a slow motion ever since she had ceased stirring it, came the head and half the body of a huge gray snake. But the witch did not look round. It grew out of the tub, waving itself backwards and forwards with a slow horizontal motion, till it reached the princess, when it laid its head upon her shoulder, and gave a low hiss in her ear. She started - but with joy; and seeing the head resting on her shoulder, drew it towards her and kissed it. Then she drew it all out of the tub, and wound it round her body. It was one of those dreadful creatures which few have ever beheld-the White Snakes of Darkness.

Then she took the keys and went down to her cellar; and as she unlocked the door she said to herself, -

"This is worth living for!"

Locking the door behind her, she descended a few steps into the cellar, and crossing it, unlocked another door into a dark, narrow passage. She locked this also behind her, and descended a few more steps. If anyone had followed the witch-princess, he would have heard her unlock exactly one hundred doors, and descend a few steps after unlocking each. When she had unlocked the last, she entered a vast cave, the roof of which was supported by huge natural pillars of rock. Now this roof was the under side of the bottom of the lake.

She then untwined the snake from her body, and held it by the tail high above her. The hideous creature stretched up its head towards the roof of the cavern, which it was just able to reach. It then began to move its head backwards and forwards, with a slow oscillating motion, as if looking for something. At the same moment the witch began to walk round and round the cavern, coming nearer to the centre every circuit; while the head of the snake described the same path over the roof that she did over the floor, for she kept holding it up. And still it kept slowly oscillating. Round and round the cavern they went, ever lessening the circuit, till at last the snake made a sudden dart, and clung to the roof with its mouth.

"That's right, my beauty!" cried the princess; "drain it dry."

She let it go, left it hanging, and sat down on a great stone, with her black cat, which had followed her all round the cave, by her side. Then she began to knit and mutter awful words. The snake hung like a huge leech, sucking at the stone; the cat stood with his back arched, and his tail like a piece of cable, looking up at the snake; and the old woman sat and knitted and muttered. Seven days and seven nights they remained thus; when suddenly the serpent dropped from the roof as if exhausted, and shriveled up till it was again like a piece of dried seaweed. The witch started to her feet, picked it up, put it in her pocket, and looked up at the roof. One drop of water was trembling on the spot where the snake had been sucking. As soon as she saw that, she turned and fled, followed by her cat. Shutting the door in a terrible hurry, she locked it, and having muttered some frightful words, sped to the next, which also she locked and muttered over; and so with all the hundred doors, till she arrived in her own cellar. There she sat down on the floor ready to faint, but listening with malicious delight to the rushing of the water, which she could hear distinctly through all the hundred doors.

But this was not enough. Now that she had tasted revenge, she lost her patience. Without further measures, the lake would be too long in disappearing. So the next night, with the last shred of the dying old moon rising, she took some of the water in which she had revived the snake, put it in a bottle, and set out, accompanied by her cat. Before morning she had made the entire circuit of the lake, muttering fearful words as she crossed every stream, and casting into it some of the water out of her bottle. When she had finished the circuit she muttered yet again, and flung a handful of water towards the moon. Thereupon every spring in the country ceased to throb and bubble, dying away like the pulse of a dying man. The next day there was no sound of falling water to be heard along the borders of the lake. The very courses were dry; and the mountains showed no silvery streaks down their dark sides. And not alone had the fountains of mother Earth ceased to flow; for all the babies throughout the country were crying dreadfully-only without tears.

12. WHERE IS THE PRINCE?

Never since the night when the princess left him so abruptly had the prince had a single interview with her. He had seen her once or twice in the lake; but as far as he could discover, she had not been in it any more at night. He had sat and sung, and looked in vain for his Nereid; while she, like a true Nereid, was wasting away with her lake, sinking as it sank, withering as it dried. When at length he discovered the change that was taking place in the level of the water, he was in great alarm and perplexity. He could not tell whether the lake was dying because the lady had forsaken it; or whether the lady would not come because the lake had begun to sink. But he resolved to know so much at least.

He disguised himself, and, going to the palace, requested to see the lord chamberlain. His appearance at once gained his request; and the lord chamberlain, being a man of some insight, perceived that there was more in the prince's solicitation than met the ear. He felt likewise that no one could tell whence a solution of the present difficulties might arise. So he granted the prince's prayer to be made shoe-black to the princess. It was rather cunning in the prince to request such an easy post, for the princess could not possibly soil as many shoes as other princesses. He soon learned all that could be learned about the princess. He went nearly distracted; but after roaming about the lake for days, and diving in every depth that remained, all that he could do was to put an extra polish on the dainty pair of boots that was never called for.

For the princess kept her room, with the curtains drawn to shut out the dying lake. But she could not shut it out of her mind for a moment. It haunted her imagination so that she felt as if the lake were her soul, drying up within her, first to mud, then to madness and death. She thus brooded over the change, with all its dreadful accompaniments, till she was nearly distracted. As for the prince, she had forgotten him. However much she had enjoyed his company in the water, she did not care for him without it. But she seemed to have forgotten her father and mother too. The lake went on sinking. Small slimy spots began to appear, which glittered steadily amidst the changeful shine of the water. These grew to broad patches of mud, which widened and spread, with rocks here and there, and floundering fishes and crawling eels swarming. The people went everywhere catching these, and looking for anything that might have dropped from the royal boats.

At length the lake was all but gone, only a few of the deepest pools remaining unexhausted.

It happened one day that a party of youngsters found themselves on the brink of one of these pools in the very centre of the lake. It was a rocky basin of considerable depth. Looking in, they saw at the bottom something that shone yellow in the sun. A little boy jumped in and dived for it. It was a plate of gold covered with writing. They carried it to the king.

On one side of it stood these words: -

"Death alone from death can save.

Love is death, and so is brave.

Love can fill the deepest grave.

Love loves on beneath the wave."

Now this was enigmatical enough to the king and courtiers. But the reverse of the plate explained it a little. Its writing amounted to this: -

"If the lake should disappear, they must find the hole through which the water ran. But it would be useless to try to stop it by any ordinary means. There was but one effectual mode.-The body of a living man could alone stanch the flow. The man must give himself of his own will; and the lake must take his life as it filled. Otherwise the offering would be of no avail. If the nation could not provide one hero, it was time it should perish."

13. HERE I AM

This was a very disheartening revelation to the king-not that he was unwilling to sacrifice a subject, but that he was hopeless of finding a man willing to sacrifice himself. No time was to be lost, however, for the princess was lying motionless on her bed, and taking no nourishment but lake -water, which was now none of the best. Therefore the king caused the contents of the wonderful plate of gold to be published throughout the country.

No one, however, came forward.

The prince, having gone several days' journey into the forest, to consult a hermit whom he had met there on his way to Lagobel, knew nothing of the oracle till his return.

When he had acquainted himself with all the particulars, he sat down and thought, -

"She will die if I don't do it, and life would be nothing to me without her; so I shall lose nothing by doing it. And life will be as pleasant to her as ever, for she will soon forget me. And there will be so much more beauty and happiness in the world!-To be sure, I shall not see it." (Here the poor prince gave a sigh.) "How lovely the lake will be in the moonlight, with that glorious creature sporting in it like a wild goddess!-It is rather hard to be drowned by inches, though. Let me see-that will be seventy inches of me to drown." (Here he tried to laugh, but could not.) "The longer the better, however," he resumed, "for can I not bargain that the princess shall be beside me all the time? So I shall see her once more, kiss her, perhaps,-who knows? And die looking in her eyes. It will be no death. At least, I shall not feel it. And to see the lake filling for the beauty again!-All right!

I am ready."

He kissed the princess's boot, laid it down, and hurried to the king's apartment. But feeling, as he went, that anything sentimental would be disagreeable, he resolved to carry off the whole affair with nonchalance. So he knocked at the door of the king's counting-house, where it was all but a capital crime to disturb him.

When the king heard the knock he started up, and opened the door in a rage. Seeing only the shoeblack, he drew his sword. This, I am sorry to say, was his usual mode of asserting his regality, when he thought his dignity was in danger. But the prince was not in the least alarmed.

"Please your majesty, I'm your butler," said he.

"My butler! you lying rascal? What do you mean?"

"I mean, I will cork your big bottle."

"Is the fellow mad?" bawled the king, raising the point of his sword.

"I will put a stopper-plug-what you call it, in your leaky lake, grand monarch," said the prince.

The king was in such a rage that before he could speak he had time to cool, and to reflect that it would be great waste to kill the only man who was willing to be useful in the present emergency, seeing that in the end the insolent fellow would be as dead as if he had died by his majesty's own hand. "Oh!" said he at last, putting up his sword with difficulty, it was so long; "I am obliged to you, you young fool! Take a glass of wine?"

"No, thank you," replied the prince.

"Very well," said the king. "Would you like to run and see your parents before you make your experiment?"

"No, thank you," said the prince.

"Then we will go and look for the hole at once," said his majesty, and proceeded to call some attendants.

"Stop, please your majesty; I have a condition to make," interposed the prince.

"What!" exclaimed the king, "a condition! and with me! How dare you?"

"As you please," returned the prince coolly. "I wish your majesty a good morning."

"You wretch! I will have you put in a sack, and stuck in the hole."

"Very well, your majesty," replied the prince, becoming a little more respectful, lest the wrath of the king should deprive him of the pleasure of dying for the princess. "But what good will that do your majesty? Please to remember that the oracle says the victim must offer himself."

"Well, you have offered yourself," retorted the king.

"Yes, upon one condition."

"Condition again!" roared the king, once more drawing his sword. "Be gone! Somebody else will be glad enough to take the honor off your shoulders."

"Your majesty knows it will not be easy to get another to take my place."

"Well, what is your condition?" growled the king, feeling that the prince was right.

"Only this," replied the prince: "that, as I must on no account die before I am fairly drowned, and the waiting will be rather wearisome, the princess, your daughter, shall go with me, feed me with her own hands, and look at me now and then, to comfort me; for you must confess it is rather hard. As soon as the water is up to my eyes, she may go and be happy, and forget her poor shoeblack."

Here the prince's voice faltered, and he very nearly grew sentimental, in spite of his resolution.

"Why didn't you tell me before what your condition was? Such a fuss about nothing!" exclaimed the king.

"Do you grant it?" persisted the prince.

"Of course I do," replied the king.

"Very well. I am ready."

"Go and have some dinner, then, while I set my people to find the place."

The king ordered out his guards, and gave directions to the officers to find the hole in the lake at once. So the bed of the lake was marked out in divisions and thoroughly examined, and in an hour or so the hole was discovered. It was in the middle of a stone, near the centre of the lake, in the very pool where the golden plate had been found. It was a three-cornered hole of no great size. There was water all round the stone, but very little was flowing through the hole.

14. THIS IS VERY KIND OF YOU.

The prince went to dress for the occasion, for he was resolved to die like a prince.

When the princess heard that a man had offered to die for her, she was so transported that she jumped off the bed, feeble as she was, and danced about the room for joy. She did not care who the man was; that was nothing to her. The hole wanted stopping; and if only a man would do, why, take one. In an hour or two more everything was ready. Her maid dressed her in haste, and they carried her to the side of the lake. When she saw it she shrieked, and covered her face with her hands. They bore her across to the stone, where they had already placed a little boat for her. The water was not deep enough to float it, but they hoped it would be, before long. They laid her on cushions, placed in the boat wines and fruits and other nice things, and stretched a canopy over all.

In a few minutes the prince appeared. The princess recognized him at once, but did not think it worth while to acknowledge him.

"Here I am," said the prince. "Put me in."

"They told me it was a shoeblack," said the princess.

"So I am," said the prince. "I blacked your little boots three times a day, because they were all I could get of you. Put me in."

The courtiers did not resent his bluntness, except by saying to each other that he was taking it out in impudence.

But how was he to be put in? The golden plate contained no instructions on this point. The prince looked at the hole, and saw but one way. He put both his legs into it, sitting on the stone, and, stooping forward, covered the corner that remained open with his two hands. In this uncomfortable position he resolved to abide his fate, and turning to the people, said, -

"Now you can go."

The king had already gone home to dinner.

"Now you can go," repeated the princess after him, like a parrot.

The people obeyed her and went.

Presently a little wave flowed over the stone, and wetted one of the prince's knees. But he did not mind it much. He began to sing, and the song he sung was this: -

"As a world that has no well,
Darkly bright in forest dell;
As a world without the gleam
Of the downward-going stream;
As a world without the glance
Of the ocean's fair expanse;
As a world where never rain
Glittered on the sunny plain;-
Such, my heart, thy world would be,
If no love did flow in thee.

"As a world without the sound
Of the rivulets underground;
Or the bubbling of the spring
Out of darkness wandering;
Or the mighty rush and flowing
Of the river's downward going;
Or the music-showers that drop
On the outspread beech's top;
Or the ocean's mighty voice,
When his lifted waves rejoice;-
Such, my soul, thy world would be,
If no love did sing in thee.
"Lady, keep thy world's delight;
Keep the waters in thy sight.
Love hath made me strong to go,
For thy sake, to realms below,
Where the water's shine and hum
Through the darkness never come:
Let, I pray, one thought of me
Spring, a little well, in thee;
Lest thy loveless soul be found
Like a dry and thirsty ground."

"Sing again, prince. It makes it less tedious," said the princess.

But the prince was too much overcome to sing any more, and a long pause followed.

"This is very kind of you, prince," said the princess at last, quite coolly, as she lay in the boat with her eyes shut.

"I am sorry I can't return the compliment," thought the prince; "but you are worth dying for, after all."

Again a wavelet, and another, and another flowed over the stone, and wetted both the prince's knees; but he did not speak or move. Two-three-four hours passed in this way, the princess apparently asleep, and the prince very patient. But he was much disappointed in his position, for he had none of the consolation he had hoped for.

At last he could bear it no longer.

"Princess!" said he.

But at the moment up started the princess, crying,-

"I'm afloat! I'm afloat!"

And the little boat bumped against the stone.

"Princess!" repeated the prince, encouraged by seeing her wide awake and looking eagerly at the water.

"Well?" said she, without looking round.

"Your papa promised that you should look at me, and you haven't looked at me once."

"Did he? Then I suppose I must. But I am so sleepy!"

"Sleep then, darling, and don't mind me," said the poor prince.

"Really, you are very good," replied the princess. "I think I will go to sleep again."

"Just give me a glass of wine and a biscuit first," said the prince, very humbly.

"With all my heart," said the princess, and gaped as she said it.

She got the wine and the biscuit, however, and leaning over the side of the boat towards him, was compelled to look at him.

"Why, prince," she said, "you don't look well! Are you sure you don't mind it?"

"Not a bit," answered he, feeling very faint in deed. "Only I shall die before it is of any use to you, unless I have something to eat."

"There, then," said she, holding out the wine to him.

"Ah! you must feed me. I dare not move my hands. The water would run away directly."

"Good gracious!" said the princess; and she began at once to feed him with bits of biscuit and sips of wine.

As she fed him, he contrived to kiss the tips of her fingers now and then. She did not seem to mind it, one way or the other. But the prince felt better.

"Now for your own sake, princess," said he, "I cannot let you go to sleep. You must sit and look at me, else I shall not be able to keep up."

"Well, I will do anything I can to oblige you," answered she, with condescension; and, sitting down, she did look at him, and kept looking at him with wonderful steadiness, considering all things.

The sun went down, and the moon rose, and, gush after gush, the waters were rising up the prince's body. They were up to his waist now.

"Why can't we go and have a swim?" said the princess. "There seems to be water enough just about here."

"I shall never swim more," said the prince.

"Oh, I forgot," said the princess, and was silent.

So the water grew and grew, and rose up and up on the prince. And the princess sat and looked at him. She fed him now and then. The night wore on. The waters rose and rose. The moon rose likewise higher and higher, and shone full on the face of the dying prince. The water was up to his neck.

"Will you kiss me, princess?" said he, feebly. The nonchalance was all gone now.

"Yes, I will," answered the princess, and kissed him with a long, sweet, cold kiss.

"Now," said he, with a sigh of content, "I die happy."

He did not speak again. The princess gave him some wine for the last time: he was past eating. Then she sat down again, and looked at him. The water rose and rose. It touched his chin. It touched his lower lip. It touched between his lips. He shut them hard to keep it out. The princess began to feel strange. It touched his upper lip. He breathed through his nostrils. The princess looked wild. It covered his nostrils. Her eyes looked scared, and shone strange in the moonlight. His head fell back; the water closed over it, and the bubbles of his last breath bubbled up through the water. The princess gave a shriek, and sprang into the lake.

She laid hold first of one leg, and then of the other, and pulled and tugged, but she could not move either. She stopped to take breath, and that made her think that he could not get any breath. She was frantic. She got hold of him, and held his head above the water, which was possible now his hands were no longer on the hole. But it was of no use, for he was past breathing.

Love and water brought back all her strength. She got under the water, and pulled and pulled with her whole might, till at last she got one leg out. The other easily followed. How she got him into the boat she never could tell; but when she did, she fainted away. Coming to herself, she seized the oars, kept herself steady as best she could, and rowed and rowed, though she had never rowed before. Round rocks, and over shallows, and through mud she rowed, till she got to the landing-stairs of the palace. By this time her people were on the shore, for they had heard her shriek. She made them carry the prince to her own room, and lay him in her bed, and light a fire, and send for the doctors.

"But the lake, your highness!" said the chamberlain, who, roused by the noise, came in, in his nightcap.

"Go and drown yourself in it!" she said.

This was the last rudeness of which the princess was ever guilty; and one must allow that she had good cause to feel provoked with the lord chamberlain.

Had it been the king himself, he would have fared no better. But both he and the queen were fast asleep. And the chamberlain went back to his bed. Somehow, the doctors never came. So the princess and her old nurse were left with the prince. But the old nurse was a wise woman, and knew what to do.

They tried everything for a long time without success. The princess was nearly distracted between hope and fear, but she tried on and on, one thing after another, and everything over and over again.

At last, when they had all but given it up, just as the sun rose, the prince opened his eyes.

15. LOOK AT THE RAIN!

The princess burst into a passion of tears, and fell on the floor. There she lay for an hour and her tears never ceased. All the pent-up crying of her life was spent now. And a rain came on, such as had never been seen in that country. The sun shone all the time, and the great drops, which fell straight to the earth, shone likewise. The palace was in the heart of a rainbow. It was a rain of rubies, and sapphires, and emeralds, and topazes. The torrents poured from the mountains like molten gold; and if it had not been for its subterraneous outlet, the lake would have overflowed and inundated the country. It was full from shore to shore.

But the princess did not heed the lake. She lay on the floor and wept. And this rain within doors was far more wonderful than the rain out of doors. For when it abated a little, and she proceeded to rise, she found, to her astonishment, that she could not. At length, after many efforts, she succeeded in getting upon her feet. But she tumbled down again directly. Hearing her fall, her old nurse uttered a yell of delight, and ran to her, screaming, -

"My darling child! she's found her gravity!"

"Oh, that's it! is it?" said the princess, rubbing her shoulder and her knee alternately. "I consider it very unpleasant. I feel as if I should be crushed to pieces."

"Hurrah!" cried the prince from the bed. "If you've come round, princess, so have I. How's the lake?"

"Brimful," answered the nurse.

"Then we're all happy."

"That we are indeed!" answered the princess, sobbing.

And there was rejoicing all over the country that rainy day. Even the babies forgot their past troubles, and danced and crowed amazingly. And the king told stories, and the queen listened to them. And he divided the money in his box, and she the honey in her pot, to all the children. And there was such jubilation as was never heard of before.

Of course the prince and princess were betrothed at once. But the princess had to learn to walk, before they could be married with any propriety. And this was not so easy at her time of life, for she could walk no more than a baby. She was always falling down and hurting herself.

"Is this the gravity you used to make so much of?" said she one day to the prince, as he raised her from the floor. "For my part, I was a great deal more comfortable without it."

"No, no, that's not it. This is it," replied the prince, as he took her up, and carried her about like a baby, kissing her all the time. "This is gravity."

"That's better," said she. "I don't mind that so much."

And she smiled the sweetest, loveliest smile in the prince's face. And she gave him one little kiss in return for all his; and he thought them overpaid, for he was beside himself with delight. I fear she complained of her gravity more than once after this, notwithstanding.

It was a long time before she got reconciled to walking. But the pain of learning it was quite counterbalanced by two things, either of which would have been sufficient consolation. The first was, that the prince himself was her teacher; and the second, that she could tumble into the lake as often as she pleased. Still, she preferred to have the prince jump in with her; and the splash they made before was nothing to the splash they made now.

The lake never sank again. In process of time, it wore the roof of the cavern quite through, and was twice as deep as before.

The only revenge the princess took upon her aunt was to tread pretty hard on her gouty toe the next time she saw her. But she was sorry for it the very next day, when she heard that the water had undermined her house, and that it had fallen in the night, burying her in its ruins; whence no one ever ventured to dig up her body. There she lies to this day.

So the prince and princess lived and were happy; and had crowns of gold, and clothes of cloth, and shoes of leather, and children of boys and girls, not one of whom was ever known, on the most critical occasion, to lose the smallest atom of his or her due proportion of gravity.

Book Four

Phantastes
A Faerie Romance for Men and Women

CRⅇ

"In good sooth, my masters, this is no door.
Yet is it a little window, that looks upon a great world."

PREFACE

For offering this new edition of my father's Phantastes, my reasons are three. The first is to rescue the work from an edition illustrated without the author's sanction, and so unsuitably that all lovers of the book must have experienced some real grief in turning its pages. With the copyright I secured also the whole of that edition and turned it into pulp. My second reason is to pay a small tribute to my father by way of personal gratitude for this, his first prose work, which was published nearly fifty years ago. Though unknown to many lovers of his greater writings, none of these has exceeded it in imaginative insight and power of expression. To me it rings with the dominant chord of his life's purpose and work. My third reason is that wider knowledge and love of the book should be made possible. To this end I have been most happy in the help of my father's old friend, who has illustrated the book. I know of no other living artist who is capable of portraying the spirit of Phantastes; and every reader of this edition will, I believe, feel that the illustrations are a part of the romance, and will gain through them some perception of the brotherhood between George MacDonald and Arthur Hughes.

GREVILLE MACDONALD.

September 1905.

CHAPTER ONE

I awoke one morning with the usual perplexity of mind which accompanies the return of consciousness. As I lay and looked through the eastern window of my room, a faint streak of peach color, dividing a cloud that just rose above the low swell of the horizon, announced the approach of the sun. As my thoughts, which a deep and apparently dreamless sleep had dissolved, began again to assume crystalline forms, the strange events of the foregoing night presented themselves anew to my wondering consciousness. The day before had been my one-and-twentieth birthday. Among other ceremonies investing me with my legal rights, the keys of an old secretary, in which my father had kept his private papers, had been delivered up to me. As soon as I was left alone, I ordered lights in the chamber where the secretary stood, the first lights that had been there for many a year; for, since my father's death, the room had been left undisturbed. But, as if the darkness had been too long an inmate to be easily expelled, and had dyed with blackness the walls to which, bat-like, it had clung, these tapers served but ill to light up the gloomy hangings, and seemed to throw yet darker shadows into the hollows of the deep-wrought cornice. All the further portions of the room lay shrouded in a mystery whose deepest folds were gathered around the dark oak cabinet which I now approached with a strange mingling of reverence and curiosity. Perhaps, like a geologist, I was about to turn up to the light some of the buried strata of the human world, with its fossil remains charred by passion and petrified by tears. Perhaps I was to learn how my father, whose personal history was unknown to me, had woven his web of story; how he had found the world, and how the world had left him. Perhaps I was to find only the records of lands and moneys, how gotten and how secured; coming down from strange men, and through troublous times, to me, who knew little or nothing of them all. To solve my speculations, and to dispel the awe which was fast gathering around me as if the dead were drawing near, I approached the secretary; and having found the key that fitted the upper portion, I opened it with some difficulty, drew near it a heavy high-backed chair, and sat down before a multitude of little drawers and slides and pigeon-holes. But the door of a little cupboard in the centre especially attracted my interest, as if there lay the secret of this long-hidden world. Its key I found.

One of the rusty hinges cracked and broke as I opened the door: it revealed a number of small pigeon-holes. These, however, being but shallow compared with the depth of those around the little cupboard, the outer ones reaching to the back of the desk, I concluded that there must be some accessible space behind; and found, indeed, that they were formed in a separate framework, which admitted of the whole being pulled out in one piece. Behind, I found a sort of flexible portcullis of small bars of wood laid close together horizontally. After long search, and trying many ways to move it, I discovered at last a scarcely projecting point of steel on one side. I pressed this repeatedly and hard with the point of an old tool that was lying near, till at length it yielded inwards; and the little slide, flying up suddenly, disclosed a chamber—empty, except that in one corner lay a little heap of withered rose-leaves, whose long- lived scent had long since departed; and, in another, a small packet of papers, tied with a bit of ribbon, whose color had gone with the rose-scent. Almost fearing to touch them, they witnessed so mutely to the law of oblivion, I leaned back in my chair, and regarded them for a moment; when suddenly there stood on the threshold of the little chamber, as though she had just emerged from its depth, a tiny woman-form, as perfect in shape as if she had been a small Greek statuette roused to life and motion. Her dress was of a kind that could never grow old- fashioned, because it was simply natural: a robe plaited in a band around the neck, and confined by a belt about the waist, descended to her feet. It was only afterwards, however, that I took notice of her dress, although my surprise was by no means of so overpowering a degree as such an apparition might naturally be expected to excite. Seeing, however, as I suppose, some astonishment in my countenance, she came forward within a yard of me, and said, in a voice that strangely recalled a sensation of twilight, and reedy river banks, and a low wind, even in this deathly room:—

"Anodos, you never saw such a little creature before, did you?"

"No," said I; "and indeed I hardly believe I do now."

"Ah! that is always the way with you men; you believe nothing the first time; and it is foolish enough to let mere repetition convince you of what you consider in itself unbelievable. I am not going to argue with you, however, but to grant you a wish."

Here I could not help interrupting her with the foolish speech, of which, however, I had no cause to repent —

"How can such a very little creature as you grant or refuse anything?"

"Is that all the philosophy you have gained in one-and-twenty years?" said she. "Form is much, but size is nothing. It is a mere matter of relation. I suppose your six-foot lordship does not feel altogether insignificant, though to others you do look small beside your old Uncle Ralph, who rises above you a great half-foot at least. But size is of so little consequence with old me, that I may as well accommodate myself to your foolish prejudices."

So saying, she leapt from the desk upon the floor, where she stood a tall, gracious lady, with pale face and large blue eyes. Her dark hair flowed behind, wavy but uncurled, down to her waist, and against it her form stood clear in its robe of white.

"Now," said she, "you will believe me."

Overcome with the presence of a beauty which I could now perceive, and drawn towards her by an attraction irresistible as incomprehensible, I suppose I stretched out my arms towards her, for she drew back a step or two, and said —

"Foolish boy, if you could touch me, I should hurt you. Besides, I was two hundred and thirty-seven years old, last Midsummer eve; and a man must not fall in love with his grandmother, you know."

"But you are not my grandmother," said I.

"How do you know that?" she retorted. "I dare say you know something of your great-grandfathers a good deal further back than that; but you know very little about your great-grandmothers on either side. Now, to the point. Your little sister was reading a fairy-tale to you last night."

"She was."

"When she had finished, she said, as she closed the book, `Is there a fairy-country, brother?' You replied with a sigh, `I suppose there is, if one could find the way into it.'"

"I did; but I meant something quite different from what you seem to think."

"Never mind what I seem to think. You shall find the way into Fairy Land to-morrow. Now look in my eyes."

Eagerly I did so. They filled me with an unknown longing. I remembered somehow that my mother died when I was a baby. I looked deeper and deeper, till they spread around me like seas, and I sank in their waters. I forgot all the rest, till I found myself at the window, whose gloomy curtains were withdrawn, and where I stood gazing on a whole heaven of stars, small and sparkling in the moonlight. Below lay a sea, still as death and hoary in the moon, sweeping into bays and around capes and islands, away, away, I knew not whither. Alas! it was no sea, but a low bog burnished by the moon. "Surely there is such a sea somewhere!" said I to myself. A low sweet voice beside me replied —

"In Fairy Land, Anodos."

I turned, but saw no one. I closed the secretary, and went to my own room, and to bed. All this I recalled as I lay with half-closed eyes. I was soon to find the truth of the lady's promise, that this day I should discover the road into Fairy Land.

CHAPTER TWO

While these strange events were passing through my mind, I suddenly, as one awakes to the consciousness that the sea has been moaning by him for hours, or that the storm has been howling about his window all night, became aware of the sound of running water near me; and, looking out of bed, I saw that a large green marble basin, in which I was wont to wash, and which stood on a low pedestal of the same material in a corner of my room, was overflowing like a spring; and that a stream of clear water was running over the carpet, all the length of the room, finding its outlet I knew not where. And, stranger still, where this carpet, which I had myself designed to imitate a field of grass and daisies, bordered the course of the little stream, the grass blades and daisies seemed to wave in a tiny breeze that followed the water's flow; while under the rivulet they bent and swayed with every motion of the changeful current, as if they were about to dissolve with it, and, forsaking their fixed form, become fluent as the waters.

My dressing-table was an old-fashioned piece of furniture of black oak, with drawers all down the front. These were elaborately carved in foliage, of which ivy formed the chief part. The nearer end of this table remained just as it had been, but on the further end a singular change had commenced. I happened to fix my eye on a little cluster of ivy-leaves. The first of these was evidently the work of the carver; the next looked curious; the third was unmistakable ivy; and just beyond it a tendril of clematis had twined itself about the gilt handle of one of the drawers. Hearing next a slight motion above me, I looked up, and saw that the branches and leaves designed upon the curtains of my bed were slightly in motion. Not knowing what change might follow next, I thought it high time to get up; and, springing from the bed, my bare feet alighted upon a cool green sward; and although I dressed in all haste, I found myself completing my toilet under the boughs of a great tree, whose top waved in the golden stream of the sunrise with many interchanging lights, and with shadows of leaf and branch gliding over leaf and branch, as the cool morning wind swung it to and fro, like a sinking sea-wave.

After washing as well as I could in the clear stream, I rose and looked around me. The tree under which I seemed to have lain all night was one of the advanced guard of a dense forest, towards which the rivulet ran. Faint traces of a footpath, much overgrown with grass and moss, and with here and there a pimpernel even, were discernible along the right bank. "This," thought I, "must surely be the path into Fairy Land, which the lady of last night promised I should so soon find." I crossed the rivulet, and accompanied it, keeping the footpath on its right bank, until it led me, as I expected, into the wood. Here I left it, without any good reason: and with a vague feeling that I ought to have followed its course, I took a more southerly direction.

CHAPTER THREE

The trees, which were far apart where I entered, giving free passage to the level rays of the sun, closed rapidly as I advanced, so that ere long their crowded stems barred the sunlight out, forming as it were a thick grating between me and the East. I seemed to be advancing towards a second midnight. In the midst of the intervening twilight, however, before I entered what appeared to be the darkest portion of the forest, I saw a country maiden coming towards me from its very depths. She did not seem to observe me, for she was apparently intent upon a bunch of wild flowers which she carried in her hand. I could hardly see her face; for, though she came direct towards me, she never looked up. But when we met, instead of passing, she turned and walked alongside of me for a few yards, still keeping her face downwards, and busied with her flowers. She spoke rapidly, however, all the time, in a low tone, as if talking to herself, but evidently addressing the purport of her words to me.

She seemed afraid of being observed by some lurking foe. "Trust the Oak," said she; "trust the Oak, and the Elm, and the great Beech. Take care of the Birch, for though she is honest, she is too young not to be changeable. But shun the Ash and the Alder; for the Ash is an ogre,—you will know him by his thick fingers; and the Alder will smother you with her web of hair, if you let her near you at night." All this was uttered without pause or alteration of tone. Then she turned suddenly and left me, walking still with the same unchanging gait. I could not conjecture what she meant, but satisfied myself with thinking that it would be time enough to find out her meaning when there was need to make use of her warning, and that the occasion would reveal the admonition. I concluded from the flowers that she carried, that the forest could not be everywhere so dense as it appeared from where I was now walking; and I was right in this conclusion. For soon I came to a more open part, and by-and-by crossed a wide grassy glade, on which were several circles of brighter green. But even here I was struck with the utter stillness. No bird sang. No insect hummed. Not a living creature crossed my way. Yet somehow the whole environment seemed only asleep, and to wear even in sleep an air of expectation. The trees seemed all to have an expression of conscious mystery, as if they said to themselves, "we could, an' if we would." They had all a meaning look about them. Then I remembered that night is the fairies' day, and the moon their sun; and I thought—Everything sleeps and dreams now: when the night comes, it will be different. At the same time I, being a man and a child of the day, felt some anxiety as to how I should fare among the elves and other children of the night who wake when mortals dream, and find their common life in those wondrous hours that flow noiselessly over the moveless death-like forms of men and women and children, lying strewn and parted beneath the weight of the heavy waves of night, which flow on and beat them down, and hold them drowned and senseless, until the ebb tide comes, and the waves sink away, back into the ocean of the dark. But I took courage and went on. Soon, however, I became again anxious, though from another cause. I had eaten nothing that day, and for an hour past had been feeling the want of food. So I grew afraid lest I should find nothing to meet my human necessities in this strange place; but once more I comforted myself with hope and went on.

Before noon, I fancied I saw a thin blue smoke rising amongst the stems of larger trees in front of me; and soon I came to an open spot of ground in which stood a little cottage, so built that the stems of four great trees formed its corners, while their branches met and intertwined over its roof, heaping a great cloud of leaves over it, up towards the heavens. I wondered at finding a human dwelling in this neighborhood; and yet it did not look altogether human, though sufficiently so to encourage me to expect to find some sort of food. Seeing no door, I went round to the other side, and there I found one, wide open. A woman sat beside it, preparing some vegetables for dinner. This was homely and comforting. As I came near, she looked up, and seeing me, showed no surprise, but bent her head again over her work, and said in a low tone:

"Did you see my daughter?"

"I believe I did," said I. "Can you give me something to eat, for I am very hungry?" "With pleasure," she replied, in the same tone; "but do not say anything more, till you come into the house, for the Ash is watching us."

Having said this, she rose and led the way into the cottage; which, I now saw, was built of the stems of small trees set closely together, and was furnished with rough chairs and tables, from which even the bark had not been removed. As soon as she had shut the door and set a chair—

"You have fairy blood in you," said she, looking hard at me.

"How do you know that?"

"You could not have got so far into this wood if it were not so; and I am trying to find out some trace of it in your countenance. I think I see it."

"What do you see?"

"Oh, never mind: I may be mistaken in that."

"But how then do you come to live here?"

"Because I too have fairy blood in me."

Here I, in my turn, looked hard at her, and thought I could perceive, notwithstanding the coarseness of her features, and especially the heaviness of her eyebrows, a something unusual—I could hardly call it grace, and yet it was an expression that strangely contrasted with the form of her features. I noticed too that her hands were delicately formed, though brown with work and exposure.

"I should be ill," she continued, "if I did not live on the borders of the fairies' country, and now and then eat of their food. And I see by your eyes that you are not quite free of the same need; though, from your education and the activity of your mind, you have felt it less than I. You may be further removed too from the fairy race."

I remembered what the lady had said about my grandmothers.

Here she placed some bread and some milk before me, with a kindly apology for the homeliness of the fare, with which, however, I was in no humor to quarrel. I now thought it time to try to get some explanation of the strange words both of her daughter and herself.

"What did you mean by speaking so about the Ash?"

She rose and looked out of the little window. My eyes followed her; but as the window was too small to allow anything to be seen from where I was sitting, I rose and looked over her shoulder. I had just time to see, across the open space, on the edge of the denser forest, a single large ash-tree, whose foliage showed bluish, amidst the truer green of the other trees around it; when she pushed me back with an expression of impatience and terror, and then almost shut out the light from the window by setting up a large old book in it.

"In general," said she, recovering her composure, "there is no danger in the daytime, for then he is sound asleep; but there is something unusual going on in the woods; there must be some solemnity among the fairies to-night, for all the trees are restless, and although they cannot come awake, they see and hear in their sleep."

"But what danger is to be dreaded from him?"

Instead of answering the question, she went again to the window and looked out, saying she feared the fairies would be interrupted by foul weather, for a storm was brewing in the west.

"And the sooner it grows dark, the sooner the Ash will be awake," added she.

I asked her how she knew that there was any unusual excitement in the woods. She replied —

"Besides the look of the trees, the dog there is unhappy; and the eyes and ears of the white rabbit are redder than usual, and he frisks about as if he expected some fun. If the cat were at home, she would have her back up; for the young fairies pull the sparks out of her tail with bramble thorns, and she knows when they are coming. So do I, in another way."

At this instant, a grey cat rushed in like a demon, and disappeared in a hole in the wall.

"There, I told you!" said the woman.

"But what of the ash-tree?" said I, returning once more to the subject. Here, however, the young woman, whom I had met in the morning, entered. A smile passed between the mother and daughter; and then the latter began to help her mother in little household duties.

"I should like to stay here till the evening," I said; "and then go on my journey, if you will allow me."

"You are welcome to do as you please; only it might be better to stay all night, than risk the dangers of the wood then. Where are you going?"

"Nay, that I do not know," I replied, "but I wish to see all that is to be seen, and therefore I should like to start just at sundown." "You are a bold youth, if you have any idea of what you are daring; but a rash one, if you know nothing about it; and, excuse me, you do not seem very well informed about the country and its manners. However, no one comes here but for some reason, either known to himself or to those who have charge of him; so you shall do just as you wish."

Accordingly I sat down, and feeling rather tired, and disinclined for further talk, I asked leave to look at the old book which still screened the window. The woman brought it to me directly, but not before taking another look towards the forest, and then drawing a white blind over the window. I sat down opposite to it by the table, on which I laid the great old volume, and read. It contained many wondrous tales of Fairy Land, and olden times, and the Knights of King Arthur's table. I read on and on, till the shades of the afternoon began to deepen; for in the midst of the forest it gloomed earlier than in the open country. At length I came to this passage —

"Here it chanced, that upon their quest, Sir Galahad and Sir Percivale rencountered in the depths of a great forest. Now, Sir Galahad was dight all in harness of silver, clear and shining; the which is a delight to look upon, but full hasty to tarnish, and withouten the labor of a ready squire, uneath to be kept fair and clean. And yet withouten squire or page, Sir Galahad's armor shone like the moon. And he rode a great white mare, whose bases and other housings were black, but all besprent with fair lilys of silver sheen. Whereas Sir Percivale bestrode a red horse, with a tawny mane and tail; whose trappings were all tosmirched with mud and mire; and his armor was wondrous rosty to behold, ne could he by any art furbish it again; so that as the sun in his going down shone twixt the bare trunks of the trees, full upon the knights twain, the one did seem all shining with light, and the other all to glow with ruddy fire. Now it came about in this wise. For Sir Percivale, after his escape from the demon lady, whenas the cross on the handle of his sword smote him to the heart, and he rove himself through the thigh, and escaped away, he came to a great wood; and, in nowise cured of his fault, yet bemoaning the same, the damosel of the alder tree encountered him, right fair to see; and with her fair words and false countenance she comforted him and beguiled him, until he followed her where she led him to a —"

Here a low hurried cry from my hostess caused me to look up from the book, and I read no more.

"Look there!" she said; "look at his fingers!"

Just as I had been reading in the book, the setting sun was shining through a cleft in the clouds piled up in the west; and a shadow as of a large distorted hand, with thick knobs and humps on the fingers, so that it was much wider across the fingers than across the undivided part of the hand, passed slowly over the little blind, and then as slowly returned in the opposite direction.

"He is almost awake, mother; and greedier than usual to-night."

"Hush, child; you need not make him more angry with us than he is; for you do not know how soon something may happen to oblige us to be in the forest after nightfall."

"But you are in the forest," said I; "how is it that you are safe here?"

"He dares not come nearer than he is now," she replied; "for any of those four oaks, at the corners of our cottage, would tear him to pieces; they are our friends. But he stands there and makes awful faces at us sometimes, and stretches out his long arms and fingers, and tries to kill us with fright; for, indeed, that is his favorite way of doing. Pray, keep out of his way to- night."

"Shall I be able to see these things?" said I.

"That I cannot tell yet, not knowing how much of the fairy nature there is in you. But we shall soon see whether you can discern the fairies in my little garden, and that will be some guide to us."

"Are the trees fairies too, as well as the flowers?" I asked.

"They are of the same race," she replied; "though those you call fairies in your country are chiefly the young children of the flower fairies. They are very fond of having fun with the thick people, as they call you; for, like most children, they like fun better than anything else."

"Why do you have flowers so near you then? Do they not annoy you?"

"Oh, no, they are very amusing, with their mimicries of grown people, and mock solemnities. Sometimes they will act a whole play through before my eyes, with perfect composure and assurance, for they are not afraid of me. Only, as soon as they have done, they burst into peals of tiny laughter, as if it was such a joke to have been serious over anything. These I speak of, however, are the fairies of the garden. They are more staid and educated than those of the fields and woods. Of course they have near relations amongst the wild flowers, but they patronize them, and treat them as country cousins, who know nothing of life, and very little of manners. Now and then, however, they are compelled to envy the grace and simplicity of the natural flowers."

"Do they live in the flowers?" I said.

"I cannot tell," she replied. "There is something in it I do not understand. Sometimes they disappear altogether, even from me, though I know they are near. They seem to die always with the flowers they resemble, and by whose names they are called; but whether they return to life with the fresh flowers, or, whether it be new flowers, new fairies, I cannot tell. They have as many sorts of dispositions as men and women, while their moods are yet more variable; twenty different expressions will cross their little faces in half a minute. I often amuse myself with watching them, but I have never been able to make personal acquaintance with any of them. If I speak to one, he or she looks up in my face, as if I were not worth heeding, gives a little laugh, and runs away." Here the woman started, as if suddenly recollecting herself, and said in a low voice to her daughter, "Make haste — go and watch him, and see in what direction he goes."

I may as well mention here, that the conclusion I arrived at from the observations I was afterwards able to make, was, that the flowers die because the fairies go away; not that the fairies disappear because the flowers die. The flowers seem a sort of houses for them, or outer bodies, which they can put on or off when they please. Just as you could form some idea of the nature of a man from the kind of house he built, if he followed his own taste, so you could, without seeing the fairies, tell what any one of them is like, by looking at the flower till you feel that you understand it. For just what the flower says to you, would the face and form of the fairy say; only so much more plainly as a face and human figure can express more than a flower. For the house or the clothes, though like the inhabitant or the wearer, cannot be wrought into an equal power of utterance. Yet you would see a strange resemblance, almost oneness, between the flower and the fairy, which you could not describe, but which described itself to you. Whether all the flowers have fairies, I cannot determine, any more than I can be sure whether all men and women have souls.

The woman and I continued the conversation for a few minutes longer. I was much interested by the information she gave me, and astonished at the language in which she was able to convey it. It seemed that intercourse with the fairies was no bad education in itself. But now the daughter returned with the news, that the Ash had just gone away in a south-westerly direction; and, as my course seemed to lie eastward, she hoped I should be in no danger of meeting him if I departed at once. I looked out of the little window, and there stood the ash-tree, to my eyes the same as before; but I believed that they knew better than I did, and prepared to go. I pulled out my purse, but to my dismay there was nothing in it. The woman with a smile begged me not to trouble myself, for money was not of the slightest use there; and as I might meet with people in my journeys whom I could not recognize to be fairies, it was well I had no money to offer, for nothing offended them so much.

"They would think," she added, "that you were making game of them; and that is their peculiar privilege with regard to us." So we went together into the little garden which sloped down towards a lower part of the wood.

Here, to my great pleasure, all was life and bustle. There was still light enough from the day to see a little; and the pale half-moon, halfway to the zenith, was reviving every moment. The whole garden was like a carnival, with tiny, gaily decorated forms, in groups, assemblies, processions, pairs or trios, moving stately on, running about wildly, or sauntering hither or thither. From the cups or bells of tall flowers, as from balconies, some looked down on the masses below, now bursting with laughter, now grave as owls; but even in their deepest solemnity, seeming only to be waiting for the arrival of the next laugh. Some were launched on a little marshy stream at the bottom, in boats chosen from the heaps of last year's leaves that lay about, curled and withered. These soon sank with them; whereupon they swam ashore and got others. Those who took fresh rose-leaves for their boats floated the longest; but for these they had to fight; for the fairy of the rose-tree complained bitterly that they were stealing her clothes, and defended her property bravely.

"You can't wear half you've got," said some.

"Never you mind; I don't choose you to have them: they are my property."

"All for the good of the community!" said one, and ran off with a great hollow leaf. But the rose-fairy sprang after him (what a beauty she was! only too like a drawing-room young lady), knocked him heels-over-head as he ran, and recovered her great red leaf. But in the meantime twenty had hurried off in different directions with others just as good; and the little creature sat down and cried, and then, in a pet, sent a perfect pink snowstorm of petals from her tree, leaping from branch to branch, and stamping and shaking and pulling. At last, after another good cry, she chose the biggest she could find, and ran away laughing, to launch her boat amongst the rest.

But my attention was first and chiefly attracted by a group of fairies near the cottage, who were talking together around what seemed a last dying primrose. They talked singing, and their talk made a song, something like this:

"Sister Snowdrop died

Before we were born."

"She came like a bride

In a snowy morn."

"What's a bride?"

"What is snow?

"Never tried."

"Do not know."

"Who told you about her?"

"Little Primrose there

Cannot do without her."

"Oh, so sweetly fair!"

"Never fear,

She will come,

Primrose dear."

"Is she dumb?"

"She'll come by-and-by."

"You will never see her."

"She went home to dies,

"Till the new year."

"Snowdrop!" "'Tis no good

To invite her."

"Primrose is very rude,

"I will bite her."

"Oh, you naughty Pocket!

"Look, she drops her head."

"She deserved it, Rocket,

"And she was nearly dead."

"To your hammock—off with you!"

"And swing alone."

"No one will laugh with you."

"No, not one."

"Now let us moan."

"And cover her o'er."

"Primrose is gone."

"All but the flower."

"Here is a leaf."

"Lay her upon it."

"Follow in grief."

"Pocket has done it."

"Deeper, poor creature!

Winter may come."

"He cannot reach her—

That is a hum."

"She is buried, the beauty!"

"Now she is done."

"That was the duty."

"Now for the fun."

And with a wild laugh they sprang away, most of them towards the cottage. During the latter part of the song-talk, they had formed themselves into a funeral procession, two of them bearing poor Primrose, whose death Pocket had hastened by biting her stalk, upon one of her own great leaves. They bore her solemnly along some distance, and then buried her under a tree. Although I say HER I saw nothing but the withered primrose-flower on its long stalk. Pocket, who had been expelled from the company by common consent, went sulkily away towards her hammock, for she was the fairy of the calceolaria, and looked rather wicked. When she reached its stem, she stopped and looked round. I could not help speaking to her, for I stood near her. I said, "Pocket, how could you be so naughty?"

"I am never naughty," she said, half-crossly, half-defiantly; "only if you come near my hammock, I will bite you, and then you will go away."

"Why did you bite poor Primrose?"

"Because she said we should never see Snowdrop; as if we were not good enough to look at her, and she was, the proud thing! — served her right!"

"Oh, Pocket, Pocket," said I; but by this time the party which had gone towards the house, rushed out again, shouting and screaming with laughter. Half of them were on the cat's back, and half held on by her fur and tail, or ran beside her; till, more coming to their help, the furious cat was held fast; and they proceeded to pick the sparks out of her with thorns and pins, which they handled like harpoons. Indeed, there were more instruments at work about her than there could have been sparks in her. One little fellow who held on hard by the tip of the tail, with his feet planted on the ground at an angle of forty-five degrees, helping to keep her fast, administered a continuous flow of admonitions to Pussy.

"Now, Pussy, be patient. You know quite well it is all for your good. You cannot be comfortable with all those sparks in you; and, indeed, I am charitably disposed to believe" (here he became very pompous) "that they are the cause of all your bad temper; so we must have them all out, every one; else we shall be reduced to the painful necessity of cutting your claws, and pulling out your eye-teeth. Quiet! Pussy, quiet!"

But with a perfect hurricane of feline curses, the poor animal broke loose, and dashed across the garden and through the hedge, faster than even the fairies could follow. "Never mind, never mind, we shall find her again; and by that time she will have laid in a fresh stock of sparks. Hooray!" And off they set, after some new mischief.

But I will not linger to enlarge on the amusing display of these frolicsome creatures. Their manners and habits are now so well known to the world, having been so often described by eyewitnesses, that it would be only indulging self-conceit, to add my account in full to the rest. I cannot help wishing, however, that my readers could see them for themselves. Especially do I desire that they should see the fairy of the daisy; a little, chubby, round-eyed child, with such innocent trust in his look! Even the most mischievous of the fairies would not tease him, although he did not belong to their set at all, but was quite a little country bumpkin. He wandered about alone, and looked at everything, with his hands in his little pockets, and a white night-cap on, the darling! He was not so beautiful as many other wild flowers I saw afterwards, but so dear and loving in his looks and little confident ways.

CHAPTER FOUR

By this time, my hostess was quite anxious that I should be gone. So, with warm thanks for their hospitality, I took my leave, and went my way through the little garden towards the forest. Some of the garden flowers had wandered into the wood, and were growing here and there along the path, but the trees soon became too thick and shadowy for them. I particularly noticed some tall lilies, which grew on both sides of the way, with large dazzlingly white flowers, set off by the universal green. It was now dark enough for me to see that every flower was shining with a light of its own. Indeed it was by this light that I saw them, an internal, peculiar light, proceeding from each, and not reflected from a common source of light as in the daytime. This light sufficed only for the plant itself, and was not strong enough to cast any but the faintest shadows around it, or to illuminate any of the neighboring objects with other than the faintest tinge of its own individual hue. From the lilies above mentioned, from the campanulas, from the foxgloves, and every bell-shaped flower, curious little figures shot up their heads, peeped at me, and drew back. They seemed to inhabit them, as snails their shells but I was sure some of them were intruders, and belonged to the gnomes or goblin-fairies, who inhabit the ground and earthy creeping plants. From the cups of Arum lilies, creatures with great heads and grotesque faces shot up like Jack-in-the-box, and made grimaces at me; or rose slowly and silly over the edge of the cup, and spouted water at me, slipping suddenly back, like those little soldier-crabs that inhabit the shells of sea-snails. Passing a row of tall thistles, I saw them crowded with little faces, which peeped every one from behind its flower, and drew back as quickly; and I heard them saying to each other, evidently intending me to hear, but the speaker always hiding behind his tuft, when I looked in his direction, "Look at him! Look at him! He has begun a story without a beginning, and it will never have any end. He! he! he! Look at him!"

But as I went further into the wood, these sights and sounds became fewer, giving way to others of a different character. A little forest of wild hyacinths was alive with exquisite creatures, who stood nearly motionless, with drooping necks, holding each by the stem of her flower, and swaying gently with it, whenever a low breath of wind swung the crowded floral belfry. In like manner, though differing of course in form and meaning, stood a group of harebells, like little angels waiting, ready, till they were wanted to go on some yet unknown message. In darker nooks, by the mossy roots of the trees, or in little tufts of grass, each dwelling in a globe of its own green light, weaving a network of grass and its shadows, glowed the glowworms.

They were just like the glowworms of our own land, for they are fairies everywhere; worms in the day, and glowworms at night, when their own can appear, and they can be themselves to others as well as themselves. But they had their enemies here. For I saw great strong-armed beetles, hurrying about with most unwieldy haste, awkward as elephant-calves, looking apparently for glowworms; for the moment a beetle espied one, through what to it was a forest of grass, or an underwood of moss, it pounced upon it, and bore it away, in spite of its feeble resistance. Wondering what their object could be, I watched one of the beetles, and then I discovered a thing I could not account for. But it is no use trying to account for things in Fairy Land; and one who travels there soon learns to forget the very idea of doing so, and takes everything as it comes; like a child, who, being in a chronic condition of wonder, is surprised at nothing. What I saw was this. Everywhere, here and there over the ground, lay little, dark-looking lumps of something more like earth than anything else, and about the size of a chestnut. The beetles hunted in couples for these; and having found one, one of them stayed to watch it, while the other hurried to find a glowworm. By signals, I presume, between them, the latter soon found his companion again: they then took the glowworm and held its luminous tail to the dark earthly pellet; when lo, it shot up into the air like a sky-rocket, seldom, however, reaching the height of the highest tree. Just like a rocket too, it burst in the air, and fell in a shower of the most gorgeously colored sparks of every variety of hue; golden and red, and purple and green, and blue and rosy fires crossed and inter-crossed each other, beneath the shadowy heads, and between the columnar stems of the forest trees. They never used the same glowworm twice, I observed; but let him go, apparently uninjured by the use they had made of him.

In other parts, the whole of the immediately surrounding foliage was illuminated by the interwoven dances in the air of splendidly colored fire-flies, which sped hither and thither, turned, twisted, crossed, and recrossed, entwining every complexity of intervolved motion. Here and there, whole mighty trees glowed with an emitted phosphorescent light. You could trace the very course of the great roots in the earth by the faint light that came through; and every twig, and every vein on every leaf was a streak of pale fire.

All this time, as I went through the wood, I was haunted with the feeling that other shapes, more like my own size and mien, were moving about at a little distance on all sides of me. But as yet I could discern none of them, although the moon was high enough to send a great many of her rays down between the trees, and these rays were unusually bright, and sight-giving, notwithstanding she was only a half-moon. I constantly imagined, however, that forms were visible in all directions except that to which my gaze was turned; and that they only became invisible, or resolved themselves into other woodland shapes, the moment my looks were directed towards them. However this may have been, except for this feeling of presence, the woods seemed utterly bare of anything like human companionship, although my glance often fell on some object which I fancied to be a human form; for I soon found that I was quite deceived; as, the moment I fixed my regard on it, it showed plainly that it was a bush, or a tree, or a rock.

Soon a vague sense of discomfort possessed me. With variations of relief, this gradually increased; as if some evil thing were wandering about in my neighborhood, sometimes nearer and sometimes further off, but still approaching. The feeling continued and deepened, until all my pleasure in the shows of various kinds that everywhere betokened the presence of the merry fairies vanished by degrees, and left me full of anxiety and fear, which I was unable to associate with any definite object whatever. At length the thought crossed my mind with horror: "Can it be possible that the Ash is looking for me? Or that, in his nightly wanderings, his path is gradually verging towards mine?" I comforted myself, however, by remembering that he had started quite in another direction; one that would lead him, if he kept it, far apart from me; especially as, for the last two or three hours, I had been diligently journeying eastward. I kept on my way, therefore, striving by direct effort of the will against the encroaching fear; and to this end occupying my mind, as much as I could, with other thoughts. I was so far successful that, although I was conscious, if I yielded for a moment, I should be almost overwhelmed with horror, I was yet able to walk right on for an hour or more. What I feared I could not tell. Indeed, I was left in a state of the vaguest uncertainty as regarded the nature of my enemy, and knew not the mode or object of his attacks; for, somehow or other, none of my questions had succeeded in drawing a definite answer from the dame in the cottage. How then to defend myself I knew not; nor even by what sign I might with certainty recognize the presence of my foe; for as yet this vague though powerful fear was all the indication of danger I had. To add to my distress, the clouds in the west had risen nearly to the top of the skies, and they and the moon were traveling slowly towards each other. Indeed, some of their advanced guard had already met her, and she had begun to wade through a filmy vapor that gradually deepened.

At length she was for a moment almost entirely obscured. When she shone out again, with a brilliancy increased by the contrast, I saw plainly on the path before me—from around which at this spot the trees receded, leaving a small space of green sward—the shadow of a large hand, with knotty joints and protuberances here and there. Especially I remarked, even in the midst of my fear, the bulbous points of the fingers. I looked hurriedly all around, but could see nothing from which such a shadow should fall. Now, however, that I had a direction, however undetermined, in which to project my apprehension, the very sense of danger and need of action overcame that stifling which is the worst property of fear. I reflected in a moment, that if this were indeed a shadow, it was useless to look for the object that cast it in any other direction than between the shadow and the moon. I looked, and peered, and intensified my vision, all to no purpose. I could see nothing of that kind, not even an ash-tree in the neighborhood. Still the shadow remained; not steady, but moving to and fro, and once I saw the fingers close, and grind themselves close, like the claws of a wild animal, as if in uncontrollable longing for some anticipated prey. There seemed but one mode left of discovering the substance of this shadow. I went forward boldly, though with an inward shudder which I would not heed, to the spot where the shadow lay, threw myself on the ground, laid my head within the form of the hand, and turned my eyes towards the moon Good heavens! what did I see? I wonder that ever I arose, and that the very shadow of the hand did not hold me where I lay until fear had frozen my brain. I saw the strangest figure; vague, shadowy, almost transparent, in the central parts, and gradually deepening in substance towards the outside, until it ended in extremities capable of casting such a shadow as fell from the hand, through the awful fingers of which I now saw the moon. The hand was uplifted in the attitude of a paw about to strike its prey. But the face, which throbbed with fluctuating and pulsatory visibility — not from changes in the light it reflected, but from changes in its own conditions of reflecting power, the alterations being from within, not from without—it was horrible. I do not know how to describe it. It caused a new sensation. Just as one cannot translate a horrible odor, or a ghastly pain, or a fearful sound, into words, so I cannot describe this new form of awful hideousness. I can only try to describe something that is not it, but seems somewhat parallel to it; or at least is suggested by it. It reminded me of what I had heard of vampires; for the face resembled that of a corpse more than anything else I can think of; especially when I can conceive such a face in motion, but not suggesting any life as the source of the motion. The features were rather handsome than otherwise, except the mouth, which had scarcely a curve in it. The lips were of equal thickness; but the thickness was not at all remarkable, even although they looked slightly swollen. They seemed fixedly open, but were not wide apart. Of course I did not REMARK these lineaments at the time: I was too horrified for that. I noted them afterwards, when the form returned on my inward sight with a vividness too intense to admit of my doubting the accuracy of the reflex. But the most awful of the features were the eyes. These were alive, yet not with life.

They seemed lighted up with an infinite greed. A gnawing voracity, which devoured the devourer, seemed to be the indwelling and propelling power of the whole ghostly apparition. I lay for a few moments simply imbruted with terror; when another cloud, obscuring the moon, delivered me from the immediately paralyzing effects of the presence to the vision of the object of horror, while it added the force of imagination to the power of fear within me; inasmuch as, knowing far worse cause for apprehension than before, I remained equally ignorant from what I had to defend myself, or how to take any precautions: he might be upon me in the darkness any moment. I sprang to my feet, and sped I knew not whither, only away from the specter. I thought no longer of the path, and often narrowly escaped dashing myself against a tree, in my headlong flight of fear.

Great drops of rain began to patter on the leaves. Thunder began to mutter, then growl in the distance. I ran on. The rain fell heavier. At length the thick leaves could hold it up no longer; and, like a second firmament, they poured their torrents on the earth. I was soon drenched, but that was nothing. I came to a small swollen stream that rushed through the woods. I had a vague hope that if I crossed this stream, I should be in safety from my pursuer; but I soon found that my hope was as false as it was vague. I dashed across the stream, ascended a rising ground, and reached a more open space, where stood only great trees. Through them I directed my way, holding eastward as nearly as I could guess, but not at all certain that I was not moving in an opposite direction. My mind was just reviving a little from its extreme terror, when, suddenly, a flash of lightning, or rather a cataract of successive flashes, behind me, seemed to throw on the ground in front of me, but far more faintly than before, from the extent of the source of the light, the shadow of the same horrible hand. I sprang forward, stung to yet wilder speed; but had not run many steps before my foot slipped, and, vainly attempting to recover myself, I fell at the foot of one of the large trees. Half-stunned, I yet raised myself, and almost involuntarily looked back. All I saw was the hand within three feet of my face. But, at the same moment, I felt two large soft arms thrown round me from behind; and a voice like a woman's said: "Do not fear the goblin; he dares not hurt you now." With that, the hand was suddenly withdrawn as from a fire, and disappeared in the darkness and the rain. Overcome with the mingling of terror and joy, I lay for some time almost insensible. The first thing I remember is the sound of a voice above me, full and low, and strangely reminding me of the sound of a gentle wind amidst the leaves of a great tree. It murmured over and over again: "I may love him, I may love him; for he is a man, and I am only a beech-tree." I found I was seated on the ground, leaning against a human form, and supported still by the arms around me, which I knew to be those of a woman who must be rather above the human size, and largely proportioned. I turned my head, but without moving otherwise, for I feared lest the arms should untwine themselves; and clear, somewhat mournful eyes met mine. At least that is how they impressed me; but I could see very little of color or outline as we sat in the dark and rainy shadow of the tree. The face seemed very lovely, and solemn from its stillness; with the aspect of one who is quite content, but waiting for something. I saw my conjecture from her arms was correct: she was above the human scale throughout, but not greatly.

"Why do you call yourself a beech-tree?" I said.

"Because I am one," she replied, in the same low, musical, murmuring voice.

"You are a woman," I returned.

"Do you think so? Am I very like a woman then?"

"You are a very beautiful woman. Is it possible you should not know it?"

"I am very glad you think so. I fancy I feel like a woman sometimes. I do so to-night—and always when the rain drips from my hair. For there is an old prophecy in our woods that one day we shall all be men and women like you. Do you know anything about it in your region? Shall I be very happy when I am a woman? I fear not, for it is always in nights like these that I feel like one. But I long to be a woman for all that."

I had let her talk on, for her voice was like a solution of all musical sounds. I now told her that I could hardly say whether women were happy or not. I knew one who had not been happy; and for my part, I had often longed for Fairy Land, as she now longed for the world of men. But then neither of us had lived long, and perhaps people grew happier as they grew older. Only I doubted it.

I could not help sighing. She felt the sigh, for her arms were still round me. She asked me how old I was.

"Twenty-one," said I.

"Why, you baby!" said she, and kissed me with the sweetest kiss of winds and odors. There was a cool faithfulness in the kiss that revived my heart wonderfully. I felt that I feared the dreadful Ash no more.

"What did the horrible Ash want with me?" I said.

"I am not quite sure, but I think he wants to bury you at the foot of his tree. But he shall not touch you, my child."

"Are all the ash-trees as dreadful as he?"

"Oh, no. They are all disagreeable selfish creatures — (what horrid men they will make, if it be true!) — but this one has a hole in his heart that nobody knows of but one or two; and he is always trying to fill it up, but he cannot. That must be what he wanted you for. I wonder if he will ever be a man. If he is, I hope they will kill him."

"How kind of you to save me from him!"

"I will take care that he shall not come near you again. But there are some in the wood more like me, from whom, alas! I cannot protect you. Only if you see any of them very beautiful, try to walk round them."

"What then?"

"I cannot tell you more. But now I must tie some of my hair about you, and then the Ash will not touch you. Here, cut some off. You men have strange cutting things about you."

She shook her long hair loose over me, never moving her arms.

"I cannot cut your beautiful hair. It would be a shame."

"Not cut my hair! It will have grown long enough before any is wanted again in this wild forest. Perhaps it may never be of any use again—not till I am a woman." And she sighed.

As gently as I could, I cut with a knife a long tress of flowing, dark hair, she hanging her beautiful head over me. When I had finished, she shuddered and breathed deep, as one does when an acute pain, steadfastly endured without sign of suffering, is at length relaxed. She then took the hair and tied it round me, singing a strange, sweet song, which I could not understand, but which left in me a feeling like this —

"I saw thee ne'er before;

I see thee never more;

But love, and help, and pain, beautiful one,

Have made thee mine, till all my years are done."

I cannot put more of it into words. She closed her arms about me again, and went on singing. The rain in the leaves, and a light wind that had arisen, kept her song company. I was wrapt in a trance of still delight. It told me the secret of the woods, and the flowers, and the birds. At one time I felt as if I was wandering in childhood through sunny spring forests, over carpets of primroses, anemones, and little white starry things — I had almost said creatures, and finding new wonderful flowers at every turn. At another, I lay half dreaming in the hot summer noon, with a book of old tales beside me, beneath a great beech; or, in autumn, grew sad because I trod on the leaves that had sheltered me, and received their last blessing in the sweet odors of decay; or, in a winter evening, frozen still, looked up, as I went home to a warm fireside, through the netted boughs and twigs to the cold, snowy moon, with her opal zone around her. At last I had fallen asleep; for I know nothing more that passed till I found myself lying under a superb beech-tree, in the clear light of the morning, just before sunrise. Around me was a girdle of fresh beech-leaves. Alas! I brought nothing with me out of Fairy Land, but memories — memories. The great boughs of the beech hung drooping around me. At my head rose its smooth stem, with its great sweeps of curving surface that swelled like undeveloped limbs. The leaves and branches above kept on the song which had sung me asleep; only now, to my mind, it sounded like a farewell and a speedwell. I sat a long time, unwilling to go; but my unfinished story urged me on. I must act and wander. With the sun well risen, I rose, and put my arms as far as they would reach around the beech-tree, and kissed it, and said goodbye. A trembling went through the leaves; a few of the last drops of the night's rain fell from off them at my feet; and as I walked slowly away, I seemed to hear in a whisper once more the words: "I may love him, I may love him; for he is a man, and I am only a beech-tree."

CHAPTER FIVE

"And she was smooth and full, as if one gush Of life had washed her, or as if a sleep Lay on her eyelid, easier to sweep Than bee from daisy."

BEDDOIS' Pygmalion.

"Sche was as whyt as lylye yn May, Or snow that sneweth yn wynterys day." Romance of Sir Launfal.

I walked on, in the fresh morning air, as if new-born. The only thing that damped my pleasure was a cloud of something between sorrow and delight that crossed my mind with the frequently returning thought of my last night's hostess. "But then," thought I, "if she is sorry, I could not help it; and she has all the pleasures she ever had. Such a day as this is surely a joy to her, as much at least as to me. And her life will perhaps be the richer, for holding now within it the memory of what came, but could not stay. And if ever she is a woman, who knows but we may meet somewhere? there is plenty of room for meeting in the universe." Comforting myself thus, yet with a vague compunction, as if I ought not to have left her, I went on. There was little to distinguish the woods to-day from those of my own land; except that all the wild things, rabbits, birds, squirrels, mice, and the numberless other inhabitants, were very tame; that is, they did not run away from me, but gazed at me as I passed, frequently coming nearer, as if to examine me more closely. Whether this came from utter ignorance, or from familiarity with the human appearance of beings who never hurt them, I could not tell. As I stood once, looking up to the splendid flower of a parasite, which hung from the branch of a tree over my head, a large white rabbit cantered slowly up, put one of its little feet on one of mine, and looked up at me with its red eyes, just as I had been looking up at the flower above me. I stooped and stroked it; but when I attempted to lift it, it banged the ground with its hind feet and scampered off at a great rate, turning, however, to look at me several times before I lost sight of it. Now and then, too, a dim human figure would appear and disappear, at some distance, amongst the trees, moving like a sleep-walker. But no one ever came near me.

This day I found plenty of food in the forest—strange nuts and fruits I had never seen before. I hesitated to eat them; but argued that, if I could live on the air of Fairy Land, I could live on its food also. I found my reasoning correct, and the result was better than I had hoped; for it not only satisfied my hunger, but operated in such a way upon my senses that I was brought into far more complete relationship with the things around me. The human forms appeared much more dense and defined; more tangibly visible, if I may say so. I seemed to know better which direction to choose when any doubt arose. I began to feel in some degree what the birds meant in their songs, though I could not express it in words, any more than you can some landscapes. At times, to my surprise, I found myself listening attentively, and as if it were no unusual thing with me, to a conversation between two squirrels or monkeys. The subjects were not very interesting, except as associated with the individual life and necessities of the little creatures: where the best nuts were to be found in the neighborhood, and who could crack them best, or who had most laid up for the winter, and such like; only they never said where the store was. There was no great difference in kind between their talk and our ordinary human conversation. Some of the creatures I never heard speak at all, and believe they never do so, except under the impulse of some great excitement. The mice talked; but the hedgehogs seemed very phlegmatic; and though I met a couple of moles above ground several times, they never said a word to each other in my hearing. There were no wild beasts in the forest; at least, I did not see one larger than a wild cat. There were plenty of snakes, however, and I do not think they were all harmless; but none ever bit me.

Soon after mid-day I arrived at a bare rocky hill, of no great size, but very steep; and having no trees — scarcely even a bush — upon it, entirely exposed to the heat of the sun. Over this my way seemed to lie, and I immediately began the ascent. On reaching the top, hot and weary, I looked around me, and saw that the forest still stretched as far as the sight could reach on every side of me. I observed that the trees, in the direction in which I was about to descend, did not come so near the foot of the hill as on the other side, and was especially regretting the unexpected postponement of shelter, because this side of the hill seemed more difficult to descend than the other had been to climb, when my eye caught the appearance of a natural path, winding down through broken rocks and along the course of a tiny stream, which I hoped would lead me more easily to the foot. I tried it, and found the descent not at all laborious; nevertheless, when I reached the bottom, I was very tired and exhausted with the heat. But just where the path seemed to end, rose a great rock, quite overgrown with shrubs and creeping plants, some of them in full and splendid blossom: these almost concealed an opening in the rock, into which the path appeared to lead. I entered, thirsting for the shade which it promised. What was my delight to find a rocky cell, all the angles rounded away with rich moss, and every ledge and projection crowded with lovely ferns, the variety of whose forms, and groupings, and shades wrought in me like a poem; for such a harmony could not exist, except they all consented to some one end! A little well of the clearest water filled a mossy hollow in one corner. I drank, and felt as if I knew what the elixir of life must be; then threw myself on a mossy mound that lay like a couch along the inner end. Here I lay in a delicious reverie for some time; during which all lovely forms, and colors, and sounds seemed to use my brain as a common hall, where they could come and go, unbidden and unexcused. I had never imagined that such capacity for simple happiness lay in me, as was now awakened by this assembly of forms and spiritual sensations, which yet were far too vague to admit of being translated into any shape common to my own and another mind. I had lain for an hour, I should suppose, though it may have been far longer, when, the harmonious tumult in my mind having somewhat relaxed, I became aware that my eyes were fixed on a strange, time-worn bas-relief on the rock opposite to me. This, after some pondering, I concluded to represent Pygmalion, as he awaited the quickening of his statue. The sculptor sat more rigid than the figure to which his eyes were turned. That seemed about to step from its pedestal and embrace the man, who waited rather than expected.

"A lovely story," I said to myself. "This cave, now, with the bushes cut away from the entrance to let the light in, might be such a place as he would choose, withdrawn from the notice of men, to set up his block of marble, and mould into a visible body the thought already clothed with form in the unseen hall of the sculptor's brain. And, indeed, if I mistake not," I said, starting up, as a sudden ray of light arrived at that moment through a crevice in the roof, and lighted up a small portion of the rock, bare of vegetation, "this very rock is marble, white enough and delicate enough for any statue, even if destined to become an ideal woman in the arms of the sculptor."

I took my knife and removed the moss from a part of the block on which I had been lying; when, to my surprise, I found it more like alabaster than ordinary marble, and soft to the edge of the knife. In fact, it was alabaster. By an inexplicable, though by no means unusual kind of impulse, I went on removing the moss from the surface of the stone; and soon saw that it was polished, or at least smooth, throughout. I continued my labor; and after clearing a space of about a couple of square feet, I observed what caused me to prosecute the work with more interest and care than before. For the ray of sunlight had now reached the spot I had cleared, and under its luster the alabaster revealed its usual slight transparency when polished, except where my knife had scratched the surface; and I observed that the transparency seemed to have a definite limit, and to end upon an opaque body like the more solid, white marble. I was careful to scratch no more. And first, a vague anticipation gave way to a startling sense of possibility; then, as I proceeded, one revelation after another produced the entrancing conviction, that under the crust of alabaster lay a dimly visible form in marble, but whether of man or woman I could not yet tell. I worked on as rapidly as the necessary care would permit; and when I had uncovered the whole mass, and rising from my knees, had retreated a little way, so that the effect of the whole might fall on me, I saw before me with sufficient plainness — though at the same time with considerable indistinctness, arising from the limited amount of light the place admitted, as well as from the nature of the object itself—a block of pure alabaster enclosing the form, apparently in marble, of a reposing woman. She lay on one side, with her hand under her cheek, and her face towards me; but her hair had fallen partly over her face, so that I could not see the expression of the whole. What I did see appeared to me perfectly lovely; more near the face that had been born with me in my soul, than anything I had seen before in nature or art. The actual outlines of the rest of the form were so indistinct, that the more than semi-opacity of the alabaster seemed insufficient to account for the fact; and I conjectured that a light robe added its obscurity. Numberless histories passed through my mind of change of substance from enchantment and other causes, and of imprisonments such as this before me. I thought of the Prince of the Enchanted City, half marble and half a man; of Ariel; of Niobe; of the Sleeping Beauty in the Wood; of the bleeding trees; and many other histories. Even my adventure of the preceding evening with the lady of the beech-tree contributed to arouse the wild hope, that by some means life might be given to this form also, and that, breaking from her alabaster tomb, she might glorify my eyes with her presence. "For," I argued, "who can tell but this cave may be the home of Marble, and this, essential Marble — that spirit of marble which, present throughout, makes it capable of being molded into any form? Then if she should awake! But how to awake her? A kiss awoke the Sleeping Beauty! a kiss cannot reach her through the incrusting alabaster." I kneeled, however, and kissed the pale coffin; but she slept on. I bethought me of Orpheus, and the following stones — that trees should follow his music seemed nothing surprising now. Might not a song awake this form, that the glory of motion might for a time displace the loveliness of rest? Sweet sounds can go where kisses may not enter. I sat and thought. Now, although always delighting in music, I had never been gifted with the power of song, until I entered the fairy forest. I had a voice, and I had a true sense of sound; but when I tried to sing, the one would not content the other, and so I remained silent. This morning, however, I had found myself, ere I was aware, rejoicing in a song; but whether it was before or after I had eaten of the fruits of the forest, I could not satisfy myself. I concluded it was after, however; and that the increased impulse to sing I now felt, was in part owing to having drunk of the little well, which shone like a brilliant eye in a corner of the cave. It saw down on the ground by the "antenatal tomb," leaned upon it with my face towards the head of the figure within, and sang — the words and tones coming together, and inseparably connected, as if word and tone formed one thing; or, as if each word could be uttered only in that tone, and was incapable of distinction from it, except in idea, by an acute analysis. I sang something like this: but the words are only a dull representation of a state whose very elevation precluded the possibility of remembrance; and in which I presume the words really employed were as far above these, as that state transcended this wherein I recall it:

"Marble woman, vainly sleeping

In the very death of dreams!

Wilt thou — slumber from thee sweeping,

All but what with vision teems —

Hear my voice come through the golden

Mist of memory and hope;

And with shadowy smile embolden

Me with primal Death to cope?

"Thee the sculptors all pursuing,

Have embodied but their own;

Round their visions, form enduring,

Marble vestments thou hast thrown;

But thyself, in silence winding,

Thou hast kept eternally;

Thee they found not, many finding —

I have found thee: wake for me."

As I sang, I looked earnestly at the face so vaguely revealed before me. I fancied, yet believed it to be but fancy, that through the dim veil of the alabaster, I saw a motion of the head as if caused by a sinking sigh. I gazed more earnestly, and concluded that it was but fancy. Nevertheless I could not help singing again —

"Rest is now filled full of beauty,
And can give thee up, I ween;
Come thou forth, for other duty
Motion pineth for her queen.

"Or, if needing years to wake thee
From thy slumbrous solitudes,
Come, sleep-walking, and betake thee
To the friendly, sleeping woods.

Sweeter dreams are in the forest,
Round thee storms would never rave;
And when need of rest is sorest,
Glide thou then into thy cave.

"Or, if still thou chooses rather
Marble, be its spell on me;
Let thy slumber round me gather,
Let another dream with thee!"

Again I paused, and gazed through the stony shroud, as if, by very force of penetrative sight, I would clear every lineament of the lovely face. And now I thought the hand that had lain under the cheek, had slipped a little downward. But then I could not be sure that I had at first observed its position accurately. So I sang again; for the longing had grown into a passionate need of seeing her alive —

"Or art thou Death, O woman? for since I
Have set me singing by thy side,
Life hath forsook the upper sky,
And all the outer world hath died.

"Yea, I am dead; for thou hast drawn

My life all downward unto thee.

Dead moon of love! let twilight dawn:

Awake! and let the darkness flee.

"Cold lady of the lovely stone!

Awake! or I shall perish here;

And thou be never more alone,

My form and I for ages near.

"But words are vain; reject them all —

They utter but a feeble part:

Hear thou the depths from which they call,

The voiceless longing of my heart."

There arose a slightly crashing sound. Like a sudden apparition that comes and is gone, a white form, veiled in a light robe of whiteness, burst upwards from the stone, stood, glided forth, and gleamed away towards the woods. For I followed to the mouth of the cave, as soon as the amazement and concentration of delight permitted the nerves of motion again to act; and saw the white form amidst the trees, as it crossed a little glade on the edge of the forest where the sunlight fell full, seeming to gather with intenser radiance on the one object that floated rather than flitted through its lake of beams. I gazed after her in a kind of despair; found, freed, lost! It seemed useless to follow, yet follow I must. I marked the direction she took; and without once looking round to the forsaken cave, I hastened towards the forest.

CHAPTER SIX

But as I crossed the space between the foot of the hill and the forest, a vision of another kind delayed my steps. Through an opening to the westward flowed, like a stream, the rays of the setting sun, and overflowed with a ruddy splendor the open space where I was. And riding as it were down this stream towards me, came a horseman in what appeared red armor. From frontlet to tail, the horse likewise shone red in the sunset. I felt as if I must have seen the knight before; but as he drew near, I could recall no feature of his countenance. Ere he came up to me, however, I remembered the legend of Sir Percival in the rusty armor, which I had left unfinished in the old book in the cottage: it was of Sir Percival that he reminded me. And no wonder; for when he came close up to me, I saw that, from crest to heel, the whole surface of his armor was covered with a light rust. The golden spurs shone, but the iron greaves glowed in the sunlight. The MORNING STAR, which hung from his wrist, glittered and glowed with its silver and bronze. His whole appearance was terrible; but his face did not answer to this appearance. It was sad, even to gloominess; and something of shame seemed to cover it. Yet it was noble and high, though thus beclouded; and the form looked lofty, although the head drooped, and the whole frame was bowed as with an inward grief. The horse seemed to share in his master's dejection, and walked spiritless and slow. I noticed, too, that the white plume on his helmet was discolored and drooping. "He has fallen in a joust with spears," I said to myself; "yet it becomes not a noble knight to be conquered in spirit because his body hath fallen." He appeared not to observe me, for he was riding past without looking up, and started into a warlike attitude the moment the first sound of my voice reached him. Then a flush, as of shame, covered all of his face that the lifted beaver disclosed. He returned my greeting with distant courtesy, and passed on. But suddenly, he reined up, sat a moment still, and then turning his horse, rode back to where I stood looking after him.

"I am ashamed," he said, "to appear a knight, and in such a guise; but it behooves me to tell you to take warning from me, lest the same evil, in his kind, overtake the singer that has befallen the knight. Hast thou ever read the story of Sir Percival and the" — (here he shuddered, that his armor rang) — "Maiden of the Alder-tree?"

"In part, I have," said I; "for yesterday, at the entrance of this forest, I found in a cottage the volume wherein it is recorded." "Then take heed," he rejoined; "for, see my armor—I put it off; and as it befell to him, so has it befallen to me. I that was proud am humble now. Yet is she terribly beautiful — beware. Never," he added, raising his head, "shall this armor be furbished, but by the blows of knightly encounter, until the last speck has disappeared from every spot where the battle-axe and sword of evil-doers, or noble foes, might fall; when I shall again lift my head, and say to my squire, `Do thy duty once more, and make this armor shine.'"

Before I could inquire further, he had struck spurs into his horse and galloped away, shrouded from my voice in the noise of his armor. For I called after him, anxious to know more about this fearful enchantress; but in vain — he heard me not. "Yet," I said to myself, "I have now been often warned; surely I shall be well on my guard; and I am fully resolved I shall not be ensnared by any beauty, however beautiful. Doubtless, some one man may escape, and I shall be he." So I went on into the wood, still hoping to find, in some one of its mysterious recesses, my lost lady of the marble. The sunny afternoon died into the loveliest twilight. Great bats began to flit about with their own noiseless flight, seemingly purposeless, because its objects are unseen. The monotonous music of the owl issued from all unexpected quarters in the half-darkness around me. The glowworm was alight here and there, burning out into the great universe. The night-hawk heightened all the harmony and stillness with his oft-recurring, discordant jar. Numberless unknown sounds came out of the unknown dusk; but all were of twilight-kind, oppressing the heart as with a condensed atmosphere of dreamy undefined love and longing. The odors of night arose, and bathed me in that luxurious mournfulness peculiar to them, as if the plants whence they floated had been watered with bygone tears. Earth drew me towards her bosom; I felt as if I could fall down and kiss her. I forgot I was in Fairy Land, and seemed to be walking in a perfect night of our own old nursing earth. Great stems rose about me, uplifting a thick multitudinous roof above me of branches, and twigs, and leaves — the bird and insect world uplifted over mine, with its own landscapes, its own thickets, and paths, and glades, and dwellings; its own bird-ways and insect-delights. Great boughs crossed my path; great roots based the tree-columns, and mightily clasped the earth, strong to lift and strong to uphold. It seemed an old, old forest, perfect in forest ways and pleasures. And when, in the midst of this ecstasy, I remembered that under some close canopy of leaves, by some giant stem, or in some mossy cave, or beside some leafy well, sat the lady of the marble, whom my songs had called forth into the outer world, waiting (might it not be?) to meet and thank her deliverer in a twilight which would veil her confusion, the whole night became one dream-realm of joy, the central form of which was everywhere present, although unbeheld. Then, remembering how my songs seemed to have called her from the marble, piercing through the pearly shroud of alabaster—"Why," thought I, "should not my voice reach her now, through the ebon night that inwraps her." My voice burst into song so spontaneously that it seemed involuntarily.

"Not a sound

But, echoing in me,

Vibrates all around

With a blind delight,

Till it breaks on Thee,

Queen of Night!

Every tree,

Overshadowing with gloom,

Seems to cover thee

Secret, dark, love-stilled,

In a holy room

Silence-filled.

"Let no moon

Creep up the heaven to-night;

I in darksome noon

Walking hopefully,

Seek my shrouded light —

Grope for thee!

"Darker grow

The borders of the dark!

Through the branches glow,

From the roof above,

Star and diamond-sparks

Light for love."

Scarcely had the last sounds floated away from the hearing of my own ears, when I heard instead a low delicious laugh near me. It was not the laugh of one who would not be heard, but the laugh of one who has just received something long and patiently desired—a laugh that ends in a low musical moan. I started, and, turning sideways, saw a dim white figure seated beside an intertwining thicket of smaller trees and underwood.

"It is my white lady!" I said, and flung myself on the ground beside her; striving, through the gathering darkness, to get a glimpse of the form which had broken its marble prison at my call.

"It is your white lady!" said the sweetest voice, in reply, sending a thrill of speechless delight through a heart which all the love-charms of the preceding day and evening had been tempering for this culminating hour. Yet, if I would have confessed it, there was something either in the sound of the voice, although it seemed sweetness itself, or else in this yielding which awaited no gradation of gentle approaches, that did not vibrate harmoniously with the beat of my inward music. And likewise, when, taking her hand in mine, I drew closer to her, looking for the beauty of her face, which, indeed, I found too plenteously, a cold shiver ran through me; but "it is the marble," I said to myself, and heeded it not.

She withdrew her hand from mine, and after that would scarce allow me to touch her. It seemed strange, after the fullness of her first greeting, that she could not trust me to come close to her. Though her words were those of a lover, she kept herself withdrawn as if a mile of space interposed between us.

"Why did you run away from me when you woke in the cave?" I said.

"Did I?" she returned. "That was very unkind of me; but I did not know better."

"I wish I could see you. The night is very dark."

"So it is. Come to my grotto. There is light there."

"Have you another cave, then?"

"Come and see."

But she did not move until I rose first, and then she was on her feet before I could offer my hand to help her. She came close to my side, and conducted me through the wood. But once or twice, when, involuntarily almost, I was about to put my arm around her as we walked on through the warm gloom, she sprang away several paces, always keeping her face full towards me, and then stood looking at me, slightly stooping, in the attitude of one who fears some half-seen enemy. It was too dark to discern the expression of her face. Then she would return and walk close beside me again, as if nothing had happened. I thought this strange; but, besides that I had almost, as I said before, given up the attempt to account for appearances in Fairy Land, I judged that it would be very unfair to expect from one who had slept so long and had been so suddenly awakened, a behavior correspondent to what I might unreflectingly look for. I knew not what she might have been dreaming about. Besides, it was possible that, while her words were free, her sense of touch might be exquisitely delicate.

At length, after walking a long way in the woods, we arrived at another thicket, through the intertexture of which was glimmering a pale rosy light.

"Push aside the branches," she said, "and make room for us to enter."

I did as she told me.

"Go in," she said; "I will follow you."

I did as she desired, and found myself in a little cave, not very unlike the marble cave. It was festooned and draperied with all kinds of green that cling to shady rocks. In the furthest corner, half-hidden in leaves, through which it glowed, mingling lovely shadows between them, burned a bright rosy flame on a little earthen lamp. The lady glided round by the wall from behind me, still keeping her face towards me, and seated herself in the furthest corner, with her back to the lamp, which she hid completely from my view. I then saw indeed a form of perfect loveliness before me. Almost it seemed as if the light of the rose-lamp shone through her (for it could not be reflected from her); such a delicate shade of pink seemed to shadow what in itself must be a marbly whiteness of hue. I discovered afterwards, however, that there was one thing in it I did not like; which was, that the white part of the eye was tinged with the same slight roseate hue as the rest of the form. It is strange that I cannot recall her features; but they, as well as her somewhat girlish figure, left on me simply and only the impression of intense loveliness. I lay down at her feet, and gazed up into her face as I lay. She began, and told me a strange tale, which, likewise, I cannot recollect; but which, at every turn and every pause, somehow or other fixed my eyes and thoughts upon her extreme beauty; seeming always to culminate in something that had a relation, revealed or hidden, but always operative, with her own loveliness. I lay entranced. It was a tale which brings back a feeling as of snows and tempests; torrents and water-sprites; lovers parted for long, and meeting at last; with a gorgeous summer night to close up the whole. I listened till she and I were blended with the tale; till she and I were the whole history. And we had met at last in this same cave of greenery, while the summer night hung round us heavy with love, and the odors that crept through the silence from the sleeping woods were the only signs of an outer world that invaded our solitude. What followed I cannot clearly remember. The succeeding horror almost obliterated it. I woke as a grey dawn stole into the cave. The damsel had disappeared; but in the shrubbery, at the mouth of the cave, stood a strange horrible object. It looked like an open coffin set up on one end; only that the part for the head and neck was defined from the shoulder-part. In fact, it was a rough representation of the human frame, only hollow, as if made of decaying bark torn from a tree.

It had arms, which were only slightly seamed, down from the shoulder- blade by the elbow, as if the bark had healed again from the cut of a knife. But the arms moved, and the hand and the fingers were tearing asunder a long silky tress of hair. The thing turned round—it had for a face and front those of my enchantress, but now of a pale greenish hue in the light of the morning, and with dead lustreless eyes. In the horror of the moment, another fear invaded me. I put my hand to my waist, and found indeed that my girdle of beech-leaves was gone. Hair again in her hands, she was tearing it fiercely. Once more, as she turned, she laughed a low laugh, but now full of scorn and derision; and then she said, as if to a companion with whom she had been talking while I slept, "There he is; you can take him now." I lay still, petrified with dismay and fear; for I now saw another figure beside her, which, although vague and indistinct, I yet recognized but too well. It was the Ash-tree. My beauty was the Maid of the Alder! and she as giving me, spoiled of my only availing defense, into the hands of bent his Gorgon-head, and entered the cave. I could not stir. He drew near me. His ghoul-eyes and his ghastly face fascinated me. He came stooping, with the hideous hand outstretched, like a beast of prey. I had given myself up to a death of unfathomable horror, when, suddenly, and just as he was on the point of seizing me, the dull, heavy blow of an axe echoed through the wood, followed by others in quick repetition. The Ash shuddered and groaned, withdrew the outstretched hand, retreated backwards to the mouth of the cave, then turned and disappeared amongst the trees. The other walking Death looked at me once, with a careless dislike on her beautifully molded features; then, heedless any more to conceal her hollow deformity, turned her frightful back and likewise vanished amid the green obscurity without. I lay and wept. The Maid of the Alder-tree had befooled me—nearly slain me—in spite of all the warnings I had received from those who knew my danger.

CHAPTER SEVEN

But I could not remain where I was any longer, though the daylight was hateful to me, and the thought of the great, innocent, bold sunrise unendurable. Here there was no well to cool my face, smarting with the bitterness of my own tears. Nor would I have washed in the well of that grotto, had it flowed clear as the rivers of Paradise. I rose, and feebly left the sepulchral cave. I took my way I knew not whither, but still towards the sunrise. The birds were singing; but not for me. All the creatures spoke a language of their own, with which I had nothing to do, and to which I cared not to find the key any more.

I walked listlessly along. What distressed me most—more even than my own folly—was the perplexing question, How can beauty and ugliness dwell so near? Even with her altered complexion and her face of dislike; disenchanted of the belief that clung around her; known for a living, walking sepulcher, faithless, deluding, traitorous; I felt notwithstanding all this, that she was beautiful. Upon this I pondered with undiminished perplexity, though not without some gain. Then I began to make surmises as to the mode of my deliverance; and concluded that some hero, wandering in search of adventure, had heard how the forest was infested; and, knowing it was useless to attack the evil thing in person, had assailed with his battle-axe the body in which he dwelt, and on which he was dependent for his power of mischief in the wood. "Very likely," I thought, "the repentant-knight, who warned me of the evil which has befallen me, was busy retrieving his lost honor, while I was sinking into the same sorrow with himself; and, hearing of the dangerous and mysterious being, arrived at his tree in time to save me from being dragged to its roots, and buried like carrion, to nourish him for yet deeper insatiableness." I found afterwards that my conjecture was correct. I wondered how he had fared when his blows recalled the Ash himself, and that too I learned afterwards.

I walked on the whole day, with intervals of rest, but without food; for I could not have eaten, had any been offered me; till, in the afternoon, I seemed to approach the outskirts of the forest, and at length arrived at a farm-house. An unspeakable joy arose in my heart at beholding an abode of human beings once more, and I hastened up to the door, and knocked. A kind-looking, matronly woman, still handsome, made her appearance; who, as soon as she saw me, said kindly, "Ah, my poor boy, you have come from the wood! Were you in it last night?"

I should have ill endured, the day before, to be called BOY; but now the motherly kindness of the word went to my heart; and, like a boy indeed, I burst into tears. She soothed me right gently; and, leading me into a room, made me lie down on a settle, while she went to find me some refreshment. She soon returned with food, but I could not eat. She almost compelled me to swallow some wine, when I revived sufficiently to be able to answer some of her questions. I told her the whole story.

"It is just as I feared," she said; "but you are now for the night beyond the reach of any of these dreadful creatures. It is no wonder they could delude a child like you. But I must beg you, when my husband comes in, not to say a word about these things; for he thinks me even half crazy for believing anything of the sort. But I must believe my senses, as he cannot believe beyond his, which give him no intimations of this kind. I think he could spend the whole of Midsummer-eve in the wood and come back with the report that he saw nothing worse than himself. Indeed, good man, he would hardly find anything better than himself, if he had seven more senses given him."

"But tell me how it is that she could be so beautiful without any heart at all — without any place even for a heart to live in."

"I cannot quite tell," she said; "but I am sure she would not look so beautiful if she did not take means to make herself look more beautiful than she is. And then, you know, you began by being in love with her before you saw her beauty, mistaking her for the lady of the marble—another kind altogether, I should think. But the chief thing that makes her beautiful is this: that, although she loves no man, she loves the love of any man; and when she finds one in her power, her desire to bewitch him and gain his love (not for the sake of his love either, but that she may be conscious anew of her own beauty, through the admiration he manifests), makes her very lovely — with a self destructive beauty, though; for it is that which is constantly wearing her away within, till, at last, the decay will reach her face, and her whole front, when all the lovely mask of nothing will fall to pieces, and she be vanished for ever. So a wise man, whom she met in the wood some years ago, and who, I think, for all his wisdom, fared no better than you, told me, when, like you, he spent the next night here, and recounted to me his adventures."

I thanked her very warmly for her solution, though it was but partial; wondering much that in her, as in woman I met on my first entering the forest, there should be such superiority to her apparent condition. Here she left me to take some rest; though, indeed, I was too much agitated to rest in any other way than by simply ceasing to move.

In half an hour, I heard a heavy step approach and enter the house. A jolly voice, whose slight huskiness appeared to proceed from overmuch laughter, called out "Betsy, the pigs' trough is quite empty, and that is a pity. Let them swill, lass! They're of no use but to get fat. Ha! ha! ha! Gluttony is not forbidden in their commandments. Ha! ha! ha!" The very voice, kind and jovial, seemed to disrobe the room of the strange look which all new places wear — to disenchant it out of the realm of the ideal into that of the actual. It began to look as if I had known every corner of it for twenty years; and when, soon after, the dame came and fetched me to partake of their early supper, the grasp of his great hand, and the harvest-moon of his benevolent face, which was needed to light up the rotundity of the globe beneath it, produced such a reaction in me, that, for a moment, I could hardly believe that there was a Fairy Land; and that all I had passed through since I left home, had not been the wandering dream of a diseased imagination, operating on a too mobile frame, not merely causing me indeed to travel, but peopling for me with vague phantoms the regions through which my actual steps had led me. But the next moment my eye fell upon a little girl who was sitting in the chimney-corner, with a little book open on her knee, from which she had apparently just looked up to fix great inquiring eyes upon me. I believed in Fairy Land again. She went on with her reading, as soon as she saw that I observed her looking at me. I went near, and peeping over her shoulder, saw that she was reading "The History of Graciosa and Percinet."

"Very improving book, sir," remarked the old farmer, with a good humored laugh. "We are in the very hottest corner of Fairy Land here. Ha! ha! Stormy night, last night, sir."

"Was it, indeed?" I rejoined. "It was not so with me. A lovelier night I never saw." "Indeed! Where were you last night?"

"I spent it in the forest. I had lost my way."

"Ah! then, perhaps, you will be able to convince my good woman, that there is nothing very remarkable about the forest; for, to tell the truth, it bears but a bad name in these parts. I dare say you saw nothing worse than yourself there?"

"I hope I did," was my inward reply; but, for an audible one, I contented myself with saying, "Why, I certainly did see some appearances I could hardly account for; but that is nothing to be wondered at in an unknown wild forest, and with the uncertain light of the moon alone to go by."

"Very true! you speak like a sensible man, sir. We have but few sensible folks round about us. Now, you would hardly credit it, but my wife believes every fairy-tale that ever was written. I cannot account for it. She is a most sensible woman in everything else."

"But should not that make you treat her belief with something of respect, though you cannot share in it yourself?"

"Yes, that is all very well in theory; but when you come to live every day in the midst of absurdity, it is far less easy to behave respectfully to it. Why, my wife actually believes the story of the 'White Cat.' You know it, I dare say."

"I read all these tales when a child, and know that one especially well."

"But, father," interposed the little girl in the chimney-corner, "you know quite well that mother is descended from that very princess who was changed by the wicked fairy into a white cat. Mother has told me so a many times, and you ought to believe everything she says."

"I can easily believe that," rejoined the farmer, with another fit of laughter; "for, the other night, a mouse came gnawing and scratching beneath the floor, and would not let us go to sleep. Your mother sprang out of bed, and going as near it as she could, mewed so infernally like a great cat, that the noise ceased instantly. I believe the poor mouse died of the fright, for we have never heard it again. Ha! ha! ha!"

The son, an ill-looking youth, who had entered during the conversation, joined in his father's laugh; but his laugh was very different from the old man's: it was polluted with a sneer. I watched him, and saw that, as soon as it was over, he looked scared, as if he dreaded some evil consequences to follow his presumption. The woman stood near, waiting till we should seat ourselves at the table, and listening to it all with an amused air, which had something in it of the look with which one listens to the sententious remarks of a pompous child. We sat down to supper, and I ate heartily. My bygone distresses began already to look far off.

"In what direction are you going?" asked the old man.

"Eastward," I replied; nor could I have given a more definite answer. "Does the forest extend much further in that direction?"

"Oh! for miles and miles; I do not know how far. For although I have lived on the borders of it all my life, I have been too busy to make journeys of discovery into it. Nor do I see what I could discover. It is only trees and trees, till one is sick of them. By the way, if you follow the eastward track from here, you will pass close to what the children say is the very house of the ogre that Hop-o'-my-Thumb visited, and ate his little daughters with the crowns of gold."

"Oh, father! ate his little daughters! No; he only changed their gold crowns for nightcaps; and the great long-toothed ogre killed them in mistake; but I do not think even he ate them, for you know they were his own little ogresses."

"Well, well, child; you know all about it a great deal better than I do. However, the house has, of course, in such a foolish neighborhood as this, a bad enough name; and I must confess there is a woman living in it, with teeth long enough, and white enough too, for the lineal descendant of the greatest ogre that ever was made. I think you had better not go near her."

In such talk as this the night wore on. When supper was finished, which lasted some time, my hostess conducted me to my chamber.

"If you had not had enough of it already," she said, "I would have put you in another room, which looks towards the forest; and where you would most likely have seen something more of its inhabitants. For they frequently pass the window, and even enter the room sometimes. Strange creatures spend whole nights in it, at certain seasons of the year. I am used to it, and do not mind it. No more does my little girl, who sleeps in it always. But this room looks southward towards the open country, and they never show themselves here; at least I never saw any."

I was somewhat sorry not to gather any experience that I might have, of the inhabitants of Fairy Land; but the effect of the farmer's company, and of my own later adventures, was such, that I chose rather an undisturbed night in my more human quarters; which, with their clean white curtains and white linen, were very inviting to my weariness.

In the morning I awoke refreshed, after a profound and dreamless sleep. The sun was high, when I looked out of the window, shining over a wide, undulating, cultivated country. Various garden-vegetables were growing beneath my window. Everything was radiant with clear sunlight. The dew-drops were sparkling their busiest; the cows in a near-by field were eating as if they had not been at it all day yesterday; the maids were singing at their work as they passed to and fro between the out-houses: I did not believe in Fairy Land. I went down, and found the family already at breakfast. But before I entered the room where they sat, the little girl came to me, and looked up in my face, as though she wanted to say something to me. I stooped towards her; she put her arms round my neck, and her mouth to my ear, and whispered —

"A white lady has been flitting about the house all night."

"No whispering behind doors!" cried the farmer; and we entered together. "Well, how have you slept? No bogies, eh?"

"Not one, thank you; I slept uncommonly well."

"I am glad to hear it. Come and breakfast."

After breakfast, the farmer and his son went out; and I was left alone with the mother and daughter.

"When I looked out of the window this morning," I said, "I felt almost certain that Fairy Land was all a delusion of my brain; but whenever I come near you or your little daughter, I feel differently. Yet I could persuade myself, after my last adventures, to go back, and have nothing more to do with such strange beings."

"How will you go back?" said the woman.

"Nay, that I do not know."

"Because I have heard, that, for those who enter Fairy Land, there is no way of going back. They must go on, and go through it. How, I do not in the least know."

"That is quite the impression on my own mind. Something compels me to go on, as if my only path was onward, but I feel less inclined this morning to continue my adventures."

"Will you come and see my little child's room? She sleeps in the one I told you of, looking towards the forest."

"Willingly," I said.

So we went together, the little girl running before to open the door for us. It was a large room, full of old-fashioned furniture, that seemed to have once belonged to some great house. The window was built with a low arch, and filled with lozenge-shaped panes. The wall was very thick, and built of solid stone. I could see that part of the house had been erected against the remains of some old castle or abbey, or other great building; the fallen stones of which had probably served to complete it. But as soon as I looked out of the window, a gush of wonderment and longing flowed over my soul like the tide of a great sea. Fairy Land lay before me, and drew me towards it with an irresistible attraction. The trees bathed their great heads in the waves of the morning, while their roots were planted deep in gloom; save where on the borders the sunshine broke against their stems, or swept in long streams through their avenues, washing with brighter hue all the leaves over which it flowed; revealing the rich brown of the decayed leaves and fallen pine-cones, and the delicate greens of the long grasses and tiny forests of moss that covered the channel over which it passed in motionless rivers of light. I turned hurriedly to bid my hostess farewell without further delay. She smiled at my haste, but with an anxious look.

"You had better not go near the house of the ogre, I think. My son will show you into another path, which will join the first beyond it."

Not wishing to be headstrong or too confident any more, I agreed; and having taken leave of my kind entertainers, went into the wood, accompanied by the youth. He scarcely spoke as we went along; but he led me through the trees till we struck upon a path. He told me to follow it, and, with a muttered "good morning" left me.

CHAPTER EIGHT

My spirits rose as I went deeper; into the forest; but I could not regain my former elasticity of mind. I found cheerfulness to be like life itself—not to be created by any argument. Afterwards I learned, that the best way to manage some kinds of pain fill thoughts, is to dare them to do their worst; to let them lie and gnaw at your heart till they are tired; and you find you still have a residue of life they cannot kill. So, better and worse, I went on, till I came to a little clearing in the forest. In the middle of this clearing stood a long, low hut, built with one end against a single tall cypress, which rose like a spire to the building. A vague misgiving crossed my mind when I saw it; but I must needs go closer, and look through a little half-open door, near the opposite end from the cypress. Window I saw none. On peeping in, and looking towards the further end, I saw a lamp burning, with a dim, reddish flame, and the head of a woman, bent downwards, as if reading by its light. I could see nothing more for a few moments. At length, as my eyes got used to the dimness of the place, I saw that the part of the rude building near me was used for household purposes; for several rough utensils lay here and there, and a bed stood in the corner.

An irresistible attraction caused me to enter. The woman never raised her face, the upper part of which alone I could see distinctly; but, as soon as I stepped within the threshold, she began to read aloud, in a low and not altogether unpleasing voice, from an ancient little volume which she held open with one hand on the table upon which stood the lamp. What she read was something like this:

"So, then, as darkness had no beginning, neither will it ever have an end. So, then, is it eternal. The negation of aught else, is its affirmation. Where the light cannot come, there abides the darkness. The light does but hollow a mine out of the infinite extension of the darkness. And ever upon the steps of the light treads the darkness; yea, springs in fountains and wells amidst it, from the secret channels of its mighty sea. Truly, man is but a passing flame, moving un-quietly amid the surrounding rest of night; without which he yet could not be, and whereof he is in part compounded."

As I drew nearer, and she read on, she moved a little to turn a leaf of the dark old volume, and I saw that her face was sallow and slightly forbidding. Her forehead was high, and her black eyes repressedly quiet. But she took no notice of me. This end of the cottage, if cottage it could be called, was destitute of furniture, except the table with the lamp, and the chair on which the woman sat. In one corner was a door, apparently of a cupboard in the wall, but which might lead to a room beyond. Still the irresistible desire which had made me enter the building urged me: I must open that door, and see what was beyond it. I approached, and laid my hand on the rude latch. Then the woman spoke, but without lifting her head or looking at me: "You had better not open that door." This was uttered quite quietly; and she went on with her reading, partly in silence, partly aloud; but both modes seemed equally intended for herself alone. The prohibition, however, only increased my desire to see; and as she took no further notice, I gently opened the door to its full width, and looked in. At first, I saw nothing worthy of attention. It seemed a common closet, with shelves on each hand, on which stood various little necessaries for the humble uses of a cottage. In one corner stood one or two brooms, in another a hatchet and other common tools; showing that it was in use every hour of the day for household purposes. But, as I looked, I saw that there were no shelves at the back, and that an empty space went in further; its termination appearing to be a faintly glimmering wall or curtain, somewhat less, however, than the width and height of the doorway where I stood. But, as I continued looking, for a few seconds, towards this faintly luminous limit, my eyes came into true relation with their object. All at once, with such a shiver as when one is suddenly conscious of the presence of another in a room where he has, for hours, considered himself alone, I saw that the seemingly luminous extremity was a sky, as of night, beheld through the long perspective of a narrow, dark passage, through what, or built of what, I could not tell. As I gazed, I clearly discerned two or three stars glimmering faintly in the distant blue. But, suddenly, and as if it had been running fast from a far distance for this very point, and had turned the corner without abating its swiftness, a dark figure sped into and along the passage from the blue opening at the remote end. I started back and shuddered, but kept looking, for I could not help it. On and on it came, with a speedy approach but delayed arrival; till, at last, through the many gradations of approach, it seemed to come within the sphere of myself, rushed up to me, and passed me into the cottage. All I could tell of its appearance was, that it seemed to be a dark human figure. Its motion was entirely noiseless, and might be called a gliding, were it not that it appeared that of a runner, but with ghostly feet. I had moved back yet a little to let him pass me, and looked round after him instantly. I could not see him.

"Where is he?" I said, in some alarm, to the woman, who still sat reading.

"There, on the floor, behind you," she said, pointing with her arm half-outstretched, but not lifting her eyes. I turned and looked, but saw nothing. Then with a feeling that there was yet something behind me, I looked round over my shoulder; and there, on the ground, lay a black shadow, the size of a man. It was so dark, that I could see it in the dim light of the lamp, which shone full upon it, apparently without thinning at all the intensity of its hue.

"I told you," said the woman, "you had better not look into that closet."

"What is it?" I said, with a growing sense of horror.

"It is only your shadow that has found you," she replied. Everybody's shadow is ranging up and down looking for him. I believe you call it by a different name in your world: yours has found you, as every person's is almost certain to do who looks into that closet, especially after meeting one in the forest, whom I dare say you have met."

Here, for the first time, she lifted her head, and looked full at me: her mouth was full of long, white, shining teeth; and I knew that I was in the house of the ogre. I could not speak, but turned and left the house, with the shadow at my heels. "A nice sort of valet to have," I said to myself bitterly, as I stepped into the sunshine, and, looking over my shoulder, saw that it lay yet blacker in the full blaze of the sunlight. Indeed, only when I stood between it and the sun, was the blackness at all diminished. I was so bewildered— stunned—both by the event itself and its suddenness, that I could not at all realize to myself what it would be to have such a constant and strange attendance; but with a dim conviction that my present dislike would soon grow to loathing, I took my dreary way through the wood.

Chapter Nine

From this time, until I arrived at the palace of Fairy Land, I can attempt no consecutive account of my wanderings and adventures. Everything, henceforward, existed for me in its relation to my attendant. What influence he exercised upon everything into contact with which I was brought, may be understood from a few detached instances. To begin with this very day on which he first joined me: after I had walked heartlessly along for two or three hours, I was very weary, and lay down to rest in a most delightful part of the forest, carpeted with wild flowers. I lay for half an hour in a dull repose, and then got up to pursue my way. The flowers on the spot where I had lain were crushed to the earth: but I saw that they would soon lift their heads and rejoice again in the sun and air. Not so those on which my shadow had lain. The very outline of it could be traced in the withered lifeless grass, and the scorched and shriveled flowers which stood there, dead, and hopeless of any resurrection. I shuddered, and hastened away with sad forebodings.

In a few days, I had reason to dread an extension of its baleful influences from the fact, that it was no longer confined to one position in regard to myself. Hitherto, when seized with an irresistible desire to look on my evil demon (which longing would unaccountably seize me at any moment, returning at longer or shorter intervals, sometimes every minute), I had to turn my head backwards, and look over my shoulder; in which position, as long as I could retain it, I was fascinated. But one day, having come out on a clear grassy hill, which commanded a glorious prospect, though of what I cannot now tell, my shadow moved round, and came in front of me. And, presently, a new manifestation increased my distress. For it began to coruscate, and shoot out on all sides a radiation of dim shadow. These rays of gloom issued from the central shadow as from a black sun, lengthening and shortening with continual change. But wherever a ray struck, that part of earth, or sea, or sky, became void, and desert, and sad to my heart. On this, the first development of its new power, one ray shot out beyond the rest, seeming to lengthen infinitely, until it smote the great sun on the face, which withered and darkened beneath the blow. I turned away and went on. The shadow retreated to its former position; and when I looked again, it had drawn in all its spears of darkness, and followed like a dog at my heels.

Once, as I passed by a cottage, there came out a lovely fairy child, with two wondrous toys, one in each hand. The one was the tube through which the fairy-gifted poet looks when he beholds the same thing everywhere; the other that through which he looks when he combines into new forms of loveliness those images of beauty which his own choice has gathered from all regions wherein he has traveled. Round the child's head was an aureole of emanating rays. As I looked at him in wonder and delight, round crept from behind me the something dark, and the child stood in my shadow. Straightway he was a commonplace boy, with a rough broad-brimmed straw hat, through which brim the sun shone from behind. The toys he carried were a multiplying-glass and a kaleidoscope. I sighed and departed.

One evening, as a great silent flood of western gold flowed through an avenue in the woods, down the stream, just as when I saw him first, came the sad knight, riding on his chestnut steed.

But his armor did not shine half so red as when I saw him first.

Many a blow of mighty sword and axe, turned aside by the strength of his mail, and glancing adown the surface, had swept from its path the fretted rust, and the glorious steel had answered the kindly blow with the thanks of returning light. These streaks and spots made his armor look like the floor of a forest in the sunlight. His forehead was higher than before, for the contracting wrinkles were nearly gone; and the sadness that remained on his face was the sadness of a dewy summer twilight, not that of a frosty autumn morn. He, too, had met the Alder-maiden as I, but he had plunged into the torrent of mighty deeds, and the stain was nearly washed away. No shadow followed him. He had not entered the dark house; he had not had time to open the closet door. "Will he ever look in?" I said to myself. "MUST his shadow find him some day?" But I could not answer my own questions.

We traveled together for two days, and I began to love him. It was plain that he suspected my story in some degree; and I saw him once or twice looking curiously and anxiously at my attendant gloom, which all this time had remained very obsequiously behind me; but I offered no explanation, and he asked none. Shame at my neglect of his warning, and a horror which shrunk from even alluding to its cause, kept me silent; till, on the evening of the second day, some noble words from my companion roused all my heart; and I was at the point of falling on his neck, and telling him the whole story; seeking, if not for helpful advice, for of that I was hopeless, yet for the comfort of sympathy — when round slid the shadow and inwrapt my friend; and I could not trust him.

The glory of his brow vanished; the light of his eye grew cold; and I held my peace. The next morning we parted.

But the most dreadful thing of all was, that I now began to feel something like satisfaction in the presence of the shadow. I began to be rather vain of my attendant, saying to myself, "In a land like this, with so many illusions everywhere, I need his aid to disenchant the things around me. He does away with all appearances, and shows me things in their true color and form. And I am not one to be fooled with the vanities of the common crowd. I will not see beauty where there is none. I will dare to behold things as they are. And if I live in a waste instead of a paradise, I will live knowing where I live." But of this a certain exercise of his power which soon followed quite cured me, turning my feelings towards him once more into loathing and distrust. It was thus:

One bright noon, a little maiden joined me, coming through the wood in a direction at right angles to my path. She came along singing and dancing, happy as a child, though she seemed almost a woman. In her hands — now in one, now in another — she carried a small globe, bright and clear as the purest crystal. This seemed at once her plaything and her greatest treasure. At one moment, you would have thought her utterly careless of it, and at another, overwhelmed with anxiety for its safety. But I believe she was taking care of it all the time, perhaps not least when least occupied about it. She stopped by me with a smile, and bade me good day with the sweetest voice. I felt a wonderful liking to the child — for she produced on me more the impression of a child, though my understanding told me differently. We talked a little, and then walked on together in the direction I had been pursuing. I asked her about the globe she carried, but getting no definite answer, I held out my hand to take it. She drew back, and said, but smiling almost invitingly the while, "You must not touch it;" — then, after a moment's pause — "Or if you do, it must be very gently." I touched it with a finger. A slight vibratory motion arose in it, accompanied, or perhaps manifested, by a faint sweet sound. I touched it again, and the sound increased. I touched it the third time: a tiny torrent of harmony rolled out of the little globe. She would not let me touch it any more.

We traveled on together all that day. She left me when twilight came on; but next day, at noon, she met me as before, and again we traveled till evening. The third day she came once more at noon, and we walked on together. Now, though we had talked about a great many things connected with Fairy Land, and the life she had led hitherto, I had never been able to learn anything about the globe. This day, however, as we went on, the shadow glided round and inwrapt the maiden. It could not change her. But my desire to know about the globe, which in his gloom began to waver as with an inward light, and to shoot out flashes of many-colored flame, grew irresistible. I put out both my hands and laid hold of it. It began to sound as before. The sound rapidly increased, till it grew a low tempest of harmony, and the globe trembled, and quivered, and throbbed between my hands. I had not the heart to pull it away from the maiden, though I held it in spite of her attempts to take it from me; yes, I shame to say, in spite of her prayers, and, at last, her tears. The music went on growing in, intensity and complication of tones, and the globe vibrated and heaved; till at last it burst in our hands, and a black vapor broke upwards from out of it; then turned, as if blown sideways, and enveloped the maiden, hiding even the shadow in its blackness. She held fast the fragments, which I abandoned, and fled from me into the forest in the direction whence she had come, wailing like a child, and crying, "You have broken my globe; my globe is broken — my globe is broken!" I followed her, in the hope of comforting her; but had not pursued her far, before a sudden cold gust of wind bowed the tree-tops above us, and swept through their stems around us; a great cloud overspread the day, and a fierce tempest came on, in which I lost sight of her. It lies heavy on my heart to this hour. At night, ere I fall asleep, often, whatever I may be thinking about, I suddenly hear her voice, crying out, "You have broken my globe; my globe is broken; ah, my globe!"

Here I will mention one more strange thing; but whether this peculiarity was owing to my shadow at all, I am not able to assure myself. I came to a village, the inhabitants of which could not at first sight be distinguished from the dwellers in our land. They rather avoided than sought my company, though they were very pleasant when I addressed them. But at last I observed, that whenever I came within a certain distance of any one of them, which distance, however, varied with different individuals, the whole appearance of the person began to change; and this change increased in degree as I approached. When I receded to the former distance, the former appearance was restored. The nature of the change was grotesque, following no fixed rule. The nearest resemblance to it that I know, is the distortion produced in your countenance when you look at it as reflected in a concave or convex surface — say, either side of a bright spoon. Of this phenomenon I first became aware in rather a ludicrous way. My host's daughter was a very pleasant pretty girl, who made herself more agreeable to me than most of those about me. For some days my companion-shadow had been less obtrusive than usual; and such was the reaction of spirits occasioned by the simple mitigation of torment, that, although I had cause enough besides to be gloomy, I felt light and comparatively happy. My impression is, that she was quite aware of the law of appearances that existed between the people of the place and myself, and had resolved to amuse herself at my expense; for one evening, after some jesting and raillery, she, somehow or other, provoked me to attempt to kiss her. But she was well defended from any assault of the kind. Her countenance became, of a sudden, absurdly hideous; the pretty mouth was elongated and otherwise amplified sufficiently to have allowed of six simultaneous kisses. I started back in bewildered dismay; she burst into the merriest fit of laughter, and ran from the room. I soon found that the same indefinable law of change operated between me and all the other villagers; and that, to feel I was in pleasant company, it was absolutely necessary for me to discover and observe the right focal distance between myself and each one with whom I had to do. This done, all went pleasantly enough. Whether, when I happened to neglect this precaution, I presented to them an equally ridiculous appearance, I did not ascertain; but I presume that the alteration was common to the approximating parties. I was likewise unable to determine whether I was a necessary party to the production of this strange transformation, or whether it took place as well, under the given circumstances, between the inhabitants themselves.

CHAPTER TEN

After leaving this village, where I had rested for nearly a week, I traveled through a desert region of dry sand and glittering rocks, peopled principally by goblin-fairies. When I first entered their domains, and, indeed, whenever I fell in with another tribe of them, they began mocking me with offered handfuls of gold and jewels, making hideous grimaces at me, and performing the most antic homage, as if they thought I expected reverence, and meant to humor me like a maniac. But ever, as soon as one cast his eyes on the shadow behind me, he made a wry face, partly of pity, partly of contempt, and looked ashamed, as if he had been caught doing something inhuman; then, throwing down his handful of gold, and ceasing all his grimaces, he stood aside to let me pass in peace, and made signs to his companions to do the like. I had no inclination to observe them much, for the shadow was in my heart as well as at my heels. I walked listlessly and almost hopelessly along, till I arrived one day at a small spring; which, bursting cool from the heart of a sun-heated rock, flowed somewhat southwards from the direction I had been taking. I drank of this spring, and found myself wonderfully refreshed. A kind of love to the cheerful little stream arose in my heart. It was born in a desert; but it seemed to say to itself, "I will flow, and sing, and lave my banks, till I make my desert a paradise." I thought I could not do better than follow it, and see what it made of it. So down with the stream I went, over rocky lands, burning with sunbeams. But the rivulet flowed not far, before a few blades of grass appeared on its banks, and then, here and there, a stunted bush. Sometimes it disappeared altogether under ground; and after I had wandered some distance, as near as I could guess, in the direction it seemed to take, I would suddenly hear it again, singing, sometimes far away to my right or left, amongst new rocks, over which it made new cataracts of watery melodies. The verdure on its banks increased as it flowed; other streams joined it; and at last, after many days' travel, I found myself, one gorgeous summer evening, resting by the side of a broad river, with a glorious horse-chestnut tree towering above me, and dropping its blossoms, milk-white and rosy-red, all about me. As I sat, a gush of joy sprang forth in my heart, and over flowed at my eyes.

Through my tears, the whole landscape glimmered in such bewildering loveliness, that I felt as if I were entering Fairy Land for the first time, and some loving hand were waiting to cool my head, and a loving word to warm my heart. Roses, wild roses, everywhere! So plentiful were they, they not only perfumed the air, they seemed to dye it a faint rose-hue. The color floated abroad with the scent, and clomb, and spread, until the whole west blushed and glowed with the gathered incense of roses. And my heart fainted with longing in my bosom.

Could I but see the Spirit of the Earth, as I saw once the in dwelling woman of the beech-tree, and my beauty of the pale marble, I should be content. Content! — Oh, how gladly would I die of the light of her eyes! Yea, I would cease to be, if that would bring me one word of love from the one mouth. The twilight sank around, and infolded me with sleep. I slept as I had not slept for months. I did not awake till late in the morning; when, refreshed in body and mind, I rose as from the death that wipes out the sadness of life, and then dies itself in the new morrow. Again I followed the stream; now climbing a steep rocky bank that hemmed it in; now wading through long grasses and wild flowers in its path; now through meadows; and anon through woods that crowded down to the very lip of the water.

At length, in a nook of the river, gloomy with the weight of overhanging foliage, and still and deep as a soul in which the torrent eddies of pain have hollowed a great gulf, and then, subsiding in violence, have left it full of a motionless, fathomless sorrow — I saw a little boat lying. So still was the water here, that the boat needed no fastening. It lay as if some one had just stepped ashore, and would in a moment return. But as there were no signs of presence, and no track through the thick bushes; and, moreover, as I was in Fairy Land where one does very much as he pleases, I forced my way to the brink, stepped into the boat, pushed it, with the help of the tree-branches, out into the stream, lay down in the bottom, and let my boat and me float whither the stream would carry us. I seemed to lose myself in the great flow of sky above me unbroken in its infinitude, except when now and then, coming nearer the shore at a bend in the river, a tree would sweep its mighty head silently above mine, and glide away back into the past, never more to fling its shadow over me. I fell asleep in this cradle, in which mother Nature was rocking her weary child; and while I slept, the sun slept not, but went round his arched way. When I awoke, he slept in the waters, and I went on my silent path beneath a round silvery moon. And a pale moon looked up from the floor of the great blue cave that lay in the abysmal silence beneath.

Why are all reflections lovelier than what we call the reality? — not so grand or so strong, it may be, but always lovelier? Fair as is the gliding sloop on the shining sea, the wavering, trembling, unresting sail below is fairer still. Yea, the reflecting ocean itself, reflected in the mirror, has a wondrousness about its waters that somewhat vanishes when I turn towards itself. All mirrors are magic mirrors. The commonest room is a room in a poem when I turn to the glass. (And this reminds me, while I write, of a strange story which I read in the fairy palace, and of which I will try to make a feeble memorial in its place.) In whatever way it may be accounted for, of one thing we may be sure, that this feeling is no cheat; for there is no cheating in nature and the simple unsought feelings of the soul. There must be a truth involved in it, though we may but in part lay hold of the meaning. Even the memories of past pain are beautiful; and past delights, though beheld only through clefts in the grey clouds of sorrow, are lovely as Fairy Land. But how have I wandered into the deeper fairyland of the soul, while as yet I only float towards the fairy palace of Fairy Land! The moon, which is the lovelier memory or reflex of the down-gone sun, the joyous day seen in the faint mirror of the brooding night, had rapt me away.

I sat up in the boat. Gigantic forest trees were about me; through which, like a silver snake, twisted and twined the great river. The little waves, when I moved in the boat, heaved and fell with a plash as of molten silver, breaking the image of the moon into a thousand morsels, fusing again into one, as the ripples of laughter die into the still face of joy. The sleeping woods, in undefined massiveness; the water that flowed in its sleep; and, above all, the enchantress moon, which had cast them all, with her pale eye, into the charmed slumber, sank into my soul, and I felt as if I had died in a dream, and should never more awake.

From this I was partly aroused by a glimmering of white, that, through the trees on the left, vaguely crossed my vision, as I gazed upwards. But the trees again hid the object; and at the moment, some strange melodious bird took up its song, and sang, not an ordinary bird-song, with constant repetitions of the same melody, but what sounded like a continuous strain, in which one thought was expressed, deepening in intensity as evolved in progress. It sounded like a welcome already overshadowed with the coming farewell. As in all sweetest music, a tinge of sadness was in every note. Nor do we know how much of the pleasures even of life we owe to the intermingled sorrows. Joy cannot unfold the deepest truths, although deepest truth must be deepest joy. Cometh white-robed Sorrow, stooping and wan, and flingeth wide the doors she may not enter. Almost we linger with Sorrow for very love.

As the song concluded the stream bore my little boat with a gentle sweep round a bend of the river; and lo! on a broad lawn, which rose from the water's edge with a long green slope to a clear elevation from which the trees receded on all sides, stood a stately palace glimmering ghostly in the moonshine: it seemed to be built throughout of the whitest marble. There was no reflection of moonlight from windows — there seemed to be none; so there was no cold glitter; only, as I said, a ghostly shimmer. Numberless shadows tempered the shine, from column and balcony and tower. For everywhere galleries ran along the face of the buildings; wings were extended in many directions; and numberless openings, through which the moonbeams vanished into the interior, and which served both for doors and windows, had their separate balconies in front, communicating with a common gallery that rose on its own pillars. Of course, I did not discover all this from the river, and in the moonlight. But, though I was there for many days, I did not succeed in mastering the inner topography of the building, so extensive and complicated was it.

Here I wished to land, but the boat had no oars on board. However, I found that a plank, serving for a seat, was unfastened, and with that I brought the boat to the bank and scrambled on shore. Deep soft turf sank beneath my feet, as I went up the ascent towards the palace.

When I reached it, I saw that it stood on a great platform of marble, with an ascent, by broad stairs of the same, all round it. Arrived on the platform, I found there was an extensive outlook over the forest, which, however, was rather veiled than revealed by the moonlight.

Entering by a wide gateway, but without gates, into an inner court, surrounded on all sides by great marble pillars supporting galleries above, I saw a large fountain of porphyry in the middle, throwing up a lofty column of water, which fell, with a noise as of the fusion of all sweet sounds, into a basin beneath; overflowing which, it ran into a single channel towards the interior of the building. Although the moon was by this time so low in the west, that not a ray of her light fell into the court, over the height of the surrounding buildings; yet was the court lighted by a second reflex from the sun of other lands. For the top of the column of water, just as it spread to fall, caught the moonbeams, and like a great pale lamp, hung high in the night air, threw a dim memory of light (as it were) over the court below. This court was paved in diamonds of white and red marble. According to my custom since I entered Fairy Land, of taking for a guide whatever I first found moving in any direction, I followed the stream from the basin of the fountain. It led me to a great open door, beneath the ascending steps of which it ran through a low arch and disappeared. Entering here, I found myself in a great hall, surrounded with white pillars, and paved with black and white. This I could see by the moonlight, which, from the other side, streamed through open windows into the hall.

Its height I could not distinctly see. As soon as I entered, I had the feeling so common to me in the woods, that there were others there besides myself, though I could see no one, and heard no sound to indicate a presence. Since my visit to the Church of Darkness, my power of seeing the fairies of the higher orders had gradually diminished, until it had almost ceased. But I could frequently believe in their presence while unable to see them. Still, although I had company, and doubtless of a safe kind, it seemed rather dreary to spend the night in an empty marble hall, however beautiful, especially as the moon was near the going down, and it would soon be dark. So I began at the place where I entered, and walked round the hall, looking for some door or passage that might lead me to a more hospitable chamber. As I walked, I was deliciously haunted with the feeling that behind some one of the seemingly innumerable pillars, one who loved me was waiting for me. Then I thought she was following me from pillar to pillar as I went along; but no arms came out of the faint moonlight, and no sigh assured me of her presence.

At length I came to an open corridor, into which I turned; notwithstanding that, in doing so, I left the light behind. Along this I walked with outstretched hands, groping my way, till, arriving at another corridor, which seemed to strike off at right angles to that in which I was, I saw at the end a faintly glimmering light, too pale even for moonshine, resembling rather a stray phosphorescence. However, where everything was white, a little light went a great way. So I walked on to the end, and a long corridor it was. When I came up to the light, I found that it proceeded from what looked like silver letters upon a door of ebony; and, to my surprise even in the home of wonder itself, the letters formed the words, THE CHAMBER OF SIR ANODOS. Although I had as yet no right to the honors of a knight, I ventured to conclude that the chamber was indeed intended for me; and, opening the door without hesitation, I entered. Any doubt as to whether I was right in so doing, was soon dispelled. What to my dark eyes seemed a blaze of light, burst upon me. A fire of large pieces of some sweet-scented wood, supported by dogs of silver, was burning on the hearth, and a bright lamp stood on a table, in the midst of a plentiful meal, apparently awaiting my arrival. But what surprised me more than all, was, that the room was in every respect a copy of my own room, the room whence the little stream from my basin had led me into Fairy Land. There was the very carpet of grass and moss and daisies, which I had myself designed; the curtains of pale blue silk, that fell like a cataract over the windows; the old-fashioned bed, with the chintz furniture, on which I had slept from boyhood. "Now I shall sleep," I said to myself. "My shadow dares not come here."

I sat down to the table, and began to help myself to the good things before me with confidence. And now I found, as in many instances before, how true the fairy tales are; for I was waited on, all the time of my meal, by invisible hands. I had scarcely to do more than look towards anything I wanted, when it was brought me, just as if it had come to me of itself. My glass was kept filled with the wine I had chosen, until I looked towards another bottle or decanter; when a fresh glass was substituted, and the other wine supplied. When I had eaten and drank more heartily and joyfully than ever since I entered Fairy Land, the whole was removed by several attendants, of whom some were male and some female, as I thought I could distinguish from the way the dishes were lifted from the table, and the motion with which they were carried out of the room. As soon as they were all taken away, I heard a sound as of the shutting of a door, and knew that I was left alone. I sat long by the fire, meditating, and wondering how it would all end; and when at length, wearied with thinking, I betook myself to my own bed, it was half with a hope that, when I awoke in the morning, I should awake not only in my own room, but in my own castle also; and that I should walk, out upon my own native soil, and find that Fairy Land was, after all, only a vision of the night. The sound of the falling waters of the fountain floated me into oblivion.

CHAPTER ELEVEN

But when, after a sleep, which, although dreamless, yet left behind it a sense of past blessedness, I awoke in the full morning, I found, indeed, that the room was still my own; but that it looked abroad upon an unknown landscape of forest and hill and dale on the one side—and on the other, upon the marble court, with the great fountain, the crest of which now flashed glorious in the sun, and cast on the pavement beneath a shower of faint shadows from the waters that fell from it into the marble basin below.

Agreeably to all authentic accounts of the treatment of travelers in Fairy Land, I found by my bedside a complete suit of fresh clothing, just such as I was in the habit of wearing; for, though varied sufficiently from the one removed, it was yet in complete accordance with my tastes. I dressed myself in this, and went out. The whole palace shone like silver in the sun. The marble was partly dull and partly polished; and every pinnacle, dome, and turret ended in a ball, or cone, or cusp of silver. It was like frost-work, and too dazzling, in the sun, for earthly eyes like mine.

I will not attempt to describe the environs, save by saying, that all the pleasures to be found in the most varied and artistic arrangement of wood and river, lawn and wild forest, garden and shrubbery, rocky hill and luxurious vale; in living creatures wild and tame, in gorgeous birds, scattered fountains, little streams, and reedy lakes — all were here. Some parts of the palace itself I shall have occasion to describe more minutely.

For this whole morning I never thought of my demon shadow; and not till the weariness which supervened on delight brought it again to my memory, did I look round to see if it was behind me: it was scarcely discernible. But its presence, however faintly revealed, sent a pang to my heart, for the pain of which, not all the beauties around me could compensate. It was followed, however, by the comforting reflection that, peradventure, I might here find the magic word of power to banish the demon and set me free, so that I should no longer be a man beside myself. The Queen of Fairy Land, thought I, must dwell here: surely she will put forth her power to deliver me, and send me singing through the further gates of her country back to my own land. "Shadow of me!" I said; "which art not me, but which representest thyself to me as me; here I may find a shadow of light which will devour thee, the shadow of darkness! Here I may find a blessing which will fall on thee as a curse, and damn thee to the blackness whence thou hast emerged unbidden." I said this, stretched at length on the slope of the lawn above the river; and as the hope arose within me, the sun came forth from a light fleecy cloud that swept across his face; and hill and dale, and the great river winding on through the still mysterious forest, flashed back his rays as with a silent shout of joy; all nature lived and glowed; the very earth grew warm beneath me; a magnificent dragon-fly went past me like an arrow from a bow, and a whole concert of birds burst into choral song.

The heat of the sun soon became too intense even for passive support. I therefore rose, and sought the shelter of one of the arcades. Wandering along from one to another of these, wherever my heedless steps led me, and wondering everywhere at the simple magnificence of the building, I arrived at another hall, the roof of which was of a pale blue, spangled with constellations of silver stars, and supported by porphyry pillars of a paler red than ordinary.—In this house (I may remark in passing), silver seemed everywhere preferred to gold, and such was the purity of the air, that it showed nowhere signs of tarnishing. — The whole of the floor of this hall, except a narrow path behind the pillars, paved with black, was hollowed into a huge basin, many feet deep, and filled with the purest, most liquid and radiant water. The sides of the basin were white marble, and the bottom was paved with all kinds of refulgent stones, of every shape and hue.

In their arrangement, you would have supposed, at first sight, that there was no design, for they seemed to lie as if cast there from careless and playful hands; but it was a most harmonious confusion; and as I looked at the play of their colors, especially when the waters were in motion, I came at last to feel as if not one little pebble could be displaced, without injuring the effect of the whole. Beneath this floor of the water, lay the reflection of the blue inverted roof, fretted with its silver stars, like a second deeper sea, clasping and upholding the first. The fairy bath was probably fed from the fountain in the court. Led by an irresistible desire, I undressed, and plunged into the water. It clothed me as with a new sense and its object both in one. The waters lay so close to me, they seemed to enter and revive my heart. I rose to the surface, shook the water from my hair, and swam as in a rainbow, amid the coruscations of the gems below seen through the agitation caused by my motion. Then, with open eyes, I dived, and swam beneath the surface. And here was a new wonder. For the basin, thus beheld, appeared to extend on all sides like a sea, with here and there groups as of ocean rocks, hollowed by ceaseless billows into wondrous caves and grotesque pinnacles. Around the caves grew sea-weeds of all hues, and the corals glowed between; while far off, I saw the glimmer of what seemed to be creatures of human form at home in the waters. I thought I had been enchanted; and that when I rose to the surface, I should find myself miles from land, swimming alone upon a heaving sea; but when my eyes emerged from the waters, I saw above me the blue spangled vault, and the red pillars around. I dived again, and found myself once more in the heart of a great sea. I then arose, and swam to the edge, where I got out easily, for the water reached the very brim, and, as I drew near washed in tiny waves over the black marble border. I dressed, and went out, deeply refreshed.

And now I began to discern faint, gracious forms, here and there throughout the building. Some walked together in earnest conversation. Others strayed alone. Some stood in groups, as if looking at and talking about a picture or a statue. None of them heeded me. Nor were they plainly visible to my eyes. Sometimes a group, or single individual, would fade entirely out of the realm of my vision as I gazed. When evening came, and the moon arose, clear as a round of a horizon-sea when the sun hangs over it in the west, I began to see them all more plainly; especially when they came between me and the moon; and yet more especially, when I myself was in the shade. But, even then, I sometimes saw only the passing wave of a white robe; or a lovely arm or neck gleamed by in the moonshine; or white feet went walking alone over the moony sward. Nor, I grieve to say, did I ever come much nearer to these glorious beings, or ever look upon the Queen of the Fairies herself. My destiny ordered otherwise.

In this palace of marble and silver, and fountains and moonshine, I spent many days; waited upon constantly in my room with everything desirable, and bathing daily in the fairy bath. All this time I was little troubled with my demon shadow I had a vague feeling that he was somewhere about the palace; but it seemed as if the hope that I should in this place be finally freed from his hated presence, had sufficed to banish him for a time. How and where I found him, I shall soon have to relate.

The third day after my arrival, I found the library of the palace; and here, all the time I remained, I spent most of the middle of the day. For it was, not to mention far greater attractions, a luxurious retreat from the noontide sun. During the mornings and afternoons, I wandered about the lovely neighborhood, or lay, lost in delicious day-dreams, beneath some mighty tree on the open lawn. My evenings were by-and-by spent in a part of the palace, the account of which, and of my adventures in connection with it, I must yet postpone for a little.

The library was a mighty hall, lighted from the roof, which was formed of something like glass, vaulted over in a single piece, and stained throughout with a great mysterious picture in gorgeous coloring.

The walls were lined from floor to roof with books and books: most of them in ancient bindings, but some in strange new fashions which I had never seen, and which, were I to make the attempt, I could ill describe. All around the walls, in front of the books, ran galleries in rows, communicating by stairs. These galleries were built of all kinds of colored stones; all sorts of marble and granite, with porphyry, jasper, lapis lazuli, agate, and various others, were ranged in wonderful melody of successive colors. Although the material, then, of which these galleries and stairs were built, rendered necessary a certain degree of massiveness in the construction, yet such was the size of the place, that they seemed to run along the walls like cords.

Over some parts of the library, descended curtains of silk of various dyes, none of which I ever saw lifted while I was there; and I felt somehow that it would be presumptuous in me to venture to look within them. But the use of the other books seemed free; and day after day I came to the library, threw myself on one of the many sumptuous eastern carpets, which lay here and there on the floor, and read, and read, until weary; if that can be designated as weariness, which was rather the faintness of rapturous delight; or until, sometimes, the failing of the light invited me to go abroad, in the hope that a cool gentle breeze might have arisen to bathe, with an airy invigorating bath, the limbs which the glow of the burning spirit within had withered no less than the glow of the blazing sun without.

One peculiarity of these books, or at least most of those I looked into, I must make a somewhat vain attempt to describe.

If, for instance, it was a book of metaphysics I opened, I had scarcely read two pages before I seemed to myself to be pondering over discovered truth, and constructing the intellectual machine whereby to communicate the discovery to my fellow men. With some books, however, of this nature, it seemed rather as if the process was removed yet a great way further back; and I was trying to find the root of a manifestation, the spiritual truth whence a material vision sprang; or to combine two propositions, both apparently true, either at once or in different remembered moods, and to find the point in which their invisibly converging lines would unite in one, revealing a truth higher than either and differing from both; though so far from being opposed to either, that it was that whence each derived its life and power. Or if the book was one of travels, I found myself the traveler. New lands, fresh experiences, novel customs, rose around me. I walked, I discovered, I fought, I suffered, I rejoiced in my success. Was it a history? I was the chief actor therein. I suffered my own blame; I was glad in my own praise. With a fiction it was the same. Mine was the whole story. For I took the place of the character who was most like myself, and his story was mine; until, grown weary with the life of years condensed in an hour, or arrived at my deathbed, or the end of the volume, I would awake, with a sudden bewilderment, to the consciousness of my present life, recognizing the walls and roof around me, and finding I joyed or sorrowed only in a book. If the book was a poem, the words disappeared, or took the subordinate position of an accompaniment to the succession of forms and images that rose and vanished with a soundless rhythm, and a hidden rime.

In one, with a mystical title, which I cannot recall, I read of a world that is not like ours. The wondrous account, in such a feeble, fragmentary way as is possible to me, I would willingly impart. Whether or not it was all a poem, I cannot tell; but, from the impulse I felt, when I first contemplated writing it, to break into rime, to which impulse I shall give way if it comes upon me again, I think it must have been, partly at least, in verse.

Chapter Twelve

They who believe in the influences of the stars over the fates of men, are, in feeling at least, nearer the truth than they who regard the heavenly bodies as related to them merely by a common obedience to an external law. All that man sees has to do with man. Worlds cannot be without an intermundane relationship. The community of the centre of all creation suggests an interradiating connection and dependence of the parts. Else a grander idea is conceivable than that which is already imbodied. The blank, which is only a forgotten life, lying behind the consciousness, and the misty splendor, which is an undeveloped life, lying before it, may be full of mysterious revelations of other connexions with the worlds around us, than those of science and poetry. No shining belt or gleaming moon, no red and green glory in a self-encircling twin-star, but has a relation with the hidden things of a man's soul, and, it may be, with the secret history of his body as well. They are portions of the living house wherein he abides.

Through the realms of the monarch Sun

Creeps a world, whose course had begun,

On a weary path with a weary pace,

Before the Earth sprang forth on her race:

But many a time the Earth had sped

Around the path she still must tread,

Ere the elder planet, on leaden wing,

Once circled the court of the planet's king.

There, in that lonely and distant star,

The seasons are not as our seasons are;

But many a year hath Autumn to dress

The trees in their matron loveliness;

As long hath old Winter in triumph to go

O'er beauties dead in his vaults below;

And many a year the Spring doth wear

Combing the icicles from her hair;

And Summer, dear Summer, hath years of June,

With large white clouds, and cool showers at noon:

And a beauty that grows to a weight like grief,

Till a burst of tears is the heart's relief.

Children, born when Winter is king,

May never rejoice in the hoping Spring;

Though their own heart-buds are bursting with joy,

And the child hath grown to the girl or boy;

But may die with cold and icy hours

Watching them ever in place of flowers.

And some who awake from their primal sleep,

When the sighs of Summer through forests creep,

Live, and love, and are loved again;

Seek for pleasure, and find its pain;

Sink to their last, their forsaken sleeping,

With the same sweet odors around them creeping.

Now the children, there, are not born as the children are born in worlds nearer to the sun. For they arrive no one knows how. A maiden, walking alone, hears a cry: for even there a cry is the first utterance; and searching about, she findeth, under an overhanging rock, or within a clump of bushes, or, it may be, betwixt gray stones on the side of a hill, or in any other sheltered and unexpected spot, a little child. This she taketh tenderly, and beareth home with joy, calling out, "Mother, mother" — if so be that her mother lives—"I have got a baby — I have found a child!" All the household gathers round to see; — "WHERE IS IT? WHAT IS IT LIKE? WHERE DID YOU FIND IT?" and such-like questions, abounding. And thereupon she relates the whole story of the discovery; for by the circumstances, such as season of the year, time of the day, condition of the air, and such like, and, especially, the peculiar and never-repeated aspect of the heavens and earth at the time, and the nature of the place of shelter wherein it is found, is determined, or at least indicated, the nature of the child thus discovered. Therefore, at certain seasons, and in certain states of the weather, according, in part, to their own fancy, the young women go out to look for children. They generally avoid seeking them, though they cannot help sometimes finding them, in places and with circumstances uncongenial to their peculiar likings. But no sooner is a child found, than its claim for protection and nurture obliterates all feeling of choice in the matter. Chiefly, however, in the season of summer, which lasts so long, coming as it does after such long intervals; and mostly in the warm evenings, about the middle of twilight; and principally in the woods and along the river banks, do the maidens go looking for children just as children look for flowers. And ever as the child grows, yea, more and more as he advances in years, will his face indicate to those who understand the spirit of Nature, and her utterances in the face of the world, the nature of the place of his birth, and the other circumstances thereof; whether a clear morning sun guided his mother to the nook whence issued the boy's low cry; or at eve the lonely maiden (for the same woman never finds a second, at least while the first lives) discovers the girl by the glimmer of her white skin, lying in a nest like that of the lark, amid long encircling grasses, and the upward-gazing eyes of the lowly daisies; whether the storm bowed the forest trees around, or the still frost fixed in silence the else flowing and babbling stream.

After they grow up, the men and women are but little together. There is this peculiar difference between them, which likewise distinguishes the women from those of the earth. The men alone have arms; the women have only wings. Resplendent wings are they, wherein they can shroud themselves from head to foot in a panoply of glistering glory. By these wings alone, it may frequently be judged in what seasons, and under what aspects, they were born. From those that came in winter, go great white wings, white as snow; the edge of every feather shining like the sheen of silver, so that they flash and glitter like frost in the sun. But underneath, they are tinged with a faint pink or rose color. Those born in spring have wings of a brilliant green, green as grass; and towards the edges the feathers are enameled like the surface of the grass-blades. These again are white within. Those that are born in summer have wings of a deep rose-color, lined with pale gold. And those born in autumn have purple wings, with a rich brown on the inside. But these colors are modified and altered in all varieties, corresponding to the mood of the day and hour, as well as the season of the year; and sometimes I found the various colors so intermingled, that I could not determine even the season, though doubtless the hieroglyphic could be deciphered by more experienced eyes. One splendor, in particular, I remember — wings of deep carmine, with an inner down of warm gray, around a form of brilliant whiteness.

She had been found as the sun went down through a low sea- fog, casting crimson along a broad sea-path into a little cave on the shore, where a bathing maiden saw her lying.

But though I speak of sun and fog, and sea and shore, the world there is in some respects very different from the earth whereon men live. For instance, the waters reflect no forms. To the unaccustomed eye they appear, if undisturbed, like the surface of a dark metal, only that the latter would reflect indistinctly, whereas they reflect not at all, except light which falls immediately upon them. This has a great effect in causing the landscapes to differ from those on the earth. On the stillest evening, no tall ship on the sea sends a long wavering reflection almost to the feet of him on shore; the face of no maiden brightens at its own beauty in a still forest-well. The sun and moon alone make a glitter on the surface. The sea is like a sea of death, ready to engulf and never to reveal: a visible shadow of oblivion. Yet the women sport in its waters like gorgeous sea-birds. The men more rarely enter them. But, on the contrary, the sky reflects everything beneath it, as if it were built of water like ours. Of course, from its concavity there is some distortion of the reflected objects; yet wondrous combinations of form are often to be seen in the overhanging depth. And then it is not shaped so much like a round dome as the sky of the earth, but, more of an egg-shape, rises to a great towering height in the middle, appearing far more lofty than the other. When the stars come out at night, it shows a mighty cupola, "fretted with golden fires," wherein there is room for all tempests to rush and rave.

One evening in early summer, I stood with a group of men and women on a steep rock that overhung the sea. They were all questioning me about my world and the ways thereof. In making reply to one of their questions, I was compelled to say that children are not born in the Earth as with them. Upon this I was assailed with a whole battery of inquiries, which at first I tried to avoid; but, at last, I was compelled, in the vaguest manner I could invent, to make some approach to the subject in question. Immediately a dim notion of what I meant, seemed to dawn in the minds of most of the women. Some of them folded their great wings all around them, as they generally do when in the least offended, and stood erect and motionless. One spread out her rosy pinions, and flashed from the promontory into the gulf at its foot. A great light shone in the eyes of one maiden, who turned and walked slowly away, with her purple and white wings half dispread behind her. She was found, the next morning, dead beneath a withered tree on a bare hill-side, some miles inland.

They buried her where she lay, as is their custom; for, before they die, they instinctively search for a spot like the place of their birth, and having found one that satisfies them, they lie down, fold their wings around them, if they be women, or cross their arms over their breasts, if they are men, just as if they were going to sleep; and so sleep indeed. The sign or cause of coming death is an indescribable longing for something, they know not what, which seizes them, and drives them into solitude, consuming them within, till the body fails. When a youth and a maiden look too deep into each other's eyes, this longing seizes and possesses them; but instead of drawing nearer to each other, they wander away, each alone, into solitary places, and die of their desire. But it seems to me, that thereafter they are born babes upon our earth: where, if, when grown, they find each other, it goes well with them; if not, it will seem to go ill. But of this I know nothing. When I told them that the women on the Earth had not wings like them, but arms, they stared, and said how bold and masculine they must look; not knowing that their wings, glorious as they are, are but undeveloped arms.

But see the power of this book, that, while recounting what I can recall of its contents, I write as if myself had visited the far-off planet, learned its ways and appearances, and conversed with its men and women. And so, while writing, it seemed to me that I had.

The book goes on with the story of a maiden, who, born at the close of autumn, and living in a long, to her endless winter, set out at last to find the regions of spring; for, as in our earth, the seasons are divided over the globe. It begins something like this:

She watched them dying for many a day,

Dropping from off the old trees away,

One by one; or else in a shower

Crowding over the withered flower

For as if they had done some grievous wrong,

The sun, that had nursed them and loved them so long,

Grew weary of loving, and, turning back,

Hastened away on his southern track;

And helplessly hung each shriveled leaf,

Faded away with an idle grief.

And the gusts of wind, sad Autumn's sighs,

Mournfully swept through their families;

Casting away with a helpless moan

All that he yet might call his own,

As the child, when his bird is gone for ever,

Flingeth the cage on the wandering river.

And the giant trees, as bare as Death,

Slowly bowed to the great Wind's breath;

And groaned with trying to keep from groaning

Amidst the young trees bending and moaning.

And the ancient planet's mighty sea

Was heaving and falling most restlessly,

And the tops of the waves were broken and white,

Tossing about to ease their might;

And the river was striving to reach the main,

And the ripple was hurrying back again.

Nature lived in sadness now;

Sadness lived on the maiden's brow,

As she watched, with a fixed, half-conscious eye,

One lonely leaf that trembled on high,

Till it dropped at last from the desolate bough —

Sorrow, oh, sorrow! 'tis winter now.

And her tears gushed forth, though it was but a leaf,

For little will loose the swollen fountain of grief:

When up to the lip the water goes,

It needs but a drop, and it overflows.

Oh! many and many a dreary year

Must pass away ere the buds appear:

Many a night of darksome sorrow

Yield to the light of a joyless morrow,

Ere birds again, on the clothed trees,

Shall fill the branches with melodies.

She will dream of meadows with wakeful streams;

Of wavy grass in the sunny beams;

Of hidden wells that soundless spring,

Hoarding their joy as a holy thing;

Of founts that tell it all day long

To the listening woods, with exultant song;

She will dream of evenings that die into nights,

Where each sense is filled with its own delights,

And the soul is still as the vaulted sky,

Lulled with an inner harmony;

And the flowers give out to the dewy night,

Changed into perfume, the gathered light;

And the darkness sinks upon all their host,

Till the sun sail up on the eastern coast—

She will wake and see the branches bare,

Weaving a net in the frozen air.

The story goes on to tell how, at last, weary with wintriness, she traveled towards the southern regions of her globe, to meet the spring on its slow way northwards; and how, after many sad adventures, many disappointed hopes, and many tears, bitter and fruitless, she found at last, one stormy afternoon, in a leafless forest, a single snowdrop growing betwixt the borders of the winter and spring. She lay down beside it and died. I almost believe that a child, pale and peaceful as a snowdrop, was born in the Earth within a fixed season from that stormy afternoon.

CHAPTER THIRTEEN

One story I will try to reproduce. But, alas! it is like trying to reconstruct a forest out of broken branches and withered leaves. In the fairy book, everything was just as it should be, though whether in words or something else, I cannot tell. It glowed and flashed the thoughts upon the soul, with such a power that the medium disappeared from the consciousness, and it was occupied only with the things themselves. My representation of it must resemble a translation from a rich and powerful language, capable of embodying the thoughts of a splendidly developed people, into the meager and half-articulate speech of a savage tribe. Of course, while I read it, I was Cosmo, and his history was mine. Yet, all the time, I seemed to have a kind of double consciousness, and the story a double meaning. Sometimes it seemed only to represent a simple story of ordinary life, perhaps almost of universal life; wherein two souls, loving each other and longing to come nearer, do, after all, but behold each other as in a glass darkly.

As through the hard rock go the branching silver veins; as into the solid land run the creeks and gulfs from the un-resting sea; as the lights and influences of the upper worlds sink silently through the earth's atmosphere; so doth Faerie invade the world of men, and sometimes startle the common eye with an association as of cause and effect, when between the two no connecting links can be traced.

Cosmo von Wehrstahl was a student at the University of Prague. Though of a noble family, he was poor, and prided himself upon the independence that poverty gives; for what will not a man pride himself upon, when he cannot get rid of it? A favorite with his fellow students, he yet had no companions; and none of them had ever crossed the threshold of his lodging in the top of one of the highest houses in the old town. Indeed, the secret of much of that complaisance which recommended him to his fellows, was the thought of his unknown retreat, whither in the evening he could betake himself and indulge undisturbed in his own studies and reveries. These studies, besides those subjects necessary to his course at the University, embraced some less commonly known and approved; for in a secret drawer lay the works of Albertus Magnus and Cornelius Agrippa, along with others less read and more abstruse. As yet, however, he had followed these researches only from curiosity, and had turned them to no practical purpose.

His lodging consisted of one large low-ceiled room, singularly bare of furniture; for besides a couple of wooden chairs, a couch which served for dreaming on both by day and night, and a great press of black oak, there was very little in the room that could be called furniture.

But curious instruments were heaped in the corners; and in one stood a skeleton, half-leaning against the wall, half-supported by a string about its neck. One of its hands, all of fingers, rested on the heavy pommel of a great sword that stood beside it.

Various weapons were scattered about over the floor. The walls were utterly bare of adornment; for the few strange things, such as a large dried bat with wings dispread, the skin of a porcupine, and a stuffed sea-mouse, could hardly be reckoned as such. But although his fancy delighted in vagaries like these, he indulged his imagination with far different fare. His mind had never yet been filled with an absorbing passion; but it lay like a still twilight open to any wind, whether the low breath that wafts but odors, or the storm that bows the great trees till they strain and creak. He saw everything as through a rose-colored glass. When he looked from his window on the street below, not a maiden passed but she moved as in a story, and drew his thoughts after her till she disappeared in the vista. When he walked in the streets, he always felt as if reading a tale, into which he sought to weave every face of interest that went by; and every sweet voice swept his soul as with the wing of a passing angel. He was in fact a poet without words; the more absorbed and endangered, that the springing-waters were dammed back into his soul, where, finding no utterance, they grew, and swelled, and undermined. He used to lie on his hard couch, and read a tale or a poem, till the book dropped from his hand; but he dreamed on, he knew not whether awake or asleep, until the opposite roof grew upon his sense, and turned golden in the sunrise. Then he arose too; and the impulses of vigorous youth kept him ever active, either in study or in sport, until again the close of the day left him free; and the world of night, which had lain drowned in the cataract of the day, rose up in his soul, with all its stars, and dim-seen phantom shapes. But this could hardly last long. Some one form must sooner or later step within the charmed circle, enter the house of life, and compel the bewildered magician to kneel and worship.

One afternoon, towards dusk, he was wandering dreamily in one of the principal streets, when a fellow student roused him by a slap on the shoulder, and asked him to accompany him into a little back alley to look at some old armor which he had taken a fancy to possess. Cosmo was considered an authority in every matter pertaining to arms, ancient or modern. In the use of weapons, none of the students could come near him; and his practical acquaintance with some had principally contributed to establish his authority in reference to all. He accompanied him willingly.

They entered a narrow alley, and thence a dirty little court, where a low arched door admitted them into a heterogeneous assemblage of everything musty, and dusty, and old, that could well be imagined. His verdict on the armor was satisfactory, and his companion at once concluded the purchase. As they were leaving the place, Cosmo's eye was attracted by an old mirror of an elliptical shape, which leaned against the wall, covered with dust. Around it was some curious carving, which he could see but very indistinctly by the glimmering light which the owner of the shop carried in his hand. It was this carving that attracted his attention; at least so it appeared to him. He left the place, however, with his friend, taking no further notice of it. They walked together to the main street, where they parted and took opposite directions.

No sooner was Cosmo left alone, than the thought of the curious old mirror returned to him. A strong desire to see it more plainly arose within him, and he directed his steps once more towards the shop. The owner opened the door when he knocked, as if he had expected him. He was a little, old, withered man, with a hooked nose, and burning eyes constantly in a slow restless motion, and looking here and there as if after something that eluded them. Pretending to examine several other articles, Cosmo at last approached the mirror, and requested to have it taken down.

"Take it down yourself, master; I cannot reach it," said the old man.

Cosmo took it down carefully, when he saw that the carving was indeed delicate and costly, being both of admirable design and execution; containing withal many devices which seemed to embody some meaning to which he had no clue. This, naturally, in one of his tastes and temperament, increased the interest he felt in the old mirror; so much, indeed, that he now longed to possess it, in order to study its frame at his leisure. He pretended, however, to want it only for use; and saying he feared the plate could be of little service, as it was rather old, he brushed away a little of the dust from its face, expecting to see a dull reflection within. His surprise was great when he found the reflection brilliant, revealing a glass not only uninjured by age, but wondrously clear and perfect (should the whole correspond to this part) even for one newly from the hands of the maker. He asked carelessly what the owner wanted for the thing. The old man replied by mentioning a sum of money far beyond the reach of poor Cosmo, who proceeded to replace the mirror where it had stood before.

"You think the price too high?" said the old man.

"I do not know that it is too much for you to ask," replied Cosmo; "but it is far too much for me to give."

The old man held up his light towards Cosmo's face. "I like your look," said he.

Cosmo could not return the compliment. In fact, now he looked closely at him for the first time, he felt a kind of repugnance to him, mingled with a strange feeling of doubt whether a man or a woman stood before him.

"What is your name?" he continued.

"Cosmo von Wehrstahl."

"Ah, ah! I thought as much. I see your father in you. I knew your father very well, young sir. I dare say in some odd corners of my house, you might find some old things with his crest and cipher upon them still. Well, I like you: you shall have the mirror at the fourth part of what I asked for it; but upon one condition."

"What is that?" said Cosmo; for, although the price was still a great deal for him to give, he could just manage it; and the desire to possess the mirror had increased to an altogether unaccountable degree, since it had seemed beyond his reach.

"That if you should ever want to get rid of it again, you will let me have the first offer."

"Certainly," replied Cosmo, with a smile; adding, "a moderate condition indeed."

"On your honor?" insisted the seller.

"On my honor," said the buyer; and the bargain was concluded.

"I will carry it home for you," said the old man, as Cosmo took it in his hands.

"No, no; I will carry it myself," said he; for he had a peculiar dislike to revealing his residence to any one, and more especially to this person, to whom he felt every moment a greater antipathy. "Just as you please," said the old creature, and muttered to himself as he held his light at the door to show him out of the court: "Sold for the sixth time! I wonder what will be the upshot of it this time. I should think my lady had enough of it by now!"

Cosmo carried his prize carefully home. But all the way he had an uncomfortable feeling that he was watched and dogged. Repeatedly he looked about, but saw nothing to justify his suspicions. Indeed, the streets were too crowded and too ill lighted to expose very readily a careful spy, if such there should be at his heels. He reached his lodging in safety, and leaned his purchase against the wall, rather relieved, strong as he was, to be rid of its weight; then, lighting his pipe, threw himself on the couch, and was soon lapt in the folds of one of his haunting dreams.

He returned home earlier than usual the next day, and fixed the mirror to the wall, over the hearth, at one end of his long room.

He then carefully wiped away the dust from its face, and, clear as the water of a sunny spring, the mirror shone out from beneath the envious covering. But his interest was chiefly occupied with the curious carving of the frame. This he cleaned as well as he could with a brush; and then he proceeded to a minute examination of its various parts, in the hope of discovering some index to the intention of the carver. In this, however, he was unsuccessful; and, at length, pausing with some weariness and disappointment, he gazed vacantly for a few moments into the depth of the reflected room. But ere long he said, half aloud: "What a strange thing a mirror is! and what a wondrous affinity exists between it and a man's imagination! For this room of mine, as I behold it in the glass, is the same, and yet not the same. It is not the mere representation of the room I live in, but it looks just as if I were reading about it in a story I like. All its commonness has disappeared. The mirror has lifted it out of the region of fact into the realm of art; and the very representing of it to me has clothed with interest that which was otherwise hard and bare; just as one sees with delight upon the stage the representation of a character from which one would escape in life as from something unendurably wearisome. But is it not rather that art rescues nature from the weary and sated regards of our senses, and the degrading injustice of our anxious everyday life, and, appealing to the imagination, which dwells apart, reveals Nature in some degree as she really is, and as she represents herself to the eye of the child, whose every-day life, fearless and unambitious, meets the true import of the wonder-teeming world around him, and rejoices therein without questioning? That skeleton, now—I almost fear it, standing there so still, with eyes only for the unseen, like a watch-tower looking across all the waste of this busy world into the quiet regions of rest beyond. And yet I know every bone and every joint in it as well as my own fist. And that old battle-axe looks as if any moment it might be caught up by a mailed hand, and, borne forth by the mighty arm, go crashing through casque, and skull, and brain, invading the Unknown with yet another bewildered ghost. I should like to live in THAT room if I could only get into it."

Scarcely had the half-molded words floated from him, as he stood gazing into the mirror, when, striking him as with a flash of amazement that fixed him in his posture, noiseless and unannounced, glided suddenly through the door into the reflected room, with stately motion, yet reluctant and faltering step, the graceful form of a woman, clothed all in white. Her back only was visible as she walked slowly up to the couch in the further end of the room, on which she laid herself wearily, turning towards him a face of unutterable loveliness, in which suffering, and dislike, and a sense of compulsion, strangely mingled with the beauty. He stood without the power of motion for some moments, with his eyes irrecoverably fixed upon her; and even after he was conscious of the ability to move, he could not summon up courage to turn and look on her, face to face, in the veritable chamber in which he stood. At length, with a sudden effort, in which the exercise of the will was so pure, that it seemed involuntary, he turned his face to the couch. It was vacant. In bewilderment, mingled with terror, he turned again to the mirror: there, on the reflected couch, lay the exquisite lady-form. She lay with closed eyes, whence two large tears were just welling from beneath the veiling lids; still as death, save for the convulsive motion of her bosom.

Cosmo himself could not have described what he felt. His emotions were of a kind that destroyed consciousness, and could never be clearly recalled. He could not help standing yet by the mirror, and keeping his eyes fixed on the lady, though he was painfully aware of his rudeness, and feared every moment that she would open hers, and meet his fixed regard. But he was, ere long, a little relieved; for, after a while, her eyelids slowly rose, and her eyes remained uncovered, but unemployed for a time; and when, at length, they began to wander about the room, as if languidly seeking to make some acquaintance with her environment, they were never directed towards him: it seemed nothing but what was in the mirror could affect her vision; and, therefore, if she saw him at all, it could only be his back, which, of necessity, was turned towards her in the glass. The two figures in the mirror could not meet face to face, except he turned and looked at her, present in his room; and, as she was not there, he concluded that if he were to turn towards the part in his room corresponding to that in which she lay, his reflection would either be invisible to her altogether, or at least it must appear to her to gaze vacantly towards her, and no meeting of the eyes would produce the impression of spiritual proximity. By-and-by her eyes fell upon the skeleton, and he saw her shudder and close them. She did not open them again, but signs of repugnance continued evident on her countenance. Cosmo would have removed the obnoxious thing at once, but he feared to discompose her yet more by the assertion of his presence which the act would involve. So he stood and watched her. The eyelids yet shrouded the eyes, as a costly case the jewels within; the troubled expression gradually faded from the countenance, leaving only a faint sorrow behind; the features settled into an unchanging expression of rest; and by these signs, and the slow regular motion of her breathing, Cosmo knew that she slept. He could now gaze on her without embarrassment. He saw that her figure, dressed in the simplest robe of white, was worthy of her face; and so harmonious, that either the delicately molded foot, or any finger of the equally delicate hand, was an index to the whole. As she lay, her whole form manifested the relaxation of perfect repose. He gazed till he was weary, and at last seated himself near the new-found shrine, and mechanically took up a book, like one who watches by a sick-bed. But his eyes gathered no thoughts from the page before him. His intellect had been stunned by the bold contradiction, to its face, of all its experience, and now lay passive, without assertion, or speculation, or even conscious astonishment; while his imagination sent one wild dream of blessedness after another coursing through his soul. How long he sat he knew not; but at length he roused himself, rose, and, trembling in every portion of his frame, looked again into the mirror. She was gone. The mirror reflected faithfully what his room presented, and nothing more. It stood there like a golden setting whence the central jewel has been stolen away— like a night- sky without the glory of its stars. She had carried with her all the strangeness of the reflected room. It had sunk to the level of the one without.

But when the first pangs of his disappointment had passed, Cosmo began to comfort himself with the hope that she might return, perhaps the next evening, at the same hour. Resolving that if she did, she should not at least be scared by the hateful skeleton, he removed that and several other articles of questionable appearance into a recess by the side of the hearth, whence they could not possibly cast any reflection into the mirror; and having made his poor room as tidy as he could, sought the solace of the open sky and of a night wind that had begun to blow, for he could not rest where he was. When he returned, somewhat composed, he could hardly prevail with himself to lie down on his bed; for he could not help feeling as if she had lain upon it; and for him to lie there now would be something like sacrilege. However, weariness prevailed; and laying himself on the couch, dressed as he was, he slept till day.

With a beating heart, beating till he could hardly breathe, he stood in dumb hope before the mirror, on the following evening. Again the reflected room shone as through a purple vapor in the gathering twilight. Everything seemed waiting like himself for a coming splendor to glorify its poor earthliness with the presence of a heavenly joy. And just as the room vibrated with the strokes of the neighboring church bell, announcing the hour of six, in glided the pale beauty, and again laid herself on the couch. Poor Cosmo nearly lost his senses with delight. She was there once more! Her eyes sought the corner where the skeleton had stood, and a faint gleam of satisfaction crossed her face, apparently at seeing it empty. She looked suffering still, but there was less of discomfort expressed in her countenance than there had been the night before. She took more notice of the things about her, and seemed to gaze with some curiosity on the strange apparatus standing here and there in her room. At length, however, drowsiness seemed to overtake her, and again she fell asleep. Resolved not to lose sight of her this time, Cosmo watched the sleeping form. Her slumber was so deep and absorbing that a fascinating repose seemed to pass contagiously from her to him as he gazed upon her; and he started as if from a dream, when the lady moved, and, without opening her eyes, rose, and passed from the room with the gait of a somnambulist.

Cosmo was now in a state of extravagant delight. Most men have a secret treasure somewhere. The miser has his golden hoard; the virtuoso his pet ring; the student his rare book; the poet his favorite haunt; the lover his secret drawer; but Cosmo had a mirror with a lovely lady in it. And now that he knew by the skeleton, that she was affected by the things around her, he had a new object in life: he would turn the bare chamber in the mirror into a room such as no lady need disdain to call her own. This he could effect only by furnishing and adorning his. And Cosmo was poor. Yet he possessed accomplishments that could be turned to account; although, hitherto, he had preferred living on his slender allowance, to increasing his means by what his pride considered unworthy of his rank. He was the best swordsman in the University; and now he offered to give lessons in fencing and similar exercises, to such as chose to pay him well for the trouble. His proposal was heard with surprise by the students; but it was eagerly accepted by many; and soon his instructions were not confined to the richer students, but were anxiously sought by many of the young nobility of Prague and its neighborhood. So that very soon he had a good deal of money at his command. The first thing he did was to remove his apparatus and oddities into a closet in the room. Then he placed his bed and a few other necessaries on each side of the hearth, and parted them from the rest of the room by two screens of Indian fabric. Then he put an elegant couch for the lady to lie upon, in the corner where his bed had formerly stood; and, by degrees, every day adding some article of luxury, converted it, at length, into a rich boudoir.

Every night, about the same time, the lady entered. The first time she saw the new couch, she started with a half-smile; then her face grew very sad, the tears came to her eyes, and she laid herself upon the couch, and pressed her face into the silken cushions, as if to hide from everything. She took notice of each addition and each change as the work proceeded; and a look of acknowledgment, as if she knew that some one was ministering to her, and was grateful for it, mingled with the constant look of suffering. At length, after she had lain down as usual one evening, her eyes fell upon some paintings with which Cosmo had just finished adorning the walls. She rose, and to his great delight, walked across the room, and proceeded to examine them carefully, testifying much pleasure in her looks as she did so. But again the sorrowful, tearful expression returned, and again she buried her face in the pillows of her couch. Gradually, however, her countenance had grown more composed; much of the suffering manifest on her first appearance had vanished, and a kind of quiet, hopeful expression had taken its place; which, however, frequently gave way to an anxious, troubled look, mingled with something of sympathetic pity.

Meantime, how fared Cosmo? As might be expected in one of his temperament, his interest had blossomed into love, and his love — shall I call it RIPENED, or — WITHERED into passion. But, alas! he loved a shadow. He could not come near her, could not speak to her, could not hear a sound from those sweet lips, to which his longing eyes would cling like bees to their honey-founts. Ever and anon he sang to himself:

"I shall die for love of the maiden;" and ever he looked again, and died not, though his heart seemed ready to break with intensity of life and longing.

And the more he did for her, the more he loved her; and he hoped that, although she never appeared to see him, yet she was pleased to think that one unknown would give his life to her. He tried to comfort himself over his separation from her, by thinking that perhaps some day she would see him and make signs to him, and that would satisfy him; "for," thought he, "is not this all that a loving soul can do to enter into communion with another? Nay, how many who love never come nearer than to behold each other as in a mirror; seem to know and yet never know the inward life; never enter the other soul; and part at last, with but the vaguest notion of the universe on the borders of which they have been hovering for years? If I could but speak to her, and knew that she heard me, I should be satisfied." Once he contemplated painting a picture on the wall, which should, of necessity, convey to the lady a thought of himself; but, though he had some skill with the pencil, he found his hand tremble so much when he began the attempt, that he was forced to give it up.

"Who lives, he dies; who dies, he is alive."

One evening, as he stood gazing on his treasure, he thought he saw a faint expression of self-consciousness on her countenance, as if she surmised that passionate eyes were fixed upon her. This grew; till at last the red blood rose over her neck, and cheek, and brow. Cosmo's longing to approach her became almost delirious. This night she was dressed in an evening costume, resplendent with diamonds. This could add nothing to her beauty, but it presented it in a new aspect; enabled her loveliness to make a new manifestation of itself in a new embodiment. For essential beauty is infinite; and, as the soul of Nature needs an endless succession of varied forms to embody her loveliness, countless faces of beauty springing forth, not any two the same, at any one of her heart-throbs; so the individual form needs an infinite change of its environments, to enable it to uncover all the phases of its loveliness. Diamonds glittered from amidst her hair, half hidden in its luxuriance, like stars through dark rain-clouds; and the bracelets on her white arms flashed all the colors of a rainbow of lightnings, as she lifted her snowy hands to cover her burning face. But her beauty shone down all its adornment. "If I might have but one of her feet to kiss," thought Cosmo, "I should be content." Alas! he deceived himself, for passion is never content. Nor did he know that there are TWO ways out of her enchanted house. But, suddenly, as if the pang had been driven into his heart from without, revealing itself first in pain, and afterwards in definite form, the thought darted into his mind, "She has a lover somewhere. Remembered words of his bring the color on her face now. I am nowhere to her. She lives in another world all day, and all night, after she leaves me. Why does she come and make me love her, till I, a strong man, am too faint to look upon her more?" He looked again, and her face was pale as a lily. A sorrowful compassion seemed to rebuke the glitter of the restless jewels, and the slow tears rose in her eyes. She left her room sooner this evening than was her wont. Cosmo remained alone, with a feeling as if his bosom had been suddenly left empty and hollow, and the weight of the whole world was crushing in its walls. The next evening, for the first time since she began to come, she came not.

And now Cosmo was in wretched plight. Since the thought of a rival had occurred to him, he could not rest for a moment. More than ever he longed to see the lady face to face. He persuaded himself that if he but knew the worst he would be satisfied; for then he could abandon Prague, and find that relief in constant motion, which is the hope of all active minds when invaded by distress. Meantime he waited with unspeakable anxiety for the next night, hoping she would return: but she did not appear. And now he fell really ill. Rallied by his fellow students on his wretched looks, he ceased to attend the lectures. His engagements were neglected. He cared for nothing, The sky, with the great sun in it, was to him a heartless, burning desert. The men and women in the streets were mere puppets, without motives in themselves, or interest to him. He saw them all as on the ever-changing field of a camera obscura. She—she alone and altogether—was his universe, his well of life, his incarnate good. For six evenings she came not. Let his absorbing passion, and the slow fever that was consuming his brain, be his excuse for the resolution which he had taken and begun to execute, before that time had expired.

Reasoning with himself, that it must be by some enchantment connected with the mirror, that the form of the lady was to be seen in it, he determined to attempt to turn to account what he had hitherto studied principally from curiosity. "For," said he to himself, "if a spell can force her presence in that glass (and she came unwillingly at first), may not a stronger spell, such as I know, especially with the aid of her half-presence in the mirror, if ever she appears again, compel her living form to come to me here? If I do her wrong, let love be my excuse. I want only to know my doom from her own lips." He never doubted, all the time, that she was a real earthly woman; or, rather, that there was a woman, who, somehow or other, threw this reflection of her form into the magic mirror.

He opened his secret drawer, took out his books of magic, lighted his lamp, and read and made notes from midnight till three in the morning, for three successive nights. Then he replaced his books; and the next night went out in quest of the materials necessary for the conjuration. These were not easy to find; for, in love-charms and all incantations of this nature, ingredients are employed scarcely fit to be mentioned, and for the thought even of which, in connexion with her, he could only excuse himself on the score of his bitter need. At length he succeeded in procuring all he required; and on the seventh evening from that on which she had last appeared, he found himself prepared for the exercise of unlawful and tyrannical power.

He cleared the centre of the room; stooped and drew a circle of red on the floor, around the spot where he stood; wrote in the four quarters mystical signs, and numbers which were all powers of seven or nine; examined the whole ring carefully, to see that no smallest break had occurred in the circumference; and then rose from his bending posture. As he rose, the church clock struck seven; and, just as she had appeared the first time, reluctant, slow, and stately, glided in the lady. Cosmo trembled; and when, turning, she revealed a countenance worn and wan, as with sickness or inward trouble, he grew faint, and felt as if he dared not proceed. But as he gazed on the face and form, which now possessed his whole soul, to the exclusion of all other joys and griefs, the longing to speak to her, to know that she heard him, to hear from her one word in return, became so unendurable, that he suddenly and hastily resumed his preparations. Stepping carefully from the circle, he put a small brazier into its centre. He then set fire to its contents of charcoal, and while it burned up, opened his window and seated himself, waiting, beside it.

It was a sultry evening. The air was full of thunder. A sense of luxurious depression filled the brain. The sky seemed to have grown heavy, and to compress the air beneath it. A kind of purplish tinge pervaded the atmosphere, and through the open window came the scents of the distant fields, which all the vapors of the city could not quench. Soon the charcoal glowed. Cosmo sprinkled upon it the incense and other substances which he had compounded, and, stepping within the circle, turned his face from the brazier and towards the mirror. Then, fixing his eyes upon the face of the lady, he began with a trembling voice to repeat a powerful incantation. He had not gone far, before the lady grew pale; and then, like a returning wave, the blood washed all its banks with its crimson tide, and she hid her face in her hands. Then he passed to a conjuration stronger yet.

The lady rose and walked uneasily to and fro in her room. Another spell; and she seemed seeking with her eyes for some object on which they wished to rest. At length it seemed as if she suddenly espied him; for her eyes fixed themselves full and wide upon his, and she drew gradually, and somewhat unwillingly, close to her side of the mirror, just as if his eyes had fascinated her. Cosmo had never seen her so near before. Now at least, eyes met eyes; but he could not quite understand the expression of hers. They were full of tender entreaty, but there was something more that he could not interpret. Though his heart seemed to labor in his throat, he would allow no delight or agitation to turn him from his task. Looking still in her face, he passed on to the mightiest charm he knew. Suddenly the lady turned and walked out of the door of her reflected chamber. A moment after she entered his room with veritable presence; and, forgetting all his precautions, he sprang from the charmed circle, and knelt before her. There she stood, the living lady of his passionate visions, alone beside him, in a thundery twilight, and the glow of a magic fire.

"Why," said the lady, with a trembling voice, "didst thou bring a poor maiden through the rainy streets alone?"

"Because I am dying for love of thee; but I only brought thee from the mirror there."

"Ah, the mirror!" and she looked up at it, and shuddered. "Alas! I am but a slave, while that mirror exists. But do not think it was the power of thy spells that drew me; it was thy longing desire to see me, that beat at the door of my heart, till I was forced to yield."

"Canst thou love me then?" said Cosmo, in a voice calm as death, but almost inarticulate with emotion.

"I do not know," she replied sadly; "that I cannot tell, so long as I am bewildered with enchantments. It were indeed a joy too great, to lay my head on thy bosom and weep to death; for I think you love me, though I do not know; — but ——"

Cosmo rose from his knees.

"I love thee as — nay, I know not what — for since I have loved thee, there is nothing else."

He seized her hand: she withdrew it.

"No, better not; I am in thy power, and therefore I may not."

She burst into tears, and kneeling before him in her turn, said —

"Cosmo, if you love me, set me free, even from thyself; break the mirror."

"And shall I see thyself instead?"

"That I cannot tell, I will not deceive thee; we may never meet again."

A fierce struggle arose in Cosmo's bosom. Now she was in his power. She did not dislike him at least; and he could see her when he would. To break the mirror would be to destroy his very life to banish out of his universe the only glory it possessed. The whole world would be but a prison, if he annihilated the one window that looked into the paradise of love. Not yet pure in love, he hesitated.

With a wail of sorrow the lady rose to her feet. "Ah! he loves me not; he loves me not even as I love him; and alas! I care more for his love than even for the freedom I ask."

"I will not wait to be willing," cried Cosmo; and sprang to the corner where the great sword stood.

Meantime it had grown very dark; only the embers cast a red glow through the room. He seized the sword by the steel scabbard, and stood before the mirror; but as he heaved a great blow at it with the heavy pommel, the blade slipped half-way out of the scabbard, and the pommel struck the wall above the mirror. At that moment, a terrible clap of thunder seemed to burst in the very room beside them; and ere Cosmo could repeat the blow, he fell senseless on the hearth. When he came to himself, he found that the lady and the mirror had both disappeared. He was seized with a brain fever, which kept him to his couch for weeks.

When he recovered his reason, he began to think what could have become of the mirror. For the lady, he hoped she had found her way back as she came; but as the mirror involved her fate with its own, he was more immediately anxious about that. He could not think she had carried it away. It was much too heavy, even if it had not been too firmly fixed in the wall, for her to remove it. Then again, he remembered the thunder; which made him believe that it was not the lightning, but some other blow that had struck him down. He concluded that, either by supernatural agency, he having exposed himself to the vengeance of the demons in leaving the circle of safety, or in some other mode, the mirror had probably found its way back to its former owner; and, horrible to think of, might have been by this time once more disposed of, delivering up the lady into the power of another man; who, if he used his power no worse than he himself had done, might yet give Cosmo abundant cause to curse the selfish indecision which prevented him from shattering the mirror at once. Indeed, to think that she whom he loved, and who had prayed to him for freedom, should be still at the mercy, in some degree, of the possessor of the mirror, and was at least exposed to his constant observation, was in itself enough to madden a chary lover.

Anxiety to be well retarded his recovery; but at length he was able to creep abroad. He first made his way to the old broker's, pretending to be in search of something else. A laughing sneer on the creature's face convinced him that he knew all about it; but he could not see it amongst his furniture, or get any information out of him as to what had become of it. He expressed the utmost surprise at hearing it had been stolen, a surprise which Cosmo saw at once to be counterfeited; while, at the same time, he fancied that the old wretch was not at all anxious to have it mistaken for genuine. Full of distress, which he concealed as well as he could, he made many searches, but with no avail. Of course he could ask no questions; but he kept his ears awake for any remotest hint that might set him in a direction of search. He never went out without a short heavy hammer of steel about him, that he might shatter the mirror the moment he was made happy by the sight of his lost treasure, if ever that blessed moment should arrive. Whether he should see the lady again, was now a thought altogether secondary, and postponed to the achievement of her freedom. He wandered here and there, like an anxious ghost, pale and haggard; gnawed ever at the heart, by the thought of what she might be suffering—all from his fault.

One night, he mingled with a crowd that filled the rooms of one of the most distinguished mansions in the city; for he accepted every invitation, that he might lose no chance, however poor, of obtaining some information that might expedite his discovery. Here he wandered about, listening to every stray word that he could catch, in the hope of a revelation. As he approached some ladies who were talking quietly in a corner, one said to another:

"Have you heard of the strange illness of the Princess von Hohenweiss?"

"Yes; she has been ill for more than a year now. It is very sad for so fine a creature to have such a terrible malady. She was better for some weeks lately, but within the last few days the same attacks have returned, apparently accompanied with more suffering than ever. It is altogether an inexplicable story."

"Is there a story connected with her illness?"

"I have only heard imperfect reports of it; but it is said that she gave offence some eighteen months ago to an old woman who had held an office of trust in the family, and who, after some incoherent threats, disappeared. This peculiar affection followed soon after. But the strangest part of the story is its association with the loss of an antique mirror, which stood in her dressing-room, and of which she constantly made use."

Here the speaker's voice sank to a whisper; and Cosmo, although his very soul sat listening in his ears, could hear no more. He trembled too much to dare to address the ladies, even if it had been advisable to expose himself to their curiosity. The name of the Princess was well known to him, but he had never seen her; except indeed it was she, which now he hardly doubted, who had knelt before him on that dreadful night. Fearful of attracting attention, for, from the weak state of his health, he could not recover an appearance of calmness, he made his way to the open air, and reached his lodgings; glad in this, that he at least knew where she lived, although he never dreamed of approaching her openly, even if he should be happy enough to free her from her hateful bondage. He hoped, too, that as he had unexpectedly learned so much, the other and far more important part might be revealed to him ere long.

"Have you seen Steinwald lately?"

"No, I have not seen him for some time. He is almost a match for me at the rapier, and I suppose he thinks he needs no more lessons."

"I wonder what has become of him. I want to see him very much. Let me see; the last time I saw him he was coming out of that old broker's den, to which, if you remember, you accompanied me once, to look at some armor. That is fully three weeks ago."

This hint was enough for Cosmo. Von Steinwald was a man of influence in the court, well known for his reckless habits and fierce passions. The very possibility that the mirror should be in his possession was hell itself to Cosmo. But violent or hasty measures of any sort were most unlikely to succeed. All that he wanted was an opportunity of breaking the fatal glass; and to obtain this he must bide his time. He revolved many plans in his mind, but without being able to fix upon any.

At length, one evening, as he was passing the house of Von Steinwald, he saw the windows more than usually brilliant. He watched for a while, and seeing that company began to arrive, hastened home, and dressed as richly as he could, in the hope of mingling with the guests unquestioned: in effecting which, there could be no difficulty for a man of his carriage.

In a lofty, silent chamber, in another part of the city, lay a form more like marble than a living woman. The loveliness of death seemed frozen upon her face, for her lips were rigid, and her eyelids closed. Her long white hands were crossed over her breast, and no breathing disturbed their repose. Beside the dead, men speak in whispers, as if the deepest rest of all could be broken by the sound of a living voice. Just so, though the soul was evidently beyond the reach of all intimations from the senses, the two ladies, who sat beside her, spoke in the gentlest tones of subdued sorrow. "She has lain so for an hour."

"This cannot last long, I fear."

"How much thinner she has grown within the last few weeks! If she would only speak, and explain what she suffers, it would be better for her. I think she has visions in her trances, but nothing can induce her to refer to them when she is awake."

"Does she ever speak in these trances?"

"I have never heard her; but they say she walks sometimes, and once put the whole household in a terrible fright by disappearing for a whole hour, and returning drenched with rain, and almost dead with exhaustion and fright. But even then she would give no account of what had happened."

A scarce audible murmur from the yet motionless lips of the lady here startled her attendants. After several ineffectual attempts at articulation, the word "COSMO!" burst from her. Then she lay still as before; but only for a moment. With a wild cry, she sprang from the couch erect on the floor, flung her arms above her head, with clasped and straining hands, and, her wide eyes flashing with light, called aloud, with a voice exultant as that of a spirit bursting from a sepulcher, "I am free! I am free! I thank thee!" Then she flung herself on the couch, and sobbed; then rose, and paced wildly up and down the room, with gestures of mingled delight and anxiety. Then turning to her motionless attendants—"Quick, Lisa, my cloak and hood!" Then lower—"I must go to him. Make haste, Lisa! You may come with me, if you will."

In another moment they were in the street, hurrying along towards one of the bridges over the Moldau. The moon was near the zenith, and the streets were almost empty. The Princess soon outstripped her attendant, and was half-way over the bridge, before the other reached it.

"Are you free, lady? The mirror is broken: are you free?"

The words were spoken close beside her, as she hurried on. She turned; and there, leaning on the parapet in a recess of the bridge, stood Cosmo, in a splendid dress, but with a white and quivering face.

"Cosmo! — I am free—and thy servant for ever. I was coming to you now."

"And I to you, for Death made me bold; but I could get no further. Have I atoned at all? Do I love you a little — truly?"

"Ah, I know now that you love me, my Cosmo; but what do you say about death?"

He did not reply. His hand was pressed against his side. She looked more closely: the blood was welling from between the fingers. She flung her arms around him with a faint bitter wail.

When Lisa came up, she found her mistress kneeling above a wan dead face, which smiled on in the spectral moonbeams.

And now I will say no more about these wondrous volumes; though I could tell many a tale out of them, and could, perhaps, vaguely represent some entrancing thoughts of a deeper kind which I found within them. From many a sultry noon till twilight, did I sit in that grand hall, buried and risen again in these old books. And I trust I have carried away in my soul some of the exhalations of their undying leaves. In after hours of deserved or needful sorrow, portions of what I read there have often come to me again, with an unexpected comforting; which was not fruitless, even though the comfort might seem in itself groundless and vain.

CHAPTER FOURTEEN

It seemed to me strange, that all this time I had heard no music in the fairy palace. I was convinced there must be music in it, but that my sense was as yet too gross to receive the influence of those mysterious motions that beget sound. Sometimes I felt sure, from the way the few figures of which I got such transitory glimpses passed me, or glided into vacancy before me, that they were moving to the law of music; and, in fact, several times I fancied for a moment that I heard a few wondrous tones coming I knew not whence. But they did not last long enough to convince me that I had heard them with the bodily sense. Such as they were, however, they took strange liberties with me, causing me to burst suddenly into tears, of which there was no presence to make me ashamed, or casting me into a kind of trance of speechless delight, which, passing as suddenly, left me faint and longing for more.

Now, on an evening, before I had been a week in the palace, I was wandering through one lighted arcade and corridor after another. At length I arrived, through a door that closed behind me, in another vast hall of the palace. It was filled with a subdued crimson light; by which I saw that slender pillars of black, built close to walls of white marble, rose to a great height, and then, dividing into innumerable divergent arches, supported a roof, like the walls, of white marble, upon which the arches intersected intricately, forming a fretting of black upon the white, like the network of a skeleton-leaf. The floor was black.

Between several pairs of the pillars upon every side, the place of the wall behind was occupied by a crimson curtain of thick silk, hanging in heavy and rich folds. Behind each of these curtains burned a powerful light, and these were the sources of the glow that filled the hall. A peculiar delicious odor pervaded the place. As soon as I entered, the old inspiration seemed to return to me, for I felt a strong impulse to sing; or rather, it seemed as if some one else was singing a song in my soul, which wanted to come forth at my lips, imbodied in my breath. But I kept silence; and feeling somewhat overcome by the red light and the perfume, as well as by the emotion within me, and seeing at one end of the hall a great crimson chair, more like a throne than a chair, beside a table of white marble, I went to it, and, throwing myself in it, gave myself up to a succession of images of bewildering beauty, which passed before my inward eye, in a long and occasionally crowded train. Here I sat for hours, I suppose; till, returning somewhat to myself, I saw that the red light had paled away, and felt a cool gentle breath gliding over my forehead. I rose and left the hall with unsteady steps, finding my way with some difficulty to my own chamber, and faintly remembering, as I went, that only in the marble cave, before I found the sleeping statue, had I ever had a similar experience.

After this, I repaired every morning to the same hall; where I sometimes sat in the chair and dreamed deliciously, and sometimes walked up and down over the black floor. Sometimes I acted within myself a whole drama, during one of these perambulations; sometimes walked deliberately through the whole epic of a tale; sometimes ventured to sing a song, though with a shrinking fear of I knew not what. I was astonished at the beauty of my own voice as it rang through the place, or rather crept undulating, like a serpent of sound, along the walls and roof of this superb music-hall. Entrancing verses arose within me as of their own accord, chanting themselves to their own melodies, and requiring no addition of music to satisfy the inward sense. But, ever in the pauses of these, when the singing mood was upon me, I seemed to hear something like the distant sound of multitudes of dancers, and felt as if it was the unheard music, moving their rhythmic motion, that within me blossomed in verse and song. I felt, too, that could I but see the dance, I should, from the harmony of complicated movements, not of the dancers in relation to each other merely, but of each dancer individually in the manifested plastic power that moved the consenting harmonious form, understand the whole of the music on the billows of which they floated and swung.

At length, one night, suddenly, when this feeling of dancing came upon me, I bethought me of lifting one of the crimson curtains, and looking if, perchance, behind it there might not be hid some other mystery, which might at least remove a step further the bewilderment of the present one. Nor was I altogether disappointed. I walked to one of the magnificent draperies, lifted a corner, and peeped in. There, burned a great, crimson, globe-shaped light, high in the cubical centre of another hall, which might be larger or less than that in which I stood, for its dimensions were not easily perceived, seeing that floor and roof and walls were entirely of black marble.

The roof was supported by the same arrangement of pillars radiating in arches, as that of the first hall; only, here, the pillars and arches were of dark red. But what absorbed my delighted gaze, was an innumerable assembly of white marble statues, of every form, and in multitudinous posture, filling the hall throughout. These stood, in the ruddy glow of the great lamp, upon pedestals of jet black. Around the lamp shone in golden letters, plainly legible from where I stood, the two words— TOUCH NOT!

There was in all this, however, no solution to the sound of dancing; and now I was aware that the influence on my mind had ceased. I did not go in that evening, for I was weary and faint, but I hoarded up the expectation of entering, as of a great coming joy.

Next night I walked, as on the preceding, through the hall. My mind was filled with pictures and songs, and therewith so much absorbed, that I did not for some time think of looking within the curtain I had last night lifted. When the thought of doing so occurred to me first, I happened to be within a few yards of it. I became conscious, at the same moment, that the sound of dancing had been for some time in my ears. I approached the curtain quickly, and, lifting it, entered the black hall. Everything was still as death. I should have concluded that the sound must have proceeded from some other more distant quarter, which conclusion its faintness would, in ordinary circumstances, have necessitated from the first; but there was a something about the statues that caused me still to remain in doubt. As I said, each stood perfectly still upon its black pedestal: but there was about every one a certain air, not of motion, but as if it had just ceased from movement; as if the rest were not altogether of the marbly stillness of thousands of years. It was as if the peculiar atmosphere of each had yet a kind of invisible tremulousness; as if its agitated wavelets had not yet subsided into a perfect calm. I had the suspicion that they had anticipated my appearance, and had sprung, each, from the living joy of the dance, to the death-silence and blackness of its isolated pedestal, just before I entered. I walked across the central hall to the curtain opposite the one I had lifted, and, entering there, found all the appearances similar; only that the statues were different, and differently grouped. Neither did they produce on my mind that impression—of motion just expired, which I had experienced from the others. I found that behind every one of the crimson curtains was a similar hall, similarly lighted, and similarly occupied.

The next night, I did not allow my thoughts to be absorbed as before with inward images, but crept stealthily along to the furthest curtain in the hall, from behind which, likewise, I had formerly seemed to hear the sound of dancing. I drew aside its edge as suddenly as I could, and, looking in, saw that the utmost stillness pervaded the vast place. I walked in, and passed through it to the other end.

There I found that it communicated with a circular corridor, divided from it only by two rows of red columns. This corridor, which was black, with red niches holding statues, ran entirely about the statue- halls, forming a communication between the further ends of them all; further, that is, as regards the central hall of white whence they all diverged like radii, finding their circumference in the corridor.

Round this corridor I now went, entering all the halls, of which there were twelve, and finding them all similarly constructed, but filled with quite various statues, of what seemed both ancient and modern sculpture. After I had simply walked through them, I found myself sufficiently tired to long for rest, and went to my own room.

In the night I dreamed that, walking close by one of the curtains, I was suddenly seized with the desire to enter, and darted in. This time I was too quick for them. All the statues were in motion, statues no longer, but men and women—all shapes of beauty that ever sprang from the brain of the sculptor, mingled in the convolutions of a complicated dance. Passing through them to the further end, I almost started from my sleep on beholding, not taking part in the dance with the others, nor seemingly endued with life like them, but standing in marble coldness and rigidity upon a black pedestal in the extreme left corner — my lady of the cave; the marble beauty who sprang from her tomb or her cradle at the call of my songs. While I gazed in speechless astonishment and admiration, a dark shadow, descending from above like the curtain of a stage, gradually hid her entirely from my view. I felt with a shudder that this shadow was perchance my missing demon, whom I had not seen for days. I awoke with a stifled cry.

Of course, the next evening I began my journey through the halls (for I knew not to which my dream had carried me), in the hope of proving the dream to be a true one, by discovering my marble beauty upon her black pedestal. At length, on reaching the tenth hall, I thought I recognized some of the forms I had seen dancing in my dream; and to my bewilderment, when I arrived at the extreme corner on the left, there stood, the only one I had yet seen, a vacant pedestal. It was exactly in the position occupied, in my dream, by the pedestal on which the white lady stood. Hope beat violently in my heart.

"Now," said I to myself, "if yet another part of the dream would but come true, and I should succeed in surprising these forms in their nightly dance; it might be the rest would follow, and I should see on the pedestal my marble queen. Then surely if my songs sufficed to give her life before, when she lay in the bonds of alabaster, much more would they be sufficient then to give her volition and motion, when she alone of assembled crowds of marble forms, would be standing rigid and cold."

But the difficulty was, to surprise the dancers. I had found that a premeditated attempt at surprise, though executed with the utmost care and rapidity, was of no avail. And, in my dream, it was effected by a sudden thought suddenly executed. I saw, therefore, that there was no plan of operation offering any probability of success, but this: to allow my mind to be occupied with other thoughts, as I wandered around the great centre-hall; and so wait till the impulse to enter one of the others should happen to arise in me just at the moment when I was close to one of the crimson curtains. For I hoped that if I entered any one of the twelve halls at the right moment, that would as it were give me the right of entrance to all the others, seeing they all had communication behind. I would not diminish the hope of the right chance, by supposing it necessary that a desire to enter should awake within me, precisely when I was close to the curtains of the tenth hall.

At first the impulses to see recurred so continually, in spite of the crowded imagery that kept passing through my mind, that they formed too nearly a continuous chain, for the hope that any one of them would succeed as a surprise. But as I persisted in banishing them, they recurred less and less often; and after two or three, at considerable intervals, had come when the spot where I happened to be was unsuitable, the hope strengthened, that soon one might arise just at the right moment; namely, when, in walking round the hall, I should be close to one of the curtains.

At length the right moment and the impulse coincided. I darted into the ninth hall. It was full of the most exquisite moving forms. The whole space wavered and swam with the involutions of an intricate dance. It seemed to break suddenly as I entered, and all made one or two bounds towards their pedestals; but, apparently on finding that they were thoroughly overtaken, they returned to their employment (for it seemed with them earnest enough to be called such) without further heeding me. Somewhat impeded by the floating crowd, I made what haste I could towards the bottom of the hall; whence, entering the corridor, I turned towards the tenth. I soon arrived at the corner I wanted to reach, for the corridor was comparatively empty; but, although the dancers here, after a little confusion, altogether disregarded my presence, I was dismayed at beholding, even yet, a vacant pedestal. But I had a conviction that she was near me. And as I looked at the pedestal, I thought I saw upon it, vaguely revealed as if through overlapping folds of drapery, the indistinct outlines of white feet. Yet there was no sign of drapery or concealing shadow whatever. But I remembered the descending shadow in my dream. And I hoped still in the power of my songs; thinking that what could dispel alabaster, might likewise be capable of dispelling what concealed my beauty now, even if it were the demon whose darkness had overshadowed all my life.

CHAPTER FIFTEEN

And now, what song should I sing to unveil my Isis, if indeed she was present unseen? I hurried away to the white hall of Phantasy, heedless of the innumerable forms of beauty that crowded my way: these might cross my eyes, but the unseen filled my brain. I wandered long, up and down the silent space: no songs came. My soul was not still enough for songs. Only in the silence and darkness of the soul's night, do those stars of the inward firmament sink to its lower surface from the singing realms beyond, and shine upon the conscious spirit. Here all effort was unavailing. If they came not, they could not be found.

Next night, it was just the same. I walked through the red glimmer of the silent hall; but lonely as there I walked, as lonely trod my soul up and down the halls of the brain. At last I entered one of the statue-halls. The dance had just commenced, and I was delighted to find that I was free of their assembly. I walked on till I came to the sacred corner. There I found the pedestal just as I had left it, with the faint glimmer as of white feet still resting on the dead black. As soon as I saw it, I seemed to feel a presence which longed to become visible; and, as it were, called to me to gift it with self-manifestation, that it might shine on me. The power of song came to me. But the moment my voice, though I sang low and soft, stirred the air of the hall, the dancers started; the quick interweaving crowd shook, lost its form, divided; each figure sprang to its pedestal, and stood, a self-evolving life no more, but a rigid, life-like, marble shape, with the whole form composed into the expression of a single state or act. Silence rolled like a spiritual thunder through the grand space. My song had ceased, scared at its own influences. But I saw in the hand of one of the statues close by me, a harp whose chords yet quivered. I remembered that as she bounded past me, her harp had brushed against my arm; so the spell of the marble had not infolded it. I sprang to her, and with a gesture of entreaty, laid my hand on the harp. The marble hand, probably from its contact with the un-charmed harp, had strength enough to relax its hold, and yield the harp to me. No other motion indicated life. Instinctively I struck the chords and sang. And not to break upon the record of my song, I mention here, that as I sang the first four lines, the loveliest feet became clear upon the black pedestal; and ever as I sang, it was as if a veil were being lifted up from before the form, but an invisible veil, so that the statue appeared to grow before me, not so much by evolution, as by infinitesimal degrees of added height. And, while I sang, I did not feel that I stood by a statue, as indeed it appeared to be, but that a real woman-soul was revealing itself by successive stages of embodiment, and consequent manifestation and expression.

Feet of beauty, firmly planting

Arches white on rosy heel!

Whence the life-spring, throbbing, panting,

Pulses upward to reveal!

Fairest things know least despising;

Foot and earth meet tenderly:

'Tis the woman, resting, rising

Upward to sublimity,

Rise the limbs, sedately sloping,

Strong and gentle, full and free;

Soft and slow, like certain hoping,

Drawing nigh the broad firm knee.

Up to speech! As up to roses

Pants the life from leaf to flower,

So each blending change discloses,

Nearer still, expression's power.

Lo! fair sweeps, white surges, twining
Up and outward fearlessly!
Temple columns, close combining,
Lift a holy mystery.
Heart of mine! what strange surprises
Mount aloft on such a stair!
Some great vision upward rises,
Curving, bending, floating fair.

Bands and sweeps, and hill and hollow
Lead my fascinated eye;
Some apocalypse will follow,
Some new world of deity.
Zoned unseen, and outward swelling,
With new thoughts and wonders rife,
Queenly majesty foretelling,
See the expanding house of life!

Sudden heaving, un-forbidden
Sighs eternal, still the same —
Mounts of snow have summits hidden
In the mists of uttered flame.
But the spirit, dawning nearly
Finds no speech for earnest pain;
Finds a soundless sighing merely —
Builds its stairs, and mounts again.

Heart, the queen, with secret hoping,
Sends out her waiting pair;
Hands, blind hands, half blindly groping,
Half in-clasping visions rare;
And the great arms, heart ways bending;
Might of Beauty, drawing home
There returning, and re-blending,
Where from roots of love they roam.

Build thy slopes of radiance beamy
Spirit, fair with womanhood!
Tower thy precipice, white-gleamy,
Climb unto the hour of good.
Dumb space will be rent asunder,
Now the shining column stands
Ready to be crowned with wonder
By the builder's joyous hands.

All the lines abroad are spreading,
Like a fountain's falling race.
Lo, the chin, first feature, treading,
Airy foot to rest the face!
Speech is nigh; oh, see the blushing,
Sweet approach of lip and breath!
Round the mouth dim silence, hushing,
Waits to die ecstatic death.

Span across in treble curving,
Bow of promise, upper lip!
Set them free, with gracious swerving;
Let the wing-words float and dip.
DUMB ART THOU? O Love immortal,
More than words thy speech must be;
Childless yet the tender portal
Of the home of melody.

Now the nostrils open fearless,
Proud in calm unconsciousness,
Sure it must be something peerless
That the great Pan would express!
Deepens, crowds some meaning tender,
In the pure, dear lady-face.
Lo, a blinding burst of splendor! —
'Tis the free soul's issuing grace.

Two calm lakes of molten glory
Circling round unfathomed deeps!
Lightning-flashes, transitory,
Cross the gulfs where darkness sleeps.
This the gate, at last, of gladness,
To the outward striving me:
In a rain of light and sadness,
Out its loves and longings flee!

With a presence I am smitten
Dumb, with a foreknown surprise;
Presence greater yet than written
Even in the glorious eyes.
Through the gulfs, with inward gazes,
I may look till I am lost;
Wandering deep in spirit-mazes,
In a sea without a coast.

Windows open to the glorious!
Time and space, oh, far beyond!
Woman, ah! thou art victorious,
And I perish, over fond.
Springs aloft the yet Unspoken
In the forehead's endless grace,
Full of silences unbroken;
Infinite, un-featured face.

Domes above, the mount of wonder;
Height and hollow wrapt in night;
Hiding in its caverns under
Woman-nations in their might.
Passing forms, the highest Human
Faints away to the Divine
Features none, of man or woman,
Can unveil the holiest shine.

Sideways, grooved porches only

Visible to passing eye,

Stand the silent, doorless, lonely

Entrance-gates of melody.

But all sounds fly in as boldly,

Groan and song, and kiss and cry

At their galleries, lifted coldly,

Darkly, 'twixt the earth and sky.

Beauty, you are spent, you know

So, in faint, half-glad despair,

From the summit you overflow

In a fall of torrent hair;

Hiding what thou hast created

In a half-transparent shroud:

Thus, with glory soft-abated,

Shines the moon through vapory cloud.

CHAPTER SIXTEEN

Ever as I sang, the veil was uplifted; ever as I sang, the signs of life grew; till, when the eyes dawned upon me, it was with that sunrise of splendor which my feeble song attempted to re-imbody.

The wonder is, that I was not altogether overcome, but was able to complete my song as the unseen veil continued to rise. This ability came solely from the state of mental elevation in which I found myself. Only because uplifted in song, was I able to endure the blaze of the dawn. But I cannot tell whether she looked more of statue or more of woman; she seemed removed into that region of phantasy where all is intensely vivid, but nothing clearly defined. At last, as I sang of her descending hair, the glow of soul faded away, like a dying sunset. A lamp within had been extinguished, and the house of life shone blank in a winter morn. She was a statue once more—but visible, and that was much gained. Yet the revulsion from hope and fruition was such, that, unable to restrain myself, I sprang to her, and, in defiance of the law of the place, flung my arms around her, as if I would tear her from the grasp of a visible Death, and lifted her from the pedestal down to my heart. But no sooner had her feet ceased to be in contact with the black pedestal, than she shuddered and trembled all over; then, writhing from my arms, before I could tighten their hold, she sprang into the corridor, with the reproachful cry, "You should not have touched me!" darted behind one of the exterior pillars of the circle, and disappeared. I followed almost as fast; but ere I could reach the pillar, the sound of a closing door, the saddest of all sounds sometimes, fell on my ear; and, arriving at the spot where she had vanished, I saw, lighted by a pale yellow lamp which hung above it, a heavy, rough door, altogether unlike any others I had seen in the palace; for they were all of ebony, or ivory, or covered with silver-plates, or of some odorous wood, and very ornate; whereas this seemed of old oak, with heavy nails and iron studs. Notwithstanding the precipitation of my pursuit, I could not help reading, in silver letters beneath the lamp: "NO ONE ENTERS HERE WITHOUT THE LEAVE OF THE QUEEN." But what was the Queen to me, when I followed my white lady? I dashed the door to the wall and sprang through. Lo! I stood on a waste windy hill. Great stones like tombstones stood all about me. No door, no palace was to be seen. A white figure gleamed past me, wringing her hands, and crying, "Ah! you should have sung to me; you should have sung to me!" and disappeared behind one of the stones. I followed. A cold gust of wind met me from behind the stone; and when I looked, I saw nothing but a great hole in the earth, into which I could find no way of entering. Had she fallen in? I could not tell. I must wait for the daylight. I sat down and wept, for there was no help.

Chapter Seventeen

When the daylight came, it brought the possibility of action, but with it little of consolation. With the first visible increase of light, I gazed into the chasm, but could not, for more than an hour, see sufficiently well to discover its nature. At last I saw it was almost a perpendicular opening, like a roughly excavated well, only very large. I could perceive no bottom; and it was not till the sun actually rose, that I discovered a sort of natural staircase, in many parts little more than suggested, which led round and round the gulf, descending spirally into its abyss. I saw at once that this was my path; and without a moment's hesitation, glad to quit the sunlight, which stared at me most heartlessly, I commenced my tortuous descent. It was very difficult. In some parts I had to cling to the rocks like a bat. In one place, I dropped from the track down upon the next returning spire of the stair; which being broad in this particular portion, and standing out from the wall at right angles, received me upon my feet safe, though somewhat stupefied by the shock. After descending a great way, I found the stair ended at a narrow opening which entered the rock horizontally. Into this I crept, and, having entered, had just room to turn round. I put my head out into the shaft by which I had come down, and surveyed the course of my descent. Looking up, I saw the stars; although the sun must by this time have been high in the heavens. Looking below, I saw that the sides of the shaft went sheer down, smooth as glass; and far beneath me, I saw the reflection of the same stars I had seen in the heavens when I looked up. I turned again, and crept inwards some distance, when the passage widened, and I was at length able to stand and walk upright. Wider and loftier grew the way; new paths branched off on every side; great open halls appeared; till at last I found myself wandering on through an underground country, in which the sky was of rock, and instead of trees and flowers, there were only fantastic rocks and stones. And ever as I went, darker grew my thoughts, till at last I had no hope whatever of finding the white lady: I no longer called her to myself MY white lady. Whenever a choice was necessary, I always chose the path which seemed to lead downwards.

At length I began to find that these regions were inhabited. From behind a rock a peal of harsh grating laughter, full of evil humor, rang through my ears, and, looking round, I saw a queer, goblin creature, with a great head and ridiculous features, just such as those described, in German histories and travels, as Kobolds. "What do you want with me?" I said. He pointed at me with a long forefinger, very thick at the root, and sharpened to a point, and answered, "He! he! he! what do YOU want here?" Then, changing his tone, he continued, with mock humility—"Honored sir, vouchsafe to withdraw from thy slaves the luster of thy august presence, for thy slaves cannot support its brightness." A second appeared, and struck in: "You are so big, you keep the sun from us. We can't see for you, and we're so cold." Thereupon arose, on all sides, the most terrific uproar of laughter, from voices like those of children in volume, but scrannel and harsh as those of decrepit age, though, unfortunately, without its weakness. The whole pandemonium of fairy devils, of all varieties of fantastic ugliness, both in form and feature, and of all sizes from one to four feet, seemed to have suddenly assembled about me. At length, after a great babble of talk among themselves, in a language unknown to me, and after seemingly endless gesticulation, consultation, elbow-nudging, and unmitigated peals of laughter, they formed into a circle about one of their number, who scrambled upon a stone, and, much to my surprise, and somewhat to my dismay, began to sing, in a voice corresponding in its nature to his talking one, from beginning to end, the song with which I had brought the light into the eyes of the white lady. He sang the same air too; and, all the time, maintained a face of mock entreaty and worship; accompanying the song with the travestied gestures of one playing on the lute. The whole assembly kept silence, except at the close of every verse, when they roared, and danced, and shouted with laughter, and flung themselves on the ground, in real or pretended convulsions of delight. When he had finished, the singer threw himself from the top of the stone, turning heels over head several times in his descent; and when he did alight, it was on the top of his head, on which he hopped about, making the most grotesque gesticulations with his legs in the air. Inexpressible laughter followed, which broke up in a shower of tiny stones from innumerable hands. They could not materially injure me, although they cut me on the head and face. I attempted to run away, but they all rushed upon me, and, laying hold of every part that afforded a grasp, held me tight. Crowding about me like bees, they shouted an insect-swarm of exasperating speeches up into my face, among which the most frequently recurring were—"You shan't have her; you shan't have her; he! he! he! She's for a better man; how he'll kiss her! How he'll kiss her!"

The galvanic torrent of this battery of malevolence stung to life within me a spark of nobleness, and I said aloud, "Well, if he is a better man, let him have her."

They instantly let go their hold of me, and fell back a step or two, with a whole broadside of grunts and humphs, as of unexpected and disappointed approbation. I made a step or two forward, and a lane was instantly opened for me through the midst of the grinning little antics, who bowed most politely to me on every side as I passed. After I had gone a few yards, I looked back, and saw them all standing quite still, looking after me, like a great school of boys; till suddenly one turned round, and with a loud whoop, rushed into the midst of the others. In an instant, the whole was one writhing and tumbling heap of contortion, reminding me of the live pyramids of intertwined snakes of which travelers make report. As soon as one was worked out of the mass, he bounded off a few paces, and then, with a somersault and a run, threw himself gyrating into the air, and descended with all his weight on the summit of the heaving and struggling chaos of fantastic figures. I left them still busy at this fierce and apparently aimless amusement. And as I went, I sang —

If a nobler waits for thee,

I will weep aside;

It is well that you should be,

Of the nobler, bride.

For if love builds up the home,

Where the heart is free,

Homeless yet the heart must roam,

That has not found thee.

One must suffer: I, for her

Yield in her my part
Take her, thou art worthier —
Still I be still, my heart!

Gift ungotten! largess high
Of a frustrate will!
But to yield it lovingly
Is a something still.

Then a little song arose of itself in my soul; and I felt for the moment, while it sank sadly within me, as if I was once more walking up and down the white hall of Phantasy in the Fairy Palace. But this lasted no longer than the song; as will be seen.

Do not vex thy violet
Perfume to afford:
Else no odor you wilt get
From its little hoard.

In thy lady's gracious eyes
Look not thou too long;
Else from them the glory flies,
And thou dost her wrong.

Come not thou too near the maid,
Clasp her not too wild;
Else the splendor is allayed,
And thy heart beguiled.

A crash of laughter, more discordant and deriding than any I had yet heard, invaded my ears. Looking on in the direction of the sound, I saw a little elderly woman, much taller, however, than the goblins I had just left, seated upon a stone by the side of the path. She rose, as I drew near, and came forward to meet me.

She was very plain and commonplace in appearance, without being hideously ugly. Looking up in my face with a stupid sneer, she said: "Isn't it a pity you haven't a pretty girl to walk all alone with you through this sweet country? How different everything would look? wouldn't it?

Strange that one can never have what one would like best! How the roses would bloom and all that, even in this infernal hole! wouldn't they, Anodos? Her eyes would light up the old cave, wouldn't they?"

"That depends on who the pretty girl should be," replied I.

"Not so very much matter that," she answered; "look here."

I had turned to go away as I gave my reply, but now I stopped and looked at her. As a rough unsightly bud might suddenly blossom into the most lovely flower; or rather, as a sunbeam bursts through a shapeless cloud, and transfigures the earth; so burst a face of resplendent beauty, as it were THROUGH the unsightly visage of the woman, destroying it with light as it dawned through it. A summer sky rose above me, gray with heat; across a shining slumberous landscape, looked from afar the peaks of snow-capped mountains; and down from a great rock beside me fell a sheet of water mad with its own delight.

"Stay with me," she said, lifting up her exquisite face, and looking full in mine.

I drew back. Again the infernal laugh grated upon my ears; again the rocks closed in around me, and the ugly woman looked at me with wicked, mocking hazel eyes.

"You shall have your reward," said she. "You shall see your white lady again."

"That lies not with you," I replied, and turned and left her.

She followed me with shriek upon shriek of laughter, as I went on my way.

I may mention here, that although there was always light enough to see my path and a few yards on every side of me, I never could find out the source of this sad sepulchral illumination.

CHAPTER EIGHTEEN

How I got through this dreary part of my travels, I do not know. I do not think I was upheld by the hope that any moment the light might break in upon me; for I scarcely thought about that. I went on with a dull endurance, varied by moments of uncontrollable sadness; for more and more the conviction grew upon me that I should never see the white lady again. It may seem strange that one with whom I had held so little communion should have so engrossed my thoughts; but benefits conferred awaken love in some minds, as surely as benefits received in others. Besides being delighted and proud that my songs had called the beautiful creature to life, the same fact caused me to feel a tenderness unspeakable for her, accompanied with a kind of feeling of property in her; for so the goblin Selfishness would reward the angel Love. When to all this is added, an overpowering sense of her beauty, and an unquestioning conviction that this was a true index to inward loveliness, it may be understood how it came to pass that my imagination filled my whole soul with the play of its own multitudinous colors and harmonies around the form which yet stood, a gracious marble radiance, in the midst of ITS white hall of phantasy. The time passed by unheeded; for my thoughts were busy. Perhaps this was also in part the cause of my needing no food, and never thinking how I should find any, during this subterraneous part of my travels. How long they endured I could not tell, for I had no means of measuring time; and when I looked back, there was such a discrepancy between the decisions of my imagination and my judgment, as to the length of time that had passed, that I was bewildered, and gave up all attempts to arrive at any conclusion on the point.

A gray mist continually gathered behind me. When I looked back towards the past, this mist was the medium through which my eyes had to strain for a vision of what had gone by; and the form of the white lady had receded into an unknown region. At length the country of rock began to close again around me, gradually and slowly narrowing, till I found myself walking in a gallery of rock once more, both sides of which I could touch with my outstretched hands. It narrowed yet, until I was forced to move carefully, in order to avoid striking against the projecting pieces of rock. The roof sank lower and lower, until I was compelled, first to stoop, and then to creep on my hands and knees. It recalled terrible dreams of childhood; but I was not much afraid, because I felt sure that this was my path, and my only hope of leaving Fairy Land, of which I was now almost weary.

At length, on getting past an abrupt turn in the passage, through which I had to force myself, I saw, a few yards ahead of me, the long- forgotten daylight shining through a small opening, to which the path, if path it could now be called, led me. With great difficulty I accomplished these last few yards, and came forth to the day. I stood on the shore of a wintry sea, with a wintry sun just a few feet above its horizon-edge. It was bare, and waste, and gray. Hundreds of hopeless waves rushed constantly shore-wards, falling exhausted upon a beach of great loose stones, that seemed to stretch miles and miles in both directions. There was nothing for the eye but mingling shades of gray; nothing for the ear but the rush of the coming, the roar of the breaking, and the moan of the retreating wave. No rock lifted up a sheltering severity above the dreariness around; even that from which I had myself emerged rose scarcely a foot above the opening by which I had reached the dismal day, more dismal even than the tomb I had left. A cold, death-like wind swept across the shore, seeming to issue from a pale mouth of cloud upon the horizon. Sign of life was nowhere visible. I wandered over the stones, up and down the beach, a human imbodiment of the nature around me. The wind increased; its keen waves flowed through my soul; the foam rushed higher up the stones; a few dead stars began to gleam in the east; the sound of the waves grew louder and yet more despairing. A dark curtain of cloud was lifted up, and a pale blue rent shone between its foot and the edge of the sea, out from which rushed an icy storm of frozen wind, that tore the waters into spray as it passed, and flung the billows in raving heaps upon the desolate shore. I could bear it no longer.

"I will not be tortured to death," I cried; "I will meet it half-way. The life within me is yet enough to bear me up to the face of Death, and then I die unconquered."

Before it had grown so dark, I had observed, though without any particular interest, that on one part of the shore a low platform of rock seemed to run out far into the midst of the breaking waters.

Towards this I now went, scrambling over smooth stones, to which scarce even a particle of sea-weed clung; and having found it, I got on it, and followed its direction, as near as I could guess, out into the tumbling chaos. I could hardly keep my feet against the wind and sea. The waves repeatedly all but swept me off my path; but I kept on my way, till I reached the end of the low promontory, which, in the fall of the waves, rose a good many feet above the surface, and, in their rise, was covered with their waters. I stood one moment and gazed into the heaving abyss beneath me; then plunged headlong into the mounting wave below. A blessing, like the kiss of a mother, seemed to alight on my soul; a calm, deeper than that which accompanies a hope deferred, bathed my spirit. I sank far into the waters, and sought not to return. I felt as if once more the great arms of the beech-tree were around me, soothing me after the miseries had passed through, and telling me, like a little sick child, that I should be better to-morrow. The waters of themselves lifted me, as with loving arms, to the surface. I breathed again, but did not unclose my eyes. I would not look on the wintry sea, and the pitiless gray sky. Thus I floated, till something gently touched me. It was a little boat floating beside me. How it came there I could not tell; but it rose and sank on the waters, and kept touching me in its fall, as if with a human will to let me know that help was by me. It was a little gay-colored boat, seemingly covered with glistering scales like those of a fish, all of brilliant rainbow hues. I scrambled into it, and lay down in the bottom, with a sense of exquisite repose.

Then I drew over me a rich, heavy, purple cloth that was beside me; and, lying still, knew, by the sound of the waters, that my little bark was fleeting rapidly onwards. Finding, however, none of that stormy motion which the sea had manifested when I beheld it from the shore, I opened my eyes;

and, looking first up, saw above me the deep violet sky of a warm southern night; and then, lifting my head, saw that I was sailing fast upon a summer sea, in the last border of a southern twilight. The aureole of the sun yet shot the extreme faint tips of its longest rays above the horizon- waves, and withdrew them not. It was a perpetual twilight. The stars, great and earnest, like children's eyes, bent down lovingly towards the waters; and the reflected stars within seemed to float up, as if longing to meet their embraces. But when I looked down, a new wonder met my view. For, vaguely revealed beneath the wave, I floated above my whole Past. The fields of my childhood flitted by; the halls of my youthful labors; the streets of great cities where I had dwelt; and the assemblies of men and women wherein I had wearied myself seeking for rest. But so indistinct were the visions, that sometimes I thought I was sailing on a shallow sea, and that strange rocks and forests of sea-plants beguiled my eye, sufficiently to be transformed, by the magic of the phantasy, into well-known objects and regions. Yet, at times, a beloved form seemed to lie close beneath me in sleep; and the eyelids would tremble as if about to forsake the conscious eye; and the arms would heave upwards, as if in dreams they sought for a satisfying presence. But these motions might come only from the heaving of the waters between those forms and me. Soon I fell asleep, overcome with fatigue and delight. In dreams of unspeakable joy — of restored friendships; of revived embraces; of love which said it had never died; of faces that had vanished long ago, yet said with smiling lips that they knew nothing of the grave; of pardons implored, and granted with such bursting floods of love, that I was almost glad I had sinned — thus I passed through this wondrous twilight. I awoke with the feeling that I had been kissed and loved to my heart's content; and found that my boat was floating motionless by the grassy shore of a little island.

CHAPTER NINETEEN

The water was deep to the very edge; and I sprang from the little boat upon a soft grassy turf. The island seemed rich with a profusion of all grasses and low flowers. All delicate lowly things were most plentiful; but no trees rose skywards, not even a bush overtopped the tall grasses, except in one place near the cottage I am about to describe, where a few plants of the gum-cistus, which drops every night all the blossoms that the day brings forth, formed a kind of natural arbor. The whole island lay open to the sky and sea. It rose nowhere more than a few feet above the level of the waters, which flowed deep all around its border. Here there seemed to be neither tide nor storm. A sense of persistent calm and fullness arose in the mind at the sight of the slow, pulse-like rise and fall of the deep, clear, un-rippled waters against the bank of the island, for shore it could hardly be called, being so much more like the edge of a full, solemn river. As I walked over the grass towards the cottage, which stood at a little distance from the bank, all the flowers of childhood looked at me with perfect child-eyes out of the grass. My heart, softened by the dreams through which it had passed, overflowed in a sad, tender love towards them. They looked to me like children impregnably fortified in a helpless confidence. The sun stood half- way down the western sky, shining very soft and golden; and there grew a second world of shadows amidst the world of grasses and wild flowers.

The cottage was square, with low walls, and a high pyramidal roof thatched with long reeds, of which the withered blossoms hung over all the eaves. It is noticeable that most of the buildings I saw in Fairy Land were cottages. There was no path to a door, nor, indeed, was there any track worn by footsteps in the island.

The cottage rose right out of the smooth turf. It had no windows that I could see; but there was a door in the centre of the side facing me, up to which I went. I knocked, and the sweetest voice

I had ever heard said, "Come in." I entered. A bright fire was burning on a hearth in the centre of the earthen floor, and the smoke found its way out at an opening in the centre of the pyramidal roof.

Over the fire hung a little pot, and over the pot bent a woman-face, the most wonderful, I thought, that I had ever beheld. For it was older than any countenance I had ever looked upon. There was not a spot in which a wrinkle could lie, where a wrinkle lay not. And the skin was ancient and brown, like old parchment. The woman's form was tall and spare: and when she stood up to welcome me, I saw that she was straight as an arrow. Could that voice of sweetness have issued from those lips of age? Mild as they were, could they be the portals whence flowed such melody? But the moment I saw her eyes, I no longer wondered at her voice: they were absolutely young—those of a woman of five-and- twenty, large, and of a clear gray. Wrinkles had beset them all about; the eyelids themselves were old, and heavy, and worn; but the eyes were very incarnations of soft light. She held out her hand to me, and the voice of sweetness again greeted me, with the single word, "Welcome." She set an old wooden chair for me, near the fire, and went on with her cooking. A wondrous sense of refuge and repose came upon me. I felt like a boy who has got home from school, miles across the hills, through a heavy storm of wind and snow. Almost, as I gazed on her, I sprang from my seat to kiss those old lips. And when, having finished her cooking, she brought some of the dish she had prepared, and set it on a little table by me, covered with a snow- white cloth, I could not help laying my head on her bosom, and bursting into happy tears. She put her arms round me, saying, "Poor child; poor child!"

As I continued to weep, she gently disengaged herself, and, taking a spoon, put some of the food (I did not know what it was) to my lips, entreating me most endearingly to swallow it. To please her, I made an effort, and succeeded. She went on feeding me like a baby, with one arm round me, till I looked up in her face and smiled: then she gave me the spoon and told me to eat, for it would do me good. I obeyed her, and found myself wonderfully refreshed. Then she drew near the fire an old-fashioned couch that was in the cottage, and making me lie down upon it, sat at my feet, and began to sing. Amazing store of old ballads rippled from her lips, over the pebbles of ancient tunes; and the voice that sang was sweet as the voice of a tuneful maiden that sings ever from very fullness of song. The songs were almost all sad, but with a sound of comfort. One I can faintly recall. It was something like this:

Sir Aglovaile through the churchyard rode;

SING, ALL ALONE I LIE:

Little recked he where'er he yode,

ALL ALONE, UP IN THE SKY.

Swerved his courser, and plunged with fear

ALL ALONE I LIE:

His cry might have wakened the dead men near,

ALL ALONE, UP IN THE SKY.

The very dead that lay at his feet,

Lapt in the mouldy winding-sheet.

But he curbed him and spurred him, until he stood

Still in his place, like a horse of wood,

With nostrils uplift, and eyes wide and wan;
But the sweat in streams from his fetlocks ran.

A ghost grew out of the shadowy air,
And sat in the midst of her moony hair.

In her gleamy hair she sat and wept;
In the dreamful moon they lay and slept;

The shadows above, and the bodies below,
Lay and slept in the moonbeams slow.

And she sang, like the moan of an autumn wind
Over the stubble left behind:

Alas, how easily things go wrong
! A sigh too much, or a kiss too long,
And there follows a mist and a weeping rain,
And life is never the same again.

Alas, how hardly things go right!
'Tis hard to watch on a summer night,
For the sigh will come and the kiss will stay,
And the summer night is a winter day.

"Oh, lovely ghosts my heart is woes
To see thee weeping and wailing so.

Oh, lovely ghost," said the fearless knight,
"Can the sword of a warrior set it right?

Or prayer of bedesman, praying mild,
As a cup of water a feverish child,

Sooth thee at last, in dreamless mood
To sleep the sleep a dead lady should?

Thine eyes they fill me with longing sore,
As if I had known thee for evermore.

Oh, lovely ghost, I could leave the day
To sit with thee in the moon away

If thou wouldst trust me, and lay thy head
To rest on a bosom that is not dead."
The lady sprang up with a strange ghost-cry,
And she flung her white ghost-arms on high:

And she laughed a laugh that was not gay,
And it lengthened out till it died away;

And the dead beneath turned and moaned,
And the yew-trees above they shuddered and groaned.

"Will he love me twice with a love that is vain?
Will he kill the poor ghost yet again?

I thought thou wert good; but I said, and wept:
`Can I have dreamed who have not slept?'

And I knew, alas! or ever I would,
Whether I dreamed, or thou wert good.

When my baby died, my brain grew wild.
I awoke, and found I was with my child."

"If thou art the ghost of my Adelaide,
How is it? Thou wert but a village maid,

And thou seemest an angel lady white,
Though thin, and wan, and past delight."

The lady smiled a flickering smile,
And she pressed her temples hard the while.

"Thou seest that Death for a woman can

Do more than knighthood for a man."

"But show me the child thou callest mine,
Is she out to-night in the ghost's sunshine?"

"In St. Peter's Church she is playing on,
At hide-and-seek, with Apostle John.

When the moonbeams right through the window go,
Where the twelve are standing in glorious show,

She says the rest of them do not stir,
But one comes down to play with her.

Then I can go where I list, and weep,
For good St. John my child will keep."

"Thy beauty filleth the very air,
Never saw I a woman so fair."

"Come, if thou darest, and sit by my side;
But do not touch me, or woe will betide.

Alas, I am weak: I might well know
This gladness betokens some further woe.

Yet come. It will come. I will bear it. I can.
For you love me yet—though but as a man."

The knight dismounted in earnest speed;
Away through the tombstones thundered the steed,

And fell by the outer wall, and died.
But the knight he kneeled by the lady's side;

Kneeled beside her in wondrous bliss,
Rapt in an everlasting kiss:

Though never his lips come the lady nigh,
And his eyes alone on her beauty lie.

All the night long, till the cock crew loud,
He kneeled by the lady, lapt in her shroud.

And what they said, I may not say:
Dead night was sweeter than living day.

How she made him so blissful glad
Who made her and found her so ghostly sad,

I may not tell; but it needs no touch
To make them blessed who love so much.

"Come every night, my ghost, to me;
And one night I will come to thee.
'Tis good to have a ghostly wife:
She will not tremble at clang of strife;

She will only hearken, amid the din,
Behind the door, if he cometh in."
And this is how Sir Aglovaile
Often walked in the moonlight pale.

And oft when the crescent but thinned the gloom,
Full orbed moonlight filled his room;

And through beneath his chamber door,
Fell a ghostly gleam on the outer floor;

And they that passed, in fear averred
That murmured words they often heard.

'Twas then that the eastern crescent shone
Through the chancel window, and good St. John

Played with the ghost-child all the night,
And the mother was free till the morning light,

And sped through the dawning night, to stay
With Aglovaile till the break of day.

And their love was a rapture, lone and high,
And dumb as the moon in the topmost sky.

One night Sir Aglovaile, weary, slept
And dreamed a dream wherein he wept.

A warrior he was, not often wept he,
But this night he wept full bitterly.

He woke—beside him the ghost-girl shone
Out of the dark: 'twas the eve of St. John.
He had dreamed a dream of a still, dark wood,
Where the maiden of old beside him stood;

But a mist came down, and caught her away,
And he sought her in vain through the pathless day,

Till he wept with the grief that can do no more,
And thought he had dreamt the dream before.

From bursting heart the weeping flowed on;
And lo! beside him the ghost-girl shone;

Shone like the light on a harbour's breast,
Over the sea of his dream's unrest;

Shone like the wondrous, nameless boon,

That the heart seeks ever, night or noon:

Warnings forgotten, when needed most,
He clasped to his bosom the radiant ghost.

She wailed aloud, and faded, and sank.
With upturn'd white face, cold and blank,

In his arms lay the corpse of the maiden pale,
And she came no more to Sir Aglovaile.

Only a voice, when winds were wild,
Sobbed and wailed like a chidden child.

Alas, how easily things go wrong!
A sigh too much, or a kiss too long,
And there follows a mist and a weeping rain,
And life is never the same again.

This was one of the simplest of her songs, which, perhaps, is the cause of my being able to remember it better than most of the others. While she sung, I was in Elysium, with the sense of a rich soul upholding, embracing, and overhanging mine, full of all plenty and bounty. I felt as if she could give me everything I wanted; as if I should never wish to leave her, but would be content to be sung to and fed by her, day after day, as years rolled by. At last I fell asleep while she sang.

When I awoke, I knew not whether it was night or day. The fire had sunk to a few red embers, which just gave light enough to show me the woman standing a few feet from me, with her back towards me, facing the door by which I had entered. She was weeping, but very gently and plentifully. The tears seemed to come freely from her heart. Thus she stood for a few minutes; then, slowly turning at right angles to her former position, she faced another of the four sides of the cottage. I now observed, for the first time, that here was a door likewise; and that, indeed, there was one in the centre of every side of the cottage.

When she looked towards the second door, her tears ceased to flow, but sighs took their place. She often closed her eyes as she stood; and every time she closed her eyes, a gentle sigh seemed to be born in her heart, and to escape at her lips. But when her eyes were open, her sighs were deep and very sad, and shook her whole frame. Then she turned towards the third door, and a cry as of fear or suppressed pain broke from her; but she seemed to hearten herself against the dismay, and to front it steadily; for, although I often heard a slight cry, and sometimes a moan, yet she never moved or bent her head, and I felt sure that her eyes never closed. Then she turned to the fourth door, and I saw her shudder, and then stand still as a statue; till at last she turned towards me and approached the fire. I saw that her face was white as death. But she gave one look upwards, and smiled the sweetest, most child-innocent smile; then heaped fresh wood on the fire, and, sitting down by the blaze, drew her wheel near her, and began to spin. While she spun, she murmured a low strange song, to which the hum of the wheel made a kind of infinite symphony. At length she paused in her spinning and singing, and glanced towards me, like a mother who looks whether or not her child gives signs of waking. She smiled when she saw that my eyes were open. I asked her whether it was day yet. She answered, "It is always day here, so long as I keep my fire burning."

I felt wonderfully refreshed; and a great desire to see more of the island awoke within me. I rose, and saying that I wished to look about me, went towards the door by which I had entered.

"Stay a moment," said my hostess, with some trepidation in her voice. "Listen to me. You will not see what you expect when you go out of that door. Only remember this: whenever you wish to come back to me, enter wherever you see this mark."

She held up her left hand between me and the fire. Upon the palm, which appeared almost transparent, I saw, in dark red, a mark like this — which I took care to fix in my mind.

She then kissed me, and bade me good-bye with a solemnity that awed me; and bewildered me too, seeing I was only going out for a little ramble in an island, which I did not believe larger than could easily be compassed in a few hours' walk at most. As I went she resumed her spinning.

I opened the door, and stepped out. The moment my foot touched the smooth sward, I seemed to issue from the door of an old barn on my father's estate, where, in the hot afternoons, I used to go and lie amongst the straw, and read. It seemed to me now that I had been asleep there. At a little distance in the field, I saw two of my brothers at play. The moment they caught sight of me, they called out to me to come and join them, which I did; and we played together as we had done years ago, till the red sun went down in the west, and the gray fog began to rise from the river. Then we went home together with a strange happiness. As we went, we heard the continually renewed larum of a landrail in the long grass. One of my brothers and I separated to a little distance, and each commenced running towards the part whence the sound appeared to come, in the hope of approaching the spot where the bird was, and so getting at least a sight of it, if we should not be able to capture the little creature. My father's voice recalled us from trampling down the rich long grass, soon to be cut down and laid aside for the winter. I had quite forgotten all about Fairy Land, and the wonderful old woman, and the curious red mark.

My favorite brother and I shared the same bed. Some childish dispute arose between us; and our last words, ere we fell asleep, were not of kindness, notwithstanding the pleasures of the day. When I woke in the morning, I missed him. He had risen early, and had gone to bathe in the river. In another hour, he was brought home drowned. Alas! alas! if we had only gone to sleep as usual, the one with his arm about the other! Amidst the horror of the moment, a strange conviction flashed across my mind, that I had gone through the very same once before.

I rushed out of the house, I knew not why, sobbing and crying bitterly. I ran through the fields in aimless distress, till, passing the old barn, I caught sight of a red mark on the door. The merest trifles sometimes rivet the attention in the deepest misery; the intellect has so little to do with grief. I went up to look at this mark, which I did not remember ever to have seen before. As I looked at it, I thought I would go in and lie down amongst the straw, for I was very weary with running about and weeping. I opened the door; and there in the cottage sat the old woman as I had left her, at her spinning-wheel.

"I did not expect you quite so soon," she said, as I shut the door behind me. I went up to the couch, and threw myself on it with that fatigue wherewith one awakes from a feverish dream of hopeless grief. The old woman sang:

The great sun, benighted,

May faint from the sky;

But love, once uplighted,

Will never more die.

Form, with its brightness,

From eyes will depart:

It walketh, in whiteness,

The halls of the heart.

Ere she had ceased singing, my courage had returned. I started from the couch, and, without taking leave of the old woman, opened the door of Sighs, and sprang into what should appear.

I stood in a lordly hall, where, by a blazing fire on the hearth, sat a lady, waiting, I knew, for some one long desired. A mirror was near me, but I saw that my form had no place within its depths, so I feared not that I should be seen. The lady wonderfully resembled my marble lady, but was altogether of the daughters of men, and I could not tell whether or not it was she.

It was not for me she waited. The tramp of a great horse rang through the court without. It ceased, and the clang of armor told that his rider alighted, and the sound of his ringing heels approached the hall. The door opened; but the lady waited, for she would meet her lord alone. He strode in: she flew like a home-bound dove into his arms, and nestled on the hard steel. It was the knight of the soiled armor. But now the armor shone like polished glass; and strange to tell, though the mirror reflected not my form, I saw a dim shadow of myself in the shining steel.

"O my beloved, thou art come, and I am blessed."

Her soft fingers speedily overcame the hard clasp of his helmet; one by one she undid the buckles of his armor; and she toiled under the weight of the mail, as she WOULD carry it aside. Then she unclasped his greaves, and unbuckled his spurs; and once more she sprang into his arms, and laid her head where she could now feel the beating of his heart. Then she disengaged herself from his embrace, and, moving back a step or two, gazed at him. He stood there a mighty form, crowned with a noble head, where all sadness had disappeared, or had been absorbed in solemn purpose. Yet I suppose that he looked more thoughtful than the lady had expected to see him, for she did not renew her caresses, although his face glowed with love, and the few words he spoke were as mighty deeds for strength; but she led him towards the hearth, and seated him in an ancient chair, and set wine before him, and sat at his feet.

"I am sad," he said, "when I think of the youth whom I met twice in the forests of Fairy Land; and who, you say, twice, with his songs, roused you from the death-sleep of an evil enchantment. There was something noble in him, but it was a nobleness of thought, and not of deed. He may yet perish of vile fear."

"Ah!" returned the lady, "you saved him once, and for that I thank you; for may I not say that I somewhat loved him? But tell me how you fared, when you struck your battle-axe into the ash-tree, and he came and found you; for so much of the story you had told me, when the beggar-child came and took you away."

"As soon as I saw him," rejoined the knight, "I knew that earthly arms availed not against such as he; and that my soul must meet him in its naked strength. So I unclasped my helm, and flung it on the ground; and, holding my good axe yet in my hand, gazed at him with steady eyes. On he came, a horror indeed, but I did not flinch. Endurance must conquer, where force could not reach. He came nearer and nearer, till the ghastly face was close to mine. A shudder as of death ran through me; but I think I did not move, for he seemed to quail, and retreated. As soon as he gave back, I struck one more sturdy blow on the stem of his tree, that the forest rang; and then looked at him again. He writhed and grinned with rage and apparent pain, and again approached me, but retreated sooner than before. I heeded him no more, but hewed with a will at the tree, till the trunk creaked, and the head bowed, and with a crash it fell to the earth. Then I looked up from my labor, and lo! the specter had vanished, and I saw him no more; nor ever in my wanderings have I heard of him again."

"Well struck! well withstood! my hero," said the lady.

"But," said the knight, somewhat troubled, "dost thou love the youth still?"

"Ah!" she replied, "how can I help it? He woke me from worse than death; he loved me. I had never been for thee, if he had not sought me first. But I love him not as I love thee. He was but the moon of my night; thou art the sun of my clay, O beloved." "Thou art right," returned the noble man. "It were hard, indeed, not to have some love in return for such a gift as he hath given thee. I, too, owe him more than words can speak."

Humbled before them, with an aching and desolate heart, I yet could not restrain my words:

"Let me, then, be the moon of thy night still, O woman! And when thy day is beclouded, as the fairest days will be, let some song of mine comfort thee, as an old, withered, half-forgotten thing, that belongs to an ancient mournful hour of uncompleted birth, which yet was beautiful in its time."

They sat silent, and I almost thought they were listening. The color of the lady's eyes grew deeper and deeper; the slow tears grew, and filled them, and overflowed. They rose, and passed, hand in hand, close to where I stood; and each looked towards me in passing. Then they disappeared through a door which closed behind them; but, ere it closed, I saw that the room into which it opened was a rich chamber, hung with gorgeous arras. I stood with an ocean of sighs frozen in my bosom. I could remain no longer. She was near me, and I could not see her; near me in the arms of one loved better than I, and I would not see her, and I would not be by her. But how to escape from the nearness of the best beloved? I had not this time forgotten the mark; for the fact that I could not enter the sphere of these living beings kept me aware that, for me, I moved in a vision, while they moved in life. I looked all about for the mark, but could see it nowhere; for I avoided looking just where it was. There the dull red cipher glowed, on the very door of their secret chamber. Struck with agony, I dashed it open, and fell at the feet of the ancient woman, who still spun on, the whole dissolved ocean of my sighs bursting from me in a storm of tearless sobs. Whether I fainted or slept, I do not know; but, as I returned to consciousness, before I seemed to have power to move, I heard the woman singing, and could distinguish the words:

O light of dead and of dying days!

O Love! in thy glory go,

In a rosy mist and a moony maze,

O'er the pathless peaks of snow.

But what is left for the cold gray soul,

That moans like a wounded dove?

One wine is left in the broken bowl!—

'Tis — TO LOVE, AND LOVE AND LOVE.

Now I could weep. When she saw me weeping, she sang:

Better to sit at the waters' birth,

Than a sea of waves to win;

To live in the love that floweth forth,

Than the love that cometh in.

Be thy heart a well of love, my child,

Flowing, and free, and sure;

For a cistern of love, though undefiled,

Keeps not the spirit pure.

I rose from the earth, loving the white lady as I had never loved her before.

Then I walked up to the door of Dismay, and opened it, and went out. And lo! I came forth upon a crowded street, where men and women went to and fro in multitudes. I knew it well; and, turning to one hand, walked sadly along the pavement. Suddenly I saw approaching me, a little way off, a form well known to me (WELL-KNOWN! — alas, how weak the word!) in the years when I thought my boyhood was left behind, and shortly before I entered the realm of Fairy Land. Wrong and Sorrow had gone together, hand-in-hand as it is well they do.

Unchangeably dear was that face. It lay in my heart as a child lies in its own white bed; but I could not meet her.

"Anything but that," I said, and, turning aside, sprang up the steps to a door, on which I fancied I saw the mystic sign. I entered — not the mysterious cottage, but her home. I rushed wildly on, and stood by the door of her room.

"She is out," I said, "I will see the old room once more."

I opened the door gently, and stood in a great solemn church. A deep-toned bell, whose sounds throbbed and echoed and swam through the empty building, struck the hour of midnight. The moon shone through the windows of the clerestory, and enough of the ghostly radiance was diffused through the church to let me see, walking with a stately, yet somewhat trailing and stumbling step, down the opposite aisle, for I stood in one of the transepts, a figure dressed in a white robe, whether for the night, or for that longer night which lies too deep for the day, I could not tell. Was it she? and was this her chamber? I crossed the church, and followed. The figure stopped, seemed to ascend as it were a high bed, and lay down. I reached the place where it lay, glimmering white. The bed was a tomb. The light was too ghostly to see clearly, but I passed my hand over the face and the hands and the feet, which were all bare. They were cold—they were marble, but I knew them. It grew dark. I turned to retrace my steps, but found, ere long, that I had wandered into what seemed a little chapel. I groped about, seeking the door. Everything I touched belonged to the dead. My hands fell on the cold effigy of a knight who lay with his legs crossed and his sword broken beside him. He lay in his noble rest, and I lived on in ignoble strife. I felt for the left hand and a certain finger; I found there the ring I knew: he was one of my own ancestors. I was in the chapel over the burial-vault of my race. I called aloud: "If any of the dead are moving here, let them take pity upon me, for I, alas! am still alive; and let some dead woman comfort me, for I am a stranger in the land of the dead, and see no light." A warm kiss alighted on my lips through the dark. And I said, "The dead kiss well; I will not be afraid." And a great hand was reached out of the dark, and grasped mine for a moment, mightily and tenderly. I said to myself: "The veil between, though very dark, is very thin."

Groping my way further, I stumbled over the heavy stone that covered the entrance of the vault: and, in stumbling, descried upon the stone the mark, glowing in red fire. I caught the great ring. All my effort could not have moved the huge slab; but it opened the door of the cottage, and I threw myself once more, pale and speechless, on the couch beside the ancient dame. She sang once more:

Thou dreamest: on a rock thou art,

High o'er the broken wave;

Thou fallest with a fearful start

But not into thy grave;

For, waking in the morning's light,

Thou smilest at the vanished night

So wilt thou sink, all pale and dumb,

Into the fainting gloom;

But ere the coming terrors come,

Thou wak'st — where is the tomb?

Thou wak'st — the dead ones smile above,

With hovering arms of sleepless love.

She paused; then sang again:

We weep for gladness, weep for grief;

The tears they are the same;

We sigh for longing, and relief;

The sighs have but one name,

And mingled in the dying strife,

Are moans that are not sad

The pangs of death are throbs of life,

Its sighs are sometimes glad.

The face is very strange and white:

It is Earth's only spot

That feebly flickers back the light

The living seeth not.

I fell asleep, and slept a dreamless sleep, for I know not how long. When I awoke, I found that my hostess had moved from where she had been sitting, and now sat between me and the fourth door.

I guessed that her design was to prevent my entering there. I sprang from the couch, and darted past her to the door. I opened it at once and went out. All I remember is a cry of distress from the woman: "Don't go there, my child! Don't go there!" But I was gone.

I knew nothing more; or, if I did, I had forgot it all when I awoke to consciousness, lying on the floor of the cottage, with my head in the lap of the woman, who was weeping over me, and stroking my hair with both hands, talking to me as a mother might talk to a sick and sleeping, or a dead child. As soon as I looked up and saw her, she smiled through her tears; smiled with withered face and young eyes, till her countenance was irradiated with the light of the smile. Then she bathed my head and face and hands in an icy cold, colorless liquid, which smelt a little of damp earth. Immediately I was able to sit up. She rose and put some food before me. When I had eaten, she said: "Listen to me, my child. You must leave me directly!"

"Leave you!" I said. "I am so happy with you. I never was so happy in my life."

"But you must go," she rejoined sadly. "Listen! What do you hear?"

"I hear the sound as of a great throbbing of water."

"Ah! you do hear it? Well, I had to go through that door—the door of the Timeless" (and she shuddered as she pointed to the fourth door)— "to find you; for if I had not gone, you would never have entered again; and because I went, the waters around my cottage will rise and rise, and flow and come, till they build a great firmament of waters over my dwelling. But as long as I keep my fire burning, they cannot enter. I have fuel enough for years; and after one year they will sink away again, and be just as they were before you came. I have not been buried for a hundred years now." And she smiled and wept.

"Alas! alas!" I cried. "I have brought this evil on the best and kindest of friends, who has filled my heart with great gifts."

"Do not think of that," she rejoined. "I can bear it very well. You will come back to me some day, I know. But I beg you, for my sake, my dear child, to do one thing. In whatever sorrow you may be, however inconsolable and irremediable it may appear, believe me that the old woman in the cottage, with the young eyes" (and she smiled), "knows something, though she must not always tell it, that would quite satisfy you about it, even in the worst moments of your distress.

Now you must go."

"But how can I go, if the waters are all about, and if the doors all lead into other regions and other worlds?"

"This is not an island," she replied; "but is joined to the land by a narrow neck; and for the door, I will lead you myself through the right one."

She took my hand, and led me through the third door; whereupon I found myself standing in the deep grassy turf on which I had landed from the little boat, but upon the opposite side of the cottage. She pointed out the direction I must take, to find the isthmus and escape the rising waters.

Then putting her arms around me, she held me to her bosom; and as I kissed her, I felt as if I were leaving my mother for the first time, and could not help weeping bitterly. At length she gently pushed me away, and with the words, "Go, my son, and do something worth doing," turned back, and, entering the cottage, closed the door behind her. I felt very desolate as I went.

CHAPTER TWENTY

I had not gone very far before I felt that the turf beneath my feet was soaked with the rising waters. But I reached the isthmus in safety. It was rocky, and so much higher than the level of the peninsula, that I had plenty of time to cross. I saw on each side of me the water rising rapidly, altogether without wind, or violent motion, or broken waves, but as if a slow strong fire were glowing beneath it. Ascending a steep acclivity, I found myself at last in an open, rocky country. After traveling for some hours, as nearly in a straight line as I could, I arrived at a lonely tower, built on the top of a little hill, which overlooked the whole neighboring country. As I approached, I heard the clang of an anvil; and so rapid were the blows, that I despaired of making myself heard till a pause in the work should ensue. It was some minutes before a cessation took place; but when it did, I knocked loudly, and had not long to wait; for, a moment after, the door was partly opened by a noble-looking youth, half-undressed, glowing with heat, and begrimed with the blackness of the forge. In one hand he held a sword, so lately from the furnace that it yet shone with a dull fire. As soon as he saw me, he threw the door wide open, and standing aside, invited me very cordially to enter. I did so; when he shut and bolted the door most carefully, and then led the way inwards. He brought me into a rude hall, which seemed to occupy almost the whole of the ground floor of the little tower, and which I saw was now being used as a workshop. A huge fire roared on the hearth, beside which was an anvil. By the anvil stood, in similar undress, and in a waiting attitude, hammer in hand, a second youth, tall as the former, but far more slightly built. Reversing the usual course of perception in such meetings, I thought them, at first sight, very unlike; and at the second glance, knew that they were brothers. The former, and apparently the elder, was muscular and dark, with curling hair, and large hazel eyes, which sometimes grew wondrously soft. The second was slender and fair, yet with a countenance like an eagle, and an eye which, though pale blue, shone with an almost fierce expression. He stood erect, as if looking from a lofty mountain crag, over a vast plain outstretched below. As soon as we entered the hall, the elder turned to me, and I saw that a glow of satisfaction shone on both their faces. To my surprise and great pleasure, he addressed me thus:

"Brother, will you sit by the fire and rest, till we finish this part of our work?"

I signified my assent; and, resolved to await any disclosure they might be inclined to make, seated myself in silence near the hearth.

The elder brother then laid the sword in the fire, covered it well over, and when it had attained a sufficient degree of heat, drew it out and laid it on the anvil, moving it carefully about, while the younger, with a succession of quick smart blows, appeared either to be welding it, or hammering one part of it to a consenting shape with the rest. Having finished, they laid it carefully in the fire; and, when it was very hot indeed, plunged it into a vessel full of some liquid, whence a blue flame sprang upwards, as the glowing steel entered.

There they left it; and drawing two stools to the fire, sat down, one on each side of me.

"We are very glad to see you, brother. We have been expecting you for some days," said the dark-haired youth.

"I am proud to be called your brother," I rejoined; "and you will not think I refuse the name, if I desire to know why you honor me with it?"

"Ah! then he does not know about it," said the younger. "We thought you had known of the bond betwixt us, and the work we have to do together. You must tell him, brother, from the first."

So the elder began:

"Our father is king of this country. Before we were born, three giant brothers had appeared in the land. No one knew exactly when, and no one had the least idea whence they came. They took possession of a ruined castle that had stood unchanged and unoccupied within the memory of any of the country people. The vaults of this castle had remained uninjured by time, and these, I presume, they made use of at first. They were rarely seen, and never offered the least injury to any one; so that they were regarded in the neighborhood as at least perfectly harmless, if not rather benevolent beings. But it began to be observed, that the old castle had assumed somehow or other, no one knew when or how, a somewhat different look from what it used to have. Not only were several breaches in the lower part of the walls built up, but actually some of the battlements which yet stood, had been repaired, apparently to prevent them from falling into worse decay, while the more important parts were being restored. Of course, every one supposed the giants must have a hand in the work, but no one ever saw them engaged in it. The peasants became yet more uneasy, after one, who had concealed himself, and watched all night, in the neighborhood of the castle, reported that he had seen, in full moonlight, the three huge giants working with might and main, all night long, restoring to their former position some massive stones, formerly steps of a grand turnpike stair, a great portion of which had long since fallen, along with part of the wall of the round tower in which it had been built. This wall they were completing, foot by foot, along with the stair. But the people said they had no just pretext for interfering: although the real reason for letting the giants alone was, that everybody was far too much afraid of them to interrupt them.

"At length, with the help of a neighboring quarry, the whole of the external wall of the castle was finished. And now the country folks were in greater fear than before. But for several years the giants remained very peaceful. The reason of this was afterwards supposed to be the fact, that they were distantly related to several good people in the country; for, as long as these lived, they remained quiet; but as soon as they were all dead the real nature of the giants broke out. Having completed the outside of their castle, they proceeded, by spoiling the country houses around them, to make a quiet luxurious provision for their comfort within. Affairs reached such a pass, that the news of their robberies came to my father's ears; but he, alas! was so crippled in his resources, by a war he was carrying on with a neighboring prince, that he could only spare a very few men, to attempt the capture of their stronghold. Upon these the giants issued in the night, and slew every man of them. And now, grown bolder by success and impunity, they no longer confined their depredations to property, but began to seize the persons of their distinguished neighbors, knights and ladies, and hold them in durance, the misery of which was heightened by all manner of indignity, until they were redeemed by their friends, at an exorbitant ransom. Many knights have adventured their overthrow, but to their own instead; for they have all been slain, or captured, or forced to make a hasty retreat. To crown their enormities, if any man now attempts their destruction, they, immediately upon his defeat, put one or more of their captives to a shameful death, on a turret in sight of all passers-by; so that they have been much less molested of late; and we, although we have burned, for years, to attack these demons and destroy them, dared not, for the sake of their captives, risk the adventure, before we should have reached at least our earliest manhood. Now, however, we are preparing for the attempt; and the grounds of this preparation are these. Having only the resolution, and not the experience necessary for the undertaking, we went and consulted a lonely woman of wisdom, who lives not very far from here, in the direction of the quarter from which you have come. She received us most kindly, and gave us what seems to us the best of advice. She first inquired what experience we had had in arms. We told her we had been well exercised from our boyhood, and for some years had kept ourselves in constant practice, with a view to this necessity.

"'But you have not actually fought for life and death?' said she.

"We were forced to confess we had not.

"'So much the better in some respects,' she replied. 'Now listen to me. Go first and work with an armorer, for as long time as you find needful to obtain a knowledge of his craft; which will not be long, seeing your hearts will be all in the work. Then go to some lonely tower, you two alone. Receive no visits from man or woman. There forge for yourselves every piece of armor that you wish to wear, or to use, in your coming encounter. And keep up your exercises.

"As, however, two of you can be no match for the three giants, I will find you, if I can, a third brother, who will take on himself the third share of the fight, and the preparation. Indeed, I have already seen one who will, I think, be the very man for your fellowship, but it will be some time before he comes to me. He is wandering now without an aim. I will show him to you in a glass, and, when he comes, you will know him at once. If he will share your endeavors, you must teach him all you know, and he will repay you well, in present song, and in future deeds.'

"She opened the door of a curious old cabinet that stood in the room. On the inside of this door was an oval convex mirror. Looking in it for some time, we at length saw reflected the place where we stood, and the old dame seated in her chair. Our forms were not reflected. But at the feet of the dame lay a young man, yourself, weeping.

"'Surely this youth will not serve our ends,' said I, 'for he weeps.'

"The old woman smiled. 'Past tears are present strength,' said she.

"'Oh!' said my brother, 'I saw you weep once over an eagle you shot.'

"'That was because it was so like you, brother,' I replied; 'but indeed, this youth may have better cause for tears than that—I was wrong.'

"'Wait a while,' said the woman; 'if I mistake not, he will make you weep till your tears are dry for ever. Tears are the only cure for weeping. And you may have need of the cure, before you go forth to fight the giants. You must wait for him, in your tower, till he comes.'

"Now if you will join us, we will soon teach you to make your armor; and we will fight together, and work together, and love each other as never three loved before. And you will sing to us, will you not?"

"That I will, when I can," I answered; "but it is only at times that the power of song comes upon me. For that I must wait; but I have a feeling that if I work well, song will not be far off to enliven the labor."

This was all the compact made: the brothers required nothing more, and I did not think of giving anything more. I rose, and threw off my upper garments.

"I know the uses of the sword," I said. "I am ashamed of my white hands beside yours so nobly soiled and hard; but that shame will soon be wiped away."

"No, no; we will not work to-day. Rest is as needful as toil. Bring the wine, brother; it is your turn to serve to-day."

The younger brother soon covered a table with rough viands, but good wine; and we ate and drank heartily, beside our work. Before the meal was over, I had learned all their story. Each had something in his heart which made the conviction, that he would victoriously perish in the coming conflict, a real sorrow to him. Otherwise they thought they would have lived enough. The causes of their trouble were respectively these:

While they wrought with an armorer, in a city famed for workmanship in steel and silver, the elder had fallen in love with a lady as far beneath him in real rank, as she was above the station he had as apprentice to an armorer. Nor did he seek to further his suit by discovering himself; but there was simply so much manhood about him, that no one ever thought of rank when in his company. This is what his brother said about it. The lady could not help loving him in return. He told her when he left her, that he had a perilous adventure before him, and that when it was achieved, she would either see him return to claim her, or hear that he had died with honor. The younger brother's grief arose from the fact, that, if they were both slain, his old father, the king, would be childless. His love for his father was so exceeding, that to one unable to sympathize with it, it would have appeared extravagant. Both loved him equally at heart; but the love of the younger had been more developed, because his thoughts and anxieties had not been otherwise occupied. When at home, he had been his constant companion; and, of late, had ministered to the infirmities of his growing age. The youth was never weary of listening to the tales of his sire's youthful adventures; and had not yet in the smallest degree lost the conviction, that his father was the greatest man in the world. The grandest triumph possible to his conception was, to return to his father, laden with the spoils of one of the hated giants. But they both were in some dread, lest the thought of the loneliness of these two might occur to them, in the moment when decision was most necessary, and disturb, in some degree, the self-possession requisite for the success of their attempt. For, as I have said, they were yet untried in actual conflict. "Now," thought I, "I see to what the powers of my gift must minister." For my own part, I did not dread death, for I had nothing to care to live for; but I dreaded the encounter because of the responsibility connected with it. I resolved however to work hard, and thus grow cool, and quick, and forceful.

The time passed away in work and song, in talk and ramble, in friendly fight and brotherly aid. I would not forge for myself armor of heavy mail like theirs, for I was not so powerful as they, and depended more for any success I might secure, upon nimbleness of motion, certainty of eye, and ready response of hand. Therefore I began to make for myself a shirt of steel plates and rings; which work, while more troublesome, was better suited to me than the heavier labor. Much assistance did the brothers give me, even after, by their instructions, I was able to make some progress alone. Their work was in a moment abandoned, to render any required aid to mine. As the old woman had promised, I tried to repay them with song; and many were the tears they both shed over my ballads and dirges. The songs they liked best to hear were two which I made for them. They were not half so good as many others I knew, especially some I had learned from the wise woman in the cottage; but what comes nearest to our needs we like the best.

The king sat on his throne

Glowing in gold and red;

The crown in his right hand shone,

And the gray hairs crowned his head.

His only son walks in,
And in walls of steel he stands:
Make me, O father, strong to win,
With the blessing of holy hands."

He knelt before his sire,
Who blessed him with feeble smile
His eyes shone out with a kingly fire,
But his old lips quivered the while.

"Go to the fight, my son,
Bring back the giant's head;
And the crown with which my brows have done,
Shall glitter on thine instead."

"My father, I seek no crowns,
But unspoken praise from thee;
For thy people's good, and thy renown,
I will die to set them free."

The king sat down and waited there,
And rose not, night nor day;
Till a sound of shouting filled the air,
And cries of a sore dismay.

Then like a king he sat once more,
With the crown upon his head;
And up to the throne the people bore
A mighty giant dead.

And up to the throne the people bore
A pale and lifeless boy.
The king rose up like a prophet of yore,
In a lofty, deathlike joy.

He put the crown on the chilly brow:

"You should have reigned with me
But Death is the king of both, and now
I go to obey with thee.

"Surely some good in me there lay,
To beget the noble one."
The old man smiled like a winter day,
And fell beside his son.

"O lady, thy lover is dead," they cried;
"He is dead, but hath slain the foe;
He hath left his name to be magnified
In a song of wonder and woe."

"Alas! I am well repaid," said she,
"With a pain that stings like joy:
For I feared, from his tenderness to me,
That he was but a feeble boy.

"Now I shall hold my head on high,
The queen among my kind;
If ye hear a sound, 'tis only a sigh
For a glory left behind."

The first three times I sang these songs they both wept passionately. But after the third time, they wept no more. Their eyes shone, and their faces grew pale, but they never wept at any of my songs again.

CHAPTER TWENTY-ONE

At length, with much toil and equal delight, our armor was finished. We armed each other, and tested the strength of the defense, with many blows of loving force. I was inferior in strength to both my brothers, but a little more agile than either; and upon this agility, joined to precision in hitting with the point of my weapon, I grounded my hopes of success in the ensuing combat. I likewise labored to develop yet more the keenness of sight with which I was naturally gifted; and, from the remarks of my companions, I soon learned that my endeavors were not in vain.

The morning arrived on which we had determined to make the attempt, and succeed or perish—perhaps both. We had resolved to fight on foot; knowing that the mishap of many of the knights who had made the attempt, had resulted from the fright of their horses at the appearance of the giants; and believing with Sir Gawain, that, though mare's sons might be false to us, the earth would never prove a traitor. But most of our preparations were, in their immediate aim at least, frustrated.

We rose, that fatal morning, by daybreak. We had rested from all labor the day before, and now were fresh as the lark. We bathed in cold spring water, and dressed ourselves in clean garments, with a sense of preparation, as for a solemn festivity. When we had broken our fast, I took an old lyre, which I had found in the tower and had myself repaired, and sung for the last time the two ballads of which I have said so much already. I followed them with this, for a closing song:

Oh, well for him who breaks his dream
With the blow that ends the strife
And, waking, knows the peace that flows
Around the pain of life!

We are dead, my brothers! Our bodies clasp,
As an armor, our souls about;
This hand is the battle-axe I grasp,
And this my hammer stout.

Fear not, my brothers, for we are dead;
No noise can break our rest;
The calm of the grave is about the head,
And the heart heaves not the breast.

And our life we throw to our people back,
To live with, a further store;
We leave it them, that there be no lack
In the land where we live no more.

Oh, well for him who breaks his dream
With the blow that ends the strife
And, waking, knows the peace that flows
Around the noise of life!

As the last few tones of the instrument were following, like a dirge, the death of the song, we all sprang to our feet. For, through one of the little windows of the tower, towards which I had looked as I sang, I saw, suddenly rising over the edge of the slope on which our tower stood, three enormous heads. The brothers knew at once, by my looks, what caused my sudden movement. We were utterly unarmed, and there was no time to arm.

But we seemed to adopt the same resolution simultaneously; for each caught up his favorite weapon, and, leaving his defense behind, sprang to the door. I snatched up a long rapier, abruptly, but very finely pointed, in my sword-hand, and in the other a saber; the elder brother seized his heavy battle-axe; and the younger, a great, two-handed sword, which he wielded in one hand like a feather. We had just time to get clear of the tower, embrace and say good-bye, and part to some little distance, that we might not encumber each other's motions, ere the triple giant-brotherhood drew near to attack us. They were about twice our height, and armed to the teeth. Through the visors of their helmets their monstrous eyes shone with a horrible ferocity. I was in the middle position, and the middle giant approached me. My eyes were busy with his armor, and I was not a moment in settling my mode of attack. I saw that his body- armor was somewhat clumsily made, and that the overlappings in the lower part had more play than necessary; and I hoped that, in a fortunate moment, some joint would open a little, in a visible and accessible part. I stood till he came near enough to aim a blow at me with the mace, which has been, in all ages, the favorite weapon of giants, when, of course, I leaped aside, and let the blow fall upon the spot where I had been standing. I expected this would strain the joints of his armor yet more. Full of fury, he made at me again; but I kept him busy, constantly eluding his blows, and hoping thus to fatigue him. He did not seem to fear any assault from me, and I attempted none as yet; but while I watched his motions in order to avoid his blows, I, at the same time, kept equal watch upon those joints of his armor, through some one of which I hoped to reach his life. At length, as if somewhat fatigued, he paused a moment, and drew himself slightly up; I bounded forward, foot and hand, ran my rapier right through to the armor of his back, let go the hilt, and passing under his right arm, turned as he fell, and flew at him with my saber. At one happy blow I divided the band of his helmet, which fell off, and allowed me, with a second cut across the eyes, to blind him quite; after which I clove his head, and turned, uninjured, to see how my brothers had fared. Both the giants were down, but so were my brothers. I flew first to the one and then to the other couple. Both pairs of combatants were dead, and yet locked together, as in the death-struggle. The elder had buried his battle-axe in the body of his foe, and had fallen beneath him as he fell. The giant had strangled him in his own death-agonies. The younger had nearly hewn off the left leg of his enemy; and, grappled with in the act, had, while they rolled together on the earth, found for his dagger a passage betwixt the gorget and cuirass of the giant, and stabbed him mortally in the throat. The blood from the giant's throat was yet pouring over the hand of his foe, which still grasped the hilt of the dagger sheathed in the wound. They lay silent. I, the least worthy, remained the sole survivor in the lists.

As I stood exhausted amidst the dead, after the first worthy deed of my life, I suddenly looked behind me, and there lay the Shadow, black in the sunshine. I went into the lonely tower, and there lay the useless armor of the noble youths—supine as they.

Ah, how sad it looked! It was a glorious death, but it was death. My songs could not comfort me now. I was almost ashamed that I was alive, when they, the true-hearted, were no more. And yet I breathed freer to think that I had gone through the trial, and had not failed. And perhaps I may be forgiven, if some feelings of pride arose in my bosom, when I looked down on the mighty form that lay dead by my hand.

"After all, however," I said to myself, and my heart sank, "it was only skill. Your giant was but a blunderer."

I left the bodies of friends and foes, peaceful enough when the death- fight was over, and, hastening to the country below, roused the peasants. They came with shouting and gladness, bringing wagons to carry the bodies. I resolved to take the princes home to their father, each as he lay, in the arms of his country's foe. But first I searched the giants, and found the keys of their castle, to which I repaired, followed by a great company of the people. It was a place of wonderful strength. I released the prisoners, knights and ladies, all in a sad condition, from the cruelties and neglects of the giants. It humbled me to see them crowding round me with thanks, when in truth the glorious brothers, lying dead by their lonely tower, were those to whom the thanks belonged. I had but aided in carrying out the thought born in their brain, and uttered in visible form before ever I laid hold thereupon. Yet I did count myself happy to have been chosen for their brother in this great dead.

After a few hours spent in refreshing and clothing the prisoners, we all commenced our journey towards the capital. This was slow at first; but, as the strength and spirits of the prisoners returned, it became more rapid; and in three days we reached the palace of the king. As we entered the city gates, with the huge bulks lying each on a wagon drawn by horses, and two of them inextricably intertwined with the dead bodies of their princes, the people raised a shout and then a cry, and followed in multitudes the solemn procession.

I will not attempt to describe the behavior of the grand old king. Joy and pride in his sons overcame his sorrow at their loss. On me he heaped every kindness that heart could devise or hand execute. He used to sit and question me, night after night, about everything that was in any way connected with them and their preparations. Our mode of life, and relation to each other, during the time we spent together, was a constant theme. He entered into the minutest details of the construction of the armor, even to a peculiar mode of riveting some of the plates, with unwearying interest. This armor I had intended to beg of the king, as my sole memorials of the contest; but, when I saw the delight he took in contemplating it, and the consolation it appeared to afford him in his sorrow, I could not ask for it; but, at his request, left my own, weapons and all, to be joined with theirs in a trophy, erected in the grand square of the palace. The king, with gorgeous ceremony, dubbed me knight with his own old hand, in which trembled the sword of his youth.

During the short time I remained, my company was, naturally, much courted by the young nobles. I was in a constant round of gaiety and diversion, notwithstanding that the court was in mourning. For the country was so rejoiced at the death of the giants, and so many of their lost friends had been restored to the nobility and men of wealth, that the gladness surpassed the grief. "Ye have indeed left your lives to your people, my great brothers!" I said.

But I was ever and ever haunted by the old shadow, which I had not seen all the time that I was at work in the tower. Even in the society of the ladies of the court, who seemed to think it only their duty to make my stay there as pleasant to me as possible, I could not help being conscious of its presence, although it might not be annoying me at the time. At length, somewhat weary of uninterrupted pleasure, and nowise strengthened thereby, either in body or mind, I put on a splendid suit of armor of steel inlaid with silver, which the old king had given me, and, mounting the horse on which it had been brought to me, took my leave of the palace, to visit the distant city in which the lady dwelt, whom the elder prince had loved. I anticipated a sore task, in conveying to her the news of his glorious fate: but this trial was spared me, in a manner as strange as anything that had happened to me in Fairy Land.

CHAPTER TWENTY-TWO

On the third day of my journey, I was riding gently along a road, apparently little frequented, to judge from the grass that grew upon it. I was approaching a forest. Everywhere in Fairy Land forests are the places where one may most certainly expect adventures. As I drew near, a youth, unarmed, gentle, and beautiful, who had just cut a branch from a yew growing on the skirts of the wood, evidently to make himself a bow, met me, and thus accosted me:

"Sir knight, be careful as you ride through this forest; for it is said to be strangely enchanted, in a sort which even those who have been witnesses of its enchantment can hardly describe."

I thanked him for his advice, which I promised to follow, and rode on. But the moment I entered the wood, it seemed to me that, if enchantment there was, it must be of a good kind; for the Shadow, which had been more than usually dark and distressing, since I had set out on this journey, suddenly disappeared. I felt a wonderful elevation of spirits, and began to reflect on my past life, and especially on my combat with the giants, with such satisfaction, that I had actually to remind myself, that I had only killed one of them; and that, but for the brothers, I should never have had the idea of attacking them, not to mention the smallest power of standing to it. Still I rejoiced, and counted myself amongst the glorious knights of old; having even the unspeakable presumption — my shame and self condemnation at the memory of it are such, that I write it as the only and sorest penance I can perform — to think of myself (will the world believe it?) as side by side with Sir Galahad! Scarcely had the thought been born in my mind, when, approaching me from the left, through the trees, I espied a resplendent knight, of mighty size, whose armor seemed to shine of itself, without the sun. When he drew near, I was astonished to see that this armor was like my own; nay, I could trace, line for line, the correspondence of the inlaid silver to the device on my own. His horse, too, was like mine in color, form, and motion; save that, like his rider, he was greater and fiercer than his counterpart. The knight rode with beaver up. As he halted right opposite to me in the narrow path, barring my way, I saw the reflection of my countenance in the centre plate of shining steel on his breastplate. Above it rose the same face — his face — only, as I have said, larger and fiercer. I was bewildered. I could not help feeling some admiration of him, but it was mingled with a dim conviction that he was evil, and that I ought to fight with him.

"Let me pass," I said.

"When I will," he replied.

Something within me said: "Spear in rest, and ride at him! Else thou art for ever a slave."

I tried, but my arm trembled so much, that I could not couch my lance. To tell the truth, I, who had overcome the giant, shook like a coward before this knight. He gave a scornful laugh, that echoed through the wood, turned his horse, and said, without looking round, "Follow me."

I obeyed, abashed and stupefied. How long he led, and how long I followed, I cannot tell. "I never knew misery before," I said to myself. "Would that I had at least struck him, and had had my death- blow in return! Why, then, do I not call to him to wheel and defend himself? Alas! I know not why, but I cannot. One look from him would cow me like a beaten hound." I followed, and was silent.

At length we came to a dreary square tower, in the middle of a dense forest. It looked as if scarce a tree had been cut down to make room for it. Across the very door, diagonally, grew the stem of a tree, so large that there was just room to squeeze past it in order to enter. One miserable square hole in the roof was the only visible suggestion of a window. Turret or battlement, or projecting masonry of any kind, it had none. Clear and smooth and massy, it rose from its base, and ended with a line straight and unbroken. The roof, carried to a centre from each of the four walls, rose slightly to the point where the rafters met. Round the base lay several little heaps of either bits of broken branches, withered and peeled, or half- whitened bones; I could not distinguish which. As I approached, the ground sounded hollow beneath my horse's hoofs. The knight took a great key from his pocket, and reaching past the stem of the tree, with some difficulty opened the door. "Dismount," he commanded. I obeyed. He turned my horse's head away from the tower, gave him a terrible blow with the flat side of his sword, and sent him madly tearing through the forest.

"Now," said he, "enter, and take your companion with you."

I looked round: knight and horse had vanished, and behind me lay the horrible shadow. I entered, for I could not help myself; and the shadow followed me. I had a terrible conviction that the knight and he were one. The door closed behind me.

Now I was indeed in pitiful plight. There was literally nothing in the tower but my shadow and me. The walls rose right up to the roof; in which, as I had seen from without, there was one little square opening. This I now knew to be the only window the tower possessed. I sat down on the floor, in listless wretchedness. I think I must have fallen asleep, and have slept for hours; for I suddenly became aware of existence, in observing that the moon was shining through the hole in the roof. As she rose higher and higher, her light crept down the wall over me, till at last it shone right upon my head. Instantaneously the walls of the tower seemed to vanish away like a mist. I sat beneath a beech, on the edge of a forest, and the open country lay, in the moonlight, for miles and miles around me, spotted with glimmering houses and spires and towers. I thought with myself, "Oh, joy! it was only a dream; the horrible narrow waste is gone, and I wake beneath a beech-tree, perhaps one that loves me, and I can go where I will." I rose, as I thought, and walked about, and did what I would, but ever kept near the tree; for always, and, of course, since my meeting with the woman of the beech-tree far more than ever, I loved that tree. So the night wore on. I waited for the sun to rise, before I could venture to renew my journey. But as soon as the first faint light of the dawn appeared, instead of shining upon me from the eye of the morning, it stole like a fainting ghost through the little square hole above my head; and the walls came out as the light grew, and the glorious night was swallowed up of the hateful day. The long dreary day passed. My shadow lay black on the floor. I felt no hunger, no need of food. The night came. The moon shone. I watched her light slowly descending the wall, as I might have watched, adown the sky, the long, swift approach of a helping angel. Her rays touched me, and I was free. Thus night after night passed away. I should have died but for this. Every night the conviction returned, that I was free. Every morning I sat wretchedly disconsolate. At length, when the course of the moon no longer permitted her beams to touch me, the night was dreary as the day.

When I slept, I was somewhat consoled by my dreams; but all the time I dreamed, I knew that I was only dreaming. But one night, at length, the moon, a mere shred of pallor, scattered a few thin ghostly rays upon me; and I think I fell asleep and dreamed. I sat in an autumn night before the vintage, on a hill overlooking my own castle. My heart sprang with joy. Oh, to be a child again, innocent, fearless, without shame or desire! I walked down to the castle. All were in consternation at my absence. My sisters were weeping for my loss. They sprang up and clung to me, with incoherent cries, as I entered. My old friends came flocking round me. A gray light shone on the roof of the hall. It was the light of the dawn shining through the square window of my tower. More earnestly than ever, I longed for freedom after this dream; more drearily than ever, crept on the next wretched day. I measured by the sunbeams, caught through the little window in the trap of my tower, how it went by, waiting only for the dreams of the night.

About noon, I started as if something foreign to all my senses and all my experience, had suddenly invaded me; yet it was only the voice of a woman singing. My whole frame quivered with joy, surprise, and the sensation of the unforeseen. Like a living soul, like an incarnation of Nature, the song entered my prison-house. Each tone folded its wings, and laid itself, like a caressing bird, upon my heart. It bathed me like a sea; inwrapt me like an odorous vapor; entered my soul like a long draught of clear spring-water; shone upon me like essential sunlight; soothed me like a mother's voice and hand. Yet, as the clearest forest-well tastes sometimes of the bitterness of decayed leaves, so to my weary, prisoned heart, its cheerfulness had a sting of cold, and its tenderness unmanned me with the faintness of long-departed joys. I wept half-bitterly, half-luxuriously; but not long. I dashed away the tears, ashamed of a weakness which I thought I had abandoned. Ere I knew, I had walked to the door, and seated myself with my ears against it, in order to catch every syllable of the revelation from the unseen outer world. And now I heard each word distinctly. The singer seemed to be standing or sitting near the tower, for the sounds indicated no change of place. The song was something like this:

The sun, like a golden knot on high,
Gathers the glories of the sky,
And binds them into a shining tent,
Roofing the world with the firmament.
And through the pavilion the rich winds blow,
And through the pavilion the waters go.
And the birds for joy, and the trees for prayer,
Bowing their heads in the sunny air,
And for thoughts, the gently talking springs,
That come from the centre with secret things —
All make a music, gentle and strong,
Bound by the heart into one sweet song.
And amidst them all, the mother Earth
Sits with the children of her birth;
She tendeth them all, as a mother hen
Her little ones round her, twelve or ten:
Oft she sitteth, with hands on knee,
Idle with love for her family.
Go forth to her from the dark and the dust,
And weep beside her, if weep thou must;
If she may not hold thee to her breast,
Like a weary infant, that cries for rest
At least she will press thee to her knee,
And tell a low, sweet tale to thee,
Till the hue to thy cheeky and the light to thine eye,
Strength to thy limbs, and courage high
To thy fainting heart, return amain,
And away to work thou goest again.
From the narrow desert, O man of pride,
Come into the house, so high and wide.

Hardly knowing what I did, I opened the door. Why had I not done so before? I do not know.

At first I could see no one; but when I had forced myself past the tree which grew across the entrance, I saw, seated on the ground, and leaning against the tree, with her back to my prison, a beautiful woman. Her countenance seemed known to me, and yet unknown. She looked at me and smiled, when I made my appearance.

"Ah! were you the prisoner there? I am very glad I have wiled you out."

"Do you know me then?" "Do you not know me? But you hurt me, and that, I suppose, makes it easy for a man to forget. You broke my globe. Yet I thank you. Perhaps I owe you many thanks for breaking it. I took the pieces, all black, and wet with crying over them, to the Fairy Queen. There was no music and no light in them now. But she took them from me, and laid them aside; and made me go to sleep in a great hall of white, with black pillars, and many red curtains. When I woke in the morning, I went to her, hoping to have my globe again, whole and sound; but she sent me away without it, and I have not seen it since. Nor do I care for it now. I have something so much better. I do not need the globe to play to me; for I can sing. I could not sing at all before. Now I go about everywhere through Fairy Land, singing till my heart is like to break, just like my globe, for very joy at my own songs. And wherever I go, my songs do good, and deliver people. And now I have delivered you, and I am so happy."

She ceased, and the tears came into her eyes.

All this time, I had been gazing at her; and now fully recognized the face of the child, glorified in the countenance of the woman.

I was ashamed and humbled before her; but a great weight was lifted from my thoughts. I knelt before her, and thanked her, and begged her to forgive me.

"Rise, rise," she said; "I have nothing to forgive; I thank you. But now I must be gone, for I do not know how many may be waiting for me, here and there, through the dark forests; and they cannot come out till I come."

She rose, and with a smile and a farewell, turned and left me. I dared not ask her to stay; in fact, I could hardly speak to her. Between her and me, there was a great gulf. She was uplifted, by sorrow and well-doing, into a region I could hardly hope ever to enter. I watched her departure, as one watches a sunset. She went like a radiance through the dark wood, which was henceforth bright to me, from simply knowing that such a creature was in it.

She was bearing the sun to the un-sunned spots. The light and the music of her broken globe were now in her heart and her brain. As she went, she sang; and I caught these few words of her song;

and the tones seemed to linger and wind about the trees after she

had disappeared:

> Thou goest thine, and I go mine —
>
> Many ways we wend;
>
> Many days, and many ways,
>
> Ending in one end.

Many a wrong, and its curing song;

Many a road, and many an inn;

Room to roam, but only one home

For all the world to win.

And so she vanished. With a sad heart, soothed by humility, and the knowledge of her peace and gladness, I bethought me what now I should do. First, I must leave the tower far behind me, lest, in some evil moment, I might be once more caged within its horrible walls. But it was ill walking in my heavy armor; and besides I had now no right to the golden spurs and the resplendent mail, fitly dulled with long neglect. I might do for a squire; but I honored knighthood too highly, to call myself any longer one of the noble brotherhood. I stripped off all my armor, piled it under the tree, just where the lady had been seated, and took my unknown way, eastward through the woods. Of all my weapons, I carried only a short axe in my hand.

Then first I knew the delight of being lowly; of saying to myself, "I am what I am, nothing more." "I have failed," I said, "I have lost myself—would it had been my shadow." I looked round: the shadow was nowhere to be seen. Ere long, I learned that it was not myself, but only my shadow, that I had lost. I learned that it is better, a thousand-fold, for a proud man to fall and be humbled, than to hold up his head in his pride and fancied innocence. I learned that he that will be a hero, will barely be a man; that he that will be nothing but a doer of his work, is sure of his manhood. In nothing was my ideal lowered, or dimmed, or grown less precious; I only saw it too plainly, to set myself for a moment beside it. Indeed, my ideal soon became my life; whereas, formerly, my life had consisted in a vain attempt to behold, if not my ideal in myself, at least myself in my ideal. Now, however, I took, at first, what perhaps was a mistaken pleasure, in despising and degrading myself. Another self seemed to arise, like a white spirit from a dead man, from the dumb and trampled self of the past. Doubtless, this self must again die and be buried, and again, from its tomb, spring a winged child; but of this my history as yet bears not the record.

Self will come to life even in the slaying of self; but there is ever something deeper and stronger than it, which will emerge at last from the unknown abysses of the soul: will it be as a solemn gloom, burning with eyes? or a clear morning after the rain? or a smiling child, that finds itself nowhere, and everywhere?

CHAPTER TWENTY-THREE

I had not gone far, for I had but just lost sight of the hated tower, when a voice of another sort, sounding near or far, as the trees permitted or intercepted its passage, reached me. It was a full, deep, manly voice, but withal clear and melodious. Now it burst on the ear with a sudden swell, and anon, dying away as suddenly, seemed to come to me across a great space. Nevertheless, it drew nearer; till, at last, I could distinguish the words of the song, and get transient glimpses of the singer, between the columns of the trees. He came nearer, dawning upon me like a growing thought. He was a knight, armed from head to heel, mounted upon a strange-looking beast, whose form I could not understand. The words which I heard him sing were like these:

Heart be stout,

And eye be true;

Good blade out!
And ill shall rue.

Courage, horse!
Thou lackst no skill;
Well thy force
Hath matched my will.

For the foe
With fiery breath,
At a blow,
It still in death.

Gently, horse!
Tread fearlessly;
'Tis his corse
That burdens thee.

The sun's eye
Is fierce at noon;
Thou and I
Will rest full soon.

And new strength
New work will meet;
Till, at length,
Long rest is sweet.

And now horse and rider had arrived near enough for me to see, fastened by the long neck to the hinder part of the saddle, and trailing its hideous length on the ground behind, the body of a great dragon. It was no wonder that, with such a drag at his heels, the horse could make but slow progress, notwithstanding his evident dismay. The horrid, serpent-like head, with its black tongue, forked with red, hanging out of its jaws, dangled against the horse's side. Its neck was covered with long blue hair, its sides with scales of green and gold. Its back was of corrugated skin, of a purple hue. Its belly was similar in nature, but its color was leaden, dashed with blotches of livid blue. Its skinny, bat-like wings and its tail were of a dull gray. It was strange to see how so many gorgeous colors, so many curving lines, and such beautiful things as wings and hair and scales, combined to form the horrible creature, intense in ugliness.

The knight was passing me with a salutation; but, as I walked towards him, he reined up, and I stood by his stirrup. When I came near him, I saw to my surprise and pleasure likewise, although a sudden pain, like a birth of fire, sprang up in my heart, that it was the knight of the soiled armor, whom I knew before, and whom I had seen in the vision, with the lady of the marble. But I could have thrown my arms around him, because she loved him. This discovery only strengthened the resolution I had formed, before I recognized him, of offering myself to the knight, to wait upon him as a squire, for he seemed to be unattended. I made my request in as few words as possible. He hesitated for a moment, and looked at me thoughtfully. I saw that he suspected who I was, but that he continued uncertain of his suspicion. No doubt he was soon convinced of its truth; but all the time I was with him, not a word crossed his lips with reference to what he evidently concluded I wished to leave unnoticed, if not to keep concealed.

"Squire and knight should be friends," said he: "can you take me by the hand?" And he held out the great gauntleted right hand. I grasped it willingly and strongly. Not a word more was said. The knight gave the sign to his horse, which again began his slow march, and I walked beside and a little behind.

We had not gone very far before we arrived at a little cottage; from which, as we drew near, a woman rushed out with the cry:

"My child! my child! have you found my child?"

"I have found her," replied the knight, "but she is sorely hurt. I was forced to leave her with the hermit, as I returned. You will find her there, and I think she will get better. You see I have brought you a present. This wretch will not hurt you again." And he undid the creature's neck, and flung the frightful burden down by the cottage door.

The woman was now almost out of sight in the wood; but the husband stood at the door, with speechless thanks in his face.

"You must bury the monster," said the knight. "If I had arrived a moment later, I should have been too late. But now you need not fear, for such a creature as this very rarely appears, in the same part, twice during a lifetime."

"Will you not dismount and rest you, Sir Knight?" said the peasant, who had, by this time, recovered himself a little.

"That I will, thankfully," said he; and, dismounting, he gave the reins to me, and told me to unbridle the horse, and lead him into the shade. "You need not tie him up," he added; "he will not run away."

When I returned, after obeying his orders, and entered the cottage, I saw the knight seated, without his helmet, and talking most familiarly with the simple host. I stood at the open door for a moment, and, gazing at him, inwardly justified the white lady in preferring him to me. A nobler countenance I never saw. Loving-kindness beamed from every line of his face. It seemed as if he would repay himself for the late arduous combat, by indulging in all the gentleness of a womanly heart. But when the talk ceased for a moment, he seemed to fall into a reverie. Then the exquisite curves of the upper lip vanished. The lip was lengthened and compressed at the same moment. You could have told that, within the lips, the teeth were firmly closed. The whole face grew stern and determined, all but fierce; only the eyes burned on like a holy sacrifice, uplift on a granite rock.

The woman entered, with her mangled child in her arms. She was pale as her little burden. She gazed, with a wild love and despairing tenderness, on the still, all but dead face, white and clear from loss of blood and terror.

The knight rose. The light that had been confined to his eyes, now shone from his whole countenance. He took the little thing in his arms, and, with the mother's help, undressed her, and looked to her wounds. The tears flowed down his face as he did so. With tender hands he bound them up, kissed the pale cheek, and gave her back to her mother. When he went home, all his tale would be of the grief and joy of the parents; while to me, who had looked on, the gracious countenance of the armed man, beaming from the panoply of steel, over the seemingly dead child, while the powerful hands turned it and shifted it, and bound it, if possible even more gently than the mother's, formed the centre of the story.

After we had partaken of the best they could give us, the knight took his leave, with a few parting instructions to the mother as to how she should treat the child.

I brought the knight his steed, held the stirrup while he mounted, and then followed him through the wood. The horse, delighted to be free of his hideous load, bounded beneath the weight of man and armor, and could hardly be restrained from galloping on. But the knight made him time his powers to mine, and so we went on for an hour or two. Then the knight dismounted, and compelled me to get into the saddle, saying: "Knight and squire must share the labor."

Holding by the stirrup, he walked along by my side, heavily clad as he was, with apparent ease. As we went, he led a conversation, in which I took what humble part my sense of my condition would permit me.

"Somehow or other," said he, "notwithstanding the beauty of this country of Faerie, in which we are, there is much that is wrong in it. If there are great splendors, there are corresponding horrors; heights and depths; beautiful women and awful fiends; noble men and weaklings. All a man has to do, is to better what he can. And if he will settle it with himself, that even renown and success are in themselves of no great value, and be content to be defeated, if so be that the fault is not his; and so go to his work with a cool brain and a strong will, he will get it done; and fare none the worse in the end, that he was not burdened with provision and precaution."

"But he will not always come off well," I ventured to say.

"Perhaps not," rejoined the knight, "in the individual act; but the result of his lifetime will content him."

"So it will fare with you, doubtless," thought I; "but for me——"

Venturing to resume the conversation after a pause, I said, hesitatingly:

"May I ask for what the little beggar-girl wanted your aid, when she came to your castle to find you?"

He looked at me for a moment in silence, and then said —

"I cannot help wondering how you know of that; but there is something about you quite strange enough to entitle you to the privilege of the country; namely, to go unquestioned. I, however, being only a man, such as you see me, am ready to tell you anything you like to ask me, as far as I can. The little beggar-girl came into the hall where I was sitting, and told me a very curious story, which I can only recollect very vaguely, it was so peculiar. What I can recall is, that she was sent to gather wings. As soon as she had gathered a pair of wings for herself, she was to fly away, she said, to the country she came from; but where that was, she could give no information.

She said she had to beg her wings from the butterflies and moths; and wherever she begged, no one refused her. But she needed a great many of the wings of butterflies and moths to make a pair for her; and so she had to wander about day after day, looking for butterflies, and night after night, looking for moths; and then she begged for their wings. But the day before, she had come into a part of the forest, she said, where there were multitudes of splendid butterflies flitting about, with wings which were just fit to make the eyes in the shoulders of hers; and she knew she could have as many of them as she liked for the asking; but as soon as she began to beg, there came a great creature right up to her, and threw her down, and walked over her. When she got up, she saw the wood was full of these beings stalking about, and seeming to have nothing to do with each other. As soon as ever she began to beg, one of them walked over her; till at last in dismay, and in growing horror of the senseless creatures, she had run away to look for somebody to help her. I asked her what they were like. She said, like great men, made of wood, without knee- or elbow-joints, and without any noses or mouths or eyes in their faces. I laughed at the little maiden, thinking she was making child's game of me; but, although she burst out laughing too, she persisted in asserting the truth of her story.

"`Only come, knight, come and see; I will lead you.'

"So I armed myself, to be ready for anything that might happen, and followed the child; for, though I could make nothing of her story, I could see she was a little human being in need of some help or other. As she walked before me, I looked attentively at her. Whether or not it was from being so often knocked down and walked over, I could not tell, but her clothes were very much torn, and in several places her white skin was peeping through. I thought she was hump-backed; but on looking more closely, I saw, through the tatters of her frock—do not laugh at me—a bunch on each shoulder, of the most gorgeous colors. Looking yet more closely, I saw that they were of the shape of folded wings, and were made of all kinds of butterfly-wings and moth-wings, crowded together like the feathers on the individual butterfly pinion; but, like them, most beautifully arranged, and producing a perfect harmony of color and shade. I could now more easily believe the rest of her story; especially as I saw, every now and then, a certain heaving motion in the wings, as if they longed to be uplifted and outspread. But beneath her scanty garments complete wings could not be concealed, and indeed, from her own story, they were yet unfinished.

"After walking for two or three hours (how the little girl found her way, I could not imagine), we came to a part of the forest, the very air of which was quivering with the motions of multitudes of resplendent butterflies; as gorgeous in color, as if the eyes of peacocks' feathers had taken to flight, but of infinite variety of hue and form, only that the appearance of some kind of eye on each wing predominated. `There they are, there they are!' cried the child, in a tone of victory mingled with terror. Except for this tone, I should have thought she referred to the butterflies, for I could see nothing else. But at that moment an enormous butterfly, whose wings had great eyes of blue surrounded by confused cloudy heaps of more dingy coloring, just like a break in the clouds on a stormy day towards evening, settled near us. The child instantly began murmuring: `Butterfly, butterfly, give me your wings'; when, the moment after, she fell to the ground, and began crying as if hurt. I drew my sword and heaved a great blow in the direction in which the child had fallen. It struck something, and instantly the most grotesque imitation of a man became visible. You see this Fairy Land is full of oddities and all sorts of incredibly ridiculous things, which a man is compelled to meet and treat as real existences, although all the time he feels foolish for doing so. This being, if being it could be called, was like a block of wood roughly hewn into the mere outlines of a man; and hardly so, for it had but head, body, legs, and arms— the head without a face, and the limbs utterly formless. I had hewn off one of its legs, but the two portions moved on as best they could, quite independent of each other; so that I had done no good. I ran after it, and clove it in twain from the head downwards; but it could not be convinced that its vocation was not to walk over people; for, as soon as the little girl began her begging again, all three parts came bustling up; and if I had not interposed my weight between her and them, she would have been trampled again under them. I saw that something else must be done. If the wood was full of the creatures, it would be an endless work to chop them so small that they could do no injury; and then, besides, the parts would be so numerous, that the butterflies would be in danger from the drift of flying chips. I served this one so, however; and then told the girl to beg again, and point out the direction in which one was coming. I was glad to find, however, that I could now see him myself, and wondered how they could have been invisible before. I would not allow him to walk over the child; but while I kept him off, and she began begging again, another appeared; and it was all I could do, from the weight of my armor, to protect her from the stupid, persevering efforts of the two. But suddenly the right plan occurred to me. I tripped one of them up, and, taking him by the legs, set him up on his head, with his heels against a tree. I was delighted to find he could not move.

Meantime the poor child was walked over by the other, but it was for the last time. Whenever one appeared, I followed the same plan— tripped him up and set him on his head; and so the little beggar was able to gather her wings without any trouble, which occupation she continued for several hours in my company."

"What became of her?" I asked.

"I took her home with me to my castle, and she told me all her story; but it seemed to me, all the time, as if I were hearing a child talk in its sleep. I could not arrange her story in my mind at all, although it seemed to leave hers in some certain order of its own. My wife —"

Here the knight checked himself, and said no more. Neither did I urge the conversation farther.

Thus we journeyed for several days, resting at night in such shelter as we could get; and when no better was to be had, lying in the forest under some tree, on a couch of old leaves.

I loved the knight more and more. I believe never squire served his master with more care and joyfulness than I. I tended his horse; I cleaned his armor; my skill in the craft enabled me to repair it when necessary; I watched his needs; and was well repaid for all by the love itself which I bore him.

"This," I said to myself, "is a true man. I will serve him, and give him all worship, seeing in him the embodiment of what I would fain become. If I cannot be noble myself, I will yet be servant to his nobleness." He, in return, soon showed me such signs of friendship and respect, as made my heart glad; and I felt that, after all, mine would be no lost life, if I might wait on him to the world's end, although no smile but his should greet me, and no one but him should say, "Well done! he was a good servant!" at last. But I burned to do something more for him than the ordinary routine of a squire's duty permitted.

One afternoon, we began to observe an appearance of roads in the wood. Branches had been cut down, and openings made, where footsteps had worn no path below. These indications increased as we passed on, till, at length, we came into a long, narrow avenue, formed by felling the trees in its line, as the remaining roots evidenced. At some little distance, on both hands, we observed signs of similar avenues, which appeared to converge with ours, towards one spot. Along these we indistinctly saw several forms moving, which seemed, with ourselves, to approach the common centre. Our path brought us, at last, up to a wall of yew-trees, growing close together, and intertwining their branches so, that nothing could be seen beyond it. An opening was cut in it like a door, and all the wall was trimmed smooth and perpendicular. The knight dismounted, and waited till I had provided for his horse's comfort; upon which we entered the place together.

It was a great space, bare of trees, and enclosed by four walls of yew, similar to that through which we had entered. These trees grew to a very great height, and did not divide from each other till close to the top, where their summits formed a row of conical battlements all around the walls. The space contained was a parallelogram of great length. Along each of the two longer sides of the interior, were ranged three ranks of men, in white robes, standing silent and solemn, each with a sword by his side, although the rest of his costume and bearing was more priestly than soldierly. For some distance inwards, the space between these opposite rows was filled with a company of men and women and children, in holiday attire. The looks of all were directed inwards, towards the further end. Far beyond the crowd, in a long avenue, seeming to narrow in the distance, went the long rows of the white-robed men. On what the attention of the multitude was fixed, we could not tell, for the sun had set before we arrived, and it was growing dark within. It grew darker and darker. The multitude waited in silence. The stars began to shine down into the enclosure, and they grew brighter and larger every moment. A wind arose, and swayed the pinnacles of the tree-tops; and made a strange sound, half like music, half like moaning, through the close branches and leaves of the tree-walls. A young girl who stood beside me, clothed in the same dress as the priests, bowed her head, and grew pale with awe.

The knight whispered to me, "How solemn it is! Surely they wait to hear the voice of a prophet. There is something good near!"

But I, though somewhat shaken by the feeling expressed by my master, yet had an unaccountable conviction that here was something bad. So I resolved to be keenly on the watch for what should follow.

Suddenly a great star, like a sun, appeared high in the air over the temple, illuminating it throughout; and a great song arose from the men in white, which went rolling round and round the building, now receding to the end, and now approaching, down the other side, the place where we stood. For some of the singers were regularly ceasing, and the next to them as regularly taking up the song, so that it crept onwards with gradations produced by changes which could not themselves be detected, for only a few of those who were singing ceased at the same moment. The song paused; and I saw a company of six of the white-robed men walk up the centre of the human avenue, surrounding a youth gorgeously attired beneath his robe of white, and wearing a chaplet of flowers on his head. I followed them closely, with my keenest observation; and, by accompanying their slow progress with my eyes, I was able to perceive more clearly what took place when they arrived at the other end. I knew that my sight was so much more keen than that of most people, that I had good reason to suppose I should see more than the rest could, at such a distance. At the farther end a throne stood upon a platform, high above the heads of the surrounding priests. To this platform I saw the company begin to ascend, apparently by an inclined plane or gentle slope. The throne itself was elevated again, on a kind of square pedestal, to the top of which led a flight of steps. On the throne sat a majestic- looking figure, whose posture seemed to indicate a mixture of pride and benignity, as he looked down on the multitude below. The company ascended to the foot of the throne, where they all kneeled for some minutes; then they rose and passed round to the side of the pedestal upon which the throne stood. Here they crowded close behind the youth, putting him in the foremost place, and one of them opened a door in the pedestal, for the youth to enter. I was sure I saw him shrink back, and those crowding behind pushed him in. Then, again, arose a burst of song from the multitude in white, which lasted some time. When it ceased, a new company of seven commenced its march up the centre. As they advanced, I looked up at my master: his noble countenance was full of reverence and awe. Incapable of evil himself, he could scarcely suspect it in another, much less in a multitude such as this, and surrounded with such appearances of solemnity. I was certain it was the really grand accompaniments that overcame him; that the stars overhead, the dark towering tops of the yew-trees, and the wind that, like an unseen spirit, sighed through their branches, bowed his spirit to the belief, that in all these ceremonies lay some great mystical meaning which, his humility told him, his ignorance prevented him from understanding.

More convinced than before, that there was evil here, I could not endure that my master should be deceived; that one like him, so pure and noble, should respect what, if my suspicions were true, was worse than the ordinary deceptions of priest-craft. I could not tell how far he might be led to countenance, and otherwise support their doings, before he should find cause to repent bitterly of his error. I watched the new procession yet more keenly, if possible, than the former. This time, the central figure was a girl; and, at the close, I observed, yet more indubitably, the shrinking back, and the crowding push. What happened to the victims, I never learned; but I had learned enough, and I could bear it no longer. I stooped, and whispered to the young girl who stood by me, to lend me her white garment. I wanted it, that I might not be entirely out of keeping with the solemnity, but might have at least this help to passing unquestioned. She looked up, half-amused and half-bewildered, as if doubting whether I was in earnest or not. But in her perplexity, she permitted me to unfasten it, and slip it down from her shoulders.

I easily got possession of it; and, sinking down on my knees in the crowd, I rose apparently in the habit of one of the worshippers.

Giving my battle-axe to the girl, to hold in pledge for the return of her stole, for I wished to test the matter unarmed, and, if it was a man that sat upon the throne, to attack him with hands bare, as I supposed his must be, I made my way through the crowd to the front, while the singing yet continued, desirous of reaching the platform while it was unoccupied by any of the priests. I was permitted to walk up the long avenue of white robes unmolested, though I saw questioning looks in many of the faces as I passed. I presume my coolness aided my passage; for I felt quite indifferent as to my own fate; not feeling, after the late events of my history, that I was at all worth taking care of; and enjoying, perhaps, something of an evil satisfaction, in the revenge I was thus taking upon the self which had fooled me so long. When I arrived on the platform, the song had just ceased, and I felt as if all were looking towards me. But instead of kneeling at its foot, I walked right up the stairs to the throne, laid hold of a great wooden image that seemed to sit upon it, and tried to hurl it from its seat. In this I failed at first, for I found it firmly fixed. But in dread lest, the first shock of amazement passing away, the guards would rush upon me before I had effected my purpose, I strained with all my might; and, with a noise as of the cracking, and breaking, and tearing of rotten wood, something gave way, and I hurled the image down the steps. Its displacement revealed a great hole in the throne, like the hollow of a decayed tree, going down apparently a great way. But I had no time to examine it, for, as I looked into it, up out of it rushed a great brute, like a wolf, but twice the size, and tumbled me headlong with itself, down the steps of the throne. As we fell, however, I caught it by the throat, and the moment we reached the platform, a struggle commenced, in which I soon got uppermost, with my hand upon its throat, and knee upon its heart. But now arose a wild cry of wrath and revenge and rescue. A universal hiss of steel, as every sword was swept from its scabbard, seemed to tear the very air in shreds. I heard the rush of hundreds towards the platform on which I knelt. I only tightened my grasp of the brute's throat. His eyes were already starting from his head, and his tongue was hanging out. My anxious hope was, that, even after they had killed me, they would be unable to undo my gripe of his throat, before the monster was past breathing. I therefore threw all my will, and force, and purpose, into the grasping hand. I remember no blow. A faintness came over me, and my consciousness departed.

CHAPTER TWENTY-FOUR

I was dead, and right content. I lay in my coffin, with my hands folded in peace. The knight, and the lady I loved, wept over me.

Her tears fell on my face.

"Ah!" said the knight, "I rushed amongst them like a madman. I hewed them down like brushwood. Their swords battered on me like hail, but hurt me not. I cut a lane through to my friend. He was dead. But he had throttled the monster, and I had to cut the handful out of its throat, before I could disengage and carry off his body. They dared not molest me as I brought him back."

"He has died well," said the lady.

My spirit rejoiced. They left me to my repose. I felt as if a cool hand had been laid upon my heart, and had stilled it. My soul was like a summer evening, after a heavy fall of rain, when the drops are yet glistening on the trees in the last rays of the down-going sun, and the wind of the twilight has begun to blow. The hot fever of life had gone by, and I breathed the clear mountain-air of the land of Death. I had never dreamed of such blessedness. It was not that I had in any way ceased to be what I had been. The very fact that anything can die, implies the existence of something that cannot die; which must either take to itself another form, as when the seed that is sown dies, and arises again; or, in conscious existence, may, perhaps, continue to lead a purely spiritual life. If my passions were dead, the souls of the passions, those essential mysteries of the spirit which had imbodied themselves in the passions, and had given to them all their glory and wonderment, yet lived, yet glowed, with a pure, undying fire. They rose above their vanishing earthly garments, and disclosed themselves angels of light. But oh, how beautiful beyond the old form! I lay thus for a time, and lived as it were an unradiating existence; my soul a motionless lake, that received all things and gave nothing back; satisfied in still contemplation, and spiritual consciousness.

Ere long, they bore me to my grave. Never tired child lay down in his white bed, and heard the sound of his playthings being laid aside for the night, with a more luxurious satisfaction of repose than I knew, when I felt the coffin settle on the firm earth, and heard the sound of the falling mould upon its lid. It has not the same hollow rattle within the coffin, that it sends up to the edge of the grave. They buried me in no graveyard. They loved me too much for that, I thank them; but they laid me in the grounds of their own castle, amid many trees; where, as it was spring-time, were growing primroses, and blue-bells, and all the families of the woods

Now that I lay in her bosom, the whole earth, and each of her many births, was as a body to me, at my will. I seemed to feel the great heart of the mother beating into mine, and feeding me with her own life, her own essential being and nature. I heard the footsteps of my friends above, and they sent a thrill through my heart. I knew that the helpers had gone, and that the knight and the lady remained, and spoke low, gentle, tearful words of him who lay beneath the yet wounded sod. I rose into a single large primrose that grew by the edge of the grave, and from the window of its humble, trusting face, looked full in the countenance of the lady. I felt that I could manifest myself in the primrose; that it said a part of what I wanted to say; just as in the old time, I had used to betake myself to a song for the same end. The flower caught her eye. She stooped and plucked it, saying, "Oh, you beautiful creature!" and, lightly kissing it, put it in her bosom. It was the first kiss she had ever given me. But the flower soon began to wither, and I forsook it.

It was evening. The sun was below the horizon; but his rosy beams yet illuminated a feathery cloud, that floated high above the world. I arose, I reached the cloud; and, throwing myself upon it, floated with it in sight of the sinking sun. He sank, and the cloud grew gray; but the grayness touched not my heart. It carried its rose-hue within; for now I could love without needing to be loved again. The moon came gliding up with all the past in her wan face. She changed my couch into a ghostly pallor, and threw all the earth below as to the bottom of a pale sea of dreams. But she could not make me sad. I knew now, that it is by loving, and not by being loved, that one can come nearest the soul of another; yea, that, where two love, it is the loving of each other, and not the being loved by each other, that originates and perfects and assures their blessedness. I knew that love gives to him that loves, power over any soul beloved, even if that soul know him not, bringing him inwardly close to that spirit; a power that cannot be but for good; for in proportion as selfishness intrudes, the love ceases, and the power which springs there from dies. Yet all love will, one day, meet with its return. All true love will, one day, behold its own image in the eyes of the beloved, and be humbly glad. This is possible in the realms of lofty Death. "Ah! my friends," thought I, "how I will tend you, and wait upon you, and haunt you with my love."

My floating chariot bore me over a great city. Its faint dull sound steamed up into the air — a sound — how composed?" How many hopeless cries," thought I, "and how many mad shouts go to make up the tumult, here so faint where I float in eternal peace, knowing that they will one day be stilled in the surrounding calm, and that despair dies into infinite hope, and the seeming impossible there, is the law here!

But, O pale-faced women, and gloomy-browed men, and forgotten children, how I will wait on you, and minister to you, and, putting my arms about you in the dark, think hope into your hearts, when you fancy no one is near! Soon as my senses have all come back, and have grown accustomed to this new blessed life, I will be among you with the love that healeth." With this, a pang and a terrible shudder went through me; a writhing as of death convulsed me; and I became once again conscious of a more limited, even a bodily and earthly life.

CHAPTER TWENTY-FIVE

Sinking from such a state of ideal bliss, into the world of shadows which again closed around and infolded me, my first dread was, not unnaturally, that my own shadow had found me again, and that my torture had commenced anew. It was a sad revulsion of feeling. This, indeed, seemed to correspond to what we think death is, before we die. Yet I felt within me a power of calm endurance to which I had hitherto been a stranger. For, in truth, that I should be able if only to think such things as I had been thinking, was an unspeakable delight. An hour of such peace made the turmoil of a lifetime worth striving through.

I found myself lying in the open air, in the early morning, before sunrise. Over me rose the summer heaven, expectant of the sun. The clouds already saw him, coming from afar; and soon every dewdrop would rejoice in his individual presence within it.

I lay motionless for a few minutes; and then slowly rose and looked about me. I was on the summit of a little hill; a valley lay beneath, and a range of mountains closed up the view upon that side. But, to my horror, across the valley, and up the height of the opposing mountains, stretched, from my very feet, a hugely expanding shade. There it lay, long and large, dark and mighty. I turned away with a sick despair; when lo! I beheld the sun just lifting his head above the eastern hill, and the shadow that fell from me, lay only where his beams fell not. I danced for joy. It was only the natural shadow, that goes with every man who walks in the sun. As he arose, higher and higher, the shadow-head sank down the side of the opposite hill, and crept in across the valley towards my feet.

Now that I was so joyously delivered from this fear, I saw and recognized the country around me. In the valley below, lay my own castle, and the haunts of my childhood were all about me hastened home. My sisters received me with unspeakable joy; but I suppose they observed some change in me, for a kind of respect, with a slight touch of awe in it, mingled with their joy, and made me ashamed. They had been in great distress about me. On the morning of my disappearance, they had found the floor of my room flooded; and, all that day, a wondrous and nearly impervious mist had hung about the castle and grounds. I had been gone, they told me, twenty- one days. To me it seemed twenty-one years. Nor could I yet feel quite secure in my new experiences. When, at night, I lay down once more in my own bed, I did not feel at all sure that when I awoke, I should not find myself in some mysterious region of Fairy Land. My dreams were incessant and perturbed; but when I did awake, I saw clearly that I was in my own home.

My mind soon grew calm; and I began the duties of my new position, somewhat instructed, I hoped, by the adventures that had befallen me in Fairy Land. Could I translate the experience of my travels there, into common life? This was the question. Or must I live it all over again, and learn it all over again, in the other forms that belong to the world of men, whose experience yet runs parallel to that of Fairy Land? These questions I cannot answer yet. But I fear.

Even yet, I find myself looking round sometimes with anxiety, to see whether my shadow falls right away from the sun or no. I have never yet discovered any inclination to either side. And if I am not unfrequently sad, I yet cast no more of a shade on the earth, than most men who have lived in it as long as I. I have a strange feeling sometimes, that I am a ghost, sent into the world to minister to my fellow men, or, rather, to repair the wrongs I have already done.

May the world be brighter for me, at least in those portions of it, where my darkness falls not.

Thus I, who set out to find my Ideal, came back rejoicing that I had lost my Shadow.

When the thought of the blessedness I experienced, after my death in Fairy Land, is too high for me to lay hold upon it and hope in it, I often think of the wise woman in the cottage, and of her solemn assurance that she knew something too good to be told. When I am oppressed by any sorrow or real perplexity, I often feel as if I had only left her cottage for a time, and would soon return out of the vision, into it again. Sometimes, on such occasions, I find myself, unconsciously almost, looking about for the mystic mark of red, with the vague hope of entering her door, and being comforted by her wise tenderness. I then console myself by saying: "I have come through the door of Dismay; and the way back from the world into which that has led me, is through my tomb. Upon that the red sign lies, and I shall find it one day, and be glad."

I will end my story with the relation of an incident which befell me a few days ago. I had been with my reapers, and, when they ceased their work at noon, I had lain down under the shadow of a great, ancient beech-tree, that stood on the edge of the field. As I lay, with my eyes closed, I began to listen to the sound of the leaves overhead. At first, they made sweet inarticulate music alone; but, by-and-by, the sound seemed to begin to take shape, and to be gradually molding itself into words; till, at last, I seemed able to distinguish these, half-dissolved in a little ocean of circumfluent tones: "A great good is coming — is coming — is coming to thee, Anodos"; and so over and over again. I fancied that the sound reminded me of the voice of the ancient woman, in the cottage that was four-square. I opened my eyes, and, for a moment, almost believed that I saw her face, with its many wrinkles and its young eyes, looking at me from between two hoary branches of the beech overhead. But when I looked more keenly, I saw only twigs and leaves, and the infinite sky, in tiny spots, gazing through between. Yet I know that good is coming to me — that good is always coming; though few have at all times the simplicity and the courage to believe it. What we call evil, is the only and best shape, which, for the person and his condition at the time, could be assumed by the best good. And so, FAREWELL.

Book Five

The Giant's Heart

༺☙༻

There was once a giant who lived on the borders of Giantland where it touched on the country of common people.

Everything in Giantland was so big that the common people saw only a mass of awful mountains and clouds; and no living man had ever come from it, as far as anybody knew, to tell what he had seen in it.

Somewhere near these borders, on the other side, by the edge of a great forest, lived a laborer with his wife and a great many children. One day Tricksey-Wee, as they called her, teased her brother Buffy-Bob, till he could not bear it any longer, and gave her a box on the ear. Tricksey-Wee cried; and Buffy-Bob was so sorry and so ashamed of himself that he cried too, and ran off into the wood. He was so long gone that Tricksey-Wee began to be frightened, for she was very fond of her brother; and she was so distressed that she had first teased him and then cried, that at last she ran into the wood to look for him, though there was more chance of losing herself than of finding him. And, indeed, so it seemed likely to turn out; for, running on without looking, she at length found herself in a valley she knew nothing about. And no wonder; for what she thought was a valley with round, rocky sides, was no other than the space between two of the roots of a great tree that grew on the borders of Giantland. She climbed over the side of it, and went towards what she took for a black, round-topped mountain, far away; but which she soon discovered to be close to her, and to be a hollow place so great that she could not tell what it was hollowed out of. Staring at it, she found that it was a doorway; and going nearer and staring harder, she saw the door, far in, with a knocker of iron upon it, a great many yards above her head, and as large as the anchor of a big ship. Now, nobody had ever been unkind to Tricksey-Wee, and therefore she was not afraid of anybody. For

Buffy-Bob's box on the ear she did not think worth considering. So spying a little hole at the bottom of the door which had been nibbled by some giant mouse, she crept through it, and found herself in an enormous hall. She could not have seen the other end of it at all, except for the great fire that was burning there, diminished to a spark in the distance. Towards this fire she ran as fast as she could, and was not far from it when something fell before her with a great clatter, over which she tumbled, and went rolling on the floor. She was not much hurt however, and got up in a moment. Then she saw that what she had fallen over was not unlike a great iron bucket. When she examined it more closely, she discovered that it was a thimble; and looking up to see who had dropped it, beheld a huge face, with spectacles as big as the round windows in a church, bending over her, and looking everywhere for the thimble. Tricksey-Wee immediately laid hold of it in both her arms, and lifted it about an inch nearer to the nose of the peering giantess. This movement made the old lady see where it was, and, her finger popping into it, it vanished from the eyes of Tricksey-Wee, buried in the folds of a white stocking like a cloud in the sky, which Mrs. Giant was busy darning. For it was Saturday night, and her husband would wear nothing but white stockings on Sunday. To be sure he did eat little children, but only very little ones; and if ever it crossed his mind that it was wrong to do so, he always said to himself that he wore whiter stockings on Sunday than any other giant in all Giantland.

At the same instant Tricksey-Wee heard a sound like the wind in a tree full of leaves, and could not think what it could be; till, looking up, she found that it was the giantess whispering to her; and when she tried very hard she could hear what she said well enough.

"Run away, dear little girl," she said, "as fast as you can; for my husband will be home in a few minutes."

"But I've never been naughty to your husband," said Tricksey-Wee, looking up in the giantess's face.

"That doesn't matter. You had better go. He is fond of little children, particularly little girls."

"Oh, then he won't hurt me."

"I am not sure of that. He is so fond of them that he eats them up; and I am afraid he couldn't help hurting you a little. He's a very good man though."

"Oh! then—" began Tricksey-Wee, feeling rather frightened; but before she could finish her sentence she heard the sound of footsteps very far apart and very heavy. The next moment, who should come running towards her, full speed, and as pale as death, but Buffy-Bob. She held out her arms, and he ran into them. But when she tried to kiss him, she only kissed the back of his head; for his white face and round eyes were turned to the door.

"Run, children; run and hide!" said the giantess.

"Come, Buffy," said Tricksey; "yonder's a great brake; we'll hide in it."

The brake was a big broom; and they had just got into the bristles of it when they heard the door open with a sound of thunder, and in stalked the giant. You would have thought you saw the whole earth through the door when he opened it, so wide was it; and when he closed it, it was like nightfall.

"Where is that little boy?" he cried, with a voice like the bellowing of a cannon. "He looked a very nice boy indeed. I am almost sure he crept through the mouse hole at the bottom of the door. Where is he, my dear?"

"I don't know," answered the giantess.

"But you know it is wicked to tell lies; don't you, my dear?" retorted the giant.

"Now, you ridiculous old Thunderthump!" said his wife, with a smile as broad as the sea in the sun, "how can I mend your white stockings and look after little boys? You have got plenty to last you over Sunday, I am sure. Just look what good little boys they are!"

Tricksey-Wee and Buffy-Bob peered through the bristles, and discovered a row of little boys, about a dozen, with very fat faces and goggle eyes, sitting before the fire, and looking stupidly into it. Thunderthump intended the most of these for pickling, and was feeding them well before salting them. Now and then, however, he could not keep his teeth off them, and would eat one by the bye, without salt.

He strode up to the wretched children. Now, what made them very wretched indeed was, that they knew if they could only keep from eating, and grow thin, the giant would dislike them, and turn them out to find their way home; but notwithstanding this, so greedy were they, that they ate as much as ever they could hold. The giantess, who fed them, comforted herself with thinking that they were not real boys and girls, but only little pigs pretending to be boys and girls.

"Now tell me the truth," cried the giant, bending his face down over them. They shook with terror, and every one hoped it was somebody else the giant liked best. "Where is the little boy that ran into the hall just now? Whoever tells me a lie shall be instantly boiled."

"He's in the broom," cried one dough-faced boy. "He's in there, and a little girl with him."

"The naughty children," cried the giant, "to hide from _me_!" And he made a stride towards the broom.

"Catch hold of the bristles, Bobby. Get right into a tuft, and hold on," cried Tricksey-Wee, just in time.

The giant caught up the broom, and seeing nothing under it, set it down again with a force that threw them both on the floor. He then made two strides to the boys, caught the dough-faced one by the neck, took the lid off a great pot that was boiling on the fire, popped him in as if he had been a trussed chicken, put the lid on again, and saying, "There, boys! See what comes of lying!" asked no more questions; for, as he always kept his word, he was afraid he might have to do the same to them all; and he did not like boiled boys. He like to eat them crisp, as radishes, whether forked or not, ought to be eaten. He then sat down, and asked his wife if his supper was ready. She looked into the pot, and throwing the boy out with the ladle, as if he had been a black beetle that had tumbled in and had had the worst of it, answered that she thought it was. Whereupon he rose to help her; and taking the pot from the fire, poured the whole contents, bubbling and splashing, into a dish like a vat. Then they sat down to supper. The children in the broom could not see what they had; but it seemed to agree with them, for the giant talked like thunder, and the giantess answered like the sea, and they grew chattier and chattier. At length the giant said,—

"I don't feel quite comfortable about that heart of mine." And as he spoke, instead of laying his hand on his bosom, he waved it away towards the corner where the children were peeping from the broom-bristles, like frightened little mice.

"Well, you know, my darling Thunderthump," answered his wife, "I always thought it ought to be nearer home. But you know best, of course."

"Ha! ha! You don't know where it is, wife. I moved it a month ago."

"What a man you are, Thunderthump! You trust any creature alive rather than your wife."

Here the giantess gave a sob which sounded exactly like a wave going flop into the mouth of a cave up to the roof.

"Where have you got it now?" she resumed, checking her emotion.

"Well, Doodlem, I don't mind telling _you_," answered the giant, soothingly. "The great she-eagle has got it for a nest egg. She sits on it night and day, and thinks she will bring the greatest eagle out of it that ever sharpened his beak on the rocks of Mount Skycrack. I can warrant no one else will touch it while she has got it. But she is rather capricious, and I confess I am not easy about it; for the least scratch of one of her claws would do for me at once. And she has claws."

I refer anyone who doubts this part of my story to certain chronicles of Giantland preserved among the Celtic nations. It was quite a common thing for a giant to put his heart out to nurse, because he did not like the trouble and responsibility of doing it himself; although I must confess it was a dangerous sort of plan to take, especially with such a delicate viscus as the heart.

All this time Buffy-Bob and Tricksey-Wee were listening with long ears.

"Oh!" thought Tricksey-Wee, "if I could but find the giant's cruel heart, wouldn't I give it a squeeze!"

The giant and giantess went on talking for a long time. The giantess kept advising the giant to hide his heart somewhere in the house; but he seemed afraid of the advantage it would give her over him.

"You could hide it at the bottom of the flour-barrel," said she.

"That would make me feel chokey," answered he.

"Well, in the coal-cellar. Or in the dust-hole—that's the place! No one would think of looking for your heart in the dust-hole."

"Worse and worse!" cried the giant.

"Well, the water-butt," suggested she.

"No, no; it would grow spongy there," said he.

"Well, what will you do with it?"

"I will leave it a month longer where it is, and then I will give it to the Queen of the Kangaroos, and she will carry it in her pouch for me. It is best to change its place, you know, lest my enemies should scent it out. But, dear Doodlem, it's a fretting care to have a heart of one's own to look after. The responsibility is too much for me. If it were not for a bite of a radish now and then, I never could bear it."

Here the giant looked lovingly towards the row of little boys by the fire, all of whom were nodding, or asleep on the floor.

"Why don't you trust it to me, dear Thunderthump?" said his wife. "I would take the best possible care of it."

"I don't doubt it, my love. But the responsibility would be too much for you. You would no longer be my darling, light-hearted, airy, laughing Doodlem. It would transform you into a heavy, oppressed woman, weary of life — as I am."

The giant closed his eyes and pretended to go to sleep. His wife got his stockings, and went on with her darning. Soon the giant's pretence became reality, and the giantess began to nod over her work.

"Now, Buffy," whispered Tricksey-Wee, "now's our time. I think it's moonlight, and we had better be off. There's a door with a hole for the cat just behind us."

"All right," said Bob; "I'm ready."

So they got out of the broom-brake and crept to the door. But to their great disappointment, when they got through it, they found themselves in a sort of shed. It was full of tubs and things, and, though it was built of wood only, they could not find a crack.

"Let us try this hole," said Tricksey; for the giant and giantess were sleeping behind them, and they dared not go back.

"All right," said Bob.

He seldom said anything else than "All right".

Now this hole was in a mound that came in through the wall of the shed, and went along the floor for some distance. They crawled into it, and found it very dark. But groping their way along, they soon came to a small crack, through which they saw grass, pale in the moonshine. As they crept on, they found the hole began to get wider and lead upwards.

"What is that noise of rushing?" said Buffy-Bob.

"I can't tell," replied Tricksey; "for, you see, I don't know what we are in."

The fact was, they were creeping along a channel in the heart of a giant tree; and the noise they heard was the noise of the sap rushing along in its wooden pipes. When they laid their ears to the wall, they heard it gurgling along with a pleasant noise.

"It sounds kind and good," said Tricksey. "It is water running. Now it must be running from somewhere to somewhere. I think we had better go on, and we shall come somewhere."

It was now rather difficult to go on, for they had to climb as if they were climbing a hill; and now the passage was wide. Nearly worn out, they saw light overhead at last, and creeping through a crack into the open air, found themselves on the fork of a huge tree. A great, broad, uneven space lay around them, out of which spread boughs in every direction, the smallest of them as big as the biggest tree in the country of common people. Overhead were leaves enough to supply all the trees they had ever seen. Not much moonlight could come through, but the leaves would glimmer white in the wind at times. The tree was full of giant birds. Every now and then, one would sweep through, with a great noise. But, except an occasional chirp, sounding like a shrill pipe in a great organ, they made no noise. All at once an owl began to hoot. He thought he was singing. As soon as he began, other birds replied, making rare game of him. To their astonishment, the children found they could understand every word they sang. And what they sang was something like this:

"I will sing a song.
I'm the Owl."
"Sing a song, you Sing-song
Ugly fowl!
What will you sing about,
Night in and Day out?"

"Sing about the night;
I'm the Owl."
"You could not see for the light,
Stupid fowl."
"Oh! the Moon! and the Dew!
And the Shadows!—tu-whoo!"

The owl spread out his silent, soft, sly wings, and lighting between Tricksey-Wee and Buffy-Bob, nearly smothered them, closing up one under each wing. It was like being buried in a down bed. But the owl did not like anything between his sides and his wings, so he opened his wings again, and the children made haste to get out. Tricksey-Wee immediately went in front of the bird, and looking up into his huge face, which was as round as the eyes of the giantess's spectacles, and much bigger, dropped a pretty courtesy, and said, — "Please, Mr. Owl, I want to whisper to you."

"Very well, small child," answered the owl, looking important, and stooping his ear towards her. "What is it?"

"Please tell me where the eagle lives that sits on the giant's heart."

"Oh, you naughty child! That's a secret. For shame!"

And with a great hiss that terrified them, the owl flew into the tree. All birds are fond of secrets; but not many of them can keep them so well as the owl.

So the children went on because they did not know what else to do. They found the way very rough and difficult, the tree was so full of humps and hollows. Now and then they plashed into a pool of rain; now and then they came upon twigs growing out of the trunk where they had no business, and they were as large as full-grown poplars. Sometimes they came upon great cushions of soft moss, and on one of them they lay down and rested. But they had not lain long before they spied a large nightingale sitting on a branch, with its bright eyes looking up at the moon. In a moment more he began to sing, and the birds about him began to reply, but in a different tone from that in which they had replied to the owl. Oh, the birds did call the nightingale such pretty names! The nightingale sang, and the birds replied like this:

"I will sing a song.

I'm the nightingale."

"Sing a song, long, long,

Little Never fail!

What will you sing about,

Light in or light out?"

"Sing about the light

Gone away;

Down, away, and out of sight —

Poor lost Day!

Mourning for the Day dead,

O'er his dim bed."

The nightingale sang so sweetly, that the children would have fallen asleep but for fear of losing any of the song. When the nightingale stopped they got up and wandered on. They did not know where they were going, but they thought it best to keep going on, because then they might come upon something or other. They were very sorry they had forgotten to ask the nightingale about the eagle's nest, but his music had put everything else out of their heads. They resolved, however, not to forget the next time they had a chance. So they went on and on, till they were both tired, and Tricksey-Wee said at last, trying to laugh,

"I declare my legs feel just like a Dutch doll's."

"Then here's the place to go to bed in," said Buffy-Bob.

They stood at the edge of a last year's nest, and looked down with delight into the round, mossy cave. Then they crept gently in, and, lying down in each other's arms, found it so deep, and warm, and comfortable, and soft, that they were soon fast asleep.

Now, close beside them, in a hollow, was another nest, in which lay a lark and his wife; and the children were awakened, very early in the morning, by a dispute between Mr. and Mrs. Lark.

"Let me up," said the lark.

"It is not time," said the lark's wife.

"It is," said the lark, rather rudely. "The darkness is quite thin. I can almost see my own beak."

"Nonsense!" said the lark's wife. "You know you came home yesterday morning quite worn out. You had to fly so very high before you saw him. I am sure he would not mind if you took it a little easier. Do be quiet and go to sleep again."

"That's not it at all," said the lark. "He doesn't want me. I want him. Let me up, I say."

He began to sing; and Tricksey-Wee and Buffy-Bob, having now learned the way, answered him:

"I will sing a song.
I'm the Lark."
"Sing, sing, Throat-strong,
Little Kill-the-dark.
What will you sing about,
Now the night is out?"

"I can only call;
I can't think.
Let me up—that's all.
Let me drink!
Thirsting all the long night
For a drink of light."

By this time the lark was standing on the edge of his nest and looking at the children.

"Poor little things! You can't fly," said the lark.

"No; but we can look up," said Tricksey.

"Ah, you don't know what it is to see the very first of the sun."

"But we know what it is to wait till he comes. He's no worse for your seeing him first, is he?"

"Oh no, certainly not," answered the lark, with condescension, and then, bursting into his Jubilate, he sprang aloft, clapping his wings like a clock running down.

"Tell us where —" began Buffy-Bob.

But the lark was out of sight. His song was all that was left of him. That was everywhere, and he was nowhere.

"Selfish bird!" said Buffy. "It's all very well for larks to go hunting the sun, but they have no business to despise their neighbors, for all that."

"Can I be of any use to you?" said a sweet bird-voice out of the nest.

This was the lark's wife, who stayed at home with the young larks while her husband went to church.

"Oh! thank you. If you please," answered Tricksey-Wee.

And up popped a pretty brown head; and then up came a brown feathery body; and last of all came the slender legs on to the edge of the nest. There she turned, and, looking down into the nest, from which came a whole litany of chirpings for breakfast, said, "Lie still, little ones." Then she turned to the children.

"My husband is King of the Larks," she said.

Buffy-Bob took off his cap, and Tricksey-Wee curtsied very low.

"Oh, it's not me," said the bird, looking very shy. "I am only his wife. It's my husband." And she looked up after him into the sky, whence his song was still falling like a shower of musical hailstones. Perhaps she could see him.

"He's a splendid bird," said Buffy-Bob; "only you know he will get up a little too early."

"Oh, no! he doesn't. It's only his way, you know. But tell me what I can do for you."

"Tell us, please, Lady Lark, where the she-eagle lives that sits on Giant Thunderthump's heart."

"Oh! that is a secret."

"Did you promise not to tell?"

"No; but larks ought to be discreet. They see more than other birds."

"But you don't fly up high like your husband, do you?"

"Not often. But it's no matter. I come to know things for all that."

"Do tell me, and I will sing you a song," said Tricksey-Wee.

"Can you sing too?—You have got no wings!"

"Yes. And I will sing you a song I learned the other day about a lark and his wife."

"Please do," said the lark's wife. "Be quiet, children, and listen."

Tricksey-Wee was very glad she happened to know a song which would please the lark's wife, at least, whatever the lark himself might have thought of it, if he had heard it. So she sang,

"Good morrow, my lord!' in the sky alone,

Sang the lark, as the sun ascended his throne.
'Shine on me, my lord; I only am come,
Of all your servants, to welcome you home.
I have flown a whole hour, right up, I swear,
To catch the first shine of your golden hair!'

"Must I thank you, then,' said the king, 'Sir Lark,
For flying so high, and hating the dark?
You ask a full cup for half a thirst:
Half is love of me, and half love to be first.
There's many a bird that makes no haste,
But waits till I come. That's as much to my taste.

"And the king hid his head in a turban of cloud;
And the lark stopped singing, quite vexed and cowed.
But he flew up higher, and thought, 'Anon,
The wrath of the king will be over and gone,
And his crown, shining out of its cloudy fold,
Will change my brown feathers to a glory of gold.'

"So he flew, with the strength of a lark he flew.
But as he rose, the cloud rose too;
And not a gleam of the golden hair
Came through the depth of the misty air;
Till, weary with flying, with sighing sore,
The strong sun-seeker could do no more.

"His wings had had no chrism of gold,
And his feathers felt withered and worn and old;
So he quivered and sank, and dropped like a stone.
And there on his nest, where he left her, alone,
Sat his little wife on her little eggs,
Keeping them warm with wings and legs.

"Did I say alone? Ah, no such thing!
Full in her face was shining the king.
'Welcome, Sir Lark! You look tired,' said he.

'Up is not always the best way to me.

While you have been singing so high and away,

I've been shining to your little wife all day.'

"He had set his crown all about the nest,

And out of the midst shone her little brown breast;

And so glorious was she in russet gold,

That for wonder and awe Sir Lark grew cold.

He popped his head under her wing, and lay

As still as a stone, till the king was away."

As soon as Tricksey-Wee had finished her song, the lark's wife began a low, sweet, modest little song of her own; and after she had piped away for two or three minutes, she said,

"You dear children, what can I do for you?"

"Tell us where the she-eagle lives, please," said Tricksey-Wee.

"Well, I don't think there can be much harm in telling such wise, good children," said Lady Lark; "I am sure you don't want to do any mischief."

"Oh, no; quite the contrary," said Buffy-Bob.

"Then I'll tell you. She lives on the very topmost peak of Mount Skycrack; and the only way to get up is to climb on the spiders' webs that cover it from top to bottom."

"That's rather serious," said Tricksey-Wee.

"But you don't want to go up, you foolish little thing! You can't go. And what do you want to go up for?"

"That is a secret," said Tricksey-Wee.

"Well, it's no business of mine," rejoined Lady Lark, a little offended, and quite vexed that she had told them. So she flew away to find some breakfast for her little ones, who by this time were chirping very impatiently. The children looked at each other, joined hands, and walked off.

In a minute more the sun was up, and they soon reached the outside of the tree. The bark was so knobby and rough, and full of twigs, that they managed to get down, though not without great difficulty. Then, far away to the north, they saw a huge peak, like the spire of a church, going right up into the sky. They thought this must be Mount Skycrack, and turned their faces towards it. As they went on, they saw a giant or two, now and then, striding about the fields or through the woods, but they kept out of their way. Nor were they in much danger; for it was only one or two of the border giants that were so very fond of children.

At last they came to the foot of Mount Skycrack. It stood in a plain alone, and shot right up, I don't know how many thousand feet, into the air, a long, narrow, spearlike mountain. The whole face of it, from top to bottom, was covered with a network of spiders' webs, with threads of various sizes, from that of silk to that of whipcord. The webs shook and quivered, and waved in the sun, glittering like silver. All about ran huge greedy spiders, catching huge silly flies, and devouring them.

Here they sat down to consider what could be done. The spiders did not heed them, but ate away at the flies. — Now, at the foot of the mountain, and all round it, was a ring of water, not very broad, but very deep. As they sat watching them, one of the spiders, whose web was woven across this water, somehow or other lost his hold, and fell in on his back. Tricksey-Wee and Buffy-Bob ran to his assistance, and laying hold each of one of his legs, succeeded, with the help of the other legs, which struggled spiderfully, in getting him out upon dry land. As soon as he had shaken himself, and dried himself a little, the spider turned to the children, saying,

"And now, what can I do for you?"

"Tell us, please," said they, "how we can get up the mountain to the she-eagle's nest."

"Nothing is easier," answered the spider. "Just run up there, and tell them all I sent you, and nobody will mind you."

"But we haven't got claws like you, Mr. Spider," said Buffy.

"Ah! no more you have, poor unprovided creatures! Still, I think we can manage it. Come home with me."

"You won't eat us, will you?" said Buffy.

"My dear child," answered the spider, in a tone of injured dignity, "I eat nothing but what is mischievous or useless. You have helped me, and now I will help you."

The children rose at once, and climbing as well as they could, reached the spider's nest in the centre of the web. Nor did they find it very difficult; for whenever too great a gap came, the spider spinning a strong cord stretched it just where they would have chosen to put their feet next. He left them in his nest, after bringing them two enormous honey-bags, taken from bees that he had caught; but presently about six of the wisest of the spiders came back with him. It was rather horrible to look up and see them all round the mouth of the nest, looking down on them in contemplation, as if wondering whether they would be nice eating. At length one of them said, — "Tell us truly what you want with the eagle, and we will try to help you."

Then Tricksey-Wee told them that there was a giant on the borders who treated little children no better than radishes, and that they had narrowly escaped being eaten by him; that they had found out that the great she-eagle of Mount Skycrack was at present sitting on his heart; and that, if they could only get hold of the heart, they would soon teach the giant better behavior.

"But," said their host, "if you get at the heart of the giant, you will find it as large as one of your elephants. What can you do with it?"

"The least scratch will kill it," replied Buffy-Bob.

"Ah! but you might do better than that," said the spider. — "Now we have resolved to help you. Here is a little bag of spider-juice. The giants cannot bear spiders, and this juice is dreadful poison to them. We are all ready to go up with you, and drive the eagle away. Then you must put the heart into this other bag, and bring it down with you; for then the giant will be in your power."

"But how can we do that?" said Buffy. "The bag is not much bigger than a pudding-bag."

"But it is as large as you will be able to carry."

"Yes; but what are we to do with the heart?"

"Put it in the bag, to be sure. Only, first, you must squeeze a drop out of the other bag upon it. You will see what will happen."

"Very well; we will do as you tell us," said Tricksey-Wee. "And now, if you please, how shall we go?"

"Oh, that's our business," said the first spider. "You come with me, and my grandfather will take your brother. Get up."

So Tricksey-Wee mounted on the narrow part of the spider's back, and held fast. And Buffy-Bob got on the grandfather's back. And up they scrambled, over one web after another, up and up — so fast! And every spider followed; so that, when Tricksey-Wee looked back, she saw a whole army of spiders scrambling after them.

"What can we want with so many?" she thought; but she said nothing.

The moon was now up, and it was a splendid sight below and around them. All Giantland was spread out under them, with its great hills, lakes, trees, and animals. And all above them was the clear heaven, and Mount Skycrack rising into it, with its endless ladders of spider-webs, glittering like cords made of moonbeams. And up the moonbeams went, crawling, and scrambling, and racing, a huge army of huge spiders.

At length they reached all but the very summit, where they stopped. Tricksey-Wee and Buffy-Bob could see above them a great globe of feathers, that finished off the mountain like an ornamental knob.

"But how shall we drive her off?" said Buffy.

"We'll soon manage that," answered the grandfather-spider. "Come on you, down there."

Up rushed the whole army, past the children, over the edge of the nest, on to the she-eagle, and buried themselves in her feathers. In a moment she became very restless, and went pecking about with her beak. All at once she spread out her wings, with a sound like a whirlwind, and flew off to bathe in the sea; and then the spiders began to drop from her in all directions on their gossamer wings. The children had to hold fast to keep the wind of the eagle's flight from blowing them off. As soon as it was over, they looked into the nest, and there lay the giant's heart—an awful and ugly thing.

"Make haste, child!" said Tricksey's spider.

So Tricksey took her bag, and squeezed a drop out of it upon the heart. She thought she heard the giant give a far-off roar of pain, and she nearly fell from her seat with terror. The heart instantly began to shrink. It shrunk and shriveled till it was nearly gone; and Buffy-Bob caught it up and put it into his bag. Then the two spiders turned and went down again as fast as they could. Before they got to the bottom, they heard the shrieks of the she-eagle over the loss of her egg; but the spiders told them not to be alarmed, for her eyes were too big to see them. — By the time they reached the foot of the mountain, all the spiders had got home, and were busy again catching flies, as if nothing had happened.

After renewed thanks to their friends, the children set off, carrying the giant's heart with them.

"If you should find it at all troublesome, just give it a little more spider-juice directly," said the grandfather, as they took their leave.

Now, the giant had given an awful roar of pain the moment they anointed his heart, and had fallen down in a fit, in which he lay so long that all the boys might have escaped if they had not been so fat. One did, and got home in safety. For days the giant was unable to speak. The first words he uttered were, —

"Oh, my heart! my heart!"

"Your heart is safe enough, dear Thunderstump," said his wife. "Really, a man of your size ought not to be so nervous and apprehensive. I am ashamed of you."

"You have no heart, Doodlem," answered he. "I assure you that at this moment mine is in the greatest danger. It has fallen into the hands of foes, though who they are I cannot tell."

Here he fainted again; for Tricksey-Wee, finding the heart begin to swell a little, had given it the least touch of spider-juice.

Again he recovered, and said,

"Dear Doodlem, my heart is coming back to me. It is coming nearer and nearer."

After lying silent for hours, he exclaimed,

"It is in the house, I know!"

And he jumped up and walked about, looking in every corner.

As he rose, Tricksey-Wee and Buffy-Bob came out of the hole in the tree-root, and through the cat-hole in the door, and walked boldly towards the giant. Both kept their eyes busy watching him. Led by the love of his own heart, the giant soon spied them, and staggered furiously towards them.

"I will eat you, you vermin!" he cried. "Here with my heart!"

Tricksey gave the heart a sharp pinch. Down fell the giant on his knees, blubbering, and crying, and begging for his heart.

"You shall have it, if you behave yourself properly," said Tricksey.

"How shall I behave myself properly?" asked he, whimpering.

"Take all those boys and girls, and carry them home at once."

"I'm not able; I'm too ill. I should fall down."

"Take them up directly."

"I can't, till you give me my heart."

"Very well!" said Tricksey; and she gave the heart another pinch.

The giant jumped to his feet, and catching up all the children, thrust some into his waistcoat pockets, some into his breast pocket, put two or three into his hat, and took a bundle of them under each arm. Then he staggered to the door.

All this time poor Doodlem was sitting in her arm-chair, crying, and mending a white stocking.

The giant led the way to the borders. He could not go so fast but that Buffy and Tricksey managed to keep up with him. When they reached the borders, they thought it would be safer to let the children find their own way home. So they told him to set them down. He obeyed.

"Have you put them all down, Mr. Thunderthump?" asked Tricksey-Wee.

"Yes," said the giant.

"That's a lie!" squeaked a little voice; and out came a head from his waistcoat pocket.

Tricksey-Wee pinched the heart till the giant roared with pain.

"You're not a gentleman. You tell stories," she said.

"He was the thinnest of the lot," said Thunderthump, crying.

"Are you all there now, children?" asked Tricksey.

"Yes, ma'am," returned they, after counting themselves very carefully, and with some difficulty; for they were all stupid children.

"Now," said Tricksey-Wee to the giant, "will you promise to carry off no more children, and never to eat a child again all you life?"

"Yes, yes! I promise," answered Thunderthump, sobbing.

"And you will never cross the borders of Giantland?"

"Never."

"And you shall never again wear white stockings on a Sunday, all your life long.—Do you promise?"

The giant hesitated at this, and began to expostulate; but Tricksey-Wee, believing it would be good for his morals, insisted; and the giant promised.

Then she required of him, that, when she gave him back his heart, he should give it to his wife to take care of for him for ever after.

The poor giant fell on his knees, and began again to beg. But Tricksey-Wee giving the heart a slight pinch, he bawled out,

"Yes, yes! Doodlem shall have it, I swear. Only she must not put it in the flour-barrel, or in the dust-hole."

"Certainly not. Make your own bargain with her.—And you promise not to interfere with my brother and me, or to take any revenge for what we have done?"

"Yes, yes, my dear children; I promise everything. Do, pray, make haste and give me back my poor heart."

"Wait there, then, till I bring it to you."

"Yes, yes. Only make haste, for I feel very faint."

Tricksey-Wee began to undo the mouth of the bag. But Buffy-Bob, who had got very knowing on his travels, took out his knife with the pretence of cutting the string; but, in reality, to be prepared for any emergency.

No sooner was the heart out of the bag, than it expanded to the size of a bullock; and the giant, with a yell of rage and vengeance, rushed on the two children, who had stepped sideways from the terrible heart. But Buffy-Bob was too quick for Thunderthump. He sprang to the heart, and buried his knife in it, up to the hilt. A fountain of blood spouted from it; and with a dreadful groan the giant fell dead at the feet of little Tricksey-Wee, who could not help being sorry for him after all.

Book Six

At the Back of the North Wind

ᏅᎬᏅ

1. THE HAY LOFT

I have been asked to tell you about the back of the north wind. An old Greek writer mentions a people who lived there, and were so comfortable that they could not bear it any longer, and drowned themselves. My story is not the same as his. I do not think Herodotus had got the right account of the place. I am going to tell you how it fared with a boy who went there.

He lived in a low room over a coach-house; and that was not by any means at the back of the north wind, as his mother very well knew. For one side of the room was built only of boards, and the boards were so old that you might run a penknife through into the north wind. And then let them settle between them which was the sharper! I know that when you pulled it out again the wind would be after it like a cat after a mouse, and you would know soon enough you were not at the back of the north wind. Still, this room was not very cold, except when the north wind blew stronger than usual: the room I have to do with now was always cold, except in summer, when the sun took the matter into his own hands. Indeed, I am not sure whether I ought to call it a room at all; for it was just a loft where they kept hay and straw and oats for the horses.

And when little Diamond — but stop: I must tell you that his father, who was a coachman, had named him after a favorite horse, and his mother had had no objection: — when little Diamond, then, lay there in bed, he could hear the horses under him munching away in the dark, or moving sleepily in their dreams. For Diamond's father had built him a bed in the loft with boards all round it, because they had so little room in their own end over the coach-house; and Diamond's father put old Diamond in the stall under the bed, because he was a quiet horse, and did not go to sleep standing, but lay down like a reasonable creature. But, although he was a surprisingly reasonable creature, yet, when young Diamond woke in the middle of the night, and felt the bed shaking in the blasts of the north wind, he could not help wondering whether, if the wind should blow the house down, and he were to fall through into the manger, old Diamond mightn't eat him up before he knew him in his night-gown. And although old Diamond was very quiet all night long, yet when he woke he got up like an earthquake, and then young Diamond knew what o'clock it was, or at least what was to be done next, which was — to go to sleep again as fast as he could.

There was hay at his feet and hay at his head, piled up in great trusses to the very roof. Indeed it was sometimes only through a little lane with several turnings, which looked as if it had been sawn out for him, that he could reach his bed at all. For the stock of hay was, of course, always in a state either of slow ebb or of sudden flow. Sometimes the whole space of the loft, with the little panes in the roof for the stars to look in, would lie open before his open eyes as he lay in bed; sometimes a yellow wall of sweet-smelling fibers closed up his view at the distance of half a yard. Sometimes, when his mother had undressed him in her room, and told him to trot to bed by himself, he would creep into the heart of the hay, and lie there thinking how cold it was outside in the wind, and how warm it was inside there in his bed, and how he could go to it when he pleased, only he wouldn't just yet; he would get a little colder first. And ever as he grew colder, his bed would grow warmer, till at last he would scramble out of the hay, shoot like an arrow into his bed, cover himself up, and snuggle down, thinking what a happy boy he was. He had not the least idea that the wind got in at a chink in the wall, and blew about him all night. For the back of his bed was only of boards an inch thick, and on the other side of them was the north wind.

Now, as I have already said, these boards were soft and crumbly. To be sure, they were tarred on the outside, yet in many places they were more like tinder than timber. Hence it happened that the soft part having worn away from about it, little Diamond found one night, after he lay down, that a knot had come out of one of them, and that the wind was blowing in upon him in a cold and rather imperious fashion. Now he had no fancy for leaving things wrong that might be set right; so he jumped out of bed again, got a little strike of hay, twisted it up, folded it in the middle, and, having thus made it into a cork, stuck it into the hole in the wall. But the wind began to blow loud and angrily, and, as Diamond was falling asleep, out blew his cork and hit him on the nose, just hard enough to wake him up quite, and let him hear the wind whistling shrill in the hole. He searched for his hay-cork, found it, stuck it in harder, and was just dropping off once more, when, pop! with an angry whistle behind it, the cork struck him again, this time on the cheek. Up he rose once more, made a fresh stopple of hay, and corked the hole severely. But he was hardly down again before — pop! it came on his forehead. He gave it up, drew the clothes above his head, and was soon fast asleep.

Although the next day was very stormy, Diamond forgot all about the hole, for he was busy making a cave by the side of his mother's fire with a broken chair, a three-legged stool, and a blanket, and then sitting in it. His mother, however, discovered it, and pasted a bit of brown paper over it, so that, when Diamond had snuggled down the next night, he had no occasion to think of it.

Presently, however, he lifted his head and listened. Who could that be talking to him? The wind was rising again, and getting very loud, and full of rushes and whistles. He was sure some one was talking — and very near him, too, it was. But he was not frightened, for he had not yet learned how to be; so he sat up and hearkened. At last the voice, which, though quite gentle, sounded a little angry, appeared to come from the back of the bed. He crept nearer to it, and laid his ear against the wall. Then he heard nothing but the wind, which sounded very loud indeed. The moment, however, that he moved his head from the wall, he heard the voice again, close to his ear. He felt about with his hand, and came upon the piece of paper his mother had pasted over the hole. Against this he laid his ear, and then he heard the voice quite distinctly. There was, in fact, a little corner of the paper loose, and through that, as from a mouth in the wall, the voice came.

"What do you mean, little boy—closing up my window?"

"What window?" asked Diamond.

"You stuffed hay into it three times last night. I had to blow it out again three times."

"You can't mean this little hole! It isn't a window; it's a hole in my bed."

"I did not say it was a window: I said it was my window."

"But it can't be a window, because windows are holes to see out of."

"Well, that's just what I made this window for."

"But you are outside: you can't want a window."

"You are quite mistaken. Windows are to see out of, you say. Well, I'm in my house, and I want windows to see out of it."

"But you've made a window into my bed."

"Well, your mother has got three windows into my dancing room, and you have three into my garret."

"But I heard father say, when my mother wanted him to make a window through the wall, that it was against the law, for it would look into Mr. Dyves's garden."

The voice laughed.

"The law would have some trouble to catch me!" it said.

"But if it's not right, you know," said Diamond, "that's no matter. You shouldn't do it."

"I am so tall I am above that law," said the voice.

"You must have a tall house, then," said Diamond.

"Yes; a tall house: the clouds are inside it."

"Dear me!" said Diamond, and thought a minute. "I think, then, you can hardly expect me to keep a window in my bed for you. Why don't you make a window into Mr. Dyves's bed?"

"Nobody makes a window into an ash-pit," said the voice, rather sadly. "I like to see nice things out of my windows."

"But he must have a nicer bed than I have, though mine is very nice — so nice that I couldn't wish a better."

"It's not the bed I care about: it's what is in it. — But you just open that window."

"Well, mother says I shouldn't be disobliging; but it's rather hard. You see the north wind will blow right in my face if I do."

"I am the North Wind."

"O-o-oh!" said Diamond, thoughtfully. "Then will you promise not to blow on my face if I open your window?"

"I can't promise that."

"But you'll give me the toothache. Mother's got it already."

"But what's to become of me without a window?"

"I'm sure I don't know. All I say is, it will be worse for me than for you."

"No; it will not. You shall not be the worse for it—I promise you that. You will be much the better for it. Just you believe what I say, and do as I tell you."

"Well, I can pull the clothes over my head," said Diamond, and feeling with his little sharp nails, he got hold of the open edge of the paper and tore it off at once.

In came a long whistling spear of cold, and struck his little naked chest. He scrambled and tumbled in under the bedclothes, and covered himself up: there was no paper now between him and the voice, and he felt a little — not frightened exactly — I told you he had not learned that yet—but rather queer; for what a strange person this North Wind must be that lived in the great house — "called Out-of-Doors, I suppose," thought Diamond — and made windows into people's beds! But the voice began again; and he could hear it quite plainly, even with his head under the bed-clothes. It was a still more gentle voice now, although six times as large and loud as it had been, and he thought it sounded a little like his mother's.

"What is your name, little boy?" it asked.

"Diamond," answered Diamond, under the bed-clothes.

"What a funny name!"

"It's a very nice name," returned its owner.

"I don't know that," said the voice.

"Well, I do," retorted Diamond, a little rudely.

"Do you know to whom you are speaking?"

"No," said Diamond.

And indeed he did not. For to know a person's name is not always to know the person's self.

"Then I must not be angry with you.—You had better look and see, though."

"Diamond is a very pretty name," persisted the boy, vexed that it should not give satisfaction.

"Diamond is a useless thing rather," said the voice.

"That's not true. Diamond is very nice — as big as two — and so quiet all night! And doesn't he make a jolly row in the morning, getting upon his four great legs! It's like thunder."

"You don't seem to know what a diamond is."

"Oh, don't I just! Diamond is a great and good horse; and he sleeps right under me. He is old Diamond, and I am young Diamond; or, if you like it better, for you're very particular, Mr. North Wind, he's big Diamond, and I'm little Diamond; and I don't know which of us my father likes best."

A beautiful laugh, large but very soft and musical, sounded somewhere beside him, but Diamond kept his head under the clothes.

"I'm not Mr. North Wind," said the voice.

"You told me that you were the North Wind," insisted Diamond.

"I did not say Mister North Wind," said the voice.

"Well, then, I do; for mother tells me I ought to be polite."

"Then let me tell you I don't think it at all polite of you to say Mister to me."

"Well, I didn't know better. I'm very sorry."

"But you ought to know better."

"I don't know that."

"I do. You can't say it's polite to lie there talking — with your head under the bed-clothes, and never look up to see what kind of person you are talking to. — I want you to come out with me."

"I want to go to sleep," said Diamond, very nearly crying, for he did not like to be scolded, even when he deserved it.

"You shall sleep all the better to-morrow night."

"Besides," said Diamond, "you are out in Mr. Dyves's garden, and I can't get there. I can only get into our own yard."

"Will you take your head out of the bed-clothes?" said the voice, just a little angrily.

"No!" answered Diamond, half peevish, half frightened.

The instant he said the word, a tremendous blast of wind crashed in a board of the wall, and swept the clothes off Diamond. He started up in terror. Leaning over him was the large, beautiful, pale face of a woman. Her dark eyes looked a little angry, for they had just begun to flash; but a quivering in her sweet upper lip made her look as if she were going to cry. What was the most strange was that away from her head streamed out her black hair in every direction, so that the darkness in the hay-loft looked as if it were made of her, hair but as Diamond gazed at her in speechless amazement, mingled with confidence — for the boy was entranced with her mighty beauty — her hair began to gather itself out of the darkness, and fell down all about her again, till her face looked out of the midst of it like a moon out of a cloud. From her eyes came all the light by which Diamond saw her face and her, hair; and that was all he did see of her yet. The wind was over and gone.

"Will you go with me now, you little Diamond? I am sorry I was forced to be so rough with you," said the lady.

"I will; yes, I will," answered Diamond, holding out both his arms. "But," he added, dropping them, "how shall I get my clothes? They are in mother's room, and the door is locked."

"Oh, never mind your clothes. You will not be cold. I shall take care of that. Nobody is cold with the north wind."

"I thought everybody was," said Diamond.

"That is a great mistake. Most people make it, however. They are cold because they are not with the north wind, but without it."

If Diamond had been a little older, and had supposed himself a good deal wiser, he would have thought the lady was joking. But he was not older, and did not fancy himself wiser, and therefore understood her well enough. Again he stretched out his arms. The lady's face drew back a little.

"Follow me, Diamond," she said.

"Yes," said Diamond, only a little ruefully.

"You're not afraid?" said the North Wind.

"No, ma'am; but mother never would let me go without shoes: she never said anything about clothes, so I dare say she wouldn't mind that."

"I know your mother very well," said the lady. "She is a good woman. I have visited her often. I was with her when you were born. I saw her laugh and cry both at once. I love your mother, Diamond."

"How was it you did not know my name, then, ma'am? Please am I to say ma'am to you, ma'am?"

"One question at a time, dear boy. I knew your name quite well, but I wanted to hear what you would say for it. Don't you remember that day when the man was finding fault with your name — how I blew the window in?"

"Yes, yes," answered Diamond, eagerly. "Our window opens like a door, right over the coach-house door. And the wind — you, ma'am — came in, and blew the Bible out of the man's hands, and the leaves went all flutter, flutter on the floor, and my mother picked it up and gave it back to him open, and there ——"

"Was your name in the Bible — the sixth stone in the high priest's breastplate."

"Oh! — a stone, was it?" said Diamond. "I thought it had been a horse — I did."

"Never mind. A horse is better than a stone any day. Well, you see, I know all about you and your mother."

"Yes. I will go with you."

"Now for the next question: you're not to call me ma'am. You must call me just my own name — respectfully, you know — just North Wind."

"Well, please, North Wind, you are so beautiful, I am quite ready to go with you."

"You must not be ready to go with everything beautiful all at once, Diamond."

"But what's beautiful can't be bad. You're not bad, North Wind?"

"No; I'm not bad. But sometimes beautiful things grow bad by doing bad, and it takes some time for their badness to spoil their beauty. So little boys may be mistaken if they go after things because they are beautiful."

"Well, I will go with you because you are beautiful and good, too."

"Ah, but there's another thing, Diamond:—What if I should look ugly without being bad — look ugly myself because I am making ugly things beautiful? — What then?"

"I don't quite understand you, North Wind. You tell me what then."

"Well, I will tell you. If you see me with my face all black, don't be frightened. If you see me flapping wings like a bat's, as big as the whole sky, don't be frightened. If you hear me raging ten times worse than Mrs. Bill, the blacksmith's wife — even if you see me looking in at people's windows like Mrs. Eve Dropper, the gardener's wife — you must believe that I am doing my work. Nay, Diamond, if I change into a serpent or a tiger, you must not let go your hold of me, for my hand will never change in yours if you keep a good hold. If you keep a hold, you will know who I am all the time, even when you look at me and can't see me the least like the North Wind. I may look something very awful. Do you understand?"

"Quite well," said little Diamond.

"Come along, then," said North Wind, and disappeared behind the mountain of hay.

Diamond crept out of bed and followed her.

2. THE LAWN

When Diamond got round the corner of the hay, for a moment he hesitated. The stair by which he would naturally have gone down to the door was at the other side of the loft, and looked very black indeed; for it was full of North Wind's hair, as she descended before him. And just beside him was the ladder going straight down into the stable, up which his father always came to fetch the hay for Diamond's dinner. Through the opening in the floor the faint gleam of the-stable lantern was enticing, and Diamond thought he would run down that way.

The stair went close past the loose-box in which Diamond the horse lived. When Diamond the boy was half-way down, he remembered that it was of no use to go this way, for the stable-door was locked. But at the same moment there was horse Diamond's great head poked out of his box on to the ladder, for he knew boy Diamond although he was in his night-gown, and wanted him to pull his ears for him. This Diamond did very gently for a minute or so, and patted and stroked his neck too, and kissed the big horse, and had begun to take the bits of straw and hay out of his mane, when all at once he recollected that the Lady North Wind was waiting for him in the yard.

"Good night, Diamond," he said, and darted up the ladder, across the loft, and down the stair to the door. But when he got out into the yard, there was no lady.

Now it is always a dreadful thing to think there is somebody and find nobody. Children in particular have not made up their minds to it; they generally cry at nobody, especially when they wake up at night. But it was an especial disappointment to Diamond, for his little heart had been beating with joy: the face of the North Wind was so grand! To have a lady like that for a friend — with such long hair, too! Why, it was longer than twenty Diamonds' tails! She was gone. And there he stood, with his bare feet on the stones of the paved yard.

It was a clear night overhead, and the stars were shining. Orion in particular was making the most of his bright belt and golden sword. But the moon was only a poor thin crescent. There was just one great, jagged, black and gray cloud in the sky, with a steep side to it like a precipice; and the moon was against this side, and looked as if she had tumbled off the top of the cloud-hill, and broken herself in rolling down the precipice. She did not seem comfortable, for she was looking down into the deep pit waiting for her. At least that was what Diamond thought as he stood for a moment staring at her. But he was quite wrong, for the moon was not afraid, and there was no pit she was going down into, for there were no sides to it, and a pit without sides to it is not a pit at all. Diamond, however, had not been out so late before in all his life, and things looked so strange about him! — just as if he had got into Fairyland, of which he knew quite as much as anybody; for his mother had no money to buy books to set him wrong on the subject. I have seen this world — only sometimes, just now and then, you know — look as strange as ever I saw Fairyland. But I confess that I have not yet seen Fairyland at its best. I am always going to see it so some time. But if you had been out in the face and not at the back of the North Wind, on a cold rather frosty night, and in your night-gown, you would have felt it all quite as strange as Diamond did. He cried a little, just a little, he was so disappointed to lose the lady: Of course, you, little man, wouldn't have done that! But for my part, I don't mind people crying so much as I mind what they cry about, and how they cry — whether they cry quietly like ladies and gentlemen, or go shrieking like vulgar emperors, or ill-natured cooks; for all emperors are not gentlemen, and all cooks are not ladies—nor all queens and princesses for that matter, either.

But it can't be denied that a little gentle crying does one good. It did Diamond good; for as soon as it was over he was a brave boy again.

"She shan't say it was my fault, anyhow!" said Diamond. "I daresay she is hiding somewhere to see what I will do. I will look for her."

So he went round the end of the stable towards the kitchen-garden. But the moment he was clear of the shelter of the stable, sharp as a knife came the wind against his little chest and his bare legs. Still he would look in the kitchen-garden, and went on. But when he got round the weeping-ash that stood in the corner, the wind blew much stronger, and it grew stronger and stronger till he could hardly fight against it. And it was so cold! All the flashy spikes of the stars seemed to have got somehow into the wind. Then he thought of what the lady had said about people being cold because they were not with the North Wind. How it was that he should have guessed what she meant at that very moment I cannot tell, but I have observed that the most wonderful thing in the world is how people come to understand anything. He turned his back to the wind, and trotted again towards the yard; whereupon, strange to say, it blew so much more gently against his calves than it had blown against his shins that he began to feel almost warm by contrast.

You must not think it was cowardly of Diamond to turn his back to the wind: he did so only because he thought Lady North Wind had said something like telling him to do so. If she had said to him that he must hold his face to it, Diamond would have held his face to it. But the most foolish thing is to fight for no good, and to please nobody.

Well, it was just as if the wind was pushing Diamond along. If he turned round, it grew very sharp on his legs especially, and so he thought the wind might really be Lady North Wind, though he could not see her, and he had better let her blow him wherever she pleased. So she blew and blew, and he went and went, until he found himself standing at a door in a wall, which door led from the yard into a little belt of shrubbery, flanking Mr. Coleman's house. Mr. Coleman was his father's master, and the owner of Diamond. He opened the door, and went through the shrubbery, and out into the middle of the lawn, still hoping to find North Wind. The soft grass was very pleasant to his bare feet, and felt warm after the stones of the yard; but the lady was nowhere to be seen. Then he began to think that after all he must have done wrong, and she was offended with him for not following close after her, but staying to talk to the horse, which certainly was neither wise nor polite.

There he stood in the middle of the lawn, the wind blowing his night-gown till it flapped like a loose sail. The stars were very shiny over his head; but they did not give light enough to show that the grass was green; and Diamond stood alone in the strange night, which looked half solid all about him. He began to wonder whether he was in a dream or not. It was important to determine this; "for," thought Diamond, "if I am in a dream, I am safe in my bed, and I needn't cry. But if I'm not in a dream, I'm out here, and perhaps I had better cry, or, at least, I'm not sure whether I can help it." He came to the conclusion, however, that, whether he was in a dream or not, there could be no harm in not crying for a little while longer: he could begin whenever he liked.

The back of Mr. Coleman's house was to the lawn, and one of the drawing-room windows looked out upon it. The ladies had not gone to bed; for the light was still shining in that window. But they had no idea that a little boy was standing on the lawn in his night-gown, or they would have run out in a moment. And as long as he saw that light, Diamond could not feel quite lonely. He stood staring, not at the great warrior Orion in the sky, nor yet at the disconsolate, neglected moon going down in the west, but at the drawing-room window with the light shining through its green curtains. He had been in that room once or twice that he could remember at Christmas times; for the Colemans were kind people, though they did not care much about children.

All at once the light went nearly out: he could only see a glimmer of the shape of the window. Then, indeed, he felt that he was left alone. It was so dreadful to be out in the night after everybody was gone to bed! That was more than he could bear. He burst out crying in good earnest, beginning with a wail like that of the wind when it is waking up.

Perhaps you think this was very foolish; for could he not go home to his own bed again when he liked? Yes; but it looked dreadful to him to creep up that stair again and lie down in his bed again, and know that North Wind's window was open beside him, and she gone, and he might never see her again. He would be just as lonely there as here. Nay, it would be much worse if he had to think that the window was nothing but a hole in the wall.

At the very moment when he burst out crying, the old nurse who had grown to be one of the family, for she had not gone away when Miss Coleman did not want any more nursing, came to the back door, which was of glass, to close the shutters. She thought she heard a cry, and, peering out with a hand on each side of her eyes like Diamond's blinkers, she saw something white on the lawn. Too old and too wise to be frightened, she opened the door, and went straight towards the white thing to see what it was. And when Diamond saw her coming he was not frightened either, though Mrs. Crump was a little cross sometimes; for there is a good kind of crossness that is only disagreeable, and there is a bad kind of crossness that is very nasty indeed. So she came up with her neck stretched out, and her head at the end of it, and her eyes foremost of all, like a snail's, peering into the night to see what it could be that went on glimmering white before her. When she did see, she made a great exclamation, and threw up her hands. Then without a word, for she thought Diamond was walking in his sleep, she caught hold of him, and led him towards the house. He made no objection, for he was just in the mood to be grateful for notice of any sort, and Mrs. Crump led him straight into the drawing-room.

Now, from the neglect of the new housemaid, the fire in Miss Coleman's bedroom had gone out, and her mother had told her to brush her hair by the drawing-room fire—a disorderly proceeding which a mother's wish could justify. The young lady was very lovely, though not nearly so beautiful as North Wind; and her hair was extremely long, for it came down to her knees—though that was nothing at all to North Wind's hair. Yet when she looked round, with her hair all about her, as Diamond entered, he thought for one moment that it was North Wind, and, pulling his hand from Mrs. Crump's, he stretched out his arms and ran towards Miss Coleman. She was so pleased that she threw down her brush, and almost knelt on the floor to receive him in her arms. He saw the next moment that she was not Lady North Wind, but she looked so like her he could not help running into her arms and bursting into tears afresh. Mrs. Crump said the poor child had walked out in his sleep, and Diamond thought she ought to know, and did not contradict her for anything he knew, it might be so indeed. He let them talk on about him, and said nothing; and when, after their astonishment was over, and Miss Coleman had given him a sponge-cake, it was decreed that Mrs. Crump should take him to his mother, he was quite satisfied.

His mother had to get out of bed to open the door when Mrs. Crump knocked. She was indeed surprised to see her, boy; and having taken him in her arms and carried him to his bed, returned and had a long confabulation with Mrs. Crump, for they were still talking when Diamond fell fast asleep, and could hear them no longer.

3. OLD DIAMOND

Diamond woke very early in the morning, and thought what a curious dream he had had. But the memory grew brighter and brighter in his head, until it did not look altogether like a dream, and he began to doubt whether he had not really been abroad in the wind last night. He came to the conclusion that, if he had really been brought home to his mother by Mrs. Crump, she would say something to him about it, and that would settle the matter. Then he got up and dressed himself, but, finding that his father and mother were not yet stirring, he went down the ladder to the stable. There he found that even old Diamond was not awake yet, for he, as well as young Diamond, always got up the moment he woke, and now he was lying as flat as a horse could lie upon his nice trim bed of straw.

"I'll give old Diamond a surprise," thought the, boy; and creeping up very softly, before the horse knew, he was astride of his back. Then it was young Diamond's turn to have more of a surprise than he had expected; for as with an earthquake, with a rumbling and a rocking hither and thither, a sprawling of legs and heaving as of many backs, young Diamond found himself hoisted up in the air, with both hands twisted in the horse's mane. The next instant old Diamond lashed out with both his hind legs, and giving one cry of terror young Diamond found himself lying on his neck, with his arms as far round it as they would go. But then the horse stood as still as a stone, except that he lifted his head gently up to let the boy slip down to his back. For when he heard young Diamond's cry he knew that there was nothing to kick about; for young Diamond was a good boy, and old Diamond was a good horse, and the one was all right on the back of the other.

As soon as Diamond had got himself comfortable on the saddle place, the horse began pulling at the hay, and the boy began thinking. He had never mounted Diamond himself before, and he had never got off him without being lifted down. So he sat, while the horse ate, wondering how he was to reach the ground.

But while he meditated, his mother woke, and her first thought was to see her boy. She had visited him twice during the night, and found him sleeping quietly. Now his bed was empty, and she was frightened.

"Diamond! Diamond! Where are you, Diamond?" she called out.

Diamond turned his head where he sat like a knight on his steed in enchanted stall, and cried aloud,—

"Here, mother!"

"Where, Diamond?" she returned.

"Here, mother, on Diamond's back."

She came running to the ladder, and peeping down, saw him aloft on the great horse.

"Come down, Diamond," she said.

"I can't," answered Diamond.

"How did you get up?" asked his mother.

"Quite easily," answered he; "but when I got up, Diamond would get up too, and so here I am."

His mother thought he had been walking in his sleep again, and hurried down the ladder. She did not much like going up to the horse, for she had not been used to horses; but she would have gone into a lion's den, not to say a horse's stall, to help her boy. So she went and lifted him off Diamond's back, and felt braver all her life after. She carried him in her arms up to her room; but, afraid of frightening him at his own sleep-walking, as she supposed it, said nothing about last night. Before the next day was over, Diamond had almost concluded the whole adventure a dream.

For a week his mother watched him very carefully — going into the loft several times a night — as often, in fact, as she woke. Every time she found him fast asleep.

All that week it was hard weather. The grass showed white in the morning with the hoar-frost which clung like tiny comfits to every blade. And as Diamond's shoes were not good, and his mother had not quite saved up enough money to get him the new pair she so much wanted for him, she would not let him run out. He played all his games over and over indoors, especially that of driving two chairs harnessed to the baby's cradle; and if they did not go very fast, they went as fast as could be expected of the best chairs in the world, although one of them had only three legs, and the other only half a back.

At length his mother brought home his new shoes, and no sooner did she find they fitted him than she told him he might run out in the yard and amuse himself for an hour.

The sun was going down when he flew from the door like a bird from its cage. All the world was new to him. A great fire of sunset burned on the top of the gate that led from the stables to the house; above the fire in the sky lay a large lake of green light, above that a golden cloud, and over that the blue of the wintry heavens. And Diamond thought that, next to his own home, he had never seen any place he would like so much to live in as that sky. For it is not fine things that make home a nice place, but your mother and your father.

As he was looking at the lovely colors, the gates were thrown open, and there was old Diamond and his friend in the carriage, dancing with impatience to get at their stalls and their oats. And in they came. Diamond was not in the least afraid of his father driving over him, but, careful not to spoil the grand show he made with his fine horses and his multitudinous cape, with a red edge to every fold, he slipped out of the way and let him dash right on to the stables. To be quite safe he had to step into the recess of the door that led from the yard to the shrubbery.

As he stood there he remembered how the wind had driven him to this same spot on the night of his dream. And once more he was almost sure that it was no dream. At all events, he would go in and see whether things looked at all now as they did then. He opened the door, and passed through the little belt of shrubbery. Not a flower was to be seen in the beds on the lawn. Even the brave old chrysanthemums and Christmas roses had passed away before the frost. What? Yes! There was one! He ran and knelt down to look at it.

It was a primrose — a dwarfish thing, but perfect in shape — a baby-wonder. As he stooped his face to see it close, a little wind began to blow, and two or three long leaves that stood up behind the flower shook and waved and quivered, but the primrose lay still in the green hollow, looking up at the sky, and not seeming to know that the wind was blowing at all. It was just a one eye that the dull black wintry earth had opened to look at the sky with. All at once Diamond thought it was saying its prayers, and he ought not to be staring at it so. He ran to the stable to see his father make Diamond's bed. Then his father took him in his arms, carried him up the ladder, and set him down at the table where they were going to have their tea.

"Miss is very poorly," said Diamond's father. "Mis'ess has been to the doctor with her to-day, and she looked very glum when she came out again. I was a-watching of them to see what doctor had said."

"And didn't Miss look glum too?" asked his mother.

"Not half as glum as Mis'ess," returned the coachman. "You see —"

But he lowered his voice, and Diamond could not make out more than a word here and there. For Diamond's father was not only one of the finest of coachmen to look at, and one of the best of drivers, but one of the most discreet of servants as well. Therefore he did not talk about family affairs to any one but his wife, whom he had proved better than himself long ago, and was careful that even Diamond should hear nothing he could repeat again concerning master and his family.

It was bed-time soon, and Diamond went to bed and fell fast asleep.

He awoke all at once, in the dark.

"Open the window, Diamond," said a voice.

Now Diamond's mother had once more pasted up North Wind's window.

"Are you North Wind?" said Diamond: "I don't hear you blowing."

"No; but you hear me talking. Open the window, for I haven't overmuch time."

"Yes," returned Diamond. "But, please, North Wind, where's the use? You left me all alone last time."

He had got up on his knees, and was busy with his nails once more at the paper over the hole in the wall. For now that North Wind spoke again, he remembered all that had taken place before as distinctly as if it had happened only last night.

"Yes, but that was your fault," returned North Wind. "I had work to do; and, besides, a gentleman should never keep a lady waiting."

"But I'm not a gentleman," said Diamond, scratching away at the paper.

"I hope you won't say so ten years after this."

"I'm going to be a coachman, and a coachman is not a gentleman," persisted Diamond.

"We call your father a gentleman in our house," said North Wind.

"He doesn't call himself one," said Diamond.

"That's of no consequence: every man ought to be a gentleman, and your father is one."

Diamond was so pleased to hear this that he scratched at the paper like ten mice, and getting hold of the edge of it, tore it off. The next instant a young girl glided across the bed, and stood upon the floor.

"Oh dear!" said Diamond, quite dismayed; "I didn't know — who are you, please?"

"I'm North Wind."

"Are you really?"

"Yes. Make haste."

"But you're no bigger than me."

"Do you think I care about how big or how little I am? Didn't you see me this evening? I was less then."

"No. Where was you?"

"Behind the leaves of the primrose. Didn't you see them blowing?"

"Yes."

"Make haste, then, if you want to go with me."

"But you are not big enough to take care of me. I think you are only Miss North Wind."

"I am big enough to show you the way, anyhow. But if you won't come, why, you must stay."

"I must dress myself. I didn't mind with a grown lady, but I couldn't go with a little girl in my night-gown."

"Very well. I'm not in such a hurry as I was the other night. Dress as fast as you can, and I'll go and shake the primrose leaves till you come."

"Don't hurt it," said Diamond.

North Wind broke out in a little laugh like the breaking of silver bubbles, and was gone in a moment. Diamond saw — for it was a starlit night, and the mass of hay was at a low ebb now — the gleam of something vanishing down the stair, and, springing out of bed, dressed himself as fast as ever he could. Then he crept out into the yard, through the door in the wall, and away to the primrose. Behind it stood North Wind, leaning over it, and looking at the flower as if she had been its mother.

"Come along," she said, jumping up and holding out her hand.

Diamond took her hand. It was cold, but so pleasant and full of life, it was better than warm. She led him across the garden. With one bound she was on the top of the wall. Diamond was left at the foot.

"Stop, stop!" he cried. "Please, I can't jump like that."

"You don't try" said North Wind, who from the top looked down a foot taller than before.

"Give me your hand again, and I will, try" said Diamond.

She reached down, Diamond laid hold of her hand, gave a great spring, and stood beside her.

"This is nice!" he said.

Another bound, and they stood in the road by the river. It was full tide, and the stars were shining clear in its depths, for it lay still, waiting for the turn to run down again to the sea. They walked along its side. But they had not walked far before its surface was covered with ripples, and the stars had vanished from its bosom.

And North Wind was now tall as a full-grown girl. Her hair was flying about her head, and the wind was blowing a breeze down the river. But she turned aside and went up a narrow lane, and as she went her hair fell down around her.

"I have some rather disagreeable work to do to-night," she said, "before I get out to sea, and I must set about it at once. The disagreeable work must be looked after first."

So saying, she laid hold of Diamond and began to run, gliding along faster and faster. Diamond kept up with her as well as he could. She made many turnings and windings, apparently because it was not quite easy to get him over walls and houses. Once they ran through a hall where they found back and front doors open. At the foot of the stair North Wind stood still, and Diamond, hearing a great growl, started in terror, and there, instead of North Wind, was a huge wolf by his side. He let go his hold in dismay, and the wolf bounded up the stair. The windows of the house rattled and shook as if guns were firing, and the sound of a great fall came from above. Diamond stood with white face staring up at the landing.

"Surely," he thought, "North Wind can't be eating one of the children!" Coming to himself all at once, he rushed after her with his little fist clenched. There were ladies in long trains going up and down the stairs, and gentlemen in white neckties attending on them, who stared at him, but none of them were of the people of the house, and they said nothing. Before he reached the head of the stair, however, North Wind met him, took him by the hand, and hurried down and out of the house.

"I hope you haven't eaten a baby, North Wind!" said Diamond, very solemnly.

North Wind laughed merrily, and went tripping on faster. Her grassy robe swept and swirled about her steps, and wherever it passed over withered leaves, they went fleeing and whirling in spirals, and running on their edges like wheels, all about her feet.

"No," she said at last, "I did not eat a baby. You would not have had to ask that foolish question if you had not let go your hold of me. You would have seen how I served a nurse that was calling a child bad names, and telling her she was wicked. She had been drinking. I saw an ugly gin bottle in a cupboard."

"And you frightened her?" said Diamond.

"I believe so!" answered North Wind laughing merrily. "I flew at her throat, and she tumbled over on the floor with such a crash that they ran in. She'll be turned away to-morrow—and quite time, if they knew as much as I do."

"But didn't you frighten the little one?"

"She never saw me. The woman would not have seen me either if she had not been wicked."

"Oh!" said Diamond, dubiously.

"Why should you see things," returned North Wind, "that you wouldn't understand or know what to do with? Good people see good things; bad people, bad things."

"Then are you a bad thing?"

"No. For you see me, Diamond, dear," said the girl, and she looked down at him, and Diamond saw the loving eyes of the great lady beaming from the depths of her falling hair.

"I had to make myself look like a bad thing before she could see me. If I had put on any other shape than a wolf's she would not have seen me, for that is what is growing to be her own shape inside of her."

"I don't know what you mean," said Diamond, "but I suppose it's all right."

They were now climbing the slope of a grassy ascent. It was Primrose Hill, in fact, although Diamond had never heard of it. The moment they reached the top, North Wind stood and turned her face towards London The stars were still shining clear and cold overhead. There was not a cloud to be seen. The air was sharp, but Diamond did not find it cold.

"Now," said the lady, "whatever you do, do not let my hand go. I might have lost you the last time, only I was not in a hurry then: now I am in a hurry."

Yet she stood still for a moment.

4. NORTH WIND

And as she stood looking towards London, Diamond saw that she was trembling.

"Are you cold, North Wind?" he asked.

"No, Diamond," she answered, looking down upon him with a smile; "I am only getting ready to sweep one of my rooms. Those careless, greedy, untidy children make it in such a mess."

As she spoke he could have told by her voice, if he had not seen with his eyes, that she was growing larger and larger. Her head went up and up towards the stars; and as she grew, still trembling through all her body, her hair also grew — longer and longer, and lifted itself from her head, and went out in black waves. The next moment, however, it fell back around her, and she grew less and less till she was only a tall woman. Then she put her hands behind her head, and gathered some of her hair, and began weaving and knotting it together. When she had done, she bent down her beautiful face close to his, and said —

"Diamond, I am afraid you would not keep hold of me, and if I were to drop you, I don't know what might happen; so I have been making a place for you in my hair. Come."

Diamond held out his arms, for with that grand face looking at him, he believed like a baby. She took him in her hands, threw him over her shoulder, and said, "Get in, Diamond."

And Diamond parted her hair with his hands, crept between, and feeling about soon found the woven nest. It was just like a pocket, or like the shawl in which gipsy women carry their children. North Wind put her hands to her back, felt all about the nest, and finding it safe, said —

"Are you comfortable, Diamond?"

"Yes, indeed," answered Diamond.

The next moment he was rising in the air. North Wind grew towering up to the place of the clouds. Her hair went streaming out from her, till it spread like a mist over the stars. She flung herself abroad in space.

Diamond held on by two of the twisted ropes which, parted and interwoven, formed his shelter, for he could not help being a little afraid. As soon as he had come to himself, he peeped through the woven meshes, for he did not dare to look over the top of the nest. The earth was rushing past like a river or a sea below him. Trees and water and green grass hurried away beneath. A great roar of wild animals rose as they rushed over the Zoological Gardens, mixed with a chattering of monkeys and a screaming of birds; but it died away in a moment behind them. And now there was nothing but the roofs of houses, sweeping along like a great torrent of stones and rocks. Chimney-pots fell, and tiles flew from the roofs; but it looked to him as if they were left behind by the roofs and the chimneys as they scudded away. There was a great roaring, for the wind was dashing against London like a sea; but at North Wind's back Diamond, of course, felt nothing of it all. He was in a perfect calm. He could hear the sound of it, that was all.

By and by he raised himself and looked over the edge of his nest. There were the houses rushing up and shooting away below him, like a fierce torrent of rocks instead of water. Then he looked up to the sky, but could see no stars; they were hidden by the blinding masses of the lady's hair which swept between. He began to wonder whether she would hear him if he spoke. He would try.

"Please, North Wind," he said, "what is that noise?"

From high over his head came the voice of North Wind, answering him, gently —

"The noise of my besom. I am the old woman that sweeps the cobwebs from the, sky; only I'm busy with the floor now."

"What makes the houses look as if they were running away?"

"I am sweeping so fast over them."

"But, please, North Wind, I knew London was very big, but I didn't know it was so big as this. It seems as if we should never get away from it."

"We are going round and round, else we should have left it long ago."

"Is this the way you sweep, North Wind?"

"Yes; I go round and round with my great besom."

"Please, would you mind going a little slower, for I want to see the streets?"

"You won't see much now."

"Why?"

"Because I have nearly swept all the people home."

"Oh! I forgot," said Diamond, and was quiet after that, for he did not want to be troublesome.

But she dropped a little towards the roofs of the houses, and Diamond could see down into the streets. There were very few people about, though. The lamps flickered and flared again, but nobody seemed to want them.

Suddenly Diamond espied a little girl coming along a street. She was dreadfully blown by the wind, and a broom she was trailing behind her was very troublesome. It seemed as if the wind had a spite at her — it kept worrying her like a wild beast, and tearing at her rags. She was so lonely there!

"Oh! please, North Wind," he cried, "won't you help that little girl?"

"No, Diamond; I mustn't leave my work."

"But why shouldn't you be kind to her?"

"I am kind to her. I am sweeping the wicked smells away."

"But you're kinder to me, dear North Wind. Why shouldn't you be as kind to her as you are to me?"

"There are reasons, Diamond. Everybody can't be done to all the same. Everybody is not ready for the same thing."

"But I don't see why I should be kinder used than she."

"Do you think nothing's to be done but what you can see, Diamond, you silly! It's all right. Of course you can help her if you like. You've got nothing particular to do at this moment; I have."

"Oh! do let me help her, then. But you won't be able to wait, perhaps?"

"No, I can't wait; you must do it yourself. And, mind, the wind will get a hold of you, too."

"Don't you want me to help her, North Wind?"

"Not without having some idea what will happen. If you break down and cry, that won't be much of a help to her, and it will make a goose of little Diamond."

"I want to go," said Diamond. "Only there's just one thing— how am I to get home?"

"If you're anxious about that, perhaps you had better go with me. I am bound to take you home again, if you do."

"There!" cried Diamond, who was still looking after the little girl. "I'm sure the wind will blow her over, and perhaps kill her. Do let me go."

They had been sweeping more slowly along the line of the street. There was a lull in the roaring.

"Well, though I cannot promise to take you home," said North Wind, as she sank nearer and nearer to the tops of the houses, "I can promise you it will be all right in the end. You will get home somehow. Have you made up your mind what to do?"

"Yes; to help the little girl," said Diamond firmly.

The same moment North Wind dropt into the street and stood, only a tall lady, but with her hair flying up over the housetops. She put her hands to her back, took Diamond, and set him down in the street. The same moment he was caught in the fierce coils of the blast, and all but blown away. North Wind stepped back a step, and at once towered in stature to the height of the houses. A chimney-pot clashed at Diamond's feet. He turned in terror, but it was to look for the little girl, and when he turned again the lady had vanished, and the wind was roaring along the street as if it had been the bed of an invisible torrent. The little girl was scudding before the blast, her hair flying too, and behind her she dragged her broom. Her little legs were going as fast as ever they could to keep her from falling. Diamond crept into the shelter of a doorway, thinking to stop her; but she passed him like a bird, crying gently and pitifully.

"Stop! stop! little girl," shouted Diamond, starting in pursuit.

"I can't," wailed the girl, "the wind won't leave go of me."

Diamond could run faster than she, and he had no broom. In a few moments he had caught her by the frock, but it tore in his hand, and away went the little girl. So he had to run again, and this time he ran so fast that he got before her, and turning round caught her in his arms, when down they went both together, which made the little girl laugh in the midst of her crying.

"Where are you going?" asked Diamond, rubbing the elbow that had stuck farthest out. The arm it belonged to was twined round a lamp-post as he stood between the little girl and the wind.

"Home," she said, gasping for breath.

"Then I will go with you," said Diamond.

And then they were silent for a while, for the wind blew worse than ever, and they had both to hold on to the lamp-post.

"Where is your crossing?" asked the girl at length.

"I don't sweep," answered Diamond.

"What do you do, then?" asked she. "You ain't big enough for most things."

"I don't know what I do do," answered he, feeling rather ashamed. "Nothing, I suppose. My father's Mr. Coleman's coachman."

"Have you a father?" she said, staring at him as if a boy with a father was a natural curiosity.

"Yes. Haven't you?" returned Diamond.

"No; nor mother neither. Old Sal's all I've got." And she began to cry again.

"I wouldn't go to her if she wasn't good to me," said Diamond.

"But you must go somewheres."

"Move on," said the voice of a policeman behind them.

"I told you so," said the girl. "You must go somewheres. They're always at it."

"But old Sal doesn't beat you, does she?"

"I wish she would."

"What do you mean?" asked Diamond, quite bewildered.

"She would if she was my mother. But she wouldn't lie abed a-cuddlin' of her ugly old bones, and laugh to hear me crying at the door."

"You don't mean she won't let you in to-night?"

"It'll be a good chance if she does."

"Why are you out so late, then?" asked Diamond.

"My crossing's a long way off at the West End, and I had been indulgin' in door-steps and mewses."

"We'd better have a try anyhow," said Diamond. "Come along."

As he spoke Diamond thought he caught a glimpse of North Wind turning a corner in front of them; and when they turned the corner too, they found it quiet there, but he saw nothing of the lady.

"Now you lead me," he said, taking her hand, "and I'll take care of you."

The girl withdrew her hand, but only to dry her eyes with her frock, for the other had enough to do with her broom. She put it in his again, and led him, turning after turning, until they stopped at a cellar-door in a very dirty lane. There she knocked.

"I shouldn't like to live here," said Diamond.

"Oh, yes, you would, if you had nowhere else to go to," answered the girl. "I only wish we may get in."

"I don't want to go in," said Diamond.

"Where do you mean to go, then?"

"Home to my home."

"Where's that?"

"I don't exactly know."

"Then you're worse off than I am."

"Oh no, for North Wind —" began Diamond, and stopped, he hardly knew why.

"What?" said the girl, as she held her ear to the door listening.

But Diamond did not reply. Neither did old Sal.

"I told you so," said the girl. "She is wide awake hearkening. But we don't get in."

"What will you do, then?" asked Diamond.

"Move on," she answered.

"Where?"

"Oh, anywheres. Bless you, I'm used to it."

"Hadn't you better come home with me, then?"

"That's a good joke, when you don't know where it is. Come on."

"But where?"

"Oh, nowheres in particular. Come on."

Diamond obeyed. The wind had now fallen considerably. They wandered on and on, turning in this direction and that, without any reason for one way more than another, until they had got out of the thick of the houses into a waste kind of place. By this time they were both very tired. Diamond felt a good deal inclined to cry, and thought he had been very silly to get down from the back of North Wind; not that he would have minded it if he had done the girl any good; but he thought he had been of no use to her. He was mistaken there, for she was far happier for having Diamond with her than if she had been wandering about alone. She did not seem so tired as he was.

"Do let us rest a bit," said Diamond.

"Let's see," she answered. "There's something like a railway there. Perhaps there's an open arch."

They went towards it and found one, and, better still, there was an empty barrel lying under the arch.

"Hallo! here we are!" said the girl. "A barrel's the jolliest bed going—on the tramp, I mean. We'll have forty winks, and then go on again."

She crept in, and Diamond crept in beside her. They put their arms round each other, and when he began to grow warm, Diamond's courage began to come back.

"This is jolly!" he said. "I'm so glad!"

"I don't think so much of it," said the girl. "I'm used to it, I suppose. But I can't think how a kid like you comes to be out all alone this time o' night."

She called him a kid, but she was not really a month older than he was; only she had had to work for her bread, and that so soon makes people older.

"But I shouldn't have been out so late if I hadn't got down to help you," said Diamond. "North Wind is gone home long ago."

"I think you must ha' got out o' one o' them Hidget Asylms," said the girl. "You said something about the north wind afore that I couldn't get the rights of."

So now, for the sake of his character, Diamond had to tell her the whole story.

She did not believe a word of it. She said he wasn't such a flat as to believe all that bosh. But as she spoke there came a great blast of wind through the arch, and set the barrel rolling. So they made haste to get out of it, for they had no notion of being rolled over and over as if they had been packed tight and wouldn't hurt, like a barrel of herrings.

"I thought we should have had a sleep," said Diamond; "but I can't say I'm very sleepy after all. Come, let's go on again."

They wandered on and on, sometimes sitting on a door-step, but always turning into lanes or fields when they had a chance.

They found themselves at last on a rising ground that sloped rather steeply on the other side. It was a waste kind of spot below, bounded by an irregular wall, with a few doors in it. Outside lay broken things in general, from garden rollers to flower-pots and wine-bottles. But the moment they reached the brow of the rising ground, a gust of wind seized them and blew them down hill as fast as they could run. Nor could Diamond stop before he went bang against one of the doors in the wall. To his dismay it burst open. When they came to themselves they peeped in. It was the back door of a garden.

"Ah, ah!" cried Diamond, after staring for a few moments, "I thought so! North Wind takes nobody in! Here I am in master's garden! I tell you what, little girl, you just bore a hole in old Sal's wall, and put your mouth to it, and say, "Please, North Wind, mayn't I go out with you?" and then you'll see what'll come."

"I daresay I shall. But I'm out in the wind too often already to want more of it."

"I said with the North Wind, not in it."

"It's all one."

"It's not all one."

"It is all one."

"But I know best."

"And I know better. I'll box your ears," said the girl.

Diamond got very angry. But he remembered that even if she did box his ears, he musn't box hers again, for she was a girl, and all that boys must do, if girls are rude, is to go away and leave them. So he went in at the door.

"Good-bye, mister" said the girl.

This brought Diamond to his senses.

"I'm sorry I was cross," he said. "Come in, and my mother will give you some breakfast."

"No, thank you. I must be off to my crossing. It's morning now."

"I'm very sorry for you," said Diamond.

"Well, it is a life to be tired of—what with old Sal, and so many holes in my shoes."

"I wonder you're so good. I should kill myself."

"Oh, no, you wouldn't! When I think of it, I always want to see what's coming next, and so I always wait till next is over. Well! I suppose there's somebody happy somewheres. But it ain't in them carriages. Oh my! how they do look sometimes—fit to bite your head off! Good-bye!"

She ran up the hill and disappeared behind it. Then Diamond shut the door as he best could, and ran through the kitchen-garden to the stable. And wasn't he glad to get into his own blessed bed again!

5. THE SUMMER-HOUSE

Diamond said nothing to his mother about his adventures. He had half a notion that North Wind was a friend of his mother, and that, if she did not know all about it, at least she did not mind his going anywhere with the lady of the wind. At the same time he doubted whether he might not appear to be telling stories if he told all, especially as he could hardly believe it himself when he thought about it in the middle of the day, although when the twilight was once half-way on to night he had no doubt about it, at least for the first few days after he had been with her. The girl that swept the crossing had certainly refused to believe him. Besides, he felt sure that North Wind would tell him if he ought to speak.

It was some time before he saw the lady of the wind again. Indeed nothing remarkable took place in Diamond's history until the following week. This was what happened then. Diamond the horse wanted new shoes, and Diamond's father took him out of the stable, and was just getting on his back to ride him to the forge, when he saw his little boy standing by the pump, and looking at him wistfully. Then the coachman took his foot out of the stirrup, left his hold of the mane and bridle, came across to his boy, lifted him up, and setting him on the horse's back, told him to sit up like a man. He then led away both Diamonds together.

The boy atop felt not a little tremulous as the great muscles that lifted the legs of the horse knotted and relaxed against his legs, and he cowered towards the withers, grasping with his hands the bit of mane worn short by the collar; but when his father looked back at him, saying once more, "Sit up, Diamond," he let the mane go and sat up, notwithstanding that the horse, thinking, I suppose, that his master had said to him, "Come up, Diamond," stepped out faster. For both the Diamonds were just grandly obedient. And Diamond soon found that, as he was obedient to his father, so the horse was obedient to him. For he had not ridden far before he found courage to reach forward and catch hold of the bridle, and when his father, whose hand was upon it, felt the boy pull it towards him, he looked up and smiled, and, well pleased, let go his hold, and left Diamond to guide Diamond; and the boy soon found that he could do so perfectly. It was a grand thing to be able to guide a great beast like that. And another discovery he made was that, in order to guide the horse, he had in a measure to obey the horse first. If he did not yield his body to the motions of the horse's body, he could not guide him; he must fall off.

The blacksmith lived at some distance, deeper into London. As they crossed the angle of a square, Diamond, who was now quite comfortable on his living throne, was glancing this way and that in a gentle pride, when he saw a girl sweeping a crossing scuddingly before a lady. The lady was his father's mistress, Mrs. Coleman, and the little girl was she for whose sake he had got off North Wind's back. He drew Diamond's bridle in eager anxiety to see whether her outstretched hand would gather a penny from Mrs. Coleman. But she had given one at the last crossing, and the hand returned only to grasp its broom. Diamond could not bear it. He had a penny in his pocket, a gift of the same lady the day before, and he tumbled off his horse to give it to the girl. He tumbled off, I say, for he did tumble when he reached the ground. But he got up in an instant, and ran, searching his pocket as he ran. She made him a pretty courtesy when he offered his treasure, but with a bewildered stare. She thought first: "Then he was on the back of the North Wind after all!" but, looking up at the sound of the horse's feet on the paved crossing, she changed her idea, saying to herself, "North Wind is his father's horse! That's the secret of it! Why couldn't he say so?" And she had a mind to refuse the penny. But his smile put it all right, and she not only took his penny but put it in her mouth with a "Thank you, mister. Did they wollop you then?"

"Oh no!" answered Diamond. "They never wollops me."

"Lor!" said the little girl, and was speechless.

Meantime his father, looking up, and seeing the horse's back bare, suffered a pang of awful dread, but the next moment catching sight of him, took him up and put him on, saying —

"Don't get off again, Diamond. The horse might have put his foot on you."

"No, father," answered the boy, and rode on in majestic safety.

The summer drew near, warm and splendid. Miss Coleman was a little better in health, and sat a good deal in the garden. One day she saw Diamond peeping through the shrubbery, and called him. He talked to her so frankly that she often sent for him after that, and by degrees it came about that he had leave to run in the garden as he pleased. He never touched any of the flowers or blossoms, for he was not like some boys who cannot enjoy a thing without pulling it to pieces, and so preventing every one from enjoying it after them.

A week even makes such a long time in a child's life, that Diamond had begun once more to feel as if North Wind were a dream of some far-off year.

One hot evening, he had been sitting with the young mistress, as they called her, in a little summer-house at the bottom of the lawn — a wonderful thing for beauty, the boy thought, for a little window in the side of it was made of colored glass. It grew dusky, and the lady began to feel chill, and went in, leaving the boy in the summer-house. He sat there gazing out at a bed of tulips, which, although they had closed for the night, could not go quite asleep for the wind that kept waving them about. All at once he saw a great bumble-bee fly out of one of the tulips.

"There! that is something done," said a voice — a gentle, merry, childish voice, but so tiny. "At last it was. I thought he would have had to stay there all night, poor fellow! I did."

Diamond could not tell whether the voice was near or far away, it was so small and yet so clear. He had never seen a fairy, but he had heard of such, and he began to look all about for one. And there was the tiniest creature sliding down the stem of the tulip!

"Are you the fairy that herds the bees?" he asked, going out of the summer-house, and down on his knees on the green shore of the tulip-bed.

"I'm not a fairy," answered the little creature.

"How do you know that?"

"It would become you better to ask how you are to know it."

"You've just told me."

"Yes. But what's the use of knowing a thing only because you're told it?"

"Well, how am I to know you are not a fairy? You do look very like one."

"In the first place, fairies are much bigger than you see me."

"Oh!" said Diamond reflectively; "I thought they were very little."

"But they might be tremendously bigger than I am, and yet not very big. Why, I could be six times the size I am, and not be very huge. Besides, a fairy can't grow big and little at will, though the nursery-tales do say so: they don't know better. You stupid Diamond! have you never seen me before?"

And, as she spoke, a moan of wind bent the tulips almost to the ground, and the creature laid her hand on Diamond's shoulder. In a moment he knew that it was North Wind.

"I am very stupid," he said; "but I never saw you so small before, not even when you were nursing the primrose."

"Must you see me every size that can be measured before you know me, Diamond?"

"But how could I think it was you taking care of a great stupid bumble-bee?"

"The more stupid he was the more need he had to be taken care of. What with sucking honey and trying to open the door, he was nearly dated; and when it opened in the morning to let the sun see the tulip's heart, what would the sun have thought to find such a stupid thing lying there — with wings too?"

"But how do you have time to look after bees?"

"I don't look after bees. I had this one to look after. It was hard work, though."

"Hard work! Why, you could blow a chimney down, or — or a boy's cap off," said Diamond.

"Both are easier than to blow a tulip open. But I scarcely know the difference between hard and easy. I am always able for what I have to do. When I see my work, I just rush at it — and it is done. But I mustn't chatter. I have got to sink a ship to-night."

"Sink a ship! What! with men in it?"

"Yes, and women too."

"How dreadful! I wish you wouldn't talk so."

"It is rather dreadful. But it is my work. I must do it."

"I hope you won't ask me to go with you."

"No, I won't ask you. But you must come for all that."

"I won't then."

"Won't you?" And North Wind grew a tall lady, and looked him in the eyes, and Diamond said:

"Please take me. You cannot be cruel."

"No; I could not be cruel if I would. I can do nothing cruel, although I often do what looks like cruel to those who do not know what I really am doing. The people they say I drown, I only carry away to — to — to — well, the back of the North Wind — that is what they used to call it long ago, only I never saw the place."

"How can you carry them there if you never saw it?"

"I know the way."

"But how is it you never saw it?"

"Because it is behind me."

"But you can look round."

"Not far enough to see my own back. No; I always look before me. In fact, I grow quite blind and deaf when I try to see my back. I only mind my work."

"But how does it be your work?"

"Ah, that I can't tell you. I only know it is, because when I do it I feel all right, and when I don't I feel all wrong. East Wind says— only one does not exactly know how much to believe of what she says, for she is very naughty sometimes—she says it is all managed by a baby; but whether she is good or naughty when she says that, I don't know. I just stick to my work. It is all one to me to let a bee out of a tulip, or to sweep the cobwebs from the sky. You would like to go with me to-night?"

"I don't want to see a ship sunk."

"But suppose I had to take you?"

"Why, then, of course I must go."

"There's a good Diamond.—I think I had better be growing a bit. Only you must go to bed first. I can't take you till you're in bed. That's the law about the children. So I had better go and do something else first."

"Very well, North Wind," said Diamond. "What are you going to do first, if you please?"

"I think I may tell you. Jump up on the top of the wall, there."

"I can't."

"Ah! and I can't help you — you haven't been to bed yet, you see. Come out to the road with me, just in front of the coach-house, and I will show you."

North Wind grew very small indeed, so small that she could not have blown the dust off a dusty miller, as the Scotch children call a yellow auricula. Diamond could not even see the blades of grass move as she flitted along by his foot. They left the lawn, went out by the wicket in the-coach-house gates, and then crossed the road to the low wall that separated it from the river.

"You can get up on this wall, Diamond," said North Wind.

"Yes; but my mother has forbidden me."

"Then don't," said North Wind.

"But I can see over," said Diamond.

"Ah! to be sure. I can't."

So saying, North Wind gave a little bound, and stood on the top of the wall. She was just about the height a dragon-fly would be, if it stood on end.

"You darling!" said Diamond, seeing what a lovely little toy-woman she was.

"Don't be impertinent, Master Diamond," said North Wind. "If there's one thing makes me more angry than another, it is the way you humans judge things by their size. I am quite as respectable now as I shall be six hours after this, when I take an East Indiaman by the royals, twist her round, and push her under. You have no right to address me in such a fashion."

But as she spoke, the tiny face wore the smile of a great, grand woman. She was only having her own beautiful fun out of Diamond, and true woman's fun never hurts.

"But look there!" she resumed. "Do you see a boat with one man in it— a green and white boat?"

"Yes; quite well."

"That's a poet."

"I thought you said it was a bo-at."

"Stupid pet! Don't you know what a poet is?"

"Why, a thing to sail on the water in."

"Well, perhaps you're not so far wrong. Some poets do carry people over the sea. But I have no business to talk so much. The man is a poet."

"The boat is a boat," said Diamond.

"Can't you spell?" asked North Wind.

"Not very well."

"So I see. A poet is not a bo-at, as you call it. A poet is a man who is glad of something, and tries to make other people glad of it too."

"Ah! now I know. Like the man in the sweety-shop."

"Not very. But I see it is no use. I wasn't sent to tell you, and so I can't tell you. I must be off. Only first just look at the man."

"He's not much of a rower" said Diamond —"paddling first with one fin and then with the other."

"Now look here!" said North Wind.

And she flashed like a dragon-fly across the water, whose surface rippled and puckered as she passed. The next moment the man in the boat glanced about him, and bent to his oars. The boat flew over the rippling water. Man and boat and river were awake. The same instant almost, North Wind perched again upon the river wall.

"How did you do that?" asked Diamond.

"I blew in his face," answered North Wind. "I don't see how that could do it," said Diamond. "I daresay not. And therefore you will say you don't believe it could."

"No, no, dear North Wind. I know you too well not to believe you."

"Well, I blew in his face, and that woke him up."

"But what was the good of it?"

"Why! don't you see? Look at him — how he is pulling. I blew the mist out of him."

"How was that?"

"That is just what I cannot tell you."

"But you did it."

"Yes. I have to do ten thousand things without being able to tell how."

"I don't like that," said Diamond.

He was staring after the boat. Hearing no answer, he looked down to the wall.

North Wind was gone. Away across the river went a long ripple— what sailors call a cat's paw. The man in the boat was putting up a sail. The moon was coming to herself on the edge of a great cloud, and the sail began to shine white. Diamond rubbed his eyes, and wondered what it was all about. Things seemed going on around him, and all to understand each other, but he could make nothing of it. So he put his hands in his pockets, and went in to have his tea. The night was very hot, for the wind had fallen again.

"You don't seem very well to-night, Diamond," said his mother.

"I am quite well, mother," returned Diamond, who was only puzzled.

"I think you had better go to bed," she added.

"Very well, mother," he answered.

He stopped for one moment to look out of the window. Above the moon the clouds were going different ways. Somehow or other this troubled him, but, notwithstanding, he was soon fast asleep.

He woke in the middle of the night and the darkness. A terrible noise was rumbling overhead, like the rolling beat of great drums echoing through a brazen vault. The roof of the loft in which he lay had no ceiling; only the tiles were between him and the sky. For a while he could not come quite awake, for the noise kept beating him down, so that his heart was troubled and fluttered painfully. A second peal of thunder burst over his head, and almost choked him with fear. Nor did he recover until the great blast that followed, having torn some tiles off the roof, sent a spout of wind down into his bed and over his face, which brought him wide awake, and gave him back his courage. The same moment he heard a mighty yet musical voice calling him.

"Come up, Diamond," it said. "It's all ready. I'm waiting for you."

He looked out of the bed, and saw a gigantic, powerful, but most lovely arm—with a hand whose fingers were nothing the less ladylike that they could have strangled a boa-constrictor, or choked a tigress off its prey—stretched down through a big hole in the roof. Without a moment's hesitation he reached out his tiny one, and laid it in the grand palm before him.

6. OUT IN THE STORM

The hand felt its way up his arm, and, grasping it gently and strongly above the elbow, lifted Diamond from the bed. The moment he was through the hole in the roof, all the winds of heaven seemed to lay hold upon him, and buffet him hither and thither. His hair blew one way, his night-gown another, his legs threatened to float from under him, and his head to grow dizzy with the swiftness of the invisible assailant. Cowering, he clung with the other hand to the huge hand which held his arm, and fear invaded his heart.

"Oh, North Wind!" he murmured, but the words vanished from his lips as he had seen the soap-bubbles that burst too soon vanish from the mouth of his pipe. The wind caught them, and they were nowhere. They couldn't get out at all, but were torn away and strangled. And yet North Wind heard them, and in her answer it seemed to Diamond that just because she was so big and could not help it, and just because her ear and her mouth must seem to him so dreadfully far away, she spoke to him more tenderly and graciously than ever before. Her voice was like the bass of a deep organ, without the groan in it; like the most delicate of violin tones without the wail in it; like the most glorious of trumpet-ejaculations without the defiance in it; like the sound of falling water without the clatter and clash in it: it was like all of them and neither of them — all of them without their faults, each of them without its peculiarity: after all, it was more like his mother's voice than anything else in the world.

"Diamond, dear," she said, "be a man. What is fearful to you is not the least fearful to me."

"But it can't hurt you," murmured Diamond, "for you're it."

"Then if I'm it, and have you in my arms, how can it hurt you?"

"Oh yes! I see," whispered Diamond. "But it looks so dreadful, and it pushes me about so."

"Yes, it does, my dear. That is what it was sent for."

At the same moment, a peal of thunder which shook Diamond's heart against the sides of his bosom hurtled out of the heavens: I cannot say out of the sky, for there was no sky. Diamond had not seen the lightning, for he had been intent on finding the face of North Wind. Every moment the folds of her garment would sweep across his eyes and blind him, but between, he could just persuade himself that he saw great glories of woman's eyes looking down through rifts in the mountainous clouds over his head.

He trembled so at the thunder, that his knees failed him, and he sunk down at North Wind's feet, and clasped her round the column of her ankle. She instantly stooped, lifted him from the roof — up — up into her bosom, and held him there, saying, as if to an inconsolable child-

"Diamond, dear, this will never do."

"Oh yes, it will," answered Diamond. "I am all right now— quite comfortable, I assure you, dear North Wind. If you will only let me stay here, I shall be all right indeed."

"But you will feel the wind here, Diamond."

"I don't mind that a bit, so long as I feel your arms through it," answered Diamond, nestling closer to her grand bosom.

"Brave boy!" returned North Wind, pressing him closer.

"No," said Diamond, "I don't see that. It's not courage at all, so long as I feel you there."

"But hadn't you better get into my hair? Then you would not feel the wind; you will here."

"Ah, but, dear North Wind, you don't know how nice it is to feel your arms about me. It is a thousand times better to have them and the wind together, than to have only your hair and the back of your neck and no wind at all."

"But it is surely more comfortable there?"

"Well, perhaps; but I begin to think there are better things than being comfortable."

"Yes, indeed there are. Well, I will keep you in front of me. You will feel the wind, but not too much. I shall only want one arm to take care of you; the other will be quite enough to sink the ship."

"Oh, dear North Wind! how can you talk so?"

"My dear boy, I never talk; I always mean what I say."

"Then you do mean to sink the ship with the other hand?"

"Yes."

"It's not like you."

"How do you know that?"

"Quite easily. Here you are taking care of a poor little boy with one arm, and there you are sinking a ship with the other. It can't be like you."

"Ah! but which is me? I can't be two mes, you know."

"No. Nobody can be two mes."

"Well, which me is me?"

"Now I must think. There looks to be two."

"Yes. That's the very point. You can't be knowing the thing you don't know, can you?"

"No."

"Which me do you know?"

"The kindest, goodest, best me in the world," answered Diamond, clinging to North Wind.

"Why am I good to you?"

"I don't know."

"Have you ever done anything for me?"

"No."

"Then I must be good to you because I choose to be good to you."

"Yes."

"Why should I choose?"

"Because — because — because you like."

"Why should I like to be good to you?"

"I don't know, except it be because it's good to be good to me."

"That's just it; I am good to you because I like to be good."

"Then why shouldn't you be good to other people as well as to me?"

"That's just what I don't know. Why shouldn't I?"

"I don't know either. Then why shouldn't you?"

"Because I am."

"There it is again," said Diamond. "I don't see that you are. It looks quite the other thing."

"Well, but listen to me, Diamond. You know the one me, you say, and that is good."

"Yes."

"Do you know the other me as well?"

"No. I can't. I shouldn't like to."

"There it is. You don't know the other me. You are sure of one of them?"

"Yes."

"And you are sure there can't be two mes?"

"Yes."

"Then the me you don't know must be the same as the me you do know,— else there would be two mes?"

"Yes."

"Then the other me you don't know must be as kind as the me you do know?"

"Yes."

"Besides, I tell you that it is so, only it doesn't look like it. That I confess freely. Have you anything more to object?"

"No, no, dear North Wind; I am quite satisfied."

"Then I will tell you something you might object. You might say that the me you know is like the other me, and that I am cruel all through."

"I know that can't be, because you are so kind."

"But that kindness might be only a pretence for the sake of being more cruel afterwards."

Diamond clung to her tighter than ever, crying —

"No, no, dear North Wind; I can't believe that. I don't believe it. I won't believe it. That would kill me. I love you, and you must love me, else how did I come to love you? How could you know how to put on such a beautiful face if you did not love me and the rest? No. You may sink as many ships as you like, and I won't say another word. I can't say I shall like to see it, you know."

"That's quite another thing," said North Wind; and as she spoke she gave one spring from the roof of the hay-loft, and rushed up into the clouds, with Diamond on her left arm close to her heart. And as if the clouds knew she had come, they burst into a fresh jubilation of thunderous light. For a few moments, Diamond seemed to be borne up through the depths of an ocean of dazzling flame; the next, the winds were writhing around him like a storm of serpents. For they were in the midst of the clouds and mists, and they of course took the shapes of the wind, eddying and wreathing and whirling and shooting and dashing about like grey and black water, so that it was as if the wind itself had taken shape, and he saw the grey and black wind tossing and raving most madly all about him. Now it blinded him by smiting him upon the eyes; now it deafened him by bellowing in his ears; for even when the thunder came he knew now that it was the billows of the great ocean of the air dashing against each other in their haste to fill the hollow scooped out by the lightning; now it took his breath quite away by sucking it from his body with the speed of its rush. But he did not mind it. He only gasped first and then laughed, for the arm of North Wind was about him, and he was leaning against her bosom. It is quite impossible for me to describe what he saw. Did you ever watch a great wave shoot into a winding passage amongst rocks? If you ever did, you would see that the water rushed every way at once, some of it even turning back and opposing the rest; greater confusion you might see nowhere except in a crowd of frightened people. Well, the wind was like that, except that it went much faster, and therefore was much wilder, and twisted and shot and curled and dodged and clashed and raved ten times more madly than anything else in creation except human passions. Diamond saw the threads of the lady's hair streaking it all. In parts indeed he could not tell which was hair and which was black storm and vapor. It seemed sometimes that all the great billows of mist-muddy wind were woven out of the crossing lines of North Wind's infinite hair, sweeping in endless intertwistings. And Diamond felt as the wind seized on his hair, which his mother kept rather long, as if he too was a part of the storm, and some of its life went out from him. But so sheltered was he by North Wind's arm and bosom that only at times, in the fiercer onslaught of some curl-billowed eddy, did he recognize for a moment how wild was the storm in which he was carried, nestling in its very core and formative centre.

It seemed to Diamond likewise that they were motionless in this centre, and that all the confusion and fighting went on around them. Flash after flash illuminated the fierce chaos, revealing in varied yellow and blue and grey and dusky red the vaporous contention; peal after peal of thunder tore the infinite waste; but it seemed to Diamond that North Wind and he were motionless, all but the hair. It was not so. They were sweeping with the speed of the wind itself towards the sea.

7. THE CATHEDRAL

I must not go on describing what cannot be described, for nothing is more wearisome.

Before they reached the sea, Diamond felt North Wind's hair just beginning to fall about him.

"Is the storm over, North Wind?" he called out.

"No, Diamond. I am only waiting a moment to set you down. You would not like to see the ship sunk, and I am going to give you a place to stop in till I come back for you."

"Oh! thank you," said Diamond. "I shall be sorry to leave you, North Wind, but I would rather not see the ship go down. And I'm afraid the poor people will cry, and I should hear them. Oh, dear!"

"There are a good many passengers on board; and to tell the truth, Diamond, I don't care about your hearing the cry you speak of. I am afraid you would not get it out of your little head again for a long time."

"But how can you bear it then, North Wind? For I am sure you are kind. I shall never doubt that again."

"I will tell you how I am able to bear it, Diamond: I am always hearing, through every noise, through all the noise I am making myself even, the sound of a far-off song. I do not exactly know where it is, or what it means; and I don't hear much of it, only the odor of its music, as it were, flitting across the great billows of the ocean outside this air in which I make such a storm; but what I do hear is quite enough to make me able to bear the cry from the drowning ship. So it would you if you could hear it."

"No, it wouldn't," returned Diamond, stoutly. "For they wouldn't hear the music of the far-away song; and if they did, it wouldn't do them any good. You see you and I are not going to be drowned, and so we might enjoy it."

"But you have never heard the psalm, and you don't know what it is like. Somehow, I can't say how, it tells me that all is right; that it is coming to swallow up all cries."

"But that won't do them any good—the people, I mean," persisted Diamond.

"It must. It must," said North Wind, hurriedly. "It wouldn't be the song it seems to be if it did not swallow up all their fear and pain too, and set them singing it themselves with the rest. I am sure it will. And do you know, ever since I knew I had hair, that is, ever since it began to go out and away, that song has been coming nearer and nearer. Only I must say it was some thousand years before I heard it."

"But how can you say it was coming nearer when you did not hear it?" asked doubting little Diamond.

"Since I began to hear it, I know it is growing louder, therefore I judge it was coming nearer and nearer until I did hear it first. I'm not so very old, you know—a few thousand years only—and I was quite a baby when I heard the noise first, but I knew it must come from the voices of people ever so much older and wiser than I was. I can't sing at all, except now and then, and I can never tell what my song is going to be; I only know what it is after I have sung it.— But this will never do. Will you stop here?"

"I can't see anywhere to stop," said Diamond. "Your hair is all down like a darkness, and I can't see through it if I knock my eyes into it ever so much."

"Look, then," said North Wind; and, with one sweep of her great white arm, she swept yards deep of darkness like a great curtain from before the face of the boy.

And lo! it was a blue night, lit up with stars. Where it did not shine with stars it shimmered with the milk of the stars, except where, just opposite to Diamond's face, the grey towers of a cathedral blotted out each its own shape of sky and stars.

"Oh! what's that?" cried Diamond, struck with a kind of terror, for he had never seen a cathedral, and it rose before him with an awful reality in the midst of the wide spaces, conquering emptiness with grandeur.

"A very good place for you to wait in," said North Wind. "But we shall go in, and you shall judge for yourself."

There was an open door in the middle of one of the towers, leading out upon the roof, and through it they passed. Then North Wind set Diamond on his feet, and he found himself at the top of a stone stair, which went twisting away down into the darkness for only a little light came in at the door. It was enough, however, to allow Diamond to see that North Wind stood beside him. He looked up to find her face, and saw that she was no longer a beautiful giantess, but the tall gracious lady he liked best to see. She took his hand, and, giving him the broad part of the spiral stair to walk on, led him down a good way; then, opening another little door, led him out upon a narrow gallery that ran all round the central part of the church, on the ledges of the windows of the clerestory, and through openings in the parts of the wall that divided the windows from each other. It was very narrow, and except when they were passing through the wall, Diamond saw nothing to keep him from falling into the church. It lay below him like a great silent gulf hollowed in stone, and he held his breath for fear as he looked down.

"What are you trembling for, little Diamond?" said the lady, as she walked gently along, with her hand held out behind her leading him, for there was not breadth enough for them to walk side by side.

"I am afraid of falling down there," answered Diamond. "It is so deep down."

"Yes, rather," answered North Wind; "but you were a hundred times higher a few minutes ago."

"Ah, yes, but somebody's arm was about me then," said Diamond, putting his little mouth to the beautiful cold hand that had a hold of his.

"What a dear little warm mouth you've got!" said North Wind.

"It is a pity you should talk nonsense with it. Don't you know I have a hold of you?"

"Yes; but I'm walking on my own legs, and they might slip. I can't trust myself so well as your arms."

"But I have a hold of you, I tell you, foolish child."

"Yes, but somehow I can't feel comfortable."

"If you were to fall, and my hold of you were to give way, I should be down after you in a less moment than a lady's watch can tick, and catch you long before you had reached the ground."

"I don't like it though," said Diamond.

"Oh! oh! oh!" he screamed the next moment, bent double with terror, for North Wind had let go her hold of his hand, and had vanished, leaving him standing as if rooted to the gallery.

She left the words, "Come after me," sounding in his ears.

But move he dared not. In a moment more he would from very terror have fallen into the church, but suddenly there came a gentle breath of cool wind upon his face, and it kept blowing upon him in little puffs, and at every puff Diamond felt his faintness going away, and his fear with it. Courage was reviving in his little heart, and still the cool wafts of the soft wind breathed upon him, and the soft wind was so mighty and strong within its gentleness, that in a minute more Diamond was marching along the narrow ledge as fearless for the time as North Wind herself.

He walked on and on, with the windows all in a row on one side of him, and the great empty nave of the church echoing to every one of his brave strides on the other, until at last he came to a little open door, from which a broader stair led him down and down and down, till at last all at once he found himself in the arms of North Wind, who held him close to her, and kissed him on the forehead. Diamond nestled to her, and murmured into her bosom,—"Why did you leave me, dear North Wind?"

"Because I wanted you to walk alone," she answered.

"But it is so much nicer here!" said Diamond.

"I daresay; but I couldn't hold a little coward to my heart. It would make me so cold!"

"But I wasn't brave of myself," said Diamond, whom my older readers will have already discovered to be a true child in this, that he was given to metaphysics. "It was the wind that blew in my face that made me brave. Wasn't it now, North Wind?"

"Yes: I know that. You had to be taught what courage was. And you couldn't know what it was without feeling it: therefore it was given you. But don't you feel as if you would try to be brave yourself next time?"

"Yes, I do. But trying is not much."

"Yes, it is — a very great deal, for it is a beginning. And a beginning is the greatest thing of all. To try to be brave is to be brave. The coward who tries to be brave is before the man who is brave because he is made so, and never had to try."

"How kind you are, North Wind!"

"I am only just. All kindness is but justice. We owe it."

"I don't quite understand that."

"Never mind; you will some day. There is no hurry about understanding it now."

"Who blew the wind on me that made me brave?"

"I did."

"I didn't see you."

"Therefore you can believe me."

"Yes, yes; of course. But how was it that such a little breath could be so strong?"

"That I don't know."

"But you made it strong?"

"No: I only blew it. I knew it would make you strong, just as it did the man in the boat, you remember. But how my breath has that power I cannot tell. It was put into it when I was made. That is all I know. But really I must be going about my work."

"Ah! the poor ship! I wish you would stop here, and let the poor ship go."

"That I dare not do. Will you stop here till I come back?"

"Yes. You won't be long?"

"Not longer than I can help. Trust me, you shall get home before the morning."

In a moment North Wind was gone, and the next Diamond heard a moaning about the church, which grew and grew to a roaring. The storm was up again, and he knew that North Wind's hair was flying.

The church was dark. Only a little light came through the windows, which were almost all of that precious old stained glass which is so much lovelier than the new. But Diamond could not see how beautiful they were, for there was not enough of light in the stars to show the colors of them. He could only just distinguish them from the walls, He looked up, but could not see the gallery along which he had passed. He could only tell where it was far up by the faint glimmer of the windows of the clerestory, whose sills made part of it. The church grew very lonely about him, and he began to feel like a child whose mother has forsaken it. Only he knew that to be left alone is not always to be forsaken.

He began to feel his way about the place, and for a while went wandering up and down. His little footsteps waked little answering echoes in the great house. It wasn't too big to mind him. It was as if the church knew he was there, and meant to make itself his house. So it went on giving back an answer to every step, until at length Diamond thought he should like to say something out loud, and see what the church would answer. But he found he was afraid to speak. He could not utter a word for fear of the loneliness. Perhaps it was as well that he did not, for the sound of a spoken word would have made him feel the place yet more deserted and empty. But he thought he could sing. He was fond of singing, and at home he used to sing, to tunes of his own, all the nursery rhymes he knew. So he began to try `Hey diddle diddle', but it wouldn't do. Then he tried `Little Boy Blue', but it was no better. Neither would `Sing a Song of Sixpence' sing itself at all. Then he tried `Poor old Cockytoo', but he wouldn't do. They all sounded so silly! and he had never thought them silly before. So he was quiet, and listened to the echoes that came out of the dark corners in answer to his footsteps.

At last he gave a great sigh, and said, "I'm so tired." But he did not hear the gentle echo that answered from far away over his head, for at the same moment he came against the lowest of a few steps that stretched across the church, and fell down and hurt his arm. He cried a little first, and then crawled up the steps on his hands and knees. At the top he came to a little bit of carpet, on which he lay down; and there he lay staring at the dull window that rose nearly a hundred feet above his head.

Now this was the eastern window of the church, and the moon was at that moment just on the edge of the horizon. The next, she was peeping over it. And lo! with the moon, St. John and St. Paul, and the rest of them, began to dawn in the window in their lovely garments. Diamond did not know that the wonder-working moon was behind, and he thought all the light was coming out of the window itself, and that the good old men were appearing to help him, growing out of the night and the darkness, because he had hurt his arm, and was very tired and lonely, and North Wind was so long in coming. So he lay and looked at them backwards over his head, wondering when they would come down or what they would do next. They were very dim, for the moonlight was not strong enough for the colors, and he had enough to do with his eyes trying to make out their shapes. So his eyes grew tired, and more and more tired, and his eyelids grew so heavy that they would keep tumbling down over his eyes. He kept lifting them and lifting them, but every time they were heavier than the last. It was no use: they were too much for him. Sometimes before he had got them half up, down they were again; and at length he gave it up quite, and the moment he gave it up, he was fast asleep.

8. THE EAST WINDOW

That Diamond had fallen fast asleep is very evident from the strange things he now fancied as taking place. For he thought he heard a sound as of whispering up in the great window. He tried to open his eyes, but he could not. And the whispering went on and grew louder and louder, until he could hear every word that was said. He thought it was the Apostles talking about him. But he could not open his eyes.

"And how comes he to be lying there, St. Peter?" said one.

"I think I saw him a while ago up in the gallery, under the Nicodemus window. Perhaps he has fallen down.

"What do you think, St. Matthew?"

"I don't think he could have crept here after falling from such a height. He must have been killed."

"What are we to do with him? We can't leave him lying there. And we could not make him comfortable up here in the window: it's rather crowded already. What do you say, St. Thomas?"

"Let's go down and look at him."

There came a rustling, and a chinking, for some time, and then there was a silence, and Diamond felt somehow that all the Apostles were standing round him and looking down on him. And still he could not open his eyes.

"What is the matter with him, St. Luke?" asked one.

"There's nothing the matter with him," answered St. Luke, who must have joined the company of the Apostles from the next window, one would think. "He's in a sound sleep."

"I have it," cried another. "This is one of North Wind's tricks. She has caught him up and dropped him at our door, like a withered leaf or a foundling baby. I don't understand that woman's conduct, I must say. As if we hadn't enough to do with our money, without going taking care of other people's children! That's not what our forefathers built cathedrals for."

Now Diamond could not bear to hear such things against North Wind, who, he knew, never played anybody a trick. She was far too busy with her own work for that. He struggled hard to open his eyes, but without success.

"She should consider that a church is not a place for pranks, not to mention that we live in it," said another.

"It certainly is disrespectful of her. But she always is disrespectful. What right has she to bang at our windows as she has been doing the whole of this night? I daresay there is glass broken somewhere. I know my blue robe is in a dreadful mess with the rain first and the dust after. It will cost me shillings to clean it."

Then Diamond knew that they could not be Apostles, talking like this. They could only be the sextons and vergers and such-like, who got up at night, and put on the robes of deans and bishops, and called each other grand names, as the foolish servants he had heard his father tell of call themselves lords and ladies, after their masters and mistresses. And he was so angry at their daring to abuse North Wind, that he jumped up, crying — "North Wind knows best what she is about. She has a good right to blow the cobwebs from your windows, for she was sent to do it. She sweeps them away from grander places, I can tell you, for I've been with her at it."

This was what he began to say, but as he spoke his eyes came wide open, and behold, there were neither Apostles nor vergers there — not even a window with the effigies of holy men in it, but a dark heap of hay all about him, and the little panes in the roof of his loft glimmering blue in the light of the morning. Old Diamond was coming awake down below in the stable. In a moment more he was on his feet, and shaking himself so that young Diamond's bed trembled under him.

"He's grand at shaking himself," said Diamond. "I wish I could shake myself like that. But then I can wash myself, and he can't. What fun it would be to see Old Diamond washing his face with his hoofs and iron shoes! Wouldn't it be a picture?"

So saying, he got up and dressed himself. Then he went out into the garden. There must have been a tremendous wind in the night, for although all was quiet now, there lay the little summer-house crushed to the ground, and over it the great elm-tree, which the wind had broken across, being much decayed in the middle. Diamond almost cried to see the wilderness of green leaves, which used to be so far up in the blue air, tossing about in the breeze, and liking it best when the wind blew it most, now lying so near the ground, and without any hope of ever getting up into the deep air again.

"I wonder how old the tree is!" thought Diamond. "It must take a long time to get so near the sky as that poor tree was."

"Yes, indeed," said a voice beside him, for Diamond had spoken the last words aloud.

Diamond started, and looking around saw a clergyman, a brother of Mrs. Coleman, who happened to be visiting her. He was a great scholar, and was in the habit of rising early.

"Who are you, my man?" he added.

"Little Diamond," answered the boy.

"Oh! I have heard of you. How do you come to be up so early?"

"Because the sham Apostles talked such nonsense, they waked me up."

The clergyman stared. Diamond saw that he had better have held his tongue, for he could not explain things.

"You must have been dreaming, my little man," said he. "Dear! dear!" he went on, looking at the tree, "there has been terrible work here. This is the north wind's doing. What a pity! I wish we lived at the back of it, I'm sure."

"Where is that sir?" asked Diamond.

"Away in the Hyperborean regions," answered the clergyman, smiling.

"I never heard of the place," returned Diamond.

"I daresay not," answered the clergyman; "but if this tree had been there now, it would not have been blown down, for there is no wind there."

"But, please, sir, if it had been there," said Diamond, "we should not have had to be sorry for it."

"Certainly not."

"Then we shouldn't have had to be glad for it, either."

"You're quite right, my boy," said the clergyman, looking at him very kindly, as he turned away to the house, with his eyes bent towards the earth. But Diamond thought within himself, "I will ask North Wind next time I see her to take me to that country. I think she did speak about it once before."

9. How Diamond Got To The Back Of The North Wind

When Diamond went home to breakfast, he found his father and mother already seated at the table. They were both busy with their bread and butter, and Diamond sat himself down in his usual place. His mother looked up at him, and, after watching him for a moment, said:

"I don't think the boy is looking well, husband."

"Don't you? Well, I don't know. I think he looks pretty bobbish. How do you feel yourself, Diamond, my boy?"

"Quite well, thank you, father; at least, I think I've got a little headache."

"There! I told you," said his father and mother both at once.

"The child's very poorly" added his mother.

"The child's quite well," added his father.

And then they both laughed.

"You see," said his mother, "I've had a letter from my sister at Sandwich."

"Sleepy old hole!" said his father.

"Don't abuse the place; there's good people in it," said his mother.

"Right, old lady," returned his father; "only I don't believe there are more than two pair of carriage-horses in the whole blessed place."

"Well, people can get to heaven without carriages—or coachmen either, husband. Not that I should like to go without my coachman, you know. But about the boy?"

"What boy?"

"That boy, there, staring at you with his goggle-eyes."

"Have I got goggle-eyes, mother?" asked Diamond, a little dismayed.

"Not too goggle," said his mother, who was quite proud of her boy's eyes, only did not want to make him vain.

"Not too goggle; only you need not stare so."

"Well, what about him?" said his father.

"I told you I had got a letter."

"Yes, from your sister; not from Diamond."

"La, husband! you've got out of bed the wrong leg first this morning, I do believe."

"I always get out with both at once," said his father, laughing.

"Well, listen then. His aunt wants the boy to go down and see her."

"And that's why you want to make out that he ain't looking well."

"No more he is. I think he had better go."

"Well, I don't care, if you can find the money," said his father.

"I'll manage that," said his mother; and so it was agreed that Diamond should go to Sandwich.

I will not describe the preparations Diamond made. You would have thought he had been going on a three months' voyage. Nor will I describe the journey, for our business is now at the place. He was met at the station by his aunt, a cheerful middle-aged woman, and conveyed in safety to the sleepy old town, as his father called it. And no wonder that it was sleepy, for it was nearly dead of old age.

Diamond went about staring with his beautiful goggle-eyes, at the quaint old streets, and the shops, and the houses. Everything looked very strange, indeed; for here was a town abandoned by its nurse, the sea, like an old oyster left on the shore till it gaped for weariness. It used to be one of the five chief seaports in England, but it began to hold itself too high, and the consequence was the sea grew less and less intimate with it, gradually drew back, and kept more to itself, till at length it left it high and dry: Sandwich was a seaport no more; the sea went on with its own tide-business a long way off, and forgot it. Of course it went to sleep, and had no more to do with ships. That's what comes to cities and nations, and boys and girls, who say, "I can do without your help. I'm enough for myself."

Diamond soon made great friends with an old woman who kept a toyshop, for his mother had given him two pence for pocket-money before he left, and he had gone into her shop to spend it, and she got talking to him. She looked very funny, because she had not got any teeth, but Diamond liked her, and went often to her shop, although he had nothing to spend there after the two pence was gone.

One afternoon he had been wandering rather wearily about the streets for some time. It was a hot day, and he felt tired. As he passed the toyshop, he stepped in.

"Please may I sit down for a minute on this box?" he said, thinking the old woman was somewhere in the shop. But he got no answer, and sat down without one. Around him were a great many toys of all prices, from a penny up to shillings. All at once he heard a gentle whirring somewhere amongst them. It made him start and look behind him. There were the sails of a windmill going round and round almost close to his ear. He thought at first it must be one of those toys which are wound up and go with clockwork; but no, it was a common penny toy, with the windmill at the end of a whistle, and when the whistle blows the windmill goes. But the wonder was that there was no one at the whistle end blowing, and yet the sails were turning round and round— now faster, now slower, now faster again.

"What can it mean?" said Diamond, aloud.

"It means me," said the tiniest voice he had ever heard.

"Who are you, please?" asked Diamond.

"Well, really, I begin to be ashamed of you," said the voice. "I wonder how long it will be before you know me; or how often I might take you in before you got sharp enough to suspect me. You are as bad as a baby that doesn't know his mother in a new bonnet."

"Not quite so bad as that, dear North Wind," said Diamond, "for I didn't see you at all, and indeed I don't see you yet, although I recognize your voice. Do grow a little, please."

"Not a hair's-breadth," said the voice, and it was the smallest voice that ever spoke. "What are you doing here?"

"I am come to see my aunt. But, please, North Wind, why didn't you come back for me in the church that night?"

"I did. I carried you safe home. All the time you were dreaming about the glass Apostles, you were lying in my arms."

"I'm so glad," said Diamond. "I thought that must be it, only I wanted to hear you say so. Did you sink the ship, then?"

"Yes."

"And drown everybody?"

"Not quite. One boat got away with six or seven men in it."

"How could the boat swim when the ship couldn't?"

"Of course I had some trouble with it. I had to contrive a bit, and manage the waves a little. When they're once thoroughly waked up, I have a good deal of trouble with them sometimes. They're apt to get stupid with tumbling over each other's heads. That's when they're fairly at it. However, the boat got to a desert island before noon next day."

"And what good will come of that?"

"I don't know. I obeyed orders. Good bye."

"Oh! stay, North Wind, do stay!" cried Diamond, dismayed to see the windmill get slower and slower.

"What is it, my dear child?" said North Wind, and the windmill began turning again so swiftly that Diamond could scarcely see it. "What a big voice you've got! and what a noise you do make with it? What is it you want? I have little to do, but that little must be done."

"I want you to take me to the country at the back of the north wind."

"That's not so easy," said North Wind, and was silent for so long that Diamond thought she was gone indeed. But after he had quite given her up, the voice began again.

"I almost wish old Herodotus had held his tongue about it. Much he knew of it!"

"Why do you wish that, North Wind?"

"Because then that clergyman would never have heard of it, and set you wanting to go. But we shall see. We shall see. You must go home now, my dear, for you don't seem very well, and I'll see what can be done for you. Don't wait for me. I've got to break a few of old Goody's toys; she's thinking too much of her new stock. Two or three will do. There! go now."

Diamond rose, quite sorry, and without a word left the shop, and went home.

It soon appeared that his mother had been right about him, for that same afternoon his head began to ache very much, and he had to go to bed.

He awoke in the middle of the night. The lattice window of his room had blown open, and the curtains of his little bed were swinging about in the wind.

"If that should be North Wind now!" thought Diamond.

But the next moment he heard some one closing the window, and his aunt came to his bedside. She put her hand on his face, and said —

"How's your head, dear?"

"Better, auntie, I think."

"Would you like something to drink?"

"Oh, yes! I should, please."

So his aunt gave him some lemonade, for she had been used to nursing sick people, and Diamond felt very much refreshed, and laid his head down again to go very fast asleep, as he thought. And so he did, but only to come awake again, as a fresh burst of wind blew the lattice open a second time. The same moment he found himself in a cloud of North Wind's hair, with her beautiful face, set in it like a moon, bending over him.

"Quick, Diamond!" she said. "I have found such a chance!"

"But I'm not well," said Diamond.

"I know that, but you will be better for a little fresh air. You shall have plenty of that."

"You want me to go, then?"

"Yes, I do. It won't hurt you."

"Very well," said Diamond; and getting out of the bed-clothes, he jumped into North Wind's arms.

"We must make haste before your aunt comes," said she, as she glided out of the open lattice and left it swinging.

The moment Diamond felt her arms fold around him he began to feel better. It was a moonless night, and very dark, with glimpses of stars when the clouds parted.

"I used to dash the waves about here," said North Wind, "where cows and sheep are feeding now; but we shall soon get to them. There they are."

And Diamond, looking down, saw the white glimmer of breaking water far below him.

"You see, Diamond," said North Wind, "it is very difficult for me to get you to the back of the north wind, for that country lies in the very north itself, and of course I can't blow northwards."

"Why not?" asked Diamond.

"You little silly!" said North Wind. "Don't you see that if I were to blow northwards I should be South Wind, and that is as much as to say that one person could be two persons?"

"But how can you ever get home at all, then?"

"You are quite right — that is my home, though I never get farther than the outer door. I sit on the doorstep, and hear the voices inside. I am nobody there, Diamond."

"I'm very sorry."

"Why?"

"That you should be nobody."

"Oh, I don't mind it. Dear little man! you will be very glad some day to be nobody yourself. But you can't understand that now, and you had better not try; for if you do, you will be certain to go fancying some egregious nonsense, and making yourself miserable about it."

"Then I won't," said Diamond.

"There's a good boy. It will all come in good time."

"But you haven't told me how you get to the doorstep, you know."

"It is easy enough for me. I have only to consent to be nobody, and there I am. I draw into myself and there I am on the doorstep. But you can easily see, or you have less sense than I think, that to drag you, you heavy thing, along with me, would take centuries, and I could not give the time to it."

"Oh, I'm so sorry!" said Diamond.

"What for now, pet?"

"That I'm so heavy for you. I would be lighter if I could, but I don't know how."

"You silly darling! Why, I could toss you a hundred miles from me if I liked. It is only when I am going home that I shall find you heavy."

"Then you are going home with me?"

"Of course. Did I not come to fetch you just for that?"

"But all this time you must be going southwards."

"Yes. Of course I am."

"How can you be taking me northwards, then?"

"A very sensible question. But you shall see. I will get rid of a few of these clouds — only they do come up so fast! It's like trying to blow a brook dry. There! What do you see now?"

"I think I see a little boat, away there, down below."

"A little boat, indeed! Well! She's a yacht of two hundred tons; and the captain of it is a friend of mine; for he is a man of good sense, and can sail his craft well. I've helped him many a time when he little thought it. I've heard him grumbling at me, when I was doing the very best I could for him. Why, I've carried him eighty miles a day, again and again, right north."

"He must have dodged for that," said Diamond, who had been watching the vessels, and had seen that they went other ways than the wind blew.

"Of course he must. But don't you see, it was the best I could do? I couldn't be South Wind. And besides it gave him a share in the business. It is not good at all — mind that, Diamond — to do everything for those you love, and not give them a share in the doing. It's not kind. It's making too much of yourself, my child. If I had been South Wind, he would only have smoked his pipe all day, and made himself stupid."

"But how could he be a man of sense and grumble at you when you were doing your best for him?"

"Oh! you must make allowances," said North Wind, "or you will never do justice to anybody. — You do understand, then, that a captain may sail north ——"

"In spite of a north wind — yes," supplemented Diamond.

"Now, I do think you must be stupid, my, dear" said North Wind. "Suppose the north wind did not blow where would he be then?"

"Why then the south wind would carry him."

"So you think that when the north wind stops the south wind blows. Nonsense. If I didn't blow, the captain couldn't sail his eighty miles a day. No doubt South Wind would carry him faster, but South Wind is sitting on her doorstep then, and if I stopped there would be a dead calm. So you are all wrong to say he can sail north in spite of me; he sails north by my help, and my help alone. You see that, Diamond?"

"Yes, I do, North Wind. I am stupid, but I don't want to be stupid."

"Good boy! I am going to blow you north in that little craft, one of the finest that ever sailed the sea. Here we are, right over it. I shall be blowing against you; you will be sailing against me; and all will be just as we want it. The captain won't get on so fast as he would like, but he will get on, and so shall we. I'm just going to put you on board. Do you see in front of the tiller— that thing the man is working, now to one side, now to the other— a round thing like the top of a drum?"

"Yes," said Diamond.

"Below that is where they keep their spare sails, and some stores of that sort. I am going to blow that cover off. The same moment I will drop you on deck, and you must tumble in. Don't be afraid, it is of no depth, and you will fall on sail-cloth. You will find it nice and warm and dry-only dark; and you will know I am near you by every roll and pitch of the vessel. Coil yourself up and go to sleep. The yacht shall be my cradle and you shall be my baby."

"Thank you, dear North Wind. I am not a bit afraid," said Diamond.

In a moment they were on a level with the bulwarks, and North Wind sent the hatch of the after-store rattling away over the deck to leeward. The next, Diamond found himself in the dark, for he had tumbled through the hole as North Wind had told him, and the cover was replaced over his head. Away he went rolling to leeward, for the wind began all at once to blow hard. He heard the call of the captain, and the loud trampling of the men over his head, as they hauled at the main sheet to get the boom on board that they might take in a reef in the mainsail. Diamond felt about until he had found what seemed the most comfortable place, and there he snuggled down and lay.

Hours after hours, a great many of them, went by; and still Diamond lay there. He never felt in the least tired or impatient, for a strange pleasure filled his heart. The straining of the masts, the creaking of the boom, the singing of the ropes, the banging of the blocks as they put the vessel about, all fell in with the roaring of the wind above, the surge of the waves past her sides, and the thud with which every now and then one would strike her; while through it all Diamond could hear the gurgling, rippling, talking flow of the water against her planks, as she slipped through it, lying now on this side, now on that—like a subdued air running through the grand music his North Wind was making about him to keep him from tiring as they sped on towards the country at the back of her doorstep.

How long this lasted Diamond had no idea. He seemed to fall asleep sometimes, only through the sleep he heard the sounds going on. At length the weather seemed to get worse. The confusion and trampling of feet grew more frequent over his head; the vessel lay over more and more on her side, and went roaring through the waves, which banged and thumped at her as if in anger. All at once arose a terrible uproar. The hatch was blown off; a cold fierce wind swept in upon him; and a long arm came with it which laid hold of him and lifted him out. The same moment he saw the little vessel far below him righting herself. She had taken in all her sails and lay now tossing on the waves like a sea-bird with folded wings. A short distance to the south lay a much larger vessel, with two or three sails set, and towards it North Wind was carrying Diamond. It was a German ship, on its way to the North Pole.

"That vessel down there will give us a lift now," said North Wind; "and after that I must do the best I can."

She managed to hide him amongst the flags of the big ship, which were all snugly stowed away, and on and on they sped towards the north. At length one night she whispered in his ear, "Come on deck, Diamond;" and he got up at once and crept on deck. Everything looked very strange. Here and there on all sides were huge masses of floating ice, looking like cathedrals, and castles, and crags, while away beyond was a blue sea.

"Is the sun rising or setting?" asked Diamond.

"Neither or both, which you please. I can hardly tell which myself. If he is setting now, he will be rising the next moment."

"What a strange light it is!" said Diamond. "I have heard that the sun doesn't go to bed all the summer in these parts. Miss Coleman told me that. I suppose he feels very sleepy, and that is why the light he sends out looks so like a dream."

"That will account for it well enough for all practical purposes," said North Wind.

Some of the icebergs were drifting northwards; one was passing very near the ship. North Wind seized Diamond, and with a single bound lighted on one of them—a huge thing, with sharp pinnacles and great clefts. The same instant a wind began to blow from the south. North Wind hurried Diamond down the north side of the iceberg, stepping by its jags and splintering; for this berg had never got far enough south to be melted and smoothed by the summer sun. She brought him to a cave near the water, where she entered, and, letting Diamond go, sat down as if weary on a ledge of ice.

Diamond seated himself on the other side, and for a while was enraptured with the color of the air inside the cave. It was a deep, dazzling, lovely blue, deeper than the deepest blue of the sky. The blue seemed to be in constant motion, like the blackness when you press your eyeballs with your fingers, boiling and sparkling. But when he looked across to North Wind he was frightened; her face was worn and livid.

"What is the matter with you, dear North Wind?" he said.

"Nothing much. I feel very faint. But you mustn't mind it, for I can bear it quite well. South Wind always blows me faint. If it were not for the cool of the thick ice between me and her, I should faint altogether. Indeed, as it is, I fear I must vanish."

Diamond stared at her in terror, for he saw that her form and face were growing, not small, but transparent, like something dissolving, not in water, but in light. He could see the side of the blue cave through her very heart. And she melted away till all that was left was a pale face, like the moon in the morning, with two great lucid eyes in it.

"I am going, Diamond," she said.

"Does it hurt you?" asked Diamond.

"It's very uncomfortable," she answered; "but I don't mind it, for I shall come all right again before long. I thought I should be able to go with you all the way, but I cannot. You must not be frightened though. Just go straight on, and you will come all right. You'll find me on the doorstep."

As she spoke, her face too faded quite away, only Diamond thought he could still see her eyes shining through the blue. When he went closer, however, he found that what he thought her eyes were only two hollows in the ice. North Wind was quite gone; and Diamond would have cried, if he had not trusted her so thoroughly. So he sat still in the blue air of the cavern listening to the wash and ripple of the water all about the base of the iceberg, as it sped on and on into the open sea northwards. It was an excellent craft to go with the current, for there was twice as much of it below water as above. But a light south wind was blowing too, and so it went fast.

After a little while Diamond went out and sat on the edge of his floating island, and looked down into the ocean beneath him. The white sides of the berg reflected so much light below the water, that he could see far down into the green abyss. Sometimes he fancied he saw the eyes of North Wind looking up at him from below, but the fancy never lasted beyond the moment of its birth. And the time passed he did not know how, for he felt as if he were in a dream. When he got tired of the green water, he went into the blue cave; and when he got tired of the blue cave he went out and gazed all about him on the blue sea, ever sparkling in the sun, which kept wheeling about the sky, never going below the horizon. But he chiefly gazed northwards, to see whether any land were appearing. All this time he never wanted to eat. He broke off little bits of the berg now and then and sucked them, and he thought them very nice.

At length, one time he came out of his cave, he spied far off on the horizon, a shining peak that rose into the sky like the top of some tremendous iceberg; and his vessel was bearing him straight towards it. As it went on the peak rose and rose higher and higher above the horizon; and other peaks rose after it, with sharp edges and jagged ridges connecting them. Diamond thought this must be the place he was going to; and he was right; for the mountains rose and rose, till he saw the line of the coast at their feet and at length the iceberg drove into a little bay, all around which were lofty precipices with snow on their tops, and streaks of ice down their sides. The berg floated slowly up to a projecting rock. Diamond stepped on shore, and without looking behind him began to follow a natural path which led windingly towards the top of the precipice.

When he reached it, he found himself on a broad table of ice, along which he could walk without much difficulty. Before him, at a considerable distance, rose a lofty ridge of ice, which shot up into fantastic pinnacles and towers and battlements. The air was very cold, and seemed somehow dead, for there was not the slightest breath of wind.

In the centre of the ridge before him appeared a gap like the opening of a valley. But as he walked towards it, gazing, and wondering whether that could be the way he had to take, he saw that what had appeared a gap was the form of a woman seated against the ice front of the ridge, leaning forwards with her hands in her lap, and her hair hanging down to the ground.

"It is North Wind on her doorstep," said Diamond joyfully, and hurried on.

He soon came up to the place, and there the form sat, like one of the great figures at the door of an Egyptian temple, motionless, with drooping arms and head. Then Diamond grew frightened, because she did not move nor speak. He was sure it was North Wind, but he thought she must be dead at last. Her face was white as the snow, her eyes were blue as the air in the ice-cave, and her hair hung down straight, like icicles. She had on a greenish robe, like the color in the hollows of a glacier seen from far off.

He stood up before her, and gazed fearfully into her face for a few minutes before he ventured to speak. At length, with a great effort and a trembling voice, he faltered out—

"North Wind!"

"Well, child?" said the form, without lifting its head.

"Are you ill, dear North Wind?"

"No. I am waiting."

"What for?"

"Till I'm wanted."

"You don't care for me any more," said Diamond, almost crying now.

"Yes I do. Only I can't show it. All my love is down at the bottom of my heart. But I feel it bubbling there."

"What do you want me to do next, dear North Wind?" said Diamond, wishing to show his love by being obedient.

"What do you want to do yourself?"

"I want to go into the country at your back."

"Then you must go through me."

"I don't know what you mean."

"I mean just what I say. You must walk on as if I were an open door, and go right through me."

"But that will hurt you."

"Not in the least. It will hurt you, though."

"I don't mind that, if you tell me to do it."

"Do it," said North Wind.

Diamond walked towards her instantly. When he reached her knees, he put out his hand to lay it on her, but nothing was there save an intense cold. He walked on. Then all grew white about him;

and the cold stung him like fire. He walked on still, groping through the whiteness. It thickened about him. At last, it got into his heart, and he lost all sense. I would say that he fainted—only whereas in common faints all grows black about you, he felt swallowed up in whiteness. It was when he reached North Wind's heart that he fainted and fell. But as he fell, he rolled over the threshold, and it was thus that Diamond got to the back of the north wind.

10. AT THE BACK OF THE NORTH WIND

I have now come to the most difficult part of my story. And why? Because I do not know enough about it. And why should I not know as much about this part as about any other part? For of course I could know nothing about the story except Diamond had told it; and why should not Diamond tell about the country at the back of the north wind, as well as about his adventures in getting there? Because, when he came back, he had forgotten a great deal, and what he did remember was very hard to tell. Things there are so different from things here! The people there do not speak the same language for one thing. Indeed, Diamond insisted that there they do not speak at all. I do not think he was right, but it may well have appeared so to Diamond. The fact is, we have different reports of the place from the most trustworthy people. Therefore we are bound to believe that it appears somewhat different to different people. All, however, agree in a general way about it.

I will tell you something of what two very different people have reported, both of whom knew more about it, I believe, than Herodotus. One of them speaks from his own experience, for he visited the country; the other from the testimony of a young peasant girl who came back from it for a month's visit to her friends. The former was a great Italian of noble family, who died more than five hundred years ago; the latter a Scotch shepherd who died not forty years ago.

The Italian, then, informs us that he had to enter that country through a fire so hot that he would have thrown himself into boiling glass to cool himself. This was not Diamond's experience, but then Durante—that was the name of the Italian, and it means Lasting, for his books will last as long as there are enough men in the world worthy of having them—Durante was an elderly man, and Diamond was a little boy, and so their experience must be a little different. The peasant girl, on the other hand, fell fast asleep in a wood, and woke in the same country.

In describing it, Durante says that the ground everywhere smelt sweetly, and that a gentle, even-tempered wind, which never blew faster or slower, breathed in his face as he went, making all the leaves point one way, not so as to disturb the birds in the tops of the trees, but, on the contrary, sounding a bass to their song. He describes also a little river which was so full that its little waves, as it hurried along, bent the grass, full of red and yellow flowers, through which it flowed. He says that the purest stream in the world beside this one would look as if it were mixed with something that did not belong to it, even although it was flowing ever in the brown shadow of the trees, and neither sun nor moon could shine upon it. He seems to imply that it is always the month of May in that country. It would be out of place to describe here the wonderful sights he saw, for the music of them is in another key from that of this story, and I shall therefore only add from the account of this traveler, that the people there are so free and so just and so healthy, that every one of them has a crown like a king and a mitre like a priest.

The peasant girl—Kilmeny was her name—could not report such grand things as Durante, for, as the shepherd says, telling her story as I tell Diamond's—

"Kilmeny had been she knew not where,

And Kilmeny had seen what she could not declare;

Kilmeny had been where the cock never crew,

Where the rain never fell, and the wind never blew.

But it seemed as the harp of the sky had rung,

And the airs of heaven played round her tongue,

When she spoke of the lovely forms she had seen,

And a land where sin had never been;

A land of love and a land of light,

Withouten sun, or moon, or night;

Where the river swayed a living stream,

And the light a pure and cloudless beam:

The land of vision it would seem,

And still an everlasting dream.”

The last two lines are the shepherd's own remark, and a matter of opinion. But it is clear, I think, that Kilmeny must have described the same country as Durante saw, though, not having his experience, she could neither understand nor describe it so well.

Now I must give you such fragments of recollection as Diamond was able to bring back with him.

When he came to himself after he fell, he found himself at the back of the north wind. North Wind herself was nowhere to be seen. Neither was there a vestige of snow or of ice within sight. The sun too had vanished; but that was no matter, for there was plenty of a certain still rayless light. Where it came from he never found out; but he thought it belonged to the country itself. Sometimes he thought it came out of the flowers, which were very bright, but had no strong color. He said the river — for all agree that there is a river there — flowed not only through, but over grass: its channel, instead of being rock, stones, pebbles, sand, or anything else, was of pure meadow grass, not over long. He insisted that if it did not sing tunes in people's ears, it sung tunes in their heads, in proof of which I may mention that, in the troubles which followed, Diamond was often heard singing; and when asked what he was singing, would answer, “One of the tunes the river at the back of the north wind sung.” And I may as well say at once that Diamond never told these things to any one but—no, I had better not say who it was; but whoever it was told me, and I thought it would be well to write them for my child-readers.

He could not say he was very happy there, for he had neither his father nor mother with him, but he felt so still and quiet and patient and contented, that, as far as the mere feeling went, it was something better than mere happiness. Nothing went wrong at the back of the north wind. Neither was anything quite right, he thought. Only everything was going to be right some day. His account disagreed with that of Durante, and agreed with that of Kilmeny, in this, that he protested there was no wind there at all. I fancy he missed it. At all events we could not do without wind. It all depends on how big our lungs are whether the wind is too strong for us or not.

When the person he told about it asked him whether he saw anybody he knew there, he answered, “Only a little girl belonging to the gardener, who thought he had lost her, but was quite mistaken, for there she was safe enough, and was to come back some day, as I came back, if they would only wait."

"Did you talk to her, Diamond?"

"No. Nobody talks there. They only look at each other, and understand everything."

"Is it cold there?"

"No."

"Is it hot?"

"No."

"What is it then?"

"You never think about such things there."

"What a queer place it must be!"

"It's a very good place."

"Do you want to go back again?"

"No; I don't think I have left it; I feel it here, somewhere."

"Did the people there look pleased?"

"Yes — quite pleased, only a little sad."

"Then they didn't look glad?"

"They looked as if they were waiting to be gladder some day."

This was how Diamond used to answer questions about that country. And now I will take up the story again, and tell you how he got back to this country.

11. How Diamond Got Home Again

When one at the back of the north wind wanted to know how things were going with any one he loved, he had to go to a certain tree, climb the stem, and sit down in the branches. In a few minutes, if he kept very still, he would see something at least of what was going on with the people he loved.

One day when Diamond was sitting in this tree, he began to long very much to get home again, and no wonder, for he saw his mother crying. Durante says that the people there may always follow their wishes, because they never wish but what is good. Diamond's wish was to get home, and he would fain follow his wish.

But how was he to set about it? If he could only see North Wind! But the moment he had got to her back, she was gone altogether from his sight. He had never seen her back. She might be sitting on her doorstep still, looking southwards, and waiting, white and thin and blue-eyed, until she was wanted. Or she might have again become a mighty creature, with power to do that which was demanded of her, and gone far away upon many missions. She must be somewhere, however. He could not go home without her, and therefore he must find her. She could never have intended to leave him always away from his mother. If there had been any danger of that, she would have told him, and given him his choice about going. For North Wind was right honest. How to find North Wind, therefore, occupied all his thoughts.

In his anxiety about his mother, he used to climb the tree every day, and sit in its branches. However many of the dwellers there did so, they never incommoded one another; for the moment one got into the tree, he became invisible to every one else; and it was such a wide-spreading tree that there was room for every one of the people of the country in it, without the least interference with each other. Sometimes, on getting down, two of them would meet at the root, and then they would smile to each other more sweetly than at any other time, as much as to say, "Ah, you've been up there too!"

One day he was sitting on one of the outer branches of the tree, looking southwards after his home. Far away was a blue shining sea, dotted with gleaming and sparkling specks of white. Those were the icebergs. Nearer he saw a great range of snow-capped mountains, and down below him the lovely meadow-grass of the country, with the stream flowing and flowing through it, away towards the sea. As he looked he began to wonder, for the whole country lay beneath him like a map, and that which was near him looked just as small as that which he knew to be miles away. The ridge of ice which encircled it appeared but a few yards off, and no larger than the row of pebbles with which a child will mark out the boundaries of the kingdom he has appropriated on the sea-shore. He thought he could distinguish the vapory form of North Wind, seated as he had left her, on the other side. Hastily he descended the tree, and to his amazement found that the map or model of the country still lay at his feet. He stood in it. With one stride he had crossed the river; with another he had reached the ridge of ice; with the third he stepped over its peaks, and sank wearily down at North Wind's knees. For there she sat on her doorstep. The peaks of the great ridge of ice were as lofty as ever behind her, and the country at her back had vanished from Diamond's view.

North Wind was as still as Diamond had left her. Her pale face was white as the snow, and her motionless eyes were as blue as the caverns in the ice. But the instant Diamond touched her, her face began to change like that of one waking from sleep. Light began to glimmer from the blue of her eyes.

A moment more, and she laid her hand on Diamond's head, and began playing with his hair. Diamond took hold of her hand, and laid his face to it. She gave a little start.

"How very alive you are, child!" she murmured. "Come nearer to me."

By the help of the stones all around he clambered up beside her, and laid himself against her bosom. She gave a great sigh, slowly lifted her arms, and slowly folded them about him, until she clasped him close. Yet a moment, and she roused herself, and came quite awake; and the cold of her bosom, which had pierced Diamond's bones, vanished.

"Have you been sitting here ever since I went through you, dear North Wind?" asked Diamond, stroking her hand.

"Yes," she answered, looking at him with her old kindness.

"Ain't you very tired?"

"No; I've often had to sit longer. Do you know how long you have been?"

"Oh! years and years," answered Diamond.

"You have just been seven days," returned North Wind.

"I thought I had been a hundred years!" exclaimed Diamond.

"Yes, I daresay," replied North Wind. "You've been away from here seven days; but how long you may have been in there is quite another thing. Behind my back and before my face things are so different! They don't go at all by the same rule."

"I'm very glad," said Diamond, after thinking a while.

"Why?" asked North Wind.

"Because I've been such a long time there, and such a little while away from mother. Why, she won't be expecting me home from Sandwich yet!"

"No. But we mustn't talk any longer. I've got my orders now, and we must be off in a few minutes."

Next moment Diamond found himself sitting alone on the rock. North Wind had vanished. A creature like a great humble-bee or cockchafer flew past his face; but it could be neither, for there were no insects amongst the ice. It passed him again and again, flying in circles around him, and he concluded that it must be North Wind herself, no bigger than Tom Thumb when his mother put him in the nutshell lined with flannel. But she was no longer vapoury and thin. She was solid, although tiny. A moment more, and she perched on his shoulder.

"Come along, Diamond," she said in his ear, in the smallest and highest of treble voices; "it is time we were setting out for Sandwich."

Diamond could just see her, by turning his head towards his shoulder as far as he could, but only with one eye, for his nose came between her and the other.

"Won't you take me in your arms and carry me?" he said in a whisper, for he knew she did not like a loud voice when she was small.

"Ah! you ungrateful boy," returned North Wind, smiling "how dare you make game of me? Yes, I will carry you, but you shall walk a bit for your impertinence first. Come along."

She jumped from his shoulder, but when Diamond looked for her upon the ground, he could see nothing but a little spider with long legs that made its way over the ice towards the south. It ran very fast indeed for a spider, but Diamond ran a long way before it, and then waited for it. It was up with him sooner than he had expected, however, and it had grown a good deal. And the spider grew and grew and went faster and faster, till all at once Diamond discovered that it was not a spider, but a weasel; and away glided the weasel, and away went Diamond after it, and it took all the run there was in him to keep up with the weasel. And the weasel grew, and grew, and grew, till all at once Diamond saw that the weasel was not a weasel but a cat. And away went the cat, and Diamond after it. And when he had run half a mile, he found the cat waiting for him, sitting up and washing her face not to lose time. And away went the cat again, and Diamond after it. But the next time he came up with the cat, the cat was not a cat, but a hunting-leopard. And the hunting-leopard grew to a jaguar, all covered with spots like eyes. And the jaguar grew to a Bengal tiger. And at none of them was Diamond afraid, for he had been at North Wind's back, and he could be afraid of her no longer whatever she did or grew. And the tiger flew over the snow in a straight line for the south, growing less and less to Diamond's eyes till it was only a black speck upon the whiteness; and then it vanished altogether. And now Diamond felt that he would rather not run any farther, and that the ice had got very rough. Besides, he was near the precipices that bounded the sea, so he slackened his pace to a walk, saying aloud to himself:

"When North Wind has punished me enough for making game of her, she will come back to me; I know she will, for I can't go much farther without her."

"You dear boy! It was only in fun. Here I am!" said North Wind's voice behind him.

Diamond turned, and saw her as he liked best to see her, standing beside him, a tall lady.

"Where's the tiger?" he asked, for he knew all the creatures from a picture book that Miss Coleman had given him. "But, of course," he added, "you were the tiger. I was puzzled and forgot. I saw it such a long way off before me, and there you were behind me. It's so odd, you know."

"It must look very odd to you, Diamond: I see that. But it is no more odd to me than to break an old pine in two."

"Well, that's odd enough," remarked Diamond.

"So it is! I forgot. Well, none of these things are odder to me than it is to you to eat bread and butter."

"Well, that's odd too, when I think of it," persisted Diamond. "I should just like a slice of bread and butter! I'm afraid to say how long it is — how long it seems to me, that is — since I had anything to eat."

"Come then," said North Wind, stooping and holding out her arms. "You shall have some bread and butter very soon. I am glad to find you want some."

Diamond held up his arms to meet hers, and was safe upon her bosom. North Wind bounded into the air. Her tresses began to lift and rise and spread and stream and flow and flutter; and with a roar from her hair and an answering roar from one of the great glaciers beside them, whose slow torrent tumbled two or three icebergs at once into the waves at their feet, North Wind and Diamond went flying southwards.

12. Who Met Diamond At Sandwich

As they flew, so fast they went that the sea slid away from under them like a great web of shot silk, blue shot with grey, and green shot with purple. They went so fast that the stars themselves appeared to sail away past them overhead, "like golden boats," on a blue sea turned upside down. And they went so fast that Diamond himself went the other way as fast—I mean he went fast asleep in North Wind's arms.

When he woke, a face was bending over him; but it was not North Wind's; it was his mother's. He put out his arms to her, and she clasped him to her bosom and burst out crying. Diamond kissed her again and again to make her stop. Perhaps kissing is the best thing for crying, but it will not always stop it.

"What is the matter, mother?" he said.

"Oh, Diamond, my darling! you have been so ill!" she sobbed.

"No, mother dear. I've only been at the back of the north wind," returned Diamond.

"I thought you were dead," said his mother.

But that moment the doctor came in.

"Oh! there!" said the doctor with gentle cheerfulness; "we're better to-day, I see."

Then he drew the mother aside, and told her not to talk to Diamond, or to mind what he might say; for he must be kept as quiet as possible. And indeed Diamond was not much inclined to talk, for he felt very strange and weak, which was little wonder, seeing that all the time he had been away he had only sucked a few lumps of ice, and there could not be much nourishment in them.

Now while he is lying there, getting strong again with chicken broth and other nice things, I will tell my readers what had been taking place at his home, for they ought to be told it.

They may have forgotten that Miss Coleman was in a very poor state of health. Now there were three reasons for this. In the first place, her lungs were not strong. In the second place, there was a gentleman somewhere who had not behaved very well to her. In the third place, she had not anything particular to do. These three nots together are enough to make a lady very ill indeed. Of course she could not help the first cause; but if the other two causes had not existed, that would have been of little consequence; she would only have to be a little careful. The second she could not help quite; but if she had had anything to do, and had done it well, it would have been very difficult for any man to behave badly to her. And for this third cause of her illness, if she had had anything to do that was worth doing, she might have borne his bad behavior so that even that would not have made her ill. It is not always easy, I confess, to find something to do that is worth doing, but the most difficult things are constantly being done, and she might have found something if she had tried. Her fault lay in this, that she had not tried. But, to be sure, her father and mother were to blame that they had never set her going. Only then again, nobody had told her father and mother that they ought to set her going in that direction. So as none of them would find it out of themselves, North Wind had to teach them.

We know that North Wind was very busy that night on which she left Diamond in the cathedral. She had in a sense been blowing through and through the Colemans' house the whole of the night. First, Miss Coleman's maid had left a chink of her mistress's window open, thinking she had shut it, and North Wind had wound a few of her hairs round the lady's throat. She was considerably worse the next morning. Again, the ship which North Wind had sunk that very night belonged to Mr. Coleman. Nor will my readers understand what a heavy loss this was to him until I have informed them that he had been getting poorer and poorer for some time. He was not so successful in his speculations as he had been, for he speculated a great deal more than was right, and it was time he should be pulled up. It is a hard thing for a rich man to grow poor; but it is an awful thing for him to grow dishonest, and some kinds of speculation lead a man deep into dishonesty before he thinks what he is about. Poverty will not make a man worthless — he may be worth a great deal more when he is poor than he was when he was rich; but dishonesty goes very far indeed to make a man of no value — a thing to be thrown out in the dust-hole of the creation, like a bit of a broken basin, or a dirty rag. So North Wind had to look after Mr. Coleman, and try to make an honest man of him. So she sank the ship which was his last venture, and he was what himself and his wife and the world called ruined.

Nor was this all yet. For on board that vessel Miss Coleman's lover was a passenger; and when the news came that the vessel had gone down, and that all on board had perished, we may be sure she did not think the loss of their fine house and garden and furniture the greatest misfortune in the world.

Of course, the trouble did not end with Mr. Coleman and his family. Nobody can suffer alone. When the cause of suffering is most deeply hidden in the heart, and nobody knows anything about it but the man himself, he must be a great and a good man indeed, such as few of us have known, if the pain inside him does not make him behave so as to cause all about him to be more or less uncomfortable. But when a man brings money-troubles on himself by making haste to be rich, then most of the people he has to do with must suffer in the same way with himself. The elm-tree which North Wind blew down that very night, as if small and great trials were to be gathered in one heap, crushed Miss Coleman's pretty summer-house: just so the fall of Mr. Coleman crushed the little family that lived over his coach-house and stable. Before Diamond was well enough to be taken home, there was no home for him to go to. Mr. Coleman — or his creditors, for I do not know the particulars — had sold house, carriage, horses, furniture, and everything. He and his wife and daughter and Mrs. Crump had gone to live in a small house in Hoxton, where he would be unknown, and whence he could walk to his place of business in the City. For he was not an old man, and hoped yet to retrieve his fortunes. Let us hope that he lived to retrieve his honesty, the tail of which had slipped through his fingers to the very last joint, if not beyond it.

Of course, Diamond's father had nothing to do for a time, but it was not so hard for him to have nothing to do as it was for Miss Coleman. He wrote to his wife that, if her sister would keep her there till he got a place, it would be better for them, and he would be greatly obliged to her. Meantime, the gentleman who had bought the house had allowed his furniture to remain where it was for a little while.

Diamond's aunt was quite willing to keep them as long as she could. And indeed Diamond was not yet well enough to be moved with safety.

When he had recovered so far as to be able to go out, one day his mother got her sister's husband, who had a little pony-cart, to carry them down to the sea-shore, and leave them there for a few hours. He had some business to do further on at Ramsgate, and would pick them up as he returned. A whiff of the sea-air would do them both good, she said, and she thought besides she could best tell Diamond what had happened if she had him quite to herself.

13. THE SEASIDE

Diamond and his mother sat down upon the edge of the rough grass that bordered the sand. The sun was just far enough past its highest not to shine in their eyes when they looked eastward. A sweet little wind blew on their left side, and comforted the mother without letting her know what it was that comforted her. Away before them stretched the sparkling waters of the ocean, every wave of which flashed out its own delight back in the face of the great sun, which looked down from the stillness of its blue house with glorious silent face upon its flashing children. On each hand the shore rounded outwards, forming a little bay. There were no white cliffs here, as further north and south, and the place was rather dreary, but the sky got at them so much the better. Not a house, not a creature was within sight. Dry sand was about their feet, and under them thin wiry grass, that just managed to grow out of the poverty-stricken shore.

"Oh dear!" said Diamond's mother, with a deep sigh, "it's a sad world!"

"Is it?" said Diamond. "I didn't know."

"How should you know, child? You've been too well taken care of, I trust."

"Oh yes, I have," returned Diamond. "I'm sorry! I thought you were taken care of too. I thought my father took care of you. I will ask him about it. I think he must have forgotten."

"Dear boy!" said his mother. "your father's the best man in the world."

"So I thought!" returned Diamond with triumph. "I was sure of it! — Well, doesn't he take very good care of you?"

"Yes, yes, he does," answered his mother, bursting into tears. "But who's to take care of him? And how is he to take care of us if he's got nothing to eat himself?"

"Oh dear!" said Diamond with a gasp; "hasn't he got anything to eat? Oh! I must go home to him."

"No, no, child. He's not come to that yet. But what's to become of us, I don't know."

"Are you very hungry, mother? There's the basket. I thought you put something to eat in it."

"O you darling stupid! I didn't say I was hungry," returned his mother, smiling through her tears.

"Then I don't understand you at all," said Diamond. "Do tell me what's the matter."

"There are people in the world who have nothing to eat, Diamond."

"Then I suppose they don't stop in it any longer. They — they — what you call — die —don't they?"

"Yes, they do. How would you like that?"

"I don't know. I never tried. But I suppose they go where they get something to eat."

"Like enough they don't want it," said his mother, petulantly.

"That's all right then," said Diamond, thinking I daresay more than he chose to put in words.

"Is it though? Poor boy! how little you know about things! Mr. Coleman's lost all his money, and your father has nothing to do, and we shall have nothing to eat by and by."

"Are you sure, mother?"

"Sure of what?"

"Sure that we shall have nothing to eat."

"No, thank Heaven! I'm not sure of it. I hope not."

"Then I can't understand it, mother. There's a piece of gingerbread in the basket, I know."

"O you little bird! You have no more sense than a sparrow that picks what it wants, and never thinks of the winter and the frost and, the snow."

"Ah — yes — I see. But the birds get through the winter, don't they?"

"Some of them fall dead on the ground."

"They must die some time. They wouldn't like to be birds always. Would you, mother?"

"What a child it is!" thought his mother, but she said nothing.

"Oh! now I remember," Diamond went on. "Father told me that day I went to Epping Forest with him, that the rose-bushes, and the may-bushes, and the holly-bushes were the bird's barns, for there were the hips, and the haws, and the holly-berries, all ready for the winter."

"Yes; that's all very true. So you see the birds are provided for. But there are no such barns for you and me, Diamond."

"Ain't there?"

"No. We've got to work for our bread."

"Then let's go and work," said Diamond, getting up.

"It's no use. We've not got anything to do."

"Then let's wait."

"Then we shall starve."

"No. There's the basket. Do you know, mother, I think I shall call that basket the barn."

"It's not a very big one. And when it's empty — where are we then?"

"At auntie's cupboard," returned Diamond promptly.

"But we can't eat auntie's things all up and leave her to starve."

"No, no. We'll go back to father before that. He'll have found a cupboard somewhere by that time."

"How do you know that?"

"I don't know it. But I haven't got even a cupboard, and I've always had plenty to eat. I've heard you say I had too much, sometimes."

"But I tell you that's because I've had a cupboard for you, child."

"And when yours was empty, auntie opened hers."

"But that can't go on."

"How do you know? I think there must be a big cupboard somewhere, out of which the little cupboards are filled, you know, mother."

"Well, I wish I could find the door of that cupboard," said his mother. But the same moment she stopped, and was silent for a good while. I cannot tell whether Diamond knew what she was thinking, but I think I know. She had heard something at church the day before, which came back upon her — something like this, that she hadn't to eat for tomorrow as well as for to-day; and that what was not wanted couldn't be missed. So, instead of saying anything more, she stretched out her hand for the basket, and she and Diamond had their dinner.

And Diamond did enjoy it. For the drive and the fresh air had made him quite hungry; and he did not, like his mother, trouble himself about what they should dine off that day week. The fact was he had lived so long without any food at all at the back of the north wind, that he knew quite well that food was not essential to existence; that in fact, under certain circumstances, people could live without it well enough.

His mother did not speak much during their dinner. After it was over she helped him to walk about a little, but he was not able for much and soon got tired. He did not get fretful, though. He was too glad of having the sun and the wind again, to fret because he could not run about. He lay down on the dry sand, and his mother covered him with a shawl. She then sat by his side, and took a bit of work from her pocket. But Diamond felt rather sleepy, and turned on his side and gazed sleepily over the sand. A few yards off he saw something fluttering.

"What is that, mother?" he said.

"Only a bit of paper," she answered.

"It flutters more than a bit of paper would, I think," said Diamond.

"I'll go and see if you like," said his mother. "My eyes are none of the best."

So she rose and went and found that they were both right, for it was a little book, partly buried in the sand. But several of its leaves were clear of the sand, and these the wind kept blowing about in a very flutterful manner. She took it up and brought it to Diamond.

"What is it, mother?" he asked.

"Some nursery rhymes, I think," she answered.

"I'm too sleepy," said Diamond. "Do read some of them to me."

"Yes, I will," she said, and began one.—"But this is such nonsense!" she said again. "I will try to find a better one."

She turned the leaves searching, but three times, with sudden puffs, the wind blew the leaves rustling back to the same verses.

"Do read that one," said Diamond, who seemed to be of the same mind as the wind. "It sounded very nice. I am sure it is a good one."

So his mother thought it might amuse him, though she couldn't find any sense in it. She never thought he might understand it, although she could not.

Now I do not exactly know what the mother read, but this is what Diamond heard, or thought afterwards that he had heard. He was, however, as I have said, very sleepy. And when he thought he understood the verses he may have been only dreaming better ones. This is how they went —

I know a river

whose waters run asleep

run run ever

singing in the shallows

dumb in the hollows

sleeping so deep

and all the swallows

that dip their feathers

in the hollows

or in the shallows

are the merriest swallows of all

for the nests they bake

with the clay they cake

with the water they shake

from their wings that rake

the water out of the shallows

or the hollows

will hold together

in any weather

and so the swallows

are the merriest fellows

and have the merriest children

and are built so narrow

like the head of an arrow

to cut the air

and go just where

the nicest water is flowing

and the nicest dust is blowing

for each so narrow

like head of an arrow

is only a barrow

to carry the mud he makes

from the nicest water flowing

and the nicest dust that is blowing

to build his nest

for her he loves best

with the nicest cakes

which the sunshine bakes

all for their merry children

all so callow

with beaks that follow

gaping and hollow

wider and wider

after their father

or after their mother

the food-provider

who brings them a spider

or a worm the poor hider

down in the earth

so there's no dearth

for their beaks as yellow

as the buttercups growing

beside the flowing

of the singing river

always and ever

growing and blowing

for fast as the sheep

awake or asleep

crop them and crop them

they cannot stop them

but up they creep

and on they go blowing

and so with the daisies

the little white praises

they grow and they blow

and they spread out their crown

and they praise the sun

and when he goes down

their praising is done

and they fold up their crown

and they sleep every one

till over the plain

he's shining amain

and they're at it again

praising and praising

such low songs raising

that no one hears them

but the sun who rears them

and the sheep that bite them

are the quietest sheep

awake or asleep

with the merriest bleat

and the little lambs

are the merriest lambs

they forget to eat

for the frolic in their feet

and the lambs and their dams

are the whitest sheep

with the woolliest wool

and the longest wool

and the trailingest tails

and they shine like snow

in the grasses that grow

by the singing river

that sings for ever

and the sheep and the lambs

are merry for ever

because the river

sings and they drink it

and the lambs and their dams

are quiet

and white

because of their diet

for what they bite
is buttercups yellow
and daisies white
and grass as green
as the river can make it
with wind as mellow
to kiss it and shake it
as never was seen
but here in the hollows
beside the river
where all the swallows
are merriest of fellows
for the nests they make
with the clay they cake
in the sunshine bake
till they are like bone
as dry in the wind
as a marble stone
so firm they bind
the grass in the clay
that dries in the wind
the sweetest wind
that blows by the river
flowing for ever
but never you find
whence comes the wind
that blows on the hollows
and over the shallows
where dip the swallows
alive it blows
the life as it goes
awake or asleep
into the river
that sings as it flows
and the life it blows
into the sheep awake or asleep
with the woolliest wool

and the trailingest tails
and it never fails
gentle and cool
to wave the wool
and to toss the grass
as the lambs and the sheep
over it pass
and tug and bite
with their teeth so white
and then with the sweep
of their trailing tails
smooth it again
and it grows amain
and amain it grows
and the wind as it blows
tosses the swallows
over the hollows
and down on the shallows
till every feather
doth shake and quiver
and all their feathers
go all together
blowing the life
and the joy so rife
into the swallows
that skim the shallows
and have the yellowest children
for the wind that blows
is the life of the river
flowing for ever
that washes the grasses
still as it passes
and feeds the daisies
the little white praises
and buttercups bonny
so golden and sunny
with butter and honey

that whiten the sheep

awake or asleep

that nibble and bite

and grow whiter than white

and merry and quiet

on the sweet diet

fed by the river

and tossed for ever

by the wind that tosses

the swallow that crosses

over the shallows

dipping his wings

to gather the water

and bake the cake

that the wind shall make

as hard as a bone

as dry as a stone

it's all in the wind

that blows from behind

and all in the river

that flows for ever

and all in the grasses

and the white daisies

and the merry sheep

awake or asleep

and the happy swallows

skimming the shallows

and it's all in the wind

that blows from behind

Here Diamond became aware that his mother had stopped reading.

"Why don't you go on, mother dear?" he asked.

"It's such nonsense!" said his mother. "I believe it would go on for ever."

"That's just what it did," said Diamond.

"What did?" she asked.

"Why, the river. That's almost the very tune it used to sing."

His mother was frightened, for she thought the fever was coming on again. So she did not contradict him.

"Who made that poem?" asked Diamond.

"I don't know," she answered. "Some silly woman for her children, I suppose—and then thought it good enough to print."

"She must have been at the back of the north wind some time or other, anyhow," said Diamond. "She couldn't have got a hold of it anywhere else. That's just how it went." And he began to chant bits of it here and there; but his mother said nothing for fear of making him, worse; and she was very glad indeed when she saw her brother-in-law jogging along in his little cart. They lifted Diamond in, and got up themselves, and away they went, "home again, home again, home again," as Diamond sang. But he soon grew quiet, and before they reached Sandwich he was fast asleep and dreaming of the country at the back of the north wind.

14. OLD DIAMOND

After this Diamond recovered so fast, that in a few days he was quite able to go home as soon as his father had a place for them to go. Now his father having saved a little money, and finding that no situation offered itself, had been thinking over a new plan. A strange occurrence it was which turned his thoughts in that direction. He had a friend in the Bloomsbury region, who lived by letting out cabs and horses to the cabmen. This man, happening to meet him one day as he was returning from an unsuccessful application, said to him:

"Why don't you set up for yourself now — in the cab line, I mean?"

"I haven't enough for that," answered Diamond's father.

"You must have saved a goodish bit, I should think. Just come home with me now and look at a horse I can let you have cheap. I bought him only a few weeks ago, thinking he'd do for a Hansom, but I was wrong. He's got bone enough for a waggon, but a waggon ain't a Hansom. He ain't got go enough for a Hansom. You see parties as takes Hansoms wants to go like the wind, and he ain't got wind enough, for he ain't so young as he once was. But for a four-wheeler as takes families and their luggage, he's the very horse. He'd carry a small house any day. I bought him cheap, and I'll sell him cheap."

"Oh, I don't want him," said Diamond's father. "A body must have time to think over an affair of so much importance. And there's the cab too. That would come to a deal of money."

"I could fit you there, I daresay," said his friend. "But come and look at the animal, anyhow."

"Since I lost my own old pair, as was Mr. Coleman's," said Diamond's father, turning to accompany the cab-master, "I ain't almost got the heart to look a horse in the face. It's a thousand pities to part man and horse."

"So it is," returned his friend sympathetically.

But what was the ex-coachman's delight, when, on going into the stable where his friend led him, he found the horse he wanted him to buy was no other than his own old Diamond, grown very thin and bony and long-legged, as if they, had been doing what they could to fit him for Hansom work!

"He ain't a Hansom horse," said Diamond's father indignantly.

"Well, you're right. He ain't handsome, but he's a good un" said his owner.

"Who says he ain't handsome? He's one of the handsomest horses a gentleman's coachman ever druv," said Diamond's father; remarking to himself under his breath—"though I says it as shouldn't" — for he did not feel inclined all at once to confess that his own old horse could have sunk so low.

"Well," said his friend, "all I say is — There's a animal for you, as strong as a church; an'll go like a train, leastways a parly," he added, correcting himself.

But the coachman had a lump in his throat and tears in his eyes. For the old horse, hearing his voice, had turned his long neck, and when his old friend went up to him and laid his hand on his side, he whinnied for joy, and laid his big head on his master's breast. This settled the matter. The coachman's arms were round the horse's neck in a moment, and he fairly broke down and cried. The cab-master had never been so fond of a horse himself as to hug him like that, but he saw in a moment how it was. And he must have been a good-hearted fellow, for I never heard of such an idea coming into the head of any other man with a horse to sell: instead of putting something on to the price because he was now pretty sure of selling him, he actually took a pound off what he had meant to ask for him, saying to himself it was a shame to part old friends.

Diamond's father, as soon as he came to himself, turned and asked how much he wanted for the horse.

"I see you're old friends," said the owner.

"It's my own old Diamond. I liked him far the best of the pair, though the other was good. You ain't got him too, have you?"

"No; nothing in the stable to match him there."

"I believe you," said the coachman. "But you'll be wanting a long price for him, I know."

"No, not so much. I bought him cheap, and as I say, he ain't for my work."

The end of it was that Diamond's father bought old Diamond again, along with a four-wheeled cab. And as there were some rooms to be had over the stable, he took them, wrote to his wife to come home, and set up as a cabman.

15. THE MEWS

It was late in the afternoon when Diamond and his mother and the baby reached London. I was so full of Diamond that I forgot to tell you a baby had arrived in the meantime. His father was waiting for them with his own cab, but they had not told Diamond who the horse was; for his father wanted to enjoy the pleasure of his surprise when he found it out. He got in with his mother without looking at the horse, and his father having put up Diamond's carpet-bag and his mother's little trunk, got upon the box himself and drove off; and Diamond was quite proud of riding home in his father's own carriage. But when he got to the mews, he could not help being a little dismayed at first; and if he had never been to the back of the north wind, I am afraid he would have cried a little. But instead of that, he said to himself it was a fine thing all the old furniture was there. And instead of helping his mother to be miserable at the change, he began to find out all the advantages of the place; for every place has some advantages, and they are always better worth knowing than the disadvantages. Certainly the weather was depressing, for a thick, dull, persistent rain was falling by the time they reached home. But happily the weather is very changeable; and besides, there was a good fire burning in the room, which their neighbor with the drunken husband had attended to for them; and the tea-things were put out, and the kettle was boiling on the fire. And with a good fire, and tea and bread and butter, things cannot be said to be miserable.

Diamond's father and mother were, notwithstanding, rather miserable, and Diamond began to feel a kind of darkness beginning to spread over his own mind. But the same moment he said to himself, "This will never do. I can't give in to this. I've been to the back of the north wind. Things go right there, and so I must try to get things to go right here. I've got to fight the miserable things. They shan't make me miserable if I can help it." I do not mean that he thought these very words. They are perhaps too grown-up for him to have thought, but they represent the kind of thing that was in his heart and his head. And when heart and head go together, nothing can stand before them.

"What nice bread and butter this is!" said Diamond.

"I'm glad you like it, my dear" said his father. "I bought the butter myself at the little shop round the corner."

"It's very nice, thank you, father. Oh, there's baby waking! I'll take him."

"Sit still, Diamond," said his mother. "Go on with your bread and butter. You're not strong enough to lift him yet."

So she took the baby herself, and set him on her knee. Then Diamond began to amuse him, and went on till the little fellow was shrieking with laughter. For the baby's world was his mother's arms; and the drizzling rain, and the dreary mews, and even his father's troubled face could not touch him. What cared baby for the loss of a hundred situations? Yet neither father nor mother thought him hard-hearted because he crowed and laughed in the middle of their troubles. On the contrary, his crowing and laughing were infectious. His little heart was so full of merriment that it could not hold it all, and it ran over into theirs. Father and mother began to laugh too, and Diamond laughed till he had a fit of coughing which frightened his mother, and made them all stop. His father took the baby, and his mother put him to bed.

But it was indeed a change to them all, not only from Sandwich, but from their old place, instead of the great river where the huge barges with their mighty brown and yellow sails went tacking from side to side like little pleasure-skiffs, and where the long thin boats shot past with eight and sometimes twelve rowers, their windows now looked out upon a dirty paved yard. And there was no garden more for Diamond to run into when he pleased, with gay flowers about his feet, and solemn sun-filled trees over his head. Neither was there a wooden wall at the back of his bed with a hole in it for North Wind to come in at when she liked. Indeed, there was such a high wall, and there were so many houses about the mews, that North Wind seldom got into the place at all, except when something must be done, and she had a grand cleaning out like other housewives; while the partition at the head of Diamond's new bed only divided it from the room occupied by a cabman who drank too much beer, and came home chiefly to quarrel with his wife and pinch his children. It was dreadful to Diamond to hear the scolding and the crying. But it could not make him miserable, because he had been at the back of the north wind.

If my reader find it hard to believe that Diamond should be so good, he must remember that he had been to the back of the north wind. If he never knew a boy so good, did he ever know a boy that had been to the back of the north wind? It was not in the least strange of Diamond to behave as he did; on the contrary, it was thoroughly sensible of him.

We shall see how he got on.

16. DIAMOND MAKES A BEGINNING

The wind blew loud, but Diamond slept a deep sleep, and never heard it. My own impression is that every time when Diamond slept well and remembered nothing about it in the morning, he had been all that night at the back of the north wind. I am almost sure that was how he woke so refreshed, and felt so quiet and hopeful all the day. Indeed he said this much, though not to me—that always when he woke from such a sleep there was a something in his mind, he could not tell what—could not tell whether it was the last far-off sounds of the river dying away in the distance, or some of the words of the endless song his mother had read to him on the sea-shore. Sometimes he thought it must have been the twittering of the swallows — over the shallows, you, know; but it may have been the chirping of the dingy sparrows picking up their breakfast in the yard - how can I tell? I don't know what I know, I only know what I think; and to tell the truth, I am more for the swallows than the sparrows. When he knew he was coming awake, he would sometimes try hard to keep hold of the words of what seemed a new song, one he had not heard before—a song in which the words and the music somehow appeared to be all one; but even when he thought he had got them well fixed in his mind, ever as he came awaker — as he would say — one line faded away out of it, and then another, and then another, till at last there was nothing left but some lovely picture of water or grass or daisies, or something else very common, but with all the commonness polished off it, and the lovely soul of it, which people so seldom see, and, alas! yet seldomer believe in, shining out. But after that he would sing the oddest, loveliest little songs to the baby — of his own making, his mother said; but Diamond said he did not make them; they were made somewhere inside him, and he knew nothing about them till they were coming out.

When he woke that first morning he got up at once, saying to himself, "I've been ill long enough, and have given a great deal of trouble; I must try and be of use now, and help my mother." When he went into her room he found her lighting the fire, and his father just getting out of bed. They had only the one room, besides the little one, not much more than a closet, in which Diamond slept. He began at once to set things to rights, but the baby waking up, he took him, and nursed him till his mother had got the breakfast ready. She was looking gloomy, and his father was silent; and indeed except Diamond had done all he possibly could to keep out the misery that was trying to get in at doors and windows, he too would have grown miserable, and then they would have been all miserable together. But to try to make others comfortable is the only way to get right comfortable ourselves, and that comes partly of not being able to think so much about ourselves when we are helping other people. For our Selves will always do pretty well if we don't pay them too much attention. Our Selves are like some little children who will be happy enough so long as they are left to their own games, but when we begin to interfere with them, and make them presents of too nice playthings, or too many sweet things, they begin at once to fret and spoil.

"Why, Diamond, child!" said his mother at last, "you're as good to your mother as if you were a girl — nursing the baby, and toasting the bread, and sweeping up the hearth! I declare a body would think you had been among the fairies."

Could Diamond have had greater praise or greater pleasure? You see when he forgot his Self his mother took care of his Self, and loved and praised his Self. Our own praises poison our Selves, and puff and swell them up, till they lose all shape and beauty, and become like great toadstools. But the praises of father or mother do our Selves good, and comfort them and make them beautiful. They never do them any harm. If they do any harm, it comes of our mixing some of our own praises with them, and that turns them nasty and slimy and poisonous.

When his father had finished his breakfast, which he did rather in a hurry, he got up and went down into the yard to get out his horse and put him to the cab.

"Won't you come and see the cab, Diamond?" he said.

"Yes, please, father — if mother can spare me a minute," answered Diamond.

"Bless the child! I don't want him," said his mother cheerfully.

But as he was following his father out of the door, she called him back.

"Diamond, just hold the baby one minute. I have something to say to your father."

So Diamond sat down again, took the baby in his lap, and began poking his face into its little body, laughing and singing all the while, so that the baby crowed like a little bantam. And what he sang was something like this—such nonsense to those that couldn't understand it! but not to the baby, who got all the good in the world out of it:—

baby's a-sleeping wake up baby for all the swallows are the merriest fellows and have the yellowest children who would go sleeping and snore like a gaby disturbing his mother and father and brother and all a-boring their ears with his snoring snoring snoring for himself and no other for himself in particular wake up baby sit up perpendicular hark to the gushing hark to the rushing where the sheep are the woolliest and the lambs the unruliest and their tails the whitest and their eyes the brightest and baby's the bonniest and baby's the funniest and baby's the shiniest and baby's the tiniest and baby's the merriest and baby's the worriest of all the lambs that plague their dams and mother's the whitest of all the dams that feed the lambs that go crop-cropping without stop-stopping and father's the best of all the swallows that build their nest out of the shining shallows and he has the merriest children that's baby and Diamond and Diamond and baby and baby and Diamond and Diamond and baby

Here Diamond's knees went off in a wild dance which tossed the baby about and shook the laughter out of him in immoderate peals. His mother had been listening at the door to the last few lines of his song, and came in with the tears in her eyes. She took the baby from him, gave him a kiss, and told him to run to his father.

By the time Diamond got into the yard, the horse was between the shafts, and his father was looping the traces on. Diamond went round to look at the horse. The sight of him made him feel very queer. He did not know much about different horses, and all other horses than their own were very much the same to him. But he could not make it out. This was Diamond and it wasn't Diamond. Diamond didn't hang his head like that; yet the head that was hanging was very like the one that Diamond used to hold so high. Diamond's bones didn't show through his skin like that; but the skin they pushed out of shape so was very like Diamond's skin; and the bones might be Diamond's bones, for he had never seen the shape of them. But when he came round in front of the old horse, and he put out his long neck, and began sniffing at him and rubbing his upper lip and his nose on him, then Diamond saw it could be no other than old Diamond, and he did just as his father had done before — put his arms round his neck and cried—but not much.

"Ain't it jolly, father?" he said. "Was there ever anybody so lucky as me? Dear old Diamond!"

And he hugged the horse again, and kissed both his big hairy cheeks. He could only manage one at a time, however—the other cheek was so far off on the other side of his big head.

His father mounted the box with just the same air, as Diamond thought, with which he had used to get upon the coach-box, and Diamond said to himself, "Father's as grand as ever anyhow." He had kept his brown livery-coat, only his wife had taken the silver buttons off and put brass ones instead, because they did not think it polite to Mr. Coleman in his fallen fortunes to let his crest be seen upon the box of a cab. Old Diamond had kept just his collar; and that had the silver crest upon it still, for his master thought nobody would notice that, and so let it remain for a memorial of the better days of which it reminded him — not unpleasantly, seeing it had been by no fault either of his or of the old horse's that they had come down in the world together.

"Oh, father, do let me drive a bit," said Diamond, jumping up on the box beside him.

His father changed places with him at once, putting the reins into his hands. Diamond gathered them up eagerly.

"Don't pull at his mouth," said his father. "just feel, at it gently to let him know you're there and attending to him. That's what I call talking to him through the reins."

"Yes, father, I understand," said Diamond. Then to the horse he said, "Go on Diamond." And old Diamond's ponderous bulk began at once to move to the voice of the little boy.

But before they had reached the entrance of the mews, another voice called after young Diamond, which, in his turn, he had to obey, for it was that of his mother. "Diamond! Diamond!" it cried; and Diamond pulled the reins, and the horse stood still as a stone.

"Husband," said his mother, coming up, "you're never going to trust him with the reins—a baby like that?"

"He must learn some day, and he can't begin too soon. I see already he's a born coachman," said his father proudly. "And I don't see well how he could escape it, for my father and my grandfather, that's his great-grandfather, was all coachmen, I'm told; so it must come natural to him, any one would think. Besides, you see, old Diamond's as proud of him as we are our own selves, wife. Don't you see how he's turning round his ears, with the mouths of them open, for the first word he speaks to tumble in? He's too well bred to turn his head, you know."

"Well, but, husband, I can't do without him to-day. Everything's got to be done, you know. It's my first day here. And there's that baby!"

"Bless you, wife! I never meant to take him away—only to the bottom of Endell Street. He can watch his way back."

"No thank you, father; not to-day," said Diamond. "Mother wants me. Perhaps she'll let me go another day."

"Very well, my man," said his father, and took the reins which Diamond was holding out to him.

Diamond got down, a little disappointed of course, and went with his mother, who was too pleased to speak. She only took hold of his hand as tight as if she had been afraid of his running away instead of glad that he would not leave her.

Now, although they did not know it, the owner of the stables, the same man who had sold the horse to his father, had been standing just inside one of the stable-doors, with his hands in his pockets, and had heard and seen all that passed; and from that day John Stonecrop took a great fancy to the little boy. And this was the beginning of what came of it.

The same evening, just as Diamond was feeling tired of the day's work, and wishing his father would come home, Mr. Stonecrop knocked at the door. His mother went and opened it.

"Good evening, ma'am," said he. "Is the little master in?"

"Yes, to be sure he is—at your service, I'm sure, Mr. Stonecrop," said his mother.

"No, no, ma'am; it's I'm at his service. I'm just a-going out with my own cab, and if he likes to come with me, he shall drive my old horse till he's tired."

"It's getting rather late for him," said his mother thoughtfully. "You see he's been an invalid."

Diamond thought, what a funny thing! How could he have been an invalid when he did not even know what the word meant? But, of course, his mother was right.

"Oh, well," said Mr. Stonecrop, "I can just let him drive through Bloomsbury Square, and then he shall run home again."

"Very good, sir. And I'm much obliged to you," said his mother. And Diamond, dancing with delight, got his cap, put his hand in Mr. Stonecrop's, and went with him to the yard where the cab was waiting. He did not think the horse looked nearly so nice as Diamond, nor Mr. Stonecrop nearly so grand as his father; but he was none, the less pleased. He got up on the box, and his new friend got up beside him.

"What's the horse's name?" whispered Diamond, as he took the reins from the man.

"It's not a nice name," said Mr. Stonecrop. "You needn't call him by it. I didn't give it him. He'll go well enough without it. Give the boy a whip, Jack. I never carries one when I drive old——"

He didn't finish the sentence. Jack handed Diamond a whip, with which, by holding it half down the stick, he managed just to flack the haunches of the horse; and away he went.

"Mind the gate," said Mr. Stonecrop; and Diamond did mind the gate, and guided the nameless horse through it in safety, pulling him this way and that according as was necessary. Diamond learned to drive all the sooner that he had been accustomed to do what he was told, and could obey the smallest hint in a moment. Nothing helps one to get on like that. Some people don't know how to do what they are told; they have not been used to it, and they neither understand quickly nor are able to turn what they do understand into action quickly. With an obedient mind one learns the rights of things fast enough; for it is the law of the universe, and to obey is to understand.

"Look out!" cried Mr. Stonecrop, as they were turning the corner into Bloomsbury Square.

It was getting dusky now. A cab was approaching rather rapidly from the opposite direction, and Diamond pulling aside, and the other driver pulling up, they only just escaped a collision. Then they knew each other.

"Why, Diamond, it's a bad beginning to run into your own father," cried the driver.

"But, father, wouldn't it have been a bad ending to run into your own son?" said Diamond in return; and the two men laughed heartily.

"This is very kind of you, I'm sure, Stonecrop," said his father.

"Not a bit. He's a brave fellow, and'll be fit to drive on his own hook in a week or two. But I think you'd better let him drive you home now, for his mother don't like his having over much of the night air, and I promised not to take him farther than the square."

"Come along then, Diamond," said his father, as he brought his cab up to the other, and moved off the box to the seat beside it. Diamond jumped across, caught at the reins, said "Good-night, and thank you, Mr. Stonecrop," and drove away home, feeling more of a man than he had ever yet had a chance of feeling in all his life. Nor did his father find it necessary to give him a single hint as to his driving. Only I suspect the fact that it was old Diamond, and old Diamond on his way to his stable, may have had something to do with young Diamond's success.

"Well, child," said his mother, when he entered the room, "you've not been long gone."

"No, mother; here I am. Give me the baby."

"The baby's asleep," said his mother.

"Then give him to me, and I'll lay him down."

But as Diamond took him, he woke up and began to laugh. For he was indeed one of the merriest children. And no wonder, for he was as plump as a plum-pudding, and had never had an ache or a pain that lasted more than five minutes at a time. Diamond sat down with him and began to sing to him.

Baby baby babbing your father's gone a-cabbing to catch a shilling for its pence to make the baby babbing dance for old Diamond's a duck they say he can swim but the duck of diamonds is baby that's him and of all the swallows the merriest fellows that bake their cake with the water they shake out of the river flowing for ever and make dust into clay on the shiniest day to build their nest father's the best and mother's the whitest and her eyes are the brightest of all the dams that watch their lambs cropping the grass where the waters pass singing for ever and of all the lambs with the shakingest tails and the jumpingest feet baby's the funniest baby's the bonniest and he never wails and he's always sweet and Diamond's his nurse and Diamond's his nurse and Diamond's his nurse

When Diamond's rhymes grew scarce, he always began dancing the baby. Some people wondered that such a child could rhyme as he did, but his rhymes were not very good, for he was only trying to remember what he had heard the river sing at the back of the north wind.

17. DIAMOND GOES ON

Diamond became a great favorite with all the men about the mews. Some may think it was not the best place in the world for him to be brought up in; but it must have been, for there he was. At first, he heard a good many rough and bad words; but he did not like them, and so they did him little harm. He did not know in the least what they meant, but there was something in the very sound of them, and in the tone of voice in which they were said, which Diamond felt to be ugly. So they did not even stick to him, not to say get inside him. He never took any notice of them, and his face shone pure and good in the middle of them, like a primrose in a hailstorm. At first, because his face was so quiet and sweet, with a smile always either awake or asleep in his eyes, and because he never heeded their ugly words and rough jokes, they said he wasn't all there, meaning that he was half an idiot, whereas he was a great deal more there than they had the sense to see. And before long the bad words found themselves ashamed to come out of the men's mouths when Diamond was near. The one would nudge the other to remind him that the boy was within hearing, and the words choked themselves before they got any farther. When they talked to him nicely he had always a good answer, sometimes a smart one, ready, and that helped much to make them change their minds about him.

One day Jack gave him a curry-comb and a brush to try his hand upon old Diamond's coat. He used them so deftly, so gently, and yet so thoroughly, as far as he could reach, that the man could not help admiring him.

"You must make haste and, grow" he said. "It won't do to have a horse's belly clean and his back dirty, you know."

"Give me a leg," said Diamond, and in a moment he was on the old horse's back with the comb and brush. He sat on his withers, and reaching forward as he ate his hay, he curried and he brushed, first at one side of his neck, and then at the other. When that was done he asked for a dressing-comb, and combed his mane thoroughly. Then he pushed himself on to his back, and did his shoulders as far down as he could reach. Then he sat on his croup, and did his back and sides; then he turned around like a monkey, and attacked his hind-quarters, and combed his tail. This last was not so easy to manage, for he had to lift it up, and every now and then old Diamond would whisk it out of his hands, and once he sent the comb flying out of the stable door, to the great amusement of the men. But Jack fetched it again, and Diamond began once more, and did not leave off until he had done the whole business fairly well, if not in a first-rate, experienced fashion. All the time the old horse went on eating his hay, and, but with an occasional whisk of his tail when Diamond tickled or scratched him, took no notice of the proceeding. But that was all a pretence, for he knew very well who it was that was perched on his back, and rubbing away at him with the comb and the brush. So he was quite pleased and proud, and perhaps said to himself something like this—

"I'm a stupid old horse, who can't brush his own coat; but there's my young godson on my back, cleaning me like an angel."

I won't vouch for what the old horse was thinking, for it is very difficult to find out what any old horse is thinking.

"Oh dear!" said Diamond when he had done, "I'm so tired!"

And he laid himself down at full length on old Diamond's back.

By this time all the men in the stable were gathered about the two Diamonds, and all much amused. One of them lifted him down, and from that time he was a greater favorite than before. And if ever there was a boy who had a chance of being a prodigy at cab-driving, Diamond was that boy, for the strife came to be who should have him out with him on the box.

His mother, however, was a little shy of the company for him, and besides she could not always spare him. Also his father liked to have him himself when he could; so that he was more desired than enjoyed among the cabmen.

But one way and another he did learn to drive all sorts of horses, and to drive them well, and that through the most crowded streets in London City. Of course there was the man always on the box-seat beside him, but before long there was seldom the least occasion to take the reins from out of his hands. For one thing he never got frightened, and consequently was never in too great a hurry. Yet when the moment came for doing something sharp, he was always ready for it. I must once more remind my readers that he had been to the back of the north wind.

One day, which was neither washing-day, nor cleaning-day nor marketing-day, nor Saturday, nor Monday — upon which consequently Diamond could be spared from the baby — his father took him on his own cab. After a stray job or two by the way, they drew up in the row upon the stand between Cockspur Street and Pall Mall. They waited a long time, but nobody seemed to want to be carried anywhere. By and by ladies would be going home from the Academy exhibition, and then there would be a chance of a job.

"Though, to be sure," said Diamond's father — with what truth I cannot say, but he believed what he said — "some ladies is very hard, and keeps you to the bare sixpence a mile, when every one knows that ain't enough to keep a family and a cab upon. To be sure it's the law; but mayhap they may get more law than they like some day themselves."

As it was very hot, Diamond's father got down to have a glass of beer himself, and give another to the old waterman. He left Diamond on the box.

A sudden noise got up, and Diamond looked round to see what was the matter.

There was a crossing near the cab-stand, where a girl was sweeping. Some rough young imps had picked a quarrel with her, and were now hauling at her broom to get it away from her. But as they did not pull all together, she was holding it against them, scolding and entreating alternately.

Diamond was off his box in a moment, and running to the help of the girl. He got hold of the broom at her end and pulled along with her. But the boys proceeded to rougher measures, and one of them hit Diamond on the nose, and made it bleed; and as he could not let go the broom to mind his nose, he was soon a dreadful figure. But presently his father came back, and missing Diamond, looked about. He had to look twice, however, before he could be sure that that was his boy in the middle of the tumult. He rushed in, and sent the assailants flying in all directions. The girl thanked Diamond, and began sweeping as if nothing had happened, while his father led him away. With the help of old Tom, the waterman, he was soon washed into decency, and his father set him on the box again, perfectly satisfied with the account he gave of the cause of his being in a fray.

"I couldn't let them behave so to a poor girl—could I, father?" he said.

"Certainly not, Diamond," said his father, quite pleased, for Diamond's father was a gentleman.

A moment after, up came the girl, running, with her broom over her shoulder, and calling, "Cab, there! cab!"

Diamond's father turned instantly, for he was the foremost in the rank, and followed the girl. One or two other passing cabs heard the cry, and made for the place, but the girl had taken care not to call till she was near enough to give her friends the first chance. When they reached the curbstone—who should it be waiting for the cab but Mrs. and Miss Coleman! They did not look at the cabman, however. The girl opened the door for them; they gave her the address, and a penny; she told the cabman, and away they drove.

When they reached the house, Diamond's father got down and rang the bell. As he opened the door of the cab, he touched his hat as he had been wont to do. The ladies both stared for a moment, and then exclaimed together:

"Why, Joseph! can it be you?"

"Yes, ma'am; yes, miss," answered he, again touching his hat, with all the respect he could possibly put into the action. "It's a lucky day which I see you once more upon it."

"Who would have thought it?" said Mrs. Coleman. "It's changed times for both of us, Joseph, and it's not very often we can have a cab even; but you see my daughter is still very poorly, and she can't bear the motion of the omnibuses. Indeed we meant to walk a bit first before we took a cab, but just at the corner, for as hot as the sun was, a cold wind came down the street, and I saw that Miss Coleman must not face it. But to think we should have fallen upon you, of all the cabmen in London! I didn't know you had got a cab."

"Well, you see, ma'am, I had a chance of buying the old horse, and I couldn't resist him. There he is, looking at you, ma'am. Nobody knows the sense in that head of his."

The two ladies went near to pat the horse, and then they noticed Diamond on the box.

"Why, you've got both Diamonds with you," said Miss Coleman. "How do you do, Diamond?"

Diamond lifted his cap, and answered politely.

"He'll be fit to drive himself before long," said his father, proudly. "The old horse is a-teaching of him."

"Well, he must come and see us, now you've found us out. Where do you live?"

Diamond's father gave the ladies a ticket with his name and address printed on it; and then Mrs. Coleman took out her purse, saying:

"And what's your fare, Joseph?"

"No, thank you, ma'am," said Joseph. "It was your own old horse as took you; and me you paid long ago."

He jumped on his box before she could say another word, and with a parting salute drove off, leaving them on the pavement, with the maid holding the door for them.

It was a long time now since Diamond had seen North Wind, or even thought much about her. And as his father drove along, he was thinking not about her, but about the crossing-sweeper, and was wondering what made him feel as if he knew her quite well, when he could not remember anything of her. But a picture arose in his mind of a little girl running before the wind and dragging her broom after her; and from that, by degrees, he recalled the whole adventure of the night when he got down from North Wind's back in a London street. But he could not quite satisfy himself whether the whole affair was not a dream which he had dreamed when he was a very little boy. Only he had been to the back of the north wind since—there could be no doubt of that; for when he woke every morning, he always knew that he had been there again. And as he thought and thought, he recalled another thing that had happened that morning, which, although it seemed a mere accident, might have something to do with what had happened since. His father had intended going on the stand at King's Cross that morning, and had turned into Gray's Inn Lane to drive there, when they found the way blocked up, and upon inquiry were informed that a stack of chimneys had been blown down in the night, and had fallen across the road. They were just clearing the rubbish away. Diamond's father turned, and made for Charing Cross.

That night the father and mother had a great deal to talk about.

"Poor things!" said the mother. "it's worse for them than it is for us. You see they've been used to such grand things, and for them to come down to a little poky house like that — it breaks my heart to think of it."

"I don't know" said Diamond thoughtfully, "whether Mrs. Coleman had bells on her toes."

"What do you mean, child?" said his mother.

"She had rings on her fingers, anyhow," returned Diamond.

"Of course she had, as any lady would. What has that to do with it?"

"When we were down at Sandwich," said Diamond, "you said you would have to part with your mother's ring, now we were poor."

"Bless the child; he forgets nothing," said his mother. "Really, Diamond, a body would need to mind what they say to you."

"Why?" said Diamond. "I only think about it."

"That's just why," said the mother.

"Why is that why?" persisted Diamond, for he had not yet learned that grown-up people are not often so much grown up that they never talk like children—and spoilt ones too.

"Mrs. Coleman is none so poor as all that yet. No, thank Heaven! she's not come to that."

"Is it a great disgrace to be poor?" asked Diamond, because of the tone in which his mother had spoken.

But his mother, whether conscience-stricken I do not know hurried him away to bed, where after various attempts to understand her, resumed and resumed again in spite of invading sleep, he was conquered at last, and gave in, murmuring over and over to himself, "Why is why?" but getting no answer to the question.

18. THE DRUNKEN CABMAN

A few nights after this, Diamond woke up suddenly, believing he heard North Wind thundering along. But it was something quite different. South Wind was moaning round the chimneys, to be sure, for she was not very happy that night, but it was not her voice that had wakened Diamond. Her voice would only have lulled him the deeper asleep. It was a loud, angry voice, now growling like that of a beast, now raving like that of a madman; and when Diamond came a little wider awake, he knew that it was the voice of the drunken cabman, the wall of whose room was at the head of his bed. It was anything but pleasant to hear, but he could not help hearing it. At length there came a cry from the woman, and then a scream from the baby. Thereupon Diamond thought it time that somebody did something, and as himself was the only somebody at hand, he must go and see whether he could not do something. So he got up and put on part of his clothes, and went down the stair, for the cabman's room did not open upon their stair, and he had to go out into the yard, and in at the next door. This, fortunately, the cabman, being drunk, had left open. By the time he reached their stair, all was still except the voice of the crying baby, which guided him to the right door. He opened it softly, and peeped in. There, leaning back in a chair, with his arms hanging down by his sides, and his legs stretched out before him and supported on his heels, sat the drunken cabman. His wife lay in her clothes upon the bed, sobbing, and the baby was wailing in the cradle. It was very miserable altogether.

Now the way most people do when they see anything very miserable is to turn away from the sight, and try to forget it. But Diamond began as usual to try to destroy the misery. The little boy was just as much one of God's messengers as if he had been an angel with a flaming sword, going out to fight the devil. The devil he had to fight just then was Misery. And the way he fought him was the very best. Like a wise soldier, he attacked him first in his weakest point — that was the, baby; for Misery can never get such a hold of a baby as of a grown person. Diamond was knowing in babies, and he knew he could do something to make the baby, happy; for although he had only known one baby as yet, and although not one baby is the same as another, yet they are so very much alike in some things, and he knew that one baby so thoroughly, that he had good reason to believe he could do something for any other. I have known people who would have begun to fight the devil in a very different and a very stupid way. They would have begun by scolding the idiotic cabman; and next they would make his wife angry by saying it must be her fault as well as his, and by leaving ill-bred though well-meant shabby little books for them to read, which they were sure to hate the sight of; while all the time they would not have put out a finger to touch the wailing baby. But Diamond had him out of the cradle in a moment, set him up on his knee, and told him to look at the light. Now all the light there was came only from a lamp in the yard, and it was a very dingy and yellow light, for the glass of the lamp was dirty, and the gas was bad; but the light that came from it was, notwithstanding, as certainly light as if it had come from the sun itself, and the baby knew that, and smiled to it; and although it was indeed a wretched room which that lamp lighted — so dreary, and dirty, and empty, and hopeless! — there in the middle of it sat Diamond on a stool, smiling to the baby, and the baby on his knees smiling to the lamp. The father of him sat staring at nothing, neither asleep nor awake, not quite lost in stupidity either, for through it all he was dimly angry with himself, he did not know why. It was that he had struck his wife. He had forgotten it, but was miserable about it, notwithstanding. And this misery was the voice of the great Love that had made him and his wife and the baby and Diamond, speaking in his heart, and telling him to be good. For that great Love speaks in the most wretched and dirty hearts; only the tone of its voice depends on the echoes of the place in which it sounds. On Mount Sinai, it was thunder; in the cabman's heart it was misery; in the soul of St. John it was perfect blessedness.

By and by he became aware that there was a voice of singing in the room. This, of course, was the voice of Diamond singing to the baby — song after song, every one as foolish as another to the cabman, for he was too tipsy to part one word from another: all the words mixed up in his ear in a gurgle without division or stop; for such was the way he spoke himself, when he was in this horrid condition. But the baby was more than content with Diamond's songs, and Diamond himself was so contented with what the songs were all about, that he did not care a bit about the songs themselves, if only baby liked them. But they did the cabman good as well as the baby and Diamond, for they put him to sleep, and the sleep was busy all the time it lasted, smoothing the wrinkles out of his temper.

At length Diamond grew tired of singing, and began to talk to the baby instead. And as soon as he stopped singing, the cabman began to wake up. His brain was a little clearer now, his temper a little smoother, and his heart not quite so dirty. He began to listen and he went on listening, and heard Diamond saying to the baby something like this, for he thought the cabman was asleep:

"Poor daddy! Baby's daddy takes too much beer and gin, and that makes him somebody else, and not his own self at all. Baby's daddy would never hit baby's mammy if he didn't take too much beer. He's very fond of baby's mammy, and works from morning to night to get her breakfast and dinner and supper, only at night he forgets, and pays the money away for beer. And they put nasty stuff in beer, I've heard my daddy say, that drives all the good out, and lets all the bad in. Daddy says when a man takes a drink, there's a thirsty devil creeps into his inside, because he knows he will always get enough there. And the devil is always crying out for more drink, and that makes the man thirsty, and so he drinks more and more, till he kills himself with it. And then the ugly devil creeps out of him, and crawls about on his belly, looking for some other cabman to get into, that he may drink, drink, drink. That's what my daddy says, baby. And he says, too, the only way to make the devil come out is to give him plenty of cold water and tea and coffee, and nothing at all that comes from the public-house; for the devil can't abide that kind of stuff, and creeps out pretty soon, for fear of being drowned in it. But your daddy will drink the nasty stuff, poor man! I wish he wouldn't, for it makes mammy cross with him, and no wonder! and then when mammy's cross, he's crosser, and there's nobody in the house to take care of them but baby; and you do take care of them, baby — don't you, baby? I know you do. Babies always take care of their fathers and mothers — don't they, baby? That's what they come for — isn't it, baby? And when daddy stops drinking beer and nasty gin with turpentine in it, father says, then mammy will be so happy, and look so pretty! and daddy will be so good to baby! and baby will be as happy as a swallow, which is the merriest fellow! And Diamond will be so happy too! And when Diamond's a man, he'll take baby out with him on the box, and teach him to drive a cab."

He went on with chatter like this till baby was asleep, by which time he was tired, and father and mother were both wide awake — only rather confused — the one from the beer, the other from the blow — and staring, the one from his chair, the other from her bed, at Diamond. But he was quite unaware of their notice, for he sat half-asleep, with his eyes wide open, staring in his turn, though without knowing it, at the cabman, while the cabman could not withdraw his gaze from Diamond's white face and big eyes. For Diamond's face was always rather pale, and now it was paler than usual with sleeplessness, and the light of the street-lamp upon it. At length he found himself nodding, and he knew then it was time to put the baby down, lest he should let him fall. So he rose from the little three-legged stool, and laid the baby in the cradle, and covered him up—it was well it was a warm night, and he did not want much covering — and then he all but staggered out of the door, he was so tipsy himself with sleep.

"Wife," said the cabman, turning towards the bed, "I do somehow believe that wur a angel just gone. Did you see him, wife? He warn't wery big, and he hadn't got none o' them wingses, you know. It wur one o' them baby-angels you sees on the gravestones, you know."

"Nonsense, hubby!" said his wife; "but it's just as good. I might say better, for you can ketch hold of him when you like. That's little Diamond as everybody knows, and a duck o' diamonds he is! No woman could wish for a better child than he be."

"I ha' heerd on him in the stable, but I never see the brat afore. Come, old girl, let bygones be bygones, and gie us a kiss, and we'll go to bed."

The cabman kept his cab in another yard, although he had his room in this. He was often late in coming home, and was not one to take notice of children, especially when he was tipsy, which was oftener than not. Hence, if he had ever seen Diamond, he did not know him. But his wife knew him well enough, as did every one else who lived all day in the yard. She was a good-natured woman. It was she who had got the fire lighted and the tea ready for them when Diamond and his mother came home from Sandwich. And her husband was not an ill-natured man either, and when in the morning he recalled not only Diamond's visit, but how he himself had behaved to his wife, he was very vexed with himself, and gladdened his poor wife's heart by telling her how sorry he was. And for a whole week after, he did not go near the public-house, hard as it was to avoid it, seeing a certain rich brewer had built one, like a trap to catch souls and bodies in, at almost every corner he had to pass on his way home. Indeed, he was never quite so bad after that, though it was some time before he began really to reform.

19. DIAMOND'S FRIENDS

One day when old Diamond was standing with his nose in his bag between Pall Mall and Cockspur Street, and his master was reading the newspaper on the box of his cab, which was the last of a good many in the row, little Diamond got down for a run, for his legs were getting cramped with sitting. And first of all he strolled with his hands in his pockets up to the crossing, where the girl and her broom were to be found in all weathers. Just as he was going to speak to her, a tall gentleman stepped upon the crossing. He was pleased to find it so clean, for the streets were muddy, and he had nice boots on; so he put his hand in his pocket, and gave the girl a penny. But when she gave him a sweet smile in return, and made him a pretty courtesy, he looked at her again, and said:

"Where do you live, my child?"

"Paradise Row," she answered; "next door to the Adam and Eve — down the area."

"Whom do you live with?" he asked.

"My wicked old grannie," she replied.

"You shouldn't call your grannie wicked," said the gentleman.

"But she is," said the girl, looking up confidently in his face. "If you don't believe me, you can come and take a look at her."

The words sounded rude, but the girl's face looked so simple that the gentleman saw she did not mean to be rude, and became still more interested in her.

"Still you shouldn't say so," he insisted.

"Shouldn't I? Everybody calls her wicked old grannie—even them that's as wicked as her. You should hear her swear. There's nothing like it in the Row. Indeed, I assure you, sir, there's ne'er a one of them can shut my grannie up once she begins and gets right a-going. You must put her in a passion first, you know. It's no good till you do that—she's so old now. How she do make them laugh, to be sure!"

Although she called her wicked, the child spoke so as plainly to indicate pride in her grannie's pre-eminence in swearing.

The gentleman looked very grave to hear her, for he was sorry that such a nice little girl should be in such bad keeping. But he did not know what to say next, and stood for a moment with his eyes on the ground. When he lifted them, he saw the face of Diamond looking up in his.

"Please, sir," said Diamond, "her grannie's very cruel to her sometimes, and shuts her out in the streets at night, if she happens to be late."

"Is this your brother?" asked the gentleman of the girl.

"No, sir."

"How does he know your grandmother, then? He does not look like one of her sort."

"Oh no, sir! He's a good boy — quite."

Here she tapped her forehead with her finger in a significant manner.

"What do you mean by that?" asked the gentleman, while Diamond looked on smiling.

"The cabbies call him God's baby," she whispered. "He's not right in the head, you know. A tile loose."

Still Diamond, though he heard every word, and understood it too, kept on smiling. What could it matter what people called him, so long as he did nothing he ought not to do? And, besides, God's baby was surely the best of names!

"Well, my little man, and what can you do?" asked the gentleman, turning towards him — just for the sake of saying something.

"Drive a cab," said Diamond.

"Good; and what else?" he continued; for, accepting what the girl had said, he regarded the still sweetness of Diamond's face as a sign of silliness, and wished to be kind to the poor little fellow.

"Nurse a baby," said Diamond.

"Well — and what else?"

"Clean father's boots, and make him a bit of toast for his tea."

"You're a useful little man," said the gentleman. "What else can you do?"

"Not much that I know of," said Diamond. "I can't curry a horse, except somebody puts me on his back. So I don't count that."

"Can you read?"

"No. But mother can and father can, and they're going to teach me some day soon."

"Well, here's a penny for you."

"Thank you, sir."

"And when you have learned to read, come to me, and I'll give you sixpence and a book with fine pictures in it."

"Please, sir, where am I to come?" asked Diamond, who was too much a man of the world not to know that he must have the gentleman's address before he could go and see him.

"You're no such silly!" thought he, as he put his hand in his pocket, and brought out a card. "There," he said, "your father will be able to read that, and tell you where to go."

"Yes, sir. Thank you, sir," said Diamond, and put the card in his pocket.

The gentleman walked away, but turning round a few paces off, saw Diamond give his penny to the girl, and, walking slower heard him say:

"I've got a father, and mother, and little brother, and you've got nothing but a wicked old grannie. You may have my penny."

The girl put it beside the other in her pocket, the only trustworthy article of dress she wore. Her grandmother always took care that she had a stout pocket.

"Is she as cruel as ever?" asked Diamond.

"Much the same. But I gets more coppers now than I used to, and I can get summats to eat, and take browns enough home besides to keep her from grumbling. It's a good thing she's so blind, though."

"Why?" asked Diamond.

"'Cause if she was as sharp in the eyes as she used to be, she would find out I never eats her broken wittles, and then she'd know as I must get something somewheres."

"Doesn't she watch you, then?"

"O' course she do. Don't she just! But I make believe and drop it in my lap, and then hitch it into my pocket."

"What would she do if she found you out?"

"She never give me no more."

"But you don't want it!"

"Yes, I do want it."

"What do you do with it, then?"

"Give it to cripple Jim."

"Who's cripple Jim?"

"A boy in the Row. His mother broke his leg when he wur a kid, so he's never come to much; but he's a good boy, is Jim, and I love Jim dearly. I always keeps off a penny for Jim —leastways as often as I can. — But there I must sweep again, for them busses makes no end o' dirt."

"Diamond! Diamond!" cried his father, who was afraid he might get no good by talking to the girl; and Diamond obeyed, and got up again upon the box. He told his father about the gentleman, and what he had promised him if he would learn to read, and showed him the gentleman's card.

"Why, it's not many doors from the Mews!" said his father, giving him back the card. "Take care of it, my boy, for it may lead to something. God knows, in these hard times a man wants as many friends as he's ever likely to get."

"Haven't you got friends enough, father?" asked Diamond.

"Well, I have no right to complain; but the more the better, you know."

"Just let me count," said Diamond.

And he took his hands from his pockets, and spreading out the fingers of his left hand, began to count, beginning at the thumb.

"There's mother, first, and then baby, and then me. Next there's old Diamond—and the cab — no, I won't count the cab, for it never looks at you, and when Diamond's out of the shafts, it's nobody. Then there's the man that drinks next door, and his wife, and his baby."

"They're no friends of mine," said his father.

"Well, they're friends of mine," said Diamond.

His father laughed.

"Much good they'll do you!" he said.

"How do you know they won't?" returned Diamond.

"Well, go on," said his father.

"Then there's Jack and Mr. Stonecrop, and, deary me! not to have mentioned Mr. Coleman and Mrs. Coleman, and Miss Coleman, and Mrs. Crump. And then there's the clergyman that spoke to me in the garden that day the tree was blown down."

"What's his name!"

"I don't know his name."

"Where does he live?"

"I don't know."

"How can you count him, then?"

"He did talk to me, and very kindlike too."

His father laughed again.

"Why, child, you're just counting everybody you know. That don't make 'em friends."

"Don't it? I thought it did. Well, but they shall be my friends. I shall make 'em."

"How will you do that?"

"They can't help themselves then, if they would. If I choose to be their friend, you know, they can't prevent me. Then there's that girl at the crossing."

"A fine set of friends you do have, to be sure, Diamond!"

"Surely she's a friend anyhow, father. If it hadn't been for her, you would never have got Mrs. Coleman and Miss Coleman to carry home."

His father was silent, for he saw that Diamond was right, and was ashamed to find himself more ungrateful than he had thought.

"Then there's the new gentleman," Diamond went on.

"If he do as he say," interposed his father.

"And why shouldn't he? I daresay sixpence ain't too much for him to spare. But I don't quite understand, father: is nobody your friend but the one that does something for you?"

"No, I won't say that, my boy. You would have to leave out baby then."

"Oh no, I shouldn't. Baby can laugh in your face, and crow in your ears, and make you feel so happy. Call you that nothing, father?"

The father's heart was fairly touched now. He made no answer to this last appeal, and Diamond ended off with saying:

"And there's the best of mine to come yet — and that's you, daddy —

except it be mother, you know. You're my friend, daddy, ain't you? And I'm your friend, ain't I?"

"And God for us all," said his father, and then they were both silent for that was very solemn.

20. DIAMOND LEARNS TO READ

The question of the tall gentleman as to whether Diamond could read or not set his father thinking it was high time he could; and as soon as old Diamond was suppered and bedded, he began the task that very night. But it was not much of a task to Diamond, for his father took for his lesson-book those very rhymes his mother had picked up on the sea-shore; and as Diamond was not beginning too soon, he learned very fast indeed. Within a month he was able to spell out most of the verses for himself.

But he had never come upon the poem he thought he had heard his mother read from it that day. He had looked through and through the book several times after he knew the letters and a few words, fancying he could tell the look of it, but had always failed to find one more like it than another. So he wisely gave up the search till he could really read. Then he resolved to begin at the beginning, and read them all straight through. This took him nearly a fortnight. When he had almost reached the end, he came upon the following verses, which took his fancy much, although they were certainly not very like those he was in search of.

Little Boy Blue

Little Boy Blue lost his way in a wood.
Sing apples and cherries, roses and honey;
He said, "I would not go back if I could,
It's all so jolly and funny."

He sang, "This wood is all my own,
Apples and cherries, roses and honey;
So here I'll sit, like a king on my throne,
All so jolly and funny."

A little snake crept out of the tree,
Apples and cherries, roses and honey;
"Lie down at my feet, little snake," said he,
All so jolly and funny.

A little bird sang in the tree overhead,
Apples and cherries, roses and honey;
"Come and sing your song on my finger instead,
All so jolly and funny."

The snake coiled up; and the bird flew down,
And sang him the song of Birdie Brown.

Little Boy Blue found it tiresome to sit,
And he thought he had better walk on a bit.

So up he got, his way to take,
And he said, "Come along, little bird and snake."

And waves of snake o'er the damp leaves passed,
And the snake went first and Birdie Brown last;

By Boy Blue's head, with flutter and dart,
Flew Birdie Brown with its song in its heart.

He came where the apples grew red and sweet:
"Tree, drop me an apple down at my feet."

He came where the cherries hung plump and red:
"Come to my mouth, sweet kisses," he said.

And the boughs bow down, and the apples they dapple
The grass, too many for him to grapple.

And the cheeriest cherries, with never a miss,
Fall to his mouth, each a full-grown kiss.

He met a little brook singing a song.
He said, "Little brook, you are going wrong.

"You must follow me, follow me, follow, I say

Do as I tell you, and come this way."

And the song-singing, sing-songing forest brook
Leaped from its bed and after him took,

Followed him, followed. And pale and wan,
The dead leaves rustled as the water ran.

And every bird high up on the bough,
And every creature low down below,

He called, and the creatures obeyed the call,
Took their legs and their wings and followed him all;

Squirrels that carried their tails like a sack,
Each on his own little humpy brown back;

Householder snails, and slugs all tails,
And butterflies, flutterbies, ships all sails;

And weasels, and ousels, and mice, and larks,
And owls, and rere-mice, and harkydarks,

All went running, and creeping, and flowing,
After the merry boy fluttering and going;

The dappled fawns fawning, the fallow-deer following,
The swallows and flies, flying and swallowing;

Cockchafers, henchafers, cockioli-birds,
Cockroaches, henroaches, cuckoos in herds.

The spider forgot and followed him spinning,
And lost all his thread from end to beginning.

The gay wasp forgot his rings and his waist,
He never had made such undignified haste.

The dragon-flies melted to mist with their hurrying.
The mole in his moleskins left his barrowing burrowing.

The bees went buzzing, so busy and beesy,
And the midges in columns so upright and easy.

But Little Boy Blue was not content,
Calling for followers still as he went,

Blowing his horn, and beating his drum,
And crying aloud, "Come all of you, come!"

He said to the shadows, "Come after me;"
And the shadows began to flicker and flee,

And they flew through the wood all flattering and fluttering,
Over the dead leaves flickering and muttering.

And he said to the wind, "Come, follow; come, follow,
With whistle and pipe, and rustle and hollo."

And the wind wound round at his desire,
As if he had been the gold cock on the spire.

And the cock itself flew down from the church,
And left the farmers all in the lurch.

They run and they fly, they creep and they come,
Everything, everything, all and some.

The very trees they tugged at their roots,
Only their feet were too fast in their boots,

After him leaning and straining and bending,
As on through their boles he kept walking and wending,

Till out of the wood he burst on a lea,

Shouting and calling, "Come after me!"

And then they rose up with a leafy hiss,
And stood as if nothing had been amiss.

Little Boy Blue sat down on a stone,
And the creatures came round him every one.

And he said to the clouds, "I want you there."
And down they sank through the thin blue air.

And he said to the sunset far in the West,
"Come here; I want you; I know best."

And the sunset came and stood up on the wold,
And burned and glowed in purple and gold.

Then Little Boy Blue began to ponder:
"What's to be done with them all, I wonder."

Then Little Boy Blue, he said, quite low,
"What to do with you all I am sure I don't know."

Then the clouds clouded down till dismal it grew;
The snake sneaked close; round Birdie Brown flew;

The brook sat up like a snake on its tail;
And the wind came up with a what-will-you wail;

And all the creatures sat and stared;
The mole opened his very eyes and glared;

And for rats and bats and the world and his wife,
Little Boy Blue was afraid of his life.

Then Birdie Brown began to sing,
And what he sang was the very thing:

"You have brought us all hither, Little Boy Blue,
Pray what do you want us all to do?"

"Go away! go away!" said Little Boy Blue;
"I'm sure I don't want you — get away — do."

"No, no; no, no; no, yes, and no, no,"
Sang Birdie Brown, "it mustn't be so.

"We cannot for nothing come here, and away.
Give us some work, or else we stay."

"Oh dear! and oh dear!" with sob and with sigh,
Said Little Boy Blue, and began to cry.

But before he got far, he thought of a thing;
And up he stood, and spoke like a king.

"Why do you hustle and jostle and bother?
Off with you all! Take me back to my mother."

The sunset stood at the gates of the west.
"Follow me, follow me" came from Birdie Brown's breast.

"I am going that way as fast as I can,"
Said the brook, as it sank and turned and ran.

Back to the woods fled the shadows like ghosts:
"If we stay, we shall all be missed from our posts."

Said the wind with a voice that had changed its cheer,
"I was just going there, when you brought me here."

"That's where I live," said the sack-backed squirrel,
And he turned his sack with a swing and a swirl.

Said the cock of the spire, "His father's churchwarden."

Said the brook running faster, "I run through his garden."

Said the mole, "Two hundred worms — there I caught 'em
Last year, and I'm going again next autumn."

Said they all, "If that's where you want us to steer for,
What in earth or in water did you bring us here for?"

"Never you mind," said Little Boy Blue;
"That's what I tell you. If that you won't do,

"I'll get up at once, and go home without you.
I think I will; I begin to doubt you."

He rose; and up rose the snake on its tail,
And hissed three times, half a hiss, half a wail.

Little Boy Blue he tried to go past him;
But wherever he turned, sat the snake and faced him.

"If you don't get out of my way," he said,
"I tell you, snake, I will break your head."

The snake he neither would go nor come;
So he hit him hard with the stick of his drum.

The snake fell down as if he were dead,
And Little Boy Blue set his foot on his head.

And all the creatures they marched before him,
And marshalled him home with a high cockolorum.

And Birdie Brown sang Twirrrr twitter twirrrr twee —
Apples and cherries, roses and honey;
Little Boy Blue has listened to me —
All so jolly and funny.

21. SAL'S NANNY

Diamond managed with many blunders to read this rhyme to his mother.

"Isn't it nice, mother?" he said.

"Yes, it's pretty," she answered.

"I think it means something," returned Diamond.

"I'm sure I don't know what," she said.

"I wonder if it's the same boy — yes, it must be the same — Little Boy Blue, you know. Let me see — how does that rhyme go?

Little Boy Blue, come blow me your horn —

Yes, of course it is — for this one went 'blowing his horn and beating his drum.' He had a drum too.

Little Boy Blue, come blow me your horn;
The sheep's in the meadow, the cow's in the corn,

He had to keep them out, you know. But he wasn't minding his work. It goes —

Where's the little boy that looks after the sheep?
He's under the haystack, fast asleep.

There, you see, mother! And then, let me see —

Who'll go and wake him? No, not I;
For if I do, he'll be sure to cry.

So I suppose nobody did wake him. He was a rather cross little boy, I daresay, when woke up. And when he did wake of himself, and saw the mischief the cow had done to the corn, instead of running home to his mother, he ran away into the wood and lost himself. Don't you think that's very likely, mother?"

"I shouldn't wonder," she answered.

"So you see he was naughty; for even when he lost himself he did not want to go home. Any of the creatures would have shown him the way if he had asked it—all but the snake. He followed the snake, you know, and he took him farther away. I suppose it was a young one of the same serpent that tempted Adam and Eve. Father was telling us about it last Sunday, you remember."

"Bless the child!" said his mother to herself; and then added aloud, finding that Diamond did not go on, "Well, what next?"

"I don't know, mother. I'm sure there's a great deal more, but what it is I can't say. I only know that he killed the snake. I suppose that's what he had a drumstick for. He couldn't do it with his horn."

"But surely you're not such a silly as to take it all for true, Diamond?"

"I think it must be. It looks true. That killing of the snake looks true. It's what I've got to do so often."

His mother looked uneasy. Diamond smiled full in her face, and added—

"When baby cries and won't be happy, and when father and you talk about your troubles, I mean."

This did little to reassure his mother; and lest my reader should have his qualms about it too, I venture to remind him once more that Diamond had been to the back of the north wind.

Finding she made no reply, Diamond went on —

"In a week or so, I shall be able to go to the tall gentleman and tell him I can read. And I'll ask him if he can help me to understand the rhyme."

But before the week was out, he had another reason for going to Mr. Raymond.

For three days, on each of which, at one time or other, Diamond's father was on the same stand near the National Gallery, the girl was not at her crossing, and Diamond got quite anxious about her, fearing she must be ill. On the fourth day, not seeing her yet, he said to his father, who had that moment shut the door of his cab upon a fare —

"Father, I want to go and look after the girl, She can't be well."

"All right," said his father. "Only take care of yourself, Diamond."

So saying he climbed on his box and drove off.

He had great confidence in his boy, you see, and would trust him anywhere. But if he had known the kind of place in which the girl lived, he would perhaps have thought twice before he allowed him to go alone. Diamond, who did know something of it, had not, however, any fear. From talking to the girl he had a good notion of where about it was, and he remembered the address well enough; so by asking his way some twenty times, mostly of policemen, he came at length pretty near the place. The last policeman he questioned looked down upon him from the summit of six feet two inches, and replied with another question, but kindly:

"What do you want there, my small kid? It ain't where you was bred, I guess."

"No sir" answered Diamond. "I live in Bloomsbury."

"That's a long way off," said the policeman.

"Yes, it's a good distance," answered Diamond; "but I find my way about pretty well. Policemen are always kind to me."

"But what on earth do you want here?"

Diamond told him plainly what he was about, and of course the man believed him, for nobody ever disbelieved Diamond. People might think he was mistaken, but they never thought he was telling a story.

"It's an ugly place," said the policeman.

"Is it far off?" asked Diamond.

"No. It's next door almost. But it's not safe."

"Nobody hurts me," said Diamond.

"I must go with you, I suppose."

"Oh, no! please not," said Diamond. "They might think I was going to meddle with them, and I ain't, you know."

"Well, do as you please," said the man, and gave him full directions.

Diamond set off, never suspecting that the policeman, who was a kind-hearted man, with children of his own, was following him close, and watching him round every corner. As he went on, all at once he thought he remembered the place, and whether it really was so, or only that he had laid up the policeman's instructions well in his mind, he went straight for the cellar of old Sal.

"He's a sharp little kid, anyhow, for as simple as he looks," said the man to himself. "Not a wrong turn does he take! But old Sal's a rum un for such a child to pay a morning visit to. She's worse when she's sober than when she's half drunk. I've seen her when she'd have torn him in pieces."

Happily then for Diamond, old Sal had gone out to get some gin. When he came to her door at the bottom of the area-stair and knocked, he received no answer. He laid his ear to the door, and thought he heard a moaning within. So he tried the door, and found it was not locked! It was a dreary place indeed, — and very dark, for the window was below the level of the street, and covered with mud, while over the grating which kept people from falling into the area, stood a chest of drawers, placed there by a dealer in second-hand furniture, which shut out almost all the light. And the smell in the place was dreadful. Diamond stood still for a while, for he could see next to nothing, but he heard the moaning plainly enough now, When he got used to the darkness, he discovered his friend lying with closed eyes and a white suffering face on a heap of little better than rags in a corner of the den. He went up to her and spoke; but she made him no answer. Indeed, she was not in the least aware of his presence, and Diamond saw that he could do nothing for her without help. So taking a lump of barley-sugar from his pocket, which he had bought for her as he came along, and laying it beside her, he left the place, having already made up his mind to go and see the tall gentleman, Mr. Raymond, and ask him to do something for Sal's Nanny, as the girl was called.

By the time he got up the area-steps, three or four women who had seen him go down were standing together at the top waiting for him. They wanted his clothes for their children; but they did not follow him down lest Sal should find them there. The moment he appeared, they laid their hands on him, and all began talking at once, for each wanted to get some advantage over her neighbors. He told them quite quietly, for he was not frightened, that he had come to see what was the matter with Nanny.

"What do you know about Nanny?" said one of them fiercely. "Wait till old Sal comes home, and you'll catch it, for going prying into her house when she's out. If you don't give me your jacket directly, I'll go and fetch her."

"I can't give you my jacket," said Diamond. "It belongs to my father and mother, you know. It's not mine to give. Is it now? You would not think it right to give away what wasn't yours — would you now?"

"Give it away! No, that I wouldn't; I'd keep it," she said, with a rough laugh. "But if the jacket ain't yours, what right have you to keep it? Here, Cherry, make haste. It'll be one go apiece."

They all began to tug at the jacket, while Diamond stooped and kept his arms bent to resist them. Before they had done him or the jacket any harm, however, suddenly they all scampered away; and Diamond, looking in the opposite direction, saw the tall policeman coming towards him.

"You had better have let me come with you, little man," he said, looking down in Diamond's face, which was flushed with his resistance.

"You came just in the right time, thank you," returned Diamond. "They've done me no harm."

"They would have if I hadn't been at hand, though."

"Yes; but you were at hand, you know, so they couldn't."

Perhaps the answer was deeper in purport than either Diamond or the policeman knew. They walked away together, Diamond telling his new friend how ill poor Nanny was, and that he was going to let the tall gentleman know. The policeman put him in the nearest way for Bloomsbury, and stepping out in good earnest, Diamond reached Mr. Raymond's door in less than an hour. When he asked if he was at home, the servant, in return, asked what he wanted.

"I want to tell him something."

"But I can't go and trouble him with such a message as that."

"He told me to come to him—that is, when I could read — and I can."

"How am I to know that?"

Diamond stared with astonishment for one moment, then answered:

"Why, I've just told you. That's how you know it."

But this man was made of coarser grain than the policeman, and, instead of seeing that Diamond could not tell a lie, he put his answer down as impudence, and saying, "Do you think I'm going to take your word for it?" shut the door in his face.

Diamond turned and sat down on the doorstep, thinking with himself that the tall gentleman must either come in or come out, and he was therefore in the best possible position for finding him. He had not waited long before the door opened again; but when he looked round, it was only the servant once more.

"Get, away" he said. "What are you doing on the doorstep?"

"Waiting for Mr. Raymond," answered Diamond, getting up.

"He's not at home."

"Then I'll wait till he comes," returned Diamond, sitting down again with a smile.

What the man would have done next I do not know, but a step sounded from the hall, and when Diamond looked round yet again, there was the tall gentleman.

"Who's this, John?" he asked.

"I don't know, sir. An imperent little boy as will sit on the doorstep."

"Please sir" said Diamond, "he told me you weren't at home, and I sat down to wait for you."

"Eh, what!" said Mr. Raymond. "John! John! This won't do. Is it a habit of yours to turn away my visitors? There'll be some one else to turn away, I'm afraid, if I find any more of this kind of thing. Come in, my little man. I suppose you've come to claim your sixpence?"

"No, sir, not that."

"What! can't you read yet?"

"Yes, I can now, a little. But I'll come for that next time. I came to tell you about Sal's Nanny."

"Who's Sal's Nanny?"

"The girl at the crossing you talked to the same day."

"Oh, yes; I remember. What's the matter? Has she got run over?"

Then Diamond told him all.

Now Mr. Raymond was one of the kindest men in London. He sent at once to have the horse put to the brougham, took Diamond with him, and drove to the Children's Hospital. There he was well known to everybody, for he was not only a large subscriber, but he used to go and tell the children stories of an afternoon. One of the doctors promised to go and find Nanny, and do what could be done — have her brought to the hospital, if possible.

That same night they sent a litter for her, and as she could be of no use to old Sal until she was better, she did not object to having her removed. So she was soon lying in the fever ward — for the first time in her life in a nice clean bed. But she knew nothing of the whole affair. She was too ill to know anything.

22. MR RAYMOND'S RIDDLE

Mr. Raymond took Diamond home with him, stopping at the Mews to tell his mother that he would send him back soon. Diamond ran in with the message himself, and when he reappeared he had in his hand the torn and crumpled book which North Wind had given him.

"Ah! I see," said Mr. Raymond: "you are going to claim your sixpence now."

"I wasn't thinking of that so much as of another thing," said Diamond. "There's a rhyme in this book I can't quite understand. I want you to tell me what it means, if you please."

"I will if I can," answered Mr. Raymond. "You shall read it to me when we get home, and then I shall see."

Still with a good many blunders, Diamond did read it after a fashion. Mr. Raymond took the little book and read it over again.

Now Mr. Raymond was a poet himself, and so, although he had never been at the back of the north wind, he was able to understand the poem pretty well. But before saying anything about it, he read it over aloud, and Diamond thought he understood it much better already.

"I'll tell you what I think it means," he then said. "It means that people may have their way for a while, if they like, but it will get them into such troubles they'll wish they hadn't had it."

"I know, I know!" said Diamond. "Like the poor cabman next door. He drinks too much."

"Just so," returned Mr. Raymond. "But when people want to do right, things about them will try to help them. Only they must kill the snake, you know."

"I was sure the snake had something to do with it," cried Diamond triumphantly.

A good deal more talk followed, and Mr. Raymond gave Diamond his sixpence.

"What will you do with it?" he asked.

"Take it home to my mother," he answered. "She has a teapot — such a black one! —with a broken spout, and she keeps all her money in it. It ain't much; but she saves it up to buy shoes for me. And there's baby coming on famously, and he'll want shoes soon. And every sixpence is something — ain't it, sir?"

"To be sure, my man. I hope you'll always make as good a use of your money."

"I hope so, sir," said Diamond.

"And here's a book for you, full of pictures and stories and poems. I wrote it myself, chiefly for the children of the hospital where I hope Nanny is going. I don't mean I printed it, you know. I made it," added Mr. Raymond, wishing Diamond to understand that he was the author of the book.

"I know what you mean. I make songs myself. They're awfully silly, but they please baby, and that's all they're meant for."

"Couldn't you let me hear one of them now?" said Mr. Raymond.

"No, sir, I couldn't. I forget them as soon as I've done with them. Besides, I couldn't make a line without baby on my knee. We make them together, you know. They're just as much baby's as mine. It's he that pulls them out of me."

"I suspect the child's a genius," said the poet to himself, "and that's what makes people think him silly."

Now if any of my child readers want to know what a genius is — shall I try to tell them, or shall I not? I will give them one very short answer: It means one who understands things without any other body telling him what they mean. God makes a few such now and then to teach the rest of us.

"Do you like riddles?" asked Mr. Raymond, turning over the leaves of his own book.

"I don't know what a riddle is," said Diamond.

"It's something that means something else, and you've got to find out what the something else is."

Mr. Raymond liked the old-fashioned riddle best, and had written a few — one of which he now read.

I have only one foot, but thousands of toes;
My one foot stands, but never goes.
I have many arms, and they're mighty all;
And hundreds of fingers, large and small.
From the ends of my fingers my beauty grows.
I breathe with my hair, and I drink with my toes.
I grow bigger and bigger about the waist,
And yet I am always very tight laced.
None e'er saw me eat — I've no mouth to bite;
Yet I eat all day in the full sunlight.
In the summer with song I shave and quiver,
But in winter I fast and groan and shiver.

"Do you know what that means, Diamond?" he asked, when he had finished.

"No, indeed, I don't," answered Diamond.

"Then you can read it for yourself, and think over it, and see if you can find out," said Mr. Raymond, giving him the book. "And now you had better go home to your mother. When you've found the riddle, you can come again."

If Diamond had had to find out the riddle in order to see Mr. Raymond again, I doubt if he would ever have seen him.

"Oh then," I think I hear some little reader say, "he could not have been a genius, for a genius finds out things without being told."

I answer, "Genius finds out truths, not tricks." And if you do not understand that, I am afraid you must be content to wait till you grow older and know more.

23. THE EARLY BIRD

When Diamond got home he found his father at home already, sitting by the fire and looking rather miserable, for his head ached and he felt sick. He had been doing night work of late, and it had not agreed with him, so he had given it up, but not in time, for he had taken some kind of fever. The next day he was forced to keep his bed, and his wife nursed him, and Diamond attended to the baby. If he had not been ill, it would have been delightful to have him at home; and the first day Diamond sang more songs than ever to the baby, and his father listened with some pleasure. But the next he could not bear even Diamond's sweet voice, and was very ill indeed; so Diamond took the baby into his own room, and had no end of quiet games with him there. If he did pull all his bedding on the floor, it did not matter, for he kept baby very quiet, and made the bed himself again, and slept in it with baby all the next night, and many nights after.

But long before his father got well, his mother's savings were all but gone. She did not say a word about it in the hearing of her husband, lest she should distress him; and one night, when she could not help crying, she came into Diamond's room that his father might not hear her. She thought Diamond was asleep, but he was not. When he heard her sobbing, he was frightened, and said —

"Is father worse, mother?"

"No, Diamond," she answered, as well as she could; "he's a good bit better."

"Then what are you crying for, mother?"

"Because my money is almost all gone," she replied.

"O mammy, you make me think of a little poem baby and I learned out of North Wind's book to-day. Don't you remember how I bothered you about some of the words?"

"Yes, child," said his mother heedlessly, thinking only of what she should do after to-morrow.

Diamond began and repeated the poem, for he had a wonderful memory.

A little bird sat on the edge of her nest;

Her yellow-beaks slept as sound as tops;

That day she had done her very best,

And had filled every one of their little crops.

She had filled her own just over-full,

And hence she was feeling a little dull.

"Oh, dear!" she sighed, as she sat with her head
Sunk in her chest, and no neck at all,
While her crop stuck out like a feather bed
Turned inside out, and rather small;
"What shall I do if things don't reform?
I don't know where there's a single worm.

"I've had twenty to-day, and the children five each,
Besides a few flies, and some very fat spiders:
No one will say I don't do as I preach —
I'm one of the best of bird-providers;
But where's the use? We want a storm —
I don't know where there's a single worm."

"There's five in my crop," said a wee, wee bird,
Which woke at the voice of his mother's pain;
"I know where there's five." And with the word
He tucked in his head, and went off again.
"The folly of childhood," sighed his mother,
"Has always been my especial bother."

The yellow-beaks they slept on and on —
They never had heard of the bogy To-morrow;
But the mother sat outside, making her moan —
She'll soon have to beg, or steal, or borrow.
For she never can tell the night before,
Where she shall find one red worm more.

The fact, as I say, was, she'd had too many;
She couldn't sleep, and she called it virtue,
Motherly foresight, affection, any
Name you may call it that will not hurt you,
So it was late ere she tucked her head in,
And she slept so late it was almost a sin.

But the little fellow who knew of five

Nor troubled his head about any more,

Woke very early, felt quite alive,

And wanted a sixth to add to his store:

He pushed his mother, the greedy elf,

Then thought he had better try for himself.

When his mother awoke and had rubbed her eyes,

Feeling less like a bird, and more like a mole,

She saw him — fancy with what surprise —

Dragging a huge worm out of a hole!

'Twas of this same hero the proverb took form:

'Tis the early bird that catches the worm.

"There, mother!" said Diamond, as he finished; "ain't it funny?"

"I wish you were like that little bird, Diamond, and could catch worms for yourself," said his mother, as she rose to go and look after her husband.

Diamond lay awake for a few minutes, thinking what he could do to catch worms. It was very little trouble to make up his mind, however, and still less to go to sleep after it.

24. ANOTHER EARLY BIRD

He got up in the morning as soon as he heard the men moving in the yard. He tucked in his little brother so that he could not tumble out of bed, and then went out, leaving the door open, so that if he should cry his mother might hear him at once. When he got into the yard he found the stable-door just opened.

"I'm the early bird, I think," he said to himself. "I hope I shall catch the worm."

He would not ask any one to help him, fearing his project might meet with disapproval and opposition. With great difficulty, but with the help of a broken chair he brought down from his bedroom, he managed to put the harness on Diamond. If the old horse had had the least objection to the proceeding, of course he could not have done it; but even when it came to the bridle, he opened his mouth for the bit, just as if he had been taking the apple which Diamond sometimes gave him. He fastened the cheek-strap very carefully, just in the usual hole, for fear of choking his friend, or else letting the bit get amongst his teeth. It was a job to get the saddle on; but with the chair he managed it. If old Diamond had had an education in physics to equal that of the camel, he would have knelt down to let him put it on his back, but that was more than could be expected of him, and then Diamond had to creep quite under him to get hold of the girth. The collar was almost the worst part of the business; but there Diamond could help Diamond. He held his head very low till his little master had got it over and turned it round, and then he lifted his head, and shook it on to his shoulders. The yoke was rather difficult; but when he had laid the traces over the horse's neck, the weight was not too much for him. He got him right at last, and led him out of the stable.

By this time there were several of the men watching him, but they would not interfere, they were so anxious to see how he would get over the various difficulties. They followed him as far as the stable-door, and there stood watching him again as he put the horse between the shafts, got them up one after the other into the loops, fastened the traces, the belly-band, the breeching, and the reins.

Then he got his whip. The moment he mounted the box, the men broke into a hearty cheer of delight at his success. But they would not let him go without a general inspection of the harness; and although they found it right, for not a buckle had to be shifted, they never allowed him to do it for himself again all the time his father was ill.

The cheer brought his mother to the window, and there she saw her little boy setting out alone with the cab in the gray of morning. She tugged at the window, but it was stiff; and before she could open it, Diamond, who was in a great hurry, was out of the mews, and almost out of the street. She called "Diamond! Diamond!" but there was no answer except from Jack.

"Never fear for him, ma'am," said Jack. "It 'ud be only a devil as would hurt him, and there ain't so many o' them as some folk 'ud have you believe. A boy o' Diamond's size as can 'arness a 'oss t'other Diamond's size, and put him to, right as a trivet — if he do upset the keb —'ll fall on his feet, ma'am."

"But he won't upset the cab, will he, Jack?"

"Not he, ma'am. Leastways he won't go for to do it."

"I know as much as that myself. What do you mean?"

"I mean he's a little likely to do it as the oldest man in the stable. How's the gov'nor to-day, ma'am?"

"A good deal better, thank you," she answered, closing the window in some fear lest her husband should have been made anxious by the news of Diamond's expedition. He knew pretty well, however, what his boy was capable of, and although not quite easy was less anxious than his mother. But as the evening drew on, the anxiety of both of them increased, and every sound of wheels made his father raise himself in his bed, and his mother peep out of the window.

Diamond had resolved to go straight to the cab-stand where he was best known, and never to crawl for fear of getting annoyed by idlers. Before he got across Oxford Street, however, he was hailed by a man who wanted to catch a train, and was in too great a hurry to think about the driver. Having carried him to King's Cross in good time, and got a good fare in return, he set off again in great spirits, and reached the stand in safety. He was the first there after all.

As the men arrived they all greeted him kindly, and inquired after his father.

"Ain't you afraid of the old 'oss running away with you?" asked one.

"No, he wouldn't run away with me," answered Diamond. "He knows I'm getting the shillings for father. Or if he did he would only run home."

"Well, you're a plucky one, for all your girl's looks!" said the man; "and I wish ye luck."

"Thank you, sir," said Diamond. "I'll do what I can. I came to the old place, you see, because I knew you would let me have my turn here."

In the course of the day one man did try to cut him out, but he was a stranger; and the shout the rest of them raised let him see it would not do, and made him so far ashamed besides, that he went away crawling.

Once, in a block, a policeman came up to him, and asked him for his number. Diamond showed him his father's badge, saying with a smile:

"Father's ill at home, and so I came out with the cab. There's no fear of me. I can drive. Besides, the old horse could go alone."

"Just as well, I daresay. You're a pair of 'em. But you are a rum 'un for a cabby—ain't you now?" said the policeman. "I don't know as I ought to let you go."

"I ain't done nothing," said Diamond. "It's not my fault I'm no bigger. I'm big enough for my age."

"That's where it is," said the man. "You ain't fit."

"How do you know that?" asked Diamond, with his usual smile, and turning his head like a little bird.

"Why, how are you to get out of this ruck now, when it begins to move?"

"Just you get up on the box," said Diamond, "and I'll show you. There, that van's a-moving now. Jump up."

The policeman did as Diamond told him, and was soon satisfied that the little fellow could drive.

"Well," he said, as he got down again, "I don't know as I should be right to interfere. Good luck to you, my little man!"

"Thank you, sir," said Diamond, and drove away.

In a few minutes a gentleman hailed him.

"Are you the driver of this cab?" he asked.

"Yes, sir" said Diamond, showing his badge, of which, he was proud.

"You're the youngest cabman I ever saw. How am I to know you won't break all my bones?"

"I would rather break all my own," said Diamond. "But if you're afraid, never mind me; I shall soon get another fare."

"I'll risk it," said the gentleman; and, opening the door himself, he jumped in.

He was going a good distance, and soon found that Diamond got him over the ground well. Now when Diamond had only to go straight ahead, and had not to mind so much what he was about, his thoughts always turned to the riddle Mr. Raymond had set him; and this gentleman looked so clever that he fancied he must be able to read it for him. He had given up all hope of finding it out for himself, and he could not plague his father about it when he was ill. He had thought of the answer himself, but fancied it could not be the right one, for to see how it all fitted required some knowledge of physiology. So, when he reached the end of his journey, he got down very quickly, and with his head just looking in at the window, said, as the gentleman gathered his gloves and newspapers:

"Please, sir, can you tell me the meaning of a riddle?"

"You must tell me the riddle first," answered the gentleman, amused.

Diamond repeated the riddle.

"Oh! that's easy enough," he returned. "It's a tree."

"Well, it ain't got no mouth, sure enough; but how then does it eat all day long?"

"It sucks in its food through the tiniest holes in its leaves," he answered. "Its breath is its food. And it can't do it except in the daylight."

"Thank you, sir, thank you," returned Diamond. "I'm sorry I couldn't find it out myself; Mr. Raymond would have been better pleased with me."

"But you needn't tell him any one told you."

Diamond gave him a stare which came from the very back of the north wind, where that kind of thing is unknown.

"That would be cheating," he said at last.

"Ain't you a cabby, then?"

"Cabbies don't cheat."

"Don't they? I am of a different opinion."

"I'm sure my father don't."

"What's your fare, young innocent?"

"Well, I think the distance is a good deal over three miles — that's two shillings. Only father says sixpence a mile is too little, though we can't ask for more."

"You're a deep one. But I think you're wrong. It's over four miles — not much, but it is."

"Then that's half-a-crown," said Diamond.

"Well, here's three shillings. Will that do?"

"Thank you kindly, sir. I'll tell my father how good you were to me — first to tell me my riddle, then to put me right about the distance, and then to give me sixpence over. It'll help father to get well again, it will."

"I hope it may, my man. I shouldn't wonder if you're as good as you look, after all."

As Diamond returned, he drew up at a stand he had never been on before: it was time to give Diamond his bag of chopped beans and oats. The men got about him, and began to chaff him. He took it all good-humouredly, until one of them, who was an ill-conditioned fellow, began to tease old Diamond by poking him roughly in the ribs, and making general game of him. That he could not bear, and the tears came in his eyes. He undid the nose-bag, put it in the boot, and was just going to mount and drive away, when the fellow interfered, and would not let him get up. Diamond endeavored to persuade him, and was very civil, but he would have his fun out of him, as he said. In a few minutes a group of idle boys had assembled, and Diamond found himself in a very uncomfortable position. Another cab drew up at the stand, and the driver got off and approached the assemblage.

"What's up here?" he asked, and Diamond knew the voice. It was that of the drunken cabman.

"Do you see this young oyster? He pretends to drive a cab," said his enemy.

"Yes, I do see him. And I sees you too. You'd better leave him alone. He ain't no oyster. He's a angel come down on his own business. You be off, or I'll be nearer you than quite agreeable."

The drunken cabman was a tall, stout man, who did not look one to take liberties with.

"Oh! if he's a friend of yours," said the other, drawing back.

Diamond got out the nose-bag again. Old Diamond should have his feed out now.

"Yes, he is a friend o' mine. One o' the best I ever had. It's a pity he ain't a friend o' yourn. You'd be the better for it, but it ain't no fault of hisn."

When Diamond went home at night, he carried with him one pound one shilling and sixpence, besides a few coppers extra, which had followed some of the fares.

His mother had got very anxious indeed — so much so that she was almost afraid, when she did hear the sound of his cab, to go and look, lest she should be yet again disappointed, and should break down before her husband. But there was the old horse, and there was the cab all right, and there was Diamond in the box, his pale face looking triumphant as a full moon in the twilight.

When he drew up at the stable-door, Jack came out, and after a good many friendly questions and congratulations, said:

"You go in to your mother, Diamond. I'll put up the old 'oss. I'll take care on him. He do deserve some small attention, he do."

"Thank you, Jack," said Diamond, and bounded into the house, and into the arms of his mother, who was waiting him at the top of the stair.

The poor, anxious woman led him into his own room, sat down on his bed, took him on her lap as if he had been a baby, and cried.

"How's father?" asked Diamond, almost afraid to ask.

"Better, my child," she answered, "but uneasy about you, my dear."

"Didn't you tell him I was the early bird gone out to catch the worm?"

"That was what put it in your head, was it, you monkey?" said his mother, beginning to get better.

"That or something else," answered Diamond, so very quietly that his mother held his head back and stared in his face.

"Well! of all the children!" she said, and said no more.

"And here's my worm," resumed Diamond.

But to see her face as he poured the shillings and sixpences and pence into her lap! She burst out crying a second time, and ran with the money to her husband.

And how pleased he was! It did him no end of good. But while he was counting the coins, Diamond turned to baby, who was lying awake in his cradle, sucking his precious thumb, and took him up, saying:

"Baby, baby! I haven't seen you for a whole year."

And then he began to sing to him as usual. And what he sang was this, for he was too happy either to make a song of his own or to sing sense. It was one out of Mr. Raymond's book.

The True Story Of The Cat And The Fiddle

Hey, diddle, diddle!

The cat and the fiddle!
He played such a merry tune,
That the cow went mad
With the pleasure she had,
And jumped right over the moon.
But then, don't you see?
Before that could be,
The moon had come down and listened.
The little dog hearkened,
So loud that he barkened,
"There's nothing like it, there isn't."

Hey, diddle, diddle!
Went the cat and the fiddle,
Hey diddle, diddle, dee, dee!
The dog laughed at the sport
Till his cough cut him short,
It was hey diddle, diddle, oh me!
And back came the cow
With a merry, merry low,
For she'd humbled the man in the moon.
The dish got excited,
The spoon was delighted,
And the dish waltzed away with the spoon.

But the man in the moon,
Coming back too soon
From the famous town of Norwich,
Caught up the dish,
Said, "It's just what I wish
To hold my cold plum-porridge!"
Gave the cow a rat-tat,
Flung water on the cat,
And sent him away like a rocket.
Said, "O Moon there you are!"
Got into her car,
And went off with the spoon in his pocket

Hey ho! diddle, diddle!

The wet cat and wet fiddle,

They made such a caterwauling,

That the cow in a fright

Stood bolt upright

Bellowing now, and bawling;

And the dog on his tail,

Stretched his neck with a wail.

But "Ho! ho!" said the man in the moon —

"No more in the South

Shall I burn my mouth,

For I've found a dish and a spoon."

25. Diamond's Dream

"There, baby!" said Diamond; "I'm so happy that I can only sing nonsense. Oh, father, think if you had been a poor man, and hadn't had a cab and old Diamond! What should I have done?"

"I don't know indeed what you could have done," said his father from the bed.

"We should have all starved, my precious Diamond," said his mother, whose pride in her boy was even greater than her joy in the shillings. Both of them together made her heart ache, for pleasure can do that as well as pain.

"Oh no! we shouldn't," said Diamond. "I could have taken Nanny's crossing till she came back; and then the money, instead of going for Old Sal's gin, would have gone for father's beef-tea. I wonder what Nanny will do when she gets well again. Somebody else will be sure to have taken the crossing by that time. I wonder if she will fight for it, and whether I shall have to help her. I won't bother my head about that. Time enough yet! Hey diddle! hey diddle! hey diddle diddle! I wonder whether Mr. Raymond would take me to see Nanny. Hey diddle! hey diddle! hey diddle diddle! The baby and fiddle! O, mother, I'm such a silly! But I can't help it. I wish I could think of something else, but there's nothing will come into my head but hey diddle diddle! the cat and the fiddle! I wonder what the angels do — when they're extra happy, you know — when they've been driving cabs all day and taking home the money to their mothers. Do you think they ever sing nonsense, mother?"

"I daresay they've got their own sort of it," answered his mother, "else they wouldn't be like other people." She was thinking more of her twenty-one shillings and sixpence, and of the nice dinner she would get for her sick husband next day, than of the angels and their nonsense, when she said it. But Diamond found her answer all right.

"Yes, to be sure," he replied. "They wouldn't be like other people if they hadn't their nonsense sometimes. But it must be very pretty nonsense, and not like that silly hey diddle diddle! the cat and the fiddle! I wish I could get it out of my head. I wonder what the angels' nonsense is like. Nonsense is a very good thing, ain't it, mother? — a little of it now and then; more of it for baby, and not so much for grown people like cabmen and their mothers? It's like the pepper and salt that goes in the soup — that's it — isn't it, mother? There's baby fast asleep! Oh, what a nonsense baby it is — to sleep so much! Shall I put him down, mother?"

Diamond chattered away. What rose in his happy little heart ran out of his mouth, and did his father and mother good. When he went to bed, which he did early, being more tired, as you may suppose, than usual, he was still thinking what the nonsense could be like which the angels sang when they were too happy to sing sense. But before coming to any conclusion he fell fast asleep. And no wonder, for it must be acknowledged a difficult question.

That night he had a very curious dream which I think my readers would like to have told them. They would, at least, if they are as fond of nice dreams as I am, and don't have enough of them of their own.

He dreamed that he was running about in the twilight in the old garden. He thought he was waiting for North Wind, but she did not come. So he would run down to the back gate, and see if she were there. He ran and ran. It was a good long garden out of his dream, but in his dream it had grown so long and spread out so wide that the gate he wanted was nowhere. He ran and ran, but instead of coming to the gate found himself in a beautiful country, not like any country he had ever been in before. There were no trees of any size; nothing bigger in fact than hawthorns, which were full of may-blossom. The place in which they grew was wild and dry, mostly covered with grass, but having patches of heath. It extended on every side as far as he could see. But although it was so wild, yet wherever in an ordinary heath you might have expected furze bushes, or holly, or broom, there grew roses — wild and rare — all kinds. On every side, far and near, roses were glowing. There too was the gum-cistus, whose flowers fall every night and come again the next morning, lilacs and syringas and laburnums, and many shrubs besides, of which he did not know the names; but the roses were everywhere. He wandered on and on, wondering when it would come to an end. It was of no use going back, for there was no house to be seen anywhere. But he was not frightened, for you know Diamond was used to things that were rather out of the way. He threw himself down under a rose-bush, and fell asleep.

He woke, not out of his dream, but into it, thinking he heard a child's voice, calling "Diamond, Diamond!" He jumped up, but all was still about him. The rose-bushes were pouring out their odors in clouds. He could see the scent like mists of the same color as the rose, issuing like a slow fountain and spreading in the air till it joined the thin rosy vapor which hung over all the wilderness. But again came the voice calling him, and it seemed to come from over his head. He looked up, but saw only the deep blue sky full of stars — more brilliant, however, than he had seen them before; and both sky and stars looked nearer to the earth.

While he gazed up, again he heard the cry. At the same moment he saw one of the biggest stars over his head give a kind of twinkle and jump, as if it went out and came in again. He threw himself on his back, and fixed his eyes upon it. Nor had he gazed long before it went out, leaving something like a scar in the blue. But as he went on gazing he saw a face where the star had been — a merry face, with bright eyes. The eyes appeared not only to see Diamond, but to know that Diamond had caught sight of them, for the face withdrew the same moment. Again came the voice, calling "Diamond, Diamond;" and in jumped the star to its place.

Diamond called as loud as he could, right up into the sky:

"Here's Diamond, down below you. What do you want him to do?"

The next instant many of the stars round about that one went out, and many voices shouted from the sky, —

"Come up; come up. We're so jolly! Diamond! Diamond!"

This was followed by a peal of the merriest, kindliest laughter, and all the stars jumped into their places again.

"How am I to come up?" shouted Diamond.

"Go round the rose-bush. It's got its foot in it," said the first voice.

Diamond got up at once, and walked to the other side of the rose-bush.

There he found what seemed the very opposite of what he wanted — a stair down into the earth. It was of turf and moss. It did not seem to promise well for getting into the sky, but Diamond had learned to look through the look of things. The voice must have meant that he was to go down this stair; and down this stair Diamond went, without waiting to think more about it.

It was such a nice stair, so cool and soft — all the sides as well as the steps grown with moss and grass and ferns! Down and down Diamond went — a long way, until at last he heard the gurgling and splashing of a little stream; nor had he gone much farther before he met it — yes, met it coming up the stairs to meet him, running up just as naturally as if it had been doing the other thing. Neither was Diamond in the least surprised to see it pitching itself from one step to another as it climbed towards him: he never thought it was odd — and no more it was, there. It would have been odd here. It made a merry tune as it came, and its voice was like the laughter he had heard from the sky. This appeared promising; and he went on, down and down the stair, and up and up the stream, till at last he came where it hurried out from under a stone, and the stair stopped altogether. And as the stream bubbled up, the stone shook and swayed with its force; and Diamond thought he would try to lift it. Lightly it rose to his hand, forced up by the stream from below; and, by what would have seemed an unaccountable perversion of things had he been awake, threatened to come tumbling upon his head. But he avoided it, and when it fell, got upon it. He now saw that the opening through which the water came pouring in was over his head, and with the help of the stone he scrambled out by it, and found himself on the side of a grassy hill which rounded away from him in every direction, and down which came the brook which vanished in the hole. But scarcely had he noticed so much as this before a merry shouting and laughter burst upon him, and a number of naked little boys came running, every one eager to get to him first. At the shoulders of each fluttered two little wings, which were of no use for flying, as they were mere buds; only being made for it they could not help fluttering as if they were flying. Just as the foremost of the troop reached him, one or two of them fell, and the rest with shouts of laughter came tumbling over them till they heaped up a mound of struggling merriment. One after another they extricated themselves, and each as he got free threw his arms round Diamond and kissed him. Diamond's heart was ready to melt within him from clear delight. When they had all embraced him, —

"Now let us have some fun," cried one, and with a shout they all scampered hither and thither, and played the wildest gambols on the grassy slopes. They kept constantly coming back to Diamond, however, as the centre of their enjoyment, rejoicing over him as if they had found a lost playmate.

There was a wind on the hillside which blew like the very embodiment of living gladness. It blew into Diamond's heart, and made him so happy that he was forced to sit down and cry.

"Now let's go and dig for stars," said one who seemed to be the captain of the troop.

They all scurried away, but soon returned, one after another, each with a pickaxe on his shoulder and a spade in his hand. As soon as they were gathered, the captain led them in a straight line to another part of the hill. Diamond rose and followed.

"Here is where we begin our lesson for to-night," he said. "Scatter and dig."

There was no more fun. Each went by himself, walking slowly with bent shoulders and his eyes fixed on the ground. Every now and then one would stop, kneel down, and look intently, feeling with his hands and parting the grass. One would get up and walk on again, another spring to his feet, catch eagerly at his pickaxe and strike it into the ground once and again, then throw it aside, snatch up his spade, and commence digging at the loosened earth. Now one would sorrowfully shovel the earth into the hole again, trample it down with his little bare white feet, and walk on. But another would give a joyful shout, and after much tugging and loosening would draw from the hole a lump as big as his head, or no bigger than his fist; when the under side of it would pour such a blaze of golden or bluish light into Diamond's eyes that he was quite dazzled. Gold and blue were the commoner colors: the jubilation was greater over red or green or purple. And every time a star was dug up all the little angels dropped their tools and crowded about it, shouting and dancing and fluttering their wing-buds.

When they had examined it well, they would kneel down one after the other and peep through the hole; but they always stood back to give Diamond the first look. All that diamond could report, however, was, that through the star-holes he saw a great many things and places and people he knew quite well, only somehow they were different — there was something marvelous about them — he could not tell what. Every time he rose from looking through a star-hole, he felt as if his heart would break for, joy; and he said that if he had not cried, he did not know what would have become of him.

As soon as all had looked, the star was carefully fitted in again, a little mould was strewn over it, and the rest of the heap left as a sign that the star had been discovered.

At length one dug up a small star of a most lovely color — a color Diamond had never seen before. The moment the angel saw what it was, instead of showing it about, he handed it to one of his neighbors, and seated himself on the edge of the hole, saying:

"This will do for me. Good-bye. I'm off."

They crowded about him, hugging and kissing him; then stood back with a solemn stillness, their wings lying close to their shoulders. The little fellow looked round on them once with a smile, and then shot himself headlong through the star-hole. Diamond, as privileged, threw himself on the ground to peep after him, but he saw nothing. "It's no use," said the captain. "I never saw anything more of one that went that way."

"His wings can't be much use," said Diamond, concerned and fearful, yet comforted by the calm looks of the rest.

"That's true," said the captain. "He's lost them by this time. They all do that go that way. You haven't got any, you see."

"No," said Diamond. "I never did have any."

"Oh! didn't you?" said the captain.

"Some people say," he added, after a pause, "that they come again. I don't know. I've never found the color I care about myself. I suppose I shall some day."

Then they looked again at the star, put it carefully into its hole, danced around it and over it— but solemnly, and called it by the name of the finder.

"Will you know it again?" asked Diamond.

"Oh, yes. We never forget a star that's been made a door of."

Then they went on with their searching and digging.

422   C3 George MacDonald

Diamond having neither pickaxe nor spade, had the more time to think.

"I don't see any little girls," he said at last.

The captain stopped his shoveling, leaned on his spade, rubbed his forehead thoughtfully with his left hand — the little angels were all left-handed—repeated the words "little girls," and then, as if a thought had struck him, resumed his work, saying —

"I think I know what you mean. I've never seen any of them, of course; but I suppose that's the sort you mean. I'm told — but mind I don't say it is so, for I don't know—that when we fall asleep, a troop of angels very like ourselves, only quite different, goes round to all the stars we have discovered, and discovers them after us. I suppose with our shoveling and handling we spoil them a bit; and I daresay the clouds that come up from below make them smoky and dull sometimes. They say—mind, I say they say — these other angels take them out one by one, and pass each round as we do, and breathe over it, and rub it with their white hands, which are softer than ours, because they don't do any pick-and-spade work, and smile at it, and put it in again: and that is what keeps them from growing dark."

"How jolly!" thought Diamond. "I should like to see them at their work too.—When do you go to sleep?" he asked the captain.

"When we grow sleepy," answered the captain. "They do say — but mind I say they say — that it is when those others — what do you call them? I don't know if that is their name; I am only guessing that may be the sort you mean — when they are on their rounds and come near any troop of us we fall asleep. They live on the west side of the hill. None of us have ever been to the top of it yet."

Even as he spoke, he dropped his spade. He tumbled down beside it, and lay fast asleep. One after the other each of the troop dropped his pickaxe or shovel from his listless hands, and lay fast asleep by his work.

"Ah!" thought Diamond to himself, with delight, "now the girl-angels are coming, and I, not being an angel, shall not fall asleep like the rest, and I shall see the girl-angels."

But the same moment he felt himself growing sleepy. He struggled hard with the invading power. He put up his fingers to his eyelids and pulled them open. But it was of no use. He thought he saw a glimmer of pale rosy light far up the green hill, and ceased to know.

When he awoke, all the angels were starting up wide awake too. He expected to see them lift their tools, but no, the time for play had come. They looked happier than ever, and each began to sing where he stood. He had not heard them sing before.

"Now," he thought, "I shall know what kind of nonsense the angels sing when they are merry. They don't drive cabs, I see, but they dig for stars, and they work hard enough to be merry after it."

And he did hear some of the angels' nonsense; for if it was all sense to them, it had only just as much sense to Diamond as made good nonsense of it. He tried hard to set it down in his mind, listening as closely as he could, now to one, now to another, and now to all together. But while they were yet singing he began, to his dismay, to find that he was coming awake — faster and faster. And as he came awake, he found that, for all the goodness of his memory, verse after verse of the angels' nonsense vanished from it. He always thought he could keep the last, but as the next began he lost the one before it, and at length awoke, struggling to keep hold of the last verse of all. He felt as if the effort to keep from forgetting that one verse of the vanishing song nearly killed him. And yet by the time he was wide awake he could not be sure of that even. It was something like this:

White hands of whiteness

Wash the stars' faces,

Till glitter, glitter, glit, goes their brightness

Down to poor places.

This, however, was so near sense that he thought it could not be really what they did sing.

26. DIAMOND TAKES A FARE THE WRONG WAY RIGHT

The next morning Diamond was up almost as early as before. He had nothing to fear from his mother now, and made no secret of what he was about. By the time he reached the stable, several of the men were there. They asked him a good many questions as to his luck the day before, and he told them all they wanted to know. But when he proceeded to harness the old horse, they pushed him aside with rough kindness, called him a baby, and began to do it all for him. So Diamond ran in and had another mouthful of tea and bread and butter; and although he had never been so tired as he was the night before, he started quite fresh this morning. It was a cloudy day, and the wind blew hard from the north — so hard sometimes that, perched on the box with just his toes touching the ground, Diamond wished that he had some kind of strap to fasten himself down with lest he should be blown away. But he did not really mind it.

His head was full of the dream he had dreamed; but it did not make him neglect his work, for his work was not to dig stars but to drive old Diamond and pick up fares. There are not many people who can think about beautiful things and do common work at the same time. But then there are not many people who have been to the back of the north wind.

There was not much business doing. And Diamond felt rather cold, notwithstanding his mother had herself put on his comforter and helped him with his greatcoat. But he was too well aware of his dignity to get inside his cab as some do. A cabman ought to be above minding the weather — at least so Diamond thought. At length he was called to a neighboring house, where a young woman with a heavy box had to be taken to Wapping for a coast-steamer.

He did not find it at all pleasant, so far east and so near the river; for the roughs were in great force. However, there being no block, not even in Nightingale Lane, he reached the entrance of the wharf, and set down his passenger without annoyance. But as he turned to go back, some idlers, not content with chaffing him, showed a mind to the fare the young woman had given him. They were just pulling him off the box, and Diamond was shouting for the police, when a pale-faced man, in very shabby clothes, but with the look of a gentleman somewhere about him, came up, and making good use of his stick, drove them off.

"Now, my little man," he said, "get on while you can. Don't lose any time. This is not a place for you."

But Diamond was not in the habit of thinking only of himself. He saw that his new friend looked weary, if not ill, and very poor.

"Won't you jump in, sir?" he said. "I will take you wherever you like."

"Thank you, my man; but I have no money; so I can't."

"Oh! I don't want any money. I shall be much happier if you will get in. You have saved me all I had. I owe you a lift, sir."

"Which way are you going?"

"To Charing Cross; but I don't mind where I go."

"Well, I am very tired. If you will take me to Charing Cross, I shall be greatly obliged to you. I have walked from Gravesend, and had hardly a penny left to get through the tunnel."

So saying, he opened the door and got in, and Diamond drove away.

But as he drove, he could not help fancying he had seen the gentleman — for Diamond knew he was a gentleman — before. Do all he could, however, he could not recall where or when. Meantime his fare, if we may call him such, seeing he was to pay nothing, whom the relief of being carried had made less and less inclined to carry himself, had been turning over things in his mind, and, as they passed the Mint, called to Diamond, who stopped the horse, got down and went to the window.

"If you didn't mind taking me to Chiswick, I should be able to pay you when we got there. It's a long way, but you shall have the whole fare from the Docks — and something over."

"Very well, sir" said Diamond. "I shall be most happy."

He was just clambering up again, when the gentleman put his head out of the window and said —

"It's The Wilderness — Mr. Coleman's place; but I'll direct you when we come into the neighborhood."

It flashed upon Diamond who he was. But he got upon his box to arrange his thoughts before making any reply.

The gentleman was Mr. Evans, to whom Miss Coleman was to have been married, and Diamond had seen him several times with her in the garden. I have said that he had not behaved very well to Miss Coleman. He had put off their marriage more than once in a cowardly fashion, merely because he was ashamed to marry upon a small income, and live in a humble way. When a man thinks of what people will say in such a case, he may love, but his love is but a poor affair. Mr. Coleman took him into the firm as a junior partner, and it was in a measure through his influence that he entered upon those speculations which ruined him. So his love had not been a blessing. The ship which North Wind had sunk was their last venture, and Mr. Evans had gone out with it in the hope of turning its cargo to the best advantage. He was one of the single boat-load which managed to reach a desert island, and he had gone through a great many hardships and sufferings since then. But he was not past being taught, and his troubles had done him no end of good, for they had made him doubt himself, and begin to think, so that he had come to see that he had been foolish as well as wicked. For, if he had had Miss Coleman with him in the desert island, to build her a hut, and hunt for her food, and make clothes for her, he would have thought himself the most fortunate of men; and when he was at home, he would not marry till he could afford a man-servant. Before he got home again, he had even begun to understand that no man can make haste to be rich without going against the will of God, in which case it is the one frightful thing to be successful. So he had come back a more humble man, and longing to ask Miss Coleman to forgive him. But he had no idea what ruin had fallen upon them, for he had never made himself thoroughly acquainted with the firm's affairs. Few speculative people do know their own affairs. Hence he never doubted he should find matters much as he left them, and expected to see them all at The Wilderness as before. But if he had not fallen in with Diamond, he would not have thought of going there first.

What was Diamond to do? He had heard his father and mother drop some remarks concerning Mr. Evans which made him doubtful of him. He understood that he had not been so considerate as he might have been. So he went rather slowly till he should make up his mind. It was, of course, of no use to drive Mr. Evans to Chiswick. But if he should tell him what had befallen them, and where they lived now, he might put off going to see them, and he was certain that Miss Coleman, at least, must want very much to see Mr. Evans. He was pretty sure also that the best thing in any case was to bring them together, and let them set matters right for themselves.

The moment he came to this conclusion, he changed his course from westward to northward, and went straight for Mr. Coleman's poor little house in Hoxton. Mr. Evans was too tired and too much occupied with his thoughts to take the least notice of the streets they passed through, and had no suspicion, therefore, of the change of direction.

By this time the wind had increased almost to a hurricane, and as they had often to head it, it was no joke for either of the Diamonds. The distance, however, was not great. Before they reached the street where Mr. Coleman lived it blew so tremendously, that when Miss Coleman, who was going out a little way, opened the door, it dashed against the wall with such a bang, that she was afraid to venture, and went in again. In five minutes after, Diamond drew up at the door. As soon as he had entered the street, however, the wind blew right behind them, and when he pulled up, old Diamond had so much ado to stop the cab against it, that the breeching broke. Young Diamond jumped off his box, knocked loudly at the door, then turned to the cab and said—before Mr. Evans had quite begun to think something must be amiss:

"Please, sir, my harness has given away. Would you mind stepping in here for a few minutes? They're friends of mine. I'll take you where you like after I've got it mended. I shan't be many minutes, but you can't stand in this wind."

Half stupid with fatigue and want of food, Mr. Evans yielded to the boy's suggestion, and walked in at the door which the maid held with difficulty against the wind. She took Mr. Evans for a visitor, as indeed he was, and showed him into the room on the ground-floor. Diamond, who had followed into the hall, whispered to her as she closed the door—

"Tell Miss Coleman. It's Miss Coleman he wants to see."

"I don't know" said the maid. "He don't look much like a gentleman."

"He is, though; and I know him, and so does Miss Coleman."

The maid could not but remember Diamond, having seen him when he and his father brought the ladies home. So she believed him, and went to do what he told her.

What passed in the little parlor when Miss Coleman came down does not belong to my story, which is all about Diamond. If he had known that Miss Coleman thought Mr. Evans was dead, perhaps he would have managed differently. There was a cry and a running to and fro in the house, and then all was quiet again.

Almost as soon as Mr. Evans went in, the wind began to cease, and was now still. Diamond found that by making the breeching just a little tighter than was quite comfortable for the old horse he could do very well for the present; and, thinking it better to let him have his bag in this quiet place, he sat on the box till the old horse should have eaten his dinner. In a little while Mr. Evans came out, and asked him to come in. Diamond obeyed, and to his delight Miss Coleman put her arms round him and kissed him, and there was payment for him! Not to mention the five precious shillings she gave him, which he could not refuse because his mother wanted them so much at home for his father. He left them nearly as happy as they were themselves.

The rest of the day he did better, and, although he had not so much to take home as the day before, yet on the whole the result was satisfactory. And what a story he had to tell his father and mother about his adventures, and how he had done, and what was the result! They asked him such a multitude of questions! Some of which he could answer, and some of which he could not answer; and his father seemed ever so much better from finding that his boy was already not only useful to his family but useful to other people, and quite taking his place as a man who judged what was wise, and did work worth doing.

For a fortnight Diamond went on driving his cab, and keeping his family. He had begun to be known about some parts of London, and people would prefer taking his cab because they liked what they heard of him. One gentleman who lived near the mews engaged him to carry him to the City every morning at a certain hour; and Diamond was punctual as clockwork — though to effect that required a good deal of care, for his father's watch was not much to be depended on, and had to be watched itself by the clock of St. George's church. Between the two, however, he did make a success of it.

After that fortnight, his father was able to go out again. Then Diamond went to make inquiries about Nanny, and this led to something else.

27. THE CHILDREN'S HOSPITAL

The first day his father resumed his work, Diamond went with him as usual. In the afternoon, however, his father, having taken a fare to the neighborhood, went home, and Diamond drove the cab the rest of the day. It was hard for old Diamond to do all the work, but they could not afford to have another horse. They contrived to save him as much as possible, and fed him well, and he did bravely.

The next morning his father was so much stronger that Diamond thought he might go and ask Mr. Raymond to take him to see Nanny. He found him at home. His servant had grown friendly by this time, and showed him in without any cross-questioning. Mr. Raymond received him with his usual kindness, consented at once, and walked with him to the Hospital, which was close at hand. It was a comfortable old-fashioned house, built in the reign of Queen Anne, and in her day, no doubt, inhabited by rich and fashionable people: now it was a home for poor sick children, who were carefully tended for love's sake. There are regions in London where a hospital in every other street might be full of such children, whose fathers and mothers are dead, or unable to take care of them.

When Diamond followed Mr. Raymond into the room where those children who had got over the worst of their illness and were growing better lay, he saw a number of little iron bedsteads, with their heads to the walls, and in every one of them a child, whose face was a story in itself. In some, health had begun to appear in a tinge upon the cheeks, and a doubtful brightness in the eyes, just as out of the cold dreary winter the spring comes in blushing buds and bright crocuses. In others there were more of the signs of winter left. Their faces reminded you of snow and keen cutting winds, more than of sunshine and soft breezes and butterflies; but even in them the signs of suffering told that the suffering was less, and that if the spring-time had but arrived, it had yet arrived.

Diamond looked all round, but could see no Nanny. He turned to Mr. Raymond with a question in his eyes.

"Well?" said Mr. Raymond.

"Nanny's not here," said Diamond.

"Oh, yes, she is."

"I don't see her."

"I do, though. There she is."

He pointed to a bed right in front of where Diamond was standing.

"That's not Nanny," he said.

"It is Nanny. I have seen her many times since you have. Illness makes a great difference."

"Why, that girl must have been to the back of the north wind!" thought Diamond, but he said nothing, only stared; and as he stared, something of the old Nanny began to dawn through the face of the new Nanny. The old Nanny, though a good girl, and a friendly girl, had been rough, blunt in her speech, and dirty in her person. Her face would always have reminded one who had already been to the back of the north wind of something he had seen in the best of company, but it had been coarse notwithstanding, partly from the weather, partly from her living amongst low people, and partly from having to defend herself: now it was so sweet, and gentle, and refined, that she might have had a lady and gentleman for a father and mother. And Diamond could not help thinking of words which he had heard in the church the day before: "Surely it is good to be afflicted;" or something like that. North Wind, somehow or other, must have had to do with her! She had grown from a rough girl into a gentle maiden.

Mr. Raymond, however, was not surprised, for he was used to see such lovely changes — something like the change which passes upon the crawling, many-footed creature, when it turns sick and ill, and revives a butterfly, with two wings instead of many feet. Instead of her having to take care of herself, kind hands ministered to her, making her comfortable and sweet and clean, soothing her aching head, and giving her cooling drink when she was thirsty; and kind eyes, the stars of the kingdom of heaven, had shone upon her; so that, what with the fire of the fever and the dew of tenderness, that which was coarse in her had melted away, and her whole face had grown so refined and sweet that Diamond did not know her. But as he gazed, the best of the old face, all the true and good part of it, that which was Nanny herself, dawned upon him, like the moon coming out of a cloud, until at length, instead of only believing Mr. Raymond that this was she, he saw for himself that it was Nanny indeed — very worn but grown beautiful.

He went up to her. She smiled. He had heard her laugh, but had never seen her smile before.

"Nanny, do you know me?" said Diamond.

She only smiled again, as if the question was amusing.

She was not likely to forget him; for although she did not yet know it was he who had got her there, she had dreamed of him often, and had talked much about him when delirious. Nor was it much wonder, for he was the only boy except Joe who had ever shown her kindness.

Meantime Mr. Raymond was going from bed to bed, talking to the little people. Every one knew him, and every one was eager to have a look, and a smile, and a kind word from him.

Diamond sat down on a stool at the head of Nanny's bed. She laid her hand in his. No one else of her old acquaintance had been near her.

Suddenly a little voice called aloud —

"Won't Mr. Raymond tell us a story?"

"Oh, yes, please do! please do!" cried several little voices which also were stronger than the rest. For Mr. Raymond was in the habit of telling them a story when he went to see them, and they enjoyed it far more than the other nice things which the doctor permitted him to give them.

"Very well," said Mr. Raymond, "I will. What sort of a story shall it be?"

"A true story," said one little girl.

"A fairy tale," said a little boy.

"Well," said Mr. Raymond, "I suppose, as there is a difference, I may choose. I can't think of any true story just at this moment, so I will tell you a sort of a fairy one."

"Oh, jolly!" exclaimed the little boy who had called out for a fairy tale.

"It came into my head this morning as I got out of bed," continued Mr. Raymond; "and if it turns out pretty well, I will write it down, and get somebody to print it for me, and then you shall read it when you like."

"Then nobody ever heard it before?" asked one older child.

"No, nobody."

"Oh!" exclaimed several, thinking it very grand to have the first telling; and I daresay there might be a peculiar freshness about it, because everything would be nearly as new to the story-teller himself as to the listeners.

Some were only sitting up and some were lying down, so there could not be the same busy gathering, bustling, and shifting to and fro with which children generally prepare themselves to hear a story; but their faces, and the turning of their heads, and many feeble exclamations of expected pleasure, showed that all such preparations were making within them.

Mr. Raymond stood in the middle of the room, that he might turn from side to side, and give each a share of seeing him. Diamond kept his place by Nanny's side, with her hand in his. I do not know how much of Mr. Raymond's story the smaller children understood; indeed, I don't quite know how much there was in it to be understood, for in such a story every one has just to take what he can get. But they all listened with apparent satisfaction, and certainly with great attention. Mr. Raymond wrote it down afterwards, and here it is — somewhat altered no doubt, for a good story-teller tries to make his stories better every time he tells them. I cannot myself help thinking that he was somewhat indebted for this one to the old story of The Sleeping Beauty.

28. LITTLE DAYLIGHT

No house of any pretension to be called a palace is in the least worthy of the name, except it has a wood near it — very near it — and the nearer the better. Not all round it — I don't mean that, for a palace ought to be open to the sun and wind, and stand high and brave, with weathercocks glittering and flags flying; but on one side of every palace there must be a wood. And there was a very grand wood indeed beside the palace of the king who was going to be Daylight's father; such a grand wood, that nobody yet had ever got to the other end of it. Near the house it was kept very trim and nice, and it was free of brushwood for a long way in; but by degrees it got wild, and it grew wilder, and wilder, and wilder, until some said wild beasts at last did what they liked in it. The king and his courtiers often hunted, however, and this kept the wild beasts far away from the palace.

One glorious summer morning, when the wind and sun were out together, when the vanes were flashing and the flags frolicking against the blue sky, little Daylight made her appearance from somewhere — nobody could tell where — a beautiful baby, with such bright eyes that she might have come from the sun, only by and by she showed such lively ways that she might equally well have come out of the wind. There was great jubilation in the palace, for this was the first baby the queen had had, and there is as much happiness over a new baby in a palace as in a cottage.

But there is one disadvantage of living near a wood: you do not know quite who your neighbors may be. Everybody knew there were in it several fairies, living within a few miles of the palace, who always had had something to do with each new baby that came; for fairies live so much longer than we, that they can have business with a good many generations of human mortals. The curious houses they lived in were well known also, — one, a hollow oak; another, a birch-tree, though nobody could ever find how that fairy made a house of it; another, a hut of growing trees intertwined, and patched up with turf and moss. But there was another fairy who had lately come to the place, and nobody even knew she was a fairy except the other fairies. A wicked old thing she was, always concealing her power, and being as disagreeable as she could, in order to tempt people to give her offence, that she might have the pleasure of taking vengeance upon them. The people about thought she was a witch, and those who knew her by sight were careful to avoid offending her. She lived in a mud house, in a swampy part of the forest.

In all history we find that fairies give their remarkable gifts to prince or princess, or any child of sufficient importance in their eyes, always at the christening. Now this we can understand, because it is an ancient custom amongst human beings as well; and it is not hard to explain why wicked fairies should choose the same time to do unkind things; but it is difficult to understand how they should be able to do them, for you would fancy all wicked creatures would be powerless on such an occasion. But I never knew of any interference on the part of the wicked fairy that did not turn out a good thing in the end. What a good thing, for instance, it was that one princess should sleep for a hundred years! Was she not saved from all the plague of young men who were not worthy of her? And did she not come awake exactly at the right moment when the right prince kissed her? For my part, I cannot help wishing a good many girls would sleep till just the same fate overtook them. It would be happier for them, and more agreeable to their friends.

Of course all the known fairies were invited to the christening. But the king and queen never thought of inviting an old witch. For the power of the fairies they have by nature; whereas a witch gets her power by wickedness. The other fairies, however, knowing the danger thus run, provided as well as they could against accidents from her quarter. But they could neither render her powerless, nor could they arrange their gifts in reference to hers beforehand, for they could not tell what those might be.

Of course the old hag was there without being asked. Not to be asked was just what she wanted, that she might have a sort of reason for doing what she wished to do. For somehow even the wickedest of creatures likes a pretext for doing the wrong thing.

Five fairies had one after the other given the child such gifts as each counted best, and the fifth had just stepped back to her place in the surrounding splendor of ladies and gentlemen, when, mumbling a laugh between her toothless gums, the wicked fairy hobbled out into the middle of the circle, and at the moment when the archbishop was handing the baby to the lady at the head of the nursery department of state affairs, addressed him thus, giving a bite or two to every word before she could part with it:

"Please your Grace, I'm very deaf: would your Grace mind repeating the princess's name?"

"With pleasure, my good woman," said the archbishop, stooping to shout in her ear: "the infant's name is little Daylight."

"And little daylight it shall be," cried the fairy, in the tone of a dry axle, "and little good shall any of her gifts do her. For I bestow upon her the gift of sleeping all day long, whether she will or not. Ha, ha! He, he! Hi, hi!"

Then out started the sixth fairy, who, of course, the others had arranged should come after the wicked one, in order to undo as much as she might.

"If she sleep all day," she said, mournfully, "she shall, at least, wake all night."

"A nice prospect for her mother and me!" thought the poor king; for they loved her far too much to give her up to nurses, especially at night, as most kings and queens do—and are sorry for it afterwards.

"You spoke before I had done," said the wicked fairy. "That's against the law. It gives me another chance."

"I beg your pardon," said the other fairies, all together.

"She did. I hadn't done laughing," said the crone. "I had only got to Hi, hi! and I had to go through Ho, ho! and Hu, hu! So I decree that if she wakes all night she shall wax and wane with its mistress, the moon. And what that may mean I hope her royal parents will live to see. Ho, ho! Hu, hu!"

But out stepped another fairy, for they had been wise enough to keep two in reserve, because every fairy knew the trick of one.

"Until," said the seventh fairy, "a prince comes who shall kiss her without knowing it."

The wicked fairy made a horrid noise like an angry cat, and hobbled away. She could not pretend that she had not finished her speech this time, for she had laughed Ho, ho! and Hu, hu!

"I don't know what that means," said the poor king to the seventh fairy.

"Don't be afraid. The meaning will come with the thing itself," said she.

The assembly broke up, miserable enough — the queen, at least, prepared for a good many sleepless nights, and the lady at the head of the nursery department anything but comfortable in the prospect before her, for of course the queen could not do it all. As for the king, he made up his mind, with what courage he could summon, to meet the demands of the case, but wondered whether he could with any propriety require the First Lord of the Treasury to take a share in the burden laid upon him.

I will not attempt to describe what they had to go through for some time. But at last the household settled into a regular system — a very irregular one in some respects. For at certain seasons the palace rang all night with bursts of laughter from little Daylight, whose heart the old fairy's curse could not reach; she was Daylight still, only a little in the wrong place, for she always dropped asleep at the first hint of dawn in the east. But her merriment was of short duration. When the moon was at the full, she was in glorious spirits, and as beautiful as it was possible for a child of her age to be. But as the moon waned, she faded, until at last she was wan and withered like the poorest, sickliest child you might come upon in the streets of a great city in the arms of a homeless mother. Then the night was quiet as the day, for the little creature lay in her gorgeous cradle night and day with hardly a motion, and indeed at last without even a moan, like one dead. At first they often thought she was dead, but at last they got used to it, and only consulted the almanac to find the moment when she would begin to revive, which, of course, was with the first appearance of the silver thread of the crescent moon. Then she would move her lips, and they would give her a little nourishment; and she would grow better and better and better, until for a few days she was splendidly well. When well, she was always merriest out in the moonlight; but even when near her worst, she seemed better when, in warm summer nights, they carried her cradle out into the light of the waning moon. Then in her sleep she would smile the faintest, most pitiful smile.

For a long time very few people ever saw her awake. As she grew older she became such a favorite, however, that about the palace there were always some who would contrive to keep awake at night, in order to be near her. But she soon began to take every chance of getting away from her nurses and enjoying her moonlight alone. And thus things went on until she was nearly seventeen years of age. Her father and mother had by that time got so used to the odd state of things that they had ceased to wonder at them. All their arrangements had reference to the state of the Princess Daylight, and it is amazing how things contrive to accommodate themselves. But how any prince was ever to find and deliver her, appeared inconceivable.

As she grew older she had grown more and more beautiful, with the sunniest hair and the loveliest eyes of heavenly blue, brilliant and profound as the sky of a June day. But so much more painful and sad was the change as her bad time came on. The more beautiful she was in the full moon, the more withered and worn did she become as the moon waned. At the time at which my story has now arrived, she looked, when the moon was small or gone, like an old woman exhausted with suffering. This was the more painful that her appearance was unnatural; for her hair and eyes did not change. Her wan face was both drawn and wrinkled, and had an eager hungry look. Her skinny hands moved as if wishing, but unable, to lay hold of something. Her shoulders were bent forward, her chest went in, and she stooped as if she were eighty years old. At last she had to be put to bed, and there await the flow of the tide of life. But she grew to dislike being seen, still more being touched by any hands, during this season. One lovely summer evening, when the moon lay all but gone upon the verge of the horizon, she vanished from her attendants, and it was only after searching for her a long time in great terror, that they found her fast asleep in the forest, at the foot of a silver birch, and carried her home.

A little way from the palace there was a great open glade, covered with the greenest and softest grass. This was her favorite haunt; for here the full moon shone free and glorious, while through a vista in the trees she could generally see more or less of the dying moon as it crossed the opening. Here she had a little rustic house built for her, and here she mostly resided. None of the court might go there without leave, and her own attendants had learned by this time not to be officious in waiting upon her, so that she was very much at liberty. Whether the good fairies had anything to do with it or not I cannot tell, but at last she got into the way of retreating further into the wood every night as the moon waned, so that sometimes they had great trouble in finding her; but as she was always very angry if she discovered they were watching her, they scarcely dared to do so. At length one night they thought they had lost her altogether. It was morning before they found her. Feeble as she was, she had wandered into a thicket a long way from the glade, and there she lay — fast asleep, of course.

Although the fame of her beauty and sweetness had gone abroad, yet as everybody knew she was under a bad spell, no king in the neighborhood had any desire to have her for a daughter-in-law. There were serious objections to such a relation.

About this time in a neighboring kingdom, in consequence of the wickedness of the nobles, an insurrection took place upon the death of the old king, the greater part of the nobility was massacred, and the young prince was compelled to flee for his life, disguised like a peasant. For some time, until he got out of the country, he suffered much from hunger and fatigue; but when he got into that ruled by the princess's father, and had no longer any fear of being recognized, he fared better, for the people were kind. He did not abandon his disguise, however. One tolerable reason was that he had no other clothes to put on, and another that he had very little money, and did not know where to get any more. There was no good in telling everybody he met that he was a prince, for he felt that a prince ought to be able to get on like other people, else his rank only made a fool of him. He had read of princes setting out upon adventure; and here he was out in similar case, only without having had a choice in the matter. He would go on, and see what would come of it.

For a day or two he had been walking through the palace-wood, and had had next to nothing to eat, when he came upon the strangest little house, inhabited by a very nice, tidy, motherly old woman. This was one of the good fairies. The moment she saw him she knew quite well who he was and what was going to come of it; but she was not at liberty to interfere with the orderly march of events. She received him with the kindness she would have shown to any other traveler, and gave him bread and milk, which he thought the most delicious food he had ever tasted, wondering that they did not have it for dinner at the palace sometimes. The old woman pressed him to stay all night. When he awoke he was amazed to find how well and strong he felt. She would not take any of the money he offered, but begged him, if he found occasion of continuing in the neighborhood, to return and occupy the same quarters.

"Thank you much, good mother," answered the prince; "but there is little chance of that. The sooner I get out of this wood the better."

"I don't know that," said the fairy.

"What do you mean?" asked the prince.

"Why, how should I know?" returned she.

"I can't tell," said the prince.

"Very well," said the fairy.

"How strangely you talk!" said the prince.

"Do I?" said the fairy.

"Yes, you do," said the prince.

"Very well," said the fairy.

The prince was not used to be spoken to in this fashion, so he felt a little angry, and turned and walked away. But this did not offend the fairy. She stood at the door of her little house looking after him till the trees hid him quite. Then she said "At last!" and went in.

The prince wandered and wandered, and got nowhere. The sun sank and sank and went out of sight, and he seemed no nearer the end of the wood than ever. He sat down on a fallen tree, ate a bit of bread the old woman had given him, and waited for the moon; for, although he was not much of an astronomer, he knew the moon would rise some time, because she had risen the night before. Up she came, slow and slow, but of a good size, pretty nearly round indeed; whereupon, greatly refreshed with his piece of bread, he got up and went — he knew not whither.

After walking a considerable distance, he thought he was coming to the outside of the forest; but when he reached what he thought the last of it, he found himself only upon the edge of a great open space in it, covered with grass. The moon shone very bright, and he thought he had never seen a more lovely spot. Still it looked dreary because of its loneliness, for he could not see the house at the other side. He sat down, weary again, and gazed into the glade. He had not seen so much room for several days.

All at once he spied something in the middle of the grass. What could it be? It moved; it came nearer. Was it a human creature, gliding across — a girl dressed in white, gleaming in the moonshine? She came nearer and nearer. He crept behind a tree and watched, wondering. It must be some strange being of the wood — a nymph whom the moonlight and the warm dusky air had enticed from her tree. But when she came close to where he stood, he no longer doubted she was human — for he had caught sight of her sunny hair, and her clear blue eyes, and the loveliest face and form that he had ever seen. All at once she began singing like a nightingale, and dancing to her own music, with her eyes ever turned towards the moon. She passed close to where he stood, dancing on by the edge of the trees and away in a great circle towards the other side, until he could see but a spot of white in the yellowish green of the moonlit grass. But when he feared it would vanish quite, the spot grew, and became a figure once more. She approached him again, singing and dancing, and waving her arms over her head, until she had completed the circle. Just opposite his tree she stood, ceased her song, dropped her arms, and broke out into a long clear laugh, musical as a brook. Then, as if tired, she threw herself on the grass, and lay gazing at the moon. The prince was almost afraid to breathe lest he should startle her, and she should vanish from his sight. As to venturing near her, that never came into his head.

She had lain for a long hour or longer, when the prince began again to doubt concerning her. Perhaps she was but a vision of his own fancy. Or was she a spirit of the wood, after all? If so, he too would haunt the wood, glad to have lost kingdom and everything for the hope of being near her. He would build him a hut in the forest, and there he would live for the pure chance of seeing her again. Upon nights like this at least she would come out and bask in the moonlight, and make his soul blessed. But while he thus dreamed she sprang to her feet, turned her face full to the moon, and began singing as she would draw her down from the sky by the power of her entrancing voice. She looked more beautiful than ever. Again she began dancing to her own music, and danced away into the distance. Once more she returned in a similar manner; but although he was watching as eagerly as before, what with fatigue and what with gazing, he fell fast asleep before she came near him. When he awoke it was broad daylight, and the princess was nowhere.

He could not leave the place. What if she should come the next night! He would gladly endure a day's hunger to see her yet again: he would buckle his belt quite tight. He walked round the glade to see if he could discover any prints of her feet. But the grass was so short, and her steps had been so light, that she had not left a single trace behind her. He walked half-way round the wood without seeing anything to account for her presence. Then he spied a lovely little house, with thatched roof and low eaves, surrounded by an exquisite garden, with doves and peacocks walking in it. Of course this must be where the gracious lady who loved the moonlight lived. Forgetting his appearance, he walked towards the door, determined to make inquiries, but as he passed a little pond full of gold and silver fishes, he caught sight of himself and turned to find the door to the kitchen. There he knocked, and asked for a piece of bread. The good-natured cook brought him in, and gave him an excellent breakfast, which the prince found nothing the worse for being served in the kitchen. While he ate, he talked with his entertainer, and learned that this was the favorite retreat of the Princess Daylight. But he learned nothing more, both because he was afraid of seeming inquisitive, and because the cook did not choose to be heard talking about her mistress to a peasant lad who had begged for his breakfast.

As he rose to take his leave, it occurred to him that he might not be so far from the old woman's cottage as he had thought, and he asked the cook whether she knew anything of such a place, describing it as well as he could. She said she knew it well enough, adding with a smile —

"It's there you're going, is it?"

"Yes, if it's not far off."

"It's not more than three miles. But mind what you are about, you know."

"Why do you say that?"

"If you're after any mischief, she'll make you repent it."

"The best thing that could happen under the circumstances," remarked the prince.

"What do you mean by that?" asked the cook.

"Why, it stands to reason," answered the prince "that if you wish to do anything wrong, the best thing for you is to be made to repent of it."

"I see," said the cook. "Well, I think you may venture. She's a good old soul."

"Which way does it lie from here?" asked the prince.

She gave him full instructions; and he left her with many thanks.

Being now refreshed, however, the prince did not go back to the cottage that day: he remained in the forest, amusing himself as best he could, but waiting anxiously for the night, in the hope that the princess would again appear. Nor was he disappointed, for, directly the moon rose, he spied a glimmering shape far across the glade. As it drew nearer, he saw it was she indeed — not dressed in white as before: in a pale blue like the sky, she looked lovelier still. He thought it was that the blue suited her yet better than the white; he did not know that she was really more beautiful because the moon was nearer the full. In fact the next night was full moon, and the princess would then be at the zenith of her loveliness.

The prince feared for some time that she was not coming near his hiding-place that night; but the circles in her dance ever widened as the moon rose, until at last they embraced the whole glade, and she came still closer to the trees where he was hiding than she had come the night before. He was entranced with her loveliness, for it was indeed a marvelous thing. All night long he watched her, but dared not go near her. He would have been ashamed of watching her too, had he not become almost incapable of thinking of anything but how beautiful she was. He watched the whole night long, and saw that as the moon went down she retreated in smaller and smaller circles, until at last he could see her no more.

Weary as he was, he set out for the old woman's cottage, where he arrived just in time for her breakfast, which she shared with him. He then went to bed, and slept for many hours. When he awoke the sun was down, and he departed in great anxiety lest he should lose a glimpse of the lovely vision. But, whether it was by the machinations of the swamp-fairy, or merely that it is one thing to go and another to return by the same road, he lost his way. I shall not attempt to describe his misery when the moon rose, and he saw nothing but trees, trees, trees.

She was high in the heavens before he reached the glade. Then indeed his troubles vanished, for there was the princess coming dancing towards him, in a dress that shone like gold, and with shoes that glimmered through the grass like fireflies. She was of course still more beautiful than before. Like an embodied sunbeam she passed him, and danced away into the distance.

Before she returned in her circle, the clouds had begun to gather about the moon. The wind rose, the trees moaned, and their lighter branches leaned all one way before it. The prince feared that the princess would go in, and he should see her no more that night. But she came dancing on more jubilant than ever, her golden dress and her sunny hair streaming out upon the blast, waving her arms towards the moon, and in the exuberance of her delight ordering the clouds away from off her face. The prince could hardly believe she was not a creature of the elements, after all.

By the time she had completed another circle, the clouds had gathered deep, and there were growlings of distant thunder. Just as she passed the tree where he stood, a flash of lightning blinded him for a moment, and when he saw again, to his horror, the princess lay on the ground. He darted to her, thinking she had been struck; but when she heard him coming, she was on her feet in a moment.

"What do you want?" she asked.

"I beg your pardon. I thought—the lightning" said the prince, hesitating.

"There's nothing the matter," said the princess, waving him off rather haughtily.

The poor prince turned and walked towards the wood.

"Come back," said Daylight: "I like you. You do what you are told. Are you good?"

"Not so good as I should like to be," said the prince.

"Then go and grow better," said the princess.

Again the disappointed prince turned and went.

"Come back," said the princess.

He obeyed, and stood before her waiting.

"Can you tell me what the sun is like?" she asked.

"No," he answered. "But where's the good of asking what you know?"

"But I don't know," she rejoined.

"Why, everybody knows."

"That's the very thing: I'm not everybody. I've never seen the sun."

"Then you can't know what it's like till you do see it."

"I think you must be a prince," said the princess.

"Do I look like one?" said the prince.

"I can't quite say that."

"Then why do you think so?"

"Because you both do what you are told and speak the truth. — Is the sun so very bright?"

"As bright as the lightning."

"But it doesn't go out like that, does it?"

"Oh, no. It shines like the moon, rises and sets like the moon, is much the same shape as the moon, only so bright that you can't look at it for a moment."

"But I would look at it," said the princess.

"But you couldn't," said the prince.

"But I could," said the princess.

"Why don't you, then?"

"Because I can't."

"Why can't you?"

"Because I can't wake. And I never shall wake until —"

Here she hid her face in her hands, turned away, and walked in the slowest, stateliest manner towards the house. The prince ventured to follow her at a little distance, but she turned and made a repellent gesture, which, like a true gentleman-prince, he obeyed at once. He waited a long time, but as she did not come near him again, and as the night had now cleared, he set off at last for the old woman's cottage.

It was long past midnight when he reached it, but, to his surprise, the old woman was paring potatoes at the door. Fairies are fond of doing odd things. Indeed, however they may dissemble, the night is always their day. And so it is with all who have fairy blood in them.

"Why, what are you doing there, this time of the night, mother?" said the prince; for that was the kind way in which any young man in his country would address a woman who was much older than himself.

"Getting your supper ready, my son," she answered.

"Oh, I don't want any supper," said the prince.

"Ah! you've seen Daylight," said she.

"I've seen a princess who never saw it," said the prince.

"Do you like her?" asked the fairy.

"Oh! don't I?" said the prince. "More than you would believe, mother."

"A fairy can believe anything that ever was or ever could be," said the old woman.

"Then are you a fairy?" asked the prince.

"Yes," said she.

"Then what do you do for things not to believe?" asked the prince.

"There's plenty of them — everything that never was nor ever could be."

"Plenty, I grant you," said the prince. "But do you believe there could be a princess who never saw the daylight? Do you believe that now?"

This the prince said, not that he doubted the princess, but that he wanted the fairy to tell him more. She was too old a fairy, however, to be caught so easily.

"Of all people, fairies must not tell secrets. Besides, she's a princess."

"Well, I'll tell you a secret. I'm a prince."

"I know that."

"How do you know it?"

"By the curl of the third eyelash on your left eyelid."

"Which corner do you count from?"

"That's a secret."

"Another secret? Well, at least, if I am a prince, there can be no harm in telling me about a princess."

"It's just the princes I can't tell."

"There ain't any more of them — are there?" said the prince.

"What! you don't think you're the only prince in the world, do you?"

"Oh, dear, no! not at all. But I know there's one too many just at present, except the princess—"

"Yes, yes, that's it," said the fairy.

"What's it?" asked the prince.

But he could get nothing more out of the fairy, and had to go to bed unanswered, which was something of a trial.

Now wicked fairies will not be bound by the law which the good fairies obey, and this always seems to give the bad the advantage over the good, for they use means to gain their ends which the others will not. But it is all of no consequence, for what they do never succeeds; nay, in the end it brings about the very thing they are trying to prevent. So you see that somehow, for all their cleverness, wicked fairies are dreadfully stupid, for, although from the beginning of the world they have really helped instead of thwarting the good fairies, not one of them is a bit wiser for it. She will try the bad thing just as they all did before her; and succeeds no better of course.

The prince had so far stolen a march upon the swamp-fairy that she did not know he was in the neighborhood until after he had seen the princess those three times. When she knew it, she consoled herself by thinking that the princess must be far too proud and too modest for any young man to venture even to speak to her before he had seen her six times at least. But there was even less danger than the wicked fairy thought; for, however much the princess might desire to be set free, she was dreadfully afraid of the wrong prince. Now, however, the fairy was going to do all she could.

She so contrived it by her deceitful spells, that the next night the prince could not by any endeavor find his way to the glade. It would take me too long to tell her tricks. They would be amusing to us, who know that they could not do any harm, but they were something other than amusing to the poor prince. He wandered about the forest till daylight, and then fell fast asleep. The same thing occurred for seven following days, during which neither could he find the good fairy's cottage. After the third quarter of the moon, however, the bad fairy thought she might be at ease about the affair for a fortnight at least, for there was no chance of the prince wishing to kiss the princess during that period. So the first day of the fourth quarter he did find the cottage, and the next day he found the glade. For nearly another week he haunted it. But the princess never came. I have little doubt she was on the farther edge of it some part of every night, but at this period she always wore black, and, there being little or no light, the prince never saw her. Nor would he have known her if he had seen her. How could he have taken the worn decrepit creature she was now, for the glorious Princess Daylight?

At last, one night when there was no moon at all, he ventured near the house. There he heard voices talking, although it was past midnight; for her women were in considerable uneasiness, because the one whose turn it was to watch her had fallen asleep, and had not seen which way she went, and this was a night when she would probably wander very far, describing a circle which did not touch the open glade at all, but stretched away from the back of the house, deep into that side of the forest — a part of which the prince knew nothing. When he understood from what they said that she had disappeared, and that she must have gone somewhere in the said direction, he plunged at once into the wood to see if he could find her. For hours he roamed with nothing to guide him but the vague notion of a circle which on one side bordered on the house, for so much had he picked up from the talk he had overheard.

It was getting towards the dawn, but as yet there was no streak of light in the sky, when he came to a great birch-tree, and sat down weary at the foot of it. While he sat — very miserable, you may be sure — full of fear for the princess, and wondering how her attendants could take it so quietly, he bethought himself that it would not be a bad plan to light a fire, which, if she were anywhere near, would attract her. This he managed with a tinder-box, which the good fairy had given him. It was just beginning to blaze up, when he heard a moan, which seemed to come from the other side of the tree. He sprung to his feet, but his heart throbbed so that he had to lean for a moment against the tree before he could move. When he got round, there lay a human form in a little dark heap on the earth. There was light enough from his fire to show that it was not the princess. He lifted it in his arms, hardly heavier than a child, and carried it to the flame. The countenance was that of an old woman, but it had a fearfully strange look. A black hood concealed her hair, and her eyes were closed. He laid her down as comfortably as he could, chafed her hands, put a little cordial from a bottle, also the gift of the fairy, into her mouth; took off his coat and wrapped it about her, and in short did the best he could. In a little while she opened her eyes and looked at him — so pitifully! The tears rose and flowed from her grey wrinkled cheeks, but she said never a word. She closed her eyes again, but the tears kept on flowing, and her whole appearance was so utterly pitiful that the prince was near crying too. He begged her to tell him what was the matter, promising to do all he could to help her; but still she did not speak. He thought she was dying, and took her in his arms again to carry her to the princess's house, where he thought the good-natured cook might be able to do something for her. When he lifted her, the tears flowed yet faster, and she gave such a sad moan that it went to his very heart.

"Mother, mother!" he said. "Poor mother!" and kissed her on the withered lips.

She started; and what eyes they were that opened upon him! But he did not see them, for it was still very dark, and he had enough to do to make his way through the trees towards the house.

Just as he approached the door, feeling more tired than he could have imagined possible — she was such a little thin old thing — she began to move, and became so restless that, unable to carry her a moment longer, he thought to lay her on the grass. But she stood upright on her feet. Her hood had dropped, and her hair fell about her. The first gleam of the morning was caught on her face: that face was bright as the never-aging Dawn, and her eyes were lovely as the sky of darkest blue. The prince recoiled in overmastering wonder. It was Daylight herself whom he had brought from the forest! He fell at her feet, nor dared to look up until she laid her hand upon his head. He rose then.

"You kissed me when I was an old woman: there! I kiss you when I am a young princess," murmured Daylight. — "Is that the sun coming?"

29. RUBY

The children were delighted with the story, and made many amusing remarks upon it. Mr. Raymond promised to search his brain for another, and when he had found one to bring it to them. Diamond having taken leave of Nanny, and promised to go and see her again soon, went away with him.

Now Mr. Raymond had been turning over in his mind what he could do both for Diamond and for Nanny. He had therefore made some acquaintance with Diamond's father, and had been greatly pleased with him. But he had come to the resolution, before he did anything so good as he would like to do for them, to put them all to a certain test. So as they walked away together, he began to talk with Diamond as follows: —

"Nanny must leave the hospital soon, Diamond."

"I'm glad of that, sir."

"Why? Don't you think it's a nice place?"

"Yes, very. But it's better to be well and doing something, you know, even if it's not quite so comfortable."

"But they can't keep Nanny so long as they would like. They can't keep her till she's quite strong. There are always so many sick children they want to take in and make better. And the question is, What will she do when they send her out again?"

"That's just what I can't tell, though I've been thinking of it over and over, sir. Her crossing was taken long ago, and I couldn't bear to see Nanny fighting for it, especially with such a poor fellow as has taken it. He's quite lame, sir."

"She doesn't look much like fighting, now, does she, Diamond?"

"No, sir. She looks too like an angel. Angels don't fight — do they, sir?"

"Not to get things for themselves, at least," said Mr. Raymond.

"Besides," added Diamond, "I don't quite see that she would have any better right to the crossing than the boy who has got it. Nobody gave it to her; she only took it. And now he has taken it."

"If she were to sweep a crossing — soon at least — after the illness she has had, she would be laid up again the very first wet day," said Mr. Raymond.

"And there's hardly any money to be got except on the wet days," remarked Diamond reflectively. "Is there nothing else she could do, sir?"

"Not without being taught, I'm afraid."

"Well, couldn't somebody teach her something?"

"Couldn't you teach her, Diamond?"

"I don't know anything myself, sir. I could teach her to dress the, baby; but nobody would give her anything for doing things like that: they are so easy. There wouldn't be much good in teaching her to drive a cab, for where would she get the cab to drive? There ain't fathers and old Diamonds everywhere. At least poor Nanny can't find any of them, I doubt."

"Perhaps if she were taught to be nice and clean, and only speak gentle words"

"Mother could teach her that," interrupted Diamond.

"And to dress babies, and feed them, and take care of them," Mr. Raymond proceeded, "she might get a place as a nurse somewhere, you know. People do give money for that."

"Then I'll ask mother," said Diamond.

"But you'll have to give her her food then; and your father, not being strong, has enough to do already without that."

"But here's me," said Diamond: "I help him out with it. When he's tired of driving, up I get. It don't make any difference to old Diamond. I don't mean he likes me as well as my father — of course he can't, you know — nobody could; but he does his duty all the same. It's got to be done, you know, sir; and Diamond's a good horse — isn't he, sir?"

"From your description I should say certainly; but I have not the pleasure of his acquaintance myself."

"Don't you think he will go to heaven, sir?"

"That I don't know anything about," said Mr. Raymond. "I confess I should be glad to think so," he added, smiling thoughtfully.

"I'm sure he'll get to the back of the north wind, anyhow," said Diamond to himself; but he had learned to be very careful of saying such things aloud.

"Isn't it rather too much for him to go in the cab all day and every day?" resumed Mr. Raymond.

"So father says, when he feels his ribs of a morning. But then he says the old horse do eat well, and the moment he's had his supper, down he goes, and never gets up till he's called; and, for the legs of him, father says that makes no end of a differ. Some horses, sir! They won't lie down all night long, but go to sleep on their four pins, like a haystack, father says. I think it's very stupid of them, and so does old Diamond. But then I suppose they don't know better, and so they can't help it. We mustn't be too hard upon them, father says."

"Your father must be a good man, Diamond." Diamond looked up in Mr. Raymond's face, wondering what he could mean.

"I said your father must be a good man, Diamond."

"Of course," said Diamond. "How could he drive a cab if he wasn't?"

"There are some men who drive cabs who are not very good," objected Mr. Raymond.

Diamond remembered the drunken cabman, and saw that his friend was right.

"Ah, but," he returned, "he must be, you know, with such a horse as old Diamond."

"That does make a difference," said Mr. Raymond. "But it is quite enough that he is a good man without our trying to account for it. Now, if you like, I will give you a proof that I think him a good man. I am going away on the Continent for a while — for three months, I believe — and I am going to let my house to a gentleman who does not want the use of my brougham. My horse is nearly as old, I fancy, as your Diamond, but I don't want to part with him, and I don't want him to be idle; for nobody, as you say, ought to be idle; but neither do I want him to be worked very hard. Now, it has come into my head that perhaps your father would take charge of him, and work him under certain conditions."

"My father will do what's right," said Diamond. "I'm sure of that."

"Well, so I think. Will you ask him when he comes home to call and have a little chat with me — to-day, some time?"

"He must have his dinner first," said Diamond. "No, he's got his dinner with him to-day. It must be after he's had his tea."

"Of course, of course. Any time will do. I shall be at home all day."

"Very well, sir. I will tell him. You may be sure he will come. My father thinks you a very kind gentleman, and I know he is right, for I know your very own self, sir."

Mr. Raymond smiled, and as they had now reached his door, they parted, and Diamond went home. As soon as his father entered the house, Diamond gave him Mr. Raymond's message, and recounted the conversation that had preceded it. His father said little, but took thought-sauce to his bread and butter, and as soon as he had finished his meal, rose, saying:

"I will go to your friend directly, Diamond. It would be a grand thing to get a little more money. We do want it." Diamond accompanied his father to Mr. Raymond's door, and there left him.

He was shown at once into Mr. Raymond's study, where he gazed with some wonder at the multitude of books on the walls, and thought what a learned man Mr. Raymond must be.

Presently Mr. Raymond entered, and after saying much the same about his old horse, made the following distinct proposal — one not over-advantageous to Diamond's father, but for which he had reasons — namely, that Joseph should have the use of Mr. Raymond's horse while he was away, on condition that he never worked him more than six hours a day, and fed him well, and that, besides, he should take Nanny home as soon as she was able to leave the hospital, and provide for her as one of his own children, neither better nor worse—so long, that is, as he had the horse.

Diamond's father could not help thinking it a pretty close bargain. He should have both the girl and the horse to feed, and only six hours' work out of the horse.

"It will save your own horse," said Mr. Raymond.

"That is true," answered Joseph; "but all I can get by my own horse is only enough to keep us, and if I save him and feed your horse and the girl — don't you see, sir?"

"Well, you can go home and think about it, and let me know by the end of the week. I am in no hurry before then."

So Joseph went home and recounted the proposal to his wife, adding that he did not think there was much advantage to be got out of it.

"Not much that way, husband," said Diamond's mother; "but there would be an advantage, and what matter who gets it!"

"I don't see it," answered her husband. "Mr. Raymond is a gentleman of property, and I don't discover any much good in helping him to save a little more. He won't easily get one to make such a bargain, and I don't mean he shall get me. It would be a loss rather than a gain — I do think — at least if I took less work out of our own horse."

"One hour would make a difference to old Diamond. But that's not the main point. You must think what an advantage it would be to the poor girl that hasn't a home to go to!"

"She is one of Diamond's friends," thought his father.

"I could be kind to her, you know," the mother went on, "and teach her housework, and how to handle a baby; and, besides, she would help me, and I should be the stronger for it, and able to do an odd bit of charing now and then, when I got the chance."

"I won't hear of that," said her husband. "Have the girl by all means. I'm ashamed I did not think of both sides of the thing at once. I wonder if the horse is a great eater. To be sure, if I gave Diamond two hours' additional rest, it would be all the better for the old bones of him, and there would be four hours extra out of the other horse. That would give Diamond something to do every day. He could drive old Diamond after dinner, and I could take the other horse out for six hours after tea, or in the morning, as I found best. It might pay for the keep of both of them, — that is, if I had good luck. I should like to oblige Mr. Raymond, though he be rather hard, for he has been very kind to our Diamond, wife. Hasn't he now?"

"He has indeed, Joseph," said his wife, and there the conversation ended.

Diamond's father went the very next day to Mr. Raymond, and accepted his proposal; so that the week after having got another stall in the same stable, he had two horses instead of one. Oddly enough, the name of the new horse was Ruby, for he was a very red chestnut. Diamond's name came from a white lozenge on his forehead. Young Diamond said they were rich now, with such a big diamond and such a big ruby.

30. Nanny's Dream

Nanny was not fit to be moved for some time yet, and Diamond went to see her as often as he could. But being more regularly engaged now, seeing he went out every day for a few hours with old Diamond, and had his baby to mind, and one of the horses to attend to, he could not go so often as he would have liked.

One evening, as he sat by her bedside, she said to him:

"I've had such a beautiful dream, Diamond! I should like to tell it you."

"Oh! do," said Diamond; "I am so fond of dreams!"

"She must have been to the back of the north wind," he said to himself.

"It was a very foolish dream, you know. But somehow it was so pleasant! What a good thing it is that you believe the dream all the time you are in it!"

My readers must not suppose that poor Nanny was able to say what she meant so well as I put it down here. She had never been to school, and had heard very little else than vulgar speech until she came to the hospital. But I have been to school, and although that could never make me able to dream so well as Nanny, it has made me able to tell her dream better than she could herself. And I am the more desirous of doing this for her that I have already done the best I could for Diamond's dream, and it would be a shame to give the boy all the advantage.

"I will tell you all I know about it," said Nanny. "The day before yesterday, a lady came to see us — a very beautiful lady, and very beautifully dressed. I heard the matron say to her that it was very kind of her to come in blue and gold; and she answered that she knew we didn't like dull colors. She had such a lovely shawl on, just like redness dipped in milk, and all worked over with flowers of the same color. It didn't shine much, it was silk, but it kept in the shine. When she came to my bedside, she sat down, just where you are sitting, Diamond, and laid her hand on the counterpane. I was sitting up, with my table before me ready for my tea. Her hand looked so pretty in its blue glove, that I was tempted to stroke it. I thought she wouldn't be angry, for everybody that comes to the hospital is kind. It's only in the streets they ain't kind. But she drew her hand away, and I almost cried, for I thought I had been rude. Instead of that, however, it was only that she didn't like giving me her glove to stroke, for she drew it off, and then laid her hand where it was before. I wasn't sure, but I ventured to put out my ugly hand."

"Your hand ain't ugly, Nanny," said Diamond; but Nanny went on —

"And I stroked it again, and then she stroked mine, — think of that! And there was a ring on her finger, and I looked down to see what it was like. And she drew it off, and put it upon one of my fingers. It was a red stone, and she told me they called it a ruby."

"Oh, that is funny!" said Diamond. "Our new horse is called Ruby. We've got another horse — a red one — such a beauty!"

But Nanny went on with her story.

"I looked at the ruby all the time the lady was talking to me, — it was so beautiful! And as she talked I kept seeing deeper and deeper into the stone. At last she rose to go away, and I began to pull the ring off my finger; and what do you think she said? — "Wear it all night, if you like. Only you must take care of it. I can't give it you, for some one gave it to me; but you may keep it till to-morrow." Wasn't it kind of her? I could hardly take my tea, I was so delighted to hear it; and I do think it was the ring that set me dreaming; for, after I had taken my tea, I leaned back, half lying and half sitting, and looked at the ring on my finger. By degrees I began to dream. The ring grew larger and larger, until at last I found that I was not looking at a red stone, but at a red sunset, which shone in at the end of a long street near where Grannie lives. I was dressed in rags as I used to be, and I had great holes in my shoes, at which the nasty mud came through to my feet. I didn't use to mind it before, but now I thought it horrid. And there was the great red sunset, with streaks of green and gold between, standing looking at me. Why couldn't I live in the sunset instead of in that dirt? Why was it so far away always? Why did it never come into our wretched street? It faded away, as the sunsets always do, and at last went out altogether. Then a cold wind began to blow, and flutter all my rags about —"

"That was North Wind herself," said Diamond.

"Eh?" said Nanny, and went on with her story.

"I turned my back to it, and wandered away. I did not know where I was going, only it was warmer to go that way. I don't think it was a north wind, for I found myself in the west end at last. But it doesn't matter in a dream which wind it was."

"I don't know that," said Diamond. "I believe North Wind can get into our dreams —yes, and blow in them. Sometimes she has blown me out of a dream altogether."

"I don't know what you mean, Diamond," said Nanny.

"Never mind," answered Diamond. "Two people can't always understand each other. They'd both be at the back of the north wind directly, and what would become of the other places without them?"

"You do talk so oddly!" said Nanny. "I sometimes think they must have been right about you."

"What did they say about me?" asked Diamond.

"They called you God's baby."

"How kind of them! But I knew that."

"Did you know what it meant, though? It meant that you were not right in the head."

"I feel all right," said Diamond, putting both hands to his head, as if it had been a globe he could take off and set on again.

"Well, as long as you are pleased I am pleased," said Nanny.

"Thank you, Nanny. Do go on with your story. I think I like dreams even better than fairy tales. But they must be nice ones, like yours, you know."

"Well, I went on, keeping my back to the wind, until I came to a fine street on the top of a hill. How it happened I don't know, but the front door of one of the houses was open, and not only the front door, but the back door as well, so that I could see right through the house — and what do you think I saw? A garden place with green grass, and the moon shining upon it! Think of that! There was no moon in the street, but through the house there was the moon. I looked and there was nobody near: I would not do any harm, and the grass was so much nicer than the mud! But I couldn't think of going on the grass with such dirty shoes: I kicked them off in the gutter, and ran in on my bare feet, up the steps, and through the house, and on to the grass; and the moment I came into the moonlight, I began to feel better."

"That's why North Wind blew you there," said Diamond.

"It came of Mr. Raymond's story about Princess Daylight," returned Nanny. "Well, I lay down upon the grass in the moonlight without thinking how I was to get out again. Somehow the moon suited me exactly. There was not a breath of the north wind you talk about; it was quite gone."

"You didn't want her any more, just then. She never goes where she's not wanted," said Diamond. "But she blew you into the moonlight, anyhow."

"Well, we won't dispute about it," said Nanny: "you've got a tile loose, you know."

"Suppose I have," returned Diamond, "don't you see it may let in the moonlight, or the sunlight for that matter?"

"Perhaps yes, perhaps no," said Nanny.

"And you've got your dreams, too, Nanny."

"Yes, but I know they're dreams."

"So do I. But I know besides they are something more as well."

"Oh! do you?" rejoined Nanny. "I don't."

"All right," said Diamond. "Perhaps you will some day."

"Perhaps I won't," said Nanny.

Diamond held his peace, and Nanny resumed her story.

"I lay a long time, and the moonlight got in at every tear in my clothes, and made me feel so happy —"

"There, I tell you!" said Diamond.

"What do you tell me?" returned Nanny.

"North Wind —"

"It was the moonlight, I tell you," persisted Nanny, and again Diamond held his peace.

"All at once I felt that the moon was not shining so strong. I looked up, and there was a cloud, all crapey and fluffy, trying to drown the beautiful creature. But the moon was so round, just like a whole plate, that the cloud couldn't stick to her. She shook it off, and said there and shone out clearer and brighter than ever. But up came a thicker cloud, — and "You shan't," said the moon; and "I will," said the cloud, — but it couldn't: out shone the moon, quite laughing at its impudence. I knew her ways, for I've always been used to watch her. She's the only thing worth looking at in our street at night."

"Don't call it your street," said Diamond. "You're not going back to it. You're coming to us, you know."

"That's too good to be true," said Nanny.

"There are very few things good enough to be true," said Diamond; "but I hope this is. Too good to be true it can't be. Isn't true good? and isn't good good? And how, then, can anything be too good to be true? That's like old Sal — to say that."

"Don't abuse Grannie, Diamond. She's a horrid old thing, she and her gin bottle; but she'll repent some day, and then you'll be glad not to have said anything against her."

"Why?" said Diamond.

"Because you'll be sorry for her."

"I am sorry for her now."

"Very well. That's right. She'll be sorry too. And there'll be an end of it."

"All right. You come to us," said Diamond.

"Where was I?" said Nanny.

"Telling me how the moon served the clouds."

"Yes. But it wouldn't do, all of it. Up came the clouds and the clouds, and they came faster and faster, until the moon was covered up. You couldn't expect her to throw off a hundred of them at once — could you?"

"Certainly not," said Diamond.

"So it grew very dark; and a dog began to yelp in the house. I looked and saw that the door to the garden was shut. Presently it was opened — not to let me out, but to let the dog in — yelping and bounding. I thought if he caught sight of me, I was in for a biting first, and the police after. So I jumped up, and ran for a little summer-house in the corner of the garden. The dog came after me, but I shut the door in his face. It was well it had a door — wasn't it?"

"You dreamed of the door because you wanted it," said Diamond.

"No, I didn't; it came of itself. It was there, in the true dream."

"There — I've caught you!" said Diamond. "I knew you believed in the dream as much as I do."

"Oh, well, if you will lay traps for a body!" said Nanny. "Anyhow, I was safe inside the summer-house. And what do you think? — There was the moon beginning to shine again — but only through one of the panes — and that one was just the color of the ruby. Wasn't it funny?"

"No, not a bit funny," said Diamond.

"If you will be contrary!" said Nanny.

"No, no," said Diamond; "I only meant that was the very pane I should have expected her to shine through."

"Oh, very well!" returned Nanny.

What Diamond meant, I do not pretend to say. He had curious notions about things.

"And now," said Nanny, "I didn't know what to do, for the dog kept barking at the door, and I couldn't get out. But the moon was so beautiful that I couldn't keep from looking at it through the red pane. And as I looked it got larger and larger till it filled the whole pane and outgrew it, so that I could see it through the other panes; and it grew till it filled them too and the whole window, so that the summer-house was nearly as bright as day."

"The dog stopped barking, and I heard a gentle tapping at the door, like the wind blowing a little branch against it."

"Just like her," said Diamond, who thought everything strange and beautiful must be done by North Wind.

"So I turned from the window and opened the door; and what do you think I saw?"

"A beautiful lady," said Diamond.

"No — the moon itself, as big as a little house, and as round as a ball, shining like yellow silver. It stood on the grass — down on the very grass: I could see nothing else for the brightness of it:

And as I stared and wondered, a door opened in the side of it, near the ground, and a curious little old man, with a crooked thing over his shoulder, looked out, and said: 'Come along, Nanny; my lady wants you. We're come to fetch you." I wasn't a bit frightened. I went up to the beautiful bright thing, and the old man held down his hand, and I took hold of it, and gave a jump, and he gave me a lift, and I was inside the moon. And what do you think it was like? It was such a pretty little house, with blue windows and white curtains! At one of the windows sat a beautiful lady, with her head leaning on her hand, looking out. She seemed rather sad, and I was sorry for her, and stood staring at her.

"'You didn't think I had such a beautiful mistress as that!' said the queer little man. 'No, indeed!' I answered: 'who would have thought it?' 'Ah! who indeed? But you see you don't know everything.' The little man closed the door, and began to pull at a rope which hung behind it with a weight at the end. After he had pulled a while, he said — 'There, that will do; we're all right now.' Then he took me by the hand and opened a little trap in the floor, and led me down two or three steps, and I saw like a great hole below me. 'Don't be frightened,' said the tittle man. 'It's not a hole. It's only a window. Put your face down and look through.' I did as he told me, and there was the garden and the summer-house, far away, lying at the bottom of the moonlight. 'There!' said the little man; 'we've brought you off! Do you see the little dog barking at us down there in the garden?' I told him I couldn't see anything so far. 'Can you see anything so small and so far off?' I said. 'Bless you, child!' said the little man; 'I could pick up a needle out of the grass if I had only a long enough arm. There's one lying by the door of the summer-house now.' I looked at his eyes. They were very small, but so bright that I think he saw by the light that went out of them. Then he took me up, and up again by a little stair in a corner of the room, and through another trapdoor, and there was one great round window above us, and I saw the blue sky and the clouds, and such lots of stars, all so big and shining as hard as ever they could!"

"The little girl-angels had been polishing them," said Diamond.

"What nonsense you do talk!" said Nanny.

"But my nonsense is just as good as yours, Nanny. When you have done, I'll tell you my dream. The stars are in it — not the moon, though. She was away somewhere. Perhaps she was gone to fetch you then. I don't think that, though, for my dream was longer ago than yours. She might have been to fetch some one else, though; for we can't fancy it's only us that get such fine things done for them. But do tell me what came next."

Perhaps one of my child-readers may remember whether the moon came down to fetch him or her the same night that Diamond had his dream. I cannot tell, of course. I know she did not come to fetch me, though I did think I could make her follow me when I was a boy — not a very tiny one either.

"The little man took me all round the house, and made me look out of every window. Oh, it was beautiful! There we were, all up in the air, in such a nice, clean little house! 'Your work will be to keep the windows bright,' said the little man. 'You won't find it very difficult, for there ain't much dust up here. Only, the frost settles on them sometimes, and the drops of rain leave marks on them.' 'I can easily clean them inside,' I said; 'but how am I to get the frost and rain off the outside of them?' 'Oh!' he said, 'it's quite easy. There are ladders all about. You've only got to go out at the door, and climb about. There are a great many windows you haven't seen yet, and some of them look into places you don't know anything about. I used to clean them myself, but I'm getting rather old, you see. Ain't I now?' 'I can't tell,' I answered. 'You see I never saw you when you were younger.' 'Never saw the man in the moon?' said he. 'Not very near,' I answered, 'not to tell how young or how old he looked. I have seen the bundle of sticks on his back.' For Jim had pointed that out to me. Jim was very fond of looking at the man in the moon. Poor Jim! I wonder he hasn't been to see me. I'm afraid he's ill too."

"I'll try to find out," said Diamond, "and let you know."

"Thank you," said Nanny. "You and Jim ought to be friends."

"But what did the man in the moon say, when you told him you had seen him with the bundle of sticks on his back?"

"He laughed. But I thought he looked offended too. His little nose turned up sharper, and he drew the corners of his mouth down from the tips of his ears into his neck. But he didn't look cross, you know."

"Didn't he say anything?"

"Oh, yes! He said: `That's all nonsense. What you saw was my bundle of dusters. I was going to clean the windows. It takes a good many, you know. Really, what they do say of their superiors down there!' `It's only because they don't know better,' I ventured to say. `Of course, of course,' said the little man. `Nobody ever does know better. Well, I forgive them, and that sets it all right, I hope.' `It's very good of you,' I said. `No!' said he, `it's not in the least good of me. I couldn't be comfortable otherwise.' After this he said nothing for a while, and I laid myself on the floor of his garret, and stared up and around at the great blue beautifulness. I had forgotten him almost, when at last he said: `Ain't you done yet?' `Done what?' I asked. `Done saying your prayers,' says he. `I wasn't saying my prayers,' I answered. `Oh, yes, you were,' said he, `though you didn't know it! And now I must show you something else.'

"He took my hand and led me down the stair again, and through a narrow passage, and through another, and another, and another. I don't know how there could be room for so many passages in such a little house. The heart of it must be ever so much farther from the sides than they are from each other. How could it have an inside that was so independent of its outside? There's the point. It was funny — wasn't it, Diamond?"

"No," said Diamond. He was going to say that that was very much the sort of thing at the back of the north wind; but he checked himself and only added, "All right. I don't see it. I don't see why the inside should depend on the outside. It ain't so with the crabs. They creep out of their outsides and make new ones. Mr. Raymond told me so."

"I don't see what that has got to do with it," said Nanny.

"Then go on with your story, please," said Diamond. "What did you come to, after going through all those winding passages into the heart of the moon?"

"I didn't say they were winding passages. I said they were long and narrow. They didn't wind. They went by corners."

"That's worth knowing," remarked Diamond. "For who knows how soon he may have to go there? But the main thing is, what did you come to at last?"

"We came to a small box against the wall of a tiny room. The little man told me to put my ear against it. I did so, and heard a noise something like the purring of a cat, only not so loud, and much sweeter. `What is it?' I asked. `Don't you know the sound?' returned the little man. `No,' I answered. `Don't you know the sound of bees?' he said. I had never heard bees, and could not know the sound of them. `Those are my lady's bees,' he went on. I had heard that bees gather honey from the flowers. `But where are the flowers for them?' I asked. `My lady's bees gather their honey from the sun and the stars,' said the little man. `Do let me see them,' I said. `No. I daren't do that,' he answered. 'I have no business with them. I don't understand them. Besides, they are so bright that if one were to fly into your eye, it would blind you altogether.' 'Then you have seen them?' 'Oh, yes! Once or twice, I think. But I don't quite know: they are so very bright — like buttons of lightning. Now I've showed you all I can to-night, and we'll go back to the room.' I followed him, and he made me sit down under a lamp that hung from the roof, and gave me some bread and honey.

"The lady had never moved. She sat with her forehead leaning on her hand, gazing out of the little window, hung like the rest with white cloudy curtains. From where I was sitting I looked out of it too, but I could see nothing. Her face was very beautiful, and very white, and very still, and her hand was as white as the forehead that leaned on it. I did not see her whole face — only the side of it, for she never moved to turn it full upon me, or even to look at me.

"How long I sat after I had eaten my bread and honey, I don't know. The little man was busy about the room, pulling a string here, and a string there, but chiefly the string at the back of the door. I was thinking with some uneasiness that he would soon be wanting me to go out and clean the windows, and I didn't fancy the job. At last he came up to me with a great armful of dusters. 'It's time you set about the windows,' he said; 'for there's rain coming, and if they're quite clean before, then the rain can't spoil them.' I got up at once. 'You needn't be afraid,' he said. 'You won't tumble off. Only you must be careful. Always hold on with one hand while you rub with the other.' As he spoke, he opened the door. I started back in a terrible fright, for there was nothing but blue air to be seen under me, like a great water without a bottom at all. But what must be must, and to live up here was so much nicer than down in the mud with holes in my shoes, that I never thought of not doing as I was told. The little man showed me how and where to lay hold while I put my foot round the edge of the door on to the first round of a ladder. 'Once you're up,' he said, 'you'll see how you have to go well enough.' I did as he told me, and crept out very carefully. Then the little man handed me the bundle of dusters, saying, 'I always carry them on my reaping hook, but I don't think you could manage it properly. You shall have it if you like.' I wouldn't take it, however, for it looked dangerous.

"I did the best I could with the dusters, and crawled up to the top of the moon. But what a grand sight it was! The stars were all over my head, so bright and so near that I could almost have laid hold of them. The round ball to which I clung went bobbing and floating away through the dark blue above and below and on every side. It was so beautiful that all fear left me, and I set to work diligently. I cleaned window after window. At length I came to a very little one, in at which I peeped. There was the room with the box of bees in it! I laid my ear to the window, and heard the musical hum quite distinctly. A great longing to see them came upon me, and I opened the window and crept in. The little box had a door like a closet. I opened it — the tiniest crack — when out came the light with such a sting that I closed it again in terror — not, however, before three bees had shot out into the room, where they darted about like flashes of lightning. Terribly frightened, I tried to get out of the window again, but I could not: there was no way to the outside of the moon but through the door; and that was in the room where the lady sat. No sooner had I reached the room, than the three bees, which had followed me, flew at once to the lady, and settled upon her hair. Then first I saw her move. She started, put up her hand, and caught them; then rose and, having held them into the flame of the lamp one after the other, turned to me. Her face was not so sad now as stern. It frightened me much. 'Nanny, you have got me into trouble,' she said. 'You have been letting out my bees, which it is all I can do to manage. You have forced me to burn them. It is a great loss, and there will be a storm.' As she spoke, the clouds had gathered all about us. I could see them come crowding up white about the windows. 'I am sorry to find,' said the lady, 'that you are not to be trusted. You must go home again — you won't do for us.' Then came a great clap of thunder, and the moon rocked and swayed. All grew dark about me, and I fell on the floor and lay half-stunned. I could hear everything but could see nothing. `Shall I throw her out of the door, my lady?' said the little man. `No,' she answered; `she's not quite bad enough for that. I don't think there's much harm in her; only she'll never do for us. She would make dreadful mischief up here. She's only fit for the mud. It's a great pity. I am sorry for her. Just take that ring off her finger. I am sadly afraid she has stolen it.' The little man caught hold of my hand, and I felt him tugging at the ring. I tried to speak what was true about it, but, after a terrible effort, only gave a groan. Other things began to come into my head. Somebody else had a hold of me. The little man wasn't there. I opened my eyes at last, and saw the nurse. I had cried out in my sleep, and she had come and waked me. But, Diamond, for all it was only a dream, I cannot help being ashamed of myself yet for opening the lady's box of bees."

"You woudn't do it again—would you — if she were to take you back?" said Diamond.

"No. I don't think anything would ever make me do it again. But where's the good? I shall never have the chance."

"I don't know that," said Diamond.

"You silly baby! It was only a dream," said Nanny.

"I know that, Nanny, dear. But how can you tell you mayn't dream it again?"

"That's not a bit likely."

"I don't know that," said Diamond.

"You're always saying that," said Nanny. "I don't like it."

"Then I won't say it again — if I don't forget." said Diamond. "But it was such a beautiful dream! — wasn't it, Nanny? What a pity you opened that door and let the bees out! You might have had such a long dream, and such nice talks with the moon-lady. Do try to go again, Nanny. I do so want to hear more."

But now the nurse came and told him it was time to go; and Diamond went, saying to himself, "I can't help thinking that North Wind had something to do with that dream. It would be tiresome to lie there all day and all night too — without dreaming. Perhaps if she hadn't done that, the moon might have carried her to the back of the north wind — who knows?"

31. THE NORTH WIND DOTH BLOW

It was a great delight to Diamond when at length Nanny was well enough to leave the hospital and go home to their house. She was not very strong yet, but Diamond's mother was very considerate of her, and took care that she should have nothing to do she was not quite fit for. If Nanny had been taken straight from the street, it is very probable she would not have been so pleasant in a decent household, or so easy to teach; but after the refining influences of her illness and the kind treatment she had had in the hospital, she moved about the house just like some rather sad pleasure haunting the mind. As she got better, and the color came back to her cheeks, her step grew lighter and quicker, her smile shone out more readily, and it became certain that she would soon be a treasure of help. It was great fun to see Diamond teaching her how to hold the baby, and wash and dress him, and often they laughed together over her awkwardness. But she had not many such lessons before she was able to perform those duties quite as well as Diamond himself.

Things however did not go well with Joseph from the very arrival of Ruby. It almost seemed as if the red beast had brought ill luck with him. The fares were fewer, and the pay less. Ruby's services did indeed make the week's income at first a little beyond what it used to be, but then there were two more to feed. After the first month he fell lame, and for the whole of the next Joseph dared not attempt to work him. I cannot say that he never grumbled, for his own health was far from what it had been; but I can say that he tried to do his best. During all that month, they lived on very short commons indeed, seldom tasting meat except on Sundays, and poor old Diamond, who worked hardest of all, not even then — so that at the end of it he was as thin as a clothes-horse, while Ruby was as plump and sleek as a bishop's cob.

Nor was it much better after Ruby was able to work again, for it was a season of great depression in business, and that is very soon felt amongst the cabmen. City men look more after their shillings, and their wives and daughters have less to spend. It was besides a wet autumn, and bread rose greatly in price. When I add to this that Diamond's mother was but poorly, for a new baby was coming, you will see that these were not very jolly times for our friends in the mews.

Notwithstanding the depressing influences around him, Joseph was able to keep a little hope alive in his heart; and when he came home at night, would get Diamond to read to him, and would also make Nanny produce her book that he might see how she was getting on. For Diamond had taken her education in hand, and as she was a clever child, she was very soon able to put letters and words together.

Thus the three months passed away, but Mr. Raymond did not return. Joseph had been looking anxiously for him, chiefly with the desire of getting rid of Ruby — not that he was absolutely of no use to him, but that he was a constant weight upon his mind. Indeed, as far as provision went, he was rather worse off with Ruby and Nanny than he had been before, but on the other hand, Nanny was a great help in the house, and it was a comfort to him to think that when the new baby did come, Nanny would be with his wife.

Of God's gifts a baby is of the greatest; therefore it is no wonder that when this one came, she was as heartily welcomed by the little household as if she had brought plenty with her. Of course she made a great difference in the work to be done — far more difference than her size warranted, but Nanny was no end of help, and Diamond was as much of a sunbeam as ever, and began to sing to the new baby the first moment he got her in his arms. But he did not sing the same songs to her that he had sung to his brother, for, he said, she was a new baby and must have new songs; and besides, she was a sister-baby and not a brother-baby, and of course would not like the same kind of songs. Where the difference in his songs lay, however, I do not pretend to be able to point out. One thing I am sure of, that they not only had no small share in the education of the little girl, but helped the whole family a great deal more than they were aware.

How they managed to get through the long dreary expensive winter, I can hardly say. Sometimes things were better, sometimes worse. But at last the spring came, and the winter was over and gone, and that was much. Still, Mr. Raymond did not return, and although the mother would have been able to manage without Nanny now, they could not look for a place for her so long as they had Ruby; and they were not altogether sorry for this. One week at last was worse than they had yet had. They were almost without bread before it was over. But the sadder he saw his father and mother looking, the more Diamond set himself to sing to the two babies.

One thing which had increased their expenses was that they had been forced to hire another little room for Nanny. When the second baby came, Diamond gave up his room that Nanny might be at hand to help his mother, and went to hers, which, although a fine place to what she had been accustomed to, was not very nice in his eyes. He did not mind the change though, for was not his mother the more comfortable for it? And was not Nanny more comfortable too? And indeed was not Diamond himself more comfortable that other people were more comfortable? And if there was more comfort every way, the change was a happy one.

32. DIAMOND AND RUBY

It was Friday night, and Diamond, like the rest of the household, had had very little to eat that day. The mother would always pay the week's rent before she laid out anything even on food. His father had been very gloomy — so gloomy that he had actually been cross to his wife. It is a strange thing how pain of seeing the suffering of those we love will sometimes make us add to their suffering by being cross with them. This comes of not having faith enough in God, and shows how necessary this faith is, for when we lose it, we lose even the kindness which alone can soothe the suffering. Diamond in consequence had gone to bed very quiet and thoughtful — a little troubled indeed.

It had been a very stormy winter. And even now that the spring had come, the north wind often blew. When Diamond went to his bed, which was in a tiny room in the roof, he heard it like the sea moaning; and when he fell asleep he still heard the moaning. All at once he said to himself, "Am I awake, or am I asleep?" But he had no time to answer the question, for there was North Wind calling him. His heart beat very fast, it was such a long time since he had heard that voice. He jumped out of bed, and looked everywhere, but could not see her. Diamond, come here," she said again and again; but where the here was he could not tell. To be sure the room was all but quite dark, and she might be close beside him.

"Dear North Wind," said Diamond, "I want so much to go to you, but I can't tell where."

"Come here, Diamond," was all her answer.

Diamond opened the door, and went out of the room, and down the stair and into the yard. His little heart was in a flutter, for he had long given up all thought of seeing her again. Neither now was he to see her. When he got out, a great puff of wind came against him, and in obedience to it he turned his back, and went as it blew. It blew him right up to the stable-door, and went on blowing.

"She wants me to go into the stable," said Diamond to himself. "but the door is locked."

He knew where the key was, in a certain hole in the wall — far too high for him to get at. He ran to the place, however: just as he reached it there came a wild blast, and down fell the key clanging on the stones at his feet. He picked it up, and ran back and opened the stable-door, and went in. And what do you think he saw?

A little light came through the dusty window from a gas-lamp, sufficient to show him Diamond and Ruby with their two heads up, looking at each other across the partition of their stalls. The light showed the white mark on Diamond's forehead, but Ruby's eye shone so bright, that he thought more light came out of it than went in. This is what he saw.

But what do you think he heard?

He heard the two horses talking to each other—in a strange language, which yet, somehow or other, he could understand, and turn over in his mind in English. The first words he heard were from Diamond, who apparently had been already quarrelling with Ruby.

"Look how fat you are Ruby!" said old Diamond. "You are so plump and your skin shines so, you ought to be ashamed of yourself."

"There's no harm in being fat," said Ruby in a deprecating tone. "No, nor in being sleek. I may as well shine as not."

"No harm?" retorted Diamond. "Is it no harm to go eating up all poor master's oats, and taking up so much of his time grooming you, when you only work six hours — no, not six hours a day, and, as I hear, get along no faster than a big dray-horse with two tons behind him?   So   they   tell me."

"Your master's not mine," said Ruby. "I must attend to my own master's interests, and eat all that is given me, and be sleek and fat as I can, and go no faster than I need."

"Now really if the rest of the horses weren't all asleep, poor things — they work till they're tired — I do believe they would get up and kick you out of the stable. You make me ashamed of being a horse. You dare to say my master ain't your master! That's your gratitude for the way he feeds you and spares you! Pray where would your carcass be if it weren't for him?"

"He doesn't do it for my sake. If I were his own horse, he would work me as hard as he does you."

"And I'm proud to be so worked. I wouldn't be as fat as you — not for all you're worth. You're a disgrace to the stable. Look at the horse next you. He's something like a horse — all skin and bone. And his master ain't over kind to him either. He put a stinging lash on his whip last week. But that old horse knows he's got the wife and children to keep — as well as his drunken master — and he works like a horse. I daresay he grudges his master the beer he drinks, but I don't believe he grudges anything else."

"Well, I don't grudge yours what he gets by me," said Ruby.

"Gets!" retorted Diamond. "What he gets isn't worth grudging. It comes to next to nothing — what with your fat and shine. "Well, at least you ought to be thankful you're the better for it. You get a two hours' rest a day out of it."

"I thank my master for that — not you, you lazy fellow! You go along like a buttock of beef upon castors — you do."

"Ain't you afraid I'll kick, if you go on like that, Diamond?"

"Kick! You couldn't kick if you tried. You might heave your rump up half a foot, but for lashing out — oho! If you did, you'd be down on your belly before you could get your legs under you again. It's my belief, once out, they'd stick out for ever. Talk of kicking! Why don't you put one foot before the other now and then when you're in the cab? The abuse master gets for your sake is quite shameful. No decent horse would bring it on him. Depend upon it, Ruby, no cabman likes to be abused any more than his fare. But his fares, at least when you are between the shafts, are very much to be excused. Indeed they are."

"Well, you see, Diamond, I don't want to go lame again."

"I don't believe you were so very lame after all — there!"

"Oh, but I was."

"Then I believe it was all your own fault. I'm not lame. I never was lame in all my life. You don't take care of your legs. You never lay them down at night. There you are with your huge carcass crushing down your poor legs all night long. You don't even care for your own legs — so long as you can eat, eat, and sleep, sleep. You a horse indeed!"

"But I tell you I was lame."

"I'm not denying there was a puffy look about your off-pastern. But my belief is, it wasn't even grease — it was fat."

"I tell you I put my foot on one of those horrid stones they make the roads with, and it gave my ankle such a twist."

"Ankle indeed! Why should you ape your betters? Horses ain't got any ankles: they're only pasterns. And so long as you don't lift your feet better, but fall asleep between every step, you'll run a good chance of laming all your ankles as you call them, one after another. It's not your lively horse that comes to grief in that way. I tell you I believe it wasn't much, and if it was, it was your own fault. There! I've done. I'm going to sleep. I'll try to think as well of you as I can. If you would but step out a bit and run off a little of your fat!" Here Diamond began to double up his knees; but Ruby spoke again, and, as young Diamond thought, in a rather different tone.

"I say, Diamond, I can't bear to have an honest old horse like you think of me like that. I will tell you the truth: it was my own fault that I fell lame."

"I told you so," returned the other, tumbling against the partition as he rolled over on his side to give his legs every possible privilege in their narrow circumstances.

"I meant to do it, Diamond."

At the words, the old horse arose with a scramble like thunder, shot his angry head and glaring eye over into Ruby's stall, and said —

"Keep out of my way, you unworthy wretch, or I'll bite you. You a horse! Why did you do that?"

"Because I wanted to grow fat."

"You grease-tub! Oh! my teeth and tail! I thought you were a humbug! Why did you want to get fat? There's no truth to be got out of you but by cross-questioning. You ain't fit to be a horse."

"Because once I am fat, my nature is to keep fat for a long time; and I didn't know when master might come home and want to see me."

"You conceited, good-for-nothing brute! You're only fit for the knacker's yard. You wanted to look handsome, did you? Hold your tongue, or I'll break my halter and be at you —with your handsome fat!"

"Never mind, Diamond. You're a good horse. You can't hurt me."

"Can't hurt you! Just let me once try."

"No, you can't."

"Why then?"

"Because I'm an angel."

"What's that?"

"Of course you don't know."

"Indeed I don't."

"I know you don't. An ignorant, rude old human horse, like you, couldn't know it. But there's young Diamond listening to all we're saying; and he knows well enough there are horses in heaven for angels to ride upon, as well as other animals, lions and eagles and bulls, in more important situations. The horses the angels ride, must be angel-horses, else the angels couldn't ride upon them. Well, I'm one of them."

"You ain't."

"Did you ever know a horse tell a lie?"

"Never before. But you've confessed to shamming lame."

"Nothing of the sort. It was necessary I should grow fat, and necessary that good Joseph, your master, should grow lean. I could have pretended to be lame, but that no horse, least of all an angel-horse would do. So I must be lame, and so I sprained my ankle — for the angel-horses have ankles — they don't talk horse-slang up there — and it hurt me very much, I assure you, Diamond, though you mayn't be good enough to be able to believe it."

Old Diamond made no reply. He had lain down again, and a sleepy snort, very like a snore, revealed that, if he was not already asleep, he was past understanding a word that Ruby was saying. When young Diamond found this, he thought he might venture to take up the dropt shuttlecock of the conversation.

"I'm good enough to believe it, Ruby," he said.

But Ruby never turned his head, or took any notice of him. I suppose he did not understand more of English than just what the coachman and stableman were in the habit of addressing him with. Finding, however, that his companion made no reply, he shot his head over the partition and looking down at him said —

"You just wait till to-morrow, and you'll see whether I'm speaking the truth or not. — I declare the old horse is fast asleep! — Diamond! — No I won't."

Ruby turned away, and began pulling at his hayrack in silence.

Diamond gave a shiver, and looking round saw that the door of the stable was open. He began to feel as if he had been dreaming, and after a glance about the stable to see if North Wind was anywhere visible, he thought he had better go back to bed.

33. THE PROSPECT BRIGHTENS

The next morning, Diamond's mother said to his father, "I'm not quite comfortable about that child again."

"Which child, Martha?" asked Joseph. "You've got a choice now."

"Well, Diamond I mean. I'm afraid he's getting into his queer ways again. He's been at his old trick of walking in his sleep. I saw him run up the stair in the middle of the night."

"Didn't you go after him, wife?"

"Of course I did — and found him fast asleep in his bed. It's because he's had so little meat for the last six weeks, I'm afraid."

"It may be that. I'm very sorry. But if it don't please God to send us enough, what am I to do, wife?"

"You can't help it, I know, my dear good man," returned Martha. "And after all I don't know. I don't see why he shouldn't get on as well as the rest of us. There I'm nursing baby all this time, and I get along pretty well. I'm sure, to hear the little man singing, you wouldn't think there was much amiss with him."

For at that moment Diamond was singing like a lark in the clouds. He had the new baby in his arms, while his mother was dressing herself. Joseph was sitting at his breakfast — a little weak tea, dry bread, and very dubious butter — which Nanny had set for him, and which he was enjoying because he was hungry. He had groomed both horses, and had got old Diamond harnessed ready to put to.

"Think of a fat angel, Dulcimer!" said Diamond.

The baby had not been christened yet, but Diamond, in reading his Bible, had come upon the word dulcimer, and thought it so pretty that ever after he called his sister Dulcimer!

"Think of a red, fat angel, Dulcimer!" he repeated; "for Ruby's an angel of a horse, Dulcimer. He sprained his ankle and got fat on purpose."

"What purpose, Diamond?" asked his father.

"Ah! that I can't tell. I suppose to look handsome when his master comes," answered Diamond. —" "What do you think, Dulcimer? It must be for some good, for Ruby's an angel."

"I wish I were rid of him, anyhow," said his father; "for he weighs heavy on my mind."

"No wonder, father: he's so fat," said Diamond. "But you needn't be afraid, for everybody says he's in better condition than when you had him."

"Yes, but he may be as thin as a tin horse before his owner comes. It was too bad to leave him on my hands this way."

"Perhaps he couldn't help it," suggested Diamond. "I daresay he has some good reason for it."

"So I should have said," returned his father, "if he had not driven such a hard bargain with me at first."

"But we don't know what may come of it yet, husband," said his wife. "Mr. Raymond may give a little to boot, seeing you've had more of the bargain than you wanted or reckoned upon."

"I'm afraid not: he's a hard man," said Joseph, as he rose and went to get his cab out.

Diamond resumed his singing. For some time he carolled snatches of everything or anything; but at last it settled down into something like what follows. I cannot tell where or how he got it.

Where did you come from, baby dear?
Out of the everywhere into here.

Where did you get your eyes so blue?
Out of the sky as I came through.

What makes the light in them sparkle and spin?
Some of the starry spikes left in.

Where did you get that little tear?
I found it waiting when I got here.

What makes your forehead so smooth and high?
A soft hand stroked it as I went by.

What makes your cheek like a warm white rose?
I saw something better than any one knows.

Whence that three-cornered smile of bliss?
Three angels gave me at once a kiss.

Where did you get this pearly ear?
God spoke, and it came out to hear.

Where did you get those arms and hands?
Love made itself into hooks and bands.

Feet, whence did you come, you darling things?
From the same box as the cherubs' wings.

How did they all just come to be you?
God thought about me, and so I grew.

But how did you come to us, you dear?
God thought about you, and so I am here.

"You never made that song, Diamond," said his mother.

"No, mother. I wish I had. No, I don't. That would be to take it from somebody else. But it's mine for all that."

"What makes it yours?"

"I love it so."

"Does loving a thing make it yours?"

"I think so, mother — at least more than anything else can. If I didn't love baby (which couldn't be, you know) she wouldn't be mine a bit. But I do love baby, and baby is my very own Dulcimer."

"The baby's mine, Diamond."

"That makes her the more mine, mother."

"How do you make that out?"

"Because you're mine, mother."

"Is that because you love me?"

"Yes, just because. Love makes the only myness," said Diamond.

When his father came home to have his dinner, and change Diamond for Ruby, they saw him look very sad, and he told them he had not had a fare worth mentioning the whole morning.

"We shall all have to go to the workhouse, wife," he said.

"It would be better to go to the back of the north wind," said Diamond, dreamily, not intending to say it aloud.

"So it would," answered his father. "But how are we to get there, Diamond?"

"We must wait till we're taken," returned Diamond.

Before his father could speak again, a knock came to the door, and in walked Mr. Raymond with a smile on his face. Joseph got up and received him respectfully, but not very cordially. Martha set a chair for him, but he would not sit down.

"You are not very glad to see me," he said to Joseph. "You don't want to part with the old horse."

"Indeed, sir, you are mistaken there. What with anxiety about him, and bad luck, I've wished I were rid of him a thousand times. It was only to be for three months, and here it's eight or nine."

"I'm sorry to hear such a statement," said Mr. Raymond. "Hasn't he been of service to you?"

"Not much, not with his lameness"

"Ah!" said Mr. Raymond, hastily – "you've been laming him—have you? That accounts for it. I see, I see."

"It wasn't my fault, and he's all right now. I don't know how it happened, but"

"He did it on purpose," said Diamond. "He put his foot on a stone just to twist his ankle."

"How do you know that, Diamond?" said his father, turning to him. "I never said so, for I could not think how it came."

"I heard it — in the stable," answered Diamond.

"Let's have a look at him," said Mr. Raymond.

"If you'll step into the yard," said Joseph, "I'll bring him out."

They went, and Joseph, having first taken off his harness, walked Ruby into the middle of the yard.

"Why," said Mr. Raymond, "you've not been using him well."

"I don't know what you mean by that, sir. I didn't expect to hear that from you. He's sound in wind and limb — as sound as a barrel."

"And as big, you might add. Why, he's as fat as a pig! You don't call that good usage!"

Joseph was too angry to make any answer.

"You've not worked him enough, I say. That's not making good use of him. That's not doing as you'd be done by."

"I shouldn't be sorry if I was served the same, sir."

"He's too fat, I say."

"There was a whole month I couldn't work him at all, and he did nothing but eat his head off. He's an awful eater. I've taken the best part of six hours a day out of him since, but I'm always afraid of his coming to grief again, and so I couldn't make the most even of that. I declare to you, sir, when he's between the shafts, I sit on the box as miserable as if I'd stolen him. He looks all the time as if he was a bottling up of complaints to make of me the minute he set eyes on you again. There! look at him now, squinting round at me with one eye! I declare to you, on my word, I haven't laid the whip on him more than three times."

"I'm glad to hear it. He never did want the whip."

"I didn't say that, sir. If ever a horse wanted the whip, he do. He's brought me to beggary almost with his snail's pace. I'm very glad you've come to rid me of him."

"I don't know that," said Mr. Raymond. "Suppose I were to ask you to buy him of me — cheap."

"I wouldn't have him in a present, sir. I don't like him. And I wouldn't drive a horse that I didn't like — no, not for gold. It can't come to good where there's no love between 'em."

"Just bring out your own horse, and let me see what sort of a pair they'd make."

Joseph laughed rather bitterly as he went to fetch Diamond.

When the two were placed side by side, Mr. Raymond could hardly keep his countenance, but from a mingling of feelings. Beside the great, red, round barrel, Ruby, all body and no legs, Diamond looked like a clothes-horse with a skin thrown over it. There was hardly a spot of him where you could not descry some sign of a bone underneath. Gaunt and grim and weary he stood, kissing his master, and heeding no one else.

"You haven't been using him well," said Mr. Raymond.

"I must say," returned Joseph, throwing an arm round his horse's neck, "that the remark had better have been spared, sir. The horse is worth three of the other now."

"I don't think so. I think they make a very nice pair. If the one's too fat, the other's too lean — so that's all right. And if you won't buy my Ruby, I must buy your Diamond."

"Thank you, sir," said Joseph, in a tone implying anything but thanks.

"You don't seem to like the proposal," said Mr. Raymond.

"I don't," returned Joseph. "I wouldn't part with my old Diamond for his skin as full of nuggets as it is of bones."

"Who said anything about parting with him?"

"You did now, sir."

"No; I didn't. I only spoke of buying him to make a pair with Ruby. We could pare Ruby and patch Diamond a bit. And for height, they are as near a match as I care about. Of course you would be the coachman — if only you would consent to be reconciled to Ruby."

Joseph stood bewildered, unable to answer.

"I've bought a small place in Kent," continued Mr. Raymond, "and I must have a pair to my carriage, for the roads are hilly thereabouts. I don't want to make a show with a pair of high-steppers. I think these will just do. Suppose, for a week or two, you set yourself to take Ruby down and bring Diamond up. If we could only lay a pipe from Ruby's sides into Diamond's, it would be the work of a moment. But I fear that wouldn't answer."

A strong inclination to laugh intruded upon Joseph's inclination to cry, and made speech still harder than before.

"I beg your pardon, sir," he said at length. "I've been so miserable, and for so long, that I never thought you was only a chaffing of me when you said I hadn't used the horses well. I did grumble at you, sir, many's the time in my trouble; but whenever I said anything, my little Diamond would look at me with a smile, as much as to say: "I know him better than you, father;" and upon my word, I always thought the boy must be right."

"Will you sell me old Diamond, then?"

"I will, sir, on one condition — that if ever you want to part with him or me, you give me the option of buying him. I could not part with him, sir. As to who calls him his, that's nothing; for, as Diamond says, it's only loving a thing that can make it yours — and I do love old Diamond, sir, dearly."

"Well, there's a cheque for twenty pounds, which I wrote to offer you for him, in case I should find you had done the handsome thing by Ruby. Will that be enough?"

"It's too much, sir. His body ain't worth it — shoes and all. It's only his heart, sir — that's worth millions — but his heart'll be mine all the same — so it's too much, sir."

"I don't think so. It won't be, at least, by the time we've got him fed up again. You take it and welcome. Just go on with your cabbing for another month, only take it out of Ruby and let Diamond rest; and by that time I shall be ready for you to go down into the country."

"Thank you, sir. thank you. Diamond set you down for a friend, sir, the moment he saw you. I do believe that child of mine knows more than other people."

"I think so, too," said Mr. Raymond as he walked away.

He had meant to test Joseph when he made the bargain about Ruby, but had no intention of so greatly prolonging the trial. He had been taken ill in Switzerland, and had been quite unable to return sooner. He went away now highly gratified at finding that he had stood the test, and was a true man.

Joseph rushed in to his wife who had been standing at the window anxiously waiting the result of the long colloquy. When she heard that the horses were to go together in double harness, she burst forth into an immoderate fit of laughter. Diamond came up with the baby in his arms and made big anxious eyes at her, saying —

"What is the matter with you, mother dear? Do cry a little. It will do you good. When father takes ever so small a drop of spirits, he puts water to it."

"You silly darling!" said his mother; "how could I but laugh at the notion of that great fat Ruby going side by side with our poor old Diamond?"

"But why not, mother? With a month's oats, and nothing to do, Diamond'll be nearer Ruby's size than you will father's. I think it's very good for different sorts to go together. Now Ruby will have a chance of teaching Diamond better manners."

"How dare you say such a thing, Diamond?" said his father, angrily. "To compare the two for manners, there's no comparison possible. Our Diamond's a gentleman."

"I don't mean to say he isn't, father; for I daresay some gentlemen judge their neighbours unjustly. That's all I mean. Diamond shouldn't have thought such bad things of Ruby. He didn't try to make the best of him."

"How do you know that, pray?"

"I heard them talking about it one night."

"Who?"

"Why Diamond and Ruby. Ruby's an angel."

Joseph stared and said no more. For all his new gladness, he was very gloomy as he re-harnessed the angel, for he thought his darling Diamond was going out of his mind.

He could not help thinking rather differently, however, when he found the change that had come over Ruby. Considering his fat, he exerted himself amazingly, and got over the ground with incredible speed. So willing, even anxious, was he to go now, that Joseph had to hold him quite tight.

Then as he laughed at his own fancies, a new fear came upon him lest the horse should break his wind, and Mr. Raymond have good cause to think he had not been using him well. He might even suppose that he had taken advantage of his new instructions, to let out upon the horse some of his pent-up dislike; whereas in truth, it had so utterly vanished that he felt as if Ruby, too, had been his friend all the time.

34. IN THE COUNTRY

Before the end of the month, Ruby had got respectably thin, and Diamond respectably stout. They really began to look fit for double harness.

Joseph and his wife got their affairs in order, and everything ready for migrating at the shortest notice; and they felt so peaceful and happy that they judged all the trouble they had gone through well worth enduring. As for Nanny, she had been so happy ever since she left the hospital, that she expected nothing better, and saw nothing attractive in the notion of the country. At the same time, she had not the least idea of what the word country meant, for she had never seen anything about her but streets and gas-lamps. Besides, she was more attached to Jim than to Diamond: Jim was a reasonable being, Diamond in her eyes at best only an amiable, over-grown baby, whom no amount of expostulation would ever bring to talk sense, not to say think it. Now that she could manage the baby as well as he, she judged herself altogether his superior. Towards his father and mother, she was all they could wish.

Diamond had taken a great deal of pains and trouble to find Jim, and had at last succeeded through the help of the tall policeman, who was glad to renew his acquaintance with the strange child. Jim had moved his quarters, and had not heard of Nanny's illness till some time after she was taken to the hospital, where he was too shy to go and inquire about her. But when at length she went to live with Diamond's family, Jim was willing enough to go and see her. It was after one of his visits, during which they had been talking of her new prospects, that Nanny expressed to Diamond her opinion of the country.

"There ain't nothing in it but the sun and moon, Diamond."

"There's trees and flowers," said Diamond.

"Well, they ain't no count," returned Nanny.

"Ain't they? They're so beautiful, they make you happy to look at them."

"That's because you're such a silly."

Diamond smiled with a far-away look, as if he were gazing through clouds of green leaves and the vision contented him. But he was thinking with himself what more he could do for Nanny; and that same evening he went to find Mr. Raymond, for he had heard that he had returned to town.

"Ah! how do you do, Diamond?" said Mr. Raymond; "I am glad to see you."

And he was indeed, for he had grown very fond of him. His opinion of him was very different from Nanny's.

"What do you want now, my child?" he asked.

"I'm always wanting something, sir," answered Diamond.

"Well, that's quite right, so long as what you want is right. Everybody is always wanting something; only we don't mention it in the right place often enough. What is it now?"

"There's a friend of Nanny's, a lame boy, called Jim."

"I've heard of him," said Mr. Raymond. "Well?"

"Nanny doesn't care much about going to the country, sir."

"Well, what has that to do with Jim?"

"You couldn't find a corner for Jim to work in — could you, sir?"

"I don't know that I couldn't. That is, if you can show good reason for it."

"He's a good boy, sir."

"Well, so much the better for him."

"I know he can shine boots, sir."

"So much the better for us."

"You want your boots shined in the country—don't you, sir?"

"Yes, to be sure."

"It wouldn't be nice to walk over the flowers with dirty boots — would it, sir?"

"No, indeed."

"They wouldn't like it — would they?"

"No, they wouldn't."

"Then Nanny would be better pleased to go, sir."

"If the flowers didn't like dirty boots to walk over them, Nanny wouldn't mind going to the country? Is that it? I don't quite see it."

"No, sir; I didn't mean that. I meant, if you would take Jim with you to clean your boots, and do odd jobs, you know, sir, then Nanny would like it better. She's so fond of Jim!"

"Now you come to the point, Diamond. I see what you mean, exactly. I will turn it over in my mind. Could you bring Jim to see me?"

"I'll try, sir. But they don't mind me much. They think I'm silly," added Diamond, with one of his sweetest smiles.

What Mr. Raymond thought, I dare hardly attempt to put down here. But one part of it was, that the highest wisdom must ever appear folly to those who do not possess it.

"I think he would come though — after dark, you know," Diamond continued. "He does well at shining boots. People's kind to lame boys, you know, sir. But after dark, there ain't so much doing."

Diamond succeeded in bringing Jim to Mr. Raymond, and the consequence was that he resolved to give the boy a chance. He provided new clothes for both him and Nanny; and upon a certain day, Joseph took his wife and three children, and Nanny and Jim, by train to a certain station in the county of Kent, where they found a cart waiting to carry them and their luggage to The Mound, which was the name of Mr. Raymond's new residence. I will not describe the varied feelings of the party as they went, or when they arrived. All I will say is, that Diamond, who is my only care, was full of quiet delight—a gladness too deep to talk about.

Joseph returned to town the same night, and the next morning drove Ruby and Diamond down, with the carriage behind them, and Mr. Raymond and a lady in the carriage. For Mr. Raymond was an old bachelor no longer: he was bringing his wife with him to live at The Mound. The moment Nanny saw her, she recognized her as the lady who had lent her the ruby-ring. That ring had been given her by Mr. Raymond.

The weather was very hot, and the woods very shadowy. There were not a great many wild flowers, for it was getting well towards autumn, and the most of the wild flowers rise early to be before the leaves, because if they did not, they would never get a glimpse of the sun for them. So they have their fun over, and are ready to go to bed again by the time the trees are dressed. But there was plenty of the loveliest grass and daisies about the house, and Diamond's chief pleasure seemed to be to lie amongst them, and breathe the pure air. But all the time, he was dreaming of the country at the back of the north wind, and trying to recall the songs the river used to sing. For this was more like being at the back of the north wind than anything he had known since he left it. Sometimes he would have his little brother, sometimes his little sister, and sometimes both of them in the grass with him, and then he felt just like a cat with her first kittens, he said, only he couldn't purr — all he could do was to sing.

These were very different times from those when he used to drive the cab, but you must not suppose that Diamond was idle. He did not do so much for his mother now, because Nanny occupied his former place; but he helped his father still, both in the stable and the harness-room, and generally went with him on the box that he might learn to drive a pair, and be ready to open the carriage-door. Mr. Raymond advised his father to give him plenty of liberty.

"A boy like that," he said, "ought not to be pushed."

Joseph assented heartily, smiling to himself at the idea of pushing Diamond. After doing everything that fell to his share, the boy had a wealth of time at his disposal. And a happy, sometimes a merry time it was. Only for two months or so, he neither saw nor heard anything of North Wind.

35. I Make Diamond's Acquaintance

Mr. Raymond's house was called The Mound, because it stood upon a little steep knoll, so smooth and symmetrical that it showed itself at once to be artificial. It had, beyond doubt, been built for Queen Elizabeth as a hunting tower — place, namely, from the top of which you could see the country for miles on all sides, and so be able to follow with your eyes the flying deer and the pursuing hounds and horsemen. The mound had been cast up to give a good basement-advantage over the neighboring heights and woods. There was a great quarry-hole not far off, brim-full of water, from which, as the current legend stated, the materials forming the heart of the mound — a kind of stone unfit for building — had been dug. The house itself was of brick, and they said the foundations were first laid in the natural level, and then the stones and earth of the mound were heaped about and between them, so that its great height should be well buttressed.

Joseph and his wife lived in a little cottage a short way from the house. It was a real cottage, with a roof of thick thatch, which, in June and July, the wind sprinkled with the red and white petals it shook from the loose topmost sprays of the rose-trees climbing the walls. At first Diamond had a nest under this thatch — a pretty little room with white muslin curtains, but afterwards Mr. and Mrs. Raymond wanted to have him for a page in the house, and his father and mother were quite pleased to have him employed without his leaving them. So he was dressed in a suit of blue, from which his pale face and fair hair came out like the loveliest blossom, and took up his abode in the house.

"Would you be afraid to sleep alone, Diamond?" asked his mistress.

"I don't know what you mean, ma'am," said Diamond. "I never was afraid of anything that I can recollect — not much, at least."

"There's a little room at the top of the house — all alone," she returned; "perhaps you would not mind sleeping there?"

"I can sleep anywhere, and I like best to be high up. Should I be able to see out?"

"I will show you the place," she answered; and taking him by the hand, she led him up and up the oval-winding stair in one of the two towers.

Near the top they entered a tiny little room, with two windows from which you could see over the whole country. Diamond clapped his hands with delight.

"You would like this room, then, Diamond?" said his mistress.

"It's the grandest room in the house," he answered. "I shall be near the stars, and yet not far from the tops of the trees. That's just what I like."

I daresay he thought, also, that it would be a nice place for North Wind to call at in passing; but he said nothing of that sort. Below him spread a lake of green leaves, with glimpses of grass here and there at the bottom of it. As he looked down, he saw a squirrel appear suddenly, and as suddenly vanish amongst the topmost branches.

"Aha! little squirrel," he cried, "my nest is built higher than yours."

"You can be up here with your books as much as you like," said his mistress. "I will have a little bell hung at the door, which I can ring when I want you. Half-way down the stair is the drawing-room."

So Diamond was installed as page, and his new room got ready for him.

It was very soon after this that I came to know Diamond. I was then a tutor in a family whose estate adjoined the little property belonging to The Mound. I had made the acquaintance of Mr. Raymond in London some time before, and was walking up the drive towards the house to call upon him one fine warm evening, when I saw Diamond for the first time. He was sitting at the foot of a great beech-tree, a few yards from the road, with a book on his knees. He did not see me. I walked up behind the tree, and peeping over his shoulder, saw that he was reading a fairy-book.

"What are you reading?" I said, and spoke suddenly, with the hope of seeing a startled little face look round at me. Diamond turned his head as quietly as if he were only obeying his mother's voice, and the calmness of his face rebuked my unkind desire and made me ashamed of it.

"I am reading the story of the Little Lady and the Goblin Prince," said Diamond.

"I am sorry I don't know the story," I returned. "Who is it by?"

"Mr. Raymond made it."

"Is he your uncle?" I asked at a guess.

"No. He's my master."

"What do you do for him?" I asked respectfully.

"Anything he wishes me to do," he answered. "I am busy for him now. He gave me this story to read. He wants my opinion upon it."

"Don't you find it rather hard to make up your mind?"

"Oh dear no! Any story always tells me itself what I'm to think about it. Mr. Raymond doesn't want me to say whether it is a clever story or not, but whether I like it, and why I like it. I never can tell what they call clever from what they call silly, but I always know whether I like a story or not."

"And can you always tell why you like it or not?"

"No. Very often I can't at all. Sometimes I can. I always know, but I can't always tell why. Mr. Raymond writes the stories, and then tries them on me. Mother does the same when she makes jam. She's made such a lot of jam since we came here! And she always makes me taste it to see if it'll do. Mother knows by the face I make whether it will or not."

At this moment I caught sight of two more children approaching. One was a handsome girl, the other a pale-faced, awkward-looking boy, who limped much on one leg. I withdrew a little, to see what would follow, for they seemed in some consternation. After a few hurried words, they went off together, and I pursued my way to the house, where I was as kindly received by Mr. and Mrs. Raymond as I could have desired. From them I learned something of Diamond, and was in consequence the more glad to find him, when I returned, seated in the same place as before.

"What did the boy and girl want with you, Diamond?" I asked.

"They had seen a creature that frightened them."

"And they came to tell you about it?"

"They couldn't get water out of the well for it. So they wanted me to go with them."

"They're both bigger than you."

"Yes, but they were frightened at it."

"And weren't you frightened at it?"

"No."

"Why?"

"Because I'm silly. I'm never frightened at things."

I could not help thinking of the old meaning of the word silly.

"And what was it?" I asked.

"I think it was a kind of an angel — a very little one. It had a long body and great wings, which it drove about it so fast that they grew a thin cloud all round it. It flew backwards and forwards over the well, or hung right in the middle, making a mist of its wings, as if its business was to take care of the water."

"And what did you do to drive it away?"

"I didn't drive it away. I knew, whatever the creature was, the well was to get water out of. So I took the jug, dipped it in, and drew the water."

"And what did the creature do?"

"Flew about."

"And it didn't hurt you?"

"No. Why should it? I wasn't doing anything wrong."

"What did your companions say then?"

"They said — `Thank you, Diamond. What a dear silly you are!'"

"And weren't you angry with them?"

"No! Why should I? I should like if they would play with me a little; but they always like better to go away together when their work is over. They never heed me. I don't mind it much, though. The other creatures are friendly. They don't run away from me. Only they're all so busy with their own work, they don't mind me much."

"Do you feel lonely, then?"

"Oh, no! When nobody minds me, I get into my nest, and look up. And then the sky does mind me, and thinks about me."

"Where is your nest?"

He rose, saying, "I will show you," and led me to the other side of the tree.

There hung a little rope-ladder from one of the lower boughs. The boy climbed up the ladder and got upon the bough. Then he climbed farther into the leafy branches, and went out of sight.

After a little while, I heard his voice coming down out of the tree.

"I am in my nest now," said the voice.

"I can't see you," I returned.

"I can't see you either, but I can see the first star peeping out of the sky. I should like to get up into the sky. Don't you think I shall, some day?"

"Yes, I do. Tell me what more you see up there."

"I don't see anything more, except a few leaves, and the big sky over me. It goes swinging about. The earth is all behind my back. There comes another star! The wind is like kisses from a big lady. When I get up here I feel as if I were in North Wind's arms."

This was the first I heard of North Wind.

The whole ways and look of the child, so full of quiet wisdom, yet so ready to accept the judgment of others in his own dispraise, took hold of my heart, and I felt myself wonderfully drawn towards him. It seemed to me, somehow, as if little Diamond possessed the secret of life, and was himself what he was so ready to think the lowest living thing — an angel of God with something special to say or do. A gush of reverence came over me, and with a single goodnight, I turned and left him in his nest.

I saw him often after this, and gained so much of his confidence that he told me all I have told you. I cannot pretend to account for it. I leave that for each philosophical reader to do after his own fashion. The easiest way is that of Nanny and Jim, who said often to each other that Diamond had a tile loose. But Mr. Raymond was much of my opinion concerning the boy; while Mrs. Raymond confessed that she often rang her bell just to have once more the pleasure of seeing the lovely stillness of the boy's face, with those blue eyes which seemed rather made for other people to look into than for himself to look out of.

It was plainer to others than to himself that he felt the desertion of Nanny and Jim. They appeared to regard him as a mere toy, except when they found he could minister to the scruple of using him — generally with success. They were, however, well-behaved to a wonderful degree; while I have little doubt that much of their good behavior was owing to the unconscious influence of the boy they called God's baby.

One very strange thing is that I could never find out where he got some of his many songs. At times they would be but bubbles blown out of a nursery rhyme, as was the following, which I heard him sing one evening to his little Dulcimer. There were about a score of sheep feeding in a paddock near him, their white wool dyed a pale rose in the light of the setting sun. Those in the long shadows from the trees were dead white; those in the sunlight were half glorified with pale rose.

Little Bo Peep, she lost her sheep,

And didn't know where to find them;

They were over the height and out of sight,

Trailing their tails behind them.

Little Bo Peep woke out of her sleep,

Jumped up and set out to find them:

"The silly things, they've got no wings,

And they've left their trails behind them:

"They've taken their tails, but they've left their trails,

And so I shall follow and find them;"

For wherever a tail had dragged a trail,

The long grass grew behind them.

And day's eyes and butter-cups, cow's lips and crow's feet

Were glittering in the sun.

She threw down her book, and caught up her crook,

And after her sheep did run.

She ran, and she ran, and ever as she ran,

The grass grew higher and higher;

Till over the hill the sun began

To set in a flame of fire.

She ran on still — up the grassy hill,
And the grass grew higher and higher;
When she reached its crown, the sun was down,
And had left a trail of fire.

The sheep and their tails were gone, all gone —
And no more trail behind them!
Yes, yes! they were there — long-tailed and fair,
But, alas! she could not find them.

Purple and gold, and rosy and blue,
With their tails all white behind them,
Her sheep they did run in the trail of the sun;
She saw them, but could not find them.

After the sun, like clouds they did run,
But she knew they were her sheep:
She sat down to cry, and look up at the sky,
But she cried herself asleep.

And as she slept the dew fell fast,
And the wind blew from the sky;
And strange things took place that shun the day's face,
Because they are sweet and shy.

Nibble, nibble, crop! she heard as she woke:
A hundred little lambs
Did pluck and eat the grass so sweet
That grew in the trails of their dams.

Little Bo Peep caught up her crook,
And wiped the tears that did blind her.
And nibble, nibble crop! without a stop!
The lambs came eating behind her.

Home, home she came, both tired and lame,

With three times as many sheep.

In a month or more, they'll be as big as before,

And then she'll laugh in her sleep.

But what would you say, if one fine day,

When they've got their bushiest tails,

Their grown up game should be just the same,

And she have to follow their trails?

Never weep, Bo Peep, though you lose your sheep,

And do not know where to find them;

'Tis after the sun the mothers have run,

And there are their lambs behind them.

I confess again to having touched up a little, but it loses far more in Diamond's sweet voice singing it than it gains by a rhyme here and there.

Some of them were out of books Mr. Raymond had given him. These he always knew, but about the others he could seldom tell. Sometimes he would say, "I made that one." but generally he would say, "I don't know; I found it somewhere;" or "I got it at the back of the north wind."

One evening I found him sitting on the grassy slope under the house, with his Dulcimer in his arms and his little brother rolling on the grass beside them. He was chanting in his usual way, more like the sound of a brook than anything else I can think of. When I went up to them he ceased his chant.

"Do go on, Diamond. Don't mind me," I said.

He began again at once. While he sang, Nanny and Jim sat a little way off, one hemming a pocket-handkerchief, and the other reading a story to her, but they never heeded Diamond. This is as near what he sang as I can recollect, or reproduce rather.

What would you see if I took you up

To my little nest in the air?

You would see the sky like a clear blue cup

Turned upside downwards there.

What would you do if I took you there

To my little nest in the tree?

My child with cries would trouble the air,

To get what she could but see.

What would you get in the top of the tree

For all your crying and grief?

Not a star would you clutch of all you see —

You could only gather a leaf.

But when you had lost your greedy grief,

Content to see from afar,

You would find in your hand a withering leaf,

In your heart a shining star.

As Diamond went on singing, it grew very dark, and just as he ceased there came a great flash of lightning, that blinded us all for a moment. Dulcimer crowed with pleasure; but when the roar of thunder came after it, the little brother gave a loud cry of terror. Nanny and Jim came running up to us, pale with fear. Diamond's face, too, was paler than usual, but with delight. Some of the glory seemed to have clung to it, and remained shining.

"You're not frightened — are you, Diamond?" I said.

"No. Why should I be?" he answered with his usual question, looking up in my face with calm shining eyes.

"He ain't got sense to be frightened," said Nanny, going up to him and giving him a pitying hug.

"Perhaps there's more sense in not being frightened, Nanny," I returned. "Do you think the lightning can do as it likes?"

"It might kill you," said Jim.

"Oh, no, it mightn't!" said Diamond.

As he spoke there came another great flash, and a tearing crack.

"There's a tree struck!" I said; and when we looked round, after the blinding of the flash had left our eyes, we saw a huge bough of the beech-tree in which was Diamond's nest hanging to the ground like the broken wing of a bird.

"There!" cried Nanny; "I told you so. If you had been up there you see what would have happened, you little silly!"

"No, I don't," said Diamond, and began to sing to Dulcimer. All I could hear of the song, for the other children were going on with their chatter, was —

The clock struck one,

And the mouse came down.

Dickery, dickery, dock!

Then there came a blast of wind, and the rain followed in straight-pouring lines, as if out of a watering-pot. Diamond jumped up with his little Dulcimer in his arms, and Nanny caught up the little boy, and they ran for the cottage. Jim vanished with a double shuffle, and I went into the house.

When I came out again to return home, the clouds were gone, and the evening sky glimmered through the trees, blue, and pale-green towards the west, I turned my steps a little aside to look at the stricken beech. I saw the bough torn from the stem, and that was all the twilight would allow me to see. While I stood gazing, down from the sky came a sound of singing, but the voice was neither of lark nor of nightingale: it was sweeter than either: it was the voice of Diamond, up in his airy nest: —

The lightning and thunder,

They go and they come;

But the stars and the stillness

Are always at home.

And then the voice ceased.

"Good-night, Diamond," I said.

"Good-night, sir," answered Diamond.

As I walked away pondering, I saw the great black top of the beech swaying about against the sky in an upper wind, and heard the murmur as of many dim half-articulate voices filling the solitude around Diamond's nest.

36. DIAMOND QUESTIONS NORTH WIND

My readers will not wonder that, after this, I did my very best to gain the friendship of Diamond. Nor did I find this at all difficult, the child was so ready to trust. Upon one subject alone was he reticent — the story of his relations with North Wind. I fancy he could not quite make up his mind what to think of them. At all events it was some little time before he trusted me with this, only then he told me everything. If I could not regard it all in exactly the same light as he did, I was, while guiltless of the least pretence, fully sympathetic, and he was satisfied without demanding of me any theory of difficult points involved. I let him see plainly enough, that whatever might be the explanation of the marvelous experience, I would have given much for a similar one myself.

On an evening soon after the thunderstorm, in a late twilight, with a half-moon high in the heavens, I came upon Diamond in the act of climbing by his little ladder into the beech-tree.

"What are you always going up there for, Diamond?" I heard Nanny ask, rather rudely, I thought.

"Sometimes for one thing, sometimes for another, Nanny," answered Diamond, looking skywards as he climbed.

"You'll break your neck some day," she said.

"I'm going up to look at the moon to-night," he added, without heeding her remark.

"You'll see the moon just as well down here," she returned.

"I don't think so."

"You'll be no nearer to her up there."

"Oh, yes! I shall. I must be nearer her, you know. I wish I could dream as pretty dreams about her as you can, Nanny."

"You silly! you never have done about that dream. I never dreamed but that one, and it was nonsense enough, I'm sure."

"It wasn't nonsense. It was a beautiful dream — and a funny one too, both in one."

"But what's the good of talking about it that way, when you know it was only a dream? Dreams ain't true."

"That one was true, Nanny. You know it was. Didn't you come to grief for doing what you were told not to do? And isn't that true?"

"I can't get any sense into him," exclaimed Nanny, with an expression of mild despair. "Do you really believe, Diamond, that there's a house in the moon, with a beautiful lady and a crooked old man and dusters in it?"

"If there isn't, there's something better," he answered, and vanished in the leaves over our heads.

I went into the house, where I visited often in the evenings. When I came out, there was a little wind blowing, very pleasant after the heat of the day, for although it was late summer now, it was still hot. The tree-tops were swinging about in it. I took my way past the beech, and called up to see if Diamond were still in his nest in its rocking head.

"Are you there, Diamond?" I said.

"Yes, sir," came his clear voice in reply.

"Isn't it growing too dark for you to get down safely?"

"Oh, no, sir — if I take time to it. I know my way so well, and never let go with one hand till I've a good hold with the other."

"Do be careful," I insisted — foolishly, seeing the boy was as careful as he could be already.

"I'm coming," he returned. "I've got all the moon I want to-night."

I heard a rustling and a rustling drawing nearer and nearer. Three or four minutes elapsed, and he appeared at length creeping down his little ladder. I took him in my arms, and set him on the ground.

"Thank you, sir," he said. "That's the north wind blowing, isn't it, sir?"

"I can't tell," I answered. "It feels cool and kind, and I think it may be. But I couldn't be sure except it were stronger, for a gentle wind might turn any way amongst the trunks of the trees."

"I shall know when I get up to my own room," said Diamond. "I think I hear my mistress's bell. Good-night, sir."

He ran to the house, and I went home.

His mistress had rung for him only to send him to bed, for she was very careful over him and I daresay thought he was not looking well. When he reached his own room, he opened both his windows, one of which looked to the north and the other to the east, to find how the wind blew. It blew right in at the northern window. Diamond was very glad, for he thought perhaps North Wind herself would come now: a real north wind had never blown all the time since he left London. But, as she always came of herself, and never when he was looking for her, and indeed almost never when he was thinking of her, he shut the east window, and went to bed. Perhaps some of my readers may wonder that he could go to sleep with such an expectation; and, indeed, if I had not known him, I should have wondered at it myself; but it was one of his peculiarities, and seemed nothing strange in him. He was so full of quietness that he could go to sleep almost any time, if he only composed himself and let the sleep come. This time he went fast asleep as usual.

But he woke in the dim blue night. The moon had vanished. He thought he heard a knocking at his door. "Somebody wants me," he said to himself, and jumping out of bed, ran to open it.

But there was no one there. He closed it again, and, the noise still continuing, found that another door in the room was rattling. It belonged to a closet, he thought, but he had never been able to open it. The wind blowing in at the window must be shaking it. He would go and see if it was so.

The door now opened quite easily, but to his surprise, instead of a closet he found a long narrow room. The moon, which was sinking in the west, shone in at an open window at the further end. The room was low with a coved ceiling, and occupied the whole top of the house, immediately under the roof. It was quite empty. The yellow light of the half-moon streamed over the dark floor. He was so delighted at the discovery of the strange, desolate, moonlit place close to his own snug little room, that he began to dance and skip about the floor. The wind came in through the door he had left open, and blew about him as he danced, and he kept turning towards it that it might blow in his face. He kept picturing to himself the many places, lovely and desolate, the hill-sides and farm-yards and tree-tops and meadows, over which it had blown on its way to The Mound. And as he danced, he grew more and more delighted with the motion and the wind; his feet grew stronger, and his body lighter, until at length it seemed as if he were borne up on the air, and could almost fly. So strong did his feeling become, that at last he began to doubt whether he was not in one of those precious dreams he had so often had, in which he floated about on the air at will. But something made him look up, and to his unspeakable delight, he found his uplifted hands lying in those of North Wind, who was dancing with him, round and round the long bare room, her hair now falling to the floor, now filling the arched ceiling, her eyes shining on him like thinking stars, and the sweetest of grand smiles playing breezily about her beautiful mouth. She was, as so often before, of the height of a rather tall lady. She did not stoop in order to dance with him, but held his hands high in hers. When he saw her, he gave one spring, and his arms were about her neck, and her arms holding him to her bosom. The same moment she swept with him through the open window in at which the moon was shining, made a circuit like a bird about to alight, and settled with him in his nest on the top of the great beech-tree. There she placed him on her lap and began to hush him as if he were her own baby, and Diamond was so entirely happy that he did not care to speak a word. At length, however, he found that he was going to sleep, and that would be to lose so much, that, pleasant as it was, he could not consent.

"Please, dear North Wind," he said, "I am so happy that I'm afraid it's a dream. How am I to know that it's not a dream?"

"What does it matter?" returned North Wind.

"I should, cry" said Diamond.

"But why should you cry? The dream, if it is a dream, is a pleasant one — is it not?"

"That's just why I want it to be true."

"Have you forgotten what you said to Nanny about her dream?"

"It's not for the dream itself — I mean, it's not for the pleasure of it," answered Diamond, "for I have that, whether it be a dream or not; it's for you, North Wind; I can't bear to find it a dream, because then I should lose you. You would be nobody then, and I could not bear that. You ain't a dream, are you, dear North Wind? Do say No, else I shall cry, and come awake, and you'll be gone for ever. I daren't dream about you once again if you ain't anybody."

"I'm either not a dream, or there's something better that's not a dream, Diamond," said North Wind, in a rather sorrowful tone, he thought.

"But it's not something better — it's you I want, North Wind," he persisted, already beginning to cry a little.

She made no answer, but rose with him in her arms and sailed away over the tree-tops till they came to a meadow, where a flock of sheep was feeding.

"Do you remember what the song you were singing a week ago says about Bo-Peep —how she lost her sheep, but got twice as many lambs?" asked North Wind, sitting down on the grass, and placing him in her lap as before.

"Oh yes, I do, well enough," answered Diamond; "but I never just quite liked that rhyme."

"Why not, child?"

"Because it seems to say one's as good as another, or two new ones are better than one that's lost. I've been thinking about it a great deal, and it seems to me that although any one sixpence is as good as any other sixpence, not twenty lambs would do instead of one sheep whose face you knew. Somehow, when once you've looked into anybody's eyes, right deep down into them, I mean, nobody will do for that one any more. Nobody, ever so beautiful or so good, will make up for that one going out of sight. So you see, North Wind, I can't help being frightened to think that perhaps I am only dreaming, and you are nowhere at all. Do tell me that you are my own, real, beautiful North Wind."

Again she rose, and shot herself into the air, as if uneasy because she could not answer him; and Diamond lay quiet in her arms, waiting for what she would say. He tried to see up into her face, for he was dreadfully afraid she was not answering him because she could not say that she was not a dream; but she had let her hair fall all over her face so that he could not see it. This frightened him still more.

"Do speak, North Wind," he said at last.

"I never speak when I have nothing to say," she replied.

"Then I do think you must be a real North Wind, and no dream," said Diamond.

"But I'm looking for something to say all the time."

"But I don't want you to say what's hard to find. If you were to say one word to comfort me that wasn't true, then I should know you must be a dream, for a great beautiful lady like you could never tell a lie."

"But she mightn't know how to say what she had to say, so that a little boy like you would understand it," said North Wind. "Here, let us get down again, and I will try to tell you what I think. You musn't suppose I am able to answer all your questions, though. There are a great many things I don't understand more than you do."

She descended on a grassy hillock, in the midst of a wild furzy common. There was a rabbit-warren underneath, and some of the rabbits came out of their holes, in the moonlight, looking very sober and wise, just like patriarchs standing in their tent-doors, and looking about them before going to bed. When they saw North Wind, instead of turning round and vanishing again with a thump of their heels, they cantered slowly up to her and snuffled all about her with their long upper lips, which moved every way at once. That was their way of kissing her; and, as she talked to Diamond, she would every now and then stroke down their furry backs, or lift and play with their long ears. They would, Diamond thought, have leaped upon her lap, but that he was there already.

"I think," said she, after they had been sitting silent for a while, "that if I were only a dream, you would not have been able to love me so. You love me when you are not with me, don't you?"

"Indeed I do," answered Diamond, stroking her hand. "I see! I see! How could I be able to love you as I do if you weren't there at all, you know? Besides, I couldn't be able to dream anything half so beautiful all out of my own head; or if I did, I couldn't love a fancy of my own like that, could I?"

"I think not. You might have loved me in a dream, dreamily, and forgotten me when you woke, I daresay, but not loved me like a real being as you love me. Even then, I don't think you could dream anything that hadn't something real like it somewhere. But you've seen me in many shapes, Diamond: you remember I was a wolf once — don't you?"

"Oh yes — a good wolf that frightened a naughty drunken nurse."

"Well, suppose I were to turn ugly, would you rather I weren't a dream then?"

"Yes; for I should know that you were beautiful inside all the same. You would love me, and I should love you all the same. I shouldn't like you to look ugly, you know. But I shouldn't believe it a bit."

"Not if you saw it?"

"No, not if I saw it ever so plain."

"There's my Diamond! I will tell you all I know about it then. I don't think I am just what you fancy me to be. I have to shape myself various ways to various people. But the heart of me is true. People call me by dreadful names, and think they know all about me. But they don't. Sometimes they call me Bad Fortune, sometimes Evil Chance, sometimes Ruin; and they have another name for me which they think the most dreadful of all."

"What is that?" asked Diamond, smiling up in her face.

"I won't tell you that name. Do you remember having to go through me to get into the country at my back?"

"Oh yes, I do. How cold you were, North Wind! and so white, all but your lovely eyes! My heart grew like a lump of ice, and then I forgot for a while."

"You were very near knowing what they call me then. Would you be afraid of me if you had to go through me again?"

"No. Why should I? Indeed I should be glad enough, if it was only to get another peep of the country at your back."

"You've never seen it yet."

"Haven't I, North Wind? Oh! I'm so sorry! I thought I had. What did I see then?"

"Only a picture of it. The real country at my real back is ever so much more beautiful than that. You shall see it one day — perhaps before very long."

"Do they sing songs there?"

"Don't you remember the dream you had about the little boys that dug for the stars?"

"Yes, that I do. I thought you must have had something to do with that dream, it was so beautiful."

"Yes; I gave you that dream."

"Oh! thank you. Did you give Nanny her dream too — about the moon and the bees?"

"Yes. I was the lady that sat at the window of the moon."

"Oh, thank you. I was almost sure you had something to do with that too. And did you tell Mr. Raymond the story about the Princess Daylight?"

"I believe I had something to do with it. At all events he thought about it one night when he couldn't sleep. But I want to ask you whether you remember the song the boy-angels sang in that dream of yours."

"No. I couldn't keep it, do what I would, and I did try."

"That was my fault."

"How could that be, North Wind?"

"Because I didn't know it properly myself, and so I couldn't teach it to you. I could only make a rough guess at something like what it would be, and so I wasn't able to make you dream it hard enough to remember it. Nor would I have done so if I could, for it was not correct. I made you dream pictures of it, though. But you will hear the very song itself when you do get to the back of—"

"My own dear North Wind," said Diamond, finishing the sentence for her, and kissing the arm that held him leaning against her.

"And now we've settled all this — for the time, at least," said North Wind.

"But I can't feel quite sure yet," said Diamond.

"You must wait a while for that. Meantime you may be hopeful, and content not to be quite sure. Come now, I will take you home again, for it won't do to tire you too much."

"Oh, no, no. I'm not the least tired," pleaded Diamond.

"It is better, though."

"Very well; if you wish it," yielded Diamond with a sigh.

"You are a dear good, boy" said North Wind. "I will come for you again to-morrow night and take you out for a longer time. We shall make a little journey together, in fact. We shall start earlier. And as the moon will be, later, we shall have a little moonlight all the way."

She rose, and swept over the meadow and the trees. In a few moments the Mound appeared below them. She sank a little, and floated in at the window of Diamond's room. There she laid him on his bed, covered him over, and in a moment he was lapt in a dreamless sleep.

37. ONCE MORE

The next night Diamond was seated by his open window, with his head on his hand, rather tired, but so eagerly waiting for the promised visit that he was afraid he could not sleep. But he started suddenly, and found that he had been already asleep. He rose, and looking out of the window saw something white against his beech-tree. It was North Wind. She was holding by one hand to a top branch. Her hair and her garments went floating away behind her over the tree, whose top was swaying about while the others were still.

"Are you ready, Diamond?" she asked.

"Yes," answered Diamond, "quite ready."

In a moment she was at the window, and her arms came in and took him. She sailed away so swiftly that he could at first mark nothing but the speed with which the clouds above and the dim earth below went rushing past. But soon he began to see that the sky was very lovely, with mottled clouds all about the moon, on which she threw faint colors like those of mother-of-pearl, or an opal. The night was warm, and in the lady's arms he did not feel the wind which down below was making waves in the ripe corn, and ripples on the rivers and lakes. At length they descended on the side of an open earthy hill, just where, from beneath a stone, a spring came bubbling out.

"I am going to take you along this little brook," said North Wind. "I am not wanted for anything else to-night, so I can give you a treat."

She stooped over the stream and holding Diamond down close to the surface of it, glided along level with its flow as it ran down the hill. And the song of the brook came up into Diamond's ears, and grew and grew and changed with every turn. It seemed to Diamond to be singing the story of its life to him. And so it was. It began with a musical tinkle which changed to a babble and then to a gentle rushing. Sometimes its song would almost cease, and then break out again, tinkle, babble, and rush, all at once. At the bottom of the hill they came to a small river, into which the brook flowed with a muffled but merry sound. Along the surface of the river, darkly clear below them in the moonlight, they floated; now, where it widened out into a little lake, they would hover for a moment over a bed of water-lilies, and watch them swing about, folded in sleep, as the water on which they leaned swayed in the presence of North Wind; and now they would watch the fishes asleep among their roots below. Sometimes she would hold Diamond over a deep hollow curving into the bank, that he might look far into the cool stillness. Sometimes she would leave the river and sweep across a clover-field. The bees were all at home, and the clover was asleep. Then she would return and follow the river. It grew wider and wider as it went. Now the armies of wheat and of oats would hang over its rush from the opposite banks; now the willows would dip low branches in its still waters; and now it would lead them through stately trees and grassy banks into a lovely garden, where the roses and lilies were asleep, the tender flowers quite folded up, and only a few wide-awake and sending out their life in sweet, strong odors. Wider and wider grew the stream, until they came upon boats lying along its banks, which rocked a little in the flutter of North Wind's garments. Then came houses on the banks, each standing in a lovely lawn, with grand trees; and in parts the river was so high that some of the grass and the roots of some of the trees were under water, and Diamond, as they glided through between the stems, could see the grass at the bottom of the water. Then they would leave the river and float about and over the houses, one after another — beautiful rich houses, which, like fine trees, had taken centuries to grow. There was scarcely a light to be seen, and not a movement to be heard: all the people in them lay fast asleep.

"What a lot of dreams they must be dreaming!" said Diamond.

"Yes," returned North Wind. "They can't surely be all lies — can they?"

"I should think it depends a little on who dreams them," suggested Diamond.

"Yes," said North Wind. "The people who think lies, and do lies, are very likely to dream lies. But the people who love what is true will surely now and then dream true things. But then something depends on whether the dreams are home-grown, or whether the seed of them is blown over somebody else's garden-wall. Ah! there's some one awake in this house!"

They were floating past a window in which a light was burning. Diamond heard a moan, and looked up anxiously in North Wind's face.

"It's a lady," said North Wind. "She can't sleep for pain."

"Couldn't you do something for her?" said Diamond.

"No, I can't. But you could."

"What could I do?"

"Sing a little song to her."

"She wouldn't hear me."

"I will take you in, and then she will hear you."

"But that would be rude, wouldn't it? You can go where you please, of course, but I should have no business in her room."

"You may trust me, Diamond. I shall take as good care of the lady as of you. The window is open. Come."

By a shaded lamp, a lady was seated in a white wrapper, trying to read, but moaning every minute. North Wind floated behind her chair, set Diamond down, and told him to sing something. He was a little frightened, but he thought a while, and then sang:

The sun is gone down,

And the moon's in the sky;

But the sun will come up,

And the moon be laid by.

The flower is asleep

But it is not dead;

When the morning shines,

It will lift its head.

When winter comes,

It will die — no, no;

It will only hide

From the frost and the snow.

Sure is the summer,

Sure is the sun;

The night and the winter

Are shadows that run.

The lady never lifted her eyes from her book, or her head from her hand.

As soon as Diamond had finished, North Wind lifted him and carried him away.

"Didn't the lady hear me?" asked Diamond when they were once more floating down the river.

"Oh, yes, she heard you," answered North Wind.

"Was she frightened then?"

"Oh, no."

"Why didn't she look to see who it was?"

"She didn't know you were there."

"How could she hear me then?"

"She didn't hear you with her ears."

"What did she hear me with?"

"With her heart."

"Where did she think the words came from?"

"She thought they came out of the book she was reading. She will search all through it to-morrow to find them, and won't be able to understand it at all."

"Oh, what fun!" said Diamond. "What will she do?"

"I can tell you what she won't do: she'll never forget the meaning of them; and she'll never be able to remember the words of them."

"If she sees them in Mr. Raymond's book, it will puzzle her, won't it?"

"Yes, that it will. She will never be able to understand it."

"Until she gets to the back of the north wind," suggested Diamond.

"Until she gets to the back of the north wind," assented the lady.

"Oh!" cried Diamond, "I know now where we are. Oh! do let me go into the old garden, and into mother's room, and Diamond's stall. I wonder if the hole is at the back of my bed still. I should like to stay there all the rest of the night. It won't take you long to get home from here, will it, North Wind?"

"No," she answered; "you shall stay as long as you like."

"Oh, how jolly," cried Diamond, as North Wind sailed over the house with him, and set him down on the lawn at the back.

Diamond ran about the lawn for a little while in the moonlight. He found part of it cut up into flower-beds, and the little summer-house with the colored glass and the great elm-tree gone. He did not like this, and ran into the stable. There were no horses there at all. He ran upstairs. The rooms were empty. The only thing left that he cared about was the hole in the wall where his little bed had stood; and that was not enough to make him wish to stop. He ran down the stair again, and out upon the lawn. There he threw himself down and began to cry. It was all so dreary and lost!

"I thought I liked the place so much," said Diamond to himself, "but I find I don't care about it. I suppose it's only the people in it that make you like a place, and when they're gone, it's dead, and you don't care a bit about it. North Wind told me I might stop as long as I liked, and I've stopped longer already. North Wind!" he cried aloud, turning his face towards the sky.

The moon was under a cloud, and all was looking dull and dismal. A star shot from the sky, and fell in the grass beside him. The moment it lighted, there stood North Wind.

"Oh!" cried Diamond, joyfully, "were you the shooting star?"

"Yes, my child."

"Did you hear me call you then?"

"Yes."

"So high up as that?"

"Yes; I heard you quite well."

"Do take me home."

"Have you had enough of your old home already?"

"Yes, more than enough. It isn't a home at all now."

"I thought that would be it," said North Wind. "Everything, dreaming and all, has got a soul in it, or else it's worth nothing, and we don't care a bit about it. Some of our thoughts are worth nothing, because they've got no soul in them. The brain puts them into the mind, not the mind into the brain."

"But how can you know about that, North Wind? You haven't got a body."

"If I hadn't you wouldn't know anything about me. No creature can know another without the help of a body. But I don't care to talk about that. It is time for you to go home."

So saying, North Wind lifted Diamond and bore him away.

38. AT THE BACK OF THE NORTH WIND

I did not see Diamond for a week or so after this, and then he told me what I have now told you. I should have been astonished at his being able even to report such conversations as he said he had had with North Wind, had I not known already that some children are profound in metaphysics. But a fear crosses me, lest, by telling so much about my friend, I should lead people to mistake him for one of those consequential, priggish little monsters, who are always trying to say clever things, and looking to see whether people appreciate them. When a child like that dies, instead of having a silly book written about him, he should be stuffed like one of those awful big-headed fishes you see in museums. But Diamond never troubled his head about what people thought of him. He never set up for knowing better than others. The wisest things he said came out when he wanted one to help him with some difficulty he was in. He was not even offended with Nanny and Jim for calling him a silly. He supposed there was something in it, though he could not quite understand what. I suspect however that the other name they gave him, God's Baby, had some share in reconciling him to it.

Happily for me, I was as much interested in metaphysics as Diamond himself, and therefore, while he recounted his conversations with North Wind, I did not find myself at all in a strange sea, although certainly I could not always feel the bottom, being indeed convinced that the bottom was miles away.

"Could it be all dreaming, do you think, sir?" he asked anxiously.

"I daren't say, Diamond," I answered. "But at least there is one thing you may be sure of, that there is a still better love than that of the wonderful being you call North Wind. Even if she be a dream, the dream of such a beautiful creature could not come to you by chance."

"Yes, I know," returned Diamond; "I know."

Then he was silent, but, I confess, appeared more thoughtful than satisfied.

The next time I saw him, he looked paler than usual.

"Have you seen your friend again?" I asked him.

"Yes," he answered, solemnly.

"Did she take you out with her?"

"No. She did not speak to me. I woke all at once, as I generally do when I am going to see her, and there she was against the door into the big room, sitting just as I saw her sit on her own doorstep, as white as snow, and her eyes as blue as the heart of an iceberg. She looked at me, but never moved or spoke."

"Weren't you afraid?" I asked.

"No. Why should I have been?" he answered. "I only felt a little cold."

"Did she stay long?"

"I don't know. I fell asleep again. I think I have been rather cold ever since though," he added with a smile.

I did not quite like this, but I said nothing.

Four days after, I called again at the Mound. The maid who opened the door looked grave, but I suspected nothing. When I reached the drawing-room, I saw Mrs. Raymond had been crying.

"Haven't you heard?" she said, seeing my questioning looks.

"I've heard nothing," I answered.

"This morning we found our dear little Diamond lying on the floor of the big attic-room, just outside his own door — fast asleep, as we thought. But when we took him up, we did not think he was asleep. We saw that —"

Here the kind-hearted lady broke out crying afresh.

"May I go and see him?" I asked.

"Yes," she sobbed. "You know your way to the top of the tower."

I walked up the winding stair, and entered his room. A lovely figure, as white and almost as clear as alabaster, was lying on the bed. I saw at once how it was. They thought he was dead. I knew that he had gone to the back of the north wind.

Book Seven

The Golden Key

ഇ൫ഭ

There was a boy who used to sit in the twilight and listen to his great-aunt's stories.

She told him that if he could reach the place where the end of the rainbow stands he would find there a golden key.

"And what is the key for?" the boy would ask. "What is it the key of? What will it open?"

"That nobody knows," his aunt would reply. "He has to find that out."

"I suppose, being gold," the boy once said, thoughtfully, "that I could get a good deal of money for it if I sold it."

"Better never find it than sell it," returned his aunt. And then the boy went to bed and dreamed about the golden key.

Now, all that his great-aunt told the boy about the golden key would have been nonsense, had it not been that their little house stood on the borders of Fairyland. For it is perfectly well known that out of Fairyland nobody ever can find where the rainbow stands. The creature takes such good care of its golden key, always flitting from place to place, lest anyone should find it! But in Fairyland it is quite different. Things that look real in this country look very thin indeed in Fairyland, while some of the things that here cannot stand still for a moment, will not move there. So it was not in the least absurd of the old lady to tell her nephew such things about the golden key.

"Did you ever know anybody find it?" he asked one evening.

"Yes. Your father, I believe, found it."

"And what did he do with it, can you tell me?"

"He never told me."

"What was it like?"

"He never showed it to me."

"How does a new key come there always?"

"I don't know. There it is."

"Perhaps it is the rainbow's egg."

"Perhaps it is. You will be a happy boy if you find the nest."

"Perhaps it comes tumbling down the rainbow from the sky."

"Perhaps it does."

One evening, in summer, he went into his own room, and stood at the lattice-window, and gazed into the forest which fringed the outskirts of Fairyland. It came close up to his great-aunt's garden, and, indeed, sent some straggling trees into it. The forest lay to the east, and the sun, which was setting behind the cottage, looked straight into the dark wood with his level red eye. The trees were all old, and had few branches below, so that the sun could see a great way into the forest; and the boy, being keen-sighted, could see almost as far as the sun. The trunks stood like rows of red columns in the shine of the red sun, and he could see down aisle after aisle in the vanishing distance. And as he gazed into the forest he began to feel as if the trees were all waiting for him, and had something they could not go on with till he came to them. But he was hungry, and wanted his supper. So he lingered.

Suddenly, far among the trees, as far as the sun could shine, he saw a glorious thing. It was the end of a rainbow, large and brilliant. He could count all the seven colors, and could see shade after shade beyond the violet; while before the red stood a color more gorgeous and mysterious still. It was a color he had never seen before. Only the spring of the rainbow-arch was visible. He could see nothing of it above the trees.

"The golden key!" he said to himself, and darted out of the house, and into the wood.

He had not gone far before the sun set. But the rainbow only glowed the brighter: for the rainbow of Fairyland is not dependent upon the sun as ours is. The trees welcomed him. The bushes made way for him. The rainbow grew larger and brighter; and at length he found himself within two trees of it.

It was a grand sight, burning away there in silence, with its gorgeous, its lovely, its delicate colors, each distinct, all combining. He could now see a great deal more of it. It rose high into the blue heavens, but bent so little that he could not tell how high the crown of the arch must reach. It was still only a small portion of a huge bow.

He stood gazing at it till he forgot himself with delight — even forgot the key which he had come to seek. And as he stood it grew more wonderful still. For in each of the colors, which was as large as the column of a church, he could faintly see beautiful forms slowly ascending as if by the steps of a winding stair. The forms appeared irregularly—now one, now many, now several, now none — men and women and children — all different, all beautiful.

He drew nearer to the rainbow. It vanished. He started back a step in dismay. It was there again, as beautiful as ever. So he contented himself with standing as near it as he might, and watching the forms that ascended the glorious colors towards the unknown height of the arch, which did not end abruptly, but faded away in the blue air, so gradually that he could not say where it ceased.

When the thought of the golden key returned, the boy very wisely proceeded to mark out in his mind the space covered by the foundation of the rainbow, in order that he might know where to search, should the rainbow disappear. It was based chiefly upon a bed of moss.

Meantime it had grown quite dark in the wood. The rainbow alone was visible by its own light. But the moment the moon rose the rainbow vanished. Nor could any change of place restore the vision to the boy's eyes. So he threw himself down upon the mossy bed, to wait till the sunlight would give him a chance of finding the key. There he fell fast asleep.

When he woke in the morning the sun was looking straight into his eyes. He turned away from it, and the same moment saw a brilliant little thing lying on the moss within a foot of his face. It was the golden key. The pipe of it was of plain gold, as bright as gold could be. The handle was curiously wrought and set with sapphires. In a terror of delight he put out his hand and took it, and had it.

He lay for a while, turning it over and over, and feeding his eyes upon its beauty. Then he jumped to his feet, remembering that the pretty thing was of no use to him yet. Where was the lock to which the key belonged? It must be somewhere, for how could anybody be so silly as make a key for which there was no lock? Where should he go to look for it? He gazed about him, up into the air, down to the earth, but saw no keyhole in the clouds, in the grass, or in the trees.

Just as he began to grow disconsolate, however, he saw something glimmering in the wood. It was a mere glimmer that he saw, but he took it for a glimmer of rainbow, and went towards it.— And now I will go back to the borders of the forest.

Not far from the house where the boy had lived there was another house, the owner of which was a merchant, who was much away from home. He had lost his wife some years before, and had only one child, a little girl, whom he left to the charge of two servants, who were very idle and careless. So she was neglected and left untidy, and was sometimes ill-used besides.

Now, it is well known that the little creatures commonly called fairies, though there are many different kinds of fairies in Fairyland, have an exceeding dislike to untidiness. Indeed, they are quite spiteful to slovenly people. Being used to all the lovely ways of the trees and flowers, and to the neatness of the birds and all woodland creatures, it makes them feel miserable, even in their deep woods and on their grassy carpets, to think that within the same moonlight lies a dirty, uncomfortable, slovenly house. And this makes them angry with the people that live in it, and they would gladly drive them out of the world if they could. They want the whole earth nice and clean. So they pinch the maids black and blue, and play them all manner of uncomfortable tricks.

But this house was quite a shame, and the fairies in the forest could not endure it. They tried everything on the maids without effect, and at last resolved upon making a clean riddance, beginning with the child. They ought to have known that it was not her fault, but they have little principle and much mischief in them, and they thought that if they got rid of her the maids would be sure to be turned away.

So one evening, the poor little girl having been put to bed early, before the sun was down, the servants went off to the village, locking the door behind them. The child did not know she was alone, and lay contentedly looking out of her window towards the forest, of which, however, she could not see much, because of the ivy and other creeping plants which had straggled across her window. All at once she saw an ape making faces at her out of the mirror, and the heads carved upon a great old wardrobe grinning fearfully. Then two old spider-legged chairs came forward into the middle of the room, and began to dance a queer, old-fashioned dance. This set her laughing, and she forgot the ape and the grinning heads. So the fairies saw they had made a mistake, and sent the chairs back to their places. But they knew that she had been reading the story of Silverhair all day. So the next moment she heard the voices of the three bears upon the stair, big voice, middle voice, and little voice, and she heard their soft, heavy tread, as if they had had stockings over their boots, coming nearer and nearer to the door of her room, till she could bear it no longer. She did just as Silverhair did, and as the fairies wanted her to do: she darted to the window, pulled it open, got upon the ivy, and so scrambled to the ground. She then fled to the forest as fast as she could run.

Now, although she did not know it, this was the very best way she could have gone; for nothing is ever so mischievous in its own place as it is out of it; and, besides, these mischievous creatures were only the children of Fairyland, as it were, and there are many other beings there as well; and if a wanderer gets in among them, the good ones will always help him more than the evil ones will be able to hurt him.

The sun was now set, and the darkness coming on, but the child thought of no danger but the bears behind her. If she had looked round, however, she would have seen that she was followed by a very different creature from a bear. It was a curious creature, made like a fish, but covered, instead of scales, with feathers of all colors, sparkling like those of a humming-bird. It had fins, not wings, and swam through the air as a fish does through the water. Its head was like the head of a small owl.

After running a long way, and as the last of the light was disappearing, she passed under a tree with drooping branches. It dropped its branches to the ground all about her, and caught her as in a trap. She struggled to get out, but the branches pressed her closer and closer to the trunk. She was in great terror and distress, when the air-fish, swimming into the thicket of branches, began tearing them with its beak. They loosened their hold at once, and the creature went on attacking them, till at length they let the child go. Then the air-fish came from behind her, and swam on in front, glittering and sparkling all lovely colors; and she followed.

It led her gently along till all at once it swam in at a cottage-door. The child followed still. There was a bright fire in the middle of the floor, upon which stood a pot without a lid, full of water that boiled and bubbled furiously. The air-fish swam straight to the pot and into the boiling water, where it lay quiet. A beautiful woman rose from the opposite side of the fire and came to meet the girl. She took her up in her arms, and said, —

"Ah, you are come at last! I have been looking for you a long time."

She sat down with her on her lap, and there the girl sat staring at her. She had never seen anything so beautiful. She was tall and strong, with white arms and neck, and a delicate flush on her face. The child could not tell what was the color of her hair, but could not help thinking it had a tinge of dark green. She had not one ornament upon her, but she looked as if she had just put off quantities of diamonds and emeralds. Yet here she was in the simplest, poorest little cottage, where she was evidently at home. She was dressed in shining green.

The girl looked at the lady, and the lady looked at the girl.

"What is your name?" asked the lady.

"The servants always call me Tangle."

"Ah, that was because your hair was so untidy. But that was their fault, the naughty women! Still it is a pretty name, and I will call you Tangle too. You must not mind my asking you questions, for you may ask me the same questions, every one of them, and any others that you like. How old are you?"

"Ten," answered Tangle.

"You don't look like it," said the lady.

"How old are you, please?" returned Tangle.

"Thousands of years old," answered the lady.

"You don't look like it," said Tangle.

"Don't I? I think I do. Don't you see how beautiful I am?"

And her great blue eyes looked down on the little Tangle, as if all the stars in the sky were melted in them to make their brightness.

"Ah! but," said Tangle, "when people live long they grow old. At least I always thought so."

"I have no time to grow old," said the lady. "I am too busy for that. It is very idle to grow old.— But I cannot have my little girl so untidy. Do you know I can't find a clean spot on your face to kiss?"

"Perhaps," suggested Tangle, feeling ashamed, but not too much so to say a word for herself — "perhaps that is because the tree made me cry so."

"My poor darling!" said the lady, looking now as if the moon were melted in her eyes, and kissing her little face, dirty as it was, "the naughty tree must suffer for making a girl cry."

"And what is your name, please?" asked Tangle.

"Grandmother," answered the lady.

"Is it really?"

"Yes, indeed. I never tell stories, even in fun."

"How good of you!"

"I couldn't if I tried. It would come true if I said it, and then I should be punished enough." And she smiled like the sun through a summer-shower.

"But now," she went on, "I must get you washed and dressed, and then we shall have some supper."

"Oh! I had supper long ago," said Tangle.

"Yes, indeed you had," answered the lady — "three years ago. You don't know that it is three years since you ran away from the bears. You are thirteen and more now."

Tangle could only stare. She felt quite sure it was true.

"You will not be afraid of anything I do with you — will you?" said the lady.

"I will try very hard not to be; but I can't be certain, you know," replied Tangle.

"I like your saying so, and I shall be quite satisfied," answered the lady.

She took off the girl's night-gown, rose with her in her arms, and going to the wall of the cottage, opened a door. Then Tangle saw a deep tank, the sides of which were filled with green plants, which had flowers of all colors. There was a roof over it like the roof of the cottage. It was filled with beautiful clear water, in which swam a multitude of such fishes as the one that had led her to the cottage. It was the light their colors gave that showed the place in which they were.

The lady spoke some words Tangle could not understand, and threw her into the tank.

The fishes came crowding about her. Two or three of them got under her head and kept it up. The rest of them rubbed themselves all over her, and with their wet feathers washed her quite clean. Then the lady, who had been looking on all the time, spoke again; whereupon some thirty or forty of the fishes rose out of the water underneath Tangle, and so bore her up to the arms the lady held out to take her. She carried her back to the fire, and, having dried her well, opened a chest, and taking out the finest linen garments, smelling of grass and lavender, put them upon her, and over all a green dress, just like her own, shining like hers, and soft like hers, and going into just such lovely folds from the waist, where it was tied with a brown cord, to her bare feet.

"Won't you give me a pair of shoes too, Grandmother?" said Tangle.

"No, my dear; no shoes. Look here. I wear no shoes."

So saying she lifted her dress a little, and there were the loveliest white feet, but no shoes. Then Tangle was content to go without shoes too. And the lady sat down with her again, and combed her hair, and brushed it, and then left it to dry while she got the supper.

First she got bread out of one hole in the wall; then milk out of another; then several kinds of fruit out of a third; and then she went to the pot on the fire, and took out the fish, now nicely cooked, and, as soon as she had pulled off its feathered skin, ready to be eaten.

"But," exclaimed Tangle. And she stared at the fish, and could say no more.

"I know what you mean," returned the lady. "You do not like to eat the messenger that brought you home. But it is the kindest return you can make. The creature was afraid to go until it saw me put the pot on, and heard me promise it should be boiled the moment it returned with you. Then it darted out of the door at once. You saw it go into the pot of itself the moment it entered, did you not?"

"I did," answered Tangle, "and I thought it very strange; but then I saw you, and forgot all about the fish."

"In Fairyland," resumed the lady, as they sat down to the table, "the ambition of the animals is to be eaten by the people; for that is their highest end in that condition. But they are not therefore destroyed. Out of that pot comes something more than the dead fish, you will see."

Tangle now remarked that the lid was on the pot. But the lady took no further notice of it till they had eaten the fish, which Tangle found nicer than any fish she had ever tasted before. It was as white as snow, and as delicate as cream. And the moment she had swallowed a mouthful of it, a change she could not describe began to take place in her. She heard a murmuring all about her, which became more and more articulate, and at length, as she went on eating, grew intelligible. By the time she had finished her share, the sounds of all the animals in the forest came crowding through the door to her ears; for the door still stood wide open, though it was pitch dark outside; and they were no longer sounds only; they were speech, and speech that she could understand. She could tell what the insects in the cottage were saying to each other too. She had even a suspicion that the trees and flowers all about the cottage were holding midnight communications with each other; but what they said she could not hear.

As soon as the fish was eaten, the lady went to the fire and took the lid off the pot. A lovely little creature in human shape, with large white wings, rose out of it, and flew round and round the roof of the cottage; then dropped, fluttering, and nestled in the lap of the lady. She spoke to it some strange words, carried it to the door, and threw it out into the darkness. Tangle heard the flapping of its wings die away in the distance.

"Now have we done the fish any harm?" she said, returning.

"No," answered Tangle, "I do not think we have. I should not mind eating one every day."

"They must wait their time, like you and me too, my little Tangle."

And she smiled a smile which the sadness in it made more lovely.

"But," she continued, "I think we may have one for supper to-morrow."

So saying she went to the door of the tank, and spoke; and now Tangle understood her perfectly.

"I want one of you," she said, — "the wisest."

Thereupon the fishes got together in the middle of the tank, with their heads forming a circle above the water, and their tails a larger circle beneath it. They were holding a council, in which their relative wisdom should be determined. At length one of them flew up into the lady's hand, looking lively and ready.

"You know where the rainbow stands?" she asked.

"Yes, Mother, quite well," answered the fish.

"Bring home a young man you will find there, who does not know where to go."

The fish was out of the door in a moment. Then the lady told Tangle it was time to go to bed; and, opening another door in the side of the cottage, showed her a little arbor, cool and green, with a bed of purple heath growing in it, upon which she threw a large wrapper made of the feathered skins of the wise fishes, shining gorgeous in the firelight.

Tangle was soon lost in the strangest, loveliest dreams. And the beautiful lady was in every one of her dreams.

In the morning she woke to the rustling of leaves over her head, and the sound of running water. But, to her surprise, she could find no door — nothing but the moss-grown wall of the cottage. So she crept through an opening in the arbor, and stood in the forest. Then she bathed in a stream that ran merrily through the trees, and felt happier; for having once been in her grandmother's pond, she must be clean and tidy ever after; and, having put on her green dress, felt like a lady.

She spent that day in the wood, listening to the birds and beasts and creeping things. She understood all that they said, though she could not repeat a word of it; and every kind had a different language, while there was a common though more limited understanding between all the inhabitants of the forest. She saw nothing of the beautiful lady, but she felt that she was near her all the time; and she took care not to go out of sight of the cottage. It was round, like a snow-hut or a wigwam; and she could see neither door nor window in it. The fact was, it had no windows; and though it was full of doors, they all opened from the inside, and could not even be seen from the outside.

She was standing at the foot of a tree in the twilight, listening to a quarrel between a mole and a squirrel, in which the mole told the squirrel that the tail was the best of him, and the squirrel called the mole Spade-fists, when, the darkness having deepened around her, she became aware of something shining in her face, and looking round, saw that the door of the cottage was open, and the red light of the fire flowing from it like a river through the darkness. She left Mole and Squirrel to settle matters as they might, and darted off to the cottage. Entering, she found the pot boiling on the fire, and the grand, lovely lady sitting on the other side of it.

"I've been watching you all day," said the lady. "You shall have something to eat by and by, but we must wait till our supper comes home."

She took Tangle on her knee, and began to sing to her—such songs as made her wish she could listen to them for ever. But at length in rushed the shining fish, and snuggled down in the pot. It was followed by a youth who had outgrown his worn garments. His face was ruddy with health, and in his hand he carried a little jewel, which sparkled in the firelight.

The first words the lady said were, —

"What is that in your hand, Mossy?"

Now Mossy was the name his companions had given him, because he had a favorite stone covered with moss, on which he used to sit whole days reading; and they said the moss had begun to grow upon him too.

Mossy held out his hand. The moment the lady saw that it was the golden key, she rose from her chair, kissed Mossy on the forehead, made him sit down on her seat, and stood before him like a servant. Mossy could not bear this, and rose at once. But the lady begged him, with tears in her beautiful eyes, to sit, and let her wait on him.

"But you are a great, splendid, beautiful lady," said Mossy.

"Yes, I am. But I work all day long — that is my pleasure; and you will have to leave me so soon!"

"How do you know that, if you please, madam?" asked Mossy.

"Because you have got the golden key."

"But I don't know what it is for. I can't find the key-hole. Will you tell me what to do?"

"You must look for the key-hole. That is your work. I cannot help you. I can only tell you that if you look for it you will find it."

"What kind of box will it open? What is there inside?"

"I do not know. I dream about it, but I know nothing."

"Must I go at once?"

"You may stop here to-night, and have some of my supper. But you must go in the morning. All I can do for you is to give you clothes. Here is a girl called Tangle, whom you must take with you."

"That will be nice," said Mossy.

"No, no!" said Tangle. "I don't want to leave you, please, Grandmother."

"You must go with him, Tangle. I am sorry to lose you, but it will be the best thing for you. Even the fishes, you see, have to go into the pot, and then out into the dark. If you fall in with the Old Man of the Sea, mind you ask him whether he has not got some more fishes ready for me. My tank is getting thin."

So saying, she took the fish from the pot, and put the lid on as before. They sat down and ate the fish, and then the winged creature rose from the pot, circled the roof, and settled on the lady's lap. She talked to it, carried it to the door, and threw it out into the dark. They heard the flap of its wings die away in the distance.

The lady then showed Mossy into just such another chamber as that of Tangle; and in the morning he found a suit of clothes laid beside him. He looked very handsome in them. But the wearer of Grandmother's clothes never thinks about how he or she looks, but thinks always how handsome other people are.

Tangle was very unwilling to go.

"Why should I leave you? I don't know the young man," she said to the lady.

"I am never allowed to keep my children long. You need not go with him except you please, but you must go some day; and I should like you to go with him, for he has the golden key. No girl need be afraid to go with a youth that has the golden key. You will take care of her, Mossy, will you not?"

"That I will," said Mossy.

And Tangle cast a glance at him, and thought she should like to go with him.

"And," said the lady, "if you should lose each other as you go through the – the — I never can remember the name of that country, — do not be afraid, but go on and on."

She kissed Tangle on the mouth and Mossy on the forehead, led them to the door, and waved her hand eastward. Mossy and Tangle took each other's hand and walked away into the depth of the forest. In his right hand Mossy held the golden key.

They wandered thus a long way, with endless amusement from the talk of the animals. They soon learned enough of their language to ask them necessary questions. The squirrels were always friendly, and gave them nuts out of their own hoards; but the bees were selfish and rude, justifying themselves on the ground that Tangle and Mossy were not subjects of their queen, and charity must begin at home, though indeed they had not one drone in their poorhouse at the time. Even the blinking moles would fetch them an earth-nut or a truffle now and then, talking as if their mouths, as well as their eyes and ears, were full of cotton wool, or their own velvety fur. By the time they got out of the forest they were very fond of each other, and Tangle was not in the least sorry that her grandmother had sent her away with Mossy.

At length the trees grew smaller, and stood farther apart, and the ground began to rise, and it got more and more steep, till the trees were all left behind, and the two were climbing a narrow path with rocks on each side. Suddenly they came upon a rude doorway, by which they entered a narrow gallery cut in the rock. It grew darker and darker, till it was pitch-dark, and they had to feel their way. At length the light began to return, and at last they came out upon a narrow path on the face of a lofty precipice. This path went winding down the rock to a wide plain, circular in shape, and surrounded on all sides by mountains. Those opposite to them were a great way off, and towered to an awful height, shooting up sharp, blue, ice-enameled pinnacles. An utter silence reigned where they stood. Not even the sound of water reached them.

Looking down, they could not tell whether the valley below was a grassy plain or a great still lake. They had never seen any space look like it. The way to it was difficult and dangerous, but down the narrow path they went, and reached the bottom in safety. They found it composed of smooth, light-colored sandstone, undulating in parts, but mostly level. It was no wonder to them now that they had not been able to tell what it was, for this surface was everywhere crowded with shadows. The mass was chiefly made up of the shadows of leaves innumerable, of all lovely and imaginative forms, waving to and fro, floating and quivering in the breath of a breeze whose motion was unfelt, whose sound was unheard. No forests clothed the mountain-sides, no trees were anywhere to be seen, and yet the shadows of the leaves, branches, and stems of all various trees covered the valley as far as their eyes could reach. They soon spied the shadows of flowers mingled with those of the leaves, and now and then the shadow of a bird with open beak, and throat distended with song. At times would appear the forms of strange, graceful creatures, running up and down the shadow-boles and along the branches, to disappear in the wind-tossed foliage. As they walked they waded knee-deep in the lovely lake. For the shadows were not merely lying on the surface of the ground, but heaped up above it like substantial forms of darkness, as if they had been cast upon a thousand different planes of the air. Tangle and Mossy often lifted their heads and gazed upwards to discry whence the shadows came; but they could see nothing more than a bright mist spread above them, higher than the tops of the mountains, which stood clear against it. No forests, no leaves, no birds were visible.

After a while, they reached more open spaces, where the shadows were thinner; and came even to portions over which shadows only flitted, leaving them clear for such as might follow. Now a wonderful form, half bird-like half human, would float across on outspread sailing pinions. Anon an exquisite shadow group of gambolling children would be followed by the loveliest female form, and that again by the grand stride of a Titanic shape, each disappearing in the surrounding press of shadowy foliage. Sometimes a profile of unspeakable beauty or grandeur would appear for a moment and vanish. Sometimes they seemed lovers that passed linked arm in arm, sometimes father and son, sometimes brothers in loving contest, sometimes sisters entwined in gracefullest community of complex form. Sometimes wild horses would tear across, free, or bestrode by noble shadows of ruling men. But some of the things which pleased them most they never knew how to describe.

About the middle of the plain they sat down to rest in the heart of a heap of shadows. After sitting for a while, each, looking up, saw the other in tears: they were each longing after the country whence the shadows fell.

"We must find the country from which the shadows come," said Mossy.

"We must, dear Mossy," responded Tangle. "What if your golden key should be the key to it?"

"Ah! that would be grand," returned Mossy. — "But we must rest here for a little, and then we shall be able to cross the plain before night."

So he lay down on the ground, and about him on every side, and over his head, was the constant play of the wonderful shadows. He could look through them, and see the one behind the other, till they mixed in a mass of darkness. Tangle, too, lay admiring, and wondering, and longing after the country whence the shadows came. When they were rested they rose and pursued their journey.

How long they were in crossing this plain I cannot tell; but before night Mossy's hair was streaked with gray, and Tangle had got wrinkles on her forehead.

As evening grew on, the shadows fell deeper and rose higher. At length they reached a place where they rose above their heads, and made all dark around them. Then they took hold of each other's hand, and walked on in silence and in some dismay. They felt the gathering darkness, and something strangely solemn besides, and the beauty of the shadows ceased to delight them. All at once Tangle found that she had not a hold of Mossy's hand, though when she lost it she could not tell.

"Mossy, Mossy!" she cried aloud in terror.

But no Mossy replied.

A moment after, the shadows sank to her feet, and down under her feet, and the mountains rose before her. She turned towards the gloomy region she had left, and called once more upon Mossy. There the gloom lay tossing and heaving, a dark, stormy, foamless sea of shadows, but no Mossy rose out of it, or came climbing up the hill on which she stood. She threw herself down and wept in despair.

Suddenly she remembered that the beautiful lady had told them, if they lost each other in a country of which she could not remember the name, they were not to be afraid, but to go straight on.

"And besides," she said to herself, "Mossy has the golden key, and so no harm will come to him, I do believe."

She rose from the ground, and went on.

Before long she arrived at a precipice, in the face of which a stair was cut. When she had ascended half-way, the stair ceased, and the path led straight into the mountain. She was afraid to enter, and turning again towards the stair, grew giddy at sight of the depth beneath her, and was forced to throw herself down in the mouth of the cave.

When she opened her eyes, she saw a beautiful little figure with wings standing beside her, waiting.

"I know you," said Tangle. "You are my fish."

"Yes. But I am a fish no longer. I am an aeranth now."

"What is that?" asked Tangle.

"What you see I am," answered the shape. "And I am come to lead you through the mountain."

"Oh! thank you, dear fish — aeranth, I mean," returned Tangle, rising.

Thereupon the aeranth took to his wings, and flew on through the long, narrow passage, reminding Tangle very much of the way he had swum on before her when he was a fish. And the moment his white wings moved, they began to throw off a continuous shower of sparks of all colors, which lighted up the passage before them.—All at once he vanished, and Tangle heard a low, sweet sound, quite different from the rush and crackle of his wings. Before her was an open arch, and through it came light, mixed with the sound of sea-waves.

She hurried out, and fell, tired and happy, upon the yellow sand of the shore. There she lay, half asleep with weariness and rest, listening to the low plash and retreat of the tiny waves, which seemed ever enticing the land to leave off being land, and become sea. And as she lay, her eyes were fixed upon the foot of a great rainbow standing far away against the sky on the other side of the sea. At length she fell fast asleep.

When she awoke, she saw an old man with long white hair down to his shoulders, leaning upon a stick covered with green buds, and so bending over her.

"What do you want here, beautiful woman?" he said.

"Am I beautiful? I am so glad!" said Tangle, rising. "My grandmother is beautiful."

"Yes. But what do you want?" he repeated, kindly.

"I think I want you. Are not you the Old Man of the Sea?"

"I am."

"Then Grandmother says, have you any more fishes ready for her?"

"We will go and see, my dear," answered the old man, speaking yet more kindly than before. "And I can do something for you, can I not?"

"Yes — show me the way up to the country from which the shadows fall," said Tangle.

For there she hoped to find Mossy again.

"Ah! indeed, that would be worth doing," said the old man. "But I cannot, for I do not know the way myself. But I will send you to the Old Man of the Earth. Perhaps he can tell you. He is much older than I am."

Leaning on his staff, he conducted her along the shore to a steep rock, that looked like a petrified ship turned upside down. The door of it was the rudder of a great vessel, ages ago at the bottom of the sea. Immediately within the door was a stair in the rock, down which the old man went, and Tangle followed. At the bottom the old man had his house, and there he lived.

As soon as she entered it, Tangle heard a strange noise, unlike anything she had ever heard before. She soon found that it was the fishes talking. She tried to understand what they said; but their speech was so old-fashioned, and rude, and undefined, that she could not make much of it.

"I will go and see about those fishes for my daughter," said the Old Man of the Sea.

And moving a slide in the wall of his house, he first looked out, and then tapped upon a thick piece of crystal that filled the round opening. Tangle came up behind him, and peeping through the window into the heart of the great deep green ocean, saw the most curious creatures, some very ugly, all very odd, and with especially queer mouths, swimming about everywhere, above and below, but all coming towards the window in answer to the tap of the Old Man of the Sea. Only a few could get their mouths against the glass; but those who were floating miles away yet turned their heads towards it. The old man looked through the whole flock carefully for some minutes, and then turning to Tangle, said, —

"I am sorry I have not got one ready yet. I want more time than she does. But I will send some as soon as I can."

He then shut the slide.

Presently a great noise arose in the sea. The old man opened the slide again, and tapped on the glass, whereupon the fishes were all as still as sleep.

"They were only talking about you," he said. "And they do speak such nonsense!—To-morrow," he continued, "I must show you the way to the Old Man of the Earth. He lives a long way from here."

"Do let me go at once," said Tangle.

"No. That is not possible. You must come this way first."

He led her to a hole in the wall, which she had not observed before. It was covered with the green leaves and white blossoms of a creeping plant.

"Only white-blossoming plants can grow under the sea," said the old man. "In there you will find a bath, in which you must lie till I call you."

Tangle went in, and found a smaller room or cave, in the further corner of which was a great basin hollowed out of a rock, and half-full of the clearest sea-water. Little streams were constantly running into it from cracks in the wall of the cavern. It was polished quite smooth inside, and had a carpet of yellow sand in the bottom of it. Large green leaves and white flowers of various plants crowded up and over it, draping and covering it almost entirely.

No sooner was she undressed and lying in the bath, than she began to feel as if the water were sinking into her, and she were receiving all the good of sleep without undergoing its forgetfulness. She felt the good coming all the time. And she grew happier and more hopeful than she had been since she lost Mossy. But she could not help thinking how very sad it was for a poor old man to live there all alone, and have to take care of a whole seaful of stupid and riotous fishes.

After about an hour, as she thought, she heard his voice calling her, and rose out of the bath. All the fatigue and aching of her long journey had vanished. She was as whole, and strong, and well as if she had slept for seven days.

Returning to the opening that led into the other part of the house, she started back with amazement, for through it she saw the form of a grand man, with a majestic and beautiful face, waiting for her.

"Come," he said; "I see you are ready."

She entered with reverence.

"Where is the Old Man of the Sea?" she asked, humbly.

"There is no one here but me," he answered, smiling. "Some people call me the Old Man of the Sea. Others have another name for me, and are terribly frightened when they meet me taking a walk by the shore. Therefore I avoid being seen by them, for they are so afraid, that they never see what I really am. You see me now. — But I must show you the way to the Old Man of the Earth."

He led her into the cave where the bath was, and there she saw, in the opposite corner, a second opening in the rock.

"Go down that stair, and it will bring you to him," said the Old Man of the Sea.

With humble thanks Tangle took her leave. She went down the winding stair, till she began to fear there was no end to it. Still down and down it went, rough and broken, with springs of water bursting out of the rocks and running down the steps beside her. It was quite dark about her, and yet she could see. For after being in that bath, people's eyes always give out a light they can see by. There were no creeping things in the way. All was safe and pleasant though so dark and damp and deep.

At last there was not one step more, and she found herself in a glimmering cave. On a stone in the middle of it sat a figure with its back towards her — the figure of an old man bent double with age. From behind she could see his white beard spread out on the rocky floor in front of him. He did not move as she entered, so she passed round that she might stand before him and speak to him.

The moment she looked in his face, she saw that he was a youth of marvelous beauty. He sat entranced with the delight of what he beheld in a mirror of something like silver, which lay on the floor at his feet, and which from behind she had taken for his white beard. He sat on, heedless of her presence, pale with the joy of his vision. She stood and watched him. At length, all trembling, she spoke. But her voice made no sound. Yet the youth lifted up his head. He showed no surprise, however, at seeing her — only smiled a welcome.

"Are you the Old Man of the Earth?" Tangle had said.

And the youth answered, and Tangle heard him, though not with her ears: —

"I am. What can I do for you?"

"Tell me the way to the country whence the shadows fall."

"Ah! that I do not know. I only dream about it myself. I see its shadows sometimes in my mirror: the way to it I do not know. But I think the Old Man of the Fire must know. He is much older than I am. He is the oldest man of all."

"Where does he live?"

"I will show you the way to his place. I never saw him myself."

So saying, the young man rose, and then stood for a while gazing at Tangle.

"I wish I could see that country too," he said. "But I must mind my work."

He led her to the side of the cave, and told her to lay her ear against the wall.

"What do you hear?" he asked.

"I hear," answered Tangle, "the sound of a great water running inside the rock."

"That river runs down to the dwelling of the oldest man of all — the Old Man of the Fire. I wish I could go to see him. But I must mind my work. That river is the only way to him."

Then the Old Man of the Earth stooped over the floor of the cave, raised a huge stone from it, and left it leaning. It disclosed a great hole that went plumb-down.

"That is the way," he said.

"But there are no stairs."

"You must throw yourself in. There is no other way."

She turned and looked him full in the face — stood so for a whole minute, as she thought: it was a whole year — then threw herself headlong into the hole.

When she came to herself, she found herself gliding down fast and deep. Her head was under water, but that did not signify, for, when she thought about it, she could not remember that she had breathed once since her bath in the cave of the Old Man of the Sea. When she lifted up her head a sudden and fierce heat struck her, and she sank it again instantly, and went sweeping on.

Gradually the stream grew shallower. At length she could hardly keep her head under. Then the water could carry her no farther. She rose from the channel, and went step for step down the burning descent. The water ceased altogether. The heat was terrible. She felt scorched to the bone, but it did not touch her strength. It grew hotter and hotter. She said, "I can bear it no longer." Yet she went on.

At the long last, the stair ended at a rude archway in an all but glowing rock. Through this archway Tangle fell exhausted into a cool mossy cave. The floor and walls were covered with moss—green, soft, and damp. A little stream spouted from a rent in the rock and fell into a basin of moss. She plunged her face into it and drank. Then she lifted her head and looked around. Then she rose and looked again. She saw no one in the cave. But the moment she stood upright she had a marvelous sense that she was in the secret of the earth and all its ways. Everything she had seen, or learned from books; all that her grandmother had said or sung to her; all the talk of the beasts, birds, and fishes; all that had happened to her on her journey with Mossy, and since then in the heart of the earth with the Old man and the Older man — all was plain: she understood it all, and saw that everything meant the same thing, though she could not have put it into words again.

The next moment she descried, in a corner of the cave, a little naked child sitting on the moss. He was playing with balls of various colors and sizes, which he disposed in strange figures upon the floor beside him. And now Tangle felt that there was something in her knowledge which was not in her understanding. For she knew there must be an infinite meaning in the change and sequence and individual forms of the figures into which the child arranged the balls, as well as in the varied harmonies of their colors, but what it all meant she could not tell. He went on busily, tirelessly, playing his solitary game, without looking up, or seeming to know that there was a stranger in his deep-withdrawn cell. Diligently as a lace-maker shifts her bobbins, he shifted and arranged his balls. Flashes of meaning would now pass from them to Tangle, and now again all would be not merely obscure, but utterly dark. She stood looking for a long time, for there was fascination in the sight; and the longer she looked the more an indescribable vague intelligence went on rousing itself in her mind. For seven years she had stood there watching the naked child with his colored balls, and it seemed to her like seven hours, when all at once the shape the balls took, she knew not why, ⸻ninded her of the Valley of Shadows, and she spoke: —

)ld Man of the Fire?" she said.

)e indebted to Novalis for these geometrical figures.

answered the child, rising and leaving his balls on the moss. "What can I do for

There was such an awfulness of absolute repose on the face of the child that Tangle stood dumb before him. He had no smile, but the love in his large gray eyes was deep as the centre. And with the repose there lay on his face a shimmer as of moonlight, which seemed as if any moment it might break into such a ravishing smile as would cause the beholder to weep himself to death. But the smile never came, and the moonlight lay there unbroken. For the heart of the child was too deep for any smile to reach from it to his face.

"Are you the oldest man of all?" Tangle at length, although filled with awe, ventured to ask.

"Yes, I am. I am very, very old. I am able to help you, I know. I can help everybody." And the child drew near and looked up in her face so that she burst into tears.

"Can you tell me the way to the country the shadows fall from?" she sobbed.

"Yes. I know the way quite well. I go there myself sometimes. But you could not go my way; you are not old enough. I will show you how you can go."

"Do not send me out into the great heat again," prayed Tangle.

"I will not," answered the child.

And he reached up, and put his little cool hand on her heart.

"Now," he said, "you can go. The fire will not burn you. Come."

He led her from the cave, and following him through another archway, she found herself in a vast desert of sand and rock. The sky of it was of rock, lowering over them like solid thunderclouds; and the whole place was so hot that she saw, in bright rivulets, the yellow gold and white silver and red copper trickling molten from the rocks. But the heat never came near her.

When they had gone some distance, the child turned up a great stone, and took something like an egg from under it. He next drew a long curved line in the sand with his finger, and laid the egg in it. He then spoke something Tangle could not understand. The egg broke, a small snake came out, and, lying in the line in the sand, grew and grew till he filled it. The moment he was thus full-grown, he began to glide away, undulating like a sea-wave.

"Follow that serpent," said the child. "He will lead you the right way."

Tangle followed the serpent. But she could not go far without looking back at the marvelous child. He stood alone in the midst of the glowing desert, beside a fountain of red flame that had burst forth at his feet, his naked whiteness glimmering a pale rosy red in the torrid fire. There he stood, looking after her, till, from the lengthening distance, she could see him no more. The serpent went straight on, turning neither to the right nor left.

Meantime Mossy had got out of the Lake of Shadows, and, following his mournful, lonely way, had reached the sea-shore. It was a dark, stormy evening. The sun had set. The wind was blowing from the sea. The waves had surrounded the rock within which lay the old man's house. A deep water rolled between it and the shore, upon which a majestic figure was walking alone.

Mossy went up to him and said,—

"Will you tell me where to find the Old Man of the Sea?"

"I am the Old Man of the Sea," the figure answered.

"I see a strong kingly man of middle age," returned Mossy.

Then the old man looked at him more intently, and said, —

"Your sight, young man, is better than that of most who take this way. The night is stormy: come to my house and tell me what I can do for you."

Mossy followed him. The waves flew from before the footsteps of the Old Man of the Sea, and Mossy followed upon dry sand.

When they had reached the cave, they sat down and gazed at each other.

Now Mossy was an old man by this time. He looked much older than the Old Man of the Sea, and his feet were very weary.

After looking at him for a moment, the old man took him by the hand and led him into his inner cave. There he helped him to undress, and laid him in the bath. And he saw that one of his hands Mossy did not open.

"What have you in that hand?" he asked.

Mossy opened his hand, and there lay the golden key.

"Ah!" said the old man, "that accounts for your knowing me. And I know the way you have to go."

"I want to find the country whence the shadows fall," said Mossy.

"I dare say you do. So do I. But meantime, one thing is certain.—What is that key for, do you think?"

"For a key-hole somewhere. But I don't know why I keep it. I never could find the key-hole. And I have lived a good while, I believe," said Mossy, sadly. "I'm not sure that I'm not old. I know my feet ache."

"Do they?" said the old man, as if he really meant to ask the question; and Mossy, who was still lying in the bath, watched his feet for a moment before he replied,—"No, they do not. Perhaps I am not old either."

"Get up and look at yourself in the water."

He rose and looked at himself in the water, and there was not a gray hair on his head or a wrinkle on his skin.

"You have tasted of death now," said the old man. "Is it good?"

"It is good," said Mossy. "It is better than life."

"No, said the old man: it is only more life.—Your feet will make no holes in the water now."

"What do you mean?"

"I will show you that presently."

They returned to the outer cave, and sat and talked together for a long time. At length the Old Man of the Sea rose, and said to Mossy, —

"Follow me."

He led him up the stair again, and opened another door. They stood on the level of the raging sea, looking towards the east. Across the waste of waters, against the bosom of a fierce black cloud, stood the foot of a rainbow, glowing in the dark.

"This indeed is my way," said Mossy, as soon as he saw the rainbow, and stepped out upon the sea. His feet made no holes in the water. He fought the wind, and climbed the waves, and went on towards the rainbow.

The storm died away. A lovely day and a lovelier night followed. A cool wind blew over the wide plain of the quiet ocean. And still Mossy journeyed eastward. But the rainbow had vanished with the storm.

Day after day he held on, and he thought he had no guide. He did not see how a shining fish under the water directed his steps. He crossed the sea, and came to a great precipice of rock, up which he could discover but one path. Nor did this lead him farther than half-way up the rock, where it ended on a platform. Here he stood and pondered.—It could not be that the way stopped here, else what was the path for? It was a rough path, not very plain, yet certainly a path. — He examined the face of the rock. It was smooth as glass. But as his eyes kept roving hopelessly over it, something glittered, and he caught sight of a row of small sapphires. They bordered a little hole in the rock.

"The key-hole!" he cried.

He tried the key. It fitted. It turned. A great clang and clash, as of iron bolts on huge brazen caldrons, echoed thunderously within. He drew out the key. The rock in front of him began to fall. He retreated from it as far as the breadth of the platform would allow. A great slab fell at his feet. In front was still the solid rock, with this one slab fallen forward out of it. But the moment he stepped upon it, a second fell, just short of the edge of the first, making the next step of a stair, which thus kept dropping itself before him as he ascended into the heart of the precipice. It led him into a hall fit for such an approach—irregular and rude in formation, but floor, sides, pillars, and vaulted roof, all one mass of shining stones of every color that light can show. In the centre stood seven columns, ranged from red to violet. And on the pedestal of one of them sat a woman, motionless, with her face bowed upon her knees. Seven years had she sat there waiting. She lifted her head as Mossy drew near. It was Tangle. Her hair had grown to her feet, and was rippled like the windless sea on broad sands. Her face was beautiful, like her grandmother's, and as still and peaceful as that of the Old Man of the Fire. Her form was tall and noble. Yet Mossy knew her at once.

"How beautiful you are, Tangle!" he said, in delight and astonishment.

"Am I?" she returned. "Oh, I have waited for you so long! But you, you are like the Old Man of the Sea. No. You are like the Old Man of the Earth. No, no. You are like the oldest man of all. You are like them all. And yet you are my own old Mossy! How did you come here? What did you do after I lost you? Did you find the key-hole? Have you got the key still?"

She had a hundred questions to ask him, and he a hundred more to ask her. They told each other all their adventures, and were as happy as man and woman could be. For they were younger and better, and stronger and wiser, than they had ever been before.

It began to grow dark. And they wanted more than ever to reach the country whence the shadows fall. So they looked about them for a way out of the cave. The door by which Mossy entered had closed again, and there was half a mile of rock between them and the sea. Neither could Tangle find the opening in the floor by which the serpent had led her thither. They searched till it grew so dark that they could see nothing, and gave it up.

After a while, however, the cave began to glimmer again. The light came from the moon, but it did not look like moonlight, for it gleamed through those seven pillars in the middle, and filled the place with all colors. And now Mossy saw that there was a pillar beside the red one, which he had not observed before. And it was of the same new color that he had seen in the rainbow when he saw it first in the fairy forest. And on it he saw a sparkle of blue. It was the sapphires round the key-hole.

He took his key. It turned in the lock to the sound of Aeolian music. A door opened upon slow hinges, and disclosed a winding stair within. The key vanished from his fingers. Tangle went up. Mossy followed. The door closed behind them. They climbed out of the earth; and, still climbing, rose above it. They were in the rainbow. Far abroad, over ocean and land, they could see through its transparent walls the earth beneath their feet. Stairs beside stairs wound up together, and beautiful beings of all ages climbed along with them.

They knew that they were going up to the country whence the shadows fall.

And by this time I think they must have got there.

Book Eight

Lilith

ᏳᎬ᎒Ꮢ

FORWARD

I took a walk on Spaulding's Farm the other afternoon. I saw the setting sun lighting up the opposite side of a stately pine wood. Its golden rays straggled into the aisles of the wood as into some noble hall. I was impressed as if some ancient and altogether admirable and shining family had settled there in that part of the land called Concord, unknown to me, — to whom the sun was servant, — who had not gone into society in the village, — who had not been called on. I saw their park, their pleasure-ground, beyond through the wood, in Spaulding's cranberry-meadow. The pines furnished them with gables as they grew. Their house was not obvious to vision; their trees grew through it. I do not know whether I heard the sounds of a suppressed hilarity or not. They seemed to recline on the sunbeams. They have sons and daughters. They are quite well. The farmer's cart-path, which leads directly through their hall, does not in the least put them out, — as the muddy bottom of a pool is sometimes seen through the reflected skies. They never heard of Spaulding, and do not know that he is their neighbor, — notwithstanding I heard him whistle as he drove his team through the house. Nothing can equal the serenity of their lives. Their coat of arms is simply a lichen. I saw it painted on the pines and oaks. Their attics were in the tops of the trees. They are of no politics. There was no noise of labor. I did not perceive that they were weaving or spinning. Yet I did detect, when the wind lulled and hearing was done away, the finest imaginable sweet musical hum, — as of a distant hive in May, which perchance was the sound of their thinking. They had no idle thoughts, and no one without could see their work, for their industry was not as in knots and excrescences embayed.

But I find it difficult to remember them. They fade irrevocably out of my mind even now while I speak and endeavor to recall them, and recollect myself. It is only after a long and serious effort to recollect my best thoughts that I become again aware of their cohabitancy. If it were not for such families as this, I think I should move out of Concord.

Thoreau: "WALKING."

1. The Library

I had just finished my studies at Oxford, and was taking a brief holiday from work before assuming definitely the management of the estate. My father died when I was yet a child; my mother followed him within a year; and I was nearly as much alone in the world as a man might find himself.

I had made little acquaintance with the history of my ancestors. Almost the only thing I knew concerning them was, that a notable number of them had been given to study. I had myself so far inherited the tendency as to devote a good deal of my time, though, I confess, after a somewhat desultory fashion, to the physical sciences. It was chiefly the wonder they woke that drew me. I was constantly seeing, and on the outlook to see, strange analogies, not only between the facts of different sciences of the same order, or between physical and metaphysical facts, but between physical hypotheses and suggestions glimmering out of the metaphysical dreams into which I was in the habit of falling. I was at the same time much given to a premature indulgence of the impulse to turn hypothesis into theory. Of my mental peculiarities there is no occasion to say more.

The house as well as the family was of some antiquity, but no description of it is necessary to the understanding of my narrative. It contained a fine library, whose growth began before the invention of printing, and had continued to my own time, greatly influenced, of course, by changes of taste and pursuit. Nothing surely can more impress upon a man the transitory nature of possession than his succeeding to an ancient property! Like a moving panorama mine has passed from before many eyes, and is now slowly flitting from before my own.

The library, although duly considered in many alterations of the house and additions to it, had nevertheless, like an encroaching state, absorbed one room after another until it occupied the greater part of the ground floor. Its chief room was large, and the walls of it were covered with books almost to the ceiling; the rooms into which it overflowed were of various sizes and shapes, and communicated in modes as various — by doors, by open arches, by short passages, by steps up and steps down.

In the great room I mainly spent my time, reading books of science, old as well as new; for the history of the human mind in relation to supposed knowledge was what most of all interested me. Ptolemy, Dante, the two Bacons, and Boyle were even more to me than Darwin or Maxwell, as so much nearer the vanished van breaking into the dark of ignorance.

In the evening of a gloomy day of August I was sitting in my usual place, my back to one of the windows, reading. It had rained the greater part of the morning and afternoon, but just as the sun was setting, the clouds parted in front of him, and he shone into the room. I rose and looked out of the window. In the centre of the great lawn the feathering top of the fountain column was filled with his red glory. I turned to resume my seat, when my eye was caught by the same glory on the one picture in the room — a portrait, in a sort of niche or little shrine sunk for it in the expanse of book-filled shelves. I knew it as the likeness of one of my ancestors, but had never even wondered why it hung there alone, and not in the gallery, or one of the great rooms, among the other family portraits. The direct sunlight brought out the painting wonderfully; for the first time I seemed to see it, and for the first time it seemed to respond to my look. With my eyes full of the light reflected from it, something, I cannot tell what, made me turn and cast a glance to the farther end of the room, when I saw, or seemed to see, a tall figure reaching up a hand to a bookshelf. The next instant, my vision apparently rectified by the comparative dusk, I saw no one, and concluded that my optic nerves had been momentarily affected from within.

I resumed my reading, and would doubtless have forgotten the vague, evanescent impression, had it not been that, having occasion a moment after to consult a certain volume, I found but a gap in the row where it ought to have stood, and the same instant remembered that just there I had seen, or fancied I saw, the old man in search of a book. I looked all about the spot but in vain. The next morning, however, there it was, just where I had thought to find it! I knew of no one in the house likely to be interested in such a book.

Three days after, another and yet odder thing took place.

In one of the walls was the low, narrow door of a closet, containing some of the oldest and rarest of the books. It was a very thick door, with a projecting frame, and it had been the fancy of some ancestor to cross it with shallow shelves, filled with book-backs only. The harmless trick may be excused by the fact that the titles on the sham backs were either humorously original, or those of books lost beyond hope of recovery. I had a great liking for the masked door.

To complete the illusion of it, some inventive workman apparently had shoved in, on the top of one of the rows, a part of a volume thin enough to lie between it and the bottom of the next shelf: he had cut away diagonally a considerable portion, and fixed the remnant with one of its open corners projecting beyond the book-backs. The binding of the mutilated volume was limp vellum, and one could open the corner far enough to see that it was manuscript upon parchment.

Happening, as I sat reading, to raise my eyes from the page, my glance fell upon this door, and at once I saw that the book described, if book it may be called, was gone. Angrier than any worth I knew in it justified, I rang the bell, and the butler appeared. When I asked him if he knew what had befallen it, he turned pale, and assured me he did not. I could less easily doubt his word than my own eyes, for he had been all his life in the family, and a more faithful servant never lived. He left on me the impression, nevertheless, that he could have said something more.

In the afternoon I was again reading in the library, and coming to a point which demanded reflection, I lowered the book and let my eyes go wandering. The same moment I saw the back of a slender old man, in a long, dark coat, shiny as from much wear, in the act of disappearing through the masked door into the closet beyond. I darted across the room, found the door shut, pulled it open, looked into the closet, which had no other issue, and, seeing nobody, concluded, not without uneasiness, that I had had a recurrence of my former illusion, and sat down again to my reading.

Naturally, however, I could not help feeling a little nervous, and presently glancing up to assure myself that I was indeed alone, started again to my feet, and ran to the masked door —for there was the mutilated volume in its place! I laid hold of it and pulled: it was firmly fixed as usual!

I was now utterly bewildered. I rang the bell; the butler came; I told him all I had seen, and he told me all he knew.

He had hoped, he said, that the old gentleman was going to be forgotten; it was well no one but myself had seen him. He had heard a good deal about him when first he served in the house, but by degrees he had ceased to be mentioned, and he had been very careful not to allude to him.

"The place was haunted by an old gentleman, was it?" I said.

He answered that at one time everybody believed it, but the fact that I had never heard of it seemed to imply that the thing had come to an end and was forgotten.

I questioned him as to what he had seen of the old gentleman.

He had never seen him, he said, although he had been in the house from the day my father was eight years old. My grandfather would never hear a word on the matter, declaring that whoever alluded to it should be dismissed without a moment's warning: it was nothing but a pretext of the maids, he said, for running into the arms of the men! but old Sir Ralph believed in nothing he could not see or lay hold of. Not one of the maids ever said she had seen the apparition, but a footman had left the place because of it.

An ancient woman in the village had told him a legend concerning a Mr. Raven, long time librarian to "that Sir Upward whose portrait hangs there among the books." Sir Upward was a great reader, she said — not of such books only as were wholesome for men to read, but of strange, forbidden, and evil books; and in so doing, Mr. Raven, who was probably the devil himself, encouraged him. Suddenly they both disappeared, and Sir Upward was never after seen or heard of, but Mr. Raven continued to show himself at uncertain intervals in the library. There were some who believed he was not dead; but both he and the old woman held it easier to believe that a dead man might revisit the world he had left, than that one who went on living for hundreds of years should be a man at all.

He had never heard that Mr. Raven meddled with anything in the house, but he might perhaps consider himself privileged in regard to the books. How the old woman had learned so much about him he could not tell; but the description she gave of him corresponded exactly with the figure I had just seen.

"I hope it was but a friendly call on the part of the old gentleman!" he concluded, with a troubled smile.

I told him I had no objection to any number of visits from Mr. Raven, but it would be well he should keep to his resolution of saying nothing about him to the servants. Then I asked him if he had ever seen the mutilated volume out of its place; he answered that he never had, and had always thought it a fixture. With that he went to it, and gave it a pull: it seemed immovable.

2. THE MIRROR

Nothing more happened for some days. I think it was about a week after, when what I have now to tell took place. I had often thought of the manuscript fragment, and repeatedly tried to discover some way of releasing it, but in vain: I could not find out what held it fast.

But I had for some time intended a thorough overhauling of the books in the closet, its atmosphere causing me uneasiness as to their condition. One day the intention suddenly became a resolve, and I was in the act of rising from my chair to make a beginning, when I saw the old librarian moving from the door of the closet toward the farther end of the room. I ought rather to say only that I caught sight of something shadowy from which I received the impression of a slight, stooping man, in a shabby dress-coat reaching almost to his heels, the tails of which, disparting a little as he walked, revealed thin legs in black stockings, and large feet in wide, slipper-like shoes.

At once I followed him: I might be following a shadow, but I never doubted I was following something. He went out of the library into the hall, and across to the foot of the great staircase, then up the stairs to the first floor, where lay the chief rooms. Past these rooms, I following close, he continued his way, through a wide corridor, to the foot of a narrower stair leading to the second floor. Up that he went also, and when I reached the top, strange as it may seem, I found myself in a region almost unknown to me. I never had brother or sister to incite to such romps as make children familiar with nook and cranny; I was a mere child when my guardian took me away; and I had never seen the house again until, about a month before, I returned to take possession.

Through passage after passage we came to a door at the bottom of a winding wooden stair, which we ascended. Every step creaked under my foot, but I heard no sound from that of my guide. Somewhere in the middle of the stair I lost sight of him, and from the top of it the shadowy shape was nowhere visible. I could not even imagine I saw him. The place was full of shadows, but he was not one of them.

I was in the main garret, with huge beams and rafters over my head, great spaces around me, a door here and there in sight, and long vistas whose gloom was thinned by a few lurking cobwebbed windows and small dusky skylights. I gazed with a strange mingling of awe and pleasure: the wide expanse of garret was my own, and unexplored!

In the middle of it stood an unpainted enclosure of rough planks, the door of which was ajar. Thinking Mr. Raven might be there, I pushed the door, and entered.

The small chamber was full of light, but such as dwells in places deserted: it had a dull, disconsolate look, as if it found itself of no use, and regretted having come. A few rather dim sunrays, marking their track through the cloud of motes that had just been stirred up, fell upon a tall mirror with a dusty face, old-fashioned and rather narrow — in appearance an ordinary glass. It had an ebony frame, on the top of which stood a black eagle, with outstretched wings, in his beak a golden chain, from whose end hung a black ball.

I had been looking at rather than into the mirror, when suddenly I became aware that it reflected neither the chamber nor my own person. I have an impression of having seen the wall melt away, but what followed is enough to account for any uncertainty: — could I have mistaken for a mirror the glass that protected a wonderful picture?

I saw before me a wild country, broken and heathy. Desolate hills of no great height, but somehow of strange appearance, occupied the middle distance; along the horizon stretched the tops of a far-off mountain range; nearest me lay a tract of moorland, flat and melancholy.

Being short-sighted, I stepped closer to examine the texture of a stone in the immediate foreground, and in the act espied, hopping toward me with solemnity, a large and ancient raven, whose purply black was here and there softened with gray. He seemed looking for worms as he came. Nowise astonished at the appearance of a live creature in a picture, I took another step forward to see him better, stumbled over something — doubtless the frame of the mirror — and stood nose to beak with the bird: I was in the open air, on a houseless heath!

3. The Raven

I turned and looked behind me: all was vague and uncertain, as when one cannot distinguish between fog and field, between cloud and mountain-side. One fact only was plain — that I saw nothing I knew. Imagining myself involved in a visual illusion, and that touch would correct sight, I stretched my arms and felt about me, walking in this direction and that, if haply, where I could see nothing, I might yet come in contact with something; but my search was vain. Instinctively then, as to the only living thing near me, I turned to the raven, which stood a little way off, regarding me with an expression at once respectful and quizzical. Then the absurdity of seeking counsel from such a one struck me, and I turned again, overwhelmed with bewilderment, not unmingled with fear. Had I wandered into a region where both the material and psychical relations of our world had ceased to hold? Might a man at any moment step beyond the realm of order, and become the sport of the lawless? Yet I saw the raven, felt the ground under my feet, and heard a sound as of wind in the lowly plants around me!

"How did I get here?" I said — apparently aloud, for the question was immediately answered.

"You came through the door," replied an odd, rather harsh voice.

I looked behind, then all about me, but saw no human shape. The terror that madness might be at hand laid hold upon me: must I henceforth place no confidence either in my senses or my consciousness? The same instant I knew it was the raven that had spoken, for he stood looking up at me with an air of waiting. The sun was not shining, yet the bird seemed to cast a shadow, and the shadow seemed part of himself.

I beg my reader to aid me in the endeavor to make myself intelligible — if here understanding be indeed possible between us. I was in a world, or call it a state of things, an economy of conditions, an idea of existence, so little correspondent with the ways and modes of this world — which we are apt to think the only world, that the best choice I can make of word or phrase is but an adumbration of what I would convey. I begin indeed to fear that I have undertaken an impossibility, undertaken to tell what I cannot tell because no speech at my command will fit the forms in my mind. Already I have set down statements I would gladly change did I know how to substitute a truer utterance; but as often as I try to fit the reality with nearer words, I find myself in danger of losing the things themselves, and feel like one in process of awaking from a dream, with the thing that seemed familiar gradually yet swiftly changing through a succession of forms until its very nature is no longer recognizable.

I bethought me that a bird capable of addressing a man must have the right of a man to a civil answer; perhaps, as a bird, even a greater claim.

A tendency to croak caused a certain roughness in his speech, but his voice was not disagreeable, and what he said, although conveying little enlightenment, did not sound rude.

"I did not come through any door," I rejoined.

"I saw you come through it! — saw you with my own ancient eyes!" asserted the raven, positively but not disrespectfully.

"I never saw any door!" I persisted.

"Of course not!" he returned; "all the doors you had yet seen – and you haven't seen many — were doors in; here you came upon a door out! The strange thing to you," he went on thoughtfully, "will be, that the more doors you go out of, the farther you get in!"

"Oblige me by telling me where I am."

"That is impossible. You know nothing about whereness. The only way to come to know where you are is to begin to make yourself at home."

"How am I to begin that where everything is so strange?"

"By doing something."

"What?"

"Anything; and the sooner you begin the better! for until you are at home, you will find it as difficult to get out as it is to get in."

"I have, unfortunately, found it too easy to get in; once out I shall not try again!"

"You have stumbled in, and may, possibly, stumble out again. Whether you have got in UNFORTUNATELY remains to be seen."

"Do you never go out, sir?"

"When I please I do, but not often, or for long. Your world is such a half-baked sort of place, it is at once so childish and so self-satisfied — in fact, it is not sufficiently developed for an old raven — at your service!"

"Am I wrong, then, in presuming that a man is superior to a bird?"

"That is as it may be. We do not waste our intellects in generalizing, but take man or bird as we find him. — I think it is now my turn to ask you a question!"

"You have the best of rights," I replied, "in the fact that you CAN do so!"

"Well answered!" he rejoined. "Tell me, then, who you are – if you happen to know."

"How should I help knowing? I am myself, and must know!"

"If you know you are yourself, you know that you are not somebody else; but do you know that you are yourself? Are you sure you are not your own father? — or, excuse me, your own fool? — Who are you, pray?"

I became at once aware that I could give him no notion of who I was. Indeed, who was I? It would be no answer to say I was who! Then I understood that I did not know myself, did not know what I was, had no grounds on which to determine that I was one and not another. As for the name I went by in my own world, I had forgotten it, and did not care to recall it, for it meant nothing, and what it might be was plainly of no consequence here. I had indeed almost forgotten that there it was a custom for everybody to have a name! So I held my peace, and it was my wisdom; for what should I say to a creature such as this raven, who saw through accident into entity?

"Look at me," he said, "and tell me who I am."

As he spoke, he turned his back, and instantly I knew him. He was no longer a raven, but a man above the middle height with a stoop, very thin, and wearing a long black tail-coat. Again he turned, and I saw him a raven.

"I have seen you before, sir," I said, feeling foolish rather than surprised.

"How can you say so from seeing me behind?" he rejoined. "Did you ever see yourself behind? You have never seen yourself at all! — Tell me now, then, who I am."

"I humbly beg your pardon," I answered: "I believe you were once the librarian of our house, but more WHO I do not know."

"Why do you beg my pardon?"

"Because I took you for a raven," I said — seeing him before me as plainly a raven as bird or man could look.

"You did me no wrong," he returned. "Calling me a raven, or thinking me one, you allowed me existence, which is the sum of what one can demand of his fellow-beings. Therefore, in return, I will give you a lesson: — No one can say he is himself, until first he knows that he IS, and then what HIMSELF is. In fact, nobody is himself, and himself is nobody. There is more in it than you can see now, but not more than you need to see. You have, I fear, got into this region too soon, but none the less you must get to be at home in it; for home, as you may or may not know, is the only place where you can go out and in. There are places you can go into, and places you can go out of; but the one place, if you do but find it, where you may go out and in both, is home."

He turned to walk away, and again I saw the librarian. He did not appear to have changed, only to have taken up his shadow. I know this seems nonsense, but I cannot help it.

I gazed after him until I saw him no more; but whether distance hid him, or he disappeared among the heather, I cannot tell.

Could it be that I was dead, I thought, and did not know it? Was I in what we used to call the world beyond the grave? and must I wander about seeking my place in it? How was I to find myself at home? The raven said I must do something: what could I do here? — And would that make me somebody? for now, alas, I was nobody!

I took the way Mr. Raven had gone, and went slowly after him. Presently I saw a wood of tall slender pine-trees, and turned toward it. The odor of it met me on my way, and I made haste to bury myself in it.

Plunged at length in its twilight glooms, I spied before me something with a shine, standing between two of the stems. It had no color, but was like the translucent trembling of the hot air that rises, in a radiant summer noon, from the sun-baked ground, vibrant like the smitten chords of a musical instrument. What it was grew no plainer as I went nearer, and when I came close up, I ceased to see it, only the form and color of the trees beyond seemed strangely uncertain. I would have passed between the stems, but received a slight shock, stumbled, and fell. When I rose, I saw before me the wooden wall of the garret chamber. I turned, and there was the mirror, on whose top the black eagle seemed but that moment to have perched.

Terror seized me, and I fled. Outside the chamber the wide garret spaces had an UNCANNY look. They seemed to have long been waiting for something; it had come, and they were waiting again! A shudder went through me on the winding stair: the house had grown strange to me! something was about to leap upon me from behind! I darted down the spiral, struck against the wall and fell, rose and ran. On the next floor I lost my way, and had gone through several passages a second time ere I found the head of the stair. At the top of the great stair I had come to myself a little, and in a few moments I sat recovering my breath in the library.

Nothing should ever again make me go up that last terrible stair! The garret at the top of it pervaded the whole house! It sat upon it, threatening to crush me out of it! The brooding brain of the building, it was full of mysterious dwellers, one or other of whom might any moment appear in the library where I sat! I was nowhere safe! I would let, I would sell the dreadful place, in which an aërial portal stood ever open to creatures whose life was other than human! I would purchase a crag in Switzerland, and thereon build a wooden nest of one story with never a garret above it, guarded by some grand old peak that would send down nothing worse than a few tons of whelming rock!

I knew all the time that my thinking was foolish, and was even aware of a certain undertone of contemptuous humor in it; but suddenly it was checked, and I seemed again to hear the croak of the raven.

"If I know nothing of my own garret," I thought, "what is there to secure me against my own brain? Can I tell what it is even now generating? — what thought it may present me the next moment, the next month, or a year away? What is at the heart of my brain? What is behind my THINK? Am I there at all? — Who, what am I?"

I could no more answer the question now than when the raven put it to me in – at —"Where in? - -where at?" I said, and gave myself up as knowing anything of myself or the universe.

I started to my feet, hurried across the room to the masked door, where the mutilated volume, sticking out from the flat of soulless, bodiless, non-existent books, appeared to beckon me, went down on my knees, and opened it as far as its position would permit, but could see nothing. I got up again, lighted a taper, and peeping as into a pair of reluctant jaws, perceived that the manuscript was verse. Further I could not carry discovery. Beginnings of lines were visible on the left-hand page, and ends of lines on the other; but I could not, of course, get at the beginning and end of a single line, and was unable, in what I could read, to make any guess at the sense. The mere words, however, woke in me feelings which to describe was, from their strangeness, impossible. Some dreams, some poems, some musical phrases, some pictures, wake feelings such as one never had before, new in color and form — spiritual sensations, as it were, hitherto unproved: here, some of the phrases, some of the senseless half-lines, some even of the individual words affected me in similar fashion — as with the aroma of an idea, rousing in me a great longing to know what the poem or poems might, even yet in their mutilation, hold or suggest.

I copied out a few of the larger shreds attainable, and tried hard to complete some of the lines, but without the least success. The only thing I gained in the effort was so much weariness that, when I went to bed, I fell asleep at once and slept soundly.

In the morning all that horror of the empty garret spaces had left me.

4. Somewhere Or Nowhere

The sun was very bright, but I doubted if the day would long be fine, and looked into the milky sapphire I wore, to see whether the star in it was clear. It was even less defined than I had expected. I rose from the breakfast-table, and went to the window to glance at the stone again. There had been heavy rain in the night, and on the lawn was a thrush breaking his way into the shell of a snail.

As I was turning my ring about to catch the response of the star to the sun, I spied a keen black eye gazing at me out of the milky misty blue. The sight startled me so that I dropped the ring, and when I picked it up the eye was gone from it. The same moment the sun was obscured; a dark vapor covered him, and in a minute or two the whole sky was clouded. The air had grown sultry, and a gust of wind came suddenly. A moment more and there was a flash of lightning, with a single sharp thunder-clap. Then the rain fell in torrents.

I had opened the window, and stood there looking out at the precipitous rain, when I descried a raven walking toward me over the grass, with solemn gait, and utter disregard of the falling deluge. Suspecting who he was, I congratulated myself that I was safe on the ground-floor. At the same time I had a conviction that, if I were not careful, something would happen.

He came nearer and nearer, made a profound bow, and with a sudden winged leap stood on the window-sill. Then he stepped over the ledge, jumped down into the room, and walked to the door. I thought he was on his way to the library, and followed him, determined, if he went up the stair, not to take one step after him. He turned, however, neither toward the library nor the stair, but to a little door that gave upon a grass-patch in a nook between two portions of the rambling old house. I made haste to open it for him. He stepped out into its creeper-covered porch, and stood looking at the rain, which fell like a huge thin cataract; I stood in the door behind him. The second flash came, and was followed by a lengthened roll of more distant thunder. He turned his head over his shoulder and looked at me, as much as to say, "You hear that?" then swiveled it round again, and anew contemplated the weather, apparently with approbation. So human were his pose and carriage and the way he kept turning his head, that I remarked almost involuntarily,

"Fine weather for the worms, Mr. Raven!"

"Yes," he answered, in the rather croaky voice I had learned to know, "the ground will be nice for them to get out and in! — It must be a grand time on the steppes of Uranus!" he added, with a glance upward; "I believe it is raining there too; it was, all the last week!"

"Why should that make it a grand time?" I asked.

"Because the animals there are all burrowers," he answered, " – like the field-mice and the moles here. — They will be, for ages to come."

"How do you know that, if I may be so bold?" I rejoined.

"As any one would who had been there to see," he replied. "It is a great sight, until you get used to it, when the earth gives a heave, and out comes a beast. You might think it a hairy elephant or a deinotherium — but none of the animals are the same as we have ever had here. I was almost frightened myself the first time I saw the dry-bog-serpent come wallowing out —such a head and mane! and SUCH eyes! — but the shower is nearly over. It will stop directly after the next thunder-clap. There it is!"

A flash came with the words, and in about half a minute the thunder. Then the rain ceased.

"Now we should be going!" said the raven, and stepped to the front of the porch.

"Going where?" I asked.

"Going where we have to go," he answered. "You did not surely think you had got home? I told you there was no going out and in at pleasure until you were at home!"

"I do not want to go," I said.

"That does not make any difference — at least not much," he answered. "This is the way!"

"I am quite content where I am."

"You think so, but you are not. Come along."

He hopped from the porch onto the grass, and turned, waiting.

"I will not leave the house to-day," I said with obstinacy.

"You will come into the garden!" rejoined the raven.

"I give in so far," I replied, and stepped from the porch.

The sun broke through the clouds, and the raindrops flashed and sparkled on the grass. The raven was walking over it.

"You will wet your feet!" I cried.

"And mire my beak," he answered, immediately plunging it deep in the sod, and drawing out a great wriggling red worm. He threw back his head, and tossed it in the air. It spread great wings, gorgeous in red and black, and soared aloft.

"Tut! tut!" I exclaimed; "you mistake, Mr. Raven: worms are not the larvæ of butterflies!"

"Never mind," he croaked; "it will do for once! I'm not a reading man at present, but sexton at the — at a certain graveyard — cemetery, more properly – in – at — no matter where!"

"I see! you can't keep your spade still: and when you have nothing to bury, you must dig something up! Only you should mind what it is before you make it fly! No creature should be allowed to forget what and where it came from!"

"Why?" said the raven.

"Because it will grow proud, and cease to recognize its superiors."

No man knows it when he is making an idiot of himself.

"Where DO the worms come from?" said the raven, as if suddenly grown curious to know.

"Why, from the earth, as you have just seen!" I answered.

"Yes, last!" he replied. "But they can't have come from it first — for that will never go back to it!" he added, looking up.

I looked up also, but could see nothing save a little dark cloud, the edges of which were red, as if with the light of the sunset.

"Surely the sun is not going down!" I exclaimed, struck with amazement.

"Oh, no!" returned the raven. "That red belongs to the worm."

"You see what comes of making creatures forget their origin!" I cried with some warmth.

"It is well, surely, if it be to rise higher and grow larger!" he returned. "But indeed I only teach them to find it!"

"Would you have the air full of worms?"

"That is the business of a sexton. If only the rest of the clergy understood it as well!"

In went his beak again through the soft turf, and out came the wriggling worm. He tossed it in the air, and away it flew.

I looked behind me, and gave a cry of dismay: I had but that moment declared I would not leave the house, and already I was a stranger in the strange land!

"What right have you to treat me so, Mr. Raven?" I said with deep offence. "Am I, or am I not, a free agent?"

"A man is as free as he chooses to make himself, never an atom freer," answered the raven.

"You have no right to make me do things against my will!"

"When you have a will, you will find that no one can."

"You wrong me in the very essence of my individuality!" I persisted.

"If you were an individual I could not, therefore now I do not. You are but beginning to become an individual."

All about me was a pine-forest, in which my eyes were already searching deep, in the hope of discovering an unaccountable glimmer, and so finding my way home. But, alas! how could I any longer call that house HOME, where every door, every window opened into OUT, and even the garden I could not keep inside!

I suppose I looked discomfited.

"Perhaps it may comfort you," said the raven, "to be told that you have not yet left your house, neither has your house left you. At the same time it cannot contain you, or you inhabit it!"

"I do not understand you," I replied. "Where am I?"

"In the region of the seven dimensions," he answered, with a curious noise in his throat, and a flutter of his tail. "You had better follow me carefully now for a moment, lest you should hurt some one!"

"There is nobody to hurt but yourself, Mr. Raven! I confess I should rather like to hurt you!"

"That you see nobody is where the danger lies. But you see that large tree to your left, about thirty yards away?"

"Of course I do: why should I not?" I answered testily.

"Ten minutes ago you did not see it, and now you do not know where it stands!"

"I do."

"Where do you think it stands?"

"Why THERE, where you know it is!"

"Where is THERE?"

"You bother me with your silly questions!" I cried. "I am growing tired of you!"

"That tree stands on the hearth of your kitchen, and grows nearly straight up its chimney," he said.

"Now I KNOW you are making game of me!" I answered, with a laugh of scorn.

"Was I making game of you when you discovered me looking out of your star-sapphire yesterday?"

"That was this morning — not an hour ago!"

"I have been widening your horizon longer than that, Mr. Vane; but never mind!"

"You mean you have been making a fool of me!" I said, turning from him.

"Excuse me: no one can do that but yourself!"

"And I decline to do it."

"You mistake."

"How?"

"In declining to acknowledge yourself one already. You make yourself such by refusing what is true, and for that you will sorely punish yourself."

"How, again?"

"By believing what is not true."

"Then, if I walk to the other side of that tree, I shall walk through the kitchen fire?"

"Certainly. You would first, however, walk through the lady at the piano in the breakfast-room. That rosebush is close by her. You would give her a terrible start!"

"There is no lady in the house!"

"Indeed! Is not your housekeeper a lady? She is counted such in a certain country where all are servants, and the liveries one and multitudinous!"

"She cannot use the piano, anyhow!"

"Her niece can: she is there — a well-educated girl and a capital musician."

"Excuse me; I cannot help it: you seem to me to be talking sheer nonsense!"

"If you could but hear the music! Those great long heads of wild hyacinth are inside the piano, among the strings of it, and give that peculiar sweetness to her playing! — Pardon me: I forgot your deafness!"

"Two objects," I said, "cannot exist in the same place at the same time!"

"Can they not? I did not know! — I remember now they do teach that with you. It is a great mistake — one of the greatest ever wiseacre made! No man of the universe, only a man of the world could have said so!"

"You a librarian, and talk such rubbish!" I cried. "Plainly, you did not read many of the books in your charge!"

"Oh, yes! I went through all in your library — at the time, and came out at the other side not much the wiser. I was a bookworm then, but when I came to know it, I woke among the butterflies. To be sure I have given up reading for a good many years — ever since I was made sexton. — There! I smell Grieg's Wedding March in the quiver of those rose-petals!"

I went to the rose-bush and listened hard, but could not hear the thinnest ghost of a sound; I only smelt something I had never before smelt in any rose. It was still rose-odor, but with a difference, caused, I suppose, by the Wedding March.

When I looked up, there was the bird by my side.

"Mr. Raven," I said, "forgive me for being so rude: I was irritated. Will you kindly show me my way home? I must go, for I have an appointment with my bailiff. One must not break faith with his servants!"

"You cannot break what was broken days ago!" he answered.

"Do show me the way," I pleaded.

"I cannot," he returned. "To go back, you must go through yourself, and that way no man can show another."

Entreaty was vain. I must accept my fate! But how was life to be lived in a world of which I had all the laws to learn? There would, however, be adventure! that held consolation; and whether I found my way home or not, I should at least have the rare advantage of knowing two worlds!

I had never yet done anything to justify my existence; my former world was nothing the better for my sojourn in it: here, however, I must earn, or in some way find, my bread! But I reasoned that, as I was not to blame in being here, I might expect to be taken care of here as well as there! I had had nothing to do with getting into the world I had just left, and in it I had found myself heir to a large property! If that world, as I now saw, had a claim upon me because I had eaten, and could eat again, upon this world I had a claim because I must eat—when it would in return have a claim on me!

"There is no hurry," said the raven, who stood regarding me; "we do not go much by the clock here. Still, the sooner one begins to do what has to be done, the better! I will take you to my wife."

"Thank you. Let us go!" I answered, and immediately he led the way.

5. THE OLD CHURCH

I followed him deep into the pine-forest. Neither of us said much while yet the sacred gloom of it closed us round. We came to larger and yet larger trees — older, and more individual, some of them grotesque with age. Then the forest grew thinner.

"You see that hawthorn?" said my guide at length, pointing with his beak.

I looked where the wood melted away on the edge of an open heath.

"I see a gnarled old man, with a great white head," I answered.

"Look again," he rejoined: "it is a hawthorn."

"It seems indeed an ancient hawthorn; but this is not the season for the hawthorn to blossom!" I objected.

"The season for the hawthorn to blossom," he replied, "is when the hawthorn blossoms. That tree is in the ruins of the church on your home-farm. You were going to give some directions to the bailiff about its churchyard, were you not, the morning of the thunder?"

"I was going to tell him I wanted it turned into a wilderness of rose-trees, and that the plough must never come within three yards of it."

"Listen!" said the raven, seeming to hold his breath.

I listened, and heard — was it the sighing of a far-off musical wind — or the ghost of a music that had once been glad? Or did I indeed hear anything?

"They go there still," said the raven.

"Who goes there? and where do they go?" I asked.

"Some of the people who used to pray there, go to the ruins still," he replied. "But they will not go much longer, I think."

"What makes them go now?"

"They need help from each other to get their thinking done, and their feelings hatched, so they talk and sing together; and then, they say, the big thought floats out of their hearts like a great ship out of the river at high water."

"Do they pray as well as sing?"

"No; they have found that each can best pray in his own silent heart . — Some people are always at their prayers. — Look! look! There goes one!"

He pointed right up into the air. A snow-white pigeon was mounting, with quick and yet quicker wing-flap, the unseen spiral of an ethereal stair. The sunshine flashed quivering from its wings.

"I see a pigeon!" I said.

"Of course you see a pigeon," rejoined the raven, "for there is the pigeon! I see a prayer on its way. — I wonder now what heart is that dove's mother! Some one may have come awake in my cemetery!"

"How can a pigeon be a prayer?" I said. "I understand, of course, how it should be a fit symbol or likeness for one; but a live pigeon to come out of a heart!"

"It MUST puzzle you! It cannot fail to do so!"

"A prayer is a thought, a thing spiritual!" I pursued.

"Very true! But if you understood any world besides your own, you would understand your own much better. — When a heart is really alive, then it is able to think live things. There is one heart all whose thoughts are strong, happy creatures, and whose very dreams are lives. When some pray, they lift heavy thoughts from the ground, only to drop them on it again; others send up their prayers in living shapes, this or that, the nearest likeness to each. All live things were thoughts to begin with, and are fit therefore to be used by those that think. When one says to the great Thinker: — "Here is one of thy thoughts: I am thinking it now!" that is a prayer — a word to the big heart from one of its own little hearts. — Look, there is another!"

This time the raven pointed his beak downward — to something at the foot of a block of granite. I looked, and saw a little flower. I had never seen one like it before, and cannot utter the feeling it woke in me by its gracious, trusting form, its color, and its odor as of a new world that was yet the old. I can only say that it suggested an anemone, was of a pale rose-hue, and had a golden heart.

"That is a prayer-flower," said the raven.

"I never saw such a flower before!" I rejoined.

"There is no other such. Not one prayer-flower is ever quite like another," he returned.

"How do you know it a prayer-flower?" I asked.

"By the expression of it," he answered. "More than that I cannot tell you. If you know it, you know it; if you do not, you do not."

"Could you not teach me to know a prayer-flower when I see it?" I said.

"I could not. But if I could, what better would you be? you would not know it of YOURSELF and ITself! Why know the name of a thing when the thing itself you do not know? Whose work is it but your own to open your eyes? But indeed the business of the universe is to make such a fool of you that you will know yourself for one, and so begin to be wise!"

But I did see that the flower was different from any flower I had ever seen before; therefore I knew that I must be seeing a shadow of the prayer in it; and a great awe came over me to think of the heart listening to the flower.

6. THE SEXTON'S COTTAGE

We had been for some time walking over a rocky moorland covered with dry plants and mosses, when I descried a little cottage in the farthest distance. The sun was not yet down, but he was wrapt in a gray cloud. The heath looked as if it had never been warm, and the wind blew strangely cold, as if from some region where it was always night.

"Here we are at last!" said the raven. "What a long way it is! In half the time I could have gone to Paradise and seen my cousin — him, you remember, who never came back to Noah! Dear! dear! it is almost winter!"

"Winter!" I cried; "it seems but half a day since we left home!"

"That is because we have traveled so fast," answered the raven. "In your world you cannot pull up the plumb-line you call gravitation, and let the world spin round under your feet! But here is my wife's house! She is very good to let me live with her, and call it the sexton's cottage!"

"But where is your churchyard — your cemetery — where you make your graves, I mean?" said I, seeing nothing but the flat heath.

The raven stretched his neck, held out his beak horizontally, turned it slowly round to all the points of the compass, and said nothing.

I followed the beak with my eyes, and lo, without church or graves, all was a churchyard! Wherever the dreary wind swept, there was the raven's cemetery! He was sexton of all he surveyed! lord of all that was laid aside! I stood in the burial-ground of the universe; its compass the unenclosed heath, its wall the gray horizon, low and starless! I had left spring and summer, autumn and sunshine behind me, and come to the winter that waited for me! I had set out in the prime of my youth, and here I was already! — But I mistook. The day might well be long in that region, for it contained the seasons. Winter slept there, the night through, in his winding-sheet of ice; with childlike smile, Spring came awake in the dawn; at noon, Summer blazed abroad in her gorgeous beauty; with the slow-changing afternoon, old Autumn crept in, and died at the first breath of the vaporous, ghosty night.

As we drew near the cottage, the clouded sun was rushing down the steepest slope of the west, and he sank while we were yet a few yards from the door. The same instant I was assailed by a cold that seemed almost a material presence, and I struggled across the threshold as if from the clutches of an icy death. A wind swelled up on the moor, and rushed at the door as with difficulty I closed it behind me. Then all was still, and I looked about me.

A candle burned on a deal table in the middle of the room, and the first thing I saw was the lid of a coffin, as I thought, set up against the wall; but it opened, for it was a door, and a woman entered. She was all in white — as white as new-fallen snow; and her face was as white as her dress, but not like snow, for at once it suggested warmth. I thought her features were perfect, but her eyes made me forget them. The life of her face and her whole person was gathered and concentrated in her eyes, where it became light. It might have been coming death that made her face luminous, but the eyes had life in them for a nation — large, and dark with a darkness ever deepening as I gazed. A whole night-heaven lay condensed in each pupil; all the stars were in its blackness, and flashed; while round it for a horizon lay coiled an iris of the eternal twilight. What any eye IS, God only knows: her eyes must have been coming direct out of his own! the still face might be a primeval perfection; the live eyes were a continuous creation.

"Here is Mr. Vane, wife!" said the raven.

"He is welcome," she answered, in a low, rich, gentle voice. Treasures of immortal sound seemed to he buried in it.

I gazed, and could not speak.

"I knew you would be glad to see him!" added the raven.

She stood in front of the door by which she had entered, and did not come nearer.

"Will he sleep?" she asked.

"I fear not," he replied; "he is neither weary nor heavy laden."

"Why then have you brought him?"

"I have my fears it may prove precipitate."

"I do not quite understand you," I said, with an uneasy foreboding as to what she meant, but a vague hope of some escape. "Surely a man must do a day's work first!"

I gazed into the white face of the woman, and my heart fluttered. She returned my gaze in silence.

"Let me first go home," I resumed, "and come again after I have found or made, invented, or at least discovered something!"

"He has not yet learned that the day begins with sleep!" said the woman, turning to her husband. "Tell him he must rest before he can do anything!"

"Men," he answered, "think so much of having done, that they fall asleep upon it. They cannot empty an egg but they turn into the shell, and lie down!"

The words drew my eyes from the woman to the raven.

I saw no raven, but the librarian — the same slender elderly man, in a rusty black coat, large in the body and long in the tails. I had seen only his back before; now for the first time I saw his face. It was so thin that it showed the shape of the bones under it, suggesting the skulls his last-claimed profession must have made him familiar with. But in truth I had never before seen a face so alive, or a look so keen or so friendly as that in his pale blue eyes, which yet had a haze about them as if they had done much weeping.

"You knew I was not a raven!" he said with a smile.

"I knew you were Mr. Raven," I replied; "but somehow I thought you a bird too!"

"What made you think me a bird?"

"You looked a raven, and I saw you dig worms out of the earth with your beak."

"And then?"

"Toss them in the air." "And then?"

"They grew butterflies, and flew away."

"Did you ever see a raven do that? I told you I was a sexton!"

"Does a sexton toss worms in the air, and turn them into butterflies?"

"Yes."

"I never saw one do it!"

"You saw me do it! — But I am still librarian in your house, for I never was dismissed, and never gave up the office. Now I am librarian here as well."

"But you have just told me you were sexton here!"

"So I am. It is much the same profession. Except you are a true sexton, books are but dead bodies to you, and a library nothing but a catacomb!"

"You bewilder me!"

"That's all right!"

A few moments he stood silent. The woman, moveless as a statue, stood silent also by the coffin-door.

"Upon occasion," said the sexton at length, "it is more convenient to put one's bird-self in front. Every one, as you ought to know, has a beast-self — and a bird-self, and a stupid fish-self, ay, and a creeping serpent-self too — which it takes a deal of crushing to kill! In truth he has also a tree-self and a crystal-self, and I don't know how many selves more — all to get into harmony. You can tell what sort a man is by his creature that comes oftenest to the front."

He turned to his wife, and I considered him more closely. He was above the ordinary height, and stood more erect than when last I saw him. His face was, like his wife's, very pale; its nose handsomely encased the beak that had retired within it; its lips were very thin, and even they had no color, but their curves were beautiful, and about them quivered a shadowy smile that had humor in it as well as love and pity.

"We are in want of something to eat and drink, wife," he said; "we have come a long way!"

"You know, husband," she answered, "we can give only to him that asks."

She turned her unchanging face and radiant eyes upon mine.

"Please give me something to eat, Mrs. Raven," I said, "and something — what you will — to quench my thirst."

"Your thirst must be greater before you can have what will quench it," she replied; "but what I can give you, I will gladly."

She went to a cupboard in the wall, brought from it bread and wine, and set them on the table.

We sat down to the perfect meal; and as I ate, the bread and wine seemed to go deeper than the hunger and thirst. Anxiety and discomfort vanished; expectation took their place.

I grew very sleepy, and now first felt weary.

"I have earned neither food nor sleep, Mrs. Raven," I said, "but you have given me the one freely, and now I hope you will give me the other, for I sorely need it."

"Sleep is too fine a thing ever to be earned," said the sexton; "it must be given and accepted, for it is a necessity. But it would be perilous to use this house as a half-way hostelry—for the repose of a night, that is, merely."

A wild-looking little black cat jumped on his knee as he spoke. He patted it as one pats a child to make it go to sleep: he seemed to me patting down the sod upon a grave — patting it lovingly, with an inward lullaby.

"Here is one of Mara's kittens!" he said to his wife: "will you give it something and put it out? she may want it!"

The woman took it from him gently, gave it a little piece of bread, and went out with it, closing the door behind her.

"How then am I to make use of your hospitality?" I asked.

"By accepting it to the full," he answered.

"I do not understand."

"In this house no one wakes of himself."

"Why?"

"Because no one anywhere ever wakes of himself. You can wake yourself no more than you can make yourself."

"Then perhaps you or Mrs. Raven would kindly call me!" I said, still nowise understanding, but feeling afresh that vague foreboding.

"We cannot."

"How dare I then go to sleep?" I cried.

"If you would have the rest of this house, you must not trouble yourself about waking. You must go to sleep heartily, altogether and outright." My soul sank within me.

The sexton sat looking me in the face. His eyes seemed to say, "Will you not trust me?" I returned his gaze, and answered,

"I will."

"Then come," he said; "I will show you your couch."

As we rose, the woman came in. She took up the candle, turned to the inner door, and led the way. I went close behind her, and the sexton followed.

7. THE CEMETERY

The air as of an ice-house met me crossing the threshold. The door fell-to behind us. The sexton said something to his wife that made her turn toward us. — What a change had passed upon her! It was as if the splendor of her eyes had grown too much for them to hold, and, sinking into her countenance, made it flash with a loveliness like that of Beatrice in the white rose of the redeemed. Life itself, life eternal, immortal, streamed from it, an unbroken lightning. Even her hands shone with a white radiance, every "pearl-shell helmet" gleaming like a moonstone. Her beauty was overpowering; I was glad when she turned it from me.

But the light of the candle reached such a little way, that at first I could see nothing of the place. Presently, however, it fell on something that glimmered, a little raised from the floor. Was it a bed? Could live thing sleep in such a mortal cold? Then surely it was no wonder it should not wake of itself! Beyond that appeared a fainter shine; and then I thought I descried uncertain gleams on every side.

A few paces brought us to the first; it was a human form under a sheet, straight and still — whether of man or woman I could not tell, for the light seemed to avoid the face as we passed.

I soon perceived that we were walking along an aisle of couches, on almost every one of which, with its head to the passage, lay something asleep or dead, covered with a sheet white as snow. My soul grew silent with dread. Through aisle after aisle we went, among couches innumerable. I could see only a few of them at once, but they were on all sides, vanishing, as it seemed, in the infinite. — Was it here lay my choice of a bed? Must I go to sleep among the unwaking, with no one to rouse me? Was this the sexton's library? were these his books? Truly it was no half-way house, this chamber of the dead!

"One of the cellars I am placed to watch!" remarked Mr. Raven — in a low voice, as if fearing to disturb his silent guests. "Much wine is set here to ripen! — But it is dark for a stranger!" he added.

"The moon is rising; she will soon be here," said his wife, and her clear voice, low and sweet, sounded of ancient sorrow long bidden adieu.

Even as she spoke the moon looked in at an opening in the wall, and a thousand gleams of white responded to her shine. But not yet could I descry beginning or end of the couches. They stretched away and away, as if for all the disparted world to sleep upon. For along the far receding narrow ways, every couch stood by itself, and on each slept a lonely sleeper. I thought at first their sleep was death, but I soon saw it was something deeper still — a something I did not know.

The moon rose higher, and shone through other openings, but I could never see enough of the place at once to know its shape or character; now it would resemble a long cathedral nave, now a huge barn made into a dwelling of tombs. She looked colder than any moon in the frostiest night of the world, and where she shone direct upon them, cast a bluish, icy gleam on the white sheets and the pallid countenances — but it might be the faces that made the moon so cold!

Of such as I could see, all were alike in the brotherhood of death, all unlike in the character and history recorded upon them. Here lay a man who had died — for although this was not death, I have no other name to give it — in the prime of manly strength; his dark beard seemed to flow like a liberated stream from the glacier of his frozen countenance; his forehead was smooth as polished marble; a shadow of pain lingered about his lips, but only a shadow. On the next couch lay the form of a girl, passing lovely to behold. The sadness left on her face by parting was not yet absorbed in perfect peace, but absolute submission possessed the placid features, which bore no sign of wasting disease, of "killing care or grief of heart": if pain had been there, it was long charmed asleep, never again to wake. Many were the beautiful that there lay very still — some of them mere children; but I did not see one infant. The most beautiful of all was a lady whose white hair, and that alone, suggested her old when first she fell asleep. On her stately countenance rested — not submission, but a right noble acquiescence, an assurance, firm as the foundations of the universe, that all was as it should be. On some faces lingered the almost obliterated scars of strife, the marrings of hopeless loss, the fading shadows of sorrows that had seemed inconsolable: the aurora of the great morning had not yet quite melted them away; but those faces were few, and every one that bore such brand of pain seemed to plead, "Pardon me: I died only yesterday!" or, "Pardon me: I died but a century ago!" That some had been dead for ages I knew, not merely by their unutterable repose, but by something for which I have neither word nor symbol.

We came at last to three empty couches, immediately beyond which lay the form of a beautiful woman, a little past the prime of life. One of her arms was outside the sheet, and her hand lay with the palm upward, in its centre a dark spot. Next to her was the stalwart figure of a man of middle age. His arm too was outside the sheet, the strong hand almost closed, as if clenched on the grip of a sword. I thought he must be a king who had died fighting for the truth.

"Will you hold the candle nearer, wife?" whispered the sexton, bending down to examine the woman's hand.

"It heals well," he murmured to himself: "the nail found in her nothing to hurt!"

At last I ventured to speak.

"Are they not dead?" I asked softly.

"I cannot answer you," he replied in a subdued voice. "I almost forget what they mean by DEAD in the old world. If I said a person was dead, my wife would understand one thing, and you would imagine another. — This is but one of my treasure vaults," he went on, "and all my guests are not laid in vaults: out there on the moor they lie thick as the leaves of a forest after the first blast of your winter — thick, let me say rather, as if the great white rose of heaven had shed its petals over it. All night the moon reads their faces, and smiles."

"But why leave them in the corrupting moonlight?" I asked.

"Our moon," he answered, "is not like yours—the old cinder of a burnt-out world; her beams embalm the dead, not corrupt them. You observe that here the sexton lays his dead on the earth; he buries very few under it! In your world he lays huge stones on them, as if to keep them down; I watch for the hour to ring the resurrection-bell, and wake those that are still asleep. Your sexton looks at the clock to know when to ring the dead-alive to church; I hearken for the cock on the spire to crow; `AWAKE, THOU THAT SLEEPEST, AND ARISE FROM THE DEAD!'"

I began to conclude that the self-styled sexton was in truth an insane parson: the whole thing was too mad! But how was I to get away from it? I was helpless! In this world of the dead, the raven and his wife were the only living I had yet seen: whither should I turn for help? I was lost in a space larger than imagination; for if here two things, or any parts of them, could occupy the same space, why not twenty or ten thousand? — But I dared not think further in that direction.

"You seem in your dead to see differences beyond my perception!" I ventured to remark.

"None of those you see," he answered, "are in truth quite dead yet, and some have but just begun to come alive and die. Others had begun to die, that is to come alive, long before they came to us; and when such are indeed dead, that instant they will wake and leave us. Almost every night some rise and go. But I will not say more, for I find my words only mislead you! — This is the couch that has been waiting for you," he ended, pointing to one of the three.

"Why just this?" I said, beginning to tremble, and anxious by parley to delay.

"For reasons which one day you will be glad to know," he answered.

"Why not know them now?"

"That also you will know when you wake."

"But these are all dead, and I am alive!" I objected, shuddering.

"Not much," rejoined the sexton with a smile, "— not nearly enough! Blessed be the true life that the pauses between its throbs are not death!"

"The place is too cold to let one sleep!" I said.

"Do these find it so?" he returned. "They sleep well — or will soon. Of cold they feel not a breath: it heals their wounds. — Do not be a coward, Mr. Vane. Turn your back on fear, and your face to whatever may come. Give yourself up to the night, and you will rest indeed. Harm will not come to you, but a good you cannot foreknow."

The sexton and I stood by the side of the couch, his wife, with the candle in her hand, at the foot of it. Her eyes were full of light, but her face was again of a still whiteness; it was no longer radiant.

"Would they have me make of a charnel-house my bed-chamber?" I cried aloud. "I will not. I will lie abroad on the heath; it cannot be colder there!"

"I have just told you that the dead are there also,

'Thick as autumnal leaves that strow the brooks In Vallombrosa,' said the librarian.

"I will NOT," I cried again; and in the compassing dark, the two gleamed out like spectres that waited on the dead; neither answered me; each stood still and sad, and looked at the other.

"Be of good comfort; we watch the flock of the great shepherd," said the sexton to his wife.

Then he turned to me.

"Didst thou not find the air of the place pure and sweet when thou enteredst it?" he asked.

"Yes; but oh, so cold!" I answered.

"Then know," he returned, and his voice was stern, "that thou who callest thyself alive, hast brought into this chamber the odors of death, and its air will not be wholesome for the sleepers until thou art gone from it!"

They went farther into the great chamber, and I was left alone in the moonlight with the dead.

I turned to escape.

What a long way I found it back through the dead! At first I was too angry to be afraid, but as I grew calm, the still shapes grew terrible. At last, with loud offence to the gracious silence, I ran, I fled wildly, and, bursting out, flung-to the door behind me. It closed with an awful silence.

I stood in pitch-darkness. Feeling about me, I found a door, opened it, and was aware of the dim light of a lamp. I stood in my library, with the handle of the masked door in my hand.

Had I come to myself out of a vision? — or lost myself by going back to one? Which was the real — what I now saw, or what I had just ceased to see? Could both be real, interpenetrating yet unmingling?

I threw myself on a couch, and fell asleep.

In the library was one small window to the east, through which, at this time of the year, the first rays of the sun shone upon a mirror whence they were reflected on the masked door: when I woke, there they shone, and thither they drew my eyes. With the feeling that behind it must lie the boundless chamber I had left by that door, I sprang to my feet, and opened it. The light, like an eager hound, shot before me into the closet, and pounced upon the gilded edges of a large book.

"What idiot," I cried, "has put that book in the shelf the wrong way?"

But the gilded edges, reflecting the light a second time, flung it on a nest of drawers in a dark corner, and I saw that one of them was half open.

"More meddling!" I cried, and went to close the drawer.

It contained old papers, and seemed more than full, for it would not close. Taking the topmost one out, I perceived that it was in my father's writing and of some length. The words on which first my eyes fell, at once made me eager to learn what it contained. I carried it to the library, sat down in one of the western windows, and read what follows.

8. MY FATHER'S MANUSCRIPT

I am filled with awe of what I have to write. The sun is shining golden above me; the sea lies blue beneath his gaze; the same world sends its growing things up to the sun, and its flying things into the air which I have breathed from my infancy; but I know the outspread splendor a passing show, and that at any moment it may, like the drop-scene of a stage, be lifted to reveal more wonderful things.

Shortly after my father's death, I was seated one morning in the library. I had been, somewhat listlessly, regarding the portrait that hangs among the books, which I knew only as that of a distant ancestor, and wishing I could learn something of its original. Then I had taken a book from the shelves and begun to read.

Glancing up from it, I saw coming toward me — not between me and the door, but between me and the portrait — a thin pale man in rusty black. He looked sharp and eager, and had a notable nose, at once reminding me of a certain jug my sisters used to call Mr. Crow.

"Finding myself in your vicinity, Mr. Vane, I have given myself the pleasure of calling," he said, in a peculiar but not disagreeable voice. "Your honored grandfather treated me — I may say it without presumption — as a friend, having known me from childhood as his father's librarian."

It did not strike me at the time how old the man must be.

"May I ask where you live now, Mr. Crow?" I said.

He smiled an amused smile.

"You nearly hit my name," he rejoined, "which shows the family insight. You have seen me before, but only once, and could not then have heard it!"

"Where was that?"

"In this very room. You were quite a child, however!"

I could not be sure that I remembered him, but for a moment I fancied I did, and I begged him to set me right as to his name.

"There is such a thing as remembering without recognizing the memory in it," he remarked. "For my name — which you have near enough — it used to be Raven."

I had heard the name, for marvelous tales had brought it me.

"It is very kind of you to come and see me," I said. "Will you not sit down?"

He seated himself at once.

"You knew my father, then, I presume?"

"I knew him," he answered with a curious smile, "but he did not care about my acquaintance, and we never met. — That gentleman, however," he added, pointing to the portrait, — "old Sir Up'ard, his people called him, — was in his day a friend of mine yet more intimate than ever your grandfather became."

Then at length I began to think the interview a strange one. But in truth it was hardly stranger that my visitor should remember Sir Upward, than that he should have been my great-grandfather's librarian!

"I owe him much," he continued; "for, although I had read many more books than he, yet, through the special direction of his studies, he was able to inform me of a certain relation of modes which I should never have discovered of myself, and could hardly have learned from any one else."

"Would you mind telling me all about that?" I said.

"By no means — as much at least as I am able: there are not such things as willful secrets," he answered — and went on.

"That closet held his library — a hundred manuscripts or so, for printing was not then invented. One morning I sat there, working at a catalogue of them, when he looked in at the door, and said, `Come.' I laid down my pen and followed him — across the great hall, down a steep rough descent, and along an underground passage to a tower he had lately built, consisting of a stair and a room at the top of it. The door of this room had a tremendous lock, which he undid with the smallest key I ever saw. I had scarcely crossed the threshold after him, when, to my eyes, he began to dwindle, and grew less and less. All at once my vision seemed to come right, and I saw that he was moving swiftly away from me. In a minute more he was the merest speck in the distance, with the tops of blue mountains beyond him, clear against a sky of paler blue. I recognized the country, for I had gone there and come again many a time, although I had never known this way to it.

"Many years after, when the tower had long disappeared, I taught one of his descendants what Sir Upward had taught me; and now and then to this day I use your house when I want to go the nearest way home. I must indeed — without your leave, for which I ask your pardon — have by this time well established a right of way through it—not from front to back, but from bottom to top!"

"You would have me then understand, Mr. Raven," I said, "that you go through my house into another world, heedless of disparting space?"

"That I go through it is an incontrovertible acknowledgement of space," returned the old librarian.

"Please do not quibble, Mr. Raven," I rejoined. "Please to take my question as you know I mean it."

"There is in your house a door, one step through which carries me into a world very much another than this."

"A better?"

"Not throughout; but so much another that most of its physical, and many of its mental laws are different from those of this world. As for moral laws, they must everywhere be fundamentally the same."

"You try my power of belief!" I said.

"You take me for a madman, probably?"

"You do not look like one."

"A liar then?"

"You give me no ground to think you such."

"Only you do not believe me?"

"I will go out of that door with you if you like: I believe in you enough to risk the attempt."

"The blunder all my children make!" he murmured. "The only door out is the door in!"

I began to think he must be crazy. He sat silent for a moment, his head resting on his hand, his elbow on the table, and his eyes on the books before him.

"A book," he said louder, "is a door in, and therefore a door out. — I see old Sir Up'ard," he went on, closing his eyes, "and my heart swells with love to him: — what world is he in?"

"The world of your heart!" I replied; "— that is, the idea of him is there."

"There is one world then at least on which your hall-door does not open?"

"I grant you so much; but the things in that world are not things to have and to hold."

"Think a little farther," he rejoined: "did anything ever become yours, except by getting into that world? — The thought is beyond you, however, at present!—I tell you there are more worlds, and more doors to them, than you will think of in many years!"

He rose, left the library, crossed the hall, and went straight up to the garret, familiar evidently with every turn. I followed, studying his back. His hair hung down long and dark, straight and glossy. His coat was wide and reached to his heels. His shoes seemed too large for him.

In the garret a light came through at the edges of the great roofing slabs, and showed us parts where was no flooring, and we must step from joist to joist: in the middle of one of these spaces rose a partition, with a door: through it I followed Mr. Raven into a small, obscure chamber, whose top contracted as it rose, and went slanting through the roof.

"That is the door I spoke of," he said, pointing to an oblong mirror that stood on the floor and leaned against the wall. I went in front of it, and saw our figures dimly reflected in its dusty face. There was something about it that made me uneasy. It looked old-fashioned and neglected, but, notwithstanding its ordinary seeming, the eagle, perched with outstretched wings on the top, appeared threatful.

"As a mirror," said the librarian, "it has grown dingy with age; but that is no matter: its doorness depends on the light."

"Light!" I rejoined; "there is no light here!"

He did not answer me, but began to pull at a little chain on the opposite wall. I heard a creaking: the top of the chamber was turning slowly round. He ceased pulling, looked at his watch, and began to pull again.

"We arrive almost to the moment!" he said; "it is on the very stroke of noon!"

The top went creaking and revolving for a minute or so. Then he pulled two other chains, now this, now that, and returned to the first. A moment more and the chamber grew much clearer: a patch of sunlight had fallen upon a mirror on the wall opposite that against which the other leaned, and on the dust I saw the path of the reflected rays to the mirror on the ground. But from the latter none were returned; they seemed to go clean through; there was nowhere in the chamber a second patch of light!

"Where are the sunrays gone?" I cried.

"That I cannot tell," returned Mr. Raven; "—back, perhaps, to where they came from first. They now belong, I fancy, to a sense not yet developed in us."

He then talked of the relations of mind to matter, and of senses to qualities, in a way I could only a little understand, whence he went on to yet stranger things which I could not at all comprehend. He spoke much about dimensions, telling me that there were many more than three, some of them concerned with powers which were indeed in us, but of which as yet we knew absolutely nothing. His words, however, I confess, took little more hold of me than the light did of the mirror, for I thought he hardly knew what he was saying.

Suddenly I was aware that our forms had gone from the mirror, which seemed full of a white mist. As I gazed I saw, growing gradually visible beyond the mist, the tops of a range of mountains, which became clearer and clearer. Soon the mist vanished entirely, uncovering the face of a wide heath, on which, at some distance, was the figure of a man moving swiftly away. I turned to address my companion; he was no longer by my side. I looked again at the form in the mirror, and recognized the wide coat flying, the black hair lifting in a wind that did not touch me. I rushed in terror from the place.

9. I REPENT

I laid the manuscript down, consoled to find that my father had had a peep into that mysterious world, and that he knew Mr. Raven.

Then I remembered that I had never heard the cause or any circumstance of my father's death, and began to believe that he must at last have followed Mr. Raven, and not come back; whereupon I speedily grew ashamed of my flight. What wondrous facts might I not by this time have gathered concerning life and death, and wide regions beyond ordinary perception! Assuredly the Ravens were good people, and a night in their house would nowise have hurt me! They were doubtless strange, but it was faculty in which the one was peculiar, and beauty in which the other was marvelous! And I had not believed in them! had treated them as unworthy of my confidence, as harboring a design against me! The more I thought of my behavior to them, the more disgusted I became with myself. Why should I have feared such dead? To share their holy rest was an honor of which I had proved myself unworthy! What harm could that sleeping king, that lady with the wound in her palm, have done me? I fell a longing after the sweet and stately stillness of their two countenances, and wept. Weeping I threw myself on a couch, and suddenly fell asleep.

As suddenly I woke, feeling as if some one had called me. The house was still as an empty church. A blackbird was singing on the lawn. I said to myself, "I will go and tell them I am ashamed, and will do whatever they would have me do!" I rose, and went straight up the stairs to the garret.

The wooden chamber was just as when first I saw it, the mirror dimly reflecting everything before it. It was nearly noon, and the sun would be a little higher than when first I came: I must raise the hood a little, and adjust the mirrors accordingly! If I had but been in time to see Mr. Raven do it!

I pulled the chains, and let the light fall on the first mirror. I turned then to the other: there were the shapes of the former vision — distinguishable indeed, but tremulous like a landscape in a pool ruffled by "a small pipling wind!" I touched the glass; it was impermeable.

Suspecting polarization as the thing required, I shifted and shifted the mirrors, changing their relation, until at last, in a great degree, so far as I was concerned, by chance, things came right between them, and I saw the mountains blue and steady and clear. I stepped forward, and my feet were among the heather.

All I knew of the way to the cottage was that we had gone through a pine-forest. I passed through many thickets and several small fir-woods, continually fancying afresh that I recognized something of the country; but I had come upon no forest, and now the sun was near the horizon, and the air had begun to grow chill with the coming winter, when, to my delight, I saw a little black object coming toward me: it was indeed the raven!

I hastened to meet him.

"I beg your pardon, sir, for my rudeness last night," I said. "Will you take me with you now? I heartily confess I do not deserve it."

"Ah!" he returned, and looked up. Then, after a brief pause, "My wife does not expect you to-night," he said. "She regrets that we at all encouraged your staying last week."

"Take me to her that I may tell her how sorry I am," I begged humbly.

"It is of no use," he answered. "Your night was not come then, or you would not have left us. It is not come now, and I cannot show you the way. The dead were rejoicing under their daisies – they all lie among the roots of the flowers of heaven — at the thought of your delight when the winter should be past, and the morning with its birds come: ere you left them, they shivered in their beds. When the spring of the universe arrives, — but that cannot be for ages yet! how many, I do not know—and do not care to know."

"Tell me one thing, I beg of you, Mr. Raven: is my father with you? Have you seen him since he left the world?"

"Yes; he is with us, fast asleep. That was he you saw with his arm on the coverlet, his hand half closed."

"Why did you not tell me? That I should have been so near him, and not know!"

"And turn your back on him!" corrected the raven.

"I would have lain down at once had I known!"

"I doubt it. Had you been ready to lie down, you would have known him! — Old Sir Up'ard," he went on, "and your twice great-grandfather, both are up and away long ago. Your great-grandfather has been with us for many a year; I think he will soon begin to stir. You saw him last night, though of course you did not know him."

"Why OF COURSE?"

"Because he is so much nearer waking than you. No one who will not sleep can ever wake."

"I do not at all understand you!"

"You turned away, and would not understand!" I held my peace. — But if I did not say something, he would go!

"And my grandfather — is he also with you?" I asked.

"No; he is still in the Evil Wood, fighting the dead."

"Where is the Evil Wood, that I may find him?"

"You will not find him; but you will hardly miss the wood. It is the place where those who will not sleep, wake up at night, to kill their dead and bury them."

"I cannot understand you!"

"Naturally not. Neither do I understand you; I can read neither your heart nor your face. When my wife and I do not understand our children, it is because there is not enough of them to be understood. God alone can understand foolishness."

"Then," I said, feeling naked and very worthless, "will you be so good as show me the nearest way home? There are more ways than one, I know, for I have gone by two already."

"There are indeed many ways."

"Tell me, please, how to recognize the nearest."

"I cannot," answered the raven; "you and I use the same words with different meanings. We are often unable to tell people what they NEED to know, because they WANT to know something else, and would therefore only misunderstand what we said. Home is ever so far away in the palm of your hand, and how to get there it is of no use to tell you. But you will get there; you must get there; you have to get there. Everybody who is not at home, has to go home. You thought you were at home where I found you: if that had been your home, you could not have left it. Nobody can leave home. And nobody ever was or ever will be at home without having gone there."

"Enigma treading on enigma!" I exclaimed. "I did not come here to be asked riddles."

"No; but you came, and found the riddles waiting for you! Indeed you are yourself the only riddle. What you call riddles are truths, and seem riddles because you are not true."

"Worse and worse!" I cried.

"And you MUST answer the riddles!" he continued. "They will go on asking themselves until you understand yourself. The universe is a riddle trying to get out, and you are holding your door hard against it."

"Will you not in pity tell me what I am to do — where I must go?"

"How should I tell YOUR to-do, or the way to it?"

"If I am not to go home, at least direct me to some of my kind."

"I do not know of any. The beings most like you are in that direction."

He pointed with his beak. I could see nothing but the setting sun, which blinded me.

"Well," I said bitterly, "I cannot help feeling hardly treated — taken from my home, abandoned in a strange world, and refused instruction as to where I am to go or what I am to do!"

"You forget," said the raven, "that, when I brought you and you declined my hospitality, you reached what you call home in safety: now you are come of yourself! Good night."

He turned and walked slowly away, with his beak toward the ground. I stood dazed. It was true I had come of myself, but had I not come with intent of atonement? My heart was sore, and in my brain was neither quest nor purpose, hope nor desire. I gazed after the raven, and would have followed him, but felt it useless.

All at once he pounced on a spot, throwing the whole weight of his body on his bill, and for some moments dug vigorously. Then with a flutter of his wings he threw back his head, and something shot from his bill, cast high in the air. That moment the sun set, and the air at once grew very dusk, but the something opened into a soft radiance, and came pulsing toward me like a fire-fly, but with a much larger and a yellower light. It flew over my head. I turned and followed it.

Here I interrupt my narrative to remark that it involves a constant struggle to say what cannot be said with even an approach to precision, the things recorded being, in their nature and in that of the creatures concerned in them, so inexpressibly different from any possible events of this economy, that I can present them only by giving, in the forms and language of life in this world, the modes in which they affected me — not the things themselves, but the feelings they woke in me. Even this much, however, I do with a continuous and abiding sense of failure, finding it impossible to present more than one phase of a multitudinously complicated significance, or one concentric sphere of a graduated embodiment. A single thing would sometimes seem to be and mean many things, with an uncertain identity at the heart of them, which kept constantly altering their look. I am indeed often driven to set down what I know to be but a clumsy and doubtful representation of the mere feeling aimed at, none of the communicating media of this world being fit to convey it, in its peculiar strangeness, with even an approach to clearness or certainty. Even to one who knew the region better than myself, I should have no assurance of transmitting the reality of my experience in it. While without a doubt, for instance, that I was actually regarding a scene of activity, I might be, at the same moment, in my consciousness aware that I was perusing a metaphysical argument.

10. The Bad Burrow

As the air grew black and the winter closed swiftly around me, the fluttering fire blazed out more luminous, and arresting its flight, hovered waiting. So soon as I came under its radiance, it flew slowly on, lingering now and then above spots where the ground was rocky. Every time I looked up, it seemed to have grown larger, and at length gave me an attendant shadow. Plainly a bird-butterfly, it flew with a certain swallowy double. Its wings were very large, nearly square, and flashed all the colors of the rainbow. Wondering at their splendor, I became so absorbed in their beauty that I stumbled over a low rock, and lay stunned. When I came to myself, the creature was hovering over my head, radiating the whole chord of light, with multitudinous gradations and some kinds of color I had never before seen. I rose and went on, but, unable to take my eyes off the shining thing to look to my steps, I struck my foot against a stone. Fearing then another fall, I sat down to watch the little glory, and a great longing awoke in me to have it in my hand. To my unspeakable delight, it began to sink toward me. Slowly at first, then swiftly it sank, growing larger as it came nearer. I felt as if the treasure of the universe were giving itself to me — put out my hand, and had it. But the instant I took it, its light went out; all was dark as pitch; a dead book with boards outspread lay cold and heavy in my hand. I threw it in the air — only to hear it fall among the heather. Burying my face in my hands, I sat in motionless misery.

But the cold grew so bitter that, fearing to be frozen, I got up. The moment I was on my feet, a faint sense of light awoke in me. "Is it coming to life?" I cried, and a great pang of hope shot through me. Alas, no! it was the edge of a moon peering up keen and sharp over a level horizon! She brought me light — but no guidance! SHE would not hover over me, would not wait on my faltering steps! She could but offer me an ignorant choice!

With a full face she rose, and I began to see a little about me. Westward of her, and not far from me, a range of low hills broke the horizon-line: I set out for it.

But what a night I had to pass ere I reached it! The moon seemed to know something, for she stared at me oddly. Her look was indeed icy-cold, but full of interest, or at least curiosity. She was not the same moon I had known on the earth; her face was strange to me, and her light yet stranger. Perhaps it came from an unknown sun! Every time I looked up, I found her staring at me with all her might! At first I was annoyed, as at the rudeness of a fellow creature; but soon I saw or fancied a certain wondering pity in her gaze: why was I out in her night? Then first I knew what an awful thing it was to be awake in the universe: I WAS, and could not help it!

As I walked, my feet lost the heather, and trod a bare spongy soil, something like dry, powdery peat. To my dismay it gave a momentary heave under me; then presently I saw what seemed the ripple of an earthquake running on before me, shadowy in the low moon. It passed into the distance; but, while yet I stared after it, a single wave rose up, and came slowly toward me. A yard or two away it burst, and from it, with a scramble and a bound, issued an animal like a tiger. About his mouth and ears hung clots of mould, and his eyes winked and flamed as he rushed at me, showing his white teeth in a soundless snarl. I stood fascinated, unconscious of either courage or fear. He turned his head to the ground, and plunged into it.

"That moon is affecting my brain," I said as I resumed my journey. "What life can be here but the phantasmic — the stuff of which dreams are made? I am indeed walking in a vain show!"

Thus I strove to keep my heart above the waters of fear, nor knew that she whom I distrusted was indeed my defense from the realities I took for phantoms: her light controlled the monsters, else had I scarce taken a second step on the hideous ground. "I will not be appalled by that which only seems!" I said to myself, yet felt it a terrible thing to walk on a sea where such fishes disported themselves below. With that, a step or two from me, the head of a worm began to come slowly out of the earth, as big as that of a polar bear and much resembling it, with a white mane to its red neck. The drawing wriggles with which its huge length extricated itself were horrible, yet I dared not turn my eyes from them. The moment its tail was free, it lay as if exhausted, wallowing in feeble effort to burrow again.

"Does it live on the dead," I wondered, "and is it unable to hurt the living? If they scent their prey and come out, why do they leave me unharmed?"

I know now it was that the moon paralyzed them.

All the night through as I walked, hideous creatures, no two alike, threatened me. In some of them, beauty of color enhanced loathliness of shape: one large serpent was covered from head to distant tail with feathers of glorious hues.

I became at length so accustomed to their hurtless menaces that I fell to beguiling the way with the invention of monstrosities, never suspecting that I owed each moment of life to the staring moon. Though hers was no primal radiance, it so hampered the evil things, that I walked in safety. For light is yet light, if but the last of a countless series of reflections! How swiftly would not my feet have carried me over the restless soil, had I known that, if still within their range when her lamp ceased to shine on the cursed spot, I should that moment be at the mercy of such as had no mercy, the centre of a writhing heap of hideousness, every individual of it as terrible as before it had but seemed! Fool of ignorance, I watched the descent of the weary, solemn, anxious moon down the widening vault above me, with no worse uneasiness than the dread of losing my way — where as yet I had indeed no way to lose.

I was drawing near the hills I had made my goal, and she was now not far from their sky-line, when the soundless wallowing ceased, and the burrow lay motionless and bare. Then I saw, slowly walking over the light soil, the form of a woman. A white mist floated about her, now assuming, now losing to reassume the shape of a garment, as it gathered to her or was blown from her by a wind that dogged her steps.

She was beautiful, but with such a pride at once and misery on her countenance that I could hardly believe what yet I saw. Up and down she walked, vainly endeavoring to lay hold of the mist and wrap it around her. The eyes in the beautiful face were dead, and on her left side was a dark spot, against which she would now and then press her hand, as if to stifle pain or sickness. Her hair hung nearly to her feet, and sometimes the wind would so mix it with the mist that I could not distinguish the one from the other; but when it fell gathering together again, it shone a pale gold in the moonlight.

Suddenly pressing both hands on her heart, she fell to the ground, and the mist rose from her and melted in the air. I ran to her. But she began to writhe in such torture that I stood aghast. A moment more and her legs, hurrying from her body, sped away serpents. From her shoulders fled her arms as in terror, serpents also. Then something flew up from her like a bat, and when I looked again, she was gone. The ground rose like the sea in a storm; terror laid hold upon me; I turned to the hills and ran.

I was already on the slope of their base, when the moon sank behind one of their summits, leaving me in its shadow. Behind me rose a waste and sickening cry, as of frustrate desire — the only sound I had heard since the fall of the dead butterfly; it made my heart shake like a flag in the wind. I turned, saw many dark objects bounding after me, and made for the crest of a ridge on which the moon still shone. She seemed to linger there that I might see to defend myself. Soon I came in sight of her, and climbed the faster.

Crossing the shadow of a rock, I heard the creatures panting at my heels. But just as the foremost threw himself upon me with a snarl of greedy hate, we rushed into the moon together. She flashed out an angry light, and he fell from me a bodiless blotch. Strength came to me, and I turned on the rest. But one by one as they darted into the light, they dropped with a howl; and I saw or fancied a strange smile on the round face above me.

I climbed to the top of the ridge: far away shone the moon, sinking to a low horizon. The air was pure and strong. I descended a little way, found it warmer, and sat down to wait the dawn.

The moon went below, and the world again was dark.

11. THE EVIL WOOD

I fell fast asleep, and when I woke the sun was rising. I went to the top again, and looked back: the hollow I had crossed in the moonlight lay without sign of life. Could it be that the calm expanse before me swarmed with creatures of devouring greed?

I turned and looked over the land through which my way must lie. It seemed a wide desert, with a patch of a different color in the distance that might be a forest. Sign of presence, human or animal, was none—smoke or dust or shadow of cultivation. Not a cloud floated in the clear heaven; no thinnest haze curtained any segment of its circling rim.

I descended, and set out for the imaginable forest: something alive might be there; on this side of it could not well be anything!

When I reached the plain, I found it, as far as my sight could go, of rock, here flat and channeled, there humped and pinnacled — evidently the wide bed of a vanished river, scored by innumerable water-runs, without a trace of moisture in them. Some of the channels bore a dry moss, and some of the rocks a few lichens almost as hard as themselves. The air, once "filled with pleasant noise of waters," was silent as death. It took me the whole day to reach the patch, — which I found indeed a forest—but not a rudiment of brook or runnel had I crossed! Yet through the glowing noon I seemed haunted by an aural mirage, hearing so plainly the voice of many waters that I could hardly believe the opposing testimony of my eyes.

The sun was approaching the horizon when I left the river-bed, and entered the forest. Sunk below the tree-tops, and sending his rays between their pillar-like boles, he revealed a world of blessed shadows waiting to receive me. I had expected a pine-wood, but here were trees of many sorts, some with strong resemblances to trees I knew, others with marvelous differences from any I had ever seen. I threw myself beneath the boughs of what seemed a eucalyptus in blossom: its flowers had a hard calyx much resembling a skull, the top of which rose like a lid to let the froth-like bloom-brain overfoam its cup. From beneath the shadow of its falchion-leaves my eyes went wandering into deep after deep of the forest.

Soon, however, its doors and windows began to close, shutting up aisle and corridor and roomier glade. The night was about me, and instant and sharp the cold. Again what a night I found it! How shall I make my reader share with me its wild ghostiness?

The tree under which I lay rose high before it branched, but the boughs of it bent so low that they seemed ready to shut me in as I leaned against the smooth stem, and let my eyes wander through the brief twilight of the vanishing forest. Presently, to my listless roving gaze, the varied outlines of the clumpy foliage began to assume or imitate — say rather SUGGEST other shapes than their own. A light wind began to blow; it set the boughs of a neighbor tree rocking, and all their branches a swing, every twig and every leaf blending its individual motion with the sway of its branch and the rock of its bough. Among its leafy shapes was a pack of wolves that struggled to break from a wizard's leash: greyhounds would not have strained so savagely! I watched them with an interest that grew as the wind gathered force, and their motions life.

Another mass of foliage, larger and more compact, presented my fancy with a group of horses' heads and forequarters projecting caparisoned from their stalls. Their necks kept moving up and down, with an impatience that augmented as the growing wind broke their vertical rhythm with a wilder swaying from side to side. What heads they were! how gaunt, how strange! — several of them bare skulls — one with the skin tight on its bones! One had lost the under jaw and hung low, looking unutterably weary — but now and then hove high as if to ease the bit. Above them, at the end of a branch, floated erect the form of a woman, waving her arms in imperious gesture. The definiteness of these and other leaf masses first surprised and then discomposed me: what if they should overpower my brain with seeming reality? But the twilight became darkness; the wind ceased; every shape was shut up in the night; I fell asleep.

It was still dark when I began to be aware of a far-off, confused, rushing noise, mingled with faint cries. It grew and grew until a tumult as of gathering multitudes filled the wood. On all sides at once the sounds drew nearer; the spot where I lay seemed the centre of a commotion that extended throughout the forest. I scarce moved hand or foot lest I should betray my presence to hostile things.

The moon at length approached the forest, and came slowly into it: with her first gleam the noises increased to a deafening uproar, and I began to see dim shapes about me. As she ascended and grew brighter, the noises became yet louder, and the shapes clearer. A furious battle was raging around me. Wild cries and roars of rage, shock of onset, struggle prolonged, all mingled with words articulate, surged in my ears. Curses and credos, snarls and sneers, laughter and mockery, sacred names and howls of hate, came huddling in chaotic interpenetration. Skeletons and phantoms fought in maddest confusion. Swords swept through the phantoms: they only shivered. Maces crashed on the skeletons, shattering them hideously: not one fell or ceased to fight, so long as a single joint held two bones together. Bones of men and horses lay scattered and heaped; grinding and crunching them under foot fought the skeletons. Everywhere charged the bone-gaunt white steeds; everywhere on foot or on wind-blown misty battle-horses, raged and ravened and raved the indestructible spectres; weapons and hoofs clashed and crushed; while skeleton jaws and phantom-throats swelled the deafening tumult with the war-cry of every opinion, bad or good, that had bred strife, injustice, cruelty in any world. The holiest words went with the most hating blow. Lie-distorted truths flew hurtling in the wind of javelins and bones. Every moment some one would turn against his comrades, and fight more wildly than before, THE TRUTH! THE TRUTH! still his cry. One I noted who wheeled ever in a circle, and smote on all sides. Wearied out, a pair would sit for a minute side by side, then rise and renew the fierce combat. None stooped to comfort the fallen, or stepped wide to spare him.

The moon shone till the sun rose, and all the night long I had glimpses of a woman moving at her will above the strife-tormented multitude, now on this front now on that, one outstretched arm urging the fight, the other pressed against her side. "Ye are men: slay one another!" she shouted. I saw her dead eyes and her dark spot, and recalled what I had seen the night before.

Such was the battle of the dead, which I saw and heard as I lay under the tree.

Just before sunrise, a breeze went through the forest, and a voice cried, "Let the dead bury their dead!" At the word the contending thousands dropped noiseless, and when the sun looked in, he saw never a bone, but here and there a withered branch.

I rose and resumed my journey, through as quiet a wood as ever grew out of the quiet earth. For the wind of the morning had ceased when the sun appeared, and the trees were silent. Not a bird sang, not a squirrel, mouse, or weasel showed itself, not a belated moth flew athwart my path. But as I went I kept watch over myself, nor dared let my eyes rest on any forest-shape. All the time I seemed to hear faint sounds of mattock and spade and hurtling bones: any moment my eyes might open on things I would not see! Daylight prudence muttered that perhaps, to appear, ten thousand phantoms awaited only my consenting fancy.

In the middle of the afternoon I came out of the wood — to find before me a second net of dry water-courses. I thought at first that I had wandered from my attempted line, and reversed my direction; but I soon saw it was not so, and concluded presently that I had come to another branch of the same river-bed. I began at once to cross it, and was in the bottom of a wide channel when the sun set.

I sat down to await the moon, and growing sleepy, stretched myself on the moss. The moment my head was down, I heard the sounds of rushing streams—all sorts of sweet watery noises. The veiled melody of the molten music sang me into a dreamless sleep, and when I woke the sun was already up, and the wrinkled country widely visible. Covered with shadows it lay striped and mottled like the skin of some wild animal. As the sun rose the shadows diminished, and it seemed as if the rocks were re-absorbing the darkness that had oozed out of them during the night.

Hitherto I had loved my Arab mare and my books more, I fear, than live man or woman; now at length my soul was athirst for a human presence, and I longed even after those inhabitants of this alien world whom the raven had so vaguely described as nearest my sort. With heavy yet hoping heart, and mind haunted by a doubt whether I was going in any direction at all, I kept wearily traveling "north-west and by south."

12. Friends And Foes

Coming, in one of the channels, upon what seemed a little shrub, the outlying picket, I trusted, of an army behind it, I knelt to look at it closer. It bore a small fruit, which, as I did not recognize it, I feared to gather and eat. Little I thought that I was watched from behind the rocks by hundreds of eyes eager with the question whether I would or would not take it.

I came to another plant somewhat bigger, then to another larger still, and at length to clumps of a like sort; by which time I saw that they were not shrubs but dwarf-trees. Before I reached the bank of this second branch of the river-bed, I found the channels so full of them that it was with difficulty I crossed such as I could not jump. In one I heard a great rush, as of a multitude of birds from an ivied wall, but saw nothing.

I came next to some large fruit-bearing trees, but what they bore looked coarse. They stood on the edge of a hollow, which evidently had once been the basin of a lake. From the left a forest seemed to flow into and fill it; but while the trees above were of many sorts, those in the hollow were almost entirely fruit-bearing.

I went a few yards down the slope of grass mingled with moss, and stretched myself upon it weary. A little farther down stood a tiny tree full of rosiest apples no bigger than small cherries, its top close to my hand; I pulled and ate one of them. Finding it delicious, I was in the act of taking another, when a sudden shouting of children, mingled with laughter clear and sweet as the music of a brook, startled me with delight.

"He likes our apples! He likes our apples! He's a good giant! He's a good giant!" cried many little voices.

"He's a giant!" objected one.

"He is rather big," assented another, "but littleness isn't everything! It won't keep you from growing big and stupid except you take care!"

I rose on my elbow and stared. Above and about and below me stood a multitude of children, apparently of all ages, some just able to run alone, and some about twelve or thirteen. Three or four seemed older. They stood in a small knot, a little apart, and were less excited than the rest. The many were chattering in groups, declaiming and contradicting, like a crowd of grown people in a city, only with greater merriment, better manners, and more sense.

I gathered that, by the approach of my hand to a second apple, they knew that I liked the first; but how from that they argued me good, I did not see, nor wondered that one of them at least should suggest caution. I did not open my mouth, for I was afraid of frightening them, and sure I should learn more by listening than by asking questions. For I understood nearly all they said — at which I was not surprised: to understand is not more wonderful than to love.

There came a movement and slight dispersion among them, and presently a sweet, innocent-looking, lovingly roguish little fellow handed me a huge green apple. Silence fell on the noisy throng; all waited expectant.

"Eat, good giant," he said.

I sat up, took the apple, smiled thanks, and would have eaten; but the moment I bit into it, I flung it far away.

Again rose a shout of delight; they flung themselves upon me, so as nearly to smother me; they kissed my face and hands; they laid hold of my legs; they clambered about my arms and shoulders, embracing my head and neck. I came to the ground at last, overwhelmed with the lovely little goblins.

"Good, good giant!" they cried. "We knew you would come! Oh you dear, good, strong giant!"

The babble of their talk sprang up afresh, and ever the jubilant shout would rise anew from hundreds of clear little throats.

Again came a sudden silence. Those around me drew back; those atop of me got off and began trying to set me on my feet. Upon their sweet faces, concern had taken the place of merriment.

"Get up, good giant!" said a little girl. "Make haste! much haste! He saw you throw his apple away!"

Before she ended, I was on my feet. She stood pointing up the slope. On the brow of it was a clownish, bad-looking fellow, a few inches taller than myself. He looked hostile, but I saw no reason to fear him, for he had no weapon, and my little friends had vanished every one.

He began to descend, and I, in the hope of better footing and position, to go up. He growled like a beast as he turned toward me.

Reaching a more level spot, I stood and waited for him. As he came near, he held out his hand. I would have taken it in friendly fashion, but he drew it back, threatened a blow, and held it out again. Then I understood him to claim the apple I had flung away, whereupon I made a grimace of dislike and a gesture of rejection.

He answered with a howl of rage that seemed to say, "Do you dare tell me my apple was not fit to eat?"

"One bad apple may grow on the best tree," I said.

Whether he perceived my meaning I cannot tell, but he made a stride nearer, and I stood on my guard. He delayed his assault, however, until a second giant, much like him, who had been stealing up behind me, was close enough, when he rushed upon me. I met him with a good blow in the face, but the other struck me on the back of the head, and between them I was soon overpowered.

They dragged me into the wood above the valley, where their tribe lived — in wretched huts, built of fallen branches and a few stones. Into one of these they pushed me, there threw me on the ground, and kicked me. A woman was present, who looked on with indifference.

I may here mention that during my captivity I hardly learned to distinguish the women from the men, they differed so little. Often I wondered whether I had not come upon a sort of fungoid people, with just enough mind to give them motion and the expressions of anger and greed. Their food, which consisted of tubers, bulbs, and fruits, was to me inexpressibly disagreeable, but nothing offended them so much as to show dislike to it. I was cuffed by the women and kicked by the men because I would not swallow it.

I lay on the floor that night hardly able to move, but I slept a good deal, and woke a little refreshed. In the morning they dragged me to the valley, and tying my feet, with a long rope, to a tree, put a flat stone with a saw-like edge in my left hand. I shifted it to the right; they kicked me, and put it again in the left; gave me to understand that I was to scrape the bark off every branch that had no fruit on it; kicked me once more, and left me.

I set about the dreary work in the hope that by satisfying them I should be left very much to myself — to make my observations and choose my time for escape. Happily one of the dwarf-trees grew close by me, and every other minute I plucked and ate a small fruit, which wonderfully refreshed and strengthened me.

13. THE LITTLE ONES

I had been at work but a few moments, when I heard small voices near me, and presently the Little Ones, as I soon found they called themselves, came creeping out from among the tiny trees that like brushwood filled the spaces between the big ones. In a minute there were scores and scores about me. I made signs that the giants had but just left me, and were not far off; but they laughed, and told me the wind was quite clean.

"They are too blind to see us," they said, and laughed like a multitude of sheep-bells.

"Do you like that rope about your ankles?" asked one.

"I want them to think I cannot take it off," I replied.

"They can scarcely see their own feet!" he rejoined. "Walk with short steps and they will think the rope is all right."

As he spoke, he danced with merriment.

One of the bigger girls got down on her knees to untie the clumsy knot. I smiled, thinking those pretty fingers could do nothing with it, but in a moment it was loose.

They then made me sit down, and fed me with delicious little fruits; after which the smaller of them began to play with me in the wildest fashion, so that it was impossible for me to resume my work. When the first grew tired, others took their places, and this went on until the sun was setting, and heavy steps were heard approaching. The little people started from me, and I made haste to put the rope round my ankles.

"We must have a care," said the girl who had freed me; "a crush of one of their horrid stumpy feet might kill a very little one!"

"Can they not perceive you at all then?"

"They might see something move; and if the children were in a heap on the top of you, as they were a moment ago, it would be terrible; for they hate every live thing but themselves. — Not that they are much alive either!"

She whistled like a bird. The next instant not one of them was to be seen or heard, and the girl herself had disappeared.

It was my master, as doubtless he counted himself, come to take me home. He freed my ankles, and dragged me to the door of his hut; there he threw me on the ground, again tied my feet, gave me a kick, and left me.

Now I might at once have made my escape; but at length I had friends, and could not think of leaving them. They were so charming, so full of winsome ways, that I must see more of them! I must know them better! "To-morrow," I said to myself with delight, "I shall see them again!" But from the moment there was silence in the huts until I fell asleep, I heard them whispering all about me, and knew that I was lovingly watched by a multitude. After that, I think they hardly ever left me quite alone.

I did not come to know the giants at all, and I believe there was scarcely anything in them to know. They never became in the least friendly, but they were much too stupid to invent cruelties. Often I avoided a bad kick by catching the foot and giving its owner a fall, upon which he never, on that occasion, renewed his attempt.

But the little people were constantly doing and saying things that pleased, often things that surprised me. Every day I grew more loath to leave them. While I was at work, they would keep coming and going, amusing and delighting me, and taking all the misery, and much of the weariness out of my monotonous toil. Very soon I loved them more than I can tell. They did not know much, but they were very wise, and seemed capable of learning anything. I had no bed save the bare ground, but almost as often as I woke, it was in a nest of children — one or other of them in my arms, though which I seldom could tell until the light came, for they ordered the succession among themselves. When one crept into my bosom, unconsciously I clasped him there, and the rest lay close around me, the smaller nearer. It is hardly necessary to say that I did not suffer much from the nightly cold! The first thing they did in the morning, and the last before sunset, was to bring the good giant plenty to eat.

One morning I was surprised on waking to find myself alone. As I came to my senses, however, I heard subdued sounds of approach, and presently the girl already mentioned, the tallest and gravest of the community, and regarded by all as their mother, appeared from the wood, followed by the multitude in jubilation manifest — but silent lest they should rouse the sleeping giant at whose door I lay. She carried a boy-baby in her arms: hitherto a girl-baby, apparently about a year old, had been the youngest. Three of the bigger girls were her nurses, but they shared their treasure with all the rest. Among the Little Ones, dolls were unknown; the bigger had the smaller, and the smaller the still less, to tend and play with.

Lona came to me and laid the infant in my arms. The baby opened his eyes and looked at me, closed them again, and fell asleep.

"He loves you already!" said the girl.

"Where did you find him?" I asked.

"In the wood, of course," she answered, her eyes beaming with delight, "— where we always find them. Isn't he a beauty? We've been out all night looking for him. Sometimes it is not easy to find!"

"How do you know when there is one to find?" I asked.

"I cannot tell," she replied. "Every one makes haste to tell the other, but we never find out who told first. Sometimes I think one must have said it asleep, and another heard it half-awake. When there is a baby in the wood, no one can stop to ask questions; and when we have found it, then it is too late."

"Do more boy or girl babies come to the wood?"

"They don't come to the wood; we go to the wood and find them."

"Are there more boys or girls of you now?"

I had found that to ask precisely the same question twice, made them knit their brows.

"I do not know," she answered.

"You can count them, surely!"

"We never do that. We shouldn't like to be counted."

"Why?"

"It wouldn't be smooth. We would rather not know."

"Where do the babies come from first?"

"From the wood — always. There is no other place they can come from."

She knew where they came from last, and thought nothing else was to be known about their advent.

"How often do you find one?"

"Such a happy thing takes all the glad we've got, and we forget the last time. You too are glad to have him — are you not, good giant?"

"Yes, indeed, I am!" I answered. "But how do you feed him?"

"I will show you," she rejoined, and went away — to return directly with two or three ripe little plums. She put one to the baby's lips.

"He would open his mouth if he were awake," she said, and took him in her arms.

She squeezed a drop to the surface, and again held the fruit to the baby's lips. Without waking he began at once to suck it, and she went on slowly squeezing until nothing but skin and stone were left.

"There!" she cried, in a tone of gentle triumph. "A big-apple world it would be with nothing for the babies! We wouldn't stop in it — would we, darling? We would leave it to the bad giants!"

"But what if you let the stone into the baby's mouth when you were feeding him?" I said.

"No mother would do that," she replied. "I shouldn't be fit to have a baby!"

I thought what a lovely woman she would grow. But what became of them when they grew up? Where did they go? That brought me again to the question — where did they come from first?

"Will you tell me where you lived before?" I said.

"Here," she replied.

"Have you NEVER lived anywhere else?" I ventured.

"Never. We all came from the wood. Some think we dropped out of the trees."

"How is it there are so many of you quite little?"

"I don't understand. Some are less and some are bigger. I am very big."

"Baby will grow bigger, won't he?"

"Of course he will!"

"And will you grow bigger?"

"I don't think so. I hope not. I am the biggest. It frightens me sometimes."

"Why should it frighten you?"

She gave me no answer.

"How old are you?" I resumed.

"I do not know what you mean. We are all just that."

"How big will the baby grow?"

"I cannot tell. — Some," she added, with a trouble in her voice, "begin to grow after we think they have stopped. — That is a frightful thing. We don't talk about it!"

"What makes it frightful?"

She was silent for a moment, then answered,

"We fear they may be beginning to grow giants."

"Why should you fear that?"

"Because it is so terrible. — I don't want to talk about it!"

She pressed the baby to her bosom with such an anxious look that I dared not further question her.

Before long I began to perceive in two or three of the smaller children some traces of greed and selfishness, and noted that the bigger girls cast on these a not infrequent glance of anxiety.

None of them put a hand to my work: they would do nothing for the giants! But they never relaxed their loving ministrations to me. They would sing to me, one after another, for hours; climb the tree to reach my mouth and pop fruit into it with their dainty little fingers; and they kept constant watch against the approach of a giant.

Sometimes they would sit and tell me stories — mostly very childish, and often seeming to mean hardly anything. Now and then they would call a general assembly to amuse me. On one such occasion a moody little fellow sang me a strange crooning song, with a refrain so pathetic that, although unintelligible to me, it caused the tears to run down my face. This phenomenon made those who saw it regard me with much perplexity. Then first I bethought myself that I had not once, in that world, looked on water, falling or lying or running. Plenty there had been in some long vanished age — that was plain enough—but the Little Ones had never seen any before they saw my tears! They had, nevertheless, it seemed, some dim, instinctive perception of their origin; for a very small child went up to the singer, shook his clenched pud in his face, and said something like this: "'Ou skeeze ze juice out of ze good giant's seeberries! Bad giant!"

"How is it," I said one day to Lona, as she sat with the baby in her arms at the foot of my tree, "that I never see any children among the giants?"

She stared a little, as if looking in vain for some sense in the question, then replied,

"They are giants; there are no little ones."

"Have they never any children?" I asked.

"No; there are never any in the wood for them. They do not love them. If they saw ours, they would stamp them."

"Is there always the same number of the giants then? I thought, before I had time to know better, that they were your fathers and mothers."

She burst into the merriest laughter, and said,

"No, good giant; WE are THEIR firsters."

But as she said it, the merriment died out of her, and she looked scared.

I stopped working, and gazed at her, bewildered.

"How CAN that be?" I exclaimed.

"I do not say; I do not understand," she answered. "But we were here and they not. They go from us. I am sorry, but we cannot help it. THEY could have helped it."

"How long have you been here?" I asked, more and more puzzled – in the hope of some side-light on the matter.

"Always, I think," she replied. "I think somebody made us always."

I turned to my scraping.

She saw I did not understand.

"The giants were not made always," she resumed. "If a Little One doesn't care, he grows greedy, and then lazy, and then big, and then stupid, and then bad. The dull creatures don't know that they come from us. Very few of them believe we are anywhere. They say NONSENSE! — Look at little Blunty: he is eating one of their apples! He will be the next! Oh! oh! he will soon be big and bad and ugly, and not know it!"

The child stood by himself a little way off, eating an apple nearly as big as his head. I had often thought he did not look so good as the rest; now he looked disgusting.

"I will take the horrid thing from him!" I cried.

"It is no use," she answered sadly. "We have done all we can, and it is too late! We were afraid he was growing, for he would not believe anything told him; but when he refused to share his berries, and said he had gathered them for himself, then we knew it! He is a glutton, and there is no hope of him. — It makes me sick to see him eat!"

"Could not some of the boys watch him, and not let him touch the poisonous things?"

"He may have them if he will: it is all one — to eat the apples, and to be a boy that would eat them if he could. No; he must go to the giants! He belongs to them. You can see how much bigger he is than when first you came! He is bigger since yesterday."

"He is as like that hideous green lump in his hand as boy could look!"

"It suits what he is making himself."

"His head and it might change places!"

"Perhaps they do!"

"Does he want to be a giant?"

"He hates the giants, but he is making himself one all the same: he likes their apples! Oh baby, baby, he was just such a darling as you when we found him!"

"He will be very miserable when he finds himself a giant!"

"Oh, no; he will like it well enough! That is the worst of it."

"Will he hate the Little Ones?"

"He will be like the rest; he will not remember us — most likely will not believe there are Little Ones. He will not care; he will eat his apples."

"Do tell me how it will come about. I understand your world so little! I come from a world where everything is different."

"I do not know about WORLD. What is it? What more but a word in your beautiful big mouth? — That makes it something!"

"Never mind about the word; tell me what next will happen to Blunty."

"He will wake one morning and find himself a giant — not like you, good giant, but like any other bad giant. You will hardly know him, but I will tell you which. He will think he has been a giant always, and will not know you, or any of us. The giants have lost themselves, Peony says, and that is why they never smile. I wonder whether they are not glad because they are bad, or bad because they are not glad. But they can't be glad when they have no babies! I wonder what BAD means, good giant!"

"I wish I knew no more about it than you!" I returned. "But I try to be good, and mean to keep on trying."

"So do I — and that is how I know you are good."

A long pause followed.

"Then you do not know where the babies come from into the wood?" I said, making one attempt more.

"There is nothing to know there," she answered. "They are in the wood; they grow there."

"Then how is it you never find one before it is quite grown?" I asked.

She knitted her brows and was silent a moment:

"They're not there till they're finished," she said.

"It is a pity the little sillies can't speak till they've forgotten everything they had to tell!" I remarked.

"Little Tolma, the last before this baby, looked as if she had something to tell, when I found her under a beech-tree, sucking her thumb, but she hadn't. She only looked up at me —oh, so sweetly! SHE will never go bad and grow big! When they begin to grow big they care for nothing but bigness; and when they cannot grow any bigger, they try to grow fatter. The bad giants are very proud of being fat."

"So they are in my world," I said; "only they do not say FAT there, they say RICH."

"In one of their houses," continued Lona, "sits the biggest and fattest of them — so proud that nobody can see him; and the giants go to his house at certain times, and call out to him, and tell him how fat he is, and beg him to make them strong to eat more and grow fat like him."

The rumor at length reached my ears that Blunty had vanished. I saw a few grave faces among the bigger ones, but he did not seem to be much missed.

The next morning Lona came to me and whispered,

"Look! look there — by that quince-tree: that is the giant that was Blunty! — Would you have known him?"

"Never," I answered. "— But now you tell me, I could fancy it might be Blunty staring through a fog! He DOES look stupid!"

"He is for ever eating those apples now!" she said. "That is what comes of Little Ones that WON'T be little!"

"They call it growing-up in my world!" I said to myself. "If only she would teach me to grow the other way, and become a Little One! — Shall I ever be able to laugh like them?"

I had had the chance, and had flung it from me! Blunty and I were alike! He did not know his loss, and I had to be taught mine!

14. A CRISIS

For a time I had no desire save to spend my life with the Little Ones. But soon other thoughts and feelings began to influence me. First awoke the vague sense that I ought to be doing something; that I was not meant for the fattening of boors! Then it came to me that I was in a marvelous world, of which it was assuredly my business to discover the ways and laws; and that, if I would do anything in return for the children's goodness, I must learn more about them than they could tell me, and to that end must be free. Surely, I thought, no suppression of their growth can be essential to their loveliness and truth and purity! Not in any world could the possibility exist of such a discord between constitution and its natural outcome! Life and law cannot be so at variance that perfection must be gained by thwarting development! But the growth of the Little Ones WAS arrested! something interfered with it: what was it? Lona seemed the eldest of them, yet not more than fifteen, and had been long in charge of a multitude, in semblance and mostly in behavior merest children, who regarded her as their mother! Were they growing at all? I doubted it. Of time they had scarcely the idea; of their own age they knew nothing! Lona herself thought she had lived always! Full of wisdom and empty of knowledge, she was at once their Love and their Law! But what seemed to me her ignorance might in truth be my own lack of insight! Her one anxiety plainly was, that her Little Ones should not grow, and change into bad giants! Their "good giant" was bound to do his best for them: without more knowledge of their nature, and some knowledge of their history, he could do nothing, and must therefore leave them! They would only be as they were before; they had in no way become dependent on me; they were still my protectors, I was not theirs; my presence but brought them more in danger of their idiotic neighbors! I longed to teach them many things: I must first understand more of those I would teach! Knowledge no doubt made bad people worse, but it must make good people better! I was convinced they would learn mathematics; and might they not be taught to write down the dainty melodies they murmured and forgot?

The conclusion was, that I must rise and continue my travels, in the hope of coming upon some elucidation of the fortunes and destiny of the bewitching little creatures.

My design, however, would not so soon have passed into action, but for what now occurred.

To prepare them for my temporary absence, I was one day telling them while at work that I would long ago have left the bad giants, but that I loved the Little Ones so much—when, as by one accord, they came rushing and crowding upon me; they scrambled over each other and up the tree and dropped on my head, until I was nearly smothered. With three very little ones in my arms, one on each shoulder clinging to my neck, one standing straight up on my head, four or five holding me fast by the legs, others grappling my body and arms, and a multitude climbing and descending upon these, I was helpless as one overwhelmed by lava. Absorbed in the merry struggle, not one of them saw my tyrant coming until he was almost upon me. With just one cry of "Take care, good giant!"

they ran from me like mice, they dropped from me like hedgehogs, they flew from me up the tree like squirrels, and the same moment, sharp round the stem came the bad giant, and dealt me such a blow on the head with a stick that I fell to the ground. The children told me afterwards that they sent him "such a many bumps of big apples and stones" that he was frightened, and ran blundering home.

When I came to myself it was night. Above me were a few pale stars that expected the moon. I thought I was alone. My head ached badly, and I was terribly athirst.

I turned wearily on my side. The moment my ear touched the ground, I heard the gushing and gurgling of water, and the soft noises made me groan with longing. At once I was amid a multitude of silent children, and delicious little fruits began to visit my lips. They came and came until my thirst was gone.

Then I was aware of sounds I had never heard there before; the air was full of little sobs.

I tried to sit up. A pile of small bodies instantly heaped itself at my back. Then I struggled to my feet, with much pushing and pulling from the Little Ones, who were wonderfully strong for their size.

"You must go away, good giant," they said. "When the bad giants see you hurt, they will all trample on you."

"I think I must," I answered.

"Go and grow strong, and come again," they said.

"I will," I replied — and sat down.

"Indeed you must go at once!" whispered Lona, who had been supporting me, and now knelt beside me.

"I listened at his door," said one of the bigger boys, "and heard the bad giant say to his wife that he had found you idle, talking to a lot of moles and squirrels, and when he beat you, they tried to kill him. He said you were a wizard, and they must knock you, or they would have no peace."

"I will go at once," I said, "and come back as soon as I have found out what is wanted to make you bigger and stronger."

"We don't want to be bigger," they answered, looking very serious. "We WON'T grow bad giants! — We are strong now; you don't know how much strong!"

It was no use holding them out a prospect that had not any attraction for them! I said nothing more, but rose and moved slowly up the slope of the valley. At once they formed themselves into a long procession; some led the way, some walked with me helping me, and the rest followed. They kept feeding me as we went.

"You are broken," they said, "and much red juice has run out of you: put some in."

When we reached the edge of the valley, there was the moon just lifting her forehead over the rim of the horizon.

"She has come to take care of you, and show you the way," said Lona.

I questioned those about me as we walked, and learned there was a great place with a giant-girl for queen. When I asked if it was a city, they said they did not know. Neither could they tell how far off, or in what direction it was, or what was the giant-girl's name; all they knew was, that she hated the Little Ones, and would like to kill them, only she could not find them. I asked how they knew that; Lona answered that she had always known it. If the giant-girl came to look for them, they must hide hard, she said. When I told them I should go and ask her why she hated them, they cried out,

"No, no! she will kill you, good giant; she will kill you! She is an awful bad-giant witch!"

I asked them where I was to go then. They told me that, beyond the baby-forest, away where the moon came from, lay a smooth green country, pleasant to the feet, without rocks or trees. But when I asked how I was to set out for it,

"The moon will tell you, we think," they said.

They were taking me up the second branch of the river bed: when they saw that the moon had reached her height, they stopped to return.

"We have never gone so far from our trees before," they said. "Now mind you watch how you go, that you may see inside your eyes how to come back to us."

"And beware of the giant-woman that lives in the desert," said one of the bigger girls as they were turning, "I suppose you have heard of her!"

"No," I answered.

"Then take care not to go near her. She is called the Cat-woman. She is awfully ugly —AND SCRATCHES."

As soon as the bigger ones stopped, the smaller had begun to run back. The others now looked at me gravely for a moment, and then walked slowly away. Last to leave me, Lona held up the baby to be kissed, gazed in my eyes, whispered, "The Cat-woman will not hurt YOU," and went without another word. I stood a while, gazing after them through the moonlight, then turned and, with a heavy heart, began my solitary journey. Soon the laughter of the Little Ones overtook me, like sheep-bells innumerable, rippling the air, and echoing in the rocks about me. I turned again, and again gazed after them: they went gamboling along, with never a care in their sweet souls. But Lona walked apart with her baby.

Pondering as I went, I recalled many traits of my little friends.

Once when I suggested that they should leave the country of the bad giants, and go with me to find another, they answered, "But that would be to NOT ourselves!" —so strong in them was the love of place that their country seemed essential to their very being! Without ambition or fear, discomfort or greed, they had no motive to desire any change; they knew of nothing amiss; and, except their babies, they had never had a chance of helping any one but myself: — How were they to grow? But again, Why should they grow? In seeking to improve their conditions, might I not do them harm, and only harm? To enlarge their minds after the notions of my world — might it not be to distort and weaken them? Their fear of growth as a possible start for gianthood might be instinctive!

The part of philanthropist is indeed a dangerous one; and the man who would do his neighbor good must first study how not to do him evil, and must begin by pulling the beam out of his own eye.

15. A STRANGE HOSTESS

I traveled on attended by the moon. As usual she was full — I had never seen her other — and to-night as she sank I thought I perceived something like a smile on her countenance.

When her under edge was a little below the horizon, there appeared in the middle of her disc, as if it had been painted upon it, a cottage, through the open door and window of which she shone; and with the sight came the conviction that I was expected there. Almost immediately the moon was gone, and the cottage had vanished; the night was rapidly growing dark, and my way being across a close succession of small ravines, I resolved to remain where I was and expect the morning. I stretched myself, therefore, in a sandy hollow, made my supper off the fruits the children had given me at parting, and was soon asleep.

I woke suddenly, saw above me constellations unknown to my former world, and had lain for a while gazing at them, when I became aware of a figure seated on the ground a little way from and above me. I was startled, as one is on discovering all at once that he is not alone. The figure was between me and the sky, so that I saw its outline well. From where I lay low in the hollow, it seemed larger than human.

It moved its head, and then first I saw that its back was toward me.

"Will you not come with me?" said a sweet, mellow voice, unmistakably a woman's.

Wishing to learn more of my hostess,

"I thank you," I replied, "but I am not uncomfortable here. Where would you have me go? I like sleeping in the open air."

"There is no hurt in the air," she returned; "but the creatures that roam the night in these parts are not such as a man would willingly have about him while he sleeps."

"I have not been disturbed," I said.

"No; I have been sitting by you ever since you lay down."

"That is very kind of you! How came you to know I was here? Why do you show me such favor?"

"I saw you," she answered, still with her back to me, "in the light of the moon, just as she went down. I see badly in the day, but at night perfectly. The shadow of my house would have hidden you, but both its doors were open. I was out on the waste, and saw you go into this hollow. You were asleep, however, before I could reach you, and I was not willing to disturb you. People are frightened if I come on them suddenly. They call me the Cat-woman. It is not my name."

I remembered what the children had told me — that she was very ugly, and scratched. But her voice was gentle, and its tone a little apologetic: she could not be a bad giantess!

"You shall not hear it from me," I answered, "Please tell me what I MAY call you!"

"When you know me, call me by the name that seems to you to fit me," she replied: "that will tell me what sort you are. People do not often give me the right one. It is well when they do."

"I suppose, madam, you live in the cottage I saw in the heart of the moon?"

"I do. I live there alone, except when I have visitors. It is a poor place, but I do what I can for my guests, and sometimes their sleep is sweet to them."

Her voice entered into me, and made me feel strangely still.

"I will go with you, madam," I said, rising.

She rose at once, and without a glance behind her led the way. I could see her just well enough to follow. She was taller than myself, but not so tall as I had thought her. That she never turned her face to me made me curious — nowise apprehensive, her voice rang so true. But how was I to fit her with a name who could not see her? I strove to get alongside of her, but failed: when I quickened my pace she quickened hers, and kept easily ahead of me. At length I did begin to grow a little afraid. Why was she so careful not to be seen? Extraordinary ugliness would account for it: she might fear terrifying me! Horror of an inconceivable monstrosity began to assail me: was I following through the dark an unheard of hideousness? Almost I repented of having accepted her hospitality.

Neither spoke, and the silence grew unbearable. I MUST break it!

"I want to find my way," I said, "to a place I have heard of, but whose name I have not yet learned. Perhaps you can tell it me!"

"Describe it, then, and I will direct you. The stupid Bags know nothing, and the careless little Lovers forget almost everything."

"Where do those live?"

"You are just come from them!"

"I never heard those names before!"

"You would not hear them. Neither people knows its own name!"

"Strange!"

"Perhaps so! but hardly any one anywhere knows his own name! It would make many a fine gentleman stare to hear himself addressed by what is really his name!"

I held my peace, beginning to wonder what my name might be.

"What now do you fancy yours?" she went on, as if aware of my thought. "But, pardon me, it is a matter of no consequence."

I had actually opened my mouth to answer her, when I discovered that my name was gone from me. I could not even recall the first letter of it! This was the second time I had been asked my name and could not tell it!

"Never mind," she said; "it is not wanted. Your real name, indeed, is written on your forehead, but at present it whirls about so irregularly that nobody can read it. I will do my part to steady it. Soon it will go slower, and, I hope, settle at last."

This startled me, and I was silent.

We had left the channels and walked a long time, but no sign of the cottage yet appeared.

"The Little Ones told me," I said at length, "of a smooth green country, pleasant to the feet!"

"Yes?" she returned.

"They told me too of a girl giantess that was queen somewhere: is that her country?"

"There is a city in that grassy land," she replied, "where a woman is princess. The city is called Bulika. But certainly the princess is not a girl! She is older than this world, and came to it from yours — with a terrible history, which is not over yet. She is an evil person, and prevails much with the Prince of the Power of the Air. The people of Bulika were formerly simple folk, tilling the ground and pasturing sheep. She came among them, and they received her hospitably. She taught them to dig for diamonds and opals and sell them to strangers, and made them give up tillage and pasturage and build a city. One day they found a huge snake and killed it; which so enraged her that she declared herself their princess, and became terrible to them. The name of the country at that time was THE LAND OF WATERS; for the dry channels, of which you have crossed so many, were then overflowing with live torrents; and the valley, where now the Bags and the Lovers have their fruit-trees, was a lake that received a great part of them. But the wicked princess gathered up in her lap what she could of the water over the whole country, closed it in an egg, and carried it away. Her lap, however, would not hold more than half of it; and the instant she was gone, what she had not yet taken fled away underground, leaving the country as dry and dusty as her own heart. Were it not for the waters under it, every living thing would long ago have perished from it. For where no water is, no rain falls; and where no rain falls, no springs rise. Ever since then, the princess has lived in Bulika, holding the inhabitants in constant terror, and doing what she can to keep them from multiplying. Yet they boast and believe themselves a prosperous, and certainly are a self-satisfied people — good at bargaining and buying, good at selling and cheating; holding well together for a common interest, and utterly treacherous where interests clash; proud of their princess and her power, and despising every one they get the better of; never doubting themselves the most honorable of all the nations, and each man counting himself better than any other. The depth of their worthlessness and height of their vainglory no one can understand who has not been there to see, who has not learned to know the miserable misgoverned and self-deceived creatures."

"I thank you, madam. And now, if you please, will you tell me something about the Little Ones — the Lovers? I long heartily to serve them. Who and what are they? and how do they come to be there? Those children are the greatest wonder I have found in this world of wonders."

"In Bulika you may, perhaps, get some light on those matters. There is an ancient poem in the library of the palace, I am told, which of course no one there can read, but in which it is plainly written that after the Lovers have gone through great troubles and learned their own name, they will fill the land, and make the giants their slaves."

"By that time they will have grown a little, will they not?" I said.

"Yes, they will have grown; yet I think too they will not have grown. It is possible to grow and not to grow, to grow less and to grow bigger, both at once — yes, even to grow by means of not growing!"

"Your words are strange, madam!" I rejoined. "But I have heard it said that some words, because they mean more, appear to mean less!"

"That is true, and such words HAVE to be understood. It were well for the princess of Bulika if she heard what the very silence of the land is shouting in her ears all day long! But she is far too clever to understand anything."

"Then I suppose, when the little Lovers are grown, their land will have water again?"

"Not exactly so: when they are thirsty enough, they will have water, and when they have water, they will grow. To grow, they must have water. And, beneath, it is flowing still."

"I have heard that water twice," I said; "—once when I lay down to wait for the moon —and when I woke the sun was shining! and once when I fell, all but killed by the bad giant. Both times came the voices of the water, and healed me."

The woman never turned her head, and kept always a little before me, but I could hear every word that left her lips, and her voice much reminded me of the woman's in the house of death. Much of what she said, I did not understand, and therefore cannot remember. But I forgot that I had ever been afraid of her.

We went on and on, and crossed yet a wide tract of sand before reaching the cottage. Its foundation stood in deep sand, but I could see that it was a rock. In character the cottage resembled the sexton's, but had thicker walls. The door, which was heavy and strong, opened immediately into a large bare room, which had two little windows opposite each other, without glass. My hostess walked in at the open door out of which the moon had looked, and going straight to the farthest corner, took a long white cloth from the floor, and wound it about her head and face. Then she closed the other door, in at which the moon had looked, trimmed a small horn lantern that stood on the hearth, and turned to receive me.

"You are very welcome, Mr. Vane!" she said, calling me by the name I had forgotten. "Your entertainment will be scanty, but, as the night is not far spent, and the day not at hand, it is better you should be indoors. Here you will be safe, and a little lack is not a great misery."

"I thank you heartily, madam," I replied. "But, seeing you know the name I could not tell you, may I not now know yours?"

"My name is Mara," she answered.

Then I remembered the sexton and the little black cat.

"Some people," she went on, "take me for Lot's wife, lamenting over Sodom; and some think I am Rachel, weeping for her children; but I am neither of those."

"I thank you again, Mara," I said. "—May I lie here on your floor till the morning?"

"At the top of that stair," she answered, "you will find a bed – on which some have slept better than they expected, and some have waked all the night and slept all the next day. It is not a very soft one, but it is better than the sand — and there are no hyenas sniffing about it!"

The stair, narrow and steep, led straight up from the room to an unceiled and unpartitioned garret, with one wide, low dormer window. Close under the sloping roof stood a narrow bed, the sight of which with its white coverlet made me shiver, so vividly it recalled the couches in the chamber of death. On the table was a dry loaf, and beside it a cup of cold water. To me, who had tasted nothing but fruit for months, they were a feast.

"I must leave you in the dark," my hostess called from the bottom of the stair. "This lantern is all the light I have, and there are things to do to-night."

"It is of no consequence, thank you, madam," I returned. "To eat and drink, to lie down and sleep, are things that can be done in the dark."

"Rest in peace," she said.

I ate up the loaf, drank the water every drop, and laid myself down. The bed was hard, the covering thin and scanty, and the night cold: I dreamed that I lay in the chamber of death, between the warrior and the lady with the healing wound.

I woke in the middle of the night, thinking I heard low noises of wild animals.

"Creatures of the desert scenting after me, I suppose!" I said to myself, and, knowing I was safe, would have gone to sleep again. But that instant a rough purring rose to a howl under my window, and I sprang from my bed to see what sort of beast uttered it.

Before the door of the cottage, in the full radiance of the moon, a tall woman stood, clothed in white, with her back toward me. She was stooping over a large white animal like a panther, patting and stroking it with one hand, while with the other she pointed to the moon half-way up the heaven, then drew a perpendicular line to the horizon. Instantly the creature darted off with amazing swiftness in the direction indicated. For a moment my eyes followed it, then sought the woman; but she was gone, and not yet had I seen her face! Again I looked after the animal, but whether I saw or only fancied a white speck in the distance, I could not tell. —What did it mean? What was the monster-cat sent off to do? I shuddered, and went back to my bed. Then I remembered that, when I lay down in the sandy hollow outside, the moon was setting; yet here she was, a few hours after, shining in all her glory! "Everything is uncertain here," I said to myself, "—even the motions of the heavenly bodies!"

I learned afterward that there were several moons in the service of this world, but the laws that ruled their times and different orbits I failed to discover.

Again I fell asleep, and slept undisturbed.

When I went down in the morning, I found bread and water waiting me, the loaf so large that I ate only half of it. My hostess sat muffled beside me while I broke my fast, and except to greet me when I entered, never opened her mouth until I asked her to instruct me how to arrive at Bulika. She then told me to go up the bank of the river-bed until it disappeared; then verge to the right until I came to a forest — in which I might spend a night, but which I must leave with my face to the rising moon. Keeping in the same direction, she said, until I reached a running stream, I must cross that at right angles, and go straight on until I saw the city on the horizon.

I thanked her, and ventured the remark that, looking out of the window in the night, I was astonished to see her messenger understand her so well, and go so straight and so fast in the direction she had indicated.

"If I had but that animal of yours to guide me—" I went on, hoping to learn something of its mission, but she interrupted me, saying,

"It was to Bulika she went—the shortest way."

"How wonderfully intelligent she looked!"

"Astarte knows her work well enough to be sent to do it," she answered.

"Have you many messengers like her?"

"As many as I require."

"Are they hard to teach?"

"They need no teaching. They are all of a certain breed, but not one of the breed is like another. Their origin is so natural it would seem to you incredible."

"May I not know it?"

"A new one came to me last night—from your head while you slept."

I laughed.

"All in this world seem to love mystery!" I said to myself. "Some chance word of mine suggested an idea — and in this form she embodies the small fact!"

"Then the creature is mine!" I cried.

"Not at all!" she answered. "That only can be ours in whose existence our will is a factor."

"Ha! a metaphysician too!" I remarked inside, and was silent.

"May I take what is left of the loaf?" I asked presently.

"You will want no more to-day," she replied.

"To-morrow I may!" I rejoined.

She rose and went to the door, saying as she went,

"It has nothing to do with to-morrow — but you may take it if you will."

She opened the door, and stood holding it. I rose, taking up the bread — but lingered, much desiring to see her face.

"Must I go, then?" I asked.

"No one sleeps in my house two nights together!" she answered.

"I thank you, then, for your hospitality, and bid you farewell!" I said, and turned to go.

"The time will come when you must house with me many days and many nights," she murmured sadly through her muffling.

"Willingly," I replied.

"Nay, NOT willingly!" she answered.

I said to myself that she was right — I would not willingly be her guest a second time! but immediately my heart rebuked me, and I had scarce crossed the threshold when I turned again.

She stood in the middle of the room; her white garments lay like foamy waves at her feet, and among them the swathings of her face: it was lovely as a night of stars. Her great gray eyes looked up to heaven; tears were flowing down her pale cheeks. She reminded me not a little of the sexton's wife, although the one looked as if she had not wept for thousands of years, and the other as if she wept constantly behind the wrappings of her beautiful head. Yet something in the very eyes that wept seemed to say, "Weeping may endure for a night, but joy cometh in the morning."

I had bowed my head for a moment, about to kneel and beg her forgiveness, when, looking up in the act, I found myself outside a doorless house. I went round and round it, but could find no entrance.

I had stopped under one of the windows, on the point of calling aloud my repentant confession, when a sudden wailing, howling scream invaded my ears, and my heart stood still. Something sprang from the window above my head, and lighted beyond me. I turned, and saw a large gray cat, its hair on end, shooting toward the river-bed. I fell with my face in the sand, and seemed to hear within the house the gentle sobbing of one who suffered but did not repent.

16. A GRUESOME DANCE

I rose to resume my journey, and walked many a desert mile. How I longed for a mountain, or even a tall rock, from whose summit I might see across the dismal plain or the dried-up channels to some bordering hope! Yet what could such foresight have availed me? That which is within a man, not that which lies beyond his vision, is the main factor in what is about to befall him: the operation upon him is the event. Foreseeing is not understanding, else surely the prophecy latent in man would come oftener to the surface!

The sun was half-way to the horizon when I saw before me a rugged rocky ascent; but ere I reached it my desire to climb was over, and I longed to lie down. By that time the sun was almost set, and the air had begun to grow dark. At my feet lay a carpet of softest, greenest moss, couch for a king: I threw myself upon it, and weariness at once began to ebb, for, the moment my head was down, the third time I heard below me many waters, playing broken airs and ethereal harmonies with the stones of their buried channels. Loveliest chaos of music-stuff the harp aquarian kept sending up to my ears! What might not a Händel have done with that ever-recurring gurgle and bell-like drip, to the mingling and mutually destructive melodies their common refrain!

As I lay listening, my eyes went wandering up and down the rocky slope abrupt above me, reading on its face the record that down there, ages ago, rushed a cataract, filling the channels that had led me to its foot. My heart swelled at the thought of the splendid tumult, where the waves danced revelling in helpless fall, to mass their music in one organ-roar below. But soon the hidden brooks lulled me to sleep, and their lullabies mingled with my dreams.

I woke before the sun, and eagerly climbed to see what lay beyond. Alas, nothing but a desert of finest sand! Not a trace was left of the river that had plunged adown the rocks! The powdery drift had filled its course to the level of the dreary expanse! As I looked back I saw that the river had divided into two branches as it fell, that whose bank I had now followed to the foot of the rocky scaur, and that which first I crossed to the Evil Wood. The wood I descried between the two on the far horizon. Before me and to the left, the desert stretched beyond my vision, but far to the right I could see a lift in the sky-line, giving hope of the forest to which my hostess had directed me.

I sat down, and sought in my pocket the half-loaf I had brought with me — then first to understand what my hostess had meant concerning it. Verily the bread was not for the morrow: it had shrunk and hardened to a stone! I threw it away, and set out again.

About noon I came to a few tamarisk and juniper trees, and then to a few stunted firs. As I went on, closer thickets and larger firs met me, and at length I was in just such a forest of pines and other trees as that in which the Little Ones found their babies, and believed I had returned upon a farther portion of the same. But what mattered WHERE while EVERYWHERE was the same as NOWHERE! I had not yet, by doing something in it, made ANYWHERE into a place! I was not yet alive; I was only dreaming I lived! I was but a consciousness with an outlook! Truly I had been nothing else in the world I had left, but now I knew the fact! I said to myself that if in this forest I should catch the faint gleam of the mirror, I would turn far aside lest it should entrap me unawares, and give me back to my old existence: here I might learn to be something by doing something! I could not endure the thought of going back, with so many beginnings and not an end achieved. The Little Ones would meet what fate was appointed them; the awful witch I should never meet; the dead would ripen and arise without me; I should but wake to know that I had dreamed, and that all my going was nowhither! I would rather go on and on than come to such a close!

I went deeper into the wood: I was weary, and would rest in it.

The trees were now large, and stood in regular, almost geometric, fashion, with roomy spaces between. There was little undergrowth, and I could see a long way in every direction. The forest was like a great church, solemn and silent and empty, for I met nothing on two feet or four that day. Now and then, it is true, some swift thing, and again some slow thing, would cross the space on which my eye happened that moment to settle; but it was always at some distance, and only enhanced the sense of wideness and vacancy. I heard a few birds, and saw plenty of butterflies, some of marvelously gorgeous coloring and combinations of color, some of a pure and dazzling whiteness.

Coming to a spot where the pines stood farther apart and gave room for flowering shrubs, and hoping it a sign of some dwelling near, I took the direction where yet more and more roses grew, for I was hungry after the voice and face of my kind — after any live soul, indeed, human or not, which I might in some measure understand. What a hell of horror, I thought, to wander alone, a bare existence never going out of itself, never widening its life in another life, but, bound with the cords of its poor peculiarities, lying an eternal prisoner in the dungeon of its own being! I began to learn that it was impossible to live for oneself even, save in the presence of others — then, alas, fearfully possible! evil was only through good! selfishness but a parasite on the tree of life! In my own world I had the habit of solitary song; here not a crooning murmur ever parted my lips! There I sang without thinking; here I thought without singing! there I had never had a bosom-friend; here the affection of an idiot would be divinely welcome! "If only I had a dog to love!" I sighed — and regarded with wonder my past self, which preferred the company of book or pen to that of man or woman; which, if the author of a tale I was enjoying appeared, would wish him away that I might return to his story. I had chosen the dead rather than the living, the thing thought rather than the thing thinking! "Any man," I said now, "is more than the greatest of books!" I had not cared for my live brothers and sisters, and now I was left without even the dead to comfort me!

The wood thinned yet more, and the pines grew yet larger, sending up huge stems, like columns eager to support the heavens. More trees of other kinds appeared; the forest was growing richer! The roses wore now trees, and their flowers of astonishing splendor.

Suddenly I spied what seemed a great house or castle; but its forms were so strangely indistinct, that I could not be certain it was more than a chance combination of tree-shapes. As I drew nearer, its lines yet held together, but neither they nor the body of it grew at all more definite; and when at length I stood in front of it, I remained as doubtful of its nature as before. House or castle habitable, it certainly was not; it might be a ruin overgrown with ivy and roses! Yet of building hid in the foliage, not the poorest wall-remnant could I discern. Again and again I seemed to descry what must be building, but it always vanished before closer inspection. Could it be, I pondered, that the ivy had embraced a huge edifice and consumed it, and its interlaced branches retained the shapes of the walls it had assimilated? — I could be sure of nothing concerning the appearance.

Before me was a rectangular vacancy — the ghost of a doorway without a door: I stepped through it, and found myself in an open space like a great hall, its floor covered with grass and flowers, its walls and roof of ivy and vine, mingled with roses.

There could be no better place in which to pass the night! I gathered a quantity of withered leaves, laid them in a corner, and threw myself upon them. A red sunset filled the hall, the night was warm, and my couch restful; I lay gazing up at the live ceiling, with its tracery of branches and twigs, its clouds of foliage, and peeping patches of loftier roof. My eyes went wading about as if tangled in it, until the sun was down, and the sky beginning to grow dark. Then the red roses turned black, and soon the yellow and white alone were visible. When they vanished, the stars came instead, hanging in the leaves like live topazes, throbbing and sparkling and flashing many colors: I was canopied with a tree from Aladdin's cave!

Then I discovered that it was full of nests, whence tiny heads, nearly indistinguishable, kept popping out with a chirp or two, and disappearing again. For a while there were rustlings and stirrings and little prayers; but as the darkness grew, the small heads became still, and at last every feathered mother had her brood quiet under her wings, the talk in the little beds was over, and God's bird-nursery at rest beneath the waves of sleep. Once more a few flutterings made me look up: an owl went sailing across. I had only a glimpse of him, but several times felt the cool wafture of his silent wings. The mother birds did not move again; they saw that he was looking for mice, not children.

About midnight I came wide awake, roused by a revelry, whose noises were yet not loud. Neither were they distant; they were close to me, but attenuate. My eyes were so dazzled, however, that for a while I could see nothing; at last they came to themselves.

I was lying on my withered leaves in the corner of a splendid hall. Before me was a crowd of gorgeously dressed men and gracefully robed women, none of whom seemed to see me. In dance after dance they vaguely embodied the story of life, its meetings, its passions, its partings. A student of Shakespeare, I had learned something of every dance alluded to in his plays, and hence partially understood several of those I now saw — the minuet, the pavin, the hey, the coranto, the lavolta. The dancers were attired in fashion as ancient as their dances.

A moon had risen while I slept, and was shining through the countless-windowed roof; but her light was crossed by so many shadows that at first I could distinguish almost nothing of the faces of the multitude; I could not fail, however, to perceive that there was something odd about them: I sat up to see them better. — Heavens! could I call them faces? They were skull fronts! — hard, gleaming bone, bare jaws, truncated noses, lipless teeth which could no more take part in any smile! Of these, some flashed set and white and murderous; others were clouded with decay, broken and gapped, colored of the earth in which they seemed so long to have lain! Fear fuller yet, the eye-sockets were not empty; in each was a lidless living eye! In those wrecks of faces, glowed or flashed or sparkled eyes of every color, shape, and expression. The beautiful, proud eye, dark and lustrous, condescending to whatever it rested upon, was the more terrible; the lovely, languishing eye, the more repulsive; while the dim, sad eyes, less at variance with their setting, were sad exceedingly, and drew the heart in spite of the horror out of which they gazed.

I rose and went among the apparitions, eager to understand something of their being and belongings. Were they souls, or were they and their rhythmic motions but phantasms of what had been? By look nor by gesture, not by slightest break in the measure, did they show themselves aware of me; I was not present to them: how much were they in relation to each other? Surely they saw their companions as I saw them! Or was each only dreaming itself and the rest? Did they know each how they appeared to the others — a death with living eyes? Had they used their faces, not for communication, not to utter thought and feeling, not to share existence with their neighbors, but to appear what they wished to appear, and conceal what they were? and, having made their faces masks, were they therefore deprived of those masks, and condemned to go without faces until they repented?

"How long must they flaunt their facelessness in faceless eyes?" I wondered. "How long will the frightful punition endure? Have they at length begun to love and be wise? Have they yet yielded to the shame that has found them?"

I heard not a word, saw not a movement of one naked mouth. Were they because of lying bereft of speech? With their eyes they spoke as if longing to be understood: was it truth or was it falsehood that spoke in their eyes? They seemed to know one another: did they see one skull beautiful, and another plain? Difference must be there, and they had had long study of skulls!

My body was to theirs no obstacle: was I a body, and were they but forms? or was I but a form, and were they bodies? The moment one of the dancers came close against me, that moment he or she was on the other side of me, and I could tell, without seeing, which, whether man or woman, had passed through my house.

On many of the skulls the hair held its place, and however dressed, or in itself however beautiful, to my eyes looked frightful on the bones of the forehead and temples. In such case, the outer ear often remained also, and at its tip, the jewel of the ear as Sidney calls it, would hang, glimmering, gleaming, or sparkling, pearl or opal or diamond—under the night of brown or of raven locks, the sunrise of golden ripples, or the moonshine of pale, inter-clouded, fluffy cirri — lichenous all on the ivory-white or damp-yellow naked bone. I looked down and saw the daintily domed instep; I looked up and saw the plump shoulders basing the spring of the round full neck — which withered at half-height to the fluted shaft of a gibbose cranium.

The music became wilder, the dance faster and faster; eyes flared and flashed, jewels twinkled and glittered, casting color and fire on the pallid grins that glode through the hall, weaving a ghastly rhythmic woof in intricate maze of multitudinous motion, when sudden came a pause, and every eye turned to the same spot: — in the doorway stood a woman, perfect in form, in holding, and in hue, regarding the company as from the pedestal of a goddess, while the dancers stood "like one forbid," frozen to a new death by the vision of a life that killed. "Dead things, I live!" said her scornful glance. Then, at once, like leaves in which an instant wind awakes, they turned each to another, and broke afresh into melodious consorted motion, a new expression in their eyes, late solitary, now filled with the interchange of a common triumph. "Thou also," they seemed to say, "wilt soon become weak as we! thou wilt soon become like unto us!" I turned mine again to the woman—and saw upon her side a small dark shadow.

She had seen the change in the dead stare; she looked down; she understood the talking eyes; she pressed both her lovely hands on the shadow, gave a smothered cry, and fled. The birds moved rustling in their nests, and a flash of joy lit up the eyes of the dancers, when suddenly a warm wind, growing in strength as it swept through the place, blew out every light. But the low moon yet glimmered on the horizon with "sick assay" to shine, and a turbid radiance yet gleamed from so many eyes, that I saw well enough what followed. As if each shape had been but a snow-image, it began to fall to pieces, ruining in the warm wind. In papery flakes the flesh peeled from its bones, dropping like soiled snow from under its garments; these fell fluttering in rags and strips, and the whole white skeleton, emerging from garment and flesh together, stood bare and lank amid the decay that littered the floor. A faint rattling shiver went through the naked company; pair after pair the lamping eyes went out; and the darkness grew round me with the loneliness. For a moment the leaves were still swept fluttering all one way; then the wind ceased, and the owl floated silent through the silent night.

Not for a moment had I been afraid. It is true that whoever would cross the threshold of any world, must leave fear behind him; but, for myself, I could claim no part in its absence. No conscious courage was operant in me; simply, I was not afraid. I neither knew why I was not afraid, nor wherefore I might have been afraid. I feared not even fear — which of all dangers is the most dangerous.

I went out into the wood, at once to resume my journey. Another moon was rising, and I turned my face toward it.

17. A GROTESQUE TRAGEDY

I had not gone ten paces when I caught sight of a strange-looking object, and went nearer to know what it might be. I found it a moldering carriage of ancient form, ruinous but still upright on its heavy wheels. On each side of the pole, still in its place, lay the skeleton of a horse; from their two grim white heads ascended the shriveled reins to the hand of the skeleton-coachman seated on his tattered hammer-cloth; both doors had fallen away; within sat two skeletons, each leaning back in its corner.

Even as I looked, they started awake, and with a cracking rattle of bones, each leaped from the door next it. One fell and lay; the other stood a moment, its structure shaking perilously; then with difficulty, for its joints were stiff, crept, holding by the back of the carriage, to the opposite side, the thin leg-bones seeming hardly strong enough to carry its weight, where, kneeling by the other, it sought to raise it, almost falling itself again in the endeavor.

The prostrate one rose at length, as by a sudden effort, to the sitting posture. For a few moments it turned its yellowish skull to this side and that; then, heedless of its neighbor, got upon its feet by grasping the spokes of the hind wheel. Half erected thus, it stood with its back to the other, both hands holding one of its knee-joints. With little less difficulty and not a few contortions, the kneeling one rose next, and addressed its companion.

"Have you hurt yourself, my lord?" it said, in a voice that sounded far-off, and ill-articulated as if blown aside by some spectral wind.

"Yes, I have," answered the other, in like but rougher tone. "You would do nothing to help me, and this cursed knee is out!"

"I did my best, my lord."

"No doubt, my lady, for it was bad! I thought I should never find my feet again! — But, bless my soul, madam! are you out in your bones?"

She cast a look at herself.

"I have nothing else to be out in," she returned; "— and YOU at least cannot complain! But what on earth does it mean? Am I dreaming?"

"YOU may be dreaming, madam — I cannot tell; but this knee of mine forbids me the grateful illusion. — Ha! I too, I perceive, have nothing to walk in but bones! — Not so unbecoming to a man, however! I trust to goodness they are not MY bones! every one aches worse than another, and this loose knee worst of all! The bed must have been damp—and I too drunk to know it!"

"Probably, my lord of Cokayne!"

"What! what! — You make me think I too am dreaming — aches and all! How do YOU know the title my roistering bullies give me? I don't remember you! — Anyhow, you have no right to take liberties! My name is — I am lord — tut, tut! What do you call me when I'm – I mean when you are sober? I cannot — at the moment, — Why, what IS my name? — I must have been VERY drunk when I went to bed! I often am!"

"You come so seldom to mine, that I do not know, my lord; but I may take your word for THAT!"

"I hope so!"

"— if for nothing else!" "Hoity toity! I never told you a lie in my life!"

"You never told me anything but lies."

"Upon my honor! — Why, I never saw the woman before!"

"You knew me well enough to lie to, my lord!"

"I do seem to begin to dream I have met you before, but, upon my oath, there is nothing to know you by! Out of your clothes, who is to tell who you may not be? — One thing I MAY swear — that I never saw you so much undressed before! — By heaven, I have no recollection of you!"

"I am glad to hear it: my recollections of you are the less distasteful! — Good morning, my lord!"

She turned away, hobbled, clacking, a few paces, and stood again.

"You are just as heartless as – as — any other woman, madam! – Where in this hell of a place shall I find my valet? — What was the cursed name I used to call the fool?"

He turned his bare noddle this way and that on its creaking pivot, still holding his knee with both hands.

"I will be your valet for once, my lord," said the lady, turning once more to him. "—What can I do for you? It is not easy to tell!"

"Tie my leg on, of course, you fool! Can't you see it is all but off? Heigho, my dancing days!"

She looked about with her eyeless sockets and found a piece of fibrous grass, with which she proceeded to bind together the adjoining parts that had formed the knee. When she had done, he gave one or two carefully tentative stamps.

"You used to stamp rather differently, my lord!" she said, as she rose from her knees.

"Eh? what! — Now I look at you again, it seems to me I used to hate you! — Eh?"

"Naturally, my lord! You hated a good many people! — your wife, of course, among the rest!"

"Ah, I begin, I be-gin – But – I must have been a long time somewhere! — I really forget! — There! your damned, miserable bit of grass is breaking! — We used to get on PRETTY well together—eh?"

"Not that I remember, my lord. The only happy moments I had in your company were scattered over the first week of our marriage."

"Was that the way of it? Ha! ha! — Well, it's over now, thank goodness!"

"I wish I could believe it! Why were we sitting there in that carriage together? It wakes apprehension!"

"I think we were divorced, my lady!"

"Hardly enough: we are still together!"

"A sad truth, but capable of remedy: the forest seems of some extent!"

"I doubt! I doubt!"

"I am sorry I cannot think of a compliment to pay you — without lying, that is. To judge by your figure and complexion you have lived hard since I saw you last! I cannot surely be QUITE so naked as your ladyship! — I beg your pardon, madam! I trust you will take it I am but jesting in a dream! It is of no consequence, however; dreaming or waking, all's one — all merest appearance! You can't be certain of anything, and that's as good as knowing there is nothing! Life may teach any fool that!"

"It has taught me the fool I was to love you!"

"You were not the only fool to do that! Women had a trick of falling in love with me: —I had forgotten that you were one of them!" "I did love you, my lord — a little — at one time!"

"Ah, there was your mistake, my lady! You should have loved me much, loved me devotedly, loved me savagely — loved me eternally! Then I should have tired of you the sooner, and not hated you so much afterward! — But let bygones be bygones! — WHERE are we? Locality is the question! To be or not to be, is NOT the question!"

"We are in the other world, I presume!"

"Granted! — but in which or what sort of other world? This can't be hell!"

"It must: there's marriage in it! You and I are damned in each other."

"Then I'm not like Othello, damned in a fair wife! — Oh, I remember my Shakespeare, madam!"

She picked up a broken branch that had fallen into a bush, and steadying herself with it, walked away, tossing her little skull.

"Give that stick to me," cried her late husband; "I want it more than you."

She returned him no answer.

"You mean to make me beg for it?"

"Not at all, my lord. I mean to keep it," she replied, continuing her slow departure.

"Give it me at once; I mean to have it! I require it."

"Unfortunately, I think I require it myself!" returned the lady, walking a little quicker, with a sharper cracking of her joints and clinking of her bones.

He started to follow her, but nearly fell: his knee-grass had burst, and with an oath he stopped, grasping his leg again.

"Come and tie it up properly!" he would have thundered, but he only piped and whistled!

She turned and looked at him.

"Come and tie it up instantly!" he repeated.

She walked a step or two farther from him.

"I swear I will not touch you!" he cried.

"Swear on, my lord! there is no one here to believe you. But, pray, do not lose your temper, or you will shake yourself to pieces, and where to find string enough to tie up all your crazy joints, is more than I can tell."

She came back, and knelt once more at his side — first, however, laying the stick in dispute beyond his reach and within her own.

The instant she had finished retying the joint, he made a grab at her, thinking, apparently, to seize her by the hair; but his hard fingers slipped on the smooth poll.

"Disgusting!" he muttered, and laid hold of her upper arm-bone.

"You will break it!" she said, looking up from her knees.

"I will, then!" he answered, and began to strain at it.

"I shall not tie your leg again the next time it comes loose!" she threatened.

He gave her arm a vicious twist, but happily her bones were in better condition than his. She stretched her other hand toward the broken branch.

"That's right: reach me the stick!" he grinned.

She brought it round with such a swing that one of the bones of the sounder leg snapped. He fell, choking with curses. The lady laughed.

"Now you will have to wear splints always!" she said; "such dry bones never mend!"

"You devil!" he cried.

"At your service, my lord! Shall I fetch you a couple of wheel-spokes? Neat—but heavy, I fear!"

He turned his bone-face aside, and did not answer, but lay and groaned. I marveled he had not gone to pieces when he fell. The lady rose and walked away — not all ungracefully, I thought.

"What can come of it?" I said to myself. "These are too wretched for any world, and this cannot be hell, for the Little Ones are in it, and the sleepers too! What can it all mean? Can things ever come right for skeletons?"

"There are words too big for you and me: ALL is one of them, and EVER is another," said a voice near me which I knew.

I looked about, but could not see the speaker.

"You are not in hell," it resumed. "Neither am I in hell. But those skeletons are in hell!"

Ere he ended I caught sight of the raven on the bough of a beech, right over my head. The same moment he left it, and alighting on the ground, stood there, the thin old man of the library, with long nose and long coat.

"The male was never a gentleman," he went on, "and in the bony stage of retrogression, with his skeleton through his skin, and his character outside his manners, does not look like one. The female is less vulgar, and has a little heart. But, the restraints of society removed, you see them now just as they are and always were!"

"Tell me, Mr. Raven, what will become of them," I said.

"We shall see," he replied. "In their day they were the handsomest couple at court; and now, even in their dry bones, they seem to regard their former repute as an inalienable possession; to see their faces, however, may yet do something for them! They felt themselves rich too while they had pockets, but they have already begun to feel rather pinched! My lord used to regard my lady as a worthless encumbrance, for he was tired of her beauty and had spent her money; now he needs her to cobble his joints for him! These changes have roots of hope in them. Besides, they cannot now get far away from each other, and they see none else of their own kind: they must at last grow weary of their mutual repugnance, and begin to love one another! for love, not hate, is deepest in what Love `loved into being.'"

"I saw many more of their kind an hour ago, in the hall close by!" I said.

"Of their kind, but not of their sort," he answered. "For many years these will see none such as you saw last night. Those are centuries in advance of these. You saw that those could even dress themselves a little! It is true they cannot yet retain their clothes so long as they would — only, at present, for a part of the night; but they are pretty steadily growing more capable, and will by and by develop faces; for every grain of truthfulness adds a fiber to the show of their humanity. Nothing but truth can appear; and whatever is must seem."

"Are they upheld by this hope?" I asked.

"They are upheld by hope, but they do not in the least know their hope; to understand it, is yet immeasurably beyond them," answered Mr. Raven.

His unexpected appearance had caused me no astonishment. I was like a child, constantly wondering, and surprised at nothing.

"Did you come to find me, sir?" I asked.

"Not at all," he replied. "I have no anxiety about you. Such as you always come back to us."

"Tell me, please, who am I such as?" I said.

"I cannot make my friend the subject of conversation," he answered, with a smile.

"But when that friend is present!" I urged.

"I decline the more strongly," he rejoined.

"But when that friend asks you!" I persisted.

"Then most positively I refuse," he returned.

"Why?"

"Because he and I would be talking of two persons as if they were one and the same. Your consciousness of yourself and my knowledge of you are far apart!"

The lapels of his coat flew out, and the lappets lifted, and I thought the metamorphosis of HOMO to CORVUS was about to take place before my eyes. But the coat closed again in front of him, and he added, with seeming inconsequence,

"In this world never trust a person who has once deceived you. Above all, never do anything such a one may ask you to do."

"I will try to remember," I answered; "— but I may forget!"

"Then some evil that is good for you will follow."

"And if I remember?"

"Some evil that is not good for you, will not follow."

The old man seemed to sink to the ground, and immediately I saw the raven several yards from me, flying low and fast.

18. DEAD OR ALIVE?

I went walking on, still facing the moon, who, not yet high, was staring straight into the forest. I did not know what ailed her, but she was dark and dented, like a battered disc of old copper, and looked dispirited and weary. Not a cloud was nigh to keep her company, and the stars were too bright for her. "Is this going to last for ever?" she seemed to say. She was going one way and I was going the other, yet through the wood we went a long way together. We did not commune much, for my eyes were on the ground; but her disconsolate look was fixed on me: I felt without seeing it. A long time we were together, I and the moon, walking side by side, she the dull shine, and I the live shadow.

Something on the ground, under a spreading tree, caught my eye with its whiteness, and I turned toward it. Vague as it was in the shadow of the foliage, it suggested, as I drew nearer, a human body. "Another skeleton!" I said to myself, kneeling and laying my hand upon it. A body it was, however, and no skeleton, though as nearly one as body could well be. It lay on its side, and was very cold — not cold like a stone, but cold like that which was once alive, and is alive no more. The closer I looked at it, the oftener I touched it, the less it seemed possible it should be other than dead. For one bewildered moment, I fancied it one of the wild dancers, a ghostly Cinderella, perhaps, that had lost her way home, and perished in the strange night of an out-of-door world! It was quite naked, and so worn that, even in the shadow, I could, peering close, have counted without touching them, every rib in its side. All its bones, indeed, were as visible as if tight-covered with only a thin elastic leather. Its beautiful yet terrible teeth, unseemly disclosed by the retracted lips, gleamed ghastly through the dark. Its hair was longer than itself, thick and very fine to the touch, and black as night.

It was the body of a tall, probably graceful woman. — How had she come there? Not of herself, and already in such wasted condition, surely! Her strength must have failed her; she had fallen, and lain there until she died of hunger! But how, even so, could she be thus emaciated? And how came she to be naked? Where were the savages to strip and leave her? or what wild beasts would have taken her garments? That her body should have been left was not wonderful!

I rose to my feet, stood, and considered. I must not, could not let her lie exposed and forsaken! Natural reverence forbade it. Even the garment of a woman claims respect; her body it were impossible to leave uncovered! Irreverent eyes might look on it! Brutal claws might toss it about! Years would pass ere the friendly rains washed it into the soil! — But the ground was hard, almost solid with interlacing roots, and I had but my bare hands!

At first it seemed plain that she had not long been dead: there was not a sign of decay about her! But then what had the slow wasting of life left of her to decay?

Could she be still alive? Might she not? What if she were! Things went very strangely in this strange world! Even then there would be little chance of bringing her back, but I must know she was dead before I buried her!

As I left the forest-hall, I had spied in the doorway a bunch of ripe grapes, and brought it with me, eating as I came: a few were yet left on the stalk, and their juice might possibly revive her! Anyhow it was all I had with which to attempt her rescue! The mouth was happily a little open; but the head was in such an awkward position that, to move the body, I passed my arm under the shoulder on which it lay, when I found the pine-needles beneath it warm: she could not have been any time dead, and MIGHT still be alive, though I could discern no motion of the heart, or any indication that she breathed! One of her hands was clenched hard, apparently inclosing something small. I squeezed a grape into her mouth, but no swallowing followed.

To do for her all I could, I spread a thick layer of pine-needles and dry leaves, laid one of my garments over it, warm from my body, lifted her upon it, and covered her with my clothes and a great heap of leaves: I would save the little warmth left in her, hoping an increase to it when the sun came back. Then I tried another grape, but could perceive no slightest movement of mouth or throat.

"Doubt," I said to myself, "may be a poor encouragement to do anything, but it is a bad reason for doing nothing." So tight was the skin upon her bones that I dared not use friction.

I crept into the heap of leaves, got as close to her as I could, and took her in my arms. I had not much heat left in me, but what I had I would share with her! Thus I spent what remained of the night, sleepless, and longing for the sun. Her cold seemed to radiate into me, but no heat to pass from me to her.

Had I fled from the beautiful sleepers, I thought, each on her "dim, straight" silver couch, to lie alone with such a bedfellow! I had refused a lovely privilege: I was given over to an awful duty! Beneath the sad, slow-setting moon, I lay with the dead, and watched for the dawn.

The darkness had given way, and the eastern horizon was growing dimly clearer, when I caught sight of a motion rather than of anything that moved — not far from me, and close to the ground. It was the low undulating of a large snake, which passed me in an unswerving line. Presently appeared, making as it seemed for the same point, what I took for a roebuck-doe and her calf. Again a while, and two creatures like bear-cubs came, with three or four smaller ones behind them. The light was now growing so rapidly that when, a few minutes after, a troop of horses went trotting past, I could see that, although the largest of them were no bigger than the smallest Shetland pony, they must yet be full-grown, so perfect were they in form, and so much had they all the ways and action of great horses. They were of many breeds. Some seemed models of cart-horses, others of chargers, hunters, racers. Dwarf cattle and small elephants followed.

"Why are the children not here!" I said to myself. "The moment I am free of this poor woman, I must go back and fetch them!"

Where were the creatures going? What drew them? Was this an exodus, or a morning habit? I must wait for the sun! Till he came I must not leave the woman! I laid my hand on the body, and could not help thinking it felt a trifle warmer. It might have gained a little of the heat I had lost! it could hardly have generated any! What reason for hope there was had not grown less!

The forehead of the day began to glow, and soon the sun came peering up, as if to see for the first time what all this stir of a new world was about. At sight of his great innocent splendor, I rose full of life, strong against death. Removing the handkerchief I had put to protect the mouth and eyes from the pine-needles, I looked anxiously to see whether I had found a priceless jewel, or but its empty case.

The body lay motionless as when I found it. Then first, in the morning light, I saw how drawn and hollow was the face, how sharp were the bones under the skin, how every tooth shaped itself through the lips. The human garment was indeed worn to its threads, but the bird of heaven might yet be nestling within, might yet awake to motion and song!

But the sun was shining on her face! I re-arranged the handkerchief, laid a few leaves lightly over it, and set out to follow the creatures. Their main track was well beaten, and must have long been used — likewise many of the tracks that, joining it from both sides, merged in, and broadened it. The trees retreated as I went, and the grass grew thicker. Presently the forest was gone, and a wide expanse of loveliest green stretched away to the horizon. Through it, along the edge of the forest, flowed a small river, and to this the track led. At sight of the water a new though undefined hope sprang up in me. The stream looked everywhere deep, and was full to the brim, but nowhere more than a few yards wide. A bluish mist rose from it, vanishing as it rose. On the opposite side, in the plentiful grass, many small animals were feeding. Apparently they slept in the forest, and in the morning sought the plain, swimming the river to reach it. I knelt and would have drunk, but the water was hot, and had a strange metallic taste.

I leapt to my feet: here was the warmth I sought — the first necessity of life! I sped back to my helpless charge.

Without well considering my solitude, no one will understand what seemed to lie for me in the redemption of this woman from death. "Prove what she may," I thought with myself, "I shall at least be lonely no more!" I had found myself such poor company that now first I seemed to know what hope was. This blessed water would expel the cold death, and drown my desolation!

I bore her to the stream. Tall as she was, I found her marvelously light, her bones were so delicate, and so little covered them. I grew yet more hopeful when I found her so far from stiff that I could carry her on one arm, like a sleeping child, leaning against my shoulder. I went softly, dreading even the wind of my motion, and glad there was no other.

The water was too hot to lay her at once in it: the shock might scare from her the yet fluttering life! I laid her on the bank, and dipping one of my garments, began to bathe the pitiful form. So wasted was it that, save from the plentifulness and blackness of the hair, it was impossible even to conjecture whether she was young or old. Her eyelids were just not shut, which made her look dead the more: there was a crack in the clouds of her night, at which no sun shone through!

The longer I went on bathing the poor bones, the less grew my hope that they would ever again be clothed with strength, that ever those eyelids would lift, and a soul look out; still I kept bathing continuously, allowing no part time to grow cold while I bathed another; and gradually the body became so much warmer, that at last I ventured to submerge it: I got into the stream and drew it in, holding the face above the water, and letting the swift, steady current flow all about the rest. I noted, but was able to conclude nothing from the fact, that, for all the heat, the shut hand never relaxed its hold.

After about ten minutes, I lifted it out and laid it again on the bank, dried it, and covered it as well as I could, then ran to the forest for leaves.

The grass and soil were dry and warm; and when I returned I thought it had scarcely lost any of the heat the water had given it. I spread the leaves upon it, and ran for more — then for a third and a fourth freight.

I could now leave it and go to explore, in the hope of discovering some shelter. I ran up the stream toward some rocky hills I saw in that direction, which were not far off.

When I reached them, I found the river issuing full grown from a rock at the bottom of one of them. To my fancy it seemed to have run down a stair inside, an eager cataract, at every landing wild to get out, but only at the foot finding a door of escape.

It did not fill the opening whence it rushed, and I crept through into a little cave, where I learned that, instead of hurrying tumultuously down a stair, it rose quietly from the ground at the back like the base of a large column, and ran along one side, nearly filling a deep, rather narrow channel. I considered the place, and saw that, if I could find a few fallen boughs long enough to lie across the channel, and large enough to bear a little weight without bending much, I might, with smaller branches and plenty of leaves, make upon them a comfortable couch, which the stream under would keep constantly warm. Then I ran back to see how my charge fared.

She was lying as I had left her. The heat had not brought her to life, but neither had it developed anything to check farther hope. I got a few boulders out of the channel, and arranged them at her feet and on both sides of her.

Running again to the wood, I had not to search long ere I found some small boughs fit for my purpose — mostly of beech, their dry yellow leaves yet clinging to them. With these I had soon laid the floor of a bridge-bed over the torrent. I crossed the boughs with smaller branches, interlaced these with twigs, and buried all deep in leaves and dry moss.

When thus at length, after not a few journeys to the forest, I had completed a warm, dry, soft couch, I took the body once more, and set out with it for the cave. It was so light that now and then as I went I almost feared lest, when I laid it down, I should find it a skeleton after all; and when at last I did lay it gently on the pathless bridge, it was a greater relief to part with that fancy than with the weight. Once more I covered the body with a thick layer of leaves; and trying again to feed her with a grape, found to my joy that I could open the mouth a little farther. The grape, indeed, lay in it unheeded, but I hoped some of the juice might find its way down.

After an hour or two on the couch, she was no longer cold. The warmth of the brook had interpenetrated her frame — truly it was but a frame! — and she was warm to the touch; —not, probably, with the warmth of life, but with a warmth which rendered it more possible, if she were alive, that she might live. I had read of one in a trance lying motionless for weeks!

In that cave, day after day, night after night, seven long days and nights, I sat or lay, now waking now sleeping, but always watching. Every morning I went out and bathed in the hot stream, and every morning felt thereupon as if I had eaten and drunk — which experience gave me courage to lay her in it also every day. Once as I did so, a shadow of discoloration on her left side gave me a terrible shock, but the next morning it had vanished, and I continued the treatment — every morning, after her bath, putting a fresh grape in her mouth.

I too ate of the grapes and other berries I found in the forest; but I believed that, with my daily bath in that river, I could have done very well without eating at all.

Every time I slept, I dreamed of finding a wounded angel, who, unable to fly, remained with me until at last she loved me and would not leave me; and every time I woke, it was to see, instead of an angel-visage with lustrous eyes, the white, motionless, wasted face upon the couch. But Adam himself, when first he saw her asleep, could not have looked more anxiously for Eve's awaking than I watched for this woman's. Adam knew nothing of himself, perhaps nothing of his need of another self; I, an alien from my fellows, had learned to love what I had lost! Were this one wasted shred of womanhood to disappear, I should have nothing in me but a consuming hunger after life! I forgot even the Little Ones: things were not amiss with them! here lay what might wake and be a woman! Might actually open eyes, and look out of them upon me!

Now first I knew what solitude meant — now that I gazed on one who neither saw nor heard, neither moved nor spoke. I saw now that a man alone is but a being that may become a man — that he is but a need, and therefore a possibility. To be enough for himself, a being must be an eternal, self-existent worm! So superbly constituted, so simply complicate is man; he rises from and stands upon such a pedestal of lower physical organisms and spiritual structures, that no atmosphere will comfort or nourish his life, less divine than that offered by other souls; nowhere but in other lives can he breathe. Only by the reflex of other lives can he ripen his specialty, develop the idea of himself, the individuality that distinguishes him from every other. Were all men alike, each would still have an individuality, secured by his personal consciousness, but there would be small reason why there should be more than two or three such; while, for the development of the differences which make a large and lofty unity possible, and which alone can make millions into a church, an endless and measureless influence and reaction are indispensable. A man to be perfect — complete, that is, in having reached the spiritual condition of persistent and universal growth, which is the mode wherein he inherits the infinitude of his Father — must have the education of a world of fellow-men. Save for the hope of the dawn of life in the form beside me, I should have fled for fellowship to the beasts that grazed and did not speak. Better to go about with them — infinitely better—than to live alone! But with the faintest prospect of a woman to my friend, I, poorest of creatures, was yet a possible man!

19. THE WHITE LEECH

I woke one morning from a profound sleep, with one of my hands very painful. The back of it was much swollen, and in the centre of the swelling was a triangular wound, like the bite of a leech. As the day went on, the swelling subsided, and by the evening the hurt was all but healed. I searched the cave, turning over every stone of any size, but discovered nothing I could imagine capable of injuring me.

Slowly the days passed, and still the body never moved, never opened its eyes. It could not be dead, for assuredly it manifested no sign of decay, and the air about it was quite pure. Moreover, I could imagine that the sharpest angles of the bones had begun to disappear, that the form was everywhere a little rounder, and the skin had less of the parchment-look: if such change was indeed there, life must be there! the tide which had ebbed so far toward the infinite, must have begun again to flow! Oh joy to me, if the rising ripples of life's ocean were indeed burying under lovely shape the bones it had all but forsaken! Twenty times a day I looked for evidence of progress, and twenty times a day I doubted — sometimes even despaired; but the moment I recalled the mental picture of her as I found her, hope revived.

Several weeks had passed thus, when one night, after lying a long time awake, I rose, thinking to go out and breathe the cooler air; for, although from the running of the stream it was always fresh in the cave, the heat was not seldom a little oppressive. The moon outside was full, the air within shadowy clear, and naturally I cast a lingering look on my treasure ere I went. "Bliss eternal!" I cried aloud, "do I see her eyes?" Great orbs, dark as if cut from the sphere of a starless night, and luminous by excess of darkness, seemed to shine amid the glimmering whiteness of her face. I stole nearer, my heart beating so that I feared the noise of it startling her. I bent over her. Alas, her eyelids were close shut! Hope and Imagination had wrought mutual illusion! my heart's desire would never be! I turned away, threw myself on the floor of the cave, and wept. Then I bethought me that her eyes had been a little open, and that now the awful chink out of which nothingness had peered, was gone: it might be that she had opened them for a moment, and was again asleep! — it might be she was awake and holding them close! In either case, life, less or more, must have shut them! I was comforted, and fell fast asleep.

That night I was again bitten, and awoke with a burning thirst.

In the morning I searched yet more thoroughly, but again in vain. The wound was of the same character, and, as before, was nearly well by the evening. I concluded that some large creature of the leech kind came occasionally from the hot stream. "But, if blood be its object," I said to myself, "so long as I am there, I need hardly fear for my treasure!"

That same morning, when, having peeled a grape as usual and taken away the seeds, I put it in her mouth, her lips made a slight movement of reception, and I KNEW she lived!

My hope was now so much stronger that I began to think of some attire for her: she must be able to rise the moment she wished! I betook myself therefore to the forest, to investigate what material it might afford, and had hardly begun to look when fibrous skeletons, like those of the leaves of the prickly pear, suggested themselves as fit for the purpose. I gathered a stock of them, laid them to dry in the sun, pulled apart the reticulated layers, and of these had soon begun to fashion two loose garments, one to hang from her waist, the other from her shoulders. With the stiletto-point of an aloe-leaf and various filaments, I sewed together three thicknesses of the tissue.

During the week that followed, there was no farther sign except that she more evidently took the grapes. But indeed all the signs became surer: plainly she was growing plumper, and her skin fairer. Still she did not open her eyes; and the horrid fear would at times invade me, that her growth was of some hideous fungoid nature, the few grapes being nowise sufficient to account for it.

Again I was bitten; and now the thing, whatever it was, began to pay me regular visits at intervals of three days. It now generally bit me in the neck or the arm, invariably with but one bite, always while I slept, and never, even when I slept, in the daytime. Hour after hour would I lie awake on the watch, but never heard it coming, or saw sign of its approach. Neither, I believe, did I ever feel it bite me. At length I became so hopeless of catching it, that I no longer troubled myself either to look for it by day, or lie in wait for it at night. I knew from my growing weakness that I was losing blood at a dangerous rate, but I cared little for that: in sight of my eyes death was yielding to life; a soul was gathering strength to save me from loneliness; we would go away together, and I should speedily recover!

The garments were at length finished, and, contemplating my handiwork with no small satisfaction, I proceeded to mat layers of the fiber into sandals.

One night I woke suddenly, breathless and faint, and longing after air, and had risen to crawl from the cave, when a slight rustle in the leaves of the couch set me listening motionless.

"I caught the vile thing," said a feeble voice, in my mother-tongue; "I caught it in the very act!"

She was alive! she spoke! I dared not yield to my transport lest I should terrify her.

"What creature?" I breathed, rather than said.

"The creature," she answered, "that was biting you."

"What was it?"

"A great white leech."

"How big?" I pursued, forcing myself to be calm.

"Not far from six feet long, I should think," she answered.

"You have saved my life, perhaps! — But how could you touch the horrid thing! How brave of you!" I cried.

"I did!" was all her answer, and I thought she shuddered.

"Where is it? What could you do with such a monster?"

"I threw it in the river."

"Then it will come again, I fear!"

"I do not think I could have killed it, even had I known how!—I heard you moaning, and got up to see what disturbed you; saw the frightful thing at your neck, and pulled it away. But I could not hold it, and was hardly able to throw it from me. I only heard it splash in the water!"

"We'll kill it next time!" I said; but with that I turned faint, sought the open air, but fell.

When I came to myself the sun was up. The lady stood a little way off, looking, even in the clumsy attire I had fashioned for her, at once grand and graceful. I HAD seen those glorious eyes! Through the night they had shone! Dark as the darkness primeval, they now outshone the day! She stood erect as a column, regarding me. Her pale cheek indicated no emotion, only question. I rose.

"We must be going!" I said. "The white leech —"

I stopped: a strange smile had flickered over her beautiful face.

"Did you find me there?" she asked, pointing to the cave.

"No; I brought you there," I replied.

"You brought me?"

"Yes."

"From where?"

"From the forest."

"What have you done with my clothes — and my jewels?"

"You had none when I found you."

"Then why did you not leave me?"

"Because I hoped you were not dead."

"Why should you have cared?"

"Because I was very lonely, and wanted you to live."

"You would have kept me enchanted for my beauty!" she said, with proud scorn.

Her words and her look roused my indignation.

"There was no beauty left in you," I said.

"Why, then, again, did you not let me alone?"

"Because you were of my own kind."

"Of YOUR kind?" she cried, in a tone of utter contempt.

"I thought so, but find I was mistaken!"

"Doubtless you pitied me!"

"Never had woman more claim on pity, or less on any other feeling!"

With an expression of pain, mortification, and anger unutterable, she turned from me and stood silent. Starless night lay profound in the gulfs of her eyes: hate of him who brought it back had slain their splendor. The light of life was gone from them.

"Had you failed to rouse me, what would you have done?" she asked suddenly without moving.

"I would have buried it."

"It! What? — You would have buried THIS?" she exclaimed, flashing round upon me in a white fury, her arms thrown out, and her eyes darting forks of cold lightning.

"Nay; that I saw not! That, weary weeks of watching and tending have brought back to you," I answered — for with such a woman I must be plain! "Had I seen the smallest sign of decay, I would at once have buried you."

"Dog of a fool!" she cried, "I was but in a trance—Samoil! What a fate! — Go and fetch the she-savage from whom you borrowed this hideous disguise."

"I made it for you. It is hideous, but I did my best."

She drew herself up to her tall height.

"How long have I been insensible?" she demanded. "A woman could not have made that dress in a day!"

"Not in twenty days," I rejoined, "hardly in thirty!"

"Ha! How long do you pretend I have lain unconscious? — Answer me at once."

"I cannot tell how long you had lain when I found you, but there was nothing left of you save skin and bone: that is more than three months ago. — Your hair was beautiful, nothing else! I have done for it what I could."

"My poor hair!" she said, and brought a great armful of it round from behind her; "— it will be more than a three-months' care to bring YOU to life again! — I suppose I must thank you, although I cannot say I am grateful!"

"There is no need, madam: I would have done the same for any woman—yes, or for any man either!"

"How is it my hair is not tangled?" she said, fondling it.

"It always drifted in the current."

"How? — What do you mean?"

"I could not have brought you to life but by bathing you in the hot river every morning."

She gave a shudder of disgust, and stood for a while with her gaze fixed on the hurrying water. Then she turned to me:

"We must understand each other!" she said. "— You have done me the two worst of wrongs — compelled me to live, and put me to shame: neither of them can I pardon!"

She raised her left hand, and flung it out as if repelling me. Something ice-cold struck me on the forehead. When I came to myself, I was on the ground, wet and shivering.

20. Gone! But How?

I rose, and looked around me, dazed at heart. For a moment I could not see her: she was gone, and loneliness had returned like the cloud after the rain! She whom I brought back from the brink of the grave, had fled from me, and left me with desolation! I dared not one moment remain thus hideously alone. Had I indeed done her a wrong? I must devote my life to sharing the burden I had compelled her to resume!

I descried her walking swiftly over the grass, away from the river, took one plunge for a farewell restorative, and set out to follow her. The last visit of the white leech, and the blow of the woman, had enfeebled me, but already my strength was reviving, and I kept her in sight without difficulty.

"Is this, then, the end?" I said as I went, and my heart brooded a sad song. Her angry, hating eyes haunted me. I could understand her resentment at my having forced life upon her, but how had I further injured her? Why should she loathe me? Could modesty itself be indignant with true service? How should the proudest woman, conscious of my every action, cherish against me the least sense of disgracing wrong? How reverently had I not touched her! As a father his motherless child, I had borne and tended her! Had all my labor, all my despairing hope gone to redeem only ingratitude? "No," I answered myself; "beauty must have a heart! However profoundly hidden, it must be there! The deeper buried, the stronger and truer will it wake at last in its beautiful grave! To rouse that heart were a better gift to her than the happiest life! It would be to give her a nobler, a higher life!"

She was ascending a gentle slope before me, walking straight and steady as one that knew whither, when I became aware that she was increasing the distance between us. I summoned my strength, and it came in full tide. My veins filled with fresh life! My body seemed to become ethereal, and, following like an easy wind, I rapidly overtook her.

Not once had she looked behind. Swiftly she moved, like a Greek goddess to rescue, but without haste. I was within three yards of her, when she turned sharply, yet with grace unbroken, and stood. Fatigue or heat she showed none. Her paleness was not a pallor, but a pure whiteness; her breathing was slow and deep. Her eyes seemed to fill the heavens, and give light to the world. It was nearly noon, but the sense was upon me as of a great night in which an invisible dew makes the stars look large.

"Why do you follow me?" she asked, quietly but rather sternly, as if she had never before seen me.

"I have lived so long," I answered, "on the mere hope of your eyes, that I must want to see them again!"

"You WILL not be spared!" she said coldly. "I command you to stop where you stand."

"Not until I see you in a place of safety will I leave you," I replied.

"Then take the consequences," she said, and resumed her swift-gliding walk.

But as she turned she cast on me a glance, and I stood as if run through with a spear. Her scorn had failed: she would kill me with her beauty!

Despair restored my volition; the spell broke; I ran, and overtook her.

"Have pity upon me!" I cried.

She gave no heed. I followed her like a child whose mother pretends to abandon him. "I will be your slave!" I said, and laid my hand on her arm.

She turned as if a serpent had bit her. I cowered before the blaze of her eyes, but could not avert my own.

"Pity me," I cried again.

She resumed her walking.

The whole day I followed her. The sun climbed the sky, seemed to pause on its summit, went down the other side. Not a moment did she pause, not a moment did I cease to follow. She never turned her head, never relaxed her pace.

The sun went below, and the night came up. I kept close to her: if I lost sight of her for a moment, it would be for ever!

All day long we had been walking over thick soft grass: abruptly she stopped, and threw herself upon it. There was yet light enough to show that she was utterly weary. I stood behind her, and gazed down on her for a moment.

Did I love her? I knew she was not good! Did I hate her? I could not leave her! I knelt beside her.

"Be gone! Do not dare touch me," she cried.

Her arms lay on the grass by her sides as if paralyzed.

Suddenly they closed about my neck, rigid as those of the torture-maiden. She drew down my face to hers, and her lips clung to my cheek. A sting of pain shot somewhere through me, and pulsed. I could not stir a hair's breadth. Gradually the pain ceased. A slumberous weariness, a dreamy pleasure stole over me, and then I knew nothing.

All at once I came to myself. The moon was a little way above the horizon, but spread no radiance; she was but a bright thing set in blackness. My cheek smarted; I put my hand to it, and found a wet spot. My neck ached: there again was a wet spot! I sighed heavily, and felt very tired. I turned my eyes listlessly around me — and saw what had become of the light of the moon: it was gathered about the lady! she stood in a shimmering nimbus! I rose and staggered toward her.

"Down!" she cried imperiously, as to a rebellious dog. "Follow me a step if you dare!"

"I will!" I murmured, with an agonized effort.

"Set foot within the gates of my city, and my people will stone you: they do not love beggars!"

I was deaf to her words. Weak as water, and half awake, I did not know that I moved, but the distance grew less between us. She took one step back, raised her left arm, and with the clenched hand seemed to strike me on the forehead. I received as it were a blow from an iron hammer, and fell.

I sprang to my feet, cold and wet, but clear-headed and strong. Had the blow revived me? it had left neither wound nor pain! — But how came I wet? — I could not have lain long, for the moon was no higher!

The lady stood some yards away, her back toward me. She was doing something, I could not distinguish what. Then by her sudden gleam I knew she had thrown off her garments, and stood white in the dazed moon. One moment she stood — and fell forward.

A streak of white shot away in a swift-drawn line. The same instant the moon recovered herself, shining out with a full flash, and I saw that the streak was a long-bodied thing, rushing in great, low-curved bounds over the grass. Dark spots seemed to run like a stream adown its back, as if it had been fleeting along under the edge of a wood, and catching the shadows of the leaves.

"God of mercy!" I cried, "is the terrible creature speeding to the night-infolded city?" and I seemed to hear from afar the sudden burst and spread of out crying terror, as the pale savage bounded from house to house, rending and slaying.

While I gazed after it fear-stricken, past me from behind, like a swift, all but noiseless arrow, shot a second large creature, pure white. Its path was straight for the spot where the lady had fallen, and, as I thought, lay. My tongue clave to the roof of my mouth. I sprang forward pursuing the beast. But in a moment the spot I made for was far behind it.

"It was well," I thought, "that I could not cry out: if she had risen, the monster would have been upon her!"

But when I reached the place, no lady was there; only the garments she had dropped lay dusk in the moonlight.

I stood staring after the second beast. It tore over the ground with yet greater swiftness than the former — in long, level, skimming leaps, the very embodiment of wasteless speed. It followed the line the other had taken, and I watched it grow smaller and smaller, until it disappeared in the uncertain distance.

But where was the lady? Had the first beast surprised her, creeping upon her noiselessly? I had heard no shriek! and there had not been time to devour her! Could it have caught her up as it ran, and borne her away to its den? So laden it could not have run so fast! and I should have seen that it carried something!

Horrible doubts began to wake in me. After a thorough but fruitless search, I set out in the track of the two animals.

21. THE FUGITIVE MOTHER

As I hastened along, a cloud came over the moon, and from the gray dark suddenly emerged a white figure, clasping a child to her bosom, and stooping as she ran. She was on a line parallel with my own, but did not perceive me as she hurried along, terror and anxiety in every movement of her driven speed.

"She is chased!" I said to myself. "Some prowler of this terrible night is after her!"

To follow would have added to her fright: I stepped into her track to stop her pursuer.

As I stood for a moment looking after her through the dusk, behind me came a swift, soft-footed rush, and ere I could turn, something sprang over my head, struck me sharply on the forehead, and knocked me down. I was up in an instant, but all I saw of my assailant was a vanishing whiteness. I ran after the beast, with the blood trickling from my forehead; but had run only a few steps, when a shriek of despair tore the quivering night. I ran the faster, though I could not but fear it must already be too late.

In a minute or two I spied a low white shape approaching me through the vapor-dusted moonlight. It must be another beast, I thought at first, for it came slowly, almost crawling, with strange, floundering leaps, as of a creature in agony! I drew aside from its path, and waited. As it neared me, I saw it was going on three legs, carrying its left fore-paw high from the ground. It had many dark, oval spots on a shining white skin, and was attended by a low rushing sound, as of water falling upon grass. As it went by me, I saw something streaming from the lifted paw.

"It is blood!" I said to myself, "some readier champion than I has wounded the beast!" But, strange to tell, such a pity seized me at sight of the suffering creature, that, though an axe had been in my hand I could not have struck at it. In a broken succession of hobbling leaps it went out of sight, its blood, as it seemed, still issuing in a small torrent, which kept flowing back softly through the grass beside me. "If it go on bleeding like that," I thought, "it will soon be hurtless!"

I went on, for I might yet be useful to the woman, and hoped also to see her deliverer.

I descried her a little way off, seated on the grass, with her child in her lap.

"Can I do anything for you?" I asked.

At the sound of my voice she started violently, and would have risen. I threw myself on the ground.

"You need not be frightened," I said. "I was following the beast when happily you found a nearer protector! It passed me now with its foot bleeding so much that by this time it must be all but dead!"

"There is little hope of that!" she answered, trembling. "Do you not know whose beast she is?"

Now I had certain strange suspicions, but I answered that I knew nothing of the brute, and asked what had become of her champion.

"What champion?" she rejoined. "I have seen no one."

"Then how came the monster to grief?"

"I pounded her foot with a stone — as hard as I could strike. Did you not hear her cry?"

"Well, you are a brave woman!" I answered. "I thought it was you gave the cry!"

"It was the leopardess."

"I never heard such a sound from the throat of an animal! it was like the scream of a woman in torture!"

"My voice was gone; I could not have shrieked to save my baby! When I saw the horrid mouth at my darling's little white neck, I caught up a stone and mashed her lame foot."

"Tell me about the creature," I said; "I am a stranger in these parts."

"You will soon know about her if you are going to Bulika!" she answered. "Now, I must never go back there!"

"Yes, I am going to Bulika," I said, "— to see the princess."

"Have a care; you had better not go! — But perhaps you are! The princess is a very good, kind woman!"

I heard a little movement. Clouds had by this time gathered so thick over the moon that I could scarcely see my companion: I feared she was rising to run from me.

"You are in no danger of any sort from me," I said. "What oath would you like me to take?"

"I know by your speech that you are not of the people of Bulika," she replied; "I will trust you! — I am not of them, either, else I should not be able: they never trust any one—If only I could see you! But I like your voice! — There, my darling is asleep! The foul beast has not hurt her! — Yes: it was my baby she was after!" she went on, caressing the child. "And then she would have torn her mother to pieces for carrying her off! — Some say the princess has two white leopardesses," she continued: "I know only one — with spots. Everybody knows HER! If the princess hear of a baby, she sends her immediately to suck its blood, and then it either dies or grows up an idiot. I would have gone away with my baby, but the princess was from home, and I thought I might wait until I was a little stronger. But she must have taken the beast with her, and been on her way home when I left, and come across my track. I heard the SNIFF-SNUFF of the leopardess behind me, and ran; — oh, how I ran! — But my darling will not die! There is no mark on her!"

"Where are you taking her?"

"Where no one ever tells!"

"Why is the princess so cruel?"

"There is an old prophecy that a child will be the death of her. That is why she will listen to no offer of marriage, they say."

"But what will become of her country if she kill all the babies?"

"She does not care about her country. She sends witches around to teach the women spells that keep babies away, and give them horrible things to eat. Some say she is in league with the Shadows to put an end to the race. At night we hear the questing beast, and lie awake and shiver. She can tell at once the house where a baby is coming, and lies down at the door, watching to get in. There are words that have power to shoo her away, only they do not always work — But here I sit talking, and the beast may by this time have got home, and her mistress be sending the other after us!"

As thus she ended, she rose in haste.

"I do not think she will ever get home. — Let me carry the baby for you!" I said, as I rose also.

She returned me no answer, and when I would have taken it, only clasped it the closer.

"I cannot think," I said, walking by her side, "how the brute could be bleeding so much!"

"Take my advice, and don't go near the palace," she answered. "There are sounds in it at night as if the dead were trying to shriek, but could not open their mouths!"

She bade me an abrupt farewell. Plainly she did not want more of my company; so I stood still, and heard her footsteps die away on the grass.

22. Bulika

I had lost all notion of my position, and was walking about in pure, helpless impatience, when suddenly I found myself in the path of the leopardess, wading in the blood from her paw. It ran against my ankles with the force of a small brook, and I got out of it the more quickly because of an unshaped suspicion in my mind as to whose blood it might be. But I kept close to the sound of it, walking up the side of the stream, for it would guide me in the direction of Bulika.

I soon began to reflect, however, that no leopardess, no elephant, no hugest animal that in our world preceded man, could keep such a torrent flowing, except every artery in its body were open, and its huge system went on filling its vessels from fields and lakes and forests as fast as they emptied themselves: it could not be blood! I dipped a finger in it, and at once satisfied myself that it was not. In truth, however it might have come there, it was a softly murmuring rivulet of water that ran, without channel, over the grass! But sweet as was its song, I dared not drink of it; I kept walking on, hoping after the light, and listening to the familiar sound so long unheard — for that of the hot stream was very different. The mere wetting of my feet in it, however, had so refreshed me, that I went on without fatigue till the darkness began to grow thinner, and I knew the sun was drawing nigh. A few minutes more, and I could discern, against the pale aurora, the wall-towers of a city — seemingly old as time itself. Then I looked down to get a sight of the brook.

It was gone. I had indeed for a long time noted its sound growing fainter, but at last had ceased to attend to it. I looked back: the grass in its course lay bent as it had flowed, and here and there glimmered a small pool. Toward the city, there was no trace of it. Near where I stood, the flow of its fountain must at least have paused!

Around the city were gardens, growing many sorts of vegetables, hardly one of which I recognized. I saw no water, no flowers, no sign of animals. The gardens came very near the walls, but were separated from them by huge heaps of gravel and refuse thrown from the battlements.

I went up to the nearest gate, and found it but half-closed, nowise secured, and without guard or sentinel. To judge by its hinges, it could not be farther opened or shut closer. Passing through, I looked down a long ancient street. It was utterly silent, and with scarce an indication in it of life present. Had I come upon a dead city? I turned and went out again, toiled a long way over the dust-heaps, and crossed several roads, each leading up to a gate: I would not re-enter until some of the inhabitants should be stirring.

What was I there for? what did I expect or hope to find? what did I mean to do?

I must see, if but once more, the woman I had brought to life! I did not desire her society: she had waked in me frightful suspicions; and friendship, not to say love, was wildly impossible between us! But her presence had had a strange influence upon me, and in her presence I must resist, and at the same time analyze that influence! The seemingly inscrutable in her I would fain penetrate: to understand something of her mode of being would be to look into marvels such as imagination could never have suggested! In this I was too daring: a man must not, for knowledge, of his own will encounter temptation! On the other hand, I had reinstated an evil force about to perish, and was, to the extent of my opposing faculty, accountable for what mischief might ensue! I had learned that she was the enemy of children: the Little Ones might be in her danger! It was in the hope of finding out something of their history that I had left them; on that I had received a little light: I must have more; I must learn how to protect them!

Hearing at length a little stir in the place, I walked through the next gate, and thence along a narrow street of tall houses to a little square, where I sat down on the base of a pillar with a hideous bat-like creature atop. Ere long, several of the inhabitants came sauntering past. I spoke to one: he gave me a rude stare and ruder word, and went on.

I got up and went through one narrow street after another, gradually filling with idlers, and was not surprised to see no children. By and by, near one of the gates, I encountered a group of young men who reminded me not a little of the bad giants. They came about me staring, and presently began to push and hustle me, then to throw things at me. I bore it as well as I could, wishing not to provoke enmity where wanted to remain for a while. Oftener than once or twice I appealed to passers-by whom I fancied more benevolent-looking, but none would halt a moment to listen to me.

I looked poor, and that was enough: to the citizens of Bulika, as to house-dogs, poverty was an offence! Deformity and sickness were taxed; and no legislation of their princess was more heartily approved of than what tended to make poverty subserve wealth.

I took to my heels at last, and no one followed me beyond the gate. A lumbering fellow, however, who sat by it eating a hunch of bread, picked up a stone to throw after me, and happily, in his stupid eagerness, threw, not the stone but the bread. I took it, and he did not dare follow to reclaim it: beyond the walls they were cowards every one. I went off a few hundred yards, threw myself down, ate the bread, fell asleep, and slept soundly in the grass, where the hot sunlight renewed my strength.

It was night when I woke. The moon looked down on me in friendly fashion, seeming to claim with me old acquaintance. She was very bright, and the same moon, I thought, that saw me through the terrors of my first night in that strange world. A cold wind blew from the gate, bringing with it an evil odor; but it did not chill me, for the sun had plenished me with warmth. I crept again into the city. There I found the few that were still in the open air crouched in corners to escape the shivering blast.

I was walking slowly through the long narrow street, when, just before me, a huge white thing bounded across it, with a single flash in the moonlight, and disappeared. I turned down the next opening, eager to get sight of it again.

It was a narrow lane, almost too narrow to pass through, but it led me into a wider street. The moment I entered the latter, I saw on the opposite side, in the shadow, the creature I had followed, itself following like a dog what I took for a man. Over his shoulder, every other moment, he glanced at the animal behind him, but neither spoke to it, nor attempted to drive it away. At a place where he had to cross a patch of moonlight, I saw that he cast no shadow, and was himself but a flat superficial shadow, of two dimensions. He was, nevertheless, an opaque shadow, for he not merely darkened any object on the other side of him, but rendered it, in fact, invisible. In the shadow he was blacker than the shadow; in the moonlight he looked like one who had drawn his shadow up about him, for not a suspicion of it moved beside or under him; while the gleaming animal, which followed so close at his heels as to seem the white shadow of his blackness, and which I now saw to be a leopardess, drew her own gliding shadow black over the ground by her side. When they passed together from the shadow into the moonlight, the Shadow deepened in blackness, the animal flashed into radiance. I was at the moment walking abreast of them on the opposite side, my bare feet sounding on the flat stones: the leopardess never turned head or twitched ear; the shadow seemed once to look at me, for I lost his profile, and saw for a second only a sharp upright line. That instant the wind found me and blew through me: I shuddered from head to foot, and my heart went from wall to wall of my bosom, like a pebble in a child's rattle.

23. A Woman Of Bulika

I turned aside into an alley, and sought shelter in a small archway. In the mouth of it I stopped, and looked out at the moonlight which filled the alley. The same instant a woman came gliding in after me, turned, trembling, and looked out also. A few seconds passed; then a huge leopard, its white skin dappled with many blots, darted across the archway. The woman pressed close to me, and my heart filled with pity. I put my arm round her.

"If the brute come here, I will lay hold of it," I said, "and you must run."

"Thank you!" she murmured.

"Have you ever seen it before?" I asked.

"Several times," she answered, still trembling. "She is a pet of the princess's. You are a stranger, or you would know her!"

"I am a stranger," I answered. "But is she, then, allowed to run loose?"

"She is kept in a cage, her mouth muzzled, and her feet in gloves of crocodile leather. Chained she is too; but she gets out often, and sucks the blood of any child she can lay hold of. Happily there are not many mothers in Bulika!"

Here she burst into tears.

"I wish I were at home!" she sobbed. "The princess returned only last night, and there is the leopardess out already! How am I to get into the house? It is me she is after, I know! She will be lying at my own door, watching for me! — But I am a fool to talk to a stranger!"

"All strangers are not bad!" I said. "The beast shall not touch you till she has done with me, and by that time you will be in. You are happy to have a house to go to! What a terrible wind it is!"

"Take me home safe, and I will give you shelter from it," she rejoined. "But we must wait a little!"

I asked her many questions. She told me the people never did anything except dig for precious stones in their cellars. They were rich, and had everything made for them in other towns.

"Why?" I asked.

"Because it is a disgrace to work," she answered. "Everybody in Bulika knows that!"

I asked how they were rich if none of them earned money. She replied that their ancestors had saved for them, and they never spent. When they wanted money they sold a few of their gems.

"But there must be some poor!" I said.

I suppose there must be, but we never think of such people. When one goes poor, we forget him. That is how we keep rich. We mean to be rich always."

"But when you have dug up all your precious stones and sold them, you will have to spend your money, and one day you will have none left!"

"We have so many, and there are so many still in the ground, that that day will never come," she replied.

"Suppose a strange people were to fall upon you, and take everything you have!"

"No strange people will dare; they are all horribly afraid of our princess. She it is who keeps us safe and free and rich!"

Every now and then as she spoke, she would stop and look behind her.

I asked why her people had such a hatred of strangers. She answered that the presence of a stranger defiled the city.

"How is that?" I said.

"Because we are more ancient and noble than any other nation. — Therefore," she added, "we always turn strangers out before night."

"How, then, can you take me into your house?" I asked.

"I will make an exception of you," she replied.

"Is there no place in the city for the taking in of strangers?"

"Such a place would be pulled down, and its owner burned. How is purity to be preserved except by keeping low people at a proper distance? Dignity is such a delicate thing!"

She told me that their princess had reigned for thousands of years; that she had power over the air and the water as well as the earth — and, she believed, over the fire too; that she could do what she pleased, and was answerable to nobody.

When at length she was willing to risk the attempt, we took our way through lanes and narrow passages, and reached her door without having met a single live creature. It was in a wider street, between two tall houses, at the top of a narrow, steep stair, up which she climbed slowly, and I followed. Ere we reached the top, however, she seemed to take fright, and darted up the rest of the steps: I arrived just in time to have the door closed in my face, and stood confounded on the landing, where was about length enough, between the opposite doors of the two houses, for a man to lie down.

Weary, and not scrupling to defile Bulika with my presence, I took advantage of the shelter, poor as it was.

24. THE WHITE LEOPARDESS

At the foot of the stair lay the moonlit street, and I could hear the unwholesome, inhospitable wind blowing about below. But not a breath of it entered my retreat, and I was composing myself to rest, when suddenly my eyes opened, and there was the head of the shining creature I had seen following the Shadow, just rising above the uppermost step! The moment she caught sight of my eyes, she stopped and began to retire, tail foremost. I sprang up; whereupon, having no room to turn, she threw herself backward, head over tail, scrambled to her feet, and in a moment was down the stair and gone. I followed her to the bottom, and looked all up and down the street. Not seeing her, I went back to my hard couch.

There were, then, two evil creatures prowling about the city, one with, and one without spots! I was not inclined to risk much for man or woman in Bulika, but the life of a child might well be worth such a poor one as mine, and I resolved to keep watch at that door the rest of the night.

Presently I heard the latch move, slow, slow: I looked up, and seeing the door half-open, rose and slid softly in. Behind it stood, not the woman I had befriended, but the muffled woman of the desert. Without a word she led me a few steps to an empty stone-paved chamber, and pointed to a rug on the floor. I wrapped myself in it, and once more lay down. She shut the door of the room, and I heard the outer door open and close again. There was no light save what came from the moonlit air.

As I lay sleepless, I began to hear a stifled moaning. It went on for a good while, and then came the cry of a child, followed by a terrible shriek. I sprang up and darted into the passage: from another door in it came the white leopardess with a new-born baby in her mouth, carrying it like a cub of her own. I threw myself upon her, and compelled her to drop the infant, which fell on the stone slabs with a piteous wail.

At the cry appeared the muffled woman. She stepped over us, the beast and myself, where we lay struggling in the narrow passage, took up the child, and carried it away. Returning, she lifted me off the animal, opened the door, and pushed me gently out. At my heels followed the leopardess.

"She too has failed me!" thought I; "— given me up to the beast to be settled with at her leisure! But we shall have a tussle for it!"

I ran down the stair, fearing she would spring on my back, but she followed me quietly. At the foot I turned to lay hold of her, but she sprang over my head; and when again I turned to face her, she was crouching at my feet! I stooped and stroked her lovely white skin; she responded by licking my bare feet with her hard dry tongue. Then I patted and fondled her, a well of tenderness overflowing in my heart: she might be treacherous too, but if I turned from every show of love lest it should be feigned, how was I ever to find the real love which must be somewhere in every world?

I stood up; she rose, and stood beside me.

A bulky object fell with a heavy squelch in the middle of the street, a few yards from us. I ran to it, and found a pulpy mass, with just form enough left to show it the body of a woman. It must have been thrown from some neighboring window! I looked around me: the Shadow was walking along the other side of the way, with the white leopardess again at his heel!

I followed and gained upon them, urging in my heart for the leopardess that probably she was not a free agent. When I got near them, however, she turned and flew at me with such a hideous snarl, that instinctively I drew back: instantly she resumed her place behind the Shadow. Again I drew near; again she flew at me, her eyes flaming like live emeralds. Once more I made the experiment: she snapped at me like a dog, and bit me. My heart gave way, and I uttered a cry; whereupon the creature looked round with a glance that plainly meant—"Why WOULD you make me do it?"

I turned away angry with myself: I had been losing my time ever since I entered the place! night as it was I would go straight to the palace! From the square I had seen it — high above the heart of the city, compassed with many defenses, more a fortress than a palace!

But I found its fortifications, like those of the city, much neglected, and partly ruinous. For centuries, clearly, they had been of no account! It had great and strong gates, with something like a drawbridge to them over a rocky chasm; but they stood open, and it was hard to believe that water had ever occupied the hollow before them. All was so still that sleep seemed to interpenetrate the structure, causing the very moonlight to look discordantly awake. I must either enter like a thief, or break a silence that rendered frightful the mere thought of a sound!

Like an outcast dog I was walking about the walls, when I came to a little recess with a stone bench: I took refuge in it from the wind, lay down, and in spite of the cold fell fast asleep.

I was wakened by something leaping upon me, and licking my face with the rough tongue of a feline animal. "It is the white leopardess!" I thought. "She is come to suck my blood! — and why should she not have it? — it would cost me more to defend than to yield it!" So I lay still, expecting a shoot of pain. But the pang did not arrive; a pleasant warmth instead began to diffuse itself through me. Stretched at my back, she lay as close to me as she could lie, the heat of her body slowly penetrating mine, and her breath, which had nothing of the wild beast in it, swathing my head and face in a genial atmosphere. A full conviction that her intention toward me was good, gained possession of me. I turned like a sleepy boy, threw my arm over her, and sank into profound unconsciousness.

When I began to come to myself, I fancied I lay warm and soft in my own bed. "Is it possible I am at home?" I thought. The well-known scents of the garden seemed to come crowding in. I rubbed my eyes, and looked out: I lay on a bare stone, in the heart of a hateful city!

I sprang from the bench. Had I indeed had a leopardess for my bedfellow, or had I but dreamed it? She had but just left me, for the warmth of her body was with me yet!

I left the recess with a new hope, as strong as it was shapeless. One thing only was clear to me: I must find the princess! Surely I had some power with her, if not over her! Had I not saved her life, and had she not prolonged it at the expense of my vitality? The reflection gave me courage to encounter her, be she what she might.

25. THE PRINCESS

Making a circuit of the castle, I came again to the open gates, crossed the ravine-like moat, and found myself in a paved court, planted at regular intervals with towering trees like poplars. In the centre was one taller than the rest, whose branches, near the top, spread a little and gave it some resemblance to a palm. Between their great stems I got glimpses of the palace, which was of a style strange to me, but suggested Indian origin. It was long and low, with lofty towers at the corners, and one huge dome in the middle, rising from the roof to half the height of the towers. The main entrance was in the centre of the front — a low arch that seemed half an ellipse. No one was visible, the doors stood wide open, and I went unchallenged into a large hall, in the form of a longish ellipse. Toward one side stood a cage, in which couched, its head on its paws, a huge leopardess, chained by a steel collar, with its mouth muzzled and its paws muffled. It was white with dark oval spots, and lay staring out of wide-open eyes, with canoe-shaped pupils, and great green irids. It appeared to watch me, but not an eyeball, not a foot, not a whisker moved, and its tail stretched out behind it rigid as an iron bar. I could not tell whether it was a live thing or not.

From this vestibule two low passages led; I took one of them, and found it branch into many, all narrow and irregular. At a spot where was scarce room for two to pass, a page ran against me. He started back in terror, but having scanned me, gathered impudence, puffed himself out, and asked my business.

"To see the princess," I answered.

"A likely thing!" he returned. "I have not seen her highness this morning myself!"

I caught him by the back of the neck, shook him, and said, "Take me to her at once, or I will drag you with me till I find her. She shall know how her servants receive her visitors."

He gave a look at me, and began to pull like a blind man's dog, leading me thus to a large kitchen, where were many servants, feebly busy, and hardly awake. I expected them to fall upon me and drive me out, but they stared instead, with wide eyes — not at me, but at something behind me, and grew more ghastly as they stared. I turned my head, and saw the white leopardess, regarding them in a way that might have feared stouter hearts.

Presently, however, one of them, seeing, I suppose, that attack was not imminent, began to recover himself; I turned to him, and let the boy go.

"Take me to the princess," I said.

"She has not yet left her room, your lordship," he replied.

"Let her know that I am here, waiting audience of her."

"Will your lordship please to give me your name?"

"Tell her that one who knows the white leech desires to see her."

"She will kill me if I take such a message: I must not. I dare not."

"You refuse?"

He cast a glance at my attendant, and went.

The others continued staring — too much afraid of her to take their eyes off her. I turned to the graceful creature, where she stood, her muzzle dropped to my heel, white as milk, a warm splendor in the gloomy place, and stooped and patted her. She looked up at me; the mere movement of her head was enough to scatter them in all directions. She rose on her hind legs, and put her paws on my shoulders; I threw my arms round her. She pricked her ears, broke from me, and was out of sight in a moment.

The man I had sent to the princess entered.

"Please to come this way, my lord," he said.

My heart gave a throb, as if bracing itself to the encounter. I followed him through many passages, and was at last shown into a room so large and so dark that its walls were invisible. A single spot on the floor reflected a little light, but around that spot all was black. I looked up, and saw at a great height an oval aperture in the roof, on the periphery of which appeared the joints between blocks of black marble. The light on the floor showed close fitting slabs of the same material. I found afterward that the elliptical wall as well was of black marble, absorbing the little light that reached it. The roof was the long half of an ellipsoid, and the opening in it was over one of the foci of the ellipse of the floor. I fancied I caught sight of reddish lines, but when I would have examined them, they were gone.

All at once, a radiant form stood in the centre of the darkness, flashing a splendor on every side. Over a robe of soft white, her hair streamed in a cataract, black as the marble on which it fell. Her eyes were a luminous blackness; her arms and feet like warm ivory. She greeted me with the innocent smile of a girl — and in face, figure, and motion seemed but now to have stepped over the threshold of womanhood. "Alas," thought I, "ill did I reckon my danger! Can this be the woman I rescued — she who struck me, scorned me, left me?" I stood gazing at her out of the darkness; she stood gazing into it, as if searching for me.

She disappeared. "She will not acknowledge me!" I thought. But the next instant her eyes flashed out of the dark straight into mine. She had descried me and come to me!

"You have found me at last!" she said, laying her hand on my shoulder. "I knew you would!"

My frame quivered with conflicting consciousnesses, to analyze which I had no power. I was simultaneously attracted and repelled: each sensation seemed either.

"You shiver!" she said. "This place is cold for you! Come."

I stood silent: she had struck me dumb with beauty; she held me dumb with sweetness.

Taking me by the hand, she drew me to the spot of light, and again flashed upon me. An instant she stood there.

"You have grown brown since last I saw you," she said.

"This is almost the first roof I have been under since you left me," I replied.

"Whose was the other?" she rejoined.

"I do not know the woman's name."

"I would gladly learn it! The instinct of hospitality is not strong in my people!" She took me again by the hand, and led me through the darkness many steps to a curtain of black. Beyond it was a white stair, up which she conducted me to a beautiful chamber.

"How you must miss the hot flowing river!" she said. "But there is a bath in the corner with no white leeches in it! At the foot of your couch you will find a garment. When you come down, I shall be in the room to your left at the foot of the stair."

I stood as she left me, accusing my presumption: how was I to treat this lovely woman as a thing of evil, who behaved to me like a sister? — Whence the marvelous change in her? She left me with a blow; she received me almost with an embrace! She had reviled me; she said she knew I would follow and find her! Did she know my doubts concerning her — how much I should want explained? COULD she explain all? Could I believe her if she did? As to her hospitality, I had surely earned and might accept that — at least until I came to a definite judgment concerning her!

Could such beauty as I saw, and such wickedness as I suspected, exist in the same person? If they could, HOW was it possible? Unable to answer the former question, I must let the latter wait!

Clear as crystal, the water in the great white bath sent a sparkling flash from the corner where it lay sunk in the marble floor, and seemed to invite me to its embrace. Except the hot stream, two draughts in the cottage of the veiled woman, and the pools in the track of the wounded leopardess, I had not seen water since leaving home: it looked a thing celestial. I plunged in.

Immediately my brain was filled with an odor strange and delicate, which yet I did not altogether like. It made me doubt the princess afresh: had she medicated it? had she enchanted it? was she in any way working on me unlawfully? And how was there water in the palace, and not a drop in the city? I remembered the crushed paw of the leopardess, and sprang from the bath.

What had I been bathing in? Again I saw the fleeing mother, again I heard the howl, again I saw the limping beast. But what matter whence it flowed? was not the water sweet? Was it not very water the pitcher-plant secreted from its heart, and stored for the weary traveler? Water came from heaven: what mattered the well where it gathered, or the spring whence it burst? But I did not re-enter the bath.

I put on the robe of white wool, embroidered on the neck and hem, that lay ready for me, and went down the stair to the room whither my hostess had directed me. It was round, all of alabaster, and without a single window: the light came through everywhere, a soft, pearly shimmer rather than shine. Vague shadowy forms went flitting about over the walls and low dome, like loose rain-clouds over a grey-blue sky.

The princess stood waiting me, in a robe embroidered with argentine rings and discs, rectangles and lozenges, close together — a silver mail. It fell unbroken from her neck and hid her feet, but its long open sleeves left her arms bare.

In the room was a table of ivory, bearing cakes and fruit, an ivory jug of milk, a crystal jug of wine of a pale rose-color, and a white loaf.

"Here we do not kill to eat," she said; "but I think you will like what I can give you."

I told her I could desire nothing better than what I saw. She seated herself on a couch by the table, and made me a sign to sit by her.

She poured me out a bowlful of milk, and, handing me the loaf, begged me to break from it such a piece as I liked. Then she filled from the wine-jug two silver goblets of grotesquely graceful workmanship.

"You have never drunk wine like this!" she said.

I drank, and wondered: every flower of Hybla and Hymettus must have sent its ghost to swell the soul of that wine!

"And now that you will be able to listen," she went on, "I must do what I can to make myself intelligible to you. Our natures, however, are so different, that this may not be easy. Men and women live but to die; we, that is such as I — we are but a few — live to live on. Old age is to you a horror; to me it is a dear desire: the older we grow, the nearer we are to our perfection. Your perfection is a poor thing, comes soon, and lasts but a little while; ours is a ceaseless ripening. I am not yet ripe, and have lived thousands of your years — how many, I never cared to note. The everlasting will not be measured.

"Many lovers have sought me; I have loved none of them: they sought but to enslave me; they sought me but as the men of my city seek gems of price. — When you found me, I found a man! I put you to the test; you stood it; your love was genuine! — It was, however, far from ideal — far from such love as I would have. You loved me truly, but not with true love. Pity has, but is not love. What woman of any world would return love for pity? Such love as yours was then, is hateful to me. I knew that, if you saw me as I am, you would love me — like the rest of them — to have and to hold: I would none of that either! I would be otherwise loved! I would have a love that outlived hopelessness, out measured indifference, hate, scorn! Therefore did I put on cruelty, despite, ingratitude. When I left you, I had shown myself such as you could at least no longer follow from pity: I was no longer in need of you! But you must satisfy my desire or set me free — prove yourself priceless or worthless! To satisfy the hunger of my love, you must follow me, looking for nothing, not gratitude, not even pity in return! — follow and find me, and be content with merest presence, with scantest forbearance! — I, not you, have failed; I yield the contest."

She looked at me tenderly, and hid her face in her hands. But I had caught a flash and a sparkle behind the tenderness, and did not believe her. She laid herself out to secure and enslave me; she only fascinated me!

"Beautiful princess," I said, "let me understand how you came to be found in such evil plight."

"There are things I cannot explain," she replied, "until you have become capable of understanding them — which can only be when love is grown perfect. There are many things so hidden from you that you cannot even wish to know them; but any question you can put, I can in some measure answer.

"I had set out to visit a part of my dominions occupied by a savage dwarf-people, strong and fierce, enemies to law and order, opposed to every kind of progress — an evil race. I went alone, fearing nothing, unaware of the least necessity for precaution. I did not know that upon the hot stream beside which you found me, a certain woman, by no means so powerful as myself, not being immortal, had cast what you call a spell — which is merely the setting in motion of a force as natural as any other, but operating primarily in a region beyond the ken of the mortal who makes use of the force.

"I set out on my journey, reached the stream, bounded across it,—"

A shadow of embarrassment darkened her cheek: I understood it, but showed no sign. Checked for the merest moment, she went on:

"— you know what a step it is in parts! — But in the very act, an indescribable cold invaded me. I recognized at once the nature of the assault, and knew it could affect me but temporarily. By sheer force of will I dragged myself to the wood — nor knew anything more until I saw you asleep, and the horrible worm at your neck. I crept out, dragged the monster from you, and laid my lips to the wound. You began to wake; I buried myself among the leaves."

She rose, her eyes flashing as never human eyes flashed, and threw her arms high over her head.

"What you have made me is yours!" she cried. "I will repay you as never yet did woman! My power, my beauty, my love are your own: take them."

She dropt kneeling beside me, laid her arms across my knees, and looked up in my face.

Then first I noted on her left hand a large clumsy glove. In my mind's eye I saw hair and claws under it, but I knew it was a hand shut hard — perhaps badly bruised. I glanced at the other: it was lovely as hand could be, and I felt that, if I did less than loathe her, I should love her. Not to dally with usurping emotions, I turned my eyes aside.

She started to her feet. I sat motionless, looking down.

"To me she may be true!" said my vanity. For a moment I was tempted to love a lie.

An odor, rather than the gentlest of airy pulses, was fanning me. I glanced up. She stood erect before me, waving her lovely arms in seemingly mystic fashion.

A frightful roar made my heart rebound against the walls of its cage. The alabaster trembled as if it would shake into shivers. The princess shuddered visibly.

"My wine was too strong for you!" she said, in a quavering voice; "I ought not to have let you take a full draught! Go and sleep now, and when you wake ask me what you please. — I will go with you: come."

As she preceded me up the stair,—

"I do not wonder that roar startled you!" she said. "It startled me, I confess: for a moment I feared she had escaped. But that is impossible."

The roar seemed to me, however — I could not tell why—to come from the WHITE leopardess, and to be meant for me, not the princess.

With a smile she left me at the door of my room, but as she turned I read anxiety on her beautiful face.

26. A BATTLE ROYAL

I threw myself on the bed, and began to turn over in my mind the tale she had told me. She had forgotten herself, and, by a single incautious word, removed one perplexity as to the condition in which I found her in the forest! The leopardess BOUNDED over; the princess lay prostrate on the bank: the running stream had dissolved her self-enchantment! Her own account of the object of her journey revealed the danger of the Little Ones then imminent: I had saved the life of their one fearful enemy!

I had but reached this conclusion when I fell asleep. The lovely wine may not have been quite innocent.

When I opened my eyes, it was night. A lamp, suspended from the ceiling, cast a clear, although soft light through the chamber. A delicious languor infolded me. I seemed floating, far from land, upon the bosom of a twilight sea. Existence was in itself pleasure. I had no pain. Surely I was dying!

No pain! — ah, what a shoot of mortal pain was that! what a sickening sting! It went right through my heart! Again! That was sharpness itself! — and so sickening! I could not move my hand to lay it on my heart; something kept it down!

The pain was dying away, but my whole body seemed paralyzed. Some evil thing was upon me! — something hateful! I would have struggled, but could not reach a struggle. My will agonized, but in vain, to assert itself. I desisted, and lay passive. Then I became aware of a soft hand on my face, pressing my head into the pillow, and of a heavy weight lying across me.

I began to breathe more freely; the weight was gone from my chest; I opened my eyes.

The princess was standing above me on the bed, looking out into the room, with the air of one who dreamed. Her great eyes were clear and calm. Her mouth wore a look of satisfied passion; she wiped from it a streak of red.

She caught my gaze, bent down, and struck me on the eyes with the handkerchief in her hand: it was like drawing the edge of a knife across them, and for a moment or two I was blind.

I heard a dull heavy sound, as of a large soft-footed animal alighting from a little jump. I opened my eyes, and saw the great swing of a long tail as it disappeared through the half-open doorway. I sprang after it.

The creature had vanished quite. I shot down the stair, and into the hall of alabaster. The moon was high, and the place like the inside of a faint, sun-blanched moon. The princess was not there. I must find her: in her presence I might protect myself; out of it I could not! I was a tame animal for her to feed upon; a human fountain for a thirst demoniac! She showed me favor the more easily to use me! My waking eyes did not fear her, but they would close, and she would come! Not seeing her, I felt her everywhere, for she might be anywhere — might even now be waiting me in some secret cavern of sleep! Only with my eyes upon her could I feel safe from her!

Outside the alabaster hall it was pitch-dark, and I had to grope my way along with hands and feet. At last I felt a curtain, put it aside, and entered the black hall. There I found a great silent assembly. How it was visible I neither saw nor could imagine, for the walls, the floor, the roof, were shrouded in what seemed an infinite blackness, blacker than the blackest of moonless, starless nights; yet my eyes could separate, although vaguely, not a few of the individuals in the mass interpenetrated and divided, as well as surrounded, by the darkness. It seemed as if my eyes would never come quite to themselves. I pressed their balls and looked and looked again, but what I saw would not grow distinct. Blackness mingled with form, silence and undefined motion possessed the wide space. All was a dim, confused dance, filled with recurrent glimpses of shapes not unknown to me. Now appeared a woman, with glorious eyes looking out of a skull; now an armed figure on a skeleton horse; now one now another of the hideous burrowing phantasms. I could trace no order and little relation in the mingling and crossing currents and eddies. If I seemed to catch the shape and rhythm of a dance, it was but to see it break, and confusion prevail. With the shifting colors of the seemingly more solid shapes, mingled a multitude of shadows, independent apparently of originals, each moving after its own free shadow-will. I looked everywhere for the princess, but throughout the wildly changing kaleidoscopic scene, could not see her nor discover indication of her presence. Where was she? What might she not be doing? No one took the least notice of me as I wandered hither and thither seeking her. At length losing hope, I turned away to look elsewhere. Finding the wall, and keeping to it with my hand, for even then I could not see it, I came, groping along, to a curtained opening into the vestibule.

Dimly moonlighted, the cage of the leopardess was the arena of what seemed a desperate although silent struggle. Two vastly differing forms, human and bestial, with entangled confusion of mingling bodies and limbs, writhed and wrestled in closest embrace. It had lasted but an instant when I saw the leopardess out of the cage, walking quietly to the open door. As I hastened after her I threw a glance behind me: there was the leopardess in the cage, couching motionless as when I saw her first.

The moon, half-way up the sky, was shining round and clear; the bodiless shadow I had seen the night before, was walking through the trees toward the gate; and after him went the leopardess, swinging her tail. I followed, a little way off, as silently as they, and neither of them once looked round. Through the open gate we went down to the city, lying quiet as the moonshine upon it. The face of the moon was very still, and its stillness looked like that of expectation.

The Shadow took his way straight to the stair at the top of which I had lain the night before. Without a pause he went up, and the leopardess followed. I quickened my pace, but, a moment after, heard a cry of horror. Then came the fall of something soft and heavy between me and the stair, and at my feet lay a body, frightfully blackened and crushed, but still recognizable as that of the woman who had led me home and shut me out. As I stood petrified, the spotted leopardess came bounding down the stair with a baby in her mouth. I darted to seize her ere she could turn at the foot; but that instant, from behind me, the white leopardess, like a great bar of glowing silver, shot through the moonlight, and had her by the neck. She dropped the child; I caught it up, and stood to watch the battle between them.

What a sight it was — now the one, now the other uppermost, both too intent for any noise beyond a low growl, a whimpered cry, or a snarl of hate — followed by a quicker scrambling of claws, as each, worrying and pushing and dragging, struggled for foothold on the pavement! The spotted leopardess was larger than the white, and I was anxious for my friend; but I soon saw that, though neither stronger nor more active, the white leopardess had the greater endurance. Not once did she lose her hold on the neck of the other. From the spotted throat at length issued a howl of agony, changing, by swift-crowded gradations, into the long-drawn CRESCENDO of a woman's uttermost wail. The white one relaxed her jaws; the spotted one drew herself away, and rose on her hind legs. Erect in the moonlight stood the princess, a confused rush of shadows careering over her whiteness — the spots of the leopard crowding, hurrying, fleeing to the refuge of her eyes, where merging they vanished. The last few, out sped and belated, mingled with the cloud of her streamy hair, leaving her radiant as the moon when a legion of little vapors has flown, wind-hunted, off her silvery disc – save that, adown the white column of her throat, a thread of blood still trickled from every wound of her adversary's terrible teeth. She turned away, took a few steps with the gait of a Hecate, fell, covered afresh with her spots, and fled at a long, stretching gallop.

The white leopardess turned also, sprang upon me, pulled my arms asunder, caught the baby as it fell, and flew with it along the street toward the gate

27. THE SILENT FOUNTAIN

I turned and followed the spotted leopardess, catching but one glimpse of her as she tore up the brow of the hill to the gate of the palace. When I reached the entrance-hall, the princess was just throwing the robe around her which she had left on the floor. The blood had ceased to flow from her wounds, and had dried in the wind of her flight.

When she saw me, a flash of anger crossed her face, and she turned her head aside. Then, with an attempted smile, she looked at me, and said,

"I have met with a small accident! Happening to hear that the cat-woman was again in the city, I went down to send her away. But she had one of her horrid creatures with her: it sprang upon me, and had its claws in my neck before I could strike it!"

She gave a shiver, and I could not help pitying her, although I knew she lied, for her wounds were real, and her face reminded me of how she looked in the cave. My heart began to reproach me that I had let her fight unaided, and I suppose I looked the compassion I felt.

"Child of folly!" she said, with another attempted smile, "— not crying, surely! — Wait for me here; I am going into the black hall for a moment. I want you to get me something for my scratches."

But I followed her close. Out of my sight I feared her.

The instant the princess entered, I heard a buzzing sound as of many low voices, and, one portion after another, the assembly began to be shiftingly illuminated, as by a ray that went traveling from spot to spot. Group after group would shine out for a space, then sink back into the general vagueness, while another part of the vast company would grow momently bright.

Some of the actions going on when thus illuminated, were not unknown to me; I had been in them, or had looked on them, and so had the princess: present with every one of them I now saw her. The skull-headed dancers footed the grass in the forest-hall: there was the princess looking in at the door! The fight went on in the Evil Wood: there was the princess urging it! Yet I was close behind her all the time, she standing motionless, her head sunk on her bosom. The confused murmur continued, the confused commotion of colors and shapes; and still the ray went shifting and showing. It settled at last on the hollow in the heath, and there was the princess, walking up and down, and trying in vain to wrap the vapor around her! Then first I was startled at what I saw: the old librarian walked up to her, and stood for a moment regarding her; she fell; her limbs forsook her and fled; her body vanished.

A wild shriek rang through the echoing place, and with the fall of her eidolon, the princess herself, till then standing like a statue in front of me, fell heavily, and lay still. I turned at once and went out: not again would I seek to restore her! As I stood trembling beside the cage, I knew that in the black ellipsoid I had been in the brain of the princess! — I saw the tail of the leopardess quiver once.

While still endeavoring to compose myself, I heard the voice of the princess beside me.

"Come now," she said; "I will show you what I want you to do for me."

She led the way into the court. I followed in dazed compliance.

The moon was near the zenith, and her present silver seemed brighter than the gold of the absent sun. She brought me through the trees to the tallest of them, the one in the centre. It was not quite like the rest, for its branches, drawing their ends together at the top, made a clump that looked from beneath like a fir-cone. The princess stood close under it, gazing up, and said, as if talking to herself,

"On the summit of that tree grows a tiny blossom which would at once heal my scratches! I might be a dove for a moment and fetch it, but I see a little snake in the leaves whose bite would be worse to a dove than the bite of a tiger to me! — How I hate that cat-woman!"

She turned to me quickly, saying with one of her sweetest smiles,

"Can you climb?"

The smile vanished with the brief question, and her face changed to a look of sadness and suffering. I ought to have left her to suffer, but the way she put her hand to her wounded neck went to my heart.

I considered the tree. All the way up to the branches, were projections on the stem like the remnants on a palm of its fallen leaves.

"I can climb that tree," I answered.

"Not with bare feet!" she returned.

In my haste to follow the leopardess disappearing, I had left my sandals in my room.

"It is no matter," I said; "I have long gone barefoot!"

Again I looked at the tree, and my eyes went wandering up the stem until my sight lost itself in the branches. The moon shone like silvery foam here and there on the rugged bole, and a little rush of wind went through the top with a murmurous sound as of water falling softly into water. I approached the tree to begin my ascent of it. The princess stopped me.

"I cannot let you attempt it with your feet bare!" she insisted. "A fall from the top would kill you!"

"So would a bite from the snake!" I answered — not believing, I confess, that there was any snake.

"It would not hurt YOU!" she replied. "— Wait a moment."

She tore from her garment the two wide borders that met in front, and kneeling on one knee, made me put first my left foot, then my right on the other, and bound them about with the thick embroidered strips.

"You have left the ends hanging, princess!" I said.

"I have nothing to cut them off with; but they are not long enough to get entangled," she replied.

I turned to the tree, and began to climb.

Now in Bulika the cold after sundown was not so great as in certain other parts of the country — especially about the sexton's cottage; yet when I had climbed a little way, I began to feel very cold, grew still colder as I ascended, and became coldest of all when I got among the branches. Then I shivered, and seemed to have lost my hands and feet.

There was hardly any wind, and the branches did not sway in the least, yet, as I approached the summit, I became aware of a peculiar unsteadiness: every branch on which I placed foot or laid hold, seemed on the point of giving way. When my head rose above the branches near the top, and in the open moonlight I began to look about for the blossom, that instant I found myself drenched from head to foot. The next, as if plunged in a stormy water, I was flung about wildly, and felt myself sinking. Tossed up and down, tossed this way and tossed that way, rolled over and over, checked, rolled the other way and tossed up again, I was sinking lower and lower. Gasping and gurgling and choking, I fell at last upon a solid bottom.

"I told you so!" croaked a voice in my ear.

28. I Am Silenced

I rubbed the water out of my eyes, and saw the raven on the edge of a huge stone basin. With the cold light of the dawn reflected from his glossy plumage, he stood calmly looking down upon me. I lay on my back in water, above which, leaning on my elbows, I just lifted my face. I was in the basin of the large fountain constructed by my father in the middle of the lawn. High over me glimmered the thick, steel-shiny stalk, shooting, with a torrent uprush, a hundred feet into the air, to spread in a blossom of foam.

Nettled at the coolness of the raven's remark,

"You told me nothing!" I said.

"I told you to do nothing any one you distrusted asked you!"

"Tut! how was mortal to remember that?"

"You will not forget the consequences of having forgotten it!" replied Mr. Raven, who stood leaning over the margin of the basin, and stretched his hand across to me.

I took it, and was immediately beside him on the lawn, dripping and streaming.

"You must change your clothes at once!" he said. "A wetting does not signify where you come from — though at present such an accident is unusual; here it has its inconveniences!"

He was again a raven, walking, with something stately in his step, toward the house, the door of which stood open.

"I have not much to change!" I laughed; for I had flung aside my robe to climb the tree.

"It is a long time since I moulted a feather!" said the raven.

In the house no one seemed awake. I went to my room, found a dressing-gown, and descended to the library.

As I entered, the librarian came from the closet. I threw myself on a couch. Mr. Raven drew a chair to my side and sat down. For a minute or two neither spoke. I was the first to break the silence.

"What does it all mean?" I said.

"A good question!" he rejoined: "nobody knows what anything is; a man can learn only what a thing means! Whether he do, depends on the use he is making of it."

"I have made no use of anything yet!"

"Not much; but you know the fact, and that is something! Most people take more than a lifetime to learn that they have learned nothing, and done less! At least you have not been without the desire to be of use!"

"I did want to do something for the children — the precious Little Ones, I mean."

"I know you did — and started the wrong way!"

"I did not know the right way."

"That is true also — but you are to blame that you did not."

"I am ready to believe whatever you tell me — as soon as I understand what it means."

"Had you accepted our invitation, you would have known the right way. When a man will not act where he is, he must go far to find his work."

"Indeed I have gone far, and got nowhere, for I have not found my work! I left the children to learn how to serve them, and have only learned the danger they are in."

"When you were with them, you were where you could help them: you left your work to look for it! It takes a wise man to know when to go away; a fool may learn to go back at once!"

"Do you mean, sir, I could have done something for the Little Ones by staying with them?"

"Could you teach them anything by leaving them?"

"No; but how could I teach them? I did not know how to begin. Besides, they were far ahead of me!"

"That is true. But you were not a rod to measure them with! Certainly, if they knew what you know, not to say what you might have known, they would be ahead of you — out of sight ahead! but you saw they were not growing — or growing so slowly that they had not yet developed the idea of growing! they were even afraid of growing!—You had never seen children remain children!"

"But surely I had no power to make them grow!"

"You might have removed some of the hindrances to their growing!"

"What are they? I do not know them. I did think perhaps it was the want of water!"

"Of course it is! they have none to cry with!"

"I would gladly have kept them from requiring any for that purpose!"

"No doubt you would — the aim of all stupid philanthropists! Why, Mr. Vane, but for the weeping in it, your world would never have become worth saving! You confess you thought it might be water they wanted: why did not you dig them a well or two?"

"That never entered my mind!"

"Not when the sounds of the waters under the earth entered your ears?"

"I believe it did once. But I was afraid of the giants for them. That was what made me bear so much from the brutes myself!"

"Indeed you almost taught the noble little creatures to be afraid of the stupid Bags! While they fed and comforted and worshipped you, all the time you submitted to be the slave of bestial men! You gave the darlings a seeming coward for their hero! A worse wrong you could hardly have done them. They gave you their hearts; you owed them your soul! — You might by this time have made the Bags hewers of wood and drawers of water to the Little Ones!"

"I fear what you say is true, Mr. Raven! But indeed I was afraid that more knowledge might prove an injury to them — render them less innocent, less lovely."

"They had given you no reason to harbor such a fear!"

"Is not a little knowledge a dangerous thing?"

"That is one of the pet falsehoods of your world! Is man's greatest knowledge more than a little? or is it therefore dangerous? The fancy that knowledge is in itself a great thing, would make any degree of knowledge more dangerous than any amount of ignorance. To know all things would not be greatness."

"At least it was for love of them, not from cowardice that I served the giants!"

"Granted. But you ought to have served the Little Ones, not the giants! You ought to have given the Little Ones water; then they would soon have taught the giants their true position. In the meantime you could yourself have made the giants cut down two-thirds of their coarse fruit-trees to give room to the little delicate ones! You lost your chance with the Lovers, Mr. Vane! You speculated about them instead of helping them!"

29. THE PERSIAN CAT

I sat in silence and shame. What he said was true: I had not been a wise neighbor to the Little Ones!

Mr. Raven resumed:

"You wronged at the same time the stupid creatures themselves. For them slavery would have been progress. To them a few such lessons as you could have given them with a stick from one of their own trees, would have been invaluable."

"I did not know they were cowards!"

"What difference does that make? The man who grounds his action on another's cowardice, is essentially a coward himself. — I fear worse will come of it! By this time the Little Ones might have been able to protect themselves from the princess, not to say the giants – they were always fit enough for that; as it was they laughed at them! but now, through your relations with her,—"

"I hate her!" I cried.

"Did you let her know you hated her?"

Again I was silent.

"Not even to her have you been faithful! — But hush! we were followed from the fountain, I fear!"

"No living creature did I see! — except a disreputable-looking cat that bolted into the shrubbery."

"It was a magnificent Persian — so wet and draggled, though, as to look what she was —worse than disreputable!"

"What do you mean, Mr. Raven?" I cried, a fresh horror taking me by the throat. "—There was a beautiful blue Persian about the house, but she fled at the very sound of water! —Could she have been after the goldfish?"

"We shall see!" returned the librarian. "I know a little about cats of several sorts, and there is that in the room which will unmask this one, or I am mistaken in her."

He rose, went to the door of the closet, brought from it the mutilated volume, and sat down again beside me. I stared at the book in his hand: it was a whole book, entire and sound!

"Where was the other half of it?" I gasped.

"Sticking through into my library," he answered.

I held my peace. A single question more would have been a plunge into a bottomless sea, and there might be no time!

"Listen," he said: "I am going to read a stanza or two. There is one present who, I imagine, will hardly enjoy the reading!" He opened the vellum cover, and turned a leaf or two. The parchment was discolored with age, and one leaf showed a dark stain over two-thirds of it. He slowly turned this also, and seemed looking for a certain passage in what appeared a continuous poem. Somewhere about the middle of the book he began to read.

But what follows represents — not what he read, only the impression it made upon me. The poem seemed in a language I had never before heard, which yet I understood perfectly, although I could not write the words, or give their meaning save in poor approximation. These fragments, then, are the shapes which those he read have finally taken in passing again through my brain:—

> "But if I found a man that could believe
> In what he saw not, felt not, and yet knew,
> From him I should take substance, and receive
> Firmness and form relate to touch and view;
> Then should I clothe me in the likeness true
> Of that idea where his soul did cleave!"

He turned a leaf and read again: —

> "In me was every woman. I had power
> Over the soul of every living man,
> Such as no woman ever had in dower —
> Could what no woman ever could, or can;
> All women, I, the woman, still outran,
> Outsoared, out sank, out reigned, in hall or bower.
>
> "For I, though me he neither saw nor heard,
> Nor with his hand could touch finger of mine,
> Although not once my breath had ever stirred
> A hair of him, could trammel brain and spine
> With rooted bonds which Death could not untwine—
> Or life, though hope were evermore deferred."

Again he paused, again turned a leaf, and again began: —

> "For by his side I lay, a bodiless thing;
> I breathed not, saw not, felt not, only thought,
> And made him love me — with a hungering
> After he knew not what — if it was aught

Or but a nameless something that was wrought

By him out of himself; for I did sing

"A song that had no sound into his soul;

I lay a heartless thing against his heart,

Giving him nothing where he gave his whole

Being to clothe me human, every part:

That I at last into his sense might dart,

Thus first into his living mind I stole.

"Ah, who was ever conquering Love but I!

Who else did ever throne in heart of man!

To visible being, with a gladsome cry

Waking, life's tremor through me throbbing ran!"

A strange, repulsive feline wail arose somewhere in the room. I started up on my elbow and stared about me, but could see nothing.

Mr. Raven turned several leaves, and went on: —

"Sudden I woke, nor knew the ghastly fear

That held me — not like serpent coiled about,

But like a vapor moist, corrupt, and drear,

Filling heart, soul, and breast and brain throughout;

My being lay motionless in sickening doubt,

Nor dared to ask how came the horror here.

"My past entire I knew, but not my now;

I understood nor what I was, nor where;

I knew what I had been: still on my brow

I felt the touch of what no more was there!

I was a fainting, dead, yet live Despair;

A life that flouted life with mop and mow!

"That I was a queen I knew right well,

And sometimes wore a splendor on my head

Whose flashing even dead darkness could not quell —

The like on neck and arms and girdle-stead;

And men declared a light my closed eyes shed

That killed the diamond in its silver cell."

Again I heard the ugly cry of feline pain. Again I looked, but saw neither shape nor motion. Mr. Raven seemed to listen a moment, but again turned several pages, and resumed: —

"Hideously wet, my hair of golden hue

Fouled my fair hands: to have it swiftly shorn

I had given my rubies, all for me dug new —

No eyes had seen, and such no waist had worn!

For a draught of water from a drinking horn,

For one blue breath, I had given my sapphires blue!

"Nay, I had given my opals for a smock,

A peasant-maiden's garment, coarse and clean:

My shroud was rotting! Once I heard a cock

Lustily crow upon the hillock green

Over my coffin. Dulled by space between,

Came back an answer like a ghostly mock."

Once more arose the bestial wail.

"I thought some foul thing was in the room!" said the librarian, casting a glance around him; but instantly he turned a leaf or two, and again read: —

"For I had bathed in milk and honey-dew,

In rain from roses shook, that ne'er touched earth,

And ointed me with nard of amber hue;

Never had spot me spotted from my birth,

Or mole, or scar of hurt, or fret of dearth;

Never one hair superfluous on me grew.

"Fleeing cold whiteness, I would sit alone —

Not in the sun — I feared his bronzing light,

But in his radiance back around me thrown

By fulgent mirrors tempering his might;

Thus bathing in a moon-bath not too bright,

My skin I tinted slow to ivory tone.

"But now, all round was dark, dark all within!

My eyes not even gave out a phantom-flash;

My fingers sank in pulp through pulpy skin;

My body lay death-weltered in a mash

Of slimy horrors —"

With a fearsome yell, her clammy fur staring in clumps, her tail thick as a cable, her eyes flashing green as a chrysoprase, her distended claws entangling themselves so that she floundered across the carpet, a huge white cat rushed from somewhere, and made for the chimney. Quick as thought the librarian threw the manuscript between her and the hearth. She crouched instantly, her eyes fixed on the book. But his voice went on as if still he read, and his eyes seemed also fixed on the book: —

"Ah, the two worlds! so strangely are they one,

And yet so measurelessly wide apart!

Oh, had I lived the bodiless alone

And from defiling sense held safe my heart,

Then had I scaped the canker and the smart,

Scaped life-in-death, scaped misery's endless moan!"

At these words such a howling, such a prolonged yell of agony burst from the cat, that we both stopped our ears. When it ceased, Mr. Raven walked to the fire-place, took up the book, and, standing between the creature and the chimney, pointed his finger at her for a moment. She lay perfectly still. He took a half-burnt stick from the hearth, drew with it some sign on the floor, put the manuscript back in its place, with a look that seemed to say, "Now we have her, I think!" and, returning to the cat, stood over her and said, in a still, solemn voice: —

"Lilith, when you came here on the way to your evil will, you little thought into whose hands you were delivering yourself! — Mr. Vane, when God created me, — not out of Nothing, as say the unwise, but out of His own endless glory — He brought me an angelic splendor to be my wife: there she lies! For her first thought was POWER; she counted it slavery to be one with me, and bear children for Him who gave her being. One child, indeed, she bore; then, puffed with the fancy that she had created her, would have me fall down and worship her! Finding, however, that I would but love and honor, never obey and worship her, she poured out her blood to escape me, fled to the army of the aliens, and soon had so ensnared the heart of the great Shadow, that he became her slave, wrought her will, and made her queen of Hell. How it is with her now, she best knows, but I know also. The one child of her body she fears and hates, and would kill, asserting a right, which is a lie, over what God sent through her into His new world. Of creating, she knows no more than the crystal that takes its allotted shape, or the worm that makes two worms when it is cloven asunder. Vilest of God's creatures, she lives by the blood and lives and souls of men. She consumes and slays, but is powerless to destroy as to create."

The animal lay motionless, its beryl eyes fixed flaming on the man: his eyes on hers held them fixed that they could not move from his.

"Then God gave me another wife — not an angel but a woman—who is to this as light is to darkness."

The cat gave a horrible screech, and began to grow bigger. She went on growing and growing. At last the spotted leopardess uttered a roar that made the house tremble. I sprang to my feet. I do not think Mr. Raven started even with his eyelids.

"It is but her jealousy that speaks," he said, "jealousy self-kindled, foiled and fruitless; for here I am, her master now whom she, would not have for her husband! while my beautiful Eve yet lives, hoping immortally! Her hated daughter lives also, but beyond her evil ken, one day to be what she counts her destruction — for even Lilith shall be saved by her childbearing. Meanwhile she exults that my human wife plunged herself and me in despair, and has borne me a countless race of miserables; but my Eve repented, and is now beautiful as never was woman or angel, while her groaning, travailing world is the nursery of our Father's children. I too have repented, and am blessed. — Thou, Lilith, hast not yet repented; but thou must. — Tell me, is the great Shadow beautiful? Knowest thou how long thou wilt thyself remain beautiful?—Answer me, if thou knowest."

Then at last I understood that Mr. Raven was indeed Adam, the old and the new man; and that his wife, ministering in the house of the dead, was Eve, the mother of us all, the lady of the New Jerusalem.

The leopardess reared; the flickering and fleeing of her spots began; the princess at length stood radiant in her perfect shape.

"I AM beautiful — and immortal!" she said—and she looked the goddess she would be.

"As a bush that burns, and is consumed," answered he who had been her husband. "—What is that under thy right hand?"

For her arm lay across her bosom, and her hand was pressed to her side.

A swift pang contorted her beautiful face, and passed.

"It is but a leopard-spot that lingers! it will quickly follow those I have dismissed," she answered.

"Thou art beautiful because God created thee, but thou art the slave of sin: take thy hand from thy side."

Her hand sank away, and as it dropt she looked him in the eyes with a quailing fierceness that had in it no surrender.

He gazed a moment at the spot.

"It is not on the leopard; it is in the woman!" he said. "Nor will it leave thee until it hath eaten to thy heart, and thy beauty hath flowed from thee through the open wound!"

She gave a glance downward, and shivered.

"Lilith," said Adam, and his tone had changed to a tender beseeching, "hear me, and repent, and He who made thee will cleanse thee!"

Her hand returned quivering to her side. Her face grew dark. She gave the cry of one from whom hope is vanishing. The cry passed into a howl. She lay writhing on the floor, a leopardess covered with spots.

"The evil thou meditatest," Adam resumed, "thou shalt never compass, Lilith, for Good and not Evil is the Universe. The battle between them may last for countless ages, but it must end: how will it fare with thee when Time hath vanished in the dawn of the eternal morn? Repent, I beseech thee; repent, and be again an angel of God!"

She rose, she stood upright, a woman once more, and said,

"I will not repent. I will drink the blood of thy child." My eyes were fastened on the princess; but when Adam spoke, I turned to him: he stood towering above her; the form of his visage was altered, and his voice was terrible.

"Down!" he cried; "or by the power given me I will melt thy very bones."

She flung herself on the floor, dwindled and dwindled, and was again a gray cat. Adam caught her up by the skin of her neck, bore her to the closet, and threw her in. He described a strange figure on the threshold, and closing the door, locked it.

Then he returned to my side the old librarian, looking sad and worn, and furtively wiping tears from his eyes.

30. ADAM EXPLAINS

"We must be on our guard," he said, "or she will again outwit us. She would befool the very elect!"

"How are we to be on our guard?" I asked.

"Every way," he answered. "She fears, therefore hates her child, and is in this house on her way to destroy her. The birth of children is in her eyes the death of their parents, and every new generation the enemy of the last. Her daughter appears to her an open channel through which her immortality — which yet she counts self-inherent — is flowing fast away: to fill it up, almost from her birth she has pursued her with an utter enmity. But the result of her machinations hitherto is, that in the region she claims as her own, has appeared a colony of children, to which that daughter is heart and head and sheltering wings. My Eve longed after the child, and would have been to her as a mother to her first-born, but we were then unfit to train her: she was carried into the wilderness, and for ages we knew nothing of her fate. But she was divinely fostered, and had young angels for her playmates; nor did she ever know care until she found a baby in the wood, and the mother-heart in her awoke. One by one she has found many children since, and that heart is not yet full. Her family is her absorbing charge, and never children were better mothered. Her authority over them is without appeal, but it is unknown to herself, and never comes to the surface except in watchfulness and service. She has forgotten the time when she lived without them, and thinks she came herself from the wood, the first of the family.

"You have saved the life of her and their enemy; therefore your life belongs to her and them. The princess was on her way to destroy them, but as she crossed that stream, vengeance overtook her, and she would have died had you not come to her aid. You did; and ere now she would have been raging among the Little Ones, had she dared again cross the stream. But there was yet a way to the blessed little colony through the world of the three dimensions; only, from that, by the slaying of her former body, she had excluded herself, and except in personal contact with one belonging to it, could not re-enter it. You provided the opportunity: never, in all her long years, had she had one before. Her hand, with lightest touch, was on one or other of your muffled feet, every step as you climbed. In that little chamber, she is now watching to leave it as soon as ever she may."

"She cannot know anything about the door! — she cannot at least know how to open it!" I said; but my heart was not so confident as my words.

"Hush, hush!" whispered the librarian, with uplifted hand; "she can hear through anything! — You must go at once, and make your way to my wife's cottage. I will remain to keep guard over her."

"Let me go to the Little Ones!" I cried.

"Beware of that, Mr. Vane. Go to my wife, and do as she tells you."

His advice did not recommend itself: why haste to encounter measureless delay? If not to protect the children, why go at all? Alas, even now I believed him only enough to ask him questions, not to obey him!

"Tell me first, Mr. Raven," I said, "why, of all places, you have shut her up there! The night I ran from your house, it was immediately into that closet!"

"The closet is no nearer our cottage, and no farther from it, than any or every other place."

"But," I returned, hard to persuade where I could not understand, "how is it then that, when you please, you take from that same door a whole book where I saw and felt only a part of one? The other part, you have just told me, stuck through into your library: when you put it again on the shelf, will it not again stick through into that? Must not then the two places, in which parts of the same volume can at the same moment exist, lie close together? Or can one part of the book be in space, or SOMEWHERE, and the other out of space, or NOWHERE?"

"I am sorry I cannot explain the thing to you," he answered; "but there is no provision in you for understanding it. Not merely, therefore, is the phenomenon inexplicable to you, but the very nature of it is inapprehensible by you. Indeed I but partially apprehend it myself. At the same time you are constantly experiencing things which you not only do not, but cannot understand. You think you understand them, but your understanding of them is only your being used to them, and therefore not surprised at them. You accept them, not because you understand them, but because you must accept them: they are there, and have unavoidable relations with you! The fact is, no man understands anything; when he knows he does not understand, that is his first tottering step — not toward understanding, but toward the capability of one day understanding. To such things as these you are not used, therefore you do not fancy you understand them. Neither I nor any man can here help you to understand; but I may, perhaps, help you a little to believe!"

He went to the door of the closet, gave a low whistle, and stood listening. A moment after, I heard, or seemed to hear, a soft whir of wings, and, looking up, saw a white dove perch for an instant on the top of the shelves over the portrait, thence drop to Mr. Raven's shoulder, and lay her head against his cheek. Only by the motions of their two heads could I tell that they were talking together; I heard nothing. Neither had I moved my eyes from them, when suddenly she was not there, and Mr. Raven came back to his seat.

"Why did you whistle?" I asked. "Surely sound here is not sound there!"

"You are right," he answered. "I whistled that you might know I called her. Not the whistle, but what the whistle meant reached her. — There is not a minute to lose: you must go!"

"I will at once!" I replied, and moved for the door.

"You will sleep to-night at my hostelry!" he said — not as a question, but in a tone of mild authority.

"My heart is with the children," I replied. "But if you insist—"

"I do insist. You can otherwise effect nothing. — I will go with you as far as the mirror, and see you off."

He rose. There came a sudden shock in the closet. Apparently the leopardess had flung herself against the heavy door. I looked at my companion.

"Come; come!" he said.

Ere we reached the door of the library, a howling yell came after us, mingled with the noise of claws that scored at the hard oak. I hesitated, and half turned.

"To think of her lying there alone," I murmured, "— with that terrible wound!"

"Nothing will ever close that wound," he answered, with a sigh. "It must eat into her heart! Annihilation itself is no death to evil. Only good where evil was, is evil dead. An evil thing must live with its evil until it chooses to be good. That alone is the slaying of evil."

I held my peace until a sound I did not understand overtook us.

"If she should break loose!" I cried.

"Make haste!" he rejoined. "I shall hurry down the moment you are gone, and I have disarranged the mirrors."

We ran, and reached the wooden chamber breathless. Mr. Raven seized the chains and adjusted the hood. Then he set the mirrors in their proper relation, and came beside me in front of the standing one. Already I saw the mountain range emerging from the mist.

Between us, wedging us asunder, darted, with the yell of a demon, the huge bulk of the spotted leopardess. She leaped through the mirror as through an open window, and settled at once into a low, even, swift gallop.

I cast a look of dismay at my companion, and sprang through to follow her. He came after me leisurely.

"You need not run," he called; "you cannot overtake her. This is our way."

As he spoke he turned in the opposite direction.

"She has more magic at her finger-tips than I care to know!" he added quietly.

"We must do what we can!" I said, and ran on, but sickening as I saw her dwindle in the distance, stopped, and went back to him.

"Doubtless we must," he answered. "But my wife has warned Mara, and she will do her part; you must sleep first: you have given me your word!"

"Nor do I mean to break it. But surely sleep is not the first thing! Surely, surely, action takes precedence of repose!"

"A man can do nothing he is not fit to do. — See! did I not tell you Mara would do her part?"

I looked whither he pointed, and saw a white spot moving at an acute angle with the line taken by the leopardess.

"There she is!" he cried. "The spotted leopardess is strong, but the white is stronger!"

"I have seen them fight: the combat did not appear decisive as to that."

"How should such eyes tell which have never slept? The princess did not confess herself beaten — that she never does — but she fled! When she confesses her last hope gone, that it is indeed hard to kick against the goad, then will her day begin to dawn! Come; come! He who cannot act must make haste to sleep!"

31. The Sexton's Old Horse

I stood and watched the last gleam of the white leopardess melt away, then turned to follow my guide — but reluctantly. What had I to do with sleep? Surely reason was the same in every world, and what reason could there be in going to sleep with the dead, when the hour was calling the live man? Besides, no one would wake me, and how could I be certain of waking early — of waking at all? — the sleepers in that house let morning glide into noon, and noon into night, nor ever stirred! I murmured, but followed, for I knew not what else to do.

The librarian walked on in silence, and I walked silent as he. Time and space glided past us. The sun set; it began to grow dark, and I felt in the air the spreading cold of the chamber of death. My heart sank lower and lower. I began to lose sight of the lean, long-coated figure, and at length could no more hear his swishing stride through the heather. But then I heard instead the slow-flapping wings of the raven; and, at intervals, now a firefly, now a gleaming butterfly rose into the rayless air.

By and by the moon appeared, slow crossing the far horizon.

"You are tired, are you not, Mr. Vane?" said the raven, alighting on a stone. "You must make acquaintance with the horse that will carry you in the morning!"

He gave a strange whistle through his long black beak. A spot appeared on the face of the half-risen moon. To my ears came presently the drumming of swift, soft-galloping hoofs, and in a minute or two, out of the very disc of the moon, low-thundered the terrible horse. His mane flowed away behind him like the crest of a wind-fighting wave, torn seaward in hoary spray, and the whisk of his tail kept blinding the eye of the moon. Nineteen hands he seemed, huge of bone, tight of skin, hard of muscle — a steed the holy Death himself might choose on which to ride abroad and slay! The moon seemed to regard him with awe; in her scary light he looked a very skeleton, loosely roped together. Terrifically large, he moved with the lightness of a winged insect. As he drew near, his speed slackened, and his mane and tail drifted about him settling.

Now I was not merely a lover of horses, but I loved every horse I saw. I had never spent money except upon horses, and had never sold a horse. The sight of this mighty one, terrible to look at, woke in me longing to possess him. It was pure greed, nay, rank covetousness, an evil thing in all the worlds. I do not mean that I could have stolen him, but that, regardless of his proper place, I would have bought him if I could. I laid my hands on him, and stroked the protuberant bones that humped a hide smooth and thin, and shiny as satin—so shiny that the very shape of the moon was reflected in it; I fondled his sharp-pointed ears, whispered words in them, and breathed into his red nostrils the breath of a man's life. He in return breathed into mine the breath of a horse's life, and we loved one another. What eyes he had! Blue-filmy like the eyes of the dead, behind each was a glowing coal! The raven, with wings half extended, looked on pleased at my love-making to his magnificent horse.

"That is well! be friends with him," he said: "he will carry you all the better to-morrow!—Now we must hurry home!"

My desire to ride the horse had grown passionate.

"May I not mount him at once, Mr. Raven?" I cried.

"By all means!" he answered. "Mount, and ride him home."

The horse bent his head over my shoulder lovingly. I twisted my hands in his mane and scrambled onto his back, not without aid from certain protuberant bones.

"He would out speed any leopard in creation!" I cried.

"Not that way at night," answered the raven; "the road is difficult. — But come; loss now will be gain then! To wait is harder than to run, and its meed is the fuller. Go on, my son —straight to the cottage. I shall be there as soon as you. It will rejoice my wife's heart to see son of hers on that horse!"

I sat silent. The horse stood like a block of marble.

"Why do you linger?" asked the raven.

"I long so much to ride after the leopardess," I answered, "that I can scarce restrain myself!"

"You have promised!"

"My debt to the Little Ones appears, I confess, a greater thing than my bond to you."

"Yield to the temptation and you will bring mischief upon them — and on yourself also."

"What matters it for me? I love them; and love works no evil. I will go."

But the truth was, I forgot the children, infatuate with the horse.

Eyes flashed through the darkness, and I knew that Adam stood in his own shape beside me. I knew also by his voice that he repressed an indignation almost too strong for him.

"Mr. Vane," he said, "do you not know why you have not yet done anything worth doing?"

"Because I have been a fool," I answered.

"Wherein?"

"In everything."

"Which do you count your most indiscreet action?"

"Bringing the princess to life: I ought to have left her to her just fate."

"Nay, now you talk foolishly! You could not have done otherwise than you did, not knowing she was evil! — But you never brought any one to life! How could you, yourself dead?"

"I dead?" I cried.

"Yes," he answered; "and you will be dead, so long as you refuse to die."

"Back to the old riddling!" I returned scornfully.

"Be persuaded, and go home with me," he continued gently. "The most — nearly the only foolish thing you ever did, was to run from our dead."

I pressed the horse's ribs, and he was off like a sudden wind. I gave him a pat on the side of the neck, and he went about in a sharp-driven curve, "close to the ground, like a cat when scratchingly she wheels about after a mouse," leaning sideways till his mane swept the tops of the heather.

Through the dark I heard the wings of the raven. Five quick flaps I heard, and he perched on the horse's head. The horse checked himself instantly, ploughing up the ground with his feet.

"Mr. Vane," croaked the raven, "think what you are doing! Twice already has evil befallen you — once from fear, and once from heedlessness: breach of word is far worse; it is a crime."

"The Little Ones are in frightful peril, and I brought it upon them!" I cried. "— But indeed I will not break my word to you. I will return, and spend in your house what nights —what days — what years you please."

"I tell you once more you will do them other than good if you go to-night," he insisted.

But a false sense of power, a sense which had no root and was merely vibrated into me from the strength of the horse, had, alas, rendered me too stupid to listen to anything he said!

"Would you take from me my last chance of reparation?" I cried. "This time there shall be no shirking! It is my duty, and I will go — if I perish for it!"

"Go, then, foolish boy!" he returned, with anger in his croak. "Take the horse, and ride to failure! May it be to humility!"

He spread his wings and flew. Again I pressed the lean ribs under me.

"After the spotted leopardess!" I whispered in his ear.

He turned his head this way and that, snuffing the air; then started, and went a few paces in a slow, undecided walk. Suddenly he quickened his walk; broke into a trot; began to gallop, and in a few moments his speed was tremendous. He seemed to see in the dark; never stumbled, not once faltered, not once hesitated. I sat as on the ridge of a wave. I felt under me the play of each individual muscle: his joints were so elastic, and his every movement glided so into the next, that not once did he jar me. His growing swiftness bore him along until he flew rather than ran. The wind met and passed us like a tornado.

Across the evil hollow we sped like a bolt from an arblast. No monster lifted its neck; all knew the hoofs that thundered over their heads! We rushed up the hills, we shot down their farther slopes; from the rocky chasms of the river-bed he did not swerve; he held on over them his fierce, terrible gallop. The moon, half-way up the heaven, gazed with a solemn trouble in her pale countenance. Rejoicing in the power of my steed and in the pride of my life, I sat like a king and rode.

We were near the middle of the many channels, my horse every other moment clearing one, sometimes two in his stride, and now and then gathering himself for a great bounding leap, when the moon reached the key-stone of her arch. Then came a wonder and a terror: she began to descend rolling like the nave of Fortune's wheel bowled by the gods, and went faster and faster. Like our own moon, this one had a human face, and now the broad forehead now the chin was uppermost as she rolled. I gazed aghast.

Across the ravines came the howling of wolves. An ugly fear began to invade the hollow places of my heart; my confidence was on the wane! The horse maintained his headlong swiftness, with ears pricked forward, and thirsty nostrils exulting in the wind his career created. But there was the moon jolting like an old chariot-wheel down the hill of heaven, with awful boding! She rolled at last over the horizon-edge and disappeared, carrying all her light with her.

The mighty steed was in the act of clearing a wide shallow channel when we were caught in the net of the darkness. His head dropped; its impetus carried his helpless bulk across, but he fell in a heap on the margin, and where he fell he lay. I got up, kneeled beside him, and felt him all over. Not a bone could I find broken, but he was a horse no more. I sat down on the body, and buried my face in my hands.

32. THE LOVERS AND THE BAGS

Bitterly cold grew the night. The body froze under me. The cry of the wolves came nearer; I heard their feet soft-padding on the rocky ground; their quick panting filled the air. Through the darkness I saw the many glowing eyes; their half-circle contracted around me. My time was come! I sprang to my feet. — Alas, I had not even a stick!

They came in a rush, their eyes flashing with fury of greed, their black throats agape to devour me. I stood hopelessly waiting them. One moment they halted over the horse — then came at me.

With a sound of swiftness all but silence, a cloud of green eyes came down on their flank. The heads that bore them flew at the wolves with a cry feebler yet fiercer than their howling snarl, and by the cry I knew them: they were cats, led by a huge gray one. I could see nothing of him but his eyes, yet I knew him — and so knew his color and bigness. A terrific battle followed, whose tale alone came to me through the night. I would have fled, for surely it was but a fight which should have me! — only where was the use? my first step would be a fall! and my foes of either kind could both see and scent me in the dark!

All at once I missed the howling, and the caterwauling grew wilder. Then came the soft padding, and I knew it meant flight: the cats had defeated the wolves! In a moment the sharpest of sharp teeth were in my legs; a moment more and the cats were all over me in a live cataract, biting wherever they could bite, furiously scratching me anywhere and everywhere. A multitude clung to my body; I could not flee. Madly I fell on the hateful swarm, every finger instinct with destruction. I tore them off me, I throttled at them in vain: when I would have flung them from me, they clung to my hands like limpets. I trampled them under my feet, thrust my fingers in their eyes, caught them in jaws stronger than theirs, but could not rid myself of one. Without cease they kept discovering upon me space for fresh mouthfuls; they hauled at my skin with the widespread, horribly curved pincers of clutching claws; they hissed and spat in my face — but never touched it until, in my despair, I threw myself on the ground, when they forsook my body, and darted at my face. I rose, and immediately they left it, the more to occupy themselves with my legs. In an agony I broke from them and ran, careless whither, cleaving the solid dark. They accompanied me in a surrounding torrent, now rubbing, now leaping up against me, but tormenting me no more. When I fell, which was often, they gave me time to rise; when from fear of falling I slackened my pace, they flew afresh at my legs. All that miserable night they kept me running — but they drove me by a comparatively smooth path, for I tumbled into no gully, and passing the Evil Wood without seeing it, left it behind in the dark. When at length the morning appeared, I was beyond the channels, and on the verge of the orchard valley. In my joy I would have made friends with my persecutors, but not a cat was to be seen. I threw myself on the moss, and fell fast asleep.

I was waked by a kick, to find myself bound hand and foot, once more the thrall of the giants!

"What fitter?" I said to myself; "to whom else should I belong?" and I laughed in the triumph of self-disgust. A second kick stopped my false merriment; and thus recurrently assisted by my captors, I succeeded at length in rising to my feet.

Six of them were about me. They undid the rope that tied my legs together, attached a rope to each of them, and dragged me away. I walked as well as I could, but, as they frequently pulled both ropes at once, I fell repeatedly, whereupon they always kicked me up again. Straight to my old labor they took me, tied my leg-ropes to a tree, undid my arms, and put the hateful flint in my left hand. Then they lay down and pelted me with fallen fruit and stones, but seldom hit me. If I could have freed my legs, and got hold of a stick I spied a couple of yards from me, I would have fallen upon all six of them! "But the Little Ones will come at night!" I said to myself, and was comforted.

All day I worked hard. When the darkness came, they tied my hands, and left me fast to the tree. I slept a good deal, but woke often, and every time from a dream of lying in the heart of a heap of children. With the morning my enemies reappeared, bringing their kicks and their bestial company.

It was about noon, and I was nearly failing from fatigue and hunger, when I heard a sudden commotion in the brushwood, followed by a burst of the bell-like laughter so dear to my heart. I gave a loud cry of delight and welcome. Immediately rose a trumpeting as of baby-elephants, a neighing as of foals, and a bellowing as of calves, and through the bushes came a crowd of Little Ones, on diminutive horses, on small elephants, on little bears; but the noises came from the riders, not the animals. Mingled with the mounted ones walked the bigger of the boys and girls, among the latter a woman with a baby crowing in her arms. The giants sprang to their lumbering feet, but were instantly saluted with a storm of sharp stones; the horses charged their legs; the bears rose and hugged them at the waist; the elephants threw their trunks round their necks, pulled them down, and gave them such a trampling as they had sometimes given, but never received before. In a moment my ropes were undone, and I was in the arms, seemingly innumerable, of the Little Ones. For some time I saw no more of the giants.

They made me sit down, and my Lona came, and without a word began to feed me with the loveliest red and yellow fruits. I sat and ate, the whole colony mounting guard until I had done. Then they brought up two of the largest of their elephants, and having placed them side by side, hooked their trunks and tied their tails together. The docile creatures could have untied their tails with a single shake, and unhooked their trunks by forgetting them; but tails and trunks remained as their little masters had arranged them, and it was clear the elephants understood that they must keep their bodies parallel. I got up, and laid myself in the hollow between their two backs; when the wise animals, counteracting the weight that pushed them apart, leaned against each other, and made for me a most comfortable litter. My feet, it is true, projected beyond their tails, but my head lay pillowed on an ear of each. Then some of the smaller children, mounting for a bodyguard, ranged themselves in a row along the back of each of my bearers; the whole assembly formed itself in train; and the procession began to move.

Whither they were carrying me, I did not try to conjecture; I yielded myself to their pleasure, almost as happy as they. Chattering and laughing and playing glad tricks innumerable at first, the moment they saw I was going to sleep, they became still as judges.

I woke: a sudden musical uproar greeted the opening of my eyes.

We were traveling through the forest in which they found the babies, and which, as I had suspected, stretched all the way from the valley to the hot stream.

A tiny girl sat with her little feet close to my face, and looked down at me coaxingly for a while, then spoke, the rest seeming to hang on her words.

"We make a petisson to king," she said.

"What is it, my darling?" I asked.

"Sut eyes one minute," she answered.

"Certainly I will! Here goes!" I replied, and shut my eyes close.

"No, no! not fore I tell oo!" she cried.

I opened them again, and we talked and laughed together for quite another hour.

"Close eyes!" she said suddenly.

I closed my eyes, and kept them close. The elephants stood still. I heard a soft scurry, a little rustle, and then a silence — for in that world SOME silences ARE heard.

"Open eyes!" twenty voices a little way off shouted at once; but when I obeyed, not a creature was visible except the elephants that bore me. I knew the children marvelously quick in getting out of the way — the giants had taught them that; but when I raised myself, and looking about in the open shrubless forest, could descry neither hand nor heel, I stared in "blank astonishment."

The sun was set, and it was fast getting dark, yet presently a multitude of birds began to sing. I lay down to listen, pretty sure that, if I left them alone, the hiders would soon come out again.

The singing grew to a little storm of bird-voices. "Surely the children must have something to do with it! — And yet how could they set the birds singing?" I said to myself as I lay and listened. Soon, however, happening to look up into the tree under which my elephants stood, I thought I spied a little motion among the leaves, and looked more keenly. Sudden white spots appeared in the dark foliage, the music died down, a gale of childish laughter rippled the air, and white spots came out in every direction: the trees were full of children! In the wildest merriment they began to descend, some dropping from bough to bough so rapidly that I could scarce believe they had not fallen. I left my litter, and was instantly surrounded — a mark for all the artillery of their jubilant fun. With stately composure the elephants walked away to bed.

"But," said I, when their uproarious gladness had had scope for a while, "how is it that I never before heard you sing like the birds? Even when I thought it must be you, I could hardly believe it!"

"Ah," said one of the wildest, "but we were not birds then! We were run-creatures, not fly-creatures! We had our hide-places in the bushes then; but when we came to no-bushes, only trees, we had to build nests! When we built nests, we grew birds, and when we were birds, we had to do birds! We asked them to teach us their noises, and they taught us, and now we are real birds! — Come and see my nest. It's not big enough for king, but it's big enough for king to see me in it!"

I told him I could not get up a tree without the sun to show me the way; when he came, I would try.

"Kings seldom have wings!" I added.

"King! king!" cried one, "oo knows none of us hasn't no wings — foolis feddery tings! Arms and legs is better."

"That is true. I can get up without wings—and carry straws in my mouth too, to build my nest with!"

"Oo knows!" he answered, and went away sucking his thumb.

A moment after, I heard him calling out of his nest, a great way up a walnut tree of enormous size,

"Up adain, king! Dood night! I seepy!"

And I heard no more of him till he woke me in the morning.

33. LONA'S NARRATIVE

I lay down by a tree, and one and one or in little groups, the children left me and climbed to their nests. They were always so tired at night and so rested in the morning, that they were equally glad to go to sleep and to get up again. I, although tired also, lay awake: Lona had not bid me good night, and I was sure she would come.

I had been struck, the moment I saw her again, with her resemblance to the princess, and could not doubt her the daughter of whom Adam had told me; but in Lona the dazzling beauty of Lilith was softened by childlikeness, and deepened by the sense of motherhood. "She is occupied probably," I said to myself, "with the child of the woman I met fleeing!" who, she had already told me, was not half mother enough.

She came at length, sat down beside me, and after a few moments of silent delight, expressed mainly by stroking my face and hands, began to tell me everything that had befallen since I went. The moon appeared as we talked, and now and then, through the leaves, lighted for a quivering moment her beautiful face — full of thought, and a care whose love redeemed and glorified it. How such a child should have been born of such a mother — such a woman of such a princess, was hard to understand; but then, happily, she had two parents — say rather, three! She drew my heart by what in me was likest herself, and I loved her as one who, grow to what perfection she might, could only become the more a child. I knew now that I loved her when I left her, and that the hope of seeing her again had been my main comfort. Every word she spoke seemed to go straight to my heart, and, like the truth itself, make it purer.

She told me that after I left the orchard valley, the giants began to believe a little more in the actual existence of their neighbors, and became in consequence more hostile to them. Sometimes the Little Ones would see them trampling furiously, perceiving or imagining some indication of their presence, while they indeed stood beside, and laughed at their foolish rage. By and by, however, their animosity assumed a more practical shape: they began to destroy the trees on whose fruit the Little Ones lived. This drove the mother of them all to meditate counteraction. Setting the sharpest of them to listen at night, she learned that the giants thought I was hidden somewhere near, intending, as soon as I recovered my strength, to come in the dark and kill them sleeping. Thereupon she concluded that the only way to stop the destruction was to give them ground for believing that they had abandoned the place. The Little Ones must remove into the forest — beyond the range of the giants, but within reach of their own trees, which they must visit by night! The main objection to the plan was, that the forest had little or no undergrowth to shelter — or conceal them if necessary.

But she reflected that where birds, there the Little Ones could find habitation. They had eager sympathies with all modes of life, and could learn of the wildest creatures: why should they not take refuge from the cold and their enemies in the tree-tops? why not, having lain in the low brushwood, seek now the lofty foliage? Why not build nests where it would not serve to scoop hollows? All that the birds could do, the Little Ones could learn — except, indeed, to fly!

She spoke to them on the subject, and they heard with approval. They could already climb the trees, and they had often watched the birds building their nests! The trees of the forest, although large, did not look bad! They went up much nearer the sky than those of the giants, and spread out their arms — some even stretched them down — as if inviting them to come and live with them! Perhaps, in the top of the tallest, they might find that bird that laid the baby-eggs, and sat upon them till they were ripe, then tumbled them down to let the little ones out! Yes; they would build sleep-houses in the trees, where no giant would see them, for never by any chance did one throw back his dull head to look up! Then the bad giants would be sure they had left the country, and the Little Ones would gather their own apples and pears and figs and mesples and peaches when they were asleep!

Thus reasoned the Lovers, and eagerly adopted Lona's suggestion — with the result that they were soon as much at home in the tree-tops as the birds themselves, and that the giants came ere long to the conclusion that they had frightened them out of the country –whereupon they forgot their trees, and again almost ceased to believe in the existence of their small neighbors.

Lona asked me whether I had not observed that many of the children were grown. I answered I had not, but could readily believe it. She assured me it was so, but said the certain evidence that their minds too had grown since their migration upward, had gone far in mitigation of the alarm the discovery had occasioned her.

In the last of the short twilight, and later when the moon was shining, they went down to the valley, and gathered fruit enough to serve them the next day; for the giants never went out in the twilight: that to them was darkness; and they hated the moon: had they been able, they would have extinguished her. But soon the Little Ones found that fruit gathered in the night was not altogether good the next day; so the question arose whether it would not be better, instead of pretending to have left the country, to make the bad giants themselves leave it.

They had already, she said, in exploring the forest, made acquaintance with the animals in it, and with most of them personally. Knowing therefore how strong as well as wise and docile some of them were, and how swift as well as manageable many others, they now set themselves to secure their aid against the giants, and with loving, playful approaches, had soon made more than friends of most of them, from the first addressing horse or elephant as Brother or Sister Elephant, Brother or Sister Horse, until before long they had an individual name for each. It was some little time longer before they said Brother or Sister Bear, but that came next, and the other day she had heard one little fellow cry, "Ah, Sister Serpent!" to a snake that bit him as he played with it too roughly. Most of them would have nothing to do with a caterpillar, except watch it through its changes; but when at length it came from its retirement with wings, all would immediately address it as Sister Butterfly, congratulating it on its metamorphosis — for which they used a word that meant something like REPENTANCE — and evidently regarding it as something sacred.

One moonlit evening, as they were going to gather their fruit, they came upon a woman seated on the ground with a baby in her lap — the woman I had met on my way to Bulika. They took her for a giantess that had stolen one of their babies, for they regarded all babies as their property. Filled with anger they fell upon her multitudinously, beating her after a childish, yet sufficiently bewildering fashion. She would have fled, but a boy threw himself down and held her by the feet. Recovering her wits, she recognized in her assailants the children whose hospitality she sought, and at once yielded the baby. Lona appeared, and carried it away in her bosom.

But while the woman noted that in striking her they were careful not to hurt the child, the Little Ones noted that, as she surrendered her, she hugged and kissed her just as they wanted to do, and came to the conclusion that she must be a giantess of the same kind as the good giant. The moment Lona had the baby, therefore, they brought the mother fruit, and began to show her every sort of childish attention.

Now the woman had been in perplexity whither to betake herself, not daring to go back to the city, because the princess was certain to find out who had lamed her leopardess: delighted with the friendliness of the little people, she resolved to remain with them for the present: she would have no trouble with her infant, and might find some way of returning to her husband, who was rich in money and gems, and very seldom unkind to her.

Here I must supplement, partly from conjecture, what Lona told me about the woman. With the rest of the inhabitants of Bulika, she was aware of the tradition that the princess lived in terror of the birth of an infant destined to her destruction. They were all unacquainted, however, with the frightful means by which she preserved her youth and beauty; and her deteriorating physical condition requiring a larger use of those means, they took the apparent increase of her hostility to children for a sign that she saw her doom approaching. This, although no one dreamed of any attempt against her, nourished in them hopes of change.

Now arose in the mind of the woman the idea of furthering the fulfillment of the shadowy prediction, or of using the myth at least for her own restoration to her husband. For what seemed more probable than that the fate foretold lay with these very children? They were marvelously brave, and the Bulikans cowards, in abject terror of animals! If she could rouse in the Little Ones the ambition of taking the city, then in the confusion of the attack, she would escape from the little army, reach her house unrecognized, and there lying hidden, await the result!

Should the children now succeed in expelling the giants, she would begin at once, while they were yet flushed with victory, to suggest the loftier aim! By disposition, indeed, they were unfit for warfare; they hardly ever quarreled, and never fought; loved every live thing, and hated either to hurt or to suffer. Still, they were easily influenced, and could certainly be taught any exercise within their strength! — At once she set some of the smaller ones throwing stones at a mark; and soon they were all engrossed with the new game, and growing skilful in it.

The first practical result was their use of stones in my rescue. While gathering fruit, they found me asleep, went home, held a council, came the next day with their elephants and horses, overwhelmed the few giants watching me, and carried me off. Jubilant over their victory, the smaller boys were childishly boastful, the bigger boys less ostentatious, while the girls, although their eyes flashed more, were not so talkative as usual. The woman of Bulika no doubt felt encouraged.

We talked the greater part of the night, chiefly about the growth of the children, and what it might indicate. With Lona's power of recognising truth I had long been familiar; now I began to be astonished at her practical wisdom. Probably, had I been more of a child myself, I should have wondered less.

It was yet far from morning when I became aware of a slight fluttering and scrambling. I rose on my elbow, and looking about me, saw many Little Ones descend from their nests. They disappeared, and in a few moments all was again still.

"What are they doing?" I asked.

"They think," answered Lona, "that, stupid as they are, the giants will search the wood, and they are gone to gather stones with which to receive them. Stones are not plentiful in the forest, and they have to scatter far to find enow. They will carry them to their nests, and from the trees attack the giants as they come within reach. Knowing their habits, they do not expect them before the morning. If they do come, it will be the opening of a war of expulsion: one or the other people must go. The result, however, is hardly doubtful. We do not mean to kill them; indeed, their skulls are so thick that I do not think we could! — not that killing would do them much harm; they are so little alive! If one were killed, his giantess would not remember him beyond three days!"

"Do the children then throw so well that the thing MIGHT happen?" I asked.

"Wait till you see them!" she answered, with a touch of pride. "— But I have not yet told you," she went on, "of a strange thing that happened the night before last! — We had come home from gathering our fruit, and were asleep in our nests, when we were roused by the horrid noises of beasts fighting. The moon was bright, and in a moment our trees glittered with staring little eyes, watching two huge leopardesses, one perfectly white, the other covered with black spots, which worried and tore each other with I do not know how many teeth and claws. To judge by her back, the spotted creature must have been climbing a tree when the other sprang upon her. When first I saw them, they were just under my own tree, rolling over and over each other. I got down on the lowest branch, and saw them perfectly. The children enjoyed the spectacle, siding some with this one, some with that, for we had never seen such beasts before, and thought they were only at play. But by degrees their roaring and growling almost ceased, and I saw that they were in deadly earnest, and heartily wished neither might be left able to climb a tree. But when the children saw the blood pouring from their flanks and throats, what do you think they did? They scurried down to comfort them, and gathering in a great crowd about the terrible creatures, began to pat and stroke them. Then I got down as well, for they were much too absorbed to heed my calling to them; but before I could reach them, the white one stopped fighting, and sprang among them with such a hideous yell that they flew up into the trees like birds. Before I got back into mine, the wicked beasts were at it again tooth and claw. Then Whitey had the best of it; Spotty ran away as fast as she could run, and Whitey came and lay down at the foot of my tree. But in a minute or two she was up again, and walking about as if she thought Spotty might be lurking somewhere. I waked often, and every time I looked out, I saw her. In the morning she went away."

"I know both the beasts," I said. "Spotty is a bad beast. She hates the children, and would kill every one of them. But Whitey loves them. She ran at them only to frighten them away, lest Spotty should get hold of any of them. No one needs be afraid of Whitey!"

By this time the Little Ones were coming back, and with much noise, for they had no care to keep quiet now that they were at open war with the giants, and laden with good stones. They mounted to their nests again, though with difficulty because of their burdens, and in a minute were fast asleep. Lona retired to her tree. I lay where I was, and slept the better that I thought most likely the white leopardess was still somewhere in the wood.

I woke soon after the sun, and lay pondering. Two hours passed, and then in truth the giants began to appear, in straggling companies of three and four, until I counted over a hundred of them. The children were still asleep, and to call them would draw the attention of the giants: I would keep quiet so long as they did not discover me. But by and by one came blundering upon me, stumbled, fell, and rose again. I thought he would pass heedless, but he began to search about. I sprang to my feet, and struck him in the middle of his huge body. The roar he gave roused the children, and a storm as of hail instantly came on, of which not a stone struck me, and not one missed the giant. He fell and lay. Others drew near, and the storm extended, each purblind creature becoming, as he entered the range of a garrisoned tree, a target for converging stones. In a short time almost every giant was prostrate, and a jubilant pæan of bird-song rose from the tops of fifty trees.

Many elephants came hurrying up, and the children descending the trees like monkeys, in a moment every elephant had three or four of them on his back, and thus loaded, began to walk over the giants, who lay and roared. Losing patience at length with their noise, the elephants gave them a few blows of their trunks, and left them.

Until night the bad giants remained where they had fallen, silent and motionless. The next morning they had disappeared every one, and the children saw no more of them. They removed to the other end of the orchard valley, and never after ventured into the forest.

34. PREPARATION

Victory thus gained, the woman of Bulika began to speak about the city, and talked much of its defenseless condition, of the wickedness of its princess, of the cowardice of its inhabitants. In a few days the children chattered of nothing but Bulika, although indeed they had not the least notion of what a city was. Then first I became aware of the design of the woman, although not yet of its motive.

The idea of taking possession of the place, recommended itself greatly to Lona — and to me also. The children were now so rapidly developing faculty, that I could see no serious obstacle to the success of the enterprise. For the terrible Lilith — woman or leopardess, I knew her one vulnerable point, her doom through her daughter, and the influence the ancient prophecy had upon the citizens: surely whatever in the enterprise could be called risk, was worth taking! Successful, — and who could doubt their success? – must not the Little Ones, from a crowd of children, speedily become a youthful people, whose government and influence would be all for righteousness? Ruling the wicked with a rod of iron, would they not be the redemption of the nation?

At the same time, I have to confess that I was not without views of personal advantage, not without ambition in the undertaking. It was just, it seemed to me, that Lona should take her seat on the throne that had been her mother's, and natural that she should make of me her consort and minister. For me, I would spend my life in her service; and between us, what might we not do, with such a core to it as the Little Ones, for the development of a noble state?

I confess also to an altogether foolish dream of opening a commerce in gems between the two worlds — happily impossible, for it could have done nothing but harm to both.

Calling to mind the appeal of Adam, I suggested to Lona that to find them water might perhaps expedite the growth of the Little Ones. She judged it prudent, however, to leave that alone for the present, as we did not know what its first consequences might be; while, in the course of time, it would almost certainly subject them to a new necessity.

"They are what they are without it!" she said: "when we have the city, we will search for water!"

We began, therefore, and pushed forward our preparations, constantly reviewing the merry troops and companies. Lona gave her attention chiefly to the commissariat, while I drilled the little soldiers, exercised them in stone-throwing, taught them the use of some other weapons, and did all I could to make warriors of them. The main difficulty was to get them to rally to their flag the instant the call was sounded. Most of them were armed with slings, some of the bigger boys with bows and arrows. The bigger girls carried aloe-spikes, strong as steel and sharp as needles, fitted to longish shafts — rather formidable weapons. Their sole duty was the charge of such as were too small to fight.

Lona had herself grown a good deal, but did not seem aware of it: she had always been, as she still was, the tallest! Her hair was much longer, and she was become almost a woman, but not one beauty of childhood had she outgrown. When first we met after our long separation, she laid down her infant, put her arms round my neck, and clung to me silent, her face glowing with gladness: the child whimpered; she sprang to him, and had him in her bosom instantly. To see her with any thoughtless, obstinate, or irritable little one, was to think of a tender grandmother. I seemed to have known her for ages — for always — from before time began! I hardly remembered my mother, but in my mind's eye she now looked like Lona; and if I imagined sister or child, invariably she had the face of Lona! My every imagination flew to her; she was my heart's wife! She hardly ever sought me, but was almost always within sound of my voice. What I did or thought, I referred constantly to her, and rejoiced to believe that, while doing her work in absolute independence, she was most at home by my side. Never for me did she neglect the smallest child, and my love only quickened my sense of duty. To love her and to do my duty, seemed, not indeed one, but inseparable. She might suggest something I should do; she might ask me what she ought to do; but she never seemed to suppose that I, any more than she, would like to do, or could care about anything except what must be done.

Her love overflowed upon me — not in caresses, but in a closeness of recognition which I can compare to nothing but the devotion of a divine animal.

I never told her anything about her mother.

The wood was full of birds, the splendor of whose plumage, while it took nothing from their song, seemed almost to make up for the lack of flowers — which, apparently, could not grow without water. Their glorious feathers being everywhere about in the forest, it came into my heart to make from them a garment for Lona. While I gathered, and bound them in overlapping rows, she watched me with evident appreciation of my choice and arrangement, never asking what I was fashioning, but evidently waiting expectant the result of my work. In a week or two it was finished — a long loose mantle, to fasten at the throat and waist, with openings for the arms.

I rose and put it on her. She rose, took it off, and laid it at my feet — I imagine from a sense of propriety. I put it again on her shoulders, and showed her where to put her arms through. She smiled, looked at the feathers a little and stroked them — again took it off and laid it down, this time by her side. When she left me, she carried it with her, and I saw no more of it for some days. At length she came to me one morning wearing it, and carrying another garment which she had fashioned similarly, but of the dried leaves of a tough evergreen. It had the strength almost of leather, and the appearance of scale-armor. I put it on at once, and we always thereafter wore those garments when on horseback.

For, on the outskirts of the forest, had appeared one day a troop of full-grown horses, with which, as they were nowise alarmed at creatures of a shape so different from their own, I had soon made friends, and two of the finest I had trained for Lona and myself. Already accustomed to ride a small one, her delight was great when first she looked down from the back of an animal of the giant kind; and the horse showed himself proud of the burden he bore. We exercised them every day until they had such confidence in us as to obey instantly and fear nothing; after which we always rode them at parade and on the march.

The undertaking did indeed at times appear to me a foolhardy one, but the confidence of the woman of Bulika, real or simulated, always overcame my hesitancy. The princess's magic, she insisted, would prove powerless against the children; and as to any force she might muster, our animal-allies alone would assure our superiority: she was herself, she said, ready, with a good stick, to encounter any two men of Bulika. She confessed to not a little fear of the leopardess, but I was myself ready for her. I shrank, however, from carrying ALL the children with us.

"Would it not be better," I said, "that you remained in the forest with your baby and the smallest of the Little Ones?"

She answered that she greatly relied on the impression the sight of them would make on the women, especially the mothers.

"When they see the darlings," she said, "their hearts will be taken by storm; and I must be there encouraging them to make a stand! If there be a remnant of hardihood in the place, it will be found among the women!"

"YOU must not encumber yourself," I said to Lona, "with any of the children; you will be wanted everywhere!"

For there were two babies besides the woman's, and even on horseback she had almost always one in her arms.

"I do not remember ever being without a child to take care of," she answered; "but when we reach the city, it shall be as you wish!"

Her confidence in one who had failed so unworthily, shamed me. But neither had I initiated the movement, nor had I any ground for opposing it; I had no choice, but must give it the best help I could! For myself, I was ready to live or die with Lona. Her humility as well as her trust humbled me, and I gave myself heartily to her purposes.

Our way lying across a grassy plain, there was no need to take food for the horses, or the two cows which would accompany us for the infants; but the elephants had to be provided for. True, the grass was as good for them as for those other animals, but it was short, and with their one-fingered long noses, they could not pick enough for a single meal. We had, therefore, set the whole colony to gather grass and make hay, of which the elephants themselves could carry a quantity sufficient to last them several days, with the supplement of what we would gather fresh every time we halted. For the bears we stored nuts, and for ourselves dried plenty of fruits. We had caught and tamed several more of the big horses, and now having loaded them and the elephants with these provisions, we were prepared to set out.

Then Lona and I held a general review, and I made them a little speech. I began by telling them that I had learned a good deal about them, and knew now where they came from. "We did not come from anywhere," they cried, interrupting me; "we are here!"

I told them that every one of them had a mother of his own, like the mother of the last baby; that I believed they had all been brought from Bulika when they were so small that they could not now remember it; that the wicked princess there was so afraid of babies, and so determined to destroy them, that their mothers had to carry them away and leave them where she could not find them; and that now we were going to Bulika, to find their mothers, and deliver them from the bad giantess.

"But I must tell you," I continued, "that there is danger before us, for, as you know, we may have to fight hard to take the city."

"We can fight! we are ready!" cried the boys.

"Yes, you can," I returned, "and I know you will: mothers are worth fighting for! Only mind, you must all keep together." "Yes, yes; we'll take care of each other," they answered. "Nobody shall touch one of us but his own mother!"

"You must mind, every one, to do immediately what your officers tell you!"

"We will, we will! — Now we're quite ready! Let us go!"

"Another thing you must not forget," I went on: "when you strike, be sure you make it a downright swinging blow; when you shoot an arrow, draw it to the head; when you sling a stone, sling it strong and straight."

"That we will!" they cried with jubilant, fearless shout.

"Perhaps you will be hurt!"

"We don't mind that! — Do we, boys?"

"Not a bit!"

"Some of you may very possibly be killed!" I said.

"I don't mind being killed!" cried one of the finest of the smaller boys: he rode a beautiful little bull, which galloped and jumped like a horse.

"I don't either! I don't either!" came from all sides.

Then Lona, queen and mother and sister of them all, spoke from her big horse by my side:

"I would give my life," she said, "to have my mother! She might kill me if she liked! I should just kiss her and die!"

"Come along, boys!" cried a girl. "We're going to our mothers!"

A pang went through my heart. — But I could not draw back; it would be moral ruin to the Little Ones!

35. THE LITTLE ONES IN BULIKA

It was early in the morning when we set out, making, between the blue sky and the green grass, a gallant show on the wide plain. We would travel all the morning, and rest the afternoon; then go on at night, rest the next day, and start again in the short twilight. The latter part of our journey we would endeavor so to divide as to arrive at the city with the first of the morning, and be already inside the gates when discovered.

It seemed as if all the inhabitants of the forest would migrate with us. A multitude of birds flew in front, imagining themselves, no doubt, the leading division; great companies of butterflies and other insects played about our heads; and a crowd of four-footed creatures followed us. These last, when night came, left us almost all; but the birds and the butterflies, the wasps and the dragon-flies, went with us to the very gates of the city.

We halted and slept soundly through the afternoon: it was our first real march, but none were tired. In the night we went faster, because it was cold. Many fell asleep on the backs of their beasts, and woke in the morning quite fresh. None tumbled off. Some rode shaggy, shambling bears, which yet made speed enough, going as fast as the elephants. Others were mounted on different kinds of deer, and would have been racing all the way had I not prevented it. Those atop of the hay on the elephants, unable to see the animals below them, would keep talking to them as long as they were awake. Once, when we had halted to feed, I heard a little fellow, as he drew out the hay to give him, commune thus with his "darling beast":

"Nosy dear, I am digging you out of the mountain, and shall soon get down to you: be patient; I'm a coming! Very soon now you'll send up your nose to look for me, and then we'll kiss like good elephants, we will!"

The same night there burst out such a tumult of elephant-trumpeting, horse-neighing, and child-imitation, ringing far over the silent levels, that, uncertain how near the city might not be, I quickly stilled the uproar lest it should give warning of our approach.

Suddenly, one morning, the sun and the city rose, as it seemed, together. To the children the walls appeared only a great mass of rock, but when I told them the inside was full of nests of stone, I saw apprehension and dislike at once invade their hearts: for the first time in their lives, I believe — many of them long little lives — they knew fear. The place looked to them bad: how were they to find mothers in such a place? But they went on bravely, for they had confidence in Lona — and in me too, little as I deserved it.

We rode through the sounding archway. Sure never had such a drumming of hoofs, such a padding of paws and feet been heard on its old pavement! The horses started and looked scared at the echo of their own steps; some halted a moment, some plunged wildly and wheeled about; but they were soon quieted, and went on. Some of the Little Ones shivered, and all were still as death.

The three girls held closer the infants they carried. All except the bears and butterflies manifested fear.

On the countenance of the woman lay a dark anxiety; nor was I myself unaffected by the general dread, for the whole army was on my hands and on my conscience: I had brought it up to the danger whose shadow was now making itself felt! But I was supported by the thought of the coming kingdom of the Little Ones, with the bad giants its slaves, and the animals its loving, obedient friends! Alas, I who dreamed thus, had not myself learned to obey! Untrusting, unfaithful obstinacy had set me at the head of that army of innocents! I was myself but a slave, like any king in the world I had left who does or would do only what pleases him! But Lona rode beside me a child indeed, therefore a free woman — calm, silent, watchful, not a whit afraid!

We were nearly in the heart of the city before any of its inhabitants became aware of our presence. But now windows began to open, and sleepy heads to look out. Every face wore at first a dull stare of wonderless astonishment, which, as soon as the starers perceived the animals, changed to one of consternation. In spite of their fear, however, when they saw that their invaders were almost all children, the women came running into the streets, and the men followed. But for a time all of them kept close to the houses, leaving open the middle of the way, for they durst not approach the animals.

At length a boy, who looked about five years old, and was full of the idea of his mother, spying in the crowd a woman whose face attracted him, threw himself upon her from his antelope, and clung about her neck; nor was she slow to return his embrace and kisses. But the hand of a man came over her shoulder, and seized him by the neck. Instantly a girl ran her sharp spear into the fellow's arm. He sent forth a savage howl, and immediately stabbed by two or three more, fled yelling.

"They are just bad giants!" said Lona, her eyes flashing as she drove her horse against one of unusual height who, having stirred up the little manhood in him, stood barring her way with a club. He dared not abide the shock, but slunk aside, and the next moment went down, struck by several stones. Another huge fellow, avoiding my charger, stepped suddenly, with a speech whose rudeness alone was intelligible, between me and the boy who rode behind me. The boy told him to address the king; the giant struck his little horse on the head with a hammer, and he fell. Before the brute could strike again, however, one of the elephants behind laid him prostrate, and trampled on him so that he did not attempt to get up until hundreds of feet had walked over him, and the army was gone by.

But at sight of the women what a dismay clouded the face of Lona! Hardly one of them was even pleasant to look upon! Were her darlings to find mothers among such as these?

Hardly had we halted in the central square, when two girls rode up in anxious haste, with the tidings that two of the boys had been hurried away by some women. We turned at once, and then first discovered that the woman we befriended had disappeared with her baby.

But at the same moment we descried a white leopardess come bounding toward us down a narrow lane that led from the square to the palace. The Little Ones had not forgotten the fight of the two leopardesses in the forest: some of them looked terrified, and their ranks began to waver; but they remembered the order I had just given them, and stood fast.

We stopped to see the result; when suddenly a small boy, called Odu, remarkable for his speed and courage, who had heard me speak of the goodness of the white leopardess, leaped from the back of his bear, which went shambling after him, and ran to meet her. The leopardess, to avoid knocking him down, pulled herself up so suddenly that she went rolling over and over: when she recovered her feet she found the child on her back. Who could doubt the subjugation of a people which saw an urchin of the enemy bestride an animal of which they lived in daily terror? Confident of the effect on the whole army, we rode on.

As we stopped at the house to which our guides led us, we heard a scream; I sprang down, and thundered at the door. My horse came and pushed me away with his nose, turned about, and had begun to batter the door with his heels, when up came little Odu on the leopardess, and at sight of her he stood still, trembling. But she too had heard the cry, and forgetting the child on her back, threw herself at the door; the boy was dashed against it, and fell senseless. Before I could reach him, Lona had him in her arms, and as soon as he came to himself, set him on the back of his bear, which had still followed him.

When the leopardess threw herself the third time against the door, it gave way, and she darted in. We followed, but she had already vanished. We sprang up a stair, and went all over the house, to find no one. Darting down again, we spied a door under the stair, and got into a labyrinth of excavations. We had not gone far, however, when we met the leopardess with the child we sought across her back.

He told us that the woman he took for his mother threw him into a hole, saying she would give him to the leopardess. But the leopardess was a good one, and took him out.

Following in search of the other boy, we got into the next house more easily, but to find, alas, that we were too late: one of the savages had just killed the little captive! It consoled Lona, however, to learn which he was, for she had been expecting him to grow a bad giant, from which worst of fates death had saved him. The leopardess sprang upon his murderer, took him by the throat, dragged him into the street, and followed Lona with him, like a cat with a great rat in her jaws.

"Let us leave the horrible place," said Lona; "there are no mothers here! This people is not worth delivering."

The leopardess dropped her burden, and charged into the crowd, this way and that, wherever it was thickest. The slaves cried out and ran, tumbling over each other in heaps.

When we got back to the army, we found it as we had left it, standing in order and ready.

But I was far from easy: the princess gave no sign, and what she might be plotting we did not know! Watch and ward must be kept the night through!

The Little Ones were such hardy creatures that they could repose anywhere: we told them to lie down with their animals where they were, and sleep till they were called. In one moment they were down, and in another lapt in the music of their sleep, a sound as of water over grass, or a soft wind among leaves. Their animals slept more lightly, ever on the edge of waking. The bigger boys and girls walked softly hither and thither among the dreaming multitude. All was still; the whole wicked place appeared at rest.

36. MOTHER AND DAUGHTER

Lona was so disgusted with the people, and especially with the women, that she wished to abandon the place as soon as possible; I, on the contrary, felt very strongly that to do so would be to fail willfully where success was possible; and, far worse, to weaken the hearts of the Little Ones, and so bring them into much greater danger. If we retreated, it was certain the princess would not leave us un-assailed! if we encountered her, the hope of the prophecy went with us! Mother and daughter must meet: it might be that Lona's loveliness would take Lilith's heart by storm! if she threatened violence, I should be there between them! If I found that I had no other power over her, I was ready, for the sake of my Lona, to strike her pitilessly on the closed hand! I knew she was doomed: most likely it was decreed that her doom should now be brought to pass through us!

Still without hint of the relation in which she stood to the princess, I stated the case to Lona as it appeared to me. At once she agreed to accompany me to the palace.

From the top of one of its great towers, the princess had, in the early morning, while the city yet slept, descried the approach of the army of the Little Ones. The sight awoke in her an over-mastering terror: she had failed in her endeavor to destroy them, and they were upon her! The prophecy was about to be fulfilled!

When she came to herself, she descended to the black hall, and seated herself in the north focus of the ellipse, under the opening in the roof.

For she must think! Now what she called THINKING required a clear consciousness of herself, not as she was, but as she chose to believe herself; and to aid her in the realization of this consciousness, she had suspended, a little way from and above her, itself invisible in the darkness of the hall, a mirror to receive the full sunlight reflected from her person. For the resulting vision of herself in the splendor of her beauty, she sat waiting the meridional sun.

Many a shadow moved about her in the darkness, but as often as, with a certain inner eye which she had, she caught sight of one, she refused to regard it. Close under the mirror stood the Shadow which attended her walks, but, self-occupied, him she did not see.

The city was taken; the inhabitants were cowering in terror; the Little Ones and their strange cavalry were encamped in the square; the sun shone upon the princess, and for a few minutes she saw herself glorious. The vision passed, but she sat on. The night was now come, and darkness clothed and filled the glass, yet she did not move. A gloom that swarmed with shadows, wallowed in the palace; the servants shivered and shook, but dared not leave it because of the beasts of the Little Ones; all night long the princess sat motionless: she must see her beauty again! She must try again to think! But courage and will had grown weary of her, and would dwell with her no more!

In the morning we chose twelve of the tallest and bravest of the boys to go with us to the palace. We rode our great horses, and they small horses and elephants.

The princess sat waiting the sun to give her the joy of her own presence. The tide of the light was creeping up the shore of the sky, but until the sun stood overhead, not a ray could enter the black hall.

He rose to our eyes, and swiftly ascended. As we climbed the steep way to the palace, he climbed the dome of its great hall. He looked in at the eye of it — and with sudden radiance the princess flashed upon her own sight. But she sprang to her feet with a cry of despair: alas her whiteness! The spot covered half her side, and was black as the marble around her! She clutched her robe, and fell back in her chair. The Shadow glided out, and she saw him go.

We found the gate open as usual, passed through the paved grove up to the palace door, and entered the vestibule. There in her cage lay the spotted leopardess, apparently asleep or lifeless. The Little Ones paused a moment to look at her. She leaped up rampant against the cage. The horses reared and plunged; the elephants retreated a step. The next instant she fell supine, writhed in quivering spasms, and lay motionless. We rode into the great hall.

The princess yet leaned back in her chair in the shaft of sunlight, when from the stones of the court came to her ears the noise of the horses' hoofs. She started, listened, and shook: never had such sound been heard in her palace! She pressed her hand to her side, and gasped. The trampling came nearer and nearer; it entered the hall itself; moving figures that were not shadows approached her through the darkness!

For us, we saw a splendor, a glorious woman centring the dark. Lona sprang from her horse, and bounded to her. I sprang from mine, and followed Lona.

"Mother! mother!" she cried, and her clear, lovely voice echoed in the dome.

The princess shivered; her face grew almost black with hate, her eyebrows met on her forehead. She rose to her feet, and stood.

"Mother! mother!" cried Lona again, as she leaped on the daïs, and flung her arms around the princess.

An instant more and I should have reached them! — in that instant I saw Lona lifted high, and dashed on the marble floor. Oh, the horrible sound of her fall! At my feet she fell, and lay still. The princess sat down with the smile of a demoness.

I dropped on my knees beside Lona, raised her from the stones, and pressed her to my bosom. With indignant hate I glanced at the princess; she answered me with her sweetest smile. I would have sprung upon her, taken her by the throat, and strangled her, but love of the child was stronger than hate of the mother, and I clasped closer my precious burden. Her arms hung helpless; her blood trickled over my hands, and fell on the floor with soft, slow little plashes.

The horses scented it — mine first, then the small ones. Mine reared, shivering and wild-eyed, went about, and thundered blindly down the dark hall, with the little horses after him. Lona's stood gazing down at his mistress, and trembling all over. The boys flung themselves from their horses' backs, and they, not seeing the black wall before them, dashed themselves, with mine, to pieces against it. The elephants came on to the foot of the daïs, and stopped, wildly trumpeting; the Little Ones sprang upon it, and stood horrified; the princess lay back in her seat, her face that of a corpse, her eyes alone alive, wickedly flaming. She was again withered and wasted to what I found in the wood, and her side was as if a great branding hand had been laid upon it. But Lona saw nothing, and I saw but Lona.

"Mother! mother!" she sighed, and her breathing ceased.

I carried her into the court: the sun shone upon a white face, and the pitiful shadow of a ghostly smile. Her head hung back. She was "dead as earth."

I forgot the Little Ones, forgot the murdering princess, forgot the body in my arms, and wandered away, looking for my Lona. The doors and windows were crowded with brute-faces jeering at me, but not daring to speak, for they saw the white leopardess behind me, hanging her head close at my heel. I spurned her with my foot. She held back a moment, and followed me again.

I reached the square: the little army was gone! Its emptiness roused me. Where were the Little Ones, HER Little Ones? I had lost her children! I stared helpless about me, staggered to the pillar, and sank upon its base.

But as I sat gazing on the still countenance, it seemed to smile a live momentary smile. I never doubted it an illusion, yet believed what it said: I should yet see her alive! It was not she, it was I who was lost, and she would find me!

I rose to go after the Little Ones, and instinctively sought the gate by which we had entered. I looked around me, but saw nothing of the leopardess.

The street was rapidly filling with a fierce crowd. They saw me encumbered with my dead, but for a time dared not assail me. Ere I reached the gate, however, they had gathered courage. The women began to hustle me; I held on heedless. A man pushed against my sacred burden: with a kick I sent him away howling. But the crowd pressed upon me, and fearing for the dead that was beyond hurt, I clasped my treasure closer, and freed my right arm. That instant, however, a commotion arose in the street behind me; the crowd broke; and through it came the Little Ones I had left in the palace. Ten of them were upon four of the elephants; on the two other elephants lay the princess, bound hand and foot, and quite still, save that her eyes rolled in their ghastly sockets. The two other Little Ones rode behind her on Lona's horse. Every now and then the wise creatures that bore her threw their trunks behind and felt her cords.

I walked on in front, and out of the city. What an end to the hopes with which I entered the evil place! We had captured the bad princess, and lost our all-beloved queen! My life was bare! My heart was empty!

37. THE SHADOW

A murmur of pleasure from my companions roused me: they had caught sight of their fellows in the distance! The two on Lona's horse rode on to join them. They were greeted with a wavering shout — which immediately died away. As we drew near, the sound of their sobs reached us like the breaking of tiny billows.

When I came among them, I saw that something dire had befallen them: on their childish faces was the haggard look left by some strange terror. No possible grief could have wrought the change. A few of them came slowly round me, and held out their arms to take my burden. I yielded it; the tender hopelessness of the smile with which they received it, made my heart swell with pity in the midst of its own desolation. In vain were their sobs over their mother-queen; in vain they sought to entice from her some recognition of their love; in vain they kissed and fondled her as they bore her away: she would not wake! On each side one carried an arm, gently stroking it; as many as could get near, put their arms under her body; those who could not, crowded around the bearers. On a spot where the grass grew thicker and softer they laid her down, and there all the Little Ones gathered sobbing.

Outside the crowd stood the elephants, and I near them, gazing at my Lona over the many little heads between. Those next me caught sight of the princess, and stared trembling. Odu was the first to speak.

"I have seen that woman before!" he whispered to his next neighbor. "It was she who fought the white leopardess, the night they woke us with their yelling!"

"Silly!" returned his companion. "That was a wild beast, with spots!"

"Look at her eyes!" insisted Odu. "I know she is a bad giantess, but she is a wild beast all the same. I know she is the spotted one!"

The other took a step nearer; Odu drew him back with a sharp pull.

"Don't look at her!" he cried, shrinking away, yet fascinated by the hate-filled longing in her eyes. "She would eat you up in a moment! It was HER shadow! She is the wicked princess!"

"That cannot be! They said she was beautiful!"

"Indeed it is the princess!" I interposed. "Wickedness has made her ugly!"

She heard, and what a look was hers!

"It was very wrong of me to run away!" said Odu thoughtfully.

"What made you run away?" I asked. "I expected to find you where I left you!"

He did not reply at once.

"I don't know what made me run," answered another. "I was frightened!"

"It was a man that came down the hill from the palace," said a third.

"How did he frighten you?"

"I don't know."

"He wasn't a man," said Odu; "he was a shadow; he had no thick to him!"

"Tell me more about him."

"He came down the hill very black, walking like a bad giant, but spread flat. He was nothing but blackness. We were frightened the moment we saw him, but we did not run away; we stood and watched him. He came on as if he would walk over us. But before he reached us, he began to spread and spread, and grew bigger end bigger, till at last he was so big that he went out of our sight, and we saw him no more, and then he was upon us!"

"What do you mean by that?"

"He was all black through between us, and we could not see one another; and then he was inside us."

"How did you know he was inside you?"

"He did me quite different. I felt like bad. I was not Odu any more — not the Odu I knew. I wanted to tear Sozo to pieces — not really, but like!"

He turned and hugged Sozo.

"It wasn't me, Sozo," he sobbed. "Really, deep down, it was Odu, loving you always! And Odu came up, and knocked Naughty away. I grew sick, and thought I must kill myself to get out of the black. Then came a horrible laugh that had heard my think, and it set the air trembling about me. And then I suppose I ran away, but I did not know I had run away until I found myself running, fast as could, and all the rest running too. I would have stopped, but I never thought of it until I was out of the gate among the grass. Then I knew that I had run away from a shadow that wanted to be me and wasn't, and that I was the Odu that loved Sozo. It was the shadow that got into me, and hated him from inside me; it was not my own self me! And now I know that I ought not to have run away! But indeed I did not quite know what I was doing until it was done! My legs did it, I think: they grew frightened, and forgot me, and ran away! Naughty legs! There! and there!"

Thus ended Odu, with a kick to each of his naughty legs.

"What became of the shadow?" I asked.

"I do not know," he answered. "I suppose he went home into the night where there is no moon."

I fell a wondering where Lona was gone, and dropping on the grass, took the dead thing in my lap, and whispered in its ear, "Where are you, Lona? I love you!" But its lips gave no answer. I kissed them, not quite cold, laid the body down again, and appointing a guard over it, rose to provide for the safety of Lona's people during the night.

Before the sun went down, I had set a watch over the princess outside the camp, and sentinels round it: intending to walk about it myself all night long, I told the rest of the army to go to sleep. They threw themselves on the grass and were asleep in a moment.

When the moon rose I caught a glimpse of something white; it was the leopardess. She swept silently round the sleeping camp, and I saw her pass three times between the princess and the Little Ones. Thereupon I made the watch lie down with the others, and stretched myself beside the body of Lona.

38. TO THE HOUSE OF BITTERNESS

In the morning we set out, and made for the forest as fast as we could. I rode Lona's horse, and carried her body. I would take it to her father: he would give it a couch in the chamber of his dead! or, if he would not, seeing she had not come of herself, I would watch it in the desert until it mouldered away! But I believed he would, for surely she had died long ago! Alas, how bitterly must I not humble myself before him!

To Adam I must take Lilith also. I had no power to make her repent! I had hardly a right to slay her — much less a right to let her loose in the world! and surely I scarce merited being made for ever her gaoler!

Again and again, on the way, I offered her food; but she answered only with a look of hungering hate. Her fiery eyes kept rolling to and fro, nor ever closed, I believe, until we reached the other side of the hot stream. After that they never opened until we came to the House of Bitterness.

One evening, as we were camping for the night, I saw a little girl go up to her, and ran to prevent mischief. But ere I could reach them, the child had put something to the lips of the princess, and given a scream of pain.

"Please, king," she whimpered, "suck finger. Bad giantess make hole in it!"

I sucked the tiny finger.

"Well now!" she cried, and a minute after was holding a second fruit to a mouth greedy of other fare. But this time she snatched her hand quickly away, and the fruit fell to the ground. The child's name was Luva.

The next day we crossed the hot stream. Again on their own ground, the Little Ones were jubilant. But their nests were still at a great distance, and that day we went no farther than the ivy-hall, where, because of its grapes, I had resolved to spend the night. When they saw the great clusters, at once they knew them good, rushed upon them, ate eagerly, and in a few minutes were all fast asleep on the green floor and in the forest around the hall. Hoping again to see the dance, and expecting the Little Ones to sleep through it, I had made them leave a wide space in the middle. I lay down among them, with Lona by my side, but did not sleep.

The night came, and suddenly the company was there. I was wondering with myself whether, night after night, they would thus go on dancing to all eternity, and whether I should not one day have to join them because of my stiff-neckedness, when the eyes of the children came open, and they sprang to their feet, wide awake. Immediately every one caught hold of a dancer, and away they went, bounding and skipping. The spectres seemed to see and welcome them: perhaps they knew all about the Little Ones, for they had themselves long been on their way back to childhood! Anyhow, their innocent gambols must, I thought, bring refreshment to weary souls who, their present taken from them and their future dark, had no life save the shadow of their vanished past. Many a merry but never a rude prank did the children play; and if they did at times cause a momentary jar in the rhythm of the dance, the poor spectres, who had nothing to smile withal, at least manifested no annoyance.

Just ere the morning began to break, I started to see the skeleton-princess in the doorway, her eyes open and glowing, the fearful spot black on her side. She stood for a moment, then came gliding in, as if she would join the dance. I sprang to my feet. A cry of repugnant fear broke from the children, and the lights vanished. But the low moon looked in, and I saw them clinging to each other. The ghosts were gone — at least they were no longer visible. The princess too had disappeared. I darted to the spot where I had left her: she lay with her eyes closed, as if she had never moved.   I returned to the hall. The Little Ones were already on the floor, composing themselves to sleep.

The next morning, as we started, we spied, a little way from us, two skeletons moving about in a thicket. The Little Ones broke their ranks, and ran to them. I followed; and, although now walking at ease, without splint or ligature, I was able to recognize the pair I had before seen in that neighborhood. The children at once made friends with them, laying hold of their arms, and stroking the bones of their long fingers; and it was plain the poor creatures took their attentions kindly. The two seemed on excellent terms with each other. Their common deprivation had drawn them together! the loss of everything had been the beginning of a new life to them!

Perceiving that they had gathered handfuls of herbs, and were looking for more —presumably to rub their bones with, for in what other way could nourishment reach their system so rudimentary? — the Little Ones, having keenly examined those they held, gathered of the same sorts, and filled the hands the skeletons held out to receive them. Then they bid them goodbye, promising to come and see them again, and resumed their journey, saying to each other they had not known there were such nice people living in the same forest.

When we came to the nest-village, I remained there a night with them, to see them resettled; for Lona still looked like one just dead, and there seemed no need of haste.

The princess had eaten nothing, and her eyes remained shut: fearing she might die ere we reached the end of our journey, I went to her in the night, and laid my bare arm upon her lips. She bit into it so fiercely that I cried out. How I got away from her I do not know, but I came to myself lying beyond her reach. It was then morning, and immediately I set about our departure.

Choosing twelve Little Ones, not of the biggest and strongest, but of the sweetest and merriest, I mounted them on six elephants, and took two more of the wise CLUMSIES, as the children called them, to bear the princess. I still rode Lona's horse, and carried her body wrapt in her cloak before me. As nearly as I could judge I took the direct way, across the left branch of the river-bed, to the House of Bitterness, where I hoped to learn how best to cross the broader and rougher branch, and how to avoid the basin of monsters: I dreaded the former for the elephants, the latter for the children.

I had one terrible night on the way — the third, passed in the desert between the two branches of the dead river.

We had stopped the elephants in a sheltered place, and there let the princess slip down between them, to lie on the sand until the morning. She seemed quite dead, but I did not think she was. I laid myself a little way from her, with the body of Lona by my other side, thus to keep watch at once over the dead and the dangerous. The moon was half-way down the west, a pale, thoughtful moon, mottling the desert with shadows. Of a sudden she was eclipsed, remaining visible, but sending forth no light: a thick, diaphanous film covered her patient beauty, and she looked troubled. The film swept a little aside, and I saw the edge of it against her clearness — the jagged outline of a bat-like wing, torn and hooked. Came a cold wind with a burning sting — and Lilith was upon me. Her hands were still bound, but with her teeth she pulled from my shoulder the cloak Lona made for me, and fixed them in my flesh. I lay as one paralyzed.

Already the very life seemed flowing from me into her, when I remembered, and struck her on the hand. She raised her head with a gurgling shriek, and I felt her shiver. I flung her from me, and sprang to my feet.

She was on her knees, and rocked herself to and fro. A second blast of hot-stinging cold enveloped us; the moon shone out clear, and I saw her face — gaunt and ghastly, besmeared with red.

"Down, devil!" I cried.

"Where are you taking me?" she asked, with the voice of a dull echo from a sepulchre.

"To your first husband," I answered.

"He will kill me!" she moaned.

"At least he will take you off my hands!"

"Give me my daughter," she suddenly screamed, grinding her teeth.

"Never! Your doom is upon you at last!"

"Loose my hands for pity's sake!" she groaned. "I am in torture. The cords are sunk in my flesh."

"I dare not. Lie down!" I said.

She threw herself on the ground like a log.

The rest of the night passed in peace, and in the morning she again seemed dead.

Before evening we came in sight of the House of Bitterness, and the next moment one of the elephants came alongside of my horse.

"Please, king, you are not going to that place?" whispered the Little One who rode on his neck.

"Indeed I am! We are going to stay the night there," I answered.

"Oh, please, don't! That must be where the cat-woman lives!"

"If you had ever seen her, you would not call her by that name!"

"Nobody ever sees her: she has lost her face! Her head is back and side all round."

"She hides her face from dull, discontented people! — Who taught you to call her the cat-woman?"

"I heard the bad giants call her so."

"What did they say about her?"

"That she had claws to her toes."

"It is not true. I know the lady. I spent a night at her house."

"But she MAY have claws to her toes! You might see her feet, and her claws be folded up inside their cushions!"

"Then perhaps you think that I have claws to my toes?"

"Oh, no; that can't be! You are good!"

"The giants might have told you so!" I pursued.

"We shouldn't believe them about you!"

"Are the giants good?"

"No; they love lying."

"Then why do you believe them about her? I know the lady is good; she cannot have claws."

"Please how do you know she is good?"

"How do you know I am good?"

I rode on, while he waited for his companions, and told them what I had said.

They hastened after me, and when they came up,—

"I would not take you to her house if I did not believe her good," I said.

"We know you would not," they answered.

"If I were to do something that frightened you — what would you say?"

"The beasts frightened us sometimes at first, but they never hurt us!" answered one.

"That was before we knew them!" added another.

"Just so!" I answered. "When you see the woman in that cottage, you will know that she is good. You may wonder at what she does, but she will always be good. I know her better than you know me. She will not hurt you, — or if she does, ——"

"Ah, you are not sure about it, king dear! You think she MAY hurt us!"

"I am sure she will never be unkind to you, even if she do hurt you!"

They were silent for a while.

"I'm not afraid of being hurt — a little! — a good deal!" cried Odu. "But I should not like scratches in the dark! The giants say the cat-woman has claw-feet all over her house!"

"I am taking the princess to her," I said.

"Why?"

"Because she is her friend."

"How can she be good then?"

"Little Tumbledown is a friend of the princess," I answered; "so is Luva: I saw them both, more than once, trying to feed her with grapes!"

"Little Tumbledown is good! Luva is very good!"

"That is why they are her friends."

"Will the cat-woman — I mean the woman that isn't the cat-woman, and has no claws to her toes — give her grapes?"

"She is more likely to give her scratches!"

"Why? — You say she is her friend!"

"That is just why. — A friend is one who gives us what we need, and the princess is sorely in need of a terrible scratching."

They were silent again.

"If any of you are afraid," I said, "you may go home; I shall not prevent you. But I cannot take one with me who believes the giants rather than me, or one who will call a good lady the cat-woman!"

"Please, king," said one, "I'm so afraid of being afraid!"

"My boy," I answered, "there is no harm in being afraid. The only harm is in doing what Fear tells you. Fear is not your master! Laugh in his face and he will run away."

"There she is — in the door waiting for us!" cried one, and put his hands over his eyes.

"How ugly she is!" cried another, and did the same.

"You do not see her," I said; "her face is covered!"

"She has no face!" they answered.

"She has a very beautiful face. I saw it once. — It is indeed as beautiful as Lona's!" I added with a sigh.

"Then what makes her hide it?"

"I think I know: — anyhow, she has some good reason for it!"

"I don't like the cat-woman! she is frightful!"

"You cannot like, and you ought not to dislike what you have never seen. — Once more, you must not call her the cat-woman!"

"What are we to call her then, please?"

"Lady Mara."

"That is a pretty name!" said a girl; "I will call her 'lady Mara'; then perhaps she will show me her beautiful face!"

Mara, drest and muffled in white, was indeed standing in the doorway to receive us.

"At last!" she said. "Lilith's hour has been long on the way, but it is come! Everything comes. Thousands of years have I waited — and not in vain!"

She came to me, took my treasure from my arms, carried it into the house, and returning, took the princess. Lilith shuddered, but made no resistance. The beasts lay down by the door. We followed our hostess, the Little Ones looking very grave. She laid the princess on a rough settle at one side of the room, unbound her, and turned to us.

"Mr. Vane," she said, "and you, Little Ones, I thank you! This woman would not yield to gentler measures; harder must have their turn. I must do what I can to make her repent!"

The pitiful-hearted Little Ones began to sob sorely.

"Will you hurt her very much, lady Mara?" said the girl I have just mentioned, putting her warm little hand in mine.

"Yes; I am afraid I must; I fear she will make me!" answered Mara. "It would be cruel to hurt her too little. It would have all to be done again, only worse."

"May I stop with her?"

"No, my child. She loves no one, therefore she cannot be WITH any one. There is One who will be with her, but she will not be with Him."

"Will the shadow that came down the hill be with her?"

"The great Shadow will be in her, I fear, but he cannot be WITH her, or with any one. She will know I am beside her, but that will not comfort her."

"Will you scratch her very deep?" asked Odu, going near, and putting his hand in hers. "Please, don't make the red juice come!"

She caught him up, turned her back to the rest of us, drew the muffling down from her face, and held him at arms' length that he might see her.

As if his face had been a mirror, I saw in it what he saw. For one moment he stared, his little mouth open; then a divine wonder arose in his countenance, and swiftly changed to intense delight. For a minute he gazed entranced, then she set him down. Yet a moment he stood looking up at her, lost in contemplation — then ran to us with the face of a prophet that knows a bliss he cannot tell. Mara rearranged her mufflings, and turned to the other children.

"You must eat and drink before you go to sleep," she said; "you have had a long journey!"

She set the bread of her house before them, and a jug of cold water. They had never seen bread before, and this was hard and dry, but they ate it without sign of distaste. They had never seen water before, but they drank without demur, one after the other looking up from the draught with a face of glad astonishment. Then she led away the smallest, and the rest went trooping after her. With her own gentle hands, they told me, she put them to bed on the floor of the garret.

39. THAT NIGHT

Their night was a troubled one, and they brought a strange report of it into the day. Whether the fear of their sleep came out into their waking, or their waking fear sank with them into their dreams, awake or asleep they were never at rest from it. All night something seemed going on in the house — something silent, something terrible, something they were not to know. Never a sound awoke; the darkness was one with the silence, and the silence was the terror.

Once, a frightful wind filled the house, and shook its inside, they said, so that it quivered and trembled like a horse shaking himself; but it was a silent wind that made not even a moan in their chamber, and passed away like a soundless sob.

They fell asleep. But they woke again with a great start. They thought the house was filling with water such as they had been drinking. It came from below, and swelled up until the garret was full of it to the very roof. But it made no more sound than the wind, and when it sank away, they fell asleep dry and warm.

The next time they woke, all the air, they said, inside and out, was full of cats. They swarmed — up and down, along and across, everywhere about the room. They felt their claws trying to get through the night-gowns lady Mara had put on them, but they could not; and in the morning not one of them had a scratch. Through the dark suddenly, came the only sound they heard the night long — the far-off howl of the huge great-grandmother-cat in the desert: she must have been calling her little ones, they thought, for that instant the cats stopped, and all was still. Once more they fell fast asleep, and did not wake till the sun was rising.

Such was the account the children gave of their experiences. But I was with the veiled woman and the princess all through the night: something of what took place I saw; much I only felt; and there was more which eye could not see, and heart only could in a measure understand.

As soon as Mara left the room with the children, my eyes fell on the white leopardess: I thought we had left her behind us, but there she was, cowering in a corner. Apparently she was in mortal terror of what she might see. A lamp stood on the high chimney-piece, and sometimes the room seemed full of lamp-shadows, sometimes of cloudy forms. The princess lay on the settle by the wall, and seemed never to have moved hand or foot. It was a fearsome waiting.

When Mara returned, she drew the settle with Lilith upon it to the middle of the room, then sat down opposite me, at the other side of the hearth. Between us burned a small fire.

Something terrible was on its way! The cloudy presences flickered and shook. A silvery creature like a slowworm came crawling out from among them, slowly crossed the clay floor, and crept into the fire. We sat motionless. The something came nearer.

But the hours passed, midnight drew nigh, and there was no change. The night was very still. Not a sound broke the silence, not a rustle from the fire, not a crack from board or beam. Now and again I felt a sort of heave, but whether in the earth or in the air or in the waters under the earth, whether in my own body or in my soul — whether it was anywhere, I could not tell. A dread sense of judgment was upon me. But I was not afraid, for I had ceased to care for aught save the thing that must be done.

Suddenly it was midnight. The muffled woman rose, turned toward the settle, and slowly unwound the long swathes that hid her face: they dropped on the ground, and she stepped over them. The feet of the princess were toward the hearth; Mara went to her head, and

turning, stood behind it. Then I saw her face. It was lovely beyond speech — white and sad, heart-and-soul sad, but not unhappy, and I knew it never could be unhappy. Great tears were running down her cheeks: she wiped them away with her robe; her countenance grew very still, and she wept no more. But for the pity in every line of her expression, she would have seemed severe. She laid her hand on the head of the princess — on the hair that grew low on the forehead, and stooping, breathed on the sallow brow. The body shuddered.

"Will you turn away from the wicked things you have been doing so long?" said Mara gently.

The princess did not answer. Mara put the question again, in the same soft, inviting tone.

Still there was no sign of hearing. She spoke the words a third time.

Then the seeming corpse opened its mouth and answered, its words appearing to frame themselves of something else than sound. — I cannot shape the thing further: sounds they were not, yet they were words to me.

"I will not," she said. "I will be myself and not another!"

"Alas, you are another now, not yourself! Will you not be your real self?"

"I will be what I mean myself now."

"If you were restored, would you not make what amends you could for the misery you have caused?"

"I would do after my nature."

"You do not know it: your nature is good, and you do evil!"

"I will do as my Self pleases — as my Self desires."

"You will do as the Shadow, overshadowing your Self inclines you?"

"I will do what I will to do."

"You have killed your daughter, Lilith!"

"I have killed thousands. She is my own!"

"She was never yours as you are another's."

"I am not another's; I am my own, and my daughter is mine."

"Then, alas, your hour is come!"

"I care not. I am what I am; no one can take from me myself!"

"You are not the Self you imagine."

"So long as I feel myself what it pleases me to think myself, I care not. I am content to be to myself what I would be. What I choose to seem to myself makes me what I am. My own thought makes me me; my own thought of myself is me. Another shall not make me!"

"But another has made you, and can compel you to see what you have made yourself. You will not be able much longer to look to yourself anything but what he sees you! You will not much longer have satisfaction in the thought of yourself. At this moment you are aware of the coming change!"

"No one ever made me. I defy that Power to unmake me from a free woman! You are his slave, and I defy you! You may be able to torture me — I do not know, but you shall not compel me to anything against my will!"

"Such a compulsion would be without value. But there is a light that goes deeper than the will, a light that lights up the darkness behind it: that light can change your will, can make it truly yours and not another's — not the Shadow's. Into the created can pour itself the creating will, and so redeem it!"

"That light shall not enter me: I hate it! — Be gone, slave!"

"I am no slave, for I love that light, and will with the deeper will which created mine. There is no slave but the creature that wills against its creator. Who is a slave but her who cries, 'I am free,' yet cannot cease to exist!"

"You speak foolishness from a cowering heart! You imagine me given over to you: I defy you! I hold myself against you! What I choose to be, you cannot change. I will not be what you think me — what you say I am!"

"I am sorry: you must suffer!"

"But be free!"

"She alone is free who would make free; she loves not freedom who would enslave: she is herself a slave. Every life, every will, every heart that came within your ken, you have sought to subdue: you are the slave of every slave you have made — such a slave that you do not know it! — See your own self!"

She took her hand from the head of the princess, and went two backward paces from her.

A soundless presence as of roaring flame possessed the house — the same, I presume, that was to the children a silent wind. Involuntarily I turned to the hearth: its fire was a still small moveless glow. But I saw the worm-thing come creeping out, white-hot, vivid as incandescent silver, the live heart of essential fire. Along the floor it crawled toward the settle, going very slow. Yet more slowly it crept up on it, and laid itself, as unwilling to go further, at the feet of the princess. I rose and stole nearer. Mara stood motionless, as one that waits an event foreknown. The shining thing crawled on to a bare bony foot: it showed no suffering, neither was the settle scorched where the worm had lain. Slowly, very slowly, it crept along her robe until it reached her bosom, where it disappeared among the folds.

The face of the princess lay stonily calm, the eyelids closed as over dead eyes; and for some minutes nothing followed. At length, on the dry, parchment-like skin, began to appear drops as of the finest dew: in a moment they were as large as seed-pearls, ran together, and began to pour down in streams. I darted forward to snatch the worm from the poor withered bosom, and crush it with my foot. But Mara, Mother of Sorrow, stepped between, and drew aside the closed edges of the robe: no serpent was there — no searing trail; the creature had passed in by the centre of the black spot, and was piercing through the joints and marrow to the thoughts and intents of the heart. The princess gave one writhing, contorted shudder, and I knew the worm was in her secret chamber.

"She is seeing herself!" said Mara; and laying her hand on my arm, she drew me three paces from the settle.

Of a sudden the princess bent her body upward in an arch, then sprang to the floor, and stood erect. The horror in her face made me tremble lest her eyes should open, and the sight of them overwhelm me. Her bosom heaved and sank, but no breath issued. Her hair hung and dripped; then it stood out from her head and emitted sparks; again hung down, and poured the sweat of her torture on the floor.

I would have thrown my arms about her, but Mara stopped me.

"You cannot go near her," she said. "She is far away from us, afar in the hell of her self-consciousness. The central fire of the universe is radiating into her the knowledge of good and evil, the knowledge of what she is. She sees at last the good she is not, the evil she is. She knows that she is herself the fire in which she is burning, but she does not know that the Light of Life is the heart of that fire. Her torment is that she is what she is. Do not fear for her; she is not forsaken. No gentler way to help her was left. Wait and watch."

It may have been five minutes or five years that she stood thus — I cannot tell; but at last she flung herself on her face.

Mara went to her, and stood looking down upon her. Large tears fell from her eyes on the woman who had never wept, and would not weep.

"Will you change your way?" she said at length.

"Why did he make me such?" gasped Lilith. "I would have made myself — oh, so different! I am glad it was he that made me and not I myself! He alone is to blame for what I am! Never would I have made such a worthless thing! He meant me such that I might know it and be miserable! I will not be made any longer!"

"Unmake yourself, then," said Mara.

"Alas, I cannot! You know it, and mock me! How often have I not agonized to cease, but the tyrant keeps me being! I curse him! — Now let him kill me!"

The words came in jets as from a dying fountain.

"Had he not made you," said Mara, gently and slowly, "you could not even hate him. But he did not make you such. You have made yourself what you are. — Be of better cheer: he can remake you."

"I will not be remade!"

"He will not change you; he will only restore you to what you were."

"I will not be aught of his making."

"Are you not willing to have that set right which you have set wrong?"

She lay silent; her suffering seemed abated.

"If you are willing, put yourself again on the settle."

"I will not," she answered, forcing the words through her clenched teeth.

A wind seemed to wake inside the house, blowing without sound or impact; and a water began to rise that had no lap in its ripples, no sob in its swell. It was cold, but it did not benumb. Unseen and noiseless it came. It smote no sense in me, yet I knew it rising. I saw it lift at last and float her. Gently it bore her, unable to resist, and left rather than laid her on the settle. Then it sank swiftly away.

The strife of thought, accusing and excusing, began afresh, and gathered fierceness. The soul of Lilith lay naked to the torture of pure interpenetrating inward light. She began to moan, and sigh deep sighs, then murmur as holding colloquy with a dividual self: her queendom was no longer whole; it was divided against itself. One moment she would exult as over her worst enemy, and weep; the next she would writhe as in the embrace of a friend whom her soul hated, and laugh like a demon. At length she began what seemed a tale about herself, in a language so strange, and in forms so shadowy, that I could but here and there understand a little. Yet the language seemed the primeval shape of one I knew well, and the forms to belong to dreams which had once been mine, but refused to be recalled. The tale appeared now and then to touch upon things that Adam had read from the disparted manuscript, and often to make allusion to influences and forces — vices too, I could not help suspecting — with which I was unacquainted.

She ceased, and again came the horror in her hair, the sparkling and flowing alternate. I sent a beseeching look to Mara.

"Those, alas, are not the tears of repentance!" she said. "The true tears gather in the eyes. Those are far more bitter, and not so good. Self-loathing is not sorrow. Yet it is good, for it marks a step in the way home, and in the father's arms the prodigal forgets the self he abominates. Once with his father, he is to himself of no more account. It will be so with her."

She went nearer and said,

"Will you restore that which you have wrongfully taken?"

"I have taken nothing," answered the princess, forcing out the words in spite of pain, "that I had not the right to take. My power to take manifested my right."

Mara left her.

Gradually my soul grew aware of an invisible darkness, a something more terrible than aught that had yet made itself felt. A horrible Nothingness, a Negation positive infolded her; the border of its being that was yet no being, touched me, and for one ghastly instant I seemed alone with Death Absolute! It was not the absence of everything I felt, but the presence of Nothing. The princess dashed herself from the settle to the floor with an exceeding great and bitter cry. It was the recoil of Being from Annihilation.

"For pity's sake," she shrieked, "tear my heart out, but let me live!"

With that there fell upon her, and upon us also who watched with her, the perfect calm as of a summer night. Suffering had all but reached the brim of her life's cup, and a hand had emptied it! She raised her head, half rose, and looked around her. A moment more, and she stood erect, with the air of a conqueror: she had won the battle! Dareful she had met her spiritual foes; they had withdrawn defeated! She raised her withered arm above her head, a pæan of unholy triumph in her throat — when suddenly her eyes fixed in a ghastly stare. — What was she seeing?

I looked, and saw: before her, cast from unseen heavenly mirror, stood the reflection of herself, and beside it a form of splendent beauty, She trembled, and sank again on the floor helpless. She knew the one what God had intended her to be, the other what she had made herself.

The rest of the night she lay motionless altogether.

With the gray dawn growing in the room, she rose, turned to Mara, and said, in prideful humility, "You have conquered. Let me go into the wilderness and bewail myself."

Mara saw that her submission was not feigned, neither was it real. She looked at her a moment, and returned:

"Begin, then, and set right in the place of wrong."

"I know not how," she replied — with the look of one who foresaw and feared the answer.

"Open thy hand, and let that which is in it go."

A fierce refusal seemed to struggle for passage, but she kept it prisoned.

"I cannot," she said. "I have no longer the power. Open it for me."

She held out the offending hand. It was more a paw than a hand. It seemed to me plain that she could not open it.

Mara did not even look at it.

"You must open it yourself," she said quietly.

"I have told you I cannot!"

"You can if you will — not indeed at once, but by persistent effort. What you have done, you do not yet wish undone — do not yet intend to undo!"

"You think so, I dare say," rejoined the princess with a flash of insolence, "but I KNOW that I cannot open my hand!"

"I know you better than you know yourself, and I know you can. You have often opened it a little way. Without trouble and pain you cannot open it quite, but you CAN open it. At worst you could beat it open! I pray you, gather your strength, and open it wide."

"I will not try what I know impossible. It would be the part of a fool!"

"Which you have been playing all your life! Oh, you are hard to teach!"

Defiance reappeared on the face of the princess. She turned her back on Mara, saying, "I know what you have been tormenting me for! You have not succeeded, nor shall you succeed! You shall yet find me stronger than you think! I will yet be mistress of myself! I am still what I have always known myself — queen of Hell, and mistress of the worlds!"

Then came the most fearful thing of all. I did not know what it was; I knew myself unable to imagine it; I knew only that if it came near me I should die of terror! I now know that it was LIFE IN DEATH — life dead, yet existent; and I knew that Lilith had had glimpses, but only glimpses of it before: it had never been with her until now.

She stood as she had turned. Mara went and sat down by the fire. Fearing to stand alone with the princess, I went also and sat again by the hearth. Something began to depart from me. A sense of cold, yet not what we call cold, crept, not into, but out of my being, and pervaded it. The lamp of life and the eternal fire seemed dying together, and I about to be left with naught but the consciousness that I had been alive. Mercifully, bereavement did not go so far, and my thought went back to Lilith.

Something was taking place in her which we did not know. We knew we did not feel what she felt, but we knew we felt something of the misery it caused her. The thing itself was in her, not in us; its reflex, her misery, reached us, and was again reflected in us: she was in the outer darkness, we present with her who was in it! We were not in the outer darkness; had we been, we could not have been WITH her; we should have been timelessly, spacelessly, absolutely apart. The darkness knows neither the light nor itself; only the light knows itself and the darkness also. None but God hates evil and understands it.

Something was gone from her, which then first, by its absence, she knew to have been with her every moment of her wicked years. The source of life had withdrawn itself; all that was left her of conscious being was the dregs of her dead and corrupted life.

She stood rigid. Mara buried her head in her hands. I gazed on the face of one who knew existence but not love — knew nor life, nor joy, nor good; with my eyes I saw the face of a live death! She knew life only to know that it was dead, and that, in her, death lived. It was not merely that life had ceased in her, but that she was consciously a dead thing. She had killed her life, and was dead — and knew it. She must DEATH IT for ever and ever! She had tried her hardest to unmake herself, and could not! She was a dead life! She could not cease! She must BE! In her face I saw and read beyond its misery — saw in its dismay that the dismay behind it was more than it could manifest. It sent out a livid gloom; the light that was in her was darkness, and after its kind it shone. She was what God could not have created. She had usurped beyond her share in self-creation, and her part had undone His! She saw now what she had made, and behold, it was not good! She was as a conscious corpse, whose coffin would never come to pieces, never set her free! Her bodily eyes stood wide open, as if gazing into the heart of horror essential — her own indestructible evil. Her right hand also was now clenched — upon existent Nothing — her inheritance!

But with God all things are possible: He can save even the rich!

Without change of look, without sign of purpose, Lilith walked toward Mara. She felt her coming, and rose to meet her.

"I yield," said the princess. "I cannot hold out. I am defeated. — Not the less, I cannot open my hand."

"Have you tried?"

"I am trying now with all my might."

"I will take you to my father. You have wronged him worst of the created, therefore he best of the created can help you."

"How can HE help me?"

"He will forgive you."

"Ah, if he would but help me to cease! Not even that am I capable of! I have no power over myself; I am a slave! I acknowledge it. Let me die."

"A slave thou art that shall one day be a child!" answered Mara. — "Verily, thou shalt die, but not as thou thinkest. Thou shalt die out of death into life. Now is the Life for, that never was against thee!"

Like her mother, in whom lay the motherhood of all the world, Mara put her arms around Lilith, and kissed her on the forehead. The fiery-cold misery went out of her eyes, and their fountains filled. She lifted, and bore her to her own bed in a corner of the room, laid her softly upon it, and closed her eyes with caressing hands.

Lilith lay and wept. The Lady of Sorrow went to the door and opened it.

Morn, with the Spring in her arms, waited outside. Softly they stole in at the opened door, with a gentle wind in the skirts of their garments. It flowed and flowed about Lilith, rippling the unknown, upwaking sea of her life eternal; rippling and to ripple it, until at length she who had been but as a weed cast on the dry sandy shore to wither, should know herself an inlet of the everlasting ocean, henceforth to flow into her for ever, and ebb no more. She answered the morning wind with reviving breath, and began to listen. For in the skirts of the wind had come the rain — the soft rain that heals the mown, the many-wounded grass —soothing it with the sweetness of all music, the hush that lives between music and silence. It bedewed the desert places around the cottage, and the sands of Lilith's heart heard it, and drank it in. When Mara returned to sit by her bed, her tears were flowing softer than the rain, and soon she was fast asleep.

40. THE HOUSE OF DEATH

The Mother of Sorrows rose, muffled her face, and went to call the Little Ones. They slept as if all the night they had not moved, but the moment she spoke they sprang to their feet, fresh as if new-made. Merrily down the stair they followed her, and she brought them where the princess lay, her tears yet flowing as she slept. Their glad faces grew grave. They looked from the princess out on the rain, then back at the princess.

"The sky is falling!" said one.

"The white juice is running out of the princess!" cried another, with an awed look.

"Is it rivers?" asked Odu, gazing at the little streams that flowed adown her hollow cheeks.

"Yes," answered Mara, " — the most wonderful of all rivers."

"I thought rivers was bigger, and rushed, like a lot of Little Ones, making loud noises!" he returned, looking at me, from whom alone he had heard of rivers.

"Look at the rivers of the sky!" said Mara. "See how they come down to wake up the waters under the earth! Soon will the rivers be flowing everywhere, merry and loud, like thousands and thousands of happy children. Oh, how glad they will make you, Little Ones! You have never seen any, and do not know how lovely is the water!"

"That will be the glad of the ground that the princess is grown good," said Odu. "See the glad of the sky!"

"Are the rivers the glad of the princess?" asked Luva. "They are not her juice, for they are not red!"

"They are the juice inside the juice," answered Mara.

Odu put one finger to his eye, looked at it, and shook his head.

"Princess will not bite now!" said Luva.

"No; she will never do that again," replied Mara. "— But now we must take her nearer home."

"Is that a nest?" asked Sozo.

"Yes; a very big nest. But we must take her to another place first."

"What is that?"

"It is the biggest room in all this world. — But I think it is going to be pulled down: it will soon be too full of little nests. — Go and get your clumsies."

"Please are there any cats in it?"

"Not one. The nests are too full of lovely dreams for one cat to get in."

"We shall be ready in a minute," said Odu, and ran out, followed by all except Luva.

Lilith was now awake, and listening with a sad smile.

"But her rivers are running so fast!" said Luva, who stood by her side and seemed unable to take her eyes from her face. "Her robe is all — I don't know what. Clumsies won't like it!"

"They won't mind it," answered Mara. "Those rivers are so clean that they make the whole world clean."

I had fallen asleep by the fire, but for some time had been awake and listening, and now rose.

"It is time to mount, Mr. Vane," said our hostess.

"Tell me, please," I said, "is there not a way by which to avoid the channels and the den of monsters?"

"There is an easy way across the river-bed, which I will show you," she answered; "but you must pass once more through the monsters."

"I fear for the children," I said.

"Fear will not once come nigh them," she rejoined.

We left the cottage. The beasts stood waiting about the door. Odu was already on the neck of one of the two that were to carry the princess. I mounted Lona's horse; Mara brought her body, and gave it me in my arms. When she came out again with the princess, a cry of delight arose from the children: she was no longer muffled! Gazing at her, and entranced with her loveliness, the boys forgot to receive the princess from her; but the elephants took Lilith tenderly with their trunks, one round her body and one round her knees, and, Mara helping, laid her along between them.

"Why does the princess want to go?" asked a small boy. "She would keep good if she staid here!"

"She wants to go, and she does not want to go: we are helping her," answered Mara. "She will not keep good here."

"What are you helping her to do?" he went on.

"To go where she will get more help — help to open her hand, which has been closed for a thousand years."

"So long? Then she has learned to do without it: why should she open it now?"

"Because it is shut upon something that is not hers."

"Please, lady Mara, may we have some of your very dry bread before we go?" said Luva.

Mara smiled, and brought them four loaves and a great jug of water.

"We will eat as we go," they said. But they drank the water with delight.

"I think," remarked one of them, "it must be elephant-juice! It makes me so strong!"

We set out, the Lady of Sorrow walking with us, more beautiful than the sun, and the white leopardess following her. I thought she meant but to put us in the path across the channels, but I soon found she was going with us all the way. Then I would have dismounted that she might ride, but she would not let me.

"I have no burden to carry," she said. "The children and I will walk together."

It was the loveliest of mornings; the sun shone his brightest, and the wind blew his sweetest, but they did not comfort the desert, for it had no water.

We crossed the channels without difficulty, the children gamboling about Mara all the way, but did not reach the top of the ridge over the bad burrow until the sun was already in the act of disappearing. Then I made the Little Ones mount their elephants, for the moon might be late, and I could not help some anxiety about them.

The Lady of Sorrow now led the way by my side; the elephants followed — the two that bore the princess in the centre; the leopardess brought up the rear; and just as we reached the frightful margin, the moon looked up and showed the shallow basin lying before us untroubled. Mara stepped into it; not a movement answered her tread or the feet of my horse. But the moment that the elephants carrying the princess touched it, the seemingly solid earth began to heave and boil, and the whole dread brood of the hellish nest was commoved. Monsters uprose on all sides, every neck at full length, every beak and claw outstretched, every mouth agape. Long-billed heads, horribly jawed faces, knotty tentacles innumerable, went out after Lilith. She lay in an agony of fear, nor dared stir a finger. Whether the hideous things even saw the children, I doubt; certainly not one of them touched a child; not one loathly member passed the live rampart of her body-guard, to lay hold of her.

"Little Ones," I cried, "keep your elephants close about the princess. Be brave; they will not touch you."

"What will not touch us? We don't know what to be brave at!" they answered; and I perceived they were unaware of one of the deformities around them.

"Never mind then," I returned; "only keep close."

They were panoplied in their blindness! Incapacity to see was their safety. What they could nowise be aware of, could not hurt them.

But the hideous forms I saw that night! Mara was a few paces in front of me when a solitary, bodiless head bounced on the path between us. The leopardess came rushing under the elephants from behind, and would have seized it, but, with frightful contortions of visage and a loathsome howl, it gave itself a rapid rotatory twist, sprang from her, and buried itself in the ground. The death in my arms assoiling me from fear, I regarded them all unmoved, although never, sure, was elsewhere beheld such a crew accursed!

Mara still went in front of me, and the leopardess now walked close behind her, shivering often, for it was very cold, when suddenly the ground before me to my left began to heave, and a low wave of earth came slinking toward us. It rose higher as it drew hear; out of it slouched a dreadful head with fleshy tubes for hair, and opening a great oval mouth, snapped at me. The leopardess sprang, but fell baffled beyond it.

Almost under our feet, shot up the head of an enormous snake, with a lamping wallowing glare in its eyes. Again the leopardess rushed to the attack, but found nothing. At a third monster she darted with like fury, and like failure — then sullenly ceased to heed the phantom-horde. But I understood the peril and hastened the crossing — the rather that the moon was carrying herself strangely. Even as she rose she seemed ready to drop and give up the attempt as hopeless; and since, I saw her sink back once fully her own breadth. The arc she made was very low, and now she had begun to descend rapidly.

We were almost over, when, between us and the border of the basin, arose a long neck, on the top of which, like the blossom of some Stygian lily, sat what seemed the head of a corpse, its mouth half open, and full of canine teeth. I went on; it retreated, then drew aside. The lady stepped on the firm land, but the leopardess between us, roused once more, turned, and flew at the throat of the terror. I remained where I was to see the elephants, with the princess and the children, safe on the bank. Then I turned to look after the leopardess. That moment the moon went down, For an instant I saw the leopardess and the snake-monster convolved in a cloud of dust; then darkness hid them. Trembling with fright, my horse wheeled, and in three bounds overtook the elephants.

As we came up with them, a shapeless jelly dropped on the princess. A white dove dropped immediately on the jelly, stabbing it with its beak. It made a squelching, sucking sound, and fell off. Then I heard the voice of a woman talking with Mara, and I knew the voice.

"I fear she is dead!" said Mara.

"I will send and find her," answered the mother. "But why, Mara, shouldst thou at all fear for her or for any one? Death cannot hurt her who dies doing the work given her to do."

"I shall miss her sorely; she is good and wise. Yet I would not have her live beyond her hour!"

"She has gone down with the wicked; she will rise with the righteous. We shall see her again ere very long."

"Mother," I said, although I did not see her, "we come to you many, but most of us are Little Ones. Will you be able to receive us all?"

"You are welcome every one," she answered. "Sooner or later all will be little ones, for all must sleep in my house! It is well with those that go to sleep young and willing! — My husband is even now preparing her couch for Lilith. She is neither young nor quite willing, but it is well indeed that she is come."

I heard no more. Mother and daughter had gone away together through the dark. But we saw a light in the distance, and toward it we went stumbling over the moor.

Adam stood in the door, holding the candle to guide us, and talking with his wife, who, behind him, laid bread and wine on the table within.

"Happy children," I heard her say, "to have looked already on the face of my daughter! Surely it is the loveliest in the great world!"

When we reached the door, Adam welcomed us almost merrily. He set the candle on the threshold, and going to the elephants, would have taken the princess to carry her in; but she repulsed him, and pushing her elephants asunder, stood erect between them. They walked from beside her, and left her with him who had been her husband — ashamed indeed of her gaunt uncomeliness, but unsubmissive. He stood with a welcome in his eyes that shone through their severity.

"We have long waited for thee, Lilith!" he said.

She returned him no answer.

Eve and her daughter came to the door.

"The mortal foe of my children!" murmured Eve, standing radiant in her beauty.

"Your children are no longer in her danger," said Mara; "she has turned from evil."

"Trust her not hastily, Mara," answered her mother; "she has deceived a multitude!"

"But you will open to her the mirror of the Law of Liberty, mother, that she may go into it, and abide in it! She consents to open her hand and restore: will not the great Father restore her to inheritance with His other children?"

"I do not know Him!" murmured Lilith, in a voice of fear and doubt.

"Therefore it is that thou art miserable," said Adam.

"I will go back whence I came!" she cried, and turned, wringing her hands, to depart.

"That is indeed what I would have thee do, where I would have thee go — to Him from whom thou camest! In thy agony didst thou not cry out for Him?"

"I cried out for Death — to escape Him and thee!"

"Death is even now on his way to lead thee to Him. Thou knowest neither Death nor the Life that dwells in Death! Both befriend thee. I am dead, and would see thee dead, for I live and love thee. Thou art weary and heavy-laden: art thou not ashamed? Is not the being thou hast corrupted become to thee at length an evil thing? Wouldst thou yet live on in disgrace eternal? Cease thou canst not: wilt thou not be restored and BE?"

She stood silent with bowed head.

"Father," said Mara, "take her in thine arms, and carry her to her couch. There she will open her hand, and die into life."

"I will walk," said the princess.

Adam turned and led the way. The princess walked feebly after him into the cottage.

Then Eve came out to me where I sat with Lona in my bosom. She reached up her arms, took her from me, and carried her in. I dismounted, and the children also. The horse and the elephants stood shivering; Mara patted and stroked them every one; they lay down and fell asleep. She led us into the cottage, and gave the Little Ones of the bread and wine on the table. Adam and Lilith were standing there together, but silent both.

Eve came from the chamber of death, where she had laid Lona down, and offered of the bread and wine to the princess.

"Thy beauty slays me! It is death I would have, not food!" said Lilith, and turned from her.

"This food will help thee to die," answered Eve.

But Lilith would not taste of it.

"If thou wilt nor eat nor drink, Lilith," said Adam, "come and see the place where thou shalt lie in peace."

He led the way through the door of death, and she followed submissive. But when her foot crossed the threshold she drew it back, and pressed her hand to her bosom, struck through with the cold immortal.

A wild blast fell roaring on the roof, and died away in a moan. She stood ghastly with terror.

"It is he!" said her voiceless lips: I read their motion.

"Who, princess!" I whispered.

"The great Shadow," she murmured.

"Here he cannot enter," said Adam. "Here he can hurt no one. Over him also is power given me."

"Are the children in the house?" asked Lilith, and at the word the heart of Eve began to love her.

"He never dared touch a child," she said. "Nor have you either ever hurt a child. Your own daughter you have but sent into the loveliest sleep, for she was already a long time dead when you slew her. And now Death shall be the atone maker; you shall sleep together."

"Wife," said Adam, "let us first put the children to bed, that she may see them safe!"

He came back to fetch them. As soon as he was gone, the princess knelt to Eve, clasped her knees, and said,

"Beautiful Eve, persuade your husband to kill me: to you he will listen! Indeed I would but cannot open my hand."

"You cannot die without opening it. To kill you would not serve you," answered Eve. "But indeed he cannot! no one can kill you but the Shadow; and whom he kills never knows she is dead, but lives to do his will, and thinks she is doing her own."

"Show me then to my grave; I am so weary I can live no longer. I must go to the Shadow — yet I would not!"

She did not, could not understand!

She struggled to rise, but fell at the feet of Eve. The Mother lifted, and carried her inward.

I followed Adam and Mara and the children into the chamber of death. We passed Eve with Lilith in her arms, and went farther in.

"You shall not go to the Shadow," I heard Eve say, as we passed them. "Even now is his head under my heel!"

The dim light in Adam's hand glimmered on the sleeping faces, and as he went on, the darkness closed over them. The very air seemed dead: was it because none of the sleepers breathed it? Profoundest sleep filled the wide place. It was as if not one had waked since last I was there, for the forms I had then noted lay there still. My father was just as I had left him, save that he seemed yet nearer to a perfect peace. The woman beside him looked younger.

The darkness, the cold, the silence, the still air, the faces of the lovely dead, made the hearts of the children beat softly, but their little tongues would talk — with low, hushed voices.

"What a curious place to sleep in!" said one, "I would rather be in my nest!" "It is SO cold!" said another.

"Yes, it is cold," answered our host; "but you will not be cold in your sleep."

"Where are our nests?" asked more than one, looking round and seeing no couch unoccupied.

"Find places, and sleep where you choose," replied Adam.

Instantly they scattered, advancing fearlessly beyond the light, but we still heard their gentle voices, and it was plain they saw where I could not.

"Oh," cried one, "here is such a beautiful lady! — may I sleep beside her? I will creep in quietly, and not wake her."

"Yes, you may," answered the voice of Eve behind us; and we came to the couch while the little fellow was yet creeping slowly and softly under the sheet. He laid his head beside the lady's, looked up at us, and was still. His eyelids fell; he was asleep.

We went a little farther, and there was another who had climbed up on the couch of a woman.

"Mother! Mother!" he cried, kneeling over her, his face close to hers. "— She's so cold she can't speak," he said, looking up to us; "but I will soon make her warm!"

He lay down, and pressing close to her, put his little arm over her. In an instant he too was asleep, smiling an absolute content.

We came to a third Little One; it was Luva. She stood on tiptoe, leaning over the edge of a couch.

"My own mother wouldn't have me," she said softly: "will you?"

Receiving no reply, she looked up at Eve. The great mother lifted her to the couch, and she got at once under the snowy covering.

Each of the Little Ones had by this time, except three of the boys, found at least an unobjecting bedfellow, and lay still and white beside a still, white woman. The little orphans had adopted mothers! One tiny girl had chosen a father to sleep with, and that was mine. A boy lay by the side of the beautiful matron with the slow-healing hand. On the middle one of the three couches hitherto unoccupied, lay Lona.

Eve set Lilith down beside it. Adam pointed to the vacant couch on Lona's right hand, and said,

"There, Lilith, is the bed I have prepared for you!"

She glanced at her daughter lying before her like a statue carved in semi-transparent alabaster, and shuddered from head to foot. "How cold it is!" she murmured.

"You will soon begin to find comfort in the cold," answered Adam.

"Promises to the dying are easy!" she said.

"But I know it: I too have slept. I am dead!"

"I believed you dead long ago; but I see you alive!"

"More alive than you know, or are able to understand. I was scarce alive when first you knew me. Now I have slept, and am awake; I am dead, and live indeed!"

"I fear that child," she said, pointing to Lona: "she will rise and terrify me!"

"She is dreaming love to you."

"But the Shadow!" she moaned; "I fear the Shadow! he will be wroth with me!"

"He at sight of whom the horses of heaven start and rear, dares not disturb one dream in this quiet chamber!"

"I shall dream then?"

"You will dream."

"What dreams?"

"That I cannot tell, but none HE can enter into. When the Shadow comes here, it will be to lie down and sleep also. His hour will come, and he knows it will."

"How long shall I sleep?"

"You and he will be the last to wake in the morning of the universe."

The princess lay down, drew the sheet over her, stretched herself out straight, and lay still with open eyes.

Adam turned to his daughter. She drew near.

"Lilith," said Mara, "you will not sleep, if you lie there a thousand years, until you have opened your hand, and yielded that which is not yours to give or to withhold."

"I cannot," she answered. "I would if I could, and gladly, for I am weary, and the shadows of death are gathering about me."

"They will gather and gather, but they cannot infold you while yet your hand remains unopened. You may think you are dead, but it will be only a dream; you may think you have come awake, but it will still be only a dream. Open your hand, and you will sleep indeed — then wake indeed."

"I am trying hard, but the fingers have grown together and into the palm."

"I pray you put forth the strength of your will. For the love of life, draw together your forces and break its bonds!"

"I have struggled in vain; I can do no more. I am very weary, and sleep lies heavy upon my lids."

"The moment you open your hand, you will sleep. Open it, and make an end."

A tinge of color arose in the parchment-like face; the contorted hand trembled with agonized effort. Mara took it, and sought to aid her.

"Hold, Mara!" cried her father. "There is danger!"

The princess turned her eyes upon Eve, beseechingly.

"There was a sword I once saw in your husband's hands," she murmured. "I fled when I saw it. I heard him who bore it say it would divide whatever was not one and indivisible!"

"I have the sword," said Adam. "The angel gave it me when he left the gate."

"Bring it, Adam," pleaded Lilith, "and cut me off this hand that I may sleep."

"I will," he answered.

He gave the candle to Eve, and went. The princess closed her eyes.

In a few minutes Adam returned with an ancient weapon in his hand. The scabbard looked like vellum grown dark with years, but the hilt shone like gold that nothing could tarnish. He drew out the blade. It flashed like a pale blue northern streamer, and the light of it made the princess open her eyes. She saw the sword, shuddered, and held out her hand. Adam took it. The sword gleamed once, there was one little gush of blood, and he laid the severed hand in Mara's lap. Lilith had given one moan, and was already fast asleep. Mara covered the arm with the sheet, and the three turned away.

"Will you not dress the wound?" I said.

"A wound from that sword," answered Adam, "needs no dressing. It is healing and not hurt."

"Poor lady!" I said, "she will wake with but one hand!"

"Where the dead deformity clung," replied Mara, "the true, lovely hand is already growing."

We heard a childish voice behind us, and turned again. The candle in Eve's hand shone on the sleeping face of Lilith, and the waking faces of the three Little Ones, grouped on the other side of her couch. "How beautiful she is grown!" said one of them.

"Poor princess!" said another; "I will sleep with her. She will not bite any more!"

As he spoke he climbed into her bed, and was immediately fast asleep. Eve covered him with the sheet.

"I will go on her other side," said the third. "She shall have two to kiss her when she wakes!"

"And I am left alone!" said the first mournfully.

"I will put you to bed," said Eve.

She gave the candle to her husband, and led the child away.

We turned once more to go back to the cottage. I was very sad, for no one had offered me a place in the house of the dead. Eve joined us as we went, and walked on before with her husband. Mara by my side carried the hand of Lilith in the lap of her robe.

"Ah, you have found her!" we heard Eve say as we stepped into the cottage.

The door stood open; two elephant-trunks came through it out of the night beyond.

"I sent them with the lantern," she went on to her husband, "to look for Mara's leopardess: they have brought her."

I followed Adam to the door, and between us we took the white creature from the elephants, and carried her to the chamber we had just left, the women preceding us, Eve with the light, and Mara still carrying the hand. There we laid the beauty across the feet of the princess, her fore-paws outstretched, and her head couching between them.

41. I AM SENT

Then I turned and said to Eve,

"Mother, one couch next to Lona is empty: I know I am unworthy, but may I not sleep this night in your chamber with my dead? Will you not pardon both my cowardice and my self-confidence, and take me in? I give me up. I am sick of myself, and would fain sleep the sleep!"

"The couch next to Lona is the one already prepared for you," she answered; "but something waits to be done ere you sleep."

"I am ready," I replied.

"How do you know you can do it?" she asked with a smile.

"Because you require it," I answered. "What is it?"

She turned to Adam:

"Is he forgiven, husband?"

"From my heart."

"Then tell him what he has to do."

Adam turned to his daughter.

"Give me that hand, Mara, my child."

She held it out to him in her lap. He took it tenderly.

"Let us go to the cottage," he said to me; "there I will instruct you."

As we went, again arose a sudden stormful blast, mingled with a great flapping on the roof, but it died away as before in a deep moan.

When the door of the death-chamber was closed behind us, Adam seated himself, and I stood before him.

"You will remember," he said, "how, after leaving my daughter's house, you came to a dry rock, bearing the marks of an ancient cataract; you climbed that rock, and found a sandy desert: go to that rock now, and from its summit walk deep into the desert. But go not many steps ere you lie down, and listen with your head on the sand. If you hear the murmur of water beneath, go a little farther, and listen again. If you still hear the sound, you are in the right direction. Every few yards you must stop, lie down, and hearken. If, listening thus, at any time you hear no sound of water, you are out of the way, and must hearken in every direction until you hear it again. Keeping with the sound, and careful not to retrace your steps, you will soon hear it louder, and the growing sound will lead you to where it is loudest: that is the spot you seek. There dig with the spade I will give you, and dig until you come to moisture: in it lay the hand, cover it to the level of the desert, and come home. — But give good heed, and carry the hand with care. Never lay it down, in what place of seeming safety soever; let nothing touch it; stop nor turn aside for any attempt to bar your way; never look behind you; speak to no one, answer no one, walk straight on. — It is yet dark, and the morning is far distant, but you must set out at once."

He gave me the hand, and brought me a spade.

"This is my gardening spade," he said; "with it I have brought many a lovely thing to the sun."

I took it, and went out into the night.

It was very cold, and pitch-dark. To fall would be a dread thing, and the way I had to go was a difficult one even in the broad sunlight! But I had not set myself the task, and the minute I started I learned that I was left to no chance: a pale light broke from the ground at every step, and showed me where next to set my foot. Through the heather and the low rocks I walked without once even stumbling. I found the bad burrow quite still; not a wave arose, not a head appeared as I crossed it.

A moon came, and herself showed me the easy way: toward morning I was almost over the dry channels of the first branch of the river-bed, and not far, I judged, from Mara's cottage.

The moon was very low, and the sun not yet up, when I saw before me in the path, here narrowed by rocks, a figure covered from head to foot as with a veil of moonlit mist. I kept on my way as if I saw nothing. The figure threw aside its veil.

"Have you forgotten me already?" said the princess — or what seemed she.

I neither hesitated nor answered; I walked straight on.

"You meant then to leave me in that horrible sepulcher! Do you not yet understand that where I please to be, there I am? Take my hand: I am alive as you!"

I was on the point of saying, "Give me your left hand," but bethought myself, held my peace, and steadily advanced.

"Give me my hand," she suddenly shrieked, "or I will tear you in pieces: you are mine!"

She flung herself upon me. I shuddered, but did not falter. Nothing touched me, and I saw her no more.

With measured tread along the path, filling it for some distance, came a body of armed men. I walked through them — nor know whether they gave way to me, or were bodiless things. But they turned and followed me; I heard and felt their march at my very heels; but I cast no look behind, and the sound of their steps and the clash of their armor died away.

A little farther on, the moon being now close to the horizon and the way in deep shadow, I descried, seated where the path was so narrow that I could not pass her, a woman with muffled face.

"Ah," she said, "you are come at last! I have waited here for you an hour or more! You have done well! Your trial is over. My father sent me to meet you that you might have a little rest on the way. Give me your charge, and lay your head in my lap; I will take good care of both until the sun is well risen. I am not bitterness always, neither to all men!"

Her words were terrible with temptation, for I was very weary. And what more likely to be true! If I were, through slavish obedience to the letter of the command and lack of pure insight, to trample under my feet the very person of the Lady of Sorrow! My heart grew faint at the thought, then beat as if it would burst my bosom.

Nevertheless my will hardened itself against my heart, and my step did not falter. I took my tongue between my teeth lest I should unawares answer, and kept on my way. If Adam had sent her, he could not complain that I would not heed her! Nor would the Lady of Sorrow love me the less that even she had not been able to turn me aside!

Just ere I reached the phantom, she pulled the covering from her face: great indeed was her loveliness, but those were not Mara's eyes! no lie could truly or for long imitate them! I advanced as if the thing were not there, and my foot found empty room.

I had almost reached the other side when a Shadow — I think it was The Shadow, barred my way. He seemed to have a helmet upon his head, but as I drew closer I perceived it was the head itself I saw — so distorted as to bear but a doubtful resemblance to the human. A cold wind smote me, dank and sickening — repulsive as the air of a charnel-house; firmness forsook my joints, and my limbs trembled as if they would drop in a helpless heap. I seemed to pass through him, but I think now that he passed through me: for a moment I was as one of the damned. Then a soft wind like the first breath of a new-born spring greeted me, and before me arose the dawn.

My way now led me past the door of Mara's cottage. It stood wide open, and upon the table I saw a loaf of bread and a pitcher of water. In or around the cottage was neither howl nor wail.

I came to the precipice that testified to the vanished river. I climbed its worn face, and went on into the desert. There at last, after much listening to and fro, I determined the spot where the hidden water was loudest, hung Lilith's hand about my neck, and began to dig. It was a long labour, for I had to make a large hole because of the looseness of the sand; but at length I threw up a damp spadeful. I flung the sexton-tool on the verge, and laid down the hand. A little water was already oozing from under its fingers. I sprang out, and made haste to fill the grave. Then, utterly fatigued, I dropped beside it, and fell asleep.

42. I SLEEP THE SLEEP

When I woke, the ground was moist about me, and my track to the grave was growing a quicksand. In its ancient course the river was swelling, and had begun to shove at its burden. Soon it would be roaring down the precipice, and, divided in its fall, rushing with one branch to re-submerge the orchard valley, with the other to drown perhaps the monster horde, and between them to isle the Evil Wood. I set out at once on my return to those who sent me.

When I came to the precipice, I took my way betwixt the branches, for I would pass again by the cottage of Mara, lest she should have returned: I longed to see her once more ere I went to sleep; and now I knew where to cross the channels, even if the river should have overtaken me and filled them. But when I reached it, the door stood open still; the bread and the water were still on the table; and deep silence was within and around it. I stopped and called aloud at the door, but no voice replied, and I went my way.

A little farther, I came where sat a gray headed man on the sand, weeping.

"What ails you, sir?" I asked. "Are you forsaken?"

"I weep," he answered, "because they will not let me die. I have been to the house of death, and its mistress, notwithstanding my years, refuses me. Intercede for me, sir, if you know her, I pray you."

"Nay, sir," I replied, "that I cannot; for she refuses none whom it is lawful for her to receive."

"How know you this of her? You have never sought death! you are much too young to desire it!"

"I fear your words may indicate that, were you young again, neither would you desire it."

"Indeed, young sir, I would not! And certain I am that you cannot."

"I may not be old enough to desire to die, but I am young enough to desire to live indeed! Therefore I go now to learn if she will at length take me in. You wish to die because you do not care to live: she will not open her door to you, for no one can die who does not long to live."

"It ill becomes your youth to mock a friendless old man. Pray, cease your riddles!"

"Did not then the Mother tell you something of the same sort?"

"In truth I believe she did; but I gave little heed to her excuses."

"Ah, then, sir," I rejoined, "it is but too plain you have not yet learned to die, and I am heartily grieved for you. Such had I too been but for the Lady of Sorrow. I am indeed young, but I have wept many tears; pardon me, therefore, if I presume to offer counsel: — Go to the Lady of Sorrow, and `take with both hands' what she will give you. Yonder lies her cottage. She is not in it now, but her door stands open, and there is bread and water on her table. Go in; sit down; eat of the bread; drink of the water; and wait there until she appear. Then ask counsel of her, for she is true, and her wisdom is great."

He fell to weeping afresh, and I left him weeping. What I said, I fear he did not heed. But Mara would find him!

The sun was down, and the moon un-risen, when I reached the abode of the monsters, but it was still as a stone till I passed over. Then I heard a noise of many waters, and a great cry behind me, but I did not turn my head.

Ere I reached the house of death, the cold was bitter and the darkness dense; and the cold and the darkness were one, and entered into my bones together. But the candle of Eve, shining from the window, guided me, and kept both frost and murk from my heart.

The door stood open, and the cottage lay empty. I sat down disconsolate.

And as I sat, there grew in me such a sense of loneliness as never yet in my wanderings had I felt. Thousands were near me, not one was with me! True, it was I who was dead, not they; but, whether by their life or by my death, we were divided! They were alive, but I was not dead enough even to know them alive: doubt WOULD come. They were, at best, far from me, and helpers I had none to lay me beside them!

Never before had I known, or truly imagined desolation! In vain I took myself to task, saying the solitude was but a seeming: I was awake, and they slept — that was all! it was only that they lay so still and did not speak! they were with me now, and soon, soon I should be with them!

I dropped Adam's old spade, and the dull sound of its fall on the clay floor seemed reverberated from the chamber beyond: a childish terror seized me; I sat and stared at the coffin-door. But father Adam, mother Eve, sister Mara would soon come to me, and then — welcome the cold world and the white neighbors! I forgot my fears, lived a little, and loved my dead.

Something did move in the chamber of the dead! There came from it what was LIKE a dim, far-off sound, yet was not what I knew as sound. My soul sprang into my ears. Was it a mere thrill of the dead air, too slight to be heard, but quivering in every spiritual sense? I KNEW without hearing, without feeling it!

The something was coming! it drew nearer! In the bosom of my desertion awoke an infant hope. The noiseless thrill reached the coffin-door — became sound, and smote on my ear.

The door began to move — with a low, soft creaking of its hinges. It was opening! I ceased to listen, and stared expectant.

It opened a little way, and a face came into the opening. It was Lona's. Its eyes were closed, but the face itself was upon me, and seemed to see me. It was white as Eve's, white as Mara's, but did not shine like their faces. She spoke, and her voice was like a sleepy night-wind in the grass.

"Are you coming, king?" it said. "I cannot rest until you are with me, gliding down the river to the great sea, and the beautiful dream-land. The sleepiness is full of lovely things: come and see them."

"Ah, my darling!" I cried. "Had I but known! — I thought you were dead!"

She lay on my bosom — cold as ice frozen to marble. She threw her arms, so white, feebly about me, and sighed —

"Carry me back to my bed, king. I want to sleep."

I bore her to the death-chamber, holding her tight lest she should dissolve out of my arms. Unaware that I saw, I carried her straight to her couch.

"Lay me down," she said, "and cover me from the warm air; it hurts — a little. Your bed is there, next to mine. I shall see you when I wake."

She was already asleep. I threw myself on my couch — blessed as never was man on the eve of his wedding.

"Come, sweet cold," I said, "and still my heart speedily."

But there came instead a glimmer of light in the chamber, and I saw the face of Adam approaching. He had not the candle, yet I saw him. At the side of Lona's couch, he looked down on her with a questioning smile, and then greeted me across it.

"We have been to the top of the hill to hear the waters on their way," he said. "They will be in the den of the monsters to-night. — But why did you not await our return?"

"My child could not sleep," I answered.

"She is fast asleep!" he rejoined.

"Yes, now!" I said; "but she was awake when I laid her down."

"She was asleep all the time!" he insisted. "She was perhaps dreaming about you — and came to you?"

"She did."

"And did you not see that her eyes were closed?"

"Now I think of it, I did."

"If you had looked ere you laid her down, you would have seen her asleep on the couch."

"That would have been terrible!"

"You would only have found that she was no longer in your arms."

"That would have been worse!"

"It is, perhaps, to think of; but to see it would not have troubled you."

"Dear father," I said, "how is it that I am not sleepy? I thought I should go to sleep like the Little Ones the moment I laid my head down!"

"Your hour is not quite come. You must have food ere you sleep."

"Ah, I ought not to have lain down without your leave, for I cannot sleep without your help! I will get up at once!"

But I found my own weight more than I could move.

"There is no need: we will serve you here," he answered. "— You do not feel cold, do you?"

"Not too cold to lie still, but perhaps too cold to eat!"

He came to the side of my couch, bent over me, and breathed on my heart. At once I was warm.

As he left me, I heard a voice, and knew it was the Mother's. She was singing, and her song was sweet and soft and low, and I thought she sat by my bed in the dark; but ere it ceased, her song soared aloft, and seemed to come from the throat of a woman-angel, high above all the region of larks, higher than man had ever yet lifted up his heart. I heard every word she sang, but could keep only this:—

"Many a wrong, and its curing song;
Many a road, and many an inn;

Room to roam, but only one home

For all the world to win!"

And I thought I had heard the song before.

Then the three came to my couch together, bringing me bread and wine, and I sat up to partake of it. Adam stood on one side of me, Eve and Mara on the other.

"You are good indeed, father Adam, mother Eve, sister Mara," I said, "to receive me! In my soul I am ashamed and sorry!"

"We knew you would come again!" answered Eve.

"How could you know it?" I returned.

"Because here was I, born to look after my brothers and sisters!" answered Mara with a smile.

"Every creature must one night yield himself and lie down," answered Adam: "he was made for liberty, and must not be left a slave!"

"It will be late, I fear, ere all have lain down!" I said.

"There is no early or late here," he rejoined. "For him the true time then first begins who lays himself down. Men are not coming home fast; women are coming faster. A desert, wide and dreary, parts him who lies down to die from him who lies down to live. The former may well make haste, but here is no haste."

"To our eyes," said Eve, "you were coming all the time: we knew Mara would find you, and you must come!"

"How long is it since my father lay down?" I asked.

"I have told you that years are of no consequence in this house," answered Adam; "we do not heed them. Your father will wake when his morning comes. Your mother, next to whom you are lying,——"

"Ah, then, it IS my mother!" I exclaimed.

"Yes — she with the wounded hand," he assented; "— she will be up and away long ere your morning is ripe."

"I am sorry."

"Rather be glad."

"It must be a sight for God Himself to see such a woman come awake!"

"It is indeed a sight for God, a sight that makes her Maker glad! He sees of the travail of His soul, and is satisfied! — Look at her once more, and sleep."

He let the rays of his candle fall on her beautiful face.

"She looks much younger!" I said.

"She IS much younger," he replied. "Even Lilith already begins to look younger!"

I lay down, blissfully drowsy.

"But when you see your mother again," he continued, "you will not at first know her. She will go on steadily growing younger until she reaches the perfection of her womanhood — a splendor beyond foresight. Then she will open her eyes, behold on one side her husband, on the other her son — and rise and leave them to go to a father and a brother more to her than they."

I heard as one in a dream. I was very cold, but already the cold caused me no suffering. I felt them put on me the white garment of the dead. Then I forgot everything. The night about me was pale with sleeping faces, but I was asleep also, nor knew that I slept.

43. THE DREAMS THAT CAME

I grew aware of existence, aware also of the profound, the infinite cold. I was intensely blessed — more blessed, I know, than my heart, imagining, can now recall. I could not think of warmth with the least suggestion of pleasure. I knew that I had enjoyed it, but could not remember how. The cold had soothed every care, dissolved every pain, comforted every sorrow. COMFORTED? Nay; sorrow was swallowed up in the life drawing nigh to restore every good and lovely thing a hundredfold! I lay at peace, full of the quietest expectation, breathing the damp odors of Earth's bountiful bosom, aware of the souls of primroses, daisies and snowdrops, patiently waiting in it for the Spring.

How convey the delight of that frozen, yet conscious sleep! I had no more to stand up! had only to lie stretched out and still! How cold I was, words cannot tell; yet I grew colder and colder — and welcomed the cold yet more and more. I grew continuously less conscious of myself, continuously more conscious of bliss, unimaginable yet felt. I had neither made it nor prayed for it: it was mine in virtue of existence! And existence was mine in virtue of a Will that dwelt in mine.

Then the dreams began to arrive — and came crowding. — I lay naked on a snowy peak. The white mist heaved below me like a billowy sea. The cold moon was in the air with me, and above the moon and me the colder sky, in which the moon and I dwelt. I was Adam, waiting for God to breathe into my nostrils the breath of life. — I was not Adam, but a child in the bosom of a mother white with a radiant whiteness. I was a youth on a white horse, leaping from cloud to cloud of a blue heaven, hasting calmly to some blessed goal. For centuries I dreamed — or was it chiliads? Or only one long night? — But why ask? for time had nothing to do with me; I was in the land of thought — farther in, higher up than the seven dimensions, the ten senses: I think I was where I am — in the heart of God. — I dreamed away dim cycles in the centre of a melting glacier, the spectral moon drawing nearer and nearer, the wind and the welter of a torrent growing in my ears. I lay and heard them: the wind and the water and the moon sang a peaceful waiting for a redemption drawing nigh. I dreamed cycles, I say, but, for aught I knew or can tell, they were the solemn, æonian march of a second, pregnant with eternity.

Then, of a sudden, but not once troubling my conscious bliss, all the wrongs I had ever done, from far beyond my earthly memory down to the present moment, were with me. Fully in every wrong lived the conscious I, confessing, abjuring, lamenting the dead, making atonement with each person I had injured, hurt, or offended. Every human soul to which I had caused a troubled thought, was now grown unspeakably dear to me, and I humbled myself before it, agonizing to cast from between us the clinging offence. I wept at the feet of the mother whose commands I had slighted; with bitter shame I confessed to my father that I had told him two lies, and long forgotten them: now for long had remembered them, and kept them in memory to crush at last at his feet. I was the eager slave of all whom I had thus or anyhow wronged. Countless services I devised to render them! For this one I would build such a house as had never grown from the ground! For that one I would train such horses as had never yet been seen in any world! For a third I would make such a garden as had never bloomed, haunted with still pools, and alive with running waters! I would write songs to make their hearts swell, and tales to make them glow! I would turn the forces of the world into such channels of invention as to make them laugh with the joy of wonder! Love possessed me! Love was my life! Love was to me, as to him that made me, all in all!

Suddenly I found myself in a solid blackness, upon which the ghost of light that dwells in the caverns of the eyes could not cast one fancied glimmer. But my heart, which feared nothing and hoped infinitely, was full of peace. I lay imagining what the light would be when it came, and what new creation it would bring with it — when, suddenly, without conscious volition, I sat up and stared about me.

The moon was looking in at the lowest, horizontal, crypt-like windows of the death-chamber, her long light slanting, I thought, across the fallen, but still ripening sheaves of the harvest of the great husbandman. — But no; that harvest was gone! Gathered in, or swept away by chaotic storm, not a sacred sheaf was there! My dead were gone! I was alone! — In desolation dread lay depths yet deeper than I had hitherto known! — Had there never been any ripening dead? Had I but dreamed them and their loveliness? Why then these walls? Why the empty couches? No; they were all up! they were all abroad in the new eternal day, and had forgotten me! They had left me behind, and alone! Tenfold more terrible was the tomb its inhabitants away! The quiet ones had made me quiet with their presence — had pervaded my mind with their blissful peace; now I had no friend, and my lovers were far from me! A moment I sat and stared horror-stricken. I had been alone with the moon on a mountain top in the sky; now I was alone with her in a huge cenotaph: she too was staring about, seeking her dead with ghastly gaze! I sprang to my feet, and staggered from the fearful place.

The cottage was empty. I ran out into the night.

No moon was there! Even as I left the chamber, a cloudy rampart had risen and covered her. But a broad shimmer came from far over the heath, mingled with a ghostly murmuring music, as if the moon were raining a light that plashed as it fell. I ran stumbling across the moor, and found a lovely lake, margined with reeds and rushes: the moon behind the cloud was gazing upon the monsters' den, full of clearest, brightest water, and very still. — But the musical murmur went on, filling the quiet air, and drawing me after it.

I walked round the border of the little mere, and climbed the range of hills. What a sight rose to my eyes! The whole expanse where, with hot, aching feet, I had crossed and re-crossed the deep-scored channels and ravines of the dry river-bed, was alive with streams, with torrents, with still pools —"a river deep and wide"! How the moon flashed on the water! How the water answered the moon with flashes of its own — white flashes breaking everywhere from its rock-encountered flow! And a great jubilant song arose from its bosom, the song of new-born liberty. I stood a moment gazing, and my heart also began to exult: my life was not all a failure! I had helped to set this river free! — My dead were not lost! I had but to go after and find them! I would follow and follow until I came whither they had gone! Our meeting might be thousands of years away, but at last — AT LAST I should hold them! Wherefore else did the floods clap their hands?

I hurried down the hill: my pilgrimage was begun! In what direction to turn my steps I knew not, but I must go and go till I found my living dead! A torrent ran swift and wide at the foot of the range: I rushed in, it laid no hold upon me; I waded through it. The next I sprang across; the third I swam; the next I waded again.

I stopped to gaze on the wondrous loveliness of the ceaseless flash and flow, and to hearken to the multitudinous broken music. Every now and then some incipient air would seem about to draw itself clear of the dulcet confusion, only to merge again in the consorted roar. At moments the world of waters would invade as if to overwhelm me — not with the force of its seaward rush, or the shouting of its liberated throng, but with the greatness of the silence wandering into sound.

As I stood lost in delight, a hand was laid on my shoulder. I turned, and saw a man in the prime of strength, beautiful as if fresh from the heart of the glad creator, young like him who cannot grow old. I looked: it was Adam. He stood large and grand, clothed in a white robe, with the moon in his hair.

"Father," I cried, "where is she? Where are the dead? Is the great resurrection come and gone? The terror of my loneliness was upon me; I could not sleep without my dead; I ran from the desolate chamber. — Whither shall I go to find them?"

"You mistake, my son," he answered, in a voice whose very breath was consolation. "You are still in the chamber of death, still upon your couch, asleep and dreaming, with the dead around you."

"Alas! when I but dream how am I to know it? The dream best dreamed is the likest to the waking truth!"

"When you are quite dead, you will dream no false dream. The soul that is true can generate nothing that is not true, neither can the false enter it."

"But, sir," I faltered, "how am I to distinguish betwixt the true and the false where both alike seem real?"

"Do you not understand?" he returned, with a smile that might have slain all the sorrows of all his children. "You CANNOT perfectly distinguish between the true and the false while you are not yet quite dead; neither indeed will you when you are quite dead — that is, quite alive, for then the false will never present itself. At this moment, believe me, you are on your bed in the house of death."

"I am trying hard to believe you, father. I do indeed believe you, although I can neither see nor feel the truth of what you say."

"You are not to blame that you cannot. And because even in a dream you believe me, I will help you. — Put forth your left hand open, and close it gently: it will clasp the hand of your Lona, who lies asleep where you lie dreaming you are awake."

I put forth my hand: it closed on the hand of Lona, firm and soft and deathless.

"But, father," I cried, "she is warm!"

"Your hand is as warm to hers. Cold is a thing unknown in our country. Neither she nor you are yet in the fields of home, but each to each is alive and warm and healthful."

Then my heart was glad. But immediately supervened a sharp-stinging doubt.

"Father," I said, "forgive me, but how am I to know surely that this also is not a part of the lovely dream in which I am now walking with thyself?"

"Thou doubtest because thou lovest the truth. Some would willingly believe life but a phantasm, if only it might for ever afford them a world of pleasant dreams: thou art not of such! Be content for a while not to know surely. The hour will come, and that ere long, when, being true, thou shalt behold the very truth, and doubt will be for ever dead. Scarce, then, wilt thou be able to recall the features of the phantom. Thou wilt then know that which thou canst not now dream. Thou hast not yet looked the Truth in the face, hast as yet at best but seen him through a cloud. That which thou seest not, and never didst see save in a glass darkly — that which, indeed, never can be known save by its innate splendor shining straight into pure eyes—that thou canst not but doubt, and art blameless in doubting until thou seest it face to face, when thou wilt no longer be able to doubt it. But to him who has once seen even a shadow only of the truth, and, even but hoping he has seen it when it is present no longer, tries to obey it —to him the real vision, the Truth himself, will come, and depart no more, but abide with him for ever."

"I think I see, father," I said; "I think I understand."

"Then remember, and recall. Trials yet await thee, heavy, of a nature thou knowest not now. Remember the things thou hast seen. Truly thou knowest not those things, but thou knowest what they have seemed, what they have meant to thee! Remember also the things thou shalt yet see. Truth is all in all; and the truth of things lies, at once hid and revealed, in their seeming."

"How can that be, father?" I said, and raised my eyes with the question; for I had been listening with down bent head, aware of nothing but the voice of Adam.

He was gone; in my ears was nought but the sounding silence of the swift-flowing waters. I stretched forth my hands to find him, but no answering touch met their seeking. I was alone — alone in the land of dreams! To myself I seemed wide awake, but I believed I was in a dream, because he had told me so.

Even in a dream, however, the dreamer must do something! he cannot sit down and refuse to stir until the dream grow weary of him and depart: I took up my wandering, and went on.

Many channels I crossed, and came to a wider space of rock; there, dreaming I was weary, I laid myself down, and longed to be awake.

I was about to rise and resume my journey, when I discovered that I lay beside a pit in the rock, whose mouth was like that of a grave. It was deep and dark; I could see no bottom.

Now in the dreams of my childhood I had found that a fall invariably woke me, and would, therefore, when desiring to discontinue a dream, seek some eminence whence to cast myself down that I might wake: with one glance at the peaceful heavens, and one at the rushing waters, I rolled myself over the edge of the pit.

For a moment consciousness left me. When it returned, I stood in the garret of my own house, in the little wooden chamber of the cowl and the mirror.

Unspeakable despair, hopelessness blank and dreary, invaded me with the knowledge: between me and my Lona lay an abyss impassable! Stretched a distance no chain could measure! Space and Time and Mode of Being, as with walls of adamant unscalable, impenetrable, shut me in from that gulf! True, it might yet be in my power to pass again through the door of light, and journey back to the chamber of the dead; and if so, I was parted from that chamber only by a wide heath, and by the pale, starry night betwixt me and the sun, which alone could open for me the mirror-door, and was now far away on the other side of the world! But an immeasurably wider gulf sank between us in this — that she was asleep and I was awake! That I was no longer worthy to share with her that sleep, and could no longer hope to awake from it with her! For truly I was much to blame: I had fled from my dream! The dream was not of my making, any more than was my life: I ought to have seen it to the end! And in fleeing from it, I had left the holy sleep itself behind me! — I would go back to Adam, tell him the truth, and bow to his decree!

I crept to my chamber, threw myself on my bed, and passed a dreamless night.

I rose, and listlessly sought the library. On the way I met no one; the house seemed dead. I sat down with a book to await the noontide: not a sentence could I understand! The mutilated manuscript offered itself from the masked door: the sight of it sickened me; what to mewas the princess with her devilry!

I rose and looked out of a window. It was a brilliant morning. With a great rush the fountain shot high, and fell roaring back. The sun sat in its feathery top. Not a bird sang, not a creature was to be seen. Raven nor librarian came near me. The world was dead about me. I took another book, sat down again, and went on waiting.

Noon was near. I went up the stairs to the dumb, shadowy roof. I closed behind me the door into the wooden chamber, and turned to open the door out of a dreary world.

I left the chamber with a heart of stone. Do what I might, all was fruitless. I pulled the chains; adjusted and re-adjusted the hood; arranged and re-arranged the mirrors; no result followed. I waited and waited to give the vision time; it would not come; the mirror stood blank; nothing lay in its dim old depth but the mirror opposite and my haggard face.

I went back to the library. There the books were hateful to me — for I had once loved them.

That night I lay awake from down-lying to uprising, and the next day renewed my endeavors with the mystic door. But all was yet in vain. How the hours went I cannot think. No one came nigh me; not a sound from the house below entered my ears. Not once did I feel weary — only desolate, drearily desolate.

I passed a second sleepless night. In the morning I went for the last time to the chamber in the roof, and for the last time sought an open door: there was none. My heart died within me. I had lost my Lona!

Was she anywhere? Had she ever been, save in the mouldering cells of my brain? "I must die one day," I thought, "and then, straight from my death-bed, I will set out to find her! If she is not, I will go to the Father and say — 'Even thou canst not help me: let me cease, I pray thee!'"

44. THE WAKING

The fourth night I seemed to fall asleep, and that night woke indeed. I opened my eyes and knew, although all was dark around me, that I lay in the house of death, and that every moment since there I fell asleep I had been dreaming, and now first was awake. "At last!" I said to my heart, and it leaped for joy. I turned my eyes; Lona stood by my couch, waiting for me! I had never lost her! — only for a little time lost the sight of her! Truly I needed not have lamented her so sorely!

It was dark, as I say, but I saw her: SHE was not dark! Her eyes shone with the radiance of the Mother's, and the same light issued from her face — nor from her face only, for her death-dress, filled with the light of her body now tenfold awake in the power of its resurrection, was white as snow and glistering. She fell asleep a girl; she awoke a woman, ripe with the loveliness of the life essential. I folded her in my arms, and knew that I lived indeed.

"I woke first!" she said, with a wondering smile.

"You did, my love, and woke me!"

"I only looked at you and waited," she answered.

The candle came floating toward us through the dark, and in a few moments Adam and Eve and Mara were with us. They greeted us with a quiet good-morning and a smile: they were used to such wakings!

"I hope you have had a pleasant darkness!" said the Mother.

"Not very," I answered, "but the waking from it is heavenly."

"It is but begun," she rejoined; "you are hardly yet awake!"

"He is at least clothed-upon with Death, which is the radiant garment of Life," said Adam.

He embraced Lona his child, put an arm around me, looked a moment or two inquiringly at the princess, and patted the head of the leopardess.

"I think we shall meet you two again before long," he said, looking first at Lona, then at me.

"Have we to die again?" I asked.

"No," he answered, with a smile like the Mother's; "you have died into life, and will die no more; you have only to keep dead. Once dying as we die here, all the dying is over. Now you have only to live, and that you must, with all your blessed might. The more you live, the stronger you become to live."

"But shall I not grow weary with living so strong?" I said. "What if I cease to live with all my might?"

"It needs but the will, and the strength is there!" said the Mother. "Pure life has no weakness to grow weary withal. THE Life keeps generating ours. Those who will not die, die many times, die constantly, keep dying deeper, never have done dying; here all is upwardness and love and gladness."

She ceased with a smile and a look that seemed to say, "We are mother and son; we understand each other! Between us no farewell is possible."

Mara kissed me on the forehead, and said, gayly,

"I told you, brother, all would be well! — When next you would comfort, say, `What will be well, is even now well.'"

She gave a little sigh, and I thought it meant, "But they will not believe you!"

"You know me now!" she ended, with a smile like her mother's.

"I know you!" I answered: "you are the voice that cried in the wilderness before ever the Baptist came! You are the shepherd whose wolves hunt the wandering sheep home ere the shadow rise and the night grow dark!"

"My work will one day be over," she said, "and then I shall be glad with the gladness of the great shepherd who sent me."

"All the night long the morning is at hand," said Adam.

"What is that flapping of wings I hear?" I asked.

"The Shadow is hovering," replied Adam: "there is one here whom he counts his own! But ours once, never more can she be his!"

I turned to look on the faces of my father and mother, and kiss them ere we went: their couches were empty save of the Little Ones who had with love's boldness appropriated their hospitality! For an instant that awful dream of desolation overshadowed me, and I turned aside.

"What is it, my heart?" said Lona.

"Their empty places frightened me," I answered.

"They are up and away long ago," said Adam. "They kissed you ere they went, and whispered, `Come soon.'"

"And I neither to feel nor hear them!" I murmured.

"How could you — far away in your dreary old house! You thought the dreadful place had you once more! Now go and find them. Your parents, my child," he added, turning to Lona, "must come and find you!"

The hour of our departure was at hand. Lona went to the couch of the mother who had slain her, and kissed her tenderly — then laid herself in her father's arms.

"That kiss will draw her homeward, my Lona!" said Adam.

"Who were her parents?" asked Lona.

"My father," answered Adam, "is her father also."

She turned and laid her hand in mine.

I kneeled and humbly thanked the three for helping me to die. Lona knelt beside me, and they all breathed upon us.

"Hark! I hear the sun," said Adam.

I listened: he was coming with the rush as of a thousand times ten thousand far-off wings, with the roar of a molten and flaming world millions upon millions of miles away. His approach was a crescendo chord of a hundred harmonies.

The three looked at each other and smiled, and that smile went floating heavenward a three-pedaled flower, the family's morning thanksgiving. From their mouths and their faces it spread over their bodies and shone through their garments. Ere I could say, "Lo, they change!" Adam and Eve stood before me the angels of the resurrection, and Mara was the Magdalene with them at the sepulcher. The countenance of Adam was like lightning, and Eve held a napkin that flung flakes of splendor about the place.

A wind began to moan in pulsing gusts.

"You hear his wings now!" said Adam; and I knew he did not mean the wings of the morning.

"It is the great Shadow stirring to depart," he went on. "Wretched creature, he has himself within him, and cannot rest!"

"But is there not in him something deeper yet?" I asked.

"Without a substance," he answered, "a shadow cannot be — yea, or without a light behind the substance!"

He listened for a moment, then called out, with a glad smile, "Hark to the golden cock! Silent and motionless for millions of years has he stood on the clock of the universe; now at last he is flapping his wings! Now will he begin to crow! And at intervals will men hear him until the dawn of the day eternal."

I listened. Far away — as in the heart of an æonian silence, I heard the clear jubilant outcry of the golden throat. It hurled defiance at death and the dark; sang infinite hope, and coming calm. It was the "expectation of the creature" finding at last a voice; the cry of a chaos that would be a kingdom!

Then I heard a great flapping.

"The black bat is flown!" said Mara.

"Amen, golden cock, bird of God!" cried Adam, and the words rang through the house of silence, and went up into the airy regions.

At his AMEN — like doves arising on wings of silver from among the potsherds, up sprang the Little Ones to their knees on their beds, calling aloud,

"Crow! crow again, golden cock!" — as if they had both seen and heard him in their dreams.

Then each turned and looked at the sleeping bedfellow, gazed a moment with loving eyes, kissed the silent companion of the night, and sprang from the couch. The Little Ones who had lain down beside my father and mother gazed blank and sad for a moment at their empty places, then slid slowly to the floor. There they fell each into the other's arms, as if then first, each by the other's eyes, assured they were alive and awake. Suddenly spying Lona, they came running, radiant with bliss, to embrace her. Odu, catching sight of the leopardess on the feet of the princess, bounded to her next, and throwing an arm over the great sleeping head, fondled and kissed it.

"Wake up, wake up, darling!" he cried; "it is time to wake!"

The leopardess did not move.

"She has slept herself cold!" he said to Mara, with an upcast look of appealing consternation.

"She is waiting for the princess to wake, my child," said Mara.

Odu looked at the princess, and saw beside her, still asleep, two of his companions. He flew at them.

"Wake up! wake up!" he cried, and pushed and pulled, now this one, now that.

But soon he began to look troubled, and turned to me with misty eyes.

"They will not wake!" he said. "And why are they so cold?"

"They too are waiting for the princess," I answered.

He stretched across, and laid his hand on her face.

"She is cold too! What is it?" he cried — and looked round in wondering dismay.

Adam went to him.

"Her wake is not ripe yet," he said: "she is busy forgetting. When she has forgotten enough to remember enough, then she will soon be ripe, and wake."

"And remember?"

"Yes — but not too much at once though."

"But the golden cock has crown!" argued the child, and fell again upon his companions.

"Peter! Peter! Crispy!" he cried. "Wake up, Peter! wake up, Crispy! We are all awake but you two! The gold cock has crown SO loud! The sun is awake and coming! Oh, why WON'T you wake?"

But Peter would not wake, neither would Crispy, and Odu wept outright at last.

"Let them sleep, darling!" said Adam. "You would not like the princess to wake and find nobody? They are quite happy. So is the leopardess."

He was comforted, and wiped his eyes as if he had been all his life used to weeping and wiping, though now first he had tears wherewith to weep — soon to be wiped altogether away.

We followed Eve to the cottage. There she offered us neither bread nor wine, but stood radiantly desiring our departure. So, with never a word of farewell, we went out. The horse and the elephants were at the door, waiting for us. We were too happy to mount them, and they followed us.

45. The Journey Home

It had ceased to be dark; we walked in a dim twilight, breathing through the dimness the breath of the spring. A wondrous change had passed upon the world — or was it not rather that a change more marvelous had taken place in us? Without light enough in the sky or the air to reveal anything, every heather-bush, every small shrub, every blade of grass was perfectly visible — either by light that went out from it, as fire from the bush Moses saw in the desert, or by light that went out of our eyes. Nothing cast a shadow; all things interchanged a little light. Every growing thing showed me, by its shape and color, its indwelling idea — the informing thought, that is, which was its being, and sent it out. My bare feet seemed to love every plant they trod upon. The world and my being, its life and mine, were one. The microcosm and macrocosm were at length atoned, at length in harmony! I lived in everything; everything entered and lived in me. To be aware of a thing, was to know its life at once and mine, to know whence we came, and where we were at home — was to know that we are all what we are, because Another is what he is! Sense after sense, hitherto asleep, awoke in me — sense after sense indescribable, because no correspondent words, no likenesses or imaginations exist, wherewithal to describe them. Full indeed — yet ever expanding, ever making room to receive — was the conscious being where things kept entering by so many open doors! When a little breeze brushing a bush of heather set its purple bells a ringing, I was myself in the joy of the bells, myself in the joy of the breeze to which responded their sweet TIN-TINNING, myself in the joy of the sense, and of the soul that received all the joys together. To everything glad I lent the hall of my being wherein to revel. I was a peaceful ocean upon which the ground-swell of a living joy was continually lifting new waves; yet was the joy ever the same joy, the eternal joy, with tens of thousands of changing forms. Life was a cosmic holiday.

Now I knew that life and truth were one; that life mere and pure is in itself bliss; that where being is not bliss, it is not life, but life-in-death. Every inspiration of the dark wind that blew where it listed, went out a sigh of thanksgiving. At last I was! I lived, and nothing could touch my life! My darling walked beside me, and we were on our way home to the Father!

So much was ours ere ever the first sun rose upon our freedom: what must not the eternal day bring with it!

We came to the fearful hollow where once had wallowed the monsters of the earth: it was indeed, as I had beheld it in my dream, a lovely lake. I gazed into its pellucid depths. A whirlpool had swept out the soil in which the abortions burrowed, and at the bottom lay visible the whole horrid brood: a dim greenish light pervaded the crystalline water, and revealed every hideous form beneath it. Coiled in spires, folded in layers, knotted on themselves, or "extended long and large," they weltered in motionless heaps — shapes more fantastic in ghoulish, blasting dismay, than ever wine-sodden brain of exhausted poet fevered into misbeing. He who dived in the swirling Maelstrom saw none to compare with them in horror: tentacular convolutions, tumid bulges, glaring orbs of sepian deformity, would have looked to him innocence beside such incarnations of hatefulness — every head the wicked flower that, bursting from an abominable stalk, perfected its evil significance.

Not one of them moved as we passed. But they were not dead. So long as exist men and women of unwholesome mind, that lake will still be peopled with loathsomenesses.

But hark the herald of the sun, the auroral wind, softly trumpeting his approach! The master-minister of the human tabernacle is at hand! Heaping before his prow a huge ripple-fretted wave of crimson and gold, he rushes aloft, as if new launched from the urging hand of his maker into the upper sea — pauses, and looks down on the world. White-raving storm of molten metals, he is but a coal from the altar of the Father's never-ending sacrifice to his children. See every little flower straighten its stalk, lift up its neck, and with outstretched head stand expectant: something more than the sun, greater than the light, is coming, is coming —none the less surely coming that it is long upon the road! What matters to-day, or to-morrow, or ten thousand years to Life himself, to Love himself! He is coming, is coming, and the necks of all humanity are stretched out to see him come! Every morning will they thus outstretch themselves, every evening will they droop and wait — until he comes. — Is this but an air-drawn vision? When he comes, will he indeed find them watching thus?

It was a glorious resurrection-morning. The night had been spent in preparing it!

The children went gamboling before, and the beasts came after us. Fluttering butterflies, darting dragon-flies hovered or shot hither and thither about our heads, a cloud of colors and flashes, now descending upon us like a snow-storm of rainbow flakes, now rising into the humid air like a rolling vapor of embodied odors. It was a summer-day more like itself, that is, more ideal, than ever man that had not died found summer-day in any world. I walked on the new earth, under the new heaven, and found them the same as the old, save that now they opened their minds to me, and I saw into them. Now, the soul of everything I met came out to greet me and make friends with me, telling me we came from the same, and meant the same. I was going to him, they said, with whom they always were, and whom they always meant; they were, they said, lightnings that took shape as they flashed from him to his. The dark rocks drank like sponges the rays that showered upon them; the great world soaked up the light, and sent out the living. Two joy-fires were Lona and I. Earth breathed heavenward her sweet-savored smoke; we breathed homeward our longing desires. For thanksgiving, our very consciousness was that.

We came to the channels, once so dry and wearyful: they ran and flashed and foamed with living water that shouted in its gladness! Far as the eye could see, all was a rushing, roaring, dashing river of water made vocal by its rocks.

We did not cross it, but "walked in glory and in joy" up its right bank, until we reached the great cataract at the foot of the sandy desert, where, roaring and swirling and dropping sheer, the river divided into its two branches. There we climbed the height — and found no desert: through grassy plains, between grassy banks, flowed the deep, wide, silent river full to the brim. Then first to the Little Ones was revealed the glory of God in the limpid flow of water. Instinctively they plunged and swam, and the beasts followed them.

The desert rejoiced and blossomed as the rose. Wide forests had sprung up, their whole undergrowth flowering shrubs peopled with song-birds. Every thicket gave birth to a rivulet, and every rivulet to its water-song.

The place of the buried hand gave no sign. Beyond and still beyond, the river came in full volume from afar. Up and up we went, now along grassy margin, and now through forest of gracious trees. The grass grew sweeter and its flowers more lovely and various as we went; the trees grew larger, and the wind fuller of messages.

We came at length to a forest whose trees were greater, grander, and more beautiful than any we had yet seen. Their live pillars upheaved a thick embowed roof, betwixt whose leaves and blossoms hardly a sunbeam filtered. Into the rafters of this aerial vault the children climbed, and through them went scrambling and leaping in a land of bloom, shouting to the unseen elephants below, and hearing them trumpet their replies. The conversations between them Lona understood while I but guessed at them blunderingly. The Little Ones chased the squirrels, and the squirrels, frolicking, drew them on — always at length allowing themselves to be caught and petted. Often would some bird, lovely in plumage and form, light upon one of them, sing a song of what was coming, and fly away. Not one monkey of any sort could they see.

46. THE CITY

Lona and I, who walked below, heard at last a great shout overhead, and in a moment or two the Little Ones began to come dropping down from the foliage with the news that, climbing to the top of a tree yet taller than the rest, they had descried, far across the plain, a curious something on the side of a solitary mountain — which mountain, they said, rose and rose, until the sky gathered thick to keep it down, and knocked its top off.

"It may be a city," they said, "but it is not at all like Bulika."

I went up to look, and saw a great city, ascending into blue clouds, where I could not distinguish mountain from sky and cloud, or rocks from dwellings. Cloud and mountain and sky, palace and precipice mingled in a seeming chaos of broken shadow and shine.

I descended, the Little Ones came with me, and together we sped on faster. They grew yet merrier as they went, leading the way, and never looking behind them. The river grew lovelier and lovelier, until I knew that never before had I seen real water. Nothing in this world is more than LIKE it.

By and by we could from the plain see the city among the blue clouds. But other clouds were gathering around a lofty tower — or was it a rock? — that stood above the city, nearer the crest of the mountain. Gray, and dark gray, and purple, they writhed in confused, contrariant motions, and tossed up a vaporous foam, while spots in them gyrated like whirlpools. At length issued a dazzling flash, which seemed for a moment to play about the Little Ones in front of us. Blinding darkness followed, but through it we heard their voices, low with delight.

"Did you see?"

"I saw."

"What did you see?"

"The beautifullest man."

"I heard him speak!"

"I didn't: what did he say?"

Here answered the smallest and most childish of the voices — that of Luva:—

"He said, `'Ou's all mine's, 'ickle ones: come along!'"

I had seen the lightning, but heard no words; Lona saw and heard with the children. A second flash came, and my eyes, though not my ears, were opened. The great quivering light was compact of angel-faces. They lamped themselves visible, and vanished.

A third flash came; its substance and radiance were human.

"I see my mother!" I cried.

"I see lots o' mothers!" said Luva.

Once more the cloud flashed — all kinds of creatures — horses and elephants, lions and dogs — oh, such beasts! And such birds! Great birds whose wings gleamed singly every color gathered in sunset or rainbow! little birds whose feathers sparkled as with all the precious stones of the hoarding earth! Silvery cranes; red flamingoes; opal pigeons; peacocks gorgeous in gold and green and blue; jewelly humming birds! Great-winged butterflies; lithe-volumed creeping things — all in one heavenly flash!

"I see that serpents grow birds here, as caterpillars used to grow butterflies!" remarked Lona.

"I saw my white pony, that died when I was a child. I needn't have been so sorry; I should just have waited!" I said.

Thunder, clap or roll, there had been none. And now came a sweet rain, filling the atmosphere with a caressing coolness. We breathed deep, and stepped out with stronger strides. The falling drops flashed the colors of all the waked up gems of the earth, and a mighty rainbow spanned the city.

The blue clouds gathered thicker; the rain fell in torrents; the children exulted and ran; it was all we could do to keep them in sight.

With silent, radiant roll, the river swept onward, filling to the margin its smooth, soft, yielding channel. For, instead of rock or shingle or sand, it flowed over grass in which grew primroses and daisies, crocuses and narcissi, pimpernels and anemones, a starry multitude, large and bright through the brilliant water. The river had gathered no turbid cloudiness from the rain, not even a tinge of yellow or brown; the delicate mass shone with the pale berylline gleam that ascended from its deep, dainty bed.

Drawing nearer to the mountain, we saw that the river came from its very peak, and rushed in full volume through the main street of the city. It descended to the gate by a stair of deep and wide steps, mingled of porphyry and serpentine, which continued to the foot of the mountain. There arriving we found shallower steps on both banks, leading up to the gate, and along the ascending street. Without the briefest halt, the Little Ones ran straight up the stair to the gate, which stood open.

Outside, on the landing, sat the portress, a woman-angel of dark visage, leaning her shadowed brow on her idle hand. The children rushed upon her, covering her with caresses, and ere she understood, they had taken heaven by surprise, and were already in the city, still mounting the stair by the side of the descending torrent. A great angel, attended by a company of shining ones, came down to meet and receive them, but merrily evading them all, up still they ran. In merry dance, however, a group of woman-angels descended upon them, and in a moment they were fettered in heavenly arms. The radiants carried them away, and I saw them no more.

"Ah!" said the mighty angel, continuing his descent to meet us who were now almost at the gate and within hearing of his words, "this is well! These are soldiers to take heaven itself by storm! — I hear of a horde of black bats on the frontiers: these will make short work with such!"

Seeing the horse and the elephants clambering up behind us —

"Take those animals to the royal stables," he added; "there tend them; then turn them into the king's forest."

"Welcome home!" he said to us, bending low with the sweetest smile.

Immediately he turned and led the way higher. The scales of his armor flashed like flakes of lightning.

Thought cannot form itself to tell what I felt, thus received by the officers of heaven. All I wanted and knew not, must be on its way to me!

We stood for a moment at the gate whence issued roaring the radiant river. I know not whence came the stones that fashioned it, but among them I saw the prototypes of all the gems I had loved on earth — far more beautiful than they, for these were living stones — such in which I saw, not the intent alone, but the intender too; not the idea alone, but the imbodier present, the operant outsender: nothing in this kingdom was dead; nothing was mere; nothing only a thing.

We went up through the city and passed out. There was no wall on the upper side, but a huge pile of broken rocks, upsloping like the moraine of an eternal glacier; and through the openings between the rocks, the river came billowing out. On their top I could dimly discern what seemed three or four great steps of a stair, disappearing in a cloud white as snow; and above the steps I saw, but with my mind's eye only, as it were a grand old chair, the throne of the Ancient of Days. Over and under and between those steps issued, plenteously, unceasingly new-born, the river of the water of life.

The great angel could guide us no farther: those rocks we must ascend alone!

My heart beating with hope and desire, I held faster the hand of my Lona, and we began to climb; but soon we let each other go, to use hands as well as feet in the toilsome ascent of the huge stones. At length we drew near the cloud, which hung down the steps like the borders of a garment, passed through the fringe, and entered the deep folds. A hand, warm and strong, laid hold of mine, and drew me to a little door with a golden lock. The door opened; the hand let mine go, and pushed me gently through. I turned quickly, and saw the board of a large book in the act of closing behind me. I stood alone in my library.

47. THE "ENDLESS ENDING"

As yet I have not found Lona, but Mara is much with me. She has taught me many things, and is teaching me more.

Can it be that that last waking also was in the dream? That I am still in the chamber of death, asleep and dreaming, not yet ripe enough to wake? Or can it be that I did not go to sleep outright and heartily, and so have come awake too soon? If that waking was itself but a dream, surely it was a dream of a better waking yet to come, and I have not been the sport of a false vision! Such a dream must have yet lovelier truth at the heart of its dreaming!

In moments of doubt I cry,

"Could God Himself create such lovely things as I dreamed?"

"Whence then came thy dream?" answers Hope.

"Out of my dark self, into the light of my consciousness."

"But whence first into thy dark self?" rejoins Hope.

"My brain was its mother, and the fever in my blood its father."

"Say rather," suggests Hope, "thy brain was the violin whence it issued, and the fever in thy blood the bow that drew it forth. — But who made the violin? And who guided the bow across its strings? Say rather, again — who set the song birds each on its bough in the tree of life, and startled each in its order from its perch? Whence came the fantasia? And whence the life that danced thereto? Didst THOU say, in the dark of thy own unconscious self, `Let beauty be; let truth seem!' and straightway beauty was, and truth but seemed?"

Man dreams and desires; God broods and wills and quickens.

When a man dreams his own dream, he is the sport of his dream; when Another gives it him, that Other is able to fulfill it.

I have never again sought the mirror. The hand sent me back: I will not go out again by that door! "All the days of my appointed time will I wait till my change come."

Now and then, when I look round on my books, they seem to waver as if a wind rippled their solid mass, and another world were about to break through. Sometimes when I am abroad, a like thing takes place; the heavens and the earth, the trees and the grass appear for a moment to shake as if about to pass away; then, lo, they have settled again into the old familiar face! At times I seem to hear whisperings around me, as if some that loved me were talking of me; but when I would distinguish the words, they cease, and all is very still. I know not whether these things rise in my brain, or enter it from without. I do not seek them; they come, and I let them go.

Strange dim memories, which will not abide identification, often, through misty windows of the past, look out upon me in the broad daylight, but I never dream now. It may be, notwithstanding, that, when most awake, I am only dreaming the more! But when I wake at last into that life which, as a mother her child, carries this life in its bosom, I shall know that I wake, and shall doubt no more.

I wait; asleep or awake, I wait.

Novalis says, "Our life is no dream, but it should and will perhaps become one."

9 780978 891435